VOLUME II

—————— HERITAGE OF ——————
AMERICAN LITERATURE
——— CIVIL WAR TO THE PRESENT ———

VOLUME II

HERITAGE OF
AMERICAN LITERATURE
CIVIL WAR TO THE PRESENT

James E. Miller, Jr.
The University of Chicago

With the assistance of
Kathleen Farley

Harcourt Brace Jovanovich, Publishers

San Diego   New York   Chicago   Austin   Washington, D.C.

London   Sydney   Tokyo   Toronto

HERITAGE OF AMERICAN LITERATURE, Volume II

ISBN: 0-15-535698-4

Library of Congress Catalog Card Number: 90-82129

Printed in the United States of America

Copyrights and Acknowledgments and Illustration Credits appear on pages 2177–86, which constitute a continuation of the copyright page.

PREFACE

Heritage of American Literature presents a survey of the travel narratives, exploration and discovery accounts, religious and political tracts, formal and informal essays, humor and wit, fiction, poetry, and drama inspired by America from Columbus's "discovery" in 1492 up to the 1990s. It stretches from Captain John Smith, William Bradford, Ann Bradstreet, and Phillis Wheatley to T. S. Eliot, William Faulkner, Ralph Ellison, and Flannery O'Connor. In the opening pages may be found Dekanawidah's *Iroquois Constitution* alongside Columbus's Letter on Discovery, and in the closing pages may be found poems, fiction, and drama by Gary Soto, Maxine Hong Kingston, and Sam Shepard. In these 500 years, the country has not ceased to elicit the awe and wonder expressed by Columbus on first setting eyes on its virgin lands. And in this long stretch of time, the American imagination has not yet provided final answers to such nagging questions as that posed by St. John de Crèvecoeur in the eighteenth century: "What is an American?"

Whereas Crèvecoeur introduced the notion of the new country as a "melting pot," the contemporary imagination is more likely to compare America to a vari-colored patchwork quilt. In a world beset by so many upheavals and disruptions, Americans are more likely now to set off in search of their roots than to leave them lost in the soil of the past. Whatever the truth of these metaphors—melting pot, patchwork quilt, roots—there can be no gainsaying that American writers and their works are made up of a multiplicity and variety that constitute their unique character and richness. Americans may be justly proud of their literature, and moreover will come to know themselves and discover their identity through encountering and experiencing that literature extensively and deeply. This anthology was designed to provide such an encounter, such an experience. Its special features include the following:

1. *Interrelated Clusters of Literary Works.* Instead of arranging selections haphazardly in accord with the authors' birth years, *Heritage of American Literature* groups them in clusters where, read together, they explicate, complement, or give resonance to each other. For example, in Volume I will be found a cluster entitled "Personal Accounts of High Adventure," which brings Mary Rowlandson's exciting account of her Indian captivity together with Sarah Kemble Knight's later hazardous trip alone from Boston to New York. Also in Volume I, "Emerging Feminist Perspectives" presents a group of important, innovative, and often skeptical or ironic women writers, ranging from Margaret Fuller and Elizabeth Cady Stanton to Rebecca Harding Davis and Louisa May Alcott. Volume I concludes with the cluster "Slavery and the Civil War," bringing together the protests and slave narratives of such gifted writers as David Walker, Frederick Douglass, and Harriet A. Jacobs, and concluding with Abraham Lincoln and Walt Whitman. Similar groupings found in Volume II include "Emerging Feminist Fiction" (from Constance Fenimore Woolson to Charlotte Perkins Gilman), "Personal Voice and View: Diaries, Autobiographies, Essays" (from Sarah Winnemucca Hopkins to William James), and "Autobiographies: Modes of Remembering" (from Gertrude Stein to Richard Wright).

2. *Balance in Selections between the Traditional and the New. Heritage of American Literature* includes, as the names listed above suggest, many writers from the past

who are new to the canon, especially women and minority writers (Native Americans, blacks, Chicanos, Asian-Americans, and others). They are represented generously in both Volumes I and II, but not at the sacrifice of writers who have long had a place in the canon, such as the familiar nineteenth-century traditional poets William Cullen Bryant, Henry Wadsworth Longfellow, John Greenleaf Whittier, Oliver Wendell Holmes, James Russell Lowell, and even the less familiar Jones Very and Frederick Goddard Tuckerman. *Heritage* is organized in such a way as to make possible a variety of approaches by the reader. For example, such central nineteenth-century writers as Edgar Allan Poe, Nathaniel Hawthorne, Herman Melville, Ralph Waldo Emerson, Walt Whitman, and Emily Dickinson are represented fully enough to satisfy those who wish to concentrate on the major writers in their approach. For the modernist period, although numerous poets, novelists, and essayists are represented, copious space is reserved for such leading figures in poetry as Ezra Pound, T. S. Eliot, Robert Frost, Wallace Stevens, William Carlos Williams, Marianne Moore, Hart Crane, and Langston Hughes, and in fiction for Willa Cather, Sherwood Anderson, Katherine Anne Porter, Jean Toomer, F. Scott Fitzgerald, William Faulkner, Ernest Hemingway, John Steinbeck, and Eudora Welty.

3. *Integrity of Individual Selections. Heritage of American Literature* has opted for novellas and one-act plays over space-gulping novels and full-length plays in the conviction that, in a literary survey, variety is of the essence. Thus Stephen Crane's *Maggie: A Girl of the Streets*, Willa Cather's "Neighbour Rosicky," William Faulkner's "Spotted Horses," Saul Bellow's "A Silver Dish," Carson McCullers's *Ballad of the Sad Café*, and John Updike's "Pigeon Feathers" are all included. By presenting only one-act dramas, *Heritage* offers more dramatists than any other anthology of American literature, including Susan Glaspell, Eugene O'Neill, Thornton Wilder, Tennessee Williams, Arthur Miller, Edward Albee, and Sam Shepard. *Heritage* includes no excerpts of novels for the sake of sampling, but rather chooses whole works in the belief that only a work in its totality can offer a genuine experience on which to base a critical or value judgment. Wherever possible, *Heritage* adopts the same approach to poems, and thus includes the whole not only of T. S. Eliot's *The Waste Land*, but also of Ezra Pound's *Hugh Selwyn Mauberley*, William Carlos Williams's *Desert Music*, Allen Tate's "Ode to the Confederate Dead," Robert Lowell's "for the Union Dead," and Charles Wright's *Tattoos*.

4. *Supportive Editorial Apparatus*. All of the introductions, biographies, headnotes, and footnotes in *Heritage* are aimed at assisting students in the reading and understanding of literary texts. Enough history, social and political background, and literary currents and movements are covered in the six section introductions to clarify questions that naturally arise out of the selections. For example, it is important to understand something of the nature of Calvinism as carried to America by the Puritans in order to comprehend Cotton Mather, Jonathan Edwards, and even Benjamin Franklin. A similar understanding of the nature of naturalism as it was discussed in Stephen Crane's day is useful to the reading of *Maggie: A Girl of the Streets*. The introductions are thus meant to support and enhance the reader's experience of the literature. The biographies serve the same purpose: the personal lives of the authors are dealt with fully and frankly, but focus is generally on the aesthetic or artistic ideas and principles espoused by the writers. Often these theories or notions help in the understanding of a work far more than details of the writer's daily life. When a work seems to assume or demand some background before beginning the reading, *Heritage* provides a comprehensive headnote—as, for example, in the case of Benjamin

Franklin's *Autobiography*, T. S. Eliot's *The Waste Land*, and Hart Crane's *The Bridge*. Commentary by authors on specific stories, poems or essays — sometimes on whole works, sometimes on particular lines, stanzas, characters, or events — may be found in headnotes or footnotes. Footnotes themselves, defining, explaining, or clarifying, have been supplied in quantity to be sure that they are there when they are wanted. In short, the editorial apparatus is included to be used when it is needed by a reader determined to experience the literary selections to the full.

Note on Titles, Texts, Dates, and Headnotes: Titles of selections are originals as bestowed by the authors except for those in brackets, which have been supplied by the editor. Texts of some selections from the seventeenth and eighteenth centuries, identified in each instance, have been modernized in spelling, punctuation, and syntax, either by the editors of editions reprinted here or by the editor of this anthology. Omissions from texts are indicated by ellipses. The dates of first publication are listed after selections to the right; if more than one date is found in this position, the first indicates the year of magazine publication and the second date indicates the first appearance in book form; the dates of composition, if they are known, are placed after the selections to the left; exceptions to this pattern of dating are indicated with the texts. Headnotes are flagged by the appearance of a dingbat (❧).

Heritage of American Literature has, in a sense, been forty years in the making. I had my first experience with the survey of American literature while a student at the University of Oklahoma (1939–42). When I left the University of Chicago with my graduate degrees and started my academic career at the University of Michigan in 1949, I began to teach both halves of the survey of American literature, and when I went to the University of Nebraska in 1953, I continued to teach the survey. Moreover, I taught the survey abroad, in Italy, Japan, and France. When, coming full circle, I returned to the University of Chicago in 1962, I again taught the survey, and this very year I have taught American literature from the Civil War (Whitman) to the present (Pynchon).

Many years ago, I began a plan for compiling an anthology of American literature, but the idea was set aside for other more pressing projects. I decided to return to the notion of making an anthology some five years ago because I suddenly had a yearning to see the field in its totality or wholeness, and in depth, as I had once glimpsed it years ago as a graduate student. The making of this anthology has been a kind of return to intellectual roots and a labor of academic love. In creating it, I began to remember my graduate courses in American literature at the University of Chicago with Professors Walter Blair, Napier Wilt, and Robert Streeter. Something of their eclecticism, pragmatism, common sense, and humor have helped shape the project.

But *Heritage of American Literature* has the stamp of my particular perspective on it throughout. By sheer force of will, I turned myself into a generalist, absorbing what I could from the scholarship and criticism of others, but always coming back in the end to my own feelings, sensibility, and field of vision. I began with the conviction that an anthology created from beginning to end out of a single, continuous, and coherent point of view — that is, my own — would have its own value. I have finished the anthology with that conviction intact.

To express gratitude to all of those who have in some way contributed to the making of this anthology would require me to write my autobiography. This I cannot do. But I can name those who have been most immediately helpful. They belong (or belonged) to the editorial and production staff of Harcourt Brace Jovanovich—Paul Nockleby, Bill McLane, Karen Allanson, Robert Watrous, Eleanor Garner, Don Fujimoto, Diane Southworth, Michael Kleist, Pat Gonzalez, Diana Reynolds, Candy Young, and Diane Pella. My thanks go also to those reviewers who provided valuable critiques of this anthology—Thomas Buell, Portland State University; Philip Furia, University of Minnesota; Frank Hodgins, University of Illinois, Urbana; Virginia M. Kouidis, Auburn University; Jerome Loving, Texas A & M University; Mitchel E. Summerlin, John C. Calhoun State Community College; and Patricia Lee Yongue, University of Houston. My collaborator and constant assistant, Kathleen Farley, has helped at every turn and crisis in the project, and has offered emotional support as well as technical assistance throughout. She has thus earned her place on the title page. In an enterprise as complicated and vast as this one, it would be absurd to claim for myself all the anthology's merits; but it would be equally absurd to imply that the blemishes belong to anyone else but myself.

JAMES E. MILLER, JR.
1990

CONTENTS

PART I

INNOVATIONS AND NEW DEPARTURES: CIVIL WAR TO THE FIRST WORLD WAR (1865–1914)

ADRIFT IN A STRANGE WORLD

After living through a trial by fire in the Civil War (1861–65), America felt it had passed triumphant through a supreme test and emerged with a new sense of itself and its place in the world. Walt Whitman spoke of what the Civil War revealed "as by flashes of lightning, with emotional depths . . . sounded and arous'd." He thought of the war as the "real parturition years (more than 1776–'83) of this henceforth homogeneous Union." James Russell Lowell represented a widespread view when he depicted the war as resolving any doubt about America's place as an equal among the world's great nations:

> Who now shall sneer?
> Who dare again to say we trace
> Our lines to a plebeian race?

Henry Adams spoke for most Americans when he said of himself and his associates that, after the war, they found themselves "set adrift in a world they would find altogether strange."

Assuming itself to have achieved a new maturity through the ordeal of the war, America went on a spree of self-exploitation. Hardheaded, rugged individualism permeated every level of the American social structure. On the intellectual level this philosophy was the fulfillment of Ralph Waldo Emerson's call for "Self-Reliance"; on the practical level the philosophy was warped into a rationalization for the grossest kinds of self-indulgence and even outright, if legalized, thievery. The "robber barons" were accumulating staggering fortunes that their descendants would spend their lives giving away. It was inevitable that historians would dub the period "The Gilded Age," after the 1873 novel by Mark Twain and Charles Dudley Warner, about the post–Civil War explosion of energy concentrated in the drive to accumulate great private wealth. Showman P. T. Barnum expressed a prevailing view: "Money-getters are the benefactors of the human race."

Some fifty years or so after the Civil War, America would emerge from the First World War universally recognized as a world power. This period witnessed the transformation of the country from an agrarian to an industrial society, with all the problems and possibilities that such a society inevitably entails. In 1869, the transcontinental railroad was completed, linking America by rail from the Atlantic to the Pacific. The massive dynamo, able to convert mechanical into electric energy, was displayed at the Columbian Exposition in Chicago in 1893 as the symbol of the miraculous new power for a new age. By the end of this period, the population of the country had tripled, to some 106,000,000. The westward movement had scattered settlements all the way to the Pacific shore, and the great plains and deserts had been carved into governable segments. The number of states within the Union increased to forty-eight, stretching between the two great oceans.

THE POLITICAL SCENE

The Civil War, along with the assassination of Abraham Lincoln in April 1865, just as the war was drawing to a close, left the country physically and emotionally exhausted. Lincoln alive had been a controversial figure. After his death there was almost universal recognition of his genius in preserving the Union and ending slavery. His achievement left a deep imprint on the country's psyche. Those who succeeded him in the presidency for the next two decades, all Republicans, left little imprint at all.

Andrew Johnson (1865–69), Lincoln's vice president from Tennessee, was scandalously drunk at his inaugural ceremony; and he was almost thrown out of office by a vindictive Congress when he tried to carry out Lincoln's conciliatory reconstruction policies. Ulysses S. Grant (1869–77) came into the office of the presidency with all the prestige of his great military victories; by the conclusion of his two terms, his reputation had been sullied by the extensive graft and corruption of his administration, even though he himself remained innocent of wrongdoing. Rutherford B. Hayes (1877–81), another general of the Union Army, entered office with fewer popular votes than his opponent and his final majority of one electoral vote was ambiguous if not fraudulent. Hayes gave way to James A. Garfield (1881), still another Union Army general; his assassination only a few months after his election brought Vice President Chester A. Arthur (1881–85) into the presidency. With a reputation as a political hack, Arthur surprised everyone after taking office, not by his mediocrity (which was confirmed), but by his restrained honesty.

Democrat Grover Cleveland's election to the presidency in 1885 ended the line of continuous Republican presidencies. Cleveland was a reform president, opposing the machine politics of the big cities and attacking the spoils system by reforming the civil service; he was the most impressive national leader during this somewhat dry period in American politics. In his bid for reelection against Benjamin Harrison, he won the popular vote but lost in the electoral college. Harrison (1889–93) was conscientious but lacked the force to resist the greedy machine politicians of the Republican party who had helped elect him and who were eager for the spoils of victory. Cleveland defeated Harrison in a renewed contest and won a second term as president (1893–97). By the time Cleveland assumed office again, the country was experiencing one of its worst depressions, accompanied by much civil unrest and many strikes. When he called out federal troops to intervene in the Pullman strike of 1894, Cleveland aroused the hostility of labor. By the end of his second four years in office, he had lost the support of his own party.

In the election of 1896, Republican William McKinley, popularly known as an ardent protectionist and author in Congress of the McKinley Tariff Act of 1890, was pitted against Democrat William Jennings Bryan, known for his populist agrarian views and his advocacy of the free coinage of silver (as against maintaining a "gold standard"). McKinley won by his tactic of refusing to debate the eloquent Bryan and by holding a series of interviews on the front porch of his home. And as was predictable, his administration supported the mercantile and imperialistic interests of his backers. He led the country into the Spanish-American War of 1898.

In 1895, Cuba had rebelled against Spanish rule. The sinking of an American battleship, the U.S.S. *Maine*, in Havana harbor in 1898 gave America an excuse for intervention. Theodore Roosevelt (then Assistant Secretary of War) led his "Rough Riders" up San Juan Hill in Cuba for a key battle victory. And half a world away in the Philippines, U.S. troops attacked and defeated the Spanish. In the end, the Spanish fleet was destroyed, and America had established itself as an imperialistic power. The war fever inspired both patriotism and protest; the latter took literary form in such works as William Vaughn Moody's bitterly satiric "On a Soldier Fallen in the Philippines."

McKinley was elected to a second term, but his assassination shortly after his second inauguration in 1901 brought into office Vice President Theodore (Teddy) Roosevelt. Roosevelt distinguished himself in the presidency by reversing many of the policies of his predecessor Republicans. He denounced "malefactors of great wealth," initiated an era of "trust-busting," promoted regulations of corporations, railroads, and banks, and supported measures for the conservation of much of America's unspoiled lands and parks. After serving an additional term to which he was elected "in his own right," Roosevelt was succeeded by William Howard Taft (1909–13). Although Taft had vowed to continue Roosevelt's progressive policies, after taking office he appeared to lapse into the conservative ways of the old guard Republicans, supporting a protective tariff and bungling the conservation program initiated by Roosevelt.

Sixteen years of Republican rule came to an end when the Democrats recaptured the presidency with Woodrow Wilson (1913–21), primarily because two candidates, Roosevelt (running as a Progressive) and Taft, split the Republican vote. It was Wilson's fate, like Lincoln's, to preside over a nation at war. When the First World War broke out in 1914, Wilson set a course determined to keep America neutral, and it remained so in spite of German provocations. Wilson won reelection in 1916 on the slogan, "He kept us out of war." But in 1917, in the face of Germany's submarine attacks on American ships, Wilson called for a declaration of war that would "make the world safe for democracy." Although it did not achieve that purpose, the war did bring an end to one era and gave birth to another, radically different.

THE SOCIAL SCENE

The latter half of the nineteenth century witnessed the creation of a number of great family fortunes, some of them familiar today through their legacy of such institutions as Carnegie public libraries and the Rockefeller Foundation. Andrew Carnegie (1835–1919) built his steel empire, which he sold to United States Steel Corporation in 1901 for $250,000,000. John D. Rockefeller (1839–1937) acquired his vast oil kingdom (his personal fortune had reached $1 billion by 1911). James Fisk (1834–1872) and Jay Gould (1836–1892) manipulated the stock market to take over control of many of the principal railroad lines and attempted to corner the gold market, causing the Black Friday panic of September 24, 1869.

At the same time that these rugged individualists battled each other for control over the nation's wealth, vast numbers of people failed to earn their daily bread. Successive depressions made life not only hard but sometimes desperate for laborers and farmers. The financial panic of 1873, brought on by wild speculation in railroad construction, led to the bloody railroad strike of 1877. The depression of 1884–87 reached its peak of violence in the Chicago Haymarket Riot of 1886. A strike at the McCormick Harvester Company led to a struggle between strikers and police in which a number of workers were killed or wounded; next day at a protest rally, a bomb was thrown into the police ranks, killing seven and injuring many more. The judge was unable to find those guilty of the actual deed, but he sentenced seven "rioters" to death for inciting the killing. The financial slump that began in 1893, following collapse of the stock market caused by European withdrawal of investments in the United States, led to a railroad strike which President Cleveland suppressed by the use of U.S. troops.

No social programs, and little governmental concern, existed for the down and out, the unemployed, the homeless. Jane Addams (1860–1935) and an associate opened Hull House in Chicago in 1889, a pioneer "settlement house" providing social services for the poor. Addams, in her *Twenty Years at Hull-House* (1910), gave an account of the conditions of the time by focusing on individual episodes to which she had been an eyewitness, as in the following: "The . . . lack of organization among the charitable forces of the city was painfully revealed in that terrible winter after the World's Fair [the Columbian Exposition of 1893], when the general financial depression throughout the country was much intensified in Chicago by the numbers of unemployed stranded at the close of the exposition. When the first cold weather came the police stations and the very corridors of the city hall were crowded by men who could afford no other lodging."

Paralleling the unstable, often manipulated economic life of the country was a rising interest, among those who suffered in the recurrent depressions, in banding together for strength. During this era, great and powerful labor and farm organizations came into existence, precarious at first but gradually consolidated. The Noble Order of the Knights of Labor, created by the garment workers of Philadelphia in 1869, led a fragile existence for a time but resulted in the founding of the Federation of Organized Trades and Labor Unions in Pittsburgh in 1881 and the organization of the American Federation of Labor (AFL) in Columbus, Ohio, in 1886. Samuel Gompers (1850–1924), president of the AFL from its founding until his death (except for 1895), became the first major labor leader of the country.

In 1867 the Patrons of Husbandry was founded under federal government sponsorship; out of this organization grew the local Granges, numbering some 20,000 by 1875. The Granges assisted the farmers in banding together in their own interest to fight monopolies and sponsored cooperative stores of various kinds. By 1880, the Grange movement having spent a good deal of its force, the Farmers Alliance came to the fore. More directly political, the Alliance reached the peak of its power in 1890 when it became the Populist party, polling over 1,000,000 votes in the 1892 election. But as an agrarian political movement that had failed to attract the sympathy of industrial centers, the Populists were doomed to disintegration, many of them turning to the Democrats and their 1896 candidate, William Jennings Bryan (1860–1925).

In his influential and popular economic treatise *The Theory of the Leisure Class* (1899), Thorstein Veblen asserted that the medieval division of classes still prevailed, with a lower class laboring in industry and an exploitive leisure class in control and practicing "conspicuous consumption." This period saw the emergence of a consumer society together with the rise of advertising, described by historian Daniel J. Boorstin as the "most characteristic, and most remunerative form of American literature." Palace-like department stores—Wanamaker's of Philadelphia, Lord and Taylor of New York, Marshall Field's of Chicago—were built to display goods, gadgets, and baubles in glittering settings. Sears, Roebuck and Company (1893) built a vast mail-order business, reaching rural markets with their catalogues, known as the "Farmer's Bible," and guaranteeing "satisfaction or your money back."

The literature of this period naturally reflected the materialistic conquests, the pathos of poverty, and the social unrest. The popular novelist Horatio Alger, Jr., following the pattern Benjamin Franklin had established in his *Autobiography* (reissued in 1867 in a definitive edition), described the way from "rags to riches" in an outpouring of books for boys in his *Ragged Dick Series* (1867), *Luck and Pluck Series* (1869), and *Tattered Tom Series* (1871). Novelists like Hamlin Garland, Frank Norris, Stephen Crane, and Theodore Dreiser were, by the end of the century, portraying the debasement and dehumanization of the downtrodden and the poor. Theodore Dreiser wrote of the ruthless tycoon in such novels as *The Financier* (1912) and *The Titan* (1914). Frank Norris, in his "Epic of Wheat" (*The Octopus*, 1901; *The Pit*, 1903) exposed the tooth-and-claw nature of the forces speculating on and profiting from this "staff of life" itself, exerting control over production, marketing, and consumption. Hamlin Garland portrayed the brutalizing nature of scrabble-farm drudgery in *Main Travelled Roads* (1891), while Stephen Crane explored the degradation of the city's poor in *Maggie: A Girl of the Streets* (1893).

THE LURE OF THE FRONTIER

During the first half of the nineteenth century, America was busy adding immense continental land areas to its territory; during the second half, Americans were busy settling those lands. The frontier had always acted as a social safety valve, luring the excess population to a new beginning in the wilderness. But, of course, America had been a frontier from the very start, and its history up to the close of the nineteenth century had been the story of the steady taming of the wilderness across the continent, from the Atlantic to the Pacific. The population figures soared to unprecedented heights as immigrants were encouraged to help conquer the forests and prairies, mountains and deserts. In 1800 there were about 5,300,000 Americans; by 1900 there were almost 76,000,000. During this same period, urban population rose from 16 to 30 percent of the total. Great cities like Detroit, Cleveland, and Chicago sprouted in America's heartland.

The closing of the frontier was quietly announced in 1890 by the Superintendent of the Census: "Up to and including 1880 the country had a frontier of settlement, but at present the unsettled area has been so broken into isolated bodies of settlement that there can hardly be said to be a frontier line. In the discussion of its extent, its westward movement, etc., it cannot, therefore, any longer have a place in the census report." In 1893 the historian Frederick Jackson Turner published "The Frontier in American History," the first of his essays assessing the impact of the frontier on the development and shaping of America. The Turner frontier thesis asserted essentially that the recurring necessity for "civilization" to establish and create institutions anew at each advance into the western wilderness gave America its unique and distinctive qualities.

There was an important reason for those "isolated bodies of settlement" in the West mentioned in the census report. The pioneers on the way to California looked at the grass-covered Great Plains as dreary stretches to cross rapidly. But the discovery was made that those wild grasses were a veritable gold mine in cattle feed. Whereas in the East, feed for cattle was a costly harvest, in the West it grew miraculously free of charge. Soon the area was teeming with entrepreneurs, cattle, and cowboys. The longhorns of Texas thrived on the prairie grass. Up north, the Union Pacific Railroad was completed into Wyoming after the Civil War, and Cheyenne was suddenly a boom town. Moving the cattle north to the railroad required cowboys to ride herd during long and arduous cattle drives threatened by predatory animals, rustlers, and Indians. The cattle were then shipped to the stockyards of Chicago, which became the beef and "hog butcher for the world" (as Carl Sandburg was later to write). From Chicago the meat was sent in Gustavus Swift's refrigerated railway cars to the East. Thus was born the lore of the cowboy and the "lone prairie," which was to supply the American imagination with some of its most enduring legends, images, and myths, all embodied in countless ballads, stories, and films.

THE LURE OF EUROPE

The lure of the frontier was counterbalanced in part by the lure of Europe. The voyage across the Atlantic was frequently made by Americans in search of culture or adventure. If the frontier acted as a safety valve in offering to the poor a new beginning, Europe was especially alluring to the well-to-do, particularly those newly rich searching for something money had not been able to buy at home. Many of the ultrarich tried to buy and bring back to America the European past. The most notorious latter-day example is William Randolph Hearst (1863–1951), on whom Orson Welles (1915–1985) based his classic movie *Citizen Kane* (1941). Hearst collected antique furniture, art objects, and even entire rooms from old monastaries to install in his palatial San Simeon estate overlooking the Pacific in California. Both Mark Twain and Henry James made the "international theme" their own, Twain by caricaturing it for comic purposes, James by probing deeply its serious revelations about national character.

In *The Innocents Abroad; or, The New Pilgrim's Progress* (1869), Twain wrote an account of a tour of Europe and the Holy Land by a group of American "pilgrims" sailing on the *Quaker City*. Over and over again, Twain found himself underwhelmed when the European guides showed off their most awesome sights, works of art, or religious relics. The latter he found particularly troublesome: "We find a piece of the true cross in every old church we go into, and some of the nails that held it together. I would like to be positive, but I think we have seen as much as a keg of nails." And he found Italy's celebrated Lake Como less impressive than America's Lake Tahoe on the Nevada-California Line.

Unlike Twain, James had come to know Europe as a boy from the time he travelled there with his family. Later he lived in France and Italy for periods of time, and finally settled in England. He made the "international theme" his own in such works as *The American* (1877), "Daisy Miller" (1879), *The Portrait of a Lady* (1881), and *The Ambassadors* (1903). In these and other stories and novels, James transplanted his hero or heroine to a European setting, where the American's personal naiveté and social informality contrasted sharply with the European's personal shrewdness and social sophistication. Whatever superiority the Europeans enjoyed in these encounters, the Americans nevertheless emerged in subtle ways as somehow freer, more beguilingly innocent, and fresher in spirit.

James was not the only American writer to live abroad. Before him James Fenimore Cooper and Washington Irving spent many years in Europe, writing some of their most popular books there. Even Nathaniel Hawthorne spent time as U.S. consul in Liverpool, England, and later lived in Italy where he found the materials for his last novel, *The Marble Faun* (1860), portraying Americans in Rome. When Hawthorne later wrote about England, he entitled the work, significantly, *Our Old Home* (1863). James's friends, Constance Fenimore Woolson and Edith Wharton, both settled in Europe, the first in Italy, the second in France, and both continued productive literary careers there, often treating in their fiction some aspect of the "international theme."

THE THEORY OF EVOLUTION

In 1859 the English naturalist Charles Darwin (1809–1882) published *On the Origin of Species by Means of Natural Selection, or the Preservation of Favoured Races in the Struggle for Life*. The ultimate impact of the book intellectually, theologically, and emotionally was incalculable. The theory of Copernicus (1473–1543) as confirmed by Galileo (1564–1642) and elaborated in a system of cosmic laws by Newton (1642–1727) had wrought an earlier intellectual revolution forcing humankind to abandon the idea that they and their world were at the center of the cosmos. As it had been startling to discover that humanity was on a relatively insignificant planet revolving about a minor star in one of innumerable galaxies of the universe, so it was alarming to discover from Darwin that human origins were not from divinity but from the primordial oceans of the far distant past, and that our close relations were not the angels but the apes. The connection with God was becoming very remote indeed, and it sometimes seemed that science was religion's enemy.

The fundamentalists were not won over easily. As late as 1925 at the famous Scopes trial in Tennessee, William Jennings Bryan won the fundamentalist's case against the teacher who had taught evolution in the public schools. And even as late as 1988, the Supreme Court had to rule that "creationism" did not deserve equal time in the schools alongside the theory of evolution. Clearly the "great agnostic" Robert Ingersoll (1833–1899) did not make much headway in his extended campaign for a rationalistic look at the Bible in such lectures as "Some Mistakes of Moses" (1879) and "Superstition" (1898).

It was the British philosopher Herbert Spencer (1820–1903) who transfigured Darwin's scientific theory into a comprehensive evolutionary philosophy, coining the term "survival of the fittest." As man had evolved biologically, so he had developed socially, economically, politically, psychologically, progressing ever and always toward greater complexity and harmony. Spencer asserted, "Progress is not an accident but a necessity. What we call evil and immorality must disappear. . . . Always towards perfection is the mighty movement—towards a complete development and a more unmixed good." While Thomas Huxley (1825–1895) became the great exponent of evolution in England, John Fiske (1842–1901), in such works as *The Outline of Cosmic Philosophy* (1874), spread the views of Darwin and Spencer on this side of the Atlantic. And the idea of an inevitable progression turned up in literature in such works as Whitman's "Song of the Universal" (1876) where it was called "mystic evolution":

> Out of the bulk, the morbid and the shallow,
> Out of the bad majority, the varied countless frauds of men and states,
> Electric, antiseptic yet, cleaving, suffusing all,
> Only the good is universal.

Whitman in some sense served as a bridge between the transcendentalism of the early part of the century and the philosophy of evolution in the latter half. Whitman's vision of cosmic evolution together with the social Darwinians' views of perfectibility provided an alternative optimism, however mild, to the pessimism felt by those who, because of the discoveries of Darwin, had lost all faith in traditional religion.

VARIETIES OF DETERMINISM: CALVINISM AND NATURALISM

By the end of the nineteenth century, a belief astonishingly close to the determinism of Calvinism came into fashion. In the eighteenth century, Calvinism had declined and faded, or simply fallen apart like the one-hoss-shay in Oliver Wendell Holmes's "The Deacon's Masterpiece." The Age of Reason had raised great objections to Calvinism, one of which was that in its doctrine of the elect, an individual was not granted free will and self-determination. Individuals ought to have, indeed must have, control over their own fate—or so the age had reasoned.

When examining the self and society in the late 1800s in attempts to diagnose the devastating illnesses besetting both, novelists like France's proponent of naturalism, Émile Zola, found themselves again and again confronted with the dark conclusion that individuals had little control over their destiny, that they were caught in a "system" which evolved blindly and ruthlessly without regard for human beings. Those like the latter-day Transcendentalist Walt Whitman or the social Darwinian Herbert Spencer, who found their way to a belief in mystic or creative evolution, were led into a kind of determinism, an optimistic determinism that led onward and upward to perfection or toward universal good. The determinism of the American novelists sometimes labelled "naturalists"—Frank Norris, Stephen Crane, Theodore Dreiser—whether economic or social, biological or cosmic, was pessimistic in tone and essence. The Calvinists had God; the mystic evolutionists had a future ideal; for the pessimistic determinists there was nothing.

It may surprise some readers, familiar only with the early Mark Twain of *Tom Sawyer* and *Huckleberry Finn*, to find that probably the best literary example of this kind of determinism is Twain's later work. When Twain was once asked to describe the turning point of his life, he kept going back in time from event to event until he reached the Garden of Eden and the constitution of Adam's temperament. Along the way, Twain described the inability of individuals to control their lives:

> Circumstances do the planning for us all, no doubt, by the help of our temperaments. I see no difference between a man and a watch, except that the man is conscious and a watch isn't, and the man *tries* to plan things and the watch doesn't. The watch doesn't wind itself and doesn't regulate itself—these things are done exteriorly. Outside influences, outside circumstances, wind the *man* and regulate him. Left to himself, he wouldn't get regulated at all, and the sort of time he would keep would not be valuable. Some rare men are wonderful watches, with gold cases, compensation balance, and all those things, and some men are only simple and sweet and humble Waterburys. I am a Waterbury. A Waterbury of that kind, some say.

Envisioning man as a mechanical watch is indeed a far cry from viewing him as the center of the universe, related to the angels. The determinists often pictured the individual or the universe in mechanical terms. Nature was no longer the benevolent gift of God but an alien and indifferent force. In Stephen Crane's "The Open Boat" (1897), in the struggle to survive after being cast adrift at sea, one of the characters muses about "the serenity of nature amid the struggles of the individual—nature in the wind, and nature in the vision of men. She did not seem cruel to him then, nor beneficent, nor treacherous, nor wise. But she was indifferent, flatly indifferent." Frank Norris, Jack London, Theodore Dreiser, and other novelists of the time share with Crane the vision of overpowering and uncontrollable forces shaping human destiny.

MODES OF PESSIMISM: ENERGY AND ENTROPY

Henry Adams, who could count two presidents among his ancestors, was an indefatigable searcher for the meaning of history and human experience. It is perhaps significant that, with all his family and personal endowment, with all his brilliance and achievement, he was one of the deepest pessimists of the age. Adams's search through history led him to the Middle Ages, which he described in *Mont-Saint-Michel and Chartres* (1904) as having a significant unity long since lost to modern man. In *The Education of Henry Adams* (1907), a spiritual and psychological autobiography, Adams gradually formulated his basic concept of history, not as a sequence of men, of societies, of time, or of thought, but as a "sequence of force." Through such a theory he was able to link in a meaningful way the earlier worship of the Virgin with the contemporary worship of the dynamo.

In a little-known work, "A Letter to American Teachers of History," published in 1910 (and reprinted in *The Degradation of the Democratic Dogma*, 1919), Adams sounded the alarm to fellow historians by pointing to their ignorance of developments in physics that would radically alter their concept of history. He cited the publication in 1852 of William Thomson's "On a Universal Tendency in Nature to the Dissipation of Mechanical Energy," a work that traced out the consequences of the "second law of thermodynamics." In effect this "law" codified the "universal tendency to the dissipation of mechanical energy" in the "material world"; the code word for this process was "entropy." The law thus undermined the relevance of the physical law (postulated by Newton) of the conservation of energy (energy could be transformed but never lost); the new law simply pointed out that such energy, though it might never be lost, would become unusable. By proclaiming the reality of entropy and thus foreseeing a time when the earth would be "unfit for habitation," Adams said, Thomson had "tossed the universe into the ash-heap." Moreover, he saw the applicability of this law of "dissipation" or "degradation" in social and political spheres—leading to stasis (or paralysis) in human relations, organizations, and structures. Adams went on to point out that those social Darwinians, who saw in the "survival of the fittest" the eternal improvement of humankind and society, had not reckoned with entropy, which suggested the precise opposite.

Adams seems not to have had much impact on his fellow historians. But his pessimism constitutes a link with the literature of a later period—particularly post–Second World War fiction. Thomas Pynchon, first with his short story "Entropy" (1960) and then with a series of novels, including *The Crying of Lot 49* (1966), brought the word and its doomsday vision into fiction. And it has recurred increasingly in contemporary fiction and criticism. Pynchon has cited, among others, Henry Adams as a writer who influenced his work.

THE PHILOSOPHY OF PRAGMATISM

Pragmatism, introduced in the 1870s by the philosopher Charles S. Peirce, seems in some respects a natural outgrowth of the philosophy of evolution, but certainly without the implied determinism of some of the evolutionary theories. Pragmatism is a down-to-earth, commonsense philosophy created in part out of a reaction against the intuitive philosophy of transcendentalism, largely a spent force by the latter nineteenth century. Pragmatism seemed much more responsive to the practical, hardheaded times than idealistic philosophy. But this new commonsense philosophy shared with transcendentalism an emphasis on such so-called American traits as self-reliance, individuality, curiosity, and even a certain kind of practicality.

Pragmatism was codified as a philosophy by William James in *Pragmatism: A New Name for Some Old Ways of Thinking* (1907). The pragmatists conceived truth not as absolute and fixed, as had the transcendentalists, but as relative and dynamic. Truth was, to put it bluntly, what worked. The test of the value of any theory was its application. James conceived pragmatism as a great mediator among philosophic systems. "The pragmatic method," he wrote,

> is primarily a method of settling metaphysical disputes that otherwise might be interminable. Is the world one or many?—fated or free?—material or spiritual?—here are notions either of which may or may not hold good of the world; and disputes over such notions are unending. The pragmatic method in such cases is to try to interpret each notion by tracing its respective practical consequences. What difference would it practically make to anyone if this notion rather than that notion were true? If no practical difference whatever can be traced, then the alternatives mean practically the same thing, and all dispute is idle.

It is easy to see how some Europeans would seize upon pragmatism as another example of America's gross materialism. One thinker, Giovanni Papini, asserted that pragmatism was not so much a philosophy as a method of doing without one.

But in spite of its critics, pragmatism flourished and found its way into many facets of American life. John Dewey (1859–1952) was the great propagator. While William James had remained largely in the area of philosophic speculation, Dewey focused on practical problems to benefit mankind and strengthen a democratic society, calling his adaptation of pragmatism "instrumentalism." His influential series of books encompassed almost all the fields of practical affairs, especially education; they include *The School and Society* (1899), *The Child and the Curriculum* (1902), *Moral Principles in Education* (1909), *Democracy and Education* (1916), *Experience and Education* (1938), and *Art as Experience* (1934).

INNOVATIONS IN POETRY

Walt Whitman privately published the first edition of *Leaves of Grass* in 1855, and tradition tells us the day was July 4. This is a legend we ought to believe, for *Leaves of Grass* appears to us today as less imitative and more genuinely native than any body of poetry produced before 1855 in America. By 1881 *Leaves of Grass* had assumed the size and shape we know today. Whitman's poems were like a breath of fresh air let into a room crowded with people in formal attire where the air is slightly stale, faintly perfumed. Whitman himself characterized the poets acclaimed by the age as "dapper little gentlemen from abroad, who flood us with their thin sentiment of parlors, parasols, piano-songs, tinkling rhymes, the five-hundredth importation—or whimpering and crying about something, chasing one aborted conceit after another, and forever occupied in dyspeptic amours with dyspeptic women."

As the modernist poet William Carlos Williams would say later, Whitman broke the dominance of iambic pentameter and brought into being "free verse" (Williams saw it as related to what he termed the "variable foot" of his own verse), proving beyond doubt its immense possibilities. Somehow the liberty of the lines sweeping across the page, the freedom of the verses breaking out of the regularities of rhythm and rhyme and stanzaic patterns, seemed to reinforce his bold outcries and defiant assertions. Taking as his three primary themes democracy, science, and, above all, religion, Whitman wrote poetry about these conventional subjects in a refreshingly unconventional way. And he celebrated the innocence of sex in a number of poems of procreation that he had the courage to defend against attack. His poetic genius quickened in the individual line with its vivid and sometimes startling images seeming to surge up from a teeming unconscious.

While Whitman was sounding his "barbaric yawp" in New York in a succession of published editions of his poetry, Emily Dickinson in her room overlooking the garden in the family house in Amherst, Massachusetts, was jotting down her miniature masterpieces on any scrap of paper that came handy. Dickinson and Whitman, though destined never to read each other, had similar fates in several respects: they were both remarkable—and natural—poetic geniuses, they were both generally ignored in their own time (their reputations as the two greatest American poets of the nineteenth century came in the twentieth), and they both had a powerful impact through their own distinctive styles on modern American poetry.

For reasons not yet entirely clear, Emily Dickinson published only ten poems during her lifetime. The history of her manuscripts and their gradual publication over a sixty-year period is a fascinating tale in itself, and the ending is happy: a definitive edition appeared in 1955, a three-volume collection of some 1,775 poems. If Whitman's lines sweep across the page spilling forth multitudes of meanings, Dickinson's stand between wide margins in the middle of the page, like mysterious runic inscriptions waiting to be deciphered. If Whitman openly cast off all the bonds of regularity, Dickinson more subtly undermined them with her slant rhymes, unconventional syntax, and enigmatic dashes.

Dickinson herself seldom defined or discussed her major themes, except through her poems, and critics have been sorting and searching through them ever since her death. Her first editors in the early 1890s (she died in 1886) grouped her poems under the titles "Life," "Love," "Nature," and "Time and Eternity." And though these subject headings are deficient—after all, what poem is not about life?—they do serve to suggest the range of her curiosity and concern. In one poem, she wrote:

> Tell all the truth but tell it slant—
> Success in Circuit lies
> Too bright for our infirm Delight
> The Truth's superb surprise.

Dickinson's "slant rhymes" often support, and reenforce, the obliqueness of her "slant meanings." Her ubiquitous dashes seem both to connect and to separate elements (cryptic images, metaphors, phrases), frequently offering two or more possible interpretations. Her demands on the reader are not small, but the rewards of probing her poems to their depths are indeed great.

Dickinson has inspired many poets as different as William Carlos Williams, W. H. Auden, and Sylvia Plath, but she has had few successful imitators. The contemporary American novelist Joyce Carol Oates has found perhaps the best explanation: "Emily Dickinson really leads nowhere since she herself is the highest embodiment of the experimental method she developed. Genius of her kind is simply inimitable."

Sidney Lanier in many ways resembles his fellow southerner of the previous age, Edgar Allan Poe. Lanier did not have Poe's macabre imagination, but he did share Poe's fascination for the melody of verse. In his work on prosody, *The Science of English Verse* (1880), Lanier attempted to translate poetic rhythm into musical terms. The relationship between music and poetry had always been one of his primary interests, as revealed by such works as the poem sequence, "The Hymns of the Marshes."

Lanier is at his best in his personal and subtly religious poetry, as in his masterpiece "The Marshes of Glynn." It is the most moving of "The Hymns of the Marshes," and represents a kind of mystic ecstasy as the poet responds with intensity and profundity to the live oaks and the marshes at the ocean's edge. There is a sweep to some of Lanier's lines not unlike Whitman's, but they are almost always richly embroidered, sometimes to the point of excess. There can be no doubt that Lanier had a touch of poetic genius, but beset by long illness and taken by early death, he had neither the energy nor the time to realize his potential.

INNOVATIONS IN FICTION

The most significant development in fiction in this period was the "rise" of realism. The names associated with this development are many, but three stand out above all others: William Dean Howells, Mark Twain, and Henry James. Realism was in part a reaction against romanticism and placed emphasis on the here and now as opposed to the long ago and far away. In the minds of many people, realism was simply the fictional attempt to embody things as they actually are, without distortion or falsification. But both Howells and James realized that to define realism usefully at all required some concept of the nature of reality.

During his lifetime William Dean Howells was probably the most influential of these three novelists in shaping literary opinion in America. As a magazine editor, Howells was in a position, first on *The Atlantic Monthly* and afterward on *Harper's*, to encourage and promote the realistic writers he admired, such as Mark Twain and Henry James. Moreover, Howells formulated in his critical writing a theory of realism that was widely admired. One of the most startling elements of it was Howells's advice to the American realist to dwell on the "more smiling aspects" of life in the United States, inasmuch as these were the norm or average. Howells's practice in encouraging such young writers as Frank Norris and Stephen Crane, and in publishing established realists and naturalists both native and foreign, seems curiously out of line with this dimension of his theory.

In addition to his role as editor and critic, Howells was a prolific novelist, and such novels as *A Modern Instance* (1882) and *The Rise of Silas Lapham* (1885) are widely read today as examples of realism of the time that was attempting, successfully, to treat middle-class American life truthfully. But much of Howells's work appears to us now almost as romantic as it is realistic. Although he was a great proponent of realism during his time, he was, paradoxically, attacked by the later generation of the 1920s as a symbol of the genteel tradition against whose conformity and conventionality he himself had rebelled.

Mark Twain did not, like Howells, have to work at being a realist; he seemed one by instinct. Samuel Langhorne Clemens, like the literary comedians before him, acquired a pen name for himself. Clemens found his name in the Mississippi steamboatman's cry indicating the channel depth. And he also found on the great continental river the basic material for his masterpieces. Never before had there been stories about boys like *The Adventures of Tom Sawyer* (1876) and *Adventures of Huckleberry Finn* (1884). Children in literature had tended to be angelic and goody-goody, sometimes nauseatingly so. Tom and Huck were refreshingly bad and scandalously antiauthoritarian. But of course these novels were more than simply stories about boys. *Huckleberry Finn* especially engaged fundamental moral and social themes, including slavery, in profound ways.

If Twain later was to view the human scene through darker and darker glasses, particularly with his growing belief in a deterministic universe, he was always honest to the world as he saw it. But the later work never reached the heights of *Tom Sawyer, Huckleberry Finn*, or *Life on the Mississippi* (1883; known as *Old Times on the Mississippi* in its shorter and, in ways, better version published in the *Atlantic Monthly* in 1875). All of these works grew out of Twain's remembrance of things as they were on the great river when the boy Clemens was first longing and then learning to be a steamboat pilot.

Henry James was a great fictional theorist not only in his critical essays but particularly in a series of prefaces he wrote for the successive volumes of his collected works (1907–09). Although his literary theory never had as popular an impact as Howells's genial commentary, James's critical works and prefaces have always attracted a devoted and intelligent audience, particularly among novelists themselves. James said that the writer to be realistic (and there was nothing inherently wrong in being romantic) must somehow conform to the sense of the "way things happen." He defined a novel as a "personal, a direct impression of life," preserving in the words *personal* and *direct* the two components (imagination and reality) vital to fiction.

If Howells would limit the subject matter of the realist to a treatment of middle-class or "average" life, James would place no limitation on subject at all. "The house of fiction," he wrote, "has . . . not one window, but a million" and more— all of varying shapes and sizes. James's own fiction tended to portray people endowed with the freedom that wealth gives to face moral and cultural problems on their own terms. Nevertheless, James probed deeply into American culture by transporting his Americans to the European scene.

He probed deeply, too, into the human mind, for in its intricacies he discovered the significant reality. He was close to his older brother, the psychologist-philosopher William James, who produced a pioneer work in his field, *Principles of Psychology*, in 1890; in it he described the concept and coined the term "stream of consciousness." Henry James himself used the term "drama of consciousness" to describe the "center of interest" of many of his novels, especially those of his later phase. Although surpassed in popularity in his time by both Howells and Twain, James came into his own after his death. It is recognized now that in such works as *The Turn of the Screw* (1898), *The Ambassadors* (1903), and *The Golden Bowl* (1904), he moved the novel forward to the edge of the great experiments in psychological fiction of the modernist period.

LOCAL COLOR AND AN EMERGING FEMINIST FICTION

One of the vigorous fictional movements to emerge after the Civil War was dubbed the "local color" movement after its tendency to embody elements that were peculiar to a particular region of the country. In *Crumbling Idols* (1894), Hamlin Garland provided a definition that remains valid today: "Local color in a novel means that it has such quality of texture and back-ground that it could not have been written in any other place or by anyone else than a native." The distinctive elements might be embodied in the dialect of the characters, folklore, superstitions, customs, or features of the landscape. Bret Harte is credited with initiating the form in his stories set in the mining towns of California, with "The Luck of Roaring Camp" in 1868 and "The Outcasts of Poker Flat" in 1869. The stories appeared in *Overland Monthly*, a California regional magazine, and became sensational successes back East, where people were hungry for information about the West.

Soon after, almost every section of the country was appearing in fictional accounts, its distinctive characteristics highlighted or sometimes caricatured. The South was especially adaptable for such portrayal. George Washington Cable began publishing his stories of New Orleans in 1873, bringing out *Old Creole Days* in 1879. And Joel Chandler Harris began printing his Uncle Remus stories in the Atlanta *Constitution*, publishing his first volume, *Uncle Remus: His Songs and Sayings*, in 1880. A northern black writer, Charles Waddell Chesnutt, began to publish short stories featuring a narrator speaking in dialect describing slavery to a northern employer in the 1880s; the stories were brought together in *The Conjure Woman* in 1890.

The nineteenth century saw a tremendous growth in writings by women. So prolific and successful were they by 1855 that Hawthorne felt compelled to dismiss them as "a damned mob of scribbling women." But women writing in the local color tradition were breaking out of the romantic and sentimental molds that had dominated popular fiction, and were at the same time pioneering in an emerging feminist tradition of women's literature. Constance Fenimore Woolson, Sarah Orne Jewett, Kate Chopin, Mary E. Wilkins Freeman, and Charlotte Perkins Gilman began to incorporate a feminist point of view, often subtly, but sometimes quite openly, in their work. Capturing authentic regional details, dialect, and characters, these writers also portrayed a universal condition in women as they struggled for independence amidst hardship or convention.

THE PERSONAL VOICE AND VIEW

The period from the Civil War to the First World War was rich in the literature of the "personal voice and view"—journals, diaries, debates, autobiographies, and essays. In Sarah Winnemucca Hopkins's *Life Among the Piutes* (1883), we experience the effect of the westward expansion on an Indian tribe as she movingly depicts the displacement of the "inheritor" by the "invader." In Alice James's *Diary* (privately published in 1892, and reissued in 1964), we look in on a mind sensitively analyzing her consciousness. Despite her invalid state, she demonstrated that she is indeed a "most interesting being"—"one," in the famous words of her brother Henry James, "on whom nothing is lost."

Two important black autobiographies appeared during this era. The first was *Up from Slavery: An Autobiography* (1901) by Booker T. Washington; the second was *The Souls of Black Folk* (1903) by William E. B. DuBois. These works contained a famous exchange between the two black leaders. Washington's "Atlanta Exposition Address," delivered in 1895, called for blacks to prove themselves worthy of civil rights and social equality first through education and diligence in work. DuBois disputed Washington's general theme in a chapter of his book entitled "Of Mr. Booker T. Washington and Others," which took exception to what DuBois considered a call for black capitulation to white racism.

The historian Henry Adams and the psychologist William James demonstrated the wide-ranging interests of alert and restless minds venturing quite beyond the confines of narrow specialization in works that are fascinatingly if obliquely personal. Adams in "The Dynamo and the Virgin," from his *Education of Henry Adams* (privately printed for limited circulation in 1907), explored the notion of history as the sequence not of individuals, societies, or ideas, but of forces or energies. Adams's comments on the second law of thermodynamics, which tossed "the universe into the ash-heap" (in his "Letter to American Teachers of History," 1910), showed his alarm over the prevailing ignorance among intellectuals about entropy, which foretells a doom for the earth and its inhabitants more bleak than that of medieval visions of the last judgment.

William James in "On a Certain Blindness in Human Beings," from his *Talks to Teachers in Psychology and to Students on Some of Life's Ideals* (1899), dwelt on the narrow perspectives with which all human beings encountered the world and how little they understood of the inner lives of others—all of which was said in the service of James's "pluralistic or individualistic philosophy." The piece is interesting especially in its turning to poets such as Walt Whitman for demonstration of how hermetically sealed the consciousness of one individual can be to another—until it is revealed in a masterwork of literature; great poetry offers a way for the "blindness" to be replaced by insight. In "The Pragmatic Method," from his *Pragmatism* (1907), James offered a simple solution for ending the endless debates over traditional—and insoluble—metaphysical questions.

FICTION AND POETRY IN TRANSITION

At the end of this period appeared a number of important novelists and poets whose work now seems mainly transitional in nature, absorbing the developments of the past and looking toward the achievements that lay ahead. In a variety of unique ways, the works of these writers bridge the gap separating the realism, naturalism, and impressionism of their own period from the modernist experiments that follow, especially in the 1920s. They are sometimes lost in literary history because their work often evades neat classification.

In fact, these writers vary widely in themes, subjects, and techniques. In such works as *Main-Travelled Roads* (1891), Hamlin Garland exposed the brutalizing effects of farm life in the sparse-yielding lands of some areas of the mid-continent. Edith Wharton probed the social conventions of old New York society in such novels as *The House of Mirth* (1905) and *The Age of Innocence* (1920); but she also showed herself adept in treating the "international theme" in such works as *The Custom of the Country* (1913). Jack London seemed to be at his best in portraying primitive life in the Canadian-Alaskan Klondike country, in such novels as *The Call of the Wild* (1903).

The term *naturalism* has been applied to writers as different as Frank Norris, Stephen Crane, and Theodore Dreiser. The term came from France, where it was popularized by Émile Zola (1840–1902), who called for a fiction of scrupulous scientific objectivity and no moral judgment in *Le Roman expérimental* (*The Experimental Novel*, 1880). Naturalistic fiction tended to focus on social outcasts or the downtrodden, including the often sordid street life in the poorest districts of cities. It portrayed nature as neither for nor against but totally indifferent to human life. And it dramatized characters who had no control over their own destiny, but were instead the puppets of an indifferent universe, shaped by psychological, economic, and social forces. This determinism made for a somber and pessimistic fiction.

Although some of these elements turn up in the work of Crane, Dreiser, and Norris, these writers cannot be wholly contained within the narrow prescriptions of naturalism. Crane's *Maggie: A Girl of the Streets* (1893) has been aptly called America's first naturalistic novel; but few critics would agree that labelling *The Red Badge of Courage* (1895) as naturalistic gets at the novel's complex psychological portrait of a soldier in battle. Naturalist elements are to be found in Frank Norris's *McTeague* (1899), but they can hardly account for the poetic sweep and epic vision of his story of wheat in *The Octopus* (1901) and *The Pit* (1903). And similarly, Dreiser's best works—*Sister Carrie* (1900), *The Financier* (1912), and *An American Tragedy* (1925)—contain many of the features we recognize as naturalistic, but these massively detailed accounts of modern life constantly escape from any simplistic naturalistic formula and take on a powerful life of their own.

Just as the novelists of this transitional period prefigured the dark vision of much modernist fiction, so the "transitional" poets foreshadowed the disenchantment and disillusion of much modernist poetry. William Vaughn Moody masked his indignation at the human plight in a sardonic, often bitterly satiric tone in such meditative lyrics as "The Menagerie" (1901), exploring the implications of the Darwinian view of the interrelatedness of animal and human species; although Moody's style is identifiably traditional, his attitudes and concerns are distinctly modern. Edwin Arlington Robinson provided character studies of the isolated and alienated inhabitants of his fictional Tilbury Town in Maine in haunting rhythms—as in "Richard Cory" (1897) and "Miniver Cheevy" (1907). Edgar Lee Masters in his *Spoon River Anthology* (1915) brought back the dead from Spoon River's cemetery to reveal lives lived mostly in spiritual isolation, loneliness, and despair.

Paul Laurence Dunbar and James Weldon Johnson anticipated the revival of black literature during the "Harlem Renaissance" of the late 1920s. In proclaiming (in his poem "Sympathy," 1893), "I know what the caged bird feels," Dunbar found a way for black writers to protest their ostracism and at the same time to impress a wide audience with their literary power. Johnson captured and preserved something vital in the black cultural heritage in recreating the sermons of a Negro preacher, catching the emotional tone and rhythms of the preacher's voice, as in "The Creation" (1920); he demonstrated how the black idiom could be used for purposes other than comic. The tragically short-lived Adelaide Crapsey, in her personally invented short "cinquains" (similar to the Japanese short poetic forms), proved herself an imagist before the appearance of the imagist credo in *Some Imagist Poets* (1915). Her frank treatment of her fatal illness in her poems looked further ahead to the confessional poets who appeared after the Second World War.

Although presented here as transitional figures, all of these poets and novelists stand perfectly well on their own. And in the vitality of their individual works, they are useful reminders that literary periods are artificial, after-the-fact creations, imperfect at best, and at their most mischievous, unduly hard on writers that seem to come before (or after) "their time."

ADDITIONAL READING

SPECIAL STUDIES

Fred Lewis Pattee, *The Development of the American Short Story*, 1923.
Van Wyck Brooks, *New England: Indian Summer*, 1940.
Henry Nash Smith, *Virgin Land: The American West as Symbol and Myth*, 1950.
Henry Steele Commager, *The American Mind: An Interpretation of American Thought and Character Since the 1880s*, 1950.
Charles C. Walcutt, *American Literary Naturalism: A Divided Stream*, 1956.
Richard Chase, *The American Novel and Its Tradition*, 1957.
Roy Harvey Pearce, *The Continuity of American Poetry*, 1961.
Leo Marx, *The Machine in the Garden: Technology and the Pastoral Ideal in America*, 1964.
Tony Tanner, *The Reign of Wonder: Naivety and Reality in American Literature*, 1965.
Warner Berthoff, *The Ferment of Realism, 1884–1919*, 1965.
Donald Pizer, *Realism and Naturalism in Nineteenth-Century American Literature*, 1966.
Larzar Ziff, *The American 1890s: Life and Times of a Lost Generation*, 1966.
Richard Bridgman, *The Colloquial Style in America*, 1966.
Jay Martin, *Harvests of Change: American Literature, 1865–1914*, 1967.
Hyatt H. Waggoner, *American Poets from the Puritans to the Present*, 1968.
Harold Kolb, *The Illusion of Life: American Realism as a Literary Form*, 1969.
Edwin Cady, *The Light of Common Day: Realism in American Fiction*, 1971.
Howard Mumford Jones, *The Age of Energy: Varieties of American Experience, 1865–1915*, 1971.
Daniel Aaron, *The Unwritten War: American Writers and the Civil War*, 1973, 1987.
Daniel Boorstin, *The Americans: The Democratic Experience*, 1973.
Anette Kolodny, *The Lay of the Land: Metaphor as Experience and History*, 1975.
David Perkins, *A History of Modern Poetry: From the 1890s to the High Modernist Mode*, 1976.
Henry Nash Smith, *Democracy and the Novel: Popular Resistance to Classic American Writers*, 1978.
Sandra M. Gilbert and Susan Gubar, *The Madwoman in the Attic: The Woman Writer and the Nineteenth-Century Literary Imagination*, 1979.
T. J. Jackson Lears, *No Place of Grace: Antimodernism and the Transformation of American Culture, 1880–1920*, 1981.
Glen A. Love, *The Westerner and the Modern Experience in the American Novel*, 1982.
Janet Holmgrin McKay, *Narration and Discourse in American Realistic Fiction*, 1982.
Eric J. Sundquist, ed., *American Realism: New Essays*, 1982.
Josephine Donovan, *New England Local Color Literature: A Woman's Tradition*, 1983.
Alfred Kazin, *An American Procession*, 1984.
Sandra M. Gilbert and Susan Gubar, *No Man's Land: The Place of the Woman Writer in the Twentieth Century*, Vol. 1: *The War of Words*, 1988; Vol. 2: *Sexchanges*, 1989.

COMPREHENSIVE HISTORIES

Vernon L. Parrington, *Main Currents in American Thought: An Interpretation of American Literature from the Beginnings to 1920*, 3 vols., 1927–30.
Robert E. Spiller et al., eds., *Literary History of the United States*, 3 vols., 1948, 1953, 1963; bibliographical vol. covering 1958–70, 1972.
Emory Elliott, ed., *Columbia History of the United States*, 1988.

BIBLIOGRAPHIES

James Woodress et al., eds., *Eight American Authors*, 1956, 1963, 1971, 1977.
Robert A. Rees and Earl N. Harbert, eds., *15 American Authors Before 1900*, 1971, rev. 1984.
Jackson R. Bryer, ed., *Fifteen Modern American Authors*, 1969; rev. and updated as *Sixteen Modern American Authors*, 1973.
James Woodress, ed., *American Literary Scholarship: An Annual*, 1963–present (editors after Woodress include Warren French, J. Albert Robbins).

INNOVATIONS
IN POETRY

WALT WHITMAN   SIDNEY LANIER
EMILY DICKINSON

"... I fain confront the fact, the need of powerful native philosophs and orators and bards, these States, as rallying points to come, in times of danger, and to fend off ruin and defection. For history is long, long, long. Shift and turn the combinations of the statement as we may, the problem of the future of America is in certain respects as dark as it is vast. Pride, competition, segregation, vicious wilfulness, and license beyond example, brood already upon us. Unwieldly and immense, who shall hold in behemoth? who bridle leviathan? Flaunt it as we choose, athwart and over the roads of our progress loom huge uncertainty, and dreadful, threatening gloom. It is useless to deny it: Democracy grows rankly up the thickest, noxious, deadliest plants and fruits of all—brings worse and worse invaders—needs newer, larger, stronger, keener compensations and compellers."

Walt Whitman, *Democratic Vistas*

WALT WHITMAN

(1819–1892)

On July 4, 1855, a slender green volume entitled *Leaves of Grass* was published in New York. The author's picture, slouching in shirt sleeves with one hand in a pocket, appeared as frontispiece. But the author's name appeared neither on the cover nor the title page; it was inserted in a line of one of the twelve poems, later to be called "Song of Myself": "Walt Whitman, an American, one of the roughs, a kosmos."

Although that book after achieving full growth would become one of the most celebrated volumes of poetry ever to be published, at birth it created scarcely a ripple. One anonymous reviewer, however, began: "An American bard at last!" The author of this laudatory review (along with others) turned out to be Whitman himself. He christened *Leaves of Grass* as "the great psalm of the republic." With all his braggadocio, he turned out to be not far from the truth.

Walter Whitman was born on a Long Island farm, the second of nine children. Both his mother and father, uneducated people of modest means, had Quaker leanings. Whitman had only a few years of schooling in Brooklyn, where his father worked for a time as a carpenter. Whitman himself worked variously as an office boy, a printer's devil and printer, a rural school teacher, and a carpenter. As a printer, Whitman was connected with several publications and began to contribute stories and poems. It was natural for him to move next into editing, serving on several Long Island and Brooklyn newspapers. In 1842, he published his one novel, *Franklin Evans; or, The Inebriate: A Tale of the Times*, a temperance novel of almost no consequence.

Whitman served as editor of the *Brooklyn Daily Eagle* from 1846 to 1848, a position of considerable consequence for a young man Whitman's age. Much of Whitman's writing was devoted to reviewing books—some 200 of them during this period. But as his views against slavery moved him to support the Free-Soil party (which opposed new states becoming slave states), he found himself at odds with his Democratic paper and lost his position.

Offered a job on the *New Orleans Crescent*, Whitman started out with his brother Jeff on the arduous journey to the thriving southern city in 1848. The trip took him through the heart of America—over the mountains to Cumberland Gap, by boat down the Ohio, and down the great muddy Mississippi to the Gulf of Mexico. He was gone from New York only some six months, but the experience was to be vital to his imaginative grasp of America.

On his return to New York, Whitman tried his hand at several trades, including journalism and carpentry, but he was secretly nourishing deep within himself the embryonic beginnings of what was to become in 1855 *Leaves of Grass*. As he was the book's printer, so he also became its publicist. He sent copies to the famous poets of the day. John Greenleaf Whittier was said to have thrown his copy in the fire in outrage at the book's obscenity.

But Ralph Waldo Emerson was stunned by the book's power and energy. He wrote the unknown author a letter that helped change the course of American literature: "I am not blind to the worth of the wonderful gift of *Leaves of Grass*. I find it the most extraordinary piece of wit and wisdom that America has yet contributed." Whitman clearly was thrilled by these comments from America's most distinguished man of letters. In preparing the format for his 1856 edition of *Leaves of Grass*, including many new poems, he included a line from the letter ("I greet you at the beginning of a great career") on the spine of the book and he published the entire letter in the volume together with a long reply addressed to "Dear Master"—all without asking Emerson's permission.

Emerson's passion chilled, but interest in Whitman's *Leaves* surged. Henry David Thoreau and Bronson Alcott sought Whitman out for a visit. By the time Whitman was ready to bring out his third edition in 1860, he found for the first time a commercial publisher in Boston ready to undertake publication. Whitman went to Boston to read proof, and there went for a walk with Emerson on Boston Commons. Emerson suggested that Whitman drop the sexual poems in his book, especially those gathered into the cluster, "Enfans d'Adam" (later, "Children of Adam"). Whitman listened, and then refused, citing as support Emerson's own doctrine of "self-reliance."

The encounter took place on the eve of the Civil War. Soon Whitman's publisher was bankrupt, and Whitman's life profoundly changed by the war itself. He was too old for combat, but he was sent by the family to the battlefield to find his brother George, wounded in battle. In passing through Washington to get to Virginia, he observed the masses of wounded in the makeshift hospitals. After finding and helping his brother, Whitman decided to remain in Washington in voluntary service of the maimed and dying, filling the role of comforter, comrade, and wound-dresser.

He issued his Civil War poems in 1865 as *Drum-Taps*, and shortly after Abraham Lincoln's assassination in April, added a sequel ("Memories of President Lincoln"). This sequel included the great elegy "When Lilacs Last in the Dooryard Bloom'd." Later these poems were integrated into the one book that Whitman spent a lifetime writing, *Leaves of Grass*. Editions continued to appear throughout Whitman's career—1871 (with the appearance for the first time of "Passage to India"), 1876 (actually a reprint, but known as the Centennial Edition, in two volumes), 1881 (published and banned in Boston and then reissued in Philadelphia), and 1891–92 (known as the "Death-Bed edition" but really a reprint). Throughout this period, Whitman tinkered with texts, shifted poems around, added and dropped passages—shaping a structure that followed the contours of his life and times, creating a new form of American epic with himself as a new kind of epic hero.

"I lean and loafe at my ease observing a spear of summer grass"; "Urge and urge and urge,/ Always the procreant urge of the world"; "Voices of sexes and lusts, voices veil'd and I remove the veil"; "I think I could turn and live with the animals, they're so placid and self-contain'd"; "I am an acme of things accomplish'd, and I an encloser of things to be"; "I tramp a perpetual journey, (come listen all!)"; "I sound my barbaric yawp over the rooftops of the world." These lines and others like them throughout *Leaves of Grass* still give off sparks as they did in Whitman's day, causing Emerson to wonder at Whitman's "long foreground" that made such power possible.

Critics have ransacked Whitman's biography and his times, searching for the secret sources of *Leaves of Grass*'s poetic energy. Whitman's was a time of great oratory, as it was also a period of opulence in opera production (Whitman attended frequently in New York). Whitman's own background encompassed rural and farm life, sea-shore experiences, as well as experiences of the city's "populous pavements." His reading in the Bible, the Hindu sacred texts, Homer, Virgil, and other great national epics left its mark and memory. But finally, Whitman's sources remain a mystery—the mystery of genius.

Whitman was the first to free poetry of the constraints of traditional meters and stanzaic patterns. His ingenious use of free verse, with its own organic rhythms and music, underscored his themes of individuality and brotherhood, freedom and democracy. His sexual themes running throughout *Leaves of Grass* and flashing boldly forth in the "Children of Adam" and "Calamus" clusters inspired both outrage and adulation. Whitman's expansive sexual vision reached to encompass hetero-, homo-, and autosexual feelings, and can only be finally comprehended as omnisexual in nature.

As in his poetry he forged a new style, so in his prose he turned away from conventional journalistic writing to a style that seemed gnarled and entangling, capable of diving to depths and soaring to heights outside the reach of correct and traditional prose. His 1855 Preface to *Leaves of Grass* was a remarkable manifesto setting an agenda for American poetry for years to come. In *Democratic Vistas* (1871) he called for American bards to step forth to counter the gross materialism he feared might be America's doom.

In *Specimen Days* (1882) he offered prose snapshots of his early life, his Civil War experiences, and his later life with its disabling illnesses. In 1873 he suffered two blows—a paralytic stroke and the death of his mother. "Well-begotten, and rais'd by a perfect mother," he had written in "Starting from Paumanok." Forced to find a refuge, he moved from Washington, D.C., to his brother's house in Camden, New Jersey, and later into his own house.

His reputation in England, which dated from 1867 with the publication of a volume of his poems selected by William Michael Rosetti, inspired British writers to seek him out in Camden, including Edward Carpenter, Oscar Wilde, and Edmund Gosse. Although he had strong American supporters such as W. D. O'Connor, whose *Good Gray Poet* appeared in 1866, and John Burroughs, whose *Notes on Walt Whitman* was issued in 1867, Whitman never gained the popular audience he yearned for ("To have great poets, there must be great audiences, too").

After making a final revision of *Leaves of Grass* in 1891 and giving it his imprimatur ("I wish to say that I prefer and recommend this present [edition]"), Whitman seemed prepared for death when it came in 1892. His work had by then been translated into several languages, including French, German, and Italian. And he could look to the future for the ideal reader he had so ardently sought:

> Camerado, this is no book,
> Who touches this touches a man,
> (Is it night? are we here together alone?)
> It is I you hold and who holds you,
> I spring from the pages into your arms—decease calls me forth.

ADDITIONAL READING

The Collected Writings of Walt Whitman, ed. Gay Wilson Allen and Sculley Bradley, 1963–.

Newton Arvin, *Whitman*, 1938; Henry Seidel Canby, *Walt Whitman, An American*, 1943; Robert D. Faner, *Walt Whitman and Opera*, 1951; Gay Wilson Allen, *The Solitary Singer: A Critical Biography of Walt Whitman*, 1955, rev. 1967; Richard Chase, *Walt Whitman Reconsidered*, 1955; James E. Miller, Jr., *A Critical Guide to Leaves of Grass*, 1957; Roger Asselineau, *The Evolution of Walt Whitman*, 2 vols., 1960, 1962; James E. Miller, Jr., *Walt Whitman*, 1962, rev. 1990; Roy Harvey Pearce, ed., *Whitman: A Collection of Critical Essays*, 1962; R. W. B. Lewis, ed., *The Presence of Walt Whitman*, 1962; John C. Broderick, ed., *Whitman the Poet*, 1962; James E. Miller, Jr., *Whitman's "Song of Myself": Origin, Growth, Meaning*, 1964; Edwin H. Miller, *Walt Whitman's Poetry: A Psychological Journey*, 1968; Edwin H. Miller, ed., *A Century of Whitman Criticism*, 1969; Gay Wilson Allen, *A Reader's Guide to Walt Whitman*, 1970; Milton Hindus, ed., *Whitman: The Critical Heritage*, 1971; Joseph Jay Rubin, *The Historic Whitman*, 1973; Arthur Golden, ed., *Walt Whitman: A Collection of Criticism*, 1974; Floyd Stovall, *The Foreground of Leaves of Grass*, 1974; Jerome M. Loving, ed., *Civil War Letters of George Washington Whitman*, 1975; Gay Wilson Allen, *The New Walt Whitman Handbook*, 1975, updated 1986; Randall H. Waldron, *Mattie: The Letters of*

Martha Mitchell Whitman, 1978; James E. Miller, Jr., *The American Quest for a Supreme Fiction: Whitman's Legacy in the Personal Epic,* 1979; Justin Kaplan, *Walt Whitman: A Life,* 1980; Harold Aspiz, *Walt Whitman and the Body Beautiful,* 1980; Betsy Erkkila, *Walt Whitman among the French,* 1980; Jim Perlman, Ed Folson, Dan Campion, eds., *Walt Whitman: The Measure of His Song,* 1981; Jerome Loving, *Emerson, Whitman, and the American Muse,* 1982; C. Carroll Hollis, *Language and Style in Leaves of Grass,* 1983; James Woodress, ed., *Critical Essays on Walt Whitman,* 1983; Paul Zweig, *Walt Whitman: The Making of the Poet,* 1984; Dennis Berthold and Kenneth Price, eds., *Dear Brother Walt: The Letters of Thomas Jefferson Whitman,* 1984; David Cavitch, *My Soul and I: The Inner Life of Walt Whitman,* 1985; Joann P. Krieg, ed., *Walt Whitman: Here and Now,* 1985; George B. Hutchinson, *The Ecstatic Whitman: Literary Shamanism and the Crisis of the Union,* 1986; M. Wynn Thomas, *The Lunar Light of Whitman's Poetry,* 1987; Charley Shively, ed., *Calamus Lovers: Walt Whitman's Working-Class Camerados,* 1987; Neeli Cherkovski, *Whitman's Wild Children,* 1988; Kerry C. Larson, *Whitman's Drama of Consensus,* 1988; Edwin Haviland Miller, *Walt Whitman's "Song of Myself": A Mosaic of Interpretations,* 1989; M. Jimmie Killingsworth, *Whitman's Poetry of the Body,* 1989; Thomas Gardner, *Discovering Ourselves in Whitman: The Contemporary American Long Poem,* 1989; Jeffrey Walker, *Bardic Ethos and the American Epic Poem: Whitman, Pound, Crane, Williams, Olson,* 1989; Thomas B. Byers, *What I Cannot Say: Self, Word, and World in Whitman, Stevens, and Merwin,* 1989; Betsy Erkkila, *Whitman the Political Poet,* 1989; David Kuebrich, *Minor Prophecy: Walt Whitman's New American Religion,* 1989; Kenneth M. Price, *Whitman and Tradition,* 1990.

TEXTS

Poetry from *Leaves of Grass,* 1891–92; 1855 Preface from *Leaves of Grass,* 1855; "Slang in America" from Volume VI of *The Complete Writings,* ed. Richard M. Bucke et al., 1902; other prose from *Complete Prose Works,* 1892.

Preface to the 1855
Edition of *Leaves of Grass*[1]

America does not repel the past or what it has produced under its forms or amid other politics or the idea of castes or the old religions . . . . accepts the lesson with calmness . . . is not so impatient as has been supposed that the slough still sticks to opinions and manners and literature while the life which served its requirements has passed into the new life of the new forms . . . perceives that the corpse is slowly borne from the eating and sleeping rooms of the house . . . perceives that it waits a little while in the door . . . that it was fittest for its days . . . that its action has descended to the stalwart and wellshaped heir who approaches . . . and that he shall be fittest for his days.

The Americans of all nations at any time upon the earth have probably the fullest poetical nature. The United States themselves are essentially the greatest poem. In the history of the earth hitherto the largest and most stirring appear tame and orderly to their ampler largeness and stir. Here at last is something in the doings of man that corresponds with the broadcast doings of the day and night. Here is not merely a nation but a teeming nation of nations. Here is action untied from strings necessarily blind to particulars and details magnificently moving in vast masses. Here is the hospitality which forever indicates heroes . . . . Here are the roughs and beards and space and ruggedness and nonchalance that the soul loves. Here the performance disdaining the trivial unapproached in the tremendous audacity of its crowds and groupings and the push of its perspective spreads with crampless and flowing breadth and showers its prolific and splendid extravagance. One sees it must indeed own the riches of the summer and winter, and need never be bankrupt while corn

---

[1] This Preface was Whitman's manifesto calling for American bards to fill the role of cosmic poets in the development of a great literature commensurate with a great democratic nation. Parts of it were incorporated with very little change in the poem "By Blue Ontario's Shore." The ellipses (. . .) are Whitman's.

grows from the ground or the orchards drop apples or the bays contain fish or men beget children upon women.

Other states indicate themselves in their deputies . . . . but the genius of the United States is not best or most in its executives or legislatures, nor in its ambassadors or authors or colleges or churches or parlors, nor even in its newspapers or inventors . . . but always most in the common people. Their manners speech dress friendships—the freshness and candor of their physiognomy—the picturesque looseness of their carriage . . . their deathless attachment to freedom—their aversion to anything indecorous or soft or mean—the practical acknowledgment of the citizens of one state by the citizens of all other states—the fierceness of their roused resentment—their curiosity and welcome of novelty—their self-esteem and wonderful sympathy—their susceptibility to a slight—the air they have of persons who never knew how it felt to stand in the presence of superiors—the fluency of their speech—their delight in music, the sure symptom of manly tenderness and native elegance of soul . . . their good temper and openhandedness—the terrible significance of their elections—the President's taking off his hat to them not they to him—these too are unrhymed poetry. It awaits the gigantic and generous treatment worthy of it.

The largeness of nature or the nation were monstrous without a corresponding largeness and generosity of the spirit of the citizen. Not nature nor swarming states nor streets and steamships nor prosperous business nor farms nor capital nor learning may suffice for the ideal of man . . . nor suffice the poet. No reminiscences may suffice either. A live nation can always cut a deep mark and can have the best authority the cheapest . . . namely from its own soul. This is the sum of the profitable uses of individuals or states and of present action and grandeur and of the subjects of poets.—As if it were necessary to trot back generation after generation to the eastern records! As if the beauty and sacredness of the demonstrable must fall behind that of the mythical! As if men do not make their mark out of any times! As if the opening of the western continent by discovery and what has transpired since in North and South America were less than the small theatre of the antique or the aimless sleepwalking of the middle ages! The pride of the United States leaves the wealth and finesse of the cities and all returns of commerce and agriculture and all the magnitude of geography or shows of exterior victory to enjoy the breed of fullsized men or one fullsized man unconquerable and simple.

The American poets are to enclose old and new for America is the race of races. Of them a bard is to be commensurate with a people. To him the other continents arrive as contributions . . . he gives them reception for their sake and his own sake. His spirit responds to his country's spirit . . . . he incarnates its geography and natural life and rivers and lakes. Mississippi with annual freshets and changing chutes, Missouri and Columbia and Ohio and Saint Lawrence with the falls and beautiful masculine Hudson, do not embouchure[2] where they spend themselves more than they embouchure into him. The blue breadth over the inland sea of Virginia and Maryland and the sea off Massachusetts and Maine and over Manhattan bay and over Champlain and Erie and over Ontario and Huron and Michigan and Superior, and over the Texan and Mexican and Floridian and Cuban seas and over the seas off California and Oregon, is not tallied by the blue breadth of the waters below more than the breadth of above and below is tallied by him. When the long Atlantic coast stretches longer and the Pacific coast stretches longer he easily stretches with them north or south. He spans between them also from east to west and reflects what is between them. On him rise solid growths that offset the growths of pine and cedar and hemlock and liveoak and locust and chestnut and cypress and hickory and limetree and cottonwood and tuliptree and cactus and wildvine and tamarind and per-

---

[2]Pour, or empty; one of Whitman's adaptations from the French (*embouchure*: mouth, as of a river).

simmon . . . . and tangles as tangled as any canebrake or swamp . . . . and forests coated with transparent ice and icicles hanging from the boughs and crackling in the wind . . . . and sides and peaks of mountains . . . . and pasturage sweet and free as savannah or upland or prairie . . . . with flights and songs and screams that answer those of the wildpigeon and highhold[3] and orchard-oriole and coot and surf-duck and redshouldered-hawk and fish-hawk and white-ibis and indian-hen and cat-owl and water-pheasant and qua-bird[4] and pied-sheldrake and blackbird and mockingbird and buzzard and condor and night-heron and eagle. To him the hereditary countenance descends both mother's and father's. To him enter the essences of the real things and past and present events—of the enormous diversity of temperature and agriculture and mines—the tribes of red aborigines—the weatherbeaten vessels entering new ports or making landings on rocky coasts—the first settlements north or south—the rapid stature and muscle—the haughty defiance of '76, and the war and peace and formation of the constitution . . . . the union always surrounded by blatherers and always calm and impregnable—the perpetual coming of immigrants—the wharfhem'd cities and superior marine—the unsurveyed interior—the loghouses and clearings and wild animals and hunters and trappers . . . . the free commerce—the fisheries and whaling and gold-digging—the endless gestation of new states—the convening of Congress every December,[5] the members duly coming up from all climates and the uttermost parts . . . . the noble character of the young mechanics and of all free American workmen and workwomen . . . . the general ardor and friendliness and enterprise—the perfect equality of the female with the male . . . . the large amativeness[6]—the fluid movement of the population—the factories and mercantile life and laborsaving machinery—the Yankee swap[7]—the New-York firemen and the target excursion[8]—the southern plantation life—the character of the northeast and of the northwest and southwest—slavery and the tremulous spreading of hands to protect it, and the stern opposition to it which shall never cease till it ceases or the speaking of tongues and the moving of lips cease. For such the expression of the American poet is to be transcendent and new. It is to be indirect and not direct or descriptive or epic. Its quality goes through these to much more. Let the age and wars of other nations be chanted and their eras and characters be illustrated and that finish the verse. Not so the great psalm of the republic. Here the theme is creative and has vista. Here comes one among the wellbeloved stonecutters and plans with decision and science and sees the solid and beautiful forms of the future where there are now no solid forms.

Of all nations the United States with veins full of poetical stuff most needs poets and will doubtless have the greatest and use them the greatest. Their Presidents shall not be their common referee so much as their poets shall. Of all mankind the great poet is the equable man. Not in him but off from him things are grotesque or eccentric or fail of their sanity. Nothing out of its place is good and nothing in its place is bad. He bestows on every object or quality its fit proportions neither more nor less. He is the arbiter of the diverse and he is the key. He is the equalizer of his age and land . . . . he supplies what wants supplying and checks what wants checking. If peace is the routine out of him speaks the spirit of peace, large, rich, thrifty, building vast and populous cities, encouraging agriculture and the arts and commerce—lighting the study of man, the soul, immortality—federal, state or municipal government, marriage, health, freetrade, intertravel by land and sea . . . . nothing too close, nothing too far off . . . the stars not too far off. In war he is the most deadly force of the war. Who recruits him recruits horse and foot . . . he fetches parks of artillery the best

---

[3]Variant of "highhole," a gold-winged woodpecker.
[4]Black-crowned night heron.
[5]Before 1933 and the Twentieth Amendment, the new Congress convened in December; now a new Congress convenes in January.

[6]Phrenological term: capacity for love between the sexes.
[7]Shrewd or clever bargain.
[8]Trip for gun practice.

that engineer ever knew. If the time becomes slothful and heavy he knows how to arouse it . . . he can make every word he speaks draw blood. Whatever stagnates in the flat[9] of custom or obedience or legislation he never stagnates. Obedience does not master him, he masters it. High up out of reach he stands turning a concentrated light . . . he turns the pivot with his finger . . . he baffles the swiftest runners as he stands and easily overtakes and envelops them. The time straying toward infidelity and confections and persiflage he withholds by his steady faith . . . he spreads out his dishes . . . he offers the sweet firmfibred meat that grows men and women. His brain is the ultimate brain. He is no arguer . . . he is judgment. He judges not as the judge judges but as the sun falling around a helpless thing. As he sees the farthest he has the most faith. His thoughts are the hymns of the praise of things. In the talk on the soul and eternity and God off of his equal plane he is silent. He sees eternity less like a play with a prologue and denouement . . . . he sees eternity in men and women . . . he does not see men and women as dreams or dots. Faith is the antiseptic of the soul . . . it pervades the common people and preserves them . . . they never give up believing and expecting and trusting. There is that indescribable freshness and unconscious-ness about an illiterate person that humbles and mocks the power of the noblest expressive genius. The poet sees for a certainty how one not a great artist may be just as sacred and perfect as the greatest artist. . . . . . The power to destroy or remould is freely used by him but never the power of attack. What is past is past. If he does not expose superior models and prove himself by every step he takes he is not what is wanted. The presence of the greatest poet conquers . . . not parleying or struggling or any prepared attempts. Now he has passed that way see after him! there is not left any vestige of despair or misanthropy or cunning or exclusiveness or the ignominy of a nativity or color or delusion of hell or the necessity of hell . . . . . and no man thence-forward shall be degraded for ignorance or weakness or sin.

The greatest poet hardly knows pettiness or triviality. If he breathes into any thing that was before thought small it dilates with the grandeur and life of the uni-verse. He is a seer . . . . he is individual . . . he is complete in himself . . . . the others are as good as he, only he sees it and they do not. He is not one of the chorus . . . . he does not stop for any regulation . . . he is the president of regulation. What the eyesight does to the rest he does to the rest. Who knows the curious mystery of the eyesight? The other senses corroborate themselves, but this is removed from any proof but its own and foreruns the identities of the spiritual world. A single glance of it mocks all the investigations of man and all the instruments and books of the earth and all reasoning. What is marvellous? what is unlikely? what is impossible or baseless or vague? after you have once just opened the space of a peachpit and given audience to far and near and to the sunset and had all things enter with electric swiftness softly and duly without confusion or jostling or jam.

The land and sea, the animals fishes and birds, the sky of heaven and the orbs, the forests mountains and rivers, are not small themes . . . but folks expect of the poet to indicate more than the beauty and dignity which always attach to dumb real ob-jects . . . . they expect him to indicate the path between reality and their souls. Men and women perceive the beauty well enough . . probably as well as he. The passionate tenacity of hunters, woodmen, early risers, cultivators of gardens and orchards and fields, the love of healthy women for the manly form, seafaring persons, drivers of horses, the passion for light and the open air, all is an old varied sign of the unfailing perception of beauty and of a residence of the poetic in outdoor people. They can never be assisted by poets to perceive . . . some may but they never can. The poetic quality is not marshalled in rhyme or uniformity or abstract addresses to things nor in melancholy complaints or good precepts, but is the life of these and much else and

---

[9]Marshy land.

is in the soul. The profit of rhyme is that it drops seeds of a sweeter and more luxuriant rhyme, and of uniformity that it conveys itself into its own roots in the ground out of sight. The rhyme and uniformity of perfect poems show the free growth of metrical laws and bud from them as unerringly and loosely as lilacs or roses on a bush, and take shapes as compact as the shapes of chestnuts and oranges and melons and pears, and shed the perfume impalpable to form. The fluency and ornaments of the finest poems or music or orations or recitations are not independent but dependent. All beauty comes from beautiful blood and a beautiful brain. If the greatnesses are in conjunction in a man or woman it is enough . . . . the fact will prevail through the universe . . . . but the gaggery[10] and gilt of a million years will not prevail. Who troubles himself about his ornaments or fluency is lost. This is what you shall do: Love the earth and sun and the animals, despise riches, give alms to every one that asks, stand up for the stupid and crazy, devote your income and labor to others, hate tyrants, argue not concerning God, have patience and indulgence toward the people, take off your hat to nothing known or unknown or to any man or number of men, go freely with powerful uneducated persons and with the young and with the mothers of families, read these leaves in the open air every season of every year of your life, re-examine all you have been told at school or church or in any book, dismiss whatever insults your own soul, and your very flesh shall be a great poem and have the richest fluency not only in its words but in the silent lines of its lips and face and between the lashes of your eyes and in every motion and joint of your body. . . . . The poet shall not spend his time in unneeded work. He shall know that the ground is always ready ploughed and manured . . . . others may not know it but he shall. He shall go directly to the creation. His trust shall master the trust of everything he touches . . . . and shall master all attachment.

The known universe has one complete lover and that is the greatest poet. He consumes an eternal passion and is indifferent which chance happens and which possible contingency of fortune or misfortune and persuades daily and hourly his delicious pay. What balks or breaks others is fuel for his burning progress to contact and amorous joy. Other proportions of the reception of pleasure dwindle to nothing to his proportions. All expected from heaven or from the highest he is rapport with in the sight of the daybreak or a scene of the winter woods or the presence of children playing or with his arm round the neck of a man or woman. His love above all love has leisure and expanse . . . . he leaves room ahead of himself. He is no irresolute or suspicious lover . . . he is sure . . . he scorns intervals. His experience and the showers and thrills are not for nothing. Nothing can jar him . . . . suffering and darkness cannot—death and fear cannot. To him complaint and jealousy and envy are corpses buried and rotten in the earth . . . . he saw them buried. The sea is not surer of the shore or the shore of the sea than he is of the fruition of his love and of all perfection and beauty.

The fruition of beauty is no chance of hit or miss . . . it is inevitable as life . . . . it is exact and plumb as gravitation. From the eyesight proceeds another eyesight and from the hearing proceeds another hearing and from the voice proceeds another voice eternally curious of the harmony of things with man. To these respond perfections not only in the committees that were supposed to stand for the rest but in the rest themselves just the same. These understand the law of perfection in masses and floods . . . that its finish is to each for itself and onward from itself . . . that it is profuse and impartial . . . that there is not a minute of the light or dark nor an acre of the earth or sea without it—nor any direction of the sky nor any trade or employment nor any turn of events. This is the reason that about the proper expression of beauty there is precision and balance . . . one part does not need to be thrust above another.

---

[10]Hoaxing.

The best singer is not the one who has the most lithe and powerful organ . . . the pleasure of poems is not in them that take the handsomest measure and similes and sound.

Without effort and without exposing in the least how it is done the greatest poet brings the spirit of any or all events and passions and scenes and persons some more and some less to bear on your individual character as you hear or read. To do this well is to compete with the laws that pursue and follow time. What is the purpose must surely be there and the clue of it must be there . . . . and the faintest indication is the indication of the best and then becomes the clearest indication. Past and present and future are not disjoined but joined. The greatest poet forms the consistence of what is to be from what has been and is. He drags the dead out of their coffins and stands them again on their feet . . . . he says to the past, Rise and walk before me that I may realize you. He learns the lesson . . . . he places himself where the future becomes present. The greatest poet does not only dazzle his rays over character and scenes and passions . . . he finally ascends and finishes all . . . he exhibits the pinnacles that no man can tell what they are for or what is beyond . . . . he glows a moment on the extremest verge. He is most wonderful in his last half-hidden smile or frown . . . by that flash of the moment of parting the one that sees it shall be encouraged or terrified afterward for many years. The greatest poet does not moralize or make applications of morals . . . he knows the soul. The soul has that measureless pride which consists in never acknowledging any lessons but its own. But it has sympathy as measureless as its pride and the one balances the other and neither can stretch too far while it stretches in company with the other. The inmost secrets of art sleep with the twain. The greatest poet has lain close betwixt both and they are vital in his style and thoughts.

The art of art, the glory of expression and the sunshine of the light of letters is simplicity. Nothing is better than simplicity . . . . nothing can make up for excess or for the lack of definiteness. To carry on the heave of impulse and pierce intellectual depths and give all subjects their articulations are powers neither common nor very uncommon. But to speak in literature with the perfect rectitude and insouciance[11] of the movements of animals and the unimpeachableness of the sentiment of trees in the woods and grass by the roadside is the flawless triumph of art. If you have looked on him who has achieved it you have looked on one of the masters of the artists of all nations and times. You shall not contemplate the flight of the graygull over the bay or the mettlesome action of the blood horse or the tall leaning of sunflowers on their stalk or the appearance of the sun journeying through heaven or the appearance of the moon afterward with any more satisfaction than you shall contemplate him. The greatest poet has less a marked style and is more the channel of thoughts and things without increase or diminution, and is the free channel of himself. He swears to his art, I will not be meddlesome, I will not have in my writing any elegance or effect or originality to hang in the way between me and the rest like curtains. I will have nothing hang in the way, not the richest curtains. What I tell I tell for precisely what it is. Let who may exalt or startle or fascinate or sooth[12] I will have purposes as health or heat or snow has and be as regardless of observation. What I experience or portray shall go from my composition without a shred of my composition. You shall stand by my side and look in the mirror with me.

The old red blood and stainless gentility of great poets will be proved by their unconstraint. A heroic person walks at his ease through and out of that custom or precedent or authority that suits him not. Of the traits of the brotherhood of writers savans[13] musicians inventors and artists nothing is finer than silent defiance advanc-

---

[11]Calm and carefree.
[12]Variant of "soothe."
[13]Whitman's variant for savants, wise persons.

ing from new free forms. In the need of poems philosophy politics mechanism science behaviour, the craft of art, an appropriate native grand-opera, shipcraft, or any craft, he is greatest forever and forever who contributes the greatest original practical example. The cleanest expression is that which finds no sphere worthy of itself and makes one.

The messages of great poets to each man and woman are, Come to us on equal terms, Only then can you understand us, We are no better than you, What we enclose you enclose, What we enjoy you may enjoy. Did you suppose there could be only one Supreme? We affirm there can be unnumbered Supremes, and that one does not countervail another any more than one eyesight countervails another . . and that men can be good or grand only of the consciousness of their supremacy within them. What do you think is the grandeur of storms and dismemberments and the deadliest battles and wrecks and the wildest fury of the elements and the power of the sea and the motion of nature and of the throes of human desires and dignity and hate and love? It is that something in the soul which says, Rage on, Whirl on, I tread master here and everywhere, Master of the spasms of the sky and of the shatter of the sea, Master of nature and passion and death, And of all terror and all pain.

The American bards shall be marked for generosity and affection and for encouraging competitors . . They shall be kosmos[14] . . without monopoly or secresy[15] . . glad to pass any thing to any one . . hungry for equals night and day. They shall not be careful of riches and privilege . . . . they shall be riches and privilege . . . . they shall perceive who the most affluent man is. The most affluent man is he that confronts all the shows he sees by equivalents out of the stronger wealth of himself. The American bard shall delineate no class of persons nor one or two out of the strata of interests nor love most nor truth most nor the soul most nor the body most . . . . and not be for the eastern states more than the western or the northern states more than the southern.

Exact science and its practical movements are no checks on the greatest poet but always his encouragement and support. The outset and remembrance are there . . there the arms that lifted him first and brace[16] him best . . . . there he returns after all his goings and comings. The sailor and traveler . . the anatomist chemist astronomer geologist phrenologist spiritualist mathematician historian and lexicographer are not poets, but they are the lawgivers of poets and their construction underlies the structure of every perfect poem. No matter what rises or is uttered they sent the seed of the conception of it . . . of them and by them stand the visible proofs of souls . . . . . always of their fatherstuff must be begotten the sinewy races of bards. If there shall be love and content between the father and the son and if the greatness of the son is the exuding of the greatness of the father there shall be love between the poet and the man of demonstrable science. In the beauty of poems are the tuft and final applause of science.

Great is the faith of the flush of knowledge and of the investigation of the depths of qualities and things. Cleaving and circling here swells the soul of the poet yet it president of itself always. The depths are fathomless and therefore calm. The innocence and nakedness are resumed . . . they are neither modest nor immodest. The whole theory of the special and supernatural and all that was twined with it or educed out of it departs as a dream.What has ever happened . . . . what happens and whatever may or shall happen, the vital laws enclose all . . . . they are sufficient for any case and for all cases . . . none to be hurried or retarded . . . . any miracle of affairs or persons inadmissible in the vast clear scheme where every motion and every spear of grass and the frames and spirits of men and women and all that concerns them are

---

[14]Variant of cosmos, harmoniously ordered universe.
[15]Variant of "secrecy."
[16]I.e., "braced."

unspeakably perfect miracles all referring to all and each distinct and in its place. It is also not consistent with the reality of the soul to admit that there is anything in the known universe more divine than men and women.

Men and women and the earth and all upon it are simply to be taken as they are, and the investigation of their past and present and future shall be unintermitted and shall be done with perfect candor. Upon this basis philosophy speculates ever looking toward the poet, ever regarding the eternal tendencies of all toward happiness never inconsistent with what is clear to the senses and to the soul. For the eternal tendencies of all toward happiness make the only point of sane philosophy. Whatever comprehends less than that . . . whatever is less than the laws of light and of astronomical motion . . . or less than the laws that follow the thief the liar the glutton and the drunkard through this life and doubtless afterward . . . . . . or less than vast stretches of time or the slow formation of density or the patient upheaving of strata—is of no account. Whatever would put God in a poem or system of philosophy as contending against some being or influence is also of no account. Sanity and ensemble characterise the great master . . . spoilt in one principle all is spoilt. The great master has nothing to do with miracles. He sees health for himself in being one of the mass . . . . he sees the hiatus in singular eminence. To the perfect shape comes common ground. To be under the general law is great for that is to correspond with it. The master knows that he is unspeakably great and that all are unspeakably great . . . . that nothing for instance is greater than to conceive children and bring them up well . . . that to be is just as great as to perceive or tell.

In the make of the great masters the idea of political liberty is indispensible. Liberty takes the adherence of heroes wherever men and women exist . . . . but never takes any adherence or welcome from the rest more than from poets. They are the voice and exposition of liberty. They out of ages are worthy the grand idea . . . . to them it is confided and they must sustain it. Nothing has precedence of it and nothing can warp or degrade it. The attitude of great poets is to cheer up slaves and horrify despots. The turn of their necks, the sound of their feet, the motions of their wrists, are full of hazard to the one and hope to the other. Come nigh them awhile and though they neither speak or advise you shall learn the faithful American lesson. Liberty is poorly served by men whose good intent is quelled from one failure or two failures or any number of failures, or from the casual indifference or ingratitude of the people, or from the sharp show of the tushes[17] of power, or the bringing to bear soldiers and cannon or any penal statutes. Liberty relies upon itself, invites no one, promises nothing, sits in calmness and light, is positive and composed, and knows no discouragement. The battle rages with many a loud alarm and frequent advance and retreat . . . . the enemy triumphs . . . . the prison, the handcuffs, the iron necklace and anklet, the scaffold, garrote and leadballs do their work . . . . the cause is asleep . . . . the strong throats are choked with their own blood . . . . the young men drop their eyelashes toward the ground when they pass each other . . . . and is liberty gone out of that place? No never. When liberty goes it is not the first to go nor the second or third to go . . it waits for all the rest to go . . it is the last. . . When the memories of the old martyrs are faded utterly away . . . . when the large names of patriots are laughed at in the public halls from the lips of the orators . . . . when the boys are no more christened after the same but christened after tyrants and traitors instead . . . . when the laws of the free are grudgingly permitted and laws for informers and blood-money are sweet to the taste of the people . . . . when I and you walk abroad upon the earth stung with compassion at the sight of numberless brothers answering our equal friendship and calling no man master—and when we are elated with noble joy at the

---

[17]Variant of tusks (teeth).

sight of slaves . . . . when the soul retires in the cool communion of the night and surveys its experience and has much extasy over the word and deed that put back a helpless innocent person into the gripe of the gripers or into any cruel inferiority . . . . when those in all parts of these states who could easier realize the true American character but do not yet—when the swarms of cringers, suckers, doughfaces,[18] lice of politics, planners of sly involutions for their own preferment to city offices or state legislatures or the judiciary or congress or the presidency, obtain a response of love and natural deference from the people whether they get the offices or no . . . . when it is better to be a bound booby[19] and rogue in office at a high salary than the poorest free mechanic or farmer with his hat unmoved from his head and firm eyes and a candid and generous heart . . . . and when servility by town or state or the federal government or any oppression on a large scale or small scale can be tried on without its own punishment following duly after in exact proportion against the smallest chance of escape . . . . or rather when all life and all the souls of men and women are discharged from any part of the earth—then only shall the instinct of liberty be discharged from that part of the earth.

As the attributes of the poets of the kosmos concentre in the real body and soul and in the pleasure of things they possess the superiority of genuineness over all fiction and romance. As they emit themselves facts are showered over with light . . . . the daylight is lit with more volatile light . . . . also the deep between the setting and rising sun goes deeper many fold. Each precise object or condition or combination or process exhibits a beauty . . . . the multiplication table its[20]—old age its—the carpenter's trade its—the grand-opera its . . . . the hugehulled cleanshaped New-York clipper at sea under steam or full sail gleams with unmatched beauty . . . . the American circles and large harmonies of government gleam with theirs . . . . and the commonest definite intentions and actions with theirs. The poets of the kosmos advance through all interpositions and coverings and turmoils and stratagems to first principles. They are of use . . . . they dissolve poverty from its need and riches from its conceit. You large proprietor they say shall not realize or perceive more than any one else. The owner of the library is not he who holds a legal title to it having bought and paid for it. Any one and every one is owner of the library who can read the same through all the varieties of tongues and subjects and styles, and in whom they enter with ease and take residence and force toward paternity and maternity, and make supple and powerful and rich and large. . . . . These American states strong and healthy and accomplished shall receive no pleasure from violations of natural models and must not permit them. In paintings or mouldings or carvings in mineral or wood, or in the illustrations of books or newspapers, or in any comic or tragic prints, or in the patterns of woven stuffs or any thing to beautify rooms or furniture or costumes, or to put upon cornices or monuments or on the prows or sterns of ships, or to put anywhere before the human eye indoors or out, that which distorts honest shapes or which creates unearthly beings or places or contingencies is a nuisance and revolt. Of the human form especially it is so great it must never be made ridiculous. Of ornaments to a work nothing outre[21] can be allowed . . but those ornaments can be allowed that conform to the perfect facts of the open air and that flow out of the nature of the work and come irrepressibly from it and are necessary to the completion of the work. Most works are most beautiful without ornament . . . Exaggerations will be revenged in human physiology. Clean and vigorous children are jetted[22] and conceived only in those communities where the models of natural forms are public every day. . . . . . Great genius and the people of these states must

---

[18]Suckers: blackmailers; doughfaces: northern congressmen who were not anti-slavery (hence, unprincipled people).
[19]Politician bought by special interests.

[20]I.e., its beauty.
[21]Bizarre, extravagant.
[22]I.e., through ejaculation of semen.

never be demeaned to romances.[23] As soon as histories are properly told there is no more need of romances.

The great poets are also to be known by the absence in them of tricks and by the justification of perfect personal candor. Then folks echo a new cheap joy and a divine voice leaping from their brains: How beautiful is candor! All faults may be forgiven of him who has perfect candor. Henceforth let no man of us lie, for we have seen that openness wins the inner and outer world and that there is no single exception, and that never since our earth gathered itself in a mass have deceit or subterfuge or prevarication attracted its smallest particle or the faintest tinge of a shade—and that through the enveloping wealth and rank of a state or the whole republic of states a sneak or sly person shall be discovered and despised . . . . and that the soul has never been once fooled and never can be fooled . . . . and thrift without the loving nod of the soul is only a fœtid puff . . . . and there never grew up in any of the continents of the globe nor upon any planet or satellite or star, nor upon the asteroids, nor in any part of ethereal space, nor in the midst of density, nor under the fluid wet of the sea, nor in that condition which precedes the birth of babes, nor at any time during the changes of life, nor in that condition that follows what we term death, nor in any stretch of abeyance or action afterward of vitality, nor in any process of formation or reformation anywhere, a being whose instinct hated the truth.

Extreme caution or prudence, the soundest organic health, large hope and comparison and fondness for women and children, large alimentiveness and destructiveness and causality,[24] with a perfect sense of the oneness of nature and the propriety of the same spirit applied to human affairs . . . these are called up of the float[25] of the brain of the world to be parts of the greatest poet from his birth out of his mother's womb and from her birth out of her mother's. Caution seldom goes far enough. It has been thought that the prudent citizen was the citizen who applied himself to solid gains and did well for himself and his family and completed a lawful life without debt or crime. The greatest poet sees and admits these economies as he sees the economies of food and sleep, but has higher notions of prudence than to think he gives much when he gives a few slight attentions at the latch of the gate. The premises of the prudence of life are not the hospitality of it or the ripeness and harvest of it. Beyond the independence of a little sum laid aside for burial-money, and of a few clapboards around and shingles overhead on a lot of American soil owned, and the easy dollars that supply the year's plain clothing and meals, the melancholy prudence of the abandonment of such a great being as a man is to the toss and pallor of years of moneymaking with all their scorching days and icy nights and all their stifling deceits and underhanded dodgings, or infinitessimals of parlors, or shameless stuffing while others starve . . and all the loss of the bloom and odor of the earth and of the flowers and atmosphere and of the sea and of the true taste of the women and men you pass or have to do with in youth or middle age, and the issuing sickness and desperate revolt at the close of a life without elevation or naivete, and the ghastly chatter of a death without serenity or majesty, is the great fraud upon modern civilization and forethought, blotching the surface and system which civilization undeniably drafts, and moistening with tears the immense features it spreads and spreads with such velocity before the reached kisses of the soul . . . . Still the right explanation remains to be made about prudence. The prudence of the mere wealth and respectability of the most esteemed life appears too faint for the eye to observe at all when little and large alike drop quietly aside at the thought of the prudence suitable for

---

[23]Cheap, artificial, debased art.
[24]Phrenological terms: "alimentiveness," appetite or taste for food and drink; "destructiveness," capacity for involvement in or witnessing violence of nature or man; "causality," comprehension of cause and effect.

[25]I.e., that which has been suspended in water or air; the primordial brain stuff waiting and ready for creation of individual geniuses or artists.

immortality. What is wisdom that fills the thinness of a year or seventy or eighty years to wisdom spaced out by ages and coming back at a certain time with strong reinforcements and rich presents and the clear faces of wedding-guests as far as you can look in every direction running gaily toward you? Only the soul is of itself . . . . all else has reference to what ensues. All that a person does or thinks is of consequence. Not a move can a man or woman make that affects him or her in a day or a month or any part of the direct lifetime or the hour of death but the same affects him or her onward afterward through the indirect lifetime. The indirect is always as great and real as the direct. The spirit receives from the body just as much as it gives to the body. Not one name of word or deed . . not of venereal sores or discolorations . . not the privacy of the onanist[26] . . not of the putrid veins of gluttons or rumdrinkers . . . not peculation[27] or cunning or betrayal or murder . . no serpentine poison of those that seduce women . . not the foolish yielding of women . . not prostitution . . not of any depravity of young men . . not of the attainment of gain by discreditable means . . not any nastiness of appetite . . not any harshness of officers to men or judges to prisoners or fathers to sons or sons to fathers or of husbands to wives or bosses to their boys . . not of greedy looks or malignant wishes . . . nor any of the wiles practised by people upon themselves . . . . ever is or ever can be stamped on the programme but it is duly realized and returned, and that returned in further performances . . . and they returned again. Nor can the push of charity or personal force ever be any thing else than the profoundest reason, whether it bring arguments to hand or no. No specification is necessary . . to add or subtract or divide is in vain. Little or big, learned or unlearned, white or black, legal or illegal, sick or well, from the first inspiration down the windpipe to the last expiration out of it, all that a male or female does that is vigorous and benevolent and clean is so much sure profit to him or her in the unshakable order of the universe and through the whole scope of it forever. If the savage or felon is wise it is well . . . . if the greatest poet or savan is wise it is simply the same . . . if the President or chief justice is wise it is the same . . . if the young mechanic or farmer is wise it is no more or less . . if the prostitute is wise it is no more nor less. The interest will come round . . all will come round. All the best actions of war and peace . . . all help given to relatives and strangers and the poor and old and sorrowful and young children and widows and the sick, and to all shunned persons . . all furtherance of fugitives and of the escape of slaves . . all the self-denial that stood steady and aloof on wrecks and saw others take the seats of the boats . . . all offering of substance or life for the good old cause, or for a friend's sake or opinion's sake . . . all pains of enthusiasts scoffed at by their neighbors . . all the vast sweet love and precious suffering of mothers . . . all honest men baffled in strifes recorded or unrecorded . . . . all the grandeur and good of the few ancient nations whose fragments of annals we inherit . . and all the good of the hundreds of far mightier and more ancient nations unknown to us by name or date or location . . . . all that was ever manfully begun, whether it succeeded or no . . . . all that has at any time been well suggested out of the divine heart of man or by the divinity of his mouth or by the shaping of his great hands . . and all that is well thought or done this day on any part of the surface of the globe . . or on any of the wandering stars or fixed stars by those there as we are here . . or that is henceforth to be well thought or done by you whoever you are, or by any one—these singly and wholly inured at their time and inure now and will inure always to the identities from which they sprung or shall spring. . . Did you guess any of them lived only its moment? The world does not so exist . . no parts palpable or impalpable so exist . . . no result exists now without being from its long antecedent result, and that from its antecedent, and so backward without the farthest mentionable spot coming a bit nearer the beginning than any other

---

[26]Masturbator (from the sin of Onan in Genesis 38:9).
[27]Embezzlement.

spot. . . . . Whatever satisfies the soul is truth. The prudence of the greatest poet answers at last the craving and glut of the soul, is not contemptuous of less ways of prudence if they conform to its ways, puts off nothing, permits no let-up for its own case or any case, has no particular sabbath or judgment-day, divides not the living from the dead or the righteous from the unrighteous, is satisfied with the present, matches every thought or act by its correlative, knows no possible forgiveness or deputed atonement . . knows that the young man who composedly periled his life and lost it has done exceeding well for himself, while the man who has not periled his life and retains it to old age in riches and case has perhaps achieved nothing for himself worth mentioning . . and that only that person has no great prudence to learn who has learnt to prefer real longlived things, and favors body and soul the same, and perceives the indirect assuredly following the direct, and what evil or good he does leaping onward and waiting to meet him again—and who in his spirit in any emergency whatever neither hurries or avoids death.

The direct trial of him who would be the greatest poet is today. If he does not flood himself with the immediate age as with vast oceanic tides . . . . . and if he does not attract his own land body and soul to himself and hang on its neck with incomparable love and plunge his semitic[28] muscle into its merits and demerits . . . and if he be not himself the age transfigured . . . . and if to him is not opened the eternity which gives similitude to all periods and locations and processes and animate and inanimate forms, and which is the bond of time, and rises up from its inconceivable vagueness and infiniteness in the swimming shape of today, and is held by the ductile anchors of life, and makes the present spot the passage from what was to what shall be, and commits itself to the representation of this wave of an hour and this one of the sixty beautiful children[29] of the wave—let him merge in the general run and wait his development. . . . . . . Still the final test of poems or any character or work remains. The prescient poet projects himself centuries ahead and judges performer or performance after the changes of time. Does it live through them? Does it still hold on untired? Will the same style and the direction of genius to similar points be satisfactory now? Has no new discovery in science or arrival at superior planes of thought and judgment and behaviour fixed him or his so that either can be looked down upon? Have the marches of tens and hundreds and thousands of years made willing detours to the right hand and the left hand for his sake? Is he beloved long and long after he is buried? Does the young man think often of him? and the young woman think often of him? and do the middleaged and the old think of him?

A great poem is for ages and ages in common and for all degrees and complexions and all departments and sects and for a woman as much as a man and a man as much as a woman. A great poem is no finish to a man or woman but rather a beginning. Has any one fancied he could sit at last under some due authority and rest satisfied with explanations and realize and be content and full? To no such terminus does the greatest poet bring . . . he brings neither cessation or sheltered fatness and ease. The touch of him tells in action. Whom he takes he takes with firm sure grasp into live regions previously unattained . . . . thenceforward is no rest . . . . they see the space and ineffable sheen that turn the old spots and lights into dead vacuums. The companion of him beholds the birth and progress of stars and learns one of the meanings. Now there shall be a man cohered out of tumult and chaos . . . . the elder encourages the younger and shows him how . . . they two shall launch off fearlessly together till the new world fits an orbit for itself and looks unabashed on the lesser orbits of the stars and sweeps through the ceaseless rings and shall never be quiet again.

---

[28]Whitman's variant for "seminal"; i.e., the phallus.
[29]I.e., minutes.

There will soon be no more priests. Their work is done. They may wait awhile . . perhaps a generation or two . . dropping off by degrees. A superior breed shall take their place . . . . the gangs of kosmos[30] and prophets en masse shall take their place. A new order shall arise and they shall be the priests of man, and every man shall be his own priest. The churches built under their umbrage shall be the churches of men and women. Through the divinity of themselves shall the kosmos and the new breed of poets be interpreters of men and women and of all events and things. They shall find their inspiration in real objects today, symptoms of the past and future . . . . They shall not deign to defend immortality or God or the perfection of things or liberty or the exquisite beauty and reality of the soul. They shall arise in America and be responded to from the remainder of the earth.

The English language befriends the grand American expression . . . . it is brawny enough and limber and full enough. On the tough stock of a race who through all change of circumstance was never without the idea of political liberty, which is the animus of all liberty, it has attracted the terms of daintier and gayer and subtler and more elegant tongues.[31] It is the powerful language of resistance . . . it is the dialect of common sense. It is the speech of the proud and melancholy races and of all who aspire. It is the chosen tongue to express growth faith self-esteem freedom justice equality friendliness amplitude prudence decision and courage. It is the medium that shall well nigh express the inexpressible.

No great literature nor any like style of behaviour or oratory or social intercourse or household arrangements or public institutions or the treatment by bosses of employed people, nor executive detail or detail of the army or navy, nor spirit of legislation or courts or police or tuition or architecture or songs or amusements of the costumes of young men, can long elude the jealous and passionate instinct of American standards. Whether or no the sign appears from the mouths of the people, it throbs a live interrogation in every freeman's and freewoman's heart after that which passes by or this built to remain. Is it uniform with my country? Are its disposals without ignominious distinctions? Is it for the evergrowing communes of brothers and lovers, large, well-united, proud beyond the old models, generous beyond all models? Is it something grown fresh out of the fields or drawn from the sea for use to me today here? I know that what answers for me an American must answer for any individual or nation that serves for a part of my materials. Does this answer? or is it without reference to universal needs? or sprung of the needs of the less developed society of special ranks? or old needs of pleasure overlaid by modern science and forms? Does this acknowledge liberty with audible and absolute acknowledgement, and set slavery at nought for life and death? Will it help breed one goodshaped and wellhung man, and a woman to be his perfect and independent mate? Does it improve manners? Is it for the nursing of the young of the republic? Does it solve[32] readily with the sweet milk of the nipples of the breasts of the mother of many children? Has it too the old ever-fresh forbearance and impartiality? Does it look with the same love on the last born and on those hardening toward stature, and on the errant, and on those who disdain all strength of assault outside of their own?

The poems distilled from other poems will probably pass away. The coward will surely pass away. The expectation of the vital and great can only be satisfied by the demeanor of the vital and great. The swarms of the polished deprecating and reflectors and the polite float off and leave no remembrance. America prepares with composure and goodwill for the visitors that have sent word. It is not intellect that is to be their warrant and welcome. The talented, the artist, the ingenious, the editor, the statesman, the erudite . . they are not unappreciated . . they fall in their place and do

---

[30]I.e., large numbers of poets in tune with the harmonious universe (cosmos).
[31]Italian, French, and Spanish from which Whitman often borrows or adapts words.
[32]Variant of "dissolve."

their work. The soul of the nation also does its work. No disguise can pass on it . . no disguise can conceal from it. It rejects none, it permits all. Only toward as good as itself and toward the like of itself will it advance half-way. An individual is as superb as a nation when he has the qualities which make a superb nation. The soul of the largest and wealthiest and proudest nation may well go half-way to meet that of its poets. The signs are effectual. There is no fear of mistake. If the one is true the other is true. The proof of a poet is that his country absorbs him as affectionately as he has absorbed it.

1855

from Leaves of Grass[1]

from INSCRIPTIONS
One's-Self I Sing

One's-self I sing, a simple separate person,
Yet utter the word Democratic, the word En-Masse.[2]

Of physiology from top to toe I sing,
Not physiognomy alone nor brain alone is worthy for the Muse, I say the
    Form complete is worthier far,
The Female equally with the Male I sing.   5

Of Life immense in passion, pulse, and power,
Cheerful, for freest action form'd under the laws divine,
The Modern Man I sing.

1867, 1871

I Hear America Singing

I hear America singing, the varied carols I hear,
Those of mechanics, each one singing his as it should be blithe and strong,
The carpenter singing his as he measures his plank or beam,
The mason singing his as he makes ready for work, or leaves off work,
The boatman singing what belongs to him in his boat, the deck-hand singing
    on the steamboat deck,   5
The shoemaker singing as he sits on his bench, the hatter singing as he
    stands,
The wood-cutter's song, the ploughboy's on his way in the morning, or at
    noon intermission or at sundown,
The delicious singing of the mother, or of the young wife at work, or of the
    girl sewing or washing,
Each singing what belongs to him or her and to none else,

---

[1]The two dates below the poems indicate first appearance in print (on the left) and final version (or placement) in *Leaves of Grass* (on the right).

[2]"All together, as a whole" (French).

The day what belongs to the day—at night the party of young fellows,
    robust, friendly,   10
Singing with open mouths their strong melodious songs.

1860, 1867

Poets to Come

Poets to come! orators, singers, musicians to come!
Not to-day is to justify me and answer what I am for,
But you, a new brood, native, athletic, continental, greater than before
    known,
Arouse! for you must justify me.

I myself but write one or two indicative words for the future,   5
I but advance a moment only to wheel and hurry back in the darkness.

I am a man who, sauntering along without fully stopping, turns a casual
    look upon you and then averts his face,
Leaving it to you to prove and define it,
Expecting the main things from you.

1860, 1867

Song of Myself¹

1

I celebrate myself, and sing myself,
And what I assume you shall assume,
For every atom belonging to me as good belongs to you.

I loafe and invite my soul,
I lean and loafe at my ease observing a spear of summer grass.   5

My tongue, every atom of my blood, form'd from this soil, this air,
Born here of parents born here from parents the same, and their parents
    the same,
I, now thirty-seven years old in perfect health begin,
Hoping to cease not till death.

Creeds and schools in abeyance,   10
Retiring back a while suffced at what they are, but never forgotten,
I harbor for good or bad, I permit to speak at every hazard,
Nature without check with original energy.

---

¹When this poem appeared in the 1855 edition, it was the lead poem and was entitled (like all the other eleven poems in the book) "Leaves of Grass." It was titled "Poem of Walt Whitman, An American" (1856) and "Walt Whitman" (1860) and went through many revisions before its final version and title appeared in the 1881 edition of a vastly expanded *Leaves of Grass*. The text here is of the last revised edition.

2

Houses and rooms are full of perfumes, the shelves are crowded with
    perfumes,
I breathe the fragrance myself and know it and like it,   15
The distillation would intoxicate me also, but I shall not let it.

The atmosphere is not a perfume, it has no taste of the distillation, it is
    odorless,
It is for my mouth forever, I am in love with it,
I will go to the bank by the wood and become undisguised and naked,
I am mad for it to be in contact with me.   20

The smoke of my own breath,
Echoes, ripples, buzz'd whispers, love-root, silk-thread, crotch and vine,
My respiration and inspiration, the beating of my heart, the passing of blood
    and air through my lungs,
The sniff of green leaves and dry leaves, and of the shore and dark-color'd
    sea-rocks, and of hay in the barn,
The sound of the belch'd words of my voice loos'd to the eddies of the wind,   25
A few light kisses, a few embraces, a reaching around of arms,
The play of shine and shade on the trees as the supple boughs wag,
The delight alone or in the rush of the streets, or along the fields and hill-
    sides,
The feeling of health, the full-noon trill, the song of me rising from bed and
    meeting the sun.

Have you reckon'd a thousand acres much? have you reckon'd the earth
    much?   30
Have you practis'd so long to learn to read?
Have you felt so proud to get at the meaning of poems?

Stop this day and night with me and you shall possess the origin of all
    poems,
You shall possess the good of the earth and sun, (there are millions of suns
    left,)
You shall no longer take things at second or third hand, nor look through
    the eyes of the dead, nor feed on the spectres in books,   35
You shall not look through my eyes either, nor take things from me,
You shall listen to all sides and filter them from your self.

3

I have heard what the talkers were talking, the talk of the beginning and the
    end,
But I do not talk of the beginning or the end.

There was never any more inception than there is now,   40
Nor any more youth or age than there is now,
And will never be any more perfection than there is now,
Nor any more heaven or hell than there is now.

Urge and urge and urge,
Always the procreant urge of the world.   45

Out of the dimness opposite equals advance, always substance and increase,
    always sex,
Always a knit of identity, always distinction, always a breed of life.

To elaborate is no avail, learn'd and unlearn'd feel that it is so.

Sure as the most certain sure, plumb in the uprights, well entretied,[2] braced
    in the beams,
Stout as a horse, affectionate, haughty, electrical,   50
I and this mystery here we stand.

Clear and sweet is my soul, and clear and sweet is all that is not my soul.

Lack one lacks both, and the unseen is proved by the seen,
Till that becomes unseen and receives proof in its turn.

Showing the best and dividing it from the worst age vexes age,   55
Knowing the perfect fitness and equanimity of things, while they discuss I
    am silent, and go bathe and admire myself.

Welcome is every organ and attribute of me, and of any man hearty and
    clean,
Not an inch nor a particle of an inch is vile, and none shall be less familiar
    than the rest.

I am satisfied—I see, dance, laugh, sing;
As the hugging and loving bed-fellow[3] sleeps at my side through the night,
    and withdraws at the peep of the day with stealthy tread,   60
Leaving me baskets cover'd with white towels swelling the house with their
    plenty,
Shall I postpone my acceptation and realization and scream at my eyes,
That they turn from gazing after and down the road,
And forthwith cipher and show me to a cent,
Exactly the value of one and exactly the value of two, and which is ahead?   65

4

Trippers and askers surround me,
People I meet, the effect upon me of my early life or the ward and city I live
    in, or the nation,
The latest dates, discoveries, inventions, societies, authors old and new,
My dinner, dress, associates, looks, compliments, dues,
The real or fancied indifference of some man or woman I love,   70
The sickness of one of my folks or of myself, or ill-doing or loss or lack of
    money, or depressions or exaltations,
Battles, the horrors of fratricidal war, the fever of doubtful news, the fitful
    events;
These come to me days and nights and go from me again,
But they are not the Me myself.

Apart from the pulling and hauling stands what I am,   75
Stands amused, complacent, compassionating, idle, unitary,
Looks down, is erect, or bends an arm on an impalpable certain rest,
Looking with side-curved head curious what will come next,
Both in and out of the game and watching and wondering at it.

Backward I see in my own days where I sweated through fog with linguists
    and contenders,
I have no mockings or arguments, I witness and wait.   80

2"Self-supported," a carpenter's term (from the French *en-*   3Named as God in the first edition.
tretenir, "to hold together").

5

I believe in you my soul, the other I am must not abase itself to you,
And you must not be abased to the other.

Loafe with me on the grass, loose the stop from your throat,
Not words, not music or rhyme I want, not custom or lecture, not even the
    best,   85
Only the lull I like, the hum of your valvèd voice.

I mind how once we lay such a transparent summer morning,
How you settled your head athwart my hips and gently turn'd over upon me,
And parted the shirt from my bosom-bone, and plunged your tongue to my
    bare-stript heart,
And reach'd till you felt my beard, and reach'd till you held my feet.   90

Swiftly arose and spread around me the peace and knowledge that pass all
    the argument of the earth,
And I know that the hand of God is the promise of my own,
And I know that the spirit of God is the brother of my own,
And that all the men ever born are also my brothers, and the women my
    sisters and lovers,
And that a kelson[4] of the creation is love,   95
And limitless are leaves stiff or drooping in the fields,
And brown ants in the little wells beneath them,
And mossy scabs of the worm fence,[5] heap'd stones, elder, mullein and
    poke-weed.

6

A child said *What is the grass?* fetching it to me with full hands,
How could I answer the child? I do not know what it is any more than he.   100

I guess it must be the flag of my disposition, out of hopeful green stuff
    woven.

Or I guess it is the handkerchief of the Lord,
A scented gift and remembrancer designedly dropt,
Bearing the owner's name someway in the corners, that we may see and
    remark, and say *Whose?*

Or I guess the grass is itself a child, the produced babe of the vegetation.   105

Or I guess it is a uniform hieroglyphic,
And it means, Sprouting alike in broad zones and narrow zones,
Growing among black folks as among white,
Kanuck,[6] Tuckahoe,[7] Congressman, Cuff,[8] I give them the same, I receive
    them the same.

And now it seems to me the beautiful uncut hair of graves.   110

Tenderly will I use you curling grass,
It may be you transpire from the breasts of young men,
It may be if I had known them I would have loved them,

---

[4]A line of jointed timbers in a ship that support and brace the
keel, the ship's basic structure.
[5]Zigzagging rail fence.

[6]French Canadian.
[7]Virginian from coastal area.
[8]Black.

It may be you are from old people, or from offspring taken soon out of
    their mothers' laps.
And here you are the mothers' laps.   115

This grass is very dark to be from the white heads of old mothers,
Darker than the colorless beards of old men,
Dark to come from under the faint red roofs of mouths.

O I perceive after all so many uttering tongues,
And I perceive they do not come from the roofs of mouths for nothing.   120

I wish I could translate the hints about the dead young men and women,
And the hints about old men and mothers, and the offspring taken soon out
    of their laps.

What do you think has become of the young and old men?
And what do you think has become of the women and children?

They are alive and well somewhere,   125
The smallest sprout shows there is really no death,
And if ever there was it led forward life, and does not wait at the end to
    arrest it,
And ceas'd the moment life appear'd.

All goes onward and outward, nothing collapses,
And to die is different from what any one supposed, and luckier.   130

7

Has any one supposed it lucky to be born?
I hasten to inform him or her it is just as lucky to die, and I know it.

I pass death with the dying and birth with the new-wash'd babe, and am not
    contain'd between my hat and boots,
And peruse manifold objects, no two alike and every one good,
The earth good and the stars good, and their adjuncts all good.   135

I am not an earth nor an adjunct of an earth,
I am the mate and companion of people, all just as immortal and fathomless
    as myself,
(They do not know how immortal, but I know.)

Every kind for itself and its own, for me mine male and female,
For me those that have been boys and that love women,   140
For me the man that is proud and feels how it stings to be slighted,
For me the sweet-heart and the old maid, for me mothers and the mothers
    of mothers,
For me lips that have smiled, eyes that have shed tears,
For me children and the begetters of children.

Undrape! you are not guilty to me, nor stale nor discarded,   145
I see through the broadcloth and gingham whether or no,
And am around, tenacious, acquisitive, tireless, and cannot be shaken away.

8

The little one sleeps in its cradle,
I lift the gauze and look a long time, and silently brush away flies with my
    hand.

The youngster and the red-faced girl turn aside up the bushy hill,   150
I peeringly view them from the top.

The suicide sprawls on the bloody floor of the bedroom,
I witness the corpse with its dabbled hair, I note where the pistol has fallen.

The blab of the pave,[9] tires of carts, sluff[10] of boot-soles, talk of the
    promenaders,
The heavy omnibus, the driver with his interrogating thumb, the clank of
    the shod horses on the granite floor,   155
The snow-sleighs, clinking, shouted jokes, pelts of snow-balls,
The hurrahs for popular favorites, the fury of rous'd mobs,
The flap of the curtain'd litter, a sick man inside borne to the hospital,
The meeting of enemies, the sudden oath, the blows and fall,
The excited crowd, the policeman with his star quickly working his passage
    to the centre of the crowd,   160
The impassive stones that receive and return so many echoes,
What groans of over-fed or half-starv'd who fall sunstruck or in fits,
What exclamations of women taken suddenly who hurry home and give
    birth to babes,
What living and buried speech is always vibrating here, what howls restrain'd
    by decorum,
Arrests of criminals, slights, adulterous offers made, acceptances, rejections
    with convex lips,   165
I mind them or the show or resonance of them—I come and I depart.

9

The big doors of the country barn stand open and ready,
The dried grass of the harvest-time loads the slow-drawn wagon,
The clear light plays on the brown gray and green intertinged,
The armfuls are pack'd to the sagging mow.   170

I am there, I help, I came stretch'd atop of the load,
I felt its soft jolts, one leg reclined on the other,
I jump from the cross-beams and seize the clover and timothy,[11]
And roll over heels and tangle my hair full of wisps.

10

Alone far in the wilds and mountains I hunt,   175
Wandering amazed at my own lightness and glee,
In the late afternoon choosing a safe spot to pass the night,
Kindling a fire and broiling the fresh-kill'd game,
Falling asleep on the gather'd leaves with my dog and gun by my side.

The Yankee clipper[12] is under her sky-sails, she cuts the sparkle and scud,[13]   180
My eyes settle the land, I bend at her prow or shout joyously from the deck.

The boatmen and clam-diggers arose early and stopt for me,
I tuck'd my trowser-ends in my boots and went and had a good time;
You should have been with us that day round the chowder-kettle.

---

[9]Idle talk of the street (pavement).
[10]Variant of "slough," in this case probably the sound of shuffling, sliding, or gripping.
[11]A grass, known in England as meadow cat's tail.

[12]Fast sailing vessel, produced in America beginning about
1840.
[13]Foam.

I saw the marriage of the trapper in the open air in the far west, the bride
    was a red girl,   185
Her father and his friends sat near cross-legged and dumbly smoking, they
    had moccasins to their feet and large thick blankets hanging from their
    shoulders,
On a bank lounged the trapper, he was drest mostly in skins, his luxuriant
    beard and curls protected his neck, he held his bride by the hand,
She had long eyelashes, her head was bare, her coarse straight locks
    descended upon her voluptuous limbs and reach'd to her feet.

The runaway slave came to my house and stopt outside,
I heard his motions crackling the twigs of the woodpile,   190
Through the swung half-door of the kitchen I saw him, limpsy[14] and weak,
And went where he sat on a log and led him in and assured him,
And brought water and fill'd a tub for his sweated body and bruis'd feet,
And gave him a room that enter'd from my own, and gave him some coarse
    clean clothes,
And remember perfectly well his revolving eyes and his awkwardness,   195
And remember putting plasters on the galls of his neck and ankles;
He staid with me a week before he was recuperated and pass'd north,
I had him sit next me at table, my fire-lock[15] lean'd in the corner.

11

Twenty-eight young men bathe by the shore,
Twenty-eight young men and all so friendly;   200
Twenty-eight years of womanly life and all so lonesome.

She owns the fine house by the rise of the bank,
She hides handsome and richly drest aft the blinds of the window.

Which of the young men does she like the best?
Ah the homeliest of them is beautiful to her.   205

Where are you off to, lady? for I see you,
You splash in the water there, yet stay stock still in your room.

Dancing and laughing along the beach came the twenty-ninth bather,
The rest did not see her, but she saw them and loved them.

The beards of the young men glisten'd with wet, it ran from their long hair,   210
Little streams pass'd all over their bodies.

An unseen hand also pass'd over their bodies,
It descended tremblingly from their temples and ribs.

The young men float on their backs, their white bellies bulge to the sun,
    they do not ask who seizes fast to them,
They do not know who puffs and declines with pendant and bending arch,   215
They do not think whom they souse with spray.

12

The butcher-boy puts off his killing-clothes, or sharpens his knife at the stall
    in the market,
I loiter enjoying his repartee and his shuffle and break-down.[16]

---

[14]Limp.
[15]Gun.

[16]Shuffle: slow dance with sliding steps; break-down: rollicking dance.

Blacksmiths with grimed and hairy chests environ the anvil,
Each has his main-sledge, they are all out, there is a great heat in the fire.   220

From the cinder-strew'd threshold I follow their movements,
The lithe sheer[17] of their waists plays even with their massive arms,
Overhand the hammers swing, overhand so slow, overhand so sure,
They do not hasten, each man hits in his place.

13

The negro holds firmly the reins of his four horses, the block swags[18]
    underneath on its tied-over chain,   225
The negro that drives the long dray[19] of the stone-yard, steady and tall he
    stands pois'd on one leg on the string-piece,[20]
His blue shirt exposes his ample neck and breast and loosens over his hip-
    band,
His glance is calm and commanding, he tosses the slouch of his hat away
    from his forehead,
The sun falls on his crispy hair and mustache, falls on the black of his
    polish'd and perfect limbs.

I behold the picturesque giant and love him, and I do not stop there,   230
I go with the team also.

In me the caresser of life wherever moving, backward as well as forward
    sluing,[21]
To niches aside and junior bending, not a person or object missing,
Absorbing all to myself and for this song.

Oxen that rattle the yoke and chain or halt in the leafy shade, what is that
    you express in your eyes?   235
It seems to me more than all the print I have read in my life.

My tread scares the wood-drake and wood-duck on my distant and day-long
    ramble,
They rise together, they slowly circle around.

I believe in those wing'd purposes,
And acknowledge red, yellow, white, playing within me,   240
And consider green and violet and the tufted crown intentional,
And do not call the tortoise unworthy because she is not something else,
And the jay in the woods never studied the gamut,[22] yet trills pretty well to
    me,
And the look of the bay mare shames silliness out of me.

14

The wild gander leads his flock through the cool night,   245
Ya-honk he says, and sounds it down to me like an invitation,
The pert may suppose it meaningless, but I listening close,
Find its purpose and place up there toward the wintry sky.

The sharp-hoof'd moose of the north, the cat on the house-sill, the
    chickadee, the prairie-dog,
The litter of the grunting sow as they tug at her teats,   250

17Curve.
18Sways or lurches.
19Low, sturdy cart.
20A long, horizontal timber to support a framework (of the

cart).
21Turning, pivoting.
22Musical scale.

The brood of the turkey-hen and she with her half-spread wings,
I see in them and myself the same old law.

The press of my foot to the earth springs a hundred affections,
They scorn the best I can do to relate them.

I am enamour'd of growing out-doors,   255
Of men that live among cattle or taste of the ocean or woods,
Of the builders and steerers of ships and the wielders of axes and mauls,
   and the drivers of horses,
I can eat and sleep with them week in and week out.

What is commonest, cheapest, nearest, easiest, is Me,
Me going in for my chances, spending for vast returns,   260
Adorning myself to bestow myself on the first that will take me,
Not asking the sky to come down to my good will,
Scattering it freely forever.

15

The pure contralto sings in the organ loft,
The carpenter dresses his plank, the tongue of his foreplane whistles its wild
   ascending lisp,   265
The married and unmarried children ride home to their Thanksgiving
   dinner,
The pilot seizes the king-pin, he heaves down with a strong arm,
The mate stands braced in the whale-boat, lance and harpoon are ready,
The duck-shooter walks by silent and cautious stretches,
The deacons are ordain'd with cross'd hands at the altar,   270
The spinning-girl retreats and advances to the hum of the big wheel,
The farmer stops by the bars[23] as he walks on a First-day[24] loafe and looks
   at the oats and rye,
The lunatic is carried at last to the asylum a confirm'd case,
(He will never sleep any more as he did in the cot in his mother's bed-room;)
The jour[25] printer with gray head and gaunt jaws works at his case,[26]   275
He turns his quid of tobacco while his eyes blurr with the manuscript;
The malform'd limbs are tied to the surgeon's table,
What is removed drops horribly in a pail;
The quadroon girl is sold at the auction-stand, the drunkard nods by the
   bar-room stove,
The machinist rolls up his sleeves, the policeman travels his beat, the gate-
   keeper marks who pass,   280
The young fellow drives the express-wagon, (I love him, though I do not
   know him;)
The half-breed straps on his light boots to compete in the race,
The western turkey-shooting draws old and young, some lean on their rifles,
   some sit on logs,
Out from the crowd steps the marksman, takes his position, levels his piece;
The groups of newly-come immigrants cover the wharf or levee,   285
As the woolly-pates[27] hoe in the sugar-field, the overseer views them from
   his saddle,
The bugle calls in the ball-room, the gentlemen run for their partners, the
   dancers bow to each other,

---

[23]Removable fence rails.
[24]Sunday (used by Quakers to avoid pagan names of the days
of the week).

[25]Journeyman (a worker who has learned his trade).
[26]Case of type.
[27]Blacks.

The youth lies awake in the cedar-roof'd garret and harks to the musical
    rain,
The Wolverine[28] sets traps on the creek that helps fill the Huron,
The squaw wrapt in her yellow-hemm'd cloth is offering moccasins and
    bead-bags for sale,   290
The connoisseur peers along the exhibition-gallery with half-shut eyes bent
    sideways,
As the deck-hands make fast the steamboat the plank is thrown for the
    shore-going passengers,
The young sister holds out the skein while the elder sister winds it off in a
    ball, and stops now and then for the knots,
The one-year wife is recovering and happy having a week ago borne her
    first child,
The clean-hair'd Yankee girl works with her sewing-machine or in the
    factory or mill,   295
The paving-man leans on his two-handed rammer, the reporter's lead flies
    swiftly over the note-book, the sign-painter is lettering with blue and gold,
The canal boy trots on the tow-path,[29] the book-keeper counts at his desk,
    the shoemaker waxes his thread,
The conductor beats time for the band and all the performers follow him,
The child is baptized, the convert is making his first professions,
The regatta is spread on the bay, the race is begun, (how the white sails
    sparkle!)   300
The drover watching his drove sings out to them that would stray,
The pedler sweats with his pack on his back, (the purchaser higgling[30] about
    the odd cent;)
The bride unrumples her white dress, the minute-hand of the clock moves
    slowly,
The opium-eater reclines with rigid head and just-open'd lips,
The prostitute draggles her shawl, her bonnet bobs on her tipsy and
    pimpled neck,   305
The crowd laugh at her blackguard oaths, the men jeer and wink to each
    other,
(Miserable! I do not laugh at your oaths nor jeer you;)
The President holding a cabinet council is surrounded by the great
    Secretaries,
On the piazza walk three matrons stately and friendly with twined arms,
The crew of the fish-smack pack repeated layers of halibut in the hold,   310
The Missourian crosses the plains toting his wares and his cattle,
As the fare-collector goes through the train he gives notice by the jingling of
    loose change,
The floor-men are laying the floor, the tinners are tinning the roof, the
    masons are calling for mortar,
In single file each shouldering his hod pass onward the laborers;
Seasons pursuing each other the indescribable crowd is gather'd, it is the
    fourth of Seventh-month,[31] (what salutes of cannon and small arms!)   315
Seasons pursuing each other the plougher ploughs, the mower mows, and
    the winter-grain falls in the ground;
Off on the lakes the pike-fisher watches and waits by the hole in the frozen
    surface,
The stumps stand thick round the clearing, the squatter strikes deep with
    his axe,
Flatboatmen make fast towards dusk near the cotton-wood or pecan-trees,

---

[28]Michigan inhabitant.   [30]Bargaining.
[29]Path on shore used for animals to pull the canal boats.   [31]July.

Coon-seekers[32] go through the regions of the Red river[33] or through those
    drain'd by the Tennessee,[34] or through those of the Arkansas,[35]   320
Torches shine in the dark that hangs on the Chattahooche or Altamahaw,[36]
Patriarchs sit at supper with sons and grandsons and great grandsons
    around them,
In walls of adobie, in canvas tents, rest hunters and trappers after their day's
    sport,
The city sleeps and the country sleeps,
The living sleep for their time, the dead sleep for their time,   325
The old husband sleeps by his wife and the young husband sleeps by his
    wife;
And these tend inward to me, and I tend outward to them,
And such as it is to be of these more or less I am,
And of these one and all I weave the song of myself.

16

I am of old and young, of the foolish as much as the wise,   330
Regardless of others, ever regardful of others,
Maternal as well as paternal, a child as well as a man,
Stuff'd with the stuff that is coarse and stuff'd with the stuff that is fine,
One of the Nation of many nations, the smallest the same and the largest the
    same,
A Southerner soon as a Northerner, a planter nonchalant and hospitable
    down by the Oconee[37] I live,   335
A Yankee bound my own way ready for trade, my joints the limberest joints
    on earth and the sternest joints on earth,
A Kentuckian walking the vale of the Elkhorn[38] in my deerskin leggings, a
    Louisianian or Georgian,
A boatman over lakes or bays or along coasts, a Hoosier, Badger, Buckeye;[39]
At home on Kanadian[40] snow-shoes or up in the bush, or with fishermen off
    Newfoundland,
At home in the fleet of ice-boats, sailing with the rest and tacking,   340
At home on the hills of Vermont or in the woods of Maine, or the Texan
    ranch,
Comrade of Californians, comrade of free North-Westerners, (loving their
    big proportions,)
Comrade of raftsmen and coalmen, comrade of all who shake hands and
    welcome to drink and meat,
A learner with the simplest, a teacher of the thoughtfullest,
A novice beginning yet experient of myriads of seasons,   345
Of every hue and caste am I, of every rank and religion,
A farmer, mechanic, artist, gentleman, sailor, quaker,
Prisoner, fancy-man,[41] rowdy, lawyer, physician, priest.

I resist any thing better than my own diversity,
Breathe the air but leave plenty after me,
And am not stuck up, and am in my place.   350

(The moth and the fish-eggs are in their place,
The bright suns I see and the dark suns I cannot see are in their place,
The palpable is in its place and the impalpable in its place.)

---

[32]Raccoon hunters.
[33]River between Texas and Oklahoma.
[34]River that runs from Tennessee through Alabama and Kentucky into the Ohio.
[35]River that flows from Colorado to the Mississippi.
[36]Georgia rivers flowing into the Gulf of Mexico.

[37]Georgia river.
[38]Nebraska river.
[39]Inhabitants of Indiana, Wisconsin, and Ohio.
[40]Canadian (Whitman often substituted initial "K" for "C").
[41]Pimp.

17

These are really the thoughts of all men in all ages and lands, they are not
    original with me,   355
If they are not yours as much as mine they are nothing, or next to nothing,
If they are not the riddle and the untying of the riddle they are nothing,
If they are not just as close as they are distant they are nothing.

This is the grass that grows wherever the land is and the water is,
This the common air that bathes the globe.   360

18

With music strong I come, with my cornets and my drums,
I play not marches for accepted victors only, I play marches for conquer'd
    and slain persons.

Have you heard that it was good to gain the day?
I also say it is good to fall, battles are lost in the same spirit in which they are
    won.

I beat and pound for the dead,   365
I blow through my embouchures[42] my loudest and gayest for them.

Vivas[43] to those who have fail'd!
And to those whose war-vessels sank in the sea!
And to those themselves who sank in the sea!
And to all generals that lost engagements, and all overcome heroes!   370
And the numberless unknown heroes equal to the greatest heroes known!

19

This is the meal equally set, this the meat for natural hunger,
It is for the wicked just the same as the righteous, I make appointments with
    all,
I will not have a single person slighted or left away,
The kept-woman, sponger, thief, are hereby invited,   375
The heavy-lipp'd slave is invited, the venerealee[44] is invited;
There shall be no difference between them and the rest.

This is the press of a bashful hand, this the float and odor of hair,
This the touch of my lips to yours, this the murmur of yearning,
This the far-off depth and height reflecting my own face,   380
This the thoughtful merge of myself, and the outlet again.

Do you guess I have some intricate purpose?
Well I have, for the Fourth-month[45] showers have, and the mica on the side
    of a rock has.

Do you take it I would astonish?
Does the daylight astonish? does the early redstart twittering through the
    woods?   385
Do I astonish more than they?

This hour I tell things in confidence,
I might not tell everybody, but I will tell you.

---

[42]Mouthpieces of musical instruments.   [44]One with sexual disease (Whitman's coinage).
[43]Salutes ("Long live," from Italian or Spanish).   [45]April.

20

Who goes there? hankering, gross, mystical, nude;
How is it I extract strength from the beef I eat?   390

What is a man anyhow? what am I? what are you?

All I mark as my own you shall offset it with your own,
Else it were time lost listening to me.

I do not snivel that snivel the world over,
The months are vacuums and the ground but wallow and filth.   395

Whimpering and truckling fold with powders for invalids,[46] conformity goes
    to the fourth-remov'd,
I wear my hat as I please indoors or out.

Why should I pray? why should I venerate and be ceremonious?

Having pried through the strata, analyzed to a hair, counsel'd with doctors
    and calculated close,
I find no sweeter fat than sticks to my own bones.   400

In all people I see myself, none more and not one a barley-corn less,
And the good or bad I say of myself I say of them.

I know I am solid and sound,
To me the converging objects of the universe perpetually flow,
All are written to me, and I must get what the writing means.   405

I know I am deathless,
I know this orbit of mine cannot be swept by a carpenter's compass,
I know I shall not pass like a child's carlacue[47] cut with a burnt stick at night.

I know I am august,
I do not trouble my spirit to vindicate itself or be understood,   410
I see that the elementary laws never apologize,
(I reckon I behave no prouder than the level[48] I plant my house by, after
    all.)

I exist as I am, that is enough,
If no other in the world be aware I sit content,
And if each and all be aware I sit content.   415

One world is aware and by far the largest to me, and that is myself,
And whether I come to my own to-day or in ten thousand or ten million
    years,
I can cheerfully take it now, or with equal cheerfulness I can wait.

My foothold is tenon'd and mortis'd[49] in granite,
I laugh at what you call dissolution,   420
And I know the amplitude of time.

---

[46]I.e., crying and cringing should be folded in the packets of medicine for the sick.
[47]Variant of "curlicue," a fancy curve or flourish (made by a glowing stick temporarily in the dark).
[48]I.e., carpenter's level.
[49]I.e., in carpentry, the tenon (or projection) of one piece of wood fits into the mortise (corresponding cavity) of another piece of wood, forming a tight joint.

21

I am the poet of the Body and I am the poet of the Soul,
The pleasures of heaven are with me and the pains of hell are with me,
The first I graft and increase upon myself, the latter I translate into a new
    tongue.

I am the poet of the woman the same as the man,   425
And I say it is as great to be a woman as to be a man,
And I say there is nothing greater than the mother of men.

I chant the chant of dilation or pride,
We have had ducking and deprecating about enough,
I show that size is only development.   430

Have you outstript the rest? are you the President?
It is a trifle, they will more than arrive there every one, and still pass on.

I am he that walks with the tender and growing night,
I call to the earth and sea half-held by the night.

Press close bare-bosom'd night—press close magnetic nourishing night!   435
Night of south winds—night of the large few stars!
Still nodding night—mad naked summer night.

Smile O voluptuous cool-breath'd earth!
Earth of the slumbering and liquid trees!
Earth of departed sunset—earth of the mountains misty-topt!   440
Earth of the vitreous[50] pour of the full moon just tinged with blue!
Earth of shine and dark mottling the tide of the river!
Earth of the limpid gray of clouds brighter and clearer for my sake!
Far-swooping elbow'd earth—rich apple-blossom'd earth!
Smile, for your lover comes.   445

Prodigal, you have given me love—therefore I to you give love!
O unspeakable passionate love.

22

You sea! I resign myself to you also—I guess what you mean,
I behold from the beach your crooked inviting fingers,
I believe you refuse to go back without feeling of me,   450
We must have a turn together, I undress, hurry me out of sight of the land,
Cushion me soft, rock me in billowy drowse,
Dash me with amorous wet, I can repay you.

Sea of stretch'd ground-swells,
Sea breathing broad and convulsive breaths,   455
Sea of the brine of life and of unshovell'd yet always-ready graves,
Howler and scooper of storms, capricious and dainty sea,
I am integral with you, I too am of one phase and of all phases.

Partaker of influx and efflux I, extoller of hate and conciliation,
Extoller of amies[51] and those that sleep in each others' arms,   460
I am he attesting sympathy,

---

[50]Glass-like.
[51]"Friends," "lovers" (French).

(Shall I make my list of things in the house and skip the house that supports
   them?)

I am not the poet of goodness only, I do not decline to be the poet of
   wickedness also.

What blurt is this about virtue and about vice?
Evil propels me and reform of evil propels me, I stand indifferent,   465
My gait is no fault-finder's or rejecter's gait,
I moisten the roots of all that has grown.

Did you fear some scrofula[52] out of the unflagging pregnancy?
Did you guess the celestial laws are yet to be work'd over and rectified?

I find one side a balance and the antipodal side a balance,   470
Soft doctrine as steady help as stable doctrine,
Thoughts and deeds of the present our rouse and early start.

This minute that comes to me over the past decillions,[53]
There is no better than it and now.

What behaved well in the past or behaves well to-day is not such a wonder,   475
The wonder is always and always how there can be a mean man or an
   infidel.

23

Endless unfolding of words of ages!
And mine a word of the modern, the word En-Masse.[54]

A word of the faith that never balks,
Here or henceforward it is all the same to me, I accept Time absolutely.   480

It alone is without flaw, it alone rounds and completes all,
That mystic baffling wonder alone completes all.

I accept Reality and dare not question it,
Materialism first and last imbuing.

Hurrah for positive science! long live exact demonstration!   485
Fetch stonecrop[55] mixt with cedar and branches of lilac,
This is the lexicographer, this the chemist, this made a grammar of the old
   cartouches,[56]
These mariners put the ship through dangerous unknown seas,
This is the geologist, this works with the scalpel, and this is a mathematician.

Gentlemen, to you the first honors always!   490
Your facts are useful, and yet they are not my dwelling,
I but enter by them to an area of my dwelling.

Less the reminders of properties told my words,
And more the reminders they of life untold, and of freedom and
   extrication,
And make short account of neuters and geldings, and favor men and
   women fully equipt,   495

---

[52]Disease of the lymphatic glands, characterized by
enlargement.
[53]The number constituted by 1 followed by 33 zeros.

[54]"All together, as a whole" (French).
[55]An herb that grows in masses of rock, used in medicine.
[56]Frames to hold inscriptions.

And beat the gong of revolt, and stop with fugitives and them that plot and
    conspire.

24

Walt Whitman, a kosmos,[57] of Manhattan the son,
Turbulent, fleshy, sensual, eating, drinking and breeding,
No sentimentalist, no stander above men and women or apart from them,
No more modest than immodest.   500

Unscrew the locks from the doors!
Unscrew the doors themselves from their jambs!

Whoever degrades another degrades me,
And whatever is done or said returns at last to me.

Through me the afflatus[58] surging and surging, through me the current
    and index.   505

I speak the pass-word primeval, I give the sign of democracy,
By God! I will accept nothing which all cannot have their counterpart of on
    the same terms.

Through me many long dumb voices,
Voices of the interminable generations of prisoners and slaves,
Voices of the diseas'd and despairing and of thieves and dwarfs,   510
Voices of cycles of preparation and accretion,
And of the threads that connect the stars, and of wombs and of the father-
    stuff,[59]
And of the rights of them the others are down upon,
Of the deform'd, trivial, flat, foolish, despised,
Fog in the air, beetles rolling balls of dung.   515

Through me forbidden voices,
Voices of sexes and lusts, voices veil'd and I remove the veil,
Voices indecent by me clarified and transfigur'd.

I do not press my fingers across my mouth,
I keep as delicate around the bowels as around the head and heart,   520
Copulation is no more rank to me than death is.

I believe in the flesh and the appetites,
Seeing, hearing, feeling, are miracles, and each part and tag of me is a
    miracle.

Divine am I inside and out, and I make holy whatever I touch or am touch'd
    from,
The scent of these arm-pits aroma finer than prayer,   525
This head more than churches, bibles, and all the creeds.

If I worship one thing more than another it shall be the spread of my own
    body, or any part of it,
Translucent mould of me it shall be you!
Shaded ledges and rests it shall be you!

---

[57]Cosmos, harmonious universe.
[58]Poetic inspiration.
[59]Semen.

Firm masculine colter[60] it shall be you!   530
Whatever goes to the tilth[61] of me it shall be you!
You my rich blood! your milky stream pale strippings of my life!
Breast that presses against other breasts it shall be you!
My brain it shall be your occult convolutions!
Root of wash'd sweet-flag![62] timorous pond-snipe! nest of guarded duplicate
    eggs! it shall be you!   535
Mix'd tussled hay of head, beard, brawn, it shall be you!
Trickling sap of maple, fibre of manly wheat, it shall be you!
Sun so generous it shall be you!
Vapors lighting and shading my face it shall be you!
You sweaty brooks and dews it shall be you!   540
Winds whose soft-tickling genitals rub against me it shall be you!
Broad muscular fields, branches of live oak, loving lounger in my winding
    paths, it shall be you!
Hands I have taken, face I have kiss'd, mortal I have ever touch'd, it shall be
    you.

I dote on myself, there is that lot of me and all so luscious,
Each moment and whatever happens thrills me with joy,   545
I cannot tell how my ankles bend, nor whence the cause of my faintest wish,
Nor the cause of the friendship I emit, nor the cause of the friendship I take
    again.

That I walk up my stoop, I pause to consider if it really be,
A morning-glory at my window satisfies me more than the metaphysics of
    books.

To behold the day-break!   550
The little light fades the immense and diaphanous shadows,
The air tastes good to my palate.

Hefts[63] of the moving world at innocent gambols silently rising, freshly
    exuding,
Scooting obliquely high and low.

Something I cannot see puts upward libidinous prongs,   555
Seas of bright juice suffuse heaven.

The earth by the sky staid with, the daily close of their junction,
The heav'd challenge from the east that moment over my head,
The mocking taunt, See then whether you shall be master!

                                    25

Dazzling and tremendous how quick the sun-rise would kill me,   560
If I could not now and always send sun-rise out of me.

We also ascend dazzling and tremendous as the sun,
We found our own O my soul in the calm and cool of the day-break.

My voice goes after what my eyes cannot reach,
With the twirl of my tongue I encompass worlds and volumes of worlds.   565

---

[60]Iron blade attached to the front of a plough.   structure and root.
[61]Cultivation.   [63]Mass, bulk, or main parts.
[62]Calamus, a flower that grows near ponds, with phallic-like

Speech is the twin of my vision, it is unequal to measure itself,
It provokes me forever, it says sarcastically,
Walt you contain enough, why don't you let it out then?

Come now I will not be tantalized, you conceive too much of articulation,
Do you not know O speech how the buds beneath you are folded? 570
Waiting in gloom, protected by frost,
The dirt receding before my prophetical screams,
I underlying causes to balance them at last,
My knowledge my live parts, it keeping tally with the meaning of all things,
Happiness, (which whoever hears me let him or her set out in search of this
    day.) 575

My final merit I refuse you, I refuse putting from me what I really am,
Encompass worlds, but never try to encompass me,
I crowd your sleekest and best by simply looking toward you.

Writing and talk do not prove me,
I carry the plenum[64] of proof and every thing else in my face, 580
With the hush of my lips I wholly confound the skeptic.

26

Now I will do nothing but listen,
To accrue what I hear into this song, to let sounds contribute toward it.

I hear bravuras of birds, bustle of growing wheat, gossip of flames, clack of
    sticks cooking my meals,
I hear the sound I love, the sound of the human voice, 585
I hear all sounds running together, combined, fused or following,
Sounds of the city and sounds out of the city, sounds of the day and night,
Talkative young ones to those that like them, the loud laugh of work-people
    at their meals,
The angry base[65] of disjointed friendship, the faint tones of the sick,
The judge with hands tight to the desk, his pallid lips pronouncing a death-
    sentence, 590
The heave'e'yo of stevedores unlading ships by the wharves, the refrain of
    the anchor-lifters,
The ring of alarm-bells, the cry of fire, the whirr of swift-streaking engines
    and hose-carts with premonitory tinkles and color'd lights,
The steam-whistle, the solid roll of the train of approaching cars,
The slow march play'd at the head of the association marching two and two,
(They go to guard some corpse, the flag-tops are draped with black muslin.) 595

I hear the violoncello, ('tis the young man's heart's complaint,)
I hear the key'd cornet, it glides quickly in through my ears,
It shakes mad-sweet pangs through my belly and breast.

I hear the chorus, it is a grand opera,
Ah this indeed is music—this suits me. 600

A tenor large and fresh as the creation fills me,
The orbic flex of his mouth is pouring and filling me full.

64Condition of fullness.
65Variant of "bass."

I hear the train'd soprano (what work with hers is this?)
The orchestra whirls me wider than Uranus[66] flies,
It wrenches such ardors from me I did not know I possess'd them,   605
It sails me, I dab with bare feet, they are lick'd by the indolent waves,
I am cut by bitter and angry hail, I lose my breath,
Steep'd amid honey'd morphine, my windpipe throttled in fakes[67] of death,
At length let up again to feel the puzzle of puzzles,
And that we call Being.   610

27

To be in any form, what is that?
(Round and round we go, all of us, and ever come back thither,)
If nothing lay more develop'd the quahaug[68] in its callous shell were
   enough.

Mine is no callous shell,
I have instant conductors all over me whether I pass or stop,   615
They seize every object and lead it harmlessly through me.

I merely stir, press, feel with my fingers, and am happy,
To touch my person to some one else's is about as much as I can stand.

28

Is this then a touch? quivering me to a new identity,
Flames and ether making a rush for my veins,   620
Treacherous tip of me reaching and crowding to help them,
My flesh and blood playing out lightning to strike what is hardly different
   from myself,
On all sides prurient provokers stiffening my limbs,
Straining the udder of my heart for its withheld drip,
Behaving licentious toward me, taking no denial,   625
Depriving me of my best as for a purpose,
Unbuttoning my clothes, holding me by the bare waist,
Deluding my confusion with the calm of the sunlight and pasture-fields,
Immodestly sliding the fellow-senses away,
They bribed to swap off with touch and go and graze at the edges of me,   630
No consideration, no regard for my draining strength or my anger,
Fetching the rest of the herd around to enjoy them a while,
Then all uniting to stand on a headland and worry me.

The sentries desert every other part of me,
They have left me helpless to a red marauder,   635
They all come to the headland to witness and assist against me.

I am given up by traitors,
I talk wildly, I have lost my wits, I and nobody else am the greatest traitor,
I went myself first to the headland, my own hands carried me there.

You villain touch! what are you doing? my breath is tight in its throat,   640
Unclench your floodgates, you are too much for me.

---

[66]Remote planet with large orbit.
[67]Rope coils.
[68]Atlantic clam.

29

Blind loving wrestling touch, sheath'd hooded sharp-tooth'd touch!
Did it make you ache so, leaving me?

Parting track'd by arriving, perpetual payment of perpetual loan,
Rich showering rain, and recompense richer afterward.   645

Sprouts take and accumulate, stand by the curb prolific and vital,
Landscapes projected masculine, full-sized and golden.

30

All truths wait in all things,
They neither hasten their own delivery nor resist it,
They do not need the obstetric forceps of the surgeon,   650
The insignificant is as big to me as any,
(What is less or more than a touch?)

Logic and sermons never convince,
The damp of the night drives deeper into my soul.

(Only what proves itself to every man and woman is so,   655
Only what nobody denies is so.)

A minute and a drop of me settle my brain,
I believe the soggy clods shall become lovers and lamps,
And a compend[69] of compends is the meat of a man or woman,
And a summit and flower there is the feeling they have for each other,   660
And they are to branch boundlessly out of that lesson until it becomes
    omnific,[70]
And until one and all shall delight us, and we them.

31

I believe a leaf of grass is no less than the journey-work of the stars,
And the pismire[71] is equally perfect, and a grain of sand, and the egg of the
    wren,
And the tree-toad is a chef-d'œuvre[72] for the highest,   665
And the running blackberry would adorn the parlors of heaven,
And the narrowest hinge in my hand puts to scorn all machinery,
And the cow crunching with depress'd head surpasses any statue,
And a mouse is miracle enough to stagger sextillions[73] of infidels.

I find I incorporate gneiss,[74] coal, long-threaded moss, fruits, grains,
    esculent roots,   670
And am stucco'd with quadrupeds and birds all over,
And have distanced what is behind me for good reasons,
But call any thing back again when I desire it.

In vain the speeding or shyness,
In vain the plutonic rocks[75] send their old heat against my approach, 675
In vain the mastodon retreats beneath its own powder'd bones,
In vain objects stand leagues off and assume manifold shapes,

---

[69]Compendium, summary, epitome.
[70]All-creating, making all things.
[71]Ant.
[72]"Masterpiece" (French).

[73]The number constituted by 1 followed by 21 zeros.
[74]Metamorphic rock, consisting of alternating layers of different minerals.
[75]Igneous, granite-like rock.

In vain the ocean settling in hollows and the great monsters lying low,
In vain the buzzard houses herself with the sky,
In vain the snake slides through the creepers and logs,   680
In vain the elk takes to the inner passes of the woods,
In vain the razor-bill'd auk sails far north to Labrador,
I follow quickly, I ascend to the nest in the fissure of the cliff.

32

I think I could turn and live with animals, they're so placid and self-
  contain'd,
I stand and look at them long and long.   685

They do not sweat and whine about their condition,
They do not lie awake in the dark and weep for their sins,
They do not make me sick discussing their duty to God,
Not one is dissatisfied, not one is demented with the mania of owning
  things,
Not one kneels to another, nor to his kind that lived thousands of years ago,   690
Not one is respectable or unhappy over the whole earth.

So they show their relations to me and I accept them,
They bring me tokens of myself, they evince them plainly in their
  possession.

I wonder where they get those tokens,
Did I pass that way huge times ago and negligently drop them?   695

Myself moving forward then and now and forever,
Gathering and showing more always and with velocity,
Infinite and omnigenous,[76] and the like of these among them,
Not too exclusive toward the reachers of my remembrancers,
Picking out here one that I love, and now go with him on brotherly terms.   700

A gigantic beauty of a stallion, fresh and responsive to my caresses,
Head high in the forehead, wide between the ears,
Limbs glossy and supple, tail dusting the ground,
Eyes full of sparkling wickedness, ears finely cut, flexibly moving.

His nostrils dilate as my heels embrace him,   705
His well-built limbs tremble with pleasure as we race around and return.

I but use you a minute, then I resign you, stallion,
Why do I need your paces when I myself out-gallop them?
Even as I stand or sit passing faster than you.

33

Space and Time! now I see it is true, what I guess'd at,   710
What I guess'd when I loaf'd on the grass,
What I guess'd while I lay alone in my bed,
And again as I walk'd the beach under the paling stars of the morning.

My ties and ballasts leave me, my elbows rest in sea-gaps,
I skirt sierras, my palms cover continents,   715
I am afoot with my vision.

---

[76]Of all kinds.

By the city's quadrangular houses—in log huts, camping with lumbermen,
Along the ruts of the turnpike, along the dry gulch and rivulet bed,
Weeding my onion-patch or hoeing rows of carrots and parsnips, crossing
    savannas, trailing in forests,
Prospecting, gold-digging, girdling the trees of a new purchase,   720
Scorch'd ankle-deep by the hot sand, hauling my boat down the shallow
    river,
Where the panther walks to and fro on a limb overhead, where the buck
    turns furiously at the hunter,
Where the rattlesnake suns his flabby length on a rock, where the otter is
    feeding on fish,
Where the alligator in his tough pimples sleeps by the bayou,
Where the black bear is searching for roots or honey, where the beaver pats
    the mud with his paddle-shaped tail;   725
Over the growing sugar, over the yellow-flower'd cotton plant, over the rice
    in its low moist field,
Over the sharp-peak'd farm house, with its scallop'd scum[77] and slender
    shoots from the gutters,
Over the western persimmon, over the long-leav'd corn, over the delicate
    blue-flower flax,
Over the white and brown buckwheat, a hummer and buzzer[78] there with
    the rest,
Over the dusky green of the rye as it ripples and shades in the breeze;   730
Scaling mountains, pulling myself cautiously up, holding on by low
    scragged[79] limbs,
Walking the path worn in the grass and beat through the leaves of the
    brush,
Where the quail is whistling betwixt the woods and the wheat-lot,
Where the bat flies in the Seventh-month eve, where the great gold-bug[80]
    drops through the dark,
Where the brook puts out of the roots of the old tree and flows to the
    meadow,   735
Where cattle stand and shake away flies with the tremulous shuddering of
    their hides,
Where the cheese-cloth hangs in the kitchen, where andirons straddle the
    hearth-slab, where cobwebs fall in festoons from the rafters;
Where trip-hammers crash, where the press is whirling its cylinders,
Where the human heart beats with terrible throes under its ribs,
Where the pear-shaped balloon is floating aloft, (floating in it myself and
    looking composedly down,)   740
Where the life-car[81] is drawn on the slip-noose, where the heat hatches pale-
    green eggs in the dented sand,
Where the she-whale swims with her calf and never forsakes it,
Where the steam-ship trails hind-ways its long pennant of smoke,
Where the fin of the shark cuts like a black chip out of the water,
Where the half-burn'd brig is riding on unknown currents,   745
Where shells grow to her slimy deck, where the dead are corrupting below;
Where the dense-starr'd flag is borne at the head of the regiments,
Approaching Manhattan up by the long-stretching island,
Under Niagara, the cataract falling like a veil over my countenance,
Upon a door-step, upon the horse-block[82] of hard wood outside,   750
Upon the race-course, or enjoying picnics or jigs or a good game of base-
    ball,

---

[77]Froth.
[78]Hummingbird and bumblebee.
[79]Scraggy, stunted.
[80]Goldsmith beetle.

[81]Water-tight vessel moved by rope from wrecked ship to shore.
[82]Block used as step in mounting.

At he-festivals, with blackguard jibes, ironical license, bull-dances,[83] drinking, laughter,

At the cider-mill tasting the sweets of the brown mash, sucking the juice through a straw,

At apple-peelings wanting kisses for all the red fruit I find,

At musters,[84] beach-parties, friendly bees, huskings, house-raisings,   755

Where the mocking-bird sounds his delicious gurgles, cackles, screams, weeps,

Where the hay-rick stands in the barn-yard, where the dry-stalks are scatter'd, where the brood-cow waits in the hovel,

Where the bull advances to do his masculine work, where the stud to the mare, where the cock is treading the hen,

Where the heifers browse, where geese nip their food with short jerks,

Where sun-down shadows lengthen over the limitless and lonesome prairie,   760

Where herds of buffalo make a crawling spread of the square miles far and near,

Where the humming-bird shimmers, where the neck of the long-lived swan is curving and winding,

Where the laughing-gull scoots by the shore, where she laughs her near-human laugh,

Where bee-hives range on a gray bench in the garden half hid by the high weeds,

Where bank-neck'd partridges roost in a ring on the ground with their heads out,   765

Where burial coaches enter the arch'd gates of a cemetery,

Where winter wolves bark amid wastes of snow and icicled trees,

Where the yellow-crown'd heron comes to the edge of the marsh at night and feeds upon small crabs,

Where the splash of swimmers and divers cools the warm noon,

Where the katy-did works her chromatic reed on the walnut-tree over the well,   770

Through patches of citrons[85] and cucumbers with silver-wired leaves,

Through the salt-lick or orange glade, or under conical firs,

Through the gymnasium, through the curtain'd saloon, through the office or public hall;

Pleas'd with the native and pleas'd with the foreign, pleas'd with the new and old,

Pleas'd with the homely woman as well as the handsome,   775

Pleas'd with the quakeress as she puts off her bonnet and talks melodiously,

Pleas'd with the tune of the choir of the whitewash'd church,

Pleas'd with the earnest words of the sweating Methodist preacher, impress'd seriously at the camp-meeting;

Looking in at the shop-windows of Broadway the whole forenoon, flatting the flesh of my nose on the thick plate glass,

Wandering the same afternoon with my face turn'd up to the clouds, or down a lane or along the beach,   780

My right and left arms round the sides of two friends, and I in the middle;

Coming home with the silent and dark-cheek'd bush-boy,[86] (behind me he rides at the drape of the day,)

Far from the settlements studying the print of animals' feet, or the moccasin print,

By the cot in the hospital reaching lemonade to a feverish patient,

Nigh the coffin'd corpse when all is still, examining with a candle;   785

Voyaging to every port to dicker and adventure,

---

[83]Indian buffalo dance.
[84]Assemblies, gatherings.
[85]Kind of watermelon.
[86]Boy of the wilderness.

Hurrying with the modern crowd as eager and fickle as any,
Hot toward one I hate, ready in my madness to knife him,
Solitary at midnight in my back yard, my thoughts gone from me a long
    while,
Walking the old hills of Judæa[87] with the beautiful gentle God by my side,   790
Speeding through space, speeding through heaven and the stars,
Speeding amid the seven satellites and the broad ring, and the diameter of
    eighty thousand miles,[88]
Speeding with tail'd meteors, throwing fire-balls like the rest,
Carrying the crescent child that carries its own full mother in its belly,[89]
Storming, enjoying, planning, loving, cautioning,   795
Backing and filling, appearing and disappearing,
I tread day and night such roads.

I visit the orchards of spheres and look at the product,
And look at quintillions[90] ripen'd and look at quintillions green.

I fly those flights of a fluid and swallowing soul,   800
My course runs below the soundings of plummets.

I help myself to material and immaterial,
No guard can shut me off, no law prevent me.

I anchor my ship for a little while only,
My messengers continually cruise away or bring their returns to me.   805

I go hunting polar furs and the seal, leaping chasms with a pike-pointed
    staff, clinging to topples[91] of brittle and blue.

I ascend to the foretruck,[92]
I take my place late at night in the crow's-nest,
We sail the arctic sea, it is plenty light enough,
Through the clear atmosphere I stretch around on the wonderful beauty,   810
The enormous masses of ice pass me and I pass them, the scenery is plain in
    all directions,
The white-topt mountains show in the distance, I fling out my fancies
    toward them,
We are approaching some great battle-field in which we are soon to be
    engaged,
We pass the colossal outposts of the encampment, we pass with still feet and
    caution,
Or we are entering by the suburbs some vast and ruin'd city,   815
The blocks and fallen architecture more than all the living cities of the
    globe.

I am a free companion, I bivouac by invading watchfires,
I turn the bridegroom out of bed and stay with the bride myself,
I tighten her all night to my thighs and lips.

My voice is the wife's voice, the screech by the rail of the stairs,   820
They fetch my man's body up dripping and drown'd.

I understand the large hearts of heroes,
The courage of present times and all times,

---

[87]Southern Palestine, scene of Jesus' ministry.
[88]The planet Saturn.
[89]The new moon.
[90]The number constituted by 1 followed by 18 zeros.
[91]That which has toppled or fallen (as ice).
[92]Variant of foretop, platform on the foremast near the top.

How the skipper saw the crowded and rudderless wreck of the steamship,
  and Death chasing it up and down the storm,
How he knuckled tight and gave not back an inch, and was faithful of days
  and faithful of nights,   825
And chalk'd in large letters on a board, *Be of good cheer, we will not desert you;*
How he follow'd with them and tack'd with them three days and would not
  give it up,
How he saved the drifting company at last,
How the lank loose-gown'd women look'd when boated from the side of
  their prepared graves,
How the silent old-faced infants and the lifted sick, and the sharp-lipp'd
  unshaved men;   830
All this I swallow, it tastes good, I like it well, it becomes mine,
I am the man, I suffer'd, I was there.[93]

The disdain and calmness of martyrs,
The mother of old, condemn'd for a witch, burnt with dry wood, her
  children gazing on,
The hounded slave that flags in the race, leans by the fence, blowing, cover'd
  with sweat,   835
The twinges that sting like needles his legs and neck, the murderous
  buckshot and the bullets,
All these I feel or am.

I am the hounded slave, I wince at the bite of the dogs,
Hell and despair are upon me, crack and again crack the marksmen,
I clutch the rails of the fence, my gore dribs,[94] thinn'd with the ooze of my
  skin,   840
I fall on the weeds and stones,
The riders spur their unwilling horses, haul close,
Taunt my dizzy ears and beat me violently over the head with whipstocks.

Agonies are one of my changes of garments.
I do not ask the wounded person how he feels, I myself become the
  wounded person,   845
My hurts turn livid upon me as I lean on a cane and observe.

I am the mash'd fireman with breast-bone broken,
Tumbling walls buried me in their debris,
Heat and smoke I inspired,[95] I heard the yelling shouts of my comrades,
I heard the distant click of their picks and shovels,   850
They have clear'd the beams away, they tenderly lift me forth.

I lie in the night air in my red shirt, the pervading hush is for my sake,
Painless after all I lie exhausted but not so unhappy,
White and beautiful are the faces around me, the heads are bared of their
  fire-caps,
The kneeling crowd fades with the light of the torches.   855

Distant and dead resuscitate,
They show me as the dial or move as the hands of me, I am the clock myself.

I am an old artillerist, I tell of my fort's bombardment,
I am there again.

---

[93]Based on the shipwreck of the *San Francisco*, out of New   [94]Falls in drops.
York Harbor, December 23–24, 1853.   [95]Inhaled.

Again the long roll of the drummers,   860
Again the attacking cannon, mortars,
Again to my listening ears the cannon responsive.

I take part, I see and hear the whole,
The cries, curses, roar, the plaudits for well-aim'd shots,
The ambulanza[96] slowly passing trailing its red drip,   865
Workmen searching after damages, making indispensable repairs,
The fall of grenades through the rent roof, the fan-shaped explosion,
The whizz of limbs, heads, stone, wood, iron, high in the air.

Again gurgles the mouth of my dying general, he furiously waves with his
   hand,
He gasps through the clot *Mind not me—mind—the entrenchments.*   870

34

Now I tell what I knew in Texas in my early youth,
(I tell not the fall of Alamo,[97]
Not one escaped to tell the fall of Alamo,
The hundred and fifty are dumb yet at Alamo,)
'Tis the tale of the murder in cold blood of four hundred and twelve young
   men.[98]   875

Retreating they had form'd in a hollow square with their baggage for
   breastworks,
Nine hundred lives out of the surrounding enemy's, nine times their
   number, was the price they took in advance,
Their colonel was wounded and their ammunition gone,
They treated for an honorable capitulation, receiv'd writing and seal, gave
   up their arms and march'd back prisoners of war.

They were the glory of the race of rangers,   880
Matchless with horse, rifle, song, supper, courtship,
Large, turbulent, generous, handsome, proud, and affectionate,
Bearded, sunburnt, drest in the free costume of hunters,
Not a single one over thirty years of age.

The second First-day morning they were brought out in squads and
   massacred, it was beautiful early summer,   885
The work commenced about five o'clock and was over by eight.

None obey'd the command to kneel,
Some made a mad and helpless rush, some stood stark and straight,
A few fell at once, shot in the temple or heart, the living and dead lay
   together,
The maim'd and mangled dug in the dirt, the new-comers saw them there,   890
Some half-kill'd attempted to crawl away,
These were despatch'd with bayonets or batter'd with the blunts of muskets,
A youth not seventeen years old seiz'd his assassin till two more came to
   release him,
The three were all torn and cover'd with the boy's blood.

At eleven o'clock began the burning of the bodies;   895
That is the tale of the murder of the four hundred and twelve young men.

---

[96]"Ambulance" (Italian).
[97]A mission turned into a fortress in San Antonio, Texas, in which all the defending troops were killed by the Mexican forces on March 6, 1836, in the Texas war for independence.
[98]In the same war, Mexican forces wiped out Col. James W. Fannin and his troops at Goliad, Texas, March 27, 1836.

35

Would you hear of an old-time sea-fight?
Would you learn who won by the light of the moon and stars?
List to the yarn, as my grandmother's father the sailor told it to me.[99]

Our foe was no skulk in his ship I tell you, (said he,)   900
His was the surly English pluck, and there is no tougher or truer, and never
   was, and never will be;
Along the lower'd eve he came horribly raking us.

We closed with him, the yards entangled, the cannon touch'd,
My captain lash'd fast with his own hands.

We had receiv'd some eighteen pound shots under the water,   905
On our lower-gun-deck two large pieces had burst at the first fire, killing all
   around and blowing up overhead.

Fighting at sun-down, fighting at dark,
Ten o'clock at night, the full moon well up, our leaks on the gain, and five
   feet of water reported,
The master-at-arms loosing the prisoners confined in the after-hold to give
   them a chance for themselves.

The transit to and from the magazine is now stopt by the sentinels,   910
They see so many strange faces they do not know whom to trust.

Our frigate takes fire,
The other asks if we demand quarter?[1]
If our colors are struck and the fighting done?

Now I laugh content, for I hear the voice of my little captain,   915
We have not struck, he composedly cries, *we have just begun our part of the
   fighting.*

Only three guns are in use,
One is directed by the captain himself against the enemy's main-mast,
Two well serv'd with grape[2] and canister[3] silence his musketry and clear his
   decks.

The tops alone second the fire of this little battery, especially the main-top, 920
They hold out bravely during the whole of the action.

Not a moment's cease,
The leaks gain fast on the pumps, the fire eats toward the powder-magazine.

One of the pumps has been shot away, it is generally thought we are sinking.

Serene stands the little captain,   925
He is not hurried, his voice is neither high nor low,
His eyes give more light to us than our battle-lanterns.

Toward twelve there in the beams of the moon they surrender to us.

---

[99]Story based on the American naval victory in the Revolu-
tionary War in 1778, when John Paul Jones, commanding the
Bonhomme Richard, defeated the British warship *Serapis*.
Jones's famous words were, "We have just begun to fight."

[1]Ask for mercy.
[2]Grape-shot, small cast-iron balls.
[3]Canister-shot, a collection of projectiles in a case.

36

Stretch'd and still lies the midnight,
Two great hulls motionless on the breast of the darkness,   930
Our vessel riddled and slowly sinking, preparations to pass to the one we
    have conquer'd,
The captain on the quarter-deck coldly giving his orders through a
    countenance white as a sheet,
Near by the corpse of the child that serv'd in the cabin,
The dead face of an old salt with long white hair and carefully curl'd
    whiskers,
The flames spite of all that can be done flickering aloft and below,   935
The husky voices of the two or three officers yet fit for duty,
Formless stacks of bodies and bodies by themselves, dabs of flesh upon the
    masts and spars,
Cut of cordage, dangle of rigging, slight shock of the soothe of waves,
Black and impassive guns, litter of powder-parcels, strong scent,
A few large stars overhead, silent and mournful shining,   940
Delicate sniffs of sea-breeze, smells of sedgy grass and fields by the shore,
    death-messages given in charge to survivors,
The hiss of the surgeon's knife, the gnawing teeth of his saw,
Wheeze, cluck, swash[4] of falling blood, short wild scream, and long, dull,
    tapering groan,
These so, these irretrievable.

37

You laggards there on guard! look to your arms!   945
In at the conquer'd doors they crowd! I am possess'd!
Embody all presences outlaw'd or suffering,
See myself in prison shaped like another man,
And feel the dull unintermitted pain.

For me the keepers of convicts shoulder their carbines and keep watch,   950
It is I let out in the morning and barr'd at night.

Not a mutineer walks handcuff'd to jail but I am handcuff'd to him and walk
    by his side,
(I am less the jolly one there, and more the silent one with sweat on my
    twitching lips.)

Not a youngster is taken for larceny but I go up too, and am tried and
    sentenced.

Not a cholera patient lies at the last gasp but I also lie at the last gasp,   955
My face is ash-color'd, my sinews gnarl, away from me people retreat.

Askers embody themselves in me and I am embodied in them,
I project my hat, sit shame-faced, and beg.

38

Enough! enough! enough!
Somehow I have been stunn'd. Stand back!   960
Give me a little time beyond my cuff'd head, slumbers, dreams, gaping,
I discover myself on the verge of a usual mistake.

_____
[4]Wet refuse.

That I could forget the mockers and insults!
That I could forget the trickling tears and the blows of the bludgeons and
   hammers!
That I could look with a separate look on my own crucifixion and bloody
   crowning![5]   965

I remember now,
I resume the overstaid fraction,[6]
The grave of rock multiplies what has been confided to it, or to any graves,
Corpses rise, gashes heal, fastenings roll from me.

I troop forth replenish'd with supreme power, one of an average unending
   procession,   970
Inland and sea-coast we go, and pass all boundary lines,
Our swift ordinances[7] on their way over the whole earth,
The blossoms we wear in our hats the growth of thousands of years.

Eleves,[8] I salute you! come forward!
Continue your annotations, continue your questionings.   975

39

The friendly and flowing savage, who is he?
Is he waiting for civilization, or past it and mastering it?

Is he some Southwesterner rais'd out-doors? is he Kanadian?
Is he from the Mississippi country? Iowa, Oregon, California?
The mountains? prairie-life, bush-life? or sailor from the sea?   980

Wherever he goes men and women accept and desire him,
They desire he should like them, touch them, speak to them, stay with them.

Behavior lawless as snow-flakes, words simple as grass, uncomb'd head,
   laughter, and naivetè,
Slow-stepping feet, common features, common modes and emanations,
They descend in new forms from the tips of his fingers,   985
They are wafted with the odor of his body or breath, they fly out of the
   glance of his eyes.

40

Flaunt of the sunshine I need not your bask—lie over!
You light surfaces only, I force surfaces and depths also.

Earth! you seem to look for something at my hands,
Say, old top-knot,[9] what do you want?   990

Man or woman, I might tell how I like you, but cannot,
And might tell what it is in me and what it is in you, but cannot,
And might tell that pining I have, that pulse of my nights and days.

Behold, I do not give lectures or a little charity,
When I give I give myself.   995

---

[5]Whitman identifies with Christ.
[6]I.e., "I bring back into the calculation a part temporarily set
aside."
[7]Authoritative affirmations, spiritual counsel.
[8]"Pupils" (French).
[9]Tuft of hair on crown of the head (Indian).

You there, impotent, loose in the knees,
Open your scarf'd[10] chops till I blow grit within you,
Spread your palms and lift the flaps of your pockets,
I am not to be denied, I compel, I have stores plenty and to spare,
And any thing I have I bestow.   1000

I do not ask who you are, that is not important to me,
You can do nothing and be nothing but what I will infold you.

To cotton-field drudge or cleaner of privies I lean,
On his right cheek I put the family kiss,
And in my soul I swear I never will deny him.   1005

On women fit for conception I start bigger and nimbler babes,
(This day I am jetting the stuff of far more arrogant republics.)

To any one dying, thither I speed and twist the knob of the door,
Turn the bed-clothes toward the foot of the bed,
Let the physician and the priest go home.   1010

I seize the descending man and raise him with resistless will,
O despairer, here is my neck,
By God, you shall not go down! hang your whole weight upon me.

I dilate you with tremendous breath, I buoy you up,
Every room of the house do I fill with an arm'd force,   1015
Lovers of me, bafflers of graves.

Sleep—I and they keep guard all night,
Not doubt, not decease shall dare to lay finger upon you,
I have embraced you, and henceforth possess you to myself,
And when you rise in the morning you will find what I tell you is so. 1020

41

I am he bringing help for the sick as they pant on their backs,
And for strong upright men I bring yet more needed help.

I heard what was said of the universe,
Heard it and heard it of several thousand years;
It is middling well as far as it goes—but is that all?   1025

Magnifying and applying come I,
Outbidding at the start the old cautious hucksters,[11]
Taking myself the exact dimensions of Jehovah,
Lithographing Kronos, Zeus his son, and Hercules his grandson,
Buying drafts of Osiris, Isis, Belus, Brahma, Buddha,   1030
In my portfolio placing Manito loose, Allah on a leaf, the crucifix engraved,
With Odin and the hideous-faced Mexitli and every idol and image,[12]
Taking them all for what they are worth and not a cent more,
Admitting they were alive and did the work of their days,

---

[10]Bound up with scarf.
[11]Hawkers of wares.
[12]The deities listed include those of the Hebrews, Greeks, Egyptians (Osiris, Isis), Babylonians (Belus), Hindus (Brahma), Buddhists, Algonquian Indians (Manito), Muhammadans (Allah), Norse (Odin), and Aztec Indians (Mexitli).

(They bore mites as for unfledg'd birds who have now to rise and fly and
  sing for themselves,) 1035
Accepting the rough deific[13] sketches to fill out better in myself, bestowing
  them freely on each man and woman I see,
Discovering as much or more in a framer framing a house,
Putting higher claims for him there with his roll'd-up sleeves driving the
  mallet and chisel,
Not objecting to special revelations, considering a curl of smoke or a hair on
  the back of my hand just as curious as any revelation,
Lads ahold of fire-engines and hook-and-ladder ropes no less to me than the
  gods of the antique wars, 1040
Minding their voices peal through the crash of destruction,
Their brawny limbs passing safe over charr'd laths, their white foreheads
  whole and unhurt out of the flames;
By the mechanic's wife with her babe at her nipple interceding for every
  person born,
Three scythes at harvest whizzing in a row from three lusty angels with
  shirts bagg'd out at their waists,
The snag-tooth'd hostler[14] with red hair redeeming sins past and to come, 1045
Selling all he possesses, traveling on foot to fee lawyers for his brother and
  sit by him while he is tried for forgery;
What was strewn in the amplest strewing the square rod about me, and not
  filling the square rod then,
The bull and the bug never worshipp'd half enough,
Dung and dirt more admirable than was dream'd,
The supernatural of no account, myself waiting my time to be one of the
  supremes, 1050
The day getting ready for me when I shall do as much good as the best, and
  be as prodigious;
By my life-lumps![15] becoming already a creator,
Putting myself here and now to the ambush'd womb of the shadows.

42

A call in the midst of the crowd,
My own voice, orotund sweeping and final. 1055

Come my children,
Come my boys and girls, my women, household and intimates,
Now the performer launches his nerve, he has pass'd his prelude on the
  reeds within.

Easily written loose-finger'd chords—I feel the thrum of your climax and
  close.

My head slues round on my neck, 1060
Music rolls, but not from the organ,
Folks are around me, but they are no household of mine.

Ever the hard unsunk ground,
Ever the eaters and drinkers, ever the upward and downward sun, ever the
  air and the ceaseless tides,

---

[13]Deity-related, divine.
[14]Groom for horses at an inn.
[15]Testicles.

Ever myself and my neighbors, refreshing, wicked, real,   1065
Ever the old inexplicable query, ever that thorn'd thumb, that breath of
    itches and thirsts,
Ever the vexer's *hoot! hoot!* till we find where the sly one hides and bring him
    forth,
Ever love, ever the sobbing liquid of life,
Ever the bandage under the chin, ever the trestles[16] of death.

Here and there with dimes on the eyes[17] walking,   1070
To feed the greed of the belly the brains liberally spooning,
Tickets buying, taking, selling, but in to the feast never once going,
Many sweating, ploughing, thrashing, and then the chaff for payment
    receiving,
A few idly owning, and they the wheat continually claiming.

This is the city and I am one of the citizens,   1075
Whatever interests the rest interests me, politics, wars, markets, newspapers,
    schools,
The mayor and councils, banks, tariffs, steamships, factories, stocks, stores,
    real estate and personal estate.

The little plentiful manikins skipping around in collars and tail'd coats,
I am aware who they are, (they are positively not worms or fleas,)
I acknowledge the duplicates of myself, the weakest and shallowest is
    deathless with me,   1080
What I do and say the same waits for them,
Every thought that flounders in me the same flounders in them.

I know perfectly well my own egotism,
Know my omnivorous lines and must not write any less,
And would fetch you whoever you are flush with myself.   1085

Not words of routine this song of mine,
But abruptly to question, to leap beyond yet nearer bring;
This printed and bound book—but the printer and the printing-office boy?
The well-taken photographs—but your wife or friend close and solid in
    your arms?
The black ship mail'd with iron, her mighty guns in her turrets—but the
    pluck of the captain and engineers?   1090
In the houses the dishes and fare and furniture—but the host and hostess,
    and the look out of their eyes?
The sky up there—yet here or next door, or across the way?
The saints and sages in history—but you yourself?
Sermons, creeds, theology—but the fathomless human brain,
And what is reason? and what is love? and what is life?   1095

43

I do not despise you priests, all time, the world over,
My faith is the greatest of faiths and the least of faiths,
Enclosing worship ancient and modern and all between ancient and
    modern,

---

[16]Coffin-supports.
[17]Eyelids of the dead were closed by use of coins; the greedy
have coins in the eye.

Believing I shall come again upon the earth after five thousand years,
Waiting responses from oracles, honoring the gods, saluting the sun,   1100
Making a fetich[18] of the first rock or stump, powowing with sticks in the
    circle of obis,[19]
Helping the llama or brahmin as he trims the lamps of the idols,
Dancing yet through the streets in a phallic procession, rapt and austere in
    the woods a gymnosophist,[20]
Drinking mead from the skull-cup, to Shastas and Vedas admirant, minding
    the Koran,[21]
Walking the teokallis,[22] spotted with gore from the stone and knife, beating
    the serpent-skin drum,   1105
Accepting the Gospels, accepting him that was crucified, knowing assuredly
    that he is divine,
To the mass kneeling or the puritan's prayer rising, or sitting patiently in a
    pew,
Ranting and frothing in my insane crisis, or waiting dead-like till my spirit
    arouses me,
Looking forth on pavement and land, or outside of pavement and land,
Belonging to the winders of the circuit of circuits.   1110

One of that centripetal and centrifugal gang I turn and talk like a man
    leaving charges before a journey.

Down-hearted doubters, dull and excluded,
Frivolous, sullen, moping, angry, affected, dishearten'd, atheistical,
I know every one of you, I know the sea of torment, doubt, despair and
    unbelief.

How the flukes[23] splash!   1115
How they contort rapid as lightning, with spasms and spouts of blood!

Be at peace bloody flukes of doubters and sullen mopers,
I take my place among you as much as among any,
The past is the push of you, me, all, precisely the same,
And what is yet untried and afterward is for you, me, all, precisely the same.   1120

I do not know what is untried and afterward,
But I know it will in its turn prove sufficient, and cannot fail.

Each who passes is consider'd, each who stops is consider'd, not a single one
    can it fail.

It cannot fail the young man who died and was buried,
Nor the young woman who died and was put by his side,   1125
Nor the little child that peep'd in at the door, and then drew back and was
    never seen again,
Nor the old man who has lived without purpose, and feels it with bitterness
    worse than gall,
Nor him in the poor house tubercled by rum and the bad disorder,[24]

---

[18]Fetish: inanimate object worshipped as having magical powers.
[19]I.e., obeah, sorcery originating in West Africa.
[20]Ancient Hindu philosopher of ascetic habits.
[21]Sacred texts of the Hindus (Shastras and Vedas) and of the Muhammadans (Koran).
[22]Aztec temple in pyramidal form (on top of a pyramid).
[23]Tail of a whale.
[24]One with skin disfigurations caused by liquor and cirrhosis.

Nor the numberless slaughter'd and wreck'd, nor the brutish koboo[25] call'd
    the ordure[26] of humanity,
Nor the sacs[27] merely floating with open mouths for food to slip in,   1130
Nor any thing in the earth, or down in the oldest graves of the earth,
Nor any thing in the myriads of spheres, nor the myriads of myriads that
    inhabit them,
Nor the present, nor the least wisp that is known.

44

It is time to explain myself—let us stand up.

What is known I strip away,   1135
I launch all men and women forward with me into the Unknown.

The clock indicates the moment—but what does eternity indicate?

We have thus far exhausted trillions of winters and summers,
There are trillions ahead, and trillions ahead of them.

Births have brought us richness and variety,   1140
And other births will bring us richness and variety.

I do not call one greater and one smaller,
That which fills its period and place is equal to any.

Were mankind murderous or jealous upon you, my brother, my sister?
I am sorry for you, they are not murderous or jealous upon me,   1145
All has been gentle with me, I keep no account with lamentation,
(What have I to do with lamentation?)

I am an acme of things accomplish'd, and I an encloser of things to be.

My feet strike an apex of the apices[28] of the stairs,
On every step bunches of ages, and larger bunches between the steps,   1150
All below duly travel'd, and still I mount and mount.

Rise after rise bow the phantoms behind me,
Afar down I see the huge first Nothing, I know I was even there,
I waited unseen and always, and slept through the lethargic mist,
And took my time, and took no hurt from the fetid carbon.[29]   1155

Long I was hugg'd close—long and long.

Immense have been the preparations for me,
Faithful and friendly the arms that have help'd me.

Cycles ferried my cradle, rowing and rowing like cheerful boatmen,
For room to me stars kept aside in their own rings,   1160
They sent influences to look after what was to hold me.

Before I was born out of my mother generations guided me,
My embryo has never been torpid, nothing could overlay it.[30]

---

[25]A primitive people of Palembang, capital of South Sumatra province.
[26]Excrement.
[27]Flower-like water animals with mouth fringed with tentacles: polyps.

[28]Plural of apex.
[29]Ancient vegetation turned to coal.
[30]Smother it.

For it the nebula cohered to an orb,
The long slow strata piled to rest it on,   1165
Vast vegetables gave it sustenance,
Monstrous sauroids[31] transported it in their mouths and deposited it with
    care.

All forces have been steadily employ'd to complete and delight me,
Now on this spot I stand with my robust soul.

45

O span of youth! ever-push'd elasticity.   1170
O manhood, balanced, florid and full.

My lovers suffocate me,
Crowding my lips, thick in the pores of my skin,
Jostling me through streets and public halls, coming naked to me at night,
Crying by day *Ahoy!* from the rocks of the river, swinging and chirping over
    my head,   1175
Calling my name from flower-beds, vines, tangled underbrush,
Lighting on every moment of my life,
Bussing[32] my body with soft balsamic[33] busses,
Noiselessly passing handfuls out of their hearts and giving them to be mine.

Old age superbly rising! O welcome, ineffable grace of dying days!   1180
Every condition promulges[34] not only itself, it promulges what grows after
    and out of itself,
And the dark hush promulges as much as any.

I open my scuttle[35] at night and see the far-sprinkled systems,
And all I see multiplied as high as I can cipher edge but the rim of the
    farther systems.

Wider and wider they spread, expanding, always expanding,   1185
Outward and outward and forever outward.

My sun has his sun and round him obediently wheels,
He joins with his partners a group of superior circuit,
And greater sets follow, making specks of the greatest inside them.

There is no stoppage and never can be stoppage,   1190
If I, you, and the worlds, and all beneath or upon their surfaces, were this
    moment reduced back to a pallid float,[36] it would not avail in the long
    run,
We should surely bring up again where we now stand,
And surely go as much farther, and then farther and farther.

A few quadrillions of eras, a few octillions[37] of cubic leagues, do not hazard
    the span or make it impatient,
They are but parts, any thing is but a part.   1195

See ever so far, there is limitless space outside of that,
Count ever so much, there is limitless time around that.

---

[31]Prehistoric and gigantic lizards.
[32]Kissing.
[33]Aromatic, soothing.
[34]Procreates, generates.

[35]An opening in a roof with a shutter or lid.
[36]Matter's primordial state of suspension throughout space
as particles suspended in water.
[37]The number constituted by 1 followed by 27 zeros.

My rendezvous is appointed, it is certain,
The Lord will be there and wait till I come on perfect terms,
The great Camerado,[38] the lover true for whom I pine will be there.   1200

46

I know I have the best of time and space, and was never measured and
    never will be measured.

I tramp a perpetual journey, (come listen all!)
My signs are a rain-proof coat, good shoes, and a staff cut from the woods,
No friend of mine takes his ease in my chair,
I have no chair, no church, no philosophy,   1205
I lead no man to a dinner-table, library, exchange,
But each man and each woman of you I lead upon a knoll,
My left hand hooking you round the waist,
My right hand pointing to landscapes of continents and the public road.

Not I, not any one else can travel that road for you,   1210
You must travel it for yourself.

It is not far, it is within reach,
Perhaps you have been on it since you were born and did not know,
Perhaps it is everywhere on water and on land.

Shoulder your duds dear son, and I will mine, and let us hasten forth,   1215
Wonderful cities and free nations we shall fetch[39] as we go.

If you tire, give me both burdens, and rest the chuff[40] of your hand on my
    hip,
And in due time you shall repay the same service to me,
For after we start we never lie by again.

This day before dawn I ascended a hill and look'd at the crowded heaven,   1220
And I said to my spirit *When we become the enfolders of those orbs, and the*
    pleasure and knowledge of every thing in them, shall we be fill'd and satisfied then?
And my spirit said *No, we but level that lift*[41] *to pass and continue beyond.*

You are also asking me questions and I hear you,
I answer that I cannot answer, you must find out for yourself.

Sit a while dear son,   1225
Here are biscuits to eat and here is milk to drink,
But as soon as you sleep and renew yourself in sweet clothes, I kiss you with
    a good-by kiss and open the gate for your egress[42] hence.

Long enough have you dream'd contemptible dreams,
Now I wash the gum from your eyes,
You must habit yourself to the dazzle of the light and of every moment of
    your life.   1230

Long have you timidly waded holding a plank by the shore,
Now I will you to be a bold swimmer,

---

[38]Intimate companion and sharer; cf. Spanish *Camarada*, bed
or chamber mate.
[39]Reach.
[40]Heel (fleshy part of the hand).
[41]Rise in ground.
[42]Exit.

To jump off in the midst of the sea, rise again, nod to me, shout, and
    laughingly dash with your hair.

47

I am the teacher of athletes,
He that by me spreads a wider breast than my own proves the width of my
    own,   1235
He most honors my style who learns under it to destroy the teacher.

The boy I love, the same becomes a man not through derived power, but in
    his own right,
Wicked rather than virtuous out of conformity or fear,
Fond of his sweetheart, relishing well his steak,
Unrequited love or a slight cutting him worse than sharp steel cuts,   1240
First-rate to ride, to fight, to hit the bull's eye, to sail a skiff, to sing a song or
    play on the banjo,
Preferring scars and the beard and faces pitted with small-pox over all
    latherers,
And those well-tann'd to those that keep out of the sun.

I teach straying from me, yet who can stray from me?
I follow you whoever you are from the present hour,   1245
My words itch at your ears till you understand them.

I do not say these things for a dollar or to fill up the time while I wait for a
    boat,
(It is you talking just as much as myself, I act as the tongue of you,
Tied in your mouth, in mine it begins to be loosen'd.)

I swear I will never again mention love or death inside a house,   1250
And I swear I will never translate myself at all, only to him or her who
    privately stays with me in the open air.

If you would understand me go to the heights or water-shore,
The nearest gnat is an explanation, and a drop or motion of waves a key,
The maul, the oar, the hand-saw, second my words.

No shutter'd room or school can commune with me,   1255
But roughs and little children better than they.

The young mechanic is closest to me, he knows me well,
The woodman that takes his axe and jug with him shall take me with him all
    day,
The farm-boy ploughing in the field feels good at the sound of my voice,
In vessels that sail my words sail, I go with fishermen and seamen and love
    them.   1260

The soldier camp'd or upon the march is mine,
On the night ere the pending battle many seek me, and I do not fail them,
On that solemn night (it may be their last) those that know me seek me.

My face rubs to the hunter's face when he lies down alone in his blanket,
The driver thinking of me does not mind the jolt of his wagon,   1265
The young mother and old mother comprehend me,
The girl and the wife rest the needle a moment and forget where they are,
They and all would resume what I have told them.

48

I have said that the soul is not more than the body,
And I have said that the body is not more than the soul,   1270
And nothing, not God, is greater to one than one's self is,
And whoever walks a furlong without sympathy walks to his own funeral
    drest in his shroud,
And I or you pocketless of a dime may purchase the pick of the earth,
And to glance with an eye or show a bean in its pod confounds the learning
    of all times,
And there is no trade or employment but the young man following it may
    become a hero,   1275
And there is no object so soft but it makes a hub for the wheel'd universe,
And I say to any man or woman, Let your soul stand cool and composed
    before a million universes.

And I say to mankind, Be not curious about God,
For I who am curious about each am not curious about God,
(No array of terms can say how much I am at peace about God and about
    death.)   1280

I hear and behold God in every object, yet understand God not in the least,
Nor do I understand who there can be more wonderful than myself.

Why should I wish to see God better than this day?
I see something of God each hour of the twenty-four, and each moment
    then,
In the faces of men and women I see God, and in my own face in the glass,   1285
I find letters from God dropt in the street, and every one is sign'd by God's
    name,
And I leave them where they are, for I know that wheresoe'er I go
Others will punctually come for ever and ever.

49

And as to you Death, and you bitter hug of mortality, it is idle to try to alarm
    me.

To his work without flinching the accoucheur[43] comes,   1290
I see the elder-hand[44] pressing receiving supporting,
I recline by the sills of the exquisite flexible doors,
And mark the outlet, and mark the relief and escape.

And as to you Corpse I think you are good manure, but that does not
    offend me,
I smell the white roses sweet-scented and growing,   1295
I reach to the leafy lips, I reach to the polish'd breasts of melons.

And as to you Life I reckon you are the leavings of many deaths,
(No doubt I have died myself ten thousand times before.)

I hear you whispering there O stars of heaven,
O suns—O grass of graves—O perpetual transfers and promotions,   1300
If you do not say any thing how can I say any thing?

---

[43]Midwife or obstetrician.
[44]Left hand.

Of the turbid pool that lies in the autumn forest,
Of the moon that descends the steeps of the soughing twilight,
Toss, sparkles of day and dusk—toss on the black stems that decay in the
    muck,
Toss to the moaning gibberish of the dry limbs.   1305

I ascend from the moon, I ascend from the night,
I perceive that the ghastly glimmer is noonday sunbeams reflected,
And debouch[45] to the steady and central from the offspring great or small.

50

There is that in me—I do not know what it is—but I know it is in me.

Wrench'd and sweaty—calm and cool then my body becomes,   1310
I sleep—I sleep long.

I do not know it—it is without name—it is a word unsaid,
It is not in any dictionary, utterance, symbol.

Something it swings on more than the earth I swing on,
To it the creation is the friend whose embracing awakes me.   1315

Perhaps I might tell more. Outlines! I plead for my brothers and sisters.

Do you see O my brothers and sisters?
It is not chaos or death—it is form, union, plan—it is eternal life—it is
    Happiness.

51

The past and present wilt[46]—I have fill'd them, emptied them,
And proceed to fill my next fold of the future.   1320

Listener up there! what have you to confide to me?
Look in my face while I snuff the sidle[47] of evening,
(Talk honestly, no one else hears you, and I stay only a minute longer.)

Do I contradict myself?
Very well then I contradict myself,   1325
(I am large, I contain multitudes.)

I concentrate toward them that are nigh, I wait on the door-slab.

Who has done his day's work? who will soonest be through with his supper?
Who wishes to walk with me?

Will you speak before I am gone? will you prove already too late? 1330

52

The spotted hawk swoops by and accuses me, he complains of my gab and
    my loitering.

45To issue from narrow to wide space.
46Lose energy or vigor.
47As the light day fades, the evening is moving obliquely (sid-
ling) out, replaced by night; to "snuff the sidle" is to put out
(as with a candle) or momentarily arrest this cyclic movement
of time.

I too am not a bit tamed, I too am untranslatable,
I sound my barbaric yawp[48] over the roofs of the world.

The last scud[49] of day holds back for me,
It flings my likeness after the rest and true as any on the shadow'd wilds,   1335
It coaxes me to the vapor and the dusk.

I depart as air, I shake my white locks at the runaway sun,
I effuse[50] my flesh in eddies, and drift it in lacy jags.

I bequeath myself to the dirt to grow from the grass I love,
If you want me again look for me under your boot-soles.   1340

You will hardly know who I am or what I mean,
But I shall be good health to you nevertheless,
And filter and fibre your blood.

Failing to fetch me at first keep encouraged,
Missing me one place search another,   1345
I stop somewhere waiting for you.

1855, 1881

from CHILDREN OF ADAM[1]

To the Garden the World

To the garden the world anew ascending,
Potent mates, daughters, sons, preluding,
The love, the life of their bodies, meaning and being,
Curious here behold my resurrection after slumber,
The revolving cycles in their wide sweep having brought me again,   5
Amorous, mature, all beautiful to me, all wondrous,
My limbs and the quivering fire that ever plays through them, for reasons,
    most wondrous,
Existing I peer and penetrate still,
Content with the present, content with the past,
By my side or back of me Eve following,   10
Or in front, and I following her just the same.

1860, 1867

From Pent-up Aching Rivers

From pent-up aching rivers,
From that of myself without which I were nothing,

---

[48]Loud, animal-like cry.
[49]Light, wind-driven clouds.
[50]Pour out.
[1]Originally entitled "Enfans d'Adam" in the 1860 edition of *Leaves of Grass*, this cluster of poems appears to have been conceived as linked by contrast with the "Calamus" cluster, written first. Whitman jotted down in a manuscript note:

"Theory of a Cluster of Poems the same *to the passion of Woman-love* as the *Calamus-Leaves* are to adhesiveness, manly love. Full of animal-fire, tender, burning,—the tremulous ache, delicious, yet such a torment. The swelling elate and vehement, that will not be denied. Adam, as a central figure and type."

From what I am determin'd to make illustrious, even if I stand sole among
    men,
From my own voice resonant, singing the phallus,
Singing the song of procreation,   5
Singing the need of superb children and therein superb grown people,
Singing the muscular urge and the blending,
Singing the bedfellow's song, (O resistless yearning!
O for any and each the body correlative attracting!
O for you whoever you are your correlative body! O it, more than all else,
    you delighting!)   10
From the hungry gnaw that eats me night and day,
From native moments, from bashful pains, singing them,
Seeking something yet unfound though I have diligently sought it many a
    long year,
Singing the true song of the soul fitful at random,
Renascent with grossest Nature or among animals,   15
Of that, of them and what goes with them my poems informing,
Of the smell of apples and lemons, of the pairing of birds,
Of the wet of woods, of the lapping of waves,
Of the mad pushes of waves upon the land, I them chanting,
The overture lightly sounding, the strain anticipating,   20
The welcome nearness, the sight of the perfect body,
The swimmer swimming naked in the bath, or motionless on his back lying
    and floating,
The female form approaching, I pensive, love-flesh tremulous aching,
The divine list for myself or you or for any one making,
The face, the limbs, the index from head to foot, and what it arouses,   25
The mystic deliria, the madness amorous, the utter abandonment,
(Hark close and still what I now whisper to you,
I love you, O you entirely possess me,
O that you and I escape from the rest and go utterly off, free and lawless,
Two hawks in the air, two fishes swimming in the sea not more lawless
    than we;)   30
The furious storm through me careering, I passionately trembling,
The oath of the inseparableness of two together, of the woman that loves me
    and whom I love more than my life, that oath swearing,
(O I willingly stake all for you,
O let me be lost if it must be so!
O you and I! what is it to us what the rest do or think?   35
What is all else to us? only that we enjoy each other and exhaust each other
    if it must be so;)
From the master, the pilot I yield the vessel to,
The general commanding me, commanding all, from him permission
    taking,
From time the programme hastening, (I have loiter'd too long as it is,)
From sex, from the warp and from the woof,[2]   40
From privacy, from frequent repinings alone,
From plenty of persons near and yet the right person not near,
From the soft sliding of hands over me and thrusting of fingers through my
    hair and beard,
From the long sustain'd kiss upon the mouth or bosom,
From the close pressure that makes me or any man drunk, fainting with
    excess,   45

---

[2]Vertical threads (warp) and horizontal threads (woof) woven
into a fabric.

From what the divine husband knows, from the work of fatherhood,
From exultation, victory and relief from the bedfellow's embrace in the
    night,
From the act-poems of eyes, hands, hips and bosoms,
From the cling of the trembling arm,
From the bending curve and the clinch,   50
From side by side the pliant coverlet off-throwing,
From the one so unwilling to have me leave, and me just as unwilling to
    leave,
(Yet a moment O tender waiter, and I return,)
From the hour of shining stars and dropping dews,
From the night a moment I emerging flitting out,   55
Celebrate you act divine and you children prepared for,
And you stalwart loins.

                                                              1860, 1881

Spontaneous Me

Spontaneous me, Nature,
The loving day, the mounting sun, the friend I am happy with,
The arm of my friend hanging idly over my shoulder,
The hillside whiten'd with blossoms of the mountain ash,
The same late in autumn, the hues of red, yellow, drab, purple, and light
    and dark green,   5
The rich coverlet of the grass, animals and birds, the private untrimm'd
    bank, the primitive apples, the pebble-stones,
Beautiful dripping fragments, the negligent list of one after another as I
    happen to call them to me or think of them,
The real poems, (what we call poems being merely pictures,)
The poems of the privacy of the night, and of men like me,
This poem drooping shy and unseen that I always carry, and that all men
    carry,   10
(Know once for all, avow'd on purpose, wherever are men like me, are our
    lusty lurking masculine poems,)
Love-thoughts, love-juice, love-odor, love-yielding, love-climbers, and the
    climbing sap,
Arms and hands of love, lips of love, phallic thumb of love, breasts of love,
    bellies press'd and glued together with love,
Earth of chaste love, life that is only life after love,
The body of my love, the body of the woman I love, the body of the man,
    the body of the earth,   15
Soft forenoon airs that blow from the south-west,
The hairy wild-bee that murmurs and hankers up and down, that gripes the
    full-grown lady-flower, curves upon her with amorous firm legs, takes his
    will of her, and holds himself tremulous and tight till he is satisfied;
The wet of woods through the early hours,
Two sleepers at night lying close together as they sleep, one with an arm
    slanting down across and below the waist of the other,
The smell of apples, aromas from crush'd sage-plant, mint, birch-bark,   20
The boy's longings, the glow and pressure as he confides to me what he was
    dreaming,
The dead leaf whirling its spiral whirl and falling still and content to the
    ground,

The no-form'd stings that sights, people, objects, sting me with,
The hubb'd sting of myself, stinging me as much as it ever can any one,
The sensitive, orbic, underlapp'd brothers, that only privileged feelers may
    be intimate where they are,   25
The curious roamer the hand roaming all over the body, the bashful
    withdrawing of flesh where the fingers soothingly pause and edge
    themselves,
The limpid liquid within the young man,
The vex'd corrosion so pensive and so painful,
The torment, the irritable tide that will not be at rest,
The like of the same I feel, the like of the same in others,   30
The young man that flushes and flushes, and the young woman that flushes
    and flushes,
The young man that wakes deep at night, the hot hand seeking to repress
    what would master him,
The mystic amorous night, the strange half-welcome pangs, visions, sweats,
The pulse pounding through palms and trembling encircling fingers, the
    young man all color'd, red, ashamed, angry;
The souse upon me of my lover the sea, as I lie willing and naked,   35
The merriment of the twin babies that crawl over the grass in the sun, the
    mother never turning her vigilant eyes from them,
The walnut-trunk, the walnut-husks, and the ripening or ripen'd long-round
    walnuts,
The continence of vegetables, birds, animals,
The consequent meanness of me should I skulk or find myself indecent,
    while birds and animals never once skulk or find themselves indecent,
The great chastity of paternity, to match the great chastity of maternity,   40
The oath of procreation I have sworn, my Adamic and fresh daughters,
The greed that eats me day and night with hungry gnaw, till I saturate what
    shall produce boys to fill my place when I am through,
The wholesome relief, repose, content,
And this bunch pluck'd at random from myself,
It has done its work—I toss it carelessly to fall where it may.   45

1856, 1867

Native Moments

Native moments—when you come upon me—ah you are here now,
Give me now libidinous joys only,
Give me the drench of my passions, give me life coarse and rank,
To-day I go consort with Nature's darlings, to-night too,
I am for those who believe in loose delights, I share the midnight orgies of
    young men,   5
I dance with the dancers and drink with the drinkers,
The echoes ring with our indecent calls, I pick out some low person for my
    dearest friend,
He shall be lawless, rude, illiterate, he shall be one condemned by others for
    deeds done,
I will play a part no longer, why should I exile myself from my companions?
O you shunn'd persons, I at least do not shun you,   10
I come forthwith in your midst, I will be your poet,
I will be more to you than to any of the rest.

1860, 1881

Facing West from California's Shores

Facing west from California's shores,
Inquiring, tireless, seeking what is yet unfound,
I, a child, very old, over waves, towards the house of maternity, the land of
    migrations, look afar,
Look off the shores of my Western sea, the circle almost circled;
For starting westward from Hindustan, from the vales of Kashmere,   5
From Asia, from the north, from the God, the sage, and the hero,
From the south, from the flowery peninsulas and the spice islands,
Long having wander'd since, round the earth having wander'd,
Now I face home again, very pleas'd and joyous,
(But where is what I started for so long ago?   10
And why is it yet unfound?)

1860, 1867

from CALAMUS[1]

In Paths Untrodden

In paths untrodden,
In the growth by margins of pond-waters,
Escaped from the life that exhibits itself,
From all the standards hitherto publish'd, from the pleasures, profits,
    conformities,
Which too long I was offering to feed my soul,   5
Clear to me now standards yet not publish'd, clear to me that my soul,
That the soul of the man I speak for rejoices in comrades,
Here by myself away from the clank of the world,
Tallying and talk'd to here by tongues aromatic,
No longer abash'd, (for in this secluded spot I can respond as I would not
    dare elsewhere,)   10
Strong upon me the life that does not exhibit itself, yet contains all the rest,
Resolv'd to sing no songs to-day but those of manly attachment,
Projecting them along that substantial life,
Bequeathing hence types of athletic love,
Afternoon this delicious Ninth-month[2] in my forty-first year,   15
I proceed for all who are or have been young men,
To tell the secret of my nights and days,
To celebrate the need of comrades.

1860, 1867

For You O Democracy

Come, I will make the continent indissoluble,
I will make the most splendid race the sun ever shone upon,

---

[1]Whitman described this plant: "Calamus is the very large and aromatic grass, or rush, growing about water ponds in the valleys—spears about three feet high; often called Sweet Flag; grows all over the Northern and Middle States. The recherché or ethereal sense of the term, as used in my book, arises probably from the actual Calamus presenting the biggest, gest and hardiest kind of spears of grass, and their fresh, aquatic, pungent bouquet." [2]September (Quaker usage).

I will make divine magnetic lands,
    With the love of comrades,
        With the life-long love of comrades.   5

I will plant companionship thick as trees along all the rivers of America, and
  along the shores of the great lakes, and all over the prairies,
I will make inseparable cities with their arms about each other's necks,
    By the love of comrades,
        By the manly love of comrades,

For you these from me, O Democracy, to serve you ma femme![3]   10
For you, for you I am trilling these songs.

                            1860, 1881

When I Heard at the Close of the Day

When I heard at the close of the day how my name had been receiv'd with
  plaudits in the capitol, still it was not a happy night for me that follow'd,
And else when I carous'd, or when my plans were accomplish'd, still I was
  not happy,
But the day when I rose at dawn from the bed of perfect health, refresh'd,
  singing, inhaling the ripe breath of autumn,
When I saw the full moon in the west grow pale and disappear in the
  morning light,
When I wander'd alone over the beach, and undressing bathed, laughing
  with the cool waters, and saw the sun rise,   5
And when I thought how my dear friend my lover was on his way coming,
    O then I was happy,
O then each breath tasted sweeter, and all that day my food nourish'd me
  more, and the beautiful day pass'd well,
And the next came with equal joy, and with the next at evening came my
  friend,
And that night while all was still I heard the waters roll slowly continually up
  the shores,
I heard the hissing rustle of the liquid and sands as directed to me
  whispering to congratulate me,   10
For the one I love most lay sleeping by me under the same cover in the cool
  night,
In the stillness in the autumn moonbeams his face was inclined toward me,
And his arm lay lightly around my breast—and that night I was happy.

                            1860, 1867

Here the Frailest Leaves of Me

Here the frailest leaves of me and yet my strongest lasting,
Here I shade and hide my thoughts, I myself do not expose them,
And yet they expose me more than all my other poems.

                            1860, 1871

---

[3]"My woman, wife" (French).

Fast-Anchor'd Eternal O Love!

Fast-anchor'd eternal O love! O woman I love!
O bride! O wife! more resistless than I can tell, the thought of you!
Then separate, as disembodied or another born,
Ethereal, the last athletic reality, my consolation,
I ascend, I float in the regions of your love O man,   5
O sharer of my roving life.

                                                              1860, 1867

Crossing Brooklyn Ferry[1]

1

Flood-tide below me! I see you face to face!
Clouds of the west—sun there half an hour high—I see you also face to
   face.

Crowds of men and women attired in the usual costumes, how curious you
   are to me!
On the ferry-boats the hundreds and hundreds that cross, returning home,
   are more curious to me than you suppose,
And you that shall cross from shore to shore years hence are more to me,
   and more in my meditations, than you might suppose.   5

2

The impalpable sustenance of me from all things at all hours of the day,
The simple, compact, well-join'd scheme, myself disintegrated, every one
   disintegrated yet part of the scheme,
The similitudes[2] of the past and those of the future,
The glories strung like beads on my smallest sights and hearings, on the
   walk in the street and the passage over the river,
The current rushing so swiftly and swimming with me far away,   10
The others that are to follow me, the ties between me and them,
The certainty of others, the life, love, sight, hearing of others.

Others will enter the gates of the ferry and cross from shore to shore,
Others will watch the run of the flood-tide,
Others will see the shipping of Manhattan north and west, and the heights
   of Brooklyn to the south and east,
Others will see the islands large and small;   15
Fifty years hence, others will see them as they cross, the sun half an hour
   high,
A hundred years hence, or ever so many hundred years hence, others will
   see them,
Will enjoy the sunset, the pouring-in of the flood-tide, the falling-back to the
   sea of the ebb-tide.

---

[1]On its first appearance in 1856, this poem was entitled "Sun-Down Poem." It was Thoreau's favorite poem by Whitman, and was one of those in *Leaves of Grass* that inspired him to ask Whitman, on his 1856 visit, whether he had read the Orien-

tals. Whitman's reply ("No. Tell me about them.") must not be taken at face value. The poem reached its final version in the 1881 edition, the version used here.
[2]Similarities.

3

It avails not, time nor place—distance avails not,   20
I am with you, you men and women of a generation, or ever so many
   generations hence,
Just as you feel when you look on the river and sky, so I felt,
Just as any of you is one of a living crowd, I was one of a crowd,
Just as you are refresh'd by the gladness of the river and the bright flow, I
   was refresh'd,
Just as you stand and lean on the rail, yet hurry with the swift current, I
   stood yet was hurried,   25
Just as you look on the numberless masts of ships and the thick-stemm'd
   pipes of steamboats, I look'd.

I too many and many a time cross'd the river of old,
Watched the Twelfth-month[3] sea-gulls, saw them high in the air floating
   with motionless wings, oscillating their bodies,
Saw how the glistening yellow lit up parts of their bodies and left the rest in
   strong shadow,
Saw the slow-wheeling circles and the gradual edging toward the south,   30
Saw the reflection of the summer sky in the water,
Had my eyes dazzled by the shimmering track of beams,
Look'd at the fine centrifugal spokes of light round the shape of my head in
   the sunlit water,
Look'd on the haze on the hills southward and south-westward,
Look'd on the vapor as it flew in fleeces tinged with violet,   35
Look'd toward the lower bay to notice the vessels arriving,
Saw their approach, saw aboard those that were near me,
Saw the white sails of schooners and sloops, saw the ships at anchor,
The sailors at work in the rigging or out astride the spars,
The round masts, the swinging motion of the hulls, the slender serpentine
   pennants,   40
The large and small steamers in motion, the pilots in their pilot-houses,
The white wake left by the passage, the quick tremulous whirl of the wheels,
The flags of all nations, the falling of them at sunset,
The scallop-edged waves in the twilight, the ladled cups, the frolicsome
   crests and glistening,
The stretch afar growing dimmer and dimmer, the gray walls of the granite
   storehouses by the docks,   45
On the river the shadowy group, the big steam-tug closely flank'd on each
   side by the barges, the hay-boat, the belated lighter,
On the neighboring shore the fires from the foundry chimneys burning
   high and glaringly into the night,
Casting their flicker of black contrasted with wild red and yellow light over
   the tops of houses, and down into the clefts of streets.

4

These and all else were to me the same as they are to you,
I loved well those cities, loved well the stately and rapid river,   50
The men and women I saw were all near to me,
Others the same—others who look back on me because I look'd forward to
   them,
(The time will come, though I stop here to-day and to-night.)

_____

[3]December.

5

What is it then between us?
What is the count of the scores or hundreds of years between us?   55

Whatever it is, it avails not—distance avails not, and place avails not,
I too lived, Brooklyn of ample hills was mine,
I too walk'd the streets of Manhattan island, and bathed in the waters
    around it,
I too felt the curious abrupt questionings stir within me,
In the day among crowds of people sometimes they came upon me,   60
In my walks home late at night or as I lay in my bed they came upon me,
I too had been struck from the float[4] forever held in solution,
I too had receiv'd identity by my body,
That I was I knew was of my body, and what I should be I knew I should be
    of my body.

6

It is not upon you alone the dark patches fall,   65
The dark threw its patches down upon me also,
The best I had done seem'd to me blank and suspicious,
My great thoughts as I supposed them, were they not in reality meagre?
Nor is it you alone who know what it is to be evil,
I am he who knew what it was to be evil,   70
I too knitted the old knot of contrariety,[5]
Blabb'd,[6] blush'd, resented, lied, stole, grudg'd,
Had guile, anger, lust, hot wishes I dared not speak,
Was wayward, vain, greedy, shallow, sly, cowardly, malignant,
The wolf, the snake, the hog, not wanting in me,   75
The cheating look, the frivolous word, the adulterous wish, not wanting,
Refusals, hates, postponements, meanness, laziness, none of these wanting,
Was one with the rest, the days and haps[7] of the rest,
Was call'd by my nighest[8] name by clear loud voices of young men as they
    saw me approaching or passing,
Felt their arms on my neck as I stood, or the negligent leaning of their flesh
    against me as I sat,   80
Saw many I loved in the street or ferry-boat or public assembly, yet never
    told them a word,
Lived the same life with the rest, the same old laughing, gnawing, sleeping,
Play'd the part that still looks back on the actor or actress,
The same old role, the role that is what we make it, as great as we like,
Or as small as we like, or both great and small.   85

7

Closer yet I approach you,
What thought you have of me now, I had as much of you—I laid in my
    stores in advance,
I consider'd long and seriously of you before you were born.

Who was to know what should come home to me?
Who knows but I am enjoying this?   90
Who knows, for all the distance, but I am as good as looking at you now, for
    all you cannot see me?

---

[4]Primordial matter spread evenly throughout the universe,   [6]Talked indiscreetly.
as suspended in water.   [7]Chance happenings.
[5]Related to "contrary" as willful or evil.   [8]Most familiar.

8

Ah, what can ever be more stately and admirable to me than mast-hemm'd
    Manhattan?
River and sunset and scallop-edg'd waves of flood-tide?
The sea-gulls oscillating their bodies, the hay-boat in the twilight, and the
    belated lighter?
What gods can exceed these that clasp me by the hand, and with voices I
    love call me promptly and loudly by my nighest name as I approach?   95
What is more subtle than this which ties me to the woman or man that looks
    in my face?
Which fuses me into you now, and pours my meaning into you?

We understand then do we not?
What I promis'd without mentioning it, have you not accepted?
What the study could not teach—what the preaching could not accomplish
    is accomplish'd, is it not?   100

9

Flow on, river! flow with the flood-tide, and ebb with the ebb-tide!
Frolic on, crested and scallop-edg'd waves!
Gorgeous clouds of the sunset! drench with your splendor me, or the men
    and women generations after me!
Cross from shore to shore, countless crowds of passengers!
Stand up, tall masts of Mannahatta! stand up, beautiful hills of Brooklyn!   105
Throb, baffled and curious brain! throw out questions and answers!
Suspend here and everywhere, eternal float of solution!
Gaze, loving and thirsting eyes, in the house or street or public assembly!
Sound out, voices of young men! loudly and musically call me by my nighest
    name!
Live, old life! play the part that looks back on the actor or actress!   110
Play the old role, the role that is great or small according as one makes it!
Consider, you who peruse me, whether I may not in unknown ways be
    looking upon you;
Be firm, rail over the river, to support those who lean idly, yet haste with the
    hasting current;
Fly on, sea-birds! fly sideways, or wheel in large circles high in the air;
Receive the summer sky, you water, and faithfully hold it till all downcast
    eyes have time to take it from you!   115
Diverge, fine spokes of light, from the shape of my head, or any one's head,
    in the sunlit water!
Come on, ships from the lower bay! pass up or down, white-sail'd schooners,
    sloops, lighters!
Flaunt away, flags of all nations! be duly lower'd at sunset!
Burn high your fires, foundry chimneys! cast black shadows at nightfall! cast
    red and yellow light over the tops of the houses!
Appearances, now or henceforth, indicate what you are,   120
You necessary film, continue to envelop the soul,
About my body for me, and your body for you, be hung our divinest
    aromas,
Thrive, cities—bring your freight, bring your shows, ample and sufficient
    rivers,
Expand, being than which none else is perhaps more spiritual,
Keep your places, objects than which none else is more lasting.   125

You have waited, you always wait, you dumb, beautiful ministers,[9]
We receive you with free sense at last, and are insatiate henceforward,
Not you any more shall be able to foil us, or withhold yourselves from us,
We use you, and do not cast you aside—we plant you permanently within us,
We fathom you not—we love you—there is perfection in you also,   130
You furnish your parts toward eternity,
Great or small, you furnish your parts toward the soul.

1856, 1881

from SEA-DRIFT

Out of the Cradle Endlessly Rocking[1]

Out of the cradle endlessly rocking,
Out of the mocking-bird's throat, the musical shuttle,
Out of the Ninth-month[2] midnight,
Over the sterile sands and the fields beyond, where the child leaving his bed
    wander'd alone, bareheaded, barefoot,
Down from the shower'd halo,   5
Up from the mystic play of shadows twining and twisting as if they were
    alive,
Out from the patches of briers and blackberries,
From the memories of the bird that chanted to me,
From your memories sad brother, from the fitful risings and fallings I
    heard,
From under that yellow half-moon late-risen and swollen as if with tears,   10
From those beginning notes of yearning and love there in the mist,
From the thousand responses of my heart never to cease,
From the myriad thence-arous'd words,
From the word stronger and more delicious than any,
From such as now they start the scene revisiting,   15
As a flock, twittering, rising, or overhead passing,
Borne hither, ere all eludes me, hurriedly,
A man, yet by these tears a little boy again,
Throwing myself on the sand, confronting the waves,
I, chanter of pains and joys, uniter of here and hereafter,   20
Taking all hints to use them, but swiftly leaping beyond them,
A reminiscence sing.

Once Paumanok,[3]
When the lilac-scent was in the air and Fifth-month[4] grass was growing,
Up this seashore in some briers,   25
Two feather'd guests from Alabama, two together,
And their nest, and four light-green eggs spotted with brown,
And every day the he-bird to and fro near at hand,
And every day the she-bird crouch'd on her nest, silent, with bright eyes,

---

[9]I.e., the tangible and intangible contents of the environment just catalogued.
[1]Entitled "A Child's Reminiscence" when it first appeared in *Saturday Press* in 1859 and "A Word Out of the Sea" in the 1860 and 1867 *Leaves*, the present title was added in 1871. The version printed here is that last revised, in the 1881

edition. Originally, the first line read: "Out of the rocked cradle."
[2]September.
[3]Indian name for Long Island.
[4]May.

And every day I, a curious boy, never too close, never disturbing them,   30
Cautiously peering, absorbing, translating.

Shine! shine! shine!
Pour down your warmth, great sun!
While we bask, we two together.
Two together!   35
Winds blow south, or winds blow north,
Day come white, or night come black,
Home, or rivers and mountains from home,
Singing all time, minding no time,
While we two keep together.   40

Till of a sudden,
May-be kill'd, unknown to her mate,
One forenoon the she-bird crouch'd not on the nest,
Nor return'd that afternoon, nor the next,
Nor ever appear'd again.   45

And thenceforward all summer in the sound of the sea,
And at night under the full of the moon in calmer weather,
Over the hoarse surging of the sea,
Or flitting from brier to brier by day,
I saw, I heard at intervals the remaining one, the he-bird,   50
The solitary guest from Alabama.

Blow! blow! blow!
Blow up sea-winds along Paumanok's shore;
I wait and I wait till you blow my mate to me.

Yes, when the stars glisten'd,   55
All night long on the prong of a moss-scallop'd stake,
Down almost amid the slapping waves,
Sat the lone singer wonderful causing tears.

He call'd on his mate,
He pour'd forth the meanings which I of all men know.   60

Yes my brother I know,
The rest might not, but I have treasur'd every note,
For more than once dimly down to the beach gliding,
Silent, avoiding the moonbeams, blending myself with the shadows,
Recalling now the obscure shapes, the echoes, the sounds and sights after
   their sorts,   65
The white arms out in the breakers tirelessly tossing,
I, with bare feet, a child, the wind wafting my hair,
Listen'd long and long.

Listen'd to keep, to sing, now translating the notes,
Following you my brother.   70

Soothe! soothe! soothe!
Close on its wave soothes the wave behind,
And again another behind embracing and lapping, every one close,
But my love soothes not me, not me.

Low hangs the moon, it rose late,
It is lagging[5]*—O I think it is heavy with love, with love.*   75

O madly the sea pushes upon the land,
With love, with love.

O night! do I not see my love fluttering out among the breakers?
What is that little black thing I see there in the white?   80

Loud! loud! loud!
Loud I call to you, my love!
High and clear I shoot my voice over the waves,
Surely you must know who is here, is here,
You must know who I am, my love.   85

Low-hanging moon!
What is that dusky spot in your brown yellow?
O it is the shape, the shape of my mate!
O moon do not keep her from me any longer.

Land! land! O land!   90
Whichever way I turn, O I think you could give me my mate back again if you only
*   would,*
For I am almost sure I see her dimly whichever way I look.

O rising stars!
Perhaps the one I want so much will rise, will rise with some of you.

O throat! O trembling throat!   95
Sound clearer through the atmosphere!
Pierce the woods, the earth,
Somewhere listening to catch you must be the one I want.

Shake out carols!
Solitary here, the night's carols!   100
Carols of lonesome love! death's carols!
Carols under that lagging, yellow, waning moon!
O under that moon where she droops almost down into the sea!
O reckless despairing carols.

But soft! sink low!   105
Soft! let me just murmur,
And do you wait a moment you husky-nois'd sea,
For somewhere I believe I heard my mate responding to me,
So faint, I must be still, be still to listen,
But not altogether still, for then she might not come immediately to me.   110

Hither my love!
Here I am! here!
With this just-sustain'd note I announce myself to you,
This gentle call is for you my love, for you.

Do not be decoy'd elsewhere,   115
That is the whistle of the wind, it is not my voice,

---

[5]Loitering.

That is the fluttering, the fluttering of the spray,
Those are the shadows of leaves.

O darkness! O in vain!
O I am very sick and sorrowful.   120

O brown halo in the sky near the moon, drooping upon the sea!
O troubled reflection in the sea!
O throat! O throbbing heart!
And I singing uselessly, uselessly all the night.

O past! O happy life! O songs of joy!   125
In the air, in the woods, over fields,
Loved! loved! loved! loved! loved!
But my mate no more, no more with me!
We two together no more.

The aria[6] sinking,   130
All else continuing, the stars shining,
The winds blowing, the notes of the bird continuous echoing,
With angry moans the fierce old mother incessantly moaning,
On the sands of Paumanok's shore gray and rustling,
The yellow half-moon enlarged, sagging down, drooping, the face of the sea
     almost touching,   135
The boy ecstatic, with his bare feet the waves, with his hair the atmosphere
     dallying,
The love in the heart long pent, now loose, now at last tumultuously
     bursting,
The aria's meaning, the ears, the soul, swiftly depositing,
The strange tears down the cheeks coursing,
The colloquy there, the trio,[7] each uttering,   140
The undertone, the savage old mother incessantly crying,
To the boy's soul's questions sullenly timing, some drown'd secret hissing,
To the outsetting bard.

Demon or bird! (said the boy's soul,)
Is it indeed toward your mate you sing? or is it really to me?   145
For I, that was a child, my tongue's use sleeping, now I have heard you,
Now in a moment I know what I am for, I awake,
And already a thousand singers, a thousand songs, clearer, louder and more
     sorrowful than yours,
A thousand warbling echoes have started to life within me, never to die.

O you singer solitary, singing by yourself, projecting me,   150
O solitary me listening, never more shall I cease perpetuating you,
Never more shall I escape, never more the reverberations,
Never more the cries of unsatisfied love be absent from me,
Never again leave me to be the peaceful child I was before what there in the
     night,
By the sea under the yellow and sagging moon,   155
The messenger there arous'd, the fire, the sweet hell within,
The unknown want, the destiny of me.

6An air or melody for solo performance in an opera.
7I.e., the bird, the ocean, the boy.

O give me the clew!⁸ (it lurks in the night here somewhere,)
O if I am to have so much, let me have more!

A word then, (for I will conquer it,)   160
The word final, superior to all,
Subtle, sent up—what is it?—I listen;
Are you whispering it, and have been all the time, you sea-waves?
Is that it from your liquid rims and wet sands?

Whereto answering, the sea,   165
Delaying not, hurrying not,
Whisper'd me through the night, and very plainly before daybreak,
Lisp'd to me the low and delicious word death,
And again death, death, death, death,
Hissing melodious, neither like the bird nor like my arous'd child's heart,   170
But edging near as privately for me rustling at my feet,
Creeping thence steadily up to my ears and laving me softly all over,
Death, death, death, death, death.

Which I do not forget,
But fuse the song of my dusky demon and brother,   175
That he sang to me in the moonlight on Paumanok's gray beach,
With the thousand responsive songs at random,
My own songs awaked from that hour,
And with them the key, the word up from the waves,
The word of the sweetest song and all songs,   180
That strong and delicious word which, creeping to my feet,
(Or like some old crone rocking the cradle, swathed in sweet garments,
    bending aside,)
The sea whisper'd me.

1859, 1881

As I Ebb'd with the Ocean of Life

1

As I ebb'd with the ocean of life,
As I wended the shores I know,
As I walk'd where the ripples continually wash you Paumanok,¹
Where they rustle up hoarse and sibilant,
Where the fierce old mother endlessly cries for her castaways,   5
I musing late in the autumn day, gazing off southward,
Held by this electric self out of the pride of which I utter poems,
Was seiz'd by the spirit that trails in the lines underfoot,
The rim, the sediment that stands for all the water and all the land of the
    globe.

Fascinated, my eyes reverting from the south, dropt, to follow those slender
    windrows,   10
Chaff, straw, splinters of wood, weeds, and the sea-gluten,

---

⁸Variant of "clue," a lead or hint that helps solve a puzzle.
¹Indian name for Long Island.

Scum, scales from shining rocks, leaves of salt-lettuce, left by the tide,
Miles walking, the sound of breaking waves the other side of me,
Paumanok there and then as I thought the old thought of likenesses,
These you presented to me you fish-shaped island,   15
As I wended the shores I know,
As I walk'd with that electric self seeking types.

2

As I wend to the shores I know not,
As I list to the dirge, the voices of men and women wreck'd,
As I inhale the impalpable breezes that set in upon me,   20
As the ocean so mysterious rolls toward me closer and closer,
I too but signify at the utmost a little wash'd-up drift,
A few sands and dead leaves to gather,
Gather, and merge myself as part of the sands and drift.

O baffled, balk'd, bent to the very earth,   25
Oppress'd with myself that I have dared to open my mouth,
Aware now that amid all that blab[2] whose echoes recoil upon me I have not
    once had the least idea who or what I am,
But that before all my arrogant poems the real Me stands yet untouch'd,
    untold, altogether unreach'd,
Withdrawn far, mocking me with mock-congratulatory signs and bows,
With peals of distant ironical laughter at every word I have written,   30
Pointing in silence to these songs, and then to the sand beneath.

I perceive I have not really understood any thing, not a single object, and
    that no man ever can,
Nature here in sight of the sea taking advantage of me to dart upon me and
    sting me,
Because I have dared to open my mouth to sing at all.

3

You oceans both, I close with you,   35
We murmur alike reproachfully rolling sands and drift, knowing not why,
These little shreds indeed standing for you and me and all.

You friable[3] shore with trails of debris,
You fish-shaped island, I take what is underfoot,
What is yours is mine my father.   40

I too Paumanok,
I too have bubbled up, floated the measureless float,[4] and been wash'd on
    your shores,
I too am but a trail of drift and debris,
I too leave little wrecks upon you, you fish-shaped island.

I throw myself upon your breast my father,   45
I cling to you so that you cannot unloose me,
I hold you so firm till you answer me something.

Kiss me my father,
Touch me with your lips as I touch those I love,
Breathe to me while I hold you close the secret of the murmuring I envy.   50

___

[2]Loose talk.
[3]Crumbling.
[4]Held in diffused suspension (as in liquid or air).

4

Ebb, ocean of life, (the flow will return,)
Cease not your moaning you fierce old mother,
Endlessly cry for your castaways, but fear not, deny not me,
Rustle not up so hoarse and angry against my feet as I touch you or gather
    from you.

I mean tenderly by you and all,   55
I gather for myself and for this phantom looking down where we lead, and
    following me and mine.

Me and mine, loose windrows, little corpses,
Froth, snowy white, and bubbles,
(See, from my dead lips the ooze exuding at last,
See, the prismatic colors glistening and rolling,)   60
Tufts of straw, sands, fragments,
Buoy'd hither from many moods, one contradicting another,
From the storm, the long calm, the darkness, the swell,
Musing, pondering, a breath, a briny tear, a dab of liquid or soil,
Up just as much out of fathomless workings fermented and thrown,   65
A limp blossom or two, torn, just as much over waves floating, drifted at
    random,
Just as much for us that sobbing dirge of Nature,
Just as much whence we come that blare of the cloud-trumpets,
We, capricious, brought hither we know not whence, spread out before you,
You up there walking or sitting,   70
Whoever you are, we too lie in drifts at your feet.

                                                                                1860, 1881

from BY THE ROADSIDE

When I Heard the Learn'd Astronomer

When I heard the learn'd astronomer,
When the proofs, the figures, were ranged in columns before me,
When I was shown the charts and diagrams, to add, divide, and measure
    them,
When I sitting heard the astronomer where he lectured with much applause
    in the lecture-room,
How soon unaccountable I became tired and sick,   5
Till rising and gliding out I wander'd off by myself,
In the mystical moist night air, and from time to time,
Look'd up in perfect silence at the stars.

                                                                                1865, 1867

I Sit and Look Out

I sit and look out upon all the sorrows of the world, and upon all oppression
    and shame,
I hear secret convulsive sobs from young men at anguish with themselves,
    remorseful after deeds done,

I see in low life the mother misused by her children, dying, neglected,
   gaunt, desperate,
I see the wife misused by her husband, I see the treacherous seducer of
   young women,
I mark the ranklings of jealousy and unrequited love attempted to be hid, I
   see these sights on the earth,   5
I see the workings of battle, pestilence, tyranny, I see martyrs and prisoners,
I observe a famine at sea, I observe the sailors casting lots who shall be kill'd
   to preserve the lives of the rest,
I observe the slights and degradations cast by arrogant persons upon
   laborers, the poor, and upon negroes, and the like;
All these—all the meanness and agony without end I sitting look out upon,
See, hear, and am silent.   10

1860, 1871

The Dalliance of the Eagles

Skirting the river road, (my forenoon walk, my rest,)
Skyward in air a sudden muffled sound, the dalliance of the eagles,
The rushing amorous contact high in space together,
The clinching interlocking claws, a living, fierce, gyrating wheel,
Four beating wings, two beaks, a swirling mass tight grappling,   5
In tumbling turning clustering loops, straight downward falling,
Till o'er the river pois'd, the twain yet one, a moment's lull,
A motionless still balance in the air, then parting, talons loosing,
Upward again on slow-firm pinions slanting, their separate diverse flight,
She hers, he his, pursuing.   10

1880, 1881

from DRUM-TAPS[1]

Cavalry Crossing a Ford

A line in long array where they wind betwixt green islands,
They take a serpentine course, their arms flash in the sun—hark to the
   musical clank,
Behold the silvery river, in it the splashing horses loitering stop to drink,
Behold the brown-faced men, each group, each person a picture, the
   negligent rest on the saddles,
Some emerge on the opposite bank, others are just entering the ford—
   while,   5
Scarlet and blue and snowy white,
The guidon flags[2] flutter gayly in the wind.

1865, 1871

---

[1]Whitman was over forty when the Civil War began in 1861, and thus too old to be taken as a soldier. But his brother George went to the war and was wounded in 1862 in Virginia. Whitman went to find him and became involved for the duration of the war as an unofficial nurse, visiting hospitals in Washington, D.C., cheering the living and comforting the dying. During his "wound-dresser" period, Whitman wrote "Drum-Taps," a cluster of poems touching on his feelings about and experiences in the war. *Drum-Taps* appeared as a book in 1865, and was reissued with "Sequel to Drum-Taps" in 1866 (containing poems written on the assassination of President Abraham Lincoln). The poems were added as annexes to a reissue of *Leaves of Grass* in 1867 and were then integrated with the whole of the new edition of *Leaves of Grass* that appeared in 1870–71.
[2]Flags identifying particular units.

Bivouac on a Mountain Side

I see before me now a traveling army halting,
Below a fertile valley spread, with barns and the orchards of summer,
Behind, the terraced sides of a mountain, abrupt, in places rising high,
Broken, with rocks, with clinging cedars, with tall shapes dingily seen,
The numerous camp-fires scatter'd near and far, some away up on the
    mountain,   5
The shadowy forms of men and horses, looming, large-sized, flickering,
And over all the sky—the sky! far, far out of reach, studded, breaking out,
    the eternal stars.

                                                                    1865, 1871

By the Bivouac's Fitful Flame

By the bivouac's fitful flame,
A procession winding around me, solemn and sweet and slow—but first I
    note,
The tents of the sleeping army, the fields' and woods' dim outline,
The darkness lit by spots of kindled fire, the silence,
Like a phantom far or near an occasional figure moving,   5
The shrubs and trees, (as I lift my eyes they seem to be stealthily watching
    me,)
While wind in procession thoughts, O tender and wondrous thoughts,
Of life and death, of home and the past and loved, and of those that are far
    away;
A solemn and slow procession there as I sit on the ground,
By the bivouac's fitful flame.   10

                                                                    1865, 1867

Vigil Strange I Kept on the Field One Night

Vigil strange I kept on the field one night;
When you my son and my comrade dropt at my side that day,
One look I but gave which your dear eyes return'd with a look I shall never
    forget,
One touch of your hand to mine O boy, reach'd up as you lay on the
    ground,
Then onward I sped in the battle, the even-contested battle,   5
Till late in the night reliev'd to the place at last again I made my way,
Found you in death so cold dear comrade, found your body son of
    responding kisses, (never again on earth responding,)
Bared your face in the starlight, curious the scene, cool blew the moderate
    night-wind,
Long there and then in vigil I stood, dimly around me the battlefield
    spreading,
Vigil wondrous and vigil sweet there in the fragrant silent night,   10
But not a tear fell, not even a long-drawn sigh, long, long I gazed,

Then on the earth partially reclining sat by your side leaning my chin in my
    hands,
Passing sweet hours, immortal and mystic hours with you dearest comrade—
    not a tear, not a word,
Vigil of silence, love and death, vigil for you my son and my soldier,
As onward silently stars aloft, eastward new ones upward stole,   15
Vigil final for you brave boy, (I could not save you, swift was your death,
I faithfully loved you and cared for you living, I think we shall surely meet
    again,)
Till at latest lingering of the night, indeed just as the dawn appear'd,
My comrade I wrapt in his blanket, envelop'd well his form,
Folded the blanket well, tucking it carefully over head and carefully under
    feet,   20
And there and then and bathed by the rising sun, my son in his grave, in his
    rude-dug grave I deposited,
Ending my vigil strange with that, vigil of night and battle-field dim,
Vigil for boy of responding kisses, (never again on earth responding,)
Vigil for comrade swiftly slain, vigil I never forget, how as day brighten'd,
I rose from the chill ground and folded my soldier well in his blanket,   25
And buried him where he fell.

1865, 1867

A March in the Ranks
Hard-Prest, and the Road Unknown

A march in the ranks hard-prest, and the road unknown,
A route through a heavy wood with muffled steps in the darkness,
Our army foil'd with loss severe, and the sullen remnant retreating,
Till after midnight glimmer upon us the lights of a dim-lighted building,
We come to an open space in the woods, and halt by the dim-lighted
    building,   5
'Tis a large old church at the crossing roads, now an impromptu hospital,
Entering but for a minute I see a sight beyond all the pictures and poems
    ever made,
Shadows of deepest, deepest black, just lit by moving candles and lamps,
And by one great pitchy torch stationary with wild red flame and clouds of
    smoke,
By these, crowds, groups of forms vaguely I see on the floor, some in the
    pews laid down,   10
At my feet more distinctly a soldier, a mere lad, in danger of bleeding to
    death, (he is shot in the abdomen,)
I stanch the blood temporarily, (the youngster's face is white as a lily,)
Then before I depart I sweep my eyes o'er the scene fain[3] to absorb it all,
Faces, varieties, postures beyond description, most in obscurity, some of
    them dead,
Surgeons operating, attendants holding lights, the smell of ether, the odor
    of blood,   15
The crowd, O the crowd of the bloody forms, the yard outside also fill'd,
Some on the bare ground, some on planks or stretchers, some in the death-
    spasm sweating,

---

[3]Reluctantly ready.

An occasional scream or cry, the doctor's shouted orders or calls,
The glisten of the little steel instruments catching the glint of the torches,
These I resume as I chant, I see again the forms, I smell the odor,   20
Then hear outside the orders given, *Fall in, my men, fall in*;
But first I bend to the dying lad, his eyes open, a half-smile gives he me,
Then the eyes close, calmly close, and I speed forth to the darkness,
Resuming, marching, ever in darkness marching, on in the ranks,
The unknown road still marching.   25

                                                                     1865, 1867

A Sight in Camp
in the Daybreak Gray and Dim

A sight in camp in the daybreak gray and dim,
As from my tent I emerge so early sleepless,
As slow I walk in the cool fresh air the path near by the hospital tent,
Three forms I see on stretchers lying, brought out there untended lying,
Over each the blanket spread, ample brownish woolen blanket,   5
Gray and heavy blanket, folding, covering all.

Curious I halt and silent stand,
Then with light fingers I from the face of the nearest the first just lift the
    blanket;
Who are you elderly man so gaunt and grim, with well-gray'd hair, and flesh
    all sunken about the eyes?
Who are you my dear comrade?   10

Then to the second I step—and who are you my child and darling?
Who are you sweet boy with cheeks yet blooming?

Then to the third—a face nor child nor old, very calm, as of beautiful
    yellow-white ivory;
Young man I think I know you—I think this face is the face of the Christ
    himself,
Dead and divine and brother of all, and here again he lies.   15

                                                                     1865, 1867

As Toilsome
I Wander'd Virginia's Woods

As toilsome I wander'd Virginia's woods,
To the music of rustling leaves kick'd by my feet, (for 'twas autumn,)
I mark'd at the foot of a tree the grave of a soldier;
Mortally wounded he and buried on the retreat, (easily all could I
    understand,)
The halt of a mid-day hour, when up! no time to lose—yet this sign left,   5
On a tablet scrawl'd and nail'd on the tree by the grave,
Bold, cautious, true, and my loving comrade.

Long, long I muse, then on my way go wandering,
Many a changeful season to follow, and many a scene of life,
Yet at times through changeful season and scene, abrupt, alone, or in the
    crowded street,   10
Comes before me the unknown soldier's grave, comes the inscription rude in
    Virginia's woods,
Bold, cautious, true, and my loving comrade.

                                                                                        1865, 1867

The Wound-Dresser

1

An old man bending I come among new faces,
Years looking backward resuming in answer to children,
Come tell us old man, as from young men and maidens that love me,
(Arous'd and angry, I'd thought to beat the alarum, and urge relentless war,
But soon my fingers fail'd me, my face droop'd and I resign'd myself   5
To sit by the wounded and soothe them, or silently watch the dead;)
Years hence of these scenes, of these furious passions, these chances,
Of unsurpass'd heroes, (was one side so brave? the other was equally brave;)
Now be witness again, paint the mightiest armies of earth,
Of those armies so rapid so wondrous what saw you to tell us?   10
What stays with you latest and deepest? of curious panics,
Of hard-fought engagements or sieges tremendous what deepest remains?

2

O maidens and young men I love and that love me,
What you ask of my days those the strangest and sudden your talking
    recalls,
Soldier alert I arrive after a long march cover'd with sweat and dust,   15
In the nick of time I come, plunge in the fight, loudly shout in the rush of
    successful charge,
Enter the captur'd works—yet lo, like a swift-running river they fade,
Pass and are gone they fade—I dwell not on soldiers' perils or soldiers' joys,
(Both I remember well—many of the hardships, few the joys, yet I was
    content.)

But in silence, in dreams' projections,   20
While the world of gain and appearance and mirth goes on,
So soon what is over forgotten, and waves wash the imprints off the sand,
With hinged knees returning I enter the doors, (while for you up there,
Whoever you are, follow without noise and be of strong heart.)

Bearing the bandages, water and sponge,   25
Straight and swift to my wounded I go,
Where they lie on the ground after the battle brought in,
Where their priceless blood reddens the grass the ground,
Or to the rows of the hospital tent, or under the roof'd hospital,
To the long rows of cots up and down each side I return,   30
To each and all one after another I draw near, not one do I miss,
An attendant follows holding a tray, he carries a refuse pail,
Soon to be fill'd with clotted rags and blood, emptied, and fill'd again.

I onward go, I stop,
With hinged knees and steady hand to dress wounds,   35
I am firm with each, the pangs are sharp yet unavoidable,
One turns to me his appealing eyes—poor boy! I never knew you,
Yet I think I could not refuse this moment to die for you, if that would save
    you.

                                     3

On, on I go, (open doors of time! open hospital doors!)
The crush'd head I dress, (poor crazed hand tear not the bandage away,)   40
The neck of the cavalry-man with the bullet through and through I
    examine,
Hard the breathing rattles, quite glazed already the eye, yet life struggles
    hard,
(Come sweet death! be persuaded O beautiful death!
In mercy come quickly.)

From the stump of the arm, the amputated hand,   45
I undo the clotted lint, remove the slough, wash off the matter and blood,
Back on his pillow the soldier bends with curv'd neck and side falling head,
His eyes are closed, his face is pale, he dares not look on the bloody stump,
And has not yet look'd on it.

I dress a wound in the side, deep, deep,   50
But a day or two more, for see the frame all wasted and sinking,
And the yellow-blue countenance see.

I dress the perforated shoulder, the foot with the bullet-wound,
Cleanse the one with a gnawing and putrid gangrene, so sickening, so
    offensive,
While the attendant stands behind aside me holding the tray and pail.   55

I am faithful, I do not give out,
The fractur'd thigh, the knee, the wound in the abdomen,
These and more I dress with impassive hand, (yet deep in my breast a fire, a
    burning flame.)

                                     4

Thus in silence in dreams' projections,
Returning, resuming, I thread my way through the hospitals,   60
The hurt and wounded I pacify with soothing hand,
I sit by the restless all the dark night, some are so young,
Some suffer so much, I recall the experience sweet and sad,
(Many a soldier's loving arms about this neck have cross'd and rested,
Many a soldier's kiss dwells on these bearded lips.)   65

                                                        1865, 1881

The Artilleryman's Vision

While my wife at my side lies slumbering, and the wars are over long,
And my head on the pillow rests at home, and the vacant midnight passes,
And through the stillness, through the dark, I hear, just hear, the breath of
    my infant,
There in the room as I wake from sleep this vision presses upon me;

The engagement opens there and then in fantasy unreal, 5
The skirmishers begin, they crawl cautiously ahead, I hear the irregular
   snap! snap!
I hear the sounds of the different missiles, the short *t-h-t! t-h-t!* of the rifle-
   balls,
I see the shells exploding leaving small white clouds, I hear the great shells
   shrieking as they pass,
The grape[4] like the hum and whirr of wind through the trees, (tumultuous
   now the contest rages,)
All the scenes at the batteries rise in detail before me again, 10
The crashing and smoking, the pride of the men in their pieces,
The chief-gunner ranges and sights his piece and selects a fuse of the right
   time,
After firing I see him lean aside and look eagerly off to note the effect;
Elsewhere I hear the cry of a regiment charging, (the young colonel leads
   himself this time with brandish'd sword,)
I see the gaps cut by the enemy's volleys, (quickly fill'd up, no delay,) 15
I breathe the suffocating smoke, then the flat clouds hover low concealing
   all;
Now a strange lull for a few seconds, not a shot fired on either side,
Then resumed the chaos louder than ever, with eager calls and orders of
   officers,
While from some distant part of the field the wind wafts to my ears a shout
   of applause, (some special success,)
And ever the sound of the cannon far or near, (rousing even in dreams a
   devilish exultation and all the old mad joy in the depths of my soul,) 20
And ever the hastening of infantry shifting positions, batteries, cavalry,
   moving hither and thither,
(The falling, dying, I heed not, the wounded dripping and red I heed not,
   some to the rear are hobbling,)
Grime, heat, rush, aides-de-camp galloping by or on a full run,
With the patter of small arms, the warning *s-s-t* of the rifles, (these in my
   vision I hear or see,)
And bombs bursting in air, and at night the vari-color'd rockets. 25

1865, 1881

Look Down Fair Moon

Look down fair moon and bathe this scene,
Pour softly down night's nimbus floods on faces ghastly, swollen, purple,
On the dead on their backs with arms toss'd wide,
Pour down your unstinted nimbus sacred moon.

1865, 1881

Reconciliation

Word over all, beautiful as the sky,
Beautiful that war and all its deeds of carnage must in time be utterly lost,

---

[4]Grape-shot.

That the hands of the sisters Death and Night incessantly softly wash again,
    and ever again, this soil'd world;
For my enemy is dead, a man divine as myself is dead,
I look where he lies white-faced and still in the coffin—I draw near,   5
Bend down and touch lightly with my lips the white face in the coffin.

1865–66, 1881

How Solemn as One by One

(Washington City, 1865)

How solemn as one by one,
As the ranks returning worn and sweaty, as the men file by where I stand,
As the faces the masks appear, as I glance at the faces studying the masks,
(As I glance upward out of this page studying you, dear friend, whoever you
    are,)
How solemn the thought of my whispering soul to each in the ranks, and to
    you!   5
I see behind each mask that wonder a kindred soul,
O the bullet could never kill what you really are, dear friend,
Nor the bayonet stab what you really are;
The soul! yourself I see, great as any, good as the best,
Waiting secure and content, which the bullet could never kill,   10
Nor the bayonet stab O friend.

1865–66, 1871

As I Lay with My Head
in Your Lap Camerado[5]

As I lay with my head in your lap camerado,
The confession I made I resume, what I said to you and the open air I
    resume,
I know I am restless and make others so,
I know my words are weapons full of danger, full of death,
For I confront peace, security, and all the settled laws, to unsettle them,   5
I am more resolute because all have denied me than I could ever have been
    had all accepted me,
I heed not and have never heeded either experience, cautions, majorities,
    nor ridicule,
And the threat of what is call'd hell is little or nothing to me,
And the lure of what is call'd heaven is little or nothing to me;
Dear camerado! I confess I have urged you onward with me, and still urge
    you, without the least idea what is our destination,   10
Or whether we shall be victorious, or utterly quell'd and defeated.

1865–66, 1881

---

[5]Close companion; cf. *Camarada* (Spanish), chambermate.

MEMORIES OF PRESIDENT LINCOLN

When Lilacs Last in the Dooryard Bloom'd[1]

1

When lilacs last in the dooryard bloom'd,
And the great star[2] early droop'd in the western sky in the night,
I mourn'd, and yet shall mourn with ever-returning spring.

Ever-returning spring, trinity sure to me you bring,
Lilac blooming perennial and drooping star in the west,   5
And thought of him I love.

2

O powerful western fallen star!
O shades of night—O moody, tearful night!
O great star disappear'd—O the black murk that hides the star!
O cruel hands that hold me powerless—O helpless soul of me!   10
O harsh surrounding cloud that will not free my soul.

3

In the dooryard fronting an old farm-house near the white-wash'd palings,
Stands the lilac-bush tall-growing with heart-shaped leaves of rich green,
With many a pointed blossom rising delicate, with the perfume strong I love,
With every leaf a miracle—and from this bush in the dooryard,   15
With delicate-color'd blossoms and heart-shaped leaves of rich green,
A sprig with its flower I break.

4

In the swamp in secluded recesses,
A shy and hidden bird is warbling a song.

Solitary the thrush,   20
The hermit withdrawn to himself, avoiding the settlements,
Sings by himself a song.

Song of the bleeding throat,
Death's outlet song of life, (for well dear brother I know,
If thou wast not granted to sing thou would'st surely die.)   25

5

Over the breast of the spring, the land, amid cities,
Amid lanes and through old woods, where lately the violets peep'd from the
    ground, spotting the gray debris,
Amid the grass in the fields each side of the lanes, passing the endless grass,
Passing the yellow-spear'd wheat, every grain from its shroud in the dark-
    brown fields uprisen.

---

[1]President Abraham Lincoln was shot by an assassin on April 14, 1865, and died the next day. The murder shocked the nation; it happened only a few weeks after Lincoln's inauguration for a second term, and only a few days after the Confederacy's General Lee surrendered his armies to the Union's General Grant at Appomattox Court House, effectively ending the Civil War. Whitman wrote in *Specimen Days*: "The day of the murder we heard the news very early in the morning. Mother prepared breakfast—and other meals afterward—as usual; but not a mouthful was eaten all day by either of us. We each drank half a cup of coffee; that was all. We got every newspaper morning and evening, and the frequent extras of that period, and pass'd them silently to each other." April is the month for lilacs in America.
[2]Venus.

Passing the apple-tree blows of white and pink in the orchards,   30
Carrying a corpse to where it shall rest in the grave,
Night and day journeys a coffin.[3]

6

Coffin that passes through lanes and streets,
Through day and night with the great cloud darkening the land,
With the pomp of the inloop'd flags with the cities draped in black,   35
With the show of the States themselves as of crape-veil'd women standing,
With processions long and winding and the flambeaus of the night,
With the countless torches lit, with the silent sea of faces and the unbared
    heads,
With the waiting depot, the arriving coffin, and the sombre faces,
With dirges through the night, with the thousand voices rising strong and
    solemn,   40
With all the mournful voices of the dirges pour'd around the coffin,
The dim-lit churches and the shuddering organs—where amid these you
    journey,
With the tolling tolling bells' perpetual clang,
Here, coffin that slowly passes,
I give you my sprig of lilac.   45

7

(Nor for you, for one alone,
Blossoms and branches green to coffins all I bring,
For fresh as the morning, thus would I chant a song for you O sane and
    sacred death.

All over bouquets of roses,
O death, I cover you over with roses and early lilies,   50
But mostly and now the lilac that blooms the first,
Copious I break, I break the sprigs from the bushes,
With loaded arms I come, pouring for you,
For you and the coffins all of you O death.)

8

O western orb sailing the heaven,   55
Now I know what you must have meant as a month since I walk'd,
As I walk'd in silence the transparent shadowy night,
As I saw you had something to tell as you bent to me night after night,
As you droop'd from the sky low down as if to my side, (while the other stars
    all look'd on,)
As we wander'd together the solemn night, (for something I know not what
    kept me from sleep,)   60
As the night advanced, and I saw on the rim of the west how full you were
    of woe,
As I stood on the rising ground in the breeze in the cool transparent night,
As I watch'd where you pass'd and was lost in the netherward black of the
    night,
As my soul in its trouble dissatisfied sank, as where you sad orb,
Concluded, dropt in the night, and was gone.   65

9

Sing on there in the swamp,
O singer bashful and tender, I hear your notes, I hear your call,

---

[3]Lincoln's coffin was placed on a train which first went to New
York and then to Springfield, Illinois, for burial.

I hear, I come presently, I understand you,
But a moment I linger, for the lustrous star has detain'd me,
The star my departing comrade holds and detains me.   70

10

O how shall I warble myself for the dead one there I loved?
And how shall I deck my song for the large sweet soul that has gone?
And what shall my perfume be for the grave of him I love?

Sea-winds blown from east and west,
Blown from the Eastern sea and blown from the Western sea, till there on
   the prairies meeting,   75
These and with these and the breath of my chant,
I'll perfume the grave of him I love.

11

O what shall I hang on the chamber walls?
And what shall the pictures be that I hang on the walls,
To adorn the burial-house of him I love?   80

Pictures of growing spring and farms and homes,
With the Fourth-month[4] eve at sundown, and the gray smoke lucid and
   bright,
With floods of the yellow gold of the gorgeous, indolent, sinking sun,
   burning, expanding the air,
With the fresh sweet herbage under foot, and the pale green leaves of the
   trees prolific,
In the distance the flowing glaze, the breast of the river, with a wind-dapple
   here and there,   85
With ranging hills on the banks, with many a line against the sky, and
   shadows,
And the city at hand with dwellings so dense, and stacks of chimneys,
And all the scenes of life and the workshops, and the workmen homeward
   returning.

12

Lo, body and soul—this land,
My own Manhattan with spires, and the sparkling and hurrying tides, and
   the ships,   90
The varied and ample land, the South and the North in the light, Ohio's
   shores and flashing Missouri,
And ever the far-spreading prairies cover'd with grass and corn.

Lo, the most excellent sun so calm and haughty,
The violet and purple morn with just-felt breezes,
The gentle soft-born measureless light,   95
The miracle spreading bathing all, the fulfill'd noon,
The coming eve delicious, the welcome night and the stars,
Over my cities shining all, enveloping man and land.

13

Sing on, sing on you gray-brown bird,
Sing from the swamps, the recesses, pour your chant from the bushes,   100
Limitless out of the dusk, out of the cedars and pines.

---

[4]April.

Sing on dearest brother, warble your reedy song,
Loud human song, with voice of uttermost woe.

O liquid and free and tender!
O wild and loose to my soul—O wondrous singer,   105
You only I hear—yet the star holds me, (but will soon depart,)
Yet the lilac with mastering odor holds me.

14

Now while I sat in the day and look'd forth,
In the close of the day with its light and the fields of spring, and the farmers
    preparing their crops,
In the large unconscious scenery of my land with its lakes and forests,   110
In the heavenly aerial beauty, (after the perturb'd winds and the storms,)
Under the arching heavens of the afternoon swift passing, and the voices of
    children and women,
The many-moving sea-tides, and I saw the ships how they sail'd,
And the summer approaching with richness, and the fields all busy with
    labor,
And the infinite separate houses, how they all went on, each with its meals
    and minutia of daily usages,   115
And the streets how their throbbings throbb'd, and the cities pent—lo, then
    and there,
Falling upon them all and among them all, enveloping me with the rest,
Appear'd the cloud, appear'd the long black trail,
And I knew death, its thought, and the sacred knowledge of death.

Then with the knowledge of death as walking one side of me,   120
And the thought of death close-walking the other side of me,
And I in the middle as with companions, and as holding the hands of
    companions,
I fled forth to the hiding receiving night that talks not,
Down to the shores of the water, the path by the swamp in the dimness,
To the solemn shadowy cedars and ghostly pines so still.   125

And the singer so shy to the rest receiv'd me,
The gray-brown bird I know receiv'd us comrades three,
And he sang the carol of death, and a verse for him I love.

From deep secluded recesses,
From the fragrant cedars and the ghostly pines so still,   130
Came the carol of the bird.

And the charm of the carol rapt me,
As I held as if by their hands my comrades in the night,
And the voice of my spirit tallied the song of the bird.

Come lovely and soothing death,   135
Undulate round the world, serenely arriving, arriving,
In the day, in the night, to all, to each,
Sooner or later delicate death.

Prais'd be the fathomless universe,
For life and joy, and for objects and knowledge curious,   140
And for love, sweet love—but praise! praise! praise!
For the sure-enwinding arms of cool-enfolding death.

Dark mother always gliding near with soft feet,
Have none chanted for thee a chant of fullest welcome?
Then I chant it for thee, I glorify thee above all,   145
I bring thee a song that when thou must indeed come, come unfalteringly.

Approach strong deliveress,
When it is so, when thou hast taken them I joyously sing the dead,
Lost in the loving floating ocean of thee,
Laved in the flood of thy bliss O death.   150

From me to thee glad serenades,
Dances for thee I propose saluting thee, adornments and feastings for thee,
And the sights of the open landscape and the high-spread sky are fitting,
And life and the fields, and the huge and thoughtful night.

The night in silence under many a star,   155
The ocean shore and the husky whispering wave whose voice I know,
And the soul turning to thee O vast and well-veil'd death,
And the body gratefully nestling close to thee.

Over the tree-tops I float thee a song,
Over the rising and sinking waves, over the myriad fields and the prairies wide,   160
Over the dense-pack'd cities all and the teeming wharves and ways,
I float this carol with joy, with joy to thee O death.

15

To the tally of my soul,
Loud and strong kept up the gray-brown bird,
With pure deliberate notes spreading filling the night.   165

Loud in the pines and cedars dim,
Clear in the freshness moist and the swamp-perfume,
And I with my comrades there in the night.

While my sight that was bound in my eyes unclosed,
As to long panoramas of visions.   170

And I saw askant[5] the armies,
I saw as in noiseless dreams hundreds of battle-flags,
Borne through the smoke of the battles and pierc'd with missiles I saw them,
And carried hither and yon through the smoke, and torn and bloody,
And at last but a few shreds left on the staffs, (and all in silence,)   175
And the staffs all splinter'd and broken.

I saw battle-corpses, myriads of them,
And the white skeletons of young men, I saw them,
I saw the debris and debris of all the slain soldiers of the war,
But I saw they were not as was thought,   180
They themselves were fully at rest, they suffer'd not,
The living remain'd and suffer'd, the mother suffer'd,
And the wife and the child and the musing comrade suffer'd,
And the armies that remain'd suffer'd.

---

[5]With mistrust.

16

Passing the visions, passing the night,   185
Passing, unloosing the hold of my comrade's hands,
Passing the song of the hermit bird and the tallying song of my soul,
Victorious song, death's outlet song, yet varying ever-altering song,
As low and wailing, yet clear the notes, rising and falling, flooding the night,
Sadly sinking and fainting, as warning and warning, and yet again bursting
    with joy,   190
Covering the earth and filling the spread of the heaven,
As that powerful psalm in the night I heard from recesses,
Passing, I leave thee lilac with heart-shaped leaves,
I leave thee there in the door-yard, blooming, returning with spring.

I cease from my song for thee,   195
From my gaze on thee in the west, fronting the west, communing with thee,
O comrade lustrous with silver face in the night.

Yet each to keep and all, retrievements out of the night,
The song, the wondrous chant of the gray-brown bird,
And the tallying chant, the echo arous'd in my soul,   200
With the lustrous and drooping star with the countenance full of woe,
With the holders holding my hand nearing the call of the bird,
Comrades mine and I in the midst, and their memory ever to keep, for the
    dead I loved so well,
For the sweetest, wisest soul of all my days and lands—and this for his dear
    sake,
Lilac and star and bird twined with the chant of my soul,   205
There in the fragrant pines and the cedars dusk and dim.

1865–66, 1881

O Captain! My Captain![1]

O Captain! my Captain! our fearful trip is done,
The ship has weather'd every rack, the prize we sought is won,
The port is near, the bells I hear, the people all exulting,
While follow eyes the steady keel, the vessel grim and daring;
        But O heart! heart! heart!   5
            O the bleeding drops of red,
                Where on the deck my Captain lies,
                    Fallen cold and dead.

O Captain! my Captain! rise up and hear the bells;
Rise up—for you the flag is flung—for you the bugle trills,   10
For you bouquets and ribbon'd wreaths—for you the shores a-crowding,
For you they call, the swaying mass, their eager faces turning;
        Here Captain! dear father!
            This arm beneath your head!
                It is some dream that on the deck,   15
                    You've fallen cold and dead.

---

[1]This poem was for a long time Whitman's most popular. It is a kind of public elegy written for public declamation, while "Lilacs" is more private, more effective in working through genuine grief to some kind of comprehension and reconciliation.

My Captain does not answer, his lips are pale and still,
My father does not feel my arm, he has no pulse nor will,
The ship is anchor'd safe and sound, its voyage closed and done,
From fearful trip the victor ship comes in with object won: 20
      Exult O shores, and ring O bells!
          But I with mournful tread,
              Walk the deck my Captain lies,
                Fallen cold and dead.

1865, 1871

Hush'd Be the Camps To-day

(May 4, 1865)

Hush'd be the camps to-day,
And soldiers let us drape our war-worn weapons,
And each with musing soul retire to celebrate,
Our dear commander's death.

No more for him life's stormy conflicts,   5
Nor victory, nor defeat—no more time's dark events,
Charging like ceaseless clouds across the sky.

But sing poet in our name,
Sing of the love we bore him—because you,—dweller in camps, know it
  truly.

As they invault the coffin there,   10
Sing—as they close the doors of earth upon him—one verse,
For the heavy hearts of soldiers.

1865, 1871

This Dust Was Once the Man

This dust was once the man,
Gentle, plain, just and resolute, under whose cautious hand,
Against the foulest crime in history known in any land or age,
Was saved the Union of these States.

1871, 1871

from AUTUMN RIVULETS

There Was a Child Went Forth

There was a child went forth every day,
And the first object he look'd upon, that object he became,

And that object became part of him for the day or a certain part of the day,
Or for many years or stretching cycles of years.

The early lilacs became part of this child,   5
And grass and white and red morning-glories, and white and red clover,
    and the song of the phœbe-bird,
And the Third-month[1] lambs and the sow's pink-faint litter, and the mare's
    foal and the cow's calf,
And the noisy brood of the barnyard or by the mire of the pond-side,
And the fish suspending themselves so curiously below there, and the
    beautiful curious liquid,
And the water-plants with their graceful flat heads, all became part of him.   10

The field-sprouts of Fourth-month and Fifth-month[2] became part of him,
Winter-grain sprouts and those of the light-yellow corn, and the esculent
    roots of the garden,
And the apple-trees cover'd with blossoms and the fruit afterward, and
    wood-berries, and the commonest weeds by the road,
And the old drunkard staggering home from the outhouse of the tavern
    whence he had lately risen,
And the schoolmistress that pass'd on her way to the school,   15
And the friendly boys that pass'd, and the quarrelsome boys,
And the tidy and fresh-cheek'd girls, and the barefoot negro boy and girl,
And all the changes of city and country wherever he went.

His own parents, he that had father'd him and she that had conceiv'd him in
    her womb and birth'd him,
They gave this child more of themselves than that,   20
They gave him afterward every day, they became part of him.

The mother at home quietly placing the dishes on the supper-table,
The mother with mild words, clean her cap and gown, a wholesome odor
    falling off her person and clothes as she walks by,
The father, strong, self-sufficient, manly, mean, anger'd, unjust,
The blow, the quick loud word, the tight bargain, the crafty lure,   25
The family usages, the language, the company, the furniture, the yearning
    and swelling heart,
Affection that will not be gainsay'd, the sense of what is real, the thought if
    after all it should prove unreal,
The doubts of day-time and the doubts of night-time, the curious whether
    and how,
Whether that which appears so is so, or is it all flashes and specks?
Men and women crowding fast in the streets, if they are not flashes and
    specks what are they?   30
The streets themselves and the façades of houses, and goods in the windows,
Vehicles, teams, the heavy-plank'd wharves, the huge crossing at the ferries,
The village on the highland seen from afar at sunset, the river between,
Shadows, aureola[3] and mist, the light falling on roofs and gables of white or
    brown two miles off,
The schooner near by sleepily dropping down the tide, the little boat slack-
    tow'd astern,   35
The hurrying tumbling waves, quick-broken crests, slapping,

---

[1]March (Quaker usage).
[2]April and May.
[3]Light-fringe around the sun in a mist.

The strata of color'd clouds, the long bar of maroon-tint away solitary by
   itself, the spread of purity it lies motionless in,
The horizon's edge, the flying sea-crow, the fragrance of salt marsh and
   shore mud,
These became part of that child who went forth every day, and who now
   goes, and will always go forth every day.

1855, 1871

To a Common Prostitute

Be composed—be at ease with me—I am Walt Whitman, liberal and lusty as
   Nature,
Not till the sun excludes you do I exclude you,
Not till the waters refuse to glisten for you and the leaves to rustle for you,
   do my words refuse to glisten and rustle for you.

My girl I appoint with you an appointment, and I charge you that you make
   preparation to be worthy to meet me,
And I charge you that you be patient and perfect till I come.   5

Till then I salute you with a significant look that you do not forget me.

1860, 1860

Sparkles from the Wheel

Where the city's ceaseless crowd moves on the livelong day,
Withdrawn I join a group of children watching, I pause aside with them.

By the curb toward the edge of the flagging,
A knife-grinder works at his wheel sharpening a great knife,
Bending over he carefully holds it to the stone, by foot and knee,   5
With measur'd tread he turns rapidly, as he presses with light but firm hand,
Forth issue then in copious golden jets,
Sparkles from the wheel.

The scene and all its belongings, how they seize and affect me,
The sad sharp-chinn'd old man with worn clothes and broad shoulder-band
   of leather,   10
Myself effusing[4] and fluid, a phantom curiously floating, now here absorb'd
   and arrested,
The group, (an unminded point set in a vast surrounding,)
The attentive, quiet children, the loud, proud, restive base of the streets,
The low hoarse purr of the whirling stone, the light-press'd blade,
Diffusing, dropping, sideways-darting, in tiny showers of gold,   15
Sparkles from the wheel.

1871, 1871

---

[4]Pouring forth.

Passage to India

1

Singing my days,
Singing the great achievements of the present,
Singing the strong light works of engineers,
Our modern wonders, (the antique ponderous Seven[1] outvied,)
In the Old World the east the Suez canal,   5
The New by its mighty railroad spann'd,
The seas inlaid with eloquent gentle wires;[2]
Yet first to sound, and ever sound, the cry with thee O soul,
The Past! the Past! the Past!

The Past—the dark unfathom'd retrospect!   10
The teeming gulf—the sleepers and the shadows!
The past—the infinite greatness of the past!
For what is the present after all but a growth out of the past?
(As a projectile form'd, impell'd, passing a certain line, still keeps on,
So the present, utterly form'd, impell'd by the past.)   15

2

Passage O soul to India!
Eclaircise[3] the myths Asiatic, the primitive fables.

Not you alone proud truths of the world,
Nor you alone ye facts of modern science,
But myths and fables of eld,[4] Asia's, Africa's fables,   20
The far-darting beams of the spirit, the unloos'd dreams,
The deep diving bibles and legends,
The daring plots of the poets, the elder religions;
O you temples fairer than lilies pour'd over by the rising sun!
O you fables spurning the known, eluding the hold of the known, mounting
    to heaven!   25
You lofty and dazzling towers, pinnacled, red as roses, burnish'd with gold!
Towers of fables immortal fashion'd from mortal dreams!
You too I welcome and fully the same as the rest!
You too with joy I sing.

Passage to India!   30
Lo, soul, seest thou not God's purpose from the first?
The earth to be spann'd, connected by network,
The races, neighbors, to marry and be given in marriage,
The oceans to be cross'd, the distant brought near,
The lands to be welded together.   35

A worship new I sing,
You captains, voyagers, explorers, yours,
You engineers, you architects, machinists, yours,

---

[1]The Seven Wonders of the Ancient World were the Egyptian pyramids, the Hanging Gardens of Babylon, the Mausoleum at Halicarnassus, the temple of Artemis at Ephesus; the Colossus of Rhodes, the statue of Zeus (by Phidias) at Olympia, and the Pharos (lighthouse) at Alexandria.
[2]The Suez Canal connecting the Red Sea and the Mediterra-nean was opened in 1869; the Union Pacific and Central Pacific railroads completed the tracks spanning America in 1869; the trans-Atlantic cable was laid in 1866.
[3]Clarify.
[4]Antiquity.

You, not for trade or transportation only,
But in God's name, and for thy sake O soul.   40

3

Passage to India!
Lo soul for thee of tableaus twain,
I see in one the Suez canal initiated, open'd,
I see the procession of steamships, the Empress Eugenie's[5] leading the van,
I mark from on deck the strange landscape, the pure sky, the level sand in
    the distance,   45
I pass swiftly the picturesque groups, the workmen gather'd,
The gigantic dredging machines.

In one again, different, (yet thine, all thine, O soul, the same,)
I see over my own continent the Pacific railroad surmounting every barrier,
I see continual trains of cars winding along the Platte[6] carrying freight and
    passengers,   50
I hear the locomotives rushing and roaring, and the shrill steam-whistle,
I hear the echoes reverberate through the grandest scenery in the world,
I cross the Laramie plains, I note the rocks in grotesque shapes, the buttes,
I see the plentiful larkspur and wild onions, the barren, colorless, sage-
    deserts,
I see in glimpses afar or towering immediately above me the great
    mountains, I see the Wind river and the Wahsatch mountains,   55
I see the Monument mountain and the Eagle's Nest, I pass the Promontory,
    I ascend the Nevadas,
I scan the noble Elk mountain and wind around its base,
I see the Humboldt range, I thread the valley and cross the river,
I see the clear waters of lake Tahoe, I see forests of majestic pines,
Or crossing the great desert, the alkaline plains, I behold enchanting
    mirages of waters and meadows,   60
Marking through these and after all, in duplicate slender lines,
Bridging the three or four thousand miles of land travel,
Tying the Eastern to the Western sea,
The road between Europe and Asia.

(Ah Genoese[7] thy dream! thy dream!   65
Centuries after thou art laid in thy grave,
The shore thou foundest verifies thy dream.)

4

Passage to India!
Struggles of many a captain, tales of many a sailor dead,
Over my mood stealing and spreading they come,   70
Like clouds and cloudlets in the unreach'd sky.

Along all history, down the slopes,
As a rivulet running, sinking now, and now again to the surface rising,
A ceaseless thought, a varied train—lo, soul, to thee, thy sight, they rise,
The plans, the voyages again, the expeditions,   75
Again Vasco de Gama[8] sails forth,
Again the knowledge gain'd, the mariner's compass,

---

[5]The wife of France's Napoleon III, aboard the leading ship opening the Suez Canal.
[6]Lines 50–64 contain place names along the route of the transcontinental railroad from Nebraska to California.
[7]Christopher Columbus (1451–1506), born in Genoa, Italy.
[8]Vasco da Gama (*c.* 1469–1524), Portuguese navigator, sailed to India by rounding Africa's Cape of Good Hope.

Lands found and nations born, thou born America,
For purpose vast, man's long probation fill'd,
Thou rondure[9] of the world at last accomplish'd.   80

5

O vast Rondure, swimming in space,
Cover'd all over with visible power and beauty,
Alternate light and day and the teeming spiritual darkness,
Unspeakable high processions of sun and moon and countless stars above,
Below, the manifold grass and waters, animals, mountains, trees,   85
With inscrutable purpose, some hidden prophetic intention,
Now first it seems my thought begins to span thee.

Down from the gardens of Asia descending radiating,
Adam and Eve appear, then their myriad progeny after them,
Wandering, yearning, curious, with restless explorations,   90
With questionings, baffled, formless, feverish, with never-happy hearts,
With that sad incessant refrain, *Wherefore unsatisfied soul?* and *Whither O
    mocking life?*

Ah who shall soothe these feverish children?
Who justify these restless explorations?
Who speak the secret of impassive earth?   95
Who bind it to us? what is this separate Nature so unnatural?
What is this earth to our affections? (unloving earth, without a throb to
    answer ours,
Cold earth, the place of graves.)

Yet soul be sure the first intent remains, and shall be carried out,
Perhaps even now the time has arrived.   100

After the seas are all cross'd, (as they seem already cross'd,)
After the great captains and engineers have accomplish'd their work,
After the noble inventors, after the scientists, the chemist, the geologist,
    ethnologist,
Finally shall come the poet worthy that name,
The true son of God shall come singing his songs.   105

Then not your deeds only O voyagers, O scientists and inventors, shall be
    justified,
All these hearts as of fretted children shall be sooth'd,
All affection shall be fully responded to, the secret shall be told,
All these separations and gaps shall be taken up and hook'd and link'd
    together,
The whole earth, this cold, impassive, voiceless earth, shall be completely
    justified,   110
Trinitas[10] divine shall be gloriously accomplish'd and compacted by the true
    son of God, the poet,
(He shall indeed pass the straits and conquer the mountains,
He shall double the cape of Good Hope to some purpose,)
Nature and Man shall be disjoin'd and diffused no more,
The true son of God shall absolutely fuse them.   115

---

[9]Roundness.
[10]Cf. *Trinitad* (Spanish), i.e., Holy Trinity.

6

Year at whose wide-flung door I sing!
Year of the purpose accomplish'd!
Year of the marriage of continents, climates and oceans!
(No mere doge of Venice now wedding the Adriatic,)[11]
I see O year in you the vast terraqueous globe given and giving all,   120
Europe to Asia, Africa join'd, and they to the New World,
The lands, geographies, dancing before you, holding a festival garland,
As brides and bridegrooms hand in hand.

Passage to India!
Cooling airs from Caucasus[12] far, soothing cradle of man,   125
The river Euphrates[13] flowing, the past lit up again.

Lo soul, the retrospect brought forward,
The old, most populous, wealthiest of earth's lands,
The streams of the Indus and the Ganges[14] and their many affluents,
(I my shores of America walking to-day behold, resuming all,)   130
The tale of Alexander[15] on his warlike marches suddenly dying,
On one side China and on the other side Persia and Arabia,
To the south the great seas and the bay of Bengal,
The flowing literatures, tremendous epics, religions, castes,
Old occult Brahma interminably far back, the tender and junior Buddha,   135
Central and southern empires and all their belongings, possessors,
The wars of Tamerlane,[16] the reign of Aurungzebe,[17]
The traders, rulers, explorers, Moslems, Venetians, Byzantium, the Arabs,
   Portuguese,
The first travelers famous yet, Marco Polo, Batouta the Moor,[18]
Doubts to be solv'd, the map incognita,[19] blanks to be fill'd,   140
The foot of man unstay'd, the hands never at rest,
Thyself O soul that will not brook a challenge.

The mediæval navigators rise before me,
The world of 1492, with its awaken'd enterprise,
Something swelling in humanity now like the sap of the earth in spring,   145
The sunset splendor of chivalry declining.

And who art thou sad shade?
Gigantic, visionary, thyself a visionary,
With majestic limbs and pious beaming eyes,
Spreading around with every look of thine a golden world,   150
Enhuing it with gorgeous hues.

As the chief histrion,[20]
Down to the footlights walks in some great scena,[21]

[11]The Doge (ruler) of Venice threw a ring into the Adriatic each year to symbolize the wedding of the city and the sea.
[12]Region in Russia from the Black Sea to the Caspian Sea.
[13]River running from Turkey to the Persian Gulf; the Euphrates valley was the legendary site of the origin of Western races.
[14]Rivers of India.
[15]Alexander the Great (356–323 B.C.), world conqueror, died suddenly of a fever at the age of thirty-three at the peak of his power.
[16]Tamerlane (*c.* 1336–1405), Mongol warrior who con-
quered an area from the Volga River to the Persian Gulf.
[17]Aurungzebe, also Aurangzeb (1618–1707), emperor of Hindustan (area of modern day India and Pakistan) and world conqueror.
[18]Marco Polo (*c.* 1254–1324), a Venetian traveller who explored the Orient, including China; Batouta, variant of Patouta (1303–1377), traveller in Africa and Asia.
[19]Unknown.
[20]Actor, i.e. Christopher Columbus.
[21]Scene.

Dominating the rest I see the Admiral himself,
(History's type of courage, action, faith,)   155
Behold him sail from Palos[22] leading his little fleet,
His voyage behold, his return, his great fame,
His misfortunes, calumniators, behold him a prisoner, chain'd,
Behold his dejection, poverty, death.

(Curious in time I stand, noting the efforts of heroes,   160
Is the deferment long? bitter the slander, poverty, death?
Lies the seed unreck'd[23] for centuries in the ground? lo, to God's due
      occasion,
Uprising in the night, it sprouts, blooms,
And fills the earth with use and beauty.)

7

Passage indeed O soul to primal thought,   165
Not lands and seas alone, thy own clear freshness,
The young maturity of brood and bloom,
To realms of budding bibles.

O soul, repressless, I with thee and thou with me,
Thy circumnavigation of the world begin,   170
Of man, the voyage of his mind's return,
To reason's early paradise,
Back, back to wisdom's birth, to innocent intuitions,
Again with fair creation.

8

O we can wait no longer,   175
We too take ship O soul,
Joyous we too launch out on trackless seas,
Fearless for unknown shores on waves of ecstasy to sail,
Amid the wafting winds, (thou pressing me to thee, I thee to me, O soul,)
Caroling free, singing our song of God,   180
Chanting our chant of pleasant exploration.

With laugh and many a kiss,
(Let others deprecate, let others weep for sin, remorse, humiliation,)
O soul, thou pleasest me, I thee.

Ah more than any priest O soul we too believe in God,   185
But with the mystery of God we dare not dally.

O soul thou pleasest me, I thee,
Sailing these seas or on the hills, or waking in the night,
Thoughts, silent thoughts, of Time and Space and Death, like waters
      flowing,
Bear me indeed as through the regions infinite,   190
Whose air I breathe, whose ripples hear, lave me all over,
Bathe me O God in thee, mounting to thee,
I and my soul to range in range of thee.

---

[22]Spanish port from which Columbus began his voyage of   [23]Unreckoned or unnoticed.
discovery in 1492.

O Thou transcendent,
Nameless, the fibre and the breath,   195
Light of the light, shedding forth universes, thou centre of them,
Thou mightier centre of the true, the good, the loving,
Thou moral, spiritual fountain—affection's source—thou reservoir,
(O pensive soul of me—O thirst unsatisfied—waitest not there?
Waitest not haply for us somewhere there the Comrade perfect?)   200
Thou pulse—thou motive of the stars, suns, systems,
That, circling, move in order, safe, harmonious,
Athwart the shapeless vastnesses of space,
How should I think, how breathe a single breath, how speak, if, out of
      myself,
I could not launch, to those, superior universes?   205

Swiftly I shrivel at the thought of God,
At Nature and its wonders, Time and Space and Death,
But that I, turning, call to thee O soul, thou actual Me,
And lo, thou gently masterest the orbs,
Thou matest Time, smilest content at Death,   210
And fillest, swellest full the vastnesses of Space.

Greater than stars or suns,
Bounding O soul thou journeyest forth;
What love than thine and ours could wider amplify?
What aspirations, wishes, outvie thine and ours O soul?   215
What dreams of the ideal? what plans of purity, perfection, strength,
What cheerful willingness for others' sake to give up all?
For others' sake to suffer all?

Reckoning ahead O soul, when thou, the time achiev'd,
The seas all cross'd, weather'd the capes, the voyage done,   220
Surrounded, copest, frontest God, yieldest, the aim attain'd,
As fill'd with friendship, love complete, the Elder Brother found,
The Younger melts in fondness in his arms.

9

Passage to more than India!
Are thy wings plumed indeed for such far flights?   225
O soul, voyagest thou indeed on voyages like those?
Disportest thou on waters such as those?
Soundest below the Sanscrit and the Vedas?[24]
Then have thy bent[25] unleash'd.

Passage to you, your shores, ye aged fierce enigmas!   230
Passage to you, to mastership of you, ye strangling problems!
You, strew'd with the wrecks of skeletons, that, living, never reach'd you.

Passage to more than India!
O secret of the earth and sky!
Of you O waters of the sea! O winding creeks and rivers!   235
Of you O woods and fields! of you strong mountains of my land!
Of you O prairies! of you gray rocks!

---

[24]Sacred Hindu scriptures, written in Sanskrit.
[25]Energy, impetus.

O morning red! O clouds! O rain and snows!
O day and night, passage to you!

O sun and moon and all you stars! Sirius and Jupiter!   240
Passage to you!

Passage, immediate passage! the blood burns in my veins!
Away O soul! hoist instantly the anchor!
Cut the hawsers—haul out—shake out every sail!
Have we not stood here like trees in the ground long enough?   245
Have we not grovel'd here long enough, eating and drinking like mere
    brutes?
Have we not darken'd and dazed ourselves with books long enough?

Sail forth—steer for the deep waters only,
Reckless O soul, exploring, I with thee, and thou with me,
For we are bound where mariner has not yet dared to go,   250
And we will risk the ship, ourselves and all.

O my brave soul!
O farther farther sail!
O daring joy, but safe! are they not all the seas of God?
O farther, farther, farther sail!   255

1871, 1881

The Sleepers

1

I wander all night in my vision,
Stepping with light feet, swiftly and noiselessly stepping and stopping,
Bending with open eyes over the shut eyes of sleepers,
Wandering and confused, lost to myself, ill-assorted, contradictory,
Pausing, gazing, bending, and stopping.   5

How solemn they look there, stretch'd and still,
How quiet they breathe, the little children in their cradles.

The wretched features of ennuyés,[1] the white features of corpses, the livid
    faces of drunkards, the sick-gray faces of onanists,[2]
The gash'd bodies on battle-fields, the insane in their strong-door'd rooms,
    the sacred idiots, the new-born emerging from gates, and the dying
    emerging from gates,
The night pervades them and infolds them.   10

The married couple sleep calmly in their bed, he with his palm on the hip of
    the wife, and she with her palm on the hip of the husband,
The sisters sleep lovingly side by side in their bed,

---

[1]"Bored persons" (French).
[2]Masturbators.

The men sleep lovingly side by side in theirs,
And the mother sleeps with her little child carefully wrapt.

The blind sleep, and the deaf and dumb sleep,   15
The prisoner sleeps well in the prison, the runaway son sleeps,
The murderer that is to be hung next day, how does he sleep?
And the murder'd person, how does he sleep?

The female that loves unrequited sleeps,
And the male that loves unrequited sleeps,   20
The head of the money-maker that plotted all day sleeps,
And the enraged and treacherous dispositions, all, all sleep.

I stand in the dark with drooping eyes by the worst-suffering and the most
    restless,
I pass my hands soothingly to and fro a few inches from them,
The restless sink in their beds, they fitfully sleep.   25

Now I pierce the darkness, new beings appear,
The earth recedes from me into the night,
I saw that it was beautiful, and I see that what is not the earth is beautiful.

I go from bedside to bedside, I sleep close with the other sleepers each in
    turn,
I dream in my dream all the dreams of the other dreamers,   30
And I become the other dreamers.

I am a dance—play up there! the fit is whirling me fast!

I am the ever-laughing—it is new moon and twilight,
I see the hiding of douceurs,[3] I see nimble ghosts whichever way I look,
Cache[4] and cache again deep in the ground and sea, and where it is neither
    ground nor sea.   35

Well do they do their jobs those journeymen divine,
Only from me can they hide nothing, and would not if they could,
I reckon I am their boss and they make me a pet besides,
And surround me and lead me and run ahead when I walk,
To lift their cunning covers to signify[5] me with stretch'd arms, and resume
    the way;   40
Onward we move, a gay gang of blackguards! with mirth-shouting music
    and wild-flapping pennants of joy!

I am the actor, the actress, the voter, the politician,
The emigrant and the exile, the criminal that stood in the box,[6]
He who has been famous and he who shall be famous after to-day,
The stammerer, the well-formed person, the wasted or feeble person.   45

I am she who adorn'd herself and folded her hair expectantly,
My truant lover has come, and it is dark.

Double yourself and receive me darkness,
Receive me and my lover too, he will not let me go without him.

3"Pleasures, as sexual delights" (French).   5Signal or invite.
4Hide (or hiding place).   6Witness stand in courtroom.

I roll myself upon you as upon a bed, I resign myself to the dusk.   50

He whom I call answers me and takes the place of my lover,
He rises with me silently from the bed.

Darkness, you are gentler than my lover, his flesh was sweaty and panting,
I feel the hot moisture yet that he left me.

My hands are spread forth, I pass them in all directions,   55
I would sound up the shadowy shore to which you are journeying.

Be careful darkness! already what was it touch'd me?
I thought my lover had gone, else darkness and he are one,
I hear the heart-beat, I follow, I fade away.

2

I descend my western course,[7] my sinews are flaccid,   60
Perfume and youth course through me and I am their wake.

It is my face yellow and wrinkled instead of the old woman's,
I sit low in a straw-bottom chair and carefully darn my grandson's stockings.

It is I too, the sleepless widow looking out on the winter midnight,
I see the sparkles of starshine on the icy and pallid earth.   65

A shroud I see and I am the shroud, I wrap a body and lie in the coffin,
It is dark here under ground, it is not evil or pain here, it is blank here, for
    reasons.

(It seems to me that every thing in the light and air ought to be happy,
Whoever is not in his coffin and the dark grave let him know he has
    enough.)

3

I see a beautiful gigantic swimmer swimming naked through the eddies of
    the sea,   70
His brown hair lies close and even to his head, he strikes out with
    courageous arms, he urges himself with his legs,
I see his white body, I see his undaunted eyes,
I hate the swift-running eddies that would dash him head-foremost on the
    rocks.

What are you doing you ruffianly red-trickled waves?
Will you kill the courageous giant? will you kill him in the prime of his
    middle age?   75

Steady and long he struggles,
He is baffled, bang'd, bruis'd, he holds out while his strength holds out,
The slapping eddies are spotted with his blood, they bear him away, they roll
    him, swing him, turn him,
His beautiful body is borne in the circling eddies, it is continually bruis'd on
    rocks,
Swiftly and out of sight is borne the brave corpse.   80

---

[7]Grow old (by analogy with sunset).

4

I turn but do not extricate myself,
Confused, a past-reading, another, but with darkness yet.

The beach is cut by the razory ice-wind, the wreck-guns[8] sound,
The tempest lulls, the moon comes floundering through the drifts.

I look where the ship helplessly heads end on, I hear the burst as she strikes,
  I hear the howls of dismay, they grow fainter and fainter.   85

I cannot aid with my wringing fingers,
I can but rush to the surf and let it drench me and freeze upon me.

I search with the crowd, not one of the company is wash'd to us alive,
In the morning I help pick up the dead and lay them in rows in a barn.

5

Now of the older war-days, the defeat at Brooklyn,[9]   90
Washington stands inside the lines, he stands on the intrench'd hills amid a
  crowd of officers,
His face is cold and damp, he cannot repress the weeping drops,
He lifts the glass perpetually to his eyes, the color is blanch'd from his
  cheeks,
He sees the slaughter of the southern braves confided to him by their
  parents.

The same at last and at last when peace is declared,   95
He stands in the room of the old tavern, the well-belov'd soldiers all pass
  through,
The officers speechless and slow draw near in their turns,
The chief encircles their necks with his arm and kisses them on the cheek,
He kisses lightly the wet cheeks one after another, he shakes hands and bids
  good-by to the army.[10]

6

Now what my mother told me one day as we sat at dinner together,   100
Of when she was a nearly grown girl living home with her parents on the
  old homestead.

A red squaw came one breakfast-time to the old homestead,
On her back she carried a bundle of rushes for rush-bottoming chairs,
Her hair, straight, shiny, coarse, black, profuse, half-envelop'd her face,
Her step was free and elastic, and her voice sounded exquisitely as she
  spoke.   105

My mother look'd in delight and amazement at the stranger,
She look'd at the freshness of her tall-borne face and full and pliant limbs,
The more she look'd upon her she loved her,
Never before had she seen such wonderful beauty and purity,
She made her sit on a bench by the jamb of the fireplace, she cook'd food
  for her,   110
She had no work to give her, but she gave her remembrance and fondness.

---

[8]Shore-based guns used to propel a line to a damaged vessel.
[9]In the Battle of Brooklyn Heights in August 1776, Washington and his troops were defeated at the beginning of the Revolutionary War.

[10]Washington bade farewell to his troops in Fraunces Tavern in New York City at the end of the Revolutionary War in 1783.

The red squaw staid all the forenoon, and toward the middle of the
   afternoon she went away,
O my mother was loth[11] to have her go away,
All the week she thought of her, she watch'd for her many a month,
She remember'd her many a winter and many a summer,   115
But the red squaw never came nor was heard of there again.

7

A show of the summer softness—a contact of something unseen—an amour
   of the light and air,
I am jealous and overwhelm'd with friendliness,
And will go gallivant with the light and air myself.

O love and summer, you are in the dreams and in me,   120
Autumn and winter are in the dreams, the farmer goes with his thrift,
The droves[12] and crops increase, the barns are well-fill'd.

Elements merge in the night, ships make tacks in the dreams,
The sailor sails, the exile returns home,
The fugitive returns unharm'd, the immigrant is back beyond months and
   years,   125
The poor Irishman lives in the simple house of his childhood with the well-
   known neighbors and faces,
They warmly welcome him, he is barefoot again, he forgets he is well off,
The Dutchman voyages home, and the Scotchman and Welshman voyage
   home, and the native of the Mediterranean voyages home,
To every port of England, France, Spain, enter well-fill'd ships,
The Swiss foots it toward his hills, the Prussian goes his way, the Hungarian
   his way, and the Pole his way,   130
The Swede returns, and the Dane and Norwegian return.

The homeward bound and the outward bound,
The beautiful lost swimmer, the ennuyé, the onanist, the female that loves
   unrequited, the money-maker,
The actor and actress, those through with their parts and those waiting to
   commence,
The affectionate boy, the husband and wife, the voter, the nominee that is
   chosen and the nominee that has fail'd,   135
The great already known and the great any time after to-day,
The stammerer, the sick, the perfect-form'd, the homely,
The criminal that stood in the box, the judge that sat and sentenced him,
   the fluent lawyers, the jury, the audience,
The laugher and weeper, the dancer, the midnight widow, the red squaw,
The consumptive, the erysipalite,[13] the idiot, he that is wrong'd,   140
The antipodes,[14] and every one between this and them in the dark,
I swear they are averaged now—one is no better than the other,
The night and sleep have liken'd them and restored them.

I swear they are all beautiful,
Every one that sleeps is beautiful, every thing in the dim light is beautiful, 145
The wildest and bloodiest is over, and all is peace.

Peace is always beautiful,
The myth of heaven indicates peace and night.

11Variant of loath (reluctant).
12Herds of cattle.
13Victim of skin disease, erysipelas.

14Two places diametrically opposite to each other on the
earth's surface.

The myth of heaven indicates the soul,
The soul is always beautiful, it appears more or it appears less, it comes or it
    lags behind,   150
It comes from its embower'd garden and looks pleasantly on itself and
    encloses the world,
Perfect and clean the genitals previously jetting, and perfect and clean the
    womb cohering,
The head well-grown proportion'd and plumb, and the bowels and joints
    proportion'd and plumb.

The soul is always beautiful,
The universe is duly in order, every thing is in its place,   155
What has arrived is in its place and what waits shall be in its place,
The twisted skull waits, the watery or rotten blood waits,
The child of the glutton or venerealee waits long, and the child of the
    drunkard waits long, and the drunkard himself waits long,
The sleepers that lived and died wait, the far advanced are to go on in their
    turns, and the far behind are to come on in their turns,
The diverse shall be no less diverse, but they shall flow and unite—they
    unite now.   160

8

The sleepers are very beautiful as they lie unclothed,
They flow hand in hand over the whole earth from east to west as they lie
    unclothed,
The Asiatic and African are hand in hand, the European and American are
    hand in hand,
Learn'd and unlearn'd are hand in hand, and male and female are hand in
    hand,
The bare arm of the girl crosses the bare breast of her lover, they press close
    without lust, his lips press her neck,   165
The father holds his grown or ungrown son in his arms with measureless
    love, and the son holds the father in his arms with measureless love,
The white hair of the mother shines on the white wrist of the daughter,
The breath of the boy goes with the breath of the man, friend is inarm'd by
    friend,
The scholar kisses the teacher and the teacher kisses the scholar, the
    wrong'd is made right,
The call of the slave is one with the master's call, and the master salutes the
    slave,   170
The felon steps forth from the prison, the insane becomes sane, the
    suffering of sick persons is reliev'd,
The sweatings and fevers stop, the throat that was unsound is sound, the
    lungs of the consumptive are resumed, the poor distress'd head is free,
The joints of the rheumatic move as smoothly as ever, and smoother than
    ever,
Stiflings and passages open, the paralyzed become supple,
The swell'd and convuls'd and congested awake to themselves in condition,   175
They pass the invigoration of the night and the chemistry of the night, and
    awake.

I too pass from the night,
I stay a while away O night, but I return to you again and love you.

Why should I be afraid to trust myself to you?
I am not afraid, I have been well brought forward by you,   180
I love the rich running day, but I do not desert her in whom I lay so long,

I know not how I came of you and I know not where I go with you, but I
    know I came well and shall go well.

I will stop only a time with the night, and rise betimes,
I will duly pass the day O my mother, and duly return to you.

1855, 1881

from WHISPERS OF HEAVENLY DEATH

Chanting the Square Deific

1

Chanting the square deific, out of the One advancing, out of the sides
Out of the old and new, out of the square entirely divine,
Solid, four-sided, (all the sides needed,) from this side Jehovah am I,
Old Brahm I, and I Saturnius am;[1]
Not Time affects me—I am Time, old, modern as any,   5
Unpersuadable, relentless, executing righteous judgments,
As the Earth, the Father, the brown old Kronos,[2] with laws,
Aged beyond computation, yet ever new, ever with those mighty laws rolling,
Relentless I forgive no man—whoever sins dies—I will have that man's life;
Therefore let none expect mercy—have the seasons, gravitation, the
    appointed days, mercy? no more have I,   10
But as the seasons and gravitation, and as all the appointed days that forgive
    not,
I dispense from this side judgments inexorable without the least remorse.

2

Consolator most mild, the promis'd one advancing,
With gentle hand extended, the mightier God am I,
Foretold by prophets and poets in their most rapt prophecies and poems,   15
From this side, lo! the Lord Christ gazes—lo! Hermes[3] I—lo! mine is
    Hercules'[4] face,
All sorrow, labor, suffering, I, tallying it, absorb in myself,
Many times have I been rejected, taunted, put in prison, and crucified, and
    many times shall be again,
All the world have I given up for my dear brothers' and sisters' sake, for the
    soul's sake,
Wending my way through the homes of men, rich or poor, with the kiss of
    affection,   20
For I am affection, I am the cheer-bringing God, with hope and all-
    enclosing charity,
With indulgent words as to children, with fresh and sane words, mine only,
Young and strong I pass knowing well I am destin'd myself to an early
    death;
But my charity has no death—my wisdom dies not, neither early nor late,
And my sweet love bequeath'd here and elsewhere never dies.   25

---

[1]Jehovah, Brahma, and Saturn are Hebrew, Hindu, and Roman deities.
[2]Variant of Cronus, Greek god identified with time, father of

Zeus.
[3]Messenger of the gods in Greek mythology.
[4]Hero of Greek myth renowned for his great strength.

3

Aloof, dissatisfied, plotting revolt,
Comrade of criminals, brother of slaves,
Crafty, despised, a drudge, ignorant,
With sudra[5] face and worn brow, black, but in the depths of my heart,
    proud as any,
Lifted now and always against whoever scorning assumes to rule me,   30
Morose, full of guile, full of reminiscences, brooding, with many wiles,
(Though it was thought I was baffled and dispel'd, and my wiles done, but
    that will never be,)

Defiant, I, Satan, still live, still utter words, in new lands duly appearing,
    (and old ones also,)
Permanent here from my side, warlike, equal with any, real as any,
Nor time nor change shall ever change me or my words.   35

4

Santa Spirita,[6] breather, life,
Beyond the light, lighter than light,
Beyond the flames of hell, joyous, leaping easily above hell,
Beyond Paradise, perfumed solely with mine own perfume,
Including all life on earth, touching, including God, including Saviour and
    Satan,   40
Ethereal, pervading all, (for without me what were all? what were God?)
Essence of forms, life of the real identities, permanent, positive, (namely the
    unseen,)
Life of the great round world, the sun and stars, and of man, I, the general
    soul,
Here the square finishing, the solid, I the most solid,
Breathe my breath also through these songs.   45

1865, 1881

A Noiseless Patient Spider

A noiseless patient spider,
I mark'd where on a little promontory it stood isolated,
Mark'd how to explore the vacant vast surrounding,
It launch'd forth filament, filament, filament, out of itself,
Ever unreeling them, ever tirelessly speeding them.   5

And you O my soul where you stand,
Surrounded, detached, in measureless oceans of space,
Ceaselessly musing, venturing, throwing, seeking the spheres to connect
    them,
Till the bridge you will need be form'd, till the ductile anchor hold,
Till the gossamer thread you fling catch somewhere, O my soul.   10

1868, 1881

5Lowest Hindu caste.
6Holy Spirit.

from FROM NOON TO STARRY NIGHT

To a Locomotive in Winter

Thee for my recitative,
Thee in the driving storm even as now, the snow, the winter-day declining,
Thee in thy panoply,[1] thy measur'd dual throbbing and thy beat convulsive,
Thy black cylindric body, golden brass and silvery steel,
Thy ponderous side-bars, parallel and connecting rods, gyrating, shuttling
    at thy sides,   5
Thy metrical, now swelling pant and roar, now tapering in the distance,
Thy great protruding head-light fix'd in front,
Thy long, pale, floating vapor-pennants, tinged with delicate purple,
The dense and murky clouds out-belching from thy smoke-stack,
Thy knitted frame, thy springs and valves, the tremulous twinkle of thy
    wheels,   10
Thy train of cars behind, obedient, merrily following,
Through gale or calm, now swift, now slack, yet steadily careering;
Type of the modern—emblem of motion and power—pulse of the
    continent,
For once come serve the Muse and merge in verse, even as here I see thee,
With storm and buffeting gusts of wind and falling snow,   15
By day thy warning ringing bell to sound its notes,
By night thy silent signal lamps to swing.

Fierce-throated beauty!
Roll through my chant with all thy lawless music, thy swinging lamps at
    night,
Thy madly-whistled laughter, echoing, rumbling like an earthquake, rousing
    all,   20
Law of thyself complete, thine own track firmly holding,
(No sweetness debonair of tearful harp or glib piano thine,)
Thy trills of shrieks by rocks and hills return'd,
Launch'd o'er the prairies wide, across the lakes,
To the free skies unpent and glad and strong.   25

1876, 1881

from SONGS OF PARTING

So Long!

To conclude, I announce what comes after me.

I remember I said before my leaves sprang at all,
I would raise my voice jocund and strong with reference to consummations.

When America does what was promis'd,
When through these States walk a hundred millions of superb persons,   5
When the rest part away for superb persons and contribute to them,
When breeds of the most perfect mothers denote America,
Then to me and mine our due fruition.

---

[1]Complete suit of armor.

I have press'd through in my own right,
I have sung the body and the soul, war and peace have I sung, and the songs
   of life and death,   10
And the songs of birth, and shown that there are many births.

I have offer'd my style to every one, I have journey'd with confident step;
While my pleasure is yet at the full I whisper *So long!*
And take the young woman's hand and the young man's hand for the last
   time.

I announce natural persons to arise,   15
I announce justice triumphant,
I announce uncompromising liberty and equality,
I announce the justification of candor and the justification of pride.

I announce that the identity of these States is a single identity only,
I announce the Union more and more compact, indissoluble,   20
I announce splendors and majesties to make all the previous politics of the
   earth insignificant.

I announce adhesiveness,[1] I say it shall be limitless, unloosen'd,
I say you shall yet find the friend you were looking for.

I announce a man or woman coming, perhaps you are the one, (*So long!*)
I announce the great individual, fluid as Nature, chaste, affectionate,
   compassionate, fully arm'd.   25

I announce a life that shall be copious, vehement, spiritual, bold,
I announce an end that shall lightly and joyfully meet its translation.

I announce myriads of youths, beautiful, gigantic, sweet-blooded,
I announce a race of splendid and savage old men.

O thicker and faster—(*So long!*)   30
O crowding too close upon me,
I foresee too much, it means more than I thought,
It appears to me I am dying.

Hasten throat and sound your last,
Salute me—salute the days once more. Peal the old cry once more.   35

Screaming electric, the atmosphere using,
At random glancing, each as I notice absorbing,
Swiftly on, but a little while alighting,
Curious envelop'd messages delivering,
Sparkles hot, seed ethereal down in the dirt dropping,   40
Myself unknowing, my commission obeying, to question it never daring,
To ages and ages yet the growth of the seed leaving,
To troops out of the war arising, they the tasks I have set promulging,
To women certain whispers of myself bequeathing, their affection me more
   clearly explaining,
To young men my problems offering—no dallier I—I the muscle of their
   brains trying,   45
So I pass, a little time vocal, visible, contrary,

---

[1]Phrenological term denoting friendship, companionship,
fraternity.

Afterward a melodious echo, passionately bent for, (death making me really
  undying,)
The best of me then when no longer visible, for toward that I have been
  incessantly preparing.

What is there more, that I lag[2] and pause and crouch extended with unshut
  mouth?
Is there a single final farewell?   50

My songs cease, I abandon them,
From behind the screen where I hid I advance personally solely to you.

Camerado,[3] this is no book,
Who touches this touches a man,
(Is it night? are we here together alone?)   55
It is I you hold and who holds you,
I spring from the pages into your arms—decease calls me forth.

O how your fingers drowse me,
Your breath falls around me like dew, your pulse lulls the tympans of my
  ears,
I feel immerged[4] from head to foot,   60
Delicious, enough.

Enough O deed impromptu and secret,
Enough O gliding present—enough O summ'd-up past.

Dear friend whoever you are take this kiss,
I give it especially to you, do not forget me,   65
I feel like one who has done work for the day to retire awhile,
I receive now again of my many translations, from my avataras[5] ascending,
  while others doubtless await me,
An unknown sphere more real than I dream'd, more direct, darts
  awakening rays about me, *So long!*
Remember my words, I may again return,
I love you, I depart from materials,   70
I am as one disembodied, triumphant, dead.

                                                              1860, 1881

from Democratic Vistas

[Diagnosing Some Deep Disease]

It may be claim'd (and I admit the weight of the claim) that common and general
worldly prosperity, and a populace well to do, and with all life's material comforts, is
the main thing, and is enough. It may be argued that our republic is, in performance,
really enacting to-day the grandest arts, poems, &c., by beating up the wilderness
into fertile farms, and in her railroads, ships, machinery, &c. And it may be ask'd,
Are these not better, indeed, for America, than any utterances even of greatest rhap-
sode,[1] artist, or literatus?

---

[2]Loiter, linger.
[3]Close companion; cf. *Camarada* (Spanish), chambermate.
[4]Immersed, covered completely.

[5]"Incarnations" (Sanskrit).
[1]Cf. rhapsodist, one who in ancient Greece recited epic
poems.

I too hail those achievements with pride and joy: then answer that the soul of man will not with such only—nay, not with such at all—be finally satisfied; but needs what (standing on these and on all things, as the feet stand on the ground) is address'd to the loftiest, to itself alone.

Out of such considerations, such truths, arises for treatment in these Vistas the important question of character, of an American stock-personality, with literatures and arts for outlets and return-expressions, and, of course, to correspond, within outlines common to all. To these, the main affair, the thinkers of the United States, in general so acute, have either given feeblest attention, or have remain'd, and remain, in a state of somnolence.

For my part, I would alarm and caution even the political and business reader, and to the utmost extent, against the prevailing delusion that the establishment of free political institutions, and plentiful intellectual smartness, with general good order, physical plenty, industry, &c. (desirable and precious advantages as they all are), do, of themselves, determine and yield to our experiment of democracy the fruitage of success. With such advantages at present fully, or almost fully, possess'd—the Union just issued,[2] victorious, from the struggle with the only foes it need ever fear (namely, those within itself, the interior ones), and with unprecedented materialistic advancement—society, in these States, is canker'd, crude, superstitious, and rotten. Political, or law-made society is, and private, or voluntary society, is also. In any vigor, the element of the moral conscience, the most important, the verteber[3] to State or man, seems to me either entirely lacking, or seriously enfeebled or ungrown.

I say we had best look our times and lands searchingly in the face, like a physician diagnosing some deep disease. Never was there, perhaps, more hollowness at heart than at present, and here in the United States. Genuine belief seems to have left us. The underlying principles of the States are not honestly believ'd in (for all this hectic glow, and these melodramatic screamings), nor is humanity itself believ'd in. What penetrating eye does not everywhere see through the mask? The spectacle is appalling. We live in an atmosphere of hypocrisy throughout. The men believe not in the women, nor the women in the men. A scornful superciliousness rules in literature. The aim of all the *littérateurs*[4] is to find something to make fun of. A lot of churches, sects, &c., the most dismal phantasms I know, usurp the name of religion. Conversation is a mass of badinage. From deceit in the spirit, the mother of all false deeds, the offspring is already incalculable. An acute and candid person, in the revenue department in Washington, who is led by the course of his employment to regularly visit the cities, North, South and West, to investigate frauds, has talk'd much with me about his discoveries. The depravity of the business classes of our country is not less than has been supposed, but infinitely greater. The official services of America, national, state, and municipal, in all their branches and departments, except the judiciary, are saturated in corruption, bribery, falsehood, mal-administration; and the judiciary is tainted. The great cities reek with respectable as much as non-respectable robbery and scoundrelism. In fashionable life, flippancy, tepid amours, weak infidelism, small aims, or no aims at all, only to kill time. In business (this all-devouring modern word, business), the one sole object is, by any means, pecuniary gain. The magician's serpent in the fable ate up all the other serpents; and money-making is our magician's serpent, remaining to-day sole master of the field. The best class we show is but a mob of fashionably dress'd speculators and vulgarians. True, indeed, behind this fantastic farce, enacted on the visible stage of society, solid things and stupendous labors are to be discover'd, existing crudely and going on in the background, to advance and tell themselves in time. Yet the truths are none the less terrible. I say that our New World democracy, however great a success in uplifting the masses out

---

[2]I.e., the Union had just been preserved by the North's defeat of the South in the Civil War.

[3]Backbone (vertebrae).
[4]"Authors" (French).

of their sloughs, in materialistic development, products, and in a certain highly-deceptive superficial popular intellectuality, is, so far, an almost complete failure in its social aspects, and in really grand religious, moral, literary, and esthetic results. In vain do we march with unprecedented strides to empire so colossal, outvying the antique, beyond Alexander's, beyond the proudest sway of Rome. In vain have we annex'd Texas, California, Alaska, and reach north for Canada and south for Cuba.[5] It is as if we were somehow being endow'd with a vast and more and more thoroughly-appointed body, and then left with little or no soul.

Let me illustrate further, as I write, with current observations, localities, &c. The subject is important, and will bear repetition. After an absence, I am now again (September, 1870) in New York City and Brooklyn, on a few weeks' vacation. The splendor, picturesqueness, and oceanic amplitude and rush of these great cities, the unsurpass'd situation, rivers and bay, sparkling sea-tides, costly and lofty new buildings, façades of marble and iron, of original grandeur and elegance of design, with the masses of gay color, the preponderance of white and blue, the flags flying, the endless ships, the tumultuous streets, Broadway, the heavy, low, musical roar, hardly ever intermitted, even at night; the jobbers'[6] houses, the rich shops, the wharves, the great Central Park, and the Brooklyn Park of hills (as I wander among them this beautiful fall weather, musing, watching, absorbing)—the assemblages of the citizens in their groups, conversations, trades, evening amusements, or along the by-quarters—these, I say, and the like of these, completely satisfy my senses of power, fulness, motion, &c., and give me, through such senses and appetites, and through my esthetic conscience, a continued exaltation and absolute fulfilment. Always and more and more, as I cross the East and North rivers, the ferries, or with the pilots in their pilot-houses, or pass an hour in Wall Street, or the gold exchange, I realize (if we must admit such partialisms) that not Nature alone is great in her fields of freedom and the open air, in her storms, the shows of night and day, the mountains, forests, seas—but in the artificial, the work of man too is equally great—in this profusion of teeming humanity—in these ingenuities, streets, goods, houses, ships—these hurrying, feverish, electric crowds of men, their complicated business genius (not least among the geniuses) and all this mighty, many-threaded wealth and industry concentrated here.

But sternly discarding, shutting our eyes to the glow and grandeur of the general superficial effect, coming down to what is of the only real importance, Personalities, and examining minutely, we question, we ask, Are there, indeed, *men* here worthy the name? Are there athletes? Are there perfect women, to match the general material luxuriance? Is there a pervading atmosphere of beautiful manners? Are there crops of fine youths, and majestic old persons? Are there arts worthy freedom and a rich people? Is there a great moral and religious civilization—the only justification of a great material one? Confess that to severe eyes, using the moral microscope upon humanity, a sort of dry and flat Sahara appears, these cities, crowded with petty grotesques, malformations, phantoms, playing meaningless antics. Confess that everywhere, in shop, street, church, theatre, bar-room, official chair, are pervading flippancy and vulgarity, low cunning, infidelity—everywhere the youth puny, impudent, foppish, prematurely ripe—everywhere an abnormal libidinousness, unhealthy forms, male, female, painted, padded, dyed, chignon'd, muddy complexions, bad blood, the capacity for good motherhood deceasing or deceas'd, shallow notions of beauty, with a range of manners, or rather lack of manners (considering the advantages enjoy'd), probably the meanest to be seen in the world.

Of all this, and these lamentable conditions, to breathe into them the breath recu-

---

[5]Texas was annexed in 1845, a major cause of the Mexican War (1846–48), which resulted in Mexico ceding California to the United States; Alaska was purchased from Russia in 1867; the disputed line between the United States and Canada was not finally fixed until 1846; in the Ostend Manifesto (1854), southern congressmen proposed to annex Cuba for more slave territory either by buying it from Spain or seizing it, but were repudiated.

[6]Persons buying merchandise from manufacturers and selling it to retailers.

perative of sane and heroic life, I say a new founded literature, not merely to copy and reflect existing surfaces, or pander to what is called taste—not only to amuse, pass away time, celebrate the beautiful, the refined, the past, or exhibit technical, rhythmic, or grammatical dexterity—but a literature underlying life, religious, consistent with science, handling the elements and forces with competent power, teaching and training men—and, as perhaps the most precious of its results, achieving the entire redemption of woman out of these incredible holds and webs of silliness, millinery, and every kind of dyspeptic depletion—and thus insuring to the States a strong and sweet Female Race, a race of perfect Mothers—is what is needed.

. . . . .

[The Need of Powerful Native Bards]

. . . That which really balances and conserves the social and political world is not so much legislation, police, treaties, and dread of punishment, as the latent eternal intuitional sense, in humanity, of fairness, manliness, decorum, &c. Indeed, this perennial regulation, control, and oversight, by self-suppliance, is *sine qua non*[1] to democracy; and a highest widest aim of democratic literature may well be to bring forth, cultivate, brace, and strengthen this sense, in individuals and society. A strong mastership of the general inferior self by the superior self is to be aided, secured, indirectly, but surely, by the literatus,[2] in his works, shaping, for individual or aggregate democracy, a great passionate body, in and along with which goes a great masterful spirit.

And still, providing for contingencies, I fain confront the fact, the need of powerful native philosophs and orators and bards, these States, as rallying points to come, in times of danger, and to fend off ruin and defection. For history is long, long, long. Shift and turn the combinations of the statement as we may, the problem of the future of America is in certain respects as dark as it is vast. Pride, competition, segregation, vicious wilfulness, and license beyond example, brood already upon us. Unwieldly and immense, who shall hold in behemoth? who bridle leviathan? Flaunt it as we choose, athwart and over the roads of our progress loom huge uncertainty, and dreadful, threatening gloom. It is useless to deny it: Democracy grows rankly up the thickest, noxious, deadliest plants and fruits of all—brings worse and worse invaders—needs newer, larger, stronger, keener compensations and compellers.

Our lands, embracing so much (embracing indeed the whole, rejecting none), hold in their breast that flame also, capable of consuming themselves, consuming us all. Short as the span of our national life has been, already have death and downfall crowded close upon us—and will again crowd close, no doubt, even if warded off. Ages to come may never know, but I know, how narrowly during the late Secession War[3]—and more than once, and more than twice or thrice—our Nationality (wherein bound up, as in a ship in a storm, depended, and yet depend, all our best life, all hope, all value), just grazed, just by a hair escaped destruction. Alas! to think of them! the agony and bloody sweat of certain of those hours! those cruel, sharp, suspended crises!

Even to-day, amid these whirls, incredible flippancy, and blind fury of parties, infidelity, entire lack of first-class captains and leaders, added to the plentiful meanness and vulgarity of the ostensible masses—that problem, the labor question, beginning to open like a yawning gulf, rapidly widening every year—what prospect have we? We sail a dangerous sea of seething currents, cross and under-currents, vortices—all so dark, untried—and whither shall we turn? It seems as if the Almighty had spread before this nation charts of imperial destinies, dazzling as the sun, yet

---

[1]"Without which not," essential condition (Latin).
[2]Writer or poet.
[3]Civil War (1861–65).

with many a deep intestine difficulty, and human aggregate of cankerous imperfection—saying, lo! the roads, the only plans of development, long and varied with all terrible balks and ebullitions. You said in your soul, I will be empire of empires, overshadowing all else, past and present, putting the history of Old-World dynasties, conquests behind me, as of no account—making a new history, a history of democracy, making old history a dwarf—I alone inaugurating largeness, culminating time. If these, O lands of America, are indeed the prizes, the determinations of your soul, be it so. But behold the cost, and already specimens of the cost. Thought you greatness was to ripen for you like a pear? If you would have greatness, know that you must conquer it through ages, centuries—must pay for it with a proportionate price. For you too, as for all lands, the struggle, the traitor, the wily person in office, scrofulous wealth, the surfeit of prosperity, the demonism of greed, the hell of passion, the decay of faith, the long postponement, the fossil-like lethargy, the ceaseless need of revolutions, prophets, thunder-storms, deaths, births, new projections and invigorations of ideas and men.

Yet I have dream'd, merged in that hidden-tangled problem of our fate, whose long unraveling stretches mysteriously through time—dream'd out, portray'd, hinted already—a little or a larger band—a band of brave and true, unprecedented yet—arm'd and equipt at every point—the members separated, it may be, by different dates and States, or south, or north, or east, or west—Pacific, Atlantic, Southern, Canadian—a year, a century here, and other centuries there—but always one, compact in soul, conscience-conserving, God-inculcating, inspired achievers, not only in literature, the greatest art, but achievers in all art—a new, undying order, dynasty, from age to age transmitted—a band, a class, at least as fit to cope with current years, our dangers, needs, as those who, for their times, so long, so well, in armor or in cowl, upheld and made illustrious, that far-back feudal, priestly world. To offset chivalry, indeed, those vanish'd countless knights, old altars, abbeys, priests, ages and strings of ages, a knightlier and more sacred cause to-day demands, and shall supply, in a New World, to larger, grander work, more than the counterpart and tally of them.

Arrived now, definitely, at an apex for these Vistas, I confess that the promulgation and belief in such a class or institution—a new and greater literatus order—its possibility (nay certainty) underlies these entire speculations—and that the rest, the other parts, as superstructures, are all founded upon it. It really seems to me the condition, not only of our future national and democratic development, but of our perpetuation. In the highly artificial and materialistic bases of modern civilization, with the corresponding arrangements and methods of living, the force-infusion of intellect alone, the depraving influences of riches just as much as poverty, the absence of all high ideals in character—with the long series of tendencies, shapings, which few are strong enough to resist, and which now seem, with steam-engine speed, to be everywhere turning out the generations of humanity like uniform iron castings—all of which, as compared with the feudal ages, we can yet do nothing better than accept, make the best of, and even welcome, upon the whole, for their oceanic practical grandeur, and their restless wholesale kneading of the masses—I say of all this tremendous and dominant play of solely materialistic bearings upon current life in the United States, with the results as already seen, accumulating, and reaching far into the future, that they must either be confronted and met by at least an equally subtle and tremendous force-infusion for purposes of spiritualization, for the pure conscience, for genuine esthetics, and for absolute and primal manliness and womanliness—or else our modern civilization, with all its improvements, is in vain, and we are on the road to a destiny, a status, equivalent, in its real world, to that of the fabled damned.

Prospecting thus the coming unsped days, and that new order in them—marking the endless train of exercise, development, unwind, in nation as in man, which life is for—we see, fore-indicated, amid these prospects and hopes, new law-forces of spoken and written language—not merely the pedagogue-forms, correct, regular, familiar with precedents, made for matters of outside propriety, fine words, thoughts definitely told out—but a language fann'd by the breath of Nature, which leaps overhead, cares mostly for impetus and effects, and for what it plants and invigorates to grow—tallies life and character, and seldomer tells a thing than suggests or necessitates it. In fact, a new theory of literary composition for imaginative works of the very first class, and especially for highest poems, is the sole course open to these States. Books are to be call'd for, and supplied, on the assumption that the process of reading is not a half-sleep, but, in highest sense, an exercise, a gymnast's struggle; that the reader is to do something for himself, must be on the alert, must himself or herself construct indeed the poem, argument, history, metaphysical essay—the text furnishing the hints, the clue, the start or frame-work. Not the book needs so much to be the complete thing, but the reader of the book does. That were to make a nation of supple and athletic minds, well-train'd, intuitive, used to depend on themselves, and not on a few coteries of writers.

Investigating here, we see, not that it is a little thing we have, in having the bequeath'd libraries, countless shelves of volumes, records, &c.; yet how serious the danger, depending entirely on them, of the bloodless vein, the nerveless arm, the false application, at second or third hand. We see that the real interest of this people of ours in the theology, history, poetry, politics, and personal models of the past (the British islands, for instance, and indeed all the past), is not necessarily to mould ourselves or our literature upon them, but to attain fuller, more definite comparisons, warnings, and the insight to ourselves, our own present, and our own far grander, different, future history, religion, social customs, &c. We see that almost everything that has been written, sung, or stated, of old, with reference to humanity under the feudal and Oriental institutes, religions, and for other lands, needs to be rewritten, re-sung, re-stated, in terms consistent with the institution of these States, and to come in range and obedient uniformity with them.

We see, as in the universes of the material kosmos, after meteorological, vegetable, and animal cycles, man at last arises, born through them, to prove them, concentrate them, to turn upon them with wonder and love—to command them, adorn them, and carry them upward into superior realms—so, out of the series of the preceding social and political universes, now arise these States. We see that while any were supposing things establish'd and completed, really the grandest things always remain; and discover that the work of the New World is not ended, but only fairly begun.

We see our land, America, her literature, esthetics, &c., as, substantially, the getting in form, or effusement and statement, of deepest basic elements and loftiest final meanings, of history and man—and the portrayal (under the eternal laws and conditions of beauty) of our own physiognomy, the subjective tie and expression of the objective, as from our own combination, continuation, and points of view—and the deposit and record of the national mentality, character, appeals, heroism, wars, and even liberties—where these, and all, culminate in native literary and artistic formulation, to be perpetuated; and not having which native, first-class formulation, she will flounder about, and her other, however imposing, eminent greatness, prove merely a passing gleam; but truly having which, she will understand herself, live nobly, nobly contribute, emanate, and, swinging, poised safely on herself, illumin'd and illuming, become a full-form'd world, and divine Mother not only of material but spiritual worlds, in ceaseless succession through time—the main thing being the average, the bodily, the concrete, the democratic, the popular, on which all the superstructures of the future are to permanently rest.

1867–68   *1871*

Slang in America[1]

View'd freely, the English language is the accretion and growth of every dialect, race, and range of time, and is both the free and compacted composition of all. From this point of view, it stands for Language in the largest sense, and is really the greatest of studies. It involves so much; is indeed a sort of universal absorber, combiner, and conqueror. The scope of its etymologies is the scope not only of man and civilization, but the history of Nature in all departments, and of the organic Universe, brought up to date; for all are comprehended in words, and their backgrounds. This is when words become vitaliz'd, and stand for things, as they unerringly and soon come to do, in the mind that enters on their study with fitting spirit, grasp, and appreciation.

Slang, profoundly consider'd, is the lawless germinal element, below all words and sentences, and behind all poetry, and proves a certain perennial rankness and protestantism in speech. As the United States inherit by far their most precious possession—the language they talk and write—from the Old World, under and out of its feudal institutes, I will allow myself to borrow a simile even of those forms farthest removed from American Democracy. Considering Language then as some mighty potentate, into the majestic audience-hall of the monarch ever enters a personage like one of Shakspere's clowns, and takes position there, and plays a part even in the stateliest ceremonies. Such is Slang, or indirection, an attempt of common humanity to escape from bald literalism, and express itself illimitably, which in highest walks produces poets and poems, and doubtless in pre-historic times gave the start to, and perfected, the whole immense tangle of the old mythologies. For, curious as it may appear, it is strictly the same impulse-source, the same thing. Slang, too, is the wholesome fermentation or eructation of those processes eternally active in language, by which froth and specks are thrown up, mostly to pass away; though occasionally to settle and permanently crystallize.

To make it plainer, it is certain that many of the oldest and solidest words we use, were originally generated from the daring and license of slang. In the processes of word-formation, myriads die, but here and there the attempt attracts superior meanings, becomes valuable and indispensable, and lives forever. Thus the term *right* means literally only straight. *Wrong* primarily meant twisted, distorted. *Integrity* means oneness. *Spirit* meant breath, or flame. A *supercilious* person was one who rais'd his eyebrows. To *insult* was to leap against. If you *influenc'd* a man, you but flow'd into him. The Hebrew word which is translated *prophesy* meant to bubble up and pour forth as a fountain. The enthusiast bubbles up with the Spirit of God within him, and it pours forth from him like a fountain. The word "prophecy" is misunderstood. Many suppose that it is limited to mere prediction; that is but the lesser portion of prophecy. The greater work is to reveal God. Every true religious enthusiast is a prophet.

Language, be it remember'd, is not an abstract construction of the learn'd, or of dictionary-makers, but is something arising out of the work, needs, ties, joys, affections, tastes, of long generations of humanity, and has its bases broad and low, close to the ground. Its final decisions are made by the masses, people nearest the concrete, having most to do with actual land and sea. It impermeates all, the Past as well as the Present, and is the grandest triumph of the human intellect. "Those mighty works of art," says Addington Symonds,[2] "which we call languages, in the construction of which whole peoples unconsciously co-operated, the forms of which were

---

[1]Whitman once remarked in his old age to his friend Horace Traubel (who preserved the comments of the poet in a series of volumes entitled *With Walt Whitman in Camden*): "I sometimes think the *Leaves* is only a language experiment." Whitman's fascination with and shrewd perception of the nature of language are evident in this pioneering piece on American slang.

[2]John Addington Symonds (1840–1893), English historian, classical scholar, critic, poet, and translator, was an early admirer of Whitman.

determin'd not by individual genius, but by the instincts of successive generations, acting to one end, inherent in the nature of the race—those poems of pure thought and fancy, cadenced not in words, but in living imagery, fountain-heads of inspiration, mirrors of the mind of nascent nations, which we call Mythologies—these surely are more marvellous in their infantine spontaneity than any more mature production of the races which evolv'd them. Yet we are utterly ignorant of their embryology; the true science of Origins is yet in its cradle."

Daring as it is to say so, in the growth of Language it is certain that the retrospect of slang from the start would be the recalling from their nebulous conditions of all that is poetical in the stores of human utterance. Moreover, the honest delving, as of late years, by the German and British workers in comparative philology, has pierc'd and dispers'd many of the falsest bubbles of centuries; and will disperse many more. It was long recorded that in Scandinavian mythology the heroes in the Norse Paradise drank out of the skulls of their slain enemies. Later investigation proves the word taken for skulls to mean *horns* of beasts slain in the hunt. And what reader had not been exercis'd over the traces of that feudal custom, by which *seigneurs*[3] warm'd their feet in the bowels of serfs, the abdomen being open'd for the purpose? It now is made to appear that the serf was only required to submit his unharm'd abdomen as a foot cushion while his lord supp'd, and was required to chafe the legs of the seigneur with his hands.

It is, curiously, in embryons and childhood and among the illiterate, we always find the groundwork and start of this great science, and its noblest products. What a relief most people have in speaking of a man not by his true and formal name, with a "Mister" to it, but by some odd or homely appellative. The propensity to approach a meaning not directly and squarely, but by circuitous styles of expression, seems indeed a born quality of the common people everywhere, evidenced by nicknames, and the inveterate determination of the masses to bestow sub-titles, sometimes ridiculous, sometimes very apt. Always among the soldiers during the secession war, one heard of "Little Mac" (Gen. McClellan), or of "Uncle Billy" (Gen. Sherman).[4] "The old man" was, of course, very common. Among the rank and file, both armies, it was very general to speak of the different States they came from by their slang names. Those from Maine were call'd Foxes; New Hampshire, Granite Boys; Massachusetts, Bay Staters; Vermont, Green Mountain Boys; Rhode Island, Gun Flints; Connecticut, Wooden Nutmegs; New York, Knickerbockers; New Jersey, Clam Catchers; Pennsylvania, Logher Heads; Delaware, Muskrats; Maryland, Claw Thumpers; Virginia, Beagles; North Carolina, Tar Boilers; South Carolina, Weasels; Georgia, Buzzards; Louisiana, Creoles; Alabama, Lizards; Kentucky, Corn Crackers; Ohio, Buckeyes; Michigan, Wolverines; Indiana, Hoosiers; Illinois, Suckers; Missouri, Pukes; Mississippi, Tadpoles; Florida, Fly up the Creeks; Wisconsin, Badgers; Iowa, Hawkeyes; Oregon, Hard Cases. Indeed I am not sure but slang names have more than once made Presidents. "Old Hickory" (Gen. Jackson) is one case in point. "Tippecanoe, and Tyler too," another.[5]

I find the same rule in the people's conversations everywhere. I heard this among the men of the city horse-cars, where the conductor is often call'd a "snatcher" (*i.e.* because his characteristic duty is to constantly pull or snatch the bell-strap, to stop or go on). Two young fellows are having a friendly talk, amid which, says 1st conductor, "What did you do before you was a snatcher?" Answer of 2d conductor, "Nail'd."

---

[3]"Lords" (French).

[4]General George McClellan (1826–1885) served as general in chief of the Union armies during early years of the Civil War; General William Sherman (1820–1891) was a Union general during the Civil War who made a famous "march to the sea" through Georgia.

[5]General Andrew Jackson (1767–1845), dubbed "Old Hickory" by his soldiers because of his hardiness, was elected president (1829–37). William Henry Harrison (1773–1841) won the battle of Tippecanoe against Indians led by Tecumseh in 1811 and in the presidential election of 1840 selected John Tyler (1790–1862) as his running mate; their campaign slogan was "Tippecanoe and Tyler too."

(Translation of answer: "I work'd as carpenter.") "What is a 'boom?'" says one editor to another. "Esteem'd contemporary," says the other, "a boom is a bulge." "Barefoot whiskey" is the Tennessee name for the undiluted stimulant. In the slang of the New York common restaurant waiters a plate of ham and beans is known as "stars and stripes," codfish balls as "sleeve-buttons," and hash as "mystery."

The Western States of the Union are, however, as may be supposed, the special areas of slang, not only in conversation, but in names of localities, towns, rivers, etc. A late Oregon traveller says:

"On your way to Olympia by rail, you cross a river called the Shookum-Chuck; your train stops at places named Newaukum, Tumwater, and Toutle; and if you seek further you will hear of whole counties labell'd Wahkiakum, or Snohomish, or Kitsar, or Klikatat; and Cowlitz, Hookium, and Nenolelops greet and offend you. They complain in Olympia that Washington Territory gets but little immigration; but what wonder? What man, having the whole American continent to choose from, would willingly date his letters from the county of Snohomish or bring up his children in the city of Nenolelops? The village of Tumwater is, as I am ready to bear witness, very pretty indeed; but surely an emigrant would think twice before he establish'd himself either there or at Toutle. Seattle is sufficiently barbarous; Stelicoom is no better; and I suspect that the Northern Pacific Railroad terminus has been fixed at Tacoma because it is one of the few places on Puget Sound whose name does not inspire horror."

Then a Nevada paper chronicles the departure of a mining party from Reno:

"The toughest set of roosters that ever shook the dust off any town left Reno yesterday for the new mining district of Cornucopia. They came here from Virginia. Among the crowd were four New York cock-fighters, two Chicago murderers, three Baltimore bruisers, one Philadelphia prize-fighter, four San Francisco hoodlums, three Virginia beats, two Union Pacific roughs, and two check guerrillas."

Among the far-west newspapers, have been, or are, *The Fairplay* (Colorado) *Flume, The Solid Muldoon,* of Ouray, *The Tombstone Epitaph,* of Nevada, *The Jimplecute,* of Texas, and *The Bazoo,* of Missouri. Shirttail Bend, Whiskey Flat, Puppytown, Wild Yankee Ranch, Squaw Flat, Rawhide Ranch, Loafer's Ravine, Squitch Gulch, Toenail Lake, are a few of the names of places in Butte County, Cal.

Perhaps indeed no place or term gives more luxuriant illustrations of the fermentation processes I have mention'd, and their froth and specks, than those Mississippi and Pacific coast regions, at the present day. Hasty and grotesque as are some of the names, others are of an appropriateness and originality unsurpassable. This applies to the Indian words, which are often perfect. Oklahoma is proposed in Congress for the name of one of our new Territories. Hog-eye, Lickskillet, Rake-pocket and Steal-easy are the names of some Texan towns. Miss Bremer[6] found among the aborigines the following names: *Men's,* Horn-point; Round-Wind; Stand-and-look-out; The-Cloud-that-goes-aside; Iron-toe; Seek-the-sun; Iron-flash; Red-bottle; White-spindle; Black-dog; Two-feathers-of-honor; Gray-grass; Bushy-tail; Thunder-face; Go-on-the-burning-Sod; Spirits-of-the-dead. *Women's,* Keep-the-fire; Spiritual-woman; Second-daughter-of-the-house; Blue-bird.

Certainly philologists have not given enough attention to this element and its results, which, I repeat, can probably be found working everywhere to-day, amid modern conditions, with as much life and activity as in far-back Greece or India,

---

[6]In *The Homes of the New World* (1853, 2 vols.), Swedish novelist Frederika Bremer (1801–1865) provided a detailed account of her travels throughout the United States, including a substantial list of Indian words and names.

under prehistoric ones. Then the wit—the rich flashes of humor and genius and poetry—darting out often from a gang of laborers, railroad-men, miners, drivers or boatmen! How often have I hover'd at the edge of a crowd of them, to hear their repartees and impromptus! You get more real fun from half an hour with them than from the books of all "the American humorists."

The science of language has large and close analogies in geological science, with its ceaseless evolution, its fossils, and its numberless submerged layers and hidden strata, the infinite go-before of the present. Or, perhaps Language is more like some vast living body, or perennial body of bodies. And slang not only brings the first feeders of it, but is afterward the start of fancy, imagination and humor, breathing into its nostrils the breath of life.

1885

EMILY DICKINSON
(1830–1886)

At the age of twenty, in a remarkable declaration of personal independence, Emily Dickinson took her stand against conventional religious belief. Religious revivals recurred in New England during the 1840s, and Dickinson had previously passed by opportunities "to convert." But the Awakening that swept Amherst, Massachusetts, in 1850 was especially strong—strong enough to claim her younger sister, Lavinia, and then her strong-willed father, Edward Dickinson. Emily Dickinson wrote to a friend, "How lonely this world is growing. . . . I am standing alone in rebellion." Her rebellion against traditional belief—her quarrel with God—would persist throughout her life, inspiring and inspiriting much of her poetry. And she would stand bravely "alone in rebellion" in other spheres of human experience.

Emily Dickinson was born, grew up, and died in Amherst, Massachusetts. The first Dickinsons were among the Puritans who came to America with John Winthrop in 1630. One of Amherst's leading citizens, her grandfather, Samuel Fowler Dickinson, was a public spirited lawyer and a founder of Amherst Academy (a primary school) and Amherst College. His son, Edward Dickinson, married the shy, submissive Emily Norcross after establishing his own law practice. Born on December 10, 1830, Emily was the second of three children. Her older brother Austin became a lawyer, settling in the house next door, while her younger sister "Vinnie," like Emily Dickinson, never married, remaining all her life in the Homestead.

The woman who would later be known as the "Myth of Amherst," shunning society for her second-story room, led a happy and normal girlhood. In her fifteenth year, she wrote a friend, "I expect I shall be the belle of Amherst when I reach my 17th year." Dickinson's education, for women of her day, was superior. As a student at Amherst Academy from 1840 to 1847 and then during one year at Mount Holyoke Female Seminary, she demonstrated her intelligence, scholarship, wit, and fiercely independent spirit. When Mount Holyoke's founder Mary Lyons asked all to rise who wanted to be Christians, Emily Dickinson alone refused. "They thought it queer I didn't rise," she recalled to a friend, "I thought a lie would be queerer." Her sister Lavinia remembered: "Emily was never floored. When the Euclid examination came and she had never studied it, she went to the blackboard and gave such a glib exposition of imaginary figures that the dazed teacher passed her with the highest mark."

Although Dickinson's formal education ended on her departure from Mount Holyoke, her passionate commitment to books endured throughout her life. Benjamin Newton, who read law in her father's law office, became her "tutor" and guided her reading. His death in 1853 was a deeply felt loss. Her father was an avid reader and recommended works for her perusal; but he was especially concerned that she read only books suitable for young ladies. References in her letters to the Bible, Shakespeare, Sir Thomas Browne, Keats, Robert and Elizabeth Barrett Browning, Emily and Charlotte Bronte, George Eliot, Ruskin, Lowell, Emerson, and many more suggest that her range and depth of reading were extraordinary.

Edward Dickinson was elected to Congress in 1852. Accompanied by her mother and sister, Emily Dickinson went to Washington to spend a few weeks in January 1855, returning by way of Philadelphia to visit a friend. There it has been assumed she met the Reverend Charles Wadsworth and perhaps heard him preach. This trip would be the only time that she would leave Massachusetts.

Sometime in the 1850s, probably earlier than critics have heretofore realized, Dickinson turned seriously to the writing of poetry. In March 1853, she wrote to her brother Austin, "I've been in the habit *myself* of writing some few things." She wrote her poems on whatever paper was handy, often jotting down lists of alternate words for the ones she used. In 1858, she began to copy her poems onto folded sheets of paper and bind sheets together, making fascicles or "books" (a kind of private publication). The original manuscripts from which she copied have disappeared. Thus the dates of the poems in the fascicles, established by modern editorial methods, are not necessarily the dates of composition of the poems.

"Publication—is the Auction / Of the Mind of Man," she wrote in one poem: "Poverty—be justifying / For so foul a thing." On the surface this appears to be an injunction to herself. Although a childhood friend, Helen Hunt Jackson, the successful author of *Romona*, enthusiastically supported Dickinson, urging the poet to publish, Dickinson declined. During her lifetime only ten poems (out of almost 1800 written) appeared in print, often without her consent, and usually in a text revised or regularized by various editors. But she wrote in another poem, "This is my letter to the World / That never wrote to Me," suggesting that she anticipated publication of her poetry.

In 1862 Dickinson read a "Letter to a Young Contributor" in the *Atlantic Monthly*, by a leading critic of the time, Thomas Wentworth Higginson, giving advice to aspiring poets. She sent him four poems, asking, "Are you too deeply occupied to see if my Verse is alive?" Instead of signing the letter, she included her name inserted in a smaller envelope with the letter.

Higginson remembered his reaction many years later: "The impression of a wholly new and original poetic genius was as distinct on my mind at the first reading of those four poems as it is now, after thirty years of further knowledge." He replied to her letter with suggestions and questions. In answer to a query about her family, she wrote: "My Mother does not care for thought—and Father, too busy with his Briefs—. . . ." To Higginson's mention of Whitman, she said: "I never read his Book—but was told that he was disgraceful."

Dickinson continued to write Higginson and to send him poems for the rest of her life, the letters resembling the poems in their startlingly fresh use of language. He was her one firm link to the literary world from which she lived apart. He urged her to visit him in Boston, but she demurred, and asked him, "Is it more far to Amherst?" Finally, in 1870, Higginson visited her at her home, finding the description of herself that she had sent him quite apt—"small, like the Wren, and my Hair is bold, like the Chestnut Bur—and my eyes, like the Sherry in the Glass, that the Guest leaves."

Higginson was astonished to find that "she went on talking constantly" and that her conversation was "quaint and aphoristic," like her poems. He later recorded what he could remember, including this observation: "If I read a book and it makes my whole body so cold no fire ever can warm me, I know *that* is poetry. If I feel physically as if the top of my head were taken off, I know *that* is poetry. These are the only way I know it. Is there any other way[?]"

From Higginson's report of his visit, we may conclude that Dickinson's dazzling use of language was displayed not only in her poems and letters, but also in her conversation. Indeed, her "lexicon" (or dictionary) was a constant companion, and her awe of words, love of language, and devotion to books are manifested in many poems. She suffered from a congenital eye disease and was treated for it at length in Boston during 1864 and again in 1865. Her greatest fear was to be deprived the means of reading. As she expressed it to a friend: "Some years ago I had a woe, the only one that ever made me tremble. It was a shutting out of all the dearest ones of time, the strongest friends of the soul—BOOKS."

Many of Emily Dickinson's poems are passionate love poems, and there are three equally passionate love letters (probably never sent) addressed simply "Dear Master." Yet no biographer has found a candidate universally accepted by Dickinson scholars and critics as the object of her love. Several candidates have been proposed, especially the Reverend Charles Wadsworth. But the evidence is very tenuous, and plausible cases have been made for her early "tutor" Benjamin Newton; for the editor of the *Springfield Republican* and family friend, Samuel Bowles; and for an elderly widower and friend, Judge Otis P. Lord. Psychoanalytic critics have not been reticent in pointing to Emily's brother Austin or Catherine Anthon (a friend of Austin's wife, Sue).

The search for a lost lover has most often been based on the assumption that success in the search would lead to discovery of Dickinson's secret sources of poetic inspiration. In this assumption the search seems woefully misguided. It appears to deny Emily Dickinson a native power of poetic genius, insisting on an external stimulant and source. Anyone reading through her poems and letters will find a continuity of passion running not only through the love poems, but also through poems on nature, on identity, on grief and anguish, on doubt and faith. Moreover the epistolary language of friendship in the nineteenth century is easily translated into love in the twentieth. And finally, Dickinson could simply have imagined herself passionately in love with any number of people—and found her consummation of that love in her poetry. She was certainly aware of the artist's license to assume a pose—or persona—when she wrote to Higginson: "When I state myself, as the Representative of the Verse—it does not mean— me—but a supposed person."

Of one love affair there can be no denial—her love affair with the English language. In one poem ("Many a phrase has the English language") she hovers on the verge of sexually explicit metaphor to embody her passionate feelings. "I love you" is the only phrase the poet hears from the English language, which becomes personified in the poem as "Saxon." Awakened from her "simple sleep" by the intimate phrase's "bright Orthography" and "Thundering . . . Prospective," the poet *stirs* and *weeps* for the ecstatic "push of Joy," pleading, "Say it again, Saxon! / Hush—Only to me!" In poems such as this one are to be found the deepest sources of her creative vitality and poetic energy.

As Emily Dickinson became more and more detached from the world beyond her house and garden, she began to exhibit those traits of behavior that led some to doubt her sanity. "I do not cross my Father's ground to any house in town," she wrote to Higginson in June 1869. On Higginson's visit in 1870, she was dressed in white (by then her constant color), and she brought him two day lilies, saying, "These are my introduction." Higginson was perceptive enough to note that there was not a "trace of affectation" in her manner and shrewd enough to detect the genius beneath the quaintness.

Genius, not neurosis, accounts for Emily Dickinson's withdrawal from society. In that small room of her own, she freed herself to write her poems, to sound the deepest psychological depths, to explore the most puzzling metaphysical mysteries. As she once said to her niece who had been confined to a room for punishment, "Matty, child, no one could ever punish a Dickinson by shutting her up alone."

There was much to give her grief during her latter days. Her father died suddenly in 1874, and the following year her mother was paralyzed. Throughout the 1870s and 1880s, Dickinson continued to write poems, even up to the year of her death (of a kidney disease) in 1886.

When her sister Lavinia discovered all the poems—nearly 1800—that Emily Dickinson left behind her, she sought help in obtaining publication from Mabel Loomis Todd, wife of an Amherst professor and family friend. Higginson consented to aid in the enterprise. Todd and Higginson worked together to publish volumes in 1890, 1891, and 1896. But the poems did not appear as originally written. As Dickinson's letters to Higginson show, he had found her "uncontrolled," "wayward," "her gait 'spasmodic,'" "Beyond [his] knowledge." And thus her poems were given titles that often violated their meaning; her slant rhymes and innovative rhythms were regularized; and her eccentric syntax, punctuation, and usage were corrected. Enough of the poetry's original power remained, however, to launch Dickinson's reputation.

Other volumes appeared sporadically—in 1914, 1937, and 1945. But not until 1955 did a scholarly variorum edition in three volumes appear, edited by Thomas H. Johnson. It was based on the extant manuscripts and dropped the "improvements" made by previous editors. The poems were given numbers, roughly in what was perceived to be the order of composition, and these numbers have been universally adopted, along with first lines, to identify the titleless poems. Johnson also edited three volumes of letters in 1958.

In preparing these various editions, the several editors separated the sheets that Dickinson had brought together in fascicles or "books," disjoining poems that she had juxtaposed. Moreover, some critics thought that the length of the dashes in the manuscript might provide clues to rhetorical emphasis or syntactical relationships. To make available to readers as closely as possible the poems as Dickinson left them, the fascicles were meticulously restored and the texts presented in a facsimile edition in 1981, edited by R. W. Franklin.

Virtually unknown as a poet in her lifetime, Emily Dickinson has come by now to occupy her rightful place beside Whitman as one of the two greatest of American poets, and, indeed, as one of the greatest poets writing in English. Her "Business" was "Circumference," and we have not yet taken the full measure of her song.

ADDITIONAL READING

The Manuscript Books of Emily Dickinson, 2 vols., ed. Ralph W. Franklin, 1981.

George F. Whicher, *This Was a Poet*, 1938; Millicent Todd Bingham, *Ancestor's Brocades*, 1945; Henry W. Wells, *Introduction to Emily Dickinson*, 1947; Richard Chase, *Emily Dickinson*, 1951; Charles R. Anderson, *Emily Dickinson's Poetry: Stairway to Surprise*, 1960; Jay Leyda, *The Years and Hours of Emily Dickinson*, 2 vols., 1960; Thomas Johnson, *Emily Dickinson: An Interpretive Biography*, 1963; Richard B. Sewall, *Emily Dickinson: A Collection of Critical Essays*, 1963; Clark Griffith, *The Long Shadow: Emily Dickinson's Tragic Poetry*, 1964; Caesar R. Blake and Carlton F. Wells, eds., *The Recognition of Emily Dickinson*, 1964; Douglas Duncan, *Emily Dickinson*, 1965; Richard B. Sewall, *The Lyman Letters: New Light on Emily Dickinson and Her Family*, 1965; Albert Gelpi, *Emily Dickinson: The Mind of the Poet*, 1965; David T. Porter, *The Art of Emily Dickinson's Early Poetry*, 1966; Jack L. Capps, *Emily Dickinson's Reading, 1836–1886*, 1966; John B. Pickard, *Emily Dickinson: An Introduction and Interpretation*, 1967; David Higgins, *Portrait of Emily Dickinson*, 1967; R. W. Franklin, *The Editions of Emily Dickinson*, 1967; Ruth Miller, *The Poetry of Emily Dickinson*, 1968; Brita Lindberg-Seyersted, *The Voice of the Poet: Aspects of Style in the Poetry of Emily Dickinson*, 1968; John Cody, *The Inner Life of Emily Dickinson*, 1971; John Evangelist Walsh, *The Hidden Life of Emily Dickinson*, 1971; Richard B. Sewall, *The Life of Emily Dickinson*, 1974; Robert Weisbuch, *Emily Dickinson's Poetry*, 1975; Karl Keller, *The Only Kangaroo Among the Beauty: Emily Dickinson and America*, 1979; Sharon Cameron, *Lyric Time: Dickinson and the Limits of Genre*, 1980; Joanne F. Diehl, *Dickinson and the Romantic Imagination*, 1981; David Porter, *Dickinson: The Modern Idiom*, 1981; Suzanne Juhasz, *The Undiscovered Continent: Emily Dickinson and the Space of the Mind*, 1983; William H. Shurr, *The Marriage of Emily Dickinson: A Study of the Fascicles*, 1983; Vivian R. Pollak, *Dickinson: The Anxiety of Gender*, 1984; Barton Levi St. Armand, *Emily Dickinson and Her Culture: The Soul's Society*, 1984; Christopher E. G. Benfey, *Emily Dickinson and the Problem of Others*, 1984; Donna Dickenson, *Emily Dickinson*, 1985; Jerome Loving, *Emily Dickinson: The Poet on the Second Story*, 1986; Cynthia Griffin Wolff, *Emily Dickinson*, 1986; Christanne Miller, *Emily Dickinson: A Poet's Grammar*, 1987.

TEXTS

The Poems of Emily Dickinson, Including Variant Readings Critically Compared with All Known Manuscripts, 3 vols., ed. Thomas H. Johnson, 1955; poems 196, 214, 288, 494, 501, 520, 585, 642, 754, 997, 1072, 1452, 1624, 1732 from *The Complete Poems of Emily Dickinson*, ed. Thomas H. Johnson, 1960 (the text of the 3-vol. edition, with the variant readings omitted and minor corrections in spelling and misplaced apostrophes); *The Letters of Emily Dickinson*, 3 vols., ed. Thomas H. Johnson and Theodora Ward, 1958.

Emily Dickinson's Poems

Although Emily Dickinson's editor, Thomas H. Johnson, has provided probable dates for composition of her poems, he was often working with later rather than first drafts, many of which have disappeared. Thus the dates are not wholly reliable. In the following selection of poems, from almost 1800 that survived, the poems are not arranged in the order in which he placed them but are grouped in accord with their thematic focus: Poems on Language and Poetry; Poems on the Self; Poems on Nature; Poems on Love, Heavenly and Earthly; Poems of Anguish, Agony, Despair; Poems on Death; Poems of Faith and Doubt. These clusters by no means stand independently separated by high walls. A poem on love may also contain religious vision, a poem on poetry touch on the essence of life, a poem on self reflect a view of society. But the thematically related clusters, drawn from the entire span of her life, provide sustained experiences in the several areas of her major interests, concerns, and passionate intensities. When they are read in related groups, the poems reflect on each other and gain resonance. A reader quickly sees that a single poem is never a definitive treatment of its theme in Dickinson's work. And a glance through the entire body of her poetry will light upon many more poems that might have been added to these combinations.

❧

POEMS ON LANGUAGE AND POETRY

276

Many a phrase has the English language—
I have heard but one—
Low as the laughter of the Cricket,
Loud, as the Thunder's Tongue—

Murmuring, like old Caspian[1] Choirs,   5
When the Tide's a' lull—
Saying itself in new inflection—
Like a Whippowil—

Breaking in bright Orthography
On my simple sleep—   10
Thundering its Prospective—
Till I stir, and weep—

Not for the Sorrow, done me—
But the push of Joy—
Say it again, Saxon![2]   15
Hush—Only to me!

c. 1861   *1935*

441

This is my letter to the World
That never wrote to Me—
The simple News that Nature told—
With tender Majesty

Her Message is committed   5
To Hands I cannot see—
For love of Her—Sweet—countrymen—
Judge tenderly—of Me

c. 1862   *1890*

448

This was a Poet—It is That
Distills amazing sense
From ordinary Meanings—
And Attar[1] so immense

---

[1]The Caspian Sea, the largest inland sea, lies within the U.S.S.R. and Iran; evocative of old Russian Orthodox choirs.
[2]Personification of the English language, derived from ancient Anglo-Saxon tribes. On the manuscript Dickinson wrote "English language" as a variant for "Saxon." See Letter 265 for another use of "Saxon."
[1]Essential oil or perfume obtained from flower petals.

From the familiar species   5
That perished by the Door—
We wonder it was not Ourselves
Arrested it—before—

Of Pictures, the Discloser—
The Poet—it is He—   10
Entitles Us—by Contrast—
To ceaseless Poverty—

Of Portion—so unconscious—
The Robbing—could not harm—
Himself—to Him—a Fortune—   15
Exterior—to Time—

c. 1862   *1929*

505

I would not paint—a picture—
I'd rather be the One
Its bright impossibility
To dwell—delicious—on—
And wonder how the fingers feel   5
Whose rare—celestial—stir—
Evokes so sweet a Torment—
Such sumptuous—Despair—

I would not talk, like Cornets—
I'd rather be the One   10
Raised softly to the Ceilings—
And out, and easy on—
Through Villages of Ether—
Myself endued Balloon
By but a lip of Metal—   15
The pier to my Pontoon—

Nor would I be a Poet—
It's finer—own the Ear—
Enamored—impotent—content—
The License to revere,   20
A privilege so awful
What would the Dower be,
Had I the Art to stun myself
With Bolts of Melody!

c. 1862   *1945*

569

I reckon—when I count at all—
First—Poets—Then the Sun—
Then Summer—Then the Heaven of God—
And then—the List is done—

But, looking back—the First so seems   5
To Comprehend the Whole—

The Others look a needless Show—
So I write—Poets—All—

Their Summer—lasts a Solid Year—
They can afford a Sun   10
The East—would deem extravagant—
And if the Further Heaven—

Be Beautiful as they prepare
For Those who worship Them—
It is too difficult a Grace—   15
To justify the Dream—

c. 1862   *1929*

657

I dwell in Possibility—
A fairer House than Prose—
More numerous of Windows—
Superior—for Doors—

Of Chambers as the Cedars—   5
Impregnable of Eye—
And for an Everlasting Roof
The Gambrels[1] of the Sky—

Of Visiters—the fairest—
For Occupation—This—   10
The spreading wide my narrow Hands
To gather Paradise—

c. 1862   *1929*

709

Publication—is the Auction
Of the Mind of Man—
Poverty—be justifying
For so foul a thing

Possibly—but We—would rather   5
From Our Garret go
White—Unto the White Creator—
Than invest—Our Snow—

Thought belong to Him who gave it—
Then—to Him Who bear   10
Its Corporeal illustration—Sell
The Royal Air—

In the Parcel—Be the Merchant
Of the Heavenly Grace—
But reduce no Human Spirit   15
To Disgrace of Price—

c. 1863   *1929*

---

[1]Roofs whose sides have two slopes, the lower one being the
steeper.

883

The Poets light but Lamps—
Themselves—go out—
The Wicks they stimulate—
If vital Light

Inhere as do the Suns—   5
Each Age a Lens
Disseminating their
Circumference—

c. 1864   *1945*

1126

Shall I take thee, the Poet said
To the propounded word?
Be stationed with the Candidates
Till I have finer tried—

The Poet searched Philology[1]   5
And was about to ring
for the suspended Candidate
There came unsummoned in—

That portion of the Vision
The Word applied to fill   10
Not unto nomination
The Cherubim reveal—

c. 1868   *1945*

1129

Tell all the Truth but tell it slant—
Success in Circuit lies
Too bright for our infirm Delight
The Truth's superb surprise
As Lightning to the Children eased   5
With explanation kind
The Truth must dazzle gradually
Or every man be blind—

c. 1868   *1945*

1452

Your thoughts don't have words every day
They come a single time
Like signal esoteric sips
Of the communion Wine
Which while you taste so native seems   5
So easy so to be
You cannot comprehend its price
Nor its infrequency

c. 1878   *1945*

---

[1]Language.

POEMS ON THE SELF

196

We don't cry—Tim and I,
We are far too grand—
But we bolt the door tight
To prevent a friend—

Then we hide our brave face   5
Deep in our hand—
Not to cry—Tim and I—
We are far too grand—

Nor to dream—he and me—
Do we condescend—   10
We just shut our brown eye
To see to the end—

Tim—see Cottages—
But, Oh, so high!
Then—we shake—Tim and I—   15
And lest I—cry—

Tim—reads a little Hymn—
And we both pray—
Please, Sir, I and Tim—
Always lost the way!   20

We must die—by and by—
Clergymen say—
Tim—shall—if I—do—
I—too—if he—

How shall we arrange it—   25
Tim—was—so—shy?
Take us simultaneous—Lord—
I—"Tim"—and—Me!

c. 1860   *1945*

288

I'm Nobody! Who are you?
Are you—Nobody—Too?
Then there's a pair of us?
Don't tell! they'd advertise—you know!

How dreary—to be—Somebody!   5
How public—like a Frog—
To tell one's name—the livelong June—
To an admiring Bog!

c. 1861   *1891*

303

The Soul selects her own Society—
Then—shuts the Door—

To her divine Majority—
Present no more—

Unmoved—she notes the Chariots—pausing—   5
At her low Gate—
Unmoved—an Emperor be kneeling
Upon her Mat—

I've known her—from an ample nation—
Choose One—   10
Then—close the Valves of her attention—
Like Stone—

c. 1862   1890

435

Much Madness is divinest Sense—
To a discerning Eye—
Much Sense—the starkest Madness—
'Tis the Majority
In this, as All, prevail—   5
Assent—and you are sane—
Demur—you're straightway dangerous—
And handled with a Chain—

c. 1862   1890

609

I Years had been from Home
And now before the Door
I dared not enter, lest a Face
I never saw before

Stare stolid into mine   5
And ask my Business there—
"My Business but a Life I left
Was such remaining there?"

I leaned upon the Awe—
I lingered with Before—   10
The Second like an Ocean rolled
And broke against my ear—

I laughed a crumbling Laugh
That I could fear a Door
Who Consternation compassed   15
And never winced before.

I fitted to the Latch
My Hand, with trembling care
Lest back the awful Door should spring
And leave me in the Floor—   20

Then moved my Fingers off
As cautiously as Glass

And held my ears, and like a Thief
Fled gasping from the House—

c. 1872   1891

612

It would have starved a Gnat—
To live so small as I—
And yet I was a living Child—
With Food's necessity

Upon me—like a Claw—   5
I could no more remove
Than I could coax a Leech away—
Or make a Dragon—move—

Nor like the Gnat—had I—
The privilege to fly   10
And seek a Dinner for myself—
How mightier He—than I—

Nor like Himself—the Art
Upon the Window Pane
To gad[1] my little Being out—   15
And not begin—again—

c. 1862   1945

642

Me from Myself—to banish—
Had I Art—
Impregnable my Fortress
Unto All Heart—

But since Myself—assault Me—   5
How have I peace
Except by subjugating
Consciousness?

And since We're mutual Monarch
How this be   10
Except by Abdication—
Me—of Me?

c. 1862   1929

670

One need not be a Chamber—to be Haunted—
One need not be a House—
The Brain has Corridors—surpassing
Material Place—

Far safer, of a Midnight Meeting   5
External Ghost

---

[1]Goad.

Than its interior Confronting—
That Cooler Host.

Far safer, through an Abbey gallop,
The Stones a'chase—
Than Unarmed, one's a'self encounter—
In lonesome Place—

Ourself behind ourself, concealed—
Should startle most—
Assassin hid in our Apartment
Be Horror's least.

The Body—borrows a Revolver—
He bolts the Door—
O'erlooking a superior spectre—
Or More—

c. 1863   1891

754

My Life had stood—a Loaded Gun—
In Corners—till a Day
The Owner passed—identified—
And carried Me away—

And now We roam in Sovereign Woods—
And now We hunt the Doe—
And every time I speak for Him—
The Mountains straight reply—

And do I smile, such cordial light
Upon the Valley glow—
It is as a Vesuvian[1] face
Had let its pleasure through—

And when at Night—Our good Day done—
I guard My Master's Head—
'Tis better than the Eider-Duck's
Deep Pillow—to have shared—

To foe of His—I'm deadly foe—
None stir the second time—
On whom I lay a Yellow Eye—
Or an emphatic Thumb—

Though I than He—may longer live
He longer must—than I—
For I have but the power to kill,
Without—the power to die—

c. 1863   1929

---

[1]Like the volcano, Mount Vesuvius.

POEMS ON NATURE

130

These are the days when Birds come back—
A very few—a Bird or two—
To take a backward look.

These are the days when skies resume
The old—old sophistries of June—   5
A blue and gold mistake.

Oh fraud that cannot cheat the Bee—
Almost thy plausibility
Induces my belief.

Till ranks of seeds their witness bear—   10
And softly thro' the altered air
Hurries a timid leaf.

Oh Sacrament of summer days,
Oh Last Communion in the Haze—
Permit a child to join.   15

Thy sacred emblems to partake—
Thy consecrated bread to take
And thine immortal wine!

c. 1859   *1864*

214

I taste a liquor never brewed—
From Tankards scooped in Pearl—
Not all the Vats upon the Rhine[1]
Yield such an Alcohol!

Inebriate of Air—am I—   5
And Debauchee of Dew—
Reeling—thro endless summer days—
From inns of Molten Blue—

When "Landlords" turn the drunken Bee
Out of the Foxglove's door—   10
When Butterflies—renounce their "drams"—
I shall but drink the more!

Till Seraphs swing their snowy Hats—
And Saints—to windows run—
To see the little Tippler   15
Leaning against the—Sun—[2]

c. 1860   *1861*

---

[1]Variant line for "Not all the Frankfort Berries." Both "Vats" and "Berries" (grapes) refer to German Rhine wine.

[2]Variant line for "From Manzanilla come!" Manzanilla is a Spanish sherry.

328

A Bird came down the Walk—
He did not know I saw—
He bit an Angleworm in halves
And ate the fellow, raw,

And then he drank a Dew   5
From a convenient Grass—
And then hopped sidewise to the Wall
To let a Beetle pass—

He glanced with rapid eyes
That hurried all around—   10
They looked like frightened Beads, I thought—
He stirred his Velvet Head

Like one in danger, Cautious,
I offered him a Crumb
And he unrolled his feathers   15
And rowed him softer home—

Than Oars divide the Ocean,
Too silver for a seam—
Or Butterflies, off Banks of Noon
Leap, plashless as they swim.   20

c. 1862   *1891*

520

I started Early—Took my Dog—
And visited the Sea—
The Mermaids in the Basement
Came out to look at me—

And Frigates—in the Upper Floor   5
Extended Hempen Hands—
Presuming Me to be a Mouse—
Aground—upon the Sands—

But no Man moved Me—till the Tide
Went past my simple Shoe—   10
And past my Apron—and my Belt
And past my Bodice—too—

And made as He would eat me up—
As wholly as a Dew
Upon a Dandelion's Sleeve—   15
And then—I started—too—

And He—He followed—close behind—
I felt His Silver Heel
Upon my Ankle—Then my Shoes
Would overflow with Pearl—   20

Until We met the Solid Town—
No One He seemed to know—

And bowing—with a Mighty look—
At me—The Sea withdrew—

c. 1862   *1891*

585[1]

I like to see it lap the Miles—
And lick the Valleys up—
And stop to feed itself at Tanks—
And then—prodigious step

Around a Pile of Mountains—   5
And supercilious peer
In Shanties—by the sides of Roads—
And then a Quarry pare

To fit its Ribs
And crawl between   10
Complaining all the while
In horrid—hooting stanza—
Then chase itself down Hill—

And neigh like Boanerges[2]—
Then—punctual as a Star   15
Stop—docile and omnipotent
At its own stable door—

c. 1862   *1891*

812

A Light exists in Spring
Not present on the Year
At any other period—
When March is scarcely here

A Color stands abroad   5
On Solitary Fields
That Science cannot overtake
But Human Nature feels.

It waits upon the Lawn,
It shows the furthest Tree   10
Upon the furthest Slope you know
It almost speaks to you.

Then as Horizons step
Or Noons report away
Without the Formula of sound   15
It passes and we stay—

A quality of loss
Affecting our Content

---

[1]In this poem, as George F. Whicher notes, Dickinson "wrote as simply and directly of the locomotive as of any bird in her garden."

[2]"Sons of thunder" (Hebrew), the name given by Jesus to two zealous apostles (Mark 3:17) and since applied to any loud-voiced preacher or orator.

As Trade had suddenly encroached
Upon a Sacrament.   20

c. 1864   *1896*

986

A narrow Fellow in the Grass
Occasionally rides—
You may have met Him—did you not
His notice sudden is—

The Grass divides as with a Comb—   5
A spotted shaft is seen—
And then it closes at your feet
And opens further on—

He likes a Boggy Acre
A Floor too cool for Corn—   10
Yet when a Boy, and Barefoot—
I more than once at Noon
Have passed, I thought, a Whip lash
Unbraiding in the Sun
When stooping to secure it   15
It wrinkled, and was gone—

Several of Nature's People
I know, and they know me—
I feel for them a transport
Of cordiality—   20

But never met this Fellow
Attended, or alone
Without a tighter breathing
And Zero at the Bone—

c. 1865   *1866*

1068

Further in Summer than the Birds
Pathetic from the Grass
A minor Nation celebrates
Its unobtrusive Mass.

No Ordinance[1] be seen   5
So gradual the Grace
A pensive Custom it becomes
Enlarging Loneliness.

Antiquest felt at Noon
When August burning low   10
Arise this spectral Canticle[2]
Repose to typify

---

[1]Religious ceremony; especially, Holy Communion.
[2]Song or hymn with words taken from the bible.

Remit as yet no Grace
No Furrow on the Glow
Yet a Druidic[3] Difference   15
Enhances Nature now

c. 1866   *1891*

1138

A Spider sewed at Night
Without a Light
Upon an Arc of White.

If Ruff it was of Dame
Or Shroud of Gnome   5
Himself himself inform.

Of Immortality
His Strategy
Was Physiognomy.

c. 1869   *1891*

1463

A Route of Evanescence
With a revolving Wheel—
A Resonance of Emerald—
A Rush of Cochineal[1]—
And every Blossom on the Bush   5
Adjusts its tumbled Head—
The mail from Tunis,[2] probably,
An easy Morning's Ride—

c. 1879   *1891*

1540

As imperceptibly as Grief
The Summer lapsed away—
Too imperceptible at last
To seem like Perfidy—

A Quietness distilled   5
As Twilight long begun,
Or Nature spending with herself
Sequestered Afternoon—
The Dusk drew earlier in—
The Morning foreign shone—   10
A courteous, yet harrowing Grace,
As Guest, that would be gone—
And thus, without a Wing
Or service of a Keel
Our Summer made her light escape   15
Into the Beautiful.

c. 1865   *1891*

---

[3]I.e., related to the Druids, a learned ancient Celtic priest-
hood, venerating nature, depicted as magicians, soothsayers,
and wizards.

[1]Red dye.
[2]On the northern coast of Africa.

1755

To make a prairie it takes a clover and one bee,
One clover, and a bee,
And revery.
The revery alone will do,
If bees are few.   5

?   *1896*

POEMS ON LOVE, HEAVENLY AND EARTHLY

209

With thee, in the Desert—
With thee in the thirst—
With thee in the Tamarind[1] wood—
Leopard breathes—at last!

c. 1860   *1945*

211

Come slowly—Eden!
Lips unused to Thee—
Bashful—sip thy Jessamines[1]—
As the fainting Bee—

Reaching late his flower,   5
Round her chamber hums—
Counts his nectars—
Enters—and is lost in Balms.[2]

c. 1860   *1890*

249

Wild Nights—Wild Nights!
Were I with thee
Wild Nights should be
Our luxury!

Futile—the Winds—   5
To a Heart in port—
Done with the Compass—
Done with the Chart!

Rowing in Eden—
Ah, the Sea!
Might I but moor—Tonight—   10
In Thee!

c. 1861   *1891*

322

There came a Day at Summer's full,
Entirely for me—

---

[1] Tropical tree.
[1] Variant of jasmines, fragrant flowers.
[2] Perfumes.

I thought that such were for the Saints,
Where Resurrections—be—

The Sun, as common, went abroad,   5
The flowers, accustomed, blew,[1]
As if no soul the solstice passed
That maketh all things new—

The time was scarce profaned, by speech—
The symbol of a word   10
Was needless, as at Sacrament,
The Wardrobe—of our Lord—

Each was to each The Sealed Church,
Permitted to commune this—time—
Lest we too awkward show   15
At Supper of the Lamb.

The Hours slid fast—as Hours will,
Clutched tight, by greedy hands—
So faces on two Decks, look back,
Bound to opposing lands—   20

And so when all the time had leaked,
Without external sound
Each bound the Other's Crucifix—
We gave no other Bond—

Sufficient troth, that we shall rise—   25
Deposed—at length, the Grave—
To that new Marriage,
Justified—through Calvaries of Love—

c. 1861   *1890*

494

Going to Him! Happy letter!
Tell Him—
Tell Him the page I didn't write—
Tell Him—I only said the Syntax—
And left the Verb and the pronoun out—   5
Tell Him just how the fingers hurried—
Then—how they waded—slow—slow—
And then you wished you had eyes in your pages—
So you could see what moved them so—

Tell Him—it wasn't a Practised Writer—   10
You guessed—from the way the sentence toiled—
You could hear the Bodice tug, behind you—
As if it held but the might of a child—
You almost pitied it—you—it worked so—
Tell Him—no—you may quibble there—   15
For it would split His Heart, to know it—
And then you and I, were silenter.

----

[1]Blossomed.

Tell Him—Night finished—before we finished—
And the Old Clock kept neighing "Day"!
And you—got sleepy—and begged to be ended—   20
What could it hinder so—to say?
Tell Him—just how she sealed you—Cautious!
But—if He ask where you are hid
Until tomorrow—Happy letter!
Gesture Coquette—and shake your Head!   25

Version I
c. 1862   *1891*

494

Going—to—Her!
Happy—Letter! Tell Her—
Tell Her—the page I never wrote!
Tell Her, I only said—the Syntax—
And left the Verb and the Pronoun—out!   5
Tell Her just how the fingers—hurried—
Then—how they—stammered—slow—slow—
And then—you wished you had eyes—in your pages—
So you could see—what moved—them—so—

Tell Her—it wasn't a practised writer—   10
You guessed—
From the way the sentence—toiled—
You could hear the Bodice—tug—behind you—
As if it held but the might of a child!
You almost pitied—it—you—it worked so—   15
Tell Her—No—you may quibble—there—
For it would split Her Heart—to know it—
And then—you and I—were silenter!

Tell Her—Day—finished—before we—finished—
And the old Clock kept neighing—"Day"!   20
And you—got sleepy—and begged to be ended—
What could—it hinder so—to say?
Tell Her—just how she sealed—you—Cautious!
But—if she ask "where you are hid"—until the evening—
Ah! Be bashful!   25

Gesture Coquette—
And shake your Head!

Version II
c. 1862   *1955*

508

I'm ceded—I've stopped being Theirs—
The name They dropped upon my face
With water, in the country church
Is finished using, now,
And They can put it with my Dolls,   5
My childhood, and the string of spools,
I've finished threading—too—

Baptized, before, without the choice,
But this time, consciously, of Grace—

Unto supremest name—
Called to my Full—The Crescent dropped—
Existence's whole Arc, filled up,[1]   10
With one small Diadem.

My second Rank—too small the first—
Crowned—Crowing—on my Father's breast—   15
A half unconscious Queen—
But this time—Adequate—Erect,
With Will to choose, or to reject,
And I choose, just a Crown—

c. 1862   *1890*

511

If you were coming in the Fall,
I'd brush the Summer by
With half a smile, and half a spurn,
As Housewives do, a Fly.

If I could see you in a year,   5
I'd wind the months in balls—
And put them each in separate Drawers,
For fear the numbers fuse—

If only Centuries, delayed,
I'd count them on my Hand,   10
Subtracting, till my fingers dropped
Into Van Dieman's Land.[1]

If certain, when this life was out—
That yours and mine, should be
I'd toss it yonder, like a Rind,   15
And take Eternity—

But, now, uncertain of the length
Of this, that is between,
It goads me, like the Goblin Bee—
That will not state—it's sting.   20

c. 1862   *1890*

528

Mine—by the Right of the White Election!
Mine—by the Royal Seal!
Mine—by the Sign in the Scarlet prison—
Bars—cannot conceal!

Mine—here—in Vision—and in Veto!   5
Mine—by the Grave's Repeal—
Titled—Confirmed—
Delirious Charter!
Mine—long as Ages steal!

c. 1862   *1890*

---

[1]I.e., just as the crescent moon gives way to the full moon, so the partial self moves into fullness of being.
[1]Former name (1642–1855) of Tasmania, an island off southeastern Australia; symbolic of a remote, far-distant place.

640

I cannot live with You—
It would be Life—
And Life is over there—
Behind the Shelf

The Sexton[1] keeps the Key to—   5
Putting up
Our Life—His Porcelain—
Like a Cup—

Discarded of the Housewife—
Quaint—or Broke—   10
A newer Sevres[2] pleases—
Old Ones crack—

I could not die—with You—
For One must wait
To shut the Other's Gaze down—   15
You—could not—

And I—Could I stand by
And see You—freeze—
Without my Right of Frost—
Death's privilege?   20

Nor could I rise—with You—
Because Your Face
Would put out Jesus'—
That New Grace

Glow plain—and foreign   25.
On my homesick Eye—
Except that You than He
Shone closer by—

They'd judge Us—How—
For You—served Heaven—You know,   30
Or sought to—
I could not—

Because You saturated Sight—
And I had no more Eyes
For sordid excellence   35
As Paradise

And were You lost, I would be—
Though My Name
Rang loudest
On the Heavenly fame—   40

And were You—saved—
And I—condemned to be

---

[1]Church caretaker, sometimes responsible for grave digging.
[2]Fine porcelain from Sèvres, France.

Where You were not—
That self—were Hell to Me—

So We must meet apart—   45
You there—I—here—
With just the Door ajar
That Oceans are—and Prayer—
And that White Sustenance—
Despair—   50

c. 1862   *1890*

664

Of all the Souls that stand create—
I have elected—One—
When Sense from Spirit—files away—
And Subterfuge—is done—
When that which is—and that which was—   5
Apart—intrinsic—stand—
And this brief Tragedy of Flesh—
Is shifted—like a Sand—
When Figures show their royal Front—
And Mists—are carved away,   10
Behold the Atom—I preferred—
To all the lists of Clay!

c. 1862   *1891*

732

She rose to His Requirement—dropt
The Playthings of Her Life
To take the honorable Work
Of Woman, and of Wife—

If ought She missed in Her new Day,   5
Of Amplitude, or Awe—
Or first Prospective—Or the Gold
In using, wear away,

It lay unmentioned—as the Sea
Develop Pearl, and Weed,   10
But only to Himself—be known
The Fathoms they abide—

c. 1863   *1890*

1072

Title divine—is mine!
The Wife—without the Sign!
Acute Degree—conferred on me—
Empress of Calvary![1]
Royal—all but the Crown!   5
Betrothed—without the swoon
God sends us Women—
When you—hold—Garnet[2] to Garnet—

---

[1]The hill where Jesus was crucified.
[2]Dark red gemstone.

Gold—to Gold—
Born—Bridalled—Shrouded—   10
In a Day—
Tri Victory
"My Husband"—women say—
Stroking the Melody—
Is *this*—the way?   15

c. 1862   *1924*

1732

My life closed twice before its close —
It yet remains to see
If Immortality unveil
A third event to me

So huge, so hopeless to conceive   5
As these that twice befell.

Parting is all we know of heaven,
And all we need of hell.

?   *1896*

1737

Rearrange a "Wife's" affection!
When they dislocate my Brain!
Amputate my freckled Bosom!
Make me bearded like a man!

Blush, my spirit, in thy Fastness—   5
Blush, my unacknowledged clay—
Seven years of troth[1] have taught thee
More than Wifehood ever may!

Love that never leaped its socket—
Trust entrenched in narrow pain—   10
Constancy thro' fire—awarded—
Anguish—bare of anodyne![2]

Burden—borne so far triumphant—
None suspect me of the crown,
For I wear the "Thorns" till *Sunset*—   15
Then—my Diadem put on.

Big my Secret but it's *bandaged*—
It will never get away
Till the Day its Weary Keeper
Leads it through the Grave to thee.   20

?   *1945*

POEMS OF ANGUISH, AGONY, DESPAIR

67

Success is counted sweetest
By those who ne'er succeed.

---
[1]Faithfulness; betrothal.
[2]Pain reliever.

To comprehend a nectar
Requires sorest need.

Not one of all the purple Host   5
Who took the Flag today
Can tell the definition
So clear of Victory

As he defeated—dying—
On whose forbidden ear   10
The distant strains of triumph
Burst agonized and clear!

c. 1859   *1864*

241

I like a look of Agony,
Because I know it's true—
Men do not sham Convulsion,
Nor simulate, a Throe—

The Eyes glaze once—and that is Death—   5
Impossible to feign
The Beads upon the Forehead
By homely Anguish strung.

c. 1861   *1890*

258

There's a certain Slant of light,
Winter Afternoons—
That oppresses, like the Heft
Of Cathedral Tunes—

Heavenly Hurt, it gives us—   5
We can find no scar,
But internal difference,
Where the Meanings, are—

None may teach it—Any—
'Tis the Seal Despair—   10
An imperial affliction
Sent us of the Air—

When it comes, the Landscape listens—
Shadows—hold their breath—
When it goes, 'tis like the Distance   15
On the look of Death—

c. 1861   *1890*

280

I felt a Funeral, in my Brain,
And Mourners to and fro
Kept treading—treading—till it seemed
That Sense was breaking through—

And when they all were seated,   5
A Service, like a Drum—
Kept beating—beating—till I thought
My Mind was going numb—

And then I heard them lift a Box
And creak across my Soul   10
With those same Boots of Lead, again,
Then Space—began to toll,

As all the Heavens were a Bell,
And Being, but an Ear,
And I, and Silence, some strange Race   15
Wrecked, solitary, here—

And then a Plank in Reason, broke,
And I dropped down, and down—
And hit a World, at every plunge,
And Finished knowing—then—   20

c. 1861   *1896*

341

After great pain, a formal feeling comes—
The Nerves sit ceremonious, like Tombs—
The stiff Heart questions was it He, that bore,
And Yesterday, or Centuries before?

The Feet, mechanical, go round—   5
Of Ground, or Air, or Ought—
A Wooden way
Regardless grown,
A Quartz contentment, like a stone—

This is the Hour of Lead—   10
Remembered, if outlived,
As Freezing persons, recollect the Snow—
First—Chill—then Stupor—then the letting go—

c. 1862   *1929*

510

It was not Death, for I stood up,
And all the Dead, lie down—
It was not Night, for all the Bells
Put out their Tongues, for Noon.

It was not Frost, for on my Flesh   5
I felt Siroccos[1]—crawl—
Nor Fire—for just my Marble feet
Could keep a Chancel,[2] cool—

And yet, it tasted, like them all,
The Figures I have seen   10

---

[1]Hot, humid, oppressive Mediterranean winds from the
Sahara.
[2]Part of a church containing the altar and sanctuary.

Set orderly, for Burial,
Reminded me, of mine—

As if my life were shaven,
And fitted to a frame,
And could not breathe without a key,   15
And 'twas like Midnight, some—

When everything that ticked—has stopped—
And Space stares all around—
Or Grisly frosts—first Autumn morns,
Repeal the Beating Ground—   20

But, most, like Chaos—Stopless—cool—
Without a Chance, or Spar—
Or even a Report of Land—
To justify—Despair.

c. 1862   *1891*

561

I measure every Grief I meet
With narrow, probing, Eyes—
I wonder if It weighs like Mine—
Or has an Easier size.

I wonder if They bore it long—   5
Or did it just begin—
I could not tell the Date of Mine—
It feels so old a pain—

I wonder if it hurts to live—
And if They have to try—   10
And whether—could They choose between—
It would not be—to die—

I note that Some—gone patient long—
At length, renew their smile—
An imitation of a Light   15
That has so little Oil—

I wonder if when Years have piled—
Some Thousands—on the Harm—
That hurt them early—such a lapse
Could give them any Balm—   20

Or would they go on aching still
Through Centuries of Nerve—
Enlightened to a larger Pain—
In Contrast with the Love—

The Grieved—are many—I am told—   25
There is the various Cause—
Death—is but one—and comes but once—
And only nails the eyes—

There's Grief of Want—and Grief of Cold—
A sort they call "Despair"—   30
There's Banishment from native Eyes—
In sight of Native Air—

And though I may not guess the kind—
Correctly—yet to me
A piercing Comfort it affords   35
In passing Calvary—

To note the fashions—of the Cross—
And how they're mostly worn—
Still fascinated to presume
That Some—are like My Own—   40

c. 1862   *1896*

650

Pain—has an Element of Blank—
It cannot recollect
When it begun—or if there were
A time when it was not—

It has no Future—but itself—   5
Its Infinite contain
Its Past—enlightened to perceive
New Periods—of Pain.

c. 1862   *1890*

764

Presentiment—is that long Shadow—on the Lawn—
Indicative that Suns go down—

The Notice to the startled Grass
That Darkness—is about to pass—

c. 1863   *1890*

937

I felt a Cleaving in my Mind—
As if my Brain had split—
I tried to match it—Seam by Seam—
But could not make them fit.

The thought behind, I strove to join   5
Unto the thought before—
But Sequence ravelled out of Sound
Like Balls—upon a Floor.

c. 1864   *1896*

997

Crumbling is not an instant's Act
A fundamental pause
Dilapidation's processes
Are organized Decays.

'Tis first a Cobweb on the Soul   5
A Cuticle of Dust
A Borer in the Axis
An Elemental Rust—

Ruin is formal—Devil's work
Consecutive and slow—   10
Fail in an instant, no man did
Slipping—is Crash's law.

c. 1865   *1945*

1670

In Winter in my Room
I came upon a Worm
Pink lank and warm
But as he was a worm
And worms presume   5
Not quite with him at home
Secured him by a string
To something neighboring
And went along.

A Trifle afterward   10
A thing occurred
I'd not believe it if I heard
But state with creeping blood
A snake with mottles rare
Surveyed my chamber floor   15
In feature as the worm before
But ringed with power
The very string with which
I tied him—too
When he was mean and new   20
That string was there—

I shrank—"How fair you are"!
Propitiation's claw—
"Afraid he hissed
Of me"?   25
"No cordiality"—
He fathomed me—
Then to a Rhythm *Slim*
Secreted in his Form
As Patterns swim   30
Projected him.

That time I flew
Both eyes his way
Lest he pursue
Nor ever ceased to run   35
Till in a distant Town
Towns on from mine
I set me down
This was a dream—

?   *1914*

POEMS ON DEATH

153

Dust is the only Secret—
Death, the only One
You cannot find out all about
In his "native town."

Nobody knew "his Father"—   5
Never was a Boy—
Had'nt any playmates,
Or "Early history"—

Industrious! Laconic!
Punctual! Sedate!   10
Bold as a Brigand![1]
Stiller than a Fleet!

Builds, like a Bird, too!
Christ robs the Nest—
Robin after Robin   15
Smuggled to Rest!

c. 1860   *1914*

216

Safe in their Alabaster[1] Chambers—
Untouched by Morning
And untouched by Noon—
Sleep the meek members of the Resurrection—
Rafter of satin,   5
And Roof of stone.

Light laughs the breeze
In her Castle above them—
Babbles the Bee in a stolid Ear,
Pipe the Sweet Birds in ignorant cadence—   10
Ah, what sagacity perished here!

Version of 1859   *1862*

216

Safe in their Alabaster Chambers—
Untouched by Morning—
And untouched by Noon—
Lie the meek members of the Resurrection—
Rafter of Satin—and Roof of Stone!   5

Grand go the Years—in the Crescent—above them—
Worlds scoop their Arcs—
And Firmaments—row—

---

[1]Bandit.
[1]Smooth, translucent, white material.

Diadems—drop—and Doges[2]—surrender—
Soundless as dots—on a Disc of Snow—   10

Version of 1861   *1890*

449

I died for Beauty—but was scarce
Adjusted in the Tomb
When One who died for Truth, was lain
In an adjoining Room—

He questioned softly "Why I failed"?   5
"For Beauty," I replied—
"And I—for Truth—Themself are One—
We Bretheren, are," He said—

And so, as Kinsmen, met a Night—
We talked between the Rooms—   10
Until the Moss had reached our lips—
And covered up—our names—

c. 1862   *1890*

465

I heard a Fly buzz—when I died—
The Stillness in the Room
Was like the Stillness in the Air—
Between the Heaves of Storm—

The Eyes around—had wrung them dry—   5
And Breaths were gathering firm
For that last Onset—when the King
Be witnessed—in the Room—

I willed my Keepsakes—Signed away
What portion of me be   10
Assignable—and then it was
There interposed a Fly—

With Blue—uncertain stumbling Buzz—
Between the light—and me—
And then the Windows failed—and then   15
I could not see to see—

c. 1862   *1896*

712

Because I could not stop for Death—
He kindly stopped for me—
The Carriage held but just Ourselves—
And Immortality.

We slowly drove—He knew no haste   5
And I had put away
My labor and my leisure too,
For His Civility—

2Chief magistrates of Venice (697–1797) and Genoa (1339–
1797).

We passed the School, where Children strove
At Recess—in the Ring— 　　　　　　　　　　10
We passed the Fields of Gazing Grain—
We passed the Setting Sun—

Or rather—He passed Us—
The Dews drew quivering and chill—
For only Gossamer, my Gown— 　　　　　　　15
My Tippet[1]—only Tulle—

We paused before a House that seemed
A Swelling of the Ground—
The Roof was scarcely visible—
The Cornice—in the Ground— 　　　　　　　20

Since then—'tis Centuries—and yet
Feels shorter than the Day
I first surmised the Horses Heads
Were toward Eternity—

c. 1863 　　　　　　　　　　　　　　　　　*1890*

949

Under the Light, yet under,
Under the Grass and the Dirt,
Under the Beetle's Cellar
Under the Clover's Root,

Further than Arm could stretch 　　　　　　5
Were it Giant long,
Further than Sunshine could
Were the Day Year long,

Over the Light, yet over,
Over the Arc of the Bird— 　　　　　　　　10
Over the Comet's chimney—
Over the Cubit's Head,

Further than Guess can gallop
Further than Riddle ride—
Oh for a Disc to the Distance 　　　　　　15
Between Ourselves and the Dead!

c. 1864 　　　　　　　　　　　　　　　　　*1945*

1078

The Bustle in a House
The Morning after Death
Is solemnest of industries
Enacted upon Earth—

The Sweeping up the Heart 　　　　　　　　5
And putting Love away
We shall not want to use again
Until Eternity.

c. 1866 　　　　　　　　　　　　　　　　　*1890*

---

[1]Tippet: shoulder covering. Tulle: fine net.

1100

The last Night that She lived
It was a Common Night
Except the Dying—this to Us
Made Nature different

We noticed smallest things—   5
Things overlooked before
By this great light upon our Minds
Italicized—as 'twere.

As We went out and in
Between Her final Room   10
And Rooms where Those to be alive
Tomorrow were, a Blame

That Others could exist
While She must finish quite
A Jealousy for Her arose   15
So nearly infinite—

We waited while She passed—
It was a narrow time—
Too jostled were Our Souls to speak
At length the notice came.   20

She mentioned, and forgot—
Then lightly as a Reed
Bent to the Water, struggled scarce—
Consented, and was dead—

And We—We placed the Hair—   25
And drew the Head erect—
And then an awful leisure was
Belief to regulate—

c. 1866   *1890*

1136

The Frost of Death was on the Pane—
"Secure your Flower" said he.
Like Sailors fighting with a Leak
We fought Mortality.

Our passive Flower we held to Sea—   5
To Mountain—To the Sun—
Yet even on his Scarlet shelf
To crawl the Frost begun—

We pried him back
Ourselves we wedged   10
Himself and her between,
Yet easy as the narrow Snake
He forked his way along

Till all her helpless beauty bent
And then our wrath begun—   15

We hunted him to his Ravine
We chased him to his Den—

We hated Death and hated Life
And nowhere was to go—
Than Sea and continent there is   20
A larger—it is Woe

c. 1869   *1945*

POEMS OF FAITH AND DOUBT

185

"Faith" is a fine invention
When Gentlemen can *see*—
But *Microscopes* are prudent
In an Emergency.

c. 1860   *1891*

254

"Hope" is the thing with feathers—
That perches in the soul—
And sings the tune without the words—
And never stops—at all—

And sweetest—in the Gale—is heard—   5
And sore must be the storm—
That could abash the little Bird
That kept so many warm—

I've heard it in the chillest land—
And on the strangest Sea—   10
Yet, never, in Extremity,
It asked a crumb—of Me.

c. 1861   *1891*

301

I reason, Earth is short—
And Anguish—absolute—
And many hurt,
But, what of that?

I reason, we could die—   5
The best Vitality
Cannot excel Decay,
But, what of that?

I reason, that in Heaven—
Somehow, it will be even—   10
Some new Equation, given—
But, what of that?

c. 1862   *1890*

324

Some keep the Sabbath going to Church—
I keep it, staying at Home—

With a Bobolink for a Chorister—
And an Orchard, for a Dome—

Some keep the Sabbath in Surplice—   5
I just wear my Wings—
And instead of tolling the Bell, for Church,
Our little Sexton—sings.

God preaches, a noted Clergyman—
And the sermon is never long,   10
So instead of getting to Heaven, at last—
I'm going, all along.'

c. 1860   1864

338

I know that He exists.
Somewhere—in Silence—
He has hid his rare life
From our gross eyes.

'Tis an instant's play.   5
'Tis a fond Ambush—
Just to make Bliss
Earn her own surprise!

But—should the play
Prove piercing earnest—   10
Should the glee—glaze—
In Death's—stiff—stare—

Would not the fun
Look too expensive!
Would not the jest—   15
Have crawled too far!

c. 1862   1891

501

This World is not Conclusion.
A Species stands beyond—
Invisible, as Music—
But positive, as Sound—
It beckons, and it baffles—   5
Philosophy—don't know—
And through a Riddle, at the last—
Sagacity, must go—
To guess it, puzzles scholars—
To gain it, Men have borne   10
Contempt of Generations
And Crucifixion, shown—
Faith slips—and laughs, and rallies—
Blushes, if any see—
Plucks at a twig of Evidence—   15
And asks a Vane, the way—
Much Gesture, from the Pulpit—
Strong Hallelujahs roll—

Narcotics cannot still the Tooth
That nibbles at the soul—   20

c. 1862   1896

632

The Brain—is wider than the Sky—
For—put them side by side—
The one the other will contain
With ease—and You—beside—

The Brain is deeper than the sea—   5
For—hold them—Blue to Blue—
The one the other will absorb—
As Sponges—Buckets—do—

The Brain is just the weight of God—
For—Heft them—Pound for Pound—   10
And they will differ—if they do—
As Syllable from Sound—

c. 1862   1896

721

Behind Me—dips Eternity—
Before Me—Immortality—
Myself—the Term between—
Death but the Drift of Eastern Gray,
Dissolving into Dawn away,   5
Before the West begin—

'Tis Kingdoms—afterward—they say—
In perfect—pauseless Monarchy—
Whose Prince—is Son of None—
Himself—His Dateless Dynasty—   10
Himself—Himself diversify—
In Duplicate divine—

'Tis Miracle before Me—then—
'Tis Miracle behind—between—
A Crescent in the Sea—   15
With Midnight to the North of Her—
And Midnight to the South of Her—
And Maelstrom[1]—in the Sky—

c. 1863   1929

1052

I never saw a Moor—
I never saw the Sea—
Yet know I how the Heather looks
And what a Billow be.

I never spoke with God   5
Nor visited in Heaven—

---

[1]A violent whirlpool.

Yet certain am I of the spot
As if the Checks[1] were given—

c. 1865   1890

1461

"Heavenly Father"—take to thee
The supreme iniquity
Fashioned by thy candid Hand
In a moment contraband—
Though to trust us—seem to us   5
More respectful—"We are Dust"—
We apologize to thee
For thine own Duplicity—

c. 1879   1914

1545

The Bible is an antique Volume—
Written by faded Men
At the suggestion of Holy Spectres—
Subjects—Bethlehem—
Eden—the ancient Homestead—   5
Satan—the Brigadier—
Judas—the Great Defaulter—
David—the Troubadour—
Sin—a distinguished Precipice
Others must resist—   10
Boys that "believe" are very lonesome—
Other Boys are "lost"—
Had but the Tale a warbling Teller—
All the Boys would come—
Orpheus'[1] Sermon captivated—   15
It did not condemn—

c. 1882   1924

1551

Those—dying then,
Knew where they went—
They went to God's Right Hand—
That Hand is amputated now
And God cannot be found—   5

The abdication of Belief
Makes the Behavior small—
Better an ignis fatuus[1]
Than no illume at all—

c. 1882   1945

---

[1]Used here "in the accepted colloquial sense of railroad tickets" (Johnson).
[1]Son of the Greek god Apollo and the muse Calliope, Orpheus charmed not only men but even wild beasts, trees, and stones with his poetry and music.
[1]A phosphorescent light flitting over marshes caused by the spontaneous combustion of gases from decaying organic matter; hence, a deceptive light.

1624

Apparently with no surprise
To any happy Flower
The Frost beheads it at its play—
In accidental power—
The blonde Assassin passes on—
The Sun proceeds unmoved
To measure off another Day
For an Approving God.

c. 1884   *1890*

1760

Elysium[1] is as far as to
The very nearest Room
If in that Room a Friend await
Felicity or Doom—

What fortitude the Soul contains,
That it can so endure
The accent of a coming Foot—
The opening of a Door—

c. 1882   *1890*

Letters to
Thomas Wentworth Higginson[1]

260 ["Say If My Verse Is Alive"]

15 April 1862

Mr Higginson,

Are you too deeply occupied to say if my Verse is alive?

The Mind is so near itself—it cannot see, distinctly—and I have none to ask—

Should you think it breathed—and had you the leisure to tell me, I should feel quick gratitude—

If I make the mistake—that you dared to tell me—would give me sincerer honor—toward you—

I enclose my name—asking you, if you please—Sir—to tell me what is true?

That you will not betray me—it is needless to ask—since Honor is it's own pawn—

---

[1]In classical myth, the abode of the blessed dead; place or condition of perfect happiness.

[1]Liberal thinker and ardent reformer, working against slavery and for labor and women's rights, Thomas Wentworth Higginson (1823–1911) had resigned his Unitarian pulpit to become an esteemed writer and critic. When his "Letter to a Young Contributor" appeared in the April 1862 *Atlantic Monthly*, Dickinson read his admonition not to ignore "the magnificent mystery of words. . . . There may be years of crowded passion in a word, and half a life in a sentence. Such

being the majesty of the art you seek to practise, you can at least take time and deliberation before dishonoring it. . . . Charge your style with life." Her letter to him in reply began a lifelong correspondence and vital relationship. With it she enclosed an envelope containing her signature on a card and four poems: "Safe in their Alabaster Chambers" (216, version of 1861); "The nearest Dream recedes unrealized" (319); "We play at Paste" (320); and "I'll tell you how the Sun rose" (318).

261 ["MY STORY"]

25 April 1862

Mr Higginson,

Your kindness claimed earlier gratitude—but I was ill—and write today, from my pillow.

Thank you for the surgery—it was not so painful as I supposed. I bring you others[1]—as you ask—though they might not differ—

While my thought is undressed—I can make the distinction, but when I put them in the Gown—they look alike, and numb.

You asked how old I was? I made no verse—but one or two[2]—until this winter—Sir—

I had a terror—since September—I could tell to none—and so I sing, as the Boy does by the Burying Ground—because I am afraid—You inquire my Books—For Poets—I have Keats—and Mr and Mrs Browning. For Prose—Mr Ruskin—Sir Thomas Browne—and the Revelations.[3] I went to school—but in your manner of the phrase—had no education. When a little Girl, I had a friend,[4] who taught me Immortality—but venturing too near, himself—he never returned—Soon after, my Tutor, died—and for several years, my Lexicon—was my only companion—Then I found one more[5]—but he was not contented I be his scholar—so he left the Land.

You ask of my Companions Hills—Sir—and the Sundown—and a Dog—large as myself, that my Father bought me—They are better than Beings—because they know—but do not tell—and the noise in the Pool, at Noon—excels my Piano. I have a Brother and Sister—My Mother does not care for thought—and Father, too busy with his Briefs—to notice what we do—He buys me many Books—but begs me not to read them—because he fears they joggle the Mind. They are religious—except me—and address an Eclipse, every morning—whom they call their "Father." But I fear my story fatigues you—I would like to learn—Could you tell me how to grow—or is it unconveyed—like Melody—or Witchcraft?

You speak of Mr Whitman—I never read his Book—but was told that he was disgraceful[6]—

I read Miss Prescott's "Circumstance,"[7] but it followed me, in the Dark—so I avoided her—

Two Editors of Journals[8] came to my Father's House, this winter—and asked me for my Mind—and when I asked them "Why," they said I was penurious—and they, would use it for the World—

I could not weigh myself—Myself—

My size felt small—to me—I read your Chapters in the Atlantic—and experienced honor for you—I was sure you would not reject a confiding question—

Is this—Sir—what you asked me to tell you?

Your friend,

E—Dickinson.

---

[1]The enclosures were "There came a Day at Summer's full" (322), "Of all the Sounds despatched abroad" (321), and "South Winds jostle them" (86).

[2]She had in fact written almost 300 poems. As Johnson notes, "She was writing to Higginson, not as a novice, but as an artist."

[3]John Keats (1795–1821), English romantic poet; Robert Browning (1812–1889) and Elizabeth Barrett Browning (1806–1861), English poets; John Ruskin (1819–1900), English art critic and essayist; Sir Thomas Browne (1605–1682), English physician and writer; and Revelation, the apocalyptic last book of the New Testament.

[4]Usually taken to be Benjamin Franklin Newton (1821–1853), who had studied law in her father's law office (1847–50).

[5]Possibly the Reverend Charles Wadsworth (1814–1882),

who sailed on May 1 for a California pastorate, though he left Philadelphia in April.

[6]Among the contemporary reviews attacking *Leaves of Grass* by the American poet Walt Whitman was one published by a Dickinson friend entitled "'Leaves of Grass'—Smut in Them" (*Springfield Daily Republican*, 1860).

[7]The popular Gothic thriller by Harriet Prescott (Spofford, 1835–1921) in the *Atlantic Monthly* of May 1860.

[8]Probably close friends Samuel Bowles (1826–1878), editor of the *Springfield Daily Republican*, and Josiah G. Holland (1819–1881), his associate. Two of her poems had earlier been anonymously printed (with editorial alterations) in the *Republican*: "I taste a liquor never brewed" (214) as "The May-Wine" in May 1861; and "Safe in their Alabaster Chambers" (216, version of 1859) as "The Sleeping" in March 1862.

265 ["My Barefoot-Rank Is Better"]

7 June 1862

Dear friend.

Your letter gave no Drunkenness, because I tasted Rum before—Domingo[1] comes but once—yet I have had few pleasures so deep as your opinion, and if I tried to thank you, my tears would block my tongue—

My dying Tutor told me that he would like to live till I had been a poet, but Death was much of Mob[2] as I could master—then—And when far afterward—a sudden light on Orchards, or a new fashion in the wind troubled my attention—I felt a palsy, here—the Verses just relieve—

Your second letter surprised me, and for a moment, swung—I had not supposed it. Your first—gave no dishonor, because the True—are not ashamed—I thanked you for your justice—but could not drop the Bells whose jingling cooled my Tramp—Perhaps the Balm, seemed better, because you bled me, first.

I smile when you suggest that I delay "to publish"—that being foreign to my thought, as Firmament to Fin—

If fame belonged to me, I could not escape her—if she did not, the longest day would pass me on the chase—and the approbation of my Dog, would forsake me—then—My Barefoot-Rank is better—

You think my gait "spasmodic"[3]—I am in danger—Sir—

You think me "uncontrolled"—I have no Tribunal.

Would you have time to be the "friend" you should think I need? I have a little shape—it would not crowd your Desk—nor make much Racket as the Mouse, that dents your Galleries—

If I might bring you what I do—not so frequent to trouble you—and ask you if I told it clear—'twould be control, to me—

The Sailor cannot see the North—but knows the Needle can—

The "hand you stretch me in the Dark," I put mine in, and turn away—I have no Saxon,[4] now—

> As if I asked a common Alms,
> And in my wondering hand
> A Stranger pressed a Kingdom,
> And I, bewildered, stand—
> As if I asked the Orient
> Had it for me a Morn—
> And it should lift it's purple Dikes,
> And shatter me with Dawn!

But, will you be my Preceptor, Mr Higginson?

Your friend
E Dickinson—

268 ["My Business Is Circumference"]

July 1862

Could you believe me—without? I had no portrait, now, but am small, like the Wren, and my Hair is bold, like the Chestnut Bur—and my eyes, like the Sherry in the Glass, that the Guest leaves—Would this do just as well?

---

[1]Santo Domingo, in the West Indies, source of rum.
[2]Audience.

[3]I.e., her poetry defied regular metrical patterns.
[4]"Language fails me" (Johnson's note). See poem 276.

It often alarms Father—He says Death might occur, and he has Molds[1] of all the rest—but has no Mold of me, but I noticed the Quick wore off those things, in a few days, and forestall the dishonor—You will think no caprice of me—

You said "Dark." I know the Butterfly—and the Lizard—and the Orchis[2]— Are not those *your* Countrymen?[3]

I am happy to be your scholar, and will deserve the kindness, I cannot repay.

If you truly consent, I recite, now[4]—

Will you tell me my fault, frankly as to yourself, for I had rather wince, than die. Men do not call the surgeon, to commend—the Bone, but to set it, Sir, and fracture within, is more critical. And for this, Preceptor, I shall bring you—Obedience—the Blossom from my Garden, and every gratitude I know. Perhaps you smile at me. I could not stop for that—My Business is Circumference[5]—An ignorance, not of Customs, but if caught with the Dawn—or the Sunset see me—Myself the only Kangaroo among the Beauty, Sir, if you please, it afflicts me, and I thought that instruction would take it away.

Because you have much business, beside the growth of me—you will appoint, yourself, how often I shall come—without your inconvenience. And if at any time— you regret you received me, or I prove a different fabric to that you supposed—you must banish me—

When I state myself, as the Representative of the Verse—it does not mean—me— but a supposed person. You are true, about the "perfection."

Today, makes Yesterday mean.

You spoke of Pippa Passes[6]—I never heard anybody speak of Pippa Passes— before.

You see my posture is benighted.

To thank you, baffles me. Are you perfectly powerful? Had I a pleasure you had not, I could delight to bring it.

Your Scholar

271 ["My Little Force Explodes"]

August 1862

Dear friend—

Are these[1] more orderly? I thank you for the Truth—

I had no Monarch in my life, and cannot rule myself, and when I try to organize— my little Force explodes—and leaves me bare and charred—

I think you called me "Wayward." Will you help me improve?

I suppose the pride that stops the Breath, in the Core of Woods, is not of Ourself—

You say I confess the little mistake,[2] and omit the large—Because I can see Orthography—but the Ignorance out of sight—is my Preceptor's charge—

Of "shunning Men and Women"—they talk of Hallowed things, aloud—and embarrass my Dog—He and I dont object to them, if they'll exist their side. I think

---

[1]Pictures of daguerrotypes, which darken when exposed to air.
[2]Orchid.
[3]Dickinson had read his nature essays.
[4]The enclosures were "Of Tribulation these are they" (325), with the note, "I spelled Ankle—wrong"; "Your Riches taught me poverty" (299); "Some keep the Sabbath going to Church" (324); and "Success is counted sweetest" (67).
[5]This complex, key word has provoked much illuminating

critical discussion, including Johnson's definition: "a projection of her imagination into all relationships of man, nature, and spirit." Cf. Ralph Waldo Emerson's essay "Circles."
[6]Robert Browning's dramatic poem (1841).

[1]The enclosures were "Before I got my Eye put out" (327) and "I cannot dance upon my Toes" (326).
[2]I.e., she had admitted misspelling a word on a poem sent with the previous letter.

Carl[o] would please you—He is dumb, and brave—I think you would like the Chestnut Tree, I met in my walk. It hit my notice suddenly—and I thought the Skies were in Blossom—

Then there's a noiseless noise in the Orchard—that I let persons hear—You told me in one letter, you could not come to see me, "now," and I made no answer, not because I had none, but did not think myself the price that you should come so far—

I do not ask so large a pleasure, lest you might deny me—

You say "Beyond your knowledge." You would not jest with me, because I believe you—but Preceptor—you cannot mean it? All men say "What" to me, but I thought it a fashion—

When much in the Woods as a little Girl, I was told that the Snake would bite me, that I might pick a poisonous flower, or Goblins kidnap me, but I went along and met no one but Angels, who were far shyer of me, than I could be of them, so I hav'nt that confidence in fraud which many exercise.

I shall observe your precept—though I dont understand it, always.

I marked a line in One Verse—because I met it after I made it[3]—and never consciously touch a paint, mixed by another person—

I do not let go it, because it is mine.

Have you the portrait of Mrs Browning?[4] Persons sent me three—If you had none, will you have mine?

Your Scholar—

Letters from T. W. Higginson to His Wife

342A [E.D. "SAYING MANY THINGS"]

[16 August 1870]

I shan't sit up tonight to write you all about E.D. dearest but if you had read Mrs. Stoddard's novels[1] you could understand a house where each member runs his or her own selves. Yet I only saw her.

A large county lawyer's house, brown brick, with great trees & a garden—I sent up my card. A parlor dark & cool & stiffish, a few books & engravings & an open piano—Malbone & O D [Out Door] Papers[2] among other books.

A step like a pattering child's in entry & in glided a little plain woman with two smooth bands of reddish hair & a face a little like Belle Dove's; not plainer—with no good feature—in a very plain & exquisitely clean white pique & a blue net worsted shawl. She came to me with two day lilies which she put in a sort of childlike way into my hand & said "These are my introduction" in a soft frightened breathless childlike voice—& added under her breath Forgive me if I am frightened; I never see strangers & hardly know what I say—but she talked soon & thenceforward continuously—& deferentially—sometimes stopping to ask me to talk instead of her—but readily recommencing. Manner between Angie Tilton & Mr. Alcott[3]—but thoroughly ingenuous & simple which they are not & saying many things which you

---

[3]I.e., she set a line in quotation marks because she later found it in print.
[4]Elizabeth Barrett Browning (1806–1861), English poet admired by Dickinson, who wrote three poems in her memory.
[1]Elizabeth Drew Stoddard (1823–1902) defied prevailing sentimental norms in realistic works like *The Morgesons* (1862), depicting unconventional individuals confined by New England family life and society.

[2]Higginson's *Malbone: An Oldport Romance* (1869) and *Out-Door Papers* (1863), a collection of his nature essays.
[3]Amos Bronson Alcott (1799–1888), progressive educator, author, mystic, utopian, was called the most transcendental of the Transcendentalists; his informal, masterful "conversations" powerfully influenced people. Angie Tilton is unidentified.

would have thought foolish & I wise—& some things you wd. hv. liked. I add a few over the page.

. . . . .

I got here at 2 & leave at 9. E.D. dreamed all night of *you* (not me) & next day got my letter proposing to come here!! She only knew of you through a mention in my notice of Charlotte Hawes.[4]

"Women talk: men are silent: that is why I dread women.

"My father only reads on Sunday—he reads *lonely* & *rigorous* books."

"If I read a book [and] it makes my whole body so cold no fire ever can warm me I know *that* is poetry. If I feel physically as if the top of my head were taken off, I know *that* is poetry. These are the only way I know it. Is there any other way?"

"How do most people live without any thoughts. There are many people in the world (you must have noticed them in the street) How do they live. How do they get strength to put on their clothes in the morning"

"When I lost the use of my Eyes[5] it was a comfort to think there were so few real *books* that I could easily find some one to read me all of them"

"Truth is such a *rare* thing it is delightful to tell it."

"I find ecstasy in living—the mere sense of living is joy enough"

I asked if she never felt want of employment, never going off the place & never seeing any visitor "I never thought of conceiving that I could ever have the slightest approach to such a want in all future time" (& added) "I feel that I have not expressed myself strongly enough."

She makes all the bread for her father only likes hers & says "& people must have puddings" this *very* dreamily, as if they were comets—so she makes them.

342B ["E D AGAIN"]

[17 August 1870]

. . . . . .

She said to me at parting "Gratitude is the only secret that cannot reveal itself."

I talked with Prest Stearns[1] of Amherst about her—& found him a very pleasant companion in the cars. Before leaving today, I got in to the Museums & enjoyed them much; saw a meteoric stone almost as long as my arm & weighing 436 lbs! a big slice of some other planet. It fell in Colorado. The collection of bird tracks of extinct birds in stone is very wonderful & unique & other good things. I saw Mr. Dickinson this morning a little—thin dry & speechless—I saw what her life has been. Dr. S. says her sister is proud of her.[2]

. . . . . .

E D again

"Could you tell me what home is"

"I never had a mother. I suppose a mother is one to whom you hurry when you are troubled."

---

[4]A young magazine writer from Worcester, Massachusetts, to whom Higginson paid tribute in a memorial piece in the *Radical*, January 1867.
[5]Dickinson underwent treatment for an eye condition in Boston in 1864 and 1865.

[1]William Augustus Stearns (1805–1876), Congregational clergyman and president of Amherst College.
[2]Lavinia Norcross Dickinson (1833–1899), discovering the poems after her sister's death, was the driving force behind their first publication (1890).

"I never knew how to tell time by the clock till I was 15. My father thought he had taught me but I did not understand & I was afraid to say I did not & afraid to ask any one else lest he should know."

Her father was not severe I should think but remote. He did not wish them to read anything but the Bible. One day her brother brought home Kavanagh[3] hid it under the piano cover & made signs to her & they read it: her father at last found it & was displeased. Perhaps it was before this that a student of his was amazed that they had never heard of Mrs. [Lydia Maria] Child[4] & used to bring them books & hide in a bush by the door. They were then little things in short dresses with their feet on the rungs of the chair. After the first book she thought in ecstasy "This then is a book! And there are more of them!"

"Is it oblivion or absorption when things pass from our minds?"

Major Hunt[5] interested her more than any man she ever saw. She remembered two things he said—that her great dog "understood gravitation" & when he said he should come again "in a year. If I say a shorter time it will be longer."

When I said I would come again *some time* she said "Say in a long time, that will be nearer. Some time is nothing."

After long disuse of her eyes she read Shakespeare & thought why is any other book needed.

I never was with any one who drained my nerve power so much. Without touching her, she drew from me. I am glad not to live near her. She often thought me *tired* & seemed very thoughtful of others.

SIDNEY LANIER
(1842–1881)

Sidney Lanier lived just a little under forty years, and during that time he gave up many years in service to the Confederate Army, in a Union prison, in drudge-work to support a growing family, and in seeking a cure for a debilitating illness. And yet he left a handful of poems that are extraordinary in their originality and intensity. He shares with Walt Whitman and Emily Dickinson a poetic gift for mystical engagement with nature. But the sonorous music of his best poems have the magic or mesmerizing effect of the most melodious poems of Tennyson and Swinburne.

Lanier was born in the little southern town of Macon, Georgia, in 1842, the son of a cultured and well-read lawyer. He attended Oglethorpe University, near Milledgeville, Georgia, from 1857 to 1860. As a star student, he was preparing for an academic career there when he was caught up in the Civil War. He joined the Macon Volunteers in 1861, saw battle in 1862 in Virginia, and, in 1864, was captured by Union forces.

Lanier was imprisoned at Point Lookout, Maryland, spending some four months in captivity. The major in charge of prisoners was notorious for his brutality, and the captured southerners were crammed into old tents with little food and suffered much dysentery, scurvy, and other illnesses. Of a delicate

---

[3]Prose tale (1849) by Longfellow.
[4]Mrs. Child (1802–1880), abolitionist and author of the historical novels *Hobomok* (1824), *The Rebels; or Boston before the Revolution* (1825), *The History of the Condition of Women* (1835), and the influential *Appeal in Favor of that Class of Americans*

Called Africans (1833).
[5]Edward B. Hunt (d. 1863), first husband of Helen Fiske Hunt Jackson (1830–1885), noted novelist and poet who later became an enthusiastic admirer of Dickinson's poetry, urging publication.

nature to begin with, Lanier developed lung trouble and prolonged fever that would eventually contribute to his death from tuberculosis.

Out of his prison experiences, Lanier wrote a novel, *Tiger Lilies*, published in 1867. This same year he married and began a family, which was to grow to four sons. Although he settled into law practice with his father, he felt drawn to an artistic career, torn between music and poetry. He had been a flute player since boyhood, even entertaining his fellow prisoners with his music. In 1873 he became first flutist for the Peabody Orchestra in Baltimore, Maryland.

Lanier divided his time between his two chief interests, combining them where he could. His first major poem, "Corn," appeared in 1875, launching his reputation as a poet. Lanier was fully aware of the risks he was taking in writing on such a mundane subject as the title announced. He wrote to a friend to whom he sent the poem, "I have endeavored to carry some very prosaic matters up to a loftier plane." His inspiration, he said, came from the "deserted homesteads and gullied hills" in the older counties of Georgia which he had seen. Lanier's sympathies in the poem are with the bankrupt farmer who finds himself finally "A gamester's catspaw and a banker's slave."

Later in 1875, he published the long poem "Symphony," a remarkable experiment in rendering different orchestral instruments by onomatopoetic expressions. At the same time he had the instruments speak in protest against the dehumanization of rampant trade and industrialism. The poem concluded with a distillation of Lanier's philosophical vision: "O'er the modern waste a dove hath whirred: / Music is Love in search of a word."

Lanier wrote and published what is universally considered his masterpiece, "The Marshes of Glynn," in 1878. The work is set in the sea marshes of Glynn County, Georgia. Planned as the first of six "Hymns of the Marshes," the poem is one of the three that Lanier completed. His fascination with the symbolic meeting point of land and ocean as poetic material parallels Whitman's in such poems as "Out of the Cradle Endlessly Rocking." Underlying Lanier's encounter with the marshes that link earth and sea is a mystical vision of death, which appears a kind of intuitional preparation for his own death that came only a few short years later ("I will fly in the greatness of God as the marsh-hen flies").

In lecturing on English literature, Lanier attracted the attention of the newly established Johns Hopkins University in Baltimore. He accepted a position on the faculty in 1879 and indulged his long-standing interest in the relationship of music and poetry, resulting in the publication in 1880 of *The Science of English Verse*. This book is a pioneer exploration of the sources and nature of poetic music. Claiming that the laws of poetry and music are the same, Lanier developed a special method of scansion that used musical notes. In his emphasis on the metronome, he was following a direction radically different from Whitman's, who was firmly embarked in the direction of free verse, with music too subtle for any kind of traditional scansion or notation.

Though well situated in his new career, free at last to pursue his own interests, Lanier was overtaken by the disease that had intensified since his Civil War imprisonment. He died of tuberculosis in September 1881. Among Lanier's poem outlines are these two lines that appear a summation of his own defiant determination in the face of his approaching fate:

I will sing against thee, Death, as the brood does,
I will make thee into music which does not die.

ADDITIONAL READING

The Letters of Sidney Lanier, 1866–1881, ed. Henry Lanier, 1899; Selected Poems of Sidney Lanier, ed. Stark Young, 1947.

Edwin Mims, Sidney Lanier, 1905; Aubrey H. Starke, Sidney Lanier: A Biographical and Critical Study, 1933; Lincoln Lorenz, The Life of Sidney Lanier, 1935; Philip Graham and Joseph Jones, A Concordance to the Poems of Sidney Lanier, 1939; Richard Webb and Edwin R. Coulson, Sidney Lanier, Poet and Prosodist, 1941; Edd Winfield Parks, Sidney Lanier: The Man, the Poet, the Critic, 1968; Jack de Bellis, Sidney Lanier, 1972; Jane S. Gabin, A Living Minstrelsy: The Poetry and Music of Sidney Lanier, 1985.

TEXT

The Centennial Edition of the Works of Sidney Lanier, 10 vols., ed. Charles R. Anderson, 1945.

The Ship of Earth

Thou Ship of Earth, with Death, and Birth, and Life, and Sex aboard,
    And fires of Desires burning hotly in the hold,
I fear thee, O! I fear thee, for I hear the tongue and sword
    At battle on the deck, and the wild mutineers are bold!

The dewdrop morn may fall from off the petal of the sky,   5
    But all the deck is wet with blood and stains the crystal red.
A pilot, GOD, a pilot! for the helm is left awry,
    And the best sailors in the ship lie there among the dead!

1868   1868

Evening Song

Look off, dear Love, across the sallow sands,
    And mark yon meeting of the sun and sea;
How long they kiss, in sight of all the lands!
        Ah, longer, longer, we.

Now in the sea's red vintage melts the sun,   5
    As Egypt's pearl dissolved in rosy wine,
And Cleopatra Night drinks all.[1] 'Tis done!
        Love, lay thine hand in mine.

Come forth, sweet stars, and comfort Heaven's heart;
    Glimmer, ye waves, round else unlighted sands;   10
O Night, divorce our sun and sky apart—
        Never our lips, our hands.

1876   1877

---

[1]According to tradition, Egyptian Queen Cleopatra dissolved a pearl in the drink used to toast Mark Antony.

The Marshes of Glynn[1]

Glooms of the live-oaks, beautiful-braided and woven
With intricate shades of the vines that myriad-cloven
  Clamber the forks of the multiform boughs,—
     Emerald twilights,—
     Virginal shy lights,   5
Wrought of the leaves to allure to the whisper of vows,
When lovers pace timidly down through the green colonnades
  Of the dim sweet woods, of the dear dark woods,
    Of the heavenly woods and glades,
  That run to the radiant marginal sand-beach within   10
    The wide sea-marshes of Glynn;—

Beautiful glooms, soft dusks in the noon-day fire,—
Wildwood privacies, closets of lone desire,
Chamber from chamber parted with wavering arras[2] of leaves,—
Cells for the passionate pleasure of prayer to the soul that grieves,   15
  Pure with a sense of the passing of saints through the wood,
  Cool for the dutiful weighing of ill with good;—

O braided dusks of the oak and woven shades of the vine,
While the riotous noon-day sun of the June-day long did shine,
Ye held me fast in your heart and I held you fast in mine;   20
  But now when the noon is no more, and riot is rest,
  And the sun is a-wait at the ponderous gate of the West,
    And the slant yellow beam down the wood-aisle doth seem
    Like a lane into heaven that leads from a dream,—
Ay, now, when my soul all day hath drunken the soul of the oak,   25
And my heart is at ease from men, and the wearisome sound of the stroke
  Of the scythe of time and the trowel of trade is low,
  And belief overmasters doubt, and I know that I know,
  And my spirit is grown to a lordly great compass within,
    That the length and the breadth and the sweep of the marshes of Glynn 30
    Will work me no fear like the fear they have wrought me of yore
      When length was fatigue, and when breadth was but bitterness sore,
      And when terror and shrinking and dreary unnamable pain
      Drew over me out of the merciless miles of the plain,—
        Oh, now, unafraid, I am fain to face   35
        The vast sweet visage of space.
        To the edge of the wood I am drawn, I am drawn,
      Where the gray beach glimmering runs, as a belt of the dawn,
         For a mete and a mark[3]
         To the forest-dark:—   40
          So:
        Affable live-oak, leaning low,—
      Thus—with your favor—soft, with a reverent hand,
      (Not lightly touching your person, Lord of the land!)
      Bending your beauty aside, with a step I stand   45
        On the firm-packed sand,
         Free
      By a world of marsh that borders a world of sea.

---

[1] Glynn County, Georgia, on the Atlantic coast near Brunswick.
[2] Tapestry.
[3] Limit and boundary.

Sinuous southward and sinuous northward the shimmering band
Of the sand-beach fastens the fringe of the marsh to the folds of the land.   50
Inward and outward to northward and southward the beach-lines linger and
          curl
As a silver-wrought garment that clings to and follows the firm sweet limbs
          of a girl.
Vanishing, swerving, evermore curving again into sight,
Softly the sand-beach wavers away to a dim gray looping of light.
And what if behind me to westward the wall of the woods stands high?   55
The world lies east: how ample, the marsh and the sea and the sky!
A league and a league of marsh-grass, waist-high, broad in the blade,
Green, and all of a height, and unflecked with a light or a shade,
          Stretch leisurely off, in a pleasant plain,
          To the terminal blue of the main.   60

          Oh, what is abroad in the marsh and the terminal sea?
              Somehow my soul seems suddenly free
          From the weighing of fate and the sad discussion of sin,
              By the length and the breadth and the sweep of the marshes of Glynn.
Ye marshes, how candid and simple and nothing-withholding and free   65
Ye publish yourselves to the sky and offer yourselves to the sea!
Tolerant plains, that suffer the sea and the rains and the sun,
Ye spread and span like the catholic[4] man who hath mightily won
          God out of knowledge and good out of infinite pain
          And sight out of blindness and purity out of a stain.   70

          As the marsh-hen secretly builds on the watery sod,
          Behold I will build me a nest on the greatness of God:
          I will fly in the greatness of God as the marsh-hen flies
          In the freedom that fills all the space 'twixt the marsh and the skies:
          By so many roots as the marsh-grass sends in the sod   75
          I will heartily lay me a-hold on the greatness of God:
          Oh, like to the greatness of God is the greatness within
          The range of the marshes, the liberal marshes of Glynn.

And the sea lends large, as the marsh: lo, out of his plenty the sea
          Pours fast: full soon the time of the flood-tide must be: 80
              Look how the grace of the sea doth go
          About and about through the intricate channels that flow
              Here and there,
              Everywhere,
Till his waters have flooded the uttermost creeks and the low-lying lanes,   85
          And the marsh is meshed with a million veins,
          That like as with rosy and silvery essences flow
              In the rose-and-silver evening glow.
                  Farewell, my lord Sun!
          The creeks overflow: a thousand rivulets run   90
          'Twixt the roots of the sod; the blades of the marsh-grass stir;
Passeth a hurrying sound of wings that westward whirr;
Passeth, and all is still; and the currents cease to run;
              And the sea and the marsh are one.

4Universal.

How still the plains of the waters be!   95
The tide is in his ecstasy.
The tide is at his highest height:
     And it is night.

And now from the Vast of the Lord will the waters of sleep
     Roll in on the souls of men,   100
But who will reveal to our waking ken
The forms that swim and the shapes that creep
     Under the waters of sleep?
And I would I could know what swimmeth below when the tide comes in
On the length and the breadth of the marvellous marshes of Glynn.   105

1878   *1878*

INNOVATIONS IN FICTION

MARK TWAIN   HENRY JAMES

WILLIAM DEAN HOWELLS

"The more we consider it the more we feel that the prose picture can never be at the end of its tether until it loses the sense of what it can do. It can do simply everything, and that is its strength and its life. Its plasticity, its elasticity are infinite; there is no color, no extension it may not take from the nature of its subject or the temper of its craftsman. It has the extraordinary advantage—a piece of luck scarcely credible—that, while capable of giving an impression of the highest perfection and the rarest finish, it moves in a luxurious independence of rules and restrictions. Think as we may, there is nothing we can mention as a consideration outside itself with which it must square, nothing we can name as one of its peculiar obligations or interdictions."

Henry James, "The Future of the Novel"

MARK TWAIN
(1835–1910)

"Twain . . . reveals himself to be one of those writers, of whom there are not a great many in any literature, who have discovered a new way of writing, valid not only for themselves but for others. I should place him . . . as one of those rare writers who have brought their language up to date, and in so doing, 'purified the dialect of the tribe.'" This assessment by the author of *The Waste Land* (1922), T. S. Eliot, is extraordinary only in that it comes from the most influential American poet of the modernist period. In making his comment, Eliot was echoing what Ernest Hemingway had said ("all modern American literature comes from one book by Mark Twain") and what William Faulkner had endorsed ("of course Mark Twain is all our grandfather").

No doubt Twain would have been surprised by such praise. During his lifetime he had a large popular audience, but little recognition from the literary establishment. He was considered a "funny man" or humorist, not a man of letters. He had a number of literary friends (Artemus Ward, Bret Harte, William Dean Howells), but by and large he was a literary loner, mining materials out of his middle-western boyhood on the Mississippi or his contemporary travels at home or abroad with all the innocence of an unrestrained natural, native genius.

Samuel Langhorne Clemens was born in Florida, Missouri, in 1835, into a large family. His father dreamed the American dream of great wealth, but lived always on the edge of bankruptcy. In 1839 he settled his family in Hannibal, Missouri, on the Mississippi River, in hopes of improving the family fortunes. His sudden death in 1847 forced the eleven-year-old Sam to leave school and go to work to contribute to family finances.

He became an apprentice printer and later worked on his older brother Orion's weekly newspaper, started in 1850. He did not launch out on his own until 1853, when he left Hannibal to roam around the country from one printing job to another. But the Hannibal of his boyhood and the great muddy Mississippi would remain deep and restive in the recesses of his imagination, awaiting the time when they would be called forth for the creation of Mark Twain's master works.

In 1856, Sam Clemens headed for New Orleans with vague plans to go to South America to find his fortune on another great continental river, the Amazon. In New Orleans he found no ship to take him on this venture, and soon he ran out of money. He then persuaded a pilot he had met on the trip down to take him on as an apprentice pilot on a Mississippi steamboat, fulfilling a boyhood dream. He learned the river, became a pilot, and prospered—until the Civil War interrupted all traffic on the river.

In 1861, Clemens joined Confederate forces in Missouri as a second lieutenant, but resigned after two weeks, stating that he was "incapacitated by fatigue" through "persistent retreat." His brother Orion, appointed secretary to the territorial governor of Nevada, took his younger brother with him to Carson City as his secretary. Finding that he had no duties and no salary, Sam cut out on his own, trying his hand as a prospector and miner, but turning finally to journalism. He adopted the pseudonym "Mark Twain," the river term called out to the pilot to inform him the river was "two-fathoms deep."

It was in a mining camp in Calaveras County, California, that Twain picked up the tall tale of the "Notorious Jumping Frog." He made it his own by ingenious attention to structure, colloquial speech, and metaphor, and found him-self famous overnight as the story was picked up by the press across the country. He was sent by a newspaper to Hawaii (then the Sandwich Islands) to write an account of what he found, and he soon began to lecture after the fashion of the literary comedians of the day such as Artemus Ward.

In 1867, after publishing his first book, *The Celebrated Jumping Frog of Cal-averas County, and Other Sketches*, Twain joined a group of American "pilgrims" sailing from New York on the *Quaker City* to Europe and the Holy Land. He was commissioned by San Francisco and New York newspapers to send back regular accounts of their adventures abroad. The dispatches were beguilingly exotic and extraordinarily comic and, when turned into *The Innocents Abroad* in 1869, solidi-fied Mark Twain's fame. Always ambivalent about their relation to the "old world," American readers found Mark Twain's role as the naive, often ignorant but always shrewd American abroad gratifyingly funny, especially as he and the others, often duped by the crafty guides, reciprocated by bamboozling the bamboozlers.

This success demonstrated to Twain that he could have a rewarding career in journalism and literature. Through a fellow voyager on the *Quaker City*, who had shown Twain a picture of his sister, Twain met, courted, and (after a decent lapse of time) married Olivia Langdon in 1870. At the age of thirty-five he thus gave up his vagabond, frontier life for family and children in genteel eastern society. But his western adventures constituted a kind of capital on which his imagina-tion would draw for the rest of his literary career.

In 1872 he published *Roughing It*, exploiting his journey west to Nevada with his brother, his experiences in the mining communities there and in California, and his trip to Hawaii. This work repeated the success of *The Innocents Abroad*. By this time Twain had settled into a large house in Hartford, Connecticut, having something of the aura and shape of a Mississippi steamboat. Together with a neighbor, Charles Dudley Warner, Twain published *The Gilded Age* in 1873, a satiric tale of post–Civil War boom times and rampant speculative schemes to get rich quick.

In 1874, Twain was casting about for a topic to turn to next. In conversation with a friend, he began to reminisce about the steamboat days on the Mississippi. With the friend's encouragement, Twain wrote to William Dean Howells, then editor of *The Atlantic Monthly*, who was enthusiastic. The result was *Old Times on the Mississippi*, which Twain wrote out of the memories of his boyhood days in Hannibal and his life as a steamboat pilot on the river. It appeared in seven installments in *The Atlantic Monthly*, his most unified work to date held together by its subject, the heyday of steamboating on the Mississippi, and by its emo-tional intensity, evoked by Twain's recollections of a lost past. At the center is the young Twain, experiencing his initiation into the mysteries of the great conti-nental river and the challenges of piloting a steamboat through her treacherous waters.

This brilliant work opened up a world of new material for Twain's imagina-tion. In 1876 appeared *The Adventures of Tom Sawyer*, which turned out to be preparation for his masterpiece published in 1884, *Adventures of Huckleberry Finn*. Both books were steeped in Twain's memories of his boyhood experiences in Hannibal and its environs, including the great muddy Mississippi flowing past and the bluffs along its banks honeycombed with mysterious crevices and caves. But in the second work, Twain let Huck, a disreputable, homeless kid living a vagabond life, tell the tale in American vernacular; and he let the Mississippi

River structure the work, alternating scenes between shore and Huck's raft as it floated down the turbulent currents. In language and material, Twain touched on archetypal elements deeply embedded in the American psyche in a book read widely around the world as rooted in American reality.

Nowhere else was Twain to sound the depths he reached in *Huckleberry Finn*. In such travel books as *A Tramp Abroad* (1880) and such historical fantasies as *The Prince and the Pauper* (1882) and *A Connecticut Yankee in King Arthur's Court* (1889), his imagination did not appear to be in touch with his profoundest feelings. Even his expansion of *Old Times on the Mississippi* into *Life on the Mississippi* (1883), introducing materials from his adult return to boyhood scenes, represented a decline in imaginative vigor.

Twain's obsession with inventions and gadgets in the hopes of finding fabulous wealth led him into financial disaster in the 1890s. His publishing house, which had flourished with the publication of Ulysses S. Grant's *Personal Memoirs*, in 1885–86, went into bankruptcy in 1894. Twain set out on the honorable path to repay all his many debts. He went on a speaking tour around the world, publishing *Following the Equator* in 1897. But the drain on his energy took its toll physically and psychically.

Twain's last years saw his wit and humor gradually replaced by a darkening world-view and a sardonic bitterness. The death of his wife Livy in 1904 intensified his melancholy. Many of his works, challenging traditional religious beliefs and notions of man's basic goodness, were set aside without publication as too inflammatory for the times. In such works as *The Mysterious Stranger* (1916) and *Letters from the Earth* (1962), Twain could best convey his bleak vision of humankind and the world through the persona of an ironically portrayed Satan.

When Twain died in 1910, he was ladened with honors from around the world, including an honorary degree bestowed by England's Oxford University in 1907. Such recognition from the literary establishment must have gratified the barefoot boy that endured within the aging man. With all its failures, his life proved a remarkable triumph. He was one of those rare American authors able to achieve both great popularity and critical acclaim in work destined to live on beyond his personal presence.

ADDITIONAL READING

The Writings of Mark Twain, 37 vols., ed. Albert Bigelow Paine, 1922–25. In progress: *The Mark Twain Papers*, ed. Robert Hirst et al., 1967–; and *The Works of Mark Twain*, ed. John Gerber et al., 1972–.

William Dean Howells, *My Mark Twain*, 1910; Albert Bigelow Paine, *Mark Twain: A Biography*, 3 vols., 1912; Van Wyck Brooks, *The Ordeal of Mark Twain*, 1920; Bernard De Voto, *Mark Twain's America*, 1932; Bernard De Voto, *Mark Twain at Work*, 1942; De Lancey Ferguson, *Mark Twain, Man and Legend*, 1943; Dixon Wector, *Sam Clemens of Hannibal*, 1952; Kenneth A. Lynn, *Mark Twain and Southwestern Humor*, 1959; Walter Blair, *Mark Twain and "Huck Finn,"* 1960; Paul Fatout, *Mark Twain on the Lecture Circuit*, 1960; Henry Nash Smith, *Mark Twain: The Development of a Writer*, 1962; Louis Budd, *Mark Twain: Social Philosopher*, 1962; Justin Kaplan, *Mr. Clemens and Mark Twain*, 1966; James M. Cox, *Mark Twain: The Fate of Humor*, 1966; Maxwell Geismar, *Mark Twain: An American Prophet*, 1970; Hamlin Hill, *Mark Twain: God's Fool*, 1973; William Gibson, *The Art of Mark Twain*, 1976; David E. E. Sloane, *Mark Twain as a Literary Comedian*, 1979; James L. Johnson, *Mark Twain and the Limits of Power: Emerson's God in Ruins*, 1982; Louis J. Budd, *Our Mark Twain: The Making of His Public Personality*, 1983; Sara D. Davis and Philip D. Beidler, eds., *Mythologizing of Mark Twain*, 1984; Everett Emerson, *The Authentic Mark Twain: A Literary Biography of Samuel L. Clemens*, 1984; John Lauber, *The Making of Mark Twain: A Biography*, 1985; Kenneth E. Eble, *Old Clemens and W. D. H.: The Story of a Remarkable Friendship*, 1985; E. Hudson Long and J. R. LeMaster, *The New Mark Twain Handbook*, 1985; James D. Wilson, *A*

Reader's Guide to the Short Stories of Mark Twain, 1987; Susan Gillman, *Dark Twins: Imposture and Identity in Mark Twain's America*, 1989; Sherwood Cummings, *Mark Twain and Science: Adventures of a Mind*, 1989.

TEXTS

"The Notorious Jumping Frog of Calaveras County" from *Mark Twain's Sketches, New and Old*, 1875; *Innocents Abroad*, 1869; "The Late Benjamin Franklin" from *Sketches New and Old*, 1875; "The Story of the Old Ram" from *Roughing It*, 1872; *Old Times on the Mississippi* from *The Atlantic Monthly*, 1875; "Baker's Blue-Jay Yarn" from *A Tramp Abroad*, 1880; "How to Tell a Story" and "Fenimore Cooper's Literary Offences" from *How to Tell a Story and Other Essays*, 1897; "The War Prayer" from *Europe and Elsewhere*, 1923; "Letter IV," "Letters from the Earth" from *What Is Man? and Other Philosophical Writings*, vol. 19 of *The Works of Mark Twain*, ed. Paul Baender, 1973.

The Notorious Jumping
Frog of Calaveras[1] County

In compliance with the request of a friend of mine, who wrote me from the East, I called on good-natured, garrulous old Simon Wheeler, and inquired after my friend's friend, Leonidas W. Smiley, as requested to do, and I hereunto append the result. I have a lurking suspicion that *Leonidas W.* Smiley is a myth; that my friend never knew such a personage; and that he only conjectured that if I asked old Wheeler about him, it would remind him of his infamous *Jim* Smiley, and he would go to work and bore me to death with some exasperating reminiscence of him as long and as tedious as it should be useless to me. If that was the design, it succeeded.

I found Simon Wheeler dozing comfortably by the bar-room stove of the dilapidated tavern in the decayed mining camp of Angel's, and I noticed that he was fat and bald-headed, and had an expression of winning gentleness and simplicity upon his tranquil countenance. He roused up, and gave me good-day. I told him a friend of mine had commissioned me to make some inquiries about a cherished companion of his boyhood named *Leonidas W.* Smiley—*Rev. Leonidas W.* Smiley, a young minister of the Gospel, who he had heard was at one time a resident of Angel's Camp. I added that if Mr. Wheeler could tell me anything about this Rev. Leonidas W. Smiley, I would feel under many obligations to him.

Simon Wheeler backed me into a corner and blockaded me there with his chair, and then sat down and reeled off the monotonous narrative which follows this paragraph. He never smiled, he never frowned, he never changed his voice from the gentle-flowing key to which he tuned his initial sentence, he never betrayed the slightest suspicion of enthusiasm; but all through the interminable narrative there ran a vein of impressive earnestness and sincerity, which showed me plainly that, so far from his imagining that there was anything ridiculous or funny about his story, he regarded it as a really important matter, and admired its two heroes as men of transcendent genius in *finesse*. I let him go on in his own way, and never interrupted him once.

"Rev. Leonidas W. H'm, Reverend Le—well, there was a feller here once by the name of *Jim* Smiley, in the winter of '49—or may be it was the spring of '50—I don't recollect exactly, somehow, though what makes me think it was one or the other is because I remember the big flume warn't finished when he first come to the camp; but any way, he was the curiosest man about always betting on anything that turned

---

[1] "Pronounced Cal-e-*va*-ras" (Twain's note).

up you ever see, if he could get anybody to bet on the other side; and if he couldn't he'd change sides. Any way that suited the other man would suit *him*—any way just so's he got a bet, *he* was satisfied. But still he was lucky, uncommon lucky; he most always come out winner. He was always ready and laying for a chance; there couldn't be no solit'ry thing mentioned but that feller'd offer to bet on it, and take ary side you please, as I was just telling you. If there was a horse-race, you'd find him flush or you'd find him busted at the end of it; if there was a dog-fight, he'd bet on it; if there was a cat-fight, he'd bet on it; if there was a chicken-fight, he'd bet on it; why, if there was two birds setting on a fence, he would bet you which one would fly first; or if there was a camp-meeting, he would be there reg'lar to bet on Parson Walker, which he judged to be the best exhorter about here, and so he was too, and a good man. If he even see a straddle-bug start to go anywheres, he would bet you how long it would take him to get to—to wherever he was going to, and if you took him up, he would foller that straddle-bug to Mexico but what he would find out where he was bound for and how long he was on the road. Lots of the boys here has seen that Smiley, and can tell you about him. Why, it never made no difference to *him*—he'd bet on *any* thing—the dangdest feller. Parson Walker's wife laid very sick once, for a good while, and it seemed as if they warn't going to save her; but one morning he come in, and Smiley up and asked him how she was, and he said she was considable better—thank the Lord for his inf'nit mercy—and coming on so smart that with the blessing of Prov'dence she'd get well yet; and Smiley, before he thought says, "Well, I'll resk two-and-a-half she don't anyway."

Thish-yer Smiley had a mare—the boys called her the fifteen-minute nag, but that was only in fun, you know, because of course she was faster than that—and he used to win money on that horse, for all she was so slow and always had the asthma, or the distemper, or the consumption, or something of that kind. They used to give her two or three hundred yards' start, and then pass her under way; but always at the fag-end of the race she'd get excited and desperate-like, and come cavorting and straddling up, and scattering her legs around limber, sometimes in the air, and sometimes out to one side amongst the fences, and kicking up m-o-r-e dust and raising m-o-r-e racket with her coughing and sneezing and blowing her nose—and *always* fetch up at the stand just about a neck ahead, as near as you could cipher it down.

And he had a little small bull-pup, that to look at him you'd think he warn't worth a cent but to set around and look ornery and lay for a chance to steal something. But as soon as money was up on him he was a different dog; his under-jaw'd begin to stick out like the fo'castle of a steamboat, and his teeth would uncover and shine like the furnaces. And a dog might tackle him and bully-rag him, and bite him, and throw him over his shoulder two or three times, and Andrew Jackson—which was the name of the pup—Andrew Jackson would never let on but what *he* was satisfied, and hadn't expected nothing else—and the bets being doubled and doubled on the other side all the time, till the money was all up; and then all of a sudden he would grab that other dog jest by the j'int of his hind leg and freeze to it—not chaw, you understand, but only just grip and hang on till they throwed up the sponge, if it was a year. Smiley always come out winner on that pup, till he harnessed a dog once that didn't have no hind legs, because they'd been sawed off in a circular saw, and when the thing had gone along far enough, and the money was all up, and he come to make a snatch for his pet holt, he see in a minute how he'd been imposed on, and how the other dog had him in the door, so to speak, and he 'peared surprised, and then he looked sorter discouraged-like, and didn't try no more to win the fight, and so he got shucked out bad. He give Smiley a look, as much as to say his heart was broke, and it was *his* fault, for putting up a dog that hadn't no hind legs for him to take holt of, which was his main dependence in a fight, and then he limped off a piece and laid down and died. It was a good pup, was that Andrew Jackson, and would have made a name for hisself if he'd lived, for the stuff was in him and he had genius—I know it, because he hadn't no opportunities to speak of, and it don't stand to reason that a dog could make such a fight as he could under them circumstances if he hadn't no talent. It always makes me feel sorry when I think of that last fight of his'n, and the way it turned out.

Well, thish-yer Smiley had rat-tarriers, and chicken cocks, and tom-cats and all them kind of things, till you couldn't rest, and you couldn't fetch nothing for him to bet on but he'd match you. He ketched a frog one day, and took him home, and said he cal'lated to educate him; and so he never done nothing for three months but set in his back yard and learn that frog to jump. And you bet you he *did* learn him, too. He'd give him a little punch behind, and the next minute you'd see that frog whirling in the air like a doughnut—see him turn one summerset, or may be a couple, if he got a good start, and come down flat-footed and all right, like a cat. He got him up so in the matter of ketching flies, and kep' him in practice so constant, that he'd nail a fly every time as fur as he could see him. Smiley said all a frog wanted was education, and he could do 'most anything—and I believe him. Why, I've seen him set Dan'l Webster down here on this floor—Dan'l Webster was the name of the frog—and sing out, "Flies, Dan'l, flies!" and quicker'n you could wink he'd spring straight up and snake a fly off'n the counter there, and flop down on the floor ag'in as solid as a gob of mud, and fall to scratching the side of his head with his hind foot as indifferent as if he hadn't no idea he'd been doin' any more'n any frog might do. You never see a frog so modest and straightfor'ard as he was, for all he was so gifted. And when it come to fair and square jumping on a dead level, he could get over more ground at one straddle than any animal of his breed you ever see. Jumping on a dead level was his strong suit, you understand; and when it come to that, Smiley would ante up money on him as long as he had a red. Smiley was monstrous proud of his frog, and well he might be, for fellers that had traveled and been everywheres, all said he laid over any frog that ever *they* see.

Well, Smiley kep' the beast in a little lattice box, and he used to fetch him down town sometimes and lay for a bet. One day a feller—a stranger in the camp, he was—come acrost him with his box, and says:

"What might it be that you've got in the box?"

And Smiley says, sorter indifferent-like, "It might be a parrot, or it might be a canary, maybe, but it ain't—it's only just a frog."

And the feller took it, and looked at it careful, and turned it round this way and that, and says, "H'm—so 'tis. Well, what's *he* good for?"

"Well," Smiley says, easy and careless, "he's good enough for *one* thing, I should judge—he can outjump any frog in Calaveras county."

The feller took the box again, and took another long, particular look, and give it back to Smiley, and says, very deliberate, "Well," he says, "I don't see no p'ints about that frog that's any better'n any other frog."

"Maybe you don't," Smiley says. "Maybe you understand frogs and maybe you don't understand 'em; maybe you've had experience, and maybe you ain't only a amature, as it were. Anyways, I've got *my* opinion and I'll resk forty dollars that he can outjump any frog in Calaveras county."

And the feller studied a minute, and then says, kinder sad like, "Well, I'm only a stranger here, and I ain't got no frog; but if I had a frog, I'd bet you."

And then Smiley says, "That's all right—that's all right—if you'll hold my box a minute, I'll go and get you a frog." And so the feller took the box, and put up his forty dollars along with Smiley's, and set down to wait.

So he set there a good while thinking and thinking to hisself, and then he got the frog out and prized his mouth open and took a teaspoon and filled him full of quail shot—filled him pretty near up to his chin—and set him on the floor. Smiley he went to the swamp and slopped around in the mud for a long time, and finally he ketched a frog, and fetched him in, and give him to this feller, and says:

"Now, if you're ready, set him alongside of Dan'l, with his fore-paws just even with Dan'l's, and I'll give the word." Then he says, "One—two—three—*git!*" and him and the feller touched up the frogs from behind, and the new frog hopped off lively, but

Dan'l give a heave, and hysted up his shoulders—so—like a Frenchman, but it warn't no use—he couldn't budge; he was planted as solid as a church, and he couldn't no more stir than if he was anchored out. Smiley was a good deal surprised, and he was disgusted too, but he didn't have no idea what the matter was, of course.

The feller took the money and started away; and when he was going out at the door, he sorter jerked his thumb over his shoulder—so—at Dan'l, and says again, very deliberate, "Well," he says "*I* don't see no p'ints about that frog that's any better'n any other frog."

Smiley he stood scratching his head and looking down at Dan'l a long time, and at last he says, "I do wonder what in the nation[2] that frog throw'd off for—I wonder if there ain't something the matter with him—he 'pears to look mighty baggy, somehow." And he ketched Dan'l by the nap of the neck, and hefted him, and says, "Why blame my cats if he don't weigh five pound!" and turned him upside down and he belched out a double handful of shot. And then he see how it was, and he was the maddest man—he set the frog down and took out after that feller, but he never ketched him. And—"

[Here Simon Wheeler heard his name called from the front yard, and got up to see what was wanted.] And turning to me as he moved away, he said: "Just set where you are, stranger, and rest easy—I ain't going to be gone a second."

But, by your leave, I did not think that a continuation of the history of the enterprising vagabond *Jim* Smiley would be likely to afford me much information concerning the Rev. *Leonidas W.* Smiley, and so I started away.

At the door I met the sociable Wheeler returning, and he button-holed me and re-commenced:

"Well,thish-yer Smiley had a yaller one-eyed cow that didn't have no tail, only jest a short stump like a bannanner, and—"

However, lacking both time and inclination, I did not wait to hear about the afflicted cow, but took my leave.

1865

from Innocents Abroad[1]

[THE OLD MASTERS]

Here, in Milan, in an ancient tumble-down ruin of a church, is the mournful wreck of the most celebrated painting in the world—"The Last Supper," by Leonardo da Vinci.[2] We are not infallible judges of pictures, but of course we went there to see this wonderful painting, once so beautiful, always so worshipped by masters in art, and forever to be famous in song and story. And the first thing that occurred was the infliction on us of a placard fairly reeking with wretched English. Take a morsel of it:

> "Bartholomew (that is the first figure on the left hand side at the spectator,) uncertain and doubtful about what he thinks to have heard, and upon which he wants to be assured by himself at Christ and by no others."

----

[2]Polite form of "damnation."

[1]In 1867 Twain sailed with other tourists (all American "innocents") on the steamship *Quaker City* to visit European countries, Egypt, and the Holy Land. Twain's way was paid by newspapers in return for accounts of the journey that he sent them. *The Innocents Abroad, or The New Pilgrim's Progress* was published in 1869. Excerpts appearing here are taken from

Chapters 19 and 53.

[2]Leonardo da Vinci (1452–1519), Italian Renaissance master, painted "The Last Supper" (1495–98?) on the refectory wall of Santa Maria delle Grazie, Milan. It depicts the agitation among the twelve apostles at hearing from Jesus that one of them would betray him. The apostles included Bartholomew, Peter, and Judas Iscariot, the betrayer.

Good, isn't it? And then Peter is described as "argumenting in a threatening and angrily condition at Judas Iscariot."

This paragraph recalls the picture. "The Last Supper" is painted on the dilapidated wall of what was a little chapel attached to the main church in ancient times, I suppose. It is battered and scarred in every direction, and stained and discolored by time, and Napoleon's horses kicked the legs off most the disciples when they (the horses, not the disciples,) were stabled there more than half a century ago.

I recognized the old picture in a moment—the Saviour with bowed head seated at the centre of a long, rough table with scattering fruits and dishes upon it, and six disciples on either side in their long robes, talking to each other—the picture from which all engravings and all copies have been made for three centuries. Perhaps no living man has ever known an attempt to paint the Lord's Supper differently. The world seems to have become settled in the belief, long ago, that it is not possible for human genius to outdo this creation of Da Vinci's. I suppose painters will go on copying it as long as any of the original is left visible to the eye. There were a dozen easels in the room, and as many artists transferring the great picture to their canvases. Fifty proofs of steel engravings and lithographs were scattered around, too. And as usual, I could not help noticing how superior the copies were to the original, that is, to my inexperienced eye. Wherever you find a Raphael, a Rubens, a Michael Angelo, a Caracci,[3] or a Da Vinci (and we see them every day,) you find artists copying them, and the copies are always the handsomest. May be the originals were handsome when they were new, but they are not now.

This picture is about thirty feet long, and ten or twelve high, I should think, and the figures are at least life size. It is one of the largest paintings in Europe.

The colors are dimmed with age; the countenances are scaled and marred, and nearly all expression is gone from them; the hair is a dead blur upon the wall, and there is no life in the eyes. Only the attitudes are certain.

People come here from all parts of the world, and glorify this masterpiece. They stand entranced before it with bated breath and parted lips, and when they speak, it is only in the catchy ejaculations of rapture:

"O, wonderful!"

"Such expression!"

"Such grace of attitude!"

"Such dignity!"

"Such faultless drawing!"

"Such matchless coloring!"

"Such feeling!"

"What delicacy of touch!"

"What sublimity of conception!"

"A vision! a vision!"

I only envy these people; I envy them their honest admiration, if it be honest—their delight, if they feel delight. I harbor no animosity toward any of them. But at the same time the thought *will* intrude itself upon me, How can they see what is not visible? What would you think of a man who looked at some decayed, blind, toothless, pock-marked Cleopatra,[4] and said: "What matchless beauty! What soul! What expression!" What would you think of a man who gazed upon a dingy, foggy sunset, and said: "What sublimity! what feeling! what richness of coloring!" What would you think of a man who stared in ecstasy upon a desert of stumps and said: "Oh, my soul, my beating heart, what a noble forest is here!"

You would think that those men had an astonishing talent for seeing things that had already passed away. It was what I thought when I stood before the Last Supper

---

[3]Master painters, Raphael (1483–1520), Italian; Rubens (1577–1640), Flemish; Michaelangelo (1475–1564), Italian; and the Carracci family of Italian painters.

[4]Egyptian Queen Cleopatra (69–30 B.C.) was famed for her beauty.

and heard men apostrophizing wonders, and beauties and perfections which had faded out of the picture and gone, a hundred years before they were born. We can imagine the beauty that was once in an aged face; we can imagine the forest if we see the stumps; but we can not absolutely *see* these things when they are not there. I am willing to believe that the eye of the practiced artist can rest upon the Last Supper and renew a lustre where only a hint of it is left, supply a tint that has faded away, restore an expression that is gone; patch, and color, and add, to the dull canvas until at last its figures shall stand before him aglow with the life, the feeling, the freshness, yea, with all the noble beauty that was theirs when first they came from the hand of the master. But *I* can not work this miracle. Can those other uninspired visitors do it, or do they only happily imagine they do?

After reading so much about it, I am satisfied that the Last Supper was a very miracle of art once. But it was three hundred years ago.

It vexes me to hear people talk so glibly of "feeling," "expression," "tone," and those other easily acquired and inexpensive technicalities of art that make such a fine show in conversations concerning pictures. There is not one man in seventy-five hundred that can tell *what* a pictured face is intended to express. There is not one man in five hundred that can go into a court-room and be sure that he will not mistake some harmless innocent of a juryman for the black-hearted assassin on trial. Yet such people talk of "character" and presume to interpret "expression" in pictures. There is an old story that Matthews,[5] the actor, was once lauding the ability of the human face to express the passions and emotions hidden in the breast. He said the countenance could disclose what was passing in the heart plainer than the tongue could.

"Now," he said, "observe my face—what does it express?"

"Despair!"

"Bah, it expresses peaceful resignation! What does *this* express?"

"Rage!"

"Stuff! it means terror! *This!*"

"Imbecility!"

"Fool! It is smothered ferocity! Now *this!*"

"Joy!"

"Oh, perdition! *Any* ass can see it means insanity!"

Expression! People coolly pretend to read it who would think themselves presumptuous if they pretended to interpret the hieroglyphics on the obelisks of Luxor[6]—yet they are fully as competent to do the one thing as the other. I have heard two very intelligent critics speak of Murillo's Immaculate Conception (now in the museum at Seville,)[7] within the past few days. One said:

"Oh, the Virgin's face is full of the ecstasy of a joy that is complete—that leaves nothing more to be desired on earth!"

The other said:

"Ah, that wonderful face is so humble, so pleading—it says as plainly as words could say it: 'I fear; I tremble; I am unworthy. But Thy will be done; sustain Thou Thy servant!'"

The reader can see the picture in any drawing-room; it can be easily recognized: the Virgin (the only young and really beautiful Virgin that was ever painted by one of the old masters, some of us think,) stands in the crescent of the new moon, with a multitude of cherubs hovering about her, and more coming; her hands are crossed upon her breast, and upon her uplifted countenance falls a glory out of the heavens. The reader may amuse himself, if he chooses, in trying to determine which of these gentlemen read the Virgin's "expression" aright, or if either of them did it.

---

[5]Charles Matthews (1776–1835), English comedian whose entertainment included songs, recitations, and imitations.
[6]Occupies now a part of the site of ancient Egyptian Thebes, on the banks of the Nile; contains many ruins.
[7]Bartolomé Esteban Murillo (1617–1682), Spanish painter, one of whose masterpieces is the "Immaculate Conception."

Any one who is acquainted with the old masters will comprehend how much the Last Supper is damaged when I say that the spectator can not really tell, now, whether the disciples are Hebrews or Italians. These ancient painters never succeeded in denationalizing themselves. The Italian artists painted Italian Virgins, the Dutch painted Dutch Virgins, the Virgins of the French painters were Frenchwomen—none of them ever put into the face of the Madonna that indescribable something which proclaims the Jewess, whether you find her in New York, in Constantinople, in Paris, Jerusalem, or in the Empire of Morocco. I saw in the Sandwich Islands, once, a picture, copied by a talented German artist from an engraving in one of the American illustrated papers. It was an allegory, representing Mr. Davis[8] in the act of signing a secession act or some such document. Over him hovered the ghost of Washington in warning attitude, and in the background a troop of shadowy soldiers in Continental uniform were limping with shoeless, bandaged feet through a driving snow-storm. Valley Forge was suggested, of course. The copy seemed accurate, and yet there was a discrepancy somewhere. After a long examination I discovered what it was—the shadowy soldiers were all Germans! Jeff. Davis was a German! even the hovering ghost was a German ghost! The artist had unconsciously worked his nationality into the picture. To tell the truth, I am getting a little perplexed about John the Baptist and his portraits. In France I finally grew reconciled to him as a Frenchman; here he is unquestionably an Italian. What next? Can it be possible that the painters make John the Baptist a Spaniard in Madrid and an Irishman in Dublin?

[THE TOMB OF ADAM]

The Greek Chapel is the most roomy, the richest and the showiest chapel in the Church of the Holy Sepulchre. Its altar, like that of all the Greek churches, is a lofty screen that extends clear across the chapel, and is gorgeous with gilding and pictures. The numerous lamps that hang before it are of gold and silver, and cost great sums.

But the feature of the place is a short column that rises from the middle of the marble pavement of the chapel, and marks the exact *centre of the earth*. The most reliable traditions tell us that this was known to be the earth's centre, ages ago, and that when Christ was upon earth he set all doubts upon the subject at rest forever, by stating with his own lips that the tradition was correct. Remember, He said that that particular column stood upon the centre of the world. If the centre of the world changes, the column changes its position accordingly. This column has moved three different times, of its own accord. This is because, in great convulsions of nature, at three different times, masses of the earth—whole ranges of mountains, probably—have flown off into space, thus lessening the diameter of the earth, and changing the exact locality of its centre by a point or two. This is a very curious and interesting circumstance, and is a withering rebuke to those philosophers who would make us believe that it is not possible for any portion of the earth to fly off into space.

To satisfy himself that this spot was really the centre of the earth, a sceptic once paid well for the privilege of ascending to the dome of the church to see if the sun gave him a shadow at noon. He came down perfectly convinced. The day was very cloudy and the sun threw no shadows at all; but the man was satisfied that if the sun had come out and made shadows it could not have made any for him. Proofs like these are not to be set aside by the idle tongues of cavilers.[1] To such as are not bigoted, and are willing to be convinced, they carry a conviction that nothing can ever shake.

---

[8]Jefferson Davis (1808–1889), president of the Confederate States of America, which seceded from the Union, causing the Civil War (1861–65).
[1]Quibbling critics.

If even greater proofs than those I have mentioned are wanted, to satisfy the headstrong and the foolish that this is the genuine centre of the earth, they are here. The greatest of them lies in the fact that from under this very column was taken the *dust from which Adam was made.* This can surely be regarded in the light of a settler. It is not likely that the original first man would have been made from an inferior quality of earth when it was entirely convenient to get first quality from the world's centre. This will strike any reflecting mind forcibly. That Adam was formed of dirt procured in this very spot is amply proven by the fact that in six thousand years no man has ever been able to prove that the dirt was *not* procured here whereof he was made.

It is a singular circumstance that right under the roof of this same great church, and not far away from that illustrious column, Adam himself, the father of the human race, lies buried. There is no question that he is actually buried in the grave which is pointed out as his—there can be none—because it has never yet been proven that that grave is not the grave in which he is buried.

The tomb of Adam! How touching it was, here in a land of strangers, far away from home, and friends, and all who cared for me, thus to discover the grave of a blood relation. True, a distant one, but still a relation. The unerring instinct of nature thrilled its recognition. The fountain of my filial affection was stirred to its profoundest depths, and I gave way to tumultuous emotion. I leaned upon a pillar and burst into tears. I deem it no shame to have wept over the grave of my poor dead relative. Let him who would sneer at my emotion close this volume here, for he will find little to his taste in my journeyings through Holy Land. Noble old man—he did not live to see me—he did not live to see his child. And I—I—alas, I did not live to see *him.* Weighed down by sorrow and disappointment, he died before I was born— six thousand brief summers before I was born. But let us try to bear it with fortitude. Let us trust that he is better off, where he is. Let us take comfort in the thought that his loss is our eternal gain.

1869

The Late Benjamin Franklin

["Never put off till to-morrow what you can do day
after to-morrow just as well."—B. F.][1]

This party was one of those persons whom they call Philosophers. He was twins, being born simultaneously in two different houses in the city of Boston. These houses remain unto this day, and have signs upon them worded in accordance with the facts. The signs are considered well enough to have, though not necessary, because the inhabitants point out the two birth-places to the stranger anyhow, and sometimes as often as several times in the same day. The subject of this memoir was of a vicious disposition, and early prostituted his talents to the invention of maxims and aphorisms calculated to inflict suffering upon the rising generation of all subsequent ages. His simplest acts, also, were contrived with a view to their being held up for the emulation of boys for ever—boys who might otherwise have been happy. It was in this spirit that he became the son of a soap-boiler, and probably for no other reason than that the efforts of all future boys who tried to be anything might be looked upon with suspicion unless they were the sons of soap-boilers. With a malevolence which is without parallel in history, he would work all day, and then sit up

---

[1]In *Poor Richard's Almanack* (1733–58) and in *The Way to Wealth* (1758), Benjamin Franklin (1706–1790) compiled and created many pithy maxims, including "Have you somewhat to do tomorrow, do it today."

nights, and let on to be studying algebra by the light of a smouldering fire, so that all other boys might have to do that also, or else have Benjamin Franklin thrown up to them. Not satisfied with these proceedings, he had a fashion of living wholly on bread and water, and studying astronomy at meal time—a thing which has brought affliction to millions of boys since, whose fathers had read Franklin's pernicious biography.[2]

His maxims were full of animosity towards boys. Nowadays a boy cannot follow out a single natural instinct without tumbling over some of those everlasting aphorisms and hearing from Franklin on the spot. If he buys two cents' worth of peanuts, his father says, "Remember what Franklin has said, my son—'A groat a day's a penny a year;'"[3] and the comfort is all gone out of those peanuts. If he wants to spin his top when he has done work, his father quotes, "Procrastination is the thief of time." If he does a virtuous action, he never gets any thing for it, because "Virtue is its own reward." And that boy is hounded to death and robbed of his natural rest, because Franklin said once, in one of his inspired flights of malignity—

"Early to bed and early to rise
Makes a man healthy and wealthy and wise."

As if it were any object to a boy to be healthy and wealthy and wise on such terms. The sorrow that that maxim has cost me through my parents' experimenting on me with it, tongue cannot tell. The legitimate result is my present state of general debility, indigence, and mental aberration. My parents used to have me up before nine o'clock in the morning, sometimes, when I was a boy. If they had let me take my natural rest, where would I have been now? Keeping store, no doubt, and respected by all.

And what an adroit old adventurer the subject of this memoir was! In order to get a chance to fly his kite on Sunday he used to hang a key on the string and let on to be fishing for lightning. And a guileless public would go home chirping about the "wisdom" and the "genius" of the hoary Sabbath-breaker. If anybody caught him playing "mumble-peg"[4] by himself, after the age of sixty, he would immediately appear to be ciphering out how the grass grew—as if it was any of his business. My grandfather knew him well, and he says Franklin was always fixed—always ready. If a body, during his old age, happened on him unexpectedly when he was catching flies, or making mud pies, or sliding on a cellar-door, he would immediately look wise, and rip out a maxim, and walk off with his nose in the air and his cap turned wrong side before, trying to appear absent-minded and eccentric. He was a hard lot.

He invented a stove that would smoke your head off in four hours by the clock. One can see the almost devilish satisfaction he took in it by his giving it his name.

He was always proud of telling how he entered Philadelphia for the first time, with nothing in the world but two shillings in his pocket and four rolls of bread under his arm. But really, when you come to examine it critically, it was nothing. Anybody could have done it.

To the subject of this memoir belongs the honor of recommending the army to go back to bows and arrows in place of bayonets and muskets. He observed, with his customary force, that the bayonet was very well under some circumstances, but that he doubted whether it could be used with accuracy at a long range.

---

[2]Franklin wrote his unfinished *Autobiography* in separate stages, beginning in 1771. Parts of the work appeared abroad in translation before an American edition—incomplete— was issued in 1818. The complete work, with accurate text, was published in English for the first time in 1867. In the work, addressed to his son, Franklin described his rise from "poverty and obscurity" to "a state of affluence and some degree of reputation in the world" through hard work, skill, personal restraint, and an ingratiating personality.

[3]In the 1737 *Almanack*, Franklin wrote: "A Penny sav'd is Twopence clear, A pin a day is a Groat a Year. Save & have. Every little makes a mickle" (pin: little; groat: British coin worth fourpence; mickle: great).

[4]Variant of mumblety-peg, a game in which a knife is thrown from various positions so that the blade sticks in the ground. The loser would have to pull a peg from the ground with his teeth.

Benjamin Franklin did a great many notable things for his country, and made her young name to be honored in many lands as the mother of such a son. It is not the idea of this memoir to ignore that or cover it up. No; the simple idea of it is to snub those pretentious maxims of his, which he worked up with a great show of originality out of truisms that had become wearisome platitudes as early as the dispersion from Babel;[5] and also to snub his stove, and his military inspirations, his unseemly endeavor to make himself conspicuous when he entered Philadelphia, and his flying his kite and fooling away his time in all sorts of such ways when he ought to have been foraging for soapfat, or constructing candles. I merely desired to do away with somewhat of the prevalent calamitous idea among heads of families that Franklin *acquired* his great genius by working for nothing, studying by moonlight, and getting up in the night instead of waiting till morning like a Christian; and that this programme, rigidly inflicted, will make a Franklin of every father's fool. It is time these gentlemen were finding out that these execrable eccentricities of instinct and conduct are only the *evidences* of genius, not the *creators* of it. I wish I had been the father of my parents long enough to make them comprehend this truth, and thus prepare them to let their son have an easier time of it. When I was a child I had to boil soap, notwithstanding my father was wealthy, and I had to get up early and study geometry at breakfast, and peddle my own poetry, and do everything just as Franklin did, in the solemn hope that I would be a Franklin some day. And here I am.

c. 1870   *1875*

from **Roughing It**[1]

THE STORY OF THE OLD RAM

CHAPTER LIII

Every now and then, in these days, the boys used to tell me I ought to get one Jim Blaine to tell me the stirring story of his grandfather's old ram—but they always added that I must not mention the matter unless Jim was drunk at the time—just comfortably and sociably drunk. They kept this up until my curiosity was on the rack to hear the story. I got to haunting Blaine; but it was of no use, the boys always found fault with his condition; he was often moderately but never satisfactorily drunk. I never watched a man's condition with such absorbing interest, such anxious solicitude; I never so pined to see a man uncompromisingly drunk before. At last, one evening I hurried to his cabin, for I learned that this time his situation was such that even the most fastidious could find no fault with it—he was tranquilly, serenely, symmetrically drunk—not a hiccup to mar his voice, not a cloud upon his brain thick enough to obscure his memory. As I entered, he was sitting upon an empty powder-keg, with a clay pipe in one hand and the other raised to command silence. His face was round, red, and very serious; his throat was bare and his hair tumbled; in general appearance and costume he was a stalwart miner of the period. On the pine table stood a candle, and its dim light revealed "the boys" sitting here and there on bunks, candle-boxes, powder-kegs, etc. They said:

"Sh—! Don't speak—he's going to commence."

---

[5]A reference to the Biblical explanation for the diversity of languages. For their arrogance in building a tower at Babel to reach the heavens, the Lord confused the speech of men and dispersed them over the earth (Genesis 11:1–9).
[1]*Roughing It* was based on Twain's journey from St. Louis to the American West—including Nevada, Mormon country, Virginia City, San Francisco—and the Sandwich Islands (now the Hawaiian Islands). The work is chock full of frontier stories, character sketches, and tall tales.

THE STORY OF THE OLD RAM

I found a seat at once, and Blaine said:

"I don't reckon them times will ever come again. There never was a more bullier old ram than what he was. Grandfather fetched him from Illinois—got him of a man by the name of Yates—Bill Yates—maybe you might have heard of him; his father was a deacon—Baptist—and he was a rustler, too; a man had to get up ruther early to get the start of old Thankful Yates; it was him that put the Greens up to jining teams with my grandfather when he moved west. Seth Green was prob'ly the pick of the flock; he married a Wilkerson—Sarah Wilkerson—good cretur, she was—one of the likeliest heifers that was ever raised in old Stoddard, everybody said that knowed her. She could heft a bar'l of flour as easy as I can flirt a flapjack. And spin? Don't mention it! Independent? Humph! When Sile Hawkins come a browsing around her, she let him know that for all his tin he couldn't trot in harness alongside of *her*. You see, Sile Hawkins was—no, it warn't Sile Hawkins, after all—it was a galoot by the name of Filkins—I disremember his first name; but he *was* a stump—come into pra'r meeting drunk, one night, hooraying for Nixon, becuz he thought it was a primary; and old deacon Ferguson up and scooted him through the window and he lit on old Miss Jefferson's head, poor old filly. She was a good soul—had a glass eye and used to lend it to old Miss Wagner, that hadn't any, to receive company in; it warn't big enough, and when Miss Wagner warn't noticing, it would get twisted around in the socket, and look up, maybe, or out to one side, and every which way, while t' other one was looking as straight ahead as a spy-glass. Grown people didn't mind it, but it most always made the children cry, it was so sort of scary. She tried packing it in raw cotton, but it wouldn't work, somehow—the cotton would get loose and stick out and look so kind of awful that the children couldn't stand it no way. She was always dropping it out, and turning up her old dead-light on the company empty, and making them oncomfortable, becuz *she* never could tell when it hopped out, being blind on that side, you see. So somebody would have to hunch her and say, 'Your game eye has fetched loose, Miss Wagner dear'—and then all of them would have to sit and wait till she jammed it in again—wrong side before, as a general thing, and green as a bird's egg, being a bashful cretur and easy sot back before company. But being wrong side before warn't much difference, anyway, becuz her own eye was sky-blue and the glass one was yaller on the front side, so whichever way she turned it it didn't match nohow. Old Miss Wagner was considerable on the borrow, she was. When she had a quilting, or Dorcas S'iety[2] at her house she gen'ally borrowed Miss Higgins's wooden leg to stump around on; it was considerable shorter than her other pin, but much *she* minded that. She said she couldn't abide crutches when she had company, becuz they were so slow; said when she had company and things had to be done, she wanted to get up and hump herself. She was as bald as a jug, and so she used to borrow Miss Jacops's wig—Miss Jacops was the coffin-peddler's wife—a ratty old buzzard, he was, that used to go roosting around where people was sick, waiting for 'em; and there that old rip would sit all day, in the shade, on a coffin that he judged would fit the can'idate; and if it was a slow customer and kind of uncertain, he'd fetch his rations and blanket along and sleep in the coffin nights. He was anchored out that way, in frosty weather, for about three weeks, once, before old Robbins's place, waiting for him; and after that, for as much as two years, Jacops was not on speaking terms with the old man, on account of his disapp'inting him. He got one of his feet froze, and lost money, too, becuz old Robbins took a favorable turn and got well. The next time Robbins got sick, Jacops tried to make up with him, and varnished up the same old coffin and fetched it along; but old Robbins was too many for

---

[2]Sewing society that made clothes for the poor, named after the Biblical Dorcas (Acts 9:36–41) who made garments for the needy.

him; he had him in, and 'peared to be powerful weak; he bought the coffin for ten dollars and Jacops was to pay it back and twenty-five more besides if Robbins didn't like the coffin after he'd tried it. And then Robbins died, and at the funeral he bursted off the lid and riz up in his shroud and told the parson to let up on the performances, becuz he could *not* stand such a coffin as that. You see he had been in a trance once before, when he was young, and he took the chances on another, cal'lating that if he made the trip it was money in his pocket, and if he missed fire he couldn't lose a cent. And by George he sued Jacops for the rhino[3] and got jedgment; and he set up the coffin in his back parlor and said he 'lowed to take his time, now. It was always an aggravation to Jacops, the way that miserable old thing acted. He moved back to Indiany pretty soon—went to Wellsville—Wellsville was the place the Hogadorns was from. Mighty fine family. Old Maryland stock. Old Squire Hogadorn could carry around more mixed licker, and cuss better than most any man I ever see. His second wife was the widder Billings—she that was Becky Martin; her dam was deacon Dunlap's first wife. Her oldest child, Maria, married a missionary and died in grace—et up by the savages. They et *him*, too, poor feller—biled him. It warn't the custom, so they say, but they explained to friends of his'n that went down there to bring away his things, that they'd tried missionaries every other way and never could get any good out of 'em—and so it annoyed all his relations to find out that that man's life was fooled away just out of a dern'd experiment, so to speak. But mind you, there ain't anything ever reely lost; everything that people can't understand and don't see the reason of does good if you only hold on and give it a fair shake; Prov'dence don't fire no blank ca'tridges, boys. That there missionary's substance, unbeknowns to himself, actu'ly converted every last one of them heathens that took a chance at the barbacue. Nothing ever fetched them but that. Don't tell *me* it was an accident that he was biled. There ain't no such a thing as an accident. When my uncle Lem was leaning up agin a scaffolding once, sick, or drunk, or suthin, an Irishman with a hod full of bricks fell on him out of the third story and broke the old man's back in two places. People said it was an accident. Much accident there was about that. He didn't know what he was there for, but he was there for a good object. If he hadn't been there the Irishman would have been killed. Nobody can ever make me believe anything different from that. Uncle Lem's dog was there. Why didn't the Irishman fall on the dog? Becuz the dog would a seen him a coming and stood from under. That's the reason the dog warn't appinted. A dog can't be depended on to carry out a special providence. Mark my words it was a put-up thing. Accidents don't happen, boys. Uncle Lem's dog—I wish you could a seen that dog. He was a reglar shepherd—or ruther he was part bull and part shepherd—splendid animal; belonged to parson Hagar before Uncle Lem got him. Parson Hagar belonged to the Western Reserve Hagars; prime family; his mother was a Watson; one of his sisters married a Wheeler; they settled in Morgan county, and he got nipped by the machinery in a carpet factory and went through in less than a quarter of a minute; his widder bought the piece of carpet that had his remains wove in, and people come a hundred mile to 'tend the funeral. There was fourteen yards in the piece. She wouldn't let them roll him up, but planted him just so—full length. The church was middling small where they preached the funeral, and they had to let one end of the coffin stick out of the window. They didn't bury him—they planted one end, and let him stand up, same as a monument. And they nailed a sign on it and put—put on— put on it—sacred to—the m-e-m-o-r-y—of fourteen y-a-r-d-s—of three-ply—car - - - pet—containing all that was—m-o-r-t-a-l—of—of—W-i-l-l-i-a-m— W-h-e—"

Jim Blaine had been growing gradually drowsy and drowsier—his head nodded, once, twice, three times—dropped peacefully upon his breast, and he fell tranquilly

---

[3]Money.

asleep. The tears were running down the boys' cheeks—they were suffocating with suppressed laughter—and had been from the start, though I had never noticed it. I perceived that I was "sold." I learned then that Jim Blaine's peculiarity was that whenever he reached a certain stage of intoxication, no human power could keep him from setting out, with impressive unction, to tell about a wonderful adventure which he had once had with his grandfather's old ram—and the mention of the ram in the first sentence was as far as any man had ever heard him get, concerning it. He always maundered off, interminably, from one thing to another, till his whisky got the best of him and he fell asleep. What the thing was that happened to him and his grandfather's old ram is a dark mystery to this day, for nobody has ever yet found out.

1872

from Old Times on the Mississippi¹

I

"Cub" Wants to Be a Pilot

When I was a boy, there was but one permanent ambition among my comrades in our village² on the west bank of the Mississippi River. That was, to be a steamboatman. We had transient ambitions of other sorts, but they were only transient. When a circus came and went, it left us all burning to become clowns; the first negro minstrel show that came to our section left us all suffering to try that kind of life; now and then we had a hope that if we lived and were good, God would permit us to be pirates. These ambitions faded out, each in its turn; but the ambition to be a steamboatman always remained.

Once a day a cheap, gaudy packet arrived upward from St. Louis, and another downward from Keokuk.³ Before these events had transpired, the day was glorious with expectancy; after they had transpired, the day was a dead and empty thing. Not only the boys, but the whole village, felt this. After all these years I can picture that old time to myself now, just as it was then: the white town drowsing in the sunshine of a summer's morning; the streets empty, or pretty nearly so; one or two clerks sitting in front of the Water Street stores, with their splint-bottomed chairs tilted back against the wall, chins on breasts, hats slouched over their faces, asleep—with shingle-shavings enough around to show what broke them down; a sow and a litter of pigs loafing along the sidewalk, doing a good business in water-melon rinds and seeds; two or three lonely little freight piles scattered about the "levee;" a pile of "skids" on the slope of the stone-paved wharf, and the fragrant town drunkard asleep in the shadow of them; two or three wood flats at the head of the wharf, but nobody to listen to the peaceful lapping of the wavelets against them; the great Mississippi, the majestic, the magnificent Mississippi, rolling its mile-wide tide along, shining in the sun; the dense forest away on the other side; the "point" above the

---

¹In October 1874, Twain wrote to the editor of the *Atlantic Monthly*, William Dean Howells, that he had been talking to a friend about "old Mississippi days of steamboating glory and grandeur" as he saw them during five years *"from the pilot house."* The friend, the Rev. Joseph Twichell, exclaimed: "What a virgin subject to hurl into a magazine." Howells was enthusiastic and the result was *Old Times on the Mississippi*, which appeared in seven installments in the *Atlantic Monthly*, January–July 1875. The ease with which Twain reconstructed his Mississippi days demonstrated to him that he had, locked in his memory, a great mass of material that could be mined for future books—as *The Adventures of Tom Sawyer* (1876), and *Adventures of Huckleberry Finn* (1885). In 1883, Twain revisited the scenes of his boyhood and youth and wrote *Life on the Mississippi*. The earlier work, however, has emotional unity and imaginative energy that time has not dispelled. It deserves to be read by itself as one of Twain's greatest books, perhaps his most impressive narrative of initiation.
²Hannibal, Missouri.
³River City in Iowa.

town, and the "point" below, bounding the river-glimpse and turning it into a sort of sea, and withal a very still and brilliant and lonely one. Presently a film of dark smoke appears above one of those remote "points;" instantly a negro drayman,[4] famous for his quick eye and prodigious voice, lifts up the cry, "S-t-e-a-m-boat a-comin'!" and the scene changes! The town drunkard stirs, the clerks wake up, a furious clatter of drays follows, every house and store pours out a human contribution, and all in a twinkling the dead town is alive and moving. Drays, carts, men, boys, all go hurrying from many quarters to a common centre, the wharf. Assembled there, the people fasten their eyes upon the coming boat as upon a wonder they are seeing for the first time. And the boat *is* rather a handsome sight, too. She is long and sharp and trim and pretty; she has two tall, fancy-topped chimneys, with a gilded device of some kind swung between them; a fanciful pilot-house, all glass and "gingerbread," perched on top of the "texas" deck[5] behind them; the paddle-boxes are gorgeous with a picture or with gilded rays above the boat's name; the boiler deck, the hurricane deck, and the texas deck are fenced and ornamented with clean white railings; there is a flag gallantly flying from the jack-staff; the furnace doors are open and the fires glaring bravely; the upper decks are black with passengers; the captain stands by the big bell, calm, imposing, the envy of all; great volumes of the blackest smoke are rolling and tumbling out of the chimneys—a husbanded grandeur created with a bit of pitch pine just before arriving at a town; the crew are grouped on the forecastle; the broad stage is run far out over the port bow, and an envied deck-hand stands picturesquely on the end of it with a coil of rope in his hand; the pent steam is screaming through the gauge-cocks; the captain lifts his hand, a bell rings, the wheels stop; then they turn back, churning the water to foam, and the steamer is at rest. Then such a scramble as there is to get aboard, and to get ashore, and to take in freight and to discharge freight, all at one and the same time; and such a yelling and cursing as the mates facilitate it all with! Ten minutes later the steamer is under way again, with no flag on the jack-staff and no black smoke issuing from the chimneys. After ten more minutes the town is dead again, and the town drunkard asleep by the skids once more.

My father was a justice of the peace, and I supposed he possessed the power of life and death over all men and could hang anybody that offended him. This was distinction enough for me as a general thing; but the desire to be a steamboatman kept intruding, nevertheless. I first wanted to be a cabin-boy, so that I could come out with a white apron on and shake a table-cloth over the side, where all my old comrades could see me; later I thought I would rather be the deck-hand who stood on the end of the stage-plank with the coil of rope in his hand, because he was particularly conspicuous. But these were only daydreams—they were too heavenly to be contemplated as real possibilities. By and by one of our boys went away. He was not heard of for a long time. At last he turned up as apprentice engineer or "striker" on a steamboat. This thing shook the bottom out of all my Sunday-school teachings. That boy had been notoriously worldly, and I just the reverse; yet he was exalted to this eminence, and I left in obscurity and misery. There was nothing generous about this fellow in his greatness. He would always manage to have a rusty bolt to scrub while his boat tarried at our town, and he would sit on the inside guard and scrub it, where we could all see him and envy him and loathe him. And whenever his boat was laid up he would come home and swell around the town in his blackest and greasiest clothes, so that nobody could help remembering that he was a steamboatman; and he used all sorts of steamboat technicalities in his talk, as if he were so used to them that he forgot common people could not understand them. He would speak of the "lab-

---

[4]Cart driver.
[5]Deck over the officer's quarters (called the "texas" because they were the largest on board).

board" side of a horse in an easy, natural way that would make one wish he was dead. And he was always talking about "St. Looy" like an old citizen; he would refer casually to occasions when he "was coming down Fourth Street," or when he was "passing by the Planter's House," or when there was a fire and he took a turn on the brakes of "the old Big Missouri;" and then he would go on and lie about how many towns the size of ours were burned down there that day. Two or three of the boys had long been persons of consideration among us because they had been to St. Louis once and had a vague general knowledge of its wonders, but the day of their glory was over now. They lapsed into a humble silence, and learned to disappear when the ruthless "cub"-engineer approached. This fellow had money, too, and hair oil. Also an ignorant silver watch and a showy brass watch chain. He wore a leather belt and used no suspenders. If ever a youth was cordially admired and hated by his comrades, this one was. No girl could withstand his charms. He "cut out" every boy in the village. When his boat blew up at last, it diffused a tranquil contentment among us such as we had not known for months. But when he came home the next week, alive, renowned, and appeared in church all battered up and bandaged, a shining hero, stared at and wondered over by everybody, it seemed to us that the partiality of Providence for an undeserving reptile had reached a point where it was open to criticism.

This creature's career could produce but one result, and it speedily followed. Boy after boy managed to get on the river. The minister's son became an engineer. The doctor's and the postmaster's sons became "mud clerks;" the wholesale liquor dealer's son became a bar-keeper on a boat; four sons of the chief merchant, and two sons of the county judge, became pilots. Pilot was the grandest position of all. The pilot, even in those days of trivial wages, had a princely salary—from a hundred and fifty to two hundred and fifty dollars a month, and no board to pay. Two months of his wages would pay a preacher's salary for a year. Now some of us were left disconsolate. We could not get on the river—at least our parents would not let us.

So by and by I ran away. I said I never would come home again till I was a pilot and could come in glory. But somehow I could not manage it. I went meekly aboard a few of the boats that lay packed together like sardines at the long St. Louis wharf, and very humbly inquired for the pilots, but got only a cold shoulder and short words from mates and clerks. I had to make the best of this sort of treatment for the time being, but I had comforting day-dreams of a future when I should be a great and honored pilot, with plenty of money, and could kill some of these mates and clerks and pay for them.

Months afterward the hope within me struggled to a reluctant death, and I found myself without an ambition. But I was ashamed to go home. I was in Cincinnati, and I set to work to map out a new career. I had been reading about the recent exploration of the river Amazon by an expedition sent out by our government. It was said that the expedition, owing to difficulties, had not thoroughly explored a part of the country lying about the head-waters, some four thousand miles from the mouth of the river. It was only about fifteen hundred miles from Cincinnati to New Orleans, where I could doubtless get a ship. I had thirty dollars left; I would go and complete the exploration of the Amazon. This was all the thought I gave to the subject. I never was great in matters of detail. I packed my valise, and took passage on an ancient tub called the Paul Jones, for New Orleans. For the sum of sixteen dollars I had the scarred and tarnished splendors of "her" main saloon principally to myself, for she was not a creature to attract the eye of wiser travelers.

When we presently got under way and went poking down the broad Ohio, I became a new being, and the subject of my own admiration. I was a traveler! A word never had tasted so good in my mouth before. I had an exultant sense of being bound for mysterious lands and distant climes which I never have felt in so uplifting a degree since. I was in such a glorified condition that all ignoble feelings departed out of me, and I was able to look down and pity the untraveled with a compassion that had hardly a trace of contempt in it. Still, when we stopped at villages and wood-yards, I could not help lolling carelessly upon the railings of the boiler deck to enjoy the envy of the country boys on the bank. If they did not seem to discover me, I presently sneezed to attract their attention, or moved to a position where they could not help seeing me. And as soon as I knew they saw me I gaped and stretched, and gave other signs of being mightily bored with traveling.

I kept my hat off all the time, and stayed where the wind and the sun could strike me, because I wanted to get the bronzed and weather-beaten look of an old traveler. Before the second day was half gone, I experienced a joy which filled me with the purest gratitude; for I saw that the skin had begun to blister and peel off my face and neck. I wished that the boys and girls at home could see me now.

We reached Louisville in time—at least the neighborhood of it. We stuck hard and fast on the rocks in the middle of the river and lay there four days. I was now begin-ning to feel a strong sense of being a part of the boat's family, a sort of infant son to the captain and younger brother to the officers. There is no estimating the pride I took in this grandeur, or the affection that began to swell and grow in me for those people. I could not know how the lordly steamboatman scorns that sort of presump-tion in a mere landsman. I particularly longed to acquire the least trifle of notice from the big stormy mate, and I was on the alert for an opportunity to do him a service to that end. It came at last. The riotous powwow of setting a spar was going on down on the forecastle, and I went down there and stood around in the way—or mostly skipping out of it—till the mate suddenly roared a general order for some-body to bring him a capstan bar. I sprang to his side and said: "Tell me where it is— I'll fetch it!"

If a rag-picker had offered to do a diplomatic service for the Emperor of Russia, the monarch could not have been more astounded than the mate was. He even stopped swearing. He stood and stared down at me. It took him ten seconds to scrape his disjointed remains together again. Then he said impressively: "Well, if this don't beat hell!" and turned to his work with the air of a man who had been confronted with a problem too abstruse for solution.

I crept away, and courted solitude for the rest of the day. I did not go to dinner; I stayed away from supper until everybody else had finished. I did not feel so much like a member of the boat's family now as before. However, my spirits returned, in installments, as we pursued our way down the river. I was sorry I hated the mate so, because it was not in (young) human nature not to admire him. He was huge and muscular, his face was bearded and whiskered all over; he had a red woman and a blue woman tattooed on his right arm,—one on each side of a blue anchor with a red rope to it; and in the matter of profanity he was perfect. When he was getting out cargo at a landing, I was always where I could see and hear. He felt all the sublimity of his great position, and made the world feel it, too. When he gave even the simplest order, he discharged it like a blast of lightning, and sent a long, reverberating peal of profanity thundering after it. I could not help contrasting the way in which the average landsman would give an order, with the mate's way of doing it. If the lands-man should wish the gangplank moved a foot farther forward, he would probably say: "James, or William, one of you push that plank forward, please;" but put the mate in his place, and he would roar out: "Here, now, start that gang-plank for'ard! Lively, now! *What*'re you about! Snatch it! *snatch* it! There! there! Aft again! aft again! Don't you hear me? Dash it to dash! are you going to *sleep* over it! '*Vast* heaving. '*Vast* heaving, I tell you! Going to heave it clear astern? WHERE 're you going with that barrel! *for'ard* with it 'fore I make you swallow it, you dash-dash-dash-*dashed* split between a tired mud-turtle and a crippled hearse-horse!"

I wished I could talk like that.

When the soreness of my adventure with the mate had somewhat worn off, I began timidly to make up to the humblest official connected with the boat—the night watchman. He snubbed my advances at first, but I presently ventured to offer him a new chalk pipe, and that softened him. So he allowed me to sit with him by the big bell on the hurricane deck, and in time he melted into conversation. He could not well have helped it, I hung with such homage on his words and so plainly showed that I felt honored by his notice. He told me the names of dim capes and shadowy islands as we glided by them in the solemnity of the night, under the winking stars, and by and by got to talking about himself. He seemed oversentimental for a man whose salary was six dollars a week—or rather he might have seemed so to an older person than I. But I drank in his words hungrily, and with a faith that might have moved mountains if it had been applied judiciously. What was it to me that he was soiled and seedy and fragrant with gin? What was it to me that his grammar was bad, his construction worse, and his profanity so void of art that it was an element of weakness rather than strength in his conversation? He was a wronged man, a man who had seen trouble, and that was enough for me. As he mellowed into his plaintive history his tears dripped upon the lantern in his lap, and I cried, too, from sympathy. He said he was the son of an English nobleman—either an earl or an alderman, he could not remember which, but believed he was both; his father, the nobleman, loved him, but his mother hated him from the cradle; and so while he was still a little boy he was sent to "one of them old, ancient colleges"—he couldn't remember which; and by and by his father died and his mother seized the property and "shook" him, as he phrased it. After his mother shook him, members of the nobility with whom he was acquainted used their influence to get him the position of "lob-lolly-boy[6] in a ship;" and from that point my watchman threw off all trammels of date and locality and branched out into a narrative that bristled all along with incredible adventures; a narrative that was so reeking with bloodshed and so crammed with hair-breadth escapes and the most engaging and unconscious personal villainies, that I sat speechless, enjoying, shuddering, wondering, worshiping.

It was a sore blight to find out afterwards that he was a low, vulgar, ignorant, sentimental, half-witted humbug, an untraveled native of the wilds of Illinois, who had absorbed wildcat literature and appropriated its marvels, until in time he had woven odds and ends of the mess into this yarn, and then gone on telling it to fledgelings like me, until he had come to believe it himself.

II

A "CUB" PILOT'S EXPERIENCE; OR, LEARNING THE RIVER

What with lying on the rocks four days at Louisville, and some other delays, the poor old Paul Jones fooled away about two weeks in making the voyage from Cincinnati to New Orleans. This gave me a chance to get acquainted with one of the pilots, and he taught me how to steer the boat, and thus made the fascination of river life more potent than ever for me.

It also gave me a chance to get acquainted with a youth who had taken deck passage—more 's the pity; for he easily borrowed six dollars of me on a promise to return to the boat and pay it back to me the day after we should arrive. But he probably died or forgot, for he never came. It was doubtless the former, since he had said his parents were wealthy, and he only traveled deck passage because it was cooler.[1]

I soon discovered two things. One was that a vessel would not be likely to sail for the mouth of the Amazon under ten or twelve years; and the other was that the nine or ten dollars still left in my pocket would not suffice for so imposing an exploration

---

[6]Attendant of a ship's doctor.
[1]"'Deck' passage—*i.e.*, steerage passage" (Twain's note).

as I had planned, even if I could afford to wait for a ship. Therefore it followed that I must contrive a new career. The Paul Jones was now bound for St. Louis. I planned a siege against my pilot, and at the end of three hard days he surrendered. He agreed to teach me the Mississippi River from New Orleans to St. Louis for five hundred dollars, payable out of the first wages I should receive after graduating. I entered upon the small enterprise of "learning" twelve or thirteen hundred miles of the great Mississippi River with the easy confidence of my time of life. If I had really known what I was about to require of my faculties, I should not have had the courage to begin. I supposed that all a pilot had to do was to keep his boat in the river, and I did not consider that that could be much of a trick, since it was so wide.

The boat backed out from New Orleans at four in the afternoon, and it was "our watch" until eight. Mr. B——,[2] my chief, "straightened her up," plowed her along past the sterns of the other boats that lay at the Levee, and then said, "Here, take her; shave those steamships as close as you'd peel an apple." I took the wheel, and my heart went down into my boots; for it seemed to me that we were about to scrape the side off every ship in the line, we were so close. I held my breath and began to claw the boat away from the danger; and I had my own opinion of the pilot who had known no better than to get us into such peril, but I was too wise to express it. In half a minute I had a wide margin of safety intervening between the Paul Jones and the ships; and within ten seconds more I was set aside in disgrace, and Mr. B—— was going into danger again and flaying me alive with abuse of my cowardice. I was stung, but I was obliged to admire the easy confidence with which my chief loafed from side to side of his wheel, and trimmed the ships so closely that disaster seemed ceaselessly imminent. When he had cooled a little he told me that the easy water was close ashore and the current outside, and therefore we must hug the bank, up-stream, to get the benefit of the former, and stay well out, down-stream, to take advantage of the latter. In my own mind I resolved to be a down-stream pilot and leave the up-streaming to people dead to prudence.

Now and then Mr. B—— called my attention to certain things. Said he, "This is Six-Mile Point." I assented. It was pleasant enough information, but I could not see the bearing of it. I was not conscious that it was a matter of any interest to me. Another time he said, "This is Nine-Mile Point." Later he said, "This is Twelve-Mile Point." They were all about level with the water's edge; they all looked about alike to me; they were monotonously unpicturesque. I hoped Mr. B—— would change the subject. But no; he would crowd up around a point, hugging the shore with affection, and then say: "The slack water ends here, abreast this bunch of China-trees; now we cross over." So he crossed over. He gave me the wheel once or twice, but I had no luck. I either came near chipping off the edge of a sugar plantation, or else I yawed too far from shore, and so I dropped back into disgrace again and got abused.

The watch was ended at last, and we took supper and went to bed. At midnight the glare of a lantern shone in my eyes, and the night watchman said:—

"Come! turn out!"

And then he left. I could not understand this extraordinary procedure; so I presently gave up trying to, and dozed off to sleep. Pretty soon the watchman was back again, and this time he was gruff. I was annoyed. I said:—

"What do you want to come bothering around here in the middle of the night for? Now as like as not I'll not get to sleep again to-night."

The watchman said:—

"Well, if this an't good, I'm blest."

The "off-watch" was just turning in, and I heard some brutal laughter from them, and such remarks as "Hello, watchman! an't the new cub turned out yet? He's deli-

[2]Identified in *Life on the Mississippi* as Horace Bixby, one of the well-known steamboat pilots of the time.

cate, likely. Give him some sugar in a rag and send for the chambermaid to sing rock-a-by-baby to him."

About this time Mr. B—— appeared on the scene. Something like a minute later I was climbing the pilot-house steps with some of my clothes on and the rest in my arms. Mr. B—— was close behind, commenting. Here was something fresh—this thing of getting up in the middle of the night to go to work. It was a detail in piloting that had never occurred to me at all. I knew that boats ran all night, but somehow I had never happened to reflect that somebody had to get up out of a warm bed to run them. I began to fear that piloting was not quite so romantic as I had imagined it was; there was something very real and work-like about this new phase of it.

It was a rather dingy night, although a fair number of stars were out. The big mate was at the wheel, and he had the old tub pointed at a star and was holding her straight up the middle of the river. The shores on either hand were not much more than a mile apart, but they seemed wonderfully far away and ever so vague and indistinct. The mate said:—

"We've got to land at Jones's plantation, sir."

The vengeful spirit in me exulted. I said to myself, I wish you joy of your job, Mr. B——; you'll have a good time finding Mr. Jones's plantation such a night as this; and I hope you never *will* find it as long as you live.

Mr. B—— said to the mate:—

"Upper end of the plantation, or the lower?"

"Upper."

"I can't do it. The stumps there are out of water at this stage. It's no great distance to the lower, and you'll have to get along with that."

"All right, sir. If Jones don't like it he'll have to lump it, I reckon."

And then the mate left. My exultation began to cool and my wonder to come up. Here was a man who not only proposed to find this plantation on such a night, but to find either end of it you preferred. I dreadfully wanted to ask a question, but I was carrying about as many short answers as my cargo-room would admit of, so I held my peace. All I desired to ask Mr. B—— was the simple question whether he was ass enough to really imagine he was going to find that plantation on a night when all plantations were exactly alike and all the same color. But I held in. I used to have fine inspirations of prudence in those days.

Mr. B—— made for the shore and soon was scraping it, just the same as if it had been daylight. And not only that, but singing—

> "Father in heaven the day is declining," etc.

It seemed to me that I had put my life in the keeping of a peculiarly reckless outcast. Presently he turned on me and said:—

"What's the name of the first point above New Orleans?"

I was gratified to be able to answer promptly, and I did. I said I didn't know.

"Don't *know*?"

This manner jolted me. I was down at the foot again, in a moment. But I had to say just what I had said before.

"Well, you're a smart one," said Mr. B——. "What's the name of the *next* point?"

Once more I didn't know.

"Well this beats anything. Tell me the name of *any* point or place I told you."

I studied a while and decided that I couldn't.

"Look-a-here! What do you start out from, above Twelve-Mile Point, to cross over?"

"I—I—don't know."

"You—you—don't know?" mimicking my drawling manner of speech.

"What *do* you know?"

"I—I—nothing, for certain."

"By the great Cæsar's ghost I believe you! You're the stupidest dunderhead I ever saw or ever heard of, so help me Moses! The idea of *you* being a pilot—*you*! Why, you don't know enough to pilot a cow down a lane."

Oh, but his wrath was up! He was a nervous man, and he shuffled from one side of his wheel to the other as if the floor was hot. He would boil a while to himself, and then overflow and scald me again.

"Look-a-here! What do you suppose I told you the names of those points for?"

I tremblingly considered a moment, and then the devil of temptation provoked me to say:—

"Well—to—to—be entertaining, I thought."

This was a red rag to the bull. He raged and stormed so (he was crossing the river at the time) that I judge it made him blind, because he ran over the steering-oar of a trading-scow. Of course the traders sent up a volley of red-hot profanity. Never was a man so grateful as Mr. B—— was: because he was brim full, and here were subjects who would *talk back*. He threw open a window, thrust his head out, and such an irruption followed as I never had heard before. The fainter and farther away the scowmen's curses drifted, the higher Mr. B—— lifted his voice and the weightier his adjectives grew. When he closed the window he was empty. You could have drawn a seine through his system and not caught curses enough to disturb your mother with. Presently he said to me in the gentlest way:—

"My boy, you must get a little memorandum-book, and every time I tell you a thing, put it down right away. There's only one way to be a pilot, and that is to get this entire river by heart. You have to know it just like A B C."

That was a dismal revelation to me; for my memory was never loaded with anything but blank cartridges. However, I did not feel discouraged long. I judged that it was best to make some allowances, for doubtless Mr. B—— was "stretching." Presently he pulled a rope and struck a few strokes on the big bell. The stars were all gone, now, and the night was as black as ink. I could hear the wheels churn along the bank, but I was not entirely certain that I could see the shore. The voice of the invisible watchman called up from the hurricane deck:—

"What's this, sir?"

"Jones's plantation."

I said to myself, I wish I might venture to offer a small bet that it is n't. But I did not chirp. I only waited to see. Mr. B—— handled the engine bells, and in due time the boat's nose came to the land, a torch glowed from the forecastle, a man skipped ashore, a darky's voice on the bank said, "Gimme de carpet-bag, Mars' Jones," and the next moment we were standing up the river again, all serene. I reflected deeply a while, and then said,—but not aloud,—Well, the finding of that plantation was the luckiest accident that ever happened; but it could n't happen again in a hundred years. And I fully believed it *was* an accident, too.

By the time we had gone seven or eight hundred miles up the river, I had learned to be a tolerably plucky upstream steersman, in daylight, and before we reached St. Louis I had made a trifle of progress in night-work, but only a trifle. I had a notebook that fairly bristled with the names of towns, "points," bars, islands, bends, reaches, etc.; but the information was to be found only in the note-book—none of it was in my head. It made my heart ache to think I had only got half of the river set down; for as our watch was four hours off and four hours on, day and night, there was a long four-hour gap in my book for every time I had slept since the voyage began.

My chief was presently hired to go on a big New Orleans boat, and I packed my satchel and went with him. She was a grand affair. When I stood in her pilot-house I was so far above the water that I seemed perched on a mountain; and her decks stretched so far away, fore and aft, below me, that I wondered how I could ever have considered the little Paul Jones a large craft. There were other differences, too. The Paul Jones's pilot-house was a cheap, dingy, battered rattle-trap, cramped for room: but here was a sumptuous glass temple; room enough to have a dance in; showy red and gold window-curtains; an imposing sofa; leather cushions and a back to the high bench where visiting pilots sit, to spin yarns and "look at the river;" bright, fanciful "cuspadores" instead of a broad wooden box filled with sawdust; nice new oil-cloth on the floor; a hospitable big stove for winter; a wheel as high as my head, costly with inlaid work; a wire tiller-rope; bright brass knobs for the bells; and a tidy, white-aproned, black "texas-tender," to bring up tarts and ices and coffee during mid-watch, day and night. Now this was "something like;" and so I began to take heart once more to believe that piloting was a romantic sort of occupation after all. The moment we were under way I began to prowl about the great steamer and fill myself with joy. She was as clean and as dainty as a drawing-room; when I looked down her long, gilded saloon, it was like gazing through a splendid tunnel; she had an oil-picture, by some gifted sign-painter, on every state-room door; she glittered with no end of prism-fringed chandeliers; the clerk's office was elegant, the bar was mar-velous, and the bar-keeper had been barbered and upholstered at incredible cost. The boiler deck (*i.e.*, the second story of the boat, so to speak) was as spacious as a church, it seemed to me; so with the forecastle; and there was no pitiful handful of deckhands, firemen, and roust-abouts down there, but a whole battalion of men. The fires were fiercely glaring from a long row of furnaces, and over them were eight huge boilers! This was unutterable pomp. The mighty engines—but enough of this. I had never felt so fine before. And when I found that the regiment of natty servants respectfully "sir'd" me, my satisfaction was complete.

When I returned to the pilot-house St. Louis was gone and I was lost. Here was a piece of river which was all down in my book, but I could make neither head nor tail of it: you understand, it was turned around. I had seen it, when coming up-stream, but I had never faced about to see how it looked when it was behind me. My heart broke again, for it was plain that I had got to learn this troublesome river *both ways*.

The pilot-house was full of pilots, going down to "look at the river." What is called the "upper river" (the two hundred miles between St. Louis and Cairo, where the Ohio comes in) was low; and the Mississippi changes its channel so constantly that the pilots used to always find it necessary to run down to Cairo to take a fresh look, when their boats were to lie in port a week, that is, when the water was at a low stage. A deal of this "looking at the river" was done by poor fellows who seldom had a berth, and whose only hope of getting one lay in their being always freshly posted and therefore ready to drop into the shoes of some reputable pilot, for a single trip, on account of such pilot's sudden illness, or some other necessity. And a good many of them con-stantly ran up and down inspecting the river, not because they ever really hoped to get a berth, but because (they being guests of the boat) it was cheaper to "look at the river" than stay ashore and pay board. In time these fellows grew dainty in their tastes, and only infested boats that had an established reputation for setting good tables. All visiting pilots were useful, for they were always ready and willing, winter or summer, night or day, to go out in the yawl and help buoy the channel or assist the boat's pilots in any way they could. They were likewise welcome because all pilots are tireless talkers, when gathered together, and as they talk only about the river they are always understood and are always interesting. Your true pilot cares nothing about anything on earth but the river, and his pride in his occupation surpasses the pride of kings.

We had a fine company of these river-inspectors along, this trip. There were eight or ten; and there was abundance of room for them in our great pilot-house. Two or three of them wore polished silk hats, elaborate shirt-fronts, diamond breastpins, kid gloves, and patent-leather boots. They were choice in their English, and bore them-selves with a dignity proper to men of solid means and prodigious reputation as pilots. The others were more or less loosely clad, and wore upon their heads tall felt cones that were suggestive of the days of the Commonwealth.[3]

I was a cipher in this august company, and felt subdued, not to say torpid. I was not even of sufficient consequence to assist at the wheel when it was necessary to put the tiller hard down in a hurry; the guest that stood nearest did that when occasion required—and this was pretty much all the time, because of the crookedness of the channel and the scant water. I stood in a corner; and the talk I listened to took the hope all out of me. One visitor said to another:—

"Jim, how did you run Plum Point, coming up?"

"It was in the night, there, and I ran it the way one of the boys on the Diana told me; started out about fifty yards above the wood pile on the false point, and held on the cabin under Plum Point till I raised the reef—quarter less twain—then straightened up for the middle bar till I got well abreast the old one-limbed cotton-wood in the bend, then got my stern on the cotton-wood and head on the low place above the point, and came through a-booming—nine and a half."

"Pretty square crossing, an't it?"

"Yes, but the upper bar's working down fast."

Another pilot spoke up and said:—

"I had better water than that, and ran it lower down; started out from the false point—mark twain—raised the second reef abreast the big snag in the bend, and had quarter less twain."

One of the gorgeous ones remarked: "I don't want to find fault with your leadsmen, but that's a good deal of water for Plum Point, it seems to me."

There was an approving nod all around as this quiet snub dropped on the boaster and "settled" him. And so they went on talk-talk-talking. Meantime, the thing that was running in my mind was, "Now if my ears hear aright, I have not only to get the names of all the towns and islands and bends, and so on, by heart, but I must even get up a warm personal acquaintanceship with every old snag and one-limbed cotton-wood and obscure wood pile that ornaments the banks of this river for twelve hundred miles; and more than that, I must actually know where these things are in the dark, unless these guests are gifted with eyes that can pierce through two miles of solid blackness; I wish the piloting business was in Jericho and I had never thought of it."

At dusk Mr. B—— tapped the big bell three times (the signal to land), and the captain emerged from his drawing-room in the forward end of the texas, and looked up inquiringly. Mr. B—— said:—

"We will lay up here all night, captain."

"Very well, sir."

That was all. The boat came to shore and was tied up for the night. It seemed to me a fine thing that the pilot could do as he pleased without asking so grand a captain's permission. I took my supper and went immediately to bed, discouraged by my day's observations and experiences. My late voyage's note-booking was but a confusion of meaningless names. It had tangled me all up in a knot every time I had looked at it in the daytime. I now hoped for respite in sleep; but no, it reveled all through my head till sunrise again, a frantic and tireless nightmare.

Next morning I felt pretty rusty and low-spirited. We went booming along, taking a good many chances, for we were anxious to "get out of the river" (as getting out to Cairo was called) before night should overtake us. But Mr. B——'s partner, the other pilot, presently grounded the boat, and we lost so much time getting her off that it was plain the darkness would overtake us a good long way above the mouth. This was

---

[3]Hats in the shape of cones like hats worn by the Puritans during the time of the British Commonwealth, in the mid-seventeenth century.

a great misfortune, especially to certain of our visiting pilots, whose boats would have to wait for their return, no matter how long that might be. It sobered the pilothouse talk a good deal. Coming upstream, pilots did not mind low water or any kind of darkness; nothing stopped them but fog. But down-stream work was different; a boat was too nearly helpless, with a stiff current pushing behind her; so it was not customary to run downstream at night in low water.

There seemed to be one small hope, however: if we could get through the intricate and dangerous Hat Island crossing before night, we could venture the rest, for we would have plainer sailing and better water. But it would be insanity to attempt Hat Island at night. So there was a great deal of looking at watches all the rest of the day, and a constant ciphering upon the speed we were making; Hat Island was the eternal subject; sometimes hope was high and sometimes we were delayed in a bad crossing, and down it went again. For hours all hands lay under the burden of this suppressed excitement; it was even communicated to me, and I got to feeling so solicitous about Hat Island, and under such an awful pressure of responsibility, that I wished I might have five minutes on shore to draw a good, full, relieving breath, and start over again. We were standing no regular watches. Each of our pilots ran such portions of the river as he had run when coming upstream, because of his greater familiarity with it; but both remained in the pilot-house constantly.

An hour before sunset, Mr. B—— took the wheel and Mr. W—— stepped aside. For the next thirty minutes every man held his watch in his hand and was restless, silent, and uneasy. At last somebody said, with a doomful sigh.

"Well, yonder's Hat Island—and we can't make it."

All the watches closed with a snap, everybody sighed and muttered something about its being "too bad, too bad—ah, if we could *only* have got here half an hour sooner!" and the place was thick with the atmosphere of disappointment. Some started to go out, but loitered, hearing no bell-tap to land. The sun dipped behind the horizon, the boat went on. Inquiring looks passed from one guest to another; and one who had his hand on the doorknob, and had turned it, waited, then presently took away his hand and let the knob turn back again. We bore steadily down the bend. More looks were exchanged, and nods of surprised admiration—but no words. Insensibly the men drew together behind Mr. B—— as the sky darkened and one or two dim stars came out. The dead silence and sense of waiting became oppressive. Mr. B—— pulled the cord, and two deep, mellow notes from the big bell floated off on the night. Then a pause, and one more note was struck. The watchman's voice followed, from the hurricane deck:—

"Labboard lead, there! Stabboard lead!"

The cries of the leadsmen began to rise out of the distance, and were gruffly repeated by the word-passers on the hurricane deck.

"M-a-r-k three! M-a-r-k three! Quarter-less-three! Half twain! Quarter twain! M-a-r-k twain! Quarter-less"—

Mr. B—— pulled two bell-ropes, and was answered by faint jinglings far below in the engine-room, and our speed slackened. The steam began to whistle through the gauge-cocks. The cries of the leadsmen went on—and it is a weird sound, always, in the night. Every pilot in the lot was watching, now, with fixed eyes, and talking under his breath. Nobody was calm and easy but Mr. B——. He would put his wheel down and stand on a spoke, and as the steamer swung into her (to me) utterly invisible marks—for we seemed to be in the midst of a wide and gloomy sea—he would meet and fasten her there. Talk was going on, now, in low voices:—

"There; she 's over the first reef all right!"

After a pause, another subdued voice:—

"Her stern 's coming down just *exactly* right, by *George!* Now she 's in the marks; over she goes!"

Somebody else muttered:—

"Oh, it was done beautiful—*beautiful!*"

Now the engines were stopped altogether, and we drifted with the current. Not that I could see the boat drift, for I could not, the stars being all gone by this time. This drifting was the dismalest work; it held one's heart still. Presently I discovered a blacker gloom than that which surrounded us. It was the head of the island. We were closing right down upon it. We entered its deeper shadow, and so imminent seemed the peril that I was likely to suffocate; and I had the strongest impulse to do *something*, anything, to save the vessel. But still Mr. B—— stood by his wheel, silent, intent as a cat, and all the pilots stood shoulder to shoulder at his back.

"She 'll not make it!" somebody whispered.

The water grew shoaler and shoaler by the leadsmen's cries, till it was down to—

"Eight-and-a-half! E-i-g-h-t feet! E-i-g-h-t feet! Seven-and"—

Mr. B—— said warningly through his speaking tube to the engineer: —

"Stand by, now!"

"Aye-aye, sir."

"Seven-and-a-half! Seven feet! *Six*-and"—

We touched bottom! Instantly Mr. B—— set a lot of bells ringing, shouted through the tube, "*Now* let her have it—every ounce you've got!" then to his partner, "Put her hard down! snatch her! snatch her!" The boat rasped and ground her way through the sand, hung upon the apex of disaster a single tremendous instant, and then over she went! And such a shout as went up at Mr. B——'s back never loosened the roof of a pilot-house before!

There was no more trouble after that. Mr. B—— was a hero that night; and it was some little time, too, before his exploit ceased to be talked about by river men.

Fully to realize the marvelous precision required in laying the great steamer in her marks in that murky waste of water, one should know that not only must she pick her intricate way through snags and blind reefs, and then shave the head of the island so closely as to brush the overhanging foliage with her stern, but at one place she must pass almost within arm's reach of a sunken and invisible wreck that would snatch the hull timbers from under her if she should strike it, and destroy a quarter of a million dollars' worth of steamboat and cargo in five minutes, and maybe a hundred and fifty human lives into the bargain.

The last remark I heard that night was a compliment to Mr. B——, uttered in soliloquy and with unction by one of our guests. He said:—

"By the Shadow of Death, but he 's a lightning pilot!"

III

THE CONTINUED PERPLEXITIES OF "CUB" PILOTING

At the end of what seemed a tedious while, I had managed to pack my head full of islands, towns, bars, "points," and bends; and a curiously inanimate mass of lumber it was, too. However, inasmuch as I could shut my eyes and reel off a good long string of these names without leaving out more than ten miles of river in every fifty, I began to feel that I could take a boat down to New Orleans if I could make her skip those little gaps. But of course my complacency could hardly get start enough to lift my nose a trifle into the air, before Mr. B—— would think of something to fetch it down again. One day he turned on me suddenly with this settler:—

"What is the shape of Walnut Bend?"

He might as well have asked me my grandmother's opinion of protoplasm. I reflected respectfully, and then said I did n't know it had any particular shape. My gunpowdery chief went off with a bang, of course, and then went on loading and firing until he was out of adjectives.

I had learned long ago that he only carried just so many rounds of ammunition, and was sure to subside into a very placable and even remorseful old smooth-bore as soon as they were all gone. That word "old" is merely affectionate; he was not more than thirty-four. I waited. By and by he said,—

"My boy, you've got to know the *shape* of the river perfectly. It is all there is left to steer by on a very dark night. Everything else is blotted out and gone. But mind you, it hasn't the same shape in the night that it has in the day-time."

"How on earth am I ever going to learn it, then?"

"How do you follow a hall at home in the dark? Because you know the shape of it. You can't see it."

"Do you mean to say that I've got to know all the million trifling variations of shape in the banks of this interminable river as well as I know the shape of the front hall at home?"

"On my honor you've got to know them *better* than any man ever did know the shapes of the halls in his own house."

"I wish I was dead!"

"Now I don't want to discourage you, but"—

"Well, pile it on me; I might as well have it now as another time."

"You see, this has got to be learned; there isn't any getting around it. A clear starlight night throws such heavy shadows that if you did n't know the shape of a shore perfectly you would claw away from every bunch of timber, because you would take the black shadow of it for a solid cape; and you see you would be getting scared to death every fifteen minutes by the watch. You would be fifty yards from shore all the time when you ought to be within twenty feet of it. You can't see a snag in one of those shadows, but you know exactly where it is, and the shape of the river tells you when you are coming to it. Then there's your pitch dark night; the river is a very different shape on a pitch dark night from what it is on a starlight night. All shores seem to be straight lines, then, and mighty dim ones, too; and you'd *run* them for straight lines, only you know better. You boldly drive your boat right into what seems to be a solid, straight wall (you knowing very well that in reality there is a curve there), and that wall falls back and makes way for you. Then there's your gray mist. You take a night when there's one of these grisly, drizzly, gray mists, and then there is n't *any* particular shape to a shore. A gray mist would tangle the head of the oldest man that ever lived. Well, then, different kinds of *moonlight* change the shape of the river in different ways. You see"—

"Oh, don't say any more, please! Have I got to learn the shape of the river according to all these five hundred thousand different ways? If I tried to carry all that cargo in my head it would make me stoop-shouldered."

"*No!* you only learn *the* shape of the river; and you learn it with such absolute certainty that you can always steer by the shape that's *in your head*, and never mind the one that's before your eyes."

"Very well, I'll try it; but after I have learned it can I depend on it? Will it keep the same form and not go fooling around?"

Before Mr. B—— could answer, Mr. W—— came in to take the watch, and he said,—

"B——, you'll have to look out for President's Island and all that country clear away up above the Old Hen and Chickens. The banks are caving and the shape of the shores changing like everything. Why, you wouldn't know the point above 40. You can go up inside the old sycamore snag, now."[1]

So that question was answered. Here were leagues of shore changing shape. My spirits were down in the mud again. Two things seemed pretty apparent to me. One

---

[1] "It may not be necessary, but still it can do no harm to explain that 'inside' means between the snag and the shore" (Twain's note).

was, that in order to be a pilot a man had got to learn more than any one man ought to be allowed to know; and the other was, that he must learn it all over again in a different way every twenty-four hours.

That night we had the watch until twelve. Now it was an ancient river custom for the two pilots to chat a bit when the watch changed. While the relieving pilot put on his gloves and lit his cigar, his partner, the retiring pilot, would say something like this:—

"I judge the upper bar is making down a little at Hale's Point; had quarter twain with the lower lead and mark twain[2] with the other."

"Yes, I thought it was making down a little, last trip. Meet any boats?"

"Met one abreast the head of 21, but she was away over hugging the bar, and I couldn't make her out entirely. I took her for the Sunny South—had n't any skylights forward of the chimneys."

And so on. And as the relieving pilot took the wheel his partner[3] would mention that we were in such-and-such a bend, and say we were abreast of such-and-such a man's wood-yard or plantation. This was courtesy; I supposed it was *necessity*. But Mr. W—— came on watch full twelve minutes late, on this particular night—a tremendous breach of etiquette; in fact, it is the unpardonable sin among pilots. So Mr. B—— gave him no greeting whatever, but simply surrendered the wheel and marched out of the pilot-house without a word. I was appalled; it was a villainous night for blackness, we were in a particularly wide and blind part of the river, where there was no shape or substance to anything, and it seemed incredible that Mr. B—— should have left that poor fellow to kill the boat trying to find out where he was. But I resolved that I would stand by him any way. He should find that he was not wholly friendless. So I stood around, and waited to be asked where we were. But Mr. W—— plunged on serenely through the solid firmament of black cats that stood for an atmosphere, and never opened his mouth. Here is a proud devil, thought I; here is a limb of Satan that would rather send us all to destruction than put himself under obligations to me, because I am not yet one of the salt of the earth and privileged to snub captains and lord it over everything dead and alive in a steamboat. I presently climbed up on the bench; I did not think it was safe to go to sleep while this lunatic was on watch.

However, I must have gone to sleep in the course of time, because the next thing I was aware of was the fact that day was breaking, Mr. W—— gone, and Mr. B—— at the wheel again. So it was four o'clock and all well—but me; I felt like a skinful of dry bones and all of them trying to ache at once.

Mr. B—— asked me what I had stayed up there for. I confessed that it was to do Mr. W—— a benevolence: tell him where he was. It took five minutes for the entire preposterousness of the thing to filter into Mr. B——'s system, and then I judge it filled him nearly up to the chin; because he paid me a compliment—and not much of a one either. He said,—

"Well, taking you by-and-large, you do seem to be more different kinds of an ass than any creature I ever saw before. What did you suppose he wanted to know for?"

I said I thought it might be a convenience to him.

"Convenience! Dash! Didn't I tell you that a man's got to know the river in the night the same as he'd know his own front hall?"

"Well, I can follow the front hall in the dark if I know it *is* the front hall; but suppose you set me down in the middle of it in the dark and not tell me which hall it is; how am *I* to know?"

"Well, you've *got* to, on the river!"

---

[2] "Two fathoms. Quarter twain is 2¼ fathoms, 13½ feet.
Mark three is three fathoms" (Twain's note).
[3] "'Partner' is technical for 'the other pilot'" (Twain's note).

"All right. Then I'm glad I never said anything to Mr. W——."

"I should say so. Why, he'd have slammed you through the window and utterly ruined a hundred dollars' worth of window-sash and stuff."

I was glad this damage had been saved, for it would have made me unpopular with the owners. They always hated anybody who had the name of being careless, and injuring things.

I went to work, now, to learn the shape of the river; and of all the eluding and ungraspable objects that ever I tried to get mind or hands on, that was the chief. I would fasten my eyes upon a sharp, wooded point that projected far into the river some miles ahead of me, and go to laboriously photographing its shape upon my brain; and just as I was beginning to succeed to my satisfaction, we would draw up toward it and the exasperating thing would begin to melt away and fold back into the bank! If there had been a conspicuous dead tree standing upon the very point of the cape, I would find that tree inconspicuously merged into the general forest, and occupying the middle of a straight shore, when I got abreast of it! No prominent hill would stick to its shape long enough for me to make up my mind what its form really was, but it was as dissolving and changeful as if it had been a mountain of butter in the hottest corner of the tropics. Nothing ever had the same shape when I was coming down-stream that it had borne when I went up. I mentioned these little difficulties to Mr. B——. He said,—

"That's the very main virtue of the thing. If the shapes didn't change every three seconds they wouldn't be of any use. Take this place where we are now, for instance. As long as that hill over yonder is only one hill, I can boom right along the way I'm going; but the moment it splits at the top and forms a V, I know I've got to scratch to starboard in a hurry, or I'll bang this boat's brains out against a rock; and then the moment one of the prongs of the V swings behind the other, I've got to waltz to larboard again, or I'll have a misunderstanding with a snag that would snatch the keelson out of this steamboat as neatly as if it were a sliver in your hand. If that hill didn't change its shape on bad nights there would be an awful steamboat grave-yard around here inside of a year."

It was plain that I had got to learn the shape of the river in all the different ways that could be thought of,—upside down, wrong end first, inside out, fore-and-aft, and "thortships,"—and then know what to do on gray nights when it hadn't any shape at all. So I set about it. In the course of time I began to get the best of this knotty lesson, and my self-complacency moved to the front once more. Mr. B—— was all fixed, and ready to start it to the rear again. He opened on me after this fashion:—

"How much water did we have in the middle crossing at Hole-in-the-Wall, trip before last?"

I considered this an outrage. I said:

"Every trip, down and up, the leadsmen are singing through that tangled place for three quarters of an hour on a stretch. How do you reckon I can remember such a mess as that?"

"My boy, you've got to remember it. You've got to remember the exact spot and the exact marks the boat lay in when we had the shoalest water, in every one of the two thousand shoal places between St. Louis and New Orleans; and you mustn't get the shoal soundings and marks of one trip mixed up with the shoal soundings and marks of another, either, for they're not often twice alike. You must keep them separate."

When I came to myself again, I said,—

"When I get so that I can do that, I'll be able to raise the dead, and then I won't have to pilot a steamboat in order to make a living. I want to retire from this business. I want a slush-bucket and a brush; I'm only fit for a roustabout. I have n't got brains enough to be a pilot; and if I had I would n't have strength enough to carry them around, unless I went on crutches."

"Now drop that! When I say I'll learn[4] a man the river, I mean it. And you can depend on it I'll learn him or kill him."

There was no use in arguing with a person like this. I promptly put such a strain on my memory that by and by even the shoal water and the countless crossing-marks began to stay with me. But the result was just the same. I never could more than get one knotty thing learned before another presented itself. Now I had often seen pilots gazing at the water and pretending to read it as if it were a book; but it was a book that told me nothing. A time came at last, however, when Mr. B—— seemed to think me far enough advanced to bear a lesson on water-reading. So he began:—

"Do you see that long slanting line on the face of the water? Now that's a reef. Moreover, it's a bluff reef. There is a solid sand-bar under it that is nearly as straight up and down as the side of a house. There is plenty of water close up to it, but mighty little on top of it. If you were to hit it you would knock the boat's brains out. Do you see where the line fringes out at the upper end and begins to fade away?"

"Yes, sir."

"Well, that is a low place; that is the head of the reef. You can climb over there, and not hurt anything. Cross over, now, and follow along close under the reef—easy water there—not much current."

I followed the reef along till I approached the fringed end. Then Mr. B—— said,—

"Now get ready. Wait till I give the word. She won't want to mount the reef; a boat hates shoal water. Stand by—wait—wait—keep her well in hand. *Now* cramp her down! Snatch her! snatch her!"

He seized the other side of the wheel and helped to spin it around until it was hard down, and then we held it so. The boat resisted and refused to answer for a while, and next she came surging to starboard, mounted the reef, and sent a long, angry ridge of water foaming away from her bows.

"Now watch her; watch her like a cat, or she'll get away from you. When she fights strong and the tiller slips a little, in a jerky, greasy sort of way, let up on her a trifle; it is the way she tells you at night that the water is too shoal; but keep edging her up, little by little, toward the point. You are well up on the bar, now; there is a bar under every point, because the water that comes down around it forms an eddy and allows the sediment to sink. Do you see those fine lines on the face of the water that branch out like the ribs of a fan? Well, those are little reefs; you want to just miss the ends of them, but run them pretty close. Now look out—look out! Don't you crowd that slick, greasy-looking place; there ain't nine feet there; she won't stand it. She begins to smell it; look sharp, I tell you! Oh blazes, there you go! Stop the starboard wheel! Quick! Ship up to back! Set her back!"

The engine bells jingled and the engines answered promptly, shooting white columns of steam far aloft out of the scape pipes, but it was too late. The boat had "smelt" the bar in good earnest; the foamy ridges that radiated from her bows suddenly disappeared, a great dead swell came rolling forward and swept ahead of her, she careened far over to larboard, and went tearing away toward the other shore as if she were about scared to death. We were a good mile from where we ought to have been, when we finally got the upper hand of her again.

During the afternoon watch the next day, Mr. B—— asked me if I knew how to run the next few miles. I said:—

"Go inside the first snag above the point, outside the next one, start out from the lower end of Higgins's woodyard, make a square crossing and"—

"That's all right. I'll be back before you close up on the next point."

But he was n't. He was still below when I rounded it and entered upon a piece of river which I had some misgivings about. I did not know that he was hiding behind a

---

4"'Teach' is not in the river vocabulary" (Twain's note).

chimney to see how I would perform. I went gayly along, getting prouder and prouder, for he had never left the boat in my sole charge such a length of time before. I even got to "setting" her and letting the wheel go, entirely, while I vain-gloriously turned my back and inspected the stern marks and hummed a tune, a sort of easy indifference which I had prodigiously admired in B—— and other great pilots. Once I inspected rather long, and when I faced to the front again my heart flew into my mouth so suddenly that if I had n't clapped my teeth together I would have lost it. One of those frightful bluff reefs was stretching its deadly length right across our bows! My head was gone in a moment; I did not know which end I stood on; I gasped and could not get my breath; I spun the wheel down with such rapidity that it wove itself together like a spider's web; the boat answered and turned square away from the reef, but the reef followed her! I fled, and still it followed—still it kept right across my bows! I never looked to see where I was going, I only fled. The awful crash was imminent—why did n't that villain come! If I committed the crime of ringing a bell, I might get thrown overboard. But better that than kill the boat. So in blind desperation I started such a rattling "shivaree" down below as never had as-tounded an engineer in this world before, I fancy. Amidst the frenzy of the bells the engines began to back and fill in a furious way, and my reason forsook its throne—we were about to crash into the woods on the other side of the river. Just then Mr. B—— stepped calmly into view on the hurricane deck. My soul went out to him in grati-tude. My distress vanished; I would have felt safe on the brink of Niagara, with Mr. B—— on the hurricane deck. He blandly and sweetly took his tooth-pick out of his mouth between his fingers, as if it were a cigar,—we were just in the act of climbing an overhanging big tree, and the passengers were scudding astern like rats,—and lifted up these commands to me ever so gently:—

"Stop the starboard. Stop the larboard. Set her back on both."

The boat hesitated, halted, pressed her nose among the boughs a critical instant, then reluctantly began to back away.

"Stop the larboard. Come ahead on it. Stop the starboard. Come ahead on it. Point her for the bar."

I sailed away as serenely as a summer's morning. Mr. B—— came in and said, with mock simplicity,—

"When you have a hail, my boy, you ought to tap the big bell three times before you land, so that the engineers can get ready."

I blushed under the sarcasm, and said I had n't had any hail.

"Ah! Then it was for wood, I suppose. The officer of the watch will tell you when he wants to wood up."

I went on consuming, and said I was n't after wood.

"Indeed? Why, what could you want over here in the bend, then? Did you ever know of a boat following a bend up-stream at this stage of the river?"

"No, sir,—and *I* was n't trying to follow it. I was getting away from a bluff reef."

"No, it was n't a bluff reef; there is n't one within three miles of where you were."

"But I saw it. It was as bluff as that one yonder."

"Just about. Run over it!"

"Do you give it as an order?"

"Yes. Run over it."

"If I don't, I wish I may die."

"All right; I am taking the responsibility."

I was just as anxious to kill the boat, now, as I had been to save her before. I impressed my orders upon my memory, to be used at the inquest, and made a straight break for the reef. As it disappeared under our bows I held my breath; but we slid over it like oil.

"Now don't you see the difference? It was n't anything but a wind reef. The wind does that."

"So I see. But it is exactly like a bluff reef. How am I ever going to tell them apart?"

"I can't tell you. It is an instinct. By and by you will just naturally *know* one from the other, but you never will be able to explain why or how you know them apart."

It turned out to be true. The face of the water, in time, became a wonderful book—a book that was a dead language to the uneducated passenger, but which told its mind to me without reserve, delivering its most cherished secrets as clearly as if it uttered them with a voice. And it was not a book to be read once and thrown aside, for it had a new story to tell every day. Throughout the long twelve hundred miles there was never a page that was void of interest, never one that you could leave unread without loss, never one that you would want to skip, thinking you could find higher enjoyment in some other thing. There never was so wonderful a book written by man; never one whose interest was so absorbing, so unflagging, so sparkingly renewed with every re-perusal. The passenger who could not read it was charmed with a peculiar sort of faint dimple on its surface (on the rare occasions when he did not overlook it altogether); but to the pilot that was an *italicized* passage; indeed, it was more than that, it was a legend of the largest capitals with a string of shouting exclamation points at the end of it; for it meant that a wreck or a rock was buried there that could tear the life out of the strongest vessel that ever floated. It is the faintest and simplest expression the water ever makes, and the most hideous to a pilot's eye. In truth, the passenger who could not read this book saw nothing but all manner of pretty pictures in it, painted by the sun and shaded by the clouds, whereas to the trained eye these were not pictures at all, but the grimmest and most dead-earnest of reading-matter.

Now when I had mastered the language of this water and had come to know every trifling feature that bordered the great river as familiarly as I knew the letters of the alphabet, I had made a valuable acquisition. But I had lost something, too. I had lost something which could never be restored to me while I lived. All the grace, the beauty, the poetry had gone out of the majestic river! I still keep in mind a certain wonderful sunset which I witnessed when steamboating was new to me. A broad expanse of the river was turned to blood; in the middle distance the red hue bright-ened into gold, through which a solitary log came floating, black and conspicuous; in one place a long, slanting mark lay sparkling upon the water; in another the surface was broken by boiling, tumbling rings, that were as many-tinted as an opal; where the ruddy flush was faintest, was a smooth spot that was covered with graceful circles and radiating lines, ever so delicately traced; the shore on our left was densely wooded, and the sombre shadow that fell from this forest was broken in one place by a long, ruffled trail that shone like silver; and high above the forest wall a clean-stemmed dead tree waved a single leafy bough that glowed like a flame in the unobstructed splendor that was flowing from the sun. There were graceful curves, reflected im-ages, woody heights, soft distances; and over the whole scene, far and near, the dissolving lights drifted steadily, enriching it, every passing moment, with new mar-vels of coloring.

I stood like one bewitched. I drank it in, in a speechless rapture. The world was new to me, and I had never seen anything like this at home. But as I have said, a day came when I began to cease noting the glories and the charms which the moon and the sun and the twilight wrought upon the river's face; another day came when I ceased altogether to note them. Then, if that sunset scene had been repeated, I would have looked upon it without rapture, and would have commented upon it, inwardly, after this fashion: This sun means that we are going to have wind to-morrow; that floating log means that the river is rising, small thanks to it; that slant-ing mark on the water refers to a bluff reef which is going to kill somebody's steam-boat one of these nights, if it keeps on stretching out like that; those tumbling "boils" show a dissolving bar and a changing channel there; the lines and circles in the slick water over yonder are a warning that that execrable place is shoaling up dangerously; that silver streak in the shadow of the forest is the "break" from a new snag, and he has located himself in the very best place he could have found to fish for steamboats; that tall, dead tree, with a single living branch, is not going to last long, and then how is a body ever going to get through this blind place at night without the friendly old landmark?

No, the romance and the beauty were all gone from the river. All the value any feature of it had for me now was the amount of usefulness it could furnish toward compassing the safe piloting of a steamboat. Since those days, I have pitied doctors from my heart. What does the lovely flush in a beauty's cheek mean to a doctor but a "break" that ripples above some deadly disease? Are not all her visible charms sown thick with what are to him the signs and symbols of hidden decay? Does he ever see her beauty at all, or doesn't he simply view her professionally, and comment upon her unwholesome condition all to himself? And doesn't he sometimes wonder whether he has gained most or lost most by learning his trade?

IV

THE "CUB" PILOT'S EDUCATION NEARLY COMPLETED

Whosoever has done me the courtesy to read my chapters which have preceded this may possibly wonder that I deal so minutely with piloting as a science. It was the prime purpose of these articles; and I am not quite done yet. I wish to show, in the most patient and painstaking way, what a wonderful science it is. Ship channels are buoyed and lighted, and therefore it is a comparatively easy undertaking to learn to run them; clear-water rivers, with gravel bottoms, change their channels very gradually, and therefore one needs to learn them but once; but piloting becomes another matter when you apply it to vast streams like the Mississippi and the Missouri, whose alluvial banks[1] cave and change constantly, whose snags are always hunting up new quarters, whose sand-bars are never at rest, whose channels are forever dodging and shirking, and whose obstructions must be confronted in all nights and all weathers without the aid of a single light-house or a single buoy; for there is neither light nor buoy to be found anywhere in all this three or four thousand miles of villainous river. I feel justified in enlarging upon this great science for the reason that I feel sure no one has ever yet written a paragraph about it who had piloted a steamboat himself, and so had a practical knowledge of the subject. If the theme were hackneyed, I should be obliged to deal gently with the reader; but since it is wholly new, I have felt at liberty to take up a considerable degree of room with it.

When I had learned the name and position of every visible feature of the river; when I had so mastered its shape that I could shut my eyes and trace it from St. Louis to New Orleans; when I had learned to read the face of the water as one would cull the news from the morning paper; and finally, when I had trained my dull memory to treasure up an endless array of soundings and crossing-marks, and keep fast hold of them, I judged that my education was complete: so I got to tilting my cap to the side of my head, and wearing a toothpick in my mouth at the wheel. Mr. B—— had his eye on these airs. One day he said,—

"What is the height of that bank yonder, at Burgess's?"

"How can I tell, sir? It is three quarters of a mile away."

"Very poor eye—very poor. Take the glass."

I took the glass, and presently said,—

"I can't tell. I suppose that that bank is about a foot and a half high."

"Foot and a half! That's a six-foot bank. How high was the bank along here last trip?"

---

[1]Made up of sand or clay deposited by flowing water.

"I don't know; I never noticed."

"You did n't? Well, you must always do it hereafter."

"Why?"

"Because you 'll have to know a good many things that it tells you. For one thing, it tells you the stage of the river—tells you whether there's more water or less in the river along here than there was last trip."

"The leads tell me that." I rather thought I had the advantage of him there.

"Yes, but suppose the leads lie? The bank would tell you so, and then you'd stir those leadsmen up a bit. There was a ten-foot bank here last trip, and there is only a six-foot bank now. What does that signify?"

"That the river is four feet higher than it was last trip."

"Very good. Is the river rising or falling?"

"Rising."

"No it ain't."

"I guess I am right, sir. Yonder is some drift-wood floating down the stream."

"A rise *starts* the drift-wood, but then it keeps on floating a while after the river is done rising. Now the bank will tell you about this. Wait till you come to a place where it shelves a little. Now here; do you see this narrow belt of fine sediment? That was deposited while the water was higher. You see the drift-wood begins to strand, too. The bank helps in other ways. Do you see that stump on the false point?"

"Ay, ay, sir."

"Well, the water is just up to the roots of it. You must make a note of that."

"Why?"

"Because that means that there 's seven feet in the chute of 103."

"But 103 is a long way up the river yet."

"That's where the benefit of the bank comes in. There is water enough in 103 *now*, yet there may not be by the time we get there; but the bank will keep us posted all along. You don't run close chutes on a falling river, up-stream, and there are precious few of them that you are allowed to run at all down-stream. There's a law of the United States against it. The river may be rising by the time we get to 103, and in that case we 'll run it. We are drawing—how much?"

"Six feet aft,—six and a half forward."

"Well, you do seem to know something."

"But what I particularly want to know is, if I have got to keep up an everlasting measuring of the banks of this river, twelve hundred miles, month in and month out?"

"Of course!"

My emotions were too deep for words for a while. Presently I said,—

"And how about these chutes? Are there many of them?"

"I should say so. I fancy we shan't run any of the river this trip as you 've ever seen it run before—so to speak. If the river begins to rise again, we'll go up behind bars that you 've always seen standing out of the river, high and dry like the roof of a house; we'll cut across low places that you 've never noticed at all, right through the middle of bars that cover fifty acres of river; we 'll creep through cracks where you 've always thought was solid land; we 'll dart through the woods and leave twenty-five miles of river off to one side; we 'll see the hind-side of every island between New Orleans and Cairo."

"Then I 've got to go to work and learn just as much more river as I already know."

"Just about twice as much more, as near as you can come at it."

"Well, one lives to find out. I think I was a fool when I went into this business."

"Yes, that is true. And you are yet. But you'll not be when you 've learned it."

"Ah, I never can learn it."

"I will see that you *do*."

By and by I ventured again:—

"Have I got to learn all this thing just as I know the rest of the river—shapes and all—and so I can run it at night?"

"Yes. And you 've got to have good fair marks from one end of the river to the other, that will help the bank tell you when there is water enough in each of these countless places,—like that stump, you know. When the river first begins to rise, you can run half a dozen of the deepest of them; when it rises a foot more you can run another dozen; the next foot will add a couple of dozen, and so on: so you see you have to know your banks and marks to a dead moral certainty, and never get them mixed; for when you start through one of those cracks, there's no backing out again, as there is in the big river; you 've got to go through, or stay there six months if you get caught on a falling river. There are about fifty of these cracks which you can 't run at all except when the river is brim full and over the banks."

"This new lesson is a cheerful prospect."

"Cheerful enough. And mind what I 've just told you; when you start into one of those places you 've got to go through. They are too narrow to turn around in, too crooked to back out of, and the shoal water is always *up at the head*; never elsewhere. And the head of them is always likely to be filling up, little by little, so that the marks you reckon their depth by, this season, may not answer for next."

"Learn a new set, then, every year?"

"Exactly. Cramp her up to the bar! What are you standing up through the middle of the river for?"

The next few months showed me strange things. On the same day that we held the conversation above narrated, we met a great rise coming down the river. The whole vast face of the stream was black with drifting dead logs, broken boughs, and great trees that had caved in and been washed away. It required the nicest steering to pick one's way through this rushing raft, even in the day-time, when crossing from point to point; and at night the difficulty was mightily increased; every now and then a huge log, lying deep in the water, would suddenly appear right under our bows, coming head-on; no use to try to avoid it then; we could only stop the engines, and one wheel would walk over that log from one end to the other, keeping up a thundering racket and careening the boat in a way that was very uncomfortable to passengers. Now and then we would hit one of these sunken logs a rattling bang, dead in the centre, with a full head of steam, and it would stun the boat as if she had hit a continent. Sometimes this log would lodge and stay right across our nose, and back the Mississippi up before it; we would have to do a little craw-fishing, then, to get away from the obstruction. We often hit *white* logs, in the dark, for we could not see them till we were right on them; but a black log is a pretty distinct object at night. A white snag is an ugly customer when the daylight is gone.

Of course, on the great rise, down came a swarm of prodigious timber-rafts from the head waters of the Mississippi, coal barges from Pittsburgh, little trading scows from everywhere, and broad-horns from "Posey County," Indiana, freighted with "fruit and furniture"—the usual term for describing it, though in plain English the freight thus aggrandized was hoop-poles and pumpkins. Pilots bore a mortal hatred to these craft; and it was returned with usury. The law required all such helpless traders to keep a light burning, but it was a law that was often broken. All of a sudden, on a murky night, a light would hop up, right under our bows, almost, and an agonized voice, with the backwoods "whang" to it, would wail out:

"Whar 'n the—you goin' to! Cain't you see nothin', you dash-dashed aig-suckin', sheep-stealin', one-eyed son of a stuffed monkey!"

Then for an instant, as we whistled by, the red glare from our furnaces would reveal the scow and the form of the gesticulating orator as if under a lightning-flash, and in that instant our firemen and deck-hands would send and receive a tempest of missiles and profanity, one of our wheels would walk off with the crashing fragments of a steering-oar, and down the dead blackness would shut again. And that flatboatman would be sure to go into New Orleans and sue our boat, swearing stoutly that he had a light burning all the time, when in truth his gang had the lantern down below to sing and lie and drink and gamble by, and no watch on deck. Once, at night, in one of those forest-bordered crevices (behind an island) which steamboatmen intensely describe with the phrase "as dark as the inside of a cow," we should have eaten up a Posey County family, fruit, furniture, and all, but that they happened to be fiddling down below and we just caught the sound of the music in time to sheer off, doing no serious damage, unfortunately, but coming so near it that we had good hopes for a moment. These people brought up their lantern, then, of course; and as we backed and filled to get away, the precious family stood in the light of it—both sexes and various ages—and cursed us till everything turned blue. Once a coal-boatman sent a bullet through our pilot-house when we borrowed a steering-oar of him, in a very narrow place.

During this big rise these small-fry craft were an intolerable nuisance. We were running chute after chute,—a new world to me,—and if there was a particularly cramped place in a chute, we would be pretty sure to meet a broad-horn there; and if he failed to be there, we would find him in a still worse locality, namely, the head of the chute, on the shoal water. And then there would be no end of profane cordialities exchanged.

Sometimes, in the big river, when we would be feeling our way cautiously along through a fog, the deep hush would suddenly be broken by yells and a clamor of tin pans, and all in an instant a log raft would appear vaguely through the webby veil, close upon us; and then we did not wait to swap knives, but snatched our engine bells out by the roots and piled on all the steam we had, to scramble out of the way! One does n't hit a rock or a solid log raft with a steamboat when he can get excused.

You will hardly believe it, but many steamboat clerks always carried a large assortment of religious tracts with them in those old departed steamboating days. Indeed they did. Twenty times a day we would be cramping up around a bar, while a string of these small-fry rascals were drifting down into the head of the bend away above and beyond us a couple of miles. Now a skiff would dart away from one of them and come fighting its laborious way across the desert of water. It would "ease all," in the shadow of our forecastle, and the panting oarsmen would shout, "Gimme a pa-a-per!" as the skiff drifted swiftly astern. The clerk would throw over a file of New Orleans journals. If these were picked up *without comment*, you might notice that now a dozen other skiffs had been drifting down upon us without saying anything. You understand, they had been waiting to see how No. 1 was going to fare. No. 1 making no comment, all the rest would bend to their oars and come on, now; and as fast as they came the clerk would heave over neat bundles of religious tracts tied to shingles. The amount of hard swearing which twelve packages of religious literature will command when impartially divided up among twelve raftsmen's crews, who have pulled a heavy skiff two miles on a hot day to get them, is simply incredible.

As I have said, the big rise brought a new world under my vision. By the time the river was over its banks we had forsaken our old paths and were hourly climbing over bars that had stood ten feet out of water before; we were shaving stumpy shores, like that at the foot of Madrid Bend, which I had always seen avoided before; we were clattering through chutes like that of 82, where the opening at the foot was an unbroken wall of timber till our nose was almost at the very spot. Some of these chutes were utter solitudes. The dense, untouched forest overhung both banks of the crooked little crack, and one could believe that human creatures had never intruded there before. The swinging grape-vines, the grassy nooks and vistas glimpsed as we swept by, the flowering creepers waving their red blossoms from the tops of dead trunks, and all the spendthrift richness of the forest foliage, were wasted and thrown away there. The chutes were lovely places to steer in; they were deep, except at the head; the current was gentle; under the "points" the water was absolutely dead, and the invisible banks so bluff that where the tender willow thickets projected you could bury your boat's broadside in them as you tore along, and then you seemed fairly to fly.

Behind other islands we found wretched little farms, and wretcheder little log-cabins; there were crazy rail fences sticking a foot or two above the water, with one or two jeans-clad, chills-racked, yellow-faced male miserables roosting on the top-rail, elbows on knees, jaws in hands, grinding tobacco and discharging the result at floating chips through crevices left by lost milk-teeth; while the rest of the family and the few farm-animals were huddled together in an empty wood-flat riding at her moorings close at hand. In this flatboat the family would have to cook and eat and sleep for a lesser or greater number of days (or possibly weeks), until the river should fall two or three feet and let them get back to their log-cabin and their chills again—chills being a merciful provision of an all-wise Providence to enable them to take exercise without exertion. And this sort of watery camping out was a thing which these people were rather liable to be treated to a couple of times a year: by the December rise out of the Ohio, and the June rise out of the Mississippi. And yet these were kindly dispensations, for they at least enabled the poor things to rise from the dead now and then, and look upon life when a steamboat went by. They appreciated the blessing, too, for they spread their mouths and eyes wide open and made the most of these occasions. Now what *could* these banished creatures find to do to keep from dying of the blues during the low-water season!

Once, in one of these lovely island chutes, we found our course completely bridged by a great fallen tree. This will serve to show how narrow some of the chutes were. The passengers had an hour's recreation in a virgin wilderness, while the boat-hands chopped the bridge away; for there was no such thing as turning back, you comprehend.

From Cairo to Baton Rouge, when the river is over its banks, you have no particular trouble in the night, for the thousand-mile wall of dense forest that guards the two banks all the way is only gapped with a farm or wood-yard opening at intervals, and so you can't "get out of the river" much easier than you could get out of a fenced lane; but from Baton Rouge to New Orleans it is a different matter. The river is more than a mile wide, and very deep—as much as two hundred feet, in places. Both banks, for a good deal over a hundred miles, are shorn of their timber and bordered by continuous sugar plantations, with only here and there a scattering sapling or row of ornamental China-trees. The timber is shorn off clear to the rear of the plantations, from two to four miles. When the first frost threatens to come, the planters snatch off their crops in a hurry. When they have finished grinding the cane, they form the refuse of the stalks (which they call *bagasse*) into great piles and set fire to them, though in other sugar countries the bagasse[2] is used for fuel in the furnaces of the sugar mills. Now the piles of damp bagasse burn slowly, and smoke like Satan's own kitchen.

An embankment ten or fifteen feet high guards both banks of the Mississippi all the way down that lower end of the river, and this embankment is set back from the edge of the shore from ten to perhaps a hundred feet, according to circumstances; say thirty or forty feet, as a general thing. Fill that whole region with an impenetrable gloom of smoke from a hundred miles of burning bagasse piles, when the river is over the banks, and turn a steamboat loose along there at midnight and see how she will feel. And see how you will feel, too! You find yourself away out in the midst of a vague dim sea that is shoreless, that fades out and loses itself in the murky distances; for you cannot discern the thin rib of embankment, and you are always imagining you see a straggling tree when you don't. The plantations themselves are transformed by the smoke and look like a part of the sea. All through your watch you are tortured with the exquisite misery of uncertainty. You hope you are keeping in the river, but you do not know. All that you are sure about is that you are likely to be

---

[2]The part of sugar cane (or sugar beets) left after the juice has been extracted.

within six feet of the bank *and* destruction, when you think you are a good half-mile from shore. And you are sure, also, that if you chance suddenly to fetch up against the embankment and topple your chimneys overboard, you will have the small comfort of knowing that it is about what you were expecting to do. One of the great Vicksburg packets darted out into a sugar plantation one night, at such a time, and had to stay there a week. But there was no novelty about it; it had often been done before.

I thought I had finished this number, but I wish to add a curious thing, while it is in my mind. It is only relevant in that it is connected with piloting. There used to be an excellent pilot on the river, a Mr. X., who was a somnambulist. It was said that if his mind was troubled about a bad piece of river, he was pretty sure to get up and walk in his sleep and do strange things. He was once fellow-pilot for a trip or two with George E——, on a great New Orleans passenger packet. During a considerable part of the first trip George was uneasy, but got over it by and by, as X. seemed content to stay in his bed when asleep. Late one night the boat was approaching Helena, Arkansas; the water was low, and the crossing above the town in a very blind and tangled condition. X. had seen the crossing since E—— had, and as the night was particularly drizzly, sullen, and dark, E—— was considering whether he had not better have X. called to assist in running the place, when the door opened and X. walked in. Now on very dark nights, light is a deadly enemy to piloting; you are aware that if you stand in a lighted room, on such a night, you cannot see things in the street to any purpose; but if you put out the lights and stand in the gloom you can make out objects in the street pretty well. So, on very dark nights, pilots do not smoke; they allow no fire in the pilot-house stove if there is a crack which can allow the least ray to escape; they order the furnaces to be curtained with huge tarpaulins and the sky-lights to be closely blinded. Then no light whatever issues from the boat. The undefinable shape that now entered the pilot-house had Mr. X.'s voice. This said,—

"Let me take her, Mr. E——; I've seen this place since you have, and it is so crooked that I reckon I can run it myself easier than I could tell you how to do it."

"It is kind of you, and I swear *I* am willing. I haven't got another drop of perspiration left in me. I have been spinning around and around the wheel like a squirrel. It is so dark I can't tell which way she is swinging till she is coming around like a whirligig."

So E—— took a seat on the bench, panting and breathless. The black phantom assumed the wheel without saying anything, steadied the waltzing steamer with a turn or two, and then stood at ease, coaxing her a little to this side and then to that, as gently and as sweetly as if the time had been noonday. When E—— observed this marvel of steering, he wished he had not confessed! He stared, and wondered, and finally said,—

"Well, I thought I knew how to steer a steamboat, but that was another mistake of mine."

X. said nothing, but went serenely on with his work. He rang for the leads; he rang to slow down the steam; he worked the boat carefully and neatly into invisible marks, then stood at the centre of the wheel and peered blandly out into the blackness, fore and aft, to verify his position; as the leads shoaled more and more, he stopped the engines entirely, and the dead silence and suspense of "drifting" followed; when the shoalest water was struck, he cracked on the steam, carried her handsomely over, and then began to work her warily into the next system of shoal marks; the same patient, heedful use of leads and engines followed, the boat slipped through without touching bottom, and entered upon the third and last intricacy of the crossing; imperceptibly she moved through the gloom, crept by inches into her marks, drifted tediously till the shoalest water was cried, and then, under a tremendous head of steam, went swinging over the reef and away into deep water and safety!

E—— let his long-pent breath pour out in a great, relieving sigh, and said:

"That 's the sweetest piece of piloting that was ever done on the Mississippi River! I would n't believed it could be done, if I had n't seen it."

There was no reply, and he added:—

"Just hold her five minutes longer, partner, and let me run down and get a cup of coffee."

A minute later E—— was biting into a pie, down in the "texas,"[3] and comforting himself with coffee. Just then the night watchman happened in, and was about to happen out again, when he noticed E—— and exclaimed,—

"Who is at the wheel, sir?"

"X."

"Dart for the pilot-house, quicker than lightning!"

The next moment both men were flying up the pilot-house companion-way, three steps at a jump! Nobody there! The great steamer was whistling down the middle of the river at her own sweet will! The watchman shot out of the place again; E—— seized the wheel, set an engine back with power, and held his breath while the boat reluctantly swung away from a "towhead"[4] which she was about to knock into the middle of the Gulf of Mexico!

By and by the watchman came back and said,—

"Did n't that lunatic tell you he was asleep, when he first came up here?"

"No."

"Well, he was. I found him walking along on top of the railings, just as unconcerned as another man would walk a pavement; and I put him to bed; now just this minute there he was again, away astern, going through that sort of tight-rope deviltry the same as before."

"Well, I think I'll stay by, next time he has one of those fits. But I hope he'll have them often. You just ought to have seen him take this boat through Helena crossing. *I* never saw anything so gaudy before. And if he can do such gold-leaf, kid-glove, diamond-breastpin piloting when he is sound asleep, what *couldn't* he do if he was dead!"

from V

"SOUNDING" FACULTIES PECULIARLY NECESSARY TO A PILOT

• • • • • • •

A pilot must have a memory; but there are two higher qualities which he must also have. He must have good and quick judgment and decision, and a cool, calm courage that no peril can shake. Give a man the merest trifle of pluck to start with, and by the time he has become a pilot he cannot be unmanned by any danger a steamboat can get into; but one cannot quite say the same for judgment. Judgment is a matter of brains, and a man must *start* with a good stock of that article or he will never succeed as a pilot.

The growth of courage in the pilot-house is steady all the time, but it does not reach a high and satisfactory condition until some time after the young pilot has been "standing his own watch," alone and under the staggering weight of all the responsibilities connected with the position. When an apprentice has become pretty thoroughly acquainted with the river, he goes clattering along so fearlessly with his steamboat, night or day, that he presently begins to imagine that it is *his* courage that

---

[3]Officer's quarters.
[4]Sandbar on which trees are growing.

animates him; but the first time the pilot steps out and leaves him to his own devices he finds out it was the other man's. He discovers that the article has been left out of his own cargo altogether. The whole river is bristling with exigencies in a moment; he is not prepared for them; he does not know how to meet them; all his knowledge forsakes him; and within fifteen minutes he is as white as a sheet and scared almost to death. Therefore pilots wisely train these cubs by various strategic tricks to look danger in the face a little more calmly. A favorite way of theirs is to play a friendly swindle upon the candidate.

Mr. B—— served me in this fashion once, and for years afterward I used to blush even in my sleep when I thought of it. I had become a good steersman; so good, indeed, that I had all the work to do on our watch, night and day; Mr. B—— seldom made a suggestion to me; all he ever did was to take the wheel on particularly bad nights or in particularly bad crossings, land the boat when she needed to be landed, play gentleman of leisure nine tenths of the watch, and collect the wages. The lower river was about bank-full, and if anybody had questioned my ability to run any crossing between Cairo and New Orleans without help or instruction, I should have felt irreparably hurt. The idea of being afraid of any crossing in the lot, in the *day-time*, was a thing too preposterous for contemplation. Well, one matchless summer's day I was bowling down the bend above island 66, brim full of self-conceit and carrying my nose as high as a giraffe's, when Mr. B—— said,—

"I am going below a while. I suppose you know the next crossing?"

This was almost an affront. It was about the plainest and simplest crossing in the whole river. One couldn't come to any harm, whether he ran it right or not; and as for depth, there never had been any bottom there. I knew all this, perfectly well.

"Know how to *run* it? Why, I can run it with my eyes shut."

"How much water is there in it?"

"Well, that is an odd question. I could n't get bottom there with a church steeple."

"You think so, do you?"

The very tone of the question shook my confidence. That was what Mr. B—— was expecting. He left, without saying anything more. I began to imagine all sorts of things. Mr. B——, unknown to me, of course, sent somebody down to the forecastle with some mysterious instructions to the leadsmen, another messenger was sent to whisper among the officers, and then Mr. B—— went into hiding behind a smoke-stack where he could observe results. Presently the captain stepped out on the hurricane deck; next the chief mate appeared; then a clerk. Every moment or two a straggler was added to my audience; and before I got to the head of the island I had fifteen or twenty people assembled down there under my nose. I began to wonder what the trouble was. As I started across, the captain glanced aloft at me and said, with a sham uneasiness in his voice,—

"Where is Mr. B——?"

"Gone below, sir."

But that did the business for me. My imagination began to construct dangers out of nothing, and they multiplied faster than I could keep the run of them. All at once I imagined I saw shoal water ahead! The wave of coward agony that surged through me then came near dislocating every joint in me. All my confidence in that crossing vanished. I seized the bell-rope; dropped it, ashamed; seized it again; dropped it once more; clutched it tremblingly once again, and pulled it so feebly that I could hardly hear the stroke myself. Captain and mate sang out instantly, and both together,—

"Starboard lead there! and quick about it!"

This was another shock. I began to climb the wheel like a squirrel; but I would hardly get the boat started to port before I would see new dangers on that side, and away I would spin to the other; only to find perils accumulating to starboard, and be crazy to get to port again. Then came the leadsman's sepulchral cry:—

"D-e-e-p four!"

Deep four in a bottomless crossing! The terror of it took my breath away.

"M-a-r-k three! M-a-r-k three! Quarter less three! Half twain!"

This was frightful! I seized the bell-ropes and stopped the engines.

"Quarter twain! Quarter twain! *Mark* twain!"

I was helpless. I did not know what in the world to do. I was quaking from head to foot, and I could have hung my hat on my eyes, they stuck out so far.

"Quarter *less* twain! Nine and a *half*!"

We were *drawing* nine! My hands were in a nerveless flutter. I could not ring a bell intelligibly with them. I flew to the speaking-tube and shouted to the engineer,—

"Oh, Ben, if you love me, *back* her! Quick, Ben! Oh, back the immortal *soul* out of her!"

I heard the door close gently. I looked around, and there stood Mr. B——, smiling a bland, sweet smile. Then the audience on the hurricane deck sent up a shout of humiliating laughter. I saw it all, now, and I felt meaner than the meanest man in human history. I laid in the lead, set the boat in her marks, came ahead on the engines, and said,—

"It was a fine trick to play on an orphan, *was n't* it? I suppose I'll never hear the last of how I was ass enough to heave the lead at the head of 66."

"Well, no, you won't, maybe. In fact I hope you won't; for I want you to learn something by that experience. Didn't you *know* there was no bottom in that crossing?"

"Yes, sir, I did."

"Very well, then. You shouldn't have allowed me or anybody else to shake your confidence in that knowledge. Try to remember that. And another thing: when you get into a dangerous place, don't turn coward. That isn't going to help matters any."

It was a good enough lesson, but pretty hardly learned. Yet about the hardest part of it was that for months I so often had to hear a phrase which I had conceived a particular distaste for. It was, "Oh, Ben, if you love me, back her!"

1875

from A Tramp Abroad

BAKER'S BLUE-JAY YARN

Animals talk to each other, of course. There can be no question about that; but I suppose there are very few people who can understand them. I never knew but one man who could. I knew he could, however, because he told me so himself. He was a middle-aged, simple-hearted miner who had lived in a lonely corner of California, among the woods and mountains, a good many years, and had studied the ways of his only neighbors, the beasts and the birds, until he believed he could accurately translate any remark which they made. This was Jim Baker. According to Jim Baker, some animals have only a limited education, and use only very simple words, and scarcely ever a comparison or a flowery figure; whereas, certain other animals have a large vocabulary, a fine command of language and a ready and fluent delivery; consequently these latter talk a great deal; they like it; they are conscious of their talent, and they enjoy "showing off." Baker said, that after long and careful observation, he had come to the conclusion that the blue-jays were the best talkers he had found among birds and beasts. Said he:—

"There's more *to* a blue-jay than any other creature. He has got more moods, and more different kinds of feelings than other creature; and mind you, whatever a blue-jay feels, he can put into language. And no mere commonplace language, either, but rattling, out-and-out book-talk—and bristling with metaphor, too—just bristling! And as for command of language—why *you* never see a blue-jay get stuck for a word.

No man ever did. They just boil out of him! And another thing: I've noticed a good deal, and there's no bird, or cow, or anything that uses as good grammar as a blue-jay. You may say a cat uses good grammar. Well, a cat does—but you let a cat get excited, once; you let a cat get to pulling fur with another cat on a shed, nights, and you'll hear grammar that will give you the lockjaw. Ignorant people think it's the *noise* which fighting cats make that is so aggravating, but it ain't so; it's the sickening grammar they use. Now I've never heard a jay use bad grammar but very seldom; and when they do, they are as ashamed as a human; they shut right down and leave.

"You may call a jay a bird. Well, so he is, in a measure—because he's got feathers on him, and don't belong to no church, perhaps; but otherwise he is just as much a human as you be. And I'll tell you for why. A jay's gifts, and instincts, and feelings, and interests, cover the whole ground. A jay hasn't got any more principle than a Congressman. A jay will lie, a jay will steal, a jay will deceive, a jay will betray; and four times out of five, a jay will go back on his solemnest promise. The sacredness of an obligation is a thing which you can't cram into no blue-jay's head. Now on top of all this, there's another thing: a jay can out-swear any gentleman in the mines. You think a cat can swear. Well, a cat can; but you give a blue-jay a subject that calls for his reserve-powers, and where is your cat? Don't talk to *me*—I know too much about this thing. And there's yet another thing: in the one little particular of scolding—just good, clean, out-and-out scolding—a blue-jay can lay over anything, human or divine. Yes, sir, a jay is everything that a man is. A jay can cry, a jay can laugh, a jay can feel shame, a jay can reason and plan and discuss, a jay likes gossip and scandal, a jay has got a sense of humor, a jay knows when he is an ass just as well as you do—maybe better. If a jay ain't human, he better take in his sign, that's all. Now I'm going to tell you a perfectly true fact about some blue-jays."

"When I first begun to understand jay language correctly, there was a little incident happened here. Seven years ago, the last man in this region but me, moved away. There stands his house,—been empty ever since; a log house, with a plank roof—just one big room, and no more; no ceiling—nothing between the rafters and the floor. Well, one Sunday morning I was sitting out here in front of my cabin, with my cat, taking the sun, and looking at the blue hills, and listening to the leaves rustling so lonely in the trees, and thinking of the home away yonder in the States, that I hadn't heard from in thirteen years, when a blue jay lit on that house, with an acorn in his mouth, and says, 'Hello, I reckon I've struck something.' When he spoke, the acorn dropped out of his mouth and rolled down the roof, of course, but he didn't care; his mind was all on the thing he had struck. It was a knot-hole in the roof. He cocked his head to one side, shut one eye and put the other one to the hole, like a 'possum looking down a jug; then he glanced up with his bright eyes, gave a wink or two with his wings—which signifies gratification, you understand,—and says, 'It looks like a hole, it's located like a hole,—blamed if I don't believe it *is* a hole!'

"Then he cocked his head down and took another look; he glances up perfectly joyful, this time; winks his wings and his tail both, and says, 'O, no, this ain't no fat thing, I reckon! If I ain't in luck!—why it's a perfectly elegant hole!' So he flew down and got that acorn, and fetched it up and dropped it in, and was just tilting his head back, with the heavenliest smile on his face, when all of a sudden he was paralyzed into a listening attitude and that smile faded gradually out of his countenance like breath off'n a razor, and the queerest look of surprise took its place. Then he says, 'Why I didn't hear it fall!' He cocked his eye at the hole again, and took a long look; raised up and shook his head; stepped around to the other side of the hole and took another look from that side; shook his head again. He studied a while, then he just went into the *de*tails—walked round and round the hole and spied into it from every point of the compass. No use. Now he took a thinking attitude on the comb of the roof and scratched the back of his head with his right foot a minute, and finally says, 'Well, it's too many for *me*, that's certain; must be a mighty long hole; however, I ain't got no time to fool around here, I got to 'tend to business; I reckon it's all right—chance it, anyway.'

"So he flew off and fetched another acorn and dropped it in, and tried to flirt his eye to the hole quick enough to see what become of it, but he was too late. He held his eye there as much as a minute; then he raised up and sighed, and says, 'Consound it, I don't seem to understand this thing, no way; however, I'll tackle her again.' He fetched another acorn, and done his level best to see what become of it, but he couldn't. He says, 'Well, *I* never struck no such a hole as this, before; I'm of the opinion it's a totally new kind of a hole.' Then he begun to get mad. He held in for a spell, walking up and down the comb of the roof and shaking his head and muttering to himself; but his feelings got the upper hand of him, presently, and he broke loose and cussed himself black in the face. I never see a bird take on so about a little thing. When he got through he walks to the hole and looks in again for half a minute; then he says, 'Well, you're a long hole, and a deep hole, and a mighty singular hole altogether—but I've started in to fill you, and I'm d—d if I *don't* fill you, if it takes a hundred years!'

"And with that, away he went. You never see a bird work so since you was born. He laid into his work like a nigger, and the way he hove acorns into that hole for about two hours and a half was one of the most exciting and astonishing spectacles I ever struck. He never stopped to take a look any more—he just hove 'em in and went for more. Well at last he could hardly flop his wings, he was so tuckered out. He comes a-drooping down, once more, sweating like an ice-pitcher, drops his acorn in and says, '*Now* I guess I've got the bulge on you by this time!' So he bent down for a look. If you'll believe me, when his head come up again he was just pale with rage. He says, 'I've shoveled acorns enough in there to keep the family thirty years, and if I can see a sign of one of 'em I wish I may land in a museum with a belly full of sawdust in two minutes!'

"He just had strength enough to crawl up on to the comb and lean his back agin the chimbly, and then he collected his impressions and begun to free his mind. I see in a second that what I had mistook for profanity in the mines was only just the rudiments, as you may say.

"Another jay was going by, and heard him doing his devotions, and stops to inquire what was up. The sufferer told him the whole circumstance, and says, 'Now yonder's the hole, and if you don't believe me, go and look for yourself.' So this fellow went and looked, and comes back and says, 'How many did you say you put in there?' 'Not any less than two tons,' says the sufferer. The other jay went and looked again. He couldn't seem to make it out, so he raised a yell, and three more jays come. They all examined the hole, they all made the sufferer tell it over again, then they all discussed it, and got off as many leather-headed opinions about it as an average crowd of humans could have done.

"They called in more jays; then more and more, till pretty soon this whole region 'peared to have a blue flush about it. There must have been five thousand of them; and such another jawing and disputing and ripping and cussing, you never heard. Every jay in the whole lot put his eye to the hole and delivered a more chuckle-headed opinion about the mystery than the jay that went there before him. They examined the house all over, too. The door was standing half open, and at last one old jay happened to go and light on it and look in. Of course that knocked the mystery galley-west in a second. There lay the acorns, scattered all over the floor. He flopped his wings and raised a whoop. 'Come here!' he says, 'Come here, everybody; hang'd if this fool hasn't been trying to fill up a house with acorns!' They all came a-swooping down like a blue cloud, and as each fellow lit on the door and took a glance, the whole absurdity of the contract that that first jay had tackled hit him home and he fell over backwards suffocating with laughter, and the next jay took his place and done the same.

"Well, sir, they roosted around here on the house-top and the trees for an hour, and guffawed over that thing like human beings. It ain't any use to tell me a blue-jay hasn't got a sense of humor, because I know better. And memory, too. They brought jays here from all over the United States to look down that hole, every summer for three years. Other birds too. And they could all see the point, except an owl that come from Nova Scotia to visit the Yo Semite, and he took this thing in on his way back. He said he couldn't see anything funny in it. But then he was a good deal disappointed about Yo Semite, too."

1880

How to Tell a Story

THE HUMOROUS STORY AN AMERICAN DEVELOPMENT.—ITS DIFFERENCE FROM COMIC AND WITTY STORIES.

I do not claim that I can tell a story as it ought to be told. I only claim to know how a story ought to be told, for I have been almost daily in the company of the most expert story-tellers for many years.

There are several kinds of stories, but only one difficult kind—the humorous. I will talk mainly about that one. The humorous story is American, the comic story is English, the witty story is French. The humorous story depends for its effect upon the *manner* of the telling; the comic story and the witty story upon the *matter*.

The humorous story may be spun out to great length, and may wander around as much as it pleases, and arrive nowhere in particular; but the comic and witty stories must be brief and end with a point. The humorous story bubbles gently along, the others burst.

The humorous story is strictly a work of art—high and delicate art—and only an artist can tell it; but no art is necessary in telling the comic and the witty story; anybody can do it. The art of telling a humorous story—understand, I mean by word of mouth, not print—was created in America, and has remained at home.

The humorous story is told gravely; the teller does his best to conceal the fact that he even dimly suspects that there is anything funny about it; but the teller of the comic story tells you beforehand that it is one of the funniest things he has ever heard, then tells it with eager delight, and is the first person to laugh when he gets through. And sometimes, if he has had good success, he is so glad and happy that he will repeat the "nub" of it and glance around from face to face, collecting applause, and then repeat it again. It is a pathetic thing to see.

Very often, of course, the rambling and disjointed humorous story finishes with a nub, point, snapper, or whatever you like to call it. Then the listener must be alert, for in many cases the teller will divert attention from that nub by dropping it in a carefully casual and indifferent way, with the pretence that he does not know it is a nub.

Artemus Ward[1] used that trick a good deal; then when the belated audience presently caught the joke he would look up with innocent surprise, as if wondering what they had found to laugh at. Dan Setchell[2] used it before him, Nye and Riley[3] and others use it to-day.

---

[1]Pseudonym of Charles Farrar Browne (1834–1867), born in Maine, a literary comedian and famed lecturer and story-teller about backwoods characters.
[2]Dan Setchell, comic actor who appeared frequently during the 1850s and 1860s.

[3]Edgar Wilson Nye (1850–1896), known as Bill Nye, born in Maine but brought up in the West, a journalist turned frontier humorist and literary comedian; James Whitcomb Riley (1849–1916), Indiana poet who often wrote humorous poems in rustic dialect.

But the teller of the comic story does not slur the nub; he shouts it at you—every time. And when he prints it, in England, France, Germany, and Italy, he italicizes it, puts some whooping exclamation-points after it, and sometimes explains it in a parenthesis. All of which is very depressing, and makes one want to renounce joking and lead a better life.

Let me set down an instance of the comic method, using an anecdote which has been popular all over the world for twelve or fifteen hundred years. The teller tells it in this way:

THE WOUNDED SOLDIER

In the course of a certain battle a soldier whose leg had been shot off appealed to another soldier who was hurrying by to carry him to the rear, informing him at the same time of the loss which he had sustained; whereupon the generous son of Mars, shouldering the unfortunate, proceeded to carry out his desire. The bullets and cannon-balls were flying in all directions, and presently one of the latter took the wounded man's head off—without, however, his deliverer being aware of it. In no long time he was hailed by an officer, who said:

"Where are you going with that carcass?"

"To the rear, sir—he's lost his leg!"

"His leg, forsooth?" responded the astonished officer; "you mean his head, you booby."

Whereupon the soldier dispossessed himself of his burden, and stood looking down upon it in great perplexity. At length he said:

"It is true, sir, just as you have said." Then after a pause he added, "*But he* TOLD *me* IT WAS HIS LEG! ! ! ! !"

Here the narrator bursts into explosion after explosion of thunderous horse-laughter, repeating that nub from time to time through his gaspings and shriekings and suffocatings.

It takes only a minute and a half to tell that in its comic-story form; and isn't worth the telling, after all. Put into the humorous-story form it takes ten minutes, and is about the funniest thing I have ever listened to—as James Whitcomb Riley tells it.

He tells it in the character of a dull-witted old farmer who has just heard it for the first time, thinks it is unspeakably funny, and is trying to repeat it to a neighbor. But he can't remember it; so he gets all mixed up and wanders helplessly round and round, putting in tedious details that don't belong in the tale and only retard it; taking them out conscientiously and putting in others that are just as useless; making minor mistakes now and then and stopping to correct them and explain how he came to make them; remembering things which he forgot to put in in their proper place and going back to put them in there; stopping his narrative a good while in order to try to recall the name of the soldier that was hurt, and finally remembering that the soldier's name was not mentioned, and remarking placidly that the name is of no real importance, anyway—better, of course, if one knew it, but not essential, after all—and so on, and so on, and so on.

The teller is innocent and happy and pleased with himself, and has to stop every little while to hold himself in and keep from laughing outright; and does hold in, but his body quakes in a jelly-like way with interior chuckles; and at the end of the ten minutes the audience have laughed until they are exhausted, and the tears are running down their faces.

The simplicity and innocence and sincerity and unconsciousness of the old farmer are perfectly simulated, and the result is a performance which is thoroughly charming and delicious. This is art—and fine and beautiful, and only a master can compass it; but a machine could tell the other story.

To string incongruities and absurdities together in a wandering and sometimes purposeless way, and seem innocently unaware that they are absurdities, is the basis of the American art, if my position is correct. Another feature is the slurring of the point. A third is the dropping of a studied remark apparently without knowing it, as if one were thinking aloud. The fourth and last is the pause.

Artemus Ward dealt in numbers three and four a good deal. He would begin to tell with great animation something which he seemed to think was wonderful; then lose confidence, and after an apparently absent-minded pause add an incongruous remark in a soliloquizing way; and that was the remark intended to explode the mine—and it did.

For instance, he would say eagerly, excitedly, "I once knew a man in New Zealand who hadn't a tooth in his head"—here his animation would die out; a silent, reflective pause would follow, then he would say dreamily, and as if to himself, "and yet that man could beat a drum better than any man I ever saw."

The pause is an exceedingly important feature in any kind of story, and a frequently recurring feature, too. It is a dainty thing, and delicate, and also uncertain and treacherous; for it must be exactly the right length—no more and no less—or it fails of its purpose and makes trouble. If the pause is too short the impressive point is passed, and the audience have had time to divine that a surprise is intended—and then you can't surprise them, of course.

On the platform I used to tell a negro ghost story that had a pause in front of the snapper on the end, and that pause was the most important thing in the whole story. If I got it the right length precisely, I could spring the finishing ejaculation with effect enough to make some impressible girl deliver a startled little yelp and jump out of her seat—and that was what I was after. This story was called "The Golden Arm," and was told in this fashion. You can practise with it yourself—and mind you look out for the pause and get it right.

THE GOLDEN ARM

Once 'pon a time dey wuz a monsus mean man, en he live 'way out in de prairie all 'lone by hisself, 'cep'n he had a wife. En bimeby she died, en he tuck en toted her way out dah in de prairie en buried her. Well, she had a golden arm—all solid gold, fum de shoulder down. He wuz pow'ful mean—pow'ful; en dat night he couldn't sleep, caze he want dat golden arm so bad.

When it come midnight he couldn't stan' it no mo'; so he git up, he did, en tuck his lantern en shoved out thoo de storm en dug her up en got de golden arm; en he bent his head down 'gin de win', en plowed en plowed en plowed thoo de snow. Den all on a sudden he stop (make a considerable pause here, and look startled, and take a listening attitude) en say: "My *lan'*, what's dat!"

En he listen—en listen—en de win' say (set your teeth together and imitate the wailing and wheezing singsong of the wind), "Bzzz-z-zzz"—en den, way back yonder whah de grave is, he hear a *voice!*—he hear a voice all mix' up in de win'—can't hardly tell 'em 'part—"Bzzz-zz—W-h-o—g-o-t—m-y—g-o-l-d-e-n *arm?*—zzz—zzz—W-h-o g-o-t m-y g-o-l-d-e-n *arm?* (You must begin to shiver violently now.)

En he begin to shiver en shake, en say, "Oh, my! *Oh*, my lan'!" en de win' blow de lantern out, en de snow en sleet blow in his face en mos' choke him, en he start a-plowin' knee-deep towards home mos' dead, he so sk'yerd—en pooty soon he hear de voice agin, en (pause) it 'us comin' *after* him! "Bzzz—zzz—zzz—W-h-o—g-o-t—m-y—g-o-l-d-e-n—*arm?*"

When he git to de pasture he hear it agin—closter now, en a-*comin'!*—a-comin' back dah in de dark en de storm—(repeat the wind and the voice). When he git to de house he rush up-stairs en jump in de bed en kiver up, head and years, en lay dah shiverin' en shakin'—en den way out dah he hear it *agin*—en a-*comin'!* En bimeby he hear (pause—awed, listening attitude)—pat—pat—pat—hit's a-comin' up-stairs! Den he hear de latch, en he *know* it's in de room!

Den pooty soon he know it's a-*stannin' by de bed!* (Pause.) Den—he know it's a-*bendin' down over him*—en he cain't skasely git his breath! Den—den— he seem to feel someth'n *c-o-l-d*, right down 'most agin his head! (Pause.)

Den de voice say, *right at his year*—"W-h-o—g-o-t—m-y—g-o-l-d-e-n *arm?*" (You must wail it out very plaintively and accusingly; then you stare steadily and impressively into the face of the farthest-gone auditor—a girl, preferably—and let that awe-inspiring pause begin to build itself in the deep hush. When it has reached exactly the right length, jump suddenly at that girl and yell, "*You've* got it!"

If you've got the *pause* right, she'll fetch a dear little yelp and spring right out of her shoes. But you *must* get the pause right; and you will find it the most troublesome and aggravating and uncertain thing you ever undertook.)

1895

Fenimore Cooper's[1] Literary Offences

The Pathfinder and *The Deerslayer* stand at the head of Cooper's novels as artistic creations. There are others of his works which contain parts as perfect as are to be found in these, and scenes even more thrilling. Not one can be compared with either of them as a finished whole.

The defects in both of these tales are comparatively slight. They were pure works of art.—*Prof. Lounsbury.*[2]

The five tales reveal an extraordinary fulness of invention.

. . . One of the very greatest characters in fiction, Natty Bumppo. . . .

The craft of the woodsman, the tricks of the trapper, all the delicate art of the forest, were familiar to Cooper from his youth up.—*Prof. Brander Matthews.*[3]

Cooper is the greatest artist in the domain of romantic fiction yet produced by America.—*Wilkie Collins.*[4]

It seems to me that it was far from right for the Professor of English Literature in Yale, the Professor of English Literature in Columbia, and Wilkie Collins to deliver opinions on Cooper's literature without having read some of it. It would have been much more decorous to keep silent and let persons talk who have read Cooper.

Cooper's art has some defects. In one place in *Deerslayer*, and in the restricted space of two-thirds of a page, Cooper has scored 114 offences against literary art out of a possible 115. It breaks the record.

---

[1]James Fenimore Cooper (1789–1851), popular American novelist of the conflict of white men and Indians in the American migration westward, especially in the five Leather-Stocking Tales, which included *The Pathfinder* (1840), *The Deerslayer* (1841), and *The Last of the Mohicans* (1826), and portrayed the frontiersman Natty Bumppo as the hero.

[2]Thomas R. Lounsbury (1838–1915), Yale English professor whose biography of Cooper appeared in 1882.
[3]Brander Matthews (1852–1929), Columbia literature professor, playwright, and critic.
[4]Wilkie Collins (1824–1889), British author, especially of detective or mystery novels.

There are nineteen rules governing literary art in the domain of romantic fiction—some say twenty-two. In *Deerslayer* Cooper violated eighteen of them. These eighteen require:

1. That a tale shall accomplish something and arrive somewhere. But the *Deerslayer* tale accomplishes nothing and arrives in the air.

2. They require that the episodes of a tale shall be necessary parts of the tale, and shall help to develop it. But as the *Deerslayer* tale is not a tale, and accomplishes nothing and arrives nowhere, the episodes have no rightful place in the work, since there was nothing for them to develop.

3. They require that the personages in a tale shall be alive, except in the case of corpses, and that always the reader shall be able to tell the corpses from the others. But this detail has often been overlooked in the *Deerslayer* tale.

4. They require that the personages in a tale, both dead and alive, shall exhibit a sufficient excuse for being there. But this detail also has been overlooked in the *Deerslayer* tale.

5. They require that when the personages of a tale deal in conversation, the talk shall sound like human talk, and be talk such as human beings would be likely to talk in the given circumstances, and have a discoverable meaning, also a discoverable purpose, and a show of relevancy, and remain in the neighborhood of the subject in hand, and be interesting to the reader, and help out the tale, and stop when the people cannot think of anything more to say. But this requirement has been ignored from the beginning of the *Deerslayer* tale to the end of it.

6. They require that when the author describes the character of a personage in his tale, the conduct and conversation of that personage shall justify said description. But this law gets little or no attention in the *Deerslayer* tale, as Natty Bumppo's case will amply prove.

7. They require that when a personage talks like an illustrated, gilt-edged, tree-calf, hand-tooled, seven-dollar Friendship's Offering[5] in the beginning of a paragraph, he shall not talk like a negro minstrel in the end of it. But this rule is flung down and danced upon in the *Deerslayer* tale.

8. They require that crass stupidities shall not be played upon the reader as "the craft of the woodsman, the delicate art of the forest," by either the author or the people in the tale. But this rule is persistently violated in the *Deerslayer* tale.

9. They require that the personages of a tale shall confine themselves to possibilities and let miracles alone; or, if they venture a miracle, the author must so plausibly set it forth as to make it look possible and reasonable. But these rules are not respected in the *Deerslayer* tale.

10. They require that the author shall make the reader feel a deep interest in the personages of his tale and in their fate; and that he shall make the reader love the good people in the tale and hate the bad ones. But the reader of the *Deerslayer* tale dislikes the good people in it, is indifferent to the others, and wishes they would all get drowned together.

11. They require that the characters in a tale shall be so clearly defined that the reader can tell beforehand what each will do in a given emergency. But in the *Deerslayer* tale this rule is vacated.

In addition to these large rules there are some little ones. They require that the author shall

12. *Say* what he is proposing to say, not merely come near it.

13. Use the right word, not its second cousin.

14. Eschew surplusage.

15. Not omit necessary details.

---

[5]Book bound in elegant tree-calf, calfskin chemically treated so as to take on a tree-like design.

16. Avoid slovenliness of form.

17. Use good grammar.

18. Employ a simple and straightforward style.

Even these seven are coldly and persistently violated in the *Deerslayer* tale.

Cooper's gift in the way of invention was not a rich endowment; but such as it was he liked to work it, he was pleased with the effects, and indeed he did some quite sweet things with it. In his little box of stage properties he kept six or eight cunning devices, tricks, artifices for his savages and woodsmen to deceive and circumvent each other with, and he was never so happy as when he was working these innocent things and seeing them go. A favorite one was to make a moccasined person tread in the tracks of the moccasined enemy, and thus hide his own trail. Cooper wore out barrels and barrels of moccasins in working that trick. Another stage-property that he pulled out of his box pretty frequently was his broken twig. He prized his broken twig above all the rest of his effects, and worked it the hardest. It is a restful chapter in any book of his when somebody doesn't step on a dry twig and alarm all the reds and whites for two hundred yards around. Every time a Cooper person is in peril, and absolute silence is worth four dollars a minute, he is sure to step on a dry twig. There may be a hundred handier things to step on, but that wouldn't satisfy Cooper. Cooper requires him to turn out and find a dry twig; and if he can't do it, go and borrow one. In fact, the Leather Stocking Series ought to have been called the Broken Twig Series.

I am sorry there is not room to put in a few dozen instances of the delicate art of the forest, as practised by Natty Bumppo and some of the other Cooperian experts. Perhaps we may venture two or three samples. Cooper was a sailor—a naval officer; yet he gravely tells us how a vessel, driving towards a lee shore in a gale, is steered for a particular spot by her skipper because he knows of an *undertow* there which will hold her back against the gale and save her. For just pure woodcraft, or sailorcraft, or whatever it is, isn't that neat? For several years Cooper was daily in the society of artillery, and he ought to have noticed that when a cannon-ball strikes the ground it either buries itself or skips a hundred feet or so; skips again a hundred feet or so— and so on, till finally it gets tired and rolls. Now in one place he loses some "females"—as he always calls women—in the edge of a wood near a plain at night in a fog, on purpose to give Bumppo a chance to show off the delicate art of the forest before the reader. These mislaid people are hunting for a fort. They hear a cannon-blast, and a cannon-ball presently comes rolling into the wood and stops at their feet. To the females this suggests nothing. The case is very different with the admirable Bumppo. I wish I may never know peace again if he doesn't strike out promptly and *follow the track* of that cannon-ball across the plain through the dense fog and find the fort. Isn't it a daisy? If Cooper had any real knowledge of Nature's ways of doing things, he had a most delicate art in concealing the fact. For instance: one of his acute Indian experts, Chingachgook[6] (pronounced Chicago, I think), has lost the trail of a person he is tracking through the forest. Apparently that trail is hopelessly lost. Neither you nor I could ever have guessed out the way to find it. It was very different with Chicago. Chicago was not stumped for long. He turned a running stream out of its course, and there, in the slush in its old bed, were that person's moccasin-tracks. The current did not wash them away, as it would have done in all other like cases— no, even the eternal laws of Nature have to vacate when Cooper wants to put up a delicate job of woodcraft on the reader.

We must be a little wary when Brander Matthews tells us that Cooper's books "reveal an extraordinary fulness of invention." As a rule, I am quite willing to accept Brander Matthews's literary judgments and applaud his lucid and graceful phrasing

---

[6]Indian friend of Natty Bumppo in the Leather-Stocking Tales.

of them; but that particular statement needs to be taken with a few tons of salt. Bless your heart, Cooper hadn't any more invention than a horse; and I don't mean a high-class horse, either; I mean a clothes-horse. It would be very difficult to find a really clever "situation" in Cooper's books, and still more difficult to find one of any kind which he has failed to render absurd by his handling of it. Look at the episodes of "the caves"; and at the celebrated scuffle between Maqua and those others on the table-land a few days later; and at Hurry Harry's queer water-transit from the castle to the ark; and at Deerslayer's half-hour with his first corpse; and at the quarrel between Hurry Harry and Deerslayer later; and at—but choose for yourself; you can't go amiss.

If Cooper had been an observer his inventive faculty would have worked better; not more interestingly, but more rationally, more plausibly. Cooper's proudest creations in the way of "situations" suffer noticeably from the absence of the observer's protecting gift. Cooper's eye was splendidly inaccurate. Cooper seldom saw anything correctly. He saw nearly all things as through a glass eye, darkly.[7] Of course a man who cannot see the commonest little every-day matters accurately is working at a disadvantage when he is constructing a "situation." In the *Deerslayer* tale Cooper has a stream which is fifty feet wide where it flows out of a lake; it presently narrows to twenty as it meanders along for no given reason, and yet when a stream acts like that it ought to be required to explain itself. Fourteen pages later the width of the brook's outlet from the lake has suddenly shrunk thirty feet, and become "the narrowest part of the stream." This shrinkage is not accounted for. The stream has bends in it, a sure indication that it has alluvial banks and cuts them; yet these bends are only thirty and fifty feet long. If Cooper had been a nice[8] and punctilious observer he would have noticed that the bends were oftener nine hundred feet long than short of it.

Cooper made the exit of that stream fifty feet wide, in the first place, for no particular reason; in the second place, he narrowed it to less than twenty to accommodate some Indians. He bends a "sapling" to the form of an arch over this narrow passage, and conceals six Indians in its foliage. They are "laying" for a settler's scow or ark which is coming up the stream on its way to the lake; it is being hauled against the stiff current by a rope whose stationary end is anchored in the lake; its rate of progress cannot be more than a mile an hour. Cooper describes the ark, but pretty obscurely. In the matter of dimensions "it was little more than a modern canal-boat." Let us guess, then, that it was about one hundred and forty feet long. It was of "greater breadth than common." Let us guess, then, that it was about sixteen feet wide. This leviathan had been prowling down bends which were but a third as long as itself, and scraping between banks where it had only two feet of space to spare on each side. We cannot too much admire this miracle. A low-roofed log dwelling occupies "two-thirds of the ark's length"—a dwelling ninety feet long and sixteen feet wide, let us say—a kind of vestibule train. The dwelling has two rooms—each forty-five feet long and sixteen feet wide, let us guess. One of them is the bedroom of the Hutter girls, Judith and Hetty; the other is the parlor in the daytime, at night it is papa's bed-chamber. The ark is arriving at the stream's exit now, whose width has been reduced to less than twenty feet to accommodate the Indians—say to eighteen. There is a foot to spare on each side of the boat. Did the Indians notice that there was going to be a tight squeeze there? Did they notice that they could make money by climbing down out of that arched sapling and just stepping aboard when the ark scraped by? No, other Indians would have noticed these things, but Cooper's Indians never notice anything. Cooper thinks they are marvelous creatures for noticing, but

---

[7]Cf. 1 Corinthians 13:12: "For now we see through a glass, darkly."
[8]I.e., discriminating.

he was almost always in error about his Indians. There was seldom a sane one among them.

The ark is one hundred and forty feet long; the dwelling is ninety feet long. The idea of the Indians is to drop softly and secretly from the arched sapling to the dwelling as the ark creeps along under it at the rate of a mile an hour, and butcher the family. It will take the ark a minute and a half to pass under. It will take the ninety foot dwelling a minute to pass under. Now, then, what did the six Indians do? It would take you thirty years to guess, and even then you would have to give it up, I believe. Therefore, I will tell you what the Indians did. Their chief, a person of quite extraordinary intellect for a Cooper Indian, warily watched the canal-boat as it squeezed along under him, and when he had got his calculations fined down to exactly the right shade, as he judged, he let go and dropped. And *missed the house!* That is actually what he did. He missed the house, and landed in the stern of the scow. It was not much of a fall, yet it knocked him silly. He lay there unconscious. If the house had been ninety-seven feet long he would have made the trip. The fault was Cooper's, not his. The error lay in the construction of the house. Cooper was no architect.

There still remained in the roost five Indians. The boat has passed under and is now out of their reach. Let me explain what the five did—you would not be able to reason it out for yourself. No. 1 jumped for the boat, but fell in the water astern of it. Then No. 2 jumped for the boat, but fell in the water still farther astern of it. Then No. 3 jumped for the boat, and fell a good way astern of it. Then No. 4 jumped for the boat, and fell in the water *away* astern. Then even No. 5 made a jump for the boat—for he was a Cooper Indian. In the matter of intellect, the difference between a Cooper Indian and the Indian that stands in front of the cigar-shop is not spacious. The scow episode is really a sublime burst of invention; but it does not thrill, because the inaccuracy of the details throws a sort of air of fictitiousness and general improbability over it. This comes of Cooper's inadequacy as an observer.

The reader will find some examples of Cooper's high talent for inaccurate observation in the account of the shooting-match in *The Pathfinder.*

> "A common wrought nail was driven lightly into the target, its head having been first touched with paint."

The color of the paint is not stated—an important omission, but Cooper deals freely in important omissions. No, after all, it was not an important omission; for this nail-head is *a hundred yards from* the marksmen, and could not be seen by them at that distance, no matter what its color might be. How far can the best eye see a common house-fly? A hundred yards? It is quite impossible. Very well; eyes that cannot see a house-fly that is a hundred yards away cannot see an ordinary nail-head at that distance, for the size of the two objects is the same. It takes a keen eye to see a fly or a nail-head at fifty yards—one hundred and fifty feet. Can the reader do it?

The nail was lightly driven, its head painted, and game called. Then the Cooper miracles began. The bullet of the first marksman chipped an edge of the nail-head; the next man's bullet drove the nail a little way into the target—and removed all the paint. Haven't the miracles gone far enough now? Not to suit Cooper; for the purpose of this whole scheme is to show off his prodigy, Deerslayer-Hawkeye-Long-Rifle-Leather-Stocking-Pathfinder-Bumppo before the ladies.

> "'Be all ready to clench it, boys!' cried out Pathfinder, stepping into his friend's tracks the instant they were vacant. 'Never mind a new nail; I can see that, though the paint is gone, and what I can see I can hit at a hundred yards, though it were only a mosquito's eye. Be ready to clench!'
>
> "The rifle cracked, the bullet sped its way, and the head of the nail was buried in the wood, covered by the piece of flattened lead."

There, you see, is a man who could hunt flies with a rifle, and command a ducal salary in a Wild West show to-day if we had him back with us.

The recorded feat is certainly surprising just as it stands; but it is not surprising enough for Cooper. Cooper adds a touch. He has made Pathfinder do this miracle with another man's rifle; and not only that, but Pathfinder did not have even the advantage of loading it himself. He had everything against him, and yet he made that impossible shot; and not only made it, but did it with absolute confidence, saying, "Be ready to clench." Now a person like that would have undertaken that same feat with a brickbat, and with Cooper to help he would have achieved it, too.

Pathfinder showed off handsomely that day before the ladies. His very first feat was a thing which no Wild West show can touch. He was standing with the group of marksmen, observing—a hundred yards from the target, mind; one Jasper raised his rifle and drove the centre of the bull's-eye. Then the Quartermaster fired. The target exhibited no result this time. There was a laugh. "It's a dead miss," said Major Lundie. Pathfinder waited an impressive moment or two; then said, in that calm, indifferent, know-it-all way of his, "No, Major, he has covered Jasper's bullet, as will be seen if any one will take the trouble to examine the target."

Wasn't it remarkable! How *could* he see that little pellet fly through the air and enter that distant bullet-hole? Yet that is what he did; for nothing is impossible to a Cooper person. Did any of those people have any deep-seated doubts about this thing? No; for that would imply sanity, and these were all Cooper people.

> "The respect for Pathfinder's skill and for his *quickness and accuracy of sight*" (the italics are mine) "was so profound and general, that the instant he made this declaration the spectators began to distrust their own opinions, and a dozen rushed to the target in order to ascertain the fact. There, sure enough, it was found that the Quartermaster's bullet had gone through the hole made by Jasper's, and that, too, so accurately as to require a minute examination to be certain of the circumstance, which, however, was soon clearly established by discovering one bullet over the other in the stump against which the target was placed."

They made a "minute" examination; but never mind, how could they know that there were two bullets in that hole without digging the latest one out? for neither probe nor eyesight could prove the presence of any more than one bullet. Did they dig? No; as we shall see. It is the Pathfinder's turn now; he steps out before the ladies, takes aim, and fires.

But, alas! here is a disappointment; an incredible, an unimaginable disappointment—for the target's aspect is unchanged; there is nothing there but that same old bullet-hole!

> "'If one dared to hint at such a thing,' cried Major Duncan, 'I should say that the Pathfinder has also missed the target!'"

As nobody had missed it yet, the "also" was not necessary; but never mind about that, for the Pathfinder is going to speak.

> "'No, no, Major,' said he, confidently, 'that *would* be a risky declaration. I didn't load the piece, and can't say what was in it; but if it was lead, you will find the bullet driving down those of the Quartermaster and Jasper, else is not my name Pathfinder.'
> "A shout from the target announced the truth of this assertion."

Is the miracle sufficient as it stands? Not for Cooper. The Pathfinder speaks again, as he "now slowly advances towards the stage occupied by the females":

"'That's not all, boys, that's not all; if you find the target touched at all, I'll own to a miss. The Quartermaster cut the wood, but you'll find no wood cut by that last messenger.'"

The miracle is at last complete. He knew—doubtless *saw*—at the distance of a hundred yards—that his bullet had passed into the hole *without fraying the edges*. There were now three bullets in that one hole—three bullets embedded processionally in the body of the stump back of the target. Everybody knew this—somehow or other—and yet nobody had dug any of them out to make sure. Cooper is not a close observer, but he is interesting. He is certainly always that, no matter what happens. And he is more interesting when he is not noticing what he is about than when he is. This is a considerable merit.

The conversations in the Cooper books have a curious sound in our modern ears. To believe that such talk really ever came out of people's mouths would be to believe that there was a time when time was of no value to a person who thought he had something to say; when it was the custom to spread a two-minute remark out to ten; when a man's mouth was a rolling-mill, and busied itself all day long in turning four-foot pigs[9] of thought into thirty-foot bars of conversational railroad iron by attenuation; when subjects were seldom faithfully stuck to, but the talk wandered all around and arrived nowhere; when conversations consisted mainly of irrelevancies, with here and there a relevancy, a relevancy with an embarrassed look, as not being able to explain how it got there.

Cooper was certainly not a master in the construction of dialogue. Inaccurate observation defeated him here as it defeated him in so many other enterprises of his. He even failed to notice that the man who talks corrupt English six days in the week must and will talk it on the seventh, and can't help himself. In the *Deerslayer* story he lets Deerslayer talk the showiest kind of book-talk sometimes, and at other times the basest of base dialects. For instance, when some one asks him if he has a sweet-heart, and if so, where she abides, this is his majestic answer:

> "'She's in the forest—hanging from the boughs of the trees, in a soft rain—in the dew on the open grass—the clouds that float about in the blue heavens—the birds that sing in the woods—the sweet springs where I slake my thirst—and in all the other glorious gifts that come from God's Providence!'"

And he preceded that, a little before, with this:

> "'It consarns me as all things that touches a fri'nd consarns a fri'nd.'"

And this is another of his remarks:

> "'If I was Injin born, now, I might tell of this, or carry in the scalp and boast of the expl'ite afore the whole tribe; or if my inimy had only been a bear'"—and so on.

We cannot imagine such a thing as a veteran Scotch Commander-in-Chief comporting himself in the field like a windy melodramatic actor, but Cooper could. On one occasion Alice and Cora were being chased by the French through a fog in the neighborhood of their father's fort:

> "'*Point de quartier aux coquins!*'[10] cried an eager pursuer, who seemed to direct the operations of the enemy.
> "'Stand firm and be ready, my gallant 60ths!' suddenly exclaimed a voice above them; 'wait to see the enemy; fire low, and sweep the glacis.'[11]

9Cf. pig iron, crude iron as it comes from a blast furnace.
10"Give the rascals no quarter" (French).
11I.e., gradual slope.

"'Father! father!' exclaimed a piercing cry from out the mist; 'it is I! Alice! thy own Elsie! spare, O! save your daughters!'

"'Hold!' shouted the former speaker, in the awful tones of parental agony, the sound reaching even to the woods, and rolling back in solemn echo. 'Tis she! God has restored me my children! Throw open the sally-port;[12] to the field, 60ths, to the field! pull not a trigger, lest ye kill my lambs! Drive off these dogs of France with your steel!'"

Cooper's word-sense was singularly dull. When a person has a poor ear for music he will flat and sharp right along without knowing it. He keeps near the tune, but it is *not* the tune. When a person has a poor ear for words, the result is a literary flatting and sharping; you perceive what he is intending to say, but you also perceive that he doesn't *say* it. This is Cooper. He was not a word-musician. His ear was satisfied with the *approximate* word. I will furnish some circumstantial evidence in support of this charge. My instances are gathered from half a dozen pages of the tale called *Deerslayer*. He uses "verbal," for "oral"; "precision," for "facility"; "phenomena," for "marvels"; "necessary," for "predetermined"; "unsophisticated," for "primitive"; "preparation," for "expectancy"; "rebuked," for "subdued"; "dependent on," for "resulting from"; "fact," for "condition"; "fact," for "conjecture"; "precaution," for "caution"; "explain," for "determine"; "mortified," for "disappointed"; "meretricious," for "factitious"; "materially," for "considerably"; "decreasing," for "deepening"; "increasing," for "disappearing"; "embedded," for "enclosed"; "treacherous," for "hostile"; "stood," for "stooped"; "softened," for "replaced"; "rejoined," for "remarked"; "situation," for "condition"; "different," for "differing"; "insensible," for "unsentient"; "brevity," for "celerity"; "distrusted," for "suspicious"; "mental imbecility," for "imbecility"; "eyes," for "sight"; "counteracting," for "opposing"; "funeral obsequies," for "obsequies."

There have been daring people in the world who claimed that Cooper could write English, but they are all dead now—all dead but Lounsbury. I don't remember that Lounsbury makes the claim in so many words, still he makes it, for he says that *Deerslayer* is a "pure work of art." Pure, in that connection, means faultless—faultless in all details—and language is a detail. If Mr. Lounsbury had only compared Cooper's English with the English which he writes himself—but it is plain that he didn't; and so it is likely that he imagines until this day that Cooper's is as clean and compact as his own. Now I feel sure, deep down in my heart, that Cooper wrote about the poorest English that exists in our language, and that the English of *Deerslayer* is the very worst that even Cooper ever wrote.

I may be mistaken, but it does seem to me that *Deerslayer* is not a work of art in any sense; it does seem to me that it is destitute of every detail that goes to the making of a work of art; in truth, it seems to me that *Deerslayer* is just simply a literary *delirium tremens*.[13]

A work of art? It has no invention; it has no order, system, sequence, or result; it has no life-likeness, no thrill, no stir, no seeming of reality; its characters are confusedly drawn, and by their acts and words they prove that they are not the sort of people the author claims that they are; its humor is pathetic; its pathos is funny; its conversations are—oh! indescribable; its love-scenes odious; its English a crime against the language.

Counting these out, what is left is Art. I think we must all admit that.

1895

---

[12]Large passage into a fortification.
[13]Violent shaking and hallucinating caused by excess alcohol.

The War Prayer

(DICTATED 1904–05)

It was a time of great and exalting excitement. The country was up in arms, the war was on, in every breast burned the holy fire of patriotism; the drums were beating, the bands playing, the toy pistols popping, the bunched firecrackers hissing and spluttering; on every hand and far down the receding and fading spread of roofs and balconies a fluttering wilderness of flags flashed in the sun; daily the young volunteers marched down the wide avenue gay and fine in their new uniforms, the proud fathers and mothers and sisters and sweethearts cheering them with voices choked with happy emotion as they swung by; nightly the packed mass meetings listened, panting, to patriot oratory which stirred the deepest deeps of their hearts, and which they interrupted at briefest intervals with cyclones of applause, the tears running down their cheeks the while; in the churches the pastors preached devotion to flag and country, and invoked the God of Battles, beseeching His aid in our good cause in outpouring of fervid eloquence which moved every listener. It was indeed a glad and gracious time, and the half dozen rash spirits that ventured to disapprove of the war and cast a doubt upon its righteousness straightway got such a stern and angry warning that for their personal safety's sake they quickly shrank out of sight and offended no more in that way.

Sunday morning came—next day the battalions would leave for the front; the church was filled; the volunteers were there, their young faces alight with martial dreams—visions of the stern advance, the gathering momentum, the rushing charge, the flashing sabers, the flight of the foe, the tumult, the enveloping smoke, the fierce pursuit, the surrender!—them home from the war, bronzed heroes, welcomed, adored, submerged in golden seas of glory! With the volunteers sat their dear ones, proud, happy, and envied by the neighbors and friends who had no sons and brothers to send forth to the field of honor, there to win for the flag, or, failing, die the noblest of noble deaths. The service proceeded; a war chapter from the Old Testament was read; the first prayer was said; it was followed by an organ burst that shook the building, and with one impulse the house rose, with glowing eyes and beating hearts, and poured out that tremendous invocation—

> "God the all-terrible!   Thou who ordainest,
> Thunder thy clarion and lightning thy sword!"

Then came the "long" prayer. None could remember the like of it for passionate pleading and moving and beautiful language. The burden of its supplication was, that an ever-merciful and benignant Father of us all would watch over our noble young soldiers, and aid, comfort, and encourage them in their patriotic work; bless them, shield them in the day of battle and the hour of peril, bear them in His mighty hand, make them strong and confident, invincible in the bloody onset; help them to crush the foe, grant to them and to their flag and country imperishable honor and glory—

An aged stranger entered and moved with slow and noiseless step up the main aisle, his eyes fixed upon the minister, his long body clothed in a robe that reached to his feet, his head bare, his white hair descending in a frothy cataract to his shoulders, his seamy face unnaturally pale, pale even to ghastliness. With all eyes following him and wondering, he made his silent way; without pausing, he ascended to the preacher's side and stood there, waiting. With shut lids the preacher, unconscious of his presence, continued his moving prayer, and at last finished it with the words, uttered in fervent appeal, "Bless our arms, grant us the victory, O Lord our God, Father and Protector of our land and flag!"

The stranger touched his arm, motioned him to step aside—which the startled minister did—and took his place. During some moments he surveyed the spellbound audience with solemn eyes, in which burned an uncanny light; then in a deep voice he said:

"I come from the Throne—bearing a message from Almighty God!" The words smote the house with a shock; if the stranger perceived it he gave no attention. "He has heard the prayer of His servant your shepherd, and will grant it if such shall be your desire after I, His messenger, shall have explained to you its import—that is to say, its full import. For it is like unto many of the prayers of men, in that it asks for more than he who utters it is aware of—except he pause and think.

"God's servant and yours has prayed his prayer. Has he paused and taken thought? Is it one prayer? No, it is two—one uttered, the other not. Both have reached the ear of Him Who heareth all supplications, the spoken and the unspoken. Ponder this—keep it in mind. If you would beseech a blessing upon yourself, beware! lest without intent you invoke a curse upon a neighbor at the same time. If you pray for the blessing of rain upon your crop which needs it, by that act you are possibly praying for a curse upon some neighbor's crop which may not need rain and can be injured by it.

"You have heard your servant's prayer—the uttered part of it. I am commissioned of God to put into words the other part of it—that part which the pastor—and also you in your hearts—fervently prayed silently. And ignorantly and unthinkingly? God grant that it was so! You heard these words: 'Grant us the victory, O Lord our God!' That is sufficient. The *whole* of the uttered prayer is compact into those pregnant words. Elaborations were not necessary. When you have prayed for victory you have prayed for many unmentioned results which follow victory—*must* follow it, cannot help but follow it. Upon the listening spirit of God the Father fell also the unspoken part of the prayer. He commandeth me to put it into words. Listen!

"O Lord our Father, our young patriots, idols of our hearts, go forth to battle—be Thou near them! With them—in spirit—we also go forth from the sweet peace of our beloved firesides to smite the foe. O Lord our God, help us to tear their soldiers to bloody shreds with our shells; help us to cover their smiling fields with the pale forms of their patriot dead; help us to drown the thunder of the guns with the shrieks of their wounded, writhing in pain; help us to lay waste their humble homes with a hurricane of fire; help us to wring the hearts of their unoffending widows with unavailing grief; help us to turn them out roofless with their little children to wander unfriended the wastes of their desolated land in rags and hunger and thirst, sports of the sun flames of summer and the icy winds of winter, broken in spirit, worn with travail, imploring Thee for the refuge of the grave and denied it—for our sakes who adore Thee, Lord, blast their hopes, blight their lives, protract their bitter pilgrimage, make heavy their steps, water their way with their tears, stain the white snow with the blood of their wounded feet! We ask it, in the spirit of love, of Him Who is the Source of Love, and Who is the ever-faithful refuge and friend of all that are sore beset and seek His aid with humble and contrite hearts. Amen."

(*After a pause.*) "Ye have prayed it; if ye still desire it, speak! The messenger of the Most High waits."

It was believed afterward that the man was a lunatic, because there was no sense in what he said.

from Letters from the Earth[1]

LETTER IV[2]

[THE HUMAN RACE'S IMAGINED HEAVEN]

I have told you nothing about man that is not true. You must pardon me if I repeat that remark now and then in these letters; I want you to take seriously the things I am telling you, and I feel that if I were in your place and you in mine, I should need that reminder from time to time, to keep my credulity from flagging.

For there is nothing about Man that is not strange to an Immortal. He looks at nothing as we look at it, his sense of proportion is quite different from ours, and his sense of values is so widely divergent from ours, that with all our large intellectual powers it is not likely that even the most gifted among us would ever be quite able to understand it.

For instance, take this sample: he has imagined a heaven, and has left entirely out of it the supremest of all his delights, the one ecstasy that stands first and foremost in the heart of every individual of his race—and of ours—sexual intercourse!

It is as if a lost and perishing person in a roasting desert should be told by a rescuer he might choose and have all longed-for things but one, and he should elect to leave out water!

His heaven is like himself: strange, interesting, astonishing, grotesque. I give you my word, it has not a single feature in it that he *actually values*. It consists—utterly and entirely—of diversions which he cares next to nothing about, here in the earth, yet is quite sure he will like in heaven. Isn't it curious? Isn't it interesting? You must not think I am exaggerating, for it is not so. I will give you details.

Most men do not sing, most men cannot sing, most men will not stay where others are singing if it be continued more than two hours. Note that.

Only about two men in a hundred can play upon a musical instrument, and not four in a hundred have any wish to learn how. Set that down.

Many men pray, not many of them like to do it. A few pray long, the others make a short cut.

More men go to church than want to.

To forty-nine men in fifty the Sabbath Day is a dreary, dreary bore.

Of all the men in a church on a Sunday, two-thirds are tired when the service is half over, and the rest before it is finished.

The gladdest moment for all of them is when the preacher uplifts his hands for the benediction. You can hear the soft rustle of relief that sweeps the house, and you recognize that it is eloquent with gratitude.

All nations look down upon all other nations.

All nations dislike all other nations.

All white nations despise all colored nations, of whatever hue, and oppress them when they can.

White men will not associate with "niggers," nor marry them.

They will not allow them in their schools and churches.

All the world hates the Jew, and will not endure him except when he is rich.

I ask you to note all those particulars.

---

[1]Twain wrote *Letters from the Earth* in 1909, but believed it too controversial for publication at that time. It was prepared for publication in 1939 by Bernard DeVoto, but set aside at the request of Twain's daughter Clara Clemens. Finally in 1962 it appeared, with Henry Nash Smith overseeing publication of the DeVoto edition.

[2]The archangel Satan has been temporarily banished from heaven and has decided to visit earth to observe the curious human race. His letters reporting his observations are sent back to his fellow archangels, Michael and Gabriel.

Further. All sane people detest noise.

All sane people, sane or insane, like to have variety in their life. Monotony quickly wearies them.

Every man, according to the mental equipment that has fallen to his share, exercises his intellect constantly, ceaselessly, and this exercise makes up a vast and valued and essential part of his life. The lowest intellect, like the highest, possesses a skill of some kind and takes a keen pleasure in testing it, proving it, perfecting it. The urchin who is his comrade's superior in games is as diligent and as enthusiastic in his practice as are the sculptor, the painter, the pianist, the mathematician and the rest. Not one of them could be happy if his talent were put under an interdict.

Now then, you have the facts. You know what the human race enjoys, and what it doesn't enjoy. It has invented a heaven, out of its own head, all by itself: guess what it is like! In fifteen hundred eternities you couldn't do it. The ablest mind known to you or me in fifty million aeons couldn't do it. Very well, I will tell you about it.

II

1. First of all, I recall to your attention the extraordinary fact with which I began. To-wit, that the human being, like the immortals, naturally places sexual intercourse far and away above all other joys—yet he has left it out of his heaven! The very thought of it excites him; opportunity sets him wild; in this state he will risk life, reputation, everything—even his queer heaven itself—to make good that opportunity and ride it to the overwhelming climax. From youth to middle age all men and all women prize copulation above all other pleasures combined, yet it is actually as I have said: it is not in their heaven, prayer takes its place.

They prize it thus highly; yet, like all their so-called "boons," it is a poor thing. At its very best and longest the act is brief beyond imagination—the imagination of an immortal, I mean. In the matter of repetition the man is limited—oh, quite beyond immortal conception. We who continue the act *and* its supremest ecstasies unbroken and without withdrawal for centuries, will never be able to understand or adequately pity the awful poverty of these people in that rich gift which, possessed as we possess it, makes all other possessions trivial and not worth the trouble of invoicing.

2. In man's heaven *everybody sings*! There are no exceptions. The man who did not sing on earth, sings there; the man who could not sing on earth is able to do it there. This universal singing is not casual, not occasional, not relieved by intervals of quiet, it goes on, all day long, and every day, during a stretch of twelve hours. And *everybody stays*; whereas in the earth the place would be empty in two hours. The singing is of hymns alone. Nay, it is of *one* hymn alone. The words are always the same, in number they are only about a dozen, there is no rhyme, there is no poetry: "Hosannah, hosannah, hosannah, Lord God of Sabaoth, 'rah! 'rah! 'rah!—ssht!—boom! . . . . . a-a-ah!"

3. Meantime, *every person* is playing on a harp—those millions and millions! whereas not more than twenty in the thousand of them could play an instrument in the earth, or ever *wanted* to.

Consider the deafening hurricane of sound—millions and millions of voices screaming at once, and millions and millions of harps gritting their teeth at the same time! I ask you—is it hideous, is it odious, is it horrible?

Consider further: it is a *praise* service; a service of compliment, of flattery, of adulation! Do you ask who it is that is willing to endure this strange compliment, this insane compliment; and who not only endures it but likes it, enjoys it, requires it, *commands* it? Hold your breath!

It is God! This race's God, I mean. He sits on his throne, attended by his four and twenty elders and some other dignitaries pertaining to his court, and looks out over his miles and miles of tempestuous worshippers, and smiles, and purrs, and nods his satisfaction northward, eastward, southward; as quaint and naif a spectacle as has yet been imagined in this universe, I take it.

It is easy to see that the inventor of the heaven did not originate the idea, but copied it from the show-ceremonies of some sorry little sovereign State up in the back settlements of the Orient somewhere.

All sane white people *hate noise*; yet they have tranquilly accepted this kind of a heaven—without thinking, without reflection, without examination—and they actually want to go to it! Profoundly devout old gray-headed men put in a large part of their time dreaming of the happy day when they will lay down the cares of this life and enter into the joys of that place. Yet you can see how unreal it is to them, and how little it takes a grip upon them as being *fact*, for they make no practical preparation for the great change: you never see one of them with a harp, you never hear one of them sing.

As you have seen, that singular show is a service of divine worship—a service of praise: praise by hymn, praise by instrumental ecstasies, praise by prostration. It takes the place of "church." Now then, in the earth these people cannot stand much church—an hour and a quarter is the limit, and they draw the line at one a week. That is to say, Sunday. One day in seven; and even then they do not look forward to it with longing. And so—consider what their heaven provides for them: "church" that lasts forever, and a *Sabbath that has no end*! They quickly weary of this brief hebdomadal[3] Sabbath here, yet they long for that eternal one; they dream of it, they talk about it, they *think* they think they are going to enjoy it—with all their simple hearts they think they think they are going to be happy in it!

It is because they do not think *at all*; they only think they think. Whereas they can't think; not two human beings in ten thousand have anything to think with. And as to imagination—oh, well, look at their heaven! They accept it, they approve it, they admire it. That gives you their intellectual measure.

4. The inventor of their heaven empties into it all the nations of the earth, in one common jumble. All are on an equality absolute, no one of them ranking another; they have to be "brothers;" they have to mix together, pray together, harp together, hosannah together—whites, niggers, Jews, everybody—there's no distinction. Here in the earth all nations hate each other, every one of them hates the Jew. Yet every pious person adores that heaven and wants to get into it. He really does. And when he is in a holy rapture he thinks he thinks that if he were only there he would take all the populace to his heart, and hug, and hug, and hug!

He is a marvel—man is! I would I knew who invented him.

5. Every man in the earth possesses some share of intellect, large or small; and be it large or be it small he takes a pride in it. Also his heart swells at mention of the names of the majestic intellectual chiefs of his race, and he loves the tale of their splendid achievements. For he is of their blood, and in honoring themselves they have honored him. Lo, what the mind of man can do! he cries; and calls the roll of the illustrious of all the ages; and points to the imperishable literatures they have given to the world, and the mechanical wonders they have invented, and the glories wherewith they have clothed science and the arts; and to them he uncovers, as to kings, and gives to them the profoundest homage and the sincerest his exultant heart can furnish—thus exalting intellect above all things else in his world, and enthroning it there under the arching skies in a supremacy unapproachable. And then he contrives a heaven that hasn't a rag of intellectuality in it anywhere!

Is it odd, is it curious, is it puzzling? It is exactly as I have said, incredible as it may sound. This sincere adorer of intellect and prodigal rewarder of its mighty services

---

[3]Weekly, every seven days.

here in the earth has invented a religion and a heaven which pay no compliments to intellect, offer it no distinctions, fling to it no largess: in fact, never even mention it.

By this time you will have noticed that the human being's heaven has been thought out and constructed upon an absolutely definite plan; and that this plan is, that it shall contain, in labored detail, each and every imaginable thing that is repulsive to a man, and not a single thing he likes!

Very well, the further we proceed the more will this curious fact be apparent.

Make a note of it: in man's heaven there are no exercises for the intellect, nothing for it to live upon. It would rot there in a year—rot and stink. Rot and stink—and at that stage become holy. A blessed thing; for only the holy can stand the joys of that bedlam.

1909   *1962*

WILLIAM DEAN HOWELLS
(1837–1920)

William Dean Howells was a leading "man of letters" of the latter half of the nineteenth century whose endorsement could assure literary success. He was a renowned novelist in his own right, and as an editor, first of *The Atlantic Monthly*, later of *Harper's Monthly*, and still later of *Harper's Weekly* (leading magazines of the day), he championed such innovative writers as Hamlin Garland, Stephen Crane, and Frank Norris. He was passionately committed to realism, but his conception of it was elastic enough to embrace both Henry James and Mark Twain. He counted the two of them as personal friends: he published *My Mark Twain* shortly after Twain died in 1910 and he had an essay in progress on Henry James when he himself died in 1920.

No one would have predicted that the boy who was born and grew up in the river towns of Ohio would reach such eminence. Howells's father was a printer and newspaper man who moved from town to town in search of a new job, a new opportunity. He settled his family in Hamilton, Ohio, on the Miami River, in 1840. There they remained for eight years, until William was eleven. These formative years of midwest boyhood Howells later recreated in a lyrical reminiscence, *A Boy's Town* (1890).

Howells's formal education was meager, but by the age of seven he was helping his father set type in the print shop. He became an enthusiastic reader of books early and indulged his enthusiasm all his long life. In 1895, he published *My Literary Passions*, an account of his reading showing an astonishing range of interest: Oliver Goldsmith, Cervantes, Shakespeare, the British and American poets and novelists, but including also the Italians (Dante), the Germans (Goethe), the French (Zola), and the Russians (Tolstoy).

At the age of twenty-one, Howells was established in a journalistic career as an editor on the *Ohio State Journal* in Columbus. In 1859, he published his first book, *Poems of Two Friends*, together with John J. Piatt. Few copies sold, and Howells discovered his career was in prose, not poetry. In 1860, he was assigned by an Ohio publisher to write a campaign biography of Abraham Lincoln. Howells wrote it hastily and got it out before competitors, winning the attention of a large public, including Lincoln himself.

Because of the biography, Howells was offered the consulship in Venice. Before going to Italy, he met and became engaged to Elinor Mead, from Vermont, whom he would marry in Paris in 1861. Travelling east, Howells visited Boston, eager to meet the writers he had read in *The Atlantic Monthly*, which had published some of his poetry. Later, in *Literary Friends and Acquaintance* (1900), Howells described his dining with James Russell Lowell, Oliver Wendell Holmes, and James T. Fields in Boston, and his meeting Nathaniel Hawthorne and Henry David Thoreau in Concord. Clearly Howells found the literary life of the East dazzling.

From 1861 to 1865, Howells served as American consul in Venice. The duties were not arduous, and Howells had time to become fluent in Italian and to become knowledgeable in Italian literature, displayed later in *Venetian Life* (1866), *Italian Journeys* (1867), and *Modern Italian Poets* (1887). By the time Howells returned to America at the end of the Civil War, his Ohio days were behind him and he found openings for his career in the East, briefly in New York as contributing editor to the *Nation*, and then in Boston as assistant editor of *The Atlantic Monthly*. Howells's association with the *Atlantic* was to last from 1866 to 1881; he became its editor-in-chief in 1871.

During this period, and later when he became associated with *Harper's Monthly* (writing the "Editor's Study" essays beginning in 1886) and with *Harper's Weekly* (writing the "Life and Letters" column beginning in 1895), Howells was at the center of American literary culture, in a position to make decisions affecting the fate of beginning writers. Perhaps his greatest asset was his eclectic taste, enabling him to see virtues in innovative writers—like the French and American naturalists—that others in that genteel age condemned.

But the remarkable thing about Howells's career was his own productivity—some 135 volumes, including 35 novels. When he retired from the *Atlantic* in 1881, it was to devote himself seriously to the writing of fiction. Then came the handful of novels for which he is chiefly remembered: *A Modern Instance* (1882), detailing the break-up of a stormy marriage; *The Rise of Silas Lapham* (1885), focusing on the friction between the newly rich and the established old guard of Boston; and *A Hazard of New Fortunes* (1890), portraying the start-up of a new literary magazine in New York backed by a newly rich entrepreneur, but introducing as background the clash between workers and capitalists in the form of a violent streetcar strike.

Howells's concern for social issues is best exemplified when, in 1886, he became incensed over the police reaction to the Haymarket Square bombing in Chicago. There had been a strike at the McCormick Reaper plant during which police fired on and killed strikers. At a meeting called to protest the firing, a bomb was thrown into the ranks of police, killing several. In the ensuing melee, a number of strikers were arrested and sentenced to die. Howells wrote a letter to the *New York Tribune* condemning the executions, but they were carried out in spite of public protest. The episode contributed to Howells's portrayal of police violence in *A Hazard of New Fortunes*, and it inspired the writing of *A Traveler from Altruria* (1892–93), more a socialist tract than a novel, describing a society freed from poverty by transfiguring competition into cooperation.

Howells's total body of work includes five volumes of sketches and stories, more than thirty publications of dramas (farces, light comedies, serious verse drama), some eleven books of travel, plus volumes of poetry, criticism, autobiography, and biography (his life of Ohio's Rutherford B. Hayes, U.S. president, 1877–81, appeared in 1876). One of his most significant works was *Criti-*

cism and Fiction (1890), pieced together from columns he wrote for the "Editor's Study" in *Harper's Monthly*. "Each new author," he wrote, should be considered "not in his proportion to any other author or artist, but in his relation to the human nature, known to us all, which it is his high privilege, his high duty, to interpret." But he also proposed that since the reality of a country lay not in its social extremes but in its average, and since America was blessed by a "broad level of prosperity," American novelists should "concern themselves with the more smiling aspects of life, which are the more American." Although Howells's thinking was advanced at the time, and indeed he was maligned by the romanticists who felt themselves under attack (as they were), his language in some passages of *Criticism and Fiction* would be used against him by many of the writers for whom he paved the way by his militant realism.

Harvard, Yale, and Oxford awarded the degreeless Howells honorary degrees during his closing years. And in 1912, at his seventy-fifth birthday in New York, President William Howard Taft turned up as a guest. But Howells began to feel himself an anachronism. He wrote to Henry James before James's death in 1916, "on the whole I should say your worship was spreading among us. I am comparatively a dead cult with my statues cut down and the grass growing over them in the pale moonlight."

Howells died in 1920, at the edge of a decade that would explode with literary innovation dedicated to the overthrow of the genteel tradition, which revered conformity and conventionality. Howells became a target, with little recognition for the literary battle scars that he himself bore from an earlier revolution. When Sinclair Lewis delivered his Nobel Prize acceptance speech in 1930, he said: "Mr. Howells was one of the gentlest, sweetest, and most honest of men, but he had the code of a pious old maid whose greatest delight was to have tea at the vicarage." Lewis himself, of course, was later to suffer a fate similar to that of Howells.

Lewis's casual judgment is too flip. A number of Howells's novels continue in print to this day. And no doubt they will continue in print as long as readers are interested in obtaining glimpses into latter nineteenth-century life and manners in America. In 1912, James wrote a public letter to Howells on his seventy-fifth birthday: "They make a great array, a literature in themselves, your studies of American life, so acute, so direct, so disinterested, so preoccupied but with the fine truth of the case; and the more attaching to me, always, for their referring themselves to a time and an order when we knew together what American life *was*." In assuring Howells that his "really beautiful time will come," Henry James deserves the last word.

ADDITIONAL READING

Life in Letters of William Dean Howells, 2 vols., ed. Mildred Howells, 1928; *The Correspondence of Samuel L. Clemens and William Dean Howells, 1872–1910*, 2 vols., ed. Henry Nash Smith and William M. Gibson, 1960; *The Complete Plays of W. D. Howells*, ed. Walter J. Meserve, 1960; *A Selected Edition of W. D. Howells*, 41 vols. projected, ed. Edwin H. Cady, 1968–; *W. D. Howells as Critic*, ed. Edwin H. Cady, 1973.

Clara and Rudolph Kirk, "Introduction," *William Dean Howells: Representative Selections*, 1950; James Woodress, *Howells and Italy*, 1952; Everett Carter, *Howells and the Age of Realism*, 1954; Edwin H. Cady, *The Road to Realism: The Early Years, 1837–1885*, 1956, and *The Realist at War: The Mature Years, 1885–1920*, 1958; Olov W. Fryckstedt, *In Quest of America: A Study of Howells' Early Development*, 1958; Van Wyck Brooks, *Howells: His Life and Work*, 1959; Robert L. Hough, *Quiet Rebel: William Dean Howells as a Social Commentator*, 1959; George N. Bennett, *William Dean Howells: The Development of a Novelist*, 1959; Clara and Rudolph Kirk, *William Dean*

Howells, 1962, and *Traveller from Altruria*, 1962; Kenneth E. Eble, ed., *Howells, A Century of Criticism*, 1962; Clara M. Kirk, *W. D. Howells and Art in His Time*, 1965; George Carrington, *The Immense Complex Drama: The World and Art of the Howells Novel*, 1966; William McMurray, *The Literary Realism of William Dean Howells*, 1967; Kermit Vanderbilt, *The Achievement of William Dean Howells: A Reinterpretation*, 1968; Edward Wagenknect, *William Dean Howells: The Friendly Eyes*, 1969; James L. Dean, *Howells' Travels Toward Art*, 1970; Kenneth Lynn, *William Dean Howells: An American Life*, 1971; George N. Bennett, *The Realism of William Dean Howells*, 1973; Ulrich Halfmann, *Interviews with William Dean Howells*, 1973; George C. Carrington, Jr., and Idiko de Papp, *Plots and Characters in the Fiction of William Dean Howells*, 1976; William Alexander, *William Dean Howells: The Realist as Humorist*, 1981; Kenneth E. Eble, *William Dean Howells*, 1982; Elizabeth Stevens Prioleau, *The Circle of Eros: Sexuality in the Work of William Dean Howells*, 1983; Edwin H. and Norma W. Cady, eds., *Critical Essays on W. D. Howells, 1886–1920*, 1983; Kenneth E. Eble, *Old Clemens and W.D.H.: The Story of a Remarkable Friendship*, 1985; John W. Crowley, *The Black Heart's Truth: The Early Career of W. D. Howells*, 1985; Elsa Nettles, *Language, Race, and Social Class in Howells's America*, 1988.

TEXTS

"The River" from *A Boy's Town*, 1890; "Editha" from *Between the Dark and the Daylight*, 1907; *Criticism and Fiction*, 1891.

from A Boy's Town[1]

from "THE RIVER"

It seems to me that the best way to get at the heart of any boy's town is to take its different watercourses and follow them into it.

The house where my boy first lived was not far from the river, and he must have seen it often before he noticed it. But he was not aware of it till he found it under the bridge. Without the river there could not have been a bridge; the fact of the bridge may have made him look for the river; but the bridge is foremost in his mind. It is a long wooden tunnel, with two roadways, and a foot-path on either side of these; there is a toll-house at each end, and from one to the other it is about as far as from the Earth to the planet Mars. On the western shore of the river is a smaller town than the Boy's Town, and in the perspective the entrance of the bridge on that side is like a dim little doorway. The timbers are of a hugeness to strike fear into the heart of the boldest little boy; and there is something awful even about the dust in the roadways; soft and thrillingly cool to the boy's bare feet, it lies thick in a perpetual twilight, streaked at intervals by the sun that slants in at the high, narrow windows under the roof; it has a certain potent, musty smell. The bridge has three piers, and at low water hardier adventurers than he wade out to the middle pier; some heroes even fish there, standing all day on the loose rocks about the base of the pier. He shudders to see them, and aches with wonder how they will get ashore. Once he is there when a big boy wades back from the middle pier, where he has been to rob a goose's nest; he has some loose silver change in his wet hand, and my boy understands that it has come out of one of the goose eggs. This fact, which he never thought of questioning,

[1]Howells was three years old in 1840 when his family moved to Hamilton, Ohio, and eleven when the family moved on. Hamilton during Howells's boyhood is the subject of *A Boy's Town*, published in 1890. In the first chapter of the book, Howells wrote: "I call it Boy's Town because I wish it to appear to the reader as a town appears to a boy from his third to his eleventh year, when he seldom, if ever, catches a glimpse of life much higher than the middle of a man, and has the most distorted and mistaken views of most things. . . . It had a river, the great Miami River, which was as blue as the sky when it was not as yellow as gold; and it had another river, called the Old River, which was the Miami's former channel, and which held an island in its sluggish loop; the boys called it The Island; and it must have been the size of Australia; perhaps it was not so large." "The River" is Chapter III from *A Boy's Town*.

gets mixed up in his mind with an idea of riches, of treasure-trove, in the cellar of an old house that has been torn down near the end of the bridge.

On the bridge he first saw the crazy man who belongs in every boy's town. In this one he was a hapless, harmless creature, whom the boys knew as Solomon Whistler, perhaps because his name was Whistler, perhaps because he whistled; though when my boy met him midway of the bridge, he marched swiftly and silently by, with his head high and looking neither to the right nor to the left, with an insensibility to the boy's presence that froze his blood and shrivelled him up with terror. As his fancy early became the sport of playfellows not endowed with one so vivid, he was taught to expect that Solomon Whistler would get him some day, though what he would do with him when he had got him his anguish must have been too great even to let him guess. Some of the boys said Solomon had gone crazy from fear of being drafted in the war of 1812; others that he had been crossed in love; but my boy did not quite know then what either meant. He only knew that Solomon Whistler lived at the poorhouse beyond the eastern border of the town, and that he ranged between this sojourn and the illimitable wilderness north of the town on the western shore of the river. The crazy man was often in the boy's dreams, the memories of which blend so with the memories of real occurrences: he could not tell later whether he once crossed the bridge when the footway had been partly taken up, and he had to walk on the girders, or whether he only dreamed of that awful passage. It was quite fearful enough to cross when the footway was all down, and he could see the blue gleam of the river far underneath through the cracks between the boards. It made his brain reel; and he felt that he took his life in his hand whenever he entered the bridge, even when he had grown old enough to be making an excursion with some of his playmates to the farm of an uncle of theirs who lived two miles up the river. The farmer gave them all the watermelons they wanted to eat, and on the way home, when they lay resting under the sycamores on the river-bank, Solomon Whistler passed by in the middle of the road, silent, swift, straight onward. I do not know why the sight of this afflicted soul did not slay my boy on the spot, he was so afraid of him; but the crazy man never really hurt any one, though the boys followed and mocked him as soon as he got by.

The boys knew little or nothing of the river south of the bridge, and frequented mainly the mile-long stretch of it between the bridge and the dam, beyond which there was practically nothing for many years; afterwards they came to know that this strange region was inhabited. Just above the bridge the Hydraulic emptied into the river with a heart-shaking plunge over an immense mill-wheel; and there was a cluster of mills at this point, which were useful in accumulating the waters into fishing-holes before they rushed through the gates upon the wheel. The boys used to play inside the big mill-wheel before the water was let into the Hydraulic, and my boy caught his first fish in the pool below the wheel. The mills had some secondary use in making flour and the like, but this could not concern a small boy. They were as simply a part of his natural circumstance as the large cottonwood-tree which hung over the river from a point near by, and which seemed to have always an oriole singing in it. All along there the banks were rather steep, and to him they looked very high. The blue clay that formed them was full of springs, which the boys dammed up in little ponds and let loose in glassy falls upon their flutter-mills. As with everything that boys do, these mills were mostly failures; the pins which supported the wheels were always giving way; and though there were instances of boys who started their wheels at recess and found them still fluttering away at noon when they came out of school, none ever carried his enterprise so far as to spin the cotton blowing from the balls of the cottonwood-tree by the shore, as they all meant to do. They met such disappointments with dauntless cheerfulness, and lightly turned from some bursting bubble to some other where the glory of the universe was still mirrored. The river shore was strewn not only with waste cotton, but with drift which the water had made porous, and which they called smokewood. They made cigars for their own use out of it, and it seemed to them that it might be generally introduced as a cheap and simple substitute for tobacco; but they never got any of it into the market, not even the market of that world where the currency was pins.

· · · · · ·

I do not know why my boy's associations with Delorac's Island were especially wild in their character, for nothing more like outlawry than the game of mumble-the-peg[2] occurred there. Perhaps it was because the boys had to get to it by water that it seemed beyond the bounds of civilization. They might have reached it by the bridge, but the temper of the boys on the western shore was uncertain; they would have had to run the gauntlet of their river-guard on the way up to it; and they might have been friendly or they might not; it would have depended a good deal on the size and number of the interlopers. Besides, it was more glorious to wade across to the island from their side of the river. They undressed and gathered their clothes up into a bundle, which they put on their heads and held there with one hand, while they used the other for swimming, when they came to a place beyond their depth. Then they dressed again, and stretched themselves under the cottonwood-trees and sycamores, and played games and told stories, and longed for a gun to kill the blackbirds which nested in the high tops, and at nightfall made such a clamor in getting to roost that it almost deafened you.

My boy never distinctly knew what formed that island, but as there was a mill there, it must have been made by the mill-race leaving and rejoining the river. It was enough for him to know that the island was there, and that a parrot—a screaming, whistling, and laughing parrot, which was a Pretty Poll, and always Wanted a Cracker—dwelt in a pretty cottage, almost hidden in trees, just below the end of the island. This parrot had the old Creole gentleman living with it who owned the island, and whom it had brought from New Orleans. The boys met him now and then as he walked abroad, with a stick, and his large stomach bowed in front of him. For no reason under the sun they were afraid of him; perhaps they thought he resented their parleys with the parrot. But he and the parrot existed solely to amuse and to frighten them; and on their own side of the river, just opposite the island, there were established some small industries for their entertainment and advantage, on a branch of the Hydraulic. I do not know just what it was they did with a mustard-mill that was there, but the turning-shop supplied them with a deep bed of elastic shavings just under the bank, which they turned somersaults into, when they were not turning them into the river.

I wonder what sign the boys who read this have for challenging or inviting one another to go in swimming. The boys in the Boy's Town used to make the motion of swimming with both arms; or they held up the forefinger and middle-finger in the form of a swallow-tail; they did this when it was necessary to be secret about it, as in school, and when they did not want the whole crowd of boys to come along; and often when they just pretended they did not want some one to know. They really had to be secret at times, for some of the boys were not allowed to go in at all; others were forbidden to go in more than once or twice a day; and as they all *had* to go in at least three or four times a day, some sort of sign had to be used that was understood among themselves alone. Since this is a true history, I had better own that they nearly all, at one time or other, must have told lies about it, either before or after the fact, some habitually, some only in great extremity. Here and there a boy, like my boy's elder brother, would not tell lies at all, even about going in swimming; but by far the

---

[2]Variant of "mumbletypeg," a boy's game in which a pocket knife is tossed, blade up, from various positions (nose, chin, elbow, etc.) and must land with the blade in the earth.

greater number bowed to their hard fate, and told them. They promised that they would not go in, and then they said that they had not been in; but Sin, for which they had made this sacrifice, was apt to betray them. Either they got their shirts on wrong side out in dressing, or else, while they were in, some enemy came upon them and tied their shirts. There are few cruelties which public opinion in the boys' world condemns, but I am glad to remember, to their honor, that there were not many in that Boy's Town who would tie shirts; and I fervently hope that there is no boy now living who would do it. As the crime is probably extinct I will say that in those wicked days, if you were such a miscreant, and there was some boy you hated, you stole up and tied the hardest kind of a knot in one arm or both arms of his shirt. Then, if the Evil One put it into your heart, you soaked the knot in water, and pounded it with a stone.

I am glad to know that in the days when he was thoughtless and senseless enough, my boy never was guilty of any degree of this meanness. It was his brother, I suppose, who taught him to abhor it; and perhaps it was his own suffering from it in part; for he, too, sometimes shed bitter tears over such a knot, as I have seen hapless little wretches do, tearing at it with their nails and gnawing at it with their teeth, knowing that the time was passing when they could hope to hide the fact that they had been in swimming, and foreseeing no remedy but to cut off the sleeve above the knot, or else put on their clothes without the shirt, and trust to untying the knot when it got dry.

There must have been a lurking anxiety in all the boys' hearts when they went in without leave, or, as my boy was apt to do, when explicitly forbidden. He was not apt at lying, I dare say, and so he took the course of open disobedience. He could not see the danger that filled the home hearts with fear for him, and he must have often broken the law and been forgiven, before Justice one day appeared for him on the riverbank and called him away from his stolen joys. It was an awful moment, and it covered him with shame before his mates, who heartlessly rejoiced, as children do, in the doom which they are escaping. That sin, at least, he fully expiated; and I will whisper to the Young People here at the end of the chapter, that somehow, soon or late, our sins do overtake us, and insist upon being paid for. That is not the best reason for not sinning, but it is well to know it, and to believe it in our acts as well as our thoughts. You will find people to tell you that things only happen so and so. It may be; only, I know that no good thing ever happened to happen to me when I had done wrong.

1890

Editha

The air was thick with the war feeling,[1] like the electricity of a storm which has not yet burst. Editha sat looking out into the hot spring afternoon, with her lips parted, and panting with the intensity of the question whether she could let him go. She had decided that she could not let him stay, when she saw him at the end of the still leafless avenue, making slowly up towards the house, with his head down and his figure relaxed. She ran impatiently out on the veranda, to the edge of the steps, and imperatively demanded greater haste of him with her will before she called aloud to him: "George!"

---

[1] I.e., relating to the Spanish-American War of 1898 over Cuba.

He had quickened his pace in mystical response to her mystical urgence, before he could have heard her; now he looked up and answered, "Well?"

"Oh, how united we are!" she exulted, and then she swooped down the steps to him. "What is it?" she cried.

"It's war," he said, and he pulled her up to him and kissed her.

She kissed him back intensely, but irrelevantly, as to their passion, and uttered from deep in her throat. "How glorious!"

"It's war," he repeated, without consenting to her sense of it; and she did not know just what to think at first. She never knew what to think of him; that made his mystery, his charm. All through their courtship, which was contemporaneous with the growth of the war feeling, she had been puzzled by his want of seriousness about it. He seemed to despise it even more than he abhorred it. She could have understood his abhorring any sort of bloodshed; that would have been a survival of his old life when he thought he would be a minister, and before he changed and took up the law. But making light of a cause so high and noble seemed to show a want of earnestness at the core of his being. Not but that she felt herself able to cope with a congenital defect of that sort, and make his love for her save him from himself. Now perhaps the miracle was already wrought in him. In the presence of the tremendous fact that he announced, all triviality seemed to have gone out of him; she began to feel that. He sank down on the top step, and wiped his forehead with his handkerchief, while she poured out upon him her question of the origin and authenticity of his news.

All the while, in her duplex emotioning, she was aware that now at the very beginning she must put a guard upon herself against urging him, by any word or act, to take the part that her whole soul willed him to take, for the completion of her ideal of him. He was very nearly perfect as he was, and he must be allowed to perfect himself. But he was peculiar, and he might very well be reasoned out of his peculiarity. Before her reasoning went her emotioning: her nature pulling upon his nature, her womanhood upon his manhood, without her knowing the means she was using to the end she was willing. She had always supposed that the man who won her would have done something to win her; she did not know what, but something. George Gearson had simply asked her for her love, on the way home from a concert, and she gave her love to him, without, as it were, thinking. But now, it flashed upon her, if he could do something worthy to *have* won her—be a hero, *her* hero—it would be even better than if he done it before asking her; it would be grander. Besides, she had believed in the war from the beginning.

"But don't you see, dearest," she said, "that it wouldn't have come to this if it hadn't been in the order of Providence? And I call any war glorious that is for the liberation of people who have been struggling for years against the cruelest oppression. Don't you think so, too?"

"I suppose so," he returned, languidly. "But war! Is it glorious to break the peace of the world?"

"That ignoble peace! It was no peace at all, with that crime and shame at our very gates." She was conscious of parroting the current phrases of the newspapers, but it was no time to pick and choose her words. She must sacrifice anything to the high ideal she had for him, and after a good deal of rapid argument she ended with the climax: "But now it doesn't matter about the how or why. Since the war has come, all that is gone. There are no two sides any more. There is nothing now but our country."

He sat with his eyes closed and his head leant back against the veranda, and he remarked, with a vague smile, as if musing aloud, "Our country—right or wrong."[2]

"Yes, right or wrong!" she returned, fervidly. "I'll go and get you some lemonade."

---

[2]The words of the American naval officer Stephen Decatur
(1779–1820) in a speech delivered in 1816.

She rose rustling, and whisked away; when she came back with two tall glasses of clouded liquid on a tray, and the ice clucking in them, he still sat as she had left him, and she said, as if there had been no interruption: "But there is no question of wrong in this case. I call it a sacred war. A war for liberty and humanity, if ever there was one. And I know you will see it just as I do, yet."

He took half the lemonade at a gulp, and he answered as he set the glass down: "I know you always have the highest ideal. When I differ from you I ought to doubt myself."

A generous sob rose in Editha's throat for the humility of a man, so very nearly perfect, who was willing to put himself below her.

Besides, she felt, more subliminally, that he was never so near slipping through her fingers as when he took that meek way.

"You shall not say that! Only, for once I happen to be right." She seized his hand in her two hands, and poured her soul from her eyes into his. "Don't you think so?" she entreated him.

He released his hand and drank the rest of his lemonade, and she added, "Have mine, too," but he shook his head in answering, "I've no business to think so, unless I act so, too."

Her heart stopped a beat before it pulsed on with leaps that she felt in her neck. She had noticed that strange thing in men: they seemed to feel bound to do what they believed, and not think a thing was finished when they said it, as girls did. She knew what was in his mind, but she pretended not, and she said, "Oh, I am not sure," and then faltered.

He went on as if to himself, without apparently heeding her: "There's only one way of proving one's faith in a thing like this."

She could not say that she understood, but she did understand.

He went on again. "If I believed—if I felt as you do about this war— Do you wish me to feel as you do?"

Now she was really not sure; so she said: "George, I don't know what you mean."

He seemed to muse away from her as before. "There is a sort of fascination in it. I suppose that at the bottom of his heart every man would like at times to have his courage tested, to see how he would act."

"How can you talk in that ghastly way?"

"It *is* rather morbid. Still, that's what it comes to, unless you're swept away by ambition or driven by conviction. I haven't the conviction or the ambition, and the other thing is what it comes to with me. I ought to have been a preacher, after all; then I couldn't have asked it of myself, as I must, now I'm a lawyer. And you believe it's a holy war, Editha?" he suddenly addressed her. "Oh, I know you do! But you wish me to believe so, too?"

She hardly knew whether he was mocking or not, in the ironical way he always had with her plainer mind. But the only thing was to be outspoken with him.

"George, I wish you to believe whatever you think is true, at any and every cost. If I've tried to talk you into anything, I take it all back."

"Oh, I know that, Editha. I know how sincere you are, and how— I wish I had your undoubting spirit! I'll think it over; I'd like to believe as you do. But I don't, now; I don't, indeed. It isn't this war alone; though this seems peculiarly wanton and needless; but it's every war—so stupid; it makes me sick. Why shouldn't this thing have been settled reasonably?"

"Because," she said, very throatily again, "God meant it to be war."

"You think it was God? Yes, I suppose that is what people will say."

"Do you suppose it would have been war if God hadn't meant it?"

"I don't know. Sometimes it seems as if God had put this world into men's keeping to work it as they pleased."

"Now, George, that is blasphemy."

"Well, I won't blaspheme. I'll try to believe in your pocket Providence," he said, and then he rose to go.

"Why don't you stay to dinner?" Dinner at Balcom's Works was at one o'clock.

"I'll come back to supper, if you'll let me. Perhaps I shall bring you a convert."

"Well, you may come back, on that condition."

"All right. If I don't come, you'll understand."

He went away without kissing her, and she felt it a suspension of their engagement. It all interested her intensely; she was undergoing a tremendous experience, and she was being equal to it. While she stood looking after him, her mother came out through one of the long windows onto the veranda, with a catlike softness and vagueness.

"Why didn't he stay to dinner?"

"Because—because—war has been declared," Editha pronounced, without turning.

Her mother said, "Oh, my!" and then said nothing more until she had sat down in one of the large Shaker chairs[3] and rocked herself for some time. Then she closed whatever tacit passage of thought there had been in her mind with the spoken words: "Well, I hope *he* won't go."

"And *I* hope he *will*," the girl said, and confronted her mother with a stormy exaltation that would have frightened any creature less unimpressionable than a cat.

Her mother rocked herself again for an interval of cogitation. What she arrived at in speech was: "Well, I guess you've done a wicked thing, Editha Balcom."

The girl said, as she passed indoors through the same window her mother had come out by: "I haven't done anything—yet."

In her room, she put together all her letters and gifts from Gearson, down to the withered petals of the first flower he had offered, with that timidity of his veiled in that irony of his. In the heart of the packet she enshrined her engagement ring which she had restored to the pretty box he had brought it her in. Then she sat down, if not calmly yet strongly, and wrote:

> "GEORGE:—I understood when you left me. But I think we had better emphasize your meaning that if we cannot be one in everything we had better be one in nothing. So I am sending these things for your keeping till you have made up your mind.
>
> "I shall always love you, and therefore I shall never marry any one else. But the man I marry must love his country first of all, and be able to say to me,
>
>> "'I could not love thee, dear, so much,
>> Loved I not honor more.'[4]
>
> "There is no honor above America with me. In this great hour there is no other honor.
>
> "Your heart will make my words clear to you. I had never expected to say so much, but it has come upon me that I must say the utmost. EDITHA."

She thought she had worded her letter well, worded it in a way that could not be bettered; all had been implied and nothing expressed.

She had it ready to send with the packet she had tied with red, white, and blue ribbon, when it occurred to her that she was not just to him, that she was not giving him a fair chance. He had said he would go and think it over, and she was not waiting.

---

[3]Chairs made by a Shaker religious community; Shakers were noted for their excellent woodwork and simplicity of design.

[4]From "To Lucasta, on Going to the Wars," by British poet Richard Lovelace (1618–1658).

She was pushing, threatening, compelling. That was not a woman's part. She must leave him free, free, free. She could not accept for her country or herself a forced sacrifice.

In writing her letter she had satisfied the impulse from which it sprang; she could well afford to wait till he had thought it over. She put the packet and the letter by, and rested serene in the consciousness of having done what was laid upon her by her love itself to do, and yet used patience, mercy, justice.

She had her reward. Gearson did not come to tea, but she had given him till morning, when, late at night there came up from the village the sound of a fife and drum, with a tumult of voices, in shouting, singing, and laughing. The noise drew nearer and nearer; it reached the street end of the avenue; there it silenced itself, and one voice, the voice she knew best, rose over the silence. It fell; the air was filled with cheers; the fife and drum struck up, with the shouting, singing, and laughing again, but now retreating; and a single figure came hurrying up the avenue.

She ran down to meet her lover and clung to him. He was very gay, and he put his arm round her with a boisterous laugh. "Well, you must call me Captain now; or Cap, if you prefer; that's what the boys call me. Yes, we've had a meeting at the town-hall, and everybody has volunteered; and they selected me for captain, and I'm going to the war, the big war, the glorious war, the holy war ordained by the pocket Providence that blesses butchery. Come along; let's tell the whole family about it. Call them from their downy beds, mother, Aunt Hitty, and all the folks!"

But when they mounted the veranda steps he did not wait for a larger audience; he poured the story out upon Editha alone.

"There was a lot of speaking, and then some of the fools set up a shout for me. It was all going one way, and I thought it would be a good joke to sprinkle a little cold water on them. But you can't do that with a crowd that adores you. The first thing I knew I was sprinkling hell-fire on them. 'Cry havoc, and let slip the dogs of war.'[5] That was the style. Now that it had come to the fight, there were no two parties; there was one country, and the thing was to fight to a finish as quick as possible. I suggested volunteering then and there, and I wrote my name first of all on the roster. Then they elected me—that's all. I wish I had some ice-water."

She left him walking up and down the veranda, while she ran for the ice-pitcher and a goblet, and when she came back he was still walking up and down, shouting the story he had told her to her father and mother, who had come out more sketchily dressed than they commonly were by day. He drank goblet after goblet of the ice-water without noticing who was giving it, and kept on talking, and laughing through his talk wildly. "It's astonishing," he said, "how well the worse reason looks when you try to make it appear the better. Why, I believe I was the first convert to the war in that crowd to-night! I never thought I should like to kill a man; but now I shouldn't care; and the smokeless powder lets you see the man drop that you kill. It's all for the country! What a thing it is to have a country that *can't* be wrong, but if it is, is right, anyway!"

Editha had a great, vital thought, an inspiration. She set down the ice-pitcher on the veranda floor, and ran up-stairs and got the letter she had written him. When at last he noisily bade her father and mother, "Well, good-night. I forgot I woke you up; I sha'n't want any sleep myself," she followed him down the avenue to the gate. There, after the whirling words that seemed to fly away from her thoughts and refuse to serve them, she made a last effort to solemnize the moment that seemed so crazy, and pressed the letter she had written upon him.

---

[5]From Antony's soliloquy after the murder of Caesar in
Shakespeare's *Julius Caesar*, III, i, 273.

"What's this?" he said. "Want me to mail it?"

"No, no. It's for you. I wrote it after you went this morning. Keep it—keep it—and read it sometime—" She thought, and then her inspiration came: "Read it if ever you doubt what you've done, or fear that I regret your having done it. Read it after you've started."

They strained each other in embraces that seemed as ineffective as their words, and he kissed her face with quick, hot breaths that were so unlike him, that made her feel as if she had lost her old lover and found a stranger in his place. The stranger said: "What a gorgeous flower you are, with your red hair, and your blue eyes that look black now, and your face with the color painted out by the white moonshine! Let me hold you under the chin, to see whether I love blood, you tiger-lily!" Then he laughed Gearson's laugh, and released her, scared and giddy. Within her wilfulness she had been frightened by a sense of subtler force in him, and mystically mastered as she had never been before.

She ran all the way back to the house, and mounted the steps panting. Her mother and father were talking of the great affair. Her mother said: "Wa'n't Mr. Gearson in rather of an excited state of mind? Didn't you think he acted curious?"

"Well, not for a man who'd just been elected captain and had set 'em up for the whole of Company A," her father chuckled back.

"What in the world do you mean, Mr. Balcom? Oh! There's Editha!" She offered to follow the girl indoors.

"Don't come, mother!" Editha called, vanishing.

Mrs. Balcom remained to reproach her husband. "I don't see much of anything to laugh at."

"Well, it's catching. Caught it from Gearson. I guess it won't be much of a war, and I guess Gearson don't think so, either. The other fellows will back down as soon as they see we mean it. I wouldn't lose any sleep over it. I'm going back to bed, myself."

Gearson came again next afternoon, looking pale and rather sick, but quite himself, even to his languid irony. "I guess I'd better tell you, Editha, that I consecrated myself to your god of battles last night by pouring too many libations to him down my own throat. But I'm all right now. One has to carry off the excitement, somehow."

"Promise me," she commanded, "that you'll never touch it again!"

"What! Not let the cannikin clink? Not let the soldier drink?[6] Well, I promise."

"You don't belong to yourself now; you don't even belong to *me*. You belong to your country, and you have a sacred charge to keep yourself strong and well for your country's sake. I have been thinking, thinking all night and all day long."

"You look as if you had been crying a little, too," he said, with his queer smile.

"That's all past. I've been thinking, and worshipping *you*. Don't you suppose I know all that you've been through, to come to this? I've followed you every step from your old theories and opinions."

"Well, you've had a long row to hoe."

"And I know you've done this from the highest motives—"

"Oh, there won't be much pettifogging to do till this cruel war is—"

"And you haven't simply done it for my sake. I couldn't respect you if you had."

"Well, then we'll say I haven't. A man that hasn't got his own respect intact wants the respect of all the other people he can corner. But we won't go into that. I'm in for the thing now, and we've got to face our future. My idea is that this isn't going to be a very protracted struggle; we shall just scare the enemy to death before it comes to a

---

[6]An allusion to a soldier's drinking song in Shakespeare's *Othello*, II, iii, 71–75.

fight at all. But we must provide for contingencies, Editha. If anything happens to me—"

"Oh, George!" She clung to him, sobbing.

"I don't want you to feel foolishly bound to my memory. I should hate that, wherever I happened to be."

"I am yours, for time and eternity—time and eternity." She liked the words; they satisfied her famine for phrases.

"Well, say eternity; that's all right; but time's another thing; and I'm talking about time. But there is something! My mother! If anything happens—"

She winced, and he laughed. "You're not the bold soldier-girl of yesterday!" Then he sobered. "If anything happens, I want you to help my mother out. She won't like my doing this thing. She brought me up to think war a fool thing as well as a bad thing. My father was in the Civil War; all through it; lost his arm in it." She thrilled with the sense of the arm round her; what if that should be lost? He laughed as if divining her: "Oh, it doesn't run in the family, as far as I know!" Then he added, gravely: "He came home with misgivings about war, and they grew on him. I guess he and mother agreed between them that I was to be brought up in his final mind about it; but that was before my time. I only knew him from my mother's report of him and his opinions; I don't know whether they were hers first; but they were hers last. This will be a blow to her. I shall have to write and tell her—"

He stopped, and she asked: "Would you like me to write, too, George?"

"I don't believe that would do. No, I'll do the writing. She'll understand a little if I say that I thought the way to minimize it was to make war on the largest possible scale at once—that I felt I must have been helping on the war somehow if I hadn't helped keep it from coming, and I knew I hadn't; when it came, I had no right to stay out of it."

Whether his sophistries satisfied him or not, they satisfied her. She clung to his breast, and whispered, with closed eyes and quivering lips: "Yes, yes, yes!"

"But if anything should happen, you might go to her and see what you could do for her. You know? It's rather far off; she can't leave her chair—"

"Oh, I'll go, if it's the ends of the earth! But nothing will happen! Nothing *can*! I—"

She felt herself lifted with his rising, and Gearson was saying, with his arm still round her, to her father: "Well, we're off at once, Mr. Balcom. We're to be formally accepted at the capital, and then bunched up with the rest somehow, and sent into camp somewhere, and got to the front as soon as possible. We all want to be in the van, of course; we're the first company to report to the Governor. I came to tell Editha, but I hadn't got round to it."

She saw him again for a moment at the capital, in the station, just before the train started southward with his regiment. He looked well, in his uniform, and very soldierly, but somehow girlish, too, with his clean-shaven face and slim figure. The manly eyes and the strong voice satisfied her, and his preoccupation with some unexpected details of duty flattered her. Other girls were weeping and bemoaning themselves, but she felt a sort of noble distinction in the abstraction, the almost unconsciousness, with which they parted. Only at the last moment he said: "Don't forget my mother. It mayn't be such a walk-over as I supposed," and he laughed at the notion.

He waved his hand to her as the train moved off—she knew it among a score of hands that were waved to other girls from the platform of the car, for it held a letter which she knew was hers. Then he went inside the car to read it, doubtless, and she did not see him again. But she felt safe for him through the strength of what she called her love. What she called her God, always speaking the name in a deep voice and with the implication of a mutual understanding, would watch over him and keep him and bring him back to her. If with an empty sleeve, then he should have three arms instead of two, for both of hers should be his for life. She did not see, though, why she should always be thinking of the arm his father had lost.

There were not many letters from him, but they were such as she could have wished, and she put her whole strength into making hers such as she imagined he could have wished, glorifying and supporting him. She wrote to his mother glorifying him as their hero, but the brief answer she got was merely to the effect that Mrs. Gearson was not well enough to write herself, and thanking her for her letter by the hand of some one who called herself "Yrs truly, Mrs. W. J. Andrews."

Editha determined not to be hurt, but to write again quite as if the answer had been all she expected. Before it seemed as if she could have written, there came news of the first skirmish, and in the list of the killed, which was telegraphed as a trifling loss on our side, was Gearson's name. There was a frantic time of trying to make out that it might be, must be, some other Gearson; but the name and the company and the regiment and the State were too definitely given.

Then there was a lapse into depths out of which it seemed as if she never could rise again; then a lift into clouds far above all grief, black clouds, that blotted out the sun, but where she soared with him, with George—George! She had the fever that she expected of herself, but she did not die in it; she was not even delirious, and it did not last long. When she was well enough to leave her bed, her one thought was of George's mother, of his strangely worded wish that she should go to her and see what she could do for her. In the exaltation of the duty laid upon her—it buoyed her up instead of burdening her—she rapidly recovered.

Her father went with her on the long railroad journey from northern New York to western Iowa; he had business out at Davenport, and he said he could just as well go then as any other time; and he went with her to the little country town where George's mother lived in a little house on the edge of the illimitable cornfields, under trees pushed to a top of the rolling prairie. George's father had settled there after the Civil War, as so many other old soldiers had done; but they were Eastern people, and Editha fancied touches of the East in the June rose overhanging the front door, and the garden with early summer flowers stretching from the gate of the paling fence.

It was very low inside the house, and so dim, with the closed blinds, that they could scarcely see one another: Editha tall and black in her crapes which filled the air with the smell of their dyes; her father standing decorously apart with his hat on his forearm, as at funerals; a woman rested in a deep arm-chair, and the woman who had let the strangers in stood behind the chair.

The seated woman turned her head round and up, and asked the woman behind her chair: "*Who* did you say?"

Editha, if she had done what she expected of herself, would have gone down on her knees at the feet of the seated figure and said, "I am George's Editha," for answer.

But instead of her own voice she heard that other woman's voice, saying: "Well, I don't know as I *did* get the name just right. I guess I'll have to make a little more light in here," and she went and pushed two of the shutters ajar.

Then Editha's father said, in his public will-now-address-a-few-remarks tone: "My name is Balcom, ma'am—Junius H. Balcom, of Balcom's Works, New York; my daughter—"

"Oh!" the seated woman broke in, with a powerful voice, the voice that always surprised Editha from Gearson's slender frame. "Let me see you. Stand round where the light can strike on your face," and Editha dumbly obeyed. "So, you're Editha Balcom," she sighed.

"Yes," Editha said, more like a culprit than a comforter.

"What did you come for?" Mrs. Gearson asked.

Editha's face quivered and her knees shook. "I came—because—because George—" She could go no further.

"Yes," the mother said, "he told me he had asked you to come if he got killed. You didn't expect that, I suppose, when you sent him."

"I would rather have died myself than done it!" Editha said, with more truth in her deep voice than she ordinarily found in it. "I tried to leave him free—"

"Yes, that letter of yours, that came back with his other things, left him free."

Editha saw now where George's irony came from.

"It was not to be read before—unless—until— I told him so," she faltered.

"Of course, he wouldn't read a letter of yours, under the circumstances, till he thought you wanted him to. Been sick?" the woman abruptly demanded.

"Very sick," Editha said, with self-pity.

"Daughter's life," her father interposed, "was almost despaired of, at one time."

Mrs. Gearson gave him no heed. "I suppose you would have been glad to die, such a brave person as you! I don't believe *he* was glad to die. He was always a timid boy, that way; he was afraid of a good many things; but if he was afraid he did what he made up his mind to. I suppose he made up his mind to go, but I knew what it cost him by what it cost me when I heard of it. I had been through *one* war before. When you sent him you didn't expect he would get killed."

The voice seemed to compassionate Editha, and it was time. "No," she huskily murmured.

"No, girls don't; women don't, when they give their men up to their country. They think they'll come marching back, somehow, just as gay as they went, or if it's an empty sleeve, or even an empty pantaloon, it's all the more glory, and they're so much the prouder of them, poor things!"

The tears began to run down Editha's face; she had not wept till then; but it was now such a relief to be understood that the tears came.

"No, you didn't expect him to get killed," Mrs. Gearson repeated, in a voice which was startlingly like George's again. "You just expected him to kill some one else, some of those foreigners, that weren't there because they had any say about it, but because they had to be there, poor wretches—conscripts, or whatever they call 'em. You thought it would be all right for my George, *your* George, to kill the sons of those miserable mothers and the husbands of those girls that you would never see the faces of." The woman lifted her powerful voice in a psalmlike note. "I thank my God he didn't live to do it! I thank my God they killed him first, and that he ain't livin' with their blood on his hands!" She dropped her eyes, which she had raised with her voice, and glared at Editha. "What you got that black on for?" She lifted herself by her powerful arms so high that her helpless body seemed to hang limp its full length. "Take it off, take it off, before I tear it from your back!"

The lady who was passing the summer near Balcom's Works was sketching Editha's beauty, which lent itself wonderfully to the effects of a colorist. It had come to that confidence which is rather apt to grow between artist and sitter, and Editha had told her everything.

"To think of your having such a tragedy in your life!" the lady said. She added: "I suppose there are people who feel that way about war. But when you consider the good this war has done—how much it has done for the country! I can't understand such people for my part. And when you had come all the way out there to console her—got up out of a sick-bed! Well!"

"I think," Editha said, magnanimously, "she wasn't quite in her right mind; and so did papa."

"Yes," the lady said, looking at Editha's lips in nature and then at her lips in art, and giving an empirical touch to them in the picture. "But how dreadful of her! How perfectly—excuse me—how *vulgar!*"

A light broke upon Editha in the darkness which she felt had been without a gleam of brightness for weeks and months. The mystery that had bewildered her was solved by the word; and from that moment she rose from grovelling in shame and self-pity, and began to live again in the ideal.

1905

from Criticism and Fiction

from CHAPTER XXI

[THE "MORE SMILING ASPECTS" OF AMERICAN LIFE]

It is the difference of the American novelist's ideals from those of the English novelist that gives him his advantage, and seems to promise him the future. The love of the passionate and the heroic, as the Englishman has it, is such a crude and un-wholesome thing, so deaf and blind to all the most delicate and important facts of art and life, so insensible to the subtle values in either that its presence or absence makes the whole difference, and enables one who is not obsessed by it to thank Heaven that he is not as that other man is.

There can be little question that many refinements of thought and spirit which every American is sensible of in the fiction of this continent, are necessarily lost upon our good kin beyond seas, whose thumb-fingered apprehension requires something gross and palpable for its assurance of reality. This is not their fault, and I am not sure that it is wholly their misfortune: they are made so as not to miss what they do not find, and they are simply content without those subtleties of life and character which it gives us so keen a pleasure to have noted in literature. If they perceive them at all it is as something vague and diaphanous, something that filmily wavers before their sense and teases them, much as the beings of an invisible world might mock one of our material frame by intimations of their presence. It is with reason, therefore, on the part of an Englishman, that Mr. Henley[1] complains of our fiction as a shadow-land, though we find more and more in it the faithful report of our life, its motives and emotions, and all the comparatively etherealized passions and ideals that influence it.

In fact, the American who chooses to enjoy his birthright to the full, lives in a world wholly different from the Englishman's, and speaks (too often through his nose) another language: he breathes a rarified and nimble air full of shining possi-bilities and radiant promises which the fog-and-soot-clogged lungs of those less-favored islanders struggle in vain to fill themselves with. But he ought to be modest in his advantage, and patient with the coughing and sputtering of his cousin who complains of finding himself in an exhausted receiver[2] on plunging into one of our novels. To be quite just to the poor fellow, I have had some such experience as that myself in the atmosphere of some of our more attenuated romances.

Yet every now and then I read a book with perfect comfort and much exhilara-tion, whose scenes the average Englishman would gasp in. Nothing happens; that is, nobody murders or debauches anybody else; there is no arson or pillage of any sort; there is not a ghost, or a ravening beast, or a hair-breadth escape, or a shipwreck, or a monster of self-sacrifice, or a lady five thousand years old in the whole course of the story; "no promenade, no band of music, nossing!" as Mr. Du Maurier's Frenchman said of the meet for a fox-hunt.[3] Yet it is all alive with the keenest interest for those

---

[1] William Ernest Henley (1849–1903), English poet, editor, and critic.
[2] A vacuum glass (chemistry).

[3] Scene in *Pictures of English Society* (1884) by George du Maurier (1834–1896), English novelist; author of the popu-lar *Trilby* (1894).

who enjoy the study of individual traits and general conditions as they make themselves known to American experience.

These conditions have been so favorable hitherto (though they are becoming always less so) that they easily account for the optimistic faith of our novel which Mr. Hughes[4] notices. It used to be one of the disadvantages of the practice of romance in America, which Hawthorne more or less whimsically lamented,[5] that there were so few shadows and inequalities in our broad level of prosperity; and it is one of the reflections suggested by Dostoïevsky's novel, The Crime and the Punishment,[6] that whoever struck a note so profoundly tragic in American fiction would do a false and mistaken thing—as false and as mistaken in its way as dealing in American fiction with certain nudities which the Latin peoples seem to find edifying. Whatever their deserts, very few American novelists have been led out to be shot, or finally exiled to the rigors of a winter at Duluth; and in a land where journeymen carpenters and plumbers strike for four dollars a day the sum of hunger and cold is comparatively small, and the wrong from class to class has been almost inappreciable, though all this is changing for the worse. Our novelists, therefore, concern themselves with the more smiling aspects of life, which are the more American, and seek the universal in the individual rather than the social interests. It is worth while, even at the risk of being called commonplace, to be true to our well-to-do actualities; the very passions themselves seem to be softened and modified by conditions which formerly at least could not be said to wrong any one, to cramp endeavor, or to cross lawful desire. Sin and suffering and shame there must always be in the world, I suppose, but I believe that in this new world of ours it is still mainly from one to another one, and oftener still from one to one's self. We have death too in American, and a great deal of disagreeable and painful disease, which the multiplicity of our patent medicines does not seem to cure; but this is tragedy that comes in the very nature of things, and is not peculiarly American, as the large, cheerful average of health and success and happy life is. It will not do to boast, but it is well to be true to the facts, and to see that, apart from these purely mortal troubles, the race here has enjoyed conditions in which most of the ills that have darkened its annals might be averted by honest work and unselfish behavior.

CHAPTER XXIV

[FICTION AND THE FACTS OF LIFE]

One of the great newspapers the other day invited the prominent American authors to speak their minds upon a point in the theory and practice of fiction which had already vexed some of them. It was the question of how much or how little the American novel ought to deal with certain facts of life which are not usually talked of before young people, and especially young ladies. Of course the question was not decided, and I forget just how far the balance inclined in favor of a larger freedom in the matter. But it certainly inclined that way; one or two writers of the sex which is somehow supposed to have purity in its keeping (as if purity were a thing that did not practically concern the other sex, preoccupied with serious affairs) gave it a rather vigorous tilt to that side. In view of this fact it would not be the part of prudence to make an effort to dress the balance; and indeed I do not know that I was going to make any such effort. But there are some things to say, around and about the subject, which I should like to have some one else say, and which I may myself possibly be safe in suggesting.

---

[4]Eilian Hughes, English critic and author of "Present Day Novels: American versus English" in his *Some Aspects of Humanity* (1889).
[5]In the Preface to *The Marble Faun* (1860).
[6]Feodor Dostoyevski (1821–1881), Russian novelist, author of *Crime and Punishment* (1886). Because of his involvement in the revolutionary movement, he was sent to Siberia and placed before a firing squad, but his death sentence was commuted at the last moment.

One of the first of these is the fact, generally lost sight of by those who censure the Anglo-Saxon novel for its prudishness, that it is really not such a prude after all; and that if it is sometimes apparently anxious to avoid those experiences of life not spoken of before young people, this may be an appearance only. Sometimes a novel which has this shuffling air, this effect of truckling to propriety, might defend itself, if it could speak for itself, by saying that such experiences happened not to come within its scheme, and that, so far from maiming or mutilating itself in ignoring them, it was all the more faithfully representative of the tone of modern life in dealing with love that was chaste, and with passion so honest that it could be openly spoken of before the tenderest society bud at dinner. It might say that the guilty intrigue, the betrayal, the extreme flirtation even, was the exceptional thing in life, and unless the scheme of the story necessarily involved it, that it would be bad art to lug it in, and as bad taste as to introduce such topics in a mixed company. It could say very justly that the novel in our civilization now always addresses a mixed company, and that the vast majority of the company are ladies, and that very many, if not most, of these ladies are young girls. If the novel were written for men and for married women alone, as in continental Europe, it might be altogether different. But the simple fact is that it is not written for them alone among us, and it is a question of writing, under cover of our universal acceptance, things for young girls to read which you would be put out-of-doors for saying to them, or of frankly giving notice of your intention, and so cutting yourself off from the pleasure—and it is a very high and sweet one—of appealing to these vivid, responsive intelligences, which are none the less brilliant and admirable because they are innocent.

One day a novelist who liked, after the manner of other men, to repine at his hard fate, complained to his friend, a critic, that he was tired of the restriction he had put upon himself in this regard; for it is a mistake, as can be readily shown, to suppose that others impose it. "See how free those French fellows are!" he rebelled. "Shall we always be shut up to our tradition of decency?"

"Do you think it's much worse than being shut up to their tradition of indecency?" said his friend.

Then that novelist began to reflect, and he remembered how sick the invariable motive of the French novel made him. He perceived finally that, convention for convention, ours was not only more tolerable, but on the whole was truer to life, not only to its complexion, but also to its texture. No one will pretend that there is not vicious love beneath the surface of our society; if he did, the fetid explosions of the divorce trials would refute him; but if he pretended that it was in any just sense characteristic of our society, he could be still more easily refuted. Yet it exists, and it is unquestionably the material of tragedy, the stuff from which intense effects are wrought. The question, after owning this fact, is whether these intense effects are not rather cheap effects. I incline to think they are, and I will try to say why I think so, if I may do so without offence. The material itself, the mere mention of it, has an instant fascination; it arrests, it detains, till the last word is said, and while there is anything to be hinted. This is what makes a love intrigue of some sort all but essential to the popularity of any fiction. Without such an intrigue the intellectual equipment of the author must be of the highest, and then he will succeed only with the highest class of readers. But any author who will deal with a guilty love intrigue holds all readers in his hand, the highest with the lowest, as long as he hints the slightest hope of the smallest potential naughtiness. He need not at all be a great author; he may be a very shabby wretch, if he has but the courage or the trick of that sort of thing. The critics will call him "virile" and "passionate;" decent people will be ashamed to have been limed by him; but the low average will only ask another chance of flocking into his net. If he happens to be an able writer, his really fine and costly work will be unheeded, and the lure to the appetite will be chiefly remembered. There may be other qualities which make reputations for other men, but in his case they will count for nothing. He pays this penalty for his success in that kind; and every one pays some such penalty who deals with some such material. It attaches in like manner to the triumphs of the writers who now almost form a school among us, and who may be said to have established themselves in an easy popularity simply by the study of erotic shivers and fervors. They may find their account in the popularity, or they may not; there is no question of the popularity.

But I do not mean to imply that their case covers the whole ground. So far as it goes, though, it ought to stop the mouths of those who complain that fiction is enslaved to propriety among us. It appears that of a certain kind of impropriety it is free to give us all it will, and more. But this is not what serious men and women writing fiction mean when they rebel against the limitations of their art in our civilization. They have no desire to deal with nakedness, as painters and sculptors freely do in the worship of beauty; or with certain facts of life, as the stage does, in the service of sensation. But they ask why, when the conventions of the plastic and histrionic arts liberate their followers to the portrayal of almost any phase of the physical or of the emotional nature, an American novelist may not write a story on the lines of Anna Karenina or Madame Bovary.[1] Sappho they put aside, and from Zola's work they avert their eyes.[2] They do not condemn him or Daudet, necessarily, or accuse their motives; they leave them out of the question; they do not want to do that kind of thing. But they do sometimes wish to do another kind, to touch one of the most serious and sorrowful problems of life in the spirit of Tolstoï and Flaubert, and they ask why they may not. At one time, they remind us, the Anglo-Saxon novelist did deal with such problems—De Foe in his spirit, Richardson in his, Goldsmith in his.[3] At what moment did our fiction lose this privilege? In what fatal hour did the Young Girl arise and seal the lips of Fiction, with a touch of her finger, to some of the most vital interests of life?

Whether I wished to oppose them in their aspiration for greater freedom, or whether I wished to encourage them, I should begin to answer them by saying that the Young Girl had never done anything of the kind. The manners of the novel have been improving with those of its readers; that is all. Gentlemen no longer swear or fall drunk under the table, or abduct young ladies and shut them up in lonely country-houses, or so habitually set about the ruin of their neighbors' wives, as they once did. Generally, people now call a spade an agricultural implement; they have not grown decent without having also grown a little squeamish, but they have grown comparatively decent; there is no doubt about that. They require of a novelist whom they respect unquestionable proof of his seriousness, if he proposes to deal with certain phases of life; they require a sort of scientific decorum. He can no longer expect to be received on the ground of entertainment only; he assumes a higher function, something like that of a physician or a priest, and they expect him to be bound by laws as sacred as those of such professions; they hold him solemnly pledged not to betray them or abuse their confidence. If he will accept the conditions, they give him their confidence, and he may then treat to his greater honor, and not at all to his disadvantage, of such experiences, such relations of men and women as George Eliot treats in Adam Bede, in Daniel Deronda, in Romola,[4] in almost all her books; such as Hawthorne treats in the Scarlet Letter; such as Dickens treats in David Copperfield; such as Thackeray treats in Pendennis,[5] and glances at in every one of his fictions; such as

---

[1]Both novels deal with adultery committed by wives of men prominent in their communities; *Anna Karenina* (1875–76) by Russian novelist Count Leo Tolstoi (1828–1910); *Madame Bovary* (1857) by French novelist Gustave Flaubert (1821–1880).

[2]*Sappho* (1884) by French novelist Alphonse Daudet (1840–1897) portrays a prostitute; the French novelist Émile Zola (1840–1902) wrote *Nana* (1880), the story of a courtesan (or prostitute).

[3]Daniel Defoe (1660–1731), English author of *Moll Flanders* (1722); Samuel Richardson (1689–1761), English author of *Pamela* (1740–42) and *Clarissa Harlowe* (1747–48); Oliver

Goldsmith (1728–1774), English author of *The Vicar of Wakefield* (1766). Each of these novels deals with seduction or illicit love.

[4]George Eliot, pen name of Mary Ann Evans (1819–1880), English novelist and author of *Adam Bede* (1859), *Daniel Deronda* (1876), and *Romola* (1863).

[5]Nathaniel Hawthorne (1804–1864), American author of *The Scarlet Letter* (1850); Charles Dickens (1812–1870), English author of *David Copperfield* (1849–50); William Makepeace Thackeray (1811–1863), English author of *Pendennis* (1848–50).

most of the masters of English fiction have at some time treated more or less openly. It is quite false or quite mistaken to suppose that our novels have left untouched these most important realities of life. They have only not made them their stock in trade; they have kept a true perspective in regard to them; they have relegated them in their pictures of life to the space and place they occupy in life itself, as we know it in England and America. They have kept a correct proportion, knowing perfectly well that unless the novel is to be a map, with everything scrupulously laid down in it, a faithful record of life in far the greater extent could be made to the exclusion of guilty love and all its circumstances and consequences.

I justify them in this view not only because I hate what is cheap and meretricious, and hold in peculiar loathing the cant of the critics who require "passion" as something in itself admirable and desirable in a novel, but because I prize fidelity in the historian of feeling and character. Most of these critics who demand "passion" would seem to have no conception of any passion but one. Yet there are several other passions: the passion of grief, the passion of avarice, the passion of pity, the passion of ambition, the passion of hate, the passion of envy, the passion of devotion, the passion of friendship; and all these have a greater part in the drama of life than the passion of love, and infinitely greater than the passion of guilty love. Wittingly or unwittingly, English fiction and American fiction have recognized this truth, not fully, not in the measure it merits, but in greater degree than most other fiction.

1891

HENRY JAMES
(1843–1916)

It is perhaps a tribute to a culture's pluralism and vitality that it could produce two such dissimilar major novelists as Mark Twain and Henry James, the one a "provincial" American genius, the other a "cosmopolitan" American genius. Ironically, the two found subjects in common. Twain's great popular comic success *The Innocents Abroad* (1869) portrayed Americans repeatedly conned by, and in turn shrewdly conning, their European guides. In novel after novel, James, too, portrayed American innocents abroad in quest of culture, frequently falling prey to scheming European aristocrats scenting easy fortune. Whereas Twain's innocents triumphed through buffoonery, James's innocents triumphed through their transcendent moral spirit expressed often in their sacrificial renunciation. James had no high regard for Twain's work, and Twain once said of a James novel, *The Bostonians*, "I would rather be damned to John Bunyan's heaven than read that."

James was born in New York City in 1843, the second child in a family of five. The father had inherited modest wealth from *his* father, an Irish immigrant who had settled in Albany, New York, and become a highly successful merchant. Henry James, Sr., distrusted the schools as too bent on imposing intellectual conformity and passivity. He undertook through various means, including private tutors, the education of his children. An important part of that education was travel abroad. For three years (1855–58), the James children attended school and worked under tutors in Geneva, London, and Paris.

The education obviously worked. Of the five children, three made their mark in the world. Henry's older brother, William, went on to become a renowned psychologist and philosopher. The younger sister, Alice, though suffering from various nervous ailments, left a *Diary* at her early death in 1892 recognized now as an important contribution to the genre of personal accounts. And, of course, Henry developed into a novelist with an international reputation. Their father set them a fast pace. He was a philosopher in his own right, steeped in the mystical thought of the eighteenth-century Swedish theologian Emanuel Swedenborg. He published several books on religious and social subjects, and was friends with Ralph Waldo Emerson, Thomas Carlyle, and other leading literary figures of the day.

The James family fortune enabled the children to find careers that suited them. After a year at Harvard Law School, Henry turned to the writing of fiction, placing his first story in *The Continental Monthly* in 1864. He published his first novel, *Watch and Ward*, in 1870. Like that of most developing writers, James's early fiction was derivative and little noticed. But he found himself passionately committed, embarked on his lifetime career. His commitment was total, his devotion to his art absolute. No alliance or relationship was to come between him and his work.

James continued his travels to Europe begun in his childhood, and out of experiences as an American abroad he found his most productive material for his fiction. His first successes—*The American* in 1877 and *Daisy Miller* in 1879—treated this "international" theme, portraying naive but morally sensitive citizens of the New World caught up in the hide-bound traditions and social machinations of the Old. James's first masterpiece, *The Portrait of a Lady* (1881), represented a classic handling of the theme in all its complexity and subtlety and brought to a close the first phase of James's development.

More and more James was attracted to the literary scene in Europe, spending a year in Paris in 1874–75, and coming to know Gustave Flaubert, Edmond de Goncourt, Émile Zola, and the Russian novelist, Ivan Turgenev. James took the measure of these and other writers in *French Poets and Novelists* (1878). Clearly James's literary horizons were extended by these French encounters, but the novelist he found most temperamentally compatible was the Europeanized Russian, Turgenev.

In 1876 James settled in England. Although he was to make extended visits to America, particularly in 1882–83 when his parents died, he remained abroad for the rest of his life. First he took an apartment in London, but in 1897 he moved into his own house in the village of Rye. Wherever he lived, James continued to write short stories, nouvelles (long tales), and novels in great numbers.

During his middle phase, James turned to social questions for the subject of his major works: in *The Bostonians* (1886), the nineteenth-century feminist movement centered in Boston; in *The Princess Casamassima* (1886), the underground revolutionary movement in London; and in *The Tragic Muse* (1889–90), the conflict between political and artistic careers in London. The failure of these works to attain popular success left James somewhat puzzled and not a little embittered.

Next James turned to the theater, and spent some five years (1890–95) writing plays and seeing them through production. He dramatized his own novel, *The American*, but it did not succeed. He continued to try and try again, until on the opening night of his *Guy Domville* in 1895 he answered the call after the play for "author, author," and appeared on stage—only to be booed. Then he threw it all over and turned back to fiction.

But the dramatic period left its imprint on his narratives. More and more he related his stories by alternating rhythmically between preparation and scene, preparation and scene. In his *Notebooks* he exhorted himself to "Dramatize, dramatize!" This method vivified his fiction of the late 1890s, which includes such remarkable and enduring short works as *The Spoils of Poynton* (1897), *What Maisie Knew* (1897), and *The Turn of the Screw* (1898).

At this time James was more prolific than ever, his imagination seemingly inexhaustible. He had also turned to dictating to a secretary, who then typed out his stories on the newly developed typewriter. Perhaps in part because of this method of composition, his style became more complex, luxuriant, capable of the most extraordinary subtleties. Some wits have claimed that the James of the three periods of his work might be labelled James the First, James the Second, and James the Old Pretender (after a succession of British monarchs).

But James's last period, which was once characterized as self-indulgent and tedious, has turned out to be, according to contemporary critics, his greatest period, quite deserving of the title "The Major Phase." For his subject James turned back to his early "international" theme, focusing on Americans confronting their destiny in Europe. Three masterpieces appeared in quick succession: *The Wings of the Dove* (1902), *The Ambassadors* (1903), and *The Golden Bowl* (1904).

Throughout his career, James had written several travel books. In 1904–05, he made a prolonged tour of America, travelling extensively on the East coast and then going cross-country to Chicago and on to California. He gathered his impressions with care and elaborated them in *The American Scene* in 1907. James's keen eye missed little on this trip and his probing account of America—past, present, and future—has proved of enduring interest.

Now in his sixties, James undertook to review the entire body of his work, revising meticulously and writing prefaces for each of the volumes as they appeared. James's interest in the theory of fiction had been made manifest earlier in the classic little essay he published in 1884, "The Art of Fiction." The prefaces to the New York Edition of his work (1907–09), published separately in 1934 as *The Art of the Novel*, constitute one of the most remarkable collections of theoretical statements on fiction ever written by a novelist. These works, together with James's *Notebooks* (1947), his numerous critical essays, and the large number of stories he wrote about writers (such as "The Figure in the Carpet") make James an imposing theorist to be reckoned with in literary history.

In the last years of his life, especially after the death of his brother William in 1910, James turned to the writing of reminiscences—*A Small Boy and Others* (1913) and *Notes of a Son and Brother* (1914). As a protest against America's early refusal to become involved in the First World War, which James saw as a threat to the survival of civilization, he became a British citizen in 1915. And when he died in 1916, he left fragments of two unfinished novels and an autobiographical account, *The Middle Years*.

In his art James has proved to be more a figure of the twentieth century than the nineteenth. It has been said with some justification of the two James brothers that William was a psychologist who wrote like a novelist, and James was a novelist who wrote like a psychologist. William James was the inventor of the term "stream of consciousness" (in his *Principles of Psychology*, 1890). In developing and elaborating "dramas of consciousness" in his fiction, especially in his later great works, Henry James moved the novel from its focus on exterior reality to a focus on an interior reality; he moved it from its foundation in nineteenth-century realism to the edge of modernism's exploitation of the "stream of consciousness" and "interior monologue," as in James Joyce's *Ulysses* (1922), Virginia Woolf's *Mrs. Dalloway* (1925), and William Faulkner's *The Sound and the Fury* (1929). Instead of fading into the past, James has come to be recognized as the master he was in the art of fiction, his work a touchstone by which new and innovative works might be measured.

ADDITIONAL READING

The Notebooks of Henry James, ed. F. O. Matthiessen and Kenneth B. Murdock, 1947, 1981; *The Complete Plays of Henry James*, ed. Leon Edel, 1949; *The Art of Travel*, ed. Morton D. Zabel, 1958; *Theory of Fiction: Henry James*, ed. James E. Miller, Jr., 1972; *Henry James Letters*, 4 vols., ed. Leon Edel, 1974–84; *The Art of Criticism*, ed. William Veeder and Susan M. Griffin, 1986; *The Complete Notebooks of Henry James*, ed. Leon Edel and Lyall H. Powers, 1987.

Joseph Warren Beach, *Henry James: Man and Author*, 1927; F. O. Matthiessen, *Henry James: The Major Phase*, 1944; F. W. Dupee, *The Question of Henry James*, 1945; F. O. Matthiessen, *The James Family*, 1947; Leon Edel, *Henry James*, 5 vols., 1953–72 (revised into one volume, *Henry James: A Life*, 1985); Quentin Anderson, *The American Henry James*, 1957; Richard Poirier, *The Comic Sense of Henry James*, 1960; Oscar Cargill, *The Novels of Henry James*, 1961; Walter F. Wright, *The Madness of Art*, 1962; Dorothea Krook, *The Ordeal of Consciousness in Henry James*, 1962; Maxwell Geismar, *Henry James and the Jacobites*, 1963; Laurence B. Holland, *The Expense of Vision*, 1964; Robert L. Gale, *The Caught Image: Figurative Language in the Fiction of Henry James*, 1964; Bruce R. McElderry, Jr., *Henry James*, 1965; S. Gorley Putt, *Henry James: A Reader's Guide*, 1966; Ora Segal, *The Lucid Re-Reflector*, 1969; Tony Tanner, ed., *Modern Judgments: Henry James*, 1969; Viola Hopkins Winner, *Henry James and the Visual Arts*, 1970; Lyall H. Powers, *Henry James and the Naturalist Movement*, 1971; Martha Banta, *Henry James and the Occult*, 1972; William Veeder, *Henry James — The Lessons of the Master*, 1975; Ruth Bernard Yeazell, *Language and Knowledge in the Late Novels of Henry James*, 1976; Sergio Perosa, *Henry James and the Experimental Novel*, 1978; Mary Doyle Springer, *A Rhetoric of Literary Character: Some Women in Henry James*, 1978; Susanne Kappeler, *Writing and Reading in Henry James*, 1980; Daniel Mark Fogel, *Henry James and the Structure of the Romantic Imagination*, 1981; R. B. J. Wilson, *Henry James's Ultimate Narrative: The Golden Bowl*, 1981; Susan Reibel Moore, *The Drama of Discrimination in Henry James*, 1982; Paul B. Armstrong, *The Phenomenology of Henry James*, 1983; Edward Wagenknecht, *The Novels of Henry James*, 1983; Robert Emmet Long, *Henry James: The Early Novels*, 1983; Marcia Jacobson, *Henry James and the Mass Market*, 1983; R. P. Blackmur, *Studies in Henry James*, ed. Veronica A. Makowsky, 1983; Carron Kaston, *Imagination and Desire in the Novels of Henry James*, 1984; Mark Seltzer, *Henry James's American Girl: The Embroidery on the Canvas*, 1984; Elizabeth Allen, *A Woman's Place in the Novels of Henry James*, 1984; Edward Wagenknecht, *The Tales of Henry James*, 1984; Anne T. Margolis, *Henry James and the Problem of Audience*, 1985; Tony Tanner, *Henry James: The Writer and His Work*, 1985; Ian F. A. Bell, *Henry James: Fiction as History*, 1985; Susan Carlson, *Women of Grace: James's Plays and the Comedy of Manners*, 1985; Vivien Jones, *James the Critic*, 1985; James W. Gargano, ed., *Critical Essays on Henry James: The Late Novels*, 1987; Adeline R. Tintner, *The Book World of Henry James*, 1988; Leon Edel and Adeline R. Tintner, eds., *The Library of Henry James*, 1988; Miranda Seymour, *A Ring of Conspirators: Henry James and His Literary Circle 1895–1915*, 1989.

TEXTS

All the tales and excerpts from Prefaces are from the "New York Edition," *The Novels and Tales of Henry James*, 1907–09 (in 1918, after James's death, the publisher added two volumes in a reissue of the edition, dating them 1917); *Hawthorne*, 1879; "The Art of Fiction" from *Partial Portraits*, 1888; "Criticism" from *New Review*, May 1891.

Daisy Miller[1]

I

At the little town of Vevey, in Switzerland, there is a particularly comfortable hotel; there are indeed many hotels, since the entertainment of tourists is the business of the place, which, as many travellers will remember, is seated upon the edge of

---

[1] "Daisy Miller," published in two installments in *Cornhill Magazine* in 1878, created a stir because of what one reader called its "outrage on American girlhood." William Dean Howells came to James's defense, declaring "so far as the average American girl was studied at all in 'Daisy Miller,' her inde- structible innocence, her invulnerable new-worldliness, had never been so delicately appreciated." The stir created by the work helped to make it, James said, the "most prosperous child of my invention."

a remarkably blue lake[2] — a lake that it behoves every tourist to visit. The shore of the lake presents an unbroken array of establishments of this order, of every category, from the "grand hotel" of the newest fashion, with a chalk-white front, a hundred balconies, and a dozen flags flying from its roof, to the small Swiss pension of an elder day, with its name inscribed in German-looking lettering upon a pink or yellow wall and an awkward summer-house in the angle of the garden. One of the hotels at Vevey, however, is famous, even classical, being distinguished from many of its up-start neighbours by an air both of luxury and of maturity. In this region, through the month of June, American travellers are extremely numerous; it may be said indeed that Vevey assumes at that time some of the characteristics of an American watering-place. There are sights and sounds that evoke a vision, an echo, of Newport and Saratoga.[3] There is a flitting hither and thither of "stylish" young girls, a rustling of muslin flounces, a rattle of dance-music in the morning hours, a sound of high-pitched voices at all times. You receive an impression of these things at the excellent inn of the "Trois Couronnes,"[4] and are transported in fancy to the Ocean House or to Congress Hall.[5] But at the "Trois Couronnes," it must be added, there are other features much at variance with these suggestions: neat German waiters who look like secretaries of legation; Russian princesses sitting in the garden; little Polish boys walking about, held by the hand, and with their governors; a view of the snowy crest of the Dent du Midi[6] and the picturesque towers of the Castle of Chillon.[7]

I hardly know whether it was the analogies or the differences that were upper-most in the mind of a young American, who, two or three years ago, sat in the garden of the "Trois Couronnes," looking about him rather idly at some of the graceful objects I have mentioned. It was a beautiful summer morning, and in whatever fash-ion the young American looked at things they must have seemed to him charming. He had come from Geneva the day before, by the little steamer, to see his aunt, who was staying at the hotel — Geneva having been for a long time his place of residence. But his aunt had a headache — his aunt had almost always a headache — and she was now shut up in her room smelling camphor, so that he was at liberty to wander about. He was some seven-and-twenty years of age; when his friends spoke of him they usually said that he was at Geneva "studying." When his enemies spoke of him they said — but after all he had no enemies: he was extremely amiable and generally liked. What I should say is simply that when certain persons spoke of him they conveyed that the reason of his spending so much time at Geneva was that he was extremely devoted to a lady who lived there — a foreign lady, a person older than himself. Very few Americans — truly I think none — had ever seen this lady, about whom there were some singular stories. But Winterbourne had an old attachment for the little capital of Calvinism;[8] he had been put to school there as a boy and had afterwards even gone, on trial — trial of the grey old "Academy"[9] on the steep and stony hillside — to college there; circumstances which had led to his forming a great many youthful friendships. Many of these he had kept, and they were a source of great satisfaction to him.

After knocking at his aunt's door and learning that she was indisposed he had taken a walk about the town and then he had come in to his breakfast. He had now finished that repast, but was enjoying a small cup of coffee which had been served him on a little table in the garden by one of the waiters who looked like *attachés*. At last he finished his coffee and lit a cigarette. Presently a small boy came walking along the path — an urchin or nine or ten. The child, who was diminutive for his years, had an

[2]Lake Geneva.
[3]Socially popular summer resorts of the time, one in Rhode Island, the other in New York.
[4]"Three crowns" (French).
[5]Resort hotels in Newport and Saratoga.
[6]Tall mountain of the Swiss Alps.
[7]Castle on Lake Geneva that serves as the scene for Byron's poem, "The Prisoner of Chillon" (1816).
[8]I.e., Geneva, where John Calvin (1509–1564) lived in exile from France, leading his Protestant attack on Catholicism.
[9]The University of Geneva.

aged expression of countenance, a pale complexion and sharp little features. He was dressed in knickerbockers and had red stockings that displayed his poor little spindleshanks; he also wore a brilliant red cravat. He carried in his hand a long alpenstock, the sharp point of which he thrust into everything he approached—the flower-beds, the garden-benches, the trains of the ladies' dresses. In front of Winterbourne he paused, looking at him with a pair of bright and penetrating little eyes.

"Will you give me a lump of sugar?" he asked in a small sharp hard voice—a voice immature and yet somehow not young.

Winterbourne glanced at the light table near him, on which his coffee-service rested, and saw that several morsels of sugar remained. "Yes, you may take one," he answered; "but I don't think too much sugar good for little boys."

This little boy stepped forward and carefully selected three of the covered fragments, two of which he buried in the pocket of his knickerbockers, depositing the other as promptly in another place. He poked his alpenstock, lance-fashion, into Winterbourne's bench and tried to crack the lump of sugar with his teeth.

"Oh blazes; it's har-r-d!" he exclaimed, divesting vowel and consonants, pertinently enough, of any taint of softness.

Winterbourne had immediately gathered that he might have the honour of claiming him as a countryman. "Take care you don't hurt your teeth," he said paternally.

"I have n't got any teeth to hurt. They've all come out. I've only got seven teeth. Mother counted them last night, and one came out right afterwards. She said she'd slap me if any more came out. I can't help it. It's this old Europe. It's the climate that makes them come out. In America they did n't come out. It's these hotels."

Winterbourne was much amused. "If you eat three lumps of sugar your mother will certainly slap you," he ventured.

"She's got to give me some candy then," rejoined his young interlocutor. "I can't get any candy here—any American candy. American candy's the best candy."

"And are American little boys the best little boys?" Winterbourne asked.

"I don't know. *I'm* an American boy," said the child.

"I see you're one of the best!" the young man laughed.

"Are you an American man?" pursued this vivacious infant. And then on his friend's affirmative reply, "American men are the best," he declared with assurance.

His companion thanked him for the compliment, and the child, who had now got astride of his alpenstock, stood looking about him while he attacked another lump of sugar. Winterbourne wondered if he himself had been like this in his infancy, for he had been brought to Europe at about the same age.

"Here comes my sister!" cried his young compatriot. "She's an American girl, you bet!"

Winterbourne looked along the path and saw a beautiful young lady advancing. "American girls are the best girls," he thereupon cheerfully remarked to his visitor.

"My sister ain't the best!" the child promptly returned. "She's always blowing[10] at me."

"I imagine that's your fault, not hers," said Winterbourne. The young lady meanwhile had drawn near. She was dressed in white muslin, with a hundred frills and flounces and knots of pale-coloured ribbon. Bareheaded, she balanced in her hand a large parasol with a deep border of embroidery; and she was strikingly, admirably pretty. "How pretty they are!" thought our friend, who straightened himself in his seat as if he were ready to rise.

The young lady paused in front of his bench, near the parapet of the garden, which overlooked the lake. The small boy had now converted his alpenstock into a vaulting-pole, by the aid of which he was springing about in the gravel and kicking it up not a little. "Why Randolph," she freely began, "what *are* you doing?"

---

[10]I.e., nagging.

"I'm going up the Alps!" cried Randolph. "This is the way!" And he gave another extravagant jump, scattering the pebbles about Winterbourne's ears.

"That's the way they come down," said Winterbourne.

"He's an American man!" proclaimed Randolph in his harsh little voice.

The young lady gave no heed to this circumstance, but looked straight at her brother. "Well, I guess you'd better be quiet," she simply observed.

It seemed to Winterbourne that he had been in a manner presented. He got up and stepped slowly toward the charming creature, throwing away his cigarette. "This little boy and I have made acquaintance," he said with great civility. In Geneva, as he had been perfectly aware, a young man was n't at liberty to speak to a young unmarried lady save under certain rarely-occuring conditions; but here at Vevey what conditions could be better than these?—a pretty American girl, coming to stand in front of you in a garden with all the confidence in life. This pretty American girl, whatever that might prove, on hearing Winterbourne's observation simply glanced at him; she then turned her head and looked over the parapet, at the lake and the opposite mountains. He wondered whether he had gone too far, but decided that he must gallantly advance rather than retreat. While he was thinking of something else to say the young lady turned again to the little boy, whom she addressed quite as if they were alone together. "I should like to know where you got that pole."

"I bought it!" Randolph shouted.

"You don't mean to say you're going to take it to Italy!"

"Yes, I'm going to take it t' Italy!" the child rang out.

She glanced over the front of her dress and smoothed out a knot or two of ribbon. Then she gave her sweet eyes to the prospect again. "Well, I guess you'd better leave it somewhere," she dropped after a moment.

"Are you going to Italy?" Winterbourne now decided very respectfully to enquire.

She glanced at him with lovely remoteness. "Yes, sir," she then replied. And she said nothing more.

"And are you—a—thinking of the Simplon?"[11] he pursued with a slight drop of assurance.

"I don't know," she said. "I suppose it's some mountain. Randolph, what mountain are we thinking of?"

"Thinking of?"—the boy stared.

"Why going right over."

"Going to where?" he demanded.

"Why right down to Italy"—Winterbourne felt vague emulations.

"I don't know," said Randolph. "I don't want to go t' Italy. I want to go to America."

"Oh Italy's a beautiful place!" the young man laughed.

"Can you get candy there?" Randolph asked of all the echoes.

"I hope not," said his sister. "I guess you've had enough candy, and mother thinks so too."

"I have n't had any for ever so long—for a hundred weeks!" cried the boy, still jumping about.

The young lady inspected her flounces and smoothed her ribbons again; and Winterbourne presently risked an observation on the beauty of the view. He was ceasing to be in doubt, for he had begun to perceive that she was really not in the least embarrassed. She might be cold, she might be austere, she might even be prim; for that was apparently—he had already so generalised—what the most "distant" American girls did: they came and planted themselves straight in front of you to show how rigidly unapproachable they were. There had n't been the slightest flush in her fresh fairness however; so that she was clearly neither offended nor fluttered. Only she was composed—he had seen that before too—of charming little parts that did n't match

---

[11]Famous mountain pass between Switzerland and Italy.

and that made no *ensemble*; and if she looked another way when he spoke to her, and seemed not particularly to hear him, this was simply her habit, her manner, the result of her having no idea whatever of "form" (with such a tell-tale appendage as Randolph where in the world would she have got it?) in any such connexion. As he talked a little more and pointed out some of the objects of interest in the view, with which she appeared wholly unacquainted, she gradually, none the less, gave him more of the benefit of her attention; and then he saw that act unqualified by the faintest shadow of reserve. It was n't however what would have been called a "bold" front she presented, for her expression was as decently limpid as the very cleanest water. Her eyes were the very prettiest conceivable, and indeed Winterbourne had n't for a long time seen anything prettier than his fair countrywoman's various features — her complexion, her nose, her ears, her teeth. He took a great interest generally in that range of effects and was addicted to noting and, as it were, recording them; so that in regard to this young lady's face he made several observations. It was n't at all insipid, yet at the same time was n't pointedly — what point, on earth, could she ever make? — expressive; and though it offered such a collection of small finenesses and neatnesses he mentally accused it — very forgivingly — of a want of finish. He thought nothing more likely than that its wearer would have had her own experience of the action of her charms, as she would certainly have acquired a resulting confidence; but even should she depend on this for her main amusement her bright sweet superficial little visage gave out neither mockery nor irony. Before long it became clear that, however these things might be, she was much disposed to conversation. She remarked to Winterbourne that they were going to Rome for the winter — she and her mother and Randolph. She asked him if he was a "real American"; she would n't have taken him for one; he seemed more like a German — this flower was gathered as from a large field of comparison — especially when he spoke. Winterbourne, laughing, answered that he had met Germans who spoke like Americans, but not, so far as he remembered, any American with the resemblance she noted. Then he asked her if she might n't be more at ease should she occupy the bench he had just quitted. She answered that she liked hanging round, but she none the less resignedly, after a little while, dropped to the bench. She told him she was from New York State — "if you know where that is"; but our friend really quickened this current by catching hold of her small slippery brother and making him stand a few minutes by his side.

"Tell me your honest name, my boy." So he artfully proceeded.

In response to which the child was indeed unvarnished truth. "Randolph C. Miller. And I'll tell you hers." With which he levelled his alpenstock at his sister.

"You had better wait till you're asked!" said this young lady quite at her leisure.

"I should like very much to know *your* name," Winterbourne made free to reply.

"Her name's Daisy Miller!" cried the urchin. "But that ain't her real name; that ain't her name on her cards."

"It's a pity you have n't got one of my cards!" Miss Miller quite as naturally remarked.

"Her real name's Annie P. Miller," the boy went on.

It seemed, all amazingly, to do her good. "Ask him *his* now" — and she indicated their friend.

But to this point Randolph seemed perfectly indifferent; he continued to supply information with regard to his own family. "My father's name is Ezra B. Miller. My father ain't in Europe — he's in a better place than Europe." Winterbourne for a moment supposed this the manner in which the child had been taught to intimate that Mr. Miller had been removed to the sphere of celestial rewards. But Randolph immediately added: "My father's in Schenectady. He's got a big business. My father's rich, you bet."

"Well!" ejaculated Miss Miller, lowering her parasol and looking at the embroidered border. Winterbourne presently released the child, who departed, dragging his alpenstock along the path. "He don't like Europe," said the girl as with an artless instinct for historic truth. "He wants to go back."

"To Schenectady, you mean?"

"Yes, he wants to go right home. He has n't got any boys here. There's one boy here, but he always goes round with a teacher. They won't let him play."

"And your brother has n't any teacher?" Winterbourne enquired.

It tapped, at a touch, the spring of confidence. "Mother thought of getting him one — to travel round with us. There was a lady told her of a very good teacher; an American lady — perhaps you know her — Mrs. Sanders. I think she came from Boston. She told her of this teacher, and we thought of getting him to travel round with us. But Randolph said he did n't want a teacher travelling round with us. He said he would n't have lessons when he was in the cars.[12] And we *are* in the cars about half the time. There was an English lady we met in the cars — I think her name was Miss Featherstone; perhaps you know her. She wanted to know why I did n't give Randolph lessons — give him 'instruction,' she called it. I guess he could give me more instruction than I could give him. He's very smart."

"Yes," said Winterbourne; "he seems very smart."

"Mother's going to get a teacher for him as soon as we get t' Italy. Can you get good teachers in Italy?"

"Very good, I should think," Winterbourne hastened to reply.

"Or else she's going to find some school. He ought to learn some more. He's only nine. He's going to college." And in this way Miss Miller continued to converse upon the affairs of her family and upon other topics. She sat there with her extremely pretty hands, ornamented with very brilliant rings, folded in her lap, and with her pretty eyes now resting upon those of Winterbourne, now wandering over the garden, the people who passed before her and the beautiful view. She addressed her new acquaintance as if she had known him a long time. He found it very pleasant. It was many years since he had heard a young girl talk so much. It might have been said of this wandering maiden who had come and sat down beside him upon a bench that she chattered. She was very quiet, she sat in a charming tranquil attitude; but her lips and her eyes were constantly moving. She had a soft slender agreeable voice, and her tone was distinctly sociable. She gave Winterbourne a report of her movements and intentions, and those of her mother and brother, in Europe, and enumerated in particular the various hotels at which they had stopped. "That English lady in the cars," she said — "Miss Featherstone — asked me if we did n't all live in hotels in America. I told her I had never been in so many hotels in my life as since I came to Europe. I've never seen so many — it's nothing but hotels." But Miss Miller made this remark with no querulous accent; she appeared to be in the best humour with everything. She declared that the hotels were very good when once you got used to their ways and that Europe was perfectly entrancing. She was n't disappointed — not a bit. Perhaps it was because she had heard so much about it before. She had ever so many intimate friends who had been there ever so many times, and that way she had got thoroughly posted. And then she had had ever so many dresses and things from Paris. Whenever she put on a Paris dress she felt as if she were in Europe.

"It was a kind of a wishing-cap," Winterbourne smiled.

"Yes," said Miss Miller at once and without examining this analogy; "it always made me wish I was here. But I need n't have done that for dresses. I'm sure they send all the pretty ones to America; you see the most frightful things here. The only thing I don't like," she proceeded, "is the society. There ain't any society — or if there is I don't know where it keeps itself. Do you? I suppose there's some society somewhere, but I have n't seen anything of it. I'm very fond of society and I've always had plenty of it. I don't mean only in Schenectady, but in New York. I used to go to New

---

[12]Railway cars.

York every winter. In New York I had lots of society. Last winter I had seventeen dinners given me, and three of them were by gentlemen," added Daisy Miller. "I've more friends in New York than in Schenectady — more gentlemen friends; and more young lady friends too," she resumed in a moment. She paused again for an instant; she was looking at Winterbourne with all her prettiness in her frank gay eyes and in her clear rather uniform smile. "I've always had," she said, "a great deal of gentlemen's society."

Poor Winterbourne was amused and perplexed — above all he was charmed. He had never yet heard a young girl express herself in just this fashion; never at least save in cases where to say such things was to have at the same time some rather complicated consciousness about them. And yet was he to accuse Miss Daisy Miller of an actual or a potential *arrière-pensée*,[13] as they said at Geneva? He felt he had lived at Geneva so long as to have got morally muddled; he had lost the right sense for the young American tone. Never indeed since he had grown old enough to appreciate things had he encountered a young compatriot of so "strong" a type as this. Certainly she was very charming, but how extraordinarily communicative and how tremendously easy! Was she simply a pretty girl from New York State — were they all like that, the pretty girls who had had a good deal of gentlemen's society? Or was she also a designing, an audacious, in short an expert young person? Yes, his instinct for such a question had ceased to serve him, and his reason could but mislead. Miss Daisy Miller looked extremely innocent. Some people had told him that after all American girls *were* exceedingly innocent, and others had told him that after all they were n't. He must on the whole take Miss Daisy Miller for a flirt — a pretty American flirt. He had never as yet had relations with representatives of that class. He had known here in Europe two or three women — persons older than Miss Daisy Miller and provided, for respectability's sake, with husbands — who were great coquettes; dangerous terrible women with whom one's light commerce might indeed take a serious turn. But this charming apparition was n't a coquette in that sense; she was very unsophisticated; she was only a pretty American flirt. Winterbourne was almost grateful for having found the formula that applied to Miss Daisy Miller. He leaned back in his seat; he remarked to himself that she had the finest little nose he had ever seen; he wondered what were the regular conditions and limitations of one's intercourse with a pretty American flirt. It presently became apparent that he was on the way to learn.

"Have you been to that old castle?" the girl soon asked, pointing with her parasol to the far-shining walls of the Château de Chillon.

"Yes, formerly, more than once," said Winterbourne. "You too, I suppose, have seen it?"

"No, we have n't been there. I want to go there dreadfully. Of course I mean to go there. I would n't go away from here without having seen that old castle."

"It's a very pretty excursion," the young man returned, "and very easy to make. You can drive, you know, or you can go by the little steamer."

"You can go in the cars," said Miss Miller.

"Yes, you can go in the cars," Winterbourne assented.

"Our courier[14] says they take you right up to the castle," she continued. "We were going last week, but mother gave out. She suffers dreadfully from dyspepsia. She said she could n't any more go — !" But this sketch of Mrs. Miller's plea remained unfinished. "Randolph would n't go either; he says he don't think much of old castles. But I guess we'll go this week if we can get Randolph."

"Your brother is n't interested in ancient monuments?" Winterbourne indulgently asked.

---

[13] "Underlying design" (French).
[14] An accompanying guide.

He now drew her, as he guessed she would herself have said, every time. "Why no, he says he don't care much about old castles. He's only nine. He wants to stay at the hotel. Mother's afraid to leave him alone, and the courier won't stay with him; so we have n't been to many places. But it will be too bad if we don't go up there." And Miss Miller pointed again at the Château de Chillon.

"I should think it might be arranged," Winterbourne was thus emboldened to reply. "Could n't you get some one to stay—for the afternoon—with Randolph?"

Miss Miller looked at him a moment, and then with all serenity, "I wish *you'd* stay with him!" she said.

He pretended to consider it. "I'd much rather go to Chillon with you."

"With me?" she asked without a shadow of emotion.

She did n't rise blushing, as a young person at Geneva would have done; and yet, conscious that he had gone very far, he thought it possible she had drawn back. "And with your mother," he answered very respectfully.

But it seemed that both his audacity and his respect were lost on Miss Daisy Miller. "I guess mother would n't go—for *you,*" she smiled. "And she ain't much *bent* on going, anyway. She don't like to ride round in the afternoon." After which she familiarly proceeded: "But did you really mean what you said just now—that you'd like to go up there?"

"Most earnestly I meant it," Winterbourne declared.

"Then we may arrange it. If mother will stay with Randolph I guess Eugenio will."

"Eugenio?" the young man echoed.

"Eugenio's our courier. He does n't like to stay with Randolph—he's the most fastidious man I ever saw. But he's a splendid courier. I guess he'll stay at home with Randolph if mother does, and then we can go to the castle."

Winterbourne reflected for an instant as lucidly as possible: "we" could only mean Miss Miller and himself. This prospect seemed almost too good to believe; he felt as if he ought to kiss the young lady's hand. Possibly he would have done so,—and quite spoiled his chance; but at this moment another person—presumably Eugenio—appeared. A tall handsome man, with superb whiskers and wearing a velvet morning-coat and a voluminous watch-guard, approached the young lady, looking sharply at her companion. "Oh Eugenio!" she said with the friendliest accent.

Eugenio had eyed Winterbourne from head to foot; he now bowed gravely to Miss Miller. "I have the honour to inform Mademoiselle that luncheon's on the table."

Mademoiselle slowly rose. "See here, Eugenio, I'm going to that old castle anyway."

"To the Château de Chillon, Mademoiselle?" the courier enquired. "Mademoiselle has made arrangements?" he added in a tone that struck Winterbourne as impertinent.

Eugenio's tone apparently threw, even to Miss Miller's own apprehension, a slightly ironical light on her position. She turned to Winterbourne with the slightest blush. "You won't back out?"

"I shall not be happy till we go!" he protested.

"And you're staying in this hotel?" she went on. "And you're really American?"

The courier still stood there with an effect of offence for the young man so far as the latter saw in it a tacit reflexion on Miss Miller's behaviour and an insinuation that she "picked up" acquaintances. "I shall have the honour of presenting to you a person who'll tell you all about me," he said, smiling, and referring to his aunt.

"Oh well, we'll go some day," she beautifully answered; with which she gave him a smile and turned away. She put up her parasol and walked back to the inn beside Eugenio. Winterbourne stood watching her, and as she moved away, drawing her muslin furbelows[15] over the walk, he spoke to himself of her natural elegance.

---

[15]Flounces or ruffles.

II

He had, however, engaged to do more than proved feasible in promising to present his aunt, Mrs. Costello, to Miss Daisy Miller. As soon as that lady had got better of her headache he waited on her in her apartment and, after a show of the proper solicitude about her health, asked if she had noticed in the hotel an American family — a mamma, a daughter and an obstreperous little boy.

"An obstreperous little boy and a preposterous big courier?" said Mrs. Costello. "Oh yes, I've noticed them. Seen them, heard them and kept out of their way." Mrs. Costello was a widow of fortune, a person of much distinction and who frequently intimated that if she had n't been so dreadfully liable to sick-headaches she would probably have left a deeper impress on her time. She had a long pale face, a high nose and a great deal of very striking white hair, which she wore in large puffs and over the top of her head. She had two sons married in New York and another who was now in Europe. This young man was amusing himself at Homburg[16] and, though guided by his taste, was rarely observed to visit any particular city at the moment selected by his mother for her appearance there. Her nephew, who had come to Vevey expressly to see her, was therefore more attentive than, as she said, her very own. He had imbibed at Geneva the idea that one must be irreproachable in all such forms. Mrs. Costello had n't seen him for many years and was now greatly pleased with him, manifesting her approbation by initiating him into many of the secrets of that social sway which, as he could see she would like him to think, she exerted from her stronghold in Forty-Second Street. She admitted that she was very exclusive, but if he had been better acquainted with New York he would see that one had to be. And her picture of the minutely hierarchical constitution of the society of that city, which she presented to him in many different lights, was, to Winterbourne's imagination, almost oppressively striking.

He at once recognised from her tone that Miss Daisy Miller's place in the social scale was low. "I'm afraid you don't approve of them," he pursued in reference to his new friends.

"They're horribly common" — it was perfectly simple. "They're the sort of Americans that one does one's duty by just ignoring."

"Ah you just ignore them?" — the young man took it in.

"I can't *not*, my dear Frederick. I would n't if I had n't to, but I have to."

"The little girl's very pretty," he went on in a moment.

"Of course she's very pretty. But she's of the last crudity."

"I see what you mean of course," he allowed after another pause.

"She has that charming look they all have," his aunt resumed. "I can't think where they pick it up; and she dresses in perfection — no, you don't know how well she dresses. I can't think where they get their taste."

"But, my dear aunt, she's not, after all, a Comanche savage."

"She is a young lady," said Mrs. Costello, "who has an intimacy with her mamma's courier?"

"An 'intimacy' with him?" Ah there it was!

"There's no other name for such a relation. But the skinny little mother's just as bad! They treat the courier as a familiar friend — as a gentleman and a scholar. I should n't wonder if he dines with them. Very likely they've never seen a man with such good manners, such fine clothes, so *like* a gentleman — or a scholar. He probably corresponds to the young lady's idea of a count. He sits with them in the garden of an evening. I think he smokes in their faces."

Winterbourne listened with interest to these disclosures; they helped him to make up his mind about Miss Daisy. Evidently she was rather wild. "Well," he said, "I'm not a courier and I did n't smoke in her face, and yet she was very charming to me."

---

[16]German resort.

"You had better have mentioned at first," Mrs. Costello returned with dignity, "that you had made her valuable acquaintance."

"We simply met in the garden and talked a bit."

"By appointment—no? Ah that's still to come! Pray what did you say?"

"I said I should take the liberty of introducing her to my admirable aunt."

"Your admirable aunt's a thousand times obliged to you."

"It was to guarantee my respectability."

"And pray who's to guarantee hers?"

"Ah you're cruel!" said the young man. "She's a very innocent girl."

"You don't say that as if you believed it," Mrs. Costello returned.

"She's completely uneducated," Winterbourne acknowledged, "but she's wonderfully pretty, and in short she's very nice. To prove I believe it I'm going to take her to the Château de Chillon."

Mrs. Costello made a wondrous face. "You two are going off there together? I should say it proved just the contrary. How long had you known her, may I ask, when this interesting project was formed? You have n't been twenty-four hours in the house."

"I had known her half an hour!" Winterbourne smiled.

"Then she's just what I supposed."

"And what do you suppose?"

"Why that she's a horror."

Our youth was silent for some moments. "You really think then," he presently began, and with a desire for trustworthy information, "you really think that—" But he paused again while his aunt waited.

"Think what, sir?"

"That she's the sort of young lady who expects a man sooner or later to—well, we'll call it carry her off?"

"I have n't the least idea what such young ladies expect a man to do. But I really consider you had better not meddle with little American girls who are uneducated, as you mildly put it. You've lived too long out of the country. You'll be sure to make some great mistake. You're too innocent."

"My dear aunt, not so much as that comes to!" he protested with a laugh and a curl of his moustache.

"You're too guilty then!"

He continued all thoughtfully to finger the ornament in question. "You won't let the poor girl know you then?" he asked at last.

"Is it literally true that she's going to the Château de Chillon with you?"

"I've no doubt she fully intends it."

"Then, my dear Frederick," said Mrs. Costello, "I must decline the honour of her acquaintance. I'm an old woman, but I'm not too old—thank heaven—to be honestly shocked!"

"But don't they all do these things—the little American girls at home?" Winterbourne enquired.

Mrs. Costello stared a moment. "I should like to see my granddaughters do them!" she then grimly returned.

This seemed to throw some light on the matter, for Winterbourne remembered to have heard his pretty cousins in New York, the daughters of this lady's two daughters, called "tremendous flirts." If therefore Miss Daisy Miller exceeded the liberal licence allowed to these young women it was probable she did go even by the American allowance rather far. Winterbourne was impatient to see her again, and it vexed, it even a little humiliated him, that he should n't by instinct appreciate her justly.

Though so impatient to see her again he hardly knew what ground he should give for his aunt's refusal to become acquainted with her; but he discovered promptly enough that with Miss Daisy Miller there was no great need of walking on tiptoe. He found her that evening in the garden, wandering about in the warm starlight after the manner of an indolent sylph and swinging to and fro the largest fan he had ever beheld. It was ten o'clock. He had dined with his aunt, had been sitting with her since dinner, and had just taken leave of her till the morrow. His young friend frankly rejoiced to renew their intercourse; she pronounced it the stupidest evening she had ever passed.

"Have you been all alone?" he asked with no intention of an epigram and no effect of her perceiving one.

"I've been walking round with mother. But mother gets tired walking round," Miss Miller explained.

"Has she gone to bed?"

"No, she does n't like to go to bed. She does n't sleep scarcely any—not three hours. She says she does n't know how she lives. She's dreadfully nervous. I guess she sleeps more than she thinks. She's gone somewhere after Randolph; she wants to try to get him to go to bed. He does n't like to go to bed."

The soft impartiality of her *constatations*,[17] as Winterbourne would have termed them, was a thing by itself—exquisite little fatalist as they seemed to make her. "Let us hope she'll persuade him," he encouragingly said.

"Well, she'll talk to him all she can—but he does n't like her to talk to him": with which Miss Daisy opened and closed her fan. "She's going to try to get Eugenio to talk to him. But Randolph ain't afraid of Eugenio. Eugenio's a splendid courier, but he can't make much impression on Randolph! I don't believe he'll go to bed before eleven." Her detachment from any invidious judgement of this was, to her companion's sense, inimitable; and it appeared that Randolph's vigil was in fact triumphantly prolonged, for Winterbourne attended her in her stroll for some time without meeting her mother. "I've been looking round for that lady you want to introduce me to," she resumed—"I guess she's your aunt." Then on his admitting the fact and expressing some curiosity as to how she had learned it, she said she had heard all about Mrs. Costello from the chambermaid. She was very quiet and very *comme il faut*;[18] she wore white puffs; she spoke to no one and she never dined at the common table. Every two days she had a headache. "I think that's a lovely description, headache and all!" said Miss Daisy, chattering along in her thin gay voice. "I want to know her ever so much. I know just what *your* aunt would be; I know I'd like her. She'd be very exclusive. I like a lady to be exclusive; I'm dying to be exclusive myself. Well, I guess we *are* exclusive, mother and I. We don't speak to any one—or they don't speak to us. I suppose it's about the same thing. Anyway, I shall be ever so glad to meet your aunt."

Winterbourne was embarrassed—he could but trump up some evasion. "She'd be most happy, but I'm afraid those tiresome headaches are always to be reckoned with."

The girl looked at him through the fine dusk. "Well, I suppose she does n't have a headache every day."

He had to make the best of it. "She tells me she wonderfully does." He did n't know what else to say.

Miss Miller stopped and stood looking at him. Her prettiness was still visible in the darkness; she kept flapping to and fro her enormous fan. "She does n't want to know me!" she then lightly broke out. "Why don't you say so? You need n't be afraid. *I'm* not afraid!" And she quite crowed for the fun of it.

Winterbourne distinguished however a wee false note in this: he was touched, shocked, mortified by it. "My dear young lady, she knows no one. She goes through life immured. It's her wretched health."

The young girl walked on a few steps in the glee of the thing. "You need n't be afraid," she repeated. "Why should she want to know me?" Then she paused again; she was close to the parapet of the garden, and in front of her was the starlit lake.

---

[17]"Declarations," "claims" (French).
[18]"Proper" (French).

There was a vague sheen on its surface, and in the distance were dimly-seen mountain forms. Daisy Miller looked out at these great lights and shades and again proclaimed a gay indifference—"Gracious! she *is* exclusive!" Winterbourne wondered if she were seriously wounded and for a moment almost wished her sense of injury might be such as to make it becoming in him to reassure and comfort her. He had a pleasant sense that she would be all accessible to a respectful tenderness at that moment. He felt quite ready to sacrifice his aunt—conversationally; to acknowledge she was a proud rude woman and to make the point that they need n't mind her. But before he had time to commit himself to this questionable mixture of gallantry and impiety, the young lady, resuming her walk, gave an exclamation in quite another tone. "Well, here's mother! I guess she *has n't* got Randolph to go to bed." The figure of a lady appeared, at a distance, very indistinct in the darkness; it advanced with a slow and wavering step and then suddenly seemed to pause.

"Are you sure it's your mother? Can you make her out in this thick dusk?" Winterbourne asked.

"Well," the girl laughed, "I guess I know my own mother! And when she has got on my shawl too. She's always wearing my things."

The lady in question, ceasing now to approach, hovered vaguely about the spot at which she had checked her steps.

"I'm afraid your mother does n't see you," said Winterbourne. "Or perhaps," he added—thinking, with Miss Miller, the joke permissible—"perhaps she feels guilty about your shawl."

"Oh it's a fearful old thing!" his companion placidly answered. "I told her she could wear it if she did n't mind looking like a fright. She won't come here because she sees you."

"Ah then," said Winterbourne, "I had better leave you."

"Oh no—come on!" the girl insisted.

"I'm afraid your mother does n't approve of my walking with you."

She gave him, he thought, the oddest glance. "It is n't for me; it's for you—that is it's for *her*. Well, I don't know who it's for! But mother does n't like any of my gentlemen friends. She's right down timid. She always makes a fuss if I introduce a gentleman. But I *do* introduce them—almost always. If I did n't introduce my gentlemen friends to mother," Miss Miller added, in her small flat monotone, "I should n't think I was natural."

"Well, to introduce me," Winterbourne remarked, "you must know my name." And he proceeded to pronounce it.

"Oh my—I can't say all that!" cried his companion, much amused. But by this time they had come up to Mrs. Miller, who, as they drew near, walked to the parapet of the garden and leaned on it, looking intently at the lake and presenting her back to them. "Mother!" said the girl in a tone of decision—upon which the elder lady turned round. "Mr. Frederick Forsyth Winterbourne," said the latter's young friend, repeating his lesson of a moment before and introducing him very frankly and prettily. "Common" she might be, as Mrs. Costello had pronounced her; yet what provision was made by that epithet for her queer little native grace?

Her mother was a small spare light person, with a wandering eye, a scarce perceptible nose, and, as to make up for it, an unmistakeable forehead, decorated—but too far back, as Winterbourne mentally described it—with thin much-frizzled hair. Like her daughter Mrs. Miller was dressed with extreme elegance; she had enormous diamonds in her ears. So far as the young man could observe, she gave him no greeting—she certainly was n't looking at him. Daisy was near her, pulling her shawl straight. "What are you doing, poking round here?" this young lady enquired—yet by no means with the harshness of accent her choice of words might have implied.

"Well, I don't know"—and the new-comer turned to the lake again.

"I should n't think you'd want that shawl!" Daisy familiarly proceeded.

"Well — I do!" her mother answered with a sound that partook for Winterbourne of an odd strain between mirth and woe.

"Did you get Randolph to go to bed?" Daisy asked.

"No, I could n't induce him" — and Mrs. Miller seemed to confess to the same mild fatalism as her daughter. "He wants to talk to the waiter. He *likes* to talk to that waiter."

"I was just telling Mr. Winterbourne," the girl went on; and to the young man's ear her tone might have indicated that she had been uttering his name all her life.

"Oh yes!" he concurred — "I've the pleasure of knowing your son."

Randolph's mamma was silent; she kept her attention on the lake. But at last a sigh broke from her. "Well, I don't see how he lives!"

"Anyhow, it is n't so bad as it was at Dover,"[19] Daisy at least opined.

"And what occurred at Dover?" Winterbourne desired to know.

"He would n't go to bed at all. I guess he sat up all night — in the public parlour. He was n't in bed at twelve o'clock: it seemed as if he could n't budge."

"It was half-past twelve when *I* gave up," Mrs. Miller recorded with passionless accuracy.

It was of great interest to Winterbourne. "Does he sleep much during the day?"

"I guess he does n't sleep *very* much," Daisy rejoined.

"I wish he just *would*!" said her mother. "It seems as if he *must* make it up somehow."

"Well, I guess it's we that make it up. I think he's real tiresome," Daisy pursued.

After which, for some moments, there was silence. "Well, Daisy Miller," the elder lady then unexpectedly broke out, "I should n't think you'd want to talk against your own brother!"

"Well he *is* tiresome, mother," said the girl, but with no sharpness of insistence.

"Well, he's only nine," Mrs. Miller lucidly urged.

"Well, he would n't go up to that castle, anyway," her daughter replied as for accommodation. "I'm going up there with Mr. Winterbourne."

To this announcement, very placidly made, Daisy's parent offered no response. Winterbourne took for granted on this that she opposed such a course; but he said to himself at the same time that she was a simple easily-managed person and that a few deferential protestations would modify her attitude. "Yes," he therefore interposed, "your daughter has kindly allowed me the honour of being her guide."

Mrs. Miller's wandering eyes attached themselves with an appealing air to her other companion, who, however, strolled a few steps further, gently humming to herself. "I presume you'll go in the cars," she then quite colorlessly remarked.

"Yes, or in the boat," said Winterbourne.

"Well, of course I don't know," Mrs. Miller returned. "I've never been up to that castle."

"It is a pity you should n't go," he observed, beginning to feel reassured as to her opposition. And yet he was quite prepared to find that as a matter of course she meant to accompany her daughter.

It was on this view accordingly that light was projected for him. "We've been thinking ever so much about going, but it seems as if we could n't. Of course Daisy — she wants to go round everywhere. But there's a lady here — I don't know her name — she says she should n't think we'd want to go to see castles *here*; she should think we'd want to wait till we got t' Italy. It seems as if there would be so many there," continued Mrs. Miller with an air of increasing confidence. "Of course we only want to see the principal ones. We visited several in England," she presently added.

"Ah yes, in England there are beautiful castles," said Winterbourne. "But Chillon here is very well worth seeing."

"Well, if Daisy feels up to it —" said Mrs. Miller in a tone that seemed to break

---

[19]English port city across the Channel.

under the burden of such conceptions. "It seems as if there's nothing she won't undertake."

"Oh I'm pretty sure she'll enjoy it!" Winterbourne declared. And he desired more and more to make it a certainty that he was to have the privilege of a *tête-à-tête*[20] with the young lady who was still strolling along in front of them and softly vocalising. "You're not disposed, madam," he enquired, "to make the so interesting excursion yourself?"

So addressed Daisy's mother looked at him an instant with a certain scared obliquity and then walked forward in silence. Then, "I guess she had better go alone," she said simply.

It gave him occasion to note that this was a very different type of maternity from that of the vigilant matrons who massed themselves in the forefront of social intercourse in the dark old city at the other end of the lake. But his meditations were interrupted by hearing his name very distinctly pronounced by Mrs. Miller's unprotected daughter. "Mr. Winterbourne!" she piped from a considerable distance.

"Mademoiselle!" said the young man.

"Don't you want to take me out in a boat?"

"At present?" he asked.

"Why of course!" she gaily returned.

"Well, Annie Miller!" exclaimed her mother.

"I beg you, madam, to let her go," he hereupon eagerly pleaded; so instantly had he been struck with the romantic side of this chance to guide through the summer starlight a skiff freighted with a fresh and beautiful young girl.

"I should n't think she'd want to," said her mother. "I should think she'd rather go indoors."

"I'm sure Mr. Winterbourne wants to *take* me," Daisy declared. "He's so awfully devoted!"

"I'll row you over to Chillon under the stars."

"I don't believe it!" Daisy laughed.

"Well!" the elder lady again gasped, as in rebuke of this freedom.

"You have n't spoken to me for half an hour," her daughter went on.

"I've been having some very pleasant conversation with your mother," Winterbourne replied.

"Oh pshaw! I want you to take me out in a boat!" Daisy went on as if nothing else had been said. They had all stopped and she had turned round and was looking at her friend. Her face wore a charming smile, her pretty eyes gleamed in the darkness, she swung her great fan about. No, he felt, it was impossible to be prettier than that.

"There are half a dozen boats moored at that landing-place," and he pointed to a range of steps that descended from the garden to the lake. "If you'll do me the honour to accept my arm we'll go and select one of them."

She stood there smiling; she threw back her head; she laughed as for the drollery of this. "I like a gentleman to be formal!"

"I assure you it's a formal offer."

"I was bound I'd make you say something," Daisy agreeably mocked.

"You see it's not very difficult," said Winterbourne. "But I'm afraid you're chaffing me."

"I think not, sir," Mrs. Miller shyly pleaded.

"Do then let me give you a row," he persisted to Daisy.

"It's quite lovely, the way you say that!" she cried in reward.

"It will be still more lovely to do it."

"Yes, it would be lovely!" But she made no movement to accompany him; she only remained an elegant image of free light irony.

---

[20] "Intimate talk" (French).

"I guess you'd better find out what time it is," her mother impartially contributed.

"It's eleven o'clock, Madam," said a voice with a foreign accent out of the neighbouring darkness; and Winterbourne, turning, recognised the florid personage he had already seen in attendance. He had apparently just approached.

"Oh Eugenio," said Daisy, "I'm going out with Mr. Winterbourne in a boat!"

Eugenio bowed. "At this hour of the night, Mademoiselle?"

"I'm going with Mr. Winterbourne," she repeated with her shining smile. "I'm going this very minute."

"Do tell her she can't, Eugenio," Mrs. Miller said to the courier.

"I think you had better not go out in a boat, Mademoiselle," the man declared.

Winterbourne wished to goodness this pretty girl were not on such familiar terms with her courier; but he said nothing, and she meanwhile added to his ground. "I suppose you don't think it's proper! My!" she wailed; "Eugenio does n't think anything's proper."

"I'm nevertheless quite at your service," Winterbourne hastened to remark.

"Does Mademoiselle propose to go alone?" Eugenio asked of Mrs. Miller.

"Oh no, with this gentleman!" cried Daisy's mamma for reassurance.

"I *meant* alone with the gentleman." The courier looked for a moment at Winterbourne—the latter seemed to make out in his face a vague presumptuous intelligence as at the expense of their companions—and then solemnly and with a bow, "As Mademoiselle pleases!" he said.

But Daisy broke off at this. "Oh I hoped you'd make a fuss! I don't care to go now."

"Ah but I myself shall make a fuss if you don't go," Winterbourne declared with spirit.

"That's all I want—a little fuss!" With which she began to laugh again.

"Mr. Randolph has retired for the night!" the courier hereupon importantly announced.

"Oh Daisy, now we can go then!" cried Mrs. Miller.

Her daughter turned away from their friend, all lighted with her odd perversity. "Good-night—I hope you're disappointed or disgusted or something!"

He looked at her gravely, taking her by the hand she offered. "I'm puzzled, if you want to know!" he answered.

"Well, I hope it won't keep you awake!" she said very smartly; and, under the escort of the privileged Eugenio, the two ladies passed toward the house.

Winterbourne's eyes followed them; he was indeed quite mystified. He lingered beside the lake a quarter of an hour, baffled by the question of the girl's sudden familiarities and caprices. But the only very definite conclusion he came to was that he should enjoy deucedly "going off" with her somewhere.

Two days later he went off with her to the Castle of Chillon. He waited for her in the large hall of the hotel, where the couriers, the servants, the foreign tourists were lounging about and staring. It was n't the place he would have chosen for a tryst, but she had placidly appointed it. She came tripping downstairs, buttoning her long gloves, squeezing her folded parasol against her pretty figure, dressed exactly in the way that consorted best, to his fancy, with their adventure. He was a man of imagination and, as our ancestors used to say, of sensibility;[21] as he took in her charming air and caught from the great staircase her impatient confiding step the note of some small sweet strain of romance, not intense but clear and sweet, seemed to sound for their start. He could have believed he was *really* going "off" with her. He led her out through all the idle people assembled—they all looked at her straight and hard: she had begun to chatter as soon as she joined him. His preference had been that they should be conveyed to Chillon in a carriage, but she expressed a lively wish to go in the little steamer—there would be such a lovely breeze upon the water and they

---

[21]I.e., delicate feeling.

should see such lots of people. The sail was n't long, but Winterbourne's companion found time for many characteristic remarks and other demonstrations, not a few of which were, from the extremity of their candour, slightly disconcerting. To the young man himself their small excursion showed so for delightfully irregular and incongruously intimate that, even allowing for her habitual sense of freedom, he had some expectation of seeing her appear to find in it the same savour. But it must be confessed that he was in this particular rather disappointed. Miss Miller was highly animated, she was in the brightest spirits; but she was clearly not at all in a nervous flutter—as she should have been to match *his* tension; she avoided neither his eyes nor those of any one else; she neither coloured from an awkward consciousness when she looked at him nor when she saw that people were looking at herself. People continued to look at her a great deal, and Winterbourne could at least take pleasure in his pretty companion's distinguished air. He had been privately afraid she would talk loud, laugh overmuch, and even perhaps desire to move extravagantly about the boat. But he quite forgot his fears; he sat smiling with his eyes on her face while, without stirring from her place, she delivered herself of a great number of original reflexions. It was the most charming innocent prattle he had ever heard, for, by his own experience hitherto, when young persons were so ingenuous they were less articulate and when they were so confident were more sophisticated. If he had assented to the idea that she was "common," at any rate, *was* she proving so, after all, or was he simply getting used to her commonness? Her discourse was for the most part of what immediately and superficially surrounded them, but there were moments when it threw out a longer look or took a sudden straight plunge.

"What on *earth* are you so solemn about?" she suddenly demanded, fixing her agreeable eyes on her friend's.

"*Am* I solemn?" he asked. "I had an idea I was grinning from ear to ear."

"You look as if you were taking me to a prayer-meeting or a funeral. If that's a grin your ears are very near together."

"Should you like me to dance a hornpipe on the deck?"

"Pray do, and I'll carry round your hat. It will pay the expenses of our journey."

"I never was better pleased in my life," Winterbourne returned.

She looked at him a moment, then let it renew her amusement. "I like to make you say those things. You're a queer mixture!"

In the castle, after they had landed, nothing could exceed the light independence of her humour. She tripped about the vaulted chambers, rustled her skirts in the corkscrew staircases, flirted back with a pretty little cry and a shudder from the edge of the oubliettes[22] and turned a singularly well-shaped ear to everything Winterbourne told her about the place. But he saw she cared little for mediæval history and that the grim ghosts of Chillon loomed but faintly before her. They had the good fortune to have been able to wander without other society than that of their guide; and Winterbourne arranged with this companion that they should n't be hurried—that they should linger and pause wherever they chose. He interpreted the bargain generously—Winterbourne on his side had been generous—and ended by leaving them quite to themselves. Miss Miller's observations were marked by no logical consistency; for anything she wanted to say she was sure to find a pretext. She found a great many, in the tortuous passages and rugged embrasures of the place, for asking her young man sudden questions about himself, his family, his previous history, his tastes, his habits, his designs, and for supplying information on corresponding points in her own situation. Of her own tastes, habits and designs the charming creature was prepared to give the most definite and indeed the most favourable account.

"Well, I hope you know enough!" she exclaimed after Winterbourne had sketched

[22]"Dungeon of oblivion" (French); underground cell with a trap door or bars in the ceiling.

for her something of the story of the unhappy Bonnivard.[23] "I never saw a man that knew so much!" The history of Bonnivard had evidently, as they say, gone into one ear and out of the other. But this easy erudition struck her none the less as wonderful, and she was soon quite sure she wished Winterbourne would travel with them and "go round" with them: they too in that case might learn something about something. "Don't you want to come and teach Randolph?" she asked; "I guess he'd improve with a gentleman teacher." Winterbourne was certain that nothing could possibly please him so much, but that he had unfortunately other occupations. "Other occupations? I don't believe a speck of it!" she protested. "What do you mean now? You're not in business." The young man allowed that he was not in business, but he had engagements which even within a day or two would necessitate his return to Geneva. "Oh bother!" she panted, "I don't believe it!" and she began to talk about something else. But a few moments later, when he was pointing out to her the interesting design of an antique fireplace, she broke out irrelevantly: "You don't mean to say you're going back to Geneva?"

"It is a melancholy fact that I shall have to report myself there to-morrow."

She met it with a vivacity that could only flatter him. "Well, Mr. Winterbourne, I think you're horrid!"

"Oh don't say such dreadful things!" he quite sincerely pleaded—"just at the last."

"The last?" the girl cried; "I call it the very first! I've half a mind to leave you here and go straight back to the hotel alone." And for the next ten minutes she did nothing but call him horrid. Poor Winterbourne was fairly bewildered; no young lady had as yet done him the honour to be so agitated by the mention of his personal plans. His companion, after this, ceased to pay any attention to the curiosities of Chillon or the beauties of the lake; she opened fire on the special charmer in Geneva whom she appeared to have instantly taken it for granted that he was hurrying back to see. How did Miss Daisy Miller know of that agent of his fate in Geneva? Winterbourne, who denied the existence of such a person, was quite unable to discover; and he was divided between amazement at the rapidity of her induction and amusement at the directness of her criticism. She struck him afresh, in all this, as an extraordinary mixture of innocence and crudity. "Does she never allow you more than three days at a time?" Miss Miller wished ironically to know. "Does n't she give you a vacation in summer? there's no one so hard-worked but they can get leave to go off somewhere at this season. I suppose if you stay another day she'll come right after you in the boat. Do wait over till Friday and I'll go down to the landing to see her arrive!" He began at last even to feel he had been wrong to be disappointed in the temper in which his young lady had embarked. If he had missed the personal accent, the personal accent was now making its appearance. It sounded very distinctly, toward the end, in her telling him she'd stop "teasing" him if he'd promise her solemnly to come down to Rome that winter.

"That's not a difficult promise to make," he hastened to acknowledge. "My aunt has taken an apartment in Rome from January and has already asked me to come and see her."

"I don't want you to come for your aunt," said Daisy; "I want you just to come for me." And this was the only allusion he was ever to hear her make again to his invidious kinswoman. He promised her that at any rate he would certainly come, and after this she forbore from teasing. Winterbourne took a carriage and they drove back to Vevey in the dusk; the girl at his side, her animation a little spent, was now quite distractingly passive.

In the evening he mentioned to Mrs. Costello that he had spent the afternoon at Chillon with Miss Daisy Miller.

---

[23]François de Bonnivard (1496–1570), Swiss patriot imprisoned for seven years in the Castle of Chillon; the hero of Byron's "The Prisoner of Chillon."

"The American—of the courier?" asked this lady.

"Ah happily the courier stayed at home."

"She went with you all alone?"

"All alone."

Mrs. Costello sniffed a little at her smelling-bottle. "And that," she exclaimed, "is the little abomination you wanted me to know!"

III

Winterbourne, who had returned to Geneva the day after his excursion to Chillon, went to Rome toward the end of January. His aunt had been established there a considerable time and he had received from her a couple of characteristic letters. "Those people you were so devoted to last summer at Vevey have turned up here, courier and all," she wrote. "They seem to have made several acquaintances, but the courier continues to be the most *intime*.[24] The young lady, however, is also very intimate with various third-rate Italians, with whom she rackets about in a way that makes much talk. Bring me that pretty novel of Cherbuliez's—'Paule Méré'[25]—and don't come later than the 23d."

Our friend would in the natural course of events, on arriving in Rome, have presently ascertained Mrs. Miller's address at the American banker's and gone to pay his compliments to Miss Daisy. "After what happened at Vevey I certainly think I may call upon them," he said to Mrs. Costello.

"If after what happens—at Vevey and everywhere—you desire to keep up the acquaintance, you're very welcome. Of course you're not squeamish—a man may know every one. Men are welcome to the privilege!"

"Pray what is it then that 'happens'—here for instance?" Winterbourne asked.

"Well, the girl tears about alone with her unmistakeably low foreigners. As to what happens further you must apply elsewhere for information. She has picked up half a dozen of the regular Roman fortune-hunters of the inferior sort and she takes them about to such houses as she may put *her* nose into. When she comes to a party—such a party as she can come to—she brings with her a gentleman with a good deal of manner and a wonderful moustache."

"And where's the mother?"

"I have n't the least idea. They're very dreadful people."

Winterbourne thought them over in these new lights. "They're very ignorant—very innocent only, and utterly uncivilised. Depend on it they're not 'bad.'"

"They're hopelessly vulgar," said Mrs. Costello. "Whether or no being hopelessly vulgar is being 'bad' is a question for the metaphysicians. They're bad enough to blush for, at any rate; and for this short life that's quite enough."

The news that his little friend the child of nature of the Swiss lakeside was now surrounded by half a dozen wonderful moustaches checked Winterbourne's impulse to go straightway to see her. He had perhaps not definitely flattered himself that he had made an ineffaceable impression upon her heart, but he was annoyed at hearing of a state of affairs so little in harmony with an image that had lately flitted in and out of his own meditations; the image of a very pretty girl looking out of an old Roman window and asking herself urgently when Mr. Winterbourne would arrive. If, however, he determined to wait a little before reminding this young lady of his claim to her faithful remembrance, he called with more promptitude on two or three other friends. One of these friends was an American lady who had spent several winters at Geneva, where she had placed her children at school. She was a very accomplished woman and she lived in Via Gregoriana.[26] Winterbourne found her in a little crimson drawing-room on a third floor; the room was filled with southern sunshine. He

[24]"Intimate" (French).
[25]Victor Cherbuliez (1829–1899), French author of *Paule Méré* (1864).
[26]A Roman street.

had n't been there ten mintues when the servant, appearing in the doorway, announced complacently "Madame Mila!" This announcement was presently followed by the entrance of little Randolph Miller, who stopped in the middle of the room and stood staring at Winterbourne. An instant later his pretty sister crossed the threshold; and then, after a considerable interval, the parent of the pair slowly advanced.

"I guess I know you!" Randolph broke ground without delay.

"I'm sure you know a great many things"—and his old friend clutched him all interestedly by the arm. "How's your education coming on?"

Daisy was engaged in some pretty babble with her hostess, but when she heard Winterbourne's voice she quickly turned her head with a "Well, I declare!" which he met smiling. "I told you I should come, you know."

"Well, I did n't believe it," she answered.

"I'm much obliged to you for that," laughed the young man.

"You might have come to see me then," Daisy went on as if they had parted the week before.

"I arrived only yesterday."

"I don't believe any such thing!" the girl declared afresh.

Winterbourne turned with a protesting smile to her mother, but this lady evaded his glance and, seating herself, fixed her eyes on her son. "We've got a bigger place than this," Randolph hereupon broke out. "It's all gold on the walls."

Mrs. Miller, more of a fatalist apparently than ever, turned uneasily in her chair. "I told you if I was to bring you you'd say something!" she stated as for the benefit of such of the company as might hear it.

"I told *you*!" Randolph retorted. "I tell *you*, sir!" he added jocosely, giving Winterbourne a thump on the knee. "It *is* bigger too!"

As Daisy's conversation with her hostess still occupied her Winterbourne judged it becoming to address a few words to her mother—such as "I hope you've been well since we parted at Vevey."

Mrs. Miller now certainly looked at him—at his chin. "Not very well, sir," she answered.

"She's got the dyspepsia," said Randolph. "I've got it too. Father's got it bad. But I've got it worst!"

This proclamation, instead of embarrassing Mrs. Miller, seemed to soothe her by reconstituting the environment to which she was most accustomed. "I suffer from the liver," she amiably whined to Winterbourne. "I think it's this climate; it's less bracing than Schenectady, especially in the winter season. I don't know whether you know we reside at Schenectady. I was saying to Daisy that I certainly had n't found any one like Dr. Davis and I did n't believe I *would*. Oh up in Schenectady, he stands first; they think everything of Dr. Davis. He has so much to do, and yet there was nothing he would n't do for *me*. He said he never saw anything like my dyspepsia, but he was bound to get at it. I'm sure there was nothing he would n't try, and I did n't care what he did to me if he only brought me relief. He was just going to try something new, and I just longed for it, when we came right off. Mr. Miller felt as if he wanted Daisy to see Europe for herself. But I could n't help writing the other day that I supposed it was all right for Daisy, but that I did n't know as I *could* get on much longer without Dr. Davis. At Schenectady he stands at the very top; and there's a great deal of sickness there too. It affects my sleep."

Winterbourne had a good deal of pathological gossip with Dr. Davis's patient, during which Daisy chattered unremittingly to her own companion. The young man asked Mrs. Miller how she was pleased with Rome. "Well, I must say I'm disappointed," she confessed. "We had heard so much about it—I suppose we had heard too much. But we could n't help that. We had been led to expect something different."

Winterbourne, however, abounded in reassurance. "Ah wait a little, and you'll grow very fond of it."

"I hate it worse and worse every day!" cried Randolph.

"You're like the infant Hannibal,"[27] his friend laughed.

"No I ain't—like any infant!" Randolph declared at a venture.

"Well, that's so—and you never *were*!" his mother concurred. "But we've seen places," she resumed, "that I'd put a long way ahead of Rome." And in reply to Winterbourne's interrogation, "There's Zürich—up there in the mountains," she instanced; "I think Zürich's real lovely, and we had n't heard half so much about it."

"The best place we've seen's the *City of Richmond*!" said Randolph.

"He means the ship," Mrs. Miller explained. "We crossed in that ship. Randolph had a good time on the *City of Richmond*."

"It's the best place *I've* struck," the child repeated. "Only it was turned the wrong way."

"Well, we've got to turn the right way sometime," said Mrs. Miller with strained but weak optimism. Winterbourne expressed the hope that her daughter at least appreciated the so various interest of Rome, and she declared with some spirit that Daisy was quite carried away. "It's on account of the society—the society's splendid. She goes round everywhere; she has made a great number of acquaintances. Of course she goes round more than I do. I must say they've all been very sweet—they've taken her right in. And then she knows a great many gentlemen. Oh she thinks there's nothing like Rome. Of course it's a great deal pleasanter for a young lady if she knows plenty of gentlemen."

By this time Daisy had turned her attention again to Winterbourne, but in quite the same free form. "I've been telling Mrs. Walker how mean you were!"

"And what's the evidence you've offered?" he asked, a trifle disconcerted, for all his superior gallantry, by her inadequate measure of the zeal of an admirer who on his way down to Rome had stopped neither at Bologna nor at Florence, simply because of a certain sweet appeal to his fond fancy, not to say to his finest curiosity. He remembered how a cynical compatriot had once told him that American women—the pretty ones, and this gave a largeness to the axiom—were at once the most exacting in the world and the least endowed with a sense of indebtedness.

"Why you were awfully mean up at Vevey," Daisy said. "You would n't do most anything. You would n't stay there when I asked you."

"Dearest young lady," cried Winterbourne, with generous passion, "have I come all the way to Rome only to be riddled by your silver shafts?"

"Just hear him say that!"—and she gave an affectionate twist to a bow on her hostess's dress. "Did you ever hear anything so quaint?"

"So 'quaint,' my dear?" echoed Mrs. Walker more critically—quite in the tone of a partisan of Winterbourne.

"Well, I don't know"—and the girl continued to finger her ribbons. "Mrs. Walker, I want to tell you something."

"Say, mother-r," broke in Randolph with his rough ends to his words, "I tell you you've got to go. Eugenio'll raise something!"

"I'm not afraid of Eugenio," said Daisy with a toss of her head. "Look here, Mrs. Walker," she went on, "you know I'm coming to your party."

"I'm delighted to hear it."

"I've got a lovely dress."

"I'm very sure of that."

"But I want to ask a favour—permission to bring a friend."

"I shall be happy to see any of your friends," said Mrs. Walker, who turned with a smile to Mrs. Miller.

"Oh they're not my friends," cried that lady, squirming in shy repudiation. "It seems as if they did n't take to *me*—I never spoke to one of them!"

---

[27]Carthaginian general (247–183 B.C.) who took his hatred of Rome from his father, also a Carthaginian general.

"It's an intimate friend of mine, Mr. Giovanelli," Daisy pursued without a tremor in her young clearness or a shadow on her shining bloom.

Mrs. Walker had a pause and gave a rapid glance at Winterbourne. "I shall be glad to see Mr. Giovanelli," she then returned.

"He's just the finest kind of Italian," Daisy pursued with the prettiest serenity. "He's a great friend of mine and the handsomest man in the world—except Mr. Winterbourne! He knows plenty of Italians, but he wants to know some Americans. It seems as if he was crazy about Americans. He's tremendously bright. He's perfectly lovely!"

It was settled that this paragon should be brought to Mrs. Walker's party, and then Mrs. Miller prepared to take her leave. "I guess we'll go right back to the hotel," she remarked with a confessed failure of the larger imagination.

"You may go back to the hotel, mother," Daisy replied, "but I'm just going to walk round."

"She's going to go it with Mr. Giovanelli," Randolph unscrupulously commented.

"I'm going to go it on the Pincio,"[28] Daisy peaceably smiled, while the way that she "condoned" these things almost melted Winterbourne's heart.

"Alone, my dear—at this hour?" Mrs. Walker asked. The afternoon was drawing to a close—it was the hour for the throng of carriages and of contemplative pedestrians. "I don't consider it's safe, Daisy," her hostess firmly asserted.

"Neither do I then," Mrs. Miller thus borrowed confidence to add. "You'll catch the fever as sure as you live. Remember what Dr. Davis told you!"

"Give her some of that medicine before she starts in," Randolph suggested.

The company had risen to its feet; Daisy, still showing her pretty teeth, bent over and kissed her hostess. "Mrs. Walker, you're too perfect," she simply said. "I'm not going alone; I'm going to meet a friend."

"Your friend won't keep you from catching the fever even if it *is* his own second nature," Mrs. Miller observed.

"Is it Mr. Giovanelli that's the dangerous attraction?" Mrs. Walker asked without mercy.

Winterbourne was watching the challenged girl; at this question his attention quickened. She stood there smiling and smoothing her bonnet-ribbons; she glanced at Winterbourne. Then, while she glanced and smiled, she brought out all affirmatively and without a shade of hesitation: "Mr. Giovanelli—the beautiful Giovanelli."

"My dear young friend"—and, taking her hand, Mrs. Walker turned to pleading—"don't prowl off to the Pincio at this hour to meet a beautiful Italian."

"Well, he speaks first-rate English," Mrs. Miller incoherently mentioned.

"Gracious me," Daisy piped up, "I don't want to do anything that's going to affect my health—or my character either! There's an easy way to settle it." Her eyes continued to play over Winterbourne. "The Pincio's only a hundred yards off, and if Mr. Winterbourne were as polite as he pretends he'd offer to walk right in with me!"

Winterbourne's politeness hastened to proclaim itself, and the girl gave him gracious leave to accompany her. They passed downstairs before her mother, and at the door he saw Mrs. Miller's carriage drawn up, with the ornamental courier whose acquaintance he had made at Vevey seated within. "Goodbye, Eugenio," cried Daisy; "I'm going to take a walk!" The distance from Via Gregoriana to the beautiful garden at the other end of the Pincian Hill is in fact rapidly traversed. As the day was splendid, however, and the concourse of vehicles, walkers and loungers numerous, the young Americans found their progress much delayed. This fact was highly agreeable to Winterbourne, in spite of his consciousness of his singular situation. The slow-moving, idly-gazing Roman crowd bestowed much attention on the extremely pretty young woman of English race who passed through it, with some difficulty, on his

---

[28]A hill within the Roman walls overlooking the city.

arm; and he wondered what on earth had been in Daisy's mind when she proposed to exhibit herself unattended to its appreciation. His own mission, to her sense, was apparently to consign her to the hands of Mr. Giovanelli; but, at once annoyed and gratified, he resolved that he would do no such thing.

"Why have n't you been to see me?" she meanwhile asked. "You can't get out of that."

"I've had the honour of telling you that I've only just stepped out of the train."

"You must have stayed in the train a good while after it stopped!" she derisively cried. "I suppose you were asleep. You've had time to go to see Mrs. Walker."

"I knew Mrs. Walker—" Winterbourne began to explain.

"I know where you knew her. You knew her at Geneva. She told me so. Well, you knew me at Vevey. That's just as good. So you ought to have come." She asked him no other question than this; she began to prattle about her own affairs. "We've got splendid rooms at the hotel; Eugenio says they're the best rooms in Rome. We're going to stay all winter—if we don't die of the fever; and I guess we'll stay then! It's a great deal nicer than I thought; I thought it would be fearfully quiet—in fact I was sure it would be deadly pokey. I foresaw we should be going round all the time with one of those dreadful old men who explain about the pictures and things. But we only had about a week of that, and now I'm enjoying myself. I know ever so many people, and they're all so charming. The society's extremely select. There are all kinds—English and Germans and Italians. I think I like the English best. I like their style of conversation. But there are some lovely Americans. I never saw anything so hospitable. There's something or other every day. There's not much dancing—but I must say I never thought dancing was everything. I was always fond of conversation. I guess I'll have plenty at Mrs. Walker's—her rooms are so small." When they had passed the gate of the Pincian Gardens Miss Miller began to wonder where Mr. Giovanelli might be. "We had better go straight to that place in front, where you look at the view."

Winterbourne took a stand. "I certainly shan't help you to find him."

"Then I shall find him without you," Daisy said with spirit.

"You certainly won't leave me!" he protested.

She burst into her familiar little laugh. "Are you afraid you'll get lost—or run over? But there's Giovanelli leaning against that tree. He's staring at the women in the carriages: did you ever see anything so cool?"

Winterbourne descried hereupon at some distance a little figure that stood with folded arms and nursing its cane. It had a handsome face, a hat artfully poised, a glass in one eye and a nosegay in its buttonhole. Daisy's friend looked at it a moment and then said: "Do you mean to speak to that thing?"

"Do I mean to speak to him? Why you don't suppose I mean to communicate by signs!"

"Pray understand then," the young man returned, "that I intend to remain with you."

Daisy stopped and looked at him without a sign of troubled consciousness, with nothing in her face but her charming eyes, her charming teeth and her happy dimples. "Well, she's a cool one!" he thought.

"I don't like the way you say that," she declared. "It's too imperious."

"I beg your pardon if I say it wrong. The main point's to give you an idea of my meaning."

The girl looked at him more gravely, but with eyes that were prettier than ever. "I've never allowed a gentleman to dictate to me or to interfere with anything I do."

"I think that's just where your mistake has come in," he retorted. "You should sometimes listen to a gentleman—the right one."

At this she began to laugh again. "I do nothing but listen to gentlemen! Tell me if Mr. Giovanelli is the right one."

The gentleman with the nosegay in his bosom had now made out our two friends and was approaching Miss Miller with obsequious rapidity. He bowed to Winterbourne as well as to the latter's compatriot; he seemed to shine, in his coxcombical way, with the desire to please and the fact of his own intelligent joy, though Winterbourne thought him not a bad-looking fellow. But he nevertheless said to Daisy: "No, he's not the right one."

She had clearly a natural turn for free introductions; she mentioned with the easiest of grace the name of each of her companions to the other. She strolled forward with one of them on either hand; Mr. Giovanelli, who spoke English very cleverly—Winterbourne afterwards learned that he had practised the idiom upon a great many American heiresses—addressed her a great deal of very polite nonsense. He had the best possible manners, and the young American, who said nothing, reflected on that depth of Italian subtlety, so strangely opposed to Anglo-Saxon simplicity, which enables people to show a smoother surface in proportion as they're more acutely displeased. Giovanelli of course had counted upon something more intimate—he had not bargained for a party of three; but he kept his temper in a manner that suggested far-stretching intentions. Winterbourne flattered himself he had taken his measure. "He's anything but a gentleman," said the young American; "he isn't even a very plausible imitation of one. He's a music-master or a penny-a-liner[29] or a third-rate artist. He's awfully on his good behaviour, but damn his fine eyes!" Mr. Giovanelli had indeed great advantages; but it was deeply disgusting to Daisy's other friend that something in her shouldn't have instinctively discriminated against such a type. Giovanelli chattered and jested and made himself agreeable according to his honest Roman lights. It was true that if he was an imitation the imitation was studied. "Nevertheless," Winterbourne said to himself, "a nice girl ought to know!" And then he came back to the dreadful question of whether this *was* in fact a nice girl. Would a nice girl—even allowing for her being a little American flirt—make a rendezvous with a presumably low-lived foreigner? The rendezvous in this case indeed had been in broad daylight and in the most crowded corner of Rome; but wasn't it possible to regard the choice of these very circumstances as a proof more of vulgarity than of anything else? Singular though it may seem, Winterbourne was vexed that the girl, in joining her *amoroso*,[30] shouldn't appear more impatient of his own company, and he was vexed precisely because of his inclination. It was impossible to regard her as a wholly unspotted flower—she lacked a certain indispensable fineness; and it would therefore much simplify the situation to be able to treat her as the subject of one of the visitations known to romancers as "lawless passions." That she should seem to wish to get rid of him would have helped him to think more lightly of her, just as to be able to think more lightly of her would have made her less perplexing. Daisy at any rate continued on this occasion to present herself as an inscrutable combination of audacity and innocence.

She had been walking some quarter of an hour, attended by her two cavaliers and responding in a tone of very childish gaiety, as it after all struck one of them, to the pretty speeches of the other, when a carriage that had detached itself from the revolving train drew up beside the path. At the same moment Winterbourne noticed that his friend Mrs. Walker—the lady whose house he had lately left—was seated in the vehicle and was beckoning to him. Leaving Miss Miller's side, he hastened to obey her summons—and all to find her flushed, excited, scandalised. "It's really too dreadful"—she earnestly appealed to him. "That crazy girl mustn't do this sort of thing. She mustn't walk here with you two men. Fifty people have remarked her."

Winterbourne—suddenly and rather oddly rubbed the wrong way by this—raised his grave eyebrows. "I think it's a pity to make too much fuss about it."

"It's a pity to let the girl ruin herself!"

"She's very innocent," he reasoned in his own troubled interest.

"She's very reckless," cried Mrs. Walker, "and goodness knows how far—left to

---

[29]Hack writer.
[30]"Lover" (Italian).

itself—it may go. Did you ever," she proceeded to enquire, "see anything so blatantly imbecile as the mother? After you had all left me just now I could n't sit still for thinking of it. It seemed too pitiful not even to attempt to save them. I ordered the carriage and put on my bonnet and came here as quickly as possible. Thank heaven I've found you!"

"What do you propose to do with us?" Winterbourne uncomfortably smiled.

"To ask her to get in, to drive her about here for half an hour—so that the world may see she's not running absolutely wild—and then take her safely home."

"I don't think it's a very happy thought," he said after reflexion, "but you're at liberty to try."

Mrs. Walker accordingly tried. The young man went in pursuit of their young lady who had simply nodded and smiled, from her distance, at her recent patroness in the carriage and then had gone her way with her own companion. On learning, in the event, that Mrs. Walker had followed her, she retraced her steps, however, with a perfect good grace and with Mr. Giovanelli at her side. She professed herself "enchanted" to have a chance to present this gentleman to her good friend, and immediately achieved the introduction; declaring with it, and as if it were of as little importance, that she had never in her life seen anything so lovely as that lady's carriage-rug.

"I'm glad you admire it," said her poor pursuer, smiling sweetly. "Will you get in and let me put it over you?"

"Oh no, thank you!"—Daisy knew her mind. "I'll admire it ever so much more as I see you driving round with it."

"Do get in and drive round *with* me," Mrs. Walker pleaded.

"That would be charming, but it's so fascinating just as I am!"—with which the girl radiantly took in the gentlemen on either side of her.

"It may be fascinating, dear child, but it's not the custom here," urged the lady of the victoria,[31] leaning forward in this vehicle with her hands devoutly clasped.

"Well, it ought to be then!" Daisy unperturbably laughed. "If I did n't walk I'd expire."

"You should walk with your mother, dear," cried Mrs. Walker with a loss of patience.

"With my mother dear?" the girl amusedly echoed. Winterbourne saw she scented interference. "My mother never walked ten steps in her life. And then, you know," she blandly added, "I'm more than five years old."

"You're old enough to be more reasonable. You're old enough, dear Miss Miller, to be talked about."

Daisy wondered to extravagance. "Talked about? What do you mean?"

"Come into my carriage and I'll tell you."

Daisy turned shining eyes again from one of the gentlemen beside her to the other. Mr. Giovanelli was bowing to and fro, rubbing down his gloves and laughing irresponsibly; Winterbourne thought the scene the most unpleasant possible. "I don't think I want to know what you mean," the girl presently said. "I don't think I should like it."

Winterbourne only wished Mrs. Walker would tuck up her carriage-rug and drive away; but this lady, as she afterwards told him, did n't feel she could "rest there." "Should you prefer being thought a very reckless girl?" she accordingly asked.

"Gracious me!" exclaimed Daisy. She looked again at Mr. Giovanelli, then she turned to her other companion. There was a small pink flush in her cheek; she was tremendously pretty. "Does Mr. Winterbourne think," she put to him with a wonderful bright intensity of appeal, "that—to save my reputation—I ought to get into the carriage?"

It really embarrassed him; for an instant he cast about—so strange was it to hear

---

[31]A horse-drawn carriage for two with a seat for a driver.

her speak that way of her "reputation." But he himself in fact had to speak in accordance with gallantry. The finest gallantry here was surely just to tell her the truth; and the truth, for our young man, as the few indications I have been able to give have made him known to the reader, was that his charming friend should listen to the voice of civilised society. He took in again her exquisite prettiness and then said more distinctly: "I think you should get into the carriage."

Daisy gave the rein to her amusement. "I never heard anything so stiff! If this is improper, Mrs. Walker," she pursued, "then I'm *all* improper, and you had better give me right up. Good-bye; I hope you'll have a lovely ride!"—and with Mr. Giovanelli, who made a triumphantly obsequious saltue, she turned away.

Mrs. Walker sat looking after her, and there were tears in Mrs. Walker's eyes. "Get in here, sir," she said to Winterbourne, indicating the place beside her. The young man answered that he felt bound to accompany Miss Miller; whereupon the lady of the victoria declared that if he refused her this favour she would never speak to him again. She was evidently wound up. He accordingly hastened to overtake Daisy and her more faithful ally, and, offering her his hand, told her that Mrs. Walker had made a stringent claim on his presence. He had expected her to answer with something rather free, something still more significant of the perversity from which the voice of society, through the lips of their distressed friend, had so earnestly endeavoured to dissuade her. But she only let her hand slip, as she scarce looked at him, through his slightly awkward grasp; while Mr. Giovanelli, to make it worse, bade him farewell with too emphatic a flourish of the hat.

Winterbourne was not in the best possible humour as he took his seat beside the author of his sacrifice. "That was not clever of you," he said candidly, as the vehicle mingled again with the throng of carriages.

"In such a case," his companion answered, "I don't want to be clever—I only want to be *true!*"

"Well, your truth has only offended the strange little creature—it has only put her off."

"It has happened very well"—Mrs. Walker accepted her work. "If she's so perfectly determined to compromise herself the sooner one knows it the better—one can act accordingly."

"I suspect she meant no great harm, you know," Winterbourne maturely opined.

"So I thought a month ago. But she has been going too far."

"What has she been doing?"

"Everything that's not done here. Flirting with any man she can pick up; sitting in corners with mysterious Italians; dancing all the evening with the same partners; receiving visits at eleven o'clock at night. Her mother melts away when the visitors come."

"But her brother," laughed Winterbourne, "sits up till two in the morning."

"He must be edified by what he sees. I'm told that at their hotel every one's talking about her and that a smile goes round among the servants when a gentleman comes and asks for Miss Miller."

"Ah we need n't mind the servants!" Winterbourne compassionately signified. "The poor girl's only fault," he presently added, "is her complete lack of education."

"She's naturally indelicate," Mrs. Walker, on her side, reasoned. "Take that example this morning. How long had you known her at Vevey?"

"A couple of days."

"Imagine then the taste of her making it a personal matter that you should have left the place!"

He agreed that taste was n't the strong point of the Millers—after which he was silent for some moments; but only at last to add: "I suspect, Mrs. Walker, that you and I have lived too long at Geneva!" And he further noted that he should be glad to learn with what particular design she had made him enter her carriage.

"I wanted to enjoin on you the importance of your ceasing your relations with

Miss Miller; that of your not appearing to flirt with her; that of your giving her no further opportunity to expose herself; that of your in short letting her alone."

"I'm afraid I can't do anything quite so enlightened as *that*," he returned. "I like her awfully, you know."

"All the more reason you should n't help her to make a scandal."

"Well, there shall be nothing scandalous in my attentions to her," he was willing to promise.

"There certainly will be in the way she takes them. But I've said what I had on my conscience," Mrs. Walker pursued. "If you wish to rejoin the young lady I'll put you down. Here, by the way, you have a chance."

The carriage was engaged in that part of the Pincian drive which overhangs the wall of Rome and overlooks the beautiful Villa Borghese.[32] It is bordered by a large parapet, near which are several seats. One of these, at a distance, was occupied by a gentleman and a lady, toward whom Mrs. Walker gave a toss of her head. At the same moment these persons rose and walked to the parapet. Winterbourne had asked the coachman to stop; he now descended from the carriage. His companion looked at him a moment in silence and then, while he raised his hat, drove majestically away. He stood where he had alighted; he had turned his eyes toward Daisy and her cavalier. They evidently saw no one; they were too deeply occupied with each other. When they reached the low garden-wall they remained a little looking off at the great flat-topped pine-clusters of Villa Borghese; then the girl's attendant admirer seated himself familiarly on the broad ledge of the wall. The western sun in the opposite sky sent out a brilliant shaft through a couple of cloud-bars; whereupon the gallant Giovanelli took her parasol out of her hands and opened it. She came a little nearer and he held the parasol over her; then, still holding it, he let it so rest on her shoulder that both of their heads were hidden from Winterbourne. This young man stayed but a moment longer; then he began to walk. But he walked—not toward the couple united beneath the parasol, rather toward the residence of his aunt Mrs. Costello.

IV

He flattered himself on the following day that there was no smiling among the servants when he at least asked for Mrs. Miller at her hotel. This lady and her daughter, however, were not at home; and on the next day after, repeating his visit, Winterbourne again was met by a denial. Mrs. Walker's party took place on the evening of the third day, and in spite of the final reserves that had marked his last interview with that social critic our young man was among the guests. Mrs. Walker was one of those pilgrims from the younger world who, while in contact with the elder, make a point, in their own phrase, of studying European society; and she had on this occasion collected several specimens of diversely-born humanity to serve, as might be, for text-books. When Winterbourne arrived the little person he desired most to find was n't there; but in a few moments he saw Mrs. Miller come in alone, very shyly and ruefully. This lady's hair, above the dead waste of her temples, was more frizzled than ever. As she approached their hostess Winterbourne also drew near.

"You see I've come all alone," said Daisy's unsupported parent. "I'm so frightened I don't know what to do; it's the first time I've ever been to a party alone—especially in this country. I wanted to bring Randolph or Eugenio or some one, but Daisy just pushed me off by myself. I ain't used to going round alone."

"And does n't your daughter intend to favour us with her society?" Mrs. Walker impressively enquired.

"Well, Daisy's all dressed," Mrs. Miller testified with that accent of the dispassion-

---

[32]Once the summer palace of the prominent Borghese family, dating from 1605, now an art museum in the midst of one of Rome's largest and most beautiful public parks.

ate, if not of the philosophic, historian with which she always recorded the current incidents of her daughter's career. "She got dressed on purpose before dinner. But she has a friend of hers there; that gentleman — the handsomest of the Italians — that she wanted to bring. They've got going at the piano — it seems as if they could n't leave off. Mr. Giovanelli does sing splendidly. But I guess they'll come before very long," Mrs. Miller hopefully concluded.

"I'm sorry she should come — in that particular way," Mrs. Walker permitted herself to observe.

"Well, I told her there was no use in her getting dressed before dinner if she was going to wait three hours," returned Daisy's mamma. "I did n't see the use of her putting on such a dress as that to sit around with Mr. Giovanelli."

"This is most horrible!" said Mrs. Walker, turning away and addressing herself to Winterbourne. "*Elle s'affiche, la malheureuse.*[33] It's her revenge for my having ventured to remonstrate with her. When she comes I shan't speak to her."

Daisy came after eleven o'clock, but she was n't, on such an occasion, a young lady to wait to be spoken to. She rustled forward in radiant loveliness, smiling and chattering, carrying a large bouquet and attended by Mr. Giovanelli. Every one stopped talking and turned and looked at her while she floated up to Mrs. Walker. "I'm afraid you thought I never was coming, so I sent mother off to tell you. I wanted to make Mr. Giovanelli practise some things before he came; you know he sings beautifully, and I want you to ask him to sing. This is Mr. Giovanelli; you know I introduced him to you; he's got the most lovely voice and he knows the most charming set of songs. I made him go over them this evening on purpose; we had the greatest time at the hotel." Of all this Daisy delivered herself with the sweetest brightest loudest confidence, looking now at her hostess and now at all the room, while she gave a series of little pats, round her very white shoulders, to the edges of her dress. "Is there any one I know?" she as undiscourageably asked.

"I think every one knows you!" said Mrs. Walker as with a grand intention; and she gave a very cursory greeting to Mr. Giovanelli. This gentleman bore himself gallantly; he smiled and bowed and showed his white teeth, he curled his moustaches and rolled his eyes and performed all the proper functions of a handsome Italian at an evening party. He sang, very prettily, half a dozen songs, though Mrs. Walker afterwards declared that she had been quite unable to find out who asked him. It was apparently not Daisy who had set him in motion — this young lady being seated a distance from the piano and though she had publicly, as it were, professed herself his musical patroness or guarantor, giving herself to gay and audible discourse while he warbled.

"It's a pity these rooms are so small; we can't dance," she remarked to Winterbourne as if she had seen him five minutes before.

"I'm not sorry we can't dance," he candidly returned. "I'm incapable of a step."

"Of course you're incapable of a step," the girl assented. "I should think your legs *would* be stiff cooped in there so much of the time in that victoria."

"Well, they were very restless there three days ago," he amicably laughed; "all they really wanted was to dance attendance on you."

"Oh my other friend — my friend in need — stuck to me; he seems more at one with his limbs than you are — I'll say that for him. But did you ever hear anything so cool," Daisy demanded, "as Mrs. Walker's wanting me to get into her carriage and drop poor Mr. Giovanelli, and under the pretext that it was proper? People have different ideas! It would have been most unkind; he had been talking about that walk for ten days."

"He should n't have talked about it at all," Winterbourne decided to make answer on this: "he would never have proposed to a young lady of this country to walk about the streets of Rome with him."

---

[33] "She is making herself conspicuous, poor girl" (French).

"About the streets?" she cried with her pretty stare. "Where then would he have proposed to her to walk? The Pincio ain't the streets either, I guess; and I besides, thank goodness, am not a young lady of this country. The young ladies of this country have a dreadfully pokey time of it, by what I can discover; I don't see why I should change my habits for *such* stupids."

"I'm afraid your habits are those of a ruthless flirt," said Winterbourne with studied severity.

"Of course they are!"—and she hoped, evidently, by the manner of it, to take his breath away. "I'm a fearful frightful flirt! Did you ever hear of a nice girl that was n't? But I suppose you'll tell me now I'm not a nice girl."

He remained grave indeed under the shock of her cynical profession. "You're a very nice girl, but I wish you'd flirt with me, and me only."

"Ah thank you, thank you very much: you're the last man I should think of flirting with. As I've had the pleasure of informing you, you're too stiff."

"You say that too often," he resentfully remarked.

Daisy gave a delighted laugh. "If I could have the sweet hope of making you angry I'd say it again."

"Don't do that—when I'm angry I'm stiffer than ever. But if you won't flirt with me do cease at least to flirt with your friend at the piano. They don't," he declared as in full sympathy with "them," "understand that sort of thing here."

"I thought they understood nothing else!" Daisy cried with startling world-knowledge.

"Not in young unmarried women."

"It seems to me much more proper in young unmarried women than in old married ones," she retorted.

"Well," said Winterbourne, "when you deal with natives you must go by the custom of the country. American flirting is a purely American silliness; it has—in its ineptitude of innocence—no place in *this* system. So when you show yourself in public with Mr. Giovanelli and without your mother—"

"Gracious, poor mother!"—and she made it beautifully unspeakable.

Winterbourne had a touched sense for this, but it did n't alter his attitude. "Though *you* may be flirting Mr. Giovanelli is n't—he means something else."

"He is n't preaching at any rate," she returned. "And if you want very much to know, we're neither of us flirting — not a little speck. We're too good friends for that. We're real intimate friends."

He was to continue to find her thus at moments inimitable. "Ah," he then judged, "if you're in love with each other it's another affair altogether!"

She had allowed him up to this point to speak so frankly that he had no thought of shocking her by the force of his logic; yet she now none the less immediately rose, blushing visibly and leaving him mentally to exclaim that the name of little American flirts was incoherence. "Mr. Giovanelli at least," she answered, sparing but a single small queer glance for it, a queerer small glance, he felt, than he had ever yet had from her—"Mr. Giovanelli never says to me such very disagreeable things."

It had an effect on him—he stood staring. The subject of their contention had finished singing; he left the piano, and his recognition of what—a little awkwardly—did n't take place in celebration of this might nevertheless have been an acclaimed operatic tenor's series of repeated ducks before the curtain. So he bowed himself over to Daisy. "Won't you come to the other room and have some tea?" he asked—offering Mrs. Walker's slightly thin refreshment as he might have done all the kingdoms of the earth.

Daisy at last turned on Winterbourne a more natural and calculable light. He was but the more muddled by it, however, since so inconsequent a smile made nothing clear—it seemed at the most to prove in her a sweetness and softness that reverted instinctively to the pardon of offences. "It has never occurred to Mr. Winterbourne to offer me any tea," she said with her finest little intention of torment and triumph.

"I've offered you excellent advice," the young man permitted himself to growl.

"I prefer weak tea!" cried Daisy, and she went off with the brilliant Giovanelli. She sat with him in the adjoining room, in the embrasure of the window, for the rest of the evening. There was an interesting performance at the piano, but neither of these conversers gave heed to it. When Daisy came to take leave of Mrs. Walker this lady conscientiously repaired the weakness of which she had been guilty at the moment of the girl's arrival—she turned her back straight on Miss Miller and left her to depart with what grace she might. Winterbourne happened to be near the door; he saw it all. Daisy turned very pale and looked at her mother, but Mrs. Miller was humbly unconscious of any rupture of any law or of any deviation from any custom. She appeared indeed to have felt an incongruous impulse to draw attention to her own striking conformity. "Good-night, Mrs. Walker," she said; "we've had a beautiful evening. You see if I let Daisy come to parties without me I don't want her to go away without me." Daisy turned away, looking with a small white prettiness, a blighted grace, at the circle near the door: Winterbourne saw that for the first moment she was too much shocked and puzzled even for indignation. He on his side was greatly touched.

"That was very cruel," he promptly remarked to Mrs. Walker.

But this lady's face was also as a stone. "She never enters my drawing-room again."

Since Winterbourne then, hereupon, was not to meet her in Mrs. Walker's drawing-room he went as often as possible to Mrs. Miller's hotel. The ladies were rarely at home, but when he found them the devoted Giovanelli was always present. Very often the glossy little Roman, serene in success, but not unduly presumptuous, occupied with Daisy alone the florid salon enjoyed by Eugenio's care, Mrs. Miller being apparently ever of the opinion that discretion is the better part of solicitude. Winterbourne noted, at first with surprise, that Daisy on these occasions was neither embarrassed nor annoyed by his own entrance; but he presently began to feel that she had no more surprises for him and that he really liked, after all, not making out what she was "up to." She showed no displeasure for the interruption of her *tête-à-tête* with Giovanelli; she could chatter as freshly and freely with two gentlemen as with one, and this easy flow had ever the same anomaly for her earlier friend that it was so free without availing itself of its freedom. Winterbourne reflected that if she was seriously interested in the Italian it was odd she should n't take more trouble to preserve the sanctity of their interviews, and he liked her the better for her innocent-looking indifference and her inexhaustible gaiety. He could hardly have said why, but she struck him as a young person not formed for a troublesome jealousy. Smile at such a betrayal though the reader may, it was a fact with regard to the women who had hitherto interested him that, given certain contingencies, Winterbourne could see himself afraid—literally afraid—of these ladies. It pleased him to believe that even were twenty other things different and Daisy should love him and he should know it and like it, he would still never be afraid of Daisy. It must be added that this conviction was not altogether flattering to her: it represented that she was nothing every way if not light.

But she was evidently very much interested in Giovanelli. She looked at him whenever he spoke; she was perpetually telling him to do this and to do that; she was constantly chaffing and abusing him. She appeared completely to have forgotten that her other friend had said anything to displease her at Mrs. Walker's entertainment. One Sunday afternoon, having gone to Saint Peter's with his aunt, Winterbourne became aware that the young woman held in horror by that lady was strolling about the great church under escort of her coxcomb of the Corso.[34] It amused him, after a debate, to point out the exemplary pair—even at the cost, as it proved, of Mrs. Costello's saying when she had taken them in through her eye-glass: "That's what makes you so pensive in these days, eh?"

---

[34]Roman street.

"I had n't the least idea I was pensive," he pleaded.

"You're very much preoccupied; you're always thinking of something."

"And what is it," he asked, "that you accuse me of thinking of?"

"Of that young lady's, Miss Baker's, Miss Chandler's—what's her name?—Miss Miller's intrigue with that little barber's block."

"Do you call it an intrigue," he asked—"an affair that goes on with such peculiar publicity?"

"That's their folly," said Mrs. Costello, "it's not their merit."

"No," he insisted with a hint perhaps of the preoccupation to which his aunt had alluded—"I don't believe there's anything to be called an intrigue."

"Well"—and Mrs. Costello dropped her glass—"I've heard a dozen people speak of it: they say she's quite carried away by him."

"They're certainly as thick as thieves," our embarrassed young man allowed.

Mrs. Costello came back to them, however, after a little; and Winterbourne recognised in this a further illustration—than that supplied by his own condition—of the spell projected by the case. "He's certainly very handsome. One easily sees how it is. She thinks him the most elegant man in the world, the finest gentleman possible. She has never seen anything like him—he's better even than the courier. It was the courier probably who introduced him, and if he succeeds in marrying the young lady the courier will come in for a magnificent commission."

"I don't believe she thinks of marrying him," Winterbourne reasoned, "and I don't believe he hopes to marry her."

"You may be very sure she thinks of nothing at all. She romps on from day to day, from hour to hour, as they did in the Golden Age. I can imagine nothing more vulgar," said Mrs. Costello, whose figure of speech scarcely went on all fours. "And at the same time," she added, "depend upon it she may tell you any moment that she is 'engaged.'"

"I think that's more than Giovanelli really expects," said Winterbourne.

"And who is Giovanelli?"

"The shiny—but, to do him justice, not greasy—little Roman. I've asked questions about him and learned something. He's apparently a perfectly respectable little man. I believe he's in a small way a *cavaliere avvocato*.[35] But he does n't move in what are called the first circles. I think it really not absolutely impossible the courier introduced him. He's evidently immensely charmed with Miss Miller. If she thinks him the finest gentleman in the world, he, on his side, has never found himself in personal contact with such splendour, such opulence, such personal daintiness, as this young lady's. And then she must seem to him wonderfully pretty and interesting. Yes, he can't really hope to pull it off. That must appear to him too impossible a piece of luck. He has nothing but his handsome face to offer, and there's a substantial, a possibly explosive Mr. Miller in that mysterious land of dollars and six-shooters. Giovanelli's but too conscious that he has n't a title to offer. If he were only a count or a *marchese*![36] What on earth can he make of the way they've taken him up?"

"He accounts for it by his handsome face and thinks Miss Miller a young lady *qui se passe ses fantaisies*!"[37]

"It's very true," Winterbourne pursued, "that Daisy and her mamma have n't yet risen to that stage of—what shall I call it?—of culture, at which the idea of catching a count or a *marchese* begins. I believe them intellectually incapable of that conception."

"Ah but the *cavaliere avvocato* does n't believe them!" cried Mrs. Costello.

Of the observation excited by Daisy's "intrigue" Winterbourne gathered that day at Saint Peter's sufficient evidence. A dozen of the American colonists in Rome came

---

[35]"Well-bred lawyer" (Italian).
[36]Marquis (higher than a count but lower than a prince).
[37]"Who indulges her whims" (French).

to talk with his relative, who sat on a small portable stool at the base of one of the great pilasters. The vesper-service was going forward in splendid chants and organ-tones in the adjacent choir, and meanwhile, between Mrs. Costello and her friends, much was said about poor little Miss Miller's going really "too far." Winterbourne was not pleased with what he heard; but when, coming out upon the great steps of the church, he saw Daisy, who had emerged before him, get into an open cab with her accomplice and roll away through the cynical streets of Rome, the measure of her course struck him as simply there to take. He felt very sorry for her — not exactly that he believed she had completely lost her wits, but because it was painful to see so much that was pretty and undefended and natural sink so low in human estimation. He made an attempt after this to give a hint to Mrs. Miller. He met one day in the Corso a friend — a tourist like himself — who had just come out of the Doria Palace, where he had been walking through the beautiful gallery. His friend "went on" for some moments about the great portrait of Innocent X, by Velasquez,[38] suspended in one of the cabinets of the palace, and then said: "And in the same cabinet, by the way, I enjoyed sight of an image of a different kind; that little American who's so much more a work of nature than of art and whom you pointed out to me last week." In answer to Winterbourne's enquiries his friend narrated that the little American — prettier now than ever — was seated with a companion in the secluded nook in which the papal presence is enshrined.

"All alone?" the young man heard himself disingenuously ask.

"Alone with a little Italian who sports in his button-hole a stack of flowers. The girl's a charming beauty, but I thought I understood from you the other day that she's a young lady *du meilleur monde*."[39]

"So she is!" said Winterbourne; and having assured himself that his informant had seen the interesting pair but ten minutes before, he jumped into a cab and went to call on Mrs. Miller. She was at home, but she apologised for receiving him in Daisy's absence.

"She's gone out somewhere with Mr. Giovanelli. She's always going round with Mr. Giovanelli."

"I've noticed they're intimate indeed," Winterbourne concurred.

"Oh it seems as if they could n't live without each other!" said Mrs. Miller. "Well, he's a real gentleman anyhow. I guess I have the joke on Daisy — that she *must* be engaged!"

"And how does your daughter *take* the joke?"

"Oh she just says she ain't. But she might as *well* be!" this philosophic parent resumed. "She goes on as if she was. But I've made Mr. Giovanelli promise to tell me if Daisy don't. I'd want to write to Mr. Miller about it — would n't you?"

Winterbourne replied that he certainly should; and the state of mind of Daisy's mamma struck him as so unprecedented in the annals of parental vigilance that he recoiled before the attempt to educate at a single interview either her conscience or her wit.

After this Daisy was never at home and he ceased to meet her at the houses of their common acquaintance, because, as he perceived, these shrewd people had quite made up their minds as to the length she must have gone. They ceased to invite her, intimating that they wished to make, and make strongly, for the benefit of observant Europeans, the point that though Miss Daisy Miller was a pretty American girl all right, her behaviour was n't pretty at all — was in fact regarded by her compatriots as quite monstrous. Winterbourne wondered how she felt about all the cold shoulders that were turned upon her, and sometimes found himself suspecting with impatience that she simply did n't feel and did n't know. He set her down as hopelessly childish

---

[38]Diego Rodriguez de Silva y Velásquez (1599–1660), Spanish painter, one of whose principal works is the painting of   Pope Innocent X (1649).
[39]"Of the best society" (French).

and shallow, as such mere giddiness and ignorance incarnate as was powerless either to heed or to suffer. Then at other moments he could n't doubt that she carried about in her elegant and irresponsible little organism a defiant, passionate, perfectly observant consciousness of the impression she produced. He asked himself whether the defiance would come from the consciousness of innocence or from her being essentially a young person of the reckless class. Then it had to be admitted, he felt, that holding fast to a belief in her "innocence" was more and more but a matter of gallantry too fine-spun for use. As I have already had occasion to relate, he was reduced without pleasure to this chopping of logic and vexed at his poor fallability, his want of instinctive certitude as to how far her extravagance was generic and national and how far it was crudely personal. Whatever it was he had helplessly missed her, and now it was too late. She was "carried away" by Mr. Giovanelli.

A few days after his brief interview with her mother he came across her at that supreme seat of flowering desolation known as the Palace of the Cæsars. The early Roman spring had filled the air with bloom and perfume, and the rugged surface of the Palatine[40] was muffled with tender verdure. Daisy moved at her ease over the great mounds of ruin that are embanked with mossy marble and paved with monumental inscriptions. It seemed to him he had never known Rome so lovely as just then. He looked off at the enchanting harmony of line and colour that remotely encircles the city—he inhaled the softly humid odours and felt the freshness of the year and the antiquity of the place reaffirm themselves in deep interfusion. It struck him also that Daisy had never showed to the eye for so utterly charming; but this had been his conviction on every occasion of their meeting. Giovanelli was of course at her side, and Giovanelli too glowed as never before with something of the glory of his race.

"Well," she broke out upon the friend it would have been such mockery to designate as the latter's rival, "I should think you'd be quite lonesome!"

"Lonesome?" Winterbourne resignedly echoed.

"You're always going round by yourself. Can't you get any one to walk with you?"

"I'm not so fortunate," he answered, "as your gallant companion."

Giovanelli had from the first treated him with distinguished politeness; he listened with a deferential air to his remarks; he laughed punctiliously at his pleasantries; he attached such importance as he could find terms for to Miss Miller's cold compatriot. He carried himself in no degree like a jealous wooer; he had obviously a great deal of tact; he had no objection to any one's expecting a little humility of him. It even struck Winterbourne that he almost yearned at times for some private communication in the interest of his character for common sense; a chance to remark to him as another intelligent man that, bless him, *he* knew how extraordinary was their young lady and did n't flatter himself with confident—at least *too* confident and too delusive—hopes of matrimony and dollars. On this occasion he strolled away from his charming charge to pluck a sprig of almond-blossom which he carefully arranged in his button-hole.

"I know why you say that," Daisy meanwhile observed. "Because you think I go round too much with *him*!" And she nodded at her discreet attendant.

"Every one thinks so—if you care to know," was all Winterbourne found to reply.

"Of course I care to know!"—she made this point with much expression. "But I don't believe a word of it. They're only pretending to be shocked. They don't really care a straw what I do. Besides, I don't go round so much."

"I think you'll find they do care. They'll show it—disagreeably," he took on himself to state.

Daisy weighed the importance of that idea. "How—disagreeably?"

"Have n't you noticed anything?" he compassionately asked.

---

[40]One of the seven hills of Rome.

"I've noticed *you*. But I noticed you've no more 'give' than a ramrod the first time ever I saw you."

"You'll find at least that I've more 'give' than several others," he patiently smiled.

"How shall I find it?"

"By going to see the others."

"What will they do to me?"

"They'll show you the cold shoulder. Do you know what that means?"

Daisy was looking at him intently; she began to colour. "Do you mean as Mrs. Walker did the other night?"

"Exactly as Mrs. Walker did the other night."

She looked away at Giovanelli, still titivating with his almond-blossom. Then with her attention again on the important subject: "I should n't think you'd let people be so unkind!"

"How can I help it?"

"I should think you'd want to say something."

"I do want to say something" — and Winterbourne paused a moment. "I want to say that your mother tells me she believes you engaged."

"Well, I guess she does," said Daisy very simply.

The young man began to laugh. "And does Randolph believe it?"

"I guess Randolph does n't believe anything." This testimony to Randolph's scepticism excited Winterbourne to further mirth, and he noticed that Giovanelli was coming back to them. Daisy, observing it as well, addressed herself again to her countryman. "Since you've mentioned it," she said, "I *am* engaged." He looked at her hard — he had stopped laughing. "You don't believe it!" she added.

He asked himself, and it was for a moment like testing a heart-beat; after which, "Yes, I believe it!" he said.

"Oh no, you don't," she answered. "But *if* you possibly do," she still more perversely pursued — "well, I ain't!"

Miss Miller and her constant guide were on their way to the gate of the enclosure, so that Winterbourne, who had but lately entered, presently took leave of them. A week later on he went to dine at a beautiful villa on the Cælian Hill,[41] and, on arriving, dismissed his hired vehicle. The evening was perfect and he promised himself the satisfaction of walking home beneath the Arch of Constantine and past the vaguely-lighted monuments of the Forum.[42] Above was a moon half-developed, whose radiance was not brilliant but veiled in a thin cloud-curtain that seemed to diffuse and equalise it. When on his return from the villa at eleven o'clock he approached the dusky circle of the Colosseum[43] the sense of the romantic in him easily suggested that the interior, in such an atmosphere, would well repay a glance. He turned aside and walked to one of the empty arches, near which, as he observed, an open carriage — one of the little Roman street-cabs — was stationed. Then he passed in among the cavernous shadows of the great structure and emerged upon the clear and silent arena. The place had never seemed to him more impressive. One half of the gigantic circus was in deep shade while the other slept in the luminous dusk. As he stood there he began to murmur Byron's famous lines out of "Manfred";[44] but before he had finished his quotation he remembered that if nocturnal meditation thereabouts was the fruit of a rich literary culture it was none the less deprecated by medical science. The air of other ages surrounded one; but the air of other ages, coldly analysed, was no better than a villainous miasma. Winterbourne sought, how-

---

[41]Another of the hills of Rome.

[42]Ruins of ancient imperial Rome: the Arch of Constantine (A.D. 313), commemorating military victories; the Forum, the political, business, and social center.

[43]Large amphitheater, site of gladiatorial combats, animal hunts, naval battles, and martyrdom of the early Christians.

[44]See Byron's verse drama "Manfred" (1817), III, iv, 8–41, where Manfred recalls that in his youth he "stood within the Coliseum's wall,/'Midst the chief relics of almighty Rome" and, under the Moon's "tender light," "the place/Became religion, and the heart ran o'er/With silent worship of the Great of old, —/The dead, but sceptred, Sovereigns, who still rule/Our spirits from their urns."

ever, toward the middle of the arena, a further reach of vision, intending the next moment, a hasty retreat. The great cross in the centre was almost obscured; only as he drew near did he make it out distinctly. He thus also distinguished two persons stationed on the low steps that formed its base. One of these was a woman seated; her companion hovered before her.

Presently the sound of the woman's voice came to him distinctly in the warm night-air. "Well, he looks at us as one of the old lions or tigers may have looked at the Christian martyrs!" These words were winged with their accent, so that they fluttered and settled about him in the darkness like vague white doves. It was Miss Daisy Miller who had released them for flight.

"Let us hope he's not very hungry"—the bland Giovanelli fell in with her humour. "He'll have to take *me* first; you'll serve for dessert."

Winterbourne felt himself pulled up with final horror now—and, it must be added, with final relief. It was as if a sudden clearance had taken place in the ambiguity of the poor girl's appearances and the whole riddle of her contradictions had grown easy to read. She was a young lady about the *shades* of whose perversity a foolish puzzled gentleman need no longer trouble his head or his heart. That once questionable quantity *had* no shades—it was a mere black little blot. He stood there looking at her, looking at her companion too, and not reflecting that though he saw them vaguely he himself must have been more brightly presented. He felt angry at all his shiftings of view—he felt ashamed of all his tender little scruples and all his witless little mercies. He was about to advance again, and then again checked himself; not from the fear of doing her injustice, but from a sense of the danger of showing undue exhilaration for this disburdenment of cautious criticism. He turned away toward the entrance of the place; but as he did so he heard Daisy speak again.

"Why it was Mr. Winterbourne! He saw me and he cuts me dead!"

What a clever little reprobate she was, he was amply able to reflect at this, and how smartly she feigned, how promptly she sought to play off on him, a surprised and injured innocence! But nothing would induce him to cut her either "dead" or to within any measurable distance even of the famous "inch" of her life. He came forward again and went toward the great cross. Daisy had got up and Giovanelli lifted his hat. Winterbourne had now begun to think simply of the madness, on the ground of exposure and infection, of a frail young creature's lounging away such hours in a nest of malaria. What if she *were* the most plausible of little reprobates? That was no reason for her dying of the *perniciosa*.[45] "How long have you been 'fooling round' here?" he asked with conscious roughness.

Daisy, lovely in the sinister silver radiance, appraised him a moment, roughness and all. "Well, I guess all the evening." She answered with spirit and, he could see even then, with exaggeration. "I never saw anything so quaint."

"I'm afraid," he returned, "you'll not think a bad attack of Roman fever very quaint. This is the way people catch it. I wonder," he added to Giovanelli, "that you, a native Roman, should countenance such extraordinary rashness."

"Ah," said this seasoned subject, "for myself I have no fear."

"Neither have I—for you!" Winterbourne retorted in French. "I'm speaking for this young lady."

Giovanelli raised his well-shaped eyebrows and showed his shining teeth, but took his critic's rebuke with docility. "I assured Mademoiselle it was a grave indiscretion, but when was Mademoiselle ever prudent?"

"I never was sick, and I don't mean to be!" Mademoiselle declared. "I don't look like much, but I'm healthy! I was bound to see the Colosseum by moonlight—I wouldn't have wanted to go home without *that*; and we've had the most beautiful time, have

---

[45]Noxious malaria, also called Roman fever because of its prevalence in Rome.

n't we, Mr. Giovanelli? If there has been any danger Eugenio can give me some pills. Eugenio has got some splendid pills."

"*I* should advise you then," said Winterbourne, "to drive home as fast as possible and take one!"

Giovanelli smiled as for the striking happy thought. "What you say is very wise. I'll go and make sure the carriage is at hand." And he went forward rapidly.

Daisy followed with Winterbourne. He tried to deny himself the small fine anguish of looking at her, but his eyes themselves refused to spare him, and she seemed moreover not in the least embarrassed. He spoke no word; Daisy chattered over the beauty of the place: "Well, I *have* seen the Colosseum by moonlight — that's one thing I can rave about!" Then noticing her companion's silence she asked him why he was so stiff — it had always been her great word. He made no answer, but he felt his laugh an immense negation of stiffness. They passed under one of the dark archways; Giovanelli was in front with the carriage. Here Daisy stopped a moment, looking at her compatriot. "*Did* you believe I was engaged the other day?"

"It does n't matter now what I believed the other day!" he replied with infinite point.

It was a wonder how she did n't wince for it. "Well, what do you believe now?"

"I believe it makes very little difference whether you're engaged or not!"

He felt her lighted eyes fairly penetrate the thick gloom of the vaulted passage — as if to seek some access to him she had n't yet compassed. But Giovanelli, with a graceful inconsequence, was at present all for retreat. "Quick, quick; if we get in by midnight we're quite safe!"

Daisy took her seat in the carriage and the fortunate Italian placed himself beside her. "Don't forget Eugenio's pills!" said Winterbourne as he lifted his hat.

"I don't care," she unexpectedly cried out for this, "whether I have Roman fever or not!" On which the cab-driver cracked his whip and they rolled across the desultory patches of antique pavement.

Winterbourne — to do him justice, as it were — mentioned to no one that he had encountered Miss Miller at midnight in the Colosseum with a gentleman; in spite of which deep discretion, however, the fact of the scandalous adventure was known a couple of days later, with a dozen vivid details, to every member of the little American circle, and was commented accordingly. Winterbourne judged thus that the people about the hotel had been thoroughly empowered to testify, and that after Daisy's return there would have been an exchange of jokes between the porter and the cab-driver. But the young man became aware at the same moment of how thoroughly it had ceased to ruffle him that the little American flirt should be "talked about" by low-minded menials. These sources of current criticism a day or two later abounded still further: the little American flirt was alarmingly ill and the doctors now in possession of the scene. Winterbourne, when the rumour came to him, immediately went to the hotel for more news. He found that two or three charitable friends had preceded him and that they were being entertained in Mrs. Miller's salon by the all-efficient Randolph.

"It's going round at night that way, you bet — that's what has made her so sick. She's always going round at night. I should n't think she'd want to — it's so plaguey dark over here. You can't see anything over here without the moon's right up. In American they don't go round by the moon!" Mrs. Miller meanwhile wholly surrendered to her genius for unapparent uses; her salon knew her less than ever, and she was presumably now at least giving her daughter the advantage of her society. It was clear that Daisy was dangerously ill.

Winterbourne constantly attended for news from the sick-room, which reached him, however, but with worrying indirectness, though he once had speech, for a moment, of the poor girl's physician and once saw Mrs. Miller, who, sharply alarmed, struck him as thereby more happily inspired than he could have conceived and indeed as the most noiseless and light-handed of nurses. She invoked a good deal the remote shade of Dr. Davis, but Winterbourne paid her the compliment of taking her after all for less monstrous a goose. To this indulgence indeed something she further said perhaps even more insidiously disposed him. "Daisy spoke of you the other day quite pleasantly. Half the time she does n't know what she's saying, but that time I think she did. She gave me a message—she told me to tell you. She wanted you to know she never was engaged to that handsome Italian who was always round. I'm sure I'm very glad; Mr. Giovanelli has n't been near us since she was taken ill. I thought he was so much of a gentleman, but I don't call that very polite! A lady told me he was afraid I had n't approved of his being round with her so much evenings. Of course it ain't as if their evenings were as pleasant as ours—since *we* don't seem to feel that way about the poison. I guess I *don't* see the point now; but I suppose he knows I'm a lady and I'd scorn to raise a fuss. Anyway, she wants you to realise she ain't engaged. I don't know why she makes so much of it, but she said to me three times, 'Mind you tell Mr. Winterbourne.' And then she told me to ask if you remembered the time you went up to that castle in Switzerland. But I said I would n't give any such messages as *that*. Only if she ain't engaged I guess I'm glad to realise it too."

But, as Winterbourne had originally judged, the truth on this question had small actual relevance. A week after this the poor girl died; it had been indeed a terrible case of the *perniciosa*. A grave was found for her in the little Protestant cemetery, by an angle of the wall of imperial Rome, beneath the cypresses and the thick spring-flowers. Winterbourne stood there beside it with a number of other mourners; a number larger than the scandal excited by the young lady's career might have made probable. Near him stood Giovanelli, who came nearer still before Winterbourne turned away. Giovanelli, in decorous mourning, showed but a whiter face; his button-hole lacked its nosegay and he had visibly something urgent—and even to distress—to say, which he scarce knew how to "place." He decided at last to confide it with a pale convulsion to Winterbourne. "She was the most beautiful young lady I ever saw, and the most amiable." To which he added in a moment: "Also—naturally!—the most innocent."

Winterbourne sounded him with hard dry eyes, but presently repeated his words, "The most innocent?"

"The most innocent!"

It came somehow so much too late that our friend could only glare at its having come at all. "Why the devil," he asked, "did you take her to that fatal place?"

Giovanelli raised his neat shoulders and eyebrows to within suspicion of a shrug. "For myself I had no fear; and *she*—she did what she liked."

Winterbourne's eyes attached themselves to the ground. "She did what she liked!"

It determined on the part of poor Giovanelli a further pious, a further candid, confidence. "If she had lived I should have got nothing. She never would have married me."

It had been spoken as if to attest, in all sincerity, his disinterestedness, but Winterbourne scarce knew what welcome to give it. He said, however, with a grace inferior to his friend's: "I dare say not."

The latter was even by this not discouraged. "For a moment I hoped so. But no. I'm convinced."

Winterbourne took it in; he stood staring at the raw protuberance among the April daisies. When he turned round again his fellow mourner had stepped back.

He almost immediately left Rome, but the following summer he again met his aunt Mrs. Costello at Vevey. Mrs. Costello extracted from the charming old hotel there a value that the Miller family had n't mastered the secret of. In the interval Winterbourne had often thought of the most interesting member of that trio—of her mystifying manners and her queer adventure. One day he spoke of her to his aunt—said it was on his conscience he had done her injustice.

"I'm sure I don't know"—that lady showed caution. "How did your injustice affect her?"

"She sent me a message before her death which I did n't understand at the time. But I've understood it since. She would have appreciated one's esteem."

"She took an odd way to gain it! But do you mean by what you say," Mrs. Costello asked, "that she would have reciprocated one's affection?"

As he made no answer to this she after a little looked round at him—he had n't been directly within sight; but the effect of that was n't to make her repeat her question. He spoke, however, after a while. "You were right in that remark that you made last summer. I was booked to make a mistake. I've lived too long in foreign parts." And this time she herself said nothing.

Nevertheless he soon went back to live at Geneva, whence there continue to come the most contradictory accounts of his motives of sojourn: a report that he's "studying" hard—an intimation that he's much interested in a very clever foreign lady.

1878, 1909

ON "DAISY MILLER" (*from* PREFACE)
["AN OUTRAGE ON AMERICAN GIRLHOOD"]

It was in Rome during the autumn of 1877; a friend then living there but settled now in a South less weighted with appeals and memories happened to mention—which she might perfectly not have done—some simple and uninformed American lady of the previous winter, whose young daughter, a child of nature and of freedom, accompanying her from hotel to hotel, had "picked up" by the wayside, with the best conscience in the world, a good-looking Roman, of vague identity, astonished at his luck, yet (so far as might be, by the pair) all innocently, all serenely exhibited and introduced: this at least till the occurrence of some small social check, some interrupting incident, of no great gravity or dignity, and which I forget. I had never heard, save on this showing, of the amiable but not otherwise eminent ladies, who were n't in fact named, I think, and whose case had merely served to point a familiar moral; and it must have been just their want of salience that left a margin for the small pencil-mark inveterately signifying, in such connexions, "Dramatise, dramatise!" The result of my recognising a few months later the sense of my pencil-mark was the short chronicle of "Daisy Miller," which I indited in London the following spring and then addressed, with no conditions attached, as I remember, to the editor of a magazine that had its seat of publication at Philadelphia and had lately appeared to appreciate my contributions. That gentleman however (an historian of some repute) promptly returned me my missive, and with an absence of comment that struck me at the time as rather grim—as, given the circumstances, requiring indeed some explanation: till a friend to whom I appealed for light, giving him the thing to read, declared it could only have passed with the Philadelphian critic for "an outrage on American girlhood." This was verily a light, and of bewildering intensity; though I was presently to read into the matter a further helpful inference. To the fault of being outrageous this little composition added that of being essentially and pre-eminently a *nouvelle*;[1] a signal example in fact of that type, foredoomed at the best, in more cases than not, to editorial disfavour. If accordingly I was afterwards to be cradled, almost blissfully, in the conception that "Daisy" at least, among my productions, might approach "success," such success for example, on her eventual appearance, as the state of being promptly pirated in Boston—a sweet tribute I had n't yet received and was never again to know—the irony of things yet claimed its rights, I could n't but long continue to feel, in the circumstance that quite a special reproba-

---

[1]Short novel.

tion had waited on the first appearance in the world of the ultimately most prosperous child of my invention. So doubly discredited, at all events, this bantling met indulgence, with no great delay, in the eyes of my admirable friend the late Leslie Stephen and was published in two numbers of *The Cornhill Magazine* (1878).[2]

It qualified itself in that publication and afterwards as "a Study"; for reasons which I confess I fail to recapture unless they may have taken account simply of a certain flatness in my poor little heroine's literal denomination. Flatness indeed, one must have felt, was the very sum of her story; so that perhaps after all the attached epithet was meant but as a deprecation, addressed to the reader, of any great critical hope of stirring scenes. It provided for mere concentration, and on an object scant and superficially vulgar—from which, however, a sufficiently brooding tenderness might eventually extract a shy incongruous charm. I suppress at all events here the appended qualification—in view of the simple truth, which ought from the first to have been apparent to me, that my little exhibition is made to no degree whatever in critical but, quite inordinately and extravagantly, in poetical terms. It comes back to me that I was at a certain hour long afterwards to have reflected, in this connexion, on the characteristic free play of the whirligig of time. It was in Italy again—in Venice and in the prized society of an interesting friend, now dead, with whom I happened to wait, on the Grand Canal, at the animated water-steps of one of the hotels. The considerable little terrace there was so disposed as to make a salient stage for certain demonstrations on the part of two young girls, children *they*, if ever, of nature and of freedom, whose use of those resources, in the general public eye, and under our own as we sat in the gondola, drew from the lips of a second companion, sociably afloat with us, the remark that there before us, with no sign absent, were a couple of attesting Daisy Millers. Then it was that, in my charming hostess's prompt protest, the whirligig, as I have called it, at once betrayed itself. "How can you liken *those* creatures to a figure of which the only fault is touchingly to have transmuted so sorry a type and to have, by a poetic artifice, not only led our judgement of it astray but made *any* judgement quite impossible?" With which this gentle lady and admirable critic turned on the author himself. "You *know* you quite falsified, by the turn you gave it, the thing you had begun with having in mind, the thing you had had, to satiety, the chance of 'observing': your pretty perversion of it, or your unprincipled mystification of our sense of it, does it really too much honour—in spite of which, none the less, as anything charming or touching always to that extent justifies itself, we after a fashion forgive and understand you. But why *waste* your romance? There are cases, too many, in which you've done it again; in which, provoked by a spirit of observation at first no doubt sufficiently sincere, and with the measured and felt truth fairly twitching your sleeve, you have yielded to your incurable prejudice in favour of grace—to whatever it is in you that makes so inordinately for form and prettiness and pathos; not to say sometimes for misplaced drolling. Is it that you've after all too much imagination? Those awful young women capering at the hotel-door, *they* are the real little Daisy Millers that were; whereas yours in the tale is such a one, more's the pity, as—for pitch of the ingenuous, for quality of the artless—could n't possibly have been at all." My answer to all which bristled of course with more professions than I can or need report here; the chief of them inevitably to the effect that my supposedly typical little figure was of course pure poetry, and had never been anything else; since this is what helpful imagination, in however slight a dose, ever directly makes for. As for the original grossness of readers, I dare say I added, that was another matter—but one which at any rate had then quite ceased to signify. . . .

1909

---

[2]British journal then edited by Sir Leslie Stephen (1832–1904), English man of letters, father of writer Virginia Woolf.

The Real Thing

I

When the porter's wife, who used to answer the house-bell, announced "A gentle-man and a lady, sir," I had, as I often had in those days—the wish being father to the thought—an immediate vision of sitters. Sitters my visitors in this case proved to be; but not in the sense I should have preferred. There was nothing at first however to indicate that they might n't have come for a portrait. The gentleman, a man of fifty, very high and very straight, with a moustache slightly grizzled and a dark grey walk-ing-coat admirably fitted, both of which I noted professionally—I don't mean as a barber or yet as a tailor—would have struck me as a celebrity if celebrities often were striking. It was a truth of which I had for some time been conscious that a figure with a good deal of frontage[1] was, as one might say, almost never a public institution. A glance at the lady helped to remind me of this paradoxical law: she also looked too distinguished to be a "personality." Moreover one would scarcely come across two variations together.

Neither of the pair immediately spoke—they only prolonged the preliminary gaze suggesting that each wished to give the other a chance. They were visibly shy; they stood there letting me take them in—which, as I afterwards perceived, was the most practical thing they could have done. In this way their embarrassment served their cause. I had seen people painfully reluctant to mention that they desired any-thing so gross as to be represented on canvas; but the scruples of my new friends appeared almost insurmountable. Yet the gentleman might have said "I should like a portrait of my wife," and the lady might have said "I should like a portrait of my husband." Perhaps they were n't husband and wife—this naturally would make the matter more delicate. Perhaps they wished to be done together—in which case they ought to have brought a third person to break the news.

"We come from Mr. Rivet," the lady finally said with a dim smile that had the effect of a moist sponge passed over a "sunk" piece of painting,[2] as well as of a vague allusion to vanished beauty. She was as tall and straight, in her degree, as her com-panion, and with ten years less to carry. She looked as sad as a woman could look whose face was not charged with expression; that is her tinted oval mask showed waste as an exposed surface shows friction. The hand of time had played over her freely, but to an effect of elimination. She was slim and stiff, and so well-dressed, in dark blue cloth, with lappets[3] and pockets and buttons, that it was clear she employed the same tailor as her husband. The couple had an indefinable air of prosperous thrift—they evidently got a good deal of luxury for their money. If I was to be one of their luxuries it would behove me to consider my terms.

"Ah Claude Rivet recommended me?" I echoed; and I added that it was very kind of him, though I could reflect that, as he only painted landscape, this was n't a sacrifice.

The lady looked very hard at the gentleman, and the gentleman looked round the room. Then staring at the floor a moment and stroking his moustache, he rested his pleasant eyes on me with the remark: "He said you were the right one."

"I try to be, when people want to sit."

"Yes, we should like to," said the lady anxiously.

"Do you mean together?"

My visitors exchanged a glance. "If you could do anything with *me* I suppose it would be double," the gentleman stammered.

---

[1] Impressive bearing.
[2] Part of a painting whose colors have dimmed.
[3] Hanging flaps such as lace.

"Oh yes, there's naturally a higher charge for two figures than for one."

"We should like to make it pay," the husband confessed.

"That's very good of you," I returned, appreciating so unwonted a sympathy—for I supposed he meant pay the artist.

A sense of strangeness seemed to dawn on the lady. "We mean for the illustrations—Mr. Rivet said you might put one in."

"Put in—an illustration?" I was equally confused.

"Sketch her off, you know," said the gentleman, colouring.

It was only then that I understood the service Claude Rivet had rendered me; he had told them how I worked in black-and-white, for magazines, for storybooks, for sketches of contemporary life, and consequently had copious employment for models. These things were true, but it was not less true—I may confess it now; whether because the aspiration was to lead to everything or to nothing I leave the reader to guess—that I could n't get the honours, to say nothing of the emoluments, of a great painter of portraits out of my head. My "illustrations" were my pot-boilers; I looked to a different branch of art—far and away the most interesting it had always seemed to me—to perpetuate my fame. There was no shame in looking to it also to make my fortune; but that fortune was by so much further from being made from the moment my visitors wished to be "done" for nothing. I was disappointed; for in the pictorial sense I had immediately *seen* them. I had seized their type—I had already settled what I would do with it. Something that would n't absolutely have pleased them, I afterwards reflected.

"Ah you're—you're—a—?" I began as soon as I had mastered my surprise. I could n't bring out the dingy word "models": it seemed so little to fit the case.

"We have n't had much practice," said the lady.

"We've got to *do* someting, and we've thought that an artist in your line might perhaps make something of us," her husband threw off. He further mentioned that they did n't know many artists and that they had gone first, on the off-chance—he painted views of course, but sometimes put in figures; perhaps I remembered—to Mr. Rivet, whom they had met a few years before at a place in Norfolk where he was sketching.

"We used to sketch a little ourselves," the lady hinted.

"It's very awkward, but we absolutely *must* do something," her husband went on.

"Of course we're not so *very* young," she admitted with a wan smile.

With the remark that I might as well know something more about them the husband handed me a card extracted from a neat new pocket-book—their appurtenances were all of the freshest—and inscribed with the words "Major Monarch." Impressive as these words were they did n't carry my knowledge much further; but my visitor presently added: "I've left the army and we've had the misfortune to lose our money. In fact our means are dreadfully small."

"It's awfully trying—a regular strain," said Mrs. Monarch.

They evidently wished to be discreet—to take care not to swagger because they were gentlefolk. I felt them willing to recognise this as something of a drawback, at the same time that I guessed at an underlying sense—their consolation in adversity—that they *had* their points. They certainly had; but these advantages struck me as preponderantly social; such for instance as would help to make a drawing-room look well. However, a drawing-room was always, or ought to be, a picture.

In consequence of his wife's allusion to their age Major Monarch observed: "Naturally it's more for the figure that we thought of going in. We can still hold ourselves up." On the instant I saw that the figure was indeed their strong point. His "naturally" did n't sound vain, but it lighted up the question. "*She* has the best one," he continued, nodding at his wife with a pleasant after-dinner absence of circumlocution. I could only reply, as if we were in fact sitting over our wine, that this did n't prevent his own from being very good; which led him in turn to make answer: "We thought that if you ever have to do people like us we might be something like it. *She* particularly—for a lady in a book, you know."

I was so amused by them that, to get more of it, I did my best to take their point of view; and though it was an embarrassment to find myself appraising physically, as if they were animals on hire or useful blacks, a pair whom I should have expected to meet only in one of the relations in which criticism is tacit, I looked at Mrs. Monarch judicially enough to be able to exclaim after a moment with conviction: "Oh yes, a lady in a book!" She was singularly like a bad illustration.

"We'll stand up, if you like," said the Major; and he raised himself before me with a really grand air.

I could take his measure at a glance—he was six feet two and a perfect gentleman. It would have paid any club in process of formation and in want of a stamp to engage him at a salary to stand in the principal window. What struck me at once was that in coming to me they had rather missed their vocation; they could surely have been turned to better account for advertising purposes. I could n't of course see the thing in detail, but I could see them make somebody's fortune—I don't mean their own. There was something in them for a waistcoat-maker, an hotel-keeper or a soap-vendor. I could imagine "We always use it" pinned on their bosoms with the greatest effect; I had a vision of the brilliancy with which they would launch a table d'hôte.[4]

Mrs. Monarch sat still, not from pride but from shyness, and presently her husband said to her: "Get up, my dear, and show how smart you are." She obeyed, but she had no need to get up to show it. She walked to the end of the studio and then came back blushing, her fluttered eyes on the partner of her appeal. I was reminded of an incident I had accidentally had a glimpse of in Paris—being with a friend there, a dramatist about to produce a play, when an actress came to him to ask to be entrusted with a part. She went through her paces before him, walked up and down as Mrs. Monarch was doing. Mrs. Monarch did it quite as well, but I abstained from applauding. It was very odd to see such people apply for such poor pay. She looked as if she had ten thousand a year. Her husband had used the word that described her: she was in the London current jargon essentially and typically "smart." Her figure was, in the same order of ideas, conspicuously and irreproachably "good." For a woman of her age her waist was surprisingly small; her elbow moreover had the orthodox crook. She held her head at the conventional angle, but why did she come to *me*? She ought to have tried on jackets at a big shop. I feared my visitors were not only destitute but "artistic"—which would be a great complication. When she sat down again I thanked her, observing that what a draughtsman most valued in his model was the faculty of keeping quiet.

"Oh *she* can keep quiet," said Major Monarch. Then he added jocosely: "I've always kept her quiet."

"I'm not a nasty fidget, am I?" It was going to wring tears from me, I felt, the way she hid her head, ostrich-like, in the other broad bosom.

The owner of this expanse addressed his answer to me. "Perhaps it is n't out of place to mention—because we ought to be quite business-like, ought n't we?—that when I married her she was known as the Beautiful Statue."

"Oh dear!" said Mrs. Monarch ruefully.

"Of course I should want a certain amount of expression," I rejoined.

"Of *course*!"—and I had never heard such unanimity.

"And then I suppose you know that you'll get awfully tired."

"Oh we *never* get tired!" they eagerly cried.

"Have you had any kind of practice?"

They hesitated—they looked at each other. "We've been photographed—*immensely*," said Mrs. Monarch.

---

[4]Common table for hotel guests, or fixed-price menu.

"She means the fellows have asked us themselves," added the Major.

"I see—because you're so good-looking."

"I don't know what they thought, but they were always after us."

"We always got our photographs for nothing," smiled Mrs. Monarch.

"We might have brought some, my dear," her husband remarked.

"I'm not sure we have any left. We've given quantities away," she explained to me.

"With our autographs and that sort of thing," said the Major.

"Are they to be got in the shops?" I enquired as a harmless pleasantry.

"Oh yes, *hers*—they used to be."

"Not now," said Mrs. Monarch with her eyes on the floor.

II

I could fancy the "sort of thing" they put on the presentation copies of their photographs, and I was sure they wrote a beautiful hand. It was odd how quickly I was sure of everything that concerned them. If they were now so poor as to have to earn shillings and pence they could never have had much of a margin. Their good looks had been their capital, and they had good-humouredly made the most of the career that this resource marked out for them. It was in their faces, the blankness, the deep intellectual repose of the twenty years of country-house visiting that had given them pleasant intonations. I could see the sunny drawing-rooms, sprinkled with periodicals she did n't read, in which Mrs. Monarch had continuously sat; I could see the wet shrubberies in which she had walked, equipped to admiration for either exercise. I could see the rich covers[5] the Major had helped to shoot and the wonderful garments in which, late at night, he repaired to the smoking-room to talk about them. I could imagine their leggings and waterproofs, their knowing tweeds and rugs, their rolls of sticks and cases of tackle and neat umbrellas; and I could evoke the exact appearance of their servants and the compact variety of their luggage on the platforms of country stations.

They gave small tips, but they were liked; they did n't do anything themselves, but they were welcome. They looked so well everywhere; they gratified the general relish for stature, complexion and "form." They knew it without fatuity or vulgarity, and they respected themselves in consequence. They were n't superficial; they were thorough and kept themselves up—it had been their line. People with such a taste for activity had to have some line. I could feel how even in a dull house they could have been counted on for the joy of life. At present something had happened—it did n't matter what, their little income had grown less, it had grown least—and they had to do something for pocket-money. Their friends could like them, I made out, without liking to support them. There was something about them that represented credit—their clothes, their manners, their type; but if credit is a large empty pocket in which an occasional chink reverberates, the chink at least must be audible. What they wanted of me was to help to make it so. Fortunately they had no children—I soon divined that. They would also perhaps wish our relations to be kept secret: this was why it was "for the figure"—the reproduction of the face would betray them.

I liked them—I felt, quite as their friends must have done—they were so simple; and I had no objection to them if they would suit. But somehow with all their perfections I did n't easily believe in them. After all they were amateurs, and the ruling passion of my life was the detestation of the amateur. Combined with this was another perversity—an innate preference for the represented subject over the real one: the defect of the real one was so apt to be a lack of representation. I liked things that appeared; then one was sure. Whether they *were* or not was a subordinate and almost always a profitless question. There were other considerations, the first of which was that I already had two or three recruits in use, notably a young person with

---

[5]Birds or animals hunted out of their cover, or shelter.

big feet, in alpaca, from Kilburn, who for a couple of years had come to me regularly for my illustrations and with whom I was still — perhaps ignobly — satisfied. I frankly explained to my visitors how the case stood, but they had taken more precautions than I supposed. They had reasoned out their opportunity, for Claude Rivet had told them of the projected *édition de luxe* of one of the writers of our day — the rarest of the novelists — who, long neglected by the multitudinous vulgar and dearly prized by the attentive (need I mention Philip Vincent?) had had the happy fortune of seeing, late in life, the dawn and then the full light of a higher criticism; an estimate in which on the part of the public there was something really of expiation. The edition preparing, planned by a publisher of taste, was practically an act of high reparation; the wood-cuts with which it was to be enriched were the homage of English art to one of the most independent representatives of English letters. Major and Mrs. Monarch confessed to me they had hoped I might be able to work *them* into my branch of the enterprise. They knew I was to do the first of the books, "Rutland Ramsay," but I had to make clear to them that my participation in the rest of the affair — this first book was to be a test — must depend on the satisfaction I should give. If this should be limited my employers would drop me with scarce common forms. It was therefore a crisis for me, and naturally I was making special preparations, looking about for new people, should they be necessary, and securing the best types. I admitted however that I should like to settle down to two or three good models who would do for everything.

"Should we have often to — a — put on special clothes?" Mrs. Monarch timidly demanded.

"Dear yes — that's half the business."

"And should we be expected to supply our own costumes?"

"Oh no; I've got a lot of things. A painter's models put on — or put off — anything he likes."

"And you mean — a — the same?"

"The same?"

Mrs. Monarch looked at her husband again.

"Oh she was just wondering," he explained, "if the costumes are in *general* use." I had to confess that they were, and I mentioned further that some of them — I had a lot of genuine greasy last-century things — had served their time, a hundred years ago, on living world-stained men and women; on figures not perhaps so far removed, in that vanished world, from *their* type, the Monarchs', *quoi!*[6] of a breeched and be-wigged age. "We'll put on anything that *fits*," said the Major.

"Oh I arrange that — they fit in the pictures."

"I'm afraid I should do better for the modern books. I'd come as you like," said Mrs. Monarch.

"She has a lot of clothes at home: they might do for contemporary life," her husband continued.

"Oh I can fancy scenes in which you'd be quite natural." And indeed I could see the slipshod rearrangements of stale properties — the stories I tried to produce pictures for without the exasperation of reading them — whose sandy tracts the good lady might help to people. But I had to return to the fact that for this sort of work — the daily mechanical grind — I was already equipped: the people I was working with were fully adequate.

"We only thought we might be more like *some* characters," said Mrs. Monarch mildly, getting up.

Her husband also rose; he stood looking at me with a dim wistfulness that was touching in so fine a man. "Would n't it be rather a pull sometimes to have — a — to have — ?" He hung fire; he wanted me to help him by phrasing what he meant. But I

6"What!" (French).

could n't—I did n't know. So he brought it out awkwardly: "The *real* thing; a gentleman, you know, or a lady." I was quite ready to give a general assent—I admitted that there was a great deal in that. This encouraged Major Monarch to say, following up his appeal with an unacted gulp: "It's awfully hard—we've tried everything." The gulp was communicative; it proved too much for his wife. Before I knew it Mrs. Monarch had dropped again upon a divan and burst into tears. Her husband sat down beside her, holding one of her hands; whereupon she quickly dried her eyes with the other, while I felt embarrassed as she looked up at me. "There is n't a confounded job I have n't applied for—waited for—prayed for. You can fancy we'd be pretty bad first. Secretaryships and that sort of thing? You might as well ask for a peerage. I'd be *anything*—I'm strong; a messenger or a coalheaver. I'd put on a gold-laced cap and open carriage-doors in front of the haberdasher's; I'd hang about a station to carry portmanteaux;[7] I'd be a postman. But they won't *look* at you; there are thousands as good as yourself already on the ground. *Gentlemen*, poor beggars, who've drunk their wine, who've kept their hunters!"

I was as reassuring as I knew how to be, and my visitors were presently on their feet again while, for the experiment, we agreed on an hour. We were discussing it when the door opened and Miss Churm came in with a wet umbrella. Miss Churm had to take the omnibus to Maida Vale and then walk half a mile. She looked a trifle blowsy and slightly splashed. I scarcely ever saw her come in without thinking afresh how odd it was that, being so little in herself, she should yet be so much in others. She was a meagre little Miss Churm, but was such an ample heroine of romance. She was only a freckled cockney,[8] but she could represent everything, from a fine lady to a shepherdess; she had the faculty as she might have had a fine voice or long hair. She could n't spell and she loved beer, but she had two or three "points," and practice, and a knack, and mother-wit, and a whimsical sensibility, and a love of the theatre, and seven sisters, and not an ounce of respect, especially for the *h*. The first thing my visitors saw was that her umbrella was wet, and in their spotless perfection they visibly winced at it. The rain had come on since their arrival.

"I'm all in a soak; there *was* a mess of people in the 'bus. I wish you lived near a stytion," said Miss Churm. I requested her to get ready as quickly as possible, and she passed into the room in which she always changed her dress. But before going out she asked me what she was to get into this time.

"It's the Russian princess, don't you know?" I answered; "the one with the 'golden eyes,' in black velvet, for the long thing in the *Cheapside*."[9]

"Golden eyes? I *say*!" cried Miss Churm, while my companions watched her with intensity as she withdrew. She always arranged herself, when she was late, before I could turn round; and I kept my visitors a little on purpose, so that they might get an idea, from seeing her, what would be expected of themselves. I mentioned that she was quite my notion of an excellent model—she was really very clever.

"Do you think she looks like a Russian princess?" Major Monarch asked with lurking alarm.

"When I make her, yes."

"Oh if you have to *make* her—!" he reasoned, not without point.

"That's the most you can ask. There are so many who are not makeable."

"Well now, *here's* a lady"—and with a persuasive smile he passed his arm into his wife's—"who's already made!"

"Oh I'm not a Russian princess," Mrs. Monarch protested a little coldly. I could see she had known some and did n't like them. There at once was a complication of a kind I never had to fear with Miss Churm.

[7]Large travelling cases.
[8]From London's lower classes in the East End slums, speaking a dialect noted for dropped *h*'s.
[9]Imaginary journal bearing the name of a London commercial street.

This young lady came back in black velvet—the gown was rather rusty and very low on her lean shoulders—and with a Japanese fan in her red hands. I reminded her that in the scene I was doing she had to look over some one's head. "I forget whose it is; but it does n't matter. Just look over a head."

"I'd rather look over a stove," said Miss Churm; and she took her station near the fire. She fell into position, settled herself into a tall attitude, gave a certain backward inclination to her head and a certain forward droop to her fan, and looked, at least to my prejudiced sense, distinguished and charming, foreign and dangerous. We left her looking so while I went downstairs with Major and Mrs. Monarch.

"I believe I could come about as near it as that," said Mrs. Monarch.

"Oh you think she's shabby, but you must allow for the alchemy of art."

However, they went off with an evident increase of comfort founded on their demonstrable advantage in being the real thing. I could fancy them shuddering over Miss Churm. She was very droll about them when I went back, for I told her what they wanted.

"Well, if *she* can sit I'll tyke to bookkeeping," said my model.

"She's very ladylike," I replied as an innocent form of aggravation.

"So much the worse for *you*. That means she can't turn round."

"She'll do for the fashionable novels."

"Oh yes, she'll *do* for them!" my model humorously declared. "Ain't they bad enough without her?" I had often sociably denounced them to Miss Churm.

III

It was for the elucidation of a mystery in one of these works that I first tried Mrs. Monarch. Her husband came with her, to be useful if necessary—it was sufficiently clear that as a general thing he would prefer to come with her. At first I wondered if this were for "propriety's" sake—if he were going to be jealous and meddling. The idea was too tiresome, and if it had been confirmed it would speedily have brought our acquaintance to a close. But I soon saw there was nothing in it and that if he accompanied Mrs. Monarch it was—in addition to the chance of being wanted— simply because he had nothing else to do. When they were separate his occupation was gone and they never *had* been separate. I judged rightly that in their awkward situation their close union was their main comfort and that this union had no weak spot. It was a real marriage, an encouragement to the hesitating, a nut for pessimists to crack. Their address was humble—I remember afterwards thinking it had been the only thing about them that was really professional—and I could fancy the lamentable lodgings in which the Major would have been left alone. He could sit there more or less grimly with his wife—he could n't sit there anyhow without her.

He had too much tact to try and make himself agreeable when he could n't be useful; so when I was too absorbed in my work to talk he simply sat and waited. But I liked to hear him talk—it made my work, when not interrupting it, less mechanical, less special. To listen to him was to combine the excitement of going out with the economy of staying at home. There was only one hindrance—that I seemed not to know any of the people this brilliant couple had known. I think he wondered extremely, during the term of our intercourse, whom the deuce I *did* know. He had n't a stray sixpence of an idea to fumble for, so we did n't spin it very fine; we confined ourselves to questions of leather and even of liquor—saddlers and breeches-makers and how to get excellent claret cheap—and matters like "good trains" and the habits of small game. His lore on these last subjects was astonishing—he managed to interweave the station-master with the ornithologist. When he could n't talk about greater things he could talk cheerfully about smaller, and since I could n't accompany him into reminiscences of the fashionable world he could lower the conversation without a visible effort to my level.

So earnest a desire to please was touching in a man who could so easily have

knocked one down. He looked after the fire and had an opinion on the draught of
the stove without my asking him, and I could see that he thought many of my arrangements not half knowing. I remember telling him that if I were only rich I'd
offer him a salary to come and teach me how to live. Sometimes he gave a random
sigh of which the essence might have been: "Give me even such a bare old barrack as
this, and I'd do something with it!" When I wanted to use him he came alone; which
was an illustration of the superior courage of women. His wife could bear her solitary
second floor, and she was in general more discreet; showing by various small reserves
that she was alive to the propriety of keeping our relations markedly professional—
not letting them slide into sociability. She wished it to remain clear that she and the
Major were employed, not cultivated, and if she approved of me as a superior, who
could be kept in his place, she never thought me quite good enough for an equal.

She sat with great intensity, giving the whole of her mind to it, and was capable of
remaining for an hour almost as motionless as before a photographer's lens. I could
see she had been photographed often, but somehow the very habit that made her
good for that purpose unfitted her for mine. At first I was extremely pleased with her
ladylike air, and it was a satisfaction, on coming to follow her lines, to see how good
they were and how far they could lead the pencil. But after a little skirmishing I
began to find her too insurmountably stiff; do what I would with it my drawing
looked like a photograph or a copy of a photograph. Her figure had no variety of
expression—she herself had no sense of variety. You may say that this was my business and was only a question of placing her. Yet I placed her in every conceivable
position and she managed to obliterate their differences. She was always a lady certainly, and into the bargain was always the same lady. She was the real thing, but
always the same thing. There were moments when I rather writhed under the serenity of her confidence that she *was* the real thing. All her dealings with me and all her
husband's were an implication that this was lucky for *me*. Meanwhile I found myself
trying to invent types that approached her own, instead of making her own transform itself—in the clever way that was not impossible for instance to poor Miss
Churm. Arrange as I would and take the precautions I would, she always came out,
in my pictures, too tall—landing me in the dilemma of having represented a fascinating woman as seven feet high, which (out of respect perhaps to my own very much
scantier inches) was far from my idea of such a personage.

The case was worse with the Major—nothing I could do would keep *him* down, so
that he became useful only for the representation of brawny giants. I adored variety
and range, I cherished human accidents, the illustrative note; I wanted to characterise closely, and the thing in the world I most hated was the danger of being ridden
by a type. I had quarrelled with some of my friends about it; I had parted company
with them for maintaining that one *had* to be, and that if the type was beautiful—
witness Raphael and Leonardo[10]—the servitude was only a gain. I was neither
Leonardo nor Raphael—I might only be a presumptuous young modern searcher;
but I held that everything was to be sacrificed sooner than character. When they
claimed that the obsessional form could easily *be* character I retorted, perhaps superficially, "Whose?" It could n't be everybody's—it might end in being nobody's.

After I had drawn Mrs. Monarch a dozen times I felt surer even than before that
the value of such a model as Miss Churm resided precisely in the fact that she had no
positive stamp, combined of course with the other fact that what she did have was a
curious and inexplicable talent for imitation. Her usual appearance was like a curtain
which she could draw up at request for a capital performance. This performance was
simply suggestive; but it was a word to the wise—it was vivid and pretty. Sometimes
even I thought it, though she was plain herself, too insipidly pretty; I made it a

[10]Raphael Sanzio (1483–1520) and Leonardo da Vinci
(1452–1519), famed Italian Renaissance painters.

reproach to her that the figures drawn from her were monotonously (*bêtement,*[11] as we used to say) graceful. Nothing made her more angry: it was so much her pride to feel she could sit for characters that had nothing in common with each other. She would accuse me at such moments of taking away her "reputytion."

It suffered a certain shrinkage, this queer quantity, from the repeated visits of my new friends. Miss Churm was greatly in demand, never in want of employment, so I had no scruple in putting her off occasionally, to try them more at my ease. It was certainly amusing at first to do the real thing—it was amusing to do Major Monarch's trousers. They *were* the real thing, even if he did come out colossal. It was amusing to do his wife's back hair—it was so mathematically neat—and the particular "smart" tension of her tight stays. She lent herself especially to positions in which the face was somewhat averted or blurred; she abounded in ladylike back views and *profils perdus.*[12] When she stood erect she took naturally one of the attitudes in which court-painters represent queens and princesses; so that I found myself wondering whether, to draw out this accomplishment, I could n't get the editor of the *Cheapside* to publish a really royal romance, "A Tale of Buckingham Palace." Sometimes however the real thing and the make-believe came into contact; by which I mean that Miss Churm, keeping an appointment or coming to make one on days when I had much work in hand, encountered her invidious rivals. The encounter was not on their part, for they noticed her no more than if she had been the housemaid; not from intentional loftiness, but simply because as yet, professionally, they did n't know how to fraternise, as I could imagine they would have liked—or at least that the Major would. They could n't talk about the omnibus—they always walked; and they did n't know what else to try—she was n't interested in good trains or cheap claret. Besides, they must have felt—in the air—that she was amused at them, secretly derisive of their ever knowing how. She was n't a person to conceal the limits of her faith if she had had a chance to show them. On the other hand Mrs. Monarch did n't think her tidy; for why else did she take pains to say to me—it was going out of the way, for Mrs. Monarch—that she did n't like dirty women?

One day when my young lady happened to be present with my other sitters—she even dropped in, when it was convenient, for a chat—I asked her to be so good as to lend a hand in getting tea, a service with which she was familiar and which was one of a class that, living as I did in a small way, with slender domestic resources, I often appealed to my models to render. They liked to lay hands on my property, to break the sitting, and sometimes the china—it made them feel Bohemian. The next time I saw Miss Churm after this incident she surprised me greatly by making a scene about it—she accused me of having wished to humiliate her. She had n't resented the outrage at the time, but had seemed obliging and amused, enjoying the comedy of asking Mrs. Monarch, who sat vague and silent, whether she would have cream and sugar, and putting an exaggerated simper into the question. She had tried intonations—as if she too wished to pass for the real thing—till I was afraid my other visitors would take offence.

Oh they were determined not to do this, and their touching patience was the measure of their great need. They would sit by the hour, uncomplaining, till I was ready to use them; they would come back on the chance of being wanted and would walk away cheerfully if it failed. I used to go to the door with them to see in what magnificent order they retreated. I tried to find other employment for them—I introduced them to several artists. But they did n't "take," for reasons I could appreciate, and I became rather anxiously aware that after such disappointments they fell

---

[11]"Stupidly" (French).
[12]"Lost profiles" (French); i.e., incomplete profiles, showing more of the back of the head and less of the face.

back upon me with a heavier weight. They did me the honour to think me most *their* form. They were n't romantic enough for the painters, and in those days there were few serious workers in black-and-white. Besides, they had an eye to the great job I had mentioned to them—they had secretly set their hearts on supplying the right essence for my pictorial vindication of our fine novelist. They knew that for this undertaking I should want no costume-effects, none of the frippery of past ages— that it was a case in which everything would be contemporary and satirical and pre- sumably genteel. If I could work them into it their future would be assured, for the labour would of course be long and the occupation steady.

One day Mrs. Monarch came without her husband—she explained his absence by his having had to go to the City. While she sat there in her usual relaxed majesty there came at the door a knock which I immediately recognised as the subdued appeal of a model out of work. It was followed by the entrance of a young man whom I at once saw to be a foreigner and who proved in fact an Italian acquainted with no English word but my name, which he uttered in a way that made it seem to include all others. I had n't then visited his country, nor was I proficient in his tongue; but as he was not so meanly constituted—what Italian is?—as to depend only on that member for expression he conveyed to me, in familiar but graceful mimicry, that he was in search of exactly the employment in which the lady before me was engaged. I was not struck with him at first, and while I continued to draw I dropped few signs of interest or encouragement. He stood his ground however—not importunately, but with a dumb dog-like fidelity in his eyes that amounted to innocent impudence, the manner of a devoted servant—he might have been in the house for years—unjustly suspected. Suddenly it struck me that this very attitude and expression made a picture; where- upon I told him to sit down and wait till I should be free. There was another picture in the way he obeyed me, and I observed as I worked that there were others still in the way he looked wonderingly, with his head thrown back, about the high studio. He might have been crossing himself in Saint Peter's. Before I finished I said to myself "The fellow's a bankrupt orange-monger, but a treasure."

When Mrs. Monarch withdrew he passed across the room like a flash to open the door for her, standing there with the rapt pure gaze of the young Dante spellbound by the young Beatrice.[13] As I never insisted, in such situations, on the blankness of the British domestic, I reflected that he had the making of a servant—and I needed one, but could n't pay him to be only that—as well as of a model; in short I resolved to adopt my bright adventurer if he would agree to officiate in the double capacity. He jumped at my offer, and in the event my rashness—for I had really known nothing about him—was n't brought home to me. He proved a sympathetic though a desul- tory ministrant, and had in a wonderful degree the *sentiment de la pose.*[14] It was un- cultivated, instinctive, a part of the happy instinct that had guided him to my door and helped him to spell out my name on the card nailed to it. He had had no other introduction to me than a guess, from the shape of my high north window, seen outside, that my place was a studio and that as a studio it would contain an artist. He had wandered to England in search of fortune, like other itinerants, and had em- barked, with a partner and a small green hand-cart, on the sale of penny ices. The ices had melted away and the partner had dissolved in their train. My young man wore tight yellow trousers with reddish stripes and his name was Oronte. He was sallow but fair, and when I put him into some old clothes of my own he looked like an Englishman. He was as good as Miss Churm, who could look, when requested, like an Italian.

---

[13]Dante Alighieri (1265–1321), Italian poet, saw Beatrice only twice, when he was nine and eighteen, but loved her from afar, making her into his ideal lady, his inspiration, and the means of his salvation in his epic poem *The Divine Comedy*.
[14]"Intuitive notion of how to pose" (French).

IV

I thought Mrs. Monarch's face slightly convulsed when, on her coming back with her husband, she found Oronte installed. It was strange to have to recognise in a scrap of a lazzarone[15] a competitor to her magnificent Major. It was she who scented danger first, for the Major was anecdotically unconscious. But Oronte gave us tea, with a hundred eager confusions — he had never been concerned in so queer a process — and I think she thought better of me for having at last an "establishment." They saw a couple of drawings that I had made of the establishment, and Mrs. Monarch hinted that it never would have struck her he had sat for them. "Now the drawings you make from *us*, they look exactly like us," she reminded me, smiling in triumph; and I recognised that this was indeed just their defect. When I drew the Monarchs I couldn't anyhow get away from them — get into the character I wanted to represent; and I had n't the least desire my model should be discoverable in my picture. Miss Churm never was, and Mrs. Monarch thought I hid her, very properly, because she was vulgar; whereas if she was lost it was only as the dead who go to heaven are lost — in the gain of an angel the more.

By this time I had got a certain start with "Rutland Ramsay," the first novel in the great projected series; that is I had produced a dozen drawings, several with the help of the Major and his wife, and I had sent them in for approval. My understanding with the publishers, as I have already hinted, had been that I was to be left to do my work, in this particular case, as I liked, with the whole book committed to me; but my connexion with the rest of the series was only contingent. There were moments when, frankly, it *was* a comfort to have the real thing under one's hand; for there were characters in "Rutland Ramsay" that were very much like it. There were people presumably as erect as the Major and women of as good a fashion as Mrs. Monarch. There was a great deal of country-house life — treated, it is true, in a fine fanciful ironical generalised way — and there was a considerable implication of knickerbockers and kilts.[16] There were certain things I had to settle at the outset; such things for instance as the exact appearance of the hero and the particular bloom and figure of the heroine. The author of course gave me a lead, but there was a margin for interpretation. I took the Monarchs into my confidence, I told them frankly what I was about, I mentioned my embarrassments and alternatives. "Oh take *him*!" Mrs. Monarch murmured sweetly, looking at her husband; and "What could you want better than my wife?" the Major enquired with the comfortable candour that now prevailed between us.

I was n't obliged to answer these remarks — I was only obliged to place my sitters. I was n't easy in mind, and I postponed a little timidly perhaps the solving of my question. The book was a large canvas, the other figures were numerous, and I worked off at first some of the episodes in which the hero and the heroine were not concerned. When once I had set *them* up I should have to stick to them — I could n't make my young man seven feet high in one place and five feet nine in another. I inclined on the whole to the latter measurement, though the Major more than once reminded me that *he* looked about as young as any one. It was indeed quite possible to arrange him, for the figure, so that it would have been difficult to detect his age. After the spontaneous Oronte had been with me a month, and after I had given him to understand several times over that his native exuberance would presently constitute an insurmountable barrier to our further intercourse, I waked to a sense of his heroic capacity. He was only five feet seven, but the remaining inches were latent. I tried him almost secretly at first, for I was really rather afraid of the judgement my other models would pass on such a choice. If they regarded Miss Churm as little

---

[15]"Beggar" (Italian).
[16]Knickerbockers, short pants gathered at the knees; kilts, colorful, pleated knee-length skirts for men (originating in Scotland). This wear suggests country, outdoor life.

better than a snare what would they think of the representation by a person so little the real thing as an Italian street-vendor of a protagonist formed by a public school?

If I went a little in fear of them it wasn't because they bullied me, because they had got an oppressive foothold, but because in their really pathetic decorum and mysteriously permanent newness they counted on me so intensely. I was therefore very glad when Jack Hawley came home: he was always of such good counsel. He painted badly himself, but there was no one like him for putting his finger on the place. He had been absent from England for a year; he had been somewhere — I don't remember where — to get a fresh eye. I was in a good deal of dread of any such organ, but we were old friends; he had been away for months and a sense of emptiness was creeping into my life. I hadn't dodged a missile for a year.

He came back with a fresh eye, but with the same old black velvet blouse, and the first evening he spent in my studio we smoked cigarettes till the small hours. He had done no work himself, he had only got the eye; so the field was clear for the production of my little things. He wanted to see what I had produced for the *Cheapside*, but he was disappointed in the exhibition. That at least seemed the meaning of two or three comprehensive groans which, as he lounged on my big divan, his leg folded under him, looking at my latest drawings, issued from his lips with the smoke of the cigarette.

"What's the matter with you?" I asked.

"What's the matter with *you?*"

"Nothing save that I'm mystified."

"You are indeed. You're quite off the hinge. What's the meaning of this new fad?" And he tossed me, with visible irreverence, a drawing in which I happened to have depicted both my elegant models. I asked if he didn't think it good, and he replied that it struck him as execrable, given the sort of thing I had always represented myself to him as wishing to arrive at; but I let that pass — I was so anxious to see exactly what he meant. The two figures in the picture looked colossal, but I supposed this was *not* what he meant, inasmuch as, for aught he knew to the contrary, I might have been trying for some such effect. I maintained that I was working exactly in the same way as when he last had done me the honour to tell me I might do something some day. "Well, there's a screw loose somewhere," he answered; "wait a bit and I'll discover it." I depended upon him to do so: where else was the fresh eye? But he produced at last nothing more luminous than "I don't know — I don't like your types." This was lame for a critic who had never consented to discuss with me anything but the question of execution, the direction of strokes and the mystery of values.

"In the drawings you've been looking at I think my types are very handsome."

"Oh they won't do!"

"I've been working with new models."

"I see you have. *They* won't do."

"Are you sure of that?"

"Absolutely — they're stupid."

"You mean *I* am — for I ought to get round that."

"You *can't* — with such people. Who are they?"

I told him, so far as was necessary, and he concluded heartlessly: "Ce sont des gens qu'il faut mettre à la porte."[17]

"You've never seen them; they're awfully good" — I flew to their defence.

"Not seen them? Why all this recent work of yours drops to pieces with them. It's all I want to see of them."

"No one else has said anything against it — the *Cheapside* people are pleased."

"Every one else is an ass, and the *Cheapside* people the biggest asses of all. Come, don't pretend at this time of day to have pretty illusions about the public, especially

---

[17]"They are people one must show to the door" (French).

about publishers and editors. It's not for *such* animals you work—it's for those who know, *coloro che sanno*;[18] so keep straight for *me* if you can't keep straight for yourself. There was a certain sort of thing you used to try for—and a very good thing it was. But this twaddle is n't *in it*." When I talked with Hawley later about "Rutland Ramsay" and its possible successors he declared that I must get back into my boat again or I should go to the bottom. His voice in short was the voice of warning.

I noted the warning, but I did n't turn my friends out of doors. They bored me a good deal; but the very fact that they bored me admonished me not to sacrifice them—if there was anything to be done with them—simply to irritation. As I look back at this phase they seem to me to have pervaded my life not a little. I have a vision of them as most of the time in my studio, seated against the wall on an old velvet bench to be out of the way, and resembling the while a pair of patient courtiers in a royal ante-chamber. I'm convinced that during the coldest weeks of the winter they held their ground because it saved them fire. Their newness was losing its gloss, and it was impossible not to feel them objects of charity. Whenever Miss Churm arrived they went away, and after I was fairly launched in "Rutland Ramsay" Miss Churm arrived pretty often. They managed to express to me tacitly that they supposed I wanted her for the low life of the book, and I let them suppose it, since they had attempted to study the work—it was lying about the studio—without discovering that it dealt only with the highest circles. They had dipped into the most brilliant of our novelists without deciphering many passages. I still took an hour from them, now and again, in spite of Jack Hawley's warning: it would be time enough to dismiss them, if dismissal should be necessary, when the rigour of the season was over. Hawley had made their acquaintance—he had met them at my fireside—and thought them a ridiculous pair. Learning that he was a painter they tried to approach him, to show him too that they were the real thing; but he looked at them, across the big room, as if they were miles away: they were a compendium of everything he most objected to in the social system of his country. Such people as that, all convention and patent-leather, with ejaculations that stopped conversation, had no business in a studio. A studio was a place to learn to see, and how could you see through a pair of feather-beds?

The main inconvenience I suffered at their hands was that at first I was shy of letting it break upon them that my artful little servant had begun to sit to me for "Rutland Ramsay." They knew I had been odd enough—they were prepared by this time to allow oddity to artists—to pick a foreign vagabond out of the streets when I might have had a person with whiskers and credentials; but it was some time before they learned how high I rated his accomplishments. They found him in an attitude more than once, but they never doubted I was doing him as an organ-grinder. There were several things they never guessed, and one of them was that for a striking scene in the novel, in which a footman briefly figured, it occurred to me to make use of Major Monarch as the menial. I kept putting this off, I did n't like to ask him to don the livery—besides the difficulty of finding a livery to fit him. At last, one day late in the winter, when I was at work on the despised Oronte, who caught one's idea on the wing, and was in the glow of feeling myself go very straight, they came in, the Major and his wife, with their society laugh about nothing (there was less and less to laugh at); came in like country-callers—they always reminded me of that—who have walked across the park after church and are presently persuaded to stay to luncheon. Luncheon was over, but they could stay to tea—I knew they wanted it. The fit was on me, however, and I could n't let my ardour cool and my work wait, with the fading daylight, while my model prepared it. So I asked Mrs. Monarch if she would mind laying it out—a request which for an instant brought all the blood to her face. Her

---

[18]"Those who know" (Italian); said of Aristotle in Dante's *Inferno*, iv, 131.

eyes were on her husband's for a second, and some mute telegraphy passed between them. Their folly was over the next instant; his cheerful shrewdness put an end to it. So far from pitying their wounded pride, I must add, I was moved to give it as complete a lesson as I could. They bustled about together and got out the cups and saucers and made the kettle boil. I know they felt as if they were waiting on my servant, and when the tea was prepared I said: "He'll have a cup, please — he's tired." Mrs. Monarch brought him one where he stood, and he took it from her as if he had been a gentleman at a party squeezing a crush-hat with an elbow.

Then it came over me that she had made a great effort for me — made it with a kind of nobleness — and that I owed her a compensation. Each time I saw her after this I wondered what the compensation could be. I could n't go on doing the wrong thing to oblige them. Oh it *was* the wrong thing, the stamp of the work for which they sat — Hawley was not the only person to say it now. I sent in a large number of the drawings I had made for "Rutland Ramsay," and I received a warning that was more to the point than Hawley's. The artistic adviser of the house for which I was working was of the opinion that many of my illustrations were not what had been looked for. Most of these illustrations were the subjects in which the Monarchs had figured. Without going into the question of what *had* been looked for, I had to face the fact that at this rate I should n't get the other books to do. I hurled myself in despair on Miss Churm — I put her through all her paces. I not only adopted Oronte publicly as my hero, but one morning when the Major looked in to see if I did n't require him to finish a *Cheapside* figure for which he had begun to sit the week before, I told him I had changed my mind — I'd do the drawing from my man. At this my visitor turned pale and stood looking at me. "Is *he* your idea of an English gentleman?" he asked.

I was disappointed, I was nervous, I wanted to get on with my work; so I replied with irritation: "Oh my dear Major — I can't be ruined for *you!*"

It was a horrid speech, but he stood another moment — after which, without a word, he quitted the studio. I drew a long breath, for I said to myself that I should n't see him again. I had n't told him definitely that I was in danger of having my work rejected, but I was vexed at his not having felt the catastrophe in the air, read with me the moral of our fruitless collaboration, the lesson that in the deceptive atmosphere of art even the highest respectability may fail of being plastic.

I did n't owe my friends money, but I did see them again. They reappeared together three days later, and, given all the other facts, there was something tragic in that one. It was a clear proof they could find nothing else in life to do. They had threshed the matter out in a dismal conference — they had digested the bad news that they were not in for the series. If they were n't useful to me even for the *Cheapside* their function seemed difficult to determine, and I could only judge at first that they had come, forgivingly, decorously, to take a last leave. This made me rejoice in secret that I had little leisure for a scene; for I had placed both my other models in position together and I was pegging away at a drawing from which I hoped to derive glory. It had been suggested by the passage in which Rutland Ramsay, drawing up a chair to Artemisia's piano-stool, says extraordinary things to her while she ostensibly fingers out a difficult piece of music. I had done Miss Churm at the piano before — it was an attitude in which she knew how to take on an absolutely poetic grace. I wished the two figures to "compose" together with intensity, and my little Italian had entered perfectly into my conception. The pair were vividly before me, the piano had been pulled out; it was a charming show of blended youth and murmured love, which I had only to catch and keep. My visitors stood and looked at it, and I was friendly to them over my shoulder.

They made no response, but I was used to silent company and went on with my work, only a little disconcerted — even though exhilarated by the sense that *this* was at least the ideal thing — at not having got rid of them after all. Presently I heard Mrs. Monarch's sweet voice beside or rather above me: "I wish her hair were a little better done." I looked up and she was staring with a strange fixedness at Miss Churm, whose back was turned to her. "Do you mind my just touching it?" she went on — a question which made me spring up for an instant as with the instinctive fear that she might do the young lady a harm. But she quieted me with a glance I shall never forget — I confess I should like to have been able to paint *that* — and went for a moment to my model. She spoke to her softly, laying a hand on her shoulder and bending over her; and as the girl, understanding, gratefully assented, she disposed her rough curls, with a few quick passes, in such a way as to make Miss Churm's head twice as charming. It was one of the most heroic personal services I've ever seen rendered. Then Mrs. Monarch turned away with a low sigh and, looking about her as if for something to do, stooped to the floor with a noble humility and picked up a dirty rag that had dropped out of my paint-box.

The Major meanwhile had also been looking for something to do, and, wandering to the other end of the studio, saw before him my breakfast-things neglected, unremoved. "I say, can't I be useful *here*?" he called out to me with an irrepressible quaver. I assented with a laugh that I fear was awkward, and for the next ten minutes, while I worked, I heard the light clatter of china and the tinkle of spoons and glass. Mrs. Monarch assisted her husband — they washed up my crockery, they put it away. They wandered off into my little scullery, and I afterwards found that they had cleaned my knives and that my slender stock of plate had an unprecedented surface. When it came over me, the latent eloquence of what they were doing, I confess that my drawing was blurred for a moment — the picture swam. They had accepted their failure, but they couldn't accept their fate. They had bowed their heads in bewilderment to the perverse and cruel law in virtue of which the real thing could be so much less precious than the unreal; but they didn't want to starve. If my servants were my models, then my models might be my servants. They would reverse the parts — the others would sit for the ladies and gentlemen and *they* would do the work. They would still be in the studio — it was an intense dumb appeal to me not to turn them out. "Take us on," they wanted to say — "we'll do *anything*."

My pencil dropped from my hand; my sitting was spoiled and I got rid of my sitters, who were also evidently rather mystified and awestruck. Then, alone with the Major and his wife I had a most uncomfortable moment. He put their prayer into a single sentence: "I say, you know — just let *us* do for you, can't you?" I couldn't — it was dreadful to see them emptying my slops; but I pretended I could, to oblige them, for about a week. Then I gave them a sum of money to go away, and I never saw them again. I obtained the remaining books, but my friend Hawley repeats that Major and Mrs. Monarch did me a permanent harm, got me into false ways. If it be true I'm content to have paid the price — for the memory.

1892, 1909

ON "THE REAL THING" (*from* PREFACE)

[ORIGINS IN REAL LIFE]

. . . [M]y much-loved friend George du Maurier[1] had spoken to me of a call from a strange and striking couple desirous to propose themselves as artist's models for his weekly "social" illustrations to *Punch*, and the acceptance of whose services would have entailed the dismissal of an undistinguished but highly expert pair, also husband and wife, who had come to him from far back on the irregular day and whom, thanks to a happy, and to that extent lucrative, appearance of "type" on the part of

---

[1]George du Maurier (1834–1896), English novelist and illustrator, famed for his caricatures in *Punch*, an English comic weekly.

each, he had reproduced, to the best effect, in a thousand drawing-room attitudes and combinations. Exceedingly modest members of society, they earned their bread by looking and, with the aid of supplied toggery, dressing, greater favourites of fortune to the life; or, otherwise expressed, by skilfully feigning a virtue not in the least native to them. Here meanwhile were their so handsome proposed, so anxious, so almost haggard competitors, originally, by every sign, of the best condition and estate, but overtaken by reverses even while conforming impeccably to the standard of superficial "smartness" and pleading with well-bred ease and the right light tone, not to say with feverish gaiety, that (as in the interest of art itself) *they* at least should n't have to "make believe." The question thus thrown up by the two friendly critics of the rather lurid little passage was of whether their not having to make believe *would* in fact serve them, and above all serve their interpreter as well as the borrowed graces of the comparatively sordid professionals who had had, for dear life, to *know how* (which was to have learnt how) to do something. The question, I recall, struck me as exquisite, and out of a momentary fond consideration of it "The Real Thing" sprang at a bound. . . .

1909

The Figure in the Carpet[1]

I

I had done a few things and earned a few pence — I had perhaps even had time to begin to think I was finer than was perceived by the patronising; but when I take the little measure of my course (a fidgety habit, for it's none of the longest yet) I count my real start from the evening George Corvick, breathless and worried, came in to ask me a service. He had done more things than I, and earned more pence, though there were chances for cleverness I thought he sometimes missed. I could only however that evening declare to him that he never missed one for kindness. There was almost rapture in hearing it proposed to me to prepare for *The Middle*, the organ of our lucubrations, so called from the position in the week of its day of appearance, an article for which he had made himself responsible and of which, tied up with a stout string, he laid on my table the subject. I pounced upon my opportunity — that is on the first volume of it — and paid scant attention to my friend's explanation of his appeal. What explanation could be more to the point than my obvious fitness for the task? I had written on Hugh Vereker, but never a word in *The Middle*, where my dealings were mainly with the ladies and the minor poets. This was his new novel, an advance copy, and whatever much or little it should do for his reputation I was clear on the spot as to what it should do for mine. Moreover if I always read him as soon as I could get hold of him I had a particular reason for wishing to read him now: I had accepted an invitation to Bridges for the following Sunday, and it had been mentioned in Lady Jane's note that Mr. Vereker was to be there. I was young enough for a flutter at meeting a man of his renown, and innocent enough to believe the occasion would demand the display of an acquaintance with his "last."

Corvick, who had promised a review of it, had not even had time to read it; he had gone to pieces in consequence of news requiring — as on precipitate reflexion he judged — that he should catch the night-mail to Paris. He had had a telegram from Gwendolen Erme in answer to his letter offering to fly to her aid. I knew already

---

[1]One of several stories about writers that James wrote, "The Figure in the Carpet" is unique in contributing its title to criticism as an important critical term — signifying the pattern of intricately related meanings in the entire body of an author's

work. James wrote of this story that his "lively impulse" had been to "reinstate analytic appreciation . . . to its virtually forfeited rights and dignities" (see the following excerpt from Preface).

about Gwendolen Erme; I had never seen her, but I had my ideas, which were mainly to the effect that Corvick would marry her if her mother would only die. That lady seemed now in a fair way to oblige him; after some dreadful mistake about a climate or a "cure" she had suddenly collapsed on the return from abroad. Her daughter, unsupported and alarmed, desiring to make a rush for home but hesitating at the risk, had accepted our friend's assistance, and it was my secret belief that at sight of him Mrs. Erme would pull round. His own belief was scarcely to be called secret; it discernibly at any rate differed from mine. He had showed me Gwendolen's photograph with the remark that she was n't pretty but was awfully interesting; she had published at the age of nineteen a novel in three volumes, "Deep Down," about which, in *The Middle*, he had been really splendid. He appreciated my present eagerness and undertook that the periodical in question should do no less; then at the last, with his hand on the door, he said to me: "Of course you'll be all right, you know." Seeing I was a trifle vague he added: "I mean you won't be silly."

"Silly—about Vereker! Why what do I ever find him but awfully clever?"

"Well, what's that but silly? What on earth does 'awfully clever' mean? For God's sake try to get *at* him. Don't let him suffer by our arrangement. Speak of him, you know, if you can, as *I* should have spoken of him."

I wondered an instant. "You mean as far and away the biggest of the lot—that sort of thing?"

Corvick almost groaned. "Oh you know, I don't put them back to back that way; it's the infancy of art! But he gives me a pleasure so rare; the sense of"—he mused a little—"something or other."

I wondered again. "The sense, pray, of what?"

"My dear man, that's just what I want *you* to say!"

Even before he had banged the door I had begun, book in hand, to prepare myself to say it. I sat up with Vereker half the night; Corvick could n't have done more than that. He was awfully clever—I stuck to that, but he was n't a bit the biggest of the lot. I did n't allude to the lot, however; I flattered myself that I emerged on this occasion from the infancy of art. "It's all right," they declared vividly at the office; and when the number appeared I felt there was a basis on which I could meet the great man. It gave me confidence for a day or two—then that confidence dropped. I had fancied him reading it with relish, but if Corvick was n't satisfied how could Vereker himself be? I reflected indeed that the heat of the admirer was sometimes grosser even than the appetite of the scribe. Corvick at all events wrote me from Paris a little ill-humouredly. Mrs. Erme was pulling round, and I had n't at all said what Vereker gave him the sense of.

II

The effect of my visit to Bridges was to turn me out for more profundity. Hugh Vereker, as I saw him there, was of a contact so void of angles that I blushed for the poverty of imagination involved in my small precautions. If he was in spirits it was n't because he had read my review; in fact on the Sunday morning I felt sure he had n't read it, though *The Middle* had been out three days and bloomed, I assured myself, in the stiff garden of periodicals which gave one of the ormolu[2] tables the air of a stand at a station. The impression he made on me personally was such that I wished him to read it, and I corrected to this end with a surreptitious hand what might be wanting in the careless conspicuity of the sheet. I'm afraid I even watched the result of my manœuvre, but up to luncheon I watched in vain.

When afterwards, in the course of our gregarious walk, I found myself for half an hour, not perhaps without another manœuvre, at the great man's side, the result of

---

[2]Gold-colored alloy used to decorate furniture.

his affability was a still livelier desire that he should n't remain in ignorance of the peculiar justice I had done him. It was n't that he seemed to thirst for justice; on the contrary I had n't yet caught in his talk the faintest grunt of a grudge—a note for which my young experience had already given me an ear. Of late he had had more recognition, and it was pleasant, as we used to say in *The Middle*, to see how it drew him out. He was n't of course popular, but I judged one of the sources of his good humour to be precisely that his success was independent of that. He had none the less become in a manner the fashion; the critics at least had put on a spurt and caught up with him. We had found out at last how clever he was, and he had had to make the best of the loss of his mystery. I was strongly tempted, as I walked beside him, to let him know how much of that unveiling was my act; and there was a moment when I probably should have done so had not one of the ladies of our party, snatching a place at his other elbow, just then appealed to him in a spirit comparatively selfish. It was very discouraging: I almost felt the liberty had been taken with myself.

I had had on my tongue's end, for my own part, a phrase or two about the right word at the right time; but later on I was glad not to have spoken, for when on our return we clustered at tea I perceived Lady Jane, who had not been out with us, brandishing *The Middle* with her longest arm. She had taken it up at her leisure; she was delighted with what she had found, and I saw that, as a mistake in a man may often be a felicity in a woman, she would practically do for me what I had n't been able to do for myself. "Some sweet little truths that needed to be spoken," I heard her declare, thrusting the paper at rather a bewildered couple by the fireplace. She grabbed it away from them again on the reappearance of Hugh Vereker, who after our walk had been upstairs to change something. "I know you don't in general look at this kind of thing, but it's an occasion really for doing so. You *have n't* seen it? Then you must. The man has actually got *at* you, at what *I* always feel, you know." Lady Jane threw into her eyes a look evidently intended to give an idea of what she always felt; but she added that she could n't have expressed it. The man in the paper expressed it in a striking manner. "Just see there, and there, where I've dashed it, how he brings it out." She had literally marked for him the brightest patches of my prose, and if I was a little amused Vereker himself may well have been. He showed how much he was when before us all Lady Jane wanted to read someting aloud. I liked at any rate the way he defeated her purpose by jerking the paper affectionately out of her clutch. He'd take it upstairs with him and look at it on going to dress. He did this half an hour later—I saw it in the his hand when he repaired to his room. That was the moment at which, thinking to give her pleasure, I mentioned to Lady Jane that I was the author of the review. I did give her pleasure, I judged, but perhaps not quite so much as I had expected. If the author was "only me" the thing did n't seem quite so remarkable. Had n't I had the effect rather of diminishing the lustre of the article than of adding to my own? Her ladyship was subject to the most extraordinary drops. It did n't matter; the only effect I cared about was the one it would have on Vereker up there by his bedroom fire.

At dinner I watched for the signs of this impression, tried to fancy some happier light in his eyes; but to my disappointment Lady Jane gave me no chance to make sure. I had hoped she'd call triumphantly down the table, publicly demand if she had n't been right. The party was large—there were people from outside as well, but I had never seen a table long enough to deprive Lady Jane of a triumph. I was just reflecting in truth that this interminable board would deprive *me* of one when the guest next me, dear woman—she was Miss Poyle, the vicar's sister, a robust unmodulated person—had the happy inspiration and the unusual courage to address herself across it to Vereker, who was opposite, but not directly, so that when he replied they were both leaning forward. She enquired, artless body, what he thought of Lady Jane's "panegyric," which she had read—not connecting it however with her right-hand neighbour; and while I strained my ear for his reply I heard him, to my stupefaction, call back gaily, his mouth full of bread: "Oh it's all right—the usual twaddle!"

I had caught Vereker's glance as he spoke, but Miss Poyle's surprise was a fortunate cover for my own. "You mean he does n't do you justice?" said the excellent woman.

Vereker laughed out, and I was happy to be able to do the same. "It's a charming article," he tossed us.

Miss Poyle thrust her chin half across the cloth. "Oh you're so deep!" she drove home.

"As deep as the ocean! All I pretend is that the author does n't see—" But a dish was at this point passed over his shoulder, and we had to wait while he helped himself.

"Does n't see what?" my neighbour continued.

"Does n't see anything."

"Dear me—how very stupid!"

"Not a bit," Vereker laughed again. "Nobody does."

The lady on his further side appealed to him and Miss Poyle sank back to myself. "Nobody sees anything!" she cheerfully announced; to which I replied that I had often thought so too, but had somehow taken the thought for a proof on my own part of a tremendous eye. I did n't tell her the article was mine; and I observed that Lady Jane, occupied at the end of the table, had not caught Vereker's words.

I rather avoided him after dinner, for I confess he struck me as cruelly conceited, and the revelation was a pain. "The usual twaddle"—my acute little study! That one's admiration should have had a reserve or two could gall him to that point? I had thought him placid, and he was placid enough; such a surface was the hard polished glass that encased the bauble of his vanity. I was really ruffled, and the only comfort was that if nobody saw anything George Corvick was quite as much out of it as I. This comfort however was not sufficient, after the ladies had dispersed, to carry me in the proper manner—I mean in a spotted jacket and humming an air—into the smoking-room. I took my way in some dejection to bed; but in the passage I encountered Mr. Vereker, who had been up once more to change, coming out of his room. *He* was humming an air and had on a spotted jacket, and as soon as he saw me his gaiety gave a start.

"My dear young man," he exclaimed, "I'm so glad to lay hands on you! I'm afraid I most unwittingly wounded you by those words of mine at dinner to Miss Poyle. I learned but half an hour ago from Lady Jane that you're the author of the little notice in *The Middle*."

I protested that no bones were broken; but he moved with me to my own door, his hand, on my shoulder, kindly feeling for a fracture; and on hearing that I had come up to bed he asked leave to cross my threshold and just tell me in three words what his qualification of my remarks had represented. It was plain he really feared I was hurt, and the sense of his solicitude suddenly made all the difference to me. My cheap review fluttered off into space, and the best things I had said in it became flat enough beside the brilliancy of his being there. I can see him there still, on my rug, in the firelight and his spotted jacket, his fine clear face all bright with the desire to be tender to my youth. I don't know what he had at first meant to say, but I think the sight of my relief touched him, excited him, brought up words to his lips from far within. It was so these words presently conveyed to me something that, as I afterwards knew, he had never uttered to any one. I've always done justice to the generous impulse that made him speak; it was simply compunction for a snub unconsciously administered to a man of letters in a position inferior to his own, a man of letters moreover in the very act of praising him. To make the thing right he talked to me exactly as an equal and on the ground of what we both loved best. The hour, the place, the unexpectedness deepened the impression: he could n't have done anything more intensely effective.

III

"I don't quite know how to explain it to you," he said, "but it was the very fact that your notice of my book had a spice of intelligence, it was just your exceptional sharpness, that produced the feeling—a very old story with me, I beg you to believe—under the momentary influence of which I used in speaking to that good lady the words you so naturally resent. I don't read the things in the newspapers unless they're thrust upon me as that one was—it's always one's best friend who does it! But I used to read them sometimes—ten years ago. I dare say they were in general rather stupider then; at any rate it always struck me they missed my little point with a perfection exactly as admirable when they patted me on the back as when they kicked me in the shins. Whenever since I've happened to have a glimpse of them they were still blazing away—still missing it, I mean, deliciously. *You* miss it, my dear fellow, with inimitable assurance; the fact of your being awfully clever and your article's being awfully nice does n't make a hair's breadth of difference. It's quite with you rising young men," Vereker laughed, "that I feel most what a failure I am!"

I listened with keen interest; it grew keener as he talked. "*You* a failure—heavens! What then may your 'little point' happen to be?"

"Have I got to *tell* you, after all these years and labours?" There was something in the friendly reproach of this—jocosely exaggerated—that made me, as an ardent young seeker for truth, blush to the roots of my hair. I'm as much in the dark as ever, though I've grown used in a sense to my obtuseness; at that moment, however, Vereker's happy accent made me appear to myself, and probably to him, a rare dunce. I was on the point of exclaiming "Ah yes, don't tell me: for my honour, for that of the craft, don't!" when he went on in a manner that showed he had read my thought and had his own idea of the probability of our some day redeeming ourselves. "By my little point I mean—what shall I call it?—the particular thing I've written my books most *for*. Is n't there for every writer a particular thing of that sort, the thing that most makes him apply himself, the thing without the effort to achieve which he would n't write at all, the very passion of his passion, the part of the business in which, for him, the flame of art burns most intensely? Well, it's *that*!"

I considered a moment—that is I followed at a respectful distance, rather gasping. I was fascinated—easily, you'll say; but I was n't going after all to be put off my guard. "Your description's certainly beautiful, but it does n't make what you describe very distinct."

"I promise you it would be distinct if it should dawn on you at all." I saw that the charm of our topic overflowed for my companion into an emotion as lively as my own. "At any rate," he went on, "I can speak for myself: there's an idea in my work without which I would n't have given a straw for the whole job. It's the finest fullest intention of the lot, and the application of it has been, I think, a triumph of patience, of ingenuity. I ought to leave that to somebody else to say; but that nobody does say it is precisely what we're talking about. It stretches, this little trick of mine, from book to book, and everything else, comparatively, plays over the surface of it. The order, the form, the texture of my books will perhaps some day constitute for the initiated a complete representation of it. So it's naturally the thing for the critic to look for. It strikes me," my visitor added, smiling, "even as the thing for the critic to find."

This seemed a responsibility indeed. "You call it a little trick?"

"That's only my little modesty. It's really an exquisite scheme."

"And you hold that you've carried the scheme out?"

"The way I've carried it out is the thing in life I think a bit well of myself for."

I had a pause. "Don't you think you ought—just a trifle—to assist the critic?"

"Assist him? What else have I done with every stroke of my pen? I've shouted my intention in his great blank face!" At this, laughing out again, Vereker laid his hand on my shoulder to show the allusion was n't to my personal appearance.

"But you talk about the initiated. There must therefore, you see, *be* initiation."

"What else in heaven's name is criticism supposed to be?" I'm afraid I coloured at this too; but I took refuge in repeating that his account of his silver lining was poor in something or other that a plain man knows things by. "That's only becaue you've never had a glimpse of it," he returned. "If you had had one the element in question would soon have become practically all you'd see. To me it's exactly as palpable as the marble of this chimney. Besides, the critic just *is n't* a plain man: if he were, pray, what would he be doing in his neighbour's garden? You're anything but a plain man yourself, and the very *raison d'être*³ of you all is that you're little demons of subtlety. If my great affair's a secret, that's only because it's a secret in spite of itself—the amazing event has made it one. I not only never took the smallest precaution to keep it so, but never dreamed of any such accident. If I had I should n't in advance have had the heart to go on. As it was, I only became aware little by little, and meanwhile I had done my work."

"And now you quite like it?" I risked.

"My work?"

"Your secret. It's the same thing."

"Your guessing that," Vereker replied, "is a proof that you're as clever as I say!" I was encouraged by this to remark that he would clearly be pained to part with it, and he confessed that it was indeed with him now the great amusement of life. "I live almost to see if it will ever be detected." He looked at me for a jesting challenge; something far within his eyes seemed to peep out. "But I need n't worry—it won't!"

"You fire me as I've never been fired," I declared; "you make me determined to do or die." Then I asked: "Is it a kind of esoteric message?"

His countenance fell at this—he put out his hand as if to bid me good-night. "Ah my dear fellow, it can't be described in cheap journalese!"

I knew of course he'd be awfully fastidious, but our talk had made me feel how much his nerves were exposed. I was unsatisfied—I kept hold of his hand. "I won't make use of the expression then," I said, "in the article in which I shall eventually announce my discovery, though I dare say I shall have hard work to do without it. But meanwhile, just to hasten that difficult birth, can't you give a fellow a clue?" I felt much more at my ease.

"My whole lucid effort gives him the clue—every page and line and letter. The thing's as concrete there as a bird in a cage, a bait on a hook, a piece of cheese in a mouse-trap. It's stuck into every volume as your foot is stuck into your shoe. It governs every line, it chooses every word, it dots every i, it places every comma."

I scratched my head. "Is it something in the style or something in the thought? An element of form or an element of feeling?"

He indulgently shook my hand again, and I felt my questions to be crude and my distinctions pitiful. "Good-night, my dear boy—don't bother about it. After all, you do like a fellow."

"And a little intelligence might spoil it?" I still detained him.

He hesitated. "Well, you've got a heart in your body. Is that an element of form or an element of feeling? What I contend that nobody has ever mentioned in my work is the organ of life."

"I see—it's some idea *about* life, some sort of philosophy. Unless it be," I added with the eagerness of a thought perhaps still happier, "some kind of game you're up to with your style, something you're after in the language. Perhaps it's a preference for the letter P!" I ventured profanely to break out. "Papa, potatoes, prunes—that sort of thing?" He was suitably indulgent: he only said I had n't got the right letter. But his amusement was over; I could see he was bored. There was nevertheless some-

---

³"Reason for being" (French).

thing else I had absolutely to learn. "Should you be able, pen in hand, to state it clearly yourself — to name it, phrase it, formulate it?"

"Oh," he almost passionately sighed, "if I were only, pen in hand, one of *you* chaps!"

"That would be a great chance for you of course. But why should you despise us chaps for not doing what you can't do yourself?"

"Can't do?" He opened his eyes. "Have n't I done it in twenty volumes? I do it in my way," he continued. "Go *you* and don't do it in yours."

"Ours is so devilish difficult," I weakly observed.

"So's mine! We each choose our own. There's no compulsion. You won't come down and smoke?"

"No. I want to think this thing out."

"You'll tell me then in the morning that you've laid me bare?"

"I'll see what I can do; I'll sleep on it. But just one word more," I added. We had left the room — I walked again with him a few steps along the passage. "This extraordinary 'general intention,' as you call it — for that's the most vivid description I can induce you to make of it — is then, generally, a sort of buried treasure?"

His face lighted. "Yes, call it that, though it's perhaps not for me to do so."

"Nonsense!" I laughed. "You know you're hugely proud of it."

"Well, I did n't propose to tell you so; but it *is* the joy of my soul!"

"You mean it's a beauty so rare, so great?"

He waited a little again. "The loveliest thing in the world!" We had stopped, and on these words he left me; but at the end of the corridor, while I looked after him rather yearningly, he turned and caught sight of my puzzled face. It made him earnestly, indeed I thought quite anxiously, shake his head and wave his finger. "Give it up — give it up!"

This was n't a challenge — it was fatherly advice. If I had had one of his books at hand I'd have repeated my recent act of faith — I'd have spent half the night with him. At three o'clock in the morning, not sleeping, remembering moreover how indispensable he was to Lady Jane, I stole down to the library with a candle. There was n't, so far as I could discover, a line of his writing in the house.

IV

Returning to town I feverishly collected them all; I picked out each in its order and held it up to the light. This gave me a maddening month, in the course of which several things took place. One of these, the last, I may as well immediately mention, was that I acted on Vereker's advice: I renounced my ridiculous attempt. I could really make nothing of the business; it proved a dead loss. After all I had always, as he had himself noted, liked him; and what now occurred was simply that my new intelligence and vain preoccupation damaged my liking. I not only failed to run a general intention to earth, I found myself missing the subordinate intentions I had formerly enjoyed. His books did n't even remain the charming things they had been for me; the exasperation of my search put me out of conceit of them. Instead of being a pleasure the more they became a resource the less; for from the moment I was unable to follow up the author's hint I of course felt it a point of honour not to make use professionally of my knowledge of them. I *had* no knowledge — nobody had any. It was humiliating, but I could bear it — they only annoyed me now. At last they even bored me, and I accounted for my confusion — perversely, I allow — by the idea that Vereker had made a fool of me. The buried treasure was a bad joke, the general intention a monstrous *pose*.

The great point of it all is, however, that I told George Corvick what had befallen me and that my information had an immense effect on him. He had at last come back, but so, unfortunately, had Mrs. Erme, and there was as yet, I could see, no question of his nuptials. He was immensely stirred up by the anecdote I had brought from Bridges; it fell in so completely with the sense he had had from the first that there was more in Vereker than met the eye. When I remarked that the eye seemed what the printed page had been expressly invented to meet he immediately accused me of being spiteful because I had been foiled. Our commerce had always that pleasant latitude. The thing Vereker had mentioned to me was exactly the thing he, Corvick, had wanted me to speak of in my review. On my suggesting at last that with the assistance I had now given him he would doubtless be prepared to speak of it himself he admitted freely that before doing this there was more he must understand. What he would have said, had he reviewed the new book, was that there was evidently in the writer's inmost art something to *be* understood. I had n't so much as hinted at that: no wonder the writer had n't been flattered! I asked Corvick what he really considered he meant by his own supersubtlety, and, unmistakeably kindled, he replied: "It is n't for the vulgar—it is n't for the vulgar!" He had hold of the tail of something: he would pull hard, pull it right out. He pumped me dry on Vereker's strange confidence and, pronouncing me the luckiest of mortals, mentioned half a dozen questions he wished to goodness I had had the gumption to put. Yet on the other hand he did n't want to be told too much—it would spoil the fun of seeing what would come. The failure of *my* fun was at the moment of our meeting not complete, but I saw it ahead, and Corvick saw that I saw it. I, on my side, saw likewise that one of the first things he would do would be to rush off with my story to Gwendolen.

On the very day after my talk with him I was surprised by the receipt of a note from Hugh Vereker, to whom our encounter at Bridges had been recalled, as he mentioned, by his falling, in a magazine, on some article to which my signature was attached. "I read it with great pleasure," he wrote, "and remembered under its influence our lively conversation by your bedroom fire. The consequence of this has been that I begin to measure the temerity of my having saddled you with a knowledge that you may find something of a burden. Now that the fit's over I can't imagine how I came to be moved so much beyond my wont. I had never before mentioned, no matter in what state of expansion, the fact of my little secret, and I shall never speak of that mystery again. I was accidentally so much more explicit with you than it had ever entered into my game to be, that I find this game—I mean the pleasure of playing it—suffers considerably. In short, if you can understand it, I've rather spoiled my sport. I really don't want to give anybody what I believe you clever young men call the tip. That's of course a selfish solicitude, and I name it to you for what it may be worth to you. If you're disposed to humour me don't repeat my revelation. Think me demented—it's your right; but don't tell anybody why."

The sequel to this communication was that as early on the morrow as I dared I drove straight to Mr. Vereker's door. He occupied in those years one of the honest old houses in Kensington Square. He received me immediately, and as soon as I came in I saw I had n't lost my power to minister to his mirth. He laughed out at the sight of my face, which doubtless expressed my perturbation. I had been indiscreet—my compunction was great. "I *have* told somebody," I panted, "and I'm sure that person will by this time have told somebody else! It's a woman, into the bargain."

"The person you've told?"

"No, the other person. I'm quite sure he must have told her."

"For all the good it will do her—or do *me*! A woman will never find out."

"No, but she'll talk all over the place: she'll do just what you don't want."

Vereker thought a moment, but was n't so disconcerted as I had feared: he felt that if the harm was done it only served him right. "It does n't matter—don't worry."

"I'll do my best, I promise you, that your talk with me shall go no further."

"Very good; do what you can."

"In the meantime," I pursued, "George Corvick's possession of the tip may, on his part, really lead to something."

"That will be a brave day."

I told him about Corvick's cleverness, his admiration, the intensity of his interest in my anecdote; and without making too much of the divergence of our respective estimates mentioned that my friend was already of opinion that he saw much further into a certain affair than most people. He was quite as fired as I had been at Bridges. He was moreover in love with the young lady: perhaps the two together would puzzle something out.

Vereker seemed struck with this. "Do you mean they're to be married?"

"I dare say that's what it will come to."

"That may help them," he conceded, "but we must give them time!"

I spoke of my own renewed assault and confessed my difficulties; whereupon he repeated his former advice: "Give it up, give it up!" He evidently did n't think me intellectually equipped for the adventure. I stayed half an hour, and he was most good-natured, but I could n't help pronouncing him a man of unstable moods. He had been free with me in a mood, he had repented in a mood, and now in a mood he had turned indifferent. This general levity helped me to believe that, so far as the subject of the tip went, there was n't much in it. I contrived however to make him answer a few more questions about it, though he did so with visible impatience. For himself, beyond doubt, the thing we were all so blank about was vividly there. It was something, I guessed, in the primal plan; something like a complex figure in a Persian carpet. He highly approved of this image when I used it, and he used another himself. "It's the very string," he said, "that my pearls are strung on!" The reason of his note to me had been that he really did n't want to give us a grain of succour — our density was a thing too perfect in its way to touch. He had formed the habit of depending on it, and if the spell was to break it must break by some force of its own. He comes back to me from that last occasion — for I was never to speak to him again — as a man with some safe preserve for sport. I wondered as I walked away where he had got *his* tip.

V

When I spoke to George Corvick of the caution I had received he made me feel that any doubt of his delicacy would be almost an insult. He had instantly told Gwendolen, but Gwendolen's ardent response was in itself a pledge of discretion. The question would now absorb them and would offer them a pastime too precious to be shared with the crowd. They appeared to have caught instinctively at Vereker's high idea of enjoyment. Their intellectual pride, however, was not such as to make them indifferent to any further light I might throw on the affair they had in hand. They were indeed of the "artistic temperament," and I was freshly struck with my colleague's power to excite himself over a question of art. He'd call it letters, he'd call it life, but it was all one thing. In what he said I now seemed to understand that he spoke equally for Gwendolen, to whom, as soon as Mrs. Erme was sufficiently better to allow her a little leisure, he made a point of introducing me. I remember our going together one Sunday in August to a huddled house in Chelsea,[4] and my renewed envy of Corvick's possession of a friend who had some light to mingle with his own. He could say things to her that I could never say to him. She had indeed no sense of humour and, with her pretty way of holding her head on one side, was one of those persons whom you want, as the phrase is, to shake, but who have learnt Hungarian by themselves. She conversed perhaps in Hungarian with Corvick; she had remarkably little English for his friend. Corvick afterwards told me that I had chilled her by my apparent indisposition to oblige them with the detail of what Vereker had said to me. I allowed that I felt I had given thought enough to that indication: had n't I even made up my mind that it was vain and would lead nowhere? The importance they attached to it was irritating and quite envenomed my doubts.

---

[4]Residential area of London.

That statement looks unamiable, and what probably happened was that I felt humiliated at seeing other persons deeply beguiled by an experiment that had brought me only chagrin. I was out in the cold while, by the evening fire, under the lamp, they followed the chase for which I myself had sounded the horn. They did as I had done, only more deliberately and sociably—they went over their author from the beginning. There was no hurry, Corvick said—the future was before them and the fascination could only grow; they would take him page by page, as they would take one of the classics, inhale him in slow draughts and let him sink all the way in. They would scarce have got so wound up, I think, if they had n't been in love: poor Vereker's inner meaning gave them endless occasion to put and to keep their young heads together. None the less it represented the kind of problem for which Corvick had a special aptitude, drew out the particular pointed patience of which, had he lived, he would have given more striking and, it was to be hoped, more fruitful examples. He at least was, in Vereker's words, a little demon of subtlety. We had begun by disputing, but I soon saw that without my stirring a finger his infatuation would have its bad hours. He would bound off on false scents as I had done—he would clap his hands over new lights and see them blown out by the wind of the turned page. He was like nothing, I told him, but the maniacs who embrace some bedlamitical[5] theory of the cryptic character of Shakespeare. To this he replied that if we had had Shakespeare's own word for his being cryptic he would at once have accepted it. The case there was altogether different—we had nothing but the word of Mr. Snooks. I returned that I was stupefied to see him attach such importance even to the word of Mr. Vereker. He wanted thereupon to know if I treated Mr. Vereker's word as a lie. I was n't perhaps prepared, in my unhappy rebound, to go so far as that, but I insisted that till the contrary was proved I should view it as too fond an imagination. I did n't, I confess, say—I did n't at that time quite know—all I felt. Deep down, as Miss Erme would have said, I was uneasy, I was expectant. At the core of my disconcerted state—for my wonted curiosity lived in its ashes—was the sharpness of a sense that Corvick would at last probably come out somewhere. He made, in defence of his credulity, a great point of the fact that from of old, in his study of this genius, he had caught whiffs and hints of he did n't know what, faint wandering notes of a hidden music. That was just the rarity, that was the charm: it fitted so perfectly into what I reported.

If I returned on several occasions to the little house in Chelsea I dare say it was as much for news of Vereker as for news of Miss Erme's ailing parent. The hours spent there by Corvick were present to my fancy as those of a chessplayer bent with a silent scowl, all the lamplit winter, over his board and his moves. As my imagination filled it out the picture held me fast. On the other side of the table was a ghostlier form, the faint figure of an antagonist good-humouredly but a little wearily secure—an antagonist who leaned back in his chair with his hands in his pockets and a smile on his fine clear face. Close to Corvick, behind him, was a girl who had begun to strike me as pale and wasted and even, on more familiar view, as rather handsome, and who rested on his shoulder and hung on his moves. He would take up a chessman and hold it poised a while over one of the little squares, and then would put it back in its place with a long sigh of disappointment. The young lady, at this, would slightly but uneasily shift her position and look across, very hard, very long, very strangely at their dim participant. I had asked them at an early stage of the business if it might n't contribute to their success to have some closer communication with him. The special circumstances would surely be held to have given me a right to introduce them. Corvick immediately replied that he had no wish to approach the altar before he had prepared the sacrifice. He quite agreed with our friend both as to the delight and as to the honour of the chase—he would bring down the animal with his own rifle. When I asked him if Miss Erme were as keen a shot he said after thinking: "No, I'm ashamed

_____

[5]I.e., crazy (from Bedlam, a lunatic asylum in London).

to say she wants to set a trap. She'd give anything to see him; she says she requires another tip. She's really quite morbid about it. But she must play fair—she *shan't* see him!" he emphatically added. I wondered if they had n't even quarrelled a little on the subject—a suspicion not corrected by the way he more than once exclaimed to me: "She's quite incredibly literary, you know—quite fantastically!" I remember his saying of her that she felt in italics and thought in capitals. "Oh when I've run him to earth," he also said, "then, you know, I shall knock at his door. Rather—I beg you to believe. I'll have it from his own lips: 'Right you are, my boy; you've done it this time!' He shall crown me victor—with the critical laurel."

Meanwhile he really avoided the chances London life might have given him of meeting the distinguished novelist; a danger, however, that disappeared with Vereker's leaving England for an indefinite absence, as the newspapers announced—going to the south for motives connected with the health of his wife, which had long kept her in retirement. A year—more than a year—had elapsed since the incident at Bridges, but I had had no further sight of him. I think I was at bottom rather ashamed—I hated to remind him that, though I had irremediably missed his point, a reputation for acuteness was rapidly overtaking me. This scruple led me a dance; kept me out of Lady Jane's house, made me even decline, when in spite of my bad manners she was a second time so good as to make me a sign, an invitation to her beautiful seat.[6] I once became aware of her under Vereker's escort at a concert, and was sure I was seen by them, but I slipped out without being caught. I felt, as on that occasion I splashed along in the rain, that I could n't have done anything else; and yet I remember saying to myself that it was hard, was even cruel. Not only had I lost the books, but I had lost the man himself: they and their author had been alike spoiled for me. I knew too which was the loss I most regretted. I had taken to the man still more than I had ever taken to the books.

VI

Six months after our friend had left England George Corvick, who made his living by his pen, contracted for a piece of work which imposed on him an absence of some length and a journey of some difficulty, and his undertaking of which was much of a surprise to me. His brother-in-law had become editor of a great provincial paper, and the great provincial paper, in a fine flight of fancy, had conceived the idea of sending a "special commissioner" to India. Special commissioners had begun, in the "metropolitan press," to be the fashion, and the journal in question must have felt it had passed too long for a mere country cousin. Corvick had no hand, I knew, for the big brush of the correspondent, but that was his brother-in-law's affair, and the fact that a particular task was not in his line was apt to be with himself exactly a reason for accepting it. He was prepared to out-Herod[7] the metropolitan press; he took solemn precautions against priggishness, he exquisitely outraged taste. Nobody ever knew it—that offended principle was all his own. In addition to his expenses he was to be conveniently paid, and I found myself able to help him, for the usual fat book, to a plausible arrangement with the usual fat publisher. I naturally inferred that his obvious desire to make a little money was not unconnected with the prospect of a union with Gwendolen Erme. I was aware that her mother's opposition was largely addressed to his want of means and of lucrative abilities, but it so happened that, on my saying the last time I saw him something that bore on the question of his separation from our young lady, he brought out with an emphasis that startled me: "Ah I'm not a bit engaged to her, you know!"

"Not overtly," I answered, "because her mother does n't like you. But I've always taken for granted a private understanding."

[6]I.e., estate.

[7]I.e., to outdo; "To out-Herod Herod" (from Shakespeare's *Hamlet*, III, ii) means to surpass in cruelty the tyrant Herod the Great (73?–4 B.C.), King of Judea.

"Well, there *was* one. But there is n't now." That was all he said save something about Mrs. Erme's having got on her feet again in the most extraordinary way—a remark pointing, as I supposed, the moral that private understandings were of little use when the doctor did n't share them. What I took the liberty of more closely inferring was that the girl might in some way have estranged him. Well, if he had taken the turn of jealousy for instance it could scarcely be jealousy of me. In that case—over and above the absurdity of it—he would n't have gone away just to leave us together. For some time before his going we had indulged in no allusion to the buried treasure, and from his silence, which my reserve simply emulated, I had drawn a sharp conclusion. His courage had dropped, his ardour had gone the way of mine—this appearance at least he left me to scan. More than that he could n't do; he could n't face the triumph with which I might have greeted an explicit admission. He need n't have been afraid, poor dear, for I had by this time lost all need to triumph. In fact I considered I showed magnanimity in not reproaching him with his collapse, for the sense of his having thrown up the game made me feel more than ever how much I at last depended on him. If Corvick had broken down I should never know; no one would be of any use if *he* was n't. It was n't a bit true I had ceased to care for knowledge; little by little my curiosity not only had begun to ache again, but had become the familiar torment of my days and my nights. There are doubtless people to whom torments of such an order appear hardly more natural than the contortions of disease; but I don't after all know why I should in this connexion so much as mention them. For the few persons, at any rate, abnormal or not, with whom my anecdote is concerned, literature was a game of skill, and skill meant courage, and courage meant honour, and honour meant passion, meant life. The stake on the table was of a special substance and our roulette the revolving mind, but we sat round the green board as intently as the grim gamblers at Monte Carlo.[8] Gwendolen Erme, for that matter, with her white face and her fixed eyes, was of the very type of the lean ladies one had met in the temples of chance. I recognized in Corvick's absence that she made this analogy vivid. It was extravagant, I admit, the way she lived for the art of the pen. Her passion visibly preyed on her, and in her presence I felt almost tepid. I got hold of "Deep Down" again: it was a desert in which she had lost herself, but in which too she had dug a wonderful hole in the sand—a cavity out of which Corvick had still more remarkably pulled her.

Early in March I had a telegram from her, in consequence of which I repaired immediately to Chelsea, where the first thing she said to me was: "He has got it, he has got it!"

She was moved, as I could see, to such depths that she must mean the great thing. "Vereker's idea?"

"His general intention. George has cabled from Bombay."

She had the missive open there; it was emphatic though concise. "Eureka. Immense." That was all—he had saved the cost of the signature. I shared her emotion, but I was disappointed. "He does n't say what it is."

"How could he—in a telegram? He'll write it."

"But how does he know?"

"Know it's the real thing? Oh I'm sure that when you see it you do know. *Vera incessu patuit dea!*"[9]

"It's you, Miss Erme, who are a 'dear' for bringing me such news!"—I went all lengths in my high spirits. "But fancy finding our goddess in the temple of Vishnu![10] How strange of George to have been able to go into the thing again in the midst of such different and such powerful solicitations!"

"He has n't gone into it, I know; it's the thing itself, let severely alone for six months, that has simply sprung out at him like a tigress out of the jungle. He did n't

[8]Gambling casino in Monte Carlo, Monaco.
[9]"Her walk revealed her as a true goddess" (Latin; a quota-tion from Virgil's *Aeneid*, I, 405).
[10]The saviour god in Hindu religion.

take a book with him — on purpose; indeed he would n't have needed to — he knows every page, as I do, by heart. They all worked in him together, and some day somewhere, when he was n't thinking, they fell, in all their superb intricacy, into the one right combination. The figure in the carpet came out. That's the way he knew it would come and the real reason — you did n't in the least understand, but I suppose I may tell you now — why he went and why I consented to his going. We knew the change would do it — that the difference of thought, of scene, would give the needed touch, the magic shake. We had perfectly, we had admirably calculated. The elements were all in his mind, and in the *secousse*[11] of a new and intense experience they just struck light." She positively struck light herself — she was literally, facially luminous. I stammered something about unconscious cerebration, and she continued: "He'll come right home — this will bring him."

"To see Vereker, you mean?"

"To see Vereker — and to see *me*. Think what he'll have to tell me!"

I hesitated. "About India?"

"About fiddlesticks! About Vereker — about the figure in the carpet."

"But, as you say, we shall surely have that in a letter."

She thought like one inspired, and I remembered how Corvick had told me long before that her face was interesting. "Perhaps it can't be got into a letter if it's 'immense.'"

"Perhaps not if it's immense bosh. If he has hold of something that can't be got into a letter he has n't hold of *the* thing. Vereker's own statement to me was exactly that the 'figure' *would* fit into a letter."

"Well, I cabled to George an hour ago — two words," said Gwendolen.

"Is it indiscreet of me to ask what they were?"

She hung fire, but at last brought them out. "'Angel, write.'"

"Good!" I cried. "I'll make it sure — I'll send him the same."

VII

My words however were not absolutely the same — I put something instead of "angel"; and in the sequel my epithet seemed the more apt, for when eventually we heard from our traveller it was merely, it was thoroughly to be tantalised. He was magnificent in his triumph, he described his discovery as stupendous; but his ecstasy only obscured it — there were to be no particulars till he should have submitted his conception to the supreme authority. He had thrown up his commission, he had thrown up his book, he had thrown up everything but the instant need to hurry to Rapallo, on the Genoese shore,[12] where Vereker was making a stay. I wrote him a letter which was to await him at Aden[13] — I besought him to relieve my suspense. That he had found my letter was indicated by a telegram which, reaching me after weary days and in the absence of any answer to my laconic dispatch to him at Bombay, was evidently intended as a reply to both communications. Those few words were in familiar French, the French of the day, which Corvick often made use of to show he was n't a prig. It had for some persons the opposite effect, but his message may fairly be paraphrased. "Have patience; I want to see, as it breaks on you, the face you'll make!" "Tellement envie de voir ta tête!" — that was what I had to sit down with. I can certainly not be said to have sat down, for I seem to remember myself at this time as rattling constantly between the little house in Chelsea and my own. Our impatience, Gwendolen's and mine, was equal, but I kept hoping her light would be greater. We all spent during this episode, for people of our means, a great deal of money in telegrams and cabs, and I counted on the receipt of news from Rapallo immediately after the junction of the discoverer with the discovered. The interval seemed an age, but late one day I heard a hansom precipitated to my door with the

---

[11]"Shock" (French).
[12]The port city and resort, Rapallo, Italy, east of Genoa.
[13]Then a British colony on the southwest coast of the Arabian peninsula.

crash engendered by a hint of liberality. I lived with my heart in my mouth and accordingly bounded to the window—a movement which gave me a view of a young lady erect on the footboard of the vehicle and eagerly looking up at my house. At sight of me she flourished a paper with a movement that brought me straight down, the movement with which, in melodramas, handkerchiefs and reprieves are flourished at the foot of the scaffold.

"Just seen Vereker—not a note wrong. Pressed me to bosom—keeps me a month." So much I read on her paper while the cabby dropped a grin from his perch. In my excitement I paid him profusely and in hers she suffered it; then as he drove away we started to walk about and talk. We had talked, heaven knows, enough before, but this was a wondrous lift. We pictured the whole scene at Rapallo, where he would have written, mentioning my name, for permission to call; that is *I* pictured it, having more material than my companion, whom I felt hang on my lips as we stopped on purpose before shop-windows we did n't look into. About one thing we were clear: if he was staying on for fuller communication we should at least have a letter from him that would help us through the dregs of delay. We understood his staying on, and yet each of us saw, I think, that the other hated it. The letter we were clear about arrived; it was for Gwendolen, and I called on her in time to save her the trouble of bringing it to me. She did n't read it out, as was natural enough; but she repeated to me what it chiefly embodied. This consisted of the remarkable statement that he'd tell her after they were married exactly what she wanted to know.

"Only *then*, when I'm his wife—not before," she explained. "It's tantamount to saying—is n't it?—that I must marry him straight off!" She smiled at me while I flushed with disappointment, a vision of fresh delay that made me at first unconscious of my surprise. It seemed more than a hint that on me as well he would impose some tiresome condition. Suddenly, while she reported several more things from his letter, I remembered what he had told me before going away. He had found Mr. Vereker deliriously interesting and his own possession of the secret a real intoxication. The buried treasure was all gold and gems. Now that it was there it seemed to grow and grow before him; it would have been, through all time and taking all tongues, one of the most wonderful flowers of literary art. Nothing, in especial, once you were face to face with it, could show for more consummately *done*. When once it came out it came out, was there with a splendour that made you ashamed; and there had n't been, save in the bottomless vulgarity of the age, with every one tasteless and tainted, every sense stopped, the smallest reason why it should have been overlooked. It was great, yet so simple, was simple, yet so great, and the final knowledge of it was an experience quite apart. He intimated that the charm of such an experience, the desire to drain it, in its freshness, to the last drop, was what kept him there close to the source. Gwendolen, frankly radiant as she tossed me these fragments, showed the elation of a prospect more assured than my own. That brought me back to the question of her marriage, prompted me to ask if what she meant by what she had just surprised me with was that she was under an engagement.

"Of course I am!" she answered. "Did n't you know it?" She seemed astonished, but I was still more so, for Corvick had told me the exact contrary. I did n't mention this, however; I only reminded her how little I had been on that score in her confidence, or even in Corvick's, and that moreover I was n't in ignorance of her mother's interdict. At bottom I was troubled by the disparity of the two accounts; but after a little I felt Corvick's to be the one I least doubted. This simply reduced me to asking myself if the girl had on the spot improvised an engagement—vamped up an old one or dashed off a new—in order to arrive at the satisfaction she desired. She must have had resources of which I was destitute, but she made her case slightly more intelligible by returning presently: "What the state of things has been is that we felt of course bound to do nothing in mamma's lifetime."

"But now you think you'll just dispense with mamma's consent?"

"Ah it may n't come to that!" I wondered what it might come to, and she went on: "Poor dear, she may swallow the dose. In fact, you know," she added with a laugh, "she really *must!*" — a proposition of which, on behalf of every one concerned, I fully acknowledged the force.

VIII

Nothing more vexatious had ever happened to me than to become aware before Corvick's arrival in England that I should n't be there to put him through. I found myself abruptly called to Germany by the alarming illness of my younger brother, who, against my advice, had gone to Munich to study, at the feet indeed of a great master, the art of portraiture in oils. The near relative who made him an allowance had threatened to withdraw it if he should, under specious pretexts, turn for superior truth to Paris — Paris being somehow, for a Cheltenham[14] aunt, the school of evil, the abyss. I deplored this prejudice at the time, and the deep injury of it was now visible — first in the fact that it had n't saved the poor boy, who was clever frail and foolish, from congestion of the lungs, and second in the greater break with London to which the event condemned me. I'm afraid that what was uppermost in my mind during several anxious weeks was the sense that if we had only been in Paris I might have run over to see Corvick. This was actually out of the question from every point of view: my brother, whose recovery gave us both plenty to do, was ill for three months, during which I never left him and at the end of which we had to face the absolute prohibition of a return to England. The consideration of climate imposed itself, and he was in no state to meet it alone. I took him to Meran[15] and there spent the summer with him, trying to show him by example how to get back to work and nursing a rage of another sort that I tried *not* to show him.

The whole business proved the first of a series of phenomena so strangely interlaced that, taken all together — which was how I had to take them — they form as good an illustration as I can recall of the manner in which, for the good of his soul doubtless, fate sometimes deals with a man's avidity. These incidents certainly had larger bearings than the comparatively meagre consequence we are here concerned with — though I feel that consequence also a thing to speak of with some respect. It's mainly in such a light, I confess, at any rate, that the ugly fruit of my exile is at this hour present to me. Even at first indeed the spirit in which my avidity, as I have called it, made me regard that term owed no element of ease to the fact that before coming back from Rapallo George Corvick addressed me in a way I objected to. His letter had none of the sedative action I must today profess myself sure he had wished to give it, and the march of occurrences was not so ordered as to make up for what it lacked. He had begun on the spot, for one of the quarterlies, a great last word on Vereker's writings, and this exhaustive study, the only one that would have counted, have existed, was to turn on the new light, to utter — oh so quietly! — the unimagined truth. It was in other words to trace the figure in the carpet through every convolution, to reproduce it in every tint. The result, according to my friend, would be the greatest literary portrait ever painted, and what he asked of me was just to be so good as not to trouble him with questions till he should hang up his masterpiece before me. He did me the honour to declare that, putting aside the great sitter himself, all aloft in his indifference, I was individually the connoisseur he was most working for. I was therefore to be a good boy and not try to peep under the curtain before the show was ready: I should enjoy it all the more if I sat very still.

I did my best to sit very still, but I could n't help giving a jump on seeing in *The Times*, after I had been a week or two in Munich and before, as I knew, Corvick had

---

[14]English city in Gloucestershire favored by the retired because of its mineral springs.

[15]Merano, a winter resort in northern Italy.

reached London, the announcement of the sudden death of poor Mrs. Erme. I instantly, by letter, appealed to Gwendolen for particulars, and she wrote me that her mother had yielded to long-threatened failure of the heart. She did n't say, but I took the liberty of reading into her words, that from the point of view of her marriage and also of her eagerness, which was quite a match for mine, this was a solution more prompt than could have been expected and more radical than waiting for the old lady to swallow the dose. I candidly admit indeed that at the time — for I heard from her repeatedly — I read some singular things into Gwendolen's words and some still more extraordinary ones into her silences. Pen in hand, this way, I live the time over, and it brings back the oddest sense of my having been, both for months and in spite of myself, a kind of coerced spectator. All my life had taken refuge in my eyes, which the procession of events appeared to have committed itself to keep astare. There were days when I thought of writing to Hugh Vereker and simply throwing myself on his charity. But I felt more deeply that I had n't fallen quite so low — besides which, quite properly, he would send me about my business. Mrs. Erme's death brought Corvick straight home, and within the month he was united "very quietly" — as quietly, I seemed to make out, as he meant in his article to bring out his *trouvaille*[16] — to the young lady he had loved and quitted. I use this last term, I may parenthetically say, because I subsequently grew sure that at the time he went to India, at the time of his great news from Bombay, there had been no positive pledge between them whatever. There had been none at the moment she was affirming to me the very opposite. On the other hand he had certainly become engaged the day he returned. The happy pair went down to Torquay[17] for their honeymoon, and there, in a reckless hour, it occurred to poor Corvick to take his young bride a drive. He had no command of that business: this had been brought home to me of old in a little tour we had once made together in a dogcart. In a dogcart he perched his companion for a rattle over Devonshire hills, on one of the likeliest of which he brought his horse, who, it was true, had bolted, down with such violence that the occupants of the cart were hurled forward and that he fell horribly on his head. He was killed on the spot; Gwendolen escaped unhurt.

I pass rapidly over the question of this unmitigated tragedy, of what the loss of my best friend meant for me, and I complete my little history of my patience and my pain by the frank statement of my having, in a postscript to my very first letter to her after the receipt of the hideous news, asked Mrs. Corvick whether her husband might n't at least have finished the great article on Vereker. Her answer was as prompt as my question: the article, which had been barely begun, was a mere heartbreaking scrap. She explained that our friend, abroad, had just settled down to it when interrupted by her mother's death, and that then, on his return, he had been kept from work by the engrossments into which that calamity was to plunge them. The opening pages were all that existed; they were striking, they were promising, but they did n't unveil the idol. That great intellectual feat was obviously to have formed his climax. She said nothing more, nothing to enlighten me as to the state of her own knowledge — the knowledge for the acquisition of which I had fancied her prodigiously acting. This was above all what I wanted to know: had *she* seen the idol unveiled? Had there been a private ceremony for a palpitating audience of one? For what else but that ceremony had the nuptials taken place? I did n't like as yet to press her, though when I thought of what had passed between us on the subject in Corvick's absence her reticence surprised me. It was therefore not till much later, from Meran, that I risked another appeal, risked it in some trepidation, for she continued to tell me nothing. "Did you hear in those few days of your blighted bliss," I wrote, "what we desired so to hear?" I said "we" as a little hint; and she showed me she could take a little hint. "I heard everything," she replied, "and I mean to keep it to myself!"

16"Work" (French).
17Town in Devonshire on Tor Bay, a seaside resort.

IX

It was impossible not to be moved with the strongest sympathy for her, and on my return to England I showed her every kindness in my power. Her mother's death had made her means sufficient, and she had gone to live in a more convenient quarter. But her loss had been great and her visitation cruel; it never would have occurred to me moreover to suppose she could come to feel the possession of a technical tip, of a piece of literary experience, a counterpoise to her grief. Strange to say, none the less, I could n't help believing after I had seen her a few times that I caught a glimpse of some such oddity. I hasten to add that there had been other things I could n't help believing, or at least imagining; and as I never felt I was really clear about these, so, as to the point I here touch on, I give her memory the benefit of the doubt. Stricken and solitary, highly accomplished and now, in her deep mourning, her maturer grace and her uncomplaining sorrow, incontestably handsome, she presented herself as lead-ing a life of singular dignity and beauty. I had at first found a way to persuade myself that I should soon get the better of the reserve formulated, the week after the catas-trophe, in her reply to an appeal as to which I was not unconscious that it might strike her as mistimed. Certainly that reserve was something of a shock to me — certainly it puzzled me the more I thought of it and even though I tried to explain it (with moments of success) by an imputation of exalted sentiments, of superstitious scru-ples, of a refinement of loyalty. Certainly it added at the same time hugely to the price of Vereker's secret, precious as this mystery already appeared. I may as well confess abjectly that Mrs. Corvick's unexpected attitude was the final tap on the nail that was to fix fast my luckless idea, convert it into the obsession of which I'm for ever conscious.

But this only helped me the more to be artful, to be adroit, to allow time to elapse before renewing my suit. There were plenty of speculations for the interval, and one of them was deeply absorbing. Corvick had kept his information from his young friend till after the removal of the last barrier to their intimacy — then only had he let the cat out of the bag. Was it Gwendolen's idea, taking a hint from him, to liberate this animal only on the basis of the renewal of such a relation? Was the figure in the carpet traceable or describable only for husbands and wives — for lovers supremely united? It came back to me in a mystifying manner that in Kensington Square, when I men-tioned that Corvick would have told the girl he loved, some word had dropped from Vereker that gave colour to this possibility. There might be little in it, but there was enough to make me wonder if I should have to marry Mrs. Corvick to get what I wanted. Was I prepared to offer her this price for the blessing of her knowledge? Ah that way madness lay! — so I at least said to myself in bewildered hours. I could see meanwhile the torch she refused to pass on flame away in her chamber of memory — pour through her eyes a light that shone in her lonely house. At the end of six months I was fully sure of what this warm presence made up to her for. We had talked again and again of the man who had brought us together — of his talent, his character, his personal charm, his certain career, his dreadful doom, and even of his clear purpose in that great study which was to have been a supreme literary portrait, a kind of critical Vandyke or Velasquez.[18] She had conveyed to me in abundance that she was tongue-tied by her perversity, by her piety, that she would never break the silence it had not been given to the "right person," as she said, to break. The hour however finally arrived. One evening when I had been sitting with her longer than usual I laid my hand firmly on her arm. "Now at last what *is* it?"

She had been expecting me and was ready. She gave a long slow soundless head-shake, merciful only in being inarticulate. This mercy did n't prevent its hurling at me the largest finest coldest "Never!" I had yet, in the course of a life that had known

---

[18]Sir Anthony Vandyke (1599–1641), Flemish painter and court painter to Charles I of England; Diego Rodriguez de Silva y Velásquez (1599–1660), Spanish painter, renowned for his realistic portrait of Philip IV of Spain.

denials, had to take full in the face. I took it and was aware that with the hard blow the tears had come into my eyes. So for a while we sat and looked at each other; after which I slowly rose. I was wondering if some day she would accept me; but this was not what I brought out. I said as I smoothed down my hat: "I know what to think then. It's nothing!"

A remote disdainful pity for me gathered in her dim smile; then she spoke in a voice that I hear at this hour. "It's my *life*!" As I stood at the door she added: "You've insulted him!"

"Do you mean Vereker?"

"I mean the Dead!"

I recognised when I reached the street the justice of her charge. Yes, it was her life — I recognised that too; but her life none the less made room with the lapse of time for another interest. A year and a half after Corvick's death she published in a single volume her second novel, "Overmastered," which I pounced on in the hope of finding in it some tell-tale echo or some peeping face. All I found was a much better book than her younger performance, showing I thought the better company she had kept. As a tissue tolerably intricate it was a carpet with a figure of its own; but the figure was not the figure I was looking for. On sending a review of it to *The Middle* I was surprised to learn from the office that a notice was already in type. When the paper came out I had no hesitation in attributing this article, which I thought rather vulgarly overdone, to Drayton Deane, who in the old days had been something of a friend of Corvick's, yet had only within a few weeks made the acquaintance of his widow. I had had an early copy of the book, but Dean had evidently had an earlier. He lacked all the same the light hand with which Corvick had gilded the gingerbread — he laid on the tinsel in splotches.

X

Six months later appeared "The Right of Way," the last chance, though we did n't know it, that we were to have to redeem ourselves. Written wholly during Vereker's sojourn abroad, the book had been heralded, in a hundred paragraphs, by the usual ineptitudes. I carried it, as early a copy as any, I this time flattered myself, straightway to Mrs. Corvick. This was the only use I had for it; I left the inevitable tribute of *The Middle* to some more ingenious mind and some less irritated temper. "But I already have it," Gwendolen said. "Drayton Deane was so good as to bring it to me yesterday, and I've just finished it."

"Yesterday? How did he get it so soon?"

"He gets everything so soon! He's to review it in *The Middle*."

"He — Drayton Deane — review Vereker?" I could n't believe my ears.

"Why not? One fine ignorance is as good as another."

I winced but I presently said: "You ought to review him yourself!"

"I don't 'review,'" she laughed. "I'm reviewed!"

Just then the door was thrown open. "Ah yes, here's your reviewer!" Drayton Deane was there with his long legs and his tall forehead: he had come to see what she thought of "The Right of Way," and to bring the news that was singularly relevant. The evening papers were just out with a telegram on the author of that work, who, in Rome, had been ill for some days with an attack of malarial fever. It had at first not been thought grave, but had taken, in consequence of complications, a turn that might give rise to anxiety. Anxiety had indeed at the latest hour begun to be felt.

I was struck in the presence of these tidings with the fundamental detachment that Mrs. Corvick's overt concern quite failed to hide: it gave me the measure of her consummate independence. That independence rested on her knowledge, the knowledge which nothing now could destroy and which nothing could make different. The figure in the carpet might take on another twist or two, but the sentence had virtually been written. The writer might go down to his grave: she was the person in the world to whom — as if she had been his favoured heir — his continued existence was least of a need. This reminded me how I had observed at a particular moment — after Corvick's death — the drop of her desire to see him face to face. She had got what she wanted without that. I had been sure that if she had n't got it she would n't have been restrained from the endeavour to sound him personally by those superior reflexions, more conceivable on a man's part than on a woman's, which in my case had served as a deterrent. It was n't however, I hasten to add, that my case, in spite of this invidious comparison, was n't ambiguous enough. At the thought that Vereker was perhaps at that moment dying there rolled over me a wave of anguish — a poignant sense of how inconsistently I still depended on him. A delicacy that it was my one compensation to suffer to rule me had left the Alps and the Apennines[19] between us, but the sense of the waning occasion suggested that I might in my despair at last have gone to him. Of course I should really have done nothing of the sort. I remained five minutes, while my companions talked of the new book, and when Drayton Deane appealed to me for my opinion of it I made answer, getting up, that I detested Hugh Vereker and simply could n't read him. I departed with the moral certainty that as the door closed behind me Deane would brand me for awfully superficial. His hostess would n't contradict *that* at least.

I continue to trace with a briefer touch our intensely odd successions. Three weeks after this came Vereker's death, and before the year was out the death of his wife. That poor lady I had never seen, but I had had a futile theory that, should she survive him long enough to be decorously accessible, I might approach her with the feeble flicker of my plea. Did she know and if she knew would she speak? It was much to be presumed that for more reasons than one she would have nothing to say; but when she passed out of all reach I felt renouncement indeed my appointed lot. I was shut up in my obsession for ever — my gaolers[20] had gone off with the key. I find myself quite as vague as a captive in a dungeon about the time that further elapsed before Mrs. Corvick became the wife of Drayton Deane. I had foreseen, through my bars, this end of the business, though there was no indecent haste and our friendship had rather fallen off. They were both so "awfully intellectual" that it struck people as a suitable match, but I had measured better than any one the wealth of understanding the bride would contribute to the union. Never, for a marriage in literary circles — so the newspapers described the alliance — had a lady been so bravely dowered. I began with due promptness to look for the fruit of the affair — that fruit, I mean, of which the premonitory symptoms would be peculiarly visible in the husband. Taking for granted the splendour of the other party's nuptial gift, I expected to see him make a show commensurate with his increase of means. I knew what his means had been — his article on "The Right of Way" had distinctly given one the figure. As he was now exactly in the position in which still more exactly I was not I watched from month to month, in the likely periodicals, for the heavy message poor Corvick had been unable to deliver and the responsibility of which would have fallen on his successor. The widow and wife would have broken by the rekindled hearth the silence that only a widow and wife might break, and Deane would be as aflame with the knowledge as Corvick in his own hour, as Gwendolen in hers, had been. Well, he was aflame doubtless, but the fire was apparently not to become a public blaze. I scanned the periodicals in vain: Drayton Deane filled them with exuberant pages, but he withheld the page I most feverishly sought. He wrote on a thousand subjects, but never on the subject of Vereker. His special line was to tell truths that other people either "funked,"[21] as he said, or overlooked, but he never told the only truth that seemed to me in these days to signify. I met the couple in those literary circles referred to in the papers: I have sufficiently intimated that it was only in such circles we

---

[19] Major mountain ranges of south central Europe and Italy.
[20] Jailers (British spelling).
[21] Avoided out of fear.

were all constructed to revolve. Gwendolen was more than ever committed to them by the publication of her third novel, and I myself definitely classed by holding the opinion that this work was inferior to its immediate predecessor. Was it worse because she had been keeping worse company? If her secret was, as she had told me, her life—a fact discernible in her increasing bloom, an air of conscious privilege that, cleverly corrected by pretty charities, gave distinction to her appearance—it had yet not a direct influence on her work. That only made one—everything only made one—yearn the more for it; only rounded it off with a mystery finer and subtler.

XI

It was therefore from her husband I could never remove my eyes: I beset him in a manner that might have made him uneasy. I went even so far as to engage him in conversation. *Did n't* he know, had n't he come into it as a matter of course?—that question hummed in my brain. Of course he knew; otherwise he would n't return my stare so queerly. His wife had told him what I wanted and he was amiably amused at my impotence. He did n't laugh—he was n't a laugher: his system was to present to my irritation, so that I should crudely expose myself, a conversational blank as vast as his big bare brow. It always happened that I turned away with a settled conviction from these unpeopled expanses, which seemed to complete each other geographically and to symbolise together Drayton Deane's want of voice, want of form. He simply had n't the art to use what he knew; he literally was incompetent to take up the duty where Corvick had left it. I went still further—it was the only glimpse of happiness I had. I made up my mind that the duty did n't appeal to him. He was n't interested, he did n't care. Yes, it quite comforted me to believe him too stupid to have joy of the thing I lacked. He was as stupid after as he had been before, and that deepened for me the golden glory in which the mystery was wrapped. I had of course none the less to recollect that his wife might have imposed her conditions and exactions. I had above all to remind myself that with Vereker's death the major incentive dropped. He was still there to be honoured by what might be done—he was no longer there to give it his sanction. Who alas but he had the authority?

Two children were born to the pair, but the second cost the mother her life. After this stroke I seemed to see another ghost of a chance. I jumped at it in thought, but I waited a certain time for manners, and at last my opportunity arrived in a remunerative way. His wife had been dead a year when I met Drayton Deane in the smoking-room of a small club of which we both were members, but where for months—perhaps because I rarely entered it—I had n't seen him. The room was empty and the occasion propitious. I deliberately offered him, to have done with the matter for ever, that advantage for which I felt he had long been looking.

"As an older acquaintance of your late wife's than even you were," I began, "you must let me say to you something I have on my mind. I shall be glad to make any terms with you that you see fit to name for the information she must have had from George Corvick—the information, you know, that had come to *him*, poor chap, in one of the happiest hours of his life, straight from Hugh Vereker."

He looked at me like a dim phrenological bust.[22] "The information—?"

"Vereker's secret, my dear man—the general intention of his books: the string the pearls were strung on, the buried treasure, the figure in the carpet."

He began to flush—the numbers on his bumps to come out. "Vereker's books had a general intention?"

I stared in my turn. "You don't mean to say you don't know it?" I thought for a moment he was playing with me. "Mrs. Deane knew it; she had it, as I say, straight from Corvick, who had, after infinite search and to Vereker's own delight, found the

---

[22]A bust used by phrenologists to map out and number on the head or cranium the various areas of the brain whose size or capacity determines the intensity of various personality traits and mental abilities of an individual, in accord with phrenology.

very mouth of the cave. Where *is* the mouth? He told after their marriage — and told alone — the person who, when the circumstances were reproduced, must have told *you*. Have I been wrong in taking for granted that she admitted you, as one of the highest privileges of the relation in which you stood to her, to the knowledge of which she was after Corvick's death the sole depositary? All *I* know is that that knowledge is infinitely precious, and what I want you to understand is that if you'll in your turn admit me to it you'll do me a kindness for which I shall be lastingly grateful."

He had turned at last very red; I dare say he had begun by thinking I had lost my wits. Little by little he followed me; on my own side I stared with a livelier surprise. Then he spoke. "I don't know what you're talking about."

He was n't acting — it was the absurd truth. "She *did n't* tell you — ?"

"Nothing about Hugh Vereker."

I was stupefied; the room went round. It had been too good even for that! "Upon your honour?"

"Upon my honour. What the devil's the matter with you?" he growled.

"I'm astounded — I'm disappointed. I wanted to get it out of you."

"It is n't *in* me!" he awkwardly laughed. "And even if it were —"

"If it were you'd let me have it — oh yes, in common humanity. But I believe you. I see — I see!" I went on, conscious, with the full turn of the wheel, of my great delusion, my false view of the poor man's attitude. What I saw, though I could n't say it, was that his wife had n't thought him worth enlightening. This struck me as strange for a woman who had thought him worth marrying. At last I explained it by the reflexion that she could n't possibly have married him for his understanding. She had married him for something else.

He was to some extent enlightened now, but he was even more astonished, more disconcerted: he took a moment to compare my story with his quickened memories. The result of his meditation was his presently saying with a good deal of rather feeble form: "This is the first I hear of what you allude to. I think you must be mistaken as to Mrs. Drayton Deane's having had any unmentioned, and still less any unmentionable, knowledge of Hugh Vereker. She'd certainly have wished it — should it have borne on his literary character — to be used."

"It *was* used. She used it herself. She told me with her own lips that she 'lived' on it."

I had no sooner spoken than I repented of my words; he grew so pale that I felt as if I had struck him. "Ah 'lived' — !" he murmured, turning short away from me.

My compunction was real; I laid my hand on his shoulder. "I beg you to forgive me — I've made a mistake. You *don't* know what I thought you knew. You could, if I had been right, have rendered me a service; and I had my reasons for assuming that you'd be in a position to meet me."

"Your reasons?" he echoed. "What were your reasons?"

I looked at him well; I hesitated; I considered. "Come and sit down with me here and I'll tell you." I drew him to a sofa, I lighted another cigar and, beginning with the anecdote of Vereker's one descent from the clouds, I recited to him the extraordinary chain of accidents that had, in spite of the original gleam, kept me till that hour in the dark. I told him in a word just what I've written out here. He listened with deepening attention, and I became aware, to my surprise, by his ejaculations, by his questions, that he would have been after all not unworthy to be trusted by his wife. So abrupt an experience of her want of trust had now a disturbing effect on him; but I saw the immediate shock throb away little by little and then gather again into waves of wonder and curiosity — waves that promised, I could perfectly judge, to break in the end with the fury of my own highest tides. I may say that to-day as victims of unappeased desire there is n't a pin to choose between us. The poor man's state is almost my consolation; there are really moments when I feel it to be quite my revenge.

1896, 1909

ON "THE FIGURE IN THE CARPET" (*from* PREFACE)
[INTENT: "TO REINSTATE ANALYTIC APPRECIATION"]

I to *this* extent recover the acute impression that may have given birth to "The Figure in the Carpet," that no truce, in English-speaking air, had ever seemed to me really struck, or even approximately strikeable, with our so marked collective mistrust of anything like close or analytic appreciation—appreciation, to *be* appreciation, implying of course some such rudimentary zeal; and this though that fine process be the Beautiful Gate itself of enjoyment. To have become consistently aware of this odd numbness of the general sensibilty, which seemed ever to condemn it, in presence of a work of art, to a view scarce of half the intentions embodied, and moreover but to the scantest measure of these, was to have been directed from an early day to some of the possible implications of the matter, and so to have been led on by seductive steps, albeit perhaps by devious ways, to such a congruous and, as I would fain call it, fascinating case as that of Hugh Vereker and his undiscovered, not to say undiscoverable, secret. That strikes me, when all is said, as an ample indication of the starting-point of this particular portrayal. There may be links missing between the chronic consciousness I have glanced at—that of Hugh Vereker's own analytic projector, speaking through the mouth of the anonymous scribe—and the poor man's attributive dependence, for the sense of being understood and enjoyed, on some responsive reach of critical perception that he is destined never to waylay with success; but even so they scarce signify, and I may not here attempt to catch them. This too in spite of the amusement almost always yielded by such recoveries and reminiscences, or to be gathered from the manipulation of any string of evolutionary pearls. What I most remember of my proper process is the lively impulse, at the root of it, to reinstate analytic appreciation, by some ironic or fantastic stroke, so far as possible, in its virtually forfeited rights and dignities. Importunate to this end had I long found the charming idea of some artist whose most characteristic intention, or cluster of intentions, should have taken all vainly for granted the public, or at the worst the not unthinkable private, excercise of penetration. I could n't, I confess, be indifferent to those rare and beautiful, or at all events odd and attaching, elements that might be imagined to grow in the shade of so much spent intensity and so much baffled calculation. The mere quality and play of an ironic consciousness in the designer left wholly alone, amid a chattering unperceiving world, with the thing he has most wanted to do, with the design more or less realised—some effectual glimpse of that might by itself, for instance, reward one's experiment. I came to Hugh Vereker, in fine, by this travelled road of a generalisation; the habit of having noted for many years how strangely and helplessly, among us all, what we call criticism—its curiosity never emerging from the limp state—is apt to stand off from the intended sense of things, from such finely-attested matters, on the artist's part, as a spirit and a form, a bias and a logic, of his own. From my definite preliminary it was no far cry to the conception of an intent worker who should find himself to the very end in presence but of the limp curiosity. Vereker's drama indeed—or I should perhaps rather say that of the aspiring young analyst whose report we read and to whom, I ruefully grant, I have ventured to impute a developed wit—is that at a given moment the limpness begins vaguely to throb and heave, to become conscious of a comparative tension. As an effect of this mild convulsion acuteness, at several points, struggles to enter the field, and the question that accordingly comes up, the issue of the affair, can be but whether the very secret of perception has n't been lost. That is the situation, and "The Figure in the Carpet" exhibits a small group of well-meaning persons engaged in a test. The reader is, on the evidence, left to conclude. . . . .

1909

The Beast in the Jungle[1]

I

What determined the speech that startled him in the course of their encounter scarcely matters, being probably but some words spoken by himself quite without intention—spoken as they lingered and slowly moved together after their renewal of acquaintance. He had been conveyed by friends an hour or two before to the house at which she was staying; the party of visitors at the other house, of whom he was one, and thanks to whom it was his theory, as always, that he was lost in the crowd, had been invited over to luncheon. There had been after luncheon much dispersal, all in the interest of the original motive, a view of Weatherend itself and the fine things, intrinsic features, pictures, heirlooms, treasures of all the arts, that made the place almost famous; and the great rooms were so numerous that guests could wander at their will, hang back from the principal group and in cases where they took such matters with the last seriousness give themselves up to mysterious appreciations and measurements. There were persons to be observed, singly or in couples, bending toward objects in out-of-the-way corners with their hands on their knees and their heads nodding quite as with the emphasis of an excited sense of smell. When they were two they either mingled their sounds of ecstasy or melted into silences of even deeper import, so that there were aspects of the occasion that gave it for Marcher much the air of the "look round," previous to a sale highly advertised, that excites or quenches, as may be, the dream of acquisition. The dream of acquisition at Weatherend would have had to be wild indeed, and John Marcher found himself, among such suggestions, disconcerted almost equally by the presence of those who knew too much and by that of those who knew nothing. The great rooms caused so much poetry and history to press upon him that he needed some straying apart to feel in a proper relation with them, though this impulse was not, as happened, like the gloating of some of his companions, to be compared to the movements of a dog sniffing a cupboard. It had an issue promptly enough in a direction that was not to have been calculated.

It led, briefly, in the course of the October afternoon, to his closer meeting with May Bartram, whose face, a reminder, yet not quite a remembrance, as they sat much separated at a very long table, had begun merely by troubling him rather pleasantly. It affected him as the sequel of something of which he had lost the beginning. He knew it, and for the time quite welcomed it, as a continuation, but did n't know what it continued, which was an interest or an amusement the greater as he was also somehow aware—yet without a direct sign from her—that the young woman herself had n't lost the thread. She had n't lost it, but she would n't give it back to him, he saw, without some putting forth of his hand for it; and he not only saw that, but saw several things more, things odd enough in the light of the fact that at the moment some accident of grouping brought them face to face he was still merely fumbling with the idea that any contact between them in the past would have had no importance. If it had had no importance he scarcely knew why his actual impression of her should so seem to have so much; the answer to which, however, was that in such a life as they all appeared to be leading for the moment one could but take things as they came. He was satisfied, without in the least being able to say why, that this young lady might roughly have ranked in the house as a poor relation; satisfied also that she was

---

[1]This story grew, says James in a 1901 *Notebook* entry, with the "small notion that comes to me of a man haunted by the fear, more and more, throughout life, that *something will happen to him*: he doesn't quite know what." By the time James finished the entry—a kind of exploratory thinking on the page—he had outlined the essentials of the story, including the protagonist's final awareness that "what *has* happened" is that "what might have happened" *didn't*. The narrative represents one of the finest examples of what James called a "drama of consciousness," with focus not on exterior but on interior (or intellectual-emotional) action.

not there on a brief visit, but was more or less a part of the establishment—almost a working, a remunerated part. Did n't she enjoy at periods a protection that she paid for by helping, among other services, to show the place and explain it, deal with the tiresome people, answer questions about the dates of the building, the styles of the furniture, the authorship of the pictures, the favourite haunts of the ghost? It was n't that she looked as if you could have given her shillings—it was impossible to look less so. Yet when she finally drifted toward him, distinctly handsome, though ever so much older—older than when he had seen her before—it might have been as an effect of her guessing that he had, within the couple of hours, devoted more imagination to her than to all the others put together, and had thereby penetrated to a kind of truth that the others were too stupid for. She *was* there on harder terms than any one; she was there as a consequence of things suffered, one way and another, in the interval of years; and she remembered him very much as she was remembered— only a good deal better.

By the time they at last thus came to speech they were alone in one of the rooms— remarkable for a fine portrait over the chimney-place—out of which their friends had passed, and the charm of it was that even before they had spoken they had practically arranged with each other to stay behind for talk. The charm, happily, was in other things too—partly in there being scarce a spot at Weatherend without something to stay behind for. It was in the way the autumn day looked into the high windows as it waned; the way the red light, breaking at the close from under a low sombre sky, reached out in a long shaft and played over old wainscots, old tapestry, old gold, old colour. It was most of all perhaps in the way she came to him as if, since she had been turned on to deal with the simpler sort, he might, should he choose to keep the whole thing down, just take her mild attention for a part of her general business. As soon as he heard her voice, however, the gap was filled up and the missing link supplied; the slight irony he divined in her attitude lost its advantage. He almost jumped at it to get there before her. "I met you years and years ago in Rome. I remember all about it." She confessed to disappointment—she had been so sure he did n't; and to prove how well he did he began to pour forth the particular recollections that popped up as he called for them. Her face and her voice, all at his service now, worked the miracle—the impression operating like the torch of a lamplighter who touches into flame, one by one, a long row of gas-jets. Marcher flattered himself the illumination was brilliant, yet he was really still more pleased on her showing him, with amusement, that in his haste to make everything right he had got most things rather wrong. It had n't been at Rome—it had been at Naples; and it had n't been eight years before—it had been more nearly ten. She had n't been, either, with her uncle and aunt, but with her mother and her brother; in addition to which it was not with the Pembles *he* had been, but with the Boyers, coming down in their company from Rome—a point on which she insisted, a little to his confusion, and as to which she had her evidence in hand. The Boyers she had known, but did n't know the Pembles, though she had heard of them, and it was the people he was with who had made them acquainted. The incident of the thunderstorm that had raged round them with such violence as to drive them for refuge into an excavation—this incident had not occurred at the Palace of the Caesars, but at Pompeii,[2] on an occasion when they had been present there at an important find.

He accepted her amendments, he enjoyed her corrections, though the moral of them was, she pointed out, that he *really* did n't remember the least thing about her; and he only felt it as a drawback that when all was made strictly historic there did n't appear much of anything left. They lingered together still, she neglecting her of-

---

[2]The ruins of Pompeii, at the foot of Vesuvius, are near Naples, not Rome.

fice—for from the moment he was so clever she had no proper right to him—and both neglecting the house, just waiting as to see if a memory or two more would n't again breathe on them. It had n't taken them many minutes, after all, to put down on the table, like the cards of a pack, those that constituted their respective hands; only what came out was that the pack was unfortunately not perfect—that the past, invoked, invited, encouraged, could give them, naturally, no more than it had. It had made them anciently meet—her at twenty, him at twenty-five; but nothing was so strange, they seemed to say to each other, as that, while so occupied, it had n't done a little more for them. They looked at each other as with the feeling of an occasion missed; the present would have been so much better if the other, in the far distance, in the foreign land, had n't been so stupidly meagre. There were n't apparently, all counted, more than a dozen little old things that had succeeded in coming to pass between them; trivialities of youth, simplicities of freshness, stupidities of ignorance, small possible germs, but too deeply buried—too deeply (did n't it seem?) to sprout after so many years. Marcher could only feel he ought to have rendered her some service—saved her from a capsized boat in the Bay or at least recovered her dressing-bag, filched from her cab in the streets of Naples by a lazzarone[3] with a stiletto. Or it would have been nice if he could have been taken with fever all alone at his hotel, and she could have come to look after him, to write to his people, to drive him out in convalescence. *Then* they would be in possession of the something or other that their actual show seemed to lack. It yet somehow presented itself, this show, as too good to be spoiled; so that they were reduced for a few minutes more to wondering a little helplessly why—since they seemed to know a certain number of the same people— their reunion had been so long averted. They did n't use that name for it, but their delay from minute to minute to join the others was a kind of confession that they did n't quite want it to be a failure. Their attempted supposition of reasons for their not having met but showed how little they knew of each other. There came in fact a moment when Marcher felt a positive pang. It was vain to pretend she was an old friend, for all the communities were wanting, in spite of which it was as an old friend that he saw she would have suited him. He had new ones enough—was surrounded with them for instance on the stage of the other house; as a new one he probably would n't have so much as noticed her. He would have liked to invent something, get her to make-believe with him that some passage of a romantic or critical kind *had* originally occurred. He was really almost reaching out in imagination—as against time—for something that would do, and saying to himself that if it did n't come this sketch of a fresh start would show for quite awkwardly bungled. They would separate, and now for no second or third chance. They would have tried and not succeeded. Then it was, just at the turn, as he afterwards made it out to himself, that, everything else failing, she herself decided to take up the case and, as it were, save the situation. He felt as soon as she spoke that she had been consciously keeping back what she said and hoping to get on without it; a scruple in her that immensely touched him when, by the end of three or four minutes more, he was able to measure it. What she brought out, at any rate, quite cleared the air and supplied the link—the link it was so odd he should frivolously have managed to lose.

"You know you told me something I've never forgotten and that again and again has made me think of you since; it was that tremendously hot day when we went to Sorrento,[4] across the bay, for the breeze. What I allude to was what you said to me, on the way back, as we sat under the awning of the boat enjoying the cool. Have you forgotten?"

He had forgotten and was even more surprised than ashamed. But the great thing

---

[3]Beggar.
[4]Resort across from Naples on the Bay of Naples.

was that he saw in this no vulgar reminder of any "sweet" speech. The vanity of women had long memories, but she was making no claim on him of a compliment or a mistake. With another woman, a totally different one, he might have feared the recall possibly even some imbecile "offer." So, in having to say that he had indeed forgotten, he was conscious rather of a loss than of a gain; he already saw an interest in the matter of her mention. "I try to think — but I give it up. Yet I remember the Sorrento day."

"I'm not very sure you do," May Bartram after a moment said; "and I'm not very sure I ought to want you to. It's dreadful to bring a person back at any time to what he was ten years before. If you 've lived away from it," she smiled, "so much the better."

"Ah if *you* have n't why should I?" he asked.

"Lived away, you mean, from what I myself was?"

"From what *I* was. I was of course an ass," Marcher went on; "but I would rather know from you just the sort of ass I was than — from the moment you have something in your mind — not know anything."

Still, however, she hesitated. "But if you 've completely ceased to be that sort — ?"

"Why I can then all the more bear to know. Besides, perhaps I have n't."

"Perhaps. Yet if you have n't," she added, "I should suppose you'd remember. Not indeed that *I* in the least connect with my impression the invidious name you use. If I had only thought you foolish," she explained, "the thing I speak of would n't so have remained with me. It was about yourself." She waited as if it might come to him; but as, only meeting her eyes in wonder, he gave no sign, she burnt her ships. "Has it ever happened?"

Then it was that, while he continued to stare, a light broke for him and the blood slowly came to his face, which began to burn with recognition. "Do you mean I told you — ?" But he faltered, lest what came to him should n't be right, lest he should only give himself away.

"It was something about yourself that it was natural one should n't forget — that is if one remembered you at all. That 's why I ask you," she smiled, "if the thing you then spoke of has ever come to pass?"

Oh then he saw, but he was lost in wonder and found himself embarrassed. This, he also saw, made her sorry for him, as if her allusion had been a mistake. It took him but a moment, however, to feel it had n't been, much as it had been a surprise. After the first little shock of it her knowledge on the contrary began, even if rather strangely, to taste sweet to him. She was the only other person in the world then who would have it, and she had had it all these years, while the fact of his having so breathed his secret had unaccountably faded from him. No wonder they could n't have met as if nothing had happened. "I judge," he finally said, "that I know what you mean. Only I had strangely enough lost any sense of having taken you so far into my confidence."

"Is it because you've taken so many others as well?"

"I've taken nobody. Not a creature since then."

"So that I'm the only person who knows?"

"The only person in the world."

"Well," she quickly replied, "I myself have never spoken. I've never, never repeated of you what you told me." She looked at him so that he perfectly believed her. Their eyes met over it in such a way that he was without a doubt. "And I never will."

She spoke with an earnestness that, as if almost excessive, put him at ease about her possible derision. Somehow the whole question was a new luxury to him — that is from the moment she was in possession. If she did n't take the sarcastic view she clearly took the sympathetic, and that was what he had had, in all the long time, from no one whomsoever. What he felt was that he could n't at present have begun to tell her, and yet could profit perhaps exquisitely by the accident of having done so of old. "Please don't then. We're just right as it is."

"Oh I am," she laughed, "if you are!" To which she added: "Then you do still feel in the same way?"

It was impossible he should n't take to himself that she was really interested, though it all kept coming as perfect surprise. He had thought of himself so long as abominably alone, and lo he was n't alone a bit. He had n't been, it appeared, for an hour—since those moments on the Sorrento boat. It was *she* who had been, he seemed to see as he looked at her—she who had been made so by the graceless fact of his lapse of fidelity. To tell her what he had told her—what had it been but to ask something of her? something that she had given, in her charity, without his having, by a remembrance, by a return of the spirit, failing another encounter, so much as thanked her. What he had asked of her had been simply at first not to laugh at him. She had beautifully not done so for ten years, and she was not doing so now. So he had endless gratitude to make up. Only for that he must see just how he had figured to her. "What, exactly, was the account I gave—?"

"Of the way you did feel? Well, it was very simple. You said you had had from your earliest time, as the deepest thing within you, the sense of being kept for something rare and strange, possibly prodigious and terrible, that was sooner or later to happen to you, that you had in your bones the foreboding and the conviction of, and that would perhaps overwhelm you."

"Do you call that very simple?" John Marcher asked.

She thought a moment. "It was perhaps because I seemed, as you spoke, to understand it."

"You do understand it?" he eagerly asked.

Again she kept her kind eyes on him. "You still have the belief?"

"Oh!" he exclaimed helplessly. There was too much to say.

"Whatever it's to be," she clearly made out, "it has n't yet come."

He shook his head in complete surrender now. "It has n't yet come. Only, you know, it is n't anything I'm to *do*, to achieve in the world, to be distinguished or admired for. I'm not such an ass as *that*. It would be much better, no doubt, if I were."

"It's to be something you 're merely to suffer?"

"Well, say to wait for—to have to meet, to face, to see suddenly break out in my life; possibly destroying all further consciousness, possibly annihilating me; possibly, on the other hand, only altering everything, striking at the root of all my world and leaving me to the consequences, however they shape themselves."

She took this in, but the light in her eyes continued for him not to be that of mockery. "Is n't what you describe perhaps but the expectation—or at any rate the sense of danger, familiar to so many people—of falling in love?"

John Marcher wondered. "Did you ask me that before?"

"No—I was n't so free-and-easy then. But it's what strikes me now."

"Of course," he said after a moment, "it strikes you. Of course it strikes *me*. Of course what 's in store for me may be no more than that. The only thing is," he went on, "that I think if it had been that I should by this time know."

"Do you mean because you've *been* in love?" And then as he but looked at her in silence: "You 've been in love, and it has n't meant such a cataclysm, has n't proved the great affair?"

"Here I am, you see. It has n't been overwhelming."

"Then it has n't been love," said May Bartram.

"Well, I at least thought it was. I took it for that—I 've taken it till now. It was agreeable, it was delightful, it was miserable," he explained. "But it was n't strange. It was n't what *my* affair 's to be."

"You want something all to yourself—something that nobody else knows or *has* known?"

"It is n't a question of what I 'want'—God knows I don't want anything. It's only a question of the apprehension that haunts me—that I live with day by day."

He said this so lucidly and consistently that he could see it further impose itself. If she had n't been interested before she 'd have been interested now. "Is it a sense of coming violence?"

Evidently now too again he liked to talk of it. "I don't think of it as — when it does come — necessarily violent. I only think of it as natural and as of course above all unmistakeable. I think of it simply as *the* thing. *The* thing will of itself appear natural."

"Then how will it appear strange?"

Marcher bethought himself. "It won't — to *me*."

"To whom then?"

"Well," he replied, smiling at last, "say to you."

"Oh then I'm to be present?"

"Why you *are* present — since you know."

"I see." She turned it over. "But I mean at the catastrophe."

At this, for a minute, their lightness gave way to their gravity; it was as if the long look they exchanged held them together. "It will only depend on yourself — if you'll watch with me."

"Are you afraid?" she asked.

"Don't leave me *now*," he went on.

"Are you afraid?" she repeated.

"Do you think me simply out of my mind?" he pursued instead of answering. "Do I merely strike you as a harmless lunatic?"

"No," said May Bartram. "I understand you. I believe you."

"You mean you feel how my obsession — poor old thing! — may correspond to some possible reality?"

"To some possible reality."

"Then you *will* watch with me?"

She hesitated, then for the third time put her question. "Are you afraid?"

"Did I tell you I was — at Naples?"

"No, you said nothing about it."

"Then I don't know. And I should *like* to know," said John Marcher. "You'll tell me yourself whether you think so. If you'll watch with me you'll see."

"Very good then." They had been moving by this time across the room, and at the door, before passing out, they paused as for the full wind-up of their understanding. "I'll watch with you," said May Bartram.

II

The fact that she "knew" — knew and yet neither chaffed him nor betrayed him — had in a short time begun to constitute between them a goodly bond, which became more marked when, within the year that followed their afternoon at Weatherend, the opportunities for meeting multiplied. The event that thus promoted these occasions was the death of the ancient lady her great-aunt, under whose wing, since losing her mother, she had to such an extent found shelter, and who, though but the widowed mother of the new successor to the property, had succeeded — thanks to a high tone and a high temper — in not forfeiting the supreme position of the great house. The deposition of this personage arrived but with her death, which, followed by many changes, made in particular a difference for the young woman in whom Marcher's expert attention had recognised from the first a dependent with a pride that might ache though it did n't bristle. Nothing for a long time had made him easier than the thought that the aching must have been much soothed by Miss Bartram's now finding herself able to set up a small home in London. She had acquired property, to an amount that made that luxury just possible, under her aunt's extremely complicated will, and when the whole matter began to be straightened out, which indeed took time, she let him know that the happy issue was at last in view. He had seen her again before that day, both because she had more than once accompanied the ancient lady to town and because he had paid another visit to the friends who so conveniently made of Weatherend one of the charms of their own hospitality. These friends had taken him back there; he had achieved there again with Miss Bartram some quiet detachment; and he had in London succeeded in persuading her to more than one brief absence from her aunt. They went together, on these latter occasions, to the National Gallery and the South Kensington Museum,[5] where, among vivid reminders, they talked of Italy at large — not now attempting to recover, as at first, the taste of their youth and their ignorance. That recovery, the first day at Weatherend, had served its purpose well, had given them quite enough; so that they were, to Marcher's sense, no longer hovering about the headwaters of their stream, but had felt their boat pushed sharply off and down the current.

They were literally afloat together; for our gentleman this was marked, quite as marked as that the fortunate cause of it was just the buried treasure of her knowledge. He had with his own hands dug up this little hoard, brought to light — that is to within reach of the dim day constituted by their discretions and privacies — the object of value the hiding-place of which he had, after putting it into the ground himself, so strangely, so long forgotten. The rare luck of his having again just stumbled on the spot made him indifferent to any other question; he would doubtless have devoted more time to the odd accident of his lapse of memory if he had n't been moved to devote so much to the sweetness, the comfort, as he felt, for the future, that this accident itself had helped to keep fresh. It had never entered into his plan that any one should "know," and mainly for the reason that it was n't in him to tell any one. That would have been impossible, for nothing but the amusement of a cold world would have waited on it. Since, however, a mysterious fate had opened his mouth betimes, in spite of him, he would count that a compensation and profit by it to the utmost. That the right person *should* know tempered the asperity of his secret more even than his shyness had permitted him to imagine; and May Bartram was clearly right, because — well, because there she was. Her knowledge simply settled it; he would have been sure enough by this time had she been wrong. There was that in his situation, no doubt, that disposed him too much to see her as a mere confidant, taking all her light for him from the fact — the fact only — of her interest in his predicament; from her mercy, sympathy, seriousness, her consent not to regard him as the funniest of the funny. Aware, in fine, that her price for him was just in her giving him this constant sense of his being admirably spared, he was careful to remember that she had also a life of her own, with things that might happen to *her*, things that in friendship one should likewise take account of. Something fairly remarkable came to pass with him, for that matter, in this connexion — something represented by a certain passage of his consciousness, in the suddenest way, from one extreme to the other.

He had thought himself, so long as nobody knew, the most disinterested person in the world, carrying his concentrated burden, his perpetual suspense, ever so quietly, holding his tongue about it, giving others no glimpse of it nor of its effect upon his life, asking of them no allowance and only making on his side all those that were asked. He had n't disturbed people with the queerness of their having to know a haunted man, though he had had moments of rather special temptation on hearing them say they were forsooth "unsettled." If they were as unsettled as he was — he who had never been settled for an hour in his life — they would know what it meant. Yet it was n't, all the same, for him to make them, and he listened to them civilly enough. This was why he had such good — though possibly such rather colourless — manners; this was why, above all, he could regard himself, in a greedy world, as decently — as in fact perhaps even a little sublimely — unselfish. Our point is accordingly that he valued this character quite sufficiently to measure his present danger of letting it lapse,

---

[5]I.e., the Victoria and Albert Museum, founded in 1851.

against which he promised himself to be much on his guard. He was quite ready, none the less, to be selfish just a little, since surely no more charming occasion for it had come to him. "Just a little," in a word, was just as much as Miss Bartram, taking one day with another, would let him. He never would be in the lease coercive, and would keep well before him the lines on which consideration for her — the very highest — ought to proceed. He would thoroughly establish the heads under which her affairs, her requirements, her peculiarities — he went so far as to give them the latitude of that name — would come into their intercourse. All this naturally was a sign of how much he took the intercourse itself for granted. There was nothing more to be done about *that*. It simply existed; had sprung into being with her first penetrating question to him in the autumn light there at Weatherend. The real form it should have taken on the basis that stood out large was the form of their marrying. But the devil in this was that the very basis itself put marrying out of the question. His conviction, his apprehension, his obsession, in short, was n't a privilege he could invite a woman to share; and that consequence of it was precisely what was the matter with him. Something or other lay in wait for him, amid the twists and the turns of the months and the years, like a crouching beast in the jungle. It signified little whether the crouching beast were destined to slay him or to be slain. The definite point was the inevitable spring of the creature; and the definite lesson from that was that a man of feeling did n't cause himself to be accompanied by a lady on a tiger-hunt. Such was the image under which he had ended by figuring his life.

They had at first, none the less, in the scattered hours spent together, made no allusion to that view of it; which was a sign he was handsomely alert to give that he did n't expect, that he in fact did n't care, always to be talking about it. Such a feature in one's outlook was really like a hump on one's back. The difference it made every minute of the day existed quite independently of discussion. One discussed of course *like* a hunchback, for there was always, if nothing else, the hunchback face. That remained, and she was watching him; but people watched best, as a general thing, in silence, so that such would be predominantly the manner of their vigil. Yet he did n't want, at the same time, to be tense and solemn; tense and solemn was what he imagined he too much showed for with other people. The thing to be, with the one person who knew, was easy and natural — to make the reference rather than be seeming to avoid it, to avoid it rather than be seeming to make it, and to keep it, in any case, familiar, facetious even, rather than pedantic and portentous. Some such consideration as the latter was doubtless in his mind for instance when he wrote pleasantly to Miss Bartram that perhaps the great thing he had so long felt as in the lap of the gods was no more than this circumstance, which touched him so nearly, of her acquiring a house in London. It was the first allusion they had yet again made, needing any other hitherto so little; but when she replied, after having given him the news, that she was by no means satisfied with such a trifle as the climax to so special a suspense, she almost set him wondering if she had n't even a larger conception of singularity for him than he had for himself. He was at all events destined to become aware little by little, as time went by, that she was all the while looking at his life, judging it, measuring it, in the light of the thing she knew, which grew to be at last, with the consecration of the years, never mentioned between them save as "the real truth" about him. That had always been his own form of reference to it, but she adopted the form so quietly that, looking back at the end of a period, he knew there was no moment at which it was traceable that she had, as he might say, got inside his idea, or exchanged the attitude of beautifully indulging for that of still more beautifully believing him.

It was always open to him to accuse her of seeing him but as the most harmless of maniacs, and this, in the long run — since it covered so much ground — was his easiest description of their friendship. He had a screw loose for her, but she liked him in spite of it and was practically, against the rest of the world, his kind wise keeper, unremunerated but fairly amused and, in the absence of other near ties, not disreputably occupied. The rest of the world of course thought him queer, but she, she only, knew how, and above all why, queer; which was precisely what enabled her to dispose the concealing veil in the right folds. She took his gaiety from him — since it had to pass with them for gaiety — as she took everything else; but she certainly so far justified by her unerring touch his finer sense of the degree to which he had ended by convincing her. *She* at least never spoke of the secret of his life except as "the real truth about you," and she had in fact a wonderful way of making it seem, as such, the secret of her own life too. That was in fine how he so constantly felt her as allowing for him; he could n't on the whole call it anything else. He allowed for himself, but she, exactly, allowed still more; partly because, better placed for a sight of the matter, she traced his unhappy perversion through reaches of its course into which he could scarce follow it. He knew how he felt, but, besides knowing that, she knew how he *looked* as well; he knew each of the things of importance he was insidiously kept from doing, but she could add up the amount they made, understand how much, with a lighter weight on his spirit, he might have done, and thereby establish how, clever as he was, he fell short. Above all she was in the secret of the difference between the forms he went through — those of his little office under Government, those of caring for his modest patrimony, for his library, for his garden in the country, for the people in London whose invitations he accepted and repaid — and the detachment that reigned beneath them and that made of all behaviour, all that could in the least be called behaviour, a long act of dissimulation. What it had come to was that he wore a mask painted with the social simper, out of the eye-holes of which there looked eyes of an expression not in the least matching the other features. This the stupid world, even after years, had never more than half-discovered. It was only May Bartram who had, and she achieved, by an art indescribable, the feat of at once — or perhaps it was only alternately — meeting the eyes from in front and mingling her own vision, as from over his shoulder, with their peep through the apertures.

So while they grew older together she did watch with him, and so she let this association give shape and colour to her own existence. Beneath *her* forms as well detachment had learned to sit, and behaviour had become for her, in the social sense, a false account of herself. There was but one account of her that would have been true all the while and that she could give straight to nobody, least of all to John Marcher. Her whole attitude was a virtual statement, but the perception of that only seemed called to take its place for him as one of the many things necessarily crowded out of his consciousness. If she had moreover, like himself, to make sacrifices to their real truth, it was to be granted that her compensation might have affected her as more prompt and more natural. They had long periods, in this London time, during which, when they were together, a stranger might have listened to them without in the least pricking up his ears; on the other hand the real truth was equally liable at any moment to rise to the surface, and the auditor would then have wondered indeed what they were talking about. They had from an early hour made up their mind that society was, luckily, unintelligent, and the margin allowed them by this had fairly become one of their commonplaces. Yet there were still moments when the situation turned almost fresh — usually under the effect of some expression drawn from herself. Her expressions doubtless repeated themselves, but her intervals were generous. "What saves us, you know, is that we answer so completely to so usual an appearance: that of the man and woman whose friendship has become such a daily habit — or almost — as to be at last indispensable." That for instance was a remark she had frequently enough had occasion to make, though she had given it at different times different developments. What we are especially concerned with is the turn it happened to take from her one afternoon when he had come to see her in honour of her birthday. This anniversary had fallen on a Sunday, at a season of thick fog and general outward gloom; but he had brought her his customary offering, having known her now long enough to have established a hundred small traditions. It was one of his proofs to himself, the present he made her on her birthday, that he had n't sunk into real selfishness. It was mostly nothing more than a small trinket, but it was always fine of its kind, and he was regularly careful to pay for it more than he thought he could afford. "Our habit saves you at least, don't you see? because it makes you, after all, for the vulgar, indistinguishable from other men. What's the most inveterate mark of men in general? Why the capacity to spend endless time with dull women — to spend it I won't say without being bored, but without minding that they are, without being driven off at a tangent by it; which comes to the same thing. I'm your dull woman, a part of the daily bread for which you pray at church. That covers your tracks more than anything."

"And what covers yours?" asked Marcher, whom his dull woman could mostly to this extent amuse. "I see of course what you mean by your saving me, in this way and that, so far as other people are concerned — I've seen it all along. Only what is it that saves *you*? I often think, you know, of that."

She looked as if she sometimes thought of that too, but rather in a different way. "Where other people, you mean, are concerned?"

"Well, you're really so in with me, you know — as a sort of result of my being so in with yourself. I mean of my having such an immense regard for you, being so tremendously mindful of all you've done for me. I sometimes ask myself if it's quite fair. Fair I mean to have so involved and — since one may say it — interested you. I almost feel as if you had n't really had time to do anything else."

"Anything else but be interested?" she asked. "Ah what else does one ever want to be? If I've been 'watching' with you, as we long ago agreed I was to do, watching's always in itself an absorption."

"Oh certainly," John Marcher said, "if you had n't had your curiosity — ! Only does n't it sometimes come to you as time goes on that your curiosity is n't being particularly repaid?"

May Bartram had a pause. "Do you ask that, by any chance, because you feel at all that yours is n't? I mean because you have to wait so long."

Oh he understood what she meant! "For the thing to happen that never does happen? For the beast to jump out? No, I'm just where I was about it. It is n't a matter as to which I can *choose*, I can decide for a change. It is n't one as to which there *can* be a change. It 's in the lap of the gods. One's in the hands of one's law — there one is. As to the form the law will take, the way it will operate, that 's its own affair."

"Yes," Miss Bartram replied; "of course one's fate's coming, of course it *has* come in its own form and its own way, all the while. Only, you know, the form and the way in your case were to have been — well, something so exceptional and, as one may say, so particularly *your* own."

Something in this made him look at her with suspicion. "You say 'were to *have* been,' as if in your heart you had begun to doubt."

"Oh!" she vaguely protested.

"As if you believed," he went on, "that nothing will now take place."

She shook her head slowly but rather inscrutably. "You're far from my thought."

He continued to look at her. "What then is the matter with you?"

"Well," she said after another wait, "the matter with me is simply that I'm more sure than ever my curiosity, as you call it, will be but too well repaid."

They were frankly grave now; he had got up from his seat, had turned once more about the little drawing-room to which, year after year, he brought his inevitable topic; in which he had, as he might have said, tasted their intimate community with every sauce, where every object was as familiar to him as the things of his own house and the very carpets were worn with his fitful walk very much as the desks in old counting-houses are worn by the elbows of generations of clerks. The generations of his nervous moods had been at work there, and the place was the written history of his whole middle life. Under the impression of what his friend had just said he knew himself, for some reason, more aware of these things; which made him, after a moment, stop again before her. "Is it possibly that you 've grown afraid?"

"Afraid?" He thought, as she repeated the word, that his question had made her, a little, change colour; so that, lest he should have touched on a truth, he explained very kindly: "You remember that that was what you asked *me* long ago—that first day at Weatherend."

"Oh yes, and you told me you did n't know—that I was to see for myself. We 've said little about it since, even in so long a time."

"Precisely," Marcher interposed—"quite as if it were too delicate a matter for us to make free with. Quite as if we might find, on pressure, that I *am* afraid. For then," he said, "we should n't, should we? quite know what to do."

She had for the time no answer to this question. "There have been days when I thought you were. Only, of course," she added, "there have been days when we have thought almost anything."

"Everything. Oh!" Marcher softly groaned as with a gasp, half-spent, at the face, more uncovered just then than it had been for a long while, of the imagination always with them. It had always had its incalculable moments of glaring out, quite as with the very eyes of the very Beast, and used as he was to them, they could still draw from him the tribute of a sigh that rose from the depths of his being. All they had thought, first and last, rolled over him; the past seemed to have been reduced to mere barren speculation. This in fact was what the place had just struck him as so full of—the simplification of everything but the state of suspense. That remained only by seeming to hang in the void surrounding it. Even his original fear, if fear it had been, had lost itself in the desert. "I judge, however," he continued, "that you see I'm not afraid now."

"What I see, as I make it out, is that you 've achieved something almost unprecedented in the way of getting used to danger. Living with it so long and so closely you 've lost your sense of it; you know it 's there, but you 're indifferent, and you cease even, as of old, to have to whistle in the dark. Considering what the danger is," May Bartram wound up, "I'm bound to say I don't think your attitude could well be surpassed."

John Marcher faintly smiled. "It's heroic?"

"Certainly—call it that."

It was what he would have liked indeed to call it. "I *am* then a man of courage?"

"That's what you were to show me."

He still, however, wondered. "But does n't the man of courage know what he's afraid of—or *not* afraid of? I don't know *that*, you see. I don't focus it. I can't name it. I only know I'm exposed."

"Yes, but exposed—how shall I say?—so directly. So intimately. That's surely enough."

"Enough to make you feel then—as what we may call the end and the upshot of our watch—that I'm not afraid?"

"You're not afraid. But it is n't," she said, "the end of our watch. That is it is n't the end of yours. You've everything still to see."

"Then why have n't *you*?" he asked. He had had, all along, to-day, the sense of her keeping something back. As this was his first impression of that it quite made a date. The case was the more marked as she did n't at first answer; which in turn made him go on. "You know something I don't." Then his voice, for that of a man of courage, trembled a little. "You know what 's to happen." Her silence, with the face she showed, was almost a confession—it made him sure. "You know, and you're afraid to tell me. It's so bad that you're afraid I'll find out."

All this might be true, for she did look as if, unexpectedly to her, he had crossed some mystic line that she had secretly drawn round her. Yet she might, after all, not have worried; and the real climax was that he himself, at all events, need n't. "You 'll never find out."

III

It was all to have made, none the less, as I have said, a date; which came out in the fact that again and again, even after long intervals, other things that passed between them wore in relation to this hour but the character of recalls and results. Its immediate effect had been indeed rather to lighten insistence — almost to provoke a reaction; as if their topic had dropped by its own weight and as if moreover, for that matter, Marcher had been visited by one of his occasional warnings against egotism. He had kept up, he felt, and very decently on the whole, his consciousness of the importance of not being selfish, and it was true that he had never sinned in that direction without promptly enough trying to press the scales the other way. He often repaired his fault, the season permitting, by inviting his friend to accompany him to the opera; and it not infrequently thus happened that, to show he did n't wish her to have but one sort of food for her mind, he was the cause of her appearing there with him a dozen nights in the month. It even happened that, seeing her home at such times, he occasionally went in with her to finish, as he called it, the evening, and, the better to make his point, sat down to the frugal but always careful little supper that awaited his pleasure. His point was made, he thought, by his not eternally insisting with her on himself; made for instance, at such hours, when it befell that, her piano at hand and each of them familiar with it, they went over passages of the opera together. It chanced to be on one of these occasions, however, that he reminded her of her not having answered a certain question he had put to her during the talk that had taken place between them on her last birthday. "What is it that saves *you?*" — saved her, he meant, from that appearance of variation from the usual human type. If he had practically escaped remark, as she pretended, by doing, in the most important particular, what most men do — find the answer to life in patching up an alliance of a sort with a woman no better than himself — how had she escaped it, and how could the alliance, such as it was, since they must suppose it had been more or less noticed, have failed to make her rather positively talked about?

"I never said," May Bartram replied, "that it had n't made me a good deal talked about."

"Ah well then you 're not 'saved.'"

"It has n't been a question for me. If you 've had your woman I 've had," she said, "my man."

"And you mean that makes you all right?"

Oh it was always as if there were so much to say! "I don't know why it should n't make me — humanly, which is what we 're speaking of — as right as it makes you."

"I see," Marcher returned. "'Humanly,' no doubt, as showing that you 're living for something. Not, that is, just for me and my secret."

May Bartram smiled. "I don't pretend it exactly shows that I 'm not living for you. It 's my intimacy with you that 's in question."

He laughed as he saw what she meant. "Yes, but since, as you say, I 'm only, so far as people make out, ordinary, you 're — are n't you? — no more than ordinary either. You help me to pass for a man like another. So if I *am*, as I understand you, you 're not compromised. Is that it?"

She had another of her waits, but she spoke clearly enough. "That 's it. It 's all that concerns me — to help you pass for a man like another."

He was careful to acknowledge the remark handsomely. "How kind, how beautiful, you are to me! How shall I ever repay you?"

She had her last grave pause, as if there might be a choice of ways. But she chose. "By going on as you are."

It was into this going on as he was that they relapsed, and really for so long a time that the day inevitably came for a further sounding of their depths. These depths, constantly bridged over by a structure firm enough in spite of its lightness and of its occasional oscillation in the somewhat vertiginous air, invited on occasion, in the interest of their nerves, a dropping of the plummet and a measurement of the abyss. A difference had been made moreover, once for all, by the fact that she had all the while not appeared to feel the need of rebutting his charge of an idea within her that he didn't dare to express—a charge uttered just before one of the fullest of their later discussions ended. It had come up for him then that she "knew" something and that what she knew was bad—too bad to tell him. When he had spoken of it as visibly so bad that she was afraid he might find it out, her reply had left the matter too equivocal to be let alone and yet, for Marcher's special sensibility, almost too formidable again to touch. He circled about it at a distance that alternately narrowed and widened and that still wasn't much affected by the consciousness in him that there was nothing she could "know," after all, any better than he did. She had no source of knowledge he hadn't equally—except of course that she might have finer nerves. That was what women had where they were interested; they made out things, where people were concerned, that the people often couldn't have made out for themselves. Their nerves, their sensibility, their imagination, were conductors and revealers, and the beauty of May Bartram was in particular that she had given herself so to his case. He felt in these days what, oddly enough, he had never felt before, the growth of a dread of losing her by some catastrophe—some catastrophe that yet wouldn't at all be *the* catastrophe: partly because she had almost of a sudden begun to strike him as more useful to him than ever yet, and partly by reason of an appearance of uncertainty in her health, coincident and equally new. It was characteristic of the inner detachment he had hitherto so successfully cultivated and to which our whole account of him is a reference, it was characteristic that his complications, such as they were, had never yet seemed so as at this crisis to thicken about him, even to the point of making him ask himself if he were, by any chance, of a truth, within sight or sound, within touch or reach, within the immediate jurisdiction, of the thing that waited.

When the day came, as come it had to, that his friend confessed to him her fear of a deep disorder in her blood, he felt somehow the shadow of a change and the chill of a shock. He immediately began to imagine aggravations and disasters, and above all to think of her peril as the direct menace for himself of personal privation. This indeed gave him one of those partial recoveries of equanimity that were agreeable to him—it showed him that what was still first in his mind was the loss she herself might suffer. "What if she should have to die before knowing, before seeing—?" It would have been brutal, in the early stages of her trouble, to put that question to her; but it had immediately sounded for him to his own concern, and the possibility was what most made him sorry for her. If she did "know," moreover, in the sense of her having had some—what should he think?—mystical irresistible light, this would make the matter not better, but worse, inasmuch as her original adoption of his own curiosity had quite become the basis of her life. She had been living to see what would *be* to be seen, and it would quite lacerate her to have to give up before the accomplishment of the vision. These reflexions, as I say, quickened his generosity; yet, make them as he might, he saw himself, with the lapse of the period, more and more disconcerted. It lapsed for him with a strange steady sweep, and the oddest oddity was that it gave him, independently of the threat of much inconvenience, almost the only positive surprise his career, if career it could be called, had yet offered him. She kept the house as she had never done; he had to go to her to see her—she could meet him nowhere now, though there was a scarce a corner of their loved old London in which she hadn't in the past, at one time or another, done so; and he found her always seated by her fire in the deep old-fashioned chair she was less and less able to leave. He had been struck one day, after an absence exceeding his usual measure, with her suddenly looking much older to him than he had ever thought of her being; then he recognised that the suddenness was all on his side—he had just simply and suddenly noticed. She looked older because inevitably, after so many years, she *was* old, or almost; which was of course true in still greater measure of her companion. If she was old, or almost, John Marcher assuredly was, and yet it was her showing of the lesson, not his own, that brought the truth home to him. His surprises began here; when once they had begun they multiplied; they came rather with a rush: it was as if, in the oddest way in the world, they had all been kept back, sown in a thick cluster, for the late afternoon of life, the time at which for people in general the unexpected has died out.

One of them was that he should have caught himself—for he *had* done so—*really* wondering if the great accident would take form now as nothing more than his being condemned to see this charming woman, this admirable friend, pass away from him. He had never so unreservedly qualified her as while confronted in thought with such a possibility; in spite of which there was small doubt for him that as an answer to his long riddle the mere effacement of even so fine a feature of his situation would be an abject anticlimax. It would represent, as connected with his past attitude, a drop of dignity under the shadow of which his existence could only become the most grotesque of failures. He had been far from holding it a failure—long as he had waited for the appearance that was to make it a success. He had waited for quite another thing, not for such a thing as that. The breath of his good faith came short, however, as he recognised how long he had waited, or how long at least his companion had. That she, at all events, might be recorded as having waited in vain—this affected him sharply, and all the more because of his at first having done little more than amuse himself with the idea. It grew more grave as the gravity of her condition grew, and the state of mind it produced in him, which he himself ended by watching as if it had been some definite disfigurement of his outer person, may pass for another of his surprises. This conjoined itself still with another, the really stupefying consciousness of a question that he would have allowed to shape itself had he dared. What did everything mean—what, that is, did *she* mean, she and her vain waiting and her probable death and the soundless admonition of it all—unless that, at this time of day, it was simply, it was overwhelmingly too late? He had never at any stage of his queer consciousness admitted the whisper of such a correction; he had never till within these last few months been so false to his conviction as not to hold that what was to come to him had time, whether *he* struck himself as having it or not. That at last, at last, he certainly had n't it, to speak of, or had it but in the scantiest measure—such, soon enough, as things went with him, became the inference with which his old obsession had to reckon: and this it was not helped to do by the more and more confirmed appearance that the great vagueness casting the long shadow in which he had lived had, to attest itself, almost no margin left. Since it was in Time that he was to have met his fate, so it was in Time that his fate was to have acted; and as he waked up to the sense of no longer being young, which was exactly the sense of being stale, just as that, in turn, was the sense of being weak, he waked up to another matter beside. It all hung together; they were subject, he and the great vagueness, to an equal and indivisible law. When the possibilities themselves had accordingly turned stale, when the secret of the gods had grown faint, had perhaps even quite evaporated, that, and that only, was failure. It would n't have been failure to be bankrupt, dishonoured, pilloried, hanged; it was failure not to be anything. And so, in the dark valley into which his path had taken its unlooked-for twist, he wondered not a little as he groped. He did n't care what awful crash might overtake him, with what ignominy or what monstrosity he might yet be associated—since he was n't after all too utterly old to suffer—if it would only be decently proportionate to the posture he had kept, all his life, in the threatened presence of it. He had but one desire left—that he should n't have been "sold."

IV

Then it was that, one afternoon, while the spring of the year was young and new she met all in her own way his frankest betrayal of these alarms. He had gone in late to see her, but evening had n't settled and she was presented to him in that long fresh light of waning April days which affects us often with a sadness sharper than the greyest hours of autumn. The week had been warm, the spring was supposed to have begun early, and May Bartram sat, for the first time in the year, without a fire; a fact that, to Marcher's sense, gave the scene of which she formed part a smooth and ultimate look, an air of knowing, in its immaculate order and cold meaningless cheer, that it would never see a fire again. Her own aspect — he could scarce have said why — intensified this note. Almost as white as wax, with the marks and signs in her face as numerous and as fine as if they had been etched by a needle, with soft white draperies relieved by a faded green scarf on the delicate tone of which the years had further refined, she was the picture of a serene and exquisite but impenetrable sphinx, whose head, or indeed all whose person, might have been powdered with silver. She was a sphinx, yet with her white petals and green fronds she might have been a lily too — only an artificial lily, wonderfully imitated and constantly kept, without dust or stain, though not exempt from a slight droop and a complexity of faint creases, under some clear glass bell. The perfection of household care, of high polish and finish, always reigned in her rooms, but they now looked most as if everything had been wound up, tucked in, put away, so that she might sit with folded hands and with nothing more to do. She was "out of it," to Marcher's vision; her work was over; she communicated with him as across some gulf or from some island of rest that she had already reached, and it made him feel strangely abandoned. Was it — or rather was n't it — that if for so long she had been watching with him the answer to their question must have swum into her ken and taken on its name, so that her occupation was verily gone? He had as much as charged her with this in saying to her, many months before, that she even then knew something she was keeping from him. It was a point he had never since ventured to press, vaguely fearing as he did that it might become a difference, perhaps a disagreement, between them. He had in this later time turned nervous, which was what he, in all the other years had never been; and the oddity was that his nervousness should have waited till he had begun to doubt, should have held off so long as he was sure. There was something, it seemed to him, that the wrong word would bring down on his head, something that would so at least ease off his tension. But he wanted not to speak the wrong word; that would make everything ugly. He wanted the knowledge he lacked to drop on him, if drop it could, by its own august weight. If she was to forsake him it was surely for her to take leave. This was why he did n't directly ask her again what she knew; but it was also why, approaching the matter from another side, he said to her in the course of his visit: "What do you regard as the very worst that at this time of day *can* happen to me?"

He had asked her that in the past often enough; they had, with the odd irregular rhythm of their intensities and avoidances, exchanged ideas about it and then had seen the ideas washed away by cool intervals, washed like figures traced in sea-sand. It had ever been the mark of their talk that the oldest allusions in it required but a little dismissal and reaction to come out again, sounding for the hour as new. She could thus at present meet his enquiry quite freshly and patiently. "Oh yes, I 've repeatedly thought, only it always seemed to me of old that I could n't quite make up my mind. I thought of dreadful things, between which it was difficult to choose; and so must you have done."

"Rather! I feel now as I had scarce done anything else. I appear to myself to have spent my life in thinking of nothing *but* dreadful things. A great many of them I 've at different times named to you, but there were others I could n't name."

"They were too, too dreadful?"

"Too, too dreadful—some of them."

She looked at him a minute, and there came to him as he met it an inconsequent sense that her eyes, when one got their full clearness, were still as beautiful as they had been in youth, only beautiful with a strange cold light—a light that somehow was a part of the effect, if it was n't rather a part of the cause, of the pale hard sweetness of the season and the hour. "And yet," she said at last, "there are horrors we 've mentioned."

It deepened the strangeness to see her, as such a figure in such a picture, talk of "horrors," but she was to do in a few minutes something stranger yet—though even of this he was to take the full measure but afterwards—and the note of it already trembled. It was, for the matter of that, one of the signs that her eyes were having again the high flicker of their prime. He had to admit, however, what she said. "Oh yes, there were times when we did go far." He caught himself in the act of speaking as if it all were over. Well, he wished it were; and the consummation depended for him clearly more and more on his friend.

But she had now a soft smile. "Oh far—!"

It was oddly ironic. "Do you mean you 're prepared to go further?"

She was frail and ancient and charming as she continued to look at him, yet it was rather as if she had lost the thread. "Do you consider that we went far?"

"Why I thought it the point you were just making—that we *had* looked most things in the face."

"Including each other?" She still smiled. "But you 're quite right. We 've had together great imaginations, often great fears; but some of them have been unspoken."

"Then the worse—we have n't faced that. I *could* face it, I believe, if I knew what you think it. I feel," he explained, "as if I had lost my power to conceive such things." And he wondered if he looked as blank as he sounded. "It 's spent."

"Then why do you assume," she asked, "that mine is n't?"

"Because you 've given me signs to the contrary. It is n't a question for you of conceiving, imagining, comparing. It is n't a question now of choosing." At last he came out with it. "You know something I don't. You 've shown me that before."

These last words had affected her, he made out in a moment, exceedingly, and she spoke with firmness. "I 've shown you, my dear, nothing."

He shook his head. "You can't hide it."

"Oh, oh!" May Bartram sounded over what she could n't hide. It was almost a smothered groan.

"You admitted it months ago, when I spoke of it to you as of something you were afraid I should find out. Your answer was that I could n't, that I would n't, and I don't pretend I have. But you had something therefore in mind, and I now see how it must have been, how it still is, the possibility that, of all possibilities, has settled itself for you as the worst. This," he went on, "is why I appeal to you. I 'm only afraid of ignorance to-day—I 'm not afraid of knowledge." And then as for a while she said nothing: "What makes me sure is that I see in your face and feel here, in this air and amid these appearances, that you 're out of it. You 've done. You 've had your experience. You leave me to my fate."

Well, she listened, motionless and white in her chair, as on a decision to be made, so that her manner was fairly an avowal, though still, with a small fine inner stiffness, an imperfect surrender. "It *would* be the worst," she finally let herself say. "I mean the thing I 've never said."

It hushed him a moment. "More monstrous than all the monstrosities we 've named?"

"More monstrous. Is n't that what you sufficiently express," she asked, "in calling it the worst?"

Marcher thought. "Assuredly—if you mean, as I do, something that includes all the loss and all the shame that are thinkable."

"It would it if *should* happen," said May Bartram. "What we're speaking of, remember, is only my idea."

"It's your belief," Marcher returned. "That's enough for me. I feel your beliefs are right. Therefore if, having this one, you give me no more light on it, you abandon me."

"No, no!" she repeated. "I'm with you—don't you see?—still." And as to make it more vivid to him she rose from her chair—a movement she seldom risked in these days—and showed herself, all draped and all soft, in her fairness and slimness. "I have n't forsaken you."

It was really, in its effort against weakness, a generous assurance, and had the success of the impulse not, happily, been great, it would have touched him to pain more than to pleasure. But the cold charm in her eyes had spread, as she hovered before him, to all the rest of her person, so that it was for the minute almost a recovery of youth. He could n't pity her for that; he could only take her as she showed—as capable even yet of helping him. It was as if, at the same time, her light might at any instant go out; wherefore he must make the most of it. There passed before him with intensity the three or four things he wanted most to know; but the question that came of itself to his lips really covered the others. "Then tell me if I shall consciously suffer."

She promptly shook her head. "Never!"

It confirmed the authority he imputed to her, and it produced on him an extraordinary effect. "Well, what's better than that? Do you call that the worst?"

"You think nothing is better?" she asked.

She seemed to mean something so special that he again sharply wondered, though still with the dawn of a prospect of relief. "Why not, if one does n't *know*?" After which, as their eyes, over his question, met in a silence, the dawn deepened and something to his purpose came prodigiously out of her very face. His own, as he took it in, suddenly flushed to the forehead, and he gasped with the force of a perception to which, on the instant, everything fitted. The sound of his gasp filled the air; then he became articulate. "I see—if I don't suffer!"

In her own look, however, was doubt. "You see what?"

"Why what you mean—what you've always meant."

She again shook her head. "What I mean is n't what I've always meant. It's different."

"It's something new?"

She hung back from it a little. "Something new. It's not what you think. I see what you think."

His divination drew breath then; only her correction might be wrong. "It is n't that I *am* a blockhead?" he asked between faintness and grimness. "It is n't that it's all a mistake?"

"A mistake?" she pityingly echoed. *That* possibility, for her, he saw, would be monstrous; and if she guaranteed him the immunity from pain it would accordingly not be what she had in mind. "Oh no," she declared; "it's nothing of that sort. You've been right."

Yet he could n't help asking himself if she were n't, thus pressed, speaking but to save him. It seemed to him he should be most in a hole if his history should prove all a platitude. "Are you telling me the truth, so that I shan't have been a bigger idiot than I can bear to know? I *have n't* lived with a vain imagination, in the most besotted illusion? I have n't waited but to see the door shut in my face?"

She shook her head again. "However the case stands *that* is n't the truth. Whatever the reality, it *is* a reality. The door is n't shut. The door's open," said May Bartram.

"Then something's to come?"

She waited once again, always with her cold sweet eyes on him. "It's never too late." She had, with her gliding step, diminished the distance between them, and she stood nearer to him, close to him, a minute, as if still charged with the unspoken. Her movement might have been for some finer emphasis of what she was at once hesitating and deciding to say. He had been standing by the chimney-piece, fireless and sparely adorned, a small perfect old French clock and two morsels of rosy Dresden constituting all its furniture; and her hand grasped the shelf while she kept him waiting, grasped it a little as for support and encouragement. She only kept him waiting, however; that is he only waited. It had become suddenly, from her movement and attitude, beautiful and vivid to him that she had something more to give him; her wasted face delicately shone with it — it glittered almost as with the white lustre of silver in her expression. She was right, incontestably, for what he saw in her face was the truth, and strangely, without consequence, while their talk of it as dreadful was still in the air, she appeared to present it as inordinately soft. This, prompting bewilderment, made him but gape the more gratefully for her revelation, so that they continued for some minutes silent, her face shining at him, her contact imponderably pressing, and his stare all kind but all expectant. The end, none the less, was that what he had expected failed to come to him. Something else took place instead, which seemed to consist at first in the mere closing of her eyes. She gave way at the same instant to a slow fine shudder, and though he remained staring — though he stared in fact but the harder — turned off and regained her chair. It was the end of what she had been intending, but it left him thinking only of that.

"Well, you don't say — ?"

She had touched in her passage a bell near the chimney and had sunk back strangely pale. "I'm afraid I'm too ill."

"Too ill to tell me?" It sprang up sharp to him, and almost to his lips, the fear she might die without giving him light. He checked himself in time from so expressing his question, but she answered as if she had heard the words.

"Don't you know — now?"

"'Now' — ?" She had spoken as if some difference had been made within the moment. But her maid, quickly obedient to her bell, was already with them. "I know nothing." And he was afterwards to say to himself that he must have spoken with odious impatience, such an impatience as to show that, supremely disconcerted, he washed his hands of the whole question.

"Oh!" said May Bartram.

"Are you in pain?" he asked as the woman went to her.

"No," said May Bartram.

Her maid, who had put an arm round her as if to take her to her room, fixed on him eyes that appealingly contradicted her; in spite of which, however, he showed once more his mystification. "What then has happened?"

She was once more, with her companion's help, on her feet, and, feeling withdrawal imposed on him, he had blankly found his hat and gloves and had reached the door. Yet he waited for her answer. "What *was* to," she said.

V

He came back the next day, but she was then unable to see him, and as it was literally the first time this had occurred in the long stretch of their acquaintance he turned away, defeated and sore, almost angry — or feeling at least that such a break in their custom was really the beginning of the end — and wandered alone with his thoughts, especially with the one he was least able to keep down. She was dying and he would lose her; she was dying and his life would end. He stopped in the Park, into which he had passed, and stared before him at his recurrent doubt. Away from her the doubt pressed again; in her presence he had believed her, but as he felt his forlornness he threw himself into the explanation that, nearest at hand, had most of a miserable warmth for him and least of a cold torment. She had deceived him to save him—to put him off with something in which he should be able to rest. What could the thing that was to happen to him be, after all, but just this thing that had begun to happen? Her dying, her death, his consequent solitude—*that* was what he had figured as the Beast in the Jungle, that was what had been in the lap of the gods. He had had her word for it as he left her—what else on earth could she have meant? It was n't a thing of a monstrous order; not a fate rare and distinguished; not a stroke of fortune that overwhelmed and immortalised; it had only the stamp of the common doom. But poor Marcher at this hour judged the common doom sufficient. It would serve his turn, and even as the consummation of infinite waiting he would bend his pride to accept it. He sat down on a bench in the twilight. He had n't been a fool. Something had *been*, as she had said, to come. Before he rose indeed it had quite struck him that the final fact really matched with the long avenue through which he had had to reach it. As sharing his suspense and as giving herself all, giving her life, to bring it to an end, she had come with him every step of the way. He had lived by her aid, and to leave her behind would be cruelly, damnably to miss her. What could be more overwhelming than that?

Well, he was to know within the week, for though she kept him a while at bay, left him restless and wretched during a series of days on each of which he asked about her only again to have to turn away, she ended his trial by receiving him where she had always received him. Yet she had been brought out at some hazard into the presence of so many of the things that were, consciously, vainly, half their past, and there was scant service left in the gentleness of her mere desire, all too visible, to check his obsession and wind up his long trouble. That was clearly what she wanted, the one thing more for her own peace while she could still put out her hand. He was so affected by her state that, once seated by her chair, he was moved to let everything go; it was she herself therefore who brought him back, took up again, before she dismissed him, her last word of the other time. She showed how she wished to leave their business in order. "I 'm not sure you understood. You 've nothing to wait for more. It *has* come."

Oh how he looked at her! "Really?"

"Really."

"The thing that, as you said, *was* to?"

"The thing that we began in our youth to watch for."

Face to face with her once more he believed her; it was a claim to which he had so abjectly little to oppose. "You mean that it has come as a positive definite occurrence, with a name and a date?"

"Positive. Definite. I don't know about the 'name,' but oh with a date!"

He found himself again too helplessly at sea. "But come in the night—come and passed me by?"

May Bartram had her strange faint smile. "Oh no, it has n't passed you by!"

"But if I have n't been aware of it and it has n't touched me—?"

"Ah your not being aware of it"—and she seemed to hesitate an instant to deal with this—"your not being aware of it is the strangeness *in* the strangeness. It 's the wonder *of* the wonder." She spoke as with the softness almost of a sick child, yet now at last, at the end of all, with the perfect straightness of a sibyl. She visibly knew that she knew, and the effect on him was of something co-ordinate, in its high character, with the law that had ruled him. It was the true voice of the law; so on her lips would the law itself have sounded. "It *has* touched you," she went on. "It has done its office. It has made you all its own."

"So utterly without my knowing it?"

"So utterly without your knowing it." His hand, as he leaned to her, was on the arm of her chair, and, dimly smiling always now, she placed her own on it. "It 's enough if *I* know it."

"Oh!" he confusedly breathed, as she herself of late so often had done.

"What I long ago said is true. You 'll never know now, and I think you ought to be content. You 've *had* it," said May Bartram.

"But had what?"

"Why what was to have marked you out. The proof of your law. It has acted. I 'm too glad," she then bravely added, "to have been able to see what it 's *not*."

He continued to attach his eyes to her, and with the sense that it was all beyond him, and that *she* was too, he would still have sharply challenged her had n't he so felt it an abuse of her weakness to do more than take devoutly what she gave him, take it hushed as to a revelation. If he did speak, it was out of the foreknowledge of his loneliness to come. "If you 're glad of what it's 'not' it might then have been worse?"

She turned her eyes away, she looked straight before her; with which after a moment: "Well, you know our fears."

He wondered. "It's something then we never feared?"

On this slowly she turned to him. "Did we ever dream, with all our dreams, that we should sit and talk of it thus?"

He tried for a little to make out that they had; but it was as if their dreams, numberless enough, were in solution in some thick cold mist through which thought lost itself. "It might have been that we could n't talk?"

"Well" — she did her best for him — "not from this side. This, you see," she said, "is the *other* side."

"I think," poor Marcher returned, "that all sides are the same to me." Then, however, as she gently shook her head in correction: "We might n't, as it were, have got across — ?"

"To where we are — no. We 're *here* — she made her weak emphasis.

"And much good does it do us!" was her friend's frank comment.

"It does us the good it can. It does us the good that *it* is n't here. It's past. It's behind," said May Bartram. "Before —" but her voice dropped.

He had got up, not to tire her, but it was hard to combat his yearning. She after all told him nothing but that his light had failed — which he knew well enough without her. "Before —?" he blankly echoed.

"Before, you see, it was always to *come*. That kept it present."

"Oh I don't care what comes now! Besides," Marcher added, "it seems to me I liked it better present, as you say, than I can like it absent with *your* absence."

"Oh mine!" — and her pale hands made light of it.

"With the absence of everything." He had a dreadful sense of standing there before her for — so far as anything but this proved, this bottomless drop was concerned — the last time of their life. It rested on him with a weight he felt he could scarce bear, and this weight it apparently was that still pressed out what remained in him of speakable protest. "I believe you; but I can't begin to pretend I understand. *Nothing*, for me, is past; nothing *will* pass till I pass myself, which I pray my stars may be as soon as possible. Say, however," he added, "that I've eaten my cake, as you contend, to the last crumb — how can the thing I've never felt at all be the thing I was marked out to feel?"

She met him perhaps less directly, but she met him unperturbed. "You take your 'feelings' for granted. You were to suffer your fate. That was not necessarily to know it."

"How in the world — when what is such knowledge but suffering?"

She looked up at him a while in silence. "No — you don't understand."

"I suffer," said John Marcher.

"Don't, don't!"

"How can I help at least *that*?"

"*Don't!*" May Bartram repeated.

She spoke it in a tone so special, in spite of her weakness, that he stared an instant — stared as if some light, hitherto hidden, had shimmered across his vision.

Darkness again closed over it, but the gleam had already become for him an idea. "Because I have n't the right — ?"

"Don't *know* — when you need n't," she mercifully urged. "You need n't — for we should n't."

"Should n't?" If he could but know what she meant!

"No — it's too much."

"Too much?" he still asked but, with a mystification that was the next moment of a sudden to give way. Her words, if they meant something, affected him in this light — the light also of her wasted face — as meaning *all*, and the sense of what knowledge had been for herself came over him with a rush which broke through into a question. "Is it of that then you 're dying?"

She but watched him, gravely at first, as to see, with this, where he was, and she might have seen something or feared something that moved her sympathy. "I would live for you still — if I could." Her eyes closed for a little, as if, withdrawn into herself, she were for a last time trying. "But I can't!" she said as she raised them again to take leave of him.

She could n't indeed, as but too promptly and sharply appeared, and he had no vision of her after this that was anything but darkness and doom. They had parted for ever in that strange talk; access to her chamber of pain, rigidly guarded, was almost wholly forbidden him; he was feeling now moreover, in the face of doctors, nurses, the two or three relatives attracted doubtless by the presumption of what she had to "leave," how few were the rights, as they were called in such cases, that he had to put forward, and how odd it might even seem that their intimacy should n't have given him more of them. The stupidest fourth cousin had more, even though she had been nothing in such a person's life. She had been a feature of features in *his*, for what else was it to have been so indispensable? Strange beyond saying were the ways of existence, baffling for him the anomaly of his lack, as he felt it to be, of producible claim. A woman might have been, as it were, everything to him, and it might yet present him in no connexion that any one seemed held to recognise. If this was the case in these closing weeks it was the case more sharply on the occasion of the last offices rendered, in the great grey London cemetery, to what had been mortal, to what had been precious, in his friend. The concourse at her grave was not numerous, but he saw himself treated as scarce more nearly concerned with it than if there had been a thousand others. He was in short from this moment face to face with the fact that he was to profit extraordinarily little by the interest May Bartram had taken in him. He could n't quite have said what he expected, but he had n't surely expected this approach to a double privation. Not only had her interest failed him, but he seemed to feel himself unattended — and for a reason he could n't seize — by the distinction, the dignity, the propriety, if nothing else, of the man markedly bereaved. It was as if in the view of society he had not *been* markedly bereaved, as if there still failed some sign or proof of it, and as if none the less his character could never be affirmed nor the deficiency ever made up. There were moments as the weeks went by when he would have liked, by some almost aggressive act, to take his stand on the intimacy of his loss, in order that it *might* be questioned and his retort, to the relief of his spirit, so recorded; but the moments of an irritation more helpless followed fast on these, the moments during which, turning things over with a good conscience but with a bare horizon, he found himself wondering if he ought n't to have begun, so to speak, further back.

He found himself wondering indeed at many things, and this last speculation had others to keep it company. What could he have done, after all, in her lifetime, without giving them both, as it were, away? He could n't have made known she was watching him, for that would have published the superstition of the Beast. This was what closed his mouth now — now that the Jungle had been threshed to vacancy and that the Beast had stolen away. It sounded too foolish and too flat; the difference for him in this particular, the extinction in his life of the element of suspense, was such as in fact to surprise him. He could scarce have said what the effect resembled; the abrupt cessation, the positive prohibition, of music perhaps, more than anything else, in some place all adjusted and all accustomed to sonority and to attention. If he could at any rate have conceived lifting the veil from his image at some moment of the past (what had he done, after all, if not lift it to *her?*) so to do this to-day, to talk to people at large of the Jungle cleared and confide to them that he now felt it as safe, would have been not only to see them listen as to a goodwife's tale, but really to hear himself tell one. What it presently came to in truth was that poor Marcher waded through his beaten grass, where no life stirred, where no breath sounded, where no evil eye seemed to gleam from a possible lair, very much as if vaguely looking for the Beast, and still more as if acutely missing it. He walked about in an existence that had grown strangely more spacious, and, stopping fitfully in places where the undergrowth of life struck him as closer, asked himself yearningly, wondered secretly and sorely, if it would have lurked here or there. It would have at all events *sprung*; what was at least complete was his belief in the truth itself of the assurance given him. The change from his old sense to his new was absolute and final: what was to happen *had* so absolutely and finally happened that he was as little able to know a fear for his future as to know a hope; so absent in short was any question of anything still to come. He was to live entirely with the other question, that of his unidentified past, that of his having to see his fortune impenetrably muffled and masked.

The torment of this vision became then his occupation; he could n't perhaps have consented to live but for the possibility of guessing. She had told him, his friend, not to guess; she had forbidden him, so far as he might, to know, and she had even in a sort denied the power in him to learn: which were so many things, precisely, to deprive him of rest. It was n't that he wanted, he argued for fairness, that anything past and done should repeat itself; it was only that he should n't, as an anticlimax, have been taken sleeping so sound as not to be able to win back by an effort of thought the lost stuff of consciousness. He declared to himself at moments that he would either win it back or have done with consciousness for ever; he made this idea his one motive in fine, made it so much his passion that none other, to compare with it, seemed ever to have touched him. The lost stuff of consciousness became thus for him as a strayed or stolen child to an unappeasable father; he hunted it up and down very much as if he were knocking at doors and enquiring of the police. This was the spirit in which, inevitably, he set himself to travel; he started on a journey that was to be as long as he could make it; it danced before him that, as the other side of the globe could n't possibly have less to say to him, it might, by a possibility of suggestion, have more. Before he quitted London, however, he made a pilgrimage to May Bartram's grave, took his way to it through the endless avenues of the grim suburban metropolis, sought it out in the wilderness of tombs, and, though he had come but for the renewal of the act of farewell, found himself, when he had at last stood by it, beguiled into long intensities. He stood for an hour, powerless to turn away and yet powerless to penetrate the darkness of death; fixing with his eyes her inscribed name and date, beating his forehead against the fact of the secret they kept, drawing his breath, while he waited, as if some sense would in pity of him rise from the stones. He kneeled on the stones, however, in vain; they kept what they concealed; and if the face of the tomb did become a face for him it was because her two names became a pair of eyes that did n't know him. He gave them a last long look, but no palest light broke.

VI

He stayed away, after this, for a year; he visited the depths of Asia, spending himself on scenes of romantic interest, of superlative sanctity; but what was present to him everywhere was that for a man who had known what *he* had known the world was vulgar and vain. The state of mind in which he had lived for so many years shone out to him, in reflexion, as a light that coloured and refined, a light beside which the glow of the East was garish cheap and thin. The terrible truth was that he had lost — with everything else — a distinction as well; the things he saw could n't help being common when he had become common to look at them. He was simply now one of them himself — he was in the dust, without a peg for the sense of difference; and there were hours when, before the temples of gods and the sepulchres of kings, his spirit turned for nobleness of association to the barely discriminated slab in the London suburb. That had become for him, and more intensely with time and distance, his one witness of a past glory. It was all that was left to him for proof or pride, yet the past glories of Pharaohs were nothing to him as he thought of it. Small wonder then that he came back to it on the morrow of his return. He was drawn there this time as irresistibly as the other, yet with a confidence, almost, that was doubtless the effect of the many months that had elapsed. He had lived, in spite of himself, into his change of feeling, and in wandering over the earth had wandered, as might be said, from the circumference to the centre of his desert. He had settled to his safety and accepted perforce his extinction; figuring to himself, with some colour, in the likeness of certain little old men he remembered to have seen, of whom, all meagre and wizened as they might look, it was related that they had in their time fought twenty duels or been loved by ten princesses. They indeed had been wondrous for others while he was but wondrous for himself; which, however, was exactly the cause of his haste to renew the wonder by getting back, as he might put it, into his own presence. That had quickened his steps and checked his delay. If his visit was prompt it was because he had been separated so long from the part of himself that alone he now valued.

It's accordingly not false to say that he reached his goal with a certain elation and stood there again with a certain assurance. The creature beneath the sod *knew* of his rare experience, so that, strangely now, the place had lost for him its mere blankness of expression. It met him in mildness — not, as before, in mockery; it wore for him the air of conscious greeting that we find, after absence, in things that have closely belonged to us and which seem to confess of themselves to the connexion. The plot of ground, the graven tablet, the tended flowers affected him so as belonging to him that he resembled for the hour a contented landlord reviewing a piece of property. Whatever had happened — well, had happened. He had not come back this time with the vanity of that question, his former worrying "What, *what?*" now practically so spent. Yet he would none the less never again so cut himself off from the spot; he would come back to it every month, for if he did nothing else by its aid he at least held up his head. It thus grew for him, in the oddest way, a positive resource; he carried out his idea of periodical returns, which took their place at last among the most inveterate of his habits. What it all amounted to, oddly enough, was that in his finally so simplified world this garden of death gave him the few square feet of earth on which he could still most live. It was as if, being nothing anywhere else for any one, nothing even for himself, he were just everything here, and if not for a crowd of witnesses or indeed for any witness but John Marcher, then by clear right of the register that he could scan like an open page. The open page was the tomb of his friend, and *there* were the facts of the past, there the truth of his life, there the backward reaches in which he could lose himself. He did this from time to time with such effect that he seemed to wander through the old years with his hand in the arm of a companion who was, in the most extraordinary manner, his other, his younger self; and to wander, which was more extraordinary yet, round and round a third presence — not wandering she, but stationary, still, whose eyes, turning with his revolution, never ceased to follow him, and whose seat was his point, so to speak, of orientation. Thus in short he settled to live — feeding all on the sense that he once *had* lived, and dependent on it not alone for a support but for an identity.

It sufficed him in its way for months and the year elapsed; it would doubtless even have carried him further but for an accident, superficially slight, which moved him, quite in another direction, with a force beyond any of his impressions of Egypt or of India. It was a thing of the merest chance — the turn, as he afterwards felt, of a hair, though he was indeed to live to believe that if light had n't come to him in this particular fashion it would still have come in another. He was to live to believe this, I say, though he was not to live, I may not less definitely mention, to do much else. We allow him at any rate the benefit of the conviction, struggling up for him at the end, that, whatever might have happened or not happened, he would have come round of himself to the light. The incident of an autumn day had put the match to the train laid from of old by his misery. With the light before him he knew that even of late his ache had only been smothered. It was strangely drugged, but it throbbed; at the touch it began to bleed. And the touch, in the event, was the face of a fellow mortal. This face, one grey afternoon when the leaves were thick in the alleys, looked into Marcher's own, at the cemetery, with an expression like the cut of a blade. He felt it, that is, so deep down that he winced at the steady thrust. The person who so mutely assaulted him was a figure he had noticed, on reaching his own goal, absorbed by a grave a short distance away, a grave apparently fresh, so that the emotion of the visitor would probably match it for frankness. This fact alone forbade further attention, though during the time he stayed he remained vaguely conscious of his neighbour, a middle-aged man apparently, in mourning, whose bowed back, among the clustered monuments and mortuary yews, was constantly presented. Marcher's theory that these were elements in contact with which he himself revived, had suffered, on this occasion, it may be granted, a marked, an excessive check. The autumn day was dire for him as none had recently been, and he rested with a heaviness he had not yet known on the low stone table that bore May Bartram's name. He rested without power to move, as if some spring in him, some spell vouchsafed, had suddenly been broken for ever. If he could have done that moment as he wanted he would simply have stretched himself on the slab that was ready to take him, treating it as a place prepared to receive his last sleep. What in all the wide world had he now to keep awake for? He stared before him with the question, and it was then that, as one of the cemetery walks passed near him, he caught the shock of the face.

His neighbour at the other grave had withdrawn, as he himself, with force enough in him, would have done by now, and was advancing along the path on his way to one of the gates. This brought him close, and his pace was slow, so that — and all the more as there was a kind of hunger in his look — the two men were for a minute directly confronted. Marcher knew him at once for one of the deeply stricken — a perception so sharp that nothing else in the picture comparatively lived, neither his dress, his age, nor his presumable character and class; nothing lived but the deep ravage of the features he showed. He *showed* them — that was the point; he was moved, as he passed, by some impulse that was either a signal for sympathy or, more possibly, a challenge to an opposed sorrow. He might already have been aware of our friend, might at some previous hour have noticed in him the smooth habit of the scene, with which the state of his own senses so scantly consorted, and might thereby have been stirred as by an overt discord. What Marcher was at all events conscious of was in the first place that the image of scarred passion presented to him was conscious too — of something that profaned the air; and in the second that, roused, startled, shocked, he was yet the next moment looking after it, as it went, with envy. The most extraordinary thing that had happened to him — though he had given that name to other matters as well — took place, after his immediate vague stare, as a consequence of this impression. The stranger passed, but the raw glare of his grief remained, making our friend wonder in pity what wrong, what wound it expressed, what injury not to be healed. What had the man *had*, to make him by the loss of it so bleed and yet live?

Something — and this reached him with a pang — that *he*, John Marcher, had n't;

the proof of which was precisely John Marcher's arid end. No passion had ever touched him, for this was what passion meant; he had survived and maundered and pined, but where had been *his* deep ravage? The extraordinary thing we speak of was the sudden rush of the result of this question. The sight that had just met his eyes named to him, as in letters of quick flame, something he had utterly, insanely missed, and what he had missed made these things a train of fire, made them mark themselves in an anguish of inward throbs. He had seen *outside* of his life, not learned it within, the way a woman was mourned when she had been loved for herself: such was the force of his conviction of the meaning of the stranger's face, which still flared for him as a smoky torch. It had n't come to him, the knowledge, on the wings of experience; it had brushed him, jostled him, upset him, with the disrespect of chance, the insolence of accident. Now that the illumination had begun, however, it blazed to the zenith, and what he presently stood there gazing at was the sounded void of his life. He gazed, he drew breath, in pain; he turned in his dismay, and, turning, he had before him in sharper incision than ever the open page of his story. The name on the table smote him as the passage of his neighbour had done, and what it said to him, full in the face, was that *she* was what he had missed. This was the awful thought, the answer to all the past, the vision at the dread clearness of which he grew as cold as the stone beneath him. Everything fell together, confessed, explained, overwhelmed; leaving him most of all stupefied at the blindness he had cherished. The fate he had been marked for he had met with a vengeance—he had emptied the cup to the lees; he had been the man of his time, *the* man, to whom nothing on earth was to have happened. That was the rare stroke—that was his visitation. So he saw it, as we say, in pale horror, while the pieces fitted and fitted. So *she* had seen it while he did n't, and so she served at this hour to drive the truth home. It was the truth, vivid and monstrous, that all the while he had waited the wait was itself his portion. This the companion of his vigil had at a given moment made out, and she had then offered him the chance to baffle his doom. One's doom, however, was never baffled, and on the day she told him his own had come down she had seen him but stupidly stare at the escape she offered him.

The escape would have been to love her; then, *then* he would have lived. *She* had lived—who could say now with what passion?—since she had loved him for himself; whereas he had never thought of her (ah how it hugely glared at him!) but in the chill of his egotism and the light of her use. Her spoken words came back to him—the chain stretched and stretched. The Beast had lurked indeed, and the Beast, at its hour, had sprung; it had sprung in that twilight of the cold April when, pale, ill, wasted, but all beautiful, and perhaps even then recoverable, she had risen from her chair to stand before him and let him imaginably guess. It had sprung as he did n't guess; it had sprung as she hopelessly turned from him, and the mark, by the time he left her, had fallen where it *was* to fall. He had justified his fear and achieved his fate; he had failed, with the last exactitude, of all he was to fail of; and a moan now rose to his lips as he remembered she had prayed he might n't know. This horror of waking—*this* was knowledge, knowledge under the breath of which the very tears in his eyes seemed to freeze. Through them, none the less, he tried to fix it and hold it; he kept it there before him so that he might feel the pain. That at least, belated and bitter, had something of the taste of life. But the bitterness suddenly sickened him, and it was as if, horribly, he saw, in the truth, in the cruelty of his image, what had been appointed and done. He saw the Jungle of his life and saw the lurking Beast; then, while he looked, perceived it, as by a stir of the air, rise, huge and hideous, for the leap that was to settle him. His eyes darkened—it was close; and, instinctively turning, in his hallucination, to avoid it, he flung himself, face down, on the tomb.

1903, 1909

ON "THE BEAST IN THE JUNGLE" (*from* PREFACE)
[MARCHER'S CAREER: "A GREAT NEGATIVE ADVENTURE"]

. . . I meet it [the subject of "The Beast in the Jungle"], in ten lines of an old
notebook, but as a recorded conceit and an accomplished fact. . . . [John Marcher]
was to have been, after a strange fashion and from the threshold of his career, condemned to keep counting with the unreasoned prevision of some extraordinary fate;
the conviction, lodged in his brain, part and parcel of his imagination from far back,
that experience would be marked for him, and whether for good or for ill, by some
rare distinction, some incalculable violence or unprecedented stroke. So I seemed to
see him start in life — under the so mixed star of the extreme of apprehension and
the extreme of confidence; all to the logical, the quite inevitable effect of the complication aforesaid: his having to wait and wait for the right recognition; none of the
mere usual and normal human adventures, whether delights or disconcertments,
appearing to conform to the great type of his fortune. So it is that he's depicted.
No gathering appearance, no descried or interpreted promise or portent, affects
his superstitious soul either as a damnation deep enough (if damnation be in question) for his appointed *quality* of consciousness, or as a translation into bliss
sublime enough (on *that* hypothesis) to fill, in vulgar parlance, the bill. Therefore as
each item of experience comes, with its possibilities, into view, he can but dismiss
it under this sterilising habit of the failure to find it good enough and thence to appropriate it.

His one desire remains of course to meet his fate, or at least to divine it, to see it as
intelligible, to learn it, in a word; but none of its harbingers, pretended or supposed,
speak his ear in the true voice; they wait their moment at his door only to pass on
unheeded, and the years ebb while he holds his breath and stays his hand and — from
the dread not less of imputed pride than of imputed pusillanimity — stifles his distinguished secret. He perforce lets everything go — leaving all the while his general
presumption disguised and his general abstention unexplained; since he's ridden by
the idea of what things may lead to, since they mostly always lead to human communities, wider or intenser, of experience, and since, above all, in his uncertainty, he
must n't compromise others. Like the blinded seeker in the old-fashioned game he
"burns," on occasion, as with the sense of the hidden thing near — only to deviate
again however into the chill; the chill that indeed settles on him as the striking of his
hour is deferred. His career thus resolves itself into a great negative adventure, my
report of which presents, for its centre, the fine case that has caused him most tor-
mentedly to "burn," and then most unprofitably to stray. He is afraid to recognise
what he incidentally misses, since what his high belief amounts to is not that he shall
have felt and vibrated less than any one else, but that he shall have felt and vibrated
more; which no acknowledgement of the minor loss must conflict with. Such a course
of existence naturally involves a climax — the final flash of the light under which he
reads his lifelong riddle and sees his conviction proved. He has indeed been marked
and indeed suffered his fortune — which is precisely to have been the man in the
world to whom nothing whatever was to happen. My picture leaves him overwhelmed — at last he has understood; though in thus disengaging my treated theme
for the reader's benefit I seem to acknowledge that this more detached witness
may not successfully have done so. I certainly grant that any felt merit in the thing
must all depend on the clearness and charm with which the subject just noted expresses itself. . . .

1909

The Jolly Corner[1]

I

"Every one asks me what I 'think' of everything," said Spencer Brydon; "and I make answer as I can—begging or dodging the question, putting them off with any nonsense. It would n't matter to any of them really," he went on, "for, even were it possible to meet in that stand-and-deliver way so silly a demand on so big a subject, my 'thoughts' would still be almost altogether about something that concerns only myself." He was talking to Miss Staverton, with whom for a couple of months now he had availed himself of every possible occasion to talk; this disposition and this re-source, this comfort and support, as the situation in fact presented itself, having promptly enough taken the first place in the considerable array of rather unattenu-ated surprises attending his so strangely belated return to America. Everything was somehow a surprise; and that might be natural when one had so long and so consis-tently neglected everything, taken pains to give surprises so much margin for play. He had given them more than thirty years—thirty-three, to be exact; and they now seemed to him to have organised their performance quite on the scale of that licence. He had been twenty-three on leaving New York—he was fifty-six to-day: unless in-deed he were to reckon as he had sometimes, since his repatriation, found himself feeling; in which case he would have lived longer than is often allotted to man. It would have taken a century, he repeatedly said to himself, and said also to Alice Staverton, it would have taken a longer absence and a more averted mind than those even of which he had been guilty, to pile up the differences, the newnesses, the queernesses, above all the bignesses, for the better or the worse, that at present as-saulted his vision wherever he looked.

The great fact all the while however had been the incalculability; since he *had* supposed himself, from decade to decade, to be allowing, and in the most liberal and intelligent manner, for brilliancy of change. He actually saw that he had allowed for nothing; he missed what he would have been sure of finding, he found what he would never have imagined. Proportions and values were upside-down; the ugly things he had expected, the ugly things of his far-away youth, when he had too promptly waked up to a sense of the ugly—these uncanny phenomena placed him rather, as it happened, under the charm; whereas the "swagger" things, the modern, the monstrous, the famous things, those he had more particularly, like thousands of ingenuous enquirers every year, come over to see, were exactly his sources of dismay. They were as so many set traps for displeasure, above all for reaction, of which his restless tread was constantly pressing the spring. It was interesting, doubtless, the whole show, but it would have been too disconcerting had n't a certain finer truth saved the situation. He had distinctly not, in this steadier light, come over *all* for the monstrosities; he had come, not only in the last analysis but quite on the face of the act, under an impulse with which they had nothing to do. He had come—putting the thing pompously—to look at his "property," which he had thus for a third of a cen-tury not been within four thousand miles of; or, expressing it less sordidly, he had yielded to the humour of seeing again his house on the jolly corner, as he usually, and quite fondly, described it—the one in which he had first seen the light, in which various members of his family had lived and had died, in which the holidays of his overschooled boyhood had been passed and the few social flowers of his chilled ado-

---

[1]In a 1914 notebook entry, James wrote of "The Jolly Cor-ner": "my hero's adventure there takes the form so to speak of his turning the tables, as I think I called it, on a 'ghost' or whatever, a visiting or haunting apparition otherwise quali-fied to appal *him*; and thereby winning a sort of victory by the appearance, and the evidence, that this personage or pres-ence was more overwhelmingly affected by him than he by *it*."

lescence gathered, and which, alienated then for so long a period, had, through the
successive deaths of his two brothers and the termination of old arrangements, come
wholly into his hands. He was the owner of another, not quite so "good"—the jolly
corner having been, from far back, superlatively extended and consecrated; and the
value of the pair represented his main capital, with an income consisting, in these
later years, of their respective rents which (thanks precisely to their original excellent
type) had never been depressingly low. He could live in "Europe," as he had been in
the habit of living, on the product of these flourishing New York leases, and all the
better since, that of the second structure, the mere number in its long row, having
within a twelvemonth fallen in, renovation at a high advance had proved beautifully
possible.

These were items of property indeed, but he had found himself since his arrival
distinguishing more than ever between them. The house within the street, two bristling blocks westward, was already in course of reconstruction as a tall mass of flats;
he had acceded, some time before, to overtures for this conversion—in which, now
that it was going forward, it had been not the least of his astonishments to find himself able, on the spot, and though without a previous ounce of such experience, to
participate with a certain intelligence, almost with a certain authority. He had lived
his life with his back so turned to such concerns and his face addressed to those of so
different an order that he scarce knew what to make of this lively stir, in a compartment of his mind never yet penetrated, of a capacity for business and a sense for
construction. These virtues, so common all round him now, had been dormant in his
own organism—where it might be said of them perhaps that they had slept the sleep
of the just. At present, in the splendid autumn weather—the autumn at least was a
pure boon in the terrible place—he loafed about his "work" undeterred, secretly
agitated; not in the least "minding" that the whole proposition, as they said, was
vulgar and sordid, and ready to climb ladders, to walk the plank, to handle materials
and look wise about them, to ask questions, in fine, and challenge explanations and
really "go into" figures.

It amused, it verily quite charmed him; and, by the same stroke, it amused, and
even more, Alice Staverton, though perhaps charming her perceptibly less. She
was n't however going to be better-off for it, as *he* was—and so astonishingly much:
nothing was now likely, he knew, ever to make her better-off than she found herself,
in the afternoon of life, as the delicately frugal possessor and tenant of the small
house in Irving Place[2] to which she had subtly managed to cling through her almost
unbroken New York career. If he knew the way to it now better than to any other
address among the dreadful multiplied numberings which seemed to him to reduce
the whole place to some vast ledger-page, overgrown, fantastic, of rules and crisscrossed lines and figures—if he had formed, for his consolation, that habit, it was
really not a little because of the charm of his having encountered and recognised, in
the vast wilderness of the wholesale, breaking through the mere gross generalisation
of wealth and force and success, a small still scene where items and shades, all delicate
things, kept the sharpness of the notes of a high voice perfectly trained, and where
economy hung about like the scent of a garden. His old friend lived with one maid
and herself dusted her relics and trimmed her lamps and polished her silver; she
stood off, in the awful modern crush, when she could, but she sallied forth and did
battle when the challenge was really to "spirit," the spirit she after all confessed to,
proudly and a little shyly, as to that of the better time, that of *their* common, their
quite far-away and antediluvian social period and order. She made use of the street-
cars when need be, the terrible things that people scrambled for as the panic-stricken
at sea scramble for the boats; she affronted, inscrutably, under stress, all the public

---

[2]In the fashionable Grammercy Park area.

concussions and ordeals; and yet, with that slim mystifying grace of her appearance, which defied you to say if she were a fair young woman who looked older through trouble, or a fine smooth older one who looked young through successful indifference; with her precious reference, above all, to memories and histories into which he could enter, she was as exquisite for him as some pale pressed flower (a rarity to begin with), and, failing other sweetnesses, she was a sufficient reward of his effort. They had communities of knowledge, "their" knowledge (this discriminating possessive was always on her lips) of presences of the other age, presences all overlaid, in his case, by the experience of a man and the freedom of a wanderer, overlaid by pleasure, by infidelity, by passages of life that were strange and dim to her, just by "Europe" in short, but still unobscured, still exposed and cherished, under that pious visitation of the spirit from which she had never been diverted.

She had come with him one day to see how his "apartment-house" was rising; he had helped her over gaps and explained to her plans, and while they were there had happened to have, before her, a brief but lively discussion with the man in charge, the representative of the building-firm that had undertaken his work. He had found himself quite "standing-up" to this personage over a failure on the latter's part to observe some detail of one of their noted conditions, and had so lucidly argued his case that, besides ever so prettily flushing, at the time, for sympathy in his triumph, she had afterwards said to him (though to a slightly greater effect of irony) that he had clearly for too many years neglected a real gift. If he had but stayed at home he would have anticipated the inventor of the sky-scraper. If he had but stayed at home he would have discovered his genius in time really to start some new variety of awful architectural hare and run it till it burrowed in a goldmine. He was to remember these words, while the weeks elapsed, for the small silver ring they had sounded over the queerest and deepest of his own lately most disguised and most muffled vibrations.

It had begun to be present to him after the first fortnight, it had broken out with the oddest abruptness, this particular wanton wonderment: it met him there—and this was the image under which he himself judged the matter, or at least, not a little, thrilled and flushed with it—very much as he might have been met by some strange figure, some unexpected occupant, at a turn of one of the dim passages of an empty house. The quaint analogy quite hauntingly remained with him, when he did n't indeed rather improve it by a still intenser form: that of his opening a door behind which he would have made sure of finding nothing, a door into a room shuttered and void, and yet so coming, with a great suppressed start, on some quite erect confronting presence, something planted in the middle of the place and facing him through the dusk. After that visit to the house in constuction he walked with his companion to see the other and always so much the better one, which in the eastward direction formed one of the corners, the "jolly" one precisely, of the street now so generally dishonoured and disfigured in its westward reaches, and of the comparatively conservative Avenue.[3] The Avenue still had pretensions, as Miss Staverton said, to decency; the old people had mostly gone, the old names were unknown, and here and there an old association seemed to stray, all vaguely, like some very aged person, out too late, whom you might meet and feel the impulse to watch or follow, in kindness, for safe restoration to shelter.

They went in together, our friends; he admitted himself with his key, as he kept no one there, he explained, preferring, for his reasons, to leave the place empty, under a simple arrangement with a good woman living in the neighbourhood and who came for a daily hour to open windows and dust and sweep. Spencer Brydon had his reasons and was growingly aware of them; they seemed to him better each time he

---

[3]Lower Fifth Avenue near Washington Square where the James family lived.

was there, though he did n't name them all to his companion, any more than he told her as yet how often, how quite absurdly often, he himself came. He only let her see for the present, while they walked through the great blank rooms, that absolute vacancy reigned and that, from top to bottom, there was nothing but Mrs. Muldoon's broomstick, in a corner, to tempt the burglar. Mrs. Muldoon was then on the premises, and she loquaciously attended the visitors, preceding them from room to room and pushing back shutters and throwing up sashes—all to show them, as she remarked, how little there was to see. There was little indeed to see in the great gaunt shell where the main dispositions and the general apportionment of space, the style of an age of ampler allowances, had nevertheless for its master their honest pleading message, affecting him as some good old servant's, some lifelong retainer's appeal for a character, or even for a retiring-pension; yet it was also a remark of Mrs. Muldoon's that, glad as she was to oblige him by her noonday round, there was a request she greatly hoped he would never make of her. If he should wish her for any reason to come in after dark she would just tell him, if he "plased," that he must ask it of somebody else.

The fact that there was nothing to see did n't militate for the worthy woman against what one *might* see, and she put it frankly to Miss Staverton that no lady could be expected to like, could she? "craping up to thim top storeys in the ayvil hours." The gas and the electric light were off the house, and she fairly evoked a gruesome vision of her march through the great grey rooms—so many of them as there were too!—with her glimmering taper. Miss Staverton met her honest glare with a smile and the profession that she herself certainly would recoil from such an adventure. Spencer Brydon meanwhile held his peace—for the moment; the question of the "evil" hours in his old home had already become too grave for him. He had begun some time since to "crape," and he knew just why a packet of candles addressed to that pursuit had been stowed by his own hand, three weeks before, at the back of a drawer of the fine old sideboard that occupied, as a "fixture," the deep recess in the dining-room. Just now he laughed at his companions—quickly however changing the subject; for the reason that, in the first place, his laugh struck him even at that moment as starting the odd echo, the conscious human resonance (he scarce knew how to qualify it) that sounds made while he was there alone sent back to his ear or his fancy; and that, in the second, he imagined Alice Staverton for the instant on the point of asking him, with a divination, if he ever so prowled. There were divinations he was unprepared for, and he had at all events averted enquiry by the time Mrs. Muldoon had left them, passing on to other parts.

There was happily enough to say, on so consecrated a spot, that could be said freely and fairly; so that a whole train of declarations was precipitated by his friend's having herself broken out, after a yearning look round: "But I hope you don't mean they want you to pull *this* to pieces!" His answer came, promptly, with his re-awakened wrath: it was of course exactly what they wanted, and what they were "at" him for, daily, with the iteration of people who could n't for their life understand a man's liability to decent feelings. He had found the place, just as it stood and beyond what he could express, an interest and a joy. There were values other than the beastly rent-values, and in short, in short—! But it was thus Miss Staverton took him up. "In short you're to make so good a thing of your sky-scraper that, living in luxury on *those* ill-gotten gains, you can afford for a while to be sentimental here!" Her smile had for him, with the words, the particular mild irony with which he found half her talk suffused; an irony without bitterness and that came, exactly, from her having so much imagination—not, like the cheap sarcasms with which one heard most people, about the world of "society," bid for the reputation of cleverness, from nobody's really having any. It was agreeable to him at this very moment to be sure that when he had answered, after a brief demur, "Well yes: so, precisely, you may put it!" her imagination would still do him justice. He explained that even if never a dollar were to come to him from the other house he would nevertheless cherish this one; and he dwelt, further, while they lingered and wandered, on the fact of the stupefaction he was already exciting, the positive mystification he felt himself create.

He spoke of the value of all he read into it, into the mere sight of the walls, mere shapes of the rooms, mere sound of the floors, mere feel, in his hand, of the old silver-plated knobs of the several mahogany doors, which suggested the pressure of the palms of the dead; the seventy years of the past in fine that these things represented, the annals of nearly three generations, counting his grandfather's, the one that had ended there, and the impalpable ashes of his long-extinct youth, afloat in the very air like microscopic motes. She listened to everything; she was a woman who answered intimately but who utterly did n't chatter. She scattered abroad therefore no cloud of words; she could assent, she could agree, above all she could encourage, without doing that. Only at the last she went a little further than he had done himself. "And then how do you know? You may still, after all, want to live here." It rather indeed pulled him up, for it was n't what he had been thinking, at least in her sense of the words. "You mean I may decide to stay on for the sake of it?"

"Well, *with* such a home—!" But, quite beautifully, she had too much tact to dot so monstrous an *i*, and it was precisely an illustration of the way she did n't rattle. How could any one—of any wit—insist on any one else's "wanting" to live in New York?

"Oh," he said, "I *might* have lived here (since I had my opportunity early in life); I might have put in here all these years. Then everything would have been different enough—and, I dare say, 'funny' enough. But that's another matter. And then the beauty of it—I mean of my perversity, of my refusal to agree to a 'deal'—is just in the total absence of a reason. Don't you see that if I had a reason about the matter at all it would *have* to be the other way, and would then be inevitably a reason of dollars? There are no reasons here *but* of dollars. Let us therefore have none whatever—not the ghost of one."

They were back in the hall then for departure, but from where they stood the vista was large, through an open door, into the great square main saloon, with its almost antique felicity of brave spaces between windows. Her eyes came back from that reach and met his own a moment. "Are you very sure the 'ghost' of one does n't, much rather, serve—?"

He had a positive sense of turning pale. But it was as near as they were then to come. For he made answer, he believed, between a glare and a grin: "Oh ghosts—of course the place must swarm with them! I should be ashamed of it if it did n't. Poor Mrs. Muldoon's right, and it's why I have n't asked her to do more than look in."

Miss Staverton's gaze again lost itself, and things she did n't utter, it was clear, came and went in her mind. She might even for the minute, off there in the fine room, have imagined some element dimly gathering. Simplified like the death-mask of a handsome face, it perhaps produced for her just then an effect akin to the stir of an expression in the "set" commemorative plaster. Yet whatever her impression may have been she produced instead a vague platitude. "Well, if it were only furnished and lived in—!"

She appeared to imply that in case of its being still furnished he might have been a little less opposed to the idea of a return. But she passed straight into the vestibule, as if to leave her words behind her, and the next moment he had opened the house-door and was standing with her on the steps. He closed the door and, while he re-pocketed his key, looking up and down, they took in the comparatively harsh actuality of the Avenue, which reminded him of the assault of the outer light of the Desert on the traveller emerging from an Egyptian tomb. But he risked before they stepped into the street his gathered answer to her speech. "For me it *is* lived in. For me it *is* furnished." At which it was easy for her to sigh "Ah yes—!" all vaguely and discreetly; since his parents and his favourite sister, to say nothing of other kin, in numbers, had run their course and met their end there. That represented, within the walls, ineffaceable life.

It was a few days after this that, during an hour passed with her again, he had expressed his impatience of the too flattering curiosity — among the people he met — about his appreciation of New York. He had arrived at none at all that was socially producible, and as for that matter of his "thinking" (thinking the better or the worse of anything there) he was wholly taken up with one subject of thought. It was mere vain egoism, and it was moreover, if she liked, a morbid obsession. He found all things come back to the question of what he personally might have been, how he might have led his life and "turned out," if he had not so, at the outset, given it up. And confessing for the first time to the intensity within him of this absurd speculation — which but proved also, no doubt, the habit of too selfishly thinking — he affirmed the impotence there of any other source of interest, any other native appeal. "What would it have made of me, what would it have made of me? I keep for ever wondering, all idiotically; as if I could possibly know! I see what it has made of dozens of others, those I meet, and it positively aches within me, to the point of exasperation, that it would have made something of me as well. Only I can't make out *what*, and the worry of it, the small rage of curiosity never to be satisfied, brings back what I remember to have felt, once or twice, after judging best, for reasons, to burn some important letter unopened. I've been sorry, I've hated it — I've never known what was in the letter. You may of course say it's a trifle — !"

"I don't say it's a trifle," Miss Staverton gravely interrupted.

She was seated by her fire, and before her, on his feet and restless, he turned to and fro between this intensity of his idea and a fitful and unseeing inspection, through his single eye-glass, of the dear little old objects on her chimney-piece. Her interruption made him for an instant look at her harder. "I should n't care if you did!" he laughed, however; "and it's only a figure, at any rate, for the way I now feel. *Not* to have followed my perverse young course — and almost in the teeth of my father's curse, as I may say; not to have kept it up, so, 'over there,' from that day to this, without a doubt or a pang; not, above all, to have liked it, to have loved it, so much, loved it, no doubt, with such an abysmal conceit of my own preference: some variation from *that*, I say, must have produced some different effect for my life and for my 'form.' I should have stuck here — if it had been possible; and I was too young, at twenty-three, to judge, *pour deux sous*,[4] whether it *were* possible. If I had waited I might have seen it was, and then I might have been, by staying here, something nearer to one of these types who have been hammered so hard and made so keen by their conditions. It is n't that I admire them so much — the question of any charm in them, or of any charm, beyond that of the rank money-passion, exerted by their conditions *for* them, has nothing to do with the matter: it's only a question of what fantastic, yet perfectly possible, development of my own nature I may n't have missed. It comes over me that I had then a strange *alter ego* deep down somewhere within me, as the full-blown flower is in the small tight bud, and that I just took the course, I just transferred him to the climate, that blighted him for once and for ever."

"And you wonder about the flower," Miss Staverton said. "So do I, if you want to know; and so I've been wondering these several weeks. I believe in the flower," she continued, "I feel it would have been quite splendid, quite huge and monstrous."

"Monstrous above all!" her visitor echoed; "and I imagine, by the same stroke, quite hideous and offensive."

"You don't believe that," she returned; "if you did you would n't wonder. You'd know, and that would be enough for you. What you feel — and what I feel *for* you — is that you'd have had power."

"You'd have liked me that way?" he asked.

She barely hung fire. "How should I not have liked you?"

"I see. You'd have liked me, have preferred me, a billionaire!"

"How should I not have liked you?" she simply again asked.

4"For two cents" (French).

He stood before her still—her question kept him motionless. He took it in, so much there was of it; and indeed his not otherwise meeting it testified to that. "I know at least what I am," he simply went on; "the other side of the medal's clear enough. I've not been edifying—I believe I'm thought in a hundred quarters to have been barely decent. I've followed strange paths and worshipped strange gods; it must have come to you again and again—in fact you've admitted to me as much—that I was leading, at any time these thirty years, a selfish frivolous scandalous life. And you see what it has made of me."

She just waited, smiling at him. "You see what it has made of *me*."

"Oh you're a person whom nothing can have altered. You were born to be what you are, anywhere, anyway: you've the perfection nothing else could have blighted. And don't you see how, without my exile, I should n't have been waiting till now—?" But he pulled up for the strange pang.

"The great thing to see," she presently said, "seems to me to be that it has spoiled nothing. It has n't spoiled your being here at last. It has n't spoiled this. It has n't spoiled your speaking—" She also however faltered.

He wondered at everything her controlled emotion might mean. "Do you believe then—too dreadfully!—that I *am* as good as I might ever have been?"

"Oh no! Far from it!" With which she got up from her chair and was nearer to him. "But I don't care," she smiled.

"You mean I'm good enough?"

She considered a little. "Will you believe it if I say so? I mean will you let that settle your question for you?" And then as if making out in his face that he drew back from this, that he had some idea which, however absurd, he could n't yet bargain away: "Oh you don't care either—but very differently: you don't care for anything but yourself."

Spencer Brydon recognised it—it was in fact what he had absolutely professed. Yet he importantly qualified. "*He* is n't myself. He's the just so totally other person. But I do want to see him," he added. "And I can. And I shall."

Their eyes met for a minute while he guessed from something in hers that she divined his strange sense. But neither of them otherwise expressed it, and her apparent understanding, with no protesting shock, no easy derision, touched him more deeply than anything yet, constituting for his stifled perversity, on the spot, an element that was like breatheable air. What she said however was unexpected. "Well, *I've* seen him."

"You—?"

"I've seen him in a dream."

"Oh a 'dream'—!" It let him down.

"But twice over," she continued. "I saw him as I see you now."

"You've dreamed the same dream—?"

"Twice over," she repeated. "The very same."

This did somehow a little speak to him, as it also gratified him. "You dream about me at that rate?"

"Ah about *him*!" she smiled.

His eyes again sounded her. "Then you know all about him." And as she said nothing more: "What's the wretch like?"

She hesitated, and it was as if he were pressing her so hard that, resisting for reasons of her own, she had to turn away. "I'll tell you some other time!"

II

It was after this that there was most of a virtue for him, most of a cultivated charm, most of a preposterous secret thrill, in the particular form of surrender to his obsession and of address to what he more and more believed to be his privilege. It was what in these weeks he was living for—since he really felt life to begin but after Mrs.

Muldoon had retired from the scene and, visiting the ample house from attic to cellar, making sure he was alone, he knew himself in safe possession and, as he tacitly expressed it, let himself go. He sometimes came twice in the twenty-four hours; the moments he liked best were those of gathering dusk, of the short autumn twilight; this was the time of which, again and again, he found himself hoping most. Then he could, as seemed to him, most intimately wander and wait, linger and listen, feel his fine attention, never in his life before so fine, on the pulse of the great vague place: he preferred the lampless hour and only wished he might have prolonged each day the deep crepuscular spell. Later — rarely much before midnight, but then for a considerable vigil — he watched with his glimmering light; moving slowly, holding it high, playing it far, rejoicing above all, as much as he might, in open vistas, reaches of communication between rooms and by passages; the long straight chance or show, as he would have called it, for the revelation he pretended to invite. It was a practice he found he could perfectly "work" without exciting remark; no one was in the least the wiser for it; even Alice Staverton, who was moreover a well of discretion, did n't quite fully imagine.

He let himself in and let himself out with the assurance of calm proprietorship; and accident so far favoured him that, if a fat Avenue "officer" had happened on occasion to see him entering at eleven-thirty, he had never yet, to the best of his belief, been noticed as emerging at two. He walked there on the crisp November nights, arrived regularly at the evening's end; it was as easy to do this after dining out as to take his way to a club or to his hotel. When he left his club, if he had n't been dining out, it was ostensibly to go to his hotel; and when he left his hotel, if he had spent a part of the evening there, it was ostensibly to go to his club. Everything was easy in fine; everything conspired and promoted: there was truly even in the strain of his experience something that glossed over, something that salved and simplified, all the rest of consciousness. He circulated, talked, renewed, loosely and pleasantly, old relations — met indeed, so far as he could, new expectations and seemed to make out on the whole that in spite of the career, of such different contacts, which he had spoken of to Miss Staverton as ministering so little, for those who might have watched it, to edification, he was positively rather liked than not. He was a dim secondary social success — and all with people who had truly not an idea of him. It was all mere surface sound, this murmur of their welcome, this popping of their corks — just as his gestures of response were the extravagant shadows, emphatic in proportion as they meant little, of some game of *ombres chinoises*.[5] He projected himself all day, in thought, straight over the bristling line of hard unconscious heads and into the other, the real, the waiting life; the life that, as soon as he had heard behind him the click of his great house-door, began for him, on the jolly corner, as beguilingly as the slow opening bars of some rich music follows the tap of the conductor's wand.

He always caught the first effect of the steel point of his stick on the old marble of the hall pavement, large black-and-white squares that he remembered as the admiration of his childhood and that had then made in him, as he now saw, for the growth of an early conception of style. This effect was the dim reverberating tinkle as of some far-off bell hung who should say where? — in the depths of the house, of the past, of that mystical other world that might have flourished for him had he not, for weal or woe, abandoned it. On this impression he did ever the same thing; he put his stick noiselessly away in a corner — feeling the place once more in the likeness of some great glass bowl, all precious concave crystal, set delicately humming by the play of a moist finger round its edge. The concave crystal held, as it were, this mystical other world, and the indescribably fine murmur of its rim was the sigh there, the scarce audible pathetic wail to his strained ear, of all the old baffled forsworn possibilities.

---

[5] "Chinese shadows" (French); a show with shadows of puppets or persons projected on a screen.

What he did therefore by this appeal of his hushed presence was to wake them into such measure of ghostly life as they might still enjoy. They were shy, all but unappeasably shy, but they were n't really sinister; at least they were n't as he had hitherto felt them—before they had taken the Form he so yearned to make them take, the Form he at moments saw himself in the light of fairly hunting on tiptoe, the points of his evening-shoes, from room to room and from storey to storey.

That was the essence of his vision—which was all rank folly, if one would, while he was out of the house and otherwise occupied, but which took on the last verisimilitude as soon as he was placed and posted. He knew what he meant and what he wanted; it was as clear as the figure on a cheque presented in demand for cash. His *alter ego* "walked"—that was the note of his image of him, while his image of his motive for his own odd pastime was the desire to waylay him and meet him. He roamed, slowly, warily, but all restlessly, he himself did—Mrs. Muldoon had been right, absolutely, with her figure of their "craping"; and the presence he watched for would roam restlessly too. But it would be as cautious and as shifty; the conviction of its probable, in fact its already quite sensible, quite audible evasion of pursuit grew for him from night to night, laying on him finally a rigour to which nothing in his life had been comparable. It had been the theory of many superficially-judging persons, he knew, that he was wasting that life in a surrender to sensations, but he had tasted of no pleasure so fine as his actual tension, had been introduced to no sport that demanded at once the patience and the nerve of this stalking of a creature more subtle, yet at bay perhaps more formidable, than any beast of the forest. The terms, the comparisons, the very practices of the chase positively came again into play; there were even moments when passages of his occasional experience as a sportsman, stirred memories, from his younger time, of moor and mountain and desert, revived for him—and to the increase of his keenness—by the tremendous force of analogy. He found himself at moments—once he had placed his single light on some mantel-shelf or in some recess—stepping back into shelter or shade, effacing himself behind a door or in an embrasure, as he had sought of old the vantage of rock and tree; he found himself holding his breath and living in the joy of the instant, the supreme suspense created by big game alone.

He was n't afraid (though putting himself the question as he believed gentlemen on Bengal tiger-shoots or in close quarters with the great bear of the Rockies had been known to confess to having put it); and this indeed—since here at least he might be frank!—because of the impression, so intimate and so strange, that he himself produced as yet a dread, produced certainly a strain, beyond the liveliest he was likely to feel. They fell for him into categories, they fairly became familiar, the signs, for his own perception, of the alarm his presence and his vigilance created; though leaving him always to remark, portentously, on his probably having formed a relation, his probably enjoying a consciousness, unique in the experience of man. People enough, first and last, had been in terror of apparitions, but who had ever before so turned the tables and become himself, in the apparitional world, an incalculable terror? He might have found this sublime had he quite dared to think of it; but he did n't too much insist, truly, on that side of his privilege. With habit and repetition he gained to an extraordinary degree the power to penetrate the dusk of distances and the darkness of corners, to resolve back into their innocence the treacheries of uncertain light, the evil-looking forms taken in the gloom by mere shadows, by accidents of the air, by shifting effects of perspective; putting down his dim luminary he could still wander on without it, pass into other rooms and, only knowing it was there behind him in case of need, see his way about, visually project for his purpose a comparative clearness. It made him feel, this acquired faculty, like some monstrous stealthy cat; he wondered if he would have glared at these moments with large shining yellow eyes, and what it might n't verily be, for the poor hard-pressed *alter ego*, to be confronted with such a type.

He liked however the open shutters; he opened everywhere those Mrs. Muldoon had closed, closing them as carefully afterwards, so that she should n't notice: he liked—oh this he did like, and above all in the upper rooms!—the sense of the hard silver of the autumn stars through the window-panes, and scarcely less the flare of the street-lamps below, the white electric lustre which it would have taken curtains to keep out. This was human actual social; this was of the world he had lived in, and he was more at his ease certainly for the countenance, coldly general and impersonal, that all the while and in spite of his detachment it seemed to give him. He had support of course mostly in the rooms at the wide front and the prolonged side; it failed him considerably in the central shades and the parts at the back. But if he sometimes, on his rounds, was glad of his optical reach, so none the less often the rear of the house affected him as the very jungle of his prey. The place was there more subdivided; a large "extension" in particular, where small rooms for servants had been multiplied, abounded in nooks and corners, in closets and passages, in the ramifications especially of an ample back staircase over which he leaned, many a time, to look far down—not deterred from his gravity even while aware that he might, for a spectator, have figured some solemn simpleton playing at hide-and-seek. Outside in fact he might himself make that ironic *rapprochement*;[6] but within the walls, and in spite of the clear windows, his consistency was proof against the cynical light of New York.

It had belonged to that idea of the exasperated consciousness of his victim to become a real test for him; since he had quite put it to himself from the first that, oh distinctly! he could "cultivate" his whole perception. He had felt it as above all open to cultivation—which indeed was but another name for his manner of spending his time. He was bringing it on, bringing it to perfection, by practice; in consequence of which it had grown so fine that he was now aware of impressions, attestations of his general postulate, that could n't have broken upon him at once. This was the case more specifically with a phenomenon at last quite frequent for him in the upper rooms, the recognition—absolutely unmistakeable, and by a turn dating from a particular hour, his resumption of his campaign after a diplomatic drop, a calculated absence of three nights—of his being definitely followed, tracked at a distance carefully taken and to the express end that he should the less confidently, less arrogantly, appear to himself merely to pursue. It worried, it finally quite broke him up, for it proved, of all the conceivable impressions, the one least suited to his book. He was kept in sight while remaining himself—as regards the essence of his position—sightless, and his only recourse then was in abrupt turns, rapid recoveries of ground. He wheeled about, retracing his steps, as if he might so catch in his face at least the stirred air of some other quick revolution. It was indeed true that his fully dislocalised thought of these manœuvres recalled to him Pantaloon, at the Christmas farce, buffeted and tricked from behind by ubiquitous Harlequin;[7] but it left intact the influence of the conditions themselves each time he was re-exposed to them, so that in fact this association, had he suffered it to become constant, would on a certain side have but ministered to his intenser gravity. He had made, as I have said, to create on the premises the baseless sense of a reprieve, his three absences; and the result of the third was to confirm the after-effect of the second.

On his return, that night—the night succeeding his last intermission—he stood in the hall and looked up the staircase with a certainty more intimate than any he had yet known. "He's *there*, at the top, and waiting—not, as in general, falling back for disappearance. He's holding his ground, and it's the first time—which is a proof, is n't it? that something has happened for him." So Brydon argued with his hand on the banister and his foot on the lowest stair; in which position he felt as never before the air chilled by his logic. He himself turned cold in it, for he seemed of a sudden to

---

[6]"Bringing together" (French); the sense here is "connection."
[7]Pantaloon, an elderly buffoon, and Harlequin, a clown, were stock characters in pantomime comedies in Europe, originating in the Italian *commedia dell'arte*.

know what now was involved. "Harder pressed? — yes, he takes it in, with its thus making clear to him that I've come, as they say, 'to stay.' He finally does n't like and can't bear it, in the sense, I mean, that his wrath, his menaced interest, now balances with his dread. I've hunted him till he has 'turned': that, up there, is what has happened — he's the fanged or the antlered animal brought at last to bay." There came to him, as I say — but determined by an influence beyond my notation! — the acuteness of this certainty; under which however the next moment he had broken into a sweat that he would as little have consented to attribute to fear as he would have dared immediately to act upon it for enterprise. It marked none the less a prodigious thrill, a thrill that represented sudden dismay, no doubt, but also represented, and with the selfsame throb, the strangest, the most joyous, possibly the next minute almost the proudest, duplication of consciousness.

"He has been dodging, retreating, hiding, but now, worked up to anger, he'll fight!" — this intense impression made a single mouthful, as it were, of terror and applause. But what was wondrous was that the applause, for the felt fact, was so eager, since, if it was his other self he was running to earth, this ineffable identity was thus in the last resort not unworthy of him. It bristled there — somewhere near at hand, however unseen still — as the hunted thing, even as the trodden worm of the adage *must* at last bristle; and Brydon at this instant tasted probably of a sensation more complex than had ever before found itself consistent with sanity. It was as if it would have shamed him that a character so associated with his own should triumphantly succeed in just skulking, should to the end not risk the open; so that the drop of this danger was, on the spot, a great lift of the whole situation. Yet with another rare shift of the same subtlety he was already trying to measure by how much more he himself might now be in peril of fear; so rejoicing that he could, in another form, actively inspire that fear, and simultaneously quaking for the form in which he might passively know it.

The apprehension of knowing it must after a little have grown in him, and the strangest moment of his adventure perhaps, the most memorable or really most interesting, afterwards, of his crisis, was the lapse of certain instants of concentrated conscious *combat*, the sense of a need to hold on to something, even after the manner of a man slipping and slipping on some awful incline; the vivid impulse, above all, to move, to act, to charge, somehow and upon something — to show himself, in a word, that he was n't afraid. The state of "holding-on" was thus the state to which he was momentarily reduced; if there had been anything, in the great vacancy, to seize, he would presently have been aware of having clutched it as he might under a shock at home have clutched the nearest chair-back. He had been surprised at any rate — of this he *was* aware — into something unprecedented since his original appropriation of the place; he had closed his eyes, held them tight, for a long minute, as with that instinct of dismay and that terror of vision. When he opened them the room, the other contiguous rooms, extraordinarily, seemed lighter — so light, almost, that at first he took the change for day. He stood firm, however that might be, just where he had paused; his resistance had helped him — it was as if there were something he had tided over. He knew after a little what this was — it had been in the imminent danger of flight. He had stiffened his will against going; without this he would have made for the stairs, and it seemed to him that, still with his eyes closed, he would have descended them, would have known how, straight and swiftly, to the bottom.

Well, as he had held out, here he was — still at the top, among the more intricate upper rooms and with the gauntlet of the others, of all the rest of the house, still to run when it should be his time to go. He would go at his time — only at his time: did n't he go every night very much at the same hour? He took out his watch — there was light for that: it was scarcely a quarter past one, and he had never withdrawn so soon. He reached his lodgings for the most part at two — with his walk of a quarter of an hour. He would wait for the last quarter — he would n't stir till then; and he kept his watch there with his eyes on it, reflecting while he held it that this deliberate wait, a wait with an effort, which he recognised, would serve perfectly for the attestation he desired to make. It would prove his courage — unless indeed the latter might most be proved by his budging at last from his place. What he mainly felt now was that, since he had n't originally scuttled, he had his dignities — which had never in his life seemed so many — all to preserve and to carry aloft. This was before him in truth as a physical image, an image almost worthy of an age of greater romance. That remark indeed glimmered for him only to glow the next instant with a finer light; since what age of romance, after all, could have matched either the state of his mind or, "objectively," as they said, the wonder of his situation? The only difference would have been that, brandishing his dignities over his head as in a parchment scroll, he might then — that is in the heroic time — have proceeded downstairs with a drawn sword in his other grasp.

At present, really, the light he had set down on the mantel of the next room would have to figure his sword; which utensil, in the course of a minute, he had taken the requisite number of steps to possess himself of. The door between the rooms was open, and from the second another door opened to a third. These rooms, as he remembered, gave all three upon a common corridor as well, but there was a fourth, beyond them, without issue save through the preceding. To have moved, to have heard his step again, was appreciably a help; though even in recognising this he lingered once more a little by the chimney-piece on which his light had rested. When he next moved, just hesitating where to turn, he found himself considering a circumstance that, after his first and comparatively vague apprehension of it, produced in him the start that often attends some pang of recollection, the violent shock of having ceased happily to forget. He had come into sight of the door in which the brief chain of communication ended and which he now surveyed from the nearer threshold, the one not directly facing it. Placed at some distance to the left of this point, it would have admitted him to the last room of the four, the room without other approach or egress, had it not, to his intimate conviction, been closed *since* his former visitation, the matter probably of a quarter of an hour before. He stared with all his eyes at the wonder of the fact, arrested again where he stood and again holding his breath while he sounded its sense. Surely it had been *subsequently* closed — that is it had been on his previous passage indubitably open!

He took it full in the face that something had happened between — that he could n't not have noticed before (by which he meant on his original tour of all the rooms that evening) that such a barrier had exceptionally presented itself. He had indeed since that moment undergone an agitation so extraordinary that it might have muddled for him any earlier view; and he tried to convince himself that he might perhaps then have gone into the room and, inadvertently, automatically, on coming out, have drawn the door after him. The difficulty was that this exactly was what he never did; it was against his whole policy, as he might have said, the essence of which was to keep vistas clear. He had them from the first, as he was well aware, quite on the brain: the strange apparition, at the far end of one of them, of his baffled "prey" (which had become by so sharp an irony so little the term now to apply!) was the form of success his imagination had most cherished, projecting into it always a refinement of beauty. He had known fifty times the start of perception that had afterwards dropped; had fifty times gasped to himself "There!" under some fond brief hallucination. The house, as the case stood, admirably lent itself; he might wonder at the taste, the native architecture of the particular time, which could rejoice so in the multiplication of doors — the opposite extreme to the modern, the actual almost complete proscription of them; but it had fairly contributed to provoke this obsession of the presence encountered telescopically, as he might say, focussed and studied in diminishing perspective and as by a rest for the elbow.

It was with these considerations that his present attention was charged — they perfectly availed to make what he saw portentous. He *could n't*, by any lapse, have blocked that aperture; and if he had n't, if it was unthinkable, why what else was clear but that there had been another agent? Another agent? — he had been catching, as he felt, a moment back, the very breath of him; but when had he been so close as in this simple, this logical, this completely personal act? It was so logical, that is, that one might have *taken* it for personal; yet for what did Brydon take it, he asked himself, while, softly panting, he felt his eyes almost leave their sockets. Ah this time at last they *were*, the two, the opposed projections of him, in presence; and this time, as much as one would, the question of danger loomed. With it rose, as not before, the question of courage — for what he knew the blank face of the door to say to him was "Show us how much you have!" It stared, it glared back at him with that challenge; it put to him the two alternatives: should he just push it open or not? Oh to have this consciousness was to *think* — and to think, Brydon knew, as he stood there, was, with the lapsing moments, not to have acted! Not to have acted — that was the misery and the pang — was even still not to act; was in fact *all* to feel the thing in another, in a new and terrible way. How long did he pause and how long did he debate? There was presently nothing to measure it; for his vibration had already changed — as just by the effect of its intensity. Shut up there, at bay, defiant, and with the prodigy of the thing palpably proveably *done*, thus giving notice like some stark signboard — under that accession of accent the situation itself had turned; and Brydon at last remarkably made up his mind on what it had turned to.

It had turned altogether to a different admonition; to a supreme hint, for him, of the value of Discretion! This slowly dawned, no doubt — for it could take its time; so perfectly, on his threshold, had he been stayed, so little as yet had he either advanced or retreated. It was the strangest of all things that now when, by his taking ten steps and applying his hand to a latch, or even his shoulder and his knee, if necessary, to a panel, all the hunger of his prime need might have been met, his high curiosity crowned, his unrest assuaged — it was amazing, but it was also exquisite and rare, that insistence should have, at a touch, quite dropped from him. Discretion — he jumped at that; and yet not, verily, at such a pitch, because it saved his nerves or his skin, but because, much more valuably, it saved the situation. When I say he "jumped" at it I feel the consonance of this term with the fact that — at the end indeed of I know not how long — he did move again, he crossed straight to the door. He would n't touch it — it seemed now that he might *if* he would: he would only just wait there a little, to show, to prove, that he would n't. He had thus another station, close to the thin partition by which revelation was denied him; but with his eyes bent and his hands held off in a mere intensity of stillness. He listened as if there had been something to hear, but this attitude, while it lasted, was his own communication. "If you won't then — good: I spare you and I give up. You affect me as by the appeal positively for pity: you convince me that for reasons rigid and sublime — what do I know? — we both of us should have suffered. I respect them then, and, though moved and privileged as, I believe, it has never been given to man, I retire, I renounce — never, on my honour, to try again. So rest for ever — and let *me*!"

That, for Brydon, was the deep sense of this last demonstration — solemn, measured, directed, as he felt it to be. He brought it to a close, he turned away; and now verily he knew how deeply he had been stirred. He retraced his steps, taking up his candle, burnt, he observed, well-nigh to the socket, and marking again, lighten it as he would, the distinctness of his footfall; after which, in a moment, he knew himself at the other side of the house. He did here what he had not yet done at these hours — he opened half a casement, one of those in the front, and let in the air of the night; a thing he would have taken at any time previous for a sharp rupture of his spell. His spell was broken now, and it did n't matter — broken by his concession and his surrender, which made it idle henceforth that he should ever come back. The empty street — its other life so marked even by the great lamplit vacancy — was within call, within touch; he stayed there as to be in it again, high above it though he was still perched; he watched as for some comforting common fact, some vulgar human note, the passage of a scavenger or a thief, some night-bird however base. He would have blessed that sign of life; he would have welcomed positively the slow approach of his friend the policeman, whom he had hitherto only sought to avoid, and was not sure that if the patrol had come into sight he might n't have felt the impulse to get into relation with it, to hail it, on some pretext, from his fourth floor.

The pretext that would n't have been too silly or too compromising, the explanation that would have saved his dignity and kept his name, in such a case, out of the papers, was not definite to him: he was so occupied with the thought of recording his Discretion — as an effect of the vow he had just uttered to his intimate adversary — that the importance of this loomed large and something had overtaken all ironically his sense of proportion. If there had been a ladder applied to the front of the house, even one of the vertiginous perpendiculars employed by painters and roofers and sometimes left standing overnight, he would have managed somehow, astride of the window-sill, to compass by outstretched leg and arm that mode of descent. If there had been some such uncanny thing as he had found in his room at hotels, a workable fire-escape in the form of notched cable or a canvas shoot, he would have availed himself of it as a proof — well, of his present delicacy. He nursed that sentiment, as the question stood, a little in vain, and even — at the end of he scarce knew, once more, how long — found it, as by the action on his mind of the failure of response of the outer world, sinking back to vague anguish. It seemed to him he had waited an age for some stir of the great grim hush; the life of the town was itself under a spell — so unnaturally, up and down the whole prospect of known and rather ugly objects, the blankness and the silence lasted. Had they ever, he asked himself, the hard-faced houses, which had begun to look livid in the dim dawn, had they ever spoken so little to any need of his spirit? Great builded voids, great crowded stillnesses put on, often, in the heart of cities, for the small hours, a sort of sinister mask, and it was of this large collective negation that Brydon presently became conscious — all the more that the break of day was, almost incredibly, now at hand, proving to him what a night he had made of it.

He looked again at his watch, saw what had become of his time-values (he had taken hours for minutes — not, as in other tense situations, minutes for hours) and the strange air of the streets was but the weak, the sullen flush of a dawn in which everything was still locked up. His choked appeal from his own open window had been the sole note of life, and he could but break off at last as for a worse despair. Yet while so deeply demoralised he was capable again of an impulse denoting — at least by his present measure — extraordinary resolution; of retracing his steps to the spot where he had turned cold with the extinction of his last pulse of doubt as to there being in the place another presence than his own. This required an effort strong enough to sicken him; but he had his reason, which overmastered for the moment everything else. There was the whole of the rest of the house to traverse, and how should he screw himself to that if the door he had seen closed were at present open? He could hold to the idea that the closing had practically been for him an act of mercy, a chance offered him to descend, depart, get off the ground and never again profane it. This conception held together, it worked; but what it meant for him depended now clearly on the amount of forbearance his recent action, or rather his recent inaction, had engendered. The image of the "presence," whatever it was, waiting there for him to go — this image had not yet been so concrete for his nerves as when he stopped short of the point at which certainty would have come to him. For, with all his resolution, or more exactly with all his dread, he did stop short — he hung back from really seeing. The risk was too great and his fear too definite: it took at this moment an awful specific form.

He knew—yes, as he had never known anything—that, *should* he see the door open, it would all too abjectly be the end of him. It would mean that the agent of his shame—for his shame was the deep abjection—was once more at large and in general possession; and what glared him thus in the face was the act that this would determine for him. It would send him straight about to the window he had left open, and by that window, be long ladder and dangling rope as absent as they would, he saw himself uncontrollably insanely fatally take his way to the street. The hideous chance of this he at least could avert; but he could only avert it by recoiling in time from assurance. He had the whole house to deal with, this fact was still there; only he now knew that uncertainty alone could start him. He stole back from where he had checked himself—merely to do so was suddenly like safety—and, making blindly for the greater staircase, left gaping rooms and sounding passages behind. Here was the top of the stairs, with a fine large dim descent and three spacious landings to mark off. His instinct was all for mildness, but his feet were harsh on the floors, and, strangely, when he had in a couple of minutes become aware of this, it counted somehow for help. He could n't have spoken, the tone of his voice would have scared him, and the common conceit or resource of "whistling in the dark" (whether literally or figuratively) have appeared basely vulgar; yet he liked none the less to hear himself go, and when he had reached his first landing—taking it all with no rush, but quite steadily—that stage of success drew from him a gasp of relief.

The house, withal, seemed immense, the scale of space again inordinate; the open rooms, to no one of which his eyes deflected, gloomed in their shuttered state like mouths of caverns; only the high skylight that formed the crown of the deep well created for him a medium in which he could advance, but which might have been, for queerness of colour, some watery under-world. He tried to think of something noble, as that his property was really grand, a splendid possession; but this nobleness took the form too of the clear delight with which he was finally to sacrifice it. They might come in now, the builders, the destroyers—they might come as soon as they would. At the end of two flights he had dropped to another zone, and from the middle of the third, with only one more left, he recognised the influence of the lower windows, of half-drawn blinds, of the occasional gleam of street-lamps, of the glazed spaces of the vestibule. This was the bottom of the sea, which showed an illumination of its own and which he even saw paved—when at a given moment he drew up to sink a long look over the banisters—with the marble squares of his childhood. By that time indubitably he felt, as he might have said in a commoner cause, better; it had allowed him to stop and draw breath, and the ease increased with the sight of the old black-and-white slabs. But what he most felt was that now surely, with the element of impunity pulling him as by hard firm hands, the case was settled for what he might have seen above had he dared that last look. The closed door, blessedly remote now, was still closed—and he had only in short to reach that of the house.

He came down further, he crossed the passage forming the access to the last flight; and if here again he stopped an instant it was almost for the sharpness of the thrill of assured escape. It made him shut his eyes—which opened again to the straight slope of the remainder of the stairs. Here was impunity still, but impunity almost excessive; inasmuch as the side-lights and the high fan-tracery of the entrance were glimmering straight into the hall; an appearance produced, he the next instant saw, by the fact that the vestibule gaped wide, that the hinged halves of the inner door had been thrown far back. Out of that again the *question* sprang at him, making his eyes, as he felt, half-start from his head, as they had done, at the top of the house, before the sign of the other door. If he had left that one open, had n't he left this one closed, and was n't he now in *most* immediate presence of some inconceivable occult activity? It was as sharp, the question, as a knife in his side, but the answer hung fire still and seemed to lose itself in the vague darkness to which the thin admitted dawn, glimmering archwise over the whole outer door, made a semicircular margin, a cold silvery nimbus that seemed to play a little as he looked—to shift and expand and contract.

It was as if there had been something within it, protected by indistinctness and corresponding in extent with the opaque surface behind, the painted panels of the last barrier to his escape, of which the key was in his pocket. The indistinctness mocked him even while he stared, affected him as somehow shrouding or challenging certitude, so that after faltering an instant on his step he let himself go with the sense that here *was* at last something to meet, to touch, to take, to know—something all unnatural and dreadful, but to advance upon which was the condition for him either of liberation or of supreme defeat. The penumbra, dense and dark, was the virtual screen of a figure which stood in it as still as some image erect in a niche or as some black-vizored sentinel guarding a treasure. Brydon was to know afterwards, was to recall and make out, the particular thing he had believed during the rest of his descent. He saw, in its great grey glimmering margin, the central vagueness diminish, and he felt it to be taking the very form toward which, for so many days, the passion of his curiosity had yearned. It gloomed, it loomed, it was something, it was somebody, the prodigy of a personal presence.

Rigid and conscious, spectral yet human, a man of his own substance and stature waited there to measure himself with his power to dismay. This only could it be—this only till he recognised, with his advance, that what made the face dim was the pair of raised hands that covered it and in which, so far from being offered in defiance, it was buried as for dark deprecation. So Brydon, before him, took him in; with every fact of him now, in the higher light, hard and acute—his planted stillness, his vivid truth, his grizzled bent head and white masking hands, his queer actuality of evening-dress, of dangling double eye-glass, of gleaming silk lappet and white linen, of pearl button and gold watch-guard and polished shoe. No portrait by a great modern master could have presented him with more intensity, thrust him out of his frame with more art, as if there had been "treatment," of the consummate sort, in his every shade and salience. The revulsion, for our friend, had become, before he knew it, immense—this drop, in the act of apprehension, to the sense of his adversary's inscrutable manœuvre. That meaning at least, while he gaped, it offered him; for he could but gape at his other self in this other anguish, gape as a proof that *he*, standing there for the achieved, the enjoyed, the triumphant life, could n't be faced in his triumph. Was n't the proof in the splendid covering hands, strong and completely spread?—so spread and so intentional that, in spite of a special verity that surpassed every other, the fact that one of these hands had lost two fingers, which were reduced to stumps, as if accidentally shot away, the face was effectually guarded and saved.

"Saved," though, *would* it be?—Brydon breathed his wonder till the very impunity of his attitude and the very insistence of his eyes produced, as he felt, a sudden stir which showed the next instant as a deeper portent, while the head raised itself, the betrayal of a braver purpose. The hands, as he looked, began to move, to open; then, as if deciding in a flash, dropped from the face and left it uncovered and presented. Horror, with the sight, had leaped into Brydon's throat, gasping there in a sound he could n't utter; for the bared identity was too hideous as *his*, and his glare was the passion of his protest. The face, *that* face, Spencer Brydon's?—he searched it still, but looking away from it in dismay and denial, falling straight from his height of sublimity. It was unknown, inconceivable, awful, disconnected from any possibility—! He had been "sold," he inwardly moaned, stalking such game as this: the presence before him was a presence, the horror within him a horror, but the waste of his nights had been only grotesque and the success of his adventure an irony. Such an identity fitted his at *no* point, made its alternative monstrous. A thousand times yes, as it came upon him nearer now—the face was the face of a stranger. It came upon him nearer now, quite as one of those expanding fantastic images projected by the magic lantern of childhood; for the stranger, whoever he might be, evil, odious, blatant, vulgar, had advanced as for aggression, and he knew himself give ground. Then harder pressed still, sick with the force of his shock, and falling back as under the hot breath and the roused passion of a life larger than his own, a rage of personality before which his own collapsed, he felt the whole vision turn to darkness and his very feet give way. His head went round; he was going; he had gone.

III

What had next brought him back, clearly—though after how long?—was Mrs. Muldoon's voice, coming to him from quite near, from so near that he seemed presently to see her as kneeling on the ground before him while he lay looking up at her; himself not wholly on the ground, but half-raised and upheld—conscious, yes, of tenderness of support and, more particularly, of a head pillowed in extraordinary softness and faintly refreshing fragrance. He considered, he wondered, his wit but half at his service; then another face intervened, bending more directly over him, and he finally knew that Alice Staverton had made her lap an ample and perfect cushion to him, and that she had to this end seated herself on the lowest degree of the staircase, the rest of his long person remaining stretched on his old black-and-white slabs. They were cold, these marble squares of his youth; but *he* somehow was not, in this rich return of consciousness—the most wonderful hour, little by little, that he had ever known, leaving him, as it did, so gratefully, so abysmally passive, and yet as with a treasure of intelligence waiting all round him for quiet appropriation; dissolved, he might call it, in the air of the place and producing the golden glow of a late autumn afternoon. He had come back, yes—come back from further away than any man but himself had ever travelled; but it was strange how with this sense what he had come back *to* seemed really the great thing, and as if his prodigious journey had been all for the sake of it. Slowly but surely his consciousness grew, his vision of his state thus completing itself: he had been miraculously *carried* back—lifted and carefully borne as from where he had been picked up, the uttermost end of an interminable grey passage. Even with this he was suffered to rest, and what had now brought him to knowledge was the break in the long mild motion.

It had brought him to knowledge, to knowledge—yes, this was the beauty of his state; which came to resemble more and more that of a man who has gone to sleep on some news of a great inheritance, and then, after dreaming it away, after profaning it with matters strange to it, has waked up again to serenity of certitude and has only to lie and watch it grow. This was the drift of his patience—that he had only to let it shine on him. He must moreover, with intermissions, still have been lifted and borne; since why and how else should he have known himself, later on, with the afternoon glow intenser, no longer at the foot of his stairs—situated as these now seemed at that dark other end of his tunnel—but on a deep window-bench of his high saloon, over which had been spread, couch-fashion, a mantle of soft stuff lined with grey fur that was familiar to his eyes and that one of his hands kept fondly feeling as for its pledge of truth. Mrs. Muldoon's face had gone, but the other, the second he had recognised, hung over him in a way that showed how he was still propped and pillowed. He took it all in, and the more he took it the more it seemed to suffice: he was as much at peace as if he had had food and drink. It was the two women who had found him, on Mrs. Muldoon's having plied, at her usual hour, her latch-key—and on her having above all arrived while Miss Staverton still lingered near the house. She had been turning away, all anxiety, from worrying the vain bell-handle—her calculation having been of the hour of the good woman's visit; but the latter, blessedly, had come up while she was still there, and they had entered together. He had then lain, beyond the vestibule, very much as he was lying now—quite, that is, as he appeared to have fallen, but all so wondrously without bruise or gash; only in a depth of stupor. What he most took in, however, at present, with the steadier clearance, was that Alice Staverton had for a long unspeakable moment not doubted he was dead.

"It must have been that I *was*." He made it out as she held him. "Yes—I can only have died. You brought me literally to life. Only," he wondered, his eyes rising to her, "only, in the name of all the benedictions, how?"

It took her but an instant to bend her face and kiss him, and something in the manner of it, and in the way her hands clasped and locked his head while he felt the cool charity and virtue of her lips, something in all this beatitude somehow answered everything. "And now I keep you," she said.

"Oh keep me, keep me!" he pleaded while her face still hung over him: in response to which it dropped again and stayed close, clingingly close. It was the seal of their situation—of which he tasted the impress for a long blissful moment in silence. But he came back. "Yet how did you know—?"

"I was uneasy. You were to have come, you remember—and you had sent no word."

"Yes, I remember—I was to have gone to you at one to-day." It caught on to their "old" life and relation—which were so near and so far. "I was still out there in my strange darkness—where was it, what was it? I must have stayed there so long." He could but wonder at the depth and the duration of his swoon.

"Since last night?" she asked with a shade of fear for her possible indiscretion.

"Since this morning—it must have been: the cold dim dawn of to-day. Where have I been," he vaguely wailed, "where have I been?" He felt her hold him close, and it was as if this helped him now to make in all security his mild moan. "What a long dark day!"

All in her tenderness she had waited a moment. "In the cold dim dawn?" she quavered.

But he had already gone on piecing together the parts of the whole prodigy. "As I did n't turn up you came straight—?"

She barely cast about. "I went first to your hotel—where they told me of your absence. You had dined out last evening and had n't been back since. But they appeared to know you had been at your club."

"So you had the idea of *this*—?"

"Of what?" she asked in a moment.

"Well—of what has happened."

"I believed at least you'd have been here. I've known, all along," she said, "that you've been coming."

"'Known' it—?"

"Well, I've believed it. I said nothing to you after that talk we had a month ago—but I felt sure. I knew you *would*," she declared.

"That I'd persist, you mean?"

"That you'd see him."

"Ah but I did n't!" cried Brydon with his long wail. "There's somebody—an awful beast; whom I brought, too horribly, to bay. But it's not me."

At this she bent over him again, and her eyes were in his eyes. "No—it's not you." And it was as if, while her face hovered, he might have made out in it, had n't it been so near, some particular meaning blurred by a smile. "No, thank heaven," she repeated—"it's not you! Of course it was n't to have been."

"Ah but it *was*," he gently insisted. And he stared before him now as he had been staring for so many weeks. "I was to have known myself."

"You could n't!" she returned consolingly. And then reverting, and as if to account further for what she had herself done, "But it was n't only *that*, that you had n't been at home," she went on. "I waited till the hour at which we had found Mrs. Muldoon that day of my going with you; and she arrived, as I've told you, while, failing to bring any one to the door, I lingered in my despair on the steps. After a little, if she had n't come, by such a mercy, I should have found means to hunt her up. But it was n't," said Alice Staverton, as if once more with her fine intention—"it was n't only that."

His eyes, as he lay, turned back to her. "What more then?"

She met it, the wonder she had stirred. "In the cold dim dawn, you say? Well, in the cold dim dawn of this morning I too saw you."

"Saw *me*—?"

"Saw *him*," said Alice Staverton. "It must have been at the same moment."

He lay an instant taking it in—as if he wished to be quite reasonable. "At the same moment?"

"Yes—in my dream again, the same one I've named to you. He came back to me. Then I knew it for a sign. He had come to you."

At this Brydon raised himself; he had to see her better. She helped him when she understood his movement, and he sat up, steadying himself beside her there on the window-bench and with his right hand grasping her left. "*He* did n't come to me."

"You came to yourself," she beautifully smiled.

"Ah I've come to myself now—thanks to you, dearest. But this brute, with his awful face—this brute's a black stranger. He's none of *me*, even as I *might* have been," Brydon sturdily declared.

But she kept the clearness that was like the breath of infallibility. "Is n't the whole point that you'd have been different?"

He almost scowled for it. "As different as *that*—?"

Her look again was more beautiful to him than the things of this world. "Have n't you exactly wanted to know *how* different? So this morning," she said, "you appeared to me."

"Like *him*?"

"A black stranger!"

"Then how did you know it was I?"

"Because, as I told you weeks ago, my mind, my imagination, had worked so over what you might, what you might n't have been—to show you, you see, how I've thought of you. In the midst of that you came to me—that my wonder might be answered. So I knew," she went on; "and believed that, since the question held you too so fast, as you told me that day, you too would see for yourself. And when this morning I again saw I knew it would be because you had—and also then, from the first moment, because you somehow wanted me. *He* seemed to tell me of that. So why," she strangely smiled, "should n't I like him?"

It brought Spencer Brydon to his feet. "You 'like' that horror—?"

"I *could* have liked him. And to me," she said, "he was no horror. I had accepted him."

"'Accepted'—?" Brydon oddly sounded.

"Before, for the interest of his difference—yes. And as *I* did n't disown him, as *I* knew him—which you at last, confronted with him in his difference, so cruelly did n't, my dear—well, he must have been, you see, less dreadful to me. And it may have pleased him that I pitied him."

She was beside him on her feet, but still holding his hand—still with her arm supporting him. But though it all brought for him thus a dim light, "You 'pitied' him?" he grudgingly, resentfully asked.

"He has been unhappy, he has been ravaged," she said.

"And have n't I been unhappy? Am not I—you've only to look at me!—ravaged?"

"Ah I don't say I like him *better*," she granted after a thought. "But he's grim, he's worn—and things have happened to him. He does n't make shift, for sight, with your charming monocle."

"No"—it struck Brydon: "I could n't have sported mine 'downtown.' They'd have guyed me there."

"His great convex pince-nez—I saw it, I recognised the kind—is for his poor ruined sight. And his poor right hand—!"

"Ah!" Brydon winced—whether for his proved identity or for his lost fingers. Then, "He has a million a year," he lucidly added. "But he has n't you."

"And he is n't—no, he is n't—*you*!" she murmured as he drew her to his breast.

                                                                            1908, 1909

ON "THE JOLLY CORNER" (*from* PREFACE)
["A *MALAISE* SO INCONGRUOUS AND DISCORDANT"]

. . . The higher interest . . . would emphasize the note I wanted; that of the strange and sinister embroidered on the very type of the normal and easy.

This was to be again, after years, the idea entertained for "The Jolly Corner," about the composition of which there would be more to say than my space allows; almost more in fact than categorical clearness might see its way to. A very limited thing being on this occasion in question, I was moved to adopt as my motive an analysis of some one of the conceivably rarest and intensest grounds for an "unnatural" anxiety, a *malaise* so incongruous and discordant, in the given prosaic prosperous conditions, as almost to be compromising. Spencer Brydon's adventure however is one of those finished fantasies that, achieving success or not, speak best even to the critical sense for themselves—which I leave it to do. . . .

                                                                            1909

from Hawthorne
[AMERICAN ABSENCES; EUROPEAN DENSITIES][1]

I know not at what age he began to keep a diary; the first entries in the American volumes are of the summer of 1835. There is a phrase in the preface to his novel of *Transformation*,[2] which must have lingered in the minds of many Americans who have tried to write novels and to lay the scene of them in the western world. "No author, without a trial, can conceive of the difficulty of writing a romance about a country where there is no shadow, no antiquity, no mystery, no picturesque and gloomy wrong, nor anything but a commonplace prosperity, in broad and simple daylight, as is happily the case with my dear native land." The perusal of Hawthorne's American Note-Books operates as a practical commentary upon this somewhat ominous text. It does so at least to my own mind; it would be too much perhaps to say that the effect would be the same for the usual English reader. An American reads between the lines—he completes the suggestions—he constructs a picture. I think I am not guilty of any gross injustice in saying that the picture he constructs from Hawthorne's American diaries, though by no means without charms of its own, is not, on the whole, an interesting one. It is characterised by an extraordinary blankness—a curious paleness of colour and paucity of detail. Hawthorne, as I have said, has a large and healthy appetite for detail, and one is therefore the more struck with the lightness of the diet to which his observation was condemned. For myself, as I turn the

[1]From Chapter II of *Hawthorne* (1879).
[2]Title of the English edition of Hawthorne's *The Marble Faun* (1860).

pages of his journals, I seem to see the image of the crude and simple society in which he lived. I use these epithets, of course, not invidiously, but descriptively; if one desires to enter as closely as possible into Hawthorne's situation, one must endeavour to reproduce his circumstances. We are struck with the large number of elements that were absent from them, and the coldness, the thinness, the blankness, to repeat my epithet, present themselves so vividly that our foremost feeling is that of compassion for a romancer looking for subjects in such a field. It takes so many things, as Hawthorne must have felt later in life, when he made the acquaintance of the denser, richer, warmer European spectacle — it takes such an accumulation of history and custom, such a complexity of manners and types, to form a fund of suggestion for a novelist. If Hawthorne had been a young Englishman, or a young Frenchman of the same degree of genius, the same cast of mind, the same habits, his consciousness of the world around him would have been a very different affair; however obscure, however reserved, his own personal life, his sense of the life of his fellow-mortals would have been almost infinitely more various. The negative side of the spectacle on which Hawthorne looked out, in his contemplative saunterings and reveries, might, indeed, with a little ingenuity, be made almost ludicrous; one might enumerate the items of high civilization, as it exists in other countries, which are absent from the texture of American life, until it should become a wonder to know what was left. No State, in the European sense of the word, and indeed barely a specific national name. No sovereign, no court, no personal loyalty, no aristocracy, no church, no clergy, no army, no diplomatic service, no country gentlemen, no palaces, no castles, nor manors, nor old country-houses, nor parsonages, nor thatched cottages nor ivied ruins; no cathedrals, nor abbeys, nor little Norman churches; no great Universities nor public schools — no Oxford, nor Eton, nor Harrow;[3] no literature, no novels, no museums, no pictures, no political society, no sporting class — no Epsom nor Ascot![4] Some such list as that might be drawn up of the absent things in American life — especially in the American life of forty years ago, the effect of which, upon an English or a French imagination, would probably as a general thing be appalling. The natural remark, in the almost lurid light of such an indictment, would be that if these things are left out, everything is left out. The American knows that a good deal remains; what it is that remains — that is his secret, his joke, as one may say. It would be cruel, in this terrible denudation, to deny him the consolation of his national gift, that "American humour" of which of late years we have heard so much. . . .

1879   *1879*

The Art of Fiction[1]

I should not have affixed so comprehensive a title to these few remarks, necessarily wanting in any completeness upon a subject the full consideration of which would carry us far, did I not seem to discover a pretext for my temerity in the interesting pamphlet lately published under this name by Mr. Walter Besant. Mr. Besant's lecture at the Royal Institution — the original form of his pamphlet — appears to indicate that many persons are interested in the art of fiction, and are not indifferent to such remarks, as those who practise it may attempt to make about it. I am therefore

---

[3]Oxford University, dating from the twelfth century; Eton and Harrow, dating from the fifteenth and sixteenth centuries, are English private secondary boarding schools (i.e., public schools) for sons of the upper class, attended by many famous literary men.
[4]English racetracks frequented by high society.

[1]James wrote this essay, one of his most important statements on fictional theory, in answer to an essay ("Fiction as One of the Fine Arts") by English novelist and critic Walter Besant (1836–1901), which he had first delivered as a lecture in April 1884. James's essay is thus structured as a fairly detailed reply to most of Besant's points.

anxious not to lose the benefit of this favourable association, and to edge in a few words under cover of the attention which Mr. Besant is sure to have excited. There is something very encouraging in his having put into form certain of his ideas on the mystery of story-telling.

It is a proof of life and curiosity—curiosity on the part of the brotherhood of novelists as well as on the part of their readers. Only a short time ago it might have been supposed that the English novel was not what the French call *discutable*.[2] It had no air of having a theory, a conviction, a consciousness of itself behind it—of being the expression of an artistic faith, the result of choice and comparison. I do not say it was necessarily the worse for that: it would take much more courage than I possess to intimate that the form of the novel as Dickens and Thackeray (for instance) saw it had any taint of incompleteness. It was, however, *naïf* (if I may help myself out with another French word); and evidently if it be destined to suffer in any way for having lost its *naïveté* it has now an idea of making sure of the corresponding advantages. During the period I have alluded to there was a comfortable, good-humoured feeling abroad that a novel is a novel as a pudding is a pudding, and that our only business with it could be to swallow it. But within a year or two, for some reason or other, there have been signs of returning animation—the era of discussion would appear to have been to a certain extent opened. Art lives upon discussion, upon experiment, upon curiosity, upon variety of attempt, upon the exchange of views and the comparison of standpoints; and there is a presumption that those times when no one has anything particular to say about it, and has no reason to give for practice or preference, though they may be times of honour, are not times of development—are times, possibly even, a little of dulness. The successful application of any art is a delightful spectacle, but the theory too is interesting; and though there is a great deal of the latter without the former I suspect there has never been a genuine success that has not had a latent core of conviction. Discussion, suggestion, formulation, these things are fertilising when they are frank and sincere. Mr. Besant has set an excellent example in saying what he thinks, for his part, about the way in which fiction should be written, as well as about the way in which it should be published; for his view of the "art," carried on into an appendix, covers that too. Other labourers in the same field will doubtless take up the argument, they will give it the light of their experience, and the effect will surely be to make our interest in the novel a little more what it had for some time threatened to fail to be—a serious, active, inquiring interest, under protection of which this delightful study may, in moments of confidence, venture to say a little more what it thinks of itself.

It must take itself seriously for the public to take it so. The old superstition about fiction being "wicked" has doubtless died out in England; but the spirit of it lingers in a certain oblique regard directed toward any story which does not more or less admit that it is only a joke. Even the most jocular novel feels in some degree the weight of the proscription that was formerly directed against literary levity: the jocularity does not always succeed in passing for orthodoxy. It is still expected, though perhaps people are ashamed to say it, that a production which is after all only a "make-believe" (for what else is a "story"?) shall be in some degree apologetic—shall renounce the pretension of attempting really to represent life. This, of course, any sensible, wide-awake story declines to do, for it quickly perceives that the tolerance granted to it on such a condition is only an attempt to stifle it disguised in the form of generosity. The old evangelical hostility to the novel, which was as explicit as it was narrow, and which regarded it as little less favourable to our immortal part than a stage-play, was in reality far less insulting. The only reason for the existence of a novel is that it does attempt to represent life. When it relinquishes this attempt, the same attempt that we see on the canvas of the painter, it will have arrived at a very strange pass. It is not

---

[2]"Disputable" (French).

expected of the picture that it will make itself humble in order to be forgiven; and the analogy between the art of the painter and the art of the novelist is, so far as I am able to see, complete. Their inspiration is the same, their process (allowing for the different quality of the vehicle), is the same, their success is the same. They may learn from each other, they may explain and sustain each other. Their cause is the same, and the honour of one is the honour of another. The Mahometans think a picture an unholy thing, but it is a long time since any Christian did, and it is therefore the more odd that in the Christian mind the traces (dissimulated though they may be) of a suspicion of the sister art should linger to this day. The only effectual way to lay it to rest is to emphasise the analogy to which I just alluded—to insist on the fact that as the picture is reality, so the novel is history. That is the only general description (which does it justice) that we may give of the novel. But history also is allowed to represent life; it is not, any more than painting, expected to apologise. The subject-matter of fiction is stored up likewise in documents and records, and if it will not give itself away, as they say in California, it must speak with assurance, with the tone of the historian. Certain accomplished novelists have a habit of giving themselves away which must often bring tears to the eyes of people who take their fiction seriously. I was lately struck, in reading over many pages of Anthony Trollope,[3] with his want of discretion in this particular. In a digression, a parenthesis or an aside, he concedes to the reader that he and this trusting friend are only "making believe." He admits that the events he narrates have not really happened, and that he can give his narrative any turn the reader may like best. Such a betrayal of a sacred office seems to me, I confess, a terrible crime; it is what I mean by the attitude of apology, and it shocks me every whit as much in Trollope as it would have shocked me in Gibbon or Macaulay.[4] It implies that the novelist is less occupied in looking for the truth (the truth, of course I mean, that he assumes, the premises that we must grant him, whatever they may be), than the historian, and in doing so it deprives him at a stroke of all his standing-room. To represent and illustrate the past, the actions of men, is the task of either writer, and the only difference that I can see is, in proportion as he succeeds, to the honour of the novelist, consisting as it does in his having more difficulty in collecting his evidence, which is so far from being purely literary. It seems to me to give him a great character, the fact that he has at once so much in common with the philosopher and the painter; this double analogy is a magnificent heritage.

It is of all this evidently that Mr. Besant is full when he insists upon the fact that fiction is one of the *fine* arts, deserving in its turn of all the honours and emoluments that have hitherto been reserved for the successful profession of music, poetry, painting, architecture. It is impossible to insist too much on so important a truth, and the place that Mr. Besant demands for the work of the novelist may be represented, a trifle less abstractly, by saying that he demands not only that it shall be reputed artistic, but that it shall be reputed very artistic indeed. It is excellent that he should have struck this note, for his doing so indicates that there was need of it, that his proposition may be to many people a novelty. One rubs one's eyes at the thought; but the rest of Mr. Besant's essay confirms the revelation. I suspect in truth that it would be possible to confirm it still further, and that one would not be far wrong in saying that in addition to the people to whom it has never occurred that a novel ought to be artistic, there are a great many others who, if this principle were urged upon them, would be filled with an indefinable mistrust. They would find it difficult to explain their repugnance, but it would operate strongly to put them on their guard. "Art," in our Protestant communities, where so many things have got so strangely twisted about, is supposed in certain circles to have some vaguely injurious effect upon those

---

[3]English novelist (1815–1882).
[4]Edward Gibbon (1737–1794) and Thomas Macaulay (1800–
1859), English historians.

who make it an important consideration, who let it weigh in the balance. It is assumed to be opposed in some mysterious manner to morality, to amusement, to instruction. When it is embodied in the work of the painter (the sculptor is another affair!) you know what it is: it stands there before you, in the honesty of pink and green and a gilt frame; you can see the worst of it at a glance, and you can be on your guard. But when it is introduced into literature it becomes more insidious — there is danger of its hurting you before you know it. Literature should be either instructive or amusing, and there is in many minds an impression that these artistic preoccupations, the search for form, contribute to neither end, interfere indeed with both. They are too frivolous to be edifying, and too serious to be diverting; and they are moreover priggish and paradoxical and superfluous. That, I think, represents the manner in which the latent thought of many people who read novels as an exercise in skipping would explain itself if it were to become articulate. They would argue, of course, that a novel ought to be "good," but they would interpret this term in a fashion of their own, which indeed would vary considerably from one critic to another. One would say that being good means representing virtuous and aspiring characters, placed in prominent positions; another would say that it depends on a "happy ending," on a distribution at the last of prizes, pensions, husbands, wives, babies, millions, appended paragraphs, and cheerful remarks. Another still would say that it means being full of incident and movement, so that we shall wish to jump ahead, to see who was the mysterious stranger, and if the stolen will was ever found, and shall not be distracted from this pleasure by any tiresome analysis or "description." But they would all agree that the "artistic" idea would spoil some of their fun. One would hold it accountable for all the description, another would see it revealed in the absence of sympathy. Its hostility to a happy ending would be evident, and it might even in some cases render any ending at all impossible. The "ending" of a novel is, for many persons, like that of a good dinner, a course of dessert and ices, and the artist in fiction is regarded as a sort of meddlesome doctor who forbids agreeable aftertastes. It is therefore true that this conception of Mr. Besant's of the novel as a superior form encounters not only a negative but a positive indifference. It matters little that as a work of art it should really be as little or as much of its essence to supply happy endings, sympathetic characters, and an objective tone, as if it were a work of mechanics: the association of ideas, however incongruous, might easily be too much for it if an eloquent voice were not sometimes raised to call attention to the fact that it is at once as free and as serious a branch of literature as any other.

Certainly this might sometimes be doubted in presence of the enormous number of works of fiction that appeal to the credulity of our generation, for it might easily seem that there could be no great character in a commodity so quickly and easily produced. It must be admitted that good novels are much compromised by bad ones, and that the field at large suffers discredit from overcrowding. I think, however, that this injury is only superficial, and that the superabundance of written fiction proves nothing against the principle itself. It has been vulgarised, like all other kinds of literature, like everything else to-day, and it has proved more than some kinds accessible to vulgarisation. But there is as much difference as there ever was between a good novel and a bad one: the bad is swept with all the daubed canvases and spoiled marble into some unvisited limbo, or infinite rubbish-yard beneath the back-windows of the world, and the good subsists and emits its light and stimulates our desire for perfection. As I shall take the liberty of making but a single criticism of Mr. Besant, whose tone is so full of the love of his art, I may as well have done with it at once. He seems to me to mistake in attempting to say so definitely beforehand what sort of an affair the good novel will be. To indicate the danger of such an error as that has been the purpose of these few pages; to suggest that certain traditions on the subject, applied *a priori*, have already had much to answer for, and that the good health of an art which undertakes so immediately to reproduce life must demand that it be perfectly free. It lives upon exercise, and the very meaning of exercise is freedom. The only obligation to which in advance we may hold a novel, without incurring the accusation of being arbitrary, is that it be interesting. That general responsibility rests upon it, but it is the only one I can think of. The ways in which it is at liberty to accomplish this result (of interesting us) strike me as innumerable, and such as can only suffer from being marked out or fenced in by prescription. They are as various as the temperament of man, and they are successful in proportion as they reveal a particular mind, different from others. A novel is in its broadest definition a personal, a direct impression of life: that, to begin with, constitutes its value, which is greater or less according to the intensity of the impression. But there will be no intensity at all, and therefore no value, unless there is freedom to feel and say. The tracing of a line to be followed, of a tone to be taken, of a form to be filled out, is a limitation of that freedom and a suppression of the very thing that we are most curious about. The form, it seems to me, is to be appreciated after the fact: then the author's choice has been made, his standard has been indicated; then we can follow lines and directions and compare tones and resemblances. Then in a word we can enjoy one of the most charming of pleasures, we can estimate quality, we can apply the test of execution. The execution belongs to the author alone; it is what is most personal to him, and we measure him by that. The advantage, the luxury, as well as the torment and responsibility of the novelist, is that there is no limit to what he may attempt as an executant — no limit to his possible experiments, efforts, discoveries, successes. Here it is especially that he works, step by step, like his brother of the brush, of whom we may always say that he has painted his picture in a manner best known to himself. His manner is his secret, not necessarily a jealous one. He cannot disclose it as a general thing if he would; he would be at a loss to teach it to others. I say this with a due recollection of having insisted on the community of method of the artist who paints a picture and the artist who writes a novel. The painter *is* able to teach the rudiments of his practice, and it is possible, from the study of good work (granted the aptitude), both to learn how to paint and to learn how to write. Yet it remains true, without injury to the *rapprochement*,[5] that the literary artist would be obliged to say to his pupil much more than the other, "Ah, well, you must do it as you can!" It is a question of degree, a matter of delicacy. If there are exact sciences, there are also exact arts, and the grammar of painting is so much more definite that it makes the difference.

I ought to add, however, that if Mr. Besant says at the beginning of his essay that the "laws of fiction may be laid down and taught with as much precision and exactness as the laws of harmony, perspective, and proportion," he mitigates what might appear to be an extravagance by applying his remark to "general" laws, and by expressing most of these rules in a manner with which it would certainly be unaccommodating to disagree. That the novelist must write from his experience, that his "characters must be real and such as might be met with in actual life;" that "a young lady brought up in a quiet country village should avoid descriptions of garrison life," and "a writer whose friends and personal experiences belong to the lower middle-class should carefully avoid introducing his characters into society;" that one should enter one's notes in a common-place book; that one's figures should be clear in outline; that making them clear by some trick of speech or of carriage is a bad method, and "describing them at length" is a worse one; that English Fiction should have a "conscious moral purpose;" that "it is almost impossible to estimate too highly the value of careful workmanship — that is, of style;" that "the most important point of all is the story," that "the story is everything": these are principles with most of which it is surely impossible not to sympathise. That remark about the lower middle-class writer

---

5"Bringing together" (French); "comparison" in this context.

and his knowing his place is perhaps rather chilling; but for the rest I should find it difficult to dissent from any one of these recommendations. At the same time, I should find it difficult positively to assent to them, with the exception, perhaps, of the injunction as to entering one's notes in a common-place book. They scarcely seem to me to have the quality that Mr. Besant attributes to the rules of the novelist — the "precision and exactness" of "the laws of harmony, perspective, and proportion." They are suggestive, they are even inspiring, but they are not exact, though they are doubtless as much so as the case admits of: which is a proof of that liberty of inter- pretation for which I just contended. For the value of these different injunctions — so beautiful and so vague — is wholly in the meaning one attaches to them. The charac- ters, the situation, which strike one as real will be those that touch and interest one most, but the measure of reality is very difficult to fix. The reality of Don Quixote or of Mr. Micawber[6] is a very delicate shade; it is a reality so coloured by the author's vision that, vivid as it may be, one would hesitate to propose it as a model: one would expose one's self to some very embarrassing questions on the part of a pupil. It goes without saying that you will not write a good novel unless you possess the sense of reality; but it will be difficult to give you a recipe for calling that sense into being. Humanity is immense, and reality has a myriad forms; the most one can affirm is that some of the flowers of fiction have the odour of it, and others have not; as for telling you in advance how your nosegay should be composed, that is another affair. It is equally excellent and inconclusive to say that one must write from experience; to our supposititious aspirant such a declaration might savour of mockery. What kind of experience is intended, and where does it begin and end? Experience is never lim- ited, and it is never complete; it is an immense sensibility, a kind of huge spider-web of the finest silken threads suspended in the chamber of consciousness, and catching every airborne particle in its tissue. It is the very atmosphere of the mind; and when the mind is imaginative — much more when it happens to be that of a man of ge- nius — it takes to itself the faintest hints of life, it converts the very pulses of the air into revelations. The young lady living in a village has only to be a damsel upon whom nothing is lost to make it quite unfair (as it seems to me) to declare to her that she shall have nothing to say about the military. Greater miracles have been seen than that, imagination assisting, she should speak the truth about some of these gentle- men. I remember an English novelist, a woman of genius,[7] telling me that she was much commended for the impression she had managed to give in one of her tales of the nature and way of life of the French Protestant youth. She had been asked where she learned so much about this recondite being, she had been congratulated on her peculiar opportunities. These opportunities consisted in her having once, in Paris, as she ascended a staircase, passed an open door where, in the household of a *pasteur*,[8] some of the young Protestants were seated at table round a finished meal. The glimpse made a picture; it lasted only a moment, but that moment was experience. She had got her direct personal impression, and she turned out her type. She knew what youth was, and what Protestantism; she also had the advantage of having seen what it was to be French, so that she converted these ideas into a concrete image and produced a reality. Above all, however, she was blessed with the faculty which when you give it an inch takes an ell, and which for the artist is a much greater source of strength than any accident of residence or of place in the social scale. The power to guess the unseen from the seen, to trace the implication of things, to judge the whole piece by the pattern, the condition of feeling life in general so completely that you are well on your way to knowing any particular corner of it — this cluster of gifts may

[6]The idealistic naive hero of *Don Quixote de la Mancha* (1605, 1615) by Miguel de Cervantes (1547–1616); Micawber, the incurably optimistic character in *David Copperfield* (1849–50) by Charles Dickens (1812–1870).
[7]Anne Isabella Thackeray, Lady Ritchie (1837–1919), daughter of English novelist William Makepeace Thackeray (1811–1863); the reference is to her *The Story of Elizabeth* (1863).
[8]"Pastor" (French).

almost be said to constitute experience, and they occur in country and in town, and in the most differing stages of education. If experience consists of impressions, it may be said that impressions *are* experience, just as (have we not seen it?) they are the very air we breathe. Therefore, if I should certainly say to a novice, "Write from experience and experience only," I should feel that this was rather a tantalising monition if I were not careful immediately to add, "Try to be one of the people on whom nothing is lost!"

I am far from intending by this to minimise the importance of exactness — of truth of detail. One can speak best from one's own taste, and I may therefore venture to say that the air of reality (solidity of specification) seems to me to be the supreme virtue of a novel — the merit on which all its other merits (including that conscious moral purpose of which Mr. Besant speaks) helplessly and submissively depend. If it be not there they are all as nothing, and if these be there, they owe their effect to the success with which the author has produced the illusion of life. The cultivation of this success, the study of this exquisite process, form, to my taste, the beginning and the end of the art of the novelist. They are his inspiration, his despair, his reward, his torment, his delight. It is here in very truth that he competes with life; it is here that he competes with his brother the painter in *his* attempt to render the look of things, the look that conveys their meaning, to catch the colour, the relief, the expression, the surface, the substance of the human spectacle. It is in regard to this that Mr. Besant is well inspired when he bids him take notes. He cannot possibly take too many, he cannot possibly take enough. All life solicits him, and to "render" the simplest surface, to produce the most momentary illusion, is a very complicated business. His case would be easier, and the rule would be more exact, if Mr. Besant had been able to tell him what notes to take. But this, I fear, he can never learn in any manual; it is the business of his life. He has to take a great many in order to select a few, he has to work them up as he can, and even the guides and philosophers who might have most to say to him must leave him alone when it comes to the application of precepts, as we leave the painter in communion with his palette. That his characters "must be clear in outline," as Mr. Besant says — he feels that down to his boots; but how he shall make them so is a secret between his good angel and himself. It would be absurdly simple if he could be taught that a great deal of "description" would make them so, or that on the contrary the absence of description and the cultivation of dialogue, or the absence of dialogue and the multiplication of "incident," would rescue him from his difficulties. Nothing, for instance, is more possible than that he be of a turn of mind for which this odd, literal opposition of description and dialogue, incident and description, has little meaning and light. People often talk of these things as if they had a kind of internecine distinctness, instead of melting into each other at every breath, and being intimately associated parts of one general effort of expression. I cannot imagine composition existing in a series of blocks, nor conceive, in any novel worth discussing at all, of a passage of description that is not in its intention narrative, a passage of dialogue that is not in its intention descriptive, a touch of truth of any sort that does not partake of the nature of incident, or an incident that derives its interest from any other source than the general and only source of the success of a work of art — that of being illustrative. A novel is a living thing, all one and continuous, like any other organism, and in proportion as it lives will it be found, I think, that in each of the parts there is something of each of the other parts. The critic who over the close texture of a finished work shall pretend to trace a geography of items will mark some frontiers as artificial, I fear, as any that have been known to history. There is an old-fashioned distinction between the novel of character and the novel of incident which must have cost many a smile to the intending fabulist who was keen about his work. It appears to me as little to the point as the equally celebrated distinction between the novel and the romance — to answer as little to any reality. There are bad novels and good novels, as there are bad pictures and good pictures; but that is the only distinction in which I see any meaning, and I can as little imagine speaking of a novel of character as I can imagine speaking of a picture of character. When one says picture one says of character, when one says novel one says of incident, and the terms may be transposed at will. What is character but the determination of incident? What is incident but the illustration of character? What is either a picture or a novel that is *not* of character? What else do we seek in it and find in it? It is an incident for a woman to stand up with her hand resting on a table and look out at you in a certain way; or if it be not an incident I think it will be hard to say what it is. At the same time it is an expression of character. If you say you don't see it (character in *that — allons donc!*),[9] this is exactly what the artist who has reasons of his own for thinking he *does* see it undertakes to show you. When a young man makes up his mind that he has not faith enough after all to enter the church as he intended, that is an incident, though you may not hurry to the end of the chapter to see whether perhaps he doesn't change once more. I do not say that these are extraordinary or startling incidents. I do not pretend to estimate the degree of interest proceeding from them, for this will depend upon the skill of the painter. It sounds almost puerile to say that some incidents are intrinsically much more important than others, and I need not take this precaution after having professed my sympathy for the major ones in remarking that the only classification of the novel that I can understand is into that which has life and that which has it not.

The novel and the romance, the novel of incident and that of character — these clumsy separations appear to me to have been made by critics and readers for their own convenience, and to help them out of some of their occasional queer predicaments, but to have little reality or interest for the producer, from whose point of view it is of course that we are attempting to consider the art of fiction. The case is the same with another shadowy category which Mr. Besant apparently is disposed to set up — that of the "modern English novel"; unless indeed it be that in this matter he has fallen into an accidental confusion of standpoints. It is not quite clear whether he intends the remarks in which he alludes to it to be didactic or historical. It is as difficult to suppose a person intending to write a modern English as to suppose him writing an ancient English novel: that is a label which begs the question. One writes the novel, one paints the picture, of one's language and of one's time, and calling it modern English will not, alas! make the difficult task any easier. No more, unfortunately, will calling this or that work of one's fellow-artist a romance — unless it be, of course, simply for the pleasantness of the thing, as for instance when Hawthorne gave this heading to his story of *Blithedale*.[10] The French, who have brought the theory of fiction to remarkable completeness, have but one name for the novel, and have not attempted smaller things in it, that I can see, for that. I can think of no obligation to which the "romancer" would not be held equally with the novelist; the standard of execution is equally high for each. Of course it is of execution that we are talking — that being the only point of a novel that is open to contention. This is perhaps too often lost sight of, only to produce interminable confusions and cross-purposes. We must grant the artist his subject, his idea, his *donnée*:[11] our criticism is applied only to what he makes of it. Naturally I do not mean that we are bound to like it or find it interesting: in case we do not our course is perfectly simple — to let it alone. We may believe that of a certain idea even the most sincere novelist can make nothing at all, and the event may perfectly justify our belief; but the failure will have been a failure to execute, and it is in the execution that the fatal weakness is recorded. If we pretend to respect the artist at all, we must allow him his freedom of choice, in the face, in particular cases, of innumerable presumptions that the choice will not

[9] "Come on!"; "nonsense!" (French).
[10] *The Blithedale Romance* (1852).
[11] "The given," "the idea," "the theme" (French).

fructify. Art derives a considerable part of its beneficial exercise from flying in the face of presumptions, and some of the most interesting experiments of which it is capable are hidden in the bosom of common things. Gustave Flaubert has written a story about the devotion of a servant-girl to a parrot,[12] and the production, highly finished as it is, cannot on the whole be called a success. We are perfectly free to find it flat, but I think it might have been interesting; and I, for my part, am extremely glad he should have written it; it is a contribution to our knowledge of what can be done — or what cannot. Ivan Turgénieff has written a tale about a deaf and dumb serf and a lap-dog,[13] and the thing is touching, loving, a little masterpiece. He struck the note of life where Gustave Flaubert missed it — he flew in the face of a presumption and achieved a victory.

Nothing, of course, will ever take the place of the good old fashion of "liking" a work of art or not liking it: the most improved criticism will not abolish that primitive, that ultimate test. I mention this to guard myself from the accusation of intimating that the idea, the subject, of a novel or a picture, does not matter. It matters, to my sense, in the highest degree, and if I might put up a prayer it would be that artists should select none but the richest. Some as I have already hastened to admit, are much more remunerative than others, and it would be a world happily arranged in which persons intending to treat them should be exempt from confusions and mistakes. This fortunate condition will arrive only, I fear, on the same day that critics become purged from error. Meanwhile, I repeat, we do not judge the artist with fairness unless we say to him, "Oh, I grant you your starting-point, because if I did not I should seem to prescribe to you, and heaven forbid I should take that responsibility. If I pretend to tell you what you must not take, you will call upon me to tell you then what you must take; in which case I shall be prettily caught. Moreover, it isn't till I have accepted your data that I can begin to measure you. I have the standard, the pitch; I have no right to tamper with your flute and then criticise your music. Of course I may not care for your idea at all; I may think it silly, or stale, or unclean; in which case I wash my hands of you altogether. I may content myself with believing that you will not have succeeded in being interesting, but I shall, of course, not attempt to demonstrate it, and you will be as indifferent to me as I am to you. I needn't remind you that there are all sorts of tastes: who can know it better? Some people, for excellent reasons, don't like to read about carpenters; others, for reasons even better, don't like to read about courtesans. Many object to Americans. Others (I believe they are mainly editors and publishers) won't look at Italians. Some readers don't like quiet subjects; others don't like bustling ones. Some enjoy a complete illusion, others the consciousness of large concessions. They choose their novels accordingly, and if they don't care about your idea they won't, *a fortiori*,[14] care about your treatment."

So that it comes back very quickly, as I have said, to the liking: in spite of M. Zola,[15] who reasons less powerfully than he represents, and who will not reconcile himself to this absoluteness of taste, thinking that there are certain things that people ought to like, and that they can be made to like. I am quite at a loss to imagine anything (at any rate in this matter of fiction) that people *ought* to like or to dislike. Selection will be sure to take care of itself, for it has a constant motive behind it. That motive is simply experience. As people feel life, so they will feel the art that is most closely related to it. This closeness of relation is what we should never forget in talking of the effort of the novel. Many people speak of it as a factitious, artificial form, a product of ingenuity, the business of which is to alter and arrange the things that surround us, to translate them into conventional, traditional moulds. This, however, is a view of the matter

[12]*The Simple Heart* (1877) by French novelist Gustave Flaubert (1821–1880).
[13]*Mumu* (1854) by Russian novelist Ivan Turgenev (1818–1883).
[14]"All the more" (Latin).
[15]Émile Zola (1840–1902), French novelist and proponent of naturalism (or scientific realism).

which carries us but a very short way, condemns the art to an eternal repetition of a few familiar *clichés*, cuts short its development, and leads us straight up to a dead wall. Catching the very note and trick, the strange irregular rhythm of life, that is the attempt whose strenuous force keeps Fiction upon her feet. In proportion as in what she offers us we see life *without* rearrangement do we feel that we are touching the truth; in proportion as we see it *with* rearrangement do we feel that we are being put off with a substitute, a compromise and convention. It is not uncommon to hear an extraordinary assurance of remark in regard to this matter of rearranging, which is often spoken of as if it were the last word of art. Mr. Besant seems to me in danger of falling into the great error with his rather unguarded talk about "selection." Art is essentially selection, but it is a selection whose main care is to be typical, to be inclusive. For many people art means rose-coloured window-panes, and selection means picking a bouquet for Mrs. Grundy.[16] They will tell you glibly that artistic considerations have nothing to do with the disagreeable, with the ugly; they will rattle off shallow commonplaces about the province of art and the limits of art till you are moved to some wonder in return as to the province and the limits of ignorance. It appears to me that no one can ever have made a seriously artistic attempt without becoming conscious of an immense increase—a kind of revelation—of freedom. One perceives in that case—by the light of a heavenly ray—that the province of art is all life, all feeling, all observation, all vision. As Mr. Besant so justly intimates, it is all experience. That is a sufficient answer to those who maintain that it must not touch the sad things of life, who stick into its divine unconscious bosom little prohibitory inscriptions on the end of sticks, such as we see in public gardens—"It is forbidden to walk on the grass; it is forbidden to touch the flowers; it is not allowed to introduce dogs or to remain after dark; it is requested to keep to the right." The young aspirant in the line of fiction whom we continue to imagine will do nothing without taste, for in that case his freedom would be of little use to him; but the first advantage of his taste will be to reveal to him the absurdity of the little sticks and tickets. If he have taste, I must add, of course he will have ingenuity, and my disrespectful reference to that quality just now was not meant to imply that it is useless in fiction. But it is only a secondary aid; the first is a capacity for receiving straight impressions.

Mr. Besant has some remarks on the question of "the story" which I shall not attempt to criticise, though they seem to me to contain a singular ambiguity, because I do not think I understand them. I cannot see what is meant by talking as if there were a part of a novel which is the story and part of it which for mystical reasons is not—unless indeed the distinction be made in a sense in which it is difficult to suppose that any one should attempt to convey anything. "The story," if it represents anything, represents the subject, the idea, the *donnée* of the novel; and there is surely no "school"—Mr. Besant speaks of a school—which urges that a novel should be all treatment and no subject. There must assuredly be something to treat; every school is intimately conscious of that. This sense of the story being the idea, the starting-point, of the novel, is the only one that I see in which it can be spoken of as something different from its organic whole; and since in proportion as the work is successful the idea permeates and penetrates it, informs and animates it, so that every word and every punctuation-point contribute directly to the expression, in that proportion do we lose our sense of the story being a blade which may be drawn more or less out of its sheath. The story and the novel, the idea and the form, are the needle and thead, and I never heard of a guild of tailors who recommended the use of the thread without the needle, or the needle without the thread. Mr. Besant is not the only critic who may be observed to have spoken as if there were certain things in life which constitute

---

[16]I.e., capitulating to convention and prudery; Mrs. Grundy is referred to in the English comedy *Speed the Plough* (1798) by Thomas Morton (1764?–1838).

stories, and certain others which do not. I find the same odd implication in an entertaining article in the *Pall Mall Gazette*, devoted, as it happens, to Mr. Besant's lecture. "The story is the thing!" says this graceful writer, as if with a tone of opposition to some other idea. I should think it was, as every painter who, as the time for "sending in" his picture looms in the distance, finds himself still in quest of a subject—as every belated artist not fixed about his theme will heartily agree. There are some subjects which speak to us and others which do not, but he would be a clever man who should undertake to give a rule—an index expurgatorius[17]—by which the story and the no-story should be known apart. It is impossible (to me at least) to imagine any such rule which shall not be altogether arbitrary. The writer in the *Pall Mall* opposes the delightful (as I suppose) novel of *Margot la Balafrée*[18] to certain tales in which "Bostonian nymphs" appear to have "rejected English dukes for psychological reasons."[19] I am not acquainted with the romance just designated, and can scarcely forgive the *Pall Mall* critic for not mentioning the name of the author, but the title appears to refer to a lady who may have received a scar in some heroic adventure. I am inconsolable at not being acquainted with this episode, but am utterly at a loss to see why it is a story when the rejection (or acceptance) of a duke is not, and why a reason, psychological or other, is not a subject when a cicatrix[20] is. They are all particles of the multitudinous life with which the novel deals, and surely no dogma which pretends to make it lawful to touch the one and unlawful to touch the other will stand for a moment on its feet. It is the special picture that must stand or fall, according as it seem to possess truth or to lack it. Mr. Besant does not, to my sense, light up the subject by intimating that a story must, under penalty of not being a story, consist of "adventures." Why of adventures more than of green spectacles? He mentions a category of impossible things, and among them he places "fiction without adventure." Why without adventure, more than without matrimony, or celibacy, or parturition, or cholera, or hydropathy, or Jansenism?[21] This seems to me to bring the novel back to the hapless little *rôle* of being an artificial, ingenious thing—bring it down from its large, free character of an immense and exquisite correspondence with life. And what *is* adventure, when it comes to that, and by what sign is the listening pupil to recognise it? It is an adventure—an immense one—for me to write this little article; and for a Bostonian nymph to reject an English duke is an adventure only less stirring, I should say, than for an English duke to be rejected by a Bostonian nymph. I see dramas within dramas in that, and innumerable points of view. A psychological reason is, to my imagination, an object adorably pictorial; to catch the tint of its complexion—I feel as if that idea might inspire one to Titianesque[22] efforts. There are few things more exciting to me, in short, than a psychological reason, and yet, I protest, the novel seems to me the most magnificent form of art. I have just been reading, at the same time, the delightful story of *Treasure Island*, by Mr. Robert Louis Stevenson and, in a manner less consecutive, the last tale from M. Edmond de Goncourt, which is entitled *Chérie*.[23] One of these works treats of murders, mysteries, islands of dreadful renown, hairbreadth escapes, miraculous coincidences and buried doubloons. The other treats of a little French girl who lived in a fine house in Paris, and died of wounded sensibility because no one would marry her. I call *Treasure Island* delightful, because it appears to me to have succeeded wonderfully in what it attempts; and I venture to bestow no epithet upon *Chérie*, which strikes me as having failed deplorably in what it attempts—that is in tracing the development of the moral

---

[17]"Expurgatory Index" (Latin), a list of books specifying passages which must be expunged or changed before Roman Catholics can read them.
[18]A novel of 1884 by the French writer Fortuné Du Boisgobey (1821–1891); "La Balafrée" means "The scarred woman."
[19]Cf. James's own *An International Episode* (1879).
[20]Scar.

[21]Hydropathy, a method of treating disease by water; Jansenism, doctrines of the Dutch theologian Cornelius Jansen (1585–1638), Bishop of Ypres, whose heretical views on grace and predestination resembled those of Calvinism.
[22]Like Titian (1477?–1576), Italian painter, famed for his color effects.
[23]*Treasure Island* appeared in 1883, *Chérie* in 1884.

consciousness of a child. But one of these productions strikes me as exactly as much of a novel as the other, and as having a "story" quite as much. The moral consciousness of a child is as much a part of life as the islands of the Spanish Main, and the one sort of geography seems to me to have those "surprises" of which Mr. Besant speaks quite as much as the other. For myself (since it comes back in the last resort, as I say, to the preference of the individual), the picture of the child's experience has the advantage that I can at successive steps (an immense luxury, near to the "sensual pleasure" of which Mr. Besant's critic in the *Pall Mall* speaks) say Yes or No, as it may be, to what the artist puts before me. I have been a child in fact, but I have been on a quest for a buried treasure only in supposition, and it is a simple accident that with M. de Goncourt I should have for the most part to say No. With George Eliot, when she painted that country with a far other intelligence,[24] I always said Yes.

The most interesting part of Mr. Besant's lecture is unfortunately the briefest passage — his very cursory allusion to the "conscious moral purpose" of the novel. Here again it is not very clear whether he be recording a fact or laying down a principle; it is a great pity that in the latter case he should not have developed his idea. This branch of the subject is of immense importance, and Mr. Besant's few words point to considerations of the widest reach, not to be lightly disposed of. He will have treated the art of fiction but superficially who is not prepared to go every inch of the way that these considerations will carry him. It is for this reason that at the beginning of these remarks I was careful to notify the reader that my reflections on so large a theme have no pretension to be exhaustive. Like Mr. Besant, I have left the question of the morality of the novel till the last, and at the last I find I have used up my space. It is a question surrounded with difficulties, as witness the very first that meets us, in the form of a definite question, on the threshold. Vagueness, in such a discussion, is fatal, and what is the meaning of your morality and your conscious moral purpose? Will you not define your terms and explain how (a novel being a picture) a picture can be either moral or immoral? You wish to paint a moral picture or carve a moral statue: will you not tell us how you would set about it? We are discussing the Art of Fiction; questions of art are questions (in the widest sense) of execution; questions of morality are quite another affair, and will you not let us see how it is that you find it so easy to mix them up? These things are so clear to Mr. Besant that he has deduced from them a law which he sees embodied in English Fiction, and which is "a truly admirable thing and a great cause for congratulation." It is a great cause for congratulation indeed when such thorny problems become as smooth as silk. I may add that in so far as Mr. Besant perceives that in point of fact English Fiction has addressed itself preponderantly to these delicate questions he will appear to many people to have made a vain discovery. They will have been positively struck, on the contrary, with the moral timidity of the usual English novelist; with his (or with her) aversion to face the difficulties with which on every side the treatment of reality bristles. He is apt to be extremely shy (whereas the picture that Mr. Besant draws is a picture of boldness), and the sign of his work, for the most part, is a cautious silence on certain subjects. In the English novel (by which of course I mean the American as well), more than in any other, there is a traditional difference between that which people know and that which they agree to admit that they know, that which they see and that which they speak of, that which they feel to be a part of life and that which they allow to enter into literature. There is the great difference, in short, between what they talk of in conversation and what they talk of in print. The essence of moral energy is to survey the whole field, and I should directly reverse Mr. Besant's remark and say not that the English novel has a purpose, but that it has a diffidence. To what degree a purpose in a work of art is a source of corruption I shall not attempt to inquire; the one that

---

[24]Cf. *Silas Marner* (1861) by George Eliot (1819–1880), pseudonym for English novelist Mary Ann Evans.

seems to me least dangerous is the purpose of making a perfect work. As for our novel, I may say lastly on this score that as we find it in England to-day it strikes me as addressed in a large degree to "young people," and that this in itself constitutes a presumption that it will be rather shy. There are certain things which it is generally agreed not to discuss, not even to mention, before young people. That is very well, but the absence of discussion is not a symptom of the moral passion. The purpose of the English novel—"a truly admirable thing, and a great cause for congratulation"—strikes me therefore as rather negative.

There is one point at which the moral sense and the artistic sense lie very near together; that is in the light of the very obvious truth that the deepest quality of a work of art will always be the quality of the mind of the producer. In proportion as that intelligence is fine will the novel, the picture, the statue partake of the substance of beauty and truth. To be constituted of such elements is, to my vision, to have purpose enough. No good novel will ever proceed from a superficial mind; that seems to me an axiom which, for the artist in fiction, will cover all needful moral ground: if the youthful aspirant take it to heart it will illuminate for him many of the mysteries of "purpose." There are many other useful things that might be said to him, but I have come to the end of my article, and can only touch them as I pass. The critic in the *Pall Mall Gazette*, whom I have already quoted, draws attention to the danger, in speaking of the art of fiction, of generalising. The danger that he has in mind is rather, I imagine, that of particularising, for there are some comprehensive remarks which, in addition to those embodied in Mr. Besant's suggestive lecture, might without fear of misleading him be addressed to the ingenuous student. I should remind him first of the magnificence of the form that is open to him, which offers to sight so few restrictions and such innumerable opportunities. The other arts, in comparison, appear confined and hampered; the various conditions under which they are exercised are so rigid and definite. But the only condition that I can think of attaching to the composition of the novel is, as I have already said, that it be sincere. This freedom is a splendid privilege, and the first lesson of the young novelist is to learn to be worthy of it. "Enjoy it as it deserves," I should say to him; "take possession of it, explore it to its utmost extent, publish it, rejoice in it. All life belongs to you, and do not listen either to those who would shut you up into corners of it and tell you that it is only here and there that art inhabits, or to those who would persuade you that this heavenly messenger wings her way outside of life altogether, breathing a superfine air, and turning away her head from the truth of things. There is no impression of life, no manner of seeing it and feeling it, to which the plan of the novelist may not offer a place; you have only to remember that talents so dissimilar as those of Alexandre Dumas and Jane Austen,[25] Charles Dickens and Gustave Flaubert have worked in this field with equal glory. Do not think too much about optimism and pessimism; try and catch the colour of life itself. In France to-day we see a prodigious effort (that of Emile Zola, to whose solid and serious work no explorer of the capacity of the novel can allude without respect), we see an extraordinary effort vitiated by a spirit of pessimism on a narrow basis. M. Zola is magnificent, but he strikes an English reader as ignorant; he has an air of working in the dark; if he had as much light as energy, his results would be of the highest value. As for the aberrations of a shallow optimism, the ground (of English fiction especially) is strewn with their brittle particles as with broken glass. If you must indulge in conclusions, let them have the taste of a wide knowledge. Remember that your first duty is to be as complete as possible—to make as perfect a work. Be generous and delicate and pursue the prize."

1884, 1888

---

[25]Alexandre Dumas (1802–1870), French novelist noted for such works of adventure as *The Three Musketeers*; Jane Austen (1775–1817), English novelist noted for her depiction of the life and manners of the middle class in such works as *Pride and Prejudice*.

from Criticism

["CRITICISM *IS* THE CRITIC"][1]

. . . The critical sense is so far from frequent that it is absolutely rare and that the possession of the cluster of qualities that minister to it is one of the highest distinctions. It is a gift inestimably precious and beautiful; therefore, so far from thinking that it passes overmuch from hand to hand, one knows that one has only to stand by the counter an hour to see that business is done with baser coin. We have too many small schoolmasters; yet not only do I not question in literature the high utility of criticism, but I should be tempted to say that the part it plays may be the supremely beneficent one when it proceeds from deep sources, from the efficient combination of experience and perception. In this light one sees the critic as the real helper of the artist, a torch-bearing outrider, the interpreter, the brother. The more the tune is noted and the direction observed the more we shall enjoy the convenience of a critical literature. When one thinks of the outfit required for free work in this spirit one is ready to pay almost any homage to the intelligence that has put it on; and when one considers the noble figure completely equipped — armed *cap-à-pie*[2] in curiosity and sympathy — one falls in love with the apparition. It certainly represents the knight who has knelt through his long vigil and who has the piety of his office. For there is something sacrificial in his function, inasmuch as he offers himself as a general touchstone. To lend himself, to protect himself and steep himself, to feel and feel till he understands and to understand so well that he can say, to have perception at the pitch of passion and expression as embracing as the air, to be infinitely curious and incorrigibly patient, and yet plastic and inflammable and determinable, stooping to conquer and serving to direct — these are fine chances for an active mind, chances to add the idea of independent beauty to the conception of success. Just in proportion as he is sentient and restless, just in proportion as he reacts and reciprocates and penetrates, is the critic a valuable instrument; for in literature assuredly criticism *is* the critic, just as art is the artist; it being assuredly the artist who invented art and the critic who invented criticism, and not the other way round.

And it is with the kinds of criticism exactly as it is with the kinds of art — the best kind, the only kind worth speaking of, is the kind that springs from the liveliest experience. There are a hundred labels and tickets, in all this matter, that have been pasted on from the outside and appear to exist for the convenience of passers-by; but the critic who lives *in* the house, ranging through its innumerable chambers, knows nothing about the bills on the front. He only knows that the more impressions he has the more he is able to record, and that the more he is saturated, poor fellow, the more he can give out. His life, at this rate, is heroic, for it is immensely vicarious. He has to understand for others, to answer for them; he is always under arms. He knows that the whole honour of the matter, for him, besides the success in his own eyes, depends upon his being indefatigably supple, and that is a formidable order. Let me not speak, however, as if his work were a conscious grind, for the sense of effort is easily lost in the enthusiasm of curiosity. Any vocation has its hours of intensity that is so closely connected with life. That of the critic, in literature, is connected doubly, for he deals with life at second-hand as well as at first; that is he deals with the experience of others, which he resolves into his own, and not of those invented and selected others with whom the novelist makes comfortable terms, but with the uncompromising swarm of authors, the clamorous children of history. He has to make them as vivid and as free as the novelist makes *his* puppets, and yet he has, as the phrase is, to take them as they come. We must be easy with him if the picture, even when the aim has

---

[1]From an essay entitled "Criticism," first published in May 1891.
[2]"Top to toe" (French).

really been to penetrate, is sometimes confused, for there are baffling and there are thankless subjects; and we make everything up to him by the peculiar purity of our esteem when the portrait is really, like the happy portraits of the other art, a text preserved by translation.

1891

from Preface to *The American*

[The Art of Romance][1]

The only *general* attribute of projected romance that I can see, the only one that fits all its cases, is the fact of the kind of experience with which it deals—experience liberated, so to speak; experience disengaged, disembroiled, disencumbered, exempt from the conditions that we usually know to attach to it and, if we wish so to put the matter, drag upon it, and operating in a medium which relieves it, in a particular interest, of the inconvenience of a *related*, a measurable state, a state subject to all our vulgar communities. The greatest intensity may so be arrived at evidently—when the sacrifice of community, of the "related" sides of situations, has not been too rash. It must to this end not flagrantly betray itself; we must even be kept if possible, for our illusion, from suspecting any sacrifice at all. The balloon of experience is in fact of course tied to the earth, and under that necessity we swing, thanks to a rope of remarkable length, in the more or less commodious car of the imagination; but it is by the rope we know where we are, and from the moment that cable is cut we are at large and unrelated: we only swing apart from the globe—though remaining as exhilarated, naturally, as we like, especially when all goes well. The art of the romancer is, "for the fun of it," insidiously to cut the cable, to cut it without our detecting him. What I have recognised then in "The American," much to my surprise and after long years, is that the experience here represented is the disconnected and uncontrolled experience—uncontrolled by our general sense of "the way things happen"—which romance alone more or less successfully palms off on us. It is a case of Newman's[2] own intimate experience all, that being my subject, the thread of which, from beginning to end, is not once exchanged, however momentarily, for any other thread; and the experience of others concerning us, and concerning him, only so far as it touches him and as he recognises, feels or divines it. There is our general sense of the way things happen—it abides with us indefeasibly, as readers of fiction, from the moment we demand that our fiction shall be intelligible; and there is our particular sense of the way they don't happen, which is liable to wake up unless reflexion and criticism, in us, have been skilfully and successfully drugged. There are drugs enough, clearly—it is all a question of applying them with tact; in which case the way things don't happen may be artfully made to pass for the way things do.

1907

from Preface to *The Portrait of a Lady*

[The House of Fiction and the Moral Sense][1]

Trying to recover here, for recognition, the germ of my idea,[2] I see that it must have consisted not at all in any conceit of a "plot," nefarious name, in any flash, upon

---

[1]From the 1907 Preface to *The American*.
[2]Christopher Newman is the title character of *The American*.

[1]From the 1908 Preface to *The Portrait of a Lady*.
[2]I.e., for *The Portrait of a Lady*.

the fancy, of a set of relations, or in any one of those situations that, by a logic of their own, immediately fall, for the fabulist, into movement, into a march or a rush, a patter of quick steps; but altogether in the sense of a single character, the character and aspect of a particular engaging young woman, to which all the usual elements of a "subject," certainly of a setting, were to need to be super-added. Quite as interesting as the young woman herself, at her best, do I find, I must again repeat, this projection of memory upon the whole matter of the growth, in one's imagination, of some such apology for a motive. These are the fascinations of the fabulist's art, these lurking forces of expansion, these necessities of upspringing in the seed, these beautiful determinations, on the part of the idea entertained, to grow as tall as possible, to push into the light and the air and thickly flower there; and, quite as much, these fine possibilities of recovering, from some good standpoint on the ground gained, the intimate history of the business — of retracing and reconstructing its steps and stages. I have always fondly remembered a remark that I heard fall years ago from the lips of Ivan Turgenieff[3] in regard to his own experience of the usual origin of the fictive picture. It began for him almost always with the vision of some person or persons, who hovered before him, soliciting him, as the active or passive figure, interesting him and appealing to him just as they were and by what they were. He saw them, in that fashion, as *disponibles*,[4] saw them subject to the chances, the complications of existence, and saw them vividly, but then had to find for them the right relations, those that would most bring them out; to imagine, to invent and select and piece together the situations most useful and favourable to the sense of the creatures themselves, the complications they would be most likely to produce and to feel.

"To arrive at these things is to arrive at my 'story,'" he said, "and that's the way I look for it. The result is that I'm often accused of not having 'story' enough. I seem to myself to have as much as I need — to show my people, to exhibit their relations with each other; for that is all my measure. If I watch them long enough I see them come together, I see them *placed*, I see them engaged in this or that act and in this or that difficulty. How they look and move and speak and behave, always in the setting I have found for them, is my account of them — of which I dare say, alas, *que cela manque souvent d'architecture*.[5] But I would rather, I think, have too little architecture than too much — when there's danger of its interfering with my measure of the truth. The French of course like more of it than I give — having by their own genius such a hand for it; and indeed one must give all one can. As for the origin of one's wind-blown germs themselves, who shall say, as you ask, where *they* come from? We have to go too far back, too far behind, to say. Is n't it all we can say that they come from every quarter of heaven, that they are *there* at almost any turn of the road? They accumulate, and we are always picking them over, selecting among them. They are the breath of life — by which I mean that life, in its own way, breathes them upon us. They are so, in a manner prescribed and imposed — floated into our minds by the current of life. That reduces to imbecility the vain critic's quarrel, so often, with one's subject, when he has n't the wit to accept it. Will he point out then which other it should properly have been? — his office being, essentially *to* point out. *Il en serait bien embarrassé.*[6] Ah, when he points out what I've done or failed to do with it, that's another matter: there he's on his ground. I give him up my 'architecture,'" my distinguished friend concluded, "as much as he will."

So this beautiful genius, and I recall with comfort the gratitude I drew from his reference to the intensity of suggestion that may reside in the stray figure, the unattached character, the image *en disponibilité*.[7] It gave me higher warrant than I seemed then to have met for just that blest habit of one's own imagination, the trick of invest-

---

[3]Russian novelist (1818–1883) whom James met in Paris in the 1870s.
[4]"Available" (French).

[5]"It is often lacking architecture" (French).
[6]"He would be quite embarrassed by it" (French).
[7]"In the reserves" (French).

ing some conceived or encountered individual, some brace or group of individuals, with the germinal property and authority. I was myself so much more antecedently conscious of my figures than of their setting—a too preliminary, a preferential interest in which struck me as in general such a putting of the cart before the horse. I might envy, though I could n't emulate, the imaginative writer so constituted as to see his fable first and to make out its agents afterwards: I could think so little of any fable that did n't need its agents positively to launch it; I could think so little of any situation that did n't depend for its interest on the nature of the persons situated, and thereby on their way of taking it. There are methods of so-called presentation, I believe—among novelists who have appeared to flourish—that offer the situation as indifferent to that support; but I have not lost the sense of the value for me, at the time, of the admirable Russian's testimony to my not needing, all superstitiously, to try and perform any such gymnastic. Other echoes from the same source linger with me, I confess, as unfadingly—if it be not all indeed one much-embracing echo. It was impossible after that not to read, for one's uses, high lucidity into the tormented and disfigured and bemuddled question of the objective value, and even quite into that of the critical appreciation, of "subject" in the novel.

One had had from an early time, for that matter, the instinct of the right estimate of such values and of its reducing to the inane the dull dispute over the "immoral" subject and the moral. Recognising so promptly the one measure of the worth of a given subject, the question about it that, rightly answered, disposes of all others—is it valid, in a word, is it genuine, is it sincere, the result of some direct impression or perception of life?—I had found small edification, mostly, in a critical pretension that had neglected from the first all delimitation of ground and all definition of terms. The air of my earlier time shows, to memory, as darkened, all round, with that vanity—unless the difference to-day be just in one's own final impatience, the lapse of one's attention. There is, I think, no more nutritive or suggestive truth in this connexion than that of the perfect dependence of the "moral" sense of a work of art on the amount of felt life concerned in producing it. The question comes back thus, obviously, to the kind and the degree of the artist's prime sensibility, which is the soil out of which his subject springs. The quality and capacity of that soil, its ability to "grow" with due freshness and straightness any vision of life, represents, strongly or weakly, the projected morality. That element is but another name for the more or less close connexion of the subject with some mark made on the intelligence, with some sincere experience. By which, at the same time, of course, one is far from contending that this enveloping air of the artist's humanity—which gives the last touch to the worth of the work—is not a widely and wondrously varying element; being on one occasion a rich and magnificent medium and on another a comparatively poor and ungenerous one. Here we get exactly the high price of the novel as a literary form— its power not only, while preserving that form with closeness, to range through all the differences of the individual relation to its general subject-matter, all the varieties of outlook on life, of disposition to reflect and project, created by conditions that are never the same from man to man (or, so far as that goes, from man to woman), but positively to appear more true to its character in proportion as it strains, or tends to burst, with a latent extravagance, its mould.

The house of fiction has in short not one window, but a million—a number of possible windows not to be reckoned, rather; every one of which has been pierced, or is still pierceable, in its vast front, by the need of the individual vision and by the pressure of the individual will. These apertures, of dissimilar shape and size, hang so, all together, over the human scene that we might have expected of them a greater sameness of report than we find. They are but windows at the best, mere holes in a dead wall, disconnected, perched aloft; they are not hinged doors opening straight upon life. But they have this mark of their own that at each of them stands a figure with a pair of eyes, or at least with a field-glass, which forms, again and again, for observation, a unique instrument, insuring to the person making use of it an impression distinct from every other. He and his neighbours are watching the same show, but one seeing more where the other sees less, one seeing black where the other sees white, one seeing big where the other sees small, one seeing coarse where the other sees fine. And so on, and so on; there is fortunately no saying on what, for the particular pair of eyes, the window may *not* open; "fortunately" by reason, precisely, of this incalculability of range. The spreading field, the human scene, is the "choice of subject"; the pierced aperture, either broad or balconied or slit-like and low-browed, is the "literary form"; but they are, singly or together, as nothing without the posted presence of the watcher—without, in other words, the consciousness of the artist. Tell me what the artist is, and I will tell you of what he has *been* conscious. Thereby I shall express to you at once his boundless freedom and his "moral" reference. . . .

1908

REGIONAL REALISM
AND LOCAL COLOR

Bret Harte
Ambrose Bierce
George Washington Cable

Joel Chandler Harris
Charles W. Chesnutt

"Local color in fiction is demonstrably the life of fiction. It is the native element, the differentiating element. It corresponds to the endless and vital charm of individual peculiarity. It is the differences which interest us; the similarities do not please, do not forever stimulate and feed as do the differences. Literature would die of dry rot if it chronicled the similarities only, or even largely."

Hamlin Garland, "Local Color in Art"

BRET HARTE
(1836–1902)

Bret Harte for a time was the most famous western writer in America. His fiction caught the spirit of the California gold rush and the little mining towns that brought together in common greed prospectors, prostitutes, gamblers, fortune seekers, and other drifters. The irony is that Harte was not a westerner but an easterner come west; and he was never a miner and spent little if any time in the mining towns he wrote about so vividly.

Born in Albany, New York, of English, Dutch, and Jewish lineage, Harte grew up in a family so straitened that it moved six times in eight years. His father died in 1845, leaving his widow with four children. Harte left school to work at the age of thirteen, and three years later was supporting himself. In spite of these handicaps, Harte grew up an avid reader, finding ample books in his father's library. His greatest love was Charles Dickens.

Mrs. Harte went to California in 1853 and remarried. The following year, Bret Harte followed her there. He tried his hand at a number of jobs, teaching school, riding stagecoach shotgun briefly for Wells Fargo, and working as printer, writer, and editor for various magazines, to which he contributed his own writing. Two years after his marriage in 1862, he was appointed secretary to the U.S. Mint in San Francisco, a position that left him time to write. In 1867, he published a volume of parodies, *Condensed Novels and Other Papers*. He became the first editor of *The Overland Monthly* in 1868, publishing in its second number "The Luck of Roaring Camp." It was read in the East, ever hungry for literary images of the West, with great enthusiasm.

In 1869, Harte followed up with "The Outcasts of Poker Flat," which increased his fame. Hardly less popular than his stories was a poem published in 1870, "Plain Language from Truthful James" (often called "The Heathen Chinee"). Even though offered a professorship at the University of California, Harte pulled up stakes with his family and headed east in 1871, a celebrity whose every move was reported widely in the press. He was given a contract by *The Atlantic Monthly*, then edited by William Dean Howells, for the astronomical sum of $10,000 to supply twelve works for publication.

Harte's new work, however, was disappointing and his literary career started going downhill, never to be reversed. He published additional tales and novels, and in 1877 he joined with Mark Twain, whom he had met in California, in collaboration on a play, *Ah Sin*. But he had no genuine successes. He and his wife had become accustomed to living in high style, but his writing brought in too little money to support their expensive tastes.

In 1878, having received appointment as U.S. Consul in Crefeld, Prussia, Harte sailed for Europe without his family. He was never to return to America. He felt isolated in Prussia and was transferred to the consulate in Glasgow, Scotland. Then, in 1885, he lost his appointment when the administration in Washington, D.C., changed. Harte decided to settle in London, where he was still popular as a writer of the American West. He tried to live up to the British image of him, reprocessing the western materials he had already thoroughly mined, but to dwindling effect for his reputation or his purse.

Harte died in 1902, aware that his best work had been finished by the time he was thirty-five. In a handful of stories written during his early years, he was bold in his treatment of sex and love, and so skilled in depicting the American West as to give impetus to the local color writing of the later regionalists. And in his creation of shrewd, coolheaded gamblers, toughened miners with tender feelings, and hardened prostitutes with hearts of gold, he provided the country with exotic archetypal characters of the American frontier that would endure into the twentieth century in countless popular novels and films.

ADDITIONAL READING

The Letters of Bret Harte, ed. Geoffrey Bret Harte, 1926; *Bret Harte: Representative Selections*, ed. Joseph B. Harrison, 1941.

Henry W. Boynton, *Bret Harte*, 1903; Henry C. Merwin, *The Life of Bret Harte; with Some Account of the California Pioneers*, 1911; George R. Stewart, Jr., *Bret Harte: Argonaut and Exile*, 1931; Margaret Duckett, *Mark Twain and Bret Harte*, 1964; Richard O'Connor, *Bret Harte*, 1966; Patrick Morrow, *Bret Harte: Literary Critic*, 1979; Linda D. Barnett, *Bret Harte: A Reference Guide*, 1980.

TEXT

The Writings of Bret Harte, 20 vols., 1896–1914.

The Outcasts of Poker Flat

As Mr. John Oakhurst, gambler, stepped into the main street of Poker Flat on the morning of the 23d of November, 1850, he was conscious of a change in its moral atmosphere since the preceding night. Two or three men, conversing earnestly together, ceased as he approached, and exchanged significant glances. There was a Sabbath lull in the air, which, in a settlement unused to Sabbath influences, looked ominous.

Mr. Oakhurst's calm, handsome face betrayed small concern in these indications. Whether he was conscious of any predisposing cause was another question. "I reckon they're after somebody," he reflected; "likely it's me." He returned to his pocket the handkerchief with which he had been whipping the red dust of Poker Flat from his neat boots, and quietly discharged his mind of any further conjecture.

In point of fact, Poker Flat was "after somebody." It had lately suffered the loss of several thousand dollars, two valuable horses, and a prominent citizen. It was experiencing a spasm of virtuous reaction, quite as lawless and ungovernable as any of the acts that had provoked it. A secret committee[1] had determined to rid the town of all improper persons. This was done permanently in regard of two men who were then hanging from the boughs of a sycamore in the gulch, and temporarily in the banishment of certain other objectionable characters. I regret to say that some of these were ladies. It is but due to the sex, however, to state that their impropriety was professional, and it was only in such easily established standards of evil that Poker Flat ventured to sit in judgment.

Mr. Oakhurst was right in supposing that he was included in this category. A few of the committee had urged hanging him as a possible example and a sure method of reimbursing themselves from his pockets of the sums he had won from them. "It's agin justice," said Jim Wheeler, "to let this yer young man from Roaring Camp—an entire stranger—carry away our money." But a crude sentiment of equity residing in

---

[1] I.e., a vigilance committee temporarily exercising the authority of law.

the breasts of those who had been fortunate enough to win from Mr. Oakhurst over-ruled this narrower local prejudice.

Mr. Oakhurst received his sentence with philosophic calmness, none the less coolly that he was aware of the hesitation of his judges. He was too much of a gambler not to accept fate. With him life was at best an uncertain game, and he recognized the usual percentage in favor of the dealer.

A body of armed men accompanied the deported wickedness of Poker Flat to the outskirts of the settlement. Besides Mr. Oakhurst, who was known to be a coolly desperate man, and for whose intimidation the armed escort was intended, the ex-patriated party consisted of a young woman familiarly known as "The Duchess;" another who had won the title of "Mother Shipton;"[2] and "Uncle Billy," a suspected sluice-robber[3] and confirmed drunkard. The cavalcade provoked no comments from the spectators, nor was any word uttered by the escort. Only when the gulch which marked the uttermost limit of Poker Flat was reached, the leader spoke briefly and to the point. The exiles were forbidden to return at the peril of their lives.

As the escort disappeared, their pent-up feelings found vent in a few hysterical tears from the Duchess, some bad language from Mother Shipton, and a Parthian[4] volley of expletives from Uncle Billy. The philosophic Oakhurst alone remained si-lent. He listened calmly to Mother Shipton's desire to cut somebody's heart out, to the repeated statements of the Duchess that she would die in the road, and to the alarm-ing oaths that seemed to be bumped out of Uncle Billy as he rode forward. With the easy good humor characteristic of his class, he insisted upon exchanging his own riding-horse, "Five-Spot," for the sorry mule which the Duchess rode. But even this act did not draw the party into any closer sympathy. The young woman readjusted her somewhat draggled plumes with a feeble, faded coquetry; Mother Shipton eyed the possessor of "Five-Spot" with malevolence, and Uncle Billy included the whole party in one sweeping anathema.

The road to Sandy Bar—a camp that, not having as yet experienced the regener-ating influences of Poker Flat, consequently seemed to offer some invitation to the emigrants—lay over a steep mountain range. It was distant a day's severe travel. In that advanced season the party soon passed out of the moist, temperate regions of the foothills into the dry, cold, bracing air of the Sierras. The trail was narrow and difficult. At noon the Duchess, rolling out of her saddle upon the ground, declared her intention of going no farther, and the party halted.

The spot was singularly wild and impressive. A wooded amphitheatre, sur-rounded on three sides by precipitous cliffs of naked granite, sloped gently toward the crest of another precipice that overlooked the valley. It was, undoubtedly, the most suitable spot for a camp, had camping been advisable. But Mr. Oakhurst knew that scarcely half the journey to Sandy Bar was accomplished, and the party were not equipped or provisioned for delay. This fact he pointed out to his companions curtly, with a philosophic commentary on the folly of "throwing up their hand before the game was played out." But they were furnished with liquor, which in this emergency stood them in place of food, fuel, rest, and prescience. In spite of his remonstrances, it was not long before they were more or less under its influence. Uncle Billy passed rapidly from a bellicose state into one of stupor, the Duchess became maudlin, and Mother Shipton snored. Mr. Oakhurst alone remained erect, leaning against a rock, calmly surveying them.

Mr. Oakhurst did not drink. It interfered with a profession which required cool-ness, impassiveness, and presence of mind, and, in his own language, he "could n't afford it." As he gazed at his recumbent fellow exiles, the loneliness begotten of his

---

[2]Name given to a reputed witch, Ursula Southill (born c. 1488), famous for her extraordinary prophecies.
[3]A sluice was a trough in which gold was sifted from the sand.

[4]Parthians were an ancient Asian people known for their strategy of pretending flight and then suddenly turning to attack.

pariah trade, his habits of life, his very vices, for the first time seriously oppressed him. He bestirred himself in dusting his black clothes, washing his hands and face, and other acts characteristic of his studiously neat habits, and for a moment forgot his annoyance. The thought of deserting his weaker and more pitiable companions never perhaps occurred to him. Yet he could not help feeling the want of that excitement which, singularly enough, was most conducive to that calm equanimity for which he was notorious. He looked at the gloomy walls that rose a thousand feet sheer above the circling pines around him, at the sky ominously clouded, at the valley below, already deepening into shadow; and, doing so, suddenly he heard his own name called.

A horseman slowly ascended the trail. In the fresh, open face of the newcomer Mr. Oakhurst recognized Tom Simson, otherwise known as "The Innocent," of Sandy Bar. He had met him some months before over a "little game," and had, with perfect equanimity, won the entire fortune—amounting to some forty dollars—of that guileless youth. After the game was finished, Mr. Oakhurst drew the youthful speculator behind the door and thus addressed him: "Tommy, you're a good little man, but you can't gamble worth a cent. Don't try it over again." He then handed him his money back, pushed him gently from the room, and so made a devoted slave of Tom Simson.

There was a remembrance of this in his boyish and enthusiastic greeting of Mr. Oakhurst. He had started, he said, to go to Poker Flat to seek his fortune. "Alone?" No, not exactly alone; in fact (a giggle), he had run away with Piney Woods. Didn't Mr. Oakhurst remember Piney? She that used to wait on the table at the Temperance House? They had been engaged a long time, but old Jake Woods had objected, and so they had run away, and were going to Poker Flat to be married, and here they were. And they were tired out, and how lucky it was they had found a place to camp, and company. All this the Innocent delivered rapidly, while Piney, a stout, comely damsel of fifteen, emerged from behind the pine-tree, where she had been blushing unseen, and rode to the side of her lover.

Mr. Oakhurst seldom troubled himself with sentiment, still less with propriety; but he had a vague idea that the situation was not fortunate. He retained, however, his presence of mind sufficiently to kick Uncle Billy, who was about to say something, and Uncle Billy was sober enough to recognize in Mr. Oakhurst's kick a superior power that would not bear trifling. He then endeavored to dissuade Tom Simson from delaying further, but in vain. He even pointed out the fact that there was no provision, nor means of making a camp. But, unluckily, the Innocent met this objection by assuring the party that he was provided with an extra mule loaded with provisions, and by the discovery of a rude attempt at a log house near the trail. "Piney can stay with Mrs. Oakhurst," said the Innocent, pointing to the Duchess, "and I can shift for myself."

Nothing but Mr. Oakhurst's admonishing foot saved Uncle Billy from bursting into a roar of laughter. As it was, he felt compelled to retire up the cañon until he could recover his gravity. There he confided the joke to the tall pine-trees, with many slaps of his leg, contortions of his face, and the usual profanity. But when he returned to the party, he found them seated by a fire—for the air had grown strangely chill and the sky overcast—in apparently amicable conversation. Piney was actually talking in an impulsive girlish fashion to the Duchess, who was listening with an interest and animation she had not shown for many days. The Innocent was holding forth, apparently with equal effect, to Mr. Oakhurst and Mother Shipton, who was actually relaxing into amiability. "Is this yer a d—d picnic?" said Uncle Billy, with inward scorn, as he surveyed the sylvan group, the glancing firelight, and the tethered animals in the foreground. Suddenly an idea mingled with the alcoholic fumes that disturbed his brain. It was apparently of a jocular nature, for he felt impelled to slap his leg again and cram his fist into his mouth.

As the shadows crept slowly up the mountain, a slight breeze rocked the tops of the pine-trees and moaned through their long and gloomy aisles. The ruined cabin, patched and covered with pine boughs, was set apart for the ladies. As the lovers parted, they unaffectedly exchanged a kiss, so honest and sincere that it might have been heard above the swaying pines. The frail Duchess and the malevolent Mother Shipton were probably too stunned to remark upon this last evidence of simplicity, and so turned without a word to the hut. The fire was replenished, the men lay down before the door, and in a few minutes were asleep.

Mr. Oakhurst was a light sleeper. Toward morning he awoke benumbed and cold. As he stirred the dying fire, the wind, which was now blowing strongly, brought to his cheek that which caused the blood to leave it, — snow!

He started to his feet with the intention of awakening the sleepers, for there was no time to lose. But turning to where Uncle Billy had been lying, he found him gone. A suspicion leaped to his brain, and a curse to his lips. He ran to the spot where the mules had been tethered — they were no longer there. The tracks were already rapidly disappearing in the snow.

The momentary excitement brought Mr. Oakhurst back to the fire with his usual calm. He did not waken the sleepers. The Innocent slumbered peacefully, with a smile on his good-humored, freckled face; the virgin Piney slept beside her frailer sisters as sweetly as though attended by celestial guardians; and Mr. Oakhurst, drawing his blanket over his shoulders, stroked his mustaches and waited for the dawn. It came slowly in a whirling mist of snowflakes that dazzled and confused the eye. What could be seen of the landscape appeared magically changed. He looked over the valley, and summed up the present and future in two words, "Snowed in!"

A careful inventory of the provisions, which, fortunately for the party, had been stored within the hut, and so escaped the felonious fingers of Uncle Billy, disclosed the fact that with care and prudence they might last ten days longer. "That is," said Mr. Oakhurst *sotto voce*[5] to the Innocent, "if you're willing to board us. If you ain't — and perhaps you'd better not — you can wait till Uncle Billy gets back with provisions." For some occult reason, Mr. Oakhurst could not bring himself to disclose Uncle Billy's rascality, and so offered the hypothesis that he had wandered from the camp and had accidentally stampeded the animals. He dropped a warning to the Duchess and Mother Shipton, who of course knew the facts of their associate's defection. "They'll find out the truth about us *all* when they find out anything," he added significantly, "and there's no good frightening them now."

Tom Simson not only put all his worldly store at the disposal of Mr. Oakhurst, but seemed to enjoy the prospect of their enforced seclusion. "We'll have a good camp for a week, and then the snow'll melt, and we'll all go back together." The cheerful gayety of the young man and Mr. Oakhurst's calm infected the others. The Innocent, with the aid of pine boughs, extemporized a thatch for the roofless cabin, and the Duchess directed Piney in the rearrangement of the interior with a taste and tact that opened the blue eyes of that provincial maiden to their fullest extent. "I reckon now you're used to fine things at Poker Flat," said Piney. The Duchess turned away sharply to conceal something that reddened her cheeks through their professional tint, and Mother Shipton requested Piney not to "chatter." But when Mr. Oakhurst returned from a weary search for the trail, he heard the sound of happy laughter echoed from the rocks. He stopped in some alarm, and his thoughts first naturally reverted to the whiskey, which he had prudently cachéd. "And yet it don't somehow sound like whiskey," said the gambler. It was not until he caught sight of the blazing fire through the

---

[5]In a low voice.

still blinding storm, and the group around it, that he settled to the conviction that it was "square fun."

Whether Mr. Oakhurst had cachéd his cards with the whiskey as something debarred the free access of the community, I cannot say. It was certain that, in Mother Shipton's words, he "didn't say 'cards' once" during that evening. Haply the time was beguiled by an accordion, produced somewhat ostentatiously by Tom Simson from his pack. Notwithstanding some difficulties attending the manipulation of this instrument, Piney Woods managed to pluck several reluctant melodies from its keys, to an accompaniment by the Innocent on a pair of bone castanets. But the crowning festivity of the evening was reached in a rude camp-meeting hymn, which the lovers, joining hands, sang with great earnestness and vociferation. I fear that a certain defiant tone and Covenanter's swing[6] to its chorus, rather than any devotional quality, caused it speedily to infect the others, who at last joined in the refrain:—

> "I'm proud to live in the service of the Lord,
> And I'm bound to die in His army."[7]

The pines rocked, the storm eddied and whirled above the miserable group, and the flames of their altar leaped heavenward, as if in token of the vow.

At midnight the storm abated, the rolling clouds parted, and the stars glittered keenly above the sleeping camp. Mr. Oakhurst, whose professional habits had enabled him to live on the smallest possible amount of sleep, in dividing the watch with Tom Simson somehow managed to take upon himself the greater part of that duty. He excused himself to the Innocent by saying that he had "often been a week without sleep." "Doing what?" asked Tom. "Poker!" replied Oakhurst sententiously. "When a man gets a streak of luck,—nigger-luck,[8]—he don't get tired. The luck gives in first. Luck," continued the gambler reflectively, "is a mighty queer thing. All you know about it for certain is that it's bound to change. And it's finding out when it's going to change that makes you. We've had a streak of bad luck since we left Poker Flat,—you come along, and slap you get into it, too. If you can hold your cards right along you're all right. For," added the gambler, with cheerful irrelevance—

> "'I'm proud to live in the service of the Lord,
> And I'm bound to die in His army.'"

The third day came, and the sun, looking through the white-curtained valley, saw the outcasts divide their slowly decreasing store of provisions for the morning meal. It was one of the peculiarities of that mountain climate that its rays diffused a kindly warmth over the wintry landscape, as if in regretful commiseration of the past. But it revealed drift on drift of snow piled high around the hut,—a hopeless, uncharted, trackless sea of white lying below the rocky shores to which the castaways still clung. Through the marvelously clear air the smoke of the pastoral village of Poker Flat rose miles away. Mother Shipton saw it, and from a remote pinnacle of her rocky fastness hurled in that direction a final malediction. It was her last vituperative attempt, and perhaps for that reason was invested with a certain degree of sublimity. It did her good, she privately informed the Duchess. "Just you go out there and cuss, and see." She then set herself to the task of amusing "the child," as she and the Duchess were pleased to call Piney. Piney was no chicken, but it was a soothing and original theory of the pair thus to account for the fact that she didn't swear and wasn't improper.

When night crept up again through the gorges, the reedy notes of the accordion rose and fell in fitful spasms and long-drawn gasps by the flickering campfire. But

---

[6]The compelling rhythms of songs sung by Scottish Presbyterians, bound by the covenants or statements of religious belief published in 1638 and 1643; they wanted separation from the Church of England.
[7]Refrain of the spiritual "Service of the Lord."
[8]An inexplicable run of good luck.

music failed to fill entirely the aching void left by insufficient food, and a new diversion was proposed by Piney,—story-telling. Neither Mr. Oakhurst nor his female companions caring to relate their personal experiences, this plan would have failed too, but for the Innocent. Some months before he had chanced upon a stray copy of Mr. Pope's[9] ingenious translation of the Iliad. He now proposed to narrate the principal incidents of that poem—having thoroughly mastered the argument and fairly forgotten the words—in the current vernacular of Sandy Bar. And so for the rest of that night the Homeric demigods again walked the earth. Trojan bully and wily Greek wrestled in the winds, and the great pines in the cañon seemed to bow to the wrath of the son of Peleus.[10] Mr. Oakhurst listened with quiet satisfaction. Most especially was he interested in the fate of "Ash-heels,"[11] as the Innocent persisted in denominating the "swift-footed Achilles."

So, with small food and much of Homer and the accordion, a week passed over the heads of the outcasts. The sun again forsook them, and again from leaden skies the snowflakes were sifted over the land. Day by day closer around them drew the snowy circle, until at last they looked from their prison over drifted walls of dazzling white, that towered twenty feet above their heads. It became more and more difficult to replenish their fires, even from the fallen trees beside them, now half hidden in the drifts. And yet no one complained. The lovers turned from the dreary prospect and looked into each other's eyes, and were happy. Mr. Oakhurst settled himself coolly to the losing game before him. The Duchess, more cheerful than she had been, assumed the care of Piney. Only Mother Shipton—once the strongest of the party— seemed to sicken and fade. At midnight on the tenth day she called Oakhurst to her side. "I'm going," she said, in a voice of querulous weakness, "but don't say anything about it. Don't waken the kids. Take the bundle from under my head, and open it." Mr. Oakhurst did so. It contained Mother Shipton's rations for the last week, untouched. "Give 'em to the child," she said, pointing to the sleeping Piney. "You've starved yourself," said the gambler. "That's what they call it," said the woman querulously, as she lay down again, and, turning her face to the wall, passed quietly away.

The accordion and the bones were put aside that day, and Homer was forgotten. When the body of Mother Shipton had been committed to the snow, Mr. Oakhurst took the Innocent aside, and showed him a pair of snow-shoes, which he had fashioned from the old pack-saddle. "There's one chance in a hundred to save her yet," he said, pointing to Piney; "but it's there," he added, pointing toward Poker Flat. "If you can reach there in two days she's safe." "And you?" asked Tom Simson. "I'll stay here," was the curt reply.

The lovers parted with a long embrace. "You are not going, too?" said the Duchess, as she saw Mr. Oakhurst apparently waiting to accompany him. "As far as the cañon," he replied. He turned suddenly and kissed the Duchess, leaving her pallid face aflame, and her trembling limbs rigid with amazement.

Night came, but not Mr. Oakhurst. It brought the storm again and the whirling snow. Then the Duchess, feeding the fire, found that some one had quietly piled beside the hut enough fuel to last a few days longer. The tears rose to her eyes, but she hid them from Piney.

The women slept but little. In the morning, looking into each other's faces, they read their fate. Neither spoke, but Piney, accepting the position of the stronger, drew near and placed her arm around the Duchess's waist. They kept this attitude for the rest of the day. That night the storm reached its greatest fury, and, rending asunder the protecting vines, invaded the very hut.

---

[9] Alexander Pope (1688–1744), English poet whose translation of Homer's *Iliad* and *Odyssey* into heroic couplets (rhyming lines of iambic pentameter) was very popular.

[10] I.e., Achilles, a Greek hero in the Trojan War.

[11] Achilles could be wounded only in his heel; thus Oakhurst's mispronunciation contains a pun.

Toward morning they found themselves unable to feed the fire, which gradually died away. As the embers slowly blackened, the Duchess crept closer to Piney, and broke the silence of many hours: "Piney, can you pray?" "No, dear," said Piney simply. The Duchess, without knowing exactly why, felt relieved, and, putting her head upon Piney's shoulder, spoke no more. And so reclining, the younger and purer pillowing the head of her soiled sister upon her virgin breast, they fell asleep.

The wind lulled as if it feared to waken them. Feathery drifts of snow, shaken from the long pine boughs, flew like white winged birds, and settled about them as they slept. The moon through the rifted clouds looked down upon what had been the camp. But all human stain, all trace of earthly travail, was hidden beneath the spotless mantle mercifully flung from above.

They slept all that day and the next, nor did they waken when voices and footsteps broke the silence of the camp. And when pitying fingers brushed the snow from their wan faces, you could scarcely have told from the equal peace that dwelt upon them which was she that had sinned. Even the law of Poker Flat recognized this, and turned away, leaving them still locked in each other's arms.

But at the head of the gulch, on one of the largest pine-trees, they found the deuce of clubs pinned to the bark with a bowie-knife. It bore the following, written in pencil in a firm hand: —

†

BENEATH THIS TREE
LIES THE BODY
OF
JOHN OAKHURST,
WHO STRUCK A STREAK OF BAD LUCK
ON THE 23D OF NOVEMBER 1850,
AND
HANDED IN HIS CHECKS
ON THE 7TH DECEMBER, 1850.

↓

And pulseless and cold, with a Derringer[12] by his side and a bullet in his heart, though still calm as in life, beneath the snow lay he who was at once the strongest and yet the weakest of the outcasts of Poker Flat.

1869, 1870

AMBROSE BIERCE
(1842–1914)

Ambrose Bierce wrote the following definitions for *The Devil's Dictionary*: Marriage: "The state or condition of a community consisting of a master, a mistress and two slaves, making in all, two"; War: "A by-product of peace"; Pray: "To ask that the laws of the universe be annulled in behalf of a single petitioner confessedly unworthy"; Comfort: "A state of mind produced by contemplation of a neighbor's uneasiness"; Faith: "Belief without evidence in what is told by one who speaks without knowledge, of things without parallel"; Birth: "The first and direst of all disasters."

---

[12]A small, short-barrelled pistol of large caliber invented by the American gunsmith, Henry Deringer (1806–1868).

Bierce started writing *The Devil's Dictionary* as a newspaper column in 1881, and it was first published in part in 1906 as *The Cynic's Word Book*, and again in 1911 with Bierce's original title. Although the 1906 title did not have the author's approval, it provides a good description of the general tenor of Bierce as person and writer. Cynicism seemed to seep into everything he created, even the way he lived his life. His was a chronically jaundiced view of the world and human fate.

He came by such a view naturally. He was born in a log cabin on Horse Cave Creek, Meigs County, Ohio, the last of nine children in a poor rootless family. He had no education except for that gained from the reading of books wherever he could find them. At the beginning of the Civil War, Bierce joined the Union Army and participated in a number of bloody battles. He won his commission as an officer in 1862, was wounded in 1864, and demobilized in 1865. His experiences on the battlefield in the chaos of war would provide the material for his most memorable short stories.

Shortly after the war, Bierce joined a brother in San Francisco and drifted into newspaper work, becoming editor of the *News Letter*. He published his first story in *The Overland Monthly* in 1871. San Francisco was at this time a breeding ground for western writers, and Bierce encountered, among others, Mark Twain, Bret Harte, and Joaquin Miller. Bierce was married in 1871 and a few months later, in 1872, sailed with his wife to England, where he remained for four years. There he became associated with a group of artists and writers, and gained some fame from publication of a series of books, using materials that he had gathered or published in California. *Nuggets and Dust Panned Out in California* appeared in 1873, *Cobwebs from an Empty Shell* in 1874. The dark, sardonic quality of his humor gained him the epithet, "Bitter Bierce."

In 1876 Bierce returned to San Francisco and resumed his work as a journalist, introducing a column "Prattle." When William Randolph Hearst took over the *San Francisco Examiner* in 1887, Bierce moved his column to the Hearst paper. He published his first volume of short stories, *Tales of Soldiers and Civilians*, in 1892 (called *In the Midst of Life* in the English edition), and he wrote bluntly in the Preface, thanking the financial backer of the work, that the book had been "denied existence by chief publishing houses of the country."

In the late 1890s, Bierce moved to the East, working for various newspapers, including Hearst's *New York Journal*. His publication of *The Devil's Dictionary* solidified his reputation as a misanthrope with a malevolent wit. From 1908 to 1912, Bierce labored at preparing his *Collected Works*, published in twelve volumes (1909–12), but it failed to bring him the recognition he rightfully believed he deserved.

In 1913, weary of the life he was living, he decided to go to Mexico to observe the Mexican Revolution then in progress. His motivation for the trip was obscure, perhaps even to himself. He wrote to a friend:

> My plan, so far as I have one, is to go through Mexico to one of the Pacific ports, if I can *get* through without being stood up against a wall and shot as an American. Thence I hope to sail for some port in South America. Thence go across the Andes and perhaps across the continent. . . . Naturally, it is possible—even probable—that I shall not return. These be "strange countries," in which things happen; that is why I am going. And I am seventy-one!

No one knows for sure what happened. It seems likely that he was killed in Mexico in a chance encounter in the random violence of war, an ironic death somehow suitably punctuating an ironic life.

ADDITIONAL READING

   The Letters of Ambrose Bierce, ed. Bertha C. Pope, 1922, 1967; *The Enlarged Devil's Dictionary*, ed., Ernest J. Hopkins, 1967.

   Vincent Starrett, *Ambrose Bierce*, 1920; C. Harley Grattan, *Bitter Bierce: A Mystery of American Letters*, 1929; Adolphe De Castro, *Portrait of Ambrose Bierce*, 1929; Carey McWilliams, *Ambrose Bierce, A Biography*, 1929, 1967; Walter Neale, *Life of Ambrose Bierce*, 1929; Franklin Walker, *Ambrose Bierce: The Wickedest Man in San Francisco*, 1941; Paul Fatout, *Ambrose Bierce, The Devil's Lexicographer*, 1951; Paul Fatout, *Ambrose Bierce and the Black Hills*, 1956; Robert A. Wiggins, *Ambrose Bierce*, 1964; Stuart C. Woodruff, *The Short Stories of Ambrose Bierce: A Study in Polarity*, 1962; Richard O'Connor, *Ambrose Bierce: A Biography*, 1967; M. E. Grenander, *Ambrose Bierce*, 1971; Cathy N. Davidson, ed., *Critical Essays on Ambrose Bierce*, 1982; Cathy N. Davidson, *The Experimental Fictions of Ambrose Bierce: Structuring the Ineffable*, 1984.

TEXT

   The Collected Works of Ambrose Bierce, 12 vols., ed. Walter Neale, 1909–12.

An Occurrence at Owl Creek Bridge

I

   A man stood upon a railroad bridge in northern Alabama, looking down into the swift water twenty feet below. The man's hands were behind his back, the wrists bound with a cord. A rope closely encircled his neck. It was attached to a stout cross-timber above his head and the slack fell to the level of his knees. Some loose boards laid upon the sleepers[1] supporting the metals of the railway supplied a footing for him and his executioners — two private soldiers of the Federal army, directed by a sergeant who in civil life may have been a deputy sheriff. At a short remove upon the same temporary platform was an officer in the uniform of his rank, armed. He was a captain. A sentinel at each end of the bridge stood with his rifle in the position known as "support," that is to say, vertical in front of the left shoulder, the hammer resting on the forearm thrown straight across the chest — a formal and unnatural position, enforcing an erect carriage of the body. It did not appear to be the duty of these two men to know what was occurring at the centre of the bridge; they merely blockaded the two ends of the foot planking that traversed it.

   Beyond one of the sentinels nobody was in sight; the railroad ran straight away into a forest for a hundred yards, then, curving, was lost to view. Doubtless there was an outpost farther along. The other bank of the stream was open ground — a gentle acclivity topped with a stockade of vertical tree trunks, loopholed for rifles, with a single embrasure through which protruded the muzzle of a brass cannon commanding the bridge. Midway of the slope between bridge and fort were the spectators — a single company of infantry in line, at "parade rest," the butts of the rifles on the ground, the barrels inclining slightly backward against the right shoulder, the hands crossed upon the stock. A lieutenant stood at the right of the line, the point of his sword upon the ground, his left hand resting upon his right. Excepting the group of four at the centre of the bridge, not a man moved. The company faced the bridge, staring stonily, motionless. The sentinels, facing the banks of the stream, might have been statues to adorn the bridge. The captain stood with folded arms, silent, observing the work of his subordinates, but making no sign. Death is a dignitary who when

---

[1]The heavy wooden crossties supporting the iron railroad tracks.

he comes announced is to be received with formal manifestations of respect, even by those most familiar with him. In the code of military etiquette silence and fixity are forms of deference.

The man who was engaged in being hanged was apparently about thirty-five years of age. He was a civilian, if one might judge from his habit, which was that of a planter. His features were good—a straight nose, firm mouth, broad forehead, from which his long, dark hair was combed straight back, falling behind his ears to the collar of his well-fitting frock-coat. He wore a mustache and pointed beard, but no whiskers; his eyes were large and dark gray, and had a kindly expression which one would hardly have expected in one whose neck was in the hemp. Evidently this was no vulgar assassin. The liberal military code makes provision for hanging many kinds of persons, and gentlemen are not excluded.

The preparations being complete, the two private soldiers stepped aside and each drew away the plank upon which he had been standing. The sergeant turned to the captain, saluted and placed himself immediately behind that officer, who in turn moved apart one pace. These movements left the condemned man and the sergeant standing on the two ends of the same plank, which spanned three of the cross-ties of the bridge. The end upon which the civilian stood almost, but not quite, reached a fourth. This plank had been held in place by the weight of the captain; it was now held by that of the sergeant. At a signal from the former the latter would step aside, the plank would tilt and the condemned man go down between two ties. The arrangement commended itself to his judgment as simple and effective. His face had not been covered nor his eyes bandaged. He looked a moment at his "unsteadfast footing," then let his gaze wander to the swirling water of the stream racing madly beneath his feet. A piece of dancing driftwood caught his attention and his eyes followed it down the current. How slowly it appeared to move! What a sluggish stream!

He closed his eyes in order to fix his last thoughts upon his wife and children. The water, touched to gold by the early sun, the brooding mists under the banks at some distance down the stream, the fort, the soldiers, the piece of drift—all had distracted him. And now he became conscious of a new disturbance. Striking through the thought of his dear ones was a sound which he could neither ignore nor understand, a sharp, distinct, metallic percussion like the stroke of a blacksmith's hammer upon the anvil; it had the same ringing quality. He wondered what it was, and whether immeasurably distant or near by—it seemed both. Its recurrence was regular, but as slow as the tolling of a death knell. He awaited each stroke with impatience and—he knew not why—apprehension. The intervals of silence grew progressively longer; the delays became maddening. With their greater infrequency the sounds increased in strength and sharpness. They hurt his ear like the thrust of a knife; he feared he would shriek. What he heard was the ticking of his watch.

He unclosed his eyes and saw again the water below him. "If I could free my hands," he thought, "I might throw off the noose and spring into the stream. By diving I could evade the bullets and, swimming vigorously, reach the bank, take to the woods and get away home. My home, thank God, is as yet outside their lines; my wife and little ones are still beyond the invader's farthest advance."

As these thoughts, which have here to be set down in words, were flashed into the doomed man's brain rather than evolved from it the captain nodded to the sergeant. The sergeant stepped aside.

II

Peyton Farquhar was a well-to-do planter, of an old and highly respected Alabama family. Being a slave owner and like other slave owners a politician he was naturally an original secessionist and ardently devoted to the Southern cause. Circumstances of an imperious nature, which it is unnecessary to relate here, had prevented him from taking service with the gallant army that had fought the disastrous campaigns ending with the fall of Corinth,[2] and he chafed under the inglorious restraint, longing for the release of his energies, the larger life of the soldier, the opportunity for distinction. That opportunity, he felt, would come, as it comes to all in war time. Meanwhile he did what he could. No service was too humble for him to perform in aid of the South, no adventure too perilous for him to undertake if consistent with the character of a civilian who was at heart a soldier, and who in good faith and without too much qualification assented to at least a part of the frankly villainous dictum that all is fair in love and war.

One evening while Farquhar and his wife were sitting on a rustic bench near the entrance to his grounds, a gray-clad soldier rode up to the gate and asked for a drink of water. Mrs. Farquhar was only too happy to serve him with her own white hands. While she was fetching the water her husband approached the dusty horseman and inquired eagerly for news from the front.

"The Yanks are repairing the railroads," said the man, "and are getting ready for another advance. They have reached the Owl Creek bridge, put it in order and built a stockade on the north bank. The commandant has issued an order, which is posted everywhere, declaring that any civilian caught interfering with the railroad, its bridges, tunnels or trains will be summarily hanged. I saw the order."

"How far is it to the Owl Creek bridge?" Farquhar asked.

"About thirty miles."

"Is there no force on this side the creek?"

"Only a picket post half a mile out, on the railroad, and a single sentinel at this end of the bridge."

"Suppose a man—a civilian and student of hanging—should elude the picket post and perhaps get the better of the sentinel," said Farquhar, smiling, "what could he accomplish?"

The soldier reflected. "I was there a month ago," he replied. "I observed that the flood of last winter had lodged a great quantity of driftwood against the wooden pier at this end of the bridge. It is now dry and would burn like tow."

The lady had now brought the water, which the soldier drank. He thanked her ceremoniously, bowed to her husband and rode away. An hour later, after nightfall, he repassed the plantation, going northward in the direction from which he had come. He was a Federal scout.[3]

III

As Peyton Farquhar fell straight downward through the bridge he lost consciousness and was as one already dead. From this state he was awakened—ages later, it seemed to him—by the pain of a sharp pressure upon his throat, followed by a sense of suffocation. Keen, poignant agonies seemed to shoot from his neck downward through every fibre of his body and limbs. These pains appeared to flash along well-defined lines of ramification and to beat with an inconceivably rapid periodicity. They seemed like streams of pulsating fire heating him to an intolerable temperature. As to his head, he was conscious of nothing but a feeling of fulness—of congestion. These sensations were unaccompanied by thought. The intellectual part of his nature was already effaced; he had power only to feel, and feeling was torment. He was conscious of motion. Encompassed in a luminous cloud, of which he was now merely the fiery heart, without material substance, he swung through unthinkable arcs of oscillation, like a vast pendulum. Then all at once, with terrible suddenness, the light about him shot upward with the noise of a loud plash; a frightful roaring was in his ears, and all was cold and dark. The power of thought was restored; he

---

[2] A city in Mississippi taken by the Union Army in 1862.
[3] I.e., a spy for the Union Army.

knew that the rope had broken and he had fallen into the stream. There was no additional strangulation; the noose about his neck was already suffocating him and kept the water from his lungs. To die of hanging at the bottom of a river!—the idea seemed to him ludicrous. He opened his eyes in the darkness and saw above him a gleam of light, but how distant, how inaccessible! He was still sinking, for the light became fainter and fainter until it was a mere glimmer. Then it began to grow and brighten, and he knew that he was rising toward the surface—knew it with reluctance, for he was now very comfortable. "To be hanged and drowned," he thought, "that is not so bad; but I do not wish to be shot. No; I will not be shot; that is not fair."

He was not conscious of an effort, but a sharp pain in his wrist apprised him that he was trying to free his hands. He gave the struggle his attention, as an idler might observe the feat of a juggler, without interest in the outcome. What splendid effort!—what magnificent, what superhuman strength! Ah, that was a fine endeavor! Bravo! The cord fell away; his arms parted and floated upward, the hands dimly seen on each side in the growing light. He watched them with a new interest as first one and then the other pounced upon the noose at his neck. They tore it away and thrust it fiercely aside, its undulations resembling those of a water-snake. "Put it back, put it back!" He thought he shouted these words to his hands, for the undoing of the noose had been succeeded by the direst pang that he had yet experienced. His neck ached horribly; his brain was on fire; his heart, which had been fluttering faintly, gave a great leap, trying to force itself out at his mouth. His whole body was racked and wrenched with an insupportable anguish! But his disobedient hands gave no heed to the command. They beat the water vigorously with quick, downward strokes, forcing him to the surface. He felt his head emerge; his eyes were blinded by the sunlight; his chest expanded convulsively, and with a supreme and crowning agony his lungs engulfed a great draught of air, which instantly he expelled in a shriek!

He was now in full possession of his physical senses. They were, indeed, preternaturally keen and alert. Something in the awful disturbance of his organic system had so exalted and refined them that they made record of things never before perceived. He felt the ripples upon his face and heard their separate sounds as they struck. He looked at the forest on the bank of the stream, saw the individual trees, the leaves and the veining of each leaf—saw the very insects upon them: the locusts, the brilliant-bodied flies, the gray spiders stretching their webs from twig to twig. He noted the prismatic colors in all the dewdrops upon a million blades of grass. The humming of the gnats that danced above the eddies of the stream, the beating of the dragon-flies' wings, the strokes of the water-spiders' legs, like oars which had lifted their boat—all these made audible music. A fish slid along beneath his eyes and he heard the rush of its body parting the water.

He had come to the surface facing down the stream; in a moment the visible world seemed to wheel slowly round, himself the pivotal point, and he saw the bridge, the fort, the soldiers upon the bridge, the captain, the sergeant, the two privates, his executioners. They were in silhouette against the blue sky. They shouted and gesticulated, pointing at him. The captain had drawn his pistol, but did not fire; the others were unarmed. Their movements were grotesque and horrible, their forms gigantic.

Suddenly he heard a sharp report and something struck the water smartly within a few inches of his head, spattering his face with spray. He heard a second report, and saw one of the sentinels with his rifle at his shoulder, a light cloud of blue smoke rising from the muzzle. The man in the water saw the eye of the man on the bridge gazing into his own through the sights of the rifle. He observed that it was a gray eye and remembered having read that gray eyes were keenest, and that all famous marksmen had them. Nevertheless, this one had missed.

A counter-swirl had caught Farquhar and turned him half round; he was again looking into the forest on the bank opposite the fort. The sound of a clear, high voice in a monotonous singsong now rang out behind him and came across the water with a distinctness that pierced and subdued all other sounds, even the beating of the ripples in his ears. Although no soldier, he had frequented camps enough to know the dread significance of that deliberate, drawling, aspirated chant; the lieutenant on shore was taking a part in the morning's work. How coldly and pitilessly — with what an even, calm intonation, presaging, and enforcing tranquillity in the men — with what accurately measured intervals fell those cruel words:

"Attention, company! . . . Shoulder arms! . . . Ready! . . . Aim! . . . Fire!"

Farquhar dived — dived as deeply as he could. The water roared in his ears like the voice of Niagara, yet he heard the dulled thunder of the volley and, rising again toward the surface, met shining bits of metal, singularly flattened, oscillating slowly downward. Some of them touched him on the face and hands, then fell away, continuing their descent. One lodged between his collar and neck; it was uncomfortably warm and he snatched it out.

As he rose to the surface, gasping for breath, he saw that he had been a long time under water; he was perceptibly farther down stream — nearer to safety. The soldiers had almost finished reloading; the metal ramrods flashed all at once in the sunshine as they were drawn from the barrels, turned in the air, and thrust into their sockets. The two sentinels fired again, independently and ineffectually.

The hunted man saw all this over his shoulder; he was now swimming vigorously with the current. His brain was as energetic as his arms and legs; he thought with the rapidity of lightning.

"The officer," he reasoned, "will not make that martinet's error a second time. It is as easy to dodge a volley as a single shot. He has probably already given the command to fire at will. God help me, I cannot dodge them all!"

An appalling plash within two yards of him was followed by a loud, rushing sound, *diminuendo*,[4] which seemed to travel back through the air to the fort and died in an explosion which stirred the very river to its deeps! A rising sheet of water curved over him, fell down upon him, blinded him, strangled him! The cannon had taken a hand in the game. As he shook his head free from the commotion of the smitten water he heard the deflected shot humming through the air ahead, and in an instant it was cracking and smashing the branches in the forest beyond.

"They will not do that again," he thought; "the next time they will use a charge of grape.[5] I must keep my eye upon the gun; the smoke will apprise me — the report arrives too late; it lags behind the missile. That is a good gun."

Suddenly he felt himself whirled round and round — spinning like a top. The water, the banks, the forests, the now distant bridge, fort and men — all were commingled and blurred. Objects were represented by their colors only; circular horizontal streaks of color — that was all he saw. He had been caught in a vortex and was being whirled on with a velocity of advance and gyration that made him giddy and sick. In a few moments he was flung upon the gravel at the foot of the left bank of the stream — the southern bank — and behind a projecting point which concealed him from his enemies. The sudden arrest of his motion, the abrasion of one of his hands on the gravel, restored him, and he wept with delight. He dug his fingers into the sand, threw it over himself in handfuls and audibly blessed it. It looked like diamonds, rubies, emeralds; he could think of nothing beautiful which it did not resemble. The trees upon the bank were giant garden plants; he noted a definite order in their arrangement, inhaled the fragrance of their blooms. A strange, roseate light shone through the spaces among their trunks and the wind made in their branches the music of æolian harps.[6] He had no wish to perfect his escape — was content to remain in that enchanting spot until retaken.

---

[4]"Gradually diminishing in volume" (Italian).
[5]Grapeshot, a cluster of small iron balls (resembling grapes) used as cannon ammunition.

[6]Stringed instruments that produce music when wind passes over them.

A whiz and rattle of grapeshot among the branches high above his head roused him from his dream. The baffled cannoneer had fired him a random farewell. He sprang to his feet, rushed up the sloping bank, and plunged into the forest.

All that day he traveled, laying his course by the rounding sun. The forest seemed interminable; nowhere did he discover a break in it, not even a woodman's road. He had not known that he lived in so wild a region. There was something uncanny in the revelation.

By nightfall he was fatigued, footsore, famishing. The thought of his wife and children urged him on. At last he found a road which led him in what he knew to be the right direction. It was as wide and straight as a city street, yet it seemed untraveled. No fields bordered it, no dwelling anywhere. Not so much as the barking of a dog suggested human habitation. The black bodies of the trees formed a straight wall on both sides, terminating on the horizon in a point, like a diagram in a lesson in perspective. Overhead, as he looked up through this rift in the wood, shone great golden stars looking unfamiliar and grouped in strange constellations. He was sure they were arranged in some order which had a secret and malign significance. The wood on either side was full of singular noises, among which—once, twice, and again—he distinctly heard whispers in an unknown tongue.

His neck was in pain and lifting his hand to it he found it horribly swollen. He knew that it had a circle of black where the rope had bruised it. His eyes felt congested; he could no longer close them. His tongue was swollen with thirst; he relieved its fever by thrusting it forward from between his teeth into the cold air. How softly the turf had carpeted the untraveled avenue—he could no longer feel the roadway beneath his feet!

Doubtless, despite his suffering, he had fallen asleep while walking, for now he sees another scene—perhaps he has merely recovered from a delirium. He stands at the gate of his own home. All is as he left it, and all bright and beautiful in the morning sunshine. He must have traveled the entire night. As he pushes open the gate and passes up the wide white walk, he sees a flutter of female garments; his wife, looking fresh and cool and sweet, steps down from the veranda to meet him. At the bottom of the steps she stands waiting, with a smile of ineffable joy, an attitude of matchless grace and dignity. Ah, how beautiful she is! He springs forward with extended arms. As he is about to clasp her he feels a stunning blow upon the back of the neck; a blinding white light blazes all about him with a sound like the shock of a cannon—then all is darkness and silence!

Peyton Farquhar was dead; his body, with a broken neck, swung gently from side to side beneath the timbers of the Owl Creek bridge.

1890, 1892

from The Devil's Dictionary

Absurdity, *n.* A statement or belief manifestly inconsistent with one's own opinion.

Bigot, *n.* One who is obstinately and zealously attached to an opinion that you do not entertain.

Debauchee, *n.* One who has so earnestly pursued pleasure that he has had the misfortune to overtake it.

Deliberation, *n.* The act of examining one's bread to determine which side it is buttered on.

Dentist, *n.* A prestidigitator who, putting metal into your mouth, pulls coins out of your pocket.

Eat, *v. i.* To perform successively (and successfully) the functions of mastication, humectation, and deglutition.

Economy, *n.* Purchasing the barrel of whiskey that you do not need for the price of the cow that you cannot afford.

Edible, *adj.* Good to eat, and wholesome to digest, as a worm to a toad, a toad to a snake, a snake to a pig, a pig to a man, and a man to a worm.

Hand, *n.* A singular instrument worn at the end of the human arm and commonly thrust into somebody's pocket.

Man, *n.* An animal so lost in rapturous contemplation of what he thinks he is as to overlook what he indubitably ought to be. His chief occupation is extermination of other animals and his own species, which, however, multiplies with such insistent rapidity as to infest the whole habitable earth and Canada.

Marriage, *n.* The state or condition of a community consisting of a master, a mistress and two slaves, making in all, two.

Push, *n.* One of the two things mainly conducive to success, especially in politics. The other is Pull.

Railroad, *n.* The chief of many mechanical devices enabling us to get away from where we are to where we are no better off. For this purpose the railroad is held in highest favor by the optimist, for it permits him to make the transit with great expedition.

Realism, *n.* The art of depicting nature as it is seen by toads. The charm suffusing a landscape painted by a mole, or a story written by a measuring-worm.

Reason, *v. i.* To weigh probabilities in the scales of desire.

Reasonable, *adj.* Accessible to the infection of our own opinions. Hospitable to persuasion, dissuasion and evasion.

Reconsider, *v.* To seek a justification for a decision already made.

Self-esteem, *n.* An erroneous appraisement.

Self-evident, *adj.* Evident to one's self and to nobody else.

Selfish, *adj.* Devoid of consideration for the selfishness of others.

Senate, *n.* A body of elderly gentlemen charged with high duties and misdemeanors.

Yankee, *n.* In Europe, an American. In the Northern States of our Union, a New Englander. In the Southern States the word is unknown. (See Damyank.)

Year, *n.* A period of three hundred and sixty-five disappointments.

Zeal, *n.* A certain nervous disorder afflicting the young and inexperienced. A passion that goeth before a sprawl.

1911

GEORGE WASHINGTON CABLE
(1844–1925)

George Washington Cable's father was from a Virginia slave-holding family and his mother was from New England, but they met and married in Indiana in 1834, migrating later to New Orleans because of a business opening. There George, their first child, was born in 1844. After suffering repeated business reverses, the father died in 1859, leaving the fourteen-year-old boy as the head of a large family.

Cable worked at various odd jobs, and then, in 1863, joined the Mississippi Cavalry in the Civil War. Deprived of an education and with a curious, restless mind, Cable found time even in his military service to read widely. After the war, he was a journalist for a time, but then found employment as an accountant and correspondence clerk in a cotton business. With a steady job, he married a New Orleans woman and started a family, which was eventually to number seven children.

Throughout these years, Cable continued his self-education, rising early in the morning to read, study French, and explore the history of New Orleans in its archives. There he found fascinating materials, which he began to work up into narratives. He said later, "It seemed a pity to let them go to waste." Cable published his first story, "'Sieur George," in *Scribner's Monthly* in 1873. This gained him a national audience and he published other stories in *Scribner's*, followed by a collection entitled *Old Creole Days* in 1879. It was extraordinarily popular, and brought Cable independent income just as the firm he worked for was dissolved because of the death of the owner.

In quick succession Cable published *The Grandissimes* (1880), his first novel, depicting Creole life; *Madame Delphine* (1881), a novelette of miscegenation; and *The Creoles of Louisiana* (1884), a historical work. Although his first literary work seemed to flow naturally from the southern background of his father, his later work, beginning with *The Silent South* (1885), seemed more in tune with his northern heritage from his New England mother. The book, which called for justice for the blacks, antagonized the southerners.

In 1885, Cable moved his family to Northhampton, Massachusetts, where he became something of a national literary figure. He read publicly from his works, made lecture tours with Mark Twain, and continued to write. But he had exhausted the material that had inspired his best work, and he turned to social and political commentary, as in *The Negro Question* (1890) and *The Southern Struggle for Pure Government* (1890). Although he turned back to the writing of fiction in his last years, he never fully recovered the imaginative powers of his early work.

Cable's early stories, like "Belles Demoiselles Plantation," are colorful accounts of Creole characters when their fortunes and culture were in decline. Cable once explained that the word *Creole* "came to include any native of French or Spanish descent whose non-alliance with the slave race entitled him to social rank." Without deep roots, linguistically trapped between two worlds and fully at home in neither, the Creoles seemed to lead exotic lives and to cultivate quaint habits. As the subjects of fiction, they often inspired laughter, but they also evoked sympathy and pity in their trials and tribulations.

ADDITIONAL READING

The Negro Question: A Selection of Writings on Civil Rights in the South by George W. Cable, ed. Arlin Turner, 1958; *Creoles and Cajuns: Stories of Old Louisiana*, ed. Arlin Turner, 1959.

Lucy Cable Bikle, *George W. Cable, His Life and Letters*, 1928; Kjell Ekström, *George Washington Cable: A Study of His Early Life and Work*, 1950; Guy A. Caldwell, *Twins of Genius*, 1953; Arlin Turner, *George W. Cable: A Biography*, 1956; Arlin Turner, *Mark Twain and George W. Cable*, 1960; Philip Butcher, *George W. Cable*, 1962; Louis D. Rubin, *George W. Cable: The Life and Times of a Southern Heretic*, 1969; Arlin Turner, ed., *Critical Essays on George W. Cable*, 1980; Thomas J. Richardson, ed., *The Grandissimes: Centennial Essays*, 1981.

TEXT

Old Creole Days, 1879.

Belles Demoiselles Plantation

The original grantee was Count —, assume the name to be De Charleu; the old Creoles[1] never forgive a public mention. He was the French king's commissary. One day, called to France to explain the lucky accident of the commissariat having burned down with his account-books inside, he left his wife, a Choctaw Comptesse, behind.

Arrived at court, his excuses were accepted, and that tract granted him where afterwards stood Belles Demoiselles[2] Plantation. A man cannot remember everything! In a fit of forgetfulness he married a French gentlewoman, rich and beautiful, and "brought her out."[3] However, "All's well that ends well;" a famine had been in the colony, and the Choctaw Comptesse had starved, leaving nought but a half-caste orphan family lurking on the edge of the settlement, bearing our French gentlewoman's own new name, and being mentioned in Monsieur's will.

And the new Comptesse — she tarried but a twelvemonth, left Monsieur a lovely son, and departed, led out of this vain world by the swamp-fever.

From this son sprang the proud Creole family of De Charleu. It rose straight up, up, up, generation after generation, tall, branchless, slender, palm-like; and finally, in the time of which I am to tell, flowered with all the rare beauty of a century-plant, in Artemise, Innocente, Felicité, the twins Marie and Martha, Leontine and little Septima; the seven beautiful daughters for whom their home had been fitly named Belles Demoiselles.

The Count's grant had once been a long Pointe,[4] round which the Mississippi used to whirl, and seethe, and foam, that it was horrid to behold. Big whirlpools would open and wheel about in the savage eddies under the low bank, and close up again, and others open, and spin, and disappear. Great circles of muddy surface would boil up from hundreds of feet below, and gloss over, and seem to float away, — sink, come back again under water, and with only a soft hiss surge up again, and again drift off, and vanish. Every few minutes the loamy bank would tip down a great load of earth upon its besieger, and fall back a foot, — sometimes a yard, — and the writhing river would press after, until at last the Pointe was quite swallowed up, and the great river glided by in a majestic curve, and asked no more; the bank stood fast, the "caving" became a forgotten misfortune, and the diminished grant was a long, sweeping, willowy bend, rustling with miles of sugar-cane.

Coming up the Mississippi in the sailing craft of those early days, about the time one first could descry the white spires of the old St. Louis Cathedral,[5] you would be pretty sure to spy, just over to your right under the levee,[6] Belles Demoiselles Mansion, with its broad veranda and red painted cypress roof, peering over the embankment, like a bird in the nest, half hid by the avenue of willows which one of the departed De Charleus, — he that married a Marot, — had planted on the levee's crown.

The house stood unusually near the river, facing eastward, and standing foursquare, with an immense veranda about its sides, and a flight of steps in front spreading broadly downward, as we open arms to a child. From the veranda nine miles of river were seen; and in their compass, near at hand, the shady garden full of rare and beautiful flowers; farther away broad fields of cane and rice, and the distant quarters of the slaves, and on the horizon everywhere a dark belt of cypress forest.

The master was old Colonel De Charleu, — Jean Albert Henri Joseph De Charleu-Marot, and "Colonel" by the grace of the first American governor.[7] Monsieur, — he would not speak to any one who called him "Colonel," — was a hoary-headed patri-

---

[1]Descendants of the original French and Spanish settlers of Louisiana.
[2]"Beautiful young ladies" (French).
[3]Brought her from France to French Louisiana.
[4]Pointed extension of land.

[5]Built in 1794 at the center of the old French Quarter.
[6]Embankment raised to prevent flooding.
[7]I.e., an honorary title rather than a military commission, bestowed after the acquisition of the territory from France in the Louisiana Purchase (1803).

arch. His step was firm, his form erect, his intellect strong and clear, his countenance classic, serene, dignified, commanding, his manners courtly, his voice musical, — fascinating. He had had his vices, — all his life; but had borne them, as his race do, with a serenity of conscience and a cleanness of mouth that left no outward blemish on the surface of the gentleman. He had gambled in Royal street,[8] drank hard in Orleans street, run his adversary through in the duelling-ground at Slaughter-house Point,[9] and danced and quarreled at the St. Philippe-street-theatre quadroon balls.[10] Even now, with all his courtesy and bounty, and a hospitality which seemed to be entertaining angels, he was bitter-proud and penurious, and deep down in his hard-finished heart loved nothing but himself, his name, and his motherless children. But these! — their ravishing beauty was all but excuse enough for the unbounded idolatry of their father. Against these seven goddesses he never rebelled. Had they even required him to defraud old De Carlos —

I can hardly say.

Old De Carlos was his extremely distant relative on the Choctaw side. With this single exception, the narrow thread-like line of descent from the Indian wife, diminished to a mere strand by injudicious alliances, and deaths in the gutters of old New Orleans, was extinct. The name, by Spanish contact, had become De Carlos; but this one surviving bearer of it was known to all, and known only, as Injin Charlie.

One thing I never knew a Creole to do. He will not utterly go back on the ties of blood, no matter what sort of knots those ties may be. For one reason, he is never ashamed of his or his father's sins; and for another, — he will tell you — he is "all heart!"

So the different heirs of the De Charleu estate had always strictly regarded the rights and interests of the De Carloses, especially their ownership of a block of dilapidated buildings in a part of the city, which had once been very poor property, but was beginning to be valuable. This block had much more than maintained the last De Carlos through a long and lazy lifetime, and, as his household consisted only of himself, and an aged and crippled negress, the inference was irresistible that he "had money." Old Charlie, though by *alias* an "Injin," was plainly a dark white man, about as old as Colonel De Charleu, sunk in the bliss of deep ignorance, shrewd, deaf, and, by repute at least, unmerciful.

The Colonel and he always conversed in English. This rare accomplishment, which the former had learned from his Scotch wife, — the latter from up-river traders, — they found an admirable medium of communication, answering, better than French could, a similar purpose to that of the stick which we fasten to the bit of one horse and breast-gear of another, whereby each keeps his distance. Once in a while, too, by way of jest, English found its way among the ladies of Belles Demoiselles, always signifying that their sire was about to have business with old Charlie.

Now a long standing wish to buy out Charlie troubled the Colonel. He had no desire to oust him unfairly; he was proud of being always fair; yet he did long to engross the whole estate under one title. Out of his luxurious idleness he had conceived this desire, and thought little of so slight an obstacle as being already somewhat in debt to old Charlie for money borrowed, and for which Belles Demoiselles was, of course, good, ten times over. Lots, buildings, rents, all, might as well be his, he thought, to give, keep, or destroy. "Had he but the old man's heritage. Ah! he might bring that into existence which his *belles demoiselles* had been begging for, 'since many years;' a home, — and such a home, — in the gay city. Here he should tear down this row of cottages, and make his garden wall; there that long rope-walk[11] should give

---

[8]Site of many gambling houses.

[9]Setting of countless duels, now part of City Park in New Orleans.

[10]Balls attended by young women who were one-fourth black and wealthy white men.

[11]Covered path or building where ropes were made.

place to vine-covered arbors; the bakery yonder should make way for a costly conservatory; that wine warehouse should come down, and the mansion go up. It should be the finest in the State. Men should never pass it, but they should say—'the palace of the De Charleus; a family of grand descent, a people of elegance and bounty, a line as old as France, a fine old man, and seven daughters as beautiful as happy; whoever dare attempt to marry there must leave his own name behind him!'

"The house should be of stones fitly set, brought down in ships from the land of 'les Yankees,' and it should have an airy belvedere,[12] with a gilded image tip-toeing and shining on its peak, and from it you should see, far across the gleaming folds of the river, the red roof of Belles Demoiselles, the country-seat. At the big stone gate there should be a porter's lodge, and it should be a privilege even to see the ground."

Truly they were a family fine enough, and fancy-free enough to have fine wishes, yet happy enough where they were, to have had no wish but to live there always.

To those, who, by whatever fortune, wandered into the garden of Belles Demoiselles some summer afternoon as the sky was reddening towards evening, it was lovely to see the family gathered out upon the tiled pavement at the foot of the broad front steps, gaily chatting and jesting, with that ripple of laughter that comes so pleasingly from a bevy of girls. The father would be found seated in their midst, the center of attention and compliment, witness, arbiter, umpire, critic, by his beautiful children's unanimous appointment, but the single vassal, too, of seven absolute sovereigns.

Now they would draw their chairs near together in eager discussion of some new step in the dance, or the adjustment of some rich adornment. Now they would start about him with excited comments to see the eldest fix a bunch of violets in his button-hole. Now the twins would move down a walk after some unusual flower, and be greeted on their return with the high pitched notes of delighted feminine surprise.

As evening came on they would draw more quietly about their paternal center. Often their chairs were forsaken, and they grouped themselves on the lower steps, one above another, and surrendered themselves to the tender influences of the approaching night. At such an hour the passer on the river, already attracted by the dark figures of the broad-roofed mansion, and its woody garden standing against the glowing sunset, would hear the voices of the hidden group rise from the spot in the soft harmonies of an evening song; swelling clearer and clearer as the thrill of music warmed them into feeling, and presently joined by the deeper tones of the father's voice; then, as the daylight passed quite away, all would be still, and he would know that the beautiful home had gathered its nestlings under its wings.

And yet, for mere vagary, it pleased them not to be pleased.

"Arti!" called one sister to another in the broad hall, one morning,—mock amazement in her distended eyes,—"something is goin' to took place!"

"*Comm-e-n-t?*"[13]—longdrawn perplexity.

"Papa is goin' to town!"

The news passed up stairs.

"Inno!"—one to another meeting in a doorway,—"something is goin' to took place!"

"*Qu'est-ce que c'est!*"[14]—vain attempt at gruffness.

"Papa is goin' to town!"

The unusual tidings were true. It was afternoon of the same day that the Colonel tossed his horse's bridle to his groom, and stepped up to old Charlie, who was sitting on his bench under a China-tree, his head, as was his fashion, bound in a Madras handkerchief. The "old man" was plainly under the effect of spirits, and smiled a deferential salutation without trusting himself to his feet.

---

[12]An open gallery on the top of the house commanding a view.

[13]"What?" (French).
[14]"What is it?" (French).

"Eh, well Charlie!"—the Colonel raised his voice to suit his kinsman's deafness,—"how is those times with my friend Charlie?"

"Eh?" said Charlie, distractedly.

"Is that goin' well with my friend Charlie?"

"In de house,—call her,"—making a pretense of rising.

"*Non, non!* I don't want,"—the speaker paused to breathe—"ow is collection?"

"O!" said Charlie, "every day he make me more poorer!"

"What do you hask for it?" asked the planter indifferently, designating the house by a wave of his whip.

"Ask for w'at?" said Injin Charlie.

"De *house!* What you ask for it?"

"I don't believe," said Charlie.

"What you would *take* for it!" cried the planter.

"Wait for w'at?"

"What you would *take* for the whole block?"

"I don't want to sell him!"

"I'll give you *ten thousand dollah* for it."

"Ten t'ousand dollah for dis house? O, no, dat is no price. He is blame good old house,—dat old house." (Old Charlie and the Colonel never swore in presence of each other.) "Forty years dat old house didn't had to be paint! I easy can get fifty t'ousand dollah for dat old house."

"Fifty thousand picayunes;[15] yes," said the Colonel.

"She's a good house. Can make plenty money," pursued the deaf man.

"That's what make you so rich, eh, Charlie?"

"*Non*, I don't make nothing. Too blame clever, me, dat's de troub'. She's a good house,—make money fast like a steamboat,—make a barrel full in a week! Me, I lose money all de days. Too blame clever."

"Charlie!"

"Eh?"

"Tell me what you'll take?"

"Make? I don't make *nothing*. Too blame clever."

"What will you *take*?"

"Oh! I got enough already,—half drunk now."

"What will you take for the 'ouse?"

"You want to buy her?"

"I don't know,"—(shrug),—"may*be*,—if you sell it cheap."

"She's a bully old house."

There was a long silence. By and by old Charlie commenced—

"Old Injin Charlie is a low-down dog."

"*C'est vrai, oui!*[16] retorted the Colonel in an undertone.

"He's got Injin blood in him."

The Colonel nodded assent.

"But he's got some blame good blood, too, ain't it?"

The Colonel nodded impatiently.

"*Bien!*[17] Old Charlie's Injin blood says, 'sell de house, Charlie, you blame old fool!' *Mais,*[18] old Charlie's good blood says, 'Charlie! if you sell dat old house, Charlie, you low-down old dog, Charlie, what de Compte De Charleu make for you grace-gran'-muzzer, de dev' can eat you, Charlie, I don't care.'"

"But you'll sell it anyhow, won't you, old man?"

"No!" and the *no* rumbled off in muttered oaths like thunder out on the Gulf. The incensed old Colonel wheeled and started off.

---

[15] A Spanish coin equal to 6¼ cents.
[16] "Yes, that's true!" (French).
[17] "All right!" (French).
[18] "But" (French).

"Curl!" (Colonel) said Charlie, standing up unsteadily.

The planter turned with an inquiring frown.

"I'll trade with you!" said Charlie.

The Colonel was tempted. "'Ow'l you trade?" he asked.

"My house for yours!"

The old Colonel turned pale with anger. He walked very quickly back, and came close up to his kinsman.

"Charlie!" he said.

"Injin Charlie," with a tipsy nod.

But by this time self-control was returning. "Sell Belles Demoiselles to you?" he said in a high key, and then laughed "Ho, ho, ho!" and rode away.

A cloud, but not a dark one, overshadowed the spirits of Belles Demoiselles' plantation. The old master, whose beaming presence had always made him a shining Saturn, spinning and sparkling within the bright circle of his daughters, fell into musing fits, started out of frowning reveries, walked often by himself, and heard business from his overseer fretfully.

No wonder. The daughters knew his closeness in trade, and attributed to it his failure to negotiate for the Old Charlie buildings, — so to call them. They began to depreciate Belles Demoiselles. If a north wind blew, it was too cold to ride. If a shower had fallen, it was too muddy to drive. In the morning the garden was wet. In the evening the grasshopper was a burden. *Ennui*[19] was turned into capital; every headache was interpreted a premonition of ague; and when the native exuberance of a flock of ladies without a want or a care burst out in laughter in the father's face, they spread their French eyes, rolled up their little hands, and with rigid wrists and mock vehemence vowed and vowed again that they only laughed at their misery, and should pine to death unless they could move to the sweet city. "O! the theater! O! Orleans Street! O! the masquerade! the Place d'Armes![20] the ball!" and they would call upon Heaven with French irreverence, and fall into each other's arms, and whirl down the hall singing a waltz, end with a grand collision and fall, and, their eyes streaming merriment, lay the blame on the slippery floor, that would some day be the death of the whole seven.

Three times more the fond father, thus goaded, managed, by accident, — business accident, — to see old Charlie and increase his offer; but in vain. He finally went to him formally.

"Eh?" said the deaf and distant relative. "For what you want him, eh? Why you don't stay where you halways be 'appy? Dis is a blame old rat-hole, — good for old Injin Charlie, — da's all. Why you don't stay where you be halways 'appy? Why you don't buy somewheres else?"

"That's none of your business," snapped the planter. Truth was, his reasons were unsatisfactory even to himself.

A sullen silence followed. Then Charlie spoke:

"Well, now, look here; I sell you old Charlie's house."

"*Bien!*[21] and the whole block," said the Colonel.

"Hold on," said Charlie. "I sell you de 'ouse and de block. Den I go and git drunk, and go to sleep; de dev' comes along and says, 'Charlie! old Charlie, you blame low-down old dog, wake up! What you doin' here? Where's de 'ouse what Monsieur le Compte give your grace-gran-muzzer? Don't you see dat fine gentyman, De Charleu, done gone and tore him down and make him over new, you blame old fool, Charlie, you low-down old Injin dog!'"

---

[19]Boredom.
[20]The heart of the French Quarter, now Jackson Square.
[21]"Good" (French).

"I'll give you forty thousand dollars," said the Colonel.

"For de 'ouse?"

"For all."

The deaf man shook his head.

"Forty-five!" said the Colonel.

"What a lie? For what you tell me 'what a lie?' I don't tell you no lie."

"*Non, non!* I give you *forty-five!*" shouted the Colonel.

Charlie shook his head again.

"Fifty!"

He shook it again.

The figures rose and rose to—

"Seventy-five!"

The answer was an invitation to go away and let the owner alone, as he was, in certain specified respects, the vilest of living creatures, and no company for a fine gentyman.

The "fine gentyman" longed to blaspheme,—but before old Charlie!—in the name of pride, how could he? He mounted and started away.

"Tell you what I'll make wid you," said Charlie.

The other, guessing aright, turned back without dismounting, smiling.

"How much Belles Demoiselles hoes me now?" asked the deaf one.

"One hundred and eighty thousand dollars," said the Colonel, firmly.

"Yass," said Charlie. "I don't want Belles Demoiselles."

The old Colonel's quiet laugh intimated it made no difference either way.

"But me," continued Charlie, "me,—I'm got le Compte De Charleu's blood in me, any'ow,—a litt' bit, any'ow, ain't it?"

The Colonel nodded that it was.

"*Bien!* If I go out of dis place and don't go to Belles Demoiselles, de peoples will say,—day will say, 'Old Charlie he been all doze time tell a blame *lie!* He ain't no kin to his old grace-gran-muzzer, not a blame bit! He don't got nary drop of De Charleu blood to save his blame low-down old Injin soul! No, sare! What I want wid money, den? No, sare? My place for yours!"

He turned to go into the house, just too soon to see the Colonel make an ugly whisk at him with his riding-whip. Then the Colonel, too, moved off.

Two or three times over, as he ambled homeward, laughter broke through his annoyance, as he recalled old Charlie's family pride and the presumption of his offer. Yet each time he could but think better of—not the offer to swap, but the preposterous ancestral loyalty. It was so much better than he could have expected from his "low-down" relative, and not unlike his own whim withal—the proposition which went with it was forgiven.

This last defeat bore so harshly on the master of Belles Demoiselles, that the daughters, reading chagrin in his face, began to repent. They loved their father as daughters can, and when they saw their pretended dejection harassing him seriously they restrained their complaints, displayed more than ordinary tenderness, and heroically and ostentatiously concluded there was no place like Belles Demoiselles. But the new mood touched him more than the old, and only refined his discontent. Here was a man, rich without the care of riches, free from any real trouble, happiness as native to his house as perfume to his garden, deliberately, as it were with premeditated malice, taking joy by the shoulder and bidding her be gone to town, whither he might easily have followed, only that the very same ancestral nonsense that kept Injin Charlie from selling the old place for twice its value prevented him from choosing any other spot for a city home.

But by and by the charm of nature and the merry hearts around him prevailed; the fit of exalted sulks passed off, and after a while the year flared up at Christmas, flickered, and went out.

New Year came and passed; the beautiful garden of Belles Demoiselles put on its spring attire; the seven fair sisters moved from rose to rose; the cloud of discontent had warmed into invisible vapor in the rich sunlight of family affection, and on the common memory the only scar of last year's wound was old Charlie's sheer impertinence in crossing the caprice of the De Charleus. The cup of gladness seemed to fill with the filling of the river.

How high it was! Its tremendous current rolled and tumbled and spun along, hustling the long funeral flotillas of drift,—and how near shore it came! Men were out day and night, watching the levee. On windy nights even the old Colonel took part, and grew light-hearted with occupation and excitement, as every minute the river threw a white arm over the levee's top, as though it would vault over. But all held fast, and, as the summer drifted in, the water sunk down into its banks and looked quite incapable of harm.

On a summer afternoon of uncommon mildness, old Colonel Jean Albert Henri Joseph De Charleu-Marot, being in a mood for reverie, slipped the custody of his feminine rulers and sought the crown of the levee, where it was his wont to promenade. Presently he sat upon a stone bench,—a favorite seat. Before him lay his broadspread fields; near by, his lordly mansion; and being still,—perhaps by female contact,—somewhat sentimental, he fell to musing on his past. It was hardly worthy to be proud of. All its morning was reddened with mad frolic, and far toward the meridian it was marred with elegant rioting. Pride had kept him well nigh useless, and despised the honors won by valor; gaming had dimmed prosperity; death had taken his heavenly wife; voluptuous ease had mortgaged his lands; and yet his house still stood, his sweet-smelling fields were still fruitful, his name was fame enough; and yonder and yonder, among the trees and flowers, like angels walking in Eden, were the seven goddesses of his only worship.

Just then a slight sound behind him brought him to his feet. He cast his eyes anxiously to the outer edge of the little strip of bank between the levee's base and the river. There was nothing visible. He paused, with his ear toward the water, his face full of frightened expectation. Ha! There came a single plashing sound, like some great beast slipping into the river, and little waves in a wide semi-circle came out from under the bank and spread over the water!

"My God!"

He plunged down the levee and bounded through the low weeds to the edge of the bank. It was sheer, and the water about four feet below. He did not stand quite on the edge, but fell upon his knees a couple of yards away, wringing his hands, moaning and weeping, and staring through his watery eyes at a fine, long crevice just discernible under the matted grass, and curving outward on either hand toward the river.

"My God!" he sobbed aloud; "my God!" and even while he called, his God answered: the tough Bermuda grass stretched and snapped, the crevice slowly became a gape, and softly, gradually, with no sound but the closing of the water at last, a ton or more of earth settled into the boiling eddy and disappeared.

At the same instant a pulse of the breeze brought from the garden behind, the joyous, thoughtless laughter of the fair mistresses of Belles Demoiselles.

The old Colonel sprang up and clambered over the levee. Then forcing himself to a more composed movement, he hastened into the house and ordered his horse.

"Tell my children to make merry while I am gone," he left word. "I shall be back tonight," and the horse's hoofs clattered down a by-road leading to the city.

"Charlie," said the planter, riding up to a window, from which the old man's nightcap was thrust out, "what you say, Charlie,—my house for yours, eh, Charlie—what you say?"

"Ello!" said Charlie; "from where you come from dis time of to-night?"

"I come from the Exchange[22] in St. Louis-street." (A small fraction of the truth.)

---

[22]A saloon.

"What you want?" said matter-of-fact Charlie.

"I come to trade."

The low-down relative drew the worsted[23] off his ears. "Oh! yass," he said with an uncertain air.

"Well, old man Charlie, what you say: my house for yours,—like you said,—eh, Charlie?"

"I dunno," said Charlie; "it's nearly mine now. Why you don't stay dare youse'f?"

"*Because I don't want!*" said the Colonel savagely. "Is dat reason enough for you? You better take me in de notion, old man, I tell you,—yes!"

Charlie never winced; but how his answer delighted the Colonel! Quoth Charlie:

"I don't care—I take him!—*mais*, possession give right off."

"Not the whole plantation, Charlie; only—"

"I don't care," said Charlie; "we easy can fix dat. *Mais*, what for you don't want to keep him? I don't want him. You better keep him."

"Don't you try to make no fool of me, old man," cried the planter.

"Oh, no!" said the other. "Oh, no! but you make a fool of yourself, ain't it?"

The dumbfounded Colonel stared; Charlie went on:

"Yass! Belles Demoiselles is more wort' dan tree block like dis one. I pass by dare since two weeks. Oh, pritty Belles Demoiselles! De cane was wave in de wind, de garden smell like a bouquet, de white-cap was jump up and down on de river; seven *belles demoiselles* was ridin' on horses. 'Pritty, pritty, pritty!' says old Charlie. Ah! *Monsieur le père*, 'ow 'appy, 'appy, 'appy!"

"Yass!" he continued—the Colonel still staring—"le Compte De Charleu have two familie. One was low-down Choctaw, one was high up *noblesse*. He give the low-down Choctaw dis old rat-hole; he give Belles Demoiselles to your gran-fozzer; and now you don't be *satisfait*. What I'll do wid Belles Demoiselles? She'll break me in two years, yass. And what you'll do wid old Charlie's house, eh? You'll tear her down and make you'se'f a blame old fool. I rather wouldn't trade!"

The planter caught a big breathful of anger, but Charlie went straight on:

"I rather wouldn't, *mais* I will do it for you;—just the same, like Monsieur le Compte would say, 'Charlie, you old fool, I want to shange houses wid you.'"

So long as the Colonel suspected irony he was angry, but as Charlie seemed, after all, to be certainly in earnest, he began to feel conscience-stricken. He was by no means a tender man, but his lately-discovered misfortune had unhinged him, and this strange, undeserved, disinterested family fealty on the part of Charlie touched his heart. And should he still try to lead him into the pitfall he had dug? He hesitated;—no, he would show him the place by broad day-light, and if he chose to overlook the "caving bank," it would be his own fault;—a trade's a trade.

"Come," said the planter, "come at my house to-night; to-morrow we look at the place before breakfast, and finish the trade."

"For what?" said Charlie.

"Oh, because I got to come in town in the morning."

"I don't want," said Charlie. "How I'm goin' to come dere?"

"I git you a horse at the liberty stable."

"Well—anyhow—I don't care—I'll go." And they went.

When they had ridden a long time, and were on the road darkened by hedges of Cherokee rose, the Colonel called behind him to the "low-down" scion:

"Keep the road, old man."

"Eh?"

"Keep the road."

"Oh, yes; all right; I keep my word; we don't goin' to play no tricks, eh?"

But the Colonel seemed not to hear. His ungenerous design was beginning to be hateful to him. Not only old Charlie's unprovoked goodness was prevailing; the eulogy on Belles Demoiselles had stirred the depths of an intense love for his beautiful home. True, if he held to it, the caving of the bank, at its present fearful speed, would let the house into the river within three months; but were it not better to lose it so, than sell his birthright? Again — coming back to the first thought, — to betray his own blood! It was only Injin Charlie; but had not the De Charleu blood just spoken out in him? Unconsciously he groaned.

After a time they struck a path approaching the plantation in the rear, and a little after, passing from behind a clump of live-oaks, they came in sight of the villa. It looked so like a gem, shining through its dark grove, so like a great glow-worm in the dense foliage, so significant of luxury and gayety, that the poor master, from an overflowing heart, groaned again.

"What?" asked Charlie.

The Colonel only drew his rein, and, dismounting mechanically, contemplated the sight before him. The high, arched doors and windows were thrown wide to the summer air; from every opening the bright light of numerous candelabra darted out upon the sparkling foliage of magnolia and bay, and here and there in the spacious verandas a colored lantern swayed in the gentle breeze. A sound of revel fell on the ear, the music of harps; and across one window, brighter than the rest, flitted, once or twice, the shadows of dancers. But oh! the shadows flitting across the heart of the fair mansion's master!

"Old Charlie," said he, gazing fondly at his house, "you and me is both old, eh?"

"Yass," said the stolid Charlie.

"And we has both been bad enough in our time, eh, Charlie?"

Charlie, surprised at the tender tone, repeated, "Yass."

"And you and me is mighty close?"

"Blame close, yass."

"But you never know me to cheat, old man!"

"No," — impassively.

"And do you think I would cheat you now?"

"I dunno," said Charlie. "I don't believe."

"Well, old man, old man," — his voice began to quiver, — "I shan't cheat you now. My God! — old man, I tell you — you better not make the trade!"

"Because for what?" asked Charlie in plain anger; but both looked quickly toward the house! The Colonel tossed his hands wildly in the air, rushed forward a step or two, and giving one fearful scream of agony and fright, fell forward on his face in the path. Old Charlie stood transfixed with horror. Belles Demoiselles, the realm of maiden beauty, the home of merriment, the house of dancing, all in the tremor and glow of pleasure, suddenly sunk, with one short, wild wail of terror — sunk, sunk, down, down, down, into the merciless, unfathomable flood of the Mississippi.

Twelve long months were midnight to the mind of the childless father; when they were only half gone, he took his bed; and every day, and every night, old Charlie, the "low-down," the "fool," watched him tenderly, tended him lovingly, for the sake of his name, his misfortunes, and his broken heart. No woman's step crossed the floor of the sick-chamber, whose western dormer-windows overpeered the dingy architecture of old Charlie's block; Charlie and a skilled physician, the one all interest, the other all gentleness, hope, and patience — these only entered by the door; but by the window came in a sweet-scented evergreen vine, transplanted from the caving bank of Belles Demoiselles. It caught the rays of sunset in its flowery net and let them softly in upon the sick man's bed; gathered the glancing beams of the moon at midnight, and often wakened the sleeper to look, with his mindless eyes, upon their pretty silver fragments strewn upon the floor.

By and by there seemed — there was — a twinkling dawn of returning reason. Slowly, peacefully, with an increase unseen from day to day, the light of reason came into the eyes, and speech became coherent; but withal there came a failing of the wrecked body, and the doctor said that monsieur was both better and worse.

One evening, as Charlie sat by the vine-clad window with his fireless pipe in his hand, the old Colonel's eyes fell full upon his own, and rested there.

"Charl—," he said with an effort, and his delighted nurse hastened to the bed-side and bowed his best ear. There was an unsuccessful effort or two, and then he whispered, smiling with sweet sadness, ——

"We didn't trade."

The truth, in this case, was a secondary matter to Charlie; the main point was to give a pleasing answer. So he nodded his head decidedly, as who should say—"Oh yes, we did, it was a bona-fide swap!" but when he saw the smile vanish, he tried the other expedient and shook his head with still more vigor, to signify that they had not so much as approached a bargain; and the smile returned.

Charlie wanted to see the vine recognized. He stepped backward to the window with a broad smile, shook the foliage, nodded and looked smart.

"I know," said the Colonel, with beaming eyes, "—many weeks."

The next day—

"Charl—"

The best ear went down.

"Send for a priest."

The priest came, and was alone with him a whole afternoon. When he left, the patient was very haggard and exhausted, but smiled and would not suffer the crucifix to be removed from his breast.

One more morning came. Just before dawn Charlie, lying on a pallet in the room, thought he was called, and came to the bed-side.

"Old man," whispered the failing invalid, "is it caving yet?"

Charlie nodded.

"It won't pay you out."

"Oh dat makes not'ing," said Charlie. Two big tears rolled down his brown face. "Dat makes not'in."

The Colonel whispered once more:

"*Mes belles demoiselles!*—in paradise;—in the garden—I shall be with them at sunrise;" and so it was.

1874, 1879

JOEL CHANDLER HARRIS
(1848–1908)

Joel Chandler Harris was one of the most admired writers of his day. In *Life on the Mississippi* (1883), Mark Twain called him "the only master" of Negro dialect "the country has produced." President Theodore Roosevelt in 1905 credited Harris with healing differences between North and South in his stories, saying, "I regard Harris as the greatest educator in the South."

This is high praise for someone who grew up poor during the Civil War period in an area of the South devastated by Union armies, especially General Sherman's notorious march through Georgia to the sea in 1864. Harris was born to a seamstress, Mary Harris, in Eatonton, Georgia, in 1848, his father having abandoned his mother shortly before the son was born. He grew up hearing his mother reading from books and early acquired a love of literature.

Neighbors helped the struggling young mother, and in 1862 Harris found himself working as printer's devil on a weekly newspaper published on the plantation, "Turnwold," near Eatonton. From the age of thirteen to seventeen, Harris lived on the plantation where he had the run of the library. And he roamed the plantation grounds, learning the Negro speech and listening to the Negro tales, legends, and folklore. He absorbed everything he saw and heard, leaving it to lie fallow deep within him for an as yet undisclosed future use.

The advent of Sherman's army abruptly ended his life on the plantation. He held several jobs on various newspapers in Georgia, finally settling in Atlanta in 1876, by then with a wife and growing family. He soon joined *The Atlanta Constitution*, where he remained for twenty-four years, writing feature articles, book reviews, and humorous pieces. He wrote his first Uncle Remus story and published it in the *Atlanta Constitution*, October 26, 1876. In the process, he discovered that he had hidden within himself the sources for his finest creative achievement.

Harris published *Uncle Remus: His Songs and Sayings* in 1881 (but it carried an 1880 copyright). The book was immensely popular in both the North and South, and was followed by *Nights with Uncle Remus* (1883), *Uncle Remus and His Friends* (1892), and *Told by Uncle Remus* (1905). The stories have their roots in African folklore, and the animal fables of Aesop and Chaucer, but the art is all Harris's. At the heart of the dialect tales is the remarkable character of the old plantation slave, shrewd and warm-hearted, telling stories to a little white boy, who is held enthralled. Slave life and slave wisdom are captured in the animal characterizations, such as in the quick and feisty Brer Rabbit repeatedly thwarting the scheming Brer Fox. But the animals also exhibit aspects of personality—greed or generosity, ferocity or tenderness, self-centeredness or compassion—which are recognizably human, and which have made the tales universally appealing.

Harris went on to write many books, including children's stories, novels, and tales of southern life. Notable among these are *Mingo and Other Sketches in Black and White* (1884) and *Free Joe and Other Georgian Sketches* (1887). But he never again equalled the success of his Uncle Remus stories.

ADDITIONAL READING

Joel Chandler Harris, Editor and Essayist: Miscellaneous Literary, Political, and Social Writings, ed. Julia C. Harris, 1931; *The Complete Tales of Uncle Remus*, ed. Richard Chase, 1955.

Julia C. Harris, *The Life and Letters of Joel Chandler Harris*, 1918; Robert L. Wiggins, *The Life of Joel Chandler Harris from Obscurity in Boyhood to Fame in Early Manhood*, 1918; Stella Brooks, *Joel Chandler Harris—Folklorist*, 1950; Paul M. Cousins, *Joel Chandler Harris: A Biography*, 1968; R. Bruce Bickley, Jr., *Joel Chandler Harris*, 1978, 1987, and *Joel Chandler Harris: A Reference Guide*, 1978; R. Bruce Bickley, Jr., ed., *Critical Essays on Joel Chandler Harris*, 1981.

TEXT

Uncle Remus, His Songs and Sayings: The Folklore of the Old Plantation, 1881.

from Uncle Remus

I

UNCLE REMUS INITIATES THE LITTLE BOY

One evening recently, the lady whom Uncle Remus calls "Miss Sally" missed her little seven-year-old. Making search for him through the house and through the yard, she heard the sound of voices in the old man's cabin, and, looking through the window, saw the child sitting by Uncle Remus. His head rested against the old man's arm, and he was gazing with an expression of the most intense interest into the rough, weather-beaten face, that beamed so kindly upon him. This is what "Miss Sally" heard:

"Bimeby, one day, arter Brer Fox bin doin' all dat he could fer ter ketch Brer Rabbit, en Brer Rabbit bin doin' all he could fer ter keep 'im fum it, Brer Fox say to hisse'f dat he'd put up a game on Brer Rabbit, en he ain't mo'n got de wuds out'n his mouf twel Brer Rabbit come a lopin' up de big road, lookin' des ez plump, en ez fat, en ez sassy ez a Moggin hoss[1] in a barley-patch.

"'Hol' on dar, Brer Rabbit,' sez Brer Fox, sezee.

"'I ain't got time, Brer Fox,' sez Brer Rabbit, sezee, sorter mendin' his licks.[2]

"'I wanter have some confab[3] wid you, Brer Rabbit,' sez Brer Fox, sezee.

"'All right, Brer Fox, but you better holler fum whar you stan'. I'm monstus full er fleas dis mawnin',' sez Brer Rabbit, sezee.

"'I seed Brer B'ar yistiddy,' sez Brer Fox, sezee, 'en he sorter rake me over de coals kaze you en me ain't make frens en live naberly, en I tole 'im dat I'd see you.'

"Den Brer Rabbit scratch one year wid his off[4] hine-foot sorter jub'usly,[5] en den he ups en sez, sezee:

"'All a settin',[6] Brer Fox. Spose'n you drap roun' termorrer en take dinner wid me. We ain't got no great doin's at our house, but I speck de ole 'oman en de chilluns kin sorter scramble roun' en git up sump'n fer ter stay yo' stummuck.'

"'I'm 'gree'ble, Brer Rabbit,' sez Brer Fox, sezee.

"'Den I'll 'pen'[7] on you,' sez Brer Rabbit, sezee.

"Nex' day, Mr. Rabbit an' Miss Rabbit got up soon, 'fo' day, en raided on a gyarden like Miss Sally's out dar, en got some cabbiges, en some roas'n years,[8] en some sparrer-grass,[9] en dey fix up a smashin' dinner. Bimeby one er de little Rabbits, playin' out in de back-yard, come runnin' in hollerin', 'Oh, ma! oh, ma! I seed Mr. Fox a comin'!' En den Brer Rabbit he tuck de chilluns by der years en make um set down, en den him en Miss Rabbit sorter dally roun' waitin' for Brer Fox. En dey keep on waitin', but no Brer Fox ain't come. Atter 'while Brer Rabbit goes to de do', easy like, en peep out, en dar, stickin' out fum behime de cornder, wuz de tip-een' er Brer Fox tail. Den Brer Rabbit shot de do' en sot down, en put his paws behime his years en begin fer ter sing:

> "'De place wharbouts you spill de grease,
>   Right dar youer boun' ter slide,
> An' whar you fine a bunch er ha'r,
>   You'll sholy fine de hide.'

"Nex' day, Brer Fox sont word by Mr. Mink, en skuze hisse'f kaze he wuz too sick fer ter come, en he ax Brer Rabbit fer ter come en take dinner wid him, en Brer Rabbit say he wuz 'gree'ble.

"Bimeby, w'en de shadders wuz at der shortes', Brer Rabbit he sorter brush up en santer down ter Brer Fox's house, en w'en he got dar, he yer somebody groanin', en he look in de do' en dar he see Brer Fox settin' up in a rockin' cheer all wrop up wid flannil, en he look mighty weak. Brer Rabbit look all 'roun', he did, but he ain't see no dinner. De dish-pan wuz settin' on de table, en close by wuz a kyarvin' knife.

"'Look like you gwineter have chicken for dinner, Brer Fox,' sez Brer Rabbit, sezee.

"'Yes, Brer Rabbit, deyer nice, en fresh, en tender,' sez Brer Fox, sezee.

---

[1] Morgan horse, strong, light trotting horse.
[2] Going faster.
[3] Talk, confabulation.
[4] Right.
[5] Dubiously.

[6] Agreed.
[7] Depend.
[8] Roasting ears (of corn).
[9] Asparagus.

"Den Brer Rabbit sorter pull his mustarsh, en say: 'You ain't got no calamus root,[10] is you, Brer Fox? I done got so now dat I can't eat no chicken 'ceppin she's seasoned up wid calamus root.' En wid dat Brer Rabbit lipt out er de do' and dodge 'mong de bushes, en sot dar watchin' fer Brer Fox; en he ain't watch long, nudder, kaze Brer Fox flung off de flannil en crope out er de house en got whar he could cloze in on Brer Rabbit, en bimeby Brer Rabbit holler out: 'Oh, Brer Fox! I'll des put yo' calamus root out yer on dish yer stump. Better come git it while hit's fresh,' and wid dat Brer Rabbit gallop off home. En Brer Fox ain't never kotch 'im yit, en w'at's mo', honey, he ain't gwineter."

II

THE WONDERFUL TAR-BABY STORY

"Didn't the fox *never* catch the rabbit, Uncle Remus?" asked the little boy the next evening.

"He come mighty nigh it, honey, sho's you bawn—Brer Fox did. One day atter Brer Rabbit fool 'im wid dat calamus root, Brer Fox went ter wuk en got 'im some tar, en mix it wid some turkentime, en fix up a contrapshun wat he call a Tar-Baby, en he tuck dish yer[1] Tar-Baby en he sot 'er in de big road, en den he lay off in de bushes fer ter see wat de news wuz gwineter be. En he didn't hatter[2] wait long, nudder, kaze bimeby here come Brer Rabbit pacin' down de road—lippity-clippity, clippity-lip-pity—dez ez sassy ez a jay-bird. Brer Fox, he lay low. Brer Rabbit come prancin' 'long twel he spy de Tar-Baby, en den he fotch up on his behime legs like he wuz 'stonished. De Tar-Baby, she sot dar, she did, en Brer Fox, he lay low.

"'Mawnin'!' sez Brer Rabbit, sezee—'nice wedder dis mawnin',' sezee.

"Tar-Baby ain't sayin' nuthin', en Brer Fox, he lay low.

"'How duz yo' sym'tums seem ter segashuate?'[3] sez Brer Rabbit, sezee.

"Brer Fox, he wink his eye slow, en lay low, en de Tar-Baby, she ain't sayin' nuthin'.

"'How you come on, den? Is you deaf?' sez Brer Rabbit, sezee. 'Kaze if you is, I kin holler louder,' sezee.

"Tar-Baby stay still, en Brer Fox, he lay low.

"'Youer stuck up, dat's w'at you is,' says Brer Rabbit, sezee, 'en I'm gwineter kyore[4] you, dat's w'at I'm a gwineter do,' sezee.

"Brer Fox, he sorter chuckle in his stummuck, he did, but Tar-Baby ain't sayin' nuthin'.

"'I'm gwineter larn you howter talk ter 'specttubble fokes ef hit's de las' ack,' sez Brer Rabbit, sezee. 'Ef you don't take off dat hat en tell me howdy, I'm gwineter bus' you wide open,' sezee.

"Tar-Baby stay still, en Brer Fox, he lay low.

"Brer Rabbit keep on axin' 'im, en de Tar-Baby, she keep on sayin' nuthin', twel present'y Brer Rabbit draw back wid his fis', he did, en blip he tuck 'er side er de head. Right dar's whar he broke his merlasses jug. His fis' stuck, en he can't pull loose. De tar hilt 'im. But Tar-Baby, she stay still, en Brer Fox, he lay low.

"'Ef you don't lemme loose, I'll knock you agin,' sez Brer Rabbit, sezee, en wid dat he fotch 'er a wipe wid de udder han', en dat stuck. Tar-Baby, she ain't sayin' nuthin', en Brer Fox, he lay low.

"'Tu'n me loose, fo' I kick de natal stuffin' outen you,' sez Brer Rabbit, sezee, but de Tar-Baby, she ain't sayin' nuthin'. She des hilt on, en den Brer Rabbit lose de use er his feet in de same way. Brer Fox, he lay low. Den Brer Rabbit squall out dat ef de Tar-Baby don't tu'n 'im loose he butt 'er cranksided. En den he butted, en his head got

---

[10]Sweet flag, a plant with long leaves and an aromatic root.
[1]This here.
[2]Have to.

[3]I.e., how are you feeling? ("How do your symptoms seem to aggravate [you]?").
[4]Cure.

stuck. Den Brer Fox, he sa'ntered fort', lookin' des ez innercent ez wunner yo'[5] mammy's mockin'-birds.

"'Howdy, Brer Rabbit,' sez Brer Fox, sezee. 'You look sorter stuck up dis mawnin',' sezee, en den he rolled on de groun', en laft en laft twel he couldn't laff no mo'. 'I speck you'll take dinner wid me dis time, Brer Rabbit. I done laid in some calamus root, en I ain't gwineter take no skuse,' sez Brer Fox, sezee."

Here Uncle Remus paused, and drew a two-pound yam out of the ashes.

"Did the fox eat the rabbit?" asked the little boy to whom the story had been told.

"Dat's all de fur[6] de tale goes," replied the old man. "He mout, en den agin he moutent. Some say Jedge B'ar come 'long en loosed 'im — some say he didn't. I hear Miss Sally callin'. You better run 'long."

IV

HOW MR. RABBIT WAS TOO SHARP FOR MR. FOX

"Uncle Remus," said the little boy one evening, when he had found the old man with little or nothing to do, "did the fox kill and eat the rabbit when he caught him with the Tar-Baby?"

"Law, honey, ain't I tell you 'bout dat?" replied the old darkey, chuckling slyly. "I 'clar ter grashus[1] I ought er tole you dat, but ole man Nod wuz ridin' on my eyeleds 'twel a leetle mo'n I'd a dis'member'd my own name, en den on to dat here come yo' mammy hollerin' atter you.

"W'at I tell you w'en I fus' begin? I tole you Brer Rabbit wuz a monstus soon beas';[2] leas'ways dat's w'at I laid out fer ter tell you. Well, den, honey, don't you go en make no udder kalkalashuns, kaze in dem days Brer Rabbit en his fambly wuz at de head er de gang w'en enny racket wuz on han', en dar dey stayed. 'Fo' you begins fer ter wipe yo' eyes 'bout Brer Rabbit, you wait en see whar'bouts Brer Rabbit gwineter fetch up at. But dat's needer yer ner dar.

"W'en Brer Fox fine Brer Rabbit mixt up wid de Tar-Baby, he feel mighty good, en he roll on de groun' en laff. Bimeby he up'n say, sezee:

"'Well, I speck I got you dis time, Brer Rabbit,' sezee; 'maybe I ain't, but I speck I is. You been runnin' roun' here sassin' atter me a mighty long time, but I speck you done come ter de een' er de row.[3] You bin cuttin' up yo' capers en bouncin' 'roun' in dis naberhood ontwel you come ter b'leeve yo'se'f de boss er de whole gang. En den youer allers some'rs whar you got no bizness,' sez Brer Fox, sezee. 'Who ax you fer ter come en strike up a 'quaintence wid dish yer Tar-Baby? En who stuck you up dar whar you iz? Nobody in de roun' worril.[4] You des tuck en jam yo'se'f on dat Tar-Baby widout waitin' fer enny invite,' sez Brer Fox, sezee, 'en dar you is, en dar you'll stay twel I fixes up a bresh-pile and fires her up, kaze I'm gwineter bobbycue[5] you dis day, sho,' sez Brer Fox, sezee.

"Den Brer Rabbit talk mighty 'umble.

"'I don't keer w'at you do wid me, Brer Fox,' sezee, 'so you don't fling me in dat brier-patch. Roas' me, Brer Fox,' sezee, 'but don't fling me in dat brier-patch,' sezee.

"'Hit's so much trouble fer ter kindle a fier,' sez Brer Fox, sezee, 'dat I speck I'll hatter[6] hang you,' sezee.

"'Hang me des ez high as you please, Brer Fox,' sez Brer Rabbit, sezee, 'but do fer de Lord's sake don't fling me in dat brier-patch,' sezee.

"'I ain't got no string,' sez Brer Fox, sezee, 'en now I speck I'll hatter drown you,' sezee.

"'Drown me des ez deep ez you please, Brer Fox,' sez Brer Rabbit, sezee, 'but do don't fling me in dat brier-patch,' sezee.

---

[5]One of your.
[6]The further.
[1]I declare to gracious.
[2]Monstrously quick beast.

[3]End of the row.
[4]Round world.
[5]Barbecue.
[6]Have to.

"'Dey ain't no water nigh,' sez Brer Fox, sezee, 'en now I speck I'll hatter skin you,' sezee.

"'Skin me, Brer Fox,' sez Brer Rabbit, sezee, 'snatch out my eyeballs, t'ar out my years by de roots, en cut off my legs,' sezee, 'but do please, Brer Fox, don't fling me in dat brier-patch,' sezee.

"Co'se Brer Fox wanter hurt Brer Rabbit bad ez he kin, so he cotch 'im by de behime legs en slung 'im right in de middle er de brier-patch. Dar wuz a considerbul flutter whar Brer Rabbit struck de bushes, en Brer Fox sorter hang 'roun' fer ter see w'at wuz gwineter happen. Bimeby he hear somebody call 'im, en way up de hill he see Brer Rabbit settin' cross-legged on a chinkapin[7] log koamin' de pitch outen his har wid a chip. Den Brer Fox know dat he bin swop off[8] mighty bad. Brer Rabbit wuz bleedzed[9] fer ter fling back some er his sass, en he holler out:

"'Bred en bawn in a brier-patch, Brer Fox—bred en bawn in a brier-patch!' en wid dat he skip out des ez lively ez a cricket in de embers.'"

1881

CHARLES W. CHESNUTT
(1858–1932)

Charles W. Chesnutt was a light-skinned black man who could—but didn't—pass for white. When he first began publishing stories, however, his color was not revealed to the public. His early stories were narrated by a literate, apparently white character whose black servant narrated tales of Negro life in Negro dialect. The stories were ingeniously crafted so as to present a black point of view without alienating a predominantly white audience.

It had been Chesnutt's purpose from the beginning to reach a white audience. He wrote in his journal in 1880 (when he was twenty-two): "If I do write, I shall write for a purpose. . . . The object of my writings would be not so much the elevation of the colored people as the elevation of the white—for I consider the unjust spirit of caste which is so insidious as to pervade a whole nation and so powerful as to subject a whole race and all connected with it to scorn and social ostracism—I consider this a barrier to the moral progress of the American people."

Chesnutt was born in Cleveland in 1858 into a family of free blacks who had come to Ohio from North Carolina. His father served in the Union Army, and after the war decided to move his family back to the land of his birth. The family settled in Fayetteville, North Carolina. Chesnutt first was a student and then a teacher in the country schools of North Carolina. He was highly disciplined and adhered to a demanding schedule of self-education. His determined program led eventually to knowledge of French, Latin, German, legal stenography, and law.

In search of better opportunities to support his growing family, Chesnutt went North, settling finally in 1884 in Cleveland, and devoted himself to a career in legal stenography and law (he passed the Ohio bar in 1887 with the highest score). At the same time, he continued the writing that he had begun in his youth. He experienced some success in publishing in scattered newspapers and

[7]Chinquapin, dwarf chestnut tree.
[8]Swapped off, fooled.
[9]Obliged.

magazines and then a breakthrough with the publication of "The Goophered Grapevine" in *The Atlantic Monthly* in 1887.

Other stories followed, leading to the publication in 1899 of three major books that would constitute the basis of his reputation as a writer. *The Conjure Woman* contained tales in dialect of "conjuring" or magic rooted in black legend and folklore but with more complexity and authenticity than the Uncle Remus tales of Joel Chandler Harris. *The Wife of His Youth and Other Stories of the Color Line* dealt with characters of mixed blood, some of whom were light enough to "pass." The third book was a biography of the escaped slave leader Frederick Douglass.

Chesnutt continued to write, but his work became more polemical, and never again achieved the popularity of these initial books. His first novel, *The House Behind the Cedars* (1900), dealt with the "color line," a subject for which his audience was apparently not prepared. Even his supporter William Dean Howells found bitterness in *The Marrow Tradition* (1901), a novel based on the 1898 race riot in Wilmington, North Carolina. The more pessimistic work, *The Colonel's Dream* (1905), with a strong denunciatory tone, attracted little attention.

Chesnutt published no other books during his lifetime. He had completed several novels, however, by the time of his death in 1932. In 1928 he was awarded the Spingarn medal by the National Association for the Advancement of Colored People for "pioneer work as a literary artist depicting the life and struggles of Americans of Negro descent." Recent criticism has testified to the ways in which Chesnutt played a critical role in establishing a tradition of black literature to which later black writers could turn for sustenance and inspiration.

ADDITIONAL READING

The Short Fiction of Charles W. Chesnutt, ed. Sylvia L. Render, 1974, 1981.

Helen M. Chesnutt, *Charles Waddell Chesnutt: Pioneer of the Color Line*, 1952; J. Noel Heermance, *Charles W. Chesnutt: America's First Black Novelist*, 1974; Frances R. Keller, *An American Crusader: The Life of Charles Waddell Chesnutt*, 1978; Curtis W. Ellison and E. W. Metcalf, Jr., *Charles W. Chesnutt: A Reference Guide*, 1980; Sylvia L. Render, *Charles W. Chesnutt*, 1980; William L. Andrews, *The Literary Career of Charles Waddell Chesnutt*, 1980; Marjorie Pryse and Hortense J. Spillers, eds., *Conjuring: Black Women, Fiction, and Literary Tradition*, 1985.

TEXT

The Wife of His Youth and Other Stories of the Color Line, 1899.

The Sheriff's Children

Branson County, North Carolina, is in a sequestered district of one of the staidest and most conservative States of the Union. Society in Branson County is almost primitive in its simplicity. Most of the white people own the farms they till, and even before the war there were no very wealthy families to force their neighbors, by comparison, into the category of "poor whites."

To Branson County, as to most rural communities in the South, the war is the one historical event that overshadows all others. It is the era from which all local chronicles are dated, — births, deaths, marriages, storms, freshets. No description of the life of any Southern community would be perfect that failed to emphasize the all pervading influence of the great conflict.

Yet the fierce tide of war that had rushed through the cities and along the great highways of the country had comparatively speaking but slightly disturbed the sluggish current of life in this region, remote from railroads and navigable streams. To the north in Virginia, to the west in Tennessee, and all along the seaboard the war had raged; but the thunder of its cannon had not disturbed the echoes of Branson County, where the loudest sounds heard were the crack of some hunter's rifle, the baying of some deep-mouthed hound, or the yodel of some tuneful negro on his way through the pine forest. To the east, Sherman's army had passed on its march to the sea; but no straggling band of "bummers"[1] had penetrated the confines of Branson County. The war, it is true, had robbed the county of the flower of its young manhood; but the burden of taxation, the doubt and uncertainty of the conflict, and the sting of ultimate defeat, had been borne by the people with an apathy that robbed misfortune of half its sharpness.

The nearest approach to town life afforded by Branson County is found in the little village of Troy, the county seat, a hamlet with a population of four or five hundred.

Ten years make little difference in the appearance of these remote Southern towns. If a railroad is built through one of them, it infuses some enterprise; the social corpse is galvanized by the fresh blood of civilization that pulses along the farthest ramifications of our great system of commercial highways. At the period of which I write, no railroad had come to Troy. If a traveler, accustomed to the bustling life of cities, could have ridden through Troy on a summer day, he might easily have fancied himself in a deserted village. Around him he would have seen weather-beaten houses, innocent of paint, the shingled roofs in many instances covered with a rich growth of moss. Here and there he would have met a razor-backed hog lazily rooting his way along the principal thoroughfare; and more than once he would probably have had to disturb the slumbers of some yellow dog, dozing away the hours in the ardent sunshine, and reluctantly yielding up his place in the middle of the dusty road.

On Saturdays the village presented a somewhat livelier appearance, and the shade trees around the court house square and along Front Street served as hitching-posts for a goodly number of horses and mules and stunted oxen, belonging to the farmer-folk who had come in to trade at the two or three local stores.

A murder was a rare event in Branson County. Every well-informed citizen could tell the number of homicides committed in the county for fifty years back, and whether the slayer, in any given instance, had escaped, either by flight or acquittal, or had suffered the penalty of the law. So, when it became known in Troy early one Friday morning in summer, about ten years after the war, that old Captain Walker, who had served in Mexico under Scott, and had left an arm on the field of Gettysburg, had been foully murdered during the night, there was intense excitement in the village. Business was practically suspended, and the citizens gathered in little groups to discuss the murder, and speculate upon the identity of the murderer. It transpired from testimony at the coroner's inquest, held during the morning, that a strange mulatto had been seen going in the direction of Captain Walker's house the night before, and had been met going away from Troy early Friday morning, by a farmer on his way to town. Other circumstances seemed to connect the stranger with the crime. The sheriff organized a posse to search for him, and early in the evening, when most of the citizens of Troy were at supper, the suspected man was brought in and lodged in the county jail.

By the following morning the news of the capture had spread to the farthest limits of the county. A much larger number of people than usual came to town that Saturday,—bearded men in straw hats and blue homespun shirts, and butternut trousers[2]

---

[1] Union soldiers who deserted to plunder the countryside in the wake of Sherman's march; known as "Sherman's bummers."

[2] Trousers dyed a brownish color with dye obtained from the bark or roots of the butternut tree.

of great amplitude of material and vagueness of outline; women in homespun frocks and slat-bonnets, with faces as expressionless as the dreary sandhills which gave them a meagre sustenance.

The murder was almost the sole topic of conversation. A steady stream of curious observers visited the house of mourning, and gazed upon the rugged face of the old veteran, now stiff and cold in death; and more than one eye dropped a tear at the remembrance of the cheery smile, and the joke — sometimes superannuated, generally feeble, but always good-natured — with which the captain had been wont to greet his acquaintances. There was a growing sentiment of anger among these stern men, toward the murderer who had thus cut down their friend, and a strong feeling that ordinary justice was too slight a punishment for such a crime.

Toward noon there was an informal gathering of citizens in Dan Tyson's store.

"I hear it 'lowed that Square Kyahtah's too sick ter hol' co'te this evenin'," said one, "an' that the purlim'nary hearin' 'll haf ter go over 'tel nex' week."

A look of disappointment went round the crowd. "Hit's the durndes', meanes' murder ever committed in this caounty," said another, with moody emphasis.

"I s'pose the nigger 'lowed the Cap'n had some greenbacks," observed a third speaker.

"The Cap'n," said another, with an air of superior information, "has left two bairls of Confedrit money, which he 'spected 'ud be good some day er nuther."

This statement gave rise to a discussion of the speculative value of Confederate money; but in a little while the conversation returned to the murder.

"Hangin' air too good fer the murderer," said one; "he oughter be burnt, stidier bein' hung."

There was an impressive pause at this point, during which a jug of moonlight whiskey went the round of the crowd.

"Well," said a round-shouldered farmer, who, in spite of his peaceable expression and faded gray eye, was known to have been one of the most daring followers of a rebel guerrilla chieftain, "what air yer gwine ter do about it? Ef you fellers air gwine ter set down an' let a wuthless nigger kill the bes' white man in Branson, an' not say nuthin' ner do nuthin', *I'll* move outen the caounty."

This speech gave tone and direction to the rest of the conversation. Whether the fear of losing the round-shouldered farmer operated to bring about the result or not is immaterial to this narrative; but, at all events, the crowd decided to lynch the negro. They agreed that this was the least that could be done to avenge the death of their murdered friend, and that it was a becoming way in which to honor his memory. They had some vague notions of the majesty of the law and the rights of the citizen, but in the passion of the moment these sunk into oblivion; a white man had been killed by a negro.

"The Cap'n was an ole sodger," said one of his friends solemnly. "He'll sleep better when he knows that a co'te-martial has be'n hilt an' jestice done."

By agreement the lynchers were to meet at Tyson's store at five o'clock in the afternoon, and proceed thence to the jail, which was situated down the Lumberton Dirt Road (as the old turnpike antedating the plank-road was called), about half a mile south of the court-house. When the preliminaries of the lynching had been arranged, and a committee appointed to manage the affair, the crowd dispersed, some to go to their dinners, and some to secure recruits for the lynching party.

It was twenty minutes to five o'clock, when an excited negro, panting and perspiring, rushed up to the back door of Sheriff Campbell's dwelling, which stood at a little distance from the jail and somewhat farther than the latter building from the court-house. A turbaned colored woman came to the door in response to the negro's knock.

"Hoddy, Sis' Nance."

"Hoddy, Brer Sam."

"Is de shurff in," inquired the negro.

"Yas, Brer Sam, he's eatin' his dinner," was the answer.

"Will yer ax 'im ter step ter de do' a minute, Sis' Nance?"

The woman went into the dining-room, and a moment later the sheriff came to the door. He was a tall, muscular man, of a ruddier complexion than is usual among Southerners. A pair of keen, deep-set gray eyes looked out from under bushy eyebrows, and about his mouth was a masterful expression, which a full beard, once sandy in color, but now profusely sprinkled with gray, could not entirely conceal. The day was hot; the sheriff had discarded his coat and vest, and had his white shirt open at the throat.

"What do you want, Sam?" he inquired of the negro, who stood hat in hand, wiping the moisture from his face with a ragged shirt-sleeve.

"Shurff, dey gwine ter hang de pris'ner w'at's lock' up in de jail. Dey're comin' dis a-way now. I wuz layin' down on a sack er corn down at de sto', behine a pile er flour-bairls, w'en I hearn Doc' Cain en Kunnel Wright talkin' erbout it. I slip' outen de back do', en run here as fas' as I could. I hearn you say down ter de sto' once't dat you wouldn't let nobody take a pris'ner 'way fum you widout walkin' over yo' dead body, en I thought I'd let you know 'fo' dey come, so yer could pertec' de pris'ner."

The sheriff listened calmly, but his face grew firmer, and a determined gleam lit up his gray eyes. His frame grew more erect, and he unconsciously assumed the attitude of a soldier who momentarily expects to meet the enemy face to face.

"Much obliged, Sam," he answered. "I'll protect the prisoner. Who's coming?"

"I dunno who-all *is* comin'," replied the negro. "Dere's Mistah McSwayne, en Doc' Cain, en Maje' McDonal', en Kunnel Wright, en a heap er yuthers. I wuz so skeered I done furgot mo' d'n half un em. I spec' dey mus' be mos' here by dis time, so I'll git outen de way, fer I don' want nobody fer ter think I wuz mix' up in dis business." The negro glanced nervously down the road toward the town, and made a movement as if to go away.

"Won't you have some dinner first?" asked the sheriff.

The negro looked longingly in at the open door, and sniffed the appetizing odor of boiled pork and collards.

"I ain't got no time fer ter tarry, Shurff," he said, "but Sis' Nance mought gin me sump'n I could kyar in my han' en eat on de way."

A moment later Nancy brought him a huge sandwich of split corn-pone, with a thick slice of fat bacon inserted between the halves, and a couple of baked yams. The negro hastily replaced his ragged hat on his head, dropped the yams in the pocket of his capacious trousers, and, taking the sandwich in his hand, hurried across the road and disappeared in the woods beyond.

The sheriff reëntered the house, and put on his coat and hat. He then took down a double-barreled shotgun and loaded it with buckshot. Filling the chambers of a revolver with fresh cartridges, he slipped it into the pocket of the sack-coat which he wore.

A comely young woman in a calico dress watched these proceedings with anxious surprise.

"Where are you going, father?" she asked. She had not heard the conversation with the negro.

"I am goin' over to the jail," responded the sheriff. "There's a mob comin' this way to lynch the nigger we've got locked up. But they won't do it," he added, with emphasis.

"Oh, father! don't go!" pleaded the girl, clinging to his arm; "they'll shoot you if you don't give him up."

"You never mind me, Polly," said her father reassuringly, as he gently unclasped her hands from his arm. "I'll take care of myself and the prisoner, too. There ain't a man in Branson County that would shoot me. Besides, I have faced fire too often to be scared away from my duty. You keep close in the house," he continued, "and if any one disturbs you just use the old horse-pistol in the top bureau drawer. It's a little old-fashioned, but it did good work a few years ago."

The young girl shuddered at this sanguinary allusion, but made no further objection to her father's departure.

The sheriff of Branson was a man far above the average of the community in wealth, education, and social position. His had been one of the few families in the county that before the war had owned large estates and numerous slaves. He had graduated at the State University at Chapel Hill, and had kept up some acquaintance with current literature and advanced thought. He had traveled some in his youth, and was looked up to in the county as an authority on all subjects connected with the outer world. At first an ardent supporter of the Union, he had opposed the secession movement in his native State as long as opposition availed to stem the tide of public opinion. Yielding at last to the force of circumstances, he had entered the Confederate service rather late in the war, and served with distinction through several campaigns, rising in time to the rank of colonel. After the war he had taken the oath of allegiance, and had been chosen by the people as the most available candidate for the office of sheriff, to which he had been elected without opposition. He had filled the office for several terms, and was universally popular with his constituents.

Colonel or Sheriff Campbell, as he was indifferently called, as the military or civil title happened to be most important in the opinion of the person addressing him, had a high sense of the responsibility attaching to his office. He had sworn to do his duty faithfully, and he knew what his duty was, as sheriff, perhaps more clearly than he had apprehended it in other passages of his life. It was, therefore, with no uncertainty in regard to his course that he prepared his weapons and went over to the jail. He had no fears for Polly's safety.

The sheriff had just locked the heavy front door of the jail behind him when a half dozen horsemen, followed by a crowd of men on foot, came round a bend in the road and drew near the jail. They halted in front of the picket fence that surrounded the building, while several of the committee of arrangements rode on a few rods farther to the sheriff's house. One of them dismounted and rapped on the door with his riding-whip.

"Is the sheriff at home?" he inquired.

"No, he has just gone out," replied Polly, who had come to the door.

"We want the jail keys," he continued.

"They are not here," said Polly. "The sheriff has them himself." Then she added, with assumed indifference, "He is at the jail now."

The man turned away, and Polly went into the front room, from which she peered anxiously between the slats of the green blinds of a window that looked toward the jail. Meanwhile the messenger returned to his companions and announced his discovery. It looked as though the sheriff had learned of their design and was preparing to resist it.

One of them stepped forward and rapped on the jail door.

"Well, what is it?" said the sheriff, from within.

"We want to talk to you, Sheriff," replied the spokesman.

There was a little wicket in the door; this the sheriff opened, and answered through it.

"All right, boys, talk away. You are all strangers to me, and I don't know what business you can have." The sheriff did not think it necessary to recognize anybody in particular on such an occasion; the question of identity sometimes comes up in the investigation of these extra-judicial executions.

"We're a committee of citizens and we want to get into the jail."

"What for? It ain't much trouble to get into jail. Most people want to keep out."

The mob was in no humor to appreciate a joke, and the sheriff's witticism fell dead upon an unresponsive audience.

"We want to have a talk with the nigger that killed Cap'n Walker."

"You can talk to that nigger in the courthouse, when he's brought out for trial. Court will be in session here next week. I know what you fellows want, but you can't get my prisoner to-day. Do you want to take the bread out of a poor man's mouth? I get seventy-five cents a day for keeping this prisoner, and he's the only one in jail. I can't have my family suffer just to please you fellows."

One or two young men in the crowd laughed at the idea of Sheriff Campbell's suffering for want of seventy-five cents a day; but they were frowned into silence by those who stood near them.

"Ef yer don't let us in," cried a voice, "we'll bu's' the do' open."

"Bust away," answered the sheriff, raising his voice so that all could hear. "But I give you fair warning. The first man that tries it will be filled with buckshot. I'm sheriff of this county; I know my duty, and I mean to do it."

"What's the use of kicking, Sheriff?" argued one of the leaders of the mob. "The nigger is sure to hang anyhow; he richly deserves it; and we've got to do something to teach the niggers their places, or white people won't be able to live in the county."

"There's no use talking, boys," responded the sheriff. "I'm a white man outside, but in this jail I'm sheriff; and if this nigger's to be hung in this county, I propose to do the hanging. So you fellows might as well right-about-face, and march back to Troy. You've had a pleasant trip, and the exercise will be good for you. You know *me*. I've got powder and ball, and I've faced fire before now, with nothing between me and the enemy, and I don't mean to surrender this jail while I'm able to shoot." Having thus announced his determination, the sheriff closed and fastened the wicket, and looked around for the best position from which to defend the building.

The crowd drew off a little, and the leaders conversed together in low tones.

The Branson County jail was a small, two-story brick building, strongly constructed, with no attempt at architectural ornamentation. Each story was divided into two large cells by a passage running from front to rear. A grated iron door gave entrance from the passage to each of the four cells. The jail seldom had many prisoners in it, and the lower windows had been boarded up. When the sheriff had closed the wicket, he ascended the steep wooden stairs to the upper floor. There was no window at the front of the upper passage, and the most available position from which to watch the movements of the crowd below was the front window of the cell occupied by the solitary prisoner.

The sheriff unlocked the door and entered the cell. The prisoner was crouched in a corner, his yellow face, blanched with terror, looking ghastly in the semi-darkness of the room. A cold perspiration had gathered on his forehead, and his teeth were chattering with affright.

"For God's sake, Sheriff," he murmured hoarsely, "don't let 'em lynch me; I didn't kill the old man."

The sheriff glanced at the cowering wretch with a look of mingled contempt and loathing.

"Get up," he said sharply. "You will probably be hung sooner or later, but it shall not be to-day, if I can help it. I'll unlock your fetters, and if I can't hold the jail, you'll have to make the best fight you can. If I'm shot, I'll consider my responsibility at an end."

There were iron fetters on the prisoner's ankles, and handcuffs on his wrists. These the sheriff unlocked, and they fell clanking to the floor.

"Keep back from the window," said the sheriff. "They might shoot if they saw you."

The sheriff drew toward the window a pine bench which formed a part of the scanty furniture of the cell, and laid his revolver upon it. Then he took his gun in hand, and took his stand at the side of the window where he could with least exposure of himself watch the movements of the crowd below.

The lynchers had not anticipated any determined resistance. Of course they had looked for a formal protest, and perhaps a sufficient show of opposition to excuse the sheriff in the eye of any stickler for legal formalities. They had not however come prepared to fight a battle, and no one of them seemed willing to lead an attack upon the jail. The leaders of the party conferred together with a good deal of animated gesticulation, which was visible to the sheriff from his outlook, though the distance was too great for him to hear what was said. At length one of them broke away from the group, and rode back to the main body of the lynchers, who were restlessly awaiting orders.

"Well, boys," said the messenger, "we'll have to let it go for the present. The sheriff says he'll shoot, and he's got the drop on us this time. There ain't any of us that want to follow Cap'n Walker jest yet. Besides, the sheriff is a good fellow, and we don't want to hurt 'im. But," he added, as if to reassure the crowd, which began to show signs of disappointment, "the nigger might as well say his prayers, for he ain't got long to live."

There was a murmur of dissent from the mob, and several voices insisted that an attack be made on the jail. But pacific counsels finally prevailed, and the mob sullenly withdrew.

The sheriff stood at the window until they had disappeared around the bend in the road. He did not relax his watchfulness when the last one was out of sight. Their withdrawal might be a mere feint, to be followed by a further attempt. So closely, indeed, was his attention drawn to the outside, that he neither saw nor heard the prisoner creep stealthily across the floor, reach out his hand and secure the revolver which lay on the bench behind the sheriff, and creep as noiselessly back to his place in the corner of the room.

A moment after the last of the lynching party had disappeared there was a shot fired from the woods across the road; a bullet whistled by the window and buried itself in the wooden casing a few inches from where the sheriff was standing. Quick as thought, with the instinct born of a semi-guerrilla army experience, he raised his gun and fired twice at the point from which a faint puff of smoke showed the hostile bullet to have been sent. He stood a moment watching, and then rested his gun against the window, and reached behind him mechanically for the other weapon. It was not on the bench. As the sheriff realized this fact, he turned his head and looked into the muzzle of the revolver.

"Stay where you are, Sheriff," said the prisoner, his eyes glistening, his face almost ruddy with excitement.

The sheriff mentally cursed his own carelessness for allowing him to be caught in such a predicament. He had not expected anything of the kind. He had relied on the negro's cowardice and subordination in the presence of an armed white man as a matter of course. The sheriff was a brave man, but realized that the prisoner had him at an immense disadvantage. The two men stood thus for a moment, fighting a harmless duel with their eyes.

"Well, what do you mean to do?" asked the sheriff with apparent calmness.

"To get away, of course," said the prisoner, in a tone which caused the sheriff to look at him more closely, and with an involuntary feeling of apprehension; if the man was not mad, he was in a state of mind akin to madness, and quite as dangerous. The sheriff felt that he must speak the prisoner fair, and watch for a chance to turn the tables on him. The keen-eyed, desperate man before him was a different being altogether from the groveling wretch who had begged so piteously for life a few minutes before.

At length the sheriff spoke: —

"Is this your gratitude to me for saving your life at the risk of my own? If I had not done so, you would now be swinging from the limb of some neighboring tree."

"True," said the prisoner, "you saved my life, but for how long? When you came in, you said Court would sit next week. When the crowd went away they said I had not long to live. It is merely a choice of two ropes."

"While there's life there's hope," replied the sheriff. He uttered this commonplace mechanically, while his brain was busy in trying to think out some way of escape. "If you are innocent you can prove it."

The mulatto kept his eye upon the sheriff. "I did n't kill the old man," he replied; "but I shall never be able to clear myself. I was at his house at nine o'clock. I stole from it the coat that was on my back when I was taken. I would be convicted, even with a fair trial, unless the real murderer were discovered beforehand."

The sheriff knew this only too well. While he was thinking what argument next to use, the prisoner continued: —

"Throw me the keys — no, unlock the door."

The sheriff stood a moment irresolute. The mulatto's eye glittered ominously. The sheriff crossed the room and unlocked the door leading into the passage.

"Now go down and unlock the outside door."

The heart of the sheriff leaped within him. Perhaps he might make a dash for liberty, and gain the outside. He descended the narrow stairs, the prisoner keeping close behind him.

The sheriff inserted the huge iron key into the lock. The rusty bolt yielded slowly. It still remained for him to pull the door open.

"Stop!" thundered the mulatto, who seemed to divine the sheriff's purpose. "Move a muscle, and I'll blow your brains out."

The sheriff obeyed; he realized that his chance had not yet come.

"Now keep on that side of the passage, and go back upstairs."

Keeping the sheriff under cover of the revolver, the mulatto followed him up the stairs. The sheriff expected the prisoner to lock him into the cell and make his own escape. He had about come to the conclusion that the best thing he could do under the circumstances was to submit quietly, and take his chances of recapturing the prisoner after the alarm had been given. The sheriff had faced death more than once upon the battlefield. A few minutes before, well armed, and with a brick wall between him and them he had dared a hundred men to fight; but he felt instinctively that the desperate man confronting him was not to be trifled with, and he was too prudent a man to risk his life against such heavy odds. He had Polly to look after, and there was a limit beyond which devotion to duty would be quixotic and even foolish.

"I want to get away," said the prisoner, "and I don't want to be captured; for if I am I know I will be hung on the spot. I am afraid," he added somewhat reflectively, "that in order to save myself I shall have to kill you."

"Good God!" exclaimed the sheriff in involuntary terror; "you would not kill the man to whom you owe your own life."

"You speak more truly than you know," replied the mulatto. "I indeed owe my life to you."

The sheriff started. He was capable of surprise, even in that moment of extreme peril. "Who are you?" he asked in amazement.

"Tom, Cicely's son," returned the other. He had closed the door and stood talking to the sheriff through the grated opening. "Don't you remember Cicely — Cicely whom you sold, with her child, to the speculator on his way to Alabama?"

The sheriff did remember. He had been sorry for it many a time since. It had been the old story of debts, mortgages, and bad crops. He had quarreled with the mother. The price offered for her and her child had been unusually large, and he had yielded to the combination of anger and pecuniary stress.

"Good God!" he gasped, "you would not murder your own father?"

"My father?" replied the mulatto. "It were well enough for me to claim the relationship, but it comes with poor grace from you to ask anything by reason of it. What father's duty have you ever performed for me? Did you give me your name, or even your protection? Other white men gave their colored sons freedom and money, and sent them to the free States. *You* sold *me* to the rice swamps."

"I at least gave you the life you cling to," murmured the sheriff.

"Life?" said the prisoner, with a sarcastic laugh. "What kind of a life? You gave me your own blood, your own features,—no man need look at us together twice to see that,—and you gave me a black mother. Poor wretch! She died under the lash, because she had enough womanhood to call her soul her own. You gave me a white man's spirit, and you made me a slave, and crushed it out."

"But you are free now," said the sheriff. He had not doubted, could not doubt, the mulatto's word. He knew whose passions coursed beneath that swarthy skin and burned in the black eyes opposite his own. He saw in this mulatto what he himself might have become had not the safeguards of parental restraint and public opinion been thrown around him.

"Free to do what?" replied the mulatto. "Free in name, but despised and scorned and set aside by the people to whose race I belong far more than to my mother's."

"There are schools," said the sheriff. "You have been to school." He had noticed that the mulatto spoke more eloquently and used better language than most Branson County people.

"I have been to school, and dreamed when I went that it would work some marvelous change in my condition. But what did I learn? I learned to feel that no degree of learning or wisdom will change the color of my skin and that I shall always wear what in my own country is a badge of degradation. When I think about it seriously I do not care particularly for such a life. It is the animal in me, not the man, that flees the gallows. I owe you nothing," he went on, "and expect nothing of you; and it would be no more than justice if I should avenge upon you my mother's wrongs and my own. But still I hate to shoot you; I have never yet taken human life — for I did *not* kill the old captain. Will you promise to give no alarm and make no attempt to capture me until morning, if I do not shoot?"

So absorbed were the two men in their colloquy and their own tumultuous thoughts that neither of them had heard the door below move upon its hinges. Neither of them had heard a light step come stealthily up the stairs, nor seen a slender form creep along the darkening passage toward the mulatto.

The sheriff hesitated. The struggle between his love of life and his sense of duty was a terrific one. It may seem strange that a man who could sell his own child into slavery should hesitate at such a moment, when his life was trembling in the balance. But the baleful influence of human slavery poisoned the very fountains of life, and created new standards of right. The sheriff was conscientious; his conscience had merely been warped by his environment. Let no one ask what his answer would have been; he was spared the necessity of a decision.

"Stop," said the mulatto, "you need not promise. I could not trust you if you did. It is your life for mine; there is but one safe way for me; you must die."

He raised his arm to fire, when there was a flash—a report from the passage behind him. His arm fell heavily at his side, and the pistol dropped at his feet.

The sheriff recovered first from his surprise, and throwing open the door secured the fallen weapon. Then seizing the prisoner he thrust him into the cell and locked the door upon him; after which he turned to Polly, who leaned half-fainting against the wall, her hands clasped over her heart.

"Oh, father, I was just in time!" she cried hysterically, and, wildly sobbing, threw herself into her father's arms.

"I watched until they all went away," she said. "I heard the shot from the woods and I saw you shoot. Then when you did not come out I feared something had happened, that perhaps you had been wounded. I got out the other pistol and ran over here. When I found the door open, I knew something was wrong, and when I heard voices I crept upstairs, and reached the top just in time to hear him say he would kill you. Oh, it was a narrow escape!"

When she had grown somewhat calmer, the sheriff left her standing there and went back into the cell. The prisoner's arm was bleeding from a flesh wound. His bravado had given place to a stony apathy. There was no sign in his face of fear or disappointment or feeling of any kind. The sheriff sent Polly to the house for cloth, and bound up the prisoner's wound with a rude skill acquired during his army life.

"I'll have a doctor come and dress the wound in the morning," he said to the prisoner. "It will do very well until then, if you will keep quiet. If the doctor asks you how the wound was caused, you can say that you were struck by the bullet fired from the woods. It would do you no good to have it known that you were shot while attempting to escape."

The prisoner uttered no word of thanks or apology, but sat in sullen silence. When the wounded arm had been bandaged, Polly and her father returned to the house.

The sheriff was in an unusually thoughtful mood that evening. He put salt in his coffee at supper, and poured vinegar over his pancakes. To many of Polly's questions he returned random answers. When he had gone to bed he lay awake for several hours.

In the silent watches of the night, when he was alone with God, there came into his mind a flood of unaccustomed thoughts. An hour or two before, standing face to face with death, he had experienced a sensation similar to that which drowning men are said to feel—a kind of clarifying of the moral faculty, in which the veil of the flesh, with its obscuring passions and prejudices, is pushed aside for a moment, and all the acts of one's life stand out, in the clear light of truth, in their correct proportions and relations,—a state of mind in which one sees himself as God may be supposed to see him. In the reaction following his rescue, this feeling had given place for a time to far different emotions. But now, in the silence of midnight, something of this clearness of spirit returned to the sheriff. He saw that he had owed some duty to this son of his,—that neither law nor custom could destroy a responsibility inherent in the nature of mankind. He could not thus, in the eyes of God at least, shake off the consequences of his sin. Had he never sinned, this wayward spirit would never have come back from the vanished past to haunt him. As these thoughts came, his anger against the mulatto died away, and in its place there sprang up a great pity. The hand of parental authority might have restrained the passions he had seen burning in the prisoner's eyes when the desperate man spoke the words which had seemed to doom his father to death. The sheriff felt that he might have saved this fiery spirit from the slough of slavery; that he might have sent him to the free North, and given him there, or in some other land, an opportunity to turn to usefulness and honorable pursuits the talents that had run to crime, perhaps to madness; he might, still less, have given this son of his the poor simulacrum of liberty which men of his caste could possess in a slave-holding community; or least of all, but still something, he might have kept the boy on the plantation, where the burdens of slavery would have fallen lightly upon him.

The sheriff recalled his own youth. He had inherited an honored name to keep untarnished; he had had a future to make; the picture of a fair young bride had beckoned him on to happiness. The poor wretch now stretched upon a pallet of straw between the brick walls of the jail had had none of these things,—no name, no father, no mother—in the true meaning of motherhood,—and until the past few years no possible future, and then one vague and shadowy in its outline, and dependent for form and substance upon the slow solution of a problem in which there were many unknown quantities.

From what he might have done to what he might yet do was an easy transition for the awakened conscience of the sheriff. It occurred to him, purely as a hypothesis, that he might permit his prisoner to escape; but his oath of office, his duty as sheriff, stood in the way of such a course, and the sheriff dismissed the idea from his mind. He could, however, investigate the circumstances of the murder, and move Heaven and earth to discover the real criminal, for he no longer doubted the prisoner's innocence; he could employ counsel for the accused, and perhaps influence public opinion in his favor. An acquittal once secured, some plan could be devised by which the sheriff might in some degree atone for his crime against this son of his — against society — against God.

When the sheriff had reached this conclusion he fell into an unquiet slumber, from which he awoke late the next morning.

He went over to the jail before breakfast and found the prisoner lying on his pallet, his face turned to the wall; he did not move when the sheriff rattled the door.

"Good-morning," said the latter, in a tone intended to waken the prisoner.

There was no response. The sheriff looked more keenly at the recumbent figure; there was an unnatural rigidity about its attitude.

He hastily unlocked the door and, entering the cell, bent over the prostrate form. There was no sound of breathing; he turned the body over — it was cold and stiff. The prisoner had torn the bandage from his wound and bled to death during the night. He had evidently been dead several hours.

1889, 1899

EMERGING FEMINIST FICTION

Constance Fenimore Woolson
Sarah Orne Jewett
Kate Chopin

Mary E. Wilkins Freeman
Charlotte Perkins Gilman

"Worse than the check set upon the physical activities of women has been the restriction of their power to think and judge for themselves. The extended use of the human will and its decisions is conditioned upon free, voluntary action. In her rudimentary position, woman was denied the physical freedom which underlies all knowledge, she was denied the mental freedom which is the path to further wisdom, she was denied the moral freedom of being mistress of her own action and of learning by the merciful law of consequences what was right and what was wrong; and she has remained, perforce, undeveloped in the larger judgment of ethics."

Charlotte Perkins Gilman, from *Women and Economics: A Study of the Economic Relation Between Men and Women as a Factor in Social Evolution*

CONSTANCE
FENIMORE WOOLSON
(1840–1894)

On the surface, Constance Fenimore Woolson's life seemed a tranquil one, filled with achievement. Beneath the surface, however, Woolson suffered periodic bouts of melancholia, spells of hereditary depression no doubt intensified by loneliness. She spent the last fourteen years of her life in Europe, the last months in Venice. There, at the age of fifty-three, ill with influenza and typhoid fever, she jumped — or fell — from her second-story window to her death. At her death she was one of the most popular writers of her time. Her work was highly admired by such other writers as Henry James, who included an essay on her in his *Partial Portraits* (1888).

A grandniece of James Fenimore Cooper, she was born in Claremont, New Hampshire, but soon moved with her family to Cleveland, Ohio. Her father was a prosperous businessman. Woolson attended the Cleveland Seminary and graduated at age eighteen from Madame Chegary's School in New York City at the top of her class. She spent summers with her family on Mackinac Island in Lake Huron, where the family had a cottage.

Her father's death in 1869, when she was twenty-nine, was a great blow. They had enjoyed a close relationship, sharing a love of books and literature. As a young girl, she had accompanied him on trips into states bordering the Great Lakes. It was at the time of her father's death that Woolson turned seriously to writing as a vocation.

She began to publish short stories in such magazines as *Harper's* and *The Atlantic Monthly*, many of them based on her experiences on Mackinac Island. These were collected under the title *Castle Nowhere: Lake Country Sketches* in 1875. By this time she had grown familiar with the post–Civil War South, spending her winters with her mother in the Carolinas and Florida. Her experiences and observations there led to another collection of stories published in 1880, entitled *Rodman the Keeper: Southern Sketches*. Both of these early volumes were recognized as fine examples of the then popular literary genre, local color fiction.

In 1879, after the death of her mother, Woolson sailed for Europe never to return to America. Her admiration for Henry James's work led to their meeting in the early 1880s. As Leon Edel has shown in his James biography (*Henry James: The Middle Years, 1882–1895*), the attachment became an extremely close one, continued by correspondence when they were separated. In accord with an agreement between them, this correspondence was destroyed — except for four letters from Woolson to James that somehow survived.

During these last years, Woolson travelled extensively and wrote continuously — poems, stories, and novels. The novels (*Anne* and *For the Major*, 1883; *East Angels*, 1886; *Jupiter Lights*, 1889; *Horace Chase*, 1894) were all set in America, but the stories were set in Europe, many of them (like much of James's work) portraying Americans abroad.

Whatever the feelings Woolson and James had for each other in life, there can be no doubt that James was deeply shaken by news of her death in Venice. He could not bring himself to attend her funeral and burial in the Protestant Cemetery in Rome (a place chosen by her), but he was determined to be present when her possessions in Venice were collected by relatives from America. There he retrieved his letters to her and some mementoes of their relationship.

Moreover, according to Leon Edel, Woolson was to survive her death in some sense in James's fiction, as, for example, in "The Beast in the Jungle." If there is something of James himself in Marcher, the man who missed out on life waiting for an awesome event to overwhelm him, then there is something of Woolson in May Server, who offers herself even in her illness, to a man blinded to her love by his self-obsession. The final scene of that story may have drawn much of its intensity from James's visit to Woolson's grave in Rome's Protestant Cemetery some months after her burial.

The Woolson story included here, "Miss Grief," although published before she met James, prefigures some aspects of the James-Woolson relationship in its portrayal of an older woman writer calling on a successful younger writer in Rome for help in publication. It is interesting to note that James may have taken from its text the title of one of the best of his stories of artists—"The Figure in the Carpet," published in 1896.

After her death, Woolson's work fell into neglect, her books went out of print, and she seldom appeared in anthologies. Recently, however, she has enjoyed something of a revival. In a reissue of a number of her stories, *Women Artists, Women Exiles: "Miss Grief" and Other Stories* (1988), the editor Joan Myers Weimer makes the case for ranking her with Sarah Orne Jewett, Mary E. Wilkins Freeman, and Kate Chopin. She writes: "The five novels, four volumes of short stories, and numerous sketches, poems, and reviews she published in her lifetime show her to be an extraordinary observer, a superb stylist, and a shrewd and witty critic of prevailing mores and ideologies."

ADDITIONAL READING

For the Major and Selected Short Stories of Constance Fenimore Woolson, ed. Rayburn S. Moore, 1967.

Henry James, "Miss Woolson," *Partial Portraits*, 1889; Fred Lewis Pattee, *The Development of the American Short Story*, 1923; Clare Benedict, *Constance Fenimore Woolson*, 1930; John Dwight Kern, *Constance Fenimore Woolson: Literary Pioneer*, 1934; Van Wyck Brooks, *The Dream of Arcadia*, 1958; Claude M. Simpson, ed., *The Local Colorists*, 1960; Leon Edel, *Henry James: The Middle Years, 1882–1895*, 1962; Rayburn S. Moore, *Constance Fenimore Woolson*, 1963; Cheryl B. Torsney, *Constance Fenimore Woolson: The Grief of Artistry*, 1989.

TEXT

Lippincott's Magazine, May 1880.

"Miss Grief"

"A conceited fool" is a not uncommon expression. Now, I know that I am not a fool, but I also know that I am conceited. But, candidly, can it be helped if one happens to be young, well and strong, passably good-looking, with some money that one has inherited and more that one has earned—in all, enough to make life comfortable—and if upon this foundation rests also the pleasant superstructure of a literary success? The success is deserved, I think: certainly it was not lightly gained. Yet even with this I fully appreciate its rarity. Thus, I find myself very well entertained in life: I have all I wish in the way of society, and a deep, although of course carefully concealed, satisfaction in my own little fame; which fame I foster by a gentle system of non-interference. I know that I am spoken of as "that quiet young fellow who writes those delightful little studies of society, you know;" and I live up to that definition.

A year ago I was in Rome, and enjoying life particularly. There was a large number of my acquaintances there, both American and English, and no day passed without its invitation. Of course I understood it: it is seldom that you find a literary man who is good-tempered, well-dressed, sufficiently provided with money, and amiably obedient to all the rules and requirements of "society." "When found, make a note of it;"[1] and the note was generally an invitation.

One evening, upon returning to my lodgings, my man Simpson informed me that a person had called in the afternoon, and upon learning that I was absent had left not a card, but her name — "Miss Grief." The title lingered — Miss Grief! "Grief has not so far visited me here," I said to myself, dismissing Simpson and seeking my little balcony for a final smoke, "and she shall not now. I shall take care to be 'not at home' to her if she continues to call." And then I fell to thinking of Ethelind Abercrombie, in whose society I had spent that and many evenings: they were golden thoughts.

The next day there was an excursion: it was late when I reached my rooms, and again Simpson informed me that Miss Grief had called.

"Is she coming continuously?" I said, half to myself.

"Yes, sir: she mentioned that she should call again."

"How does she look?"

"Well, sir, a lady, but not so prosperous as she was, I should say," answered Simpson discreetly.

"Young?"

"No, sir."

"Alone?"

"A maid with her, sir."

But once outside in my little high-up balcony with my cigar, I again forgot Miss Grief and whatever she might represent. Who would not forget in that moonlight, with Ethelind Abercrombie's face to remember?

The stranger came a third time, and I was absent: then she let two days pass, and began again. It grew to be a regular dialogue between Simpson and myself when I came in at night: "Grief to-day?"

"Yes, sir."

"What time?"

"Four, sir."

"Happy the man," I thought, "who can keep her confined to a particular hour!"

But I should not have treated my visitor so cavalierly if I had not felt sure that she was eccentric and unconventional — qualities extremely tiresome in a woman no longer young or attractive, and without money to gild them over. If she were not eccentric she would not have persisted in coming to my door day after day in this silent way, without stating her errand, leaving a note or presenting her credentials in any shape. I made up my mind that she had something to sell — a bit of carving or some intaglio[2] supposed to be antique. It was known that I had a fancy for oddities. I said to myself, "She has read or heard of my 'Old Gold' story or else 'The Buried God,' and she thinks me an idealizing ignoramus upon whom she can impose. Her sepulchral name is at least not Italian: probably she is a sharp country-woman of mine, turning by means of æsthetic lies an honest penny when she can."

She had called seven times during a period of two weeks without seeing me, when one day I happened to be at home in the afternoon, owing to a pouring rain and a fit of doubt concerning Miss Abercrombie. For I had constructed a careful theory of that young lady's characteristics in my own mind, and she had lived up to it de-

---

[1]The favorite expression of Captain Cuttle, a character prone to clichés and inapt quotations in *Dombey and Son*   (1847–48) by Charles Dickens (1812–1870).
[2]Engraving in stone or hard metal.

lightfully until the previous evening, when with one word she had blown it to atoms and taken flight, leaving me standing, as it were, on a desolate shore, with nothing but a handful of mistaken inductions wherewith to console myself. I do not know a more exasperating frame of mind, at least for a constructor of theories. I could not write, and so I took up a French novel (I model myself a little on Balzac[3]). I had been turning over its pages but a few moments when Simpson knocked, and, entering softly, said, with just a shadow of a smile on his well-trained face, "Miss Grief." I briefly consigned Miss Grief to all the Furies,[4] and then, as he still lingered—perhaps not knowing where they resided—I asked where the visitor was.

"Outside, sir—in the hall. I told her I would see if you were at home."

"She must be unpleasantly wet if she had no carriage."

"No carriage, sir: they always come on foot. I think she *is* a little damp, sir."

"Well, let her in, but I don't want the maid. I may as well see her now, I suppose, and end the affair."

"Yes, sir."

I did not put down my book. My visitor should have a hearing, but not much more: she had sacrificed her womanly claims by her persistent attacks upon my door. Presently Simpson ushered her in. "Miss Grief," he said, and then went out, closing the curtain behind him.

A woman—yes, a lady—but shabby, unattractive and more than middle-aged.

I rose, bowed slightly, and then dropped into my chair again, still keeping the book in my hand. "Miss Grief?" I said interrogatively as I indicated a seat with my eyebrows.

"Not Grief," she answered—"Crief: my name is Crief."

She sat down, and I saw that she held a small flat box.

"Not carving, then," I thought—"probably old lace, something that belonged to Tullia or Lucrezia Borgia."[5] But as she did not speak I found myself obliged to begin: "You have been here, I think, once or twice before?"

"Seven times: this is the eighth."

A silence.

"I am often out: indeed, I may say that I am never in," I remarked carelessly.

"Yes: you have many friends."

"Who will perhaps buy old lace," I mentally added. But this time I too remained silent: why should I trouble myself to draw her out? She had sought me: let her advance her idea, whatever it was, now that entrance was gained.

But Miss Grief (I preferred to call her so) did not look as though she could advance anything: her black gown, damp with rain, seemed to retreat fearfully to her thin self, while her thin self retreated as far as possible from me, from the chair, from everything. Her eyes were cast down: an old-fashioned lace veil with a heavy border shaded her face. She looked at the floor, and I looked at her.

I grew a little impatient, but I made up my mind that I would continue silent and see how long a time she would consider necessary to give due effect to her little pantomime. Comedy? Or was it tragedy? I suppose full five minutes passed thus in our double silence; and that is a long time when two persons are sitting opposite each other alone in a small still room.

At last my visitor, without raising her eyes, said slowly, "You are very happy, are you not, with youth, health, friends, riches, fame?"

It was a singular beginning. Her voice was clear, low and very sweet as she thus

[3]Honoré de Balzac (1790–1850), French novelist renowned for his detailed studies of contemporary society, *La Comédie humaine* or *The Human Comedy* (1827–47), a series of ninety-one separate works.
[4]In classical mythology, the three avenging winged goddesses who pursued and punished the guilty who had escaped jus-

tice. They drove Orestes to madness for slaying his mother.
[5]Lucrezia Borgia (1480–1519), Duchess of Ferrara, daughter of Pope Alexander VI; Tullia, in Roman legendary history, daughter of King Seruius Tullius. Both came down through tradition as perpetrators of great evil, especially against their fathers.

enumerated my advantages one by one in a list. I was attracted by it, but repelled by her words, which seemed to me flattery both dull and bold.

"Thanks," I said, "for your kindness, but I fear it is undeserved. I seldom discuss myself even when with my friends."

"I am your friend," replied Miss Grief. Then, after a moment, she added slowly, "I have read every word you have written."

I curled the edges of my book indifferently: I am not a fop,[6] I hope, but—others have said the same.

"What is more, I know much of it by heart," continued my visitor. "Wait: I will show you;" and then, without pause, she began to repeat something of mine word for word, just as I had written it. On she went, and I—listened. I intended interrupting her after a moment, but I did not, because she was reciting so well, and also because I felt a desire gaining upon me to see what she would make of a certain conversation which I knew was coming—a conversation between two of my characters which was, to say the least, sphinx-like, and somewhat incandescent also. What won me a little, too, was the fact that the scene she was reciting (it was hardly more than that, although called a story) was secretly my favorite among all the sketches from my pen with which a gracious public had been favored. I never said so, but it was; and I had always felt a wondering annoyance that the aforesaid public, while kindly praising beyond their worth other attempts of mine, had never noticed the higher purpose of this little shaft, aimed not at the balconies and lighted windows of society, but straight up toward the distant stars. So she went on, and presently reached the conversation: my two people began to talk. She had raised her eyes now, and was looking at me soberly as she gave the words of the woman, quiet, gentle, cold, and the replies of the man, bitter, hot and scathing. Her very voice changed, and took, although always sweetly, the different tones required, while no point of meaning, however small, no breath of delicate emphasis which I had meant, but which the dull types could not give, escaped appreciative and full, almost overfull, recognition which startled me. For she had understood me—understood me almost better than I had understood myself. It seemed to me that while I had labored to interpret partially a psychological riddle, she, coming after, had comprehended its bearings better than I had, although confining herself strictly to my own words and emphasis. The scene ended (and it ended rather suddenly), she dropped her eyes, and moved her hand nervously to and fro over the box she held: her gloves were old and shabby, her hands small.

I was secretly much surprised by what I had heard, but my ill-humor was deepseated that day, and I still felt sure, besides, that the box contained something that I was expected to buy.

"You recite remarkably well," I said carelessly, "and I am much flattered also by your appreciation of my efforts. But it is not, I presume, to that alone that I owe the pleasure of this visit?"

"Yes," she answered, still looking down, "it is, for if you had not written that scene I should not have sought you. Your other sketches are interiors—exquisitely painted and delicately finished, but of small scope. *This* is a sketch in a few bold, masterly lines—work of entirely different spirit and purpose."

I was nettled by her insight. "You have bestowed so much of your kind attention upon me that I feel your debtor," I said, conventionally. "It may be that there is something I can do for you—connected, possibly, with that box?"

It was a little impertinent, but it was true, for she answered, "Yes."

I smiled, but her eyes were cast down and she did not see the smile.

"What I have to show you is a manuscript," she said after a pause which I did not break: "it is a drama. I thought that perhaps you would read it."

---

[6]Dandy.

"An authoress! This is worse than old lace," I said to myself in dismay.—Then, aloud, "My opinion would be worth nothing, Miss Crief."

"Not in a business way, I know. But it might be—an assistance personally." Her voice had sunk to a whisper: outside, the rain was pouring steadily down. She was a very depressing object to me as she sat there with her box.

"I hardly think I have the time at present—" I began.

She had raised her eyes and was looking at me: then, when I paused, she rose and came suddenly toward my chair. "Yes, you will read it," she said with her hand on my arm—"you will read it. Look at this room; look at yourself; look at all you have. Then look at me, and have pity."

I had risen, for she held my arm and her damp skirt was brushing my knees.

Her large dark eyes looked intently into mine as she went on: "I have no shame in asking. Why should I have? It is my last endeavor, but a calm and well-considered one. If you refuse I shall go away, knowing that Fate has willed it so. And I shall be content."

"She is mad," I thought. But she did not look so, and she had spoken quietly, even gently.—"Sit down," I said, moving away from her. I felt as if I had been magnetized, but it was only the nearness of her eyes to mine, and their intensity. I drew forward a chair, but she remained standing.

"I cannot," she said in the same sweet, gentle tone, "unless you promise."

"Very well, I promise; only sit down."

As I took her arm to lead her to the chair I perceived that she was trembling, but her face continued unmoved.

"You do not, of course, wish me to look at your manuscript now?" I said, temporizing: "it would be much better to leave it. Give me your address, and I will return it to you with my written opinion; although, I repeat, the latter will be of no use to you. It is the opinion of an editor or publisher that you want."

"It shall be as you please. And I will go in a moment," said Miss Grief, pressing her palms together, as if trying to control the tremor that had seized her slight frame.

She looked so pallid that I thought of offering her a glass of wine: then I remembered that if I did it might be a bait to bring her there again, and this I was desirous to prevent. She rose while the thought was passing through my mind. Her pasteboard box lay on the chair she had first occupied: she took it, wrote an address on the cover, laid it down, and then, bowing with a little air of formality, drew her black shawl around her shoulders and turned toward the door.

I followed, after touching the bell. "You will hear from me by letter," I said.

Simpson opened the door, and I caught a glimpse of the maid, who was waiting in the anteroom. She was an old woman, shorter than her mistress, equally thin, and dressed like her in rusty black. As the door opened she turned toward it a pair of small, dim blue eyes with a look of furtive suspense. Simpson dropped the curtain, shutting me into the inner room: he had no intention of allowing me to accompany my visitor farther. But I had the curiosity to go to a bay-window in an angle from whence I could command the street-door, and presently I saw them issue forth in the rain and walk away side by side, the mistress, being the taller, holding the umbrella: probably there was not much difference in rank between persons so poor and forlorn as these.

It grew dark. I was invited out for the evening, and I knew that if I went I should meet Miss Abercrombie. I said to myself that I would not go. I got out my paper for writing, I made my preparations for a quiet evening at home with myself; but it was of no use. It all ended slavishly in my going. At the last allowable moment I presented myself, and—as a punishment for my vacillation, I suppose—I never passed a more disagreeable evening. I drove homeward in a vixenish temper: it was foggy without, and very foggy within. What Ethelind really was, now that she had broken through my elaborately-built theories, I was not able to decide. There was, to tell the truth, a certain young Englishman— But that is apart from this story.

I reached home, went up to my rooms and had a supper. It was to console myself: I am obliged to console myself scientifically once in a while. I was walking up and down afterward, smoking and feeling somewhat better, when my eye fell upon the pasteboard box. I took it up: on the cover was written an address which showed that my visitor must have walked a long distance in order to see me: "A. Crief."—"A Grief," I thought; "and so she is. I positively believe she has brought all this trouble upon me: she has the evil eye." I took out the manuscript and looked at it. It was in the form of a little volume, and clearly written: on the cover was the word "Armor" in German text, and underneath a pen-and-ink sketch of a helmet, breastplate and shield.

"Grief certainly needs armor," I said to myself, sitting down by the table and turning over the pages. "I may as well look over the thing now: I could not be in a worse mood." And then I began to read.

Early the next morning Simpson took a note from me to the given address, returning with the following reply: "No; I prefer to come to you; at four; A. CRIEF." These words, with their three semicolons, were written in pencil upon a piece of coarse printing-paper, but the handwriting was as clear and delicate as that of the manuscript in ink.

"What sort of a place was it, Simpson?"

"Very poor, sir, but I did not go all the way up. The elder person came down, sir, took the note, and requested me to wait where I was."

"You had no chance, then, to make inquiries?" I said, knowing full well that he had emptied the entire neighborhood of any information it might possess concerning these two lodgers.

"Well, sir, you know how these foreigners will talk, whether one wants to hear or not. But it seems that these two persons have been there but a few weeks: they live alone, and are uncommonly silent and reserved. The people around there call them something that signifies 'the Madames American, thin and dumb.'"

At four the "Madames American" arrived: it was raining again, and they came on foot under their old umbrella. The maid waited in the anteroom, and Miss Grief was ushered into my bachelor's parlor, which was library and dining-room in one. I had thought that I should meet her with great deference, but she looked so forlorn that my deference changed to pity. It was the woman that impressed me then, more than the writer—the fragile, nerveless body more than the inspired mind. For it was inspired: I had sat up half the night over her drama, and had felt thrilled through and through more than once by its earnestness, passion and power.

No one could have been more surprised than I was to find myself thus enthusiastic. I thought I had outgrown that sort of thing. And one would have supposed, too (I myself should have supposed so the day before), that the faults of the drama, which were many and prominent, would have chilled any liking I might have felt, I being a writer myself, and therefore critical; for writers are as apt to make much of the "how," rather than the "what," as painters, who, it is well known, prefer an exquisitely rendered representation of a commonplace theme to an imperfectly executed picture of even the most striking subject. But in this case, on the contrary, the scattered rays of splendor in Miss Grief's drama had made me forget the dark spots, which were numerous and disfiguring; or, rather, the splendor had made me anxious to have the spots removed. And this also was a philanthropic state very unusual for me. Regarding unsuccessful writers my motto had been "Væ victis!"[7]

My visitor took a seat and folded her hands: I could see, in spite of her quiet

---

[7]"Woe to the vanquished!" (Latin).

manner, that she was in breathless suspense. It seemed so pitiful that she should be trembling there before me—a woman so much older than I was, a woman who possessed the divine spark of genius, which I was by no means sure, in spite of my success, had been granted to me—that I felt as if I ought to go down on my knees before her and entreat her to take her proper place of supremacy at once. But there! one does not go down on one's knees combustively, as it were, before a woman over fifty, plain in feature, thin, dejected and ill-dressed. I contented myself with taking her hands (in their miserable old gloves) in mine, while I said cordially, "Miss Crief, your drama seems to me full of original power. It has roused my enthusiasm: I sat up half the night reading it."

The hands I held shook, but something (perhaps a shame for having evaded the knees business) made me tighten my hold and bestow upon her also a reassuring smile. She looked at me for a moment, and then, suddenly and noiselessly, tears rose and rolled down her cheeks. I dropped her hands and retreated. I had not thought her tearful: on the contrary, her voice and face had seemed rigidly controlled. But now here she was bending herself over the side of the chair with her head resting on her arms, not sobbing aloud, but her whole frame shaken by the strength of her emotion. I rushed for a glass of wine: I pressed her to take it. I did not quite know what to do, but, putting myself in her place, I decided to praise the drama; and praise it I did. I do not know when I have used so many adjectives. She raised her head and began to wipe her eyes.

"Do take the wine," I said, interrupting myself in my cataract of language.

"I dare not," she answered; then added humbly, "that is, unless you have a biscuit here or a bit of bread."

I found some biscuit: she ate two, and then slowly drank the wine while I resumed my verbal Niagara. Under its influence—and that of the wine too, perhaps—she began to show new life. It was not that she looked radiant—she could not—but simply that she looked warm. I now perceived what had been the principal discomfort of her appearance heretofore: it was that she had looked all the time as if suffering from cold.

At last I could think of nothing more to say, and stopped. I really admired the drama, but I thought I had exerted myself sufficiently as an anti-hysteric, and that adjectives enough, for the present at least, had been administered. She had put down her empty wine-glass, and was resting her hands on the broad cushioned arms of her chair with a sort of expanded content.

"You must pardon my tears," she said, smiling: "it was the revulsion of feeling. My life was at a low ebb: if your sentence had been against me it would have been my end."

"Your end?"

"Yes, the end of my life: I should have destroyed myself."

"Then you would have been a weak as well as wicked woman," I said in a tone of disgust: I do hate sensationalism.

"Oh, no, you know nothing about it. I should have destroyed only this poor worn tenement of clay. But I can well understand how *you* would look upon it. Regarding the desirableness of life the prince and the beggar may have different opinions.—We will say no more of it, but talk of the drama instead." As she spoke the word "drama" a triumphant brightness came into her eyes.

I took the manuscript from a drawer and sat down beside her. "I suppose you know that there are faults," I said, expecting ready acquiescence.

"I was not aware that there were any," was her gentle reply.

Here was a beginning! After all my interest in her—and, I may say under the circumstances, my kindness—she received me in this way! However, my belief in her genius was too sincere to be altered by her whimsies; so I persevered. "Let us go over it together," I said. "Shall I read it to you, or will you read it to me?"

"I will not read it, but recite it."

"That will never do: you will recite it so well that we shall see only the good points, and what we have to concern ourselves with now is the bad ones."

"I will recite it," she repeated.

"Look here, Miss Crief," I said bluntly, "for what purpose did you come to me? Certainly not merely to recite: I am no stage-manager. In plain English, was it not your idea that I might help you in obtaining a publisher?"

"Yes, yes," she answered, looking at me apprehensively, all her old manner returning.

I followed up my advantage, opened the little paper volume and began. I first took the drama line by line, and spoke of the faults of expression and structure: then I turned back and touched upon two or three glaring impossibilities in the plot. "Your absorbed interest in the motive of the whole no doubt made you forget these blemishes," I said apologetically.

But, to my surprise, I found that she did not see the blemishes — that she appreciated nothing I had said, comprehended nothing. Such unaccountable obtuseness puzzled me. I began again, going over the whole with even greater minuteness and care. I worked hard: the perspiration stood in beads upon my forehead as I struggled with her — what shall I call it — obstinacy? But it was not exactly obstinacy. She simply could not see the faults of her own work, any more than a blind man can see the smoke that dims a patch of blue sky. When I had finished my task the second time she still remained as gently impassive as before. I leaned back in my chair exhausted and looked at her.

Even then she did not seem to comprehend (whether she agreed with it or not) what I must be thinking. "It is such a heaven to me that you like it!" she murmured dreamily, breaking the silence. Then, with more animation, "And *now* you will let me recite it?"

I was too weary to oppose her: she threw aside her shawl and bonnet, and, standing in the centre of the room, began.

And she carried me along with her: all the strong passages were doubly strong when spoken, and the faults, which seemed nothing to her, were made by her earnestness to seem nothing to me, at least for that moment. When it was ended she stood looking at me with a triumphant smile.

"Yes," I said, "I like it, and you see that I do. But I like it because my taste is peculiar. To me originality and force are everything — perhaps because I have them not to any marked degree myself — but the world at large will not overlook as I do your absolutely barbarous shortcomings on account of them. Will you trust me to go over the drama and correct it at my pleasure?" This was a vast deal for me to offer: I was surprised at myself.

"No," she answered softly, still smiling. "There shall not be so much as a comma altered." Then she sat down and fell into a reverie as though she were alone.

"Have you written anything else?" I said after a while, when I had become tired of the silence.

"Yes."

"Can I see it? Or is it *them*?"

"It is *them*. Yes, you can see all."

"I will call upon you for the purpose."

"No, you must not," she said, coming back to the present nervously: "I prefer to come to you."

At this moment Simpson entered to light the room, and busied himself rather longer than was necessary over the task. When he finally went out I saw that my visitor's manner had sunk into its former depression: the presence of the servant seemed to have chilled her.

"When did you say I might come?" I repeated, ignoring her refusal.

"I did not say it. It would be impossible."

"Well, then, when will you come here?" There was, I fear, a trace of fatigue in my tone.

"At your good pleasure, sir," she answered humbly.

My chivalry was touched by this: after all, she was a woman. "Come to-morrow," I said. "By the way, come and dine with me then: why not?" I was curious to see what she would reply.

"Why not, indeed? Yes, I will come. I am forty-three: I might have been your mother."

This was not quite true, as I am over thirty; but I look young, while she—Well, I had thought her over fifty. "I can hardly call you 'mother,' but then we might compromise upon 'aunt,'" I said, laughing. "Aunt what?"

"My name is Aaronna," she gravely answered. "My father was much disappointed that I was not a boy, and gave me as nearly as possible the name he had prepared—Aaron."

"Then come and dine with me to-morrow, and bring with you the other manuscripts, Aaronna," I said, amused at the quaint sound of the name. On the whole, I did not like "aunt."

"I will come," she answered.

It was twilight and still raining, but she refused all offers of escort or carriage, departing with her maid, as she had come, under the brown umbrella.

The next day we had the dinner. Simpson was astonished—and more than astonished, grieved—when I told him that he was to dine with the maid; but he could not complain in words, since my own guest, the mistress, was hardly more attractive. When our preparations were complete I could not help laughing: the two prim little tables, one in the parlor and one in the anteroom, and Simpson disapprovingly going back and forth between them, were irresistible.

I greeted my guest hilariously when she arrived, and, fortunately, her manner was not quite so depressed as usual: I could never have accorded myself with a tearful mood. I had thought that perhaps she would make, for the occasion, some change in her attire: I have never known a woman who had not some scrap of finery, however small, in reserve for that unexpected occasion of which she is ever dreaming. But no: Miss Grief wore the same black gown, unadorned and unaltered. I was glad that there was no rain that day, so that the skirt did not at least look so damp and rheumatic.

She ate quietly, almost furtively, yet with a good appetite, and she did not refuse the wine. Then, when the meal was over and Simpson had removed the dishes, I asked for the new manuscripts. She gave me an old green copybook filled with short poems, and a prose sketch by itself: I lit a cigar and sat down at my desk to look them over.

"Perhaps you will try a cigarette?" I suggested, more for amusement than anything else, for there was not a shade of Bohemianism about her: her whole appearance was puritanical.

"I have not yet succeeded in learning to smoke."

"You have tried?" I said, turning round.

"Yes: Serena and I tried, but we did not succeed."

"Serena is your maid?"

"She lives with me."

I was seized with inward laughter, and began hastily to look over her manuscripts with my back toward her, so that she might not see it. A vision had risen before me of those two forlorn women, alone in their room with locked doors, patiently trying to acquire the smoker's art.

But my attention was soon absorbed by the papers before me. Such a fantastic collection of words, lines and epithets I had never before seen, or even in dreams imagined. In truth, they were like the work of dreams: they were *Kubla Khan*,[8] only more so. Here and there was radiance like the flash of a diamond, but each poem, almost each verse and line, was marred by some fault or lack which seemed wilful perversity, like the work of an evil sprite. It was like a case of jeweller's wares set before you, with each ring unfinished, each bracelet too large or too small for its purpose, each breastpin without its fastening, each necklace purposely broken. I turned the pages, marvelling. When about half an hour had passed, and I was leaning back for a moment to light another cigar, I glanced toward my visitor. She was behind me, in an easy-chair before my small fire, and she was — fast asleep! In the relaxation of her unconsciousness I was struck anew by the poverty her appearance expressed: her feet were visible, and I saw the miserable worn old shoes which hitherto she had kept concealed.

After looking at her for a moment I returned to my task and took up the prose story: in prose she must be more reasonable. She was less fantastic perhaps, but hardly more reasonable. The story was that of a profligate and commonplace man forced by two of his friends, in order not to break the heart of a dying girl who loves him, to live up to a high imaginary ideal of himself which her pure but mistaken mind has formed. He has a handsome face and sweet voice, and repeats what they tell him. Her long, slow decline and happy death, and his own inward ennui and profound weariness of the rôle he has to play, made the vivid points of the story. So far, well enough, but here was the trouble: through the whole narrative moved another character, a physician of tender heart and exquisite mercy, who practised murder as a fine art, and was regarded (by the author) as a second Messiah! This was monstrous. I read it through twice, and threw it down: then, fatigued, I turned round and leaned back, waiting for her to wake. I could see her profile against the dark hue of the easy-chair.

Presently she seemed to feel my gaze, for she stirred, then opened her eyes. "I have been asleep," she said, rising hurriedly.

"No harm in that, Aaronna."

But she was deeply embarrassed and troubled, much more so than the occasion required; so much so, indeed, that I turned the conversation back upon the manuscripts as a diversion. "I cannot stand that doctor of yours," I said, indicating the prose story: "no one would. You must cut him out."

Her self-possession returned as if by magic. "Certainly not," she answered haughtily.

"Oh, if you do not care— I had labored under the impression that you were anxious these things should find a purchaser."

"I am, I am," she said, her manner changing to deep humility with wonderful rapidity. With such alternations of feeling as this sweeping over her like great waves, no wonder she was old before her time.

"Then you must take out that doctor."

"I am willing, but do not know how," she answered, pressing her hands together helplessly. "In my mind he belongs to the story so closely that he cannot be separated from it."

Here Simpson entered, bringing a note for me: it was a line from Mrs. Abercrombie inviting me for that evening — an unexpected gathering, and therefore likely to be all the more agreeable. My heart bounded in spite of me: I forgot Miss Grief and her manuscripts for the moment as completely as though they had never existed. But, bodily, being still in the same room with her, her speech brought me back to the present.

---

[8]Unfinished poem (1797) by English poet Samuel Taylor Coleridge (1772–1834) who called it "a vision in a dream" composed in an opium-induced sleep.

"You have had good news?" she said.

"Oh no, nothing especial—merely an invitation."

"But good news also," she repeated. "And now, as for me, I must go."

Not supposing that she would stay much later in any case, I had that morning ordered a carriage to come for her at about that hour. I told her this. She made no reply beyond putting on her bonnet and shawl.

"You will hear from me soon," I said: "I shall do all I can for you."

She had reached the door, but before opening it she stopped, turned and extended her hand. "You are good," she said: "I give you thanks. Do not think me ungrateful or envious. It is only that you are young, and I am so—so old." Then she opened the door and passed through the anteroom without pause, her maid accompanying her and Simpson with gladness lighting the way. They were gone. I dressed hastily and went out—to continue my studies in psychology.

Time passed: I was busy, amused and perhaps a little excited (sometimes psychology is delightful). But, although much occupied with my own affairs, I did not altogether neglect my self-imposed task regarding Miss Grief. I began by sending her prose story to a friend, the editor of a monthly magazine, with a letter making a strong plea for its admittance. It should have a chance first on its own merits. Then I forwarded the drama to a publisher, also an acquaintance, a man with a taste for phantasms and a soul above mere common popularity, as his own coffers knew to their cost. This done, I waited with conscience clear.

Four weeks passed. During this waiting period I heard nothing from Miss Grief. At last one morning came a letter from my editor. "The story has force, but I cannot stand that doctor," he wrote. "Let her cut him out, and I might print it." Just what I myself had said. The package lay there on my table, travel-worn and grimed: a returned manuscript is, I think, the most melancholy object on earth. I decided to wait, before writing to Aaronna, until the second letter was received. A week later it came. "Armor" was declined. The publisher had been "impressed" by the power displayed in certain passages, but the "impossibilities of the plot" rendered it "unavailable for publication"—in fact, would "bury it in ridicule" if brought before the public, a public "lamentably" fond of amusement, "seeking it, undaunted, even in the cannon's mouth." I doubt if he knew himself what he meant. But one thing, at any rate, was clear: "Armor" was declined.

Now, I am, as I have remarked before, a little obstinate. I was determined that Miss Grief's work should be received. I would alter and improve it myself, without letting her know: the end justified the means. Surely the sieve of my own good taste, whose mesh had been pronounced so fine and delicate, would serve for two. I began, and utterly failed.

I set to work first upon "Armor." I amended, altered, left out, put in, pieced, condensed, lengthened: I did my best, and all to no avail. I could not succeed in completing anything that satisfied me, or that approached, in truth, Miss Grief's own work just as it stood. I suppose I went over that manuscript twenty times: I covered sheets of paper with my copies. But the obstinate drama refused to be corrected: as it was it must stand or fall.

Wearied and annoyed, I threw it aside and took up the prose story: that would be easier. But, to my surprise, I found that that apparently gentle "doctor" would not out: he was so closely interwoven with every part of the tale that to take him out was like taking out one especial figure in a carpet: that is impossible unless you unravel the whole. At last I did unravel the whole, and then the story was no longer good, or Aaronna's: it was weak, and mine. All this took time, for of course I had much to do in connection with my own life and tasks. But, although slowly and at my leisure, I really did try my best as regarded Miss Grief, and without success. I was forced at last to make up my mind that either my own powers were not equal to the task, or else that her perversities were as essential a part of her work as her inspirations, and not to be separated from it. Once during this period I showed two of the short poems to Eth-elind, withholding of course the writer's name. "They were written by a woman," I explained.

"Her mind must have been disordered, poor thing!" Ethelind said in her gentle way when she returned them — "at least judging by these. They are hopelessly mixed and vague."

Now, they were not vague so much as vast. But I knew that I could not make Ethelind comprehend it, and (so complex a creature is man) I do not know that I wanted her to comprehend it. These were the only ones in the whole collection that I would have shown her, and I was rather glad that she did not like even these. Not that poor Aaronna's poems were evil: they were simply unrestrained, large, vast, like the skies or the wind. Ethelind was bounded on all sides, like a violet in a garden-bed. And I liked her so.

One afternoon, about the time when I was beginning to see that I could not "im-prove" Miss Grief, I came upon the maid. I was driving, and she had stopped on the crossing to let the carriage pass. I recognized her at a glance (by her general forlorn-ness), and called to the driver to stop. "How is Miss Crief?" I said. "I have been intending to write to her for some time."

"And your note, when it comes," answered the old woman on the crosswalk fiercely, "she shall not see."

"What?"

"I say she shall not see it. Your patronizing face shows that you have no good news, and you shall not rack and stab her any more on *this* earth, please God, while I have authority."

"Who has racked or stabbed her, Serena?"

"Serena, indeed! Rubbish! I'm no Serena: I'm her aunt. And as to who has racked and stabbed her, I say you, *you* — YOU literary men!" She had put her old head inside my carriage, and flung out these words at me in a shrill, menacing tone. "But she shall die in peace in spite of you," she continued. "Vampires! you take her ideas and fatten on them, and leave her to starve. You know you do — *you* who have had her poor manuscripts these months and months!"

"Is she ill?" I asked in real concern, gathering that much at least from the incoher-ent tirade.

"She is dying," answered the desolate old creature, her voice softening and her dim eyes filling with tears.

"Oh, I trust not. Perhaps something can be done. Can I help you in any way?"

"In all ways if you would," she said, breaking down and beginning to sob weakly, with her head resting on the sill of the carriage-window. "Oh, what have we not been through together, we two! Piece by piece I have sold all."

I am good-hearted enough, but I do not like to have old women weeping across my carriage-door. I suggested, therefore, that she should come inside and let me take her home. Her shabby old skirt was soon beside me, and, following her directions, the driver turned toward one of the most wretched quarters of the city, the abode of poverty, crowded and unclean. Here, in a large bare chamber up many flights of stairs, I found Miss Grief.

As I entered I was startled: I thought she was dead. There seemed no life present until she opened her eyes, and even then they rested upon us vaguely, as though she did not know who we were. But as I approached a sudden light came into them: she recognized me, and this sudden animation, this return of the soul to the windows of the almost deserted body, was the most wonderful thing I ever saw. "You have good news of the drama?" she whispered as I bent over her: "tell me. I *know* you have good news."

What was I to answer? Pray, what would you have answered, puritan?

"Yes, I have good news, Aaronna," I said. "The drama will appear." (And who knows? Perhaps it will in some other world.)

She smiled, and her now brilliant eyes did not leave my face.

"He knows I'm your aunt: I told him," said the old woman, coming to the bedside.

"Did you?" whispered Miss Grief, still gazing at me with a smile. "Then please, dear Aunt Martha, give me something to eat."

Aunt Martha hurried across the room, and I followed her. "It's the first time she's asked for food in weeks," she said in a husky tone.

She opened a cupboard-door vaguely, but I could see nothing within. "What have you for her?" I asked with some impatience, although in a low voice.

"Please God, nothing!" answered the poor old woman, hiding her reply and her tears behind the broad cupboard-door. "I was going out to get a little something when I met you."

"Good Heavens! is it money you need? Here, take this and send; or go yourself in the carriage waiting below."

She hurried out breathless, and I went back to the bedside, much disturbed by what I had seen and heard. But Miss Grief's eyes were full of life, and as I sat down beside her she whispered earnestly, "Tell me."

And I did tell her—a romance invented for the occasion. I venture to say that none of my published sketches could compare with it. As for the lie involved, it will stand among my few good deeds, I know, at the judgment-bar.

And she was satisfied. "I have never known what it was," she whispered, "to be fully happy until now." She closed her eyes, and when the lids fell I again thought that she had passed away. But no, there was still pulsation in her small, thin wrist. As she perceived my touch she smiled. "Yes, I am happy," she said again, although without audible sound.

The old aunt returned: food was prepared, and she took some. I myself went out after wine that should be rich and pure. She rallied a little, but I did not leave her: her eyes dwelt upon me and compelled me to stay, or rather my conscience compelled me. It was a damp night, and I had a little fire made. The wine, fruit, flowers and candles I had ordered made the bare place for the time being bright and fragrant. Aunt Martha dozed in her chair from sheer fatigue—she had watched many nights—but Miss Grief was awake, and I sat beside her.

"I make you my executor," she murmured, "as to the drama. But my other manuscripts place, when I am gone, under my head, and let them be buried with me. They are not many—those you have and these. See!"

I followed her gesture, and saw under her pillows the edges of two more copy-books like the one I had. "Do not look at them—my poor dead children!" she said tenderly. "Let them depart with me—unread, as I have been."

Later she whispered, "Did you wonder why I came to you? It was the contrast. You were young—strong—rich—praised—loved—successful: all that I was not. I wanted to look at you—and imagine how it would feel. You had success—but I had the greater power. Tell me: did I not have it?"

"Yes, Aaronna."

"It is all in the past now. But I am satisfied."

After another pause she said with a faint smile, "Do you remember when I fell asleep in your parlor? It was the good and rich food. It was so long since I had had food like that!"

I took her hand and held it, conscience-stricken, but now she hardly seemed to perceive my touch. "And the smoking?" she whispered. "Do you remember how you laughed? I saw it. But I had heard that smoking soothed—that one was no longer tired and hungry—with a cigar."

In little whispers of this sort, separated by long rests and pauses, the night passed. Once she asked if her aunt was asleep, and when I answered in the affirmative she said, "Help her to return home—to America: the drama will pay for it. I ought never to have brought her away."

I promised, and she resumed her bright-eyed silence.

I think she did not speak again. Toward morning the change came, and soon after sunrise, with her old aunt kneeling by her side, she passed away.

All was arranged as she had wished. Her manuscripts, covered with violets, formed her pillow. No one followed her to the grave save her aunt and myself: I thought she would prefer it so. Her name was not "Crief," after all, but "Moncrief:" I saw it written out by Aunt Martha for the coffin-plate, as follows: "Aaronna Moncrief, aged forty-three years two months and eight days."

I never knew more of her history than is written here. If there was more that I might have learned, it remained unlearned, for I did not ask.

And the drama? I keep it here in this locked case. I could have had it published at my own expense, but I think that now she knows its faults herself, and would not like it.

I keep it, and once in a while I read it over — not as a *memento mori*[9] exactly, but rather as a memento of my own good-fortune, for which I should continually give thanks. The want of one grain made all her work void, and that one grain was given to me. She, with the greater power, failed — I, with the less, succeeded. But no praise is due to me for that. When I die "Armor" is to be destroyed unread: not even Ethelind is to see it. For women will misunderstand each other; and, dear and precious to me as my sweet wife is, I could not bear that she or any one should cast so much as a thought of scorn upon the memory of the writer, upon my poor dead, "unavailable," unaccepted "Miss Grief."

1880, 1967

SARAH ORNE JEWETT
(1849–1909)

Sara Orne Jewett once commented: "The thing that teases the mind over and over for years and at last gets itself put down rightly on paper — whether little or great, it belongs to Literature." This seems to have been a description of her intuitive method of composition. The result was a fiction with little dramatic action but great depth of feeling and subtlety of characterization.

Jewett grew up in South Berwick, Maine, a seaport that was already in decline when she was born. One grandfather was a sea captain, the other a surgeon. Her father was a doctor who developed the habit of carrying his daughter with him on his rounds in his large practice. At an early age, Jewett began to meet the people of her country who would later become characters in her fiction.

She had the run of her father's large library — volumes of Jane Austen, George Eliot, Turgenev, Flaubert, and many others. At the age of fourteen she was deeply impressed by Harriet Beecher Stowe's *The Pearl of Orr's Island*, describing life in the settlements along the Maine coast. She would later remember her intense devotion to reading as the source of her education, not Berwick Academy, from which she graduated in 1865. When she began her first attempts to write stories, her father advised her, "Don't try to write *about* people and things, tell them just as they are!"

Jewett was only nineteen in 1869 when *The Atlantic Monthly* accepted one of

---

[9]"Reminder of death" (Latin).

her stories set in a Maine village called Deephaven. William Dean Howells, editor of the *Atlantic*, took a personal interest in her work and published other stories set in the same seaport town, clearly modelled on her own South Berwick. Later he encouraged her to bring the stories together in a book. *Deephaven* appeared in 1877 and made Sarah Orne Jewett a successful author at age twenty-eight.

She entered the larger literary world with zest, counting among her acquaintances James Russell Lowell, John Greenleaf Whittier, and James T. Fields, a Boston publisher. A friendship with Fields's wife, Annie Fields (fifteen years her senior), grew into a lasting companionship when Fields died in 1881. The two women were highly compatible, sharing the Fields residence in Boston during the winters, where they received literary figures, and travelling widely throughout Europe in the summers. There they met Tennyson, Christina Rosetti, Mark Twain (in Venice), Henry James (at Rye, in England), and many other writers.

Despite her wide travelling, most of her work — more than twenty volumes in her long career — was set in New England. In 1881, she published a volume of sketches, *Country By-Ways*, and dedicated it to her father, who had died in 1878. She tried her hand at a novel, publishing *A Country Doctor* in 1884. Based on her father's life and experience, at the same time it revealed her own earlier desire to become a doctor.

It was not, however, until 1889, with the publication of *The Country of the Pointed Firs*, that Jewett hit her stride. This series of local color sketches set in a Maine seaport established the basis for Jewett's enduring reputation. A reviewer wrote: "*The Country of the Pointed Firs* is the flower of a sweet, sane knowledge of life, and an art so elusive that it smiles up at you while you pull aside the petals, vainly probing its heart." Willa Cather, who as a young writer had sought Jewett out, wrote in the Introduction to a modern reprint of the book: "If I were asked to name three American books which have the possibility of a long, long life, I would say at once, *The Scarlet Letter, Huckleberry Finn*, and *The Country of the Pointed Firs*."

In 1901, Jewett received an honorary degree from her father's college, Bowdoin — the first such degree Bowdoin had bestowed on a woman. A fall from a carriage in 1901 resulted in injuries that were to plague her for the rest of her life, and that would deflect her from her writing career. She died in 1909 in the same house in South Berwick, Maine, where she had been born.

ADDITIONAL READING

Stories and Tales, 7 vols., 1910; *Letters of Sarah Orne Jewett*, ed. Annie Fields, 1911; *The Best Short Stories of Sarah Orne Jewett*, 2 vols., ed. Willa Cather, 1925; *Sarah Orne Jewett Letters*, ed. Richard Cary, 1956, 1967; *Deephaven and Other Stories*, ed. Richard Carey, 1966; *The Uncollected Stories of Sarah Orne Jewett*, ed. Richard Carey, 1971.

F. O. Matthiessen, *Sarah Orne Jewett*, 1929; Clara and Carl Weber, *A Bibliography of the Published Writings of Sarah Orne Jewett*, 1949; Perry D. Westbrook, *Acres of Flint: Sarah Orne Jewett and Her Contemporaries*, 1951, 1981; Richard Cary, *Sarah Orne Jewett*, 1962; Margaret Farrand Thorp, *Sarah Orne Jewett*, 1966; Richard Cary, ed., *Appreciation of Sarah Orne Jewett: 29 Interpretive Essays*, 1973; Josephine Donovan, *Sarah Orne Jewett*, 1980; Josephine Donovan, "Sarah Orne Jewett and the World of Mothers," *New England Local Color Literature: A Woman's Tradition*, 1983; Louis A. Renza, *"A White Heron" and the Question of Minor Literature*, 1984; Gwen L. Nagel, ed., *Critical Essays on Sarah Orne Jewett*, 1984; Sarah Way Sherman, *Sarah Orne Jewett, An American Persephone*, 1989.

TEXT

Tales of New England, 1890.

A White Heron[1]

I

The woods were already filled with shadows one June evening, just before eight o'clock, though a bright sunset still glimmered faintly among the trunks of the trees. A little girl was driving home her cow, a plodding, dilatory, provoking creature in her behavior, but a valued companion for all that. They were going away from the western light, and striking deep into the dark woods, but their feet were familiar with the path, and it was no matter whether their eyes could see it or not.

There was hardly a night the summer through when the old cow could be found waiting at the pasture bars; on the contrary, it was her greatest pleasure to hide herself away among the high huckleberry bushes, and though she wore a loud bell she had made the discovery that if one stood perfectly still it would not ring. So Sylvia had to hunt for her until she found her, and call Co'! Co'! with never an answering Moo, until her childish patience was quite spent. If the creature had not given good milk and plenty of it, the case would have seemed very different to her owners. Besides, Sylvia had all the time there was, and very little use to make of it. Sometimes in pleasant weather it was a consolation to look upon the cow's pranks as an intelligent attempt to play hide and seek, and as the child had no playmates she lent herself to this amusement with a good deal of zest. Though this chase had been so long that the wary animal herself had given an unusual signal of her whereabouts, Sylvia had only laughed when she came upon Mistress Moolly at the swamp-side, and urged her affectionately homeward with a twig of birch leaves. The old cow was not inclined to wander farther, she even turned in the right direction for once as they left the pasture, and stepped along the road at a good pace. She was quite ready to be milked now, and seldom stopped to browse. Sylvia wondered what her grandmother would say because they were so late. It was a great while since she had left home at half past five o'clock, but everybody knew the difficulty of making this errand a short one. Mrs. Tilley had chased the hornéd torment too many summer evenings herself to blame any one else for lingering, and was only thankful as she waited that she had Sylvia, nowadays, to give such valuable assistance. The good woman suspected that Sylvia loitered occasionally on her own account; there never was such a child for straying about out-of-doors since the world was made! Everybody said that it was a good change for a little maid who had tried to grow for eight years in a crowded manufacturing town, but, as for Sylvia herself, it seemed as if she never had been alive at all before she came to live at the farm. She thought often with wistful compassion of a wretched dry geranium that belonged to a town neighbor.

"'Afraid of folks,'" old Mrs. Tilley said to herself, with a smile, after she had made the unlikely choice of Sylvia from her daughter's houseful of children, and was returning to the farm. "'Afraid of folks,' they said! I guess she won't be troubled no great with 'em up to the old place!" When they reached the door of the lonely home and stopped to unlock it, and the cat came to purr loudly, and rub against them, a deserted pussy, indeed, but fat with young robins, Sylvia whispered that this was a beautiful place to live in, and she never should wish to go home.

The companions followed the shady woodroad, the cow taking slow steps, and the child very fast ones. The cow stopped long at the brook to drink, as if the pasture were not half a swamp, and Sylvia stood still and waited, letting her bare feet cool themselves in the shoal water, while the great twilight moths struck softly against her.

---

[1] "A White Heron" was first published in 1886 and reprinted with minor revisions in *Tales of New England* (1890), the source of this text.

She waded on through the brook as the cow moved away, and listened to the thrushes with a heart that beat fast with pleasure. There was a stirring in the great boughs overhead. They were full of little birds and beasts that seemed to be wide-awake, and going about their world, or else saying good-night to each other in sleepy twitters. Sylvia herself felt sleepy as she walked along. However, it was not much farther to the house, and the air was soft and sweet. She was not often in the woods so late as this, and it made her feel as if she were a part of the gray shadows and the moving leaves. She was just thinking how long it seemed since she first came to the farm a year ago, and wondering if everything went on in the noisy town just the same as when she was there; the thought of the great red-faced boy who used to chase and frighten her made her hurry along the path to escape from the shadow of the trees.

Suddenly this little woods-girl is horror-stricken to hear a clear whistle not very far away. Not a bird's whistle, which would have a sort of friendliness, but a boy's whistle, determined, and somewhat aggressive. Sylvia left the cow to whatever sad fate might await her, and stepped discreetly aside into the bushes, but she was just too late. The enemy had discovered her, and called out in a very cheerful and persuasive tone, "Halloa, little girl, how far is it to the road?" and trembling Sylvia answered almost inaudibly, "A good ways."

She did not dare look boldly at the tall young man, who carried a gun over his shoulder, but she came out of her bush and again followed the cow, while he walked alongside.

"I have been hunting for some birds," the stranger said kindly, "and I have lost my way, and need a friend very much. Don't be afraid," he added gallantly. "Speak up and tell me what your name is, and whether you think I can spend the night at your house, and go out gunning early in the morning."

Sylvia was more alarmed than before. Would not her grandmother consider her much to blame? But who could have foreseen such an accident as this? It did not appear to be her fault, and she hung her head as if the stem of it were broken, but managed to answer "Sylvy," with much effort when her companion again asked her name.

Mrs. Tilley was standing in the doorway when the trio came into view. The cow gave a loud moo by way of explanation.

"Yes, you'd better speak up for yourself, you old trial! Where'd she tucked herself away this time, Sylvy?" Sylvia kept an awed silence; she knew by instinct that her grandmother did not comprehend the gravity of the situation. She must be mistaking the stranger for one of the farmer-lads of the region.

The young man stood his gun beside the door, and dropped a heavy game-bag beside it; then he bade Mrs. Tilley good-evening, and repeated his wayfarer's story, and asked if he could have a night's lodging.

"Put me anywhere you like," he said. "I must be off early in the morning, before day; but I am very hungry, indeed. You can give me some milk at any rate, that's plain."

"Dear sakes, yes," responded the hostess, whose long slumbering hospitality seemed to be easily awakened. "You might fare better if you went out on the main road a mile or so, but you're welcome to what we've got. I'll milk right off, and you make yourself at home. You can sleep on husks or feathers," she proffered graciously. "I raised them all myself. There's good pasturing for geese just below here towards the ma'sh. Now step round and set a plate for the gentleman, Sylvy!" And Sylvia promptly stepped. She was glad to have something to do, and she was hungry herself.

It was a surprise to find so clean and comfortable a little dwelling in this New England wilderness. The young man had known the horrors of its most primitive housekeeping, and the dreary squalor of that level of society which does not rebel at the companionship of hens. This was the best thrift of an old-fashioned farmstead, though on such a small scale that it seemed like a hermitage. He listened eagerly to the old woman's quaint talk, he watched Sylvia's pale face and shining gray eyes with ever growing enthusiasm, and insisted that this was the best supper he had eaten for a month; then, afterward, the new-made friends sat down in the doorway together while the moon came up.

Soon it would be berry-time, and Sylvia was a great help at picking. The cow was a good milker, though a plaguy thing to keep track of, the hostess gossiped frankly, adding presently that she had buried four children, so that Sylvia's mother, and a son (who might be dead) in California were all the children she had left. "Dan, my boy, was a great hand to go gunning," she explained sadly. "I never wanted for pa'tridges or gray squer'ls while he was to home. He's been a great wand'rer, I expect, and he's no hand to write letters. There, I don't blame him, I'd ha' seen the world myself if it had been so I could.

"Sylvia takes after him," the grandmother continued affectionately, after a minute's pause. "There ain't a foot o' ground she don't know her way over, and the wild creatur's counts her one o' themselves. Squer'ls she'll tame to come an' feed right out o' her hands, and all sorts o' birds. Last winter she got the jay-birds to bangeing[2] here, and I believe she 'd 'a' scanted herself of her own meals to have plenty to throw out amongst 'em, if I had n't kep' watch. Anything but crows, I tell her, I'm willin' to help support, — though Dan he went an' tamed one o' them that did seem to have reason same as folks. It was round here a good spell after he went away. Dan an' his father they did n't hitch, — but he never held up his head ag'in after Dan had dared him an' gone off."

The guest did not notice this hint of family sorrows in his eager interest in something else.

"So Sylvy knows all about birds, does she?" he exclaimed, as he looked round at the little girl who sat, very demure but increasingly sleepy, in the moonlight. "I am making a collection of birds myself. I have been at it ever since I was a boy." (Mrs. Tilley smiled.) "There are two or three very rare ones I have been hunting for these five years. I mean to get them on my own ground if they can be found."

"Do you cage 'em up?" asked Mrs. Tilley doubtfully, in response to this enthusiastic announcement.

"Oh, no, they're stuffed and preserved, dozens and dozens of them," said the ornithologist, "and I have shot or snared every one myself. I caught a glimpse of a white heron three miles from here on Saturday, and I have followed it in this direction. They have never been found in this district at all. The little white heron, it is," and he turned again to look at Sylvia with the hope of discovering that the rare bird was one of her acquaintances.

But Sylvia was watching a hop-toad in the narrow footpath.

"You would know the heron if you saw it," the stranger continued eagerly. "A queer tall white bird with soft feathers and long thin legs. And it would have a nest perhaps in the top of a high tree, made of sticks, something like a hawk's nest."

Sylvia's heart gave a wild beat; she knew that strange white bird, and had once stolen softly near where it stood in some bright green swamp grass, away over at the other side of the woods. There was an open place where the sunshine always seemed strangely yellow and hot, where tall, nodding rushes grew, and her grandmother had warned her that she might sink in the soft black mud underneath and never be heard of more. Not far beyond were the salt marshes and beyond those was the sea, the sea which Sylvia wondered and dreamed about, but never had looked upon, though its great voice could often be heard above the noise of the woods on stormy nights.

"I can't think of anything I should like so much as to find the heron's nest," the handsome stranger was saying. "I would give ten dollars to anybody who could show it to me," he added desperately, "and I mean to spend my whole vacation hunting for

---

[2]Lounging about.

it if need be. Perhaps it was only migrating, or had been chased out of its own region by some bird of prey."

Mrs. Tilley gave amazed attention to all this, but Sylvia still watched the toad, not divining, as she might have done at some calmer time, that the creature wished to get to its hole under the doorstep, and was much hindered by the unusual spectators at that hour of the evening. No amount of thought, that night, could decide how many wished-for treasures the ten dollars, so lightly spoken of, would buy.

The next day the young sportsman hovered about the woods, and Sylvia kept him company, having lost her first fear of the friendly lad, who proved to be most kind and sympathetic. He told her many things about the birds and what they knew and where they lived and what they did with themselves. And he gave her a jack-knife, which she thought as great a treasure as if she were a desert-islander. All day long he did not once make her troubled or afraid except when he brought down some unsuspecting singing creature from its bough. Sylvia would have liked him vastly better without his gun; she could not understand why he killed the very birds he seemed to like so much. But as the day waned, Sylvia still watched the young man with loving admiration. She had never seen anybody so charming and delightful; the woman's heart, asleep in the child, was vaguely thrilled by a dream of love. Some premonition of that great power stirred and swayed these young foresters who traversed the solemn woodlands with soft-footed silent care. They stopped to listen to a bird's song; they pressed forward again eagerly, parting the branches, — speaking to each other rarely and in whispers; the young man going first and Sylvia following, fascinated, a few steps behind, with her gray eyes dark with excitement.

She grieved because the longed-for white heron was elusive, but she did not lead the guest, she only followed, and there was no such thing as speaking first. The sound of her own unquestioned voice would have terrified her, — it was hard enough to answer yes or no when there was need of that. At last evening began to fall, and they drove the cow home together, and Sylvia smiled with pleasure when they came to the place where she heard the whistle and was afraid only the night before.

II

Half a mile from home, at the farther edge of the woods, where the land was highest, a great pine-tree stood, the last of its generation. Whether it was left for a boundary mark, or for what reason, no one could say; the woodchoppers who had felled its mates were dead and gone long ago, and a whole forest of sturdy trees, pines and oaks and maples, had grown again. But the stately head of this old pine towered above them all and made a landmark for sea and shore miles and miles away. Sylvia knew it well. She had always believed that whoever climbed to the top of it could see the ocean; and the little girl had often laid her hand on the great rough trunk and looked up wistfully at those dark boughs that the wind always stirred, no matter how hot and still the air might be below. Now she thought of the tree with a new excitement, for why, if one climbed it at break of day, could not one see all the world, and easily discover whence the white heron flew, and mark the place, and find the hidden nest?

What a spirit of adventure, what wild ambition! What fancied triumph and delight and glory for the later morning when she could make known the secret! It was almost too real and too great for the childish heart to bear.

All night the door of the little house stood open, and the whippoorwills came and sang upon the very step. The young sportsman and his old hostess were sound asleep, but Sylvia's great design kept her broad awake and watching. She forgot to think of sleep. The short summer night seemed as long as the winter darkness, and at last when the whippoorwills ceased, and she was afraid the morning would after all come too soon, she stole out of the house and followed the pasture path through the woods, hastening toward the open ground beyond, listening with a sense of comfort and companionship to the drowsy twitter of a half-awakened bird, whose perch she had jarred in passing. Alas, if the great wave of human interest which flooded for the first time this dull little life should sweep away the satisfactions of an existence heart to heart with nature and the dumb life of the forest!

There was the huge tree asleep yet in the paling moonlight, and small and hopeful Sylvia began with utmost bravery to mount to the top of it, with tingling, eager blood coursing the channels of her whole frame, with her bare feet and fingers, that pinched and held like bird's claws to the monstrous ladder reaching up, up, almost to the sky itself. First she must mount the white oak tree that grew alongside, where she was almost lost among the dark branches and the green leaves heavy and wet with dew; a bird fluttered off its nest, and a red squirrel ran to and fro and scolded pettishly at the harmless housebreaker. Sylvia felt her way easily. She had often climbed there, and knew that higher still one of the oak's upper branches chafed against the pine trunk, just where its lower boughs were set close together. There, when she made the dangerous pass from one tree to the other, the great enterprise would really begin.

She crept out along the swaying oak limb at last, and took the daring step across into the old pine-tree. The way was harder than she thought; she must reach far and hold fast, the sharp dry twigs caught and held her and scratched her like angry talons, the pitch made her thin little fingers clumsy and stiff as she went round and round the tree's great stem, higher and higher upward. The sparrows and robins in the woods below were beginning to wake and twitter to the dawn, yet it seemed much lighter there aloft in the pine-tree, and the child knew that she must hurry if her project were to be of any use.

The tree seemed to lengthen itself out as she went up, and to reach farther and farther upward. It was like a great main-mast to the voyaging earth; it must truly have been amazed that morning through all its ponderous frame as it felt this determined spark of human spirit creeping and climbing from higher branch to branch. Who knows how steadily the least twigs held themselves to advantage this light, weak creature on her way! The old pine must have loved his new dependent. More than all the hawks, and bats, and moths, and even the sweet-voiced thrushes, was the brave, beating heart of the solitary gray-eyed child. And the tree stood still and held away the winds that June morning while the dawn grew bright in the east.

Sylvia's face was like a pale star, if one had seen it from the ground, when the last thorny bough was past, and she stood trembling and tired but wholly triumphant, high in the tree-top. Yes, there was the sea with the dawning sun making a golden dazzle over it, and toward that glorious east flew two hawks with slow-moving pinions. How low they looked in the air from that height when before one had only seen them far up, and dark against the blue sky. Their gray feathers were as soft as moths; they seemed only a little way from the tree, and Sylvia felt as if she too could go flying away among the clouds. Westward, the woodlands and farms reached miles and miles into the distance; here and there were church steeples, and white villages; truly it was a vast and awesome world.

The birds sang louder and louder. At last the sun came up bewilderingly bright. Sylvia could see the white sails of ships out at sea, and the clouds that were purple and rose-colored and yellow at first began to fade away. Where was the white heron's nest in the sea of green branches, and was this wonderful sight and pageant of the world the only reward for having climbed to such a giddy height? Now look down again, Sylvia, where the green marsh is set among the shining birches and dark hemlocks; there where you saw the white heron once you will see him again; look, look! a white spot of him like a single floating feather comes up from the dead hemlock and grows larger, and rises, and comes close at last, and goes by the landmark pine with steady sweep of wing and outstretched slender neck and crested head. And wait! wait! do not move a foot or a finger, little girl, do not send an arrow of light and consciousness from your two eager eyes, for the heron has perched on a pine bough not far beyond yours, and cries back to his mate on the nest, and plumes his feathers for the new day!

The child gives a long sigh a minute later when a company of shouting cat-birds comes also to the tree, and vexed by their fluttering and lawlessness the solemn heron goes away. She knows his secret now, the wild, light, slender bird that floats and wavers, and goes back like an arrow presently to his home in the green world beneath. Then Sylvia, well satisfied, makes her perilous way down again, not daring to look far below the branch she stands on, ready to cry sometimes because her fingers ache and her lamed feet slip. Wondering over and over again what the stranger would say to her, and what he would think when she told him how to find his way straight to the heron's nest.

"Sylvy, Sylvy!" called the busy old grandmother again and again, but nobody answered, and the small husk bed was empty, and Sylvia had disappeared.

The guest waked from a dream, and remembering his day's pleasure hurried to dress himself that it might sooner begin. He was sure from the way the shy little girl looked once or twice yesterday that she had at least seen the white heron, and now she must really be persuaded to tell. Here she comes now, paler than ever, and her worn old frock is torn and tattered, and smeared with pine pitch. The grandmother and the sportsman stand in the door together and question her, and the splendid moment has come to speak of the dead hemlock-tree by the green marsh.

But Sylvia does not speak after all, though the old grandmother fretfully rebukes her, and the young man's kind appealing eyes are looking straight in her own. He can make them rich with money; he has promised it, and they are poor now. He is so well worth making happy, and he waits to hear the story she can tell.

No, she must keep silence! What is it that suddenly forbids her and makes her dumb? Has she been nine years growing, and now, when the great world for the first time puts out a hand to her, must she thrust it aside for a bird's sake? The murmur of the pine's green branches is in her ears, she remembers how the white heron came flying through the golden air and how they watched the sea and the morning together, and Sylvia cannot speak; she cannot tell the heron's secret and give its life away.

Dear loyalty, that suffered a sharp pang as the guest went away disappointed later in the day, that could have served and followed him and loved him as a dog loves! Many a night Sylvia heard the echo of his whistle haunting the pasture path as she came home with the loitering cow. She forgot even her sorrow at the sharp report of his gun and the piteous sight of thrushes and sparrows dropping silent to the ground, their songs hushed and their pretty feathers stained and wet with blood. Were the birds better friends than their hunter might have been,—who can tell? Whatever treasures were lost to her, woodlands and summer-time, remember! Bring your gifts and graces and tell your secrets to this lonely country child!

1886, 1890

Miss Tempy's Watchers[1]

The time of year was April; the place was a small farming town in New Hampshire, remote from any railroad. One by one the lights had been blown out in the scattered houses near Miss Tempy Dent's; but as her neighbors took a last look out-

---

[1]"Miss Tempy's Watchers" was first published in 1888 and reprinted in *Tales of New England* (1890), the source of this text.

of-doors, their eyes turned with instinctive curiosity toward the old house, where a lamp burned steadily. They gave a little sigh. "Poor Miss Tempy!" said more than one bereft acquaintance; for the good woman lay dead in her north chamber, and the light was a watcher's light. The funeral was set for the next day, at one o'clock.

The watchers were two of the oldest friends, Mrs. Crowe and Sarah Ann Binson. They were sitting in the kitchen, because it seemed less awesome than the unused best room, and they beguiled the long hours by steady conversation. One would think that neither topics nor opinions would hold out, at that rate, all through the long spring night; but there was a certain degree of excitement just then, and the two women had risen to an unusual level of expressiveness and confidence. Each had already told the other more than once fact that she had determined to keep secret; they were again and again tempted into statements that either would have found impossible by daylight. Mrs. Crowe was knitting a blue yarn stocking for her husband; the foot was already so long that it seemed as if she must have forgotten to narrow it at the proper time. Mrs. Crowe knew exactly what she was about, however; she was of a much cooler disposition than Sister Binson, who made futile attempts at some sewing, only to drop her work into her lap whenever the talk was most engaging.

Their faces were interesting, — of the dry, shrewd, quick-witted New England type, with thin hair twisted neatly back out of the way. Mrs. Crowe could look vague and benignant, and Miss Binson was, to quote her neighbors, a little too sharp-set; but the world knew that she had need to be, with the load she must carry of supporting an inefficient widowed sister and six unpromising and unwilling nieces and nephews. The eldest boy was at last placed with a good man to learn the mason's trade. Sarah Ann Binson, for all her sharp, anxious aspect, never defended herself, when her sister whined and fretted. She was told every week of her life that the poor children never would have had to lift a finger if their father had lived, and yet she had kept her steadfast way with the little farm, and patiently taught the young people many useful things, for which, as everybody said, they would live to thank her. However pleasureless her life appeared to outward view, it was brimful of pleasure to herself.

Mrs. Crowe, on the contrary, was well to do, her husband being a rich farmer and an easy-going man. She was a stingy woman, but for all that she looked kindly; and when she gave away anything, or lifted a finger to help anybody, it was thought a great piece of beneficence, and a compliment, indeed, which the recipient accepted with twice as much gratitude as double the gift that came from a poorer and more generous acquaintance. Everybody liked to be on good terms with Mrs. Crowe. Socially she stood much higher than Sarah Ann Binson. They were both old schoolmates and friends of Temperance Dent, who had asked them, one day, not long before she died, if they would not come together and look after the house, and manage everything, when she was gone. She may have had some hope that they might become closer friends in this period of intimate partnership, and that the richer woman might better understand the burdens of the poorer. They had not kept the house the night before; they were too weary with the care of their old friend, whom they had not left until all was over.

There was a brook which ran down the hillside very near the house, and the sound of it was much louder than usual. When there was silence in the kitchen, the busy stream had a strange insistence in its wild voice, as if it tried to make the watchers understand something that related to the past.

"I declare, I can't begin to sorrow for Tempy yet. I am so glad to have her at rest," whispered Mrs. Crowe. "It is strange to set here without her, but I can't make it clear that she has gone. I feel as if she had got easy and dropped off to sleep, and I'm more scared about waking her up than knowing any other feeling."

"Yes," said Sarah Ann, "it's just like that, ain't it? But I tell you we are goin' to miss her worse than we expect. She's helped me through with many a trial, has Temperance. I ain't the only one who says the same, neither."

These words were spoken as if there were a third person listening; somebody beside Mrs. Crowe. The watchers could not rid their minds of the feeling that they were being watched themselves. The spring wind whistled in the window crack, now and then, and buffeted the little house in a gusty way that had a sort of companionable effect. Yet, on the whole, it was a very still night, and the watchers spoke in a half-whisper.

"She was the freest-handed woman that ever I knew," said Mrs. Crowe, decidedly. "According to her means, she gave away more than anybody. I used to tell her 't wa'n't right. I used really to be afraid that she went without too much, for we have a duty to ourselves."

Sister Binson looked up in a half-amused, unconscious way, and then recollected herself.

Mrs. Crowe met her look with a serious face. "It ain't so easy for me to give as it is for some," she said simply, but with an effort which was made possible only by the occasion. "I should like to say, while Tempy is laying here yet in her own house, that she has been a constant lesson to me. Folks are too kind, and shame me with thanks for what I do. I ain't such a generous woman as poor Tempy was, for all she had nothin' to do with, as one may say."

Sarah Binson was much moved at this confession, and was even pained and touched by the unexpected humility. "You have a good many calls on you" — she began, and then left her kind little compliment half finished.

"Yes, yes, but I've got means enough. My disposition's more of a cross to me as I grow older, and I made up my mind this morning that Tempy's example should be my pattern henceforth." She began to knit faster than ever.

"'T ain't no use to get morbid: that's what Tempy used to say herself," said Sarah Ann, after a minute's silence. "Ain't it strange to say 'used to say'?" and her own voice choked a little. "She never did like to hear folks git goin' about themselves."

"'T was only because they're apt to do it so as other folks will say't wasn't so, an' praise 'em up," humbly replied Mrs. Crowe, "and that ain't my object. There wa'n't a child but what Tempy set herself to work to see what she could do to please it. One time my brother's folks had been stopping here in the summer, from Massachusetts. The children was all little, and they broke up a sight of toys, and left 'em when they were going away. Tempy come right up after they rode by, to see if she couldn't help me set the house to rights, and she caught me just as I was going to fling some of the clutter into the stove. I was kind of tired out, starting 'em off in season. 'Oh, give me them!' says she, real pleading; and she wropped 'em up and took 'em home with her when she went, and she mended 'em up and stuck 'em together, and made some young one or other happy with every blessed one. You'd thought I'd done her the biggest favor. 'No thanks to me. I should ha' burnt 'em, Tempy,' says I."

"Some of 'em came to our house, I know," said Miss Binson. "She'd take a lot o' trouble to please a child, 'stead o' shoving of it out o' the way, like the rest of us when we're drove."

"I can tell you the biggest thing she ever done, and I don't know's there's anybody left but me to tell it. I don't want it forgot," Sarah Binson went on, looking up at the clock to see how the night was going. "It was that pretty-looking Trevor girl, who taught the Corners school, and married so well afterwards, out in New York State. You remember her, I dare say?"

"Certain," said Mrs. Crowe, with an air of interest.

"She was a splendid scholar, folks said, and give the school a great start; but she'd overdone herself getting her education, and working to pay for it, and she all broke down one spring, and Tempy made her come and stop with her a while, — you remember that? Well, she had an uncle, her mother's brother, out in Chicago, who was well off and friendly, and used to write to Lizzie Trevor, and I dare say make her some presents; but he was a lively, driving man, and didn't take time to stop and think about his folks. He hadn't seen her since she was a little girl. Poor Lizzie was so pale and weakly that she just got through the term o' school. She looked as if she was just going straight off in a decline. Tempy, she cosseted[2] her up a while, and then, next thing folks knew, she was tellin' round how Miss Trevor had gone to see her uncle, and meant to visit Niagary Falls on the way, and stop over night. Now I happened to know, in ways I won't dwell on to explain, that the poor girl was in debt for her schoolin' when she come here, and her last quarter's pay had just squared it off at last, and left her without a cent ahead, hardly; but it had fretted her thinking of it, so she paid it all; those might have dunned her that she owed it to. An' I taxed Tempy about the girl's goin' off on such a journey till she owned up, rather 'n have Lizzie blamed, that she'd given her sixty dollars, same's if she was rolling in riches, and sent her off to have a good rest and vacation."

"Sixty dollars!" exclaimed Mrs. Crowe. "Tempy only had ninety dollars a year that came in to her; rest of her livin' she got by helpin' about, with what she raised off this little piece o' ground, sand one side an' clay the other. An' how often I've heard her tell, years ago, that she'd rather see Niagary than any other sight in the world!"

The women looked at each other in silence; the magnitude of the generous sacrifice was almost too great for their comprehension.

"She was just poor enough to do that!" declared Mrs. Crowe at last, in an abandonment of feeling. "Say what you may, I feel humbled to the dust," and her companion ventured to say nothing. She never had given away sixty dollars at once, but it was simply because she never had it to give. It came to her very lips to say in explanation, "Tempy was so situated;" but she checked herself in time, for she would not betray her own loyal guarding of a dependent household.

"Folks say a great deal of generosity, and this one's being public-sperited, and that one free-handed about giving," said Mrs. Crowe, who was a little nervous in the silence. "I suppose we can't tell the sorrow it would be to some folks not to give, same's 't would be to me not to save. I seem kind of made for that, as if 't was what I'd got to do. I should feel sights better about it if I could make it evident what I was savin' for. If I had a child, now, Sarah Ann," and her voice was a little husky,—"if I had a child, I should think I was heapin' of it up because he was the one trained by the Lord to scatter it again for good. But here's Mr. Crowe and me, we can't do anything with money, and both of us like to keep things same's they've always been. Now Priscilla Dance was talking away like a mill-clapper,[3] week before last. She'd think I would go right off and get one o' them new-fashioned gilt-and-white papers for the best room, and some new furniture, an' a marble-top table. And I looked at her, all struck up. 'Why,' says I, 'Priscilla, that nice old velvet paper ain't hurt a mite. I shouldn't feel 't was my best room without it. Dan'el says 't is the first thing he can remember rubbin' his little baby fingers on to it, and how splendid he thought them red roses was.' I maintain," continued Mrs. Crowe stoutly, "that folks wastes sights o' good money doin' just such foolish things. Tearin' out the insides o' meetin'-houses, and fixin' the pews different; 't was good enough as 't was with mendin'; then times come, an' they want to put it all back same's 't was before."

This touched upon an exciting subject to active members of that parish. Miss Binson and Mrs. Crowe belonged to opposite parties, and had at one time come as near hard feelings as they could, and yet escape them. Each hastened to speak of others things and to show her untouched friendliness.

"I do agree with you," said Sister Binson, "that few of us know what use to make of

---

[2]Pampered.
[3]A device in a mill that makes a clapping noise as it strikes the hopper or funnel to make the grain move down to the millstones.

money, beyond every-day necessities. You've seen more o' the world than I have, and know what's expected. When it comes to taste and judgment about such things, I ought to defer to others;" and with this modest avowal the critical moment passed when there might have been an improper discussion.

In the silence that followed, the fact of their presence in a house of death grew more clear than before. There was something disturbing in the noise of a mouse gnawing at the dry boards of a closet wall near by. Both the watchers looked up anxiously at the clock; it was almost the middle of the night, and the whole world seemed to have left them alone with their solemn duty. Only the brook was awake.

"Perhaps we might give a look up-stairs now," whispered Mrs. Crowe, as if she hoped to hear some reason against their going just then to the chamber of death; but Sister Binson rose, with a serious and yet satisfied countenance, and lifted the small lamp from the table. She was much more used to watching than Mrs. Crowe, and much less affected by it. They opened the door into a small entry with a steep stairway; they climbed the creaking stairs, and entered the cold upper room on tiptoe. Mrs. Crowe's heart began to beat very fast as the lamp was put on a high bureau, and made long, fixed shadows about the walls. She went hesitatingly toward the solemn shape under its white drapery, and felt a sense of remonstrance as Sarah Ann gently, but in a business-like way, turned back the thin sheet.

"Seems to me she looks pleasanter and pleasanter," whispered Sarah Ann Binson impulsively, as they gazed at the white face with its wonderful smile. "To-morrow 't will all have faded out. I do believe they kind of wake up a day or two after they die, and it's then they go." She replaced the light covering, and they both turned quickly away; there was a chill in this upper room.

"'T is a great thing for anybody to have got through, ain't it?" said Mrs. Crowe softly, as she began to go down the stairs on tiptoe. The warm air from the kitchen beneath met them with a sense of welcome and shelter.

"I don' know why it is, but I feel as near again to Tempy down here as I do up there," replied Sister Binson. "I feel as if the air was full of her, kind of. I can sense things, now and then, that she seems to say. Now I never was one to take up with no nonsense of sperits and such, but I declare I felt as if she told me just now to put some more wood into the stove."

Mrs. Crowe preserved a gloomy silence. She had suspected before this that her companion was of a weaker and more credulous disposition than herself. "'T is a great thing to have got through," she repeated, ignoring definitely all that had last been said. "I suppose you know as well as I that Tempy was one that always feared death. Well, it's all put behind her now; she knows what 't is." Mrs. Crowe gave a little sigh, and Sister Binson's quick sympathies were stirred toward this other old friend, who also dreaded the great change.

"I'd never like to forgit almost those last words Tempy spoke plain to me," she said gently, like the comforter she truly was. "She looked up at me once or twice, that last afternoon after I come to set by her, and let Mis' Owen go home; and I says, 'Can I do anything to ease you, Tempy?' and the tears come into my eyes so I couldn't see what kind of a nod she give me. 'No, Sarah Ann, you can't, dear,' says she; and then she got her breath again, and says she, looking at me real meanin', 'I'm only a-gettin' sleepier and sleepier; that's all there is,' says she, and smiled up at me kind of wishful, and shut her eyes. I knew well enough all she meant. She'd been lookin' out for a chance to tell me, and I don' know's she ever said much afterwards."

Mrs. Crowe was not knitting; she had been listening too eagerly. "Yes, 't will be a comfort to think of that sometimes," she said, in acknowledgment.

"I know that old Dr. Prince said once, in evenin' meetin', that he'd watched by many a dyin' bed, as we well knew, and enough o' his sick folks had been scared o' dyin' their whole lives through; but when they come to the last, he'd never seen one but was willin', and most were glad, to go. ''Tis as natural as bein' born or livin' on,' he said. I don't know what had moved him to speak that night. You know he wa'n't in the habit of it, and 't was the monthly concert of prayer for foreign missions anyways," said Sarah Ann; "but 't was a great stay to the mind to listen to his words of experience."

"There never was a better man," responded Mrs. Crowe, in a really cheerful tone. She had recovered from her feeling of nervous dread, the kitchen was so comfortable with lamplight and firelight; and just then the old clock began to tell the hour of twelve with leisurely whirring strokes.

Sister Binson laid aside her work, and rose quickly and went to the cupboard. "We'd better take a little to eat," she explained. "The night will go fast after this. I want to know if you went and made some o' your nice cupcake, while you was home to-day?" she asked, in a pleased tone; and Mrs. Crowe acknowledged such a gratifying piece of thoughtfulness for this humble friend who denied herself all luxuries. Sarah Ann brewed a generous cup of tea, and the watchers drew their chairs up to the table presently, and quelled their hunger with good country appetites. Sister Binson put a spoon into a small, old-fashioned glass of preserved quince, and passed it to her friend. She was most familiar with the house, and played the part of hostess. "Spread some o' this on your bread and butter," she said to Mrs. Crowe. "Tempy wanted me to use some three or four times, but I never felt to. I know she'd like to have us comfortable now, and would urge us to make a good supper, poor dear."

"What excellent preserves she did make!" mourned Mrs. Crowe. "None of us has got her light hand at doin' things tasty. She made most o' everything, too. Now, she only had that one old quince-tree down in the far corner of the piece, but she'd go out in the spring and tend to it, and look at it so pleasant, and kind of expect the old thorny thing into bloomin'."

"She was just the same with folks," said Sarah Ann. "And she'd never git more 'n a little apernful o' quinces, but she'd have every mite o' goodness out o' those, and set the glasses up onto her best-room closet shelf, *so* pleased. 'T wa'n't but a week ago to-morrow mornin' I fetched her a little taste o' jelly in a teaspoon; and she says 'Thank ye,' and took it, an' the minute she tasted it she looked up at me as worried as could be. 'Oh, I don't want to eat that,' says she. 'I always keep that in case o' sickness.' 'You're goin' to have the good o' one tumbler yourself,' says I. 'I'd just like to know who's sick now, if you ain't!' An' she couldn't help laughin', I spoke up so smart. Oh, dear me, how I shall miss talkin' over things with her! She always sensed things, and got just the p'int you meant."

"She didn't begin to age until two or three years ago, did she?" asked Mrs. Crowe. "I never saw anybody keep her looks as Tempy did. She looked young long after I begun to feel like an old woman. The doctor used to say 't was her young heart, and I don't know but what he was right. How she did do for other folks! There was one spell she wasn't at home a day to a fortnight. She got most of her livin' so, and that made her own potatoes and things last her through. None o' the young folks could get married without her, and all the old ones was disappointed if she wa'n't round when they was down with sickness and had to go. An' cleanin', or tailorin' for boys, or rug-hookin', —there was nothin' but what she could do as handy as most. 'I do love to work,'—ain't you heard her say that twenty times a week?"

Sarah Ann Binson nodded, and began to clear away the empty plates. "We may want a taste o' somethin' more towards mornin'," she said. "There's plenty in the closet here; and in case some comes from a distance to the funeral, we'll have a little table spread after we get back to the house."

"Yes, I was busy all the mornin.' I've cooked up a sight o' things to bring over," said Mrs. Crowe. "I felt 't was the last I could do for her."

They drew their chairs near the stove again, and took up their work. Sister Binson's rocking-chair creaked as she rocked; the brook sounded louder than ever. It was more lonely when nobody spoke, and presently Mrs. Crowe returned to her thoughts of growing old.

"Yes, Tempy aged all of a sudden. I remember I asked her if she felt as well as common, one day, and she laughed at me good. There, when Mr. Crowe begun to look old, I couldn't help feeling as if somethin' ailed him, and like as not 't was somethin' he was goin' to git right over, and I dosed him for it stiddy, half of one summer."

"How many things we shall be wanting to ask Tempy!" exclaimed Sarah Ann Binson, after a long pause. "I can't make up my mind to doin' without her. I wish folks could come back just once, and tell us how 't is where they've gone. Seems then we could do without 'em better."

The brook hurried on, the wind blew about the house now and then; the house itself was a silent place, and the supper, the warm fire, and an absence of any new topics for conversation made the watchers drowsy. Sister Binson closed her eyes first, to rest them for a minute; and Mrs. Crowe glanced at her compassionately, with a new sympathy for the hard-worked little woman. She made up her mind to let Sarah Ann have a good rest, while she kept watch alone; but in a few minutes her own knitting was dropped, and she, too, fell asleep. Overhead, the pale shape of Tempy Dent, the outworn body of that generous, loving-hearted, simple soul, slept on also in its white raiment. Perhaps Tempy herself stood near, and saw her own life and its surroundings with new understanding. Perhaps she herself was the only watcher.

Later, by some hours, Sarah Ann Binson woke with a start. There was a pale light of dawn outside the small windows. Inside the kitchen, the lamp burned dim. Mrs. Crowe awoke, too.

"I think Tempy'd be the first to say 't was just as well we both had some rest," she said, not without a guilty feeling.

Her companion went to the outer door and opened it wide. The fresh air was none too cold, and the brook's voice was not nearly so loud as it had been in the midnight darkness. She could see the shapes of the hills, and the great shadows that lay across the lower country. The east was fast growing bright.

"'T will be a beautiful day for the funeral," she said, and turned again, with a sigh, to follow Mrs. Crowe up the stairs.[4]

1888, 1890

K A T E   C H O P I N

(1851–1904)

When in 1899 Kate Chopin published *The Awakening*, her classic novel of a woman's "awakening" to her sexual being and identity, it was blasted by reviewers. They found it indelicate, morbid, or unhealthy, revealing what a "cruel loathsome monster Passion can be." One critic thought it should have been labelled "poison" to protect "moral babes." Then at the height of her imaginative powers, Chopin was deflected from her writing by this hostile reaction and within five years was dead from a cerebral hemorrhage. Her work remained out

---

[4]The original 1888 version of this story included this final sentence: "The world seemed more and more empty without the kind face and helpful hands of Tempy Dent." Jewett deleted it in the 1890 reprinting.

of print and largely unread until a reissue of *The Awakening* in 1964. Since then Kate Chopin has assumed her rightful place in American literary history.

Kate O'Flaherty was born into a well-to-do St. Louis family in 1851. Her Irish father was killed in an accident in 1855, and she was brought up by her mother, a descendant of an elite French Creole family, her grandmother, and her great-grandmother — all widows. Through her great-grandmother's influence and the education she received at the St. Louis Academy of the Sacred Heart, she mastered French and became an avid reader of literature. Her main education came from reading widely in English, American, and French classics. But her love of books did not disqualify her from becoming, upon graduating from the Academy in 1868, one of the "belles of St. Louis."

In 1870 Kate O'Flaherty married a Louisianan, Oscar Chopin (French pronunciation: "show-pan"), and settled in New Orleans where her husband was a cotton merchant. On the failure of his brokerage in 1879, Oscar Chopin moved the family to his cotton plantation in Cloutiersville, Natchitoches Parish, Louisiana, situated on the Red River (which flows southeast into the Mississippi). Kate Chopin was enchanted by the exotic plantation setting, but her life there was cut short by the sudden death in 1883 of Oscar Chopin from swamp fever. She was left on her own to manage a large plantation and to raise six children.

Circumstances forced Kate Chopin to give up her beloved plantation and return to St. Louis. With the death of her mother in 1885, the lonely Chopin took the advice of her family doctor and friend and began writing fiction. For models she steeped herself in the American local colorists, Sarah Orne Jewett and Mary E. Wilkins Freeman. Skeptical of local color theorist Hamlin Garland, in his insistence on treating the "actualities" of social problems, she felt, rather, that "human impulses" did not change. She responded enthusiastically to the work of contemporary French realists, especially Guy de Maupassant, of whom she wrote: "Here was life, not fiction." In her own fiction, Chopin explored the complexities of the southern life she had found so fascinating.

Chopin published her first story in 1889; a privately printed novel, *Fault*, about marriage and divorce, followed in 1890. But it was in 1894, with *Bayou Folk*, a collection of tales about colorful Louisiana Creole characters and customs, that she established herself as a leading writer in the local color movement. It was followed by another impressive collection in 1897 entitled *A Night in Acadie*. These two volumes marked the appearance of such memorable — and daring — stories as "Désirée's Baby," "The Story of an Hour," and "A Pair of Silk Stockings."

The attacks on her following the publication of *The Awakening* in 1899 clearly were stifling to her imagination. The American writer who figures importantly in the development of that imagination — Walt Whitman — had himself suffered repeated attacks for his sexual frankness. One of Whitman's most sensuous passages in "Song of Myself" are quoted by a character in the short story "A Respectable Woman," and Whitman's lyric sensuality is a lurking presence throughout *The Awakening*, as it is also in the most daring of the short stories such as "The Storm."

But Kate Chopin was no mere follower. If Whitman was a pioneer in his poetry exploring the feelings of awakening male sexuality, Kate Chopin was equally a pioneer in her fiction portraying the feelings of an awakening feminine sexuality. It is a scandal that her work was excluded for so long from the recognition it so richly deserves. That recognition, so long in coming, has, according to her editor Per Seyerstead, "elevat[ed] her from the status of a regional writer to a pioneer realist."

ADDITIONAL READING

A *Kate Chopin Miscellany*, ed. Per Seyersted and Emily Toth, 1980.

Daniel S. Rankin, *Kate Chopin and Her Creole Stories*, 1932; Per Seyersted, *Kate Chopin: A Critical Biography*, 1969, 1980; Peggy Skaggs, *Kate Chopin*, 1985; Barbara C. Ewell, *Kate Chopin*, 1986.

TEXT

The Complete Works of Kate Chopin, 2 vols., ed. Per Seyersted, 1969.

Désirée's Baby

As the day was pleasant, Madame Valmondé drove over to L'Abri to see Désirée and the baby.

It made her laugh to think of Désirée with a baby. Why, it seemed but yesterday that Désirée was little more than a baby herself; when Monsieur in riding through the gateway of Valmondé had found her lying asleep in the shadow of the big stone pillar.

The little one awoke in his arms and began to cry for "Dada." That was as much as she could do or say. Some people thought she might have strayed there of her own accord, for she was of the toddling age. The prevailing belief was that she had been purposely left by a party of Texans, whose canvas-covered wagon, late in the day, had crossed the ferry that Coton Maïs kept, just below the plantation. In time Madame Valmondé abandoned every speculation but the one that Désirée had been sent to her by a beneficent Providence to be the child of her affection, seeing that she was without child of the flesh. For the girl grew to be beautiful and gentle, affectionate and sincere, — the idol of Valmondé.

It was no wonder, when she stood one day against the stone pillar in whose shadow she had lain asleep, eighteen years before, that Armand Aubigny riding by and seeing her there, had fallen in love with her. That was the way all the Aubignys fell in love, as if struck by a pistol shot. The wonder was that he had not loved her before; for he had known her since his father brought him home from Paris, a boy of eight, after his mother died there. The passion that awoke in him that day, when he saw her at the gate, swept along like an avalanche, or like a prairie fire, or like anything that drives headlong over all obstacles.

Monsieur Valmondé grew practical and wanted things well considered: that is, the girl's obscure origin. Armand looked into her eyes and did not care. He was reminded that she was nameless. What did it matter about a name when he could give her one of the oldest and proudest in Louisiana? He ordered the *corbeille*[1] from Paris, and contained himself with what patience he could until it arrived; then they were married.

Madame Valmondé had not seen Désirée and the baby for four weeks. When she reached L'Abri she shuddered at the first sight of it, as she always did. It was a sad looking place, which for many years had not known the gentle presence of a mistress, old Monsieur Aubigny having married and buried his wife in France, and she having loved her own land too well ever to leave it. The roof came down steep and black like a cowl, reaching out beyond the wide galleries that encircled the yellow stuccoed house. Big, solemn oaks grew close to it, and their thick-leaved, far-reaching branches shadowed it like a pall. Young Aubigny's rule was a strict one, too, and

---

[1]Wedding gifts from the groom to the bride.

under it his negroes had forgotten how to be gay, as they had been during the old master's easy-going and indulgent lifetime.

The young mother was recovering slowly, and lay full length, in her soft white muslins and laces, upon a couch. The baby was beside her, upon her arm, where he had fallen asleep, at her breast. The yellow nurse woman sat beside a window fanning herself.

Madame Valmondé bent her portly figure over Désirée and kissed her, holding her an instant tenderly in her arms. Then she turned to the child.

"This is not the baby!" she exclaimed, in startled tones. French was the language spoken at Valmondé in those days.

"I knew you would be astonished," laughed Désirée, "at the way he has grown. The little *cochon de lait*!² Look at his legs, mamma, and his hands and fingernails, — real finger-nails. Zandrine had to cut them this morning. Isn't it true, Zandrine?"

The woman bowed her turbaned head majestically, "Mais si,³ Madame."

"And the way he cries," went on Désirée, "is deafening. Armand heard him the other day as far away as La Blanche's cabin."

Madame Valmondé had never removed her eyes from the child. She lifted it and walked with it over to the window that was the lightest. She scanned the baby narrowly, then looked as searchingly at Zandrine, whose face was turned to gaze across the fields.

"Yes, the child has grown, has changed," said Madame Valmondé, slowly, as she replaced it beside its mother. "What does Armand say?"

Désirée's face became suffused with a glow that was happiness itself.

"Oh, Armand is the proudest father in the parish, I believe, chiefly because it is a boy, to bear his name; though he says not, — that he would have loved a girl as well. But I know it is n't true. I know he says that to please me. And mamma," she added, drawing Madame Valmondé's head down to her, and speaking in a whisper, "he has n't punished one of them — not one of them — since baby is born. Even Négrillon, who pretended to have burnt his leg that he might rest from work — he only laughed, and said Négrillon was a great scamp. Oh, mamma, I'm so happy; it frightens me."

What Désirée said was true. Marriage, and later the birth of his son had softened Armand Aubigny's imperious and exacting nature greatly. This was what made the gentle Désirée so happy, for she loved him desperately. When he frowned she trembled, but loved him. When he smiled, she asked no greater blessing of God. But Armand's dark, handsome face had not often been disfigured by frowns since the day he fell in love with her.

When the baby was about three months old, Désirée awoke one day to the conviction that there was something in the air menacing her peace. It was at first too subtle to grasp. It had only been a disquieting suggestion; an air of mystery among the blacks; unexpected visits from far-off neighbors who could hardly account for their coming. Then a strange, an awful change in her husband's manner, which she dared not ask him to explain. When he spoke to her, it was with averted eyes, from which the old love-light seemed to have gone out. He absented himself from home; and when there, avoided her presence and that of her child, without excuse. And the very spirit of Satan seemed suddenly to take hold of him in his dealings with the slaves. Désirée was miserable enough to die.

She sat in her room, one hot afternoon, in her *peignoir*, listlessly drawing through her fingers the strands of her long, silky brown hair that hung about her shoulders. The baby, half naked, lay asleep upon her own great mahogany bed, that was like a sumptuous throne, with its satin-lined half-canopy. One of La Blanche's little quadroon boys — half naked too — stood fanning the child slowly with a fan of peacock

---

²"Suckling-pig" (French).
³"Yes, of course" (French).

feathers. Désirée's eyes had been fixed absently and sadly upon the baby, while she was striving to penetrate the threatening mist that she felt closing about her. She looked from her child to the boy who stood beside him, and back again; over and over. "Ah!" It was a cry that she could not help; which she was not conscious of having uttered. The blood turned like ice in her veins, and a clammy moisture gathered upon her face.

She tried to speak to the little quadroon boy; but no sound would come, at first. When he heard his name uttered, he looked up, and his mistress was pointing to the door. He laid aside the great, soft fan, and obediently stole away, over the polished floor, on his bare tiptoes.

She stayed motionless, with gaze riveted upon her child, and her face the picture of fright.

Presently her husband entered the room, and without noticing her, went to a table and began to search among some papers which covered it.

"Armand," she called to him, in a voice which must have stabbed him, if he was human. But he did not notice. "Armand," she said again. Then she rose and tottered towards him. "Armand," she panted once more, clutching his arm, "look at our child. What does it mean? tell me."

He coldly but gently loosened her fingers from about his arm and thrust the hand away from him. "Tell me what it means!" she cried despairingly.

"It means," he answered lightly, "that the child is not white; it means that you are not white."

A quick conception of all that this accusation meant for her nerved her with unwonted courage to deny it. "It is a lie; it is not true, I am white! Look at my hair, it is brown; and my eyes are gray, Armand, you know they are gray. And my skin is fair," seizing his wrist. "Look at my hand; whiter than yours, Armand," she laughed hysterically.

"As white as La Blanche's," he returned cruelly; and went away leaving her alone with their child.

When she could hold a pen in her hand, she sent a despairing letter to Madame Valmondé.

"My mother, they tell me I am not white. Armand has told me I am not white. For God's sake tell them it is not true. You must know it is not true. I shall die. I must die. I cannot be so unhappy, and live."

The answer that came was as brief:

"My own Désirée: Come home to Valmondé; back to your mother who loves you. Come with your child."

When the letter reached Désirée she went with it to her husband's study, and laid it open upon the desk before which he sat. She was like a stone image: silent, white, motionless after she placed it there.

In silence he ran his cold eyes over the written words. He said nothing. "Shall I go, Armand?" she asked in tones sharp with agonized suspense.

"Yes, go."

"Do you want me to go?"

"Yes, I want you to go."

He thought Almighty God had dealt cruelly and unjustly with him; and felt, somehow, that he was paying Him back in kind when he stabbed thus into his wife's soul. Moreover he no longer loved her, because of the unconscious injury she had brought upon his home and his name.

She turned away like one stunned by a blow, and walked slowly towards the door, hoping he would call her back.

"Good-by, Armand," she moaned.

He did not answer her. That was his last blow at fate.

Désirée went in search of her child. Zandrine was pacing the sombre gallery with it. She took the little one from the nurse's arms with no word of explanation, and descending the steps, walked away, under the live-oak branches.

It was an October afternoon; the sun was just sinking. Out in the still fields the negroes were picking cotton.

Désirée had not changed the thin white garment nor the slippers which she wore. Her hair was uncovered and the sun's rays brought a golden gleam from its brown meshes. She did not take the broad, beaten road which led to the far-off plantation of Valmondé. She walked across a deserted field, where the stubble bruised her tender feet, so delicately shod, and tore her thin gown to shreds.

She disappeared among the reeds and willows that grew thick along the banks of the deep, sluggish bayou; and she did not come back again.

Some weeks later there was a curious scene enacted at L'Abri. In the centre of the smoothly swept back yard was a great bonfire. Armand Aubigny sat in the wide hall-way that commanded a view of the spectacle; and it was he who dealt out to a half dozen negroes the material which kept this fire ablaze.

A graceful cradle of willow, with all its dainty furbishings, was laid upon the pyre, which had already been fed with the richness of a priceless *layette*. Then there were silk gowns, and velvet and satin ones added to these; laces, too, and embroideries; bonnets and gloves; for the *corbeille* had been of rare quality.

The last thing to go was a tiny bundle of letters; innocent little scribblings that Désirée had sent to him during the days of their espousal. There was the remnant of one back in the drawer from which he took them. But it was not Désirée's; it was part of an old letter from his mother to his father. He read it. She was thanking God for the blessing of her husband's love: —

"But, above all," she wrote, "night and day, I thank the good God for having so arranged our lives that our dear Armand will never know that his mother, who adores him, belongs to the race that is cursed with the brand of slavery."

1892   *1893, 1894*

A Respectable Woman

Mrs. Baroda was a little provoked to learn that her husband expected his friend, Gouvernail, up to spend a week or two on the plantation.

They had entertained a good deal during the winter; much of the time had also been passed in New Orleans in various forms of mild dissipation. She was looking forward to a period of unbroken rest, now, and undisturbed tête-à-tête with her husband, when he informed her that Gouvernail was coming up to stay a week or two.

This was a man she had heard much of but never seen. He had been her husband's college friend; was now a journalist, and in no sense a society man or "a man about town," which were, perhaps, some of the reasons she had never met him. But she had unconsciously formed an image of him in her mind. She pictured him tall, slim, cynical; with eyeglasses, and his hands in his pockets; and she did not like him. Gouvernail was slim enough, but he wasn't very tall nor very cynical; neither did he wear eye-glasses nor carry his hands in his pockets. And she rather liked him when he first presented himself.

But why she liked him she could not explain satisfactorily to herself when she partly attempted to do so. She could discover in him none of those brilliant and promising traits which Gaston, her husband, had often assured her that he possessed. On the contrary, he sat rather mute and receptive before her chatty eagerness to make him feel at home and in face of Gaston's frank and wordy hospitality. His manner was as courteous toward her as the most exacting woman could require; but he made no direct appeal to her approval or even esteem.

Once settled at the plantation he seemed to like to sit upon the wide portico in the shade of one of the big Corinthian pillars, smoking his cigar lazily and listening attentively to Gaston's experience as a sugar planter.

"This is what I call living," he would utter with deep satisfaction, as the air that swept across the sugar field caressed him with its warm and scented velvety touch. It pleased him also to get on familiar terms with the big dogs that came about him, rubbing themselves sociably against his legs. He did not care to fish, and displayed no eagerness to go out and kill grosbecs[1] when Gaston proposed doing so.

Gouvernail's personality puzzled Mrs. Baroda, but she liked him. Indeed, he was a lovable, inoffensive fellow. After a few days, when she could understand him no better than at first, she gave over being puzzled and remained piqued. In this mood she left her husband and her guest, for the most part, alone together. Then finding that Gouvernail took no manner of exception to her action, she imposed her society upon him, accompanying him in his idle strolls to the mill and walks along the batture.[2] She persistently sought to penetrate the reserve in which he had unconsciously enveloped himself.

"When is he going — your friend?" she one day asked her husband. "For my part, he tires me frightfully."

"Not for a week yet, dear. I can't understand; he gives you no trouble."

"No. I should like him better if he did; if he were more like others, and I had to plan somewhat for his comfort and enjoyment."

Gaston took his wife's pretty face between his hands and looked tenderly and laughingly into her troubled eyes. They were making a bit of toilet sociably together in Mrs. Baroda's dressing-room.

"You are full of surprises, ma belle,"[3] he said to her. "Even I can never count upon how you are going to act under given conditions." He kissed her and turned to fasten his cravat before the mirror.

"Here you are," he went on, "taking poor Gouvernail seriously and making a commotion over him, the last thing he would desire or expect."

"Commotion!" she hotly resented. "Nonsense! How can you say such a thing? Commotion, indeed! But, you know, you said he was clever."

"So he is. But the poor fellow is run down by overwork now. That's why I asked him here to take a rest."

"You used to say he was a man of ideas," she retorted, unconciliated. "I expected him to be interesting, at least. I'm going to the city in the morning to have my spring gowns fitted. Let me know when Mr. Gouvernail is gone; I shall be at my Aunt Octavie's."

That night she went and sat alone upon a bench that stood beneath a live oak tree at the edge of the gravel walk.

She had never known her thoughts or her intentions to be so confused. She could gather nothing from them but the feeling of a distinct necessity to quit her home in the morning.

Mrs. Baroda heard footsteps crunching the gravel; but could discern in the darkness only the approaching red point of a lighted cigar. She knew it was Gouvernail, for her husband did not smoke. She hoped to remain unnoticed, but her white gown revealed her to him. He threw away his cigar and seated himself upon the bench beside her; without a suspicion that she might object to his presence.

---

[1] French spelling of grosbeaks, or finches.
[2] Land between the river embankment (levee) and the river at low-water level, made up of flowing river deposits.
[3] "My beauty" (French).

"Your husband told me to bring this to you, Mrs. Baroda," he said, handing her a filmy, white scarf with which she sometimes enveloped her head and shoulders. She accepted the scarf from him with a murmur of thanks, and let it lie in her lap.

He made some commonplace observation upon the baneful effect of the night air at that season. Then as his gaze reached out into the darkness, he murmured, half to himself:

> "'Night of south winds — night of the large few stars!
> Still nodding night — '"[4]

She made no reply to this apostrophe to the night, which indeed, was not addressed to her.

Gouvernail was in no sense a diffident man, for he was not a self-conscious one. His periods of reserve were not constitutional, but the result of moods. Sitting there beside Mrs. Baroda, his silence melted for the time.

He talked freely and intimately in a low, hesitating drawl that was not unpleasant to hear. He talked of the old college days when he and Gaston had been a good deal to each other; of the days of keen and blind ambitions and large intentions. Now there was left with him, at least, a philosophic acquiescence to the existing order — only a desire to be permitted to exist, with now and then a little whiff of genuine life, such as he was breathing now.

Her mind only vaguely grasped what he was saying. Her physical being was for the moment predominant. She was not thinking of his words, only drinking in the tones of his voice. She wanted to reach out her hand in the darkness and touch him with the sensitive tips of her fingers upon the face or the lips. She wanted to draw close to him and whisper against his cheek — she did not care what — as she might have done if she had not been a respectable woman.

The stronger the impulse grew to bring herself near him, the further, in fact, did she draw away from him. As soon as she could do so without an appearance of too great rudeness, she rose and left him there alone.

Before she reached the house, Gouvernail had lighted a fresh cigar and ended his apostrophe to the night.

Mrs. Baroda was greatly tempted that night to tell her husband — who was also her friend — of this folly that had seized her. But she did not yield to the temptation. Beside being a respectable woman she was a very sensible one; and she knew there are some battles in life which a human being must fight alone.

When Gaston arose in the morning, his wife had already departed. She had taken an early morning train to the city. She did not return till Gouvernail was gone from under her roof.

There was some talk of having him back during the summer that followed. That is, Gaston greatly desired it; but this desire yielded to his wife's strenuous opposition.

However, before the year ended, she proposed, wholly from herself, to have Gouvernail visit them again. Her husband was surprised and delighted with the suggestion coming from her.

"I am glad, chère amie,[5] to know that you have finally overcome your dislike for him; truly he did not deserve it."

"Oh," she told him, laughingly, after pressing a long, tender kiss upon his lips, "I have overcome everything! you will see. This time I shall be very nice to him."

1894   *1894, 1897*

---

[4]From section 21 of "Song of Myself" (1855) by Walt Whitman: "Press close bare-bosom'd night — press close magnetic nourishing night! / Night of south winds — night of the

large few stars! / Still nodding night — mad naked summer night."
[5]"Dear one" (French).

The Story of an Hour

Knowing that Mrs. Mallard was afflicted with a heart trouble, great care was taken to break to her as gently as possible the news of her husband's death.

In was her sister Josephine who told her, in broken sentences; veiled hints that revealed in half concealing. Her husband's friend Richards was there, too, near her. It was he who had been in the newspaper office when intelligence of the railroad disaster was received, with Brently Mallard's name leading the list "killed." He had only taken the time to assure himself of its truth by a second telegram, and had hastened to forestall any less careful, less tender friend in bearing the sad message.

She did not hear the story as many women have heard the same, with a paralyzed inability to accept its significance. She wept at once, with sudden, wild abandonment, in her sister's arms. When the storm of grief had spent itself she went away to her room alone. She would have no one follow her.

There stood, facing the open window, a comfortable, roomy armchair. Into this she sank, pressed down by a physical exhaustion that haunted her body and seemed to reach into her soul.

She could see in the open square before her house the tops of trees that were all aquiver with the new spring life. The delicious breath of rain was in the air. In the street below a peddler was crying his wares. The notes of a distant song which some one was singing reached her faintly, and countless sparrows were twittering in the eaves.

There were patches of blue sky showing here and there through the clouds that had met and piled one above the other in the west facing her window.

She sat with her head thrown back upon the cushion of the chair, quite motionless, except when a sob came up into her throat and shook her, as a child who has cried itself to sleep continues to sob in its dreams.

She was young, with a fair, calm face, whose lines bespoke repression and even a certain strength. But now there was a dull stare in her eyes, whose gaze was fixed away off yonder on one of those patches of blue sky. It was not a glance of reflection, but rather indicated a suspension of intelligent thought.

There was something come to her and she was waiting for it, fearfully. What was it? She did not know; it was too subtle and elusive to name. But she felt it, creeping out of the sky, reaching toward her through the sounds, the scents, the color that filled the air.

Now her bosom rose and fell tumultuously. She was beginning to recognize this thing that was approaching to possess her, and she was striving to beat it back with her will—as powerless as her two white slender hands would have been.

When she abandoned herself a little whispered word escaped her slightly parted lips. She said it over and over under her breath: "free, free, free!" The vacant stare and the look of terror that had followed it went from her eyes. They stayed keen and bright. Her pulses beat fast, and the coursing blood warmed and relaxed every inch of her body.

She did not stop to ask if it were or were not a monstrous joy that held her. A clear and exalted perception enabled her to dismiss the suggestion as trivial.

She knew that she would weep again when she saw the kind, tender hands folded in death; the face that had never looked save with love upon her, fixed and gray and dead. But she saw beyond that bitter moment a long procession of years to come that would belong to her absolutely. And she opened and spread her arms out to them in welcome.

There would be no one to live for her during those coming years; she would live for herself. There would be no powerful will bending hers in that blind persistence with which men and women believe they have a right to impose a private will upon a fellow-creature. A kind intention or a cruel intention made the act seem no less a crime as she looked upon it in that brief moment of illumination.

And yet she had loved him — sometimes. Often she had not. What did it matter! What could love, the unsolved mystery, count for in face of this possession of self-assertion which she suddenly recognized as the strongest impulse of her being!

"Free! Body and soul free!" she kept whispering.

Josephine was kneeling before the closed door with her lips to the keyhole, imploring for admission. "Louise, open the door! I beg; open the door — you will make yourself ill. What are you doing, Louise? For heaven's sake open the door."

"Go away. I am not making myself ill." No; she was drinking in a very elixir of life through that open window.

Her fancy was running riot along those days ahead of her. Spring days, and summer days, and all sorts of days that would be her own. She breathed a quick prayer that life might be long. It was only yesterday she had thought with a shudder that life might be long.

She arose at length and opened the door to her sister's importunities. There was a feverish triumph in her eyes, and she carried herself unwittingly like a goddess of Victory. She clasped her sister's waist, and together they descended the stairs. Richards stood waiting for them at the bottom.

Some one was opening the front door with a latchkey. It was Brently Mallard who entered, a little travel-stained, composedly carrying his grip-sack and umbrella. He had been far from the scene of the accident, and did not even know there had been one. He stood amazed at Josephine's piercing cry; at Richards' quick motion to screen him from the view of his wife.

But Richards was too late.

When the doctors came they said she had died of heart disease — of joy that kills.

1894   *1894*

A Pair of Silk Stockings

Little Mrs. Sommers one day found herself the unexpected possessor of fifteen dollars. It seemed to her a very large amount of money, and the way in which it stuffed and bulged her worn old *porte-mònnaie*[1] gave her a feeling of importance such as she had not enjoyed for years.

The question of investment was one that occupied her greatly. For a day or two she walked about apparently in a dreamy state, but really absorbed in speculation and calculation. She did not wish to act hastily, to do anything she might afterward regret. But it was during the still hours of the night when she lay awake revolving plans in her mind that she seemed to see her way clearly toward a proper and judicious use of the money.

A dollar or two should be added to the price usually paid for Janie's shoes, which would insure their lasting an appreciable time longer than they usually did. She would buy so and so many yards of percale for new shirt waists for the boys and Janie and Mag. She had intended to make the old ones do by skilful patching. Mag should have another gown. She had seen some beautiful patterns, veritable bargains in the shop windows. And still there would be left enough for new stockings — two pairs apiece — and what darning that would save for a while! She would get caps for the boys and sailor-hats for the girls. The vision of her little brood looking fresh and

---

[1]"Change purse" (French).

dainty and new for once in their lives excited her and made her restless and wakeful with anticipation.

The neighbors sometimes talked of certain "better days" that little Mrs. Sommers had known before she had ever thought of being Mrs. Sommers. She herself indulged in no such morbid retrospection. She had no time — no second of time to devote to the past. The needs of the present absorbed her every faculty. A vision of the future like some dim, gaunt monster sometimes appalled her, but luckily tomorrow never comes.

Mrs. Sommers was one who knew the value of bargains; who could stand for hours making her way inch by inch toward the desired object that was selling below cost. She could elbow her way if need be; she had learned to clutch a piece of goods and hold it and stick to it with persistence and determination till her turn came to be served, no matter when it came.

But that day she was a little faint and tired. She had swallowed a light luncheon — no! when she came to think of it, between getting the children fed and the place righted, and preparing herself for the shopping bout, she had actually forgotten to eat any luncheon at all!

She sat herself upon a revolving stool before a counter that was comparatively deserted, trying to gather strength and courage to charge through an eager multitude that was besieging breast-works of shirting and figured lawn.[2] An all-gone limp feeling had come over her and she rested her hand aimlessly upon the counter. She wore no gloves. By degrees she grew aware that her hand had encountered something very soothing, very pleasant to touch. She looked down to see that her hand lay upon a pile of silk stockings. A placard near by announced that they had been reduced in price from two dollars and fifty cents to one dollar and ninety-eight cents; and a young girl who stood behind the counter asked her if she wished to examine their line of silk hosiery. She smiled, just as if she had been asked to inspect a tiara of diamonds with the ultimate view of purchasing it. But she went on feeling the soft, sheeny luxurious things — with both hands now, holding them up to see them glisten, and to feel them glide serpent-like through her fingers.

Two hectic blotches came suddenly into her pale cheeks. She looked up at the girl.

"Do you think there are any eights-and-a-half among these?"

There were any number of eights-and-a-half. In fact, there were more of that size than any other. Here was a light-blue pair; there were some lavender, some all black and various shades of tan and gray. Mrs. Sommers selected a black pair and looked at them very long and closely. She pretended to be examining their texture, which the clerk assured her was excellent.

"A dollar and ninety-eight cents," she mused aloud. "Well, I'll take this pair." She handed the girl a five-dollar bill and waited for her change and for her parcel. What a very small parcel it was! It seemed lost in the depths of her shabby old shopping-bag.

Mrs. Sommers after that did not move in the direction of the bargain counter. She took the elevator, which carried her to an upper floor into the region of the ladies' waiting-rooms. Here, in a retired corner, she exchanged her cotton stockings for the new silk ones which she had just bought. She was not going through any acute mental process or reasoning with herself, nor was she striving to explain to her satisfaction the motive of her action. She was not thinking at all. She seemed for the time to be taking a rest from that laborious and fatiguing function and to have abandoned herself to some mechanical impulse that directed her actions and freed her of responsibility.

How good was the touch of the raw silk to her flesh! She felt like lying back in the cushioned chair and reveling for a while in the luxury of it. She did for a little while. Then she replaced her shoes, rolled the cotton stockings together and thrust them

---

[2]Thin linen or cotton fabric.

into her bag. After doing this she crossed straight over to the shoe department and took her seat to be fitted.

She was fastidious. The clerk could not make her out; he could not reconcile her shoes with her stockings, and she was not too easily pleased. She held back her skirts and turned her feet one way and her head another way as she glanced down at the polished, pointed-tipped boots. Her foot and ankle looked very pretty. She could not realize that they belonged to her and were a part of herself. She wanted an excellent and stylish fit, she told the young fellow who served her, and she did not mind the difference of a dollar or two more in the price so long as she got what she desired.

It was a long time since Mrs. Sommers had been fitted with gloves. On rare occasions when she had bought a pair they were always "bargains," so cheap that it would have been preposterous and unreasonable to have expected them to be fitted to the hand.

Now she rested her elbow on the cushion of the glove counter, and a pretty, pleasant young creature, delicate and deft of touch, drew a long-wristed "kid" over Mrs. Sommer's hand. She smoothed it down over the wrist and buttoned it neatly, and both lost themselves for a second or two in admiring contemplation of the little symmetrical gloved hand. But there were other places where money might be spent.

There were books and magazines piled up in the window of a stall a few paces down the street. Mrs. Sommers bought two high-priced magazines such as she had been accustomed to read in the days when she had been accustomed to other pleasant things. She carried them without wrapping. As well as she could she lifted her skirts at the crossings. Her stockings and boots and well fitting gloves had worked marvels in her bearing — had given her a feeling of assurance, a sense of belonging to the well-dressed multitude.

She was very hungry. Another time she would have stilled the cravings for food until reaching her own home, where she would have brewed herself a cup of tea and taken a snack of anything that was available. But the impulse that was guiding her would not suffer her to entertain any such thought.

There was a restaurant at the corner. She had never entered its doors; from the outside she had sometimes caught glimpses of spotless damask and shining crystal, and soft-stepping waiters serving people of fashion.

When she entered her appearance created no surprise, no consternation, as she had half feared it might. She seated herself at a small table alone, and an attentive waiter at once approached to take her order. She did not want a profusion; she craved a nice and tasty bite — a half dozen blue-points,[3] a plump chop with cress, a something sweet — a crème-frappée,[4] for instance; a glass of Rhine wine, and after all a small cup of black coffee.

While waiting to be served she removed her gloves very leisurely and laid them beside her. Then she picked up a magazine and glanced through it, cutting the pages with a blunt edge of her knife. It was all very agreeable. The damask was even more spotless than it had seemed through the window, and the crystal more sparkling. There were quiet ladies and gentlemen, who did not notice her, lunching at the small tables like her own. A soft, pleasing strain of music could be heard, and a gentle breeze was blowing through the window. She tasted a bite, and she read a word or two, and she sipped the amber wine and wiggled her toes in the silk stockings. The price of it made no difference. She counted the money out to the waiter and left an extra coin on his tray, whereupon he bowed before her as before a princess of royal blood.

There was still money in her purse, and her next temptation presented itself in the shape of a matinée poster.

---

[3] Oysters.
[4] "Frozen custard" (French).

It was a little later when she entered the theatre, the play had begun and the house seemed to her to be packed. But there were vacant seats here and there, and into one of them she was ushered, between brilliantly dressed women who had gone there to kill time and eat candy and display their gaudy attire. There were many others who were there solely for the play and acting. It is safe to say there was no one present who bore quite the attitude which Mrs. Sommers did to her surroundings. She gathered in the whole — stage and players and people in one wide impression, and absorbed it and enjoyed it. She laughed at the comedy and wept — she and the gaudy woman next to her wept over the tragedy. And they talked a little together over it. And the gaudy woman wiped her eyes and sniffled on a tiny square of filmy, perfumed lace and passed little Mrs. Sommers her box of candy.

The play was over, the music ceased, the crowd filed out. It was like a dream ended. People scattered in all directions. Mrs. Sommers went to the corner and waited for the cable car.

A man with keen eyes, who sat opposite her, seemed to like the study of her small, pale face. It puzzled him to decipher what he saw there. In truth, he saw nothing — unless he were wizard enough to detect a poignant wish, a powerful longing that the cable car would never stop anywhere, but go on and on with her forever.

1896   *1897*

The Storm

A Sequel to "The 'Cadian Ball"[1]

I

The leaves were so still that even Bibi thought it was going to rain. Bobinôt, who was accustomed to converse on terms of perfect equality with his little son, called the child's attention to certain sombre clouds that were rolling with sinister intention from the west, accompanied by a sullen, threatening roar. They were at Friedheimer's store and decided to remain there till the storm had passed. They sat within the door on two empty kegs. Bibi was four years old and looked very wise.

"Mama'll be 'fraid, yes," he suggested with blinking eyes.

"She'll shut the house. Maybe she got Sylvie helpin' her this evenin'," Bobinôt responded reassuringly.

"No; she ent got Sylvie. Sylvie was helpin' her yistiday," piped Bibi.

Bobinôt arose and going across to the counter purchased a can of shrimps, of which Calixta was very fond. Then he returned to his perch on the keg and sat stolidly holding the can of shrimps while the storm burst. It shook the wooden store and seemed to be ripping great furrows in the distant field. Bibi laid his little hand on his father's knee and was not afraid.

II

Calixta, at home, felt no uneasiness for their safety. She sat at a side window sewing furiously on a sewing machine. She was greatly occupied and did not notice the approaching storm. But she felt very warm and often stopped to mop her face on which the perspiration gathered in beads. She unfastened her white sacque[2] at the

---

[1] Written and published in 1892, "At the 'Cadian Ball" depicts the courtship of the two sets of lovers that appear in this sequel, "The Storm." Chopin never tried to publish "The Storm."
[2] A loose-fitting gown.

throat. It began to grow dark, and suddenly realizing the situation she got up hurriedly and went about closing windows and doors.

Out on the small front gallery she had hung Bobinôt's Sunday clothes to air and she hastened out to gather them before the rain fell. As she stepped outside, Alcée Laballière rode in at the gate. She had not seen him very often since her marriage, and never alone. She stood there with Bobinôt's coat in her hands, and the big rain drops began to fall. Alcée rode his horse under the shelter of a side projection where the chickens had huddled and there were plows and a harrow piled up in the corner.

"May I come and wait on your gallery till the storm is over, Calixta?" he asked.

"Come 'long in, M'sieur Alcée."

His voice and her own startled her as if from a trance, and she seized Bobinôt's vest. Alcée, mounting to the porch, grabbed the trousers and snatched Bibi's braided jacket that was about to be carried away by a sudden gust of wind. He expressed an intention to remain outside, but it was soon apparent that he might as well have been out in the open: the water beat in upon the boards in driving sheets, and he went inside, closing the door after him. It was even necessary to put something beneath the door to keep the water out.

"My! what a rain! It's good two years sence it rain' like that," exclaimed Calixta as she rolled up a piece of bagging and Alcée helped her to thrust it beneath the crack.

She was a little fuller of figure than five years before when she married; but she had lost nothing of her vivacity. Her blue eyes still retained their melting quality; and her yellow hair, dishevelled by the wind and rain, kinked more stubbornly than ever about her ears and temples.

The rain beat upon the low, shingled roof with a force and clatter that threatened to break an entrance and deluge them there. They were in the dining room—the sitting room—the general utility room. Adjoining was her bed room, with Bibi's couch along side her own. The door stood open, and the room with its white, monumental bed, its closed shutters, looked dim and mysterious.

Alcée flung himself into a rocker and Calixta nervously began to gather up from the floor the lengths of a cotton sheet which she had been sewing.

"If this keeps up, *Dieu sait*[3] if the levees[4] goin' to stan' it!" she exclaimed.

"What have you got to do with the levees?"

"I got enough to do! An' there's Bobinôt with Bibi out in the storm—if he only didn' left Friedheimer's!"

"Let us hope, Calixta, that Bobinôt's got sense enough to come in out of a cyclone."

She went and stood at the window with a greatly disturbed look on her face. She wiped the frame that was clouded with moisture. It was stiflingly hot. Alcée got up and joined her at the window, looking over her shoulder. The rain was coming down in sheets obscuring the view of far-off cabins and enveloping the distant wood in a gray mist. The playing of the lightning was incessant. A bolt struck a tall chinaberry tree at the edge of the field. It filled all visible space with a blinding glare and the crash seemed to invade the very boards they stood upon.

Calixta put her hands to her eyes, and with a cry, staggered backward. Alcée's arm encircled her, and for an instant he drew her close and spasmodically to him.

"*Bonté*!"[5] she cried, releasing herself from his encircling arm and retreating from the window, "the house'll go next! If I only knew w'ere Bibi was!" She would not compose herself; she would not be seated. Alcée clasped her shoulder and looked into her face. The contact of her warm, palpitating body when he had unthinkingly

---

[3] "God knows" (French).
[4] Embankments raised to prevent flooding.
[5] "Goodness!" (French).

drawn her into his arms, had aroused all the old-time infatuation and desire for her flesh.

"Calixta," he said, "don't be frightened. Nothing can happen. The house is too low to be struck, with so many tall trees standing about. There! aren't you going to be quiet? say, aren't you?" He pushed her hair back from her face that was warm and steaming. Her lips were as red and moist as pomegranate seed. Her white neck and a glimpse of her full, firm bosom disturbed him powerfully. As she glanced up at him the fear in her liquid blue eyes had given place to a drowsy gleam that unconsciously betrayed a sensuous desire. He looked down into her eyes and there was nothing for him to do but to gather her lips in a kiss. It reminded him of Assumption.[6]

"Do you remember — in Assumption, Calixta?" he asked in a low voice broken by passion. Oh! she remembered; for in Assumption he had kissed her and kissed and kissed her; until his senses would well nigh fail, and to save her he would resort to a desperate flight. If she was not an immaculate dove in those days, she was still inviolate; a passionate creature whose very defenselessness had made her defense, against which his honor forbade him to prevail. Now — well, now — her lips seemed in a manner free to be tasted, as well as her round, white throat and her whiter breasts.

They did not heed the crashing torrents, and the roar of the elements made her laugh as she lay in his arms. She was a revelation in that dim mysterious chamber; as white as the couch she lay upon. Her firm, elastic flesh that was knowing for the first time its birthright, was like a creamy lily that the sun invites to contribute its breath and perfume to the undying life of the world.

The generous abundance of her passion, without guile or trickery, was like a white flame which penetrated and found response in depths of his own sensuous nature that had never yet been reached.

When he touched her breasts they gave themselves up in quivering ecstasy, inviting his lips. Her mouth was a fountain of delight. And when he possessed her, they seemed to swoon together at the very borderland of life's mystery.

He stayed cushioned upon her, breathless, dazed, enervated, with his heart beating like a hammer upon her. With one hand she clasped his head, her lips lightly touching his forehead. The other hand stroked with a soothing rhythm his muscular shoulders.

The growl of the thunder was distant and passing away. The rain beat softly upon the shingles, inviting them to drowsiness and sleep. But they dared not yield.

The rain was over; and the sun was turning the glistening green world into a palace of gems. Calixta, on the gallery, watched Alcée ride away. He turned and smiled at her with a beaming face; and she lifted her pretty chin in the air and laughed aloud.

III

Bobinôt and Bibi, trudging home, stopped without at the cistern to make themselves presentable.

"My! Bibi, w'at will yo' mama say! You ought to be ashame'. You oughtn' put on those good pants. Look at 'em! An' that mud on yo' collar! How you got that mud on yo' collar, Bibi? I never saw such a boy!" Bibi was the picture of pathetic resignation. Bobinôt was the embodiment of serious solicitude as he strove to remove from his own person and his son's the signs of their tramp over heavy roads and through wet fields. He scraped the mud off Bibi's bare legs and feet with a stick and carefully

---

[6]Assumption parish, Louisiana, where the two, then unmarried, had met by chance, causing people to whisper "a breath of scandal" about Calixta (see "At the 'Cadian Ball").

removed all traces from his heavy brogans. Then, prepared for the worst — the meeting with an over-scrupulous housewife, they entered cautiously at the back door.

Calixta was preparing supper. She had set the table and was dripping coffee at the hearth. She sprang up as they came in.

"Oh, Bobinôt! You back! My! but I was uneasy. W'ere you been during the rain? An' Bibi? he ain't wet? he ain't hurt?" She had clasped Bibi and was kissing him effusively. Bobinôt's explanations and apologies which he had been composing all along the way, died on his lips as Calixta felt him to see if he were dry, and seemed to express nothing but satisfaction at their safe return.

"I brought you some shrimps, Calixta," offered Bobinôt, hauling the can from his ample side pocket and laying it on the table.

"Shrimps! Oh, Bobinôt! you too good fo' anything!" and she gave him a smacking kiss on the cheek that resounded. "*J'vous réponds,*[7] we'll have a feas' to night! umph-umph!"

Bobinôt and Bibi began to relax and enjoy themselves, and when the three seated themselves at table they laughed much and so loud that anyone might have heard them as far away as Laballière's.

IV

Alcée Laballière wrote to his wife, Clarisse, that night. It was a loving letter, full of tender solicitude. He told her not to hurry back, but if she and the babies liked it at Biloxi, to stay a month longer. He was getting on nicely; and though he missed them, he was willing to bear the separation a while longer — realizing that their health and pleasure were the first things to be considered.

V

As for Clarisse, she was charmed upon receiving her husband's letter. She and the babies were doing well. The society was agreeable; many of her old friends and acquaintances were at the bay. And the first free breath since her marriage seemed to restore the pleasant liberty of her maiden days. Devoted as she was to her husband, their intimate conjugal life was something which she was more than willing to forego for a while.

So the storm passed and every one was happy.

1898   1969

MARY E. WILKINS FREEMAN
(1852–1930)

In her marriage in 1902 at the age of forty-nine, after she had already achieved acclaim as a local color writer, Mary E. Wilkins might have made a good character-study for one of her own stories that appeared in *A New England Nun* in 1891. Her husband, Dr. Charles Manning Freeman, was a nonpracticing physician with a reputation for drinking, chasing women, and driving fast horses. The acquaintanceship and courtship had lasted for a decade. A few years after the marriage, Charles Freeman began to receive treatment for his alcoholism. And in 1919, Mary Freeman committed him to a hospital for the insane. He died some four years later, leaving the sum of one dollar to his wife in his will, which

---

[7]"I assure you" (French).

she successfully challenged. In fact, rarely do such lurid events appear in Mary Freeman's tales of village life in a New England in decline. Hers is an art of restraint and understatement, focusing more on character than on action.

She was born in Randolph, Massachusetts, and attended school there and in Brattleboro, Vermont, where her father went into a drygoods business. She attended Mount Holyoke Female Seminary in 1870–71, and then returned to live with her family in Brattleboro. In 1876, Charles Wilkins's business failed and by the early 1880s, Mary Wilkins's mother, father, and only sister were dead. Left to fend for herself, she turned to the writing of short stories. She later commented: "What directed me to the short story? I think the answer is very simple. The short story did not take so long to write, it was easier, and, of course, I was not *sure* of my own ability to write a short story, much less a novel. I consider the art of the novel as a very different affair from that of the short story. The latter can be a simple little melody; the other can be grand opera."

Although it is difficult to account, in the simple facts of her life, for Mary Wilkins's suddenly revealed talent for writing fiction, the truth is that her letters reveal her to have been well-read in literature. Her reading included the Americans Poe, Hawthorne, and Jewett, the British Fielding, Dickens, and Thackeray, the Russian Tolstoy, and the Greek classics. From these and other writers, she clearly learned the possibilities of the art of fiction.

Her stories began to appear in important magazines of the day (*Harper's Bazaar* and *Harper's Magazine*) in 1883 and 1884. Her first collection of stories, *A Humble Romance and Other Stories*, was published in 1887, followed by *A New England Nun and Other Stories* in 1891. Most of the stories by which we remember Mary E. Wilkins Freeman appeared in these two volumes of tales describing simple New England country life and hard-working people.

Most often her heroine is a poor woman, alone in effect if not in fact, confronting deprivation, neglect, or antagonism, and discovering — frequently with surprise — inner resources that enable her to endure and sometimes to triumph. Her stories focus thus on an interior rather than an exterior action. And they build to a climax — a point of sudden awareness or determination, of deep feeling and insight. The critic F. O. Matthiessen has said that she was "unsurpassed among all American writers in her ability to give the breathless intensity of a moment."

Mary Freeman continued to write and publish stories and novels until her death of a heart attack in 1930. Her books include fourteen collections of tales, thirteen novels, several children's books, essays, and poems. She was awarded the Howells Medal for Fiction by the American Academy of Arts and Letters in 1926. And that same year, she and Edith Wharton were the first women to be elected to membership in the National Institute of Arts and Letters.

ADDITIONAL READING

The Collected Ghost Stories of Mary E. Wilkins Freeman, ed. Edward Wagenknecht, 1974; *Selected Stories of Mary E. Wilkins Freeman*, ed. Marjorie Pryse, 1983; *The Infant Sphinx: Collected Letters of Mary E. Wilkins Freeman*, ed. Brent L. Kendrick, 1985.

Edward Foster, *Mary E. Wilkins Freeman*, 1956; Abigail Ann Hamblen, *The New England Art of Mary E. Wilkins Freeman*, 1966; Perry Westbrook, *Mary Wilkins Freeman*, 1967, 1988.

TEXT

A New England Nun and Other Stories, 1891.

The Revolt of "Mother"

"Father!"

"What is it?"

"What are them men diggin' over there in the field for?"

There was a sudden dropping and enlarging of the lower part of the old man's face, as if some heavy weight had settled therein; he shut his mouth tight, and went on harnessing the great bay mare. He hustled the collar on to her neck with a jerk.

"Father!"

The old man slapped the saddle upon the mare's back.

"Look here, father, I want to know what them men are diggin' over in the field for, an' I'm goin' to know."

"I wish you'd go into the house, mother, an' 'tend to your own affairs," the old man said then. He ran his words together, and his speech was almost as inarticulate as a growl.

But the woman understood; it was her most native tongue. "I ain't goin' into the house till you tell me what them men are doin' over there in the field," said she.

Then she stood waiting. She was a small woman, short and straight-waisted like a child in her brown cotton gown. Her forehead was mild and benevolent between the smooth curves of gray hair; there were meek downward lines about her nose and mouth; but her eyes, fixed upon the old man, looked as if the meekness had been the result of her own will, never of the will of another.

They were in the barn, standing before the wide open doors. The spring air, full of the smell of growing grass and unseen blossoms, came in their faces. The deep yard in front was littered with farm wagons and piles of wood; on the edges, close to the fence and the house, the grass was a vivid green, and there were some dandelions.

The old man glanced doggedly at his wife as he tightened the last buckles on the harness. She looked as immovable to him as one of the rocks in his pasture-land, bound to the earth with generations of blackberry vines. He slapped the reins over the horse, and started forth from the barn.

"*Father!*" said she.

The old man pulled up. "What is it?"

"I want to know what them men are diggin' over there in that field for."

"They're diggin' a cellar, I s'pose, if you've got to know."

"A cellar for what?"

"A barn."

"A barn? You ain't goin' to build a barn over there where we was goin' to have a house, father?"

The old man said not another word. He hurried the horse into the farm wagon, and clattered out of the yard, jouncing as sturdily on his seat as a boy.

The woman stood a moment looking after him, then she went out of the barn across a corner of the yard to the house. The house, standing at right angles with the great barn and a long reach of sheds and out-buildings, was infinitesimal compared with them. It was scarcely as commodious for people as the little boxes under the barn eaves were for doves.

A pretty girl's face, pink and delicate as a flower, was looking out of one of the house windows. She was watching three men who were digging over in the field which bounded the yard near the road line. She turned quietly when the woman entered.

"What are they digging for, mother?" said she. "Did he tell you?"

"They're diggin' for—a cellar for a new barn."

"Oh, mother, he ain't going to build another barn?"

"That's what he says."

A boy stood before the kitchen glass combing his hair. He combed slowly and painstakingly, arranging his brown hair in a smooth hillock over his forehead. He did not seem to pay any attention to the conversation.

"Sammy, did you know father was going to build a new barn?" asked the girl.

The boy combed assiduously.

"Sammy!"

He turned, and showed a face like his father's under his smooth crest of hair. "Yes, I s'pose I did," he said, reluctantly.

"How long have you known it?" asked his mother.

"'Bout three months, I guess."

"Why didn't you tell of it?"

"Didn't think 'twould do no good."

"I don't see what father wants another barn for," said the girl, in her sweet, slow voice. She turned again to the window, and stared out at the digging men in the field. Her tender, sweet face was full of a gentle distress. Her forehead was as bald and innocent as a baby's, with the light hair strained back from it in a row of curl-papers. She was quite large, but her soft curves did not look as if they covered muscles.

Her mother looked sternly at the boy. "Is he goin' to buy more cows?" said she.

The boy did not reply; he was tying his shoes.

"Sammy, I want you to tell me if he's goin' to buy more cows."

"I s'pose he is."

"How many?"

"Four, I guess."

His mother said nothing more. She went into the pantry, and there was a clatter of dishes. The boy got his cap from a nail behind the door, took an old arithmetic from the shelf, and started for school. He was lightly built, but clumsy. He went out of the yard with a curious spring in the hips, that made his loose home-made jacket tilt up in the rear.

The girl went to the sink, and began to wash the dishes that were piled up there. Her mother came promptly out of the pantry, and shoved her aside. "You wipe 'em," said she; "I'll wash. There's a good many this mornin'."

The mother plunged her hands vigorously into the water, the girl wiped the plates slowly and dreamily. "Mother," said she, "don't you think it's too bad father's going to build that new barn, much as we need a decent house to live in?"

Her mother scrubbed a dish fiercely. "You ain't found out yet we're women-folks, Nanny Penn," said she. "You ain't seen enough of men-folks yet to. One of these days you'll find it out, an' then you'll know that we know only what men-folks think we do, so far as any use of it goes, an' how we'd ought to reckon men-folks in with Providence, an' not complain of what they do any more than we do of the weather."

"I don't care; I don't believe George is anything like that, anyhow," said Nanny. Her delicate face flushed pink, her lips pouted softly, as if she were going to cry.

"You wait an' see. I guess George Eastman ain't no better than other men. You hadn't ought to judge father, though. He can't help it, 'cause he don't look at things jest the way we do. An' we've been pretty comfortable here, after all. The roof don't leak — ain't never but once — that's one thing. Father's kept it shingled right up."

"I do wish we had a parlor."

"I guess it won't hurt George Eastman any to come to see you in a nice clean kitchen. I guess a good many girls don't have as good a place as this. Nobody's ever heard me complain."

"I ain't complained either, mother."

"Well, I don't think you'd better, a good father an' a good home as you've got. S'pose your father made you go out an' work for your livin'? Lots of girls have to that ain't no stronger an' better able to than you be."

Sarah Penn washed the frying-pan with a conclusive air. She scrubbed the outside of it as faithfully as the inside. She was a masterly keeper of her box of a house. Her one living-room never seemed to have in it any of the dust which the friction of life with inanimate matter produces. She swept, and there seemed to be no dirt to go before the broom; she cleaned, and one could see no difference. She was like an artist so perfect that he has apparently no art. To-day she got out a mixing bowl and a board, and rolled some pies, and there was no more flour upon her than upon her daughter who was doing finer work. Nanny was to be married in the fall, and she was sewing on some white cambric and embroidery. She sewed industriously while her mother cooked, her soft milk-white hands and wrists showed whiter than her delicate work.

"We must have the stove moved out in the shed before long," said Mrs. Penn. "Talk about not havin' things, it's been a real blessin' to be able to put a stove up in that shed in hot weather. Father did one good thing when he fixed that stove-pipe out there."

Sarah Penn's face as she rolled her pies had that expression of meek vigor which might have characterized one of the New Testament saints. She was making mince-pies. Her husband, Adoniram Penn, liked them better than any other kind. She baked twice a week. Adoniram often liked a piece of pie between meals. She hurried this morning. It had been later than usual when she began, and she wanted to have a pie baked for dinner. However deep a resentment she might be forced to hold against her husband, she would never fail in sedulous attention to his wants.

Nobility of character manifests itself in loop-holes when it is not provided with large doors. Sarah Penn's showed itself to-day in flaky dishes of pastry. So she made the pies faithfully, while across the table she could see, when she glanced up from her work, the sight that rankled in her patient and steadfast soul—the digging of the cellar of the new barn in the place where Adoniram forty years ago had promised her their new house should stand.

The pies were done for dinner. Adoniram and Sammy were home a few minutes after twelve o'clock. The dinner was eaten with serious haste. There was never much conversation at the table in the Penn family. Adoniram asked a blessing, and they ate promptly, then rose up and went about their work.

Sammy went back to school, taking soft sly lopes out of the yard like rabbit. He wanted a game of marbles before school, and feared his father would give him some chores to do. Adoniram hastened to the door and called after him, but he was out of sight.

"I don't see what you let him go for, mother," said he. "I wanted him to help me unload that wood."

Adoniram went to work out in the yard unloading wood from the wagon. Sarah put away the dinner dishes, while Nanny took down her curl-papers and changed her dress. She was going down to the store to buy some more embroidery and thread.

When Nanny was gone, Mrs. Penn went to the door. "Father!" she called.

"Well, what is it!"

"I want to see you jest a minute, father."

"I can't leave this wood nohow. I've got to git it unloaded an' go for a load of gravel afore two o'clock. Sammy had ought to helped me. You hadn't ought to let him go to school so early."

"I want to see you jest a minute."

"I tell ye I can't, nohow, mother."

"Father, you come here." Sarah Penn stood in the door like a queen; she held her head as if it bore a crown; there was that patience which makes authority royal in her voice. Adoniram went.

Mrs. Penn led the way into the kitchen, and pointed to a chair. "Sit down, father," said she; "I've got somethin' I want to say to you."

He sat down heavily; his face was quite stolid, but he looked at her with restive eyes. "Well, what is it, mother?"

"I want to know what you're buildin' that new barn for, father?"

"I ain't got nothin' to say about it."

"It can't be you think you need another barn?"

"I tell ye I ain't got nothin' to say about it, mother; an' I ain't goin' to say nothin'."

"Be you goin' to buy more cows?"

Adoniram did not reply; he shut his mouth tight.

"I know you be, as well as I want to. Now, father, look here"—Sarah Penn had not sat down; she stood before her husband in the humble fashion of a Scripture woman—"I'm goin' to talk real plain to you; I never have sence I married you, but I'm goin' to now. I ain't never complained, an' I ain't goin' to complain now, but I'm goin' to talk plain. You see this room here, father; you look at it well. You see there ain't no carpet on the floor, an' you see the paper is all dirty, an' droppin' off the walls. We ain't had no new paper on it for ten year, an' then I put it on myself, an' it didn't cost but ninepence a roll. You see this room, father; it's all the one I've had to work in an' eat in an' sit in sence we was married. There ain't another woman in the whole town whose husband ain't got half the means you have but what's got better. It's all the room Nanny's got to have her company in; an' there ain't one of her mates but what's got better, an' their fathers not so able as hers is. It's all the room she'll have to be married in. What would you have thought, father, if we had had our weddin' in a room no better than this? I was married in my mother's parlor, with a carpet on the floor, an' stuffed furniture, an' a mahogany card-table. An' this is all the room my daughter will have to be married in. Look here, father!"

Sarah Penn went across the room as though it were a tragic stage. She flung open a door and disclosed a tiny bedroom, only large enough for a bed and bureau, with a path between. "There, father," said she—"there's all the room I've had to sleep in forty year. All my children were born there—the two that died, an' the two that's livin'. I was sick with a fever there."

She stepped to another door and opened it. It led into the small, ill-lighted pantry. "Here," said she, "is all the buttery I've got—every place I've got for my dishes, to set away my victuals in, an' to keep my milk-pans in. Father, I've been takin' care of the milk of six cows in this place, an' now you're goin' to build a new barn, an' keep more cows, an' give me more to do in it."

She threw open another door. A narrow crooked flight of stairs wound upward from it. "There, father," said she, "I want you to look at the stairs that go up to them two unfinished chambers that are all the places our son an' daughter have had to sleep in all their lives. There ain't a prettier girl in town nor a more ladylike one than Nanny, an' that's the place she has to sleep in. It ain't so good as your horse's stall; it ain't so warm an' tight."

Sarah Penn went back and stood before her husband. "Now, father," said she, "I want to know if you think you're doin' right an' accordin' to what you profess. Here, when we was married, forty year ago, you promised me faithful that we should have a new house built in that lot over in the field before the year was out. You said you had money enough, an' you wouldn't ask me to live in no such place as this. It is forty year now, an' you've been makin' more money, an' I've been savin' of it for you ever since, an' you ain't built no house yet. You've built sheds an' cow-houses an' one new barn, an' now you're goin' to build another. Father, I want to know if you think it's right. You're lodgin' your dumb beasts better than you are your own flesh an' blood. I want to know if you think it's right."

"I ain't got nothin' to say."

"You can't say nothin' without ownin' it ain't right, father. An' there's another thing—I ain't complained; I've got along forty year, an' I s'pose I should forty more, if it wa'n't for that—if we don't have another house. Nanny she can't live with us after she's married. She'll have to go somewheres else to live away from us, an' it don't seem as if I could have it so, noways, father. She wa'n't ever strong. She's got considerable color, but there wa'n't never any backbone to her. I've always took the heft of every-thing off her, an' she ain't fit to keep house an' do everything herself. She'll be all worn out inside of a year. Think of her doin' all the washin' an' ironin' an' bakin' with them soft white hands an' arms, an' sweepin'! I can't have it so, noways, father."

Mrs. Penn's face was burning; her mild eyes gleamed. She had pleaded her little cause like a Webster;[1] she had ranged from severity to pathos; but her opponent employed that obstinate silence which makes eloquence futile with mocking echoes. Adoniram arose clumsily.

"Father, ain't you got nothin' to say?" said Mrs. Penn.

"I've got to go off after that load of gravel. I can't stan' here talkin' all day."

"Father, won't you think it over, an' have a house built there instead of a barn?"

"I ain't got nothin' to say."

Adoniram shuffled out. Mrs. Penn went into her bedroom. When she came out, her eyes were red. She had a roll of unbleached cotton cloth. She spread it out on the kitchen table, and began cutting out some shirts for her husband. The men over in the field had a team to help them this afternoon; she could hear their halloos. She had a scanty pattern for the shirts; she had to plan and piece the sleeves.

Nanny came home with her embroidery, and sat down with her needlework. She had taken down her curl-papers, and there was a soft roll of fair hair like an aureole over her forehead; her face was as delicately fine and clear as porcelain. Suddenly she looked up, and the tender red flamed all over her face and neck. "Mother," said she.

"What say?"

"I've been thinking—I don't see how we're goin' to have any—wedding in this room. I'd be ashamed to have his folks come if we didn't have anybody else."

"Mebbe we can have some new paper before then; I can put it on. I guess you won't have no call to be ashamed of your belongin's."

"We might have the wedding in the new barn," said Nanny, with gentle pettish-ness. "Why, mother, what makes you look so?"

Mrs. Penn had started, and was staring at her with a curious expression. She turned again to her work, and spread out a pattern carefully on the cloth. "Nothin'," said she.

Presently Adoniram clattered out of the yard in his two-wheeled dump cart, standing as proudly upright as a Roman charioteer. Mrs. Penn opened the door and stood there a minute looking out; the halloos of the men sounded louder.

It seemed to her all through the spring months that she heard nothing but the halloos and the noises of saws and hammers. The new barn grew fast. It was a fine edifice for this little village. Men came on pleasant Sundays, in their meeting suits and clean shirt bosoms, and stood around it admiringly. Mrs. Penn did not speak of it, and Adoniram did not mention it to her, although sometimes, upon a return from inspecting it, he bore himself with injured dignity.

"It's a strange thing how your mother feels about the new barn," he said, confiden-tially, to Sammy one day.

Sammy only grunted after an odd fashion for a boy; he had learned it from his father.

The barn was all completed ready for use by the third week in July. Adoniram had planned to move his stock in on Wednesday; on Tuesday he received a letter which changed his plans. He came in with it early in the morning. "Sammy's been to the post-office," said he, "an' I've got a letter from Hiram." Hiram was Mrs. Penn's brother, who lived in Vermont.

"Well," said Mrs. Penn, "what does he say about the folks?"

"I guess they're all right. He says he thinks if I come up country right off there's a

---

[1] I.e., like American statesman Daniel Webster (1782–1852), famed orator and debater.

chance to buy jest the kind of a horse I want." He stared reflectively out of the window at the new barn.

Mrs. Penn was making pies. She went on clapping the rolling-pin into the crust, although she was very pale, and her heart beat loudly.

"I dun' know but what I'd better go," said Adoniram. "I hate to go off jest now, right in the midst of hayin', but the ten-acre lot's cut, an' I guess Rufus an' the others can git along without me three or four days. I can't get a horse round here to suit me, nohow, an' I've got to have another for all that wood-haulin' in the fall. I told Hiram to watch out, an' if he got wind of a good horse to let me know. I guess I'd better go."

"I'll get out your clean shirt an' collar," said Mrs. Penn calmly.

She laid out Adoniram's Sunday suit and his clean clothes on the bed in the little bedroom. She got his shaving-water and razor ready. At last she buttoned on his collar and fastened his black cravat.

Adoniram never wore his collar and cravat except on extra occasions. He held his head high, with a rasped dignity. When he was all ready, with his coat and hat brushed, and a lunch of pie and cheese in a paper bag, he hesitated on the threshold of the door. He looked at his wife, and his manner was defiantly apologetic. "*If* them cows come to-day, Sammy can drive 'em into the new barn," said he; "an' when they bring the hay up, they can pitch it in there."

"Well," replied Mrs. Penn.

Adoniram set his shaven face ahead and started. When he had cleared the door-step, he turned and looked back with a kind of nervous solemnity. "I shall be back by Saturday if nothin' happens," said he.

"Do be careful, father," returned his wife.

She stood in the door with Nanny at her elbow and watched him out of sight. Her eyes had a strange, doubtful expression in them; her peaceful forehead was contracted. She went in, and about her baking again. Nanny sat sewing. Her wedding-day was drawing nearer, and she was getting pale and thin with her steady sewing. Her mother kept glancing at her.

"Have you got that pain in your side this mornin'?" she asked.

"A little."

Mrs. Penn's face, as she worked, changed, her perplexed forehead smoothed, her eyes were steady, her lips firmly set. She formed a maxim for herself, although incoherently with her unlettered thoughts. "Unsolicited opportunities are the guideposts of the Lord to the new roads of life," she repeated in effect, and she made up her mind to her course of action.

"S'posin' I *had* wrote to Hiram," she muttered once, when she was in the pantry — "s'posin' I had wrote, an' asked him if he knew of any horse? But I didn't, an' father's goin' wa'n't none of my doin'. It looks like a providence." Her voice rang out quite loud at the last.

"What you talkin' about, mother?" called Nanny.

"Nothin'."

Mrs. Penn hurried her baking; at eleven o'clock it was all done. The load of hay from the west field came slowly down the cart track, and drew up at the new barn. Mrs. Penn ran out. "Stop!" she screamed — "stop!"

The men stopped and looked; Sammy upreared from the top of the load, and stared at his mother.

"Stop!" she cried out again. "Don't you put the hay in that barn; put it in the old one."

"Why, he said to put it in here," returned one of the haymakers, wonderingly. He was a young man, a neighbor's son, whom Adoniram hired by the year to help on the farm.

"Don't you put the hay in the new barn; there's room enough in the old one, ain't there?" said Mrs. Penn.

"Room enough," returned the hired man, in his thick, rustic tones. "Didn't need the new barn, nohow, far as room's concerned. Well, I s'pose he changed his mind." He took hold of the horses' bridles.

Mrs. Penn went back to the house. Soon the kitchen windows were darkened, and a fragrance like warm honey came into the room.

Nanny laid down her work. "I thought father wanted them to put the hay into the new barn?" she said, wonderingly.

"It's all right," replied her mother.

Sammy slid down from the load of hay, and came in to see if dinner was ready.

"I ain't goin' to get a regular dinner to-day, as long as father's gone," said his mother. "I've let the fire go out. You can have some bread an' milk an' pie. I thought we could get along." She set out some bowls of milk, some bread, and a pie on the kitchen table. "You'd better eat your dinner now," said she. "You might jest as well get through with it. I want you to help me afterward."

Nanny and Sammy stared at each other. There was something strange in their mother's manner. Mrs. Penn did not eat anything herself. She went into the pantry, and they heard her moving dishes while they ate. Presently she came out with a pile of plates. She got the clothesbasket out of the shed, and packed them in it. Nanny and Sammy watched. She brought out cups and saucers, and put them in with the plates.

"What you goin' to do, mother?" inquired Nanny, in a timid voice. A sense of something unusual made her tremble, as if it were a ghost. Sammy rolled his eyes over his pie.

"You'll see what I'm goin' to do," replied Mrs. Penn. "If you're through, Nanny, I want you to go up-stairs an' pack up your things; an' I want you, Sammy, to help me take down the bed in the bedroom."

"Oh, mother, what for?" gasped Nanny.

"You'll see."

During the next few hours a feat was performed by this simple, pious New England mother which was equal in its way to Wolfe's storming of the Heights of Abraham.[2] It took no more genius and audacity of bravery for Wolfe to cheer his wondering soldiers up those steep precipices, under the sleeping eyes of the enemy, than for Sarah Penn, at the head of her children, to move all their little household goods into the new barn while her husband was away.

Nanny and Sammy followed their mother's instructions without a murmur; indeed, they were overawed. There is a certain uncanny and superhuman quality about all such purely original undertakings as their mother's was to them. Nanny went back and forth with her light loads, and Sammy tugged with sober energy.

At five o'clock in the afternoon the little house in which the Penns had lived for forty years had emptied itself into the new barn.

Every builder builds somewhat for unknown purposes, and is in a measure a prophet. The architect of Adoniram Penn's barn, while he designed it for the comfort of four-footed animals, had planned better than he knew for the comfort of humans. Sarah Penn saw at a glance its possibilities. Those great box-stalls, with quilts hung before them, would make better bedrooms than the one she had occupied for forty years, and there was a tight carriage-room. The harness-room, with its chimney and shelves, would make a kitchen of her dreams. The great middle space would make a parlor, by-and-by, fit for a palace. Up stairs there was as much room as down. With partitions and windows, what a house would there be! Sarah looked at the row of stanchions before the allotted space for cows, and reflected that she would have her front entry there.

----

[2]The British, under General James Wolfe (1727–1759), captured Quebec in 1759, defeating the French on the nearby Plains of Abraham.

At six o'clock the stove was up in the harness-room, the kettle was boiling, and the table set for tea. It looked almost as home-like as the abandoned house across the yard had ever done. The young hired man milked, and Sarah directed him calmly to bring the milk to the new barn. He came gaping, dropping little blots of foam from the brimming pails on the grass. Before the next morning he had spread the story of Adoniram Penn's wife moving into the new barn all over the little village. Men assembled in the store and talked it over, women with shawls over their heads scuttled into each other's houses before their work was done. Any deviation from the ordinary course of life in this quiet town was enough to stop all progress in it. Everybody paused to look at the staid, independent figure on the side track.[3] There was a difference of opinion with regard to her. Some held her to be insane; some, of a lawless and rebellious spirit.

Friday the minister went to see her. It was in the forenoon, and she was at the barn door shelling peas for dinner. She looked up and returned his salutation with dignity, then she went on with her work. She did not invite him in. The saintly expression of her face remained fixed, but there was an angry flush over it.

The minister stood awkwardly before her, and talked. She handled the peas as if they were bullets. At last she looked up, and her eyes showed the spirit that her meek front had covered for a lifetime.

"There ain't no use talkin', Mr. Hersey," said she. "I've thought it all over an' over, an' I believe I'm doin' what's right. I've made it the subject of prayer, an' it's betwixt me an' the Lord an' Adoniram. There ain't no call for nobody else to worry about it."

"Well, of course, if you have brought it to the Lord in prayer, and feel satisfied that you are doing right, Mrs. Penn," said the minister, helplessly. His thin gray-bearded face was pathetic. He was a sickly man; his youthful confidence had cooled; he had to scourge himself up to some of his pastoral duties as relentlessly as a Catholic ascetic, and then he was prostrated by the smart.

"I think it's right jest as much as I think it was right for our forefathers to come over from the old country 'cause they didn't have what belonged to 'em," said Mrs. Penn. She arose. The barn threshold might have been Plymouth Rock from her bearing. "I don't doubt you mean well, Mr. Hersey," said she, "but there are things people hadn't ought to interfere with. I've been a member of the church for over forty year. I've got my own mind an' my own feet, an' I'm goin' to think my own thoughts an' go my own ways, an' nobody but the Lord is goin' to dictate to me unless I've a mind to have him. Won't you come in an' set down? How is Mis' Hersey?"

"She is well, I thank you," replied the minister. He added some more perplexed apologetic remarks; then he retreated.

He could expound the intricacies of every character study in the Scriptures, he was competent to grasp the Pilgrim Fathers and all historical innovators, but Sarah Penn was beyond him. He could deal with primal cases, but parallel ones worsted him. But, after all, although it was aside from his province, he wondered more how Adoniram Penn would deal with his wife than how the Lord would. Everybody shared the wonder. When Adoniram's four new cows arrived, Sarah ordered three to be put in the old barn, the other in the house shed where the cooking-stove had stood. That added to the excitement. It was whispered that all four cows were domiciled in the house.

Towards sunset on Saturday, when Adoniram was expected home, there was a knot of men in the road near the new barn. The hired man had milked, but he still hung around the premises. Sarah Penn had supper all ready. There were brown-bread and baked beans and a custard pie; it was the supper that Adoniram loved on a Saturday night. She had on a clean calico, and she bore herself imperturbably.

---

[3]Short section of track connected to the main railroad track by switches.

Nanny and Sammy kept close at her heels. Their eyes were large, and Nanny was full of nervous tremors. Still there was to them more pleasant excitement than anything else. An inborn confidence in their mother over their father asserted itself.

Sammy looked out of the harness-room window. "There he is," he announced, in an awed whisper. He and Nanny peeped around the casing. Mrs. Penn kept on about her work. The children watched Adoniram leave the new horse standing in the drive while he went to the house door. It was fastened. Then he went around to the shed. That door was seldom locked, even when the family was away. The thought how her father would be confronted by the cow flashed upon Nanny. There was a hysterical sob in her throat. Adoniram emerged from the shed and stood looking around in a dazed fashion. His lips moved; he was saying something, but they could not hear what it was. The hired man was peeping around a corner of the old barn, but nobody saw him.

Adoniram took the new horse by the bridle and led him across the yard to the new barn. Nanny and Sammy slunk close to their mother. The barn doors rolled back, and there stood Adoniram, with the long mild face of the great Canadian farm horse looking over his shoulder.

Nanny kept behind her mother, but Sammy stepped suddenly forward, and stood in front of her.

Adoniram stared at the group. "What on airth you all down here for?" said he. "What's the matter over to the house?"

"We've come here to live, father," said Sammy. His shrill voice quavered out bravely.

"What"—Adoniram sniffed—"what is it smells like cookin'?" said he. He stepped forward and looked in the open door of the harness-room. Then he turned to his wife. His old bristling face was pale and frightened. "What on airth does this mean, mother?" he gasped.

"You come in here, father," said Sarah. She led the way into the harness-room and shut the door. "Now, father," said she, "you needn't be scared. I ain't crazy. There ain't nothin' to be upset over. But we've come here to live, an' we're goin' to live here. We've got jest as good a right here as new horses an' cows. The house wa'n't fit for us to live in any longer, an' I made up my mind I wa'n't goin' to stay there. I've done my duty by you forty year, an' I'm goin' to do it now; but I'm goin' to live here. You've got to put in some windows and partitions; an' you'll have to buy some furniture."

"Why, mother!" the old man gasped.

"You'd better take your coat off an' get washed—there's the wash-basin—an' then we'll have supper."

"Why, mother!"

Sammy went past the window, leading the new horse to the old barn. The old man saw him, and shook his head speechlessly. He tried to take off his coat, but his arms seemed to lack the power. His wife helped him. She poured some water into the tin basin, and put in a piece of soap. She got the comb and brush, and smoothed his thin gray hair after he had washed. Then she put the beans, hot bread, and tea on the table. Sammy came in and the family drew up. Adoniram sat looking dazedly at his plate, and they waited.

"Ain't you goin' to ask a blessin', father?" said Sarah.

And the old man bent his head and mumbled.

All through the meal he stopped eating at intervals, and stared furtively at his wife; but he ate well. The home food tasted good to him, and his old frame was too sturdily healthy to be affected by his mind. But after supper he went out, and sat down on the step of the smaller door at the right of the barn, through which he had meant his Jerseys to pass in stately file, but which Sarah designed for her front house door, and he leaned his head on his hands.

After the supper dishes were cleared away and the milkpans washed, Sarah went out to him. The twilight was deepening. There was a clear green glow in the sky. Before them stretched the smooth level of field; in the distance was a cluster of haystacks like the huts of a village; the air was very cool and calm and sweet. The landscape might have been an ideal one of peace.

Sarah bent over and touched her husband on one of his thin, sinewy shoulders. "Father!"

The old man's shoulders heaved: he was weeping.

"Why, don't do so, father," said Sarah.

"I'll—put up the—partitions, an'—everything you—want, mother."

Sarah put her apron up to her face; she was overcome by her own triumph.

Adoniram was like a fortress whose walls had no active resistance, and went down the instant the right besieging tools were used. "Why, mother," he said, hoarsely, "I hadn't no idee you was so set on't as all this comes to."

1891

CHARLOTTE PERKINS GILMAN
(1860–1935)

In 1885 when Charlotte Gilman gave birth to a daughter the year following her first marriage (to Charles Walter Stetson), she became profoundly depressed and sought the help of a renowned physician, Dr. S. Weir Mitchell, who diagnosed her as afflicted with "hysteria." He put her under treatment for a month, and on discharging her offered this advice: "Live as domestic a life as possible. Have your child with you all the time. Lie down an hour after each meal. Have but two hours' intellectual life a day. And never touch pen, brush, or pencil as long as you live."

Seldom, surely, has such bad advice been given a patient by a physician— prescribing precisely that regimen which brought about the "hysteria" in the first place. Fortunately the patient ultimately ignored the advice and escaped the fate of the narrator in "The Yellow Wall-Paper," Gilman's short story based on her experience: that unfortunate woman descends into madness.

Charlotte Perkins was born in Hartford, Connecticut, the third of four children born to Mary Westcott and Frederick Beecher Perkins, a relative of the theologian Lyman Beecher, the minister Henry Ward Beecher, and the novelist Harriet Beecher Stowe. The father, himself a writer, deserted his family, leaving his wife to bring up the children in poverty. Charlotte's formal schooling was meager, but she educated herself by reading widely.

After attending the Rhode Island School of Design for a brief time, Charlotte Perkins turned to teaching art to support herself. In 1884 she married the artist Charles Walter Stetson, and the following year Katherine Beecher was born— bringing on the depression and "hysteria." Feeling that she might go insane, Charlotte Stetson moved to California in 1888, taking her daughter with her. Divorce followed in 1892. When Charles Stetson remarried one of her friends, she sent her daughter to live with her ex-husband and new wife.

Although Charlotte Perkins saved her sanity by disregarding her physician's advice, she continued to experience periods of depression for the rest of her life. No doubt contributing to her condition were indelible childhood experiences— the desertion of her father, who broke off all relations with his children, and the coldness of an austere mother harrassed by overwork and endless poverty. But one result of the breakdown was the writing and publication in 1892 of one of the most remarkable short stories in American literature — "The Yellow Wall-Paper," now admired as one of the classics of feminist literature, but recognized too as a powerful and chilling imaginative account of psychological disintegration.

Attracted by the socialist movement of the time, Charlotte Perkins was deeply impressed by Edward Bellamy's *Looking Backwards* (1888), a fictional account of a life in a socialist utopian society. She launched a career of lecturing and writing as a crusader for social reform, with emphasis on the oppression of women. Her most influential work was *Women and Economics* (1898), translated into many foreign languages, including Japanese.

In 1900 Charlotte Perkins married her cousin, George Houghton Gilman, a marriage that proved quite different from her first. He was apparently supportive of her career until his death in 1934. A series of works flowed from her pen, most of them exploring the institutionalized relations of men and women. Among the most important of these were *The Man-Made World* (1911), *Herland* (1915), a utopian novel, and *His Religion and Hers* (1923). She also founded and edited her own magazine, *The Forerunner* (1909–16), in which she published her essays, fiction, and poetry.

After her husband's death, Charlotte Gilman went to California to live with her daughter. Suffering from cancer, she put an end to her life by chloroform in 1935. She left a letter published posthumously in her autobiography: "My life is in Humanity — and that goes on. . . . The one predominant duty is to find one's work and do it, and I have striven mightily at that."

ADDITIONAL READING

The Living of Charlotte Perkins Gilman: An Autobiography, 1935; *The Charlotte Perkins Gilman Reader*, ed. Ann J. Lane, 1980.

Mary A. Hill, *Charlotte Perkins Gilman: The Making of a Radical Feminist, 1860–1896*, 1980; Gary Scharnhorst, *Charlotte Perkins Gilman*, 1985, and *Charlotte Perkins Gilman: A Bibliography*, 1985; Polly Wynn Allen, *Building Domestic Liberty: Charlotte Perkins Gilman's Architectural Feminism*, 1988; Ann J. Love, *To Herland and Beyond: The Life and Work of Charlotte Perkins Gilman*, 1990.

TEXT

The New England Magazine, January 1892.

The Yellow Wall-Paper

It is very seldom that mere ordinary people like John and myself secure ancestral halls for the summer.

A colonial mansion, a hereditary estate, I would say a haunted house, and reach the height of romantic felicity — but that would be asking too much of fate!

Still I will proudly declare that there is something queer about it.

Else, why should it be let so cheaply? And why have stood so long untenanted?

John laughs at me, of course, but one expects that in marriage.

John is practical in the extreme. He has no patience with faith, an intense horror of superstition, and he scoffs openly at any talk of things not to be felt and seen and put down in figures.

John is a physician, and *perhaps* — (I would not say it to a living soul, of course, but this is dead paper and a great relief to my mind—) *perhaps* that is one reason I do not get well faster.

You see he does not believe I am sick!

And what can one do?

If a physician of high standing, and one's own husband, assures friends and relatives that there is really nothing the matter with one but temporary nervous depression—a slight hysterical tendency[1]—what is one to do?

My brother is also a physician, and also of high standing, and he says the same thing.

So I take phosphates or phosphites—whichever it is, and tonics, and journeys, and air, and exercise, and am absolutely forbidden to "work" until I am well again.

Personally, I disagree with their ideas.

Personally, I believe that congenial work, with excitement and change, would do me good.

But what is one to do?

I did write for a while in spite of them; but it *does* exhaust me a good deal—having to be so sly about it, or else meet with heavy opposition.

I sometimes fancy that in my condition if I had less opposition and more society and stimulus—but John says the very worst thing I can do is to think about my condition, and I confess it always makes me feel bad.

So I will let it alone and talk about the house.

The most beautiful place! It is quite alone, standing well back from the road, quite three miles from the village. It makes me think of English places that you read about, for there are hedges and walls and gates that lock, and lots of separate little houses for the gardeners and people.

There is a *delicious* garden! I never saw such a garden—large and shady, full of box-bordered paths, and lined with long grape-covered arbors with seats under them.

There were greenhouses, too, but they are all broken now.

There was some legal trouble, I believe, something about the heirs and co-heirs; anyhow, the place has been empty for years.

That spoils my ghostliness, I am afraid, but I don't care—there is something strange about the house—I can feel it.

I even said so to John one moonlight evening, but he said what I felt was a *draught*, and shut the window.

I get unreasonably angry with John sometimes. I'm sure I never used to be so sensitive. I think it is due to this nervous condition.

But John says if I feel so, I shall neglect proper self-control; so I take pains to control myself—before him, at least, and that makes me very tired.

I don't like our room a bit. I wanted one downstairs that opened on the piazza and had roses all over the window, and such pretty old-fashioned chintz hangings! but John would not hear of it.

He said there was only one window and not room for two beds, and no near room for him if he took another.

He is very careful and loving, and hardly lets me stir without special direction.

I have a schedule prescription for each hour in the day; he takes all care from me, and so I feel basely ungrateful not to value it more.

He said we came here solely on my account, that I was to have perfect rest and all the air I could get. "Your exercise depends on your strength, my dear," said he, "and your food somewhat on your appetite; but air you can absorb all the time." So we took the nursery at the top of the house.

---

[1]Until well into the twentieth century, "hysteria" was considered a woman's disease characterized by a wide range of physical or mental symptoms, including nervousness, anxiety, depression, and fantasy.

It is a big, airy room, the whole floor nearly, with windows that look all ways, and air and sunshine galore. It was nursery first and then playroom and gymnasium, I should judge; for the windows are barred for little children, and there are rings and things in the walls.

The paint and paper look as if a boys' school had used it. It is stripped off — the paper — in great patches all around the head of my bed, about as far as I can reach, and in a great place on the other side of the room low down. I never saw a worse paper in my life.

One of those sprawling flamboyant patterns committing every artistic sin.

It is dull enough to confuse the eye in following, pronounced enough to constantly irritate and provoke study, and when you follow the lame uncertain curves for a little distance they suddenly commit suicide — plunge off at outrageous angles, destroy themselves in unheard of contradictions.

The color is repellant, almost revolting; a smouldering unclean yellow, strangely faded by the slow-turning sunlight.

It is a dull yet lurid orange in some places, a sickly sulphur tint in others.

No wonder the children hated it! I should hate it myself if I had to live in this room long.

There comes John, and I must put this away, — he hates to have me write a word.

.   .   .   .   .

We have been here two weeks, and I haven't felt like writing before, since that first day.

I am sitting by the window now, up in this atrocious nursery, and there is nothing to hinder my writing as much as I please, save lack of strength.

John is away all day, and even some nights when his cases are serious.

I am glad my case is not serious!

But these nervous troubles are dreadfully depressing.

John does not know how much I really suffer. He knows there is no *reason* to suffer, and that satisfies him.

Of course it is only nervousness. It does weigh on me so not to do my duty in any way!

I meant to be such a help to John, such a real rest and comfort, and here I am a comparative burden already!

Nobody would believe what an effort it is to do what little I am able, — to dress and entertain, and order things.

It is fortunate Mary is so good with the baby. Such a dear baby!

And yet I *cannot* be with him, it makes me so nervous.

I suppose John never was nervous in his life. He laughs at me so about this wallpaper!

At first he meant to repaper the room, but afterwards he said that I was letting it get the better of me, and that nothing was worse for a nervous patient than to give way to such fancies.

He said that after the wall-paper was changed it would be the heavy bedstead, and then the barred windows, and then the gate at the head of the stairs, and so on.

"You know the place is doing you good," he said, "and really, dear, I don't care to renovate the house just for a three months' rental."

"Then do let us go downstairs," I said, "there are such pretty rooms there."

Then he took me in his arms and called me a blessed little goose, and said he would go down cellar, if I wished, and have it whitewashed into the bargain.

But he is right enough about the beds and windows and things.

It is an airy and comfortable room as any one need wish, and, of course, I would not be so silly as to make him uncomfortable just for a whim.

I'm really getting quite fond of the big room, all but that horrid paper.

Out of one window I can see the garden, those mysterious deep-shaded arbors, the riotous old-fashioned flowers, and bushes and gnarly trees.

Out of another I get a lovely view of the bay and a little private wharf belonging to the estate. There is a beautiful shaded lane that runs down there from the house. I always fancy I see people walking in these numerous paths and arbors, but John has cautioned me not to give way to fancy in the least. He says that with my imaginative power and habit of story-making, a nervous weakness like mine is sure to lead to all manner of excited fancies, and that I ought to use my will and good sense to check the tendency. So I try.

I think sometimes that if I were only well enough to write a little it would relieve the press of ideas and rest me.

But I find I get pretty tired when I try.

It is so discouraging not to have any advice and companionship about my work. When I get really well, John says we will ask Cousin Henry and Julia down for a long visit; but he says he would as soon put fireworks in my pillow-case as to let me have those stimulating people about now.

I wish I could get well faster.

But I must not think about that. This paper looks to me as if it *knew* what a vicious influence it had!

There is a recurrent spot where the pattern lolls like a broken neck and two bulbous eyes stare at you upside down.

I get positively angry with the impertinence of it and the everlastingness. Up and down and sideways they crawl, and those absurd, unblinking eyes are everywhere. There is one place where two breaths didn't match, and the eyes go all up and down the line, one a little higher than the other.

I never saw so much expression in an inanimate thing before, and we all know how much expression they have! I used to lie awake as a child and get more entertainment and terror out of blank walls and plain furniture than most children could find in a toy-store.

I remember what a kindly wink the knobs of our big, old bureau used to have, and there was one chair that always seemed like a strong friend.

I used to feel that if any of the other things looked too fierce I could always hop into that chair and be safe.

The furniture in this room is no worse than inharmonious, however, for we had to bring it all from downstairs. I suppose when this was used as a playroom they had to take the nursery things out, and no wonder! I never saw such ravages as the children have made here.

The wall-paper, as I said before, is torn off in spots, and it sticketh closer than a brother[2]—they must have had perseverance as well as hatred.

Then the floor is scratched and gouged and splintered, the plaster itself is dug out here and there, and this great heavy bed which is all we found in the room, looks as if it had been through the wars.

But I don't mind it a bit—only the paper.

There comes John's sister. Such a dear girl as she is, and so careful of me! I must not let her find me writing.

She is a perfect and enthusiastic housekeeper, and hopes for no better profession. I verily believe she thinks it is the writing which made me sick!

But I can write when she is out, and see her a long way off from these windows.

There is one that commands the road, a lovely shaded winding road, and one that just looks off over the country. A lovely country, too, full of great elms and velvet meadows.

---

[2]Proverbs 18:24: "There is a friend that sticketh closer than a brother."

This wall-paper has a kind of sub-pattern in a different shade, a particularly irritating one, for you can only see it in certain lights, and not clearly then.

But in the places where it isn't faded and where the sun is just so—I can see a strange, provoking, formless sort of figure, that seems to skulk about behind that silly and conspicuous front design.

There's sister on the stairs!

•   •   •   •   •

Well, the Fourth of July is over! The people are all gone and I am tired out. John thought it might do me good to see a little company, so we just had mother and Nellie and the children down for a week.

Of course I didn't do a thing. Jennie sees to everything now.

But it tired me all the same.

John says if I don't pick up faster he shall send me to Weir Mitchell[3] in the fall.

But I don't want to go there at all. I had a friend who was in his hands once, and she says he is just like John and my brother, only more so!

Besides, it is such an undertaking to go so far.

I don't feel as if it was worth while to turn my hand over for anything, and I'm getting dreadfully fretful and querulous.

I cry at nothing, and cry most of the time.

Of course I don't when John is here, or anybody else, but when I am alone.

And I am alone a good deal just now. John is kept in town very often by serious cases, and Jennie is good and lets me alone when I want her to.

So I walk a little in the garden or down that lovely lane, sit on the porch under the roses, and lie down up here a good deal.

I'm getting really fond of the room in spite of the wall-paper. Perhaps *because* of the wall-paper.

It dwells in my mind so!

I lie here on this great immovable bed—it is nailed down, I believe—and follow that pattern about by the hour. It is as good as gymnastics, I assure you. I start, we'll say, at the bottom, down in the corner over there where it has not been touched, and I determine for the thousandth time that I *will* follow that pointless pattern to some sort of a conclusion.

I know a little of the principle of design, and I know this thing was not arranged on any laws of radiation, or alternation, or repetition, or symmetry, or anything else that I ever heard of.

It is repeated, of course, by the breadths, but not otherwise.

Looked at in one way each breadth stands alone, the bloated curves and flourishes—a kind of "debased Romanesque" with *delirium tremens*[4]—go waddling up and down in isolated columns of fatuity.

But, on the other hand, they connect diagonally, and the sprawling outlines run off in great slanting waves of optic horror, like a lot of wallowing seaweeds in full chase.

The whole thing goes horizontally, too, at least it seems so, and I exhaust myself in trying to distinguish the order of its going in that direction.

They have used a horizontal breadth for a frieze,[5] and that adds wonderfully to the confusion.

There is one end of the room where it is almost intact, and there, when the cross-lights fade and the low sun shines directly upon it, I can almost fancy radiation after

---

[3]Silas Weir Mitchell (1829–1914), American physician and novelist, specialized in nervous diseases and was renowned for his "rest cure."
[4]I.e., the intricate ornamentation of the Romanesque style is "debased," without order or structure, and with the violent "trembling delirium" (Latin) such as is caused by alcohol poisoning.
[5]Ornamental border.

all,—the interminable grotesque seem to form around a common centre and rush off in headlong plunges of equal distraction.

It makes me tired to follow it. I will take a nap I guess.

. . . . .

I don't know why I should write this.

I don't want to.

I don't feel able.

And I know John would think it absurd. But I *must* say what I feel and think in some way—it is such a relief!

But the effort is getting to be greater than the relief.

Half the time now I am awfully lazy, and lie down ever so much.

John says I mustn't lose my strength, and has me take cod liver oil and lots of tonics and things, to say nothing of ale and wine and rare meat.

Dear John! He loves me very dearly, and hates to have me sick. I tried to have a real earnest reasonable talk with him the other day, and tell him how I wish he would let me go and make a visit to Cousin Henry and Julia.

But he said I wasn't able to go, nor able to stand it after I got there; and I did not make out a very good case for myself, for I was crying before I had finished.

It is getting to be a great effort for me to think straight. Just this nervous weakness I suppose.

And dear John gathered me up in his arms, and just carried me upstairs and laid me on the bed, and sat by me and read to me till it tired my head.

He said I was his darling and his comfort and all he had, and that I must take care of myself for his sake, and keep well.

He says no one but myself can help me out of it, that I must use my will and self-control and not let any silly fancies run away with me.

There's one comfort, the baby is well and happy, and does not have to occupy this nursery with the horrid wall-paper.

If we had not used it, that blessed child would have! What a fortunate escape! Why, I wouldn't have a child of mine, an impressionable little thing, live in such a room for worlds.

I never thought of it before, but it is lucky that John kept me here after all, I can stand it so much easier than a baby, you see.

Of course I never mention it to them any more—I am too wise,—but I keep watch of it all the same.

There are things in that paper that nobody knows but me, or ever will.

Behind that outside pattern the dim shapes get clearer every day.

It is always the same shape, only very numerous.

And it is like a woman stooping down and creeping about behind that pattern. I don't like it a bit. I wonder—I begin to think—I wish John would take me away from here!

. . . . .

It is so hard to talk with John about my case, because he is so wise, and because he loves me so.

But I tried it last night.

It was moonlight. The moon shines in all around just as the sun does.

I hate to see it sometimes, it creeps so slowly, and always comes in by one window or another.

John was asleep and I hated to waken him, so I kept still and watched the moonlight on that undulating wall-paper till I felt creepy.

The faint figure behind seemed to shake the pattern, just as if she wanted to get out.

I got up softly and went to feel and see if the paper *did* move, and when I came back John was awake.

"What is it, little girl?" he said. "Don't go walking about like that—you'll get cold."

I thought it was a good time to talk, so I told him that I really was not gaining here, and that I wished he would take me away.

"Why, darling!" said he, "our lease will be up in three weeks, and I can't see how to leave before.

"The repairs are not done at home, and I cannot possibly leave town just now. Of course if you were in any danger, I could and would, but you really are better, dear, whether you can see it or not. I am a doctor, dear, and I know. You are gaining flesh and color, your appetite is better, I feel really much easier about you."

"I don't weigh a bit more," said I, "nor as much; and my appetite may be better in the evening when you are here, but it is worse in the morning when you are away!"

"Bless her little heart!" said he with a big hug, "she shall be as sick as she pleases! But now let's improve the shining hours[6] by going to sleep, and talk about it in the morning!"

"And you won't go away?" I asked gloomily.

"Why, how can I, dear? It is only three weeks more and then we will take a nice little trip of a few days while Jennie is getting the house ready. Really dear you are better!"

"Better in body perhaps—" I began, and stopped short, for he sat up straight and looked at me with such a stern, reproachful look that I could not say another word.

"My darling," said he, "I beg of you, for my sake and for our child's sake, as well as for your own, that you will never for one instant let that idea enter your mind! There is nothing so dangerous, so fascinating, to a temperament like yours. It is a false and foolish fancy. Can you not trust me as a physician when I tell you so?"

So of course I said no more on that score, and we went to sleep before long. He thought I was asleep first, but I wasn't, and lay there for hours trying to decide whether that front pattern and the back pattern really did move together or separately.

· · · · ·

On a pattern like this, by daylight, there is a lack of sequence, a defiance of law, that is a constant irritant to a normal mind.

The color is hideous enough, and unreliable enough, and infuriating enough, but the pattern is torturing.

You think you have mastered it, but just as you get well underway in following, it turns a back-somersault and there you are. It slaps you in the face, knocks you down, and tramples upon you. It is like a bad dream.

The outside pattern is a florid arabesque, reminding one of a fungus. If you can imagine a toadstool in joints, an interminable string of toadstools, budding and sprouting in endless convolutions—why, that is something like it.

That is, sometimes!

There is one marked peculiarity about this paper, a thing nobody seems to notice but myself, and that is that it changes as the light changes.

When the sun shoots in through the east window—I always watch for that first long, straight ray—it changes so quickly that I never can quite believe it.

That is why I watch it always.

---

[6]Cf. the lines from the children's poem "Against Idleness and Mischief" by English theologian Isaac Watts (1674–1748): "How doth the little busy bee / Improve each shining hour, / And gather honey all the day / From every opening flower!"

By moonlight—the moon shines in all night when there is a moon—I wouldn't know it was the same paper.

At night in any kind of light, in twilight, candlelight, lamplight, and worst of all by moonlight, it becomes bars! The outside pattern I mean, and the woman behind it is as plain as can be.

I didn't realize for a long time what the thing was that showed behind, that dim sub-pattern, but now I am quite sure it is a woman.

By daylight she is subdued, quiet. I fancy it is the pattern that keeps her so still. It is so puzzling. It keeps me quiet by the hour.

I lie down ever so much now. John says it is good for me, and to sleep all I can.

Indeed he started the habit by making me lie down for an hour after each meal.

It is a very bad habit I am convinced, for you see I don't sleep.

And that cultivates deceit, for I don't tell them I'm awake—O no!

The fact is I am getting a little afraid of John.

He seems very queer sometimes, and even Jennie has an inexplicable look.

It strikes me occasionally, just as a scientific hypothesis,—that perhaps it is the paper!

I have watched John when he did not know I was looking, and come into the room suddenly on the most innocent excuses, and I've caught him several times *looking at the paper*! And Jennie too. I caught Jennie with her hand on it once.

She didn't know I was in the room, and when I asked her in a quiet, a very quiet voice, with the most restrained manner possible, what she was doing with the paper—she turned around as if she had been caught stealing, and looked quite angry—asked me why I should frighten her so!

Then she said that the paper stained everything it touched, that she had found yellow smooches on all my clothes and John's, and she wished we would be more careful!

Did not that sound innocent? But I know she was studying that pattern, and I am determined that nobody shall find it out but myself!

. . . . . .

Life is very much more exciting now than it used to be. You see I have something more to expect, to look forward to, to watch. I really do eat better, and am more quiet than I was.

John is so pleased to see me improve! He laughed a little the other day, and said I seemed to be flourishing in spite of my wall-paper.

I turned it off with a laugh. I had no intention of telling him it was *because* of the wall-paper—he would make fun of me. He might even want to take me away.

I don't want to leave now until I have found it out. There is a week more, and I think that will be enough.

. . . . . .

I'm feeling ever so much better! I don't sleep much at night, for it is so interesting to watch developments; but I sleep a good deal in the daytime.

In the daytime it is tiresome and perplexing.

There are always new shoots on the fungus, and new shades of yellow all over it. I cannot keep count of them, though I have tried conscientiously.

It is the strangest yellow, that wall-paper! It makes me think of all the yellow things I ever saw—not beautiful ones like buttercups, but old foul, bad yellow things.

But there is something else about that paper—the smell! I noticed it the moment we came into the room, but with so much air and sun it was not bad. Now we have had a week of fog and rain, and whether the windows are open or not, the smell is here.

It creeps all over the house.

I find it hovering in the dining-room, skulking in the parlor, hiding in the hall, lying in wait for me on the stairs.

It gets into my hair.

Even when I go to ride, if I turn my head suddenly and surprise it—there is that smell!

Such a peculiar odor, too! I have spent hours in trying to analyze it, to find what it smelled like.

It is not bad—at first, and very gentle, but quite the subtlest, most enduring odor I ever met.

In this damp weather it is awful, I wake up in the night and find it hanging over me.

It used to disturb me at first. I thought seriously of burning the house—to reach the smell.

But now I am used to it. The only thing I can think of that it is like is the *color* of the paper! A yellow smell.

There is a very funny mark on this wall, low down, near the mopboard. A streak that runs round the room. It goes behind every piece of furniture, except the bed, a long, straight, even *smooch*, as if it had been rubbed over and over.

I wonder how it was done and who did it, and what they did it for. Round and round and round—round and round and round—it makes me dizzy!

· · · · ·

I really have discovered something at last.

Through watching so much at night, when it changes so, I have finally found out.

The front pattern *does* move—and no wonder! The woman behind shakes it!

Sometimes I think there are a great many women behind, and sometimes only one, and she crawls around fast, and her crawling shakes it all over.

Then in the very bright spots she keeps still, and in the very shady spots she just takes hold of the bars and shakes them hard.

And she is all the time trying to climb through. But nobody could climb through that pattern—it strangles so; I think that is why it has so many heads.

They get through, and then the pattern strangles them off and turns them upside down, and makes their eyes white!

If those heads were covered or taken off it would not be half so bad.

· · · · ·

I think that woman gets out in the daytime!

And I'll tell you why—privately—I've seen her!

I can see her out of every one of my windows!

It is the same woman, I know, for she is always creeping, and most women do not creep by daylight.

I see her in that long shaded lane, creeping up and down. I see her in those dark grape arbors, creeping all around the garden.

I see her on that long road under the trees, creeping along, and when a carriage comes she hides under the blackberry vines.

I don't blame her a bit. It must be very humiliating to be caught creeping by daylight!

I always lock the door when I creep by daylight. I can't do it at night, for I know John would suspect something at once.

And John is so queer now, that I don't want to irritate him. I wish he would take another room! Besides, I don't want anybody to get that woman out at night but myself.

I often wonder if I could see her out of all the windows at once.

But, turn as fast as I can, I can only see out of one at one time.

And though I always see her, she *may* be able to creep faster than I can turn!

I have watched her sometimes away off in the open country, creeping as fast as a cloud shadow in a high wind.

•   •   •   •   •

If only that top pattern could be gotten off from the under one! I mean to try it, little by little.

I have found out another funny thing, but I shan't tell it this time! It does not do to trust people too much.

There are only two more days to get this paper off, and I believe John is beginning to notice. I don't like the look in his eyes.

And I heard him ask Jennie a lot of professional questions about me. She had a very good report to give.

She said I slept a good deal in the daytime.

John knows I don't sleep very well at night, for all I'm so quiet!

He asked me all sorts of questions, too, and pretended to be very loving and kind.

As if I couldn't see through him!

Still, I don't wonder he acts so, sleeping under this paper for three months.

It only interests me, but I feel sure John and Jennie are secretly affected by it.

•   •   •   •   •

Hurrah! This is the last day, but it is enough. John to stay in town over night, and won't be out until this evening.

Jennie wanted to sleep with me—the sly thing! but I told her I should undoubtedly rest better for a night all alone.

That was clever, for really I wasn't alone a bit! As soon as it was moonlight and that poor thing began to crawl and shake the pattern, I got up and ran to help her.

I pulled and she shook, I shook and she pulled, and before morning we had peeled off yards of that paper.

A strip about as high as my head and half around the room.

And then when the sun came and that awful pattern began to laugh at me, I declared I would finish it to-day!

We go away to-morrow, and they are moving all my furniture down again to leave things as they were before.

Jennie looked at the wall in amazement, but I told her merrily that I did it out of pure spite at the vicious thing.

She laughed and said she wouldn't mind doing it herself, but I must not get tired.

How she betrayed herself that time!

But I am here, and no person touches this paper but me,—not *alive*!

She tried to get me out of the room—it was too patent! But I said it was so quiet and empty and clean now that I believed I would lie down again and sleep all I could; and not to wake me even for dinner—I would call when I woke.

So now she is gone, and the servants are gone, and the things are gone, and there is nothing left but that great bedstead nailed down, with the canvas mattress we found on it.

We shall sleep downstairs to-night, and take the boat home to-morrow.

I quite enjoy the room, now it is bare again.

How those children did tear about here!

This bedstead is fairly gnawed!

But I must get to work.

I have locked the door and thrown the key down into the front path.

I don't want to go out, and I don't want to have anybody come in, till John comes. I want to astonish him.

I've got a rope up here that even Jennie did not find. If that woman does get out, and tries to get away, I can tie her!

But I forgot I could not reach far without anything to stand on!

This bed will *not* move!

I tried to lift and push it until I was lame, and then I got so angry I bit off a little piece at one corner—but it hurt my teeth.

Then I peeled off all the paper I could reach standing on the floor. It sticks horribly and the pattern just enjoys it! All those strangled heads and bulbous eyes and waddling fungus growths just shriek with derision!

I am getting angry enough to do something desperate. To jump out of the window would be an admirable exercise, but the bars are too strong even to try.

Besides I wouldn't do it. Of course not. I know well enough that a step like that is improper and might be misconstrued.

I don't like to *look* out of the windows even—there are so many of those creeping women, and they creep so fast.

I wonder if they all come out of that wall-paper as I did?

But I am securely fastened now by my well-hidden rope—you don't get *me* out in the road there!

I suppose I shall have to get back behind the pattern when it comes night, and that is hard!

It is so pleasant to be out in this great room and creep around as I please!

I don't want to go outside. I won't, even if Jennie asks me to.

For outside you have to creep on the ground, and everything is green instead of yellow.

But here I can creep smoothly on the floor, and my shoulder just fits in that long smooch around the wall, so I cannot lose my way.

Why there's John at the door!

It is no use, young man, you can't open it!

How he does call and pound!

Now he's crying for an axe.

It would be a shame to break down that beautiful door!

"John dear!" said I in the gentlest voice, "the key is down by the front steps, under a plantain leaf!"

That silenced him for a few moments.

Then he said—very quietly indeed, "Open the door, my darling!"

"I can't," said I. "The key is down by the front door under a plantain leaf!"

And then I said it again, several times, very gently and slowly, and said it so often that he had to go and see, and he got it of course, and came in. He stopped short by the door.

"What is the matter?" he cried. "For God's sake, what are you doing!"

I kept on creeping just the same, but I looked at him over my shoulder.

"I've got out at last," said I, "in spite of you and Jane? And I've pulled off most of the paper, so you can't put me back!"

Now why should that man have fainted? But he did, and right across my path by the wall, so that I had to creep over him every time!

1892

PERSONAL VOICE AND VIEW:
DIARIES, AUTOBIOGRAPHIES, ESSAYS

SARAH WINNEMUCCA HOPKINS
ALICE JAMES
BOOKER T. WASHINGTON

WILLIAM E. B. DUBOIS
HENRY ADAMS
WILLIAM JAMES

"I think that if I get into the habit of writing a bit about what happens, or rather doesn't happen, I may lose a little of the sense of loneliness and desolation which abides with me. My circumstances allowing of nothing but the ejaculation of one-syllabled reflections, a written monologue by that most interesting being, *myself*, may have its yet to be discovered consolations. I shall at least have it all my own way and it may bring relief as an outlet to that geyser of emotions, sensations, speculations and reflections which ferments perpetually within my poor old carcass for its sins; so here goes, my first Journal!"

Alice James, *Diary*

SARAH WINNEMUCCA HOPKINS
(*c.* 1844–1891)

Sarah Winnemucca was born a Paiute Indian in Nevada, granddaughter of Captain Truckee and daughter of Chief Winnemucca, both leaders of their nomadic tribe that called themselves simply the *Numa*, or *people*. Her Indian name was Thocmetony, meaning Shell Flower. The Paiutes subsisted in a generally sparse environment by digging roots and harvesting pine nuts. They were known variously as Piute or Pi-Utah, and were called the Snake Indians in Oregon.

Sarah's grandfather, Captain Truckee, fought with General John Charles Frémont in the Mexican War (1846–48), and generally encouraged his fellow Indians to make friends with the white man. But, as her later account makes clear, his granddaughter grew up terrified of the militant whites she witnessed crossing the West on the way to California in the gold rush of 1849.

Because she became fluent in English when she was quite young, she developed into a translator and negotiator for her people in their encounters with the whites, first in Nevada and later in Oregon. In 1879 she began a speaking tour in the East on behalf of the Paiutes, making more than 300 presentations and becoming known as "Princess" Sarah. She also found time to begin writing *Life Among the Piutes: Their Wrongs and Claims*. In the East she met Mrs. Horace Mann, wife of the noted educator, who offered to edit the manuscript for her. The book appeared in 1883, with both the author's and editor's names on the title page.

Sarah Winnemucca was married twice to army lieutenants, first very briefly to Edward C. Bartlett in 1871, and later to Lewis Hopkins. Neither marriage seems to have been successful, inasmuch as both men were hard drinkers and talented at spending her money. She herself became disillusioned with governmental Indian land policies and returned to Nevada to devote herself to the development of a school for the Paiute children. Her declining health forced her to retire from this enterprise in 1887. She died four years later.

Life Among the Piutes was thought for a time to be largely the creation of Mrs. Mann, primarily because Sarah Winnemucca was unschooled and self-taught. But recent critics have established that the book is indeed its author's, not its editor's. It is remarkable because of its vivid character portrayals, its description of dramatic incidents, and its preservation of many Indian beliefs, legends, and myths. It is also eloquent in speaking out against the harsh treatment of the Indians:

> You who are educated by a Christian government in the art of war . . . covenanting with God to make this land the home of the free and the brave. Ah, then you rise from your bended knees and seizing the welcoming hands of those who are the owners of this land, which you are not, your carbines rise upon the bleak shore, and your so-called civilization sweeps inland from the ocean wave . . . leaving its pathway marked by crimson lines of blood, and strewed by the bones of two races, the inheritor and the invader; and I am crying out to you for justice. . . .

ADDITIONAL READING

Marion E. Gridley, *American Indian Women*, 1974; Paula Gunn Allen, ed., *Studies in American Indian Literature*, 1983; Gae Whitney Canfield, *Sarah Winnemucca of the Northern Paiutes*, 1983; H. David Brumble III, "Sarah Winnemucca," *American Indian Autobiography*, 1988.

TEXT

Life Among the Piutes: Their Wrongs and Claims, 1883.

from Life Among the Piutes[1]

[THE "LONG-LOOKED FOR WHITE BROTHERS"]

I was born somewhere near 1844, but am not sure of the precise time. I was a very small child when the first white people came into our country. They came like a lion, yes, like a roaring lion, and have continued so ever since, and I have never forgotten their first coming. My people were scattered at that time over nearly all the territory now known as Nevada. My grandfather was chief of the entire Piute nation, and was camped near Humboldt Lake,[2] with a small portion of his tribe, when a party travelling eastward from California was seen coming. When the news was brought to my grandfather, he asked what they looked like? When told that they had hair on their faces, and were white, he jumped up and clasped his hands together, and cried aloud,—

"My white brothers,—my long-looked for white brothers have come at last!"

He immediately gathered some of his leading men, and went to the place where the party had gone into camp. Arriving near them, he was commanded to halt in a manner that was readily understood without an interpreter. Grandpa at once made signs of friendship by throwing down his robe and throwing up his arms to show them he had no weapons; but in vain,—they kept him at a distance. He knew not what to do. He had expected so much pleasure in welcoming his white brothers to the best in the land, that after looking at them sorrowfully for a little while, he came away quite unhappy. But he would not give them up so easily. He took some of his most trustworthy men and followed them day after day, camping near them at night, and travelling in sight of them by day, hoping in this way to gain their confidence. But he was disappointed, poor dear old soul!

I can imagine his feelings, for I have drank deeply from the same cup. When I think of my past life, and the bitter trials I have endured, I can scarcely believe I live, and yet I do; and, with the help of Him who notes the sparrow's fall,[3] I mean to fight for my down-trodden race while life lasts.

Seeing they would not trust him, my grandfather left them, saying, "Perhaps they will come again next year." Then he summoned his whole people, and told them this tradition:—

"In the beginning of the world there were only four, two girls and two boys. Our forefather and mother were only two, and we are their children. You all know that a great while ago there was a happy family in this world. One girl and one boy were dark and the others were white. For a time they got along together without quarrelling, but soon they disagreed, and there was trouble. They were cross to one another and fought, and our parents were very much grieved. They prayed that their children might learn better, but it did not do any good; and afterwards the whole household was made so unhappy that the father and mother saw that they must separate their children; and then our father took the dark boy and girl, and the white boy and girl, and asked them, 'Why are you so cruel to each other?' They hung down their heads, and would not speak. They were ashamed. He said to them, 'Have I not been

---

[1] From Chapter 1. The Paiutes are two distinct Indian groups of the Shoshonean subfamily of the Uto-Aztecan language family; Hopkins belonged to the Northern Paiutes who roamed the Great Basin, now western Nevada, northeastern California, and southeastern Oregon.
[2] In northwestern Nevada, also called Humboldt Sink.
[3] Cf. Matthew 10:29.

kind to you all, and given you everything your hearts wished for? You do not have to hunt and kill your own game to live upon. You see, my dear children, I have power to call whatsoever kind of game we want to eat; and I also have the power to separate my dear children, if they are not good to each other.' So he separated his children by a word. He said, 'Depart from each other, you cruel children; — go across the mighty ocean and do not seek each other's lives.'

"So the light girl and boy disappeared by that one word, and their parents saw them no more, and they were grieved, although they knew their children were happy. And by-and-by the dark children grew into a large nation; and we believe it is the one we belong to, and that the nation that sprung from the white children will some time send some one to meet us and heal all the old trouble. Now, the white people we saw a few days ago must certainly be our white brothers, and I want to welcome them. I want to love them as I love all of you. But they would not let me; they were afraid. But they will come again, and I want you one and all to promise that, should I not live to welcome them myself, you will not hurt a hair on their heads, but welcome them as I tried to do."

How good of him to try and heal the wound, and how vain were his efforts! My people had never seen a white man, and yet they existed, and were a strong race. The people promised as he wished, and they all went back to their work.

The next year came a great emigration, and camped near Humboldt Lake. The name of the man in charge of the trains was Captain Johnson, and they stayed three days to rest their horses, as they had a long journey before them without water. During their stay my grandfather and some of his people called upon them, and they all shook hands, and when our white brothers were going away they gave my grandfather a white tin plate. Oh, what a time they had over that beautiful gift, — it was so bright! They saw that after they left, my grandfather called for all his people to come together, and he then showed them the beautiful gift which he had received from his white brothers. Everybody was so pleased; nothing like it was ever seen in our country before. My grandfather thought so much of it that he bored holes in it and fastened it on his head, and wore it as his hat. He held it in as much admiration as my white sisters hold their diamond rings or a sealskin jacket. So that winter they talked of nothing but their white brothers. The following spring there came great news down the Humboldt River,[4] saying that there were some more of the white brothers coming, and there was something among them that was burning all in a blaze. My grandfather asked them what it was like. They told him it looked like a man; it had legs and hands and a head, but the head had quit burning, and it was left quite black. There was the greatest excitement among my people everywhere about the men in a blazing fire. They were excited because they did not know there were any people in the world but the two, — that is, the Indians and the whites; they thought that was all of us in the beginning of the world, and, of course, we did not know where the others had come from, and we don't know yet. Ha! ha! oh, what a laughable thing that was! It was two negroes wearing red shirts!

The third year more emigrants came, and that summer Captain Fremont, who is now General Fremont.[5]

My grandfather met him, and they were soon friends. They met just where the railroad crosses Truckee River,[6] now called Wadsworth, Nevada. Captain Fremont gave my grandfather the name of Captain Truckee, and he also called the river after him. Truckee is an Indian word; it means *all right,* or *very well.* A party of twelve of my

[4]Nevada River, flowing southwest into Humboldt Sink.
[5]General John Charles Frémont (1813–1890), soldier, explorer, and politician, led an expedition (1843–44) through Utah to Oregon, down the length of California, and back through Nevada, Utah, and Colorado, and another (1845–46), mapping the Central Rockies and crossing into California; his detailed reports of the West encouraged and greatly aided later emigrants.
[6]River in California and Nevada flowing northeast, past Wadsworth, into Pyramid Lake, Nevada (the lake was named in 1844 by Frémont).

people went to California with Captain Fremont. I do not know just how long they were gone.

During the time my grandfather was away in California, where he staid till after the Mexican war,[7] there was a girl-baby born in our family. I can just remember it. It must have been in spring, because everything was green. I was away playing with some other children when my mother called me to come to her. So I ran to her. She then asked me to sit down, which I did. She then handed me some beautiful beads, and asked me if I would like to buy something with them. I said: —

"Yes, mother, — some pine nuts."

My mother said: —

"Would you like something else you can love and play with? Would you like to have a little sister?" I said, —

"Yes, dear mother, a little, little sister; not like my sister Mary, for she won't let me play with her. She leaves me and goes with big girls to play;" and then my mother wanted to know if I would give my pretty beads for the little sister.

Just then the baby let out such a cry it frightened me: and I jumped up and cried so that my mother took me in her arms, and said it was a little sister for me, and not to be afraid. This is all I can remember about it. . . .

The following spring, before my grandfather returned home, there was a great excitement among my people on account of fearful news coming from different tribes, that the people whom they called their white brothers were killing everybody that came in their way, and all the Indian tribes had gone into the mountains to save their lives. So my father told all his people to go into the mountains and hunt and lay up food for the coming winter. Then we all went into the mountains. There was a fearful story they told us children. Our mothers told us that the whites were killing everybody and eating them. So we were all afraid of them. Every dust that we could see blowing in the valleys we would say it was the white people. In the late fall my father told his people to go to the rivers and fish, and we all went to Humboldt River, and the women went to work gathering wild seed, which they grind between the rocks. The stones are round, big enough to hold in the hands. The women did this when they got back, and when they had gathered all they could they put it in one place and covered it with grass, and then over the grass mud. After it is covered it looks like an Indian wigwam.

Oh, what a fright we all got one morning to hear some white people were coming. Every one ran as best they could. My poor mother was left with my little sister and me. Oh, I never can forget it. My poor mother was carrying my little sister on her back, and trying to make me run; but I was so frightened I could not move my feet, and while my poor mother was trying to get me along my aunt overtook us, and she said to my mother: "Let us bury our girls, or we shall all be killed and eaten up." So they went to work and buried us, and told us if we heard any noise not to cry out, for if we did they would surely kill us and eat us. So our mothers buried me and my cousin, planted sage bushes over our faces to keep the sun from burning them, and there we were left all day.

Oh, can any one imagine my feelings *buried alive*, thinking every minute that I was to be unburied and eaten up by the people that my grandfather loved so much? With my heart throbbing, and not daring to breathe, we lay there all day. It seemed that the night would never come. Thanks be to God! the night came at last. Oh, how I cried and said: "Oh, father, have you forgotten me? Are you never coming for me?" I cried so I thought my very heartstrings would break.

[7]The Mexican War (1846–48), begun after the United States annexed Texas (1845), resulted in Mexico ceding to the United States the region from Texas to the California coast, including Nevada.

At last we heard some whispering. We did not dare to whisper to each other, so we lay still. I could hear their footsteps coming nearer and nearer. I thought my heart was coming right out of my mouth. Then I heard my mother say, "'T is right here!" Oh, can any one in this world ever imagine what were my feelings when I was dug up by my poor mother and father? My cousin and I were once more happy in our mothers' and fathers' care, and we were taken to where all the rest were.

I was once buried alive; but my second burial shall be for ever, where no father or mother will come and dig me up. It shall not be with throbbing heart that I shall listen for coming footsteps. I shall be in the sweet rest of peace, — I, the chieftain's weary daughter. . . .

["Oh, Where Will It End?"]

My father got up very early one morning, and told his people the time had come, — that we could no longer be happy as of old, as the white people we called our brothers had brought a great trouble and sorrow among us already. He went on and said, —

"These white people must be a great nation, as they have houses that move. It is wonderful to see them move along. I fear we will suffer greatly by their coming to our country; they come for no good to us, although my father said they were our brothers, but they do not seem to think we are like them. What do you all think about it? Maybe I am wrong. My dear children, there is something telling me that I am not wrong, because I am sure they have minds like us, and think as we do; and I know that they were doing wrong when they set fire to our winter supplies. They surely knew it was our food."

And this was the first wrong done to us by our white brothers.

Now comes the end of our merrymaking.

Then my father told his people his fearful dream, as he called it. He said, —

"I dreamt this same thing three nights, — the very same. I saw the greatest emigration that has yet been through our country. I looked North and South and East and West, and saw nothing but dust, and I heard a great weeping. I saw women crying, and I also saw my men shot down by the white people. They were killing my people with something that made a great noise like thunder and lightning, and I saw the blood streaming from the mouths of my men that lay all around me. I saw it as if it was real. Oh, my dear children! You may all think it is only a dream, — nevertheless, I feel that it will come to pass. And to avoid bloodshed, we must all go to the mountains during the summer, or till my father comes back from California. He will then tell us what to do. Let us keep away from the emigrant roads and stay in the mountains all summer. There are to be a great many pine nuts this summer, and we can lay up great supplies for the coming winter, and if the emigrants don't come too early, we can take a run down and fish for a month, and lay up dried fish. I know we can dry a great many in a month, and young men can go into the valleys on hunting excursions, and kill as many rabbits as they can. In that way we can live in the mountains all summer and all winter too."

So ended my father's dream. During that day one could see old women getting together talking over what they had heard my father say. They said, —

"It is true what our great chief has said, for it was shown to him by a higher power. It is not a dream. Oh, it surely will come to pass. We shall no longer be a happy people, as we now are; we shall no longer go here and there as of old; we shall no longer build our big fires as a signal to our friends, for we shall always be afraid of being seen by those bad people."

"Surely they don't eat people?"

"Yes, they do eat people, because they ate each other up in the mountains last winter."

This was the talk among the old women during the day.

"Oh, how grieved we are! Oh, where will it end?"

That evening one of our doctors called for a council, and all the men gathered together in the council-tent to hear what their medicine man had to say, for we all believe our doctor is greater than any human being living. We do not call him a medicine man because he gives medicine to the sick, as your doctors do. Our medicine man cures the sick by the laying on of hands, and we have doctresses as well as doctors. We believe that our doctors can communicate with holy spirits from heaven. We call heaven the Spirit Land.

Well, when all the men get together, of course there must be smoking the first thing. After the pipe has passed round five times to the right, it stops, and then he tells them to sing five songs. He is the leader in the song-singing. He sings heavenly songs, and he says he is singing with the angels. It is hard to describe these songs. They are all different, and he says the angels sing them to him.

Our doctors never sing war-songs, except at a war-dance, as they never go themselves on the war-path. While they were singing the last song, he said,—

"Now I am going into a trance. While I am in the trance you must smoke just as you did before; not a word must be spoken while I am in the trance."

About fifteen minutes after the smoking was over, he began to make a noise as if he was crying a great way off. The noise came nearer and nearer, until he breathed, and after he came to, he kept on crying. And then he prophesied, and told the people that my father's dream was true in one sense of the word,—that is, "Our people will not all die at the hands of our white brothers. They will kill a great many with their guns, but they will bring among us a fearful disease that will cause us to die by hundreds."

We all wept, for we believed this word came from heaven.

So ended our feast, and every family went to its own home in the pine-nut mountains, and remained there till the pine nuts were ripe. . . .

1883

ALICE JAMES
(1848–1892)

Alice James, having suffered all her life from an illness that could not be definitively diagnosed, decided at the age of thirty to commit suicide. She consulted her father, Henry James, Senior, steeped in the philosophy and mysticism of Ralph Waldo Emerson and Emanuel Swedenborg. He described Alice's crisis in a letter: "She asked me if suicide . . . was a sin. . . . I told her that so far as I was concerned she had my full permission to end her life whenever she pleased. She then remarked that . . . she could never do it now I had given her freedom. . . ."

The youngest child and only girl in a family of five children, Alice James began to be overtaken by inexplicable illnesses in adolescence. When a conversation became intense and exciting, she would faint. At times she felt deep within herself strange hostilities, even an impulse to "knock . . . off the head of the benignant pater." Doctors examined her and came up with such terms as "rheumatic gout," "spinal neurosis," "cardiac complications," and "nervous hyperaesthesia."

It was clearly not easy to grow up the invalid sister of William and Henry

James, watching them achieve extraordinary reputations in psychology and literature. But she did not waste herself in self-pity. William wrote: "Alice met all attempts at sympathy with jeers and laughter, having her own brave philosophy, which was to keep her attention turned to things outside her sick-room and away from herself."

After the death of her parents, in 1884 she went to visit Henry, then in London. By this time she had acquired a close friend, Katharine Peabody Loring, who travelled with her and who would stay with her through her last years. They remained in England because Alice had become too ill to make the journey back to America. Theirs was an intimate friendship, a sharing of feelings and intellectual interests, vital to the emotional well-being of both. In 1889, Alice began to keep a diary to alleviate her "sense of loneliness and desolation." In the diary she recorded her relief, in 1891, when she was finally diagnosed with a definable illness — breast cancer: "Ever since I have been ill, I have longed and longed for some palpable disease, no matter how conventionally dreadful a label it might have. . . ." The end was not long in coming. But Alice James remained alert to the world around her, as her diary shows. On January 6, 1892, she copied down some lines from a book of Emily Dickinson's poems, just then being published for the first time:

> How dreary to be somebody
>   How public, like a frog
> To tell your name the livelong day
>   To an admiring bog!

Her eminent brothers would have recognized in these lines the ironic laughter from their younger sister.

Alice James died in March 1892, at the age of forty-four. Her friend Katharine Loring made a final summary entry in the diary. She then had the diary privately printed, presenting copies to Alice's brothers. Henry at first had misgivings at the diary's private and family exposures. But, as he wrote to his brother William, he became "immensely impressed" with it "as a revelation of a moral and personal picture. . . . its face-to-face with the universe for-and-by herself." Henry James found confirmed in the diary what he had been "tremendously conscious of in [Alice's] lifetime . . . that her disastrous, her tragic health was in a manner the only solution for her of the practical problem of life — as it suppressed the element of equality, reciprocity, etc."

Alice James's *Diary* reveals that she lived an intellectually engaged and emotionally rich life, in spite of the seclusion imposed by her illness. That she undertook to write a daily account of her life speaks to the vitality of her spirit. That she kept it up to the very end indicates the fierce intensity of her will. In the *Diary* she has left a remarkable literary document, as moving as it is fascinating. She emerges from it as the enduring and plucky heroine of her own little — but by no means minor — tragic drama.

ADDITIONAL READING

Alice James: Her Brothers — Her Journal, ed. Anna Robeson Burr, 1934; *The Death and Letters of Alice James*, ed. Ruth Bernard Yeazell, 1981.

F. O. Matthiessen, "Alice," *The James Family*, 1947; Leon Edel, "Portrait of Alice James," *The Diary of Alice James*, 1964; Jean Strouse, *Alice James: A Biography*, 1980.

TEXT

The Diary of Alice James, ed. Leon Edel, 1964.

from The Diary of Alice James

["That Most Interesting Being, *Myself*"]

May 31st, 1889.   I think that if I get into the habit of writing a bit about what happens, or rather doesn't happen, I may lose a little of the sense of loneliness and desolation which abides with me. My circumstances allowing of nothing but the ejaculation of one-syllabled reflections, a written monologue by that most interesting being, *myself*, may have its yet to be discovered consolations. I shall at least have it all my own way and it may bring relief as an outlet to that geyser of emotions, sensations, speculations and reflections which ferments perpetually within my poor old carcass for its sins; so here goes, my first Journal!

["Flooded by One of Those Luminous Waves"]

July 12th [1889].   . . . It's amusing to see how, even on my microscopic field, minute events are perpetually taking place illustrative of the broadest facts of human nature. Yesterday Nurse and I had a good laugh but I must allow that decidedly she "had" me. I was thinking of something that interested me very much and my mind was suddenly flooded by one of those luminous waves that sweep out of consciousness all but the living sense and overpower one with joy in the rich, throbbing complexity of life, when suddenly I looked up at Nurse, who was dressing me, and saw her primitive, rudimentary expression (so common here) as of no inherited quarrel with her destiny of putting petticoats over my head; the poverty and deadness of it contrasted to the tide of speculation that was coursing thro' my brain made me exclaim, "Oh! Nurse, don't you wish you were inside of *me!*" — her look of dismay and vehement disclaimer — "Inside of you, Miss, when you have just had a sick head-ache for five days!" — gave a greater blow to my vanity, than that much battered article has ever received. The headache had gone off in the night and I had clean forgotten it — when the little wretch confronted me with it, at this sublime moment when I was feeling within me the potency of a Bismarck,[1] and left me powerless before the immutable law that however great we may seem to our own consciousness no human being would exchange his for ours, and before the fact that *my* glorious rôle was to stand for *Sick headache* to mankind! What a grotesque I am to be sure! Lying in this room, with the resistance of a thistle-down, having illusory moments of throbbing with the pulse of the Race, the Mystery to be solved at the next breath and the fountain of all Happiness within me — the sense of vitality, in short, simply proportionate to the excess of weakness! — To sit by and watch these absurdities is amusing in its way and reminds me of how I used to *listen* to my "company manners" in the days when I had 'em, and how ridiculous they sounded.

Ah! Those strange people who have the courage to be unhappy! *Are* they unhappy, by-the-way?

["A Cruel and Unnatural Fate"]

November 16th [1889].   Kath.[2] sailed on November 9th in the Umbria, and tomorrow I hope for a cable telling of her arrival today. She seems decidedly to have "interrupted the Diary, Miss," as Nurse plaintively predicted after her arrival (was ever a diary, by the way, so honoured in its own country before?) — but that calamity perhaps isn't irretrievable. Notwithstanding the wear and tear of Time and the burden of three invalids upon her soul and body she seems as large a joke as ever, an embodi-

---

[1]Otto Eduard Leopold von Bismarck (1815–1898), first chancellor of the German Empire, known as the "Iron Chancellor."
[2]Katherine Peabody Loring (1849–1943), who travelled to

England with Alice James and became her close companion during her last years.

ment of the stretchable, a purely transatlantic and modern possibility. She had, of course, an edition, up to date, of her pocket compendium of use*less* information and she reassuringly and smilingly "informed" any of the population on any subject they might desire. I feel like a creature who, after a long draught of fresh air, has crept back under an exhausted receiver closing down over her again with a hopeless and all too familiar click. But it has happened so often now since my scaffolding began to fall eight years ago, that after a few futile squirms I already breathe and live and find my suffocation being therein the natural one, for Heaven be praised! agonies do *not* repeat themselves, unless we wish it. We have each time something more to meet them with and nothing is more true than that "à force de s'élargir pour la souffrance, l'âme en arrive à des capacités prodigieuses, ce qui la comblait naguère à la faire crever en couvre à peine le fond maintenant"[3] — but my soul will never stretch itself to allowing that it is anything else than a cruel and unnatural fate for a woman to live alone, to have no one to care and "do for" daily is not only a sorrow, but a sterilizing process. This is a scientific statement, not a lament, for I am replete with the fertilization of the last three months.

[SICK OF BEING "GOOD"]

December 11th [1889]. How sick one gets of being "good," how much I should respect myself if I could burst out and make every one wretched for 24 hours; embody selfishness, as they say [two words erased] does. If it were only voluntary and one made a conscious choice, it might enrich the soul a bit, but when it has become simply automatic thro' a sense of the expedient — of the grotesque futility of the perverse — it's degrading! And then the dolts praise one for being "amiable!" just as if one didn't avoid ruffling one's feathers as one avoids plum-pudding or any other indigestible compound!

["IF I HAD HAD ANY EDUCATION . . ."]

December 12th [1889]. One day when my shawls were falling off to the left, my cushions falling out to the right and the duvet[4] off my knees, one of those crises of misery in short, which are all in the day's work for an invalid Kath. exclaimed, "What an awful pity it is that you can't say *damn*." I agreed with her from my heart. It is an immense loss to have all robust and sustaining expletives refined away from one! At such moments of trial refinement is a feeble reed to lean upon. I wonder, whether, if I had had any education, I should have been more, or less, of a fool than I am. It would have deprived me surely of those exquisite moments of mental flatulence which every now and then inflate the cerebral vacuum with a delicious sense of latent possiblities — of stretching oneself to cosmic limits, and who would ever give up the reality of dreams for relative knowledge?

["A PITCH OF BROTHERLY DEVOTION"]

March 25th [1890]. Henry[5] came on the 10th, and spent the day, Henry the patient, I should call him. Five years ago in November, I crossed the water and suspended myself like an old woman of the sea round his neck where to all appearances I shall remain for all time. I have given him endless care and anxiety but notwithstanding this and the fantastic nature of my troubles I have never seen an impatient look upon his face or heard an unsympathetic or misunderstanding sound cross his

---

[3]"By dint of enlarging itself through suffering, the soul attains a prodigious capacity, [so that] what would have overwhelmed and annihilated it not long ago, scarcely reaches its depth now" (French).
[4]Down-filled quilt.
[5]Alice's brother, the novelist Henry James (1843–1916).

lips. He comes at my slightest sign and hangs on to whatever organ may be in eruption and gives me calm and solace by assuring me that my nerves are his nerves and
my stomach his stomach—this last a pitch of brotherly devotion never before approached by the race. He has never remotely hinted that he expected me to be well at
any given moment, that burden which fond friend and relative so inevitably impose[s] upon the cherished invalid. But he has always been the same since I can
remember and has almost as strongly as Father that personal susceptibilty—what can
one call it, it seems as if it were a matter of the scarfskin,[6] as if they perceived thro'
that your mood and were saved thereby from rubbing you raw with their theory of it,
or blindness to it.

I was so pleased to come a little while ago across the following in a letter of William's to Wilkie in February, '66, after his return from Brazil:[7] "Harry, I think much
improved, he is a noble fellow—so true, delicate and honorable." All of which is as
true in 1890 as then. I was of course much gratified to find this further on, "—and
Alice has got to be quite a nice girl"—hasn't it the true fraternal condescension in its
ring! I am afraid that I have fallen from such altitudes since at various moments.
. . . H. seems cheerful about his play[8] and to be unable to grasp my flutterations
about it. What a "state" I was in when he told me six months ago as a great secret that
he had embarked. I had to tell some one about it, or have exploded, so of course
there was nothing to turn to but little Nurse. I could cry, if it were not so much better
an investment to laugh, over my poverty in the way of receptacles for my overflow—
such a contrast to the vast and responsive reservoirs of the past. Nurse undergoes it
all passively, finding it a pleasant change from the iniquities of the parson and Mr.
Balfour[9] which she has in such monotonous alternation.

["Pleasure under Difficulties"]

June 18th [1890].   It is very curious how, for the last year or two, I perpetually
come across in my reading just what I have been thinking about, curious I mean, of
course, because my reading is so haphazard. It reminds me of Wm. in old days when
his eyes were bad and I used to begin and tell him something which I thought of
interest from whatever book I might be reading, when he would invariably say, "I
glanced into the book yesterday and read that." I wonder what determines the *selection* of memory, why does one childish experience or impression stand out so luminous and solid against the, for the most part, vague and misty background? The
things we remember have a *first-timeness* about them which suggests that that may be
the reason of their survival. I must ask Wm. some day if there is any theory on the
subject, or better, whether 'tis worth a theory. I remember so distinctly the first time I
was conscious of a purely intellectual process. 'Twas the summer of '56 which we
spent in Boulogne and the parents of Mlle. Marie Boningue our governess had a
campagne[10] on the outskirts and invited us to spend the day, perhaps Marie's fête-
day.[11] A large and shabby calèche[12] came for us into which we were packed, save
Wm.; all I can remember of the drive was a never-ending ribbon of dust stretching in
front and the anguish greater even than usual of Wilky's and Bob's[13] heels grinding
into my shins. Marie told us that her father had a scar upon his face caused by a bad
scald in his youth and we must be sure and not look at him as he was very sensitive.

[6]I.e. exquisite sensitivity (from the tender skin of the cuticle).
[7]Her brother, William James (1842–1910), was a member of the expedition to Brazil (1865–66) led by the naturalist Louis Agassiz (1807–1873). Garth Wilkinson James (Wilkie) (1845–1883) was the third son of the James family. Harry is another name for Henry James.
[8]Henry James's play based on his novel *The American* (1877).
[9]Arthur James Balfour (1848–1930), British member of Par-
liament and a leader in the Conservative Party, serving as Chief Secretary for Ireland, Lord of the Treasury, and Prime Minister.
[10]"Country house" (French).
[11]Birthday.
[12]Open carriage.
[13]Bob: Robertson James (1846–1910), the fourth son.

How I remember the painful conflict between sympathy and the desire to look and the fear that my baseness should be discovered by the good man as he sat at the head of the table in charge of a big frosted-cake sprinkled o'er with those pink and white worms in which lurk the caraway seed. How easy 'twould be to picture one's youth as a perpetual escape from that abhorred object! — I wonder if it is a blight upon children still? — But to arrive at the first flowering of me Intellect! We were turned into the garden to play, a sandy or rather dusty expanse with nothing in it, as I remember, but two or three scrubby apple-trees, from one of which hung a swing. As time went on Wilky and Bob disappeared, not to my grief, and the Boningues. Harry was sitting in the swing and I came up and stood near by as the sun began to slant over the desolate expanse, as the dready h[ou]rs, with that endlessness which they have for infancy, passed, when Harry suddenly exclaimed: "This might certainly be called pleasure under difficulties!" The stir of my whole being in response to the substance and exquisite, *original* form of this remark almost makes my heart beat now with the sisterly pride which was then awakened and it came to me in a flash, the higher nature of this appeal to the mind, as compared to the rudimentary solicitations which usually produced my childish explosions of laughter; and I can also feel distinctly the sense of self-satisfaction in that I could not only perceive, but appreciate this subtlety, as if I had acquired a new sense, a sense whereby to measure intellectual things, wit as distinguished from giggling, for example.

["Unwrinkled Serenity"]

July 28th [1890].   I lay in a meadow until the unwrinkled serenity entered into my bones and made me one with the browsing kine,[14] the still greenery, the drifting clouds, and the swooping birds.

["An Infinite Succession of Conscious Abandonments"]

October 26th [1890].   William uses an excellent expression when he says in his paper on the "Hidden Self"[15] that the nervous victim "abandons" certain portions of his consciousness. It may be the word commonly used by his kind. It is just the right one at any rate, altho' I have never unfortunately been able to abandon my consciousness and get five minutes' rest. I have passed thro' an infinite succession of conscious abandonments and in looking back now I see how it began in my childhood, altho' I wasn't conscious of the necessity until '67 or '68 when I broke down first, acutely, and had violent turns of hysteria. As I lay prostrate after the storm with my mind luminous and active and susceptible of the clearest, strongest impressions, I saw so distinctly that it was a fight simply between my body and my will, a battle in which the former was to be triumphant to the end. Owing to some physical weakness, excess of nervous susceptibility, the moral power *pauses*, as it were for a moment, and refuses to maintain muscular sanity, worn out with the strain of its constabulary functions. As I used to sit immovable reading in the library with waves of violent inclination suddenly invading my muscles taking some one of their myriad forms such as throwing myself out of the window, or knocking off the head of the benignant pater[16] as he sat with his silver locks, writing at his table, it used to seem to me that the only difference between me and the insane was that I had not only all the horrors and suffering of insanity but the duties of doctor, nurse, and strait-jacket imposed upon me, too. Conceive of never being without the sense that if you let yourself go for a moment your mechanism will fall into pie and that at some given moment you must abandon

---

[14]Cows.
[15]An essay by William James which had appeared in *Scribner's*, March 1890.

[16]I.e., Alice's father, Henry James, Sr. (1811–1882), mystical thinker and writer.

it all, let the dykes break and the flood sweep in, acknowledging yourself abjectly impotent before the immutable laws. When all one's moral and natural stock in trade is a temperament forbidding the abandonment of an inch or the relaxation of a muscle, 'tis a never-ending fight. When the fancy took me of a morning at school to *study* my lessons by way of variety instead of shirking or wiggling thro' the most impossible sensations of upheaval, violent revolt in my head overtook me so that I had to "abandon" my brain, as it were. So it has always been, anything that sticks of itself is free to do so, but conscious and continuous cerebration is an impossible exercise and from just behind the eyes my head feels like a dense jungle into which no ray of light has ever penetrated. So, with the rest, you abandon the pit of your stomach, the palms of your hands, the soles of your feet, and refuse to keep them sane when you find in turn one moral impression after another producing despair in the one, terror in the other, anxiety in the third and so on until life becomes one long flight from remote suggestion and complicated eluding of the multifold traps set for your undoing.

["Going Downhill at a Steady Trot"]

May 31st [1891].   To him who waits, all things come! My aspirations may have been eccentric, but I cannot complain now, that they have not been brilliantly fulfilled. Ever since I have been ill, I have longed and longed for some palpable disease, no matter how conventionally dreadful a label it might have, but I was always driven back to stagger alone under the monstrous mass of subjective sensations, which that sympathetic being "the medical man" had no higher inspiration than to assure me I was personally responsible for, washing his hands of me with a graceful complacency under my very nose. Dr. Torry[17] was the only man who ever treated me like a rational being, who did not assume, because I was victim to many pains, that I was, of necessity, an arrested mental development too.

Notwithstanding all the happiness and comfort here, I have been going downhill at a steady trot; so they sent for Sir Andrew Clark[18] four days ago, and the blessed being has endowed me not only with cardiac complications, but says that a lump that I have had in one of my breasts for three months, which has given me a great deal of pain, is a tumour, that nothing can be done for me but to alleviate pain, that it is only a question of time, etc. This with a delicate embroidery of "the most distressing case of nervous hyperæsthesia" added to a spinal neurosis that has taken me off my legs for seven years; with attacks of rheumatic gout in my stomach for the last twenty, ought to satisfy the most inflated pathologic vanity. It is decidedly indecent to catalogue oneself in this way, but I put it down in a scientific spirit, to show that though I have no productive worth, I have a certain value as an indestructible quantity.

[The "Gastronomic Vice"]

June 17th [1891].   We were quite grateful for the Englishry of this: K saw the other day a very smart lady in a victoria[19] driving in the crowd at the canonical hour, down Piccadilly to the Park, and so far carrying out to perfection the lesson of the day, but with that homely burst of nature to which the most encrusted here are subject, she was satisfying the cravings of the stomach by eating, with the utmost complacency, in the eye of man, a huge, stodgy penny bun. The perfection in all her appointments in the way of carriage, etc — with the absence of subtlety in her palate

---

[17]Dr. John Cooper Torry, a prominent London physician, member of the Royal College of Physicians.
[18]A noted British physician and surgeon, vice president of the British Medical Association.

[19]A four-wheeled carriage for two with an elevated driver's seat; canonical hour: socially correct time; Piccadilly: London street leading to Hyde Park, a fashionable area for strolling.

as shown by the placid consumption of the bun, and complete indifference, at this very visible moment, at exhibiting her features distorted by the ugly process of masticating such an adhesive substance, had an incongruity very characteristic of the soil. They seem in matters of taste to have no sense of gradations. H. is always saying this, but it jumped at my eye from the first, and is therefore an original if not unique utterance. H., by the way, has embedded in his pages many pearls fallen from my lips, which he steals in the most unblushing way, saying, simply, that he knew they had been said by the family, so it did not matter.

I remember when I was at H.'s during the Jubilee Year,[20] having one of those longings to commit sin that come over us every now and then. All but gastronomic vice being denied by my miserable sex, I sent Nurse to Gunter's for some *éclairs*, and word was sent back that "they were a kind of *biscuit* that had to be eaten fresh, so they had to be ordered the day before!" . . .

["UNEXAMPLED GENIUS FOR FRIENDSHIP AND DEVOTION"]

January 1st, 1892. As the ugliest things go to the making of the fairest, it is not wonderful that this unholy granite substance in my breast should be the soil propitious for the perfect flowering of Katharine's unexampled genius for friendship and devotion. The story of her watchfulness, patience and untiring resource cannot be told by my feeble pen, but all the pain and discomfort seem a slender price to pay for all the happiness and peace with which she fills my days.

It must be allowed, however, that she has one most serious defect; she is most unbecoming to the race of man, and when he takes the shape of the British Doctor, the spectacle of impotent paralysis that he presents is truly pitiful. Baldwin[21] did keep his shape and colour, but even the great Sir Andrew Clark faded visibly to the eyes.

When will men pass from the illusion of the intellectual, limited to sapless reason, and bow to the intelligent, juicy with the succulent science of life.

["THIS LONG SLOW DYING"]

February 2nd [1892]. This long slow dying is no doubt instructive, but it is disappointingly free from excitements: "naturalness" being carried to its supreme expression. One sloughs off the activities one by one, and never knows that they're gone, until one suddenly finds that the months have slipped away and the sofa will never more be laid upon, the morning paper read, or the loss of the new book regretted; one revolves with equal content within the narrowing circle until the vanishing point is reached, I suppose.

Vanity, however, maintains its undisputed sway, and I take satisfaction in feeling as much myself as ever, perhaps simply a more concentrated essence in this curtailment. If I could concern myself about the fate of my soul, it would give doubtless a savor of uncertainty to the fleeting moments, but I never felt so absolutely uninterested in the poor, shabby, old thing. The fact is, I have been dead so long and it has been simply such a grim shoving of the hours behind me as I faced a ceaseless possible horror, since that hideous summer of '78, when I went down to the deep sea, its dark waters closed over me and I knew neither hope nor peace; that now it's only the shrivelling of an empty pea pod that has to be completed.

A little while ago we had rather an amusing episode with the kind and usually understanding Tuckey,[22] who was led away into assuring me that I should live a good bit still—I was terribly shocked and when he saw the havoc that he wrought, he

---

[20]Celebration of the fiftieth year of the reign of Queen Victoria (1819–1901); she became queen in 1837.
[21]Dr. W. W. Baldwin, friend of Henry James and an American expatriate physician.
[22]Dr. Charles Lloyd Tuckey, a well-known English psychiatrist who used hypnotism in his treatment.

reassuringly said: "but you'll be comfortable, too," at which I exclaimed: "Oh I don't care about that, but boo-hoo, it's so *inconvenient!*" and the poor man burst into a roar of laughter. I was glad afterwards that it happened, as I was taken quite by surprise, and was able to test the sincerity of my mortuary inclinations. I have always *thought* that I wanted to die, but I felt quite uncertain as to what my muscular demonstrations might be at the moment of transition, for I occasionally have a quiver as of an expected dentistical wrench when I fancy the actual moment. But my substance seemed equally outraged with my mind at Tuckey's dictum, so mayhap I shall be able to maintain a calm befitting so sublimated a spirit! — at any rate there is no humbuggy "strength of mind" about it, 'tis simply physical debility, 'twould be such a bore to be perturbed.

["Spiritualized into a 'District Messenger'"]

February 28th [1892].   It is taken for granted apparently that I shall be spiritualized into a "district messenger," for here comes another message for Father and Mother; imagine my dragging them, of whom I can only think as a sublimation of their qualities, into gossip about the little more or the little less faith of Tom, Dick or Harry. I do pray to Heaven that the dreadful Mrs. Piper[23] won't be let loose upon my defenceless soul. I suppose the thing "medium" has done more to degrade spiritual conception than the grossest forms of materialism or idolatry: was there ever anything transmitted but the pettiest, meanest, coarsest facts and details: anything rising above the squalid intestines of human affairs? And oh, the curious spongy minds that sop it all up and lose all sense of taste and humour!

["Ground Slowly on the Grim Grindstone"]

March 4th [1892].   I am being ground slowly on the grim grindstone of physical pain, and on two nights I had almost asked for K.'s lethal dose, but one steps hesitantly along such unaccustomed ways and endures from second to second; and I feel sure that it can't be possible but what the bewildered little hammer that keeps me going will very shortly see the decency of ending his distracted career; however this may be, physical pain however great ends in itself and falls away like dry husks from the mind, whilst moral discords and nervous horrors sear the soul. These last, Katharine has completely under the control of her rhythmic hand, so I go no longer in dread. Oh the wonderful moment when I felt myself floated for the first time into the deep sea of divine *cessation*, and saw all the dear old mysteries and miracles vanish into vapour! That first experience doesn't repeat itself, fortunately, for it might become a seduction.

Katharine can't help it, she's made that way, a simple embodiment of Health, as Baldwin called her, "the New England Professor of doing things."

Final Entry by Katharine P. Loring

[March, 1892].   All through Saturday the 5th and even in the night, Alice was making sentences. One of the last things she said to me was to make a correction in the sentence of March 4th "moral discords and nervous horrors."

This dictation of March 4th was rushing about in her brain all day, and although she was very weak and it tired her much to dictate, she could not get her head quiet until she had had it written: then she was relieved and I finished Miss Woolson's story of "Dorothy"[24] to her.

K.P.L.

---

[23]Mrs. L. E. Piper, a Boston spiritual medium who had figured in William James's investigations into spiritualism.
[24]Constance Fenimore Woolson (1840–1894), American

novelist, friend of Henry James, and author of the short story "Dorothy," which appeared in the March 1892 *Harper's*.

BOOKER T. WASHINGTON
(1856–1915)

Booker T. Washington was born in a log cabin, the son of a slave woman who served as a cook on a plantation in Virginia. It is believed that his father was a white man from a nearby plantation. He was later to remember the hard times of his childhood, especially the scarcity of food. And he was to remember, too, the advent of freedom that came in 1865 at the end of the Civil War, announced to the assembled slaves with a reading of the Emancipation Proclamation.

The freed slave family of mother Jane and four children moved to Malden, West Virginia, walking most of the way, to join Jane's husband Washington Ferguson, and to begin anew the struggle for existence. In spite of the need for all hands to work, Jane encouraged the children to learn to read. By working long hours before and after classes, Booker was able finally to attend regular elementary school, taking as his last name his stepfather's first name.

At the age of sixteen, in 1872, Washington set out for Hampton Institute, some 500 miles away in Virginia, walking and carrying a few possessions in a satchel. Hampton had been founded in 1868 by Civil War Union General Samuel Armstrong to provide education for the freed slaves in the manual arts and other vocations. When Washington arrived and applied, he was asked to clean a room. He demonstrated his thoroughness by sweeping and cleaning it three times, and was admitted. He supported himself in part for his three years at Hampton by acting as janitor. Money from northern white supporters of the Institute also helped pay his way.

Washington learned the trade of brick mason, but he also learned table manners, the use of a napkin, the use of a toothbrush, the use of bed sheets. After teaching for a time back in Malden, and spending a year in Washington, D.C., at Wayland Seminary, Washington was called back to Hampton to take charge of a dormitory housing Indian students, then being admitted by the Institute as an experiment in extending educational opportunities to Native Americans.

Washington's energy, industry, and integrity made him the natural choice of General Armstrong to recommend as the head of the newly authorized normal school at Tuskegee, Alabama. When Washington arrived in Tuskegee, in 1881, he found that no provision had been made for buildings or grounds for his school. His first challenge was to find a place to hold classes. For the next thirty-four years, to the end of his life, Washington dedicated himself to the building of Tuskegee into a first-class educational establishment. From nothing, it grew to an institution of some hundred buildings, enormous grounds, and an endowment of $2 million.

In the process of this achievement, Washington became popular as a public speaker. He was invited in 1895 to represent his race in a speech to be delivered at the Cotton States and International Exposition at Atlanta, where there was a special building devoted to the progress of Negroes after Emancipation. It was this speech, known as the "Atlanta Compromise," that made Washington a national leader and spokesman of his race. Calling for the blacks to prove their worth through education and industry before demanding civil rights and social equality, Washington advocated moderation and conciliation: "In all things that are purely social we can be as separate as the fingers, yet one as the hand in all things essential to mutual progress."

Washington published a number of books during his career, but his most popular work was his autobiography, *Up from Slavery* (1901). Rivalling Benjamin Franklin's *Autobiography* in its story of success achieved in the face of hardship and poverty, Washington's account constituted (like Franklin's) a series of moral lessons for others to follow. Pragmatism was key to the principles of both.

Washington's fame spread North and South. In 1891, he was awarded an honorary degree by Harvard University. In 1901, he was invited to dine at the White House by President Theodore Roosevelt. But there were, of course, black intellectuals who thought Washington had conceded too much to whites in exchange for vocational and economic gains. It was W. E. B. DuBois (see especially his *Souls of Black Folk*, 1903) who took the lead in righting the balance, shifting concern back to critical civil rights and social issues. But few blacks or whites would challenge Washington's extraordinary achievements in self-education and the education of his fellow blacks.

ADDITIONAL READING

The Booker T. Washington Papers, 13 vols., ed. Louis R. Harlan, 1972–84.

W. E. B. DuBois, "Of Mr. Booker T. Washington and Others," *The Souls of Black Folk*, 1903; Basil Matthews, *Booker T. Washington: Educator and Interracial Interpreter*, 1948; G. R. Spencer, *Booker T. Washington and the Negro's Place in American Life*, 1955; John Hope Franklin, *From Slavery to Freedom*, 1947, 1956, 1967; August Meier, *Negro Thought in America, 1880–1915*, 1963; John Hope Franklin, "Introduction," *Three Negro Classics*, 1965; E. L. Thornborough, *Booker T. Washington*, 1969; Louis R. Harlan, *Booker T. Washington: The Making of a Black Leader, 1865– 1901*, 1972; Arna Bontemps, *Young Booker: Booker T. Washington's Early Days*, 1972; Robert B. Stepto, "Lost in a Cause: Booker T. Washington's *Up from Slavery*," *From Behind the Veil: A Study of Afro-American Narrative*, 1979; Louis R. Harlan, *Booker T. Washington: The Wizard of Tuskegee, 1901–1915*, 1983.

TEXT

Up from Slavery: An Autobiography, 1901.

from Up from Slavery

CHAPTER XIV
THE ATLANTA EXPOSITION ADDRESS[1]

The Atlanta Exposition, at which I had been asked to make an address as a representative of the Negro race, as stated in the last chapter, was opened with a short address from Governor Bullock. After other interesting exercises, including an invocation from Bishop Nelson, of Georgia, a dedicatory ode by Albert Howell, Jr., and addresses by the President of the Exposition and Mrs. Joseph Thompson, the President of the Woman's Board, Governor Bullock introduced me with the words, "We have with us to-day a representative of Negro enterprise and Negro civilization."

When I arose to speak, there was considerable cheering, especially from the coloured people. As I remember it now, the thing that was uppermost in my mind was the desire to say something that would cement the friendship of the races and bring

---

[1] This speech catapulted Washington into national prominence as a Negro leader. It was made at the Atlanta Cotton States and International Exposition of 1895 and stressed the importance of education, and especially vocational education, for blacks, and at the same time avoided confrontational rhetoric regarding civil rights and social equality. For representation of black objection to Washington's position, see W. E. B. DuBois's "Of Mr. Booker T. Washington and Others" (from *Souls of Black Folk*, 1903).

about hearty coöperation between them. So far as my outward surroundings were concerned, the only thing that I recall distinctly now is that when I got up, I saw thousands of eyes looking intently into my face. The following is the address which I delivered: —

MR. PRESIDENT AND GENTLEMEN OF THE BOARD OF DIRECTORS AND CITIZENS.

One-third of the population of the South is of the Negro race. No enterprise seeking the material, civil, or moral welfare of this section can disregard this element of our population and reach the highest success. I but convey to you, Mr. President and Directors, the sentiment of the masses of my race when I say that in no way have the value and manhood of the American Negro been more fittingly and generously recognized than by the managers of this magnificent Exposition at every stage of its progress. It is a recognition that will do more to cement the friendship of the two races than any occurrence since the dawn of our freedom.

Not only this, but the opportunity here afforded will awaken among us a new era of industrial progress. Ignorant and inexperienced, it is not strange that in the first years of our new life we began at the top instead of at the bottom; that a seat in Congress or the state legislature was more sought than real estate or industrial skill; that the political convention or stump speaking had more attractions than starting a dairy farm or truck garden.

A ship lost at sea for many days suddenly sighted a friendly vessel. From the mast of the unfortunate vessel was seen a signal, "Water, water; we die of thirst!" The answer from the friendly vessel at once came back, "Cast down your bucket where you are." A second time the signal, "Water, water; send us water!" ran up from the distressed vessel, and was answered, "Cast down your bucket where you are." And a third and fourth signal for water was answered, "Cast down your bucket where you are." The captain of the distressed vessel, at last heeding the injunction, cast down his bucket, and it came up full of fresh, sparkling water from the mouth of the Amazon River. To those of my race who depend on bettering their condition in a foreign land or who underestimate the importance of cultivating friendly relations with the Southern white man, who is their next-door neighbour, I would say: "Cast down your bucket where you are" — cast it down in making friends in every manly way of the people of all races by whom we are surrounded.

Cast it down in agriculture, mechanics, in commerce, in domestic service, and in the professions. And in this connection it is well to bear in mind that whatever other sins the South may be called to bear, when it comes to business, pure and simple, it is in the South that the Negro is given a man's chance in the commercial world, and in nothing is this Exposition more eloquent than in emphasizing this chance. Our greatest danger is that in the great leap from slavery to freedom we may overlook the fact that the masses of us are to live by the productions of our hands, and fail to keep in mind that we shall prosper in proportion as we learn to dignify and glorify common labour and put brains and skill into the common occupations of life; shall prosper in proportion as we learn to draw the line between the superficial and the substantial, the ornamental gewgaws of life and the useful. No race can prosper till it learns that there is as much dignity in tilling a field as in writing a poem. It is at the bottom of life we must begin, and not at the top. Nor should we permit our grievances to overshadow our opportunities.

To those of the white race who look to the incoming of those of foreign birth and strange tongue and habits for the prosperity of the South, were I permitted I would repeat what I say to my own race, "Cast down your bucket where you are." Cast it down among the eight millions of Negroes whose habits you know, whose fidelity and love you have tested in days when to have proved treacherous meant the ruin of your firesides. Cast down your bucket among these people who have, without strikes and labour wars, tilled your fields, cleared your forests, builded your railroads and cities, and brought forth treasures from the bowels of the earth, and helped make possible this magnificent representation of the progress of the South. Casting down your bucket among my people, helping and encouraging them as you are doing on these grounds, and to education of head, hand, and heart, you will find that they will buy your surplus land, make blossom the waste places in your fields, and run your factories. While doing this, you can be sure in the future, as in the past, that you and your families will be surrounded by the most patient, faithful, law-abiding, and unresentful people that the world has seen. As we have proved our loyalty to you in the past, in nursing your children, watching by the sick-bed of your mothers and fathers, and often following them with tear-dimmed eyes to their graves, so in the future, in our humble way, we shall stand by you with a devotion that no foreigner can approach, ready to lay down our lives, if need be, in defence of yours, interlacing our industrial, commercial, civil, and religious life with yours in a way that shall make the interests of both races one. In all things that are purely social we can be as separate as the fingers, yet one as the hand in all things essential to mutual progress.

There is no defence or security for any of us except in the highest intelligence and development of all. If anywhere there are efforts tending to curtail the fullest growth of the Negro, let these efforts be turned into stimulating, encouraging, and making him the most useful and intelligent citizen. Effort or means so invested will pay a thousand per cent interest. These efforts will be twice blessed—"blessing him that gives and him that takes."[2]

There is no escape through law of man or God from the inevitable:—

> The laws of changeless justice bind
>   Oppressor with oppressed;
> And close as sin and suffering joined
>   We march to fate abreast.[3]

Nearly sixteen millions of hands will aid you in pulling the load upward, or they will pull against you the load downward. We shall constitute one-third and more of the ignorance and crime of the South, or one-third its intelligence and progress; we shall contribute one-third to the business and industrial prosperity of the South, or we shall prove a veritable body of death, stagnating, depressing, retarding every effort to advance the body politic.

Gentlemen of the Exposition, as we present to you our humble effort at an exhibition of our progress, you must not expect overmuch. Starting thirty years ago with ownership here and there in a few quilts and pumpkins and chickens (gathered from miscellaneous sources), remember the path that has led from these to the inventions and production of agricultural implements, buggies, steam-engines, newspapers, books, statuary, carving, paintings, the management of drug-stores and banks, has not been trodden without contact with thorns and thistles. While we take pride in what we exhibit as a result of our independent efforts, we do not for a moment forget that our part in this exhibition would fall far short of your expectations but for the constant help that has come to our educational life, not only from the Southern states, but especially from Northern philanthropists, who have made their gifts a constant stream of blessing and encouragement.

The wisest among my race understand that the agitation of questions of social equality is the extremest folly, and that progress in the enjoyment of all the privileges

---

[2]Shakespeare, *The Merchant of Venice*, IV, 1 ("It blesseth him that gives, and him that takes"), from Portia's famous "quality of mercy" speech.
[3]From "The Song of the Negro Boatmen" in the poem "At Port Royal" (1862) by John Greenleaf Whittier (1807–1892), American Quaker and antislavery poet. The first line reads, "That laws. . . ."

that will come to us must be the result of severe and constant struggle rather than of artificial forcing. No race that has anything to contribute to the markets of the world is long in any degree ostracized. It is important and right that all privileges of the law be ours, but it is vastly more important that we be prepared for the exercises of these privileges. The opportunity to earn a dollar in a factory just now is worth infinitely more than the opportunity to spend a dollar in an opera-house.

In conclusion, may I repeat that nothing in thirty years has given us more hope and encouragement, and drawn us so near to you of the white race, as this opportunity offered by the Exposition; and here bending, as it were, over the altar that represents the results of the struggles of your race and mine, both starting practically empty-handed three decades ago, I pledge that in your effort to work out the great and intricate problem which God has laid at the doors of the South, you shall have at all times the patient, sympathetic help of my race; only let this be constantly in mind, that, while from representations in these buildings of the product of field, of forest, of mine, of factory, letters, and art, much good will come, yet far above and beyond material benefits will be that higher good, that, let us pray God, will come, in a blotting out of sectional differences and racial animosities and suspicions, in a determination to administer absolute justice, in a willing obedience among all classes to the mandates of law. This, this, coupled with our material prosperity, will bring into our beloved South a new heaven and a new earth.

The first thing that I remember, after I had finished speaking, was that Governor Bullock rushed across the platform and took me by the hand, and that others did the same. I received so many and such hearty congratulations that I found it difficult to get out of the building. I did not appreciate to any degree, however, the impression which my address seemed to have made, until the next morning, when I went into the business part of the city. As soon as I was recognized, I was surprised to find myself pointed out and surrounded by a crowd of men who wished to shake hands with me. This was kept up on every street on to which I went, to an extent which embarrassed me so much that I went back to my boarding-place. The next morning I returned to Tuskegee. At the station in Atlanta, and at almost all of the stations at which the train stopped between that city and Tuskegee, I found a crowd of people anxious to shake hands with me.

The papers in all parts of the United States published the address in full, and for months afterward there were complimentary editorial references to it. Mr. Clark Howell, the editor of the Atlanta *Constitution*, telegraphed to a New York paper, among other words, the following, "I do not exaggerate when I say that Professor Booker T. Washington's address yesterday was one of the most notable speeches, both as to character and as to the warmth of its reception, ever delivered to a Southern audience. The address was a revelation. The whole speech is a platform upon which blacks and whites can stand with full justice to each other."

The Boston *Transcript* said editorially: "The speech of Booker T. Washington at the Atlanta Exposition, this week, seems to have dwarfed all the other proceedings and the Exposition itself. The sensation that it has caused in the press has never been equalled."

I very soon began receiving all kinds of propositions from lecture bureaus, and editors of magazines and papers, to take the lecture platform, and to write articles. One lecture bureau offered me fifty thousand dollars, or two hundred dollars a night and expenses, if I would place my services at its disposal for a given period. To all these communications I replied that my life-work was at Tuskegee; and that whenever I spoke it must be in the interests of the Tuskegee school and my race, and that I would enter into no arrangements that seemed to place a mere commercial value upon my services.

Some days after its delivery I sent a copy of my address to the President of the

United States, the Hon. Grover Cleveland.[4] I received from him the following auto-graph reply:—

GRAY GABLES, BUZZARD'S BAY, MASS.,
October 6, 1895.

BOOKER T. WASHINGTON, ESQ.:

MY DEAR SIR: I thank you for sending me a copy of your address delivered at the Atlanta Exposition.

I thank you with much enthusiasm for making the address. I have read it with intense interest, and I think the Exposition would be fully justified if it did not do more than furnish the opportunity for its delivery. Your words cannot fail to delight and encourage all who wish well for your race; and if our col-oured fellow-citizens do not from your utterances gather new hope and form new determinations to gain every valuable advantage offered them by their citizenship, it will be strange indeed.

Yours very truly,
GROVER CLEVELAND.

Later I met Mr. Cleveland, for the first time, when, as President, he visited the Atlanta Exposition. At the request of myself and others he consented to spend an hour in the Negro Building, for the purpose of inspecting the Negro exhibit and of giving the coloured people in attendance an opportunity to shake hands with him. As soon as I met Mr. Cleveland I became impressed with his simplicity, greatness, and rugged honesty. I have met him many times since then, both at public functions and at his private residence in Princeton, and the more I see of him the more I admire him. When he visited the Negro Building in Atlanta he seemed to give himself up wholly, for that hour, to the coloured people. He seemed to be as careful to shake hands with some old coloured "auntie" clad partially in rags, and to take as much pleasure in doing so, as if he were greeting some millionnaire. Many of the coloured people took advantage of the occasion to get him to write his name in a book or on a slip of paper. He was as careful and patient in doing this as if he were putting his signature to some great state document.

Mr. Cleveland has not only shown his friendship for me in many personal ways, but has always consented to do anything I have asked of him for our school. This he has done, whether it was to make a personal donation or to use his influence in securing the donations of others. Judging from my personal acquaintance with Mr. Cleveland, I do not believe that he is conscious of possessing any colour prejudice. He is too great for that. In my contact with people I find that, as a rule, it is only the little, narrow people who live for themselves, who never read good books, who do not travel, who never open up their souls in a way to permit them to come into contact with other souls—with the great outside world. No man whose vision is bounded by colour can come into contact with what is highest and best in the world. In meeting men, in many places, I have found that the happiest people are those who do the most for others; the most miserable are those who do the least. I have also found that few things, if any, are capable of making one so blind and narrow as race prejudice. I often say to our students, in the course of my talks to them on Sunday evenings in the chapel, that the longer I live and the more experience I have of the world, the more I am convinced that, after all, the one thing that is most worth living for—and dying for, if need be—is the opportunity of making some one else more happy and more useful.

The coloured people and the coloured newspapers at first seemed to be greatly pleased with the character of my Atlanta address, as well as with its reception. But

[4]Grover Cleveland (1837–1908) served two separated terms as U.S. president (1885–89 and 1893–97).

after the first burst of enthusiasm began to die away, and the coloured people began reading the speech in cold type, some of them seemed to feel that they had been hypnotized. They seemed to feel that I had been too liberal in my remarks toward the Southern whites, and that I had not spoken out strongly enough for what they termed the "rights" of the race. For a while there was a reaction, so far as a certain element of my own race was concerned, but later these reactionary ones seemed to have been won over to my way of believing and acting.

While speaking of changes in public sentiment, I recall that about ten years after the school at Tuskegee was established, I had an experience that I shall never forget. Dr. Lyman Abbott,[5] then the pastor of Plymouth Church, and also editor of the *Outlook* (then the *Christian Union*), asked me to write a letter for his paper giving my opinion of the exact condition, mental and moral, of the coloured ministers in the South, as based upon my observations. I wrote the letter, giving the exact facts as I conceived them to be. The picture painted was a rather black one — or, since I am black, shall I say "white"? It could not be otherwise with a race but a few years out of slavery, a race which had not had time or opportunity to produce a competent ministry.

What I said soon reached every Negro minister in the country, I think, and the letters of condemnation which I received from them were not few. I think that for a year after the publication of this article every association and every conference or religious body of any kind, of my race, that met, did not fail before adjourning to pass a resolution condemning me, or calling upon me to retract or modify what I had said. Many of these organizations went so far in their resolutions as to advise parents to cease sending their children to Tuskegee. One association even appointed a "missionary" whose duty it was to warn the people against sending their children to Tuskegee. This missionary had a son in the school, and I noticed that, whatever the "missionary" might have said or done with regard to others, he was careful not to take his son away from the institution. Many of the coloured papers, especially those that were the organs of religious bodies, joined in the general chorus of condemnation or demands for retraction.

During the whole time of the excitement, and through all the criticism, I did not utter a word of explanation or retraction. I knew that I was right, and that time and the sober second thought of the people would vindicate me. It was not long before the bishops and other church leaders began to make a careful investigation of the conditions of the ministry, and they found out that I was right. In fact, the oldest and most influential bishop in one branch of the Methodist Church said that my words were far too mild. Very soon public sentiment began making itself felt, in demanding a purifying of the ministry. While this is not yet complete by any means, I think I may say, without egotism, and I have been told by many of our most influential ministers, that my words had much to do with starting a demand for the placing of a higher type of men in the pulpit. I have had the satisfaction of having many who once condemned me thank me heartily for my frank words.

The change of the attitude of the Negro ministry, so far as regards myself, is so complete that at the present time I have no warmer friends among any class than I have among the clergymen. The improvement in the character and life of the Negro ministers is one of the most gratifying evidences of the progress of the race. My experience with them, as well as other events in my life, convince me that the thing to do, when one feels sure that he has said or done the right thing, and is condemned, is to stand still and keep quiet. If he is right, time will show it.

In the midst of the discussion which was going on concerning my Atlanta speech, I received the letter which I give below, from Dr. Gilman, the President of Johns Hop-

---

[5]Dr. Lyman Abbott (1835–1922), American Congregational clergyman, author, and editor.

kins University, who had been made chairman of the judges of award in connection with the Atlanta Exposition: —

JOHNS HOPKINS UNIVERSITY, BALTIMORE,
President's Office, September 30, 1895.

DEAR MR. WASHINGTON: Would it be agreeable to you to be one of the Judges of Award in the Department of Education at Atlanta? If so, I shall be glad to place your name upon the list. A line by telegraph will be welcomed.

Yours very truly,
D. C. GILMAN.

I think I was even more surprised to receive this invitation than I had been to receive the invitation to speak at the opening of the Exposition. It was to be a part of my duty, as one of the jurors, to pass not only upon the exhibits of the coloured schools, but also upon those of the white schools. I accepted the position, and spent a month in Atlanta in performance of the duties which it entailed. The board of jurors was a large one, consisting in all of sixty members. It was about equally divided between Southern white people and Northern white people. Among them were college presidents, leading scientists and men of letters, and specialists in many subjects. When the group of jurors to which I was assigned met for organization, Mr. Thomas Nelson Page,[6] who was one of the number, moved that I be made secretary of that division, and the motion was unanimously adopted. Nearly half of our division were Southern people. In performing my duties in the inspection of the exhibits of white schools I was in every case treated with respect, and at the close of our labours I parted from my associates with regret.

I am often asked to express myself more freely than I do upon the political condition and the political future of my race. These recollections of my experience in Atlanta give me the opportunity to do so briefly. My own belief is, although I have never before said so in so many words, that the time will come when the Negro in the South will be accorded all the political rights which his ability, character, and material possessions entitle him to. I think, though, that the opportunity to freely exercise such political rights will not come in any large degree through outside or artificial forcing, but will be accorded to the Negro by the Southern white people themselves, and that they will protect him in the exercise of those rights. Just as soon as the South gets over the old feeling that it is being forced by "foreigners," or "aliens," to do something which it does not want to do, I believe that the change in the direction that I have indicated is going to begin. In fact, there are indications that it is already beginning in a slight degree.

Let me illustrate my meaning. Suppose that some months before the opening of the Atlanta Exposition there had been a general demand from the press and public platform outside the South that a Negro be given a place on the opening programme, and that a Negro be placed upon the board of jurors of award. Would any such recognition of the race have taken place? I do not think so. The Atlanta officials went as far as they did because they felt it to be a pleasure, as well as a duty, to reward what they considered merit in the Negro race. Say what we will, there is something in human nature which we cannot blot out, which makes one man, in the end, recognize and reward merit in another, regardless of colour or race.

I believe it is the duty of the Negro — as the greater part of the race is already doing — to deport himself modestly in regard to political claims, depending upon the slow but sure influences that proceed from the possession of property, intelligence, and high character for the full recognition of his political rights. I think that the according of the full exercise of political rights is going to be a matter of natural, slow

---

[6]Thomas Nelson Page (1853–1922), Virginia novelist and diplomat.

growth, not an over-night, gourd-vine affair. I do not believe that the Negro should cease voting, for a man cannot learn the exercise of self-government by ceasing to vote, any more than a boy can learn to swim by keeping out of the water, but I do believe that in his voting he should more and more be influenced by those of intelligence and character who are his next-door neighbours.

I know coloured men who, through the encouragement, help, and advice of Southern white people, have accumulated thousands of dollars' worth of property, but who, at the same time, would never think of going to those same persons for advice concerning the casting of their ballots. This, it seems to me, is unwise and unreasonable, and should cease. In saying this I do not mean that the Negro should truckle, or not vote from principle, for the instant he ceases to vote from principle he loses the confidence and respect of the Southern white man even.

I do not believe that any state should make a law that permits an ignorant and poverty-stricken white man to vote, and prevents a black man in the same condition from voting. Such a law is not only unjust, but it will react, as all unjust laws do, in time; for the effect of such a law is to encourage the Negro to secure education and property, and at the same time it encourages the white man to remain in ignorance and poverty. I believe that in time, through the operation of intelligence and friendly race relations, all cheating at the ballot-box in the South will cease. It will become apparent that the white man who begins by cheating a Negro out of his ballot soon learns to cheat a white man out of his, and that the man who does this ends his career of dishonesty by the theft of property or by some equally serious crime. In my opinion, the time will come when the South will encourage all of its citizens to vote. It will see that it pays better, from every standpoint, to have healthy, vigorous life than to have that political stagnation which always results when one-half of the population has no share and no interest in the Government.

As a rule, I believe in universal, free suffrage, but I believe that in the South we are confronted with peculiar conditions that justify the protection of the ballot in many of the states, for a while at least, either by an educational test, a property test, or by both combined; but whatever tests are required, they should be made to apply with equal and exact justice to both races.

1901

WILLIAM E. B. DuBOIS
(1868–1963)

In 1897, W. E. B. DuBois wrote in "Strivings of the Negro People" that "this American world" yields to the black man "no true self-consciousness, but only lets him see himself through the revelation of the other world. It is a peculiar sensation, this double-consciousness. . . . One ever feels his twoness — an American, a Negro; two souls, two thoughts, two unprecedented strivings; two warring ideals in one dark body, whose dogged strength alone keeps it from being torn asunder." This insight into the Afro-American identity and destiny is but one of a great many expressed in the various stages of intellectual growth that DuBois passed through during his long life. That life began in America (Massachusetts) in 1868 and ended in Africa (Ghana) in 1963.

At the beginning, DuBois later recalled, "in general thought and conduct" he became "quite thoroughly New England." He was educated in the public schools in Great Barrington, Massachusetts, and attended Sunday School at the Congregational Church. Only gradually did he become aware of the overriding significance of his black identity. It was, however, fixed in his consciousness when he set

out in 1885 for Nashville, Tennessee, and Fisk University, an institution established after the Civil War for the education of blacks. He had his first glimpse of
the southern roots of American black culture when he taught during the summers in the black schools in the Tennessee hills, observing the poverty, the hard
work, the yearning, the hopelessness.

After graduating from Fisk in 1888, DuBois attended Harvard where he re-
ceived a second B.A. in philosophy. He studied with the philosophers George
Santayana, Josiah Royce, and William James. James was influential in turning
DuBois toward history as a discipline and social issues as a lifelong concern.
Under the historian Albert Bushnell Hart, he completed a master's degree in
history at Harvard in 1892, and then studied for two years at the University of
Berlin, Germany. He finished his Ph.D. at Harvard in 1895, and his dissertation,
The Suppression of the African Slave-Trade to the United States, was published in 1896
as the first volume in Harvard's Historical Studies series.

For a time DuBois devoted himself to university teaching. His first job was at
Wilberforce University in Ohio, teaching Latin and Greek. In 1896, he accepted
an appointment at the University of Pennsylvania for one year to prepare a study
of the urbanization of blacks in Philadelphia. His *The Philadelphia Negro* appeared in 1899. In 1897 came his appointment to the University of Atlanta,
where he taught history, sociology, and economics. He held this position until
1909, and again from 1934 to 1944.

The twenty-four years between these appointments (1910–34) were spent in
New York with the National Association for the Advancement of Colored People
(NAACP). As director of publications for the organization, DuBois founded a
monthly magazine, *Crisis*, whose circulation rose to 100,000 within ten years. It
became the most important organ for the black cause in America, reflecting
DuBois's own passionate commitment to right wrongs and replace oppression
with justice and equality.

In 1903, DuBois published the book that has assured his enduring fame — *The
Souls of Black Folk*. It combines autobiographical, historical, and fictional elements in a disarmingly supple and often lyrical style. The most influential essay
in it was "Of Mr. Booker T. Washington and Others," which had appeared earlier
as a review of Washington's *Up from Slavery*. In it DuBois took strong exception to
some of the concessions that Washington seemed to make to white racism in his
"Atlanta Exposition Address."

As he grew older, DuBois became more militant, even separating from the
NAACP because of disagreements. His political interests broadened to include
the imperialistic exploitations of Africa. He was a prolific writer, publishing
some nineteen books and great numbers of articles, poems, and novels during
his lifetime. Noteworthy are his biography of *John Brown* (1909); a book combining essays, fiction, and fact entitled *Darkwater: Voices from Within the Veil* (1920);
and a revisionist history of the South after the Civil War — *Black Reconstruction in
America* (1934).

DuBois's visit to Russia in 1926 intensified his interest in socialism and communism, and during the later years of his life he became more radical. On a
world tour in 1958–59, he visited a number of Communist countries, including
China and Russia. He was awarded the Lenin Peace Prize by Russia in 1959.

Near the very end of his career, DuBois was invited by Ghana to come to
Africa to edit the *Encyclopedia Africana*. He sailed for Ghana in 1961, when he was
ninety-three years old. In 1963, he renounced his American citizenship; a few
months later, he died. He was buried in Accra, Ghana. At the time of his death,
the civil rights movement in America was becoming its most effective, its de-

mands and demonstrations resulting in the abolition of racial segregation laws in the states and the passing of voting rights acts in the U.S. Congress. Although gone from the scene, his life had helped to make that movement possible.

ADDITIONAL READING

The Autobiography of W. E. B. DuBois: A Soliloquy on Viewing My Life from the Last Decade of Its First Century, 1968; *W. E. B. DuBois Speaks: Speeches and Addresses*, ed. Philip S. Foner, 1970; *W. E. B. DuBois: A Reader*, ed. Meyer Weinberg, 1970; *A W. E. B. DuBois Reader*, ed. Andrew G. Paschal, 1971; *The Emerging Thought of W. E. B. DuBois: Essays and Editorials from the "Crisis,"* ed. Herbert Lee Moon, 1972; *The Correspondence of W. E. B. DuBois*, 3 vols., ed. Herbert Aptheker, 1973–78.

Francis L. Broderick, *W. E. B. DuBois, Negro Leader in a Time of Crisis*, 1959; Elliot M. Rudwick, *W. E. B. DuBois: A Study in Minority Group Leadership*, 1961; August Meier, *Negro Thought in America, 1880–1915*, 1963; John Hope Franklin, *From Slavery to Freedom: A History of American Negroes*, 1947, 1956, 1967; Leslie A. Lacey, *Cheer the Lonesome Traveller: The Life of W. E. B. DuBois*, 1970; Shirley Graham, *His Day Is Marching On: A Memoir of W. E. B. DuBois*, 1971; Arnold Rampersad, *The Art and Imagination of W. E. B. DuBois*, 1976; Jack B. Moore, *W. E. B. DuBois*, 1981; William L. Andrews, ed., *Critical Essays on W. E. B. DuBois*, 1985.

TEXT

The Souls of Black Folk, 1903.

from The Souls of Black Folk

III

OF MR. BOOKER T. WASHINGTON AND OTHERS[1]

From birth till death enslaved; in word, in deed, unmanned!

. . . .

Hereditary bondsmen! Know ye not
Who would be free themselves must strike the blow?

BYRON[2]

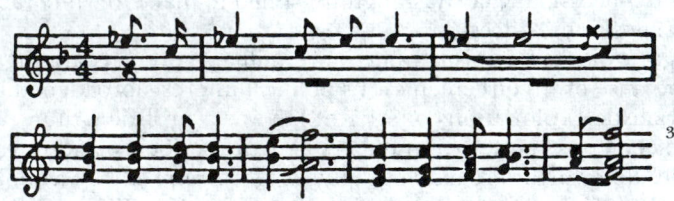

Easily the most striking thing in the history of the American Negro since 1876[4] is the ascendancy of Mr. Booker T. Washington. It began at the time when war memories and ideals were rapidly passing; a day of astonishing commercial development was

[1]Booker T. Washington (1856–1915) founded and built Tuskegee Institute in Alabama. In his "Atlanta Exposition Address" (included in this anthology), he called for Negroes to concentrate on self-education, personal improvement, and vocational training rather than demands for civil rights and social equality. His speech attracted the attention of presidents and other white leaders, but made many blacks uneasy. DuBois was the first black intellectual to articulate important reservations.
[2]From *Childe Harold's Pilgrimage* (1812), Canto II, 74, 9; 76, 1–2, by George Gordon, Lord Byron (1788–1824), British

romantic poet. Note italics in original: "*Who* would be free *themselves* must strike the blow?"
[3]From a Negro spiritual, "A Great Camp-Meetin' in de Promised Land"; the words accompanying the notes: "Going to mourn and never tire—/ mourn and never tire, mourn and never tire." See Chapter XIV, "Of Sorrow Songs," in *The Souls of Black Folk*.
[4]The period of Reconstruction in the South after the Civil War, with radical or black control of many legislatures in the deep South, lasted from 1865 to 1876. The last Federal troops were removed from the South in 1877.

dawning; a sense of doubt and hesitation overtook the freedmen's sons, — then it was that his leading began. Mr. Washington came, with a simple definite programme, at the psychological moment when the nation was a little ashamed of having bestowed so much sentiment on Negroes, and was concentrating its energies on Dollars. His programme of industrial education, conciliation of the South, and submission and silence as to civil and political rights, was not wholly original; the Free Negroes from 1830 up to war-time had striven to build industrial schools, and the American Missionary Association had from the first taught various trades; and Price[5] and others had sought a way of honorable alliance with the best of the Southerners. But Mr. Washington first indissolubly linked these things; he put enthusiasm, unlimited energy, and perfect faith into this programme, and changed it from a by-path into a veritable Way of Life. And the tale of the methods by which he did this is a fascinating study of human life.

It startled the nation to hear a Negro advocating such a programme after many decades of bitter complaint; it startled and won the applause of the South, it interested and won the admiration of the North; and after a confused murmur of protest, it silenced if it did not convert the Negroes themselves.

To gain the sympathy and coöperation of the various elements comprising the white South was Mr. Washington's first task; and this, at the time Tuskegee was founded, seemed, for a black man, well-nigh impossible. And yet ten years later it was done in the word spoken at Atlanta: "In all things purely social we can be as separate as the five fingers, and yet one as the hand in all things essential to mutual progress." This "Atlanta Compromise" is by all odds the most notable thing in Mr. Washington's career. The South interpreted it in different ways: the radicals received it as a complete surrender of the demand for civil and political equality; the conservatives, as a generously conceived working basis for mutual understanding. So both approved it, and to-day its author is certainly the most distinguished Southerner since Jefferson Davis,[6] and the one with the largest personal following.

Next to this achievement comes Mr. Washington's work in gaining place and consideration in the North. Others less shrewd and tactful had formerly essayed to sit on these two stools and had fallen between them; but as Mr. Washington knew the heart of the South from birth and training, so by singular insight he intuitively grasped the spirit of the age which was dominating the North. And so thoroughly did he learn the speech and thought of triumphant commercialism, and the ideal of material prosperity, that the picture of a lone black boy poring over a French grammar amid the weeds and dirt of a neglected home soon seemed to him the acme of absurdities. One wonders what Socrates and St. Francis of Assisi[7] would say to this.

And yet this very singleness of vision and thorough oneness with his age is a mark of the successful man. It is as though Nature must needs make men narrow in order to give them force. So Mr. Washington's cult has gained unquestioning followers, his work has wonderfully prospered, his friends are legion, and his enemies are confounded. To-day he stands as the one recognized spokesman of his ten million fellows, and one of the most notable figures in a nation of seventy millions. One hesitates, therefore, to criticise a life which, beginning with so little, has done so much. And yet the time is come when one may speak in all sincerity and utter courtesy of the mistakes and shortcomings of Mr. Washington's career, as well as of his triumphs, without being thought captious or envious, and without forgetting that it is easier to do ill than well in the world.

The criticism that has hitherto met Mr. Washington has not always been of this broad character. In the South especially has he had to walk warily to avoid the harsh-

---

[5]Thomas Frederick Price (1860–1919), Roman Catholic priest who was a founder of the American Missionary Association.
[6]Southern leader (1808–1889), served as president of the Confederate States of America during the Civil War.

[7]Socrates (470?–399 B.C.), Greek philosopher, known only through the work of his disciple, Plato; St. Francis of Assisi (1182–1226), Italian monk and founder of the Franciscan order.

est judgments, — and naturally so, for he is dealing with the one subject of deepest sensitiveness to that section. Twice — once when at the Chicago celebration of the Spanish-American War he alluded to the color-prejudice that is "eating away the vitals of the South," and once when he dined with President Roosevelt[8] — has the resulting Southern criticism been violent enough to threaten seriously his popularity. In the North the feeling has several times forced itself into words, that Mr. Washington's counsels of submission overlooked certain elements of true manhood, and that his educational programme was unnecessarily narrow. Usually, however, such criticism has not found open expression, although, too, the spiritual sons of the Abolitionists have not been prepared to acknowledge that the schools founded before Tuskegee, by men of broad ideals and self-sacrificing spirit, were wholly failures or worthy of ridicule. While, then, criticism has not failed to follow Mr. Washington, yet the prevailing public opinion of the land has been but too willing to deliver the solution of a wearisome problem into his hands, and say, "If that is all you and your race ask, take it."

Among his own people, however, Mr. Washington has encountered the strongest and most lasting opposition, amounting at times to bitterness, and even to-day continuing strong and insistent even though largely silenced in outward expression by the public opinion of the nation. Some of this opposition is, of course, mere envy; the disappointment of displaced demagogues and the spite of narrow minds. But aside from this, there is among educated and thoughtful colored men in all parts of the land a feeling of deep regret, sorrow, and apprehension at the wide currency and ascendancy which some of Mr. Washington's theories have gained. These same men admire his sincerity of purpose, and are willing to forgive much to honest endeavor which is doing something worth the doing. They coöperate with Mr. Washington as far as they conscientiously can; and, indeed, it is no ordinary tribute to this man's tact and power that, steering as he must between so many diverse interests and opinions, he so largely retains the respect of all.

But the hushing of the criticism of honest opponents is a dangerous thing. It leads some of the best of the critics to unfortunate silence and paralysis of effort, and others to burst into speech so passionately and intemperately as to lose listeners. Honest and earnest criticism from those whose interests are most nearly touched, — criticism of writers by readers, of government by those governed, of leaders by those led, — this is the soul of democracy and the safeguard of modern society. If the best of the American Negroes receive by outer pressure a leader whom they had not recognized before, manifestly there is here a certain palpable gain. Yet there is also irreparable loss, — a loss of that peculiarly valuable education which a group receives when by search and criticism it finds and commissions its own leaders. The way in which this is done is at once the most elementary and the nicest problem of social growth. History is but the record of such group-leadership; and yet how infinitely changeful is its type and character! And of all types and kinds, what can be more instructive than the leadership of a group within a group? — that curious double movement where real progress may be negative and actual advance be relative retrogression. All this is the social student's inspiration and despair.

Now in the past the American Negro has had instructive experience in the choosing of group leaders, founding thus a peculiar dynasty which in the light of present conditions is worth while studying. When sticks and stones and beasts form the sole environment of a people, their attitude is largely one of determined opposition to and conquest of natural forces. But when to earth and brute is added an environment of men and ideas, then the attitude of the imprisoned group may take three main forms, — a feeling of revolt and revenge; an attempt to adjust all thought and

---

[8]Washington was invited to dine at the White House by President Theodore Roosevelt (1858–1919) in 1901.

action to the will of the greater group; or, finally, a determined effort at self-realization and self-development despite environing opinion. The influence of all of these attitudes at various times can be traced in the history of the American Negro, and in the evolution of his successive leaders.

Before 1750, while the fire of African freedom still burned in the veins of the slaves, there was in all leadership or attempted leadership but the one motive of revolt and revenge,—typified in the terrible Maroons, the Danish blacks, and Cato of Stono,[9] and veiling all the Americas in fear of insurrection. The liberalizing tendencies of the latter half of the eighteenth century brought, along with kindlier relations between black and white, thoughts of ultimate adjustment and assimilation. Such aspiration was especially voiced in the earnest songs of Phyllis, in the martyrdom of Attucks, the fighting of Salem and Poor, the intellectual accomplishments of Banneker and Derham, and the political demands of the Cuffes.[10]

Stern financial and social stress after the war cooled much of the previous humanitarian ardor. The disappointment and impatience of the Negroes at the persistence of slavery and serfdom voiced itself in two movements. The slaves in the South, aroused undoubtedly by vague rumors of the Haytian revolt, made three fierce attempts at insurrection,—in 1800 under Gabriel in Virginia, in 1822 under Vesey in Carolina, and in 1831 again in Virginia under the terrible Nat Turner.[11] In the Free States, on the other hand, a new and curious attempt at self-development was made. In Philadelphia and New York color-prescription led to a withdrawal of Negro communicants from white churches and the formation of a peculiar socio-religious institution among the Negroes known as the African Church,—an organization still living and controlling in its various branches over a million of men.

Walker's wild appeal[12] against the trend of the times showed how the world was changing after the coming of the cotton-gin. By 1830 slavery seemed hopelessly fastened on the South, and the slaves thoroughly cowed into submission. The free Negroes of the North, inspired by the mulatto immigrants from the West Indies, began to change the basis of their demands; they recognized the slavery of slaves, but insisted that they themselves were freemen, and sought assimilation and amalgamation with the nation on the same terms with other men. Thus, Forten and Purvis of Philadelphia, Shad of Wilmington, Du Bois of New Haven, Barbadoes of Boston,[13] and others, strove singly and together as men, they said, not as slaves; as "people of color," not as "Negroes." The trend of the times, however, refused them recognition save in individual and exceptional cases, considered them as one with all the despised blacks, and they soon found themselves striving to keep even the rights they formerly had of

---

[9]"Maroons" were groups of runaway slaves in the Caribbean Islands who hid and harrassed plantation owners (later, runaway American slaves adopted the name and tactics); Danish blacks of the Danish West Indies islands, faced with hunger and severe punishment for stealing, rose up against their masters in 1733, killing many whites before being suppressed; Cato of Stono was the leader in 1739 of a slave uprising which began on a plantation near Stono, twenty miles west of Charleston, South Carolina, resulting in many deaths of both whites and blacks.
[10]Phillis Wheatley (*c.* 1753–1784), a slave in Boston and a remarkably gifted poet; Crispus Attucks (1723?–1770), black leader of the 1770 Boston Massacre, killed by the British troops; Peter Salem and Salem Poor, black soldiers who fought in the Revolutionary Army against the British, taking part in the Battle of Bunker Hill and cited for heroism; Benjamin Banneker (1731–1806), a Maryland black and accomplished mathematician and astronomer, publisher of an almanac; James Derham (1726–?), a slave who learned medicine from his master and went on to become an eminent physician in New Orleans; Paul Cuffe (1759–1817), a free Massachusetts black who became owner of a number of sailing ships and experimented at his own expense with the repatriation of blacks in Africa.

[11]The Haitian slave revolt occurred in the late eighteenth century (during the French Revolution). Toussaint L'Ouverture (1743–1803) emerged as leader of guerrilla bands of slaves and held sway until he was captured by the French (under Napoleon) in 1802; Gabriel (1775–1800) led a force of some one thousand slaves against Richmond, Virginia, in 1800, but was betrayed and hanged; Denmark Vesey (1767?–1822) of South Carolina planned a general uprising in 1822, but he and other blacks were arrested and condemned before they could put their plot into action; Nat Turner (1800–1831) led fellow blacks in a slave revolt in 1831 in Southhampton County, Virginia, and killed many plantation owners before being captured and hanged.
[12]David Walker (1785–1830) published his *Walker's Appeal* in 1829 in Boston, calling on all blacks to rise up against slavery.
[13]James Forten (1766–1842), Philadelphia sailmaker and prosperous businessman, supported the abolition movement; Robert Purvis (1810–1898), a founder of the American Anti-Slavery Society and supporter of the Underground Railroad; Abraham Shadd, another of the "Founding Fathers" of the American Anti-Slavery Society; Alexander Du-Bois, grandfather of W. E. B. DuBois and a religious leader; James G. Barbadoes attended the first National Convention of Negroes in 1830 in Philadelphia.

voting and working and moving as freemen. Schemes of migration and colonization arose among them; but these they refused to entertain, and they eventually turned to the Abolition movement as a final refuge.

Here, led by Remond, Nell, Wells-Brown, and Douglass,[14] a new period of self-assertion and self-development dawned. To be sure, ultimate freedom and assimilation was the ideal before the leaders, but the assertion of the manhood rights of the Negro by himself was the main reliance, and John Brown's raid[15] was the extreme of its logic. After the war and emancipation, the great form of Frederick Douglass, the greatest of American Negro leaders, still led the host. Self-assertion, especially in political lines, was the main programme, and behind Douglass came Elliot, Bruce, and Langston,[16] and the Reconstruction politicians, and, less conspicuous but of greater social significance Alexander Crummell and Bishop Daniel Payne.[17]

Then came the Revolution of 1876, the suppression of the Negro votes, the changing and shifting of ideals, and the seeking of new lights in the great night. Douglass, in his old age, still bravely stood for the ideals of his early manhood,— ultimate assimilation *through* self-assertion, and on no other terms. For a time Price arose as a new leader, destined, it seemed, not to give up, but to re-state the old ideals in a form less repugnant to the white South. But he passed away in his prime. Then came the new leader. Nearly all the former ones had become leaders by the silent suffrage of their fellows, had sought to lead their own people alone, and were usually, save Douglass, little known outside their race. But Booker T. Washington arose as essentially the leader not of one race but of two,— a compromiser between the South, the North, and the Negro. Naturally the Negroes resented, at first bitterly, signs of compromise which surrendered their civil and political rights, even though this was to be exchanged for larger chances of economic development. The rich and dominating North, however, was not only weary of the race problem, but was investing largely in Southern enterprises, and welcomed any method of peaceful coöperation. Thus, by national opinion, the Negroes began to recognize Mr. Washington's leadership; and the voice of criticism was hushed.

Mr. Washington represents in Negro thought the old attitude of adjustment and submission; but adjustment at such a peculiar time as to make his programme unique. This is an age of unusual economic development, and Mr. Washington's programme naturally takes an economic cast, becoming a gospel of Work and Money to such an extent as apparently almost completely to overshadow the higher aims of life. Moreover, this is an age when the more advanced races are coming in closer contact with the less developed races, and the race-feeling is therefore intensified; and Mr. Washington's programme practically accepts the alleged inferiority of the Negro races. Again, in our own land, the reaction from the sentiment of war time has given impetus to race-prejudice against Negroes, and Mr. Washington withdraws many of the high demands of Negroes as men and American citizens. In other periods of intensified prejudice all the Negro's tendency to self-assertion has been called forth; at this period a policy of submission is advocated. In the history of nearly all other races and peoples the doctrine preached at such crises has been that manly self-respect is worth more than lands and houses, and that a people who voluntarily surrender such respect, or cease striving for it, are not worth civilizing.

[14]Charles Lenox Remond (1810–1873), black leader in the abolition movement; William C. Nell (1816–1874), black author of *Services of Colored Americans in the Wars of 1776 and 1812* (1852); William Wells-Brown (1816?–1884), author of *Clotel* (1853), first novel by an American black; Frederick Douglass (1817–1895), author of *Narrative of the Life of Frederick Douglass* (1845, expanded and revised, 1892).
[15]John Brown (1800–1859), white abolitionist who led a raid at Harper's Ferry, a U.S. arsenal in Virginia. He was captured, tried and hanged.

[16]Robert Brown Elliot (1842–1884), black South Carolinian who served as congressman in the House of Representatives; Blanche K. Bruce (1841–1898), Senator from Mississippi (1875–81); John Mercer Langston (1829–1897), congressman and diplomat, represented the United States in Haiti beginning in 1877.
[17]Alexander Crummell (1819–1898), Episcopal religious leader and missionary, serving in Liberia; Bishop Daniel Payne (1811–1893), Methodist religious leader who served as president of Wilberforce University (1863–76).

In answer to this, it has been claimed that the Negro can survive only through submission. Mr. Washington distinctly asks that black people give up, at least for the present, three things,—

First, political power,

Second, insistence on civil rights,

Third, higher education of Negro youth, —

and concentrate all their energies on industrial education, the accumulation of wealth, and the conciliation of the South. This policy has been courageously and insistently advocated for over fifteen years, and has been triumphant for perhaps ten years. As a result of this tender of the palm-branch, what has been the return? In these years there have occurred:

1. The disfranchisement of the Negro.

2. The legal creation of a distinct status of civil inferiority for the Negro.

3. The steady withdrawal of aid from institutions for the higher training of the Negro.

These movements are not, to be sure, direct results of Mr. Washington's teachings; but his propaganda has, without a shadow of doubt, helped their speedier accomplishment. The question then comes: Is it possible, and probable, that nine millions of men can make effective progress in economic lines if they are deprived of political rights, made a servile caste, and allowed only the most meagre chance for developing their exceptional men? If history and reason give any distinct answer to these questions, it is an emphatic *No*. And Mr. Washington thus faces the triple paradox of his career:

1. He is striving nobly to make Negro artisans business men and property-owners; but it is utterly impossible, under modern competitive methods, for workingmen and property-owners to defend their rights and exist without the right of suffrage.

2. He insists on thrift and self-respect, but at the same time counsels a silent submission to civic inferiority such as is bound to sap the manhood of any race in the long run.

3. He advocates common-school[18] and industrial training, and depreciates institutions of higher learning; but neither the Negro common-schools, nor Tuskegee itself, could remain open a day were it not for teachers trained in Negro colleges, or trained by their graduates.

This triple paradox in Mr. Washington's position is the object of criticism by two classes of colored Americans. One class is spiritually descended from Toussaint the Savior, through Gabriel, Vesey, and Turner,[19] and they represent the attitude of revolt and revenge; they hate the white South blindly and distrust the white race generally, and so far as they agree on definite action, think that the Negro's only hope lies in emigration beyond the borders of the United States. And yet, by the irony of fate, nothing has more effectually made this programme seem hopeless than the recent course of the United States toward weaker and darker peoples in the West Indies, Hawaii, and the Philippines,—for where in the world may we go and be safe from lying and brute force?

The other class of Negroes who cannot agree with Mr. Washington has hitherto said little aloud. They deprecate the sight of scattered counsels, of internal disagreement; and especially they dislike making their just criticism of a useful and earnest man an excuse for a general discharge of venom from small-minded opponents. Nevertheless, the questions involved are so fundamental and serious that it is difficult to see how men like the Grimkes, Kelly Miller, J. W. E. Bowen,[20] and other represen-

[18]Free public schools.

[19]Toussaint L'Ouverture (1743–1803), leader of Haiti slave revolt of late eighteenth century; see note 11 for others.

[20]Archibald Henry Grimké (1849–1930), black lawyer, writer, and diplomat, who served as president of the Ameri- can Negro Academy (1903–16); Kelly Miller (1863–1939), a primary sponsor of the National Urban League, formed in 1911; J. W. E. Bowen (1855?–?), religious leader and presi- dent of the Negro Gammon Theological Seminary, Atlanta.

tatives of this group, can much longer be silent. Such men feel in conscience bound to ask of this nation three things:

1. The right to vote.
2. Civic equality.
3. The education of youth according to ability.

They acknowledge Mr. Washington's invaluable service in counselling patience and courtesy in such demands; they do not ask that ignorant black men vote when ignorant whites are debarred, or that any reasonable restrictions in the suffrage should not be applied; they know that the low social level of the mass of the race is responsible for much discrimination against it, but they also know, and the nation knows, that relentless color-prejudice is more often a cause than a result of the Negro's degradation; they seek the abatement of this relic of barbarism, and not its systematic encouragement and pampering by all agencies of social power from the Associated Press to the Church of Christ. They advocate, with Mr. Washington, a broad system of Negro common schools supplemented by thorough industrial training; but they are surprised that a man of Mr. Washington's insight cannot see that no such educational system ever has rested or can rest on any other basis than that of the well-equipped college and university, and they insist that there is a demand for a few such institutions throughout the South to train the best of the Negro youth as teachers, professional men, and leaders.

This group of men honor Mr. Washington for his attitude of conciliation toward the white South; they accept the "Atlanta Compromise" in its broadest interpretation; they recognize, with him, many signs of promise, many men of high purpose and fair judgment, in this section; they know that no easy task has been laid upon a region already tottering under heavy burdens. But, nevertheless, they insist that the way to truth and right lies in straightforward honesty, not in indiscriminate flattery; in praising those of the South who do well and criticising uncompromisingly those who do ill; in taking advantage of the opportunities at hand and urging their fellows to do the same, but at the same time in remembering that only a firm adherence to their higher ideals and aspirations will ever keep those ideals within the realm of possibility. They do not expect that the free right to vote, to enjoy civic rights, and to be educated, will come in a moment; they do not expect to see the bias and prejudices of years disappear at the blast of a trumpet; but they are absolutely certain that the way for a people to gain their reasonable rights is not by voluntarily throwing them away and insisting that they do not want them; that the way for a people to gain respect is not by continually belittling and ridiculing themselves; that, on the contrary, Negroes must insist continually, in season and out of season, that voting is necessary to modern manhood, that color discrimination is barbarism, and that black boys need education as well as white boys.

In failing thus to state plainly and unequivocally the legitimate demands of their people, even at the cost of opposing an honored leader, the thinking classes of American Negroes would shirk a heavy responsibility, — a responsibility to themselves, a responsibility to the struggling masses, a responsibility to the darker races of men whose future depends so largely on this American experiment, but especially a responsibility to this nation, — this common Fatherland. It is wrong to encourage a man or a people in evil-doing; it is wrong to aid and abet a national crime simply because it is unpopular not to do so. The growing spirit of kindliness and reconciliation between the North and South after the frightful differences of a generation ago ought to be a source of deep congratulation to all, and especially to those whose mistreatment caused the war; but if that reconciliation is to be marked by the industrial slavery and civic death of those same black men, with permanent legislation into a position of inferiority, then those black men, if they are really men, are called upon by every consideration of patriotism and loyalty to oppose such a course by all civilized methods, even though such opposition involves disagreement with Mr. Booker

T. Washington. We have no right to sit silently by while the inevitable seeds are sown for a harvest of disaster to our children, black and white.

First, it is the duty of black men to judge the South discriminatingly. The present generation of Southerners are not responsible for the past, and they should not be blindly hated or blamed for it. Furthermore, to no class is the indiscriminate endorsement of the recent course of the South toward Negroes more nauseating than to the best thought of the South. The South is not "solid"; it is a land in the ferment of social change, wherein forces of all kinds are fighting for supremacy; and to praise the ill the South is to-day perpetrating is just as wrong as to condemn the good. Discriminating and broad-minded criticism is what the South needs,—needs it for the sake of her own white sons and daughters, and for the insurance of robust, healthy mental and moral development.

To-day even the attitude of the Southern whites toward the blacks is not, as so many assume, in all cases the same; the ignorant Southerner hates the Negro, the workingmen fear his competition, the money-makers wish to use him as a laborer, some of the educated see a menace in his upward development, while others— usually the sons of the masters—wish to help him to rise. National opinion has enabled this last class to maintain the Negro common schools, and to protect the Negro partially in property, life, and limb. Through the pressure of the money-makers, the Negro is in danger of being reduced to semi-slavery, especially in the country districts; the workingmen, and those of the educated who fear the Negro, have united to disfranchise him, and some have urged his deportation; while the passions of the ignorant are easily aroused to lynch and abuse any black man. To praise this intricate whirl of thought and prejudice is nonsense; to inveigh indiscriminately against "the South" is unjust; but to use the same breath in praising Governor Aycock, exposing Senator Morgan, arguing with Mr. Thomas Nelson Page, and denouncing Senator Ben Tillman,[21] is not only sane, but the imperative duty of thinking black men.

It would be unjust to Mr. Washington not to acknowledge that in several instances he has opposed movements in the South which were unjust to the Negro; he sent memorials to the Louisiana and Alabama constitutional conventions, he has spoken against lynching, and in other ways has openly or silently set his influence against sinister schemes and unfortunate happenings. Notwithstanding this, it is equally true to assert that on the whole the distinct impression left by Mr. Washington's propaganda is, first, that the South is justified in its present attitude toward the Negro because of the Negro's degradation; secondly, that the prime cause of the Negro's failure to rise more quickly is his wrong education in the past; and, thirdly, that his future rise depends primarily on his own efforts. Each of these propositions is a dangerous half-truth. The supplementary truths must never be lost sight of: first, slavery and race-prejudice are potent if not sufficient causes of the Negro's position; second, industrial and common-school training were necessarily slow in planting because they had to await the black teachers trained by higher institutions,—it being extremely doubtful if any essentially different development was possible, and certainly a Tuskegee was unthinkable before 1880; and, third, while it is a great truth to say that the Negro must strive and strive mightily to help himself, it is equally true that unless his striving be not simply seconded, but rather aroused and encouraged, by the initiative of the richer and wiser environing group, he cannot hope for great success.

In his failure to realize and impress this last point, Mr. Washington is especially to be criticised. His doctrine has tended to make the whites, North and South, shift the burden of the Negro problem to the Negro's shoulders and stand aside as critical and

---

[21]Governor Charles Brantley Aycock (1859–1912) of North Carolina; Senator Edwin Denison Morgan (1811–1883) of New York; Thomas Nelson Page (1853–1922), Virginia novelist and diplomat; Senator Benjamin R. Tillman (1847–1918) of South Carolina.

rather pessimistic spectators; when in fact the burden belongs to the nation, and the hands of none of us are clean if we bend not our energies to righting these great wrongs.

The South ought to be led, by candid and honest criticism, to assert her better self and do her full duty to the race she has cruelly wronged and is still wronging. The North—her co-partner in guilt—cannot salve her conscience by plastering it with gold. We cannot settle this problem by diplomacy and suaveness, by "policy" alone. If worse come to worst, can the moral fibre of this country survive the slow throttling and murder of nine millions of men?

The black men of America have a duty to perform, a duty stern and delicate,—a forward movement to oppose a part of the work of their greatest leader. So far as Mr. Washington preaches Thrift, Patience, and Industrial Training for the masses, we must hold up his hands and strive with him, rejoicing in his honors and glorying in the strength of this Joshua[22] called of God and of man to lead the headless host. But so far as Mr. Washington apologizes for injustice, North or South, does not rightly value the privilege and duty of voting, belittles the emasculating effects of caste distinctions, and opposes the higher training and ambition of our brighter minds,—so far as he, the South, or the Nation, does this,—we must unceasingly and firmly oppose them. By every civilized and peaceful method we must strive for the rights which the world accords to men, clinging unwaveringly to those great words which the sons of the Fathers would fain forget: "We hold these truths to be self-evident: That all men are created equal; that they are endowed by their Creator with certain unalienable rights; that among these are life, liberty, and the pursuit of happiness."

1902   *1903*

HENRY ADAMS
(1838–1918)

Those participating in the founding of the United States in the late eighteenth century constituted something of an intellectual elite. Among those founders was the great-grandfather of Henry Adams—John Adams. He served on the committee assigned to write the Declaration of Independence, became the fledgling nation's first vice president and second president. Henry's grandfather, John Quincy Adams, became the sixth president of the United States. Henry's father, Charles Francis Adams, had a distinguished career as congressman and served as Abraham Lincoln's minister to England during the critical Civil War period.

It is perhaps no wonder that, coming along in the fourth generation of such a distinguished line of public servants, Henry Adams would come to question the practical usefulness of his scholarly, meditative life, lived largely apart from public affairs. Looking back on his birth in 1838, he remarked of himself as though he were a character in a fiction: "Probably no child, born in the year, held better cards than he. . . . As it happened, he never got to the point of playing the game at all; he lost himself in the study of it, watching the errors of the players." This is the ironic self-deprecation of America's profoundest and most eloquent pessi-

---

[22]Successor to Moses and leader of the Israelites into the Promised Land (see Joshua 1–12).

mist. As it has turned out, Henry Adams is more widely and deeply known among succeeding generations than his ancestors who were presidents.

As befitted an Adams, the young Henry was given the best education possible, including a Boston private school, Harvard, and then, for finish, a period in Europe, studying civil law in Berlin, happening on a revolution in Italy, observing the sophisticated life of Paris. On returning from Europe, Henry went to Washington, D.C., to serve as secretary to his father, elected to Congress in 1858. When his father went to England as American minister, Henry followed and did not return to America for seven years, in 1868.

During this period, Henry Adams began to write articles for the journals, especially *The North American Review*, attracting sufficient attention as to win him the offer in 1870 of an assistant professorship in medieval history at Harvard, together with editorship of *The North American Review*. Adams spent seven years in the post, instituting the first graduate seminar in history at Harvard. But he found the duties of a professor confining and decided to give himself the freedom the family means could afford.

With his wife (he had married Marian Hooper in 1872) he settled in Washington, D.C., and his home there became a social-intellectual center. Adams began to devote his time to writing biography, fiction, and history. He wrote two novels, both published under pseudonyms, and one of which became a best-seller — *Democracy* (1880). It presented an unflattering portrait of capitol life and American politics in the period after the Civil War, when under the Grant administration corruption was commonplace.

In 1885, Marian Adams, in a state of depression at her father's death, committed suicide. The event broke Adams's life in two, and for a time he referred to his "posthumous" existence. In his autobiography (*The Education*) written later, he passed over this period of deep distress in silence. But he commissioned from the American sculptor Augustus Saint-Gaudens a memorial, completed in 1891: a brooding figure in bronze, seated and half-hooded, placed in Rock Creek Cemetery, Washington, D.C.

Adams embarked on somewhat aimless travel to the Orient in 1886 in an attempt to regain emotional equilibrium. On returning to Washington, he immersed himself in a major historical study he had undertaken that was to turn out to be his major contribution in history — *History of the United States During the Administrations of Thomas Jefferson and James Madison* (9 vols., 1889–91). Jefferson and Madison had followed his great-grandfather in the presidency, and Adams's interest was personal as well as professional.

After completing this major work, Adams again turned to travel, letting his imagination for the time lie fallow. But he was gathering impressions that would inspire the two books on which his literary reputation would rest: *Mont-Saint-Michel and Chartres*, privately printed in 1904, and *The Education of Henry Adams*, privately printed in 1907. Though the first of these works is a study of the medieval period, and the second focuses on the modern age, Adams saw them as linked, the one a study of an age of unity, the other a study of an age of confusing multiplicity.

The Education of Henry Adams is a masterpiece in the genre of personal writing, not quite an autobiography and even less an objective study of contemporary times. It is dominated by the personal voice of the author writing about himself in the third person. That voice is in turn ironic, wistful, sharply critical, poignantly nostalgic, and always precariously poised on the edge of an abyss, the time yet to be — or perhaps not to be. Beginning with a complaint that his education had not prepared him for the age in which he lived, Adams quickly turned to sifting through the shards and fragments of contemporary philosophy and science, trying to fit the pieces of a puzzle together and to peer into the future. What he glimpsed dismayed him.

In one of the book's brilliant insights, Adams found the gigantic modern dynamo, which he first witnessed at the Chicago Columbian Exposition of 1893, as the present's counterpart to the Virgin of the medieval period. Both were the sources of enormous energy, the one enabling the building of soaring skyscrapers, the other enabling the construction of the magnificent cathedrals of the Middle Ages. What puzzled him was the fertility and sexuality implicit in the medieval worship of the Madonna and child, and the absence of such elements in the contemporary cult of the dynamo.

Adams found no solutions to the puzzles that fascinated him. But he foresaw that with the increasingly rapid discovery of sources of energy, the human race would soon have unlimited and fearful power at its command. Moreover, he foresaw that if human beings escaped self-destruction by the awful power under their control, there remained the inevitability of eventual doom in the generally ignored second law of thermodynamics first proclaimed in the middle of the nineteenth century. In a privately published work, "A Letter to American Teachers of History" (1910), Adams pointed out that the "entropy" resulting from the gradual dissipation of all energy envisioned by the second law of thermodynamics in effect "tossed the universe into the ash-heap": "If the entire universe, in every variety of active energy, organic and inorganic, human or divine, is to be treated as a clockwork that is running down, society can hardly go on ignoring the fact forever."

Adams's doomsday imagination might well be seen as a forerunner of T. S. Eliot's in *The Waste Land* (1922), a poem of dark vision in which the protagonist is left at the end sifting through cultures and civilizations, saying: "These fragments I have shored against my ruins." But of course, the fulfillment of cosmic entropy would find no survivors to sort through fragments. In the bleakness of his vision, Adams links himself closely to those writers who, after the Second World War, were beset by grim visions of apocalypse. One of these, Thomas Pynchon, has adopted entropy as an obsessive theme, beginning with a short story by that title published in 1960 and elaborated in such novels as *The Crying of Lot 49* (1966). Adams figures high on the list of writers that Pynchon has named as having helped to shape his imagination.

ADDITIONAL READING

The Letters of Henry Adams, 6 vols., ed. J. D. Levenson et al., 1983–88.

J. T. Adams, *Henry Adams*, 1933; Ernest Samuels, *The Young Henry Adams*, 1948, *Henry Adams: The Middle Years*, 1958, and *Henry Adams: The Major Phase*, 1964; Robert A. Hume, *Runaway Star: An Appreciation of Henry Adams*, 1951; William H. Jordy, *Henry Adams: Scientific Historian*, 1952, 1963; Elizabeth Stevenson, *Henry Adams, A Biography*, 1956; J. C. Levenson, *The Mind and Art of Henry Adams*, 1957, 1968; George Hochfield, *Henry Adams: An Introduction and Interpretation*, 1962; Vern Wagner, *The Suspension of Henry Adams: A Study of Manner and Matter*, 1969; John J. Conder, *A Formula of His Own: Henry Adams's Literary Experiment*, 1970; Ernest Scheyer, *The Circle of Henry Adams: Art and Artists*, 1970; Melvin Lyon, *Symbol and Idea in Henry Adams*, 1970; John Carlos Rowe, *Henry Adams and Henry James: The Emergence of a Modern Consciousness*, 1976; Earl N. Harbert, *The Force So Much Closer Home: Henry Adams and the Adams Family*, 1977, and *Henry Adams: A Reference Guide*, 1978; Ferman Bishop, *Henry Adams*, 1979; William Dusinberre, *Henry Adams: The Myth of Failure*, 1980; David R. Contosta, *Henry Adams and the American Experience*, 1980; Earl N. Harbert, ed., *Critical Essays on Henry Adams*, 1981; Harold Kaplan, *Henry Adams and the Naturalist Tradition in American Fiction*, 1981; Edward Chalfant, *Both Sides of the Ocean: A Biography of Henry Adams: His First Life, 1838–1862*, 1982; William Wasserstrom, *The Ironies of Progress: Henry Adams and the American Dream*, 1984.

TEXTS

   The Education of Henry Adams, ed. Ernest Samuels, 1973; *The Degradation of the Democratic Dogma*, ed. Brooks Adams, 1919.

from The Education of Henry Adams

CHAPTER XXV
THE DYNAMO AND THE VIRGIN
(1900)[1]

   Until the Great Exposition of 1900 closed its doors in November, Adams haunted it, aching to absorb knowledge, and helpless to find it. He would have liked to know how much of it could have been grasped by the best-informed man in the world. While he was thus meditating chaos, Langley[2] came by, and showed it to him. At Langley's behest, the Exhibition dropped its superfluous rags and stripped itself to the skin, for Langley knew what to study, and why, and how; while Adams might as well have stood outside in the night, staring at the Milky Way. Yet Langley said nothing new, and taught nothing that one might not have learned from Lord Bacon,[3] three hundred years before; but though one should have known the "Advancement of Science" as well as one knew the "Comedy of Errors,"[4] the literary knowledge counted for nothing until some teacher should show how to apply it. Bacon took a vast deal of trouble in teaching King James I[5] and his subjects, American or other, towards the year 1620, that true science was the development or economy of forces; yet an elderly American in 1900 knew neither the formula nor the forces; or even so much as to say to himself that his historical business in the Exposition concerned only the economies or developments of force since 1893, when he began the study at Chicago.[6]

   Nothing in education is so astonishing as the amount of ignorance it accumulates in the form of inert facts. Adams had looked at most of the accumulations of art in the storehouses called Art Museums; yet he did not know how to look at the art exhibits of 1900. He had studied Karl Marx[7] and his doctrines of history with profound attention, yet he could not apply them at Paris. Langley, with the ease of a great master of experiment, threw out of the field every exhibit that did not reveal a new application of force, and naturally threw out, to begin with, almost the whole art exhibit. Equally, he ignored almost the whole industrial exhibit. He led his pupil directly to the forces. His chief interest was in new motors to make his airship feasible, and he taught Adams the astonishing complexities of the new Daimler[8] motor, and of the automobile, which, since 1893, had become a nightmare at a hundred kilometres an hour,[9] almost as destructive as the electric tram which was only ten

---

[1]Chapter XXV of *The Education* was written after Adams visited the Paris Exposition of 1900 at which he witnessed the latest achievements in modern technology.
[2]Samuel Langley (1834–1906), American astronomer and airplane pioneer.
[3]Francis Bacon (1561–1626), English philosopher, scientist, and essayist, whose *Advancement of Learning* appeared in 1605 and was expanded in 1623 as *De Augmentis Scientiarum*.
[4]Early comedy (1594) by Shakespeare.
[5]King James I (1566–1625), king of Great Britain (1603–25).
[6]The World's Columbian Exposition was held in Chicago in 1893; Adams was deeply impressed by the scientific exhibits, especially the dynamos.
[7]Karl Marx (1818–1883), whose doctrines of history in *Das Kapital* (1867) derive from his philosophy of "dialectical materialism," embracing a belief that societies inevitably evolved through stages toward the highest or socialist-communist form.
[8]Gottlieb Daimler (1834–1900), German pioneer in the development of the automobile.
[9]I.e., about 62 miles per hour.

years older; and threatening to become as terrible as the locomotive steam-engine itself, which was almost exactly Adams's own age.

Then he showed his scholar the great hall of dynamos, and explained how little he knew about electricity or force of any kind, even of his own special sun, which spouted heat in inconceivable volume, but which, as far as he knew, might spout less or more, at any time, for all the certainty he felt in it. To him, the dynamo itself was but an ingenious channel for conveying somewhere the heat latent in a few tons of poor coal hidden in a dirty engine-house carefully kept out of sight; but to Adams the dynamo became a symbol of infinity. As he grew accustomed to the great gallery of machines, he began to feel the forty-foot dynamos as a moral force, much as the early Christians felt the Cross. The planet itself seemed less impressive, in its old-fashioned, deliberate, annual or daily revolution, than this huge wheel, revolving within arm's-length at some vertiginous speed, and barely murmuring — scarcely humming an audible warning to stand a hair's-breadth further for respect of power — while it would not wake the baby lying close against its frame. Before the end, one began to pray to it; inherited instinct taught the natural expression of man before silent and infinite force. Among the thousand symbols of ultimate energy, the dynamo was not so human as some, but it was the most expressive.

Yet the dynamo, next to the steam-engine, was the most familiar of exhibits. For Adams's objects its value lay chiefly in its occult mechanism. Between the dynamo in the gallery of machines and the engine-house outside, the break of continuity amounted to abysmal fracture for a historian's objects. No more relation could he discover between the steam and the electric current than between the Cross and the cathedral. The forces were interchangeable if not reversible, but he could see only an absolute *fiat* in electricity as in faith. Langley could not help him. Indeed, Langley seemed to be worried by the same trouble, for he constantly repeated that the new forces were anarchical, and especially that he was not responsible for the new rays, that were little short of parricidal in their wicked spirit towards science. His own rays, with which he had doubled the solar spectrum, were altogether harmless and beneficent; but Radium[10] denied its God — or, what was to Langley the same thing, denied the truths of his Science. The force was wholly new.

A historian who asked only to learn enough to be as futile as Langley or Kelvin,[11] made rapid progress under this teaching, and mixed himself up in the tangle of ideas until he achieved a sort of Paradise of ignorance vastly consoling to his fatigued senses. He wrapped himself in vibrations and rays which were new, and he would have hugged Marconi and Branly[12] had he met them, as he hugged the dynamo; while he lost his arithmetic in trying to figure out the equation between the discoveries and the economies of force. The economies, like the discoveries, were absolute, supersensual, occult; incapable of expression in horse-power. What mathematical equivalent could he suggest as the value of a Branly coherer? Frozen air, or the electric furnace, had some scale of measurement, no doubt, if somebody could invent a thermometer adequate to the purpose; but X-rays[13] had played no part whatever in man's consciousness, and the atom itself had figured only as a fiction of thought. In these seven years man had translated himself into a new universe which had no common scale of measurement with the old. He had entered a supersensual world, in which he could measure nothing except by chance collisions of movements imperceptible to his senses, perhaps even imperceptible to his instruments, but perceptible to each other, and so to some known ray at the end of the scale. Langley seemed

---

[10]In 1900 radium was a new phenomenon, having been isolated and identified some two years before by Pierre and Maria Curie in France.
[11]William Thomson, Baron Kelvin (1824–1907), British mathematician and physicist who made many basic discoveries in molecular dynamics.

[12]Guglielmo Marconi (1874–1937), Italian engineer and inventor of the wireless telegraph, leading to development of radio. Edouard Branly (1846–1940), French physicist who invented the Branley "coherer" to detect radio waves.
[13]X-rays were discovered in 1895 by German physicist Wilhelm Konrad Roentgen (1845–1923).

prepared for anything, even for an indeterminable number of universes inter-fused—physics stark mad in metaphysics.

Historians undertake to arrange sequences,—called stories, or histories—assuming in silence a relation of cause and effect. These assumptions, hidden in the depths of dusty libraries, have been astounding, but commonly unconscious and childlike; so much so, that if any captious critic were to drag them to light, historians would probably reply, with one voice, that they had never supposed themselves required to know what they were talking about. Adams, for one, had toiled in vain to find out what he meant. He had even published a dozen volumes of American history for no other purpose than to satisfy himself whether, by the severest process of stating, with the least possible comment, such facts as seemed sure, in such order as seemed rigorously consequent, he could fix for a familiar moment a necessary sequence of human movement. The result had satisfied him as little as at Harvard College. Where he saw sequence, other men saw something quite different, and no one saw the same unit of measure. He cared little about his experiments and less about his statesmen, who seemed to him quite as ignorant as himself and, as a rule, no more honest; but he insisted on a relation of sequence, and if he could not reach it by one method, he would try as many methods as science knew. Satisfied that the sequence of men led to nothing and that the sequence of their society could lead no further, while the mere sequence of time was artificial, and the sequence of thought was chaos, he turned at last to the sequence of force; and thus it happened that, after ten years' pursuit, he found himself lying in the Gallery of Machines at the Great Exposition of 1900, with his historical neck broken by the sudden irruption of forces totally new.

Since no one else showed much concern, an elderly person without other cares had no need to betray alarm. The year 1900 was not the first to upset schoolmasters. Copernicus and Galileo[14] had broken many professorial necks about 1600; Columbus[15] had stood the world on its head towards 1500; but the nearest approach to the revolution of 1900 was that of 310, when Constantine set up the Cross.[16] The rays that Langley disowned, as well as those which he fathered, were occult, supersensual, irrational; they were a revelation of mysterious energy like that of the Cross; they were what, in terms of mediæval science, were called immediate modes of the divine substance.

The historian was thus reduced to his last resources. Clearly if he was bound to reduce all these forces to a common value, this common value could have no measure but that of their attraction on his own mind. He must treat them as they had been felt; as convertible, reversible, interchangeable attractions on thought. He made up his mind to venture it; he would risk translating rays into faith. Such a reversible process would vastly amuse a chemist, but the chemist could not deny that he, or some of his fellow physicists, could feel the force of both. When Adams was a boy in Boston, the best chemist in the place had probably never heard of Venus[17] except by way of scandal, or of the Virgin[18] except as idolatry; neither had he heard of dynamos or automobiles or radium; yet his mind was ready to feel the force of all, though the rays were unborn and the women were dead.

Here opened another totally new education, which promised to be by far the most hazardous of all. The knife-edge along which he must crawl, like Sir Lancelot in the twelfth century,[19] divided two kingdoms of force which had nothing in common but

[14]Nikolaus Copernicus (1473–1543), Polish astronomer who demonstrated that the earth rotated around the sun; Galileo Galilei (1564–1642), Italian astronomer who discovered the nature of gravity and motion.

[15]Christopher Columbus (1446?–1506) discovered America in 1492.

[16]Constantine I (288?–337), Roman emperor who was converted to Christianity in 313 and conferred legality on it as a religion.

[17]Venus, the name of the Roman goddess of love, is the root word for "venereal," which a chemist (or druggist-pharmacist) would have heard about through his selling of treatments for venereal disease.

[18]The idolizing of the Virgin Mary, common in Catholic countries such as Italy and Spain, was frowned on by American Protestantism.

[19]In one chivalric tale, Sir Lancelot had to crawl along a sword-edged bridge in order to rescue the imprisoned Guinevere.

attraction. They were as different as a magnet is from gravitation, supposing one knew what a magnet was, or gravitation, or love. The force of the Virgin was still felt at Lourdes,[20] and seemed to be as potent as X-rays; but in America neither Venus nor Virgin ever had value as force—at most as sentiment. No American had ever been truly afraid of either.

This problem in dynamics gravely perplexed an American historian. The Woman had once been supreme; in France she still seemed potent, not merely as a sentiment, but as a force. Why was she unknown in America? For evidently America was ashamed of her, and she was ashamed of herself, otherwise they would not have strewn fig-leaves so profusely all over her. When she was a true force, she was ignorant of fig-leaves, but the monthly-magazine-made American female had not a feature that would have been recognized by Adam. The trait was notorious, and often humorous, but anyone brought up among Puritans knew that sex was sin. In any previous age, sex was strength. Neither art nor beauty was needed. Everyone, even among Puritans, knew that neither Diana of the Ephesians[21] nor any of the Oriental goddesses was worshipped for her beauty. She was goddess because of her force; she was the animated dynamo; she was reproduction—the greatest and most mysterious of all energies; all she needed was to be fecund. Singularly enough, not one of Adams's many schools of education had ever drawn his attention to the opening lines of Lucretius, though they were perhaps the finest in all Latin literature, where the poet invoked Venus exactly as Dante invoked the Virgin:—

"Quae quoniam rerum naturam *sola* gubernas."[22]

The Venus of Epicurean philosophy survived in the Virgin of the Schools:—

"Donna, sei tanto grande, e tanto vali,
Che qual vuol grazia, e a te non ricorre,
Sua disianza vuol volar senz' ali."[23]

All this was to American thought as though it had never existed. The true American knew something of the facts, but nothing of the feelings; he read the letter, but he never felt the law. Before this historical chasm, a mind like that of Adams felt itself helpless; he turned from the Virgin to the Dynamo as though he were a Branly coherer. On one side, at the Louvre and at Chartres,[24] as he knew by the record of work actually done and still before his eyes, was the highest energy ever known to man, the creator of four-fifths of his noblest art, exercising vastly more attraction over the human mind than all the steam-engines and dynamos ever dreamed of; and yet this energy was unknown to the American mind. An American Virgin would never dare command; an American Venus would never dare exist.

The question, which to any plain American of the nineteenth century seemed as remote as it did to Adams, drew him almost violently to study, once it was posed; and on this point Langleys were as useless as though they were Herbert Spencers[25] or dynamos. The idea survived only as art. There one turned as naturally as though the artist were himself a woman. Adams began to ponder, asking himself whether he knew of any American artist who had ever insisted on the power of sex, as every

---

[20]Lourdes is a shrine in southern France dedicated to the Virgin and celebrated for miraculous cures.
[21]Virgin fertility goddess (Artemis in Greek), whose statue at the temple in the ancient Greek city Ephesus was a cone surmounted by a bust covered with breasts.
[22]"Since thou alone dost govern the nature of things," from *On the Nature of Things* (I.21) by Roman poet and Epicurean philosopher Lucretius (c.99–55 B.C.).
[23]"Lady, thou art so great and so prevailing, / That he who wishes grace, nor runs to thee, / His aspirations without wings would fly," from *Divine Comedy*, "Paradiso" (XXXIII, ll. 13–15), by Italian poet Dante Aligheri (1265–1321); transla-

tion by Henry Wadsworth Longfellow. "Virgin of the Schools," i.e., of the medieval scholastic philosophers.
[24]The Louvre is the famous Paris art museum which contains many medieval and Renaissance masterpieces portraying the Virgin and Child (as Leonardo da Vinci's "Virgin of the Rocks"); Chartres Cathedral of Our Lady is renowned for its medieval stained glass windows, many of the most prominent portraying Virgin and Child.
[25]Herbert Spencer (1820–1903), English philosopher and social scientist famous for adapting the Darwinian theory of evolution to the social and philosophical spheres.

classic had always done; but he could think only of Walt Whitman;[26] Bret Harte,[27] as far as the magazines would let him venture; and one or two painters, for the flesh-tones. All the rest had used sex for sentiment, never for force; to them, Eve was a tender flower, and Herodias[28] an unfeminine horror. American art, like the American language and American education, was as far as possible sexless. Society regarded this victory over sex as its greatest triumph, and the historian readily admitted it, since the moral issue, for the moment, did not concern one who was studying the relations of unmoral force. He cared nothing for the sex of the dynamo until he could measure its energy.

Vaguely seeking a clue, he wandered through the art exhibit, and, in his stroll, stopped almost every day before St. Gaudens's General Sherman,[29] which had been given the central post of honor. St. Gaudens himself was in Paris, putting on the work his usual interminable last touches, and listening to the usual contradictory suggestions of brother sculptors. Of all the American artists who gave to American art whatever life it breathed in the seventies, St. Gaudens was perhaps the most sympathetic, but certainly the most inarticulate. General Grant or Don Cameron[30] had scarcely less instinct of rhetoric than he. All the others — the Hunts, Richardson, John La Farge, Stanford White[31] — were exuberant; only St. Gaudens could never discuss or dilate on an emotion, or suggest artistic arguments for giving to his work the forms that he felt. He never laid down the law, or affected the despot, or became brutalized like Whistler[32] by the brutalities of his world. He required no incense; he was no egoist; his simplicity of thought was excessive; he could not imitate, or give any form but his own to the creations of his hand. No one felt more strongly than he the strength of other men, but the idea that they could affect him never stirred an image in his mind.

This summer his health was poor and his spirits were low. For such a temper, Adams was not the best companion, since his own gaiety was not *folle;*[33] but he risked going now and then to the studio on Mont Parnasse to draw him out for a stroll in the Bois de Boulogne,[34] or dinner as pleased his moods, and in return St. Gaudens sometimes let Adams go about in his company.

Once St. Gaudens took him down to Amiens, with a party of Frenchmen, to see the cathedral.[35] Not until they found themselves actually studying the sculpture of the western portal, did it dawn on Adams's mind that, for his purposes, St. Gaudens on that spot had more interest to him than the cathedral itself. Great men before great monuments express great truths, provided they are not taken too solemnly. Adams never tired of quoting the supreme phrase of his idol Gibbon,[36] before the Gothic cathedrals: "I darted a contemptuous look on the stately monuments of superstition." Even in the footnotes of his history, Gibbon had never inserted a bit of humor more human than this, and one would have paid largely for a photograph of the fat little historian, on the background of Notre Dame of Amiens, trying to persuade his readers — perhaps himself — that he was darting a contemptuous look on the stately monument, for which he felt in fact the respect which every man of his vast

[26]Walt Whitman (1819–1892), American poet noted for his use of sexual imagery and his celebration of sexuality in *Leaves of Grass* (1855–92).

[27]Bret Harte (1836–1902), American writer whose stories (see "The Outcasts of Poker Flat") sometimes presented gamblers and prostitutes in a sympathetic light.

[28]Herodias (*c.* 14 B.C.–A.D. 40) who with her daughter Salome tricked her husband, King Herod of Judea, into beheading John the Baptist.

[29]The equestrian statue of Civil War Union General Sherman by Augustus Saint-Gaudens (1848–1907), Irish-born American sculptor; the statue is now in New York.

[30]General Ulysses S. Grant (1822–1885), the principal Union Civil War general and, later, president (1868–76); J. D. Cameron (1833–1918), served as U.S. secretary of war and as U.S. Senator from Pennsylvania.

[31]William Morris Hunt (1824–1879), painter, and Richard

Morris Hunt (1827–1895), architect; Henry H. Richardson (1838–1886), architect; John La Farge (1835–1910), painter-sculptor; Stanford White (1853–1906), architect.

[32]James McNeill Whistler (1834–1903), American expatriate artist and caustic wit, won a libel suit defending his art and published his attacks on critics in *The Gentle Art of Making Enemies* (1890).

[33]"Mad, foolish" (French).

[34]Montparnasse, an area on the Left Bank in Paris, was a gathering place for artists and intellectuals; Bois de Boulogne is a large park in a fashionable area of Paris.

[35]The Cathedral of Our Lady in Amiens, a city north of Paris, is considered to be the masterpiece of Gothic architecture.

[36]Edward Gibbon (1737–1794), English historian, author of *The Decline and Fall of the Roman Empire* (1776–88); Adams paraphrases the entry for February 21, 1763, in Gibbon's *French Journal.*

study and active mind always feels before objects worthy of it; but besides the humor, one felt also the relation. Gibbon ignored the Virgin, because in 1789 religious monuments were out of fashion. In 1900 his remark sounded fresh and simple as the green fields to ears that had heard a hundred years of other remarks, mostly no more fresh and certainly less simple. Without malice, one might find it more instructive than a whole lecture of Ruskin.[37] One sees what one brings, and at that moment Gibbon brought the French Revolution. Ruskin brought reaction against the Revolution. St. Gaudens had passed beyond all. He liked the stately monuments much more than he liked Gibbon or Ruskin; he loved their dignity; their unity; their scale; their lines; their lights and shadows; their decorative sculpture; but he was even less conscious than they of the force that created it all—the Virgin, the Woman—by whose genius "the stately monuments of superstition" were built, through which she was expressed. He would have seen more meaning in Isis[38] with the cow's horns, at Edfoo, who expressed the same thought. The art remained, but the energy was lost even upon the artist.

Yet in mind and person St. Gaudens was a survival of the 1500's; he bore the stamp of the Renaissance, and should have carried an image of the Virgin round his neck, or stuck in his hat, like Louis XI.[39] In mere time he was a lost soul that had strayed by chance into the twentieth century, and forgotten where it came from. He writhed and cursed at his ignorance, much as Adams did at his own, but in the opposite sense. St. Gaudens was a child of Benvenuto Cellini,[40] smothered in an American cradle. Adams was a quintessence of Boston, devoured by curiosity to think like Benvenuto. St. Gaudens's art was starved from birth, and Adams's instinct was blighted from babyhood. Each had but half of a nature, and when they came together before the Virgin of Amiens they ought both to have felt in her the force that made them one; but it was not so. To Adams she became more than ever a channel of force; to St. Gaudens she remained as before a channel of taste.

For a symbol of power, St. Gaudens instinctively preferred the horse, as was plain in his horse and Victory of the Sherman monument. Doubtless Sherman also felt it so. The attitude was so American that, for at least forty years, Adams had never realized that any other could be in sound taste. How many years had he taken to admit a notion of what Michael Angelo and Rubens[41] were driving at? He could not say; but he knew that only since 1895 had he begun to feel the Virgin or Venus as force, and not everywhere even so. At Chartres—perhaps at Lourdes—possibly at Cnidos if one could still find there the divinely naked Aphrodite of Praxiteles[42]—but otherwise one must look for force to the goddesses of Indian mythology. The idea died out long ago in the German and English stock. St. Gaudens at Amiens was hardly less sensitive to the force of the female energy than Matthew Arnold at the Grande Chartreuse.[43] Neither of them felt goddesses as power—only as reflected emotion, human expression, beauty, purity, taste, scarcely even as sympathy. They felt a railway train as power; yet they, and all other artists, constantly complained that the power embodied in a railway train could never be embodied in art. All the steam in the world could not, like the Virgin, build Chartres.

Yet in mechanics, whatever the mechanicians might think, both energies acted as interchangeable forces on man, and by action on man all known force may be measured. Indeed, few men of science measured force in any other way. After once

---

[37]John Ruskin (1819–1900), English critic of art and architecture, author of *The Stones of Venice* (1851–53) and *The Bible of Amiens* (1880–85), among others.

[38]Isis was an Egyptian goddess of fertility, usually depicted with cow's horns; Adams had seen her statue at Edfu in Egypt.

[39]Louis XI (1423–1483), a pious king of France.

[40]Benvenuto Cellini (1500–1571), Italian goldsmith, sculptor, and author of a celebrated *Autobiography*.

[41]Michelangelo (1475–1564), Italian sculptor and painter, created powerful nude statues, such as his famous David;

Peter Paul Rubens (1577–1640), Flemish painter noted for his voluptuous female nudes.

[42]Praxiteles (fourth century B.C.), Athenian sculptor famed for his statues of Greek gods and goddesses, including his Aphrodite at Cnidus in Greece, lost in antiquity but known through copies.

[43]Matthew Arnold (1822–1888), English poet and cultural critic, in "Stanzas from the Grande Chartreuse" (1855), grieves over the loss of faith that inspires the chant of the monks heard by him at a Carthusian monastery near Grenoble, France.

admitting that a straight line was the shortest distance between two points, no serious mathematician cared to deny anything that suited his convenience, and rejected no symbol, unproved or unproveable, that helped him to accomplish work. The symbol was force, as a compass-needle or a triangle was force, as the mechanist might prove by losing it, and nothing could be gained by ignoring their value. Symbol or energy, the Virgin had acted as the greatest force the Western world ever felt, and had drawn man's activities to herself more strongly than any other power, natural or supernatural, had ever done; the historian's business was to follow the track of the energy; to find where it came from and where it went to; its complex source and shifting channels; its values, equivalents, conversions. It could scarcely be more complex than radium; it could hardly be deflected, diverted, polarized, absorbed more perplexingly than other radiant matter. Adams knew nothing about any of them, but as a mathematical problem of influence on human progress, though all were occult, all reacted on his mind, and he rather inclined to think the Virgin easiest to handle.

The pursuit turned out be be long and tortuous, leading at last into the vast forests of scholastic science. From Zeno to Descartes, hand in hand with Thomas Aquinas, Montaigne, and Pascal,[44] one stumbled as stupidly as though one were still a German student of 1860.[45] Only with the instinct of despair could one force one's self into this old thicket of ignorance after having been repulsed at a score of entrances more promising and more popular. Thus far, no path had led anywhere, unless perhaps to an exceedingly modest living. Forty-five years of study had proved to be quite futile for the pursuit of power; one controlled no more force in 1900 than in 1850, although the amount of force controlled by society had enormously increased. The secret of education still hid itself somewhere behind ignorance, and one fumbled over it as feebly as ever. In such labyrinths, the staff is a force almost more necessary than the legs; the pen becomes a sort of blind-man's dog, to keep him from falling into the gutters. The pen works for itself, and acts like a hand, modelling the plastic material over and over again to the form that suits it best. The form is never arbitrary, but is a sort of growth like crystallization, as any artist knows too well; for often the pencil or pen runs into side-paths and shapelessness, loses its relations, stops or is bogged. Then it has to return on its trail, and recover, if it can, its line of force. The result of a year's work depends more on what is struck out than on what is left in; on the sequence of the main lines of thought, than on their play or variety. Compelled once more to lean heavily on this support, Adams covered more thousands of pages with figures as formal as though they were algebra, laboriously striking out, altering, burning, experimenting, until the year had expired, the Exposition had long been closed, and winter drawing to its end, before he sailed from Cherbourg,[46] on January 19, 1901, for home.

1907, 1918

from A Letter to American Teachers of History[1]

[ENTROPY: THE UNIVERSE TOSSED INTO THE ASH-HEAP]

The mechanical theory of the universe governed physical science for three hundred years. Directly succeeding the theological scheme of a universe existing as a

---

[44]Zeno (fourth century B.C.), Greek founder of the philosophical school of stoicism; René Descartes (1596–1650), French mathematician and thinker who moved philosophy from scholastic quibbling to scientific and practical concerns; Saint Thomas Aquinas (*c.*1225–1274), Italian philosopher and theologian, author of *Summa Theologiae*; Michel Eyquem de Montaigne (1533–1592), French essayist and skeptic;

Blaise Pascal (1623–1662), French mathematician and philosopher, author of *Pensées*, often mystical in nature.
[45]Adams studied in Germany between 1858 and 1860.
[46]Seaport on the northern coast of France.
[1]Privately printed in 1910, and reprinted in *The Degradation of the Democratic Dogma* (1919).

unity by the will of an infinite and eternal Creator, it affirmed or assumed the unity and indestructibility of Force or Energy, as a scientific dogma or Law, which was called the Law of the Conservation of Energy. Under this Law the quantity of matter in the universe remained invariable; the sum of movement remained constant; energy was indestructible; "nothing was added; nothing was lost;" nothing was created, nothing was destroyed.

Towards the middle of the nineteenth century,—that is, about 1850,—a new school of physicists appeared in Europe, dating from an "Essay on the Motive Power of Heat," published by Sadi Carnot[2] in 1824, and made famous by the names of William Thomson, Lord Kelvin, in England, and of Clausius and Helmholz in Germany,[3] who announced a second law of dynamics. The first law said that Energy was never lost; the second said that it was never saved; that, while the sum of energy in the universe might remain constant,—granting that the universe was a closed box from which nothing could escape,—the higher powers of energy tended always to fall lower, and that this process had no known limit.

The second law was briefly stated by Thomson in a paper "On a Universal Tendency in Nature to the Dissipation of Mechanical Energy," published in October, 1852, which is now as classic as Kepler's or Newton's Laws,[4] and quite as necessary to a scientific education. Quoted exactly from Thomson's "Mathematical and Physical Papers" (Cambridge, 1882, Vol. I, p. 514), the Law of Dissipation runs thus:—

1. There is at present in the material world a universal tendency to the dissipation of mechanical energy.
2. Any restoration of mechanical energy, without more than an equivalent of dissipation, is impossible in inanimate material processes, and is probably never effected by means of organized matter, either endowed with vegetable life or subjected to the will of an animated creature.
3. Within a finite period of time past, the earth must have been, and within a finite period of time to come, the earth must again be unfit for the habitation of man as at present constituted, unless operations have been, or are to be performed, which are impossible under the laws to which the known operations going on at present in the material world, are subject.

When this young man of twenty-eight thus tossed the universe into the ash-heap, few scientific authorities took him seriously; but after the first gasp of surprise physicists began to give him qualified support which soon became absolute. . . . To physicists, this law of Entropy became "a prodigiously abstract conception" . . . ; but to the vulgar and ignorant historian it meant only that the ash-heap was constantly increasing in size; while the public understood little and cared less about Entropy, and the literary class knew only that the Newtonian universe, in which they had been cradled, admitted no loss of energy in the solar system, where the planets, at the end of their planetary years, returned exactly to their positions at the beginning. Gravitation showed no waste of energy whatever, except where friction occurred, but had planets gone off like comets, and never returned, the scholar of 1860 would still have feared to question the scientific dogma which asserted resolutely, without qualification, the fact that nothing in nature was lost. . . .

No one knew anything; and yet the analogy between Heat and Vital Energy, suggested by Thomson in his Law of Dissipation,—and received by the public with sleepy indifference,—was insisted upon by the physicists in accents that became sharper with every generation, until it began to pass the bounds of scientific restraint.

[2]Nicolas-Léonard-Sadi Carnot (1796–1832), French physicist who in his essay put forward the theory that was in substance the second law of thermodynamics.
[3]William Thomson, Lord Kelvin (1824–1907), British physicist and mathematician; Rudolph Julius Emanuel Clausius (1822–1888), German mathematical physicist; Herman Ludwig Ferdinand von Helmholz (1821–1894), German physicist and professor of physiology.
[4]Johannes Kepler (1571–1630), German astronomer who discovered laws of planetary motion; Sir Isaac Newton (1642–1727), English physicist and mathematician who discovered that Kepler's laws could all be derived from the one law of gravitation.

Already in 1884, Faye,[5] in his *Origins of the World*, fairly threatened mankind with its doom:

> We must renounce those brilliant fancies by which we try to deceive our-selves in order to endow man with unlimited posterity, and to regard the uni-verse as the immense theatre on which is to be developed a spontaneous prog-ress without end. On the contrary, life must disappear, and the grandest material works of the human race will have to be effaced by degrees under the action of a few physical forces which will survive man for a time. Nothing will remain. . . .

Thus, it seemed, that whatever the universities thought or taught, the physicists regarded society as an organism in the only respect which seriously concerned historians: — It would die! If life was to disappear, the form of Vital Energy known as Social Energy, must also, presumably, go to increase the Entropy of the Universe, thus proving — at least to the degree necessary and sufficient to produce conviction in historians, — that History was a Science. . . .

Thomson's famous paper on "A Universal Tendency in Nature to the Dissipation of Energy" was published in 1852. Seven years afterwards, Charles Darwin[6] an-nounced his law of Evolution, which involved a contradiction . . . to both the laws of thermodynamics. Thomson, physicist and mathematician, had thought only of pro-viding the energy necessary to move his world; Darwin, neither physicist nor mathe-matician, took the necessary energy as given. Possibly, if he thought about it at all, he assumed the Law of Conservation as the mechanical equivalent of Lyell's[7] Law of Uniformity; but he seemed scrupulously careful to avoid asserting either principle. On his own account he never committed himself to the doctrine that, within the geological record, organization had largely advanced, or risen to higher powers, but he did assert, and permitted his followers to assert much more broadly that "the inhabitants of the world, at each successive period in its history, have beaten their predecessors in the race for life, and are, in so far, hgher in the scale"; meaning probably that they were better fitted to their conditions, but conveying the idea that their vital powers had risen from lower to higher by the spontaneous struggle of the organism for life. This popular understanding of Darwin had little to do with Dar-win, whose great service, — in the field of history, — consisted by no mean in his per-sonal theories either of natural selection, or of adaptation, or of uniform evolution; which might be all abandoned without affecting his credit for bringing all vital pro-cesses under the law of development or evolution, — whether upward or downward being immaterial to the principle that all history must be studied as a science. . . .

Thus, at the same moment, three contradictory laws of energy were in force, all equally useful to science: — 1. The Law of Conservation, that nothing could be ad-ded, and nothing lost, in the sum of energy. 2. The Law of Dissipation, that nothing could be added, but that Intensity must be lost. 3. The Law of Evolution, that Vital Energy could be added, and raised indefinitely in potential, without the smallest apparent compensaton. . . .

This teaching is explicit. Animal energies accent and emphasize the law of physics that nature, always and everywhere, tends to an equilibrium by levelling its inten-sities. Mechanical energies admit apparent exceptions, like gravitation, but animal energies admit none. All grow old and die. This is the teaching of physics, and al-though most physicists show caution in defining exactly what they mean by vital en-ergy, the law, as they announce it, is relentless. For human purposes, whatever does work is a form of energy, and since historians exist only to recount and sum up the work that society has done, either as State, or as Church, as civil or as military, as

---

[5] Hervé-Auguste-Étienne-Albans Faye (1814–1902), French astronomer.
[6] Charles Darwin (1809–1882), whose *On the Origin of Species by Means of Natural Selection*, containing his theory of evolu-tion, appeared in 1859.
[7] Sir Charles Lyell (1797–1875), British geologist whose the-ory of uniformitarianism was set forth in his *Principles of Geol-ogy* (1830–1833).

intellectual or physical, organisms, they will, if they obey the physical law, hold that society does work by degrading its energies. On the other hand, if the historian follows Haeckel[8] and the evolutionists, he should hold that vital energy, by raising itself to higher potentials, without apparent compensation, has accomplished its work in defiance of both the laws of thermodynamics.

Down to the end of the nineteenth century nothing greatly mattered, since the actual forces could be fairly well calculated or accounted for on either principle, but schools of applied mechanics are apt to get into trouble by using contradictory methods. One process or the other acquires an advantage. The weaker submits, but in this instance, the difficulty of naming the weaker was extreme. That the Evolutionist should surrender his conquests seemed quite unlikely, since he felt behind him the whole momentum of popular success and sympathy, and stood as heir-apparent to all the aspirations of mankind. About him were arranged in battalions, like an army, the energies of government, of society, of democracy, of socialism, of nearly all literature and art, as well as hope, and whatever was left of instinct, — all striving to illustrate not the Descent but the Ascent of Man. The *hostis humani generis,*[9] the outlaw and enemy, was the Degradationist,[10] who could have no friends, because he proclaimed the steady and fated enfeeblement and extinction of all nature's energies; but that he should abandon his laws seemed a still more preposterous idea. Never had he asserted them so aggressively, or with such dogmatic authority. He held undisputed possession of every technical school in the world, and even the primary schools were largely under his control. His second law of thermodynamics held its place in every text-book of science. The Universities and higher branches of education were greatly, if not wholly, controlled by his methods. The field of mathematics had become his. He had no serious intellectual rival. Few things are more difficult than to judge how far a society is looking one way and working in another, for the points are shifting and the rate of speed is uncertain. The acceleration of movement seems rapid, but the inertia, or resistance to deflection, may increase with the rapidity, so that society might pass through phase after phase of speed, like a comet, without noting deflection in its thought. If a simpler figure is needed, society may be likened to an island surrounded by a rising ocean which silently floods its defences. One after another the defences have been abandoned, and society has climbed to higher ground supposed to be out of danger. So the classic Gods were abandoned for monotheism, and the scholastic philosophy[11] was dropped in favor of the Newtonian; but the classic Gods and the scholastic philosophy were always popular, and the newer philosophies won their victories by developing compulsory force. Inertia is the law of mind as well as of matter, and inertia is a form of instinct; yet in western civilization it has never held its own.

The pessimism or unpopularity of the law will not prevent its enforcement, if it develops superior force, even if it leads where no one wants to go. The proof is that the law is already enforced in every field excepting that of human history, and even human history has not wholly escaped. In physics it rules with uncontested sway. In physiology, the old army of Evolutionists have suffered defections so serious that no discipline remains. A full account of the situation would need an amount of knowledge that is now granted to no one; but the most trifling popular science is enough for popular teachers like ourselves. . . .

If one, and by far the most extensive period of terrestrial history, is already taught in this sense by physicists [i.e., following the law of entropy and thus projecting the

---

[8]Ernest Heinrich Philipp August Haeckel (1834–1919), German biologist and philosopher who was the first German to espouse Darwin's theory of evolution; he formulated the idea that "ontogony recapitulates phylogeny"—the development of the individual organism repeats or reflects the development of the group.

[9]"Enemies of the human race" (Latin).
[10]One who believes in the principle that during any irreversible process the total energy available to do work decreases (as in the second law of thermodynamics).
[11]I.e., the religious philosophy of the medieval theologians.

extinction of the sun along with the death of life on earth], all biology, including human history, will have also to be re-edited by them according to this lugubrious plan; and the University professor of history as it has been hitherto understood, will soon have urgent need to make up his mind whether to accept or resist it. If he decides to accept it, he has only to hold his tongue, and remain quietly in the pleasant meadows of antiquarianism, protected as heretofore by the convenient and sufficient axiom of the nineteenth century that history is not a science, and society not an organism; but if this resource should fail him, his first thought will be to find allies. He will seek them among his Darwinist friends, to begin with; but he will scarcely finish the opening chapter of the last book on Transformation, Mutation, Inheritance, or whatever new name may, as one writer expresses it, dissimulate creative or destructive force under the term Evolution, without discovering that the familiar, genial dispute over the origin of species has turned into a sinister and almost lurid battle over the extinction of species, for which the Darwinian theories of survival are declared inadequate to the point of childishness. . . .

• • • • • •

. . . As long as the theory of Degradation, — as of Evolution, — was only one of the convenient tools of science, the sociologist had no just cause for complaint. Every science, — and mathematics first of all, — uses what tools it likes. The Professor of Physics is not teaching Ethics; he is training young men to handle concrete energy in one or more of its many forms, and he has no choice but to use the most convenient formulas. Unfortunately the formula most convenient for him is not at all convenient for his colleagues in sociology and history, without pressing the inquiry further, into more intimate branches of practice like medicine, jurisprudence, and politics. If the entire universe, in every variety of active energy, organic and inorganic, human or divine, is to be treated as clockwork that is running down, society can hardly go on ignoring the fact forever. Hitherto it has often happened that two systems of education, like the Scholastic and Baconian,[12] could exist side by side for centuries, — as they exist still, — in adjoining schools and universities, by no more scientific device than that of shutting their eyes to each other; but the universe has been terribly narrowed by thermodynamics. Already History and Sociology gasp for breath.

1910, 1919

WILLIAM JAMES
(1842–1910)

Long after he had become a noted psychologist, with pioneering scholarship to his credit, William James looked back at his beginnings and remarked: "I originally studied medicine in order to be a physiologist, but I drifted into psychology and philosophy from a sort of fatality. I never had any philosophic instruction, the first lecture on psychology I ever heard being the first I ever gave."

This remark outlines James's early life. The son of the Swedenborgian mystic Henry James, Sr., the oldest of five children that included novelist Henry and diarist Alice, William James was well into his thirties before he was embarked on his life's profession. After first studying art, James started medical school at

[12]Reference to the scientific philosophy of Francis Bacon (1561–1626), whose *Advancement of Learning* appeared in 1605; he emphasized inductive knowledge (derived from observation or experimentation) as opposed to deductive knowledge (derived from abstract generalizations).

Harvard in 1865. He interrupted his medical training to accompany the renowned naturalist Louis Agassiz on an expedition to Brazil. He returned home in ill health, but recovered sufficiently to go to Germany in 1867 to study physiology. Finally, in 1869, he took his medical degree at Harvard.

But he was unable to begin practice because of recurring illness, compounded by physical and spiritual debility. In his crisis he turned, according to his own testimony, to reading the French philosopher Charles Bernard Renouvier on free will, and worked his way out of his dark depression by deciding: "My first act of free will shall be to believe in free will." The episode was a turning point in his life.

In 1872, James was appointed instructor of physiology at Harvard. Gradually his interest turned to physiological psychology and philosophy. He established a ground-breaking laboratory in psychology at Harvard in 1876. And in 1879, he introduced a course in "The Philsophy of Evolution." By this time he had moved to the department of philosophy.

In 1890, James published a massive, two-volume work in his field, *The Principles of Psychology*, which quickly established itself as a basic text—and remains today of extraordinary interest. In this work, James provided the psychological rationale for the modernist focus in fiction on interior mental processes. In a chapter entitled "The Stream of Thought," he wrote: "[Consciousness] is nothing jointed; it flows. A 'river' or a 'stream' are the metaphors by which it is most naturally described. In talking of it hereafter, let us call it the stream of thought, of consciousness, or of subjective life." Out of the possibilities offered by James, later literary critics chose the term *stream of consciousness*.

On finishing *The Principles of Psychology*, James turned to philosophic and religious interests. In *The Will to Believe* (1897), he defended the position of those who accepted metaphysical concepts that could not be scientifically proven. And in *The Varieties of Religious Experience* (1902), he explored the nature and meaning of mystical experiences. In the same year that he retired from Harvard, he published *Pragmatism: A New Name for Old Ways of Thinking* (1907), setting forth the philosophical position that ideas, concepts, or propositions in conflict should be judged by their practical consequences; if such consequences are the same, dispute is pointless.

In James's last years, he was recognized as America's leading philosopher. He was a prolific writer, publishing *The Meaning of Truth* and *A Pluralistic Universe* in 1909. Several posthumous works appeared after his death in 1910, including *Some Problems in Philosophy* in 1911, *Memories and Studies* (edited by his brother Henry) in 1911, and *Essays in Radical Empiricism* in 1912.

It is hard to characterize James because his restless intellect and imagination roamed over a great many fields. But in a prefatory comment written in 1899 on one of his most important essays, "On a Certain Blindness in Human Beings," James said that the work embodied a "definite view of the world and of our moral relations to the same" which he labelled "the pluralistic or individualistic philosophy," and which was basic to all his thought. According to this view, "the truth is too great for any one actual mind . . . to know the whole of it. . . . The practical consequence of such a philosophy is the well-known democratic respect for the sacredness of individuality." James found this philosophy reflected in many poets and novelists, principal among them his fellow American and bardic poet Walt Whitman. In his wide-ranging curiosity and eclecticism, James calls to mind Ralph Waldo Emerson's ideal described in "The American Scholar": in the "distribution of functions the scholar is the delegated intellect. In the right state he is *Man Thinking*."

ADDITIONAL READING

The Letters of William James, 2 vols., ed. Henry James [his son], 1920; *The Writings of William James: A Comprehensive Edition*, ed. John J. McDermott, 1967; *The Works of William James*, ed. Frederick H. Burkhardt et al., 1975–.

Josiah Royce, *William James and Other Essays on the Philosophy of Life*, 1911; Julius Bixler, *Religion in the Philosophy of William James*, 1924; Ralph Barton Perry, *The Thought and Character of William James*, 2 vols., 1935, and *In the Spirit of William James*, 1938; F. O. Matthiessen, *The James Family*, 1947; Gay Wilson Allen, *William James: A Biography*, 1967; Bernard P. Brennan, *William James*, 1968; Richard A. Hocks, *Henry James and Pragmatic Thought: A Study in the Relationship Between the Philosophy of William James and the Literary Craft of Henry James*, 1974; Jacque Barzun, *A Stroll with William James*, 1983; Gerald E. Meyers, *William James: His Life and Thought*, 1986; Graham Bird, *William James: The Arguments of the Philosophers*, 1987.

TEXTS

Talks to Teachers in Psychology and to Students on Some of Life's Ideals, 1899; *Pragmatism: A New Name for Old Ways of Thinking*, 1907.

from On a Certain Blindness in Human Beings

When "On a Certain Blindness in Human Beings" appeared in *Talks to Teachers in Psychology and to Students on Some of Life's Ideals* in 1899, James, in the Preface, singled out the essay as one he considered central to his philosophy and one of his most important:

> I wish I were able to make . . . "On a Certain Blindness in Human Beings" more impressive. It is more than the mere piece of sentimentalism which it may seem to some readers. It connects itself with a definite view of the world and of our moral relations to the same. Those who have done me the honor of reading my volume of philosophic essays will recognize that I mean the pluralistic or individualistic philosophy. According to that philosophy, the truth is too great for any one actual mind, even though that mind be dubbed 'the Absolute,' to know the whole of it. The facts and worths of life need many cognizers to take them in. There is no point of view absolutely public and universal. Private and uncommunicable perceptions always remain over, and the worst of it is that those who look for them from the outside never know *where*.
>
> The practical consequence of such a philosophy is the well-known democratic respect for the sacredness of individuality, — is, at any rate, the outward tolerance of whatever is not itself intolerant. These phrases are so familiar that they sound now rather dead in our ears. Once they had a passionate inner meaning. Such a passionate inner meaning they may easily acquire again if the pretension of our nation to inflict its own inner ideals and institutions *vi et armis*[1] upon Orientals should meet with a resistance as obdurate as so far it has been gallant and spirited. Religiously and philosophically, our ancient national doctrine of live and let live may prove to have a far deeper meaning than our people now seem to imagine it to possess.

---

[1]"By force of arms" (Latin). James is referring to the Span-ish-American War (1898) and U.S. imperialism in conquering the Philippines.

[PRIVATE AND UNCOMMUNICABLE PERCEPTIONS]

Our judgments concerning the worth of things, big or little, depend on the *feelings* the things arouse in us. Where we judge a thing to be precious in consequence of the *idea* we frame of it, this is only because the idea is itself associated already with a feeling. If we were radically feelingless, and if ideas were the only things our mind could entertain, we should lose all our likes and dislikes at a stroke, and be unable to point to any one situation or experience in life more valuable or significant than any other.

Now the blindness in human beings, of which this discourse will treat, is the blindness with which we all are afflicted in regard to the feelings of creatures and people different from ourselves.

We are practical beings, each of us with limited functions and duties to perform. Each is bound to feel intensely the importance of his own duties and the significance of the situations that call these forth. But this feeling is in each of us a vital secret, for sympathy with which we vainly look to others. The others are too much absorbed in their own vital secrets to take an interest in ours. Hence the stupidity and injustice of our opinions, so far as they deal with the significance of alien lives. Hence the falsity of our judgments, so far as they presume to decide in an absolute way on the value of other persons' conditions or ideals.

Take our dogs and ourselves, connected as we are by a tie more intimate than most ties in this world; and yet, outside of that tie of friendly fondness, how insensible, each of us, to all that makes life significant for the other! — we to the rapture of bones under hedges, or smells of trees and lamp-posts, they to the delights of literature and art. As you sit reading the most moving romance you ever fell upon, what sort of a judge is your fox-terrier of your behavior? With all his good will toward you, the nature of your conduct is absolutely excluded from his comprehension. To sit there like a senseless statue, when you might be taking him to walk and throwing sticks for him to catch! What queer disease is this that comes over you every day, of holding things and staring at them like that for hours together, paralyzed of motion and vacant of all conscious life? The African savages came nearer the truth; but they, too, missed it, when they gathered wonderingly round one of our American travellers who, in the interior, had just come into possession of a stray copy of the New York *Commercial Advertiser*, and was devouring it column by column. When he got through, they offered him a high price for the mysterious object; and, being asked for what they wanted it, they said: "For an eye medicine," — that being the only reason they could conceive of for the protracted bath which he had given his eyes upon its surface.

The spectator's judgment is sure to miss the root of the matter, and to possess no truth. The subject judged knows a part of the world of reality which the judging spectator fails to see, knows more while the spectator knows less; and, wherever there is conflict of opinion and difference of vision, we are bound to believe that the truer side is the side that feels the more, and not the side that feels the less.

Let me take a personal example of the kind that befalls each one of us daily: —

Some years ago, while journeying in the mountains of North Carolina, I passed by a large number of 'coves,' as they call them there, or heads of small valleys between the hills, which had been newly cleared and planted. The impression on my mind was one of unmitigated squalor. The settler had in every case cut down the more manageable trees, and left their charred stumps standing. The larger trees he had girdled and killed, in order that their foliage should not cast a shade. He had then built a log cabin, plastering its chinks with clay, and had set up a tall zigzag rail fence around the scene of his havoc, to keep the pigs and cattle out. Finally, he had irregularly planted the intervals between the stumps and trees with Indian corn, which grew among the chips; and there he dwelt with his wife and babes — an axe, a gun, a few utensils, and some pigs and chickens feeding in the woods, being the sum total of his possessions.

The forest had been destroyed; and what had 'improved' it out of existence was hideous, a sort of ulcer, without a single element of artificial grace to make up for the loss of Nature's beauty. Ugly, indeed, seemed the life of the squatter, scudding, as the sailors say, under bare poles, beginning again away back where our first ancestors started, and by hardly a single item the better off for all the achievements of the intervening generations.

Talk about going back to nature! I said to myself, oppressed by the dreariness, as I drove by. Talk of a country life for one's old age and for one's children! Never thus, with nothing but the bare ground and one's bare hands to fight the battle! Never, without the best spoils of culture woven in! The beauties and commodities gained by the centuries are sacred. They are our heritage and birthright. No modern person ought to be willing to live a day in such a state of rudimentariness and denudation.

Then I said to the mountaineer who was driving me, "What sort of people are they who have to make these new clearings?" "All of us," he replied. "Why, we ain't happy here, unless we are getting one of these coves under cultivation." I instantly felt that I had been losing the whole inward significance of the situation. Because to me the clearings spoke of naught but denudation, I thought that to those whose sturdy arms and obedient axes had made them they could tell no other story. But, when *they* looked on the hideous stumps, what they thought of was personal victory. The chips, the girdled trees, and the vile split rails spoke of honest sweat, persistent toil and final reward. The cabin was a warrant of safety for self and wife and babes. In short, the clearing, which to me was a mere ugly picture on the retina, was to them a symbol redolent with moral memories and sang a very pæan of duty, struggle, and success.

I had been as blind to the peculiar ideality of their conditions as they certainly would also have been to the ideality of mine, had they had a peep at my strange indoor academic ways of life at Cambridge. . . .

[James goes on to devote much space to long literary quotations illustrating the kind of blindness he found in himself and which he attributes to all of us. His examples are taken from such writers as Robert Louis Stevenson, Ralph Waldo Emerson, and William Wordsworth. His use of the example of Whitman follows.]

Walt Whitman, for instance, is accounted by many of us a contemporary prophet. He abolishes the usual human distinctions, brings all conventionalisms into solution, and loves and celebrates hardly any human attributes save those elementary ones common to all members of the race. For this he becomes a sort of ideal tramp, a rider on omnibus-tops and ferry-boats, and, considered either practically or academically, a worthless, unproductive being. His verses are but ejaculations — things mostly without subject or verb, a succession of interjections on an immense scale. He felt the human crowd as rapturously as Wordsworth felt the mountains, felt it as an overpoweringly significant presence, simply to absorb one's mind in which should be business sufficient and worthy to fill the days of a serious man. As he crosses Brooklyn ferry, this is what he feels: —

Flood-tide below me! I watch you, face to face;
Clouds of the west! sun there half an hour high! I see you also face to face.
Crowds of men and women attired in the usual costumes! how curious you are to
  me!
On the ferry-boats, the hundreds and hundreds that cross, returning home, are
  more curious to me than you suppose;
And you that shall cross from shore to shore years hence, are more to me, and
  more in my meditations, than you might suppose.
Others will enter the gates of the ferry, and cross from shore to shore;
Others will watch the run of the flood-tide;
Others will see the shipping of Manhattan north and west, and the heights of
  Brooklyn to the south and east;

Others will see the islands large and small;
Fifty years hence, others will see them as they cross, the sun half an hour high.
A hundred years hence, or ever so many hundred years hence, others will see
  them,
Will enjoy the sunset, the pouring in of the flood-tide, the falling back to the sea of
  the ebb-tide.
It avails not, neither time or place—distance avails not.
Just as you feel when you look on the river and sky, so I felt;
Just as any of you is one of a living crowd, I was one of a crowd;
Just as you are refresh'd by the gladness of the river and the bright flow, I was
  refresh'd;
Just as you stand and lean on the rail, yet hurry with the swift current, I stood, yet
  was hurried;
Just as you look on the numberless masts of ships, and the thick-stemmed pipes of
  steamboats, I looked.
I too many and many a time cross'd the river, the sun half an hour high;
I watched the Twelfth-month sea-gulls—I saw them high in the air, with
  motionless wings, oscillating their bodies,
I saw how the glistening yellow lit up parts of their bodies, and left the rest in
  strong shadow,
I saw the slow-wheeling circles, and the gradual edging toward the south.
Saw the white sails of schooners and sloops, saw the ships at anchor,
The sailors at work in the rigging, or out astride the spars;
The scallop-edged waves in the twilight, the ladled cups, the frolicsome crests and
  glistening;
The stretch afar growing dimmer and dimmer, the gray walls of the granite store-
  houses by the docks;
On the neighboring shores, the fires from the foundry chimneys burning high . . . .
  into the night,
Casting their flicker of black . . . . into the clefts of streets.
These, and all else, were to me the same as they are to you.[1]

And so on, through the rest of a divinely beautiful poem. And, if you wish to see
what this hoary loafer considered the most worthy way of profiting by life's heaven-
sent opportunities, read the delicious volume of his letters to a young car-conductor[2]
who had become his friend:—

NEW YORK, Oct. 9, 1868.

Dear Pete,—It is splendid here this forenoon—bright and cool. I was out
early taking a short walk by the river only two squares from where I live. . . .
Shall I tell you about [my life] just to fill up? I generally spend the forenoon in
my room writing, etc., then take a bath fix up and go out about twelve and loafe
somewhere or call on someone down town or on business, or perhaps if it is
very pleasant and I feel like it ride a trip with some driver friend on Broadway
from 23rd Street to Bowling Green, three miles each way. (Every day I find I
have plenty to do, every hour is occupied with something.) You know it is a
never ending amusement and study and recreation for me to ride a couple of
hours on a pleasant afternoon on a Broadway stage[3] in this way. You see everything as you pass, a sort of living, endless panorama—shops and splendid
buildings and great windows: on the broad sidewalks crowds of women richly
dressed continually passing, altogether different, superior in style and looks
from any to be seen anywhere else—in fact a perfect stream of people—men
too dressed in high style, and plenty of foreigners—and then in the streets the

---

[1]An abridged and sometimes altered version of the first 49
lines of Walt Whitman's "Crossing Brooklyn Ferry" (see
Whitman selections).

[2]Horse-car conductor; i.e., streetcar or omnibus.
[3]Stagecoach, horse-drawn.

thick crowd of carriages, stages, carts, hotel and private coaches, and in fact all sorts of vehicles and many first class teams, mile after mile, and the splendor of such a great street and so many tall, ornamental, noble buildings many of them of white marble, and the gayety and motion on every side: you will not wonder how much attraction all this is on a fine day, to a great loafer like me, who enjoys so much seeing the busy world move by him, and exhibiting itself for his amusement, while he takes it easy and just looks on and observes.[4]

Truly a futile way of passing the time, some of you may say, and not altogether creditable to a grown-up man. And yet, from the deepest point of view, who knows the more of truth, and who knows the less, — Whitman on his omnibus-top, full of the inner joy with which the spectacle inspires him, or you, full of the disdain which the futility of his occupation excites?

When your ordinary Brooklynite or New Yorker, leading a life replete with too much luxury, or tired and careworn about his personal affairs, crosses the ferry or goes up Broadway, *his* fancy does not thus "soar away into the colors of the sunset" as did Whitman's, nor does he inwardly realize at all the indisputable fact that this world never did anywhere or at any time contain more of essential divinity, or of eternal meaning, than is embodied in the fields of vision over which his eyes so carelessly pass. There is life; and there, a step away, is death. There is the only kind of beauty there ever was. There is the old human struggle and its fruits together. There is the text and the sermon, the real and the ideal in one. . . .

· · · · · ·

And now what is the result of all these considerations and quotations? It is negative in one sense, but positive in another. It absolutely forbids us to be forward in pronouncing on the meaninglessness of forms of existence other than our own; and it commands us to tolerate, respect, and indulge those whom we see harmlessly interested and happy in their own ways, however unintelligible these may be to us. Hands off: neither the whole of truth nor the whole of good is revealed to any single observer, although each observer gains a partial superiority of insight from the peculiar position in which he stands. Even prisons and sick-rooms have their special revelations. It is enough to ask of each of us that he should be faithful to his own opportunities and make the most of his own blessings, without presuming to regulate the rest of the vast field.

1899

from Pragmatism

["The Pragmatic Method"][1]

Some years ago, being with a camping party in the mountains, I returned from a solitary ramble to find every one engaged in a ferocious metaphysical dispute, the *corpus*[2] of the dispute was a squirrel—a live squirrel supposed to be clinging to one side of a tree-trunk; while over against the tree's opposite side a human being was imagined to stand. This human witness tries to get sight of the squirrel by moving rapidly round the tree, but no matter how fast he goes, the squirrel moves as fast in the opposite direction, and always keeps the tree between himself and the man, so

---

[4]From *Calamus, A Series of Letters Written during the Years 1868–1880, By Walt Whitman to a Young Friend (Peter Doyle)*, ed. Richard Maurice Bucke (1897, pp. 41, 42).

[1]From "What Pragmatism Means" (Lecture Two).
[2]"Substance" (Latin).

that never a glimpse of him is caught. The resultant metaphysical problem now is this: *Does the man go round the squirrel or not*? He goes round the tree, sure enough, and the squirrel is on the tree; but does he go round the squirrel? In the unlimited leisure of the wilderness, discussion had been worn threadbare. Everyone had taken sides, and was obstinate; and the numbers on both sides were even. Each side, when I appeared therefore appealed to me to make it a majority. Mindful of the scholastic adage that whenever you meet a contradiction you must make a distinction, I immediately sought and found one, as follows: "Which part is right," I said, "depends on what you *practically mean* by 'going round' the squirrel. If you mean passing from the north of him to the east, then to the south, then to the west, and then to the north of him again, obviously the man does go round him, for he occupies these successive positions. But if on the contrary you mean being first in front of him, then on the right of him, then behind him, then on his left, and finally in front again, it is quite as obvious that the man fails to go round him, for by the compensating movements the squirrel makes, he keeps his belly turned towards the man all the time, and his back turned away. Make the distinction, and there is no occasion for any farther dispute. You are both right and both wrong according as you conceive the verb 'to go round' in one practical fashion or the other."

Although one or two of the hotter disputants called my speech a shuffling evasion, saying they wanted no quibbling or scholastic hair-splitting, but meant just plain honest English "round," the majority seemed to think that the distinction had assuaged the dispute.

I tell this trivial anecdote because it is a peculiarly simple example of what I wish now to speak of as *the pragmatic method*. The pragmatic method is primarily a method of settling metaphysical disputes that otherwise might be interminable. Is the world one or many?—fated or free?—material or spiritual?—here are notions either of which may or may not hold good of the world; and disputes over such notions are unending. The pragmatic method in such cases is to try to interpret each notion by tracing its respective practical consequences. What difference would it practically make to any one if this notion rather than that notion were true? If no practical difference whatever can be traced, then the alternatives mean practically the same thing, and all dispute is idle. Whenever a dispute is serious, we ought to be able to show some practical difference that must follow from one side or the other's being right. . . .

Metaphysics has usually followed a very primitive kind of quest. You know how men have always hankered after unlawful magic, and you know what a great part in magic *words* have always played. If you have his name, or the formula of incantation that binds him, you can control the spirit, genie, afrite,[3] or whatever the power may be. Solomon[4] knew the names of all the spirits, and having their names, he held them subject to his will. So the universe has always appeared to the natural mind as a kind of enigma, of which the key must be sought in the shape of some illuminating or power-bringing word or name. That word names the universe's *principle*, and to possess it is after a fashion to possess the universe itself. "God," "Matter," "Reason," "the Absolute," "Energy," are so many solving names. You can rest when you have them. You are at the end of your metaphysical quest.

But if you follow the pragmatic method, you cannot look on any such word as closing your quest. You must bring out of each word its practical cash-value, set it at work within the stream of your experience. It appears less as a solution, then, than as a program for more work, and more particularly as an indication of the ways in which existing realities may be *changed*.

---

[3] In Arabian mythology, an evil demon or monster.
[4] Tenth-century B.C. king of Israel, noted for his wealth and wisdom (See 1 Kings).

Theories thus become instruments, not answers to enigmas, in which we can rest. We don't lie back upon them, we move forward, and, on occasion, make nature over again by their aid. Pragmatism unstiffens all our theories, limbers them up and sets each one at work. Being nothing essentially new, it harmonizes with many ancient philosophic tendencies. It agrees with nominalism for instance, in always appealing to particulars; with utilitarianism in emphasizing practical aspects; with positivism in its disdain for verbal solutions, useless questions and metaphysical abstractions.

All these, you see, are *anti-intellectual* tendencies. Against rationalism as a pretension and a method pragmatism is fully armed and militant. But, at the outset, at least, it stands for no particular results. It has no dogmas, and no doctrines save its method. As the young Italian pragmatist Papini[5] has well said, it lies in the midst of our theories, like a corridor in a hotel. Innumerable chambers open out of it. In one you may find a man writing an atheistic volume; in the next some one on his knees praying for faith and strength; in a third a chemist investigating a body's properties. In a fourth a system of idealist metaphysics is being excogitated; in a fifth the impossibility of metaphysics is being shown. But they all own the corridor, and all must pass through it if they want a practicable way of getting into or out of their respective rooms.

No particular results then, so far, but only an attitude of orientation, is what the pragmatic method means. *The attitude of looking away from first things, principles, "categories," supposed necessities; and of looking towards last things, fruits, consequences, facts.* . . .

1907

---

[5]Giovanni Papini (1881–1956), Italian philosopher.

REALISM IN TRANSITION:
SOCIETY AND PSYCHOLOGY

————

HAMLIN GARLAND   STEPHEN CRANE
EDITH WHARTON   THEODORE DREISER
FRANK NORRIS   JACK LONDON

"Go out into the street and stand where the ways cross and hear the machinery of life work clashing in its grooves. Can the utmost resort of your ingenuity evolve a better story than any one of the millions that jog your elbow? Shut yourself in your closet and turn your eyes inward upon yourself—deep *into* yourself, down, down into the heart of you; and the tread of the feet upon the pavement is the systole and diastole of your own being—different only in degree. It is life; and it is that which you must have to make your book, your novel—life, not other people's novels."

Frank Norris, "The Need of a Literary Conscience"

HAMLIN GARLAND
(1860–1940)

A book of stories about farm life in the West, entitled *Main-Travelled Roads*, was published in 1891, and its author, Hamlin Garland, explained the title in the Preface: "The main-travelled road in the West (as everywhere) is hot and dusty in summer, and desolate and drear with mud in fall and spring, and in winter the winds sweep the snow across it. . . . Mainly it is long and wearyful and has a dull little town at one end, and a home of toil at the other." The six stories in the book shattered the American dream of idyllic life on a farm in the West.

Garland knew firsthand the life he described. He was born on a farm near West Salem, Wisconsin. His father, a veteran of the Civil War, had left Maine in search of the western promise of a fulfilled, independent life. He moved his family of four children from one state to another—Minnesota, Iowa, South Dakota—always in search of a better stake. The reality of farm life for all members of the family was the ceaseless drudgery that sapped the spirit and stifled intellectual energies.

Hamlin Garland thought only of escape. The little schooling he had introduced him, through the *McGuffey Reader*, to the classic authors, including Milton, Shakespeare, and Hawthorne. In 1881 he left home for the East, only to discover that the life of workers was as limiting as the life of farmers. After teaching in Illinois for a year, he returned for a brief spell to South Dakota and staked out a claim. But soon his old antipathy to farm life unsettled him and he pulled out for Boston in 1884.

In Boston Garland began a formidable program of reading to complete his education, immersing himself in the works of Walt Whitman, Charles Darwin, and Herbert Spencer (a British philosopher who applied the concept of Darwinian evolution to the philosophical and moral realm). He was deeply impressed by Henry George's *Progress and Poverty* and became a believer in George's idea of the "single tax" on land to correct social injustices. During this period Garland supported himself by sporadic teaching and lecturing.

On a brief trip back to the West in 1887, Garland found his memories of the "monotonous commonplace landscape" awakened anew—but this time he looked with a writer's eye. He gathered fresh impressions and, after returning to Boston, began to write and publish the stories that would become *Main-Travelled Roads*. The book established his reputation and was praised by William Dean Howells for its portrayal of "gaunt, grim, sordid, pathetic, ferocious figures, . . . whose blind groping for fairer conditions is . . . so menacing to the politician." Garland was less effective in the more polemical novels that followed. Perhaps the most interesting for a modern reader is *Rose of Dutcher's Coolly* (1895), condemned for its frank treatment of a young girl's sexual awakening. The novel reflects Garland's belief in equality for women.

In 1893 Garland presented a lecture at Chicago's Columbian Exposition entitled "Local Color in Fiction." He gathered this essay with others to make a book of criticism published in 1894 as *Crumbling Idols*. In it he introduced his term, *veritism*: "Art, I must insist, is an individual thing,—the question of one man facing certain facts and telling his individual relations to them. His first care must be to present his own concept. This is, I believe, the essence of veritism: 'Write of those things of which you know most, and for which you care most. By so doing you will be true to yourself, true to your locality, and true to your time.'"

As one critic, Robert Spiller, has pointed out, the "difference between realism and veritism in literature [is] exactly that between realism and impressionism in painting." That is, precise reproduction of the "out there" is not so important as representation of one's personal impressions of the "out there."

Although Garland's stories and novels after *Main-Travelled Roads* were disappointing, his venture into autobiography proved a great success. *A Son of the Middle Border* (1917) appeared finally to fulfill the promise of the earlier work, describing directly the experience of growing up in the rugged heartland of the country. There followed a number of sequels: *A Daughter of the Middle Border* (1921), *Trail-Makers of the Middle Border* (1926), and *Back-Trailers from the Middle Border* (1928). Garland was elected to the American Academy of Arts and Letters in 1918, and was awarded the Pulitzer Prize in 1921, achieving the recognition that had eluded him for so long.

In 1930 Garland moved to California where he spent the last ten years of his life, dying there of a cerebral hemorrhage. He was and is remembered as the writer who destroyed the romantic myths of frontier life on the farm.

ADDITIONAL READING

Hamlin Garland's Diary, ed. Donald Pizer, 1968; *The Works of Hamlin Garland*, 44 vols. in progress, ed. Donald Pizer.

Jean Holloway, *Hamlin Garland: A Biography*, 1960; Donald Pizer, *Hamlin Garland's Early Work and Career*, 1960; Robert Gish, *Hamlin Garland: The Far West*, 1976; Charles L. P. Silet, *Henry Blake Fuller and Hamlin Garland: A Reference Guide*, 1977; Joseph B. McCullough, *Hamlin Garland*, 1978; James Nagel, ed., *Critical Essays on Hamlin Garland*, 1982; Charles L. P. Silet, Robert E. Welch, and Richard Boudreau, eds., *The Critical Reception of Hamlin Garland, 1891–1978*, 1985.

TEXT

"Under the Lion's Paw" from *Main-Travelled Roads*, 1893; "Local Color in Art" from *Crumbling Idols*, 1894.

Under the Lion's Paw[1]

"Along this main-travelled road trailed an endless
line of prairie schooners,[2] coming into sight at the
east, and passing out of sight over the swell to the
west. We children used to wonder where they were
going and why they went."

I

It was the last of autumn and first day of winter coming together. All day long the ploughmen on their prairie farms had moved to and fro in their wide level fields through the falling snow, which melted as it fell, wetting them to the skin — all day, notwithstanding the frequent squalls of snow, the dripping, desolate clouds, and the muck of the furrows, black and tenacious as tar.

---

[1] This story first appeared in *Harper's Weekly*, September 7, 1889. The epigraph was supplied when it was collected with five other stories in *Main-Travelled Roads* (1891), roads, Garland wrote, where "the poor and the weary predominate."
[2] Canvas-covered wagons.

Under their dripping harness the horses swung to and fro silently, with that marvellous uncomplaining patience which marks the horse. All day the wild geese, honking wildly, as they sprawled sidewise down the wind, seemed to be fleeing from an enemy behind, and with neck outthrust and wings extended, sailed down the wind, soon lost to sight.

Yet the ploughman behind his plough, though the snow lay on his ragged greatcoat, and the cold clinging mud rose on his heavy boots, fettering him like gyves,[3] whistled in the very beard of the gale. As day passed, the snow, ceasing to melt, lay along the ploughed land, and lodged in the depth of the stubble, till on each slow round the last furrow stood out black and shining as jet between the ploughed land and the gray stubble.

When night began to fall, and the geese, flying low, began to alight invisibly in the near corn-field, Stephen Council was still at work "finishing a land." He rode on his sulky plough[4] when going with the wind, but walked when facing it. Sitting bent and cold but cheery under his slouch hat, he talked encouragingly to his four-in-hand.

"Come round there, boys! — Round agin! We got t' finish this land. Come in there, Dan! *Stiddy*, Kate, — stiddy! None o' y'r tantrums, Kittie. It's purty tuff, but got a be did. *Tchk! tchk!* Step along, Pete! Don't let Kate git y'r single-tree[5] on the wheel. *Once more!*"

They seemed to know what he meant, and that this was the last round, for they worked with greater vigor than before.

"Once more, boys, an' then, sez I, oats an' a nice warm stall, an' sleep f'r all."

By the time the last furrow was turned on the land it was too dark to see the house, and the snow was changing to rain again. The tired and hungry man could see the light from the kitchen shining through the leafless hedge, and he lifted a great shout, "Supper f'r a half a dozen!"

It was nearly eight o'clock by the time he had finished his chores and started for supper. He was picking his way carefully through the mud, when the tall form of a man loomed up before him with a premonitory cough.

"Waddy ye want?" was the rather startled question of the farmer.

"Well, ye see," began the stranger, in a deprecating tone, "we'd like t' git in f'r the night. We've tried every house f'r the last two miles, but they hadn't any room f'r us. My wife's jest about sick, 'n the children are cold and hungry —"

"Oh, y' want 'o stay all night, eh?"

"Yes, sir; it 'ud be a great accom—"

"Waal, I don't make it a practice t' turn anybuddy way hungry, not on sech nights as this. Drive right in. We ain't got much, but sech as it is—"

But the stranger had disappeared. And soon his steaming, weary team, with drooping heads and swinging single-trees, moved past the well to the block beside the path. Council stood at the side of the "schooner" and helped the children out — two little half-sleeping children — and then a small woman with a babe in her arms.

"There ye go!" he shouted jovially, to the children. "*Now* we're all right! Run right along to the house there, an' tell Mam' Council you wants sumpthin' t' eat. Right this way, Mis'— keep right off t' the right there. I'll go an' git a lantern. Come," he said to the dazed and silent group at his side.

"Mother," he shouted, as he neared the fragrant and warmly lighted kitchen, "here are some wayfarers an' folks who need sumpthin' t' eat an' a place t' snooze." He ended by pushing them all in.

Mrs. Council, a large, jolly, rather coarse-looking woman, took the children in her arms. "Come right in, you little rabbits. 'Most asleep, hey? Now here's a drink o' milk f'r each o' ye. I'll have s'm tea in a minute. Take off y'r things and set up t' the fire."

---

[3]Shackles, chains.
[4]One-seat plow with wheels, here drawn by four horses.

[5]Pivoted bar to which the harness straps of a horse are attached; also called whiffletree.

While she set the children to drinking milk, Council got out his lantern and went out to the barn to help the stranger about his team, where his loud, hearty voice could be heard as it came and went between the haymow and the stalls.

The woman came to light as a small, timid, and discouraged-looking woman, but still pretty, in a thin and sorrowful way.

"Land sakes! An' you've travelled all the way from Clear Lake t'-day in this mud! Waal! waal! No wonder you're all tired out. Don't wait f'r the men, Mis' —" She hesitated, waiting for the name.

"Haskins."

"Mis' Haskins, set right up to the table an' take a good swig o' tea whilst I make y' s'm toast. It's green tea, an' it's good. I tell Council as I git older I don't seem to enjoy Young Hyson n'r Gunpowder.[6] I want the reel green tea, jest as it comes off'n the vines. Seems t' have more heart in it, some way. Don't s'pose it has. Council says it's all in m' eye."

Going on in this easy way, she soon had the children filled with bread and milk and the woman thoroughly at home, eating some toast and sweet-melon pickles, and sipping the tea.

"See the little rats!" she laughed at the children. "They're full as they can stick now, and they want to go to bed. Now, don't git up, Mis' Haskins; set right where you are an' let me look after 'em. I know all about young ones, though I'm all alone now. Jane went an' married last fall. But, as I tell Council, it's lucky we keep our health. Set right there, Mis' Haskins; I won't have you stir a finger."

It was an unmeasured pleasure to sit there in the warm, homely kitchen, the jovial chatter of the housewife driving out and holding at bay the growl of the impotent, cheated wind.

The little woman's eyes filled with tears which fell down upon the sleeping baby in her arms. The world was not so desolate and cold and hopeless, after all.

"Now I hope Council won't stop out there and talk politics all night. He's the greatest man to talk politics an' read the *Tribune* — How old is it?"

She broke off and peered down at the face of the babe.

"Two months 'n' five days," said the mother, with a mother's exactness.

"Ye don't say! I want 'o know! The dear little pudzy-wudzy!" she went on, stirring it up in the neighborhood of the ribs with her fat forefinger.

"Pooty tough on 'oo to go gallivant'n' 'cross lots this way —"

"Yes, that's so; a man can't lift a mountain," said Council, entering the door. "Mother, this is Mr. Haskins, from Kansas. He's been eat up 'n' drove out by grasshoppers."

"Glad t' see yeh! — Pa, empty that wash-basin 'n' give him a chance t' wash."

Haskins was a tall man, with a thin, gloomy face. His hair was a reddish brown, like his coat, and seemed equally faded by the wind and sun, and his sallow face, though hard and set, was pathetic somehow. You would have felt that he had suffered much by the line of his mouth showing under his thin, yellow mustache.

"Hain't Ike got home yet, Sairy?"

"Hain't seen 'im."

"W-a-a-l, set right up, Mr. Haskins; wade right into what we've got; 'tain't much, but we manage to live on it — she gits fat on it," laughed Council, pointing his thumb at his wife.

After supper, while the women put the children to bed, Haskins and Council talked on, seated near the huge cooking-stove, the steam rising from their wet clothing. In the Western fashion Council told as much of his own life as he drew from his guest. He asked but few questions, but by and by the story of Haskins' struggles

---

[6]Fine varieties of green tea.

and defeat come out. The story was a terrible one, but he told it quietly, seated with his elbows on his knees, gazing most of the time at the hearth.

"I didn't like the looks of the country, anyhow," Haskins said, partly rising and glancing at his wife. "I was ust t' northern Ingyannie, where we have lots o' timber 'n' lots o' rain, 'n' I didn't like the looks o' that dry prairie. What galled me the worst was goin' s' far away acrosst so much fine land layin' all through here vacant."

"And the 'hoppers eat ye four years, hand runnin', did they?"

"Eat! They wiped us out. They chawed everything that was green. They jest set around waitin' f'r us to die t' eat us, too. My God! I ust t' dream of 'em sittin' 'round on the bedpost, six feet long, workin' their jaws. They eet the fork-handles. They got worse 'n' worse till they jest rolled on one another, piled up like snow in winter. Well, it ain't no use. If I was t' talk all winter I couldn't tell nawthin'. But all the while I couldn't help thinkin' of all that land back here that nobuddy was usin' that I ought 'o had 'stead o' bein' out there in that cussed country."

"Waal, why didn't ye stop an' settle here?" asked Ike, who had come in and was eating his supper.

"Fer the simple reason that you fellers wantid ten 'r fifteen dollars an acre fer the bare land, and I hadn't no money fer that kind o' thing."

"Yes, I do my own work," Mrs. Council was heard to say in the pause which followed. "I'm a gettin' purty heavy t' be on m' laigs all day, but we can't afford t' hire, so I keep rackin' around somehow, like a foundered horse. S' lame—I tell Council he can't tell how lame I am, f'r I'm jest as lame in one laig as t'other." And the good soul laughed at the joke on herself as she took a handful of flour and dusted the biscuit-board to keep the dough from sticking.

"Well, I hain't *never* been very strong," said Mrs. Haskins. "Our folks was Canadians an' small-boned, and then since my last child I hain't got up again fairly. I don't like t' complain. Tim has about all he can bear now—but they was days this week when I jest wanted to lay right down an' die."

"Waal, now, I'll tell ye," said Council, from his side of the stove, silencing everybody with his good-natured roar, "I'd go down and *see* Butler, *anyway*, if I was you. I guess he'd let you have his place purty cheap; the farm's all run down. He's ben anxious t' let t' somebuddy next year. It 'ud be a good chance fer you. Anyhow, you go to bed and sleep like a babe. I've got some ploughin' t' do, anyhow, an' we'll see if somethin' can't be done about your case. Ike, you go out an' see if the horses is all right, an' I'll show the folks t' bed."

When the tired husband and wife were lying under the generous quilts of the spare bed, Haskins listened a moment to the wind in the eaves, and then said, with a slow and solemn tone,

"There are people in this world who are good enough t' be angels, an' only haff t' die to *be* angels."

II

Jim Butler was one of those men called in the West "land poor." Early in the history of Rock River he had come into the town and started in the grocery business in a small way, occupying a small building in a mean part of town. At this period of his life he earned all he got, and was up early and late sorting beans, working over butter, and carting his goods to and from the station. But a change came over him at the end of the second year, when he sold a lot of land for four times what he paid for it. From that time forward he believed in land speculation as the surest way of getting rich. Every cent he could save or spare from his trade he put into land at forced sale, or mortgages on land, which were "just as good as the wheat," he was accustomed to say.

Farm after farm fell into his hands, until he was recognized as one of the leading landowners of the county. His mortgages were scattered all over Cedar County, and as they slowly but surely fell in he sought usually to retain the former owner as tenant.

He was not ready to foreclose; indeed, he had the name of being one of the "easiest" men in the town. He let the debtor off again and again, extending the time whenever possible.

"I don't want y'r land," he said. "All I'm after is the int'rest on my money—that's all. Now, if y' want 'o stay on the farm, why, I'll give y' a good chance. I can't have the land layin' vacant." And in many cases the owner remained as tenant.

In the meantime he had sold his store; he couldn't spend time in it; he was mainly occupied now with sitting around town on rainy days smoking and "gassin' with the boys," or in riding to and from his farms. In fishing-time he fished a good deal. Doc Grimes, Ben Ashley, and Cal Cheatham were his cronies on these fishing excursions or hunting trips in the time of chickens or partridges. In winter they went to Northern Wisconsin to shoot deer.

In spite of all these signs of easy life Butler persisted in saying he "hadn't enough money to pay taxes on his land," and was careful to convey the impression that he was poor in spite of his twenty farms. At one time he was said to be worth fifty thousand dollars, but land had been a little slow of sale of late, so that he was not worth so much.

A fine farm, known as the Higley place, had fallen into his hands in the usual way the previous year, and he had not been able to find a tenant for it. Poor Higley, after working himself nearly to death on it in the attempt to lift the mortgage, had gone off to Dakota, leaving the farm and his curse to Butler.

This was the farm which Council advised Haskins to apply for; and the next day Council hitched up his team and drove down town to see Butler.

"You jest let *me* do the talkin'," he said. "We'll find him wearin' out his pants on some salt barrel somew'ers; and if he thought you *wanted* a place he'd sock it to you hot and heavy. You jest keep quiet; I'll fix 'im."

Butler was seated in Ben Ashley's store telling fish yarns when Council sauntered in casually.

"Hello, But; lyin' agin, hey?"

"Hello, Steve! how goes it?"

"Oh, so-so. Too dang much rain these days. I thought it was goin' t' freeze up f'r good last night. Tight squeak if I get m' ploughin' done. How's farmin' with *you* these days?"

"Bad. Ploughin' ain't half done."

"It 'ud be a religious idee f'r you t' go out an' take a hand y'rself."

"I don't haff to," said Butler, with a wink.

"Got anybody on the Higley place?"

"No. Know of anybody?"

"Waal, no; not eggsackly. I've got a relation back t' Michigan who's ben hot an' cold on the idee o' comin' West f'r some time. *Might* come if he could get a good lay-out. What do you talk on the farm?"

"Well, I d' know. I'll rent it on shares or I'll rent it money rent."

"Waal, how much money, say?"

"Well, say ten per cent, on the price—two-fifty."

"Waal, that ain't bad. Wait on 'im till 'e thrashes?"

Haskins listened eagerly to his important question, but Council was coolly eating a dried apple which he had speared out of a barrel with his knife. Butler studied him carefully.

"Well, knocks me out of twenty-five dollars interest."

"My relation'll need all he's got t' git his crops in," said Council, in the safe, indifferent way.

"Well, all right; *say* wait," concluded Butler.

"All right; this is the man. Haskins, this is Mr. Butler—no relation to Ben[7]—the hardest-working man in Cedar County."

On the way home Haskins said: "I ain't much better off. I'd like that farm; it's a good farm, but it's all run down, an' so 'm I. I could make a good farm of it if I had half a show. But I can't stock it n'r seed it."

"Waal, now, don't you worry," roared Council in his ear. "We'll pull y' through somehow till next harvest. He's agreed t' hire it ploughed, an' you can earn a hundred dollars ploughin' an' y' c'n git the seed o' me, an' pay me back when y' can."

Haskins was silent with emotion, but at last he said, "I ain't got nothin' t' live on."

"Now, don't you worry 'bout that. You jest make your headquarters at ol' Steve Council's. Mother'll take a pile o' comfort in havin' y'r wife an' children 'round. Y' see, Jane's married off lately, an' Ike's away a good 'eal, so we'll be darn glad t' have y' stop with us this winter. Nex' spring we'll see if y' can't git a start agin." And he chirruped to the team, which sprang forward with the rumbling, clattering wagon.

"Say, looky here, Council, you can't do this. I never saw—" shouted Haskins in his neighbor's ear.

Council moved about uneasily in his seat and stopped his stammering gratitude by saying: "Hold on, now; don't make such a fuss over a little thing. When I see a man down, an' things all on top of 'm, I jest like t' kick 'em off an' help 'm up. That's the kind of religion I got, an' it's about the *only* kind."

They rode the rest of the way home in silence. And when the red light of the lamp shone out into the darkness of the cold and windy night, and he thought of this refuge for his children and wife, Haskins could have put his arm around the neck of his burly companion and squeezed him like a lover. But he contented himself with saying, "Steve Council, you'll git y'r pay f'r this some day."

"Don't want any pay. My religion ain't run on such business principles."

The wind was growing colder, and the ground was covered with a white frost, as they turned into the gate of the Council farm, and the children came rushing out, shouting, "Papa's come!" They hardly looked like the same children who had sat at the table the night before. Their torpidity, under the influence of sunshine and Mother Council, had given way to a sort of spasmodic cheerfulness, as insects in winter revive when laid on the hearth.

III

Haskins worked like a fiend, and his wife, like the heroic woman that she was, bore also uncomplainingly the most terrible burdens. They rose early and toiled without intermission till the darkness fell on the plain, then tumbled into bed, every bone and muscle aching with fatigue, to rise with the sun next morning to the same round of the same ferocity of labor.

The eldest boy drove a team all through the spring, ploughing and seeding, milked the cows, and did chores innumerable, in most ways taking the place of a man.

An infinitely pathetic but common figure—this boy on the American farm, where there is no law against child labor. To see him in his coarse clothing, his huge boots, and his ragged cap, as he staggered with a pail of water from the well, or trudged in the cold and cheerless dawn out into the frosty field behind his team, gave the city-bred visitor a sharp pang of sympathetic pain. Yet Haskins loved his boy, and would have saved him from this if he could, but he could not.

By June the first year the result of such Herculean[8] toil began to show on the

---

[7]Benjamin Franklin Butler (1818–1893), American lawyer, army officer, and politician.

[8]I.e., tremendously difficult, after Hercules, mythic hero of great strength who performed heroic labors.

farm. The yard was cleaned up and sown to grass, the garden ploughed and planted, and the house mended.

Council had given them four of his cows.

"Take 'em an' run 'em on shares. I don't want 'o milk s' many. Ike's away s' much now, Sat'd'ys an' Sund'ys, I can't stand the bother anyhow."

Other men, seeing the confidence of Council in the newcomer, had sold him tools on time; and as he was really an able farmer, he soon had round him many evidences of his care and thrift. At the advice of Council he had taken the farm for three years, with the privilege of re-renting or buying at the end of the term.

"It's a good bargain, an' y' want 'o nail it," said Council. "If you have any kind ov a crop, you c'n pay y'r debts, an' keep seed an' bread."

The new hope which now sprang up in the heart of Haskins and his wife grew great almost as a pain by the time the wide field of wheat began to wave and rustle and swirl in the winds of July. Day after day he would snatch a few moments after supper to go and look at it.

"Have ye seen the wheat t'-day, Nettie?" he asked one night as he rose from supper.

"No, Tim, I ain't had time."

"Well, take time now. Le's go look at it."

She threw an old hat on her head—Tommy's hat—and looking almost pretty in her thin, sad way, went out with her husband to the hedge.

"Ain't it grand, Nettie? Just look at it."

It was grand. Level, russet here and there, heavy-headed, wide as a lake, and full of multitudinous whispers and gleams of wealth, it stretched away before the gazers like the fabled field of the cloth of gold.

"Oh, I think—I *hope* we'll have a good crop, Tim; and oh, how good the people have been to us!"

"Yes; I don't know where we'd be t'-day if it hadn't ben f'r Council and his wife."

"They're the best people in the world," said the little woman, with a great sob of gratitude.

"We'll be in the field on Monday, sure," said Haskins, gripping the rail on the fence as if already at the work of the harvest.

The harvest came, bounteous, glorious, but the winds came and blew it into tangles, and the rain matted it here and there close to the ground, increasing the work of gathering it threefold.

Oh, how they toiled in those glorious days! Clothing dripping with sweat, arms aching, filled with briers, fingers raw and bleeding, backs broken with the weight of heavy bundles, Haskins and his man toiled on. Tommy drove the harvester, while his father and a hired man bound on the machine. In this way they cut ten acres every day, and almost every night after supper, when the hand went to bed, Haskins returned to the field shocking the bound grain in the light of the moon. Many a night he worked till his anxious wife came out at ten o'clock to call him in to rest and lunch.

At the same time she cooked for the men, took care of the children, washed and ironed, milked the cows at night, made the butter, and sometimes fed the horses and watered them while her husband kept at the shocking.

No slave in the Roman galleys could have toiled so frightfully and lived, for this man thought himself a free man, and that he was working for his wife and babes.

When he sank into his bed with a deep groan of relief, too tired to change his grimy, dripping clothing, he felt that he was getting nearer and nearer to a home of his own, and pushing the wolf of want a little farther from his door.

There is no despair so deep as the despair of a homeless man or woman. To roam the roads of the country or the streets of the city, to feel there is no rood of ground on which the feet can rest, to halt weary and hungry outside lighted windows and hear laughter and song within,—these are the hungers and rebellions that drive men to crime and women to shame.

It was the memory of this homelessness, and the fear of its coming again, that spurred Timothy Haskins and Nettie, his wife, to such ferocious labor during that first year.

<h2 style="text-align:center">IV</h2>

"'M, yes; 'm, yes; first-rate," said Butler, as his eye took in the neat garden, the pig-pen, and the well-filled barnyard. "You're gitt'n' quite a stock around yeh. Done well, eh?"

Haskins was showing Butler around the place. He had not seen it for a year, having spent the year in Washington and Boston with Ashley, his brother-in-law, who had been elected to Congress.

"Yes, I've laid out a good deal of money durin' the last three years. I've paid out three hundred dollars f'r fencin'."

"Um—h'm! I see, I see," said Butler, while Haskins went on:

"The kitchen there cost two hundred; the barn ain't cost much in money, but I've put a lot o' time on it. I've dug a new well, and I—"

"Yes, yes, I see. You've done well. Stock worth a thousand dollars," said Butler, picking his teeth with a straw.

"About that," said Haskins, modestly. "We begin to feel's if we was gitt'n' a home f'r ourselves; but we've worked hard. I tell you we begin to feel it, Mr. Butler, and we're goin' t' begin to ease up purty soon. We've been kind o' plannin' a trip back t' *her* folks after the fall ploughin's done."

"*Eggs*-actly!" said Butler, who was evidently thinking of something else. "I suppose you've kind o' calc'lated on stayin' here three years more?"

"Well, yes. Fact is, I think I c'n buy the farm this fall, if you'll give me a reasonable show."

"Um—m! What do you call a reasonable show?"

"Well, say a quarter down and three years' time."

Butler looked at the huge stacks of wheat, which filled the yard, over which the chickens were fluttering and crawling, catching grasshoppers, and out of which the crickets were singing innumerably. He smiled in a peculiar way as he said, "Oh, I won't be hard on yeh. But what did you expect to pay f'r the place?"

"Why, about what you offered it for before, two thousand five hundred, or *possibly* three thousand dollars," he added quickly, as he saw the owner shake his head.

"This farm is worth five thousand and five hundred dollars," said Butler, in a careless and decided voice.

"*What*!" almost shrieked the astounded Haskins. "What's that? Five thousand? Why, that's double what you offered it for three years ago."

"Of course, and it's worth it. It was all run down then; now it's in good shape. You've laid out fifteen hundred dollars in improvements, according to your own story."

"But *you* had nothin' t' do about that. It's my work an' my money."

"You bet it was; but it's my land."

"But what's to pay me for all my—"

"Ain't you had the use of 'em?" replied Butler, smiling calmly into his face.

Haskins was like a man struck on the head with a sandbag; he couldn't think; he stammered as he tried to say: "But—I never'd git the use—You'd rob me! More'n that: you agreed—you promised that I could buy or rent at the end of three years at—"

"That's all right. But I didn't say I'd let you carry off the improvements, nor that I'd go on renting the farm at two-fifty. The land is doubled in value, it don't matter how; it don't enter into the question; an' now you can pay me five hundred dollars a year rent, or take it on your own terms at fifty-five hundred, or—git out."

He was turning away when Haskins, the sweat pouring from his face, fronted him, saying again:

"But *you've* done nothing to make it so. You hain't added a cent. I put it all there myself, expectin' to buy. I worked an' sweat to improve it. I was workin' for myself an' babes—"

"Well, why didn't you buy when I offered to sell? What y' kickin' about?"

"I'm kickin' about payin' you twice f'r my own things,—my own fences, my own kitchen, my own garden."

Butler laughed. "You're too green t' eat, young feller. *Your* improvements! The law will sing another tune."

"But I trusted your word."

"Never trust anybody, my friend. Besides, I didn't promise not to do this thing. Why, man, don't look at me like that. Don't take me for a thief. It's the law. The reg'lar thing. Everybody does it."

"I don't care if they do. It's stealin' jest the same. You take three thousand dollars of my money—the work o' my hands and my wife's." He broke down at this point. He was not a strong man mentally. He could face hardship, ceaseless toil, but he could not face the cold and sneering face of Butler.

"But I don't take it," said Butler, coolly. "All you've got to do is to go on jest as you've been a-doin', or give me a thousand dollars down, and a mortgage at ten per cent on the rest."

Haskins sat down blindly on a bundle of oats near by, and with staring eyes and drooping head went over the situation. He was under the lion's paw. He felt a horrible numbness in his heart and limbs. He was hid in a mist, and there was no path out.

Butler walked about, looking at the huge stacks of grain, and pulling now and again a few handfuls out, shelling the heads in his hands and blowing the chaff away. He hummed a little tune as he did so. He had an accommodating air of waiting.

Haskins was in the midst of the terrible toil of the last year. He was walking again in the rain and the mud behind his plough; he felt the dust and dirt of the threshing. The ferocious husking-time, with its cutting wind and biting, clinging snows, lay hard upon him. Then he thought of his wife, how she had cheerfully cooked and baked, without holiday and without rest.

"Well, what do you think of it?" inquired the cool, mocking, insinuating voice of Butler.

"I think you're a thief and a liar!" shouted Haskins, leaping up. "A black-hearted houn'!" Butler's smile maddened him; with a sudden leap he caught a fork in his hands, and whirled it in the air. "You'll never rob another man, damn ye!" he grated through his teeth, a look of pitiless ferocity in his accusing eyes.

Butler shrank and quivered, expecting the blow; stood, held hypnotized by the eyes of the man he had a moment before despised—a man transformed into an avenging demon. But in the deadly hush between the lift of the weapon and its fall there came a gush of faint, childish laughter and then across the range of his vision, far away and dim, he saw the sun-bright head of his baby girl, as, with the pretty, tottering run of a two-year-old, she moved across the grass of the dooryard. His hands relaxed; the fork fell to the ground; his head lowered.

"Make out y'r deed an' mor'gage, an' git off'n my land, an' don't ye never cross my line agin; if y' do, I'll kill ye."

Butler backed away from the man in wild haste, and climbing into his buggy with trembling limbs drove off down the road, leaving Haskins seated dumbly on the sunny pile of sheaves, his head sunk into his hands.

1889, 1891

Local Color in Art[1]

Local color in fiction is demonstrably the life of fiction. It is the native element, the differentiating element. It corresponds to the endless and vital charm of individual peculiarity. It is the differences which interest us; the similarities do not please, do not forever stimulate and feed as do the differences. Literature would die of dry rot if it chronicled the similarities only, or even largely.

Historically, the local color of a poet or dramatist is of the greatest value. The charm of Horace is the side light he throws on the manners and customs of his time. The vital in Homer[2] lies, after all, in his local color, not in his abstractions. Because the sagas of the North delineate more exactly how men and women lived and wrought in those days, therefore they have always appealed to me with infinitely greater power than Homer.

Similarly, it is the local color of Chaucer that interests us to-day. We yawn over his tales of chivalry which were in the manner of his contemporaries, but the Miller and the Priest[3] interest us. Wherever the man of the past in literature showed us what he really lived and loved, he moves us. We understand him, and we really feel an interest in him.

Historically, local color has gained in beauty and suggestiveness and humanity from Chaucer down to the present day. Each age has embodied more and more of its actual life and social conformation until the differentiating qualities of modern art make the best paintings of Norway as distinct in local color as its fiction is vital and indigenous.

Every great moving literature to-day is full of local color. It is this element which puts the Norwegian and Russian almost at the very summit of modern novel writing, and it is the comparative lack of this distinctive flavor which makes the English and French take a lower place in truth and sincerity.

Everywhere all over the modern European world, men are writing novels and dramas as naturally as the grass or corn or flax grows. The Provençal, the Hun, the Catalonian, the Norwegian, is getting a hearing.[4] This literature is not the literature of scholars; it is the literature of lovers and doers; of men who love the modern and who have not been educated to despise common things.

These men are speaking a new word. They are not hunting themes, they are struggling to express.

Conventional criticism does not hamper or confine them. They are rooted in the soil. They stand among the corn-fields and they dig in the peat-bogs. They concern themselves with modern and very present words and themes, and they have brought a new word which is to divide in half the domain of beauty.

They have made art the re-creation of the beautiful *and the significant*. Mere beauty no longer suffices. Beauty is the world-old aristocrat who has taken for mate this mighty young plebeian Significance. Their child is to be the most human and humane literature ever seen.

It has taken the United States longer to achieve independence of English critics than it took to free itself from old-world political and economic rule. Its political freedom was won, not by its gentlemen and scholars, but by its yeomanry; and in the same way our national literature will come in its fulness when the common American rises spontaneously to the expression of his concept of life.

The fatal blight upon most American art has been, and is to-day, its imitative

---

[1]This essay first appeared in *Crumbling Idols: Twelve Essays on Art Dealing Chiefly with Literature, Painting and the Drama* (1894).
[2]Roman poet and satirist, Horace (65–8 B.C.); Greek epic poet Homer.

[3]Characters in *The Canterbury Tales* by English poet Geoffrey Chaucer (c. 1343–1400).
[4]A reference to the regional literature of southern France, Hungary or central Europe, northeastern Spain, and Norway, respectively.

quality, which has kept it characterless and factitious,—a forced rose-culture rather than the free flowering of native plants.

Our writers despised or feared the home market. They rested their immortality upon the "universal theme," which was a theme of no interest to the public and of small interest to themselves.

During the first century and a half, our literature had very little national color. It was quite like the utterance of corresponding classes in England. But at length Bryant and Cooper felt the influence of our mighty forests and prairies. Whittier uttered something of New England boy-life, and Thoreau[5] prodded about among newly discovered wonders, and the American literature got its first start.

Under the influence of Cooper came the stories of wild life from Texas, from Ohio, and from Illinois. The wild, rough settlements could not produce smooth and cultured poems or stories; they only furnished forth rough-and-ready anecdotes, but in these stories there were hints of something fine and strong and native.

As the settlements increased in size, as the pressure of the forest and the wild beast grew less, expression rose to a higher plane; men softened in speech and manner. All preparations were being made for a local literature raised to the level of art.

The Pacific slope was first in the line. By the exceptional interest which the world took in the life of the gold fields, and by the forward urge which seems always to surprise the pessimist and the scholiast,[6] two young men[7] were plunged into that wild life, led across the plains set in the shadow of Mount Shasta, and local literature received its first great marked, decided impetus.

To-day we have in America, at last, a group of writers who have no suspicion of imitation laid upon them. Whatever faults they may be supposed to have, they are at any rate, themselves. American critics can depend upon a characteristic American literature of fiction and the drama from these people.

The corn has flowered, and the cotton-boll has broken into speech.

Local color—what is it? It means that the writer spontaneously reflects the life which goes on around him. It is natural and unstrained art.

It is, in a sense, unnatural and artificial to find an American writing novels of Russia or Spain or the Holy Land. He cannot hope to do it so well as the native. The best he can look for is that poor word of praise, "He does it very well, considering he is an alien."

If a young writer complain that there are no themes at home, that he is forced to go abroad for prospective and romance, I answer there is something wrong in his education or his perceptive faculty. Often he is more anxious to win a money success than to be patiently one of art's unhurried devotees.

I can sympathize with him, however, for criticism has not helped him to be true. Criticism of the formal kind and spontaneous expression are always at war, like the old man and the youth. They may politely conceal it, but they are mutually destructive.

Old men naturally love the past; the books they read are the master-pieces; the great men are all dying off, they say; the young man should treat lofty and universal themes, as they used to do. These localisms are petty. These truths are disturbing. Youth annoys them. Spontaneousness is formlessness, and the criticism that does not call for the abstract and the ideal and the beautiful is leading to destruction, these critics say.

And yet there is a criticism which helps, which tends to keep a writer at his best; but such criticism recognizes the dynamic force of a literature, and tries to spy out tendencies. This criticism to-day sees that local color means national character, and is aiding the young writer to treat his themes in the best art.

---

[5]William Cullen Bryant (1794–1878); James Fenimore Cooper (1789–1851); John Greenleaf Whittier (1807–1892); and Henry David Thoreau (1817–1862).

[6]One of the ancient commentators on classical authors.
[7]Bret Harte (1836–1902) and Joaquin Miller (1841?–1913); Mount Shasta is in northern California.

I assert it is the most natural thing in the world for a man to love his native land and his native, intimate surroundings. Born into a web of circumstances, enmeshed in common life, the youthful artist begins to think. All the associations of that childhood and the love-life of youth combine to make that web of common affairs, threads of silver and beads of gold; the near-at-hand things are the dearest and sweetest after all.

As the reader will see, I am using local color to mean something more than a forced study of the picturesque scenery of a State.

Local color in a novel means that it has such quality of texture and back-ground that it could not have been written in any other place or by any one else than a native.

It means a statement of life as indigenous as the plant-growth. It means that the picturesque shall not be seen by the author,—that every tree and bird and mountain shall be dear and companionable and necessary, not picturesque; the tourist cannot write the local novel.

From this it follows that local color must not be put in for the sake of local color. It must go in, it *will* go in, because the writer naturally carries it with him half unconsciously, or conscious only of its significance, its interest to him.

He must not stop to think whether it will interest the reader or not. He must be loyal to himself, and put it in because he loves it. If he is an artist, he will make his reader feel it through his own emotion.

What we should stand for is not universality of theme, but beauty and strength of treatment, leaving the writer to choose his theme because he loves it.

Here is the work of the critic. Recognizing that the theme is beyond his control, let him aid the young writer to delineate simply and with unwavering strokes. Even here the critic can do little, if he is possessed of the idea that the young writer of to-day should model upon Addison or Macaulay or Swift.[8]

There are new criterions to-day in writing as in painting, and individual expression is the aim. The critic can do much to aid a young writer to *not* copy an old master or any other master. Good criticism can aid him to be vivid and simple and unhackneyed in his technique, the subject is his own affair.

I agree with him who says, Local art must be raised to the highest levels in its expression; but in aiding this perfection of technique we must be careful not to cut into the artist's spontaneity. To apply ancient dogmas of criticism to our life and literature would be benumbing to artist and fatal to his art.

1894

EDITH WHARTON
(1862–1937)

Edith Wharton was born Edith Newbold Jones into a New York family of "old money," part of an "aristocracy" that imposed on all members fixed patterns of behavior and judged their morals and manners by rigid standards. By simply growing to adulthood in this restrictive environment, the sensitive young girl absorbed the materials and themes for the works of literature that she would one day write—to the surprise (and consternation) of her family and friends. Much later, when she could look back with some objectivity on her origins, she identi-

---

[8]English writers Joseph Addison (1672–1719); Thomas Babbington Macaulay (1800–1859); and Jonathan Swift (1667–1745).

fied the virtues of this "old society" as "social amenity and financial incorruptibility." But she added: "The weakness of the social structure of my parents' day was a blind dread of innovation, an instinctive shrinking from responsibility."

Her father's inheritance enabled the family to live a life of leisure, insulated from the sordid life of work. Long periods of living abroad made ample funds go even further, and enabled the young Edith not only to become familiar with European culture but to develop fluency in French, Italian, and German. She never attended school but studied with tutors, early developing a passion for reading. She had the run of her father's library, where she read the classic works of English and French literature. By the time of her "coming out" into society at the age of eighteen, she published a cluster of poems anonymously in *The Atlantic Monthly*.

In 1885, at the age of twenty-three, she married a wealthy Bostonian, Edward ("Teddy") Wharton, thirteen years older than she. As her friend Henry James was to say of her later, she had done "an almost—or rather an utterly—inconceivable thing." It was from the beginning an unhappy marriage. They lived a life of luxury, spending part of the year in their New York house, and part in "The Mount" which they built in Lenox in the Massachusetts Berkshires. By 1907 they were living permanently in Paris, Teddy becoming increasingly unstable. And by 1913, after twenty-eight years of keeping up a front, they were finally divorced. His mental illness grew more acute and he died a few years later.

One basis for the incompatibility was Teddy Wharton's total lack of interest in literature and lack of sympathy for his wife's devotion to writing. Perhaps in part because of the state of her marriage, Edith Wharton turned more and more to this interest that could not be shared. Her first book, a collaboration with Ogden Codman, was *The Decoration of Houses* (1897), a subject for which her opulent upbringing had suitably prepared her. But in 1899, she published her first volume of short stories, *The Greater Inclination*. Its success set her firmly on the path of a career that, as it ostracized her from her social class by breaching its code, at the same time freed her from the restraints of her past and carried her into an exciting intellectual world of writers and artists.

After trying her hand at a historical novel recreating Italy of the eighteenth century (*The Valley of Decision*, 1902), Wharton finally found her natural subject in *The House of Mirth* (1905). It tells the story of a woman in New York who is first entangled in high society and then ruthlessly cast out of it. This novel was followed by *The Custom of the Country* (1913), considered by some her masterpiece, and *The Age of Innocence* (1920), which won the Pulitzer Prize. Both of these novels are set in the world she knew well and portray characters somehow trapped in that world, living diminished or unfulfilled lives. But in two novellas published during this period—*Ethan Frome* (1911) and *Summer* (1917)—Wharton departed from her usual material, providing her stories with a stark New England backdrop and portraying simple farm and village life far removed from the life of her youth. The first of these has proved one of her most popular works.

During the First World War, she was tireless in her support of France and continued to live there after the war until her death. She published book after book, including travel accounts, criticism, and poetry as well as fiction. But the critical consensus is that her best work had been done by 1920. Two books, however, deserve special attention. *The Writing of Fiction* (1925) offers insight into her ideas about the technique of constructing stories and novels. And the autobiographical *A Backward Glance* (1934) presents fascinating glimpses of her life among the literati, notably her friendship with Henry James. It took later biographers (especially R. W. B. Lewis in *Edith Wharton: A Biography*, 1975) to uncover the story of her passionate love affair with the American journalist Morton Fullerton from 1907 to 1910.

In one of the most astute of critical appraisals of Edith Wharton, the novelist Louis Auchincloss has written: "She knew her men and women of property, recently or anciently acquired, how they decorated their houses and where they spent their summers. She realized that the social game was without rules, and this realization made her one of the few novelists before Proust who could describe it with any profundity."

ADDITIONAL READING

The Edith Wharton Reader, ed. Louis Auchincloss, 1965; *The Collected Short Stories of Edith Wharton*, 2 vols., ed. R. W. B. Lewis, 1968; *The Letters of Edith Wharton*, ed. R. W. B. Lewis and Nancy Lewis, 1988.

Percy Lubbock, *Portrait of Edith Wharton*, 1947, 1969; Blake Nevius, *Edith Wharton: A Study of Her Fiction*, 1953; Marilyn Jones Lyde, *Edith Wharton: Convention and Morality in the Work of a Novelist*, 1959; Louis Auchincloss, *Edith Wharton*, 1961; Millicent Bell, *Edith Wharton and Henry James*, 1965; Geoffrey Walton, *Edith Wharton: A Critical Interpretation*, 1970, 1982; Louis Auchincloss, *Edith Wharton: A Woman in Her Time*, 1971; R. W. B. Lewis, *Edith Wharton: A Biography*, 1975; Gary H. Lindberg, *Edith Wharton and the Novel of Manners*, 1975; Margaret B. McDowell, *Edith Wharton*, 1976; Richard H. Lawson, *Edith Wharton*, 1977; Cynthia Griffin Wolff, *A Feast of Words: The Triumph of Edith Wharton*, 1977; Elizabeth Ammons, *Edith Wharton's Argument with America*, 1980; Carol Wershoven, *The Female Intruder in the Novels of Edith Wharton*, 1983; Catherine M. Rae, *Edith Wharton's New York Quartet*, 1984; Judith Fryer, *Felicitous Space: The Imaginative Structures of Edith Wharton and Willa Cather*, 1986; Harold Bloom, ed., *Edith Wharton*, 1986.

TEXTS

"The Other Two" from *The Descent of Man*, 1904; "Roman Fever" from *The World Over*, 1936; *A Backward Glance*, 1934.

The Other Two

I

Waythorn, on the drawing-room hearth, waited for his wife to come down to dinner.

It was their first night under his own roof, and he was surprised at his thrill of boyish agitation. He was not so old, to be sure—his glass gave him little more than the five-and-thirty years to which his wife confessed—but he had fancied himself already in the temperate zone; yet here he was listening for her step with a tender sense of all it symbolised, with some old trail of verse about the garlanded nuptial door-posts floating through his enjoyment of the pleasant room and the good dinner just beyond it.

They had been hastily recalled from their honeymoon by the illness of Lily Haskett, the child of Mrs. Waythorn's first marriage. The little girl, at Waythorn's desire, had been transferred to his house on the day of her mother's wedding, and the doctor, on their arrival, broke the news that she was ill with typhoid, but declared that all the symptoms were favourable. Lily could show twelve years of unblemished health, and the case promised to be a light one. The nurse spoke as reassuringly, and after a moment of alarm Mrs. Waythorn had adjusted herself to the situation. She was very fond of Lily—her affection for the child had perhaps been her decisive charm in Waythorn's eyes—but she had the perfectly balanced nerves which her little girl had inherited, and no woman ever wasted less tissue in unproductive worry. Waythorn was therefore quite prepared to see her come in presently, a little late because of a last look at Lily, but as serene and well-appointed as if her good-night kiss had been laid on the brow of health. Her composure was restful to him; it acted as ballast to his somewhat unstable sensibilities. As he pictured her bending over the child's bed he thought how soothing her presence must be in illness: her very step would prognosticate recovery.

His own life had been a gray one, from temperament rather than circumstance, and he had been drawn to her by the unperturbed gaiety which kept her fresh and elastic at an age when most women's activities are growing either slack or febrile. He knew what was said about her; for, popular as she was, there had always been a faint undercurrent of detraction. When she had appeared in New York, nine or ten years earlier, as the pretty Mrs. Haskett whom Gus Varick had unearthed somewhere— was it in Pittsburg or Utica?—society, while promptly accepting her, had reserved the right to cast a doubt on its own indiscrimination. Enquiry, however, established her undoubted connection with a socially reigning family, and explained her recent divorce as the natural result of a runaway match at seventeen; and as nothing was known of Mr. Haskett it was easy to believe the worst of him.

Alice Haskett's remarriage with Gus Varick was a passport to the set whose recognition she coveted, and for a few years the Varicks were the most popular couple in town. Unfortunately the alliance was brief and stormy, and this time the husband had his champions. Still, even Varick's stanchest supporters admitted that he was not meant for matrimony, and Mrs. Varick's grievances were of a nature to bear the inspection of the New York courts. A New York divorce is in itself a diploma of virtue, and in the semi-widowhood of this second separation Mrs. Varick took on an air of sanctity, and was allowed to confide her wrongs to some of the most scrupulous ears in town. But when it was known that she was to marry Waythorn there was a momentary reaction. Her best friends would have preferred to see her remain in the rôle of the injured wife, which was as becoming to her as crape to a rosy complexion. True, a decent time had elapsed, and it was not even suggested that Waythorn had supplanted his predecessor. People shook their heads over him, however, and one grudging friend, to whom he affirmed that he took the step with his eyes open, replied oracularly: "Yes—and with your ears shut."

Waythorn could afford to smile at these innuendoes. In the Wall Street phrase, he had "discounted" them. He knew that society has not yet adapted itself to the consequences of divorce, and that till the adaptation takes place every woman who uses the freedom the law accords her must be her own social justification. Waythorn had an amused confidence in his wife's ability to justify herself. His expectations were fulfilled, and before the wedding took place Alice Varick's group had rallied openly to her support. She took it all imperturbably: she had a way of surmounting obstacles without seeming to be aware of them, and Waythorn looked back with wonder at the trivialities over which he had worn his nerves thin. He had the sense of having found refuge in a richer, warmer nature than his own, and his satisfaction, at the moment, was humourously summed up in the thought that his wife, when she had done all she could for Lily, would not be ashamed to come down and enjoy a good dinner.

The anticipation of such enjoyment was not, however, the sentiment expressed by Mrs. Waythorn's charming face when she presently joined him. Though she had put on her most engaging teagown she had neglected to assume the smile that went with it, and Waythorn thought he had never seen her look so nearly worried.

"What is it?" he asked. "Is anything wrong with Lily?"

"No; I've just been in and she's still sleeping." Mrs. Waythorn hesitated. "But something tiresome has happened."

He had taken her two hands, and now perceived that he was crushing a paper between them.

"This letter?"

"Yes — Mr. Haskett has written — I mean his lawyer has written."

Waythorn felt himself flush uncomfortably. He dropped his wife's hands.

"What about?"

"About seeing Lily. You know the courts —"

"Yes, yes," he interrupted nervously.

Nothing was known about Haskett in New York. He was vaguely supposed to have remained in the outer darkness from which his wife had been rescued, and Waythorn was one of the few who were aware that he had given up his business in Utica and followed her to New York in order to be near his little girl. In the days of his wooing, Waythorn had often met Lily on the doorstep, rosy and smiling, on her way "to see papa."

"I am so sorry," Mrs. Waythorn murmured.

He roused himself. "What does he want?"

"He wants to see her. You know she goes to him once a week."

"Well — he doesn't expect her to go to him now, does he?"

"No — he has heard of her illness; but he expects to come here."

"*Here?*"

Mrs. Waythorn reddened under his gaze. They looked away from each other.

"I'm afraid he has the right. . . . You'll see. . . ." She made a proffer of the letter.

Waythorn moved away with a gesture of refusal. He stood staring about the softly lighted room, which a moment before had seemed so full of bridal intimacy.

"I'm so sorry," she repeated. "If Lily could have been moved —"

"That's out of the question," he returned impatiently.

"I suppose so."

Her lip was beginning to tremble, and he felt himself a brute.

"He must come, of course," he said. "When is — his day?"

"I'm afraid — to-morrow."

"Very well. Send a note in the morning."

The butler entered to announce dinner.

Waythorn turned to his wife. "Come — you must be tired. It's beastly, but try to forget about it," he said, drawing her hand through his arm.

"You're so good, dear. I'll try," she whispered back.

Her face cleared at once, and as she looked at him across the flowers, between the rosy candle-shades, he saw her lips waver back into a smile.

"How pretty everything is!" she sighed luxuriously.

He turned to the butler. "The champagne at once, please. Mrs. Waythorn is tired."

In a moment or two their eyes met above the sparkling glasses. Her own were quite clear and untroubled: he saw that she had obeyed his injunction and forgotten.

II

Waythorn, the next morning, went down town earlier than usual. Haskett was not likely to come till the afternoon, but the instinct of flight drove him forth. He meant to stay away all day — he had thoughts of dining at his club. As his door closed behind him he reflected that before he opened it again it would have admitted another man who had as much right to enter it as himself, and the thought filled him with a physical repugnance.

He caught the "elevated" at the employés' hour, and found himself crushed between two layers of pendulous humanity. At Eighth Street the man facing him wriggled out, and another took his place. Waythorn glanced up and saw that it was Gus Varick. The men were so close together that it was impossible to ignore the smile of recognition on Varick's handsome overblown face. And after all — why not? They had always been on good terms, and Varick had been divorced before Waythorn's attentions to his wife began. The two exchanged a word on the perennial grievance of the congested trains, and when a seat at their side was miraculously left empty the instinct of self-preservation made Waythorn slip into it after Varick.

The latter drew the stout man's breath of relief. "Lord—I was beginning to feel like a pressed flower." He leaned back, looking unconcernedly at Waythorn. "Sorry to hear that Sellers is knocked out again."

"Sellers?" echoed Waythorn, starting at his partner's name.

Varick looked surprised. "You didn't know he was laid up with the gout?"

"No. I've been away—I only got back last night." Waythorn felt himself reddening in anticipation of the other's smile.

"Ah—yes; to be sure. And Sellers's attack came on two days ago. I'm afraid he's pretty bad. Very awkward for me, as it happens, because he was just putting through a rather important thing for me."

"Ah?" Waythorn wondered vaguely since when Varick had been dealing in "important things." Hitherto he had dabbled only in the shallow pools of speculation, with which Waythorn's office did not usually concern itself.

It occurred to him that Varick might be talking at random, to relieve the strain of their propinquity. That strain was becoming momentarily more apparent to Waythorn, and when, at Cortlandt Street, he caught sight of an acquaintance and had a sudden vision of the picture he and Varick must present to an initiated eye, he jumped up with a muttered excuse.

"I hope you'll find Sellers better," said Varick civilly, and he stammered back: "If I can be of any use to you—" and let the departing crowd sweep him to the platform.

At his office he heard that Sellers was in fact ill with the gout, and would probably not be able to leave the house for some weeks.

"I'm sorry it should have happened so, Mr. Waythorn," the senior clerk said with affable significance. "Mr. Sellers was very much upset at the idea of giving you such a lot of extra work just now."

"Oh, that's no matter," said Waythorn hastily. He secretly welcomed the pressure of additional business, and was glad to think that, when the day's work was over, he would have to call at his partner's on the way home.

He was late for luncheon, and turned in at the nearest restaurant instead of going to his club. The place was full, and the waiter hurried him to the back of the room to capture the only vacant table. In the cloud of cigar-smoke Waythorn did not at once distinguish his neighbours: but presently, looking about him, he saw Varick seated a few feet off. This time, luckily, they were too far apart for conversation, and Varick, who faced another way, had probably not even seen him; but there was an irony in their renewed nearness.

Varick was said to be fond of good living, and as Waythorn sat despatching his hurried luncheon he looked across half enviously at the other's leisurely degustation of his meal. When Waythorn first saw him he had been helping himself with critical deliberation to a bit of Camembert at the ideal point of liquefaction, and now, the cheese removed, he was just pouring his *café double* from its little two-storied earthen pot. He poured slowly, his ruddy profile bent above the task, and one beringed white hand steadying the lid of the coffee-pot; then he stretched his other hand to the decanter of cognac at his elbow, filled a liqueur-glass, took a tentative sip, and poured the brandy into his coffee-cup.

Waythorn watched him in a kind of fascination. What was he thinking of—only of the flavour of the coffee and the liqueur? Had the morning's meeting left no more trace in his thoughts than on his face? Had his wife so completely passed out of his life that even this odd encounter with her present husband, within a week after her remarriage, was no more than an incident in his day? And as Waythorn mused, another idea struck him: had Haskett ever met Varick as Varick and he had just met?

The recollection of Haskett perturbed him, and he rose and left the restaurant, taking a circuitous way out to escape the placid irony of Varick's nod.

It was after seven when Waythorn reached home. He thought the footman who opened the door looked at him oddly.

"How is Miss Lily?" he asked in haste.

"Doing very well, sir. A gentleman—"

"Tell Barlow to put off dinner for half an hour," Waythorn cut him off, hurrying upstairs.

He went straight to his room and dressed without seeing his wife. When he reached the drawing-room she was there, fresh and radiant. Lily's day had been good; the doctor was not coming back that evening.

At dinner Waythorn told her of Sellers's illness and of the resulting complications. She listened sympathetically, adjuring him not to let himself be overworked, and asking vague feminine questions about the routine of the office. Then she gave him the chronicle of Lily's day; quoted the nurse and doctor, and told him who had called to inquire. He had never seen her more serene and unruffled. It struck him, with a curious pang, that she was very happy in being with him, so happy that she found a childish pleasure in rehearsing the trivial incidents of her day.

After dinner they went to the library, and the servant put the coffee and liqueurs on a low table before her and left the room. She looked singularly soft and girlish in her rosy pale dress, against the dark leather of one of his bachelor armchairs. A day earlier the contrast would have charmed him.

He turned away now, choosing a cigar with affected deliberation.

"Did Haskett come?" he asked, with his back to her.

"Oh, yes—he came."

"You didn't see him, of course?"

She hesitated a moment. "I let the nurse see him."

That was all. There was nothing more to ask. He swung round toward her, applying a match to his cigar. Well, the thing was over for a week, at any rate. He would try not to think of it. She looked up at him, a trifle rosier than usual, with a smile in her eyes.

"Ready for your coffee, dear?"

He leaned against the mantelpiece, watching her as she lifted the coffee-pot. The lamplight struck a gleam from her bracelets and tipped her soft hair with brightness. How light and slender she was, and how each gesture flowed into the next! She seemed a creature all compact of harmonies. As the thought of Haskett receded, Waythorn felt himself yielding again to the joy of possessorship. They were his, those white hands with their flitting motions, his the light haze of hair, the lips and eyes. . . .

She set down the coffee-pot, and reaching for the decanter of cognac, measured off a liqueur-glass and poured it into his cup.

Waythorn uttered a sudden exclamation.

"What is the matter?" she said, startled.

"Nothing; only—I don't take cognac in my coffee."

"Oh, how stupid of me," she cried.

Their eyes met, and she blushed a sudden agonised red.

III

Ten days later, Mr. Sellers, still house-bound, asked Waythorn to call on his way down town.

The senior partner, with his swaddled foot propped up by the fire, greeted his associate with an air of embarrassment.

"I'm sorry, my dear fellow; I've got to ask you to do an awkward thing for me."

Waythorn waited, and the other went on, after a pause apparently given to the arrangement of his phrases: "The fact is, when I was knocked out I had just gone into a rather complicated piece of business for—Gus Varick."

"Well?" said Waythorn, with an attempt to put him at his ease.

"Well—it's this way: Varick came to me the day before my attack. He had evidently had an inside tip from somebody, and had made about a hundred thousand. He came to me for advice, and I suggested his going in with Vanderlyn."

"Oh, the deuce!" Waythorn exclaimed. He saw in a flash what had happened. The investment was an alluring one, but required negotiation. He listened quietly while Sellers put the case before him, and, the statement ended, he said: "You think I ought to see Varick?"

"I'm afraid I can't as yet. The doctor is obdurate. And this thing can't wait. I hate to ask you, but no one else in the office knows the ins and outs of it."

Waythorn stood silent. He did not care a farthing for the success of Varick's venture, but the honour of the office was to be considered, and he could hardly refuse to oblige his partner.

"Very well," he said, "I'll do it."

That afternoon, apprised by telephone, Varick called at the office. Waythorn, waiting in his private room, wondered what the others thought of it. The newspapers, at the time of Mrs. Waythorn's marriage, had acquainted their readers with every detail of her previous matrimonial ventures, and Waythorn could fancy the clerks smiling behind Varick's back as he was ushered in.

Varick bore himself admirably. He was easy without being undignified, and Waythorn was conscious of cutting a much less impressive figure. Varick had no experience of business, and the talk prolonged itself for nearly an hour while Waythorn set forth with scrupulous precision the details of the proposed transaction.

"I'm awfully obliged to you," Varick said as he rose. "The fact is I'm not used to having much money to look after, and I don't want to make an ass of myself—" He smiled, and Waythorn could not help noticing that there was something pleasant about his smile. "It feels uncommonly queer to have enough cash to pay one's bills. I'd have sold my soul for it a few years ago!"

Waythorn winced at the allusion. He had heard it rumoured that a lack of funds had been one of the determining causes of the Varick separation, but it did not occur to him that Varick's words were intentional. It seemed more likely that the desire to keep clear of embarrassing topics had fatally drawn him into one. Waythorn did not wish to be outdone in civility.

"We'll do the best we can for you," he said. "I think this is a good thing you're in."

"Oh, I'm sure it's immense. It's awfully good of you—" Varick broke off, embarrassed. "I suppose the thing's settled now—but if—"

"If anything happens before Sellers is about, I'll see you again," said Waythorn quietly. He was glad, in the end, to appear the more self-possessed of the two.

•   •   •   •   •

The course of Lily's illness ran smooth, and as the days passed Waythorn grew used to the idea of Haskett's weekly visit. The first time the day came round, he stayed out late, and questioned his wife as to the visit on his return. She replied at once that Haskett had merely seen the nurse downstairs, as the doctor did not wish any one in the child's sick-room till after the crisis.

The following week Waythorn was again conscious of the recurrence of the day, but had forgotten it by the time he came home to dinner. The crisis of the disease came a few days later, with a rapid decline of fever, and the little girl was pronounced out of danger. In the rejoicing which ensued the thought of Haskett passed out of Waythorn's mind, and one afternoon, letting himself into the house with a latch-key, he went straight to his library without noticing a shabby hat and umbrella in the hall.

In the library he found a small effaced-looking man with a thinnish gray beard sitting on the edge of a chair. The stranger might have been a piano-tuner, or one of those mysteriously efficient persons who are summoned in emergencies to adjust some detail of the domestic machinery. He blinked at Waythorn through a pair of gold-rimmed spectacles and said mildly: "Mr. Waythorn, I presume? I am Lily's father."

Waythorn flushed. "Oh—" he stammered uncomfortably. He broke off, disliking to appear rude. Inwardly he was trying to adjust the actual Haskett to the image of him projected by his wife's reminiscences. Waythorn had been allowed to infer that Alice's first husband was a brute.

"I am sorry to intrude," said Haskett, with his over-the-counter politeness.

"Don't mention it," returned Waythorn, collecting himself. "I suppose the nurse has been told?"

"I presume so. I can wait," said Haskett. He had a resigned way of speaking, as though life had worn down his natural powers of resistance.

Waythorn stood on the threshold, nervously pulling off his gloves.

"I'm sorry you've been detained. I will send for the nurse," he said; and as he opened the door he added with an effort: "I'm glad we can give you a good report of Lily." He winced as the *we* slipped out, but Haskett seemed not to notice it.

"Thank you, Mr. Waythorn. It's been an anxious time for me."

"Ah, well, that's past. Soon she'll be able to go to you." Waythorn nodded and passed out.

In his own room he flung himself down with a groan. He hated the womanish sensibility which made him suffer so acutely from the grotesque chances of life. He had known when he married that his wife's former husbands were both living, and that amid the multiplied contacts of modern existence there were a thousand chances to one that he would run against one or the other, yet he found himself as much disturbed by his brief encounter with Haskett as though the law had not obligingly removed all difficulties in the way of their meeting.

Waythorn sprang up and began to pace the room nervously. He had not suffered half as much from his two meetings with Varick. It was Haskett's presence in his own house that made the situation so intolerable. He stood still, hearing steps in the passage.

"This way, please," he heard the nurse say. Haskett was being taken upstairs, then: not a corner of the house but was open to him. Waythorn dropped into another chair, staring vaguely ahead of him. On his dressing-table stood a photograph of Alice, taken when he had first known her. She was Alice Varick then—how fine and exquisite he had thought her! Those were Varick's pearls about her neck. At Waythorn's instance they had been returned before her marriage. Had Haskett ever given her any trinkets—and what had become of them, Waythorn wondered? He realised suddenly that he knew very little of Haskett's past or present situation; but from the man's appearance and manner of speech he could reconstruct with curious precision the surroundings of Alice's first marriage. And it startled him to think that she had, in the background of her life, a phase of existence so different from anything with which he had connected her. Varick, whatever his faults, was a gentleman, in the conventional, traditional sense of the term: the sense which at that moment seemed, oddly enough, to have most meaning to Waythorn. He and Varick had the same social habits, spoke the same language, understood the same allusions. But this other man . . . it was grotesquely uppermost in Waythorn's mind that Haskett had worn a made-up tie attached with an elastic. Why should that ridiculous detail symbolise the whole man? Waythorn was exasperated by his own paltriness, but the fact of the tie expanded, forced itself on him, became as it were the key to Alice's past. He could see her, as Mrs. Haskett, sitting in a "front parlour" furnished in plush, with a pianola,[1]

---

[1]An automatic player piano.

and a copy of "Ben Hur"[2] on the centre-table. He could see her going to the theatre with Haskett—or perhaps even to a "Church Sociable"—she in a "picture hat" and Haskett in a black frock-coat, a little creased, with the made-up tie on an elastic. On the way home they would stop and look at the illuminated shop-windows, lingering over the photographs of New York actresses. On Sunday afternoons Haskett would take her for a walk, pushing Lily ahead of them in a white enamelled perambulator, and Waythorn had a vision of the people they would stop and talk to. He could fancy how pretty Alice must have looked, in a dress adroitly constructed from the hints of a New York fashion-paper, and how she must have looked down on the other women, chafing at her life, and secretly feeling that she belonged in a bigger place.

For the moment his foremost thought was one of wonder at the way in which she had shed the phase of existence which her marriage with Haskett implied. It was as if her whole aspect, every gesture, every inflection, every allusion, were a studied negation of that period of her life. If she had denied being married to Haskett she could hardly have stood more convicted of duplicity than in this obliteration of the self which had been his wife.

Waythorn started up, checking himself in the analysis of her motives. What right had he to create a fantastic effigy of her and then pass judgment on it? She had spoken vaguely of her first marriage as unhappy, had hinted, with becoming reticence, that Haskett had wrought havoc among her young illusions. . . . It was a pity for Waythorn's peace of mind that Haskett's very inoffensiveness shed a new light on the nature of those illusions. A man would rather think that his wife has been brutalised by her first husband than that the process has been reversed.

IV

"Mr. Waythorn, I don't like that French governess of Lily's."

Haskett, subdued and apologetic, stood before Waythorn in the library, revolving his shabby hat in his hand.

Waythorn, surprised in his armchair over the evening paper, stared back perplexedly at his visitor.

"You'll excuse my asking to see you," Haskett continued. "But this is my last visit, and I thought if I could have a word with you it would be a better way than writing to Mrs. Waythorn's lawyer."

Waythorn rose uneasily. He did not like the French governess either; but that was irrelevant.

"I am not so sure of that," he returned stiffly; "but since you wish it I will give your message to—my wife." He always hesitated over the possessive pronoun in addressing Haskett.

The latter sighed. "I don't know as that will help much. She didn't like it when I spoke to her."

Waythorn turned red. "When did you see her?" he asked.

"Not since the first day I came to see Lily—right after she was taken sick. I remarked to her then that I didn't like the governess."

Waythorn made no answer. He remembered distinctly that, after that first visit, he had asked his wife if she had seen Haskett. She had lied to him then, but she had respected his wishes since; and the incident cast a curious light on her character. He was sure she would not have seen Haskett that first day if she had divined that Waythorn would object, and the fact that she did not divine it was almost as disagreeable to the latter as the discovery that she had lied to him.

"I don't like the woman," Haskett was repeating with mild persistency. "She ain't straight, Mr. Waythorn—she'll teach the child to be underhand. I've noticed a change

[2]*Ben Hur, A Tale of the Christ* (1880), the best-selling historical romance by Lew Wallace (1827–1905).

in Lily—she's too anxious to please—and she don't always tell the truth. She used to be the straightest child, Mr. Waythorn—" He broke off, his voice a little thick. "Not but what I want her to have a stylish education," he ended.

Waythorn was touched. "I'm sorry, Mr. Haskett; but frankly, I don't quite see what I can do."

Haskett hesitated. Then he laid his hat on the table, and advanced to the hearth-rug, on which Waythorn was standing. There was nothing aggressive in his manner, but he had the solemnity of a timid man resolved on a decisive measure.

"There's just one thing you can do, Mr. Waythorn," he said. "You can remind Mrs. Waythorn that, by the decree of the courts, I am entitled to have a voice in Lily's bringing up." He paused, and went on more deprecatingly: "I'm not the kind to talk about enforcing my rights, Mr. Waythorn. I don't know as I think a man is entitled to rights he hasn't known how to hold on to; but this business of the child is different. I've never let go there—and I never mean to."

· · · · · · ·

The scene left Waythorn deeply shaken. Shamefacedly, in indirect ways, he had been finding out about Haskett; and all that he had learned was favourable. The little man, in order to be near his daughter, had sold out his share in a profitable business in Utica, and accepted a modest clerkship in a New York manufacturing house. He boarded in a shabby street and had few acquaintances. His passion for Lily filled his life. Waythorn felt that this exploration of Haskett was like groping about with a dark-lantern in his wife's past; but he saw now that there were recesses his lantern had not explored. He had never enquired into the exact circumstances of his wife's first matrimonial rupture. On the surface all had been fair. It was she who had obtained the divorce, and the court had given her the child. But Waythorn knew how many ambiguities such a verdict might cover. The mere fact that Haskett retained a right over his daughter implied an unsuspected compromise. Waythorn was an idealist. He always refused to recognise unpleasant contingencies till he found himself confronted with them, and then he saw them followed by a spectral train of consequences. His next days were thus haunted, and he determined to try to lay the ghosts by conjuring them up in his wife's presence.

When he repeated Haskett's request a flame of anger passed over her face; but she subdued it instantly and spoke with a slight quiver of outraged motherhood.

"It is very ungentlemanly of him," she said.

The word grated on Waythorn. "That is neither here nor there. It's a bare question of rights."

She murmured: "It's not as if he could ever be a help to Lily—"

Waythorn flushed. This was even less to his taste. "The question is," he repeated, "what authority has he over her?"

She looked downward, twisting herself a little in her seat. "I am willing to see him—I thought you objected," she faltered.

In a flash he understood that she knew the extent of Haskett's claims. Perhaps it was not the first time she had resisted them.

"My objecting has nothing to do with it," he said coldly; "if Haskett has a right to be consulted you must consult him."

She burst into tears, and he saw that she expected him to regard her as a victim.

Haskett did not abuse his rights. Waythorn had felt miserably sure that he would not. But the governess was dismissed, and from time to time the little man demanded an interview with Alice. After the first outburst she accepted the situation with her usual adaptability. Haskett had once reminded Waythorn of the piano-tuner, and Mrs. Waythorn, after a month or two, appeared to class him with that domestic familiar. Waythorn could not but respect the father's tenacity. At first he had tried to cultivate the suspicion that Haskett might be "up to" something, that he had an object in securing a foothold in the house. But in his heart Waythorn was sure of Haskett's single-mindedness; he even guessed in the latter a mild contempt for such advantages as his relation with the Waythorns might offer. Haskett's sincerity of purpose made him invulnerable, and his successor had to accept him as a lien on the property.

· · · · · ·

Mr. Sellers was sent to Europe to recover from his gout, and Varick's affairs hung on Waythorn's hands. The negotiations were prolonged and complicated; they necessitated frequent conferences between the two men, and the interests of the firm forbade Waythorn's suggesting that his client should transfer his business to another office.

Varick appeared well in the transaction. In moments of relaxation his coarse streak appeared, and Waythorn dreaded his geniality; but in the office he was concise and clear-headed, with a flattering deference to Waythorn's judgment. Their business relations being so affably established, it would have been absurd for the two men to ignore each other in society. The first time they met in a drawing-room, Varick took up their intercourse in the same easy key, and his hostess's grateful glance obliged Waythorn to respond to it. After that they ran across each other frequently, and one evening at a ball Waythorn, wandering through the remoter rooms, came upon Varick seated beside his wife. She coloured a little, and faltered in what she was saying; but Varick nodded to Waythorn without rising, and the latter strolled on.

In the carriage, on the way home, he broke out nervously: "I didn't know you spoke to Varick."

Her voice trembled a little. "It's the first time — he happened to be standing near me; I didn't know what to do. It's so awkward, meeting everywhere — and he said you had been very kind about some business."

"That's different," said Waythorn.

She paused a moment. "I'll do just as you wish," she returned pliantly. "I thought it would be less awkward to speak to him when we meet."

Her pliancy was beginning to sicken him. Had she really no will of her own — no theory about her relation to these men? She had accepted Haskett — did she mean to accept Varick? It was "less awkward," as she had said, and her instinct was to evade difficulties or to circumvent them. With sudden vividness Waythorn saw how the instinct had developed. She was "as easy as an old shoe" — a shoe that too many feet had worn. Her elasticity was the result of tension in too many different directions. Alice Haskett — Alice Varick — Alice Waythorn — she had been each in turn, and had left hanging to each name a little of her privacy, a little of her personality, a little of the inmost self where the unknown god abides.

"Yes — it's better to speak to Varick," said Waythorn wearily.

V

The winter wore on, and society took advantage of the Waythorns' acceptance of Varick. Harassed hostesses were grateful to them for bridging over a social difficulty, and Mrs. Waythorn was held up as a miracle of good taste. Some experimental spirits could not resist the diversion of throwing Varick and his former wife together, and there were those who thought he found a zest in the propinquity. But Mrs. Waythorn's conduct remained irreproachable. She neither avoided Varick nor sought him out. Even Waythorn could not but admit that she had discovered the solution of the newest social problem.

He had married her without giving much thought to that problem. He had fancied that a woman can shed her past like a man. But now he saw that Alice was bound to hers both by the circumstances which forced her into continued relation with it, and by the traces it had left on her nature. With grim irony Waythorn compared himself to a member of a syndicate. He held so many shares in his wife's personality and his predecessors were his partners in the business. If there had been any element of passion in the transaction he would have felt less deteriorated by it. The fact that Alice took her change of husbands like a change of weather reduced the situation to mediocrity. He could have forgiven her for blunders, for excesses; for resisting Haskett, for yielding to Varick; for anything but her acquiescence and her tact. She reminded him of a juggler tossing knives; but the knives were blunt and she knew they would never cut her.

And then, gradually, habit formed a protecting surface for his sensibilities. If he paid for each day's comfort with the small change of his illusions, he grew daily to value the comfort more and set less store upon the coin. He had drifted into a dulling propinquity with Haskett and Varick and he took refuge in the cheap revenge of satirising the situation. He even began to reckon up the advantages which accrued from it, to ask himself if it were not better to own a third of a wife who knew how to make a man happy than a whole one who had lacked opportunity to acquire the art. For it *was* an art, and made up, like all others, of concessions, eliminations and embellishments; of lights judiciously thrown and shadows skilfully softened. His wife knew exactly how to manage the lights, and he knew exactly to what training she owed her skill. He even tried to trace the source of his obligations, to discriminate between the influences which had combined to produce his domestic happiness: he perceived that Haskett's commonness had made Alice worship good breeding, while Varick's liberal construction of the marriage bond had taught her to value the conjugal virtues; so that he was directly indebted to his predecessors for the devotion which made his life easy if not inspiring.

From this phase he passed into that of complete acceptance. He ceased to satirise himself because time dulled the irony of the situation and the joke lost its humour with its sting. Even the sight of Haskett's hat on the hall table had ceased to touch the springs of epigram. The hat was often seen there now, for it had been decided that it was better for Lily's father to visit her than for the little girl to go to his boarding-house. Waythorn, having acquiesced in this arrangement, had been surprised to find how little difference it made. Haskett was never obtrusive, and the few visitors who met him on the stairs were unaware of his identity. Waythorn did not know how often he saw Alice, but with himself Haskett was seldom in contact.

One afternoon, however, he learned on entering that Lily's father was waiting to see him. In the library he found Haskett occupying a chair in his usual provisional way. Waythorn always felt grateful to him for not leaning back.

"I hope you'll excuse me, Mr. Waythorn," he said rising. "I wanted to see Mrs. Waythorn about Lily, and your man asked me to wait here till she came in."

"Of course," said Waythorn, remembering that a sudden leak had that morning given over the drawing-room to the plumbers.

He opened his cigar-case and held it out to his visitor, and Haskett's acceptance seemed to mark a fresh stage in their intercourse. The spring evening was chilly, and Waythorn invited his guest to draw up his chair to the fire. He meant to find an excuse to leave Haskett in a moment; but he was tired and cold, and after all the little man no longer jarred on him.

The two were enclosed in the intimacy of their blended cigar-smoke when the door opened and Varick walked into the room. Waythorn rose abruptly. It was the first time that Varick had come to the house, and the surprise of seeing him, combined with the singular inopportuneness of his arrival, gave a new edge to Waythorn's blunted sensibilities. He stared at his visitor without speaking.

Varick seemed too preoccupied to notice his host's embarrassment.

"My dear fellow," he exclaimed in his most expansive tone, "I must apologise for tumbling in on you in this way, but I was too late to catch you down town, and so I thought—"

He stopped short, catching sight of Haskett, and his sanguine colour deepened to a flush which spread vividly under his scant blond hair. But in a moment he recovered himself and nodded slightly. Haskett returned the bow in silence, and Waythorn was still groping for speech when the footman came in carrying a tea-table.

The intrusion offered a welcome vent to Waythorn's nerves. "What the deuce are you bringing this here for?" he said sharply.

"I beg your pardon, sir, but the plumbers are still in the drawing-room, and Mrs. Waythorn said she would have tea in the library." The footman's perfectly respectful tone implied a reflection on Waythorn's reasonableness.

"Oh, very well," said the latter resignedly, and the footman proceeded to open the folding tea-table and set out its complicated appointments. While this interminable process continued the three men stood motionless, watching it with a fascinated stare, till Waythorn, to break the silence, said to Varick: "Won't you have a cigar?"

He held out the case he had just tendered to Haskett, and Varick helped himself with a smile. Waythorn looked about for a match, and finding none, proffered a light from his own cigar. Haskett, in the background, held his ground mildly, examining his cigar-tip now and then, and stepping forward at the right moment to knock its ashes into the fire.

The footman at last withdrew, and Varick immediately began: "If I could just say half a word to you about this business—"

"Certainly," stammered Waythorn; "in the dining-room—"

But as he placed his hand on the door it opened from without, and his wife appeared on the threshold.

She came in fresh and smiling, in her street dress and hat, shedding a fragrance from the boa[3] which she loosened in advancing.

"Shall we have tea in here, dear?" she began; and then she caught sight of Varick. Her smile deepened, veiling a slight tremor of surprise.

"Why, how do you do?" she said with a distinct note of pleasure.

As she shook hands with Varick she saw Haskett standing behind him. Her smile faded for a moment, but she recalled it quickly, with a scarcely perceptible side-glance at Waythorn.

"How do you do, Mr. Haskett?" she said, and shook hands with him a shade less cordially.

The three men stood awkwardly before her, till Varick, always the most self-possessed, dashed into an explanatory phrase.

"We—I had to see Waythorn a moment on business," he stammered, brick-red from chin to nape.

Haskett stepped forward with his air of mild obstinacy. "I am sorry to intrude; but you appointed five o'clock—" he directed his resigned glance to the time-piece on the mantel.

She swept aside their embarrassment with a charming gesture of hospitality.

"I'm so sorry—I'm always late; but the afternoon was so lovely." She stood drawing off her gloves; propitiatory and graceful, diffusing about her a sense of ease and familiarity in which the situation lost its grotesqueness. "But before talking business," she added brightly, "I'm sure every one wants a cup of tea."

She dropped into her low chair by the tea-table, and the two visitors, as if drawn by her smile, advanced to receive the cups she held out.

She glanced about for Waythorn, and he took the third cup with a laugh.

1904

---

[3]Long scarf of fur or feathers.

Roman Fever

I

From the table at which they had been lunching two American ladies of ripe but well-cared-for middle age moved across the lofty terrace of the Roman restaurant and, leaning on its parapet, looked first at each other, and then down on the outspread glories of the Palatine and the Forum,[1] with the same expression of vague but benevolent approval.

As they leaned there a girlish voice echoed up gaily from the stairs leading to the court below. "Well, come along, then," it cried, not to them but to an invisible companion, "and let's leave the young things to their knitting"; and a voice as fresh laughed back: "Oh, look here, Babs, not actually *knitting*—" "Well, I mean figuratively," rejoined the first. "After all, we haven't left our poor parents much else to do . . ." and at that point the turn of the stairs engulfed the dialogue.

The two ladies looked at each other again, this time with a tinge of smiling embarrassment, and the smaller and paler one shook her head and coloured slightly.

"Barbara!" she murmured, sending an unheard rebuke after the mocking voice in the stairway.

The other lady, who was fuller, and higher in colour, with a small determined nose supported by vigorous black eyebrows, gave a good-humoured laugh. "That's what our daughters think of us!"

Her companion replied by a deprecating gesture. "Not of us individually. We must remember that. It's just the collective modern idea of Mothers. And you see—" Half guiltily she drew from her handsomely mounted black hand-bag a twist of crimson silk run through by two fine knitting needles. "One never knows," she murmured. "The new system has certainly given us a good deal of time to kill; and sometimes I get tired just looking—even at this." Her gesture was now addressed to the stupendous scene at their feet.

The dark lady laughed again, and they both relapsed upon the view, contemplating it in silence, with a sort of diffused serenity which might have been borrowed from the spring effulgence of the Roman skies. The luncheon-hour was long past, and the two had their end of the vast terrace to themselves. At its opposite extremity a few groups, detained by a lingering look at the outspread city, were gathering up guide-books and fumbling for tips. The last of them scattered, and the two ladies were alone on the air-washed height.

"Well, I don't see why we shouldn't just stay here," said Mrs. Slade, the lady of the high colour and energetic brows. Two derelict basket-chairs stood near, and she pushed them into the angle of the parapet, and settled herself in one, her gaze upon the Palatine. "After all, it's still the most beautiful view in the world."

"It always will be, to me," assented her friend Mrs. Ansley, with so slight a stress on the "me" that Mrs. Slade, though she noticed it, wondered if it were not merely accidental, like the random underlinings of old-fashioned letter-writers.

"Grace Ansley was always old-fashioned," she thought; and added aloud, with a retrospective smile: "It's a view we've both been familiar with for a good many years. When we first met here we were younger than our girls are now. You remember?"

"Oh, yes, I remember," murmured Mrs. Ansley, with the same undefinable stress.—"There's that head-waiter wondering," she interpolated. She was evidently far less sure than her companion of herself and of her rights in the world.

"I'll cure him of wondering," said Mrs. Slade, stretching her hand toward a bag as

---

[1]Palatine, chief of the seven Roman hills, site of ancient Roman palaces; Forum, ruins of imperial Rome's social and political center.

discreetly opulent-looking as Mrs. Ansley's. Signing to the head-waiter, she explained that she and her friend were old lovers of Rome, and would like to spend the end of the afternoon looking down on the view—that is, if it did not disturb the service? The head-waiter, bowing over her gratuity, assured her that the ladies were most welcome, and would be still more so if they would condescend to remain for dinner. A full moon night, they would remember. . .

Mrs. Slade's black brows drew together, as though references to the moon were out-of-place and even unwelcome. But she smiled away her frown as the head-waiter retreated. "Well, why not? We might do worse. There's no knowing, I suppose, when the girls will be back. Do you even know back from *where*? I don't!"

Mrs. Ansley again coloured slightly. "I think those young Italian aviators we met at the Embassy invited them to fly to Tarquinia[2] for tea. I suppose they'll want to wait and fly back by moonlight."

"Moonlight—moonlight! What a part it still plays. Do you suppose they're as sentimental as we were?"

"I've come to the conclusion that I don't in the least know what they are," said Mrs. Ansley. "And perhaps we didn't know much more about each other."

"No; perhaps we didn't."

Her friend gave her a shy glance. "I never should have supposed you were sentimental, Alida."

"Well, perhaps I wasn't." Mrs. Slade drew her lids together in retrospect; and for a few moments the two ladies, who had been intimate since childhood, reflected how little they knew each other. Each one, of course, had a label ready to attach to the other's name; Mrs. Delphin Slade, for instance, would have told herself, or any one who asked her, that Mrs. Horace Ansley, twenty-five years ago, had been exquisitely lovely—no, you wouldn't believe it, would you? . . . though, of course, still charming, distinguished. . . Well, as a girl she had been exquisite; far more beautiful than her daughter Barbara, though certainly Babs, according to the new standards at any rate, was more effective—had more *edge*, as they say. Funny where she got it, with those two nullities as parents. Yes; Horace Ansley was—well, just the duplicate of his wife. Museum specimens of old New York. Good-looking, irreproachable, exemplary. Mrs. Slade and Mrs. Ansley had lived opposite each other—actually as well as figuratively—for years. When the drawing-room curtains in No. 20 East 73rd Street were renewed, No. 23, across the way, was always aware of it. And of all the movings, buyings, travels, anniversaries, illnesses—the tame chronicle of an estimable pair. Little of it escaped Mrs. Slade. But she had grown bored with it by the time her husband made his big *coup* in Wall Street, and when they bought in upper Park Avenue had already begun to think: "I'd rather live opposite a speak-easy[3] for a change; at least one might see it raided." The idea of seeing Grace raided was so amusing that (before the move) she launched it at a woman's lunch. It made a hit, and went the rounds—she sometimes wondered if it had crossed the street, and reached Mrs. Ansley. She hoped not, but didn't much mind. Those were the days when respectability was at a discount, and it did the irreproachable no harm to laugh at them a little.

A few years later, and not many months apart, both ladies lost their husbands. There was an appropriate exchange of wreaths and condolences, and a brief renewal of intimacy in the half-shadow of their mourning; and now, after another interval, they had run across each other in Rome, at the same hotel, each of them the modest appendage of a salient daughter. The similarity of their lot had again drawn them together, lending itself to mild jokes, and the mutual confession that, if in old days it

---

[2]Picturesque town in central Italy, dating back to the ancient
Etruscans, containing medieval ruins and churches.
[3]Place selling illegal liquor.

must have been tiring to "keep up" with daughters, it was now, at times, a little dull not to.

No doubt, Mrs. Slade reflected, she felt her unemployment more than poor Grace ever would. It was a big drop from being the wife of Delphin Slade to being his widow. She had always regarded herself (with a certain conjugal pride) as his equal in social gifts, as contributing her full share to the making of the exceptional couple they were: but the difference after his death was irremediable. As the wife of the famous corporation lawyer, always with an international case or two on hand, every day brought its exciting and unexpected obligation: the impromptu entertaining of eminent colleagues from abroad, the hurried dashes on legal business to London, Paris or Rome, where the entertaining was so handsomely reciprocated; the amusement of hearing in her wake: "What, that handsome woman with the good clothes and the eyes is Mrs. Slade — *the* Slade's wife? Really? Generally the wives of celebrities are such frumps."

Yes; being *the* Slade's widow was a dullish business after that. In living up to such a husband all her faculties had been engaged; now she had only her daughter to live up to, for the son who seemed to have inherited his father's gifts had died suddenly in boyhood. She had fought through that agony because her husband was there, to be helped and to help; now, after the father's death, the thought of the boy had become unbearable. There was nothing left but to mother her daughter; and dear Jenny was such a perfect daughter that she needed no excessive mothering. "Now with Babs Ansley I don't know that I *should* be so quiet," Mrs. Slade sometimes half-enviously reflected; but Jenny, who was younger than her brilliant friend, was that rare accident, an extremely pretty girl who somehow made youth and prettiness seem as safe as their absence. It was all perplexing — and to Mrs. Slade a little boring. She wished that Jenny would fall in love — with the wrong man, even; that she might have to be watched, out-manoeuvred, rescued. And instead, it was Jenny who watched her mother, kept her out of draughts, made sure that she had taken her tonic. . .

Mrs. Ansley was much less articulate than her friend, and her mental portrait of Mrs. Slade was slighter, and drawn with fainter touches. "Alida Slade's awfully brilliant; but not as brilliant as she thinks," would have summed it up; though she would have added, for the enlightenment of strangers, that Mrs. Slade had been an extremely dashing girl; much more so than her daughter, who was pretty, of course, and clever in a way, but had none of her mother's — well, "vividness", some one had once called it. Mrs. Ansley would take up current words like this, and cite them in quotation marks, as unheard-of audacities. No; Jenny was not like her mother. Sometimes Mrs. Ansley thought Alida Slade was disappointed; on the whole she had had a sad life. Full of failures and mistakes; Mrs. Ansley had always been rather sorry for her. . .

So these two ladies visualized each other, each through the wrong end of her little telescope.

II

For a long time they continued to sit side by side without speaking. It seemed as though, to both, there was a relief in laying down their somewhat futile activities in the presence of the vast Memento Mori[4] which faced them. Mrs. Slade sat quite still, her eyes fixed on the golden slope of the Palace of the Cæsars, and after a while Mrs. Ansley ceased to fidget with her bag, and she too sank into meditation. Like many intimate friends, the two ladies had never before had occasion to be silent together, and Mrs. Ansley was slightly embarrassed by what seemed, after so many years, a new stage in their intimacy, and one with which she did not yet know how to deal.

---

[4]"Reminder of death" (Latin).

Suddenly the air was full of that deep clangour of bells which periodically covers Rome with a roof of silver. Mrs. Slade glanced at her wrist-watch. "Five o'clock already," she said, as though surprised.

Mrs. Ansley suggested interrogatively: "There's bridge at the Embassy at five." For a long time Mrs. Slade did not answer. She appeared to be lost in contemplation, and Mrs. Ansley thought the remark had escaped her. But after a while she said, as if speaking out of a dream: "Bridge, did you say? Not unless you want to. . . But I don't think I will, you know."

"Oh, no," Mrs. Ansley hastened to assure her. "I don't care to at all. It's so lovely here; and so full of old memories, as you say." She settled herself in her chair, and almost furtively drew forth her knitting. Mrs. Slade took sideway note of this activity, but her own beautifully cared-for hands remained motionless on her knee.

"I was just thinking," she said slowly, "what different things Rome stands for to each generation of travellers. To our grandmothers, Roman fever;[5] to our mothers, sentimental dangers — how we used to be guarded! — to our daughters, no more dangers than the middle of Main Street. They don't know it — but how much they're missing!"

The long golden light was beginning to pale, and Mrs. Ansley lifted her knitting a little closer to her eyes. "Yes; how we were guarded!"

"I always used to think," Mrs. Slade continued, "that our mothers had a much more difficult job than our grandmothers. When Roman fever stalked the streets it must have been comparatively easy to gather in the girls at the danger hour; but when you and I were young, with such beauty calling us, and the spice of disobedience thrown in, and no worse risk than catching cold during the cool hour after sunset, the mothers used to be put to it to keep us in — didn't they?"

She turned again toward Mrs. Ansley, but the latter had reached a delicate point in her knitting. "One, two, three — slip two; yes, they must have been," she assented, without looking up.

Mrs. Slade's eyes rested on her with a deepened attention. "She can knit — in the face of *this*! How like her. . ."

Mrs. Slade leaned back, brooding, her eyes ranging from the ruins which faced her to the long green hollow of the Forum, the fading glow of the church fronts beyond it, and the outlying immensity of the Colosseum.[6] Suddenly she thought: "It's all very well to say that our girls have done away with sentiment and moonlight. But if Babs Ansley isn't out to catch that young aviator — the one who's a Marchese[7] — then I don't know anything. And Jenny has no chance beside her. I know that too. I wonder if that's why Grace Ansley likes the two girls to go everywhere together? My poor Jenny as a foil — !" Mrs. Slade gave a hardly audible laugh, and at the sound Mrs. Ansley dropped her knitting.

"Yes — ?"

"I — oh, nothing. I was only thinking how your Babs carries everything before her. That Campolieri boy is one of the best matches in Rome. Don't look so innocent, my dear — you know he is. And I was wondering, ever so respectfully, you understand . . . wondering how two such exemplary characters as you and Horace had managed to produce anything quite so dynamic." Mrs. Slade laughed again, with a touch of asperity.

Mrs. Ansley's hands lay inert across her needles. She looked straight out at the great accumulated wreckage of passion and splendour at her feet. But her small profile was almost expressionless. At length she said: "I think you overrate Babs, my dear."

---

[5]Malaria, prevalent in Rome.
[6]Ancient Roman amphitheater.
[7]Italian nobleman.

Mrs. Slade's tone grew easier. "No; I don't. I appreciate her. And perhaps envy you. Oh, my girl's perfect; if I were a chronic invalid I'd — well, I think I'd rather be in Jenny's hands. There must be times . . . but there! I always wanted a brilliant daughter . . . and never quite understood why I got an angel instead."

Mrs. Ansley echoed her laugh in a faint murmur. "Babs is an angel too."

"Of course — of course! But she's got rainbow wings. Well, they're wandering by the sea with their young men; and here we sit . . . and it all brings back the past a little too acutely."

Mrs. Ansley had resumed her knitting. One might almost have imagined (if one had known her less well, Mrs. Slade reflected) that, for her also, too many memories rose from the lengthening shadows of those august ruins. But no; she was simply absorbed in her work. What was there for her to worry about? She knew that Babs would almost certainly come back engaged to the extremely eligible Campolieri. "And she'll sell the New York house, and settle down near them in Rome, and never be in their way . . . she's much too tactful. But she'll have an excellent cook, and just the right people in for bridge and cocktails . . . and a perfectly peaceful old age among her grandchildren."

Mrs. Slade broke off this prophetic flight with a recoil of self-disgust. There was no one of whom she had less right to think unkindly than of Grace Ansley. Would she never cure herself of envying her? Perhaps she had begun too long ago.

She stood up and leaned against the parapet, filling her troubled eyes with the tranquillizing magic of the hour. But instead of tranquillizing her the sight seemed to increase her exasperation. Her gaze turned toward the Colosseum. Already its golden flank was drowned in purple shadow, and above it the sky curved crystal clear, without light or colour. It was the moment when afternoon and evening hang balanced in mid-heaven.

Mrs. Slade turned back and laid her hand on her friend's arm. The gesture was so abrupt that Mrs. Ansley looked up, startled.

"The sun's set. You're not afraid, my dear?"

"Afraid — ?"

"Of Roman fever or pneumonia? I remember how ill you were that winter. As a girl you had a very delicate throat, hadn't you?"

"Oh, we're all right up here. Down below, in the Forum, it does get deathly cold, all of a sudden . . . but not here."

"Ah, of course you know because you had to be so careful." Mrs. Slade turned back to the parapet. She thought: "I must make one more effort not to hate her." Aloud she said: "Whenever I look at the Forum from up here, I remember that story about a great-aunt of yours, wasn't she? A dreadfully wicked great-aunt?"

"Oh, yes; Great-aunt Harriet. The one who was supposed to have sent her young sister out to the Forum after sunset to gather a night-blooming flower for her album. All our great-aunts and grandmothers used to have albums of dried flowers."

Mrs. Slade nodded. "But she really sent her because they were in love with the same man —"

"Well, that was the family tradition. They said Aunt Harriet confessed it years afterward. At any rate, the poor little sister caught the fever and died. Mother used to frighten us with the story when we were children."

"And you frightened *me* with it, that winter when you and I were here as girls. The winter I was engaged to Delphin."

Mrs. Ansley gave a faint laugh. "Oh, did I? Really frighten you? I don't believe you're easily frightened."

"Not often; but I was then. I was easily frightened because I was too happy. I wonder if you know what that means?"

"I — yes . . ." Mrs. Ansley faltered.

"Well, I suppose that was why the story of your wicked aunt made such an impression on me. And I thought: 'There's no more Roman fever, but the Forum is deathly cold after sunset—especially after a hot day. And the Colosseum's even colder and damper'."

"The Colosseum—?"

"Yes. It wasn't easy to get in, after the gates were locked for the night. Far from easy. Still, in those days it could be managed; it *was* managed, often. Lovers met there who couldn't meet elsewhere. You knew that?"

"I—I daresay. I don't remember."

"You don't remember? You don't remember going to visit some ruins or other one evening, just after dark, and catching a bad chill? You were supposed to have gone to see the moon rise. People always said that expedition was what caused your illness."

There was a moment's silence; then Mrs. Ansley rejoined: "Did they? It was all so long ago."

"Yes. And you got well again—so it didn't matter. But I suppose it struck your friends—the reason given for your illness, I mean—because everybody knew you were so prudent on account of your throat, and your mother took such care of you. . . You *had* been out late sight-seeing, hadn't you, that night?"

"Perhaps I had. The most prudent girls aren't always prudent. What made you think of it now?"

Mrs. Slade seemed to have no answer ready. But after a moment she broke out: "Because I simply can't bear it any longer—!"

Mrs. Ansley lifted her head quickly. Her eyes were wide and very pale. "Can't bear what?"

"Why—your not knowing that I've always known why you went."

"Why I went—?"

"Yes. You think I'm bluffing, don't you? Well, you went to meet the man I was engaged to—and I can repeat every word of the letter that took you there."

While Mrs. Slade spoke Mrs. Ansley had risen unsteadily to her feet. Her bag, her knitting and gloves, slid in a panic-stricken heap to the ground. She looked at Mrs. Slade as though she were looking at a ghost.

"No, no—don't," she faltered out.

"Why not? Listen, if you don't believe me. 'My one darling, things can't go on like this. I must see you alone. Come to the Colosseum immediately after dark tomorrow. There will be somebody to let you in. No one whom you need fear will suspect'—but perhaps you've forgotten what the letter said?"

Mrs. Ansley met the challenge with an unexpected composure. Steadying herself against the chair she looked at her friend, and replied: "No; I know it by heart too."

"And the signature? 'Only *your* D.S.' Was that it? I'm right, am I? That was the letter that took you out that evening after dark?"

Mrs. Ansley was still looking at her. It seemed to Mrs. Slade that a slow struggle was going on behind the voluntarily controlled mask of her small quiet face. "I shouldn't have thought she had herself so well in hand," Mrs. Slade reflected, almost resentfully. But at this moment Mrs. Ansley spoke. "I don't know how you knew. I burnt that letter at once."

"Yes; you would, naturally—you're so prudent!" The sneer was open now. "And if you burnt the letter you're wondering how on earth I know what was in it. That's it, isn't it?"

Mrs. Slade waited, but Mrs. Ansley did not speak.

"Well, my dear, I know what was in that letter because I wrote it!"

"You wrote it?"

"Yes."

The two women stood for a minute staring at each other in the last golden light. Then Mrs. Ansley dropped back into her chair. "Oh," she murmured, and covered her face with her hands.

Mrs. Slade waited nervously for another word or movement. None came, and at length she broke out: "I horrify you."

Mrs. Ansley's hands dropped to her knee. The face they uncovered was streaked with tears. "I wasn't thinking of you. I was thinking — it was the only letter I ever had from him!"

"And I wrote it. Yes; I wrote it! But I was the girl he was engaged to. Did you happen to remember that?"

Mrs. Ansley's head drooped again. "I'm not trying to excuse myself. . . I remembered. . ."

"And still you went?"

"Still I went."

Mrs. Slade stood looking down on the small bowed figure at her side. The flame of her wrath had already sunk, and she wondered why she had ever thought there would be any satisfaction in inflicting so purposeless a wound on her friend. But she had to justify herself.

"You do understand? I'd found out — and I hated you, hated you. I knew you were in love with Delphin — and I was afraid; afraid of you, of your quiet ways, your sweet- ness . . . your . . . well, I wanted you out of the way, that's all. Just for a few weeks; just till I was sure of him. So in a blind fury I wrote that letter. . . I don't know why I'm telling you now."

"I suppose," said Mrs. Ansley slowly, "it's because you've always gone on hating me."

"Perhaps. Or because I wanted to get the whole thing off my mind." She paused. "I'm glad you destroyed the letter. Of course I never thought you'd die."

Mrs. Ansley relapsed into silence, and Mrs. Slade, leaning above her, was con- scious of a strange sense of isolation, of being cut off from the warm current of human communion. "You think me a monster!"

"I don't know. . . It was the only letter I had, and you say he didn't write it?"

"Ah, how you care for him still!"

"I cared for that memory," said Mrs. Ansley.

Mrs. Slade continued to look down on her. She seemed physically reduced by the blow — as if, when she got up, the wind might scatter her like a puff of dust. Mrs. Slade's jealousy suddenly leapt up again at the sight. All these years the woman had been living on that letter. How she must have loved him, to treasure the mere mem- ory of its ashes! The letter of the man her friend was engaged to. Wasn't it she who was the monster?

"You tried your best to get him away from me, didn't you? But you failed; and I kept him. That's all."

"Yes. That's all."

"I wish now I hadn't told you. I'd no idea you'd feel about it as you do; I thought you'd be amused. It all happened so long ago, as you say; and you must do me the justice to remember that I had no reason to think you'd ever taken it seriously. How could I, when you were married to Horace Ansley two months afterward? As soon as you could get out of bed your mother rushed you off to Florence and married you. People were rather surprised — they wondered at its being done so quickly; but I thought I knew. I had an idea you did it out of *pique*[8] — to be able to say you'd got ahead of Delphin and me. Girls have such silly reasons for doing the most serious things. And your marrying so soon convinced me that you'd never really cared."

"Yes. I suppose it would," Mrs. Ansley assented.

The clear heaven overhead was emptied of all its gold. Dusk spread over it, abruptly darkening the Seven Hills. Here and there lights began to twinkle through the foliage at their feet. Steps were coming and going on the deserted terrace — waiters looking out of the doorway at the head of the stairs, then reappearing with trays and napkins and flasks of wine. Tables were moved, chairs straightened. A feeble string of electric lights flickered out. Some vases of faded flowers were carried

---

[8]Resentment stemming from wounded pride.

away, and brought back replenished. A stout lady in a dust-coat suddenly appeared, asking in broken Italian if any one had seen the elastic band which held together her tattered Baedeker.[9] She poked with her stick under the table at which she had lunched, the waiters assisting.

The corner where Mrs. Slade and Mrs. Ansley sat was still shadowy and deserted. For a long time neither of them spoke. At length Mrs. Slade began again: "I suppose I did it as a sort of joke—"

"A joke?"

"Well, girls are ferocious sometimes, you know. Girls in love especially. And I remember laughing to myself all the evening at the idea that you were waiting around there in the dark, dodging out of sight, listening for every sound, trying to get in—. Of course I was upset when I heard you were so ill afterward."

Mrs. Ansley had not moved for a long time. But now she turned slowly toward her companion. "But I didn't wait. He'd arranged everything. He was there. We were let in at once," she said.

Mrs. Slade sprang up from her leaning position. "Delphin there? They let you in?—Ah, now you're lying!" she burst out with violence.

Mrs. Ansley's voice grew clearer, and full of surprise. "But of course he was there. Naturally he came—"

"Came? How did he know he'd find you there? You must be raving!"

Mrs. Ansley hesitated, as though reflecting. "But I answered the letter. I told him I'd be there. So he came."

Mrs. Slade flung her hands up to her face. "Oh, God—you answered! I never thought of your answering. . ."

"It's odd you never thought of it, if you wrote the letter."

"Yes. I was blind with rage."

Mrs. Ansley rose, and drew her fur scarf about her. "It is cold here. We'd better go. . . I'm sorry for you," she said, as she clasped the fur about her throat.

The unexpected words sent a pang through Mrs. Slade. "Yes; we'd better go." She gathered up her bag and cloak. "I don't know why you should be sorry for me," she muttered.

Mrs. Ansley stood looking away from her toward the dusky secret mass of the Colosseum. "Well—because I didn't have to wait that night."

Mrs. Slade gave an unquiet laugh. "Yes; I was beaten there. But I oughtn't to begrudge it to you, I suppose. At the end of all these years. After all, I had everything; I had him for twenty-five years. And you had nothing but that one letter that he didn't write."

Mrs. Ansley was again silent. At length she turned toward the door of the terrace. She took a step, and turned back, facing her companion.

"I had Barbara," she said, and began to move ahead of Mrs. Slade toward the stairway.

1934, 1936

from A Backward Glance

[HENRY JAMES AND WALT WHITMAN][1]

I think it was James who first made me understand that genius is not an indivisible element, but one variously apportioned, so that the popular system of dividing hu-

---

[9]A guidebook, one of a popular series by Karl Baedecker (1801–1859).
[1]From chapter VIII, devoted to the memories of Henry James (1843–1916), American novelist and close friend of

Wharton. This passage reveals James's love for Whitman's poetry in contrast with his attack on it in a review written when he was twenty-two.

manity into geniuses and non-geniuses is a singularly inadequate way of estimating human complexity. In connection with this, I once brought him a phrase culled in a literary review. "Mr. — — has *almost a streak* of genius." James, always an eager collector of verbal oddities, fell on the phrase with rapture, and earnest requests to every one to define the exact extent of "almost a streak" caused him amusement for months afterward. I mention this because so few people seem to have known in Henry James the ever-bubbling fountain of fun which was the delight of his intimates.

One of our joys, when the talk touched on any great example of prose or verse, was to get the book from the shelf, and ask one of the company to read the passage aloud. There were some admirable readers in the group, in whose gift I had long delighted; but I had never heard Henry James read aloud—or known that he enjoyed doing so—till one night some one alluded to Emily Brontë's poems, and I said I had never read "Remembrance." Immediately he took the volume from my hand, and, his eyes filling, and some far-away emotion deepening his rich and flexible voice, he began:

> Cold in the earth, and the deep snow piled above thee,
> Far, far removed, cold in the dreary grave,
> Have I forgot, my only Love, to love thee,
> Severed at last by Time's all-severing wave?[2]

I had never before heard poetry read as he read it; and I never have since. He chanted it, and he was not afraid to chant it, as many good readers are, who, though they instinctively feel that the genius of the English poetical idiom requires it to be spoken *as poetry*, are yet afraid of yielding to their instinct because the present-day fashion is to chatter high verse as though it were colloquial prose. James, on the contrary, far from shirking the rhythmic emphasis, gave it full expression. His stammer ceased as by magic as soon as he began to read, and his ear, so sensitive to the convolutions of an intricate prose style, never allowed him to falter over the most complex prosody but swept him forward on greater rollers of sound till the full weight of his voice fell on the last cadence.

James's reading was a thing apart, an emanation of his inmost self, unaffected by fashion or elocutionary artifice. He read from his soul, and no one who never heard him read poetry knows what that soul was. Another day some one spoke of Whitman, and it was a joy to me to discover that James thought him, as I did, the greatest of American poets. "Leaves of Grass"[3] was put into his hands, and all that evening we sat rapt while he wandered from "The Song of Myself" to "When lilacs last in the dooryard bloomed" (when he read "Lovely and soothing Death" his voice filled the hushed room like an organ adagio), and thence let himself be lured on to the mysterious music of "Out of the Cradle," reading, or rather crooning it in a mood of subdued ecstasy till the fivefold invocation to Death tolled out like the knocks in the opening bars of the Fifth Symphony.[4]

James's admiration of Whitman, his immediate response to that mighty appeal, was a new proof of the way in which, above a certain level, the most divergent intelligences walk together like gods. We talked long that night of "Leaves of Grass," tossing back and forth to each other treasure after treasure; but finally James, in one of his sudden humorous drops from the heights, flung up his hands and cried out with the old stammer and twinkle: "Oh, yes, a great genius; undoubtedly a very great genius! Only one cannot help deploring his too-extensive acquaintance with the foreign languages."

1934

---

[2]Lines 1–4 of "Remembrance" (1846) by English novelist and poet Emily Brontë (1818–1848).

[3]*Leaves of Grass* (1855–92) by Walt Whitman (1819–1892).
[4]By German composer Ludwig van Beethoven (1770–1827).

FRANK NORRIS
(1870–1902)

Frank Norris once wrote that the most difficult lesson for the "intended novelist" to learn about writing fiction "is the fact that life is better than literature. The amateur will say this with conviction, will preach it in public and practise the exact reverse in private. But it still remains true that all the temperament, all the sensitiveness to impressions, all the education in the world will not help one little, little bit in the writing of the novel if life itself, the crude, the raw, the vulgar, if you will, is not studied. An hour's experience is worth ten years of study — of reading other people's books."

The "crude," the "raw," the "vulgar" — Norris was at the forefront in opening fiction to subjects that had too often been declared off limits by the genteel. In doing so, he helped to create a native *naturalism* that, though related to the French naturalism of Émile Zola among others, had its own American accent and flavor as in the work of Stephen Crane, Theodore Dreiser, and Jack London.

Norris was born in Chicago into a well-to-do family in the jewelry business. His father had worked his way up from itinerant clock-mender and peddler; his mother had taught school and had a successful career as an actress. The family moved to California in 1884, where Frank attended a school for boys (Belmont) outside San Francisco. He showed early on an aptitude for drawing and was encouraged to study art. In 1887 the Norrises went abroad, visiting London and Paris. After seeing their son established as a student in the Atelier Julien in Paris, his parents returned to America. In 1889 Norris abruptly returned home, perhaps by this time discouraged at his progress as an artist.

In any event, he entered the University of California in 1890 and was soon determined to become a writer. After four years at the university, Norris went to Harvard in 1894 to study writing for a year. Although he had not read the French naturalists when in Paris, he began to read Émile Zola at Berkeley and at Cambridge began writing two novels, *Vandover and the Brute* (published posthumously in 1914) and *McTeague*. He incorporated in them the elements of naturalism that he observed in Zola: a portrayal of life's seamier side, with crude characters motivated primarily by greed; and a demonstration of the severe limitations placed on free will by biological, social, and economic determinism.

He then became a journalist, turning up in South Africa during the preliminary skirmishes of the Boer War. He was captured by the Boers and expelled, but an attack of African fever delayed his departure until 1896. For two years he worked for a San Francisco magazine, *The Wave*, which serialized his first novel, the sea romance *Moran of the Lady Letty* (1898). He next moved to the muckraking journal *McClure's Magazine*, serving as its correspondent covering the Spanish-American War in Cuba, where he met Stephen Crane. A bout of malaria cut this assignment short.

Although Norris wrote and published other works to put money in his purse, he spent all his serious talent in the writing of *McTeague*, published in 1899. William Dean Howells noted, in a remarkably favorable review, the novel's "Zolaesque lines," and observed: "It abounds in touches of character at once fine and free, in little miracles of observation, in vivid insight, in simple and subtle expression." Although Howells regretted that Norris's portrayal of life as "squalid and cruel and vile and hateful" left out "beauty," his regret was submerged in his praise.

Norris was elated by *McTeague*'s reception and was soon embarked on his "Epic of Wheat" trilogy. *The Octopus* (1901) dealt with the wheat farmers in conflict with the railroad trust. *The Pit* (published posthumously in 1903) dealt with the greed operative in the speculative trading in grain on the Chicago stock exchange. Norris's death in 1902 (from peritonitis following an appendectomy) prevented him from writing the third volume, *The Wolf*, about the consumption of wheat in the village of a country suffering a calamitous famine. A collection of Norris's essays, *The Responsibilities of the Novelist*, appeared in 1903.

Norris's death cut short a career of immense promise. Even in the brief time he had, he proved himself an innovator in American fiction, introducing materials and subjects that had previously been barred. Later writers — Hemingway and Faulkner, Flannery O'Connor and Ralph Ellison among them — would take advantage of the freedoms he championed and exemplified.

ADDITIONAL READING

The Complete Edition of Frank Norris, 10 vols., 1928; *The Letters of Frank Norris*, ed. Franklin Walker, 1956; *The Literary Criticism of Frank Norris*, ed. Donald Pizer, 1964.

Franklin Walker, *Frank Norris: A Biography*, 1932, 1963; Ernest Marchand, *Frank Norris: A Study*, 1942; *Frank Norris: A Bibliography*, compiled by Kenneth A. Lohf and Eugene P. Sheehy, 1959; Warren French, *Frank Norris*, 1962; Donald Pizer, *The Novels of Frank Norris*, 1966; William B. Dillingham, *Frank Norris: Instinct and Art*, 1969; Jesse S. Crisler and Joseph R. McElrath, Jr., *Frank Norris: A Reference Guide*, 1974; Don Graham, *The Fiction of Frank Norris*, 1978; Don Graham, ed., *Critical Essays on Frank Norris*, 1980; Harold Kaplan, *Power and Order: Henry Adams and the Naturalistic Tradition in American Fiction*, 1981; Joseph R. McElrath, ed., *Frank Norris: The Critical Reception*, 1981; Barbara Hochman, *The Art of Frank Norris, Storyteller*, 1988.

TEXTS

A Deal in Wheat and Other Stories of the New and Old West, 1903; *The Responsibilities of the Novelist*, 1903.

A Deal in Wheat

I
THE BEAR[1] — WHEAT AT SIXTY-TWO

As Sam Lewiston backed the horse into the shafts of his buckboard and began hitching the tugs to the whiffletree,[2] his wife came out from the kitchen door of the house and drew near, and stood for some time at the horse's head, her arms folded and her apron rolled around them. For a long moment neither spoke. They had talked over the situation so long and so comprehensively the night before that there seemed to be nothing more to say.

The time was late in the summer, the place a ranch in southwestern Kansas, and Lewiston and his wife were two of a vast population of farmers, wheat growers, who at that moment were passing through a crisis — a crisis that at any moment might culminate in tragedy. Wheat was down to sixty-six.

---

[1] In the stock exchange, both *bears* and *bulls* are speculators, out for quick and easy money, often unethical in their manipulation of the market for personal profit. A "bear" in wheat is one who sells stock for future delivery of wheat in the expectation (or knowledge) that prices will fall; he thus will pay less for the wheat than the sum for which he sold it. The "bull" buys at a low price in a market on the rise (perhaps because of his own manipulation).

[2] Pivoted bar to which the harness straps or tugs are secured.

At length Emma Lewiston spoke.

"Well," she hazarded, looking vaguely out across the ranch toward the horizon, leagues distant; "well, Sam, there's always that offer of brother Joe's. We can quit—and go to Chicago—if the worst comes."

"And give up!" exclaimed Lewiston, running the lines through the torets.[3] "Leave the ranch! Give up! After all these years!"

His wife made no reply for the moment. Lewiston climbed into the buckboard and gathered up the lines. "Well, here goes for the last try, Emmie," he said. "Good-by, girl. Maybe things will look better in town to-day."

"Maybe," she said gravely. She kissed her husband good-by and stood for some time looking after the buckboard traveling toward the town in a moving pillar of dust.

"I don't know," she murmured at length; "I don't know just how we're going to make out."

When he reached town, Lewiston tied the horse to the iron railing in front of the Odd Fellows' Hall, the ground floor of which was occupied by the post-office, and went across the street and up the stairway of a building of brick and granite—quite the most pretentious structure of the town—and knocked at a door upon the first landing. The door was furnished with a pane of frosted glass, on which, in gold letters, was inscribed, "Bridges & Co., Grain Dealers."

Bridges himself, a middle-aged man who wore a velvet skull-cap and who was smoking a Pittsburg stogie, met the farmer at the counter and the two exchanged perfunctory greetings.

"Well," said Lewiston, tentatively, after awhile.

"Well, Lewiston," said the other, "I can't take that wheat of yours at any better than sixty-two."

"Sixty-*two*."

"It's the Chicago price that does it, Lewiston. Truslow is bearing the stuff for all he's worth. It's Truslow and the bear clique that stick the knife into us. The price broke again this morning. We've just got a wire."

"Good heavens," murmured Lewiston, looking vaguely from side to side. "That—that ruins me. I *can't* carry my grain any longer—what with storage charges and—and—Bridges, I don't see just how I'm going to make out. Sixty-two cents a bushel! Why, man, what with this and with that it's cost me nearly a dollar a bushel to raise that wheat, and now Truslow—"

He turned away abruptly with a quick gesture of infinite discouragement.

He went down the stairs, and making his way to where his buckboard was hitched, got in, and, with eyes vacant, the reins slipping and sliding in his limp, half-open hands, drove slowly back to the ranch. His wife had seen him coming, and met him as he drew up before the barn.

"Well?" she demanded.

"Emmie," he said as he got out of the buckboard, laying his arm across her shoulder, "Emmie, I guess we'll take up with Joe's offer. We'll go to Chicago. We're cleaned out!"

II
THE BULL—WHEAT AT A DOLLAR-TEN

... —*and said Party of the Second Part further covenants and agrees to merchandise such wheat in foreign ports, it being understood and agreed between the Party of the First Part and the Party of the Second Part that the wheat hereinbefore mentioned is released and sold to the Party of the Second Part for export purposes only, and not for consumption or distribution within the boundaries of the United States of America or of Canada.*

---

[3]Terrets: harness rings.

"Now, Mr. Gates, if you will sign for Mr. Truslow I guess that'll be all," remarked Hornung when he had finished reading.

Hornung affixed his signature to the two documents and passed them over to Gates, who signed for his principal and client, Truslow—or, as he had been called ever since he had gone into the fight against Hornung's corner[4]—the Great Bear. Hornung's secretary was called in and witnessed the signatures, and Gates thrust the contract into his Gladstone bag and stood up, smoothing his hat.

"You will deliver the warehouse receipts for the grain," began Gates.

"I'll send a messenger to Truslow's office before noon," interrupted Hornung. "You can pay by certified check through the Illinois Trust people."

When the other had taken himself off, Hornung sat for some moments gazing abstractedly toward his office windows, thinking over the whole matter. He had just agreed to release to Truslow, at the rate of one dollar and ten cents per bushel, one hundred thousand out of the two million and odd bushels of wheat that he, Hornung, controlled, or actually owned. And for the moment he was wondering if, after all, he had done wisely in not goring the Great Bear to actual financial death. He had made him pay one hundred thousand dollars. Truslow was good for this amount. Would it not have been better to have put a prohibitive figure on the grain and forced the Bear into bankruptcy? True, Hornung would then be without his enemy's money, but Truslow would have been eliminated from the situation, and that—so Hornung told himself—was always a consummation most devoutly, strenuously and diligently to be striven for. Truslow once dead was dead, but the Bear was never more dangerous than when desperate.

"But so long as he can't get *wheat*," muttered Hornung at the end of his reflections, "he can't hurt me. And he can't get it. That I *know*."

For Hornung controlled the situation. So far back as the February of that year an "unknown bull" had been making his presence felt on the floor of the Board of Trade. By the middle of March the commercial reports of the daily press had begun to speak of "the powerful bull clique"; a few weeks later that legendary condition of affairs implied and epitomized in the magic words "Dollar Wheat" had been attained, and by the first of April, when the price had been boosted to one dollar and ten cents a bushel, Hornung had disclosed his hand, and in place of mere rumours, the definite and authoritative news that May wheat had been cornered in the Chicago pit[5] went flashing around the world from Liverpool to Odessa and from Duluth to Buenos Ayres.

It was—so the veteran operators were persuaded—Truslow himself who had made Hornung's corner possible. The Great Bear had for once over-reached himself, and, believing himself all-powerful, had hammered the price just the fatal fraction too far down. Wheat had gone to sixty-two—for the time, and under the circumstances, an abnormal price. When the reaction came it was tremendous. Hornung saw his chance, seized it, and in a few months had turned the tables, had cornered the product, and virtually driven the bear clique out of the pit.

On the same day that the delivery of the hundred thousand bushels was made to Truslow, Hornung met his broker at his lunch club.

"Well," said the latter, "I see you let go that line of stuff to Truslow."

Hornung nodded; but the broker added:

"Remember, I was against it from the very beginning. I know we've cleared up over a hundred thou'. I would have fifty times preferred to have lost twice that and *smashed Truslow dead*. Bet you what you like he makes us pay for it somehow."

"Huh!" grunted his principal. "How about insurance, and warehouse charges,

---

[4] I.e., corner, or monopoly, of wheat.
[5] A pit is the area of an exchange, here the Chicago Board of Trade, where trade in a specific commodity is carried on.

and carrying expenses on that lot? Guess we'd have had to pay those, too, if we'd held on."

But the other put up his chin, unwilling to be persuaded. "I won't sleep easy," he declared, "till Truslow is busted."

III
THE PIT

Just as Going mounted the steps on the edge of the pit the great gong struck, a roar of a hundred voices developed with the swiftness of successive explosions, the rush of a hundred men surging downward to the centre of the pit filled the air with the stamp and grind of feet, a hundred hands in eager strenuous gestures tossed upward from out the brown of the crowd, the official reporter in his cage on the margin of the pit leaned far forward with straining ear to catch the opening bid, and another day of battle was begun.

Since the sale of the hundred thousand bushels of wheat to Truslow the "Hornung crowd" had steadily shouldered the price higher until on this particular morning it stood at one dollar and a half. That was Hornung's price. No one else had any grain to sell.

But not ten minutes after the opening, Going was surprised out of all countenance to hear shouted from the other side of the pit these words:

"Sell May at one-fifty."

Going was for the moment touching elbows with Kimbark on one side and with Merriam on the other, all three belonging to the "Hornung crowd." Their answering challenge of "*Sold*" was as the voice of one man. They did not pause to reflect upon the strangeness of the circumstance. (That was for afterward.) Their response to the offer was as unconscious as reflex action and almost as rapid, and before the pit was well aware of what had happened the transaction of one thousand bushels was down upon Going's trading-card and fifteen hundred dollars had changed hands. But here was a marvel—the whole available supply of wheat cornered, Hornung master of the situation, invincible, unassailable; yet behold a man willing to sell, a Bear bold enough to raise his head.

"That was Kennedy, wasn't it, who made that offer?" asked Kimbark, as Going noted down the trade—"Kennedy, that new man?"

"Yes; who do you suppose he's selling for; who's willing to go short at this stage of the game?"

"Maybe he ain't short."

"Short! Great heavens, man; where'd he get the stuff?"

"Blamed if I know. We can account for every handful of May. Steady! Oh, there he goes again."

"Sell a thousand May at one-fifty," vociferated the bear-broker, throwing out his hand, one finger raised to indicate the number of "contracts" offered. This time it was evident that he was attacking the Hornung crowd deliberately, for, ignoring the jam of traders that swept toward him, he looked across the pit to where Going and Kimbark were shouting "*Sold! Sold!*" and nodded his head.

A second time Going made memoranda of the trade, and either the Hornung holdings were increased by two thousand bushels of May wheat or the Hornung bank account swelled by at least three thousand dollars of some unknown short's money.

Of late—so sure was the bull crowd of its position—no one had even thought of glancing at the inspection sheet on the bulletin board. But now one of Going's messengers hurried up to him with the announcement that this sheet showed receipts at Chicago for that morning of twenty-five thousand bushels, and not credited to Hornung. Some one had got hold of a line of wheat overlooked by the "clique" and was dumping it upon them.

"Wire the Chief," said Going over his shoulder to Merriam. This one struggled out of the crowd, and on a telegraph blank scribbled:

> "Strong bear movement—New man—Kennedy—Selling in lots of five contracts—Chicago receipts twenty-five thousand."

The message was despatched, and in a few moments the answer came back, laconic, of military terseness:

> "Support the market."

And Going obeyed, Merriam and Kimbark following, the new broker fairly throwing the wheat at them in thousand-bushel lots.

"Sell May at 'fifty; sell May; sell May." A moment's indecision, an instant's hesitation, the first faint suggestion of weakness, and the market would have broken under them. But for the better part of four hours they stood their ground, taking all that was offered, in constant communication with the Chief, and from time to time stimulated and steadied by his brief, unvarying command:

"Support the market."

At the close of the session they had bought in the twenty-five thousand bushels of May. Hornung's position was as stable as a rock, and the price closed even with the opening figure—one dollar and a half.

But the morning's work was the talk of all La Salle Street. Who was back of the raid? What was the meaning of this unexpected selling? For weeks the pit trading had been merely nominal. Truslow, the Great Bear, from whom the most serious attack might have been expected, had gone to his country seat at Geneva Lake, in Wisconsin, declaring himself to be out of the market entirely. He went bass-fishing every day.

IV
THE BELT LINE

On a certain day toward the middle of the month, at a time when the mysterious Bear had unloaded some eighty thousand bushels upon Hornung, a conference was held in the library of Hornung's home. His broker attended it, and also a clean-faced, bright-eyed individual whose name of Cyrus Ryder might have been found upon the pay-roll of a rather well-known detective agency. For upward of half an hour after the conference began the detective spoke, the other two listening attentively, gravely.

"Then, last of all," concluded Ryder, "I made out I was a hobo, and began stealing rides on the Belt Line Railroad. Know the road? It just circles Chicago. Truslow owns it. Yes? Well, then I began to catch on. I noticed that cars of certain numbers—thirty-one nought thirty-four, thirty-two one ninety—well, the numbers don't matter, but anyhow, these cars were always switched onto the sidings by Mr. Truslow's main elevator D soon as they came in. The wheat was shunted in, and they were pulled out again. Well, I spotted one car and stole a ride on her. Say, look here, *that car went right around the city on the Belt, and came back to D again, and the same wheat in her all the time.* The grain was re-inspected—it was raw, I tell you—and the warehouse receipts made out just as though the stuff had come in from Kansas or Iowa."

"The same wheat all the time!" interrupted Hornung.

"The same wheat—your wheat, that you sold to Truslow."

"Great snakes!" ejaculated Hornung's broker. "Truslow never took it abroad at all."

"Took it abroad! Say, he's just been running it around Chicago, like the supers in 'Shenandoah,'[6] round an' round, so you'd think it was a new lot, an' selling it back to you again."

---

[6]The supernumerary actors, "supers," in Bronson Howard's popular Civil War play *Shenandoah* (1888) gave the effect of great numbers by circling on and off stage repeatedly.

"No wonder we couldn't account for so much wheat."

"Bought it from us at one-ten, and made us buy it back—our own wheat—at one-fifty."

Hornung and his broker looked at each other in silence for a moment. Then all at once Hornung struck the arm of his chair with his fist and exploded in a roar of laughter. The broker stared for one bewildered moment, then followed his example.

"Sold! Sold!" shouted Hornung almost gleefully. "Upon my soul it's as good as a Gilbert and Sullivan show. And we—Oh, Lord! Billy, shake on it, and hats off to my distinguished friend, Truslow. He'll be President some day. Hey! What? Prosecute him? Not I."

"He's done us out of a neat hatful of dollars for all that," observed the broker, suddenly grave.

"Billy, it's worth the price."

"We've got to make it up somehow."

"Well, tell you what. We were going to boost the price to one seventy-five next week, and make that our settlement figure."

"Can't do it now. Can't afford it."

"No. Here; we'll let out a big link; we'll put wheat at two dollars, and let it go at that."

"Two it is, then," said the broker.

V
THE BREAD LINE

The street was very dark and absolutely deserted. It was a district on the "South Side," not far from the Chicago River, given up largely to wholesale stores, and after nightfall was empty of all life. The echoes slept but lightly hereabouts, and the slightest footfall, the faintest noise, woke them upon the instant and sent them clamouring up and down the length of the pavement between the iron shuttered fronts. The only light visible came from the side door of a certain "Vienna" bakery, where at one o'clock in the morning loaves of bread were given away to any who should ask. Every evening about nine o'clock the outcasts began to gather about the side door. The stragglers came in rapidly, and the line—the "bread line," as it was called—began to form. By midnight it was usually some hundred yards in length, stretching almost the entire length of the block.

Toward ten in the evening, his coat collar turned up against the fine drizzle that pervaded the air, his hands in his pockets, his elbows gripping his sides, Sam Lewiston came up and silently took his place at the end of the line.

Unable to conduct his farm upon a paying basis at the time when Truslow, the "Great Bear," had sent the price of grain down to sixty-two cents a bushel, Lewiston had turned over his entire property to his creditors, and, leaving Kansas for good, had abandoned farming, and had left his wife at her sister's boarding-house in Topeka with the understanding that she was to join him in Chicago so soon as he had found a steady job. Then he had come to Chicago and had turned workman. His brother Joe conducted a small hat factory on Archer Avenue, and for a time he found there a meager employment. But difficulties had occurred, times were bad, the hat factory was involved in debts, the repealing of a certain import duty on manufactured felt overcrowded the home market with cheap Belgian and French products, and in the end his brother had assigned[7] and gone to Milwaukee.

Thrown out of work, Lewiston drifted aimlessly about Chicago, from pillar to post, working a little, earning here a dollar, there a dime, but always sinking, sinking, till at last the ooze of the lowest bottom dragged at his feet and the rush of the great ebb went over him and engulfed him and shut him out from the light, and a park bench became his home and the "bread line" his chief makeshift of subsistence.

---

[7]Transferred his property to another.

He stood now in the enfolding drizzle, sodden, stupefied with fatigue. Before and behind stretched the line. There was no talking. There was no sound. The street was empty. It was so still that the passing of a cable-car in the adjoining thoroughfare grated like prolonged rolling explosions, beginning and ending at immeasurable distances. The drizzle descended incessantly. After a long time midnight struck.

There was something ominous and gravely impressive in this interminable line of dark figures, close-pressed, soundless; a crowd, yet absolutely still; a close-packed, silent file, waiting, waiting in the vast deserted night-ridden street; waiting without a word, without a movement, there under the night and under the slow-moving mists of rain.

Few in the crowd were professional beggars. Most of them were workmen, long since out of work, forced into idleness by long-continued "hard times," by ill luck, by sickness. To them the "bread line" was a godsend. At least they could not starve. Between jobs here in the end was something to hold them up—a small platform, as it were, above the sweep of black water, where for a moment they might pause and take breath before the plunge.

The period of waiting on this night of rain seemed endless to those silent, hungry men; but at length there was a stir. The line moved. The side door opened. Ah, at last! They were going to hand out the bread.

But instead of the usual white-aproned under-cook with his crowded hampers there now appeared in the doorway a new man—a young fellow who looked like a bookkeeper's assistant. He bore in his hand a placard, which he tacked to the outside of the door. Then he disappeared within the bakery, locking the door after him.

A shudder of poignant despair, an unformed, inarticulate sense of calamity, seemed to run from end to end of the line. What had happened? Those in the rear, unable to read the placard, surged forward, a sense of bitter disappointment clutching at their hearts.

The line broke up, disintegrated into a shapeless throng—a throng that crowded forward and collected in front of the shut door whereon the placard was affixed. Lewiston, with the others, pushed forward. On the placard he read these words:

> "Owing to the fact that the price of grain has been increased to two dollars a bushel, there will be no distribution of bread from this bakery until further notice."

Lewiston turned away, dumb, bewildered. Till morning he walked the streets, going on without purpose, without direction. But now at last his luck had turned. Overnight the wheel of his fortunes had creaked and swung upon its axis, and before noon he had found a job in the street-cleaning brigade. In the course of time he rose to be first shift-boss, then deputy inspector, then inspector, promoted to the dignity of driving in a red wagon with rubber tires and drawing a salary instead of mere wages. The wife was sent for and a new start made.

But Lewiston never forgot. Dimly he began to see the significance of things. Caught once in the cogs and wheels of a great and terrible engine, he had seen—none better—its workings. Of all the men who had vainly stood in the "bread line" on that rainy night in early summer, he, perhaps, had been the only one who had struggled up to the surface again. How many others had gone down in the great ebb? Grim question; he dared not think how many.

He had seen the two ends of a great wheat operation—a battle between Bear and Bull. The stories (subsequently published in the city's press) of Truslow's countermove in selling Hornung his own wheat, supplied the unseen section. The farmer—he who raised the wheat—was ruined upon one hand; the working-man—he who consumed it—was ruined upon the other. But between the two, the great operators, who never saw the wheat they traded in, bought and sold the world's food, gambled in the nourishment of entire nations, practised their tricks, their chicanery and oblique shifty "deals," were reconciled in their differences, and went on through their appointed way, jovial, contented, enthroned, and unassailable.

1902

A Plea for Romantic Fiction

Let us at the start make a distinction. Observe that one speaks of romanticism and not sentimentalism. One claims that the latter is as distinct from the former as is that other form of art which is called Realism. Romance has been often put upon and over-burdened by being forced to bear the onus of abuse that by right should fall to sentiment; but the two should be kept very distinct, for a very high and illustrious place will be claimed for romance, while sentiment will be handed down the scullery stairs.

Many people to-day are composing mere sentimentalism, and calling it and causing it to be called romance; so with those who are too busy to think much upon these subjects, but who none the less love honest literature, Romance, too, has fallen into disrepute. Consider now the cut-and-thrust stories. They are all labeled Romances, and it is very easy to get the impression that Romance must be an affair of cloaks and daggers, or moonlight and golden hair. But this is not so at all. The true Romance is a more serious business than this. It is not merely a conjurer's trick-box, full of flimsy quackeries, tinsel and claptraps, meant only to amuse, and relying upon deception to do even that. Is it not something better than this? Can we not see in it an instrument, keen, finely tempered, flawless—an instrument with which we may go straight through the clothes and tissues and wrappings of flesh down deep into the red, living heart of things?

Is all this too subtle, too merely speculative and intrinsic, too *précieuse*[1] and nice and "literary"? Devoutly one hopes the contrary. So much is made of so-called Romanticism in present-day fiction that the subject seems worthy of discussion, and a protest against the misuse of a really noble and honest formula of literature appeals to be timely—misuse, that is, in the sense of limited use. Let us suppose for the moment that a romance can be made out of a cut-and-thrust business. Good Heavens, are there no other things that are romantic, even in this—falsely, falsely called—humdrum world of to-day? Why should it be that so soon as the novelist addresses himself—seriously—to the consideration of contemporary life he must abandon Romance and take up that harsh, loveless, colorless, blunt tool called Realism?

Now, let us understand at once what is meant by Romance and what by Realism. Romance, I take it, is the kind of fiction that takes cognizance of variations from the type of normal life. Realism is the kind of fiction that confines itself to the type of normal life. According to this definition, then, Romance may even treat of the sordid, the unlovely—as for instance, the novels of M. Zola.[2] (Zola has been dubbed a Realist, but he is, on the contrary, the very head of the Romanticists.) Also, Realism, used as it sometimes is as a term of reproach, need not be in the remotest sense or degree offensive, but on the other hand respectable as a church and proper as a deacon—as, for instance, the novels of Mr. Howells.[3]

The reason why one claims so much for Romance, and quarrels so pointedly with

---

[1]"Affected" (French).
[2]Émile Zola (1840–1902), French naturalistic novelist.

[3]William Dean Howells (1837–1920), American novelist and editor.

Realism, is that Realism stultifies itself. It notes only the surface of things. For it, Beauty is not even skin deep, but only a geometrical plane, without dimensions and depth, a mere outside. Realism is very excellent so far as it goes, but it goes no further than the Realist himself can actually see, or actually hear. Realism is minute; it is the drama of a broken teacup, the tragedy of a walk down the block, the excitement of an afternoon call, the adventure of an invitation to dinner. It is the visit to my neighbor's house, a formal visit, from which I may draw no conclusions. I see my neighbor and his friends—very, oh, such very! probable people—and that is all. Realism bows upon the doormat and goes away and says to me, as we link arms on the sidewalk: "That is life." And I say it is not. It is not, as you would very well see if you took Romance with you to call upon your neighbor.

Lately you have been taking Romance a weary journey across the water—ages and the flood of years—and haling her into the fusby, musty, worm-eaten, moth-riddled, rust-corroded "Grandes Salles"[4] of the Middle Ages and the Renaissance, and she has found the drama of a bygone age for you there. But would you take her across the street to your neighbor's front parlor (with the bisque[5] fisher-boy on the mantel and the photograph of Niagara Falls on glass hanging in the front window); would you introduce her there? Not you. Would you take a walk with her on Fifth Avenue, or Beacon Street, or Michigan Avenue?[6] No, indeed. Would you choose her for a companion of a morning spent in Wall Street,[7] or an afternoon in the Waldorf-Astoria?[8] You just guess you would not.

She would be out of place, you say—inappropriate. She might be awkward in my neighbor's front parlor, and knock over the little bisque fisher-boy. Well, she might. If she did, you might find underneath the base of the statuette, hidden away, tucked away—what? God knows. But something that would be a complete revelation of my neighbor's secretest life.

So you think Romance would stop in the front parlor and discuss medicated flannels and mineral waters with the ladies? Not for more than five minutes. She would be off upstairs with you, prying, peeping, peering into the closets of the bedroom, into the nursery, into the sitting-room; yes, and into that little iron box screwed to the lower shelf of the closet in the library; and into those compartments and pigeon-holes of the *secrétaire*[9] in the study. She would find a heartache (maybe) between the pillows of the mistress's bed, and a memory carefully secreted in the master's deed-box. She would come upon a great hope amid the books and papers of the study-table of the young man's room, and—perhaps—who knows—an affair, or, great Heavens, an intrigue, in the scented ribbons and gloves and hairpins of the young lady's bureau. And she would pick here a little and there a little, making up a bag of hopes and fears and a package of joys and sorrows—great ones, mind you—and then come down to the front door, and, stepping out into the street, hand you the bags and package and say to you—"That is Life!"

Romance does very well in the castles of the Middle Ages and the Renaissance chateaux, and she has the *entrée* there and is very well received. That is all well and good. But let us protest against limiting her to such places and such times. You will find her, I grant you, in the chatelaine's[10] chamber and the dungeon of the man-at-arms; but, if you choose to look for her, you will find her equally at home in the brownstone house on the corner and in the office-building downtown. And this very day, in this very hour, she is sitting among the rags and wretchedness, the dirt and despair of the tenements of the East Side of New York.

"What?" I hear you say, "look for Romance—the lady of the silken robes and golden crown, our beautiful, chaste maiden of soft voice and gentle eyes—look for

---

[4]"Great halls" (French).
[5]Pottery.
[6]Fashionable streets in New York City, Boston, and Chicago.
[7]New York's financial center.

[8]Luxurious New York City hotel.
[9]Desk.
[10]Mistress of a castle or great house.

her among the vicious ruffians, male and female, of Allen Street and Mulberry Bend?"[11] I tell you she is there, and to your shame be it said you will not know her in those surroundings. You, the aristocrats, who demand the fine linen and the purple in your fiction; you, the sensitive, the delicate, who will associate with your Romance only so long as she wears a silken gown. You will not follow her to the slums, for you believe that Romance should only amuse and entertain you, singing you sweet songs and touching the harp of silver strings with rosy-tipped fingers. If haply she should call to you from the squalor of a dive, or the awful degradation of a disorderly house, crying: "Look! listen! This, too, is life. These, too, are my children! Look at them, know them and, knowing, help!" Should she call thus you would stop your ears; you would avert your eyes and you would answer, "Come from there, Romance. Your place is not there!" And you would make of her a harlequin, a tumbler, a sword-dancer, when, as a matter of fact, she should be by right divine a teacher sent from God.

She will not often wear the robe of silk, the gold crown, the jeweled shoon;[12] will not always sweep the silver harp. An iron note is hers if so she choose, and coarse garments, and stained hands; and, meeting her thus, it is for you to know her as she passes—know her for the same young queen of the blue mantle and lilies. She can teach you if you will be humble to learn—teach you by showing. God help you if at last you take from Romance her mission of teaching; if you do not believe that she has a purpose—a nobler purpose and a mightier than mere amusement, mere entertainment. Let Realism do the entertaining with its meticulous presentation of teacups, rag carpets, wall-paper and haircloth sofas, stopping with these, going no deeper than it sees, choosing the ordinary, the untroubled, the commonplace.

But to Romance belongs the wide world for range, and the unplumbed depths of the human heart, and the mystery of sex, and the problems of life, and the black, unsearched penetralia[13] of the soul of man. You, the indolent, must not always be amused. What matter the silken clothes, what matter the prince's houses? Romance, too, is a teacher, and if—throwing aside the purple—she wears the camel's-hair and feeds upon the locusts, it is to cry aloud unto the people, "Prepare ye the way of the Lord; make straight his path."[14]

1901

STEPHEN CRANE
(1871–1900)

Stephen Crane was dead before he reached the age of thirty. Yet he was firmly established as an important American writer, known especially for his classic tale of men at war, *The Red Badge of Courage*. Crane had published nothing during his first twenty years. But during his last nine years, he wrote enough to fill twelve volumes in his collected works, published in 1925–27.

Crane was, as one critic, Edwin Cady, has called him, a P. K.—a preacher's kid. He was born in Newark, New Jersey, the fourteenth (and last) child of a Methodist minister. Following the call of his ministry, the Reverend Crane established his family in a succession of New Jersey towns, including Port Jervis, which would serve later as the locale for Crane's "Whilomville" stories. Crane's father died in

---

[11]New York City slum streets.
[12]Shoes.
[13]Hidden parts.

[14]The cry of John the Baptist who was clothed in camel's hair and ate locusts and wild honey (Matthew 3:3–4).

1880, leaving the family in difficult straits. Crane attended Lafayette College as an engineering student for a brief time and then enrolled in Syracuse University, where he played catcher and shortstop on the baseball team. Clearly disillusioned with college life, Crane dropped out of Syracuse after one term. With his mother's death in 1891, he found himself on his own at the age of twenty.

Crane settled in New York City in the early 1890s, and began his exploration of its slums, gathering his impressions of the poor and outcast, the drifters and bums, the criminals and prostitutes. By this time he had awakened to his possibilities as a writer and he restlessly searched for material. He had begun a novel in his student days at Syracuse, and now he revised it in the light of his New York experience. By 1893, he was ready to publish, but no publisher would take it because of its offensive language and subject matter. Crane borrowed the money from his brother (a successful journalist) to publish *Maggie: A Girl of the Streets* under the pseudonym Johnston Smith. It was a commercial failure, but among the book's few readers were Hamlin Garland and William Dean Howells. From this time, they became Crane's promoters and champions.

Within a year, in 1894, Crane's *The Red Badge of Courage* was serialized in a large number of small newspapers throughout the country and appeared as a book in both America and England in 1895. Suddenly Crane found himself the famous author of a "war book" without ever having experienced combat or observed men in battle. Many readers with battlefield experience swore to the fidelity of Crane's descriptions. In this same year appeared Crane's first volume of poems, which he wrote after being introduced to Emily Dickinson's poetry by Howells — *The Black Rider and Other Lines*. And a commercial publisher reissued *Maggie* the following year, but only after some mutilating revisions.

In the five short years that remained to him, Crane poured forth one volume after another, astutely combining a career as a journalist with that of an imaginative writer. Out of an 1895 newspaper assignment in the West, which took Crane to Nebraska, Texas, and Mexico, came the materials for two memorable short stories, "The Blue Hotel" and "The Bride Comes to Yellow Sky." In 1895–96, covering the Cuban insurrection, Crane found himself shipwrecked off the Florida coast; out of the experience he created his most famous short story, "The Open Boat." In 1897 Crane was assigned to go to Greece to cover the Turkish War, and in 1898 to Cuba to report on the Spanish-American War. He found nothing in his firsthand observation of war to undermine his faith in his imaginative creation of the experience earlier in *The Red Badge of Courage*.

In spite of his journalistic assignments, Crane salvaged something of a personal life (and scandalized many) by forming a companionship with Cora Taylor, mistress of the "Hotel de Dream" (a "house of assignation") in Jacksonville, Florida. They went to England and settled in Surrey, in the south. There they developed friendships with a number of writers, including Joseph Conrad, Henry James, and H. G. Wells.

Finding himself ill with tuberculosis in his final years, Crane wrote with astonishing speed to pull himself out from under mounting debts. In 1899, the year before his death, he published three books, including his second book of poems, *War Is Kind*, and a volume of tales, *The Monster and Other Stories*. In a desperate attempt to find a climate benevolent to his illness, Crane went with Cora in 1900 to a sanitorium in Badenweiler, Germany. He died there in the Black Forest in June 1900.

Crane is often called a naturalist, credited with writing America's first naturalistic novel in *Maggie: A Girl of the Streets*. But he is also frequently labelled an impressionist, especially in the descriptive prose of *The Red Badge of Courage*.

And critics see his poetry as anticipating the imagist movement of Ezra Pound and others, culminating with publication of *Some Imagist Poets* (1915). For a writer who died so young, Crane appears to fill many roles in the development of American literature. But, finally, it is not any particular "ism" reflected in his work that gives it distinction. It is rather the individual stamp of his genius that enables his stories and novels to live long after the "isms" have faded from memory.

ADDITIONAL READING

The Work of Stephen Crane, 12 vols., ed. Wilson Follett, 1925–27, reprinted in 6 vols., 1963; *The Works of Stephen Crane*, 10 vols., ed. Fredson Bowers, 1969–76; *Stephen Crane: Letters*, ed. R. W. Stallman and Lillian Gilkes, 1960; *The Correspondence of Stephen Crane*, 2 vols., ed. Stanley Wertheim and Paul Sorrentino, 1988.

Thomas Beer, *Stephen Crane: A Study in American Letters*, 1923; Thomas L. Raymond, *Stephen Crane*, 1923; John Berryman, *Stephen Crane*, 1950; Daniel G. Hoffman, *The Poetry of Stephen Crane*, 1957; Edwin H. Cady, *Stephen Crane*, 1962, 1980; Eric Solomon, *Stephen Crane: From Parody to Realism*, 1966; Maurice Bassan, ed., *Stephen Crane: A Collection of Critical Essays*, 1967; R. W. Stallman, *Stephen Crane: A Biography*, 1968; Donald B. Gibson, *The Fiction of Stephen Crane*, 1968; Marston La France, *A Reading of Stephen Crane*, 1971; Joseph Katz, ed., *Stephen Crane in Transition: Centenary Essays*, 1972; Thomas A. Gullason, ed., *Stephen Crane's Career: Perspectives and Evaluations*, 1972; Robert W. Stallman, *Stephen Crane: A Critical Bibliography*, 1972; Richard M. Weatherford, ed., *Stephen Crane, The Critical Heritage*, 1973; Frank Bergon, *Stephen Crane's Artistry*, 1975; James Nagel, *Stephen Crane and Literary Impressionism*, 1980; Chester L. Wolford, *The Anger of Stephen Crane: Fiction and the Epic Tradition*, 1983; Michael Fried, *Realism, Writing, Disfiguration: On Thomas Eakins and Stephen Crane*, 1987; Bettina L. Knapp, *Stephen Crane*, 1987.

TEXTS

Maggie: A Girl of the Streets, 1893; "The Open Boat," "The Blue Hotel," and "An Episode of War" from *The Works of Stephen Crane*, ed. Fredson Bowers: Vol. 5, *Tales of Adventure*, intr. J. C. Levenson, 1970, and Vol. 6, *Tales of War*, intr. James B. Colvert, 1970; *The Poems of Stephen Crane: A Critical Edition*, ed. Joseph Katz, 1966.

Maggie: A Girl of the Streets

A STORY OF NEW YORK[1]

CHAPTER I

A very little boy stood upon a heap of gravel for the honor of Rum Alley. He was throwing stones at howling urchins from Devil's Row who were circling madly about the heap and pelting at him.

His infantile countenance was livid with fury. His small body was writhing in the delivery of great, crimson oaths.

"Run, Jimmie, run! Dey'll get yehs," screamed a retreating Rum Alley child.

---

[1]Turned down by one publisher as "Too cruel," *Maggie* was privately published by Crane in a paperbound edition in 1893 with the pseudonym of Johnston Smith. When the novel was republished in 1896 by D. Appleton and Company under his own name, Crane was asked to revise to make it more acceptable to prevailing genteel tastes. Besides dispensing "with a goodly number of damns," changing diction, correcting misprints, spelling, and punctuation, the 1896 edition deletes some significant passages in Chapter Seventeen. The text here is that of the original 1893 edition, with minor corrections of misprints, spelling, and punctuation.

On a copy of the 1893 *Maggie*, given to Hamlin Garland, Crane wrote: "It is inevitable that you will be greatly shocked by this book but continue please with all possible courage to the end. For it tries to show that environment is a tremendous thing in the world and frequently shapes lives regardless. If one proves that theory one makes room in Heaven for all sorts of souls (notably an occasional street girl) who are not confidently expected to be there by many excellent people."

"Naw," responded Jimmie with a valiant roar, "dese micks can't make me run."

Howls of renewed wrath went up from Devil's Row throats. Tattered gamins on the right made a furious assault on the gravel heap. On their small, convulsed faces there shone the grins of true assassins. As they charged, they threw stones and cursed in shrill chorus.

The little champion of Rum Alley stumbled precipitately down the other side. His coat had been torn to shreds in a scuffle, and his hat was gone. He had bruises on twenty parts of his body, and blood was dripping from a cut in his head. His wan features wore a look of a tiny, insane demon.

On the ground, children from Devil's Row closed in on their antagonist. He crooked his left arm defensively about his head and fought with cursing fury. The little boys ran to and fro, dodging, hurling stones and swearing in barbaric trebles.

From a window of an apartment house that upreared its form from amid squat, ignorant stables, there leaned a curious woman. Some laborers, unloading a scow at a dock at the river, paused for a moment and regarded the fight. The engineer of a passive tugboat hung lazily to a railing and watched. Over on the Island, a worm of yellow convicts came from the shadow of a grey ominous building and crawled slowly along the river's bank.

A stone had smashed into Jimmie's mouth. Blood was bubbling over his chin and down upon his ragged shirt. Tears made furrows on his dirt-stained cheeks. His thin legs had begun to tremble and turn weak, causing his small body to reel. His roaring curses of the first part of the fight had changed to a blasphemous chatter.

In the yells of the whirling mob of Devil's Row children there were notes of joy like songs of triumphant savagery. The little boys seemed to leer gloatingly at the blood upon the other child's face.

Down the avenue came boastfully sauntering a lad of sixteen years, although the chronic sneer of an ideal manhood already sat upon his lips. His hat was tipped with an air of challenge over his eye. Between his teeth, a cigar stump was tilted at the angle of defiance. He walked with a certain swing of the shoulders which appalled the timid. He glanced over into the vacant lot in which the little raving boys from Devil's Row seethed about the shrieking and tearful child from Rum Alley.

"Gee!" he murmured with interest, "A scrap. Gee!"

He strode over to the cursing circle, swinging his shoulders in a manner which denoted that he held victory in his fists. He approached at the back of one of the most deeply engaged of the Devil's Row children.

"Ah, what deh hell," he said, and smote the deeply-engaged one on the back of the head. The little boy fell to the ground and gave a hoarse, tremendous howl. He scrambled to his feet, and perceiving, evidently, the size of his assailant, ran quickly off, shouting alarms. The entire Devil's Row party followed him. They came to a stand a short distance away and yelled taunting oaths at the boy with the chronic sneer. The latter, momentarily, paid no attention to them.

"What deh hell, Jimmie?" he asked of the small champion.

Jimmie wiped his blood-wet features with his sleeve.

"Well, it was dis way, Pete, see! I was goin' teh lick dat Riley kid and dey all pitched on me."

Some Rum Alley children now came forward. The party stood for a moment exchanging vainglorious remarks with Devil's Row. A few stones were thrown at long distances, and words of challenge passed between small warriors. Then the Rum Alley contingent turned slowly in the direction of their home street. They began to give, each to each, distorted versions of the fight. Causes of retreat in particular cases were magnified. Blows dealt in the fight were enlarged to catapultian power, and stones thrown were alleged to have hurtled with infinite accuracy. Valor grew strong again, and the little boys began to swear with great spirit.

"Ah, we blokies kin lick deh hull damn Row," said a child, swaggering.

Little Jimmie was striving to stanch the flow of blood from his cut lips. Scowling, he turned upon the speaker.

"Ah, where deh hell was yeh when I was doin' all deh fightin'?" he demanded. "Youse kids makes me tired."

"Ah, go ahn," replied the other argumentatively.

Jimmie replied with heavy contempt. "Ah, youse can't fight. Blue Billie! I kin lick yeh wid one han'."

"Ah, go ahn," replied Billie again.

"Ah," said Jimmie threateningly.

"Ah," said the other in the same tone.

They struck at each other, clinched, and rolled over on the cobble stones.

"Smash 'im, Jimmie, kick deh damn guts out of 'im," yelled Pete, the lad with the chronic sneer, in tones of delight.

The small combatants pounded and kicked, scratched and tore. They began to weep and their curses struggled in their throats with sobs. The others little boys clasped their hands and wriggled their legs in excitement. They formed a bobbing circle about the pair.

A tiny spectator was suddenly agitated.

"Cheese it, Jimmie, cheese it! Here comes yer fader," he yelled.

The circle of little boys instantly parted. They drew away and waited in ecstatic awe for that which was about to happen. The two little boys fighting in the modes of four thousand years ago, did not hear the warning.

Up the avenue there plodded slowly a man with sullen eyes. He was carrying a dinner pail and smoking an apple-wood pipe.

As he neared the spot where the little boys strove, he regarded them listlessly. But suddenly he roared an oath and advanced upon the rolling fighters.

"Here, you Jim, git up, now, while I belt yer life out, you damned disorderly brat."

He began to kick into the chaotic mass on the ground. The boy Billie felt a heavy boot strike his head. He made a furious effort and disentangled himself from Jimmie. He tottered away, damning.

Jimmie arose painfully from the ground and confronting his father, began to curse him. His parent kicked him. "Come home, now," he cried, "an' stop yer jawin', er I'll lam the everlasting head off yehs."

They departed. The man paced placidly along with the apple-wood emblem of serenity between his teeth. The boy followed a dozen feet in the rear. He swore luridly, for he felt that it was a degradation for one who aimed to be some vague soldier, or a man of blood with a sort of sublime license, to be taken home by a father.

CHAPTER II

Eventually they entered into a dark region where, from a careening building, a dozen gruesome doorways gave up loads of babies to the streets and the gutter. A wind of early autumn raised yellow dust from cobble and swirled it against an hundred windows. Long streamers of garments fluttered from fire-escapes. In all unhandy places there were buckets, brooms, rags and bottles. In the street infants played or fought with other infants or sat stupidly in the way of vehicles. Formidable women, with uncombed hair and disordered dress, gossiped while leaning on railings, or screamed in frantic quarrels. Withered persons, in curious postures of submission to something, sat smoking pipes in obscure corners. A thousand odors of cooking food came forth to the street. The building quivered and creaked from the weight of humanity stamping about in its bowels.

A small ragged girl dragged a red, bawling infant along the crowded ways. He was hanging back, baby-like, bracing his wrinkled, bare legs.

The little girl cried out: "Ah, Tommie, come ahn. Dere's Jimmie and fader. Don't be a-pullin' me back."

She jerked the baby's arm impatiently. He fell on his face, roaring. With a second jerk she pulled him to his feet, and they went on. With the obstinacy of his order, he protested against being dragged in a chosen direction. He made heroic endeavors to keep on his legs, denounce his sister and consume a bit of orange peeling which he chewed between the times of his infantile orations.

As the sullen-eyed man, followed by the blood-covered boy, drew near, the little girl burst into reproachful cries. "Ah, Jimmie, youse bin fightin' agin."

The urchin swelled disdainfully.

"Ah, what deh hell, Mag. See?"

The little girl upbraided him. "Youse allus fightin', Jimmie, an' yeh knows it puts mudder out when yehs come home half dead, an' it's like we'll all get a poundin'."

She began to weep. The babe threw back his head and roared at his prospects.

"Ah, what deh hell!" cried Jimmie. "Shut up er I'll smack yer mout'. See?"

As his sister continued her lamentations, he suddenly swore and struck her. The little girl reeled and, recovering herself, burst into tears and quaveringly cursed him. As she slowly retreated her brother advanced dealing her cuffs. The father heard and turned about.

"Stop that, Jim, d'yeh hear? Leave yer sister alone on the street. It's like I can never beat any sense into yer damned wooden head."

The urchin raised his voice in defiance to his parent and continued his attacks. The babe bawled tremendously, protesting with great violence. During his sister's hasty manœuvres, he was dragged by the arm.

Finally the procession plunged into one of the gruesome doorways. They crawled up dark stairways and along cold, gloomy halls. At last the father pushed open a door and they entered a lighted room in which a large woman was rampant.

She stopped in a career from a seething stove to a pan-covered table. As the father and children filed in she peered at them.

"Eh, what? Been fightin' agin, by Gawd!" She threw herself upon Jimmie. The urchin tried to dart behind the others and in the scuffle the babe, Tommie, was knocked down. He protested with his usual vehemence, because they had bruised his tender shins against a table leg.

The mother's massive shoulders heaved with anger. Grasping the urchin by the neck and shoulder she shook him until he rattled. She dragged him to an unholy sink, and, soaking a rag in water, began to scrub his lacerated face with it. Jimmie screamed in pain and tried to twist his shoulders out of the clasp of the huge arms.

The babe sat on the floor watching the scene, his face in contortions like that of a woman at a tragedy. The father, with a newly-ladened pipe in his mouth, crouched on a backless chair near the stove. Jimmie's cries annoyed him. He turned about and bellowed at his wife:

"Let the damned kid alone for a minute, will yeh, Mary? Yer allus poundin' 'im. When I come nights I can't git no rest 'cause yer allus poundin' a kid. Let up, d'yeh hear? Don't be allus poundin' a kid."

The woman's operations on the urchin instantly increased in violence. At last she tossed him to a corner where he limply lay cursing and weeping.

The wife put her immense hands on her hips and with a chieftain-like stride approached her husband.

"Ho," she said, with a great grunt of contempt. "An' what in the devil are you stickin' your nose for?"

The babe crawled under the table and, turning, peered out cautiously. The ragged girl retreated and the urchin in the corner drew his legs carefully beneath him.

The man puffed his pipe calmly and put his great mudded boots on the back part of the stove.

"Go teh hell," he murmured, tranquilly.

The woman screamed and shook her fists before her husband's eyes. The rough yellow of her face and neck flared suddenly crimson. She began to howl.

He puffed imperturbably at his pipe for a time, but finally arose and began to look out at the window into the darkening chaos of back yards.

"You've been drinkin', Mary," he said. "You'd better let up on the bot', ol' woman, or you'll git done."

"You're a liar. I ain't had a drop," she roared in reply.

They had a lurid altercation, in which they damned each other's souls with frequence.

The babe was staring out from under the table, his small face working in his excitement.

The ragged girl went stealthily over to the corner where the urchin lay.

"Are yehs hurted much, Jimmie?" she whispered timidly.

"Not a damn bit! See?" growled the little boy.

"Will I wash deh blood?"

"Naw!"

"Will I"—

"When I catch dat Riley kid I'll break 'is face! Dat's right! See?"

He turned his face to the wall as if resolved to grimly bide his time.

In the quarrel between husband and wife, the woman was victor. The man grabbed his hat and rushed from the room, apparently determined upon a vengeful drunk. She followed to the door and thundered at him as he made his way down stairs.

She returned and stirred up the room until her children were bobbing about like bubbles.

"Git outa deh way," she persistently bawled, waving feet with their dishevelled shoes near the heads of her children. She shrouded herself, puffing and snorting, in a cloud of steam at the stove, and eventually extracted a frying-pan full of potatoes that hissed.

She flourished it. "Come teh yer suppers, now," she cried with sudden exasperation. "Hurry up, now, er I'll help yeh!"

The children scrambled hastily. With prodigious clatter they arranged themselves at table. The babe sat with his feet dangling high from a precarious infant chair and gorged his small stomach. Jimmie forced, with feverish rapidity, the grease-enveloped pieces between his wounded lips. Maggie, with side glances of fear of interruption, ate like a small pursued tigress.

The mother sat blinking at them. She delivered reproaches, swallowed potatoes and drank from a yellow-brown bottle. After a time her mood changed and she wept as she carried little Tommie into another room and laid him to sleep with his fists doubled in an old quilt of faded red and green grandeur. Then she came and moaned by the stove. She rocked to and fro upon a chair, shedding tears and crooning miserably to the two children about their "poor mother" and "yer fader, damn 'is soul."

The little girl plodded between the table and the chair with a dish-pan on it. She tottered on her small legs beneath burdens of dishes.

Jimmie sat nursing his various wounds. He cast furtive glances at his mother. His practised eye perceived her gradually emerge from a muddled mist of sentiment until her brain burned in drunken heat. He sat breathless.

Maggie broke a plate.

The mother started to her feet as if propelled.

"Good Gawd," she howled. Her eyes glittered on her child with sudden hatred. The fervent red of her face turned almost to purple. The little boy ran to the halls, shrieking like a monk in an earthquake.

He floundered about in darkness until he found the stairs. He stumbled, panic-stricken, to the next floor. An old woman opened a door. A light behind her threw a flare on the urchin's quivering face.

"Eh, Gawd, child, what is it dis time? Is yer fader beatin' yer mudder, or yer mudder beatin' yer fader?"

CHAPTER III

Jimmie and the old woman listened long in the hall. Above the muffled roar of conversation, the dismal wailings of babies at night, the thumping of feet in unseen corridors and rooms, mingled with the sound of varied hoarse shoutings in the street and the rattling of wheels over cobbles, they heard the screams of the child and the roars of the mother die away to a feeble moaning and a subdued bass muttering.

The old woman was a gnarled and leathery personage who could don, at will, an expression of great virtue. She possessed a small music-box capable of one tune, and a collection of "God bless yehs" pitched in assorted keys of fervency. Each day she took a position upon the stones of Fifth Avenue, where she crooked her legs under her and crouched immovable and hideous, like an idol. She received daily a small sum in pennies. It was contributed, for the most part, by persons who did not make their homes in that vicinity.

Once, when a lady had dropped her purse on the sidewalk, the gnarled woman had grabbed it and smuggled it with great dexterity beneath her cloak. When she was arrested she had cursed the lady into a partial swoon, and with her aged limbs, twisted from rheumatism, had almost kicked the stomach out of a huge policeman whose conduct upon that occasion she referred to when she said: "The police, damn 'em."

"Eh, Jimmie, it's cursed shame," she said. "Go, now, like a dear an' buy me a can, an' if yer mudder raises 'ell all night yehs can sleep here."

Jimmie took a tendered tin-pail and seven pennies and departed. He passed into the side door of a saloon and went to the bar. Straining up on his toes he raised the pail and pennies as high as his arms would let him. He saw two hands thrust down and take them. Directly the same hands let down the filled pail and he left.

In front of the gruesome doorway he met a lurching figure. It was his father, swaying about on uncertain legs.

"Give me deh can. See?" said the man, threateningly.

"Ah, come off! I got dis can fer dat ol' woman an' it 'ud be dirt teh swipe it. See?" cried Jimmie.

The father wrenched the pail from the urchin. He grasped it in both hands and lifted it to his mouth. He glued his lips to the under edge and tilted his head. His hairy throat swelled until it seemed to grow near his chin. There was a tremendous gulping movement and the beer was gone.

The man caught his breath and laughed. He hit his son on the head with the empty pail. As it rolled clanging into the street, Jimmie began to scream and kicked repeatedly at his father's shins.

"Look at deh dirt what yeh done me," he yelled. "Deh ol' woman 'ill be raisin' hell."

He retreated to the middle of the street, but the man did not pursue. He staggered toward the door.

"I'll club hell outa yeh when I ketch yeh," he shouted and disappeared.

During the evening he had been standing against a bar drinking whiskies and declaring to all comers, confidentially: "My home reg'lar livin' hell! Damndes' place! Reg'lar hell! Why do I come an' drin' whisk' here thish way? 'Cause home reg'lar livin' hell!"

Jimmie waited a long time in the street and then crept warily up through the building. He passed with great caution the door of the gnarled woman, and finally stopped outside his home and listened.

He could hear his mother moving heavily about among the furniture of the room. She was chanting in a mournful voice, occasionally interjecting bursts of volcanic wrath at the father, who, Jimmie judged, had sunk down on the floor or in a corner.

"Why deh blazes don' chere try teh keep Jim from fightin'? I'll break yer jaw," she suddenly bellowed.

The man mumbled with drunken indifference. "Ah, wha' deh hell. W'a's odds? Wha' makes kick?"

"Because he tears 'is clothes, yeh damn fool," cried the woman in supreme wrath.

The husband seemed to become aroused. "Go teh hell," he thundered fiercely in reply. There was a crash against the door and something broke into clattering fragments. Jimmie partially suppressed a howl and darted down the stairway. Below he paused and listened. He heard howls and curses, groans and shrieks, confusingly in chorus as if a battle were raging. With all was the crash of splintering furniture. The eyes of the urchin glared in fear that one of them would discover him.

Curious faces appeared in door-ways, and whispered comments passed to and fro. "Ol' Johnson's raisin' hell agin."

Jimmie stood until the noises ceased and the other inhabitants of the tenement had all yawned and shut their doors. Then he crawled upstairs with the caution of an invader of a panther den. Sounds of labored breathing came through the broken door-panels. He pushed the door opened and entered, quaking.

A glow from the fire threw red hues over the bare floor, the cracked and soiled plastering, and the overturned and broken furniture.

In the middle of the floor lay his mother asleep. In one corner of the room his father's limp body hung across the seat of a chair.

The urchin stole forward. He began to shiver in dread of awakening his parents. His mother's great chest was heaving painfully. Jimmie paused and looked down at her. Her face was inflamed and swollen from drinking. Her yellow brows shaded eyelids that had grown blue. Her tangled hair tossed in waves over her forehead. Her mouth was set in the same lines of vindictive hatred that it had, perhaps, borne during the fight. Her bare, red arms were thrown out above her head in positions of exhaustion, something, mayhap, like those of a sated villain.

The urchin bended over his mother. He was fearful lest she should open her eyes, and the dread within him was so strong, that he could not forbear to stare, but hung as if fascinated over the woman's grim face.

Suddenly her eyes opened. The urchin found himself looking straight into that expression, which, it would seem, had the power to change his blood to salt. He howled piercingly and fell backward.

The woman floundered for a moment, tossed her arms about her head as if in combat, and again began to snore.

Jimmie crawled back in the shadows and waited. A noise in the next room had followed his cry at the discovery that his mother was awake. He grovelled in the gloom, the eyes from out his drawn face riveted upon the intervening door.

He heard it creak, and then the sound of a small voice came to him. "Jimmie! Jimmie! Are yehs dere?" it whispered. The urchin started. The thin, white face of his sister looked at him from the door-way of the other room. She crept to him across the floor.

The father had not moved, but lay in the same death-like sleep. The mother writhed in uneasy slumber, her chest wheezing as if she were in the agonies of strangulation. Out at the window a florid moon was peering over dark roofs, and in the distance the waters of a river glimmered pallidly.

The small frame of the ragged girl was quivering. Her features were haggard from weeping, and her eyes gleamed from fear. She grasped the urchin's arm in her little trembling hands and they huddled in a corner. The eyes of both were drawn, by some force, to stare at the woman's face, for they thought she need only to awake and all fiends would come from below.

They crouched until the ghost-mists of dawn appeared at the window, drawing close to the panes, and looking in at the prostrate, heaving body of the mother.

CHAPTER IV

The babe, Tommie, died. He went away in a white, insignificant coffin, his small waxen hand clutching a flower that the girl, Maggie, had stolen from an Italian.

She and Jimmie lived.

The inexperienced fibres of the boy's eyes were hardened at an early age. He became a young man of leather. He lived some red years without laboring. During that time his sneer became chronic. He studied human nature in the gutter, and found it no worse than he thought he had reason to believe it. He never conceived a respect for the world, because he had begun with no idols that it had smashed.

He clad his soul in armor by means of happening hilariously in at a mission church where a man composed his sermons of "yous." While they got warm at the stove, he told his hearers just where he calculated they stood with the Lord. Many of the sinners were impatient over the pictured depths of their degradation. They were waiting for soup-tickets.

A reader of words of wind-demons might have been able to see the portions of a dialogue pass to and fro between the exhorter and his hearers.

"You are damned," said the preacher. And the reader of sounds might have seen the reply go forth from the ragged people: "Where's our soup?"

Jimmie and a companion sat in a rear seat and commented upon the things that didn't concern them, with all the freedom of English gentlemen. When they grew thirsty and went out their minds confused the speaker with Christ.

Momentarily, Jimmie was sullen with thoughts of a hopeless altitude where grew fruit. His companion said that if he should ever meet God he would ask for a million dollars and a bottle of beer.

Jimmie's occupation for a long time was to stand on street-corners and watch the world go by, dreaming blood-red dreams at the passing of pretty women. He menaced mankind at the intersections of streets.

On the corners he was in life and of life. The world was going on and he was there to perceive it.

He maintained a belligerent attitude toward all well-dressed men. To him fine raiment was allied to weakness, and all good coats covered faint hearts. He and his order were kings, to a certain extent, over the men of untarnished clothes, because these latter dreaded, perhaps, to be either killed or laughed at.

Above all things he despised obvious Christians and ciphers with the chrysanthemums of aristocracy in their button-holes. He considered himself above both of these classes. He was afraid of neither the devil nor the leader of society.

When he had a dollar in his pocket his satisfaction with existence was the greatest thing in the world. So, eventually, he felt obliged to work. His father died and his mother's years were divided up into periods of thirty days.

He became a truck driver. He was given the charge of a pains-taking pair of horses and a large rattling truck. He invaded the turmoil and tumble of the down-town streets and learned to breath maledictory defiance at the police who occasionally used to climb up, drag him from his perch and beat him.

In the lower part of the city he daily involved himself in hideous tangles. If he and his team chanced to be in the rear he preserved a demeanor of serenity, crossing his legs and bursting forth into yells when foot passengers took dangerous dives beneath the noses of his champing horses. He smoked his pipe calmly for he knew that his pay was marching on.

If in the front and the key-truck of chaos, he entered terrifically into the quarrel that was raging to and fro among the drivers on their high seats, and sometimes roared oaths and violently got himself arrested.

After a time his sneer grew so that it turned its glare upon all things. He became so sharp that he believed in nothing. To him the police were always actuated by malignant impulses and the rest of the world was composed, for the most part, of despicable creatures who were all trying to take advantage of him and with whom, in defense, he was obliged to quarrel on all possible occasions. He himself occupied a down-trodden position that had a private but distinct element of grandeur in its isolation.

The most complete cases of aggravated idiocy were, to his mind, rampant upon the front platforms of all of the street cars. At first his tongue strove with these beings, but he eventually was superior. He became immured like an African cow. In him grew a majestic contempt for those strings of street cars that followed him like intent bugs.

He fell into the habit, when starting on a long journey, of fixing his eye on a high and distant object, commanding his horses to begin, and then going into a sort of a trance of observation. Multitudes of drivers might howl in his rear, and passengers might load him with opprobrium, he would not awaken until some blue policeman turned red and began to frenziedly tear bridles and beat the soft noses of the responsible horses.

When he paused to contemplate the attitude of the police toward himself and his fellows, he believed that they were the only men in the city who had no rights. When driving about, he felt that he was held liable by the police for anything that might occur in the streets, and was the common prey of all energetic officials. In revenge, he resolved never to move out of the way of anything, until formidable circumstances, or a much larger man than himself forced him to it.

Foot-passengers were mere pestering flies with an insane disregard for their legs and his convenience. He could not conceive their maniacal desires to cross the streets. Their madness smote him with eternal amazement. He was continually storming at them from his throne. He sat aloft and denounced their frantic leaps, plunges, dives and straddles.

When they would thrust at, or parry, the noses of his champing horses, making them swing their heads and move their feet, disturbing a solid dreamy repose, he swore at the men as fools, for he himself could perceive that Providence had caused it clearly to be written, that he and his team had the unalienable right to stand in the proper path of the sun chariot, and if they so minded, obstruct its mission or take a wheel off.

And, perhaps, if the god-driver had an ungovernable desire to step down, put up his flame colored fists and manfully dispute the right of way, he would have probably been immediately opposed by a scowling mortal with two sets of very hard knuckles.

It is possible, perhaps, that this young man would have derided, in an axle-wide alley, the approach of a flying ferry boat. Yet he achieved a respect for a fire engine. As one charged toward his truck, he would drive fearfully upon a side-walk, threatening untold people with annihilation. When an engine would strike a mass of blocked trucks, splitting it into fragments, as a blow annihilates a cake of ice, Jimmie's team could usually be observed high and safe, with whole wheels, on the sidewalk. The fearful coming of the engine could break up the most intricate muddle of heavy vehicles at which the police had been swearing for the half of an hour.

A fire-engine was enshrined in his heart as an appalling thing that he loved with a distant dog-like devotion. They had been known to overturn street-cars. Those leaping horses, striking sparks from the cobbles in their forward lunge, were creatures to be ineffably admired. The clang of the gong pierced his breast like a noise of remembered war.

When Jimmie was a little boy, he began to be arrested. Before he reached a great age, he had a fair record.

He developed too great a tendency to climb down from his truck and fight with other drivers. He had been in quite a number of miscellaneous fights, and in some general barroom rows that had become known to the police. Once he had been arrested for assaulting a Chinaman. Two women in different parts of the city, and entirely unknown to each other, caused him considerable annoyance by breaking forth, simultaneously, at fateful intervals, into wailings about marriage and support and infants.

Nevertheless, he had, on a certain star-lit evening, said wonderingly and quite reverently: "Deh moon looks like hell, don't it?"

CHAPTER V

The girl, Maggie, blossomed in a mud puddle. She grew to be a most rare and wonderful production of a tenement district, a pretty girl.

None of the dirt of Rum Alley seemed to be in her veins. The philosophers up-stairs, down-stairs and on the same floor, puzzled over it.

When a child, playing and fighting with gamins in the street, dirt disguised her. Attired in tatters and grime, she went unseen.

There came a time, however, when the young men of the vicinity, said: "Dat Johnson goil is a puty good looker." About this period her brother remarked to her: "Mag, I'll tell yeh dis! See? Yeh've edder got teh go teh hell or go teh work!" Whereupon she went to work, having the feminine aversion of going to hell.

By a chance, she got a position in an establishment where they made collars and cuffs. She received a stool and a machine in a room where sat twenty girls of various shades of yellow discontent. She perched on the stool and treadled at her machine all day, turning out collars, the name of whose brand could be noted for its irrelevancy to anything in connection with collars. At night she returned home to her mother.

Jimmie grew large enough to take the vague position of head of the family. As incumbent of that office, he stumbled up-stairs late at night, as his father had done before him. He reeled about the room, swearing at his relations, or went to sleep on the floor.

The mother had gradually arisen to that degree of fame that she could bandy words with her acquaintances among the police-justices. Court-officials called her by her first name. When she appeared they pursued a course which had been theirs for months. They invariably grinned and cried out: "Hello, Mary, you here again?" Her grey head wagged in many a court. She always besieged the bench with voluble excuses, explanations, apologies and prayers. Her flaming face and rolling eyes were a sort of familiar sight on the Island. She measured time by means of sprees, and was eternally swollen and dishevelled.

One day the young man, Pete, who as a lad had smitten the Devil's Row urchin in the back of the head and put to flight the antagonists of his friend, Jimmie, strutted upon the scene. He met Jimmie one day on the street, promised to take him to a boxing match in Williamsburg, and called for him in the evening.

Maggie observed Pete.

He sat on a table in the Johnson home and dangled his checked legs with an enticing nonchalance. His hair was curled down over his forehead in an oiled bang. His rather pugged nose seemed to revolt from contact with a bristling moustache of short, wire-like hairs. His blue double-breasted coat, edged with black braid, buttoned close to a red puff tie, and his patent-leather shoes, looked like murder-fitted weapons.

His mannerisms stamped him as a man who had a correct sense of his personal superiority. There was valor and contempt for circumstances in the glance of his eye. He waved his hands like a man of the world, who dismisses religion and philosophy, and says "Fudge." He had certainly seen everything and with each curl of his lip, he declared that it amounted to nothing. Maggie thought he must be a very elegant and graceful bartender.

He was telling tales to Jimmie.

Maggie watched him furtively, with half-closed eyes, lit with a vague interest.

"Hully gee! Dey makes me tired," he said. "Mos' e'ry day some farmer comes in an' tries teh run deh shop. See? But dey gits t'rowed right out! I jolt dem right out in deh street before dey knows where dey is! See?"

"Sure," said Jimmie.

"Dere was a mug come in deh place deh odder day wid an idear he wus goin' teh own deh place! Hully gee, he wus goin' teh own deh place! I see he had a still on an' I didn' wanna giv 'im no stuff, so I says: 'Git deh hell outa here an' don' make no trouble,' I says like dat! See? 'Git deh hell outa here an' don' make no trouble'; like dat. 'Git deh hell outa here,' I says. See?"

Jimmie nodded understandingly. Over his features played an eager desire to state the amount of his valor in a similar crisis, but the narrator proceeded.

"Well, deh blokie he says: 'T'hell wid it! I ain' lookin' for no scrap,' he says (See?) 'but' he says, 'I'm spectable cit'zen an' I wanna drink an' purtydamnsoon, too.' See? 'Deh hell,' I says. Like dat! 'Deh hell,' I says. See? 'Don' make no trouble,' I says. Like dat. 'Don' make no trouble.' See? Den deh mug he squared off an' said he was fine as silk wid his dukes (See?) an' he wanned a drink damnquick. Dat's what he said. See?"

"Sure," repeated Jimmie.

Pete continued. "Say, I jes' jumped deh bar an' deh way I plunked dat blokie was great. See? Dat's right! In deh jaw! See? Hully gee, he t'rowed a spittoon true deh front windee. Say, I taut I'd drop dead. But deh boss, he comes in after an' he says, 'Pete, yehs done jes' right! Yeh've gota keep order an' it's all right.' See? 'It's all right,' he says. Dat's what he said."

The two held a technical discussion.

"Dat bloke was a dandy," said Pete, in conclusion, "but he had'n' oughta made no trouble. Dat's what I says teh dem: 'Don' come in here an' make no trouble,' I says, like dat. 'Don' make no trouble.' See."

As Jimmie and his friend exchanged tales descriptive of their prowess, Maggie leaned back in the shadow. Her eyes dwelt wonderingly and rather wistfully upon Pete's face. The broken furniture, grimy walls, and general disorder and dirt of her home of a sudden appeared before her and began to take a potential aspect. Pete's aristocratic person looked as if it might soil. She looked keenly at him, occasionally, wondering if he was feeling contempt. But Pete seemed to be enveloped in reminiscence.

"Hully gee," said he, "dose mugs can't phase me. Dey knows I kin wipe up deh street wid any t'ree of dem."

When he said, "Ah, what deh hell," his voice was burdened with disdain for the inevitable and contempt for anything that fate might compel him to endure.

Maggie perceived that here was the beau ideal of a man. Her dim thoughts were often searching for far away lands where, as God says, the little hills sing together in the morning. Under the trees of her dream-gardens there had always walked a lover.

CHAPTER VI

Pete took note of Maggie.

"Say, Mag, I'm stuck on yer shape. It's outa sight," he said, parenthetically, with an affable grin.

As he became aware that she was listening closely, he grew still more eloquent in his descriptions of various happenings in his career. It appeared that he was invincible in fights.

"Why," he said, referring to a man with whom he had had a misunderstanding, "dat mug scrapped like a damn dago. Dat's right. He was dead easy. See? He taut he was a scrapper! But he foun' out diff'ent! Hully gee."

He walked to and fro in the small room, which seemed then to grow even smaller and unfit to hold his dignity, the attribute of a supreme warrior. That swing of the shoulders that had frozen the timid when he was but a lad had increased with his growth and education at the ratio of ten to one. It, combined with the sneer upon his mouth, told mankind that there was nothing in space which could appall him. Maggie marvelled at him and surrounded him with greatness. She vaguely tried to calculate the altitude of the pinnacle from which he must have looked down upon her.

"I met a chump deh odder day way up in deh city," he said. "I was goin' teh see a frien' of mine. When I was a-crossin' deh street deh chump runned plump inteh me, an' den he turns aroun' an' says, 'Yer insolen' ruffin,' he says, like dat. 'Oh, gee,' I says, 'oh, gee, go teh hell and git off deh eart',' I says, like dat. See? 'Go teh hell an' git off deh eart',' like dat. Den deh blokie he got wild. He says I was a contempt'ble scoun'el, er someting like dat, an' he says I was doom' teh everlastin' pe'dition an' all like dat. 'Gee,' I says, 'gee! Deh hell I am,' I says. 'Deh hell I am,' like dat. An' den I slugged 'im. See?"

With Jimmie in his company, Pete departed in a sort of a blaze of glory from the Johnson home. Maggie, leaning from the window, watched him as he walked down the street.

Here was a formidable man who disdained the strength of a world full of fists. Here was one who had contempt for brass-clothed power; one whose knuckles could defiantly ring against the granite of law. He was a knight.

The two men went from under the glimmering street-lamp and passed into shadows.

Turning, Maggie contemplated the dark, dust-stained walls, and the scant and crude furniture of her home. A clock, in a splintered and battered oblong box of varnished wood, she suddenly regarded as an abomination. She noted that it ticked raspingly. The almost vanished flowers in the carpet-pattern, she conceived to be newly hideous. Some faint attempts she had made with blue ribbon, to freshen the appearance of a dingy curtain, she now saw to be piteous.

She wondered what Pete dined on.

She reflected upon the collar and cuff factory. It began to appear to her mind as a dreary place of endless grinding. Pete's elegant occupation brought him, no doubt, into contact with people who had money and manners. It was probable that he had a large acquaintance of pretty girls. He must have great sums of money to spend.

To her the earth was composed of hardships and insults. She felt instant admiration for a man who openly defied it. She thought that if the grim angel of death should clutch his heart, Pete would shrug his shoulders and say: "Oh, ev'ryt'ing goes."

She anticipated that he would come again shortly. She spent some of her week's pay in the purchase of flowered cretonne for a lambrequin.[2] She made it with infinite care and hung it to the slightly-careening mantel, over the stove, in the kitchen. She studied it with painful anxiety from different points in the room. She wanted it to look well on Sunday night when, perhaps, Jimmie's friend would come. On Sunday night, however, Pete did not appear.

Afterward the girl looked at it with a sense of humiliation. She was now convinced that Pete was superior to admiration for lambrequins.

A few evenings later Pete entered with fascinating innovations in his apparel. As she had seen him twice and he had different suits on each time, Maggie had a dim impression that his wardrobe was prodigiously extensive.

"Say, Mag," he said, "put on yer bes' duds Friday night an' I'll take yehs teh deh show. See?"

He spent a few moments in flourishing his clothes and then vanished, without having glanced at the lambrequin.

Over the eternal collars and cuffs in the factory Maggie spent the most of three days in making imaginary sketches of Pete and his daily environment. She imagined some half dozen women in love with him and thought he must lean dangerously

---

[2]An ornamental drapery for a shelf, windowtop, or door.

toward an indefinite one, whom she pictured with great charms of person, but with an altogether contemptible disposition.

She thought he must live in a blare of pleasure. He had friends, and people who were afraid of him.

She saw the golden glitter of the place where Pete was to take her. An entertainment of many hues and many melodies where she was afraid she might appear small and mouse-colored.

Her mother drank whiskey all Friday morning. With lurid face and tossing hair she cursed and destroyed furniture all Friday afternoon. When Maggie came home at half-past six her mother lay asleep amidst the wreck of chairs and a table. Fragments of various household utensils were scattered about the floor. She had vented some phase of drunken fury upon the lambrequin. It lay in a bedraggled heap in the corner.

"Hah," she snorted, sitting up suddenly, "where deh hell yeh been? Why deh hell don' yeh come home earlier? Been loafin' 'round deh streets. Yer gettin' teh be a reg'lar devil."

When Pete arrived Maggie, in a worn black dress, was waiting for him in the midst of a floor strewn with wreckage. The curtain at the window had been pulled by a heavy hand and hung by one tack, dangling to and fro in the draft through the cracks at the sash. The knots of blue ribbons appeared like violated flowers. The fire in the stove had gone out. The displaced lids and open doors showed heaps of sullen grey ashes. The remnants of a meal, ghastly, like dead flesh, lay in a corner. Maggie's red mother, stretched on the floor, blasphemed and gave her daughter a bad name.

CHAPTER VII

An orchestra of yellow silk women and bald-headed men on an elevated stage near the centre of a great green-hued hall, played a popular waltz. The place was crowded with people grouped about little tables. A battalion of waiters slid among the throng, carrying trays of beer glasses and making change from the inexhaustible vaults of their trousers pockets. Little boys, in the costumes of French chefs, paraded up and down the irregular aisles vending fancy cakes. There was a low rumble of conversation and a subdued clinking of glasses. Clouds of tobacco smoke rolled and wavered high in air about the dull gilt of the chandeliers.

The vast crowd had an air throughout of having just quitted labor. Men with calloused hands and attired in garments that showed the wear of an endless trudge for a living, smoked their pipes contentedly and spent five, ten, or perhaps fifteen cents for beer. There was a mere sprinkling of kid-gloved men who smoked cigars purchased elsewhere. The great body of the crowd was composed of people who showed that all day they strove with their hands. Quiet Germans, with maybe their wives and two or three children, sat listening to the music, with the expressions of happy cows. An occasional party of sailors from a war-ship, their faces pictures of sturdy health, spent the earlier hours of the evening at the small round tables. Very infrequent tipsy men, swollen with the value of their opinions, engaged their companions in earnest and confidential conversation. In the balcony, and here and there below, shone the impassive faces of women. The nationalities of the Bowery beamed upon the stage from all directions.

Pete aggressively walked up a side aisle and took seats with Maggie at a table beneath the balcony.

"Two beehs!"

Leaning back he regarded with eyes of superiority the scene before them. This attitude affected Maggie strongly. A man who could regard such a sight with indifference must be accustomed to very great things.

It was obvious that Pete had been to this place many times before, and was very familiar with it. A knowledge of this fact made Maggie feel little and new.

He was extremely gracious and attentive. He displayed the consideration of a cultured gentleman who knew what was due.

"Say, what deh hell? Bring deh lady a big glass! What deh hell use is dat pony?"

"Don't be fresh, now," said the waiter, with some warmth, as he departed.

"Ah, git off deh eart'," said Pete, after the other's retreating form.

Maggie perceived that Pete brought forth all his elegance and all his knowledge of high-class customs for her benefit. Her heart warmed as she reflected upon his condescension.

The orchestra of yellow silk women and bald-headed men gave vent to a few bars of anticipatory music and a girl, in a pink dress with short skirts, galloped upon the stage. She smiled upon the throng as if in acknowledgment of a warm welcome, and began to walk to and fro, making profuse gesticulations and singing, in brazen soprano tones, a song, the words of which were inaudible. When she broke into the swift rattling measures of a chorus some half tipsy men near the stage joined in the rollicking refrain and glasses were pounded rhythmically upon the tables. People leaned forward to watch her and to try to catch the words of the song. When she vanished there were long rollings of applause.

Obedient to more anticipatory bars, she reappeared amidst the half-suppressed cheering of the tipsy men. The orchestra plunged into dance music and the laces of the dancer fluttered and flew in the glare of gas jets. She divulged the fact that she was attired in some half dozen skirts. It was patent that any one of them would have proved adequate for the purpose for which skirts are intended. An occasional man bent forward, intent upon the pink stockings. Maggie wondered at the splendor of the costume and lost herself in calculations of the cost of the silks and laces.

The dancer's smile of stereotyped enthusiasm was turned for ten minutes upon the faces of her audience. In the finale she fell into some of those grotesque attitudes which were at the time popular among the dancers in the theatres up-town, giving to the Bowery public the phantasies of the aristocratic theatre-going public, at reduced rates.

"Say, Pete," said Maggie, leaning forward, "dis is great."

"Sure," said Pete, with proper complacence.

A ventriloquist followed the dancer. He held two fantastic dolls on his knees. He made them sing mournful ditties and say funny things about geography and Ireland.

"Do dose little men talk?" asked Maggie.

"Naw," said Pete, "it's some damn fake. See?"

Two girls, on the bills as sisters, came forth and sang a duet that is heard occasionally at concerts given under church auspices. They supplemented it with a dance which of course can never be seen at concerts given under church auspices.

After the duettists had retired, a woman of debatable age sang a negro melody. The chorus necessitated some grotesque waddlings supposed to be an imitation of a plantation darkey, under the influence, probably, of music and the moon. The audience was just enthusiastic enough over it to have her return and sing a sorrowful lay, whose lines told of a mother's love and a sweetheart who waited and a young man who was lost at sea under the most harrowing circumstances. From the faces of a score or so in the crowd, the self-contained look faded. Many heads were bent forward with eagerness and sympathy. As the last distressing sentiment of the piece was brought forth, it was greeted by that kind of applause which rings as sincere.

As a final effort, the singer rendered some verses which described a vision of Britain being annihilated by America, and Ireland bursting her bonds. A carefully prepared crisis was reached in the last line of the last verse, where the singer threw out her arms and cried, "The star-spangled banner." Instantly a great cheer swelled from the throats of the assemblage of the masses. There was a heavy rumble of booted feet thumping the floor. Eyes gleamed with sudden fire, and calloused hands waved frantically in the air.

After a few moments' rest, the orchestra played crashingly, and a small fat man burst out upon the stage. He began to roar a song and stamp back and forth before the footlights, wildly waving a glossy silk hat and throwing leers, or smiles, broadcast. He made his face into fantastic grimaces until he looked like a pictured devil on a Japanese kite. The crowd laughed gleefully. His short, fat legs were never still a moment. He shouted and roared and bobbed his shock of red wig until the audience broke out in excited applause.

Pete did not pay much attention to the progress of events upon the stage. He was drinking beer and watching Maggie.

Her cheeks were blushing with excitement and her eyes were glistening. She drew deep breaths of pleasure. No thoughts of the atmosphere of the collar and cuff factory came to her.

When the orchestra crashed finally, they jostled their way to the sidewalk with the crowd. Pete took Maggie's arm and pushed a way for her, offering to fight with a man or two.

They reached Maggie's home at a late hour and stood for a moment in front of the gruesome doorway.

"Say, Mag," said Pete, "give us a kiss for takin' yeh teh deh show, will yer?"

Maggie laughed, as if startled, and drew away from him.

"Naw, Pete," she said, "dat wasn't in it."

"Ah, what deh hell?" urged Pete.

The girl retreated nervously.

"Ah, what deh hell?" repeated he.

Maggie darted into the hall, and up the stairs. She turned and smiled at him, then disappeared.

Pete walked slowly down the street. He had something of an astonished expression upon his features. He paused under a lamppost and breathed a low breath of surprise.

"Gawd," he said, "I wonner if I've been played fer a duffer."

As thoughts of Pete came to Maggie's mind, she began to have an intense dislike for all of her dresses.

"What deh hell ails yeh? What makes yeh be allus fixin' and fussin'? Good Gawd," her mother would frequently roar at her.

She began to note, with more interest, the well-dressed women she met on the avenues. She envied elegance and soft palms. She craved those adornments of person which she saw every day on the street, conceiving them to be allies of vast importance to women.

Studying faces, she thought many of the women and girls she chanced to meet, smiled with serenity as though forever cherished and watched over by those they loved.

The air in the collar and cuff establishment strangled her. She knew she was gradually and surely shrivelling in the hot, stuffy room. The begrimed windows rattled incessantly from the passing of elevated trains. The place was filled with a whirl of noises and odors.

She wondered as she regarded some of the grizzled women in the room, mere mechanical contrivances sewing seams and grinding out, with heads bended over their work, tales of imagined or real girl-hood happiness, past drunks, the baby at home, and unpaid wages. She speculated how long her youth would endure. She began to see the bloom upon her cheeks as valuable.

She imagined herself, in an exasperating future, as a scrawny woman with an eternal grievance. Too, she thought Pete to be a very fastidious person concerning the appearance of women.

She felt she would love to see somebody entangle their fingers in the oily beard of the fat foreigner who owned the establishment. He was a detestable creature. He wore white socks with low shoes.

He sat all day delivering orations, in the depths of a cushioned chair. His pocket-book deprived them of the power of retort.

"What een hell do you sink I pie fife dolla a week for? Play? No, py damn!"

Maggie was anxious for a friend to whom she could talk about Pete. She would have liked to discuss his admirable mannerisms with a reliable mutual friend. At home, she found her mother often drunk and always raving.

It seems that the world had treated this woman very badly, and she took a deep revenge upon such portions of it as came within her reach. She broke furniture as if she were at last getting her rights. She swelled with virtuous indignation as she carried the lighter articles of household use, one by one under the shadows of the three gilt balls, where Hebrews chained them with chains of interest.

Jimmie came when he was obliged to by circumstances over which he had no control. His well-trained legs brought him staggering home and put him to bed some nights when he would rather have gone elsewhere.

Swaggering Pete loomed like a golden sun to Maggie. He took her to a dime museum where rows of meek freaks astonished her. She contemplated their deformities with awe and thought them a sort of chosen tribe.

Pete, raking his brains for amusement, discovered the Central Park Menagerie and the Museum of Arts. Sunday afternoons would sometimes find them at these places. Pete did not appear to be particularly interested in what he saw. He stood around looking heavy, while Maggie giggled in glee.

Once at the Menagerie he went into a trance of admiration before the spectacle of a very small monkey threatening to trash a cageful because one of them had pulled his tail and he had not wheeled about quickly enough to discover who did it. Ever after Pete knew that monkey by sight and winked at him, trying to induce him to fight with other and larger monkeys.

At the Museum, Maggie said, "Dis is outa sight."

"Oh hell," said Pete, "wait till next summer an' I'll take yehs to a picnic."

While the girl wandered in the vaulted rooms, Pete occupied himself in returning stony stare for stony stare, the appalling scrutiny of the watch-dogs of the treasures. Occasionally he would remark in loud tones: "Dat jay has got glass eyes," and sentences of the sort. When he tired of this amusement he would go to the mummies and moralize over them.

Usually he submitted with silent dignity to all which he had to go through, but, at times, he was goaded into comment.

"What deh hell," he demanded once. "Look at all dese little jugs! Hundred jugs in a row! Ten rows in a case an' 'bout a t'ousand cases! What deh blazes use is dem?"

Evenings during the week he took her to see plays in which the brain-clutching heroine was rescued from the palatial home of her guardian, who is cruelly after her bonds, by the hero with the beautiful sentiments. The latter spent most of his time out at soak in pale-green snow storms, busy with a nickel-plated revolver, rescuing aged strangers from villains.

Maggie lost herself in sympathy with the wanderers swooning in snow storms beneath happy-hued church windows. And a choir within singing "Joy to the World." To Maggie and the rest of the audience this was transcendental realism. Joy always within, and they, like the actor, inevitably without. Viewing it, they hugged themselves in ecstatic pity of their imagined or real condition.

The girl thought the arrogance and granite-heartedness of the magnate of the play was very accurately drawn. She echoed the maledictions that the occupants of the gallery showered on this individual when his lines compelled him to expose his extreme selfishness.

Shady persons in the audience revolted from the pictured villainy of the drama. With untiring zeal they hissed vice and applauded virtue. Unmistakably bad men evinced an apparently sincere admiration for virtue.

The loud gallery was overwhelmingly with the unfortunate and the oppressed. They encouraged the struggling hero with cries, and jeered the villain, hooting and calling attention to his whiskers. When anybody died in the pale-green snow storms, the gallery mourned. They sought out the painted misery and hugged it as akin.

In the hero's erratic march from poverty in the first act, to wealth and triumph in the final one, in which he forgives all the enemies that he has left, he was assisted by the gallery, which applauded his generous and noble sentiments and confounded the speeches of his opponents by making irrelevant but very sharp remarks. Those actors who were cursed with villainy parts were confronted at every turn by the gallery. If one of them rendered lines containing the most subtle distinctions between right and wrong, the gallery was immediately aware if the actor meant wickedness, and denounced him accordingly.

The last act was a triumph for the hero, poor and of the masses, the representative of the audience, over the villain and the rich man, his pockets stuffed with bonds, his heart packed with tyrannical purposes, imperturbable amid suffering.

Maggie always departed with raised spirits from the showing places of the melodrama. She rejoiced at the way in which the poor and virtuous eventually surmounted the wealthy and wicked. The theater made her think. She wondered if the culture and refinement she had seen imitated, perhaps grotesquely, by the heroine on the stage, could be acquired by a girl who lived in a tenement house and worked in a shirt factory.

CHAPTER IX

A group of urchins were intent upon the side door of a saloon. Expectancy gleamed from their eyes. They were twisting their fingers in excitement.

"Here she comes," yelled one of them suddenly.

The group of urchins burst instantly asunder and its individual fragments were spread in a wide, respectable half circle about the point of interest. The saloon door opened with a crash, and the figure of a woman appeared upon the threshold. Her grey hair fell in knotted masses about her shoulders. Her face was crimsoned and wet with perspiration. Her eyes had a rolling glare.

"Not a damn cent more of me money will yehs ever get, not a damn cent. I spent me money here fer t'ree years an' now yehs tells me yeh'll sell me no more stuff! T'hell wid yeh, Johnnie Murckre! 'Disturbance'? Disturbance be damned! T'hell wid yeh, Johnnie—"

The door received a kick of exasperation from within and the woman lurched heavily out on the sidewalk.

The gamins in the half-circle became violently agitated. They began to dance about and hoot and yell and jeer. Wide dirty grins spread over each face.

The woman made a furious dash at a particularly outrageous cluster of little boys. They laughed delightedly and scampered off a short distance, calling out over their shoulders to her. She stood tottering on the curbstone and thundered at them.

"Yeh devil's kids," she howled, shaking red fists. The little boys whooped in glee. As she started up the street they fell in behind and marched uproariously. Occasionally she wheeled about and made charges on them. They ran nimbly out of reach and taunted her.

In the frame of a gruesome doorway she stood for a moment cursing them. Her hair straggled, giving her crimson features a look of insanity. Her great fists quivered as she shook them madly in the air.

The urchins made terrific noises until she turned and disappeared. Then they filed quietly in the way they had come.

The woman floundered about in the lower hall of the tenement house and finally stumbled up the stairs. On an upper hall a door was opened and a collection of heads peered curiously out, watching her. With a wrathful snort the woman confronted the door, but it was slammed hastily in her face and the key was turned.

She stood for a few minutes, delivering a frenzied challenge at the panels.

"Come out in deh hall, Mary Murphy, damn yeh, if yehs want a row. Come ahn, yeh overgrown terrier, come ahn."

She began to kick the door with her great feet. She shrilly defied the universe to appear and do battle. Her cursing trebles brought heads from all doors save the one she threatened. Her eyes glared in every direction. The air was full of her tossing fists.

"Come ahn, deh hull damn gang of yehs, come ahn," she roared at the spectators. An oath or two, cat-calls, jeers and bits of facetious advice were given in reply. Missiles clattered about her feet.

"What deh hell's deh matter wid yeh?" said a voice in the gathered gloom, and Jimmie came forward. He carried a tin dinner-pail in his hand and under his arm a brown truckman's apron done in a bundle. "What deh hell's wrong?" he demanded.

"Come out, all of yehs, come out," his mother was howling. "Come ahn an' I'll stamp yer damn brains under me feet."

"Shet yer face, an' come home, yer damned old fool," roared Jimmie at her. She strided up to him and twirled her fingers in his face. Her eyes were darting flames of unreasoning rage and her frame trembled with eagerness for a fight.

"T'hell wid yehs! An' who deh hell are yehs? I ain't givin' a snap of me fingers fer yehs," she bawled at him. She turned her huge back in tremendous disdain and climbed the stairs to the next floor.

Jimmie followed, cursing blackly. At the top of the flight he seized his mother's arm and started to drag her toward the door of their room.

"Come home, damn yeh," he gritted between his teeth.

"Take yer hands off me! Take yer hands off me," shrieked his mother.

She raised her arm and whirled her great fist at her son's face. Jimmie dodged his head and the blow struck him in the back of the neck. "Damn yeh," gritted he again. He threw out his left hand and writhed his fingers about her middle arm. The mother and the son began to sway and struggle like gladiators.

"Whoop!" said the Rum Alley tenement house. The hall filled with interested spectators.

"Hi, ol' lady, dat was a dandy!"

"T'ree to one on deh red!"

"Ah, stop yer dam scrappin'!"

The door of the Johnson home opened and Maggie looked out. Jimmie made a supreme cursing effort and hurled his mother into the room. He quickly followed and closed the door. The Rum Alley tenement swore disappointedly and retired.

The mother slowly gathered herself up from the floor. Her eyes glittered menacingly upon her children.

"Here, now," said Jimmie, "we've had enough of dis. Sit down, an' don' make no trouble."

He grasped her arm, and twisting it, forced her into a creaking chair.

"Keep yer hands off me," roared his mother again.

"Damn yer ol' hide," yelled Jimmie, madly. Maggie shrieked and ran into the other room. To her there came the sound of a storm of crashes and curses. There was a great final thump and Jimmie's voice cried: "Dere damn yeh, stay still." Maggie opened the door now, and went warily out. "Oh, Jimmie."

He was leaning against the wall and swearing. Blood stood upon bruises on his knotty fore-arms where they had scraped against the floor or the walls in the scuffle. The mother lay screeching on the floor, the tears running down her furrowed face.

Maggie, standing in the middle of the room, gazed about her. The usual upheaval of the tables and chairs had taken place. Crockery was strewn broadcast in fragments. The stove had been disturbed on its legs, and now leaned idiotically to one side. A pail had been upset and water spread in all directions.

The door opened and Pete appeared. He shrugged his shoulders. "Oh, Gawd," he observed.

He walked over to Maggie and whispered in her ear. "Ah, what deh hell, Mag? Come ahn and we'll have a hell of a time."

The mother in the corner upreared her head and shook her tangled locks.

"Teh hell wid him and you," she said, glowering at her daughter in the gloom. Her eyes seemed to burn balefully. "Yeh've gone teh deh devil, Mag Johnson, yehs knows yehs have gone teh deh devil. Yer a disgrace teh yer people, damn yeh. An' now, git out an' go ahn wid dat doe-faced jude of yours. Go teh hell wid him, damn yeh, an' a good riddance. Go teh hell an' see how yeh likes it."

Maggie gazed long at her mother.

"Go teh hell now, an' see how yeh likes it. Git out. I won't have sech as yehs in me house! Get out, d'yeh hear! Damn yeh, git out!"

The girl began to tremble.

At this instant Pete came forward. "Oh, what deh hell, Mag, see," whispered he softly in her ear. "Dis all blows over. See? Deh ol' woman 'ill be all right in deh mornin'. Come ahn out wid me! We'll have a hell of a time."

The woman on the floor cursed. Jimmie was intent upon his bruised fore-arms. The girl cast a glance about the room filled with a chaotic mass of debris, and at the red, writhing body of her mother.

"Go teh hell an' good riddance."

She went.

CHAPTER X

Jimmie had an idea it wasn't common courtesy for a friend to come to one's home and ruin one's sister. But he was not sure how much Pete knew about the rules of politeness.

The following night he returned home from work at rather a late hour in the evening. In passing through the halls he came upon the gnarled and leathery old woman who possessed the music box. She was grinning in the dim light that drifted through dust-stained panes. She beckoned to him with a smudged forefinger.

"Ah, Jimmie, what do yehs tink I got onto las' night. It was deh funnies' ting I ever saw," she cried, coming close to him and leering. She was trembling with eagerness to tell her tale. "I was by me door las' night when yer sister and her jude feller came in late, oh, very late. An' she, the dear, she was a-cryin' as if her heart would break, she was. It was deh funnies' ting I ever saw. An' right out here by me door she asked him did he love her, did he. An' she was a-cryin' as if her heart would break, poor t'ing. An' him, I could see by deh way what he said it dat she had been askin' orften, he says: 'Oh, hell, yes,' he says, says he, 'Oh, hell, yes.'"

Storm-clouds swept over Jimmie's face, but he turned from the leathery old woman and plodded on up stairs.

"'Oh, hell, yes,'" called she after him. She laughed a laugh that was like a prophetic croak. "'Oh, hell, yes,' he says, says he, 'Oh, hell, yes.'"

There was no one in at home. The rooms showed that attempts had been made at tidying them. Parts of the wreckage of the day before had been repaired by an unskilful hand. A chair or two and the table, stood uncertainly upon legs. The floor had been newly swept. Too, the blue ribbons had been restored to the curtains, and the lambrequin, with its immense sheaves of yellow wheat and red roses of equal size, had been returned, in a worn and sorry state, to its position at the mantel. Maggie's jacket and hat were gone from the nail behind the door.

Jimmie walked to the window and began to look through the blurred glass. It occurred to him to vaguely wonder, for an instant, if some of the women of his acquaintance had brothers.

Suddenly, however, he began to swear.

"But he was me frien'! I brought 'im here! Dat's deh hell of it!"

He fumed about the room, his anger gradually rising to the furious pitch.

"I'll kill deh jay! Dat's what I'll do! I'll kill deh jay!"

He clutched his hat and sprang toward the door. But it opened and his mother's great form blocked the passage.

"What deh hell's deh matter wid yeh?" exclaimed she, coming into the rooms.

Jimmie gave vent to a sardonic curse and then laughed heavily.

"Well, Maggie's gone teh deh devil! Dat's what! See?"

"Eh?" said his mother.

"Maggie's gone teh deh devil! Are yehs deaf?" roared Jimmie, impatiently.

"Deh hell she has," murmured the mother, astounded.

Jimmie grunted, and then began to stare out at the window. His mother sat down in a chair, but a moment later sprang erect and delivered a maddened whirl of oaths. Her son turned to look at her as she reeled and swayed in the middle of the room, her fierce face convulsed with passion, her blotched arms raised high in imprecation.

"May Gawd curse her forever," she shrieked. "May she eat nothin' but stones and deh dirt in deh street. May she sleep in deh gutter an' never see deh sun shine agin. Deh damn—"

"Here, now," said her son. "Take a drop on yourself."

The mother raised lamenting eyes to the ceiling.

"She's deh devil's own chil', Jimmie," she whispered. "Ah, who would t'ink such a bad girl could grow up in our fambly, Jimmie, me son. Many deh hour I've spent in talk wid dat girl an' tol' her if she ever went on deh streets I'd see her damned. An' after all her bringin' up an' what I tol' her and talked wid her, she goes teh deh bad, like a duck teh water."

The tears rolled down her furrowed face. Her hands trembled.

"An' den when dat Sadie MacMallister next door to us was sent teh deh devil by dat feller what worked in deh soap-factory, didn't I tell our Mag dat if she—"

"Ah, dat's anudder story," interrupted the brother. "Of course, dat Sadie was nice an' all dat—but—see—it ain't dessame as if—well, Maggie was diff'ent—see—she was diff'ent."

He was trying to formulate a theory that he had always unconsciously held, that all sisters, excepting his own, could advisedly be ruined.

He suddenly broke out again. "I'll go t'ump hell outa deh mug what did her deh harm. I'll kill 'im! He t'inks he kin scrap, but when he gits me a-chasin' 'im he'll fin' out where he's wrong, deh damned duffer. I'll wipe up deh street wid 'im."

In a fury he plunged out of the doorway. As he vanished the mother raised her head and lifted both hands, entreating.

"May Gawd curse her forever," she cried.

In the darkness of the hallway Jimmie discerned a knot of women talking volubly. When he strode by they paid no attention to him.

"She allus was a bold thing," he heard one of them cry in an eager voice. "Dere wasn't a feller come teh deh house but she'd try teh mash 'im. My Annie says deh shameless t'ing tried teh ketch her feller, her own feller, what we useter know his fader."

"I could a' tol' yehs dis two years ago," said a woman, in a key of triumph. "Yesir, it was over two years ago dat I says teh my ol' man, I says, 'Dat Johnson girl ain't straight,' I says. 'Oh, hell,' he says. 'Oh, hell.' 'Dat's all right,' I says, 'but I know what I knows,' I says, 'an' it 'ill come out later. You wait an' see,' I says, 'you see.'"

"Anybody what had eyes could see dat dere was somethin' wrong wid dat girl. I didn't like her actions."

On the street Jimmie met a friend. "What deh hell?" asked the latter.

Jimmie explained. "An' I'll t'ump 'im till he can't stand."

"Oh, what deh hell," said the friend. "What's deh use!" Yeh'll git pulled in! Everybody 'ill be onto it! An' ten plunks! Gee!"

Jimmie was determined. "He t'inks he kin scrap, but he'll fin' out diff'ent."

"Gee," remonstrated the friend, "What deh hell?"

CHAPTER XI

On a corner a glass-fronted building shed a yellow glare upon the pavements. The open mouth of a saloon called seductively to passengers to enter and annihilate sorrow or create rage.

The interior of the place was papered in olive and bronze tints of imitation leather. A shining bar of counterfeit massiveness extended down the side of the room. Behind it a great mahogany-appearing sideboard reached the ceiling. Upon its shelves rested pyramids of shimmering glasses that were never disturbed. Mirrors set in the face of the sideboard multiplied them. Lemons, oranges and paper napkins, arranged with mathematical precision, sat among the glasses. Many-hued decanters of liquor perched at regular intervals on the lower shelves. A nickel-plated cash register occupied a position in the exact center of the general effect. The elementary senses of it all seemed to be opulence and geometrical accuracy.

Across from the bar a small counter held a collection of plates upon which swarmed frayed fragments of crackers, slices of boiled ham, dishevelled bits of cheese, and pickles swimming in vinegar. An odor of grasping, begrimmed hands and munching mouths pervaded.

Pete, in a white jacket, was behind the bar bending expectantly toward a quiet stranger. "A beeh," said the man. Pete drew a foam-topped glassful and set it dripping upon the bar.

At this moment the light bamboo doors at the entrance swung open and crashed against the siding. Jimmie and a companion entered. They swaggered unsteadily but belligerently toward the bar and looked at Pete with bleared and blinking eyes.

"Gin," said Jimmie.

"Gin," said the companion.

Pete slid a bottle and two glasses along the bar. He bended his head sideways as he assiduously polished away with a napkin at the gleaming wood. He had a look of watchfulness upon his features.

Jimmie and his companion kept their eyes upon the bartender and conversed loudly in tones of contempt.

"He's a dindy masher, ain't he, by Gawd?" laughed Jimmie.

"Oh, hell, yes," said the companion, sneering widely. "He's great, he is. Git onto deh mug on deh blokie. Dat's enough to make a feller turn hand-springs in 'is sleep."

The quiet stranger moved himself and his glass a trifle further away and maintained an attitude of oblivion.

"Gee! ain't he hot stuff!"

"Git onto his shape! Great Gawd!"

"Hey," cried Jimmie, in tones of command. Pete came along slowly, with a sullen dropping of the under lip.

"Well," he growled, "what's eatin' yehs?"

"Gin," said Jimmie.

"Gin," said the companion.

As Pete confronted them with the bottle and the glasses, they laughed in his face. Jimmie's companion, evidently overcome with merriment, pointed a grimy forefinger in Pete's direction.

"Say, Jimmie," demanded he, "what deh hell is dat behind deh bar?"

"Damned if I knows," replied Jimmie. They laughed loudly. Pete put down a bottle with a bang and turned a formidable face toward them. He disclosed his teeth and his shoulders heaved restlessly.

"You fellers can't guy me," he said. "Drink yer stuff an' git out an' don' make no trouble."

Instantly the laughter faded from the faces of the two men and expressions of offended dignity immediately came.

"Who deh hell has said anyt'ing teh you," cried they in the same breath.

The quiet stranger looked at the door calculatingly.

"Ah, come off," said Pete to the two men. "Don't pick me up for no jay. Drink yer rum an' git out an' don' make no trouble."

"Oh, deh hell," airily cried Jimmie.

"Oh, deh hell," airily repeated his companion.

"We goes when we git ready! See!" continued Jimmie.

"Well," said Pete in a threatening voice, "don' make no trouble."

Jimmie suddenly leaned forward with his head on one side. He snarled like a wild animal.

"Well, what if we does? See?" said he.

Dark blood flushed into Pete's face, and he shot a lurid glance at Jimmie.

"Well, den we'll see whose deh bes' man, you or me," he said.

The quiet stranger moved modestly toward the door.

Jimmie began to swell with valor.

"Don' pick me up fer no tenderfoot. When yeh tackles me yeh tackles one of deh bes' men in deh city. See? I'm a scrapper, I am. Ain't dat right, Billie?"

"Sure, Mike," responded his companion in tones of conviction.

"Oh, hell," said Pete, easily. "Go fall on yerself."

The two men again began to laugh.

"What deh hell is dat talkin'?" cried the companion.

"Damned if I knows," replied Jimmie with exaggerated contempt.

Pete made a furious gesture. "Git outa here now, an' don' make no trouble. See? Youse fellers er lookin' fer a scrap an' it's damn likely yeh'll fin' one if yeh keeps on shootin' off yer mout's. I know yehs! See? I kin lick better men dan yehs ever saw in yer lifes. Dat's right! See? Don' pick me up fer no stuff er yeh might be jolted out in deh street before yeh knows where yeh is. When I comes from behind dis bar, I t'rows yehs bote inteh deh street. See?"

"Oh, hell," cried the two men in chorus.

The glare of a panther came into Pete's eyes. "Dat's what I said! Unnerstan'?"

He came through a passage at the end of the bar and swelled down upon the two men. They stepped promptly forward and crowded close to him.

They bristled like three roosters. They moved their heads pugnaciously and kept their shoulders braced. The nervous muscles about each mouth twitched with a forced smile of mockery.

"Well, what deh hell yer goin' teh do?" gritted Jimmie.

Pete stepped warily back, waving his hands before him to keep the men from coming too near.

"Well, what deh hell yer goin' teh do?" repeated Jimmie's ally. They kept close to him, taunting and leering. They strove to make him attempt the initial blow.

"Keep back, now! Don' crowd me," ominously said Pete.

Again they chorused in contempt. "Oh, hell!"

In a small, tossing group, the three men edged for positions like frigates contemplating battle.

"Well, why deh hell don' yeh try teh t'row us out?" cried Jimmie and his ally with copious sneers.

The bravery of bull-dogs sat upon the faces of the men. Their clenched fists moved like eager weapons.

The allied two jostled the bartender's elbows, glaring at him with feverish eyes and forcing him toward the wall.

Suddenly Pete swore redly. The flash of action gleamed from his eyes. He threw back his arm and aimed a tremendous, lightning-like blow at Jimmie's face. His foot swung a step forward and the weight of his body was behind his fist. Jimmie ducked his head, Bowery-like, with the quickness of a cat. The fierce, answering blows of him and his ally crushed on Pete's bowed head.

The quiet stranger vanished.

The arms of the combatants whirled in the air like flails. The faces of the men, at first flushed to flame-colored anger, now began to fade to the pallor of warriors in the blood and heat of a battle. Their lips curled back and stretched tightly over the gums in ghoul-like grins. Through their white, gripped teeth struggled hoarse whisperings of oaths. Their eyes glittered with murderous fire.

Each head was huddled between its owner's shoulders, and arms were swinging with marvelous rapidity. Feet scraped to and fro with a loud scratching sound upon the sanded floor. Blows left crimson blotches upon pale skin. The curses of the first quarter minute of the fight died away. The breaths of the fighters came wheezingly from their lips and the three chests were straining and heaving. Pete at intervals gave vent to low, labored hisses, that sounded like a desire to kill. Jimmie's ally gibbered at times like a wounded maniac. Jimmie was silent, fighting with the face of a sacrificial priest. The rage of fear shone in all their eyes and their blood-colored fists swirled.

At a tottering moment a blow from Pete's hand struck the ally and he crashed to the floor. He wriggled instantly to his feet and grasping the quiet stranger's beer glass from the bar, hurled it at Pete's head.

High on the wall it burst like a bomb, shivering fragments flying in all directions. Then missles came to every man's hand. The place had heretofore appeared free of things to throw, but suddenly glass and bottles went singing through the air. They were thrown point blank at bobbing heads. The pyramid of shimmering glasses, that had never been disturbed, changed to cascades as heavy bottles were flung into them. Mirrors splintered to nothing.

The three frothing creatures on the floor buried themselves in a frenzy for blood. There followed in the wake of missles and fists some unknown prayers, perhaps for death.

The quiet stranger had sprawled very pyrotechnically out on the sidewalk. A laugh ran up and down the avenue for the half of a block.

"Dey've t'rowed a bloke inteh deh street."

People heard the sound of breaking glass and shuffling feet within the saloon and came running. A small group, bending down to look under the bamboo doors, watching the fall of glass, and three pairs of violent legs, changed in a moment to a crowd.

A policeman came charging down the sidewalk and bounced through the doors into the saloon. The crowd bended and surged in absorbing anxiety to see.

Jimmie caught first sight of the on-coming interruption. On his feet he had the same regard for a policeman that, when on his truck, he had for a fire engine. He howled and ran for the side door.

The officer made a terrific advance, club in hand. One comprehensive sweep of the long night stick threw the ally to the floor and forced Pete to a corner. With his disengaged hand he made a furious effort at Jimmie's coattails. Then he regained his balance and paused.

"Well, well, you are a pair of pictures. What in hell yeh been up to?"

Jimmie, with his face drenched in blood, escaped up a side street, pursued a short distance by some of the more law-loving, or excited individuals of the crowd.

Later, from a corner safely dark, he saw the policeman, the ally and the bartender emerge from the saloon. Pete locked the doors and then followed up the avenue in the rear of the crowd-encompassed policeman and his charge.

On first thoughts Jimmie, with his heart throbbing at battle heat, started to go desperately to the rescue of his friend, but he halted.

"Ah, what deh hell?" he demanded of himself.

CHAPTER XII

In a hall of irregular shape sat Pete and Maggie drinking beer. A submissive orchestra dictated to by a spectacled man with frowsy hair and a dress suit, industriously followed the bobs of his head and the waves of his baton. A ballad singer, in a dress of flaming scarlet, sang in the inevitable voice of brass. When she vanished, men seated at the tables near the front applauded loudly, pounding the polished wood with their beer glasses. She returned attired in less gown, and sang again. She received another enthusiastic encore. She reappeared in still less gown and danced. The deafening rumble of glasses and clapping of hands that followed her exit indicated an overwhelming desire to have her come on for the fourth time, but the curiosity of the audience was not gratified.

Maggie was pale. From her eyes had been plucked all look of self-reliance. She leaned with a dependent air toward her companion. She was timid, as if fearing his anger or displeasure. She seemed to beseech tenderness of him.

Pete's air of distinguished valor had grown upon him until it threatened stupendous dimensions. He was infinitely gracious to the girl. It was apparent to her that his condescension was a marvel.

He could appear to strut even while sitting still and he showed that he was a lion of lordly characteristics by the air with which he spat.

With Maggie gazing at him wonderingly, he took pride in commanding the waiters who were, however, indifferent or deaf.

"Hi, you, git a russle on yehs! What deh hell yeh's lookin' at? Two more beehs, d'yeh hear?"

He leaned back and critically regarded the person of a girl with a straw-colored wig who upon the stage was flinging her heels in somewhat awkward imitation of a well-known danseuse.

At times Maggie told Pete long confidential tales of her former home life, dwelling upon the escapades of the other members of the family and the difficulties she had to combat in order to obtain a degree of comfort. He responded in tones of philanthropy. He pressed her arm with an air of reassuring proprietorship.

"Dey was damn jays," he said, denouncing the mother and brother.

The sound of the music which, by the efforts of the frowsy-headed leader, drifted to her ears through the smoke-filled atmosphere, made the girl dream. She thought of her former Rum Alley environment and turned to regard Pete's strong protecting fists. She thought of the collar and cuff manufactory and the eternal moan of the proprietor: "What een hell do you sink I pie fife dolla a week for? Play? No, py damn." She contemplated Pete's man-subduing eyes and noted that wealth and prosperity was indicated by his clothes. She imagined a future, rose-tinted, because of its distance from all that she previously had experienced.

As to the present she perceived only vague reasons to be miserable. Her life was Pete's and she considered him worthy of the charge. She would be disturbed by no particular apprehensions, so long as Pete adored her as he now said he did. She did not feel like a bad woman. To her knowledge she had never seen any better.

At times men at other tables regarded the girl furtively. Pete, aware of it, nodded at her and grinned. He felt proud.

"Mag, yer a bloomin' good-looker," he remarked, studying her face through the haze. The men made Maggie fear, but she blushed at Pete's words as it became apparent to her that she was the apple of his eye.

Grey-headed men, wonderfully pathetic in their dissipation, stared at her through clouds. Smooth-cheeked boys, some of them with faces of stone and mouths of sin, not nearly so pathetic as the grey heads, tried to find the girl's eyes in the smoke wreaths. Maggie considered she was not what they thought her. She confined her glances to Pete and the stage.

The orchestra played negro melodies and a versatile drummer pounded, whacked, clattered and scratched on a dozen machines to make noise.

Those glances of the men, shot at Maggie from under half-closed lids, made her tremble. She thought them all to be worse men than Pete.

"Come, let's go," she said.

As they went out Maggie perceived two women seated at a table with some other men. They were painted and their cheeks had lost their roundness. As she passed them the girl, with a shrinking movement, drew back her skirts.

CHAPTER XIII

Jimmie did not return home for a number of days after the fight with Pete in the saloon. When he did, he approached with extreme caution.

He found his mother raving. Maggie had not returned home. The parent continually wondered how her daughter could come to such a pass. She had never considered Maggie as a pearl dropped unstained into Rum Alley from Heaven, but she could not conceive how it was possible for her daughter to fall so low as to bring disgrace upon her family. She was terrific in denunciation of the girl's wickedness.

The fact that the neighbors talked of it, maddened her. When women came in, and in the course of their conversation casually asked, "Where's Maggie dese days?" the mother shook her fuzzy head at them and appalled them with curses. Cunning hints inviting confidence she rebuffed with violence.

"An' wid all deh bringin' up she had, how could she?" moaningly she asked of her son. "Wid all deh talkin' wid her I did an' deh t'ings I tol' her to remember? When a girl is bringed up deh way I bringed up Maggie, how kin she go teh deh devil?"

Jimmie was transfixed by these questions. He could not conceive how under the circumstances his mother's daughter and his sister could have been so wicked.

His mother took a drink from a squdgy bottle that sat on the table. She continued her lament.

"She had a bad heart, dat girl did, Jimmie. She was wicked teh deh heart an' we never knowed it."

Jimmie nodded, admitting the fact.

"We lived in deh same house wid her an' I brought her up an' we never knowed how bad she was."

Jimmie nodded again.

"Wid a home like dis an' a mudder like me, she went teh deh bad," cried the mother, raising her eyes.

One day, Jimmie came home, sat down in a chair and began to wriggle about with a new and strange nervousness. At last he spoke shamefacedly.

"Well, look-a-here, dis t'ing queers us! See? We're queered! An' maybe it 'ud be better if I — well, I t'ink I kin look 'er up an' — maybe it 'ud be better if I fetched her home an' —"

The mother started from her chair and broke forth into a storm of passionate anger.

"What! Let 'er come an' sleep under deh same roof wid her mudder agin! Oh, yes, I will, won't I? Sure? Shame on yehs, Jimmie Johnson, fer sayin' such a t'ing teh yer own mudder — teh yer own mudder! Little did I t'ink when yehs was a babby playin' about me feet dat ye'd grow up teh say sech a t'ing teh yer mudder — yer own mudder. I never taut —"

Sobs choked her and interrupted her reproaches.

"Dere ain't nottin teh raise sech hell about," said Jimmie. "I on'y says it 'ud be better if we keep dis t'ing dark, see? It queers us! See?"

His mother laughed a laugh that seemed to ring through the city and be echoed and re-echoed by countless other laughs. "Oh, yes, I will, wont I! Sure!"

"Well, yeh must take me fer a damn fool," said Jimmie, indignant at his mother for mocking him. "I didn't say we'd make 'er inteh a little tin angel, ner nottin, but deh way it is now she can queer us! Don' che see?"

"Aye, she'll git tired of deh life atter a while an' den she'll wanna be a-comin' home, won' she, deh beast! I'll let 'er in den, won' I?"

"Well, I didn' mean none of dis prod'gal bus'ness anyway," explained Jimmie.

"It wasn't no prod'gal dauter, yeh damn fool," said the mother. "It was prod'gal son, anyhow."

"I know dat," said Jimmie.

For a time they sat in silence. The mother's eyes gloated on a scene her imagination could call before her. Her lips were set in a vindictive smile.

"Aye, she'll cry, won' she, an' carry on, an' tell how Pete, or some odder feller, beats 'er an' she'll say she's sorry an' all dat an' she ain't happy, she ain't, an' she wants to come home agin, she does."

With grim humor, the mother imitated the possible wailing notes of the daughter's voice.

"Den I'll take 'er in, won't I, deh beast. She kin cry 'er two eyes out on deh stones of deh street before I'll dirty deh place wid her. She abused an' ill-treated her own mudder—her own mudder what loved her an' she'll never git anodder chance dis side of hell."

Jimmie thought he had a great idea of women's frailty, but he could not understand why any of his kin should be victims.

"Damn her," he fervidly said.

Again he wondered vaguely if some of the women of his acquaintance had brothers. Nevertheless, his mind did not for an instant confuse himself with those brothers nor his sister with theirs. After the mother had, with great difficulty, suppressed the neighbors, she went among them and proclaimed her grief. "May Gawd forgive dat girl," was her continual cry. To attentive ears she recited the whole length and breadth of her woes.

"I bringed 'er up deh way a dauter oughta be bringed up an' dis is how she served me! She went teh deh devil deh first chance she got! May Gawd forgive her."

When arrested for drunkenness she used the story of her daughter's downfall with telling effect upon the police-justices. Finally one of them said to her, peering down over his spectacles: "Mary, the records of this and other courts show that you are the mother of forty-two daughters who have been ruined. The case is unparalleled in the annals of this court, and this court thinks—"

The mother went through life shedding large tears of sorrow. Her red face was a picture of agony.

Of course Jimmie publicly damned his sister that he might appear on a higher social plane. But, arguing with himself, stumbling about in ways that he knew not, he, once, almost came to a conclusion that his sister would have been more firmly good had she better known why. However, he felt that he could not hold such a view. He threw it hastily aside.

CHAPTER XIV

In a hilarious hall there were twenty-eight tables and twenty-eight women and a crowd of smoking men. Valiant noise was made on a stage at the end of the hall by an orchestra composed of men who looked as if they had just happened in. Soiled waiters ran to and fro, swooping down like hawks on the unwary in the throng; clattering along the aisles with trays covered with glasses; stumbling over women's skirts and charging two prices for everything but beer, all with a swiftness that blurred the view of the cocoanut palms and dusty monstrosities painted upon the walls of the room. A bouncer, with a immense load of business upon his hands, plunged about in the crowd, dragging bashful strangers to prominent chairs, ordering waiters here and there and quarreling furiously with men who wanted to sing with the orchestra.

The usual smoke cloud was present, but so dense that heads and arms seemed entangled in it. The rumble of conversation was replaced by a roar. Plenteous oaths heaved through the air. The room rang with the shrill voices of women bubbling o'er with drink-laughter. The chief element in the music of the orchestra was speed. The musicians played in intent fury. A woman was singing and smiling upon the stage, but no one took notice of her. The rate at which the piano, cornet and violins were going, seemed to impart wildness to the half-drunken crowd. Beer glasses were emptied at a gulp and conversation became a rapid chatter. The smoke eddied and swirled like a shadowy river hurrying toward some unseen falls. Pete and Maggie entered the hall and took chairs at a table near the door. The woman who was seated there made an attempt to occupy Pete's attention and, failing, went away.

Three weeks had passed since the girl had left home. The air of spaniel-like dependence had been magnified and showed its direct effect in the peculiar off-handedness and ease of Pete's ways toward her.

She followed Pete's eyes with hers, anticipating with smiles gracious looks from him.

A woman of brilliance and audacity, accompanied by a mere boy, came into the place and took seats near them.

At once Pete sprang to his feet, his face beaming with glad surprise.

"By Gawd, there's Nellie," he cried.

He went over to the table and held out an eager hand to the woman.

"Why, hello, Pete, me boy, how are you," said she, giving him her fingers.

Maggie took instant note of the woman. She perceived that her black dress fitted her to perfection. Her linen collar and cuffs were spotless. Tan gloves were stretched over her well-shaped hands. A hat of a prevailing fashion perched jauntily upon her dark hair. She wore no jewelry and was painted with no apparent paint. She looked clear-eyed through the stares of the men.

"Sit down, and call your lady-friend over," she said cordially to Pete. At his beckoning Maggie came and sat between Pete and the mere boy.

"I thought yeh were gone away fer good," began Pete, at once. "When did yeh git back? How did dat Buff'lo bus'ness turn out?"

The woman shrugged her shoulders. "Well, he didn't have as many stamps as he tried to make out, so I shook him, that's all."

"Well, I'm glad teh see yehs back in deh city," said Pete, with awkward gallantry.

He and the woman entered into a long conversation, exchanging reminiscences of days together. Maggie sat still, unable to formulate an intelligent sentence upon the conversation and painfully aware of it.

She saw Pete's eyes sparkle as he gazed upon the handsome stranger. He listened smilingly to all she said. The woman was familiar with all his affairs, asked him about mutual friends, and knew the amount of his salary.

She paid no attention to Maggie, looking toward her once or twice and apparently seeing the wall beyond.

The mere boy was sulky. In the beginning he had welcomed with acclamations the additions.

"Let's all have a drink! What'll you take, Nell? And you, Miss what's-your-name. Have a drink, Mr. ——, you, I mean."

He had shown a sprightly desire to do the talking for the company and tell all about his family. In a loud voice he declaimed on various topics. He assumed a patronizing air toward Pete. As Maggie was silent, he paid no attention to her. He made a great show of lavishing wealth upon the woman of brilliance and audacity.

"Do keep still, Freddie! You gibber like an ape, dear," said the woman to him. She turned away and devoted her attention to Pete.

"We'll have many a good time together again, eh?"

"Sure, Mike," said Pete, enthusiastic at once.

"Say," whispered she, leaning forward, "let's go over to Billie's and have a heluva time."

"Well, it's dis way! See?" said Pete. "I got dis lady frien' here."

"Oh, t'hell with her," argued the woman.

Pete appeared disturbed.

"All right," said she, nodding her head at him. "All right for you! We'll see the next time you ask me to go anywheres with you."

Pete squirmed.

"Say," he said, beseechingly, "come wid me a minit an' I'll tell yer why."

The woman waved her hand.

"Oh, that's all right, you needn't explain, you know. You wouldn't come merely because you wouldn't come, that's all there is of it."

To Pete's visible distress she turned to the mere boy, bringing him speedily from a terrific rage. He had been debating whether it would be the part of a man to pick a quarrel with Pete, or would he be justified in striking him savagely with his beer glass without warning. But he recovered himself when the woman turned to renew her smilings. He beamed upon her with an expression that was somewhat tipsy and inexpressibly tender.

"Say, shake that Bowery jay," requested he, in a loud whisper.

"Freddie, you are so droll," she replied.

Pete reached forward and touched the woman on the arm.

"Come out a minit while I tells yeh why I can't go wid yer. Yer doin' me dirt, Nell! I never taut ye'd do me dirt, Nell. Come on, will yer?" He spoke in tones of injury.

"Why, I don't see why I should be interested in your explanations," said the woman, with a coldness that seemed to reduce Pete to a pulp.

His eyes pleaded with her. "Come out a minit while I tells yeh."

The woman nodded slightly at Maggie and the mere boy, "'Scuse me."

The mere boy interrupted his loving smile and turned a shriveling glare upon Pete. His boyish countenance flushed and he spoke, in a whine, to the woman:

"Oh, I say, Nellie, this ain't a square deal, you know. You aren't goin' to leave me and go off with that duffer, are you? I should think—"

"Why, you dear boy, of course I'm not," cried the woman, affectionately. She bended over and whispered in his ear. He smiled again and settled in his chair as if resolved to wait patiently.

As the woman walked down between the rows of tables, Pete was at her shoulder talking earnestly, apparently in explanation. The woman waved her hands with studied airs of indifference. The doors swung behind them, leaving Maggie and the mere boy seated at the table.

Maggie was dazed. She could dimly perceive that something stupendous had happened. She wondered why Pete saw fit to remonstrate with the woman, pleading for forgiveness with his eyes. She thought she noted an air of submission about her leonine Pete. She was astounded.

The mere boy occupied himself with cocktails and a cigar. He was tranquilly silent for half an hour. Then he bestirred himself and spoke.

"Well," he said, sighing, "I knew this was the way it would be." There was another stillness. The mere boy seemed to be musing.

"She was pulling m'leg. That's the whole amount of it," he said, suddenly. "It's a bloomin' shame the way that girl does. Why, I've spent over two dollars in drinks tonight. And she goes off with that plug-ugly who looks as if he had been hit in the face with a coin-die. I call it rocky treatment for a fellah like me. Here, waiter, bring me a cock-tail and make it damned strong."

Maggie made no reply. She was watching the doors. "It's a mean piece of business," complained the mere boy. He explained to her how amazing it was that anybody should treat him in such a manner. "But I'll get square with her, you bet. She won't get far ahead of yours truly, you know," he added, winking. "I'll tell her plainly that it was bloomin' mean business. And she won't come it over me with any of her 'now-Freddie-dears.' She thinks my name is Freddie, you know, but of course it ain't. I always tell these people some name like that, because if they got onto your right name they might use it sometime. Understand? Oh, they don't fool me much."

Maggie was paying no attention, being intent upon the doors. The mere boy relapsed into a period of gloom, during which he exterminated a number of cock-tails with a determined air, as if replying defiantly to fate. He occasionally broke forth into sentences composed of invectives joined together in a long string.

The girl was still staring at the doors. After a time the mere boy began to see cobwebs just in front of his nose. He spurred himself into being agreeable and insisted upon her having a charlotte-russe and a glass of beer.

"They's gone," he remarked, "they's gone." He looked at her through the smoke wreaths. "Shay, lil' girl, we mightish well make bes' of it. You ain't such bad-lookin' girl, y'know. Not half bad. Can't come up to Nell, though. No, can't do it! Well, I should shay not! Nell fine-lookin' girl. F—i—n—ine. You look damn bad longsider her, but by y'self ain't so bad. Have to do anyhow. Nell gone. On'y you left. Not half bad, though."

Maggie stood up.

"I'm going home," she said.

The mere boy started.

"Eh? What? Home," he cried, struck with amazement. "I beg pardon, did hear say home?"

"I'm going home," she repeated.

"Great Gawd, what hava struck," demanded the mere boy of himself, stupefied.

In a semi-comatose state he conducted her on board an up-town car, ostentatiously paid her fare, leered kindly at her through the rear window and fell off the steps.

CHAPTER XV

A forlorn woman went along a lighted avenue. The street was filled with people desperately bound on missions. An endless crowd darted at the elevated station stairs and the horse cars were thronged with owners of bundles.

The pace of the forlorn woman was slow. She was apparently searching for some one. She loitered near the doors of saloons and watched men emerge from them. She scanned furtively the faces in the rushing stream of pedestrians. Hurrying men, bent on catching some boat or train, jostled her elbows, failing to notice her, their thoughts fixed on distant dinners.

The forlorn woman had a peculiar face. Her smile was no smile. But when in repose her features had a shadowy look that was like a sardonic grin, as if some one had sketched with cruel forefinger indelible lines about her mouth.

Jimmie came strolling up the avenue. The woman encountered him with an aggrieved air.

"Oh, Jimmie, I've been lookin' all over fer yehs—" she began.

Jimmie made an impatient gesture and quickened his pace.

"Ah, don't bodder me! Good Gawd!" he said, with the savageness of a man whose life is pestered.

The woman followed him along the sidewalk in somewhat the manner of a suppliant.

"But, Jimmie," she said, "yehs told me ye'd—"

Jimmie turned upon her fiercely as if resolved to make a last stand for comfort and peace.

"Say, fer Gawd's sake, Hattie, don' foller me from one end of deh city teh deh odder. Let up, will yehs! Give me a minute's res', can't yehs? Yehs makes me tired, allus taggin' me. See? Ain' yehs got no sense? Do yehs want people teh get onto me? Go chase yerself, fer Gawd's sake."

The woman stepped closer and laid her fingers on his arm. "But, look-a here—"

Jimmie snarled. "Oh, go teh hell."

He darted into the front door of a convenient saloon and a moment later came out into the shadows that surrounded the side door. On the brilliantly lighted avenue he perceived the forlorn woman dodging about like a scout. Jimmie laughed with an air of relief and went away.

When he arrived home he found his mother clamoring. Maggie had returned. She stood shivering beneath the torrent of her mother's wrath.

"Well, I'm damned," said Jimmie in greeting.

His mother, tottering about the room, pointed a quivering fore-finger.

"Lookut her, Jimmie, lookut here. Dere's yer sister, boy. Dere's yer sister. Lookut her! Lookut her!"

She screamed in scoffing laughter.

The girl stood in the middle of the room. She edged about as if unable to find a place on the floor to put her feet.

"Ha, ha, ha," bellowed the mother. "Dere she stands! Ain' she purty? Lookut her! Ain' she sweet, deh beast? Lookut her! Ha, ha, lookut her!"

She lurched forward and put her red and seamed hands upon her daughter's face. She bent down and peered keenly up into the eyes of the girl.

"Oh, she's jes' dessame as she ever was, ain' she? She's her mudder's purty darlin' yit, ain' she? Lookut her, Jimmie! Come here, fer Gawd's sake, and lookut her."

The loud, tremendous sneering of the mother brought the denizens of the Rum Alley tenement to their doors. Women came in the hall-ways. Children scurried to and fro.

"What's up? Dat Johnson party on anudder tear?"

"Naw! Young Mag's come home!"

"Deh hell ych say?"

Through the open doors curious eyes stared in at Maggie. Children ventured into the room and ogled her, as if they formed the front row at a theatre. Women, without, bended toward each other and whispered, nodding their heads with airs of profound philosophy. A baby, overcome with curiosity concerning this object at which all were looking, sidled forward and touched her dress, cautiously, as if investigating a red-hot stove. Its mother's voice rang out like a warning trumpet. She rushed forward and grabbed her child, casting a terrible look of indignation at the girl.

Maggie's mother paced to and fro, addressing the doorful of eyes, expounding like a glib showman at a museum. Her voice rang through the building.

"Dere she stands," she cried, wheeling suddenly and pointing with dramatic finger. "Dere she stands! Lookut her! Ain' she a dindy? An' she was so good as to come home teh her mudder, she was! Ain' she a beaut'? Ain' she a dindy? Fer Gawd's sake!"

The jeering cries ended in another burst of shrill laughter.

The girl seemed to awaken. "Jimmie—"

He drew hastily back from her.

"Well, now, yer a hell of a t'ing, ain' yeh?" he said, his lips curling in scorn. Radiant virtue sat upon his brow and his repelling hands expressed horror of contamination.

Maggie turned and went.

The crowd at the door fell back precipitately. A baby falling down in front of the door, wrenched a scream like a wounded animal from its mother. Another woman sprang forward and picked it up, with a chivalrous air, as if rescuing a human being from an oncoming express train.

As the girl passed down through the hall, she went before open doors framing more eyes strangely microscopic, and sending broad beams of inquisitive light into the darkness of her path. On the second floor she met the gnarled old woman who possessed the music box.

"So," she cried, "'ere yehs are back again, are yehs? An' dey've kicked yehs out? Well, come in an' stay wid me teh-night. I ain' got no moral standin'.'"

From above came an unceasing babble of tongues, over all of which rang the mother's derisive laughter.

CHAPTER XVI

Pete did not consider that he had ruined Maggie. If he had thought that her soul could never smile again, he would have believed the mother and brother, who were pyrotechnic over the affair, to be responsible for it.

Besides, in his world, souls did not insist upon being able to smile. "What deh hell?"

He felt a trifle entangled. It distressed him. Revelations and scenes might bring upon him the wrath of the owner of the saloon, who insisted upon respectability of an advanced type.

"What deh hell do dey wanna raise such a smoke about it fer? demanded he of himself, disgusted with the attitude of the family. He saw no necessity for anyone's losing their equilibrium merely because their sister or their daughter had stayed away from home.

Searching about in his mind for possible reasons for their conduct, he came upon the conclusion that Maggie's motives were correct, but that the two others wished to snare him. He felt pursued.

The woman of brilliance and audacity whom he had met in the hilarious hall showed a disposition to ridicule him.

"A little pale thing with no spirit," she said. "Did you note the expression of her eyes? There was something in them about pumpkin pie and virtue. That is a peculiar way the left corner of her mouth has of twitching, isn't it? Dear, dear, my cloud-compelling Pete, what are you coming to?"

Pete asserted at once that he never was very much interested in the girl. The woman interrupted him, laughing.

"Oh, it's not of the slightest consequence to me, my dear young man. You needn't draw maps for my benefit. Why should I be concerned about it?"

But Pete continued with his explanations. If he was laughed at for his tastes in women, he felt obliged to say that they were only temporary or indifferent ones.

The morning after Maggie had departed from home, Pete stood behind the bar. He was immaculate in white jacket and apron and his hair was plastered over his brow with infinite correctness. No customers were in the place. Pete was twisting his napkined fist slowly in a beer glass, softly whistling to himself and occasionally holding the object of his attention between his eyes and a few weak beams of sunlight that had found their way over the thick screens and into the shaded room.

With lingering thoughts of the woman of brilliance and audacity, the bartender raised his head and stared through the varying cracks between the swaying bamboo doors. Suddenly the whistling pucker faded from his lips. He saw Maggie walking slowly past. He gave a great start, fearing for the previously-mentioned eminent respectability of the place.

He threw a swift, nervous glance about him, all at once feeling guilty. No one was in the room.

He went hastily over to the side door. Opening it and looking out, he perceived Maggie standing, as if undecided, on the corner. She was searching the place with her eyes.

As she turned her face toward him Pete beckoned to her hurriedly, intent upon returning with speed to a position behind the bar and to the atmosphere of respectability upon which the proprietor insisted.

Maggie came to him, the anxious look disappearing from her face and a smile wreathing her lips.

"Oh, Pete —," she began brightly.

The bartender made a violent gesture of impatience.

"Oh, my Gawd," cried he, vehemently. "What deh hell do yeh wanna hang aroun' here fer? Do yeh wanna git me inteh trouble?" he demanded with an air of injury.

Astonishment swept over the girl's features.

"Why, Pete! yehs tol' me—"

Pete glanced profound irritation. His countenance reddened with the anger of a man whose respectability is being threatened.

"Say, yehs makes me tired. See? What deh hell deh yeh wanna tag aroun' atter me fer? Yeh'll git me inteh trouble wid deh ol' man an' dey'll be hell teh pay! If he sees a woman roun' here he'll go crazy an' I'll lose me job! See? Ain' yehs got not sense? Don' be allus bodderin' me. See? Yer brudder come in here an' raised hell an' deh ol' man hada put up fer it! An' now I'm done! See? I'm done."

The girl's eyes stared into his face. "Pete, don' yeh remem—"

"Oh, hell," interrupted Pete, anticipating.

The girl seemed to have a struggle with herself. She was apparently bewildered and could not find speech. Finally she asked in a low voice: "But where kin I go?"

The question exasperated Pete beyond the powers of endurance. It was a direct attempt to give him some responsibility in a matter that did not concern him. In his indignation he volunteered information.

"Oh, go teh hell," cried he. He slammed the door furiously and returned, with an air of relief, to his respectability.

Maggie went away.

She wandered aimlessly for several blocks. She stopped once and asked aloud a question of herself: "Who?"

A man who was passing near her shoulder, humorously took the questioning word as intended for him.

"Eh? What? Who? Nobody! I didn't say anything," he laughingly said, and continued his way.

Soon the girl discovered that if she walked with such apparent aimlessness, some men looked at her with calculating eyes. She quickened her step, frightened. As a protection, she adopted a demeanor of intentness as if going somewhere.

After a time she left rattling avenues and passed between rows of houses with sterness and stolidity stamped upon their features. She hung her head for she felt their eyes grimly upon her.

Suddenly she came upon a stout gentleman in a silk hat and a chaste black coat, whose decorous row of buttons reached from his chin to his knees. The girl had heard of the Grace of God and she decided to approach this man.

His beaming, chubby face was a picture of benevolence and kind-heartedness. His eyes shone good-will.

But as the girl timidly accosted him, he gave a convulsive movement and saved his respectability by a vigorous side-step. He did not risk it to save a soul. For how was he to know that there was a soul before him that needed saving?

CHAPTER XVII

Upon a wet evening, several months after the last chapter, two interminable rows of cars, pulled by slipping horses, jangled along a prominent side-street. A dozen cabs, with coat-enshrouded drivers, clattered to and fro. Electric lights, whirring softly, shed a blurred radiance. A flower dealer, his feet tapping impatiently, his nose and his wares glistening with rain-drops, stood behind an array of roses and chrysanthemums. Two or three theatres emptied a crowd upon the storm-swept pavements. Men pulled their hats over their eyebrows and raised their collars to their ears. Women shrugged impatient shoulders in their warm cloaks and stopped to arrange their skirts for a walk through the storm. People having been comparatively silent for two hours burst into a roar of conversation, their hearts still kindling from the glowings of the stage.

The pavements became tossing seas of umbrellas. Men stepped forth to hail cabs or cars, raising their fingers in varied forms of polite request or imperative demand. An endless procession wended toward elevated stations. An atmosphere of pleasure and prosperity seemed to hang over the throng, born, perhaps, of good clothes and of having just emerged from a place of forgetfulness.

In the mingled light and gloom of an adjacent park, a handful of wet wanderers, in attitudes of chronic dejection, was scattered among the benches.

A girl of the painted cohorts of the city went along the street. She threw changing glances at men who passed her, giving smiling invitations to men of rural or untaught pattern and usually seeming sedately unconscious of the men with a metropolitan seal upon their faces.

Crossing glittering avenues, she went into the throng emerging from the places of forgetness. She hurried forward through the crowd as if intent upon reaching a distant home, bending forward in her handsome cloak, daintily lifting her skirts and picking for her well-shod feet the dryer spots upon the pavements.

The restless doors of saloons, clashing to and fro, disclosed animated rows of men before bars and hurrying barkeepers.

A concert hall gave to the street faint sounds of swift, machine-like music, as if a group of phantom musicians were hastening.

A tall young man, smoking a cigarette with a sublime air, strolled near the girl. He had on evening dress, a moustache, a chrysanthemum, and a look of ennui, all of which he kept carefully under his eye. Seeing the girl walk on as if such a young man as he was not in existence, he looked back transfixed with interest. He stared glassily for a moment, but gave a slight convulsive start when he discerned that she was neither new, Parisian, nor theatrical. He wheeled about hastily and turned his stare into the air, like a sailor with a search-light.

A stout gentleman, with pompous and philanthropic whiskers, went stolidly by, the broad of his back sneering at the girl.

A belated man in business clothes, and in haste to catch a car, bounced against her shoulder. "Hi, there, Mary, I beg your pardon! Brace up, old girl." He grasped her arm to steady her, and then was away running down the middle of the street.

The girl walked on out of the realm of restaurants and saloons. She passed more glittering avenues and went into darker blocks than those where the crowd travelled.

A young man in light overcoat and derby hat received a glance shot keenly from the eyes of the girl. He stopped and looked at her, thrusting his hands in his pockets and making a mocking smile curl his lips. "Come, now, old lady," he said, "you don't mean to tell me that you sized me up for a farmer?"

A laboring man marched along with bundles under his arms. To her remarks, he replied: "It's a fine evenin', ain't it?"

She smiled squarely into the face of a boy who was hurrying by with his hand buried in his overcoat, his blonde locks bobbing on his youthful temples, and a cheery smile of unconcern upon his lips. He turned his head and smiled back at her, waving his hands.

"Not this eve — some other eve!"

A drunken man, reeling in her pathway, began to roar at her. "I ain' ga no money, dammit," he shouted, in a dismal voice. He lurched on up the street, wailing to himself, "Dammit, I ain' ga no money. Damn ba' luck. Ain' ga no more money."

The girl went into gloomy districts near the river, where the tall black factories shut in the street and only occasional broad beams of light fell across the pavements from saloons. In front of one of these places, from whence came the sound of a violin vigorously scraped, the patter of feet on boards and the ring of loud laughter, there stood a man with blotched features.

"Ah, there," said the girl.

"I've got a date," said the man.

Further on in the darkness she met a ragged being with shifting, blood-shot eyes and grimy hands. "Ah, what deh hell? T'ink I'm a millionaire?"

She went into the blackness of the final block. The shutters of the tall buildings were closed like grim lips. The structures seemed to have eyes that looked over her, beyond her, at other things. Afar off the lights of the avenues glittered as if from an impossible distance. Street car bells jingled with a sound of merriment.

When almost to the river the girl saw a great figure. On going forward she perceived it to be a huge fat man in torn and greasy garments. His grey hair straggled down over his forehead. His small, bleared eyes, sparkling from amidst great rolls of red fat, swept eagerly over the girl's upturned face. He laughed, his brown, disordered teeth gleaming under a grey, grizzled moustache from which beer-drops dripped. His whole body gently quivered and shook like that of a dead jelly fish. Chuckling and leering, he followed the girl of the crimson legions.

At their feet the river appeared a deathly black hue. Some hidden factory sent up a yellow glare, that lit for a moment the waters lapping oilily against timbers. The varied sounds of life, made joyous by distance and seeming unapproachableness, came faintly and died away to a silence.[3]

CHAPTER XVIII

In a partitioned-off section of a saloon sat a man with a half dozen women, gleefully laughing, hovering about him. The man had arrived at that stage of drunkenness where affection is felt for the universe.

"I'm good f'ler, girls," he said, convincingly. "I'm damn good f'ler. An'body treats me right, I allus trea's zem right! See?"

The women nodded their heads approvingly. "To be sure," they cried in hearty chorus. "You're the kind of a man we like, Pete. You're outa sight! What yeh goin' to buy this time, dear?"

"An'thin' yehs wants, damn it," said the man in an abandonment of good will. His countenance shone with the true spirit of benevolence. He was in the proper mode of missionaries. He would have fraternized with obscure Hottentots. And above all, he was overwhelmed in tenderness for his friends, who were all illustrious.

"An'thing yehs wants, damn it," repeated he, waving his hands with beneficent recklessness. "I'm good f'ler, girls, an' if an'body treats me right I—here," called he through an open door to a waiter, "bring girls drinks, damn it. What 'ill yehs have, girls? An'thing yehs wants, damn it!"

The waiter glanced in with the disgusted look of the man who serves intoxicants for the man who takes too much of them. He nodded his head shortly at the order from each individual, and went.

"Damn it," said the man, "we're havin' heluva time. I like you girls! Damn'd if I don't! Yer right sort! See?"

He spoke at length and with feeling, concerning the excellencies of his assembled friends.

"Don' try pull man's leg, but have a heluva time! Das right! Das way teh do! Now, if I sawght yehs tryin' work me fer drinks, wouldn' buy damn t'ing! But yer right sort, damn it! Yehs know how ter treat a f'ler, an' I stays by yehs 'til spen' las' cent! Das right! I'm good f'ler an' I knows when an'body treats me right!"

Between the times of the arrival and departure of the waiter, the man discoursed to the women on the tender regard he felt for all living things. He laid stress upon the purity of his motives in all dealings with men in the world and spoke of the fervor of

---

[3]Deleted from this chapter in the 1896 edition was the dialogue after the "man with botched features" appears: "'Ah, there,' said the girl. 'I've got a date,' said the man." Next, the response of the "ragged being" was deleted: "'Ah, what deh hell? T'ink I'm a millionaire?'" Finally, the entire penultimate paragraph was omitted, and the first sentence in the last paragraph was changed to "At the feet of the tall buildings appeared the deathly black hue of the river."

his friendship for those who were amiable. Tears welled slowly from his eyes. His voice quavered when he spoke to them.

Once when the waiter was about to depart with an empty tray, the man drew a coin from his pocket and held it forth.

"Here," said he, quite magnificently "here's quar'."

The waiter kept his hands on his tray.

"I don' want yer money," he said.

The other put forth the coin with tearful insistence.

"Here, damn it," cried he, "tak't! Yer damn goo' f'ler an' I wan' yehs tak't!"

"Come, come, now," said the waiter, with the sullen air of a man who is forced into giving advice. "Put yer mon in yer pocket! Yer loaded an' yehs on'y makes a damn fool of yerself."

As the latter passed out of the door the man turned pathetically to the women.

"He don' know I'm damn goo' f'ler," cried he, dismally.

"Never you mind, Pete, dear," said a woman of brilliance and audacity, laying her hand with great affection upon his arm. "Never you mind, old boy! We'll stay by you, dear!"

"Das ri'," cried the man, his face lighting up at the soothing tones of the woman's voice. "Das ri', I'm damn goo' f'ler an' w'en anyone trea's me' ri', I treats zem ri'! Shee!"

"Sure!" cried the women. "And we're not goin' back on you, old man."

The man turned appealing eyes to the woman of brilliance and audacity. He felt that if he could be convicted of a contemptible action he would die.

"Shay, Nell, damn it, I allus trea's yehs shquare, didn' I? I allus been goo' f'ler wi' yehs, ain't I, Nell?"

"Sure you have, Pete," assented the woman. She delivered an oration to her companions. "Yessir, that's a fact. Pete's a square fellah, he is. He never goes back on a friend. He's the right kind an' we stay by him, don't we, girls?"

"Sure," they exclaimed. Looking lovingly at him they raised their glasses and drank his health.

"Girlsh," said the man, beseechingly, "I allus trea's yehs ri', didn' I? I'm goo' f'ler, ain' I, girlsh?"

"Sure," again they chorused.

"Well," said he finally, "le's have nozzer drink, zen."

"That's right," hailed a woman, "that's right. Yer no bloomin' jay! Yer spends yer money like a man. Dat's right."

The man pounded the table with his quivering fists.

"Yessir," he cried, with deep earnestness, as if someone disputed him. "I'm damn goo' f'ler, an' w'en anyone trea's me ri', I allus trea's — le's have nozzer drink."

He began to beat the wood with his glass.

"Shay," howled he, growing suddenly impatient. As the waiter did not then come, the man swelled with wrath.

"Shay," howled he again.

The waiter appeared at the door.

"Bringsh drinksh," said the man.

The waiter disappeared with the orders.

"Zat f'ler dam fool," cried the man. "He insul' me! I'm ge'man! Can' stan' be insul'! I'm goin' lickim when comes!"

"No, no," cried the women, crowding about and trying to subdue him. "He's all right! He didn't mean anything! Let it go! He's a good fellah!"

"Din' he insul' me?" asked the man earnestly.

"No," said they. "Of course he didn't? He's all right!"

"Sure he didn' insul' me," demanded the man, with deep anxiety in his voice.

"No, no! We know him! He's a good fellah. He didn't mean anything."

"Well, zen," said the man, resolutely, "I'm go' 'pol'gize!"

When the waiter came, the man struggled to the middle of the floor.

"Girlsh shed you insul' me! I shay damn lie! I 'pol'gize!"

"All right," said the waiter.

The man sat down. He felt a sleepy but strong desire to straighten things out and have a perfect understanding with everybody.

"Nell, I allus trea's yeh shquare, din I? Yeh likes me, don' yehs, Nell? I'm goo' f'ler?"

"Sure," said the woman of brilliance and audacity.

"Yeh knows I'm stuck on yehs, don' yehs, Nell?"

"Sure," she repeated, carelessly.

Overwhelmed by a spasm of drunken adoration, he drew two or three bills from his pocket, and, with the trembling fingers of an offering priest, laid them on the table before the woman.

"Yehs knows, damn it, yehs kin have all got, 'cause I'm stuck on yehs, Nell, damn't, I—I'm stuck on yehs, Nell—buy drinksh—damn't—we're havin' heluva time—w'en anyone trea's me ri'—I—damn't, Nell—we're havin' heluva—time."

Shortly he went to sleep with his swollen face fallen forward on his chest.

The women drank and laughed, not heeding the slumbering man in the corner. Finally he lurched forward and fell groaning to the floor.

The women screamed in disgust and drew back their skirts.

"Come ahn," cried one, starting up angrily, "let's get out of here."

The woman of brilliance and audacity stayed behind, taking up the bills and stuffing them into a deep, irregularly-shaped pocket. A gutteral snore from the recumbent man caused her to turn and look down at him.

She laughed. "What a damn fool," she said, and went.

The smoke from the lamps settled heavily down in the little compartment, obscuring the way out. The smell of oil, stifling in its intensity, pervaded the air. The wine from an overturned glass dripped softly down upon the blotches on the man's neck.

CHAPTER XIX

In a room a woman sat at a table eating like a fat monk in a picture.

A soiled, unshaven man pushed open the door and entered.

"Well," said he, "Mag's dead."

"What?" said the woman, her mouth filled with bread.

"Mag's dead," repeated the man.

"Deh hell she is," said the woman. She continued her meal. When she finished her coffee she began to weep.

"I kin remember when her two feet was no bigger dan yer t'umb, and she weared worsted boots," moaned she.

"Well, whata dat?" said the man.

"I kin remember when she weared worsted boots," she cried.

The neighbors began to gather in the hall, staring in at the weeping woman as if watching the contortions of a dying dog. A dozen women entered and lamented with her. Under their busy hands the rooms took on that appalling appearance of neatness and order with which death is greeted.

Suddenly the door opened and a woman in a black gown rushed in with outstretched arms. "Ah, poor Mary," she cried, and tenderly embraced the moaning one.

"Ah, what ter'ble affliction is dis," continued she. Her vocabulary was derived from mission churches. "Me poor Mary, how I feel fer yehs! Ah, what a ter'ble affliction is a disobed'ent chil'."

Her good, motherly face was wet with tears. She trembled in eagerness to express her sympathy. The mourner sat with bowed head, rocking her body heavily to and fro, and crying out in a high, strained voice that sounded like a dirge on some forlorn pipe.

"I kin remember when she weared worsted boots an' her two feets was no bigger dan yer t'umb an' she weared worsted boots, Miss Smith," she cried, raising her streaming eyes.

"Ah, me poor Mary," sobbed the woman in black. With low, coddling cries, she sank on her knees by the mourner's chair, and put her arms about her. The other women began to groan in different keys.

"Yer poor misguided chil' is gone now, Mary, an' let us hope it's fer deh bes'. Yeh'll fergive her now, Mary, won't yehs, dear, all her disobed'ence? All her t'ankless behavior to her mudder an' all her badness? She's gone where her ter'ble sins will be judged."

The woman in black raised her face and paused. The inevitable sunlight came streaming in at the windows and shed a ghastly cheerfulness upon the faded hues of the room. Two or three of the spectators were sniffling, and one was loudly weeping. The mourner arose and staggered into the other room. In a moment she emerged with a pair of faded baby shoes held in the hollow of her hand.

"I kin remember when she used to wear dem," cried she. The women burst anew into cries as if they had all been stabbed. The mourner turned to the soiled and unshaven man.

"Jimmie, boy, go git yer sister! Go git yer sister an' we'll put deh boots on her feets!"

"Dey won't fit her now, yeh damn fool," said the man.

"Go git yer sister, Jimmie," shrieked the woman, confronting him fiercely.

The man swore sullenly. He went over to a corner and slowly began to put on his coat. He took his hat and went out, with a dragging, reluctant step.

The woman in black came forward and again besought the mourner.

"Yeh'll fergive her, Mary! Yeh'll fergive yer bad, bad chil'! Her life was a curse an' her days were black an' yeh'll fergive yer bad girl? She's gone where her sins will be judged."

"She's gone where her sins will be judged," cried the other women, like a choir at a funeral.

"Deh Lord give and deh Lord takes away," said the woman in black, raising her eyes to the sunbeams.

"Deh Lord gives and deh Lord takes away," responded the others.

"Yeh'll fergive her, Mary!" pleaded the woman in black. The mourner essayed to speak but her voice gave way. She shook her great shoulders frantically, in an agony of grief. Hot tears seemed to scald her quivering face. Finally her voice came and arose like a scream of pain.

"Oh, yes, I'll fergive her! I'll fergive her!"

1891–93   *1893*

The Open Boat

A Tale Intended to Be after the Fact.
Being the Experience of Four Men
from the Sunk Steamer *Commodore*[1]

I

None of them knew the color of the sky. Their eyes glanced level, and were fastened upon the waves that swept toward them. These waves were of the hue of slate,

---

[1]As a correspondent covering the Cuban Revolution, Crane sailed on the *Commodore*, carrying contraband munitions for the Cuban rebels. On January 2, 1897, the ship sank off the coast of Florida. Crane spent almost 30 hours at sea in a ten-foot dinghy before reaching Daytona Beach. The *New York Press* had reported him missing, but on January 7, it published "Stephen Crane's Own Story," his factual news report of the event. Afterwards, he wrote the story "The Open Boat," published in *Scribner's Magazine* in June 1897.

save for the tops, which were of foaming white, and all of the men knew the colors of the sea. The horizon narrowed and widened, and dipped and rose, and at all times its edge was jagged with waves that seemed thrust up in points like rocks.

Many a man ought to have a bath-tub larger than the boat which here rode upon the sea. These waves were most wrongfully and barbarously abrupt and tall, and each froth-top was a problem in small boat navigation.

The cook squatted in the bottom and looked with both eyes at the six inches of gunwale[2] which separated him from the ocean. His sleeves were rolled over his fat forearms, and the two flaps of his unbuttoned vest dangled as he bent to bail out the boat. Often he said: "Gawd! That was a narrow clip." As he remarked it he invariably gazed eastward over the broken sea.

The oiler,[3] steering with one of the two oars in the boat, sometimes raised himself suddenly to keep clear of water that swirled in over the stern. It was a thin little oar and it seemed often ready to snap.

The correspondent, pulling at the other oar, watched the waves and wondered why he was there.

The injured captain, lying in the bow, was at this time buried in that profound dejection and indifference which comes, temporarily at least, to even the bravest and most enduring when, willy nilly, the firm fails, the army loses, the ship goes down. The mind of the master of a vessel is rooted deep in the timbers of her, though he command for a day or a decade, and this captain had on him the stern impression of a scene in the grays of dawn of seven turned faces, and later a stump of a top-mast with a white ball on it that slashed to and fro at the waves, went low and lower, and down. Thereafter there was something strange in his voice. Although steady, it was deep with mourning, and of a quality beyond oration or tears.

"Keep'er a little more south, Billie," said he.

"'A little more south,' sir," said the oiler in the stern.

A seat in this boat was not unlike a seat upon a bucking broncho, and, by the same token, a broncho is not much smaller. The craft pranced and reared, and plunged like an animal. As each wave came, and she rose for it, she seemed like a horse making at a fence outrageously high. The manner of her scramble over these walls of water is a mystic thing, and, moreover, at the top of them were ordinarily these problems in white water, the foam racing down from the summit of each wave, requiring a new leap, and a leap from the air. Then, after scornfully bumping a crest, she would slide, and race, and splash down a long incline and arrive bobbing and nodding in front of the next menace.

A singular disadvantage of the sea lies in the fact that after successfully surmounting one wave you discover that there is another behind it just as important and just as nervously anxious to do something effective in the way of swamping boats. In a ten-foot dingey one can get an idea of the resources of the sea in the line of waves that is not probable to the average experience, which is never at sea in a dingey. As each slaty wall of water approached, it shut all else from the view of the men in the boat, and it was not difficult to imagine that this particular wave was the final outburst of the ocean, the last effort of the grim water. There was a terrible grace in the move of the waves, and they came in silence, save for the snarling of the crests.

In the wan light, the faces of the men must have been gray. Their eyes must have glinted in strange ways as they gazed steadily astern. Viewed from a balcony, the whole thing would doubtlessly have been weirdly picturesque. But the men in the boat had no time to see it, and if they had had leisure there were other things to occupy their minds. The sun swung steadily up the sky, and they knew it was broad day because the color of the sea changed from slate to emerald-green, streaked with amber lights, and the foam was like tumbling snow. The process of the breaking day

---

[2]Upper edge of a boat.
[3]One who oils machinery and engines.

was unknown to them. They were aware only of this effect upon the color of the waves that rolled toward them.

In disjointed sentences the cook and the correspondent argued as to the difference between a life-saving station and a house of refuge. The cook had said: "There's a house of refuge just north of the Mosquito Inlet Light, and as soon as they see us, they'll come off in their boat and pick us up."

"As soon as who see us?" said the correspondent.

"The crew," said the cook.

"Houses of refuge don't have crews," said the correspondent. "As I understand them, they are only places where clothes and grub are stored for the benefit of shipwrecked people. They don't carry crews."

"Oh, yes, they do," said the cook.

"No, they don't," said the correspondent.

"Well, we're not there yet, anyhow," said the oiler, in the stern.

"Well," said the cook, "perhaps it's not a house of refuge that I'm thinking of as being near Mosquito Inlet Light. Perhaps it's a life-saving station."

"We're not there yet," said the oiler, in the stern.

II

As the boat bounced from the top of each wave, the wind tore through the hair of the hatless men, and as the craft plopped her stern down again the spray slashed past them. The crest of each of these waves was a hill, from the top of which the men surveyed, for a moment, a broad tumultuous expanse, shining and wind-riven. It was probably splendid. It was probably glorious, this play of the free sea, wild with lights of emerald and white and amber.

"Bully good thing it's an on-shore wind," said the cook. "If not, where would we be? Wouldn't have a show."

"That's right," said the correspondent.

The busy oiler nodded his assent.

Then the captain, in the bow, chuckled in a way that expressed humor, contempt, tragedy, all in one. "Do you think we've got much of a show, now, boys?" said he.

Whereupon the three were silent, save for a trifle of hemming and hawing. To express any particular optimism at this time they felt to be childish and stupid, but they all doubtless possessed this sense of the situation in their mind. A young man thinks doggedly at such times. On the other hand, the ethics of their condition was decidedly against any open suggestion of hopelessness. So they were silent.

"Oh, well," said the captain, soothing his children, "we'll get ashore all right."

But there was that in his tone which made them think, so the oiler quoth: "Yes! If this wind holds!"

The cook was bailing. "Yes! If we don't catch hell in the surf."

Canton flannel[4] gulls flew near and far. Sometimes they sat down on the sea, near patches of brown sea-weed that rolled over the waves with a movement like carpets on a line in a gale. The birds sat comfortably in groups, and they were envied by some in the dingey, for the wrath of the sea was no more to them than it was to a covey of prairie chickens a thousand miles inland. Often they came very close and stared at the men with black bead-like eyes. At these times they were uncanny and sinister in their unblinking scrutiny, and the men hooted angrily at them, telling them to be gone. One came, and evidently decided to alight on the top of the captain's head. The bird flew parallel to the boat and did not circle, but made short sidelong jumps in the air in chicken-fashion. His black eyes were wistfully fixed upon the captain's head. "Ugly brute," said the oiler to the bird. "You look as if you were made with a jack-

---

[4]Heavy soft cotton, with wooly nap, originally made in Canton, China.

knife." The cook and the correspondent swore darkly at the creature. The captain naturally wished to knock it away with the end of the heavy painter,[5] but he did not dare do it, because anything resembling an emphatic gesture would have capsized this freighted boat, and so with his open hand, the captain gently and carefully waved the gull away. After it had been discouraged from the pursuit the captain breathed easier on account of his hair, and others breathed easier because the bird struck their minds at this time as being somehow grewsome and ominous.

In the meantime the oiler and the correspondent rowed. And also they rowed.

They sat together in the same seat, and each rowed an oar. Then the oiler took both oars; then the correspondent took both oars; then the oiler; then the correspondent. They rowed and they rowed. The very ticklish part of the business was when the time came for the reclining one in the stern to take his turn at the oars. By the very last star of truth, it is easier to steal eggs from under a hen than it was to change seats in the dingey. First the man in the stern slid his hand along the thwart[6] and moved with care, as if he were of Sèvres.[7] Then the man in the rowing seat slid his hand along the other thwart. It was all done with the most extraordinary care. As the two sidled past each other, the whole party kept watchful eyes on the coming wave, and the captain cried: "Look out now! Steady there!"

The brown mats of sea-weed that appeared from time to time were like islands, bits of earth. They were travelling, apparently, neither one way nor the other. They were, to all intents, stationary. They informed the men in the boat that it was making progress slowly toward the land.

The captain, rearing cautiously in the bow, after the dingey soared on a great swell, said that he had seen the light-house at Mosquito Inlet. Presently the cook remarked that he had seen it. The correspondent was at the oars, then, and for some reason he too wished to look at the light-house, but his back was toward the far shore and the waves were important, and for some time he could not seize an opportunity to turn his head. But at last there came a wave more gentle than the others, and when at the crest of it he swiftly scoured the western horizon.

"See it?" said the captain.

"No," said the correspondent, slowly, "I didn't see anything."

"Look again," said the captain. He pointed. "It's exactly in that direction."

At the top of another wave, the correspondent did as he was bid, and this time his eyes chanced on a small still thing on the edge of the swaying horizon. It was precisely like the point of a pin. It took an anxious eye to find a light-house so tiny.

"Think we'll make it, Captain?"

"If this wind holds and the boat don't swamp, we can't do much else," said the captain.

The little boat, lifted by each towering sea, and splashed viciously by the crests, made progress that in the absence of sea-weed was not apparent to those in her. She seemed just a wee thing wallowing, miraculously, top-up, at the mercy of five oceans. Occasionally, a great spread of water, like white flames, swarmed into her.

"Bail her, cook," said the captain, serenely.

"All right, Captain," said the cheerful cook.

III

It would be difficult to describe the subtle brotherhood of men that was here established on the seas. No one said that it was so. No one mentioned it. But it dwelt in the boat, and each man felt it warm him. They were a captain, an oiler, a cook, and a correspondent, and they were friends, friends in a more curiously iron-bound de-

---

[5] Bow-rope.
[6] Rower's seat.
[7] Fine china made in Sèvres, France.

gree than may be common. The hurt captain, lying against the water-jar in the bow, spoke always in a low voice and calmly, but he could never command a more ready and swiftly obedient crew than the motley three of the dingey. It was more than a mere recognition of what was best for the common safety. There was surely in it a quality that was personal and heartfelt. And after this devotion to the commander of the boat there was this comradeship that the correspondent, for instance, who had been taught to be cynical of men, knew even at the time was the best experience of his life. But no one said that it was so. No one mentioned it.

"I wish we had a sail," remarked the captain. "We might try my overcoat on the end of an oar and give you two boys a chance to rest." So the cook and the correspondent held the mast and spread wide the overcoat. The oiler steered, and the little boat made good way with her new rig. Sometimes the oiler had to scull sharply to keep a sea from breaking into the boat, but otherwise sailing was a success.

Meanwhile the light-house had been growing slowly larger. It had now almost assumed color, and appeared like a little gray shadow on the sky. The man at the oars could not be prevented from turning his head rather often to try for a glimpse of this little gray shadow.

At last, from the top of each wave the men in the tossing boat could see land. Even as the light-house was an upright shadow on the sky, this land seemed but a long black shadow on the sea. It certainly was thinner than paper. "We must be about opposite New Smyrna," said the cook, who had coasted this shore often in schooners. "Captain, by the way, I believe they abandoned that life-saving station there about a year ago."

"Did they?" said the captain.

The wind slowly died away. The cook and the correspondent were not now obliged to slave in order to hold high the oar. But the waves continued their old impetuous swooping at the dingey, and the little craft, no longer under way, struggled woundily[8] over them. The oiler or the correspondent took the oars again.

Shipwrecks are *apropos* of nothing. If men could only train for them and have them occur when the men had reached pink condition, there would be less drowning at sea. Of the four in the dingey none had slept any time worth mentioning for two days and two nights previous to embarking in the dingey, and in the excitement of clambering about the deck of a foundering ship they had also forgotten to eat heartily.

For these reasons, and for others, neither the oiler nor the correspondent was fond of rowing at this time. The correspondent wondered ingenuously how in the name of all that was sane could there be people who thought it amusing to row a boat. It was not an amusement; it was a diabolical punishment, and even a genius of mental aberrations could never conclude that it was anything but a horror of the muscles and a crime against the back. He mentioned to the boat in general how the amusement of rowing struck him, and the weary-faced oiler smiled in full sympathy. Previously to the foundering, by the way, the oiler had worked double-watch in the engine-room of the ship.

"Take her easy, now, boys," said the captain. "Don't spend yourselves. If we have to run a surf you'll need all your strength, because we'll sure have to swim for it. Take your time."

Slowly the land arose from the sea. From a black line it became a line of black and a line of white—trees and sand. Finally, the captain said that he could make out a house on the shore. "That's the house of refuge, sure," said the cook. "They'll see us before long, and come out after us."

The distant light-house reared high. "The keeper ought to be able to make us out

---

[8]Excessively.

now, if he's looking through a glass," said the captain. "He'll notify the life-saving people."

"None of those other boats could have got ashore to give word of the wreck," said the oiler, in a low voice. "Else the life-boat would be out hunting us."

Slowly and beautifully the land loomed out of the sea. The wind came again. It had veered from the northeast to the southeast. Finally, a new sound struck the ears of the men in the boat. It was the low thunder of the surf on the shore. "We'll never be able to make the light-house now," said the captain. "Swing her head a little more north, Billie."

"'A little more north,' sir," said the oiler.

Whereupon the little boat turned her nose once more down the wind, and all but the oarsman watched the shore grow. Under the influence of this expansion doubt and direful apprehension was leaving the minds of the men. The management of the boat was still most absorbing, but it could not prevent a quiet cheerfulness. In an hour, perhaps, they would be ashore.

Their back-bones had become thoroughly used to balancing in the boat and they now rode this wild colt of a dingey like circus men. The correspondent thought that he had been drenched to the skin, but happening to feel in the top pocket of his coat, he found therein eight cigars. Four of them were soaked with sea-water; four were perfectly scatheless. After a search, somebody produced three dry matches, and thereupon the four waifs rode impudently in their little boat, and with an assurance of an impending rescue shining in their eyes, puffed at the big cigars and judged well and ill of all men. Everybody took a drink of water.

IV

"Cook," remarked the captain, "there don't seem to be any signs of life about your house of refuge."

"No," replied the cook. "Funny they don't see us!"

A broad stretch of lowly coast lay before the eyes of the men. It was of dunes topped with dark vegetation. The roar of the surf was plain, and sometimes they could see the white lip of a wave as it spun up the beach. A tiny house was blocked out black upon the sky. Southward, the slim light-house lifted its little gray length.

Tide, wind, and waves were swinging the dingey northward. "Funny they don't see us," said the men.

The surf's roar was here dulled, but its tone was, nevertheless, thunderous and mighty. As the boat swam over the great rollers, the men sat listening to this roar. "We'll swamp sure," said everybody.

It is fair to say here that there was not a life-saving station within twenty miles in either direction, but the men did not know this fact and in consequence they made dark and opprobrious remarks concerning the eyesight of the nation's life-savers. Four scowling men sat in the dingey and surpassed records in the invention of epithets.

"Funny they don't see us."

The light-heartedness of a former time had completely faded. To their sharpened minds it was easy to conjure pictures of all kinds of incompetency and blindness and, indeed, cowardice. There was the shore of the populous land, and it was bitter and bitter to them that from it came no sign.

"Well," said the captain, ultimately, "I suppose we'll have to make a try for ourselves. If we stay out here too long, we'll none of us have strength left to swim after the boat swamps."

And so the oiler, who was at the oars, turned the boat straight for the shore. There was a sudden tightening of muscles. There was some thinking.

"If we don't all get ashore—" said the captain. "If we don't all get ashore, I suppose you fellows know where to send news of my finish?"

They then briefly exchanged some addresses and admonitions. As for the reflections of the men, there was a great deal of rage in them. Perchance they might be formulated thus: "If I am going to be drowned—if I am going to be drowned—if I am going to be drowned, why, in the name of the seven mad gods who rule the sea, was I allowed to come thus far and contemplate sand and trees? Was I brought here merely to have my nose dragged away as I was about to nibble the sacred cheese of life? It is preposterous. If this old ninny-woman, Fate, cannot do better than this, she should be deprived of the management of men's fortunes. She is an old hen who knows not her intention. If she has decided to drown me, why did she not do it in the beginning and save me all this trouble. The whole affair is absurd. . . . But, no, she cannot mean to drown me. She dare not drown me. She cannot drown me. Not after all this work." Afterward the man might have had an impulse to shake his fist at the clouds. "Just you drown me, now, and then hear what I call you!"

The billows that came at this time were more formidable. They seemed always just about to break and roll over the little boat in a turmoil of foam. There was a preparatory and long growl in the speech of them. No mind unused to the sea would have concluded that the dingey could ascend these sheer heights in time. The shore was still afar. The oiler was a wily surfman. "Boys," he said, swiftly, "she won't live three minutes more and we're too far out to swim. Shall I take her to sea again, Captain?"

"Yes! Go ahead!" said the captain.

This oiler, by a series of quick miracles, and fast and steady oarsmanship, turned the boat in the middle of the surf and took her safely to sea again.

There was a considerable silence as the boat bumped over the furrowed sea to deeper water. Then somebody in gloom spoke. "Well, anyhow, they must have seen us from the shore by now."

The gulls went in slanting flight up the wind toward the gray desolate east. A squall, marked by dingy clouds, and clouds brick-red, like smoke from a burning building, appeared from the southeast.

"What do you think of those life-saving people? Ain't they peaches?"

"Funny they haven't seen us."

"Maybe they think we're out here for sport! Maybe they think we're fishin'. Maybe they think we're damned fools."

It was a long afternoon. A changed tide tried to force them southward, but wind and wave said northward. Far ahead, where coast-line, sea, and sky formed their mighty angle, there were little dots which seemed to indicate a city on the shore.

"St. Augustine?"

The captain shook his head. "Too near Mosquito Inlet."

And the oiler rowed, and then the correspondent rowed. Then the oiler rowed. It was a weary business. The human back can become the seat of more aches and pains than are registered in books for the composite anatomy of a regiment. It is a limited area, but it can become the theatre of innumerable muscular conflicts, tangles, wrenches, knots, and other comforts.

"Did you ever like to row, Billie?" asked the correspondent.

"No," said the oiler. "Hang it."

When one exchanged the rowing-seat for a place in the bottom of the boat, he suffered a bodily depression that caused him to be careless of everything save an obligation to wiggle one finger. There was cold sea-water swashing to and fro in the boat, and he lay in it. His head, pillowed on a thwart, was within an inch of the swirl of a wave crest, and sometimes a particularly obstreperous sea came in-board and drenched him once more. But these matters did not annoy him. It is almost certain that if the boat had capsized he would have tumbled comfortably out upon the ocean as if he felt sure that it was a great soft mattress.

"Look! There's a man on the shore!"

"Where?"

"There! See 'im? See 'im?"

"Yes, sure! He's walking along."

"Now he's stopped. Look! He's facing us!"

"He's waving at us!"

"So he is! By thunder!"

"Ah, now, we're all right! Now we're all right! There'll be a boat out here for us in half an hour."

"He's going on. He's running. He's going up to that house there."

The remote beach seemed lower than the sea, and it required a searching glance to discern the little black figure. The captain saw a floating stick and they rowed to it. A bath-towel was by some weird chance in the boat, and, tying this on the stick, the captain waved it. The oarsman did not dare turn his head, so he was obliged to ask questions.

"What's he doing now?"

"He's standing still again. He's looking, I think. . . . There he goes again. Toward the house. . . . Now he's stopped again."

"Is he waving at us?"

"No, not now! he was, though."

"Look! There comes another man!"

"He's running."

"Look at him go, would you."

"Why, he's on a bicycle. Now he's met the other man. They're both waving at us. Look!"

"There comes something up the beach."

"What the devil is that thing?"

"Why, it looks like a boat."

"Why, certainly it's a boat."

"No, it's on wheels."

"Yes, so it is. Well, that must be the life-boat. They drag them along shore on a wagon."

"That's the life-boat, sure."

"No, by —, it's — it's an omnibus."

"I tell you it's a life-boat."

"It is not! It's an omnibus. I can see it plain. See? One of those big hotel omnibuses."

"By thunder, you're right. It's an omnibus, sure as fate. What do you suppose they are doing with an omnibus? Maybe they are going around collecting the life-crew, hey?"

"That's it, likely. Look! There's a fellow waving a little black flag. He's standing on the steps of the omnibus. There come those other two fellows. Now they're all talking together. Look at the fellow with the flag. Maybe he ain't waving it!"

"That ain't a flag, is it? That's his coat. Why, certainly, that's his coat."

"So it is. It's his coat. He's taken it off and is waving it around his head. But would you look at him swing it!"

"Oh, say, there isn't any life-saving station there. That's just a winter resort hotel omnibus that has brought over some of the boarders to see us drown."

"What's that idiot with the coat mean? What's he signaling, anyhow?"

"It looks as if he were trying to tell us to go north. There must be a life-saving station up there."

"No! He thinks we're fishing. Just giving us a merry hand. See? Ah, there, Willie."

"Well, I wish I could make something out of those signals. What do you suppose he means?"

"He don't mean anything. He's just playing."

"Well, if he'd just signal us to try the surf again, or to go to sea and wait, or go north, or go south, or go to hell — there would be some reason in it. But look at him. He just stands there and keeps his coat revolving like a wheel. The ass!"

"There come more people."

"Now there's quite a mob. Look! Isn't that a boat?"

"Where? Oh, I see where you mean. No, that's no boat."

"That fellow is still waving his coat."

"He must think we like to see him do that. Why don't he quit it. It don't mean anything."

"I don't know. I think he is trying to make us go north. It must be that there's a life-saving station there somewhere."

"Say, he ain't tired yet. Look at 'im wave."

"Wonder how long he can keep that up. He's been revolving his coat ever since he caught sight of us. He's an idiot. Why aren't they getting men to bring a boat out. A fishing boat—one of those big yawls—could come out here all right. Why don't he do something?"

"Oh, it's all right, now."

"They'll have a boat out here for us in less than no time, now that they've seen us."

A faint yellow tone came into the sky over the low land. The shadows on the sea slowly deepened. The wind bore coldness with it, and the men began to shiver.

"Holy smoke!" said one, allowing his voice to express his impious mood, "if we keep on monkeying out here! If we've got to flounder out here all night!"

"Oh, we'll never have to stay here all night! Don't you worry. They've seen us now, and it won't be long before they'll come chasing out after us."

The shore grew dusky. The man waving a coat blended gradually into this gloom, and it swallowed in the same manner the omnibus and the group of people. The spray, when it dashed uproariously over the side, made the voyagers shrink and swear like men who were being branded.

"I'd like to catch the chump who waved the coat. I feel like soaking him one, just for luck."

"Why? What did he do?"

"Oh, nothing, but then he seemed so damned cheerful."

In the meantime the oiler rowed, and then the correspondent rowed, and then the oiler rowed. Gray-faced and bowed forward, they mechanically, turn by turn, plied the leaden oars. The form of the light-house had vanished from the southern horizon, but finally a pale star appeared, just lifting from the sea. The streaked saffron in the west passed before the all-merging darkness, and the sea to the east was black. The land had vanished, and was expressed only by the low and drear thunder of the surf.

"If I am going to be drowned—if I am going to be drowned—if I am going to be drowned, why, in the name of the seven mad gods who rule the sea, was I allowed to come thus far and contemplate sand and trees? Was I brought here merely to have my nose dragged away as I was about to nibble the sacred cheese of life?"

The patient captain, drooped over the water-jar, was sometimes obliged to speak to the oarsman.

"Keep her head up! Keep her head up!"

"'Keep her head up,' sir." The voices were weary and low.

This was surely a quiet evening. All save the oarsman lay heavily and listlessly in the boat's bottom. As for him, his eyes were just capable of noting the tall black waves that swept forward in a most sinister silence, save for an occasional subdued growl of a crest.

The cook's head was on a thwart, and he looked without interest at the water under his nose. He was deep in other scenes. Finally he spoke. "Billie," he murmured, dreamfully, "what kind of pie do you like best?"

V

"Pie," said the oiler and the correspondent, agitatedly. "Don't talk about those things, blast you!"

"Well," said the cook, "I was just thinking about ham sandwiches, and—"

A night on the sea in an open boat is a long night. As darkness settled finally, the shine of the light, lifting from the sea in the south, changed to full gold. On the northern horizon a new light appeared, a small bluish gleam on the edge of the waters. These two lights were the furniture of the world. Otherwise there was nothing but waves.

Two men huddled in the stern, and distances were so magnificent in the dingey that the rower was enabled to keep his feet partly warmed by thrusting them under his companions. Their legs indeed extended far under the rowing-seat until they touched the feet of the captain forward. Sometimes, despite the efforts of the tired oarsman, a wave came piling into the boat, an icy wave of the night, and the chilling water soaked them anew. They would twist their bodies for a moment and groan, and sleep the dead sleep once more, while the water in the boat gurgled about them as the craft rocked.

The plan of the oiler and the correspondent was for one to row until he lost the ability, and then arouse the other from his sea-water couch in the bottom of the boat.

The oiler plied the oars until his head drooped forward, and the overpowering sleep blinded him. And he rowed yet afterward. Then he touched a man in the bottom of the boat, and called his name. "Will you spell me for a little while?" he said, meekly.

"Sure, Billie," said the correspondent, awakening and dragging himself to a sitting position. They exchanged places carefully, and the oiler, cuddling down in the sea-water at the cook's side, seemed to go to sleep instantly.

The particular violence of the sea had ceased. The waves came without snarling. The obligation of the man at the oars was to keep the boat headed so that the tilt of the rollers would not capsize her, and to preserve her from filling when the crests rushed past. The black waves were silent and hard to be seen in the darkness. Often one was almost upon the boat before the oarsman was aware.

In a low voice the correspondent addressed the captain. He was not sure that the captain was awake, although this iron man seemed to be always awake. "Captain, shall I keep her making for that light north, sir?"

The same steady voice answered him. "Yes. Keep it about two points off the port bow."

The cook had tied a life-belt around himself in order to get even the warmth which this clumsy cork contrivance could donate, and he seemed almost stove-like when a rower, whose teeth invariably chattered wildly as soon as he ceased his labor, dropped down to sleep.

The correspondent, as he rowed, looked down at the two men sleeping under foot. The cook's arm was around the oiler's shoulders, and, with their fragmentary clothing and haggard faces, they were the babes of the sea, a grotesque rendering of the old babes in the wood.

Later he must have grown stupid at his work, for suddenly there was a growling of water, and a crest came with a roar and a swash into the boat, and it was a wonder that it did not set the cook afloat in his life-belt. The cook continued to sleep, but the oiler sat up, blinking his eyes and shaking with the new cold.

"Oh, I'm awful sorry, Billie," said the correspondent, contritely.

"That's all right, old boy," said the oiler, and lay down again and was asleep.

Presently it seemed that even the captain dozed, and the correspondent thought that he was the one man afloat on all the oceans. The wind had a voice as it came over the waves, and it was sadder than the end.

There was a long, loud swishing astern of the boat, and a gleaming trail of phosphorescence, like blue flame, was furrowed on the black waters. It might have been made by a monstrous knife.

Then there came a stillness, while the correspondent breathed with the open mouth and looked at the sea.

Suddenly there was another swish and another long flash of bluish light, and this time it was alongside the boat, and might almost have been reached with an oar. The correspondent saw an enormous fin speed like a shadow through the water, hurling the crystalline spray and leaving the long glowing trail.

The correspondent looked over his shoulder at the captain. His face was hidden, and he seemed to be asleep. He looked at the babes of the sea. They certainly were asleep. So, being bereft of sympathy, he leaned a little way to one side and swore softly into the sea.

But the thing did not then leave the vicinity of the boat. Ahead or astern, on one side or the other, at intervals long or short, fled the long sparkling streak, and there was to be heard the whiroo of the dark fin. The speed and power of the thing was greatly to be admired. It cut the water like a gigantic and keen projectile.

The presence of this biding thing did not affect the man with the same horror that it would if he had been a picnicker. He simply looked at the sea dully and swore in an undertone.

Nevertheless, it is true that he did not wish to be alone with the thing. He wished one of his companions to awaken by chance and keep him company with it. But the captain hung motionless over the water-jar and the oiler and the cook in the bottom of the boat were plunged in slumber.

VI

"If I am going to be drowned—if I am going to be drowned—if I am going to be drowned, why, in the name of the seven mad gods who rule the sea, was I allowed to come thus far and contemplate sand and trees?"

During this dismal night, it may be remarked that a man would conclude that it was really the intention of the seven mad gods to drown him, despite the abominable injustice of it. For it was certainly an abominable injustice to drown a man who had worked so hard, so hard. The man felt it would be a crime most unnatural. Other people had drowned at sea since galleys swarmed with painted sails, but still—

When it occurs to a man that nature does not regard him as important, and that she feels she would not maim the universe by disposing of him, he at first wishes to throw bricks at the temple, and he hates deeply the fact that there are no bricks and no temples. Any visible expression of nature would surely be pelleted with his jeers.

Then, if there be no tangible thing to hoot he feels, perhaps, the desire to confront a personification and indulge in pleas, bowed to one knee, and with hands supplicant, saying: "Yes, but I love myself."

A high cold star on a winter's night is the word he feels that she says to him. Thereafter he knows the pathos of his situation.

The men in the dingey had not discussed these matters, but each had, no doubt, reflected upon them in silence and according to his mind. There was seldom any expression upon their faces save the general one of complete weariness. Speech was devoted to the business of the boat.

To chime the notes of his emotion, a verse mysteriously entered the correspondent's head. He had even forgotten that he had forgotten this verse, but it suddenly was in his mind.

> A soldier of the Legion lay dying in Algiers,
> There was lack of woman's nursing, there was dearth
>   of woman's tears;
> But a comrade stood beside him, and he took that
>   comrade's hand,
> And he said: "I never more shall see my own, my
>   native land."[9]

[9]Crane's version of lines from "Bingen on the Rhine" (1883) by English poet Caroline E. S. Norton (1808–1877).

In his childhood, the correspondent had been made acquainted with the fact that a soldier of the Legion lay dying in Algiers, but he had never regarded it as important. Myriads of his school-fellows had informed him of the soldier's plight, but the dinning had naturally ended by making him perfectly indifferent. He had never considered it his affair that a soldier of the Legion lay dying in Algiers, nor had it appeared to him as a matter for sorrow. It was less to him than the breaking of a pencil's point.

Now, however, it quaintly came to him as a human, living thing. It was no longer merely a picture of a few throes in the breast of a poet, meanwhile drinking tea and warming his feet at the grate; it was an actuality—stern, mournful, and fine.

The correspondent plainly saw the soldier. He lay on the sand with his feet out straight and still. While his pale left hand was upon his chest in an attempt to thwart the going of his life, the blood came between his fingers. In the far Algerian distance, a city of low square forms was set against a sky that was faint with the last sunset hues. The correspondent, plying the oars and dreaming of the slow and slower movement of the lips of the soldier, was moved by a profound and perfectly impersonal comprehension. He was sorry for the soldier of the Legion who lay dying in Algiers.

The thing which had followed the boat and waited had evidently grown bored at the delay. There was no longer to be heard the slash of the cut-water, and there was no longer the flame of the long trail. The light in the north still glimmered, but it was apparently no nearer to the boat. Sometimes the boom of the surf rang in the correspondent's ears, and he turned the craft seaward then and rowed harder. Southward, some one had evidently built a watch-fire on the beach. It was too low and too far to be seen, but it made a shimmering, roseate reflection upon the bluff back of it, and this could be discerned from the boat. The wind came stronger, and sometimes a wave suddenly raged out like a mountain-cat and there was to be seen the sheen and sparkle of a broken crest.

The captain, in the bow, moved on his water-jar and sat erect. "Pretty long night," he observed to the correspondent. He looked at the shore. "Those life-saving people take their time."

"Did you see that shark playing around?"

"Yes, I saw him. He was a big fellow, all right."

"Wish I had known you were awake."

Later the correspondent spoke into the bottom of the boat.

"Billie!" There was a slow and gradual disentanglement. "Billie, will you spell me?"

"Sure," said the oiler.

As soon as the correspondent touched the cold comfortable sea-water in the bottom of the boat, and had huddled close to the cook's life-belt he was deep in sleep, despite the fact that his teeth played all the popular airs. This sleep was so good to him that it was but a moment before he heard a voice call his name in a tone that demonstrated the last stages of exhaustion. "Will you spell me?"

"Sure, Billie."

The light in the north had mysteriously vanished, but the correspondent took his course from the wide-awake captain.

Later in the night they took the boat farther out to sea, and the captain directed the cook to take one oar at the stern and keep the boat facing the seas. He was to call out if he should hear the thunder of the surf. This plan enabled the oiler and the correspondent to get respite together. "We'll give those boys a chance to get into shape again," said the captain. They curled down and, after a few preliminary chatterings and trembles, slept once more the dead sleep. Neither knew they had bequeathed to the cook the company of another shark, or perhaps the same shark.

As the boat caroused on the waves, spray occasionally bumped over the side and gave them a fresh soaking, but this had no power to break their repose. The ominous slash of the wind and the water affected them as it would have affected mummies.

"Boys," said the cook, with the notes of every reluctance in his voice, "she's drifted in pretty close. I guess one of you had better take her to sea again." The correspondent, aroused, heard the crash of the toppled crests.

As he was rowing, the captain gave him some whiskey and water, and this steadied the chills out of him. "If I ever get ashore and anybody shows me even a photograph of an oar—"

At last there was a short conversation.

"Billie. . . . Billie, will you spell me?"

"Sure," said the oiler.

VII

When the correspondent again opened his eyes, the sea and the sky were each of the gray hue of the dawning. Later, carmine and gold was painted upon the waters. The morning appeared finally, in its splendor, with a sky of pure blue, and the sunlight flamed on the tips of the waves.

On the distant dunes were set many little black cottages, and a tall white wind-mill reared above them. No man, nor dog, nor bicycle appeared on the beach. The cottages might have formed a deserted village.

The voyagers scanned the shore. A conference was held in the boat. "Well," said the captain, "if no help is coming, we might better try a run through the surf right away. If we stay out here much longer we will be too weak to do anything for ourselves at all." The others silently acquiesced in this reasoning. The boat was headed for the beach. The correspondent wondered if none ever ascended the tall windtower, and if then they never looked seaward. This tower was a giant, standing with its back to the plight of the ants. It represented in a degree, to the correspondent, the serenity of nature amid the struggles of the individual—nature in the wind, and nature in the vision of men. She did not seem cruel to him then, nor beneficent, nor treacherous, nor wise. But she was indifferent, flatly indifferent. It is, perhaps, plausible that a man in this situation, impressed with the unconcern of the universe, should see the innumerable flaws of his life and have them taste wickedly in his mind and wish for another chance. A distinction between right and wrong seems absurdly clear to him, then, in this new ignorance of the grave-edge, and he understands that if he were given another opportunity he would mend his conduct and his words, and be better and brighter during an introduction, or at a tea.

"Now, boys," said the captain, "she is going to swamp sure. All we can do is to work her in as far as possible, and then when she swamps, pile out and scramble for the beach. Keep cool now, and don't jump until she swamps sure."

The oiler took the oars. Over his shoulders he scanned the surf. "Captain," he said, "I think I'd better bring her about, and keep her head-on to the seas and back her in."

"All right, Billie," said the captain. "Back her in." The oiler swung the boat then and, seated in the stern, the cook and the correspondent were obliged to look over their shoulders to contemplate the lonely and indifferent shore.

The monstrous inshore rollers heaved the boat high until the men were again enabled to see the white sheets of water scudding up the slanted beach. "We won't get in very close," said the captain. Each time a man could wrest his attention from the rollers, he turned his glance toward the shore, and in the expression of the eyes during this contemplation there was a singular quality. The correspondent, observing the others, knew that they were not afraid, but the full meaning of their glances was shrouded.

As for himself, he was too tired to grapple fundamentally with the fact. He tried to coerce his mind into thinking of it, but the mind was dominated at this time by the muscles, and the muscles said they did not care. It merely occurred to him that if he should drown it would be a shame.

There were no hurried words, no pallor, no plain agitation. The men simply looked at the shore. "Now, remember to get well clear of the boat when you jump," said the captain.

Seaward the crest of a roller suddenly fell with a thunderous crash, and the long white comber came roaring down upon the boat.

"Steady now," said the captain. The men were silent. They turned their eyes from the shore to the comber and waited. The boat slid up the incline, leaped at the furious top, bounced over it, and swung down the long back of the wave. Some water had been shipped and the cook bailed it out.

But the next crest crashed also. The tumbling boiling flood of white water caught the boat and whirled it almost perpendicular. Water swarmed in from all sides. The correspondent had his hands on the gunwale at this time, and when the water entered at that place he swiftly withdrew his fingers, as if he objected to wetting them.

The little boat, drunken with this weight of water, reeled and snuggled deeper into the sea.

"Bail her out, cook! Bail her out," said the captain.

"All right, Captain," said the cook.

"Now, boys, the next one will do for us, sure," said the oiler. "Mind to jump clear of the boat."

The third wave moved forward, huge, furious, implacable. It fairly swallowed the dingey, and almost simultaneously the men tumbled into the sea. A piece of life-belt had lain in the bottom of the boat, and as the correspondent went overboard he held this to his chest with his left hand.

The January water was icy, and he reflected immediately that it was colder than he had expected to find it off the coast of Florida. This appeared to his dazed mind as a fact important enough to be noted at the time. The coldness of the water was sad; it was tragic. This fact was somehow so mixed and confused with his opinion of his own situation that it seemed almost a proper reason for tears. The water was cold.

When he came to the surface he was conscious of little but the noisy water. Afterward he saw his companions in the sea. The oiler was ahead in the race. He was swimming strongly and rapidly. Off to the correspondent's left, the cook's great white and corked back bulged out of the water, and in the rear the captain was hanging with his one good hand to the keel of the overturned dingey.

There is a certain immovable quality to a shore, and the correspondent wondered at it amid the confusion of the sea.

It seemed also very attractive, but the correspondent knew that it was a long journey, and he paddled leisurely. The piece of life-preserver lay under him, and sometimes he whirled down the incline of a wave as if he were on a hand-sled.

But finally he arrived at a place in the sea where travel was beset with difficulty. He did not pause swimming to inquire what manner of current had caught him, but there his progress ceased. The shore was set before him like a bit of scenery on a stage, and he looked at it and understood with his eyes each detail of it.

As the cook passed, much farther to the left, the captain was calling to him, "Turn over on your back, cook! Turn over on your back and use the oar."

"All right, sir." The cook turned on his back, and, paddling with an oar, went ahead as if he were a canoe.

Presently the boat also passed to the left of the correspondent with the captain clinging with one hand to the keel. He would have appeared like a man raising himself to look over a board fence, if it were not for the extraordinary gymnastics of the boat. The correspondent marvelled that the captain could still hold to it.

They passed on, nearer to shore — the oiler, the cook, the captain — and following them went the water-jar, bouncing gayly over the seas.

The correspondent remained in the grip of this strange new enemy—a current. The shore, with its white slope of sand and its green bluff, topped with little silent cottages, was spread like a picture before him. It was very near to him then, but he was impressed as one who in a gallery looks at a scene from Brittany or Holland.

He thought: "I am going to drown? Can it be possible? Can it be possible? Can it be possible?" Perhaps an individual must consider his own death to be the final phenomenon of nature.

But later a wave perhaps whirled him out of this small deadly current, for he found suddenly that he could again make progress toward the shore. Later still, he was aware that the captain, clinging with one hand to the keel of the dingey, had his face turned away from the shore and toward him, and was calling his name. "Come to the boat! Come to the boat!"

In his struggle to reach the captain and the boat, he reflected that when one gets properly wearied, drowning must really be a comfortable arrangement, a cessation of hostilities accompanied by a large degree of relief, and he was glad of it, for the main thing in his mind for some moments had been horror of the temporary agony. He did not wish to be hurt.

Presently he saw a man running along the shore. He was undressing with most remarkable speed. Coat, trousers, shirt, everything flew magically off him.

"Come to the boat," called the captain.

"All right, Captain." As the correspondent paddled, he saw the captain let himself down to bottom and leave the boat. Then the correspondent performed his one little marvel of the voyage. A large wave caught him and flung him with ease and supreme speed completely over the boat and far beyond it. It struck him even then as an event in gymnastics, and a true miracle of the sea. An overturned boat in the surf is not a plaything to a swimming man.

The correspondent arrived in water that reached only to his waist, but his condition did not enable him to stand for more than a moment. Each wave knocked him into a heap, and the under-tow pulled at him.

Then he saw the man who had been running and undressing, and undressing and running, come bounding into the water. He dragged ashore the cook, and then waded toward the captain, but the captain waved him away, and sent him to the correspondent. He was naked, naked as a tree in winter, but a halo was about his head, and he shone like a saint. He gave a strong pull, and a long drag, and a bully heave at the correspondent's hand. The correspondent, schooled in the minor formulæ, said: "Thanks, old man." But suddenly the man cried: "What's that?" He pointed a swift finger. The correspondent said: "Go."

In the shallows, face downward, lay the oiler. His forehead touched sand that was periodically, between each wave, clear of the sea.

The correspondent did not know all that transpired afterward. When he achieved safe ground he fell, striking the sand with each particular part of his body. It was as if he had dropped from a roof, but the thud was grateful to him.

It seems that instantly the beach was populated with men with blankets, clothes, and flasks, and women with coffee-pots and all the remedies sacred to their minds. The welcome of the land to the men from the sea was warm and generous, but a still and dripping shape was carried slowly up the beach, and the land's welcome for it could only be the different and sinister hospitality of the grave.

When it came night, the white waves paced to and fro in the moonlight, and the wind brought the sound of the great sea's voice to the men on shore, and they felt that they could then be interpreters.

1897   *1897, 1898*

The Blue Hotel

I

The Palace Hotel at Fort Romper was painted a light blue, a shade that is on the legs of a kind of heron, causing the bird to declare its position against any background. The Palace Hotel, then, was always screaming and howling in a way that made the dazzling winter landscape of Nebraska seem only a gray swampish hush. It stood alone on the prairie, and when the snow was falling the town two hundred yards away was not visible. But when the traveler alighted at the railway station he was obliged to pass the Palace Hotel before he could come upon the company of low clap-board houses which composed Fort Romper, and it was not to be thought that any traveler could pass the Palace Hotel without looking at it. Pat Scully, the proprietor, had proved himself a master of strategy when he chose his paints. It is true that on clear days, when the great trans-continental expresses, long lines of swaying Pullmans, swept through Fort Romper, passengers were overcome at the sight, and the cult that knows the brown-reds and the subdivisions of the dark greens of the East expressed shame, pity, horror, in a laugh. But to the citizens of this prairie town, and to the people who would naturally stop there, Pat Scully had performed a feat. With this opulence and splendor, these creeds, classes, egotisms, that steamed through Romper on the rails day after day, they had no color in common.

As if the displayed delights of such a blue hotel were not sufficiently enticing, it was Scully's habit to go every morning and evening to meet the leisurely trains that stopped at Romper and work his seductions upon any man that he might see wavering, gripsack in hand.

One morning, when a snow-crusted engine dragged its long string of freight cars and its one passenger coach to the station, Scully performed the marvel of catching three men. One was a shaky and quick-eyed Swede, with a great shining cheap valise; one was a tall bronzed cowboy, who was on his way to a ranch near the Dakota line; one was a little silent man from the East, who didn't look it, and didn't announce it. Scully practically made them prisoners. He was so nimble and merry and kindly that each probably felt it would be the height of brutality to try to escape. They trudged off over the creaking board sidewalks in the wake of the eager little Irishman. He wore a heavy fur cap squeezed tightly down on his head. It caused his two red ears to stick out stiffly, as if they were made of tin.

At last, Scully, elaborately, with boisterous hospitality, conducted them through the portals of the blue hotel. The room which they entered was small. It seemed to be merely a proper temple for an enormous stove, which, in the center, was humming with god-like violence. At various points on its surface the iron had become luminous and glowed yellow from the heat. Beside the stove Scully's son Johnnie was playing High-Five[1] with an old farmer who had whiskers both gray and sandy. They were quarreling. Frequently the old farmer turned his face toward a box of sawdust — colored brown from tobacco juice — that was behind the stove, and spat with an air of great impatience and irritation. With a loud flourish of words Scully destroyed the game of cards, and bustled his son upstairs with part of the baggage of the new guests. He himself conducted them to three basins of the coldest water in the world. The cowboy and the Easterner burnished themselves fiery red with this water, until it seemed to be some kind of a metal polish. The Swede, however, merely dipped his fingers gingerly and with trepidation. It was notable that throughout this series of small ceremonies the three travelers were made to feel that Scully was very benevo-

---

[1] A card game known also as All-Fours, Double Pedro, or Cinch.

lent. He was conferring great favors upon them. He handed the towel from one to the other with an air of philanthropic impulse.

Afterward they went to the first room, and, sitting about the stove, listened to Scully's officious clamor at his daughters, who were preparing the midday meal. They reflected in the silence of experienced men who tread carefully amid new people. Nevertheless, the old farmer, stationary, invincible in his chair near the warmest part of the stove, turned his face from the sawdust box frequently and addressed a glowing commonplace to the strangers. Usually he was answered in short but adequate sentences by either the cowboy or the Easterner. The Swede said nothing. He seemed to be occupied in making furtive estimates of each man in the room. One might have thought that he had the sense of silly suspicion which comes to guilt. He resembled a badly frightened man.

Later, at dinner, he spoke a little, addressing his conversation entirely to Scully. He volunteered that he had come from New York, where for ten years he had worked as a tailor. These facts seemed to strike Scully as fascinating, and afterward he volunteered that he had lived at Romper for fourteen years. The Swede asked about the crops and the price of labor. He seemed barely to listen to Scully's extended replies. His eyes continued to rove from man to man.

Finally, with a laugh and a wink, he said that some of these Western communities were very dangerous; and after his statement he straightened his legs under the table, tilted his head, and laughed again, loudly. It was plain that the demonstration had no meaning to the others. They looked at him wondering and in silence.

II

As the men trooped heavily back into the front room, the two little windows presented views of a turmoiling sea of snow. The huge arms of the wind were making attempts — mighty, circular, futile — the embrace the flakes as they sped. A gate-post like a still man with a blanched face stood aghast amid this profligate fury. In a hearty voice Scully announced the presence of a blizzard. The guests of the blue hotel, lighting their pipes, assented with grunts of lazy masculine contentment. No island of the sea could be exempt in the degree of this little room with its humming stove. Johnnie, son of Scully, in a tone which defined his opinion of his ability as a card-player, challenged the old farmer of both gray and sandy whiskers to a game of High-Five. The farmer agreed with a contemptuous and bitter scoff. They sat close to the stove, and squared their knees under a wide board. The cowboy and the Easterner watched the game with interest. The Swede remained near the window, aloof, but with a countenance that showed signs of an inexplicable excitement.

The play of Johnnie and the gray-beard was suddenly ended by another quarrel. The old man arose while casting a look of heated scorn at his adversary. He slowly buttoned his coat, and then stalked with fabulous dignity from the room. In the discreet silence of all other men the Swede laughed. His laughter rang somehow childish. Men by this time had begun to look at him askance, as if they wished to inquire what ailed him.

A new game was formed jocosely. The cowboy volunteered to become the partner of Johnnie, and they all then turned to ask the Swede to throw in his lot with the little Easterner. He asked some questions about the game, and learning that it wore many names, and that he had played it when it was under an alias, he accepted the invitation. He strode toward the men nervously, as if he expected to be assaulted. Finally, seated, he gazed from face to face and laughed shrilly. This laugh was so strange that the Easterner looked up quickly, the cowboy sat intent and with his mouth open, and Johnnie paused, holding the cards with still fingers.

Afterward there was a short silence. Then Johnnie said: "Well, let's get at it. Come on now!" They pulled their chairs forward until their knees were bunched under the board. They began to play, and their interest in the game caused the others to forget the manner of the Swede.

The cowboy was a board-whacker. Each time that he held superior cards he whanged them, one by one, with exceeding force, down upon the improvised table, and took the tricks with a glowing air of prowess and pride that sent thrills of indignation into the hearts of his opponents. A game with a board-whacker in it is sure to become intense. The countenances of the Easterner and the Swede were miserable whenever the cowboy thundered down his aces and kings, while Johnnie, his eyes gleaming with joy, chuckled and chuckled.

Because of the absorbing play none considered the strange ways of the Swede. They paid strict heed to the game. Finally, during a lull caused by a new deal, the Swede suddenly addressed Johnnie: "I suppose there have been a good many men killed in this room." The jaws of the others dropped and they looked at him.

"What in hell are you talking about?" said Johnnie.

The Swede laughed again his blatant laugh, full of a kind of false courage and defiance. "Oh, you know what I mean all right," he answered.

"I'm a liar if I do!" Johnnie protested. The card was halted, and the men stared at the Swede. Johnnie evidently felt that as the son of the proprietor he should make a direct inquiry. "Now, what might you be drivin' at, mister?" he asked. The Swede winked at him. It was a wink full of cunning. His fingers shook on the edge of the board. "Oh, maybe you think I have been to nowheres. Maybe you think I'm a tenderfoot?"

"I don't know nothin' about you," answered Johnnie, "and I don't give a damn where you've been. All I got to say is that I don't know what you're driving at. There hain't never been nobody killed in this room."

The cowboy, who had been steadily gazing at the Swede, then spoke. "What's wrong with you, mister?"

Apparently it seemed to the Swede that he was formidably menaced. He shivered and turned white near the corners of his mouth. He sent an appealing glance in the direction of the little Easterner. During these moments he did not forget to wear his air of advanced pot-valor.[2] "They say they don't know what I mean," he remarked mockingly to the Easterner.

The latter answered after prolonged and cautious reflection. "I don't understand you," he said, impassively.

The Swede made a movement then which announced that he thought he had encountered treachery from the only quarter where he had expected sympathy if not help. "Oh, I see you are all against me. I see—"

The cowboy was in a state of deep stupefaction. "Say," he cried, as he tumbled in the deck violently down upon the board. "Say, what are you gittin' at, hey?"

The Swede sprang up with the celerity of a man escaping from a snake on the floor. "I don't want to fight!" he shouted. "I don't want to fight!"

The cowboy stretched his long legs indolently and deliberately. His hands were in his pockets. He spat into the sawdust box. "Well, who the hell thought you did?" he inquired.

The Swede backed rapidly toward a corner of the room. His hands were out protectingly in front of his chest, but he was making an obvious struggle to control his fright. "Gentlemen," he quavered, "I suppose I am going to be killed before I can leave this house! I suppose I am going to be killed before I can leave this house!" In his eyes was the dying swan look. Through the windows could be seen the snow turning blue in the shadow of dusk. The wind tore at the house and some loose thing beat regularly against the clap-boards like a spirit tapping.

---

[2]Drunken courage.

A door opened, and Scully himself entered. He paused in surprise as he noted the tragic attitude of the Swede. Then he said: "What's the matter here?"

The Swede answered him swiftly and eagerly: "These men are going to kill me."

"Kill you!" ejaculated Scully. "Kill you! What are you talkin'?"

The Swede made the gesture of a martyr.

Scully wheeled sternly upon his son. "What is this, Johnnie?"

The lad had grown sullen. "Damned if I know," he answered. "I can't make no sense to it." He began to shuffle the cards, fluttering them together with an angry snap. "He says a good many men have been killed in this room, or something like that. And he says he's goin' to be killed here too. I don't know what ails him. He's crazy, I shouldn't wonder."

Scully then looked for explanation to the cowboy, but the cowboy simply shrugged his shoulders.

"Kill you?" said Scully again to the Swede. "Kill you? Man, you're off your nut."

"Oh, I know," burst out the Swede. "I know what will happen. Yes, I'm crazy — yes. Yes, of course, I'm crazy — yes. But I know one thing —" There was a sort of sweat of misery and terror upon his face. "I know I won't get out of here alive."

The cowboy drew a deep breath, as if his mind was passing into the last stages of dissolution. "Well, I'm dog-goned," he whispered to himself.

Scully wheeled suddenly and faced his son. "You've been troublin' this man!"

Johnnie's voice was loud with its burden of grievance. "Why, good Gawd, I ain't done nothin' to 'im."

The Swede broke in. "Gentlemen, do not disturb yourselves. I will leave this house. I will go 'way because —" He accused them dramatically with his glance. "Because I do not want to be killed."

Scully was furious with his son. "Will you tell me what is the matter, you young divil? What's the matter, anyhow? Speak out!"

"Blame it," cried Johnnie in despair, "don't I tell you I don't know. He — he says we want to kill him, and that's all I know. I can't tell what ails him."

The Swede continued to repeat: "Never mind, Mr. Scully, never mind. I will leave this house. I will go away, because I do not wish to be killed. Yes, of course, I am crazy — yes. But I know one thing! I will go away. I will leave this house. Never mind, Mr. Scully, never mind. I will go away."

"You will not go 'way," said Scully. "You will not go 'way until I hear the reason of this business. If anybody has troubled you I will take care of him. This is my house. You are under my roof, and I will not allow any peaceable man to be troubled here." He cast a terrible eye upon Johnnie, the cowboy, and the Easterner.

"Never mind, Mr. Scully, never mind. I will go 'way. I do not wish to be killed." The Swede moved toward the door, which opened upon the stairs. It was evidently his intention to go at once for his baggage.

"No, no," shouted Scully peremptorily; but the white-faced man slid by him and disappeared. "Now," said Scully severely, "what does this mane?"

Johnnie and the cowboy cried together: "Why, we didn't do nothin' to 'im!"

Scully's eyes were cold. "No," he said, "you didn't?"

Johnnie swore a deep oath. "Why, this is the wildest loon I ever see. We didn't do nothin' at all. We were jest sittin' here playin' cards and he —"

The father suddenly spoke to the Easterner. "Mr. Blanc," he asked, "what has these boys been doin'?"

The Easterner reflected again. "I didn't see anything wrong at all," he said at last slowly.

Scully began to howl. "But what does it mane?" He stared ferociously at his son. "I have a mind to lather you for this, me boy."

Johnnie was frantic. "Well, what have I done?" he bawled at his father.

III

"I think you are tongue-tied," said Scully finally to his son, the cowboy and the Easterner, and at the end of this scornful sentence he left the room.

Upstairs the Swede was swiftly fastening the straps of his great valise. Once his back happened to be half-turned toward the door, and hearing a noise there, he wheeled and sprang up, uttering a loud cry. Scully's wrinkled visage showed grimly in the light of the small lamp he carried. This yellow effulgence, streaming upward, colored only his prominent features, and left his eyes, for instance, in mysterious shadow. He resembled a murderer.

"Man, man!" he exclaimed, "have you gone daffy?"

"Oh, no! Oh, no!" rejoined the other. "There are people in this world who know pretty nearly as much as you do—understand?"

For a moment they stood gazing at each other. Upon the Swede's deathly pale cheeks were two spots brightly crimson and sharply edged, as if they had been carefully painted. Scully placed the light on the table and sat himself on the edge of the bed. He spoke ruminatively. "By cracky, I never heard of such a thing in my life. It's a complete muddle. I can't for the soul of me think how you ever got this idea into your head." Presently he lifted his eyes and asked: "And did you sure think they were going to kill you?"

The Swede scanned the old man as if he wished to see into his mind. "I did," he said at last. He obviously suspected that this answer might precipitate an outbreak. As he pulled on a strap his whole arm shook, the elbow wavering like a bit of paper.

Scully banged his hand impressively on the foot-board of the bed. "Why, man, we're goin' to have a line of ilictric street-cars in this town next spring."

"'A line of electric street-cars,'" repeated the Swede stupidly.

"And," said Scully, "there's a new railroad goin' to be built down from Broken Arm to here. Not to mintion the four churches and the smashin' big brick school-house. Then there's the big factory, too. Why, in two years Romper'll be a met-tro-*pol*- is."

Having finished the preparation of his baggage, the Swede straightened himself. "Mr. Scully," he said with sudden hardihood, "how much do I owe you?"

"You don't owe me anythin'," said the old man angrily.

"Yes, I do," retorted the Swede. He took seventy-five cents from his pocket and tendered it to Scully; but the latter snapped his fingers in disdainful refusal. However, it happened that they both stood gazing in a strange fashion at three silver pieces on the Swede's open palm.

"I'll not take your money," said Scully at last. "Not after what's been goin' on here." Then a plan seemed to strike him. "Here," he cried, picking up his lamp and moving toward the door. "Here! Come with me a minute."

"No," said the Swede in overwhelming alarm.

"Yes," urged the old man. "Come on! I want you to come and see a picter—just across the hall—in my room."

The Swede must have concluded that his hour was come. His jaw dropped and his teeth showed like a dead man's. He ultimately followed Scully across the corridor, but he had the step of one hung in chains.

Scully flashed the light high on the wall of his own chamber. There was revealed a ridiculous photograph of a little girl. She was leaning against a balustrade of gorgeous decoration, and the formidable band to her hair was prominent. The figure was as graceful as an upright sled-stake, and, withal, it was of the hue of lead. "There," said Scully tenderly. "That's the picter of my little girl that died. Her name was Carrie. She had the purtiest hair you ever saw! I was that fond of her, she—"

Turning then he saw that the Swede was not contemplating the picture at all, but, instead, was keeping keen watch on the gloom in the rear.

"Look, man!" shouted Scully heartily. "That's the picter of my little gal that died. Her name was Carrie. And then here's the picter of my oldest boy, Michael. He's a lawyer in Lincoln an' doin' well. I gave that boy a grand eddycation, and I'm glad for it now. He's a fine boy. Look at 'im now. Ain't he bold as blazes, him there in Lincoln, an honored an' respicted gintleman. An honored an' respicted gintleman," concluded Scully with a flourish. And so saying, he smote the Swede jovially on the back.

The Swede faintly smiled.

"Now," said the old man, "there's only one more thing." He dropped suddenly to the floor and thrust his head beneath the bed. The Swede could hear his muffled voice. "I'd keep it under me piller if it wasn't for that boy Johnnie. Then there's the old woman—Where is it now? I never put it twice in the same place. Ah, now come out with you!"

Presently he backed clumsily from under the bed, dragging with him an old coat rolled into a bundle. "I've fetched him," he muttered. Kneeling on the floor he unrolled the coat and extracted from its heart a large yellow-brown whisky bottle.

His first maneuver was to hold the bottle up to the light. Reassured, apparently, that nobody had been tampering with it, he thrust it with a generous movement toward the Swede.

The weak-kneed Swede was about to eagerly clutch this element of strength, but he suddenly jerked his hand away and cast a look of horror upon Scully.

"Drink," said the old man affectionately. He had arisen to his feet, and now stood facing the Swede.

There was a silence. Then again Scully said: "Drink!"

The Swede laughed wildly. He grabbed the bottle, put it to his mouth, and as his lips curled absurdly around the opening and his throat worked, he kept his glance burning with hatred upon the old man's face.

IV

After the departure of Scully the three men, with the cardboard still upon their knees, preserved for a long time an astounded silence. Then Johnnie said: "That's the dod-dangest Swede I ever see."

"He ain't no Swede," said the cowboy scornfully.

"Well, what is he then?" cried Johnnie. "What is he then?"

"It's my opinion," replied the cowboy deliberately, "he's some kind of a Dutchman." It was a venerable custom of the country to entitle as Swedes all light-haired men who spoke with a heavy tongue. In consequence the idea of the cowboy was not without its daring. "Yes, sir," he repeated. "It's my opinion this feller is some kind of a Dutchman."

"Well, he says he's a Swede, anyhow," muttered Johnnie sulkily. He turned to the Easterner: "What do you think, Mr. Blanc?"

"Oh, I don't know," replied the Easterner.

"Well, what do you think makes him act that way?" asked the cowboy.

"Why, he's frightened!" The Easterner knocked his pipe against a rim of the stove. "He's clear frightened out of his boots."

"What at?" cried Johnnie and cowboy together.

The Easterner reflected over his answer.

"What at?" cried the others again.

"Oh, I don't know, but it seems to me this man has been reading dime-novels, and he thinks he's right out in the middle of it—the shootin' and stabbin' and all."

"But," said the cowboy, deeply scandalized, "this ain't Wyoming, ner none of them places. This is Nebrasker."

"Yes," added Johnnie, "an' why don't he wait till he gits *out West*?"

"The traveled Easterner laughed. "It isn't different there even—not in these days.

But he thinks he's right in the middle of hell."

Johnnie and the cowboy mused long.

"It's awful funny," remarked Johnnie at last.

"Yes," said the cowboy. "This is a queer game. I hope we don't git snowed in, because then we'd have to stand this here man bein' around with us all the time. That wouldn't be no good."

"I wish pop would throw him out," said Johnnie.

Presently they heard a loud stamping on the stairs, accompanied by ringing jokes in the voice of old Scully, and laughter, evidently from the Swede. The men around the stove stared vacantly at each other. "Gosh," said the cowboy. The door flew open, and old Scully, flushed and anecdotal, came into the room. He was jabbering at the Swede, who followed him, laughing bravely. It was the entry of two roysterers from a banquet hall.

"Come now," said Scully sharply to the three seated men, "move up and give us a chance at the stove." The cowboy and the Easterner obediently sidled their chairs to make room for the newcomers. Johnnie, however, simply arranged himself in a more indolent attitude, and then remained motionless.

"Come! Git over, there," said Scully.

"Plenty of room on the other side of the stove," said Johnnie.

"Do you think we want to sit in the draught?" roared the father.

But the Swede here interposed with a grandeur of confidence. "No, no. Let the boy sit where he likes," he cried in a bullying voice to the father.

"All right! All right!" said Scully deferentially. The cowboy and the Easterner exchanged glances of wonder.

The five chairs were formed in a crescent about one side of the stove. The Swede began to talk; he talked arrogantly, profanely, angrily. Johnnie, the cowboy and the Easterner maintained a morose silence, while old Scully appeared to be receptive and eager, breaking in constantly with sympathetic ejaculations.

Finally the Swede announced that he was thirsty. He moved in his chair, and said that he would go for a drink of water.

"I'll git it for you," cried Scully at once.

"No," said the Swede contemptuously. "I'll get it for myself." He arose and stalked with the air of an owner off into the executive parts of the hotel.

As soon as the Swede was out of hearing Scully sprang to his feet and whispered intensely to the others. "Upstairs he thought I was tryin' to poison 'im."

"Say," said Johnnie, "this makes me sick. Why don't you throw 'im out in the snow?"

"Why, he's all right now," declared Scully. "It was only that he was from the East and he thought this was a tough place. That's all. He's all right now."

The cowboy looked with admiration upon the Easterner. "You were straight," he said. "You were on to that there Dutchman."

"Well," said Johnnie to his father, "he may be all right now, but I don't see it. Other time he was scared, and now he's too fresh."

Scully's speech was always a combination of Irish brogue and idiom, Western twang and idiom, and scraps of curiously formal diction taken from the story-books and newspapers. He now hurled a strange mass of language at the head of his son. "What do I keep? What do I keep? What do I keep?" he demanded in a voice of thunder. He slapped his knee impressively, to indicate that he himself was going to make reply, and that all should heed. "I keep a hotel," he shouted. "A hotel, do you mind? A guest under my roof has sacred privileges. He is to be intimidated by none. Not one word shall he hear that would prijudice him in favor of goin' away. I'll not have it. There's no place in this here town where they can say they iver took in a guest of mine because he was afraid to stay here." He wheeled suddenly upon the cowboy and the Easterner. "Am I right?"

"Yes, Mr. Scully," said the cowboy, "I think you're right."

"Yes, Mr. Scully," said the Easterner, "I think you're right."

V

At six-o'clock supper, the Swede fizzed like a fire-wheel. He sometimes seemed on the point of bursting into riotous song, and in all his madness he was encouraged by old Scully. The Easterner was incased in reserve; the cowboy sat in wide-mouthed amazement, forgetting to eat, while Johnnie wrathily demolished great plates of food. The daughters of the house when they were obliged to replenish the biscuits approached as warily as Indians, and, having succeeded in their purposes, fled with ill-concealed trepidation. The Swede domineered the whole feast, and he gave it the appearance of a cruel bacchanal. He seemed to have grown suddenly taller; he gazed, brutally disdainful, into every face. His voice rang through the room. Once when he jabbed out harpoon-fashion with his fork to pinion a biscuit the weapon nearly impaled the hand of the Easterner which had been stretched quietly out for the same biscuit.

After supper, as the men filed toward the other room, the Swede smote Scully ruthlessly on the shoulder. "Well, old boy, that was a good square meal." Johnnie looked hopefully at his father; he knew that shoulder was tender from an old fall; and indeed it appeared for a moment as if Scully was going to flame out over the matter, but in the end he smiled a sickly smile and remained silent. The others understood from his manner that he was admitting his responsibility for the Swede's new viewpoint.

Johnnie, however, addressed his parent in an aside. "Why don't you license somebody to kick you downstairs?" Scully scowled darkly by a way of reply.

When they were gathered about the stove, the Swede insisted on another game of High-Five. Scully gently deprecated the plan at first, but the Swede turned a wolfish glare upon him. The old man subsided, and the Swede canvassed the others. In his tone there was always a great threat. The cowboy and the Easterner both remarked indifferently that they would play. Scully said that he would presently have to go to meet the 6.58 train, and so the Swede turned menacingly upon Johnnie. For a moment their glances crossed like blades, and then Johnnie smiled and said: "Yes, I'll play."

They formed a square with the little board on their knees. The Easterner and the Swede were again partners. As the play went on, it was noticeable that the cowboy was not board-whacking as usual. Meanwhile, Scully, near the lamp, had put on his spectacles and, with an appearance curiously like an old priest, was reading a newspaper. In time he went out to meet the 6.58 train, and, despite his precautions, a gust of polar wind whirled into the room as he opened the door. Besides scattering the cards, it chilled the players to the marrow. The Swede cursed frightfully. When Scully returned, his entrance disturbed a cozy and friendly scene. The Swede again cursed. But presently they were once more intent, their heads bent forward and their hands moving swiftly. The Swede had adopted the fashion of board-whacking.

Scully took up his paper and for a long time remained immersed in matters which were extraordinarily remote from him. The lamp burned badly, and once he stopped to adjust the wick. The newspaper as he turned from page to page rustled with a slow and comfortable sound. Then suddenly he heard three terrible words: "You are cheatin'!"

Such scenes often prove that there can be little of dramatic import in environment. Any room can present a tragic front; any room can be comic. This little den was now hideous as a torture-chamber. The new faces of the men themselves had changed it upon the instant. The Swede held a huge fist in front of Johnnie's face, while the latter looked steadily over it into the blazing orbs of his accuser. The Easterner had grown pallid; the cowboy's jaw had dropped in that expression of bovine amazement which was one of his important mannerisms. After the three words, the first sound in the room was made by Scully's paper as it floated forgotten to his feet. His spectacles had also fallen from his nose, but by a clutch he has saved them in air. His hand, grasping the spectacles, now remained poised awkwardly and near his shoulder. He stared at the card-players.

Probably the silence was while a second elapsed. Then, if the floor had been suddenly twitched out from under the men they could not have moved quicker. The five had projected themselves headlong toward a common point. It happened that Johnnie in rising to hurl himself upon the Swede had stumbled slightly because of his curiously instinctive care for the cards and the board. The loss of the moment allowed time for the arrival of Scully, and also allowed the cowboy time to give the Swede a great push which sent him staggering back. The men found tongue together, and hoarse shouts of rage, appeal or fear burst from every throat. The cowboy pushed and jostled feverishly at the Swede, and the Easterner and Scully clung wildly to Johnnie; but, through the smoky air, above the swaying bodies of the peace-compellers, the eyes of the two warriors ever sought each other in glances of challenge that were at once hot and steely.

Of course the board had been overturned, and now the whole company of cards was scattered over the floor, where the boots of the men trampled the fat and painted kings and queens as they gazed with their silly eyes at the war that was waging above them.

Scully's voice was dominating the yells. "Stop now! Stop, I say! Stop, now—"

Johnnie, as he struggled to burst through the rank formed by Scully and the Easterner, was crying: "Well, he says I cheated! He says I cheated! I won't allow no man to say I cheated! If he says I cheated, he's a —— ——!"

The cowboy was telling the Swede: "Quit, now! Quit, d'ye hear—"

The screams of the Swede never ceased. "He did cheat! I saw him! I saw him—"

As for the Easterner, he was importuning in a voice that was not heeded. "Wait a moment, can't you? Oh, wait a moment. What's the good of a fight over a game of cards? Wait a moment—"

In this tumult no complete sentences were clear. "Cheat"—"Quit"—"He says"— These fragments pierced the uproar and rang out sharply. It was remarkable that whereas Scully undoubtedly made the most noise, he was the least heard of any of the riotous band.

Then suddenly there was a great cessation. It was as if each man had paused for breath, and although the room was still lighted with the anger of men, it could be seen that there was no danger of immediate conflict, and at once Johnnie, shouldering his way forward, almost succeeded in confronting the Swede. "What did you say I cheated for? What did you say I cheated for? I don't cheat and I won't let no man say I do!"

The Swede said: "I saw you! I saw you!"

"Well," cried Johnnie, "I'll fight any man what says I cheat!"

"No, you won't," said the cowboy. "Not here."

"Ah, be still, can't you?" said Scully, coming between them.

The quiet was sufficient to allow the Easterner's voice to be heard. He was repeating: "Oh, wait a moment, can't you? What's the good of a fight over a game of cards? Wait a moment."

Johnnie, his red face appearing above his father's shoulder, hailed the Swede again. "Did you say I cheated?"

The Swede showed his teeth. "Yes."

"Then," said Johnnie, "we must fight."

"Yes, fight," roared the Swede. He was like a demoniac. "Yes, fight! I'll show you what kind of a man I am! I'll show you who you want to fight! Maybe you think I can't fight! Maybe you think I can't! I'll show you, you skin,[3] you card-sharp! Yes, you cheated! You cheated! You cheated!"

"Well, let's git at it, then, mister," said Johnnie coolly.

The cowboy's brow was beaded with sweat from his efforts in intercepting all sorts of raids. He turned in despair to Scully. "What are you goin' to do now?"

A change had come over the Celtic visage of the old man. He now seemed all eagerness; his eyes glowed.

"We'll let them fight," he answered stalwartly. "I can't put up with it any longer. I've stood this damned Swede till I'm sick. We'll let them fight."

VI

The men prepared to go out of doors. The Easterner was so nervous that he had great difficulty in getting his arms into the sleeves of his new leather-coat. As the cowboy drew his fur-cap down over his ears his hands trembled. In fact, Johnnie and old Scully were the only ones who displayed no agitation. These preliminaries were conducted without words.

Scully threw open the door. "Well, come on," he said. Instantly a terrific wind caused the flame of the lamp to struggle at its wick, while a puff of black smoke sprang from the chimney-top. The stove was in mid-current of the blast, and its voice swelled to equal the roar of the storm. Some of the scarred and bedabbled cards were caught up form the floor and dashed helplessly against the further wall. The men lowered their heads and plunged into the tempest as into a sea.

No snow was falling, but great whirls and clouds of flakes, swept up from the ground by the frantic winds, were streaming southward with the speed of bullets. The covered land was blue with the sheen of an unearthly satin, and there was no other hue save where at the low black railway station—which seemed incredibly distant—one light gleamed like a tiny jewel. As the men floundered into a thigh-deep drift, it was known that the Swede was bawling out something. Scully went to him, put a hand on his shoulder and projected an ear. "What's that you say?" he shouted.

"I say," bawled the Swede again, "I won't stand much show against this gang. I know you'll all pitch on me."

Scully smote him reproachfully on the arm. "Tut, man," he yelled. The wind tore the words from Scully's lips and scattered them far a-lee.

"You are all a gang of—" boomed the Swede, but the storm also seized the remainder of this sentence.

Immediately turning their backs upon the wind, the men had swung around a corner to the sheltered side of the hotel. It was the function of the little house to preserve here, amid this great devastation of snow, an irregular V-shape of heavily-incrusted grass, which crackled beneath the feet. One could imagine the great drifts piled against the windward side. When the party reached the comparative peace of this spot it was found that the Swede was still bellowing.

"Oh, I know what kind of a thing this is! I know you'll all pitch on me. I can't lick you all!"

Scully turned upon him panther-fashion. "You'll not have to whip all of us. You'll have to whip my son Johnnie. An' the man what troubles you durin' that time will have me to dale with."

The arrangements were swiftly made. The two men faced each other, obedient to the harsh commands of Scully, whose face, in the subtly luminous gloom, could be seen set in the austere impersonal lines that are pictured on the countenances of the Roman veterans. The Easterner's teeth were chattering, and he was hopping up and down like a mechanical toy. The cowboy stood rock-like.

---

[3]Cheat (slang).

The contestants had not stripped off any clothing. Each was in his ordinary attire. Their fists were up, and they eyed each other in a calm that had the elements of leonine cruelty in it.

During this pause, the Easterner's mind, like a film, took lasting impressions of three men—the iron-nerved master of the ceremony; the Swede, pale, motionless, terrible; and Johnnie, serene yet ferocious, brutish yet heroic. The entire prelude had in it a tragedy greater than the tragedy of action, and this aspect was accentuated by the long mellow cry of the blizzard, as if sped the tumbling and wailing flakes into the black abyss of the south.

"Now!" said Scully.

The two combatants leaped forward and crashed together like bullocks. There was heard the cushioned sound of blows, and of a curse squeezing out from between the tight teeth of one.

As for the spectators, the Easterner's pent-up breath exploded form him with a pop of relief, absolute relief from the tension of the preliminaries. The cowboy bounded into the air with a yowl. Scully was immovable as from supreme amazement and fear at the fury of the fight which he himself had permitted and arranged.

For a time the encounter in the darkness was such a perplexity of flying arms that it presented no more detail than would a swiftly-revolving wheel. Occasionally a face, as if illumined by a flash of light, would shine out, ghastly and marked with pink spots. A moment later, the men might have been known as shadows, if it were not for the involuntary utterance of oaths that came from them in whispers.

Suddenly a holocaust of warlike desire caught the cowboy, and he bolted forward with the speed of a broncho. "Go it, Johnnie; go it! Kill him! Kill him!"

Scully confronted him. "Kape back," he said; and by his glance the cowboy could tell that this man was Johnnie's father.

To the Easterner there was a monotony of unchangeable fighting that was an abomination. This confused mingling was eternal to his sense, which was concentrated in a longing for the end, the priceless end. Once the fighters lurched near him, and as he scrambled hastily backward, he heard them breathe like men on the rack.

"Kill him, Johnnie! Kill him! Kill him!" The cowboy's face was contorted like one of those agony-masks in museums.

"Keep still," said Scully icily.

Then there was a sudden loud grunt, incomplete, cut-short, and Johnnie's body swung away from the Swede and fell with sickening heaviness to the grass. The cowboy was barely in time to prevent the mad Swede from flinging himself upon his prone adversary. "No, you don't," said the cowboy, interposing an arm. "Wait a second."

Scully was at his son's side. "Johnnie! Johnnie, me boy?" His voice had a quality of melancholy tenderness. "Johnnie? Can you go on with it?" He looked anxiously down into the bloody pulpy face of his son.

There was a moment of silence, and then Johnnie answered in his ordinary voice: "Yes, I—it—yes."

Assisted by his father he struggled to his feet. "Wait a bit now till you git your wind," said the old man.

A few paces away the cowboy was lecturing the Swede. "No, you don't! Wait a second!"

The Easterner was plucking at Scully's sleeve. "Oh, this is enough," he pleaded. "This is enough! Let it go as it stands. This is enough!"

"Bill," said Scully, "git out of the road." The cowboy stepped aside. "Now." The combatants were actuated by a new caution as they advanced toward collision. They glared at each other, and then the Swede aimed a lightning blow that carried with it his entire weight. Johnnie was evidently half-stupid from weakness, but he miraculously dodged, and his fist sent the over-balanced Swede sprawling.

The cowboy, Scully and the Easterner burst into a cheer that was like a chorus of triumphant soldiery, but before its conclusion the Swede had scuffled agilely to his feet and come in berserk abandon at his foe. There was another perplexity of flying arms, and Johnnie's body again swung away and fell, even as a bundle might fall from a roof. The Swede instantly staggered to a little wind-waved tree and leaned upon it, breathing like an engine, while his savage and flame-lit eyes roamed from face to face as the men bent over Johnnie. There was a splendor of isolation in his situation at this time which the Easterner felt once when, lifting his eyes from the man on the ground, he beheld that mysterious and lonely figure, waiting.

"Are you any good yet, Johnnie?" asked Scully in a broken voice.

The son gasped and opened his eyes languidly. After a moment he answered: "No—I ain't—any good—any—more." Then, from shame and bodily ill, he began to weep, the tears furrowing down through the blood-stains on his face. "He was too—too—too heavy for me."

Scully straightened and addressed the waiting figure. "Stranger," he said, evenly, "it's all up with our side." Then his voice changed into that vibrant huskiness which is commonly the tone of the most simple and deadly announcements. "Johnnie is whipped."

Without replying, the victor moved off on the route to the front door of the hotel.

The cowboy was formulating new and unspellable blasphemies. The Easterner was startled to find that they were out in a wind that seemed to come direct from the shadowed arctic floes. He heard again the wail of the snow as it was flung to its grave in the south. He knew now that all this time the cold had been sinking into him deeper and deeper, and he wondered that he had not perished. He felt indifferent to the condition of the vanquished man.

"Johnnie, can you walk?" asked Scully.

"Did I hurt—hurt him any?" asked the son.

"Can you walk, boy? Can you walk?"

Johnnie's voice was suddenly strong. There was a robust impatience in it. "I asked you whether I hurt him any!"

"Yes, yes, Johnnie," answered the cowboy consolingly; "he's hurt a good deal."

They raised him from the ground, and as soon as he was on his feet he went tottering off, rebuffing all attempts at assistance. When the party rounded the corner they were fairly blinded by the pelting of the snow. It burned their faces like fire. The cowboy carried Johnnie through the drift to the door. As they entered some cards again rose from the floor and beat against the wall.

The Easterner rushed to the stove. He was so profoundly chilled that he almost dared to embrace the glowing iron. The Swede was not in the room. Johnnie sank into a chair, and folding his arms on his knees, buried his face in them. Scully, warming one foot and then the other at a rim of the stove, muttered to himself with Celtic mournfulness. The cowboy had removed his fur-cap, and with a dazed and rueful air he was now running one hand through his tousled locks. From overhead they could hear the creaking of boards, as the Swede trampled here and there in his room.

The sad quiet was broken by the sudden flinging open of a door that led toward the kitchen. It was instantly followed by an inrush of women. They precipitated themselves upon Johnnie amid a chorus of lamentation. Before they carried their prey off to the kitchen, there to be bathed and harangued with that mixture of sympathy and abuse which is a feat of their sex, the mother straightened herself and fixed old Scully with an eye of stern reproach. "Shame be upon you, Patrick Scully!" she cried. "Your own son, too. Shame be upon you!"

"There, now! Be quiet, now!" said the old man weakly.

"Shame be upon you, Patrick Scully!" The girls, rallying to this slogan, sniffed disdainfully in the direction of those trembling accomplices, the cowboy and the Easterner. Presently they bore Johnnie away, and left the three men to dismal reflection.

VII

"I'd like to fight this here Dutchman myself," said the cowboy, breaking a long silence.

Scully wagged his head sadly. "No, that wouldn't do. It wouldn't be right. It wouldn't be right."

"Well, why wouldn't it?" argued the cowboy. "I don't see no harm in it."

"No," answered Scully with mournful heroism. "It wouldn't be right. It was Johnnie's fight, and now we mustn't whip the man just because he whipped Johnnie."

"Yes, that's true enough," said the cowboy; "but—he better not get fresh with me, because I couldn't stand no more of it."

"You'll not say a word to him," commanded Scully, and even then they heard the tread of the Swede on the stairs. His entrance was made theatric. He swept the door back with a bang and swaggered to the middle of the room. No one looked at him. "Well," he cried, insolently, at Scully, "I s'pose you'll tell me now how much I owe you?"

The old man remained stolid. "You don't owe me nothin'."

"Huh!" said the Swede, "huh! Don't owe 'im nothin'."

The cowboy addressed the Swede. "Stranger, I don't see how you come to be so gay around here."

Old Scully was instantly alert. "Stop!" he shouted, holding his hand forth, fingers upward. "Bill, you shut up!"

The cowboy spat carelessly into the sawdust box. "I didn't say a word, did I?" he asked.

"Mr. Scully," called the Swede, "how much do I owe you?" It was seen that he was attired for departure, and that he had his valise in his hand.

"You don't owe me nothin'," repeated Scully in his same imperturbable way.

"Huh!" said the Swede. "I guess you're right. I guess if it was any way at all, you'd owe me somethin'. That's what I guess." He turned to the cowboy. "'Kill him! Kill him! Kill him!'" he mimicked, and then guffawed victoriously. "'Kill him!'" he was convulsed with ironical humor.

But he might have been jeering the dead. The three men were immovable and silent, staring with glassy eyes at the stove.

The Swede opened the door and passed into the storm, giving one derisive glance backward at the still group.

As soon as the door was closed, Scully and the cowboy leaped to their feet and began to curse. They trampled to and fro, waving their arms and smashing into the air with their fists. "Oh, but that was a hard minute!" wailed Scully. "That was a hard minute! Him there leerin' and scoffin'! One bang at his nose was worth forty dollars to me that minute! How did you stand it, Bill?"

"How did I stand it?" cried the cowboy in a quivering voice. "How did I stand it? Oh!"

The old man burst into sudden brogue. "I'd loike to take that Swade," he wailed, "and hould 'im down on a shtone flure and bate 'im to a jelly wid a shtick!"

The cowboy groaned in sympathy. "I'd like to git him by the neck and ha-ammer him"—he brought his hand down on a chair with a hoise like a pistol-shot—"hammer that there Dutchman until he couldn't tell himself from a dead coyote!"

"I'd bate 'im until he—"

"I'd show *him* some things—"

And then together they raised a yearning fanatic cry. "Oh-o-oh! if we only could—"

"Yes!"

"Yes!"

"And then I'd—"

"O-o-oh!"

VIII

The Swede, tightly gripping his valise, tacked across the face of the storm as if he carried sails. He was following a line of little naked gasping trees, which he knew must mark the way of the road. His face, fresh from the pounding of Johnnie's fists, felt more pleasure than pain in the wind and the driving snow. A number of square shapes loomed upon him finally, and he knew them as the houses of the main body of the town. He found a street and made travel along it, leaning heavily upon the wind whenever, at a corner, a terrific blast caught him.

He might have been in a deserted village. We picture the world as thick with conquering and elate humanity, but here, with the bugles of the tempest pealing, it was hard to imagine a peopled earth. One viewed the existence of man then as a marvel, and conceded a glamour of wonder to these lice which were caused to cling to a whirling, fire-smote, ice-locked, disease-stricken, space-lost bulb. The conceit of man was explained by this storm to be the very engine of life. One was a coxcomb not to die in it. However, the Swede found a saloon.

In front of it an indomitable red light was burning, and the snow-flakes were made blood-color as they flew through the circumscribed territory of the lamp's shining. The Swede pushed open the door of the saloon and entered. A sanded expanse was before him, and at the end of it four men sat about a table drinking. Down one side of the room extended a radiant bar, and its guardian was leaning upon his elbows listening to the talk of the men at the table. The Swede dropped his valise upon the floor, and, smiling fraternally upon the barkeeper, said: "Gimme some whisky, will you?" The man placed a bottle, a whisky-glass, and a glass of ice-thick water upon the bar. The Swede poured himself an abnormal portion of whisky and drank it in three gulps. "Pretty bad night," remarked the bartender indifferently. He was making the pretension of blindness, which is usually a distinction of his class; but it could have been seen that he was furtively studying the half-erased blood-stains on the face of the Swede. "Bad night," he said again.

"Oh, it's good enough for me," replied the Swede, hardily, as he poured himself some more whisky. The barkeeper took his coin and maneuvered it through its reception by the highly-nickeled cash-machine. A bell rang; a card labeled "20 cts." had appeared.

"No," continued the Swede, "this isn't too bad weather. It's good enough for me."

"So?" murmured the barkeeper languidly.

The copious drams made the Swede's eyes swim, and he breathed a trifle heavier. "Yes, I like this weather. I like it. It suits me." It was apparently his design to impart a deep significance to these words.

"So?" murmured the bartender again. He turned to gaze dreamily at the scroll-like birds and bird-like scrolls which had been drawn with soap upon the mirrors back of the bar.

"Well, I guess I'll take another drink," said the Swede presently. "Have something?"

"No, thanks; I'm not drinkin'," answered the bartender. Afterward he asked: "How did you hurt your face?"

The Swede immediately began to boast loudly. "Why, in a fight. I thumped the soul out of a man down here at Scully's hotel."

The interest of the four men at the table was at last aroused.

"Who was it?" said one.

"Johnnie Scully," blustered the Swede. "Son of the man what runs it. He will be pretty near dead for some weeks, I can tell you. I made a nice thing of him, I did. He couldn't get up. They carried him in the house. Have a drink?"

Instantly the men in some way incased themselves in reserve. "No, thanks," said one. The group was of curious formation. Two were prominent local business men; one was the district-attorney; and one was a professional gambler of the kind known as "square." But a scrutiny of the group would not have enabled an observer to pick the gambler from the men of more reputable pursuits. He was, in fact, a man so delicate in manner, when among people of fair class, and so judicious in his choice of victims, that in the strictly masculine part of the town's life he had come to be explicitly trusted and admired. People called him a thoroughbred. The fear and contempt with which his craft was regarded was undoubtedly the reason that his quiet dignity shone conspicuous above the quiet dignity of men who might be merely hatters, billiard-markers or grocery clerks. Beyond an occasional unwary traveler, who came by rail, this gambler was supposed to prey solely upon reckless and senile farmers, who, when flush with good crops, drove into town in all the pride and confidence of an absolutely invulnerable stupidity. Hearing at times in circuitous fashion of the despoilment of such a farmer, the important men of Romper invariably laughed in contempt of the victim, and if they thought of the wolf at all, it was with a kind of pride at the knowledge that he would never dare think of attacking their wisdom and courage. Besides, it was popular that this gambler had a real wife and two real children in a neat cottage in a suburb, where he led an exemplary home life, and when any one even suggested a discrepancy in his character, the crowd immediately vociferated descriptions of this virtuous family circle. Then men who led exemplary home lives, and men who did not lead exemplary home lives, all subsided in a bunch, remarking that there was nothing more to be said.

However, when a restriction was placed upon him—as, for instance, when a strong clique of members of the new Pollywog Club refused to permit him, even as a spectator, to appear in the rooms of the organization—the candor and gentleness with which he accepted the judgment disarmed many of his foes and made his friends more desperately partisan. He invariably distinguished between himself and a respectable Romper man so quickly and frankly that his manner actually appeared to be a continual broadcast compliment.

And one must not forget to declare the fundamental fact of his entire position in Romper. It is irrefutable that in all affairs outside of his business, in all matters that occur eternally and commonly between man and man, this thieving card-player was so generous, so just, so moral, that, in a contest, he could have put to flight the consciences of nine-tenths of the citizens of Romper.

And so it happened that he was seated in this saloon with the two prominent local merchants and the district-attorney.

The Swede continued to drink raw whisky, meanwhile babbling at the barkeeper and trying to induce him to indulge in potations. "Come on. Have a drink. Come on. What—no? Well, have a little one then. By gawd, I've whipped a man to-night, and I want to celebrate. I whipped him good, too. Gentlemen," the Swede cried to the men at the table, "have a drink?"

"Ssh!" said the barkeeper.

The group at the table, although furtively attentive, had been pretending to be deep in talk, but now a man lifted his eyes toward the Swede and said shortly: "Thanks. We don't want any more."

At this reply the Swede ruffled out his chest like a rooster. "Well," he exploded, "it seems I can't get anybody to drink with me in this town. Seems so, don't it? Well!"

"Ssh!" said the barkeeper.

"Say," snarled the Swede, "don't you try to shut me up. I won't have it. I'm a gentleman, and I want people to drink with me. And I want 'em to drink with me now. *Now*—do you understand?" He rapped the bar with his knuckles.

Years of experience had calloused the bartender. He merely grew sulky. "I hear you," he answered.

"Well," cried the Swede, "listen hard then. See those men over there? Well, they're going to drink with me, and don't you forget it. Now you watch."

"Hi!" yelled the barkeeper, "this won't do!"

"Why won't it?" demanded the Swede. He stalked over to the table, and by chance laid his hand upon the shoulder of the gambler. "How about this?" he asked, wrathfully. "I asked you to drink with me."

The gambler simply twisted his head and spoke over his shoulder. "My friend, I don't know you."

"Oh, hell!" answered the Swede, "come and have a drink."

"Now, my boy," advised the gambler kindly, "take your hand off my shoulder and go 'way and mind your own business." He was a little slim man, and it seemed strange to hear him use this tone of heroic patronage to the burly Swede. The other man at the table said nothing.

"What? You won't drink with me, you little dude! I'll make you then! I'll make you!" The Swede had grasped the gambler frenziedly at the throat, and was dragging him from his chair. The other men sprang up. The barkeeper dashed around the corner of his bar. There was a great tumult, and then was seen a long blade in the hand of the gambler. It shot forward, and a human body, this citadel of virtue, wisdom, power, was pierced as easily as if it had been a melon. The Swede fell with a cry of supreme astonishment.

The prominent merchants and the district-attorney must have at once tumbled out of the place backward. The bartender found himself hanging limply to the arm of a chair and gazing into the eyes of a murderer.

"Henry," said the latter, as he wiped his knife on one of the towels that hung beneath the bar-rail, "you tell 'em where to find me. I'll be home, waiting for 'em." Then he vanished. A moment afterward the barkeeper was in the street dinning through the storm for help, and, moreover, companionship.

The corpse of the Swede, alone in the saloon, had its eyes fixed upon a dreadful legend that dwelt a-top of the cash-machine. "This registers the amount of your purchase."

IX

Months later, the cowboy was frying pork over the stove of a little ranch near the Dakota line, when there was a quick thud of hoofs outside, and, presently, the Easterner entered with the letters and the papers.

"Well," said the Easterner at once, "the chap that killed the Swede has got three years. Wasn't much, was it?"

"He has? Three years?" The cowboy poised his pan of pork, while he ruminated upon the news. "Three years. That ain't much."

"No. It was a light sentence," replied the Easterner as he unbuckled his spurs. "Seems there was a good deal of sympathy for him in Romper."

"If the bartender had been any good," observed the cowboy thoughtfully, "he would have gone in and cracked that there Dutchman on the head with a bottle in the beginnin' of it and stopped all this here murderin'."

"Yes, a thousand things might have happened," said the Easterner tartly.

The cowboy returned his pan of pork to the fire, but his philosophy continued. "It's funny, ain't it? If he hadn't said Johnnie was cheatin' he'd be alive this minute. He was an awful fool. Game played for fun, too. Not for money. I believe he was crazy."

"I feel sorry for that gambler," said the Easterner.

"Oh, so do I," said the cowboy. "He don't deserve none of it for killin' who he did."

"The Swede might not have been killed if everything had been square."

"Might not have been killed?" exclaimed the cowboy. "Everythin' square? Why, when he said that Johnnie was cheatin' and acted like such a jackass? And then in the saloon he fairly walked up to git hurt?" With these arguments the cowboy browbeat the Easterner and reduced him to rage.

"You're a fool!" cried the Easterner viciously. "You're a bigger jackass than the

Swede by a million majority. Now let me tell you one thing. Let me tell you something. Listen! Johnnie *was* cheating!"

"'Johnnie,'" said the cowboy blankly. There was a minute of silence, and then he said robustly: "Why, no. The game was only for fun."

"Fun or not," said the Easterner, "Johnnie was cheating. I saw him. I know it. I saw him. And I refused to stand up and be a man. I let the Swede fight it out alone. And you — you were simply puffing around the place and wanting to fight. And then old Scully himself! We are all in it! This poor gambler isn't even a noun. He is kind of an adverb. Every sin is the result of a collaboration. We, five of us, have collaborated in the murder of this Swede. Usually there are from a dozen to forty women really involved in every murder, but in this case it seems to be only five men — you, I, Johnnie, old Scully, and that fool of an unfortunate gambler came merely as a culmination, the apex of a human movement, and gets all the punishment."

The cowboy, injured and rebellious, cried out blindly into this fog of mysterious theory. "Well, I didn't do anythin', did I?"

1898   *1898, 1899*

An Episode of War

The lieutenant's rubber blanket lay on the ground, and upon it he had poured the company's supply of coffee. Corporals and other representatives of the grimy and hot-throated men who lined the breastwork had come for each squad's portion.

The lieutenant was frowning and serious at this task of division. His lips pursed as he drew with his sword various crevices in the heap until brown square of coffee, astoundingly equal in size, appeared in the blanket. He was on the verge of a great triumph in mathematics and the corporals were thronging forward, each to reap a little square, when suddenly the lieutenant cried out and looked quickly at a man near him as if he suspected it was a case of personal assault. The others cried out also when they saw blood upon the lieutenant's sleeve.

He had winced like a man stung, swayed dangerously, and then straightened. The sound of his hoarse breathing was plainly audible. He looked sadly, mystically, over the breastwork at the green face of a wood where now were many little puffs of white smoke. During this moment, the men about him gazed statue-like and silent, astonished and awed by this catastrophe which had happened when catastrophes were not expected — when they had leisure to observe it.

As the lieutenant stared at the wood, they too swung their heads so that for another moment all hands, still silent, contemplated the distant forest as if their minds were fixed upon the mystery of a bullet's journey.

The officer had, of course, been compelled to take his sword at once into his left hand. He did not hold it by the hilt. He gripped it at the middle of the blade, awkwardly. Turning his eyes from the hostile wood, he looked at the sword as he held it there, and seemed puzzled as to what to do with it, where to put it. In short this weapon had of a sudden become a strange thing to him. He looked at it in a kind of stupefaction, as if he had been miraculously endowed with a trident, a sceptre, or a spade.

Finally, he tried to sheath it. To sheath a sword held by the left hand, at the middle of the blade, in a scabbard hung at the left hip, is a feat worthy of a sawdust ring. This wounded officer engaged in a desperate struggle with the sword and the wobbling scabbard, and during the time of it, he breathed like a wrestler.

But at this instant the men, the spectators, awoke from their stone-like poses and crowded forward sympathetically. The orderly-sergeant took the sword and tenderly placed it in the scabbard. At the time, he leaned nervously backward, and did not allow even his finger to brush the body of the lieutenant. A wound gives strange dignity to him who bears it. Well men shy from this new and terrible majesty. It is as if the wounded man's hand is upon the curtain which hangs before the revelations of all existence, the meaning of ants, potentates, wars, cities, sunshine, snow, a feather dropped from a bird's wing, and the power of it sheds radiance upon a bloody form, and makes the other men understand sometimes that they are little. His comrades look at him with large eyes thoughtfully. Moreover, they fear vaguely that the weight of a finger upon him might send him headlong, precipitate the tragedy, hurl him at once into the dim grey unknown. And so the orderly-sergeant while sheathing the sword leaned nervously backward.

There were others who proffered assistance. One timidly presented his shoulder and asked the lieutenant if he cared to lean upon it, but the latter waved him away mournfully. He wore the look of one who knows he is the victim of a terrible disease and understands his helplessness. He again stared over the breastwork at the forest, and then turning went slowly rearward. He held his right wrist tenderly in his left hand, as if the wounded arm was made of very brittle glass.

And the men in silence stared at the wood, then at the lieutenant.

As the wounded officer passed from the line of battle, he was enabled to see many things which as a participant in the fight were unknown to him. He saw a general on a black horse gazing over the lines of blue infantry at the green woods which veiled his problems. An aide galloped furiously, dragged his horse suddenly to a halt, saluted, and presented a paper. It was, for a wonder, precisely like an historical painting.

To the rear of the general and his staff, a group, composed of a bugler, two or three orderlies, and the bearer of the corps standard, all upon maniacal horses, were working like slaves to hold their ground, preserve their respectful interval, while the shells bloomed in the air about them, and caused their chargers to make furious quivering leaps.

A battery, a tumultuous and shining mass, was swirling toward the right. The wild thud of hoofs, the cries of the riders shouting blame and praise, menace and encouragement, and, last, the roar of the wheels, the slant of the glistening guns, brought the lieutenant to an intent pause. The battery swept in curves that stirred the heart; it made halts as dramatic as the crash of a wave on the rocks, and when it fled onward, this aggregation of wheels, levers, motors, had a beautiful unity, as if it were a missile. The sound of it was a war-chorus that reached into the depths of man's emotion.

The lieutenant, still holding his arm as if it were of glass, stood watching this battery until all detail of it was lost, save the figures of the riders, which rose and fell and waved lashes over the black mass.

Later he turned his eyes toward the battle where the shooting sometimes crackled like bush-fires, sometimes sputtered with exasperating irregularity, and sometimes reverberated like the thunder. He saw the smoke rolling upward and saw crowds of men who ran and cheered, or stood and blazed away at the inscrutable distance.

He came upon some stragglers and they told him how to find the field hospital. They described its exact location. In fact these men, no longer having part in the battle, knew more of it than others. They told the performance of every corps, every division, the opinion of every general. The lieutenant, carrying his wounded arm rearward, looked upon them with wonder.

At the roadside a brigade was making coffee and buzzing with talk like a girls' boarding-school. Several officers came out to him and inquired concerning things of which he knew nothing. One, seeing his arm, began to scold. "Why, man, that's no way to do. You want to fix that thing." He appropriated the lieutenant and the lieutenant's wound. He cut the sleeve and laid bare the arm, every nerve of which softly fluttered under his touch. He bound his handkerchief over the wound, scolding away in the meantime. His tone allowed one to think that he was in the habit of being wounded every day. The lieutenant hung his head, feeling, in this presence, that he did not know how to be correctly wounded.

The low white tents of the hospital were grouped around an old school-house. There was here a singular commotion. In the foreground two ambulances inter-locked wheels in the deep mud. The drivers were tossing the blame of it back and forth, gesticulating and berating, while from the ambulances, both crammed with wounded, there came an occasional groan. An interminable crowd of bandaged men were coming and going. Great numbers sat under the trees nursing heads or arms or legs. There was a dispute of some kind raging on the steps of the school-house. Sitting with his back against a tree a man with a face as grey as a new army blanket was serenely smoking a corn-cob pipe. The lieutenant wished to rush forward and in-form him that he was dying.

A busy surgeon was passing near the lieutenant. "Good morning," he said with a friendly smile. Then he caught sight of the lieutenant's arm and his face at once changed. "Well, let's have a look at it." He seemed possessed suddenly of a great contempt for the lieutenant. This wound evidently placed the latter on a very low social plane. The doctor cried out impatiently. What mutton-head had tied it up that way anyhow. The lieutenant answered: "Oh, a man."

When the wound was disclosed the doctor fingered it disdainfully. "Humph," he said. "You come along with me and I'll 'tend to you." His voice contained the same scorn as if he were saying: "You will have to go to jail."

The lieutenant had been very meek but now his face flushed, and he looked into the doctor's eyes. "I guess I won't have it amputated," he said.

"Nonsense, man! nonsense! nonsense!" cried the doctor. "Come along, now. I won't amputate it. Come along. Don't be a baby."

"Let go of me," said the lieutenant, holding back wrathfully. His glance fixed upon the door of the old school-house, as sinister to him as the portals of death.

And this is the story of how the lieutenant lost his arm. When he reached home his sisters, his mother, his wife, sobbed for a long time at the sight of the flat sleeve. "Oh, well," he said, standing shamefaced amid these tears, "I don't suppose it matters so much as all that."

1899

from **Poems**

Black Riders
Came from the Sea[1]

Black riders came from the sea.
There was clang and clang of spear and shield,
And clash and clash of hoof and heel,
Wild shouts and the wave of hair
In the rush upon the wind: 5
Thus the ride of Sin.

1895

---

[1]Crane did not title his poems; these titles, taken from the first lines, are provided by the editor.

In the Desert

In the desert
I saw a creature, naked, bestial,
Who, squatting upon the ground,
Held his heart in his hands,
And ate of it.   5
I said: "Is it good, friend?"
"It is bitter—bitter," he answered;
"But I like it
Because it is bitter,
And because it is my heart."   10

                                                                   1895

God Fashioned the
Ship of the World Carefully

God fashioned the ship of the world carefully.
With the infinite skill of an all-master
Made He the hull and the sails,
Held He the rudder
Ready for adjustment.   5
Erect stood He, scanning His work proudly.
Then—at fateful time—a wrong called,
And God turned, heeding.
Lo, the ship, at this opportunity, slipped slyly,
Making cunning noiseless travel down the ways.   10
So that, forever rudderless, it went upon the seas
Going ridiculous voyages,
Making quaint progress,
Turning as with serious purpose
Before stupid winds.   15
And there were many in the sky
Who laughed at this thing.

                                                                   1895

I Stood
upon a High Place

I stood upon a high place,
And saw, below, many devils
Running, leaping,
And carousing in sin.
One looked up, grinning,   5
And said: "Comrade! Brother!"

                                                                   1895

I Saw a Man
Pursuing the Horizon

I saw a man pursuing the horizon;
Round and round they sped.
I was disturbed at this;
I accosted the man.
"It is futile," I said,   5
"You can never—"

"You lie," he cried,
And ran on.

                                                                    1895

A Man Saw a Ball
of Gold in the Sky

A man saw a ball of gold in the sky;
He climbed for it,
And eventually he achieved it—
It was clay.

Now this is the strange part: 5
When the man went to the earth
And looked again,
Lo, there was the ball of gold.
Now this is the strange part:
It was a ball of gold.   . 10
Aye, by the heavens, it was a ball of gold.

                                                                    1895

Many Red Devils
Ran from My Heart

Many red devils ran from my heart
And out upon the page.
They were so tiny
The pen could mash them.
And many struggled in the ink.   5
It was strange
To write in this red muck
Of things from my heart.

                                                                    1895

"Think as
I Think," Said a Man

"Think as I think," said a man,
"Or you are abominably wicked,
You are a toad."

And after I had thought of it,
I said: "I will, then, be a toad."   5

                                                                                    1895

God Lay
Dead in Heaven

God lay dead in Heaven;
Angels sang the hymn of the end;
Purple winds went moaning,
Their wings drip-dripping
With blood   5
That fell upon the earth.
It, groaning thing,
Turned black and sank.
Then from the far caverns
Of dead sins   10
Came monsters, livid with desire.
They fought,
Wrangled over the world,
A morsel.
But of all sadness this was sad,—   15
A woman's arms tried to shield
The head of a sleeping man
From the jaws of the final beast.

                                                                                    1895

Do Not Weep,
Maiden, for War Is Kind

Do not weep, maiden, for war is kind.
Because your lover threw wild hands toward the sky
And the affrighted steed ran on alone,
Do not weep.
War is kind.   5

    Hoarse, booming drums of the regiment,
    Little souls who thirst for fight,
    These men were born to drill and die.

The unexplained glory flies above them,
Great is the Battle-God, great, and his Kingdom —
A field where a thousand corpses lie.

Do not weep, babe, for war is kind.
Because your father tumbled in the yellow trenches,
Raged at his breast, gulped and died,
Do not weep.
War is kind.

    Swift blazing flag of the regiment,
    Eagle with crest of red and gold,
    These men were born to drill and die.
    Point for them the virtue of slaughter,
    Make plain to them the excellence of killing
    And a field where a thousand corpses lie.

Mother whose heart hung humble as a button
On the bright splendid shroud of your son,
Do not weep.
War is kind.

1896, 1899

To the Maiden

To the maiden
The sea was blue meadow
Alive with little froth-people
Singing.

To the sailor, wrecked,
The sea was dead grey walls
Superlative in vacancy
Upon which nevertheless at fateful time
Was written
The grim hatred of nature.

1896, 1899

The Wayfarer

The wayfarer
Perceiving the pathway to truth
Was struck with astonishment.
It was thickly grown with weeds.
"Ha," he said,
"I see that none has passed here
In a long time."

Later he saw that each weed
Was a singular knife.
"Well," he mumbled at last,
"Doubtless there are other roads."   10

                                                      1899

A Slant of Sun
on Dull Brown Walls

A slant of sun on dull brown walls
A forgotten sky of bashful blue.
Toward God a mighty hymn
A song of collisions and cries
Rumbling wheels, hoof-beats, bells,   5
Welcomes, farewells, love-calls, final moans,
Voices of joy, idiocy, warning, despair,
The unknown appeals of brutes,
The chanting of flowers
The screams of cut trees,   10
The senseless babble of hens and wise men—
A cluttered incoherency that says at the stars:
"Oh, God, save us."

                                                      1895, 1899

A Man Said
to the Universe

A man said to the universe:
"Sir, I exist!"
"However," replied the universe,
"The fact has not created in me
A sense of obligation."   5

                                                      1899

A Man Adrift
on a Slim Spar

A man adrift on a slim spar
A horizon smaller than the rim of a bottle
Tented waves rearing lashy dark points
The near whine of froth in circles.
                    God is cold.   5

The incessant raise and swing of the sea
And growl after growl of crest
The sinkings, green, seething, endless
The upheaval half-completed.
              God is cold.   10

The seas are in the hollow of The Hand;
Oceans may be turned to a spray
Raining down through the stars
Because of a gesture of pity toward a babe.
Oceans may become grey ashes,   15
Die with a long moan and a roar
Amid the tumult of the fishes
And the cries of the ships,
Because The Hand beckons the mice.

A horizon smaller than a doomed assassin's cap,   20
Inky, surging tumults
A reeling, drunken sky and no sky
A pale hand sliding from a polished spar.
              God is cold.

The puff of a coat imprisoning air: 25
A face kissing the water-death
A weary slow sway of a lost hand
And the sea, the moving sea, the sea.
              God is cold.

1897   1929

THEODORE DREISER
(1871–1945)

When the Nobel Committee decided to award the literary prize to an American in 1930, the choice came down to two writers, Theodore Dreiser and Sinclair Lewis. Lewis was chosen, and he paid tribute to Dreiser in his Nobel address: "Suppose you had taken Theodore Dreiser. Now to me, as to many other American writers, Dreiser, more than any other man, is marching alone. Usually unappreciated, often hounded, he has cleared the trail from Victorian Howellsian timidity and gentility in American fiction to honesty, boldness, and passion of life. Without his pioneering I doubt if any of us could, unless we liked to be sent to jail, seek to express life, beauty and terror." In 1930, Dreiser was fifty-nine; though he lived on until seventy-four, the coveted prize was not to be his. But Sinclair Lewis's tribute turned out to be an accurate placement of Dreiser in the history of American literature.

Born in Terre Haute, Indiana, to a stern German Catholic immigrant father and a sympathetic, illiterate mother, Dreiser was the twelfth of thirteen children. Poverty propelled the family from one small Indiana town to another, and even caused it to split up for a period. By the time he was sixteen, Dreiser went to work in Chicago at one odd job after another—washing dishes, shovelling coal, collecting bills. He was rescued by a high school teacher who gave him money to attend Indiana University. He left after a year, and later observed that his studies did not "concern ordinary life at all."

At twenty, Dreiser became a reporter for the *Chicago Globe*, beginning a career in journalism that would, in a few years time, expand into magazine editing. His older brother, Paul Dresser (he changed the spelling of the last name), had achieved success in New York as a song-and-dance man and composer of popular songs—including "My Gal Sal" and "On the Banks of the Wabash." He became part owner of a music firm in New York, and Dreiser appealed to Paul to launch a magazine for him to edit. In 1895, Dreiser became editor of a successful magazine entitled *Ev'ry Month*. His magazine career lasted for over a decade and saw him as editor of several mass-circulation pulp magazines, including *Smith's Magazine*, *Broadway Magazine*, and *Delineator* (a publication of Butterick, the sewing-pattern publisher).

But Dreiser's interest had early turned to the writing of fiction. In 1900, his long novel *Sister Carrie*, set in Chicago and New York, was read by Frank Norris for Doubleday, Page & Co. He enthusiastically recommended publication, and a contract was issued to Dreiser. When the publisher's wife read the manuscript, she found the frank treatment of sex offensive. Dreiser held the publisher to the contract, but found himself defeated when the book was left, unpromoted by the publisher, to die a quiet death. His total royalties from a sale of 456 copies was $68.40. The book was reissued with greater success by another publisher in 1907, but not before Dreiser went through a period of suicidal despondency similar to that suffered by a main character in the novel.

Dreiser had drawn for his portrayal of Sister Carrie from his boyhood observations of the predicament of his own sisters and their illegitimate pregnancies. He was to use such real-life materials for all his fiction, including the *Trilogy of Desire* he launched in 1912 with *The Financier*. The model for his hero was Charles Yerkes, a Philadelphia entrepreneur who was convicted of embezzlement but who recouped his fortune by taking over the streetcar systems of Philadelphia and Chicago. The second volume of the trilogy, *The Titan*, appeared in 1914, and the third, *The Stoic*, in 1947 (after Dreiser's death). These works— together with *Jennie Gerhardt* (1911) and especially *The "Genius"* (1915), with their bold treatment of the sex relations of characters both in and out of wedlock— renewed the controversy over Dreiser's "morality." The New York Society for the Suppression of Vice succeeded in getting *The "Genius"* withdrawn, giving substance to Sinclair Lewis's later dubbing of Dreiser a "pioneer."

Although Dreiser continued to write stories, autobiographical volumes, and plays, he did not try to produce another novel after 1915 until writing *An American Tragedy*, published in 1925. He deliberately modelled his protagonist on a young man convicted of murdering his pregnant girl friend in a small New York town in 1906. Although Dreiser carefully studied the newspaper accounts of court records of the case, he shaped his narrative into an indictment of materialistic American values, pointing to the social tragedy that underlay the local crime.

This novel firmly established Dreiser, then fifty-four, as an important and successful writer. But his interests turned more and more to economic and social injustice, especially during the Great Depression of the 1930s. He spent his energies in speaking or pamphleteering for one cause or another, some of them Communist-sponsored. His indignation led him finally to join the Communist party in 1945, the year he died. His sympathies were always for the outcast, the down-trodden, the poor, and helpless.

His early reading of Charles Darwin, Thomas Huxley, and Herbert Spencer had confirmed his observation that economic, social, and psychological forces overwhelmed the power of individuals to shape their own lives, leaving them little personal responsibility for their behavior. His novels reflected this vision of the human fate. Yet his devotion to social causes seemed to suggest a belief that by making moral judgments and commitments, wrongs could be righted. What endures from his career is not the pamphleteering but the imaginative embodiment in his novels of characters driven by compulsive desires for money, sex, position, and prestige.

ADDITIONAL READING

The Letters of Theodore Dreiser, 3 vols., ed. Robert H. Elias, 1959; *Theodore Dreiser: A Selection of Uncollected Prose*, ed. Donald Pizer, 1977; *Theodore Dreiser: American Diaries, 1902–1926*, ed. Thomas P. Riggio, 1982; *Dreiser-Mencken Letters: The Correspondence of Theodore Dreiser and H. L. Mencken, 1907–1945*, ed. Thomas P. Riggio, 1986.

H. L. Mencken, "Theodore Dreiser," *A Book of Prefaces*, 1917; Dorothy Dudley, *Forgotten Frontiers: Dreiser and the Land of the Free*, 1932, 1946; Robert H. Elias, *Theodore Dreiser: Apostle of Nature*, 1949; Helen Dreiser, *My Life with Dreiser*, 1951; F. O. Matthiessen, *Theodore Dreiser*, 1951; Alfred Kazin and Charles Shapiro, eds., *The Stature of Theodore Dreiser: A Critical Survey of the Man and His Work*, 1955; Charles Shapiro, *Theodore Dreiser: Our Bitter Patriot*, 1962; Philip Gerber, *Theodore Dreiser*, 1964; W. A. Swanberg, *Dreiser*, 1965; Marguerite Tjader, *Theodore Dreiser: A New Dimension*, 1965; John J. McAleer, *Theodore Dreiser: An Introduction and Interpretation*, 1968; Ellen Moers, *Two Dreisers*, 1969; Richard Lehan, *Theodore Dreiser: His World and His Novels*, 1969; Robert Penn Warren, *Homage to Theodore Dreiser*, 1971; James Lundquist, *Theodore Dreiser*, 1974; R. N. Mookerjee, *Theodore Dreiser: His Thought and Social Criticism*, 1974; Donald Pizer, Richard W. Dowell, and Frederic E. Rusch, *Theodore Dreiser: A Primary and Secondary Bibliography*, 1975; Donald Pizer, *The Novels of Theodore Dreiser*, 1976; Voshimobu Hakutani, *Young Dreiser: A Critical Study*, 1980; Donald Pizer, ed., *Critical Essays on Theodore Dreiser*, 1981; Lawrence E. Hussman, Jr., *Dreiser and His Fiction: A Twentieth-Century Quest*, 1983; Joseph Griffin, *The Small Canvas: An Introduction to Dreiser's Short Stories*, 1985; Richard Lingeman, *Theodore Dreiser: At the Gates of the City, 1871–1907*, 1986; Jeanetta Boswell, *Theodore Dreiser and the Critics, 1911–1982: A Bibliography with Selective Annotations*, 1986.

TEXT

Free and Other Stories, 1918.

Nigger Jeff

The city editor was waiting for one of his best reporters, Elmer Davies by name, a vain and rather self-sufficient youth who was inclined to be of that turn of mind which sees in life only a fixed and ordered process of rewards and punishments. If one did not do exactly right, one did not get along well. On the contrary, if one did, one did. Only the so-called evil were really punished, only the good truly rewarded — or Mr. Davies had heard this so long in his youth that he had come nearly to believe it. Presently he appeared. He was dressed in a new spring suit, a new hat and new shoes. In the lapel of his coat was a small bunch of violets. It was one o'clock of a sunny spring afternoon, and he was feeling exceedingly well and good-natured — quite fit, indeed. The world was going unusually well with him. It seemed worth singing about.

"Read that, Davies," said the city editor, handing him the clipping. "I'll tell you afterward what I want you to do."

The reporter stood by the editorial chair and read:

Pleasant Valley, Ko., April 16.

"A most dastardly crime has just been reported here. Jeff Ingalls, a negro, this morning assaulted Ada Whitaker, the nineteen-year-old daughter of Morgan Whitaker, a well-to-do farmer, whose home is four miles south of this place. A posse, headed by Sheriff Mathews, has started in pursuit. If he is caught, it is thought he will be lynched."

The reporter raised his eyes as he finished. What a terrible crime! What evil people there were in the world! No doubt such a creature ought to be lynched, and that quickly.

"You had better go out there, Davies," said the city editor. "It looks as if something might come of that. A lynching up here would be a big thing. There's never been one in this state."

Davies smiled. He was always pleased to be sent out of town. It was a mark of appreciation. The city editor rarely sent any of the other men on these big stories. What a nice ride he would have!

As he went along, however, a few minutes later he began to meditate on this. Perhaps, as the city editor had suggested, he might be compelled to witness an actual lynching. That was by no means so pleasant in itself. In his fixed code of rewards and punishments he had no particular place for lynchings, even for crimes of the nature described, especially if he had to witness the lynching. It was too horrible a kind of reward or punishment. Once, in line of duty, he had been compelled to witness a hanging, and that had made him sick—deathly so—even though carried out as a part of the due process of law of his day and place. Now, as he looked at this fine day and his excellent clothes, he was not so sure that this was a worthwhile assignment. Why should he always be selected for such things—just because he could write? There were others—lots of men on the staff. He began to hope as he went along that nothing really serious would come of it, that they would catch the man before he got there and put him in jail—or, if the worst had to be—painful thought!—that it would be all over by the time he got there. Let's see—the telegram had been filed at nine a.m. It was now one-thirty and would be three by the time he got out there, all of that. That would give them time enough, and then, if all were well, or ill, as it were, he could just gather the details of the crime and the—aftermath—and return. The mere thought of an approaching lynching troubled him greatly, and the farther he went the less he liked it.

He found the village of Pleasant Valley a very small affair indeed, just a few dozen houses nestling between green slopes of low hills, with one small business corner and a rambling array of lanes. One or two merchants of K——, the city from which he had just arrived, lived out here, but otherwise it was very rural. He took notes of the whiteness of the little houses, the shimmering beauty of the small stream one had to cross in going from the depot. At the one main corner a few men were gathered about a typical village barroom. Davies headed for this as being the most likely source of information.

In mingling with this company at first he said nothing about his being a newspaper man, being very doubtful as to its effect upon them, their freedom of speech and manner.

The whole company was apparently tense with interest in the crime which still remained unpunished, seemingly craving excitement and desirous of seeing something done about it. No such opportunity to work up wrath and vent their stored-up animal propensities had probably occurred here in years. He took this occasion to inquire into the exact details of the attack, where it had occurred, where the Whitakers lived. Then, seeing that mere talk prevailed here, he went away thinking that he had best find out for himself how the victim was. As yet she had not been described, and it was necessary to know a little something about her. Accordingly, he sought an old man who kept a stable in the village, and procured a horse. No carriage was to be had. Davies was not an excellent rider, but he made a shift of it. The Whitaker home was not so very far away—about four miles out—and before long he was knocking at its front door, set back a hundred feet from the rough country road.

"I'm from the *Times*," he said to the tall, raw-boned woman who opened the door, with an attempt at being impressive. His position as reporter in this matter was a little dubious; he might be welcome, and he might not. Then he asked if this were Mrs. Whitaker, and how Miss Whitaker was by now.

"She's doing very well," answered the woman, who seemed decidedly stern, if repressed and nervous, a Spartan type. "Won't you come in? She's rather feverish, but the doctor says she'll probably be all right later on." She said no more.

Davies acknowledged the invitation by entering. He was very anxious to see the girl, but she was sleeping under the influence of an opiate, and he did not care to press the matter at once.

"When did this happen?" he asked.

"About eight o'clock this morning," said the woman. "She started to go over to our next door neighbor here, Mr. Edmonds, and this negro met her. We didn't know anything about it until she came crying through the gate and dropped down in here."

"Were you the first one to meet her?" asked Davies.

"Yes, I was the only one," said Mrs. Whitaker. "The men had all gone to the fields."

Davies listened to more of the details, the type and history of the man, and then rose to go. Before doing so he was allowed to have a look at the girl, who was still sleeping. She was young and rather pretty. In the yard he met a country man who was just coming to get home news. The latter imparted more information.

"They're lookin' all around south of here," he said, speaking of a crowd which was supposed to be searching. "I expect they'll make short work of him if they get him. He can't get away very well, for he's on foot, wherever he is. The sheriff's after him too, with a deputy or two, I believe. He'll be tryin' to save him an' take him over to Clayton, but I don't believe he'll be able to do it, not if the crowd catches him first."

So, thought Davies, he would probably have to witness a lynching after all. The prospect was most unhappy.

"Does any one know where this negro lived?" he asked heavily, a growing sense of his duty weighing upon him.

"Oh, right down here a little way," replied the farmer. "Jeff Ingalls was his name. We all know him around here. He worked for one and another of the farmers hereabouts, and don't appear to have had such a bad record, either, except for drinkin' a little now and then. Miss Ada recognized him, all right. You follow this road to the next crossing and turn to the right. It's a little log house that sets back off the road—something like that one you see down the lane there, only it's got lots o' chips scattered about."

Davies decided to go there first, but changed his mind. It was growing late, and he thought he had better return to the village. Perhaps by now developments in connection with the sheriff or the posse were to be learned.

Accordingly, he rode back and put the horse in the hands of its owner, hoping that all had been concluded and that he might learn of it here. At the principal corner much the same company was still present, arguing, fomenting, gesticulating. They seemed parts of different companies that earlier in the day had been out searching. He wondered what they had been doing since, and then decided to ingratiate himself by telling them he had just come from the Whitakers and what he had learned there of the present condition of the girl and the movements of the sheriff.

Just then a young farmer came galloping up. He was coatless, hatless, breathless.

"They've got him!" he shouted excitedly. "They've got him!"

A chorus of "whos," "wheres" and "whens" greeted this information as the crowd gathered about the rider.

"Why, Mathews caught him up here at his own house!" exclaimed the latter, pulling out a handkerchief and wiping his face. "He must 'a' gone back there for something. Mathews's takin' him over to Clayton, so they think, but they don't project he'll ever get there. They're after him now, but Mathews says he'll shoot the first man that tries to take him away."

"Which way'd he go?" exclaimed the men in chorus, stirring as if to make an attack.

"'Cross Sellers' Lane," said the rider." The boys think he's goin' by way of Baldwin."

"Whoopee!" yelled one of the listeners. "We'll get him away from him, all right! Are you goin', Sam?"

"You bet!" said the latter. "Wait'll I get my horse!"

"Lord!" thought Davies. "To think of being (perforce) one of a lynching party — a hired spectator!"

He delayed no longer, however, but hastened to secure his horse again. He saw that the crowd would be off in a minute to catch up with the sheriff. There would be information in that quarter, drama very likely.

"What's doin'?" inquired the liveryman as he noted Davies' excited appearance.

"They're after him," replied the latter nervously. "The sheriff's caught him. They're going now to try to take him away from him, or that's what they say. The sheriff is taking him over to Clayton, by way of Baldwin. I want to get over there if I can. Give me the horse again, and I'll give you a couple of dollars more."

The liveryman led the horse out, but not without many provisionary cautions as to the care which was to be taken of him, the damages which would ensue if it were not. He was not to be ridden beyond midnight. If one were wanted for longer than that Davies must get him elsewhere or come and get another, to all of which Davies promptly agreed. He then mounted and rode away.

When he reached the corner again several of the men who had gone for their horses were already there, ready to start. The young man who had brought the news had long since dashed off to other parts.

Davies waited to see which road this new company would take. Then through as pleasant a country as one would wish to see, up hill and down dale, with charming vistas breaking upon the gaze at every turn, he did the riding of his life. So disturbed was the reporter by the grim turn things had taken that he scarcely noted the beauty that was stretched before him, save to note that it was so. Death! Death! The proximity of involuntary and enforced death was what weighed upon him now.

In about an hour the company had come in sight of the sheriff, who, with two other men, was driving a wagon he had borrowed along a lone country road. The latter was sitting at the back, a revolver in each hand, his face toward the group, which at sight of him trailed after at a respectful distance. Excited as every one was, there was no disposition, for the time being at least, to halt the progress of the law.

"He's in that wagon," Davies heard one man say. "Don't you see they've got him in there tied and laid down?"

Davies looked.

"That's right," said another. "I see him now."

"What we ought to do," said a third, who was riding near the front, "is to take him away and hang him. That's just what he deserves, and that's what he'll get before we're through to-day."

"Yes!" called the sheriff, who seemed to have heard this. "You're not goin' to do any hangin' this day, so you just might as well go on back." He did not appear to be much troubled by the appearance of the crowd.

"Where's old man Whitaker?" asked one of the men who seemed to feel that they needed a leader. "He'd get him quick enough!"

"He's with the other crowd, down below Olney," was the reply.

"Somebody ought to go an' tell him."

"Clark's gone," assured another, who hoped for the worst.

Davies rode among the company a prey to mingled and singular feelings. He was very much excited and yet depressed by the character of the crowd which, in so far as he could see, was largely impelled to its jaunt by curiosity and yet also able under sufficient motivation on the part of some one — any one, really — to kill too. There was not so much daring as a desire to gain daring from others, an unconscious wish or impulse to organize the total strength or will of those present into one strength or one will, sufficient to overcome the sheriff and inflict death upon his charge. It was strange — almost intellectually incomprehensible — and yet so it was. The men were plainly afraid of the determined sheriff. They thought something ought to be done, but they did not feel like getting into trouble.

Mathews, a large solemn, sage, brown man in worn clothes and a faded brown hat, contemplated the recent addition to his trailers with apparent indifference. Seemingly he was determined to protect his man and avoid mob justice, come what may. A mob should not have him if he had to shoot, and if he shot it would be to kill. Finally, since the company thus added to did not dash upon him, he seemingly decided to scare them off. Apparently he thought he could do this, since they trailed like calves.

"Stop a minute!" he called to his driver.

The latter pulled up. So did the crowd behind. Then the sheriff stood over the prostrate body of the negro, who lay in the jolting wagon beneath him, and called back:

"Go 'way from here, you people! Go on, now! I won't have you follerin' after me!"

"Give us the nigger!" yelled one in a half-bantering, half-derisive tone of voice.

"I'll give ye just two minutes to go on back out o' this road," returned the sheriff grimly, pulling out his watch and looking at it. They were about a hundred feet apart. "If you don't, I'll clear you out!"

"Give us the nigger!"

"I know you, Scott," answered Mathews, recognizing the voice. "I'll arrest every last one of ye tomorrow. Mark my word!"

The company listened in silence, the horses champing and twisting.

"We've got a right to foller," answered one of the men.

"I give ye fair warning," said the sheriff, jumping from his wagon and leveling his pistols as he approached. "When I count five I'll begin to shoot!"

He was a serious and stalwart figure as he approached, and the crowd fell back a little.

"Git out o' this now!" he yelled. "One — Two —"

The company turned completely and retreated, Davies among them.

"We'll foller him when he gits further on," said one of the men in explanation.

"He's got to do it," said another. "Let him git a little ways ahead."

The sheriff returned to his wagon and drove on. He seemed, however, to realize that he would not be obeyed and that safety lay in haste alone. His wagon was traveling fast. If only he could lose them or get a good start he might possibly get to Clayton and the strong county jail by morning. His followers, however, trailed him swiftly as might be, determined not to be left behind.

"He's goin' to Baldwin," said one of the company of which Davies was a member.

"Where's that?" asked Davies.

"Over west o' here, about four miles."

"Why is he going there?"

"That's where he lives. I guess he thinks if he kin git 'im over there he kin purtect 'im till he kin git more help from Clayton. I cal'late he'll try an' take 'im over yet tonight, or early in the mornin' shore."

Davies smiled at the man's English. This countryside lingo always fascinated him.

Yet the men lagged, hesitating as to what to do. They did not want to lose sight of Mathews, and yet cowardice controlled them. They did not want to get into direct altercation with the law. It wasn't their place to hang the man, although plainly they felt that he ought to be hanged, and that it would be a stirring and exciting thing if he were. Consequently they desired to watch and be on hand—to get old Whitaker and his son Jake, if they could, who were out looking elsewhere. They wanted to see what the father and brother would do.

The quandary was solved by one of the men, who suggested that they could get to Baldwin by going back to Pleasant Valley and taking the Sand River pike, and that in the meantime they might come upon Whitaker and his son en route, or leave word at his house. It was a shorter cut than this the sheriff was taking, although he would get there first now. Possibly they could beat him at least to Clayton, if he attempted to go on. The Clayton road was back via Pleasant Valley, or near it, and easily intercepted. Therefore, while one or two remained to trail the sheriff and give the alarm in case he did attempt to go on to Clayton, the rest, followed by Davies, set off at a gallop to Pleasant Valley. It was nearly dusk now when they arrived and stopped at the corner store—supper time. The fires of evening meals were marked by upcurling smoke from chimneys. Here, somehow, the zest to follow seemed to depart. Evidently the sheriff had worsted them for the night. Morg Whitaker, the father, had not been found; neither had Jake. Perhaps they had better eat. Two or three had already secretly fallen away.

They were telling the news of what had occurred so far to one of the two store-keepers who kept the place, when suddenly Jake Whitaker, the girl's brother, and several companions came riding up. They had been scouring the territory to the north of the town, and were hot and tired. Plainly they were unaware of the developments of which the crowd had been a part.

"The sheriff's got 'im!" exclaimed one of the company, with that blatance which always accompanies the telling of great news in small rural companies. "He taken him over to Baldwin in a wagon a coupla hours ago."

"Which way did he go?" asked the son, whose hardy figure, worn, hand-me-down clothes and rakish hat showed up picturesquely as he turned here and there on his horse.

"'Cross Seller' Lane. You won't git 'em that-a-way, though, Jake. He's already over there by now. Better take the short cut."

A babble of voices now made the scene more interesting. One told how the negro had been caught, another that the sheriff was defiant, a third that men were still tracking him or over there watching, until all the chief points of the drama had been spoken if not heard.

Instantly suppers were forgotten. The whole customary order of the evening was overturned once more. The company started off on another excited jaunt, up hill and down dale, through the lovely country that lay between Baldwin and Pleasant Valley.

By now Davies was very weary of this procedure and of his saddle. He wondered when, if ever, this story was to culminate, let alone he write it. Tragic as it might prove, he could not nevertheless spend an indefinite period trailing a possibility, and yet, so great was the potentiality of the present situation, he dared not leave. By contrast with the horror impending, as he now noted, the night was so beautiful that it was all but poignant. Stars were already beginning to shine. Distant lamps twinkled like yellow eyes from the cottages in the valleys and on the hillsides. The air was fresh and tender. Some pea-fowls were crying afar off, and the east promised a golden moon.

Silently the assembled company trotted on—no more than a score in all. In the dusk, and with Jake ahead, it seemed too grim a pilgrimage for joking. Young Jake, riding silently toward the front, looked as if tragedy were all he craved. His friends seemed considerately to withdraw from him, seeing that he was the aggrieved.

After an hour's riding Baldwin came into view, lying in a sheltering cup of low hills. Already its lights were twinkling softly and there was still an air of honest firesides and cheery suppers about it which appealed to Davies in his hungry state. Still, he had no thought now of anything save this pursuit.

Once in the village, the company was greeted by calls of recognition. Everybody seemed to know what they had come for. The sheriff and his charge were still there, so a dozen citizens volunteered. The local storekeepers and loungers followed the cavalcade up the street to the sheriff's house, for the riders had now fallen into a solemn walk.

"You won't get him though, boys," said one whom Davies later learned was Seavey, the village postmaster and telegraph operator, a rather youthful person of between twenty-five and thirty, as they passed his door. "He's got two deputies in there with him, or did have, and they say he's going to take him over to Clayton."

At the first street corner they were joined by the several men who had followed the sheriff.

"He tried to give us the slip," they volunteered excitedly, "but he's got the nigger in the house, there, down in the cellar. The deputies ain't with him. They've gone somewhere for help—Clayton, maybe."

"How do you know?"

"We saw 'em go out that back way. We think we did, anyhow."

A hundred feet from the sheriff's little white cottage, which backed up against a sloping field, the men parleyed. Then Jake announced that he proposed to go boldly up to the sheriff's door and demand the negro.

"If he don't turn him out I'll break in the door an' take him!" he said.

"That's right! We'll stand by you, Whitaker," commented several.

By now the throng of unmounted natives had gathered. The whole village was up and about, its one street alive and running with people. Heads appeared at doors and windows. Riders pranced up and down, hallooing. A few revolver shots were heard. Presently the mob gathered even closer to the sheriff's gate, and Jake stepped forward as leader. Instead, however, of going boldly up to the door as at first it appeared he would, he stopped at the gate, calling to the sheriff.

"Hello, Mathews!"

"Eh, eh, eh!" bellowed the crowd.

The call was repeated. Still no answer. Apparently to the sheriff delay appeared to be his one best weapon.

Their coming, however, was not as unexpected as some might have thought. The figure of the sheriff was plainly to be seen close to one of the front windows. He appeared to be holding a double-barreled shotgun. The negro, as it developed later, was cowering and chattering in the darkest corner of the cellar, hearkening no doubt to the voices and firing of the revolvers outside.

Suddenly, and just as Jake was about to go forward, the front door of the house flew open, and in the glow of a single lamp inside appeared first the doubled-barreled end of the gun, followed immediately by the form of Mathews, who held the weapon poised ready for a quick throw to the shoulder. All except Jake fell back.

"Mr. Mathews," he called deliberately, "we want that nigger!"

"Well, you can't git 'im!" replied the sheriff. "He's not here."

"Then what you got that gun fer?" yelled a voice.

Mathews made no answer.

"Better give him up, Mathews," called another, who was safe in the crowd, "or we'll come in an' take him!"

"No you won't," said the sheriff defiantly. "I said the man wasn't here. I say it ag'in. You couldn't have him if he was, an' you can't come in my house! Now if you people don't want trouble you'd better go on away."

"He's down in the cellar!" yelled another.

"Why don't you let us see?" asked another.

Mathews waved his gun slightly.

"You'd better go away from here now," cautioned the sheriff. "I'm tellin' ye! I'll have warrants out for the lot o' ye, if ye don't mind!"

The crowd continued to simmer and stew, while Jake stood as before. He was very pale and tense, but lacked initiative.

"He won't shoot," called some one at the back of the crowd. "Why don't you go in, Jake, an' git him?"

"Sure! Rush in. That's it!" observed a second.

"He won't, eh?" replied the sheriff softly. Then he added in a lower tone, "The first man that comes inside that gate takes the consequences."

No one ventured inside the gate; many even fell back. It seemed as if the planned assault had come to nothing.

"Why not go around the back way?" called some one else.

"Try it!" replied the sheriff. "See what you find on that side! I told you you couldn't come inside. You'd better go away from here now before ye git into trouble," he repeated. "You can't come in, an' it'll only mean bloodshed."

There was more chattering and jesting while the sheriff stood on guard. He, however, said no more. Nor did he allow the banter, turmoil and lust for tragedy to disturb him. Only, he kept his eye on Jake, on whose movements the crowd seemed to hang.

Time passed, and still nothing was done. The truth was that young Jake, put to the test, was not sufficiently courageous himself, for all his daring, and felt the weakness of the crowd behind him. To all intents and purposes he was alone, for he did not inspire confidence. He finally fell back a little, observing, "I'll git 'im before mornin', all right," and now the crowd itself began to disperse, returning to its stores and homes or standing about the postoffice and the one village drugstore. Finally, Davies smiled and came away. He was sure he had the story of a defeated mob. The sheriff was to be his great hero. He proposed to interview him later. For the present, he meant to seek out Seavey, the telegraph operator, and arrange to file a message, then see if something to eat was not to be had somewhere.

After a time he found the operator and told him what he wanted—to write and file a story as he wrote it. The latter indicated a table in the little postoffice and telegraph station which he could use. He became very much interested in the reporter when he learned he was from the *Times*, and when Davies asked where he could get something to eat said he would run across the street and tell the proprietor of the only boarding house to fix him something which he could consume as he wrote. He appeared to be interested in how a newspaper man would go about telling a story of this kind over a wire.

"You start your story," he said, "and I'll come back and see if I can get the *Times* on the wire."

Davies sat down and began his account. He was intent on describing things to date, the uncertainty and turmoil, the apparent victory of the sheriff. Plainly the courage of the latter had won, and it was all so picturesque. "A foiled lynching," he began, and as he wrote the obliging postmaster, who had by now returned, picked up the pages and carefully deciphered them for himself.

"That's all right. I'll see if I can get the *Times* now," he commented.

"Very obliging postmaster," thought Davies as he wrote, but he had so often encountered pleasant and obliging people on his rounds that he soon dropped that thought.

The food was brought, and still Davies wrote on, munching as he did so. In a little while the *Times* answered an often-repeated call.

"Davies at Baldwin," ticked the postmaster, "get ready for quite a story!"

"Let 'er go!" answered the operator at the *Times*, who had been expecting this dispatch.

As the events of the day formulated themselves in his mind, Davies wrote and turned over page after page. Between whiles he looked out through the small window before him where afar off he could see a lonely light twinkling against a hillside. Not infrequently he stopped his work to see if anything new was happening, whether the situation was in any danger of changing, but apparently it was not. He then proposed to remain until all possibility of a tragedy, this night anyhow, was eliminated. The operator also wandered about, waiting for an accumulation of pages upon which he could work but making sure to keep up with the writer. The two became quite friendly.

Finally, his dispatch nearly finished, he asked the postmaster to caution the night editor at K—— to the effect, that if anything more happened before one in the morning he would file it, but not to expect anything more as nothing might happen. The reply came that he was to remain and await developments. Then he and the postmaster sat down to talk.

About eleven o'clock, when both had about convinced themselves that all was over for this night anyhow, and the lights in the village had all but vanished, a stillness of the purest, summery-est, country-est quality having settled down, a faint beating of hoofs, which seemed to suggest the approach of a large cavalcade, could be heard out on the Sand River pike as Davies by now had come to learn it was, back or northwest of the postoffice. At the sound the postmaster got up, as did Davies, both stepping outside and listening. On it came, and as the volume increased, the former said, "Might be help for the sheriff, but I doubt it. I telegraphed Clayton six times to-day. They wouldn't come that way, though. It's the wrong road." Now, thought Davies nervously, after all there might be something to add to his story, and he had so wished that it was all over! Lynchings, as he now felt, were horrible things. He wished people wouldn't do such things—take the law, which now more than ever he respected, into their own hands. It was too brutal, cruel. That negro cowering there in the dark probably, and the sheriff all taut and tense, worrying over his charge and his duty, were not happy things to contemplate in the face of such a thing as this. It was true that the crime which had been committed was dreadful, but still why couldn't people allow the law to take its course? It was so much better. The law was powerful enough to deal with cases of this kind.

"They're comin' back, all right," said the postmaster solemnly, as he and Davies stared in the direction of the sound which grew louder from moment to moment.

"It's not any help from Clayton, I'm afraid."

"By George, I think you're right!" answered the reporter, something telling him that more trouble was at hand. "Here they come!"

As he spoke there was a clattering of hoofs and crunching of saddle girths as a large company of men dashed up the road and turned into the narrow street of the village, the figure of Jake Whitaker and an older bearded man in a wide black hat riding side by side in front.

"There's Jake," said the postmaster, "and that's his father riding beside him there. The old man's a terror when he gets his dander up. Sompin's sure to happen now."

Davies realized that in his absence writing a new turn had been given to things. Evidently the son had returned to Pleasant Valley and organized a new posse or gone out to meet his father.

Instantly the place was astir again. Lights appeared in doorways and windows, and both were thrown open. People were leaning or gazing out to see what new movement was afoot. Davies noted at once that there was none of the brash enthusiasm about this company such as had characterized the previous descent. There was grimness everywhere, and he now began to feel that this was the beginning of the end. After the cavalcade had passed down the street toward the sheriff's house, which was quite dark now, he ran after it, arriving a few moments after the former which was already in part dismounted. The townspeople followed. The sheriff, as it now developed, had not relaxed any of his vigilance, however; he was not sleeping, and as the crowd reappeared the light inside reappeared.

By the light of the moon, which was almost overhead, Davies was able to make out several of his companions of the afternoon, and Jake, the son. There were many more, though, now, whom he did not know, and foremost among them this old man.

The latter was strong, iron-gray, and wore a full beard. He looked very much like a blacksmith.

"Keep your eye on the old man," advised the postmaster, who had by now come up and was standing by.

While they were still looking, the old man went boldly forward to the little front porch of the house and knocked at the door. Some one lifted a curtain at the window and peeped out.

"Hello, in there!" cried the old man, knocking again.

"What do you want?" asked a voice.

"I want that nigger!"

"Well, you can't have him! I've told you people that once."

"Bring him out or I'll break down the door!" said the old man.

"If you do it's at your own risk. I know you, Whitaker, an' you know me. I'll give ye two minutes to get off that porch!"

"I want that nigger, I tell ye!"

"If ye don't git off that porch I'll fire through the door," said the voice solemnly. "One— Two—"

The old man backed cautiously away.

"Come out, Mathews!" yelled the crowd. "You've got to give him up this time. We ain't goin' back without him."

Slowly the door opened, as if the individual within were very well satisfied as to his power to handle the mob. He had done it once before this night, why not again? It revealed his tall form, armed with his shotgun. He looked around very stolidly, and then addressed the old man as one would a friend.

"Ye can't have him, Morgan," he said. "It's ag'in' the law. You know that as well as I do."

"Law or no law," said the old man, "I want that nigger!"

"I tell you I can't let you have him, Morgan. It's ag'in' the law. You know you oughtn't to be comin' around here at this time o' night actin' so."

"Well, I'll take him then," said the old man, making a move.

"Stand back!" shouted the sheriff, leveling his gun on the instant. "I'll blow ye into kingdom come, sure as hell!"

A noticeable movement on the part of the crowd ceased. The sheriff lowered his weapon as if he thought the danger were once more over.

"You-all ought to be ashamed of yerselves," he went on, his voice sinking to a gentle neighborly reproof, "tryin' to upset the law this way."

"The nigger didn't upset no law, did he?" asked one derisively.

"Well, the law's goin' to take care of the nigger now," Mathews made answer.

"Give us that scoundrel, Mathews; you'd better do it," said the old man. "It'll save a heap o' trouble."

"I'll not argue with ye, Morgan. I said ye couldn't have him, an' ye can't. If ye want bloodshed, all right. But don't blame me. I'll kill the first man that tries to make a move this way."

He shifted his gun handily and waited. The crowd stood outside his little fence murmuring.

Presently the old man retired and spoke to several others. There was more murmuring, and then he came back to the dead line.

"We don't want to cause trouble, Mathews," he began explanatively, moving his hand oratorically, "but we think you ought to see that it won't do any good to stand out. We think that—"

Davies and the postmaster were watching young Jake, whose peculiar attitude attracted their attention. The latter was standing poised at the edge of the crowd, evidently seeking to remain unobserved. His eyes were on the sheriff, who was hearkening to the old man. Suddenly, as the father talked and when the sheriff seemed for a moment mollified and unsuspecting, he made a quick run for the porch. There was an intense movement all along the line as the life and death of the deed became apparent. Quickly the sheriff drew his gun to his shoulder. Both triggers were pressed at the same time, and the gun spoke, but not before Jake was in and under him. The latter had been in sufficient time to knock the gun barrel upward and fall upon his man. Both shots blazed harmlessly over the heads of the crowd in red puffs, and then followed a general onslaught. Men leaped the fence by tens and crowded upon the little cottage. They swarmed about every side of the house and crowded upon the porch, where four men were scuffling with the sheriff. The latter soon gave up, vowing vengeance and the law. Torches were brought, and a rope. A wagon drove up and was backed into the yard. Then began the calls for the negro.

As Davies contemplated all this he could not help thinking of the negro who during all this turmoil must have been crouching in his corner in the cellar, trembling for his fate. Now indeed he must realize that his end was near. He could not have dozed or lost consciousness during the intervening hours, but must have been cowering there, wondering and praying. All the while he must have been terrified lest the sheriff might not get him away in time. Now, at the sound of horses' feet and the new murmurs of contention, how must his body quake and his teeth chatter!

"I'd hate to be that nigger," commented the postmaster grimly, "but you can't do anything with 'em. The county oughta sent help."

"It's horrible, horrible!" was all Davies could say.

He moved closer to the house, with the crowd, eager to observe every detail of the procedure. Now it was that a number of the men, as eager in their search as bloodhounds, appeared at a low cellar entryway at the side of the house carrying a rope. Others followed with torches. Headed by father and son they began to descend into the dark hole. With impressive daring, Davies, who was by no means sure that he would be allowed but who was also determined if possible to see, followed.

Suddenly, in the farthest corner, he espied Ingalls. The latter in his fear and agony had worked himself into a crouching position, as if he were about to spring. His nails were apparently forced into the earth. His eyes were rolling, his mouth foaming.

"Oh, my Lawd, boss," he moaned, gazing almost as one blind, at the lights, "oh, my Lawd, boss, don't kill me! I won't do it no mo'. I didn't go to do it. I didn't mean to dis time. I was just drunk, boss. Oh, my Lawd! My Lawd!" His teeth chattered the while his mouth seemed to gape open. He was no longer sane really, but kept repeating monotonously, "Oh, my Lawd!"

"Here he is, boys! Pull him out," cried the father.

The negro now gave one yell of terror and collapsed, falling prone. He quite bounded as he did so, coming down with a dead chug on the earthen floor. Reason had forsaken him. He was by now a groveling, foaming brute. The last gleam of intelligence was that which notified him of the set eyes of his pursuers.

Davies, who by now had retreated to the grass outside before this sight, was standing but ten feet back when they began to reappear after seizing and binding him. Although shaken to the roots of his being, he still had all the cool observing powers of the trained and relentless reporter. Even now he noted the color values of the scene, the red, smoky heads of the torches, the disheveled appearance of the men, the scuffling and pulling. Then all at once he clapped his hands over his mouth, almost unconscious of what he was doing.

"Oh, my God!" he whispered, his voice losing power.

The sickening sight was that of the negro, foaming at the mouth, bloodshot as to his eyes, his hands working convulsively, being dragged up the cellar steps feet foremost. They had tied a rope about his waist and feet, and so had hauled him out, leaving his head to hang and drag. The black face was distorted beyond all human semblance.

"Oh, my God!" said Davies again, biting his fingers unconsciously.

The crowd gathered about now more closely than ever, more horror-stricken than gleeful at their own work. None apparently had either the courage or the charity to gainsay what was being done. With a kind of mechanical deftness now the negro was rudely lifted and like a sack of wheat thrown into the wagon. Father and son now mounted in front to drive and the crowd took to their horses, content to clatter, a silent cavalcade, behind. As Davies afterwards concluded, they were not so much hardened lynchers perhaps as curious spectators, the majority of them, eager for any variation — any excuse for one — to the dreary commonplaces of their existences. The task to most — all indeed — was entirely new. Wide-eyed and nerve-racked, Davies ran for his own horse and mounting followed. He was so excited he scarcely knew what he was doing.

Slowly the silent company now took its way up the Sand River pike whence it had come. The moon was still high, pouring down a wash of silvery light. As Davies rode he wondered how he was to complete his telegram, but decided that he could not. When this was over there would be no time. How long would it be before they would really hang him? And would they? The whole procedure seemed so unreal, so barbaric that he could scarcely believe it — that he was a part of it. Still they rode on.

"Are they really going to hang him?" he asked of one who rode beside him, a total stranger who seemed however not to resent his presence.

"That's what they got 'im fer," answered the stranger.

And think, he thought to himself, to-morrow night he would be resting in his own good bed back in K——!

Davies dropped behind again and into silence and tried to recover his nerves. He could scarcely realize that he, ordinarily accustomed to the routine of the city, its humdrum and at least outward social regularity, was a part of this. The night was so soft, the air so refreshing. The shadowy trees were stirring with a cool night wind. Why should any one have to die this way? Why couldn't the people of Baldwin or elsewhere have bestirred themselves on the side of the law before this, just let it take its course? Both father and son now seemed brutal, the injury to the daughter and sister not so vital as all this. Still, also, custom seemed to require death in this way for this. It was like some axiomatic, mathematic law — hard, but custom. The silent company, an articulated, mechanical and therefore terrible thing, moved on. It also was axiomatic, mathematic. After a time he drew near to the wagon and looked at the negro again.

The latter, as Davies was glad to note, seemed still out of his sense. He was breathing heavily and groaning, but probably not with any conscious pain. His eyes were fixed and staring, his face and hands bleeding as if they had been scratched or trampled upon. He was crumpled limply.

But Davies could stand it no longer now. He fell back, sick at heart, content to see no more. It seemed a ghastly, murderous thing to do. Still the company moved on and he followed, past fields lit white by the moon, under dark, silent groups of trees, through which the moonlight fell in patches, up low hills and down into valleys, until at last a little stream came into view, the same little stream, as it proved, which he had seen earlier to-day and for a bridge over which they were heading. Here it ran now, sparkling like electricity in the night. After a time the road drew closer to the water and then crossed directly over the bridge, which could be seen a little way ahead.

Up to this the company now rode and then halted. The wagon was driven up on the bridge, and father and son got out. All the riders, including Davies, dismounted, and a full score of them gathered about the wagon from which the negro was lifted, quite as one might a bag. Fortunately, as Davies now told himself, he was still unconscious, an accidental mercy. Nevertheless he decided now that he could not witness the end, and went down by the waterside slightly above the bridge. He was not, after all, the utterly relentless reporter. From where he stood, however, he could see long beams of iron projecting out over the water, where the bridge was braced, and some of the men fastening a rope to a beam, and then he could see that they were fixing the other end around the negro's neck.

Finally the curious company stood back, and he turned his face away.

"Have you anything to say?" a voice demanded.

There was no answer. The negro was probably lolling and groaning, quite as unconscious as he was before.

Then came the concerted action of a dozen men, the lifting of the black mass into the air, and then Davies saw the limp form plunge down and pull up with a creaking sound of rope. In the weak moonlight it seemed as if the body were struggling, but he could not tell. He watched, wide-mouthed and silent, and then the body ceased moving. Then after a time he heard the company making ready to depart, and finally it did so, leaving him quite indifferently to himself and his thoughts. Only the black mass swaying in the pale light over the glimmering water seemed human and alive, his sole companion.

He sat down upon the bank and gazed in silence. Now the horror was gone. The suffering was ended. He was no longer afraid. Everything was summery and beautiful. The whole cavalcade had disappeared; the moon finally sank. His horse, tethered to a sapling beyond the bridge, waited patiently. Still he sat. He might now have hurried back to the small post-office in Baldwin and attempted to file additional details of his story, providing he could find Seavey, but it would have done no good. It was quite too late, and anyhow what did it matter? No other reporter had been present, and he could write a fuller, sadder, more colorful story on the morrow. He wondered idly what had become of Seavey? Why had he not followed? Life seemed so sad, so strange, so mysterious, so inexplicable.

As he still sat there the light of morning broke, a tender lavender and gray in the east. Then came the roseate hues of dawn, all the wondrous coloring of celestial halls, to which the waters of the stream responded. The white pebbles shone pinkily at the bottom, the grass and sedges first black now gleamed a translucent green. Still the body hung there black and limp against the sky, and now a light breeze sprang and stirred it visibly. At last he arose, mounted his horse and made his way back to Pleasant Valley, too full of the late tragedy to be much interested in anything else. Rousing his liveryman, he adjusted his difficulties with him by telling him the whole story, assuring him of his horse's care and handing him a five-dollar bill. Then he left, to walk and think again.

Since there was no train before noon and his duty plainly called him to a portion of another day's work here, he decided to make a day of it, idling about and getting additional details as to what further might be done. Who would cut the body down? What about arresting the lynchers—the father and son, for instance? What about the sheriff now? Would he act as he threatened? If he telegraphed the main fact of the lynching his city editor would not mind, he knew, his coming late, and the day here was so beautiful. He proceeded to talk with citizens and officials, rode out to the injured girl's home, rode to Baldwin to see the sheriff. There was a singular silence and placidity in that corner. The latter assured him that he knew nearly all of those who had taken part, and proposed to swear out warrants for them, but just the same Davies noted that he took his defeat as he did his danger, philosophically. There was no real activity in that corner later. He wished to remain a popular sheriff, no doubt.

It was sundown again before he remembered that he had not discovered whether the body had been removed. Nor had he heard why the negro came back, nor exactly how he was caught. A nine o'clock evening train to the city giving him a little more time for investigation, he decided to avail himself of it. The negro's cabin was two miles out along a pine-shaded road, but so pleasant was the evening that he decided to walk. En route, the last rays of the sinking sun stretched long shadows of budding trees across his path. It was not long before he came upon the cabin, a one-story affair set well back from the road and surrounded with a few scattered trees. By now it was quite dark. The ground between the cabin and the road was open, and strewn with the chips of a woodpile. The roof was sagged, and the windows patched in places, but for all that it had the glow of a home. Through the front door, which stood open, the blaze of a wood-fire might be seen, its yellow light filling the interior with a golden glow.

Hesitating before the door, Davies finally knocked. Receiving no answer he looked in on the battered cane chairs and aged furniture with considerable interest. It was a typical negro cabin, poor beyond the need of description. After a time a door in the rear of the room opened and a little negro girl entered carrying a battered tin lamp without any chimney. She had not heard his knock and started perceptibly at the sight of his figure in the doorway. Then she raised her smoking lamp above her head in order to see better, and approached.

There was something ridiculous about her unformed figure and loose gingham dress, as he noted. Her feet and hands were so large. Her black head was strongly emphasized by little pigtails of hair done up in white twine, which stood out all over her head. Her dark skin was made apparently more so by contrast with her white teeth and the whites of her eyes.

Davies looked at her for a moment but little moved now by the oddity which ordinarily would have amused him, and asked, "Is this where Ingalls lived?"

The girl nodded her head. She was exceedingly subdued, and looked as if she might have been crying.

"Has the body been brought here?"

"Yes, suh," she answered, with a soft negro accent.

"When did they bring it?"

"Dis moanin'."

"Are you his sister?"

"Yes, suh."

"Well, can you tell me how they caught him? When did he come back, and what for?" He was feeling slightly ashamed to intrude thus.

"In de afternoon, about two."

"And what for?" repeated Davies.

"To see us," answered the girl. "To see my motha'."

"Well, did he want anything? He didn't come just to see her, did he?"

"Yes, suh," said the girl, "he come to say good-by. We doan know when dey caught him." Her voice wavered.

"Well, didn't he know he might get caught?" asked Davies sympathetically, seeing that the girl was so moved.

"Yes, suh, I think he did."

She still stood very quietly holding the poor battered lamp up, and looking down.

"Well, what did he have to say?" asked Davies.

"He didn' have nothin' much to say, suh, He said he wanted to see motha'. He was a-goin' away."

The girl seemed to regard Davies as an official of some sort, and he knew it.

"Can I have a look at the body?" he asked.

The girl did not answer, but started as if to lead the way.

"When is the funeral?" he asked.

"Tomorra'."

The girl then led him through several bare sheds of rooms strung in a row to the furthermost one of the line. This last seemed a sort of storage shed for odds and ends. It had several windows, but they were quite bare of glass and open to the moonlight save for a few wooden boards nailed across from the outside. Davies had been wondering all the while where the body was and at the lonely and forsaken air of the place. No one but this little pig-tailed girl seemed about. If they had any colored neighbors they were probably afraid to be seen here.

Now, as he stepped into this cool, dark, exposed outer room, the desolation seemed quite complete. It was very bare, a mere shed or wash-room. There was the body in the middle of the room, stretched upon an ironing board which rested on a box and a chair, and covered with a white sheet. All the corners of the room were quite dark. Only its middle was brightened by splotches of silvery light.

Davies came forward, the while the girl left him, still carrying her lamp. Evidently she thought the moon lighted up the room sufficiently, and she did not feel equal to remaining. He lifted the sheet quite boldly, for he could see well enough, and looked at the still, black form. The face was extremely distorted, even in death, and he could see where the rope had tightened. A bar of cool moonlight lay just across the face and breast. He was still looking, thinking soon to restore the covering, when a sound, half sigh, half groan, reached his ears.

At it he started as if a ghost had made it. It was so eerie and unexpected in this dark place. His muscles tightened. Instantly his heart went hammering like mad. His first impression was that it must have come from the dead.

"Oo-o-ohh!" came the sound again, this time whimpering, as if some one were crying.

Instantly he turned, for now it seemed to come from a corner of the room, the extreme corner to his right, back of him. Greatly disturbed, he approached, and then as his eyes strained he seemed to catch the shadow of something, the figure of a woman, perhaps, crouching against the walls, huddled up, dark, almost indistinguishable.

"Oh, oh, oh!" the sound now repeated itself, even more plaintively than before.

Davies began to understand. He approached slowly, then more swiftly desired to withdraw, for he was in the presence of an old black mammy, doubled up and weeping. She was in the very niche of the two walls, her head sunk on her knees, her body quite still. "Oh, oh, oh!" she repeated, as he stood there near her.

Davies drew silently back. Before such grief his intrusion seemed cold and unwarranted. The guiltlessness of the mother—her love—how could one balance that against the other? The sensation of tears came to his eyes. He instantly covered the dead and withdrew.

Out in the moonlight he struck a brisk pace, but soon stopped and looked back. The whole dreary cabin, with its one golden eye, the door, seemed such a pitiful thing. The weeping mammy, alone in her corner—and he had come back to say "Good-by!" Davies swelled with feeling. The night, the tragedy, the grief, he saw it all. But also with the cruel instinct of the budding artist that he already was, he was beginning to meditate on the character of story it would make—the color, the pathos. The knowledge now that it was not always exact justice that was meted out to all and that it was not so much the business of the writer to indict as to interpret was borne in on him with distinctness by the cruel sorrow of the mother, whose blame, if any, was infinitesimal.

"I'll get it all in!" he exclaimed feelingly, if triumphantly at last. "I'll get it all in!"

1901, 1918

JACK LONDON
(1876–1916)

Jack London once wrote to a friend about his youth:

> Do you know my childhood? . . . I was eight years old when I put on my first undershirt made or bought at a store. Duty—at ten years I was on the streets selling newspapers. Every cent was turned over to my people, and I went to school in constant shame of the hats, shoes, clothes I wore. Duty—from then on I had no childhood. Up at three o'clock in the morning to carry papers. When that was finished I did not go home but continued on to school. School out, my evening papers. Saturdays I worked on an ice wagon. Sunday I went to a bowling alley and set up pins for drunken Dutchmen. Duty—I turned over every cent and went dressed like a scarecrow.

Born out of wedlock in San Francisco in 1876, London took the name of his stepfather John London, a truck gardener. By the age of fifteen, Jack London became an oyster pirate, conducting raids on oyster beds from his sloop, the *Razzle Dazzle*. He drifted from one job to another, sometimes living as a hobo, often haunting the saloons on the Oakland waterfront. In 1893 at age seventeen, he signed on a sealer as able-bodied seaman and sailed for Japan and the waters off the Siberian coast in quest of seals. In 1894 he followed for a time an army of the unemployed marching in protest to Washington, D.C., but he soon abandoned the march for the life of a tramp. Jailed for a month in the Erie County Penitentiary on charges of vagrancy, an experience he was to call "unbelievable . . . unprintable . . . unthinkable," London upon his release "ran back to California and opened the books."

In 1895 he graduated from Oakland High School, supporting himself as a janitor. And the following year he entered the University of California. He dropped out after one semester, tried his hand unsuccessfully at writing, and was soon on his way to northern Canada, where gold had been discovered in 1896. He and his companions spent the winter of 1897–98 on the Yukon in Klondike gold country, near Alaska. Suffering from a bout with scurvy, London returned home penniless. The only gold he garnered from his episode was stored in his imagination in the form of material for the stories that would later bring him fame and fortune.

For one who had led such a physically active life, London was astonishingly well read. He had begun his reading during his grammar school days in the public library, and he remained a voracious reader throughout his life. Rudyard Kipling and Robert Louis Stevenson were among his favorite writers. He turned once again to writing on his return from the Klondike and found magazines willing to take his stories. *The Atlantic Monthly* accepted "An Odyssey of the North" in 1899, and Houghton Mifflin published a book of his stories, *The Son of the Wolf*, in 1900. He threw himself into his profession with a vengeance, writing whatever he could sell—stories, essays, poems, novels. In 1903 he published *The Call of the Wild*, the story of a domestic dog that, when taken to Alaska, reverts to savagery and joins a wolf pack. The book was an immediate success worldwide and established London, then twenty-seven, as a famous writer.

Throughout the remainder of his life, London courted adventure. In 1904 he set out to cover the Russo-Japanese War for the *San Francisco Examiner*. In 1907–09, he attempted to sail around the world in his yacht *The Snark*, but finally abandoned the voyage when he became ill in Australia. In 1914 he went to Mexico to cover the Mexican Revolution as a war correspondent for *Collier's*. Throughout these and other adventures, he read and wrote incessantly.

Through his reading of Karl Marx and his firsthand experience among the down-trodden, he had early become a committed socialist. But his reading of Charles Darwin and Herbert Spencer reenforced a natural imaginative allegiance to the primal instincts and "the survival of the fittest." He embodied these conflicting beliefs in his work, his social concerns shaping such books as *The People of the Abyss* (1903) and *War of the Classes* (1905), and his vision of life as a primitive struggle shaping such contrasting volumes as *The Call of the Wild* (1903) and *White Fang* (1906). His version of the failed American Dream in *Martin Eden* (1909), the story of the formation and destruction of a writer, has been read as London's most autobiographical novel. In all, London wrote fifty books in the sixteen years of his writing career, seven of which were published posthumously.

Shortly after his second marriage in 1905 (his first ended in divorce), London settled on a ranch-sized estate in Sonoma County, California, and spent much time overseeing the building of an enormous mansion. In 1913, before its completion, it was destroyed by a fire. Its loss was a shock to London. In his last years he made a fortune in his writing, but he was profligate in his generosity to his friends, who gathered often at his table. The more money London made, the more his debts seemed to mount and the more he wrote. He suffered from uremia, a serious and painful kidney disease, but he refused to give up lavish eating and drinking to follow the prescribed treatment. In 1916, at the age of forty, he died from an overdose of morphine, taken apparently to deaden the pain of an attack of uremia. He escaped the pain — and all the other burdens that had beset his life.

ADDITIONAL READING

Letters from Jack London, ed. King Hendricks and Irvin Shepard, 1965; *The Letters of Jack London*, 3 vols., ed. Earle Labor, Robert C. Leitz III, and I. Milo Shepard, 1988.

Joan London, *Jack London and His Times: An Unconventional Biography*, 1939; Philip S. Foner, *Jack London, American Rebel*, 1947; Franklin Walker, *Jack London and the Klondike*, 1966; Earle Labor, *Jack London*, 1974; James I. McClintock, *White Logic: Jack London's Short Stories*, 1975; Joan R. Sherman, *Jack London: A Reference Guide*, 1977; Andrew Sinclair, *Jack: A Biography of Jack London*, 1977; John Perry, *Jack London, an American Myth*, 1981; Joan D. Hedrick, *Solitary Comrade: Jack London and His Work*, 1982; Charles W. Watson, Jr., *The Novels of Jack London: A Reappraisal*, 1983; Jacqueline Tavernier-Courbin, *Critical Essays on Jack London*, 1983; James Lundquist, *Jack London: Adventures, Ideas, and Fiction*, 1987; Clarice Stasz, *American Dreamers: Charmian and Jack London*, 1988.

TEXT

Children of the Frost, 1902.

The Law of Life

Old Koskoosh listened greedily. Though his sight had long since faded, his hearing was still acute, and the slightest sound penetrated to the glimmering intelligence which yet abode behind the withered forehead, but which no longer gazed forth upon the things of the world. Ah! that was Sit-cum-to-ha, shrilly anathematizing the dogs as she cuffed and beat them into the harnesses. Sit-cum-to-ha was his daughter's daughter, but she was too busy to waste a thought upon her broken grandfather, sitting alone there in the snow, forlorn and helpless. Camp must be broken. The long trail waited while the short day refused to linger. Life called her, and the duties of life, not death. And he was very close to death now.

The thought made the old man panicky for the moment, and he stretched forth a palsied hand which wandered tremblingly over the small heap of dry wood beside him. Reassured that it was indeed there, his hand returned to the shelter of his mangy furs, and he again fell to listening. The sulky crackling of half-frozen hides told him that the chief's moose-skin lodge had been struck, and even then was being rammed and jammed into portable compass. The chief was his son, stalwart and strong, head man of the tribesmen, and a mighty hunter. As the women toiled with the camp luggage, his voice rose, chiding them for their slowness. Old Koskoosh strained his ears. It was the last time he would hear that voice. There went Geehow's lodge! And Tusken's! Seven, eight, nine; only the shaman's could be still standing. There! They were at work upon it now. He could hear the shaman grunt as he piled it on the sled. A child whimpered, and a woman soothed it with soft, crooning gutturals. Little Koo-tee, the old man thought, a fretful child, and not overstrong. It would die soon, perhaps, and they would burn a hole through the frozen tundra and pile rocks above to keep the wolverines away. Well, what did it matter? A few years at best, and as many an empty belly as a full one. And in the end, Death waited, ever-hungry and hungriest of them all.

What was that? Oh, the men lashing the sleds and drawing tight the thongs. He listened, who would listen no more. The whip-lashes snarled and bit among the dogs. Hear them whine! How they hated the work and the trail! They were off! Sled after sled churned slowly away into the silence. They were gone. They had passed out of his life, and he faced the last bitter hour alone. No. The snow crunched beneath a moccasin; a man stood beside him; upon his head a hand rested gently. His son was good to do this thing. He remembered other old men whose sons had not waited after the tribe. But his son had. He wandered away into the past, till the young man's voice brought him back.

"Is it well with you?" he asked.

And the old man answered, "It is well."

"There be wood beside you," the younger man continued, "and the fire burns bright. The morning is gray, and the cold has broken. It will snow presently. Even now is it snowing."

"Ay, even now is it snowing."

"The tribesmen hurry. Their bales are heavy, and their bellies flat with lack of feasting. The trail is long and they travel fast. I go now. It is well?"

"It is well. I am as a last year's leaf, clinging lightly to the stem. The first breath that blows, and I fall. My voice is become like an old woman's. My eyes no longer show me the way of my feet, and my feet are heavy, and I am tired. It is well."

He bowed his head in content till the last noise of the complaining snow had died away, and he knew his son was beyond recall. Then his hand crept out in haste to the wood. It alone stood between him and the eternity that yawned in upon him. At last the measure of his life was a handful of fagots. One by one they would go to feed the fire, and just so, step by step, death would creep upon him. When the last stick had surrendered up its heat, the frost would begin to gather strength. First his feet would yield, then his hands; and the numbness would travel, slowly, from the extremities to the body. His head would fall forward upon his knees, and he would rest. It was easy. All men must die.

He did not complain. It was the way of life, and it was just. He had been born close to the earth, close to the earth had he lived, and the law thereof was not new to him. It was the law of all flesh. Nature was not kindly to the flesh. She had no concern for that concrete thing called the individual. Her interest lay in the species, the race. This was the deepest abstraction old Koskoosh's barbaric mind was capable of, but he grasped it firmly. He saw it exemplified in all life. The rise of the sap, the bursting greenness of the willow bud, the fall of the yellow leaf—in this alone was told the whole history. But one task did Nature set the individual. Did he not perform it, he died. Did he perform it, it was all the same, he died. Nature did not care; there were plenty who were obedient, and it was only the obedience in this matter, not the obedient, which lived and lived always. The tribe of Koskoosh was very old. The old men he had known when a boy, had known old men before them. Therefore it was true that the tribe lived, that it stood for the obedience of all its members, way down into the forgotten past, whose very resting-places were unremembered. They did not count; they were episodes. They had passed away like clouds from a summer sky. He also was an episode, and would pass away. Nature did not care. To life she set one task, gave one law. To perpetuate was the task of life, its law was death. A maiden was a good creature to look upon, full-breasted and strong, with spring to her step and light in her eyes. But her task was yet before her. The light in her eyes brightened, her step quickened, she was now bold with the young men, now timid, and she gave them of her own unrest. And ever she grew fairer and yet fairer to look upon, till some hunter, able no longer to withhold himself, took her to his lodge to cook and toil for him and to become the mother of his children. And with the coming of her offspring her looks left her. Her limbs dragged and shuffled, her eyes dimmed and bleared, and only the little children found joy against the withered cheek of the old squaw by the fire. Her task was done. But a little while, on the first pinch of famine or the first long trail, and she would be left, as he had been left, in the snow, with a little pile of wood. Such was the law.

He placed a stick carefully upon the fire and resumed his meditations. It was the same everywhere, with all things. The mosquitoes vanished with the first frost. The little tree-squirrel crawled away to die. When age settled upon the rabbit it became slow and heavy, and could no longer outfoot its enemies. Even the big bald-face grew clumsy and blind and quarrelsome, in the end to be dragged down by a handful of yelping huskies. He remembered how he had abandoned his own father on an upper reach of the Klondike one winter, the winter before the missionary came with his talk-books and his box of medicines. Many a time had Koskoosh smacked his lips over the recollection of that box, though now his mouth refused to moisten. The "pain-killer" had been especially good. But the missionary was a bother after all, for he brought no meat into the camp, and he ate heartily, and the hunters grumbled. But he chilled his lungs on the divide by the Mayo, and the dogs afterwards nosed the stones away and fought over his bones.

Koskoosh placed another stick on the fire and harked back deeper into the past. There was the time of the Great Famine, when the old men crouched empty-bellied to the fire, and let fall from their lips dim traditions of the ancient day when the Yukon ran wide open for three winters, and then lay frozen for three summers. He had lost his mother in that famine. In the summer the salmon run had failed, and the tribe looked forward to the winter and the coming of the caribou. Then the winter came, but with it there were no caribou. Never had the like been known, not even in the lives of the old men. But the caribou did not come, and it was the seventh year, and the rabbits had not replenished, and the dogs were naught but bundles of bones. And through the long darkness the children wailed and died, and the women, and the old men; and not one in ten of the tribe lived to meet the sun when it came back in the spring. That *was* a famine!

But he had seen times of plenty, too, when the meat spoiled on their hands, and the dogs were fat and worthless with overeating—times when they let the game go unkilled, and the women were fertile, and the lodges were cluttered with sprawling men-children and women-children. Then it was the men became high-stomached, and revived ancient quarrels, and crossed the divides to the south to kill the Pellys, and to the west that they might sit by the dead fires of the Tananas. He remembered, when a boy, during a time of plenty, when he saw a moose pulled down by the wolves. Zing-ha lay with him in the snow and watched—Zing-ha, who later became the craftiest of hunters, and who, in the end, fell through an air-hole on the Yukon. They found him, a month afterward, just as he had crawled halfway out and frozen stiff to the ice.

But the moose. Zing-ha and he had gone out that day to play at hunting after the manner of their fathers. On the bed of the creek they struck the fresh track of a moose, and with it the tracks of many wolves. "An old one," Zing-ha, who was quicker at reading the sign, said—"an old one who cannot keep up with the herd. The wolves have cut him out from his brothers, and they will never leave him." And it was so. It was their way. By day and by night, never resting, snarling on his heels, snapping at his nose, they would stay by him to the end. How Zing-ha and he felt the blood-lust quicken! The finish would be a sight to see!

Eager-footed, they took the trail, and even he, Koskoosh, slow of sight and an unversed tracker, could have followed it blind, it was so wide. Hot were they on the heels of the chase, reading the grim tragedy, fresh-written, at every step. Now they came to where the moose had made a stand. Thrice the length of a grown man's body, in every direction, had the snow been stamped about and uptossed. In the midst were the deep impressions of the splay-hoofed game, and all about, everywhere, were the lighter footmarks of the wolves. Some, while their brothers harried the kill, had lain to one side and rested. The full-stretched impress of their bodies in the snow was as perfect as though made the moment before. One wolf had been caught in a wild lunge of the maddened victim and trampled to death. A few bones, well picked, bore witness.

Again, they ceased the uplift of their snowshoes at a second stand. Here the great animal had fought desperately. Twice had he been dragged down, as the snow attested, and twice had he shaken his assailants clear and gained footing once more. He had done his task long since, but none the less was life dear to him. Zing-ha said it was a strange thing, a moose once down to get free again; but this one certainly had. The shaman would see signs and wonders in this when they told him.

And yet again, they come to where the moose had made to mount the bank and gain the timber. But his foes had laid on from behind, till he reared and fell back upon them, crushing two deep into the snow. It was plain the kill was at hand, for their brothers had left them untouched. Two more stands were hurried past, brief in time-length and very close together. The trail was red now, and the clean stride of the great beast had grown short and slovenly. Then they heard the first sounds of the battle—not the full-throated chorus of the chase, but the short, snappy bark which spoke of close quarters and teeth to flesh. Crawling up the wind, Zing-ha bellied it through the snow, and with him crept he, Koskoosh, who was to be chief of the tribesmen in the years to come. Together they shoved aside the under branches of a young spruce and peered forth. It was the end they saw.

The picture, like all of youth's impressions, was still strong with him, and his dim eyes watched the end played out as vividly as in that far-off time. Koskoosh marvelled at this, for in the days which followed, when he was a leader of men and a head of councillors, he had done great deeds and made his name a curse in the mouths of the Pellys, to say naught of the strange white man he had killed, knife to knife, in open fight.

For long he pondered on the days of his youth, till the fire died down and the frost bit deeper. He replenished it with two sticks this time, and gauged his grip on life by what remained. If Sit-cum-to-ha had only remembered her grandfather, and gathered a larger armful, his hours would have been longer. It would have been easy. But she was ever a careless child, and honored not her ancestors from the time the Beaver, son of the son of Zing-ha, first cast eyes upon her. Well, what mattered it? Had he not done likewise in his own quick youth? For a while he listened to the silence. Perhaps the heart of his son might soften, and he would come back with the dogs to take his old father on with the tribe to where the caribou ran thick and the fat hung heavy upon them.

He strained his ears, his restless brain for the moment stilled. Not a stir, nothing. He alone took breath in the midst of the great silence. It was very lonely. Hark! What was that? A chill passed over his body. The familiar, long-drawn howl broke the void, and it was close at hand. Then on his darkened eyes was projected the vision of the moose—the old bull moose—the torn flanks and bloody sides, the riddled mane, and the great branching horns, down low and tossing to the last. He saw the flashing forms of gray, the gleaming eyes, the lolling tongues, the slavered fangs. And he saw the inexorable circle close in till it became a dark point in the midst of the stamped snow.

A cold muzzle thrust against his cheek, and at its touch his soul leaped back to the present. His hand shot into the fire and dragged out a burning faggot. Overcome for the nonce by his hereditary fear of man, the brute retreated, raising a prolonged call to his brothers; and greedily they answered, till a ring of crouching, jaw-slobbered gray was stretched round about. The old man listened to the drawing in of this circle. He waved his brand wildly, and sniffs turned to snarls; but the panting brutes refused to scatter. Now one wormed his chest forward, dragging his haunches after, now a second, now a third; but never a one drew back. Why should he cling to life? he asked, and dropped the blazing stick into the snow. It sizzled and went out. The circle grunted uneasily, but held its own. Again he saw the last stand of the old bull moose, and Koskoosh dropped his head wearily upon his knees. What did it matter after all? Was it not the law of life?

1901, 1902

POETRY IN
TRANSITION

William Vaughn Moody
Edwin Arlington Robinson
Edgar Lee Masters

Paul Laurence Dunbar
James Weldon Johnson
Adelaide Crapsey

"You won't find much in the way of natural description. There is very little tinkling water, and there is not a red-bellied robin in the whole collection. When it comes to 'nightingales and roses,' I am not 'in it,' nor have I the smallest desire to be. I sing, in my own particular manner, of heaven and hell and now and then of material things (supposing they exist) of a more prosy connotation than those generally admitted into the domain of metre. In short I write whatever I think is appropriate to the subject and let tradition go to the deuce."

Edwin Arlington Robinson, in a letter of 1896 referring to his first book of poems,
The Torrent and the Night Before (1896)

718

WILLIAM VAUGHN MOODY
(1869–1910)

In the first decade of the twentieth century, William Vaughn Moody was the most prominent and promising poet to come on the American scene. Although he carried the literary baggage of the nineteenth century with him in a style identifiably traditional, at the same time he introduced into his poems an ironic tone or sardonic thrust identifiably modern (or "pre-modern"). His artfully controlled indignation in "On a Soldier Fallen in the Philippines" at America's imperialistic moves to put down an insurrection in the Philippines introduces irony and historical contrast in much the way T. S. Eliot and Ezra Pound would use them later, and portrays an America whose "evil days draw near / When the nation, robed in gloom, / With its faithless past shall strive."

Moody was born and brought up in Indiana. His father died in 1886, when Moody was seventeen. In spite of the breaking up of the family, Moody found his way to Harvard in 1889 and completed his studies in three years. While there, he became an editor of the *Harvard Monthly* and associated with a group of students, including Robert Herrick and George Santayana, who would go on to become well-known writers. Following his graduation, Moody took an M.A. in English at Harvard while serving as an assistant in the department.

In 1895, Moody was appointed instructor in English at the newly established University of Chicago, where he remained for seven years. He took a year off in 1899–1900 to write poetry, publishing *The Masque of Judgment*, a verse drama, in 1900, and a book of *Poems* in 1901. As his interest in producing poems and plays grew, he longed for more time to devote to writing. In collaboration with his colleague at Chicago, Robert Morss Lovett, Moody published *A History of English Literature* (1902) — a textbook that provided the income that freed him from the classroom.

In the few years remaining to him, Moody produced an impressive body of work and established for himself a considerable literary reputation. He had his first dramatic success with a prose drama, *The Great Divide*, produced in 1906 (turned into a successful film in 1929). This was followed by *The Faith Healer*, produced in 1909 — a critical but not a popular success. He proved himself best as a poet not in the short lyric but in the longer poem, often meditative in nature, embodying passionate feelings about a personal or public issue — as in the dramatic monologue "The Menagerie" (1910), a wry and witty comment on the notion of "survival of the fittest" attributed to Darwin's theory of evolution.

Moody's death in 1910 cut him off in mid-career. Although he dominated the century's first decade, he did not live to see the American poetic renaissance that would, after taking note of the direction in which he pointed, develop momentum in the century's second decade — soon to eclipse those transitional figures left in a rapidly receding past.

ADDITIONAL READING

Some Letters of William Vaughn Moody, ed. Daniel Gregory Mason, 1913; *Selected Poems of William Vaughn Moody*, ed. Robert Morss Lovett, 1931; *Letters to Harriet by William Vaughn Moody*, ed. Percy MacKaye, 1935.

David D. Henry, *William Vaughn Moody: A Study*, 1934; Martin Halpern, *William Vaughn Moody*, 1964; Maurice F. Brown, *Estranging Dawn: The Life and Works of William Vaughn Moody*, 1973.

TEXT

The Poems and Plays of William Vaughn Moody, 2 vols., ed. John M. Manly, 1912.

On a Soldier Fallen in the Philippines[1]

Streets of the roaring town,
Hush for him, hush, be still!
He comes, who was stricken down
Doing the word of our will.
Hush! Let him have his state,   5
Give him his soldier's crown.
The grists of trade can wait
Their grinding at the mill,
But he cannot wait for his honor, now the trumpet has been blown;
Wreathe pride now for his granite brow, lay love on his breast of stone.   10

Toll! Let the great bells toll
Till the clashing air is dim.
Did we wrong this parted soul?
We will make up it to him.
Toll! Let him never guess   15
What work we set him to.
Laurel, laurel, yes;
He did what we bade him do.
Praise, and never a whispered hint but the fight he fought was good;
Never a word that the blood on his sword was his country's own heart's-
    blood.   20

A flag for the soldier's bier
Who dies that his land may live;
O, banners, banners here,
That he doubt not nor misgive!
That he heed not from the tomb   25
The evil days draw near
When the nation, robed in gloom,
With its faithless past shall strive.
Let him never dream that his bullet's scream went wide of its island mark,
Home to the heart of his darling land where she stumbled and sinned in the
    dark.   30

1901

---

[1]In the Spanish-American War (1898) the United States pushed Spain out of Cuba and the Philippine Islands, replacing Spanish dominance or control with its own. Moody was one of many Americans who criticized what they considered the imperialistic and militaristic moves of the United States to extend its power and protect its economic interests (especially the sugar industry in Cuba). "On a Soldier Fallen in the Philippines" reflects Moody's bitter opposition to American imperialism.

The Menagerie[1]

Thank God my brain is not inclined to cut
Such capers every day! I'm just about
Mellow, but then—There goes the tent-flap shut.
Rain's in the wind. I thought so: every snout
Was twitching when the keeper turned me out.   5

That screaming parrot makes my blood run cold.
Gabriel's trump![2] the big bull elephant
Squeals "Rain!" to the parched herd. The monkeys scold,
And jabber that it's rain water they want.
(It makes me sick to see a monkey pant.)   10

I'll foot it home, to try and make believe
I'm sober. After this I stick to beer,
And drop the circus when the sane folks leave.
A man's a fool to look at things too near:
They look back, and begin to cut up queer.   15

Beasts do, at any rate; especially
Wild devils caged. They have the coolest way
Of being something else than what you see:
You pass a sleek young zebra nosing hay,
A nylghau[3] looking bored and distingué,[4]—   20

And think you've seen a donkey and a bird.
Not on your life! Just glance back, if you dare.
The zebra chews, the nylghau has n't stirred;
But something's happened, Heaven knows what or where
To freeze your scalp and pompadour your hair.   25

I'm not precisely an æolian lute[5]
Hung in the wandering winds of sentiment,
But drown me if the ugliest, meanest brute
Grunting and fretting in that sultry tent
Did n't just floor me with embarrassment!   30

'T was like a thunder-clap from out the clear,—
One minute they were circus beasts, some grand,
Some ugly, some amusing, and some queer:
Rival attractions to the hobo band,
The flying jenny,[6] and the peanut stand.   35

---

[1] "The Menagerie" is a dramatic monologue in which the speaker, "A little man in trousers, slightly jagged," contemplates the perplexing meaning of Darwin's theory of evolution as it has been interpreted to mean the "survival of the fittest."

[2] The trumpet blast of the archangel Gabriel, according to tradition, will announce Christ's return and the resurrection of the dead.

[3] Indian antelope.

[4] Distinguished.

[5] Usually "aeolian harp," a stringed instrument played by the wind (after Aeolus, Greek god of the winds).

[6] Merry-go-round.

Next minute they were old hearth-mates of mine!
Lost people, eyeing me with such a stare!
Patient, satiric, devilish, divine;
A gaze of hopeless envy, squalid care,
Hatred, and thwarted love, and dim despair.   40

Within my blood my ancient kindred spoke,—
Grotesque and monstrous voices, heard afar
Down ocean caves when behemoth[7] awoke,
Or through fern forests roared the plesiosaur[8]
Locked with the giant-bat in ghastly war.   45

And suddenly, as in a flash of light,
I saw great Nature working out her plan;
Through all her shapes from mastodon to mite
Forever groping, testing, passing on
To find at last the shape and soul of Man.   50

Till in the fullness of accomplished time,
Comes brother Forepaugh,[9] upon business bent,
Tracks her through frozen and through torrid clime,
And shows us, neatly labeled in a tent,
The stages of her huge experiment;   55

Blabbing aloud her shy and reticent hours;
Dragging to light her blinking, slothful moods;
Publishing fretful seasons when her powers
Worked wild and sullen in her solitudes,
Or when her mordant laughter shook the woods.   60

Here, round about me, were her vagrant births;
Sick dreams she had, fierce projects she essayed;
Her qualms, her fiery prides, her crazy mirths;
The troublings of her spirit as she strayed,
Cringed, gloated, mocked, was lordly, was afraid,   65

On that long road she went to seek mankind;
Here were the darkling coverts that she beat
To find the Hider she was sent to find;
Here the distracted footprints of her feet
Whereby her soul's Desire she came to greet.   70

But why should they, her botch-work, turn about
And stare disdain at me, her finished job?
Why was the place one vast suspended shout
Of laughter? Why did all the daylight throb
With soundless guffaw and dumb-stricken sob?   75

Helpless I stood among those awful cages;
The beasts were walking loose, and I was bagged!
I, I, last product of the toiling ages,
Goal of heroic feet that never lagged,—
A little man in trousers, slightly jagged.[10]   80

---

[7]The great beast, possibly a hippopotamus, described by God   [9]Adam Forepaugh (1831–1890), American circus proprietor.
to Job (Job 40:15–24).   [10]Drunk.
[8]Large, long-necked marine reptile of the dinosaur age.

Deliver me from such another jury!
The Judgment-day will be a picnic to 't.
Their satire was more dreadful than their fury,
And worst of all was just a kind of brute
Disgust, and giving up, and sinking mute.   85

Survival of the fittest, adaptation,
And all their other evolution terms,
Seem to omit one small consideration,
To wit, that tumblebugs and angleworms
Have souls: there's soul in everything that squirms.   90

And souls are restless, plagued, impatient things,
All dream and unaccountable desire;
Crawling, but pestered with the thought of wings;
Spreading through every inch of earth's old mire
Mystical hanker after something higher.   95

Wishes *are* horses,[11] as I understand.
I guess a wistful polyp that has strokes
Of feeling faint to gallivant on land
Will come to be a scandal to his folks;
Legs he will sprout, in spite of threats and jokes.   100

And at the core of every life that crawls
Or runs or flies or swims or vegetates —
Churning the mammoth's heart-blood, in the galls
Of shark and tiger planting gorgeous hates,
Lighting the love of eagles for their mates;   105

Yes, in the dim brain of the jellied fish
That is and is not living — moved and stirred
From the beginning a mysterious wish,
A vision, a command, a fatal Word:
The name of Man was uttered, and they heard.   110

Upward along the æons of old war
They sought him: wing and shank-bone, claw and bill
Were fashioned and rejected; wide and far
They roamed the twilight jungles of their will;
But still they sought him, and desired him still.   115

Man they desired, but mind you, Perfect Man,
The radiant and the loving, yet to be!
I hardly wonder, when they came to scan
The upshot of their strenuosity,
They gazed with mixed emotions upon *me*.   120

Well, my advice to you is, Face the creatures,
Or spot them sideways with your weather eye,
Just to keep tab on their expansive features;
It is n't pleasant when you're stepping high
To catch a giraffe smiling on the sly.   125

---

[11]Cf. the proverb, "If wishes were horses, beggars might ride."

If nature made you graceful, don't get gay
Back-to before the hippopotamus;
If meek and godly, find some place to play
Besides right where three mad hyenas fuss:
You may hear language that we won't discuss.   130

If you're a sweet thing in a flower-bed hat,
Or her best fellow with your tie tucked in,
Don't squander love's bright springtime girding at
An old chimpanzee with an Irish chin:
There may be hidden meaning in his grin.   135

1901

EDWIN ARLINGTON ROBINSON
(1869–1935)

In 1893, the twenty-three-year-old Edwin Arlington Robinson wrote to a friend: "The people who interest me are my close associates and the creatures of my own fancy. I have a dozen or so of the latter who have kept me company for a long time. Now I want to see them on paper, and if the fates are willing I propose to before spring. Perhaps no one will see them save myself, but there will even then be the satisfaction of knowing that I have done something." Three years later, in 1896, Robinson published his first book of poems, *The Torrent and the Night Before*, followed in 1897 by *The Children of the Night*.

Titles of the poems — "Luke Havergal," "Richard Cory," "Cliff Klingen-hagen" — indicate that Robinson got down on paper those "creatures" of his "own fancy" that had kept him company for so long. From the very beginning, the writing of poems for Robinson meant the creation of characters. Although he would go on later in his career to write long narrative poems, his reputation today rests largely on those poems of character portrayal that filled his early volumes.

Robinson was born in Head Tide, Maine, in 1869, but the family soon moved to Gardiner, Maine, where Robinson spent his boyhood. After graduation from high school, Robinson went to Harvard, but his time there was limited to two years, cut short by a sudden turn in his father's fortunes. At his father's death in 1893, Robinson was left to make his own way. He remained in Gardiner, devoting himself to writing. The Tilbury Town of Robinson's work is Gardiner transfigured by his poetic imagination.

The publication of his first two books did little to ease Robinson's plight. In 1899 he moved to New York and continued his writing, even in the face of continued economic hardship. He published a third book, *Captain Craig and Other Poems*, in 1902. President Theodore Roosevelt, at the behest of his son, read *The Children of the Night* and reviewed it favorably in 1905 in *The Outlook*, a "family magazine" of the time. This review, along with Roosevelt's appointment of Robinson to a position in the New York customs service, marked a change for the better in Robinson's fortunes. Robinson felt secure enough in 1909 to resign his position, and he dedicated his 1910 volume, *The Town Down the River*, to Roosevelt.

With the publication of *The Man Against the Sky* in 1916, Robinson's reputation was secured. In 1922, he was awarded the first of three Pulitzer Prizes for his *Collected Poems*. *The Man Who Died Twice* (1924) and *Tristram* (1927) also won Pulitzers. Robinson continued to write and publish poetry until his death in 1935. Much of his creative energy was spent in the writing of a succession of long poems, three devoted to recreating Arthurian legends (*Merlin*, 1917; *Lancelot*, 1920; and *Tristram*, 1927), and others devoted to psychoanalytical character portrayals (*Cavender's House*, 1929; *The Glory of the Nightingales*, 1930; and *Matthias at the Door*, 1931).

But now Robinson is chiefly remembered for his early portraits of the people of Tilbury Town. They are individuals often unhappy, puzzled about life, concerned about death. And they wonder how — or if — they should live their lives. The wealthy Richard Cory puts a bullet through his head. The disenchanted Miniver Cheevy scratches his head and keeps on drinking. The lonely old Mr. Flood throws himself a wild and ghostly party. Robinson's dark vision of the human plight, manifested in these and other portrayals, has made a lasting imprint on the modern reader's imagination.

ADDITIONAL READING

Collected Poems of Edwin Arlington Robinson, 1921, enlarged through 1937; *Selected Poems of Edwin Arlington Robinson*, ed. Morton D. Zabel, 1965, 1966; *Uncollected Poems and Prose of Edwin Arlington Robinson*, ed. Richard Carey, 1975; *Selected Letters of Edwin Arlington Robinson*, ed. Ridgely Torrence, 1940.

Mark Van Doren, *Edwin Arlington Robinson*, 1927; Charles Beecher Hogan, *A Bibliography of Edwin Arlington Robinson*, 1927; Herman Hagedorn, *Edwin Arlington Robinson: A Bibliography*, 1938; Estelle Kaplan, *Philosophy in the Poetry of Edwin Arlington Robinson*, 1940; Yvor Winters, *Edwin Arlington Robinson*, 1946; Emery Neff, *Edwin Arlington Robinson*, 1948, 1968; Ellsworth Barnard, *Edwin Arlington Robinson: A Critical Study*, 1952; Edwin S. Fussell, *Edwin Arlington Robinson: The Literary Background of a Traditional Poet*, 1954; Louis Cox, *E. A. Robinson*, 1962; Chard Powers Smith, *Where the Light Falls: A Portrait of Edwin Arlington Robinson*, 1965; Wallace L. Anderson, *Edwin Arlington Robinson*, 1967; Hoyt C. Franchere, *Edward Arlington Robinson*, 1968; Louis O. Coxe, *Edwin Arlington Robinson: The Life of Poetry*, 1969; Ellsworth Barnard, ed., *Appreciation of Edwin Arlington Robinson: Twenty-Eight Interpretive Essays*, 1969; Francis Murphy, *Edwin Arlington Robinson: A Collection of Critical Essays*, 1970; William White, *Edwin Arlington Robinson: A Supplementary Bibliography*, 1971; Richard Cary, ed., *Early Reception of Edwin Arlington Robinson: The First Twenty Years*, 1974; Nancy Carol Joyner, ed., *Edwin Arlington Robinson: A Reference Guide*, 1978; Harold Bloom, ed., *Edwin Arlington Robinson*, 1988.

TEXT

Collected Poems of Edwin Arlington Robinson, 1937.

Luke Havergal

Go to the western gate, Luke Havergal,
There where the vines cling crimson on the wall,
And in the twilight wait for what will come.
The leaves will whisper there of her, and some,
Like flying words, will strike you as they fall;   5
But go, and if you listen she will call.
Go to the western gate, Luke Havergal —
Luke Havergal.

No, there is not a dawn in eastern skies
To rift the fiery night that's in your eyes;   10
But there, where western glooms are gathering,
The dark will end the dark, if anything:
God slays Himself with every leaf that flies,
And hell is more than half of paradise.
No, there is not a dawn in eastern skies—   15
In eastern skies.

Out of a grave I come to tell you this,
Out of a grave I come to quench the kiss
That flames upon your forehead with a glow
That blinds you to the way that you must go.   20
Yes, there is yet one way to where she is,
Bitter, but one that faith may never miss.
Out of a grave I come to tell you this—
To tell you this.

There is the western gate, Luke Havergal,   25
There are the crimson leaves upon the wall.
Go, for the winds are tearing them away,—
Nor think to riddle the dead words they say,
Nor any more to feel them as they fall;
But go, and if you trust her she will call.   30
There is the western gate, Luke Havergal—
Luke Havergal.

1896

The Clerks

I did not think that I should find them there
When I came back again; but there they stood,
As in the days they dreamed of when young blood
Was in their cheeks and women called them fair.
Be sure, they met me with an ancient air,—   5
And yes, there was a shop-worn brotherhood
About them; but the men were just as good,
And just as human as they ever were.

And you that ache so much to be sublime,
And you that feed yourselves with your descent,   10
What comes of all your visions and your fears?
Poets and kings are but the clerks of Time,
Tiering the same dull webs of discontent,
Clipping the same sad alnage[1] of the years.

1896

---

[1] A measurement of cloth.

Richard Cory

Whenever Richard Cory went down town,
We people on the pavement looked at him:
He was a gentleman from sole to crown,
Clean favored, and imperially slim.

And he was always quietly arrayed,   5
And he was always human when he talked;
But still he fluttered pulses when he said,
"Good-morning," and he glittered when he walked.

And he was rich—yes, richer than a king—
And admirably schooled in every grace: 10
In fine, we thought that he was everything
To make us wish that we were in his place.

So on we worked, and waited for the light,
And went without the meat, and cursed the bread;
And Richard Cory, one calm summer night,   15
Went home and put a bullet through his head.

1897

Cliff Klingenhagen

Cliff Klingenhagen had me in to dine
With him one day; and after soup and meat,
And all the other things there were to eat,
Cliff took two glasses and filled one with wine
And one with wormwood. Then, without a sign   5
For me to choose at all, he took the draught
Of bitterness himself, and lightly quaffed
It off, and said the other one was mine.

And when I asked him what the deuce he meant
By doing that, he only looked at me   10
And smiled, and said it was a way of his.
And though I know the fellow, I have spent
Long time a-wondering when I shall be
As happy as Cliff Klingenhagen is.

1897

Miniver Cheevy

Miniver Cheevy, child of scorn,
    Grew lean while he assailed the seasons;
He wept that he was ever born,
    And he had reasons.

Miniver loved the days of old   5
  When swords were bright and steeds were prancing;
The vision of a warrior bold
  Would set him dancing.

Miniver sighed for what was not,
  And dreamed, and rested from his labors;   10
He dreamed of Thebes and Camelot,
  And Priam's neighbors.[1]

Miniver mourned the ripe renown
  That made so many a name so fragrant;
He mourned Romance, now on the town,   15
  And Art, a vagrant.

Miniver loved the Medici,[2]
  Albeit he had never seen one;
He would have sinned incessantly
  Could he have been one.   20

Miniver cursed the commonplace
  And eyed a khaki suit with loathing;
He missed the mediæval grace
  Of iron clothing.

Miniver scorned the gold he sought,   25
  But sore annoyed was he without it;
Miniver thought, and thought, and thought,
  And thought about it.

Miniver Cheevy, born too late,
  Scratched his head and kept on thinking;   30
Miniver coughed, and called it fate,
  And kept on drinking.

                                                              1907, 1910

For a Dead Lady

No more with overflowing light
Shall fill the eyes that now are faded,
Nor shall another's fringe with night
Their woman-hidden world as they did.
No more shall quiver down the days   5
The flowing wonder of her ways,
Whereof no language may requite
The shifting and the many-shaded.

---

[1]Thebes: ancient city depicted in Greek legend and drama; Camelot: fabled site of King Arthur's court; Priam, king of Troy, the city sacked by the Greeks during the Trojan War in Homer's *Iliad*.
[2]Renaissance family of Florence, Italy, rulers and patrons of the arts.

The grace, divine, definitive,
Clings only as a faint forestalling;   10
The laugh that love could not forgive
Is hushed, and answers to no calling;
The forehead and the little ears
Have gone where Saturn keeps the years;[1]
The breast where roses could not live   15
Has done with rising and with falling.

The beauty, shattered by the laws
That have creation in their keeping,
No longer trembles at applause,
Or over children that are sleeping;   20
And we who delve in beauty's lore
Know all that we have known before
Of what inexorable cause
Makes Time so vicious in his reaping.

1909, 1910

How Annandale Went Out

"They called it Annandale—and I was there
To flourish, to find words, and to attend:
Liar, physician, hypocrite, and friend,
I watched him; and the sight was not so fair
As one or two that I have seen elsewhere: 5
An apparatus not for me to mend—
A wreck, with hell between him and the end,
Remained of Annandale; and I was there.

"I knew the ruin as I knew the man;
So put the two together, if you can,   10
Remembering the worst you know of me.
Now view yourself as I was, on the spot—
With a slight kind of engine. Do you see?
Like this . . . You wouldn't hang me? I thought not."

1910

Eros Turannos[1]

She fears him, and will always ask
   What fated her to choose him;
She meets in his engaging mask
   All reasons to refuse him;
But what she meets and what she fears   5
Are less than are the downward years,
Drawn slowly to the foamless weirs[2]
   Of age, were she to lose him.

---

[1]Roman god identified with the Greek god of maturity,
Cronus, confused with chronos (Greek for "time").

[1]"Love, the Tyrant" (Greek).
[2]River dam.

Between a blurred sagacity
   That once had power to sound him,
And Love, that will not let him be   10
   The Judas that she found him,
Her pride assuages her almost,
As if it were alone the cost.—
He sees that he will not be lost,   15
   And waits and looks around him.

A sense of ocean and old trees
   Envelops and allures him;
Tradition, touching all he sees,
   Beguiles and reassures him;   20
And all her doubts of what he says
Are dimmed with what she knows of days—
Till even prejudice delays
   And fades, and she secures him.

The falling leaf inaugurates   25
   The reign of her confusion;
The pounding wave reverberates
   The dirge of her illusion;
And home, where passion lived and died,
Becomes a place where she can hide,   30
While all the town and harbor side
   Vibrate with her seclusion.

We tell you, tapping on our brows,
   The story as it should be,—
As if the story of a house   35
   Were told, or ever could be;
We'll have no kindly veil between
Her visions and those we have seen,—
As if we guessed what hers have been,
   Or what they are or would be.   40

Meanwhile we do no harm; for they
   That with a god have striven,
Not hearing much of what we say,
   Take what the god has given;
Though like waves breaking it may be,   45
Or like a changed familiar tree,
Or like a stairway to the sea
   Where down the blind are driven.

1914, 1916

The Mill

The miller's wife had waited long,
   The tea was cold, the fire was dead;
And there might yet be nothing wrong
   In how he went and what he said:
"There are no millers any more,"   5
   Was all that she had heard him say;
And he had lingered at the door
   So long that it seemed yesterday.

Sick with a fear that had no form
   She knew that she was there at last;   10
And in the mill there was a warm
   And mealy fragrance of the past.
What else there was would only seem
   To say again what he had meant;
And what was hanging from a beam   15
   Would not have heeded where she went.

And if she thought it followed her,
   She may have reasoned in the dark
That one way of the few there were
   Would hide her and would leave no mark: 20
Black water, smooth above the weir
   Like starry velvet in the night,
Though ruffled once, would soon appear
   The same as ever to the sight.

1919, 1920

The Dark Hills

Dark hills at evening in the west,
Where sunset hovers like a sound
Of golden horns that sang to rest
Old bones of warriors under ground,
Far now from all the bannered ways   5
Where flash the legions of the sun,
You fade—as if the last of days
Were fading, and all wars were done.

1920

Mr. Flood's Party

Old Eben Flood, climbing alone one night
Over the hill between the town below
And the forsaken upland hermitage
That held as much as he should ever know
On earth again of home, paused warily.   5
The road was his with not a native near;
And Eben, having leisure, said aloud,
For no man else in Tilbury Town to hear:

"Well, Mr. Flood, we have the harvest moon
Again, and we may not have many more;   10
The bird is on the wing, the poet says,[1]
And you and I have said it here before."

---

[1] "Come, fill the Cup, and in the fire of Spring / The Winter garment of Repentance fling: / The Bird of Time has but a little way / To fly—and Lo! the Bird is on the Wing," stanza seven of *The Rubáiyát of Omar Khayyám* (1859), translated by the English poet Edward Fitzgerald (1809–1883).

Drink to the bird." He raised up to the light
The jug that he had gone so far to fill,
And answered huskily: "Well, Mr. Flood,   15
Since you propose it, I believe I will."

Alone, as if enduring to the end
A valiant armor of scarred hopes outworn,
He stood there in the middle of the road
Like Roland's ghost winding a silent horn.[2]   20
Below him, in the town among the trees,
Where friends of other days had honored him,
A phantom salutation of the dead
Rang thinly till old Eben's eyes were dim.

Then, as a mother lays her sleeping child   25
Down tenderly, fearing it may awake,
He set the jug down slowly at his feet
With trembling care, knowing that most things break;
And only when assured that on firm earth
It stood, as the uncertain lives of men   30
Assuredly did not, he paced away,
And with his hand extended paused again:

"Well, Mr. Flood, we have not met like this
In a long time; and many a change has come
To both of us, I fear, since last it was   35
We had a drop together. Welcome home!"
Convivially returning with himself,
Again he raised the jug up to the light;
And with an acquiescent quaver said:
"Well, Mr. Flood, if you insist, I might.   40

"Only a very little, Mr. Flood—
For auld lang syne. No more, sir; that will do."
So, for the time, apparently it did,
And Eben evidently thought so too;
For soon amid the silver loneliness   45
Of night he lifted up his voice and sang,
Secure, with only two moons listening,
Until the whole harmonious landscape rang—

"For auld lang syne." The weary throat gave out,
The last word wavered, and the song was done.   50
He raised again the jug regretfully
And shook his head, and was again alone.
There was not much that was ahead of him,
And there was nothing in the town below—
Where strangers would have shut the many doors   55
That many friends had opened long ago.

                                                          1920

---

[2]The proud hero of the eleventh-century French romance
Chanson de Roland refused to sound his horn for help until,
surrounded, his men dead, he blew so mightily that the veins
in his neck burst and he died.

The Sheaves

Where long the shadows of the wind had rolled,
Green wheat was yielding to the change assigned;
And as by some vast magic undivined
The world was turning slowly into gold.
Like nothing that was ever bought or sold   5
It waited there, the body and the mind;
And with a mighty meaning of a kind
That tells the more the more it is not told.

So in a land where all days are not fair,
Fair days went on till on another day   10
A thousand golden sheaves were lying there,
Shining and still, but not for long to stay—
As if a thousand girls with golden hair
Might rise from where they slept and go away.

1923, 1925

Karma[1]

Christmas was in the air and all was well
With him, but for a few confusing flaws
In divers of God's images. Because
A friend of his would neither buy nor sell,
Was he to answer for the axe that fell?   5
He pondered; and the reason for it was,
Partly, a slowly freezing Santa Claus
Upon the corner, with his beard and bell.

Acknowledging an improvident surprise,
He magnified a fancy that he wished   10
The friend whom he had wrecked were here again.
Not sure of that, he found a compromise;
And from the fulness of his heart he fished
A dime for Jesus who had died for men.

1923, 1925

New England[1]

Here where the wind is always north-north-east
And children learn to walk on frozen toes,
Wonder begets an envy of all those
Who boil elsewhere with such a lyric yeast
Of love that you will hear them at a feast   5
Where demons would appeal for some repose,
Still clamoring where the chalice overflows
And crying wildest who have drunk the least.

---

[1]In Hinduism and Buddhism, the sum of one's actions in one stage of existence that determines one's fate in the next.
[1]Responding to a critic charging him with disloyalty, Robinson said that this sonnet was meant as "an oblique attack upon all those who are forever throwing dead cats at New England for its alleged emotional and moral frigidity."

Passion is here a soilure[2] of the wits,
We're told, and Love a cross for them to bear;   10
Joy shivers in the corner where she knits
And Conscience always has the rocking-chair,
Cheerful as when she tortured into fits
The first cat that was ever killed by Care.[3]

1923, 1925

EDGAR LEE MASTERS
(1869–1950)

A book of poems entitled *Spoon River Anthology* appeared in 1915. It brought together a series of "epitaphs," or speeches from the grave, of the inhabitants of Spoon River, Illinois, now "asleep" in the cemetery on a hill outside town. The speeches revealed the dark secrets of the lonely lives of Spoon River citizens — the hatred of husband and wife, the hostility between banker and worker, the frustration, unhappiness, or anguish that marked most of the lives. The book created a sensation, angering those who claimed to recognize their portraits, fascinating others by its scandalous revelations of small town American life. By 1940 it had seen some seventy editions and translation into eight languages. Its influence is apparent on such later important works as Sherwood Anderson's *Winesburg, Ohio* (1919), Thornton Wilder's *Our Town* (1938), and Dylan Thomas's *Under Milkwood* (1959). The author was Edgar Lee Masters, a forty-six-year-old lawyer practicing in Chicago. His book was success enough to enable him to quit the law and devote himself wholly to writing. Although he was to write more than fifty books, never again was he to achieve the critical acclaim brought by *Spoon River Anthology*.

Masters was born in Kansas, but within a year of his birth, his parents returned to their farm in Illinois because the father was unsuccessful in establishing his law practice in Kansas. Soon, however, Hardin Masters turned again to law, first in Petersburg, Illinois, near the Sangamon River, and later in Lewistown, near the Spoon River. Spoon River was (and is) indeed a river, but the town of Spoon River was a creation of Edgar Lee Masters's imagination out of his boyhood memories of Illinois small towns — particularly Petersburg and Lewistown.

Masters had only one year at Knox College and was then taken in by his father to "read law." He was admitted to the bar in 1891 and was practicing law with the famed Clarence Darrow in the early 1900s. Gradually disillusion set in for a profession which had been his choice. He had always been interested in literature and he turned more and more to this interest, publishing several plays and volumes of poetry, none of them attracting much attention.

Masters had been submitting his poems to *Reedy's Mirror* in St. Louis; in 1909, the editor William Marion Reedy called his attention to J. W. Mackail's *Selected*

---

[2]Soiling.
[3]A reference to the proverbial "Let care kill a cat," expressed by merrymakers, as in *Shirburn Ballads* (*c.* 1600), XXI, stanza 2.

Epigrams from the Greek Anthology. This work contained a sequence of short poems, interconnected through cross-references, portraying speakers talking about their lives from beyond the grave. *The Greek Anthology* served as the model for Masters's Spoon River poems, which appeared first in *Reedy's Mirror* in 1914, under the pseudonym Webster Ford. Publication of the book in 1915 brought Masters immediate recognition, and his name began to be linked with other Chicago writers—Carl Sandburg, Vachel Lindsay, Sherwood Anderson—in a "Chicago Literary Renaissance."

With the success of *Spoon River Anthology*, Masters extricated himself from his law practice and an unhappy marriage, and concentrated his energies on his literary career. In 1920 he moved to New York and in the 1930s settled into the Chelsea Hotel, then a place of faded elegance. He published additional books of poetry, a sequence of autobiographical novels, and biographical studies of Lincoln, Vachel Lindsay, Walt Whitman, and Mark Twain. Of his later work, perhaps the most interesting is his autobiography, *Across Spoon River* (1936). When he died in 1950, he was remembered primarily as the author of one great book—*Spoon River Anthology*.

ADDITIONAL READING

Lois Harley, *Spoon River Revisited*, 1963; John T. Flanagan, *The Spoon River Poet and His Critics*, 1974; Hardin Wallace Masters, *Edgar Lee Masters: A Biographical Sketchbook about a Famous American Author*, 1978; Ronald Primeau, *Beyond Spoon River: The Legacy of Edgar Lee Masters*, 1981; Hilary Masters, *Last Stands: Notes from Memory*, 1982; John H. Wrenn and Margaret M. Wrenn, *Edgar Lee Masters*, 1983.

TEXT

Spoon River Anthology, 1915.

from Spoon River Anthology

Cassius Hueffer

They have chiseled on my stone the words:
"His life was gentle, and the elements so mixed in him
That nature might stand up and say to all the world,
This was a man."[1]
Those who knew me smile   5
As they read this empty rhetoric.

My epitaph should have been:
"Life was not gentle to him,
And the elements so mixed in him
That he made warfare on life,   10
In the which he was slain."

---

[1] Said of Brutus in Shakespeare's *Julius Caesar*, V. v. 73–75.

While I lived I could not cope with slanderous tongues,
Now that I am dead I must submit to an epitaph
Graven by a fool!

1914, 1915

Amanda Barker

Henry got me with child,
Knowing that I could not bring forth life
Without losing my own.
In my youth therefore I entered the portals of dust.
Traveler, it is believed in the village where I lived   5
That Henry loved me with a husband's love,
But I proclaim from the dust
That he slew me to gratify his hatred.

1914, 1915

Frank Drummer

Out of a cell into this darkened space —
The end at twenty-five!
My tongue could not speak what stirred within me,
And the village thought me a fool.
Yet at the start there was a clear vision,   5
A high and urgent purpose in my soul
Which drove me on trying to memorize
The Encyclopædia Britannica!

1914, 1915

Doc Hill

I went up and down the streets
Here and there by day and night,
Through all hours of the night caring for the poor who were sick.
Do you know why?
My wife hated me, my son went to the dogs.   5
And I turned to the people and poured out my love to them.
Sweet it was to see the crowds about the lawns on the day of my funeral,
And hear them murmur their love and sorrow.
But oh, dear God, my soul trembled — scarcely able
To hold to the railing of the new life   10
When I saw Em Stanton behind the oak tree
At the grave,
Hiding herself, and her grief!

1914, 1915

Margaret Fuller[1] Slack

I would have been as great as George Eliot[2]
But for an untoward fate.
For look at the photograph of me made by Peniwit,[3]
Chin resting on hand, and deep-set eyes —
Gray, too, and far-searching.   5
But there was the old, old problem:
Should it be celibacy, matrimony or unchastity?
Then John Slack, the rich druggist, wooed me,
Luring me with the promise of leisure for my novel,
And I married him, giving birth to eight children,   10
And had no time to write.
It was all over with me, anyway,
When I ran the needle in my hand
While washing the baby's things,
And died from lock-jaw, an ironical death.   15
Hear me, ambitious souls,
Sex is the curse of life!

1914, 1915

Lucinda Matlock[1]

I went to the dances at Chandlerville,
And played snap-out at Winchester.
One time we changed partners,
Driving home in the moonlight of middle June,
And then I found Davis.   5
We were married and lived together for seventy years,
Enjoying, working, raising the twelve children,
Eight of whom we lost
Ere I had reached the age of sixty.
I spun, I wove, I kept the house, I nursed the sick,   10
I made the garden, and for holiday
Rambled over the fields where sang the larks,
And by Spoon River gathering many a shell,
And many a flower and medicinal weed —
Shouting to the wooded hills, singing to the green valleys.
At ninety-six I had lived enough, that is all,   15
And passed to a sweet repose.
What is this I hear of sorrow and weariness,
Anger, discontent and drooping hopes?
Degenerate sons and daughters,   20
Life is too strong for you —
It takes life to love Life.

1914, 1915

[1]American editor, journalist, critic, author of the feminist *Woman in the Nineteenth Century* (1845), Margaret Fuller (1810–1850) was noted as an unorthodox, emancipated intellectual.
[2]Pen name of Mary Ann Evans (1819–1880), English novelist.

[3]Such a photograph of Fuller exists, but "Peniwit" is a Spoon River character.
[1]Based on the poet's paternal grandmother, Lucinda Masters, wife of Squire Davis Masters. Her mother's surname was Matlock.

The Village Atheist

Ye young debaters over the doctrine
Of the soul's immortality,
I who lie here was the village atheist,
Talkative, contentious, versed in the arguments
Of the infidels.   5
But through a long sickness
Coughing myself to death
I read the *Upanishads*[1] and the poetry of Jesus.
And they lighted a torch of hope and intuition
And desire which the Shadow,   10
Leading me swiftly through the caverns of darkness,
Could not extinguish.
Listen to me, ye who live in the senses
And think through the senses only:
Immortality is not a gift,   15
Immortality is an achievement;
And only those who strive mightily
Shall possess it.

1914, 1915

PAUL LAURENCE DUNBAR
(1872–1906)

Paul Laurence Dunbar's father was born a slave in Kentucky and escaped to Canada before the Civil War. In Canada he taught himself to read and returned during the war to enlist in the Union Army. He became a plasterer in Dayton, Ohio, after the war, and it was there that his son was born. The father died when his son was only twelve years old.

Dunbar was popular enough in high school to be elected president of the literary society and talented enough to edit the school magazine. But after graduation the only job he could find was that of elevator operator, earning four dollars a week. He began to publish poems in the newspapers and financed publication of his first volume of poetry, *Oak and Ivy*, in 1893. He sold copies on the elevator to pay off his debt.

His book attracted attention, and encouraged some benefactors to help in the publication of a second volume, *Majors and Minors*, in 1895. A copy found its way into the hands of William Dean Howells, who wrote an enthusiastic review of it in 1896 in *Harper's Weekly*. This same year, Dunbar published his third volume of verse with Dodd, Mead & Co., *Lyrics of Lowly Life*, with an Introduction by Howells. The work brought him considerable fame, and he became a successful lecturer and public reader of his poems, touring England in 1897. A bout with pneumonia and tuberculosis in 1899 did not deter him from writing. Although he continued to write lyric poems, more and more he turned to stories and

---

[1]Treatise on the nature of man and the universe, part of the ancient, sacred Vedic books of the Hindus.

novels, publishing some six volumes from 1900 until his death. He died in Dayton of tuberculosis in 1906.

His most popular poems were his dialect poems. But as critics Richard A. Long and Eugenia W. Collier have asserted, the "subject matter of the dialect poems is the simple pleasures and sorrows of a childlike people who could be comical or pathetic—seldom anything else." It was this dimension of black dialect poetry that James Weldon Johnson would seek to purge and purify when he came later to write the poetic sermons in *God's Trombones*.

Dunbar himself felt an uneasiness with his dialect poems, as well as puzzlement at their popularity. He wrote in "The Poet":

> He sang of love when earth was young,
>   And love, itself, was in his lays.
>   But ah, the world, it turned to praise
> A jingle in a broken tongue.

Whatever the flaws of his dialect poetry, Dunbar stands at the beginning of a vital modern tradition in black American poetry. And many of his lines—such as "I know why the caged bird sings"—while giving voice to the black experience in America, speak as well to aspects of the human condition shared by all.

ADDITIONAL READING

The Paul Laurence Dunbar Reader, ed. Jay Martin and Gossie H. Hudson, 1975.

Lida Keck Wiggins, *The Life and Works of Paul Laurence Dunbar*, 1907; Benjamin Brawley, *Paul Laurence Dunbar: Poet of His People*, 1936; Victor Lawson, *Dunbar Critically Examined*, 1941; Virginia Cunningham, *Paul Laurence Dunbar and His Song*, 1947, 1969; Addison Gayle, Jr., *Oak and Ivy: A Biography of Paul Laurence Dunbar*, 1971; E. W. Metcalf, Jr., *Paul Laurence Dunbar: A Bibliography*, 1975; Jay Martin, ed., *A Singer in the Dawn: Reinterpretations of Paul Laurence Dunbar*, 1975; Peter Revell, *Paul Laurence Dunbar*, 1979.

TEXT

The Complete Poems of Paul Laurence Dunbar, 1913.

Sympathy

I know what the caged bird feels, alas!
    When the sun is bright on the upland slopes;
When the wind stirs soft through the springing grass,
And the river flows like a stream of glass;
    When the first bird sings and the first bud opes,   5
And the faint perfume from its chalice steals—
I know what the caged bird feels!

I know why the caged bird beats his wing
    Till its blood is red on the cruel bars;
For he must fly back to his perch and cling   10
When he fain would be on the bough a-swing;
    And a pain still throbs in the old, old scars
And they pulse again with a keener sting—
I know why he beats his wing!

I know why the caged bird sings, ah me,   15
   When his wing is bruised and his bosom sore,—
When he beats his bars and he would be free;
It is not a carol of joy or glee,
   But a prayer that he sends from his heart's deep core,
But a plea, that upward to Heaven he flings—   20
I know why the caged bird sings!

                                       1893

We Wear the Mask

We wear the mask that grins and lies,
It hides our cheeks and shades our eyes,—
This debt we pay to human guile;
With torn and bleeding hearts we smile,
And mouth with myriad subtleties.   5

Why should the world be overwise,
In counting all our tears and sighs?
Nay, let them only see us, while
    We wear the mask.

We smile, but, O great Christ, our cries   10
To thee from tortured souls arise.
We sing, but oh the clay is vile
Beneath our feet, and long the mile;
But let the world dream otherwise,
    We wear the mask!   15

                                       1895

A Death Song

Lay me down beneaf de willers in de grass,
Whah de branch'll go a-singin' as it pass.
   An' w'en I's a-layin' low,
   I kin hyeah it as it go
Singin', "Sleep, my honey, tek yo' res' at las'."   5

Lay me nigh to whah hit meks a little pool,
An' de watah stan's so quiet lak an' cool,
   Whah de little birds in spring,
   Ust to come an' drink an' sing,
An' de chillen waded on dey way to school.   10

Let me settle w'en my shouldahs draps dey load
Nigh enough to hyeah de noises in de road;
   Fu' I t'ink de las' long res'
   Gwine to soothe my sperrit bes'
Ef I's layin' 'mong de t'ings I's allus knowed.   15

                                       1899

Life's Tragedy

It may be misery not to sing at all
   And to go silent through the brimming day.
It may be sorrow never to be loved,
   But deeper griefs than these beset the way.

To have come near to sing the perfect song   5
   And only by a half-tone lost the key,
There is the potent sorrow, there the grief,
   The pale, sad staring of life's tragedy.

To have just missed the perfect love,
   Not the hot passion of untempered youth,   10
But that which lays aside its vanity
   And gives thee, for thy trusting worship, truth—

This, this it is to be accursed indeed;
   For if we mortals love, or if we sing,
We count our joys not by the things we have,   15
   But by what kept us from the perfect thing.

1902

JAMES WELDON JOHNSON
(1871–1938)

In 1918, while travelling in the West for the National Society for the Advancement of Colored People (NAACP), the forty-seven-year-old black novelist, essayist, and poet James Weldon Johnson happened into one of the black churches just in time to hear a black preacher "handsome in his gigantic proportions." The congregation was bored and sleepy until the preacher began to deliver a sermon that began with the creation of the world and ended with the Judgment Day.

The effect on the congregation—and Johnson—was electrifying: "He intoned, he moaned, he pleaded—he blared, he crashed, he thundered. A woman sprang to her feet, uttered a piercing scream, threw her handbag to the pulpit, striking the preacher full in the chest, whirled round several times, and fainted. The congregation reached a state of ecstasy. I was fascinated by this exhibition; moreover, something primordial in me was stirred. Before the preacher finished, I took a slip of paper from my pocket and somewhat surreptitiously jotted down some ideas. . . ." The result was Johnson's poetic masterpiece, "The Creation," published two years later in *The Freeman*. The poem would be put together with six additional such sermons and published in 1927 as *God's Trombones: Seven Negro Sermons in Verse*.

Johnson decided, in creating the sermons, to discard "conventionalized Negro dialect" because it was not his intention "to paint the picturesque or comic aspects of the old-time Negro preacher" but rather "to interpret what was in his mind, to express, if possible, the dream to which, despite limitations, he strove to give utterance." He chose, therefore, a "loose rhythmic instead of a strict metric form" that was adaptable to the "characteristic syncopations of the primitive material."

God's Trombones marked a turning in Johnson's career, which had been very productive up to its appearance. Born in Jacksonville, Florida, to educated parents, he was raised in a secure and cultured environment. He attended Atlanta University, graduating in 1894. He taught summer school in Georgia's cotton belt and saw firsthand the hard life lived by blacks. After teaching for a time, he read law and was admitted to the Florida bar in 1897. He next discovered his talent for writing songs and teamed up with his brother J. Rosamond Johnson in New York to write the lyrics for over 200 songs, among them "Under the Bamboo Tree" (later quoted in T. S. Eliot's "Sweeney Agonistes") and "Lift Every Voice and Sing," known as the "Black National Anthem."

As a reward for supporting Theodore Roosevelt for reelection as president in 1904, Johnson entered the consular service, holding posts in Venezuela and Nicaragua from 1906 to 1912. He published his first novel, *The Autobiography of an Ex-Colored Man*, in 1912, and his first volume of poetry, *Fifty Years and Other Poems*, in 1917. From 1916 to 1930, Johnson served as field secretary (later, executive secretary) of the NAACP, taking an activist role in defending blacks against the violence of white racism.

During this period, Johnson continued his writing. He edited *The Book of American Negro Poetry* in 1922 and two volumes of Negro spirituals in 1925 and 1926. The first of these, published by the major publishing house of Harcourt, Brace, and Co., was a key volume in initiating the Harlem Renaissance, bringing to black writers themselves a consciousness of working out of a rich literary tradition and opening the possibility of bringing that tradition to a full flowering in the 1920s. Associated with the Harlem Renaissance would be such writers as Countee Cullen, Langston Hughes, and Jean Toomer. Johnson's own *God's Trombones* was counted as an important work of the movement. In 1931, Johnson revised his *Book of American Negro Poetry* to include the work of the Harlem Renaissance writers.

Johnson wrote a personal history of New York, *Black Manhattan* (1930), which is particularly valuable in its account of black theater and drama. And he published his autobiography, *Along This Way*, in 1933. By this time he had become a professor of creative literature at Fisk University. A series of his lectures was published in 1934 as *Negro Americans, What Now?* When he died in an automobile accident in 1938, his race—and America—was deprived of one of its most eloquent voices of reason as well as one of its most versatile and talented writers.

ADDITIONAL READING

Stephen H. Bronz, *Roots of Negro Racial Consciousness, The 1920's: Three Harlem Renaissance Authors*, 1964; Ellen Terry, *Young Jim: The Early Years of James Weldon Johnson*, 1967; Eugene Levy, *James Weldon Johnson: Black Leader, Black Voice*, 1973; Robert Fleming, *James Weldon Johnson and Arna Wendell Bontemps: A Reference Guide*, 1978; Robert E. Fleming, *James Weldon Johnson*, 1987.

TEXTS

"We to America" from *Saint Peter Relates an Incident: Selected Poems*, 1935; "The Creation" from *God's Trombones*, 1927.

We to America[1]

How would you have us, as we are—
Or sinking 'neath the load we bear?
Our eyes fixed forward on a star—
Or gazing empty at despair?

Rising or falling? Men or things?   5
With dragging pace or footsteps fleet?
Strong, willing sinews in your wings?
Or tightening chains about your feet?

1914   *1917*

from # God's Trombones[1]

The Creation

And God stepped out on space,
And he looked around and said:
I'm lonely—
I'll make me a world.

And far as the eye of God could see   5
Darkness covered everything,
Blacker than a hundred midnights
Down in a cypress swamp.

Then God smiled,
And the light broke,   10
And the darkness rolled up on one side,
And the light stood shining on the other,
And God said: That's good!

Then God reached out and took the light in his hands,
And God rolled the light around in his hands   15
Until he made the sun;
And he set that sun a-blazing in the heavens.
And the light that was left from making the sun
God gathered it up in a shining ball

---

[1]This poem was first published in *The Crisis* 15 (1917) as "A Negro to America."

[1]In the Preface to *God's Trombones: Seven Negro Sermons in Verse* (1927), Johnson discusses the importance and power of the "old-time Negro preacher" and the sermons, vaguely remembered from his childhood, which he planned to make into poetry. The "immediate stimulus" came in the summer of 1918 when he heard a famed black evangelist preach: "He started intoning the old folk-sermon that begins with the creation of the world and ends with Judgement Day. . . . He strode the pulpit up and down in what was actually a very rhythmic dance, and he brought into play the full gamut of his wonderful voice, a voice—what shall I say?—not of an organ or a trumpet, but rather of a trombone, the instrument possessing above all others the power to express the wide and varied range of emotions encompassed by the human voice—and with greater amplitude." Johnson was moved to write "The Creation," first published in the *Freeman*, 1920. Cf. Genesis 1 and 2.

And flung it against the darkness,   20
Spangling the night with the moon and stars.
Then down between
The darkness and the light
He hurled the world;
And God said: That's good!   25

Then God himself stepped down—
And the sun was on his right hand,
And the moon was on his left;
The stars were clustered about his head,
And the earth was under his feet.   30
And God walked, and where he trod
His footsteps hollowed the valleys out
And bulged the mountains up.

Then he stopped and looked and saw
That the earth was hot and barren.   35
So God stepped over to the edge of the world
And he spat out the seven seas—
He batted his eyes, and the lightnings flashed—
He clapped his hands, and the thunders rolled—
And the waters above the earth came down,   40
The cooling waters came down.

Then the green grass sprouted,
And the little red flowers blossomed,
The pine tree pointed his finger to the sky,
And the oak spread out his arms,   45
The lakes cuddled down in the hollows of the ground,
And the rivers ran down to the sea;
And God smiled again,
And the rainbow appeared,
And curled itself around his shoulder.   50

Then God raised his arm and he waved his hand
Over the sea and over the land,
And he said: Bring forth! Bring forth!
And quicker than God could drop his hand,
Fishes and fowls   55
And beasts and birds
Swam the rivers and the seas,
Roamed the forests and the woods,
And split the air with their wings.
And God said: That's good!   60

Then God walked around,
And God looked around
On all that he had made.
He looked at his sun,
And he looked at his moon,   65
And he looked at his little stars;
He looked on his world
With all its living things,
And God said: I'm lonely still.

Then God sat down— 70
On the side of a hill where he could think;
By a deep, wide river he sat down;
With his head in his hands,
God thought and thought,
Till he thought: I'll make me a man! 75

Up from the bed of the river
God scooped the clay;
And by the bank of the river
He kneeled him down;
And there the great God Almighty 80
Who lit the sun and fixed it in the sky,
Who flung the stars to the most far corner of the night,
Who rounded the earth in the middle of his hand;
This Great God,
Like a mammy bending over her baby, 85
Kneeled down in the dust
Toiling over a lump of clay
Till he shaped it in his own image;

Then into it he blew the breath of life,
And man became a living soul. 90
Amen. Amen.

1918 *1920, 1927*

ADELAIDE CRAPSEY
(1878–1914)

In her brief life, Adelaide Crapsey produced a body of poetry remarkable in its anticipation of the Imagists and even more remarkable for its personal account of her own dying—which connects with the poetry of the post–World War II confessional poets such as Sylvia Plath. During the long months of her last year, spent in a sanatorium suffering from tubercular meningitis, she polished the poems by which she is remembered, conceiving them (as she suggests in "Song") as her "shimmering" shroud.

Crapsey was born in 1878 in Brooklyn Heights, New York, into the large family of an Episcopal clergyman, who soon after her birth was established in a church in Rochester, New York. Adelaide studied Latin and French at a boarding school in Kenosha, Wisconsin, before entering Vassar College in 1897. There she was an excellent student, active in debate and drama, and was named class poet. In 1904 she went to Rome to study for a year at the School of Archeology.

The Reverend Algernon Sidney Crapsey became deeply concerned about the plight of the poor in Rochester, and his seemingly radical sermons attracted the attention of church officials. He was charged with heresy, and Adelaide accompanied her father to Batavia, New York, for the trial. The issue was finally resolved at the end of 1906, when the Reverend Crapsey requested his own removal from his position. The family seemed plagued with misfortune. One daughter had died of undulant fever in 1898, and another of appendicitis in

1901. An older son died in 1907 from malaria with which he had first been stricken during the Spanish-American War.

Adelaide Crapsey had shown signs of frailty as early as 1904 and found herself often beset by an inexplicable fatigue requiring rest. In spite of her recurring ill health, she went to Europe in 1909, spending time in Rome, London, and Kent. The spells of fatigue increased and she was hospitalized briefly in Rome. In 1911 she returned from abroad to an instructorship at Smith College. Soon she discovered that she was afflicted with tubercular meningitis, but she made the decision to keep the knowledge of her fatal illness from her family. She collapsed in the summer of 1913 while vacationing in Massachusetts and was sent to a nursing home at Saranac Lake, New York, where she spent the last months of her life sharing her intimate experience of dying with her poetry.

Outside her sanatorium window was a graveyard, a constant reminder of her own inevitable end. In ironic and bitter lines she scolded the dead for acquiescing so meekly in their death in "To the Dead in the Grave-Yard Under my Window: — Written in a Moment of Exasperation":

> How can you lie so still? All day I watch
> And never a blade of all the green sod moves
> To show where restlessly you toss and turn,
> And fling a desperate arm or draw up knees
> Stiffened and aching from their long disuse;
> I watch all night and not one ghost comes forth
> To take its freedom of the midnight hour.
> Oh, have you no rebellion in your bones?
> The very worms must scorn you where you lie,
> A pallid mouldering acquiescent folk,
> Meek habitants of unresented graves.

Crapsey's defiance filled the rest of the poem: "I'll not be patient! I will not lie still!"

During the last months, Crapsey spent considerable time sifting through her work, selecting poems she wanted preserved and placing them in her chosen order for publication. She alternated this activity with writing a treatise on prosody based on a scientific approach to poetic music or sounds that she had learned from her teacher at Vassar, Edith Rickert. *A Study in English Metrics* was published posthumously in 1918.

Adelaide Crapsey died in October 1914, at the age of thirty-six. Her poetry, entitled simply and austerely *Verse*, appeared in 1915 with a Foreword by Claude Bragdon, an American theosophist and architect who was her friend and a neighbor in Rochester. The poetry was well received, with special attention given to her *cinquains*, a metrical form of her own invention, consisting of five lines and resembling the short Japanese forms, such as the haiku.

Some indications of continuing interest in Adelaide Crapsey's poetry are suggested by new editions appearing in 1922 and 1934, with a definitive edition in 1977 done in accord with modern editing standards by Susan Sutton Smith. Among those praising her poetry were Edmund Wilson, Carl Sandburg, and Conrad Aiken. But it was Yvor Winters who was most lavish in his praise. He called her a "minor poet of great distinction," and described her as "certainly an immortal poet . . . who has long been one of the most famous poets of our century." Perhaps this claim should have been true, but the fact is that it was not until recently, with the new edition of her work, a critical book on her by Edward Butscher, and a biography by Karen Alkalay-Gut, that a contemporary reassessment has begun, likely to result in restoration of her to her rightful place in literary history.

ADDITIONAL READING

Sidney Algernon Crapsey, *The Last of the Heretics*, 1924 (autobiography of Crapsey's father); Mary Elizabeth Osborn, *Adelaide Crapsey*, 1933; Edward Butscher, *Adelaide Crapsey*, 1979; Karen Alkalay-Gut, "The Dying of Adelaide Crapsey," *Journal of Modern Literature*, July 1986; Karen Alkalay-Gut, *Alone in the Dawn: The Life of Adelaide Crapsey*, 1988.

TEXT

The Complete Poems and Collected Letters of Adelaide Crapsey, ed. Susan Sutton Smith, 1977.

from Cinquains[1]

November Night

Listen. .
With faint dry sound,
Like steps of passing ghosts,
The leaves, frost-crisp'd, break from the trees
And fall.   5

1911–13   *1915*

Triad

These be
Three silent things:
The falling snow. . the hour
Before the dawn. . the mouth of one
Just dead.   5

1911–13   *1915*

Susanna and the Elders[2]

"Why do
You thus devise
Evil against her?" "For that
She is beautiful, delicate:
Therefore."   5

1911–13   *1915*

---

[1]Before her death, Crapsey had arranged a group of her poems for publication, dividing them into "Part I," "Cinquains," and "Part II." The cinquain, a verse form invented by Crapsey, was defined by Sister M. Edwardine O'Connor in 1930 as a five-line stanza "built on stresses, one for the first line, two for the second, three for the third, four for the fourth, with a drop back to one for the fifth line. In the poet's opinion this made the most condensed metrical form in English that would hold together as a complete unit." Published in the posthumous editions of *Verse* (1915, 1922), the cinquains were dated by the poet as having been written between 1911 and 1913.

[2]In the Old Testament apocryphal book Susanna, the virtuous Susanna is falsely accused of adultery by the Hebrew Elders who watched her at her bath and attempted to seduce her.

The Guarded Wound

If it
Were lighter touch
Than petal of flower resting
On grass oh still too heavy it were,
Too heavy!   5

1911–13   *1915*

Amaze

I know
Not these my hands
And yet I think there was
A woman like me once had hands
Like these.   5

1911–13   *1915*

The Warning

Just now,
Out of the strange
Still dusk. . as strange, as still. .
A white moth flew. Why am I grown
So cold?   5

1911–13   *1915*

Blue Hyacinths

In your
Curled petals what ghosts
Of blue headlands and seas,
What perfumed immortal breath sighing
Of Greece.   5

1911–13   *1922*

Song

I make my shroud but no one knows,
So shimmering fine it is and fair,
With stitches set in even rows.
I make my shroud but no one knows.

In door-way where the lilac blows,   5
Humming a little wandering air,
I make my shroud and no one knows,
So shimmering fine it is and fair.

1915

Lines Addressed to My Left Lung Inconveniently Enamoured of Plant-Life[1]

It was, my lung, most strange of you,
    A freak I cannot pardon,
Thus to transform yourself into
    A vegetable-garden.

Though laking William[2] set erewhile   5
    His seal on rural fashions,
I must deplore, bewail, revile
    Your horticultural passions.

And as your ways I thus lament
    (Which, plainly, I call crazy)   10
For all I know, serene, content,
    You think yourself a daisy!

1914   *1977*

---

[1]This poem was written at the nursing home, where Crapsey was being treated for pulmonary tuberculosis, and sent with a letter to a friend in February 1914.

[2]William Wordsworth (1770–1850), romantic nature poet, lived in the Lake Country of northern England.

PART II

THE MODERNIST REVOLUTION: BETWEEN THE WORLD WARS (1914–1945)

"THE WORLD BROKE IN TWO"

The period between the two world wars has been variously called the "age of anxiety," the "age of futility," the "age of despair"; it might well have been called the "age of horrors." In the First World War, which America entered in 1917 and which was over in 1918, there were over 115,000 American deaths. In the Second World War, which lasted for America from 1941 to 1945, there were over 400,000 dead. The wounded, of course, far outnumbered the dead. And the numbers of those who served—and had their lives forever disrupted—were larger still: almost 5,000,000 in the First and over 16,000,000 in the Second.

Thus these two catastrophic wars marked deep divisions with the past. After the First, known as the Great War, the country (and the world) changed so radically that there seemed little connection with an earlier, more innocent way of life. As the American novelist Willa Cather once said, "The world broke in two in 1922 or thereabouts." Despite the war, the 1920s were boom times, when the restraints of an earlier, more reserved time were cast aside. The war had been fought, according to President Woodrow Wilson, to make the world safe for democracy. Instead, the world seemed to be made safe for totalitarianism, as fascist dictators first took control of Italy and Germany, and then Spain, and a Communist dictator took control of Russia. The boom times came to an end with a crash in 1929, which brought on the Great Depression, not to end until the advent of the Second World War. That war was ended when the United States dropped atomic bombs on Hiroshima and Nagasaki in 1945, blasting Japan out of its determination to defend every inch of its soil with the blood of its soldiers in a planned American invasion.

Though both world wars brought about precipitate and permanent change in the country as in the world, the dropping of the atomic bomb signalled an even deeper break with the past. The discovery of the secret of atomic energy and the immediate use of it for enormously destructive purposes suggested a modern Faustian pact with the devil, a pact that would lead inevitably to the dreaded doomsday the American Puritans had foreseen, but with both saints and sinners indiscriminately annihilated—an apocalypse without God. Whatever sense of futility infected the 1920s and 1930s faded in comparison with the deep, soul-sick despair arising from the knowledge that for the first time in history, human beings had the power to end life on earth and to destroy the earth itself.

This sickness of soul was intensified by the sudden awareness, coming with the revelations at the end of the war in Europe, of the "final solution" adopted by Hitler in Germany to dispose of the "Jewish problem." As the invading Allied armies came upon the concentration camps, and the news photos began to tell the story of over seven million Jews and other "undesirables" who had been systematically and efficiently killed or starved, there was worldwide nausea at the mountains of corpses still unburied. Any notion of the innate nobility of human beings appeared absurd. This holocaust burned into the modern mind the terrible knowledge of the frailty of human life in the face of the demonstrated depravity of the human spirit.

The changes that were wrought by the First World War (1914–18) in the way people thought, felt, and lived their lives had a deep impact on American literature. The even more profound changes of the Second World War (1939–45) were also reflected in literature, beginning a transformation still in progress today as we approach the beginning of the twenty-first century.

THE POLITICAL SCENE

The 1920s witnessed a series of helpless, weak, or ineffective presidencies. Woodrow Wilson (1856–1924), president from 1913 to 1921, was the second of two Democrats to hold the office between the Civil War and the First World War. He had campaigned for his second term on a platform of keeping America out of war; thus when German submarine attacks on American shipping brought America into the war, Wilson attempted to turn the struggle into a fight for the ideals of democracy and the rule of international law. As a part of the peace settlement in the Treaty of Versailles, he insisted on the creation of a League of Nations, only to find his own Congress opposing him in the name of American sovereignty. He toured the country to inspire support for the League of Nations, but in the end was defeated; the League was created without American participation. Wilson's health failed, and the country returned to a succession of Republican presidents of dubious ability.

Warren Gamaliel Harding (1865–1923), president from 1921 to 1923, had pledged in his campaign a "return to normalcy." He appointed to his cabinet a number of businessmen, later to become known as "the Ohio Gang" (Harry Daugherty and Albert Fall), who brought America the Teapot Dome scandal — essentially a theft on a grand scale of the naval oil reserves at Teapot Dome, Wyoming. Cabinet members landed in jail, as did oil entrepreneur Harry F. Sinclair. Harding himself, under immense strain, died on a return trip from Alaska, saving him from having to face the consequences of his appointment of dishonest and unscrupulous men to high office.

Calvin Coolidge (1872–1933), Harding's vice president, a taciturn New Englander, became president in 1923 and won reelection the following year to serve until 1929. He became famous for his public pronouncements, such as: "The chief business of the American people is business"; "When a lot of people are out of work, unemployment results"; "The man who builds a factory builds a temple; the man who works there worships there." Coolidge was notorious for not showing emotion. When he died in 1933, the wag Dorothy Parker asked: "How can they tell?"

The Iowan Herbert Hoover (1874–1964), who had served ably as Secretary of Commerce under Harding and Coolidge, won a hard-fought election over the New York Catholic Alfred E. Smith (1873–1944) and was inaugurated as president in 1929. Few individuals, and least of all the president, were paying attention to the signs that would make that year the cataclysmic end of a boom era, beginning with the stock market crash of October. As the economy gradually collapsed, fortunes vanished overnight, and many speculators jumped from the windows high in their skyscrapers, Hoover became notorious for his recurrent assurances that conditions were "fundamentally sound." Unemployment soared, businesses and farms failed, banks closed, and still Hoover insisted the "fundamental strength of the nation's economy [was] unimpaired."

The Democratic governor of New York, Franklin Delano Roosevelt (1882–1945), was swept into office by a landslide in 1932, to preside over the Great Depression for the decade of the 1930s and over America's involvement in the Second World War from 1941 to 1945, the longest serving president in American history. He was elected four times but died in 1945 soon after the beginning of the last term. Roosevelt, a gifted and eloquent speaker, was the first president to master mass media communications by talking directly to the people through a series of "fireside chats" over the recently invented radio. Perhaps his most famous remark, often quoted, was said in reassurance to people suffering through the Great Depression: "The only thing we have to fear is fear itself."

His program to counteract the Great Depression — called the New Deal — as well as his strategy to collaborate with the Soviet Union in the war with Germany, remained matters of controversy long after his departure from the scene. But his sudden death in 1945, shortly before the winning of the war and the establishment of the United Nations (which he ardently supported), evoked an outpouring of grief. And it brought to the presidency the feisty vice president from Missouri, Harry S. Truman (1884–1972). It was he who made the historic decision to drop the atomic bomb on Hiroshima and Nagasaki, bringing the Second World War to a close.

THE SOCIAL SCENE: GOOD TIMES AND BAD

The Census Bureau had officially announced the closing of the American frontier in 1890, based simply on the increased density of population throughout the country. By 1920, more people were living in cities than in rural areas, and America was rapidly becoming an urban nation. In 1919, in response to the temperance movement led by the Women's Christian Temperance Union (WCTU), the Eighteenth Amendment to the Constitution was adopted. It launched the prohibition era, lasting until 1933, during which time the sale of alcohol was prohibited in the United States. Illegality only made drinking more attractive. Many citizens manufactured "bathtub gin" in their own bathrooms. Others drank in the speakeasies where plenty of bootleg liquor could be bought. Instead of bringing about a period of purity and innocence, prohibition brought into being a wave of criminality in which rival gangs warred with each other for control of the lucrative bootleg trade. One Chicago gangster-bootlegger, Al "Scarface" Capone (1899–1947), became a notorious international celebrity; he was eventually jailed for income tax evasion.

In 1920 the Nineteenth Amendment gave women the right to vote. The women's suffrage movement had begun as far back as 1848, at the Seneca Falls Convention on Women's Rights. By 1920, several western states had already extended suffrage to women, but never the country at large. Recognition of women's right to vote led to recognition of other rights and freedoms. Released from many of the restraints placed on them by a genteel culture of the past, women experienced a new sexual freedom, which gave rise to a 1920s woman known as the "flapper," who bobbed her hair, smoked, and did the Charleston, or any other of the latest dance crazes. F. Scott Fitzgerald memorialized her and the age she helped to create in two volumes of short stories, *Flappers and Philosophers* (1920) and *Tales of the Jazz Age* (1922).

Wars always accelerate the developing technology of a culture. By 1920, there were about 9,000,000 automobiles on the road; by 1930, the number was close to 30,000,000. Mass production techniques developed by Henry Ford (1863–1947) had made possession of a Model-T possible for the ordinary person. A network of paved roads was making it possible to go on a joy ride to a neighboring community or into town. Closed cars became common, and were called "rooms on wheels," where privacy was immediate and young people could spark, woo, make whoopee, or make love.

By the end of the 1920s, every third household in America had a radio. For the first time in the nation's history, the whole citizenry could enjoy entertainment simultaneously — and hear the news daily, as well as political or presidential speeches. An entire country listening to one of Roosevelt's "fireside chats" became "one nation" as it had never been before. The movies, though silent, attracted large audiences and brought movie stars on the cultural scene. Toward the end of the decade, "talkies" came into being in Al Jolson's *The Jazz Singer* (1927). The period of the enormous movie palaces was beginning, showing the films that would have an incalculable effect on American society, stimulating romantic dreams and tempering the inchoate hostilities of underpaid factory workers and sales clerks.

Not all Americans shared in the riches sparked by the "Roaring Twenties," not most of the whites, and certainly not any of the blacks. Some 100,000 blacks had fought in the war, but returned home to a society as racist as before. During the war, blacks had migrated in large numbers from the rural South to the industrial North, to take jobs in defense and other industries. In the large cities of the North, great concentrations of blacks lived in unofficially segregated areas (or ghettoes), but tensions grew as they claimed their rights to use public facilities. In 1919, in Chicago, a small black boy drifted over the invisible line drawn in the water off the Chicago beaches. The boy was attacked and died in the water. A riot began that spread to all parts of the city. In 1920, a similar senseless clash took place in Tulsa, Oklahoma.

The Rising Tide of Color Against White World Supremacy, by an American author, Lothrop Stoddard, appeared in 1920, reinforcing white racist views. It is remembered today primarily because it was quoted seriously by the shallow Tom Buchanan in F. Scott Fitzgerald's *The Great Gatsby* (1925). There were, of course, other brands of prejudice widespread in America, as, for example, anti-Semitism, practiced covertly in such areas as housing or college admissions. Anti-Catholic feelings in what H. L. Mencken characterized as the Bible Belt of America (where fundamentalist Protestants were dominant) were intensified during the presidential election of 1928, when the Democratic candidate was Alfred E. Smith, the Catholic governor of New York, running against the Republican midwesterner Herbert Hoover. Fear of Catholics was inflamed by the charge against Smith (who pledged to overturn Prohibition) that he would bring "rum, Romanism, and rebellion." The Ku Klux Klan, which came into being in the South after the Civil War as the white means of controlling the freed slaves, was revived beginning in 1915, inspired in large part because of the glorification of the Klan in D. W. Griffith's Civil War motion picture epic, *Birth of a Nation*. The new Klan aimed its vilification and violence not only at blacks, but also at Jews and Catholics.

Certain events of the period became touchstones of the time. Such was the famous Sacco-Vanzetti case, in which two "anarchists," Nicola Sacco and Bartolomeo Vanzetti, were sentenced to death in 1921 for a robbery and murder at a shoe factory in Massachusetts in 1920. There was little evidence for the conviction and as a result of a campaign waged by intellectuals and writers, worldwide sympathy developed for the two men. They were executed in 1927. Many literary works were written in protest against what was widely considered a terrible miscarriage of justice, including poems by Countee Cullen and Edna St. Vincent Millay, a play by Maxwell Anderson, and a novel by John Dos Passos.

Two events of the 1920s seemed to portray the worst and the best of American culture: the Scopes trial of 1925 and the Lindbergh flight of 1927. A high school teacher in Tennessee, John T. Scopes, became a national celebrity when he violated state law by teaching the Darwinian theory of evolution in his high school biology class. The famed Nebraska orator-politician William Jennings Bryan (1860–1925) presented Tennessee's case by defending a literal interpretation of the Bible. The distinguished Chicago lawyer Clarence Darrow (1857–1938) defended Scopes by using common sense to puncture and deflate such an interpretation. Darrow won the intellectual battle but lost the case, and the fundamentalist law remained on the books. In 1955, Jerome Lawrence and Robert E. Lee turned this episode into the successful play *Inherit the Wind* and proved that the religious issues were still very much alive.

In contrast with the Scopes "monkey trial," which brought America considerable ridicule from abroad, the Lindbergh flight of 1927 brought the country praise and adulation. Charles A. Lindbergh (1902–1974), at the age of twenty-five, made the first solo flight across the Atlantic, flying nonstop from New York to Paris in a little over thirty-three hours in his monoplane "The Spirit of Saint Louis." He became an instant international hero, receiving many honors from nations around the world, and he wrote a best-selling account of his flight in *We* (1927). His youth, ingenuity, and daring seemed to display the best in the national character.

The stock market crash of October 1929 ushered in the Great Depression that lasted for the entire decade of the 1930s. By 1932, unemployment had risen to over 12,000,000, and 5,000 banks had failed; between 30,000 and 40,000 businesses had shut up shop. The country's attention focused on the hard times and President Roosevelt's New Deal and its "alphabet soup" of remedies — the PWA (Public Works Administration), the NRA (National Recovery Act), the WPA (Works Progress Administration), the NYA (National Youth Administration), and more.

Many writers who, disillusioned by the First World War, had concentrated for the most part on aesthetic problems, now found themselves galvanized by the plight of the poor and optimistically threw their support behind what they perceived to be the solution — social and political change or revolution in accord with Marxist thought. At no other time in American history was enrollment in the Communist party so high. The Party had been formed in 1919, with the help of the journalist John Reed (1887–1920), who had visited Russia and published his eyewitness account of the Russian Revolution, *Ten Days That Shook the World* (1919). Many of the members of the Communist party — often idealistic — would be devastatingly targeted by the anti-Communist witchhunting of the McCarthy years in the early 1950s. The leftist writers of the 1930s found an organ in the *Partisan Review* established in 1934, but they soon splintered into Stalinists and Trotskyites, reflecting the arcane ideological divisions in the Soviet Union.

With the distractions of the Great Depression, the populace paid little heed to the Japanese occupation of China's Manchuria in 1931, or Hitler's rise to dictatorial power in Germany in 1933, or Stalin's great purges in the Soviet Union in the mid-1930s, enslaving and killing millions. When the fascist General Francisco Franco rebelled against the Spanish Republican government in 1936, a small band of American volunteers formed the Lincoln Brigade to fight against him and his forces, but to little avail against the superior assistance extended by Nazi Germany and Fascist Italy. By the time Ernest Hemingway published his Spanish Civil War novel *For Whom the Bell Tolls* in 1940, the Second World War was already underway. America was forced into the war by the Japanese bombing of Pearl Harbor, which destroyed much of the American Pacific Fleet on December 7, 1941. The country's attention quickly shifted from domestic troubles to the very real dangers of totalitarian conquest of the world and the loss of all those freedoms nurtured, if not always honored, since the American Revolution.

INTELLECTUAL CURRENTS

The two decades of the 1920s and 1930s, though they differed sharply in the wild prosperity of the one and the Great Depression of the other, were continuous and consistent in their pessimistic views on the plight of humanity and the world. Two literary works—one published near the beginning of this period, the other near the end—may be taken as characteristic: T. S. Eliot's *The Waste Land* (1922) and John Steinbeck's *The Grapes of Wrath* (1939). The first set the intellectual tone for the 1920s, with its religious skepticism and psychological despair, and the second reflected the intellectual mood of the 1930s, with its disheartenment and despondency at the failure of social, economic, and political structures.

Given the characteristics of these two decades, it should not be surprising that the preoccupation with the ideas of Sigmund Freud (1856–1939) in the 1920s gave way in the 1930s to a commitment to the philosophy of Karl Marx (1818–1883). Though Freud focused attention on the psychological makeup of the individual and Marx on the economic structure of the society, both bequeathed systems of thought containing elements of determinism that diminished individual freedom of the will. Freud demonstrated that human behavior was shaped by events, generally in childhood, beyond the control of the individual; Marx asserted that economic and political structures were shaped by "dialectical materialism," a kind of social evolution obedient to laws as fixed as those ruling Darwin's biological evolution—and thus also beyond human control.

Other intellectual strands contributed to the general pessimism. In psychology, "behaviorism" proposed that there was no such thing as consciousness (central to Freud's concepts) but only response to stimuli—or conditioned reflexes. J. B. Watson (1878–1958) provided the foundation of American behaviorism in *Behavior: An Introduction to Comparative Psychology* (1914). A German historian, Oswald Spengler (1880–1936), predicted in his massive study *Decline of the West* (1918–22) the extinction of Western civilization. The American patrician Henry Adams, as early as 1910 in his *Letter to American Teachers of History*, had sounded the alarm about the civilization's developing loss of social and psychic energy in an entropic state similar to the "entropy," or state of stasis (decay and death), toward which all physical energy tends (as predicted by the second law of thermodynamics). In his *Education of Henry Adams*, privately printed in 1907 and posthumously published in 1918, he had also propounded his "law of acceleration" in a "Dynamic Theory of History" that envisioned a continuously accelerating pace in the unlocking of the ever more powerful sources of energy yet hidden in nature—to a point in the near future when the unleashed forces would defy human control.

The two world wars that began and ended this period were both a source and a confirmation of the pessimism that dominated the serious thought of the time. Such famous novels as F. Scott Fitzgerald's *The Great Gatsby* (1925), Ernest Hemingway's *The Sun Also Rises* (1926), John Dos Passos's *U.S.A.* (1938), and John Steinbeck's *The Grapes of Wrath* (1939) all represented, in one way or another, a questioning of accepted values and a search for sustenance, spiritual and material, for survival. Fitzgerald had captured the disillusion of the age in his first novel, *This Side of Paradise* (1920): "Here was a new generation . . . grown up to find all Gods dead, all wars fought, all faiths in man shaken." Most of the writers of the period, whether poet, dramatist, or novelist, would subscribe to the description of the act of writing given by Wallace Stevens at the beginning of his poem "Of Modern Poetry": "The poem of the mind in the act of finding / What will suffice. It has not always had / To find: the scene was set; it repeated what / Was in the script."

Scientific thought itself seemed to leave the individual filled with confusion and uncertainty about the nature of what had once been ancient and enduring realities: time and space. In publications on his theory of relativity, first in 1905 and later in 1916, the German scientist Albert Einstein (1879–1955) declared that space and time were not separate entities but a continuum and that the continuum was not flat but curved. Einstein's theories would lead ultimately (in the 1960s) to the discovery of mysterious "black holes" in the universe, in which a collapsing star may simply diminish into an infinite density, or perhaps escape into the "white hole" of another universe. At the same time that Einstein was turning the universe on its head, other scientists began exploring the precise nature of the smallest particles of matter, discovering that they were not static solids at all but little worlds of dynamic energy, ruled (according to quantum or wave mechanics) not by fixed laws but by an "uncertainty principle." Thus the traditional scientific belief in causal law gave way to theories of probability, which appeared in some sense to be an admission that chance played its part in the unfolding drama of the universe.

In the newly developed science of psychology, philosophers were exploring human consciousness for the sources of an ever-elusive reality. William James (brother of novelist Henry) had published his pioneer work *Principles of Psychology* in 1890, and coined the phrase "stream of consciousness" ("let us call it the stream of thought, of consciousness, or of subjective life"). The French philosopher Henri Bergson (1859–1941) in a series of important works (*Creative Evolution*, 1907; *Mind-Energy*, 1919; and *The Creative Mind*, 1934) proposed that change and movement (flux) were basic to all reality, that time was a continuous flow through consciousness, and that living beings were animated by an *élan vital* (or life force) which rendered intuitive or mystical insight transcendent over rationality. Such theories as those of James and Bergson were important influences on novelists using "stream of consciousness" or "interior monologue" in their fiction: Marcel Proust in France, James Joyce in (or away from) Ireland, Virginia Woolf in England, and William Faulkner in America.

Another movement of the time, more metaphysical than philosophical, revolved around a Russian writer, P. D. Ouspensky (1878–1947). In *Tertium Organum* (1920), he advocated a mystical comprehension of human experience and the world, drawing an important part of his thought from Richard Maurice

Bucke's *Cosmic Consciousness* (1901). Bucke had been a friend and biographer of Walt Whitman and had cited Whitman as one of the few people throughout history to be endowed with cosmic consciousness, a consciousness quite beyond the "self-consciousness" of ordinary people, which in turn is considerably beyond the "simple consciousness" of animals. George Gurdjieff (1874?–1949), a Greek-Russian-Armenian forerunner of Ouspensky, set up his Institute for the Harmonious Development of Man at Fontainebleau near Paris and presided there in the 1920s teaching ways of reaching the higher consciousness. Hart Crane, Jean Toomer, Gorham Munson, and other American writers read Ouspensky and were attracted to Gurdjieff when he visited the United States with his followers (who performed mysterious dances) in the early 1920s. Jean Toomer later went to France to study at Gurdjieff's institute.

While some thinkers explored the universe or the atom in search of the secrets of reality or studied the complexities of human consciousness, still others began to focus on language itself as holding secrets of its own. British philosopher Bertrand Russell (1872–1970), with coauthor Alfred North Whitehead (1861–1947), produced a seminal work, *Principia Mathematica* (1910–13), which led to the development of "analytical philosophy," concentrating not on ideas but on the language in which the ideas were expressed. An Austrian philosopher, Ludwig Wittgenstein (1889–1951), influenced by Russell (and who in turn influenced Russell), produced his highly influential *Tractatus Logico-Philosophicus* in 1922, proposing that most problems puzzling philosophy could be solved (or proved metaphysical and thus nonproblems) by linguistic analysis. A popularization of this movement appeared in 1938, entitled significantly *The Tyranny of Words*, by the American Stuart Chase.

All these currents and crosscurrents of thought, which filtered through the culture by casual references and popular accounts, became known to the many who never read the basic texts. It was inevitable that these discoveries, theories, and ideas would become influences, sometimes fundamental and shaping, on the imaginations of the writers of the time. Much of the innovativeness of modern American literature came from the new perceptions of reality inspired by the scientists, philosophers, and thinkers of the time.

THE LITTLE MAGAZINES

Although there were many magazines published in America in the early twentieth century, poetry appeared in them rarely and then only as "filler" to take up leftover space on a page. For poetry it was a demeaning position, which Harriet Monroe (1860–1936), a Chicago poet of little renown, set out to remedy when she collected enough donations from Chicago meatpackers and other entrepreneurs to publish the first issue of *Poetry: A Magazine of Verse* in 1912. Ezra Pound, already living abroad, signed on as foreign correspondent. Through his recommendations and her own good judgment, Harriet Monroe succeeded in making "porkopolis" a poetry center. She published the early work of many of the poets who would become the major poets of the time—Pound himself, T. S. Eliot, William Carlos Williams, Marianne Moore, Robert Frost, Wallace Stevens, Hart Crane, and others. She herself promoted the midwestern poets, Carl Sandburg, Edgar Lee Masters, and Vachel Lindsay.

Chicago seemed to be the literary center for a time, but there was a gravitational pull to the East, especially New York, a center in its own right. Margaret C.

Anderson (1893?–1973) established *The Little Review* in Chicago in 1914 but moved it in 1917 to New York, where it got into legal difficulties by serializing James Joyce's *Ulysses*. Finally Anderson and her magazine settled in Paris in 1924. Alfred Kreymborg (1883–1966) edited his *Others* (1915–19) in New Jersey, where he lived; it was said to be a magazine where those poets Harriet Monroe rejected for *Poetry* (the "others") could be published. Kreymborg's home became a gathering place for poets in and around New York, including William Carlos Williams, Marianne Moore, and Wallace Stevens. *The Dial*, which had been established in the 1880s in Chicago, went through several transformations and ended up in New York during the 1920s, where, in 1922, it published *The Waste Land*, and where, from 1926 to the magazine's demise in 1929, Marianne Moore served as editor. *The Fugitive* was established in Nashville, Tennessee, in 1922 and continued into 1925; it became the center for publication of southern writers such as John Crowe Ransom and Allen Tate.

Many of the little magazines, like *Broom* (1921–24) and *Secession* (1922–24), lasted only a few years, sometimes months; a very few others, like *Poetry*, are still being published. But however long they lasted, they tended to shake up the literary scene, printing the poetry and fiction considered too risky or avantgarde by the popular magazines. It is hard to imagine the modernist movement taking place without the little magazines. They offered writers a chance to experiment, to try out new techniques, to venture new voices. Some of the avantgarde writing has not survived, of course; but an astonishing amount of work that first appeared in the little magazines has come to be considered as the classic literature of the twentieth century.

A number of magazines, not quite in the "little magazine" category, became very influential during this period. *The Smart Set* had been founded in 1890, but came to life especially when H. L. Mencken became literary editor in 1908. Mencken and George Jean Nathan served as editors from 1914 to 1923, turning it into one of the most widely read magazines of the day. They published early work of such American writers as Eugene O'Neill, F. Scott Fitzgerald, and Waldo Frank. In 1924 they broke away and established their own magazine, *The American Mercury*, promising to "attempt a realistic presentation of the whole gaudy, gorgeous American scene." They published, among others, Theodore Dreiser, Sherwood Anderson, and Edgar Lee Masters. In 1925, *The New Yorker* was founded by Harold Ross, who edited it until his death in 1951, developing its reputation as the place where the best prose written in America was published. Among its writers were James Thurber, Edmund Wilson, and E. B. White. Harold Ross early developed a number of sophisticated artists to provide amusing, often satiric cartoons for each issue. He once referred to *The New Yorker* as an adult comic magazine. There can be little doubt that the often-subsidized little magazines prepared the way for these literary magazines of quality to achieve critical and popular success.

THE TRIPLE RENAISSANCE: CHICAGO, POETRY, HARLEM

The hunger for a revival in literature during this period may be judged by the number of gatherings or movements that were given the impressive label of "renaissance." Little attention was paid to the need for a "naissance" before the possibility of a "re-naissance"; poetry had had its "golden day" in the nineteenth century, but Chicago and Harlem had never previously been literary centers. It fits the exuberance of the American character that the idea of a rebirth without a prior "first birth" did not seem contradictory.

The first such movement, often called the "Chicago Renaissance," took place between 1912 and 1925. For a brief moment in time Chicago appeared to replace other literary centers (especially Boston and New York) in the vitality and innovative energy of its writers. Chicago itself had recovered from the disastrous fire of 1871 and had rebuilt with speed, introducing a new skyscraper architecture that astonished the nation. Its Columbian Exposition of 1893 had attracted worldwide attention. Midwesterners from such states as Indiana, Ohio, and Iowa escaped the restraints of small-town America by fleeing to Chicago. The naturalist Theodore Dreiser came from Indiana and set the first scenes of his *Sister Carrie* (1900) in Chicago. Sherwood Anderson came from Ohio and showed his young hero in *Winesburg, Ohio* (1919) at the end setting out for the big city. A number of Chicago poets came from the small towns of Illinois—Carl Sandburg from Galesburg, Edgar Lee Masters from Lewistown, and Vachel Lindsay from Springfield. Carl Sandburg published "Chicago" in *Poetry* in 1914 (collected in 1916 in his *Chicago Poems*), sketching the city as the "Hog Butcher for the World... / Stormy, husky brawling, / City of the Big Shoulders."

The "Poetry Renaissance" is often dated from 1912 because of the establishment of *Poetry: A Magazine of Verse* that year. Ezra Pound himself, in response to Harriet Monroe's "project for a magazine of verse," predicted an "awakening" that would "make the Italian renaissance look like a tempest in a tea-pot." *Poetry* encouraged the writing of serious verse by paying for poems, and, like the other magazines, by providing an outlet for new voices as well as a forum where poets could learn from each other. Carl Sandburg, for example, paid tribute to Pound, whom he had encountered in *Poetry*'s pages. It was *Poetry* that brought T. S. Eliot's "The Love Song of J. Alfred Prufrock" to American readers, and the *Dial* that brought *The Waste Land*.

The attention focused on the poets by the little magazines played a significant part in bringing about publication of important volumes of poetry. A mere listing of a few of the books published from 1912 to 1923 suggests the nature of the renewal poetry was undergoing—1912: Ezra Pound, *Ripostes*; 1913: Robert Frost, *A Boy's Will*, and Vachel Lindsay, *General William Booth Enters into Heaven and Other Poems*; 1915: Edgar Lee Masters, *Spoon River Anthology*, and Sara Teasdale, *Rivers to the Sea*; 1917: T. S. Eliot, *Prufrock and Other Observations*; 1920: Edna St. Vincent Millay, *A Few Figs from Thistles*, and Ezra Pound, *Hugh Selwyn Mauberly*; 1921: H. D., *Hymen*, and Marianne Moore, *Poems*; 1922: T. S. Eliot, *The Waste Land*; 1923: William Carlos Williams, *Spring and All*, and Wallace Stevens, *Harmonium*. Many more remarkable works were soon to come. It was during this period, one of the richest in America for poetry, that the international literary influences went into reverse—flowing definitively from the United States to Europe for the first time.

The "Harlem Renaissance" (sometimes called the "New Negro Renaissance") was centered in New York's black district of Harlem and flourished during the latter half of the 1920s. A signal date is 1925, when a black Howard University philosophy professor (and Rhodes scholar), Alain Locke (1886–1954), edited a collection of poetry, fiction, drama, and essays entitled *The New Negro: An Interpretation*. The Foreword opened: "This volume aims to document the New Negro culturally and socially,—to register the transformations of the inner and outer life of the Negro in America that have so significantly taken place in the last few years." The range of talent represented in the volume was extraordinary.

It included fiction by Jean Toomer and Zora Neale Hurston; poems by Countee Cullen, Claude McKay, James Weldon Johnson, and Langston Hughes; and essays by Alain Locke himself ("The Negro Spirituals") and W. E. B. DuBois ("The Negro Mind Reaches Out").

Clearly the Harlem Renaissance marked a turning point for black writers in America. There was for the first time an open celebration of blackness, including black music, black folklore, and black culture, as well as black literature. Although some writers such as Countee Cullen insisted on his rights as a poet to write on subjects other than "color," he still wrote many poems out of his black experience. But it was Langston Hughes who demonstrated for later black writers the richness of their unique cultural heritage that could inform and shape their work. All of the Harlem Renaissance writers helped to prepare the way for such later talented black writers as Richard Wright, Ralph Ellison, James Baldwin, Gwendolyn Brooks, Toni Morrison, and Alice Walker.

Another movement of the time, never distinguished by the term *renaissance*, was that of the "Southern Fugitives" (or "Agrarians"). The center for this movement was Vanderbilt University in Tennessee, where in the early 1920s the little magazine *The Fugitive* was published. John Crowe Ransom, professor at Vanderbilt, became the leader of a group of southern poets publishing in the magazine, including Allen Tate, Robert Penn Warren, and Laura Riding. A collection of work that had appeared in the magazine was published as the *Fugitive Anthology* in 1928. In 1930, these and other southern writers published a symposium, *I'll Take My Stand: The South and the Agrarian Tradition by Twelve Southerners*. Like the blacks in the Harlem Renaissance, the southerners looked to their cultural roots for their distinctive identity. They found their values in the conservative agrarian, as opposed to the liberal urban, tradition, and they tended to concentrate on the frailty and weaknesses of human nature rather than its strengths and possibilities. Their somewhat pessimistic vision became an important influence on the literature of the 1930s and beyond.

THE LOST GENERATION: EXPATRIATES

A phenomenon of American literature of this time is that a large amount of the best of it was written abroad. During the First World War, many writers-to-be (John Dos Passos, Ernest Hemingway, E. E. Cummings) had served overseas. A line from a song — "How're you goin' to keep them down on the farm after they've seen Paree?" — had much truth to it. The exodus abroad had begun earlier, when Gertrude Stein settled with her brother in Paris in 1903. It turned into something of a flood after the war. In 1922 appeared an influential work sweepingly entitled *Civilization in the United States: An Inquiry by Thirty Americans*. It was edited by a vagabond literary figure, Harold Stearns (1891–1943), and included pieces by H. L. Mencken, Van Wyck Brooks, and George Jean Nathan. The criticism of the country was savage, emphasizing its spiritual vacuity, its materialistic obsession, and the venality of its politicians. In answer to the question posed in the title of his essay, "What Should a Young Man Do?" Stearns concluded, "leave." He followed his own advice and went to Paris. Ironically, Stearns survived in literary history primarily as a minor character — a drunken bum asking for a handout — in Hemingway's *The Sun Also Rises*.

Many Americans were already there, and more were to come. Ezra Pound was the archetypal expatriate; from about 1908 on, he lived abroad, first in Italy, then London, Paris, and again Italy. T. S. Eliot spent a year studying in Paris

(1910–11) and went to study in Germany in 1914, but was forced by the outbreak of war to go to London; he was never to return to live in America. Ernest Hemingway went to Italy in 1918 to drive an ambulance for the Red Cross and settled in Paris in the early 1920s. F. Scott Fitzgerald left to live in Europe in 1924 and stayed until December 1926. Many more writers followed Harold Stearns's advice and left America for Paris to become members of the expatriate group, including Kay Boyle, Robert McAlmon, and Glenway Westcott. They were attracted, however, as much by the favorable rate of exchange as by the supposed superiority of European civilization. Of all the so-called writers who went to live abroad, particularly in Paris, many wrote very little and are now forgotten, and many wrote — or published — nothing at all.

These expatriates felt the postwar pessimism of the time and often expressed a precious sense of the "nobility of futility." The sense of futility was frequently manifested not in creative energy but in ennui and drink. Ernest Hemingway used Gertrude Stein's remark to him — "You are all a lost generation" — as an epigraph to his novel *The Sun Also Rises* (1926). It came to be used to designate the entire disillusioned and despairing postwar generation. Gertrude Stein would reveal later (in *The Autobiography of Alice B. Toklas*, 1933) that she had picked up the phrase from the proprietor of a hotel, who was referring to the young mechanic fixing Stein's car — a member of a disillusioned, disoriented, and rootless generation that had lost all sense of tradition and values.

MODERNISM AND THE AVANT-GARDE

The term *modernism*, like romanticism and realism, has been variously defined, and in its broadest sense means simply that which is of this age rather than the past. But perhaps because of the fierce determination of the principal writers of the period to renew and revitalize literature — together with their extraordinary success — "modernism" has become a label fixed in time. The outer limits of the period are vague and debatable, but the end of modernism was ordained by the appearance of what was dubbed postmodernism after the Second World War, with the gradual passing from the scene of the literary giants of the 1920s and 1930s and the gradual emergence of new writers with new subjects and techniques, especially during the 1960s. Some critics might want to argue that American modernism began with Walt Whitman and Emily Dickinson in poetry and Mark Twain and Henry James in fiction. Certainly these writers had an impact on the modernist writers. Other critics might want to argue that modernism began when William James coined the phrase, "stream of consciousness," in 1890; or when Gertrude Stein (who had studied with James) published her remarkable work of fiction *Three Lives* in 1909; or when Harriet Monroe founded *Poetry* in 1912. Any of these dates might do as long as critics are left free to find the seeds of modernism as far back as the eighteenth century and even before.

Unlike modernism, the term *avant-garde* has remained a floating and usable term for successive literary generations. So we may say that the period of American modernism, bounded roughly by the two world wars, was a time during which the avant-garde reigned. Writers of the avant-garde were those who were unorthodox, daring, and experimental, such as Ezra Pound, T. S. Eliot, Marianne Moore, William Carlos Williams, and Wallace Stevens in poetry; Gertrude Stein, F. Scott Fitzgerald, Ernest Hemingway, and William Faulkner in fiction; and in drama, the neglected Susan Glaspell, as well as the acknowledged greats, Eugene O'Neill and Thornton Wilder. All of these innovative writers eventually found acceptance by the mainstream culture, some (Hemingway and Wilder) more quickly than others; a number, such as Pound and Stein, found their readers largely among the professors and students in English departments of the universities, a small but nevertheless "orthodox" group. Such acceptance and absorption by the mainstream or orthodox culture meant, of course, that the members of the avant-garde became members of an establishment that would in its turn become the target of another rebellious antiestablishment avant-garde (as in the postmodernism after the Second World War).

The modernist movement was an international movement, with innovations in one country quickly spreading to another. "Futurism" was born in Italy in 1909, with Filippo Tommaso Marinetti (1876–1944) issuing his "Manifesto of Futurism," calling for radical change in literature and art; another futurist manifesto was issued in 1912, entitled "A Slap in the Face of Public Taste." The latter called for rebellion against conventional syntax and for a kind of anarchy in language. Such pugnacity, aimed at the entrenched establishment, was a part of most such local campaigns in the international avant-garde. "Dadaism" was founded in Zurich in 1916 by Tristan Tzara (1896–1963) and others and was aimed at subverting all traditional social, artistic, and literary values, substituting a kind of deliberate madness for reason and a designed chaos for order. André Breton (1896–1966), a Parisian dadaist, became fascinated by the unconscious, and broke from the dadaists to found "surrealism" in 1924, advocating suspension of conscious reason in favor of the unconscious in the artistic process.

The American modernists drew not only from these "campaigns" but also from the French *symboliste* movement of the last three decades of the nineteenth century, led by Arthur Rimbaud, Paul Verlaine, and Stéphane Mallarmé (all of whom had been influenced by America's Edgar Allan Poe through his French translator Charles Baudelaire). The movement, a kind of pre-surrealist movement, turned away from exterior reality to the realities of the conscious and unconscious mind and focused on highly personal and often obscure images or symbols, making for a suggestive and difficult poetry. T. S. Eliot had steeped himself in the French *symbolistes*. But he also learned from the English tradition. In "The Metaphysical Poets" (1921), he noted: "We can only say that it appears likely that poets in our civilization, as it exists at present, must be *difficult* . . . . The poet must become more and more comprehensive, more allusive, more indirect, in order to force, to dislocate if necessary, language into his meaning."

The American modernists—under the guidance of the chief exponent of "Make It New," Ezra Pound—initiated some campaigns of their own in "imagism" and "vorticism." The first of these was influenced by the aesthetic theories of the Englishman T. E. Hulme (1883–1917), called the "father of imagism," but also by the precision of Greek and Oriental poetry (especially the Japanese haiku), and the experiments of the French symbolists and practitioners of *vers libre*. Pound was the editor of *Des Imagistes*, published in 1914, the first of a series of such anthologies. He defined imagism as a poetry that focused on an image that "presents an intellectual and emotional complex in an instant of time." In articulating the principles of the movement, he stressed direct treatment of the "thing," use of no superfluous words, and composition in the sequence of the musical phrase. Pound soon grew impatient with Amy Lowell's taking over the movement as her own (Pound then called it "Amygism"), and left it to help found vorticism, an iconoclastic movement reacting to the romantic vagueness of poets like Amy Lowell, and named after the "vortex" conceived as a "radiant node . . . from which, and through which, and into which, ideas are constantly rushing." *Blast: Review of the Great English Vortex*, the movement's magazine, edited by the English writer Wyndham Lewis (1882–1957), appeared once in 1914 and again in 1915. Principal contributors were Pound and T. S. Eliot.

Such movements as imagism produced brief modernist poems sharply chiselled, but other forces, notably the epic tradition as radically transformed by Walt Whitman in *Leaves of Grass*, produced long modernist poems, seemingly fragmented, loose and baggy in structure, often open-ended or unfinished. These poems had as their closest analogies the artistic forms of the "collage" or "assemblage," or so-called "found art." If at times the shorter poems seemed classically impersonal, the longer poems seemed shaped to the lives lived by the poets. Ezra Pound provided examples of both in his two-line "In a Station of the Metro" and his unfinished *Cantos*. T. S. Eliot provided similar examples in his imagistic "Preludes" and in his epic-like *The Waste Land* and *Four Quartets*; as did William Carlos Williams in "The Red Wheelbarrow" and the open-ended *Paterson*; and H. D. in the miniature "Oread" and in her meditative *The Walls Do Not Fall* (the first part of her *Trilogy*).

Modernism might be considered a revolt against "realism," but not against "reality"; this "real" reality was to be found not in the sequence of exterior events but in the flow of consciousness in encounter with those events, actively selecting, shaping, and creating experience. The drama of human consciousness as presented in T. S. Eliot's "The Love Song of J. Alfred Prufrock" was remarkably complex, the flow endless. Even in sleep, consciousness became the unconscious and experience became dream. William Faulkner provided for American fiction its best examples of the use of the stream of consciousness in such novels as *The Sound and the Fury* (1929) and *As I Lay Dying* (1930). Eugene O'Neill adapted the interior monologue for the stage in his play *Strange Interlude* (1928). Poets, playwrights, and novelists of the period introduced these techniques or variations on them throughout their works.

THE POETRY RENAISSANCE: MAKING IT NEW

Poets by their very nature are individualistic and abhor classification. The modernist poets all had distinctive voices, but they all were participants in an enterprise whose mission was summed up by Ezra Pound in his simple yet complex advice: "Make it new." Because modernist poetry is so rich, and the poets so many, one useful way to approach them is in groups, exploring some resemblances before examining their differences. Looming as major figures who, in ways often radically different from one another, were shapers of the modern are Ezra Pound, T. S. Eliot, Robert Frost, Wallace Stevens, William Carlos Williams, Marianne Moore, Hart Crane, and Langston Hughes. In addition to writing an impressive and original body of poetry, these poets were influential in what they said about the nature of poetry and the role of the poet in society.

Pound ransacked the world and the past, including Oriental literature and history, in order to be sure that what he made was new: "My pawing over the ancients and semi-ancients has been one struggle to find out what has been done, once for all, better than it can ever be done again." In 1912, before anyone could have guessed that a genuinely new poetry would soon appear, he wrote prophetically:

> As to Twentieth-century poetry, and the poetry which I expect to see written during the next decade or so, it will, I think, move against poppycock, it will be harder and saner, it will be . . . "nearer the bone." It will be as much like granite

as it can be, its force will lie in its truth, its interpretative power (of course, poetic force does always rest there); I mean it will not try to seem forcible by rhetorical din, and luxurious riot. We will have fewer painted adjectives impeding the shock and stroke of it. At least for myself, I want it so, austere, direct, free from emotional slither.

Within the next few years, Pound began to find the kind of poetry he prophesied, and where he did not find it but suspected misdirected talent, he generously gave out advice. Of the seven poets other than Pound gathered in this group as "shapers of the modern," over half were his "discoveries" or the beneficiaries of his counsel early in their careers: Eliot, Frost, Williams, and Moore. With his position as foreign correspondent for *Poetry* and his close connections with other little magazines and presses, he was in a position to make his earlier prophecy come true. In the case of Eliot, Pound saw to the publication of "The Love Song of J. Alfred Prufrock" in *Poetry* in 1915, and was later, because of Eliot's breakdown, to serve as midwife for *The Waste Land*. Through his editorial skills, he helped it to become what he called "the justification of the 'movement,' of our modern experiment."

Pound provided more modernist manifestoes than any other poet of the time. But Eliot made critical statements in his essays that were more influential in the universities. His coined phrases — "impersonal theory of poetry," "objective correlative," "dissociation of sensibility" — became counters in the "new criticism," endlessly defined and elaborated and debated. Eliot, who had his mischievous moments, would later claim that he himself wasn't at all sure what he meant by these "notorious" terms. But that did not deter their continuing use in the academies.

In contrast with Eliot, Frost wrote little prose, but what he wrote was memorable. He said that a poem "begins in delight and ends in wisdom." And he also said that a poem "ends in a clarification of life — not necessarily a great clarification, such as sects and cults are founded on, but in a momentary stay against confusion." In these seemingly simple statements (from "The Figure a Poem Makes"), Frost defined his differences from Pound and Eliot, and also his kind of newness. His was an immediately accessible poetry, as theirs was not. He became, in his public readings, America's beloved "good gray poet." He had strong links with New England's past, drawing the title of his first book, *A Boy's Will*, from Henry Wadsworth Longfellow and borrowing many of his themes from Edwin Arlington Robinson. But whatever his connections with these predecessors, he was modern and they were not; the secret of his modernity probably lay in his simple (yet complex) notion of a poem's figure and end.

A glance through the pages of the collected poems of Wallace Stevens, William Carlos Williams, and Marianne Moore quickly reveals their startling originality. Stevens's very titles — "Thirteen Ways of Looking at a Blackbird," "The Emperor of Ice Cream," "The Man on the Dump" — suggest a kind of anti-poetry, and the texts are just as strange. Stevens's wit is stamped over all his poems, but he was deadly serious about poetry and its purpose, defining the modern poem (in "Of Modern Poetry") as "the poem of the mind in the act of finding what will suffice" in an age characterized by the loss of belief. Williams's pages in *Paterson* are filled with charts, statistics, and even personal letters (one from the young poet Allen Ginsberg); all of the initially jarring juxtapositions ultimately make sense to the reader willing to engage the poem on its own terms. Williams revealed his driving force in a slogan he inserted frequently in both his prose and poetry: "No ideas but in things." Marianne Moore's poems at first look peculiar on the page, with unfamiliar stanzaic forms of her own invention, and a language of precision that seems unpoetic. She opened her famous poem "Poetry" with the shocking revelation: "I, too, dislike it," but she went on to claim all human experience, including "business documents and school-books," as the province of a genuine poetry that cannot fail to interest the deepest skeptic.

Hart Crane's dissolute, tortured life and early death fulfilled the popular conception of the romantic poet, but his was a distinctively modern poetry, difficult, allusive, and often obscure. Most of his life was given over to the construction (as a counter to what he saw as a defeatist negativism in *The Waste Land*) of his masterpiece *The Bridge*—an embodiment of Whitman's affirmations in the ironies, gestures, and techniques of the most complicated modernist poetry. He summed up the essence of his method (and revealed the source of his poetry's difficulty) in the phrase, "the logic of metaphor," a technique replacing ordinary logic or rationality in poetry; his ideal reader would find subterranean connections between the puzzlingly dissimilar items yoked together in metaphor not in the intellect but on the unconscious level in an intuitive response to the poem.

Langston Hughes, the central figure of the Harlem Renaissance, published his manifesto in 1926, when he was only twenty-four years old: "The Negro Artist and the Racial Mountain." His way of "making it new" involved, as with the other modernists, a radical break with the past: "We younger Negro artists who create now intend to express our individual dark-skinned selves without fear or shame. If white people are pleased we are glad. If they are not, it doesn't matter. We know we are beautiful. And ugly too. The tom-tom cries and the tom-tom laughs." In stating plainly his own personal commitment as a poet, he provided a platform for black poets and artists to come: "Most of my own poems are racial in theme and treatment, derived from the life I know. In many of them I try to grasp and hold some of the meanings and rhythms of jazz." Hughes gave black writers a new sense of self, a genuine source for an individual voice. His manifesto, his poetry and fiction, and his life constituted a kind of artistic declaration of independence, useful for all writers, of whatever color or origin.

In 1935, Robert Frost described the period of his youth as an age that "ran wild in the quest of new ways to be new." The poetic experiments often involved "subtraction" or "elimination." Poetry was written, he remembered, "without punctuation," "without capital letters," "without metric frame on which to measure the rhythm," "without any images but those to the eye," "without content under the trade name of poésie pure," "without ability," and "without feeling or sentiment." Frost's descriptions are quite apt, even though the implicit negative value judgments are distorted. He no doubt had in mind his major "competitors" like Pound and Eliot, but also those presented here under "Experiments, Rebellions, and Break-Aways": Carl Sandburg, Vachel Lindsay, H. D., Robinson Jeffers, Archibald MacLeish, and E. E. Cummings. All of these poets tried one or more of the "subtractions" that Frost included on his list, and more successfully than his remarks would indicate.

Sandburg and Jeffers, two radically different poets, both wrote in the free-flowing line of Whitmanesque free verse (Frost had asserted that writing free verse was like playing tennis without a net). But Sandburg's simple faith in the people and Jeffers's chilling "inhumanism" were at radical odds with each other. Vachel Lindsay's poetry, in contrast with that of Sandburg and Jeffers, was compellingly, often savagely musical, designed to be chanted and sung. Filling the romantic role of the vagabond poet, he mesmerized audiences with his recitations of "General William Booth Enters into Heaven" and "The Congo."

Archibald MacLeish provided one of the most memorable definitions of the modernist poem in his 1926 "Ars Poetica," opening: "A poem should be palpable and mute / As a globed fruit." As first published, MacLeish's poem eliminated most punctuation; each of the two-line "stanzas" presented a sharply chiselled image, illustrating what was prescribed: "A poem should be wordless / As the flight of birds"; "A poem should be motionless in time / As the moon climbs." This influential poem concluded with its most frequently quoted lines: "A poem should not mean / But be." Although MacLeish's view of poetry would go through several transfigurations, especially in the 1930s, his "Ars Poetica" endured as a justification of the imagist movement and a favorite text of the New Critics, whose concept of poetry it essentially defined. (The New Criticism provided explications of the "hard" New Poetry by reading poems rigorously without reference to contaminating contexts of biography or history.)

The name we know Hilda Doolittle by is H. D., a creation of Ezra Pound when he signed her poems he was forwarding to *Poetry*, "H. D., *Imagiste*." Although she continued to sign her poems H. D., she went on to write a series of long poems that were considerably more than simply "*Imagiste*." These longer works (as, for example, her *Trilogy*) have only recently come to be recognized as important examples of the lyric or personal epic that flourished during the modernist period. She has, however, been traditionally identified in literary history as the Imagist par excellence. It could be argued that H. D.'s "Sea Rose," "Pear Tree," and "Oread" fulfilled MacLeish's prescriptions set forth in "Ars Poetica" more than any of his own poems.

Of all the poets who sought newness by "subtraction," E. E. Cummings eliminated the most. He gave up capital letters (signing his name e. e. cummings), punctuation, conventional word divisions and line arrangements. Few readers have failed to fall under the charming spell of the rebellious spirit of his poems, particularly as they defy many of the arbitrary rules of writing and the rigid conventions of genteel society. Often Cummings turned his poems into puzzles, scattering the letters over the page and daring the reader to make sense out of seeming chaos. The readers who succeeded in reassembling the letters into words were pleased with themselves, and felt that oneness with Cummings he encouraged when he wrote in an Introduction to his *Collected Poems*: "The poems to come are for you and me and are not for mostpeople." Some critics have observed that Cummings appeals to the adolescent rebel in all of us, but in the end most of us (perhaps the "mostpeople" he disdained) crave something more. Other critics have placed a special value on his perennial appeal to the young, and point to a number of poems that are classics of their kind—"anyone lived in a pretty how town," "my father moved through dooms of love," "pity this busy monster, manunkind."

Another group of poets of the modernist period attempted to achieve newness within the tradition—by renewing, extending, and enlarging it. This group includes Sara Teasdale, Elinor Wylie, Edna St. Vincent Millay, John Crowe Ransom, Allen Tate, and Countee Cullen. It is perhaps no accident that two members of the Southern Fugitive group, John Crowe Ransom and Allen Tate, were the chief theorists of this group. Ransom characterized himself as "in manners, aristocratic; in religion, ritualistic; in art, traditional." All of these poets placed great value on the short lyric; most wrote sonnets at some point in their careers. None attempted the kind of long poem, or epic, written by Pound, Eliot, Williams, H. D., and others.

Sara Teasdale and Elinor Wylie, like Hart Crane, lived lives that seemed to conform to popular notions about poets: they were unhappy in love. Relationships with men were surrounded by mystery or clouded by scandal; they died young, Teasdale by suicide, Wylie by stroke. Both Teasdale and Wylie defended the traditional forms within which they wrote their poems. Teasdale expressed her "joy and freedom" in using "regular rhythm, modified by variations within itself, and regular recurrence of rhymes." Wylie defended herself as a "miniature lyricist" who had "cultivated a small clean technique." Both Teasdale and Wylie wrote sonnet sequences and embodied personal emotion in their poems. But Teasdale believed that a poem must spring from deep emotion and clearly wrote out of her own sometimes turbulent feelings (a recent selection of her poems was entitled *Mirror of the Heart*). Wylie, on the other hand, often modelled her poems after the Elizabethan or Metaphysical poets she read and constructed her poems with the glitter and elegance of "enamelled snuffboxes" (her own metaphor).

Edna St. Vincent Millay was a rebel in her life but a traditionalist in her poetry. *A Few Figs from Thistles*, published in 1920, established her as the spokeswoman of the rebellious youth of the jazz age by providing highly quotable — and daring — lines: "My candle burns at both its ends; / It will not last the night; / But ah, my foes, and oh, my friends — / It gives a lovely light." Those who quoted her lines cared little that though they expressed defiance, they expressed it in thoroughly traditional forms. Millay made herself a master of the sonnet form, and in one sonnet expressed her pleasure in its imposed restraints: "I will put Chaos into fourteen lines," she said, and will keep him "in the strict confines / Of this sweet Order. . . / Till he with Order mingles and combines" in "pious rape."

John Crowe Ransom and Allen Tate produced a great deal more prose than poetry. They were severe critics of their own work and eliminated many of their early poems when they brought together their own final collections. Their poems were difficult, allusive, cryptic — in the fashion of the poetry of the major modernists; and they clearly identified with the social conservatism of poets like Pound and Eliot. But in form they were severely traditional. Ransom charged that though the "moderns. . . find the old practice trite. . . they lack any consistent conception of what a new practice might be." Tate's defense of traditional forms was blunt: "Formal versification is the primary structure of poetic order, the assurance to the reader and to the poet himself that the poet is in control of the disorder both outside him and within his own mind. . . . Yet is not much of the so-called poetry of the past twenty or more years merely anti-poetry, a parasite on the body of positive poetry. . . ?" Both Ransom and Tate at their best produced poems that seem remarkably modernist in feeling and distinctively traditionalist in form — as in Ransom's "Bells for John Whiteside's Daughter" and Tate's "Ode to the Confederate Dead."

Countee Cullen, one of the most gifted poets of the Harlem Renaissance, once provided a description of himself (in the third person): "As a poet [Cullen] is a rank conservative, loving the measured line and the skillful rhyme; but not blind to those poets who will not be circumscribed. . . ." Like Sara Teasdale and Elinor Wylie, he frequently turned to the sonnet form to contain and shape his personal emotion. Indeed, his most famous poem, "Yet Do I Marvel," is a sonnet that consists of a series of charges against God which tend to undermine the opening affirmation, "I doubt not God is good." The climactic charge, and one that Cullen clearly felt deeply, was God's role in shaping Cullen himself: "Yet do I marvel at this curious thing: / To make a poet black, and to bid him sing!" Langston Hughes could never have written these lines; he would find the source of his material and inspiration as a poet in his own black identity. But Cullen, though he wrote poems out of his black experience, claimed his right to shape poems out of his fundamentally human experience also. His favorite poet was not American, but British, to whom he addressed an important poem "To John Keats, Poet, at Springtime."

The experience of all these poets who sought and found the new in a renewal of the tradition may be symbolized by that of Allen Tate, who wrote in "Poetry Modern and Unmodern":

> I did not discover modernism, or perhaps I had better say, the shock to the twentieth-century sensibility out of which modernism developed, through Yeats, Eliot, or Pound. Without knowing what I was seeing, I saw it first in that curious Victorian poet James Thomson (B. V. [Thomson's pseudonym]), whose inflated rhetoric and echolalia merely adumbrated the center of psychic and moral interest of later and better poets. It remained to find the right language and to establish a center from which it could be spoken; for the poet is never wholly aware of his subject until his language is able to speak it, and to render it to the entire human being, to both the sensibility and the intellect.

In some way, all these poets found the "right language" and established a "center from which to speak it" within the traditional poetic forms, enabling them to avoid the sentimentality and grandiloquence of the genteel tradition against which all the modernists were rebelling.

THE NEW DRAMA

American drama came to maturity during the modernist period at a time when the "legitimate theater" was rapidly disappearing as a source of popular entertainment. America's Puritan origins, with the Puritan hostility to the theater, inhibited the development of an American drama until well into the eighteenth century, when a production in 1787 of Royall Tyler's *The Contrast* demonstrated clearly that Americans could write and enjoy stage plays. Throughout the nineteenth century and into the twentieth, an American theater flourished, with travelling theatrical companies bringing British plays (including Shakespeare's) and "adapted" European plays to the provinces. American playwrights were soon writing American plays, as for example Anna Cora Mowatt's *Fashion; or, Life in New York*, produced in 1845. Some of the most popular dramas were adaptations of American fiction, such as *Rip Van Winkle* and *Uncle Tom's Cabin*. Melodramas with hissable villains delighted the audiences, as did spectacle — the sinking of a ship or the burning of a building on stage. Most appreciated was the "well-made play," which reflected the audience's own sentiments and values — or biases. On stage the Chinese, Irish, Italians, Swedes, or Germans were turned into hilarious comic characters in servant roles and other "bit" parts. Such drama did not survive as literature, though it was frequently studied as "popular literature" for its sociological revelations.

Early in the twentieth century, at a time when the infant motion picture industry was just beginning to replace stage plays as popular fare, American drama began to mature. It was nourished and influenced by international movements in drama, especially expressionism as it had developed in Germany (1910–25), portraying the playwright's inner feelings, ideas, and emotions instead of an exterior or objective reality. The German playwright Bertold Brecht, in his youth, had been a part of this movement. The Swedish playwright August

Strindberg, who had died in 1912, had written a number of "dream plays" (such as *A Dream Play*, 1902, which gave the genre its name) helping to shape the expressionist movement and directly influencing American playwrights. Other major playwrights who exerted much influence were the Norwegian playwright Henrik Ibsen, the Italian Luigi Pirandello, and the Irishman George Bernard Shaw.

Also important in the emergence of modern American drama was the development of "little" or experimental theater groups, sometimes operating with improvised facilities. The Provincetown Players were organized in Provinceton, Massachusetts, on Cape Cod. They were soon presenting plays in a fishing shack-playhouse, the Wharf Theatre, and in a small theater in Greenwich Village in 1917. Prime movers in this little-theater group were ex-Iowans George Cram Cook, who directed plays, and his wife Susan Glaspell, who wrote them. As a young playwright, Eugene O'Neill became associated with the group, and in 1916 his one-act play *Bound East for Cardiff* appeared together with Susan Glaspell's *Trifles*. The group became for O'Neill, Glaspell, and other playwrights a laboratory to try out their dramatic ideas and played a central role in the development of modern American drama. Another experimental group, the Washington Square Players, was founded in New York's Greenwich Village in 1915; it was disrupted by the First World War but reorganized as the Theatre Guild in 1919.

The 1920s and 1930s were a time of great experimentation in the American theater. Eugene O'Neill early demonstrated that he could write traditional realistic drama, as in *Beyond the Horizon* in 1920 and *Anna Christie* in 1921. But at the same time (more or less) he brought out the expressionistic plays *The Emperor Jones* in 1920 and *The Hairy Ape* in 1922. Elmer Rice, a lawyer turned playwright, produced his first play as early as 1914, but the appearance of his *The Adding Machine* in 1923, with its hero a Mr. Zero, caused one critic to write that the play was "the best and fairest example of the newer expressionism in the theatre, that it has experienced." Rice's *Street Scene*, produced in 1929, presented a realistic slice of life from a teeming tenement area in New York. Maxwell Anderson collaborated with a world war veteran, Laurence Stallings, to produce a realistic war (or "anti-war") drama, *What Price Glory?*, in 1924.

In 1931, with the country in the middle of the Great Depression, a number of individuals broke away from the Theatre Guild because of its insistence on remaining apolitical and formed the Group Theatre. It devoted its energies to encouraging playwrights with some kind of social or political vision in tune with the hard times. One of the most important of the group's playwrights was Clifford Odets, author of the social dramas *Awake and Sing* and *Waiting for Lefty*, both produced in 1935. Even when plays were without a specific social message, in the 1930s they often dealt with the down and out or exiles and outcasts, as in John Steinbeck's story of two migrant workers, *Of Mice and Men*, produced in 1937; and in William Saroyan's account of a number of life's drifters (a bartender, a prostitute, an Indian fighter) in *The Time of Your Life*, produced in 1939. Lillian Hellman introduced a higher social level in her play about consuming greed, *The Little Foxes*, presented also in 1939. One of the most innovative playwrights of the latter part of this period was Thornton Wilder. As early as 1931, he had experimented with nonrealistic techniques in a remarkable series of short plays, including the powerful "cyclic" drama *The Long Christmas Dinner*. His *Our Town*, produced in 1938 on a bare stage with a minimum of symbolic props carried out as the Stage Manager called for them, though set in Grover's Corner, New

Hampshire, captured something cyclic and profound in the whole of human life that has made it one of the most frequently produced of American plays. Wilder's *The Skin of Our Teeth* (1942) encompassed, in a kind of surrealistic way, the whole of human history and at the same time was alternately comic and poignant. Its allegorical reach and epic sweep clearly owed something to James Joyce's massive fictional masterpiece *Finnegans Wake* (1939).

This listing of examples of the revitalization of drama during this period does not touch on such folk drama as *Porgy* (1927) by Dorothy and Dubose Heyward (the play on which George and Ira Gershwin later based their musical *Porgy and Bess*, 1935). Nor does it include any examples of that peculiarly American form of theater, musical comedy, such as the classic *Oklahoma!* (1943). Also virtually omitted is comedy, including such plays as *Life with Father* (1939) by Howard Lindsay and Russel Crouse; and *Harvey* (1944), a play about an alcoholic's imaginary rabbit, by Mary Chase. But this sampling is extensive enough to indicate that the literature of the theater was during this period as remarkable in its "newness" as was the poetry and fiction. And one playwright of the period, Eugene O'Neill, left a body of work that made him one of the most imposing of America's literary figures, as well-known abroad as at home. His later plays included *Desire Under the Elms* (1924), *The Great God Brown* (1926), *Mourning Becomes Electra* (1933), and *The Iceman Cometh* (1946). At his death in 1953, O'Neill left a number of plays which have since been produced. The autobiographical *Long Day's Journey into Night*, now considered by many his best play, was produced in 1956; *A Touch of the Poet* in 1957; *A Moon for the Misbegotten* in 1957; *Hughie* in 1964; and *More Stately Mansions* in 1964.

NEW DIMENSIONS IN PROSE

In 1916, when he was twenty years old, John Dos Passos published a short essay entitled "Against American Literature" in *The New Republic*. Surveying contemporary American fiction, he wrote: "This wholesome rice-pudding fare is, unfortunately, a strangely unstimulating diet; so we are forced to give it body — like apple jack — by a stiff infusion of a stronger product. As a result of this constant need to draw on foreign sources our literature has become a hybrid which, like the mule, is barren and must be produced afresh each time by the crossing of other strains." In conclusion he asked: "Shall we stagnate forever . . . patronizing the art of other peoples, but producing nothing from amid our jumble of races but steel and oil and grain?"

In 1937, Malcolm Cowley (a member of the "lost generation") brought together a number of essays on the literature of the 1920s by various critics and entitled the volume *After the Genteel Tradition*. He borrowed the phrase for his title from the American philosopher George Santayana (1863–1952), who had used it in the titles of two essays: "The Genteel Tradition in American Philosophy" (1911) and "The Genteel Tradition at Bay" (1931). Cowley found the phrase especially apt in identifying the target against which the writers of the 1920s were rebelling. The word *genteel* evoked a literary tradition of conventionality, polite conformity, and social correctness. John Dos Passos had attacked the genteel tradition without using the term. Ironically, Cowley described the venerable William Dean Howells, the great promoter in the past of realism and naturalism, as the essence of the genteel tradition. Howells, who died in 1920, had thus lived beyond his time; he would have been surprised to be identified as a leader of reactionary literary forces.

Within a decade after Dos Passos wrote his little piece, American fiction had gone through a revolution in which Dos Passos himself played a leading role. Almost every year introduced new works of fiction that legitimately claimed serious attention — 1918: Willa Cather, *My Antonia*; 1919: Sherwood Anderson, *Winesburg, Ohio*; 1920: F. Scott Fitzgerald, *This Side of Paradise*, and Sinclair Lewis, *Main Street*; 1921: John Dos Passos, *Three Soldiers*; 1922: Sinclair Lewis, *Babbitt*, and E. E. Cummings, *The Enormous Room*; 1923: Jean Toomer, *Cane*, and Willa Cather, *A Lost Lady*; 1924: Ernest Hemingway, *In Our Time*; 1925: F. Scott Fitzgerald, *The Great Gatsby*, John Dos Passos, *Manhattan Transfer*, Willa Cather, *The Professor's House*, Theodore Dreiser, *An American Tragedy*, and Gertrude Stein, *The Making of Americans*; 1926: Ernest Hemingway, *The Sun Also Rises*.

This is, of course, a selective list; some of these authors had published before Dos Passos wrote his piece in 1916, and all would write important works after 1926 (as, for example, Fitzgerald's *Tender Is the Night*, 1934, and John Dos Passos's three-part masterpiece, *U.S.A.*, published as a single work in 1938). And it does not reach until the end of the 1920s, thus missing 1929: William Faulkner, *The Sound and the Fury*, Ernest Hemingway, *A Farewell to Arms*, and Thomas Wolfe, *Look Homeward, Angel*. Moreover, there were some new writers that would appear in the next decade that belong to this flowering of American fiction. Katherine Anne Porter's first volume of short stories, *Flowering Judas*, appeared in 1930. John Steinbeck published throughout the 1930s, achieving acclaim in 1939 for his *The Grapes of Wrath*. Richard Wright published his first volume of short stories, *Uncle Tom's Children*, in 1938, and his remarkably successful novel *Native Son* in 1940. And Eudora Welty began publishing short stories in the latter half of the 1930s, issuing her first volume, *A Curtain of Green*, in 1941.

Nearly all of the novelists of this period wrote short stories, and those committed to the short story often tried their hand at novels. The period is as rich for the short story as it is for the novel. Any list meant to encompass the fiction writers responsible for innovations in fiction during the period would be incomplete without all of the following: Willa Cather, Sherwood Anderson, Katherine Anne Porter, Jean Toomer, F. Scott Fitzgerald, William Faulkner, Ernest Hemingway, John Steinbeck, and Eudora Welty. The range and variety of subjects and techniques represented by the work of these writers offer an excellent introduction to the major fiction of this period and may serve as a guide to the important novels that changed the course of American fiction.

Many other novelists and short story writers wrote in a variety of autobiographical modes so as to expand the meaning of the form. Gertrude Stein, Claude McKay, James Thurber, E. B. White, Thomas Wolfe, Zora Neale Hurston, and Richard Wright found various and fascinating ways — tragic, serious, and comic — of remembering their lives. They often used the techniques of fictional narrative to reconstruct their pasts out of their imaginative memories, demonstrating that the problems facing an autobiographer and a novelist are quite similar and the solutions often identical. And the rewards of reading the two genres are very much alike.

Gertrude Stein, in *The Autobiography of Alice B. Toklas* (1933), devised a technique in which she could talk without reticence about her own views and accomplishments by adopting the fiction that her companion Alice Toklas was writing *her* autobiography. James Thurber's comic talent seems, if anything, intensified when he wrote about himself in *My Life and Hard Times* (1933). E. B. White turned his personal account of a visit to Walden Pond, entitled "Walden" (1942), into an ironic contrast between his contemporary encounter with nature and

Henry David Thoreau's experience in a more innocent age. Thomas Wolfe wrote much in the same style and about the same matter in both his autobiographical sketches and his fiction. Indeed, his autobiography became his fiction with changes of the names of characters and places, and thus the first-person sketches in *From Death to Morning* (1935) are a better introduction to his four massive novels than the few short (but very long) stories he left. Claude McKay in *A Long Way from Home* (1937), Richard Wright in *Black Boy* (1945), and Zora Neale Hurston in *Dust Tracks on a Road* (1942) represent three very different black writers dealing directly, but as inventively as in fiction, with their experience growing up in, or coming to terms with, America. Nonblack readers may be struck by how being black made a radical difference in the lives of these writers, but they may be struck too at how the black experience is, essentially, the *human* experience (growing up, discovering one's identity, facing irrational hostility, confronting death) complicated many-fold by white racism.

The 1920s and 1930s saw the emergence of many extraordinarily gifted cultural and social critics, including H. L. Mencken, Sinclair Lewis, Henry Miller, Edmund Wilson, John Dos Passos, and James Agee. All but Mencken wrote fiction, but Wilson and Agee are better known and more highly praised for their literary or cultural commentary than for their fiction. Mencken's "On Being an American" (1922) explains why, during the exodus to Europe of American writers in the 1920s, he stayed in America. Wilson was important as literary critic, social commentator, and political thinker, but he was perhaps at his best as historian of contemporary literature, as exemplified in "The Literary Consequences of the Crash" (1952). James Agee's classic 1930s portrayal of the lives of southern share-croppers, *Let Us Now Praise Famous Men* (1941), remains one of the most moving accounts written of the Great Depression.

The three committed novelists in this group were also passionate social and cultural critics. Sinclair Lewis, America's first winner of the Nobel Prize in literature, provided a vivid picture of the plight of the writer in America in his astute 1930 Nobel speech, "The American Fear of Literature." The long-term expatriate Henry Miller took time out in 1940 from writing fiction (highly autobiographical in nature) to return from Paris for a new look at the America from which he had earlier fled; the result was *The Air-Conditioned Nightmare* (1945), a disillusioned examination of the state of American culture on the eve of the Second World War. John Dos Passos wrote in his masterpiece *U.S.A.* a kind of documentary fiction, including news clippings, headlines, thumbnail biographies of public figures, advertisements, and popular songs. Many passages, literary equivalents of the "assemblages" or "collages" of modern art, treat vividly, succinctly, and perhaps definitively such historical moments as the stock market crash that began the Great Depression.

During this period, the line separating various kinds of prose had grown very thin. Identical subjects and techniques carried over from what we might call imaginative fiction to imaginative nonfiction, with corresponding mixed effects on the reader. John Dos Passos adapted documentary techniques to fiction, while James Agee adapted narrative techniques to documentary accounts. All of the autobiographers used the selective techniques of fiction to achieve a predetermined effect — comic for Thurber, wonder and awe for Wolfe, indignation for Wright. Thus the generalizations that might be ventured for the fiction of the period — about language, style, tone, structure, form, plot, character, point of view, theme — might well have relevance to autobiography and social commentary.

There were two opposite tendencies in prose style during the 1920s and 1930s, one represented by the metaphor of the iceberg, as articulated by Ernest Hemingway, and the other by the metaphor of the pinhead, as elaborated by Faulkner. Early in his career, Hemingway became famous for the economy, simplicity, and austerity of his style that fit so well his constant theme of grace under pressure. It was often said that he had modelled himself on Sherwood Anderson and Gertrude Stein, known for their plain and iterative styles cast in monosyllabic vocabularies. He once explained his secret: "I always try to write on the principle of the iceberg. There is seven-eighths of it underwater for every part that shows. . . . If a writer omits something because he does not know it then there is a hole in the story."

In contrast with Hemingway's style, Faulkner's was complex, profuse, entangled and entangling, seeming to suit his complicated theme of time eternal that is present in any single moment of human experience. When asked about his run-on sentences and vague pronoun references, Faulkner answered that he was the kind of writer who wanted to "reduce all human experience onto the head of a pin as the man engraved the Lord's Prayer on the head of a pin once. He can't do that, but he is still going to try. And the obscurity, the prolixity which you find in writers is simply that desire to put all that experience into one word. Then he has got to add another word, another word becomes a sentence, but he's still trying to get it into one unstopping whole. . . ."

The naturalistic tendency surviving out of the past to produce massive slice-of-life novels, as in Theodore Dreiser's *An American Tragedy* (1925), was countered not only by Hemingway's terse, taut style but also by Willa Cather's concise, poetically suggestive style. In an essay entitled "The Novel Démeublé" ("The Novel Unfurnished"), she wrote: "How wonderful it would be if we could throw all the furniture out of the window; and along with it, all the meaningless reiterations concerning physical sensations, all the tiresome old patterns, and leave the room as bare as the stage of a Greek theatre." Her avoidance of a "tasteless amplitude" was exemplified by other writers of the time, such as Jean Toomer in his poetically shaped *Cane* (1923), by F. Scott Fitzgerald in his artfully crafted *The Great Gatsby* (1925), and by Katherine Anne Porter and Eudora Welty in numerous stories thematically explosive in their compactness.

In the novel, there was much experimentation in the representation of action, as in John Dos Passos's *Manhattan Transfer* (1925), with the weaving back and forth from character to character, most of whom had little connection with each other but whose experiences, as compositely presented, offered the portrait of a modern metropolis. William Faulkner became a master, in such novels as *The Sound and the Fury* (1929) and *Absalom, Absalom!* (1936), at disrupting chronology and scrambling time sequence for thematic ends. Even before Dos Passos and Faulkner experimented with the plotting of novels, Gertrude Stein had, in "Melanctha" (one of the *Three Lives*, 1909), discovered herself writing outside conventional chronology. In her fascinating, idiosyncratic style, she wrote later in *Composition as Explanation* (1926) about "Melanctha":

> In that there was a constant recurring and beginning there was a marked direction in the direction of being in the present although naturally I had been accustomed to past present and future, and why, because the composition forming around me was a prolonged present. A composition of a prolonged present is a natural composition in the world as it has been these thirty years it was more and more a prolonged present. I created then a prolonged present naturally I knew nothing of a continuous present but it came naturally to me to make one, it was simple it was clear to me and nobody knew why it was done like that, I did not myself although naturally to me it was natural.

In the short story during this period, the traditional focus on plot diminished or shifted. In *A Story Teller's Story* (1924), Sherwood Anderson described the situation he found when he began to write: "There was a notion that ran through all storytelling in America, that stories must be built about a plot and that absurd Anglo-Saxon notion that they must point a moral, uplift the people, make better citizens, etc. The magazines were filled with these plot stories. . . . 'The Poison Plot,' I called it. . . . What was wanted I thought was form, not plot, an altogether more elusive and difficult thing to come at. . . ." Katherine Anne Porter wrote later in "No Plot, My Dear, No Story" (1942), "a short story needed *first* a *theme*, and then a point of view, a certain knowledge of human nature and strong feeling about it, and style. . . . The greater the theme and the better the style, the better the story. . . ." Whether it was "form" (as with Anderson) or "theme" (as with Porter), some important element dislodged plot from its central role in the short story. For Eudora Welty, this something was "mystery," as she wrote in "The Reading and Writing of Short Stories" (1949): "Every good story has mystery — not the puzzle kind, but the mystery of allurement. As we understand the story better, it is likely that the mystery does not necessarily decrease; rather it simply grows more beautiful."

The focus of fiction tended to shift during this period from "outside" to "inside," from happening to consciousness. Henry James, the one significant transitional figure in the novel standing between the Victorian and the modern period, managed this shift with brilliance in the "dramas of consciousness" of his late, great period, in such novels as *The Ambassadors* (1903). It was James's brother William, who in his 1890 *Principles of Psychology*, had provided the term *stream of consciousness* for the most innovative technique in modernist fiction. But writers like Anderson, who did not use avant-garde narrative techniques, nevertheless focused on the interior dramas of his lonely and tortured characters. In the stories of Anderson and others, an important "event" tended to be psychological — a moment of intense awareness, a sudden insight, a shock of recognition. Such concerns on the part of writers made for a more subtle, a more complex, fiction.

It is perhaps good to end this discussion of the nature of the new in modernism with an eloquent reminder of the endurance of the old. It comes appropriately from one of the greatest innovators in modern fiction, William Faulkner, in his 1950 Nobel Prize acceptance speech. He spoke at a time when the world was still trying to absorb the terrible knowledge that human beings had it in their power, through the released energy of the atom, to destroy themselves and the world. He reminded beginning writers of the "old verities and truths of the heart, the old universal truths lacking which any story is ephemeral and doomed — love and honor and pity and pride and compassion and sacrifice." Faulkner refused to accept the end of the human race: "I believe that man will not merely endure: he will prevail. He is immortal, not because he alone among creatures has an inexhaustible voice, but because he has a soul, a spirit capable of compassion and sacrifice and endurance. The poet's, the writer's, duty is to write about these things."

ADDITIONAL READING

SPECIAL STUDIES

René Taupin, *The Influence of French Symbolism on Modern American Poetry*, 1929, trans. William and Anne Rich Pratt, 1985.

Frederick Lewis Allen, *Only Yesterday: An Informal History of the 1920s*, 1931.
Glenn Hughes, *Imagism and the Imagists: A Study in Modern Poetry*, 1931.
Malcolm Cowley, *Exile's Return: A Narrative of Ideas*, 1934, 1951.
Malcolm Cowley, *After the Genteel Tradition: American Writers, 1910–1930*, 1937, 1964.
Alfred Kazin, *On Native Grounds: An Interpretation of Modern American Prose Literature*, 1942.
Frederick J. Hoffman, Charles Allen, and Carolyn Ulrich, *The Little Magazine: A History and a Bibliography*, 1946.
Louise Bogan, *Achievement in American Poetry, 1900–1950*, 1951.
Alan S. Downer, *Fifty Years of American Drama*, 1951.
Edmund Wilson, *The Shores of Light: A Literary Chronicle of the Twenties and Thirties*, 1952.
Bernard Duffey, *The Chicago Renaissance in American Letters: A Critical History*, 1954.
Frederick J. Hoffman, *The Twenties: American Writing in the Postwar Decade*, 1955, 1962.
Walter Rideout, *The Radical Novel in the United States, 1900–1954*, 1956.
William E. Leuchtenburg, *The Perils of Prosperity, 1914–1932*, 1958.
John M. Bradbury, *The Fugitives: A Critical Account*, 1958.
Louise Cowan, *The Fugitive Group: A Literary History*, 1959.
Rob Roy Purdy, ed., *Fugitives' Reunion*, 1959.
Roy Harvey Pearce, *The Continuity of American Poetry*, 1961.
Daniel Aaron, *Writers on the Left*, 1961.
Austin M. Wright, *The American Short Story in the Twenties*, 1961.
J. Hillis Miller, *Poets of Reality*, 1965.
Dale Kramer, *Chicago Renaissance: The Literary Life in the Midwest*, 1966.
Harvey Swados, *The American Writer and the Great Depression*, 1966.
Nicholas Joost, *The Dial: Years of Transition, 1912–1920, 1967.*
Stanley Cooperman, *World War I and the American Novel*, 1967.
Edward Margolies, *Native Sons: A Critical Study of Twentieth-Century Negro American Authors*, 1968.
Hyatt H. Waggoner, *American Poets: From the Puritans to the Present Day*, 1968.
Jerome Mazzaro, ed., *Modern American Poetry*, 1970.
Nathan Irvin Huggins, *Harlem Renaissance*, 1971.
Hugh Kenner, *The Pound Era*, 1971.
Warren French, ed., *The Twenties: Fiction, Poetry, Drama*, 1975.
Albert Gelpi, *The Tenth Muse: The Psyche of the American Poet*, 1975.
Hugh Kenner, *A Homemade World: The American Modernist Writers*, 1975.
David Perkins, *A History of Modern Poetry: From the 1890s to the High Modernist Mode*, 1976.
Ellen Williams, *Harriet Monroe and the Poetry Renaissance: The First Ten Years of Poetry, 1912–22*, 1977.
James E. Miller, Jr., *The American Quest for a Supreme Fiction: Whitman's Legacy in the Personal Epic*, 1979.
Marie Boroff, *Language and the Poet: Verbal Artistry in the Poetry of Frost, Stevens, and Moore*, 1979.
Daniel Hoffman, ed., *Harvard Guide to Contemporary Writing*, 1979.
Helen Vendler, *Part of Nature, Part of Us: Modern American Poets*, 1980.
Marjorie Perloff, *The Poetics of Indeterminacy: Rimbaud to Cage*, 1981.
Marcus Klein, *Foreigners: The Making of American Literature, 1900–1940*, 1981.
David Levering Lewis, *When Harlem Was in Vogue*, 1981, 1989.
Geoffrey Perrett, *America in the Twenties: A History*, 1982.
Donald E. Stanford, *Revolution and Convention in Modern Poetry*, 1983.
Noel Riley Fitch, *Sylvia Beach and the Lost Generation: A Literary History of Paris in the Twenties and Thirties*, 1983.
Michael G. Cooke, *Afro-American Literature in the Twentieth Century*, 1984.
Bruce Kellner, ed., *The Harlem Renaissance: A Historical Dictionary for the Era*, 1984.
Arna Bontemps, ed., *Harlem Renaissance Remembered*, 1984.
Philip Stevick, ed., *The American Short Story, 1900–1945*, 1984.
Douglas Robinson, *American Apocalypse: The Images of the End of the World in American Literature*, 1985.
Gorham Munson, *The Awakening Twenties: A Memoir-History of a Literary Period*, 1985.
Margaret Dickie, *On the Modernist Long Poem*, 1986.
Marjorie Perloff, *The Futurist Moment: Avant-Garde, Avant Guerre, and the Language of Rupture*, 1986.
Shaari Benstock, *Women of the Left Bank: Paris, 1900–1940*, 1986.
William Drake, *Women Poets in America, 1915–1945*, 1987.
Bernard W. Bell, *The Afro-American Novel and Its Tradition*, 1987.
David Perkins, *A History of Modern Poetry: Modernism and After*, 1987.
Albert Gelpi, *A Coherent Splendor: The American Poetic Renaissance, 1910–1950*, 1987.

Cecelia Tichi, *Shifting Gears: Technology, Literature, Culture in Modernist America*, 1987.
Victor A. Kramer, ed., *The Harlem Renaissance Reexamined*, 1987.
Henry Louis Gates, Jr., *Figures in Black: Words, Signs, and the "Radical" Self*, 1987.
Melvin Dixon, *Ride Out the Wilderness: Geography and Identity in Afro-American Literature*, 1987.
William Drake, *The First Wave: Women Poets in America, 1915–1945*, 1987.
John F. Callahan, *In the African-American Grain: The Pursuit of Voice in Twentieth-Century Black Fiction*, 1988.
Ann Allen Shockley, *Afro-American Women Writers, 1746–1933: An Anthology and Critical Guide*, 1988.
James F. Knapp, *Literary Modernism and the Transformation of Work*, 1988.
Sandra M. Gilbert and Susan Gubar, *No Man's Land: The Place of the Woman Writer in the Twentieth Century:* Vol. I, *The War of the Words*, 1988; Vol. II, *Sexchanges*, 1989.
Gillian Hanscombe and Virginia L. Smyers, *Writing for Their Lives: The Modernist Women, 1910–1940*, 1989.

COMPREHENSIVE HISTORIES

Robert E. Spiller et al., eds., *Literary History of the United States*, 3 vols., 1948, 1953, 1963; bibliographical volume covering 1858–70, 1972.
Emory Elliott, ed., *Columbia Literary History of the United States*, 1988.

BIBLIOGRAPHIES

Jackson R. Bryer, *Fifteen Modern American Writers*, 1969; rev. and updated as *Sixteen Modern American Writers*, 1973.
James Woodress, ed. (and others), *American Literary Scholarship: An Annual*, 1963–present.

THE POETRY RENAISSANCE
Making It New: Shapers of the Modern

EZRA POUND   WILLIAM CARLOS WILLIAMS
T. S. ELIOT   MARIANNE MOORE
ROBERT FROST   HART CRANE
WALLACE STEVENS   LANGSTON HUGHES

AS THE SUN MAKES IT NEW
DAY BY DAY MAKE IT NEW
YET AGAIN MAKE IT NEW

from Ezra Pound's translation of the Confucian *Ta Hio*, 1928, 1947

EZRA POUND
(1885–1972)

One critic has subtitled a book on Ezra Pound: "Prime Minister of Poetry." Pound might also have been called the "Commanding General of Modernism." His battle cry, repeated throughout his poems and prose, was "Make It New!" He sent back dispatches to Harriet Monroe, editor of *Poetry* in Chicago, from his forward position at the poetic front in London, proclaiming his discoveries and victories. He heralded Robert Frost and T. S. Eliot; he sabotaged Amy Lowell and Edgar Lee Masters. He tossed out advice in his letters right and left, usually as do's and don't's: "no cliches, set phrases, stereotyped journalese"; "objectivity and again objectivity, and expression." Gertrude Stein said of him that he was "a village explainer, excellent if you were a village, but if you were not, not."

There is a grain of truth in Stein's put-down. Pound was a shrewd combination of sophisticated cosmopolitan and cracker-barrel philosopher. He was born in what he called "a half savage country"—Hailey, Idaho. Two years after his birth, the family moved to Philadelphia, where his father had a position in the U.S. Treasury's mint. Pound's upbringing was comfortably middle class. He was taken on his first tour of Europe by a great-aunt when he was thirteen.

By the time Pound reached fifteen, he had decided to become a poet. He entered the University of Pennsylvania in 1901, moving to Hamilton College, in New York, for his last two years and graduation. In 1906 he took an M. A. in romance languages back at Pennsylvania. He came to know Hilda Doolittle— with whom for a time he was in love—and William Carlos Williams during his years at the University of Pennsylvania. Throughout their divergent careers, Pound and Williams would continue an uneasy relationship, with Williams remaining in place in America, finding the universal in the local, while Pound roamed the world in restless pursuit of the elusive ideal society or culture for artists.

In 1906, Pound returned to Europe on a fellowship awarded to enable him to do research for a Ph. D. The following year he gave academic life a try when he took a position teaching French and Spanish at Wabash College, Crawfordsville, Indiana, in 1907. After only four months he lost his job when he let a stranded burlesque performer occupy his room. Impatient with the pedantry of academia and the prudery of midwestern America, Pound abandoned his graduate work and in 1908 set off again for Europe. In Venice he paid for publication of his first book of poems, *A Lume Spento* ("By the Extinguished Candle"). In London that fall, he followed with a second volume, *A Quinzaine for This Yule* (Quinzaine: "about fifteen"; there are fifteen poems in the book). By 1911, Pound had published three additional volumes, *Personae* ("Masks," or "Roles," 1909), *Exultations* (1909), and *Canzoni* ("Songs," 1911) and had come to the end of his premodernist phase, a phase in which archaisms, poetic diction, and foreign phrases peppered his pages, as in "Aux Belles Londres" ("To the Beauties of London"), which opens with the Swinburnian line: "I am aweary with the utter and beautiful weariness."

After a visit to America in 1911, Pound sailed back to England and would not return to his home country for some three decades. Within the next five years he would be radically transformed as a poet and he would become the leader of the poetic renaissance. Many factors brought about this transformation. One, as Pound himself would later confess, was the ridicule of his early poetry by the British writer Ford Madox Ford: "He felt the errors of contemporary style to the point of rolling . . . on the floor . . . when my third volume displayed me trapped, fly-papered, gummed and strapped down in a jejune provincial effort to learn . . . the stilted language that then passed for 'good English.'" The "roll," Pound observed, saved him "at least two years," and sent him back to "using the living tongue."

There were other figures who helped change Pound, including the Irish poet William Butler Yeats (for whom Pound served as secretary in 1913 and whom Pound, in turn, modernized) and the English philosopher-poet, T. E. Hulme, who led a weekly discussion group in London devoted to modernist movements in the arts. In the years 1913–15, the widow of the American Orientalist Ernest Fenellosa turned over his papers to Pound, and out of them Pound assembled four books: *Cathay* (1915), *Certain Noble Plays of Japan* (1916), *Noh, or Accomplishment* (1917), and *The Chinese Written Character as a Medium for Poetry* (1919). Thus the forms and styles of Oriental poetry had a direct conduit through Pound to flow into and help shape the new poetry.

In 1912, Pound had been appointed by Harriet Monroe "foreign correspondent" for her new magazine in Chicago, *Poetry: A Magazine of Verse*. At times Pound seemed bent on filling the entire magazine with his discoveries. He sent her a laudatory review of Robert Frost's first volume of poems, *A Boy's Will,* published in England in 1913. This same year he sent Monroe three poems by Hilda Doolittle (signed "H. D., *Imagiste*"). And Pound was responsible for the appearance of "The Love Song of J. Alfred Prufrock" in *Poetry* in 1915. Pound himself published "A Few Don'ts by an Imagiste" in *Poetry* in 1913, and in 1914 he edited a volume, *Des Imagistes: An Anthology*, containing poems by himself, H. D., Amy Lowell, William Carlos Williams, and others. But Pound shied away from the movement when Amy Lowell, to his dismay, took over the leadership and edited three additional anthologies entitled *Some Imagist Poets* (1915–17).

As *Poetry* had introduced "imagism" to the world in 1913, the British journal *Blast*, edited by Wyndham Lewis, introduced "vorticism" in 1914–15, with Pound assuming once again a leadership role. Pound had identified imagism with creation of an image "which presents an intellectual and emotional complex in an instant of time." The definition (and the examples) suggested to some practitioners and critics the diminutive and perhaps the static or momentary. Pound seems to have moved on to vorticism because he was searching for a way out of these constraints—or misconceptions. He wrote, "The image is not an idea. It is a radiant node or cluster; it is what I can, and must perforce, call a VORTEX, from which, and through which, and into which, ideas are constantly rushing." Pound's concept of vorticism, with its focus on ideas, seemed to open imagism to a more dynamic poetry than had seemed possible before. He said, "The organization of forms is a much more energetic and creative action than the copying or imitating of light on a hay stack." Pound was beginning to sound like a poet who was thinking of writing a poem of epic length: he began tentative work on *The Cantos* in 1915.

But in the meantime, Pound was continuing to publish his shorter poems, reflecting the revolution in his poetic imagination—beginning with *Ripostes* in 1912 (containing "Portrait D'Une Femme" and "The Seafarer") and *Lustra* in 1916 (containing "A Pact" and "In a Station of the Metro"). Pound himself provided a description of the critical moment that brought him to the climax of his second period, the publication of "Hugh Selwyn Mauberley" in 1920:

> At a particular date in a particular room, two authors [Pound and Eliot] . . . decided that the dilutation of *vers libre*, Amygism [Amy Lowell], Lee Masterism

[Edgar Lee Masters], general floppiness had gone too far and that some counter-current must be set going. Parallel situation centuries ago in China. Remedy prescribed "Emaux et Camees" [*Enamels and Cameos*, by Theophile Gautier] (or the Bay State Hymn Book [America's *Bay Psalm Book*, which provided rhymned versions of the Psalms for singing]). Rhyme and regular strophes. Results: Poems in Mr. Eliot's *second* volume, not contained in his first [i.e., *Poems* (1920), not *Prufrock and Other Observations* (1917)], also "[Hugh Selwyn] Mauberley." Divergence later [i.e., the epic *Cantos*, to which Pound devoted himself after 1920].

Pound's "Hugh Selwyn Mauberley" (1920) had been shaped in part by T. S. Eliot's "Love Song of J. Alfred Prufrock," which Pound had championed. But Pound's poem was more clearly a personal proclamation: he called it his "farewell to London." It was, of course, a farewell to more than a city; it was a farewell to that side of Pound (the aesthetic Mauberley-like side) attracted to an art with greater homage to beauty than to life. The outbursts in the poem against the slaughter of the First World War were a sign of his poetry in the epic to come.

When Eliot finished a long poem in 1921, at a time that he was suffering a nervous breakdown, he turned the mass of manuscripts over to the friend he would call *"il miglior fabbro"* ("the better craftsman"). Pound shaped the poem, originally entitled *He Do the Police in Different Voices*, into *The Waste Land* by severe pruning. In the process he turned a poem Eliot would always claim later was a *personal* poem into a work that seemed to most readers a piece of pessimistic social — or cosmic — commentary. In a letter written in 1922, Pound exclaimed, "It's all rubbish to pretend that art isn't didactic," and declared himself in favor of what he termed the "profounder didacticism" of such epic poets as Homer and Dante. Clearly he felt that this didacticism was contained in the epic-like poem he had made out of Eliot's manuscripts. He said (in this same letter), "Eliot's *Waste Land* is I think the justification of the 'movement,' of our modern experiment, since 1900."

By this time, of course, Pound was well launched on his own epic, *The Cantos*, which would occupy him for the rest of his life. It was a modernist work written with a didactic accent, in a variety of voices and styles ranging from the poetically prophetic to the American (or "Amur'k'n") colloquial. The final poem would consist of 109 completed cantos. The period of publication of *The Cantos* extended from 1917 (with the first three, later revised, appearing in *Poetry*) to 1969 (with *Drafts and Fragments of Cantos CX–CXVII*). A brief "Canto CXX" was added in 1972. The closest forerunner of this personal or lyric epic was Walt Whitman's *Leaves of Grass*, an epic poem that lodged early in Pound's psyche, as is indicated by his recurrent obsessive need to work out his relation to this predecessor poet and his poetry in such pieces as "What I Think of Walt Whitman" (1909), "A Pact" (1913), *The ABC of Reading* (1934), and in Cantos 74–78 (*The Pisan Cantos*, 1948).

Pound defined an epic as a "poem including history," a conveniently loose definition that enabled him to indulge a life-long interest in sifting through the world's literatures — Greek and Latin, Anglo-Saxon, Oriental, medieval, Provençal. He had said as early as 1912, "My pawing over the ancients and semi-ancients has been one struggle to find out what has been done, once for all, better than it can ever be done again, and to find out what remains for us to do." The form of *The Cantos* might be, Pound said, that of a "fugue: theme, response, contrasujet." Or it might be that of a "rag-bag to stuff" all of the modern world's "thought" in. Pound wrote of *The Cantos* in 1933: "I am not proceeding according to Aristotelian logic but according to the ideogrammic method of first heaping together the necessary components of thought." Such a method consists of the juxtaposition of elements that connect only by an imaginative leap (or dive) by the reader; grammatical logic is replaced by metaphorical logic (Hart Crane would later invent the term "logic of metaphor" for his own method).

Pound had married Dorothy Shakespear in 1914, left England for Paris in 1920, and in 1924 settled in the coastal town of Rapallo, Italy, where he would spend much of the remainder of his life. In the 1920s, he had children by both his wife and a mistress, Olga Rudge. Apparently an amicable arrangement was worked out between wife and mistress, and they often shared the same household.

In 1918, Pound had come upon the economic theories of Major C. H. Douglas, whose notion of "social credit" would enable governments to pay dividends rather than collect taxes. Pound became obsessed with economic theory and the evils of usury, and it became (as *usura*) a dominant theme in *The Cantos*. Meantime, Pound saw in the rising young Italian ruler Mussolini a political hero who could reform the economic system. In spite of Mussolini's increasingly dictatorial rule during the 1920s and 1930s, Pound remained an admirer, even through Mussolini's nakedly imperialistic takeover of Ethiopia in 1935. In 1939, Pound made a trip to America with the purpose of setting President Franklin Delano Roosevelt and other government leaders straight on the virtues of social credit and Mussolini's experiment in fascism. Such a mad mission was, of course, doomed to fail.

Embittered, Pound returned to Italy, where, during the Second World War, he made strident broadcasts against America, blaming the war on an international Jewish conspiracy and the criminality of President Roosevelt. He told American soldiers their real enemy was the U.S. government. Pound was accused of treason, and at the end of the war he was held by U.S. forces in a "cage" near Pisa (where the *Pisan Cantos* were written). On his return to the United States, Pound was declared unfit to stand trial by a board of psychiatrists and was placed in St. Elizabeths Hospital for the Criminally Insane in Washington, D.C., where he remained from 1945 to 1958.

Although Pound was confined during this period, he enjoyed considerable freedom in that he was able to read and write as he pleased and to receive visitors. He continued to work on additional cantos and on various translations. In 1949 his winning of the Bollingen Award for Poetry aroused a storm of controversy, with renewed charges of his treasonous behavior and anti-Semitism. In 1958, through the actions of Archibald MacLeish, Robert Frost, T. S. Eliot, and others, he was released from his confinement. He returned to Rapallo, giving the Fascist salute as he disembarked in Italy. Pound's pro-Fascist, anti-Semitic sentiments continued to filter through his postwar cantos.

In Italy, Pound returned to his writing and translating. In 1965 he attended funeral services for T. S. Eliot in England's Westminster Cathedral. And in 1969 he made a last visit to the United States. But more and more during his last years he seemed to withdraw into himself. He surprised friends by announcing at one gathering, in which he had been unresponsive, "I did not enter into silence; silence captured me." He died in 1972. And he remains one of the most enigmatic and controversial figures in American literature. His achievement was enormous as poet, translator, leader of literary movements, promoter of poetry and poets. But his genius was flawed by obsessions that seemed tinged with madness. He was, in short, an American original.

ADDITIONAL READING

The Letters of Ezra Pound, 1907–1941, ed. D. D. Paige, 1950; *The Translations of Ezra Pound*, ed. Hugh Kenner, 1953; *Literary Essays of Ezra Pound*, ed. T. S. Eliot, 1954; *Pound/Joyce: The Letters of Ezra Pound to James Joyce with Pound's Essays on Joyce*, ed. Forrest Read, 1967; *Ezra Pound: A Critical Anthology*, ed. J. P. Sullivan, 1970; *Ezra Pound: Selected Prose, 1909–1965*, ed. William Cookson, 1973; *Collected Early Poems of Ezra Pound*, ed. Michael John King, 1976; "*Ezra Pound Speaking,*" *Radio Speeches of World War II*, ed. Leonard W. Doob, 1978; *Ezra Pound and Dorothy Shakespear: Their Letters, 1909–1914*, ed. Omar Pound and A. Walton Litz, 1984; *Pound/Lewis: The Letters of Ezra Pound and Wyndham Lewis*, ed. Timothy Materer, 1985.

Hugh Kenner, *The Poetry of Ezra Pound*, 1951; Harold H. Watts, *Ezra Pound and the Cantos*, 1952; Lewis Leary, ed., *Motive and Method in the Cantos of Ezra Pound*, 1954; John J. Espey, *Ezra Pound's Mauberley: A Study in Composition*, 1955; John Hamilton Edwards and William Vasse, *Annotated Index to the Cantos of Ezra Pound*, 1957; Clark Emery, *Ideas into Action: A Study of Pound's Cantos*, 1958; M. L. Rosenthal, *A Primer of Ezra Pound*, 1960; Eustace Mullins, *This Difficult Individual, Ezra Pound*, 1960; Walter Sutton, ed., *Ezra Pound: A Collection of Critical Essays*, 1963; George Dekker, *Sailing After Knowledge*, 1963; J. P. Sullivan, *Ezra Pound and Sextus Propertius: A Study in Creative Translation*, 1964; Donald Davie, *Ezra Pound: Poet as Sculptor*, 1964; Noel Stock, *Reading the Cantos*, 1966; Julien Cornell, *The Trial of Ezra Pound*, 1966; Michael Reck, *Ezra Pound: A Close-Up*, 1967; Charles Norman, *The Case of Ezra Pound*, 1968; N. C. De Nagy, *The Poetry of Ezra Pound*, 1968; Earle Davis, *Vision Fugitive: Ezra Pound and Economics*, 1968; Charles Norman, *Ezra Pound*, 1969; Eva Hesse, ed., *New Approaches to Ezra Pound*, 1969; Herbert N. Schneidau, *Ezra Pound: The Image and the Real*, 1969; Hugh Witemeyer, *The Poetry of Ezra Pound: Forms and Renewal, 1908–1920*, 1969; Wai-Lim Yip, *Ezra Pound's Cathay*, 1969; Noel Stock, *The Life of Ezra Pound*, 1970; Hugh Kenner, *The Pound Era*, 1971; Christine Brooke-Rose, *A ZBC of Ezra Pound*, 1971; Sister Bernetta Quinn, *Ezra Pound: An Introduction to the Poetry*, 1972; Eric Homberger, ed., *Ezra Pound: The Critical Heritage*, 1972; Stuart Y. McDougal, *Ezra Pound and the Troubadour Tradition*, 1972; William M. Chace, *The Political Identities of Ezra Pound and T. S. Eliot*, 1973; James J. Wilhelm, *Dante and Pound: The Epic of Judgment*, 1974; Eugene Paul Nassar, *The Cantos of Ezra Pound: The Lyric Mode*, 1975; Ronald Bush, *The Genesis of Ezra Pound's Cantos*, 1976; Donald Davie, *Ezra Pound*, 1976. C. David Heyman, *Ezra Pound: The Last Rower. A Political Profile*, 1976; James J. Wilhelm, *The Later Cantos of Ezra Pound*, 1977; Michael Alexander, *The Poetic Achievement of Ezra Pound*, 1979; James F. Knapp, *Ezra Pound*, 1979; George Kearns, *Guide to Ezra Pound's Selected Cantos*, 1980; Wendy Flory, *Ezra Pound and the Cantos*, 1980; Michael André Bernstein, *The Tale of the Tribe: Ezra Pound and Modern Verse Epic*, 1980; Carrol F. Terrell, *A Companion to the Cantos of Ezra Pound* (Cantos 1–71), 1980; Peter Ackroyd, *Ezra Pound and His World*, 1981; Ian F. A. Bell, *The Modernist Poetics of Ezra Pound*, 1981; Christine Froula, *A Guide to Ezra Pound's Selected Poems*, 1983; Donald Gallup, *Ezra Pound: A Bibliography*, 1983 (rev. of 1963 ed.); Ron Thomas, *The Latin Masks of Ezra Pound*, 1983; E. Fuller Torrey, *The Roots of Treason: Ezra Pound and the Secret of St. Elizabeth's*, 1983; Ronnie Apter, *Digging for the Treasure: Translations After Pound*, 1984; Burton Raffel, *Ezra Pound: The Prime Minister of Poetry*, 1984; Carroll F. Terrell, *A Companion to the Cantos of Ezra Pound* (Cantos 74–117), 1984; Christine Froula, *To Write Paradise: Style and Error in Pound's Cantos*, 1985; James J. Wilhelm, *The American Roots of Ezra Pound*, 1985; Beatrice Ricks, *Ezra Pound: A Bibliography of Secondary Works*, 1986; Kevin M. Oderman, *Ezra Pound and the Erotic Medium*, 1986; John Steven Childs, *Modernist Form: Pound's Style in the Early Cantos*, 1986; Martin A. Kayman, *The Modernism of Ezra Pound*, 1986; Jean-Michel Rabate, *Language, Sexuality and Ideology in Ezra Pound's "Cantos,"* 1986; James Laughlin, *Pound as Wuz: Essays and Lectures on Ezra Pound*, 1988; Robert Casillo, *The Genealogy of Demons: Anti-Semitism, Fascism, and the Myths of Ezra Pound*, 1988; James Longenback, *Stone Cottage: Pound, Yeats, and Modernism*, 1988; John Tytell, *Ezra Pound: The Solitary Volcano*, 1988; Wendy Stallard Flory, *The American Ezra Pound*, 1988; Humphrey Carpenter, *A Serious Character: The Life of Ezra Pound*, 1988.

TEXTS

Personae: The Collected Shorter Poems, 1971; *The Cantos of Ezra Pound*, 1970–72; "A Retrospect," *Literary Essays of Ezra Pound*, ed. T. S. Eliot, 1935; "What I Feel About Walt Whitman," *Selected Prose, 1909–1965*, ed. William Cookson, 1973.

The Tree

I stood still and was a tree amid the wood,
Knowing the truth of things unseen before;
Of Daphne[1] and the laurel bow
And that god-feasting couple[2] old
That grew elm-oak amid the wold.[3]   5
'Twas not until the gods had been
Kindly entreated, and been brought within
Unto the hearth of their heart's home
That they might do this wonder thing;
Nathless[4] I have been a tree amid the wood   10
And many a new thing understood
That was rank folly to my head before.

1908

Sestina: Altaforte[1]

LOQUITUR:[2] *En*[3] Bertrans de Born.
    Dante Alighieri put this man in hell for that he
        was a stirrer up of strife.[4]
    Eccovi![5]
    Judge ye!
    Have I dug him up again?
The scene is at his castle, Altaforte. "Papiols" is his
        jongleur.[6]
"The Leopard," the *device*[7] of Richard Cœur de Lion.

I

Damn it all! all this our South stinks peace.
You whoreson dog, Papiols, come! Let's to music!
I have no life save when the swords clash.
But ah! when I see the standards gold, vair,[8] purple, opposing
And the broad fields beneath them turn crimson,   5
Then howl I my heart nigh mad with rejoicing.

[1]In Greek mythology, a nymph changed into a laurel tree to escape the amorous god Apollo (Ovid, *Metamorphoses*, 1).
[2]A poor old couple, Baucis and Philemon, in return for their kind hospitality to the gods Zeus and Hermes, who were disguised as weary travellers, were granted death at the same time and were changed into two intertwining trees (Ovid, *Metamorphoses*, 8).
[3]Rolling plain.
[4]Nevertheless.
[1]In this poem, Pound conveys the spirit of the twelfth-century Provençal soldier and troubadour Bertrans de Born, whose war songs he admired. In "How I Began" (1913), Pound wrote, "I had had De Born in my mind. I had found him untranslatable. Then it occurred to me that I might present him in this manner. I wanted the curious involution and recurrence of the Sestina." The sestina form, invented by the Provençal troubadour Arnaut Daniel in the twelfth century,
consists of six six-line stanzas and a three-line envoy (short concluding stanza). The six words that end the lines in the first stanza are repeated as line-end words in the other stanzas according to a set pattern, and three are to occur at the middle of each line in the envoy. Pound deviates slightly from the pattern. *Altaforte*: high and strong (Italian).
[2]"He speaks" (Latin).
[3]"Lord" (Provençal).
[4]In Dante's *Inferno*, XXVIII, de Born suffers in hell for having encouraged Prince Henry, son of Henry II, King of England, in his war against his brother Richard Cœur de Lion (the Lion-hearted), which became a rebellion against Henry II.
[5]"Look you!" (Italian).
[6]"Minstrel" (French).
[7]Heraldic emblem.
[8]Heraldic representation of a fur of cup-shaped skins sewn in rows, silver and blue alternately.

II

In hot summer have I great rejoicing
When the tempests kill the earth's foul peace,
And the lightnings from black heav'n flash crimson,
And the fierce thunders roar me their music   10
And the winds shriek through the clouds mad, opposing,
And through all the riven skies God's swords clash.

III

Hell grant soon we hear again the swords clash!
And the shrill neighs of destriers[9] in battle rejoicing,
Spiked breast to spiked breast opposing!   15
Better one hour's stour[10] than a year's peace
With fat boards, bawds, wine and frail music!
Bah! there's no wine like the blood's crimson!

IV

And I love to see the sun rise blood-crimson.
And I watch his spears through the dark clash   20
And it fills all my heart with rejoicing
And pries wide my mouth with fast music
When I see him so scorn and defy peace,
His lone might 'gainst all darkness opposing.

V

The man who fears war and squats opposing   25
My words for stour, hath no blood of crimson
But is fit only to rot in womanish peace
Far from where worth's won and the swords clash
For the death of such sluts I go rejoicing;
Yea, I fill all the air with my music.   30

VI

Papiols, Papiols, to the music!
There's no sound like to swords swords opposing,
No cry like the battle's rejoicing
When our elbows and swords drip the crimson
And our charges 'gainst "The Leopard's" rush clash.   35
May God damn for ever all who cry "Peace!"

VII

And let the music of the swords make them crimson!
Hell grant soon we hear again the swords clash!
Hell blot black for alway the thought "Peace"!

1909

---

[9]War horses.
[10]Battle.

The Seafarer[1]

From THE ANGLO-SAXON

May I for my own self song's truth reckon,
Journey's jargon, how I in harsh days
Hardship endured oft.
Bitter breast-cares have I abided,
Known on my keel many a care's hold,   5
And dire sea-surge, and there I oft spent
Narrow nightwatch nigh the ship's head
While she tossed close to cliffs. Coldly afflicted,
My feet were by frost benumbed.
Chill its chains are; chafing sighs   10
Hew my heart round and hunger begot
Mere-weary[2] mood. Lest man know not
That he on dry land loveliest liveth,
List how I, care-wretched, on ice-cold sea,
Weathered the winter, wretched outcast   15
Deprived of my kinsmen;
Hung with hard ice-flakes, where hail-scur[3] flew,
There I heard naught save the harsh sea
And ice-cold wave, at whiles the swan cries,
Did for my games the gannet's[4] clamour,   20
Sea-fowls' loudness was for me laughter,
The mews'[5] singing all my mead-drink.
Storms, on the stone-cliffs beaten, fell on the stern
In icy feathers; full oft the eagle screamed
With spray on his pinion.   25
                            Not any protector
May make merry man faring needy.
This he little believes, who aye in winsome life
Abides 'mid burghers some heavy business,
Wealthy and wine-flushed, how I weary oft   30
Must bide above brine.
Neareth nightshade, snoweth from north,
Frost froze the land, hail fell on earth then,
Corn of the coldest. Nathless[6] there knocketh now
The heart's thought that I on high streams   35
The salt-wavy tumult traverse alone.
Moaneth alway my mind's lust
That I fare forth, that I afar hence
Seek out a foreign fastness.
For this there's no mood-lofty man over earth's midst,   40
Not though he be given his good, but will have in his youth greed;
Nor his deed to the daring, nor his king to the faithful
But shall have his sorrow for sea-fare
Whatever his lord will.
He hath not heart for harping, nor in ring-having   45
Nor winsomeness to wife, nor world's delight
Nor any whit else save the wave's slash,
Yet longing comes upon him to fare forth on the water.

---

[1] Pound's translation of a thousand-year-old Anglo-Saxon poem.
[2] Sea-weary.
[3] Hail-shower.
[4] A large sea bird.
[5] Gulls.
[6] Nevertheless.

Bosque[7] taketh blossom, cometh beauty of berries,
Fields to fairness, land fares brisker,   50
All this admonisheth man eager of mood,
The heart turns to travel so that he then thinks
On flood-ways to be far departing.
Cuckoo calleth with gloomy crying,
He singeth summerward, bodeth sorrow,   55
The bitter heart's blood. Burgher knows not—
He the prosperous man—what some perform
Where wandering them widest draweth.
So that but now my heart burst from my breastlock,
My mood 'mid the mere-flood,[8]   60
Over the whale's acre, would wander wide.
On earth's shelter cometh oft to me,
Eager and ready, the crying lone-flyer,
Whets for the whale-path the heart irresistibly,
O'er tracks of ocean; seeing that anyhow   65
My lord deems to me this dead life
On loan and on land, I believe not
That any earth-weal eternal standeth
Save there be somewhat calamitous
That, ere a man's tide go, turn it to twain.   70
Disease or oldness or sword-hate
Beats out the breath from doom-gripped body.
And for this, every earl whatever, for those speaking after—
Laud of the living, boasteth some last word,
That he will work ere he pass onward,   75
Frame on the fair earth 'gainst foes his malice,
Daring ado, . . .
So that all men shall honour him after
And his laud beyond them remain 'mid the English,
Aye, for ever, a lasting life's-blast,   80
Delight 'mid the doughty.
                                    Days little durable,
And all arrogance of earthen riches,
There come now no kings nor Cæsars
Nor gold-giving lords like those gone.   85
Howe'er in mirth most magnified,
Whoe'er lived in life most lordliest,
Drear all this excellence, delights undurable!
Waneth the watch, but the world holdeth.
Tomb hideth trouble. The blade is layed low.   90
Earthly glory ageth and seareth.
No man at all going the earth's gait,
But age fares against him, his face paleth,
Grey-haired he groaneth, knows gone companions,
Lordly men, are to earth o'ergiven,   95
Nor may he then the flesh-cover, whose life ceaseth,
Nor eat the sweet nor feel the sorry,
Nor stir hand nor think in mid heart,
And though he strew the grave with gold,
His born brothers, their buried bodies   100
Be an unlikely treasure hoard.

                                                        1911, 1912

---

[7]Bush.
[8]Sea-flood.

To Whistler, American[1]

On the loan exhibit of his paintings at the Tate Gallery.[2]

You also, our first great,
Had tried all ways;
Tested and pried and worked in many fashions,
And this much gives me heart to play the game.

Here is part that's slight, and part gone wrong,   5
And much of little moment, and some few
Perfect as Dürer![3]
'In the Studio' and these two portraits,[4] if I had my choice!
And then these sketches in the mood of Greece?

You had your searches, your uncertainties,   10
And this is good to know—for us, I mean,
Who bear the brunt of our America
And try to wrench her impulse into art.

You were not always sure, not always set
To hiding night or tuning 'symphonies';[5]   15
Had not one style from birth, but tried and pried
And stretched and tampered with the media.

You and Abe Lincoln from that mass of dolts
Show us there's chance at least of winning through.

1912, 1949

Portrait d'une Femme[1]

Your mind and you are our Sargasso Sea,[2]
London has swept about you this score years
And bright ships left you this or that in fee:
Ideas, old gossip, oddments of all things,
Strange spars of knowledge and dimmed wares of price.   5
Great minds have sought you—lacking someone else.
You have been second always. Tragical?
No. You preferred it to the usual thing:
One dull man, dulling and uxorious,
One average mind—with one thought less, each year.   10
Oh, you are patient, I have seen you sit
Hours, where something might have floated up.
And now you pay one. Yes, you richly pay.

---

[1]James Abbott McNeill Whistler (1834–1903), expatriate American painter, whose devotion to "art for art's sake," rather than for social or moral purposes, embroiled him in many aesthetic controversies.
[2]In London.
[3]Albrecht Dürer (1471–1528), German painter and engraver.
[4]"Brown and Gold—de Race [Thoroughbred (French)]," "Grenat et Or—Le Petit Cardinal [Garnet and Gold—The Little Cardinal (French)]" (Pound's note). Titles of a portrait

of a young Italian boy and a portrait of a young woman wearing a deep-plum-colored cap, like that of a cardinal.
[5]Whistler's musical titles, "Nocturne" (for night scenes) or "Symphony," related harmonies of color to those in music and emphasized the abstract, nonrepresentational qualities of the paintings.
[1]"Portrait of a woman" (French).
[2]Calm area of the North Atlantic, choked with seaweed ("sargasso"), once thought to have entangled ships.

You are a person of some interest, one comes to you
And takes strange gain away: 15
Trophies fished up; some curious suggestion;
Fact that leads nowhere; and a tale or two,
Pregnant with mandrakes,[3] or with something else
That might prove useful and yet never proves,
That never fits a corner or shows use,   20
Or finds its hour upon the loom of days:
The tarnished, gaudy, wonderful old work;
Idols and ambergris[4] and rare inlays,
These are your riches, your great store; and yet
For all this sea-hoard of deciduous things,   25
Strange woods half sodden, and new brighter stuff:
In the slow float of differing light and deep,
No! there is nothing! In the whole and all,
Nothing that's quite your own.
                    Yet this is you.   30

                                                        1912

A Virginal[1]

No, no! Go from me. I have left her lately.
I will not spoil my sheath with lesser brightness,
For my surrounding air hath a new lightness;
Slight are her arms, yet they have bound me straitly
And left me cloaked as with a gauze of æther;   5
As with sweet leaves; as with subtle clearness.
Oh, I have picked up magic in her nearness
To sheathe me half in half the things that sheathe her.
No, no! Go from me. I have still the flavour,
Soft as spring wind that's come from birchen bowers.   10
Green come the shoots, aye April in the branches,
As winter's wound with her sleight hand she staunches,
Hath of the trees a likeness of the savour:
As white their bark, so white this lady's hours.

                                                        1912

The Return

See, they return; ah, see the tentative
Movements, and the slow feet,
The trouble in the pace and the uncertain
Wavering!

---

[3]An herb with a branched root, resembling the human body, believed by the ancients to have magical and aphrodisiac powers, including inducing conception in women.
[4]A waxy substance secreted by the sperm whale and found floating on the sea; used in making perfumes.

[1]A small rectangular harpsichord popular in the sixteenth and seventeenth centuries, so named because it was played by young girls; Pound admired the modern copy made by British musician Arnold Dolmetsch (1858–1940), who recreated early instruments and revived medieval music.

See, they return, one, and by one,   5
With fear, as half-awakened;
As if the snow should hesitate
And murmur in the wind,
                    and half turn back;
These were the "Wing'd-with-Awe,"   10
                    Inviolable.

Gods of the wingèd shoe!
With them the silver hounds,
                    sniffing the trace of air!

Haie! Haie!   15
        These were the swift to harry;
These the keen-scented;
These were the souls of blood.

Slow on the leash,
                    pallid the leash-men!   20

                                                        1912

Salutation

O generation of the thoroughly smug
        and thoroughly uncomfortable,
I have seen fishermen picnicking in the sun,
I have seen them with untidy families,
I have seen their smiles full of teeth   5
        and heard ungainly laughter.
And I am happier than you are,
And they were happier than I am;
And the fish swim in the lake
        and do not even own clothing.   10

                                                    1913, 1916

A Pact

I make a pact with you, Walt Whitman—
I have detested you long enough.
I come to you as a grown child
Who has had a pig-headed father;
I am old enough now to make friends.   5
It was you that broke the new wood,
Now is a time for carving.
We have one sap and one root—
Let there be commerce between us.

                                                    1913, 1916

In a Station of the Metro[1]

The apparition of these faces in the crowd;
Petals on a wet, black bough.

1913, 1916

The River-Merchant's Wife: A Letter[1]

While my hair was still cut straight across my forehead
I played about the front gate, pulling flowers.
You came by on bamboo stilts, playing horse,
You walked about my seat, playing with blue plums.
And we went on living in the village of Chōkan:[2]   5
Two small people, without dislike or suspicion.

At fourteen I married My Lord you.
I never laughed, being bashful.
Lowering my head, I looked at the wall.
Called to, a thousand times, I never looked back.   10

At fifteen I stopped scowling,
I desired my dust to be mingled with yours
Forever and forever and forever.
Why should I climb the look out?

At sixteen you departed,   15
You went into far Ku-tō-en,[3] by the river of swirling eddies,
And you have been gone five months.
The monkeys make sorrowful noise overhead.

You dragged your feet when you went out.
By the gate now, the moss is grown, the different mosses,   20
Too deep to clear them away!
The leaves fall early this autumn, in wind.
The paired butterflies are already yellow with August
Over the grass in the West garden;
They hurt me. I grow older.   25

---

[1]Pound explains the genesis of this poem in *Gaudier-Brzeska: A Memoir* (1916): "Three years ago in Paris I got out of a 'metro' train at La Concorde, and saw suddenly a beautiful face, and then another and another, and then a beautiful child's face, and then another beautiful woman, and I tried all that day to find words for what this had meant to me, and I could not find any words that seemed to me worthy, or as lovely as that sudden emotion. And that evening . . . I was still trying, and I found, suddenly, the expression. I do not mean that I found words, but there came an equation . . . not in speech, but in little splotches of colour. . . . The 'one image poem' is a form of super-position, that is to say, it is one idea set on top of another. I found it useful in getting out of the impasse in which I had been left by my metro emotion. I wrote a thirty-line poem, and destroyed it. . . . Six months later I made a poem half that length; a year later I made [one] *hokku*-like sentence. . . . In a poem of this sort one is trying to record the precise instant when a thing outward and objective transforms itself, or darts into a thing inward and subjective."

[1]A translation from the Chinese of Li Po (701–762), called Rihaku in Japanese, from the posthumous notes of the American Orientalist Ernest Fenollosa (1853–1908). With the aid of Japanese scholars, Fenollosa had written Japanese pronunciations and rough English translations beneath the Chinese characters; since Pound knew no Chinese at the time, he used the Japanese spellings for place names and the poet's name.

[2]Chinese: Ch'ang-kan, a suburb of Nanking (now Nanjing).

[3]Chinese: Ch'ü-t'ang, one of the three great gorges, with dangerous rocky shoals, through which the Yangtze River (Yangtze Kiang, as in line 26) passes.

If you are coming down through the narrows of the river Kiang,
Please let me know beforehand,
And I will come out to meet you
        As far as Chō-fū-Sa.[4]
          By Rihaku (Li T'ai Po)

                    1915

Hugh Selwyn Mauberley

(LIFE AND CONTACTS)[1]

"Vocat æstus in umbram"[2]
Nemesianus, Ec. IV.

E. P. ODE POUR L'ELECTION DE SON SEPULCHRE[3]

I

For three years, out of key with his time,
He strove to resuscitate the dead art
Of poetry; to maintain "the sublime"
In the old sense. Wrong from the start—

No, hardly, but seeing he had been born   5
In a half savage country,[4] out of date;
Bent resolutely on wringing lilies from the acorn;
Capaneus;[5] trout for factitious bait;

"Ἴδμεν γάρ τοι πάνθ', ὅσ' ἐνὶ Τροίη[6]
Caught in the unstopped ear;   10
Giving the rocks small lee-way
The chopped seas held him, therefore, that year.

His true Penelope[7] was Flaubert,[8]
He fished by obstinate isles;
Observed the elegance of Circe's[9] hair   15
Rather than the mottoes on sun-dials.

---

[4]Chinese: Ch'ang-feng-sha, a beach on the Yangtze several hundred miles from Nanking.
[1]Pound called this poem "a farewell to London" and described it as "a study in form, an attempt to condense the James novel." Christine Froula, in *A Guide to Ezra Pound's "Selected Poems"* (1983), notes that the poem "marks a crucial turning point in Pound's career: it is a farewell to the aestheticism which has played a large part in his poetry up to this point, and, at the same time, an ironic and bitter indictment of modern society.... *Mauberley* is divided into two parts. The first part opens with a mock-burial of 'E.P.,' the aesthete in Pound, followed by eleven London vignettes, and concludes with an 'Envoi,' or send-off, for the whole. The second part, subtitled 'Mauberley,' depicts the character, career, and fate of this fictional aesthete in the first four poems, and concludes with 'Medallion,' an example of Mauberley's art."
[2]"The heat calls us into the shade," from *Eclogue IV* of Nemesianus, a third-century Latin poet, native of Carthage.

[3]"E.P. [Ezra Pound] Ode on the Choice of His Tomb," adapted from "De l'Election de son sépulchre," an ode by French poet Pierre de Ronsard (1524–1585).
[4]The United States.
[5]One of the Seven against Thebes, destroyed by a thunderbolt for defying Zeus.
[6]"Idmen gar toi panth', hos' eni Troie" (Greek): "For we know all that [the Argives and Trojans have suffered] in Troy," part of the Siren's song in Homer's *Odyssey* XII.189. Odysseus stopped his shipmates' ears with wax so that they would not hear the fatally enticing song, which he experienced by lashing himself to the ship's mast.
[7]Odysseus's faithful wife to whom he returns from the Trojan War after ten years.
[8]Gustave Flaubert (1821–1880), French novelist who advocated the search for *le mot juste* (the precise word).
[9]Sorceress who detained Odysseus for one year.

Unaffected by "the march of events,"
He passed from men's memory in *l'an trentuniesme*
De son eage;[10] the case presents
No adjunct to the Muses' diadem.   20

II

The age demanded an image
Of its accelerated grimace,
Something for the modern stage,
Not, at any rate, an Attic grace;[11]

Not, not certainly, the obscure reveries   25
Of the inward gaze;
Better mendacities
Than the classics in paraphrase!

The "age demanded" chiefly a mould in plaster,
Made with no loss of time,   30
A prose kinema,[12] not, not assuredly, alabaster
Or the "sculpture" of rhyme.

III

The tea-rose tea-gown,[13] etc.
Supplants the mousseline of Cos,[14]
The pianola[15] "replaces"   35
Sappho's barbitos.[16]

Christ follows Dionysus,[17]
Phallic and ambrosial
Made way for macerations;[18]
Caliban casts out Ariel.[19]   40

All things are a flowing,
Sage Heracleitus[20] says;
But a tawdry cheapness
Shall outlast our days.

Even the Christian beauty   45
Defects — after Samothrace;[21]
We see τὸ καλόν[22]
Decreed in the market place.

---

[10]"The thirty-first year of his age" (Old French), adapted from the first line of the *Grand Testament* (1461) by the fifteenth-century French poet, beggar, and thief François Villon, whom Pound called "the first voice . . . broken by bad economics."
[11]The classical purity of ancient Athens.
[12]Motion (Greek); cf. cinema: "motion pictures."
[13]Fashionable elaborately decorated dress.
[14]Cos, a Greek island famed for its fine light cloth or muslin ("mousseline" in French), used in the classically draped ancient tunics.
[15]Player piano.
[16]Lyre (Greek), an instrument used to accompany the classi-cal lyrics of the Greek poet Sappho (sixth century B.C.).
[17]Greek god of wine and fertility celebrated in ecstatic, or-giastic rites.
[18]The fasting of Christianity; also the maceration of Christ's body in the communion wafer.
[19]Caliban, "a savage and deformed slave," and Ariel, "an airy spirit," in Shakespeare's *The Tempest*.
[20]Greek philosopher (fl. 500 B.C.) who held that all things are in constant flux, destined for ultimate dissolution.
[21]Greek island where the famous "Winged Victory" statue was found and the site of Dionysiac rites; also visited by Paul, spreading the gospel.
[22]"To kalon" (Greek): "The beautiful."

Faun's flesh is not to us,
Nor the saint's vision.   50
We have the press for wafer;
Franchise for circumcision.

All men, in law, are equals.
Free of Pisistratus,[23]
We choose a knave or an eunuch   55
To rule over us.

O bright Apollo,
τίν' ἄνδρα, τίν' ἥρωα, τινα θεόν,[24]
What god, man, or hero
Shall I place a tin wreath upon!   60

IV

These fought in any case,
and some believing,
            pro domo,[25] in any case . . .

Some quick to arm,
some for adventure,   65
some from fear of weakness,
some from fear of censure,
some for love of slaughter, in imagination,
learning later . . .
some in fear, learning love of slaughter;   70

Died some, pro patria,
            non "dulce" non "et decor"[26] . . .
walked eye-deep in hell
believing in old men's lies, then unbelieving
came home, home to a lie,   75
home to many deceits,
home to old lies and new infamy;
usury[27] age-old and age-thick
and liars in public places.

Daring as never before, wastage as never before.   80
Young blood and high blood,
fair cheeks, and fine bodies;

fortitude as never before

frankness as never before,
disillusions as never told in the old days,   85
hysterias, trench confessions,
laughter out of dead bellies.

---

[23]Athenian tyrant (d. 527 B.C.), noted for the stability of his reign and great patronage of the arts.
[24]"Tin' andra, tin' heroa, tina theon" (Greek): "What man, what hero, what god," adapted from the Olympian Ode II.2 by Greek lyric poet Pindar (c. 522–c. 433 B.C.), which reads: "What god, what hero, what man shall we loudly praise?" Pound puns on "tin" (sound of the Greek word "what") in "tin

wreath" below, which contrasts with the traditional laurel wreath bestowed on heroes.
[25]"For home" (Latin).
[26]Pound negates the phrase of Latin poet Horace (65–8 B.C.), Odes III.ii.13: Dulce et decorum est pro patria mori ("It is sweet and fitting to die for one's country").
[27]The practice of lending money at exorbitant interest rates.

V

There died a myriad,
And of the best, among them,
For an old bitch gone in the teeth,   90
For a botched civilization,

Charm, smiling at the good mouth,
Quick eyes gone under earth's lid,

For two gross of broken statues,
For a few thousand battered books.   95

YEUX GLAUQUES[28]

Gladstone[29] was still respected,
When John Ruskin produced
"Kings' Treasuries";[30] Swinburne[31]
And Rossetti still abused.

Foetid Buchanan lifted up his voice[32]   100
When that faun's head of hers
Became a pastime for
Painters and adulterers.

The Burne-Jones cartons[33]
Have preserved her eyes;   105
Still, at the Tate, they teach
Cophetua to rhapsodize;

Thin like brook-water,
With a vacant gaze.
The English Rubaiyat was still-born[34]   110
In those days.

The thin, clear gaze, the same
Still darts out faun-like from the half-ruin'd face,
Questing and passive. . . .
"Ah, poor Jenny's case" . . .   115

Bewildered that a world
Shows no surprise
At her last maquero's[35]
Adulteries.

---

[28]"Greenish-blue eyes" (French); here referring to the eyes of Elizabeth Slidall, wife and model of Dante Gabriel Rossetti (1828–1882), English poet, painter, and founder of the Pre-Raphaelite Brotherhood of artists. Slidall committed suicide in 1862, two years after their marriage.
[29]William Ewart Gladstone (1809–1898), British statesman and four times liberal prime minister in the period 1868–94, representative of conventional Victorian morality.
[30]John Ruskin (1819–1900), English art critic, social reformer, and champion of the Pre-Raphaelite artists. In "Of Kings' Treasuries" (*Sesame and Lilies*, 1865), he indicts the English for despising literature, science, art, natural scenery, and compassion.
[31]Algernon Charles Swinburne (1837–1909), English poet and critic who rebelled against Victorian social and religious conventions.
[32]Robert Buchanan (1841–1901), English critic, attacked the

Pre-Raphaelites and Swinburne for aesthetic fleshliness in "The Fleshly School of Poetry" (1871), which led to Rossetti's breakdown. Central in the attack was Rossetti's poem "Jenny," about the musings of a man-about-town on the fate of a London prostitute. Pound conjoins the painter's model ("faun's head of hers") with the prostitute ("poor Jenny's case") in his attack on a hypocritical culture that both exploits and condemns such women.
[33]Pound takes Elizabeth Slidall as the model for the prepatory drawings ("cartons," French for "cartoons") of the Pre-Raphaelite painter Sir Edward Burne-Jones (1833–1898); his painting *King Cophetua and the Beggar Maid* (1884) hangs in London's Tate Gallery.
[34]English poet Edward Fitzgerald (1809–1883) published his translation of *The Rubáiyát of Omar Khayyam* in 1859, which was ignored until discovered and praised by Rossetti.
[35]"Maquereau" (French), pimp.

"SIENA MI FE'; DISFECEMI MAREMMA"[36]

Among the pickled fœtuses and bottled bones,   120
Engaged in perfecting the catalogue,
I found the last scion of the
Senatorial families of Strasbourg, Monsieur Verog.[37]

For two hours he talked of Galliffet;[38]
Of Dowson; of the Rhymers' Club;[39]   125
Told me how Johnson (Lionel) died
By falling from a high stool in a pub . . .

But showed no trace of alcohol
At the autopsy, privately performed—
Tissue preserved—the pure mind   130
Arose toward Newman[40] as the whiskey warmed.

Dowson found harlots cheaper than hotels;
Headlam[41] for uplift; Image impartially imbued
With raptures for Bacchus, Terpsichore[42] and the Church.
So spoke the author of "The Dorian Mood,"   135

M. Verog, out of step with the decade,
Detached from his contemporaries,
Neglected by the young,
Because of these reveries.

BRENNBAUM[43]

The sky-like limpid eyes,   140
The circular infant's face,
The stiffness from spats to collar
Never relaxing into grace;

The heavy memories of Horeb, Sinai and the forty years,[44]
Showed only when the daylight fell   145
Level across the face
Of Brennbaum "The Impeccable."

---

[36]"Siena made me; Maremma unmade me" (Italian); spoken by Pia de' Tolomei of Siena, murdered by her husband in the Maremma marshes, in Dante's *Purgatorio* V.

[37]Victor Plarr (1863–1929), whose family left Strasbourg for Britain after the Franco-Prussian War (1870–71), was librarian to the Royal College of Surgeons in London. His books include a volume of poems, *In the Dorian Mood* (1896), and *Ernest Dowson 1888–1897: Reminiscences* (1914).

[38]The Marquis de Galliffet (1830–1909), a French general who led a heroic unsupported cavalry charge in the Battle of Sedan during the Franco-Prussian War.

[39]Plarr belonged to the Rhymers' Club, a group of poets who met in the 1890s at the Cheshire Cheese, a London eating-house on Fleet Street; Yeats was prominent among the group, which also included English poets Ernest Dowson (1867–1900) and Lionel Johnson (1867–1902), who actually died from a fall on the street.

[40]Johnson was a convert to Catholicism, as was John Henry Cardinal Newman (1801–1890), intellectual leader of English Catholicism.

[41]Rev. Stewart D. Headlam (1847–1924), denied a regular curacy for lecturing on and defending theater and music-halls, founded the Church and Stage Club, which was greatly aided by Selwyn Image (1849–1930), editor of a literary magazine, *Hobby-Horse.*

[42]Bacchus: Roman god of wine, music, tragedy; Terpsichore: Greek muse of dance.

[43]A modern Jew who suggests the Wandering Jew, possibly based on Max Beerbohm (1872–1956), English critic, essayist, and caricaturist, known as "The Incomparable Max," and whom Pound may have mistakenly thought Jewish.

[44]Moses was called at Mount Horeb, where the Israelites made a covenant with Jehovah; received the Ten Commandments at Mount Sinai (another name for Horeb); and for forty years led the Israelites through the wilderness to the promised land.

MR. NIXON[45]

In the cream gilded cabin of his steam yacht
Mr. Nixon advised me kindly, to advance with fewer
Dangers of delay. "Consider   150
          "Carefully the reviewer.

"I was as poor as you are;
"When I began I got, of course,
"Advance on royalties, fifty at first," said Mr. Nixon,
"Follow me, and take a column,   155
"Even if you have to work free.

"Butter reviewers. From fifty to three hundred
"I rose in eighteen months;
"The hardest nut I had to crack
"Was Dr. Dundas.   160

"I never mentioned a man but with the view
"Of selling my own works.
"The tip's a good one, as for literature
"It gives no man a sinecure.

"And no one knows, at sight, a masterpiece.   165
"And give up verse, my boy,
"There's nothing in it."

•   •   •   •   •

Likewise a friend of Blougram's[46] once advised me:
Don't kick against the pricks,[47]
Accept opinion. The "Nineties" tried your game   170
And died, there's nothing in it.

X

Beneath the sagging roof
The stylist[48] has taken shelter,
Unpaid, uncelebrated,
At last from the world's welter   175

Nature receives him;
With a placcid and uneducated mistress
He exercises his talents
And the soil meets his distress.

The haven from sophistications and contentions   180
Leaks through its thatch;
He offers succulent cooking;
The door has a creaking latch.

---

[45]Probably based on Arnold Bennett (1867–1931), commercially successful English novelist.
[46]In Robert Browning's poem "Bishop Blougram's Apology" (1855), the Bishop gives a causistic defense of his worldly success.
[47]Cf. Christ's words to Paul before his conversion in Acts 9:5, "It is hard for thee to kick against the pricks."
[48]Probably based on Ford Madox Ford (1873–1939), English poet, novelist, critic, and editor, who influenced Pound.

XI

"Conservatrix of Milésien"[49]
Habits of mind and feeling,   185
Possibly. But in Ealing[50]
With the most bank-clerkly of Englishmen?

No, "Milésian" is an exaggeration.
No instinct has survived in her
Older than those her grandmother   190
Told her would fit her station.

XII

"Daphne with her thighs in bark
Stretches toward me her leafy hands," — [51]
Subjectively. In the stuffed-satin drawing-room
I await The Lady Valentine's commands,   195

Knowing my coat has never been
Of precisely the fashion
To stimulate, in her,
A durable passion;

Doubtful, somewhat, of the value   200
Of well-gowned approbation
Of literary effort,
But never of The Lady Valentine's vocation:

Poetry, her border of ideas,
The edge, uncertain, but a means of blending   205
With other strata
Where the lower and higher have ending;

A hook to catch the Lady Jane's attention,
A modulation toward the theatre,
Also, in the case of revolution,   210
A possible friend and comforter.

                    .   .   .   .   .

Conduct, on the other hand, the soul
"Which the highest cultures have nourished"[52]
To Fleet St. where
Dr. Johnson flourished;[53]   215

Beside this thoroughfare
The sale of half-hose has
Long since superseded the cultivation
Of Pierian roses.[54]

---

[49]Pound adapts a phrase from the story "Stratagèmes" (1894) by French writer Rémy de Gourmont (1858–1915): "Women . . . these conservers of Milesian traditions." The licentious Greek *Milesian Tales* by Aristides of Miletus (second century B.C.) have not survived.
[50]A London suburb.
[51]Translated from "Le Château du Souvenir" (*Émaux et Camées*, 1852) by French poet Théophile Gautier (1811–1872). In Greek myth, the nymph Daphne prayed to escape the amorous advances of the god Apollo and was turned into a laurel tree.
[52]Translation of the first line of "Complainte des Pianos" by French poet Jules Laforgue (1860–1887).
[53]Samuel Johnson (1709–1784), English lexicographer, poet, essayist, and leading man of letters in the late eighteenth century, met with other writers on Fleet Street, a center for London journalism.
[54]An allusion to a line from the Greek poet Sappho: "For you hold no claim to the Pierian roses"; Pieria, in Greek myth, is the birthplace of the Muses.

ENVOI (1919)[55]

Go, dumb-born book,　　　　　　　　　　　　　　220
Tell her that sang me once that song of Lawes:[56]
Hadst thou but song
As thou hast subjects known,
Then were there cause in thee that should condone
Even my faults that heavy upon me lie,　　　　225
And build her glories their longevity.

Tell her that sheds
Such treasure in the air,
Recking naught else but that her graces give
Life to the moment,　　　　　　　　　　　　　230
I would bid them live
As roses might, in magic amber laid,
Red overwrought with orange and all made
One substance and one colour
Braving time.　　　　　　　　　　　　　　　235

Tell her that goes
With song upon her lips
But sings not out the song, nor knows
The maker of it, some other mouth,
May be as fair as hers,　　　　　　　　　　　240
Might, in new ages, gain her worshippers,
When our two dusts with Waller's shall be laid,
Siftings on siftings in oblivion,
Till change hath broken down
All things save Beauty alone.　　　　　　　　245

MAUBERLEY

1920

"Vacuos exercet in aera morsus."[57]

I

Turned from the "eau-forte
Par Jacquemart"[58]
To the strait head
Of Messalina:[59]

"His true Penelope　　　　　　　　　　　　　250
Was Flaubert,"[60]
And his tool
The engraver's.

---

[55]This envoi is based on the seventeenth-century *carpe-diem* song, "Go, Lovely Rose," by English poet Edmund Waller (1606–1687).
[56]Henry Lawes (1596–1662), preeminent English composer of his day, set Waller's song to music.
[57]"He bites at the empty air" (Latin), adapted from Ovid's *Metamorphoses* VII, 786, in which a dog pursues a monster ravaging Thebes, and later both are turned to stone.

[58]"Etching by Jacquemart" (French); an etching of Gautier by the French engraver Jules F. Jacquemart (1837–1880) appears in an edition of *Emaux et Camées*.
[59]Valeria Messalina, the dissolute wife of the Roman Emperor Claudius, who had her killed; her profile was engraved on ancient coins.
[60]Cf. line 13.

Firmness,
Not the full smile,   255
His art, but an art
In profile;

Colourless
Pier Francesca,[61]
Pisanello[62] lacking the skill   260
To forge Achaia.[63]

II

"Qu'est ce qu'ils savent de l'amour, et qu'est ce qu'ils
peuvent en comprendre?
    S'ils ne comprennent pas la poésie, s'ils ne sentent pas
la musique, qu'est ce qu'ils peuvent comprendre de cette
passion en comparaison avec laquelle la rose est grossière et
le parfum des violettes un tonnerre?"   CAID ALI[64]

For three years, diabolus[65] in the scale,
He drank ambrosia,[66]
All passes, ANANGKE[67] prevails,
Came end, at last, to that Arcadia.[68]   265

He had moved amid her[69] phantasmagoria,
Amid her galaxies,
NUKTOS 'AGALMA[70]

    .   .   .   .   .

Drifted . . . drifted precipitate,
Asking time to be rid of . . .   270
Of his bewilderment; to designate
His new found orchid. . . .

To be certain . . . certain . . .
(Amid ærial flowers) . . . time for arrangements—
Drifted on   275
To the final estrangement;

Unable in the supervening blankness
To sift TO AGATHON[71] from the chaff
Until he found his sieve . . .
Ultimately, his seismograph: 280

—Given that is his "fundamental passion,"
This urge to convey the relation

---

[61]Piero della Francesca (*c.* 1420–1492), Umbrian painter noted for the mathematical perfection of his forms and for his pale, soft colors.
[62]Antonio Pisanello (1395–*c.* 1455), Veronese painter and portrait medalist.
[63]Ancient region of Greece, here standing for Grecian art.
[64]Caid Ali is a Persian pseudonym of Pound's, associated with Fitzgerald's *Rubáiyát*. The French reads: "What do they know of love, and what can they understand of it? If they do not understand poetry, if they do not feel music, what can they understand of this passion compared to which the rose is coarse and the perfume of violets thunderous?"

[65]The diabolus (Latin for "devil") is the augmented fourth, a dissonant interval in the musical scale, forbidden to medieval academic composers; cf. line 1.
[66]Food of the gods.
[67]"Necessity," or "Fate" (Greek).
[68]An idyllic pastoral land in classical mythology, named after a district in ancient Greece.
[69]I.e., Night's.
[70]"Night's jewel" (Greek), from Poem IX, celebrating the evening star, by Greek poet Bion (*c.* 100 B.C.).
[71]"The Good" (Greek).

Of eye-lid and cheek-bone
By verbal manifestation;

To present the series   285
Of curious heads in medallion—

He had passed, inconscient, full gaze,
The wide-banded irides[72]
And botticellian sprays[73] implied
In their diastasis;[74]   290

Which anæthesis,[75] noted a year late,
And weighed, revealed his great affect,
(Orchid), mandate
Of Eros,[76] a retrospect.

. . . . .

Mouths biting empty air,   295
The still stone dogs,
Caught in metamorphosis, were
Left him as epilogues.

"THE AGE DEMANDED"

VIDE[77] POEM II. PAGE 794

For this agility chance found
Him of all men, unfit   300
As the red-beaked steeds of
The Cytheræan[78] for a chain bit.

The glow of porcelain
Brought no reforming sense
To his perception   305
Of the social inconsequence.

Thus, if her colour
Came against his gaze,
Tempered as if
It were through a perfect glaze   310

He made no immediate application
Of this to relation of the state
To the individual, the month was more temperate
Because this beauty had been.

The coral isle, the lion-coloured sand   315
Burst in upon the porcelain revery:
Impetuous troubling
Of his imagery.

---

[72]Plural of "iris"; here, both eyes and flowers.
[73]An allusion to the Italian painter Sandro Botticelli (*c*. 1445–1510), renowned for his delicately colored, distinctly outlined paintings, especially *The Birth of Venus*, in which the goddess rises from the foam of the sea on a shell, blown by the wind.
[74]Separation; "the divided stance of the eyes, or their dilation in erotic invitation" (Froula, 101).

[75]Insensibility.
[76]Greek god of love, son of Aphrodite (Venus), goddess of love.
[77]"See" (Latin).
[78]Epithet for Aphrodite, in Greek myth, born of the sea, who is said to have first stepped ashore on the island of Cythera; her carriage was drawn by doves.

Mildness, amid the neo-Nietzschean[79] clatter,
His sense of graduations,   320
Quite out of place amid
Resistance to current exacerbations,

Invitation, mere invitation to perceptivity
Gradually led him to the isolation
Which these presents place   325
Under a more tolerant, perhaps, examination.

By constant elimination
The manifest universe
Yielded an armour
Against utter consternation,   330

A Minoan undulation,[80]
Seen, we admit, amid ambrosial circumstances
Strengthened him against
The discouraging doctrine of chances,

And his desire for survival,   335
Faint in the most strenuous moods,
Became an Olympian *apathein*[81]
In the presence of selected perceptions.

A pale gold, in the aforesaid pattern,
The unexpected palms   340
Destroying, certainly, the artist's urge,
Left him delighted with the imaginary
Audition of the phantasmal sea-surge,

Incapable of the least utterance or composition,
Emendation, conservation of the "better tradition,"   345
Refinement of medium, elimination of superfluities,
August attraction or concentration.

Nothing, in brief, but maudlin confession,
Irresponse to human aggression,
Amid the precipitation, down-float   350
Of insubstantial manna,
Lifting the faint susurrus[82]
Of his subjective hosannah.

Ultimate affronts to
Human redundancies;   355

Non-esteem of self-styled "his betters"
Leading, as he well knew,
To his final
Exclusion from the world of letters.

---

[79]Friedrich Nietzsche (1844–1900), German philosopher, whose theories challenging systematic Western thought were fashionable at this time.
[80]An aspect of the art of the Minoan period, the high civiliza-tion of the Cretan Bronze Age (*c.* 3000–1000 B.C.), named after King Minos of Crete.
[81]"Indifference," or "lack of emotion" (Greek).
[82]"Whispering" (Latin).

IV

Scattered Moluccas[83]   360
Not knowing, day to day,
The first day's end, in the next noon;
The placid water
Unbroken by the Simoon;[84]

Thick foliage   365
Placid beneath warm suns,
Tawn fore-shores
Washed in the cobalt of oblivions;

Or through dawn-mist
The grey and rose   370
Of the juridical
Flamingoes;

A consciousness disjunct,
Being but this overblotted
Series   375
Of intermittences;

Coracle[85] of pacific voyages,
The unforecasted beach;
Then on an oar
Read this: 380

"I was
And I no more exist;
Here drifted
An hedonist."

MEDALLION

Luini[86] in porcelain!   385
The grand piano
Utters a profane
Protest with her clear soprano.

The sleek head emerges
From the gold-yellow frock   390
As Anadyomene[87] in the opening
Pages of Reinach.

Honey-red, closing the face-oval,
A basket-work of braids which seem as if they were
Spun in King Minos'[88] hall   395
From metal, or intractable amber;

---

[83]Spice Islands, near New Guinea.
[84]A hot, sandy wind from the desert.
[85]A small boat.
[86]Bernardino Luini (c. 1481–1532), Italian painter, executed a series of medallion portraits; thus, the singer is like a "Luini in porcelain."
[87]Epithet for Aphrodite meaning "foam-born"; a head of

Aphrodite is reproduced in *Apollo* (1904), a history of art by French archaeologist and art historian Salomon Reinach (1858–1932).
[88]Legendary King of Crete whose magnificent palace is at Knossos, and whose name is given to the high civilization of the Minoan period.

The face-oval beneath the glaze,
Bright in its suave bounding-line, as,
Beneath half-watt rays,
The eyes turn topaz.   400

1920

from The Cantos[1]

I[2]

And then went down to the ship,
Set keel to breakers, forth on the godly sea, and
We set up mast and sail on that swart ship,
Bore sheep aboard her, and our bodies also
Heavy with weeping, and winds from sternward   5
Bore us out onward with bellying canvas,
Circe's this craft, the trim-coifed goddess.[3]
Then sat we amidships, wind jamming the tiller,
Thus with stretched sail, we went over sea till day's end.
Sun to his slumber, shadows o'er all the ocean,   10
Came we then to the bounds of deepest water,
To the Kimmerian lands,[4] and peopled cities
Covered with close-webbed mist, unpierced ever
With glitter of sun-rays
Nor with stars stretched, nor looking back from heaven   15
Swartest night stretched over wretched men there.
The ocean flowing backward, came we then to the place
Aforesaid by Circe.
Here did they rites, Perimedes and Eurylochus,[5]
And drawing sword from my hip   20
I dug the ell-square pitkin;[6]
Poured we libations unto each the dead,
First mead and then sweet wine, water mixed with white flour.
Then prayed I many a prayer to the sickly death's-heads;
As set in Ithaca, sterile bulls of the best   25
For sacrifice, heaping the pyre with goods,

---

[1]Pound began working on *The Cantos* in 1915, publishing early versions of the first three in 1917 and the last *Drafts and Fragments* in 1969. He called his epic "a poem including history," an attempt to tell "the tale of the tribe." Presenting fragments of many cultures, literature, art, languages, myths, history, economics, historical personages in allusive juxtapositions, *The Cantos* pose a formidable challenge for the reader, but one well worth meeting. In 1966 Pound wrote that the "best introduction to the *Cantos*" might be some lines from an early draft, lines which include: ". . . say the thing's an art-form, / . . . and that the modern world / Needs such a rag-bag to stuff all its thought in. . . ."

[2]In lines 1–67, Pound adapts Book XI of Homer's *Odyssey*, describing Odysseus's voyage to the underworld, where he summons up the spirits of the dead.

[3]The goddess sorceress Circe, who has detained Odysseus and his men for a year, has granted his request to leave her island and return home to Ithaca, but instructs him to go first to the underworld and seek prophecy for his journey from the blind Theban Tiresius, who alone among the dead retains his prophetic powers.

[4]Mist-shrouded lands at the edge of the earth, near the entrance to Hades.

[5]Two of Odysseus's men.

[6]Small pit (Pound's coinage); an ell is a measure originally a forearm's length.

A sheep to Tiresias only, black and a bell-sheep.[7]
Dark blood flowed in the fosse,[8]
Souls out of Erebus,[9] cadaverous dead, of brides
Of youths and of the old who had borne much;   30
Souls stained with recent tears, girls tender,
Men many, mauled with bronze lance heads,
Battle spoil, bearing yet dreory[10] arms,
These many crowded about me; with shouting,
Pallor upon me, cried to my men for more beasts;   35
Slaughtered the herds, sheep slain of bronze;
Poured ointment, cried to the gods,
To Pluto the strong, and praised Proserpine;[11]
Unsheathed the narrow sword,
I sat to keep off the impetuous impotent dead,   40
Till I should hear Tiresias.
But first Elpenor[12] came, our friend Elpenor,
Unburied, cast on the wide earth,
Limbs that we left in the house of Circe,
Unwept, unwrapped in sepulchre, since toils urged other.   45
Pitiful spirit. And I cried in hurried speech:
"Elpenor, how art thou come to this dark coast?
"Cam'st thou afoot, outstripping seamen?"
            And he in heavy speech:
"Ill fate and abundant wine. I slept in Circe's ingle.[13]   50
"Going down the long ladder unguarded,
"I fell against the buttress,
"Shattered the nape-nerve, the soul sought Avernus.[14]
"But thou, O King, I bid remember me, unwept, unburied,
"Heap up mine arms, be tomb by sea-bord, and inscribed: 55
"*A man of no fortune, and with a name to come.*
"And set my oar up, that I swung mid fellows."

And Anticlea[15] came, whom I beat off, and then Tiresias Theban,
Holding his golden wand, knew me, and spoke first:
"A second time? why? man of ill star,   60
"Facing the sunless dead and this joyless region?
"Stand from the fosse, leave me my bloody bever[16]
"For soothsay."
            And I stepped back,
And he strong with the blood, said then: "Odysseus   65
"Shalt return through spiteful Neptune,[17] over dark seas,

---

[7]The leader of the flock.
[8]Ditch.
[9]The darkness the souls pass through before reaching Hades.
[10]Bloody (Old English: *dreorig*).
[11]Pluto, lord of the underworld, and his queen Proserpine, who revisits the earth each spring as goddess of fertility.
[12]One of Odysseus's men who had died in a drunken fall from Circe's roof and was left unburied. Odysseus will return "unto Circe" to perform the burial rites at the end of the canto.

[13]Corner.
[14]Crater near Naples; in legend, at the entrance to Hades.
[15]Mother of Odysseus, who had died during his absence from Ithaca. In the *Odyssey*, Odysseus weeps at the sight of her, but holds her off because of Circe's warning that no spirit should drink the blood, and thus speak to him, before Tiresias.
[16]Drink.
[17]God of the sea, "spiteful" because Odysseus had blinded his son, the Cyclops.

"Lose all companions." And then Anticlea came.
Lie quiet Divus. I mean, that is Andreas Divus,
In officina Wecheli, 1538, out of Homer.[18]
And he sailed, by Sirens[19] and thence outward and away   70
And unto Circe.
       Venerandam,[20]
In the Cretan's phrase, with the golden crown, Aphrodite,
Cypri munimenta sortita est,[21] mirthful, orichalchi,[22] with golden
Girdles and breast bands, thou with dark eyelids   75
Bearing the golden bough of Argicida.[23] So that:

1915   *1917, 1925*

XIII

Kung[1] walked
       by the dynastic temple
and into the cedar grove,
       and then out by the lower river,
And with him Khieu, Tchi   5
       and Tian the low speaking
And "we are unknown," said Kung,
"You will take up charioteering?
       Then you will become known,
"Or perhaps I should take up charioteering, or archery?   10
"Or the practice of public speaking?"
And Tseu-lou said, "I would put the defences in order,"
And Khieu said, "If I were lord of a province
I would put it in better order than this is."
And Tchi said, "I would prefer a small mountain temple,   15
"With order in the observances,
       with a suitable performance of the ritual,"
And Tian said, with his hand on the strings of his lute
The low sounds continuing
       after his hand left the strings,   20
And the sound went up like smoke, under the leaves,
And he looked after the sound:

---

[18]Andreas Divus, translator of a Renaissance Latin version of Homer's *Odyssey*, published in Paris "at the workshop of Wechel" (Latin) in 1538. Pound adapts this text, not the original Greek of Homer's epic.

[19]Sea nymphs whose singing lured sailors to destruction.

[20]"Venerable" (Latin). Said of Aphrodite, Greek goddess of love and beauty, in the second Homeric Hymn to Aphrodite as translated into Latin by Georgius Dartona of Crete; his translation of the Homeric Hymns (not really by Homer) was included in Pound's copy of Divus's *Odyssey*.

[21]"She was allotted the fortifications of Cyprus" (Latin).

[22]"Of copper" (Latin), referring to her earrings.

[23]This line comes from the first Homeric Hymn to Aphrodite, in which she seduces Anchises, Aeneas' father, by telling him she is a mortal carried off by the messenger god Hermes "of the golden wand." Arigicida is an epithet for Hermes meaning "Slayer of Argus," the hundred-eyed monster; it can also mean "Slayer of Greeks," referring to Aphrodite, who helped the Trojans and her son Aeneas during the Trojan War. Aeneas offered a golden bough to Proserpine when he descended to the underworld.

[1]Kung Fu-Tseu, or Confucius (551–479 B.C.), Chinese philosopher, whose social and ethical ideals function in *The Cantos* as a "backbone moral," opposed to the disorder and materialism of western society. Except for the last three lines, this canto is drawn mostly from the *Analects*, a compilation of Confucius's teachings by his followers.

                        "The old swimming hole,
    "And the boys flopping off the planks,
    "Or sitting in the underbrush playing mandolins."   25
                And Kung smiled upon all of them equally.
    And Thseng-sie desired to know:
                "Which had answered correctly?"
    And Kung said, "They have all answered correctly,
    "That is to say, each in his nature."   30
    And Kung raised his cane against Yuan Jang,
                Yuan Jang being his elder,
    For Yuan Jang sat by the roadside pretending to
                be receiving wisdom.
    And Kung said   35
                "You old fool, come out of it,
    Get up and do something useful."
                And Kung said
    "Respect a child's faculties
    "From the moment it inhales the clear air,   40
    "But a man of fifty who knows nothing
                Is worthy of no respect."
    And "When the prince has gathered about him
    "All the savants and artists, his riches will be fully employed."
    And Kung said, and wrote on the bo leaves: 45
                If a man have not order within him
    He can not spread order about him;
    And if a man have not order within him
    His family will not act with due order;
                And if the prince have not order within him   50
    He can not put order in his dominions.
    And Kung gave the words "order"
    and "brotherly deference"
    And said nothing of the "life after death."
    And he said   55
                "Anyone can run to excesses,
    It is easy to shoot past the mark,
    It is hard to stand firm in the middle."

    And they said: If a man commit murder
                Should his father protect him, and hide him?   60
    And Kung said:
                He should hide him.

    And Kung gave his daughter to Kong-Tch'ang
                Although Kong-Tch'ang was in prison.
    And he gave his niece to Nan-Young   65
                although Nan-Young was out of office.
    And Kung said, "Wang ruled with moderation,
                In his day the State was well kept,
    And even I can remember
    A day when the historians left blanks in their writings,   70
    I mean for things they didn't know,
    But that time seems to be passing."
    And Kung said, "Without character you will
                be unable to play on that instrument
    Or to execute the music fit for the Odes.   75

The blossoms of the apricot
      blow from the east to the west,
And I have tried to keep them from falling."

1924, 1925

XLV

With *Usura*[1]

With usura hath no man a house of good stone
each block cut smooth and well fitting
that design might cover their face,
with usura   5
hath no man a painted paradise on his church wall
harpes et luz[2]
or where virgin receiveth message[3]
and halo projects from incision,
with usura   10
seeth no man Gonzaga his heirs and his concubines[4]
no picture is made to endure nor to live with
but it is made to sell and sell quickly
with usura, sin against nature,
is thy bread ever more of stale rags   15
is thy bread dry as paper,
with no mountain wheat, no strong flour
with usura the line grows thick
with usura is no clear demarcation
and no man can find site for his dwelling.   20
Stonecutter is kept from his stone
weaver is kept from his loom
WITH USURA
wool comes not to market
sheep bringeth no gain with usura   25
Usura is a murrain,[5] usura
blunteth the needle in the maid's hand
and stoppeth the spinner's cunning. Pietro Lombardo[6]
came not by usura
Duccio[7] came not by usura   30

---

[1]"Usury" (Latin): the practice of lending money at exorbitant interest rates. Pound later appended a note to this canto, defining usury as: "A charge for the use of purchasing power, levied without regard to production; often without regard to the possibilities of production." The Catholic Church condemned usury until the sixteenth century when John Calvin argued against its prohibition; hence Pound draws his examples of non-usurious economics from the medieval and early Renaissance periods.

[2]"Harps and lutes" (Old French), from François Villon's "Ballade pour prier Nôtre Dame," written as a prayer for his mother to say to the Virgin: "In my parish church, I see a painted paradise where there are harps and lutes."

[3]I.e., paintings of the Annunciation.

[4]A reference to the famed portrait frescoes (1474) of the court and family of Lodovico Gonzaga (1414–1478) in the ducal palace of Mantua by the court painter Andrea Mantegna (1431–1506).

[5]Plague.

[6]Italian sculptor (1435–1515) who built the church of Santa Maria dei Miracoli, Venice, with the mermaid bas-reliefs carved by his son Tullio (1455–1532).

[7]Agostino di Duccio (1418?–1481), famed for the bas-reliefs in the Tempio Malatestiano in Rimini. Pound admired the Italian lord and soldier Sigismondo Pandolfo Malatesta (1417–1468) for employing great artists to create the Tempio (Temple), known officially as the Church of San Francesco.

nor Pier della Francesca;[8] Zuan Bellin'[9] not by usura
nor was 'La Calunnia'[10] painted.
Came not by usura Angelico;[11] came not Ambrogio Praedis,[12]
Came no church of cut stone signed: *Adamo me fecit.*[13]
Not by usura St Trophime[14]   35
Not by usura Saint Hilaire,[15]
Usura rusteth the chisel
It rusteth the craft and the craftsman
It gnaweth the thread in the loom
None learneth to weave gold in her pattern;   40
Azure hath a canker by usura; cramoisi[16] is unbroidered
Emerald findeth no Memling[17]
Usura slayeth the child in the womb
It stayeth the young man's courting
It hath brought palsey to bed, lyeth   45
between the young bride and her bridegroom
                    CONTRA NATURAM[18]
They have brought whores for Eleusis[19]
Corpses are set to banquet
at behest of usura.[20]   50

                                                            1936, 1937

from LXXXI[1]

What thou lovest well remains,
                              the rest is dross
What thou lov'st well shall not be reft from thee
What thou lov'st well is thy true heritage   135
Whose world, or mine or theirs
                    or is it of none?

---

[8]Italian painter (1420?–1492) who painted a fresco for the Tempio.
[9]Giovanni Bellini (1430–1516), Venetian painter, whose "Pietà" is in the Tempio.
[10]"Calumny" (Italian), an allegorical painting by the Italian painter Sandro Botticelli (1444–1510).
[11]Fra Angelico (1387–1455), Florentine painter.
[12]Milanese painter (1455–1508).
[13]"Adam made me" (Latin), from an inscription on a hand-hewn column in the Church of San Zeno, Verona, Italy.
[14]Romanesque church in Arles, France, famed for its double-columned cloisters.
[15]Romanesque church in Poitiers, France, admired by Pound for "its proportions."
[16]"Crimson cloth" (French).
[17]Hans Memling (1430?–1495), Flemish painter.
[18]"Against nature" (Latin).
[19]Town in ancient Greece where the sacred Eleusinian mys-

teries to Demeter, the earth mother, were celebrated. These purifying fertility rites, centering on the sorrows of Demeter at the rape of her daughter Persephone by Pluto, and the joys of her reunification with her daughter each spring, include a movement toward mystic illumination by the initiates with a hope of rebirth. Pound sees a perversion of sexuality with usura.
[20]Near the end of his life, in 1972, Pound wrote: "re USURY: I was out of focus, taking a symptom for a cause. The cause is AVARICE."
[1]Pound wrote this canto, one of the autobiographical *Pisan Cantos* (1948), in 1945 while imprisoned in a U.S. Army camp near Pisa, Italy, awaiting trial for treason for his pro-Fascist Mussolini wartime broadcasts. The canto opens with a cluster of memories, interrupted by the poet's cry of pain and loneliness. The poet is then consoled by memories of poetry and song, which usher in a vision of eyes in his tent, and lead to this excerpt, which ends the canto.

First came the seen, then thus the palpable
    Elysium,[2] though it were in the halls of hell,
What thou lovest well is thy true heritage
What thou lov'st well shall not be reft from thee

The ant's a centaur in his dragon world.
Pull down thy vanity, it is not man
Made courage, or made order, or made grace,
    Pull down thy vanity, I say pull down.
Learn of the green world what can be thy place
In scaled invention or true artistry,
Pull down thy vanity,
              Paquin[3] pull down!
The green casque[4] has outdone your elegance.

"Master thyself, then others shall thee beare"[5]
    Pull down thy vanity
Thou art a beaten dog beneath the hail,
A swollen magpie in a fitful sun,
Half black half white
Nor knowst'ou wing from tail
Pull down thy vanity
        How mean thy hates
Fostered in falsity,
        Pull down thy vanity,
Rathe[6] to destroy, niggard[7] in charity,
Pull down thy vanity,
        I say pull down.

But to have done instead of not doing
        this is not vanity
To have, with decency, knocked
That a Blunt[8] should open
      To have gathered from the air a live tradition
or from a fine old eye the unconquered flame
This is not vanity.
    Here error is all in the not done,
all in the diffidence that faltered . . .

1945   1948

---

[2]Paradise of the blest in Greek mythology.
[3]Parisian dress designer.
[4]Helmet (of a green insect).
[5]Adaptation of a line from Chaucer's "Truth: Ballade of Good Counsel."
[6]Quick.
[7]Stingy.
[8]Wilfred Scawen Blunt (1840–1922), English poet who was censured and jailed for his anti-imperialist activities. In 1914, Pound, Yeats, and a committee of poets held a testimonial dinner for him at his home.

CXVI

Came Neptunus[1]
       his mind leaping
            like dolphins,
These concepts the human mind has attained.
To make Cosmos[2] —   5
To achieve the possible —
Muss.,[3] wrecked for an error,
But the record
        the palimpsest[4] —
a little light   10
       in great darkness —
cuniculi[5] —
An old "crank" dead in Virginia.[6]
Unprepared young burdened with records,
The vision of the Madonna   15
       above the cigar butts
          and over the portal.
"Have made a mass of laws"
        (mucchio di leggi)[7]
Litterae nihil sanantes[8]   20
       Justinian's,[9]
a tangle of works unfinished.

I have brought the great ball of crystal;
      who can lift it?
Can you enter the great acorn of light?   25
      But the beauty is not the madness
Tho' my errors and wrecks lie about me.
And I am not a demigod,
I cannot make it cohere.[10]
If love be not in the house there is nothing.   30
The voice of famine unheard.
How came beauty against this blackness,
Twice beauty under the elms —
      To be saved by squirrels and bluejays?
       "plus j'aime le chien"[11]   35
Ariadne.[12]

---

[1]Roman god of the sea.
[2]A harmonious, orderly whole or universe, opposed to chaos.
[3]Benito Mussolini (1883–1945), Italian Fascist dictator, executed by partisans.
[4]Parchment or vellum written on several times, with visible traces of imperfectly erased earlier writings.
[5]"Underground passages" (Latin).
[6]Thomas Jefferson; his correspondence with John Adams was admired by Pound.
[7]"Mass of laws" (Italian), a quotation from Mussolini.

[8]"Writings cure nothing" (Latin).
[9]Justinian I (483–565), Byzantine emperor who codified Roman law.
[10]An allusion to Pound's 1956 translation of Sophocles's *Women of Trachis* and the words of the demi-god Herakles: "what / SPLENDOUR, / IT ALL COHERES."
[11]An allusion to a French saying, "Plus je vois des hommes, plus j'admire les chiens" ("The more I know of man, the more I love dogs").
[12]In Greek myth, the daughter of King Minos, who gave Theseus a thread to guide him out of the labyrinth.

Disney[13] against the metaphysicals,
and Laforgue[14] more than they thought in him,
Spire[15] thanked me in proposito[16]
And I have learned more from Jules   40
                    (Jules Laforgue) since then
deeps in him,
            and Linnaeus.[17]
                    chi crescerà i nostri[18] —
but about that terzo[19]   45
            third heaven,
                    that Venere,
again is all "paradiso"
            a nice quiet paradise
                    over the shambles,   50
and some climbing
            before the take-off,[20]
to "see again,"
the verb is "see," not "walk on"[21]
i.e. it coheres all right   55
            even if my notes do not cohere.
Many errors,
            a little rightness,
to excuse his hell
            and my paradiso.   60
And as to why they go wrong,
            thinking of rightness
And as to who will copy this palimpsest?
            al poco giorno
                    ed al gran cerchio d'ombra[22]   65
But to affirm the gold threat in the pattern
                    (Torcello)[23]
al Vicolo d'oro[24]
            (Tigullio).[25]
To confess wrong without losing rightness: 70
Charity I have had sometimes,
            I cannot make it flow thru.
A little light, like a rushlight
            to lead back to splendour.

1962, 1968

---

[13]Walt Disney (1901–1966); Pound admired "the serious side of Disney, the Confucian side. . . . It's in having taken an ethos, as he does in *Perri*, that squirrel film, where you have the values of courage and tenderness asserted in a way that everyone can understand" (*Writers at Work: The Paris Review Interviews*, Second Series, 1963).
[14]Jules Laforgue (1860–1887), whose ironic diction and free verse rhythms influenced the early poetry of Eliot and Pound.
[15]André Spire (1868–1966), French poet and Zionist.
[16]"On the subject" (Italian).
[17]Swedish botanist (1707–1778), founder of modern taxonomy.
[18]Abbreviated from the Italian "Ecco chi crescerà li nostri amori" ("Behold, one who will increase our loves"), spoken to Dante as he enters the second sphere of Paradise, Mercury,

by the radiant souls of those motivated by personal honor and glory (*Paradiso*, V, 105).
[19]"Third" (Italian); the third heaven of Paradise, governed by Venus (*Venere* in Italian), contains the souls of the amorous who have overcome physical passion for the love of God.
[20]Possibly an allusion to Dante's emergence from Hell and long climb to Mount Purgatory, where they "take-off" for the climb towards Paradise.
[21]An allusion to the last words of Dante's *Inferno*: "riveder le stelle" ("to see again the stars").
[22]"To the short day and the great circle of shadow" (Italian), the first line of a sestina by Dante.
[23]Island village in the Venetian Lagoon, whose cathedral contains Byzantine mosaics.
[24]"On the Lane of Gold" (Italian).
[25]The Bay of Tigullio off Rapallo, Italy, where Pound lived.

CXX

I have tried to write Paradise

Do not move
    Let the wind speak
        that is paradise.

Let the Gods forgive what I   5
    have made
Let those I love try to forgive
    what I have made.

1969

What I Feel about Walt Whitman[1]

From this side of the Atlantic I am for the first time able to read Whitman, and from the vantage of my education and—if it be permitted a man of my scant years—my world citizenship: I see him America's poet. The only Poet before the artists of the Carmen-Hovey[2] period, or better, the only one of the conventionally recognised 'American Poets' who is worth reading.

He *is* America. His crudity is an exceeding great stench, but it *is* America. He is the hollow place in the rock that echoes with his time. He *does* 'chant the crucial stage' and he is the 'voice triumphant.' He is disgusting. He is an exceedingly nauseating pill, but he accomplishes his mission.

Entirely free from the renaissance humanist ideal of the complete man or from the Greek idealism, he is content to be what he is, and he is his time and his people. He is a genius because he has vision of what he is and of his function. He knows that he is a beginning and not a classically finished work.

I honour him for he prophesied me while I can only recognise him as a forebear of whom I ought to be proud.

In America there is much for the healing of the nations, but woe unto him of the cultured palate who attempts the dose.

As for Whitman, I read him (in many parts) with acute pain, but when I write of certain things I find myself using his rhythms. The expression of certain things related to cosmic consciousness seems tainted with this maramis.[3]

I am (in common with every educated man) an heir of the ages and I demand my birth-right. Yet if Whitman represented his time in language acceptable to one accustomed to my standard of intellectual-artistic living he would belie his time and na-

---

[1] Written in 1909, this essay was not published until 1955. Pound's attitude toward Whitman was ambivalent, as evident in *Patria Mia* (written before 1913), "A Pact" (1913), and *ABC of Reading* (1934). In Canto LXXXII, however, written in 1945 while in a prison camp, he movingly evokes lines from Whitman's "Out of the Cradle Endlessly Rocking." This essay reveals Pound's early ambitions to be America's epic poet, later to become manifest in his writing of *The Cantos*.

[2] Bliss Carman (1861–1919), Canadian-born poet who collaborated with American poet Richard Hovey (1864–1900) on *Songs from Vagabondia* (1894) and its sequels, which broke with the anemic poetry of the time.

[3] Probably "marasmus": wasting away.

tion. And yet I am but one of his 'ages and ages' encrustations' or to be exact an encrustation of the next age. The vital part of my message, taken from the sap and fibre of America, is the same as his.

Mentally I am a Walt Whitman who has learned to wear a collar and a dress shirt (although at times inimical to both). Personally I might be a very glad to conceal my relationship to my spiritual father and brag about my more congenial ancestry–Dante, Shakespeare, Theocritus, Villon,[4] but the descent is a bit difficult to establish. And, to be frank, Whitman is to my fatherland (*Patriam quam odi et amo*[5] for no uncertain reasons) what Dante is to Italy and I at my best can only be a strife for a renaissance in America of all the lost or temporarily mislaid beauty, truth, valour, glory of Greece, Italy, England and all the rest of it.

And yet if a man has written lines like Whitman's to *Sunset Breeze*[6] one has to love him. I think we have not yet paid enough attention to the deliberate artistry of the man, not in details but in the large.

I am immortal even as he is, yet with a lesser vitality as I am the more in love with beauty (If I really do love it more than he did). Like Dante he wrote in the 'vulgar tongue,' in a new metric. The first great man to write in the language of his people.

Et ego Petrarca in lingua vetera scribo,[7] and in a tongue my people understood not.

It seems to me I should like to drive Whitman into the old world. I sledge, he drill–and to scourge America with all the old beauty. (For Beauty *is* an accusation) and with a thousand thongs from Homer to Yeats, from Theocritus to Marcel Schwob.[8] This desire is because I am young and impatient, were I old and wise I should content myself in seeing and saying that these things will come. But now, since I am by no means sure it would be true prophecy, I am fain set my own hand to the labour.

It is a great thing, reading a man to know, not 'His Tricks are not as yet my Tricks, but I can easily make them mine' but 'His message is my message. We will see that men hear it.'

1909   1955

---

from A Retrospect[1]

There has been so much scribbling about a new fashion in poetry, that I may perhaps be pardoned this brief recapitulation and retrospect.

In the spring or early summer of 1912, 'H.D.', Richard Aldington[2] and myself decided that we were agreed upon the three principles following:

1. Direct treatment of the 'thing' whether subjective or objective.

2. To use absolutely no word that does not contribute to the presentation.

3. As regarding rhythm: to compose in the sequence of the musical phrase, not in sequence of a metronome.

Upon many points of taste and of predilection we differed, but agreeing upon these three positions we thought we had as much right to a group name, at least as

---

4 Theocritus (early third century B.C.), Greek poet; François Villon (1431–?), French poet.
5 "Fatherland which I hate and love" (Latin).
6 "To the Sun-set Breeze," contained in the "Good-Bye My Fancy" cluster in *Leaves of Grass* (1891–92).
7 "And I, Petrarch, write in the old tongue" (Latin); Petrarch (1304–1374), Italian poet and scholar of classical antiquity, founder of Renaissance Humanism, decided to use Latin, not Italian, for his major writings.

8 William Butler Yeats (1865–1939), Irish poet; Marcel Schwob (1867–1905), French writer.
1 A group of early essays and notes which appeared under this title in *Pavannes and Divisions* (1918).
2 "H.D.," Hilda Doolittle (1886–1961), American poet; Richard Aldington (1892–1962), English poet. As foreign correspondent for *Poetry: A Magazine of Verse*, founded in Chicago in 1912 by Harriet Monroe (1861–1936), Pound had sent their poems for publication, identifying them as *"Imagistes."*

much right, as a number of French 'schools' proclaimed by Mr. Flint in the August number of Harold Monro's magazine for 1911.[3]

This school has since been 'joined' or 'followed' by numerous people[4] who, whatever their merits, do not show any signs of agreeing with the second specification. Indeed *vers libre*[5] has become as prolix and as verbose as any of the flaccid varieties that preceded it. It has brought faults of its own. The actual language and phrasing is often as bad as that of our elders without even the excuse that the words are shovelled in to fill a metric pattern or to complete the noise of a rhyme-sound. Whether or no the phrases followed by the followers are musical must be left to the reader's decision. At times I can find a marked metre in 'vers libres,' as stale and hackneyed as any pseudo-Swinburnian,[6] at times the writers seem to follow no musical structure whatever. But it is, on the whole, good that the field should be ploughed. Perhaps a few good poems have come from the new method, and if so it is justified.

Criticism is not a circumscription or a set of prohibitions. It provides fixed points of departure. It may startle a dull reader into alertness. That little of it which is good is mostly in stray phrases; or if it be an older artist helping a younger it is in great measure but rules of thumb, cautions gained by experience.

I set together a few phrases on practical working about the time the first remarks on imagisme were published. The first use of the word 'Imagiste' was in my note to T. E. Hulme's[7] five poems, printed at the end of my 'Ripostes' in the autumn of 1912. I reprint my cautions[8] from *Poetry* for March, 1913.

A FEW DON'TS

An 'Image' is that which presents an intellectual and emotional complex in an instant of time. I use the term 'complex' rather in the technical sense employed by the newer psychologists, such as Hart,[9] though we might not agree absolutely in our application.

It is the presentation of such a 'complex' instantaneously which gives that sense of sudden liberation; that sense of freedom from time limits and space limits; that sense of sudden growth, which we experience in the presence of the greatest works of art.

It is better to present one Image in a lifetime than to produce voluminous works.

All this, however, some may consider open to debate. The immediate necessity is to tabulate A LIST OF DON'TS for those beginning to write verses. I can not pull all of them into Mosaic negative.

To begin with, consider the three propositions (demanding direct treatment, economy of words, and the sequence of the musical phrase), not as dogma—never consider anything as dogma—but as the result of long contemplation, which, even if it is some one else's contemplation, may be worth consideration.

Pay no attention to the criticism of men who have never themselves written a notable work. Consider the discrepancies between the actual writing of the Greek poets and dramatists, and the theories of the Graeco-Roman grammarians, concocted to explain their metres.

---

[3]F. S. Flint (1885–1960), English poet, whose essay "Contemporary French Poetry" appeared in the August 1912 *Poetry Review*, published by the English poet and editor Harold Monro (1879–1932). Pound coined the French *"Imagisme"* to distinguish his group from the numerous French schools or *"ismes"* discussed by Flint.
[4]A reference to American poet Amy Lowell (1874–1925) and other poets whose work appeared in three anthologies with Lowell's help, *Some Imagist Poets* (1915–17). Pound labelled it Amygism.
[5]"Free verse" (French), poetry that replaces fixed patterns of rhyme and meter with more subtle rhythmical cadences and musical sounds.

[6]Imitator of the musical, highly abstract, poetry of Algernon Charles Swinburne (1837–1909), English poet.
[7]English writer (1883–1917), whose theories of language and art, emphasizing the image, influenced Pound.
[8]The remaining excerpt appeared in *Poetry*, along with Flint's essay "Imagisme," in response to the stir created by the poems of "H.D., *Imagiste*" in the January 1913 issue. It is the first credo of imagism, the movement T. S. Eliot called "the starting-point of modern poetry."
[9]Bernard Hart (1879–1966), English psychiatrist.

LANGUAGE

Use no superfluous word, no adjective which does not reveal something.

Don't use such an expression as 'dim lands *of peace*.' It dulls the image. It mixes an abstraction with the concrete. It comes from the writer's not realizing that the natural object is always the *adequate* symbol.

Go in fear of abstractions. Do not retell in mediocre verse what has already been done in good prose. Don't think any intelligent person is going to be deceived when you try to shirk all the difficulties of the unspeakably difficult art of good prose by chopping your composition into line lengths.

What the expert is tired of today the public will be tired of tomorrow.

Don't imagine that the art of poetry is any simpler than the art of music, or that you can please the expert before you have spent at least as much effort on the art of verse as the average piano teacher spends on the art of music.

Be influenced by as many great artists as you can, but have the decency either to acknowledge the debt outright, or to try to conceal it.

Don't allow 'influence' to mean merely that you mop up the particular decorative vocabulary of some one or two poets whom you happen to admire. A Turkish war correspondent was recently caught red-handed babbling in his despatches of 'dove-grey' hills, or else it was 'pearl-pale,' I can not remember.

Use either no ornament or good ornament.

RHYTHM AND RHYME

Let the candidate fill his mind with the finest cadences he can discover, preferably in a foreign language,[10] so that the meaning of the words may be less likely to divert his attention from the movement; e.g. Saxon charms, Hebridean Folk Songs, the verse of Dante, and the lyrics of Shakespeare — if he can dissociate the vocabulary from the cadence. Let him dissect the lyrics of Goethe[11] coldly into their component sound values, syllables long and short, stressed and unstressed, into vowels and consonants.

It is not necessary that a poem should rely on its music, but if it does rely on its music that music must be such as will delight the expert.

Let the neophyte know assonance and alliteration, rhyme immediate and delayed, simple and polyphonic, as a musician would expect to know harmony and counterpoint and all the minutiae of his craft. No time is too great to give to these matters or to any one of them, even if the artist seldom have need of them.

Don't imagine that a thing will 'go' in verse just because it's too dull to go in prose.

Don't be 'viewy' — leave that to the writers of pretty little philosophic essays. Don't be descriptive; remember that the painter can describe a landscape much better than you can, and that he has to know a deal more about it.

When Shakespeare talks of the 'Dawn in russet mantle clad' he presents something which the painter does not present. There is in this line of his nothing that one can call description; he presents.

Consider the way of the scientists rather than the way of an advertising agent for a new soap.

The scientist does not expect to be acclaimed as a great scientist until he has *discovered* something. He begins by learning what has been discovered already. He goes from that point onward. He does not bank on being a charming fellow personally. He does not expect his friends to applaud the results of his freshman class work. Freshmen in poetry are unfortunately not confined to a definite and recognizable class room. They are 'all over the shop.' Is it any wonder 'the public is indifferent to poetry?'

---

[10]"This is for rhythm, his vocabulary must of course be found in his native tongue" (Pound's note).
[11]Johann Wolfgang von Goethe (1749–1832), German poet.

Don't chop your stuff into separate *iambs*. Don't make each line stop dead at the end, and then begin every next line with a heave. Let the beginning of the next line catch the rise of the rhythm wave, unless you want a definite longish pause.

In short, behave as a musician, a good musician, when dealing with that phase of your art which has exact parallels in music. The same laws govern, and you are bound by no others.

Naturally, your rhythmic structure should not destroy the shape of your words, or their natural sound, or their meaning. It is improbable that, at the start, you will be able to get a rhythm-structure strong enough to affect them very much, though you may fall a victim to all sorts of false stopping due to line ends and cæsurae.

The Musician can rely on pitch and the volume of the orchestra. You can not. The term harmony is misapplied in poetry; it refers to simultaneous sounds of different pitch. There is, however, in the best verse a sort of residue of sound which remains in the ear of the hearer and acts more or less as an organ-base.

A rhyme must have in it some slight element of surprise if it is to give pleasure; it need not be bizarre or curious, but it must be well used if used at all.

Vide[12] further Vildrac and Duhamel's notes on rhyme in *'Technique Poétique.'*[13]

That part of your poetry which strikes upon the imaginative *eye* of the reader will lose nothing by translation into a foreign tongue; that which appeals to the ear can reach only those who take it in the original.

Consider the definiteness of Dante's presentation, as compared with Milton's rhetoric. Read as much of Wordsworth as does not seem too unutterably dull.

If you want the gist of the matter go to Sappho, Catullus, Villon, Heine[14] when he is in the vein, Gautier[15] when he is not too frigid; or, if you have not the tongues, seek out the leisurely Chaucer. Good prose will do you no harm, and there is good discipline to be had by trying to write it.

Translation is likewise good training, if you find that your original matter 'wobbles' when you try to rewrite it. The meaning of the poem to be translated can not 'wobble.'

If you are using a symmetrical form, don't put in what you want to say and then fill up the remaining vacuums with slush.

Don't mess up the perception of one sense by trying to define it in terms of another. This is usually only the result of being too lazy to find the exact word. To this clause there are possibly exceptions.

The first three simple prescriptions will throw out nine-tenths of all the bad poetry now accepted as standard and classic; and will prevent you from many a crime of production.

'. . . *Mais d'abord il faut étre un poète*,'[16] as MM. Duhamel and Vildrac have said at the end of their little book, *'Notes sur la Technique Poétique.'*

1913, 1918

T. S. ELIOT
(1888–1965)

When T. S. Eliot met Ezra Pound in London in 1914 and showed him "The Love Song of J. Alfred Prufrock," Pound was astonished. In sending the poem to

---

[12]"See" (Latin).
[13]Charles Vildrac (1882–1971) and Georges Duhamel (1884–1966), French poets and authors of *Notes sur la technique poétique* (1910).
[14]Sappho (sixth century B.C.), Greek poet; Catullus (87-54?

B.C.), Roman poet; François Villon (1431–?), French poet; Heinrich Heine (1797–1856), German poet.
[15]Théophile Gautier (1811–1872), French poet.
[16]"But first, one must be a poet" (French).

Harriet Monroe, editor of *Poetry: A Magazine of Verse* in Chicago, Pound said of Eliot: "He has sent in the best poem I have yet had from an American. . . . He has actually trained himself *and* modernized himself *on his own*." The poem's appearance in *Poetry* in 1915, and in *Prufrock and Other Observations* in 1917, and the appearance of this same poet's *The Waste Land* in 1922 marked a radical break from poetry of the past and a daring breakthrough to poetry of the future — and the literary period we now call modernism. Pound, who had severely pruned *The Waste Land* with Eliot's acquiescence, was right on mark when he wrote: "Eliot's *Waste Land* is I think the justification of the 'movement,' of our modern experiment, since 1900."

How was it that Eliot *modernized* himself? He started out writing under the influence of the romantics and the Victorians. But his vague dissatisfaction with his models became focused and intense when he read Arthur Symon's *The Symbolist Movement in Literature* (1899). Eliot later said: "But for having read this book [in 1908] I should not . . . have heard of [Jules] Laforgue or [Arthur] Rimbaud. . . . So the Symons book is one of those which affected the course of my life. . . ." Jules Laforgue, Eliot asserted on another occasion, "was the first to teach me how to speak, to teach me the poetic possibilities of my own idiom of speech." Thus Eliot found his way to the ironic tone and cynical air that filtered through "The Love Song of J. Alfred Prufrock."

It was from a forerunner of the French symbolistes, Charles Baudelaire, a poet who was a translator and promoter of the American romantic Edgar Allan Poe, that Eliot borrowed a major theme of *The Waste Land*. As he recalled later (in "What Dante Means to Me," 1950), "From Baudelaire I learned first, a precedent for the poetical possibilities, never developed by any poet writing in my own language, of the more sordid aspects of the modern metropolis, of the possibility of fusion between the sordidly realistic and the phantasmagoric, the possibility of the juxtaposition of the matter-of-fact and the fantastic." Thus it was that Eliot found his way to the poetical exploitation of what appeared "unpoetical" or even anti-poetical. Thus it was also, ironically, that Eliot was influenced at second hand by a poet he thought third-rate, Edgar Allan Poe, an imaginative connoisseur of the sordid and the phastasmagoric. Poe's works had gone through a sea-change abroad and returned home to Eliot in a French transfiguration.

This remarkable poet who changed the course of modern poetry was born in St. Louis, Missouri, in 1888. His grandfather, a Unitarian minister, had come west to this burgeoning Mississippi River town from Massachusetts in 1834 and had helped found Washington University there in 1872. Eliot's father was head of a brick company, his mother (who had taught school) a lifelong amateur poet. Eliot was educated in the best private schools, including a final finishing year at Milton Academy in Massachusetts. He attended Harvard as an undergraduate (1906–10) and (after a year in France) was a graduate student there (1911–14). Among his classmates was another aspiring poet, Conrad Aiken. And among his teachers were the philosopher George Santayana, the humanist and antiromantic scholar Irving Babbitt, and a guest professor, the eminent British philosopher and logician Bertrand Russell.

Eliot's year in France (1910–11) was important in enabling him to consolidate and exploit his keen interest in the French symbolist movement. Eliot had begun "The Love Song of J. Alfred Prufrock" at Harvard in 1910, and he finished a draft of it in 1911, at a time when he had developed a close friendship with a French medical student Jean Verdenal, who himself wrote poetry. Verdenal, who was killed in 1915 in the First World War (at the Dardanelles), became inseparably linked with "Prufrock" when, beginning in 1917, Eliot dedicated the volume in which it appeared to his friend. By 1925 a quotation from Dante accompanied the dedication: "Now you are able to comprehend the quantity of love that warms me toward you, / When I forget our emptiness / Treating shades as if they were solid."

In 1914 Eliot had reached a point in his graduate studies in philosophy when he could benefit from a fellowship for a year of study in Germany and finish his thesis on the contemporary English philosopher F. H. Bradley. He was forced, however, to go to England when war broke out on the continent. And suddenly, some two months after Verdenal had been killed at Gallipoli, Eliot married Vivienne Haigh-Wood, in June 1915. About this time, Bertrand Russell had described Eliot as an "ultracivilized," "exquisite and listless" young man lacking "vigour of life." What possessed such a decorous young man to marry so precipitately, no one has been able to say. But there is unanimous agreement that the marriage was disastrous. Most critics and biographers have blamed Vivienne and her illnesses ("hysteria" or "depression") for the friction, but the evidence is obscure.

In any event, Eliot was immediately confronted with the necessity of earning a living. He taught and lectured for a time, and then worked in the foreign department of Lloyds Bank (1917–23). Later, in 1925, he would go to work for the publisher Faber and Faber, with which he would be associated until his death in 1965. Unlike Pound but like William Carlos Williams and Wallace Stevens, Eliot would divide his life between the world of daily work and the world of literature.

As early as 1916, Eliot wrote to his friend Conrad Aiken of his wife Vivienne's illness, his friend Verdenal's death, and of his own inability to write. He then added that though he had written nothing, he had "lived through material for a score of long poems in the last six months." This appears to be the first revelation that Eliot was ambitious to write a poem of length out of his own emotional tribulations of the time. By 1921, as he seemed to be having a nervous breakdown, he had already accumulated many pages of a manuscript for the long poem that he would finish at Lausanne, Switzerland, on the banks of Lake Leman, while under the care of a fashionable psychiatrist.

When Eliot emerged from his psychiatric retreat, he turned over to Ezra Pound a sheaf of manuscripts entitled *He Do the Police in Different Voices*, a title he had taken from Charles Dickens's *Our Mutual Friend*. Correspondence indicates that Eliot did not have the nervous stamina to stand up to Pound when he disagreed with Pound's radical revisions. For example, Pound wanted to cut the epigraph, chosen by Eliot from Joseph Conrad's *Heart of Darkness*, a quotation from the narrator Marlow: "Did he [Mr. Kurtz] live his life in every detail of desire, temptation, and surrender during that supreme moment of complete knowledge? He cried in a whisper at some image, at some vision, — he cried out twice, a cry that was no more than a breath: 'The horror! The horror!'" Eliot protested that the epigraph was "elucidative"; but he capitulated and substituted a quotation from the *Satyricon*. As Pound slashed the poem, Eliot saw it losing coherence, and at one point even suggested opening it with "Gerontion." The footnotes Eliot ultimately added were in part an attempt to provide the lost cohesiveness (as in the note on Tiresias informing readers that he is "the most important personage in the poem, uniting all the rest").

Pound's revisions turned the poem into a work containing what he was attempting to incorporate in his own *Cantos* — the "profounder didacticism," which included a decrying of contemporary civilization. The widely read critic Edmund Wilson immediately interpreted the poem as social commentary, a reading that Eliot would repeatedly disavow, asserting that it "was only the relief of a personal and wholly insignificant grouse against life." Changing the title from *He Do the Police in Different Voices* to *The Waste Land* obscured the fact that all the voices of the poem originated in a single protagonist who, like the ventriloquist in Dickens, was expressing his feelings and views in a variety of imitations and intonations.

Eliot died thinking that *The Waste Land* manuscripts, which Pound had returned to him after revision, were lost. As it turned out, descendants of the American benefactor to whom Eliot had given them had sold the manuscripts to the New York Public Library, which revealed its possession of them only after Eliot's death. Since their publication in 1971, controversy has swirled over meanings that had long been assumed as unshakeable. The poem continues to be read variously—as social commentary; as a personal, even elegiac poem expressing grief for a dead friend; as an anguished response to a world without meaning or redemption; as an ultimately religious poem, finally affirming spiritual transcendence.

Eliot shook up the literary world as much by his criticism as by his poetry. He had a knack for tossing off phrases that were immediately picked up and repeatedly defined and used by critics. He introduced the "impersonal theory of poetry" in "Tradition and the Individual Talent" (1917), asserting that poetry was not "a turning loose of emotion, but an escape from emotion," not "the expression of personality, but an escape from personality." In an essay entitled "Hamlet and His Problems" (1919), Eliot said that to express emotion in art, the artist must find an "objective correlative"—"a set of objects, a situation, a chain of events" which become the "formula of that *particular* emotion."

In "The Metaphysical Poets" (1921), Eliot suggested that the early seventeenth-century poets of that designation, with their "unified sensibilities," found themselves capable of a "direct sensuous apprehension of thought," and thus were able to fuse thought and feeling in their work. In the later seventeenth century and into the eighteenth, through the "dissociation of sensibilities," the balance was tipped in favor of thought, while in the later eighteenth century and through the nineteenth, the balance was tipped in favor of feeling. The implication was that modernist poetry was restoring the balance of thought and feeling lost centuries before.

In a celebrated review of James Joyce's *Ulysses*, entitled "Ulysses, Order, and Myth," published in 1923, Eliot coined the term "mythical method" to describe how Joyce had constructed his novel: "In using myth, in manipulating a continuous parallel between contemporaneity and antiquity, Mr. Joyce is pursuing a method which others must pursue after him. . . . It is simply a way of controlling, of ordering, of giving a shape and a significance to the immense panorama of futility and anarchy which is contemporary history. . . . Instead of narrative method, we may now use the mythical method." It was not lost on Eliot's critics that the "mythical method" appeared also to apply to his own *Waste Land*, with its constant movement back and forth from a waste land present to a contrasting past.

The New Criticism that was gradually developing to cope with the new poetry of modernism found Eliot's terms indispensable in renewing literary studies, moving away from the then dominant philological, historical, and biographical approaches to a close reading or explication of poetic texts. The assumption of the New Critics was that poems were "wholes," self-contained "constructs" made up of parts which could be examined and evaluated in astute "critical analyses."

One of the ironies of literary history was the tendency of Eliot to shift his position, disavowing an earlier for a later idea or theory, often leaving his disciples holding an outmoded term and concept. His early tendency to find fault with Milton later turned to the discovery of Milton's virtues. Rudyard Kipling, who would not have survived the strictures of Eliot's early criticism, surfaced to be praised in 1941. In the latter part of his career, Eliot often referred to the critical terms invented by his younger self disparagingly, as "notorious." He said in 1961 ("To Criticize the Critic"), referring to "dissociation of sensibility" and "objective correlative": "I am not sure, at this distance of time, how valid are the two phrases. . . . They may soon go out of fashion completely." Eliot's repeated assertion that *The Waste Land* was a personal poem tended to undermine his earlier "impersonal theory of poetry." And in "The Three Voices of Poetry" (1953), Eliot described a kind of poetry written by a poet who "does not know what he has to say until he has said it. . . . he feels powerless . . . and the words, the poem he makes, are a kind of form of exorcism of this demon." Eliot often hinted that *The Waste Land* was, for him, this kind of poem. In a 1959 *Paris Review* interview, Eliot said of *The Waste Land*: "I wasn't even bothering whether I understood what I was saying."

Much of Eliot's creative energy went into the editing of influential little magazines. He worked as assistant editor of the *Egoist* from 1917 to 1919. In 1922, Eliot founded the *Criterion* and edited it until its demise in 1939. In 1925, Eliot brought his poems together in a single volume, *Poems 1909–1925*. When he was baptized as a member of the Anglican Church and became a British citizen in 1927, he declared himself a "classicist in literature, royalist in politics, and anglo-catholic in religion."

The religious theme was sounded with increasing intensity in his poetry, as in *Ash-Wednesday* (1930), the "Choruses" for the religious pageant *The Rock* (1934), and most remarkably in the successive parts of *Four Quartets*: "Burnt Norton" (1936), "East Coker" (1940), "The Dry Salvages" (1941), and "Little Gidding" (1942). These titles are all place names associated with Eliot's life, especially his spiritual journey into transcendent or mystical awareness: "Burnt Norton," a place in the Cotswolds, near Chipping Campden, where Eliot rendezvoused several times in the early 1930s with his Bostonian friend, Emily Hale (reputed to be his great, unfulfilled love), staying with her and her friends living nearby; "East Coker," a village in Somerset where his ancestors lived for two centuries; "The Dry Salvages," a group of rocks off Cape Ann, Massachusetts, with which Eliot became familiar in his boyhood vacations; and "Little Gidding," in Huntingdonshire, where a seventeenth-century religious group founded a community, destroyed by the Puritans; a restored chapel remains, and Eliot made a pilgrimage there in 1936.

The spiritual quest traced in the poem, published as a whole work in 1943, is toward "that still point of the turning world" where all contradictions and contrarieties become reconciled. The end of the quest is to arrive at the point of departure, and "know the place for the first time." *Four Quartets* proved to be Eliot's farewell to serious poetry. He continued to write, but in other forms. Eliot's critics differ as to Eliot's masterpiece — *The Waste Land* or *Four Quartets*. We might be willing to accept both as in some sense masterpieces, one a great poem of religious despair or skepticism, the other a great poem of religious search and final affirmation.

Eliot arranged with his solicitors to inform his wife in 1932, after his departure for lectures in America, of his permanent separation from her. The unhappy Vivienne died in a sanatorium in 1947, and shortly afterwards Eliot set up in an apartment with John Hayward, a young Englishman disabled by muscular dystrophy and confined to a wheelchair. If it was indeed true that Emily Hale was

Eliot's great love, he passed up an opportunity to marry her when he was finally free to do so. In 1957 when Eliot married his Faber and Faber secretary Valerie Fletcher, his separation from his roommate Hayward bore resemblances, and with similar effects, to his earlier separation from Vivienne. In 1957 Eliot was sixty-eight, Valerie Fletcher thirty.

During Eliot's latter years, as his literary commentary became less schematic, his cultural commentary grew more conservative. In such works as *The Idea of a Christian Society* (1939) and *Notes Towards a Definition of Culture* (1948), his emphasis was on faith, order, and authority. His concerns and positions seemed remote from the times, in decades that saw economic collapse and a world war fought between the democracies and the totalitarian states. At times, Eliot's references to Jews appeared in contexts in his prose, as it had earlier in his poetry, that gave rise to the charges of anti-Semitism; according to new evidence presented by Christopher Ricks in *T. S. Eliot and Prejudice* (1989), there seems to be some truth to the charges. Even should there be an agreement that the charges are true, there is little agreement as to how this should affect response to the poems. Clearly, readers must be left to determine for themselves.

Eliot had been interested in writing plays as far back as 1932, when his unfinished play "Sweeney Agonistes" was published in England. In 1935, his play *Murder in the Cathedral* was produced at the Canterbury Festival in the Chapter House of the Cathedral, where the murder of Thomas à Becket had taken place, and was an impressive success. In 1949, with the popular acclaim of *The Cocktail Party*, Eliot seemed launched on a new literary career. He appeared to have discovered the secret of writing poetic drama that could be a success commercially. With the appearance of *The Confidential Clerk* in 1954 and *The Elder Statesman* in 1959, Eliot seemed less firm in his grasp of theatrical techniques and the audiences less enthusiastic in their responses. Ironically, his witty 1939 *Old Possum's Book of Practical Cats* was in the 1980s turned into an astonishingly popular, long-running musical entitled *Cats*. It now seems likely to overshadow Eliot's own works written for the theater.

Eliot was awarded the Nobel Prize for Literature in 1948, only one of a number of honors bestowed on him in the latter part of his career. He died in 1965 in England and was buried in East Coker, the home of his English ancestors. His wife Valerie became literary executor and took over control of his manuscripts and papers. His shaping influence on modern poetry was profound, different from Pound's influence in that it was by the brilliant example of his poems. Such prominent later poets as Robert Lowell and John Berryman began under his long shadow, and finally realized they had to move out from under if they were to find their own voice, occupy their own territory.

ADDITIONAL READING

The Complete Poems and Plays of T. S. Eliot, 1969; *The Waste Land: A Facsimile and Transcript of the Original Drafts Including the Annotations of Ezra Pound*, ed. Valerie Eliot, 1971; *Selected Prose of T. S. Eliot*, ed. Frank Kermode, 1975; *The Use of Poetry and the Use of Criticism*, 1933; *On Poetry and Critics*, 1957; *Knowledge and Experience in the Philosophy of F. H. Bradley*, 1964; *To Criticize the Critic and Other Writings*, 1965; *The Letters of T. S. Eliot: Volume I, 1898–1922*, ed. Valerie Eliot, 1988.

F. R. Leavis, *New Bearings in English Poetry*, 1932; F. O. Matthiessen, *The Achievement of T. S. Eliot*, 1935, 1947, 1958; Balachandra Rajan, ed., *T. S. Eliot: A Study of His Writings by Various Hands*, 1947; Leonard Unger, ed., *T. S. Eliot: A Selected Critique*, 1948; Elizabeth Drew, *T. S. Eliot: The Design of His Poetry*, 1949; Helen Gardner, *The Art of T. S. Eliot*, 1949; D. E. S. Maxwell, *The Poetry of T. S. Eliot*, 1952; George Williamson, *A Reader's Guide to T. S. Eliot*, 1953; Grover Smith, *T. S. Eliot's Poetry and Plays*, 1956, 1974; Hugh Kenner, *The Invisible Poet: T. S. Eliot*, 1959; David E. Jones, *The Plays of T. S. Eliot*, 1960; Kristian Schmidt, *Poetry and Belief in the Work of T. S. Eliot*,

1961; Hugh Kenner, ed., *T. S. Eliot: A Collection of Critical Essays*, 1962; A. G. George, *T. S. Eliot: His Mind and His Art*, 1962; Northrop Frye, *T. S. Eliot*, 1963, 1981; Carol Smith, *T. S. Eliot's Dramatic Theory and Practice*, 1963; Robert Knoll, ed., *Storm Over the Waste Land*, 1964; Philip R. Headings, *T. S. Eliot*, 1964; Howard Howarth, *Notes of Some Figures Behind T. S. Eliot*, 1964; Helen Gardner, *T. S. Eliot: Monuments and Patterns*, 1966; Jay Martin, ed., *Twentieth-Century Interpretations of The Waste Land*, 1968; Donald C. Gallup, *T. S. Eliot: A Bibliography*, 1969; Harry Blamires, *Word Unheard: A Guide Through Eliot's Four Quartets*, 1969; Allen Austin, *T. S. Eliot: The Literary and Social Criticism*, 1971; Bernard Bergonzi, *T. S. Eliot*, 1971; Gertrude Patterson, *T. S. Eliot: Poems in the Making*, 1971; Robert Sencourt, *T. S. Eliot: A Memoir*, 1972; Roger Kojecky, *T. S. Eliot's Social Criticism*, 1972; John D. Margolis, *T. S. Eliot's Intellectual Development*, 1972; William M. Chace, *The Political Identities of Ezra Pound and T. S. Eliot*, 1973; A. Walton Litz, *Eliot in His Time*, 1973; Mowbray Allan, *T. S. Eliot's Impersonal Theory of Poetry*, 1974; Linda W. Wagner, ed., *T. S. Eliot: A Collection of Criticism*, 1974; Elizabeth Schneider, *T. S. Eliot: The Pattern in the Carpet*, 1975; Balachandra Rajan, *The Overwhelming Question: A Study of the Poetry of T. S. Eliot*, 1976; Stephen Spender, *T. S. Eliot*, 1976; Derek Traversi, *T. S. Eliot: The Longer Poems*, 1976; Helen Gardner, *The Composition of "Four Quartets,"* 1977; Lyndall Gordon, *Eliot's Early Years* (Vol. 1 of biography), 1977; James E. Miller, Jr., *T. S. Eliot's Personal Waste Land: Exorcism of the Demons*, 1977; David Newton-DeMolina, ed., *The Literary Criticism of T. S. Eliot: New Essays*, 1977; A. D. Moody, *Thomas Stearns Eliot, Poet*, 1979; Beatrice Ricks, *T. S. Eliot, A Bibliography of Secondary Works*, 1980; Michael Grant, ed., *T. S. Eliot: The Critical Heritage*, 2 vols., 1982; Caroline Behr, *T. S. Eliot: A Chronology of His Life and Work*, 1982; Eloise Knapp Hay, *T. S. Eliot's Negative Way*, 1982; Robert Canary, *T. S. Eliot: The Poet and His Critics*, 1982; Ronald Bush, *T. S. Eliot: A Study in Character and Style*, 1983; Peter Ackroyd, *T. S. Eliot*, 1984; Calvin Bedient, *He Do the Police in Different Voices: The Waste Land and Its Protagonist*, 1986; Lyndall Gordon, *Eliot's New Life* (Vol. 2 of biography), 1988; Robert F. Fleissner, *Ascending the Prufrockian Stair*, 1988; Christopher Ricks, *T. S. Eliot and Prejudice*, 1989; Jewel Spears Brooker and Joseph Bentley, *Reading The Waste Land: Modernism and the Limits of Interpretation*, 1990.

TEXTS

Selected Essays, 1951; *The Complete Poems and Plays of T. S. Eliot*, 1962; "The Death of Saint Narcissus," *Poems Written in Early Youth*, 1967.

The Death of Saint Narcissus[1]

Come under the shadow of this gray rock —
Come in under the shadow of this gray rock,
And I will show you something different from either
Your shadow sprawling over the sand at daybreak, or
Your shadow leaping behind the fire against the red rock: 5
I will show you his bloody cloth and limbs
And the gray shadow on his lips.

　　He walked once between the sea and the high cliffs
When the wind made him aware of his limbs smoothly passing each other
And of his arms crossed over his breast.   10
When he walked over the meadows
He was stifled and soothed by his own rhythm.
By the river
His eyes were aware of the pointed corners of his eyes
And his hands aware of the pointed tips of his fingers.   15

---

[1] In August 1915, Pound sent this poem to *Poetry* magazine, where it was set up in type but never published. It was probably withdrawn by Eliot, who later said that he did not care to have the poem printed in his lifetime. He did supervise its appearance in 1950 in a privately printed volume, limited to twelve copies, entitled *Poems Written in Early Youth*, republished in 1967 by Valerie Eliot. An early draft later came to light when *The Waste Land* manuscripts were discovered in 1968. The title conflates Narcissus — in Greek myth, the beautiful youth in love with his own reflection — and Saint Sebastian — the Roman martyr shot with arrows, often portrayed in Renaissance art as a beautiful, undraped young man, bound and pierced with numerous arrows. Compare the opening lines with lines 26–30 in *The Waste Land* (1922).

Struck down by such knowledge
He could not live men's ways, but became a dancer before God
If he walked in city streets
He seemed to tread on faces, convulsive thighs and knees.
So he came out under the rock.   20

   First he was sure that he had been a tree,
Twisting its branches among each other
And tangling its roots among each other.

   Then he knew that he had been a fish
With slippery white belly held tight in his own fingers,   25
Writhing in his own clutch, his ancient beauty
Caught fast in the pink tips of his new beauty.

   Then he had been a young girl
Caught in the woods by a drunken old man
Knowing at the end the taste of his own whiteness   30
The horror of his own smoothness,
And he felt drunken and old.

   So he became a dancer to God.
Because his flesh was in love with the burning arrows
He danced on the hot sand
Until the arrows came.   35
As he embraced them his white skin surrendered itself to the redness of
    blood, and satisfied him.
Now he is green, dry and stained
With the shadow in his mouth.

1967

The Love Song of J. Alfred Prufrock

> *S'io credesse che mia risposta fosse*
> *A persona che mai tornasse al mondo,*
> *Questa fiamma staria senza piu scosse.*
> *Ma perciocche giammai di questo fondo*
> *Non torno vivo alcun, s'i'odo il vero,*
> *Senza tema d'infamia ti rispondo.*[1]

Let us go, then, you and I,
When the evening is spread out against the sky
Like a patient etherised upon a table;
Let us go, through certain half-deserted streets,
The muttering retreats   5
Of restless nights in one-night cheap hotels
And sawdust restaurants with oyster-shells:
Streets that follow like a tedious argument
Of insidious intent

---

[1]From Dante's *Inferno*, XXVII, 61–66, spoken by the flame-engulfed soul of one who gave evil counsel, Guido da Motefeltro, when Dante asks his name: "If I thought that my reply might be to one who would ever return to the world, this flame would stand still with no more quiverings. But since never from this depth did any man return alive, if what I hear is true, I answer you without fear of disgrace."

To lead you to an overwhelming question. . .   10
Oh, do not ask, "What is it?"
Let us go and make our visit.

    In the room the women come and go
Talking of Michelangelo.

    The yellow fog that rubs its back upon the window-panes,   15
The yellow smoke that rubs its muzzle on the window-panes
Licked its tongue into the corners of the evening,
Lingered upon the pools that stand in drains,
Let fall upon its back the soot that falls from chimneys,
Slipped by the terrace, made a sudden leap,   20
And seeing that it was a soft October night,
Curled once about the house, and fell asleep.

    And indeed there will be time
For the yellow smoke that slides along the street,
Rubbing its back upon the window-panes;   25
There will be time, there will be time
To prepare a face to meet the faces that you meet;
There will be time to murder and create,
And time for all the works and days[2] of hands
That lift and drop a question on your plate;   30
Time for you and time for me,
And time yet for a hundred indecisions,
And for a hundred visions and revisions,
Before the taking of a toast and tea.

    In the room the women come and go   35
Talking of Michelangelo.

    And indeed there will be time
To wonder, "Do I dare?" and, "Do I dare?"
Time to turn back and descend the stair,
With a bald spot in the middle of my hair—   40
(They will say: "How his hair is growing thin!")
My morning coat, my collar mounting firmly to the chin,
My necktie rich and modest, but asserted by a simple pin—
(They will say: "But how his arms and legs are thin!")
Do I dare   45
Disturb the universe?
In a minute there is time
For decisions and revisions which a minute will reverse.

    For I have known them all already, known them all:—
Have known the evenings, mornings, afternoons,   50
I have measured out my life with coffee spoons;
I know the voices dying with a dying fall[3]
Beneath the music from a farther room.
    So how should I presume?

---

[2]The didactic poem *Works and Days*, by the Greek poet Hesiod (eighth century B.C.), recounts the rewards of living a life of honest labor.
[3]Cf. Shakespeare's *Twelfth Night*, I,i,1–4: "If music be the food of love, play on, / Give me excess of it, that, surfeiting, / The appetite may sicken, and so die. / That strain again! It had a dying fall."

And I have known the eyes already, known them all—　　　　　55
The eyes that fix you in a formulated phrase,
And when I am formulated, sprawling on a pin,
When I am pinned and wriggling on the wall,
Then how should I begin
To spit out all the butt-ends of my days and ways?　　　　　60
　　And how should I presume?

And I have known the arms already, known them all—
Arms that are braceleted and white and bare
(But in the lamplight, downed with light brown hair!)
Is it perfume from a dress　　　　　65
That makes me so digress?
Arms that lie along a table, or wrap about a shawl.
　　And should I then presume?
　　And how should I begin?

　　　　·　·　·　·　·

Shall I say, I have gone at dusk through narrow streets　　　　　70
And watched the smoke that rises from the pipes
Of lonely men in shirt-sleeves, leaning out of windows? . . .

　　I should have been a pair of ragged claws
Scuttling across the floors of silent seas.

　　　　·　·　·　·　·

And the afternoon, the evening, sleeps so peacefully!　　　　　75
Smoothed by long fingers,
Asleep . . . tired . . . or it malingers,
Stretched on the floor, here beside you and me.
Should I, after tea and cakes and ices,
Have the strength to force the moment to its crisis?　　　　　80
But though I have wept and fasted, wept and prayed,
Though I have seen my head (grown slightly bald) brought in upon a
　　platter,[4]
I am no prophet—and here's no great matter;
I have seen the moment of my greatness flicker,
And I have seen the eternal Footman hold my coat, and snicker,　　　　　85
And in short, I was afraid.

　　And would it have been worth it, after all,
After the cups, the marmalade, the tea,
Among the porcelain, among some talk of you and me,
Would it have been worth while,　　　　　90
To have bitten off the matter with a smile,
To have squeezed the universe into a ball[5]
To roll it toward some overwhelming question,
To say: "I am Lazarus,[6] come from the dead,
Come back to tell you all, I shall tell you all"—　　　　　95
If one, settling a pillow by her head,
　　Should say: "That is not what I meant at all.
　　That is not it, at all."

---

[4]The head of the prophet John the Baptist was delivered on a platter to Salome at her request, instigated by her mother Herodias, wife of King Herod (Matthew 14:1–11).
[5]Cf. "To His Coy Mistress," lines 41–44, by English poet An-
drew Marvell (1621–1678): "Let us roll all our strength and all / Our sweetness up into one ball, / And tear our pleasures with rough strife / Through the iron gates of life."
[6]Lazarus, raised from the dead by Jesus (John 11:1–44).

And would it have been worth it, after all,
Would it have been worth while,   100
After the sunsets and the dooryards and the sprinkled streets,
After the novels, after the teacups, after the skirts that trail along the floor —
And this, and so much more? —
It is impossible to say just what I mean!
But as if a magic lantern threw the nerves in patterns on a screen: 105
Would it have been worth while
If one, settling a pillow or throwing off a shawl,
And turning toward the window, should say:
    "That is not it at all,
    That is not what I meant, at all."   110

                    •   •   •   •   •

No! I am not Prince Hamlet,[7] nor was meant to be;
Am an attendant lord, one that will do
To swell a progress,[8] start a scene or two,
Advise the prince; no doubt, an easy tool,
Deferential, glad to be of use,   115
Politic, cautious, and meticulous;
Full of high sentence,[9] but a bit obtuse;
At times, indeed, almost ridiculous —
Almost, at times, the Fool.

    I grow old . . . I grow old . . .   120
I shall wear the bottoms of my trousers rolled.

    Shall I part my hair behind? Do I dare to eat a peach?
I shall wear white flannel trousers, and walk upon the beach.
I have heard the mermaids singing, each to each.

    I do not think that they will sing to me.   125

    I have seen them riding seaward on the waves
Combing the white hair of the waves blown back
When the wind blows the water white and black.

    We have lingered in the chambers of the sea
By sea-girls wreathed with seaweed red and brown   130
Till human voices wake us, and we drown.

                                                                        1915, 1917

Preludes

I

The winter evening settles down
With smell of steaks in passageways.
Six o'clock.
The burnt-out ends of smoky days.
And now a gusty shower wraps   5
The grimy scraps

---

[7]I.e., Prufrock will be like Polonius, the king's advisor in
Shakespeare's *Hamlet.*   [8]Royal procession.
[9]Opinions.

Of withered leaves about your feet
And newspapers from vacant lots;
The showers beat
On broken blinds and chimney-pots,   10
And at the corner of the street
A lonely cab-horse steams and stamps.
And then the lighting of the lamps.

II

The morning comes to consciousness
Of faint stale smells of beer   15
From the sawdust-trampled street
With all its muddy feet that press
To early coffee-stands.
With the other masquerades
That time resumes,   20
One thinks of all the hands
That are raising dingy shades
In a thousand furnished rooms.

III

You tossed a blanket from the bed,
You lay upon your back, and waited;   25
You dozed, and watched the night revealing
The thousand sordid images
Of which your soul was constituted;
They flickered against the ceiling.
And when all the world came back   30
And the light crept up between the shutters
And you heard the sparrows in the gutters,
You had such a vision of the street
As the street hardly understands;
Sitting along the bed's edge, where   35
You curled the papers from your hair,
Or clasped the yellow soles of feet
In the palms of both soiled hands.

IV

His soul stretched tight across the skies
That fade behind a city block,   40
Or trampled by insistent feet
At four and five and six o'clock;
And short square fingers stuffing pipes,
And evening newspapers, and eyes
Assured of certain certainties,   45
The conscience of a blackened street
Impatient to assume the world.

   I am moved by fancies that are curled
Around these images, and cling:
The notion of some infinitely gentle   50
Infinitely suffering thing.

   Wipe your hand across your mouth, and laugh;
The worlds revolve like ancient women
Gathering fuel in vacant lots.

1915, 1917

La Figlia Che Piange[1]

O quam te memorem virgo . . .[2]

Stand on the highest pavement of the stair —
Lean on a garden urn —
Weave, weave the sunlight in your hair —
Clasp your flowers to you with a pained surprise —
Fling them to the ground and turn   5
With a fugitive resentment in your eyes:
But weave, weave the sunlight in your hair.

So I would have had him leave,
So I would have had her stand and grieve,
So he would have left   10
As the soul leaves the body torn and bruised,
As the mind deserts the body it has used.
I should find
Some way incomparably light and deft,
Some way we both should understand,   15
Simple and faithless as a smile and shake of the hand.

She turned away, but with the autumn weather
Compelled my imagination many days,
Many days and many hours;
Her hair over her arms and her arms full of flowers.   20
And I wonder how they should have been together!
I should have lost a gesture and a pose.
Sometimes these cogitations still amaze
The troubled midnight and the noon's repose.

1916, 1917

Sweeney among the Nightingales[1]

ὤμοι, πέπληγμαι καιρίαν πληγὴν ἔσω.[2]

Apeneck Sweeney spreads his knees
Letting his arms hang down to laugh,
The zebra stripes along his jaw
Swelling to maculate[3] giraffe.

The circles of the stormy moon   5
Slide westward toward the River Plate,[4]
Death and the Raven[5] drift above
And Sweeney guards the hornèd gate.[6]

---

[1]"The girl who weeps" (Italian).
[2]"O maiden, how should I address you?" (Latin), Aeneas's words to his mother Venus in disguise in Virgil's *Aeneid*, I, 327.
[1]According to F. O. Matthiessen, "Eliot once remarked that all he consciously set out to create in [this poem] was a sense of foreboding."
[2]"Alas! I am struck a deadly blow and deep within" (Greek),

the cry of Agamemnon, murdered by his adulterous wife Clytemnestra in Aeschylus's *Agamemnon*, line 1343.
[3]Spotted.
[4]Rio de la Plata, an estuary in South America.
[5]The constellation Corvus.
[6]In the classical underworld, the abode of dreams has two gates: one of ivory, through which illusion and fantasies pass; and one of horn, through which true dreams come forth.

Gloomy Orion and the Dog[7]
Are veiled; and hushed the shrunken seas;   10
The person in the Spanish cape
Tries to sit on Sweeney's knees

Slips and pulls the table cloth
Overturns a coffee-cup,
Reorganized upon the floor   15
She yawns and draws a stocking up;

The silent man in mocha brown
Sprawls at the window-sill and gapes;
The waiter brings in oranges
Bananas figs and hothouse grapes;   20

The silent vertebrate in brown
Contracts and concentrates, withdraws;
Rachel *née* Rabinovitch
Tears at the grapes with murderous paws;

She and the lady in the cape   25
Are suspect, thought to be in league;
Therefore the man with heavy eyes
Declines the gambit, shows fatigue,

Leaves the room and reappears
Outside the window, leaning in,   30
Branches of wistaria
Circumscribe a golden grin;

The host with someone indistinct
Converses at the door apart,
The nightingales[8] are singing near   35
The Convent of the Sacred Heart,

And sang within the bloody wood
When Agamemnon cried aloud,
And let their liquid siftings fall
To stain the stiff dishonoured shroud.   40

1918, 1919

Sweeney Erect

*And the trees about me,
Let them be dry and leafless; let the rocks
Groan with continual surges; and behind me
Make all a desolation. Look, look, wenches![1]*

---

[7]The constellation Orion, the hunter killed by the goddess Diana; the Dog Star, Sirius, in the constellation Canis Major. [8]In classical myth, Philomela is raped by her sister Procne's husband, King Tereus, who cut out her tongue to insure her silence. Informed of the crime through Philomela's woven embroidery, Procne serves the flesh of her son Itys to Tereus. The outraged gods turn Tereus into a hawk, Procne into a swallow, and Philomela into a nightingale.

[1]The epigraph is from *The Maid's Tragedy*, II, ii, by Francis Beaumont (1584–1616) and John Fletcher (1579–1625). Aspatia, whose lover has left her, tells her women to use her as a model for their needlework depicting the story of Ariadne. In Greek myth, Ariadne, daughter of King Minos, gave Theseus a thread to guide him out of the Minotaur's labyrinth. Theseus married her, but later deserted her and sailed away.

Paint me a cavernous waste shore
    Cast in the unstilled Cyclades,[2]
Paint me the bold anfractuous[3] rocks
    Faced by the snarled and yelping seas.

Display me Aeolus[4] above   5
    Reviewing the insurgent gales
Which tangle Ariadne's hair
    And swell with haste the perjured sails.

Morning stirs the feet and hands
    (Nausicaa and Polypheme).[5]   10
Gesture of orang-outang
    Rises from the sheets in steam.

This withered root of knots of hair
    Slitted below and gashed with eyes,
This oval O cropped out with teeth: 15
    The sickle motion from the thighs

Jackknifes upward at the knees
    Then straightens out from heel to hip
Pushing the framework of the bed
    And clawing at the pillow slip.   20

Sweeney addressed full length to shave
    Broadbottomed, pink from nape to base,
Knows the female temperament
    And wipes the suds around his face.

(The lengthened shadow of a man   25
    Is history, said Emerson[6]
Who had not seen the silhouette
    Of Sweeney straddled in the sun.)

Tests the razor on his leg
    Waiting until the shriek subsides.   30
The epileptic on the bed
    Curves backward, clutching at her sides.

The ladies of the corridor
    Find themselves involved, disgraced,
Call witness to their principles   35
    And deprecate the lack of taste

Observing that hysteria
    Might easily be misunderstood;
Mrs. Turner intimates
    It does the house no sort of good.   40

---

[2]Greek island group.
[3]Winding, tortuous.
[4]Greek god of the winds.
[5]In Homer's *Odyssey*, Princess Nausicaa courageously befriends the unclad, shipwrecked Odysseus, giving him food, clothing, and directions to her father's court; Polyphemus is the gigantic savage cyclops, blinded by Odysseus.
[6]Loosely paraphrased from the essay "Self-Reliance" by Ralph Waldo Emerson (1803–1882).

> But Doris, towelled from the bath,
>   Enters padding on broad feet,
> Bringing sal volatile[7]
>   And a glass of brandy neat.

1919

ON READING *THE WASTE LAND*

Many comprehensive interpretations have been written for *The Waste Land*, but none of them has been established as definitive. There has, however, accumulated in the large number of explications of the poem a considerable body of information about the quotations, allusions, and references (both intellectual and personal) in particular passages and lines. Some of this information might be useful, some not. Eliot himself claimed that he often "experienced" a poem before understanding it: "The more seasoned reader . . . does not bother about understanding; not, at least, at first." In initial encounter with Eliot's poetry, or any poetry, it is important when possible to *sound* it — read it aloud — and to avoid wading too far into the swamplands of commentary.

On first encounter with *The Waste Land*, we might best read it through as a dreamlike recapitulation of a life ("mixing memory and desire"), the characters melding into each other in fragments of scenes as in a dream, but resolving into figures connected with the life lived by a central consciousness. This consciousness we might assume to belong to someone (call him "the protagonist") in a state of spiritual crisis reliving, through recollection, the deeply buried moments of "desire, temptation, and surrender" in his life (the words are in a quotation from Joseph Conrad's *Heart of Darkness* which served as epigraph of the poem until rejected by Pound; Eliot replied plaintively that the Conrad epigraph was "elucidative"). All of the poem fits into this dramatic frame, and the parts form a sequence that moves with a kind of directness and inevitability to the climactic vision ("the awful daring of a moment's surrender") brought by the Thunder's voice at the end. And the protagonist at the end has only the fragments (scraps of haunting quotations linked with the indelible moments of a life) to "shore . . . against [his] ruins."

It is possible that seeds of *The Waste Land* were planted in Eliot's mind as early as 1916. He wrote to his friend Conrad Aiken about his wife Vivienne's illness and his French friend Jean Verdenal's death in the war, and added: "I have *lived* through material for a score of long poems in the last six months." And it is true that when the poem was published in 1922, Conrad Aiken (a friend and fellow poet from Harvard who, like Eliot, settled in England) said he recognized "poems" embedded in it that Eliot had shown him many years before.

See the accompanying Eliot biography for an account of Eliot's finishing the poem while under the care of a psychiatrist in Lausanne, Switzerland, and his turning the poem over to Pound for radical revision.

The poem appeared first in *The Criterion* in London in 1922, and later the same year in *The Dial* in America. Eliot's notorious footnotes that now accompany the poem were added only for the book publication later in 1922. Eliot was to remark on them later:

> I had at first intended only to put down all the references for my quotations, with a view to spiking the guns of critics of my earlier poems who had accused

---

[7]An aromatic alcoholic solution of ammonium carbonate used as a restorative or stimulant.

me of plagiarism. Then, when it came to print *The Waste Land* as a little book . . . it was discovered that the poem was inconveniently short, so I set to work to expand the notes, in order to provide a few more pages of printed matter, with the result that they became the remarkable exposition of bogus scholarship that is still on view today. I have sometimes thought of getting rid of these notes; but now they can never be unstuck. They have had almost greater popularity than the poem itself. . . .

Critics have differed on how to take Eliot's casual dismissal of the notes, but few have been willing to banish them entirely. It is possible that he was motivated in part by a desire to impose a modicum of coherence which he felt was lost in Pound's revisions (he had proposed at one point adding "Gerontion" as a prelude).

For those who want to explore in depth some particular approach to *The Waste Land*, the following works open the way. Many critics from the beginning viewed the poem as a criticism of modern life and the modern world, an interpretation sometimes called "sociological." One of the best examples of this approach is Edmund Wilson's 1922 review in *The Dial*, "The Poetry of Drouth" (reprinted in *T. S. Eliot: The Critical Heritage*, ed. Micheal Grant, 1982, and incorporated in part in Wilson's essay on Eliot in *Axel's Castle*, 1931). Critics like I. A. Richards found that in *The Waste Land* Eliot had effected "a complete severance between poetry and *all* beliefs"; see his "The Poetry of T. S. Eliot" in *Principles of Literary Criticism* (1927). Other critics agreed with Cleanth Brooks, who found the theme of *The Waste Land* "the rehabilitation of a system of beliefs"; see his essay on Eliot in *Modern Poetry and the Tradition* (1939). A more recent tendency is to interpret *The Waste Land* as a personal poem. Following Eliot's own lead in insisting that his poem was a "personal . . . grouse against life," James E. Miller, Jr., has read the poem (focusing on the manuscript before Pound revised it), as *subtextually* a kind of elegy for his dead friend Jean Verdenal and a cry of agony in the bonds of a loveless marriage with Vivienne; see his *T. S. Eliot's Personal Waste Land: Exorcism of the Demons* (1977).

The Waste Land[1]

"Nam Sibyllam quidem Cumis ego ipse oculis meis vidi in ampulla pendere, et cum illi pueri dicerent: Σίβυλλα τί θέλεις; respondebat illa: ἀποθανεῖν θέλω."[2]

For Ezra Pound
il miglior fabbro.[3]

---

[1]Eliot's footnotes are integrated with other explanatory footnotes and are always identified as Eliot's. The following comment headed his notes: "Not only the title, but the plan and a good deal of the incidental symbolism of the poem were suggested by Miss Jessie L. Weston's book on the Grail legend: *From Ritual to Romance* (Cambridge). Indeed, so deeply am I indebted, Miss Weston's book will elucidate the difficulties of the poem much better than my notes can do; and I recommend it (apart from the great interest of the book itself) to any who think such elucidation of the poem worth the trouble. To another work of anthropology I am indebted in general, one which has influenced our generation profoundly; I mean *The Golden Bough*, I have used especially the two volumes *Adonis, Attis, Osiris*. Anyone who is acquainted with these works will immediately recognise in the poem certain references to vegetation ceremonies." Sir James Frazer (1854–1941) was a Scottish anthropologist and author of a twelve-volume work, *The Golden Bough* (1907–15). Eliot refers to the volumes dealing with the vegetation gods (Adonis, Attis, Osiris).

[2]"For in fact I myself saw with my own eyes the Sibyl of Cumae hanging in a cage; and when the boys said to her, 'Sibyl, what do you want?', she replied, 'I want to die'" (Latin/Greek from *Patronius Satyricon*, XLVIII). Sibyl, granted long life by Apollo, had forgotten to ask for eternal youth.

[3]"The better craftsman" (Italian), said of the Provençal poet Arnaut Daniel in Dante's *Purgatorio*, XXVI, 117. In this dedication, Eliot pays tribute to Pound for his editorial help in shaping *The Waste Land*.

I. THE BURIAL OF THE DEAD[4]

April is the cruellest month, breeding
Lilacs out of the dead land, mixing
Memory and desire, stirring
Dull roots with spring rain.
Winter kept us warm, covering   5
Earth in forgetful snow, feeding
A little life with dried tubers.
Summer surprised us, coming over the Starnbergersee[5]
With a shower of rain; we stopped in the colonnade,
And went on in sunlight, into the Hofgarten,[6]   10
And drank coffee, and talked for an hour.
Bin gar keine Russin, stamm' aus Litauen, echt deutsch.[7]
And when we were children, staying at the archduke's,
My cousin's, he took me out on a sled,
And I was frightened. He said, Marie,   15
Marie, hold on tight. And down we went.
In the mountains, there you feel free.
I read, much of the night, and go south in the winter.

   What are the roots that clutch, what branches grow
Out of this stony rubbish? Son of man,[8]   20
You cannot say, or guess, for you know only
A heap of broken images, where the sun beats,
And the dead tree gives no shelter, the cricket no relief,[9]
And the dry stone no sound of water. Only
There is shadow under this red rock,[10]   25
(Come in under the shadow of this red rock),
And I will show you something different from either
Your shadow at morning striding behind you
Or your shadow at evening rising to meet you;
I will show you fear in a handful of dust.[11]   30
          Frisch weht der Wind
          Der Heimat zu
          Mein Irisch Kind,
          Wo weilest du?[12]
"You gave me hyacinths[13] first a year ago;   35
"They called me the hyacinth girl."
—Yet when we came back, late, from the Hyacinth garden,
Your arms full, and your hair wet, I could not
Speak, and my eyes failed, I was neither
Living nor dead, and I knew nothing,   40

4Title of the Anglican burial service in *The Book of Common Prayer*.

5Lake near Munich, Germany.

6Park in Munich.

7"I am no Russian; I come from Lithuania, a true German" (German). In the facsimile *Waste Land*, the editor Valerie Eliot said that Eliot's "description of the sledding . . . was taken verbatim from a conversation he had with [Countess Marie Larisch], niece and confidante of the Austrian Empress Elizabeth."

8"Cf. Ezekial II, i" (Eliot's note), where God says to the prophet Ezekiel: "Son of man, stand upon thy feet, and I will speak unto thee."

9"Cf. Ecclesiastes XII, v" (Eliot's note), where the preacher speaks of the evil days "when they shall be afraid of that which is high and fears shall be in the way, and the almond tree shall flourish, and the grasshopper shall be a burden, and desire shall fail: because man goeth to his long home, and the mourners go about the streets."

10Cf. Isaiah 32:2, where a savior is described "as rivers of water in a dry place, as the shadow of a great rock in a weary land." Lines 26–30, following, echo the opening lines of "The Death of St. Narcissus," written in 1915 or earlier.

11Cf. Genesis 3:19: ". . . for dust thou art, and unto dust shalt thou return," which is recalled in the Anglican burial service.

12"V. [*vide*, see] *Tristan und Isolde*, 1, verses 5–8" (Eliot's note). In Richard Wagner's opera, Tristan sails with Isolde from Ireland to Cornwall, where she is to wed King Mark, whom she does not love. At sea, a sailor sings of a girl he left behind: "Fresh blows the wind / Homeward / My Irish Maid, / Where do you linger?" (German).

13In Greek myth, Apollo loved the handsome boy Hyacinthus, and accidentally killed him; to keep him forever, he transformed him into the flower that bears his name (not the modern flower, but a kind of iris).

Looking into the heart of light, the silence.
Oed' und leer das Meer.[14]

Madame Sosostris, famous clairvoyante,
Had a bad cold, nevertheless
Is known to be the wisest woman in Europe,   45
With a wicked pack of cards.[15] Here, said she,
Is your card, the drowned Phoenician Sailor,
(Those are pearls that were his eyes.[16] Look!)
Here is Belladonna, the Lady of the Rocks,
The lady of situations.   50
Here is the man with three staves, and here the Wheel,
And here is the one-eyed merchant, and this card,
Which is blank, is something he carries on his back,
Which I am forbidden to see. I do not find
The Hanged Man. Fear death by water.   55
I see crowds of people, walking round in a ring.
Thank you. If you see dear Mrs. Equitone,
Tell her I bring the horoscope myself:
One must be so careful these days.

Unreal City,[17]   60
Under the brown fog of a winter dawn,
A crowd flowed over London Bridge, so many,
I had not thought death had undone so many.[18]
Sighs, short and infrequent, were exhaled,[19]
And each man fixed his eyes before his feet.   65
Flowed up the hill and down King William Street,
To where Saint Mary Woolnoth[20] kept the hours
With a dead sound on the final stroke of nine.[21]
There I saw one I knew, and stopped him, crying: "Stetson![22]
"You who were with me in the ships at Mylae![23]   70
"That corpse you planted last year in your garden,
"Has it begun to sprout? Will it bloom this year?
"Or has the sudden frost disturbed its bed?
"Oh keep the Dog far hence, that's friend to men,

---

[14]"[*Tristan*] III, verse 24" (Eliot's note). The mortally wounded Tristan awaits his beloved Isolde, but a shepherd, on watch for her ship, reports, "Desolate and empty the sea" (German).

[15]The Tarot pack, used in fortune telling. Eliot refers in the following note to Frazer's *The Golden Bough* and to the "fisher king," who is the impotent ruler of the waste land described in Weston's *From Ritual to Romance* (see note 1): "I am not familiar with the exact constitution of the Tarot pack of cards, from which I have obviously departed to suit my own convenience. The Hanged Man, a member of the traditional pack, fits my purpose in two ways: because he is associated in my mind with the Hanged God of Frazer, and because I associate him with the hooded figure in the passage of the disciples to Emmaus in Part V. The Phoenician Sailor and the Merchant appear later; also the 'crowds of people,' and Death by Water is executed in Part IV. The Man with Three Staves (an authentic member of the Tarot pack) I associate, quite arbitrarily, with the Fisher King himself."

[16]From Shakespeare's *The Tempest*, I, ii, line 398. Prince Ferdinand, believing his father drowned, is puzzled, perhaps consoled, by the invisible "airy spirit" in Ariel's song containing this line, which the Prince takes to refer to his father.

[17]In a note to this line, Eliot cites lines from "Les Sept Vieil-

lards" ("The Seven Old Men" [French]), by French poet Charles Baudelaire (1821–1867), which may be translated: "Swarming city, city full of dreams, / Where a ghost in broad daylight accosts the passerby." Eliot's note: "Cf. Baudelaire: 'Fourmillante cité, cité pleine de rêves, / Où le spectre en plein jour raccroche le passant.'"

[18]"Cf. Inferno III, 55–57: 'si lunga tratta / di gente, ch'io non avrei mai creduto / che morte tanta n'avesse disfatta'" (Eliot's note): "So long a train / of people, I never should have believed / that death had undone so many" (Italian).

[19]"Cf. Inferno IV, 25–27: 'Quivi, secondo che per ascoltare, / non avea pianto, ma' che di sospiri, / che l'aura eterna facevan tremare'" (Eliot's note): "Here, as one listened, / there was no complaining, but only sighs, / which made the eternal air tremble" (Italian).

[20]London church at the corner of King William and Lombard streets.

[21]"A phenomenon which I have often noticed" (Eliot's note).

[22]Stetson was based on a bank-clerk acquaintance of Eliot's, according to Valerie Eliot (see Barbara Everett, "Eliot in and out of *The Waste Land*," *Critical Quarterly*, Spring 1975).

[23]Roman naval victory over Carthage in 260 B.C.

"Or with his nails he'll dig it up again!"[24]   75
"You! hypocrite lecteur!—mon semblable,—mon frère!"[25]

II. A GAME OF CHESS[1]

The Chair she sat in, like a burnished throne,[2]
Glowed on the marble, where the glass
Held up by standards wrought with fruited vines
From which a golden Cupidon[3] peeped out   80
(Another hid his eyes behind his wing)
Doubled the flames of sevenbranched candelabra
Reflecting light upon the table as
The glitter of her jewels rose to meet it,
From satin cases poured in rich profusion;   85
In vials of ivory and coloured glass
Unstoppered, lurked her strange synthetic perfumes,
Unguent, powdered, or liquid—troubled, confused
And drowned the sense in odours; stirred by the air
That freshened from the window, these ascended   90
In fattening the prolonged candle-flames,
Flung their smoke into the laquearia,[4]
Stirring the pattern on the coffered ceiling.
Huge sea-wood fed with copper
Burned green and orange, framed by the coloured stone,   95
In which sad light a carvèd dolphin swam.
Above the antique mantel was displayed
As though a window gave upon the sylvan scene[5]
The change of Philomel, by the barbarous king[6]
So rudely forced; yet there the nightingale[7]   100
Filled all the desert with inviolable voice
And still she cried, and still the world pursues,
"Jug Jug"[8] to dirty ears.
And other withered stumps of time
Were told upon the walls; staring forms   105
Leaned out, leaning, hushing the room enclosed.
Footsteps shuffled on the stair.
Under the firelight, under the brush, her hair
Spread out in fiery points
Glowed into words, then would be savagely still.   110

---

[24]"Cf. the Dirge in Webster's *White Devil*" (Eliot's note): "But keep the wolf far thence, that's foe to men, / For with his nails he'll dig them up again" (V, iv, 97–98). In John Webster's (1580?–1625) *The White Devil* (1612), the dirge is sung by a woman driven to distraction by the murder of one of her sons by the other. The "corpse" has been taken to refer to the fertility god, and the "sprouting" to the god's resurrection. Metaphorically, the "corpse" might be a memory buried in the unconscious.

[25]"V. [see] Baudelaire, Preface to *Fleurs du Mal* [Flowers of Evil]" (Eliot's note). This is the last line of "Au Lecteur" ("To the Reader"), describing ennui as the worst sin: "Hypocrite reader!—my double,—my brother!"

[1]The title comes from the play *A Game of Chess* by Thomas Middleton (1570?–1627), about a loveless marriage of convenience; in another Middleton play, *Women Beware Women*, the moves in a chess game in one room accompany the moves in a seduction in progress in the room next door.

[2]"Cf. *Antony and Cleopatra*, II, ii, l. 190" (Eliot's note). The beautiful passage in Shakespeare, describing Cleopatra's boat, opens: "The barge she sat in, like a burnished throne . . ."

[3]Statue of Cupid, Roman god of love.

[4]"Laquearia. V. [see] *Aeneid*, l, 726" (Eliot's note). Panelled ceiling: in Virgil, the scene in which Queen Dido gives a banquet for her lover Aeneas is described in part: "Lighted lamps hang from the fretted ceiling of gold, and flaming torches overcome the night."

[5]"Sylvan scene. V. [see] Milton, *Paradise Lost*, IV, 140" (Eliot's note). Milton describes the Garden of Eden as first seen by Satan.

[6]"V. [see] Ovid, *Metamorphoses*, VI, Philomela" (Eliot's note). Philomel is raped by her brother-in-law Tereus; to ensure her silence, he cuts out her tongue. The gods compensate by turning her into a nightingale.

[7]"Cf. Part III, l. 204" (Eliot's note). The sound of the nightingale's song is repeated in the context of a modern seduction or rape scene.

[8]Conventional representation of one note of the song of the nightingale, used especially in Elizabethan literature.

"My nerves are bad to-night. Yes, bad. Stay with me.
"Speak to me. Why do you never speak. Speak.
"What are you thinking of? What thinking? What?
"I never know what you are thinking. Think."

I think we are in rats' alley[9]   115
Where the dead men lost their bones.

"What is that noise?"
                        The wind under the door.[10]
"What is that noise now? What is the wind doing?"
                        Nothing again nothing.   120
                                              "Do
"You know nothing? Do you see nothing? Do you remember
"Nothing?"

          I remember
Those are pearls that were his eyes.   125
"Are you alive, or not? Is there nothing in your head?"[11]
                                      But

O O O O that Shakespeherian Rag—
It's so elegant
So intelligent[12]   130
"What shall I do now? What shall I do?"
"I shall rush out as I am, and walk the street
"With my hair down, so. What shall we do to-morrow?
"What shall we ever do?"
                        The hot water at ten.   135
And if it rains, a closed car at four.
And we shall play a game of chess,
Pressing lidless eyes and waiting for a knock upon the door.[13]

    When Lil's husband got demobbed,[14] I said—
I didn't mince my words, I said to her myself,   140
HURRY UP PLEASE ITS TIME[15]
Now Albert's coming back, make yourself a bit smart.
He'll want to know what you done with that money he gave you
To get yourself some teeth. He did, I was there.
You have them all out, Lil, and get a nice set,   145
He said, I swear, I can't bear to look at you.
And no more can't I, I said, and think of poor Albert,
He's been in the army four years, he wants a good time,
And if you don't give it him, there's others will, I said.
Oh is there, she said. Something o' that, I said.   150
Then I'll know who to thank, she said, and give me a straight look.

9"Cf. Part III, l. 195" (Eliot's note). The rat-image recurs.
10"Cf. Webster: 'Is the wind in that door still?'" (Eliot's note). From John Webster's *The Devil's Law Case*, III, ii, l. 162. A doctor poses the question on finding a victim of violent assault still breathing.
11"Cf. Part I, l. 37, 48" (Eliot's note). By this mysterious note, Eliot seems to suggest that the protagonist is here remembering the love scene in the hyacinth garden and a haunting death (in l. 48, the line "Those are pearls that were his eyes" is linked with the "drowned Phoenician Sailor," who is principally described in Part IV, "Death by Water"). It is useful to note that the line after l. 124 ("I remember") in the original manuscript read: "The hyacinth garden. Those are pearls that were his eyes, yes!"
12Scraps of lines from a rag-time song popular around 1912, "That Shakespearian Rag."
13"Cf. the game of chess in Middleton's *Women Beware Women*" (Eliot's note). See note 1, p. 837.
14Demobilized, discharged from military service.
15Announcement made by the barkeeper in an English pub that the closing time (enforced by law) is approaching and last drinks should be ordered.

HURRY UP PLEASE ITS TIME
If you don't like it you can get on with it, I said.
Others can pick and choose if you can't.
But if Albert makes off, it won't be for lack of telling.   155
You ought to be ashamed, I said, to look so antique.
(And her only thirty-one.)
I can't help it, she said, pulling a long face,
It's them pills I took, to bring it off, she said.
(She's had five already, and nearly died of young George.)   160
The chemist[16] said it would be all right, but I've never been the same.
You are a proper fool, I said.
Well, if Albert won't leave you alone, there it is, I said,
What you get married for if you don't want children?
HURRY UP PLEASE ITS TIME   165
Well, that Sunday Albert was home, they had a hot gammon,[17]
And they asked me in to dinner, to get the beauty of it hot—
HURRY UP PLEASE ITS TIME
HURRY UP PLEASE ITS TIME
Goonight Bill. Goonight Lou. Goonight May. Goonight.   170
Ta ta. Goonight. Goonight.
Good night, ladies, good night, sweet ladies, good night, good night.[18]

III. THE FIRE SERMON[1]

The river's tent is broken: the last fingers of leaf
Clutch and sink into the wet bank. The wind
Crosses the brown land, unheard. The nymphs are departed.   175
Sweet Thames, run softly, till I end my song.[2]
The river bears no empty bottles, sandwich papers,
Silk handkerchiefs, cardboard boxes, cigarette ends
Or other testimony of summer nights. The nymphs are departed.
And their friends, the loitering heirs of city directors;   180
Departed, have left no addresses.
By the waters of Leman I sat down and wept . . .[3]
Sweet Thames, run softly till I end my song,
Sweet Thames, run softly, for I speak not loud or long.
But at my back in a cold blast I hear[4]   185
The rattle of the bones, and chuckle spread from ear to ear.
A rat crept softly through the vegetation
Dragging its slimy belly on the bank
While I was fishing in the dull canal
On a winter evening round behind the gashouse   190
Musing upon the king my brother's wreck
And on the king my father's death before him.[5]
White bodies naked on the low damp ground

[16]I.e., pharmacist (in England).
[17]Smoked ham or bacon.
[18]Adapted from Ophelia's mad speech after Hamlet has rejected her. See *Hamlet*, IV, i, 72–74.
[1]A sermon by Gautama Buddha (563?–483? B.C.), Indian philosopher and founder of Buddhism, advising his followers to quench the fires of the passions, especially the physical, and to become detached from things of this world by living a spiritual life.
[2]"V. [see] Spenser, *Prothalamion*" (Eliot's note). The line comes from the marriage song of Edmund Spenser (1552?–1599).
[3]Leman is a lake in Switzerland, on which is located

Lausanne, where Eliot was under the care of a psychiatrist in 1921 as he was finishing *The Waste Land*. The line echoes the opening of Psalm 137, describing the Hebrews weeping for their homeland: "By the rivers of Babylon, there we sat down, yea, we wept, when we remembered Zion."
[4]Cf. "To His Coy Mistress" by Andrew Marvell (1621–1678): "But at my back I always hear / Time's wingèd chariot hurrying near."
[5]"Cf. *The Tempest*, I, ii" (Eliot's note). Ferdinand mourns because he thinks his father dead. Note especially ll. 389–391: "Sitting on a bank, / Weeping again the King my father's wreck, / This music crept by me upon the waters."

And bones cast in a little low dry garret,
Rattled by the rat's foot only, year to year.   195
But at my back from time to time I hear[6]
The sound of horns and motors, which shall bring[7]
Sweeney[8] to Mrs. Porter in the spring.
O the moon shone bright on Mrs. Porter[9]
And on her daughter   200
They wash their feet in soda water
Et O ces voix d'enfants, chantant dans la coupole![10]

  Twit twit twit
Jug jug jug jug jug jug
So rudely forc'd.   205
Tereu[11]

  Unreal City
Under the brown fog of a winter noon
Mr. Eugenides, the Smyrna[12] merchant
Unshaven, with a pocket full of currants[13]   210
C.i.f. London: documents at sight,
Asked me in demotic[14] French
To luncheon at the Cannon Street Hotel
Followed by a weekend at the Metropole.[15]

  At the violet hour, when the eyes and back   215
Turn upward from the desk, when the human engine waits
Like a taxi throbbing waiting,
I Tiresias, though blind, throbbing between two lives,[16]
Old man with wrinkled female breasts, can see
At the violet hour, the evening hour that strives   220

---

[6]"Cf. Marvell, 'To His Coy Mistress'" (Eliot's note). See note 4.

[7]"Cf. Day, *Parliament of Bees*: 'When of the sudden, listening, you shall hear, / A noise of horns and hunting, which shall bring / Actaeon to Diana in the spring, / Where all shall see her naked skin . . .'" (Eliot's note). John Day (*c.* 1574–*c.* 1640) wrote *The Parliament of Bees* (1607?). In the scene from which the lines are taken, Actaeon is spying on the naked goddess of hunting, Diana; he is turned by her into a stag to be devoured by his own dogs.

[8]Cf. other poems by Eliot (as "Sweeney Erect") in which the vulgar, lustful Sweeney appears.

[9]"I do not know the origin of the ballad from which these lines are taken: it was reported to me from Sydney, Australia" (Eliot's note). This bawdy ballad was sung by Australian troops as they fought at the Dardanelles in the First World War. A Mrs. Porter (according to C. M. Bowra in *The Creative Experiment*, 1967) kept a brothel in Cairo for the troops.

[10]"V. [see] Verlaine, *Parsifal*" (Eliot's note): "O, the voices of children singing in the choirloft!" (French). This line ends the sonnet "Parsifal" by Paul Verlaine (1844–1896), in which Parsifal is described as mastering his own lust, including an "inclination" toward the "flesh of a virgin boy." In the opera *Parsifal* by Richard Wagner (1813–1883), the knight Parsifal, in quest of the Holy Grail, withstands the attempt of an enchantress to seduce him, and, after he heals the Fisher King and becomes king, hears (at the end of the opera) the children's voices from on high praising Christ in song.

[11]A recurrence of the nightingale's song and another reminder of Tereus's rape of Philomel and her metamorphosis into a nightingale.

[12]A port in Turkey.

[13]"The currants were quoted at a price 'carriage and insurance free to London'; and the Bill of Lading etc. were to be handed to the buyer upon payment of the sight draft" (Eliot's note).

[14]The vernacular or everyday (vulgar) form.

[15]The Cannon Street Hotel, near the Cannon Street Station in London, was known as a place for homosexual encounters; the Metropole was a luxurious hotel in the seaside resort of Brighton.

[16]"Tiresias, although a mere spectator and not indeed a 'character,' is yet the most important personage in the poem, uniting all the rest. Just as the one-eyed merchant, seller of currants, melts into the Phoenician Sailor, and the latter is not wholly distinct from Ferdinand Prince of Naples, so all the women are one woman, and the two sexes meet in Tiresias. What Tiresias *sees*, in fact, is the substance of the poem. The whole passage from Ovid is of great anthropological interest" (Eliot's note). Eliot then quotes the Latin text of Ovid's *Metamorphoses*, III, 320–338, which reads in English: "It happened that Jove, heated with wine, laid care aside to jest with Juno in an idle hour. 'I insist,' he said, 'that your pleasure in love is greater than that we [males] enjoy.' She disagreed. So they decided to ask the judgment of wise Tiresias. He knew love from both sides. For once, having outraged two huge serpents mating in the forest, with a blow of his stick, he had, wonderful to say, been changed from a man into a woman, and in that shape he spent seven years. In the eighth year he saw the same serpents again and said, 'Since in striking you there is such magic power as to change the nature of the giver of the blow, now will I strike you again.' So saying, he struck the serpents and was restored to his former state and became as he was born. Therefore, being asked to arbitrate the cheerful quarrel of the gods, he took Jove's side; Saturnia [Juno] was, they say, grieved more deeply either than she should have been, or the issue deserved, and condemned the judge to perpetual blindness, but the eternal father gave Tiresias the power to know the future in return for the loss of his sight."

Homeward, and brings the sailor home from sea,[17]
The typist home at teatime, clears her breakfast, lights
Her stove, and lays out food in tins.
Out of the window perilously spread
Her drying combinations touched by the sun's last rays,   225
On the divan are piled (at night her bed)
Stockings, slippers, camisoles, and stays.[18]
I Tiresias, old man with wrinkled dugs[19]
Perceived the scene, and foretold the rest—
I too awaited the expected guest.   230
He, the young man carbuncular, arrives,
A small house agent's clerk, with one bold stare,
One of the low on whom assurance sits
As a silk hat on a Bradford[20] millionaire.
The time is now propitious, as he guesses,   235
The meal is ended, she is bored and tired,
Endeavours to engage her in caresses
Which still are unreproved, if undesired.
Flushed and decided, he assaults at once;
Exploring hands encounter no defence;   240
His vanity requires no response,
And makes a welcome of indifference.
(And I Tiresias have foresuffered all
Enacted on this same divan or bed;
I who have sat by Thebes below the wall   245
And walked among the lowest of the dead.)[21]
Bestows one final patronising kiss,
And gropes his way, finding the stairs unlit . . .

    She turns and looks a moment in the glass,
Hardly aware of her departed lover;   250
Her brain allows one half-formed thought to pass:
"Well now that's done: and I'm glad it's over."
When lovely woman stoops to folly and
Paces about her room again, alone,
She smoothes her hair with automatic hand,   255
And puts a record on the gramophone.[22]

    "This music crept by me upon the waters"[23]
And along the Strand, up Queen Victoria Street.
O City city, I can sometimes hear
Beside a public bar in Lower Thames Street,   260
The pleasant whining of a mandoline
And a clatter and a chatter from within
Where fishmen lounge at noon: where the walls

---

[17]"This may not appear as exact as Sappho's lines, but I had in mind the 'longshore' or 'dory' fisherman, who returns at nightfall" (Eliot's note): Eliot is referring to Sappho's poem to the Evening Star: "Hesperus [Evening Star] you bring home all things the bright morning dispersed—the sheep, the goat, the child to its mother." Robert Louis Stevenson echoed Sappho in his poem "Requiem": "Home is the sailor, home from the sea."
[18]Stays: corsets (chiefly British).
[19]Nipples.
[20]A northern industrial and manufacturing center, which prospered during the First World War and would have produced war millionaires.

[21]Tiresias prophesied in the market of Thebes; after his death he went to Hades, the Greek underworld of departed souls, where he continued to be available for prophesies.
[22]"V. [see] Goldsmith, the song in *The Vicar of Wakefield*" (Eliot's note). From Chapter XXIV of *The Vicar of Wakefield* by Oliver Goldsmith (1728–1774): "When lovely woman stoops to folly, / And finds too late that men betray, / What charm can soothe her melancholy? / What art can wash her guilt away? / The only art her guilt to cover, / To hide her shame from every eye, / To give repentance to her lover, / And wring his bosom—is to die."
[23]"V. [see] *The Tempest*, as above" (Eliot's note). See note 5.

Of Magnus Martyr[24] hold
Inexplicable splendour of Ionian white and gold.   265

        The river sweats[25]
Oil and tar
The barges drift
With the turning tide
Red sails   270
Wide
To leeward, swing on the heavy spar.
The barges wash
Drifting logs
Down Greenwich reach   275
Past the Isle of Dogs.[26]
            Weialala leia
            Wallala leialala

Elizabeth and Leicester[27]
Beating oars   280
The stern was formed
A gilded shell
Red and gold
The brisk swell
Rippled both shores   285
Southwest wind
Carried down stream
The peal of bells
White towers
            Weialala leia   290
            Wallala leialala

"Trams[28] and dusty trees.
Highbury bore me. Richmond and Kew
Undid me.[29] By Richmond I raised my knees
Supine on the floor of a narrow canoe."   295

    "My feet are at Moorgate,[30] and my heart
Under my feet. After the event
He wept. He promised 'a new start.'
I made no comment. What should I resent?"

    "On Margate Sands.[31]   300

---

[24]"The interior of St. Magnus Martyr is to my mind one of the finest among Wren's interiors. See *The Proposed Demolition of Nineteen City Churches*: (P. S. King & Son, Ltd.)" (Eliot's note). Sir Christopher Wren (1632–1723), the great British architect, built St. Magnus Martyr in 1676.

[25]"The Song of the (three) Thames-daughters begins here. From line 292 to 306 inclusive they speak in turn. V. [see] *Gotterdammerung*, III, i: the Rhine daughters" (Eliot's note). In Wagner's *Gotterdammerung* ("Twilight of the Gods"), the three "daughters" of the Rhine River sing a song mourning the loss of the gold in their keeping, stolen by the opera's hero, Siegfried, a theft resulting in the loss of the Rhine's beauty. Their refrain is quoted by Eliot in ll. 277–78.

[26]The isle of Dogs is a peninsula in east London formed by a bend of the Thames River, across from Greenwich, where Queen Elizabeth was born.

[27]"V. [see] Froude, *Elizabeth*, Vol. I, ch. iv, letter of De Quadra to Philip of Spain: 'In the afternoon we were in a barge,

watching the games on the river. (The queen [Queen Elizabeth I]) was alone with Lord Robert [Dudley, Earl of Leicester] and myself [De Quadra, a Catholic Bishop] on the poop, when they began to talk nonsense, and went so far that Lord Robert at last said, as I was on the spot there was no reason why they should not be married if the queen pleased'" (Eliot's note). I.e., Elizabeth and Leicester joked about getting married, but, of course, Elizabeth never married.

[28]Streetcars.

[29]"Cf. *Purgatorio*, V, 133: 'Ricorditi di me, che son la Pia; / Siena mi fe', disfecemi Maremma'" (Eliot's note): "Remember me, who am La Pia; / Siena made me, Maremma undid me" (Italian). The speaker here in Dante's *Purgatorio* is Pia de' Tolomei, born in Siena but killed in Maremma by her husband. Highbury, Richmond, and Kew are places near London.

[30]East London slum.

[31]Thames estuary resort.

I can connect
Nothing with nothing.
The broken fingernails of dirty hands.
My people humble people who expect
Nothing."   305

            la la

    To Carthage then I came[32]

    Burning burning burning burning[33]
O Lord Thou pluckest me out[34]
O Lord Thou pluckest   310

burning

IV. DEATH BY WATER[1]

Phlebas the Phoenician, a fortnight dead,   315
Forgot the cry of gulls, and the deep sea swell
And the profit and loss.
                  A current under sea   320
Picked his bones in whispers. As he rose and fell
He passed the stages of his age and youth
Entering the whirlpool.
                  Gentile or Jew
O you who turn the wheel and look to windward,
Consider Phlebas, who was once handsome and tall as you.

V. WHAT THE THUNDER SAID[1]

After the torchlight red on sweaty faces
After the frosty silence in the gardens
After the agony in stony places
The shouting and the crying   325
Prison and palace and reverberation
Of thunder of spring over distant mountains
He who was living is now dead[2]

---

[32]"V. [see] St. Augustine's *Confessions*: "to Carthage then I came, where a cauldron of unholy loves sang all about mine ears" (Eliot's note). St. Augustine (354–430) describes his life of sexual sin in Carthage.

[33]"The complete text of the Buddha's Fire Sermon (which corresponds in importance to the Sermon on the Mount) from which these words are taken, will be found translated in the late Henry Clarke Warren's *Buddhism in Translation* (Harvard Oriental Series). Mr. Warren was one of the great pioneers of Buddhist studies in the Occident" (Eliot's note).

[34]"From St. Augustine's *Confessions* again. The collocation of these two representatives of eastern and western asceticism, as the culmination of this part of the poem, is not an accident" (Eliot's note). I.e., St. Augustine expresses gratitude to the Lord for plucking him out of his sinking into sin.

[1]See Madame Sosostris's prophecy, ll. 47–48. Originally this section was much longer, concluding with the lines that remain here. Eliot was so concerned about Pound's eliminating most of the section that he asked whether perhaps the rest should be cut. Pound replied that "Phlebas is an integral part of the poem." Critics have disagreed as to the meaning of the section. Those critics who think the poem is a cry of despair, without belief, say that Phlebas's death is absolute; those who think the poem offers some ray of hope, the possibility of belief, say that Phlebas's death is some kind of renewal or rebirth. Critics who read the poem as subtextually personal see Phlebas as Jean Verdenal, killed in the Dardanelles in 1915. The line from *The Tempest* ("Those are pearls that were his eyes") is associated with the drowned Phoenician Sailor in the Madame Sosostris passage and seems to haunt the protagonist there (l. 48) and again in Part II, as the husband is listening to the fretful wife (l. 125); by his mysterious footnote to this passage, Eliot associates Phlebas also with the Hyacinth garden of line 37.

[1]"In the first part of Part V three themes are employed: the journey to Emmaus, the approach to the Chapel Perilous (see Miss Weston's book) and the present decay of eastern Europe" (Eliot's note). The Thunder represents the voice of God in the Hindu *Upanishads*, and his speech begins in l. 400. After the crucifixion and the disappearance of Jesus from the tomb, two of his disciples meet a stranger who accompanies them on their way to Emmaus (a small village near Jerusalem). When they eat with the stranger, they come to know that he is Jesus and that Jesus was resurrected. In the Grail legend, the quester must visit the Chapel Perilous and the Perilous Cemetery—very much like a visit to the regions of the dead to attain mystical insight or spiritual knowledge (a descent before the ascent).

[2]The imagery of these opening lines suggests the agony of Christ in the Garden of Gethsemane, the betrayal by Judas, the imprisonment of Christ, the judgment of Pontius Pilate (in the palace), the crucifixion and burial of Christ; the sound of thunder suggests God's awareness of these events.

We who were living are now dying
With a little patience   330

    Here is no water but only rock
Rock and no water and the sandy road
The road winding above among the mountains
Which are mountains of rock without water
If there were water we should stop and drink   335
Amongst the rock one cannot stop or think
Sweat is dry and feet are in the sand
If there were only water amongst the rock
Dead mountain mouth of carious[3] teeth that cannot spit
Here one can neither stand nor lie nor sit   340
There is not even silence in the mountains
But dry sterile thunder without rain
There is not even solitude in the mountains
But red sullen faces sneer and snarl
From doors of mudcracked houses   345
                      If there were water
   And no rock
   If there were rock
   And also water
   And water   350
   A spring
   A pool among the rock
   If there were the sound of water only
   Not the cicada
   And dry grass singing   355
   But sound of water over a rock
   Where the hermit-thrush sings in the pine trees[4]
   Drip drop drip drop drop drop drop
   But there is no water

   Who is the third who walks always beside you?[5]   360
When I count, there are only you and I together
But when I look ahead up the white road
There is always another one walking beside you
Gliding wrapt in a brown mantle, hooded
I do not know whether a man or a woman   365
—But who is that on the other side of you?

   What is that sound high in the air
Murmur of maternal lamentation
Who are those hooded hordes swarming

---

[3]Rotten or decayed.'
[4]"This is *Turdus aonalaschkae pallasii*, the hermit-thrush which
I have heard in Quebec Province. Chapman says (*Handbook of
Birds of Eastern North America*) 'it is most at home in secluded
woodland and thickety retreats. . . . Its notes are not remarkable for variety or volume, but in purity and sweetness of
tone and exquisite modulation they are unequalled.' Its
'water-dripping song' is justly celebrated" (Eliot's note). The
most famous use of the hermit-thrush in literature is by Walt
Whitman in his elegy for Abraham Lincoln, "When Lilacs
Last in the Dooryard Bloom'd," which seems relevant here
particularly because *The Waste Land* opens with the lilac image. In both poems the hermit-thrush sings from the pine

trees (also cedars in Whitman) and his song seems to contain
a spiritual message.
[5]"The following lines were stimulated by the account of one
of the Antarctic expeditions (I forget which, but I think one
of Shackleton's): it was related that the party of explorers, at
the extremity of their strength, had the constant delusion
that there was *one more member* than could actually be counted" (Eliot's note). Note also that on the journey to Emmaus,
two disciples were discussing Jesus' crucifixion and met
a stranger who "drew near, and went with them. But their
eyes were holden that they should not know him" (Luke
24:15–16).

Over endless plains, stumbling in cracked earth   370
Ringed by the flat horizon only
What is the city over the mountains
Cracks and reforms and bursts in the violet air
Falling towers
Jerusalem Athens Alexandria   375
Vienna London
Unreal[6]

A woman drew her long black hair out tight
And fiddled whisper music on those strings
And bats with baby faces in the violet light   380
Whistled, and beat their wings
And crawled head downward down a blackened wall
And upside down in air were towers
Tolling reminiscent bells, that kept the hours
And voices singing out of empty cisterns and exhausted wells.   385

In this decayed hole among the mountains
In the faint moonlight, the grass is singing
Over the tumbled graves, about the chapel
There is the empty chapel,[7] only the wind's home.
It has no windows, and the door swings,   390
Dry bones can harm no one.
Only a cock stood on the rooftree
Co co rico co co rico[8]
In a flash of lightning. Then a damp gust
Bringing rain   395

Ganga[9] was sunken, and the limp leaves
Waited for rain, while the black clouds
Gathered far distant, over Himavant.[10]
The jungle crouched, humped in silence.
Then spoke the thunder   400
DA
Datta: what have we given?[11]
My friend, blood shaking my heart
The awful daring of a moment's surrender
Which an age of prudence can never retract   405
By this, and this only, we have existed

---

[6]For ll. 367–77, Eliot provided this note: "Cf. Hermann Hesse, *Blick ins Chaos*: 'Schon ist halb Europa, schon ist zumindest der halbe Osten Europas auf dem Wege zum Chaos, fährt betrunken im heiligem Wahn am Abgrund entlang und singt dazu, singt betrunken und hymnisch wie Dmitri Karamasoff sang. Ueber diese Lieder lacht der Bürger beleidigt, der Heilige und Seher hört sie mit Tränen.'" "'Already half of Europe, already at least half of Eastern Europe, is on the way to chaos, going drunk in holy folly along the edge of the abyss and singing drunken hymns as Dimitri Karamozov did. The burgher laughs scornfully at these songs while the saint and seer hear them with tears." Herman Hesse (1877–1962), *A Glimpse into Chaos*. The reference is to Fyodor Dostoyevsky's *The Brothers Karamazov* (1879–80).

[7]I.e., the Chapel Perilous.

[8]The cock's crow announcing dawn (and perhaps, as in folklore, proclaiming the withdrawal of evil spirits of the night) is rendered in the French imitation of the sound.

[9]The Ganges, a sacred river in India.

[10]The Himayalas, a mountain range between India and Tibet.

[11]"'Datta, dayadhvam, damyata' (Give, sympathise, control). The fable of the meaning of the Thunder is found in the *Brihadaranyaka-Upanishad*, 5, 1. A translation is found in Deussen's *Sechzig Upanishads des Veda*, p. 489" (Eliot's note). In the *Upanishad*, the god Prajapati is asked by his sons of three classes—gods, men, and Asuras—to instruct them, and he does so through the voice of the Thunder, always in the same single syllable. First he says "Da," and the gods understand him to advise self-control; his next "Da" to the men they take to mean "give"; and his third "Da" to the Asuras (Hindu evil deities) they understand to mean "have compassion." As the commentator on this Upanishad points out, the uttering of the one syllable forced members of each group in turn to discover their own weaknesses within. Eliot departs from the *Upanishad*, as he inverts the order from *control yourselves, give,* and *have compassion* to *give, sympathize, control.*

Which is not to be found in our obituaries
Or in memories draped by the beneficent spider[12]
Or under seals broken by the lean solicitor
In our empty rooms   410
DA
Dayadhvam: I have heard the key
Turn in the door once and turn once only[13]
We think of the key, each in his prison
Thinking of the key, each confirms a prison   415
Only at nightfall, aethereal rumours
Revive for a moment a broken Coriolanus[14]
DA
Damyata: The boat responded
Gaily, to the hand expert with sail and oar   420
The sea was calm, your heart would have responded
Gaily, when invited, beating obedient
To controlling hands
                                    I sat upon the shore
Fishing,[15] with the arid plain behind me   425
Shall I at least set my lands in order?[16]
London Bridge is falling down falling down falling down
Poi s'ascose nel foco che gli affina[17]
Quando fiam uti chelidon—O swallow swallow[18]
Le Prince d'Aquitaine à la tour abolie[19]   430
These fragments I have shored against my ruins
Why then Ile fit you. Hieronymo's mad againe.[20]
Datta. Dayadhvam. Damyata.
        Shantih   shantih   shantih[21]

                                                    1922

---

[12]"Cf. Webster, *The White Devil*, V, vi: '. . . they'll remarry / Ere the worm pierce your winding-sheet, ere the spider / Make a thin curtain for your epitaphs'" (Eliot's note).
[13]Eliot provides this note for line 412: "Cf. *Inferno*, XXXIII, 46: 'ed io sentii chiavar l'uscio di sotto / all'orribile torre.' ["... and below I heard the door of the horrible tower being closed up," spoken by Ugalino to Dante, telling of his and his children's imprisonment by his enemies.] Also F. H. Bradley, *Appearance and Reality*, p. 346: 'My external sensations are no less private to myself than are my thoughts or my feelings. In either case my experience falls within my own circle, a circle closed on the outside; and, with all its elements alike, every sphere is opaque to the others which surround it. . . . In brief, regarded as an existence which appears in a soul, the whole world for each is peculiar and private to that soul.'"
[14]In Shakespeare's *Coriolanus*, the arrogant and proud Roman general of that name who went over to the enemy and led the attack on Rome, but then (as his mother pleaded with him) turned back and was killed for the betrayal.
[15]"V. [see] Weston: *From Ritual to Romance*; chapter on the Fisher King" (Eliot's note). It is important to note that it is not the infertility of the lands that have rendered the Fisher King impotent, but the other way around: his sexual impotence has rendered the lands infertile (the waste land within had created the waste land without). Weston writes: "Now there can be no possible doubt here, the condition of the King is sympathetically reflected on the land, the loss of virility in the one brings about a suspension of the reproductive processes of Nature on the other."
[16]Cf. Isaiah 38:1: "Thus saith the Lord, Set thine house in order: for thou shalt die, and not live."
[17]"V. [see] *Purgatorio*, XXVI, 148. 'Ara vos prec per aquella valor / que vos guida al som de l'escalina, / sovegna vos a

temps de ma dolor.' / Poi s'ascose nel foco che gli affina" (Eliot's note): "'Now I pray you by that power which guides you to the top of this stairway, be mindful of my pain in proper season.' He hid himself in the fire which refines them." The Provençal poet Arnaut Daniel is here speaking to Dante; in this Canto, he is described as in a band of the hermaphroditic lustful encountering and kissing a band of sodomites and then passing on to the refining fire.
[18]"When shall I be like the swallow—O swallow, swallow?" (Latin). "V. [see] *Pervigilium Veneris*. Cf. Philomela in Parts II and III" (Eliot's note). In *The Vigil of Venus*, the line reads: "When shall I be like the swallow and my voice no longer dumb?" I.e., the speaker needs a mate, needs love, to be able to sing.
[19]"The Prince of Aquitaine in the ruined tower" (French). "V. [see] Gerard de Nerval, Sonnet *El Descichado*" (Eliot's note). Gerard de Nerval (1808–1855), French poet, wrote in this sonnet: "I am the dark man, the disconsolate widower, / The prince of Aquitania whose tower has been torn down: / My sole *star* is dead,—and my constellated lute / Bears the black *sun* of *Melancholia*." The speaker has lost his love in death.
[20]"V. [see] Kyd's *Spanish Tragedy*" (Eliot's note). Thomas Kyd (1557?–1595), Elizabethan playwright. In his revenge tragedy, Hieronymo is driven to near madness in his grief at the murder of his son and plans his revenge when asked by the murderers to supply a play for the court. "Why then Ile fit [accommodate] you," he tells them. The murderers are killed on stage, and then Hieronymo takes his own life. "Hieronymo's mad againe" is the subtitle of the play.
[21]"Shantih. Repeated as here, a formal ending to an Upanishad. 'The Peace which passeth understanding' is our equivalent to this word" (Eliot's note).

Journey of the Magi[1]

'A cold coming we had of it,
Just the worst time of the year
For a journey, and such a long journey:
The ways deep and the weather sharp,
The very dead of winter.'[2]   5
And the camels galled, sore-footed, refractory,
Lying down in the melting snow.
There were times we regretted
The summer palaces on slopes, the terraces,
And the silken girls bringing sherbet.   10
Then the camel men cursing and grumbling
And running away, and wanting their liquor and women,
And the night-fires going out, and the lack of shelters,
And the cities hostile and the towns unfriendly
And the villages dirty and charging high prices: 15
A hard time we had of it.
At the end we preferred to travel all night,
Sleeping in snatches,
With the voices singing in our ears, saying
That this was all folly.   20

    Then at dawn we came down to a temperate valley,
Wet, below the snow line, smelling of vegetation;
With a running stream and a water-mill beating the darkness,
And three trees on the low sky,
And an old white horse galloped away in the meadow.   25
Then we came to a tavern with vine-leaves over the lintel,
Six hands at an open door dicing for pieces of silver,
And feet kicking the empty wine-skins.
But there was no information, and so we continued
And arrived at evening, not a moment too soon   30
Finding the place; it was (you may say) satisfactory.

    All this was a long time ago, I remember,
And I would do it again, but set down
This set down
This: were we led all that way for   35
Birth or Death? There was a Birth, certainly,
We had evidence and no doubt. I had seen birth and death,
But had thought they were different; this Birth was
Hard and bitter agony for us, like Death, our death.
We returned to our places, these Kingdoms,   40
But no longer at ease here, in the old dispensation,
With an alien people clutching their gods.
I should be glad of another death.[3]

1927

---

[1]The Magi were the three wise men who, by following the star of Bethlehem, arrived to bear witness to the birth of Christ. See Matthew 2:1–12.
[2]Lines based on a Christmas sermon delivered in 1622 by Lancelot Andrewes (1555–1626); in the poem, the lines are spoken by one of the wise men.
[3]I.e., the speaker's, for he is not at ease with a life amidst an "alien people clutching their [pagan] gods" and is assured of redemption by the coming of Christ.

from Four Quartets[1]

Burnt Norton

τοῦ λόγου δ'ἐόντος ξυνοῦ ζώουσιν οἱ πολλοί
ὡς ἰδίαν ἔχοντες φρόνησιν.
I. p. 77. Fr. 2.
ὁδὸς ἄνω κάτω μία καὶ ὡυτή.
I. p. 89. Fr. 60.
Diels: *Die Fragmente der Vorsokratiker* (Herakleitos).[2]

I

Time present and time past
Are both perhaps present in time future,
And time future contained in time past.
If all time is eternally present
All time is unredeemable.   5
What might have been is an abstraction
Remaining a perpetual possibility
Only in a world of speculation.
What might have been and what has been
Point to one end, which is always present.   10
Footfalls echo in the memory
Down the passage which we did not take
Towards the door we never opened
Into the rose-garden.[3] My words echo
Thus, in your mind.   15
                              But to what purpose
Disturbing the dust on a bowl of rose-leaves
I do not know.

---

[1]*Four Quartets* consists of four interrelated poems brought together as a complete work in 1943. The title suggests a musical analogy with the "quartet," a composition (sometimes labelled "chamber music") written for four instruments. Eliot remarked in *The Music of Poetry* (1942) that "the music of verse is not a line by line matter, but a question of the whole poem. . . . It is a music of imagery as well as sound." He also said that "the properties in which music concerns the poet most nearly, are the sense of rhythm and the sense of structure." The titles of the four parts of *Four Quartets* are all place names that have some personal associations for Eliot. "Burnt Norton" (1936) is a country house at Ebrington in Gloucestershire (in the West Midlands), near the village of Chipping Camden—where in 1934 and a few years thereafter Eliot stayed with the Bostonian Emily Hale and the friends she was visiting (she is thought by some biographers to be Eliot's great unfulfilled love). "East Coker" (1940) is the village in southwest England from which Eliot's ancestors emigrated to America. "The Dry Salvages" (1941), as Eliot informs the reader in a note, is "a small group of rocks" located "off the N. E. coast of Cape Ann, Massachusetts"; Eliot spent his holidays there as a boy. "Little Gidding" (1942), which Eliot visited in 1936, is in Huntingdonshire in the East Midlands and the seat of an Anglican religious community established in 1625 which was destroyed by the Puritans during the rule of Oliver Cromwell; a restored chapel remains. *Four Quartets* represents Eliot's mystic quest for the Transcendent and is filled with the language of the religious mystics whose goal is Union through release from the earthly bonds of time and space. The mystic way follows a path that leads from an Awakening of self through a Purification of the self to a first illumination; this is often followed (as in the case of St. John the Divine) by a Dark Night of the Soul that occurs just before the ecstatic Union with the Transcendent. It has been suggested that the four major sections of *Four Quartets* correspond to the four elements, air, earth, water, and fire; and also, in order, to God the Father, Christ the Son, the Virgin Mary, and the Holy Ghost. *Four Quartets* is, in many ways, Eliot's most personal poem—but subtextually, not overtly. When Eliot was revising the last quartet, "Little Gidding," Eliot significantly remarked: "The defect . . . I feel, is the lack of some acute personal reminiscence (never to be explicated, of course, but to give power from well below the surface) and I can *perhaps* supply it in Part II [containing the enigmatic scene of the "familiar compound ghost"].

[2]The epigraphs are taken from *Fragments of the Presocratics* by Hermann Diels (1848–1922), a German philologist, and are by Heraclitus, a Greek philosopher of the sixth century B.C. who taught that all things are in a state of flux and that everything is balanced by its opposite. The quotations: "But although the Word is universal, most individuals live by their own rules"; "The way up and the way down are one and the same."

[3]The rose is a traditional symbol of perfection, love, and a mystic center; it is associated with both Venus and the Virgin Mary. As a Christian symbol, for example, it is embodied in the large stained-glass rose windows of the great cathedrals.

Other echoes
Inhabit the garden. Shall we follow?   20
Quick, said the bird, find them, find them,
Round the corner. Through the first gate,
Into our first world, shall we follow
The deception of the thrush?⁴ Into our first world.
There they were, dignified, invisible,   25
Moving without pressure, over the dead leaves,
In the autumn heat, through the vibrant air,
And the bird called, in response to
The unheard music hidden in the shrubbery,
And the unseen eyebeam crossed, for the roses   30
Had the look of flowers that are looked at.
There they were as our guests, accepted and accepting.
So we moved, and they, in a formal pattern,
Along the empty alley, into the box circle,
To look down into the drained pool.   35
Dry the pool, dry concrete, brown edged,
And the pool was filled with water out of sunlight,
And the lotos rose, quietly, quietly,
The surface glittered out of heart of light,⁵
And they were behind us, reflected in the pool.   40
Then a cloud passed, and the pool was empty.
Go, said the bird, for the leaves were full of children,
Hidden excitedly, containing laughter.
Go, go, go, said the bird: human kind
Cannot bear very much reality.   45
Time past and time future
What might have been and what has been
Point to one end, which is always present.

II

Garlic and sapphires in the mud
Clot the bedded axle-tree.⁶   50
The trilling wire in the blood
Sings below inveterate scars
And reconciles forgotten wars.
The dance along the artery
The circulation of the lymph   55
Are figured in the drift of stars
Ascend to summer in the tree
We move above the moving tree
In light upon the figured leaf
And hear upon the sodden floor   60
Below, the boarhound and the boar
Pursue their pattern as before
But reconciled among the stars.

At the still point of the turning world. Neither flesh nor fleshless;
Neither from nor towards; at the still point, there the dance is,   65

---

⁴The bird here and below appears to fulfill a traditional symbolic role of leading to transcendent knowledge or insight; cf. the appearance of the hermit-thrush in the last part of *The Waste Land*.

⁵Cf. the use of "heart of light" in the hyacinth garden passage in the first part of *The Waste Land* (there associated by contrast with "heart of darkness"; Eliot's original epigraph for that poem had come from Joseph Conrad's powerful novella).

⁶An axle-tree is a bar fixed crosswise on an animal-drawn vehicle and holds the rotating wheels. Here it is the axle of the world in a passage that acknowledges through vivid imagery humankind's gross physicality alongside its transcendent spirituality.

But neither arrest nor movement. And do not call it fixity,
Where past and future are gathered. Neither movement from nor towards,
Neither ascent nor decline. Except for the point, the still point,
There would be no dance, and there is only the dance.
I can only say, *there* we have been: but I cannot say where.   70
And I cannot say, how long, for that is to place it in time.[7]

    The inner freedom from the practical desire,
The release from action and suffering, release from the inner
And the outer compulsion, yet surrounded
By a grace of sense, a white light still and moving,   75
Erhebung[8] without motion, concentration
Without elimination, both a new world
And the old made explicit, understood
In the completion of its partial ecstasy,
The resolution of its partial horror.   80
Yet the enchainment of past and future
Woven in the weakness of the changing body,
Protects mankind from heaven and damnation
Which flesh cannot endure.
                          Time past and time future   85
Allow but a little consciousness.
To be conscious is not to be in time
But only in time can the moment in the rose-garden,
The moment in the arbour where the rain beat.
The moment in the draughty church at smokefall[9]   90
Be remembered; involved with past and future.
Only through time time is conquered.

III

Here[10] is a place of disaffection
Time before and time after
In a dim light: neither daylight   95
Investing form with lucid stillness
Turning shadow into transient beauty
With slow rotation suggesting permanence
Nor darkness to purify the soul
Emptying the sensual with deprivation   100
Cleansing affection from the temporal.
Neither plenitude nor vacancy. Only a flicker
Over the strained time-ridden faces
Distracted from distraction by distraction
Filled with fancies and empty of meaning   105
Tumid apathy with no concentration
Men and bits of paper, whirled by the cold wind
That blows before and after time,
Wind in and out of unwholesome lungs
Time before and time after.   110
Eructation[11] of unhealthy souls

---

[7]Eliot's image of "the still point of the turning world" symbolizes spiritual transcendence over both time and space—the mystic's goal.

[8]"Exaltation" (German).

[9]Here the poet lists a series of "mystic moments" that transcended time, but that, paradoxically, can be remembered only in time; thus the mystic path is not an escape from time but leads *through* time.

[10]The poet appears to be on a subway; there is no daylight, and the darkness is not the kind to "purify the soul" (line 96). I.e., the experience is not on the mystic path, where the darkness is a "dark night of the soul" (spiritual struggle). Cf. Hart Crane's use of a subway ride in the next-to-last section of *The Bridge*.

[11]Discharging, as belching or expelling gas.

Into the faded air, the torpid
Driven on the wind that sweeps the gloomy hills of London,
Hampstead and Clerkenwell, Campden and Putney,
Highgate, Primrose and Ludgate. Not here   115
Not here the darkness, in this twittering world.

    Descend lower, descend only
Into the world of perpetual solitude,
World not world, but that which is not world,
Internal darkness,[12] deprivation   120
And destitution of all property,
Desiccation of the world of sense,
Evacuation of the world of fancy,
Inoperancy of the world of spirit;
This is the one way, and the other   125
Is the same, not in movement
But abstention from movement; while the world moves
In appetency,[13] on its metalled ways
Of time past and time future.

IV

Time and the bell have buried the day,   130
The black cloud[14] carries the sun away.
Will the sunflower turn to us, will the clematis[15]
Stray down, bend to us; tendril and spray
Clutch and cling?
Chill   135
Fingers of yew be curled
Down on us? After the kingfisher's wing
Has answered light to light, and is silent, the light is still
At the still point of the turning world.

V

Words move, music moves   140
Only in time; but that which is only living
Can only die. Words, after speech, reach
Into the silence. Only by the form, the pattern,
Can words or music reach
The stillness, as a Chinese jar still   145
Moves perpetually in its stillness.
Not the stillness of the violin, while the note lasts,
Not that only, but the co-existence,
Or say that the end precedes the beginning,
And the end and the beginning were always there   150
Before the beginning and after the end.
And all is always now. Words strain,
Crack and sometimes break, under the burden,
Under the tension, slip, slide, perish,
Decay with imprecision, will not stay in place,   155
Will not stay still.[16] Shrieking voices

---

[12]I.e., not the darkness of the subway ride, "distracted from
distraction" and "empty of meaning," but the true "dark
night of the soul," in which one feels the agony of being cut
off from God.
[13]I.e., filled with appetites and desires.
[14]Cf. the "black cloud" in Walt Whitman's "When Lilacs Last
in the Dooryard Bloom'd."

[15]The sunflower and clematis (one kind called "virgin's-
bower") are associated with transcendence and spiritual life,
the yew tree with death and resurrection; the kingfisher
bird, like the thrush in part one, acts as mediator with the
Transcendent.
[16]Mystics traditionally found language inadequate to the
profundity of their experience in Union with Transcendence.

Scolding, mocking, or merely chattering,
Always assail them. The Word in the desert[17]
Is most attacked by voices of temptation,
The crying shadow in the funeral dance,   160
The loud lament of the disconsolate chimera.[18]

  The detail of the pattern is movement,
As in the figure of the ten stairs.[19]
Desire itself is movement
Not in itself desirable;   165
Love is itself unmoving,
Only the cause and end of movement,
Timeless, and undesiring
Except in the aspect of time
Caught in the form of limitation   170
Between un-being and being.
Sudden in a shaft of sunlight
Even while the dust moves
There rises the hidden laughter
Of children in the foliage   175
Quick now, here, now, always—
Ridiculous the waste sad time
Stretching before and after.

                                                        1936

Tradition and the Individual Talent[1]

I

In English writing we seldom speak of tradition, though we occasionally apply its name in deploring its absence. We cannot refer to "the tradition" or to "a tradition"; at most, we employ the adjective in saying that the poetry of So-and-so is "traditional" or even "too traditional." Seldom, perhaps, does the word appear except in a phrase of censure. If otherwise, it is vaguely approbative, with the implication, as to the work approved, of some pleasing archaeological reconstruction. You can hardly make the word agreeable to English ears without this comfortable reference to the reassuring science of archaeology.

Certainly the word is not likely to appear in our appreciations of living or dead writers. Every nation, every race, has not only its own creative, but its own critical turn of mind; and is even more oblivious of the shortcomings and limitations of its critical habits than of those of its creative genius. We know, or think we know, from the enormous mass of critical writing that has appeared in the French language the critical method or habit of the French; we only conclude (we are such unconscious people) that the French are "more critical" than we, and sometimes even plume ourselves a little with the fact, as if the French were the less spontaneous. Perhaps they

---

[17]Cf. St. John 1:1: "In the beginning was the Word, and the Word was with God, and the Word was God." The allusion is to Christ's temptation in the wilderness, Luke 4:1–13.
[18]In Greek mythology, a fire-breathing monster with the head of a lion, the body of a she-goat, and the tail of a dragon or serpent. It was killed by Bellerophon with the aid of the winged horse Pegasus.

[19]Originally derived from Jacob's ladder (Genesis 28:12), on which angels moved between heaven and earth, the "ten stairs" allude to St. John of the Cross and his "Ten Degrees of the Mystical Ladder of Divine Love."
[1]Eliot published this essay in the *Egoist* in 1919 but he dated it 1917 in his *Selected Essays*. It was included in *The Sacred Wood* in 1920.

are; but we might remind ourselves that criticism is as inevitable as breathing, and that we should be none the worse for articulating what passes in our minds when we read a book and feel an emotion about it, for criticizing our own minds in their work of criticism. One of the facts that might come to light in this process is our tendency to insist, when we praise a poet, upon those aspects of his work in which he least resembles any one else. In these aspects or parts of his work we pretend to find what is individual, what is the peculiar essence of the man. We dwell with satisfaction upon the poet's difference from his predecessors, especially his immediate predecessors; we endeavour to find something that can be isolated in order to be enjoyed. Whereas if we approach a poet without this prejudice we shall often find that not only the best, but the most individual parts of his work may be those in which the dead poets, his ancestors, assert their immortality most vigorously. And I do not mean the impressionable period of adolescence, but the period of full maturity.

Yet if the only form of tradition, of handing down, consisted in following the ways of the immediate generation before us in a blind or timid adherence to its successes, "tradition" should positively be discouraged. We have seen many such simple currents soon lost in the sand; and novelty is better than repetition. Tradition is a matter of much wider significance. It cannot be inherited, and if you want it you must obtain it by great labour. It involves, in the first place, the historical sense, which we may call nearly indispensable to any one who would continue to be a poet beyond his twenty-fifth year; and the historical sense involves a perception, not only of the pastness of the past, but of its presence; the historical sense compels a man to write not merely with his own generation in his bones, but with a feeling that the whole of the literature of Europe from Homer and within it the whole of the literature of his own country has a simultaneous existence and composes a simultaneous order. This historical sense, which is a sense of the timeless as well as of the temporal and of the timeless and of the temporal together, is what makes a writer traditional. And it is at the same time what makes a writer most acutely conscious of his place in time, of his own contemporaneity.

No poet, no artist of any art, has his complete meaning alone. His significance, his appreciation is the appreciation of his relation to the dead poets and artists. You cannot value him alone; you must set him, for contrast and comparison, among the dead. I mean this as a principle of aesthetic, not merely historical, criticism. The necessity that he shall conform, that he shall cohere, is not onesided; what happens when a new work of art is created is something that happens simultaneously to all the works of art which preceded it. The existing monuments form an ideal order among themselves, which is modified by the introduction of the new (the really new) work of art among them. The existing order is complete before the new work arrives; for order to persist after the supervention of novelty, the *whole* existing order must be, if ever so slightly, altered; and so the relations, proportions, values of each work of art toward the whole are readjusted; and this is conformity between the old and the new. Whoever has approved this idea of order, of the form of European, of English literature will not find it preposterous that the past should be altered by the present as much as the present is directed by the past. And the poet who is aware of this will be aware of great difficulties and responsibilities.

In a peculiar sense he will be aware also that he must inevitably be judged by the standards of the past. I say judged, not amputated, by them; not judged to be as good as, or worse or better than, the dead; and certainly not judged by the canons of dead critics. It is a judgment, a comparison, in which two things are measured by each other. To conform merely would be for the new work not really to conform at all; it would not be new, and would therefore not be a work of art. And we do not quite say that the new is more valuable because it fits in; but its fitting in is a test of its value—a test, it is true, which can only be slowly and cautiously applied, for we are none of us infallible judges of conformity. We say: it appears to conform, and is perhaps individual, or it appears individual, and many conform; but we are hardly likely to find that it is one and not the other.

To proceed to a more intelligible exposition of the relation of the poet to the past: he can neither take the past as a lump, an indiscriminate bolus,[2] nor can he form himself wholly on one or two private admirations, nor can he form himself wholly upon one preferred period. The first course is inadmissible, the second is an important experience of youth, and the third is a pleasant and highly desirable supplement. The poet must be very conscious of the main current, which does not at all flow invariably through the most distinguished reputations. He must be quite aware of the obvious fact that art never improves, but that the material of art is never quite the same. He must be aware that the mind of Europe — the mind of his own country — a mind which he learns in time to be much more important than his own private mind — is a mind which changes, and that this change is a development which abandons nothing *en route*, which does not superannuate either Shakespeare, or Homer, or the rock drawing of the Magdalenian draughtsmen.[3] That this development, refinement perhaps, complication certainly, is not, from the point of view of the artist, any improvement. Perhaps not even an improvement from the point of view of the psychologist or not to the extent which we imagine; perhaps only in the end based upon a complication in economics and machinery. But the difference between the present and the past is that the conscious present is an awareness of the past in a way and to an extent which the past's awareness of itself cannot show.

Some one said: "The dead writers are remote from us because we *know* so much more than they did." Precisely, and they are that which we know.

I am alive to a usual objection to what is clearly part of my programme for the *métier*[4] of poetry. The objection is that the doctrine requires a ridiculous amount of erudition (pedantry), a claim which can be rejected by appeal to the lives of poets in any pantheon. It will even be affirmed that much learning deadens or perverts poetic sensibility. While, however, we persist in believing that a poet ought to know as much as will not encroach upon his necessary receptivity and necessary laziness, it is not desirable to confine knowledge to whatever can be put into a useful shape for examinations, drawing-rooms, or the still more pretentious modes of publicity. Some can absorb knowledge, the more tardy must sweat for it. Shakespeare acquired more essential history from Plutarch[5] than most men could from the whole British Museum. What is to be insisted upon is that the poet must develop or procure the consciousness of the past and that he should continue to develop this consciousness throughout his career.

What happens is a continual surrender of himself as he is at the moment to something which is more valuable. The progress of an artist is a continual self-sacrifice, a continual extinction of personality.

There remains to define this process of depersonalization and its relation to the sense of tradition. It is in this depersonalization that art may be said to approach the condition of science. I, therefore, invite you to consider, as a suggestive analogy, the action which takes place when a bit of finely filiated platinum is introduced into a chamber containing oxygen and sulphur dioxide.[6]

II

Honest criticism and sensitive appreciation are directed not upon the poet but upon the poetry. If we attend to the confused cries of the newspaper critics and the

---

[2]A round mass of medicinal material, somewhat larger than an ordinary pill.
[3]The paleolithic artists who drew the pictures on the walls of the caves in La Madeleine, southwestern France.
[4]"Craft" or "Art" (French).

[5]Greek biographer (first century A.D.), author of *Parallel Lives*, used by Shakespeare as a source for material in his history plays.
[6]The analogy is to the "catalyst" in chemistry; see the second paragraph of part II for an extension of the analogy.

susurrus[7] of popular repetition that follows, we shall hear the names of poets in great numbers; if we seek not Blue-book[8] knowledge but the enjoyment of poetry, and ask for a poem, we shall seldom find it. I have tried to point out the importance of the relation of the poem to other poems by other authors, and suggested the conception of poetry as a living whole of all the poetry that has ever been written. The other aspect of this Impersonal theory of poetry is the relation of the poem to its author. And I hinted, by an analogy, that the mind of the mature poet differs from that of the immature one not precisely in any valuation of "personality," not being necessarily more interesting, or having "more to say," but rather by being a more finely perfected medium in which special, or very varied feelings are at liberty to enter into new combinations.

The analogy was that of the catalyst. When the two gases previously mentioned are mixed in the presence of a filament of platinum, they form sulphurous acid. This combination takes place only if the platinum is present; nevertheless the newly formed acid contains no trace of platinum, and the platinum itself is apparently unaffected; has remained inert, neutral, and unchanged. The mind of the poet is the shred of platinum. It may partly or exclusively operate upon the experience of the man himself; but, the more perfect the artist, the more completely separate in him will be the man who suffers and the mind which creates; the more perfectly will the mind digest and transmute the passions which are its material.

The experience, you will notice, the elements which enter the presence of the transforming catalyst, are of two kinds: emotions and feelings. The effect of a work of art upon the person who enjoys it is an experience different in kind from any experience not of art. It may be formed out of one emotion, or may be a combination of several; and various feelings, inhering for the writer in particular words or phrases or images, may be added to compose the final result. Or great poetry may be made without the direct use of any emotion whatever: composed out of feelings solely. Canto XV of the *Inferno* (Brunetto Latini)[9] is a working up of the emotion evident in the situation; but the effect, though single as that of any work of art, is obtained by considerable complexity of detail. The last quatrain gives an image, a feeling attaching to an image, which "came," which did not develop simply out of what precedes, but which was probably in suspension in the poet's mind until the proper combination arrived for it to add itself to. The poet's mind is in fact a receptacle for seizing and storing up numberless feelings, phrases, images, which remain there until all the particles which can unite to form a new compound are present together.

If you compare several representative passages of the greatest poetry you see how great is the variety of types of combination, and also how completely any semi-ethical criterion of "sublimity" misses the mark. For it is not the "greatness," the intensity, of the emotions, the components, but the intensity of the artistic process, the pressure, so to speak, under which the fusion takes place, that counts. The episode of Paolo and Francesca[10] employs a definite emotion, but the intensity of the poetry is something quite different from whatever intensity in the supposed experience it may give the impression of. It is no more intense, furthermore, than Canto XXVI, the voyage of Ulysses,[11] which has not the direct dependence upon an emotion. Great variety is possible in the process of transmutation of emotion: the murder of Agamemnon, or the agony of Othello,[12] gives an artistic effect apparently closer to a possible original

---

[7]"Murmuring" (Latin).

[8]I.e., official government publications.

[9]Condemned for "unnatural lust," Brunetto was a Florentine philosopher assigned by Dante to eternal punishment in hell, but when Dante meets him there, they talk as friends.

[10]Famous illicit lovers treated in Canto V of Dante's *Inferno*; they were killed by Francesca's jealous husband.

[11]In Dante's *Inferno*, Canto XXVI, Ulysses tells Dante of his last voyage and death in a shipwreck; since this voyage is not described in Homer's *Odyssey*, scholars have assumed that it was invented by Dante.

[12]In the Greek tragedy *Agamemnon* by Aeschylus (525–456 B.C.), Agamemnon is murdered by his wife Clytemnestra; in Shakespeare's *Othello*, the jealous hero, believing lies about his wife's infidelity, murders her.

than the scenes from Dante. In the *Agamemnon*, the artistic emotion approximates to the emotion of an actual spectator; in *Othello* to the emotion of the protagonist himself. But the difference between art and the event is always absolute; the combination which is the murder of Agamemnon is probably as complex as that which is the voyage of Ulysses. In either case there has been a fusion of elements. The ode of Keats[13] contains a number of feelings which have nothing particular to do with the nightingale, but which the nightingale, partly, perhaps, because of its attractive name, and partly because of its reputation, served to bring together.

The point of view which I am struggling to attack is perhaps related to the metaphysical theory of the substantial unity of the soul: for my meaning is, that the poet has, not a "personality" to express, but a particular medium, which is only a medium and not a personality, in which impressions and experiences combine in peculiar and unexpected ways. Impressions and experiences which are important for the man may take no place in the poetry, and those which become important in the poetry may play quite a negligible part in the man, the personality.

I will quote a passage which is unfamiliar enough to be regarded with fresh attention in the light — or darkness — of these observations:

> And now methinks I could e'en chide myself
> For doating on her beauty, though her death
> Shall be revenged after no common action.
> Does the silkworm expend her yellow labours
> For thee? For thee does she undo herself?
> Are lordships sold to maintain ladyships
> For the poor benefit of a bewildering minute?
> Why does yon fellow falsify highways,
> And put his life between the judge's lips,
> To refine such a thing — keeps horse and men
> To beat their valours for her? . . .[14]

In this passage (as is evident if it is taken in its context) there is a combination of positive and negative emotions: an intensely strong attraction toward beauty and an equally intense fascination by the ugliness which is contrasted with it and which destroys it. This balance of contrasted emotion is in the dramatic situation to which the speech is pertinent, but that situation alone is inadequate to it. This is, so to speak, the structural emotion, provided by the drama. But the whole effect, the dominant tone, is due to the fact that a number of floating feelings, having an affinity to this emotion by no means superficially evident, have combined with it to give us a new art emotion.

It is not in his personal emotions, the emotions provoked by particular events in his life, that the poet is in any way remarkable or interesting. His particular emotions may be simple, or crude, or flat. The emotion in his poetry will be a very complex thing, but not with the complexity of the emotions of people who have very complex or unusual emotions in life. One error, in fact, of eccentricity in poetry is to seek for new human emotions to express; and in this search for novelty in the wrong place it discovers the perverse. The business of the poet is not to find new emotions, but to use the ordinary ones and, in working them up into poetry, to express feelings which are not in actual emotions at all. And emotions which he has never experienced will serve his turn as well as those familiar to him. Consequently, we must believe that "emotion recollected in tranquillity"[15] is an inexact formula. For it is neither emotion, nor recollection, nor, without distortion of meaning, tranquillity. It is a concentration, and a new thing resulting from the concentration, of a very great number of

---

[13]"Ode to a Nightingale" by John Keats (1795-1821).
[14]From *The Revenger's Tragedy*, III, v, 71-82, by Cyril Tourneur (1575?-1626).

[15]In his Preface to the second edition of *Lyrical Ballads* (1800), William Wordsworth (1774–1846) wrote that "poetry takes its origin from emotion recollected in tranquility."

experiences which to the practical and active person would not seem to be experiences at all; it is a concentration which does not happen consciously or of deliberation. These experiences are not "recollected," and they finally unite in an atmosphere which is "tranquil" only in that it is a passive attending upon the event. Of course this is not quite the whole story. There is a great deal, in the writing of poetry, which must be conscious and deliberate. In fact, the bad poet is usually unconscious where he ought to be conscious, and conscious where he ought to be unconscious. Both errors tend to make him "personal." Poetry is not a turning loose of emotion, but an escape from emotion; it is not the expression of personality, but an escape from personality. But, of course, only those who have personality and emotions know what it means to want to escape from these things.

III

ὁ δὲ νοῦς ἴσως Θειότερόν τι καὶ ἀπαθές ἐστιν.[16]

This essay proposes to halt at the frontier of metaphysics or mysticism, and confine itself to such practical conclusions as can be applied by the responsible person interested in poetry. To divert interest from the poet to the poetry is a laudable aim: for it would conduce to a juster estimation of actual poetry, good and bad. There are many people who appreciate the expression of sincere emotion in verse, and there is a smaller number of people who can appreciate technical excellence. But very few know when there is an expression of *significant* emotion, emotion which has its life in the poem and not in the history of the poet. The emotion of art is impersonal. And the poet cannot reach this impersonality without surrendering himself wholly to the work to be done. And he is not likely to know what is to be done unless he lives in what is not merely the present, but the present moment of the past, unless he is conscious, not of what is dead, but of what is already living.

1919, 1920

ROBERT FROST
(1874–1963)

In 1916, Robert Frost sent to his good friend, Louis Untermeyer, a rumination or meditation on the nature of a "good poem" and its way of coming into being. The poem, he wrote,

> *says* something, first felt and then unfolded in thought as the poem [writes] itself. That's what makes a poem. A poem is never a put-up job so to speak. It begins as a lump in the throat, a sense of wrong, a homesickness, a lovesickness. It is never a thought to begin with. It is at its best when it is a tantalizing vagueness. It finds its thought and succeeds, or doesn't find it and comes to nothing. It finds its thought or makes its thought. I suppose it finds it lying around with others not so much to its purpose in a more or less full mind. That's why it oftener comes to nothing in youth before experience has filled the mind with thoughts. It may be a big big emotion then and yet finds nothing it can embody in. It finds the thought and the thought finds the words. Let's say again: A poem particularly must not begin with thought first.

---

[16]"The mind is no doubt more divine and is not subject to emotion" (Greek); from *On the Soul*, I. 4, by Greek philosopher, Aristotle (384–322 B.C.).

At the time of setting forth this view of poetry, Frost was in his early forties and had already published two books containing some of the poems for which he is still best remembered today. His was an incorrigibly old-fashioned, somewhat romantic view of poetry. He had been shaped by the nineteenth century and held little in common with revolutionary ideas being tossed up in the twentieth-century's second decade, with its "Poetry Renaissance" seemingly determined to "make it new."

In 1935, in his early sixties, Frost wrote about this wild enthusiasm for new-ness in an introduction to a volume by Edward Arlington Robinson, who died in 1935 and for whom Frost felt a strong affinity:

> It may come to the notice of posterity . . . that this, our age, ran wild in the quest of new ways to be new. The one old way to be new no longer served. . . . Those tried were largely by subtraction—elimination. Poetry, for example, was tried without punctuation. It was tried without capital letters. It was tried without metric frame on which to measure the rhythm. It was tried without any images but those to the eye. . . . It was tried without content under the trade name of poesie pure. It was tried without phrase, epigram, coherence, logic and consis-tency. It was tried without ability. . . . It was tried without feeling or sentiment like murder for small pay in the underworld. . . .

Frost clearly identified with Robinson when he described him as content "with the old-fashioned way to be new," to "come on" (or discover) one's "difference." Frost's list of experimenters' subtractions or eliminations may be taken as a list of his own essentials—traditional poetic elements that characterize his poetry. He was one of the few poets of his time who gained and held both a critical and popular audience. He became a skilled public reader of his poetry and en-thralled audiences. As he grew old (he lived until age eighty-eight), he filled the role of America's "good gray poet" (a term first applied to Whitman) and seemed to perform as an unofficial poet laureate.

At the beginning, such a career for Frost could hardly have been foreseen. He was born not in the New England of his poems but in San Francisco, California. His parents were displaced New Englanders, his father a newspaperman as well as a drifter and drinker. The relationship between mother and father was strained, and there were separations. When William Frost died in 1885, his wife and children returned to Lawrence, Massachusetts, for the burial. They re-mained with relatives in Lawrence, where Frost attended high school. He en-tered Dartmouth College but left after one semester and held a variety of jobs—teacher, mill worker, newspaperman. His first published poem appeared in 1894 in a New York magazine, *The Independent.*

Frost married Elinor White, a high school classmate and co-valedictorian, and the first of six children was born the following year. From 1897 to 1899, Frost attended Harvard College as a special student, and then in 1900 took his family to live on a farm bought for him by his grandfather near Derry, New Hamp-shire. For the next ten years or so, Frost put in a daily stint of writing poetry, letting the manuscripts accumulate without publication. Some of his most famil-iar poems were written during this period.

In 1912, when he was thirty-eight, Frost suddenly sold his farm, uprooted his family (only four of the six children remained alive), and moved to England. Along with him came a trunk of accumulated manuscripts. Two books appeared in England in quick succession—*A Boy's Will* in 1913 and *North of Boston* in 1914.

In the meantime, Frost had met Ezra Pound, who liked his work and offered to review it in *Poetry*. A British reviewer called *North of Boston* "one of the most revolutionary books of modern times." The volume contained "Mending Wall," "After Apple-Picking," and many other poems destined to become favorites.

Frost brought his family back to America in 1915, settling on a farm in New Hampshire. A publisher brought out American editions of Frost's first two volumes, and they were well reviewed. A new volume, *Mountain Interval* (containing "The Road Not Taken" and "The Oven Bird") was published in 1916. Frost's fame began to spread, and he was elected to the National Institute of Arts and Letters. Frost's risky maneuver had worked: favorable recognition in England was followed by instant recognition in America.

But Frost was far from able to live on his income from poetry. Throughout his career, he was to put money in his purse by giving public readings of his poetry and by serving as professor of English or poet in residence at various institutions, including Amherst College in Massachusetts and the University of Michigan. In 1920 he settled on a farm in Vermont, near South Shaftsbury, and helped establish the Bread Loaf School of English at Middlebury College in Vermont.

In 1923, Frost published his *Selected Poems* and a new volume, *New Hampshire*. The latter won for Frost in 1924 the first of four Pulitzer Prizes. His *West-Running Brook* appeared in 1928, and his *Collected Poems* in 1930. The latter garnered his second Pulitzer. During the 1930s, Frost published *A Further Range* (1936), winning a third Pulitzer, and an enlarged edition of *Collected Poems* (1939). In the 1940s, he published *A Witness Tree* (1942), collecting a fourth Pulitzer, and *Steeple Bush* (1947). He also published two poetic dramas, *A Masque of Reason* (1945) and *A Masque of Mercy* (1947), introducing Biblical characters (Job, Jonah, God) in modern settings discussing religious and ethical questions. Frost's *Complete Poems* (1949) would later (after his death) incorporate *In the Clearing* (1962) to make up *The Poetry of Robert Frost* (1969).

Frost's steadily accumulating works and honors may suggest a stable life of equanimity. We know now, from Lawrance Thompson's massive biography (three volumes published in 1966, 1970, and 1976), that Frost's life was filled with emotional turbulence. During his eighty-eight years, he was forced to face many deaths—his father's in 1885, his mother's in 1900, the death of his first child (born 1896) in 1900, and the death of a daughter in the year of her birth (1907). Another daughter died of tuberculosis in 1934, and a son by suicide in 1940.

But no doubt the death that affected him most deeply was that of his wife of over forty years in 1938. Theirs had been a troubled marriage. Frost's concern for his poetic career took precedence over domestic affairs and relationships; he once remarked of his wife to his friend Louis Untermeyer: "Elinor has never been of any earthly use to me." When in a black mood about his poetic reputation, he tended to blame and abuse his family. At the end, as his wife lay dying, she refused to see her husband. Frost was filled with a complex mixture of rage and guilt and became so ill that his doctor forbade his attending the cremation.

Frost's was an egocentric and vindictive personality. He once said: "I always hold that we get forward as much by hating as by loving." His hate became manifest in his jealousy of other poets he saw as competitive or threatening. He said to a fellow poet, "I wonder do you feel as badly as I do when some other fellow does a good piece of work?" And he wrote to Louis Untermeyer, "May I be guarded and watched over always by the jealousy of a strong nature. It is better than arms around the body. Jealousy alone gives me the sense of being held."

It is possible to overemphasize the dark side of Frost, but recognition of it indicates to what extent the public personality he cultivated — that of the good gray poet — was a creation of his imagination as much as his poems, which are not so revelatory of the personal Frost as his letters. Clearly Frost savored the various honors bestowed on him — honorary degrees from Oxford and Cambridge in 1957, U.S. Senate resolutions on his seventy-fifth and eighty-fifth birthdays in 1950 and 1959, and the Bollingen Prize in Poetry in 1963. But his disappointment was deep when he was repeatedly passed over for the Nobel Prize in Literature.

His role as unofficial poet laureate was officially recognized when he read his poem "The Gift Outright" at John Kennedy's inauguration in 1961. And he went to Moscow in 1962 as cultural representative of America, where he read "Mending Wall" at a time when Russia's building of the Berlin Wall was fresh on everybody's mind in Europe and America.

When Frost died in 1963, he could indeed feel fulfilled as a poet whose "utmost of ambition is to lodge a few poems where they will be hard to get rid of." Readers are still trying to come to terms with the large body of poems he left, many choosing as favorites those that arouse nostalgia for a past rural innocence that perhaps never existed. Others hearken to Lionel Trilling, who in a 1959 landmark critical essay wrote: "I think of Robert Frost as a terrifying poet. . . . The universe that he conceives is a terrifying universe. Read the poem called 'Design' and see if you sleep the better for it. Read 'Neither Out Far nor In Deep'. . . and see if you are warmed by anything in it except the energy with which emptiness is perceived."

ADDITIONAL READING

The Letters of Robert Frost to Louis Untermeyer, 1963; *Interviews with Robert Frost*, ed. Edward Connery Lathem, 1966; *Robert Frost on Writing*, ed. Elaine Barry, 1973; *Selected Letters of Robert Frost*, ed. Lawrance Thompson, 1964.

Richard Thornton, ed., *Recognition of Robert Frost*, 1937; Lawrance Thompson, *Fire and Ice: The Art and Thought of Robert Frost*, 1942; Sidney Cox, *A Swinger of Birches*, 1957; Reginald L. Cook, *The Dimensions of Robert Frost*, 1958; Lawrance Thompson, *Robert Frost*, 1959; George W. Nitchie, *Human Values in the Poetry of Robert Frost*, 1960; John F. Lynen, *The Pastoral Art of Robert Frost*, 1960; Elizabeth Shepley Sergeant, *Robert Frost: The Trial by Existence*, 1960; Robert A. Greenberg and James G. Hepburn, eds., *Robert Frost: An Introduction*, 1961; John Robert Doyle, Jr., *The Poetry of Robert Frost*, 1962; James M. Cox, ed., *Robert Frost: A Collection of Critical Essays*, 1962; Reuben A. Brower, *The Poetry of Robert Frost: Constellations of Intentions*, 1963; Radcliffe Squires, *The Major Themes of Robert Frost*, 1963; Lawrance Thompson, *Robert Frost: The Early Years, 1874–1915*, 1966, and *Robert Frost: The Years of Triumph, 1915–1938*, 1970; Elaine Barry, *Robert Frost*, 1973; Jac L. Tharpe, ed., *Frost: Centennial Essays*, Vol. I, 1974, II, 1976, III, 1970; Frank Lentricchia, *Robert Frost: Modern Poetics and the Landscape of Self*, 1975; Frank and Melissa Lentricchia, *Robert Frost: A Bibliography*, 1976; Lawrance Thompson and R. H. Winnick, *Robert Frost: The Later Years, 1938–1963*, 1976; Richard Poirier, *Robert Frost: The Work of Knowing*, 1977; Linda W. Wagner, ed., *Robert Frost: The Critical Reception*, 1977; John C. Kemp, *Robert Frost and New England: The Poet as Regionalist*, 1979; Kathryn Gibbs Harris, *Robert Frost: Studies of the Poetry*, 1979; James L. Potter, *Robert Frost Handbook*, 1980; Philip L. Gerber, *Robert Frost*, 1982 (rev. of 1966 vol.); Philip L. Gerber, ed., *Critical Essays on Robert Frost*, 1982; Harold Bloom, ed., *Robert Frost*, 1986; George Monteiro, *Robert Frost and the New England Renaissance*, 1988.

TEXT

The Poetry of Robert Frost, ed. Edward Connery Lathem, 1969; *Selected Prose of Robert Frost*, ed. Hyde Cox and Edward Connery Lathem, 1966.

The Pasture[1]

I'm going out to clean the pasture spring;
I'll only stop to rake the leaves away
(And wait to watch the water clear, I may)
I sha'n't be gone long.—You come too.

I'm going out to fetch the little calf   5
That's standing by the mother. It's so young
It totters when she licks it with her tongue.
I sha'n't be gone long.—You come too.

1914

Mowing

There was never a sound beside the wood but one,
And that was my long scythe whispering to the ground.
What was it it whispered? I knew not well myself;
Perhaps it was something about the heat of the sun,
Something, perhaps, about the lack of sound—   5
And that was why it whispered and did not speak.
It was no dream of the gift of idle hours,
Or easy gold at the hand of fay or elf:
Anything more than the truth would have seemed too weak
To the earnest love that laid the swale in rows,   10
Not without feeble-pointed spikes of flowers
(Pale orchises), and scared a bright green snake.
The fact is the sweetest dream that labor knows.
My long scythe whispered and left the hay to make.

1913

The Tuft of Flowers

I went to turn the grass once after one
Who mowed it in the dew before the sun.

The dew was gone that made his blade so keen
Before I came to view the leveled scene.

I looked for him behind an isle of trees;   5
I listened for his whetstone on the breeze.

But he had gone his way, the grass all mown,
And I must be, as he had been—alone,

"As all must be," I said within my heart,
"Whether they work together or apart."   10

---

[1]First published as the introductory poem to *North of Boston* (1914) and later chosen by Frost to be the epigraph to his collected poems.

But as I said it, swift there passed me by
On noiseless wing a bewildered butterfly,

Seeking with memories grown dim o'er night
Some resting flower of yesterday's delight.

And once I marked his flight go round and round,   15
As where some flower lay withering on the ground.

And then he flew as far as eye could see,
And then on tremulous wing came back to me.

I thought of questions that have no reply,
And would have turned to toss the grass to dry;   20

But he turned first, and led my eye to look
As a tall tuft of flowers beside a brook,

A leaping tongue of bloom the scythe had spared
Beside a reedy brook the scythe had bared.

The mower in the dew had loved them thus,   25
By leaving them to flourish, not for us,

Nor yet to draw one thought of ours to him,
But from sheer morning gladness at the brim.

The butterfly and I had lit upon,
Nevertheless, a message from the dawn,   30

That made me hear the wakening birds around,
And hear his long scythe whispering to the ground,

And feel a spirit kindred to my own;
So that henceforth I worked no more alone;

But glad with him, I worked as with his aid,   35
And weary, sought at noon with him the shade;

And dreaming, as it were, held brotherly speech
With one whose thought I had not hoped to reach.

"Men work together," I told him from the heart,
"Whether they work together or apart."   40

1906, 1913

Mending Wall

Something there is that doesn't love a wall,
That sends the frozen-ground-swell under it
And spills the upper boulders in the sun,
And makes gaps even two can pass abreast.

The work of hunters is another thing: 5
I have come after them and made repair
Where they have left not one stone on a stone,
But they would have the rabbit out of hiding,
To please the yelping dogs. The gaps I mean,
No one has seen them made or heard them made,   10
But at spring mending-time we find them there.
I let my neighbor know beyond the hill;
And on a day we meet to walk the line
And set the wall between us once again.
We keep the wall between us as we go.   15
To each the boulders that have fallen to each.
And some are loaves and some so nearly balls
We have to use a spell to make them balance:
"Stay where you are until our backs are turned!"
We wear our fingers rough with handling them.   20
Oh, just another kind of outdoor game,
One on a side. It comes to little more:
There where it is we do not need the wall:
He is all pine and I am apple orchard.
My apple trees will never get across   25
And eat the cones under his pines, I tell him.
He only says, "Good fences make good neighbors."
Spring is the mischief in me, and I wonder
If I could put a notion in his head:
"*Why* do they make good neighbors? Isn't it   30
Where there are cows? But here there are no cows.
Before I built a wall I'd ask to know
What I was walling in or walling out,
And to whom I was like to give offense.
Something there is that doesn't love a wall,   35
That wants it down." I could say "Elves" to him,
But it's not elves exactly, and I'd rather
He said it for himself. I see him there,
Bringing a stone grasped firmly by the top
In each hand, like an old-stone savage armed.   40
He moves in darkness as it seems to me,
Not of woods only and the shade of trees.
He will not go behind his father's saying,
And he likes having thought of it so well
He says again, "Good fences make good neighbors."   45

1914

Home Burial

He saw her from the bottom of the stairs
Before she saw him. She was starting down,
Looking back over her shoulder at some fear.
She took a doubtful step and then undid it
To raise herself and look again. He spoke   5
Advancing toward her: "What is it you see
From up there always?—for I want to know."

She turned and sank upon her skirts at that,
And her face changed from terrified to dull.
He said to gain time: "What is it you see?"   10
Mounting until she cowered under him.
"I will find out now—you must tell me, dear."
She, in her place, refused him any help,
With the least stiffening of her neck and silence.
She let him look, sure that he wouldn't see,   15
Blind creature; and awhile he didn't see.
But at last he murmured, "Oh," and again, "Oh."

"What is it—what?" she said.

                                    "Just that I see."

"You don't," she challenged. "Tell me what it is."

"The wonder is I didn't see at once.   20
I never noticed it from here before.
I must be wonted to it—that's the reason.
The little graveyard where my people are!
So small the window frames the whole of it.
Not so much larger than a bedroom, is it?   25
There are three stones of slate and one of marble,
Broad-shouldered little slabs there in the sunlight
On the sidehill. We haven't to mind *those*.
But I understand: it is not the stones,
But the child's mound——"

                             "Don't, don't, don't,
    don't," she cried.   30

She withdrew, shrinking from beneath his arm
That rested on the banister, and slid downstairs;
And turned on him with such a daunting look,
He said twice over before he knew himself:
"Can't a man speak of his own child he's lost?"   35

"Not you!—Oh, where's my hat? Oh, I don't need it!
I must get out of here. I must get air.—
I don't know rightly whether any man can."

"Amy! Don't go to someone else this time.
Listen to me. I won't come down the stairs."   40
He sat and fixed his chin between his fists.
"There's something I should like to ask you, dear."

"You don't know how to ask it."

                                  "Help me, then."

Her fingers moved the latch for all reply.

"My words are nearly always an offense.   45
I don't know how to speak of anything
So as to please you. But I might be taught,

I should suppose. I can't say I see how.
A man must partly give up being a man
With womenfolk. We could have some arrangement   50
By which I'd bind myself to keep hands off
Anything special you're a-mind to name.
Though I don't like such things 'twixt those that love.
Two that don't love can't live together without them.
But two that do can't live together with them."   55
She moved the latch a little. "Don't — don't go.
Don't carry it to someone else this time.
Tell me about it if it's something human.
Let me into your grief. I'm not so much
Unlike other folks as your standing there   60
Apart would make me out. Give me my chance.
I do think, though, you overdo it a little.
What was it brought you up to think it the thing
To take your mother-loss of a first child
So inconsolably — in the face of love.   65
You'd think his memory might be satisfied——"

"There you go sneering now!"

                              "I'm not, I'm not!
You make me angry. I'll come down to you.
God, what a woman! And it's come to this,
A man can't speak of his own child that's dead."   70

"You can't because you don't know how to speak.
If you had any feelings, you that dug
With your own hand — how could you? — his little grave;
I saw you from that very window there,
Making the gravel leap and leap in air,   75
Leap up, like that, like that, and land so lightly
And roll back down the mound beside the hole.
I thought, Who is that man? I didn't know you.
And I crept down the stairs and up the stairs
To look again, and still your spade kept lifting.   80
Then you came in. I heard your rumbling voice
Out in the kitchen, and I don't know why,
But I went near to see with my own eyes.
You could sit there with the stains on your shoes
Of the fresh earth from your own baby's grave   85
And talk about your everyday concerns.
You had stood the spade up against the wall
Outside there in the entry, for I saw it."

"I shall laugh the worst laugh I ever laughed.
I'm cursed. God, if I don't believe I'm cursed."   90

"I can't repeat the very words you were saying:
'Three foggy mornings and one rainy day
Will rot the best birch fence a man can build.'
Think of it, talk like that at such a time!
What had how long it takes a birch to rot   95
To do with what was in the darkened parlor?
You *couldn't* care! The nearest friends can go

With anyone to death, comes so far short
They might as well not try to go at all.
No, from the time when one is sick to death,   100
One is alone, and he dies more alone.
Friends make pretense of following to the grave,
But before one is in it, their minds are turned
And making the best of their way back to life
And living people, and things they understand.   105
But the world's evil. I won't have grief so
If I can change it. Oh, I won't, I won't!"

"There, you have said it all and you feel better.
You won't go now. You're crying. Close the door.
The heart's gone out of it: why keep it up?   110
Amy! There's someone coming down the road!"

"*You*—oh, you think the talk is all. I must go—
Somewhere out of this house. How can I make you——"

"If—you—do!" She was opening the door wider.
"Where do you mean to go? First tell me that.   115
I'll follow and bring you back by force. I *will*!—"

                                                                      1914

After Apple-Picking

My long two-pointed ladder's sticking through a tree
Toward heaven still,
And there's a barrel that I didn't fill
Beside it, and there may be two or three
Apples I didn't pick upon some bough.   5
But I am done with apple-picking now.
Essence of winter sleep is on the night,
The scent of apples: I am drowsing off.
I cannot rub the strangeness from my sight
I got from looking through a pane of glass   10
I skimmed this morning from the drinking trough
And held against the world of hoary grass.
It melted, and I let it fall and break.
But I was well
Upon my way to sleep before it fell,   15
And I could tell
What form my dreaming was about to take.
Magnified apples appear and disappear,
Stem end and blossom end,
And every fleck of russet showing clear.   20
My instep arch not only keeps the ache,
It keeps the pressure of a ladder-round.
I feel the ladder sway as the boughs bend.
And I keep hearing from the cellar bin
The rumbling sound   25
Of load on load of apples coming in.
For I have had too much
Of apple-picking: I am overtired

Of the great harvest I myself desired.
There were ten thousand thousand fruit to touch,   30
Cherish in hand, lift down, and not let fall.
For all
That struck the earth,
No matter if not bruised or spiked with stubble,
Went surely to the cider-apple heap   35
As of no worth.
One can see what will trouble
This sleep of mine, whatever sleep it is.
Were he not gone,
The woodchuck could say whether it's like his   40
Long sleep, as I describe its coming on,
Or just some human sleep.

                                             1914

The Road Not Taken

Two roads diverged in a yellow wood,
And sorry I could not travel both
And be one traveler, long I stood
And looked down one as far as I could
To where it bent in the undergrowth;   5

Then took the other, as just as fair,
And having perhaps the better claim,
Because it was grassy and wanted wear;
Though as for that, the passing there
Had worn them really about the same,   10

And both that morning equally lay
In leaves no step had trodden black.
Oh, I kept the first for another day!
Yet knowing how way leads on to way,
I doubted if I should ever come back.   15

I shall be telling this with a sigh
Somewhere ages and ages hence:
Two roads diverged in a wood, and I—
I took the one less traveled by,
And that has made all the difference.   20

                                        1915, 1916

The Oven Bird

There is a singer everyone has heard,
Loud, a mid-summer and a mid-wood bird,
Who makes the solid tree trunks sound again.
He says that leaves are old and that for flowers
Mid-summer is to spring as one to ten.   5

He says the early petal-fall is past,
When pear and cherry bloom went down in showers
On sunny days a moment overcast;
And comes that other fall we name the fall.
He says the highway dust is over all.   10
The bird would cease and be as other birds
But that he knows in singing not to sing.
The question that he frames in all but words
Is what to make of a diminished thing.

1906–07   *1916*

Birches

When I see birches bend to left and right
Across the lines of straighter darker trees,
I like to think some boy's been swinging them.
But swinging doesn't bend them down to stay
As ice storms do. Often you must have seen them   5
Loaded with ice a sunny winter morning
After a rain. They click upon themselves
As the breeze rises, and turn many-colored
As the stir cracks and crazes their enamel.
Soon the sun's warmth makes them shed crystal shells   10
Shattering and avalanching on the snow crust—
Such heaps of broken glass to sweep away
You'd think the inner dome of heaven had fallen.
They are dragged to the withered bracken by the load,
And they seem not to break; though once they are bowed   15
So low for long, they never right themselves:
You may see their trunks arching in the woods
Years afterwards, trailing their leaves on the ground
Like girls on hands and knees that throw their hair
Before them over their heads to dry in the sun.   20
But I was going to say when Truth broke in
With all her matter of fact about the ice storm,
I should prefer to have some boy bend them
As he went out and in to fetch the cows—
Some boy too far from town to learn baseball,   25
Whose only play was what he found himself,
Summer or winter, and could play alone.
One by one he subdued his father's trees
By riding them down over and over again
Until he took the stiffness out of them,   30
And not one but hung limp, not one was left
For him to conquer. He learned all there was
To learn about not launching out too soon
And so not carrying the tree away
Clear to the ground. He always kept his poise   35
To the top branches, climbing carefully
With the same pains you use to fill a cup
Up to the brim, and even above the brim.
Then he flung outward, feet first, with a swish,
Kicking his way down through the air to the ground.   40

So was I once myself a swinger of birches.
And so I dream of going back to be.
It's when I'm weary of considerations,
And life is too much like a pathless wood
Where your face burns and tickles with the cobwebs   45
Broken across it, and one eye is weeping
From a twig's having lashed across it open.
I'd like to get away from earth awhile
And then come back to it and begin over.
May no fate willfully misunderstand me   50
And half grant what I wish and snatch me away
Not to return. Earth's the right place for love:
I don't know where it's likely to go better.
I'd like to go by climbing a birch tree,
And climb black branches up a snow-white trunk   55
Toward heaven, till the tree could bear no more,
But dipped its top and set me down again.
That would be good both going and coming back.
One could do worse than be a swinger of birches.

1913–14   1915, 1916

The Hill Wife

I. LONELINESS

HER WORD

One ought not to have to care
    So much as you and I
Care when the birds come round the house
    To seem to say good-by;

Or care so much when they come back   5
    With whatever it is they sing;
The truth being we are as much
    Too glad for the one thing

As we are too sad for the other here —
    With birds that fill their breasts   10
But with each other and themselves
    And their built or driven nests.

II. HOUSE FEAR

Always — I tell you this they learned —
Always at night when they returned
To the lonely house from far away,
To lamps unlighted and fire gone gray,
They learned to rattle the lock and key   5
To give whatever might chance to be,
Warning and time to be off in flight:
And preferring the out- to the indoor night,
They learned to leave the house door wide
Until they had lit the lamp inside.   10

III. THE SMILE

HER WORD

I didn't like the way he went away.
That smile! It never came of being gay.
Still he smiled—did you see him?—I was sure!
Perhaps because we gave him only bread
And the wretch knew from that that we were poor.   5
Perhaps because he let us give instead
Of seizing from us as he might have seized.
Perhaps he mocked at us for being wed,
Or being very young (and he was pleased
To have a vision of us old and dead).   10
I wonder how far down the road he's got.
He's watching from the woods as like as not.

IV. THE OFT-REPEATED DREAM

She had no saying dark enough
   For the dark pine that kept
Forever trying the window latch
   Of the room where they slept.

The tireless but ineffectual hands   5
   That with every futile pass
Made the great tree seem as a little bird
   Before the mystery of glass!

It never had been inside the room,
   And only one of the two   10
Was afraid in an oft-repeated dream
   Of what the tree might do.

V. THE IMPULSE

It was too lonely for her there,
   And too wild,
And since there were but two of them,
   And no child,

And work was little in the house,   5
   She was free,
And followed where he furrowed field,
   Or felled tree.

She rested on a log and tossed
   The fresh chips,   10
With a song only to herself
   On her lips.

And once she went to break a bough
   Of black alder.
She strayed so far she scarcely heard   15
   When he called her—

And didn't answer—didn't speak—
   Or return.
She stood, and then she ran and hid
   In the fern.   20

He never found her, though he looked
    Everywhere,
And he asked at her mother's house
    Was she there.

Sudden and swift and light as that   25
    The ties gave,
And he learned of finalities
    Besides the grave.

                                 1916

"Out, Out—"[1]

The buzz saw snarled and rattled in the yard
And made dust and dropped stove-length sticks of wood,
Sweet-scented stuff when the breeze drew across it.
And from there those that lifted eyes could count
Five mountain ranges one behind the other   5
Under the sunset far into Vermont.
And the saw snarled and rattled, snarled and rattled,
As it ran light, or had to bear a load.
And nothing happened: day was all but done.
Call it a day, I wish they might have said   10
To please the boy by giving him the half hour
That a boy counts so much when saved from work.
His sister stood beside them in her apron
To tell them "Supper." At the word, the saw,
As if to prove saws knew what supper meant,   15
Leaped out at the boy's hand, or seemed to leap—
He must have given the hand. However it was,
Neither refused the meeting. But the hand!
The boy's first outcry was a rueful laugh,
As he swung toward them holding up the hand,   20
Half in appeal, but half as if to keep
The life from spilling. Then the boy saw all—
Since he was old enough to know, big boy
Doing a man's work, though a child at heart—
He saw all spoiled. "Don't let him cut my hand off—   25
The doctor, when he comes. Don't let him, sister!"
So. But the hand was gone already.
The doctor put him in the dark of ether.
He lay and puffed his lips out with his breath.
And then—the watcher at his pulse took fright.   30
No one believed. They listened at his heart.
Little—less—nothing!—and that ended it.
No more to build on there. And they, since they
Were not the one dead, turned to their affairs.

                                 1916

---

[1]Cf. Shakespeare's *Macbeth*, V, v, 23–28: "Out, out, brief candle! / Life's but a walking shadow; a poor player / That struts and frets his hour upon the stage, / And then is heard no more: it is a tale / told by an idiot; full of sound and fury, / signifying nothing."

For Once, Then, Something[1]

Others taunt me with having knelt at well-curbs
Always wrong to the light, so never seeing
Deeper down in the well than where the water
Gives me back in a shining surface picture
Me myself in the summer heaven, godlike,   5
Looking out of a wreath of fern and cloud puffs.
Once, when trying with chin against a well-curb,
I discerned, as I thought, beyond the picture,
Through the picture, a something white, uncertain,
Something more of the depths — and then I lost it.   10
Water came to rebuke the too clear water.
One drop fell from a fern, and lo, a ripple
Shook whatever it was lay there at bottom,
Blurred it, blotted it out. What was that whiteness?
Truth?[2] A pebble of quartz? For once, then, something.   15

1917   *1920, 1923*

Fire and Ice

Some say the world will end in fire,
Some say in ice.
From what I've tasted of desire
I hold with those who favor fire.
But if it had to perish twice,   5
I think I know enough of hate
To say that for destruction ice
Is also great
And would suffice.

1920, 1923

The Need of Being
Versed in Country Things

The house had gone to bring again
To the midnight sky a sunset glow.
Now the chimney was all of the house that stood,
Like a pistil after the petals go.

The barn opposed across the way,   5
That would have joined the house in flame
Had it been the will of the wind, was left
To bear forsaken the place's name.

---

[1] This poem is written in hedecasyllabics, each line containing 11 syllables.
[2] Cf. Democritus, Greek philosopher of the fifth century B.C.:
"Of truth we know nothing, for truth lies at the bottom of a well" (Diogenes Laertius, *Pyrrho.* Bk. IX, sec. 72).

No more it opened with all one end
For teams that came by the stony road   10
To drum on the floor with scurrying hoofs
And brush the mow with the summer load.

The birds that came to it through the air
At broken windows flew out and in,
Their murmur more like the sigh we sigh   15
From too much dwelling on what has been.

Yet for them the lilac renewed its leaf,
And the aged elm, though touched with fire;
And the dry pump flung up an awkward arm;
And the fence post carried a strand of wire.   20

For them there was really nothing sad.
But though they rejoiced in the nest they kept,
One had to be versed in country things
Not to believe the phoebes wept.

1920, 1923

Design

I found a dimpled spider, fat and white,
On a white heal-all,[1] holding up a moth
Like a white piece of rigid satin cloth —
Assorted characters of death and blight
Mixed ready to begin the morning right,   5
Like the ingredients of a witches' broth —
A snow-drop spider, a flower like a froth,
And dead wings carried like a paper kite.

What had that flower to do with being white,
The wayside blue and innocent heal-all?   10
What brought the kindred spider to that height,
Then steered the white moth thither in the night?
What but design of darkness to appall? —
If design govern in a thing so small.

1922, 1936

Nothing Gold Can Stay

Nature's first green is gold,
Her hardest hue to hold.
Her early leaf's a flower;

---

[1] A flower, usually violet-blue, of the "self-heal" (or "heal-all")
plant, said to have healing powers.

But only so an hour.
Then leaf subsides to leaf.   5
So Eden sank to grief,
So dawn goes down to day.
Nothing gold can stay.

1923

Stopping by Woods on a Snowy Evening

Whose woods these are I think I know.
His house is in the village, though;
He will not see me stopping here
To watch his woods fill up with snow.

My little horse must think it queer   5
To stop without a farmhouse near
Between the woods and frozen lake
The darkest evening of the year.

He gives his harness bells a shake
To ask if there is some mistake.   10
The only other sound's the sweep
Of easy wind and downy flake.

The woods are lovely, dark and deep,
But I have promises to keep,
And miles to go before I sleep,   15
And miles to go before I sleep.

1923

Once by the Pacific

The shattered water made a misty din.
Great waves looked over others coming in,
And thought of doing something to the shore
That water never did to land before.
The clouds were low and hairy in the skies,   5
Like locks blown forward in the gleam of eyes.
You could not tell, and yet it looked as if
The shore was lucky in being backed by cliff,
The cliff in being backed by continent;
It looked as if a night of dark intent   10
Was coming, and not only a night, an age.
Someone had better be prepared for rage.
There would be more than ocean-water broken
Before God's last *Put out the Light* was spoken.[1]

1926, 1928

---

[1]Cf. Genesis 1:3: "And God said, Let there be light."

Acquainted with the Night

I have been one acquainted with the night.
I have walked out in rain—and back in rain.
I have outwalked the furthest city light.

I have looked down the saddest city lane.
I have passed by the watchman on his beat   5
And dropped my eyes, unwilling to explain.

I have stood still and stopped the sound of feet
When far away an interrupted cry
Came over houses from another street,

But not to call me back or say good-by;   10
And further still at an unearthly height
One luminary clock against the sky

Proclaimed the time was neither wrong nor right.
I have been one acquainted with the night.

1928

Desert Places

Snow falling and night falling fast, oh, fast
In a field I looked into going past,
And the ground almost covered smooth in snow,
But a few weeds and stubble showing last.

The woods around it have it—it is theirs.   5
All animals are smothered in their lairs.
I am too absent-spirited to count;
The loneliness includes me unawares.

And lonely as it is, that loneliness
Will be more lonely ere it will be less—   10
A blanker whiteness of benighted snow
With no expression, nothing to express.

They cannot scare me with their empty spaces
Between stars—on stars where no human race is.
I have it in me so much nearer home   15
To scare myself with my own desert places.

1934, 1936

Neither Out
Far nor In Deep

The people along the sand
All turn and look one way.
They turn their back on the land.
They look at the sea all day.

As long as it takes to pass   5
A ship keeps raising its hull;
The wetter ground like glass
Reflects a standing gull.

The land may vary more;
But wherever the truth may be—   10
The water comes ashore,
And the people look at the sea.

They cannot look out far.
They cannot look in deep.
But when was that ever a bar   15
To any watch they keep?

1934, 1936

Provide, Provide

The witch that came (the withered hag)
To wash the steps with pail and rag
Was once the beauty Abishag,[1]

The picture pride of Hollywood.
Too many fall from great and good   5
For you to doubt the likelihood.

Die early and avoid the fate.
Or if predestined to die late,
Make up your mind to die in state.

Make the whole stock exchange your own!   10
If need be occupy a throne,
Where nobody can call *you* crone.

Some have relied on what they knew,
Others on being simply true.
What worked for them might work for you.   15

---

[1]A beautiful young virgin brought in to minister to the old
and dying King David (1 Kings 1:2–4).

No memory of having starred
Atones for later disregard
Or keeps the end from being hard.

Better to go down dignified
With boughten friendship at your side   20
Than none at all. Provide, provide!

1934, 1936

The Most of It

He thought he kept the universe alone;
For all the voice in answer he could wake
Was but the mocking echo of his own
From some tree-hidden cliff across the lake.
Some morning from the boulder-broken beach   5
He would cry out on life, that what it wants
Is not its own love back in copy speech,
But counter-love, original response.
And nothing ever came of what he cried
Unless it was the embodiment that crashed   10
In the cliff's talus[1] on the other side,
And then in the far-distant water splashed,
But after a time allowed for it to swim,
Instead of proving human when it neared
And someone else additional to him,   15
As a great buck it powerfully appeared,
Pushing the crumpled water up ahead,
And landed pouring like a waterfall,
And stumbled through the rocks with horny tread,
And forced the underbrush—and that was all.   20

1942

Never Again Would
Birds' Song Be the Same

He would declare and could himself believe
That the birds there in all the garden round
From having heard the daylong voice of Eve
Had added to their own an oversound,
Her tone of meaning but without the words.   5
Admittedly an eloquence so soft
Could only have had an influence on birds
When call or laughter carried it aloft.

---

[1]Slope formed by accumulated debris.

Be that as may be, she was in their song.
Moreover her voice upon their voices crossed   10
Had now persisted in the woods so long
That probably it never would be lost.
Never again would birds' song be the same.
And to do that to birds was why she came.

1942

The Gift Outright[1]

The land was ours before we were the land's.
She was our land more than a hundred years
Before we were her people. She was ours
In Massachusetts, in Virginia,
But we were England's, still colonials,   5
Possessing what we still were unpossessed by,
Possessed by what we now no more possessed.
Something we were withholding made us weak
Until we found out that it was ourselves   10
We were withholding from our land of living,
And forthwith found salvation in surrender.
Such as we were we gave ourselves outright
(The deed of gift was many deeds of war)
To the land vaguely realizing westward,
But still unstoried, artless, unenhanced,   15
Such as she was, such as she would become.

1942

Directive

Back out of all this now too much for us,
Back in a time made simple by the loss
Of detail, burned, dissolved, and broken off
Like graveyard marble sculpture in the weather,
There is a house that is no more a house   5
Upon a farm that is no more a farm
And in a town that is no more a town.
The road there, if you'll let a guide direct you
Who only has at heart your getting lost,
May seem as if it should have been a quarry—   10
Great monolithic knees the former town
Long since gave up pretense of keeping covered.
And there's a story in a book about it:
Besides the wear of iron wagon wheels
The ledges show lines ruled southeast-northwest,   15

---

[1]Frost recited this poem at the inauguration of President
John F. Kennedy in January 1961.

The chisel work of an enormous Glacier
That braced his feet against the Arctic Pole.
You must not mind a certain coolness from him
Still said to haunt this side of Panther Mountain.
Nor need you mind the serial ordeal   20
Of being watched from forty cellar holes
As if by eye pairs out of forty firkins.[1]
As for the woods' excitement over you
That sends light rustle rushes to their leaves
Charge that to upstart inexperience.   25
Where were they all not twenty years ago?
They think too much of having shaded out
A few old pecker-fretted apple trees.
Make yourself up a cheering song of how
Someone's road home from work this once was,   30
Who may be just ahead of you on foot
Or creaking with a buggy load of grain.
The height of the adventure is the height
Of country where two village cultures faded
Into each other. Both of them are lost.   35
And if you're lost enough to find yourself
By now, pull in your ladder road behind you
And put a sign up CLOSED to all but me.
Then make yourself at home. The only field
Now left's no bigger than a harness gall.[2]   40
First there's the children's house of make-believe,
Some shattered dishes underneath a pine,
The playthings in the playhouse of the children.
Weep for what little things could make them glad.
Then for the house that is no more a house,   45
But only a belilaced cellar hole,
Now slowly closing like a dent in dough.
This was no playhouse but a house in earnest.
Your destination and your destiny's
A brook that was the water of the house,   50
Cold as a spring as yet so near its source,
Too lofty and original to rage.
(We know the valley streams that when aroused
Will leave their tatters hung on barb and thorn.)
I have kept hidden in the instep arch   55
Of an old cedar at the waterside
A broken drinking goblet like the Grail[3]
Under a spell so the wrong ones can't find it,
So can't get saved, as Saint Mark says they mustn't.[4]
(I stole the goblet from the children's playhouse.)   60
Here are your waters and your watering place.
Drink and be whole again beyond confusion.

1946, 1947

---

[1]Small wooden barrels for storing butter, cheese, or lard.
[2]Sore caused by friction of the harness.
[3]In medieval legend, the cup used by Christ at the Last Supper and the object of chivalrous quests.
[4]Cf. Mark 4:11–12, in which Jesus says to his disciples: "Unto you it is given to know the mystery of the kingdom of God: but unto them that are without, all these things were done in parables: That seeing they may see, and not perceive; and hearing they may hear, and not understand; lest at any time they should be converted, and their sins should be forgiven them." Regarding this reference to St. Mark, Frost has said, "Saint Mark says that these things of Christ are said in parables so the wrong ones won't understand them and then get saved. It seems that people weren't meant to be saved if they didn't understand figures of speech" (S. P. C. Duvall, *American Literature*, January 1960, p. 487).

The Figure a Poem Makes[1]

Abstraction is an old story with the philosophers, but it has been like a new toy in the hands of the artists of our day. Why can't we have any one quality of poetry we choose by itself? We can have in thought. Then it will go hard if we can't in practice. Our lives for it.

Granted no one but a humanist much cares how sound a poem is if it is only *a* sound. The sound is the gold in the ore. Then we will have the sound out alone and dispense with the inessential. We do till we make the discovery that the object in writing poetry is to make all poems sound as different as possible from each other, and the resources for that of vowels, consonants, punctuation, syntax, words, sentences, meter are not enough. We need the help of context—meaning—subject matter. That is the greatest help towards variety. All that can be done with words is soon told. So also with meters—particularly in our language where there are virtually but two, strict iambic and loose iambic. The ancients with many were still poor if they depended on meters for all tune. It is painful to watch our sprung-rhythmists[2] straining at the point of omitting one short from a foot for relief from monotony. The possibilities for tune from the dramatic tones of meaning struck across the rigidity of a limited meter are endless. And we are back in poetry as merely one more art of having something to say, sound or unsound. Probably better if sound, because deeper and from wider experience.

Then there is this wildness whereof it is spoken. Granted again that it has an equal claim with sound to being a poem's better half. If it is a wild tune, it is a poem. Our problem then is, as modern abstractionists, to have the wildness pure; to be wild with nothing to be wild about. We bring up as aberrationists, giving way to undirected associations and kicking ourselves from one chance suggestion to another in all directions as of a hot afternoon in the life of a grasshopper. Theme alone can steady us down. Just as the first mystery was how a poem could have a tune in such a straightness as meter, so the second mystery is how a poem can have wildness and at the same time a subject that shall be fulfilled.

It should be of the pleasure of a poem itself to tell how it can. The figure a poem makes. It begins in delight and ends in wisdom. The figure is the same as for love. No one can really hold that the ecstasy should be static and stand still in one place. It begins in delight, it inclines to the impulse, it assumes direction with the first line laid down, it runs a course of lucky events, and ends in a clarification of life—not necessarily a great clarification, such as sects and cults are founded on, but in a momentary stay against confusion. It has denouement. It has an outcome that though unforeseen was predestined from the first image of the original mood—and indeed from the very mood. It is but a trick poem and no poem at all if the best of it was thought of first and saved for the last. It finds its own name as it goes and discovers the best waiting for it in some final phrase at once wise and sad—the happy-sad blend of the drinking song.

No tears in the writer, no tears in the reader. No surprise for the writer, no surprise for the reader. For me the initial delight is in the surprise of remembering something I didn't know I knew. I am in a place, in a situation, as if I had materialized from cloud or risen out of the ground. There is a glad recognition of the long lost and the rest follows. Step by step the wonder of unexpected supply keeps growing. The impressions most useful to my purpose seem always those I was unaware of and so made no note of at the time when taken, and the conclusion is come to that like giants we are always hurling experience ahead of us to pave the future with against

---

[1]This essay was first published as an introduction to *The Collected Poems of Robert Frost* (1939).
[2]"Sprung rhythm" was coined by the English poet Gerard

Manley Hopkins (1844–1889) to describe his nontraditional metrical system of stressed and unstressed syllables within a foot.

the day when we may want to strike a line of purpose across it for somewhere. The line will have the more charm for not being mechanically straight. We enjoy the straight crookedness of a good walking stick. Modern instruments of precision are being used to make things crooked as if by eye and hand in the old days.

I tell how there may be a better wildness of logic than of inconsequence. But the logic is backward, in retrospect, after the act. It must be more felt than seen ahead like prophecy. It must be a revelation, or a series of revelations, as much for the poet as for the reader. For it to be that there must have been the greatest freedom of the material to move about in it and to establish relations in it regardless of time and space, previous relation, and everything but affinity. We prate of freedom. We call our schools free because we are not free to stay away from them till we are sixteen years of age. I have given up my democratic prejudices and now willingly set the lower classes free to be completely taken care of by the upper classes. Political freedom is nothing to me. I bestow it right and left. All I would keep for myself is the freedom of my material—the condition of body and mind now and then to summons aptly from the vast chaos of all I have lived through.

Scholars and artists thrown together are often annoyed at the puzzle of where they differ. Both work from knowledge; but I suspect they differ most importantly in the way their knowledge is come by. Scholars get theirs with conscientious thoroughness along projected lines of logic; poets theirs cavalierly and as it happens in and out of books. They stick to nothing deliberately, but let what will stick to them like burrs where they walk in the fields. No acquirement is on assignment, or even self-assignment. Knowledge of the second kind is much more available in the wild free ways of wit and art. A schoolboy may be defined as one who can tell you what he knows in the order in which he learned it. The artist must value himself as he snatches a thing from some previous order in time and space into a new order with not so much as a ligature clinging to it of the old place where it was organic.

More than once I should have lost my soul to radicalism if it had been the originality it was mistaken for by its young converts. Originality and initiative are what I ask for my country. For myself the originality need be no more than the freshness of a poem run in the way I have described: from delight to wisdom. The figure is the same as for love. Like a piece of ice on a hot stove the poem must ride on its own melting. A poem may be worked over once it is in being, but may not be worried into being. Its most precious quality will remain its having run itself and carried away the poet with it. Read it a hundred times: it will forever keep its freshness as a petal keeps its fragrance. It can never lose its sense of a meaning that once unfolded by surprise as it went.

1939

WALLACE STEVENS
(1879–1955)

In "Of Modern Poetry," Wallace Stevens was in effect describing the whole body of his poetry when he defined the modern poem as the "poem of the mind in the act of finding what will suffice." Questioned about one of his poems in 1940, he wrote: "I ought to say that it is a habit of mind with me to be thinking of some substitute for religion. I don't necessarily mean some substitute for the church, because no one believes in the church as an institution more than I do. My trouble, and the trouble of a great many people, is the loss of belief in the sort of God in Whom we were all brought up to believe." When asked to write about himself by a journal publishing some of his poems, he wrote in 1954 (the year before he died): "The author's work suggests the possibility of a supreme fiction, recognised as a fiction, in which men could propose to themselves a fulfillment. In the creation of any such fiction, poetry would have a vital significance. There are many poems relating to the interactions between reality and the imagination, which are to be regarded as marginal to this central theme."

It is easy to see, given Stevens's view of the serious role of poetry in life, that he could say and mean, "To me, poetry is not a literary activity: it is a vital activity." Yet Stevens lived the full life of a businessman and a family man, writing poetry when he found moments free from a busy schedule. He was born in Reading, Pennsylvania, to a father described by Stevens as "a lawyer, a Presbyterian, and a Democrat." He added, "I have ceased to be all these things."

Stevens graduated from high school in Reading and attended Harvard (1897–1900). There he began to write poetry, composing a sonnet that caught the attention of the philosopher-professor George Santayana, who became a lifelong influence. After leaving Harvard, Stevens worked in New York as a reporter, but soon gave in to his father's wish that he go to law school. He took a law degree in 1903 and was admitted to the New York bar in 1904.

For the next few years Stevens practiced law in New York. In 1908 he found his position secure enough to marry Elsie Kachel whom he had met in Reading a few years before. From the start there seemed to be some friction. She disliked New York and Stevens's "Bohemian" friends—Alfred Kreymborg (editor of *Others*), Carl Van Vechten, William Carlos Williams, Marianne Moore, and others. And as it turned out, she had little interest in poetry and found Stevens's passionate devotion to it puzzling if not annoying. In 1916, Stevens took an executive position with the Hartford Accident and Indemnity Company in Hartford, Connecticut, where he would remain the rest of his life, devoting himself to business and poetry. His winter vacations in Florida became the source of much of the lush, exotic imagery of his poems.

Gradually Stevens began to appear in print in the little magazines. Four poems appeared in the "War Number" of *Poetry* magazine in 1914, and an altered version of "Sunday Morning" appeared there the following year. By the early 1920s, Stevens had published enough poems to fill a volume. But he was uncertain that he was ready. After finishing his long poem "The Comedian as the Letter C" in 1922, he decided he had the "ballast" for a volume. *Harmonium* appeared in 1923. Despite enthusiastic reviews in *Poetry* and *The Dial*, sales were small, and the book was quickly remaindered.

Stevens was disappointed and seems to have quit writing poetry for the next several years. An expanded edition of *Harmonium* was published in 1931, with fourteen additional poems, and the reception (especially reviews by Morton D. Zabel and R. P. Blackmur) made it clear that Stevens was a poet who could not be ignored. *Ideas of Order*, published in 1936, contained what were to become some of Stevens's most admired poems, including "The Idea of Order at Key West." But in the middle of the Great Depression, politically conscious critics found the poetry too remote from the realities of the hard times. Stevens attempted to answer his critics in *Owl's Clover* in 1936 (especially in "Mr. Burnshaw and the Statue"), obliquely attacking the view that poetry should be the vehicle for dogma or propaganda. But Stevens himself rejected the poem when he later brought out his *Collected Poems*.

By now Stevens must have become inured to misunderstanding or negative criticism of his poems. He continued to write and publish. A major poem (and statement) appeared in 1937 in *"The Man with the Blue Guitar" and Other Poems*. The title poem was a masterpiece, using a Picasso painting of a man playing a guitar as symbolic of the artist-poet mediating with finesse and discrimination between the world of reality and the world of imagination. When pressed later to answer questions about the meaning of the poem, Stevens said: "Poetry is a passion, not a habit. This passion nourishes itself on reality. Imagination has no source except in reality, and ceases to have any value when it departs from reality. Here is a fundamental principle about the imagination: It does not create except as it transforms. There is nothing that exists exclusively by reason of the imagination, or that does not exist in some form in reality. Thus reality = the imagination, and the imagination = reality. Imagination gives, but gives in relation."

This theme, of the complicated interrelationship of imagination and reality, and the relevance of that theme to the problem of belief (the search for a "supreme fiction") became the obsessive subject of Stevens's poetry. He worked remarkable variations in treating it, but he would not let it go — or, more likely, it would not let go of him. It was sounded in a minor note in many short poems. But it came into central focus in *Notes Toward a Supreme Fiction* in 1942. This long poem is arguably Stevens's masterpiece, his most comprehensive meditation on the perplexing metaphysical questions of belief, or how to believe, or what to believe. He wrote to a friend in 1943: "I ought to say I have not defined a supreme fiction. . . . In principle there appear to be certain characteristics of a supreme fiction, *and the Notes is confined to a statement* of a few of those characteristics. As I see the subject, it could occupy a school of rabbis for the next few generations. In trying to create something as valid as the idea of God has been, and for that matter remains, the first necessity seems to be breadth."

Now in his mid-sixties, Stevens continued to write and publish. *Transport to Summer* appeared in 1947, and *The Auroras of Autumn* in 1950. In the latter year he was awarded the Bollingen Prize in Poetry. In 1951 he put together his prose in *The Necessary Angel: Essays on Reality and the Imagination*. After publishing his *Collected Poems* in 1954, he was awarded the Pulitzer Prize and the National Book Award. The year of these honors (1955) was also the year of his death.

The Collected Poems contained a final section of new poems, including his elegy to Santayana, "To an Old Philosopher in Rome," and a last poem that seemed to work variations on a William Carlos Williams saying ("No ideas but in things"); Stevens revised Williams thus: "Not Ideas About the Thing But the Thing Itself." Stevens had wanted to call this comprehensive collection *The Whole of Harmonium*, perhaps in the belief that his individual volumes brought together formed an organic whole reflecting a spiritual-intellectual journey of the twentieth century, as Walt Whitman's deathbed edition of *Leaves of Grass* of 1892 represented such a journey of the nineteenth. In any event, many long-time interpreters of Stevens believe his poetry is best encountered in the arrangement he made of it in *Collected Poems*.

William Carlos Williams had two occasions on which to do a summing up of Stevens, on Stevens's seventy-fifth birthday in 1954 and on reviewing *Opus Posthumous: Poems, Plays, Prose* when it appeared in 1957. On the two occasions he focused on language, but with different emphases. On the first he said, "It's the infinite variety of resource in the phrasing of his poetic ideas that has kept Stevens alive for us the past thirty to forty years. It was there in the first poems, and is still there in *The Auroras of Autumn. . . .*" On the second occasion Williams said: "That Stevens could stand firm once he had established his ground is attested by the aspect of the poems themselves — full of a special whimsy permitted by the solidity of his reasoning. He permitted himself to go to the adventurous limits of his vocabulary, to stand on the point of a needle because he felt perfectly secure there, knowing the rest of the universe to be unstable."

ADDITIONAL READING

Letters of Wallace Stevens, ed. Holly Stevens, 1966; *The Palm at the End of the Mind: Selected Poems and a Play*, ed. Holly Stevens, 1971.

William Van O'Connor, *The Shaping Spirit: A Study of Wallace Stevens*, 1950; Robert Pack, *Wallace Stevens: An Approach to His Poetry and Thought*, 1958; Frank Kermode, *Wallace Stevens*, 1960; Ashley Brown and Robert S. Haller, eds., *The Achievement of Wallace Stevens*, 1962; Daniel Fuchs, *The Comic Spirit of Wallace Stevens*, 1963; Marie Borroff, ed., *Wallace Stevens: A Collection of Critical Essays*, 1963; Thomas F. Walsh, *Concordance to the Poetry of Wallace Stevens*, 1963; Roy Harvey Pearce and J. Hillis Miller, eds., *The Act of the Mind: Essays on the Poetry of Wallace Stevens*, 1963; John J. Enck, *Wallace Stevens: Image and Judgments*, 1964; Joseph N. Riddel, *The Clairvoyant Eye: The Poetry and Poetics of Wallace Stevens*, 1965; Eugene Paul Nasser, *Wallace Stevens: An Anatomy of Figuration*, 1965; Louis L. Martz, *The Poem of the Mind*, 1966; Frank Doggett, *Stevens' Poetry of Thought*, 1966; Robert Buttel, *Wallace Stevens: The Making of Harmonium*, 1967; Ronald Sukenick, *Wallace Stevens: Musing the Obscure*, 1967; Frank Lentricchia, *The Gaiety of Language: An Essay on the Radical Poetics of William Butler Yeats and Wallace Stevens*, 1968; William Burney, *Wallace Stevens*, 1968; James Baird, *The Dome and the Rock: Structure in the Poetry of Wallace Stevens*, 1968; Helen Vendler, *On Extended Wings: Wallace Stevens' Longer Poems*, 1969; Samuel French Morse, *Wallace Stevens: Poetry as Life*, 1970; Irvin Ehrenpreis, ed., *Wallace Stevens: A Critical Anthology*, 1972; Michel Benamou, *Wallace Stevens and the Symbolist Imagination*, 1972; A. Walton Litz, *Introspective Voyager: The Poetic Development of Wallace Stevens*, 1972; Edward Kessler, *Images of Wallace Stevens*, 1972; J. M. Edelstein, *Wallace Stevens: A Descriptive Bibliography*, 1974; Lucy Beckett, *Wallace Stevens*, 1974; Diane Wood Middlebrook, *Walt Whitman and Wallace Stevens*, 1974; Alan Perlis, *Wallace Stevens: A World of Transforming Shapes*, 1976; Harold Bloom, *Wallace Stevens: The Poems of Our Climate*, 1977; Holly Stevens, *Souvenirs and Prophecies: The Young Wallace Stevens*, 1977; Susan B. Weston, *Wallace Stevens: An Introduction to the Poetry*, 1977; Abbie F. Willard, *Wallace Stevens: The Poet and His Critics*, 1978; Frank Doggett and Robert Buttel, eds., *Wallace Stevens: A Celebration*, 1980; Peter Brazeau, *Parts of a World: Wallace Stevens Remembered, An Oral Biography*, 1983; David M. La Guardia, *Advance on Chaos: The Sanctifying Imagination of Wallace Stevens*, 1983; Helen Vendler, *Wallace Stevens: Words Chosen Out of Desire*, 1984; Charles Doyle, ed., *Wallace Stevens: The Critical Heritage*, 1985; Albert Gelpi, ed., *Wallace Stevens: The Poetics of Modernism*, 1985; Jacqueline Vaught Brogan, *Stevens and Simile: A Theory of Language*, 1986; Milton J. Bates, *A Mythology of Self*, 1986; George Lensing, *Wallace Stevens: A Poet's Growth*, 1986; Joan Richardson, *Wallace Stevens: The Early Years, 1879–1923*, 1986; Joseph Carroll, *Wallace Stevens' Supreme Fiction: A New Romanticism*, 1987; Joan Richardson, *Wallace Stevens: The Later Years, 1928–1955*, 1988; Eleanor Cook, *Poetry, Word-Play, and Word-War in Wallace Stevens*, 1988.

TEXTS

The Collected Poems of Wallace Stevens, 1954; *The Necessary Angel: Essays on Reality and Imagination*, 1951; *Opus Posthumous: Poems, Plays, Prose*, 1957.

Sunday Morning[1]

I

Complacencies of the peignoir,[2] and late
Coffee and oranges in a sunny chair,
And the green freedom of a cockatoo
Upon a rug mingle to dissipate
The holy hush of ancient sacrifice.[3]   5
She dreams a little, and she feels the dark

---

[1]There are two voices in the poem, that of the poet (or his persona) describing the lady, and that of the lady who makes comments or asks questions (as in stanzas IV and V) answered by the poet. "This is not essentially a woman's meditation on religion and the meaning of life. It is anybody's meditation. To judge from your comment on II, you are taking the thing a little too literally. The poem is simply an expression of paganism, although, of course, I did not think that I was expressing paganism when I wrote it" (Stevens to L. W. Payne, 1928, *Letters*).
[2]Dressing gown.
[3]The crucifixion of Christ.

Encroachment of that old catastrophe,
As a calm darkens among water-lights.
The pungent oranges and bright, green wings
Seem things in some procession of the dead,   10
Winding across wide water, without sound.
The day is like wide water, without sound,
Stilled for the passing of her dreaming feet
Over the seas, to silent Palestine,
Dominion of the blood and sepulchre.[4]   15

II

Why should she give her bounty to the dead?
What is divinity if it can come
Only in silent shadows and in dreams?
Shall she not find in comforts of the sun,
In pungent fruit and bright, green wings, or else   20
In any balm or beauty of the earth,
Things to be cherished like the thought of heaven?
Divinity must live within herself:
Passions of rain, or moods in falling snow;
Grievings in loneliness, or unsubdued   25
Elations when the forest blooms; gusty
Emotions on wet roads on autumn nights;
All pleasures and all pains, remembering
The bough of summer and the winter branch.
These are the measures destined for her soul.   30

III

Jove[5] in the clouds had his inhuman birth.
No mother suckled him, no sweet land gave
Large-mannered motions to his mythy mind
He moved among us, as a muttering king,
Magnificent, would move among his hinds,   35
Until our blood, commingling, virginal,[6]
With heaven, brought such requital to desire
The very hinds[7] discerned it, in a star.
Shall our blood fail? Or shall it come to be
The blood of paradise? And shall the earth   40
Seem all of paradise that we shall know?
The sky will be much friendlier then than now,
A part of labor and a part of pain,
And next in glory to enduring love,
Not this dividing and indifferent blue.   45

IV

She says, "I am content when wakened birds,
Before they fly, test the reality
Of misty fields, by their sweet questionings;
But when the birds are gone, and their warm fields
Return no more, where, then, is paradise?"   50
There is not any haunt of prophecy,
Nor any old chimera[8] of the grave,
Neither the golden underground,[9] nor isle

[4]The burial of Christ.
[5]Supreme god in Roman mythology (Zeus in Greek).
[6]Mary became pregnant through the Holy Spirit, and thus remained virgin.
[7]Peasants.
[8]Illusion or fanciful myth.
[9]The Elysian fields of classical mythology.

Melodious,[10] where spirits gat them home,
Nor visionary south, nor cloudy palm[11]   55
Remote on heaven's hill, that has endured
As April's green endures; or will endure
Like her remembrance of awakened birds,
Or her desire for June and evening, tipped
By the consummation of the swallow's wings.   60

V

She says, "But in contentment I still feel
The need of some imperishable bliss."
Death is the mother of beauty; hence from her,
Alone, shall come fulfilment to our dreams
And our desires. Although she strews the leaves   65
Of sure obliteration on our paths,
The path sick sorrow took, the many paths
Where triumph rang its brassy phrase, or love
Whispered a little out of tenderness,
She makes the willow shiver in the sun   70
For maidens who were wont to sit and gaze
Upon the grass, relinquished to their feet.
She causes boys to pile new plums and pears
On disregarded plate.[12] The maidens taste
And stray impassioned in the littering leaves.   75

VI

Is there no change of death in paradise?
Does ripe fruit never fall? Or do the boughs
Hang always heavy in that perfect sky,
Unchanging, yet so like our perishing earth,
With rivers like our own that seek for seas   80
They never find, the same receding shores
That never touch with inarticulate pang?
Why set the pear upon those river-banks
Or spice the shores with odors of the plum?
Alas, that they should wear our colors there,   85
The silken weavings of our afternoons,
And pick the strings of our insipid lutes!
Death is the mother of beauty, mystical,
Within whose burning bosom we devise
Our earthly mothers waiting, sleeplessly.   90

VII

Supple and turbulent, a ring of men[13]
Shall chant in orgy on a summer morn
Their boisterous devotion to the sun,
Not as a god, but as a god might be,
Naked among them, like a savage source.   95
Their chant shall be a chant of paradise,
Out of their blood, returning to the sky;
And in their chant shall enter, voice by voice,

---

[10]The island Avalon where King Arthur was carried by boat after death.
[11]The palm was used in the celebration of Christ's arrival in Jerusalem; thus, Palm Sunday, the Sunday before Easter.

[12]I.e., silver (plate) dishes.
[13]When Stevens was asked by Hi Simons in 1944 if stanzas III and VII were meant to suggest a "naturalistic religion as a substitute for supernaturalism," Stevens replied, "Yes."

The windy lake wherein their lord delights,
The trees, like serafin, and echoing hills,   100
That choir among themselves long afterward.
They shall know well the heavenly fellowship
Of men that perish and of summer morn.
And whence they came and whither they shall go
The dew upon their feet shall manifest.[14]   105

VIII

She hears, upon that water without sound,
A voice that cries, "The tomb in Palestine
Is not the porch of spirits lingering.[15]
It is the grave of Jesus, where he lay."
We live in an old chaos of the sun,   110
Or old dependency of day and night,
Or island solitude, unsponsored, free,
Of that wide water, inescapable.
Deer walk upon our mountains, and the quail
Whistle about us their spontaneous cries;   115
Sweet berries ripen in the wilderness;
And, in the isolation of the sky,
At evening, casual flocks of pigeons make
Ambiguous undulations as they sink,
Downward to darkness, on extended wings.   120

1915, 1923

Peter Quince at the Clavier[1]

I

Just as my fingers on these keys
Make music, so the selfsame sounds
On my spirit make a music, too.

Music is feeling, then, not sound;
And thus it is that what I feel,   5
Here in this room, desiring you,

Thinking of your blue-shadowed silk,
Is music. It is like the strain
Waked in the elders by Susanna.[2]

Of a green evening, clear and warm,   10
She bathed in her still garden, while
The red-eyed elders watching, felt

---

[14]"Of the last two lines [of stanza VII], it is probably the last that is obscure to you. Life is as fugitive as dew upon the feet of men dancing in dew. Men do not either come from any direction or disappear in any direction. Life is as meaningless as dew" (Stevens to Payne, 1928).
[15]When the friends of Jesus found his tomb empty, an angel told them: "He is not here: for he is risen" (Matthew 28:6).
[1]Peter Quince, in Shakespeare's *Midsummer Night's Dream*, is the stage manager of the inserted play "Pyramus and Thisbe." Here he is at the keyboard (clavier), perhaps of a harmonium (a reed organ).
[2]The story of Susanna and the Elders appears in one of the Apocrypha, "The Book of Susanna," in which the elders observe Susanna (wife of Joachim) at her bath and try to seduce her; when she accuses them, they say that she lured them on. Susanna was found innocent, and the elders were executed.

The basses of their beings throb
In witching chords, and their thin blood
Pulse pizzicati of Hosanna.[3]   15

II

In the green water, clear and warm,
Susanna lay.
She searched
The touch of springs,
And found   20
Concealed imaginings.
She sighed,
For so much melody.

Upon the bank, she stood
In the cool   25
Of spent emotions.
She felt, among the leaves,
The dew
Of old devotions.

She walked upon the grass,   30
Still quavering.
The winds were like her maids,
On timid feet,
Fetching her woven scarves,
Yet wavering.   35

A breath upon her hand
Muted the night.
She turned—
A cymbal crashed,
And roaring horns.   40

III

Soon, with a noise like tambourines,
Came her attendant Byzantines.

They wondered why Susanna cried
Against the elders by her side;

And as they whispered, the refrain   45
Was like a willow swept by rain.

Anon, their lamps' uplifted flame
Revealed Susanna and her shame.

And then, the simpering Byzantines
Fled, with a noise like tambourines.   50

IV

Beauty is momentary in the mind—
The fitful tracing of a portal;

---

[3]In music, "pizzicato" means to pluck rather than to use the
bow in sounding the strings of an instrument; "Hosanna" is a
shout of praise to God.

But in the flesh it is immortal.
The body dies; the body's beauty lives.
So evenings die, in their green going,   55
A wave, interminably flowing.
So gardens die, their meek breath scenting
The cowl of winter, done repenting.
So maidens die, to the auroral
Celebration of a maiden's choral.   60
Susanna's music touched the bawdy strings
Of those white elders; but, escaping,
Left only Death's ironic scraping.
Now, in its immortality, it plays
On the clear viol of her memory,   65
And makes a constant sacrament of praise.

1915, 1923

Domination of Black[1]

At night, by the fire,
The colors of the bushes
And of the fallen leaves,
Repeating themselves,
Turned in the room,   5
Like the leaves themselves
Turning in the wind.
Yes: but the color of the heavy hemlocks
Came striding.
And I remembered the cry of the peacocks.   10

The colors of their tails
Were like the leaves themselves
Turning in the wind,
In the twilight wind.
They swept over the room,   15
Just as they flew from the boughs of the hemlocks
Down to the ground.
I heard them cry—the peacocks.
Was it a cry against the twilight
Or against the leaves themselves   20
Turning in the wind,
Turning as the flames
Turned in the fire,
Turning as the tails of the peacocks
Turned in the loud fire,   25
Loud as the hemlocks
Full of the cry of the peacocks?
Or was it a cry against the hemlocks?

---

[1]"I am sorry that a poem of this sort has to contain any ideas at all, because its sole purpose is to fill the mind with the images & sounds that it contains. A mind that examines such a poem for its prose contents gets absolutely nothing from it. You are supposed to get heavens full of the colors and full of sounds, and you are supposed to feel as you would feel if you actually got all this" (Stevens to L. W. Payne, 1928, *Letters*).

Out of the window,
I saw how the planets gathered   30
Like the leaves themselves
Turning in the wind.
I saw how the night came,
Came striding like the color of the heavy hemlocks
I felt afraid.   35
And I remembered the cry of the peacocks.

1916, 1923

Thirteen Ways of
Looking at a Blackbird[1]

I

Among twenty snowy mountains,
The only moving thing
Was the eye of the blackbird.

II

I was of three minds,
Like a tree   5
In which there are three blackbirds.

III

The blackbird whirled in the autumn winds.
It was a small part of the pantomime.

IV

A man and a woman
Are one.   10
A man and a woman and a blackbird
Are one.

V

I do not know which to prefer,
The beauty of inflections
Or the beauty of innuendoes,   15
The blackbird whistling
Or just after.

VI

Icicles filled the long window
With barbaric glass.
The shadow of the blackbird   20
Crossed it, to and fro.
The mood
Traced in the shadow
An indecipherable cause.

---

[1]I.e., an example of the ways the imagination may impose order on reality; the number thirteen has in folklore been considered a symbol of death and birth and as an unlucky number.

VII

O thin men of Haddam,[2]   25
Why do you imagine golden birds?
Do you not see how the blackbird
Walks around the feet
Of the women about you?

VIII

I know noble accents   30
And lucid, inescapable rhythms;
But I know, too,
That the blackbird is involved
In what I know.

IX

When the blackbird flew out of sight,   35
It marked the edge
Of one of many circles.

X

At the sight of blackbirds
Flying in a green light,
Even the bawds of euphony   40
Would cry out sharply.[3]

XI

He rode over Connecticut
In a glass coach.
Once, a fear pierced him,
In that he mistook   45
The shadow of his equipage
For blackbirds.

XII

The river is moving.
The blackbird must be flying.[4]

XIII

It was evening all afternoon.   50
It was snowing
And it was going to snow.
The blackbird sat
In the cedar-limbs.[5]

1917, 1923

---

[2]"The thin men of Haddam are entirely fictitious although some years ago one of the citizens of that place wrote to me to ask what I had in mind. I just like the name. It is an old whaling town, I believe. In any case, it has a completely Yankee sound" (Stevens to Renato Poggioli, 1953, *Letters*).
[3]"Bawds of euphony" may be grossly translated as "hookers (or whores) for harmony (or pleasant sounds)": i.e., poets who might be described as "academic" and who prostitute their poetry by embodying it in tinkling or agreeable sounds to please and lull readers. "What was intended by X was that the bawds of euphony would suddenly cease to be academic and express themselves sharply: naturally, with pleasure, etc." (Stevens to Henry Church, 1939, *Letters*).
[4]"The point [of XII] is the compulsion frequently back of the things that we do" (Stevens to Church, 1939).
[5]Stevens implied that XII was meant to "convey despair" when, in the 1939 letter to Henry Church, he complained that a French translation probably failed to convey it; the imagery is generally bleak, suggestive of death.

The Death of a Soldier

Life contracts and death is expected,
As in a season of autumn.
The soldier falls.

He does not become a three-days personage,
Imposing his separation,   5
Calling for pomp.

Death is absolute and without memorial,
As in a season of autumn,
When the wind stops,

When the wind stops and, over the heavens,   10
The clouds go, nevertheless,
In their direction.

1918, 1931

Nuances of a
Theme by Williams

It's a strange courage
you give me, ancient star:

Shine alone in the sunrise
toward which you lend no part![1]

I

Shine alone, shine nakedly, shine like bronze,
that reflects neither my face nor any inner part
of my being, shine like fire, that mirrors nothing.

II

Lend no part to any humanity that suffuses
you in its own light.   5
Be not chimera[2] of morning,
Half-man, half-star.
Be not an intelligence,
Like a widow's bird
Or an old horse.   10

1918, 1923

---

[1]The quotation is the whole of William Carlos Williams's poem, "El Hombre" ("The Man"). The morning star (as well as the evening star) is the planet Venus. Both the Williams and the Stevens lines, with their dominant descriptions cast in negatives ("no," "not") seem to represent a subtle distanc-ing from such romantic feelings about nature as those expressed in a poem like "Bright Star, Would I Were Stedfast as Thou Art," by John Keats (1795–1821).
[2]An illusion, a fancy.

Anecdote of the Jar

I placed a jar in Tennessee,
And round it was, upon a hill.
It made the slovenly wilderness
Surround that hill.

The wilderness rose up to it,   5
And sprawled around, no longer wild.
The jar was round upon the ground
And tall and of a port in air.

It took dominion everywhere.
The jar was gray and bare.   10
It did not give of bird or bush,
Like nothing else in Tennessee.

1919, 1923

The Snow Man[1]

One must have a mind of winter
To regard the frost and the boughs
Of the pine-trees crusted with snow;

And have been cold a long time
To behold the junipers shagged with ice,   5
The spruces rough in the distant glitter

Of the January sun; and not to think
Of any misery in the sound of the wind,
In the sound of a few leaves,

Which is the sound of the land   10
Full of the same wind
That is blowing in the same bare place

For the listener, who listens in the snow,
And, nothing himself, beholds
Nothing that is not there and the nothing that is.   15

1921, 1923

A High-Toned
Old Christian Woman

Poetry is the supreme fiction, madame.
Take the moral law and make a nave[1] of it
And from the nave build haunted heaven. Thus,

---

[1] "I shall explain The Snow Man as an example of the necessity of identifying oneself with reality in order to understand it and enjoy it" (Stevens to Hi Simons, 1944, *Letters*).

[1] The main part of a church, usually vaulted in a cathedral.

The conscience is converted into palms,
Like windy citherns[2] hankering for hymns.   5
We agree in principle. That's clear. But take
The opposing law and make a peristyle,[3]
And from the peristyle project a masque[4]
Beyond the planets. Thus, our bawdiness,[5]
Unpurged by epitaph, indulged at last,   10
Is equally converted into palms,[6]
Squiggling like saxophones. And palm for palm,
Madame, we are where we began. Allow,
Therefore, that in the planetary scene
Your disaffected flagellants,[7] well-stuffed,   15
Smacking their muzzy bellies in parade,
Proud of such novelties of the sublime,
Such tink and tank and tunk-a-tunk-tunk,
May, merely may, madame, whip from themselves
A jovial hullabaloo among the spheres.   20
This will make widows wince. But fictive things
Wink as they will. Wink most when widows wince.

1922, 1923

The Emperor of Ice-Cream[1]

Call the roller of big cigars,
The muscular one, and bid him whip
In kitchen cups concupiscent curds.[2]
Let the wenches dawdle in such dress
As they are used to wear, and let the boys   5
Bring flowers in last month's newspapers.
Let be be finale of seem.[3]
The only emperor is the emperor of ice-cream.

Take from the dresser of deal.[4]
Lacking the three glass knobs, that sheet   10
On which she embroidered fantails[5] once
And spread it so as to cover her face.
If her horny feet protrude, they come
To show how cold she is, and dumb.
Let the lamp affix its beam.   15
The only emperor is the emperor of ice-cream.

1922, 1923

---

[2]Stringed musical instrument.
[3]A colonnade around a building, usually associated with Greek temples, and thus pagan in contrast with a nave.
[4]A dramatic entertainment in the form of a revel or dance, with miming.
[5]I.e., our sexuality, intact before death, is celebrated in paganism (while called sinful by Christianity).
[6]I.e., palms used in both Christian and pagan rituals.
[7]The Christian flagellants, who whip and lacerate their bodies in religious frenzy, when become disaffected and therefore pagan, will savor and celebrate their bodies and physical pleasures.
[1]"I think I should select from my poems as my favorite The Emperor of Ice Cream. This wears a deliberately common-place costume, and yet seems to me to contain something of the essential gaudiness of poetry" (Stevens to William Rose

Benét, 1933, *Letters*).
[2]"The words 'concupiscent curds' have no genealogy; they are merely expressive: at least, I hope they are expressive. They express the concupiscence [sexual desire] of life, but by contrast with the things in relation to them in the poem, they express or accentuate life's destitution, and it is this that gives them something more than a cheap lustre" (Stevens to Leonard C. van Geyzel, 1945, *Letters*).
[3]"The true sense of Let be be the finale of seem is let being become the conclusion or denouement of appearing to be: in short, ice cream is an absolute good. The poem is obviously not about ice cream, but about being as distinguished from seeming to be" (Stevens to Henry Church, 1939, *Letters*).
[4]Fir or pine wood.
[5]"The word fantails does not mean fans, but fantail pigeons" (Stevens to Church, 1939).

The Idea of Order at Key West[1]

She sang beyond the genius of the sea.
The water never formed to mind or voice,
Like a body wholly body, fluttering
Its empty sleeves; and yet its mimic motion
Made constant cry, caused constantly a cry,   5
That was not ours although we understood,
Inhuman, of the veritable ocean.

The sea was not a mask. No more was she.
The song and water were not medleyed sound
Even if what she sang was what she heard,   10
Since what she sang was uttered word by word.
It may be that in all her phrases stirred
The grinding water and the gasping wind;
But it was she and not the sea we heard.

For she was the maker of the song she sang.   15
The ever-hooded, tragic-gestured sea
Was merely a place by which she walked to sing.
Whose spirit is this? we said, because we knew
It was the spirit that we sought and knew
That we should ask this often as she sang.   20

If it was only the dark voice of the sea
That rose, or even colored by many waves;
If it was only the outer voice of sky
And cloud, of the sunken coral water-walled,
However clear, it would have been deep air,   25
The heaving speech of air, a summer sound
Repeated in a summer without end
And sound alone. But it was more than that,
More even than her voice, and ours, among
The meaningless plungings of water and the wind,   30
Theatrical distances, bronze shadows heaped
On high horizons, mountainous atmospheres
Of sky and sea.
                      It was her voice that made
The sky acutest at its vanishing.   35
She measured to the hour its solitude.
She was the single artificer of the world
In which she sang. And when she sang, the sea,
Whatever self it had, became the self
That was her song, for she was the maker. Then we,   40
As we beheld her striding there alone,
Knew that there never was a world for her
Except the one she sang and, singing, made.

---

[1]"In 'The Idea of Order at Key West' life has ceased to be a matter of chance. It may be that every man introduces his own order into the life about him and that the idea of order in general is simply what Bishop Berkeley might have called a fortuitous concourse of personal orders. But still there is order. . . . But then, I never thought that it was a fixed philosophic proposition that life was a mass of irrelevancies any more than I now think that it is a fixed philosophic proposition that every man introduces his own order as part of a general order. These are tentative ideas for the purposes of poetry" (Stevens to Ronald Lane Latimer, 1935, *Letters*).

Ramon Fernandez,[2] tell me, if you know,
Why, when the singing ended and we turned   45
Toward the town, tell why the glassy lights,
The lights in the fishing boats at anchor there,
As the night descended, tilting in the air,
Mastered the night and portioned out the sea,
Fixing emblazoned zones and fiery poles,   50
Arranging, deepening, enchanting night.

Oh! Blessed rage for order, pale Ramon,
The maker's rage to order words of the sea,
Words of the fragrant portals, dimly-starred,
And of ourselves and of our origins,   55
In ghostlier demarcations, keener sounds.

1934, 1936

A Postcard from the Volcano[1]

Children picking up our bones
Will never know that these were once
As quick as foxes on the hill;

And that in autumn, when the grapes
Made sharp air sharper by their smell   5
These had a being, breathing frost;

And least will guess that with our bones
We left much more, left what still is
The look of things, left what we felt

At what we saw. The spring clouds blow   10
Above the shuttered mansion-house,
Beyond our gate and the windy sky

Cries out a literate despair.
We knew for long the mansion's look
And what we said of it became   15

A part of what it is . . . Children,
Still weaving budded aureoles,[2]
Will speak our speech and never know,

Will say of the mansion that it seems
As if he that lived there left behind   20
A spirit storming in blank walls,

---

[2]"Ramon Fernandez was not intended to be anyone at all. I chose two everyday Spanish names. I knew of Ramon Fernandez, the critic, and had read some of his criticisms but I did not have him in mind" (Stevens to Bernard Heringman, 1953, *Letters*). Ramon Fernandez (1894–1944), French literary critic.
[1]The poem itself is a postcard from the volcano, i.e., the destruction wrought by time and death, leaving little evidence of life as experienced by those who lived it. The title may conjure up for some the volcanic destruction—and the freezing in time—of the Italian city of Pompeii in A.D. 79; excavation of the ruins was begun in the eighteenth century and continues today.
[2]Halo-shaped headdress made of flower buds.

A dirty house in a gutted world,
A tatter of shadows peaked to white,
Smeared with the gold of the opulent sun.

1936

The Poems of Our Climate

I

Clear water in a brilliant bowl,
Pink and white carnations. The light
In the room more like a snowy air,
Reflecting snow. A newly-fallen snow
At the end of winter when afternoons return.   5
Pink and white carnations — one desires
So much more than that. The day itself
Is simplified: a bowl of white,
Cold, a cold porcelain, low and round,
With nothing more than the carnations there.   10

II

Say even that this complete simplicity
Stripped one of all one's torments, concealed
The evilly compounded, vital I
And made it fresh in a world of white,
A world of clear water, brilliant-edged,   15
Still one would want more, one would need more,
More than a world of white and snowy scents.

III

There would still remain the never-resting mind,
So that one would want to escape, come back
To what had been so long composed.   20
The imperfect is our paradise.
Note that, in this bitterness, delight,
Since the imperfect is so hot in us,
Lies in flawed words and stubborn sounds.

1938, 1942

The Man on the Dump

Day creeps down. The moon is creeping up.
The sun is a corbeil[1] of flowers the moon Blanche[2]
Places there, a bouquet. Ho-ho . . . The dump is full

---

[1]Sculptured basket of fruit used in architectural designs.
[2]"White" (French).

Of images. Days pass like papers from a press.
The bouquets come here in the papers. So the sun,   5
And so the moon, both come, and the janitor's poems
Of every day, the wrapper on the can of pears,
The cat in the paper-bag, the corset, the box
From Esthonia: the tiger chest, for tea.

The freshness of night has been fresh a long time.   10
The freshness of morning, the blowing of day, one says
That it puffs as Cornelius Nepos[3] reads, it puffs
More than, less than or it puffs like this or that.
The green smacks in the eye, the dew in the green
Smacks like fresh water in a can, like the sea   15
On a cocoanut—how many men have copied dew
For buttons, how many women have covered themselves
With dew, dew dresses, stones and chains of dew, heads
Of the floweriest flowers dewed with the dewiest dew.
One grows to hate these things except on the dump.   20

Now, in the time of spring (azaleas, trilliums,
Myrtle, viburnums, daffodils, blue phlox),
Between that disgust and this, between the things
That are on the dump (azaleas and so on)
And those that will be (azaleas and so on),   25
One feels the purifying change. One rejects
The trash.

            That's the moment when the moon creeps up
To the bubbling of bassoons. That's the time
One looks at the elephant-colorings of tires.   30
Everything is shed; and the moon comes up as the moon
(All its images are in the dump) and you see
As a man (not like an image of a man),
You see the moon rise in the empty sky.

One sits and beats an old tin can, lard pail.   35
One beats and beats for that which one believes.
That's what one wants to get near. Could it after all
Be merely oneself, as superior as the ear
To a crow's voice? Did the nightingale torture the ear,
Pack the heart and scratch the mind? And does the ear   40
Solace itself in peevish birds? Is it peace,
Is it a philosopher's honeymoon, one finds
On the dump? Is it to sit among mattresses of the dead,
Bottles, pots, shoes and grass and murmur *aptest eve*:[4]
Is it to hear the blatter of grackles and say   45
Invisible priest; is it to eject, to pull
The day to pieces and cry *stanza my stone*?
Where was it one first heard of the truth? The the.[5]

1938, 1942

---

[3]Cornelius Nepos (*c.* 100–*c.* 25 B.C.), Roman historian whose
only extant works are a few fragments.
[4]Poetic language unsuited for embodying the realities of the
dump (or of things as they are).
[5]The real realness (things as they actually are).

Of Modern Poetry

The poem of the mind in the act of finding
What will suffice. It has not always had
To find: the scene was set; it repeated what
Was in the script.
                              Then the theatre was changed   5
To something else. Its past was a souvenir.
It has to be living, to learn the speech of the place.
It has to face the men of the time and to meet
The women of the time. It has to think about war
And it has to find what will suffice. It has   10
To construct a new stage. It has to be on that stage
And, like an insatiable actor, slowly and
With meditation, speak words that in the ear,
In the delicatest ear of the mind, repeat,
Exactly, that which it wants to hear, at the sound   15
Of which, an invisible audience listens,
Not to the play, but to itself, expressed
In an emotion as of two people, as of two
Emotions becoming one. The actor is
A metaphysician in the dark, twanging   20
An instrument, twanging a wiry string that gives
Sounds passing through sudden rightnesses, wholly
Containing the mind, below which it cannot descend,
Beyond which it has no will to rise.
                              It must   25
Be the finding of a satisfaction, and may
Be of a man skating, a woman dancing, a woman
Combing. The poem of the act of the mind.

1940, 1942

The House Was Quiet
and the World Was Calm

The house was quiet and the world was calm.
The reader became the book; and summer night

Was like the conscious being of the book.
The house was quiet and the world was calm.

The words were spoken as if there was no book,   5
Except that the reader leaned above the page,

Wanted to lean, wanted much most to be
The scholar to whom his book is true, to whom

The summer night is like a perfection of thought.
The house was quiet because it had to be.   10

The quiet was part of the meaning, part of the mind:
The access of perfection to the page.

And the world was calm. The truth in a calm world,
In which there is no other meaning, itself

Is calm, itself is summer and night, itself   15
Is the reader leaning late and reading there.

                                                                1945, 1947

Large Red Man Reading

There were ghosts that returned to earth to hear his phrases,
As he sat there reading, aloud, the great blue tabulae.[1]
They were those from the wilderness of stars that had expected more.

There were those that returned to hear him read from the poem of life,
Of the pans above the stove, the pots on the table, the tulips among them.   5
They were those that would have wept to step barefoot into reality,

That would have wept and been happy, have shivered in the frost
And cried out to feel it again, have run fingers over leaves
And against the most coiled thorn, have seized on what was ugly

And laughed, as he sat there reading, from out of the purple tabulae,   10
The outlines of being and its expressings, the syllables of its law:
Poesis, poesis,[2] the literal characters, the vatic[3] lines,

Which in those ears and in those thin, those spended hearts,
Took on color, took on shape and the size of things as they are
And spoke the feeling for them, which was what they had lacked.   15

                                                                1948, 1950

Final Soliloquy of
the Interior Paramour

Light the first light of evening, as in a room
In which we rest and, for small reason, think
The world imagined is the ultimate good.

This is, therefore, the intensest rendezvous.
It is in that thought that we collect ourselves,   5
Out of all the indifferences, into one thing:

---

[1] "Writing tablets" (Latin).
[2] "Poetry" (Latin).
[3] Prophetic.

Within a single thing, a single shawl
Wrapped tightly round us, since we are poor, a warmth,
A light, a power, the miraculous influence.

Here, now, we forget each other and ourselves.   10
We feel the obscurity of an order, a whole,
A knowledge, that which arranged the rendezvous.

Within its vital boundary, in the mind.
We say God and the imagination are one . . .
How high that highest candle lights the dark.   15

Out of this same light, out of the central mind,
We make a dwelling in the evening air,
In which being there together is enough.

                                        1951, 1953

The Planet on the Table

Ariel[1] was glad he had written his poems.
They were of a remembered time
Or of something seen that he liked.

Other makings of the sun
Were waste and welter   5
And the ripe shrub writhed.

His self and the sun were one
And his poems, although makings of his self,
Were no less makings of the sun.

It was not important that they survive.   10
What mattered was that they should bear
Some lineament or character,

Some affluence, if only half-perceived,
In the poverty of their words,
Of the planet of which they were part.   15

                                        1953, 1954

Not Ideas about the
Thing but the Thing Itself[1]

At the earliest ending of winter,
In March, a scrawny cry from outside
Seemed like a sound in his mind.

---

[1]The airy, creative creature in Shakespeare's *The Tempest*;
here an archetypal or idealized poet.
[1]Stevens placed this poem last in *Collected Poems*. The title is a
variation of the poetry slogan used by William Carlos Williams: "No ideas but in things."

He knew that he heard it,
A bird's cry, at daylight or before,   5
In the early March wind.

The sun was rising at six,
No longer a battered panache[2] above snow . . .
It would have been outside.

It was not from the vast ventriloquism   10
Of sleep's faded papier-mâché[3] . . .
The sun was coming from outside.

That scrawny cry—it was
A chorister whose c[4] preceded the choir.
It was part of the colossal sun,   15

Surrounded by its choral rings,
Still far away. It was like
A new knowledge of reality.

1954

from The Noble Rider and the Sound of Words

[INTERDEPENDENCE OF IMAGINATION AND REALITY][1]

Here I am, well-advanced in my paper, with everything of interest that I started out to say remaining to be said. I am interested in the nature of poetry and I have stated its nature, from one of the many points of view from which it is possible to state it. It is an interdependence of the imagination and reality as equals. This is not a definition, since it is incomplete. But it states the nature of poetry. Then I am interested in the role of the poet and this is paramount. In this area of my subject I might be expected to speak of the social, that is to say sociological or political, obligation of the poet. He has none. That he must be contemporaneous is as old as Longinus[2] and I dare say older. But that he *is* contemporaneous is almost inevitable. How contemporaneous in the direct sense in which being contemporaneous is intended were the four great poets of whom I spoke a moment ago?[3] I do not think that a poet owes any more as a social obligation than he owes as a moral obligation, and if there is anything concerning poetry about which people agree it is that the role of the poet is not to be found in morals. I cannot say what that wide agreement amounts to because the agreement (in which I do not join) that the poet is under a social obligation is equally wide. Reality is life and life is society and the imagination and reality; that is to say, the imagination and society are inseparable. That is pre-eminently true in the case of the poetic drama. The poetic drama needs a terrible genius before it is anything more than a literary relic. Besides the theater has forgotten that it could ever be terrible. It is not one of the instruments of fate, decidedly. Yes: the all-commanding subject-matter of poetry is life, the never-ceasing source. But it is not a social obligation. One

---

[2]A plume of feathers, especially such a plume worn in a helmet.
[3]Material made of paper pulp and resin, formed into shapes.
[4]The chorister of a choir who sounds the note C on a pitch pipe to give choir members the starting key.
[1]This essay is Part 5 of "The Noble Rider and the Sound of

Words," presented as a lecture in 1941 and later included in *The Necessary Angel* (1951).
[2]Dionysius Longinus (213?–273), Greek philosopher and author of *On the Sublime*.
[3]Virgil, Dante, Shakespeare, Milton.

does not love and go back to one's ancient mother as a social obligation. One goes back out of a suasion not to be denied. Unquestionably if a social movement moved one deeply enough, its moving poems would follow. No politician can command the imagination, directing it to do this or that. Stalin[4] might grind his teeth the whole of a Russian winter and yet all the poets in the Soviets might remain silent the following spring. He might excite their imaginations by something he said or did. He would not command them. He is singularly free from that "cult of pomp," which is the comic side of the European disaster; and that means as much as anything to us. The truth is that the social obligation so closely urged is a phase of the pressure of reality which a poet (in the absence of dramatic poets) is bound to resist or evade today. Dante in Purgatory and Paradise[5] was still the voice of the Middle Ages but not through fulfilling any social obligation. Since that is the role most frequently urged, if that role is eliminated, and if a possible poet is left facing life without any categorical exactions upon him, what then? What is his function? Certainly it is not to lead people out of the confusion in which they find themselves. Nor is it, I think, to comfort them while they follow their readers to and fro. I think that his function is to make his imagination theirs and that he fulfills himself only as he sees his imagination become the light in the minds of others. His role, in short, is to help people to live their lives. Time and time again it has been said that he may not address himself to an élite. I think he may. There is not a poet whom we prize living today that does not address himself to an élite. The poet will continue to do this: to address himself to an élite even in a classless society, unless, perhaps, this exposes him to imprisonment or exile. In that event he is likely not to address himself to anyone at all. He may, like Shostakovich,[6] content himself with pretence. He will, nevertheless, still be addressing himself to an élite, for all poets address themselves to someone and it is of the essence of that instinct, and it seems to amount to an instinct, that it should be to an élite, not to a drab but to a woman with the hair of a pythoness, not to a chamber of commerce but to a gallery of one's own, if there are enough of one's own to fill a gallery. And that élite, if it responds, not out of complaisance, but because the poet has quickened it, because he has educed from it that for which it was searching in itself and in the life around it and which it had not yet quite found, will thereafter do for the poet what he cannot do for himself, that is to say, receive his poetry.

I repeat that his role is to help people to live their lives. He has had immensely to do with giving life whatever savor it possesses. He has had to do with whatever the imagination and the senses have made of the world. He has, in fact, had to do with life except as the intellect has had to do with it and, as to that, no one is needed to tell us that poetry and philosophy are akin. I want to repeat for two reasons a number of observations made by Charles Mauron.[7] The first reason is that these observations tell us what it is that a poet does to help people to live their lives and the second is that they prepare the way for a word concerning escapism. They are: that the artist transforms us into epicures; that he has to discover the possible work of art in the real world, then to extract it, when he does not himself compose it entirely; that he is *un amoreux perpétuel*[8] of the world that he contemplates and thereby enriches; that art sets out to express the human soul; and finally that everything like a firm grasp of reality is eliminated from the aesthetic field. With these aphorisms in mind, how is it possible to condemn escapism? The poetic process is psychologically an escapist process. The chatter about escapism is, to my way of thinking, merely common cant. My own remarks about resisting or evading the pressure of reality mean escapism, if

[4]Joseph Stalin (1879–1953), ruler of the Soviet Union from 1924 until his death in 1953.
[5]Dante Alighieri (1265–1321), Italian author of *The Divine Comedy*, consisting of "Inferno," "Purgatorio," and "Paradiso."
[6]Dmitri Shostakovich (1906–1975), Russian composer who fell in and out of favor with the Communist regime in the Soviet Union.
[7]Charles Mauron (1899–1966), French psychoanalytic critic, author of *Aesthetics and Psychology*, tr. Roger Fry and Katherine John (1935).
[8]"A perpetual lover" (French).

analyzed. Escapism has a pejorative sense, which it cannot be supposed that I include in the sense in which I use the word. The pejorative sense applies where the poet is not attached to reality, where the imagination does not adhere to reality, which, for my part, I regard as fundamental. If we go back to the collection of solid, static objects extended in space, which Dr. Joad[9] posited, and if we say that the space is blank space, nowhere, without color, and that the objects, though solid, have no shadows and, though static, exert a mournful power, and, without elaborating this complete poverty, if suddenly we hear a different and familiar description of the place:

> This City now doth, like a garment, wear
> The beauty of the morning, silent bare,
> Ships, towers, domes, theatres, and temples lie
> Open unto the fields, and to the sky;
> All bright and glittering in the smokeless air;[10]

if we have this experience, we know how poets help people to live their lives. This illustration must serve for all the rest. There is, in fact, a world of poetry indistinguishable from the world in which we live, or, I ought to say, no doubt, from the world in which we shall come to live, since what makes the poet the potent figure that he is, or was, or ought to be, is that he creates the world to which we turn incessantly and without knowing it and that he gives to life the supreme fictions without which we are unable to conceive of it.

And what about the sound of words? What about nobility, of which the fortunes were to be a kind of test of the value of the poet? I do not know of anything that will appear to have suffered more from the passage of time than the music of poetry and that has suffered less. The deepening need for words to express our thoughts and feelings which, we are sure, are all the truth that we shall ever experience, having no illusions, makes us listen to words when we hear them, loving them and feeling them, makes us search the sound of them, for a finality, a perfection, an unalterable vibration, which it is only within the power of the acutest poet to give them. Those of us who may have been thinking of the path of poetry, those who understand that words are thoughts and not only our own thoughts but the thoughts of men and women ignorant of what it is that they are thinking, must be conscious of this: that, above everything else, poetry is words; and that words, above everything else, are, in poetry, sounds. This being so, my time and yours might have been better spent if I had been less interested in trying to give our possible poet an identity and less interested in trying to appoint him to his place. But unless I had done these things, it might have been thought that I was rhetorical, when I was speaking in the simplest way about things of such importance that nothing is more so. A poet's words are of things that do not exist without the words. Thus, the image of the charioteer and of the winged horses, which has been held to be precious for all of time that matters, was created by words of things that never existed without the words.[11] A description of Verrocchio's statue[12] could be the integration of an illusion equal to the statue itself. Poetry is a revelation in words by means of the words. Croce[13] was not speaking of poetry in particular when he said that language is perpetual creation. About nobility I cannot be sure that the decline, not to say the disappearance of nobility is anything more

---

[9]Cyril Joad (1891–1953), British philosopher.
[10]From "Sonnet Composed upon Westminster Bridge, September 3, 1802," by William Wordsworth (1770–1850).
[11]Stevens began his essay with a quotation from Plato's *Phaedrus*: "Let our figure be of a composite nature—a pair of winged horses and a charioteer. Now the winged horses and the charioteer of the gods are all of them noble, and of noble breed, while ours are mixed; and we have a charioteer who drives them in a pair, and one of them is noble and of noble origin, and the other is ignoble and of ignoble origin; and, as

might be expected, there is a great deal of trouble in managing them."
[12]Andrea del Verrocchio (1435–1488), Italian sculptor and painter; earlier in this essay, Stevens had praised his statue of Bartolomeo Colleoni (an Italian soldier) as a work of art for its time, but added that in our time it would seem "a little overpowering, a little magnificent."
[13]Benedetto Croce (1866–1952), Italian philosopher and critic.

than a maladjustment between the imagination and reality. We have been a little insane about the truth. We have had an obsession. In its ultimate extension, the truth about which we have been insane will lead us to look beyond the truth to something in which the imagination will be the dominant complement. It is not only that the imagination adheres to reality, but, also, that reality adheres to the imagination and that the interdependence is essential. We may emerge from our *bassesse*[14] and, if we do, how would it happen if not by the intervention of some fortune of the mind? And what would that fortune of the mind happen to be? It might be only commonsense but even that, a commonsense beyond the truth, would be a nobility of long descent.

The poet refuses to allow his task to be set for him. He denies that he has a task and considers that the organization of materia poetica[15] is a contradiction in terms. Yet the imagination gives to everything that it touches a peculiarity, and it seems to me that the peculiarity of the imagination is nobility, of which there are many degrees. This inherent nobility is the natural source of another, which our extremely headstrong generation regards as false and decadent. I mean that nobility which is our spiritual height and depth; and while I know how difficult it is to express it, nevertheless I am bound to give a sense of it. Nothing could be more evasive and inaccessible. Nothing distorts itself and seeks disguise more quickly. There is a shame of disclosing it and in its definite presentations a horror of it. But there it is. The fact that it is there is what makes it possible to invite to the reading and writing of poetry men of intelligence and desire for life. I am not thinking of the ethical or the sonorous or at all of the manner of it. The manner of it is, in fact, its difficulty, which each man must feel each day differently, for himself. I am not thinking of the solemn, the portentous or demoded. On the other hand, I am evading a definition. If it is defined, it will be fixed and it must not be fixed. As in the case of an external thing, nobility resolves itself into an enormous number of vibrations, movements, changes. To fix it is to put an end to it. Let me show it to you unfixed.

Late last year Epstein[16] exhibited some of his flower paintings at the Leicester Galleries in London. A commentator in *Apollo* said: *"How with this rage can beauty hold a plea* . . . The quotation from Shakespeare's 65th sonnet prefaces the catalogue. . . . It would be apropos to any other flower paintings than Mr. Epstein's. His make no pretence to fragility. They shout, explode all over the picture space and generally oppose the rage of the world with such a rage of form and colour as no flower in nature or pigment has done since Van Gogh."[17]

What ferocious beauty the line from Shakespeare puts on when used under such circumstances! While it has its modulation of despair, it holds its plea and is noble. There is no element more conspicuously absent from contemporary poetry than nobility. There is no element that poets have sought after, more curiously and more piously, certain of its obscure existence. Its voice is one of the inarticulate voices which it is their business to overhear and to record. The nobility of rhetoric is, of course, a lifeless nobility. Pareto's[18] epigram that history is a cemetery of aristocracies easily becomes another: that poetry is a cemetery of nobilities. For the sensitive poet, conscious of negations, nothing is more difficult than the affirmations of nobility and yet there is nothing that he requires of himself more persistently, since in them and in their kind, alone, are to be found those sanctions that are the reasons for his being and for that occasional ecstasy, or ecstatic freedom of the mind, which is his special privilege.

It is hard to think of a thing more out of time than nobility. Looked at plainly it seems false and dead and ugly. To look at it at all makes us realize sharply that in our present, in the presence of our reality, the past looks false and is, therefore, dead and

---

[14]"Baseness" or "lowness" (French).

[15]"Poetic material" (Latin).

[16]Sir Jacob Epstein (1880–1959), British sculptor, whose abstract works raised a public outcry.

[17]Vincent van Gogh (1853–1890), Dutch painter, known especially for his sunflower paintings.

[18]Vilfredo Pareto (1848–1923), Italian economist and sociologist.

is, therefore, ugly; and we turn away from it as from something repulsive and particularly from the characteristic that it has a way of assuming: something that was noble in its day, grandeur that was, the rhetorical once. But as a wave is a force and not the water of which it is composed, which is never the same, so nobility is a force and not the manifestations of which it is composed, which are never the same. Possibly this description of it as a force will do more than anything else I can have said about it to reconcile you to it. It is not an artifice that the mind has added to human nature. The mind has added nothing to human nature. It is a violence from within that protects us from a violence without. It is the imagination pressing back against the pressure of reality. It seems, in the last analysis, to have something to do with our self-preservation; and that, no doubt, is why the expression of it, the sound of its words, helps us to live our lives.

1942

WILLIAM CARLOS WILLIAMS
(1883–1963)

In his *Autobiography* (1951), William Carlos Williams described the devastating effect on him and others when T. S. Eliot's *The Waste Land* appeared in 1922: "It wiped out our world as if an atom bomb had been dropped upon it. . . . To me especially it struck like a sardonic bullet. . . . Critically Eliot returned us to the classroom just at the moment when I felt that we were on the point of an escape to matters much closer to the essence of a new art form itself—rooted in the locality which should give it fruit."

The key term for Williams here is locality. He had always thought that the expatriate poets, T. S. Eliot and Ezra Pound especially, had been mistaken in pursuit of culture and the poetic muse abroad, leaving their native "locality" and becoming in effect without roots. In several places in his work Williams repeated a sentence that condensed his theory: "No ideas but in things." In a 1939 essay, "Against the Weather," he wrote: "If I succeed in keeping myself objective enough, sensual enough, I can produce the factors, the concretions of materials by which others shall understand and so be led to use—that they may the better see, touch, taste, enjoy—their own world *differing as it may* from mine. By mine, they, different, can be discovered to be the same as I, and, thrown into contrast, will see the implications of a general enjoyment through me." All his life, he added, he had "striven to emphasize . . . what was meant by the universality of the local."

At the time of the writing of his *Autobiography*, in the late 1940s, Williams's reputation was eclipsed by Eliot's and Pound's enormous reputations. But gradually in the postwar years, with the completion of the last books of his epic *Paterson* in the 1950s, Williams began to emerge as a neglected major figure, influential with a new generation of important poets, including Allen Ginsberg, Denise Levertov, Robert Creeley, and, among more traditional poets, Robert Lowell.

It is perhaps ironic that the modernist who insisted on his American roots came from foreign-born parents and himself spent some critical years of his youth being educated abroad. His father was from England and brought up in the West Indies, and his mother was born in Puerto Rico. Williams began school in Rutherford, New Jersey, where he was born, but at age fourteen went to Europe for two years to study, first in Geneva, and then at the Lycée Condorcet in Paris.

Back in the United States he attended the Horace Mann High School in New York and then attended medical school at the University of Pennsylvania (1902–06). There he came to know Ezra Pound, Hilda Doolittle, and the artist Charles Demuth, who would help Williams to realize that innovations in painting might be adaptable to poetry. Williams interned in New York City and, in 1909–10, studied pediatrics at Leipzig in Germany, ending his year abroad by travelling throughout Europe. He returned to America, married Florence (Flossie) Herman in 1910, and settled down in Rutherford for a lifetime's medical practice, during which he would deliver more than 2,000 babies.

But Williams had early decided on two careers, one as a physician, the other as a poet. His two youthful poetic enthusiasms were John Keats and Walt Whitman. His first book of poems, privately published in 1909, showed the influence of his reading in the romantic poets. Pound wrote to him that he had written some "fine lines" but, he said, "nowhere I think do you add anything to the poets you have used as models." The Keats influence would fade immediately. The Whitman connection was deeper, and Williams would cite (and often quarrel with) Whitman throughout his poetic career.

Combining poetry and medicine was no easy task, especially for one as devoted to service to his patients as Williams was. He snatched moments whenever he could from his busy schedule to write down ideas and poems on scraps of paper or even prescription forms. In 1913, Pound helped him get his second volume, *Tempers*, published in England. By this time Williams's style had changed, and he was clearly embarked on his long search for a new measure, a new form for his poems. His poems began to appear in *Poetry*, *The Dial*, and other little magazines.

By the time Williams published *Al Que Quiere!* ("To Him Who Wants It") in 1917, he had found his own distinctive voice, and the next few years saw the publication of a number of important volumes: *Kora in Hell: Improvisations* (1920), *Sour Grapes* (1921), *Spring and All* (1923), *The Descent of Winter* (1928). Some of his best-known lyrics appeared in the books, such as "Queen-Ann's-Lace," "Spring and All," and "The Red Wheelbarrow." They made clear that Williams's slogan-theory, "No ideas but in things," held much in common with imagism. Indeed, Pound had included a Williams poem in his 1914 *Des Imagistes*.

From 1920 to 1923, Williams joined with Robert McAlmon to publish a little magazine of their invention, *Contact*. It was a shoestring enterprise, the first issues mimeographed on cheap yellow paper. But it had spirit. Williams wrote in the first issue a manifesto that spoke to his own poetry: "We, *Contact*, aim to emphasize the local phase of the game of writing. . . . We want to give all our energy to the setting up of new vigors of artistic perception, invention, and expression in the United States. Only by slow growth, consciously fostered to the point of enthusiasm, will American work of the quality of Marianne Moore's best poetry come to the fore of intelligent attention and the ignorance which has made America an artistic desert be somewhat dissipated."

During the 1920s, Williams found the time to write some prose along with his poetry. His first novel, published in 1923 in Paris, was called *The Great American Novel*, an "anti-novel" which Williams described in his *Autobiography* as "a satire on the novel form in which a little (female) Ford car falls more or less in love with a Mack truck." After a trip to Europe in 1924, Williams wrote *In the American*

Grain (1925), an impressionistic essay-history of the discovery and development of America as seen (or as might have been seen) through the eyes of principal figures such as Columbus, Franklin, Poe, and Lincoln. *A Voyage to Pagany* (1928), a novel-travel book, was based on Williams's travels in 1924 throughout Europe.

Beginning in the 1930s, Williams directed still more of his creative energy into the writing of prose. His short story collections include *The Knife of the Times* (1932), *Life Along the Passaic River* (1938), *Make Light of It* (1950), and *The Farmers' Daughters* (1961). In these stories Williams wrote directly out of his experiences as a doctor treating patients. In *White Mule* (1937), *In the Money* (1940), and *The Build-Up* (1952), a fictional trilogy, Williams chronicled the life of an immigrant family from the nineteenth century to the First World War. The story was based on the experience of his wife's family, whose forebears had been German immigrants.

Williams continued to write lyric poems, publishing a poem entitled "Paterson" in the 1920s and another entitled "Paterson: Episode 17" in the 1930s, indicating by the title of the second that he had in mind a longer work. Indeed, lines of these poems were to find their way later into Williams's epic *Paterson*, the focus of Williams's creative effort in the last two decades of his life. Successive books of *Paterson* appeared in 1946, 1948, 1949, and 1951. There is clear evidence that Williams considered the poem finished with Book Four, but found himself with a compulsion to continue what he came to think of as his major poetic work. He added Book Five in 1958 and he was working on Book Six when he died in 1963. Like Whitman's *Leaves of Grass*, Williams's poem had become open-ended.

The poem is the best example of Williams's use of the local—Paterson, New Jersey, on the Passaic River—to reach the universal. The epic resembles a "collage" or "assemblage," including, as it does, "found objects" such as scraps of history, geography, snatches of conversation, overheard comments, magazine articles, newspaper stories, statistical tracts, and letters from friends and acquaintances (from the then beginning poet Allen Ginsberg, for example).

The themes are multitudinous, but cluster about a search—the search for Beautiful Thing, the search for a redeeming language (an entire library goes up in flames in Book Three), and the search for an ascent from the descent (or a search for the "hole / at the bottom of the cavern / of death"). Beautiful Thing (person, place, or thing) is ultimately found as the essence of what on the surface seems mundane (in one instance, a Negress beating a rug). A redeeming language is found in the completed poem, made up of the collage of languages that make up the poem's speech. The search for an ascent, a way up, is found in the creative imagination itself, which leads to the return from the threatening sea to the shore at the end of Book Four, and leads to the "Yo ho! ta ho! . . . dance to a measure" at the end of Book Five.

"Paterson" is a shifting identity in the poem—the city, but also a man, everyman, modern man, a poet, a doctor, and, of course, William Carlos Williams himself. As the poem progresses, the identity between the author and his poetic character becomes more firmly established and other guises drop away. In the writing of his epic, Williams came more and more to use what he called the "variable foot" (containing up to four syllables and two stresses) and the triadic line (the three parts of the line placed beneath each other and spaced across the page).

Williams used the variable foot and triadic line in many of his later poems, sometimes only occasionally, sometimes with variation. Two of his finest works from this period are the long poems *The Desert Music* (1954) and "Asphodel, That

Greeny Flower" (1955). The first of these is very much in thematic resonance with *Paterson*, finding paradoxically the "music of survival" in the great western American desert (or "waste land") and a "changeless, endless / inescapable and insistent music" in a sordid scene in a sleazy bar of a Mexican border town (Juarez). "Asphodel, That Greeny Flower" is an old age love poem from Williams to his wife, Flossie, balancing an earlier prose work—*A Novelette*, 1932—in which Williams had explored their relationship obliquely (Williams was later to call this work an attempt at "automatic writing").

Given that Williams spent his life delivering and looking after babies, the sheer bulk of his writing is astonishing. There was even a volume of plays published in 1961, *Many Loves and Other Plays*. *A Dream of Love* was produced in New York in 1949, and *Many Loves* there in 1959. Some recognition came during Williams's last years. He received the first National Book Award for poetry in 1950 for *Paterson, Book Three* (1949) and *Selected Poems* (1949). And he won the Bollingen Award for Poetry in 1953.

Williams began to suffer strokes and heart problems in the late 1940s, but continued writing to the end, publishing a new collection of poems, *Pictures from Brueghel*, in 1962 (awarded the Pulitzer Prize the following year). He died in 1963, in the place where he was born—Rutherford. A new and revised edition of *The Collected Later Poems* (first published in 1950) appeared that same year.

Wallace Stevens came near to capturing the essence of Williams in his Preface to Williams's *Collected Poems, 1921–1931* (1934): "[Williams's] passion for the anti-poetic is a blood passion and not a passion of the inkpot. The anti-poetic is his spirit's cure. He needs it as a naked man needs shelter or as an animal needs salt. To a man with a sentimental side the anti-poetic is that truth, that reality to which all of us are forever fleeing."

ADDITIONAL READING

The Selected Letters of William Carlos Williams, ed. J. C. Thirlwall, 1957, 1985; *I Wanted to Write a Poem: The Autobiography of the Works of a Poet*, reported and ed. Edith Heal, 1958; *The Collected Earlier Poems*, 1951; *The Collected Later Poems*, 1963.

Linda Wagner, *The Poems of William Carlos Williams*, 1964; J. Hillis Miller, ed., *William Carlos Williams: A Collection of Critical Essays*, 1966; Alan Ostrom, *The Poetic World of William Carlos Williams*, 1966; W. S. Peterson, *An Approach to Paterson*, 1967; John Malcolm Brinnin, *William Carlos Williams*, 1963; Thomas R. Whitaker, *William Carlos Williams*, 1968; James Guimond, *The Art of William Carlos Williams: A Discovery and Possession of America*, 1968; Sherman Paul, *The Music of Survival: A Biography of a Poem by William Carlos Williams*, 1968; Emily Mitchell Wallace, *A Bibliography of William Carlos Williams*, 1968; Bram Dijkstra, *The Hieroglyphics of a New Speech: Cubism, Stieglitz, and the Early Poetry of William Carlos Williams*, 1969; James Breslin, *William Carlos Williams: An American Artist*, 1970; Joel Conarroe, *William Carlos Williams's Paterson: Language and Landscape*, 1970; Linda Wagner, *The Prose of William Carlos Williams*, 1970; Mike Weaver, *William Carlos Williams: The American Background*, 1971; Benjamin Sankey, *A Companion to William Carlos Williams's Paterson*, 1971; Joseph N. Riddel, *The Inverted Bell: Modernism and the Counter-Poetics of William Carlos Williams*, 1974; Reed Whittemore, *William Carlos Williams; Poet from Jersey*, 1975; Jerome Mazzaro, *William Carlos Williams: The Knack of Survival in America*, 1975; Paul Mariani, *William Carlos Williams: The Poet and His Critics*, 1975; Linda Wagner, *William Carlos Williams: A Reference Guide*, 1978; Charles Doyle, ed., *William Carlos Williams: The Critical Heritage*, 1980; Paul Mariani, *William Carlos Williams: A New World Naked*, 1981; Margaret Lloyd, *William Carlos Williams's "Paterson": A Critical Reappraisal*, 1982; Charles Doyle, *William Carlos Williams and the American Poem*, 1982; Carroll F. Terrell, ed., *William Carlos Williams: Man and Poet*, 1983; Stephen Tapscott, *American Beauty: William Carlos Williams and the Modernist Whitman*, 1984; Stephen Cushman, *William Carlos Williams and the Meanings of Measure*, 1985; Audrey T. Rodgers, *Virgin and Whore: The Image of Women in the Poetry of William Carlos Williams*, 1987; Peter Schmidt, *William Carlos Williams, the Arts, and Literary Tradition*, 1988.

TEXTS

   The Collected Poems of William Carlos Williams: Volume I, 1909–1939, ed. A. Walton Litz and Christopher MacGowan, 1986; *The Collected Poems of William Carlos Williams: Volume II, 1939–1962*, ed. Christopher MacGowan, 1988; *Selected Essays of William Carlos Williams*, 1954.

Tract

I will teach you my townspeople
how to perform a funeral —
for you have it over a troop
of artists —
unless one should scour the world —   5
you have the ground sense necessary.

See! the hearse leads.
I begin with a design for a hearse.
For Christ's sake not black —
nor white either — and not polished!   10
Let it be weathered — like a farm wagon —
with gilt wheels (this could be
applied fresh at small expense)
or no wheels at all:
a rough dray to drag over the ground.   15

Knock the glass out!
My God — glass, my townspeople!
For what purpose? Is it for the dead
to look out or for us to see
how well he is housed or to see   20
the flowers or the lack of them —
or what?
To keep the rain and snow from him?
He will have a heavier rain soon:
pebbles and dirt and what not.   25
Let there be no glass —
and no upholstery, phew!
and no little brass rollers
and small easy wheels on the bottom —
my townspeople what are you thinking of?   30

A rough plain hearse then
with gilt wheels and no top at all.
On this the coffin lies
by its own weight.

                    No wreaths please —   35
especially no hot house flowers.
Some common memento is better,
something he prized and is known by:
his old clothes — a few books perhaps —
God knows what! You realize   40
how we are about these things
my townspeople —

something will be found—anything
even flowers if he had come to that.
So much for the hearse.   45

For heaven's sake though see to the driver!
Take off the silk hat! In fact
that's no place at all for him—
up there unceremoniously
dragging our friend out to his own dignity!   50
Bring him down—bring him down!
Low and inconspicuous! I'd not have him ride
on the wagon at all—damn him—
the undertaker's understrapper!
Let him hold the reins   55
and walk at the side
and inconspicuously too!

Then briefly as to yourselves:
Walk behind—as they do in France,
seventh class, or if you ride   60
Hell take curtains! Go with some show
of inconvenience; sit openly—
to the weather as to grief.
Or do you think you can shut grief in?
What—from us? We who have perhaps   65
nothing to lose? Share with us
share with us—it will be money
in your pockets.
                        Go now
I think you are ready.   70

                                        1916, 1917

The Young Housewife[1]

At ten A.M. the young housewife
moves about in negligee behind
the wooden walls of her husband's house.
I pass solitary in my car.

Then again she comes to the curb   5
to call the ice-man, fish-man, and stands
shy, uncorseted, tucking in
stray ends of hair, and I compare her
to a fallen leaf.

The noiseless wheels of my car   10
rush with a crackling sound over
dried leaves as I bow and pass smiling.

                                        1916, 1938

_____
[1]Williams commented about this poem: "Whenever a man sees a beautiful woman it's an occasion for poetry— compensating beauty with beauty" (*Collected Poems*, Vol. I, 479).

El Hombre[1]

It's a strange courage
you give me ancient star:

Shine alone in the sunrise
toward which you lend no part!

1916, 1917

Danse Russe[1]

If I when my wife is sleeping
and the baby and Kathleen
are sleeping
and the sun is a flame-white disc
in silken mists   5
above shining trees, —
if I in my north room
dance naked, grotesquely
before my mirror
waving my shirt round my head   10
and singing softly to myself:
"I am lonely, lonely.
I was born to be lonely,
I am best so!"
If I admire my arms, my face,   15
my shoulders, flanks, buttocks
against the yellow drawn shades, —

Who shall say I am not
the happy genius[2] of my household?

1916, 1917

Portrait of a Lady[1]

Your thighs are appletrees
whose blossoms touch the sky.
Which sky?[2] The sky
where Watteau[3] hung a lady's

---

[1]"The Man" (Spanish). See Wallace Stevens's "Nuances of a Theme by Williams," which elaborates on the theme of this poem.
[1]"Russian Dance" (French).
[2]I.e., "genius loci": the guardian spirit of a place.
[1]In art, a traditional title of the painting of a beautiful woman has been simply "Portrait of a Lady." Henry James used the title for one of his novels (1881) and both Ezra Pound and

T. S. Eliot wrote poems under this title.
[2]There seem to be two voices in the poem, one drawing the rather romantic portrait and the other asking skeptical and challenging questions; the two voices may be an interior dialogue of a single person.
[3]Antoine Watteau (1684–1721), French painter known for his idyllic, sensuous scenes of playful aristocrats in open air festivities.

slipper. Your knees   5
are a southern breeze—or
a gust of snow. Agh! what
sort of man was Fragonard?[4]
—as if that answered
anything. Ah, yes—below   10
the knees, since the tune
drops that way, it is
one of those white summer days,
the tall grass of your ankles
flickers upon the shore—   15
Which shore?—
the sand clings to my lips—
Which shore?
Agh, petals maybe. How
should I know?   20
Which shore? Which shore?
I said petals from an appletree.

1920, 1934

Queen-Anne's-Lace[1]

Her body is not so white as
anemone petals nor so smooth—nor
so remote a thing. It is a field
of the wild carrot taking
the field by force; the grass   5
does not raise above it.
Here is no question of whiteness,
white as can be, with a purple mole
at the center of each flower.
Each flower is a hand's span   10
of her whiteness. Wherever
his hand has lain there is
a tiny purple blemish. Each part
is a blossom under his touch
to which the fibres of her being   15
stem one by one, each to its end,
until the whole field is a
white desire, empty, a single stem,
a cluster, flower by flower,
a pious wish to whiteness gone over—   20
or nothing.

1920, 1921

---

[4]Jean-Honoré Fragonard (1732–1806), French painter of love and gallantry in idealized scenes; famous for *The Swing*, portraying a young lady rising into the sky in the swing, her slipper kicked high in the air, while her young lover languishes in the grass below. This seems to be the painting Williams has in mind.

[1]A wild plant of the carrot family, with small white flowers in flat-topped clusters, suggestive of the appearance and delicacy of lace.

The Great Figure[1]

Among the rain
and lights
I saw the figure 5
in gold
on a red   5
firetruck
moving
tense
unheeded
to gong clangs   10
siren howls
and wheels rumbling
through the dark city.

1921

Spring and All[1]

By the road to the contagious hospital
under the surge of the blue
mottled clouds driven from the
northeast — a cold wind. Beyond, the
waste of broad, muddy fields   5
brown with dried weeds, standing and fallen

patches of standing water
the scattering of tall trees

All along the road the reddish
purplish, forked, upstanding, twiggy   10
stuff of bushes and small trees
with dead, brown leaves under them
leafless vines —

Lifeless in appearance, sluggish
dazed spring approaches —   15

They enter the new world naked,
cold, uncertain of all
save that they enter. All about them
the cold, familiar wind —

[1]Williams said of this poem (in his *Autobiography*): "Once on a hot July day coming back exhausted from the Post Graduate Clinic, I dropped in as I sometimes did at Marsden [Hartley's] studio on Fifteenth Street for a talk, a little drink maybe and to see what he was doing. As I approached his number I heard a great clatter of bells and the roar of a fire engine passing the end of the street down Ninth avenue. I turned just in time to see a golden figure 5 on a red background flash by. The impression was so sudden and forceful that I took a piece of paper out of my pocket and wrote a short poem about it." Williams's friend, the painter Charles Demuth, painted a poster of the vivid image captured in the poem, entitling it "I Saw the Figure 5 in Gold" (1928).

[1]This title was first used for a volume of untitled, numbered poems interspersed among prose passages, published in 1923; Williams eventually gave titles to all the poems, giving the book's title to this poem. Williams said of this poem: "One of the best images I have ever perpetrated, which even Yvor Winters [1900–1968; poet and critic] liked. But just at this point he parted company from me for the classic forms" (*Collected Poems*, Vol. 1, p. 501).

Now the grass, tomorrow   20
the stiff curl of wildcarrot leaf

One by one objects are defined—
It quickens: clarity, outline of leaf

But now the stark dignity of
entrance—Still, the profound change   25
has come upon them: rooted, they
grip down and begin to awaken

                                                                    1923

The Red Wheelbarrow[1]

so much depends
upon

a red wheel
barrow

glazed with rain   5
water

beside the white
chickens

                                                                    1923

Paterson[1]

Before the grass is out the people are out
and bare twigs still whip the wind—
when there is nothing, in the pause between
snow and grass in the parks and at the street ends
—Say it, no ideas but in things[2]—   5
nothing but the blank faces of the houses
and cylindrical trees
bent, forked by preconception and accident
split, furrowed, creased, mottled, stained
secret—into the body of the light—   10

These are the ideas, savage and tender
somewhat of the music, et cetera
of Paterson, that great philosopher—

---

[1]Williams once said of this poem: "The wheelbarrow in question stood outside the window of an old Negro's house on a back street in the suburb where I live. It was pouring rain and there were white chickens walking about in it. The sight impressed me somehow as about the most important, the most integral that it had ever been my pleasure to gaze upon. And the meter though no more than a fragment succeeds in portraying this pleasure flawlessly, even it succeeds in denoting a certain unquenchable exaltation—in fact I find the poem quite perfect" (William Rose Benét, *Fifty Poets*, 1933).

[1]Passages from this poem found their way later into Book One of Williams's epic, *Paterson* (1946); the city of Paterson is identified with a man, also called Paterson (and Williams's persona).

[2]This slogan remained a credo for Williams and he repeated it many times in both prose and poetry throughout his career.

From above, higher than the spires, higher
even than the office towers, from oozy fields   15
abandoned to grey beds of dead grass
black sumac, withered weed stalks
mud and thickets cluttered with dead leaves—
the river comes pouring in above the city
and crashes from the edge of the gorge   20
in a recoil of spray and rainbow mists—
—Say it, no ideas but in things—
and factories crystallized from its force,
like ice from spray upon the chimney rocks

· · · · ·

Say it! No ideas but in things. Mr.   25
Paterson has gone away
to rest and write. Inside the bus one sees
his thoughts sitting and standing. His thoughts
alight and scatter—

Who are these people (how complex   30
this mathematic) among whom I see myself
in the regularly ordered plateglass of
his thoughts, glimmering before shoes and bicycles—?
They walk incommunicado, the
equation is beyond solution, yet   35
its sense is clear—that they may live
his thought is listed in the Telephone
Directory—

        and there's young Alex Shorn[3]
whose dad the boot-black bought a house   40
and painted it inside
with seascapes of a pale green monochrome—
the infant Dionysus springing from
Apollo's arm—the floors oakgrained in
Balkan fashion—Hermes' nose, the body   45
of a gourmand, the lips of Cupid, the eyes
the black eyes of Venus' sister[4]—

But who! who are these people? It is
his flesh making the traffic, cranking the car
buying the meat—   50
Defeated in achieving the solution they
fall back among cheap pictures, furniture
filled silk, cardboard shoes, bad dentistry
windows that will not open, poisonous gin
scurvy, toothache—   55

· · · · ·

But never, in despair and anxiety
forget to drive wit in, in till it

---

[3]Actual son of a bootblack in Paterson (see *Collected Poems*, Vol. I, p. 512).
[4]The decoration of the house in European fashion, using classical mythological figures, contrasts starkly with the realities of the setting and routine of lives as actually lived in Paterson.

discover that his thoughts are decorous and simple
and never forget that though his thoughts are decorous
and simple, the despair and anxiety   60

the grace and detail of
a dynamo—

Divine thought! Jacob fell backwards off the press
and broke his spine. What pathos, what mercy
of nurses (who keep birthday books)   65
and doctors who can't speak proper english—
is here correctly on a spotless bed
painless to the Nth power—the two legs
perfect without movement or sensation

Twice a month Paterson receives letters   70
from the Pope, his works are translated
into French, the clerks in the post office
ungum the rare stamps from his packages
and steal them for their children's albums

So in his high decorum he is wise   75

    •   •   •   •   •

What wind and sun of children stamping the snow
stamping the snow and screaming drunkenly
The actual, florid detail of cheap carpet
amazingly upon the floor and paid for
as no portrait ever was—Canary singing   80
and geraniums in tin cans spreading their leaves
reflecting red upon the frost—
They are the divisions and imbalances
of his whole concept, made small by pity
and desire, they are—no ideas beside the facts—   85

1927, 1938

Young Sycamore

I must tell you
this young tree
whose round and firm trunk
between the wet

pavement and the gutter   5
(where water
is trickling) rises
bodily

into the air with
one undulant   10
thrust half its height—
and then

dividing and waning
sending out
young branches on   15
all sides—

hung with cocoons—
it thins
till nothing is left of it
but two   20

eccentric knotted
twigs
bending forward
hornlike at the top

                                  1927, 1934

Poem

As the cat
climbed over
the top of

the jamcloset
first the right   5
forefoot

carefully
then the hind
stepped down

into the pit of   10
the empty
flowerpot

                                  1930, 1934

The Botticellian Trees[1]

The alphabet of
the trees

is fading in the
song of the leaves

the crossing   5
bars of the thin

---

[1]In *La Primavera* (*Spring*), the Italian painter Sandro Botticelli (1444–1510) presents an allegory of springtime, with figures of the three graces dancing, with cupid aiming his arrow at a young man gazing into the trees, and a young lover pursuing a young maiden; the trees are in leaf and bearing fruit.

letters that spelled
winter

and the cold
have been illumined   10

with
pointed green

by the rain and sun—
The strict simple

principles of   15
straight branches

are being modified
by pinched-out

ifs of color, devout
conditions   20

the smiles of love—

        •   •   •   •   •

until the stript
sentences

move as a woman's
limbs under cloth   25

and praise from secrecy
quick with desire

love's ascendancy
in summer—

In summer the song   30
sings itself

above the muffled words—

                                              1931, 1934

This Is Just to Say

I have eaten
the plums
that were in
the icebox

and which   5
you were probably
saving
for breakfast

Forgive me
they were delicious   10
so sweet
and so cold

1934

To a Poor Old Woman

munching a plum on
the street a paper bag
of them in her hand

They taste good to her
They taste good   5
to her. They taste
good to her

You can see it by
the way she gives herself
to the one half   10
sucked out in her hand

Comforted
a solace of ripe plums
seeming to fill the air
They taste good to her   15

1934, 1935

Proletarian Portrait[1]

A big young bareheaded woman
in an apron

Her hair slicked back standing
on the street

One stockinged foot toeing   5
the sidewalk

Her shoe in her hand. Looking
intently into it

[1] Williams commented: "Ezra Pound wrote that he didn't like this because of the proletarian tone. He thought it was obvious and so what? 'She might have done as well in Russia as in Passaic'" (*Collected Poems*, Vol. I, p. 540). Williams had titled it "Study for a Figure Representing Modern Culture" when it appeared in *Galaxy: An Anthology*, 1934.

She pulls out the paper insole
to find the nail   10

That has been hurting her

                                                    1935

The Yachts[1]

contend in a sea which the land partly encloses
shielding them from the too-heavy blows
of an ungoverned ocean which when it chooses

tortures the biggest hulls, the best man knows
to pit against its beatings, and sinks them pitilessly.   5
Mothlike in mists, scintillant in the minute

brilliance of cloudless days, with broad bellying sails
they glide to the wind tossing green water
from their sharp prows while over them the crew crawls

ant-like, solicitously grooming them, releasing,   10
making fast as they turn, lean far over and having
caught the wind again, side by side, head for the mark.

In a well guarded arena of open water surrounded by
lesser and greater craft which, sycophant, lumbering
and flittering follow them, they appear youthful, rare   15

as the light of a happy eye, live with the grace
of all that in the mind is fleckless, free and
naturally to be desired. Now the sea which holds them

is moody, lapping their glossy sides, as if feeling
for some slightest flaw but fails completely.   20
Today no race. Then the wind comes again. The yachts

move, jockeying for a start, the signal is set and they
are off. Now the waves strike at them but they are too
well made, they slip through, though they take in canvas.

Arms with hands grasping seek to clutch at the prows.   25
Bodies thrown recklessly in the way are cut aside.
It is a sea of faces about them in agony, in despair

---

[1]Williams commented on this poem: "I wrote the whole damn thing without a change. I was thinking of terza rima, but gave up rime —a *very* vague imitation of Dante. I was quickly carried away by my own feelings"; ". . . the yachts do not sink but go on with the race while only *in the imagination* are they seen to founder. It is a false situation which the yachts typify with the beauty of their movements while the real situation (of the poor) is desperate while 'the skillful yachts pass over'" (*Collected Poems*, Vol. I, p. 541).

until the horror of the race dawns staggering the mind,
the whole sea become an entanglement of watery bodies
lost to the world bearing what they cannot hold. Broken,   30

beaten, desolate, reaching from the dead to be taken up
they cry out, failing, failing! their cries rising
in waves still as the skillful yachts pass over.

                                                                    1935

The Poor

It's the anarchy of poverty
delights me, the old

yellow wooden house indented
among the new brick tenements

Or a cast-iron balcony   5
with panels showing oak branches
in full leaf. It fits
the dress of the children

reflecting every stage and
custom of necessity—   10
Chimneys, roofs, fences of
wood and metal in an unfenced

age and enclosing next to
nothing at all: the old man
in a sweater and soft black   15
hat who sweeps the sidewalk—

his own ten feet of it—
in a wind that fitfully
turning his corner has
overwhelmed the entire city   20

                                                                    1938

Between Walls

the back wings
of the

hospital where
nothing

will grow lie   5
cinders

    in which shine
    the broken

    pieces of a green
    bottle   10

1938

These

are the desolate, dark weeks
when nature in its barrenness
equals the stupidity of man.

The year plunges into night
and the heart plunges   5
lower than night

to an empty, windswept place
without sun, stars or moon
but a peculiar light as of thought

that spins a dark fire—   10
whirling upon itself until,
in the cold, it kindles

to make a man aware of nothing
that he knows, not loneliness
itself—Not a ghost but   15

would be embraced—emptiness,
despair—(They
whine and whistle) among

the flashes and booms of war;
houses of whose rooms   20
the cold is greater than can be thought,

the people gone that we loved,
the beds lying empty, the couches
damp, the chairs unused—

Hide it away somewhere   25
out of the mind, let it get roots
and grow, unrelated to jealous

ears and eyes—for itself.
In this mine they come to dig—all.
Is this the counterfoil to sweetest   30

music? The source of poetry that
seeing the clock stopped, says,
The clock has stopped

that ticked yesterday so well?
and hears the sound of lakewater   35
splashing — that is now stone.

1938

Burning the Christmas Greens[1]

Their time past, pulled down
cracked and flung to the fire
—go up in a roar

All recognition lost, burnt clean
clean in the flame, the green   5
dispersed, a living red,
flame red, red as blood wakes
on the ash—

and ebbs to a steady burning
the rekindled bed become   10
a landscape of flame

At the winter's midnight
we went to the trees, the coarse
holly, the balsam and
the hemlock for their green   15

At the thick of the dark
the moment of the cold's
deepest plunge we brought branches
cut from the green trees

to fill our need, and over   20
doorways, about paper Christmas
bells covered with tinfoil
and fastened by red ribbons

we stuck the green prongs
in the windows hung   25
woven wreaths and above pictures
the living green. On the

mantle we built a green forest
and among those hemlock
sprays put a herd of small   30
white deer as if they

---

[1]Williams commented on this poem: "An occurrence in our home. Certainly no one can escape the conclusion that this poem envisages a rebirth of the 'state' perhaps but certainly of the mind following the destruction of the shibboleths of tradition which often comfort it"; "As far as I know the Christmas poem was as good as anything I've ever written" (*Collected Poems*, Vol. II, pp. 460–61).

were walking there. All this!
and it seemed gentle and good
to us. Their time past,
relief! The room bare. We　　35

stuffed the dead grate
with them upon the half burnt out
log's smoldering eye, opening
red and closing under them

and we stood there looking down.　　40
Green is a solace
a promise of peace, a fort
against the cold (though we

did not say so) a challenge
above the snow's　　45
hard shell. Green (we might
have said) that, where

small birds hide and dodge
and lift their plaintive
rallying cries, blocks for them　　50
and knocks down

the unseeing bullets of
the storm. Green spruce boughs
pulled down by a weight of
snow—Transformed!　　55

Violence leaped and appeared.
Recreant! roared to life
as the flame rose through and
our eyes recoiled from it.

In the jagged flames green　　60
to red, instant and alive. Green!
those sure abutments . . . Gone!
lost to mind

and quick in the contracting
tunnel of the grate　　65
appeared a world! Black
mountains, black and red—as

yet uncolored—and ash white,
an infant landscape of shimmering
ash and flame and we, in　　70
that instant, lost,

breathless to be witnesses,
as if we stood
ourselves refreshed among
the shining fauna of that fire.　　75

1944

The Descent[1]

<pre>
The descent beckons
            as the ascent beckoned.
                        Memory is a kind
of accomplishment,
            a sort of renewal   5
                        even
an initiation, since the spaces it opens are new places
            inhabited by hordes
                        heretofore unrealized,
of new kinds —   10
            since their movements
                        are toward new objectives
(even though formerly they were abandoned).

No defeat is made up entirely of defeat — since
the world it opens is always a place   15
            formerly
                        unsuspected. A
world lost,
            a world unsuspected,
                        beckons to new places   20
and no whiteness (lost) is so white as the memory
of whiteness   .

With evening, love wakens
            though its shadows
                        which are alive by reason   25
of the sun shining —
            grow sleepy now and drop away
                        from desire   .

Love without shadows stirs now
            beginning to awaken   30
                        as night
advances.

The descent
            made up of despairs
                        and without accomplishment   35
realizes a new awakening:
            which is a reversal
of despair.
            For what we cannot accomplish, what
is denied to love,   40
            what we have lost in the anticipation —
                        a descent follows,
endless and indestructible   .
</pre>

1948, 1954

---

[1] "The Descent" was a poem embedded in Book Two of *Paterson* (1948), but Williams wanted it published separately in 1954 in *The Desert Music and Other Poems*. He wrote to his publisher, explaining: "I certainly want to include 'The Descent' in the forthcoming book. Otherwise, if I exclude it, the train of thought which induced the present format of my poems will not be completely revealed"; when "The Descent" was included in an anthology, *Poet's Choice*, ed. Paul Engle and Joseph Langland (1962), Williams supplied a note: "I write in the American idiom and for many years I have been using what I call the variable foot. 'The Descent' is the first poem in that medium that wholly satisfied me" (*Collected Poems*, Vol. II, p. 486). Williams used his "variable foot" (providing rhythm but avoiding a fixed meter) and his "triadic line" (a three-part line with each part stepping down across the page) in most of his later poetry.

The Desert Music[1]

—the dance begins: to end about a form
propped motionless—on the bridge
between Juárez and El Paso[2]—unrecognizable
in a semi-dark

                    Wait!   5

The others[3] waited while you inspected it,
on the very walk itself   .

                    Is it alive?

                              —neither a head,
legs nor arms!   10

              It isn't a sack of rags someone
has abandoned here   .   torpid against
the flange of the supporting girder   .   ?

                    an inhuman shapelessness,
knees hugged tight up into the belly   15

              Egg-shaped!

                        What a place to sleep!
on the International Boundary.   Where else,
interjurisdictional, not to be disturbed?

How shall we get said what must be said?   20

Only the poem.

Only the counted poem, to an exact measure:
to imitate, not to copy nature, not
to copy nature

NOT, prostrate, to copy nature   25
                    but a dance! to dance

---

[1]*The Desert Music* was read at a Harvard assembly, June 1951, after which Williams was made an honorary member of Phi Beta Kappa. Williams wrote in a letter to Norman Macleod: "It has taken me a month or more to write it, transcribe it, have it typed, correct it and polish it. That took about all the drive I had"; he wrote to Robert Lowell after his appearance at Harvard: "From the faces of some (not all) of those on the platform I think they must have fumigated Memorial Hall after I left. The student body was, on the other hand, delighted and showed it by their tumultuous applause after I had finished my '15 minute' poem" (*Collected Poems*, Vol. II, p. 493).

In *I Wanted to Write a Poem*, reported and edited by Edith Heal (1958), Williams commented on the book *The Desert Music and Other Poems* (1954): "There is something special about this book. Just before I had my cerebral accident, I had received an invitation to read a poem at Phi Beta Kappa exercises at Harvard. I had no poem to read them so I wrote one. I had just returned from a trip to the West and the picture of the desert country around El Paso was fresh in my mind. I'd crossed the desert and *seen* the desert. It is always important to me to be familiar with what I am writing about. I was hon-

ored by the invitation to read at Harvard (but was perhaps not so honored after I had read). The students were tickled to death but some of the gentlemen sitting on the platform disapproved. After all, it is a pretty shocking poem, speaking as it does of the whores of Juárez.

"When I recovered from the cerebral attack, I began to write again. My whole interest in poetry now was in developing the concept I had discovered—the variable foot—based on the model of the poem in *Paterson* Book Two, section three. Now, consciously, I knew what I wanted to do. I had a group of poems ready and Dave McDowell said, 'You also have the one you did for Harvard—that will make a book.' The other poems in *Desert Music* are more important than the title poem because they consciously use what I had discovered."

[2]Border towns: Juárez, Mexico; El Paso, Texas. Williams and his wife Florence (Flossie) visited there on a return trip from Los Angeles in 1950.

[3]Robert McAlmon, an American writer and one of the expatriate Paris group, together with his two brothers and their wives, joined the Williamses on the visit to Juárez.

two and two with him—
                    sequestered there asleep,
                              right end up!

        A music   30
supersedes his composure, hallooing to us
across a great distance   .   .

                              wakens the dance
who blows upon his benumbed fingers!

                              Only the poem   35
only the made poem, to get said what must
be said, not to copy nature, sticks
in our throats   .

The law?   The law gives us nothing
but a corpse, wrapped in a dirty mantle.   40
The law is based on murder and confinement,
long delayed,
but this, following the insensate music,
is based on the dance:

                    an agony of self-realization   45
bound into a whole
by that which surrounds us   .

                    I cannot escape

I cannot vomit it up

Only the poem!   50

Only the made poem, the verb calls it
                              into being.

                    —it looks too small for a man.
A woman.   Or a very shriveled old man.
Maybe dead.   They probably inspect the place   55
and will cart it away later   .

                    Heave it into the river.
A good thing.

Leaving California to return east, the fertile desert,
                    (were it to get water)   60
surrounded us, a music of survival, subdued, distant, half
                    heard; we were engulfed
by it as in the early evening, seeing the wind lift
                    and drive the sand, we
passed Yuma. All night long, heading for El Paso to   65
                    meet our friend,[4]

---

[4]Robert McAlmon; in the early 1920s Williams and
McAlmon had together edited *Contact*, a little magazine of
avant-garde writing.

we slept fitfully.   Thinking of Paris, I waked to the tick
                    of the rails.   The
jagged desert   .

                                                 — to tell   70
            what subsequently I saw and what heard

                            — to place myself (in
my nature) beside nature

                        — to imitate
nature (for to copy nature would be a   75
        shameful thing)

                    I lay myself down:

The Old Market's a good place to begin:
Let's cut through here —
                                        tequila's only   80
a nickel a slug in these side streets.
Keep out though.   Oh, it's all right at
this time of day but I saw H. terribly
beaten up in one of those joints.   He
asked for it. I thought he was going to   85
be killed.   I do
my drinking on the main drag   .

                        That's the bull ring
Oh, said Floss, after she got used to the
change of light   .   90
                    What color! Isn't it
wonderful!

            — paper flowers (*para los santos*)[5]
baked red-clay utensils, daubed
with blue, silverware,   95
dried peppers, onions, print goods, children's
clothing   .   the place deserted all but
for a few Indians squatted in the
booths, unnoticing (don't you think it)
as though they slept there   .   100

            There's a second tier.   Do you
want to go up?

            What makes Texans so tall?
We saw a woman this morning in a mink cape
six feet if she was an inch.   What a woman!   105

Probably a Broadway figure.

— tell you what else we saw: about a million
sparrows screaming their heads off
in the trees of that small park where

---

5 "For the saints" (Spanish).

the buses stop, sanctuary,   110
I suppose,
from the wind driving the sand in that way
about the city   .

                  Texas rain they call it

—and those two alligators in the fountain   .   115

There were four

         I saw only two

                 They were looking
right at you all the time   .

Penny please!   Give me penny please, mister.   120

           Don't give them anything.

                   .   instinctively
one has already drawn one's naked
wrist away from those obscene fingers
as in the mind a vague apprehension speaks   125
and the music rouses   .

                Let's get in here.
          a music!   cut off as
the bar door closes behind us.

             We've got   130
another half hour.

             —returned to the street,
the pressure moves from booth to booth along
the curb.   Opposite, no less insistent
the better stores are wide open.   Come in   135
and look around.   You don't have to buy: hats,
riding boots, blankets   .

            Look at the way,
slung from her neck with a shawl, that young
Indian woman carries her baby!   140

             —a stream of Spanish,
as she brushes by, intense, wide-
eyed in eager talk with her boy husband

—three half-grown girls, one of them eating a
pomegranate.   Laughing.   145

             and the serious tourist,
man and wife, middle-aged, middle-western,
their arms loaded with loot, whispering
together—still looking for bargains   .

and the aniline[6]   150
red and green candy at the little booth
tended by the old Indian woman.
            Do you suppose anyone actually
buys—and eats the stuff?

My feet are beginning to ache me.   155

                    We still got a few minutes.
Let's try here.   They had the mayor
up last month for taking $3000 a week from
the whorehouses of the city.   Not much left
for the girls.   There's a show on.   160

                    Only a few tables
occupied.   A conventional orchestra—this
place livens up later—playing the usual local
jing-a-jing—a boy and girl team, she
                    confidential with someone   165
off stage.   Laughing: just finishing the act.

So we drink until the next turn—a strip tease.

Do you mean it?   Wow!   Look at her.

                    You'd have to be
pretty drunk to get any kick out of that.   170
She's no Mexican.   Some worn-out trouper from
the States.   Look at those breasts   .

        There is a fascination
        seeing her shake
        the beaded sequins from   175
        a string about her hips

        She gyrates but it's
        not what you think,
        one does not laugh
        to watch her belly.   180

        One is moved but not
        at the dull show.   The
        guitarist yawns.   She
        cannot even sing.   She

        has about her painted   185
        hardihood a screen
        of pretty doves which
        flutter their wings.

        Her cold eyes perfunc-
        torily moan but do not   190
        smile.   Yet they bill

---

[6]A poisonous oily liquid, derivative of benzene, used in the
making of dyes; here, used to dye the candies.

and coo by grace of
a certain candor.   She

is heavy on her feet.
That's good.   She   195
bends forward leaning
on the table of the
balding man sitting
upright, alone, so that
everything hangs for-   200
ward.
            What the hell
are you grinning
to yourself about?   Not
at *her*?   205
            The music!
I like her.   She fits

the music   .

Why don't these Indians get over this nauseating prattle
about their souls and their loves and sing us something   210
else for a change?

            This place is rank
            with it.   She
            at least knows she's
            part of another tune,   215
            knows her customers,
            has the same
            opinion of them as I
            have.   That gives her
            one up   .   one up   220
            following the lying
            music   .

There is another music.   The bright-colored candy
of her nakedness lifts her unexpectedly
to partake of its tune   .   225

                        Andromeda[7] of those rocks,
the virgin of her mind   .   those unearthly
greens and reds
                        in her mockery of virtue
she becomes unaccountably virtuous   .   230
                        though she in no
way pretends it   .

Let's get out of this.

                  In the street it hit
me in the face as we started to walk again.   Or   235
am I merely playing the poet?   Do I merely invent
it out of whole cloth?   I thought   .

---

[7]A beautiful Ethiopian princess who had offended the
Nereids and had been chained to a rock; Perseus, son of
Zeus, rescued and married her.

What in the form of an old whore in
a cheap Mexican joint in Juárez, her bare
can waggling crazily can be   240
so refreshing to me, raise to my ear
so sweet a tune, built of such slime?

Here we are.   They'll be along any minute.
The bar is at the right of the entrance,
a few tables opposite which you have to pass   245
to get to the dining room, beyond.

A foursome, two oversize Americans, no
longer young, got up as cowboys,
hats and all, are drunk and carrying on
with their gals, drunk also,   250

especially one inciting her man, the
biggest, *Yip ee*! to dance in
the narrow space, oblivious to everything
—she is insatiable and he is trying

stumblingly to keep up with her.   255
Give it the gun, pardner!   *Yip ee*!   We
pushed by them to our table, seven
of us.   Seated about the room

were quiet family groups, some with
children, eating.   Rather a better   260
class than you notice
on the streets.   So here we are.   You

can see through into the kitchen
where one of the cooks, his shirt sleeves
rolled up, an apron over   265
the well-pressed pants of a street

suit, black hair neatly parted,
a tall
good-looking man, is working
absorbed, before a chopping block   270

Old Fashioneds all around?

                So this is William
Carlos Williams, the poet   ·

                Floss and I had half consumed
our quartered hearts of lettuce before   275
we noticed the others hadn't touched theirs   ·
You seem quite normal.   Can you tell me?   Why
does one want to write a poem?

                Because it's there to be written.

Oh.   A matter of inspiration then?   280

                                Of necessity.

Oh.   But what sets it off?

           I am that he whose brains
           are scattered
                aimlessly   285

                            —and so,
the hour done, the quail eaten, we were on
our way back to El Paso.

                  Good night.   Good
night and thank you   .   No.   Thank you.   We're   290
going to walk   .

—and so, on the naked wrist, we feel again
those insistent fingers   .

                    Penny please, mister.
Penny please.   Give me penny.

                     Here! now go away.   295

—but the music, the music has reawakened
as we leave the busier parts of the street
and come again to the bridge in the semi-dark,
pay our fee and begin again to cross   .
seeing the lights along the mountain back of El   300
Paso and pause to watch the boys calling out
to us to throw more coins to them standing
in the shallow water   .   so that's
where the incentive lay, with the annoyance
of those surprising fingers.   305

                  So you're a poet?
a good thing to be got rid of—half drunk,
a free dinner under your belt, even though you
get typhoid—and to have met people you
can at least talk to   .   310

              relief from that changeless, endless
inescapable and insistent music   .   .

             What else, Latins, do you yourselves
seek but relief!
with the expressionless ding dong you dish up   315
to us of your souls and your loves, which
we swallow. Spaniards! (though these are mostly
Indians who chase the white bastards
through the streets on their Independence Day
and try to kill them)   .   320

                    What's that?

Oh, come on.

            But what's THAT?

                                    the music! the
music! as when Casals[8] struck   325
and held a deep cello tone
and I am speechless

                        There it sat
in the projecting angle of the bridge flange
as I stood aghast and looked at it —   330
in the half-light: shapeless or rather returned
to its original shape, armless, legless,
headless, packed like the pit of a fruit into
that obscure corner — or
a fish to swim against the stream — or   335
a child in the womb prepared to imitate life,
warding its life against
a birth of awful promise.   The music
guards it, a mucus, a film that surrounds it,
a benumbing ink that stains the   340
sea of our minds — to hold us off — shed
of a shape close as it can get to no shape,
a music! a protecting music

                        I *am* a poet! I
am.   I am.   I am a poet, I reaffirmed, ashamed   345

Now the music volleys through as in
a lonely moment I hear it.   Now it is all
about me.   The dance!   The verb detaches itself
seeking to become articulate

                        And I could not help thinking   350
                        of the wonders of the brain that
                        hears that music and of our
                        skill sometimes to record it.

1951   *1951, 1954*

Introduction to *The Wedge*

[POEM: MACHINE MADE OF WORDS]

The war is the first and only thing in the world today.[1]

The arts generally are not, nor is this writing a diversion from that for relief, a turning away. It *is* the war or part of it, merely a different sector of the field.

Critics of rather better than average standing have said in recent years that after socialism has been achieved it's likely there will be no further use for poetry, that it will disappear. This comes from nothing else than a faulty definition of poetry — and the arts generally. I don't hear anyone say that mathematics is likely to be outmoded, to disappear shortly. Then why poetry?

---

[8]Pablo Casals (1876–1973), Spanish violincellist, conductor, and composer, and a virtuoso performer.

[1]The Second World War, in which America fought with the Allies from 1941 until August of 1945.

It is an error attributable to the Freudian concept[2] of the thing, that the arts are a resort from frustration, a misconception still entertained in many minds.

They speak as though action itself in all its phases were not compatible with frustration. All action the same. But Richard Coeur de Lion[3] wrote at least one of the finest lyrics of his day. Take Don Juan[4] for instance. Who isn't frustrated and does not prove it by his actions — if you want to say so? But through art the psychologically maimed may become the most distinguished man of his age. Take Freud for instance.

The making of poetry is no more an evidence of frustration than is the work of Henry Kaiser or of Timoshenko.[5] It's the war, the driving forward of desire to a complex end. And when that shall have been achieved, mathematics and the arts will turn elsewhere — beyond the atom if necessary for their reward and let's all be frustrated together.

A man isn't a block that remains stationary though the psychologists treat him so — and most take an insane pride in believing it. Consistency! He varies; Hamlet today, Caesar tomorrow;[6] here, there, somewhere — if he is to retain his sanity, and why not?

The arts have a *complex* relation to society. The poet isn't a fixed phenomenon, no more is his work. *That* might be a note on current affairs, a diagnosis, a plan for procedure, a retrospect — all in its own peculiarly enduring form. There need be nothing limited or frustrated about that. It may be a throw-off from the most violent and successful action or run parallel to it, a saga. It may be the picking out of an essential detail for memory, something to be set aside for further study, a sort of shorthand of emotional significances for later reference.

Let the metaphysical take care of itself, the arts have nothing to do with it. They will concern themselves with it if they please, among other things. To make two bald statements: There's nothing sentimental about a machine, and: A poem is a small (or large) machine made of words. When I say there's nothing sentimental about a poem I mean that there can be no part, as in any other machine, that is redundant.

Prose may carry a load of ill-defined matter like a ship. But poetry is the machine which drives it, pruned to a perfect economy. As in all machines its movement is intrinsic, undulant, a physical more than a literary character. In a poem this movement is distinguished in each case by the character of the speech from which it arises.

Therefore, each speech having its own character, the poetry it engenders will be peculiar to that speech also in its own intrinsic form. The effect is beauty, what in a single object resolves our complex feelings of propriety. One doesn't seek beauty. All that an artist or a Sperry[7] can do is to drive toward his purpose, in the nature of his materials; not to take gold where Babbit metal[8] is called for; to make: make clear the complexity of his perceptions in the medium given to him by inheritance, chance, accident or whatever it may be to work with according to his talents and the will that drives them. Don't talk about frustration fathering the arts. The bastardization of words is too widespread for that today.

My own interest in the arts has been extracurricular. Up from the gutter, so to speak. Of necessity. Each age and place to its own. But in the U.S. the necessity for

[2]Sigmund Freud (1856–1939), Austrian founder of psychoanalysis; he explored the relationship between neuroses and art, but did not proclaim any fixed laws about that relationship.

[3]Richard I, "Coeur de Lion" or "The Lion-Hearted" (1157–1199), king of England; he wrote lyric poems in French.

[4]A legendary Spaniard infamous for his many sexual adventures; a libertine.

[5]Henry Kaiser (1882–1967), American industrialist whose feats of production of needed materials during the Second World War were awesome; Semyon Timoshenko (1895–1970), Soviet army commander who halted the German drive on Moscow in the Second World War.

[6]In Shakespeare's play, the introspective Hamlet hesitates to act; Julius Caesar, on the other hand, was a forceful and decisive Roman general and statesman.

[7]Elmer Ambrose Sperry (1860–1930), American industrialist, electrical engineer, and inventor, who organized the Sperry Gyroscope Company in 1910.

[8]Babbit metal: an alloy of tin with smaller amounts of antimony and copper used in manufacturing various kinds of machinery.

recognizing this intrinsic character has been largely ignored by the various English Departments of the academies.

When a man makes a poem, makes it, mind you, he takes words as he finds them interrelated about him and composes them—without distortion which would mar their exact significances—into an intense expression of his perceptions and ardors that they may constitute a revelation in the speech that he uses. It isn't what he *says* that counts as a work of art, it's what he makes, with such intensity of perception that it lives with an intrinsic movement of its own to verify its authenticity. Your attention is called now and then to some beautiful line or sonnet-sequence because of what is said there. So be it. To me all sonnets say the same thing of no importance. What does it matter what the line "says"?

There is no poetry of distinction without formal invention, for it is in the intimate form that works of art achieve their exact meaning, in which they most resemble the machine, to give language its highest dignity, its illumination in the environment to which it is native. Such war, as the arts live and breathe by, is continuous.

It may be that my interests as expressed here are pre-art. If so I look for a development along these lines and will be satisfied with nothing else.

1944

MARIANNE MOORE
(1887–1972)

Marianne Moore has often been called the poet supreme of animals. A glance down the table of contents of her collected poems reveals such titles as "The Buffalo," "The Fish," "The Monkeys," "Snakes, Mongooses, Snake-Charmers and the Like," "A Jelly Fish," "To a Giraffe," "To a Snail," "The Pangolin," "The Paper Nautilus," "Elephants," and so on. It was not uncommon in earlier periods to write poems about or to animals—but usually the most beautiful or mysterious or spiritually evocative were chosen: nightingales, waterfowls, butterflies, bees, and even snakes. But Moore's animals are often strange or awkward-seeming creatures she has read about in books, found in magazines, newspapers, on precious art works, common shoe-polish containers, or observed at the zoo, which she loved to visit. They are described with an almost scientific precision, and their odd, unhuman traits are detailed—all in a style that is delicately balanced between wit and wisdom, poised on the edge of metaphysical insight.

Given her fascination for unlovely animals, it should not be surprising to find that her definition of poetry, one of the most famous conceived by a modernist, includes an ordinary creature sometimes considered a nuisance or even in its claminess slightly repellent. Poets, she said in "Poetry," must become "literalists of the imagination" and present "imaginary gardens with real toads in them." No one before her had ever dared to define poetry in terms of "toads"—"real toads," moreover. Note how a reversal of the items—"imaginary toads in real gardens"—diminishes the force of those "real toads" (ugh!).

Marianne Moore was born in a suburb of St. Louis, only a few months before T. S. Eliot was born in the same city. Her father abandoned the family and she grew up in the house of her grandfather, a Presbyterian minister. Her mother moved the family to Carlisle, Pennsylvania, where she had obtained a teaching job. Moore graduated from Bryn Mawr in 1909; among her classmates was

Hilda Doolittle (H.D.). In 1911 she and her mother toured France and England; in Paris they went to every museum "except two," she remembered later. Back in Carlisle, Moore obtained a job teaching business (or commercial) courses in the U.S. Indian School, working there from 1911 to 1915.

Moore had begun to write poems at Bryn Mawr, and now she started sending poems out to the little magazines — *Poetry, Others, The Egoist* (London). Her first poems began to appear in 1915. In 1918, Moore and her mother moved together with Moore's brother (a Presbyterian minister) to New York, eventually settling in Brooklyn, where Moore became, and remained for life, a passionate Brooklyn Dodgers fan. She never married, and lived with her mother all her life. For a time she taught, and from 1921 to 1925 she worked as a part-time librarian in a branch of the New York Public Library. She was soon involved in a literary circle including William Carlos Williams, Wallace Stevens, and Alfred Kreymborg (editor of *Others*).

In 1921, without Moore's authorization, H. D. and Bryher (Winifred Ellerman) brought out a volume of Moore's poems with the Egoist Press in England. When asked her reaction later, Moore replied: "To issue my slight product — conspicuously tentative — seemed to me premature." She herself brought out her poems, entitled *Observations* in 1924. Her poetry drew the praise of Ezra Pound, T. S. Eliot, Wallace Stevens, and others. William Carlos Williams would say later in his *Autobiography*, "She was like a rafter holding up the superstructure of our uncompleted building." In an interview, Moore exclaimed: "I never was a rafter holding up anyone."

In 1925 Marianne Moore became editor of *The Dial*, one of the leading art and literature journals of the time, and remained until the magazine's demise in 1929. Asked later about the editorial policy, she replied: "I think individuality was the great thing. We were not conformist to anything. We certainly didn't have a policy, except I remember hearing the word 'intensity' very often."

Work as editor slowed her in the writing of her own poetry. After her editorship of *The Dial* she became productive again, continuing in the distinctive style she had made her own, a style she claimed was shaped by the "precision, economy of statement, logic" of good prose as much as by poetry. Among the prose stylists she admired were Samuel Johnson, Henry James, and Ezra Pound.

One frequently noted characteristic of her style is the copious use of quotations culled from books, magazines, statistical works, or newspapers; she kept a large file of such material that had attracted her interest, and often a poem would take its beginning from such a scrap or fragment. She wrote in the Foreword to *A Marianne Moore Reader* (1961): "'Why the many quotation marks?' I am asked. Pardon my saying more than once, When a thing has been said so well that it could not be said better, why paraphrase it? Hence my writing is, if not a cabinet of fossils, a kind of collection of flies in amber."

In this same Foreword, Moore pointed out the rationale (or irrationality) of other characteristics of her poetic style: "Rhythm: the clue to it all . . . — something built in as in music"; "I dislike the reversed order of words; don't like to be impeded by an unnecessary capital at the beginning of every line. . . ."; "I like straight writing, end-stopped lines, an effect of flowing continuity, and after 1929 — perhaps earlier — wrote no verse that did not (in my opinion) rhyme." Although the rhymes are indeed there in her poems, they are often so subtle as to be passed over unrecognized (except perhaps at unconscious levels).

One characteristic of Moore's poems often puzzles readers — the lines as spaced and grouped on a page as to suggest a sequence of eccentric but similar if not identical stanzas. When asked about her "syllabic verse" (in which the line length is determined by the number of syllables, not by the number of stressed syllables or feet), she objected to the term:

> It never occurred to me that what I wrote was something to define. I am governed by the pull of the sentences as the pull of the fabric is governed by gravity. . . . I never "plan" a stanza. Words cluster like chromosomes, determining the procedure. I may influence an arrangement or thin it, then try to have successive stanzas identical with the first. Spontaneous initial originality — say, impetus — seems difficult to reproduce consciously later. As Stravinsky said about pitch, "If I transpose it for some reasons, I am in danger of losing the freshness of first contact and will have difficulty in recapturing its attractiveness."

Moore's *Selected Poems* appeared in 1935, and her *Collected Poems* in 1951. For the latter she was given the National Book Award, the Pulitzer Prize, the Bollingen Prize, and the Gold Medal for Poetry of the National Institute of Arts and Letters. Her lifelong interest in animals was climaxed in 1954 by publication of her translations from the French of *The Fables of La Fontaine*. Her selected essays appeared in 1955 as *Predilections*. This same year, she was asked by Ford Motor Company to suggest a name for a new car line. After a voluminous correspondence (published in *The New Yorker* in 1957), the company ignored her suggestions (among them, the Resilient Bullet, the Taper Racer, the Utopian Turtletop), and the car was named after a Ford family member, Edsel; it was one of the greatest flops in automobile history.

During her last years, Moore continued to write poetry, publishing *Like a Bulwark* in 1956, *O to Be a Dragon* in 1959, *Tell Me, Tell Me* in 1966. She published her *Complete Poems* in 1967 (reissued in 1980 with some corrections and additions). She was a rigorous reviser of her poems; one famous poem, "Poetry," was reduced from twenty-nine lines to three in *Complete Poems*. But Moore provided in her notes the whole of the original. It was in this period that she began to wear a black cape and a tricornered hat for all excursions outside her apartment. A photograph of her in this quaint attire has become the fixed public image of her.

As Morton Dauwen Zabel said in 1935, "Confronting Miss Moore's poems . . . calls for a renovation not only of the attention, but of one's habits, definitions, and prejudices; and of what these have done to one's understanding of the words, rhythms, and sentences of poetry." As early as 1923, T. S. Eliot wrote (reviewing Moore's *Poems*), "I can only, at the moment, think of five contemporary poets . . . whose work excites me as much as, or more than, Miss Moore's." And he said in 1935, in his Preface to her *Selected Poems*: "My conviction, for what it is worth, has remained unchanged for the last fourteen years: that Miss Moore's poems form part of the small body of writings, among what passes for poetry, in which an original sensibility and alert intelligence and deep feeling have been engaged in maintaining the life of the English language."

ADDITIONAL READING

Eugene P. Sheehy and Kenneth A. Lohf, eds., *The Achievement of Marianne Moore: A Bibliography, 1907–1957*, 1958; M. J. Tambimuttu, ed., *Festschrift for Marianne Moore's Seventy-Fifth Birthday — by Various Hands*, 1964; Bernard F. Engel, *Marianne Moore*, 1964; Jean Garrigue, *Marianne Moore*, 1965; Charles Tomlinson, ed., *Marianne Moore: A Collection of Critical Essays*, 1969; Donald Hall, *Marianne Moore: The Cage and the Animal*, 1970; Gary Lane, *A Concordance to the Poems of Marianne Moore*, 1972; Craig S. Abbott, *Marianne Moore: A Descriptive Bibliography*, 1977; Pamela W. Hadas, *Marianne Moore: Poet of Affection*, 1977; Laurence Stapleton, *Marianne Moore: The Poet's Advance*, 1978; Marie Borroff, *Language and the Poet: Verbal Artistry in Frost, Stevens, and Moore*, 1979; Craig S. Abbott, *Marianne Moore: A Reference Guide*, 1980; Bonnie Costello, *Marianne Moore: Imaginary Possessions*, 1981; Taffy Martin, *Marianne Moore: Subversive Modernist*,

1986; John M. Slatin, *The Savage's Romance: The Poetry of Marianne Moore*, 1986; Grace Schulman, *Marianne Moore: The Poetry of Engagement*, 1987; Margaret Holley, *The Poetry of Marianne Moore: A Study in Voice and Value*, 1987; "Marianne Moore Special Issue," *Sagetrieb*, Winter 1987; "Special issue: Marianne Moore," *William Carlos Williams Review*, Spring 1988.

TEXTS

"Poetry" from *The Collected Poems of Marianne Moore*, 1951; all other poems from *The Complete Poems of Marianne Moore*, 1981 ("Definitive Edition, with the Author's Final Revisions"); *The Complete Prose of Marianne Moore*, ed. Patricia C. Willis, 1986.

To a Steam Roller

The illustration
is nothing to you without the application.
   You lack half wit. You crush all the particles down
     into close conformity, and then walk back and forth on them.

Sparkling chips of rock   5
are crushed down to the level of the parent block.
   Were not "impersonal judgment in aesthetic
     matters, a metaphysical impossibility," you

might fairly achieve
it. As for butterflies, I can hardly conceive   10
   of one's attending upon you, but to question
     the congruence of the complement is vain, if it exists.

                                            1915, 1921

The Monkeys[1]

winked too much and were afraid of snakes. The zebras, supreme in
their abnormality; the elephants with their fog-colored skin
   and strictly practical appendages
     were there, the small cats; and the parakeet—
       trivial and humdrum on examination, destroying   5
     bark and portions of the food it could not eat.

I recall their magnificence, now not more magnificent
than it is dim. It is difficult to recall the ornament,
   speech, and precise manner of what one might
     call the minor acquaintances twenty   10
       years back; but I shall not forget him—that Gilgamesh[2] among
     the hairy carnivora—that cat with the

wedge-shaped, slate-gray marks on its forelegs and the resolute tail,
astringently remarking, "They have imposed on us with their pale

---

[1] The animals—the monkeys, the hairy carnivora, the cat, etc.—in this poem (as critics have observed) serve Moore in making a statement about critics, poets, and poetry.

[2] Legendary hero, part man and part immortal king, of the ancient Babylonian *Epic of Gilgamesh*.

half-fledged protestations, trembling about   15
   in inarticulate frenzy, saying
     it is not for us to understand art; finding it
   all so difficult, examining the thing

as if it were inconceivably arcanic, as symmet-
rically frigid as if it had been carved out of chrysoprase[3]   20
   or marble—strict with tension, malignant
     in its power over us and deeper
       than the sea when it proffers flattery in exchange for hemp,
rye, flax, horses, platinum, timber, and fur."

1917, 1921, 1935

The Fish

   wade
   through black jade.[1]
     Of the crow-blue mussel-shells, one keeps
     adjusting the ash-heaps;
       opening and shutting itself like   5

   an
   injured fan.
     The barnacles which encrust the side
     of the wave, cannot hide
       there for the submerged shafts of the   10

   sun,
   split like spun
     glass, move themselves with spotlight swiftness
     into the crevices—
       in and out, illuminating   15

   the
   turquoise sea
     of bodies. The water drives a wedge
     of iron through the iron edge
       of the cliff; whereupon the stars,[2]   20

   pink
   rice-grains, ink-
     bespattered jelly-fish, crabs like green
     lilies, and submarine
       toadstools, slide each on the other.   25

   All
   external
     marks of abuse are present on this
     defiant edifice—[3]
       all the physical features of   30

---

[3]Light-green quartz, semi-precious stone.   [2]Starfish.
[1]I.e., the dark sea.   [3]The cliff of line 20.

          ac-
          cident—lack
              of cornice, dynamite grooves, burns, and
              hatchet strokes, these things stand
                  out on it; the chasm-side[4] is   35

          dead.
          Repeated
              evidence has proved that it can live
              on what can not revive
                  its youth. The sea grows old in it.   40

                                                        1918, 1921

Poetry[1]

I, too, dislike it: there are things that are important beyond all this fiddle.
    Reading it, however, with a perfect contempt for it, one discovers in
    it after all, a place for the genuine.
        Hands that can grasp, eyes
        that can dilate, hair that can rise   5
            if it must, these things are important not because a

high-sounding interpretation can be put upon them but because they are
    useful. When they become so derivative as to become unintelligible,
    the same thing may be said for all of us, that we
        do not admire what   10
        we cannot understand: the bat
            holding on upside down or in quest of something to

eat, elephants pushing, a wild horse taking a roll, a tireless wolf under
    a tree, the immovable critic twitching his skin like a horse that feels a flea,
        the base-
    ball fan, the statistician—   15
        nor is it valid
        to discriminate against 'business documents and

school-books';[2] all these phenomena are important. One must make a
        distinction
    however: when dragged into prominence by half poets, the result is not
        poetry,
    nor till the poets among us can be   20
        'literalists of
        the imagination'[3]—above
            insolence and triviality and can present

---

[4]The side of the cliff toward the ocean.
[1]"Poetry" went through several revisions, and in its final form was extraordinarily brief: "I, too, dislike it. / Reading it, however, with a perfect contempt for it, one discovers in / it, after all, a place for the genuine." The version appearing here is from *Collected Poems*, 1951.
[2]"*Diary of Tolstoy* [1917], p. 84: 'Where the boundary between prose and poetry lies, I shall never be able to understand. The question is raised in manuals of style, yet the answer to it lies beyond me. Poetry is verse: prose is not verse. Or else poetry is everything with the exception of business documents and school books'" (Moore's note).

[3]"'Literalists of the imagination.' [William Butler] Yeats, *Ideas of Good and Evil* (A. H. Bullen, 1903), p. 182. 'The limitation of his [William Blake's] view was from the very intensity of his vision; he was a too literal realist of imagination, as others are of nature; and because he believed that the figures seen by the mind's eye, when exalted by inspiration, were "external existences," symbols of divine essences, he hated every grace of style that might obscure their lineaments'" (Moore's note). *Ideas of Good and Evil* is a book of Yeats essays. The quotation comes from Yeats's essay, "William Blake and His Illustrations to the *Divine Comedy*."

for inspection, 'imaginary gardens with real toads in them,' shall we have
 it. In the meantime, if you demand on the one hand,   25
the raw material of poetry in
  all its rawness and
  that which is on the other hand
   genuine, you are interested in poetry.

                 1919, 1921

In the Days of Prismatic Color[1]

not in the days of Adam and Eve, but when Adam
 was alone; when there was no smoke and color was
fine, not with the refinement
 of early civilization art, but because
of its originality; with nothing to modify it but the   5

mist that went up, obliqueness was a variation
 of the perpendicular, plain to see and
to account for: it is no
 longer that; nor did the blue-red-yellow band
of incandescence that was color keep its stripe: it also is one of   10

those things into which much that is peculiar can be
 read; complexity is not a crime, but carry
it to the point of murkiness
 and nothing is plain. Complexity,
moreover, that has been committed to darkness, instead of   15

granting itself to be the pestilence that it is, moves all a-
 bout as if to bewilder us with the dismal
fallacy that insistence
 is the measure of achievement and that all
truth must be dark. Principally throat, sophistication is as it al-   20

ways has been—at the antipodes from the initial great truths. "Part of it was crawling, part of it
was about to crawl, the rest
 was torpid in its lair."[2] In the short-legged, fitful advance, the gurgling and all the minutiae—we have the classic 25

multitude of feet. To what purpose! Truth is no Apollo
 Belvedere,[3] no formal thing. The wave may go over it if it likes.
Know that it will be there when it says,
 "I shall be there when the wave has gone by."

              1919, 1921, 1924

---

[1]In the mythic time when light was split into all the colors of the spectrum, as through a prism.
[2]"'Part of it was crawling,' etc. Nestor. *Greek Anthology* (Loeb Classical Library), Vol. III, p. 129" (Moore's note). Reference is to a serpent-like monster moving out of its lair.
[3]The greatest surviving statue of Apollo, in the Vatican at Rome; it is a Roman copy in marble of a Greek bronze and has been considered the epitome of form in classical art.

A Grave[1]

Man looking into the sea,
taking the view from those who have as much right to it as you have to it
    yourself,
it is human nature to stand in the middle of a thing,
but you cannot stand in the middle of this;
the sea has nothing to give but a well excavated grave.   5
The firs stand in a procession, each with an emerald turkey-foot at the top,
reserved as their contours, saying nothing;
repression, however, is not the most obvious characteristic of the sea;
the sea is a collector, quick to return a rapacious look.
There are others besides you who have worn that look —   10
whose expression is no longer a protest; the fish no longer investigate them
for their bones have not lasted:
men lower nets, unconscious of the fact that they are desecrating a grave,
and row quickly away — the blades of the oars
moving together like the feet of water-spiders as if there were no such thing
    as death.   15
The wrinkles progress among themselves in a phalanx — beautiful under
    networks of foam,
and fade breathlessly while the sea rustles in and out of the seaweed;
the birds swim through the air at top speed, emitting cat-calls as
    heretofore —
the tortoise-shell scourges about the feet of the cliffs, in motion beneath
    them;
and the ocean, under the pulsation of lighthouses and noise of bell-buoys,   20
advances as usual, looking as if it were not that ocean in which dropped
    things are bound to sink —
in which if they turn and twist, it is neither with volition nor consciousness.

1921, 1924

When I Buy Pictures

or what is closer to the truth,
when I look at that of which I may regard myself as the imaginary possessor,
I fix upon what would give me pleasure in my average moments:
the satire upon curiosity in which no more is discernible
than the intensity of the mood;   5
or quite the opposite — the old thing, the medieval decorated hat-box,
in which there are hounds with waists diminishing like the waist of the
    hour-glass,
and deer and birds and seated people;
it may be no more than a square of parquetry;[1] the literal biography
    perhaps,
in letters standing well apart upon a parchment-like expanse;   10

---

[1]Moore commented on this poem: "As for 'A Grave,' it has a significance strongly apart from the literal origin, which was a man who placed himself between my mother and me, and surf we were watching from a 'middle' ledge of rocks on Mon- hegan Island after a storm. ('Don't be annoyed,' my mother said. 'It is human nature to stand in the middle of a thing.')" (William Rose Benét, *Fifty Poets*, 1933).

[1]Inlaid woodwork in geometric forms, used for flooring.

an artichoke in six varieties of blue; the snipe-legged hieroglyphic in three
  parts;
the silver fence[2] protecting Adam's grave, or Michael taking Adam by the
  wrist.[3]
Too stern an intellectual emphasis upon this quality or that detracts from
  one's enjoyment.
It must not wish to disarm anything; nor may the approved triumph easily
  be honored—
that which is great because something else is small.   15
It comes to this: of whatever sort it is,
it must be "lit with piercing glances into the life of things";[4]
it must acknowledge the spiritual forces which have made it.

                                                          1921

To a Snail

If "compression is the first grace of style,"[1]
you have it. Contractility is a virtue
as modesty is a virtue.
It is not the acquisition of any one thing
that is able to adorn,   5
or the incidental quality that occurs
as a concomitant of something well said,
that we value in style,
but the principle that is hid:
in the absence of feet, "a method of conclusions";   10
"a knowledge of principles,"
in the curious phenomenon of your occipital[2] horn.

                                                          1924

The Steeple-Jack[1]

Dürer[2] would have seen a reason for living
  in a town like this, with eight stranded whales
to look at; with the sweet sea air coming into your house
on a fine day, from water etched
  with waves as formal as the scales   5
on a fish.

One by one in two's and three's, the seagulls keep
  flying back and forth over the town clock,

---

[2]"'Silver Fence.' 'A silver fence was erected by Constantine to enclose the grave of Adam.' *Literary Digest*, January 5, 1918; descriptive paragraph with photograph" (Moore's note).
[3]In John Milton's *Paradise Lost*, Books XI and XII, the Archangel Michael is sent to explain to Adam the sentence of expulsion from Eden, to offer some hope for the future, and to actually carry out the sentence; Michael gives Adam a vision of the future of the human race up to Noah's flood and foretells the coming of Christ.
[4]"'Lit by piercing glances . . .' A. R. Gordon, *The Poets of the*

Old Testament (Hodder and Stoughton, 1919)" (Moore's note).
[1]"'The very first grace of style is that which comes from compression.' *Demetrius on Style*, translated by W. Hamilton Fyfe (Heinemann, 1932)" (Moore's note).
[2]The occipital bone forms the back part of the skull, where the snail grows a horn.
[1]A person who climbs steeples and towers to build or repair them.
[2]Albrecht Dürer (1471–1528), German painter and engraver.

or sailing around the lighthouse without moving their wings—
rising steadily with a slight
      quiver of the body—or flock
mewing where   10

a sea of purple of the peacock's neck is
      paled to greenish azure as Dürer changed
the pine green of the Tyrol[3] to peacock blue and guinea   15
gray. You can see a twenty-five-
      pound lobster; and fish nets arranged
to dry. The

whirlwind fife-and-drum of the storm bends the salt
      marsh grass, disturbs stars in the sky and the   20
star on the steeple; it is a privilege to see so
much confusion. Disguised by what
      might seem the opposite, the sea-
side flowers and

trees are favored by the fog so that you have   25
      the tropics at first hand: the trumpet-vine,
fox-glove, giant snap-dragon, a salpiglossis[4] that has
spots and stripes; morning-glories, gourds,
      or moon-vines trained on fishing-twine
at the back door;   30

cat-tails, flags, blueberries and spiderwort,
      striped grass, lichens, sunflowers, asters, daisies—
yellow and crab-claw ragged sailors[5] with green bracts[6]—toad-plant,
petunias, ferns; pink lilies, blue
      ones, tigers; poppies; black sweet-peas.   35
The climate

is not right for the banyan, frangipani,[7] or
      jack-fruit trees; or for exotic serpent
life. Ring lizard and snake-skin for the foot, if you see fit;
but here they've cats, not cobras, to   40
      keep down the rats. The diffident
little newt

with white pin-dots on black horizontal spaced-
      out bands lives here; yet there is nothing that
ambition can buy or take away. The college student   45
named Ambrose sits on the hillside
      with his not-native books and hat
and sees boats

at sea progress white and rigid as if in
      a groove. Liking an elegance of which   50
the source is not bravado, he knows by heart the antique

---

[3]Region of the Alps in western Austria and northern Italy.
[4]A small genus of Chilean herbs having large, showily marked flowers.
[5]Blue bottle, cornflower, or bachelor's button with blue, white, pink, or purple flowers.
[6]A modified leaf, scale-like.
[7]Tropical American shrub with large, fragrant flowers.

sugar-bowl shaped summer-house of
    interlacing slats, and the pitch
of the church

spire, not true, from which a man in scarlet lets   55
    down a rope as a spider spins a thread;
he might be part of a novel, but on the sidewalk a
sign says C. J. Poole, Steeple-Jack,
    in black and white; and one in red
and white says   60

Danger. The church portico has four fluted
    columns, each a single piece of stone, made
modester by white-wash. This would be a fit haven for
waifs, children, animals, prisoners,
    and presidents who have repaid   65
sin-driven

senators by not thinking about them. The
    place has a school-house, a post-office in a
store, fish-houses, hen-houses, a three-masted schooner on
the stocks. The hero, the student,   70
    the steeple-jack, each in his way,
is at home.

It could not be dangerous to be living
    in a town like this, of simple people,
who have a steeple-jack placing danger-signs by the church   75
while he is gilding the solid-
    pointed star, which on a steeple
stands for hope.

                                      1932, 1935, 1961

No Swan So Fine[1]

"No water so still as the
    dead fountains of Versailles."[2] No swan,
with swart blind look askance
and gondoliering legs, so fine
    as the chintz china one with fawn-   5
brown eyes and toothed gold
collar on to show whose bird it was.

Lodged in the Louis Fifteenth
    candelabrum-tree of cockscomb-
tinted buttons, dahlias,   10

---

[1] "A pair of Louis XV candelabra with Dresden figures of swans belonging to Lord Balfour" (Moore's Note).
[2] "There is no water so still as in the dead fountains of Versailles.' Percy Phillip, *New York Times Magazine*, May 10, 1931" (Moore's note). Versailles: palace of the French kings, southwest of Paris.

sea-urchins, and everlastings,
    it perches on the branching foam
of polished sculptured
flowers—at ease and tall. The king is dead.

1932, 1935

The Pangolin[1]

Another armored animal—scale
    lapping scale with spruce-cone regularity until they
form the uninterrupted central
    tail-row! This near artichoke with head and legs and grit-equipped gizzard,
    the night miniature artist engineer is,   5
        yes, Leonardo da Vinci's replica—
            impressive animal and toiler of whom we seldom hear.
        Armor seems extra. But for him,
            the closing ear-ridge[2]—
                or bare ear lacking even this small   10
                eminence and similarly safe

contracting nose and eye apertures
    impenetrably closable, are not; a true ant-eater,
not cockroach-eater, who endures
    exhausting solitary trips through unfamiliar ground at night,   15
    returning before sunrise; stepping in the moonlight,
        on the moonlight peculiarly,[3] that the outside
            edges of his hands may bear the weight and save the claws
        for digging. Serpentined about
            the tree, he draws   20
                away from danger unpugnaciously,
                with no sound but a harmless hiss; keeping

the fragile grace of the Thomas-
    of-Leighton Buzzard Westminster Abbey wrought-iron vine,[4] or
rolls himself into a ball that has   25
    power to defy all effort to unroll it; strongly intailed, neat
    head for core, on neck not breaking off, with curled-in feet.
        Nevertheless he has sting-proof scales; and nest
        of rocks closed with earth from inside, which he can thus darken.
        Sun and moon and day and night and man and beast   30
            each with a splendor
                which man in all his vileness cannot
                set aside; each with an excellence!

"Fearful yet to be feared," the armored
    ant-eater met by the driver-ant does not turn back, but   35
engulfs what he can, the flattened sword-

---

[1] A mammal, also called scaly anteater, covered with broad, overlapping, horny scales; feeds on termites as well as ants; about two-feet long, and curls into a ball when threatened.
[2] "The closing ear-ridge,' and certain other detail, from 'Pangolins' by Robert T. Hatt, *Natural History*, December 1935" (Moore's note).

[3] "Stepping . . . peculiarly.' See Lyddeker's *Royal Natural History*" (Moore's note).
[4] "Thomas of Leighton Buzzard's vine: a fragment of iron-work in Westminster Abbey" (Moore's note).

edged leafpoints on the tail and artichoke set leg- and body-plates
quivering violently when it retaliates
      and swarms on him. Compact like the furled fringed frill
        on the hat-brim of Gargallo's[5] hollow iron head of a   40
   matador, he will drop and will
      then walk away
         unhurt, although if unintruded on,
         he cautiously works down the tree, helped

by his tail. The giant-pangolin-   45
      tail, graceful tool, as prop or hand or broom or ax, tipped like
an elephant's trunk with special skin,
   is not lost on this ant- and stone-swallowing uninjurable
   artichoke which simpletons thought a living fable
      whom the stones had nourished, whereas ants had done   50
        so. Pangolins are not aggressive animals; between
   dusk and day they have the not unchain-like machine-like
      form and frictionless creep of a thing
        made graceful by adversities, con-

versities. To explain grace requires   55
      a curious hand. If that which is at all were not forever,
why would those who graced the spires
   with animals and gathered there to rest, on cold luxurious
   low stone seats—a monk and monk and monk—between the thus
      ingenious roof supports, have slaved to confuse   60
        grace with a kindly manner, time in which to pay a debt,
   the cure for sins, a graceful use
      of what are yet
        approved stone mullions[6] branching out across
        the perpendiculars? A sailboat   65

was the first machine.[7] Pangolins, made
      for moving quietly also, are models of exactness,
on four legs; on hind feet plantigrade,[8]
   with certain postures of a man. Beneath sun and moon, man slaving
   to make his life more sweet, leaves half the flowers worth having,   70
      needing to choose wisely how to use his strength;
        a paper-maker like the wasp; a tractor of foodstuffs,
   like the ant; spidering a length
      of web from bluffs
        above a stream; in fighting, mechanicked   75
        like the pangolin; capsizing in

disheartenment. Bedizened[9] or stark
      naked, man, the self, the being we call human, writing-
master to this world, griffons a dark
   "Like does not like like that is obnoxious"; and writes error with four   80
   r's. Among animals, *one* has a sense of humor.

[5]Pablo Gargallo y Catalan (1881–1934), Spanish sculptor who gained recognition in the 1920s creating figurative sculptures out of thin leaves of metal.
[6]Thin vertical dividing bars between the panes of a window.
[7]"A sailboat was the first machine." See F. L. Morse, *Power: Its Application from the 17th Dynasty to the 20th Century*" (Moore's note).
[8]Walking on the whole sole of the foot, like a man or a bear.
[9]Decked out or dressed in a showy way.

Humor saves a few steps, it saves years. Unignorant,
   modest and unemotional, and all emotion,
he has everlasting vigor,
     power to grow,   85
        though there are few creatures who can make one
        breathe faster and make one erecter.

Not afraid of anything is he,
   and then goes cowering forth, tread paced to meet an obstacle
at every step. Consistent with the   90
     formula   warm blood, no gills, two pairs of hands and a few hairs—that
is a mammal; there he sits in his own habitat,
    serge-clad, strong-shod. The prey of fear, he, always
       curtailed, extinguished, thwarted by the dusk, work partly done,
says to the alternating blaze,   95
     "Again the sun!
        anew each day; and new and new and new,
        that comes into and steadies my soul."

                         1936

The Paper Nautilus[1]

    For authorities whose hopes
are shaped by mercenaries?
    Writers entrapped by
    teatime fame and by
commuters' comforts? Not for these   5
    the paper nautilus
    constructs her thin glass shell.

    Giving her perishable
souvenir of hope, a dull
    white outside and smooth-   10
    edged inner surface
glossy as the sea,[2] the watchful
    maker of it guards it
    day and night; she scarcely

    eats until the eggs are hatched.   15
Buried eightfold in her eight
    arms, for she is in
    a sense a devil-
fish, her glass ram's-horn-cradled freight
    is hid but is not crushed;   20
    as Hercules,[3] bitten

    by a crab loyal to the hydra,
    was hindered to succeed,

---

[1]A cephalopod, or mollusk, having a head with two large eyes, a beak, and with muscular tentacles about the mouth; found in warm waters, it is related to the octopus. A fragile, shell-like structure, secreted by one pair of arms (in the female only), holds the eggs in the reproductive process.

[2]I.e., the structure containing the eggs for reproduction.
[3]The second labor of Hercules was to kill the multiheaded Hydra, but the Hydra grew a new head in place of any head cut off; the goddess Hera sent a huge crab to help the Hydra.

the intensively
    watched eggs coming from   25
the shell free it when they are freed—
    leaving its wasp-nest flaws
    of white on white, and close-

laid Ionic[4] chiton-folds[5]
like the lines in the mane of   30
    a Parthenon horse,[6]
    round which the arms had
wound themselves as if they knew love
    is the only fortress
    strong enough to trust to.   35

1940, 1941

Nevertheless

you've seen a strawberry
    that's had a struggle; yet
    was, where the fragments met,

a hedgehog or a star-
    fish for the multitude   5
    of seeds. What better food

than apple-seeds—the fruit
    within the fruit—locked in
    like counter-curved twin

hazel-nuts? Frost that kills   10
    the little rubber-plant-
    leaves of *kok-saghyz*[1]-stalks, can't

harm the roots; they still grow
    in frozen ground. Once where
    there was a prickly-pear-   15

leaf clinging to barbed wire,
    a root shot down to grow
    in earth two feet below;

as carrots from mandrakes[2]
    or a ram's-horn root some-   20
    times. Victory won't come

to me unless I go
    to it; a grape-tendril
    ties a knot in knots till

---

[4]I.e., in the Greek style of architecture, characterized by ornamental scrolls.
[5]Tunic-folds.
[6]A horse sculpture on the temple of Athena, the Parthenon, built on the Acropolis in Athens.

[1]"Dandelion" (Russian).
[2]Poisonous plant of the nightshade family, with phallic-shaped root.

knotted thirty times,—so   25
    the bound twig that's under-
    gone and over-gone, can't stir.

The weak overcomes its
    menace, the strong over-
    comes itself. What is there   30

like fortitude! What sap
    went through that little thread
    to make the cherry red!

1943, 1944

The Mind Is
an Enchanting Thing

is an enchanted thing
    like the glaze on a
katydid-wing
        subdivided by sun
        till the nettings are legion.   5
Like Gieseking playing Scarlatti;[1]

like the apteryx-awl[2]
    as a beak, or the
kiwi's[3] rain-shawl
        of haired feathers, the mind   10
        feeling its way as though blind,
walks along with its eyes on the ground.

It has memory's ear
    that can hear without
having to hear.   15
        Like the gyroscope's fall,
        truly unequivocal
because trued by regnant certainty,

it is a power of
    strong enchantment. It   20
is like the dove-
        neck animated by
        sun; it is memory's eye;
it's conscientious inconsistency.

It tears off the veil; tears   25
    the temptation, the
mist the heart wears,
        from its eyes—if the heart
        has a face; it takes apart
dejection. It's fire in the dove-neck's   30

---

[1]Walter Gieseking (1895–1956), celebrated German pianist; Domenico Scarlatti (1685–1757), Italian composer, wrote operas and composed over 500 sonatas with innovative harmony and form.

[2]A bird that cannot fly, with a long awl-like beak and no tail feathers.

[3]A nonflying bird like the apteryx.

iridescence; in the
    inconsistencies
of Scarlatti.
     Unconfusion submits
      its confusion to proof; it's   35
not a Herod's oath[4] that cannot change.

1943, 1944

A Jelly-Fish

Visible, invisible,
    a fluctuating charm
an amber-tinctured amethyst
    inhabits it, your arm
approaches and it opens   5
    and it closes; you had meant
to catch it and it quivers;
    you abandon your intent.

1909   *1957, 1959*

from Foreword to *A Marianne Moore Reader*[1]

[Idiosyncrasies and Explanations]

Published: it is enough. The magazine was discontinued. The edition was small. One paragraph needs restating. Newspaper cuts on the fold or disintegrates. When was it published, and where? "The title was 'Words and . . .' something else. Could you say what it was?" I have forgotten. Happened upon years later, it seems to have been "Words and Modes of Expression." What became of "Tedium and Integrity," the unfinished manuscript of which there was no duplicate? A housekeeper is needed to assort the untidiness. For whom? A curioso or just for the author? In that case "as safe at the publisher's as if chained to the shelves of Bodley," Lamb[2] said, smiling.

Verse: prose: a specimen or so of translation for those on whom completeness would weigh as a leg-iron. How would it seem to me if someone else had written it? Does it hold the attention? "Has it human value?" Or seem as if one had ever heard of "lucidity, force, and ease" or had any help from past thinkers? Is it subservient singsong or has it "muscles"?

La Fontaine's Fables. Professor Brower[3]—if I am not inventing it—says a translator must have "depth of experience." The rhythm of a translation as motion, I think, should suggest the rhythm of the original, and the words be very nearly an equivalent of the author's meaning. After endless last choices, digressions, irrelevances, defi-

---

[4]Cf. Mark 6:26. When Salome requested the head of John the Baptist, "the king was exceeding sorry; *yet* for his oath's sake, and for their sakes which sat with him, he would not reject her."
[1]*The Marianne Moore Reader* was published in 1961 and contained a selection of Moore's poetry and prose. Moore's "Foreword" begins with questions she must have posed in looking through work and deciding what to include. The ti-

tles mentioned seem to have been unfinished or lost essays or essay fragments.
[2]Bodley: the Bodleian Library at Oxford University; Charles Lamb (1775–1834), British essayist.
[3]Moore published her translation, *The Fables of La Fontaine*, in 1954; Reuben Brower, long-time professor at Amherst College, Massachusetts.

ances, and futile imprudences, I am repaid for attempting to translate "The Grass-hopper and the Ant" by hitting upon a substitute for an error, the most offensive and meaningless of a long list: "an't you please."

> —I sang for those who might pass by chance—
> Night and day, an't you please"

for which I am substituting "Night and day. Please do not be repelled," with the ant's reply, "Sang? A delight when someone has excelled." In harmonizing notes or words, there is more room for originality than in moralizing, and "the point," prefixed or appended to a tale irresistibly told, seems redundant. Although La Fontaine's primary concern was the poetry; even so, for him and for us, indifference to being educated has been conquered, and certain lessons in these fables contrive to be indelible: *Greed:* The owner of the hen that laid the golden eggs, "cut the magic chain and she'd never lay again. / Think this when covetous!" *Ingratitude:* The reanimated adder lunged at the farmer, "Its foster father who had been its rescuer. / . . . Two strokes made three snakes of the coil—/ A body, a tail, and a head. / The pestilent thirds writhed together to the rear / But of course could no longer adhere." "Ingrates," La Fontaine says, "will always die in agony." *Be content with your lot:* A shepherd "was lured to part with his one and only flock / And invest all he'd earned, in a ship; but ah, the shock—/ Wrecked in return for all he'd paid."

Prose: mine will always be "essays" and verse of mine, observations. Of "Tedium and Integrity" the first few pages are missing—summarized sufficiently by: manner for matter; shadow for substance; ego for rapture. As antonym, integrity was suggested to me by a blossoming peach branch—a drawing by Hsieh Ho[4]—reproduced above a *New York Times Book Review* notice of *The Mustard Seed Garden Manual of Painting* formulated about 500 A.D.—translated and edited by Miss Mai-mai Sze, published by the Bollingen Foundation in 1956 and as a Modern Library paperback in 1959. The plum branch led me to *The Tao of Painting*,[5] of which "The Mustard Seed Garden" is a part, the (not "a") Tao being a way of life, a "oneness" that is tireless; whereas egotism, synonymous with ignorance in Buddhist thinking, is tedious. And the Tao led me to the dragon in the classification of primary symbols, "symbol of the power of heaven"—changing at will to the size of a silkworm; or swelling to the totality of heaven and earth;[6] at will invisible, made personal by a friend at a party— an authority on gems, finance, painting, and music—who exclaimed obligingly, as I concluded a digression on cranes, peaches, bats, and butterflies as symbols of long life and happiness, "O to be a dragon!" (The exclamation, lost sight of for a time, was appropriated as a title[7] later.)

Verse: "Why the many quotation marks?" I am asked. Pardon my saying more than once, When a thing has been said so well that it could not be said better, why paraphrase it? Hence my writing is, if not a cabinet of fossils, a kind of collection of flies in amber.

More than once after a reading, I have been asked with circumspectly hesitant delicacy, "Your . . . poem, 'Marriage';[8] would you care to . . . make a statement about it?" Gladly. The thing (I would hardly call it a poem) is no philosophic precipitate; nor does it veil anything personal in the way of triumphs, entrapments, or dangerous

---

[4]Hsieh Ho was a fifth-century Chinese painter who formulated "Six Canons of Painting."

[5]*The Tao of Painting: A Study of the Ritual Disposition of Chinese Painting*, 2 vols., translated by Mai-mai Sze from the texts dated 1679–1701, was published in 1956; it contained *The Mustard Seed Garden Manual of Painting*.

[6]"The dragon as lord of space makes relevant Miss Mai-mai Sze's emphasis on 'space as China's chief contribution to painting; the essential part of the wheel being the inner space

between its spokes; the space in a room, its usefulness' in keeping with the Manual: 'a crowded ill-arranged composition is one of the Twelve Faults of Painting'; as a man 'if he had eyes all over his body, would be a monstrosity'" (Moore's note).

[7]Moore's poem "O to Be a Dragon" was first published in 1957.

[8]Moore's poem published in 1923.

colloquies. It is a little anthology of statements that took my fancy— phrasings that I
liked.

Rhythm: The clue to it all (for me originally)—something built-in as in music.

> No man may him hyde
> From Deth holow-eyed.

I dislike the reversed order of words; don't like to be impeded by an unnecessary
capital at the beginning of every line; I don't like, here, the meaning; the cadence
coming close to being the sole reason for all that follows, the accent on "holow" rather
than on "eyed," so firmly placed that the most willful reader cannot misplace it. "A fig
for thee, O Death!"[9]—meaning the opposite—has for me the same fascination.
Appoggiaturas[10]—a charmed subject. A study of trills can be absorbing to the exclusion of everything else—"the open, over-lapping, regular. . . ." A London *Times Literary Supplement* reviewer (perforce anonymous), reviewing *The Interpretation of Bach's
Keyboard Works* by Erwin Bodky (Oxford University Press) on April 7, 1961, says,
"phrasing is rarely marked by Bach . . . except as a warning that something abnormal
is intended"—a remark which has a bearing, for prose and verse, on the matter of
"ease" alluded to earlier. I like straight writing, end-stopped lines, an effect of flowing continuity, and after 1929—perhaps earlier—wrote no verse that did not (in my
opinion) rhyme. *However,* when a friendly, businesslike, shrewd, valiant government
official in a broadcast summarizes me in handsome style—a man who feels that in
writing as in conduct I distinguish between liberty and license, agrees with me that
punctuation and syntax have a bearing on meaning, and looks at human weakness to
determine the possibilities of strength—when he says in conclusion, "She writes in
free verse," I am not irascible.

Why an inordinate interest in animals and athletes? They are subjects for art and
exemplars of it, are they not? minding their own business. Pangolins, hornbills,
pitchers, catchers, do not pry or prey—or prolong the conversation; do not make us
selfconscious; look their best when caring least; although in a Frank Buck documentary[11] I saw a leopard insult a crocodile (basking on a river bank—head only visible
on the bank)—bat the animal on the nose and continue on its way without so much as
a look back. Perhaps I really don't know. I do know that I don't know how to account
for a person who could be indifferent to miracles of dexterity, a certain feat by Don
Zimmer[12]—a Dodger at the time—making a backhand catch, of a ball coming hard
from behind on the left, fast enough to take his hand off. "The fabric of existence
weaves itself whole," as Charles Ives[13] said (*Time,* August 22, 1960). "You cannot set
art off in a corner and hope for it to have vitality, reality, and substance. My work in
music helped my business [insurance] and my work in business helped my music."

. . . "I think I might call you a moralist," the inquirer began, "or do you object?"
"No," I said, "I think perhaps I am. I do not thrust promises or deeds of mercy right
and left to write a lyric—if what I write ever is one"—a qualification received with
smiles by a specialist (or proseur turned poseur)—(leopard and crocodile). "Poetry
must not be drawn by the ears," Sidney[14] says; in either the writing or the reading. T.
S. Eliot is convinced that the work of contemporary poets should be read by students
for enjoyment, not for credits; not taught formally but out of enthusiasm—with the
classics as criterion (*New York Times,* December 30, 1960—printed a year earlier in
Chicago). He is right about it, I think.

[9]Title of a poem by American poet Edward Taylor (*c.* 1642–
1729).

[10]In music, an ornamental tone preceding another tone; a
grace note.

[11]Frank Buck (1884–1950), a big-game hunter, collecting animals for zoos; he made many motion-picture documentaries
of his expeditions.

[12]Don Zimmer (b. 1931), on the Brooklyn Dodgers baseball

team (1954–57), the L.A. Dodgers (1958–59), and the Chicago Cubs (1960–61).

[13]Charles Ives (1874–1954), American composer who used
American themes and folk music in his compositions, and
supported himself with a prosperous insurance business.

[14]Sir Philip Sidney (1554–1586), British poet and author of
An Apology for Poetry, 1595.

Prosody is a tool; poetry is "a maze, a trap, a web"—Professor Richards'[15] epitome—and the quarry is captured in his own lines, "Not No" (in *Goodbye Earth*).

> *Not mine this life that must be lived in me.*
>
> Inside as out Another's: let it be.
> Ha, Skater on the Brink!
>   Come whence,
>   Where go?
>
> Anywhere
>   Elsewhere
>   Where I would not know
> *Not mine, not mine, all this lived through in me.*
>
> Who asks? Who answers? What ventriloquy!

My favorite poem? asked not too aggressively—perhaps recalling that Henry James[16] could not name his "favorite letter of the alphabet or wave of the sea." The Book of Job,[17] I have sometimes thought—for the verity of its agony and a fidelity that contrives glory for ashes. I do not deplore it that Sir Francis Bacon[18] was often scathing, since he said, "By far the greatest obstacle . . . to advancement of anything is despair." Prizing Henry James, I take his worries for the most part with detachment; those of William James[19] to myself when he says, "man's chief difference from the brutes lies in the exuberant excess of his subjective propensities. Prune his extravagance, sober him, and you undo him."

1961

HART CRANE
(1899–1932)

Hart Crane died young, scarcely thirty-three when he flung himself off the stern of a ship in 1932; it was dark and therefore impossible to tell whether he tried to reach the life preserver that was thrown out to him. His reputation as a poet was at that time considerable, as he had published the poem he had spent most of his creative life writing, *The Bridge*, in 1930. On its appearance, one reviewer, Horace Gregory, concluded: "With the publication of *The Bridge* [Crane's] promise as an important American poet is fulfilled. His defects and merits are here, eloquently displayed. His effort to create a synthesis (himself deeply affected by the disintegrating forces that mark the work of his contemporaries) is a notable contribution to American poetry."

The seeds for Crane's impulsive suicide were planted deep within him during his troubled youth, growing up in Garretsville, Ohio—a counterpart of sorts to Sherwood Anderson's small town Winesburg, Ohio. His father was a successful candy manufacturer and his mother a strong-willed and possessive woman. It was an unhappy marriage, and at one point (in 1909) Crane was sent to live with his grandmother in Cleveland, where he attended high school. He travelled to the West Indies and to the American West with his mother, who felt no compunc-

---

[15] I. A. Richards (1893–1979), linguist, literary critic, and poet; quoted are lines 4–13 of "Not No" in *Goodbye Earth* (1958).
[16] Henry James (1843–1916), American novelist.
[17] An Old Testament book in which Job seeks from God the

meaning of all his apparently meaningless misfortunes and suffering.
[18] Sir Francis Bacon (1561–1626), English philosopher and essayist.
[19] William James (1842–1910), American psychologist.

tion in taking him out of school to provide her companionship. Crane was to become tormented throughout his life, finding no relief in his addiction to alcohol or his homosexuality.

Crane's interest in poetry developed early and he published his first poem in 1916. He did not accumulate enough credits to graduate from high school and he never attended college. But he was an omnivorous reader, especially of poetry, and was absorbing the classics at an early age. After his parents' divorce in 1916, he lived briefly in New York. In 1918, he returned to Cleveland and tried to enlist in the army (America had entered the First World War) but was turned down. He worked for a time in an advertising agency, and then went to work in one of his father's candy stores. Later, in 1920, he fulfilled his father's desire of entering the business.

In 1921 there was a final rupture with his father. Crane left the business and launched out on his own, devoting more and more time to the writing of poetry, immersing himself in the new poetry then appearing in the little magazines. He worked for advertising agencies to support his commitment to poetry, first in Cleveland and then, in 1923, in New York. He came to know Gorham Munson, Waldo Frank, Allen Tate, and other writers of the time. In 1924, he took a room that had once been the room of John Augustus Roebling, architect of the Brooklyn Bridge, within sight of the famous bridge. And for a time in 1925 he shared a home in Patterson, New York, with the Allen Tates, but Crane was not easy to live with and the arrangement ended in a quarrel.

In 1926, Crane published his first book of poems, *White Buildings*. It contained some of his best verses, the poems he had been working on over the early 1920s. Included were such impressive short lyrics as "My Grandmother's Love Letters," "Chaplinesque," and "The Wine Menagerie." Also included were two important longer poems. "For the Marriage of Faustus and Helen" was set in the sordid, urban present and, in Crane's words, built "a bridge between so-called classic experience and many divergent realities of our seething, confused cosmos of today." "Voyages" was a love sequence for Emil Opffer, a sailor who shared his room overlooking Brooklyn Bridge. Allen Tate, in his introduction to *White Buildings*, said: "It is the old poetry I am acquainted with which is at once contemporary and in the grand manner. It is an American poetry."

Allen Tate also admitted that Crane's poems were "sometimes obscure," suggesting that the "great difficulty which his poetry presents the reader is the style." Crane had tried to come to terms with this charge when Harriet Monroe had complained of obscurities in his poem "At Melville's Tomb," submitted for publication in *Poetry*. He wrote her a defense in 1926 based on what he called the "logic of metaphor," a logic not of intellect but of feeling or "sensibility": "It often happens that images, themselves totally dissociated, when joined in the circuit of a particular emotion located with specific relation to both of them, conduce to great vividness and accuracy of statement in defining that emotion."

Early in the 1920s, Crane was coming to the decision to write a poem of epic length. He had read the British classic poets, the French symbolists, and the American modernists. But two American poets figured most importantly in shaping his imagination for this ambitious undertaking — Walt Whitman and T. S. Eliot. Whitman's *Leaves of Grass*, and especially "Crossing Brooklyn Ferry" and "Passage to India," would serve as models to be modernized. T. S. Eliot's *The Waste Land* would serve as a negative model in its substance, but a positive model in its strategies and techniques. When Crane first read *The Waste Land*, he exclaimed in a letter to Gorham Munson that it was "so damned dead." In a later letter, he revealed his ambition: "I would take Eliot as a point of departure toward an almost complete reverse of direction. . . . I would apply as much of his education and technique as I can absorb and assemble toward a more positive, . . . ecstatic goal."

Thus throughout the remainder of the 1920s, Crane was obsessed with the demanding work on his ambitious epic, *The Bridge*, taking as his starting point the Brooklyn Bridge, a construction of modern technology that had replaced the ferryboat celebrated in Whitman's "Crossing Brooklyn Ferry." It was emotionally exhausting work in that it often had to be forced emotionally in a direction opposite to Crane's frequent states of depression and feelings of pessimism. These were exacerbated by his loneliness, his heavy drinking, and his successive and short-lived affairs with sailors, drifters, or other vagabonds.

Luck was with him in finding a patron in Otto Kahn, a wealthy industrialist with an interest in the arts, willing to support Crane's vague plan "to enunciate a new cultural synthesis of America." Crane's letters to Otto Kahn revealed Crane's developing plans for *The Bridge* and remain as a valuable introduction to the long poem (they are quoted in the footnotes to the poem here). Crane began with the end of the poem, "Atlantis," that "ecstatic goal" which in its spiritual affirmations would counter the dark pessimism of *The Waste Land*.

The Bridge did not appear until 1930, just at the beginning of the Great Depression. Although many critics were positive in their reactions, two that Crane respected set forth their frank reservations — Allen Tate and Yvor Winters. Both thought the culprit in Crane's vision was Whitman, saluted in *The Bridge* as "Our Meistersinger." Winters later, in an astonishing bit of reasoning, would blame Crane's suicide on his allegiance to Whitman and Ralph Waldo Emerson!

In the latter part of the 1920s, Crane wandered about the world writing *The Bridge*. He lived for different periods in New York; the Isle of Pines; Paterson, New Jersey; California; Paris. *The Bridge* was brought out first in Paris by the Black Sun Press, owned by Harry and Caresse Crosby. By the time Crane let go of it, he was calling it "an epic of the modern consciousness," and he wrote to the Crosbys: "For all I know, the *Bridge* may turn into something like the form of *Leaves of Grass*, with a number of editions, each incorporating further additions."

As it turned out, *The Bridge* would remain as first published. Crane went to Mexico, planning to write an epic on Cortez's conquest of Mexico. There he alternated between periods of concentrated writing and bouts of debauchery. He came to know, and to quarrel with, Katherine Anne Porter there. And there he lived for a time with Peggy Baird, Malcolm Cowley's ex-wife. It was on his return in 1932 that he jumped into the sea.

Since Crane's death, the voices of his detractors have tended to subside, and his serious defenders have stepped to the fore; but controversy continues. His critical fate has been thus similar to Whitman's — a fact that would not displease him. Tate's claim that *The Bridge* lacked a "coherent structure" has been undermined again and again by more recent critics, who have found a convincing subterranean coherence. But these critics would be the first to admit that the poem is not without flaws — resembling, thus, those other ambitious epic poems of the twentieth century: Eliot's *The Waste Land*, Pound's *The Cantos*, and Williams's *Paterson*.

ADDITIONAL READING

The Letters of Hart Crane, 1916–1932, ed. Brom Weber, 1952, 1965; *The Letters of Hart Crane and His Family*, ed. Thomas S. W. Lewis, 1974.

Philip Horton, *The Life of an American Poet*, 1937, 1957; Brom Weber, *Hart Crane: A Biographical and Critical Study*, 1948; L. S. Dembo, *Hart Crane's Sanscrit Charge: A Study of "The Bridge,"* 1960; Vincent Quinn, *Hart Crane*, 1963; Samuel Hazo, *Hart Crane: An Introduction and Interpretation*, 1963; Monroe Spears, *Hart Crane*, 1965; Richard W. B. Lewis, *The Poetry of Hart Crane*, 1967; Helge N. Nilson, *Hart Crane's "The Bridge": A Study in Sources and Interpretation*, 1967; Hunce Voelcker, *The Hart Crane Voyages*, 1967; Herbert A. Leibowitz, *Hart Crane: An Introduction to the Poetry*, 1968; R. W. Butterfield, *The Broken Arc: A Study of Hart Crane*, 1969; Susan Jenkins Brown, *Robber Rocks: Letters and Memories of Hart Crane, 1923–1932*, 1969; John Unterecker, *Voyager: A Life of Hart Crane*, 1969; Joseph Schwartz and Robert C. Schweik, *Hart Crane: A Descriptive Bibliography*, 1972; Gary Lane, *A Concordance to the Poems of Hart Crane*, 1972; M. D. Uroff, *Hart Crane: The Patterns of His Poetry*, 1974; Richard P. Sugg, *Hart Crane's "The Bridge,"* 1976; Samuel Hazo, *Smithareened Apart: A Critique of Hart Crane*, 1977; James E. Miller, Jr., "An Epic of the Modern Consciousness: Hart Crane's *Bridge*," *The American Quest for a Supreme Fiction*, 1979; Helge N. Nilsen, *Hart Crane's Divided Vision: An Analysis of "The Bridge,"* 1980; David R. Clark, ed., *Critical Essays on Hart Crane*, 1982; Allen Tractenberg, ed., *Hart Crane: A Collection of Critical Essays*, 1982; Joseph Schwartz, ed., *Hart Crane: A Reference Guide*, 1983; Edward Brunner, *Hart Crane and the Making of "The Bridge,"* 1985; Harold Bloom, ed., *Hart Crane*, 1986; Paul Giles, *Hart Crane: The Contexts of "The Bridge,"* 1986; Lee Edelman, *Transmemberment of Song: Hart Crane's Anatomies of Rhetoric and Desire*, 1987.

TEXT

The Complete Poems and Selected Letters and Prose of Hart Crane, ed. Brom Weber, 1966.

My Grandmother's Love Letters

There are no stars to-night
But those of memory.
Yet how much room for memory there is
In the loose girdle of soft rain.

There is even room enough   5
For the letters of my mother's mother,
Elizabeth,
That have been pressed so long
Into a corner of the roof
That they are brown and soft,   10
And liable to melt as snow.

Over the greatness of such space
Steps must be gentle.
It is all hung by an invisible white hair.
It trembles as birch limbs webbing the air.   15

And I ask myself:

"Are your fingers long enough to play
Old keys that are but echoes:
Is the silence strong enough
To carry back the music to its source   20
And back to you again
As though to her?"

Yet I would lead my grandmother by the hand
Through much of what she would not understand;

And so I stumble. And the rain continues on the roof   25
With such a sound of gently pitying laughter.

1919   *1920, 1926*

Chaplinesque[1]

We make our meek adjustments,
Contented with such random consolations
As the wind deposits
In slithered and too ample pockets.

For we can still love the world, who find   5
A famished kitten on the step, and know
Recesses for it from the fury of the street,
Or warm torn elbow coverts.

We will sidestep, and to the final smirk
Dally the doom of that inevitable thumb   10
That slowly chafes its puckered index toward us,
Facing the dull squint with what innocence
And what surprise!

And yet these fine collapses are not lies
More than the pirouettes of any pliant cane;   15
Our obsequies are, in a way, no enterprise.
We can evade you, and all else but the heart:
What blame to us if the heart live on.

The game enforces smirks; but we have seen
The moon in lonely alleys make   20
A grail of laughter of an empty ash can,
And through all sound of gaiety and quest
Have heard a kitten in the wilderness.

1921   *1921, 1926*

from Voyages[1]

I

Above the fresh ruffles of the surf
Bright striped urchins flay each other with sand.
They have contrived a conquest for shell shucks,

---

[1]After the manner of Chaplin. Crane wrote to his friend Gorham Munson that he had seen Charlie Chaplin in *The Kid* and called Chaplin a "dramatic genius"; he added: "My poem is a sympathetic attempt to put in words some of the Chaplin pantomime, so beautiful, and so full of eloquence, and so modern."

[1]Crane wrote a series of love poems, "Voyages," for Emil Opffer, Jr., a merchant seaman with whom he was living in the mid-1920s.

And their fingers crumble fragments of baked weed
Gaily digging and scattering.   5

And in answer to their treble interjections
The sun beats lightning on the waves,
The waves fold thunder on the sand;
And could they hear me I would tell them:

O brilliant kids, frisk with your dog,   10
Fondle your shells and sticks, bleached
By time and the elements; but there is a line
You must not cross nor ever trust beyond it
Spry cordage² of your bodies to caresses
Too lichen-faithful from too wide a breast.   15
The bottom of the sea is cruel.

1921–23   1923, 1926

V

Meticulous, past midnight in clear rime,
Infrangible³ and lonely, smooth as though cast
Together in one merciless white blade—
The bay estuaries fleck the hard sky limits.

—As if too brittle or too clear to touch!   5
The cables of our sleep so swiftly filed,
Already hang, shred ends from remembered stars.
One frozen trackless smile . . . What words
Can strangle this deaf moonlight? For we

Are overtaken. Now no cry, no sword   10
Can fasten or deflect this tidal wedge,
Slow tyranny of moonlight, moonlight loved
And changed . . . "There's

Nothing like this in the world," you say,
Knowing I cannot touch your hand and look   15
Too, into that godless cleft of sky
Where nothing turns but dead sands flashing.

"—And never to quite understand!" No,
In all the argosy of your bright hair I dreamed
Nothing so flagless as this piracy.   20

But now
Draw in your head, alone and too tall here.
Your eyes already in the slant of drifting foam;
Your breath sealed by the ghosts I do not know:
Draw in your head and sleep the long way home.   25

1926

²Ropes used in the rigging of ships.
³That which cannot be separated or violated.

At Melville's Tomb[1]

Often beneath the wave, wide from this ledge
The dice of drowned men's bones he saw bequeath[2]
An embassy. Their numbers as he watched,
Beat on the dusty shore and were obscured.

And wrecks passed without sound of bells,   5
The calyx of death's bounty giving back[3]
A scattered chapter, livid hieroglyph,
The portent wound in corridors of shells.

Then in the circuit calm of one vast coil,
Its lashings charmed and malice reconciled,   10
Frosted eyes there were that lifted altars;[4]
And silent answers crept across the stars.

Compass, quadrant and sextant contrive[5]
No farther tides . . . High in the azure steeps
Monody[6] shall not wake the mariner.   15
This fabulous shadow only the sea keeps.

1925–26   *1926*

To Emily Dickinson

You who desired so much — in vain to ask —
Yet fed your hunger like an endless task,
Dared dignify the labor, bless the quest —
Achieved that stillness ultimately best,

Being, of all, least sought for: Emily, hear!   5
O sweet, dead Silencer, most suddenly clear

---

[1]Crane sent this poem to Harriet Monroe, editor of *Poetry*, who raised so many questions about the meaning of certain lines that Crane replied with a defense of his use of what he called the "logic of metaphor": "It often happens that images, themselves totally dissociated, when joined in the circuit of a particular emotion located with specific relation to both of them, conduce to great vividness and accuracy of statement in defining that emotion."

[2]Crane wrote to Monroe of this line: "Dice bequeath an embassy, in the first place, by being ground (in this connection only, of course) in little cubes from the bones of drowned men by the action of the sea, and are finally thrown up on the sand, having 'numbers' but no identification. These being the bones of dead men who never completed their voyage, it seems legitimate to refer to them as the only surviving evidence of certain messages undelivered, mute evidence of certain things, experiences that the dead mariners might have had to deliver. Dice as a symbol of chance and circumstances is also implied."

[3]Crane: "This calyx refers in a double ironic sense both to a cornucopia and the vortex made by a sinking vessel. As soon as the water has closed over a ship, the whirlpool sends up broken spars, wreckage, etc., which can be alluded to as livid hieroglyphs, making a *scattered chapter* so far as any complete

record of the recent ship and her crew is concerned. In fact, about as much definite knowledge might come from all this as anyone might gain from the roar of his own veins, which is easily heard (haven't you ever done it?) by holding a shell close to one's ear."

[4]Crane: "'Frosted eyes lift altars.' Refers simply to a conviction that a man, not knowing perhaps a definite god yet being endowed with a reverence for deity — such a man naturally postulates a deity somehow, and the altar of that deity by the very *action* of the eyes *lifted* in searching."

[5]Instruments used to calculate location and distances at sea. Crane: "Hasn't it often occurred that instruments originally invented for record and computation have inadvertently so extended the concepts of the entity they were invented to measure (concepts of space, etc.) in the mind and imagination that employed them, that they may metaphorically be said to have extended the original boundaries of the entity measured? This little bit of 'relativity' ought not to be discredited in poetry now that scientists are proceeding to measure the universe on principles of pure *ratio*, quite as metaphorical, so far as previous standards of scientific method extended, as some of the axioms in *Job*."

[6]Originally in Greek literature a lyric solo; now a poem written to mourn someone's death.

When singing that Eternity possessed
And plundered momently in every breast;

— Truly no flower yet withers in your hand,
The harvest you descried and understand   10
Needs more than wit to gather, love to bind.
Some reconcilement of remotest mind —

Leaves Ormus rubyless, and Ophir[1] chill.
Else tears heap all within one clay-cold hill.

1927, 1933

ON READING *THE BRIDGE*

Crane, in a letter to his benefactor Otto Kahn, called *The Bridge* an "epic of the modern consciousness." The epic sweep of his poem embodies the American past, but not in chronological order. It was Crane's intention, in moving back and forth between present and past, to "show the continuous and living evidence of the past in the inmost vital substance of the present." Beginning with Columbus and the discovery of America, jumping next to "the harbor of 20th-century America," and then working backward through the pioneer period, always in terms of the present," Crane finally arrives at the "very core of the nature-world of the Indian." "What I am really handling," said Crane, "is the Myth of America."

Crane's descriptions of his epic poem are sufficient to prepare us to find his own consciousness, as a representative "modern consciousness," providing the cultural synthesis or assimilation he is attempting. In short, he is his own epic's hero. His consciousness is the presiding consciousness of the poem, and we must turn to it for the poem's structure. In the frame of that consciousness, the poem's duration is one day — from the dawn of the proem, "To Brooklyn Bridge," to the night of "The Tunnel" and midnight of the final section, "Atlantis." In this structure, the high noon of the poem is, then, "Cape Hatteras," which comes to focus on America's nineteenth-century epic poet Walt Whitman. Crane indicated to his publishers that he wanted a photograph of barges and a tug to come between "Cutty Sark" and "Cape Hatteras": "That is the 'center' of the book, both physically and symbolically." But of course there are many days and nights in the poem, and the structure can be envisioned as one day only if the poem is taken as a meditation, an imaginative recreation in the consciousness of the poet as he himself goes through one day of life in New York, ending at midnight in the middle of Brooklyn Bridge.

Although the poet's meditative or spiritual journey is for one day, in a sense it is forever (in the open form of the poem) and in intention it is out of space, out of time, into eternity — via the poet's cosmic consciousness. As in other such personal or lyric epics, the journey itself is the destination; voyaging is its own excuse for being. And if we experience the poem as Crane intended, we'll share his journey, including his "dark night of the soul" in "The Tunnel"; and we'll emerge with him in the concluding "Atlantis" as he steps onto the now mythic

---

[1]Ormus: Ormuz or Hormuz, near the Strait of Hormuz (in the Middle East); the old city of Hormuz was a flourishing trading center when Marco Polo visited it in the thirteenth century. Ophir was a Biblical city rich in gold; see 1 Kings 9:28.

bridge and into a mystical moment of transcendent perception and transfiguring vision.

from The Bridge

*From going to and fro in the earth,
and from walking up and down in it.*

THE BOOK OF JOB[1]

To Brooklyn Bridge

How many dawns, chill from his rippling rest
The seagull's wings shall dip and pivot him,
Shedding white rings of tumult, building high
Over the chained bay waters Liberty —

Then, with inviolate curve, forsake our eyes   5
As apparitional as sails that cross
Some page of figures to be filed away;
— Till elevators drop us from our day . . .

I think of cinemas, panoramic sleights
With multitudes bent toward some flashing scene   10
Never disclosed, but hastened to again,
Foretold to other eyes on the same screen;

And Thee,[2] across the harbor, silver-paced
As though the sun took step of thee, yet left
Some motion ever unspent in thy stride, —   15
Implicitly thy freedom staying thee!

Out of some subway scuttle, cell or loft
A bedlamite[3] speeds to thy parapets,
Tilting there momently, shrill shirt ballooning,
A jest falls from the speechless caravan.   20

Down Wall,[4] from girder into street noon leaks,
A rip-tooth of the sky's acetylene;
All afternoon the cloud-flown derricks turn . . .
Thy cables breathe the North Atlantic still.

And obscure as that heaven of the Jews,   25
Thy guerdon[5] . . . Accolade thou dost bestow
Of anonymity time cannot raise:
Vibrant reprieve and pardon thou dost show.

---

[1]The reply by Satan to the Lord when he asked Satan where he had been (see Job 1:7).
[2]Brooklyn Bridge.
[3]Insane person.
[4]Wall Street in New York City.
[5]Reward.

O harp and altar, of the fury fused,
(How could mere toil align thy choiring strings!)   30
Terrific threshold of the prophet's pledge,
Prayer of pariah, and the lover's cry,—

Again the traffic lights that skim thy swift
Unfractioned idiom, immaculate sigh of stars,
Beading thy path—condense eternity: 35
And we have seen night lifted in thine arms.

Under thy shadow by the piers I waited;
Only in darkness is thy shadow clear.
The City's fiery parcels all undone,
Already snow submerges an iron year . . .   40

O Sleepless as the river under thee,
Vaulting the sea, the prairies' dreaming sod,
Unto us lowliest sometime sweep, descend
And of the curveship lend a myth to God.[6]

I. Ave Maria[1]

Venient annis, sæcula seris,
Quibus Oceanus vincula rerum
Laxet et ingens pateat tellus
Tiphysque novos detegat orbes
Nec sit terris ultima Thule.

                              SENECA[2]

Columbus,   Be with me, Luis de San Angel,[3] now—
alone, gazing   Witness before the tides can wrest away
toward Spain,   The word I bring, O you who reined my suit
invokes the   Into the Queen's great heart that doubtful day;
presence of   For I have seen now what no perjured breath   5
two faithful   Of clown nor sage can riddle or gainsay;—
partisans of   To you, too, Juan Perez,[4] whose counsel fear
his quest . . .   And greed adjourned,—I bring you back Cathay![5]

Here waves climb into dusk on gleaming mail;
Invisible valves of the sea,—locks, tendons   10
Crested and creeping, troughing corridors
That fall back yawning to another plunge.
Slowly the sun's red caravel drops light
Once more behind us. . . . It is morning there—
O where our Indian emperies lie revealed,   15
Yet lost, all, let this keel one instant yield!

---

[6]The language used here in direct address to the bridge suggests the invocation to the muse, asking for inspiration and help, found at the beginning of the traditional epic.
[1]"Ave Maria" ("Hail Mary"), first two words of a Catholic prayer. Crane calls this section Columbus's "monologue"; it may be considered a meditative prayer.
[2]"There will come an age in the far-off years when Ocean shall unloose the bonds of things, when the whole broad earth shall be revealed, when Tethys [Jason's helmsman in his

quest for the golden fleece] shall disclose new worlds" (Latin). From the tragedy, *Medea*, by the Roman playwright Seneca (4 B.C.–A.D. 65).
[3]A Spanish Franciscan prior, collector of church revenues, who supported Columbus's request to the Spanish throne for sponsorship of his voyage to find a passage to India.
[4]Queen Isabella's court confessor and also a supporter of Columbus's request.
[5]Medieval name of China.

I thought of Genoa;[6] and this truth, now proved,
That made me exile in her streets, stood me
More absolute than ever—biding the moon
Till dawn should clear that dim frontier, first seen   20
—The Chan's[7] great continent. . . . Then faith, not fear
Nigh surged me witless. . . . Hearing the surf near—
I, wonder-breathing, kept the watch,—saw
The first palm chevron the first lighted hill.

And lowered. And they came out to us crying,   25
"The Great White Birds!" (O Madre María, still
One ship of these thou grantest safe returning;[8]
Assure us through thy mantle's ageless blue!)
And record of more, floating in a casque,[9]
Was tumbled from us under bare poles scudding;   30
And later hurricanes may claim more pawn. . . .
For here between two worlds, another, harsh,

This third, of water, tests the word; lo, here
Bewilderment and mutiny heap whelming
Laughter, and shadow cuts sleep from the heart   35
Almost as though the Moor's flung scimitar
Found more than flesh to fathom in its fall.
Yet under tempest-lash and surfeitings
Some inmost sob, half-heard, dissuades the abyss,
Merges the wind in measure to the waves,   40

Series on series, infinite,—till eyes
Starved wide on blackened tides, accrete—enclose
This turning rondure whole,[10] this crescent ring
Sun-cusped and zoned with modulated fire
Like pearls that whisper through the Doge's[11] hands   45
—Yet no delirium of jewels! O Fernando,[12]
Take of that eastern shore, this western sea,
Yet yield thy God's, thy Virgin's charity!

—Rush down the plenitude, and you shall see
Isaiah counting famine on this lee![13]   50

· · ·

An herb, a stray branch among salty teeth,
The jellied weeds that drag the shore,—perhaps
Tomorrow's moon will grant us Saltes Bar—
Palos[14] again,—a land cleared of long war.

---

[6]Columbus's birthplace in Italy.
[7]Also "Khan," emperor of China.
[8]Prayer here addressed to "Mother Mary [mother of Christ]" asking that one of Columbus's ships be permitted to survive (the *Nina*; the *Santa Maria* had been grounded and the *Pinta* lost in a storm).
[9]Cask, in which Columbus had placed the record of the voyage and set it adrift—just in case his ship did not survive.
[10]I.e., the world; Columbus's voyage proved that the world was round.
[11]The chief magistrates of Venice and Genoa, important

points on the trade route with the Orient; Columbus set out in hopes of finding a shorter trade route to India.
[12]Spain's King Ferdinand V.
[13]Cf. Isaiah 14:29–30, in which Israel's oppressors are warned: "The firstborn of the poor shall feed, and the needy shall lie down in safety: and I will kill thy root with famine, and he shall slay thy remnant." "Lee" is a protective shelter, on shipboard the side away from the wind.
[14]"Saltes Bar," a sandbar; "Palos," a Spanish Mediterranean seaport, from which Columbus began his voyage.

Some Angelus[15] environs the cordage tree;   55
Dark waters onward shake the dark prow free.

· · ·

O Thou who sleepest[16] on Thyself, apart
Like ocean athwart lanes of death and birth,
And all the eddying breath between dost search
Cruelly with love thy parable of man,—   60
aInquisitor! incognizable Word
Of Eden and the enchained Sepulchre,[17]
Into thy steep savannahs, burning blue,
Utter to loneliness the sail is true.

Who grindest oar, and arguing the mast   65
Subscribest holocaust of ships, O Thou
Within whose primal scan consummately
The glistening seignories[18] of Ganges swim;—
Who sendest greeting by the corposant,[19]
And Teneriffe's garnet—flamed it in a cloud,   70
Urging through night our passage to the Chan;—
Te Deum laudamus,[20] for thy teeming span!

Of all that amplitude that time explores,
A needle in the sight, suspended north,—
Yielding by inference and discard, faith   75
And true appointment from the hidden shoal:
This disposition that thy night relates
From Moon to Saturn in one sapphire wheel:
The orbic wake of thy once whirling feet,
Elohim,[21] still I hear thy sounding heel!   80

White toil of heaven's cordons,[22] mustering
In holy rings all sails charged to the far
Hushed gleaming fields and pendant seething wheat
Of knowledge,—round thy brows unhooded now
—The kindled Crown! acceded of the poles   85
And biassed by full sails, meridians[23] reel
Thy purpose—still one shore beyond desire!
The sea's green crying towers a-sway, Beyond

And kingdoms
                 naked in the   90
                                trembling heart—
     Te Deum laudamus
               O Thou Hand of Fire[24]

---

[15]A bell sounded morning, noon, and night to remind hearers of the time for the prayer commemorating the Incarnation.

[16]Cf. Psalms 44:23: "Awake, why sleepest thou, O Lord? arise, cast *us* not off for ever."

[17]I.e., God as manifested in the Garden of Eden and in the burial (and resurrection) of Christ.

[18]Dominions, perhaps here a metaphor for the sacred fish of the Ganges, sacred river of India.

[19]A glowing ball of fire (actually, electrical discharge) sometimes seen at the top of one of the ship's masts during storms;

one was witnessed by Columbus and his crew near Teneriffe (one of the Canary Islands).

[20]"O Lord we praise Thee" (Latin; opening of Catholic prayer).

[21]Variant name for God.

[22]Protective ranks or rows.

[23]Great circles of the earth, passing through the two poles.

[24]The corposant (literally, the "body of the saint") is transfigured here into God's "Hand of Fire" (note recurrence of the image in "The Tunnel," l. 138, and the "Bridge of Fire" in "Atlantis," l. 93).

from **II. Powhatan's Daughter**[1]

*"—Pocahuntus, a well-featured but wanton yong girle . . .
of the age of eleven or twelve years, get the boyes forth with
her into the market place, and make them wheele, falling on
their hands, turning their heels upwards, whom she would
followe, and wheele so herself, naked as she was, all the fort
over."*[2]

THE HARBOR DAWN[3]

*400 years and
more . . . or is
it from the
soundless shore
of sleep that
time*

Insistently through sleep—a tide of voices—
They meet you listening midway in your dream,
The long, tired sounds, fog-insulated noises:
Gongs in white surplices, beshrouded wails,
Far strum of fog horns . . . signals dispersed in veils.   5

And then a truck will lumber past the wharves
As winch engines begin throbbing on some deck;
Or a drunken stevedore's howl and thud below
Comes echoing alley-upward through dim snow.

And if they take your sleep away sometimes   10
They give it back again. Soft sleeves of sound
Attend the darkling harbor, the pillowed bay;
Somewhere out there in blankness steam

Spills into steam, and wanders, washed away
—Flurried by keen fifings, eddied   15
Among distant chiming buoys—adrift. The sky,
Cool feathery fold, suspends, distills
This wavering slumber. . . . Slowly—
Immemorially the window, the half-covered chair
Ask nothing but this sheath of pallid air.   20

*recalls you to
your love,
there in a
waking dream
to merge
your seed*

And you beside me, blessèd now while sirens
Sing to us, stealthily weave us into day—
Serenely now, before day claims our eyes
Your cool arms murmurously about me lay.

While myriad snowy hands are clustering at the panes—   25

    *your hands within my hands are deeds;
    my tongue upon your throat—singing
    arms close; eyes wide, undoubtful
        dark
           drink the dawn—*   30
    a forest shudders in your hair!

---

[1]"Powhatan's daughter, or Pocahontas, is the mythological nature-symbol chosen to represent the physical body of the continent, or the soil. She here takes on much the same role as the traditional Hertha of ancient Teutonic mythology" (Crane's comment in a letter to Kahn).

[2]The epigraph is taken from William Strachey, *Historie of Travaile into Virginia Britannia*, written before 1618, first published in 1849.

[3]Crane wrote to Kahn that the "movement of the verse" in "Harbor Dawn" "is in considerable contrast to that of the 'Ave Maria,' with its sea-swell crescendo and the climacteric vision of Columbus. This legato, in which images blur as objects only half apprehended on the border of sleep and consciousness, makes an admirable transition between the intervening centuries. The love-motif (in italics) carries along a symbolism of the life and ages of man (here the sowing of the seed) which is further developed in each of the subsequent sections of 'Powhatan's Daughter,' though it is never particularly stressed. In 2 ('Van Winkle') it is childhood; in 3 it is Youth; in 4, Manhood; in 5 it is Age. This motif is interwoven and tends to be implicit in the imagery rather than anywhere stressed."

—with whom? The window goes blond slowly. Frostily clears.
From Cyclopean towers[4] across Manhattan waters
—Two—three bright window-eyes aglitter, disk
The sun, released—aloft with cold gulls hither.   35

Who is the   The fog leans one last moment on the sill.
woman with   Under the mistletoe of dreams, a star—
us in the   As though to join us at some distant hill—
dawn? . . .   Turns in the waking west and goes to sleep.
whose is the
flesh our feet
have moved
upon?

VAN WINKLE[1]

Streets spread Macadam, gun-grey as the tunny's belt,
past store and Leaps from Far Rockaway to Golden Gate:[2]
factory—sped   Listen! the miles a hurdy-gurdy grinds—
by sunlight   Down gold arpeggios mile on mile unwinds.
and her
smile . . .   Times earlier, when you hurried off to school,   5
                  —It is the same hour though a later day—
                  You walked with Pizarro in a copybook,
                  And Cortes rode up,[3] reining tautly in—
                  Firmly as coffee grips the taste,—and away!

                  There was Priscilla's cheek close in the wind,   10
                  And Captain Smith,[4] all beard and certainty,
                  And Rip Van Winkle bowing by the way,—
Like Memory,   "Is this Sleepy Hollow,[5] friend—?" And he—
she is time's
truant, shall   *And Rip forgot the office hours,*
take you by   *and he forgot the pay;*   15
the hand . . .   *Van Winkle sweeps a tenement*
                              way down on Avenue A,—

                  The grind-organ says . . . Remember, remember
                  The cinder pile at the end of the backyard
                  Where we stoned the family of young   20
                  Garter snakes under . . . And the monoplanes

---

[4]Cyclops was a one-eyed giant who encountered Odysseus in Homer's *Odyssey*, IX; here the towers are tall buildings.
[1]Crane wrote to Kahn: "The protagonist has left the room with its harbor sounds, and is walking to the subway. The rhythm is quickened; it is a transition between sleep and the immanent tasks of the day. Space is filled with the music of a hand organ and fresh sunlight, and one has the impression of the whole continent—from Atlantic to Pacific—freshly arisen and moving. The walk to the subway arouses reminiscences of childhood, also the 'childhood' of the continental conquest, vis., the conquistadores, Priscilla, Capt. John Smith, etc. These parallelisms unite in the figure of Rip Van Winkle who finally becomes identified with the protagonist, as you will notice, and who really boards the subway with the reader. He becomes the 'guardian angel' of the journey into the past." Washington Irving (1783–1859), in "Rip Van Winkle," told the story of a man who wandered off into the Catskills before the Revolutionary War, encountered small creatures who plied him with liquor, and then slept for twenty years; on his return he found his wife and friends dead, his country with a different form of government, and all things changed.
[2]I.e., from a village on Long Island (Far Rockaway) to the Golden Gate Strait at the entrance to San Francisco Bay.
[3]Francisco Pizarro (1485–1547) and Hernando Cortez (1471–1541), subjects of study in the protagonist's youth, were Spanish "conquistadores" (or conquerors), Pizarro in Peru, Cortez in Mexico.
[4]Henry Wadsworth Longfellow, in "The Courtship of Miles Standish," retold (in poetry) the story of Priscilla Alden preferring Standish's emissary in courtship, John Alden, to Standish himself; Captain Smith (1580–1631) wrote several accounts of his experiences in the settlement of Jamestown, Virginia, in one of which he relates the story of the Indian Princess Pocahontas saving him when her father had ordered him killed.
[5]"The Legend of Sleepy Hollow" is another story by Washington Irving, in which the frail school teacher Ichabod Crane is frightened by a headless horseman.

We launched—with paper wings and twisted
Rubber bands . . . Recall—recall

the rapid tongues
That flittered from under the ash heap day   25
After day whenever your stick discovered
Some sunning inch of unsuspecting fibre—
It flashed back at your thrust, as clean as fire.

And Rip was slowly made aware
  that he, Van Winkle, was not here   30
nor there. He woke and swore he'd seen Broadway
  a Catskill daisy chain in May—

So memory, that strikes a rhyme out of a box,
Or splits a random smell of flowers through glass—
Is it the whip stripped from the lilac tree   35
One day in spring my father took to me,
Or is it the Sabbatical, unconscious smile
My mother almost brought me once from church
And once only, as I recall—?

It[6] flickered through the snow screen, blindly   40
It forsook her at the doorway, it was gone
Before I had left the window. It
Did not return with the kiss in the hall.

Macadam, gun-grey as the tunny's belt,
Leaps from Far Rockaway to Golden Gate. . . .   45
Keep hold of that nickel for car-change, Rip,—
Have you got your *"Times"*—?
And hurry along, Van Winkle—it's getting late!

[Crane's explanation of his overall purpose in "Powhatan's Daughter" provides a valuable summary of the parts not included here: "Powhatan's daughter, or Pocahontas, is the mythological nature-symbol chosen to represent the physical body of the continent, or the soil. She here takes on much the same role as the traditional Hertha of ancient Teutonic mythology. The five sub-sections of Part II are mainly concerned with a gradual exploration of this 'body' whose first possessor was the Indian. It seemed altogether ineffective from the poetic standpoint to approach this material from the purely chronological angle—beginning with, say, the landing of 'The Mayflower,' continuing with a résumé of the Revolution through the conquest of the West, etc. One can get that viewpoint in any history primer. What I am after is an assimilation of this experience, a more organic panorama, showing the continuous and living evidence of the past in the inmost vital substance of the present"

"The Harbor Dawn" and "Van Winkle" of "Powhatan's Daughter" are followed by three additional sub-sections entitled "The River," "The Dance," and "Indiana." Crane's poetic technique makes it very difficult to summarize his poems, but his explanations in letters to friends about his purpose in the first two of these omitted sub-sections provide a sense of their contents:

On "The River" (letter to Mrs. T. W. Simpson, July 4, 1927): "I'm trying in this part of the poem to chart the pioneer experience of our forefathers—and to tell

---
[6]The mother's smile.

the story backwards, as it were, on the 'backs' of hobos. These hobos are simply 'psychological ponies' to carry the reader across the country and back to the Mississippi, which you will notice is described as a great River of Time. I also unlatch the door to the pure Indian world which opens out in 'The Dance' section, so the reader is gradually led back in time to the pure savage world, while existing at the same time in the present."

On "The Dance" (letter to Otto H. Kahn, September 12, 1927): "Here one is on the pure mythical and smoky soil at last! Not only do I describe the conflict between the two races in this dance — I also become identified with the Indian and his world before it is over, which is the only method possible of ever really possessing the Indian and his world as a cultural factor. I think I really succeed in getting under the skin of this glorious and dying animal, in terms of expression, in symbols, which he himself would comprehend. Pocahantas (the continent) is the common basis of our meeting; she survives the extinction of the Indian, who finally, after being assumed into the elements of nature (as he understood them), persists only as a kind of 'eye' in the sky, or as a star that hangs between day and night — 'the twilight's dim perpetual throne.'"

"Indiana" in summary: This sub-section is a monologue of an Indiana farmer's widow, the time about 1860. The farmer failed in the Colorado gold rush of 1858–59 and returned to till the soil. The widow is bidding goodbye to her son, going off to sea, and remembering a moment when he was a baby and she exchanged a strange, haunting, and mystic look with an Indian woman also carrying a baby.

Following "Powhatan's Daughter" is one section of *The Bridge*, Part III ("Cutty Sark"), omitted here. Crane wrote to Otto Kahn (letter of September 12, 1927): "'Cutty Sark' is a phantasy on the period of the whalers and clipper ships. It also starts in the present and 'progresses backward.' The form of the poem may seem erratic, but it is meant to present the hallucinations incident to rum-drinking in a South Street dive, as well as the lurch of a boat in heavy seas, etc. . . . 'Cutty Sark' [name of one of the clipper ships but also a popular Scotch whiskey] is built on the plan of a fugue. Two 'voices'—that of the world of Time, and that of the world of Eternity—are interwoven in action. The Atlantis theme (that of eternity) is the transmuted voice of the nickel-slot pianola, and this voice alternates with that of the derelict sailor and the description of the action. The airy regatta of phantom clipper ships seen from Brooklyn Bridge on the way home is quite effective, I think. It was a pleasure to use historical names for these lovely ghosts. Music still haunts their names long after the wind has left their sails."]

IV. Cape Hatteras[1]

The seas all crossed,
weathered the capes, the voyage done . . .
                                        WALT WHITMAN[2]

    Imponderable the dinosaur
        sinks slow,
           the mammoth saurian
               ghoul, the eastern
                   Cape . . .   5

---

[1]Crane described this section to Kahn as a "kind of ode to Whitman." Kitty Hawk, North Carolina, on Cape Hatteras, is the place where the Wright brothers had their first successful flight of an airplane.
[2]From "Passage to India."

While rises in the west the coastwise range,
                    slowly the hushed land—
Combustion at the astral core—the dorsal change
Of energy—convulsive shift of sand . . .
But we, who round the capes, the promontories   10
Where strange tongues vary messages of surf
Below grey citadels, repeating to the stars
The ancient names—return home to our own
Hearths, there to eat an apple and recall
The songs that gypsies dealt us at Marseille   15
Or how the priests walked—slowly through Bombay—
Or to read you, Walt,—knowing us in thrall

To that deep wonderment, our native clay
Whose depth of red, eternal flesh of Pocahontas—
Those continental folded æons, surcharged   20
With sweetness below derricks, chimneys, tunnels—
Is veined by all that time has really pledged us . . .
And from above, thin squeaks of radio static,
The captured fume of space foams in our ears—
What whisperings of far watches on the main   25
Relapsing into silence, while time clears
Our lenses, lifts a focus, resurrects
A periscope to glimpse what joys or pain
Our eyes can share or answer—then deflects
Us, shunting to a labyrinth submersed   30
Where each sees only his dim past reversed . . .

But that star-glistered salver of infinity,
The circle, blind crucible of endless space,
Is sluiced by motion,—subjugated never.
Adam and Adam's answer in the forest   35
Left Hesperus[3] mirrored in the lucid pool.
Now the eagle dominates our days, is jurist
Of the ambiguous cloud. We know the strident rule
Of wings imperious . . . Space, instantaneous,
Flickers a moment, consumes us in its smile: 40
A flash over the horizon—shifting gears—
And we have laughter, or more sudden tears.
Dream cancels dream in this new realm of fact
From which we wake into the dream of act;
Seeing himself an atom in a shroud—   45
Man hears himself an engine in a cloud!

"—Recorders ages hence"[4]—ah, syllables of faith!
Walt, tell me, Walt Whitman, if infinity
Be still the same as when you walked the beach
Near Paumanok—your lone patrol—and heard the wraith   50
Through surf, its bird note there a long time falling . . .[5]
For you, the panoramas and this breed of towers,
Of you—the theme that's statured in the cliff.
O Saunterer on free ways still ahead!

---

[3]The evening star.
[4]The title of a poem in the "Calamus" section of Whitman's *Leaves of Grass.*
[5]Whitman in "Out of the Cradle Endlessly Rocking" de-

scribes himself as a young boy listening on the beach of Long Island (Paumanok) to a mockingbird's song of grief over the loss of a mate.

Not this our empire yet, but labyrinth   55
Wherein your eyes, like the Great Navigator's[6] without ship,
Gleam from the great stones of each prison crypt
Of canyoned traffic . . . Confronting the Exchange,
Surviving in a world of stocks,—they also range
Across the hills where second timber strays   60
Back over Connecticut farms, abandoned pastures,—
Sea eyes and tidal, undenying, bright with myth!

The nasal whine of power whips a new universe . . .
Where spouting pillars spoor the evening sky,
Under the looming stacks of the gigantic power house   65
Stars prick the eyes with sharp ammoniac proverbs,
New verities, new inklings in the velvet hummed
Of dynamos, where hearing's leash is strummed . . .
Power's script,—wound, bobbin-bound, refined—
Is stropped to the slap of belts on booming spools, spurred   70
Into the bulging bouillon, harnessed jelly of the stars.
Towards what? The forked crash of split thunder parts
Our hearing momentwise; but fast in whirling armatures,
As bright as frogs' eyes, giggling in the girth
Of steely gizzards—axle-bound, confined   75
In coiled precision, bunched in mutual glee
The bearings glint,—O murmurless and shined
In oilrinsed circles of blind ecstasy!

Stars scribble on our eyes the frosty sagas,
The gleaming cantos of unvanquished space . . .   80
O sinewy silver biplane, nudging the wind's withers!
There, from Kill Devils Hill at Kitty Hawk
Two brothers in their twinship left the dune;
Warping the gale, the Wright windwrestlers veered
Capeward, then blading the wind's flank, banked and spun   85
What ciphers risen from prophetic script,
What marathons new-set between the stars!
The soul, by naphtha fledged into new reaches
Already knows the closer clasp of Mars,—
New latitudes, unknotting, soon give place   90
To what fierce schedules, rife of doom apace!

Behold the dragon's covey—amphibian, ubiquitous
To hedge the seaboard, wrap the headland, ride
The blue's cloud-templed districts unto ether . . .
While Iliads glimmer[7] through eyes raised in pride   95
Hell's belt springs wider into heaven's plumed side.
O bright circumferences, heights employed to fly
War's fiery kennel masked in downy offings,—
This tournament of space, the threshed and chiselled height,
Is baited by marauding circles, bludgeon flail   100
Of rancorous grenades whose screaming petals carve us
Wounds that we wrap with theorems sharp as hail!

Wheeled swiftly, wings emerge from larval-silver hangars.
Taut motors surge, space-gnawing, into flight;

---

[6]I.e., Columbus.
[7]The feats of the airplane cause onlookers to think heroic
action is possible again, on the scale of that fabulous time of
Homer's *Iliad*.

Through sparkling visibility, outspread, unsleeping,   105
Wings clip the last peripheries of light . . .
Tellurian[8] wind-sleuths on dawn patrol,
Each plane a hurtling javelin of winged ordnance,
Bristle the heights above a screeching gale to hover;
Surely no eye that Sunward Escadrille[9] can cover!   110
There, meaningful, fledged as the Pleiades[10]
With razor sheen they zoom each rapid helix!
Up-chartered choristers of their own speeding
They, cavalcade on escapade, shear Cumulus —
Lay siege and hurdle Cirrus[11] down the skies!   115
While Cetus-like,[12] O thou Dirigible, enormous Lounger
Of pendulous auroral beaches, — satelled wide
By convoy planes, moonferrets that rejoin thee
On fleeing balconies as thou dost glide,
— Hast splintered space!   120

　　　　　　　　　　Low, shadowed of the Cape,
Regard the moving turrets! From grey decks
See scouting griffons[13] rise through gaseous crepe
Hung low . . . until a conch of thunder answers
Cloud-belfries, banging, while searchlights, like fencers,   125
Slit the sky's pancreas of foaming anthracite
Toward thee, O Corsair[14] of the typhoon, — pilot, hear!
Thine eyes bicarbonated white by speed, O Skygak,[15] see
How from thy path above the levin's lance
Thou sowest doom thou hast nor time nor chance   130
To reckon — as thy stilly eyes partake
What alcohol of space . . . ! Remember, Falcon-Ace,
Thou hast there in thy wrist a Sanskrit charge[16]
To conjugate infinity's dim marge —
Anew . . . !   135

　　　　　　　　　But first, here at this height receive
The benediction of the shell's deep, sure reprieve!
Lead-perforated fuselage, escutcheoned wings
Lift agonized quittance, tilting from the invisible brink
Now eagle-bright, now   140
　　　　　　　　　　　quarry-hid, twist-
　　　　　　　　　　　　　　　　-ing, sink with
Enormous repercussive list-
　　　　　　　　　　　　-ings down
Giddily spiralled   145
　　　　　　　　gauntlets, upturned, unlooping
In guerrilla sleights, trapped in combustion gyr-
Ing, dance the curdled depth
　　　　　　　　　　　　down whizzing
Zodiacs, dashed   150
　　　　　　　(now nearing fast the Cape!)

---

[8]Tellurian is an inhabitant of the earth.
[9]A squadron of airplanes (from the French).
[10]A constellation named after the daughters of Atlas.
[11]Cumulus is a formation of thick clouds, while Cirrus is a formation of fleecy clouds.
[12]I.e., whale-like.
[13]Wire-haired dogs (air fights are "dog fights").

[14]A privateer or pirate ship.
[15]I.e., stunt pilot.
[16]A sacred command; Sanskrit is the language of the sacred texts of Hinduism. In "Passage to India," Whitman calls for spiritual feats to match the material or technological achievements of the time.

                    down gravitation's
                vortex into crashed
. . . . dispersion . . . into mashed and shapeless debris. . . .
By Hatteras bunched the beached heap of high bravery!   155

                        • • • •

The stars have grooved our eyes with old persuasions
Of love and hatred, birth,—surcease of nations . . .
But who has held the heights more sure than thou,
O Walt!—Ascensions of thee hover in me now
As thou at junctions elegiac, there, of speed   160
With vast eternity, dost wield the rebound seed!
The competent loam, the probable grass,—travail
Of tides awash the pedestal of Everest, fail
Not less than thou in pure impulse inbred
To answer deepest soundings! O, upward from the dead   165
Thou bringest tally, and a pact, new bound
Of living brotherhood!

                Thou, there beyond—
Glacial sierras and the flight of ravens,
Hermetically past condor zones, through zenith havens   170
Past where the albatross has offered up
His last wing-pulse, and downcast as a cup
That's drained, is shivered back to earth—thy wand
Has beat a song, O Walt,—there and beyond!
And this, thine other hand, upon my heart   175
Is plummet ushered of those tears that start
What memories of vigils, bloody, by that Cape,—
Ghoul-mound of man's perversity at balk
And fraternal massacre! Thou, pallid there as chalk,
Hast kept of wounds, O Mourner, all that sum   180
That then from Appomattox stretched to Somme![17]

Cowslip and shad-blow, flaked like tethered foam
Around bared teeth of stallions, bloomed that spring
When first I read thy lines, rife as the loam
Of prairies, yet like breakers cliffward leaping!   185
O, early following thee, I searched the hill
Blue-writ and odor-firm with violets, 'til
With June the mountain laurel broke through green
And filled the forest with what clustrous sheen!
Potomac lilies,—then the Pontiac rose,   190
And Klondike edelweiss of occult snows!
White banks of moonlight came descending valleys—
How speechful on oak-vizored palisades,
As vibrantly I following down Sequoia alleys
Heard thunder's eloquence through green arcades   195
Set trumpets breathing in each clump and grass tuft—'til
Gold autumn, captured, crowned the trembling hill!

---

[17]Sites of battles of the Civil War (Appomattox) and World War I (Somme); Whitman wrote his "Drum-Taps" poems about the Civil War and his elegy "When Lilacs Last in the Dooryard Bloom'd" for Abraham Lincoln on his assassination near the end of the Civil War.

Panis Angelicus![18] Eyes tranquil with the blaze
Of love's own diametric gaze, of love's amaze!
Not greatest, thou,—not first, nor last,—but near   200
And onward yielding past my utmost year.
Familiar, thou, as mendicants in public places;
Evasive—too—as dayspring's spreading arc to trace is:—
Our Meistersinger,[19] thou set breath in steel;
And it was thou who on the boldest heel   205
Stood up and flung the span on even wing
Of that great Bridge, our Myth, whereof I sing!

Years of the Modern! Propulsions toward what capes?
But thou, *Panis Angelicus*, hast thou not seen
And passed that Barrier that none escapes—   210
But knows it leastwise as death-strife?—O, something green,
Beyond all sesames of science was thy choice
Wherewith to bind us throbbing with one voice,
New integers of Roman, Viking, Celt—
Thou, Vedic Caesar, to the greensward knelt![20]   215

And now, as launched in abysmal cupolas of space,
Toward endless terminals, Easters of speeding light—
Vast engines outward veering with seraphic grace
On clarion cylinders pass out of sight
To course that span of consciousness thou'st named   220
The Open Road[21]—thy vision is reclaimed!
What heritage thou'st signalled to our hands!

And see! the rainbow's arch—how shimmeringly stands
Above the Cape's ghoul-mound, O joyous seer!
Recorders ages hence, yes, they shall hear   225
In their own veins uncancelled thy sure tread
And read thee by the aureole 'round thy head
Of pasture-shine, *Panis Angelicus!*
                   yes, Walt,
Afoot again, and onward without halt,—   230
Not soon, nor suddenly,—no, never to let go
   My hand
      in yours,[22]
        Walt Whitman—
           so—   235

[Part V ("Three Songs") and Part VI ("QuakerHill"), which follow "Cape Hatteras," are omitted here and may be summarized briefly:

"Three Songs" are short lyic poems, each portraying a modern woman linked with a mythic or religious figure: "Southern Cross" with Eve, "National Winter Garden" with Mary Magdalene, and "Virginia" with the Virgin Mary. Crane's portrayal of a contemporary Eve, Magdalene, and Virgin, are, ultimately, celebratory in nature, finding even within the sordid modernity a sexual-procrea-

---

[18]"Bread of angels" (Latin): Whitman provides spiritual sustenance through his poetry.
[19]Master Singer (highest rank in the medieval German guild of singers and poets).
[20]The Vedas are the sacred texts of Hinduism: thus Whitman as Vedic Caesar is a spiritual leader; the "greensward"

on which he kneels is suggestive of his masterpiece, *Leaves of Grass*, in which grass is a dominant image and symbol of individuality and equality.
[21]Reference to Whitman's "Song of the Open Road."
[22]Cf. "Camerado, I give you my hand!" from the end of Whitman's "Song of the Open Road."

tional energy that is ultimately redeeming. In "Southern Cross," the protagonist's sexual longing enables him to evoke a Whitmanian scene of cosmic coupling ("The Southern Cross takes night / And lifts her girdles from her, one by one —"), but his call for a woman in the flesh "falls vainly on the wave," and the poem closes in what seems to be masturbatory loneliness. In "National Winter Garden" Magdalene is reincarnated in the "common prostitute" of a modern burlesque queen, with the protagonist picking a "blonde out neatly through the smoke." Even the vulgarity of the burlesque cannot negate its immanent vitality. And the vitality is present too in the mundane business-office world of "Virginia," with the protagonist singing the song of his Mary ("And I'm still waiting you —") and elevating her commonplace attributes into tower-dwelling mythological and shining "Cathedral Mary," a miracle of imaginative transfiguration through sexual energy.

"Quaker Hill" is a savage exposure of the emptiness of life in the resort-hotel that the modern age has made out of the old Quaker Meeting House in upstate New York. The tourists are the living dead "playing" in what was ironically the "Promised Land." In this scene, the protagonist sees "death's stare" from all four horizons, and the poem turns from the modern scene to the past, as the poet asks not "scalped Yankees" but "slain Iroquois to guide." The poet tells us that we must descend "from the hawk's eye stemming view" to "worm's eye" in order to "construe" death (and love). The section ends with the redeeming song, from the "throbbing throat" of the "whip-poor-will," which "unhusks the heart of fright, / Breaks us and saves . . . / Love from despair — when love foresees the end." Crane commented on this section (letter to Caresse Crosby, December 26, 1929): "Quaker Hill" is not . . . one of the major sections of the poem; it is rather by way of an 'accent mark' that it is valuable at all."]

VII. The Tunnel[1]

To Find the Western path
Right thro' the Gates of Wrath
BLAKE[2]

Performances, assortments, résumés —
Up Times Square to Columbus Circle lights
Channel the congresses, nightly sessions,
Refractions of the thousand theatres, faces —
Mysterious kitchens. . . . You shall search them all.   5
Someday by heart you'll learn each famous sight
And watch the curtain lift in hell's despite;
You'll find the garden in the third act dead,
Finger your knees — and wish yourself in bed
With tabloid crime-sheets perched in easy sight.   10

---

[1]Crane described this section: "Subway — the encroachment of machinery on humanity: a kind of purgatory in relation to the open sky of last section." The section portrays the protagonist's trip on the subway as a descent into hell, or even something akin to the "dark night of the soul" that mystics often experience just before the transcendent union or illumination.

[2]From "Morning" by William Blake (1757–1827); this stanza concludes: "Sweet Mercy leads me on, / With soft repentant moan / I see the break of day."

Then let you reach your hat
and go.
As usual, let you — also
walking down — exclaim
to twelve upward leaving   15
a subscription praise
for what time slays.

Or can't you quite make up your mind to ride;
A walk is better underneath the L[3] a brisk
Ten blocks or so before? But you find yourself   20
Preparing penguin flexions of the arms, —
As usual you will meet the scuttle yawn:
The subway yawns the quickest promise home.

Be minimum, then, to swim the hiving swarms
Out of the Square, the Circle burning bright —   25
Avoid the glass doors gyring at your right,
Where boxed alone a second, eyes take fright
— Quite unprepared rush naked back to light:
And down beside the turnstile press the coin
Into the slot. The gongs already rattle.   30

And so
of cities you bespeak
subways, rivered under streets
and rivers. . . . In the car
the overtone of motion   35
underground, the monotone
of motion is the sound
of other faces, also underground —

"Let's have a pencil Jimmy — living now
at Floral Park   40
Flatbush — on the fourth of July —
like a pigeon's muddy dream — potatoes
to dig in the field — travlin the town — too —
night after night — the Culver line — the
girls all shaping up — it used to be — "   45

Our tongues recant like beaten weather vanes.
This answer lives like verdigris,[4] like hair
Beyond extinction, surcease of the bone;
And repetition freezes — "What

"what do you want? getting weak on the links?   50
fandaddle daddy don't ask for change — IS THIS
FOURTEENTH? it's half past six she said — if
you don't like my gate why did you
swing on it, why *didja*
swing on it   55
anyhow — "

And somehow anyhow swing —

The phonographs of hades in the brain
Are tunnels that re-wind themselves, and love
A burnt match skating in a urinal—   60
Somewhere above Fourteenth TAKE THE EXPRESS
To brush some new presentiment of pain—

"But I want service in this office SERVICE
I said—after
the show she cried a little afterwards but—"   65

Whose head is swinging from the swollen strap?
Whose body smokes along the bitten rails,
Bursts from a smoldering bundle far behind
In back forks of the chasms of the brain,—
Puffs from a riven stump far out behind   70
In interborough fissures of the mind . . . ?

And why do I often meet your visage[5] here,
Your eyes like agate lanterns—on and on
Below the toothpaste and the dandruff ads?
—And did their riding eyes right through your side,   75
And did their eyes like unwashed platters ride?
And Death, aloft,—gigantically down
Probing through you—toward me, O evermore![6]
And when they dragged your retching flesh,
Your trembling hands that night through Baltimore—   80
That last night on the ballot rounds, did you
Shaking, did you deny the ticket, Poe?

For Gravesend Manor change at Chambers Street.
The platform hurries along to a dead stop.

The intent escalator lifts a serenade   85
Stilly
Of shoes, umbrellas, each eye attending its shoe, then
Bolting outright somewhere above where streets
Burst suddenly in rain. . . . The gongs recur:
Elbows and levers, guard and hissing door.   90
Thunder is galvothermic[7] here below. . . . The car
Wheels off. The train rounds, bending to a scream,
Taking the final level for the dive
Under the river—
And somewhat emptier than before,   95
Demented, for a hitching second, humps; then
Lets go. . . . Toward corners of the floor
Newspapers wing, revolve and wing.
Blank windows gargle signals through the roar.

And does the Dæmon take you home, also,   100
Wop washerwoman, with the bandaged hair?
After the corridors are swept, the cuspidors—
The gaunt sky-barracks cleanly now, and bare,

[5]Edgar Allan Poe, with a nightmare imagination.
[6]Cf. Poe's "To Helen" ("The agate lamp within thy hand"), "The City in the Sea" ("Death looks gigantically down"), and "The Raven" (with the refrain "Nevermore").
[7]The production of heat by galvanism (which is electricity produced by chemical action).

O Genoese,[8] do you bring mother eyes and hands
Back home to children and to golden hair?   105

Dæmon, demurring and eventful yawn!
Whose hideous laughter is a bellows mirth
— Or the muffled slaughter of a day in birth —
O cruelly to inoculate the brinking dawn
With antennæ toward worlds that glow and sink; —   110
To spoon us out more liquid than the dim
Locution of the eldest star, and pack
The conscience navelled in the plunging wind,
Umbilical to call — and straightway die!

O caught like pennies beneath soot and steam,   115
Kiss of our agony thou gatherest;
Condensed, thou takest all — shrill ganglia
Impassioned with some song we fail to keep.
And yet, like Lazarus,[9] to feel the slope,
The sod and billow breaking, — lifting ground,   120
— A sound of waters bending astride the sky
Unceasing with some Word that will not die . . . !

· · ·

A tugboat, wheezing wreaths of steam,
Lunged past, with one galvanic blare stove up the River.
I counted the echoes assembling, one after one,   125
Searching, thumbing the midnight on the piers.
Lights, coasting, left the oily tympanum of waters;
The blackness somewhere gouged glass on a sky.
And this thy harbor, O my City, I have driven under,
Tossed from the coil of ticking towers. . . . Tomorrow,   130
And to be. . . . Here by the River that is East —
Here at the waters' edge the hands drop memory;
Shadowless in that abyss they unaccounting lie.
How far away the star has pooled the sea —
Or shall the hands be drawn away, to die?   135

Kiss of our agony Thou gatherest,
O Hand of Fire[10]
gatherest —

VIII. Atlantis[1]

*Music is then the knowledge of that which relates to love in
harmony and system.*

PLATO[2]

Through the bound cable strands, the arching path
Upward, veering with light, the flight of strings, —

---

[8]The "wop washerwoman" here called, with greater sympathy, "Genoese" (that is, from Genoa, Italy, like Columbus).
[9]The brother of Mary and Martha, raised from the dead by Christ (John 11:43–44).
[10]Cf. the end of "Ave Maria."
[1]Crane described "Atlantis": "The Bridge — a sweeping dith-
yramb in which the Bridge becomes the symbol of consciousness spanning time and space." Atlantis, mentioned in Plato, was the legendary island in the Atlantic that disappeared, sinking into the sea.
[2]From *Republic*, III, 403.

Taut miles of shuttling moonlight syncopate
The whispered rush, telepathy of wires.
Up the index of night, granite and steel—   5
Transparent meshes—fleckless the gleaming staves—
Sibylline[3] voices flicker, waveringly stream
As though a god were issue of the strings. . . .

And through that cordage, threading with its call
One arc synoptic of all tides below—   10
Their labyrinthine mouths of history
Pouring reply as though all ships at sea
Complighted in one vibrant breath made cry,—
"Make thy love sure—to weave whose song we ply!"
—From black embankments, moveless soundings hailed,   15
So seven oceans answer from their dream.

And on, obliquely up bright carrier bars
New octaves trestle the twin monoliths
Beyond whose frosted capes the moon bequeaths
Two worlds of sleep (O arching strands of song!)—   20
Onward and up the crystal-flooded aisle
White tempest nets file upward, upward ring
With silver terraces the humming spars,
The loft of vision, palladium[4] helm of stars.

Sheerly the eyes, like seagulls stung with rime—   25
Slit and propelled by glistening fins of light—
Pick biting way up towering looms that press
Sidelong with flight of blade on tendon blade
—Tomorrows into yesteryear—and link
What cipher-script of time no traveller reads   30
But who, through smoking pyres of love and death,
Searches the timeless laugh of mythic spears.

Like hails, farewells—up planet-sequined heights
Some trillion whispering hammers glimmer Tyre:[5]
Serenely, sharply up the long anvil cry   35
Of inchling æons silence rivets Troy.[6]
And you, aloft there—Jason![7] hesting Shout!
Still wrapping harness to the swarming air!
Silvery the rushing wake, surpassing call,
Beams yelling Æolus![8] splintered in the straits!   40

From gulfs unfolding, terrible of drums,
Tall Vision-of-the-Voyage, tensely spare—
Bridge, lifting night to cycloramic crest
Of deepest day—O Choir, translating time
Into what multitudinous Verb the suns   45
And synergy of waters ever fuse, recast
In myriad syllables,—Psalm of Cathay![9]
O Love, thy white, pervasive Paradigm . . . !

---

[3]Prophetic (like the sibyls of mythology).
[4]A statue of Pallas Athena or a silvery-white metallic chemical element of the platinum group.
[5]Ancient seaport of Phoenicia, now in Lebanon.
[6]City destroyed in the Trojan War, described in Homer's *Iliad*.
[7]Leader of the Greek Argonauts on a successful quest to obtain the golden fleece.
[8]God of the winds on the island of Aeolia.
[9]Old name for China.

We left the haven hanging in the night—
Sheened harbor lanterns backward fled the keel.   50
Pacific here at time's end, bearing corn,—
Eyes stammer through the pangs of dust and steel.
And still the circular, indubitable frieze
Of heaven's meditation, yoking wave
To kneeling wave, one song devoutly binds—   55
The vernal strophe chimes from deathless strings!

O Thou steeled Cognizance whose leap commits
The agile precincts of the lark's return;
Within whose lariat sweep encinctured sing
In single chrysalis the many twain,—   60
Of stars Thou art the stitch and stallion glow
And like an organ, Thou, with sound of doom—
Sight, sound and flesh Thou leadest from time's realm
As love strikes clear direction for the helm.

Swift peal of secular light, intrinsic Myth   65
Whose fell unshadow is death's utter wound,—
O River-throated—iridescently upborne
Through the bright drench and fabric of our veins;
With white escarpments[10] swinging into light,
Sustained in tears the cities are endowed   70
And justified conclamant with ripe fields
Revolving through their harvests in sweet torment.

Forever Deity's glittering Pledge, O Thou
Whose canticle[11] fresh chemistry assigns
To wrapt inception and beatitude,—   75
Always through blinding cables, to our joy,
Of thy white seizure springs the prophecy:
Always through spiring cordage,[12] pyramids
Of silver sequel, Deity's young name
Kinetic of white choiring wings . . . ascends.   80

Migrations that must needs void memory,
Inventions that cobblestone the heart,—
Unspeakable Thou Bridge to Thee, O Love.
Thy pardon for this history, whitest Flower,
O Answerer of all,—Anemone,[13]—   85
Now while thy petals spend the suns about us, hold—
(O Thou whose radiance doth inherit me)
Atlantis,—hold thy floating singer late!

So to thine Everpresence, beyond time,
Like spears ensanguined of one tolling star   90
That bleeds infinity—the orphic strings,[14]
Sidereal[15] phalanxes, leap and converge:
—One Song, one Bridge of Fire! Is it Cathay,
Now pity steeps the grass and rainbows ring

---

[10]Steep slopes or cliffs.
[11]Song or chant; hymn whose words come from the Bible.
[12]Ropes in a ship's rigging.
[13]In Greek mythology, when the love affair between Aphrodite and Adonis ended with Adonis's death caused by a wild boar, Aphrodite caused the red anemone to spring from his blood; the white anemone sprang from Aphrodite's tears.
[14]Reference to Orpheus's lyre; thus, enchanting.
[15]Starry.

The serpent with the eagle in the leaves . . . ?[16]   95
Whispers antiphonal in azure swing.

1923–29   1930

The Broken Tower

The bell-rope that gathers God at dawn
Dispatches me as though I dropped down the knell
Of a spent day — to wander the cathedral lawn
From pit to crucifix, feet chill on steps from hell.

Have you not heard, have you not seen that corps   5
Of shadows in the tower, whose shoulders sway
Antiphonal carillons launched before
The stars are caught and hived in the sun's ray?

The bells, I say, the bells break down their tower;
And swing I know not where. Their tongues engrave   10
Membrane through marrow, my long-scattered score
Of broken intervals . . . And I, their sexton slave!

Oval encyclicals[1] in canyons heaping
The impasse high with choir. Banked voices slain!
Pagodas, campaniles with reveilles outleaping —   15
O terraced echoes prostrate on the plain! . . .

And so it was I entered the broken world
To trace the visionary company of love, its voice
An instant in the wind (I know not whither hurled)
But not for long to hold each desperate choice.   20

My word I poured. But was it cognate, scored
Of that tribunal monarch of the air
Whose thigh embronzes earth, strikes crystal Word
In wounds pledged once to hope — cleft to despair?

The steep encroachments of my blood left me   25
No answer (could blood hold such a lofty tower
As flings the question true?) — or is it she
Whose sweet mortality stirs latent power? —

And through whose pulse I hear, counting the strokes
My veins recall and add, revived and sure   30
The angelus[2] of wars my chest evokes:
What I hold healed, original now, and pure . . .

---

[16]The image of the serpent (time) with the eagle (space), first introduced at the end of "The Dance" in "Powhatan's Daughter," suggests a mystic fusion similar to that in Mexican Indian mythology's Quetzalcoatl, the feathered serpent (*quetzal* [bird] plus *coatl* [snake]), one of the most revered of the ancient gods. Crane lived for a time in Mexico, and he had read D. H. Lawrence's *The Plumed Serpent* (1926), a story of an attempt to restore in Mexico the ancient Aztec religion whose believers worshipped the Quetzalcoatl and lived in harmony with a mystic "blood consciousness" (rather than the intellect or reason).
[1]A letter intended for wide circulation among members of a particular group (as from the Pope to his bishops).
[2]Prayers recited morning, noon, and evening celebrating the Annunciation and Incarnation; the tolling of the Angelus bell signals the time for the prayer.

And builds, within, a tower that is not stone
(Not stone can jacket heaven) — but slip
Of pebbles, — visible wings of silence sown   35
In azure circles, widening as they dip

The matrix[3] of the heart, lift down the eye
That shrines the quiet lake and swells a tower . . .
The commodious, tall decorum of that sky
Unseals her earth, and lifts love in its shower.   40

1932   *1933*

Modern Poetry

Modern poetry has long since passed the crest of its rebellion against many of the so-called classical strictures. Indeed the primary departures of the early intransigeants were often more in a classic direction, with respect to certain neglected early European traditions, than were many of the Victorian regulations that formed the immediate butt of attack.

Revolution flourishes still, but rather as a contemporary tradition in which the original obstacles to freedom have been, if not always eradicated, at least obscured by floods of later experimentation. Indeed, to the serious artist, revolution as an all-engrossing program no longer exists. It persists at a rapid momentum in certain groups or movements, but often in forms which are more constricting than liberating, in view of a generous choice of subject matter.

The poet's concern must be, as always, self-discipline toward a formal integration of experience. For poetry is an architectural art, based not on Evolution or the idea of progress, but on the articulation of the contemporary human consciousness *sub specie æternitatis*,[1] and inclusive of all readjustments incident to science and other shifting factors related to that consciousness. The key to the process of free creative activity which Coleridge gave us in his *Lectures on Shakespeare*[2] exposes the responsibilities of every poet, modern or ancient, and cannot be improved upon. "No work of true genius," he says, "dares want its appropriate form, neither indeed is there any danger of this. As it must not, so genius can not, be lawless: for it is even this that constitutes its genius — *the power of acting creatively under laws of its own origination.*"

Poetry has at once a greater intimacy and a wider, more exact scope of implication than painting or any of the other arts. It is therefore more apt to be indicative of impending changes in other media such as painting or music. This is a logical deduction that facts do not always favor, as in the case of some modern composers such as Stravinsky,[3] the full purport of whose inspiration seems to lie beyond the reach of current literary expression. Literature has a more tangible relationship to painting; and it is highly probable that the Symbolist movement in French poetry was a considerable factor in the instigation first, of Impressionism, and later, of Cubism.[4] Both arts have had parallel and somewhat analogous tendencies toward abstract statement and metaphysical representation. In this recent preoccupation it is certain that both

---

[3]A substance or point in which something takes its origin; womb (obsolete).
[1]"In its essential or universal form or nature" (Latin).
[2]Samuel Taylor Coleridge (1772–1834); *Coleridge's Shakespearean Criticism*, 2 vols., ed. Thomas Middleton Raysor (1930).
[3]Igor Stravinsky (1882–1971), American composer of modern music, born in Russia.

[4]The symbolist poetry movement in France, during the last thirty years of the nineteenth century, represented a turning away from external to internal reality of the human psyche. Impressionism was a nineteenth-century French movement in art (primarily) with emphasis on painting from direct observation of nature. Cubism was an early twentieth-century French movement in art, reducing figures and objects to their basic geometric shapes.

media were responding to the shifting emphasis of the Western World away from religion toward science. Analysis and discovery, the two basic concerns of science, became conscious objectives of both painter and poet. A great deal of modern painting is as independent of any representational motive as a mathematical equation; while some of the most intense and eloquent current verse derives sheerly from acute psychological analysis, quite independent of any dramatic motivation.

The function of poetry in a Machine Age is identical to its function in any other age; and its capacities for presenting the most complete synthesis of human values remain essentially immune from any of the so-called inroads of science. The emotional stimulus of machinery is on an entirely different psychic plane from that of poetry. Its only menace lies in its capacities for facile entertainment, so easily accessible as to arrest the development of any but the most negligible esthetic responses. The ultimate influence of machinery in this respect remains to be seen, but its firm entrenchment in our lives has already produced a series of challenging new responsibilities for the poet.

For unless poetry can absorb the machine, i.e., *acclimatize* it as naturally and casually as trees, cattle, galleons, castles and all other human associations of the past, then poetry has failed of its full contemporary function. This process does not infer any program of lyrical pandering to the taste of those obsessed by the importance of machinery; nor does it essentially involve even the specific mention of a single mechanical contrivance. It demands, however, along with the traditional qualifications of the poet, an extraordinary capacity for surrender, at least temporarily, to the sensations of urban life. This presupposes, of course, that the poet possesses sufficient spontaneity and gusto to convert this experience into positive terms. Machinery will tend to lose its sensational glamour and appear in its true subsidiary order in human life as use and continual poetic allusion subdue its novelty. For, contrary to general prejudice, the wonderment experienced in watching nose dives is of less immediate creative promise to poetry than the familiar gesture of a motorist in the modest act of shifting gears. I mean to say that mere romantic speculation on the power and beauty of machinery keeps it at a continual remove; it can not act creatively in our lives until, like the unconscious nervous responses of our bodies, its connotations emanate from within — forming as spontaneous a terminology of poetic reference as the bucolic world of pasture, plow, and barn.

The familiar contention that science is inimical to poetry is no more tenable than the kindred notion that theology has been proverbially hostile — with the *Commedia* of Dante[5] to prove the contrary. That "truth" which science pursues is radically different from the metaphorical, extra-logical "truth" of the poet. When Blake[6] wrote that "a tear is an intellectual thing, And a sigh is the sword of an Angel King" — he was not in any logical conflict with the principles of the Newtonian Universe.[7] Similarly, poetic prophecy in the case of the seer has nothing to do with factual prediction or with futurity. It is a peculiar type of perception, capable of apprehending some absolute and timeless concept of the imagination with astounding clarity and conviction.

That the modern poet can profitably assume the roles of philosopher or theologian is questionable at best. Science, the uncanonized Deity of the times, seems to have automatically displaced the hierarchies of both Academy and Church. It is pertinent to cite the authors of the *Commedia* and *Paradise Lost*[8] as poets whose verse survives the religious dogmas and philosophies of their respective periods, but it is fallacious to assume that either of these poets could have written important religious verse without the fully developed and articulated religious dogmas that each was heir to.

---

[5]Dante's *Divine Comedy*, called the supreme expression of the Middle Ages, is based on the Thomistic cosmology and theology of its time.
[6]William Blake (1757–1827), British poet.

[7]Sir Isaac Newton's (1642–1727) theories of universal gravitation and terrestrial mechanics.
[8]John Milton (1608–1674), British poet, author of *Paradise Lost*.

The future of American poetry is too complicated a speculation to be more than approached in this limited space. Involved in it are the host of considerations relative to the comparative influences of science, machinery, and other factors which I have merely touched upon; — besides those influential traditions of early English prosody which form points of departure, at least, for any indigenous rhythms and forms which may emerge. The most typical and valid expression of the American *psychosis* seems to me still to be found in Whitman. His faults as a technician and his clumsy and indiscriminate enthusiasm are somewhat beside the point. He, better than any other, was able to coördinate those forces in America which seem most intractable, fusing them into a universal vision which takes on additional significance as time goes on. He was a revolutionist beyond the strict meaning of Coleridge's definition of genius, but his bequest is still to be realized in all its implications.

1930

LANGSTON HUGHES
(1902–1967)

In an important manifesto, "The Negro Artist and the Racial Mountain," published in *The Nation* in 1926, Langston Hughes said: "We younger Negro artists who create now intend to express our individual dark-skinned selves without fear or shame. If white people are pleased we are glad. If they are not, it doesn't matter. We know we are beautiful. And ugly too. The tom-tom cries and the tom-tom laughs. If colored people are pleased we are glad. If they are not, their displeasure doesn't matter either. We build our temples for tomorrow, strong as we know how, and we stand on top of the mountain, free within ourselves."

Langston Hughes devoted his whole life to literature, writing stories, novels, essays, autobiography, histories, biographies, plays (comedies, tragedies, operas, gospel song plays), and poetry. Especially poetry. He was the natural poet laureate of the New Negro Harlem Renaissance. It was his astonishingly fertile imagination that fueled that renaissance and kept it going.

Shortly after his birth in Joplin, Missouri, in 1902, Langston Hughes began a series of unsettling moves across the country, due to his parents' unhappy marriage. Though he would see his parents intermittently, for most of his first thirteen years he was raised by his stern maternal grandmother, a woman of Indian, French, and African ancestry, like her husband who had been killed with John Brown at Harper's Ferry. From her he heard many stories of the brave people who fought slavery, but none, he would later recall, about black folkways.

Further complicating Hughes's sense of identity was his father, who, with a long line of distinguished white ancestry, could not come to terms with his black heritage and racial discrimination. He finally left his family to live out his life in Mexico. In his autobiography *The Big Sea* (1940), Hughes wrote, "I hated my father." That hatred stemmed from his father's scorn for the black race and for his son's dedication to writing about black people. Hughes broke his ties to him in 1921, but he would use the theme of a white or partially white father rejecting his mixed blooded son (as in his play *Mulatto*, produced in 1935).

Hughes began writing verse upon his election as class poet in the eighth grade at Lincoln, Illinois. He attended high school in Cleveland and began writing for the school's *Monthly*, influenced by the free verse of Edgar Lee Masters, Vachel Lindsay, Carl Sandburg (whose populism made Sandburg his "guiding star"), and Walt Whitman. He also wrote dialect poems like those by Paul Laurence Dunbar.

After graduating in 1920, Hughes entered Columbia University, but left after his first year. He worked at odd jobs—clerk, waiter, bus boy, farm hand—but found time to continue writing poetry. In 1923–24, Hughes went to sea as a crewman and later a messboy. On the ship going to Africa, Hughes dropped overboard the books he had toted along, feeling as they fell one by one into the water that he was ridding himself of all the things "unpleasant and miserable" out of his past—the memory of his father, the poverty of his mother, the "stupidities of color-prejudice." There was one book he saved, however: Walt Whitman's *Leaves of Grass*. Whitman's book was to help Hughes find his own role as a writer and his own voice as a poet. On a voyage to Europe in 1924, Hughes left the ship and went to Paris and found a job as night club doorman. He bummed around France and Italy for a part of the year and then returned to America.

In the spring of 1925, Hughes won two prizes for his poems from two black publications—*The Crisis* and *Opportunity*. At *Opportunity*'s award banquet, James Weldon Johnson read "The Weary Blues," and afterward Hughes met the critic Carl Van Vechten, who sent his poems to the publisher Alfred A. Knopf. In December, while working at the Wardman Park Hotel in Washington, D.C., Hughes slipped some poems under the dishes served to Vachel Lindsay in the dining room. At a public reading that evening, the famous Lindsay announced he had "discovered" a Negro poet and he included Hughes's poems in his reading. The story was picked up by the newspapers nationwide.

In 1926, Hughes entered Lincoln University in Pennsylvania, graduating in 1929. During this period his fame spread as a poet. He published *The Weary Blues* in 1926 and *Fine Clothes to the Jew* in 1927. He began to give poetry readings and in 1929 made a reading tour of the South.

By the 1930s, Hughes was well embarked on a writing career, and the books flowed from his pen. In 1930, he published a novel, *Not Without Laughter*. On a trip to Russia in 1931 to make a movie, he found the plans for the movie abandoned but, in his newly acquired leisure, discovered the short stories of D. H. Lawrence, which inspired him to embark on a series of stories published in 1934, *The Ways of White Folks*. In 1935, Hughes saw his play *Mulatto* in a successful run on Broadway and a national tour. Aside from his own dramas and other theatrical writing, Hughes was active in supporting the establishment of Negro theaters across the country—the Suitcase Theater in Harlem, the Negro Art Theater in Los Angeles, and the Skyloft Theater in Chicago.

Throughout his career, Hughes continued to write and publish poems. His volumes of verse include: *The Dream Keeper and Other Poems* (1932), *Shakespeare's Harlem* (1942), *Fields of Wonder* (1947), *One-Way Ticket* (1949), *Montage of a Dream Deferred* (1951), *Ask Your Mama: 12 Moods for Jazz* (1961), and *The Panther and the Lash* (1967). In 1959, Loraine Hansberry took her title for her successful play about black life in Chicago, *A Raisin in the Sun*, from a line in a poem ("Harlem") contained in *Montage of a Dream Deferred*, perhaps the finest of all Hughes's volumes of poetry.

In 1943, Hughes published a series of sketches of what was to become his most famous fictional character, Jesse B. Simple, a street-smart ordinary black guy filled with the ordinary troubles of black folk, but able to summon to his support a rich fund of black folk-wisdom as he carries on a running dialogue with a narrator who needles and challenges him. The result: *Simple Speaks His Mind* (1950), *Simple Takes a Wife* (1953), *Simple Stakes a Claim* (1957), *The Best of Simple* (1961), and *Simple's Uncle Sam* (1965).

Hughes's two autobiographical volumes are *The Big Sea* and *I Wonder as I Wander* (1956). These are not introspective volumes, nor in any sense revelatory in the confessional mode, but accounts of the interesting life Hughes lived. He was something of a loner, never marrying; although he had many friends and companions, few or none professed to know him deeply.

From the time of publishing "The Negro Artist and the Racial Mountain" in 1926, Hughes was single-minded in his determination to write out of his own black identity. The anthologies that he put together promoted Negro culture: *First Book of Negroes* (1952), *The First Book of Jazz* (1955), *The Book of Negro Folklore* (1958), *New Negro Poets: U.S.A.* (1964), *The Book of Negro Humor* (1966), *The Best Short Stories by Negro Writers* (1967).

Although there had been talented black writers in America before Hughes, his achievement fundamentally altered the way later black writers would see themselves, their cultural resources, and their creative possibilities. As one critic (Charles S. Johnson) said in 1928, in an essay entitled "Jazz Poetry and the Blues": "The new racial poetry of the Negro is the expression of something more than an experimentation in a new technique. It marks the birth of a new racial consciousness and self-conception. It is a first frank acceptance of race, and the recognition of difference without the usual implications of disparity." Hughes had led the way in the creation of this "new racial poetry."

ADDITIONAL READING

The Langston Hughes Reader, 1958; *Arno Bontemps-Langston Hughes, Letters 1925–1967*, ed. Charles H. Nichols, 1980.

James A. Emanuel, *Langston Hughes*, 1967; Donald C. Dickinson, *A Bio-Bibliography of Langston Hughes, 1902–1967*, 1967; Therman B. O'Daniel, ed., *Langston Hughes, Black Genius: A Critical Evaluation*, 1971; Peter Mandelik and Stanley Schatt, *A Concordance to the Poetry of Langston Hughes*, 1975; James S. Haskins, *Always Movin' On: The Life of Langston Hughes*, 1976; Onwuchekwa Jemie, *Langston Hughes: An Introduction to the Poetry*, 1976; Richard K. Barksdale, *Langston Hughes: The Poet and His Critics*, 1977; R. Baxter Miller, *Langston Hughes and Gwendolyn Brooks: A Reference Guide*, 1978; Faith Berry, *Langston Hughes: Before and Beyond Harlem*, 1983; Edward J. Mullen, ed., *Critical Essays on Langston Hughes*, 1986; Arnold Rampersad, *The Life of Langston Hughes: Volume I, 1902–1941*, 1986, and *Volume II, 1940–1967*, 1988; Steven C. Tracy, *Langston Hughes and the Blues*, 1988.

TEXTS

Selected Poems, 1959; "The Negro Artist and the Racial Mountain," *The Nation* (June 23, 1926), CXXII, 692–694.

The Negro Speaks of Rivers

I've known rivers:
I've known rivers ancient as the world and older than the
    flow of human blood in human veins.

My soul has grown deep like the rivers.

I bathed in the Euphrates when dawns were young.
I built my hut near the Congo and it lulled me to sleep.   5
I looked upon the Nile and raised the pyramids above it.
I heard the singing of the Mississippi when Abe Lincoln
       went down to New Orleans, and I've seen its muddy
       bosom turn all golden in the sunset.

I've known rivers:
Ancient, dusky rivers.

My soul has grown deep like the rivers.   10

1921, 1926

Mother to Son

Well, son, I'll tell you:
Life for me ain't been no crystal stair.
It's had tacks in it,
And splinters,
And boards torn up,   5
And places with no carpet on the floor —
Bare.
But all the time
I'se been a-climbin' on,
And reachin' landin's,   10
And turnin' corners,
And sometimes goin' in the dark
Where there ain't been no light.
So boy, don't you turn back.
Don't you set down on the steps   15
'Cause you finds it's kinder hard.
Don't you fall now —
For I'se still goin', honey,
I'se still climbin',
And life for me ain't been no crystal stair.   20

1922, 1926

Dream Variations

To fling my arms wide
In some place of the sun,
To whirl and to dance
Till the white day is done.
Then rest at cool evening   5
Beneath a tall tree
While night comes on gently,
    Dark like me —
That is my dream!

To fling my arms wide   10
In the face of the sun,
Dance! Whirl! Whirl!
Till the quick day is done.
Rest at pale evening . . .
A tall, slim tree . . .   15
Night coming tenderly
      Black like me.

1924, 1926

I, Too

I, too, sing America.

I am the darker brother.
They send me to eat in the kitchen
When company comes,
But I laugh,   5
And eat well,
And grow strong.

Tomorrow,
I'll be at the table
When company comes.   10
Nobody'll dare
Say to me,
"Eat in the kitchen,"
Then.

Besides,   15
They'll see how beautiful I am
And be ashamed —

I, too, am America.

1925, 1932

The Weary Blues

Droning a drowsy syncopated tune,
Rocking back and forth to a mellow croon,
      I heard a Negro play.
Down on Lenox Avenue the other night
By the pale dull pallor of an old gas light   5
      He did a lazy sway. . . .
      He did a lazy sway. . . .
To the tune o' those Weary Blues.
With his ebony hands on each ivory key
He made that poor piano moan with melody.   10
      O Blues!
Swaying to and fro on his rickety stool

He played that sad raggy tune like a musical fool.
      Sweet Blues!
Coming from a black man's soul.   15
      O Blues!
In a deep song voice with a melancholy tone
I heard that Negro sing, that old piano moan—
      "Ain't got nobody in all this world,
      Ain't got nobody but ma self.   20
      I's gwine to quit ma frownin'
      And put ma troubles on the shelf."
Thump, thump, thump, went his foot on the floor.
He played a few chords then he sang some more—
      "I got the Weary Blues   25
      And I can't be satisfied.
      Got the Weary Blues
      And can't be satisfied—
      I ain't happy no mo'
      And I wish that I had died."   30
And far into the night he crooned that tune.
The stars went out and so did the moon.
The singer stopped playing and went to bed
While the Weary Blues echoed through his head.
He slept like a rock or a man that's dead.   35

1925, 1926

Song for a Dark Girl

Way Down South in Dixie
      (Break the heart of me)
They hung my black young lover
      To a cross roads tree.

Way Down South in Dixie   5
      (Bruised body high in air)
I asked the white Lord Jesus
      What was the use of prayer.

Way down South in Dixie
      (Break the heart of me)   10
Love is a naked shadow
      On a gnarled and naked tree.

1927

Mulatto

I am your son, white man!

Georgia dusk
And the turpentine woods.
One of the pillars of the temple fell.

You are my son!   5
Like hell!

The moon over the turpentine woods.
The Southern night
Full of stars,
Great big yellow stars.   10
  What's a body but a toy?
    Juicy bodies
    Of nigger wenches
    Blue black
    Against black fences.   15
    O, you little bastard boy,
    What's a body but a toy?
The scent of pine wood stings the soft night air.
  What's the body of your mother?
Silver moonlight everywhere.   20
  What's the body of your mother?
Sharp pine scent in the evening air.
    A nigger night,
    A nigger joy,
    A little yellow   25
    Bastard boy.

  Naw, you ain't my brother.
  Niggers ain't my brother.
  Not ever.
  Niggers ain't my brother.   30

The Southern night is full of stars,
Great big yellow stars.
    O, sweet as earth,
    Dusk dark bodies
    Give sweet birth   35
To little yellow bastard boys.

  Git on back there in the night,
  You ain't white.

The bright stars scatter everywhere.
Pine wood scent in the evening air.   40
    A nigger night,
    A nigger joy.

  I am your son, white man!

    A little yellow
    Bastard boy.   45

1927

Merry-Go-Round

Colored child at carnival:

Where is the Jim Crow section
On this merry-go-round,

Mister, cause I want to ride?
Down South where I come from   5
White and colored
Can't sit side by side.
Down South on the train
There's a Jim Crow car.
On the bus we're put in the back—   10
But there ain't no back
To a merry-go-round!
Where's the horse
For a kid that's black?

1942

Ballad of the Fortune Teller

Madam could look in your hand—
Never seen you before—
And tell you more than
You'd want to know.

She could tell you about love,   5
And money, and such.
And she wouldn't
Charge you much.

A fellow came one day.
Madam took him in.   10
She treated him like
He was her kin.

Gave him money to gamble.
She gave him bread,
And let him sleep in her   15
Walnut bed.

Friends tried to tell her
Dave meant her no good.
Looks like she could've knowed it
If she only would.   20

He mistreated her terrible,
Beat her up bad.
Then went off and left her.
Stole all she had.

She tried to find out   25
What road he took.
There wasn't a trace
No way she looked.

That woman who could foresee
What *your* future meant,   30
Couldn't tell, to save her,
Where Dave went.

1942

Still Here

I've been scarred and battered.
My hopes the wind done scattered.
Snow has friz me, sun has baked me.
    Looks like between 'em
    They done tried to make me   5
Stop laughin', stop lovin', stop livin'—
    But I don't care!
    I'm still here!

                                     1943

Uncle Tom

Within—
The beaten pride.
Without—
The grinning face,
The low, obsequious,   5
Double bow,
The sly and servile grace
Of one the white folks
Long ago
Taught well   10
To know his
Place.

                         1944–45, 1959

Trumpet Player

The Negro
With the trumpet at his lips
Has dark moons of weariness
Beneath his eyes
Where the smoldering memory   5
Of slave ships
Blazed to the crack of whips
About his thighs.

The Negro
With the trumpet at his lips   10
Has a head of vibrant hair
Tamed down,
Patent-leathered now
Until it gleams
Like jet—   15
Were jet a crown.

The music
From the trumpet at his lips

Is honey
Mixed with liquid fire.   20
The rhythm
From the trumpet at his lips
Is ecstasy
Distilled from old desire —

Desire   25
That is longing for the moon
Where the moonlight's but a spotlight
In his eyes,
Desire
That is longing for the sea   30
Where the sea's a bar-glass
Sucker size.

The Negro
With the trumpet at his lips
Whose jacket   35
Has a *fine* one-button roll,
Does not know
Upon what riff the music slips
Its hypodermic needle
To his soul —   40

But softly
As the tune comes from his throat
Trouble
Mellows to a golden note.

1947

Life Is Fine

I went down to the river,
I set down on the bank.
I tried to think but couldn't,
So I jumped in and sank.

I came up once and hollered!   5
I came up twice and cried!
If that water hadn't a-been so cold
I might've sunk and died.

    But it was
    Cold in that water!   10
    It was cold!

I took the elevator
Sixteen floors above the ground.
I thought about my baby
And thought I would jump down.   15

I stood there and I hollered!
I stood there and I cried!

If it hadn't a-been so high
I might've jumped and died.

> *But it was*   20
> *High up there!*
> *It was high!*

So since I'm still here livin',
I guess I will live on.
I could've died for love —   25
But for livin' I was born.

Though you may hear me holler,
And you may see me cry —
I'll be dogged, sweet baby,
If you gonna see me die.   30

> *Life is fine!*
> *Fine as wine!*
> *Life is fine!*

                                                                        1949

Theme for English B

The instructor said,

> *Go home and write*
> *a page tonight.*
> *And let that page come out of you —*
> *Then, it will be true.*   5

I wonder if it's that simple?
I am twenty-two, colored, born in Winston-Salem.
I went to school there, then Durham, then here
to this college on the hill above Harlem.
I am the only colored student in my class.   10
The steps from the hill lead down into Harlem,
through a park, then I cross St. Nicholas,
Eighth Avenue, Seventh, and I come to the Y,
the Harlem Branch Y, where I take the elevator
up to my room, sit down, and write this page: 15

It's not easy to know what is true for you or me
at twenty-two, my age. But I guess I'm what
I feel and see and hear, Harlem, I hear you:
hear you, hear me — we two — you, me, talk on this page.
(I hear New York, too.) Me — who?   20

Well, I like to eat, sleep, drink, and be in love.
I like to work, read, learn, and understand life.
I like a pipe for a Christmas present,
or records — Bessie,[1] bop, or Bach.
I guess being colored doesn't make me *not* like   25

---

[1] Bessie Smith (1898?–1937), black blues singer.

the same things other folks like who are other races.
So will my page be colored that I write?
Being me, it will not be white.
But it will be
a part of you, instructor.   30
You are white—
yet a part of me, as I am a part of you.
That's American.
Sometimes perhaps you don't want to be a part of me.
Nor do I often want to be a part of you.   35
But we are, that's true!
As I learn from you,
I guess you learn from me—
although you're older—and white—
and somewhat more free.   40

This is my page for English B.

1949, 1951

Low to High

How can you forget me?
But you do!
You said you was gonna take me
Up with you—
Now you've got your Cadillac,   5
you done forgot that you are black.
How can you forget me
When I'm you?

But you do.

How can you forget me,   10
fellow, say?
How can you low-rate me
this way?
You treat me like you damn well please,
Ignore me—though I pay your fees.   15
How can you forget me?

But you do.

1949, 1951

High to Low

God knows
We have our troubles, too—
One trouble is you:
you talk too loud,
cuss too loud,   5
look too black,
don't get anywhere,

and sometimes it seems
you don't even care.
The way you send your kids to school   10
stockings down,
(not Ethical Culture)
the way you shout out loud in church,
(not St. Phillips)
and the way you lounge on doorsteps   15
just as if you were down South,
(not at 409)
the way you clown—
the way, in other words,
you let me down—   20
me, trying to uphold the race
and you—
well, you can see,
we have our problems,
too, with you.   25

1949, 1951

Harlem

What happens to a dream deferred?

Does it dry up
like a raisin in the sun?
Or fester like a sore—
And then run?   5
Does it stink like rotten meat?
Or crust and sugar over—
like a syrupy sweet?

Maybe it just sags
like a heavy load.   10

Or does it explode?

1951

Nightmare Boogie

I had a dream
and I could see
a million faces
black as me!
A nightmare dream: 5
Quicker than light
All them faces
Turned dead white!
Boogie-woogie,

Rolling bass,   10
Whirling treble
of cat-gut lace.

1951

Good Morning

Good morning, daddy!
I was born here, he said,
watched Harlem grow
until colored folks spread
from river to river   5
across the middle of Manhattan
out of Penn Station
dark tenth of a nation,
planes from Puerto Rico,
and holds of boats, chico,   10
up from Cuba Haiti Jamaica,
in buses marked New York
from Georgia Florida Louisiana
to Harlem Brooklyn the Bronx
but most of all to Harlem   15
dusky sash across Manhattan
I've seen them come dark
    wondering
    wide-eyed
    dreaming   20
out of Penn Station —
but the trains are late.
The gates open —
Yet there're bars
at each gate.   25

    What happens
    to a dream deferred?

Daddy, ain't you heard?

1951

Same in Blues

I said to my baby,
Baby, take it slow.
I can't, she said, I can't!
I got to go!

    There's a certain   5
    amount of traveling
    in a dream deferred.

Lulu said to Leonard,
I want a diamond ring.
Leonard said to Lulu,
You won't get a goddamn thing!   10

    A certain
    amount of nothing
    in a dream deferred.

Daddy, daddy, daddy,   15
All I want is you.
You can have me, baby—
but my lovin' days is through.

    A certain
    amount of impotence   20
    in a dream deferred.

Three parties
On my party line—
But that third party,
Lord, ain't mine!   25

    There's liable
    to be confusion
    in a dream deferred.

From river to river,
Uptown and down,   30
There's liable to be confusion
when a dream gets kicked around.

                                         1951

Boogie: 1 a.m.

Good evening, daddy!
I know you've heard
The boogie-woogie rumble
Of a dream deferred
Trilling the treble   5
And twining the bass
Into midnight ruffles
Of cat-gut lace.

                                         1951

Café: 3 A.M.

Detectives from the vice squad
with weary sadistic eyes
spotting fairies.

Degenerates,
some folks say.   5

But God, Nature,
or somebody
made them that way.

Police lady or Lesbian
over there?   10
      Where?

                                                    1951

Motto

I play it cool
And dig all jive.
That's the reason
I stay alive.

My motto,   5
As I live and learn,
      is:
*Dig And Be Dug
In Return.*

                                                    1951

Dream Boogie

Good morning, daddy!
Ain't you heard
The boogie-woogie rumble
Of a dream deferred?

Listen closely: 5
You'll hear their feet
Beating out and beating out a—

*You think
It's a happy beat?*

Listen to it closely: 10
Ain't you heard
something underneath
like a—

What did I say?

Sure,   15
I'm happy!
Take it away!

Hey, pop!
Re-bop!
Mop!   20

Y-e-a-h!

                                                                          1951

Old Walt

Old Walt Whitman
Went finding and seeking,
Finding less than sought
Seeking more than found,
Every detail minding   5
Of the seeking or the finding.

Pleasured equally
In seeking as in finding,
Each detail minding,
Old Walt went seeking   10
And finding.

                                                                 1954, 1959

Letter

Dear Mama,
      Time I pay rent and get my food
and laundry I don't have much left
but here is five dollars for you
to show you I still appreciates you.   5
My girl-friend send her love and say
she hopes to lay eyes on you sometime in life.

Mama, it has been raining cats and dogs up
here. Well, that is all so I will close.
            Your son baby   10
                Respectably as ever,
                     Joe

                                                                       1958

The Negro Artist and the Racial Mountain

One of the most promising of the young Negro poets said to me once, "I want to
be a poet—not a Negro poet," meaning, I believe, "I want to write like a white poet";
meaning subconsciously, "I would like to be a white poet"; meaning behind that, "I
would like to be white." And I was sorry the young man said that, for no great poet
has ever been afraid of being himself. And I doubted then that, with his desire to run

away spiritually from his race, this boy would ever be a great poet. But this is the mountain standing in the way of any true Negro art in America—this urge within the race toward whiteness, the desire to pour racial individuality into the mold of American standardization, and to be as little Negro and as much American as possible.

But let us look at the immediate background of this young poet. His family is of what I suppose one would call the Negro middle class: people who are by no means rich yet never uncomfortable nor hungry—smug, contented, respectable folk, members of the Baptist church. The father goes to work every morning. He is a chief steward at a large white club. The mother sometimes does fancy sewing or supervises parties for the rich families of the town. The children go to a mixed school. In the home they read white papers and magazines. And the mother often says "Don't be like niggers" when the children are bad. A frequent phrase from the father is, "Look how well a white man does things." And so the word white comes to be unconsciously a symbol of all the virtues. It holds for the children beauty, morality, and money. The whisper of "I want to be white" runs silently through their minds. This young poet's home is, I believe, a fairly typical home of the colored middle class. One sees immediately how difficult it would be for an artist born in such a home to interest himself in interpreting the beauty of his own people. He is never taught to see that beauty. He is taught rather not to see it, or if he does, to be ashamed of it when it is not according to Caucasian patterns.

For racial culture the home of a self-styled "high-class" Negro has nothing better to offer. Instead there will perhaps be more aping of things white than in a less cultured or less wealthy home. The father is perhaps a doctor, lawyer, landowner, or politician. The mother may be a social worker, or a teacher, or she may do nothing and have a maid. Father is often dark but he has usually married the lightest woman he could find. The family attend a fashionable church where few really colored faces are to be found. And they themselves draw a color line. In the North they go to white theaters and white movies. And in the South they have at least two cars and a house "like white folks." Nordic manners, Nordic faces, Nordic hair, Nordic art (if any), and an Episcopal heaven. A very high mountain indeed for the would-be racial artist to climb in order to discover himself and his people.

But then there are the low-down folks, the so-called common element, and they are the majority—may the Lord be praised! The people who have their nip of gin on Saturday nights and are not too important to themselves or the community, or too well fed, or too learned to watch the lazy world go round. They live on Seventh Street in Washington or State Street in Chicago and they do not particularly care whether they are like white folks or anybody else. Their joy runs, bang! into ecstasy. Their religion soars to a shout. Work maybe a little today, rest a little tomorrow. Play awhile. Sing awhile. O, let's dance! These common people are not afraid of spirituals, as for a long time their more intellectual brethren were, and jazz is their child. They furnish a wealth of colorful, distinctive material for any artist because they still hold their own individuality in the face of American standardizations. And perhaps these common people will give to the world its truly great Negro artist, the one who is not afraid to be himself. Whereas the better-class Negro would tell the artist what to do, the people at least let him alone when he does appear. And they are not ashamed of him—if they know he exists at all. And they accept what beauty is their own without question.

Certainly there is, for the American Negro artist who can escape the restrictions the more advanced among his own group would put upon him, a great field of unused material ready for his art. Without going outside his race and even among the better classes with their "white" culture and conscious American manners, but still Negro enough to be different, there is sufficient matter to furnish a black artist with a lifetime of creative work. And when he chooses to touch on the relations between Negroes and whites in this country with their innumerable overtones and undertones, surely, and especially for literature and the drama, there is an inexhaustible supply of themes at hand. To these the Negro artist can give his racial individuality, his heritage of rhythm and warmth, and his incongruous humor that so often, as in the Blues, becomes ironic laughter mixed with tears. But let us look again at the mountain.

A prominent Negro clubwoman in Philadelphia paid eleven dollars to hear Raquel Meller[1] sing Andalusian popular songs. But she told me a few weeks before she would not think of going to hear "that woman," Clara Smith,[2] a great black artist, sing Negro folksongs. And many an upper-class Negro church, even now, would not dream of employing a spiritual in its services. The drab melodies in white folks' hymnbooks are much to be preferred. "We want to worship the Lord correctly and quietly. We don't believe in 'shouting.' Let's be dull like the Nordics," they say, in effect.

The road for the serious black artist, then, who would produce a racial art is most certainly rocky and the mountain is high. Until recently he received almost no encouragement for his work from either white or colored people. The fine novels of Chestnutt[3] go out of print with neither race noticing their passing. The quaint charm and humor of Dunbar's[4] dialect verse brought to him, in his day, largely the same kind of encouragement one would give a sideshow freak (A colored man writing poetry! How odd!) or a clown (How amusing!).

The present vogue in things Negro, although it may do as much harm as good for the budding colored artist, has at least done this: it has brought him forcibly to the attention of his own people among whom for so long, unless the other race had noticed him beforehand, he was a prophet with little honor. I understand that Charles Gilpin[5] acted for years in Negro theaters without any special acclaim from his own, but when Broadway gave him eight curtain calls, Negroes, too, began to beat a tin pan in his honor. I know a young colored writer, a manual worker by day, who had been writing well for the colored magazines for some years, but it was not until he recently broke into the white publications and his first book was accepted by a prominent New York publisher that the "best" Negroes in his city took the trouble to discover that he lived there. Then almost immediately they decided to give a grand dinner for him. But the society ladies were careful to whisper to his mother that perhaps she'd better not come. They were not sure she would have an evening gown.

The Negro artist works against an undertow of sharp criticism and misunderstanding from his own group and unintentional bribes from the whites. "O, be respectable, write about nice people, show how good we are," say the Negroes. "Be stereotyped, don't go too far, don't shatter our illusions about you, don't amuse us too seriously. We will pay you," say the whites. Both would have told Jean Toomer[6] not to write "Cane." The colored people did not praise it. The white people did not buy it. Most of the colored people who did read "Cane" hate it. They are afraid of it. Although the critics gave it good reviews the public remained indifferent. Yet (excepting the work of DuBois[7]) "Cane" contains the finest prose written by a Negro in America. And like the singing of Robeson,[8] it is truly racial.

But in spite of the Nordicized Negro intelligentsia and the desires of some white editors we have an honest American Negro literature already with us. Now I await the rise of the Negro theater. Our folk music, having achieved world-wide fame,

---

[1]Raquel Meller (1888–1962), Spanish screen actress and singer of regional songs of Spain.

[2]Clara Smith (1894–1935), a black blues singer who ran her own Clara Smith Theatrical Club in New York and who appeared in many musical reviews.

[3]Charles Waddell Chesnutt (1858–1932), black novelist especially known for *The Conjure Woman* (1899).

[4]Paul Laurence Dunbar (1872–1906), black poet who gained national attention with *Lyrics of Lowly Life* (1896).

[5]Charles Gilpin (1878–1930), black actor who gained wide attention playing the leading role in Eugene O'Neill's *The Em-*

peror Jones in 1920.

[6]Jean Toomer (1894–1967), black writer, author of *Cane* (1923), which portrays the language, folklore, songs, and traditions of black people in Georgia.

[7]W. E. B. DuBois (1868–1963), black historian, sociologist, journalist, poet, novelist; author of *The Souls of Black Folk* (1903).

[8]Paul Robeson (1898–1976), black singer and actor who gained attention for appearances in *The Emperor Jones* in 1925 and *Porgy* in 1928.

offers itself to the genius of the great individual American Negro composer who is to come. And within the next decade I expect to see the work of a growing school of colored artists who paint and model the beauty of dark faces and create with new technique the expressions of their own soul-world. And the Negro dancers who will dance like flame and the singers who will continue to carry our songs to all who listen — they will be with us in even greater numbers tomorrow.

Most of my own poems are racial in theme and treatment, derived from the life I know. In many of them I try to grasp and hold some of the meanings and rhythms of jazz. I am sincere as I know how to be in these poems and yet after every reading I answer questions like these from my own people: Do you think Negroes should always write about Negroes? I wish you wouldn't read some of your poems to white folks. How do you find anything interesting in a place like a cabaret? Why do you write about black people? You aren't black. What makes you do so many jazz poems?

But jazz to me is one of the inherent expressions of Negro life in America: the eternal tom-tom beating in the Negro soul — the tom-tom of revolt against weariness in a white world, a world of subway trains, and work, work, work; the tom-tom of joy and laughter, and pain swallowed in a smile. Yet the Philadelphia clubwoman is ashamed to say that her race created it and she does not like me to write about it. The old subconscious "white is best" runs through her mind. Years of study under white teachers, a lifetime of white books, pictures, and papers, and white manners, morals, and Puritan standards made her dislike the spirituals. And now she turns up her nose at jazz and all its manifestations — likewise almost everything else distinctly racial. She doesn't care for the Winold Reiss[9] portraits of Negroes because they are "too Negro." She does not want a true picture of herself from anybody. She wants the artist to flatter her, to make the white world believe that all Negroes are as smug and as near white in soul as she wants to be. But, to my mind, it is the duty of the younger Negro artist, if he accepts any duties at all from outsiders, to change through the force of his art that old whispering "I want to be white," hidden in the aspirations of his people, to "Why should I want to be white? I am a Negro — and beautiful!"

So I am ashamed for the black poet who says, "I want to be a poet, not a Negro poet," as though his own racial world were not as interesting as any other world. I am ashamed, too, for the colored artist who runs from the painting of Negro faces to the painting of sunsets after the manner of the academicians because he fears the strange un-whiteness of his own features. An artist must be free to choose what he does, certainly, but he must also never be afraid to do what he might choose.

Let the blare of Negro jazz bands and the bellowing voice of Bessie Smith[10] singing Blues penetrate the closed ears of the colored near-intellectuals until they listen and perhaps understand. Let Paul Robeson singing Water Boy, and Rudolph Fisher[11] writing about the streets of Harlem, and Jean Toomer holding the heart of Georgia in his hands, and Aaron Douglas[12] drawing strange black fantasies cause the smug Negro middle class to turn from their white, respectable, ordinary books and papers to catch a glimmer of their own beauty. We younger Negro artists who create now intend to express our individual dark-skinned selves without fear or shame. If white people are pleased we are glad. If they are not, it doesn't matter. We know we are beautiful. And ugly too. The tom-tom cries and the tom-tom laughs. If colored people are pleased we are glad. If they are not, their displeasure doesn't matter either. We build our temples for tomorrow, strong as we know how, and we stand on top of the mountain, free within ourselves.

1926

---

[9]Winold Reiss (1887–1953), white painter who depicted blacks not as stereotypes but as individuals.
[10]Bessie Smith (1898?–1937), famous black blues singer.
[11]Rudolph Fisher (1897–1934), black medical doctor and writer; his novel, *The Walls of Jericho* (1928), was a satiric portrait of Harlem.
[12]Aaron Douglas (1898–1979), well-known black painter of the Harlem Renaissance who studied under Winold Reiss.

THE POETRY RENAISSANCE
Experiments, Rebellions, Break-Aways

———

CARL SANDBURG   ROBINSON JEFFERS
VACHEL LINDSAY   ARCHIBALD MACLEISH
H. D. (HILDA DOOLITTLE)   E. E. CUMMINGS

———

Taking his position at the hub of things [the poet] contemplates the mystery of the universe;

He feeds his emotions and his mind on the great works of the past. Moving along with the four seasons, he sighs at the passing of time;

Gazing at the myriad objects, he thinks of the complexity of the world.

He sorrows over the falling leaves in virile autumn;

He takes joy in the delicate bud of fragrant spring. With awe at heart he experiences chill;

His spirit solemn, he turns his gaze to the clouds. He declaims the superb works of his predecessors;

He croons the clean fragrance of past worthies. He roams in the forest of literature, and praises the symmetry of great art. Moved, he pushes his books away and takes the writing brush, that he may express himself in letters.

• • •

We poets struggle with Non-being to force it to yield Being;
  We knock upon silence for an answering music.

We enclose boundless space in a square foot of paper;
  We pour our deluge from the inch space of the heart.

from the Wen Fu of Lu Chi,* as quoted in Archibald MacLeish, *Poetry and Experience*, 1961

———

*Lu Chi was a third-century Chinese poet who wrote a "Fu"
or "Rhymeprose" (a work containing both prose and rhymes)
about the nature of the creative process.

CARL SANDBURG
(1878–1967)

Carl Sandburg opens his *Good Morning, America* (1928) with a series of thirty-eight definitions of poetry. Some of the more arresting: "Poetry is an art practiced with the terribly plastic material of human language"; "Poetry is a fossil rock-print of a fin and wing, with an illegible oath between"; "Poetry is a shuffling of boxes of illusions buckled with a strap of facts"; "Poetry is the achievement of the synthesis of hyacinths and biscuits." These definitions suggest that Sandburg's notions of the possibilities of poetry were very broad indeed.

Sandburg was born in Galesburg, Illinois, to Swedish immigrant parents. His father worked as a blacksmith in the railroad yards and could neither read nor write. Leaving school at thirteen, Sandburg worked at a great variety of odd jobs — milkman, bottle washer, worker in an icehouse and a brickyard, painter's apprentice. For a time he was a hobo, riding the rails out west, seeing Kansas, Nebraska, and Colorado. For eight months he served in the army during the Spanish-American War (1898); he got as far as Puerto Rico, but not to Cuba.

Returning to Galesburg, Sandburg started working his way through Lombard College (later to become Knox) in Galesburg, but he left in 1902 without a degree. His first book of poems (a short pamphlet) was privately printed as *In Reckless Ecstasy* in 1904, but he would later change his poetic style and taste. He wandered about the country as a stereopticon slide salesman and worked as secretary for Milwaukee's Socialist mayor, Emil Seidel. In 1908 he met and married Lillian Steichen, sister of the noted photographer Edward Steichen, with whom Sandburg would later collaborate on a book (*The Family of Man*, 1955). In Chicago, he worked as a newspaperman, particularly for the *Chicago Daily News*.

In 1914, Harriet Monroe published Sandburg's "Chicago" and eight additional poems in *Poetry*. And a volume of poems, called *Chicago Poems*, appeared in 1916. Sandburg soon was identified with the other Midwest poets (Edgar Lee Masters and Vachel Lindsay), and the first volume was followed by others: *Cornhuskers* (1918), *Smoke and Steel* (1920), *Slabs of the Sunburnt West* (1922), and *Good Morning, America* (1928). Sandburg became a kind of wandering minstrel, accompanying himself on the guitar as he sang American folk ballads he had picked up during his years of wanderlust, reciting his poems, and commenting on life with his homespun philosophy. He published a volume of folk songs, *The American Songbag*, in 1927.

The 1930s witnessed Sandburg's popularity increase as a poet of the common man. His had always been a poetry portraying workers at ordinary, everyday jobs. The state of the country during the Great Depression appeared to confirm the authenticity of his leftist sympathies for the down-trodden, the exploited, the vagabonds, and wanderers. He had been there himself. In 1936, he published *The People, Yes*, a celebratory long poem of the endurance of the people in the face of adversity. His prosy, free-verse style seemed especially suited for such a celebration of common humanity struggling to survive.

As a native of Illinois, Sandburg had always admired Abraham Lincoln. He published the first two volumes of a Lincoln biography (*The Prairie Years*) in 1926 and four more volumes (*The War Years*) in 1939; the work won the Pulitzer Prize for history in 1940. His *Complete Poems* in 1950 won the Pulitzer Prize for poetry. In 1948 Sandburg tried his hand at a novel, *Remembrance Rock*, but its epic sweep seemed beyond the interest of most readers. However, his autobiography, *Always the Young Stranger* (1952), was and remains popular.

Sandburg was fond of quoting a speech of one of Rudyard Kipling's characters: "I will be the word of the people. Mine will be the bleeding mouth from which the gag is snatched. I will say everything." In placing his stake with the common people, Sandburg went against the grain of the main thrust of the modernist movement, with its elliptical style studded with allusions and obscure references. *The People, Yes* was stuffed with sayings, jokes, stories, and anecdotes — all taken from the common fund or lore of ordinary people. It seemed the ideal poem for the Great Depression, but it has not weathered the ravages of time as well as some of Sandburg's earlier lyrics, like the energy-filled "Chicago" ("Hog Butcher for the World . . . City of the Big Shoulders") or the ironic "Grass" and "Cool Tombs."

ADDITIONAL READING

The Letters of Carl Sandburg, ed. Herbert Mitgang, 1968; *The Poet and the Dream Girl: The Love Letters of Lillian Steichen and Carl Sandburg*, ed. Margaret Sandburg, 1987.

Rebecca West, "Introduction," *Selected Poems of Carl Sandburg*, 1926; Bruce Weirick, *From Whitman to Sandburg in American Poetry*, 1928; Karl Detzer, *Carl Sandburg*, 1941; Harry Golden, *Carl Sandburg*, 1961; Richard Crowder, *Carl Sandburg*, 1964; Hazel Durnell, *The America of Carl Sandburg*, 1965; Joseph Haas, *Carl Sandburg*, 1967; North Callahan, *Carl Sandburg, Lincoln of Our Literature*, 1969; Mark Van Doren, *Carl Sandburg, with a Bibliography of Sandburg Material in the Collections of the Library of Congress*, 1969; Gay Wilson Allen, *Carl Sandburg*, 1972; Helga Sandburg, *A Great and Glorious Romance*, 1978; North Callahan, *Carl Sandburg: His Life and Works*, 1987; Helga Sandburg, ". . . Where Love Begins," 1989.

TEXT

The Complete Poems of Carl Sandburg, 1970.

Chicago

Hog Butcher for the World,
Tool Maker, Stacker of Wheat,
Player with Railroads and the Nation's Freight Handler;
Stormy, husky, brawling,
City of the Big Shoulders: 5

They tell me you are wicked and I believe them, for I have seen your
    painted women under the gas lamps luring the farm boys.
And they tell me you are crooked and I answer: Yes, it is true I have seen the
    gunman kill and go free to kill again.
And they tell me you are brutal and my reply is: On the faces of women and
    children I have seen the marks of wanton hunger.
And having answered so I turn once more to those who sneer at this my city,
    and I give them back the sneer and say to them:
Come and show me another city with lifted head singing so proud to be alive
    and coarse and strong and cunning.   10
Flinging magnetic curses amid the toil of piling job on job, here is a tall bold
    slugger set vivid against the little soft cities;
Fierce as a dog with tongue lapping for action, cunning as a savage pitted
    against the wilderness,

      Bareheaded,
      Shoveling,
      Wrecking,   15
      Planning,
      Building, breaking, rebuilding,
Under the smoke, dust all over his mouth, laughing with white teeth,
Under the terrible burden of destiny laughing as a young man laughs,
Laughing even as an ignorant fighter laughs who has never lost a battle,   20
Bragging and laughing that under his wrist is the pulse, and under his ribs
    the heart of the people,
                    Laughing!
Laughing the stormy, husky, brawling laughter of Youth, half-naked,
    sweating, proud to be Hog Butcher, Tool Maker, Stacker of Wheat, Player
    with Railroads and Freight Handler to the Nation.

                                                1914, 1916

Fog

    The fog comes
    on little cat feet.

    It sits looking
    over harbor and city
    on silent haunches   5
    and then moves on.

                                                  1916

Cool Tombs

When Abraham Lincoln was shoveled into the tombs, he forgot the
    copperheads[1] and the assassin . . . in the dust, in the cool tombs.

And Ulysses Grant[2] lost all thought of con men and Wall Street, cash and
    collateral turned ashes . . . in the dust, in the cool tombs.

Pocahontas' body, lovely as a poplar, sweet as a red haw[3] in November or a
    pawpaw[4] in May, did she wonder? does she remember? . . . in the dust, in
    the cool tombs?

Take any streetful of people buying clothes and groceries, cheering a hero
    or throwing confetti and blowing tin horns . . . tell me if the lovers are
    losers . . . tell me if any get more than the lovers . . . in the dust . . . in the
    cool tombs.

                                                1918

---

[1] A species of poisonous snake, here a term applied during the Civil War to northerners who sided with the Confederacy in the South.
[2] Ulysses S. Grant (1822–1885) was elected twice to the presidency (in 1868 and 1872), and during his second term was betrayed by many of his own appointees who accepted bribes; Grant himself was later exploited economically and went bankrupt.
[3] Pocahontas (1595?–1617), now a mythic "Indian maiden" figure, was daughter of a chieftan and saved the life of the British adventurer-explorer Captain John Smith; a red haw: the small, red fruit of a hawthorn-like American tree.
[4] Edible fruit of the pawpaw or papaw tree.

Grass

Pile the bodies high at Austerlitz and Waterloo.[1]
Shovel them under and let me work—
   I am the grass; I cover all.

And pile them high at Gettysburg[2]
And pile them high at Ypres and Verdun.[3]   5
Shovel them under and let me work.
Two years, ten years, and passengers ask the conductor:
   What place is this?
   Where are we now?

   I am the grass.   10
   Let me work.

          1918

Four Preludes on Playthings of the Wind

"The past is a bucket of ashes."

1

The woman named Tomorrow
sits with a hairpin in her teeth
and takes her time
and does her hair the way she wants it
and fastens at last the last braid and coil   5
and puts the hairpin where it belongs
and turns and drawls: Well, what of it?
My grandmother, Yesterday, is gone.
What of it? Let the dead be dead.

2

The doors were cedar   10
and the panels strips of gold
and the girls were golden girls
and the panels read and the girls chanted:
  We are the greatest city,
  the greatest nation: 15
  nothing like us ever was.
The doors are twisted on broken hinges.
Sheets of rain swish through on the wind
  where the golden girls ran and the panels read:
  We are the greatest city,   20

---

[1]Austerlitz, in what is now Czechoslovakia, was the site in 1805 of Napoleon's great victory; Waterloo in Belgium was the site in 1815 of Napoleon's defeat.
[2]The battleground in Pennsylvania of a critical defeat of the Confederate Army in 1863.
[3]Ypres in Belgium and Verdun in France were battlegrounds in the First World War (1914–18).

the greatest nation,
nothing like us ever was.

3

It has happened before.
Strong men put up a city and got
    a nation together,   25
And paid singers to sing and women
        to warble: We are the greatest city,
            the greatest nation,
                nothing like us ever was.

And while the singers sang   30
and the strong men listened
and paid the singers well
and felt good about it all,
    there were rats and lizards who listened
    . . . and the only listeners left now   35
    . . . are . . . the rats . . . and the lizards.

And there are black crows
crying, "Caw, caw,"
bringing mud and sticks
building a nest   40
        over the words carved
        on the doors where the panels were cedar
        and the strips on the panels were gold
        and the golden girls came singing:
            We are the greatest city,   45
            the greatest nation:
            nothing like us ever was.

The only singers now are crows crying, "Caw, caw,"
And the sheets of rain whine in the wind and doorways.
And the only listeners now are . . . the rats . . . and the lizards.   50

4

The feet of the rats
scribble on the doorsills;
the hieroglyphs of the rat footprints
chatter the pedigrees of the rats
and babble of the blood   55
and gabble of the breed
of the grandfathers and the great-grandfathers
of the rats.

And the wind shifts
and the dust on a doorsill shifts   60
and even the writing of the rat footprints
tells us nothing, nothing at all
about the greatest city, the greatest nation
where the strong men listened
and the women warbled: Nothing like us ever was.   65

1920

Threes

I was a boy when I heard three red words
a thousand Frenchmen died in the streets
for: Liberty, Equality, Fraternity[1]—I asked
why men die for words.

I was older; men with mustaches, sideburns,   5
lilacs, told me the high golden words are:
Mother, Home, and Heaven[2]—other older men with
face decorations said: God, Duty, Immortality
—they sang these threes slow from deep lungs.

Years ticked off their say-so on the great clocks   10
of doom and damnation, soup and nuts: meteors flashed
their say-so: and out of great Russia came three
dusky syllables workmen took guns and went out to die
for: Bread, Peace, Land.

And I met a marine of the U. S. A., a leatherneck with a girl on his knee   15
for a memory in ports circling the earth and he said: Tell me how to say
three things and I always get by—gimme a plate of ham and eggs—how
much?—and—do you love me, kid?

1920

VACHEL LINDSAY
(1879–1931)

In 1912, Vachel Lindsay, a bachelor poet of thirty-three years, started the third of a series of walking tours (the first two had been made in the East and the South) in which he would trade poetry for food and shelter on his way from Springfield, Illinois, to California. His pamphlet of poems, entitled "Rhymes to be traded for Bread," opened with the terms: "This book is to be used in exchange for the necessities of life on a tramp-journey from the author's hometown, through the West and back, during which he will observe the following rules: (1) Keep away from the cities. (2) Keep away from the railroads. (3) Have nothing to do with money. Carry no baggage. (4) Ask for dinner about quarter after eleven. (5) Ask for supper, lodging, and breakfast about quarter of five. (6) Travel alone. (7) Be neat, truthful, civil and on the square. (8) Preach the gospel of beauty."

By the time Lindsay reached Wagon Mound, New Mexico, one thousand miles from home, confronted by a seemingly endless desert, he wired home for money and took the train to California. While on the journey, General William Booth, British founder of the Salvation Army, died. In California, Lindsay

---

[1]Motto of the French Revolution (1789–99).
[2]Old-fashioned Victorian ideals of the late nineteenth and early twentieth century.

wrote "General William Booth Enters into Heaven" and published it in Harriet Monroe's *Poetry* magazine; the poem introduced the evangelical-oratorical style that would be the basis of Lindsay's reputation as a poet. At a *Poetry* banquet in Chicago in 1914, the Irish poet William Butler Yeats saluted Lindsay as "a fellow craftsman" and praised "General William Booth" for its "strange beauty"; Lindsay responded by reciting his celebrated "The Congo." With these and other such stirring poems, together with his commitment to the restoration of what Yeats called "the primitive singing of poetry," Lindsay set out on his long career of poetry readings. He developed in his appearances a "half-chanted lyric," with a line "two-thirds spoken and one-third sung," in performances he labelled "the higher vaudeville."

Lindsay had come a long way to this turning point in his career. Born in Springfield, Illinois, in 1879, to a father who was a physician and a mother who was a devout Christian (Church of Christ, or Campbellite), Lindsay could not make up his mind on a career. After finishing high school in Springfield, he attended Hiram College in Ohio (1897–1900), intending to enter the ministry. He abandoned that ambition and studied at the Art Institute of Chicago (1901–05), becoming an artist. During this period, he began to write poems, and, later, to publish them in miscellaneous newspapers and local magazines. Lindsay's several walking tours in the South, East, and West combined his various interests in art, religion, and literature, but gradually poetry began to dominate. The success of "General William Booth Enters Heaven" in *Poetry* was followed by that of his first book of poems professionally published, *General William Booth Enters Heaven and Other Poems*, in 1913; and that of his second book, *The Congo and Other Poems*, in 1914. Lindsay was well launched on his literary career. Through Harriet Monroe, editor of *Poetry*, Lindsay met Sarah Teasdale in 1914 and began a passionate courtship with her, writing her endless romantic letters expressing his love. But in the end, she chose a financially sound St. Louis businessman over the wild-eyed poet.

Lindsay's career was to take him around the country, a modern vagabond poet willing to travel by train. His dramatic readings attracted large and admiring audiences. The height of his career came perhaps in 1920, when he read his poems at Oxford University, in England, the first American poet to receive such recognition. But there seemed to be a falling off in the quality of Lindsay's successive volumes of verse: *The Chinese Nightingale and Other Poems* (1917), and *The Golden Whales of California and Other Rhymes in the American Language* (1920). His *Collected Poems* appeared in 1923 (revised and illustrated, 1925).

In 1925, Lindsay married and lived for a time in Spokane, Washington, the home of his wife's family. But in spite of his marriage, Lindsay found himself fighting off bouts of depression, intensified, no doubt, by his discovery in a medical examination in 1924 that he suffered from epilepsy. He continued to publish volumes of poetry — *Going-to-the-Sun* (1923), *Going-to-the-Stars* and *The Candle in the Cabin* (1926), and *Every Soul Is a Circus* (1929) — but they did not capture the imagination of his readers as did the earlier volumes.

In 1929, Lindsay returned with his family, now including two children, to live in his childhood home in Springfield, Illinois. In one of his periods of despondency in December 1931, he committed suicide by drinking lysol. His complete poems, edited by Dennis Camp and published in 1984, fill two volumes with a total of 817 pages. Lindsay's legacy is his revival of poetry as a performing art, with chants and refrains, oratorical flourishes, and evangelistic fervor reconnecting poetry to its primal impulses and inspiration.

ADDITIONAL READING

Adventures: Rhymes & Designs, Including the prose volumes Adventures While Preaching the Gospel of Beauty together with Rhymes to be Traded for Bread, The Village Improvement Parade, and selections from The Village Magazine. By Vachel Lindsay, Intro. Robert F. Sayre, 1968; *Selected Poems of Vachel Lindsay,* ed. Mark Harris, 1963; *Letters of Vachel Lindsay,* ed. Marc Chénetier, 1979.

Edgar Lee Masters, *Vachel Lindsay: A Poet in America,* 1935; H. L. Mencken, *Vachel Lindsay: The True Voice of Middle America,* 1947; Eleanor Ruggles, *The West-Going Heart: A Life of Vachel Lindsay,* 1959; John T. Flanagan, ed., *Profile of Vachel Lindsay,* 1970; Ann Massa, *Vachel Lindsay: Fieldworker for the American Dream,* 1970; Glenn Joseph Wolfe, *Vachel Lindsay: The Poet as Film Theorist,* 1973.

TEXT

The Poetry of Vachel Lindsay Complete & with Lindsay's Drawings, 3 vols., ed. Dennis Camp, 1984 (Vol. III contains notes, bibliography, an appendix of prefaces, and a title index).

General William Booth Enters into Heaven[1]

(To be sung to the tune of "The Blood of the Lamb" with indicated instrument.)

I

(*Bass drum beaten loudly.*)
Booth led boldly with his big bass drum —
(Are you washed in the blood of the Lamb?)
The Saints smiled gravely and they said : "He's come."
(Are you washed in the blood of the Lamb?)
Walking lepers followed, rank on rank,   5
Lurching bravos from the ditches dank,
Drabs from the alleyways and drug fiends pale —
Minds still passion-ridden, soul-powers frail: —
Vermin-eaten saints with moldy breath,
Unwashed legions with the ways of Death —   10
(Are you washed in the blood of the Lamb?)

(*Banjos.*)
Every slum had sent its half-a-score
The round world over. (Booth had groaned for more.)
Every banner that the wide world flies
Bloomed with glory and transcendent dyes.   15

---

[1]The English Methodist preacher William Booth (1829–1912) founded the Salvation Army, which Lindsay came to know "from the inside." While tramping around the country reciting his poetry, he writes in the preface to his *Complete Poems* (1923), when he was "dead broke, and begging . . . and much confused," he slept in Salvation Army quarters several times in Georgia and New Jersey. "Certainly, at that time, the Army was struggling with what General Booth called the submerged tenth of the population. And I was with the submerged. . . . By General Booth's own story, quoted incessantly by the papers the year of his death, he went into the lowest depths of London, with malice aforethought, with deliberate intention to rescue the most notoriously degraded, those given up by policeman, physician, preacher and charity worker. He reiterated in his autobiography that he wanted to find those so low there were none lower. He put them into uniform. He put them under military discipline. He put them in authority over one another. He chose their musical instruments, and their astonishing tunes. The world has forgotten what a scandal to respectable religion the resulting army was when it began. . . . In my poem I merely turned into rhyme as well as I could, word for word, General Booth's own account of his life, and the telegraph dispatches of his death after going blind. I set it to the tune that is not a tune, but a speech, a refrain used most frequently in the meetings of the Army on any public square to this day."

Big-voiced lasses made their banjos bang,
Tranced, fanatical they shrieked and sang:—
"Are you washed in the blood of the Lamb?"
Hallelujah! It was queer to see
Bull-necked convicts with that land make free.   20
Loons with trumpets blowed a blare, blare, blare
On, on upward through the golden air!
(Are you washed in the blood of the Lamb?)

II

(*Bass drum slower and softer.*)
Booth died blind and still by faith he trod,
Eyes still dazzled by the ways of God.   25
Booth led boldly, and he looked the chief
Eagle countenance in sharp relief,
Beard a-flying, air of high command
Unabated in that holy land.

(*Sweet flute music.*)
Jesus came from out the court-house door,   30
Stretched his hands above the passing poor.
Booth saw not, but led his queer ones there
Round and round the mighty court-house square.
Then, in an instant all that blear review
Marched on spotless, clad in raiment new.   35
The lame were straightened, withered limbs uncurled
And blind eyes opened on a new, sweet world.

(*Bass drum louder.*)
Drabs and vixens in a flash made whole!
Gone was the weasel-head, the snout, the jowl!
Sages and sibyls now, and athletes clean,   40
Rulers of empires, and of forests green!

(*Grand chorus of all instruments. Tambourines
to the foreground.*)
The hosts were sandalled, and their wings were fire!
(Are you washed in the blood of the Lamb?)
But their noise played havoc with the angel-choir.
(Are you washed in the blood of the Lamb?)   45
Oh, shout Salvation! It was good to see
Kings and Princes by the Lamb set free.
The banjos rattled and the tambourines
Jing-jing-jingled in the hands of Queens.

(*Reverently sung, no instruments.*)
And when Booth halted by the curb for prayer   50
He saw his Master through the flag-filled air.
Christ came gently with a robe and crown
For Booth the soldier, while the throng knelt down.
He saw King Jesus. They were face to face,
And he knelt a-weeping in that holy place.   55
Are you washed in the blood of the Lamb?

Factory Windows Are Always Broken

Factory windows are always broken.
Somebody's always throwing bricks,
Somebody's always heaving cinders,
Playing ugly Yahoo[1] tricks.

Factory windows are always broken.   5
Other windows are let alone.
No one throws through the chapel-window
The bitter, snarling, derisive stone.

Factory windows are always broken.
Something or other is going wrong.   10
Something is rotten, I think, in Denmark.[2]
End of the factory-window song.

1914   1914

Abraham Lincoln Walks at Midnight

(*IN SPRINGFIELD, ILLINOIS*)

It is portentous, and a thing of state
That here at midnight, in our little town
A mourning figure walks, and will not rest,
Near the old court-house[1] pacing up and down.

Or by his homestead, or in shadowed yards,   5
He lingers where his children used to play,
Or through the market, on the well-worn stones
He stalks until the dawn-stars burn away.

A bronzed, lank man! His suit of ancient black,
A famous high top-hat and plain worn shawl   10
Make him the quaint great figure that men love,
The prairie-lawyer, master of us all.

He cannot sleep upon his hillside[2] now.
He is among us:—as in times before!
And we who toss and lie awake for long   15
Breathe deep, and start, to see him pass the door.

His head is bowed. He thinks on men and kings.
Yea, when the sick world cries, how can he sleep?
Too many peasants fight, they know not why,
Too many homesteads in black terror weep.   20

The sins of all the war-lords burn his heart.
He sees the dreadnaughts[3] scouring every main.

---

[1]Brutish, coarse.
[2]See Shakespeare's *Hamlet*, I, iv, 90; words spoken to Hamlet after the ghost of his father, king of Denmark, appears.
[1]Site of the Illinois General Assembly, where Lincoln served

as representative (1834–41).
[2]Oakridge Cemetery, near Springfield.
[3]Armed battleships.

He carries on his shawl-wrapped shoulders now
The bitterness, the folly and the pain.

He cannot rest until a spirit-dawn 25
Shall come;—the shining hope of Europe free:
The league of sober folk, the Workers' Earth,
Bringing long peace to Cornland, Alp and Sea.

It breaks his heart that kings must murder still,
That all his hours of travail here for men 30
Seem yet in vain. And who will bring white peace
That he may sleep upon his hill again?

1914 *1914*

The Leaden-Eyed[1]

Let not young souls be smothered out before
They do quaint deeds and fully flaunt their pride.
It is the world's one crime its babes grow dull,
Its poor are ox-like, limp and leaden-eyed.

Not that they starve, but starve so dreamlessly, 5
Not that they sow, but that they seldom reap,
Not that they serve, but have no gods to serve,
Not that they die, but that they die like sheep.

1910–12 *1917*

H. D. (HILDA DOOLITTLE)
(1886–1961)

In 1905, Ezra Pound took William Carlos Williams, both of them students at the University of Pennsylvania, to visit a young woman of Pound's acquaintance and with whom he would later become engaged. The young woman, Hilda Doolittle, was not a student, but was the daughter of a professor of astronomy. Williams described her: "There was about her that which is found in wild animals at times, a breathless impatience, almost a silly unwillingness to come to the point. . . . She fascinated me, not for her beauty, which was unquestioned if bizarre to my sense, but for a provocative indifference to rule and order which I liked."

Pound's engagement with Hilda Doolittle would come to naught. But it was he who bears some responsibility for her initial (and continuing) identity as an imagist, a label that has obscured her later achievements. They encountered each other in London in 1912, at a time when Pound was serving as the "foreign

[1]Cf. English poet John Keats's "Ode to a Nightingale" (1819), lines 26–28: "Where youth grows pale, and spectre-thin, and dies; / Where but to think is to be full of sorrow / And leaden-eyed despairs, . . ."

correspondent" for *Poetry* magazine in Chicago. Pound was promoting a new poetic movement "*Imagisme*," derived in part from modern French poetry, and when he sent three of Hilda Doolittle's poems to the editor, Harriet Monroe, he signed them simply, "H. D., *Imagiste*."

She came to be considered the quintessential imagist, primarily because of such vivid and indelible lines as those of her frequently anthologized "Heat" (written and published in her first book and in her 1983 *Collected Poems* as the second part of "Garden"):

> Fruit cannot drop
> through this thick air —
> fruit cannot fall into heat
> that presses up and blunts
> the points of pears
> and rounds the grapes.

As her one-time husband Richard Aldington commented, "the Imagist movement was H. D., and H. D., the Imagist movement." Doolittle retained the initials H. D. in signing her work throughout her life, and dropped what she called the "affectation," "*Imagiste*"; but long after imagism had passed from the scene and she had turned to writing other kinds of poetry, such as the long lyric-epic, she continued to be labelled in literary history an "Imagist."

H. D. was born Hilda Doolittle in Bethlehem, Pennsylvania, in 1886, her father an astronomer, her mother a member of the "Bohemian or Moravian Brotherhood," with a strong mystical bent. In 1904, she enrolled at Bryn Mawr College, where Marianne Moore was also a student. Ill health forced her withdrawal in 1906, and she turned to reading (including Greek and Latin), writing, and translating poetry.

William Carlos Williams's perception of her on first meeting ("provocative indifference to rule and order") was to prove right on the mark. From the time she went to Europe in 1911, she lived an unconventional, adventurous — and an intuitively feminist — life. She met the British poet Richard Aldington through her friend Pound and married him in 1913. He was literary editor of the *Egoist*, and she took over his position in 1916 when he entered the army to fight in the First World War (T. S. Eliot succeeded her the year following). Also in 1916, her first book of poems, *Sea Garden*, appeared.

By the end of the war, her personal situation had been radically changed. Her marriage with Aldington had broken up, her brother Gilbert had been killed in the war, her father had died, she became seriously ill for a time with double pneumonia, and she found herself pregnant after a brief affair in 1919 with a young acquaintance, Cecil Gray. Fortunately about this time, she met a young woman, Winifred Ellerman, who had lavishly admired *Sea Garden*. Winifred Ellerman was the illegitimate daughter of a rich English shipping magnate and went by the name of Bryher (which she took from one of the Scilly Islands).

With her abundant resources, Bryher came to H. D.'s aid, seeing her through the birth of a daughter (Perdita), travelling with her in Greece, America, and Egypt, and finally settling with her in Switzerland, in a loving, domestic relationship. Bryher also provided funds for publication of H. D.'s second volume of poems, *Hymen*, in 1921. This volume was followed by *Heliodora and Other Poems*, in 1924, and *Collected Poems of H. D.* in 1925.

From 1925 to her death in 1961, H. D. wrote prodigiously, but much of what she wrote remained unpublished at the time of her death. She published her first work of fiction, *Palimpsest*, in 1926 and followed with other related works in

Hedylus (1928) and *Bid Me to Live* (1960). In 1927 she published a verse drama, *Hippolytus Temporizes*. The three volumes of her long lyric-epic, set in London during the devastating attacks of the Second World War, appeared in 1944 (*The Walls Do Not Fall*), 1945 (*Tribute to the Angels*), and 1946 (*The Flowering of the Rod*). These works were brought together as *Trilogy*, published in 1973.

She was analyzed by Sigmund Freud in 1933–34 and wrote an account of the experience in *Tribute to Freud* (1956). In a long poem, *Helen in Egypt*, published in 1961 shortly after her death, she imagined the experiences of Helen of Troy as Helen herself (and not the men fighting over her) might have seen them. *End to Torment: A Memoir of Ezra Pound by H. D.* was published in 1979. An autobiographical novel, published in 1981, *HERmione*, described the emotional and psychic plight of a woman in love simultaneously with a man and another woman. A "novelistic memoir of childhood," *The Gift*, was published in 1982.

Since Hilda Doolittle's first published poems were signed "H. D., *Imagiste*," and since she appeared with six poems in Ezra Pound's 1914 *Des Imagistes: An Anthology*, and with additional poems in Amy Lowell's continuation of the series until 1917 (as *Some Imagist Poets: An Anthology*), it was perhaps inevitable that she would never lose the label Pound first placed after her initials. A primary reason for this fixed identification is that her early poems (like "Oread," "Pear Tree," and "Garden") offered the best examples of the movement's principles of using images to command attention and evoke feeling, of avoiding abstractions, generalizations, and exhortations, and of producing poetry that was "hard and clear, never blurred nor indefinite." In Pound's words: "Objective — no slither — direct — no excess of adjectives . . . no metaphors that won't permit examination . . . straight talk — straight as the Greek!"

Such principles were best realized in the short lyric, as Glenn Hughes emphasized in his 1931 book *Imagism & the Imagists*. In a chapter entitled "H. D. — The Perfect Imagist," Hughes wrote: "The extraordinary thing about H. D.'s poetry is that it has altered so little in the last seventeen years. It is somewhat astonishing that she should have arrived so quickly at the mastery of a difficult technique, but it is even more astonishing that a poet of her abilities should have been satisfied during so many years to labor within the bounds of one so narrow."

But of course, Glenn could not have known about H. D.'s later long poems, which have a complexity and suggestiveness of meaning that goes quite beyond the limitations of an imagist lyric. Only in the recent past has this work begun to receive critical recognition. In an important essay which appeared in 1975, entitled "Who Buried H. D.? A Poet, Her Critics, and Her Place in 'The Literary Tradition,'" Susan Friedman pointed out the bias of H. D.'s male critics, especially the Freudians who attributed her creative drive to "penis-envy," and asserted: "H. D.'s epic poetry should be compared to the *Cantos*, *Paterson*, the *Four Quartets*, and *The Bridge*, for like these poems, her work is the kind of 'cosmic poetry' the imagists swore they would never write."

In 1983, *H. D.: Collected Poems, 1912–1944* appeared, edited by Louis L. Martz, containing some two hundred pages of previously unpublished or uncollected poetry. And out of one of the "Man/Woman and Poet" conferences, held the past few years at the University of Maine, a volume of essays has been published: *H. D.: Woman and Poet* (1986), edited by Michael King. It contains over five hundred pages of critical commentary, addressed to every facet of H. D.'s work, including the long poems and the fiction. Over one hundred of the pages at the end are devoted to an invaluable annotated bibliography, compiled by Mary S. Mathis and Michael King. The critical job of assessment of H. D. as an important modernist literary figure, though delayed, seems now to be underway.

ADDITIONAL READING

Glenn Hughes, "H. D.—The Perfect Imagist," *Imagism & the Imagists*, 1931; Thomas B. Swann, *The Classical World of H. D.*, 1962; Vincent Quinn, *Hilda Doolittle*, 1967; Susan Gubar, "The Echoing Spell of H. D.'s Trilogy," *Shakespeare's Sisters*, ed. Sandra M. Gilbert and Susan Gubar, 1979; Susan Stanford Friedman, *Psyche Reborn: The Emergence of H. D.*, 1981; Janice S. Robinson, *H. D.: The Life and the Works of an American Poet*, 1982; Barbara Guest, *Herself Defined: The Poet H. D. and Her World*, 1984; Rachel Blau du Plessis, *The Struggle of That Career*, 1986; Michael King, ed., *H. D.: Woman and Poet*, 1986; Angela DiPace Fritz, *Thought and Vision: A Critical Reading of H. D.'s Poetry*, 1988.

TEXT

H. D.: Collected Poems, 1912–1944, ed. Louis L. Martz, 1983.

Orchard[1]

I saw the first pear
as it fell—
the honey-seeking, golden-banded,
the yellow swarm
was not more fleet than I,   5
(spare us from loveliness)
and I fell prostrate
crying:
you have flayed us
with your blossoms,   10
spare us the beauty
of fruit-trees.

The honey-seeking
paused not,
the air thundered their song,   15
and I alone was prostrate.

O rough-hewn
god of the orchard,
I bring you an offering—
do you, alone unbeautiful,   20
son of the god,
spare us from loveliness:

these fallen hazel-nuts,
stripped late of their green sheaths,
grapes, red-purple,   25
their berries
dripping with wine,
pomegranates already broken,
and shrunken figs
and quinces untouched,   30
I bring you as offering.

1913, 1916

---

[1]First published in *Poetry*, January 1913, with the title "Priapus/Keeper-of-Orchards." Priapus, son of Dionysus and Aphrodite, was a Greek phallic god of fertility. His statue, carved of figwood, was placed in gardens and orchards to protect the fruit against thieves, who would be punished with sexual violation.

Oread[1]

Whirl up, sea—
whirl your pointed pines,
splash your great pines
on our rocks,
hurl your green over us,   5
cover us with your pools of fir.

                                                        1914, 1924

Sea Rose

Rose, harsh rose,
marred and with stint of petals,
meagre flower, thin,
sparse of leaf,

more precious   5
than a wet rose
single on a stem—
you are caught in the drift.

Stunted, with small leaf,
you are flung on the sand,   10
you are lifted
in the crisp sand
that drives in the wind.

Can the spice-rose
drip such acrid fragrance   15
hardened in a leaf?

                                                        1916

Mid-day

The light beats upon me.
I am startled—
a split leaf crackles on the paved floor—
I am anguished—defeated.

A slight wind shakes the seed-pods—   5
my thoughts are spent
as the black seeds.
My thoughts tear me,
I dread their fever.
I am scattered in its whirl.   10

---

[1]One of a group of mountain nymphs, companions of Artemis (also called Diana).

I am scattered like
the hot shrivelled seeds.

The shrivelled seeds
are split on the path—
the grass bends with dust,   15
the grape slips
under its crackled leaf:
yet far beyond the spent seed-pods,
and the blackened stalks of mint,
the poplar is bright on the hill,   20
the poplar spreads out,
deep-rooted among trees.

O poplar, you are great
among the hill-stones,
while I perish on the path   25
among the crevices of the rocks.

                                                    1916

Garden

I

You are clear
O rose, cut in rock,
hard as the descent of hail.

I could scrape the colour
from the petals   5
like split dye from a rock.

If I could break you
I could break a tree.

If I could stir
I could break a tree—   10
I could break you.

II [Heat][1]

O wind, rend open the heat,
cut apart the heat,
rend it to tatters.

Fruit cannot drop   15
through this thick air—
fruit cannot fall into heat
that presses up and blunts
the points of pears
and rounds the grapes.   20

---

[1] Part II of "Garden" has often been reprinted as an independent poem under the title "Heat."

Cut the heat—
plough through it,
turning it on either side
of your path.

1916

Pear Tree

Silver dust
lifted from the earth,
higher than my arms reach,
you have mounted,
O silver,   5
higher than my arms reach
you front us with great mass;

no flower ever opened
so staunch a white leaf,
no flower ever parted silver   10
from such rare silver;

O white pear,
your flower-tufts
thick on the branch
bring summer and ripe fruits   15
in their purple hearts.

1916

Song

You are as gold
as the half-ripe grain
that merges to gold again,
as white as the white rain
that beats through   5
the half-opened flowers
of the great flower tufts
thick on the black limbs
of an Illyrian[1] apple bough.

Can honey distill such fragrance   10
as your bright hair—
for your face is as fair as rain,
yet as rain that lies clear
on white honey-comb,
lends radiance to the white wax,   15

---

[1]Illyria was an ancient country along the Adriatic coast.

so your hair on your brow
casts light for a shadow.

1921

Holy Satyr[1]

Most holy Satyr,
like a goat,
with horns and hooves
to match thy coat
of russet brown,   5
I make leaf-circlets
and a crown of honey-flowers
for thy throat;
where the amber petals
drip to ivory,   10
I cut and slip
each stiffened petal
in the rift
of carven petal;
honey horn   15
has wed the bright
virgin petal of the white
flower cluster: lip to lip
let them whisper,
let them lilt, quivering.   20
Most holy Satyr,
like a goat,
hear this our song,
accept our leaves,
love-offering,   25
return our hymn,
like echo fling
a sweet song,
answering note for note.

1924

from The Walls Do Not Fall

To Bryher

for Karnak 1923
from London 1942

[1]

An incident here and there,
and rails gone (for guns)
from your (and my) old town square:

---

[1]Satyrs were, in Greek mythology, riotous and lustful attendants of Dionysus, with the upper body human, but the lower a horse or goat.

mist and mist-grey, no colour,
still the Luxor[1] bee, chick and hare   5
pursue unalterable purpose

in green, rose-red, lapis;
they continue to prophesy
from the stone papyrus:[2]

there, as here,[3] ruin opens   10
the tomb, the temple; enter,
there as here, there are no doors:

the shrine lies open to the sky,
the rain falls, here, there
sand drifts; eternity endures: 15

ruin everywhere, yet as the fallen roof
leaves the sealed room
open to the air,

so, through our desolation,
thoughts stir, inspiration stalks us   20
through gloom:

unaware, Spirit announces the Presence;
shivering overtakes us,
as of old, Samuel:[4]

trembling at a known street-corner,   25
we know not nor are known;
the Pythian[5] pronounces — we pass on

to another cellar, to another sliced wall
where poor utensils show
like rare objects in a museum;   30

Pompeii[6] has nothing to teach us,
we know crack of volcanic fissure,
slow flow of terrible lava,

pressure on heart, lungs, the brain
about to burst its brittle case   35
(what the skull can endure!):

over us, Apocryphal fire,[7]
under us, the earth sway, dip of a floor,
slope of a pavement

---

[1]An ancient town on the Nile in Egypt, with temple and tombs in ruins.
[2]Papyrus, a plant native to the Nile from which a paper-like material is made on which to write.
[3]"There" is ancient Egypt; "here" is war-torn England.
[4]Biblical Hebrew prophet and judge (see his two books of the Bible).
[5]Pythia: the priestess of Apollo at Delphi who delivered the oracles.

[6]Ancient town in Italy covered by the lava from an eruption of nearby Vesuvius in A.D. 79; the lava preserved the town over the centuries, and the ruins have been excavated.
[7]The Apocrypha are rejected books of the Bible because of doubtful authenticity; in one, 2 Esdras (Chapter 13), there is a vision of the second coming of Christ in which He rises from the sea and sends forth fire from his mouth to destroy his enemies.

where men roll, drunk   40
with a new bewilderment,
sorcery, bedevilment:

the bone-frame was made for
no such shock knit within terror,
yet the skeleton stood up to it: 45

the flesh? it was melted away,
the heart burnt out, dead ember,
tendons, muscles shattered, outer husk dismembered,

yet the frame held:
we passed the flame: we wonder   50
what saved us? what for?

[2]

Evil was active in the land,
Good was impoverished and sad;

Ill promised adventure,
Good was smug and fat;   55

Dev-ill was after us,
tricked up like Jehovah;

Good was the tasteless pod,
stripped from the manna-beans, pulse, lentils:

they were angry when we were so hungry   60
for the nourishment, God;

they snatched off our amulets,[8]
charms are not, they said, grace;

but gods always face two-ways,
so let us search the old highways   65

for the true-rune, the right-spell,
recover old values;

nor listen if they shout out,
your beauty, Isis, Aset or Astarte,[9]

is a harlot; you are retrogressive,   70
zealot, hankering after old flesh-pots;

your heart, moreover,
is a dead canker,

they continue, and
your rhythm is the devil's hymn,   75

---

[8]Something worn as a protection against evil.
[9]Isis: Egyptian goddess, wife of Osiris, represented female
fertility; Astarte (or Aset): ancient Semitic goddess of fertility.

your stylus[10] is dipped in corrosive sublimate,
how can you scratch out

indelible ink of the palimpsest[11]
of past misadventure?

1944

ROBINSON JEFFERS
(1887–1962)

Robinson Jeffers was the loner of the modernist movement, remaining in his tower on the Pacific coast, dreaming of a magnificent world of nature uncontaminated by human beings. At least this is the image his pervasive philosophy of "inhumanism" conveys to many readers. In " Sign-Post," he writes:

> Turn outward, love things, not men, turn right away from humanity.
> Let that doll lie. Consider if you like how the lilies grow,
> Lean on the silent rock until you feel its divinity
> Climb the great ladder out of the pit of yourself and man.

Such chilling advice may well seem perverse to those who are inclined to sing along with Walt Whitman the song of the self or to exclaim with Carl Sandburg, "the people, yes!"

William Hamilton Jeffers was a forty-seven-year-old Presbyterian minister and professor of theology when his son Robinson Jeffers was born in 1887 in Pittsburgh. His mother was twenty-two years younger than his father. The young Jeffers grew up isolated and alone and was early set to the study of Greek and Latin. He was placed in school in Zurich, and later in Lucerne, in Leipzig, in Lausanne — mastering Italian, French, and German by the time he was twelve. He recalled later, "I had little or no companionship with other children and spent much time in day-dreams."

Retirement of the elder ailing Jeffers enabled the family to move to California for its climate in 1903. The younger Jeffers attended Occidental College, graduating in 1905 at the age of eighteen. For the next eight years, Jeffers seemed to be uncertain about a career. He tried graduate study in languages at the University of Southern California (USC), and then went abroad to the University of Zurich in 1906, studying a variety of fields, including literature, philosophy, and history. But he returned to California and in 1907 entered medical school at USC. He dropped out in 1910 and went to the University of Washington in Seattle to study forestry. The following year he returned to California and gave himself up to drifting and idleness.

By this time he was desperately in love with a married woman, Una Call Kuster, whom he had met as a fellow student at USC. After something of a local scandal, Una broke with her husband and, in 1913, married Jeffers. For a man as shy as Jeffers, the scandal must have been agonizing, but no doubt worth the winning of Una, who became his lifelong partner in his isolated career as a poet until her death in 1950.

---

[10]A marking or writing device.
[11]A parchment written on several times, with visible remnants of earlier writings imperfectly erased.

After marriage, Jeffers and his wife made plans to settle in a little village on the southern coast of England. The outbreak of the First World War forced them to change plans, and in 1914 they discovered Carmel-by-the-Sea, on the Pacific coast just south of Monterey. They fell in love with the land and ocean and were soon embarked in constructing a home (Tor House) on a height within view and sound of the sea. Later Jeffers took his time in building Hawk Tower in which he located his study. It was a formidable retreat, surrounded by a battlement and topped on the fourth floor with a turret.

Jeffers's first two volumes of poetry, *Flagons and Apples* (1912) and *Californians* (1916), were based on his personal experience in wooing Una, first his failure, and then the happiness of success. The poems were uncharacteristically affirmative, and Jeffers never included them in his later selections or collections. In 1924, Jeffers published *Tamar and Other Poems*, followed by *Roan Stallion, Tamar and Other Poems* in 1925. Immediately he was recognized as a major poetic voice with a style, form, and vision all his own. In the books he established a pattern of alternating short lyrics, often meditations on some aspect of wild nature, with long narrative poems, filled with violence and intense, frequently distorted or grotesque passions. He wrote a long flowing line, a kind of colloquial free verse, without allusions and obscure references, creating a poetry easily accessible to readers.

For three decades, the books flowed from his pen: *The Women at Point Sur* (1927), *Cawdor* (1928), *Dear Judas* (1929), *Thurso's Landing* (1932), *Give Your Heart to the Hawks* (1933), *Solstice* (1935), *Such Counsels You Gave Me* (1937), *Be Angry at the Sun* (1941), *The Double Axe* (1948), and *Hungerfield* (1953). His "free" translation of Euripides's *Medea* was produced in 1947, starring Judith Anderson, with great success.

But Jeffers's popularity, sufficient to place his picture on the cover of *Time* magazine in 1932, began to wane in the later 1930s. The distressing social upheavals of the Great Depression were not a congenial environment for a philosophy of "inhumanism." Such a time seemed to call for concentration not on wild nature but on human misery. It certainly did not seem a time "to uncenter the human mind on itself." By the time Jeffers died in 1962, with the terrible destruction of the Second World War and the potential destruction of the atom bomb a reality, Jeffers's vision of a peopleless world no longer seemed bizarre. Since his death there has been a gradual reassessment upward of his place in American literature.

ADDITIONAL READING

The Selected Letters of Robinson Jeffers, 1897–1962, ed. Ann N. Ridgeway, 1968; *The Collected Poetry of Robinson Jeffers; Vol. One, 1920–1928*, and *Vol. Two, 1928–1938*, ed. Tim Hunt, 1988 and 1989 (two more volumes projected).

George Sterling, *Robinson Jeffers: The Man and the Artist*, 1926; L. C. Powell, *Robinson Jeffers: The Man and His Work*, 1934, 1940; Radcliffe Squires, *The Loyalties of Robinson Jeffers*, 1956, 1963; M. C. Monjian, *Robinson Jeffers*, 1958; Melba Bennett, *The Stone Mason of Tor House: The Life and Work of Robinson Jeffers*, 1966; Brother Antoninus (William Everson), *Robinson Jeffers: Fragments of an Older Fury*, 1968; Arthur B. Coffin, *Robinson Jeffers: Poet of Inhumanism*, 1970; Robert Brophy, *Robinson Jeffers: Myth, Ritual, and Symbol in His Narrative Poems*, 1973; James Shebl, *In This Wild Water: The Suppressed Poems of Robinson Jeffers*, 1976; Marlan Beilke, *Shining Clarity: God and Man in the Works of Robinson Jeffers*, 1977; William H. Nolte, *Rock and Hawk: Robinson Jeffers and the Romantic Agony*, 1978; Robert Zaller, *The Cliffs of Solitude: A Reading of Robinson Jeffers*, 1983; James Karman, *Robinson Jeffers: Poet of California*, 1987; William Everson, *The Excesses of God: Robinson Jeffers as a Religious Figure*, 1988.

TEXTS

"Original Sin," "To Death" from *Robinson Jeffers: Selected Poems*, 1965; remaining poems from *The Selected Poetry of Robinson Jeffers*, 1959.

To the Stone-Cutters[1]

Stone-cutters fighting time with marble, you foredefeated
Challengers of oblivion
Eat cynical earnings, knowing rock splits, records fall down,
The square-limbed Roman letters
Scale in the thaws, wear in the rain. The poet as well   5
Builds his monument mockingly;
For man will be blotted out, the blithe earth die, the brave sun
Die blind and blacken to the heart:
Yet stones have stood for a thousand years, and pained thoughts found
The honey of peace in old poems.   10

1924

Boats in a Fog

Sports and gallantries, the stage, the arts, the antics of dancers,
The exuberant voices of music,
Have charm for children but lack nobility; it is bitter earnestness
That makes beauty; the mind
Knows, grown adult.   5
           A sudden fog-drift muffled the ocean,
A throbbing of engines moved in it,
At length, a stone's throw out, between the rocks and the vapor,
One by one moved shadows
Out of the mystery, shadows, fishing-boats, trailing each other   10
Following the cliff for guidance,
Holding a difficult path between the peril of the sea-fog
And the foam on the shore granite.
One by one, trailing their leader, six crept by me,
Out of the vapor and into it,   15
The throb of their engines subdued by the fog, patient and cautious,
Coasting all round the peninsula
Back to the buoys in Monterey harbor. A flight of pelicans
Is nothing lovelier to look at;
The flight of the planets is nothing nobler; all the arts lose virtue   20
Against the essential reality
Of creatures going about their business among the equally
Earnest elements of nature.

1925

---

[1]Jeffers said of this poem: "When I was building the walls of our house we wanted carvings of unicorn and hawk, my wife's favorite animal and mine, to build the stonework, and we persuaded the old man who used to cut the tomb-stones in Monterey to make them for us. His and our preoccupations with stones made me think of writing the verses; and they are chosen rather for love of old stones and old Scotch stone-masons than for any more arguable reason" (William Rose Benét, *Fifty Poets*, 1933).

Shine, Perishing Republic

While this America settles in the mould of its vulgarity, heavily thickening to empire,
And protest, only a bubble in the molten mass, pops and sighs out, and the mass hardens,

I sadly smiling remember that the flower fades to make fruit, the fruit rots to make earth.
Out of the mother; and through the spring exultances, ripeness and decadence; and home to the mother.

You making haste haste on decay: not blameworthy; life is good, be it stubbornly long or suddenly   5
A mortal splendor: meteors are not needed less than mountains: shine, perishing republic.

But for my children, I would have them keep their distance from the thickening center; corruption
Never has been compulsory, when the cities lie at the monster's feet there are left the mountains.

And boys, be in nothing so moderate as in love of man, a clever servant, insufferable master.
There is the trap that catches noblest spirits, that caught — they say — God, when he walked on earth.   10

1925

Hurt Hawks

I

The broken pillar of the wing jags from the clotted shoulder,
The wing trails like a banner in defeat,
No more to use the sky forever but live with famine
And pain a few days: cat nor coyote
Will shorten the week of waiting for death, there is game without talons.   5
He stands under the oak-bush and waits
The lame feet of salvation; at night he remembers freedom
And flies in a dream, the dawns ruin it.
He is strong and pain is worse to the strong, incapacity is worse.
The curs of the day come and torment him   10
At distance, no one but death the redeemer will humble that head,
The intrepid readiness, the terrible eyes.
The wild God of the world is sometimes merciful to those
That ask mercy, not often to the arrogant.
You do not know him, you communal people, or you have forgotten him;   15
Intemperate and savage, the hawk remembers him;
Beautiful and wild, the hawks, and men that are dying, remember him.

II

I'd sooner, except the penalties, kill a man than a hawk; but the great redtail
Had nothing left but unable misery
From the bone too shattered for mending, the wing that trailed under his
  talons when he moved.   20
We had fed him six weeks, I gave him freedom,
He wandered over the foreland hill and returned in the evening, asking for
  death,
Not like a beggar, still eyed with the old
Implacable arrogance. I gave him the lead gift in the twilight. What fell was
  relaxed,
Owl-downy, soft feminine feathers; but what   25
Soared: the fierce rush: the night-herons by the flooded river cried fear at its
  rising
Before it was quite unsheathed from reality.

1928

Original Sin

The man-brained and man-handed ground-ape, physically
The most repulsive of all hot-blooded animals
Up to that time of the world: they had dug a pitfall
And caught a mammoth, but how could their sticks and stones
Reach the life in that hide? They danced around the pit, shrieking   5
With ape excitement, flinging sharp flints in vain, and the stench of their
  bodies
Stained the white air of dawn; but presently one of them
Remembered the yellow dancer, wood-eating fire
That guards the cave-mouth: he ran and fetched him, and others
Gathered sticks at the wood's edge; they made a blaze   10
And pushed it into the pit, and they fed it high, around the mired sides
Of their huge prey. They watched the long hairy trunk
Waver over the stifle-trumpeting pain,
And they were happy.
                    Meanwhile the intense color and nobility of sunrise,   15
Rose and gold and amber, flowed up the sky. Wet rocks were shining, a little
  wind
Stirred the leaves of the forest and the marsh flag-flowers; the soft valley
  between the low hills
Became as beautiful as the sky; while in its midst, hour after hour, the happy
  hunters
Roasted their living meat slowly to death.
                                These are the people.   20
This is the human dawn. As for me, I would rather
Be a worm in a wild apple than a son of man.
But we are what we are, and we might remember
Not to hate any person, for all are vicious;
And not be astonished at any evil, all are deserved;   25
And not fear death; it is the only way to be cleansed.

1948

To Death

I think of you as a great king, cold and austere;
The throne is not gold but iron, the stones of the high hall are black basalt
  blocks, and the pavement also,
With blood in the corners:
Yet you are merciful; it is for you we labor,
And after a time you give us eternal peace.   5

I think of you as a mean little servant, but steward of the estate,
Pale and a hunchback, shuffling along the corridors,
Tapping at every door. You have the keys of the treasury.

You are the arbiter of the games and bestower of prizes.
For you the young men sweat and the boys play battle, for your award   10
Their hot young lives: what can they win with their lives—
Whether they bide at home or bleed on the capes of Asia,
Or add columns of figures or the fates of Europe—
But eternal peace?
You sit and watch men fighting, and to you they come.   15
You watch the victors go home, and to you they come.

You have a sister named Life, an opulent treacherous woman,
Blonde and a harlot, a great promiser, and very cruel too.
Even the meanest minds after some time
Understand her tricks and her guile. You have a cousin named Christ   20
To whom men turn; but presently all to you. To you the conquerors
And to you the pale saints. The lions of the desert
And the sky-swimming eagles flock to your feet. Athens and Rome
Turned to adore you; and America will, no doubt of that:
We are intelligent too; we shall turn and bow down our heads.   25

1951

ARCHIBALD MacLEISH
(1892–1982)

In 1926, Archibald MacLeish said in "Ars Poetica": "A poem should be palpable and mute / As a globed fruit"; and "A poem should not mean / But be." In 1941, on the eve of the Second World War, MacLeish would perceive the limitation of an exclusively aesthetic commitment: "It is this characteristic of contemporary poetry [its demand for innovation] which explains its failure to make recognizable to us our experience of our time. To write in faith and credit of such experience as ours, and to bring it to recognition, requires the responsible and dangerous language of acceptance and belief."

In changing his position on the role of poetry in life, MacLeish was simply reflecting the radical changes he was living through. After the First World War came the disillusioned 1920s, followed by the Great Depression, and then the Second World War to stay the horrors of Naziism and Fascism. MacLeish fought in the First World War, became an expatriate for a time in the 1920s, turned to the left during the Great Depression, and became a public figure in public office during the Second World War.

MacLeish was born in Glencoe, Illinois, in 1892, into an affluent family. He was educated at the exclusive Hotchkiss School in Connecticut and then took a degree at Yale in 1915. He started law school at Harvard, but dropped out to volunteer service in the army. He served in France, where he was promoted to captain in the Field Artillery. After the war he completed his law degree in 1920 and began to practice law in Boston. He had published a volume of poems, *Tower of Ivory*, in 1917, and in 1923 he followed his deepest instincts, threw over the law profession, and took his family to Paris where he would be free to write poetry.

MacLeish's period of expatriation lasted until 1928, by which time he had published four books: *The Happy Marriage* (1924), *The Pot of Earth* (1925), *Nobodaddy* (1926), and *Streets in the Moon* (1926). Shortly after his return to America in 1928, he published *The Hamlet of A. MacLeish*. His poetry of this period was thoroughly modernist, sometimes showing the influence of Ezra Pound and T. S. Eliot, and reflecting the sense of loss and futility of the lost generation.

With the advent of the Great Depression, MacLeish's poetic interests changed. In preparation for writing an epic about Cortez's conquest of Mexico, he retraced on foot, in 1928–29, the route Cortez's army took from what is now Vera Cruz to what was to become Mexico City. The long poem, *Conquistador*, appeared in 1932 and was awarded a Pulitzer Prize. MacLeish's other poems of this period, published in *New Found Land* (1930) and *Frescoes for Mr. Rockefeller's City* (1933), began to manifest social awareness and to sound social themes. In 1933, MacLeish put out a collection of his poetry entitled *Poems, 1924–1933*, suggesting by its air of closure that he was entering still another phase in his poetic development.

And indeed his interest in social issues did deepen and his concern for totalitarian aggression intensified as the events in Europe (the rise of Naziism and Hitler in Germany, and the triumph of Fascism and Franco in the Spanish Civil War) seemed to move inexorably toward another world war. MacLeish's social and political concerns were reflected in a volume of poems, *Public Speech* (1936), and in two radio plays, *The Fall of the City* (1937) and *Air Raid* (1938). In the long poem *America was Promises* (1939), MacLeish traced the country's history from its founding to the treacherous present in which the bright "promises" of the founders were endangered.

In an attempt to reach a larger audience in sounding the alarm of the threat of totalitarian countries, MacLeish turned to the writing of essays, collected in *The Irresponsibles* (1940), *A Time to Speak* (1941), and *A Time to Act* (1941). From 1930 to 1938, MacLeish had served on the editorial board of *Fortune* magazine. During the Second World War, President Franklin D. Roosevelt appointed him Librarian of Congress (1939–44) and, later, to other governmental posts. From 1949 to 1962, MacLeish taught poetry at Harvard.

Collected Poems, 1917–1952, published in 1952, won a second Pulitzer Prize as well as other awards for MacLeish. And his highly successful modern-dress dramatization of the Book of Job, entitled *J. B.* (1958), won still another Pulitzer Prize. MacLeish continued to write and publish essays, speeches, and poems during his last years. His *New and Collected Poems* appeared in 1976. He died in 1982.

Archibald MacLeish was, during this period, America's most visible poet who dedicated himself to service in public life. In radical contrast to Robinson Jeffers, who withdrew into an almost hermetically sealed privacy, MacLeish put himself and his talent in the service of just political causes as he saw them. In spite of his prominence and the prizes he won, MacLeish was a modest man without illusion as to the measure of his considerable talent.

But MacLeish's devotion to poetry was genuine. In his most thoughtful book about the art he practiced, *Poetry and Experience* (1961), he finally came to focus on the paradoxical truth of the imagination:

> The power of the mortal world over the imagination must be accepted by and for the imagination in the same breath in which one affirms the power of the imagination over the mortal world. The "beauty" of time—of experience—of what Keats called "circumstance"—of the "arable field of events"—must be accepted in the same breath in which one asserts the "truth" of those eternities the imagination can preserve from time and circumstance.... To face the truth of the passing away of the world and make song of it, make beauty of it, is not to solve the riddle of our mortal lives but perhaps to accomplish something more.

ADDITIONAL READING

Letters of Archibald MacLeish, 1907–1982, ed. R. H. Winnick, 1983.

Signi L. Falk, *Archibald MacLeish*, 1965; Grover Smith, *Archibald MacLeish*, 1971; Edward Mullaly, *Archibald MacLeish: A Checklist*, 1973; Bernard A. Drabeck and Helen E. Ellis, eds., *Archibald MacLeish: Reflections*, 1986.

TEXT

New and Collected Poems, 1976.

Ars Poetica[1]

A poem should be palpable and mute
As a globed fruit,

Dumb
As old medallions to the thumb,

Silent as the sleeve-worn stone   5
Of casement ledges where the moss has grown—

A poem should be wordless
As the flight of birds.

          ·

A poem should be motionless in time
As the moon climbs,   10

Leaving, as the moon releases
Twig by twig the night-entangled trees,

Leaving, as the moon behind the winter leaves,
Memory by memory the mind—

---

[1]"The Art of Poetry" (Latin). The Roman poet Horace (68–8 B.C.) wrote a famous epistle on poetry which bears this title.

A poem should be motionless in time   15
As the moon climbs.

                                    •

A poem should be equal to:
Not true.

For all the history of grief
An empty doorway and a maple leaf.   20

For love
The leaning grasses and two lights above the sea —

A poem should not mean
But be.

                                                                  1926

Memorial Rain

FOR KENNETH MACLEISH[1]

Ambassador Puser the ambassador
Reminds himself in French, felicitous tongue,
What these (young men no longer) lie here for
In rows that once, and somewhere else, were young . . .

        All night in Brussels the wind had tugged at my door: 5
        I had heard the wind at my door and the trees strung
        Taut, and to me who had never been before
        In that country it was a strange wind, blowing
        Steadily, stiffening the walls, the floor,
        The roof of my room. I had not slept for knowing   10
        He too, dead, was a stranger in that land
        And felt beneath the earth in the wind's flowing
        A tightening of roots and would not understand,
        Remembering lake winds in Illinois,[2]
        That strange wind. I had felt his bones in the sand   15
        Listening.

                . . . *Reflects that these enjoy*
        Their country's gratitude, that deep repose,
        That peace no pain can break, no hurt destroy,
        That rest, that sleep . . .   20

                        At Ghent[3] the wind rose.
        There was a smell of rain and a heavy drag
        Of wind in the hedges but not as the wind blows
        Over fresh water when the waves lag

---

[1]MacLeish's brother, who died in the First World War flying
in the air corps; his plane crashed in Belgium.
[2]The MacLeish brothers grew up in Glencoe, Illinois, near
Lake Michigan.
[3]Capital of East Flanders, province in Belgium.

Foaming and the willows huddle and it will rain: 25
I felt him waiting.

. . . Indicates the flag
Which (may he say) enisles in Flanders plain
This little field these happy, happy dead
Have made America . . .   30

                                   In the ripe grain
The wind coiled glistening, darted, fled,
Dragging its heavy body: at Waereghem[4]
The wind coiled in the grass above his head:
Waiting—listening . . .   35

        . . . Dedicates to them
This earth their bones have hallowed, this last gift
A grateful country . . .

                                   Under the dry grass stem
The words are blurred, are thickened, the words sift   40
Confused by the rasp of the wind, by the thin grating
Of ants under the grass, the minute shift
And tumble of dusty sand separating
From dusty sand. The roots of the grass strain,
Tighten, the earth is rigid, waits—he is waiting—   45

And suddenly, and all at once, the rain!

                                                    1925, 1926

You, Andrew Marvell[1]

And here face down beneath the sun
And here upon earth's noonward height
To feel the always coming on
The always rising of the night:

To feel creep up the curving east   5
The earthy chill of dusk and slow
Upon those under lands the vast
And ever climbing shadow grow

And strange at Ecbatan[2] the trees
Take leaf by leaf the evening strange   10
The flooding dark about their knees
The mountains over Persia change

And now at Kermanshah[3] the gate
Dark empty and the withered grass

---

[4]A Belgium town where a cemetery for Allied soldiers killed in the First World War is located.
[1]British poet (1621–1678), whose poem "To His Coy Mistress" contains two lines that are the beginning point of Mac-Leish's poem: "But at my back I always hear / Time's wingèd chariot hurrying near."
[2]Old capital of ancient Media, now in Iran.
[3]A city of ancient Persia, now Iran.

And through the twilight now the late   15
Few travelers in the westward pass

And Baghdad[4] darken and the bridge
Across the silent river gone
And through Arabia the edge
Of evening widen and steal on   20

And deepen on Palmyra's[5] street
The wheel rut in the ruined stone
And Lebanon fade out and Crete
High through the clouds and overblown

And over Sicily the air   25
Still flashing with the landward gulls
And loom and slowly disappear
The sails above the shadowy hulls

And Spain go under and the shore
Of Africa the gilded sand   30
And evening vanish and no more
The low pale light across that land

Nor now the long light on the sea:

And here face downward in the sun
To feel how swift how secretly   35
The shadow of the night comes on . . .

1930

Epistle to Be Left in the Earth

. . . It is colder now,
                        there are many stars,
                                                we are drifting
North by the Great Bear,[1]
                        the leaves are falling,   5
The water is stone in the scooped rocks,
                                                to southward
Red sun grey air:
                        the crows are
Slow on their crooked wings,   10
                        the jays have left us:
Long since we passed the flares of Orion.[2]
Each man believes in his heart he will die.
Many have written last thoughts and last letters.
None know if our deaths are now or forever: 15
None know if this wandering earth will be found.

---

[4]An ancient city made famous in the *Thousand and One Nights*, now in Iraq.
[5]Ancient city and oasis, now in Syria.
[1]Constellation of Ursa Major, containing the Big Dipper.

[2]A constellation formed by Diana to immortalize the hunter Orion whom she loved when he was accidentally killed (classical mythology).

We lie down and the snow covers our garments.
I pray you,
        you (if any open this writing)
Make in your mouths the words that were our names.   20
I will tell you all we have learned,
                I will tell you everything:
The earth is round,
         there are springs under the orchards,
The loam cuts with a blunt knife,   25
             beware of
Elms in thunder,
        the lights in the sky are stars —
We think they do not see,
          we think also   30
The trees do not know nor the leaves of the grasses hear us:
The birds too are ignorant.
           Do not listen.
Do not stand at dark in the open windows.
We before you have heard this: 35
          they are voices:
They are not words at all but the wind rising.
Also none among us has seen God.
(. . . We have thought often
The flaws of sun in the late and driving weather   40
Pointed to one tree but it was not so.)
As for the nights I warn you the nights are dangerous:
The wind changes at night and the dreams come.

It is very cold,
        there are strange stars near Arcturus,[3]   45

Voices are crying an unknown name in the sky

                1930

E. E. CUMMINGS
(1894–1962)

In an Introduction to his *Collected Poems* published in 1938, which contained poems from ten previous volumes, E. E. Cummings made explicit the tone of "exclusivity" that his poetry conveys to the captivated reader:

> The poems to come are for you and for me and are not for mostpeople
> —it's no use trying to pretend that mostpeople and ourselves are alike. Mostpeople have less in common with ourselves than the squarerootofminusone. You and I are human beings;mostpeople are snobs. . . .
> you and I are not snobs. We can never be born enough. We are human beings;for whom birth is a supremely welcome mystery,the mystery of growing: the mystery which happens only and whenever we are faithful to ourselves. You and I wear the dangerous looseness of doom and find it becoming.

---

[3]The brightest star in the constellation Boötes.

Life, for eternal us, is now; and now is much too busy being a little more than everything to seem anything,catastrophic included.

The rebellion against typographical conventions is so charming, the *YouandIness* of the vision so cozy and warm, few readers would want to have themselves counted among *mostpeople*.

E. E. Cummings was born in Cambridge, Massachusetts, to a father who was a Unitarian minister and a professor of sociology at Harvard. "My father," Cummings said later, "gave me Plato's metaphor of the cave with my mother's milk." After his father's death (by an automobile accident in 1926), Cummings wrote for him a moving elegy, "my father moved through dooms of love." His mother, whose distinguished New England ancestry included literary, religious, and political leaders, wanted her son to be a poet from birth and encouraged his early writing.

Cummings entered Harvard in 1911, and took a B.A. in 1915 and an M.A. in 1916. The most exciting discovery he made during this period was the poetry of Ezra Pound. Cummings's youthful romanticism was quickly displaced by Pound's modernism. In 1917, Cummings and a friend joined the Ambulance Corps of the American Red Cross in order to escape the draft. Before they had settled into their assignment, their letters home attracted the notice of French intelligence. They were under suspicion as traitors and sent to a detention camp, where they remained from September through December 1917.

Cummings's father succeeded, through high-level intercession, in getting them released, and they returned to America. Cummings was then drafted, but was saved from further service by the Armistice signed in 1918. Out of his prison experience, Cummings wrote *The Enormous Room* (1922), turning his outrage into art and providing an extraordinary portrait of his colorful and rebellious fellow prisoners. The book found its place among the many antiwar books published in the 1920s.

Cummings lived a bohemian life in Paris during the early 1920s, and then settled into New York's Greenwich Village. There he devoted himself to painting and poetry, interests that would last a lifetime. He published his first volume of poems, *Tulips and Chimneys*, in 1923. From the very first, Cummings experimented with typography, dropping capitals and marks of punctuation, as well as arranging and spacing poems on the page to provide a kind of visual rhythm. He not only pried phrases apart but also broke words into syllables and letters, arranging them on successive lines. He moved words into unusual positions, forcing them to function as various parts of speech.

Cummings used unusual and expressive titles for his volumes of verse: *&* *[AND]* (1925), *XLI Poems* (1925), *is 5* (1926), *W [ViVa]* (1931), *No Thanks* (1935), *1 × 1 [One Times One]* (1944). At times he simply informed the reader of the number of poems in the volume (as in *73 Poems*, 1963). His *Collected Poems* appeared in 1938; and with *Poems 1923–1954* in 1954, he won a special citation by the National Book Awards Committee. Cummings received the Bollingen Prize for Poetry in 1957.

Although Cummings wrote poetry all his life, occasionally he published works in other genres. In 1928, his play *Him* was produced by Provincetown Playhouse, puzzling critics by its enormous cast of characters and seemingly chaotic plot. In 1933 he travelled in Russia, keeping a journal of his experiences in the totalitarian state. He published an account of his trip, *Eimi* ("I am" in Greek), in 1933, as critical of the authoritarianism he found there as he had been of that he had found earlier in the French detention camp. When Cummings was invited to lecture at Harvard (1952–53), he gave instead a series of "nonlectures," published in 1953 as *i : six nonlectures.*

Cummings has attracted both adulation and skepticism. It would be surprising if there were not, in over 800 pages of *Complete Poems*, occasional lapses into sentimentality; or touches of haughtiness in holding aloof from "mostpeople" characterized as "manunkind"; or sometimes mere meaningless, adolescent fun in typographical trickery. But at their best, Cummings's poems are extraordinarily effective.

Cummings's love poems, such as "All in green went my love riding," capture the feeling of unrestrained ecstasy in a kind of verbal (and visual) dance. His poems about everyday experience, such as "anyone lived in a pretty how town," convey a poignant sense of the rapid passing of all things human. His satiric poems, like "'next to of course god America i,'" can be powerful in their savage exposure of fakery, pomposity, or phoneyness. If he may justly be characterized as the clown of the typewriter keys, his clowning often results in a biting wit, or an unnerving tug at the deeper emotions.

ADDITIONAL READING

Selected Letters of E. E. Cummings, ed. F. W. Dupee and George Stade, 1969.

Charles Norman, *The Magic Maker*, 1958, 1964; George J. Firmage, *E. E. Cummings: A Bibliography*, 1960; Norman Friedman, *E. E. Cummings: The Art of His Poetry*, 1960; S. V. Baum, ed., *E. E. Cummings and the Critics*, 1962; Norman Friedman, *E. E. Cummings: The Growth of a Writer*, 1964; Barry A. Marks, *E. E. Cummings*, 1964; Robert E. Wegner, *The Poetry and Prose of E. E. Cummings*, 1965; Eve Triem, *E. E. Cummings*, 1969; Norman Friedman, ed., *E. E. Cummings: A Collection of Critical Essays*, 1972; Bethany K. Dumas, *E. E. Cummings: A Remembrance of Miracles*, 1974; Cary Lane, *I Am: A Study of E. E. Cummings' Poems*, 1976; Paul Lauter, *E. E. Cummings: Index of First Lines and Bibliography of Works by and about the Poet*, 1976; Rushworth Kidder, *E. E. Cummings: An Introduction to the Poetry*, 1979; Guy L. Rotella, *E. E. Cummings: A Reference Guide*, 1979; Richard S. Kennedy, *Dreams in the Mirror*, 1980; Lloyd N. Dendinger, ed., *E. E. Cummings: The Critical Reception*, 1981; Kate McBride, ed., *A Concordance to the Poems of E. E. Cummings*, 1982; Guy Rotella, ed., *Critical Essays on E. E. Cummings*, 1984; Milton A. Cohen, *Poet and Painter: The Aesthetics of E. E. Cummings's Early Work*, 1987.

TEXT

Complete Poems, 1913–1962, 1972.

[All in green went my love riding]

All in green went my love riding
on a great horse of gold
into the silver dawn.

four lean hounds crouched low and smiling
the merry deer ran before.   5

Fleeter be they than dappled dreams
the swift sweet deer
the red rare deer.

Four red roebuck at a white water
the cruel bugle sang before.   10

Horn at hip went my love riding
riding the echo down
into the silver dawn.

four lean hounds crouched low and smiling
the level meadows ran before.   15

Softer be they than slippered sleep
the lean lithe deer
the fleet flown deer.

Four fleet does at a gold valley
the famished arrow sang before.   20

Bow at belt went my love riding
riding the mountain down
into the silver dawn.

four lean hounds crouched low and smiling
the sheer peaks ran before.   25

Paler be they than daunting death
the sleek slim deer
the tall tense deer.

Four tall stags at a green mountain
the lucky hunter sang before.   30

All in green went my love riding
on a great horse of gold
into the silver dawn.

four lean hounds crouched low and smiling
my heart fell dead before.   35

1916, 1923

[in Just-]

in Just-
spring   when the world is mud-
luscious   the little
lame balloonman

whistles   far   and wee   5

and eddieandbill come
running from marbles and
piracies and it's
spring

when the world is puddle-wonderful   10

the queer
old balloonman whistles
far   and   wee
and bettyandisbel come dancing

from hop-scotch and jump-rope and   15

it's
spring
and
    the

        goat-footed   20

balloonMan   whistles
far
and
wee

1920, 1923

[Buffalo Bill's]

Buffalo Bill's
defunct
      who used to
      ride a watersmooth-silver
                  stallion   5
and break onetwothreefourfive pigeonsjustlikethat
                                 Jesus

he was a handsome man
                  and what i want to know is
how do you like your blueeyed boy   10
Mister Death

1920, 1923

Poem,or Beauty Hurts Mr.Vinal

take it from me kiddo
believe me
my country,'tis of

you,land of the Cluett
Shirt Boston Garter and Spearmint   5
Girl With The Wrigley Eyes(of you
land of the Arrow Ide
and Earl &

Wilson
Collars)of you i   10
sing:land of Abraham Lincoln and Lydia E. Pinkham,
land above all of Just Add Hot Water And Serve—
from every B.V.D.

let freedom ring

amen.   i do however protest,anent the un   15
-spontaneous and otherwise scented merde which
greets one(Everywhere Why)as divine poesy per
that and this radically defunct periodical.   i would

suggest that certain ideas gestures
rhymes,like Gillette Razor Blades   20
having been used and reused
to the mystical moment of dullness emphatically are
Not To Be Resharpened.   (Case in point

if we are to believe these gently O sweetly
melancholy trillers amid the thrillers   25
these crepuscular violinists among my and your
skyscrapers—Helen & Cleopatra were Just Too Lovely,
The Snail's On The Thorn enter Morn and God's
In His andsoforth

do you get me?)according   30
to such supposedly indigenous
throstles Art is O World O Life
a formula:example,Turn Your Shirttails Into
Drawers and If It Isn't An Eastman It Isn't A
Kodak therefore my friends let   35
us now sing each and all fortissimo A-
mer
i

ca,I
love,   40
You.   And there're a
hun-dred-mil-lion-oth-ers,like
all of you successfully if
delicately gelded (or spaded)
gentlemen (and ladies)—pretty   45

littleliverpill-
hearted-Nujolneeding-There's-A-Reason
americans(who tensetendoned and with
upward vacant eyes,painfully
perpetually crouched,quivering,upon the   50
sternly allotted sandpile
—how silently
emit a tiny violetflavoured nuisance:Odor?

ono.
comes out like a ribbon lies flat on the brush   55

                                                           1922, 1926

[Spring is like a perhaps hand]

Spring is like a perhaps hand
(which comes carefully
out of Nowhere)arranging
a window,into which people look(while
people stare   5
arranging and changing placing
carefully there a strange
thing and a known thing here)and

changing everything carefully

spring is like a perhaps   10
Hand in a window
(carefully to
and fro moving New and
Old things,while
people stare carefully   15
moving a perhaps
fraction of flower here placing
an inch of air there)and

without breaking anything.

                                                                    1925

[Humanity i love you]

Humanity i love you
because you would rather black the boots of
success than enquire whose soul dangles from his
watch-chain which would be embarrassing for both

parties and because you   5
unflinchingly applaud all
songs containing the words country home and
mother when sung at the old howard

Humanity i love you because
when you're hard up you pawn your   10
intelligence to buy a drink and when
you're flush pride keeps

you from the pawn shop and
because you are continually committing
nuisances but more   15
especially in your own house

Humanity i love you because you
are perpetually putting the secret of
life in your pants and forgetting
it's there and sitting down   20

on it
and because you are
forever making poems in the lap
of death Humanity

i hate you   25

                                                                                    1925

["next to of course god america i]

"next to of course god america i
love you land of the pilgrims' and so forth oh
say can you see by the dawn's early my
country 'tis of centuries come and go
and are no more what of it we should worry   5
in every language even deafanddumb
thy sons acclaim your glorious name by gorry
by jingo by gee by gosh by gum
why talk of beauty what could be more beaut-
iful than these heroic happy dead   10
who rushed like lions to the roaring slaughter
they did not stop to think they died instead
then shall the voice of liberty be mute?"

He spoke.   And drank rapidly a glass of water

                                                                        1925, 1926

[Jimmie's got a goil]

Jimmie's got a goil
                goil
                        goil,
                                Jimmie
's got a goil and   5
she coitnly can shimmie

when you see her shake
                                shake
                                        shake,
                                                when   10
you see her shake a
shimmie how you wish that you was Jimmie.

Oh for such a gurl
                gurl
                        gurl,   15
                                oh
for such a gurl to
be a fellow's twistandtwirl

talk about your Sal-
              Sal-   20
                    Sal-,
                          talk

about your Salo
-mes but gimme Jimmie's gal.

                                                                1926

[come,gaze with me upon this dome]

come,gaze with me upon this dome
of many coloured glass,and see
his mother's pride,his father's joy,
unto whom duty whispers low

"thou must!" and who replies, "I can!"   5
—yon clean upstanding well dressed boy
that with his peers full oft hath quaffed
the wine of life and found it sweet—

a tear within his stern blue eye,
upon his firm white lips a smile,   10
one thought alone:to do or die
for God for country and for Yale

above his blond determined head
the sacred flag of truth unfurled,
in the bright heyday of his youth   15
the upper class American

unsullied stands,before the world:
with manly heart and conscience free,
upon the front steps of her home
by the high minded pure young girl   20

much kissed,by loving relatives
well fed,and fully photographed
the son of man goes forth to war
with trumpets clap and syphilis

                                                                1926

[she being Brand]

she being Brand

-new;and you
know consequently a
little stiff i was
careful of her and(having   5

thoroughly oiled the universal
joint tested my gas felt of
her radiator made sure her springs were O.

K.)i went right to it flooded-the-carburetor cranked her

up,slipped the   10
clutch(and then somehow got into reverse she
kicked what
the hell)next
minute i was back in neutral tried and

again slo-wly; bare,ly nudg.   ing(my   15

lev-er Right-
oh and her gears being in
A 1 shape passed
from low through
second-in-to-high like   20
greasedlightning)just as we turned the corner of Divinity

avenue i touched the accelerator and give

her the juice,good

                    (it
was the first ride and believe i we was   25
happy to see how nice she acted right up to
the last minute coming back down by the Public
Gardens i slammed on

the
internalexpanding   30
&
externalcontracting
brakes Bothatonce and

brought allofher tremB
-ling   35
to a:dead.

stand-
;Still)

                                        1926

[my sweet old etcetera]

        my sweet old etcetera
        aunt lucy during the recent

        war could and what
        is more did tell you just
        what everybody was fighting   5

for,
my sister

isabel created hundreds
(and
hundreds)of socks not to   10
mention shirts fleaproof earwarmers

etcetera wristers etcetera,my

mother hoped that

i would die etcetera
bravely of course my father used   15
to become hoarse talking about how it was
a privilege and if only he
could meanwhile my

self etcetera lay quietly
in the deep mud et   20

cetera
(dreaming,
et
    cetera,of
Your smile   25
eyes knees and of your Etcetera)

                                                          1926

[i sing of Olaf glad and big]

i sing of Olaf glad and big
whose warmest heart recoiled at war:
a conscientious object-or

his wellbelovéd colonel(trig
westpointer most succinctly bred)   5
took erring Olaf soon in hand;
but—though an host of overjoyed
noncoms(first knocking on the head
him)do through icy waters roll
that helplessness which others stroke   10
with brushes recently employed
anent this muddy toiletbowl,
while kindred intellects evoke
allegiance per blunt instruments—
Olaf(being to all intents   15
a corpse and wanting any rag
upon what God unto him gave)
responds,without getting annoyed
"I will not kiss your fucking flag"

straightway the silver bird looked grave   20
(departing hurriedly to shave)

but—though all kinds of officers
(a yearning nation's blueeyed pride)
their passive prey did kick and curse
until for wear their clarion   25
voices and boots were much the worse,
and egged the firstclassprivates on
his rectum wickedly to tease
by means of skilfully applied
bayonets roasted hot with heat—   30
Olaf(upon what were once knees)
does almost ceaselessly repeat
"there is some shit I will not eat"

our president,being of which
assertions duly notified   35
threw the yellowsonofabitch
into a dungeon,where he died

Christ(of His mercy infinite)
i pray to see;and Olaf,too

preponderatingly because   40
unless statistics lie he was
more brave than me:more blond than you.

                                                                    1931

[somewhere i have never travelled,gladly beyond]

somewhere i have never travelled,gladly beyond
any experience,your eyes have their silence:
in your most frail gesture are things which enclose me,
or which i cannot touch because they are too near

your slightest look easily will unclose me   5
though i have closed myself as fingers,
you open always petal by petal myself as Spring opens
(touching skilfully,mysteriously)her first rose

or if your wish to be close to me,i and
my life will shut very beautifully,suddenly,   10
as when the heart of this flower imagines
the snow carefully everywhere descending;

nothing which we are to perceive in this world equals
the power of your intense fragility:whose texture
compels me with the colour of its countries,   15
rendering death and forever with each breathing

(i do not know what it is about you that closes
and opens;only something in me understands
the voice of your eyes is deeper than all roses)
nobody,not even the rain,has such small hands   20

1931

[Space being(don't forget to remember)Curved]

Space being(don't forget to remember)Curved
(and that reminds me who said o yes Frost
Something there is which isn't fond of walls)

an electromagnetic(now I've lost
the)Einstein expanded Newton's law preserved   5
conTinuum(but we read that beFore)

of Course life being just a Reflex you
know since Everything is Relative or

to sum it All Up god being Dead(not to

mention inTerred)   10
                        LONG LIVE that Upwardlooking
Serene Illustrious and Beatific
Lord of Creation,MAN:
                        at a least crooking
of Whose compassionate digit,earth's most terrific   15

quadruped swoons into billiardBalls!

1931

[anyone lived in a pretty how town]

anyone lived in a pretty how town
(with up so floating many bells down)
spring summer autumn winter
he sang his didn't he danced his did.

Women and men(both little and small)   5
cared for anyone not at all
they sowed their isn't they reaped their same
sun moon stars rain

children guessed(but only a few
and down they forgot as up they grew   10
autumn winter spring summer)
that noone loved him more by more

when by now and tree by leaf
she laughed his joy she cried his grief
bird by snow and stir by still   15
anyone's any was all to her

someones married their everyones
laughed their cryings and did their dance
(sleep wake hope and then)they
said their nevers they slept their dream   20

stars rain sun moon
(and only the snow can begin to explain
how children are apt to forget to remember
with up so floating many bells down)

one day anyone died i guess   25
(and noone stooped to kiss his face)
busy folk buried them side by side
little by little and was by was

all by all and deep by deep
and more by more they dream their sleep   30
noone and anyone earth by april
wish by spirit and if by yes.

Women and men(both dong and ding)
summer autumn winter spring
reaped their sowing and went their came   35
sun moon stars rain

                               1940

[my father moved through dooms of love]

my father moved through dooms of love
through sames of am through haves of give,
singing each morning out of each night
my father moved through depths of height

this motionless forgetful where   5
turned at his glance to shining here;
that if(so timid air is firm)
under his eyes would stir and squirm

newly as from unburied which
floats the first who,his april touch   10
drove sleeping selves to swarm their fates
woke dreamers to their ghostly roots

and should some why completely weep
my father's fingers brought her sleep:
vainly no smallest voice might cry   15
for he could feel the mountains grow.

Lifting the valleys of the sea
my father moved through griefs of joy;
praising a forehead called the moon
singing desire into begin   20

joy was his song and joy so pure
a heart of star by him could steer
and pure so now and now so yes
the wrists of twilight would rejoice

keen as midsummer's keen beyond   25
conceiving mind of sun will stand,
so strictly(over utmost him
so hugely)stood my father's dream

his flesh was flesh his blood was blood:
no hungry man but wished him food;   30
no cripple wouldn't creep one mile
uphill to only see him smile.

Scorning the pomp of must and shall
my father moved through dooms of feel;
his anger was as right as rain   35
his pity was as green as grain

septembering arms of year extend
less humbly wealth to foe and friend
than he to foolish and to wise
offered immeasurable is   40

proudly and(by octobering flame
beckoned)as earth will downward climb,
so naked for immortal work
his shoulders marched against the dark

his sorrow was as true as bread: 45
no liar looked him in the head;
if every friend became his foe
he'd laugh and build a world with snow.

My father moved through theys of we,
singing each new leaf out of each tree   50
(and every child was sure that spring
danced when she heard my father sing)

then let men kill which cannot share,
let blood and flesh be mud and mire,
scheming imagine,passion willed,   55
freedom a drug that's bought and sold

giving to steal and cruel kind,
a heart to fear,to doubt a mind,
to differ a disease of same,
conform the pinnacle of am   60

though dull were all we taste as bright,
bitter all utterly things sweet,

maggoty minus and dumb death
all we inherit,all bequeath

and nothing quite so least as truth   65
—i say though hate were why men breathe—
because my father lived his soul
love is the whole and more than all

                                                    1940

[pity this busy monster,manunkind,]

pity this busy monster,manunkind,

not.   Progress is a comfortable disease:
your victim(death and life safely beyond)

plays with the bigness of his littleness
—electrons deify one razorblade   5
into a mountainrange;lenses extend

unwish through curving wherewhen till unwish
returns on its unself.
                              A world of made
is not a world of born—pity poor flesh   10

and trees,poor stars and stones,but never this
fine specimen of hypermagical

ultraomnipotence.   We doctors know

a hopeless case if—listen:there's a hell
of a good universe next door;let's go   15

                                        1943, 1944

[what if a much of a which of a wind]

what if a much of a which of a wind
gives the truth to summer's lie;
bloodies with dizzying leaves the sun
and yanks immortal stars awry?
Blow king to beggar and queen to seem   5
(blow friend to fiend:blow space to time)
—when skies are hanged and oceans drowned,
the single secret will still be man

what if a keen of a lean wind flays
screaming hills with sleet and snow: 10
strangles valleys by ropes of thing
and stifles forests in white ago?
Blow hope to terror;blow seeing to blind
(blow pity to envy and soul to mind)

—whose hearts are mountains,roots are trees,   15
it's they shall cry hello to the spring

what if a dawn of a doom of a dream
bites this universe in two,
peels forever out of his grave
and sprinkles nowhere with me and you?   20
Blow soon to never and never to twice
(blow life to isn't:blow death to was)
—all nothing's only our hugest home;
the most who die,the more we live

                                                    1943, 1944

[plato told]

plato told

him:he couldn't
believe it(jesus

told him;he
wouldn't believe   5
it)lao

tsze[1]
certainly told
him,and general
(yes   10

mam)
sherman;[2]
and even
(believe it
or   15

not)you
told him:i told
him;we told him
(he didn't believe it,no

sir)it took   20
a nipponized bit of
the old sixth

avenue
el;in the top of his head:to tell

him[3]   25

                                                    1944

---

[1]Lao Tse (sixth century B.C.), Chinese philosopher whose writings are the basis of Taoism.
[2]William Tecumseh Sherman (1820–1891), Union General in the Civil War who told a military academy's graduating class that "war is hell."

[3]Cummings alludes to the sale to Japan (Nippon in Japanese) in the 1930s of scrap metal from the elevated railway over New York's Sixth Avenue when it was torn down; it was converted into weapons to fight Americans during the Second World War.

[l(a]

l(a

le
af
fa

ll   5

s)
one
l

iness

1958

[but]

but

he" i
staring

into winter twi

light(whisper)"was   5
my friend" reme
mbering "&

friendship

is a
miracle"   10
his always
not imaginably

morethanmostgenerous

spirit.   Feeling
only   15
(jesus)every(god)

where

(chr
ist)

what absolute nothing   20

1963

THE POETRY RENAISSANCE
Renewal in the Tradition

Sara Teasdale
Elinor Wylie
Edna St. Vincent Millay

John Crowe Ransom
Allen Tate
Countee Cullen

"I would covet a program something like this: In manners, aristocratic; in religion, ritualistic; in art, traditional. . . .

I shall try a preliminary definition of the poet's traditional function on behalf of society: he proposed to make virtue delicious. He compounded a moral effect with an aesthetic effect. The total effect was not a pure one, but it was rich, and relished highly. The name of the moral effect was goodness; the name of the aesthetic effect was beauty. Perhaps these did not have to coexist, but the planners of society saw to it that they should; they called upon the artists to reinforce morality with charm. The artists obliged. . . .

The virtue of formal lyrics, or 'minor poems,' is one that no other literary type can manifest: they are the only complete and self-determined poetry. There the poetic object is elected by a free choice from all objects in the world, and this object, deliberately elected and carefully worked up by the adult poet, becomes his microcosm. With a serious poet each minor poem may be the symbol of a major decision. It is as ranging and comprehensive an action as the mind has ever tried."

John Crowe Ransom, *The World's Body*, 1938

SARA TEASDALE

(1884–1933)

There were some poets—and quite fine ones—who, instead of attempting to forge the new, spent their imaginative energies in renewing the old, giving new life to inherited forms and traditional themes. Sara Teasdale wrote to Harriet Monroe in 1919: "There seems to be a feeling that if more of us could free our poetry of lines having approximately the same number of syllables, and stanzas each having the same number of lines, we should be happier and better poets. But is it not evident . . . that fairly regular rhythm, modified by variations within itself, and regular recurrence of rhymes are joy and freedom, not bondage, to those poets who choose them of their own free will and who use them with ease?"

As for the source of poetry, Teasdale asserted in 1918: "If a poem is of any value it must spring directly from the experience of the writer—not necessarily from an external experience but at least from a spiritual one. If a poem is sincere and springs from deep emotion, no matter what the form, it will be of value to us." Pound and Eliot, of course, were at this same time mounting attacks against these positions.

Sara Teasdale was born in 1884 into a prosperous St. Louis, Missouri, family. She attended Hosmer Hall School in St. Louis, graduating in 1903. There she read widely in the classics and in recent literature. Among her favorite poets were Elizabeth Barrett Browning, Christina Rossetti, and A. E. Housman.

From 1903 to 1907, Teasdale was associated with a group of young women in St. Louis known as the Potters who published a literary magazine, the *Potter's Wheel*. It was probably during this period that Teasdale decided to commit her life to poetry. In 1905, Teasdale accompanied her mother on the "grand tour" of Europe, visiting the Holy Land, Greece, Italy, Spain, France, and England. In 1907, Teasdale's first volume of poems, *Sonnets to Duse* (that is, Eleonora Duse, the great Italian actress of the time), was privately printed. Much of this uneven work had appeared in the *Potter's Wheel*. The volume attracted little attention.

Teasdale published her next book, *Helen of Troy and Other Poems*, in 1911, this time with a commercial publisher. The volume opened with a series of dramatic monologues and included a cluster of "Love Poems." There was some advance in Teasdale's control of her craft in this volume, but the real breakthrough came with her next book, *Rivers to the Sea*, published in 1915. It was an immediate success critically and sold astonishingly well, requiring several new printings. Clearly Teasdale had found a voice, sometimes distant and ironic but always deeply personal, to treat her (as well as her audience's) favorite theme of love— "New Love and Old," "The Kiss," "The Old Maid."

One reason for the new strength in these poems was to be found in Teasdale's personal life. For a poet who was to make her major theme love, there was little evidence of firsthand experience in her early sheltered life. Indeed, she had always had a delicate constitution, vulnerable to inexplicable illnesses that rendered her wan, quickly upset, poised to retreat. But her situation changed in 1914, when she met the vagabond poet Vachel Lindsay. His courtship was stormy, carried out at long distance by endless letters expressing devotion.

But in 1914, Lindsay, though on his way to poetic fame, was penniless. And Teasdale had an alternative in a successful St. Louis businessman, Ernst Filsinger, who had out of admiration memorized many of her poems. They married in December 1914. In the mid-1920s, strains developed in their marriage, and Teasdale found companionship with a young college student, Margaret Conklin, in whom she seems to have seen her younger self. They travelled together in Europe in 1927, and Teasdale divorced her husband in 1929. Although the marriage turned out to be unsuccessful, it provided many of the experiences that would be the basis for her later poems.

Teasdale's successive books reflected (as her theory of poetry would suggest) her own varying states of emotional being. *Love Songs* (1917) and *Flame and Shadow* (1920) projected a self-assurance and affirmation, often celebratory. *Dark of the Moon* (1926) sounded a sobering, somber note. And her last volume, published after her death from an overdose of sleeping pills in 1933, appeared as a kind of suicide note of farewell: "Gather together, against the coming of the night, / All that we played with here. . . ." One of the poems included is "In Memory of Vachel Lindsay," who had taken his life in 1931.

When at her height of fame, Teasdale was praised by both critics and readers alike. *Love Songs* (1917) had received the first national award for poetry given in America, the Columbia Prize (precursor of the Pulitzer Prize) presented in 1918 by the Poetry Society of America. But gradually the critical acclaim grew still as the modernist movement swept all else aside. But Teasdale's *Collected Poems*, which appeared first in 1937, were reissued in 1945 and again in 1966. In an Introduction to this last edition, Marya Zaturenska claims with some justice that Teasdale is "a poet of rare distinction. . . . She has outlived many more fashionable and showier reputations. She endures because she was, *is* unique." A biography by William Drake in 1979 sparked renewed interest in her. And in 1984, Drake published *Mirror of the Heart: Poems of Sara Teasdale*, presenting fifty-one previously unpublished poems and placing these and other poems in the order of composition inasmuch as he could determine dates from the manuscripts. There is need now for a general reassessment of her place in American literature.

ADDITIONAL READING

Margaret Haley Carpenter, *Sara Teasdale: A Biography*, 1960; William Drake, *Sara Teasdale: Woman and Poet*, 1979; Carol B. Schoen, *Sara Teasdale*, 1986.

TEXT

The Collected Poems of Sara Teasdale, 1937.

I Shall Not Care

When I am dead and over me bright April
    Shakes out her rain-drenched hair,
Tho' you should lean above me broken-hearted,
    I shall not care.

I shall have peace, as leafy trees are peaceful   5
    When rain bends down the bough,
And I shall be more silent and cold-hearted
    Than you are now.

Song Making

My heart cried like a beaten child
   Ceaselessly all night long;
I had to take my own cries
   And thread them into a song.

One was a cry at black midnight   5
   And one when the first cock crew —
My heart was like a beaten child,
   But no one ever knew.

Life, you have put me in your debt
   And I must serve you long —   10
But oh, the debt is terrible
   That must be paid in song.

1916   1916, 1920

Day's Ending

(TUCSON)

Aloof as aged kings,
Wearing like them the purple,
The mountains ring the mesa
Crowned with a dusky light;
Many a time I watched   5
That coming-on of darkness
Till stars burned through the heavens
Intolerably bright.

It was not long I lived there
But I became a woman   10
Under those vehement stars,
For it was there I heard
For the first time my spirit
Forging an iron rule for me,
As though with slow cold hammers   15
Beating out word by word:

"Only yourself can heal you,
Only yourself can lead you,
The road is heavy going
And ends where no man knows;   20
Take love when love is given,
But never think to find it
A sure escape from sorrow
Or a complete repose."

1921   1926

In Memory of Vachel Lindsay

"Deep in the ages," you said, "deep in the ages,"[1]
    And, "To live in mankind is far more than to live in a name."[2]
You are deep in the ages, now, deep in the ages,
    You whom the world could not break, nor the years tame.

Fly out, fly on, eagle that is not forgotten,   5
    Fly straight to the innermost light, you who loved sun in your eyes,
Free of the fret, free of the weight of living,
    Bravest among the brave, gayest among the wise.

1931   1931, 1933

In a Darkening Garden

Gather together, against the coming of night,
    All that we played with here,
Toys and fruits, the quill from the sea-bird's flight,
    The small flute, hollow and clear;
The apple that was not eaten, the grapes untasted—   5
    Let them be put away.
They served for us, I would not have them wasted,
    They lasted out our day.

1931   1933

Moon's Ending

Moon, worn thin to the width of a quill,
    In the dawn clouds flying,
How good to go, light into light, and still
    Giving light, dying.

1928   1933

ELINOR WYLIE
(1885–1928)

In an essay revealingly entitled "Jewelled Bindings," written after she had
become praised as a poet, Elinor Wylie set forth her theory about her kind of
poetry: she believed herself a "minor" poet, one of "a group, enchanted by a

---

[1]From Vachel Lindsay's poem "The Chinese Nightingale,"
written for Sara Teasdale.   [2]From Vachel Lindsay's poem "The Eagle That Is
Forgotten."

midas-touch or a colder silver madness into workers in metal and glass, in substances hard and brittle, in crisp and sharp-edged forms," making what are in essence "enamelled snuffboxes." Such "little" or "diminutive" verse was distinguished by its "short lines, clear small stanzas, brilliant and compact": "I don't mean inferior or contemptible, or negligible. Nor do I mean great." As such a miniature lyricist, she said, "I believe that we are good workmen, dexterous and clean in our handling of gold and silver and precious — or even semi-precious — stones. . . . As to the decoration, the setting of words transparent or opaque . . . in a pattern upon our jewelled bindings, I am by no means ready to discard it. . . . And, in the remote possibility that some of us are not geniuses . . . it may be an excellent thing after all that we have cultivated a small clean technique."

Such statements reveal that Wylie clearly conceived herself as writing outside the main avant-garde currents of the time. Her aesthetic seems more compatible with the art-for-art's-sake movement of the 1890s than the modernist movement of the 1920s.

Wylie grew up in the upper-class circles of Philadelphia and Washington, D.C. Her father, Henry Hoyt, served as assistant attorney-general of the United States and as solicitor-general. Elinor Hoyt was educated at exclusive private schools and spent summers at the family vacation home in Maine. She was endowed with great beauty and all the social graces. In 1905 she married the son of an admiral, gave birth to a son in 1907, and settled into the country-club life for which she seemed destined.

But suddenly, in 1910, she eloped with Horace Wylie, an older man who was intellectual and learned, qualities notably absent in the admiral's son. Horace Wylie's wife would not give him a divorce, and he took Elinor off to England, causing one of the great scandals of the day. While in England, Elinor Wylie's first book of poems, *Incidental Numbers*, was privately printed in 1912. Its somewhat immature verses were little noticed.

The two runaway lovers returned to the United States in 1916 and were married. After travelling about, they settled in Washington, D.C., in 1919. During this period, Elinor Wylie's literary interests and reputation were expanding. She published poems in the little magazines, and in 1921 she moved to New York to enter directly — and with glittering impact — the literary scene. Her book of poems *Nets to Catch the Wind* appeared this same year, winning a prize from the Poetry Society of America, and applause from readers. In 1923, Wylie published her first novel, *Jennifer Lorn*, and a second book of poems, *Black Armour*, securing her literary reputation. This same year, she divorced her husband and married William Rose Benét, a poet-critic of considerable reputation.

For a time Wylie was poetry editor for *Vanity Fair*, and when the Literary Guild was formed, she served as editor along with Carl Van Doren and Joseph Wood Krutch. The success of her first novel inspired her to continue writing fiction, including *The Venetian Glass Nephew* (1925), *The Orphan Angel* (1926), and *Mr. Hodge and Mr. Hazard* (1928). The choice of *The Orphan Angel* as a Book-of-the-Month Club selection indicates the popularity of her witty, erudite novels, with their exotic historical settings and elegant, refined characters. The word critics found apt for her poetry — "exquisite" — they also found suitable for her fiction.

But Wylie considered herself first a poet, publishing her third volume, *Trivial Breath*, in 1928. In England in 1928, while she was working on a sonnet sequence (*One Person*), she suffered a stroke which paralyzed one side of her face. She returned to America and, in December, suffered another stroke which caused her death at the age of forty-three. *Angels and Earthly Creatures*, containing the sonnet sequence and other poems, was published in 1929.

Wylie's poetry has been described as terse, ambiguous, brilliant, sparkling "without burning." Her own metaphor, "enamelled snuff boxes," is richly suggestive. Her poems are studded with exotic, arresting phrases. And when all these work together with quiet resonance, the result is a memorable poem that can haunt the imagination. Edmund Wilson, who knew her personally, must have had this effect in mind, when he called her, in an essay on her death, "the mistress of a wonderful language, in which accuracy, vigor and splendor seem to require no study and no effort."

ADDITIONAL READING

Collected Prose of Elinor Wylie, ed. William Rose Benét, 1933; *Last Poems of Elinor Wylie*, ed. Jane D. Wise, 1943.

William Rose Benét, *The Prose and Poetry of Elinor Wylie*, 1934; Nancy Hoyt, *Elinor Wylie: Portrait of an Unknown Lady*, 1935; Thomas A. Gray, *Elinor Wylie*, 1969; Stanley Olson, *Elinor Wylie: A Life Apart*, 1979; Judith Farr, *The Life and Art of Elinor Wylie*, 1983.

TEXT

Collected Poems of Elinor Wylie, ed. William Rose Benét, 1932.

The Eagle and the Mole

Avoid the reeking herd,
Shun the polluted flock,
Live like that stoic bird,
The eagle of the rock.

The huddled warmth of crowds   5
Begets and fosters hate;
He keeps, above the clouds,
His cliff inviolate.

When flocks are folded warm,
And herds to shelter run,   10
He sails above the storm,
He stares into the sun.

If in the eagle's track
Your sinews cannot leap,
Avoid the lathered pack,   15
Turn from the steaming sheep.

If you would keep your soul
From spotted sight or sound,
Live like the velvet mole;
Go burrow underground.   20

And there hold intercourse
With roots of trees and stones,

With rivers at their source,
And disembodied bones.

                                                              1921

Velvet Shoes

Let us walk in the white snow
    In a soundless space;
With footsteps quiet and slow,
    At a tranquil pace,
    Under veils of white lace.   5

I shall go shod in silk,
    And you in wool,
White as a white cow's milk,
    More beautiful
    Than the breast of a gull.   10

We shall walk through the still town
    In a windless peace;
We shall step upon white down,
    Upon silver fleece,
    Upon softer than these.   15

We shall walk in velvet shoes:
    Wherever we go
Silence will fall like dews
    On white silence below.
    We shall walk in the snow.   20

                                                              1921

Let No Charitable Hope

Now let no charitable hope
Confuse my mind with images
Of eagle and of antelope:
I am in nature none of these.

I was, being human, born alone;   5
I am, being woman, hard beset;
I live by squeezing from a stone
The little nourishment I get.

In masks outrageous and austere
The years go by in single file;   10
But none has merited my fear,
And none has quite escaped my smile.

                                                              1923

Confession of Faith

I lack the braver mind
That dares to find
The lover friend, and kind.

I fear him to the bone;
I lie alone   5
By the beloved one,

And, breathless for suspense,
Erect defense
Against love's violence

Whose silences portend   10
A bloody end
For lover never friend.

But, in default of faith,
In futile breath,
I dream no ill of Death.   15

                              1928

from One Person[1]

VII

Would I might make subliminal my flesh
And so contrive a gentle atmosphere
To comfort you because I am not there;
Or else incorporate and carve afresh
A lady, from the chilly heaven and clear   5
Which flows around you like a stream of air,
To warm and wind you in her body's mesh.

So would I cherish you a loving twice;
Once in a mist made matter; once again
In my true substance made ethereal: 10
And yet I cannot succour you at all
Whose letter cries, "My hands are cold as ice,"
The while I kiss the colder air in vain.

XII

In our content, before the autumn came
To shower sallow droppings on the mould,
Sometimes you have permitted me to fold
Your grief in swaddling-bands, and smile to name
Yourself my infant, with an infant's claim   5
To utmost adoration as of old,

---

[1]A sonnet sequence.

Suckled with kindness, fondled from the cold,
And loved beyond philosophy or shame.

I dreamt I was the mother of a son
Who had deserved a manger for a crib;   10
Torn from your body, furbished from your rib,
I am the daughter of your skeleton,
Born of your bitter and excessive pain:
I shall not dream you are my child again.

1929

Pretty Words

Poets make pets of pretty, docile words:
I love smooth words, like gold-enamelled fish
Which circle slowly with a silken swish,
And tender ones, like downy-feathered birds:
Words shy and dappled, deep-eyed deer in herds,   5
Come to my hand, and playful if I wish,
Or purring softly at a silver dish,
Blue Persian kittens, fed on cream and curds.

I love bright words, words up and singing early;
Words that are luminous in the dark, and sing;   10
Warm lazy words, white cattle under trees;
I love words opalescent, cool, and pearly,
Like midsummer moths, and honied words like bees,
Gilded and sticky, with a little sting.

1932

EDNA ST. VINCENT MILLAY
(1892–1950)

Edna St. Vincent Millay's 1918 quatrain became the badge of the liberated, flaming youth of the 1920s:

> My candle burns at both ends;
>   It will not last the night;
> But ah, my foes, and oh, my friends—
>   It gives a lovely light!

Like F. Scott Fitzgerald, Millay symbolized the rebellion against the restraints of the genteel tradition. She was hailed as America's female Byron. But in spite of her advanced views on women, society, and sex, she was very much a traditionalist in her poetic technique. One critic called her "a twentieth-century romantic temperament in a nineteenth-century romantic vehicle."

Born in Rockland, Maine, Millay published verses in the children's magazine *St. Nicholas* and achieved recognition as a poet at the age of nineteen when her poem "Renascence" appeared in *The Lyric Year* (1912). Upon hearing "Renascence" recited by the young poet, one of the listeners was so impressed as to become her patron, enabling her to attend Vassar (1913–17). Her first book of poems, *Renascence and Other Poems*, was published the year of her graduation in 1917.

Millay went to New York, settling into the "bohemian" life of Greenwich Village, and joined the Provincetown Players, where she directed her own antiwar play, *Aria da Capo* (1920). Drama would be a continuing interest, but Millay concentrated her imaginative energies in the writing of poetry. To support herself, she wrote for magazines, including satirical sketches under the name of "Nancy Boyd," published in 1924 as *Distressing Dialogues*.

But with the poems in *A Few Figs from Thistles* (1920), the rebellious youth of the 1920s found a spokeswoman and thrust her in the role of the "free woman." She seemed to fulfill the role in her life, having a series of affairs with prominent men, including Edmund Wilson who spoke of her "intoxicating effect." In spite of her long-lasting marriage to Eugen Jan Boissevain in 1923 and her turn to other (and what she considered more serious) themes, she could never quite escape the image of flip satirist and embodiment of the Jazz Age. Her third volume of poems, *Second April* (1921), was a return to the life-affirming lyricism of the earlier *Renascence*. A fourth volume, *The Harp-Weaver and Other Poems* (1923), won her the Pulitzer Prize.

Millay was active in various causes, including the protest against the execution of the anarchists Sacco and Vanzetti in 1927. The event became the focus of a number of her poems. Later, she became concerned about the rise of totalitarianism and the dangers it posed to democracy. *Make Bright the Arrows* (1940) and *The Murder of Lidice* (1942) were expressions of her political feelings, ranging from alarm to outrage. In 1944, she suffered a nervous breakdown. In 1949, her attentive and supportive husband died; she died of a heart attack the following year.

For all her willingness to defy social conventions, Millay was astonishingly conservative in holding on to literary conventions. She found no fault with traditional poetic diction, and she preferred traditional stanzaic patterns and poetic forms. She began in "Renascence" writing in rhyming four-beat couplets. And she turned again and again to the rigorous discipline of the sonnet, exclaiming in one (included in the posthumous 1954 *Mine the Harvest*), "I will put chaos into fourteen lines." In this justification of her use of the sonnet form, she paid tribute to "the strict confines / Of this sweet Order" — in a tone of defiance in the very structure of compliance.

ADDITIONAL READING

Letters of Edna St. Vincent Millay, ed. Allan Ross Macdougall, 1952.

Elizabeth Atkins, *Edna St. Vincent Millay and Her Times*, 1936; Miriam Gurko, *Restless Spirit: The Life of Edna St. Vincent Millay*, 1957; James Gray, *Edna St. Vincent Millay*, 1967; Jean Gould, *The Poet and Her Book: A Biography of Edna St. Vincent Millay*, 1969; John Dash, *A Life of One's Own: Three Gifted Women and the Men They Married*, 1973; Anne Cheney, *Millay in Greenwich Village*, 1975; Judith Nierman, *Edna St. Vincent Millay: A Reference Guide*, 1977; Norman A. Brittin, *Edna St. Vincent Millay*, 1967, 1982.

TEXT

Collected Poems, ed. Norma Millay, 1956.

First Fig

My candle burns at both ends;
   It will not last the night;
But ah, my foes, and oh, my friends—
   It gives a lovely light!

1920

Second Fig

Safe upon the solid rock the ugly houses stand:
Come and see my shining palace built upon the sand!

1920

Thursday

And if I loved you Wednesday,
   Well, what is that to you?
I do not love you Thursday—
   So much is true.

And why you come complaining   5
   Is more than I can see.
I loved you Wednesday,—yes—but what
   Is that to me?

1920

Recuerdo[1]

We were very tired, we were very merry—
We had gone back and forth all night on the ferry.
It was bare and bright, and smelled like a stable—
But we looked into a fire, we leaned across a table,
We lay on a hill-top underneath the moon;   5
And the whistles kept blowing, and the dawn came soon.

We were very tired, we were very merry—
We had gone back and forth all night on the ferry;
And you ate an apple, and I ate a pear,
From a dozen of each we had bought somewhere;   10
And the sky went wan, and the wind came cold,
And the sun rose dripping, a bucketful of gold.

---

[1]"Memory" (Spanish).

We were very tired, we were very merry,
We had gone back and forth all night on the ferry.
We hailed, "Good morrow, mother!" to a shawl-covered head,   15
And bought a morning paper, which neither of us read;
And she wept, "God bless you!" for the apples and pears,
And we gave her all our money but our subway fares.

                                                                        1920

[What lips my lips have kissed, and where, and why]

What lips my lips have kissed, and where, and why,
I have forgotten, and what arms have lain
Under my head till morning; but the rain
Is full of ghosts tonight, that tap and sigh
Upon the glass and listen for reply,   5
And in my heart there stirs a quiet pain
For unremembered lads that not again
Will turn to me at midnight with a cry.
Thus in the winter stands the lonely tree,
Nor knows what birds have vanished one by one,   10
Yet knows its boughs more silent than before:
I cannot say what loves have come and gone,
I only know that summer sang in me
A little while, that in me sings no more.

                                                                        1923

[Euclid alone has looked on Beauty bare]

Euclid[1] alone has looked on Beauty bare.
Let all who prate of Beauty hold their peace,
And lay them prone upon the earth and cease
To ponder on themselves, the while they stare
At nothing, intricately drawn nowhere   5
In shapes of shifting lineage; let geese
Gabble and hiss, but heroes seek release
From dusty bondage into luminous air.
O blinding hour, O holy, terrible day,
When first the shaft into his vision shone   10
Of light anatomized! Euclid alone
Has looked on Beauty bare. Fortunate they
Who, though once only and then but far away,
Have heard her massive sandal set on stone.

                                                                        1923

---

[1]Euclid (*c.* 300 B.C.), Greek mathematician and genius in
geometry.

[Love is not all: it is not meat nor drink]

Love is not all: it is not meat nor drink
Nor slumber nor a roof against the rain;
Nor yet a floating spar to men that sink
And rise and sink and rise and sink again;
Love can not fill the thickened lung with breath,   5
Nor clean the blood, nor set the fractured bone;
Yet many a man is making friends with death
Even as I speak, for lack of love alone.
It well may be that in a difficult hour,
Pinned down by pain and moaning for release,   10
Or nagged by want past resolution's power,
I might be driven to sell your love for peace,
Or trade the memory of this night for food.
It well may be. I do not think I would.

1931

[Clearly my ruined garden as it stood]

Clearly my ruined garden as it stood
Before the frost came on it I recall—
Stiff marigolds, and what a trunk of wood
The zinnia had, that was the first to fall;
These pale and oozy stalks, these hanging leaves   5
Nerveless and darkened, dripping in the sun,
Cannot gainsay me, though the spirit grieves
And wrings its hands at what the frost has done.
If in a widening silence you should guess
I read the moment with recording eyes,   10
Taking your love and all your loveliness
Into a listening body hushed of sighs . . .
Though summer's rife and the warm rose in season,
Rebuke me not: I have a winter reason.

1931

[I too beneath your moon, almighty Sex,]

I too beneath your moon, almighty Sex,
Go forth at nightfall crying like a cat,
Leaving the lofty tower I laboured at
For birds to foul and boys and girls to vex
With tittering chalk; and you, and the long necks   5
Of neighbours sitting where their mothers sat
Are well aware of shadowy this and that
In me, that's neither noble nor complex.

Such as I am, however, I have brought
To what it is, this tower; it is my own;   10
Though it was reared To Beauty, it was wrought
From what I had to build with: honest bone
Is there, and anguish; pride; and burning thought;
And lust is there, and nights not spent alone.

                                                                      1939

[I will put Chaos into fourteen lines]

I will put Chaos into fourteen lines
And keep him there; and let him thence escape
If he be lucky; let him twist, and ape
Flood, fire, and demon — his adroit designs
Will strain to nothing in the strict confines   5
Of this sweet Order, where, in pious rape,
I hold his essence and amorphous shape,
Till he with Order mingles and combines.
Past are the hours, the years, of our duress,
His arrogance, our awful servitude: 10
I have him. He is nothing more nor less
Than something simple not yet understood;
I shall not even force him to confess;
Or answer. I will only make him good.

                                                                      1954

JOHN CROWE RANSOM
(1888–1974)

In an essay written in 1954, John Crowe Ransom used what he described as an "absurd figure" to describe a poem:

> Suppose we say that the poem is an organism . . . we will figure its organs . . .: the head, the heart, the feet. . . . The organs are all intelligent, and can speak. Their joint product is a poem, and it is in a language within which three persistent speakers are speaking in their individual languages; the head in an intellectual language, the heart in an affective language, the feet in a rhythmical language; and it is to be supposed that in the composite language we attend to each of them, though usually with different degrees of consciousness.

In insisting on the intellectual, emotional, and musical components of poetry joined harmoniously as a living organism, Ransom was drawing upon the past to counter contemporary one-dimensional definitions of poetry that somehow diminished its possibilities. Following T. S. Eliot's self-characterization (royalist in politics, Anglo-Catholic in religion, classicist in literature), Ransom presented himself (or his "program") as "going something like this: In manner, aristocratic; in religion, ritualistic; in art, traditional."

Ransom came by his conservatism naturally. He was born in Pulaski, Tennessee, took a B.A. from Vanderbilt University, and studied as a Rhodes Scholar

(1910–13) in England at Oxford University. On returning to America, he taught briefly at Hotchkiss School, in Connecticut, and then at Vanderbilt. He served as a lieutenant in the Field Artillery in the First World War, and wrote his first book, *Poems About God*, published in 1919.

Back at Vanderbilt after the war, Ransom became a leader in a discussion group styling itself the "Fugitives," and helped to found and edit a little magazine *The Fugitive* (1922–25). During this period Ransom wrote his best poetry, published in two volumes, *Chills and Fever* (1924) and *Two Gentlemen in Bonds* (1927). In the 1930s and later, Ransom wrote a few additional poems, but published no additional volumes. When he published his *Selected Poems* in 1945, he passed over his first book and included only thirty-seven poems from his second and third volumes, plus five new poems. Although there was little new work, Ransom revised the poems that survived his rigorous selection.

Ransom continued to write, of course, but mainly critical essays. He joined other "southern agrarians" and contributed to their volume published in 1930, *I'll Take My Stand* — a stand *against* northern industrialism and rootlessness and *for* southern agrarianism and the tradition of received culture and values. In 1937, he moved from Vanderbilt to Kenyon College in Ohio, becoming the Carnegie Professor of Poetry there, and established *The Kenyon Review*, serving as its editor until 1959. He turned it into one of the most influential little magazines of the period.

In 1938, Ransom brought together a number of his essays in criticism and in critical theory, entitled *The World's Body*, containing the important statement, "Poetry: A Note in Ontology," reclaiming ideas as a possible focus for poetry. And in 1941, he published *The New Criticism*, discussing the critical work of I. A. Richards, T. S. Eliot, Yvor Winters, and William Empson. In a final chapter, setting forth his own position, Ransom ventured to characterize the modernists — poets such as Pound, Eliot, and Stevens: "The fundamental consideration is that the moderns are well instructed in the practice of the traditionalists. But this is what has happened: they find the old practice trite, and ontologically inadequate for them. Yet they lack any consistent conception of what a new practice might be — and a new practice that would be radical enough is probably not possible — and therefore work by taking liberties with the old practice, and irregularize and desystematize it, without denying it."

In spite of his importance as a critic, Ransom is primarily remembered as the author of a handful of superbly sculpted poems containing in balance all three of those elements — the intellectual, the emotional, the musical — which come together in the making of a poem. His volume of *Selected Poems* was revised and enlarged in 1963 and won the Bollingen Prize for Poetry; on its revision and enlargement again in 1969, Ransom was given the National Book Award in Poetry. His poetry looks conventional on the page, with its stanzaic patterns and regular rhyme schemes. But a close reading reveals archaic diction, strange usages, and slant-rhymes that keep the reader off balance and attentive. Subtlety and irony are in sufficient supply to avoid sentimentality. And there is the sound of a southern voice that seems at times self-mocking in its arcane interests and meticulous concern for the seemingly insignificant.

ADDITIONAL READING

Beating the Bushes: Selected Essays, 1941–1970, 1972; *Selected Essays of John Crowe Ransom*, ed. Thomas Daniel Young and John Hindle, 1984; *Selected Letters of John Crowe Ransom*, ed. Thomas Daniel Young and George Core, 1985.

John L. Stewart, *John Crowe Ransom*, 1962; Karl F. Knight, *The Poetry of John Crowe Ransom*, 1964; Robert Buffington, *The Equilibrist: A Study of John Crowe Ransom's Poems, 1916–1963*, 1967; Thomas Daniel Young, ed., *John Crowe Ransom: Critical Essays and a Bibliography*, 1968; Thornton H. Parsons, *John Crowe Ransom*, 1969; Karl F. Knight, *The Poetry of John Crowe Ransom: A Study of Diction, Metaphor, and Symbol*, 1971; James E. Magner, Jr., *John Crowe Ransom*, 1971; Miller Williams, *The Poetry of John Crowe Ransom*, 1972; Thomas Daniel Young, *Gentleman in a Dustcoat: A Biography of John Crowe Ransom*, 1976; Thomas Daniel Young, *John Crowe Ransom: An Annotated Bibliography*, 1982.

TEXT

Selected Poems, 1969.

Dead Boy

The little cousin is dead, by foul subtraction,
A green bough from Virginia's aged tree,
And none of the county kin like the transaction,
Nor some of the world of outer dark, like me.

A boy not beautiful, nor good, nor clever,   5
A black cloud full of storms too hot for keeping,
A sword beneath his mother's heart—yet never
Woman bewept her babe as this is weeping.

A pig with a pasty face, so I had said,
Squealing for cookies, kinned by poor pretense   10
With a noble house. But the little man quite dead,
I see the forbears' antique lineaments.

The elder men have strode by the box of death
To the wide flag porch, and muttering low send round
The bruit[1] of the day. O friendly waste of breath!   15
Their hearts are hurt with a deep dynastic wound.

He was pale and little, the foolish neighbors say;
The first-fruits, saith the Preacher, the Lord hath taken;
But this was the old tree's late branch wrenched away,
Grieving the sapless limbs, the shorn and shaken.   20

1920, 1927

Spectral Lovers

By night they haunted a thicket of April mist,
Out of that black ground suddenly come to birth,
Else angels lost in each other and fallen on earth.
Lovers they knew they were, but why unclasped, unkissed?
Why should two lovers be frozen apart in fear?   5
And yet they were, they were.

---

[1]Rumor (archaic).

Over the shredding of an April blossom
Scarcely her fingers touched him, quick with care,
Yet of evasions even she made a snare.
The heart was bold that clanged within her bosom,   10
The moment perfect, the time stopped for them,
Still her face turned from him.

Strong were the batteries of the April night
And the stealthy emanations of the field;
Should the walls of her prison undefended yield   15
And open her treasure to the first clamorous knight?
"This is the mad moon, and shall I surrender all?
If he but ask it I shall."

And gesturing largely to the moon of Easter,
Mincing his steps and swishing the jubilant grass,   20
Beheading some field-flowers that had come to pass,
He had reduced his tributaries faster
Had not considerations pinched his heart
Unfitly for his art.

"Do I reel with the sap of April like a drunkard?   25
Blessed is he that taketh this richest of cities;
But it is so stainless the sack were a thousand pities.
This is that marble fortress not to be conquered,
Lest its white peace in the black flame turn to tinder
And an unutterable cinder."   30

They passed me once in April, in the mist.
No other season is it when one walks and discovers
Two tall and wandering, like spectral lovers,
White in the season's moon-gold and amethyst,
Who touch quick fingers fluttering like a bird   35
Whose songs shall never be heard.

1923, 1924

Bells for John Whiteside's Daughter

There was such speed in her little body,
And such lightness in her footfall,
It is no wonder her brown study[1]
Astonishes us all.

Her wars were bruited in our high window.   5
We looked among orchard trees and beyond
Where she took arms against her shadow,
Or harried unto the pond

The lazy geese, like a snow cloud
Dripping their snow on the green grass,   10
Tricking and stopping, sleepy and proud,
Who cried in goose, Alas,

---

[1]Reverie, deep absorption in thought.

For the tireless heart within the little
Lady with rod that made them rise
From their noon apple-dreams and scuttle   15
Goose-fashion under the skies!

But now go the bells, and we are ready,
In one house we are sternly stopped
To say we are vexed at her brown study,
Lying so primly propped.   20

                                                    1924

Piazza Piece

—I am a gentleman in a dustcoat trying
To make you hear. Your ears are soft and small
And listen to an old man not at all,
They want the young men's whispering and sighing.
But see the roses on your trellis dying   5
And hear the spectral singing of the moon;
For I must have my lovely lady soon,
I am a gentleman in a dustcoat trying.

—I am a lady young in beauty waiting
Until my truelove comes, and then we kiss.   10
But what grey man among the vines is this
Whose words are dry and faint as in a dream?
Back from my trellis, Sir, before I scream!
I am a lady young in beauty waiting.

                                                    1925, 1927

Janet Waking

Beautifully Janet slept
Till it was deeply morning. She woke then
And thought about her dainty-feathered hen,
To see how it had kept.

One kiss she gave her mother.   5
Only a small one gave she to her daddy
Who would have kissed each curl of his shining baby;
No kiss at all for her brother.

"Old Chucky, old Chucky!" she cried,
Running across the world upon the grass   10
To Chucky's house, and listening. But alas,
Her Chucky had died.

It was a transmogrifying bee
Came droning down on Chucky's old bald head
And sat and put the poison. It scarcely bled,   15
But how exceedingly

And purply did the knot
Swell with the venom and communicate
Its rigor! Now the poor comb stood up straight
But Chucky did not.   20

So there was Janet
Kneeling on the wet grass, crying her brown hen
(Translated far beyond the daughters of men)
To rise and walk upon it.

And weeping fast as she had breath   25
Janet implored us, "Wake her from her sleep!"
And would not be instructed in how deep
Was the forgetful kingdom of death.

                                          1925, 1927

The Equilibrists[1]

Full of her long white arms and milky skin
He had a thousand times remembered sin.
Alone in the press of people traveled he,
Minding her jacinth, and myrrh, and ivory.

Mouth he remembered: the quaint orifice   5
From which came heat that flamed upon the kiss,
Till cold words came down spiral from the head,
Grey doves from the officious tower illsped.

Body: it was a white field ready for love,
On her body's field, with the gaunt tower above,   10
The lilies grew, beseeching him to take,
If he would pluck and wear them, bruise and break.

Eyes talking: Never mind the cruel words,
Embrace my flowers, but not embrace the swords.
But what they said, the doves came straightway flying   15
And unsaid: Honor, Honor, they came crying.

Importunate her doves. Too pure, too wise,
Clambering on his shoulder, saying, Arise,
Leave me now, and never let us meet,
Eternal distance now command thy feet.   20

Predicament indeed, which thus discovers
Honor among thieves, Honor between lovers.
O such a little word is Honor, they feel!
But the grey word is between them cold as steel.

At length I saw these lovers fully were come   25
Into their torture of equilibrium;
Dreadfully had forsworn each other, and yet
They were bound each to each, and they did not forget.

---

[1]Acrobats or tightrope walkers.

And rigid as two painful stars, and twirled
About the clustered night their prison world,   30
They burned with fierce love always to come near,
But Honor beat them back and kept them clear.

Ah, the strict lovers, they are ruined now!
I cried in anger. But with puddled brow
Devising for those gibbeted and brave   35
Came I descanting: Man, what would you have?

For spin your period out, and draw your breath,
A kinder sæculum[2] begins with Death.
Would you ascend to Heaven and bodiless dwell?
Or take your bodies honorless to Hell?   40

In Heaven you have heard no marriage is,[3]
No white flesh tinder to your lecheries,
Your male and female tissue sweetly shaped
Sublimed away, and furious blood escaped.

Great lovers lie in Hell, the stubborn ones   45
Infatuate of the flesh upon the bones;
Stuprate,[4] they rend each other when they kiss,
The pieces kiss again, no end to this.

But still I watched them spinning, orbited nice.
Their flames were not more radiant than their ice.   50
I dug in the quiet earth and wrought the tomb
And made these lines to memorize their doom: —

EPITAPH

Equilibrists lie here; stranger, tread light;
Close, but untouching in each other's sight;
Mouldered the lips and ashy the tall skull.   55
Let them lie perilous and beautiful.

1925, 1927

ALLEN TATE
(1899–1979)

In an essay published in 1968, "Poetry Modern and Unmodern," Allen Tate revealed his preference for classical form:

> Formal versification is the primary structure of poetic order, the assurance to the reader and to the poet himself that the poet is in control of the disorder both outside him and within his own mind. Here is a theoretical difficulty that I cannot deal with any better than I could have dealt with it forty years ago. Yet is

---

[2]"Era" (Latin).
[3]Cf. Matthew 22:30.
[4]To stuprate (obsolete) is to violate or ravish (especially a woman); thus the lovers claw and tear each other, bent on their own individual pleasure.

not much of the so-called poetry of the past twenty or more years merely anti-poetry, a parasite on the body of positive poetry, without significance except that it reminds us that poetry can be written, or has been written?

Tate's conservatism was a part of his southern heritage. He was born John Orley Allen Tate in Clark County, Kentucky. He entered Vanderbilt University in 1918, at a time of great intellectual ferment. Tate's roommate was Robert Penn Warren, and he took courses with John Crowe Ransom. Ransom gathered Tate and Warren into the group called the "Fugitives," which met regularly to read and discuss their poems. For a time Tate helped to edit *The Fugitive* and published his first poems there under the pen name "Henry Feathertop."

After graduation in 1923, Tate headed for New York to make his way, by hook or crook, as a writer, or even as a man of letters. One of his jobs was writing for the quasi-pornographic magazine *Telling Tales* (competitor of *Snappy Stories*). In 1924 he married the novelist Caroline Gordon, and for a time they settled into a house in Patterson, New York. There Hart Crane came to stay and learn from Tate; he left after a quarrel over housekeeping, but the two continued an important relationship. The Tates soon moved back to New York, in Greenwich Village.

In 1928, Tate published *Mr. Pope and Other Poems*. The poetry, written in traditional stanzaic form, was difficult and the readers few. This same year Tate published *Stonewall Jackson: The Good Soldier*, his biography of the Confederate general who was killed in battle in the middle of the Civil War. The following year (1929), Tate published the biography of another southern hero who had served as president of the Confederate States of America: *Jefferson Davis: His Rise and Fall*. And to set the seal on his southern identity, Tate joined with other southerners in 1930 in writing an essay for *I'll Take My Stand: The South and the Agrarian Tradition by Twelve Southerners*.

Tate published *Poems, 1928–1931* in 1932 and *The Mediterranean and Other Poems* in 1936. In his *Selected Poems*, published in 1937, he exercised a severe self-criticism, keeping less than half the poems from his 1928 volume, most of the 1932 volume, and all of the 1936 volume. In his Preface to the 1937 *Selected Poems*, he stated that he had worked on "Ode to the Confederate Dead," his most famous and frequently anthologized poem, for some ten years. The revised, final version appeared in this selection. One of his associates from Vanderbilt days, Donald Davidson, wrote to him about the "Ode": "Your 'Elegy' is not for the Confederate dead but for your own dead emotion." Tate himself, in 1938, provided a detailed analysis of the poem in "Narcissus as Narcissus," asserting at the beginning, "I do not know its obscure origins." Tate would say later that all his poems "were about the suffering that comes from disbelief."

For a time Tate served as editor of *Hound and Horn* (1932–34), and later for *The Sewanee Review* (1944–46). In 1943–44, he held the chair of poetry in the Library of Congress. In 1951 he was appointed Professor of English at the University of Minnesota, retiring in 1968. He had converted to Catholicism in 1950 but did not always observe its personal restrictions. He divorced Caroline Gordon in 1959 and married the poet Isabella Gardner that same year. In 1966 he again divorced and remarried.

Tate published one novel, *The Fathers* (1938), and innumerable critical essays. His *Reactionary Essays on Poetry and Ideas* was published in 1936. Other volumes include *Reason in Madness* (1941), *On the Limits of Poetry: Selected Essays 1928–1948* (1948), and *The Forlorn Demon: Didactic and Critical Essays* (1953). A comprehensive collection, *Essays of Four Decades*, appeared in 1968.

Tate's poetry might be described as traditionalist or formalist, but with some linguistic elements of modernism incorporated. Tate could never use slang, like Pound, or music hall ribaldries, like Eliot, or a colloquial folksiness, like Williams. But he could pare his language to the bone, rendering it lean and hard, and achieving a stately eloquence, as in the opening of his "Ode":

> Row after row with strict impunity,
> The headstones yield their names to the elements,
> The wind whirrs without recollection. . . .

ADDITIONAL READING

The Republic of Letters in America: The Correspondence of John Peale Bishop and Allen Tate, ed. Thomas D. Young and John J. Hindle, 1981; *The Poetry Reviews of Allen Tate, 1924–1944*, ed. Ashley Brown and Frances Neel Cheney, 1983.

R. K. Meiners, *The Last Alternative: A Study of the Works of Allen Tate*, 1963; George Hemphill, *Allen Tate*, 1964; Ferman Bishop, *Allen Tate*, 1967; M. E. Bradford, *Rumors of Mortality: An Introduction to Allen Tate*, 1969; Radcliffe Squires, *Allen Tate: A Literary Biography*, 1971; Radcliffe Squires, ed., *Allen Tate and His Work: Critical Evaluations*, 1972; Robert S. Dupree, *Allen Tate and the Augustinian Imagination*, 1983; Walter Sullivan, *Allen Tate: A Recollection*, 1988.

TEXT

Collected Poems, 1919–1976, 1977.

For a Dead Citizen

He was the finest of our happy men;
He had all joys, he never thought of death;
He fiddled sometimes with his mind, and then
Shook off the tremor like a nervous wren —
Just once or twice I saw him catch his breath.   5

Or in the shimmering clatter of the streets,
Or shaking hands, or tying his cravat,
He was the quick intelligent fool one meets
Without an afterthought of charnel sheets:
He never looked at things as This or That.   10

I saw him once again. It was too late;
His pretty wife was sad; I didn't know
For I was out of town and it was fate
That the indifferent message of that date
Should be a death, the embarrassing dumb show.   15

There at the church they took him through the door,
His sweet wide mouth much as it was before,
And some said, bitterly bitterly wept his whore.

1924, 1928

Light

Last night I fled until I came
To streets where leaking casements dripped
Stale lamplight from the corpse of flame;
A nervous window bled.

The moon swagged in the air.   5
Out of the mist a girl tossed
Spittle of song; a hoarse light
Spattered the fog with heavy hair.

Damp bells in a remote tower
Sharply released the throat of God,   10
I leaned to the erect night
Dead as stiff turf in winter sod.

Then with the careless energy
Of a dream, the forward curse
Of a cold particular eye   15
In the headlong hearse.

1924, 1928

Sonnets at Christmas

I

This is the day His hour of life draws near,
Let me get ready from head to foot for it
Most handily with eyes to pick the year
For small feed to reward a feathered wit.
Some men would see it an epiphany   5
At ease, at food and drink, others at chase;
Yet I, stung lassitude, with ecstasy
Unspent argue the season's difficult case
So: Man, dull creature of enormous head,
What would he look at in the coiling sky?   10
But I must kneel again unto the Dead
While Christmas bells of paper white and red,
Figured with boys and girls spilt from a sled,
Ring out the silence I am nourished by.

II

Ah, Christ, I love you rings to the wild sky   15
And I must think a little of the past:
When I was ten I told a stinking lie
That got a black boy whipped; but now at last
The going years, caught in an after-glow,

Reverse like balls englished upon green baize[1] —   20
Let them return, let the round trumpets blow
The ancient crackle of the Christ's deep gaze.
Deafened and blind, with senses yet unfound,
Am I, untutored to the after-wit
Of knowledge, knowing a nightmare has no sound;   25
Therefore with idle hands and head I sit
In late December before the fire's daze
Punished by crimes of which I would be quit.

                                                        1934, 1936

Ode to the Confederate Dead[1]

Row after row with strict impunity
The headstones yield their names to the element,
The wind whirrs without recollection;
In the riven troughs the splayed leaves
Pile up, of nature the casual sacrament   5
To the seasonal eternity of death;
Then driven by the fierce scrutiny
Of heaven to their election in the vast breath,
They sough the rumour of mortality.

Autumn is desolation in the plot   10
Of a thousand acres where these memories grow
From the inexhaustible bodies that are not
Dead, but feed the grass row after rich row.
Think of the autumns that have come and gone! —
Ambitious November with the humors of the year,   15
With a particular zeal for every slab,
Staining the uncomfortable angels that rot
On the slabs, a wing chipped here, an arm there:
The brute curiosity of an angel's stare
Turns you, like them, to stone,   20
Transforms the heaving air
Till plunged to a heavier world below
You shift your sea-space blindly
Heaving, turning like the blind crab.[2]

---

[1]Green felt cover on a pool table; to "english" a ball is to cause it to spin by striking one side or releasing it with a sharp twist.

[1]Tate has written an extensive analysis of this poem in his essay "Narcissus as Narcissus," in which he says the poem "is 'about' solipsism, a philosophical doctrine which says that we create the world in the act of perceiving it; or about Narcissism, or any other *ism* that denotes the failure of the human personality to function objectively in nature and society." Tate adds: "Narcissism and the Confederate dead cannot be connected logically, or even historically. . . . The proof of the connection must lie, if anywhere, in the experienced conflict which is the poem itself."

[2]Tate's comment: "The structure of the Ode is simple. Figure to yourself a man stopping at the gate of a Confederate graveyard on a late autumn afternoon. The leaves are falling; his first impressions bring him the 'rumor of mortality'; and the desolation barely allows him, at the beginning of the second stanza, the conventionally heroic surmise that the dead will enrich the earth, 'where these memories grow.' From those quoted words to the end of that passage he pauses for a baroque meditation on the ravages of time, concluding with the figure of the 'blind crab.' This creature has mobility but no direction, energy but from the human point of view, no purposeful world to use it in: in the entire poem there are only two explicit symbols for the looked-in ego: the crab is the first and less explicit symbol, a mere hint, a planting of the idea that will become overt in its second instance — the jaguar towards the end. The crab is the first intimation of the nature of the moral conflict upon which the drama of the poem develops: the cut-off-ness of the modern 'intellectual man' from the world."

Dazed by the wind, only the wind   25
The leaves flying, plunge

You know who have waited by the wall
The twilight certainty of an animal,
Those midnight restitutions of the blood
You know—the immitigable pines, the smoky frieze   30
Of the sky, the sudden call: you know the rage,
The cold pool left by the mounting flood,
Of muted Zeno and Parmenides.³
You who have waited for the angry resolution
Of those desires that should be yours tomorrow,   35
You know the unimportant shrift of death
And praise the vision
And praise the arrogant circumstance
Of those who fall
Rank upon rank, hurried beyond decision—   40
Here by the sagging gate, stopped by the wall.⁴

         Seeing, seeing only the leaves
         Flying, plunge and expire

Turn your eyes to the immoderate past,
Turn to the inscrutable infantry rising   45
Demons out of the earth—they will not last.
Stonewall,⁵ Stonewall, and the sunken fields of hemp,
Shiloh, Antietam, Malvern Hill, Bull Run.⁶
Lost in that orient of the thick-and-fast
You will curse the setting sun.   50

         Cursing only the leaves crying
         Like an old man in a storm

You hear the shout, the crazy hemlocks point
With troubled fingers to the silence which
Smothers you, a mummy, in time.   55

                    The hound bitch
Toothless and dying, in a musty cellar
Hears the wind only.

                    Now that the salt of their blood
Stiffens the saltier oblivion of the sea,   60
Seals the malignant purity of the flood,

---

³Parmenides and his follower Zeno were fifth-century Greek philosophers who held that the universe was an unchanging whole and that mutability and motion were illusions.
⁴Tate's comment: "The next long passage or 'strophe' . . . states the other term of the conflict. It is the theme of heroism, not merely moral heroism, but heroism in the grand style, elevating even death from mere physical dissolution into a formal ritual: this heroism is a formal ebullience of the human spirit in an entire society, not private, romantic illusion—something better than moral heroism, great as that may be, for moral heroism being personal and individual, may be achieved by certain men in all ages, even ages of decadence. But the late Hart Crane's commentary, in a letter, is better than any I can make: he described the theme as the 'theme of chivalry, a tradition of excess (not literally excess, rather active faith) which cannot be perpetuated in the fragmentary cosmos of today—"those desires which should be yours tomorrow," but which, you know, will not persist nor find any way into action.'"
⁵Thomas Jonathan Jackson, known as "Stonewall" (1824–1863), skilled Confederate general who was killed in 1863 in a battle at Chancellorsville.
⁶Sites of crucial battles during the Civil War; the two battles of Bull Run in 1861 and 1862 were Confederate victories; the other battles listed, all in 1862, were unsuccessful for the Confederates.

What shall we who count our days and bow
Our heads with a commemorial woe
In the ribboned coats of grim felicity,
What shall we say of the bones, unclean,   65
Whose verdurous anonymity will grow?
The ragged arms, the ragged heads and eyes
Lost in these acres of the insane green?
The gray lean spiders come, they come and go;
In a tangle of willows without light   70
The singular screech-owl's tight
Invisible lyric seeds the mind
With the furious murmur of their chivalry.

       We shall say only the leaves
       Flying, plunge and expire   75

We shall say only the leaves whispering
In the improbable mist of nightfall
That flies on multiple wing;
Night is the beginning and the end
And in between the ends of distraction   80
Waits mute speculation, the patient curse
That stones the eyes, or like the jaguar leaps[7]
For his own image in a jungle pool, his victim.
What shall we say who have knowledge
Carried to the heart? Shall we take the act   85
To the grave? Shall we, more hopeful, set up the grave
In the house? The ravenous grave?

              Leave now
The shut gate and the decomposing wall:
The gentle serpent, green in the mulberry bush,   90
Riots with his tongue through the hush—
Sentinel of the grave who counts us all![8]

1926–36   *1928, 1937*

COUNTEE CULLEN

(1903–1946)

In a Foreword to an important anthology he edited in 1927, *Caroling Dusk: An Anthology of Verse by Negro Poets*, Countee Cullen said that he had deliberately avoided the term "Negro verse" in the subtitle because such a label would have been "more confusing than accurate." He added, "the attempt to corral the out-

---

[7]Tate's comment: "This figure of the jaguar is the only explicit rendering of the Narcissus motif in the poem, but instead of a youth gazing into a pool, a predatory beast stares at a jungle stream, and leaps to devour himself."
[8]Tate's comment: "The closing image, that of the serpent, is the ancient symbol of time, and I tried to give it the credibility of the commonplace by placing it in a mulberry bush—with the faint hope that the silkworm would somehow be implicit. But time is also death. If that is so, then space, or the Becoming, is life. . . ."

bursts of the ebony muse into some definite mold to which all poetry by Negroes will conform seems altogether futile and aside from the facts."

In this same volume he said of himself (writing in the third person): "As a poet [Cullen] is a rank conservative, loving the measured line and the skillful rhyme; but not blind to the virtues of those poets who will not be circumscribed. He has said perhaps with a reiteration sickening to some of his friends, that he wishes any merit that may be in his work to flow from it solely as the expression of a poet — with no racial consideration to bolster it up. He is still of the same thought."

This position of serene self-assurance Countee Cullen maintained throughout his brief career. It apparently was the source of both his strength and his weakness. According to recent scholarship, he was born in 1903 in Louisville, Kentucky (although he frequently cited his birthplace as New York). Little is known about his background until his adoption in 1918 by the Reverend and Mrs. Frederick A. Cullen, of Harlem's Salem Methodist Episcopal Church.

Cullen began writing poetry in elementary school. He attended De Witt Clinton High School in New York (where few students were black), and was vice-president of his senior class, as well as editor of the literary magazine, *The Magpie*. He began winning prizes for his poems in high school, and continued to do so during the period he attended New York University (1922–25), where he was elected to Phi Beta Kappa. The year of his graduation (1925), he won second prize for "To One Who Said Me Nay" in the Literary Contest of *Opportunity: A Journal of Negro Life* (Langston Hughes won first prize with "The Weary Blues"); and he won the John Reed Memorial Prize, given by *Poetry* magazine, for "Threnody for a Brown Girl." This same year, he published his first — and perhaps his best — book of poems, *Color*. After taking an M.A. from Harvard, Cullen went to work for *Opportunity* as assistant editor, writing a column called "The Dark Tower." In 1927, he won the Harmon Foundation Literary Award (a special award for black achievement in the arts). And he published his second volume of poems, *Copper Sun*. He was awarded a Guggenheim Fellowship in 1928.

Before going to Europe, Cullen married Yolande DuBois, daughter of W. E. B. DuBois, in a spectacular ceremony at the Salem Methodist Episcopal Church, with his father presiding. There were sixteen bridesmaids, 1,300 invited guests, and countless spectators. Cullen's best man was his lifetime friend and companion Harold Jackman, a West Indian black. The marriage turned out to be a mistake. Two months after the wedding, Cullen went to Europe not with his bride but with his best man. A divorce was arranged in 1930. Recent biographical accounts have speculated, persuasively, that Cullen was probably homosexual. But he married again in 1940 and the marriage lasted until his death in 1946.

From 1934 until he died, Cullen taught French and English at the Frederick Douglass Junior High School in Harlem. In spite of the demands of teaching, Cullen continued to write and publish. He had published *The Ballad of the Brown Girl: An Old Ballad Retold* in 1927 and *The Black Christ and Other Poems* in 1929. This was followed by *The Medea, and Some Poems* in 1937, and the posthumously published *On These I Stand: An Anthology of the Best Poems of Countee Cullen* in 1947 (he made the selection and arrangement before he died).

In addition to these works, Cullen published a Harlem novel, *One Way to Heaven*, in 1932. He wrote two volumes of light verse for children: *The Lost Zoo (A Rhyme for the Young, But Not too Young) by Christopher Cat and Countee Cullen* (1940) and *My Lives and How I Lost Them by Christopher Cat in Collaboration with Countee Cullen* (1942).

Countee Cullen followed his love of the "measured line and the skillful rhyme" to the end, and did not experiment, as did other black poets such as Langston Hughes, with verse in the black idiom or blues rhythms. But he wrote many poems on the theme of "color," some of them with biting wit, as in one of his "Epitaphs," "For a Lady I Know":

> She even thinks that up in heaven
> Her class lies late and snores,
> While poor black cherubs rise at seven
> To do celestial chores.

He followed his instincts, however, to write not simply as a black poet who was confined to one theme (color) but as a poet who happened to be black, with complete freedom to write about faith, death, or any other matter that engaged his mind and emotions. The British romantic poet John Keats was the poet he most deeply admired. Thus it was that he could conclude "Yet Do I Marvel," his most widely read poem, with a line Langston Hughes could never have written: "Yet do I marvel at this curious thing: / To make a poet black, and bid him sing!"

ADDITIONAL READING

Helen J. Dinger, *A Study of Countee Cullen*, 1953; Stephen H. Bronz, *Roots of Negro Racial Consciousness — The 1920's: Three Harlem Renaissance Authors*, 1954; Blanche E. Ferguson, *Countee Cullen and the Negro Renaissance*, 1966; Margeret Perry, *A Bio-Bibliography of Countée P. Cullen*, 1971; Darwin T. Turner, *In a Minor Chord: Three Afro-American Writers and Their Search for Identity*, 1971; Houston A. Baker, Jr., *A Many-Colored Coat of Dreams: The Poetry of Countee Cullen*, 1974; Alan R. Shucard, *Countee Cullen*, 1984; Victor A. Kramer, ed., *The Harlem Renaissance Re-examined*, 1987.

TEXT

On These I Stand: An Anthology of the Best Poems of Countee Cullen, 1947.

Yet Do I Marvel

> I doubt not God is good, well-meaning, kind,
> And did He stoop to quibble could tell why
> The little buried mole continues blind,
> Why flesh that mirrors Him must some day die,
> Make plain the reason tortured Tantalus[1]   5
> Is baited by the fickle fruit, declare
> If merely brute caprice dooms Sisyphus[2]
> To struggle up a never-ending stair.
> Inscrutable His ways are, and immune
> To catechism by a mind too strewn   10
> With petty cares to slightly understand
> What awful brain compels His awful hand.

---

[1]Tantalus suffers hunger and thirst in Hades, perpetually tantalized by a lake that dries up when he bends near and fruit that withdraws at his reach.

[2]In Hades Sisyphus is condemned to roll up a hill a huge stone that perpetually rolls down again each time.

Yet do I marvel at this curious thing:
To make a poet black, and bid him sing!

1924, 1925

From the Dark Tower

(TO CHARLES S. JOHNSON)[1]

We shall not always plant while others reap
The golden increment of bursting fruit,
Not always countenance, abject and mute,
That lesser men should hold their brothers cheap;
Not everlastingly while others sleep   5
Shall we beguile their limbs with mellow flute,
Not always bend to some more subtle brute;
We were not made eternally to weep.

The night whose sable breast relieves the stark,
White stars is no less lovely being dark,   10
And there are buds that cannot bloom at all
In light, but crumple, piteous, and fall;
So in the dark we hide the heart that bleeds,
And wait, and tend our agonizing seeds.

1924, 1927

Incident

(FOR ERIC WALROND)[1]

Once riding in old Baltimore,
    Heart-filled, head-filled with glee,
I saw a Baltimorean
    Keep looking straight at me.

Now I was eight and very small,   5
    And he was no whit bigger,
And so I smiled, but he poked out
    His tongue, and called me, "Nigger."

I saw the whole of Baltimore
    From May until December;   10
Of all the things that happened there
    That's all that I remember.

1924, 1925

---

[1]Charles S. Johnson (1893–1956), educator, editor, and one of the prime movers of the Harlem Renaissance; he founded *Opportunity: A Journal of Negro Life* in 1923 and edited it until 1928.

[1]Eric Walrond (1898–1966), black fiction writer and essayist; his protest article, "On Being Black" (1922), recounted the kinds of discrimination he had experienced.

Heritage

(FOR HAROLD JACKMAN)[1]

What is Africa to me:
Copper sun or scarlet sea,
Jungle star or jungle track,
Strong bronzed men, or regal black
Women from whose loins I sprang   5
When the birds of Eden sang?
One three centuries removed
From the scenes his fathers loved,
Spicy grove, cinnamon tree,
What is Africa to me?   10

So I lie, who all day long
Want no sound except the song
Sung by wild barbaric birds
Goading massive jungle herds,
Juggernauts of flesh that pass   15
Trampling tall defiant grass
Where young forest lovers lie,
Plighting troth beneath the sky.
So I lie, who always hear,
Though I cram against my ear   20
Both my thumbs, and keep them there,
Great drums throbbing through the air.
So I lie, whose fount of pride,
Dear distress, and joy allied,
Is my somber flesh and skin,   25
With the dark blood dammed within
Like great pulsing tides of wine
That, I fear, must burst the fine
Channels of the chafing net
Where they surge and foam and fret.   30

Africa? A book one thumbs
Listlessly, till slumber comes.
Unremembered are her bats
Circling through the night, her cats
Crouching in the river reeds,   35
Stalking gentle flesh that feeds
By the river brink; no more
Does the bugle-throated roar
Cry that monarch claws have leapt
From the scabbards where they slept.   40
Silver snakes that once a year
Doff the lovely coats you wear,
Seek no covert in your fear
Lest a mortal eye should see;
What's your nakedness to me?   45
Here no leprous flowers rear
Fierce corollas[2] in the air;
Here no bodies sleek and wet,

---

[1]Harold Jackman (*c.* 1900–1960) a West Indian black and   1928.
Cullen's close friend who accompanied him to Europe in   [2]The petals, or inner leaves, of a flower.

Dripping mingled rain and sweat,
Tread the savage measures of   50
Jungle boys and girls in love.
What is last year's snow to me,[3]
Last year's anything? The tree
Budding yearly must forget
How its past arose or set—   55
Bough and blossom, flower, fruit,
Even what shy bird with mute
Wonder at her travail there,
Meekly labored in its hair.
One three centuries removed   60
From the scenes his fathers loved,
Spicy grove, cinnamon tree,
What is Africa to me?

So I lie, who find no peace
Night or day, no slight release   65
From the unremittant beat
Made by cruel padded feet
Walking through my body's street.
Up and down they go, and back,
Treading out a jungle track.   70
So I lie, who never quite
Safely sleep from rain at night—
I can never rest at all
When the rain begins to fall;
Like a soul gone mad with pain   75
I must match its weird refrain;
Ever must I twist and squirm,
Writhing like a baited worm,
While its primal measures drip
Through my body, crying, "Strip!   80
Doff this new exuberance.
Come and dance the Lover's Dance!"
In an old remembered way
Rain works on me night and day.

Quaint, outlandish heathen gods   85
Black men fashion out of rods,
Clay, and brittle bits of stone,
In a likeness like their own,
My conversion came high-priced;
I belong to Jesus Christ,   90
Preacher of humility;
Heathen gods are naught to me.

Father, Son, and Holy Ghost,
So I make an idle boast;
Jesus of the twice-turned cheek,[4]   95
Lamb of God, although I speak
With my mouth thus, in my heart
Do I play a double part.
Ever at Thy glowing altar
Must my heart grow sick and falter,   100

---

[3]Cf. "Where are the snows of yesteryear," a refrain from a ballad by French poet François Villon (1431–1463?).

[4]See Matthew 5:39: "Whosoever shall smite thee on thy right cheek, turn to him the other also."

Wishing He I served were black,
Thinking then it would not lack
Precedent of pain to guide it,
Let who would or might deride it;
Surely then this flesh would know   105
Yours had borne a kindred woe.
Lord, I fashion dark gods, too,
Daring even to give You
Dark despairing features where,
Crowned with dark rebellious hair,   110
Patience wavers just so much as
Mortal grief compels, while touches
Quick and hot, of anger, rise
To smitten cheek and weary eyes.
Lord, forgive me if my need   115
Sometimes shapes a human creed.
All day long and all night through,
One thing only must I do:
Quench my pride and cool my blood,
Lest I perish in the flood.   120
Lest a hidden ember set
Timber that I thought was wet
Burning like the dryest flax,
Melting like the merest wax,
Lest the grave restore its dead.   125
Not yet has my heart or head
In the least way realized
They and I are civilized.

                                                  1925

To Certain Critics

Then call me traitor if you must,
Shout treason and default!
Say I betray a sacred trust
Aching beyond this vault.
I'll bear your censure as your praise,   5
For never shall the clan
Confine my singing to its ways
Beyond the ways of man.

No racial option narrows grief,
Pain is no patriot,   10
And sorrow plaits her dismal leaf
For all as lief as not.
With blind sheep groping every hill,
Searching an oriflamme,[1]
How shall the shepherd heart then thrill   15
To only the darker lamb?

                                                  1929

---

[1] Inspirational banner or standard.

THE NEW DRAMA

SUSAN GLASPELL   THORNTON WILDER
EUGENE O'NEILL

"The playwright today must dig at the roots of the sickness of today as he feels it—the death of the Old God and the failure of science and materialism to give any satisfying new One for the surviving primitive religious instinct to find a meaning for life in, and to comfort its fears of death with. It seems to me that anyone trying to do big work nowadays must have this big subject behind all the little subjects of his plays or novels, or he is simply scribbling around on the surface of things and has no more real status than a parlor entertainer."

Eugene O'Neill, letter to George Jean Nathan in Intimate Notebooks, 1932

SUSAN GLASPELL
(1876–1948)

"We were supposed to be a sort of 'special' group—radical, wild. . . . Most of us were from families who had other ideas—who wanted to make money." Thus Susan Glaspell spoke of the bohemian group involved with her in the founding and nurturing of the Provincetown Players in 1915 in Provincetown, Massachusetts. She was not only a pioneer, there at the beginning of the modern resuscitation of American drama, but went on to be hailed as "the playwright of woman's selfhood." She had travelled a long distance, both physically and psychologically, from the Middle West where she grew up.

She was born into a middle-class family in the Mississippi River town of Davenport, Iowa, in 1876 (not in 1882 as commonly thought, according to her biographer Arthur Waterman). She was something of a star in high school in Davenport, and worked for a time as a reporter on a Davenport newspaper. She later attended Drake University in Des Moines, and after graduation in 1899 she became a reporter on the *Des Moines Daily News*, covering state politics and the courts (including murder trials) for some two years. Ambitious to become a writer, she threw over her job, returned to Davenport, and devoted herself to writing fiction. She was immediately successful in placing her short stories in the popular magazines, and she published her first novel, *The Glory of the Conquered: The Story of a Great Love*, in 1909. *Lifted Masks*, a collection of her stories, appeared in 1912.

In the meantime she had come to know a radical young man with literary ambitions (and an Iowan like herself), George Cram Cook, who was sympathetic with her free spirit and appreciative of her talent. They set out for Europe in 1909 with the disapproval of their families: he was in his second marriage, with children. Glaspell and "Jig" Cook were married in 1913 in New Jersey, and were soon settled in Provincetown, Massachusetts, where they began to collaborate in the writing of drama. They helped establish the Provincetown Players there in 1915, producing plays in a fish house on a wharf, called the Wharf Theatre (or Provincetown Playhouse). The group soon had another theater in Greenwich Village. In the next few years, American drama flourished under the auspices of the Provincetown Players. Among the people associated with the Players were the radical John Reed, the poet Edna St. Vincent Millay, and the talented young playwright Eugene O'Neill.

Glaspell was asked to write a play to accompany O'Neill's one-act drama, *Bound East for Cardiff*, scheduled for production by the Provincetown Players in 1916. She recalled later her perplexity: "I went out on the wharf, sat alone on one of our wooden benches without a back, and looked for a long time at that bare little stage. After a time, the stage became a kitchen—a kitchen there all by itself. I saw just where the stove was, the table, and the steps going upstairs. Then the door at the back opened, and people all bundled up came in—two or three men, I wasn't sure which, but sure enough about the two women, who hung back, reluctant to enter that kitchen." Thus *Trifles* came into being, portraying the diminished lives of rural women surrounded by insensitive men, somewhat in the tradition of the fiction of earlier regional realists like Mary E. Wilkins Freeman and Hamlin Garland.

Trifles is a remarkably effective play and is now often cited as Glaspell's best work. She turned it into a short story entitled "Jury of Her Peers," which was selected for *The Best Short Stories of 1917*. For a time she continued to write successful one-act plays, including *Close the Book* (1917), *The Outside* (1917), and *Woman's Honor* (1918). Beginning in 1919 with *Bernice*, Glaspell began to write full-length plays, and followed with *The Inheritors* and *The Verge*, both produced in 1921. None of these gave her the satisfaction of success for which she was hoping. She wrote a succession of plays, but it was not until *Alison's House* (produced in 1930), inspired in part by episodes in the life of Emily Dickinson, that Glaspell won critical acclaim with the Pulitzer Prize, awarded in 1931.

After the professional theater world of New York had in effect taken over the experimental drama in which they had pioneered, Glaspell and her husband retreated to Greece—the land of drama's beginnings—to live in 1922. It was there that Cook suddenly died in 1924. The next year, Glaspell married Norman Matson, and collaborated with her new husband in writing drama. But much of her time she devoted to the writing of a biography of George Cram Cook, *The Road to the Temple*, published in London in 1926. Later she returned to her earlier interest in the writing of fiction, producing a succession of novels, including *Brook Evans* (1928), *The Morning Is Near Us* (1940), *Norma Ashe* (1942), and *Judd Rankin's Daughter* (1945). Although a number of her nine novels were popular successes, one becoming a movie and another becoming a Literary Guild selection, her fiction was not as innovative or experimental as her drama.

Today Glaspell is primarily remembered for her one-act play *Trifles*. One critic, C. W. E. Bigsby, has commented on its seemingly simple and artless construction: "Not the least remarkable aspect of *Trifles* is the extent to which Susan Glaspell herself makes the slightest of dramatic forms carry such a burden of meaning. Understatement proves as effective a strategy for her as it was to be for Hemingway. Just as the principal characters never make an appearance, so the crucial revelations of the play are never fully voiced: reticence becomes a style as well as a subject." In the revolution just beginning to take place in American drama, *Trifles* in 1916 played a significant role in breaking new ground both in subject and technique.

ADDITIONAL READING

Plays, 1920; *A Road to the Temple* (Glaspell's biography of George Cram Cook), 1926.

Helen Deutsch and Stella Hanau, *The Provincetown: A Story of the Theatre*, 1931; Arthur Waterman, *Susan Glaspell*, 1966; C. W. E. Bigsby, "Introduction," *Plays by Susan Glaspell*, ed. Bigsby, 1987.

TEXT

Trifles, 1916.

Trifles

A PLAY IN ONE ACT

CHARACTERS

GEORGE HENDERSON,   [*County Attorney*]
HENRY PETERS,   [*Sheriff*]
LEWIS HALE,   [*A Neighboring Farmer*]

MRS. PETERS
MRS. HALE

SCENE: The kitchen in the now abandoned farmhouse of John Wright, a gloomy kitchen, plainly left without having been put in order — unwashed pans under the sink, a loaf of bread outside the bread-box, a dish-towel on the table — other signs of incompleted work. Door opens rear and enter sheriff followed by county attorney and Hale. The sheriff and Hale are men in middle life, the county attorney is a young man; all are much bundled up and go at once to the stove. They are followed by the two women — the sheriff's wife first; she is a slight wiry woman, a thin nervous face. Mrs. Hale is larger and would ordinarily be called more comfortable looking, but she is disturbed now and looks fearfully about as she enters. The women have come in slowly, and stand close together near the door.

COUNTY ATTORNEY: *(Rubbing his hands)* This feels good. Come up to the fire, 10
ladies.

MRS. PETERS: *(Takes a step forward and looks around)* I'm not — cold.

SHERIFF: *(Unbuttoning his overcoat and stepping away from the stove as if to mark the beginning of official business)* Now, Mr. Hale, before we move things about, you explain to Mr. Henderson just what you saw when you came here yesterday morning.

COUNTY ATTORNEY: By the way, has anything been moved? Are things just as you left them yesterday?

SHERIFF: *(Looking all about)* It's just the same. When it dropped below zero last night I thought I'd better send Frank out this morning to make a fire for us — 20
no use getting pneumonia with a big case on, but I told him not to touch anything except the stove — and you know Frank.

COUNTY ATTORNEY: Somebody should have been left here yesterday.

SHERIFF: Oh — yesterday. When I had to send Frank to Morris Center for that man who went crazy — I want you to know I had my hands full yesterday. I knew you could get back from Omaha by today and as long as I went over everything here myself——

COUNTY ATTORNEY: Well, Mr. Hale, tell just what happened when you came here yesterday morning.

HALE: Harry and I had started to town with a load of potatoes. We came along 30
the road from my place and as I got here I said, "I'm going to see if I can't get John Wright to go in with me on a party telephone. I spoke to Wright about it once before and he put me off, saying folks talked too much anyway, and all he asked was peace and quiet — I guess you know about how much he talked himself, but I thought maybe if I went to the house and talked about it before his wife, though I said to Harry that I didn't know as what his wife wanted made much difference to John —

COUNTY ATTORNEY: Let's talk about that later, Mr. Hale. I do want to talk about that, but tell now just what happened when you got to the house.

HALE: I didn't hear or see anything; I knocked at the door, and still it was all 40
quiet inside. I knew they must be up, it was past eight o'clock. So I knocked again, and I thought I heard somebody say "Come in." I wasn't sure, I'm not sure yet, but I opened the door — this door *(jerking a hand backward)* and there in that rocker — *(pointing to it)* sat Mrs. Wright. *(All look at the rocker)*

COUNTY ATTORNEY: What — was she doing?

HALE: She was rockin' back and forth. She had her apron in her hand and was kind of — pleating it.

COUNTY ATTORNEY: And how did she — look?

HALE: Well, she looked queer.

COUNTY ATTORNEY: How do you mean — queer?   50

HALE: Well, as if she didn't know what she was going to do next. And kind of done up.

COUNTY ATTORNEY: How did she seem to feel about your coming?

HALE: Why, I don't think she minded — one way or other. She didn't pay much attention. I said, "How do, Mrs. Wright, it's cold, ain't it?" And she said "Is it?" — and went on kind of pleating at her apron. Well, I was surprised; she didn't ask me to come up to the stove, or to set down, but just sat there, not even looking at me, so I said, "I want to see John." And then she — laughed. I guess you would call it a laugh. I thought of Harry and the team outside, so I said a little sharp: "Can't I see John?" "No," she says, kind o' dull like. "Ain't he   60 home?" says I. "Yes," says she, "he's home." "Then why can't I see him?" I asked her, out of patience. "'Cause he's dead," says she. *"Dead?"* says I. She just nodded her head, not getting a bit excited, but rockin' back and forth. "Why — where is he?" says I, not knowing what to say. She just pointed upstairs — like that *(himself pointing to the room above)* I got up, with the idea of going up there. I walked from there to here — *(pointing)* — then I says, "Why, what did he die of?" "He died of a rope around his neck," says she, and just went on pleatin' at her apron. Well, I went out and called Harry. I thought I might — need help. We went upstairs and there he was — lyin' —

COUNTY ATTORNEY: I think I'd rather have you go into that upstairs, where you   70 can point it all out. Just go on now with the rest of the story.

HALE: Well, my first thought was to get that rope off. It looked — *(stops, his face twitches)* — but Harry, he went up to him, and he said, "No, he's dead all right, and we'd better not touch anything." So we went back down stairs. She was still sitting that same way. "Has anybody been notified?" I asked. "No," says she, unconcerned. "Who did this, Mrs. Wright?" said Harry. He said it businesslike — and she stopped pleatin' of her apron. "I don't know," she says. "You don't *know?*" says Harry. "No," says she. "Weren't you sleepin' in the bed with him?" says Harry. "Yes," says she, "but I was on the inside." "Somebody slipped a rope round his neck and strangled him and you didn't wake up?" says Harry.   80 "I didn't wake up," she said after him. We may have looked as if we didn't see how that could be, for after a minute she said, "I sleep sound." Harry was going to ask her more questions but I said maybe we ought to let her tell her story first to the coroner, or the sheriff, so Harry went fast as he could to Rivers' place, where there's a telephone.

COUNTY ATTORNEY: And what did Mrs. Wright do when she knew that you had gone for the coroner?

HALE: She moved from that chair to this one over here, *(pointing to a small chair in the corner)* and just sat there with her hands held together and looking down. I got a feeling that I ought to make some conversation, so I said I had come in to   90 see if John wanted to put in a telephone, and at that she started to laugh, and then she stopped and looked at me — scared. *(County attorney, who has had his notebook out, makes a note)* I dunno, maybe it wasn't scared. I wouldn't like to say it was. Soon Harry got back, and then Dr. Lloyd came, and you, Mr. Peters, and so I guess that's all I know that you don't.

COUNTY ATTORNEY: *(Looking around)* I guess we'll go upstairs first — and then out to the barn and around there. *(To sheriff)* You're convinced that there was nothing important here — nothing that would point to any motive?

SHERIFF: Nothing here but kitchen things.

COUNTY ATTORNEY: *(Opens the door of a cupboard closet. Gets up on a chair and looks   100 on a shelf. Pulls his hand away, sticky)* Here's a nice mess. *(The women draw nearer)*

MRS. PETERS: Oh, her fruit; it did freeze. *(To County Attorney)* She worried about that when it turned so cold. She said the fire'd go out and her jars would break.

SHERIFF: Well, can you beat the women! Held for murder and worrying about her preserves.

COUNTY ATTORNEY: *(Setting his lips firmly)* I guess before we are through she may have something more serious than preserves to worry about.

HALE: Well, women are used to worrying over trifles. *(The two women move a little closer together)*

COUNTY ATTORNEY: *(With the gallantry of a young politician)* And yet, for all their worries, what would we do without the ladies? *(The women do not unbend. He goes to sink, takes a dipperful of water from pail and pouring it into basin, washes his hands. Starts to wipe them on roller-towel, turns it for a cleaner place)* Dirty towels! *(Kicks his foot against pans under the sink)* Not much of a housekeeper, would you say, ladies? 110

MRS. HALE: *(Stiffly)* There's a great deal of work to be done on a farm.

COUNTY ATTORNEY: *(With conciliation)* To be sure. And yet *(with a little bow to her)* I know there are some Dickson county farmhouses which do not have such roller towels. *(Gives it a pull to expose its full length again.)*

MRS. HALE: Those towels get dirty awful quick. Men's hands aren't always as clean as they might be. 120

COUNTY ATTORNEY: Ah, loyal to your sex, I see. But you and Mrs. Wright were neighbors. I suppose you were friends, too.

MRS. HALE: *(Shaking her head.)* I've not seen much of her of late years. I've not been in this house—it's more than a year.

COUNTY ATTORNEY: And why was that? You didn't like her?

MRS. HALE: I liked her all well enough. Farmer's wives have their hands full, Mr. Henderson. And then—

COUNTY ATTORNEY: Yes—?

MRS. HALE: *(Looking about.)* It never seemed a very cheerful place. 130

COUNTY ATTORNEY: No—it's not cheerful. I shouldn't say she had the home-making instinct.

MRS. HALE: Well, I don't know as Wright had, either.

COUNTY ATTORNEY: You mean that they didn't get on very well?

MRS. HALE: No, I don't mean anything. But I don't think a place'd be any cheer-fuller for John Wright's being in it.

COUNTY ATTORNEY: I'd like to talk more of that a little later. I want to get the lay of things upstairs now. *(Moves to stair-door, followed by the two men)*

SHERIFF: I suppose anything Mrs. Peters does'll be all right. She was to take in some clothes for her, you know, and a few little things. We left in such a hurry yesterday. 140

COUNTY ATTORNEY: Yes, but I would like to see what you take, Mrs. Peters, and keep an eye out for anything that might be of use to us.

MRS. PETERS: Yes, Mr. Henderson. *(The women listen to the men's steps on the stairs, then look about the kitchen)*

MRS. HALE: I'd hate to have men coming into my kitchen, snooping round and criticizing. *(Arranges pans under sink which the county attorney had shoved out of place)*

MRS. PETERS: Of course it's no more than their duty.

MRS. HALE: Duty's all right, but I guess that deputy sheriff that came out to make the fire might have got a little of this on. *(Gives roller towel a pull)* Wish I'd thought of that sooner. Seems mean to talk about her for not having things slicked up when she had to come away in such a hurry. 150

MRS. PETERS: *(Going to table at side, lifts one end of towel that covers a pan)* She had bread set. *(Stands still)*

MRS. HALE: *(Her eyes fixed on loaf of bread outside bread-box. Moves slowly toward it)* She was going to put this in there. *(Picks up loaf, then abruptly drops it. In a manner of returning to familiar things)* It's a shame about her fruit. I wonder if it's all gone. (*Gets up on a chair and looks*) I think there's some here that is all right, Mrs. Peters. Yes—here; (*holding it toward the window*) this is cherries, too. (*Looking* 160 *again*) I declare I believe that's the only one. (*Gets down, bottle in her hand. Goes to sink and wipes it off on the outside*) She'll feel awful bad after all her hard work in the hot weather. I remember the afternoon I put up my cherries last summer. (*Puts bottle on table. With a sigh starts to sit down in rocking-chair. Before she is seated realizes what chair it is; with a slow look at it, steps back. The chair which she has touched rocks back and forth*)

MRS. PETERS: Well, I must get those things from the front room closet. (*Starts to door left, looks into the other room, steps back*) You coming with me, Mrs. Hale? You could help me carry them. (*Both women go out; reappear, Mrs. Peters carrying a dress and skirt, Mrs. Hale following with a pair of shoes*) 170

MRS. PETERS: My, its cold in there. (*Puts clothes on table, goes up to stove*)

MRS. HALE: (*Holding up skirt and examining it*) Wright was close. I think maybe that's why she kept so much to herself. She didn't even belong to the Ladies' Aid. I suppose she felt she couldn't do her part, and then you don't enjoy things when you feel shabby. She used to wear pretty clothes and be lively, when she was Minnie Foster, one of the town girls singing in the choir. But that was—oh, that was thirty years ago. This all you was to take in?

MRS. PETERS: She said she wanted an apron. Funny thing to want, for there isn't much to get you dirty in jail, goodness knows. But I suppose just to make her feel more natural. She said they was in the top drawer in this cupboard. Yes, 180 here. And then her little shawl that always hung behind the door. (*Looks on stair door*) Yes, here it is.

MRS. HALE: (*Abruptly moving toward her.*) Mrs. Peters?

MRS. PETERS: Yes, Mrs. Hale?

MRS. HALE: Do you think she did it?

MRS. PETERS: (*In a frightened voice*) Oh, I don't know.

MRS. HALE: Well, I don't think she did. Asking for an apron and her little shawl. Worrying about her fruit.

MRS. PETERS: (*Starts to speak, glances up, where footsteps are heard in the room above. In a low voice*) Mr. Peters says it looks bad for her. Mr. Henderson is awful sarcastic 190 in a speech and he'll make fun of her sayin' she didn't wake up.

MRS. HALE: Well, I guess John Wright didn't wake when they was slipping that rope under his neck.

MRS. PETERS: No, it's strange. It must have been done awful crafty and still. They say it was such a—funny way to kill a man, rigging it all up like that.

MRS. HALE: That's just what Mr. Hale said. There was a gun in the house. He says that's what he can't understand.

MRS. PETERS: Mr. Henderson said coming out that what was needed for the case was a motive; something to show anger, or—sudden feeling.

MRS. HALE: (*Standing by table*) Well, I don't see any signs of anger around here, 200 but (*puts hand on dish towel in middle of table, stands looking at table, one half of which is clean, the other half messy*) It's wiped to here. (*Makes a move as if to finish work, then turns and looks at loaf of bread beside the breadbox. Drops towel. In that voice of coming back to familiar things*) Wonder how they are finding things upstairs. I hope she had it a little more red-up up there. You know, it seems kind of *sneaking*. Locking her up in town and then coming out here and trying to get her own house to turn against her!

MRS. PETERS: But Mrs. Hale, the law is the law.

MRS. HALE: I spose't is. (*Unbuttoning her coat*) Better loosen up your things, Mrs. Peters. You won't feel them when you go out. 210

MRS. PETERS: (*Taking off fur tippet, goes to hang it on hook at back of room, stands looking at the under part of the small table*) She was piecing a quilt. (*Brings large sewing basket to table front and they look at the bright pieces*)

MRS. HALE: It's log cabin pattern. Pretty isn't it? I wonder if she was goin' to quilt
it or just knot it? (*Footsteps have been heard coming down the stairs. The sheriff enters
followed by Hale and Henderson*)

SHERIFF: They wonder if she was going to quilt it or just knot it. (*The men laugh,
the women look abashed*)

COUNTY ATTORNEY: (*Rubbing his hands over the stove*) Frank's fire didn't do much
up there, did it? Well, let's go out to the barn and get that cleared up. (*Exeunt* 220
men door rear)

MRS. HALE: (*Resentfully*) I don't know as there's anything so strange, our takin' up
our time with little things while we're waiting for them to get the evidence. (*Sits
down, smoothing out block with decision*) I don't see as it's anything to laugh about.

MRS. PETERS: (*Apologetically*) Of course they've got awful important things on
their minds. (*Pulls up a chair and sits by the table*)

MRS. HALE: (*Examining another block*) Mrs. Peters, look at this one. Here, this is
the one she was working on, and look at the sewing! All the rest of it has been so
nice and even. And look at this! It's all over the place! Why, it looks as if she
didn't know what she was about! (*After she has said this they look at each other, then* 230
*start to glance back at the door. After an instant Mrs. Hale has pulled at a knot and
ripped the sewing*)

MRS. PETERS: Oh, what are you doing, Mrs. Hale?

MRS. HALE: (*Mildly*) Just pulling out a stitch or two that's not sewed very good.
(*Threading a needle*) Bad sewing always made me fidgety.

MRS. PETERS: (*Nervously*) I don't think we ought to touch things.

MRS. HALE: I'll just finish up this end. (*Suddenly stopping and leaning forward*) Mrs.
Peters?

MRS. PETERS: Yes, Mrs. Hale?

MRS. HALE: What do you suppose she was so nervous about?   240

MRS. PETERS: Oh—I don't know. I don't know as she was nervous. I sometimes
sew awful queer when I'm just tired. (*Mrs. Hale starts to say something, looks at her,
compresses her lips a little, goes on sewing*) Well I must get these things wrapped up.
They may be through sooner than we think. (*Piling apron and other things up
together*) I wonder where I can find a piece of paper, and string.

MRS. HALE: In that cupboard, maybe.

MRS. PETERS: (*Looking in cupboard*) Why, here's a bird-cage. (*Holds it up*) Did she
have a bird, Mrs. Hale?

MRS. HALE: Why, I don't know whether she did or not—I've not been here for so
long. There was a man around last year selling canaries cheap, but I don't know   250
as she took one; maybe she did. She used to sing real pretty herself.

MRS. PETERS: (*Glancing around*) Seems funny to think of a bird here. But she
must have had one, or why should she have had a cage? I wonder what happened to it.

MRS. HALE: I s'pose maybe the cat got it.

MRS. PETERS: No, she didn't have a cat. She's got that feeling some people have
about cats—being afraid of them. My cat got in her room and she was real
upset and asked me to take it out.

MRS. HALE: My sister Bessie was like that. Queer, ain't it?

MRS. PETERS: (*Examining cage*) Why, look, at this door. It's broke. One hinge is   260
pulled apart.

MRS. HALE: (*Looking too*) Looks as if someone must have been rough with it.

MRS. PETERS: Why, yes. (*Puts cage on table*)

MRS. HALE: I wish if they're going to find any evidence they'd be about it. I don't
like this place.

MRS. PETERS: But I'm awful glad you came with me, Mrs. Hale. It would be
lonesome for me sitting here alone.

MRS. HALE: It would, wouldn't it? (*Dropping sewing, voice falling*) But I tell you

what I do wish, Mrs. Peters. I wish I had come over some times when *she* was
here. I —*(looking around the room)*— wish I had.   270

MRS. PETERS: But of course you were awful busy, Mrs. Hale — your house and
your children.

MRS. HALE: I could've come. I stayed away because it weren't cheerful — and
that's why I ought to have come. I — I've never liked this place. Maybe because
it's down in a hollow and you don't see the road. I dunno what it is, but it's a
lonesome place and always was. I wish I had come over to see Minnie Foster
sometimes. I can see now — *(shakes her head)*

MRS. PETERS: Well, you musn't reproach yourself, Mrs. Hale. Somehow we just
don't see how it is with other folks until — something comes up.

MRS. HALE: Not having children makes less work — but it makes a quiet house, 280
and Wright out to work all day, and no company when he did come in. Did you
know John Wright, Mrs. Peters?

MRS. PETERS: Not to know him; I've seen him in town. They say he was a good
man.

MRS. HALE: Yes — good; he didn't drink, and kept his word as well as most, I
guess, and paid his debts. But he was a hard man, Mrs. Peters. Just to pass the
time of day with him — *(shivers)* Like a raw wind that gets to the bone. *(Pauses,
her eye falling on the cage)* I should think she would 'a wanted a bird. But what do
you suppose went with it?

MRS. PETERS: I don't know, unless it got sick and died. *(She reaches over and swings* 290
the broken door, swings it again, both women watch it)

MRS. HALE: You weren't raised round here, were you? *(Mrs. Peters shakes her head)*
You didn't know — her?

MRS. PETERS: Not till they brought her yesterday.

MRS. HALE: She — come to think of it, she was kind of like a bird herself — real
sweet and pretty, but kind of timid and — fluttery. How — she — did — change.
(Silence; then as if struck by a happy thought and relieved to get back to every day things)
Tell you what, Mrs. Peters, why don't you take the quilt in with you? It might
take up her mind.

MRS. PETERS: Why, I think that's a real nice idea, Mrs. Hale. There couldn't 300
possibly be any objection to it, could there? Now, just what would I take? I
wonder if her patches are in here — and her things. *(Both look in sewing basket)*

MRS. HALE: Here's some red. I expect this has got sewing things in it. *(Brings out a
fancy box)* What a pretty box. Looks like something somebody would give you.
Maybe her scissors are in here. *(Opens box. Suddenly puts her hand to her nose.)*
Why — *(Mrs. Peters bends nearer, then turns her face away)* There's something
wrapped up in this piece of silk.

MRS. PETERS: Why, this isn't her scissors.

MRS. HALE: *(Lifting the silk)* Oh, Mrs. Peters — It's *(Mrs. Peters bends closer)*

MRS. PETERS: It's the bird.   310

MRS. HALE: *(Jumping up)* But, Mrs. Peters — look at it! It's neck! Look at its neck!
It's all — other side *to.*

MRS. PETERS: Somebody-wrung-its-neck. *(Their eyes meet. A look of growing comprehension, of horror. Steps are heard outside. Mrs. Hale slips box under quilt pieces, and
sinks into her chair. Enter Sheriff and County Attorney Mrs. Peters rises)*

COUNTY ATTORNEY: *(As one turning from serious things to little pleasantries)* Well,
ladies, have you decided whether she was going to quilt it or knot it?

MRS. PETERS: We think she was going to — knot it.

COUNTY ATTORNEY: Well, that's interesting, I am sure. *(Looking at bird-cage)* Has
the bird flown?   320

MRS. HALE: *(Piling more quilt pieces over the box)* We think the — cat got it.

COUNTY ATTORNEY: *(Preoccupied)* Is there a cat? *(Mrs. Hale glances in a quick covert
way at Mrs. Peters)*

MRS. PETERS: Well, not *now*. They're superstitious, you know. They leave.

COUNTY ATTORNEY: *(To Peters, in the manner of continuing an interrupted conversation)* No sign at all of anyone having come from the outside. Their own rope. Now let's go up again and go over it piece by piece. *(They start upstairs)* It would have to have been someone who knew just the—*(Mrs. Peters sinks into her chair. The two women sit there not looking at one another, but as if peering into something and at the same time holding back. When they talk now it is in the manner of feeling their* 330 *way over strange ground, as if afraid of what they are saying, but as if they can not help saying it)*

MRS. HALE: She liked the bird. She was going to bury it in that pretty box.

MRS. PETERS: *(In a whisper)* When I was a girl—my kitten—there was a boy took a hatchet, and before my eyes—and before I could get there—*(covers her face an instant)* If they hadn't held me back I would have—*(catches herself, looks upstairs where steps are heard, falters weakly)*—hurt him.

MRS. HALE: *(With a slow look around her.)* I wonder how it would seem never to have any children around. *(Pause)* No, Wright wouldn't like the bird—a thing that sang. She used to sing. He killed that, too.   340

MRS. PETERS: *(Moving uneasily)* We don't know who killed the bird.

MRS. HALE: I knew John Wright.

MRS. PETERS: It was an awful thing was done in this house that night, Mrs. Hale. Killing a man while he slept, slipping a rope around his neck that choked the life out of him.

MRS. HALE: His neck. Choked the life out of him. *(Her hand goes out and rests on the bird-cage)*

MRS. PETERS: *(With rising voice)* We don't know who killed him. We don't *know*.

MRS. HALE: *(Her own feeling not interrupted)* If there'd been years and years of nothing, then a bird to sing to you, it would be awful—still, after the bird was   350 still.

MRS. PETERS: *(Something within her speaking)* I know what stillness is. When we homesteaded in Dakota, and my first baby died—after he was two years old, and me with no other then—

MRS. HALE: *(Moving)* How soon do you suppose they'll be through, looking for the evidence?

MRS. PETERS: I know what stillness is. *(Pulling herself back)* The law has got to punish crime, Mrs. Hale.

MRS. HALE: *(Not as if answering that)* I wish you'd seen Minnie Foster when she wore a white dress with blue ribbons and stood up there in the choir and sang.   360 *(Suddenly looking around the room)* Oh, I *wish* I'd come over here once in a while! That was a crime! That was a crime! Who's going to punish that?

MRS. PETERS: *(Looking upstairs)* We mustn't—take on.

MRS. HALE: I might have known she needed help! I know how things can be—for women. I tell you, it's queer, Mrs. Peters. We live close together and we live far apart. We all go through the same things—it's all just a different kind of the same thing—*(Brushes her eyes, then seeing the bottle of fruit, reaches out for it)* If I was you I wouldn't tell her her fruit was gone. Tell her it *ain't*. Tell her it's all right. Take this in to prove it to her. She—she may never know whether it was broke or not.   370

MRS. PETERS: *(Picks up the bottle, looks about for something to wrap it in; takes petticoat from clothes brought from front room, very nervously begins winding that around it. In a false voice)* My, it's a good thing the men couldn't hear us. Wouldn't they just laugh! Getting all stirred up over a little thing like a—dead canary. As if that could have anything to do with—with—wouldn't they *laugh*! *(The men are heard coming down stairs)*

MRS. HALE: *(Muttering)* Maybe they would—maybe they wouldn't.

COUNTY ATTORNEY: No , Peters, it's all perfectly clear except a reason for doing it. But you know juries when it comes to women. If there was some definite thing. Something to show — something to make a story about — a thing that 380 would connect up with this strange way of doing it — *(The women's eyes meet for an instant. Enter Hale from outer door)*

HALE: Well, I've got the team around. Pretty cold out there.

COUNTY ATTORNEY: I'm going to stay here a while by myself. *(To sheriff)* You can send Frank out for me, can't you? I want to go over everything. I'm not satisfied that we can't do better.

SHERIFF: Do you want to see what Mrs. Peters is going to take in?

COUNTY ATTORNEY: *(Goes to table. Picks up apron, laughs)* Oh, I guess they're not very dangerous things the ladies have picked out. *(Moves a few things about, disturbing quilt pieces which cover the box. Steps back)* No, Mrs. Peters doesn't need 390 supervising. For that matter, a sheriff's wife is married to the law. Ever think of it that way, Mrs. Peters?

MRS. PETERS: Not — just that way.

SHERIFF: *(Chuckling)* Married to the law. *(Moves toward front room)* I just want you to come in here a minute, George. We ought to take a look at these windows.

COUNTY ATTORNEY: Oh, windows!

SHERIFF: We'll be right out, Mr. Hale. *(Exit Hale door rear. Sheriff follows County Attorney through door left. The two women's eyes follow them out. Mrs. Hale rises, hands tightly together, looking intensely at Mrs. Peters, whose eyes make a slow turn, finally meeting Mrs. Hale's. A moment Mrs. Hale holds her, then her own eyes point the way to 400 the spot where the box is concealed. Suddenly Mrs. Peters throws back quilt pieces and tries to put box in the bag she is wearing. It is too big. She opens box, starts to take bird out, cannot touch it, goes to pieces, stands there helpless. Sound of a knob turning in the other room. Mrs. Hale snatches box and puts it in the pocket of her big coat. Enter County Attorney and Sheriff.*

COUNTY ATTORNEY: *(Facetiously)* Well, Henry, at least we found out that she was not going to quilt it. She was going to — what is it you call it, ladies?

MRS. HALE: *(Hand against her pocket)* We call it — knot it, Mr. Henderson.

CURTAIN

1916

EUGENE O'NEILL
(1888–1953)

Eugene O'Neill won four Pulitzer Prizes for Drama, in 1920 for *Beyond the Horizon*, in 1921 for *Anna Christie*, in 1928 for *Strange Interlude*, and post-humously in 1957 for *Long Day's Journey into Night*. In an interview given when he was emerging as the most promising American playwright on the scene, he commented: "The theater to me *is* life. . . . [and] life is struggle, often, if not usually, unsuccessful struggle; for most of us have something within us which prevents us from accomplishing what we dream and desire. And then, as we progress, we are always seeing further than we can reach." Such was the essence of the tragic vision of O'Neill's plays.

O'Neill travelled a long and wandering road to reach the eminence he found in the early 1920s. He was born in a hotel room (as he would die in one) to an actor-father who was always on the road. James O'Neill was a successful performer who chose to spend most of his life playing the central role in a dramatic version of Alexandre Dumas's romantic novel *The Count of Monte Cristo*. It was not a creative career, but it paid well. Disliking her "backstage" role, his mother Ellen Quinlan O'Neill developed a lifetime addiction to morphine.

O'Neill was placed in Catholic boarding schools as his parents travelled the dramatic circuit, and early in life discovered the sharp pangs of aloneness and loneliness. He lost his faith and insisted on going to a non-Catholic private academy. He went to Princeton in 1906, but was soon suspended for unruly and destructive behavior while drunk. He had been schooled well in the bohemian life his father lived with his fellow actors.

In 1909 he did the honorable thing and married a girl he had made pregnant. But he immediately abandoned her by going on what he later styled a "prospecting expedition" to Honduras. This taste of foreign travel led him in 1910 to ship as a common seaman on a sailing vessel bound for Buenos Aires, Argentina, where he lived for a time as a vagabond and beachcomber. Next he shipped on a passenger liner bound for Europe and back. All these experiences he was storing in the reservoir of his imagination for later use.

Back in New York, he lived above a bar on the waterfront and resumed the dissolute, drifting life he had lived before. He accommodated his wife's desire for a divorce by arranging to be caught with a prostitute, worked for a time as a reporter, and consumed great quantities of alcohol (an ability inherited from his father). But as his health generally deteriorated, he was confined to a tuberculosis sanitarium for several months in 1913.

While recovering from his illness, O'Neill suddenly decided to become a playwright. He had always been a serious reader of books (Nietzsche was a favorite author). Now he read classic dramatists and was impressed by the Scandinavian writers Henrik Ibsen and August Strindberg—especially the latter. In 1914 he entered the famed Dramatic Workshop at Harvard, run by Professor George Pierce Baker, determined, as he put it, to be "an artist or nothing."

After a term in the Dramatic Workshop, O'Neill headed for New York, settled in Greenwich Village, and joined the experimental little theater group, the Provincetown Players of Provincetown, Massachusetts. Through the Players he saw the first production of one of his plays in 1916—*Bound East for Cardiff*. Other productions followed, including, in 1920, *Beyond the Horizon*, a full-length play which started as a little theater experiment but ended on Broadway, winning a Pulitzer Prize. Later the same year, O'Neill had a great success with *The Emperor Jones*, an expressionistic play about an ex-convict and former Pullman porter who crowns himself emperor of a West Indian island. In 1921, O'Neill won his second Pulitzer Prize for *Anna Christie*, portraying a reformed prostitute ennobled by genuine love—and incidentally giving the audience a happy ending (a change for O'Neill).

Throughout the 1920s and early 1930s, O'Neill produced play after play, surprising or shocking his audiences by introducing controversial themes and unconventional techniques: in 1922, *The Hairy Ape*, using symbolic techniques to suggest evolutionary throwbacks; in 1924, *All God's Chillun Got Wings*, dealing with interracial marriage, and *Desire Under the Elms* with incest; in 1926, *The Great God Brown*, introducing masks to delineate character; in 1927, *Lazarus Laughed*, employing masks, stylized speeches, and choral readings; in 1928, *Strange Interlude*, introducing speeches representing the "unspoken" thoughts of the characters; in 1931, *Mourning Becomes Electra*, a trilogy of plays roughly modelled on Aeschylus's *Oresteia* and touching on adultery, murder, suicide, and incest — all in one New England family. Both *Strange Interlude* and *Mourning Becomes Electra* ran for five hours, with dinner breaks for the audiences.

O'Neill's creative achievement during these years was astonishing, but gradually during the era of the Great Depression, he seemed to fade from public attention. By 1936, when he was awarded the Nobel Prize for Literature, no new plays by him were being produced. He was beset by a crippling illness, a degenerative disease of the nerves. But he continued to write plays and simply set them aside.

O'Neill appears to have waited out the Depression and the Second World War, and then, in 1946, brought to production a play written in 1939, *The Iceman Cometh*. It was not the kind of success O'Neill had repeatedly had in his earlier career, and he dropped further plans to produce his other plays. He died in 1953, unaware that before many years his reputation would be resurrected.

O'Neill's autobiographical drama *A Long Day's Journey Into Night*, written in 1940–41, was produced in 1956 and took Broadway by storm. It was declared O'Neill's finest play and was awarded a Pulitzer Prize. This same year, a revival of *The Iceman Cometh*, set in a seedy bar of the kind O'Neill lived above in his dissolute youth, was highly praised, and O'Neill again was often dubbed America's greatest playwright.

There were critics who took exception, as there had been earlier. The main charge levelled against his plays was that their language could not carry the weight of their ideas or convey the depth of their emotions and feelings. When this charge had been made against *Mourning Becomes Electra*, O'Neill answered: "It needed great language to lift it beyond itself. I haven't got that. And, by way of self-consolation, I don't think, from the evidence of all that is being written today, that great language is possible for anyone living in the discordant, broken, faithless rhythm of our time. The best one can do is to be pathetically eloquent by one's moving, dramatic inarticulations!"

Other of O'Neill's leftover plays were produced, often first abroad, particularly in Sweden, where interest in O'Neill remained strong even when it had faded in America. *A Touch of the Poet* was produced in 1957 and *More Stately Mansions* in 1962. *Hughie*, first produced in Stockholm in 1958, was to have been one of a cycle of one-act plays to be called *By Way of Obit*. From its first appearance, it has been recognized as vintage — and "top-drawer" — O'Neill. One critic, Henry Hewes, has observed: "O'Neill in 'Hughie' has written the whole cycle of life into a forty-minute piece. The wise guy and the sucker stand for all forms of human interdependence. The swing from naked truth to illusion, from isolation to communication, from bitterness to love are all basic to living. We alternate from one to the other, and this cyclic motion rather than the achievement of a goal is the stuff and richness of life."

ADDITIONAL READING

The Plays of Eugene O'Neill, 3 vols., 1951; *Selected Letters of Eugene O'Neill*, ed. Travis Bogard and Jackson R. Bryer, 1988; *The Unknown O'Neill: Unpublished or Unfamiliar Writings of Eugene O'Neill*, ed. Travis Bogard, 1988; *Eugene O'Neill: The Unfinished Plays*, ed. Virginia Floyd, 1988; *Conversations with Eugene O'Neill*, ed. Mark W. Estrin, 1990.

Barrett H. Clark, *Eugene O'Neill: The Man and His Plays*, 1926, 1947; Edwin A. Engel, *The Haunted Heroes of Eugene O'Neill*, 1953; Doris V. Falk, *Eugene O'Neill and the Tragic Tension*, 1958; Crosswell Bowen, *The Curse of the Misbegotten: A Tale of the House of O'Neill*, 1957; Oscar Cargill et al., ed., *O'Neill and His Plays: Four Decades of Criticism*, 1961; Arthur and Barbara Gelb, *O'Neill*, 1962, 1973; Doris Alexander, *The Tempering of Eugene O'Neill*, 1962; John Gassner, ed., *O'Neill: A Collection of Critical Essays*, 1964; Frederic Ives Carpenter, *Eugene O'Neill*, 1964, 1979; John Henry Raleigh, *The Plays of Eugene O'Neill*, 1965; Jordon Y. Miller, ed., *Playwright's Progress: O'Neill and the Critics*, 1965; John Gassner, *Eugene O'Neill*, 1965; Jordan Y. Miller, *Eugene O'Neill and the American Critic: A Summary and Bibliographical Checklist*, 1967, 1973; Louis Sheaffer, *O'Neill: Son and Playwright*, 1968; Egil Törnquist, *A Drama of Souls: Studies in O'Neill's Supernaturalistic Technique*, 1969; Horst Frenz, *Eugene O'Neill*, 1971; Travis Bogard, *Contour in Time: The Plays of Eugene O'Neill*, 1972, rev. 1988; Louis Sheaffer, *O'Neill: Son and Artist*, 1973; Jennifer McCabe Atkinson, *Eugene O'Neill: A Descriptive Bibliography*, 1974; Leonard Chabrower, *Ritual and Pathos: The Theater of O'Neill*, 1976; Ernest G. Griffin, ed., *Eugene O'Neill: A Collection of Criticism*, 1976; Michael Manheim, *Eugene O'Neill's New Language of Kinship*, 1982; Margaret Loftus Renald, *The Eugene O'Neill Companion*, 1984; Virginia Floyd, *The Plays of Eugene O'Neill: A New Assessment*, 1985; Judith E. Barlow, *Final Acts: The Creation of Three Late O'Neill Plays*, 1985; John H. Stoupe, ed., *Critical Approaches to O'Neill*, 1988; Ronald H. Wainscott, *Staging O'Neill*, 1988; Madeline Smith and Richard Eaton, *Eugene O'Neill: An Annotated Bibliography*, 1988; Shyamal Bagchee, ed., *Perspectives on O'Neill: New Essays*, 1988.

TEXT

Hughie, 1959.

Hughie

CHARACTERS

"ERIE" SMITH,   a teller of tales
A NIGHT CLERK

SCENE

The desk and a section of lobby of a small hotel on a West Side street in midtown New York. It is between 3 and 4 A.M. of a day in the summer of 1928.

It is one of those hotels, built in the decade 1900–10 on the side streets of the Great White Way[1] sector, which began as respectable second class but soon were forced to deteriorate in order to survive. Following the First World War and Prohibition, it had given up all pretense of respectability, and now is anything a paying guest wants it to be, a third class dump, catering to the catch-as-catch-can trade. But still it does not prosper. It has not shared in the Great Hollow Boom of the twenties. The Everlasting Opulence of the New Economic Law has overlooked it. It manages to keep running by cutting the overhead for service, repairs, and cleanliness to a minimum.   10

The desk faces left along a section of seedy lobby with shabby chairs. The street entrance is off-stage, left. Behind the desk are a telephone switchboard and the operator's stool. At right, the usual numbered tiers of mailboxes, and above them a clock.

The NIGHT CLERK *sits on the stool, facing front, his back to the switchboard. There is nothing to do. He is not thinking. He is not sleepy. He simply droops and stares acquiescently*

---

[1]The area where the New York theaters are clustered on and around Broadway.

at nothing. It would be discouraging to glance at the clock. He knows there are several hours to go before his shift is over. Anyway, he does not need to look at clocks. He has been a night clerk in New York hotels so long he can tell time by sounds in the street.

He is in his early forties. Tall, thin, with a scrawny neck and jutting Adam's apple. His 20 *face is long and narrow, greasy with perspiration, sallow, studded with pimples from ingrowing hairs. His nose is large and without character. So is his mouth. So are his ears. So is his thinning brown hair, powdered with dandruff. Behind horn-rimmed spectacles, his blank brown eyes contain no discernible expression. One would say they had even forgotten how it feels to be bored. He wears an ill-fitting blue serge suit, white shirt and collar, a blue tie. The suit is old and shines at the elbows as if it had been waxed and polished.*

Footsteps echo in the deserted lobby as someone comes in from the street. The Night Clerk rises wearily. His eyes remain empty but his gummy lips part automatically in a welcoming The-Patron-Is-Always-Right grimace, intended as a smile. His big uneven teeth are in bad condition. 30

ERIE SMITH *enters and approaches the desk. He is about the same age as the Clerk and has the same pasty, perspiry, night-life complexion. There the resemblance ends. Erie is around medium height but appears shorter because he is stout and his fat legs are too short for his body. So are his fat arms. His big head squats on a neck which seems part of his beefy shoulders. His face is round, his snub nose flattened at the tip. His blue eyes have drooping lids and puffy pouches under them. His sandy hair is falling out and the top of his head is bald. He walks to the desk with a breezy, familiar air, his gait a bit waddling because of his short legs. He carries a Panama hat and mops his face with a red and blue silk handkerchief. He wears a light grey suit cut in the extreme, tight-waisted, Broadway mode, the coat open to reveal an old and faded but expensive silk shirt in a shade of blue that sets teeth on edge, and* 40 *a gay red and blue foulard tie, its knot stained by perspiration. His trousers are held up by a braided brown leather belt with a brass buckle. His shoes are tan and white, his socks white silk.*

In manner, he is consciously a Broadway sport and a Wise Guy—the type of small fry gambler and horse player, living hand to mouth on the fringe of the rackets. Infesting corners, doorways, cheap restaurants, the bars of minor speakeasies, he and his kind imagine they are in the Real Know, cynical oracles of the One True Grapevine.

Erie usually speaks in a low, guarded tone, his droop-lidded eyes suspiciously wary of nonexistent eavesdroppers. His face is set in the prescribed pattern of gambler's dead pan. His small, pursy mouth is always crooked in the cynical leer of one who possesses superior, inside 50 *information, and his shifty once-over glances never miss the price tags he detects on everything and everybody. Yet there is something phoney about his characterization of himself, some sentimental softness behind it which doesn't belong in the hard-boiled picture.*

Erie avoids looking at the Night Clerk, as if he resented him.

ERIE [*Peremptorily.*] Key. [*Then as the Night Clerk gropes with his memory— grudgingly.*] Forgot you ain't seen me before. Erie Smith's the name. I'm an old timer in this fleabag. 492.

NIGHT CLERK [*In a tone of one who is wearily relieved when he does not have to remember anything—he plucks out the key.*] 492. Yes, sir.

ERIE [*Taking the key, gives the Clerk the once-over. He appears not unfavorably impressed* 60 *but his tone still holds resentment.*] How long you been on the job? Four, five days, huh? I been off on a drunk. Come to now, though. Tapering off. Well, I'm glad they fired that young squirt they took on when Hughie got sick. One of them fresh wise punks. Couldn't tell him nothing. Pleased to meet you, Pal. Hope you stick around. [*He shoves out his hand. The Night Clerk takes it obediently.*]

NIGHT CLERK [*With a compliant, uninterested smile.*] Glad to know you, Mr. Smith.

ERIE What's your name?

NIGHT CLERK   [*As if he had half forgotten because what did it matter, anyway?*] Hughes. Charlie Hughes.

ERIE   [*Starts.*] Huh? Hughes? Say, is that on the level?   70

NIGHT CLERK   Charlie Hughes.

ERIE   Well, I be damned! What the hell d'you know about that! [*Warming toward the Clerk.*] Say, now I notice, you don't look like Hughie, but you remind me of him somehow. You ain't by any chance related?

NIGHT CLERK   You mean to the Hughes who had this job so long and died recently? No, sir. No relation.

ERIE   [*Gloomily.*] No, that's right. Hughie told me he didn't have no relations left — except his wife and kids, of course. [*He pauses — more gloomily.*] Yeah. The poor guy croaked last week. His funeral was what started me off on a bat. [*Then boastfully, as if defending himself against gloom.*] Some drunk! I don't go on one   80 often. It's bum dope in my book. A guy gets careless and gabs about things he knows and when he comes to he's liable to find there's guys who'd feel easier if he wasn't around no more. That's the trouble with knowing things. Take my tip, Pal. Don't never know nothin'. Be a sap and stay healthy. [*His manner has become secretive, with sinister undertones. But the Night Clerk doesn't notice this. Long experience with guests who stop at his desk in the small hours to talk about themselves has given him a foolproof technique of self-defense. He appears to listen with agreeable submissiveness and be impressed, but his mind is blank and he doesn't hear unless a direct question is put to him, and sometimes not even then. Erie thinks he is impressed.*] But hell, I always keep my noggin working, booze or no booze. I'm no sucker. What   90 was I sayin'? Oh, some drunk. I sure hit the high spots. You shoulda seen the doll I made night before last. And did she take me to the cleaners! I'm a sucker for blondes. [*He pauses — giving the Night Clerk a cynical, contemptuous glance.*] You're married, ain't you?

NIGHT CLERK   [*Long ago he gave up caring whether questions were personal or not.*] Yes, sir.

ERIE   Yeah, I'd'a laid ten to one on it. You got that old look. Like Hughie had. Maybe that's the resemblance. [*He chuckles contemptuously.*] Kids, too, I bet?

NIGHT CLERK   Yes, sir. Three.

ERIE   You're worse off than Hughie was. He only had two. Three, huh? Well,   100 that's what comes of being careless! [*He laughs. The Night Clerk smiles at a guest. He had been a little offended when a guest first made that crack — must have been ten years ago — yes, Eddie, the oldest, is eleven now — or is it twelve? Erie goes on with good-natured tolerance.*] Well, I suppose marriage ain't such a bum racket, if you're made for it. Hughie didn't seem to mind it much, although if you want my low-down,[2] his wife is a bum — in spades! Oh, I don't mean cheatin'. With her puss and figure, she'd never make no one except she raided a blind asylum. [*The Night Clerk feels that he has been standing a long time and his feet are beginning to ache and he wishes 492 would stop talking and go to bed so he can sit down again and listen to the noises in the street and think about nothing. Erie gives him an amused, condescending   110 glance.*] How old are you? Wait! Let me guess. You look fifty or over but I'll lay ten to one you're forty-three or maybe forty-four.

NIGHT CLERK   I'm forty-three. [*He adds vaguely.*] Or maybe it is forty-four.

ERIE   [*Elated.*] I win, huh? I sure can call the turn on ages, Buddy. You ought to see the dolls get sored up when I work it on them! You're like Hughie. He looked like he'd never see fifty again and he was only forty-three. Me, I'm forty-five. Never think it, would you? Most of the dames don't think I've hit forty yet. [*The Night Clerk shifts his position so he can lean more on the desk. Maybe those shoes he*

---

[2] I.e., unadorned facts.

sees advertised for fallen arches — But they cost eight dollars, so that's out — Get a pair when he goes to heaven. Erie is sizing him up with another cynical, friendly glance.] I make another bet about you. Born and raised in the sticks, wasn't you? 120

NIGHT CLERK   [*Faintly aroused and defensive.*] I come originally from Saginaw, Michigan, but I've lived here in the Big Town so long I consider myself a New Yorker now. [*This is a long speech for him and he wonders sadly why he took the trouble to make it.*]

ERIE   I don't deserve no medal for picking that one. Nearly every guy I know on the Big Stem[3] — and I know most of 'em — hails from the sticks. Take me. You'd never guess it but I was dragged up in Erie, P-a. Ain't that a knockout! Erie, P-a! That's how I got my moniker. No one calls me nothing but Erie. You better call me Erie, too, Pal, or I won't know when you're talkin' to me. 130

NIGHT CLERK   All right, Erie.

ERIE   Atta Boy. [*He chuckles.*] Here's another knockout. Smith is my real name. A Broadway guy like me named Smith and it's my real name! Ain't that a knockout! [*He explains carefully so there will be no misunderstanding.*] I don't remember nothing about Erie, P-a, you understand — or want to. Some punk burg! After grammar school, my Old Man put me to work in his store, dealing out groceries. Some punk job! I stuck it out till I was eighteen before I took a run-out powder. [*The Night Clerk seems turned into a drooping waxwork, draped along the desk. This is what he used to dread before he perfected his technique of not listening: The Guest's Story of His Life. He fixes his mind on his aching feet. Erie chuckles.*] Speaking 140 of marriage, that was the big reason I ducked. A doll nearly had me hooked for the old shotgun ceremony. Closest I ever come to being played for a sucker. This doll in Erie — Daisy's her name — was one of them dumb wide-open dolls. All the guys give her a play. Then one day she wakes up and finds she's going to have a kid. I never figure she meant to frame me in particular. Way I always figured, she didn't have no idea who, so she holds a lottery all by herself. Put about a thousand guys' names in a hat — all she could remember — and drew one out and I was it. Then she told her Ma, and her Ma told her Pa, and her Pa come round looking for me. But I was no fall guy even in them days. I took it on the lam. For Saratoga, to look the bangtails[4] over. I'd started to be a horse 150 player in Erie, though I'd never seen a track. I been one ever since. [*With a touch of bravado.*] And I ain't done so bad, Pal. I've made some killings in my time the gang still gab about. I've been in the big bucks. More'n once, and I will be again. I've had tough breaks too, but what the hell, I always get by. When the horses won't run for me, there's draw or stud. When they're bad, there's a crap game. And when they're all bad, there's always bucks to pick up for little errands I ain't talkin' about, which they give a guy who can keep his clam shut. Oh, I get along, Buddy. I get along fine. [*He waits for approving assent from the Night Clerk, but the latter is not hearing so intently he misses his cue until the expectant silence crashes his ears.*] 160

NIGHT CLERK   [*Hastily, gambling on "yes."*] Yes, Sir.

ERIE   [*Bitingly.*] Sorry if I'm keeping you up, Sport. [*With an aggrieved air.*] Hughie was a wide-awake guy. He was always waiting for me to roll in. He'd say, "Hello, Erie, how'd the bangtails treat you?" Or, "How's luck?" Or, "Did you make the old bones behave?" Then I'd tell him how I'd done. He'd ask, "What's new along the Big Stem?" and I'd tell him the latest off the grapevine. [*He grins with affectionate condescension.*] It used to hand me a laugh to hear old Hughie crackin' like a sport. In all the years I knew him, he never bet a buck on nothin'.

---

[3]The biggest of two peninsulas forming Michigan.
[4]Racehorses (slang).

[*Excusingly.*] But it ain't his fault. He'd have took a chance, but how could he with his wife keepin' cases on every nickel of his salary? I showed him lots of ways he could cross her up, but he was too scared. [*He chuckles.*] The biggest knockout was when he'd kid me about dames. He'd crack, "What? No blonde to-night, Erie? You must be slippin'." Jeez, you never see a guy more bashful with a doll around than Hughie was. I used to introduce him to the tramps I'd drag home with me. I'd wise them up to kid him along and pretend they'd fell for him. In two minutes, they'd have him hanging on the ropes. His face'd be red and he'd look like he wanted to crawl under the desk and hide. Some of them dolls was raw babies. They'd make him pretty raw propositions. He'd stutter like he was paralyzed. But he ate it up, just the same. He was tickled pink. I used to hope maybe I could nerve him up to do a little cheatin'. I'd offer to fix it for him with one of my dolls. Hell, I got plenty, I wouldn't have minded. I'd tell him, "Just let that wife of yours know you're cheatin', and she'll have some respect for you." But he was too scared. [*He pauses — boastfully.*] Some queens I've brought here in my time, Brother — frails from the Follies, or the Scandals, or the Frolics,[5] that'd knock your eye out! And I still can make 'em. You watch. I ain't slippin'. [*He looks at the Night Clerk expecting reassurance, but the Clerk's mind has slipped away to the clanging bounce of garbage cans in the outer night. He is thinking: "A job I'd like. I'd bang those cans louder than they do! I'd wake up the whole damned city!" Erie mutters disgustedly to himself.*] Jesus, what a dummy! [*He makes a move in the direction of the elevator, off right front — gloomily.*] Might as well hit the hay, I guess.

NIGHT CLERK   [*Comes to — with the nearest approach to feeling he has shown in many a long night — approvingly.*] Good night, Mr. Smith. I hope you have a good rest. [*But Erie stops, glancing around the deserted lobby with forlorn distate, jiggling the room key in his hand.*]

ERIE   What a crummy dump! What did I come back for? I shoulda stayed on a drunk. You'd never guess it, Buddy, but when I first come here this was a classy hotel — and clean, can you believe it? [*He scowls.*] I've been campin' here, off and on, fifteen years, but I've got a good notion to move out. It ain't the same place since Hughie was took to the hospital. [*Gloomily.*] Hell with going to bed! I'll just lie there worrying — [*He turns back to the desk. The Clerk's face would express despair, but the last time he was able to feel despair was back around World War days when the cost of living got so high and he was out of a job for three months. Erie leans on the desk — in a dejected, confidential tone.*] Believe me, Brother, I never been a guy to worry, but this time I'm on a spot where I got to, if I ain't a sap.

NIGHT CLERK   [*In the vague tone of a corpse which admits it once overheard a favorable rumor about life.*] That's too bad, Mr. Smith. But they say most of the things we worry about never happen. [*His mind escapes to the street again to play bouncing cans with the garbage men.*]

ERIE   [*Grimly.*] This thing happens, Pal. I ain't won a bet at nothin' since Hughie was took to the hospital. I'm jinxed. And that ain't all — But to hell with it! You're right, at that. Something always turns up for me. I was born lucky. I ain't worried. Just moaning low. Hell, who don't when they're getting over a drunk? You know how it is. The Brooklyn Boys march over the bridge with blood-hounds to hunt you down. And I'm still carrying the torch for Hughie. His checking out was a real K.O. for me. Damn if I know why. Lots of guys I've been pals with, in a way, croaked from booze or something, or got rubbed out, but I always took it as part of the game. Hell, we all gotta croak. Here today, gone tomorrow, so what's the good of beefin'? When a guy's dead, he's dead. He

---

[5]Burlesque shows or stage reviews.

don't give a damn, so why should anybody else? [*But this fatalistic philosophy is no* 220 *comfort and Erie sighs.*] I miss Hughie, I guess. I guess I'd got to like him a lot. [*Again he explains carefully so there will be no misunderstanding.*] Not that I was ever real pals with him, you understand. He didn't run in my class. He didn't know none of the answers. He was just a sucker. [*He sighs again.*] But I sure am sorry he's gone. You missed a lot not knowing Hughie, Pal. He sure was one grand little guy. [*He stares at the lobby floor. The Night Clerk regards him with vacant, bulging eyes full of a vague envy for the blind. The garbage men have gone their predestined way. Time is that much older. The Clerk's mind remains in the street to greet the noise of a far-off El train. Its approach is pleasantly like a memory of hope; then it roars and rocks* 230 *and rattles past the nearby corner, and the noise pleasantly deafens memory; then it recedes and dies, and there is something melancholy about that. But there is hope. Only so many El trains pass in one night, and each one passing leaves one less to pass, so the night recedes, too, until at last it must die and join all the other long nights in Nirvana,[6] the Big Night of Nights. And that's life. "What I always tell Jess when she nags me to worry about something: 'That's life, isn't it? What can you do about it?'" Erie sighs again—then turns to the Clerk, his foolishly wary, wise-guy eyes defenseless, his poker face as self-betraying as a hurt dog's—appealingly.*] Say, you do remind me of Hughie somehow, Pal. You got the same look on your map. [*But the Clerk's mind is far away attending the obsequies of night, and it takes it some time to get back. Erie is hurt—contemptuously.*] But I guess it's only that old night clerk look! There's one of 'em 240 born every minute!

NIGHT CLERK   [*His mind arrives just in time to catch this last—with a bright grimace.*] Yes, Mr. Smith. That's what Barnum[7] said, and it's certainly true, isn't it?

ERIE   [*Grateful even for this sign of companionship, growls.*] Nix on the Mr. Smith stuff, Charlie. There's ten of *them* born every minute. Call me Erie, like I told you.

NIGHT CLERK   [*Automatically, as his mind tiptoes into the night again.*] All right, Erie.

ERIE   [*Encouraged, leans on the desk, clacking his room key like a castanet.*] Yeah. Hughie was one grand little guy. All the same, like I said, he wasn't the kind of guy you'd ever figger a guy like me would take to. Because he was a sucker, 250 see—the kind of sap you'd take to the cleaners a million times and he'd never wise up he was took. Why, night after night, just for a gag, I'd get him to shoot crap with me here on the desk. With *my* dice. And he'd never ask to give 'em the once-over. Can you beat that! [*He chuckles—then earnestly.*] Not that I'd ever ring in no phoneys on a pal. I'm no heel. [*He chuckles again.*] And anyway, I didn't need none to take Hughie because he never even made me knock 'em against nothing. Just a roll on the desk here. Boy, if they'd ever let me throw 'em that way in a real game, I'd be worth ten million dollars. [*He laughs.*] You'da thought Hughie woulda got wise something was out of order when, no matter how much he'd win on a run of luck like suckers have sometimes, I'd always take him 260 to the cleaners in the end. But he never suspicioned nothing. All he'd say was "Gosh, Erie, no wonder you took up gambling. You sure were born lucky." [*He chuckles.*] Can you beat that? [*He hastens to explain earnestly.*] Of course, like I said, it was only a gag. We'd play with real jack,[8] just to make it look real, but it was all my jack. He never had no jack. His wife dealt him four bits a day for spending money. So I'd stake him at the start to half of what I got—in chicken feed,[9] I mean. We'd pretend a cent was a buck, and a nickel was a fin and so on.

---

[6]The state of being free from cyclic personal reincarnation, a kind of Hindu heaven.
[7]P. T. Barnum (1810–1891), famous for his travelling freak show. He is supposed to have said, "There is a sucker born every minute."
[8]Money.
[9]Small amount of money.

Some big game! He got a big kick out of it. He'd get all het up. It give me a kick, too—especially when he'd say, "Gosh, Erie, I don't wonder you never worry about money, with your luck." [*He laughs.*] That guy would believe anything! Of course, I'd stall him off when he'd want to shoot nights when I didn't have a goddamned nickel. [*He chuckles.*] What laughs he used to hand me! He'd always call horses "the bangtails," like he'd known 'em all his life—and he'd never seen a race horse, not till I kidnaped him one day and took him down to Belmont. What a kick he got out of that! I got scared he'd pass out with excitement. And he wasn't doing no betting either. All he had was four bits. It was just the track, and the crowd, and the horses got him. Mostly the horses. [*With a surprised, reflective air.*] Y'know, it's funny how a dumb, simple guy like Hughie will all of a sudden get something right. He says, "They're the most beautiful things in the world, I think." And he wins! I tell you, Pal, I'd rather sleep in the same stall with old Man o' War[10] than make the whole damn Follies. What do you think? 270 280

NIGHT CLERK   [*His mind darts back from a cruising taxi and blinks bewilderedly in the light: "Say yes."*] Yes, I agree with you, Mr.—I mean, Erie.

ERIE   [*With good-natured contempt.*] Yeah? I bet you never seen one, except back at the old Fair Grounds in the sticks. I don't mean them kind of turtles. I mean a real horse. [*The Clerk wonders what horses have to do with anything—or for that matter, what anything has to do with anything—then gives it up. Erie takes up his tale.*] And what d'you think happened the next night? Damned if Hughie didn't dig two bucks out of his pants and try to slip 'em to me. "Let this ride on the nose of whatever horse you're betting on tomorrow," he told me. I got sore. "Nix," I told him, "if you're going to start playin' sucker and bettin' on horse races, you don't get no assist from me." [*He grins wryly.*] Was that a laugh! Me advising a sucker not to bet when I've spent a lot of my life tellin' saps a story to make 'em bet! I said, "Where'd you grab this dough? Outa the Little Woman's purse, huh? What tale you going to give her when you lose it? She'll start breaking up the furniture with you!" "No," he says, "she'll just cry." "That's worse," I said, "no guy can beat that racket. I had a doll cry on me once in a restaurant full of people till I had to promise her a diamond engagement ring to sober her up." Well, anyway, Hughie sneaked the two bucks back in the Little Woman's purse when he went home that morning, and that was the end of that. [*Cynically.*] Boy Scouts got nothin' on me, Pal, when it comes to good deeds. That was one I done. It's too bad I can't remember no others. [*He is well wound up now and goes on without noticing that the Night Clerk's mind has left the premises in his sole custody.*] Y'know I had Hughie sized up for a sap the first time I seen him. I'd just rolled in from Tia Juana.[11] I'd made a big killing down there and I was lousy with jack. Came all the way in a drawing room,[12] and I wasn't lonely in it neither. There was a blonde movie doll on the train—and I was lucky in them days. Used to follow the horses South every winter. I don't no more. Sick of traveling. And I ain't as lucky as I was—[*Hastily.*] Anyway, this time I'm talkin' about, soon as I hit this lobby I see there's a new night clerk, and while I'm signing up for the bridal suite I make a bet with myself he's never been nothin' but a night clerk. And I win. At first, he wouldn't open up. Not that he was cagey about gabbin' too much. But like he couldn't think of nothin' about himself worth saying. But after he'd seen me roll in here the last one every night, and I'd stop to kid him along and tell him the tale of what I'd win that day, he got friendly and talked. He'd come from a hick burg upstate. Graduated from high school, and had a shot at different jobs in the old home town but couldn't make the 290 300 310

---

[10]Famous race horse, winner of the 1920 Belmont Stakes.   United States.
[11]Tijuana, a town in northwest Mexico on the border with the   [12]Luxurious (and expensive) railroad car.

grade until he was took on as night clerk in the hotel there. Then he made good. But he wasn't satisfied. Didn't like being only a night clerk where everybody knew him. He'd read somewhere—in the Suckers' Almanac, I guess— that all a guy had to do was come to the Big Town and Old Man Success would be waitin' at the Grand Central[13] to give him the key to the city. What a gag that is! Even I believed that once, and no one could ever call me a sap. Well, anyway, he made the break and come here and the only job he could get was night clerk. Then he fell in love—or kidded himself he was—and got married. Met her on a subway train. It stopped sudden and she was jerked into him, and he put his arms around her, and they started talking, and the poor boob never stood a chance. She was a sales girl in some punk department store, and she was sick of standing on her dogs all day, and all the way home to Brooklyn, too. So, the way I figger it, knowing Hughie and dames, she proposed and said "yes" for him, and married him, and after that, of course, he never dared stop being a night clerk, even if he could. [*He pauses.*] Maybe you think I ain't giving her a square shake. Well, maybe I ain't. She never give me one. She put me down as a bad influence, and let her chips ride. And maybe Hughie couldn't have done no better. Dolls didn't call him no riot. Hughie and her seemed happy enough the time he had me out to dinner in their flat. Well, not happy. Maybe contented. No, that's boosting it, too. Resigned comes nearer, as if each was givin' the other a break by thinking, "Well, what more could I expect?" [*Abruptly he addresses the Night Clerk with contemptuous good nature.*] How d'you and your Little Woman hit it off, Brother?

NIGHT CLERK   [*His mind has been counting the footfalls of the cop on the beat as they recede, sauntering longingly toward the dawn's release. "If he'd only shoot it out with a gunman some night! Nothing exciting has happened in any night I've ever lived through!" He stammers gropingly among the echoes of Erie's last words.*] Oh—you mean *my* wife? Why, we get along all right, I guess.

ERIE   [*Disgustedly.*] Better lay off them headache pills, Pal. First thing you know, some guy is going to call you a dope. [*But the Night Clerk cannot take this seriously. It is years since he cared what anyone called him. So many guests have called him so many things. The Little Woman has, too. And, of course, he has, himself. But that's all past. Is daybreak coming now? No, too early yet. He can tell by the sound of that surface car. It is still lost in the night. Flat wheeled and tired. Distant the carbarn,[14] and far away the sleep. Erie, having soothed resentment with his wisecrack, goes on with a friendly grin.*] Well, keep hoping, Pal. Hughie was as big a dope as you until I give him some interest in life. [*Slipping back into narrative.*] That time he took me home to dinner. Was that a knockout! It took him a hell of a while to get up nerve to ask me. "Sure, Hughie," I told him, "I'll be tickled to death." I was thinking, I'd rather be shot. For one thing, he lived in Brooklyn, and I'd sooner take a trip to China. Another thing, I'm a guy that likes to eat what I order and not what somebody deals me. And he had kids and a wife, and the family racket is out of my line. But Hughie looked so tickled I couldn't welsh on him. And it didn't work out so bad. Of course, what he called home was only a dump of a cheap flat. Still, it wasn't so bad for a change. His wife had done a lot of stuff to doll it up. Nothin' with no class, you understand. Just cheap stuff to make it comfortable. And his kids wasn't the gorillas I'd expected, neither. No throwin' spitballs in my soup or them kind of gags. They was quiet like Hughie. I kinda liked 'em. After dinner I started tellin' 'em a story about a race horse a guy I know owned once. I thought it was up to me to put out something, and kids like animal

---

[13]I.e., Grand Central Station.
[14]Bus, streetcar, or train terminal.

stories, and this one was true, at that. This old turtle never wins a race, but he was as foxy as ten guys, a natural born crook, the goddamnedest thief, he'd steal anything in reach that wasn't nailed down — Well, I didn't get far. Hughie's wife butt in and stopped me cold. Told the kids it was bedtime and hustled 'em off like I was giving 'em measles. It got my goat, kinda. I coulda liked her — a little — if she'd give me a chance. Not that she was nothin' Ziegfeld[15] would want to glorify. When you call her plain, you give her all the breaks. [*Resentfully.*] Well, to hell with it. She had me tagged for a bum, and seein' me made her sure she was right. You can bet she told Hughie never invite me again, and he never did. He tried to apologize, but I shut him up quick. He says, "Irma was brought up strict. She can't help being narrow-minded about gamblers." I said, "What's it to me? I don't want to hear your dame troubles. I got plenty of my own. Remember that doll I brung home night before last? She gives me an argument I promised her ten bucks. I told her, 'Listen, Baby, I got an impediment in my speech. Maybe it sounded like ten, but it was two, and that's all you get. Hell, I don't want to buy your soul! What would I do with it?' Now she's peddling the news along Broadway I'm a rat and a chiseler, and of course all the rats and chiselers believe her. Before she's through, I won't have a friend left." [*He pauses — confidentially.*] I switched the subject on Hughie, see, on purpose. He never did beef to me about his wife again. [*He gives a forced chuckle.*] Believe me, Pal, I can stop guys that start telling me their family troubles!

NIGHT CLERK   [*His mind has hopped an ambulance clanging down Sixth, and is asking without curiosity: "Will he die, Doctor, or isn't he lucky?" "I'm afraid not, but he'll have to be absolutely quiet for months and months." "With a pretty nurse taking care of him?" "Probably not pretty." "Well, anyway, I claim he's lucky. And now I must get back to the hotel. 492 won't go to bed and insists on telling me jokes. It must have been a joke because he's chuckling." He laughs with a heartiness which has forgotten that heart is more than a word used in "Have a heart," an old slang expression.*] Ha — Ha! That's a good one, Erie. That's the best I've heard in a long time!

ERIE   [*For a moment is so hurt and depressed he hasn't the spirit to make a sarcastic crack. He stares at the floor, twirling his room key — to himself.*] Jesus, this sure is a dead dump. About as homey as the Morgue. [*He glances up at the clock.*] Gettin' late. Better beat it up to my cell and grab some shut eye. [*He makes a move to detach himself from the desk but fails and remains wearily glued to it. His eyes prowl the lobby and finally come to rest on the Clerk's glistening, sallow face. He summons up strength for a withering crack.*] Why didn't you tell me you was deaf, Buddy? I know guys is sensitive about them little afflictions, but I'll keep it confidential. [*But the Clerk's mind has rushed out to follow the siren wail of a fire engine. "A fireman's life must be exciting." His mind rides the engine, and asks a fireman with disinterested eagerness: "Where's the fire? Is it a real good one this time? Has it a good start? Will it be big enough, do you think?" Erie examines his face — bitingly.*] Take my tip, Pal, and don't never try to buy from a dope peddler. He'll tell you you had enough already. [*The Clerk's mind continues its dialogue with the fireman: "I mean, big enough to burn down the whole damn city?" "Sorry, Brother, but there's no chance. There's too much stone and steel. There'd always be something left." "Yes, I guess you're right. There's too much stone and steel. I wasn't really hoping, anyway. It really doesn't matter to me." Erie gives him up and again attempts to pry himself from the desk, twirling his key frantically as if it were a fetish which might set him free.*] Well, me for the hay. [*But he can't dislodge himself — dully.*] Christ, it's lonely. I wish Hughie was here. By God, if he was, I'd tell him a tale that'd make his eyes pop! The bigger the story the harder he'd

---

[15]Florenz Ziegfeld (1867–1932), developed a new kind of musical review in 1907 and called it the "Ziegfeld Follies"; a new "Ziegfeld Follies" was produced each year and was famous for its chorus line of beautiful girls.

fall. He was that kind of sap. He thought gambling was romantic. I guess he saw me like a sort of dream guy, the sort of guy he'd like to be if he could take a chance. I guess he lived a sort of double life listening to me gabbin' about hittin' the high spots. Come to figger it, I'll bet he even cheated on his wife that way, using me and my dolls. [*He chuckles.*] No wonder he liked me, huh? And the bigger I made myself the more he lapped it up. I went easy on him at first. I didn't lie — not any more'n a guy naturally does when he gabs about the bets he wins and the dolls he's made. But I soon see he was cryin' for more, and when a sucker cries for more, you're a dope if you don't let him have it. Every tramp I made got to be a Follies' doll. Hughie liked 'em to be Follies' dolls. Or in the Scandals or Frolics. He wanted me to be the Sheik of Araby, or something that any blonde 'd go round-heeled about. Well, I give him plenty of that. And I give him plenty of gambling tales. I explained my campin' in this dump was because I don't want to waste jack on nothin' but gambling. It was like dope to me, I told him. I couldn't quit. He lapped that up. He liked to kid himself I'm mixed up in the racket. He thought gangsters was romantic. So I fed him some baloney about highjacking I'd done once. I told him I knew all the Big Shots. Well, so I do, most of 'em, to say hello, and sometimes they hello back. Who wouldn't know 'em that hangs around Broadway and the joints? I run errands for 'em sometimes, because there's dough in it, but I'm cagey about gettin' in where it ain't healthy. Hughie wanted to think me and Legs Diamond[16] was old pals. So I give him that too. I give him anything he cried for. [*Earnestly.*] Don't get the wrong idea, Pal. What I fed Hughie wasn't all lies. The tales about gambling wasn't. They was stories of big games and killings that really happened since I've been hangin' round. Only I wasn't in on 'em like I made out — except one or two from way back when I had a run of big luck and was in the bucks for a while until I was took to the cleaners. [*He stops to pay tribute of a sigh to the memory of brave days that were and that never were — then meditatively.*] Yeah, Hughie lapped up my stories like they was duck soup, or a beakful of heroin.[17] I sure took him around with me in tales and showed him one hell of a time. [*He chuckles — then seriously.*] And, d'you know, it done me good, too, in a way. Sure. I'd get to seein' myself like he seen me. Some nights I'd come back here without a buck, feeling lower than a snake's belly, and first thing you know I'd be lousy with jack, bettin' a grand a race. Oh, I was wise I was kiddin' myself. I ain't a sap. But what the hell, Hughie loved it, and it didn't cost nobody nothin', and if every guy along Broadway who kids himself was to drop dead there wouldn't be nobody left. Ain't it the truth, Charlie? [*He again stares at the Night Clerk appealingly, forgetting past rebuffs. The Clerk's face is taut with vacancy. His mind has been trying to fasten itself to some noise in the night, but a rare and threatening pause of silence has fallen on the city, and here he is, chained behind a hotel desk forever, awake when everyone else in the world is asleep, except Room 492, and he won't go to bed, he's still talking, and there is no escape.*]

NIGHT CLERK   [*His glassy eyes stare through Erie's face. He stammers deferentially.*] Truth? I'm afraid I didn't get — What's the truth?

ERIE   [*Hopelessly.*] Nothing, Pal. Not a thing. [*His eyes fall to the floor. For a while he is too defeated even to twirl his room key. The Clerk's mind still cannot make a getaway because the city remains silent, and the night vaguely reminds him of death, and he is vaguely frightened, and now that he remembers, his feet are giving him hell, but that's no excuse not to act as if the Guest is always right: "I should have paid 492 more attention.*

---

[16]Nickname for infamous, rich gangster of the period, John
Henry Diamond (1896–1931).
[17]I.e., easy to swallow.

After all, he is company. He is awake and alive. I should use him to help me live through the night. What's he been talking about? I must have caught some of it without meaning to." The Night Clerk's forehead puckers perspiringly as he tries to remember. Erie begins talking again but this time it is obviously aloud to himself, without hope of a listener.] I 470 could tell by Hughie's face before he went to the hospital, he was through. I've seen the same look on guys' faces when they knew they was on the spot, just before guys caught up with them. I went to see him twice in the hospital. The first time, his wife was there and give me a dirty look, but he cooked up a smile and said, "Hello, Erie, how're the bangtails treating you?" I see he wants a big story to cheer him, but his wife butts in and says he's weak and he mustn't get excited. I felt like crackin', "Well, the Docs in this dump got the right dope. Just leave you with him and he'll never get excited." The second time I went, they wouldn't let me see him. That was near the end. I went to his funeral, too. There wasn't nobody but a coupla his wife's relations. I had to feel sorry for 480 her. She looked like she ought to be parked in a coffin, too. The kids was bawlin'. There wasn't no flowers but a coupla lousy wreaths. It woulda been a punk showing for poor old Hughie, if it hadn't been for my flower piece. [*He swells with pride.*] That was some display, Pal. It'd knock your eye out! Set me back a hundred bucks, and no kiddin'! A big horseshoe of red roses! I knew Hughie'd want a horseshoe because that made it look like he'd been a horse player. And around the top printed in forget-me-nots was "Good-by, Old Pal." Hughie liked to kid himself he was my pal. [*He adds sadly.*] And so he was, at that—even if he was a sucker. [*He pauses, his false poker face as nakedly forlorn as an organ grinder's monkey's. Outside, the spell of abnormal quiet presses suffocatingly upon* 490 *the street, enters the deserted, dirty lobby. The Night Clerk's mind cowers away from it. He cringes behind the desk, his feet aching like hell. There is only one possible escape. If his mind could only fasten onto something 492 has said. "What's he been talking about? A clerk should always be attentive. You even are duty bound to laugh at a guest's smutty jokes, no matter how often you've heard them. That's the policy of the hotel. 492 has been gassing[18] for hours. What's he been telling me? I must be slipping. Always before this I've been able to hear without bothering to listen, but now when I need company—Ah! I've got it! Gambling! He said a lot about gambling. That's something I've always wanted to know more about, too. Maybe he's a professional gambler. Like Arnold Rothstein."*][19]

NIGHT CLERK   [*Blurts out with an uncanny, almost lifelike eagerness.*] I beg your par- 500 don, Mr. — Erie — but did I understand you to say you are a gambler by profession? Do you, by any chance, know the Big Shot, Arnold Rothstein? [*But this time it is Erie who doesn't hear him. And the Clerk's mind is now suddenly impervious to the threat of Night and Silence as it pursues an ideal of fame and glory within itself called Arnold Rothstein.*]

ERIE   [*With mournful longing.*] Christ, I wish Hughie was alive and kickin'. I'd tell him I win ten grand from the bookies, and ten grand at stud, and ten grand in a crap game! I'd tell him I bought one of those Mercedes sport roadsters with nickel pipes sticking out of the hood! I'd tell him I lay three babes from the Follies — two blondes and one brunette! [*The Night Clerk dreams, a rapt hero wor-* 510 *ship transfiguring his pimply face: "Arnold Rothstein! He must be some guy! I read a story about him. He'll gamble for any limit on anything, and always wins. The story said he wouldn't bother playing in a poker game unless the smallest bet you could make—one white chip!—was a hundred dollars. Christ, that's going some! I'd like to have the dough to get in a game with him once! The last pot everyone would drop out but him and me. I'd say, 'Okay, Arnold, the sky's the limit,' and I'd raise him five grand, and he'd call, and I'd*

---

[18]Chattering about nothing.
[19]Rothstein (1883–1928), rich, high-stakes gambler and criminal (bank robbing, bootlegging); killed for not paying a gambling debt.

have a royal flush[20] *to his four aces. Then I'd say, 'Okay, Arnold, I'm a good sport, I'll give you a break. I'll cut you double or nothing. Just one cut. I want quick action for my dough.' And I'd cut the ace of spades and win again." Beatific vision swoons on the empty pools of the Night Clerk's eyes. He resembles a holy saint, recently elected to Paradise. Erie* [520] *breaks the silence—bitterly resigned.*] But Hughie's better off, at that, being dead. He's got all the luck. He needn't do no worryin' now. He's out of the racket. I mean, the whole goddamned racket. I mean life.

NIGHT CLERK   [*Kicked out of his dream—with detached, pleasant acquiescence.*] Yes, it is a goddamned racket when you stop to think, isn't it, 492? But we might as well make the best of it, because—Well, you can't burn it all down, can you? There's too much steel and stone. There'd always be something left to start it going again.

ERIE   [*Scowls bewilderedly.*] Say, what is this? What the hell you talkin' about?

NIGHT CLERK   [*At a loss—in much confusion.*] Why, to be frank, I really don't—Just [530] something that came into my head.

ERIE   [*Bitingly, but showing he is comforted at having made some sort of contact.*] Get it out of your head quick, Charlie, or some guys in uniform will walk in here with a butterfly net and catch you. [*He changes the subject—earnestly.*] Listen, Pal, maybe you guess I was kiddin' about that flower piece for Hughie costing a hundred bucks? Well, I ain't! I didn't give a damn what it cost. It was up to me to give Hughie a big-time send-off, because I knew nobody else would.

NIGHT CLERK   Oh, I'm not doubting your word, Erie. You won the money gambling, I suppose—I mean, I beg your pardon if I'm mistaken, but you are a gambler, aren't you? [540]

ERIE   [*Preoccupied.*] Yeah, sure, when I got scratch[21] to put up. What of it? But I don't win that hundred bucks. I don't win a bet since Hughie was took to the hospital. I had to get down on my knees and beg every guy I know for a sawbuck[22] here and a sawbuck there until I raised it.

NIGHT CLERK   [*His mind concentrated on the Big Ideal—insistently.*] Do you by any chance know—Arnold Rothstein?

ERIE   [*His train of thought interrupted—irritably.*] Arnold? What's he got to do with it? He wouldn't loan a guy like me a nickel to save my grandmother from streetwalking.

NIGHT CLERK   [*With humble awe.*] Then you do know him! [550]

ERIE   Sure I know the bastard. Who don't on Broadway? And he knows me— when he wants to. He uses me to run errands when there ain't no one else handy. But he ain't my trouble, Pal. My trouble is, some of these guys I put the bite on is dead wrong G's,[23] and they expect to be paid back next Tuesday, or else I'm outa luck and have to take it on the lam, or I'll get beat up and maybe sent to a hospital. [*He suddenly rouses himself and there is something pathetically but genuinely gallant about him.*] But what the hell. I was wise I was takin' a chance. I've always took a chance, and if I lose I pay, and no welshing! It sure was worth it to give Hughie the big send-off. [*He pauses. The Night Clerk hasn't paid any attention except to his own dream. A question is trembling on his parted lips, but before he* [560] *can get it out Erie goes on gloomily.*] But even that ain't my big worry, Charlie. My big worry is the run of bad luck I've had since Hughie got took to the hospital. Not a win. That ain't natural. I've always been a lucky guy—lucky enough to get by and pay up, I mean. I wouldn't never worry about owing guys, like I owe them guys. I'd always know I'd make a win that'd fix it. But now I got a lousy hunch when I lost Hughie I lost my luck—I mean, I've lost the old confidence.

---

[20]The five highest cards of a suit.   [22]Ten dollar bill.
[21]Money.   [23]I.e., he owes them thousands (G's: grands).

He used to give me confidence. [*He turns away from the desk.*] No use gabbin' here all night. You can't do me no good. [*He starts toward the elevator.*]

NIGHT CLERK   [*Pleadingly.*] Just a minute, Erie, if you don't mind. [*With awe.*] So you're an old friend of Arnold Rothstein! Would you mind telling me if it's   570
really true when Arnold Rothstein plays poker, one white chip is—a hundred dollars?

ERIE   [*Dully exasperated.*] Say, for Christ's sake, what's it to you—? [*He stops abruptly, staring probingly at the Clerk. There is a pause. Suddenly his face lights up with a saving revelation. He grins warmly and saunters confidently back to the desk.*] Say, Charlie, why didn't you put me wise before, you was interested in gambling? Hell, I got you all wrong, Pal. I been tellin' myself, this guy ain't like old Hughie. He ain't got no sportin' blood. He's just a dope. [*Generously.*] Now I see you're a right guy. Shake. [*He shoves out his hand which the Clerk clasps with a limp pleasure. Erie goes on with gathering warmth and self-assurance.*] That's the stuff.   580
You and me'll get along. I'll give you all the breaks, like I give Hughie.

NIGHT CLERK   [*Gratefully.*] Thank you, Erie. [*Then insistently.*] Is it true when Arnold Rothstein plays poker, one white chip—

ERIE   [*With magnificent carelessness.*] Sets you back a hundred bucks? Sure. Why not? Arnold's in the bucks, ain't he? And when you're in the bucks, a C note[24] is chicken feed. I ought to know, Pal. I was in the bucks when Arnold was a piker.[25] Why, one time down in New Orleans I lit a cigar with a C note, just for a gag, y'understand. I was with a bunch of high class dolls and I wanted to see their eyes pop out—and believe me, they sure popped! After that, I coulda made 'em one at a time or all together! Hell, I once win twenty grand on a   590
single race. That's action! A good crap game is action, too. Hell, I've been in games where there was a hundred grand in real folding money lying around the floor. That's travelin'! [*He darts a quick glance at the Clerk's face and begins to hedge warily. But he needn't. The Clerk sees him now as the Gambler in 492, the Friend of Arnold Rothstein—and nothing is incredible. Erie goes on.*] Of course, I wouldn't kid you. I'm not in the bucks now—not right this moment. You know how it is, Charlie. Down today and up tomorrow. I got some dough ridin' on the nose of a turtle in the 4th at Saratoga. I hear a story he'll be so full of hop, if the joc can keep him from jumpin' over the grandstand, he'll win by a mile. So if I roll in   600
here with a blonde that'll knock your eyes out, don't be surprised. [*He winks and chuckles.*]

NIGHT CLERK   [*Ingratiatingly pally, smiling.*] Oh, you can't surprise me that way. I've been a night clerk in New York all my life, almost. [*He tries out a wink himself.*] I'll forget the house rules, Erie.

ERIE   [*Dryly.*] Yeah. The manager wouldn't like you to remember something he ain't heard of yet. [*Then slyly feeling his way.*] How about shootin' a little crap, Charlie? I mean just in fun, like I used to with Hughie. I know you can't afford takin' no chances. I'll stake you, see? I got a coupla bucks. We gotta use real jack or it don't look real. It's all my jack, get it? You can't lose. I just want to show you how I'll take you to the cleaners. It'll give me confidence. [*He has taken two one-   610
dollar bills and some change from his pocket. He pushes most of it across to the Clerk.*] Here y'are. [*He produces a pair of dice—carelessly.*] Want to give these dice the once-over before we start?

NIGHT CLERK   [*Earnestly.*] What do you think I am? I know I can trust you.

ERIE   [*Smiles.*] You remind me a lot of Hughie, Pal. He always trusted me. Well, don't blame me if I'm lucky. [*He clicks the dice in his hand—thoughtfully.*] Y'know,

---

[24]Century note: $100 bill.
[25]Stingy, cautious gambler.

it's time I quit carryin' the torch for Hughie. Hell, what's the use? It don't do him no good. He's gone. Like we all gotta go. Him yesterday; me or you tomorrow, and who cares, and what's the difference? It's all in the racket, huh? [*His soul is purged of grief, his confidence restored.*] I shoot two bits.   620

NIGHT CLERK   [*Manfully, with an excited deadpan expression he hopes resembles Arnold Rothstein's.*] I fade you.[26]

ERIE   [*Throws the dice.*] Four's my point. [*Gathers them up swiftly and throws them again.*] Four it is. [*He takes the money.*] Easy when you got my luck—and know how. Huh, Charlie? [*He chuckles, giving the Night Clerk the slyly amused, contemptuous, affectionate wink with which a Wise Guy regales a Sucker.*]

CURTAIN

1940–41   1959

THORNTON WILDER
(1897–1975)

Though the body of Thornton Wilder's dramatic work, compared to that of Eugene O'Neill's, is relatively small, that work has been perhaps as influential as O'Neill's in shaping later American drama. Wilder's rebellion against the traditional "realistic" theater was based on his belief in the uniqueness of the dramatic form. He wrote in a 1957 preface:

> [The theater] has one foot planted firmly in the particular, since each actor before us (even when he wears a mask!) is indubitably a living, breathing "one"; yet it tends and strains to exhibit a general truth since its relation to a specific "realistic" truth is confused and undermined by the fact that it is an accumulation of untruths, pretenses and fiction. The novel is pre-eminently the vehicle of the unique occasion, the theater of the generalized one. It is through the theater's power to raise the exhibited individual action into the realm of the idea and type and universal that it is able to evoke our belief.

Wilder could speak with some authority about both the dramatic and fictional forms. By the time he wrote this preface, he had a considerable reputation as a playwright and novelist. Indeed, he had won three Pulitzer Prizes for literature.

Wilder was born in Madison, Wisconsin, where his father was editor of a newspaper. Both his mother and father came from pious Calvinistic backgrounds, and his older brother became a professor of theology. Although Wilder himself was exposed to the same influences as his brother, he grew up with a healthy skepticism of institutionalized religion. He once remarked that a debased language of "clergymen and teachers" had "rendered embarrassing and even ridiculous all the terms of the spiritual life." He came to see his aim as a writer was in part "to discover the spirit that is not unequal to the elevation of the great religious themes, yet which does not fall into repellent didacticism."

When his father entered the consulate service, Wilder attended a series of schools in Hong Kong and China, but finally graduated from Berkeley High

---

[26]Cover the bet.

School in California. He wanted to go to Yale, but his father sent him to Oberlin in Ohio, where he first began to publish in the college literary magazine. At the end of two years he transferred to Yale, and continued publishing plays and essays in the *Yale Literary Magazine;* after a brief stint of service in the Coast Artillery during the First World War, he took a degree in 1920. He studied architecture briefly in Rome, and then began to teach at the Lawrenceville School in New Jersey, where he remained until 1928.

Meantime he had published two novels. The first, *Cabala* (1926), set in modern decadent Rome, was highly praised but not widely read. The second, *The Bridge of San Luis Rey* (1927), set in Peru, opens with the death of five travellers in the collapse of a bridge; the travellers' lives are then explored in a quest for the meaning of this seemingly meaningless catastrophe. The book was a great popular and critical success, winning the Pulitzer Prize.

Wilder's income freed him from his job at Lawrenceville School and enabled him to devote himself entirely to writing. He chose, however, to accept a half-time appointment at the University of Chicago in 1930, and continued teaching there until 1936. It was there he met Gertrude Stein on her lecture tour in America in 1934–35. They became close friends, exchanging ideas about writing, and he promoted her work, providing an introduction to *Narration* (1935), her four Chicago lectures. He later visited her in France, and after her death he lectured on her theories about the creative process.

Wilder never married, and little is known about his personal life. Gilbert A. Harrison in his recent biography (*The Enthusiast*, 1983) presents the evidence of a brief homosexual affair with one Samuel Steward in Italy in 1937. Harrison speculates, however, that Wilder repressed and controlled his homosexual impulses, diverting his sexual energies into his writing.

Drama seems to have been Wilder's first love. The same year he published his first novel (1926), the American Laboratory Theatre produced his first play, *The Trumpet Shall Sound*, which had appeared in 1920 in the *Yale Literary Magazine*. The production was a failure, and Wilder abandoned the play, salvaging only what he had learned in writing and producing it. In 1928 he published a collection of plays and playlets, *The Angel That Troubled the Waters*. Written over a period of a dozen years, these works were much like laboratory exercises, in which Wilder experimented with serious, especially spiritual, themes and with non-realistic, allegorical techniques.

It was, however, in 1931, with the publication of *The Long Christmas Dinner and Other Plays*, that Wilder gave solid evidence of his skill and power in developing a new drama. Two of these plays, including the title play, were produced in 1931 at Yale and the University of Chicago. In a number of the volume's one-act plays, Wilder presented realistic characters in a symbolic setting involved in "allegorical" events that encapsulate a "general truth" about human destiny.

In *The Long Christmas Dinner*, for example, Wilder portrayed ninety years in the life of a single family, the cyclic patterns of ordinary and extraordinary events, of life and death; from one door on stage the successive generations enter as "born," while through another draped in black velvet, the dead make their exit. In achieving this ingenious integration of the "particular" with the "universal," Wilder discovered the dramatic method that best suited his vision of human life and its meaning.

The fulfillment of this method came in two plays: *Our Town*, produced in 1938, and *The Skin of Our Teeth*, in 1942. Both plays won Pulitzer Prizes. In *Our*

Town, Wilder introduced a Stage Manager who calls for and dismisses characters and stage props, and who also explains the cyclic and universal dimensions of the particularized events enacted on stage. The result is a play that is both extraordinarily poignant and profound, and one that has become an American classic. In *The Skin of Our Teeth*, Wilder used his innovative method to portray the whole of human history from Adam and Eve to the present, with humankind precariously surviving one devastating catastrophe or war after another. It spoke eloquently to a country gearing up to enter the Second World War, and it has remained popular in dramatic literature.

In these plays Wilder left his greatest literary legacy. However, *The Matchmaker*, produced in 1954, provided the material for one of the most successful musicals ever written—*Hello, Dolly!* (1964). And *The Long Christmas Dinner* inspired an opera, with music by Paul Hindemith, presented in Mannheim, Germany, in 1961. Wilder's achievement in the novel was also impressive, including *The Women of Andros* (1930), *Heaven's My Destination* (1935), *The Ides of March* (1948), *The Eighth Day* (1967), and *Theophilus North* (1973). But it is as a dramatist of a handful of plays that Wilder seems most likely to be longest remembered.

ADDITIONAL READING

American Characteristics and Other Essays by Thornton Wilder, ed. Donald Gallup, 1979; *The Journals of Thornton Wilder, 1939–1961*, ed. Donald Gallup, 1985.

Rex Burbank, *Thornton Wilder*, 1961, 1978; Bernard Grebanier, *Thornton Wilder*, 1964; Malcolm Goldstein, *The Art of Thornton Wilder*, 1965; Donald Haberman, *The Plays of Thornton Wilder*, 1967; M. C. Kuner, *Thornton Wilder: The Bright and the Dark*, 1972; Richard H. Goldstone, *Thornton Wilder: An Intimate Portrait*, 1975; Linda Simon, *Thornton Wilder: His World*, 1979; Amos Niven Wilder, *Thornton Wilder and His Public*, 1980; Gilbert A. Harrison, *The Enthusiast: A Life of Thornton Wilder*, 1983; David Castronovo, *Thornton Wilder*, 1986.

TEXT

The Long Christmas Dinner and Other Plays in One Act, 1931.

The Long Christmas Dinner

The dining-room of the Bayard home. Close to the footlights a long dining table is handsomely spread for Christmas dinner. The carver's place with a great turkey before it is at the spectator's right.

A door, left back, leads into the hall.

At the extreme left, by the proscenium pillar, is a strange portal trimmed with garlands of fruits and flowers. Directly opposite is another edged and hung with black velvet. The portals denote birth and death.

Ninety years are to be traversed in this play which represents in accelerated motion ninety Christmas dinners at the Bayard household. The actors are dressed in inconspicuous clothes and must indicate their gradual increase in years through their acting. Most of them carry wigs of white hair which they adjust upon their heads at the indicated moment, simply and without comment. The ladies may have shawls concealed beneath the table that they gradually draw up about their shoulders as they grow older. 10

Throughout the play the characters continue eating imaginary food with imaginary knives and forks.

There is no curtain. The audience arriving at the theatre sees the stage set and the table laid, though still in partial darkness. Gradually the lights in the auditorium become dim and the stage brightens until sparkling winter sunlight streams through the dining room windows.

Enter Lucia. *She inspects the table, touching here a knife and there a fork. She talks to*   20
a servant girl who is invisible to us.

LUCIA.   I reckon we're ready now, Gertrude. We won't ring the chimes today. I'll just call them myself.

She goes into the hall and calls:

Roderick. Mother Bayard. We're all ready. Come to dinner.

Enter Roderick *pushing* Mother Bayard *in a wheel chair.*

MOTHER BAYARD.   . . . and a new horse too, Roderick. I used to think that only the wicked owned two horses. A new horse and a new house and a new wife!   30

RODERICK.   Well, Mother, how do you like it? Our first Christmas dinner in the new house, hey?

MOTHER BAYARD.   Tz-Tz-Tz! I don't know what your dear father would say!

LUCIA.   Here, Mother Bayard, you sit between us.

Roderick says grace.

MOTHER BAYARD.   My dear Lucia, I can remember when there were still Indians on this very ground, and I wasn't a young girl either. I can remember when we had to cross the Mississippi on a new-made raft. I can remember when St. Louis and Kansas City were full of Indians.

LUCIA   *(tying a napkin around* Mother Bayard's *neck).* Imagine that! There! —   40
What a wonderful day for our first Christmas dinner: a beautiful sunny morning, snow, a splendid sermon. Dr. McCarthy preaches a splendid sermon. I cried and cried.

RODERICK   *(extending an imaginary carving-fork).* Come now, what'll you have, Mother? A little sliver of white?

LUCIA.   Every least twig is wrapped around with ice. You almost never see that. Can I cut it up for you, dear? *(over her shoulder)* Gertrude, I forgot the jelly. You know, — on the top shelf. — Mother Bayard, I found your mother's gravy-boat while we were moving. What was her name, dear? What were all your names? You were . . . a . . . Genevieve Wainright. Now your mother —   50

MOTHER BAYARD.   Yes, you must write it down somewhere. I was Genevieve Wainright. My mother was Faith Morrison. She was the daughter of a farmer in New Hampshire who was something of a blacksmith too. And she married young John Wainright —

LUCIA   *(memorizing on her fingers).* Genevieve Wainright. Faith Morrison.

RODERICK.   It's all down in a book somewhere upstairs. We have it all. All that kind of thing is very interesting. Come, Lucia, just a little wine. Mother, a little red wine for Christmas day. Full of iron. "Take a little wine for thy stomach's sake."

LUCIA.   Really, I can't get used to wine! What would my father say? But I suppose   60
it's all right.

Enter Cousin Brandon *from the hall. He takes his place by* Lucia.

COUSIN BRANDON   *(rubbing his hands).* Well, well, I smell turkey. My dear cousins, I can't tell you how pleasant it is to be having Christmas dinner with you all. I've lived out there in Alaska so long without relatives. Let me see, how long have you had this new house, Roderick?

RODERICK.   Why, it must be . . .

MOTHER BAYARD.   Five years. It's five years, children. You should keep a diary. This is your sixth Christmas dinner here.

LUCIA.   Think of that, Roderick. We feel as though we had lived here twenty   70
years.

COUSIN BRANDON.   At all events it still looks as good as new.

RODERICK   *(over his carving)*. What'll you have, Brandon, light or dark?—Frieda, fill up Cousin Brandon's glass.

LUCIA.   Oh, dear, I can't get used to these wines. I don't know what my father'd say, I'm sure. What'll you have, Mother Bayard?

During the following speeches Mother Bayard's *chair, without any visible propulsion, starts to draw away from the table, turns toward the right, and slowly goes toward the dark portal.*

MOTHER BAYARD.   Yes, I can remember when there were Indians on this very   80
land.

LUCIA   *(softly)*. Mother Bayard hasn't been very well lately, Roderick.

MOTHER BAYARD.   My mother was a Faith Morrison. And in New Hampshire she married a young John Wainright, who was a Congregational minister. He saw her in his congregation one day . . .

LUCIA.   Mother Bayard, hadn't you better lie down, dear?

MOTHER BAYARD.   . . . and right in the middle of his sermon he said to himself: "I'll marry that girl." And he did, and I'm their daughter.

LUCIA   *(half rising and looking after her with anxiety)*. Just a little nap, dear?

MOTHER BAYARD.   I'm all right. Just go on with your dinner. I was ten, and I said   90
to my brother—

She goes out. A very slight pause.

COUSIN BRANDON.   It's too bad it's such a cold dark day today. We almost need the lamps. I spoke to Major Lewis for a moment after church. His sciatica[1] troubles him, but he does pretty well.

LUCIA   *(dabbing her eyes)*. I know Mother Bayard wouldn't want us to grieve for her on Christmas day, but I can't forget her sitting in her wheel chair right beside us, only a year ago. And she would be so glad to know our good news.

RODERICK   *(patting her hand)*. Now, now. It's Christmas. *(formally)* Cousin Brandon, a glass of wine with you, sir.   100

COUSIN BRANDON   *(half rising, lifting his glass gallantly)*. A glass of wine with you, sir.

LUCIA.   Does the Major's sciatica cause him much pain?

COUSIN BRANDON.   Some, perhaps. But you know his way. He says it'll be all the same in a hundred years.

LUCIA.   Yes, he's a great philosopher.

RODERICK.   His wife sends you a thousand thanks for her Christmas present.

LUCIA.   I forgot what I gave her.—Oh, yes, the workbasket!

Through the entrance of birth comes a nurse wheeling a perambulator trimmed with blue ribbons. Lucia *rushes toward it, the men following.*   110

O my wonderful new baby, my darling baby! Who ever saw such a child! Quick, nurse, a boy or a girl? A boy! Roderick, what shall we call him? Really, nurse, you've never seen such a child!

RODERICK.   We'll call him Charles after your father and grandfather.

LUCIA.   But there are no Charleses in the Bible, Roderick.

RODERICK.   Of course, there are. Surely there are.

---

[1]Painful disorder extending from the hip down the back of the thigh.

LUCIA.   Roderick! — Very well, but he will always be Samuel to me. — What miraculous hands he has! Really, they are the most beautiful hands in the world. All right, nurse. Have a good nap, my darling child.

RODERICK.   Don't drop him, nurse. Brandon and I need him in our firm.   120

Exit nurse and perambulator into the hall. The others return to their chairs, Lucia *taking the place left vacant by* Mother Bayard *and* Cousin Brandon *moving up beside her.* Cousin Brandon *puts on his white hair.*

Lucia, a little white meat? Some stuffing? Cranberry sauce, anybody?

LUCIA   *(over her shoulder).* Margaret, the stuffing is very good today. — Just a little, thank you.

RODERICK.   Now something to wash it down. *(half rising)* Cousin Brandon, a glass of wine with you, sir. To the ladies, God bless them.

LUCIA.   Thank you, kind sirs.

COUSIN BRANDON.   Pity it's such an overcast day today. And no snow.   130

LUCIA.   But the sermon was lovely. I cried and cried. Dr. Spaulding does preach such a splendid sermon.

RODERICK.   I saw Major Lewis for a moment after church. He says his rheumatism comes and goes. His wife says she has something for Charles and will bring it over this afternoon.

Enter nurse again with perambulator. Pink ribbons. Same rush toward the left.

LUCIA.   O my lovely new baby! Really, it never occurred to me that it might be a girl. Why, nurse, she's perfect.

RODERICK.   Now call her what you choose. It's your turn.

LUCIA.   Looloolooloo. Aië. Aië. Yes, this time I shall have my way. She shall be   140 called Genevieve after your mother. Have a good nap, my treasure.

She looks after it as the nurse wheels the perambulator into the hall.

Imagine! Sometime she'll be grown up and say "Good morning, Mother. Good morning, Father." — Really, Cousin Brandon, you don't find a baby like that every day.

COUSIN BRANDON.   *And* the new factory.

LUCIA.   A new factory? Really? Roderick, I shall be very uncomfortable if we're going to turn out to be rich. I've been afraid of that for years. — However, we mustn't talk about such things on Christmas day. I'll just take a little piece of white meat, thank you. Roderick, Charles is destined for the ministry. I'm sure   150 of it.

RODERICK.   Woman, he's only twelve. Let him have a free mind. *We* want him in the firm, I don't mind saying. Anyway, no time passes as slowly as this when you're waiting for your urchins to grow up and settle down to business.

LUCIA.   I don't want time to go any faster, thank you. I love the children just as they are. — Really, Roderick, you know what the doctor said: One glass a meal. *(putting her hand over his glass)* No, Margaret, that will be all.

Roderick rises, glass in hand. With a look of dismay on his face he takes a few steps toward the dark portal.

RODERICK.   Now I wonder what's the matter with me.   160

LUCIA.   Roderick, do be reasonable.

RODERICK   *(tottering, but with gallant irony).* But, my dear, statistics show that we steady, moderate drinkers . . .

LUCIA   *(rises, gazing at him in anguish).* Roderick! My dear! What . . .?

RODERICK   *(returns to his seat with a frightened look of relief).* Well, it's fine to be back at table with you again. How many good Christmas dinners have I had to miss upstairs? And to be back at a fine bright one, too.

LUCIA.   O my dear, you gave us a very alarming time! Here's your glass of milk. —

Josephine, bring Mr. Bayard his medicine from the cupboard in the library.

RODERICK.   At all events, now that I'm better I'm going to start doing something 170 about the house.

LUCIA.   Roderick! You're not going to change the house?

RODERICK.   Only touch it up here and there. It looks a hundred years old.

Charles *enters casually from the hall. He kisses his mother's hair and sits down.*

LUCIA.   Charles, you carve the turkey, dear. Your father's not well. — You always said you hated carving, though you *are* so clever at it.

Father and son exchange places.

CHARLES.   It's a great blowy morning, mother. The wind comes over the hill like a lot of cannon.

LUCIA.   And such a good sermon. I cried and cried. Mother Bayard loved a good 180 sermon so. And she used to sing the Christmas hymns all around the year. Oh, dear, oh, dear, I've been thinking of her all morning!

RODERICK.   Sh, Mother. It's Christmas day. You mustn't think of such things. — You mustn't be depressed.

LUCIA.   But sad things aren't the same as depressing things. I must be getting old: I like them.

CHARLES.   Uncle Brandon, you haven't anything to eat. Pass his plate, Hilda . . . and some cranberry sauce . . .

Enter Genevieve. *She kisses her father's temple and sits down.*

GENEVIEVE.   It's glorious. Every least twig is wrapped around with ice. You al- 190 most never see that.

LUCIA.   Did you have time to deliver those presents after church, Genevieve?

GENEVIEVE.   Yes, Mama. Old Mrs. Lewis sends you a thousand thanks for hers. It was just what she wanted, she said. Give me lots, Charles, lots.

RODERICK   *(rising and starting toward the dark portal).* Statistics, ladies and gentlemen, show that we steady, moderate . . .

CHARLES.   How about a little skating this afternoon, Father?

RODERICK.   I'll live till I'm ninety.

LUCIA.   I really don't think he ought to go skating.

RODERICK   *(at the very portal, suddenly astonished).* Yes, but . . . but . . . not yet! 200
He goes out.

LUCIA   *(dabbing her eyes).* He was so young and so clever, Cousin Brandon. *(raising her voice for* Cousin Brandon's *deafness)* I say he was so young and so clever. — Never forget your father, children. He was a good man. — Well, he wouldn't want us to grieve for him today.

CHARLES.   White or dark, Genevieve? Just another sliver, Mother?

LUCIA   *(Putting on her white hair).* I can remember our first Christmas dinner in this house, Genevieve. Twenty-five years ago today. Mother Bayard was sitting here in her wheel chair. She could remember when Indians lived on this very spot and when she had to cross the river on a new-made raft. 210

CHARLES AND GENEVIEVE.   She couldn't have, Mother. That can't be true.

LUCIA.   It certainly was true — even I can remember when there was only one paved street. We were very happy to walk on boards. *(louder, to Cousin Brandon)* We can remember when there were no sidewalks, can't we, Cousin Brandon?

COUSIN BRANDON   *(delighted).* Oh, yes! And those were the days.

CHARLES AND GENEVIEVE   *(sotto voce. This is a family refrain).* Those were the days.

LUCIA.   . . . and the ball last night, Genevieve? Did you have a nice time? I hope you didn't *waltz*, dear. I think a girl in our position ought to set an example. Did Charles keep an eye on you? 220

GENEVIEVE.   He had none left. They were all on Leonora Banning. He can't conceal it any longer, Mother. I think he's engaged to marry Leonora Banning.

CHARLES.   I'm not engaged to marry anyone.

LUCIA.   Well, she's very pretty.

GENEVIEVE.   I shall never marry, Mother—I shall sit in this house beside you forever, as though life were one long, happy Christmas dinner.

LUCIA.   O my child, you mustn't say such things!

GENEVIEVE   *(playfully)*. You don't want me? You don't want me?

Lucia *bursts into tears.*

Why, Mother, how silly you are! There's nothing sad about that—what could   230
possibly be sad about that.

LUCIA   *(drying her eyes)*. Forgive me. I'm just unpredictable, that's all.

Charles *goes to the door and leads in* Leonora Banning.

LEONORA   *(kissing* Lucia's *temple)*. Good morning, Mother Bayard. Good morning, everybody. It's really a splendid Christmas day today.

CHARLES.   Little white meat? Genevieve, Mother, Leonora?

LEONORA.   Every least twig is encircled with ice.—You never see that.

CHARLES   *(shouting)*. Uncle Brandon, another?—Rogers, fill my uncle's glass.

LUCIA   *(to Charles)*. Do what your father used to do. It would please Cousin Brandon so. You know—*(pretending to raise a glass)*—"Uncle Brandon, a glass of   240
wine—"

CHARLES   *(rising)*. Uncle Brandon, a glass of wine with you, sir.

BRANDON.   A glass of wine with you, sir. To the ladies, God bless them every one.

THE LADIES.   Thank you, kind sirs.

GENEVIEVE.   And if I go to Germany for my music I promise to be back for Christmas. I wouldn't miss that.

LUCIA.   I hate to think of you over there all alone in those strange pensions.[2]

GENEVIEVE.   But, darling, the time will pass so fast that you'll hardly know I'm gone. I'll be back in the twinkling of an eye.

Enter Left, the nurse and perambulator. Green ribbons.   250

LEONORA.   Oh, what an angel! The darlingest baby in the world. Do let me hold it, nurse.

But the nurse resolutely wheels the perambulator across the stage and out the dark door.

Oh, I did love it so!

Lucia *goes to her, puts her arms around* Leonora's *shoulders, and they encircle the room whispering—*Lucia *then hands her over to* Charles *who conducts her on the same circuit.*

GENEVIEVE   *(as her mother sits down,—softly)*. Isn't there anything I can do?

LUCIA   *(raises her eyebrows, ruefully)*. No, dear. Only time, only the passing of time   260
can help in these things.

Charles *and* Leonora *return to the table.*

Don't you think we could ask Cousin Ermengarde to come and live with us here? There's plenty for everyone and there's no reason why she should go on teaching the First Grade for ever and ever. She wouldn't be in the way, would she, Charles?

CHARLES.   No, I think it would be fine.—A little more potato and gravy, anybody? A little more turkey, Mother?

Brandon *rises and starts slowly toward the dark portal.*

---

[2]Boarding houses or small hotels.

Lucia *rises and stands for a moment with her face in her hands.*   270

COUSIN BRANDON   *(muttering).* It was great to be in Alaska in those days . . .

GENEVIEVE   *(half rising, and gazing at her mother in fear).* Mother, what is . . .?

LUCIA   *(Hurriedly).* Hush, my dear. It will pass. — Hold fast to your music, you know. *(as* Genevieve *starts toward her)* No, no. I want to be alone for a few minutes.

She turns and starts after Cousin Brandon *toward the Right.*

CHARLES.   If the Republicans collected all their votes instead of going off into cliques among themselves, they might prevent his getting a second term.

GENEVIEVE.   Charles, Mother doesn't tell us, but she hasn't been very well these days.   280

CHARLES.   Come, Mother, we'll go to Florida for a few weeks.

Exit Brandon.

LUCIA   *(smiling at* Genevieve *and waving her hand).* Don't be foolish. Don't grieve.

She clasps her hands under her chin; her lips move, whispering; she walks serenely into the portal.

Genevieve *stares after her, frozen.*

At the same moment the nurse and perambulator enter from the Left. Pale yellow ribbons. Leonora *rushes to it.*

LEONORA.   O my darlings . . . twins . . . Charles, aren't they glorious! Look at them. Look at them.   290

GENEVIEVE   *(sinks down on the table her face buried in her arms).* But what will I do? What's left for me to do?

CHARLES   *(bending over the basket).* Which is which?

LEONORA.   I feel as though I were the first mother who ever had twins. — Look at them now! — But why wasn't Mother Bayard allowed to stay and see them!

GENEVIEVE   *(rising suddenly distraught, loudly).* I don't want to go on. I can't bear it.

CHARLES   *(goes to her quickly. They sit down. He whispers to her earnestly taking both her hands).* But Genevieve, Genevieve! How frightfully Mother would feel to think that . . . Genevieve!

GENEVIEVE   *(shaking her head wildly).* I never told her how wonderful she was. We   300
all treated her as though she were just a friend in the house. I thought she'd be here forever.

LEONORA   *(timidly).* Genevieve darling, do come one minute and hold my babies' hands. We shall call the girl Lucia after her grandmother, — will that please you? Do just see what adorable little hands they have.

Genevieve *collects herself and goes over to the perambulator. She smiles brokenly into the basket.*

GENEVIEVE.   They are wonderful, Leonora.

LEONORA.   Give him your finger, darling. Just let him hold it.

CHARLES.   And we'll call the boy Samuel. — Well, now everybody come and finish   310
your dinners. Don't drop them, nurse; at least don't drop the boy. We need him in the firm.

LEONORA   *(stands looking after them as the nurse wheels them into the hall).* Someday they'll be big. Imagine! They'll come in and say "Hello, Mother!" *(She makes clucking noises of rapturous consternation.)*

CHARLES.   Come, a little wine, Leonora, Genevieve? Full of iron. Eduardo, fill the ladies' glasses. It certainly is a keen, cold morning. I used to go skating with Father on mornings like this and Mother would come back from church saying—

GENEVIEVE   *(dreamily).* I know: saying "Such a splendid sermon. I cried and   320
cried."

LEONORA.   Why did she cry, dear?

GENEVIEVE.   That generation all cried at sermons. It was their way.

LEONORA.   Really, Genevieve?

GENEVIEVE.   They had had to go since they were children and I suppose sermons reminded them of their fathers and mothers, just as Christmas dinners do us. Especially in an old house like this.

LEONORA.   It really is pretty old, Charles. And so ugly, with all that ironwork filigree and that dreadful cupola.

GENEVIEVE.   Charles! You aren't going to change the house!   330

CHARLES.   No, no. I won't give up the house, but great heavens! it's fifty years old. This Spring we'll remove the cupola and build a new wing toward the tennis courts.

From now on Genevieve *is seen to change. She sits up more straightly. The corners of her mouth become fixed. She becomes a forthright and slightly disillusioned spinster.* Charles *becomes the plain business man and a little pompous.*

LEONORA.   And then couldn't we ask your dear old Cousin Ermengarde to come and live with us? She's really the self-effacing kind.

CHARLES.   Ask her now. Take her out of the First Grade.

GENEVIEVE.   We only seem to think of it on Christmas day with her Christmas   340 card staring us in the face.

Enter Left, nurse and perambulator. Blue ribbons.

LEONORA.   Another boy! Another boy! Here's a Roderick for you at last.

CHARLES.   Roderick Brandon Bayard. A regular little fighter.

LEONORA.   Goodbye, darling. Don't grow up too fast. Yes, yes. Aië, aië, aië — stay just as you are. — Thank you, nurse.

GENEVIEVE   *(who has not left the table, repeats dryly).* Stay just as you are.

Exit nurse and perambulator. The others return to their places.

LEONORA.   Now I have three children. One, two, three. Two boys and a girl. I'm collecting them. It's very exciting. *(over her shoulder)* What, Hilda? Oh, Cousin   350 Ermengarde's come! Come in, Cousin.

She goes to the hall and welcomes Cousin Ermengarde *who already wears her white hair.*

ERMENGARDE   *(shyly).* It's such a pleasure to be with you all.

CHARLES   *(pulling out her chair for her).* The twins have taken a great fancy to you already, Cousin.

LEONORA.   The baby went to her at once.

CHARLES.   Exactly how are we related, Cousin Ermengarde? — There, Genevieve, that's your specialty. — First a little more turkey and stuffing, Mother? Cranberry sauce, anybody?   360

GENEVIEVE.   I can work it out: Grandmother Bayard was your . . .

ERMENGARDE.   Your Grandmother Bayard was a second cousin of my Grandmother Haskins through the Wainrights.

CHARLES.   Well, it's all in a book somewhere upstairs. All that kind of thing is awfully interesting.

GENEVIEVE.   Nonsense. There are no such books. I collect my notes off gravestones, and you have to scrape a good deal of moss — let me tell you — to find one great-grandparent.

CHARLES.   There's a story that my Grandmother Bayard crossed the Mississippi on a raft before there were any bridges or ferryboats. She died before Ge-   370 nevieve or I were born. Time certainly goes very fast in a great new country like this. Have some more cranberry sauce, Cousin Ermengarde.

ERMENGARDE   *(timidly).* Well, time must be passing very slowly in Europe with this dreadful, dreadful war going on.

CHARLES. Perhaps an occasional war isn't so bad after all. It clears up a lot of poisons that collect in nations. It's like a boil.

ERMENGARDE. Oh, dear, oh, dear!

CHARLES *(with relish)*. Yes, it's like a boil.—Ho! ho! Here are your twins.

  The twins appear at the door into the hall. Sam *is wearing the uniform of an ensign.* Lucia *is fussing over some detail on it.* 380

LUCIA. Isn't he wonderful in it, Mother?

CHARLES. Let's get a look at you.

SAM. Mother, don't let Roderick fool with my stamp album while I'm gone.

LEONORA. Now, Sam, do write a letter once in a while. Do be a good boy about that, mind.

SAM. You might send some of those cakes of yours once in a while, Cousin Ermengarde.

ERMENGARDE *(in a flutter)*. I certainly will, my dear boy.

CHARLES. If you need any money, we have agents in Paris and London, remember. 390

SAM. Well, goodbye . . .

  Sam *goes briskly out through the dark portal, tossing his unneeded white hair through the door before him.*

  Lucia *sits down at the table with lowered eyes.*

ERMENGARDE *(after a slight pause, in a low, constrained voice, making conversation)*. I spoke to Mrs. Fairchild for a moment coming out of church. Her rheumatism's a little better, she says. She sends you her warmest thanks for the Christmas present. The workbasket, wasn't it?—It was an admirable sermon. And our stained-glass window looked so beautiful, Leonora, so beautiful. Everybody spoke of it and so affectionately of Sammy. *(Leonora's hand goes to her mouth.)* 400 Forgive me, Leonora, but it's better to speak of him than not to speak of him when we're all thinking of him so hard.

LEONORA *(rising, in anguish)*. He was a mere boy. He was a mere boy, Charles.

CHARLES. My dear, my dear.

LEONORA. I want to tell him how wonderful he was. We let him go so casually. I want to tell him how we all feel about him.—Forgive me, let me walk about a minute.—Yes, of course, Ermengarde—it's best to speak of him.

LUCIA *(in a low voice to Genevieve)*. Isn't there anything I can do?

GENEVIEVE. No, no. Only time, only the passing of time can help in these things.

  Leonora, *straying about the room finds herself near the door to the hall at the moment* 410 *that her son* Roderick *enters. He links his arm with hers and leads her back to the table.*

RODERICK. What's the matter, anyway? What are you all so glum about? The skating was fine today.

CHARLES. Sit down, young man. I have something to say to you.

RODERICK. Everybody was there. Lucia skated in the corners with Dan Creighton the whole time. When'll it be, Lucia, when'll it be?

LUCIA. I don't know what you mean.

RODERICK. Lucia's leaving us soon, Mother. Dan Creighton, of all people.

CHARLES *(ominously)*. Roderick, I have something to say to you.

RODERICK. Yes, Father. 420

CHARLES. Is it true, Roderick, that you made yourself conspicuous last night at the Country Club—at a Christmas Eve dance, too?

LEONORA. Not now, Charles, I beg of you. This is Christmas dinner.

RODERICK *(loudly)*. No, I didn't.

LUCIA. Really, Father, he didn't. It was that dreadful Johnny Lewis.

CHARLES. I don't want to hear about Johnny Lewis. I want to know whether a son of mine . . .

LEONORA.   Charles, I beg of you . . .

CHARLES.   The first family of this city!

RODERICK   *(rising)*. I hate this town and everything about it. I always did.   430

CHARLES.   You behaved like a spoiled puppy, sir, an ill-bred spoiled puppy.

RODERICK.   What did I do? What did I do that was wrong?

CHARLES.   You were drunk and you were rude to the daughters of my best friends.

GENEVIEVE   *(striking the table)*. Nothing in the world deserves an ugly scene like this. Charles, I'm ashamed of you.

RODERICK.   Great God, you gotta get drunk in this town to forget how dull it is. Time passes so slowly here that it stands still, that's what's the trouble.

CHARLES.   Well, young man, we can employ your time. You will leave the university and you will come into the Bayard factory on January second.   440

RODERICK   *(at the door into the hall)*. I have better things to do than to go into your old factory. I'm going somewhere where time passes, my God!

   He goes out into the hall.

LEONORA   *(rising)*. Roderick, Roderick, come here just a moment.—Charles where can he go?

LUCIA   *(rising)*. Sh, Mother. He'll come back. Now I have to go upstairs and pack my trunk.

LEONORA.   I won't have any children left!

LUCIA.   Sh, Mother. He'll come back. He's only gone to California or somewhere.—Cousin Ermengarde has done most of my packing—thanks a   450
thousand times, Cousin Ermengarde. *(She kisses her mother.)* I won't be long.

   She runs out into the hall.

   Genevieve *and* Leonora *put on their white hair.*

ERMENGARDE.   It's a very beautiful day. On the way home from church I stopped and saw Mrs. Foster a moment. Her arthritis comes and goes.

LEONORA.   Is she actually in pain, dear?

ERMENGARDE.   Oh, she says it'll all be the same in a hundred years!

LEONORA.   Yes, she's a brave little stoic.

CHARLES.   Come now, a little white meat, Mother?—Mary, pass my cousin's plate.   460

LEONORA.   What is it, Mary?—Oh, here's a telegram from them in Paris! "Love and Christmas greetings to all." I told them we'd be eating some of their wedding cake and thinking about them today. It seems to be all decided that they will settle down in the East, Ermengarde. I can't even have my daughter for a neighbor. They hope to build before long somewhere on the shore north of New York.

GENEVIEVE.   There is no shore north of New York.

LEONORA.   Well, East or West or whatever it is.

   Pause.

CHARLES.   My, what a dark day.   470

   He puts on his white hair. Pause.

   How slowly time passes without any young people in the house.

LEONORA.   I have three children somewhere.

CHARLES   *(blunderingly offering comfort)*. Well, one of them gave his life for his country.

LEONORA   *(sadly)*. And one of them is selling aluminum in China.

GENEVIEVE   *(slowly working herself up to a hysterical crisis)*. I can stand everything but this terrible soot everywhere. We should have moved long ago. We're surrounded by factories. We have to change the window curtains every week.

LEONORA.   Why, Genevieve!   480

GENEVIEVE. I can't stand it. I can't stand it any more. I'm going abroad. It's not only the soot that comes through the very walls of this house; it's the *thoughts*, it's the thought of what has been and what might have been here. And the feeling about this house of the years *grinding away*. My mother died yesterday—not twenty-five years ago. Oh, I'm going to live and die abroad! Yes, I'm going to be the American old maid living and dying in a pension in Munich or Florence.

ERMENGARDE. Genevieve, you're tired.

CHARLES. Come, Genevieve, take a good drink of cold water. Mary, open the window a minute.   490

GENEVIEVE. I'm sorry. I'm sorry.
    She hurries tearfully out into the hall.

ERMENGARDE. Dear Genevieve will come back to us, I think.
    She rises and starts toward the dark portal.
You should have been out today, Leonora. It was one of those days when everything was encircled with ice. Very pretty, indeed.
    Charles *rises and starts after her.*

CHARLES. Leonora, I used to go skating with Father on mornings like this.—I wish I felt a little better.

LEONORA. What! Have I got two invalids on my hands at once? Now, Cousin 500
Ermengarde, you must get better and help me nurse Charles.

ERMENGARDE. I'll do my best.
    Ermengarde *turns at the very portal and comes back to the table.*

CHARLES. Well, Leonora, I'll do what you ask. I'll write the puppy a letter of forgiveness and apology. It's Christmas day. I'll cable it. That's what I'll do.
    He goes out the dark door.

LEONORA. *(drying her eyes).* Ermengarde, it's such a comfort having you here with me. Mary, I really can't eat anything. Well, perhaps, a sliver of white meat.

ERMENGARDE. *(very old).* I spoke to Mrs. Keene for a moment coming out of church. She asked after the young people.—At church I felt very proud sitting 510
under our windows, Leonora, and our brass tablets. The Bayard aisle,—it's a regular Bayard aisle and I love it.

LEONORA. Ermengarde, would you be very angry with me if I went and stayed with the young people a little this Spring?

ERMENGARDE. Why, no. I know how badly they want you and need you. Especially now that they're about to build a new house.

LEONORA. You wouldn't be angry? This house is yours as long as you want it, remember.

ERMENGARDE. I don't see why the rest of you dislike it. I like it more than I can say.   520

LEONORA. I won't be long. I'll be back in no time and we can have some more of our readings-aloud in the evening.
    She kisses her and goes into the hall. Ermengarde *left alone, eats slowly and talks to* Mary.

ERMENGARDE. Really, Mary, I'll change my mind. If you'll ask Bertha to be good enough to make me a little eggnog. A dear little eggnog.—Such a nice letter this morning from Mrs. Bayard, Mary. Such a nice letter. They're having their first Christmas dinner in the new house. They must be very happy. They call her Mother Bayard, she says, as though she were an old lady. And she says she finds it more comfortable to come and go in a wheel chair.—Such a dear letter. 530
. . . And Mary, I can tell you a secret. It's still a great secret, mind! They're expecting a grandchild. Isn't that good news! Now I'll read a little.

She props a book up before her, still dipping a spoon into a custard from time to time. She grows from very old to immensely old. She sighs. The book falls down. She finds a cane beside her, and soon totters into the dark portal, murmuring:

"Dear little Roderick and little Lucia."

THE END

1931

NEW DIMENSIONS IN PROSE
The New Fiction

"Now listen carefully: except in emergencies, when you are trying to manufacture a quick trick and make some easy money, you don't really need a plot. If you have one, all well and good, if you know what it means and what to do with it. If you are aiming to take up the writing *trade*, you need very different equipment from that which you will need for the *art*, or even just the *profession* of writing. . . . First, have faith in your theme, then get so well acquainted with your characters that they live and grow in your imagination exactly as if you saw them in the flesh; and finally, tell their story with all the truth and tenderness and severity you are capable of; and if you have any character of your own, you will have a style of your own; it grows, as your ideas grow, and as your knowledge of your craft increases. You will discover after a great while that you are probably a writer. You may even make some money at it."

Katherine Anne Porter, "No Plot, My Dear, No Story," 1942

WILLA CATHER
(1873–1947)

In reacting against the many overstuffed naturalistic novels of her time, Willa Cather wrote "The Novel Démeublé" ("The Novel Unfurnished"), in which she exclaimed: "How wonderful it would be if we could throw all the furniture out of the window; and along with it, all the meaningless reiterations concerning physical sensations, all the tiresome old patterns, and leave the room as bare as the stage of a Greek theater, or as that house into which the glory of the pentecost descended; leave the scene bare for the play of emotions, great or little — for the nursery tale, no less than the tragedy, is killed by tasteless amplitude." By the time she wrote "The Novel Démeublé" in 1922, Cather had hit her stride as a novelist, and her economic, lucid, poetic style achieved effects that lay beyond the reach of the enumerations, repetitions, and cumulative details of the traditional naturalistic novel.

Cather did not come by her style and technique without a long apprenticeship. She was born in Virginia and at the age of nine, in 1883, moved with her family to a Great Plains farm in Nebraska at a time when the state was a sparsely settled area of the still remote West. Cather's father soon grew disenchanted with homesteading and moved his family into nearby Red Cloud, one of the typical little towns of those frontier days.

Willa Cather grew up in Red Cloud, gathering the impressions she could not then have known would find their way later into her most moving novels. She was especially fascinated by the European immigrants who had pulled up stakes in the old country and found their way to the American West in quest of a new beginning — the Czechoslovakians, Germans, Scandinavians. She encountered them as the dynamic, attractive "hired girls" working in the households of the slightly more prosperous American settlers. And she found them in their own homes, with the books, pictures, and music that they had brought with them from Europe, evoking an old world culture that both fascinated and haunted this bright young girl off the Nebraska prairie. In Red Cloud Cather discovered the world beyond the horizon and was awakened to the many wonders of its art.

Cather graduated from high school in Red Cloud in 1890 and entered the University of Nebraska in Lincoln. There she made friends with Louise Pound and Dorothy Canfield Fisher (whose father, James Canfield, was the University's president). While still a student, she began to write drama reviews for the *Nebraska State Journal*. Its editor later recalled that Cather's reviews were "of such biting frankness that she became famous among actors from coast to coast." When Stephen Crane came west on a journalistic assignment in 1895, it is likely that Cather met him through her connection with the *Journal*.

In 1896, Cather moved to Pittsburgh to take an editorial post on the *Home Monthly*, a fledgling women's magazine, where she began to publish her first stories. She was to remain in Pittsburgh for ten years, dividing her time between journalism and teaching English in high school. It was in Pittsburgh that she met Isabelle McClung, forming the deepest friendship of her life and finding in the McClung mansion a refuge where she could retreat from the world and write. Cather and Isabelle McClung travelled together to England in 1902 and were there joined by Dorothy Canfield on a trip through France. The friendship with Isabelle McClung was jolted by the latter's marriage in 1916, but survived in reality until Isabelle McClung's death in 1938.

Cather published a slender volume of poems, *April Twilights*, in 1903, and a volume of seven short stories, *The Troll Garden*, in 1905. Neither volume established Cather as a writer, but two of the stories in *The Troll Garden* turned out to be among her most popular and enduring—"The Sculptor's Funeral" and "Paul's Case." The latter, subtitled "A Study in Temperament," remains impressive as a psychological study of an adolescent boy in desperate, irrational rebellion against a drab, lower-middle-class existence for which he is inevitably destined.

Cather's writing attracted the attention of S. S. McClure, publisher of the fast-growing muckraking magazine *McClure's* in New York. She became an editor of this famous magazine in 1905. One of her early assignments was to take over for drastic revision a manuscript dealing with Mary Baker Eddy and the Christian Science movement. This assignment required her going to Boston to do some firsthand research on the movement. There she met Annie Fields, widow of the Boston publisher James T. Fields, and through her, Sarah Orne Jewett, whose work (especially *The Country of the Pointed Firs*) Cather had known and admired.

Although Cather could have had a long and successful career in magazine work, writing and editing, she found herself restless after a few years at *McClure's*, impatient to get on with her own work. She was encouraged by Sarah Orne Jewett to find her own "quiet center of life, and write from that to the world." More and more she turned to her own writing, publishing her first novel, *Alexander's Bridge* (1912), set in the East and Canada and done in the manner of Henry James (one of Cather's favorite authors). The same year she left *McClure's*, determined to make her way on her own as a writer of fiction.

In 1913, Cather published *O Pioneers!*, the first of her novels to be set on the Nebraska prairie of her youth. The favorable reviews encouraged Cather to believe that she had at last found the material that was most compatible with her poetic imagination. There followed, in 1915, *The Song of the Lark*; in 1918, *My Ántonia*; in 1920, *Youth and the Bright Medusa* (a book of short stories); and in 1923, *One of Ours*, which won a Pulitzer Prize. Cather's Great Plains experience turned up, in one form or another, in all these works. But it found its most beautiful and moving embodiment in *My Ántonia*, which H. L. Mencken described in a review: "There is not only the story of poor peasants, flung by fortune into lonely, inhospitable wilds; there is the eternal tragedy of man."

During the 1920s, Willa Cather was at the height of her powers, publishing the novels now considered among her best: *A Lost Lady* (1923); *The Professor's House* (1925); *My Mortal Enemy* (1926); and *Death Comes for the Archbishop* (1927). The most moving of these is probably *A Lost Lady*, the most complex, *The Professor's House*, and the most deeply religious and epic in scope, *Death Comes for the Archbishop*. Experimental in form and carefully crafted, all are distinguished by a style both marvelously simple and magically evocative.

By the 1930s, Cather had virtually exhausted the Nebraska materials that had inspired her greatest novels and she turned to the past for her subjects. She set *Shadows on the Rock* (1931) in seventeenth-century Quebec and *Sapphira and the Slave Girl* (1940) in pre-Civil War Virginia (including her forebears in the action). In *Obscure Destinies* (1932), she returned to her Nebraska past in three novellas, including the much admired "Neighbour Rosicky."

As early as 1896, Cather had written: "Art is not thought or emotion, but expression, expression, always expression. To keep an idea living, intact, tinged with all its original feeling, its original mood, preserving in it all the ecstasy which attended its birth, to keep it so all the way from the brain to the hand and transfer it on paper a living thing with color, odor, sound, life all in it, that is what art means, that is the greatest of all the gifts of the gods." In this statement she provided an excellent description of her remarkable achievement in her greatest work.

When Cather died in 1947, Morton D. Zabel wrote in *The Nation* perhaps the best summation of her career, touching the personal feelings that lay beneath the melancholy cast of her work: "She knew what it meant to be raised in the hinterland of privation and harsh necessities; knew what it meant to look for escape to Chicago and the world beyond; knew . . . what privileges of the richer world mean when they are approached from the outposts of life, what has to be broken away from and what has to be returned to for later nourishment, and [she knew] how little the world appears when its romantic distances and remote promise are curtailed to the dimensions of the individual destiny."

ADDITIONAL READING

The Novels and Stories of Willa Cather, 13 vols., 1937–41; *Willa Cather on Writing*, 1949; *Writings from Willa Cather's Campus Years*, ed. James Shively, 1950; *Willa Cather's Collected Short Fiction, 1892–1912*, ed. Virginia Faulkner, 1965, 1970; *The Kingdom of Art: Willa Cather's First Principles and Critical Statements, 1893–1896*, ed. Bernice Slote, 1967; *The World and the Parish: Willa Cather's Articles and Reviews, 1893–1902*, 2 vols., ed. William M. Curtin, 1970.

René Rapin, *Willa Cather*, 1930; Mildred R. Bennett, *The World of Willa Cather*, 1951, 1961; E. K. Brown and Leon Edel, *Willa Cather: A Critical Biography*, 1953; Edith Lewis, *Willa Cather Living*, 1953; John H. Randall, III, *The Landscape and the Looking Glass*, 1960, 1973; Edward A. and Lillian D. Bloom, *Willa Cather's Gift of Sympathy*, 1962; Elizabeth Shepley Sergeant, *Willa Cather: A Memoir*, 1953, 1963; Dorothy Van Ghent, *Willa Cather*, 1964; James Schroeter, ed., *Willa Cather and Her Critics*, 1967; James Woodress, *Willa Cather: Her Life and Art*, 1970; Bernice Slote and Virginia Faulkner, eds., *The Art of Willa Cather*, 1974; John J. Murphy, ed., *Five Essays on Willa Cather*, 1974; Philip Gerber, *Willa Cather*, 1975; David Stock, *Willa Cather's Imagination*, 1975; Mona Pers, *Willa Cather's Children*, 1975; Joan Crane, *Willa Cather: A Bibliography*, 1982; Phyllis C. Robinson, *Willa: The Life of Willa Cather*, 1983; Marilyn Arnold, *Willa Cather's Short Fiction*, 1984; Susan J. Rosowski, *The Voyage Perilous: Willa Cather's Romanticism*, 1986; Judith Fryer, *The Imaginative Structures of Edith Wharton and Willa Cather*, 1986; Marilyn Arnold, *Willa Cather: A Reference Guide*, 1986; Sharon O'Brien, *Willa Cather: The Emerging Voice*, 1987; James Woodress, *Willa Cather: A Literary Life*, 1987; Robert J. Nelson, *Willa Cather and France: In Search of the Lost Language*, 1988; Hermione Lee, *Willa Cather*, 1989.

TEXTS

"Paul's Case," *The Troll Garden*, 1905; "Neighbour Rosicky," *Obscure Destinies*, 1932.

Paul's Case

A Study in Temperament

It was Paul's afternoon to appear before the faculty of the Pittsburgh High School to account for his various misdemeanours. He had been suspended a week ago, and his father had called at the Principal's office and confessed his perplexity about his son. Paul entered the faculty room suave and smiling. His clothes were a trifle outgrown and the tan velvet on the collar of his open overcoat was frayed and worn; but for all that there was something of the dandy about him, and he wore an opal pin in his neatly knotted black four-in-hand,[1] and a red carnation in his buttonhole. This

---

[1] Long necktie tied by a slipknot.

latter adornment the faculty somehow felt was not properly significant of the contrite spirit befitting a boy under the ban of suspension.

Paul was tall for his age and very thin, with high, cramped shoulders and a narrow chest. His eyes were remarkable for a certain hysterical brilliancy and he continually used them in a conscious, theatrical sort of way, peculiarly offensive in a boy. The pupils were abnormally large, as though he were addicted to belladonna,[2] but there was a glassy glitter about them which that drug does not produce.

When questioned by the Principal as to why he was there, Paul stated, politely enough, that he wanted to come back to school. This was a lie, but Paul was quite accustomed to lying; found it, indeed, indispensable for overcoming friction. His teachers were asked to state their respective charges against him, which they did with such a rancour and aggrievedness as evinced that this was not a usual case. Disorder and impertinence were among the offences named, yet each of his instructors felt that it was scarcely possible to put into words the real cause of the trouble, which lay in a sort of hysterically defiant manner of the boy's; in the contempt which they all knew he felt for them, and which he seemingly made not the least effort to conceal. Once, when he had been making a synopsis of a paragraph at the blackboard, his English teacher had stepped to his side and attempted to guide his hand. Paul had started back with a shudder and thrust his hands violently behind him. The astonished woman could scarcely have been more hurt and embarrassed had he struck at her. The insult was so involuntary and definitely personal as to be unforgettable. In one way and another, he had made all his teachers, men and women alike, conscious of the same feeling of physical aversion. In one class he habitually sat with his hand shading his eyes; in another he always looked out of the window during the recitation; in another he made a running commentary on the lecture, with humorous intention.

His teachers felt this afternoon that his whole attitude was symbolized by his shrug and his flippantly red carnation flower, and they fell upon him without mercy, his English teacher leading the pack. He stood through it smiling, his pale lips parted over his white teeth. (His lips were continually twitching, and he had a habit of raising his eyebrows that was contemptuous and irritating to the last degree.) Older boys than Paul had broken down and shed tears under that baptism of fire, but his set smile did not once desert him, and his only sign of discomfort was the nervous trembling of the fingers that toyed with the buttons of his overcoat, and an occasional jerking of the other hand that held his hat. Paul was always smiling, always glancing about him, seeming to feel that people might be watching him and trying to detect something. This conscious expression, since it was as far as possible from boyish mirthfulness, was usually attributed to insolence or "smartness."

As the inquisition proceeded, one of his instructors repeated an impertinent remark of the boy's, and the Principal asked him whether he thought that a courteous speech to have made a woman. Paul shrugged his shoulders slightly and his eyebrows twitched.

"I don't know," he replied. "I didn't mean to be polite or impolite, either. I guess it's a sort of way I have of saying things regardless."

The Principal, who was a sympathetic man, asked him whether he didn't think that a way it would be well to get rid of. Paul grinned and said he guessed so. When he was told that he could go, he bowed gracefully and went out. His bow was but a repetition of the scandalous red carnation.

His teachers were in despair, and his drawing master voiced the feeling of them all when he declared there was something about the boy which none of them understood. He added: "I don't really believe that smile of his comes altogether from insolence; there's something sort of haunted about it. The boy is not strong, for one

---

[2]Drug that dilates the pupils of the eyes.

thing. I happen to know that he was born in Colorado, only a few months before his mother died out there of a long illness. There is something wrong about the fellow."

The drawing master had come to realize that, in looking at Paul, one saw only his white teeth and the forced animation of his eyes. One warm afternoon the boy had gone to sleep at his drawing-board, and his master had noted with amazement what a white, blue-veined face it was; drawn and wrinkled like an old man's about the eyes, the lips twitching even in his sleep, and stiff with a nervous tension that drew them back from his teeth.

His teachers left the building dissatisfied and unhappy; humiliated to have felt so vindictive toward a mere boy, to have uttered this feeling in cutting terms, and to have set each other on, as it were, in the grewsome game of intemperate reproach. Some of them remembered having seen a miserable street cat set at bay by a ring of tormentors.

As for Paul, he ran down the hill whistling the Soldiers' Chorus from *Faust*[3] looking wildly behind him now and then to see whether some of his teachers were not there to writhe under his light-heartedness. As it was now late in the afternoon and Paul was on duty that evening as usher at Carnegie Hall, he decided that he would not go home to supper. When he reached the concert hall the doors were not yet open and, as it was chilly outside, he decided to go up into the picture gallery—always deserted at this hour—where there were some of Raffelli's[4] gay studies of Paris streets and an airy blue Venetian scene or two that always exhilarated him. He was delighted to find no one in the gallery but the old guard, who sat in one corner, a newspaper on his knee, a black patch over one eye and the other closed. Paul possessed himself of the place and walked confidently up and down, whistling under his breath. After a while he sat down before a blue Rico[5] and lost himself. When he bethought him to look at his watch, it was after seven o'clock, and he rose with a start and ran downstairs, making a face at Augustus,[6] peering out from the castroom,[7] and an evil gesture at the Venus of Milo[8] as he passed her on the stairway.

When Paul reached the ushers' dressing-room half-a-dozen boys were there already, and he began excitedly to tumble into his uniform. It was one of the few that at all approached fitting, and Paul thought it very becoming—though he knew that the tight, straight coat accentuated his narrow chest, about which he was exceedingly sensitive. He was always considerably excited while he dressed, twanging all over to the tuning of the strings and the preliminary flourishes of the horns in the music-room; but to-night he seemed quite beside himself, and he teased and plagued the boys until, telling him that he was crazy, they put him down on the floor and sat on him.

Somewhat calmed by his suppression, Paul dashed out to the front of the house to seat the early comers. He was a model usher; gracious and smiling he ran up and down the aisles; nothing was too much trouble for him; he carried messages and brought programmes as though it were his greatest pleasure in life, and all the people in his section thought him a charming boy, feeling that he remembered and admired them. As the house filled, he grew more and more vivacious and animated, and the colour came to his cheeks and lips. It was very much as though this were a great reception and Paul were the host. Just as the musicians came out to take their places, his English teacher arrived with checks for the seats which a prominent manufacturer had taken for the season. She betrayed some embarrassment when she

[3]The opera *Faust* (1859), by Charles François Gounod (1818–1893), French composer.
[4]Jean François Raffielli (1850–1924), an impressionist French painter of Italian descent.
[5]Martin Rico y Ortega(1833–1908), Spanish artist whose landscapes of Venice are noted for their blue skies.
[6]Original name: Gaius Octavius, sometimes known as Octavianus (63 B.C.–A.D. 14), first Roman emperor (27 B.C.–A.D. 14).
[7]Room where the opera cast assembled.
[8]Famous Greek statue of the goddess Venus, found (with arms missing) on the island of Melos in 1820 and now in the Paris museum, the Louvre.

handed Paul the tickets, and a *hauteur*[9] which subsequently made her feel very foolish. Paul was startled for a moment, and had the feeling of wanting to put her out; what business had she here among all these fine people and gay colours? He looked her over and decided that she was not appropriately dressed and must be a fool to sit downstairs in such togs. The tickets had probably been sent her out of kindness, he reflected as he put down a seat for her, and she had about as much right to sit there as he had.

When the symphony began Paul sank into one of the rear seats with a long sigh of relief, and lost himself as he had done before the Rico. It was not that symphonies, as such, meant anything in particular to Paul, but the first sigh of the instruments seemed to free some hilarious and potent spirit within him; something that struggled there like the Genius in the bottle found by the Arab fisherman.[10] He felt a sudden zest of life; the lights danced before his eyes and the concert hall blazed into unimaginable splendour. When the soprano soloist came on, Paul forgot even the nastiness of his teacher's being there and gave himself up to the peculiar stimulus such personages always had for him. The soloist chanced to be a German woman, by no means in her first youth, and the mother of many children; but she wore an elaborate gown and a tiara, and above all she had that indefinable air of achievement, that world-shine upon her, which, in Paul's eyes, made her a veritable queen of Romance.

After a concert was over Paul was always irritable and wretched until he got to sleep, and to-night he was even more than usually restless. He had the feeling of not being able to let down, of its being impossible to give up this delicious excitement which was the only thing that could be called living at all. During the last number he withdrew and, after hastily changing his clothes in the dressing-room, slipped out to the side door where the soprano's carriage stood. Here he began pacing rapidly up and down the walk, waiting to see her come out.

Over yonder the Schenley, in its vacant stretch, loomed big and square through the fine rain, the windows of its twelve stories glowing like those of a lighted cardboard house under a Christmas tree. All the actors and singers of the better class stayed there when they were in the city, and a number of the big manufacturers of the place lived there in the winter. Paul had often hung about the hotel, watching the people go in and out, longing to enter and leave school-masters and dull care behind him forever.

At last the singer came out, accompanied by the conductor, who helped her into her carriage and closed the door with a cordial *auf wiedersehen*[11] which set Paul to wondering whether she were not an old sweetheart of his. Paul followed the carriage over to the hotel, walking so rapidly as not to be far from the entrance when the singer alighted and disappeared behind the swinging glass doors that were opened by a negro in a tall hat and a long coat. In the moment that the door was ajar it seemed to Paul that he, too, entered. He seemed to feel himself go after her up the steps, into the warm, lighted building, into an exotic, a tropical world of shiny, glistening surfaces and basking ease. He reflected upon the mysterious dishes that were brought into the dining-room, the green bottles in buckets of ice, as he had seen them in the supper party pictures of the *Sunday World* supplement. A quick gust of wind brought the rain down with sudden vehemence, and Paul was startled to find that he was still outside in the slush of the gravel driveway; that his boots were letting in the water and his scanty overcoat was clinging wet about him; that the lights in front of the concert hall were out, and that the rain was driving in sheets between him and the orange glow of the windows above him. There it was, what he wanted —

---

[9] "Disdainful pride" (French).
[10] See "The fisherman and the Jinni (genie or genius)" in *The Thousand Nights and a Night* (or *The Arabian Nights*) (*c*. 900–1500); a jinni is a demon or monstrous giant in Arabic folklore.
[11] "Good-bye" (German).

tangibly before him, like the fairy world of a Christmas pantomime, but mocking spirits stood guard at the doors, and, as the rain beat in his face, Paul wondered whether he were destined always to shiver in the black night outside, looking up at it.

He turned and walked reluctantly toward the car tracks. The end had to come sometime; his father in his night-clothes at the top of the stairs, explanations that did not explain, hastily improvised fictions that were forever tripping him up, his up-stairs room and its horrible yellow wall-paper, the creaking bureau with the greasy plush collar-box, and over his painted wooden bed the pictures of George Washington and John Calvin, and the framed motto, "Feed my Lambs," which had been worked in red worsted by his mother.[12]

Half an hour later, Paul alighted from his car and went slowly down one of the side streets off the main thoroughfare. It was a highly respectable street, where all the houses were exactly alike, and where business men of moderate means begot and reared large families of children, all of whom went to Sabbath-school and learned the shorter catechism, and were interested in arithmetic; all of whom were as exactly alike as their homes, and of a piece with the monotony in which they lived. Paul never went up Cordelia Street without a shudder of loathing. His home was next to the house of the Cumberland minister. He approached it to-night with the nerveless sense of defeat, the hopeless feeling of sinking back forever into ugliness and commonness that he had always had when he came home. The moment he turned into Cordelia Street he felt the waters close above his head. After each of these orgies of living, he experienced all the physical depression which follows a debauch; the loathing of respectable beds, of common food, of a house penetrated by kitchen odours; a shuddering repulsion for the flavourless, colourless mass of every-day existence; a morbid desire for cool things and soft lights and fresh flowers.

The nearer he approached the house, the more absolutely unequal Paul felt to the sight of it all; his ugly sleeping chamber; the cold bathroom with the grimy zinc tub, the cracked mirror, the dripping spiggots; his father, at the top of the stairs, his hairy legs sticking out from his night-shirt, his feet thrust into carpet slippers. He was so much later than usual that there would certainly be inquiries and reproaches. Paul stopped short before the door. He felt that he could not be accosted by his father to-night; that he could not toss again on that miserable bed. He would not go in. He would tell his father that he had no car fare, and it was raining so hard he had gone home with one of the boys and stayed all night.

Meanwhile, he was wet and cold. He went around to the back of the house and tried one of the basement windows, found it open, raised it cautiously, and scrambled down the cellar wall to the floor. There he stood, holding his breath, terrified by the noise he had made, but the floor above him was silent, and there was no creak on the stairs. He found a soap-box, and carried it over to the soft ring of light that streamed from the furnace door, and sat down. He was horribly afraid of rats, so he did not try to sleep, but sat looking distrustfully at the dark, still terrified lest he might have awakened his father. In such reactions, after one of the experiences which made days and nights out of the dreary blanks of the calendar, when his senses were deadened, Paul's head was always singularly clear. Suppose his father had heard him getting in at the window and had come down and shot him for a burglar? Then, again, suppose his father had come down, pistol in hand, and he had cried out in time to save himself, and his father had been horrified to think how nearly he had killed him? Then, again, suppose a day should come when his father would remember that night, and wish there had been no warning cry to stay his hand? With this last supposition Paul entertained himself until daybreak.

The following Sunday was fine; the sodden November chill was broken by the last

---

[12]John Calvin (1509–1564), French protestant theologian whose work figured prominently in the beliefs of the Puritan settlers of America; the "framed motto" would have been an embroidered illustration of a Biblical quotation.

flash of autumnal summer. In the morning Paul had to go to church and Sabbath-school, as always. On seasonable Sunday afternoons the burghers of Cordelia Street always sat out on their front "stoops," and talked to their neighbours on the next stoop, or called to those across the street in neighbourly fashion. The men usually sat on gay cushions placed upon the steps that led down to the sidewalk, while the women, in their Sunday "waists," sat in rockers on the cramped porches, pretending to be greatly at their ease. The children played in the streets; there were so many of them that the place resembled the recreation grounds of a kindergarten. The men on the steps — all in their shirt sleeves, their vests unbuttoned — sat with their legs well apart, their stomachs comfortably protruding, and talked of the prices of things, or told anecdotes of the sagacity of their various chiefs and overlords. They occasionally looked over the multitude of squabbling children, listened affectionately to their high-pitched, nasal voices, smiling to see their own proclivities reproduced in their offspring, and interspersed their legends of the iron kings with remarks about their sons' progress at school, their grades in arithmetic, and the amounts they had saved in their toy banks.

On this last Sunday of November, Paul sat all the afternoon on the lowest step of his "stoop," staring into the street, while his sisters, in their rockers, were talking to the minister's daughters next door about how many shirt-waists they had made in the last week, and how many waffles some one had eaten at the last church supper. When the weather was warm, and his father was in a particularly jovial frame of mind, the girls made lemonade, which was always brought out in a red-glass pitcher, orna-mented with forget-me-nots in blue enamel. This the girls thought very fine, and the neighbours always joked about the suspicious colour of the pitcher.

To-day Paul's father sat on the top step, talking to a young man who shifted a restless baby from knee to knee. He happened to be the young man who was daily held up to Paul as a model, and after whom it was his father's dearest hope that he would pattern. This young man was of a ruddy complexion, with a compressed, red mouth, and faded, near-sighted eyes, over which he wore thick spectacles, with gold bows that curved about his ears. He was clerk to one of the magnates of a great steel corporation, and was looked upon in Cordelia Street as a young man with a future. There was a story that, some five years ago — he was now barely twenty-six — he had been a trifle dissipated but in order to curb his appetites and save the loss of time and strength that a sowing of wild oats might have entailed, he had taken his chief's advice, oft reiterated to his employees, and at twenty-one had married the first woman whom he could persuade to share his fortunes. She happened to be an angu-lar school-mistress, much older than he, who also wore thick glasses, and who had now borne him four children, all near-sighted, like herself.

The young man was relating how his chief, now cruising in the Mediterranean, kept in touch with all the details of the business, arranging his office hours on his yacht just as though he were at home, and "knocking off work enough to keep two stenographers busy." His father told, in turn, the plan his corporation was consider-ing, of putting in an electric railway plant at Cairo. Paul snapped his teeth; he had an awful apprehension that they might spoil it all before he got there. Yet he rather liked to hear these legends of the iron kings, that were told and retold on Sundays and holidays; these stories of palaces in Venice, yachts on the Mediterranean, and high play at Monte Carlo appealed to his fancy, and he was interested in the triumphs of these cash boys who had become famous, though he had no mind for the cash-boy stage.

After supper was over, and he had helped to dry the dishes, Paul nervously asked his father whether he could go to George's to get some help in his geometry, and still more nervously asked for car fare. This latter request he had to repeat, as his father, on principle, did not like to hear requests for money, whether much or little. He asked Paul whether he could not go to some boy who lived nearer, and told him that he ought not to leave his school work until Sunday; but he gave him the dime. He was not a poor man, but he had a worthy ambition to come up in the world. His only reason for allowing Paul to usher was, that he thought a boy ought to be earning a little.

Paul bounded upstairs, scrubbed the greasy odour of the dish-water from his hands with the ill-smelling soap he hated, and then shook over his fingers a few drops of violet water from the bottle he kept hidden in his drawer. He left the house with his geometry conspicuously under his arm, and the moment he got out of Cordelia Street and boarded a downtown car, he shook off the lethargy of two deadening days, and began to live again.

The leading juvenile of the permanent stock company which played at one of the downtown theatres was an acquaintance of Paul's, and the boy had been invited to drop in at the Sunday-night rehearsals whenever he could. For more than a year Paul had spent every available moment loitering about Charley Edwards's dressing-room. He had won a place among Edwards's following not only because the young actor, who could not afford to employ a dresser, often found him useful, but because he recognized in Paul something akin to what churchmen term "vocation."

It was at the theatre and at Carnegie Hall that Paul really lived; the rest was but a sleep and a forgetting.[13] This was Paul's fairy tale, and it had for him all the allurement of a secret love. The moment he inhaled the gassy, painty, dusty odour behind the scenes, he breathed like a prisoner set free, and felt within him the possibility of doing or saying splendid, brilliant, poetic things. The moment the cracked orchestra beat out the overture from *Martha*,[14] or jerked at the serenade from *Rigoletto*,[15] all stupid and ugly things slid from him, and his senses were deliciously, yet delicately fired.

Perhaps it was because, in Paul's world, the natural nearly always wore the guise of ugliness, that a certain element of artificiality seemed to him necessary in beauty. Perhaps it was because his experience of life elsewhere was so full of Sabbath-school picnics, petty economies, wholesome advice as to how to succeed in life, and the unescapable odours of cooking, that he found this existence so alluring, these smartly-clad men and women so attractive, that he was so moved by these starry apple orchards that bloomed perennially under the lime-light.

It would be difficult to put it strongly enough how convincingly the stage entrance of that theatre was for Paul the actual portal of Romance. Certainly none of the company ever suspected it, least of all Charley Edwards. It was very like the old stories that used to float about London of fabulously rich Jews, who had subterranean halls there, with palms, and fountains, and soft lamps and richly apparelled women who never saw the disenchanting light of London day. So, in the midst of that smoke-palled city, enamoured of figures and grimy toil, Paul had his secret temple, his wishing carpet, his bit of blue-and-white Mediterranean shore bathed in perpetual sunshine.

Several of Paul's teachers had a theory that his imagination had been perverted by garish fiction, but the truth was that he scarcely ever read at all. The books at home were not such as would either tempt or corrupt a youthful mind, and as for reading the novels that some of his friends urged upon him — well, he got what he wanted much more quickly from music; any sort of music, from an orchestra to a barrel organ. He needed only the spark, the indescribable thrill that made his imagination master of his senses, and he could make plots and pictures enough of his own. It was equally true that he was not stage struck — not, at any rate, in the usual acceptation of that expression. He had no desire to become an actor, any more than he had to

---

[13]Reference to l. 58 of "Ode: Intimations of Immortality," by British poet William Wordsworth (1770–1850): "Our birth is but a sleep and a forgetting."

[14]Opera by German composer Griedrich von Flotow (1812–1883).

[15]Opera by Italian composer Giuseppe Verdi (1813–1901).

become a musician. He felt no necessity to do any of these things; what he wanted was to see, to be in the atmosphere, float on the wave of it, to be carried out, blue league after blue league, away from everything.

After a night behind the scenes, Paul found the school-room more than ever repulsive; the bare floors and naked walls; the prosy men who never wore frock coats, or violets in their buttonholes; the women with their dull gowns, shrill voices, and pitiful seriousness about prepositions that govern the dative. He could not bear to have the other pupils think, for a moment, that he took these people seriously; he must convey to them that he considered it all trivial, and was there only by way of a jest, anyway. He had autographed pictures of all the members of the stock company which he showed his classmates, telling them the most incredible stories of his famil-iarity with these people, of his acquaintance with the soloists who came to Carnegie Hall, his suppers with them and the flowers he sent them. When these stories lost their effect, and his audience grew listless, he became desperate and would bid all the boys good-bye, announcing that he was going to travel for a while; going to Naples, to Venice, to Egypt. Then, next Monday, he would slip back, conscious and nervously smiling; his sister was ill, and he should have to defer his voyage until spring.

Matters went steadily worse with Paul at school. In the itch to let his instructors know how heartily he despised them and their homilies, and how thoroughly he was appreciated elsewhere, he mentioned once or twice that he had no time to fool with theorems; adding—with a twitch of the eyebrows and a touch of that nervous bra-vado which so perplexed them—that he was helping the people down at the stock company; they were old friends of his.

The upshot of the matter was, that the Principal went to Paul's father, and Paul was taken out of school and put to work. The manager at Carnegie Hall was told to get another usher in his stead; the doorkeeper at the theatre was warned not to admit him to the house; and Charley Edwards remorsefully promised the boy's father not to see him again.

The members of the stock company were vastly amused when some of Paul's sto-ries reached them—especially the women. They were hardworking women, most of them supporting indigent husbands or brothers, and they laughed rather bitterly at having stirred the boy to such fervid and florid inventions. They agreed with the faculty and with his father that Paul's was a bad case.

The east-bound train was ploughing through a January snow-storm; the dull dawn was beginning to show grey when the engine whistled a mile out of Newark. Paul started up from the seat where he had lain curled in uneasy slumber, rubbed the breath-misted window glass with his hand, and peered out. The snow was whirling in curling eddies above the white bottom lands, and the drifts lay already deep in the fields and along the fences, while here and there the long dead grass and dried weed stalks protruded black above it. Lights shone from the scattered houses, and a gang of labourers who stood beside the track waved their lanterns.

Paul had slept very little, and he felt grimy and uncomfortable. He had made the all-night journey in a day coach, partly because he was ashamed, dressed as he was, to go into a Pullman, and partly because he was afraid of being seen there by some Pittsburgh business man, who might have noticed him in Denny & Carson's office. When the whistle awoke him, he clutched quickly at his breast pocket, glancing about him with an uncertain smile. But the little, clay-bespattered Italians were still sleep-ing, the slatternly women across the aisle were in open-mouthed oblivion, and even the crumby, crying babies were for the nonce stilled. Paul settled back to struggle with his impatience as best he could.

When he arrived at the Jersey City station, he hurried through his breakfast, manifestly ill at ease and keeping a sharp eye about him. After he reached the Twenty-third Street station, he consulted a cabman, and had himself driven to a men's furnishing establishment that was just opening for the day. He spent upward of two hours there, buying with endless reconsidering and great care. His new street suit he put on in the fitting-room; the frock coat and dress clothes he had bundled into the cab with his linen. Then he drove to a hatter's and a shoe house. His next errand was at Tiffany's, where he selected his silver and a new scarf-pin. He would not wait to have his silver marked, he said. Lastly, he stopped at a trunk shop on Broadway, and had his purchases packed into various travelling bags.

It was a little after one o'clock when he drove up to the Waldorf, and after settling with the cabman, went into the office. He registered from Washington; said his mother and father had been abroad, and that he had come down to await the arrival of their steamer. He told his story plausibly and had no trouble, since he volunteered to pay for them in advance, in engaging his rooms; a sleeping-room, sitting-room and bath.

Not once, but a hundred times Paul had planned this entry into New York. He had gone over every detail of it with Charley Edwards, and in his scrap book at home there were pages of description about New York hotels, cut from the Sunday papers. When he was shown to his sitting-room on the eighth floor, he saw at a glance that everything was as it should be; there was but one detail in his mental picture that the place did not realize, so he rang for the bell boy and sent him down for flowers. He moved about nervously until the boy returned, putting away his new linen and fingering it delightedly as he did so. When the flowers came, he put them hastily into water, and then tumbled into a hot bath. Presently he came out of his white bathroom, resplendent in his new silk underwear, and playing with the tassels of his red robe. The snow was whirling so fiercely outside his windows that he could scarcely see across the street, but within the air was deliciously soft and fragrant. He put the violets and jonquils on the taboret[16] beside the couch, and threw himself down, with a long sigh, covering himself with a Roman blanket. He was thoroughly tired; he had been in such haste, he had stood up to such a strain, covered so much ground in the last twenty-four hours, that he wanted to think how it had all come about. Lulled by the sound of the wind, the warm air, and the cool fragrance of the flowers, he sank into deep, drowsy retrospection.

It had been wonderfully simple; when they had shut him out of the theatre and concert hall, when they had taken away his bone, the whole thing was virtually determined. The rest was a mere matter of opportunity. The only thing that at all surprised him was his own courage—for he realized well enough that he had always been tormented by fear, a sort of apprehensive dread that, of late years, as the meshes of the lies he had told closed about him, had been pulling the muscles of his body tighter and tighter. Until now, he could not remember the time when he had not been dreading something. Even when he was a little boy, it was always there—behind him, or before, or on either side. There had always been the shadowed corner, the dark place into which he dared not look, but from which something seemed always to be watching him—and Paul had done things that were not pretty to watch, he knew.

But now he had a curious sense of relief, as though he had at last thrown down the gauntlet to the thing in the corner.

Yet it was but a day since he had been sulking in the traces; but yesterday afternoon that he had been sent to the bank with Denny & Carson's deposit, as usual—but this time he was instructed to leave the book to be balanced. There was above two thousand dollars in checks, and nearly a thousand in the bank notes which he had taken from the book and quietly transferred to his pocket. At the bank he had made out a new deposit slip. His nerves had been steady enough to permit of his returning to the office, where he had finished his work and asked for a full day's holiday to-

---

[16]Stool.

morrow, Saturday, giving a perfectly reasonable pretext. The bank book, he knew, would not be returned before Monday or Tuesday, and his father would be out of town for the next week. From the time he slipped the bank notes into his pocket until he boarded the night train for New York, he had not known a moment's hesitation. It was not the first time Paul had steered through treacherous waters.

How astonishingly easy it had all been; here he was, the thing done; and this time there would be no awakening, no figure at the top of the stairs. He watched the snow flakes whirling by his window until he fell asleep.

When he awoke, it was three o'clock in the afternoon. He bounded up with a start; half of one of his precious days gone already! He spent more than an hour in dressing, watching every stage of his toilet carefully in the mirror. Everything was quite perfect; he was exactly the kind of boy he had always wanted to be.

When he went downstairs, Paul took a carriage and drove up Fifth Avenue toward the Park. The snow had somewhat abated; carriages and tradesmen's wagons were hurrying soundlessly to and fro in the winter twilight; boys in woollen mufflers were shovelling off the doorsteps; the avenue stages made fine spots of colour against the white street. Here and there on the corners were stands, with whole flower gardens blooming under glass cases, against the sides of which the snow flakes stuck and melted; violets, roses, carnations, lilies of the valley—somehow vastly more lovely and alluring that they blossomed thus unnaturally in the snow. The Park itself was a wonderful stage winterpiece.

When he returned, the pause of the twilight had ceased, and the tune of the streets had changed. The snow was falling faster, lights streamed from the hotels that reared their dozen stories fearlessly up into the storm, defying the raging Atlantic winds. A long, black stream of carriages poured down the avenue, intersected here and there by other streams, tending horizontally. There were a score of cabs about the entrance of his hotel, and his driver had to wait. Boys in livery were running in and out of the awning stretched across the sidewalk, up and down the red velvet carpet laid from the door to the street. Above, about, within it all was the rumble and roar, the hurry and toss of thousands of human beings as hot for pleasure as himself, and on every side of him towered the glaring affirmation of the omnipotence of wealth.

The boy set his teeth and drew his shoulders together in a spasm of realization; the plot of all dramas, the text of all romances, the nerve-stuff of all sensations was whirling about him like the snow flakes. He burnt like a faggot in a tempest.

When Paul went down to dinner, the music of the orchestra came floating up the elevator shaft to greet him. His head whirled as he stepped into the thronged corridor, and he sank back into one of the chairs against the wall to get his breath. The lights, the chatter, the perfumes, the bewildering medley of colour—he had, for a moment, the feeling of not being able to stand it. But only for a moment; these were his own people, he told himself. He went slowly about the corridors, through the writing-rooms, smoking-rooms, reception-rooms, as though he were exploring the chambers of an enchanted palace, built and peopled for him alone.

When he reached the dining-room he sat down at a table near a window. The flowers, the white linen, the many-coloured wine glasses, the gay toilettes of the women, the low popping of corks, the undulating repetitions of the *Blue Danube*[17] from the orchestra, all flooded Paul's dream with bewildering radiance. When the roseate tinge of his champagne was added—that cold, precious, bubbling stuff that creamed and foamed in his glass—Paul wondered that there were honest men in the world at all. This was what all the world was fighting for, he reflected; this was what all the struggle was about. He doubted the reality of his past. Had he ever known a place

---

[17]Waltz by Vienna composer Johann Strauss the younger
(1825–1899).

called Cordelia Street, a place where fagged-looking businessmen got on the early car; mere rivets in a machine they seemed to Paul, — sickening men, with combings of children's hair always hanging to their coats, and the smell of cooking in their clothes. Cordelia Street — Ah! that belonged to another time and country; had he not always been thus, had he not sat here night after night, from as far back as he could remember, looking pensively over just such shimmering textures, and slowly twirling the stem of a glass like this one between his thumb and middle finger? He rather thought he had.

He was not in the least abashed or lonely. He had no especial desire to meet or to know any of these people; all he demanded was the right to look on and conjecture, to watch the pageant. The mere stage properties were all he contended for. Nor was he lonely later in the evening, in his loge at the Metropolitan. He was now entirely rid of his nervous misgivings, of his forced aggressiveness, of the imperative desire to show himself different from his surroundings. He felt now that his surroundings explained him. Nobody questioned the purple; he had only to wear it passively. He had only to glance down at his attire to reassure himself that here it would be impossible for anyone to humiliate him.

He found it hard to leave his beautiful sitting-room to go to bed that night, and sat long watching the raging storm from his turret window. When he went to sleep it was with the lights turned on in his bedroom; partly because of his old timidity, and partly so that, if he should wake in the night, there would be no wretched moment of doubt, no horrible suspicion of yellow wall-paper, or of Washington and Calvin above his bed.

Sunday morning the city was practically snow-bound. Paul breakfasted late, and in the afternoon he fell in with a wild San Francisco boy, a freshman at Yale, who said he had run down for a "little flyer" over Sunday. The young man offered to show Paul the night side of the town, and the two boys went out together after dinner, not returning to the hotel until seven o'clock the next morning. They had started out in the confiding warmth of a champagne friendship, but their parting in the elevator was singularly cool. The freshman pulled himself together to make his train, and Paul went to bed. He awoke at two o'clock in the afternoon, very thirsty and dizzy, and rang for ice-water, coffee, and the Pittsburgh papers.

On the part of the hotel management, Paul excited no suspicion. There was this to be said for him, that he wore his spoils with dignity and in no way made himself conspicuous. Even under the glow of his wine he was never boisterous, though he found the stuff like a magician's wand for wonder-building. His chief greediness lay in his ears and eyes, and his excesses were not offensive ones. His dearest pleasures were the grey winter twilights in his sitting-room; his quiet enjoyment of his flowers, his clothes, his wide divan, his cigarette and his sense of power. He could not remember a time when he had felt so at peace with himself. The mere release from the necessity of petty lying, lying every day and every day, restored his self-respect. He had never lied for pleasure, even at school; but to be noticed and admired, to assert his difference from other Cordelia Street boys; and he felt a good deal more manly, more honest, even, now that he had no need for boastful pretensions, now that he could, as his actor friends used to say, "dress the part." It was characteristic that remorse did not occur to him. His golden days went by without a shadow, and he made each as perfect as he could.

On the eighth day after his arrival in New York, he found the whole affair exploited in the Pittsburgh papers, exploited with a wealth of detail which indicated that local news of a sensational nature was at a low ebb. The firm of Denny & Carson announced that the boy's father had refunded the full amount of the theft, and that they had no intention of prosecuting. The Cumberland minister had been interviewed, and expressed his hope of yet reclaiming the motherless lad, and his Sabbath-school teacher declared that she would spare no effort to that end. The rumour had reached Pittsburgh that the boy had been seen in a New York hotel, and his father had gone East to find him and bring him home.

Paul had just come in to dress for dinner; he sank into a chair, weak to the knees, and clasped his head in his hands. It was to be worse than jail, even; the tepid waters of Cordelia Street were to close over him finally and forever. The grey monotony stretched before him in hopeless, unrelieved years; Sabbath-school, Young People's Meeting, the yellow-papered room, the damp dish-towels; it all rushed back upon him with a sickening vividness. He had the old feeling that the orchestra had suddenly stopped, the sinking sensation that the play was over. The sweat broke out on his face, and he sprang to his feet, looked about him with his white, conscious smile, and winked at himself in the mirror. With something of the old childish belief in miracles with which he had so often gone to class, all his lessons unlearned, Paul dressed and dashed whistling down the corridor to the elevator.

He had no sooner entered the dining-room and caught the measure of the music than his remembrance was lightened by his old elastic power of claiming the moment, mounting with it, and finding it all sufficient. The glare and glitter about him, the mere scenic accessories had again, and for the last time, their old potency. He would show himself that he was game, he would finish the thing splendidly. He doubted, more than ever, the existence of Cordelia Street, and for the first time he drank his wine recklessly. Was he not, after all, one of those fortunate beings born to the purple, was he not still himself and in his own place? He drummed a nervous accompaniment to the Pagliacci[18] music and looked about him, telling himself over and over that it had paid.

He reflected drowsily, to the swell of the music and the chill sweetness of his wine, that he might have done it more wisely. He might have caught an outbound steamer and been well out of their clutches before now. But the other side of the world had seemed too far away and too uncertain then; he could not have waited for it; his need had been too sharp. If he had to choose over again, he would do the same thing tomorrow. He looked affectionately about the dining-room, now gilded with a soft mist. Ah, it had paid indeed!

Paul was awakened next morning by a painful throbbing in his head and feet. He had thrown himself across the bed without undressing, and had slept with his shoes on. His limbs and hands were lead heavy, and his tongue and throat were parched and burnt. There came upon him one of those fateful attacks of clear-headedness that never occurred except when he was physically exhausted and his nerves hung loose. He lay still and closed his eyes and let the tide of things wash over him.

His father was in New York; "stopping at some joint or other," he told himself. The memory of successive summers on the front stoop fell upon him like a weight of black water. He had not a hundred dollars left; and he knew now, more than ever, that money was everything, the wall that stood between all he loathed and all he wanted. The thing was winding itself up; he had thought of that on his first glorious day in New York, and had even provided a way to snap the thread. It lay on his dressing-table now; he had got it out last night when he came blindly up from dinner, but the shiny metal hurt his eyes, and he disliked the looks of it.

He rose and moved about with a painful effort, succumbing now and again to attacks of nausea. It was the old depression exaggerated; all the world had become Cordelia Street. Yet somehow he was not afraid of anything, was absolutely calm; perhaps because he had looked into the dark corner at last and knew. It was bad enough, what he saw there, but somehow not so bad as his long fear of it had been. He saw everything clearly now. He had a feeling that he had made the best of it, that he had lived the sort of life he was meant to live, and for half an hour he sat staring at

---

[18]Opera by Italian composer Ruggiero Leoncavallo (1858–1919).

the revolver. But he told himself that was not the way, so he went downstairs and took a cab to the ferry.

When Paul arrived at Newark, he got off the train and took another cab, directing the driver to follow the Pennsylvania tracks out of the town. The snow lay heavy on the roadways and had drifted deep in the open fields. Only here and there the dead grass or dried weed stalks projected, singularly black, above it. Once well into the country, Paul dismissed the carriage and walked, floundering along the tracks, his mind a medley of irrelevant things. He seemed to hold in his brain an actual picture of everything he had seen that morning. He remembered every feature of both his drivers, of the toothless old woman from whom he had bought the red flowers in his coat, the agent from whom he had got his ticket, and all of his fellow-passengers on the ferry. His mind, unable to cope with vital matters near at hand, worked feverishly and deftly at sorting and grouping these images. They made for him a part of the ugliness of the world, of the ache in his head, and the bitter burning on his tongue. He stooped and put a handful of snow into his mouth as he walked, but that, too, seemed hot. When he reached a little hillside, where the tracks ran through a cut some twenty feet below him, he stopped and sat down.

The carnations in his coat were drooping with the cold, he noticed; their red glory all over. It occurred to him that all the flowers he had seen in the glass cases that first night must have gone the same way, long before this. It was only one splendid breath they had, in spite of their brave mockery at the winter outside the glass; and it was a losing game in the end, it seemed, this revolt against the homilies by which the world is run. Paul took one of the blossoms carefully from his coat and scooped a little hole in the snow, where he covered it up. Then he dozed a while, from his weak condition, seemingly insensible to the cold.

The sound of an approaching train awoke him, and he started to his feet, remembering only his resolution, and afraid lest he should be too late. He stood watching the approaching locomotive, his teeth chattering, his lips drawn away from them in a frightened smile; once or twice he glanced nervously sidewise, as though he were being watched. When the right moment came, he jumped. As he fell, the folly of his haste occurred to him with merciless clearness, the vastness of what he had left undone. There flashed through his brain, clearer than ever before, the blue of Adriatic water, the yellow of Algerian sands.

He felt something strike his chest, and that his body was being thrown swiftly through the air, on and on, immeasurably far and fast, while his limbs were gently relaxed. Then, because the picture making mechanism was crushed, the disturbing visions flashed into black, and Paul dropped back into the immense design of things.

1905

Neighbour Rosicky

I

When Doctor Burleigh told neighbour Rosicky he had a bad heart, Rosicky protested.

"So? No, I guess my heart was always pretty good. I got a little asthma, maybe. Just a awful short breath when I was pitchin' hay last summer, dat's all."

"Well now, Rosicky, if you know more about it than I do, what did you come to me for? It's your heart that makes you short of breath, I tell you. You're sixty-five years old, and you've always worked hard, and your heart's tired. You've got to be careful from now on, and you can't do heavy work any more. You've got five boys at home to do it for you."

The old farmer looked up at the Doctor with a gleam of amusement in his queer triangular-shaped eyes. His eyes were large and lively, but the lids were caught up in the middle in a curious way, so that they formed a triangle. He did not look like a sick man. His brown face was creased but not wrinkled, he had a ruddy colour in his smooth-shaven cheeks and in his lips, under his long brown moustache. His hair was thin and ragged around his ears, but very little grey. His forehead, naturally high and crossed by deep parallel lines, now ran all the way up to his pointed crown. Rosicky's face had the habit of looking interested,—suggested a contented disposition and a reflective quality that was gay rather than grave. This gave him a certain detachment, the easy manner of an onlooker and observer.

"Well, I guess you ain't got no pills fur a bad heart, Doctor Ed. I guess the only thing is fur me to git me a new one."

Doctor Burleigh swung round in his desk-chair and frowned at the old farmer. "I think if I were you I'd take a little care of the old one, Rosicky."

Rosicky shrugged. "Maybe I don't know how. I expect you mean fur me not to drink my coffee no more."

"I wouldn't, in your place. But you'll do as you choose about that. I've never yet been able to separate a Bohemian[1] from his coffee or his pipe. I've quit trying. But the sure thing is you've got to cut out farm work. You can feed the stock and do chores about the barn, but you can't do anything in the fields that makes you short of breath."

"How about shelling corn?"

"Of course not!"

Rosicky considered with puckered brows.

"I can't make my heart go no longer'n it wants to, can I, Doctor Ed?"

"I think it's good for five or six years yet, maybe more, if you'll take the strain off it. Sit around the house and help Mary. If I had a good wife like yours, I'd want to stay around the house."

His patient chuckled. "It ain't no place fur a man. I don't like no old man hanging round the kitchen too much. An' my wife, she's a awful hard worker her own self."

"That's it; you can help her a little. My Lord, Rosicky, you are one of the few men I know who has a family he can get some comfort out of; happy dispositions, never quarrel among themselves, and they treat you right. I want to see you live a few years and enjoy them."

"Oh, they're good kids, all right," Rosicky assented.

The Doctor wrote him a prescription and asked him how his oldest son, Rudolph, who had married in the spring, was getting on. Rudolph had struck out for himself, on rented land. "And how's Polly? I was afraid Mary mightn't like an American daughter-in-law, but it seems to be working out all right."

"Yes, she's a fine girl. Dat widder woman bring her daughters up very nice. Polly got lots of spunk, an' she got some style, too. Da's nice, for young folks to have some style." Rosicky inclined his head gallantly. His voice and his twinkly smile were an affectionate compliment to his daughter-in-law.

"It looks like a storm, and you'd better be getting home before it comes. In town in the car?" Doctor Burleigh rose.

"No, I'm in de wagon. When you got five boys, you ain't got much chance to ride round in de Ford. I ain't much for cars, noway."

"Well, it's a good road out to your place; but I don't want you bumping around in a wagon much. And never again on a hay-rake, remember!"

Rosicky placed the Doctor's fee delicately behind the desk-telephone, looking the other way, as if this were an absent-minded gesture. He put on his plush cap and his corduroy jacket with a sheepskin collar, and went out.

---

[1]Native of Bohemia, now a part of Czechoslovakia.

The Doctor picked up his stethoscope and frowned at it as if he were seriously annoyed with the instrument. He wished it had been telling tales about some other man's heart, some old man who didn't look the Doctor in the eye so knowingly, or hold out such a warm brown hand when he said good-bye. Doctor Burleigh had been a poor boy in the country before he went away to medical school; he had known Rosicky almost ever since he could remember, and he had a deep affection for Mrs. Rosicky.

Only last winter he had had such a good breakfast at Rosicky's, and that when he needed it. He had been out all night on a long, hard confinement case[2] at Tom Marshall's, — a big rich farm where there was plenty of stock and plenty of feed and a great deal of expensive farm machinery of the newest model, and no comfort whatever. The woman had too many children and too much work, and she was no manager. When the baby was born at last, and handed over to the assisting neighbour woman, and the mother was properly attended to, Burleigh refused any breakfast in that slovenly house, and drove his buggy — the snow was too deep for a car — eight miles to Anton Rosicky's place. He didn't know another farm-house where a man could get such a warm welcome, and such good strong coffee with rich cream. No wonder the old chap didn't want to give up his coffee!

He had driven in just when the boys had come back from the barn and were washing up for breakfast. The long table, covered with a bright oilcloth, was set out with dishes waiting for them, and the warm kitchen was full of the smell of coffee and hot biscuit and sausage. Five big handsome boys, running from twenty to twelve, all with what Burleigh called natural good manners, — they hadn't a bit of the painful self-consciousness he himself had to struggle with when he was a lad. One ran to put his horse away, another helped him off with his fur coat and hung it up, and Josephine, the youngest child and the only daughter, quickly set another place under her mother's direction.

With Mary, to feed creatures was the natural expression of affection, — her chickens, the calves, her big hungry boys. It was a rare pleasure to feed a young man whom she seldom saw and of whom she was as proud as if he belonged to her. Some country housekeepers would have stopped to spread a white cloth over the oilcloth, to change the thick cups and plates for their best china, and the wooden-handled knives for plated ones. But not Mary.

"You must take us as you find us, Doctor Ed. I'd be glad to put out my good things for you if you was expected, but I'm glad to get you any way at all."

He knew she was glad, — she threw back her head and spoke out as if she were announcing him to the whole prairie. Rosicky hadn't said anything at all; he merely smiled his twinkling smile, put some more coal on the fire, and went into his own room to pour the Doctor a little drink in a medicine glass. When they were all seated, he watched his wife's face from his end of the table and spoke to her in Czech. Then, with the instinct of politeness which seldom failed him, he turned to the Doctor and said slyly; "I was just tellin' her not to ask you no questions about Mrs. Marshall till you eat some breakfast. My wife, she's terrible fur to ask questions."

The boys laughed, and so did Mary. She watched the Doctor devour her biscuit and sausage, too much excited to eat anything herself. She drank her coffee and sat taking in everything about her visitor. She had known him when he was a poor country boy, and was boastfully proud of his success, always saying: "What do people go to Omaha for, to see a doctor, when we got the best one in the State right here?" If Mary liked people at all, she felt physical pleasure in the sight of them, personal exultation in any good fortune that came to them. Burleigh didn't know many women like that, but he knew she was like that.

---

[2]Childbirth.

When his hunger was satisfied, he did, of course, have to tell them about Mrs. Marshall, and he noticed what a friendly interest the boys took in the matter.

Rudolph, the oldest one (he was still living at home then), said: "The last time I was over there, she was lifting them big heavy milkcans, and I knew she oughtn't to be doing it."

"Yes, Rudolph told me about that when he come home, and I said it wasn't right," Mary put in warmly. "It was all right for me to do them things up to the last, for I was terrible strong, but that woman's weakly. And do you think she'll be able to nurse it, Ed?" She sometimes forgot to give him the title she was so proud of. "And to think of your being up all night and then not able to get a decent breakfast! I don't know what's the matter with such people."

"Why, Mother," said one of the boys, "if Doctor Ed had got breakfast there, we wouldn't have him here. So you ought to be glad."

"He knows I'm glad to have him, John, any time. But I'm sorry for that poor woman, how bad she'll feel the Doctor had to go away in the cold without his breakfast."

"I wish I'd been in practice when these were getting born." The doctor looked down the row of close-clipped heads. "I missed some good breakfasts by not being."

The boys began to laugh at their mother because she flushed so red, but she stood her ground and threw up her head. "I don't care, you wouldn't have got away from this house without breakfast. No doctor ever did. I'd have had something ready fixed that Anton could warm up for you."

The boys laughed harder than ever, and exclaimed at her: "I'll bet you would!" "She would, that!"

"Father, did you get breakfast for the doctor when we were born?"

"Yes, and he used to bring me my breakfast, too, mighty nice. I was always awful hungry!" Mary admitted with a guilty laugh.

While the boys were getting the Doctor's horse, he went to the window to examine the house plants. "What do you do to your geraniums to keep them blooming all winter, Mary? I never pass this house that from the road I don't see your windows full of flowers."

She snapped off a dark red one, and a ruffled new green leaf, and put them in his buttonhole. "There, that looks better. You look too solemn for a young man, Ed. Why don't you git married? I'm worried about you. Settin' at breakfast, I looked at you real hard, and I seen you've got some grey hairs already."

"Oh, yes! They're coming. Maybe they'd come faster if I married."

"Don't talk so. You'll ruin your health eating at the hotel. I could send your wife a nice loaf of nut bread, if you only had one. I don't like to see a young man getting grey. I'll tell you something, Ed; you make some strong black tea and keep it handy in a bowl, and every morning just brush it into your hair, an' it'll keep the grey from showin' much. That's the way I do!"

Sometimes the Doctor heard the gossipers in the drug-store wondering why Rosicky didn't get on faster. He was industrious, and so were his boys, but they were rather free and easy, weren't pushers, and they didn't always show good judgment. They were comfortable, they were out of debt, but they didn't get much ahead. Maybe, Doctor Burleigh reflected, people as generous and warm-hearted and affectionate as the Rosickys never got ahead much; maybe you couldn't enjoy your life and put it into the bank, too.

II

When Rosicky left Doctor Burleigh's office he went into the farm-implement store to light his pipe and put on his glasses and read over the list Mary had given him. Then he went into the general merchandise place next door and stood about until the pretty girl with the plucked eyebrows, who always waited on him, was free. Those eyebrows, two thin India-ink strokes, amused him, because he remembered how they used to be. Rosicky always prolonged his shopping by a little joking; the girl knew the old fellow admired her, and she liked to chaff with him.

"Seems to me about every other week you buy ticking, Mr. Rosicky, and always the best quality," she remarked as she measured off the heavy bolt with red stripes.

"You see, my wife is always makin' goose-fedder pillows, an' de thin stuff don't hold in dem little down-fedders."

"You must have lots of pillows at your house."

"Sure. She makes quilts of dem, too, We sleeps easy. Now she's makin' a fedder quilt for my son's wife. You know Polly, that married my Rudolph. How much my bill, Miss Pearl?"

"Eight eighty-five."

"Chust make it nine, and put in some candy fur de women."

"As usual. I never did see a man buy so much candy for his wife. First thing you know, she'll be getting too fat."

"I'd like dat. I ain't much fur all dem slim women like what de style is now."

"That's one for me, I suppose, Mr. Bohunk!" Pearl sniffed and elevated her India-ink strokes.

When Rosicky went out to his wagon, it was beginning to snow, — the first snow of the season, and he was glad to see it. He rattled out of town and along the highway through a wonderfully rich stretch of country, the finest farms in the county. He admired this High Prairie, as it was called, and always liked to drive through it. His own place lay in a rougher territory, where there was some clay in the soil and it was not so productive. When he bought his land, he hadn't the money to buy on High Prairie; so he told his boys, when they grumbled, that if their land hadn't some clay in it, they wouldn't own it at all. All the same, he enjoyed looking at these fine farms, as he enjoyed looking at a prize bull.

After he had gone eight miles, he came to the graveyard, which lay just at the edge of his own hay-land. There he stopped his horses and sat still on his wagon seat, looking about at the snowfall. Over yonder on the hill he could see his own house, crouching low, with the clump of orchard behind and the windmill before, and all down the gentle hill-slope the rows of pale gold cornstalks stood out against the white field. The snow was falling over the cornfield and the pasture and the hay-land, steadily, with very little wind, — a nice dry snow. The graveyard had only a light wire fence about it and was all overgrown with long red grass. The fine snow, settling into this red grass and upon the few little evergreens and the headstones, looked very pretty.

It was a nice graveyard, Rosicky reflected, sort of snug and homelike, not cramped or mournful, — a big sweep all round it. A man could lie down in the long grass and see the complete arch of the sky over him, hear the wagons go by; in summer the mowing-machine rattled right up to the wire fence. And it was so near home. Over there across the cornstalks his own roof and windmill looked so good to him that he promised himself to mind the Doctor and take care of himself. He was awful fond of his place, he admitted. He wasn't anxious to leave it. And it was a comfort to think that he would never have to go farther than the edge of his own hayfield. The snow, falling over his barnyard and the graveyard, seemed to draw things together like. And they were all old neighbours in the graveyard, most of them friends; there was nothing to feel awkward or embarrassed about. Embarrassment was the most disagreeable feeling Rosicky knew. He didn't often have it, — only with certain people whom he didn't understand at all.

Well, it was a nice snowstorm; a fine sight to see the snow falling so quietly and graciously over so much open country. On his cap and shoulders, on the horses' backs and manes, light, delicate, mysterious it fell; and with it a dry cool fragrance was released into the air. It meant rest for vegetation and men and beasts, for the ground itself; a season of long nights for sleep, leisurely breakfasts, peace by the fire. This and much more went through Rosicky's mind, but he merely told himself that winter was coming, clucked to his horses, and drove on.

When he reached home, John, the youngest boy, ran out to put away his team for him, and he met Mary coming up from the outside cellar with her apron full of carrots. They went into the house together. On the table, covered with oilcloth figured with clusters of blue grapes, a place was set, and he smelled hot coffee-cake of some kind. Anton never lunched in town; he thought that extravagant, and anyhow he didn't like the food. So Mary always had something ready for him when he got home.

After he was settled in his chair, stirring his coffee in a big cup, Mary took out of the oven a pan of *kolache* stuffed with apricots, examined them anxiously to see whether they had got too dry, put them beside his plate, and then sat down opposite him.

Rosicky asked her in Czech if she wasn't going to have any coffee.

She replied in English, as being somehow the right language for transacting business: "Now what did Doctor Ed say, Anton? You tell me just what."

"He said I was to tell you some compliments, but I forgot 'em." Rosicky's eyes twinkled.

"About you, I mean. What did he say about your asthma?"

"He says I ain't go no asthma." Rosicky took one of the little rolls in his broad brown fingers. The thickened nail of his right thumb told the story of his past.

"Well, what is the matter? And don't try to put me off."

"He don't say nothing much, only I'm a little older, and my heart ain't so good like it used to be."

Mary started and brushed her hair back from her temples with both hands as if she were a little out of her mind. From the way she glared, she might have been in a rage with him.

"He says there's something the matter with your heart? Doctor Ed says so?"

"Now don't yell at me like I was a hog in de garden, Mary. You know I always did like to hear a woman talk soft. He didn't say anything de matter wid my heart, only it ain't so young like it used to be, an' he tell me not to pitch hay or run de corn-sheller."

Mary wanted to jump up, but she sat still. She admired the way he never under any circumstances raised his voice or spoke roughly. He was city-bred, and she was country-bred; she often said she wanted her boys to have their papa's nice ways.

"You never have no pain there, do you? It's your breathing and your stomach that's been wrong. I wouldn't believe nobody but Doctor Ed about it. I guess I'll go see him myself. Didn't he give you no advice?"

"Chust to take it easy like, an' stay round de house dis winter. I guess you got some carpenter work for me to do. I kin make some new shelves for you, and I want dis long time to build a closet in de boys' room and make dem two little fellers keep dere clo'es hung up."

Rosicky drank his coffee from time to time, while he considered. His moustache was of the soft long variety and came down over his mouth like the teeth of a buggy-rake over a bundle of hay. Each time he put down his cup, he ran his blue handkerchief over his lips. When he took a drink of water, he managed very neatly with the back of his hand.

Mary sat watching him intently, trying to find any change in his face. It is hard to see anyone who has become like your own body to you. Yes, his hair had got thin, and his high forehead had deep lines running from left to right. But his neck, always clean shaved except in the busiest seasons, was not loose or baggy. It was burned a dark reddish brown, and there were deep creases in it, but it looked firm and full of blood. His cheeks had a good colour. On either side of his mouth there was a half-moon down the length of his cheek, not wrinkles, but two lines that had come there from his habitual expression. He was shorter and broader than when she married him; his back had grown broad and curved, a good deal like the shell of an old turtle, and his arms and legs were short.

He was fifteen years older than Mary, but she had hardly ever thought about it before. He was her man, and the kind of man she liked. She was rough, and he was gentle, — city-bred, as she always said. They had been shipmates on a rough voyage and had stood by each other in trying times. Life had gone well with them because, at bottom, they had the same ideas about life. They agreed, without discussion, as to what was most important and what was secondary. They didn't often exchange opinions, even in Czech, — it was as if they had thought the same thought together. A good deal had to be sacrificed and thrown overboard in a hard life like theirs, and they had never disagreed as to the things that could go. It had been a hard life, and a soft life, too. There wasn't anything brutal in the short, broad-backed man with the three-cornered eyes and the forehead that went on to the top of his skull. He was a city man, a gentle man, and though he had married a rough farm girl, he had never touched her without gentleness.

They had been at one accord not to hurry through life, not to be always skimping and saving. They saw their neighbours buy more land and feed more stock than they did, without discontent. Once when the creamery agent came to the Rosickys to persuade them to sell him their cream, he told them how much money the Fasslers, their nearest neighbours, had made on their cream last year.

"Yes," said Mary, "and look at them Fassler children! Pale, pinched little things, they look like skimmed milk. I'd rather put some colour into my children's faces than put money into the bank."

The agent shrugged and turned to Anton.

"I guess we'll do like she says," said Rosicky.

III

Mary very soon got into town to see Doctor Ed, and then she had a talk with her boys and set a guard over Rosicky. Even John, the youngest, had his father on his mind. If Rosicky went to throw hay down from the loft, one of the boys ran up the ladder and took the fork from him. He sometimes complained that though he was getting to be an old man, he wasn't an old woman yet.

That winter he stayed in the house in the afternoons and carpentered, or sat in the chair between the window full of plants and the wooden bench where the two pails of drinking-water stood. This spot was called "Father's corner," though it was not a corner at all. He had a shelf there, where he kept his Bohemian papers and his pipes and tobacco, and his shears and needles and thread and tailor's thimble. Having been a tailor in his youth, he couldn't bear to see a woman patching at his clothes, or at the boys'. He liked tailoring, and always patched all the overalls and jackets and work shirts. Occasionally he made over a pair of pants one of the older boys had outgrown, for the little fellow.

While he sewed, he let his mind run back over his life. He had a good deal to remember, really; life in three countries. The only part of his youth he didn't like to remember was the two years he had spent in London, in Cheapside, working for a German tailor who was wretchedly poor. Those days, when he was nearly always hungry, when his clothes were dropping off him for dirt, and the sound of a strange language kept him in continual bewilderment, had left a sore spot in his mind that wouldn't bear touching.

He was twenty when he landed at Castle Garden in New York,[3] and he had a

---

[3]Before Ellis Island, the processing place for immigrants.

protector who got him work in a tailor shop in Vesey Street, down near the Washington Market. He looked upon that part of his life as very happy. He became a good workman, he was industrious, and his wages were increased from time to time. He minded his own business and envied nobody's good fortune. He went to night school and learned to read English. He often did overtime work and was well paid for it, but somehow he never saved anything. He couldn't refuse a loan to a friend, and he was self-indulgent. He liked a good dinner, and a little went for beer, a little for tobacco; a good deal went to the girls. He often stood through an opera on Saturday nights; he could get standing-room for a dollar. Those were the great days of opera in New York, and it gave a fellow something to think about for the rest of the week. Rosicky had a quick ear, and a childish love of all the stage splendour; the scenery, the costumes, the ballet. He usually went with a chum, and after the performance they had beer and maybe some oysters somewhere. It was a fine life; for the first five years or so it satisfied him completely. He was never hungry or cold or dirty, and everything amused him: a fire, a dog fight, a parade, a storm, a ferry ride. He thought New York the finest, richest, friendliest city in the world.

Moreover, he had what he called a happy home life. Very near the tailor shop was a small furniture-factory, where an old Austrian, Loeffler, employed a few skilled men and made unusual furniture, most of it to order, for the rich German housewives up-town. The top floor of Loeffler's five-storey factory was a loft, where he kept his choice lumber and stored the odd pieces of furniture left on his hands. One of the young workmen he employed was a Czech, and he and Rosicky became fast friends. They persuaded Loeffler to let them have a sleeping-room in one corner of the loft. They bought good beds and bedding and had their pick of the furniture kept up there. The loft was low-pitched, but light and airy, full of windows, and good-smelling by reason of the fine lumber put up there to season. Old Loeffler used to go down to the docks and buy wood from South America and the East from the sea captains. The young men were as foolish about their house as a bridal pair. Zichec, the young cabinet-maker, devised every sort of convenience, and Rosicky kept their clothes in order. At night and on Sundays, when the quiver of machinery underneath was still, it was the quietest place in the world, and on summer nights all the sea winds blew in. Zichec often practised on his flute in the evening. They were both fond of music and went to the opera together. Rosicky thought he wanted to live like that for ever.

But as the years passed, all alike, he began to get a little restless. When spring came round, he would begin to feel fretted, and he got to drinking. He was likely to drink too much of a Saturday night. On Sunday he was languid and heavy, getting over his spree. On Monday he plunged into work again. So he never had time to figure out what ailed him, though he knew something did. When the grass turned green in Park Place, and the lilac hedge at the back of Trinity churchyard put out its blossoms, he was tormented by a longing to run away. That was why he drank too much; to get a temporary illusion of freedom and wide horizons.

Rosicky, the old Rosicky, could remember as if it were yesterday the day when the young Rosicky found out what was the matter with him. It was on a Fourth of July afternoon, and he was sitting in Park Place in the sun. The lower part of New York was empty. Wall Street, Liberty Street, Broadway, all empty. So much stone and asphalt with nothing going on, so many empty windows. The emptiness was intense, like the stillness in a great factory when the machinery stops and the belts and bands cease running. It was too great a change, it took all the strength out of one. Those blank buildings, without the stream of life pouring through them, were like empty jails. It struck young Rosicky that this was the trouble with big cities; they built you in from the earth itself, cemented you away from any contact with the ground. You lived in an unnatural world, like the fish in an aquarium, who were probably much more comfortable than they ever were in the sea.

On that very day he began to think seriously about the articles he had read in the Bohemian papers, describing prosperous Czech farming communities in the West. He believed he would like to go out there as a farm hand; it was hardly possible that he could ever have land of his own. His people had always been workmen; his father and grandfather had worked in shops. His mother's parents had lived in the country, but they rented their farm and had a hard time to get along. Nobody in his family had ever owned any land,—that belonged to a different station of life altogether. Anton's mother died when he was little, and he was sent into the country to her parents. He stayed with them until he was twelve, and formed those ties with the earth and the farm animals and growing things which are never made at all unless they are made early. After his grandfather died, he went back to live with his father and stepmother, but she was very hard on him, and his father helped him to get passage to London.

After that Fourth of July day in Park Place, the desire to return to the country never left him. To work on another man's farm would be all he asked; to see the sun rise and set and to plant things and watch them grow. He was a very simple man. He was like a tree that has not many roots, but one tap-root that goes down deep. He subscribed for a Bohemian paper printed in Chicago, then for one printed in Omaha. His mind got farther and farther west. He began to save a little money to buy his liberty. When he was thirty-five, there was a great meeting in New York of Bohemian athletic societies, and Rosicky left the tailor shop and went home with the Omaha delgates to try his fortune in another part of the world.

IV

Perhaps the fact that his own youth was well over before he began to have a family was one reason why Rosicky was so fond of his boys. He had almost a grandfather's indulgence for them. He had never had to worry about any of them—except, just now, a little about Rudolph.

On Saturday night the boys always piled into the Ford, took little Josephine, and went to town to the moving-picture show. One Saturday morning they were talking at the breakfast table about starting early that evening, so that they would have an hour or so to see the Christmas things in the stores before the show began. Rosicky looked down the table.

"I hope you boys ain't disappointed, but I want you to let me have de car tonight. Maybe some of you can go in with de neighbours."

Their faces fell. They worked hard all week, and they were still like children. A new jackknife or a box of candy pleased the older ones as much as the little fellow.

"If you and Mother are going to town," Frank said, "maybe you could take a couple of us along with you, anyway."

"No, I want to take de car down to Rudolph's, and let him an' Polly go in to de show. She don't git into town enough, an' I'm afraid she's gettin' lonesome, an' he can't afford no car yet."

That settled it. The boys were a good deal dashed. Their father took another piece of apple-cake and went on: "Maybe next Saturday night de two little fellers can go along wid dem."

"Oh, is Rudolph going to have the car every Saturday night?"

Rosicky did not reply at once; then he began to speak seriously: "Listen, boys; Polly ain't lookin' so good. I don't like to see nobody lookin' sad. It comes hard fur a town girl to be a farmer's wife. I don't want no trouble to start in Rudolph's family. When it starts, it ain't so easy to stop. An American girl don't git used to our ways all at once. I like to tell Polly she and Rudolph can have the car every Saturday night till after New Year's, if it's all right with you boys."

"Sure it's all right, Papa," Mary cut in. "And it's good you thought about that. Town girls is used to more than country girls. I lay awake nights, scared she'll make Rudolph discontented with the farm."

The boys put as good a face on it as they could. They surely looked forward to their Saturday nights in town. That evening Rosicky drove the car the half-mile down to Rudolph's new, bare little house.

Polly was in a short-sleeved gingham dress, clearing away the supper dishes. She was a trim, slim little thing, with blue eyes and shingled yellow hair, and her eyebrows were reduced to a mere brush-stroke, like Miss Pearl's.

"Good evening, Mr. Rosicky. Rudolph's at the barn, I guess." She never called him father, or Mary mother. She was sensitive about having married a foreigner. She never in the world would have done it if Rudolph hadn't been such a handsome, persuasive fellow and such a gallant lover. He had graduated in her class in the high school in town, and their friendship began in the ninth grade.

Rosicky went in, though he wasn't exactly asked. "My boys ain't goin' to town tonight, an' I brought de car over fur you two to go in to de picture show."

Polly, carrying dishes to the sink, looked over her shoulder at him. "Thank you. But I'm late with my work tonight, and pretty tired. Maybe Rudolph would like to go in with you."

"Oh, I don't go to de shows! I'm too old-fashioned. You won't feel so tired after you ride in de air a ways. It's a nice clear night, an' it ain't cold. You go an' fix yourself up, Polly, an' I'll wash de dishes an' leave everything nice fur you."

Polly blushed and tossed her bob. "I couldn't let you do that, Mr. Rosicky. I wouldn't think of it."

Rosicky said nothing. He found a bib apron on a nail behind the kitchen door. He slipped it over his head and then took Polly by her two elbows and pushed her gently toward the door of her own room. "I washed up de kitchen many times for my wife, when de babies was sick or somethin'. You go an' make yourself look nice. I like you to look prettier'n any of dem town girls when you go in. De young folks must have some fun, an' I'm goin' to look out fur you, Polly."

That kind, reassuring grip on her elbows, the old man's funny bright eyes, made Polly want to drop her head on his shoulder for a second. She restrained herself, but she lingered in his grasp at the door of her room, murmuring tearfully: "You always lived in the city when you were young, didn't you? Don't you ever get lonesome out here?"

As she turned round to him, her hand fell naturally into his, and he stood holding it and smiling into her face with his peculiar, knowing, indulgent smile without a shadow of reproach in it. "Dem big cities is all right fur de rich, but dey is terrible hard fur de poor."

"I don't know. Sometimes I think I'd like to take a chance. You lived in New York, didn't you?"

"An' London. Da's bigger still. I learned my trade dere. Here's Rudolph comin', you better hurry."

"Will you tell me about London some time?"

"Maybe. Only I ain't no talker, Polly. Run an' dress yourself up."

The bedroom door closed behind her, and Rudolph came in from the outside, looking anxious. He had seen the car and was sorry any of his family should come just then. Supper hadn't been a very pleasant occasion. Halting in the doorway, he saw his father in a kitchen apron, carrying dishes to the sink. He flushed crimson and something flashed in his eye. Rosicky held up a warning finger.

"I brought de car over fur you an' Polly to go to de picture show, an' I made her let me finish here so you won't be late. You go put on a clean shirt, quick!"

"But don't the boys want the car, Father?"

"Not tonight dey don't." Rosicky fumbled under his apron and found his pants pocket. He took out a silver dollar and said in a hurried whisper: "You go an' buy dat girl some ice cream an' candy tonight, like you was courtin'. She's awful good friends wid me."

Rudolph was very short of cash, but he took the money as if it hurt him. There had been a crop failure all over the county. He had more than once been sorry he'd married this year.

In a few minutes the young people came out, looking clean and a little stiff. Rosicky hurried them off, and then he took his own time with the dishes. He scoured the pots and pans and put away the milk and swept the kitchen. He put some coal in the stove and shut off the draughts, so the place would be warm for them when they got home late at night. Then he sat down and had a pipe and listened to the clock tick.

Generally speaking, marrying an American girl was certainly a risk. A Czech should marry a Czech. It was lucky that Polly was the daughter of a poor widow woman; Rudolph was proud, and if she had a prosperous family to throw up at him, they could never make it go. Polly was one of four sisters, and they all worked; one was book-keeper in the bank, one taught music, and Polly and her younger sister had been clerks, like Miss Pearl. All four of them were musical, had pretty voices, and sang in the Methodist choir, which the eldest sister directed.

Polly missed the sociability of a store position. She missed the choir, and the company of her sisters. She didn't dislike housework, but she disliked so much of it. Rosicky was a little anxious about this pair. He was afraid Polly would grow so discontented that Rudy would quit the farm and take a factory job in Omaha. He had worked for a winter up there, two years ago, to get money to marry on. He had done very well, and they would always take him back at the stockyards. But to Rosicky that meant the end of everything for his son. To be a landless man was to be a wage-earner, a slave, all your life; to have nothing, to be nothing.

Rosicky thought he would come over and do a little carpentering for Polly after the New Year. He guessed she needed jollying. Rudolph was a serious sort of chap, serious in love and serious about his work.

Rosicky shook out his pipe and walked home across the fields. Ahead of him the lamplight shone from his kitchen windows. Suppose he were still in a tailor shop on Vesey Street, with a bunch of pale, narrow-chested sons working on machines, all coming home tired and sullen to eat supper in a kitchen that was a parlour also; with another crowded, angry family quarrelling just across the dumb-waiter shaft, and squeaking pulleys at the windows where dirty washings hung on dirty lines above a court full of old brooms and mops and ash-cans. . . .

He stopped by the windmill to look up at the frosty winter stars and draw a long breath before he went inside. That kitchen with the shining windows was dear to him; but the sleeping fields and bright stars and the noble darkness were dearer still.

V

On the day before Christmas the weather set in very cold; no snow, but a bitter, biting wind that whistled and sang over the flat land and lashed one's face like fine wires. There was baking going on in the Rosicky kitchen all day, and Rosicky sat inside, making over a coat that Albert had outgrown into an overcoat for John. Mary had a big red geranium in bloom for Christmas, and a row of Jerusalem cherry trees, full of berries. It was the first year she had ever grown these; Doctor Ed brought her the seeds from Omaha when he went to some medical convention. They reminded Rosicky of plants he had seen in England; and all afternoon, as he stitched, he sat thinking about those two years in London, which his mind usually shrank from even after all this while.

He was a lad of eighteen when he dropped down into London, with no money and no connexions except the address of a cousin who was supposed to be working at a confectioner's. When he went to the pastry shop, however, he found that the cousin had gone to America. Anton tramped the streets for several days, sleeping in door-ways and on the Embankment,[4] until he was in utter despair. He knew no English, and the sound of the strange language all about him confused him. By chance he met a poor German tailor who had learned his trade in Vienna, and could speak a little Czech. This tailor, Lifschnitz, kept a repair shop in a Cheapside[5] basement, under-neath a cobbler. He didn't much need an apprentice, but he was sorry for the boy and took him in for no wages but his keep and what he could pick up. The pickings were supposed to be coppers given you when you took work home to a customer. But most of the customers called for their clothes themselves, and the coppers that came Anton's way were very few. He had, however, a place to sleep. The tailor's family lived upstairs in three rooms; a kitchen, a bedroom, where Lifschnitz and his wife and five children slept, and a living-room. Two corners of this living-room were curtained off for lodgers; in one Rosicky slept on an old horsehair sofa, with a feather quilt to wrap himself in. The other corner was rented to a wretched, dirty boy, who was studying the violin. He actually practised there. Rosicky was dirty, too. There was no way to be anything else. Mrs. Lifschnitz got the water she cooked and washed with from a pump in a brick court, four flights down. There were bugs in the place, and multi-tudes of fleas, though the poor woman did the best she could. Rosicky knew she often went empty to give another potato or a spoonful of dripping to the two hungry, sad-eyed boys who lodged with her. He used to think he would never get out of there, never get a clean shirt to his back again. What would he do, he wondered, when his clothes actually dropped to pieces and the worn cloth wouldn't hold patches any longer?

It was still early when the old farmer put aside his sewing and his recollections. The sky had been a dark grey all day, with not a gleam of sun, and the light failed at four o'clock. He went to shave and change his shirt while the turkey was roasting. Rudolph and Polly were coming over for supper.

After supper they sat round in the kitchen, and the younger boys were saying how sorry they were it hadn't snowed. Everybody was sorry. They wanted a deep snow that would lie long and keep the wheat warm, and leave the ground soaked when it melted.

"Yes, sir!" Rudolph broke out fiercely; "if we have another dry year like last year, there's going to be hard times in this country."

Rosicky filled his pipe. "You boys don't know what hard times is. You don't owe nobody, you got plenty to eat an' keep warm, an' plenty water to keep clean. When you got them, you can't have it very hard."

Rudolph frowned, opened and shut his big right hand, and dropped it clenched upon his knee. "I've got to have a good deal more than that, Father, or I'll quit this farming gamble. I can always make good wages railroading, or at the packing house, and be sure of my money."

"Maybe so," his father answered dryly.

Mary, who had just come in from the pantry and was wiping her hands on the roller towel, thought Rudy and his father were getting too serious. She brought her darning-basket and sat down in the middle of the group.

"I ain't much afraid of hard times, Rudy," she said heartily. "We've had a plenty, but we've always come through. Your father wouldn't never take nothing very hard, not even hard times. I got a mind to tell you a story on him. Maybe you boys can't hardly remember the year we had that terrible hot wind, that burned everything up on the Fourth of July? All the corn an' the gardens. An' that was in the days when we didn't have alfalfa yet,—I guess it wasn't invented."

[4]Area of London alongside the Thames River.
[5]London street, originally a market place.

"Well, that very day your father was out cultivatin' corn, and I was here in the kitchen makin' plum preserves. We had bushels of plums that year. I noticed it was terrible hot, but it's always hot in the kitchen when you're preservin', an' I was too busy with my plums to mind. Anton come in from the field about three o'clock, an' I asked him what was the matter.

"'Nothin',' he says, 'but it's pretty hot, an' I think I won't work no more today.' He stood round for a few minutes, an' then he says: 'Ain't you near through? I want you should git up a nice supper for us tonight. It's Fourth of July.'

"I told him to git along, that I was right in the middle of preservin', but the plums would taste good on hot biscuit. 'I'm goin' to have fried chicken, too,' he says, and he went off an' killed a couple. You three oldest boys was little fellers, playin' round outside, real hot an' sweaty, an' your father took you to the horse tank down by the windmill an' took off your clothes an' put you in. Them two box-elder trees was little then, but they made shade over the tank. Then he took off all his own clothes, an' got in with you. While he was playin' in the water with you, the Methodist preacher drove into our place to say how all the neighbours was goin' to meet at the schoolhouse that night, to pray for rain. He drove right to the windmill, of course, and there was your father and you three with no clothes on. I was in the kitchen door, an' I had to laugh, for the preacher acted like he ain't never seen a naked man before. He surely was embarrassed, an' your father couldn't git to his clothes; they was all hangin' up on the windmill to let the sweat dry out of 'em. So he laid in the tank where he was, an' put one of you boys on top of him to cover him up a little, an' talked to the preacher.

"When you got through playin' in the water, he put clean clothes on you and a clean shirt on himself, an' by that time I'd begun to get supper. He says: 'It's too hot in here to eat comfortable. Let's have a picnic in the orchard. We'll eat our supper behind the mulberry hedge, under them linden trees.'

"So he carried our supper down, an' a bottle of my wild-grape wine, an' everything tasted good, I can tell you. The wind got cooler as the sun was goin' down, and it turned out pleasant, only I noticed how the leaves was curled up on the linden trees. That made me think, an' I asked your father if that hot wind all day hadn't been terrible hard on the gardens an' the corn.

"'Corn,' he says, 'there ain't no corn.'

"'What you talkin' about?' I said. 'Ain't we got forty acres?'

"'We ain't got an ear,' he says, 'nor nobody else ain't got none. All the corn in this country was cooked by three o'clock today, like you'd roasted it in an oven.'

"'You mean you won't get no crop at all?' I asked him. I couldn't believe it, after he'd worked so hard.

"'No crop this year,' he says. 'That's why we're havin' a picnic. We might as well enjoy what we got.'

"An' that's how your father behaved, when all the neighbours was so discouraged they couldn't look you in the face. An' we enjoyed ourselves that year, poor as we was, an' our neighbours wasn't a bit better off for bein' miserable. Some of 'em grieved till they got poor digestions and couldn't relish what they did have."

The younger boys said they thought their father had the best of it. But Rudolph was thinking that, all the same, the neighbours had managed to get ahead more, in the fifteen years since that time. There must be something wrong about his father's way of doing things. He wished he knew what was going on in the back of Polly's mind. He knew she liked his father, but he knew, too, that she was afraid of something. When his mother sent over coffee-cake or prune tarts or a loaf of fresh bread, Polly seemed to regard them with a certain suspicion. When she observed to him that his brothers had nice manners, her tone implied that it was remarkable they should have. With his mother she was stiff and on her guard. Mary's hearty frankness and gusts of good humour irritated her. Polly was afraid of being unusual or conspicuous in any way, of being "ordinary," as she said!

When Mary had finished her story, Rosicky laid aside his pipe.

"You boys like me to tell you about some of dem hard times I been through in London?" Warmly encouraged, he sat rubbing his forehead along the deep creases. It was bothersome to tell a long story in English (he nearly always talked to the boys in Czech), but he wanted Polly to hear this one.

"Well, you know about dat tailor shop I worked in in London? I had one Christmas dere I ain't never forgot. Times was awful bad before Christmas; de boss ain't got much work, an' have it awful hard to pay his rent. It ain't so much fun, bein' poor in a big city like London, I'll say! All de windows is full of good t'ings to eat, an' all de pushcarts in de streets is full, an' you smell 'em all de time, an' you ain't got no money,—not a damn bit. I didn't mind de cold so much, though I didn't have no overcoat, chust a short jacket I'd outgrowed so it wouldn't meet on me, an' my hands was chapped raw. But I always had a good appetite, like you all know, an' de sight of dem pork pies in de windows was awful fur me!

"Day before Christmas was terrible foggy dat year, an' dat fog gits into your bones and makes you all damp like. Mrs. Lifschnitz didn't give us nothin' but a little bread an' drippin' for supper, because she was savin' to try for to give us a good dinner on Christmas Day. After supper de boss say I can go an' enjoy myself, so I went into de streets to listen to de Christmas singers. Dey sing old songs an' make very nice music, an' I run round after dem a good ways, till I got awful hungry. I t'ink maybe if I go home, I can sleep till morning an' forgit my belly.

"I went into my corner real quiet, and roll up in my fedder quilt. But I ain't got my head down, till I smell somet'ing good. Seem like it git stronger an' stronger, an' I can't git to sleep noway. I can't understand dat smell. Dere was a gas light in a hall across de court, dat always shine in at my window a little. I got up an' look round. I got a little wooden box in my corner fur a stool, 'cause I ain't got no chair. I picks up dat box, and under it dere is a roast goose on a platter! I can't believe my eyes. I carry it to de window where de light comes in, an' touch it and smell it to find out, an' den I taste it to be sure. I say, I will eat chust one little bite of dat goose, so I can go to sleep, and tomorrow I won't eat none at all. But I tell you, boys, when I stop, one half of dat goose was gone!"

The narrator bowed his head, and the boys shouted. But little Josephine slipped behind his chair and kissed him on the neck beneath his ear.

"Poor little Papa, I don't want him to be hungry!"

"Da's long ago, child. I ain't never been hungry since I had your mudder to cook fur me."

"Go on and tell us the rest, please," said Polly.

"Well, when I come to realize what I done, of course, I felt terrible. I felt better in de stomach, but very bad in de heart. I set on my bed wid dat platter on my knees, an' it all come to me; how hard dat poor woman save to buy dat goose, and how she get some neighbour to cook it dat got more fire, an' how she put it in my corner to keep it away from dem hungry children. Dey was a old carpet hung up to shut my corner off, an' de children wasn't allowed to go in dere. An' I know she put it in my corner because she trust me more'n she did de violin boy. I can't stand it to face her after I spoil de Christmas. So I put on my shoes and go out into de city. I tell myself I better throw myself in de river; but I guess I ain't dat kind of a boy.

"It was after twelve o'clock, an' terrible cold, an' I start out to walk about London all night. I walk along de river awhile, but dey was lots of drunks all along; men, and women too. I chust move along to keep away from de police. I git onto de Strand, an' den over to New Oxford Street, where dere was a big German restaurant on de ground floor, wid big windows all fixed up fine, an' I could see de people havin' parties inside. While I was lookin' in, two men and two ladies come out, laughin' and talkin' and feelin' happy about all dey been eatin' an' drinkin', and dey was speakin' Czech,—not like de Austrians, but like de home folks talk it.

"I guess I went crazy, an' I done what I ain't never done before nor since. I went right up to dem gay people an' begun to beg dem: 'Fellow-countrymen, for God's sake give me money enough to buy a goose!'

"Dey laugh, of course, but de ladies speak awful kind to me, an' dey take me back into de restaurant and give me hot coffee and cakes, an' make me tell all about how I happened to come to London, an' what I was doin' dere. Dey take my name and where I work down on paper, an' both of dem ladies give me ten shillings.

"De big market at Covent Garden[6] ain't very far away, an' by dat time it was open. I go dere an' buy a big goose an' some pork pies, an' potatoes and onions, an' cakes an' oranges fur de children,—all I could carry! When I git home, everybody is still asleep. I pile all I bought on de kitchen table, an' go in an' lay down on my bed, an' I ain't waken up till I hear dat woman scream when she come out into her kitchen. My goodness, but she was surprise! She laugh an' cry at de same time, an' hug me and waken all de children. She ain't stop fur no breakfast; she git de Christmas dinner ready dat morning, and we all sit down an' eat all we can hold. I ain't never seen dat violin boy have all he can hold before.

"Two three days after dat, de two men come to hunt me up, an' dey ask my boss, and he give me a good report an' tell dem I was a steady boy all right. One of dem Bohemians was very smart an' run a Bohemian newspaper in New York, an' de odder was a rich man, in de importing business, an' dey been travelling togedder. Dey told me how t'ings was easier in New York, an' offered to pay my passage when dey was goin' home soon on a boat. My boss say to me: 'You go. You ain't got no chance here, an' I like to see you git ahead, fur you always been a good boy to my woman, and fur dat fine Christmas dinner you give us all.' An' da's how I got to New York."

That night when Rudolph and Polly, arm in arm, were running home across the fields with the bitter wind at their backs, his heart leaped for joy when she said she thought they might have his family come over for supper on New Year's Eve. "Let's get up a nice supper, and not let your mother help at all; make her be company for once."

"That would be lovely of you, Polly," he said humbly. He was a very simple, modest boy, and he, too, felt vaguely that Polly and her sisters were more experienced and worldly than his people.

VI

The winter turned out badly for farmers. It was bitterly cold, and after the first light snows before Christmas there was no snow at all,—and no rain. March was as bitter as February. On those days when the wind fairly punished the country, Rosicky sat by his window. In the fall he and the boys had put in a big wheat planting, and now the seed had frozen in the ground. All that land would have to be ploughed up and planted over again, planted in corn. It had happened before, but he was younger then, and he never worried about what had to be. He was sure of himself and of Mary; he knew they could bear what they had to bear, that they would always pull through somehow. But he was not so sure about the young ones, and he felt troubled because Rudolph and Polly were having such a hard start.

Sitting beside his flowering window while the panes rattled and the wind blew in under the door, Rosicky gave himself to reflection as he had not done since those Sundays in the loft of the furniture-factory in New York, long ago. Then he was trying to find what he wanted in life for himself; now he was trying to find what he wanted for his boys, and why it was he so hungered to feel sure they would be here, working this very land, after he was gone.

---

[6]London market area and site of famous theater/opera house.

They would have to work hard on the farm, and probably they would never do much more than make a living. But if he could think of them as staying here on the land, he wouldn't have to fear any great unkindness for them. Hardships, certainly; it was a hardship to have the wheat freeze in the ground when seed was so high; and to have to sell your stock because you had no feed. But there would be other years when everything came along right, and you caught up. And what you had was your own. You didn't have to choose between bosses and strikers, and go wrong either way. You didn't have to do with dishonest and cruel people. They were the only things in his experience he had found terrifying and horrible; the look in the eyes of a dishonest and crafty man, of a scheming and rapacious woman.

In the country, if you had a mean neighbour, you could keep off his land and make him keep off yours. But in the city, all the foulness and misery and brutality of your neighbours was part of your life. The worst things he had come upon in his journey through the world were human,—depraved and poisonous specimens of man. To this day he could recall certain terrible faces in the London streets. There were mean people everywhere, to be sure, even in their own country town here. But they weren't tempered, hardened, sharpened, like the treacherous people in cities who live by grinding or cheating or poisoning their fellow-men. He had helped to bury two of his fellow-workmen in the tailoring trade, and he was distrustful of the organized industries that see one out of the world in big cities. Here, if you were sick, you had Doctor Ed to look after you; and if you died, fat Mr. Haycock, the kindest man in the world, buried you.

It seemed to Rosicky that for good, honest boys like his, the worst they could do on the farm was better than the best they would be likely to do in the city. If he'd had a mean boy, now, one who was crooked and sharp and tried to put anything over on his brothers, then town would be the place for him. But he had no such boy. As for Rudolph, the discontented one, he would give the shirt off his back to anyone who touched his heart. What Rosicky really hoped for his boys was that they could get through the world without ever knowing much about the cruelty of human beings. "Their mother and me ain't prepared them for that," he sometimes said to himself.

These thoughts brought him back to a grateful consideration of his own case. What an escape he had had, to be sure! He, too, in his time, had had to take money for repair work from the hand of a hungry child who let it go so wistfully; because it was money due his boss. And now, in all these years, he had never had to take a cent from anyone in bitter need,—never had to look at the face of a woman become like a wolf's from struggle and famine. When he thought of these things, Rosicky would put on his cap and jacket and slip down to the barn and give his work-horses a little extra oats, letting them eat it out of his hand in their slobbery fashion. It was his way of expressing what he felt, and made him chuckle with pleasure.

The spring came warm, with blue skies,—but dry, dry as a bone. The boys began ploughing up the wheat-fields to plant them over in corn. Rosicky would stand at the fence corner and watch them, and the earth was so dry it blew up in clouds of brown dust that hid the horses and the sulky plough and the driver. It was a bad outlook.

The big alfalfa-field that lay between the home place and Rudolph's came up green, but Rosicky was worried because during that open windy winter a great many Russian thistle plants had blown in there and lodged. He kept asking the boys to rake them out; he was afraid their seed would root and "take the alfalfa." Rudolph said that was nonsense. The boys were working so hard planting corn, their father felt he couldn't insist about the thistles, but he set great store by that big alfalfa field. It was a feed you could depend on,—and there was some deeper reason, vague, but strong. The peculiar green of that clover woke early memories in old Rosicky, went back to something in his childhood in the old world. When he was a little boy, he had played in fields of that strong blue-green colour.

One morning, when Rudolph had gone to town in the car, leaving a work-team idle in his barn, Rosicky went over to his son's place, put the horses to the buggy-rake, and set about quietly raking up those thistles. He behaved with guilty caution, and rather enjoyed stealing a march on Doctor Ed, who was just then taking his first vacation in seven years of practice and was attending a clinic in Chicago. Rosicky got the thistles raked up, but did not stop to burn them. That would take some time, and his breath was pretty short, so he thought he had better get the horses back to the barn.

He got them into the barn and to their stalls, but the pain had come on so sharp in his chest that he didn't try to take the harness off. He started for the house, bending lower with every step. The cramp in his chest was shutting him up like a jack-knife. When he reached the windmill, he swayed and caught at the ladder. He saw Polly coming down the hill, running with the swiftness of a slim greyhound. In a flash she had her shoulder under his armpit.

"Lean on me, Father, hard! Don't be afraid. We can get to the house all right."

Somehow they did, though Rosicky became blind with pain; he could keep on his legs, but he couldn't steer his course. The next thing he was conscious of was lying on Polly's bed, and Polly bending over him wringing out bath towels in hot water and putting them on his chest. She stopped only to throw coal into the stove, and she kept the tea-kettle and the black pot going. She put these hot applications on him for nearly an hour, she told him afterwards, and all that time he was drawn up stiff and blue, with the sweat pouring off him.

As the pain gradually loosed its grip, the stiffness went out of his jaws, the black circles round his eyes disappeared, and a little of his natural colour came back. When his daughter-in-law buttoned his shirt over his chest at last, he sighed.

"Da's fine, de way I feel now, Polly. It was a awful bad spell, an' I was so sorry it all come on you like it did."

Polly was flushed and excited. "Is the pain really gone? Can I leave you long enough to telephone over to your place?"

Rosicky's eyelids fluttered. "Don't telephone, Polly. It ain't no use to scare my wife. It's nice and quiet here, an' if I ain't too much trouble to you, just let me lay still till I feel like myself. I ain't got no pain now. It's nice here."

Polly bent over him and wiped the moisture from his face. "Oh, I'm so glad it's over!" she broke out impulsively. "It just broke my heart to see you suffer so, Father."

Rosicky motioned her to sit down on the chair where the tea-kettle had been, and looked up at her with that lively affectionate gleam in his eyes. "You was awful good to me, I won't never forget dat. I hate it to be sick on you like dis. Down at de barn I say to myself, dat young girl ain't had much experience in sickness, I don't want to scare her, an' maybe she's got a baby comin' or somet'ing."

Polly took his hand. He was looking at her so intently and affectionately and confidingly; his eyes seemed to caress her face, to regard it with pleasure. She frowned with her funny streaks of eyebrows, and then smiled back at him.

"I guess maybe there is something of that kind going to happen. But I haven't told anyone yet, not my mother or Rudolph. You'll be the first to know."

His hand pressed hers. She noticed that it was warm again. The twinkle in his yellow-brown eyes seemed to come nearer.

"I like mighty well to see dat little child, Polly," was all he said. Then he closed his eyes and lay half-smiling. But Polly sat still, thinking hard. She had a sudden feeling that nobody in the world, not her mother, not Rudolph, or anyone, really loved her as much as old Rosicky did. It perplexed her. She sat frowning and trying to puzzle it out. It was as if Rosicky had a special gift for loving people, something that was like an ear for music or an eye for colour. It was quiet, unobtrusive; it was merely there. You saw it in his eyes, — perhaps that was why they were merry. You felt it in his hands, too. After he dropped off to sleep, she sat holding his warm, broad, flexible brown hand. She had never seen another in the least like it. She wondered if it wasn't a kind of gypsy hand, it was so alive and quick and light in its communications,—very strange in a farmer. Nearly all the farmers she knew had huge lumps of fists, like mauls,[7] or they were knotty and bony and uncomfortable-looking, with stiff fingers. But Rosicky's was like quick-silver, flexible, muscular, about the colour of a pale cigar, with deep, deep creases across the palm. It wasn't nervous, it wasn't a stupid lump; it was a warm brown human hand, with some cleverness in it, a great deal of generosity, and something else which Polly could only call "gypsy-like,"—something nimble and lively and sure, in the way that animals are.

Polly remembered that hour long afterwards; it had been like an awakening to her. It seemed to her that she had never learned so much about life from anything as from old Rosicky's hand. It brought her to herself; it communicated some direct and untranslatable message.

When she heard Rudolph coming in the car, she ran out to meet him.

"Oh, Rudy, your father's been awful sick! He raked up those thistles he's been worrying about, and afterwards he could hardly get to the house. He suffered so I was afraid he was going to die."

Rudolph jumped to the ground. "Where is he now?"

"On the bed. He's asleep. I was terribly scared, because, you know, I'm so fond of your father." She slipped her arm through his and they went into the house. That afternoon they took Rosicky home and put him to bed, though he protested that he was quite well again.

The next morning he got up and dressed and sat down to breakfast with his family. He told Mary that his coffee tasted better than usual to him, and he warned the boys not to bear any tales to Doctor Ed when he got home. After breakfast he sat down by his window to do some patching and asked Mary to thread several needles for him before she went to feed her chickens,—her eyes were better than his, and her hands steadier. He lit his pipe and took up John's overalls. Mary had been watching him anxiously all morning, and as she went out of the door with her bucket of scraps, she saw that he was smiling. He was thinking, indeed, about Polly, and how he might never have known what a tender heart she had if he hadn't got sick over there. Girls nowadays didn't wear their heart on their sleeve. But now he knew Polly would make a fine woman after the foolishness wore off. Either a woman had that sweetness at her heart or she hadn't. You couldn't always tell by the look of them; but if they had that, everything came out right in the end.

After he had taken a few stitches, the cramp began in his chest, like yesterday. He put his pipe cautiously down on the window-sill and bent over to ease the pull. No use,—he had better try to get to his bed if he could. He rose and groped his way across the familiar floor, which was rising and falling like the deck of a ship. At the door he fell. When Mary came in, she found him lying there, and the moment she touched him she knew that he was gone.

Doctor Ed was away when Rosicky died, and for the first few weeks after he got home he was hard driven. Every day he said to himself that he must get out to see that family that had lost their father. One soft, warm moonlight night in early summer he started for the farm. His mind was on other things, and not until his road ran by the graveyard did he realize that Rosicky wasn't over there on the hill where the red lamplight shone, but here, in the moonlight. He stopped his car, shut off the engine, and sat there for a while.

---

[7]Heavy wooden hammers.

A sudden hush had fallen on his soul. Everything here seemed strangely moving and significant, though signifying what, he did not know. Close by the wire fence stood Rosicky's mowing-machine, where one of the boys had been cutting hay that afternoon; his own work-horses had been going up and down there. The new-cut hay perfumed all the night air. The moonlight silvered the long, billowy grass that grew over the graves and hid the fence; the few little evergreens stood out black in it, like shadows in a pool. The sky was very blue and soft, the stars rather faint because the moon was full.

For the first time it struck Doctor Ed that this was really a beautiful graveyard. He thought of city cemeteries; acres of shrubbery and heavy stone, so arranged and lonely and unlike anything in the living world. Cities of the dead, indeed; cities of the forgotten, of the "put away." But this was open and free, this little square of long grass which the wind for ever stirred. Nothing but the sky overhead, and the many-coloured fields running on until they met that sky. The horses worked here in summer; the neighbours passed on their way to town; and over yonder, in the cornfield, Rosicky's own cattle would be eating fodder as winter came on. Nothing could be more undeathlike than this place; nothing could be more right for a man who had helped to do the work of great cities and had always longed for the open country and had got to it at last. Rosicky's life seemed to him complete and beautiful.

1928   *1930, 1932*

SHERWOOD ANDERSON
(1876–1941)

In 1924, in *A Story Teller's Story*, Sherwood Anderson noted that when he started writing, there was a belief that "stories must be built about a plot and that . . . they must point a moral, uplift the people, make better citizens. . . . 'The Poison Plot,' I called it in conversation with my friends as the plot notion did seem to me to poison all storytelling. What I wanted I thought was form, not plot, an altogether more elusive and difficult thing to come at. . . ." These words, from one of the writers most responsible for the change of the nature of the short story in the twentieth century, reveal the essence of that change: a shift of focus from plot and action to form and style. William Faulkner, who first came to know Anderson in New Orleans in 1925, would express the opinion of many when he said later of Anderson, "he's the father of all my generation—Hemingway . . . , Thomas Wolfe, Dos Passos."

In Anderson's beginning there seemed to be little chance that he could "father" any writer, let alone a generation. Until he was thirty-six years old, he lived the typical American success story. Born of a harness maker who moved from small town to small town in mid-America, Anderson did not come to live in the original of Winesburg—Clyde, Ohio—until 1884, when he was eight years old; and he left Clyde for Chicago in 1896, ready to begin earning his living as a laborer in a warehouse.

In 1898–99, he was caught up as a soldier in the army during the Spanish-American War, serving briefly in Cuba after the fighting was over. After taking a degree at Wittenberg Academy in Springfield, Illinois (he attended only one year), he turned up again in Chicago and got a job writing advertising copy.

After his first marriage in 1904, his business career prospered. He became president of United Factories Company in Cleveland in 1906, and the very next year became head of his own paint business in Elyria, Ohio.

At the pinnacle of his business career, having proved to himself his business ability, some dissatisfaction began to take shape inside him to taunt and torture him. He began to write novels at night while still tending his paint business during the day, living a kind of divided life. At last, in 1912, when he was thirty-six, something snapped: while dictating a business letter, he suddenly stopped and left his office, disappearing for several days. He was found in Cleveland, confused and disoriented, but he was never to go back to the business world.

Anderson returned to Chicago, intent on combining a literary career with a job in advertising. He found himself in the middle of what was later to be styled the Chicago Renaissance, including such writers as Theodore Dreiser, Carl Sandburg, and Ben Hecht. In 1916, Anderson published an autobiographical novel he had finished earlier — *Windy McPherson's Son. Marching Men* (1917), based in part on his army experience, was followed by *Mid-American Chants* (1918), a series of prose-poems after the manner of Walt Whitman.

It was not, however, until the appearance of *Winesburg, Ohio*, in 1919, that Anderson found his individual voice and style. One of the enduring classics of American literature, *Winesburg, Ohio* is part of a familiar tradition sometimes called the "flight from the village." This tradition, dating back to the nineteenth century, portrayed heroes scheming to escape the stifling social structures of small-town America and moving to the big cities — only too often to find a life of loneliness, poverty, and degradation. Stories embodying this pattern simply worked variations on the social realities of a time when America was changing from a rural to an urban society.

Winesburg, Ohio presents an indelible portrait of an American town, showing people living diminished and repressed lives, lives of "quiet desperation." Their loneliness is intense, their unspoken longing and yearning palpable. When some gesture of protest is attempted, it manifests itself in grotesque behavior that remains inexplicable to observers. It was Anderson's genius to spin the "adventures" of these characters in a web of poetic prose that ensnares the reader in an enlightened sympathy for the warped individuals committing the most bizarre deeds.

Anderson published additional volumes of short stories — *The Triumph of the Egg* (1921), *Horses and Men* (1923), and *Death in the Woods and Other Stories* (1933). All of these contain fine tales, but the individual volumes cannot compare in power with Anderson's masterpiece. Moreover, Anderson was never able to transfer his talent in the shorter forms to the longer. His novels include *Poor White* (1920), *Many Marriages* (1923), *Dark Laughter* (1925), *Beyond Desire* (1932), and *Kit Brandon* (1936). It was *Dark Laughter*, a tale of primal instincts winning out over social proprieties, that inspired Ernest Hemingway to write a wicked parody of Anderson and others (including Gertrude Stein) in *Torrents of Spring* (1926).

In the late 1920s, Anderson settled on a farm near Marion, Virginia, and bought two local newspapers, one Republican, the other Democratic. He lived out his life there, remote from the national literary scene. But he continued to write and publish. *Hello Towns* (1929) brought together a collection of his sketches written for his two papers; *Puzzled America* (1935) consisted of essays composed while on a journey through America during the Great Depression. By the time Anderson died in 1941, he had completed the third of his three volumes of autobiography: *A Story-Teller's Story* (1924), *Tar: A Midwest Childhood* (1926), and *Sherwood Anderson's Memoirs* (1942).

ADDITIONAL READING

Letters of Sherwood Anderson, ed. Howard Mumford Jones and Walter Rideout, 1953; *Sherwood Anderson: Selected Letters*, ed. Charles E. Modlin, 1983.

Irving Howe, *Sherwood Anderson*, 1951; James Schevill, *Sherwood Anderson: His Life and Work*, 1951; Eugene P. Seehy and Kenneth A. Lohf, *Sherwood Anderson: A Bibliography*, 1960; Rex Burbank, *Sherwood Anderson*, 1964; Brom Weber, *Sherwood Anderson*, 1964; R. L. White, ed., *The Achievement of Sherwood Anderson: Essays in Criticism*, 1966; David D. Anderson, *Sherwood Anderson: An Introduction and Interpretation*, 1967; Paul P. Appel, ed., *Homage to Sherwood Anderson*, 1970; Walter Rideout, ed., *Sherwood Anderson: A Collection of Critical Essays*, 1974; David Anderson, ed., *Critical Essays on Sherwood Anderson*, 1981; Kim Townsend, *Sherwood Anderson: A Biography*, 1987.

TEXT

Winesburg, Ohio, 1919.

from Winesburg, Ohio

THE BOOK OF THE GROTESQUE[1]

The writer, an old man with a white mustache, had some difficulty in getting into bed. The windows of the house in which he lived were high and he wanted to look at the trees when he awoke in the morning. A carpenter came to fix the bed so that it would be on a level with the window.

Quite a fuss was made about the matter. The carpenter, who had been a soldier in the Civil War, came into the writer's room and sat down to talk of building a platform for the purpose of raising the bed. The writer had cigars lying about and the carpenter smoked.

For a time the two men talked of the raising of the bed and then they talked of other things. The soldier got on the subject of the war. The writer, in fact, led him to that subject. The carpenter had once been a prisoner in Andersonville prison[2] and had lost a brother. The brother had died of starvation, and whenever the carpenter got upon that subject he cried. He, like the old writer, had a white mustache, and when he cried he puckered up his lips and the mustache bobbed up and down. The weeping old man with the cigar in his mouth was ludicrous. The plan the writer had for the raising of his bed was forgotten and later the carpenter did it in his own way and the writer, who was past sixty, had to help himself with a chair when he went to bed at night.

In his bed the writer rolled over on his side and lay quite still. For years he had been beset with notions concerning his heart. He was a hard smoker and his heart fluttered. The idea had got into his mind that he would some time die unexpectedly and always when he got into bed he thought of that. It did not alarm him. The effect in fact was quite a special thing and not easily explained. It made him more alive, there in bed, than at any other time. Perfectly still he lay and his body was old and not

---

[1] The first chapter of *Winesburg, Ohio*, "The Book of the Grotesque," suggests the nature of the characters in the stories that follow. At one time, Anderson had entitled the work in progress *The Book of the Grotesque*.
[2] Andersonville, Georgia, site of the infamous Confederate prison in which many Union soldiers died.

of much use any more, but something inside him was altogether young. He was like a pregnant woman, only that the thing inside him was not a baby but a youth. No, it wasn't a youth, it was a woman, young, and wearing a coat of mail like a knight. It is absurd, you see, to try to tell what was inside the old writer as he lay on his high bed and listened to the fluttering of his heart. The thing to get at is what the writer, or the young thing within the writer, was thinking about.

The old writer, like all of the people in the world, had got, during his long life, a great many notions in his head. He had once been quite handsome and a number of women had been in love with him. And then, of course, he had known people, many people, known them in a peculiarly intimate way that was different from the way in which you and I know people. At least that is what the writer thought and the thought pleased him. Why quarrel with an old man concerning his thoughts?

In the bed the writer had a dream that was not a dream. As he grew somewhat sleepy but was still conscious, figures began to appear before his eyes. He imagined the young indescribable thing within himself was driving a long procession of figures before his eyes.

You see the interest in all this lies in the figures that went before the eyes of the writer. They were all grotesques. All of the men and women the writer had ever known had become grotesques.

The grotesques were not all horrible. Some were amusing, some almost beautiful, and one, a woman all drawn out of shape, hurt the old man by her grotesqueness. When she passed he made a noise like a small dog whimpering. Had you come into the room you might have supposed the old man had unpleasant dreams or perhaps indigestion.

For an hour the procession of grotesques passed before the eyes of the old man, and then, although it was a painful thing to do, he crept out of bed and began to write. Some one of the grotesques had made a deep impression on his mind and he wanted to describe it.

At his desk the writer worked for an hour. In the end he wrote a book which he called "The Book of the Grotesque." It was never published, but I saw it once and it made an indelible impression on my mind. The book had one central thought that is very strange and has always remained with me. By remembering it I have been able to understand many people and things that I was never able to understand before. The thought was involved but a simple statement of it would be something like this:

That in the beginning when the world was young there were a great many thoughts but no such thing as a truth. Man made the truths himself and each truth was a composite of a great many vague thoughts. All about in the world were the truths and they were all beautiful.

The old man had listed hundreds of the truths in his book. I will not try to tell you of all of them. There was the truth of virginity and the truth of passion, the truth of wealth and of poverty, of thrift and of profligacy, of carelessness and abandon. Hundreds and hundreds were the truths and they were all beautiful.

And then the people came along. Each as he appeared snatched up one of the truths and some who were quite strong snatched up a dozen of them.

It was the truths that made the people grotesques. The old man had quite an elaborate theory concerning the matter. It was his notion that the moment one of the people took one of the truths to himself, called it his truth, and tried to live his life by it, he became a grotesque and the truth he embraced became a falsehood.

You can see for yourself how the old man, who had spent all of his life writing and was filled with words, would write hundreds of pages concerning this matter. The subject would become so big in his mind that he himself would be in danger of becoming a grotesque. He didn't, I suppose, for the same reason that he never published the book. It was the young thing inside him that saved the old man.

Concerning the old carpenter who fixed the bed for the writer, I only mentioned him because he, like many of what are called very common people, became the nearest thing to what is understandable and lovable of all the grotesques in the writer's book.

ADVENTURE

Alice Hindman, a woman of twenty-seven when George Willard[1] was a mere boy, had lived in Winesburg all her life. She clerked in Winney's Dry Goods Store and lived with her mother who had married a second husband.

Alice's step-father was a carriage painter, and given to drink. His story is an odd one. It will be worth telling some day.

At twenty-seven Alice was tall and somewhat slight. Her head was large and overshadowed her body. Her shoulders were a little stooped and her hair and eyes brown. She was very quiet but beneath a placid exterior a continual ferment went on.

When she was a girl of sixteen and before she began to work in the store, Alice had an affair with a young man. The young man, named Ned Currie, was older than Alice. He, like George Willard, was employed on the *Winesburg Eagle* and for a long time he went to see Alice almost every evening. Together the two walked under the trees through the streets of the town and talked of what they would do with their lives. Alice was then a very pretty girl and Ned Currie took her into his arms and kissed her. He became excited and said things he did not intend to say and Alice, betrayed by her desire to have something beautiful come into her rather narrow life, also grew excited. She also talked. The outer crust of her life, all of her natural diffidence and reserve, was torn away and she gave herself over to the emotions of love. When, late in the fall of her sixteenth year, Ned Currie went away to Cleveland where he hoped to get a place on a city newspaper and rise in the world, she wanted to go with him. With a trembling voice she told him what was in her mind. "I will work and you can work," she said. "I do not want to harness you to a needless expense that will prevent your making progress. Don't marry me now. We will get along without that and we can be together. Even though we live in the same house no one will say anything. In the city we will be unknown and people will pay no attention to us."

Ned Currie was puzzled by the determination and abandon of his sweetheart and was also deeply touched. He had wanted the girl to become his mistress but changed his mind. He wanted to protect and care for her. "You don't know what you're talking about," he said sharply; "you may be sure I'll let you do no such thing. As soon as I get a good job I'll come back. For the present you'll have to stay here. It's the only thing we can do."

On the evening before he left Winesburg to take up his new life in the city, Ned Currie went to call on Alice. They walked about through the streets for an hour and then got a rig from Wesley Moyer's livery and went for a drive in the country. The moon came up and they found themselves unable to talk. In his sadness the young man forgot the resolutions he had made regarding his conduct with the girl.

They got out of the buggy at a place where a long meadow ran down to the bank of Wine Creek and there in the dim light became lovers. When at midnight they returned to town they were both glad. It did not seem to them that anything that could happen in the future could blot out the wonder and beauty of the thing that had happened. "Now we will have to stick to each other, whatever happens we will have to do that," Ned Currie said as he left the girl at her father's door.

The young newspaper man did not succeed in getting a place on a Cleveland paper and went west to Chicago. For a time he was lonely and wrote to Alice almost

---

[1]George Willard's story of growing up in Winesburg and, at the end, leaving the small town, is told in *Winesburg, Ohio*, but in many of the book's stories such as this one he fades into the background (see "Sophistication," following).

every day. Then he was caught up by the life of the city; he began to make friends and found new interests in life. In Chicago he boarded at a house where there were several women. One of them attracted his attention and he forgot Alice in Winesburg. At the end of a year he had stopped writing letters, and only once in a long time, when he was lonely or when he went into one of the city parks and saw the moon shining on the grass as it had shone that night on the meadow by Wine Creek, did he think of her at all.

In Winesburg the girl who had been loved grew to be a woman. When she was twenty-two years old her father, who owned a harness repair shop, died suddenly. The harness maker was an old soldier, and after a few months his wife received a widow's pension. She used the first money she got to buy a loom and became a weaver of carpets, and Alice got a place in Winney's store. For a number of years nothing could have induced her to believe that Ned Currie would not in the end return to her.

She was glad to be employed because the daily round of toil in the store made the time of waiting seem less long and uninteresting. She began to save money, thinking that when she had saved two or three hundred dollars she would follow her lover to the city and try if her presence would not win back his affections.

Alice did not blame Ned Currie for what had happened in the moonlight in the field, but felt that she could never marry another man. To her the thought of giving to another what she still felt could belong only to Ned seemed monstrous. When other young men tried to attract her attention she would have nothing to do with them. "I am his wife and shall remain his wife whether he comes back or not," she whispered to herself, and for all of her willingness to support herself could not have understood the growing modern idea of a woman's owning herself and giving and taking for her own ends in life.

Alice worked in the dry goods store from eight in the morning until six at night and on three evenings a week went back to the store to stay from seven until nine. As time passed and she became more and more lonely she began to practice the devices common to lonely people. When at night she went upstairs into her own room she knelt on the floor to pray and in her prayers whispered things she wanted to say to her lover. She became attached to inanimate objects, and because it was her own, could not bear to have anyone touch the furniture of her room. The trick of saving money, begun for a purpose, was carried on after the scheme of going to the city to find Ned Currie had been given up. It became a fixed habit, and when she needed new clothes she did not get them. Sometimes on rainy afternoons in the store she got out her bank book and, letting it lie open before her, spent hours dreaming impossible dreams of saving money enough so that the interest would support both herself and her future husband.

"Ned always liked to travel about," she thought. "I'll give him the chance. Some day when we are married and I can save both his money and my own, we will be rich. Then we can travel together all over the world."

In the dry goods store weeks ran into months and months into years as Alice waited and dreamed of her lover's return. Her employer, a grey old man with false teeth and a thin grey mustache that drooped down over his mouth, was not given to conversation, and sometimes, on rainy days and in the winter when a storm raged in Main Street, long hours passed when no customers came in. Alice arranged and rearranged the stock. She stood near the front window where she could look down the deserted street and thought of the evenings when she had walked with Ned Currie and of what he had said. "We will have to stick to each other now." The words echoed and re-echoed through the mind of the maturing woman. Tears came into her eyes. Sometimes when her employer had gone out and she was alone in the store she put her head on the counter and wept. "Oh, Ned, I am waiting," she whispered over and over, and all the time the creeping fear that he would never come back grew stronger within her.

In the spring when the rains have passed and before the long hot days of summer have come, the country about Winesburg is delightful. The town lies in the midst of open fields, but beyond the fields are pleasant patches of woodlands. In the wooded places are many little cloistered nooks, quiet places where lovers go to sit on Sunday afternoons. Through the trees they look out across the fields and see farmers at work about the barns or people driving up and down on the roads. In the town bells ring and occasionally a train passes, looking like a toy thing in the distance.

For several years after Ned Currie went away Alice did not go into the wood with other young people on Sunday, but one day after he had been gone for two or three years and when her loneliness seemed unbearable, she put on her best dress and set out. Finding a little sheltered place from which she could see the town and a long stretch of the fields, she sat down. Fear of age and ineffectuality took possession of her. She could not sit still, and arose. As she stood looking out over the land something, perhaps the thought of never ceasing life as it expresses itself in the flow of the seasons, fixed her mind on the passing years. With a shiver of dread, she realized that for her the beauty and freshness of youth had passed. For the first time she felt that she had been cheated. She did not blame Ned Currie and did not know what to blame. Sadness swept over her. Dropping to her knees, she tried to pray, but instead of prayers words of protest came to her lips. "It is not going to come to me. I will never find happiness. Why do I tell myself lies?" she cried, and an odd sense of relief came with this, her first bold attempt to face the fear that had become a part of her everyday life.

In the year when Alice Hindman became twenty-five two things happened to disturb the dull uneventfulness of her days. Her mother married Bush Milton, the carriage painter of Winesburg, and she herself became a member of the Winesburg Methodist Church. Alice joined the church because she had become frightened by the loneliness of her position in life. Her mother's second marriage had emphasized her isolation. "I am becoming old and queer. If Ned comes he will not want me. In the city where he is living men are perpetually young. There is so much going on that they do not have time to grow old," she told herself with a grim little smile, and went resolutely about the business of becoming acquainted with people. Every Thursday evening when the store had closed she went to a prayer meeting in the basement of the church and on Sunday evening attended a meeting of an organization called The Epworth League.

When Will Hurley, a middle-aged man who clerked in a drug store and who also belonged to the church, offered to walk home with her she did not protest. "Of course I will not let him make a practice of being with me, but if he comes to see me once in a long time there can be no harm in that," she told herself, still determined in her loyalty to Ned Currie.

Without realizing what was happening, Alice was trying feebly at first, but with growing determination, to get a new hold upon life. Beside the drug clerk she walked in silence, but sometimes in the darkness as they went stolidly along she put out her hand and touched softly the folds of his coat. When he left her at the gate before her mother's house she did not go indoors, but stood for a moment by the door. She wanted to call to the drug clerk, to ask him to sit with her in the darkness on the porch before the house, but was afraid he would not understand. "It is not him that I want," she told herself; "I want to avoid being so much alone. If I am not careful I will grow unaccustomed to being with people."

· · · · ·

During the early fall of her twenty-seventh year a passionate restlessness took possession of Alice. She could not bear to be in the company of the drug clerk, and when, in the evening, he came to walk with her she sent him away. Her mind became intensely active and when, weary from the long hours of standing behind the counter in the store, she went home and crawled into bed, she could not sleep. With staring eyes she looked into the darkness. Her imagination, like a child awakened from long sleep, played about the room. Deep within her there was something that would not be cheated by phantasies and that demanded some definite answer from life.

Alice took a pillow into her arms and held it tightly against her breasts. Getting out of bed, she arranged a blanket so that in the darkness it looked like a form lying between the sheets and, kneeling beside the bed, she caressed it, whispering words over and over, like a refrain. "Why doesn't something happen? Why am I left here alone?" she muttered. Although she sometimes thought of Ned Currie, she no longer depended on him. Her desire had grown vague. She did not want Ned Currie or any other man. She wanted to be loved, to have something answer the call that was growing louder and louder within her.

And then one night when it rained Alice had an adventure. It frightened and confused her. She had come home from the store at nine and found the house empty. Bush Milton had gone off to town and her mother to the house of a neighbor. Alice went upstairs to her room and undressed in the darkness. For a moment she stood by the window hearing the rain beat against the glass and then a strange desire took possession of her. Without stopping to think of what she intended to do, she ran downstairs through the dark house and out into the rain. As she stood on the little grass plot before the house and felt the cold rain on her body a mad desire to run naked through the streets took possession of her.

She thought that the rain would have some creative and wonderful effect on her body. Not for years had she felt so full of youth and courage. She wanted to leap and run, to cry out, to find some other lonely human and embrace him. On the brick sidewalk before the house a man stumbled homeward. Alice started to run. A wild, desperate mood took possession of her. "What do I care who it is. He is alone, and I will go to him," she thought; and then without stopping to consider the possible result of her madness, called softly. "Wait!" she cried. "Don't go away. Whoever you are, you must wait."

The man on the sidewalk stopped and stood listening. He was an old man and somewhat deaf. Putting his hand to his mouth, he shouted: "What? What say?" he called.

Alice dropped to the ground and lay trembling. She was so frightened at the thought of what she had done that when the man had gone on his way she did not dare get to her feet, but crawled on hands and knees through the grass to the house. When she got to her own room she bolted the door and drew her dressing table across the doorway. Her body shook as with a chill and her hands trembled so that she had difficulty getting into her nightdress. When she got into bed she buried her face in the pillow and wept brokenheartedly. "What is the matter with me? I will do something dreadful if I am not careful," she thought, and turning her face to the wall, began trying to force herself to face bravely the fact that many people must live and die alone, even in Winesburg.

SOPHISTICATION

It was early evening of a day in the late fall and the Winesburg County Fair had brought crowds of country people into town. The day had been clear and the night came on warm and pleasant. On the Trunion Pike, where the road after it left town stretched away between berry fields now covered with dry brown leaves, the dust from passing wagons arose in clouds. Children, curled into little balls, slept on the straw scattered on wagon beds. Their hair was full of dust and their fingers black and sticky. The dust rolled away over the fields and the departing sun set it ablaze with colors.

In the main street of Winesburg crowds filled the stores and the sidewalks. Night came on, horses whinnied, the clerks in the stores ran madly about, children became lost and cried lustily, an American town worked terribly at the task of amusing itself.

Pushing his way through the crowds in Main Street, young George Willard concealed himself in the stairway leading to Doctor Reefy's office and looked at the people. With feverish eyes he watched the faces drifting past under the store lights. Thoughts kept coming into his head and he did not want to think. He stamped impatiently on the wooden steps and looked sharply about. "Well, is she going to stay with him all day? Have I done all this waiting for nothing?" he muttered.

George Willard, the Ohio village boy, was fast growing into manhood and new thoughts had been coming into his mind. All that day, amid the jam of people at the Fair, he had gone about feeling lonely. He was about to leave Winesburg to go away to some city where he hoped to get work on a city newspaper and he felt grown up. The mood that had taken possession of him was a thing known to men and unknown to boys. He felt old and a little tired. Memories awoke in him. To his mind his new sense of maturity set him apart, made of him a half-tragic figure. He wanted someone to understand the feeling that had taken possession of him after his mother's death.

There is a time in the life of every boy when he for the first time takes the backward view of life. Perhaps that is the moment when he crosses the line into manhood. The boy is walking through the street of his town. He is thinking of the future and of the figure he will cut in the world. Ambitions and regrets awake within him. Suddenly something happens; he stops under a tree and waits as for a voice calling his name. Ghosts of old things creep into his consciousness; the voices outside of himself whisper a message concerning the limitations of life. From being quite sure of himself and his future he becomes not at all sure. If he be an imaginative boy a door is torn open and for the first time he looks out upon the world, seeing, as though they marched in procession before him, the countless figures of men who before his time have come out of nothingness into the world, lived their lives and again disappeared into nothingness. The sadness of sophistication has come to the boy. With a little gasp he sees himself as merely a leaf blown by the wind through the streets of his village. He knows that in spite of all the stout talk of his fellows he must live and die in uncertainty, a thing blown by the winds, a thing destined like corn to wilt in the sun. He shivers and looks eagerly about. The eighteen years he has lived seem but a moment, a breathing space in the long march of humanity. Already he hears death calling. With all his heart he wants to come close to some other human, touch someone with his hands, be touched by the hand of another. If he prefers that the other be a woman, that is because he believes that a woman will be gentle, that she will understand. He wants, most of all, understanding.

When the moment of sophistication came to George Willard his mind turned to Helen White, the Winesburg banker's daughter. Always he had been conscious of the girl growing into womanhood as he grew into manhood. Once on a summer night when he was eighteen, he had walked with her on a country road and in her presence had given way to an impulse to boast, to make himself appear big and significant in her eyes. Now he wanted to see her for another purpose. He wanted to tell her of the new impulses that had come to him. He had tried to make her think of him as a man when he knew nothing of manhood and now he wanted to be with her and to try to make her feel the change he believed had taken place in his nature.

As for Helen White, she also had come to a period of change. What George felt, she in her young woman's way felt also. She was no longer a girl and hungered to reach into the grace and beauty of womanhood. She had come home from Cleveland, where she was attending college, to spend a day at the Fair. She also had begun to have memories. During the day she sat in the grand-stand with a young man, one of the instructors from the college, who was a guest of her mother's. The young man was of a pedantic turn of mind and she felt at once he would not do for her purpose.

At the Fair she was glad to be seen in his company as he was well dressed and a stranger. She knew that the fact of his presence would create an impression. During the day she was happy, but when night came on she began to grow restless. She wanted to drive the instructor away, to get out of his presence. While they sat together in the grand-stand and while the eyes of former schoolmates were upon them, she paid so much attention to her escort that he grew interested. "A scholar needs money. I should marry a woman with money," he mused.

Helen White was thinking of George Willard even as he wandered gloomily through the crowds thinking of her. She remembered the summer evening when they had walked together and wanted to walk with him again. She thought that the months she had spent in the city, the going to theatres and the seeing of great crowds wandering in lighted thoroughfares, had changed her profoundly. She wanted him to feel and be conscious of the change in her nature.

The summer evening together that had left its mark on the memory of both the young man and woman had, when looked at quite sensibly, been rather stupidly spent. They had walked out of town along a country road. Then they had stopped by a fence near a field of young corn and George had taken off his coat and let it hang on his arm. "Well, I've stayed here in Winesburg—yes—I've not gone away but I'm growing up," he had said. "I've been reading books and I've been thinking. I'm going to try to amount to something in life.

"Well," he explained, "that isn't the point. Perhaps I'd better quit talking."

The confused boy put his hand on the girl's arm. His voice trembled. The two started to walk back along the road toward town. In his desperation George boasted, "I'm going to be a big man, the biggest that ever lived here in Winesburg," he declared. "I want you to do something, I don't know what. Perhaps it is none of my business. I want you to try to be different from other women. You see the point. It's none of my business I tell you. I want you to be a beautiful woman. You see what I want."

The boy's voice failed and in silence the two came back into town and went along the street to Helen White's house. At the gate he tried to say something impressive. Speeches he had thought out came into his head, but they seemed utterly pointless. "I thought—I used to think—I had it in my mind you would marry Seth Richmond. Now I know you won't," was all he could find to say as she went through the gate and toward the door of her house.

On the warm fall evening as he stood in the stairway and looked at the crowd drifting through Main Street, George thought of the talk beside the field of young corn and was ashamed of the figure he had made of himself. In the street the people surged up and down like cattle confined in a pen. Buggies and wagons almost filled the narrow thoroughfare. A band played and small boys raced along the sidewalk, diving between the legs of men. Young men with shining red faces walked awkwardly about with girls on their arms. In a room above one of the stores, where a dance was to be held, the fiddlers tuned their instruments. The broken sounds floated down through an open window and out across the murmur of voices and the loud blare of the horns of the band. The medley of sounds got on young Willard's nerves. Everywhere, on all sides, the sense of crowding, moving life closed in about him. He wanted to run away by himself and think. "If she wants to stay with that fellow she may. Why should I care? What difference does it make to me?" he growled and went along Main Street and through Hern's grocery into a side street.

George felt so utterly lonely and dejected that he wanted to weep but pride made him walk rapidly along, swinging his arms. He came to Westley Moyer's livery barn and stopped in the shadows to listen to a group of men who talked of a race Westley's stallion, Tony Tip, had won at the Fair during the afternoon. A crowd had gathered in front of the barn and before the crowd walked Westley, prancing up and down and boasting. He held a whip in his hand and kept tapping the ground. Little puffs of dust arose in the lamplight. "Hell, quit your talking," Westley exclaimed. "I wasn't afraid, I knew I had 'em beat all the time. I wasn't afraid."

Ordinarily George Willard would have been intensely interested in the boasting of Moyer, the horseman. Now it made him angry. He turned and hurried away along the street. "Old windbag," he sputtered. "Why does he want to be bragging? Why don't he shut up?"

George went into a vacant lot and as he hurried along, fell over a pile of rubbish. A nail protruding from an empty barrel tore his trousers. He sat down on the ground and swore. With a pin he mended the torn place and then arose and went on. "I'll go to Helen White's house, that's what I'll do. I'll walk right in. I'll say that I want to see her. I'll walk right in and sit down, that's what I'll do," he declared, climbing over a fence and beginning to run.

· · · · ·

On the veranda of Banker White's house Helen was restless and distraught. The instructor sat between the mother and daughter. His talk wearied the girl. Although he had also been raised in an Ohio town, the instructor began to put on the airs of the city. He wanted to appear cosmopolitan. "I like the chance you have given me to study the background out of which most of our girls come," he declared. "It was good of you, Mrs. White, to have me down for the day." He turned to Helen and laughed. "Your life is still bound up with the life of this town?" he asked. "There are people here in whom you are interested?" To the girl his voice sounded pompous and heavy.

Helen arose and went into the house. At the door leading to a garden at the back she stopped and stood listening. Her mother began to talk. "There is no one here fit to associate with a girl of Helen's breeding," she said.

Helen ran down a flight of stairs at the back of the house and into the garden. In the darkness she stopped and stood trembling. It seemed to her that the world was full of meaningless people saying words. Afire with eagerness she ran through a garden gate and turning a corner by the banker's barn, went into a little side street. "George! Where are you, George?" she cried, filled with nervous excitement. She stopped running, and leaned against a tree to laugh hysterically. Along the dark little street came George Willard, still saying words. "I'm going to walk right into her house. I'll go right in and sit down," he declared as he came up to her. He stopped and stared stupidly. "Come on," he said and took hold of her hand. With hanging heads they walked away along the street under the trees. Dry leaves rustled under foot. Now that he had found her George wondered what he had better do and say.

· · · · ·

At the upper end of the fair ground, in Winesburg, there is a half decayed old grand-stand. It has never been painted and the boards are all warped out of shape. The fair ground stands on top of a low hill rising out of the valley of Wine Creek and from the grand-stand one can see at night, over a cornfield, the lights of the town reflected against the sky.

George and Helen climbed the hill to the fair ground, coming by the path past Waterworks Pond. The feeling of loneliness and isolation that had come to the young man in the crowded streets of his town was both broken and intensified by the presence of Helen. What he felt was reflected in her.

In youth there are always two forces fighting in people. The warm unthinking little animal struggles against the thing that reflects and remembers, and the older, the more sophisticated thing had possession of George Willard. Sensing his mood, Helen walked beside him filled with respect. When they got to the grand-stand they climbed up under the roof and sat down on one of the long bench-like seats.

There is something memorable in the experience to be had by going into a fair ground that stands at the edge of a Middle Western town on a night after the annual fair has been held. The sensation is one never to be forgotten. On all sides are ghosts, not of the dead, but of living people. Here, during the day just passed, have come the people pouring in from the town and the country around. Farmers with their wives and children and all the people from the hundreds of little frame houses have gathered within these board walls. Young girls have laughed and men with beards have talked of the affairs of their lives. The place has been filled to overflowing with life. It has itched and squirmed with life and now it is night and the life has all gone away. The silence is almost terrifying. One conceals oneself standing silently beside the trunk of a tree and what there is of a reflective tendency in his nature is intensified. One shudders at the thought of the meaninglessness of life while at the same instant, and if the people of the town are his people, one loves life so intensely that tears come into the eyes.

In the darkness under the roof of the grand-stand, George Willard sat beside Helen White and felt very keenly his own insignificance in the scheme of existence. Now that he had come out of town where the presence of the people stirring about, busy with a multitude of affairs, had been so irritating the irritation was all gone. The presence of Helen renewed and refreshed him. It was as though her woman's hand was assisting him to make some minute readjustment of the machinery of his life. He began to think of the people in the town where he had always lived with something like reverence. He had reverence for Helen. He wanted to love and to be loved by her, but he did not want at the moment to be confused by her womanhood. In the darkness he took hold of her hand and when she crept close put a hand on her shoulder. A wind began to blow and he shivered. With all his strength he tried to hold and to understand the mood that had come upon him. In that high place in the darkness the two oddly sensitive human atoms held each other tightly and waited. In the mind of each was the same thought. "I have come to this lonely place and here is this other," was the substance of the thing felt.

In Winesburg the crowded day had run itself out into the long night of the late fall. Farm horses jogged away along lonely country roads pulling their portion of weary people. Clerks began to bring samples of goods in off the sidewalks and lock the doors of stores. In the Opera House a crowd had gathered to see a show and further down Main Street the fiddlers, their instruments tuned, sweated and worked to keep the feet of youth flying over a dance floor.

In the darkness in the grand-stand Helen White and George Willard remained silent. Now and then the spell that held them was broken and they turned and tried in the dim light to see into each other's eyes. They kissed but that impulse did not last. At the upper end of the fair ground a half dozen men worked over horses that had raced during the afternoon. The men had built a fire and were heating kettles of water. Only their legs could be seen as they passed back and forth in the light. When the wind blew the little flames of the fire danced crazily about.

George and Helen arose and walked away into the darkness. They went along a path past a field of corn that had not yet been cut. The wind whispered among the dry corn blades. For a moment during the walk back into town the spell that held them was broken. When they had come to the crest of Waterworks Hill they stopped by a tree and George again put his hands on the girl's shoulders. She embraced him eagerly and then again they drew quickly back from that impulse. They stopped kissing and stood a little apart. Mutual respect grew big in them. They were both embarrassed and to relieve their embarrassment dropped into the animalism of youth. They laughed and began to pull and haul at each other. In some way chastened and purified by the mood they had been in they became, not man and woman, not boy and girl, but excited little animals.

It was so they went down the hill. In the darkness they played like two splendid young things in a young world. Once, running swiftly forward, Helen tripped George and he fell. He squirmed and shouted. Shaking with laughter, he rolled down the hill. Helen ran after him. For just a moment she stopped in the darkness. There is no way of knowing what woman's thoughts went through her mind but, when the bottom of the hill was reached and she came up to the boy, she took his arm and walked beside him in dignified silence. For some reason they could not have explained they had both got from their silent evening together the thing needed. Man or boy, woman or girl, they had for a moment taken hold of the thing that makes the mature life of men and women in the modern world possible.

1919

KATHERINE ANNE PORTER
(1890–1980)

When she was in her seventies, Katherine Anne Porter told an interviewer the secret for her of the creative process in writing a story:

> Sometimes an idea starts completely inarticulately. You're not thinking in images or words or — well, it's exactly like a dark cloud moving in your head. You keep wondering what will come out of this. . . . You begin to think directly in words. Abstractly. Then the words transform themselves into images. By the time I write the story my people are up and alive and walking around and taking things into their own hands. They exist as independently inside my head as you do before me now. I have been criticized for not enough detail in describing my characters, and not enough furniture in the house. And the odd thing is that I see it all so clearly.

This description of the writing process confirms that Porter was an intuitive writer, *possessed by* the creative moment. The closing "furniture" image suggests that she followed the credo of Willa Cather in "The Novel Démeublé" ("The Novel Unfurnished"). Porter's 1952 essay, "Reflections on Willa Cather," was a tribute to a writer who had exerted strong influence on her.

In a number of casual remarks in interviews, Porter invented a biography for herself that for long misled literary scholars. She had, she said, grown up in a large house of plantation proportions attended by a number of former slaves, she had been educated at southern convent schools, she had run away from home and eloped at sixteen, she had "bolted" again at twenty-one, going to Chicago, where, by accident, she "went into the movies." None of these nor other such fabrications were true. She was born Callie Porter in a log cabin in Indian Creek, Texas, in 1890 and grew up in poverty, the daughter of a marginal dirt-farmer. Her mother died in 1892, and her grandmother (who had taken over the role of mother) died in 1901. Her only formal schooling was limited to one year at a private school in San Antonio, with some training in acting. At sixteen she contracted a marriage that, though disastrous, lasted for nine years. The only permanent legacy from this marriage, except the interior scars, was Porter's conversion in 1910 to Catholicism, her husband's religion. In 1914 she went to Chicago to find work in the movies and was employed for a brief time. In 1916 she entered a sanatorium in Texas for treatment of her tuberculosis. Although cured of this serious disease, she almost died in Denver in the influenza epidemic that swept the country near the end of the First World War, an experience evoked in her story "Pale Horse, Pale Rider." During 1920–21, she went to Mexico on a magazine assignment and was firsthand witness to the inauguration of

Alvaro Obregon as a freely elected president, promising stability in a time of revolutionary upheaval.

All through her early years, Porter was an omnivorous reader, crediting as her educators Henry James, James Joyce, W. B. Yeats, T. S. Eliot, and Ezra Pound. In one interview she listed books that she admired, including Emily Bronte's *Wuthering Heights*, E. M. Forster's *A Passage to India*, and Virginia Woolf's *To the Lighthouse*. In learning her craft, she said, "I wrote a pastiche of other people, imitating Dr. Johnson and Laurence Sterne, and Petrarch and Shakespeare's sonnets, and then I tried writing my own way." She said she always knew she was to be a writer: "I did not choose this vocation and if I had any say in the matter, I would not have chosen it. . . . I spent fifteen years wandering about, weighted horribly with masses of paper and little else. Yet for this vocation I was and am willing to live and die and I consider very few other things of the slightest importance."

Porter published her first story, "María Concepción," in *Century Magazine* in 1922. Her first collection of stories, *Flowering Judas*, appeared in 1930, and contained six stories, including "The Jilting of Granny Weatherall." Only 600 copies were printed, primarily because the publisher (Harcourt, Brace) did not believe the book would sell. Perhaps its greatest success was in winning for Porter in 1931 a Guggenheim Fellowship, which she spent in Mexico. There she met and quarreled with Hart Crane.

When *Flowering Judas and Other Stories* appeared in 1935, it contained four additional stories and proved popular enough to appear in a Modern Library edition in 1940. Meantime, Porter brought out *Pale Horse, Pale Rider: Three Short Novels* in 1939, containing, in addition to the title story, "Old Mortality" and "Noon Wine." The reviews were extravagant, comparing her to Nathaniel Hawthorne, Gustave Flaubert, and Henry James.

During her long life, Porter published only two other books of fiction—*The Leaning Tower and Other Stories* (1944), containing "The Grave," and the novel *Ship of Fools* (1962), which began as a short story in 1936 entitled "Promised Land." *Ship of Fools*, based on a 1931 voyage Porter took from Vera Cruz, Mexico, to Bremerhaven, Germany, became a bestseller and popular movie; and it made Porter rich. But critics consistently rated it below her other work in artistic finish.

Porter once told Malcolm Cowley that she had had four husbands and thirty-seven lovers. However much fabrication there was in the statement (four marriages are a matter of record), the truth seems to be that Porter placed her art above her relations with men. When America's "lost generation" was going to France, she went to Mexico. When the exiles were returning from France in the 1930s, she went to Europe, living in Berlin, Madrid, Basel, and Paris. But always she dedicated herself to writing and rewriting, distilling from a large accumulation only a little for publication. Her *Collected Stories*, published in 1965, contains twenty-six works. Although this is a small body of work, critics agree that it is strong enough to support the large reputation that rightfully belongs to Katherine Anne Porter.

ADDITIONAL READING

The Collected Essays and Occasional Writings of Katherine Anne Porter, 1970.

Edward Schwarz, ed., *Katherine Anne Porter, A Critical Bibliography: Bulletin of the New York Public Library*, 1953; Harry John Mooney, Jr., *The Fiction and Criticism of Katherine Anne Porter*, 1957, rev. 1962; Ray B. West, *Katherine Anne Porter*, 1963; William L. Nance, S. M., *Katherine Anne Porter and the Art of Rejection*, 1964; George Hendrick, *Katherine Anne Porter*, 1965; W. S.

Emmon, *Katherine Anne Porter: The Regional Stories*, 1967; Louise Waldrip and Shirley Ann Bauer, eds., *A Bibliography of the Works of Katherine Anne Porter*, 1969; Lodwick Hartley and George Core, eds., *Katherine Anne Porter: A Critical Symposium*, 1969; Paul R. Baumgarten, *Katherine Anne Porter*, 1969; M. M. Liberman, *Katherine Anne Porter's Fiction*, 1971; John L. Hardy, *Katherine Anne Porter*, 1973; Robert F. Kiernan, *Katherine Anne Porter and Carson McCullers: A Reference Guide*, 1976; Robert Penn Warren, ed., *Katherine Anne Porter: A Collection of Critical Essays*, 1979; Enrique Hank Lopez, *Conversations with Katherine Anne Porter, Refugee from Indian Creek*, 1981; Joan Givner, *Katherine Anne Porter: A Life*, 1982; Jane Krause Demouey, *Katherine Anne Porter's Women: The Eye of Her Fiction*, 1983; Darlene Harbour Unrue, *Truth and Vision in Katherine Anne Porter's Fiction*, 1985; Joan Givner, ed., *Katherine Anne Porter: Conversations*, 1987; Darlene Harbour Unrue, *Understanding Katherine Anne Porter*, 1988.

TEXT

The Collected Stories of Katherine Anne Porter, 1965.

The Jilting of Granny Weatherall

She flicked her wrist neatly out of Doctor Harry's pudgy careful fingers and pulled the sheet up to her chin. The brat ought to be in knee breeches. Doctoring around the country with spectacles on his nose! "Get along now, take your schoolbooks and go. There's nothing wrong with me."

Doctor Harry spread a warm paw like a cushion on her forehead where the forked green vein danced and made her eyelids twitch. "Now, now, be a good girl, and we'll have you up in no time."

"That's no way to speak to a woman nearly eighty years old just because she's down. I'd have you respect your elders, young man."

"Well, Missy, excuse me." Doctor Harry patted her cheek. "But I've got to warn you, haven't I? You're a marvel, but you must be careful or you're going to be good and sorry."

"Don't tell me what I'm going to be. I'm on my feet now, morally speaking. It's Cornelia. I had to go to bed to get rid of her."

Her bones felt loose, and floated around in her skin, and Doctor Harry floated like a balloon around the foot of the bed. He floated and pulled down his waistcoat and swung his glasses on a cord. "Well, stay where you are, it certainly can't hurt you."

"Get along and doctor your sick," said Granny Weatherall. "Leave a well woman alone. I'll call for you when I want you. . . . Where were you forty years ago when I pulled through milk-leg and double pneumonia? You weren't even born. Don't let Cornelia lead you on," she shouted, because Doctor Harry appeared to float up to the ceiling and out. "I pay my own bills, and I don't throw my money away on nonsense!"

She meant to wave good-by, but it was too much trouble. Her eyes closed of themselves, it was like a dark curtain drawn around the bed. The pillow rose and floated under her, pleasant as a hammock in a light wind. She listened to the leaves rustling outside the window. No, somebody was swishing newspapers: no, Cornelia and Doctor Harry were whispering together. She leaped broad awake, thinking they whispered in her ear.

"She was never like this, *never* like this!" "Well, what can we expect?" "Yes, eighty years old. . . ."

Well, and what if she was? She still had ears. It was like Cornelia to whisper around doors. She always kept things secret in such a public way. She was always being tactful and kind. Cornelia was dutiful; that was the trouble with her. Dutiful and good: "So good and dutiful," said Granny, "that I'd like to spank her." She saw herself spanking Cornelia and making a fine job of it.

"What'd you say, Mother?"

Granny felt her face tying up in hard knots.

"Can't a body think, I'd like to know?"

"I thought you might want something."

"I do. I want a lot of things. First off, go away and don't whisper."

She lay and drowsed, hoping in her sleep that the children would keep out and let her rest a minute. It had been a long day. Not that she was tired. It was always pleasant to snatch a minute now and then. There was always so much to be done, let me see: tomorrow.

Tomorrow was far away and there was nothing to trouble about. Things were finished somehow when the time came; thank God there was always a little margin over for peace: then a person could spread out the plan of life and tuck in the edges orderly. It was good to have everything clean and folded away, with the hair brushes and tonic bottles sitting straight on the white embroidered linen: the day started without fuss and the pantry shelves laid out with rows of jelly glasses and brown jugs and white stone-china jars with blue whirligigs and words painted on them: coffee, tea, sugar, ginger, cinnamon, allspice: and the bronze clock with the lion on top nicely dusted off. The dust that lion could collect in twenty-four hours! The box in the attic with all those letters tied up, well, she'd have to go through that tomorrow. All those letters—George's letters and John's letters and her letters to them both—lying around for the children to find afterwards made her uneasy. Yes, that would be tomorrow's business. No use to let them know how silly she had been once.

While she was rummaging around she found death in her mind and it felt clammy and unfamiliar. She had spent so much time preparing for death there was no need for bringing it up again. Let it take care of itself now. When she was sixty she had felt very old, finished, and went around making farewell trips to see her children and grandchildren, with a secret in her mind: This is the very last of your mother, children! Then she made her will and came down with a long fever. That was all just a notion like a lot of other things, but it was lucky too, for she had once for all got over the idea of dying for a long time. Now she couldn't be worried. She hoped she had better sense now. Her father had lived to be one hundred and two years old and had drunk a noggin of strong hot toddy on his last birthday. He told the reporters it was his daily habit, and he owed his long life to that. He had made quite a scandal and was very pleased about it. She believed she'd just plague Cornelia a little.

"Cornelia! Cornelia!" No footsteps, but a sudden hand on her cheek. "Bless you, where have you been?"

"Here, Mother."

"Well, Cornelia, I want a noggin of hot toddy."

"Are you cold, darling?"

"I'm chilly, Cornelia. Lying in bed stops the circulation. I must have told you that a thousand times."

Well, she could just hear Cornelia telling her husband that Mother was getting a little childish and they'd have to humor her. The thing that most annoyed her was that Cornelia thought she was deaf, dumb, and blind. Little hasty glances and tiny gestures tossed around her and over her head saying, "Don't cross her, let her have her way, she's eighty years old," and she sitting there as if she lived in a thin glass cage. Sometimes Granny almost made up her mind to pack up and move back to her own house where nobody could remind her every minute that she was old. Wait, wait, Cornelia, till your own children whisper behind your back!

In her day she had kept a better house and had got more work done. She wasn't too old yet for Lydia to be driving eighty miles for advice when one of the children jumped the track, and Jimmy still dropped in and talked things over: "Now, Mammy, you've a good business head, I want to know what you think of this? . . ." Old. Cornelia couldn't change the furniture around without asking. Little things, little things!

They had been so sweet when they were little. Granny wished the old days were back again with the children young and everything to be done over. It had been a hard pull, but not too much for her. When she thought of all the food she had cooked, and all the clothes she had cut and sewed, and all the gardens she had made—well, the children showed it. There they were, made out of her, and they couldn't get away from that. Sometimes she wanted to see John again and point to them and say, Well, I didn't do so badly, did I? But that would have to wait. That was for tomorrow. She used to think of him as a man, but now all the children were older than their father, and he would be a child beside her if she saw him now. It seemed strange and there was something wrong in the idea. Why, he couldn't possibly recognize her. She had fenced in a hundred acres once, digging the post holes herself and clamping the wires with just a negro boy to help. That changed a woman. John would be looking for a young woman with the peaked Spanish comb in her hair and the painted fan. Digging post holes changed a woman. Riding country roads in the winter when women had their babies was another thing: sitting up nights with sick horses and sick negroes and sick children and hardly ever losing one. John, I hardly ever lost one of them! John would see that in a minute, that would be something he could understand, she wouldn't have to explain anything!

It made her feel like rolling up her sleeves and putting the whole place to rights again. No matter if Cornelia was determined to be everywhere at once, there were a great many things left undone on this place. She would start tomorrow and do them. It was good to be strong enough for everything, even if all you made melted and changed and slipped under your hands, so that by the time you finished you almost forgot what you were working for. What was it I set out to do? she asked herself intently, but she could not remember. A fog rose over the valley, she saw it marching across the creek swallowing the trees and moving up the hill like an army of ghosts. Soon it would be at the near edge of the orchard, and then it was time to go in and light the lamps. Come in, children, don't stay out in the night air.

Lighting the lamps had been beautiful. The children huddled up to her and breathed like little calves waiting at the bars in the twilight. Their eyes followed the match and watched the flame rise and settle in a blue curve, then they moved away from her. The lamp was lit, they didn't have to be scared and hang on to mother any more. Never, never, never more. God, for all my life I thank Thee. Without Thee, my God, I could never have done it. Hail, Mary, full of grace.[1]

I want you to pick all the fruit this year and see that nothing is wasted. There's always someone who can use it. Don't let good things rot for want of using. You waste life when you waste good food. Don't let things get lost. It's bitter to lose things. Now, don't let me get to thinking, not when I am tired and taking a little nap before supper. . . .

The pillow rose about her shoulders and pressed against her heart and the memory was being squeezed out of it: oh, push down the pillow, somebody: it would smother her if she tried to hold it. Such a fresh breeze blowing and such a green day with no threats in it. But he had not come, just the same. What does a woman do when she has put on the white veil and set out the white cake for a man and he doesn't come? She tried to remember. No, I swear he never harmed me but in that. He never harmed me but in that . . . and what if he did? There was the day, the day, but a whirl of dark smoke rose and covered it, crept up and over into the bright field where everything was planted so carefully in orderly rows. That was hell, she knew hell when she saw it. For sixty years she had prayed against remembering him and against losing her soul in the deep pit of hell, and now the two things were mingled in one

---

[1] First line of a common Catholic prayer.

and the thought of him was a smoky cloud from hell that moved and crept in her head when she had just got rid of Doctor Harry and was trying to rest a minute. Wounded vanity, Ellen, said a sharp voice in the top of her mind. Don't let your wounded vanity get the upper hand of you. Plenty of girls get jilted. You were jilted, weren't you? Then stand up to it. Her eyelids wavered and let in streamers of blue-gray light like tissue paper over her eyes. She must get up and pull the shades down or she'd never sleep. She was in bed again and the shades were not down. How could that happen? Better turn over, hide from the light, sleeping in the light gave you nightmares. "Mother, how do you feel now?" and a stinging wetness on her forehead. But I don't like having my face washed in cold water!

Hapsy? George? Lydia? Jimmy?[2] No, Cornelia, and her features were swollen and full of little puddles. "They're coming, darling, they'll all be here soon." Go wash your face, child, you look funny.

Instead of obeying, Cornelia knelt down and put her head on the pillow. She seemed to be talking but there was no sound. "Well, are you tongue-tied? Whose birthday is it? Are you going to give a party?"

Cornelia's mouth moved urgently in strange shapes. "Don't do that, you bother me, daughter."

"Oh, no, Mother. Oh, no. . . ."

Nonsense. It was strange about children. They disputed your every word. "No what, Cornelia?"

"Here's Doctor Harry."

"I won't see that boy again. He just left five minutes ago."

"That was this morning, Mother. It's night now. Here's the nurse."

"This is Doctor Harry, Mrs. Weatherall. I never saw you look so young and happy!"

"Ah, I'll never be young again—but I'd be happy if they'd let me lie in peace and get rested."

She thought she spoke up loudly, but no one answered. A warm weight on her forehead, a warm bracelet on her wrist, and a breeze went on whispering, trying to tell her something. A shuffle of leaves in the everlasting hand of God, He blew on them and they danced and rattled. "Mother, don't mind, we're going to give you a little hypodermic." "Look here, daughter, how do ants get in this bed? I saw sugar ants yesterday." Did you send for Hapsy too?

It was Hapsy she really wanted. She had to go a long way back through a great many rooms to find Hapsy standing with a baby on her arm. She seemed to herself to be Hapsy also, and the baby on Hapsy's arm was Hapsy and himself and herself, all at once, and there was no surprise in the meeting. Then Hapsy melted from within and turned flimsy as gray gauze and the baby was a gauzy shadow, and Hapsy came up close and said, "I thought you'd never come," and looked at her very searchingly and said, "You haven't changed a bit!" They leaned forward to kiss, when Cornelia began whispering from a long way off, "Oh, is there anything you want to tell me? Is there anything I can do for you?"

Yes, she had changed her mind after sixty years and she would like to see George. I want you to find George. Find him and be sure to tell him I forgot him. I want him to know I had my husband just the same and my children and my house like any other woman. A good house too and a good husband that I loved and fine children out of him. Better than I hoped for even. Tell him I was given back everything he took away and more. Oh, no, oh, God, no, there was something else besides the house

---

[2]Children of Granny Weatherall. The man who jilted her was George. She later married John, and named her first child George. Her last child she called Hapsy, diminutive for Happiness: the child she wanted from George.

and the man and the children. Oh, surely they were not all? What was it? Something not given back. . . . Her breath crowded down under her ribs and grew into a monstrous frightening shape with cutting edges; it bored up into her head, and the agony was unbelievable: Yes, John, get the Doctor now, no more talk, my time has come.

When this one was born it should be the last. The last. It should have been born first, for it was the one she had truly wanted. Everything came in good time. Nothing left out, left over. She was strong, in three days she would be as well as ever. Better. A woman needed milk in her to have her full health.

"Mother, do you hear me?"

"I've been telling you—"

"Mother, Father Connolly's here."

"I went to Holy Communion only last week. Tell him I'm not so sinful as all that."

"Father just wants to speak to you."

He could speak as much as he pleased. It was like him to drop in and inquire about her soul as if it were a teething baby, and then stay on for a cup of tea and a round of cards and gossip. He always had a funny story of some sort, usually about an Irishman who made his little mistakes and confessed them, and the point lay in some absurd thing he would blurt out in the confessional showing his struggles between native piety and original sin. Granny felt easy about her soul. Cornelia, where are your manners? Give Father Connolly a chair. She had her secret comfortable understanding with a few favorite saints who cleared a straight road to God for her. All as surely signed and sealed as the papers for the new Forty Acres. Forever . . . heirs and assigns forever. Since the day the wedding cake was not cut, but thrown out and wasted. The whole bottom dropped out of the world, and there she was blind and sweating with nothing under her feet and the walls falling away. His hand had caught her under the breast, she had not fallen, there was the freshly polished floor with the green rug on it, just as before. He had cursed like a sailor's parrot and said, "I'll kill him for you." Don't lay a hand on him, for my sake leave something to God. "Now, Ellen, you must believe what I tell you. . . ."

So there was nothing, nothing to worry about any more, except sometimes in the night one of the children screamed in a nightmare, and they both hustled out shaking and hunting for the matches and calling, "There, wait a minute, here we are!" John, get the doctor now, Hapsy's time has come. But there was Hapsy standing by the bed in a white cap. "Cornelia, tell Hapsy to take off her cap. I can't see her plain."

Her eyes opened very wide and the room stood out like a picture she had seen somewhere. Dark colors with the shadows rising towards the ceiling in long angles. The tall black dresser gleamed with nothing on it but John's picture, enlarged from a little one, with John's eyes very black when they should have been blue. You never saw him, so how do you know how he looked? But the man insisted the copy was perfect, it was very rich and handsome. For a picture, yes, but it's not my husband. The table by the bed had a linen cover and a candle and a crucifix. The light was blue from Cornelia's silk lampshades. No sort of light at all, just frippery. You had to live forty years with kerosene lamps to appreciate honest electricity. She felt very strong and she saw Doctor Harry with a rosy nimbus around him.

"You look like a saint, Doctor Harry, and I vow that's as near as you'll ever come to it."

"She's saying something."

"I heard you, Cornelia. What's all this carrying-on?"

"Father Connolly's saying—"

Cornelia's voice staggered and bumped like a cart in a bad road. It rounded corners and turned back again and arrived nowhere. Granny stepped up in the cart very lightly and reached for the reins, but a man sat beside her and she knew him by his hands, driving the cart. She did not look in his face, for she knew without seeing, but looked instead down the road where the trees leaned over and bowed to each other and a thousand birds were singing a Mass. She felt like singing too, but she put her hand in the bosom of her dress and pulled out a rosary, and Father Connolly murmured Latin in a very solemn voice and tickled her feet.[3] My God, will you stop that nonsense? I'm a married woman. What if he did run away and leave me to face the priest by myself? I found another a whole world better. I wouldn't have exchanged my husband for anybody except St. Michael himself, and you may tell him that for me with a thank you in the bargain.

Light flashed on her closed eyelids, and a deep roaring shook her. Cornelia, is that lightning? I hear thunder. There's going to be a storm. Close all the windows. Call the children in. . . . "Mother, here we are, all of us." "Is that you, Hapsy?" "Oh, no, I'm Lydia. We drove as fast as we could." Their faces drifted above her, drifted away. The rosary fell out of her hands and Lydia put it back. Jimmy tried to help, their hands fumbled together, and Granny closed two fingers around Jimmy's thumb. Beads wouldn't do, it must be something alive. She was so amazed her thoughts ran round and round. So, my dear Lord, this is my death and I wasn't even thinking about it. My children have come to see me die. But I can't, it's not time. Oh, I always hated surprises. I wanted to give Cornelia the amethyst set—Cornelia, you're to have the amethyst set, but Hapsy's to wear it when she wants, and, Doctor Harry, do shut up. Nobody sent for you. Oh, my dear Lord, do wait a minute. I meant to do something about the Forty Acres, Jimmy doesn't need it and Lydia will later on, with that worthless husband of hers. I meant to finish the altar cloth and send six bottles of wine to Sister Borgia for her dyspepsia. I want to send six bottles of wine to Sister Borgia, Father Connolly, now don't let me forget.

Cornelia's voice made short turns and tilted over and crashed. "Oh, Mother, oh, Mother, oh, Mother. . . ."

"I'm not going, Cornelia. I'm taken by surprise. I can't go."

You'll see Hapsy again. What about her? "I thought you'd never come." Granny made a long journey outward, looking for Hapsy. What if I don't find her? What then? Her heart sank down and down, there was no bottom to death, she couldn't come to the end of it. The blue light from Cornelia's lampshade drew into a tiny point in the center of her brain, it flickered and winked like an eye, quietly it fluttered and dwindled. Granny lay curled down within herself, amazed and watchful, staring at the point of light that was herself; her body was now only a deeper mass of shadow in an endless darkness and this darkness would curl around the light and swallow it up. God, give a sign!

For the second time there was no sign. Again no bridegroom and the priest in the house. She could not remember any other sorrow because this grief wiped them all away. Oh, no, there's nothing more cruel than this—I'll never forgive it. She stretched herself with a deep breath and blew out the light.

1929, 1930

The Grave

The grandfather, dead for more than thirty years, had been twice disturbed in his long repose by the constancy and possessiveness of his widow. She removed his bones first to Louisiana and then to Texas as if she had set out to find her own burial place, knowing well she would never return to the places she had left. In Texas she set up a small cemetery in a corner of her first farm, and as the family connection grew, and

---

[3]The priest is administering the last rites, which involves anointing the feet.

oddments of relations came over from Kentucky to settle, it contained at last about twenty graves. After the grandmother's death, part of her land was to be sold for the benefit of certain of her children, and the cemetery happened to lie in the part set aside for sale. It was necessary to take up the bodies and bury them again in the family plot in the big new public cemetery, where the grandmother had been buried. At last her husband was to lie beside her for eternity, as she had planned.

The family cemetery had been a pleasant small neglected garden of tangled rose bushes and ragged cedar trees and cypress, the simple flat stones rising out of un-cropped sweet-smelling wild grass. The graves were lying open and empty one burn-ing day when Miranda and her brother Paul, who often went together to hunt rabbits and doves, propped their twenty-two Winchester rifles[1] carefully against the rail fence, climbed over and explored among the graves. She was nine years old and he was twelve.

They peered into the pits all shaped alike with such purposeful accuracy, and looking at each other with pleased adventurous eyes, they said in solemn tones: "These were graves!" trying by words to shape a special, suitable emotion in their minds, but they felt nothing except an agreeable thrill of wonder: they were seeing a new sight, doing something they had not done before. In them both there was also a small disappointment at the entire common-placeness of the actual spectacle. Even if it had once contained a coffin for years upon years, when the coffin was gone a grave was just a hole in the ground. Miranda leaped into the pit that had held her grand-father's bones. Scratching around aimlessly and pleasurably as any young animal, she scooped up a lump of earth and weighed it in her palm. It had a pleasantly sweet, corrupt smell, being mixed with cedar needles and small leaves, and as the crumbs fell apart, she saw a silver dove no larger than a hazel nut, with spread wings and a neat fan-shaped tail. The breast had a deep round hollow in it. Turning it up to the fierce sunlight, she saw that the inside of the hollow was cut in little whorls. She scrambled out, over the pile of loose earth that had fallen back into one end of the grave, calling to Paul that she had found something, he must guess what . . . His head appeared smiling over the rim of another grave. He waved a closed hand at her. "I've got something too!" They ran to compare treasures, making a game of it, so many guesses each, all wrong, and a final showdown with opened palms. Paul had found a thin wide gold ring carved with intricate flowers and leaves. Miranda was smitten at sight of the ring and wished to have it. Paul seemed more impressed by the dove. They made a trade, with some little bickering. After he had got the dove in his hand, Paul said, "Don't you know what this is? This is a screw head for a *coffin!* . . . I'll bet nobody else in the world has one like this!"

Miranda glanced at it without covetousness. She had the gold ring on her thumb; it fitted perfectly. "Maybe we ought to go now," she said, "maybe one of the niggers 'll see us and tell somebody." They knew the land had been sold, the cemetery was no longer theirs, and they felt like trespassers. They climbed back over the fence, slung their rifles loosely under their arms—they had been shooting at targets with various kinds of firearms since they were seven years old—and set out to look for the rabbits and doves or whatever small game might happen along. On these expeditions Mir-anda always followed at Paul's heels along the path, obeying instructions about han-dling her gun when going through fences; learning how to stand it up properly so it would not slip and fire unexpectedly; how to wait her time for a shot and not just bang away in the air without looking, spoiling shots for Paul, who really could hit things if given a chance. Now and then, in her excitement at seeing birds whizz up suddenly before her face, or a rabbit leap across her very toes, she lost her head, and almost without sighting she flung her rifle up and pulled the trigger. She hardly ever

---

[1] A rifle manufactured by Winchester's using a cartridge .22 inches in diameter.

hit any sort of mark. She had no proper sense of hunting at all. Her brother would be often completely disgusted with her. "You don't care whether you get your bird or not," he said. "That's no way to hunt." Miranda could not understand his indignation. She had seen him smash his hat and yell with fury when he had missed his aim. "What I like about shooting," said Miranda, with exasperating inconsequence, "is pulling the trigger and hearing the noise."

"Then, by golly," said Paul, "whyn't you go back to the range and shoot at bulls-eyes?"

"I'd just as soon," said Miranda, "only like this, we walk around more."

"Well, you just stay behind and stop spoiling my shots," said Paul, who, when he made a kill, wanted to be certain he had made it. Miranda, who alone brought down a bird once in twenty rounds, always claimed as her own any game they got when they fired at the same moment. It was tiresome and unfair and her brother was sick of it.

"Now, the first dove we see, or the first rabbit, is mine," he told her. "And the next will be yours. Remember that and don't get smarty."

"What about snakes?" asked Miranda idly. "Can I have the first snake?"

Waving her thumb gently and watching her gold ring glitter, Miranda lost interest in shooting. She was wearing her summer roughing outfit: dark blue overalls, a light blue shirt, a hired-man's straw hat, and thick brown sandals. Her brother had the same outfit except his was a sober hickory-nut color. Ordinarily Miranda preferred her overalls to any other dress, though it was making rather a scandal in the country-side, for the year was 1903, and in the back country the law of female decorum had teeth in it. Her father had been criticized for letting his girls dress like boys and go careering around astride barebacked horses. Big sister Maria, the really independent and fearless one, in spite of her rather affected ways, rode at a dead run with only a rope knotted around her horse's nose. It was said the motherless family was running down, with the Grandmother no longer there to hold it together. It was known that she had discriminated against her son Harry in her will, and that he was in straits about money. Some of his old neighbors reflected with vicious satisfaction that now he would probably not be so stiffnecked, nor have any more high-stepping horses either. Miranda knew this, though she could not say how. She had met along the road old women of the kind who smoked corn-cob pipes, who had treated her grand-mother with most sincere respect. They slanted their gummy old eyes side-ways at the granddaughter and said, "Ain't you ashamed of yoself, Missy? It's against the Scriptures to dress like that. Whut yo Pappy thinkin about?" Miranda, with her pow-erful social sense, which was like a fine set of antennae radiating from every pore of her skin, would feel ashamed because she knew well it was rude and ill-bred to shock anybody, even bad-tempered old crones, though she had faith in her father's judg-ment and was perfectly comfortable in the clothes. Her father had said, "They're just what you need, and they'll save your dresses for school . . ." This sounded quite simple and natural to her. She had been brought up in rigorous economy. Wastefulness was vulgar. It was also a sin. These were truths; she had heard them repeated many times and never once disputed.

Now the ring, shining with the serene purity of fine gold on her rather grubby thumb, turned her feelings against her overalls and sockless feet, toes sticking through the thick brown leather straps. She wanted to go back to the farmhouse, take a good cold bath, dust herself with plenty of Maria's violet talcum powder—provided Maria was not present to object, of course—put on the thinnest, most becoming dress she owned, with a big sash, and sit in a wicker chair under the trees . . . These things were not all she wanted, of course; she had vague stirrings of desire for luxury and a grand way of living which could not take precise form in her imagination but were founded on family legend of past wealth and leisure. These immediate comforts were what she could have, and she wanted them at once. She lagged rather far be-hind Paul, and once she thought of just turning back without a word and going home. She stopped, thinking that Paul would never do that to her, and so she would have to tell him. When a rabbit leaped, she let Paul have it without dispute. He killed it with one shot.

When she came up with him, he was already kneeling, examining the wound, the rabbit trailing from his hands. "Right through the head," he said complacently, as if he had aimed for it. He took out his sharp, competent bowie knife and started to skin the body. He did it very cleanly and quickly. Uncle Jimbilly knew how to prepare the skins so that Miranada always had fur coats for her dolls, for though she never cared much for her dolls she liked seeing them in fur coats. The children knelt facing each other over the dead animal. Miranda watched admiringly while her brother stripped the skin away as if he were taking off a glove. The flayed flesh emerged dark scarlet, sleek, firm; Miranda with thumb and finger felt the long fine muscles with the silvery flat strips binding them to the joints. Brother lifted the oddly bloated belly. "Look," he said, in a low amazed voice. "It was going to have young ones."

Very carefully he slit the thin flesh from the center ribs to the flanks, and a scarlet bag appeared. He slit again and pulled the bag open, and there lay a bundle of tiny rabbits, each wrapped in a thin scarlet veil. The brother pulled these off and there they were, dark gray, their sleek wet down lying in minute even ripples, like a baby's head just washed, their unbelievably small delicate ears folded close, their little blind faces almost featureless.

Miranda said, "Oh, I want to *see*," under her breath. She looked and looked— excited but not frightened, for she was accustomed to the sight of animals killed in hunting—filled with pity and astonishment and a kind of shocked delight in the wonderful little creatures for their own sakes, they were so pretty. She touched one of them ever so carefully, "Ah, there's blood running over them," she said and began to tremble without knowing why. Yet she wanted most deeply to see and to know. Having seen, she felt at once as if she had known all along. The very memory of her former ignorance faded, she had always known just this. No one had ever told her anything outright, she had been rather unobservant of the animal life around her because she was so accustomed to animals. They seemed simply disorderly and unaccountably rude in their habits, but altogether natural and not very interesting. Her brother had spoken as if he had known about everything all along. He may have seen all this before. He had never said a word to her, but she knew now a part at least of what he knew. She understood a little of the secret, formless intuitions in her own mind and body, which had been clearing up, taking form, so gradually and so steadily she had not realized that she was learning what she had to know. Paul said cautiously, as if he were talking about something forbidden: "They were just about ready to be born." His voice dropped on the last word. "I know," said Miranda, "like kittens. I know, like babies." She was quietly and terribly agitated, standing again with her rifle under her arm, looking down at the bloody heap. "I don't want the skin," she said, "I won't have it." Paul buried the young rabbits again in their mother's body, wrapped the skin around her, carried her to a clump of sage bushes, and hid her away. He came out again at once and said to Miranda, with an eager friendliness, a confidential tone quite unusual in him, as if he were taking her into an important secret on equal terms: "Listen now. Now you listen to me, and don't ever forget. Don't you ever tell a living soul that you saw this. Don't tell a soul. Don't tell Dad because I'll get into trouble. He'll say I'm leading you into things you ought not to do. He's always saying that. So now don't you go and forget and blab out something the way you're always doing . . . Now, that's a secret. Don't you tell."

Miranda never told, she did not even wish to tell anybody. She thought about the whole worrisome affair with confused unhappiness for a few days. Then it sank quietly into her mind and was heaped over by accumulated thousands of impressions, for nearly twenty years. One day she was picking her path among the puddles and crushed refuse of a market street in a strange city of a strange country, when without warning, plain and clear in its true colors as if she looked through a frame upon a scene that had not stirred nor changed since the moment it happened, the episode of that far-off day leaped from its burial place before her mind's eye. She was so reasonlessly horrified she halted suddenly staring, the scene before her eyes dimmed by the vision back of them. An Indian vendor had held up before her a tray of dyed sugar sweets, in the shapes of all kinds of small creatures: birds, baby chicks, baby rabbits, lambs, baby pigs. They were in gay colors and smelled of vanilla, maybe. . . . It was a very hot day and the smell in the market, with its piles of raw flesh and wilting flowers, was like the mingled sweetness and corruption she had smelled that other day in the empty cemetery at home: the day she had remembered always until now vaguely as the time she and her brother had found treasure in the opened graves. Instantly upon this thought the dreadful vision faded, and she saw clearly her brother, whose childhood face she had forgotten, standing again in the blazing sunshine, again twelve years old, a pleased sober smile in his eyes, turning the silver dove over and over in his hands.

1935, 1940

JEAN TOOMER
(1894–1967)

In 1922 at a time when he was at work on his masterpiece *Cane*, Jean Toomer wrote to Sherwood Anderson: "Your images are clean, glowing, healthy, vibrant: sunlight on forks of trees, on mellow piles of pine boards. . . . Your Yea! to life is one of the clear fine tones in our medley of harsh discordant sounds. Life is measured by your own glowing, and you find life, you find its possibilities deeply hopeful and beautiful. It seems to me that art in our day, other than in its purely aesthetic phase, has a sort of religious function."

Toomer was twenty-eight years old in 1922, at the first flood of his creative powers. The years that brought him to this moment were filled with much wandering and great uncertainty, a fate perhaps inevitable for one caught ambiguously between black and white worlds. Toomer was born in Washington, D.C., of a father who was a southern planter and a mother who was the daughter of P. B. S. Pinchback, who became acting governor of Louisiana during Reconstruction.

This grandfather was to be the central force in Toomer's life, particularly as his father disappeared the year after his birth. Toomer was later (1922) to describe his heritage in a biographical sketch: "Racially, I seem to have (who knows for sure) seven blood mixtures: French, Dutch, Welsh, Negro, German, Jewish, and Indian. Because of these, my position in America has been a curious one. I have lived equally amid the two race groups. Now white, now colored. From my own point of view I am naturally and inevitably an American."

After living for a time with his mother and stepfather in New Rochelle, New York, Toomer returned to live with his grandfather in Washington, D.C., where he finished high school in 1914. He then enrolled in succession at a number of universities without ever taking a degree—the University of Wisconsin for a year, studying agriculture; the American College of Physical Training in Chicago for several months; the University of Chicago, in the premedical program; New York University, studying sociology; the City College of New York, studying history. Dropping out of school, Toomer volunteered for service in the First

World War, but was rejected because of poor eyesight and a hernia. He then turned to a succession of miscellaneous jobs but was unhappy in all of them and increasingly disenchanted with his lot. No doubt a major reason for his restlessness was his attraction to literature. He wrote of this period:

> At all possible times I was either writing or reading. I read all of Waldo Frank, most of Dostoevsky, much of Tolstoy, Flaubert, Baudelaire, Sinclair Lewis, Dreiser, most all of the American poets, Coleridge, Blake, Pater,—in fine, a good portion of the modern writers of all western countries. In addition—Freud, and the psychoanalysts, and a miscellany of scientific and philosophic works. And I began reading these magazines: *The Dial, Poetry, The Liberator, The Nation* and *The New Republic*, etc.

In 1921, Toomer was hired as a temporary principal of Georgia Normal and Industrial Institute at Sparta, Georgia. This was Toomer's first experience of the Deep South, and it affected him deeply. He wrote later: "The setting was crude in a way, but strangely rich and beautiful. . . . There was a valley, the valley of 'Cane,' with smoke-wreaths during the day and mist at night. A family of back-country Negroes had only recently moved into a shack not too far away. They sang. And this was the first time I'd ever heard the folk-songs and spirituals. They were very rich and sad and joyous and beautiful." Toomer learned that some Negroes in the town objected to the songs, calling them "shouting." He sensed that what he was witnessing and hearing "would be certain to die out," and its death would be a tragic loss: "And this feeling I put into *Cane. Cane* was a swan-song. It was a song of an end. And why no one has seen and felt that, why people have expected me to write a second and a third and a fourth book like *Cane*, is one of the queer misunderstandings of my life."

Published in 1923, *Cane* has three parts: a series of rural Georgia sketches interspersed with poems, followed by tales of blacks in the urban North uncertain of their identity, and concluding with a long story in dramatic form ("Kabnis") about a northern mulatto who went South ostensibly to teach but in search of self and the meaning of the black heritage. Although *Cane* was no bestseller, it established Toomer as an innovative, imaginative writer. He settled in New York that summer, and, as he put it, "stepped into the literary world. [Waldo] Frank, Gorham Munson, Kenneth Burke, Hart Crane, Matthew Josephson, Malcolm Cowley, Paul Rosenfeld, Van Wyck Brooks, Robert Littell—*Broom*, the *Dial*, the *New Republic* and many more. . . . it was an extraordinary summer."

As it turned out, that summer was the peak of Toomer's literary career. He felt that those who expected more fiction from him like that of his first book simply did not understand *Cane*. His writing could come only from his deepest feelings. And as he moved on in his restless spiritual quest, he became interested (as did Hart Crane and others) in the mystical teachings of P. D. Ouspensky, set forth in such philosophical books as his *Tertium Organum: A Key to the Enigmas of the World* (1920).

Through Ouspensky, Toomer was drawn to the teachings of George Ivanovitch Gurdjieff, and went to France for two summers in the mid-1920s to study with him in his school at Fontainebleau. He himself became a teacher of Gurdjieff's mystical doctrines and practices, and belief in cosmic consciousness. Toomer spread the word in Harlem, Chicago, Taos, New Mexico, Portage, Wisconsin, and Carmel, California. He once wrote: "I am not sure I have a soul. . . but if I have then Gurdjieff has penetrated the shell and written upon the kernel indelibly." Later in his life, Toomer was drawn to the Quakers, and joined the Society of Friends in 1940. He died in 1967 in Pennsylvania.

Toomer was generally forgotten except as a footnote in literary history until the republication of *Cane* in 1969, with an introduction by the writer Arna Bontemps, the so-called "keeper of the flame" of the Harlem Renaissance. Again the book was hailed as a classic, and this time took its place among the major works of the modern period. Scholars and critics have sifted through the fiction, poetry, plays, essays, autobiographical writings, and aphorisms left in manuscript at Toomer's death and published a small fraction of the material. A full assessment of Toomer's career must await fuller publication of these works, now on deposit at Fisk University in Nashville, Tennessee.

ADDITIONAL READING

The Wayward and the Seeking: A Collection of Writings by Jean Toomer, ed. Darwin T. Turner, 1980; *The Collected Poems of Jean Toomer*, ed. Robert B. Jones and Margery Toomer Latimer, 1988.

Darwin T. Turner, "Jean Toomer: Exile," *In a Minor Chord: Three Afro-American Writers and Their Search for Identity*, 1971; Frank Durham, ed., *Studies in Cane*, 1971; "A Special Number" on Jean Toomer, *College Language Association Journal*, XVII, No. 4 (June 1974); Fritz Gysin, "Jean Toomer," *The Grotesque in American Negro Fiction*, 1975; Brian Joseph Benson and Mabel Mayle Dillard, *Jean Toomer*, 1980; Nellie Y. McKay, *Jean Toomer, Artist*, 1984; Cynthia Earl Kerman and Richard Eldridge, *The Lives of Jean Toomer*, 1988; Therman B. O'Daniel, *Jean Toomer: A Critical Evaluation*, 1988.

TEXT

Cane, 1969.

from Cane

KARINTHA

Her skin is like dusk on the eastern horizon,
O cant you see it, O cant you see it,
Her skin is like dusk on the eastern horizon
. . . When the sun goes down.

Men had always wanted her, this Karintha, even as a child, Karintha carrying beauty, perfect as dusk when the sun goes down. Old men rode her hobby-horse upon their knees. Young men danced with her at frolics when they should have been dancing with their grownup girls. God grant us youth, secretly prayed the old men. The young fellows counted the time to pass before she would be old enough to mate with them. This interest of the male, who wishes to ripen a growing thing too soon, could mean no good to her.

Karintha, at twelve, was a wild flash that told the other folks just what it was to live. At sunset, when there was no wind, and the pine-smoke from over by the sawmill hugged the earth, and you couldnt see more than a few feet in front, her sudden darting past you was a bit of vivid color, like a black bird that flashes in light. With the other children one could hear, some distance off, their feet flopping in the two-inch dust. Karintha's running was a whir. It had the sound of the red dust that sometimes makes a spiral in the road. At dusk, during the hush just after the sawmill had closed down, and before any of the women had started their supper-getting-ready songs, her voice, high-pitched, shrill, would put one's ears to itching. But no one ever thought to make her stop because of it. She stoned the cows, and beat her dog, and fought the other children. . . . Even the preacher, who caught her at mischief, told himself that she was as innocently lovely as a November cotton flower. Already, rumors were out about her. Homes in Georgia are most often built on the two-room plan. In one, you cook and eat, in the other you sleep, and there love goes on. Karintha had seen or heard, perhaps she had felt her parents loving. One could but imitate one's parents, for to follow them was the way of God. She played "home" with a small boy who was not afraid to do her bidding. That started the whole thing. Old men could no longer ride her hobby-horse upon their knees. But young men counted faster.

> Her skin is like dusk,
> O cant you see it,
> Her skin is like dusk,
> When the sun goes down.

Karintha is a woman. She who carries beauty, perfect as dusk when the sun goes down. She has been married many times. Old men remind her that a few years back they rode her hobby-horse upon their knees. Karintha smiles, and indulges them when she is in the mood for it. She has contempt for them. Karintha is a woman. Young men run stills to make her money. Young men go to the big cities and run on the road. Young men go away to college. They all want to bring her money. These are the young men who thought that all they had to do was to count time. But Karintha is a woman, and she has had a child. A child fell out of her womb onto a bed of pine-needles in the forest. Pine-needles are smooth and sweet. They are elastic to the feet of rabbits. . . . A sawmill was nearby. Its pyramidal sawdust pile smouldered. It is a year before one completely burns. Meanwhile, the smoke curls up and hangs in odd wraiths about the trees, curls up, and spreads itself out over the valley. . . Weeks after Karintha returned home the smoke was so heavy you tasted it in water. Some one made a song:

> Smoke is on the hills. Rise up.
> Smoke is on the hills, O rise
> And take my soul to Jesus.

Karintha is a woman. Men do not know that the soul of her was a growing thing ripened too soon. They will bring their money; they will die not having found it out. . . Karintha at twenty, carrying beauty, perfect as dusk when the sun goes down. Karintha. . .

> Her skin is like dusk on the eastern horizon,
> O cant you see it, O cant you see it,
> Her skin is like dusk on the eastern horizon
> . . . When the sun goes down.

Goes down. . .

1923

BLOOD-BURNING MOON

1

Up from the skeleton stone walls, up from the rotting floor boards and the solid hand-hewn beams of oak of the pre-war cotton factory, dusk came. Up from the dusk the full moon came. Glowing like a fired pine-knot, it illumined the great door and soft showered the Negro shanties aligned along the single street of factory town. The full moon in the great door was an omen. Negro women improvised songs against its spell.

Louisa sang as she came over the crest of the hill from the white folks' kitchen.

Her skin was the color of oak leaves on young trees in fall. Her breasts, firm and up-pointed like ripe acorns. And her singing had the low murmur of winds in fig trees. Bob Stone, younger son of the people she worked for, loved her. By the way the world reckons things, he had won her. By measure of that warm glow which came into her mind at thought of him, he had won her. Tom Burwell, whom the whole town called Big Boy, also loved her. But working in the fields all day, and far away from her, gave him no chance to show it. Though often enough of evenings he had tried to. Somehow, he never got along. Strong as he was with hands upon the ax or plow, he found it difficult to hold her. Or so he thought. But the fact was that he held her to factory town more firmly than he thought for. His black balanced, and pulled against, the white of Stone, when she thought of them. And her mind was vaguely upon them as she came over the crest of the hill, coming from the white folks' kitchen. As she sang softly at the evil face of the full moon.

A strange stir was in her. Indolently, she tried to fix upon Bob or Tom as the cause of it. To meet Bob in the canebrake, as she was going to do an hour or so later, was nothing new. And Tom's proposal which she felt on its way to her could be indefi-nitely put off. Separately, there was no unusual significance to either one. But for some reason, they jumbled when her eyes gazed vacantly at the rising moon. And from the jumble came the stir that was strangely within her. Her lips trembled. The slow rhythm of her song grew agitant and restless. Rusty black and tan spotted hounds, lying in the dark corners of porches or prowling around back yards, put their noses in the air and caught its tremor. They began plaintively to yelp and howl. Chickens woke up and cackled. Intermittently, all over the countryside dogs barked and roosters crowed as if heralding a weird dawn or some ungodly awakening. The women sang lustily. Their songs were cotton-wads to stop their ears. Louisa came down into factory town and sank wearily upon the step before her home. The moon was rising towards a thick cloud-bank which soon would hide it.

> Red nigger moon. Sinner!
> Blood-burning moon. Sinner!
> Come out that fact'ry door.

2

Up from the deep dusk of a cleared spot on the edge of the forest a mellow glow arose and spread fan-wise into the low-hanging heavens. And all around the air was heavy with the scent of boiling cane. A large pile of cane-stalks lay like ribboned shadows upon the ground. A mule, harnessed to a pole, trudged lazily round and round the pivot of the grinder. Beneath a swaying oil lamp, a Negro alternately whipped out at the mule, and fed cane-stalks to the grinder. A fat boy waddled pails of fresh ground juice between the grinder and the boiling stove. Steam came from the copper boiling pan. The scent of cane came from the copper pan and drenched the forest and the hill that sloped to factory town, beneath its fragrance. It drenched the men in circle seated around the stove. Some of them chewed at the white pulp of stalks, but there was no need for them to, if all they wanted was to taste the cane. One tasted it in factory town. And from factory town one could see the soft haze thrown by the glowing stove upon the low-hanging heavens.

Old David Georgia stirred the thickening syrup with a long ladle, and ever so often drew it off. Old David Georgia tended his stove and told tales about the white folks, about moonshining and cotton picking, and about sweet nigger gals, to the men who sat there about his stove to listen to him. Tom Burwell chewed cane-stalk and laughed with the others till someone mentioned Louisa. Till some one said some-thing about Louisa and Bob Stone, about the silk stockings she must have gotten from him. Blood ran up Tom's neck hotter than the glow that flooded from the stove. He sprang up. Glared at the men and said, "She's my gal." Will Manning laughed.

Tom strode over to him. Yanked him up and knocked him to the ground. Several of Manning's friends got up to fight for him. Tom whipped out a long knife and would have cut them to shreds if they hadnt ducked into the woods. Tom had had enough. He nodded to Old David Georgia and swung down the path to factory town. Just then, the dogs started barking and the roosters began to crow. Tom felt funny. Away from the fight, away from the stove, chill got to him. He shivered. He shuddered when he saw the full moon rising towards the cloud-bank. He who didnt give a godam for the fears of old women. He forced his mind to fasten on Louisa. Bob Stone. Better not be. He turned into the street and saw Louisa sitting before her home. He went towards her, ambling, touched the brim of a marvelously shaped, spotted, felt hat, said he wanted to say something to her, and then found that he didnt know what he had to say, or if he did, that he couldnt say it. He shoved his big fists in his overalls, grinned, and started to move off.

"Youall want me, Tom?"

"Thats what us wants, sho, Louisa."

"Well, here I am—"

"An here I is, but that aint ahelpin none, all th same."

"You wanted to say something? . ."

"I did that, sho. But words is like th spots on dice: no matter how y fumbles em, there's times when they jes wont come. I dunno why. Seems like th love I feels fo yo done stole m tongue. I got it now. Whee! Louisa, honey, I oughtnt tell y, I feel I oughtnt cause yo is young an goes t church an I has had other gals, but Louisa I sho do love y. Lil gal, Ise watched y from them first days when youall sat right here befo yo door befo th well an sang sometimes in a way that like t broke m heart. Ise carried y with me into th fields, day after day, an after that, an I sho can plow when yo is there, an I can pick cotton. Yassur! Come near beatin Barlo yesterday. I sho did. Yassur! An next year if ole Stone'll trust me, I'll have a farm. My own. My bales will buy yo what y gets from white folks now. Silk stockings an purple dresses—course I dont believe what some folks been whisperin as t how y gets them things now. White folks always did do for niggers what they likes. An they jes cant help alikin yo, Louisa. Bob Stone likes y. Course he does. But not th way folks is awhisperin. Does he, hon?"

"I dont know what you mean, Tom."

"Course y dont. Ise already cut two niggers. Had t hon, t tell em so. Niggers always tryin t make somethin out a nothin. An then besides, white folks aint up t them tricks so much nowadays. Godam better not be. Leastawise not with yo. Cause I wouldnt stand f it. Nassur."

"What would you do, Tom?"

"Cut him jes like I cut a nigger."

"No, Tom—"

"I said I would an there aint no mo to it. But that aint th talk f now. Sing, honey Louisa, an while I'm listenin t y I'll be makin love."

Tom took her hand in his. Against the tough thickness of his own, hers felt soft and small. His huge body slipped down the step beside her. The full moon sank upward into the deep purple of the cloud-bank. An old woman brought a lighted lamp and hung it on the common well whose bulky shadow squatted in the middle of the road, opposite Tom and Louisa. The old woman lifted the well-lid, took hold the chain, and began drawing up the heavy bucket. As she did so, she sang. Figures shifted, restlesslike, between lamp and window in the front rooms of the shanties. Shadows of the figures fought each other on the gray dust of the road. Figures raised the windows and joined the old woman in song. Louisa and Tom, the whole street, singing:

> Red nigger moon. Sinner!
> Blood-burning moon. Sinner!
> Come out that fact'ry door.

3

Bob Stone sauntered from his veranda out into the gloom of fir trees and magnolias. The clear white of his skin paled, and the flush of his cheeks turned purple. As if to balance this outer change, his mind became consciously a white man's. He passed the house with its huge open hearth which, in the days of slavery, was the plantation cookery. He saw Louisa bent over that hearth. He went in as a master should and took her. Direct, honest, bold. None of this sneaking that he had to go through now. The contrast was repulsive to him. His family had lost ground. Hell no, his family still owned the niggers, practically. Damned if they did, or he wouldnt have to duck around so. What would they think if they knew? His mother? His sister? He shouldnt mention them, shouldnt think of them in this connection. There in the dusk he blushed at doing so. Fellows about town were all right, but how about his friends up North? He could see them incredible, repulsed. They didnt know. The thought first made him laugh. Then, with their eyes still upon him, he began to feel embarrassed. He felt the need of explaining things to them. Explain hell. They wouldnt understand, and moreover, who ever heard of a Southerner getting on his knees to any Yankee, or anyone. No sir. He was going to see Louisa to-night, and love her. She was lovely—in her way. Nigger way. What way was that? Damned if he knew. Must know. He'd known her long enough to know. Was there something about niggers that you couldnt know? Listening to them at church didnt tell you anything. Looking at them didnt tell you anything. Talking to them didnt tell you anything—unless it was gossip, unless they wanted to talk. Of course, about farming, and licker, and craps—but those werent nigger. Nigger was something more. How much more? Something to be afraid of, more? Hell no. Who ever heard of being afraid of a nigger? Tom Burwell. Cartwell had told him that Tom went with Louisa after she reached home. No sir. No nigger had ever been with his girl. He'd like to see one try. Some position for him to be in. Him, Bob Stone, of the old Stone family, in a scrap with a nigger over a nigger girl. In the good old days. . . Ha! Those were the days. His family had lost ground. Not so much, though. Enough for him to have to cut through old Lemon's canefield by way of the woods, that he might meet her. She was worth it. Beautiful nigger gal. Why nigger? Why not, just gal? No, it was because she was nigger that he went to her. Sweet. . . The scent of boiling cane came to him. Then he saw the rich glow of the stove. He heard the voices of the men circled around it. He was about to skirt the clearing when he heard his own name mentioned. He stopped. Quivering. Leaning against a tree, he listened.

   "Bad nigger. Yassur, he sho is one bad nigger when he gets started."

   "Tom Burwell's been on th gang three times fo cuttin men."

   "What y think he's agwine t do t Bob Stone?"

   "Dunno yet. He aint found out. When he does— Baby!"

   "Aint no tellin."

   "Young Stone aint no quitter an I ken tell y that. Blood of the old uns in his veins."

   "Thats right. He'll scrap, sho."

   "Be gettin too hot f niggers round this away."

   "Shut up, nigger. Y dont know what y talkin bout."

Bob Stone's ears burned as though he had been holding them over the stove. Sizzling heat welled up within him. His feet felt as if they rested on red-hot coals. They stung him to quick movement. He circled the fringe of the glowing. Not a twig cracked beneath his feet. He reached the path that led to factory town. Plunged furiously down it. Halfway along, a blindness within him veered him aside. He crashed into the bordering canebrake. Cane leaves cut his face and lips. He tasted blood. He threw himself down and dug his fingers in the ground. The earth was cool. Cane-roots took the fever from his hands. After a long while, or so it seemed to him, the thought came to him that it must be time to see Louisa. He got to his feet and walked calmly to their meeting place. No Louisa. Tom Burwell had her. Veins in his forehead bulged and distended. Saliva moistened the dried blood on his lips. He bit down on his lips. He tasted blood. Not his own blood; Tom Burwell's blood. Bob drove through the cane and out again upon the road. A hound swung down the path before him towards factory town. Bob couldnt see it. The dog loped aside to let him pass. Bob's blind rushing made him stumble over it. He fell with a thud that dazed him. The hound yelped. Answering yelps came from all over the countryside. Chickens cackled. Roosters crowed, heralding the bloodshot eyes of southern awakening. Singers in the town were silenced. They shut their windows down. Palpitant between the rooster crows, a chill hush settled upon the huddled forms of Tom and Louisa. A figure rushed from the shadow and stood before them. Tom popped to his feet.

"Whats y want?"

"I'm Bob Stone."

"Yassur—an I'm Tom Burwell. Whats y want?"

Bob lunged at him. Tom side-stepped, caught him by the shoulder, and flung him to the ground. Straddled him.

"Let me up."

"Yassur—but watch yo doins, Bob Stone."

A few dark figures, drawn by the sound of scuffle, stood about them. Bob sprang to his feet.

"Fight like a man, Tom Burwell, an I'll lick y."

Again he lunged. Tom side-stepped and flung him to the ground. Straddled him.

"Get off me, you godam nigger you."

"Yo sho has started somethin now. Get up."

Tom yanked him up and began hammering at him. Each blow sounded as if it smashed into a precious, irreplaceable soft something. Beneath them, Bob staggered back. He reached in his pocket and whipped out a knife.

"Thats my game, sho."

Blue flash, a steel blade slashed across Bob Stone's throat. He had a sweetish sick feeling. Blood began to flow. Then he felt a sharp twitch of pain. He let his knife drop. He slapped one hand against his neck. He pressed the other on top of his head as if to hold it down. He groaned. He turned, and staggered towards the crest of the hill in the direction of white town. Negroes who had seen the fight slunk into their homes and blew the lamps out. Louisa, dazed, hysterical, refused to go indoors. She slipped, crumbled, her body loosely propped against the woodwork of the well. Tom Burwell leaned against it. He seemed rooted there.

Bob reached Broad Street. White men rushed up to him. He collapsed in their arms.

"Tom Burwell. . . ."

White men like ants upon a forage rushed about. Except for the taut hum of their moving, all was silent. Shotguns, revolvers, rope, kerosene, torches. Two high-powered cars with glaring search-lights. They came together. The taut hum rose to a low roar. Then nothing could be heard but the flop of their feet in the thick dust of the road. The moving body of their silence preceded them over the crest of the hill into factory town. It flattened the Negroes beneath it. It rolled to the wall of the factory, where it stopped. Tom knew that they were coming. He couldnt move. And then he saw the search-lights of the two cars glaring down on him. A quick shock went through him. He stiffened. He started to run. A yell went up from the mob. Tom wheeled about and faced them. They poured down on him. They swarmed. A large man with dead-white face and flabby cheeks came to him and almost jabbed a gun-barrel through his guts.

"Hands behind y, nigger."

Tom's wrist were bound. The big man shoved him to the well. Burn him over it, and when the woodwork caved in, his body would drop to the bottom. Two deaths for

a godam nigger. Louisa was driven back. The mob pushed in. Its pressure, its momentum was too great. Drag him to the factory. Wood and stakes already there. Tom
moved in the direction indicated. But they had to drag him. They reached the great
door. Too many to get in there. The mob divided and flowed around the walls to
either side. The big man shoved him through the door. The mob pressed in from the
sides. Taut humming. No words. A stake was sunk into the ground. Rotting floor
boards piled around it. Kerosene poured on the rotting floor boards. Tom bound to
the stake. His breast was bare. Nails scratches let little lines of blood trickle down and
mat into the hair. His face, his eyes were set and stony. Except for irregular breathing, one would have thought him already dead. Torches were flung unto the pile. A
great flare muffled in black smoke shot upward. The mob yelled. The mob was silent.
Now Tom could be seen within the flames. Only his head, erect, lean, like a blackened
stone. Stench of burning flesh soaked the air. Tom's eyes popped. His head settled
downward. The mob yelled. Its yell echoed against the skeleton stone walls and
sounded like a hundred yells. Like a hundred mobs yelling. Its yell thudded against
the thick front wall and fell back. Ghost of a yell slipped through the flames and out
the great door of the factory. It fluttered like a dying thing down the single street of
factory town. Louisa, upon the step before her home, did not hear it, but her eyes
opened slowly. They saw the full moon glowing in the great door. The full moon, an
evil thing, an omen, soft showering the homes of folks she knew. Where were they,
these people? She'd sing, and perhaps they'd come out and join her. Perhaps Tom
Burwell would come. At any rate, the full moon in the great door was an omen which
she must sing to:

> Red nigger moon. Sinner!
> Blood-burning moon. Sinner!
> Come out that fact'ry door.

1923

F. SCOTT FITZGERALD
(1896–1940)

On the verge of publishing his third novel and masterpiece, *The Great Gatsby*
(1925), F. Scott Fitzgerald commented in an interview: "Five years ago the new
American novels needed comment by the author. . . . But now there is an intelligent body of opinion guided by such men as [H. L.] Mencken, Edmund Wilson
and Van Wyck Brooks, comment should be unnecessary; and the writer, if he has
any aspirations toward art, should try to convey the feel of his scenes, places and
people directly — as Conrad does, as a few Americans (notably Willa Cather) are
already trying to do."

Fitzgerald was clearly accurate in seeing himself and his new novel as part of a
modernist movement, in which Joseph Conrad, with his ingenious use of multiple narrators (or observers), and Willa Cather, with her stripping the excess furniture from the stage of her fictions (as advised in "The Novel Démeublé"), were
major makers and shapers. Fitzgerald was one of the few significant writers of
the period who could dedicate himself simultaneously to art and popular appeal
and succeed handsomely in both.

Francis Scott Key Fitzgerald was so christened because he was a descendent of
the composer of the American national anthem. Although born in St. Paul, Minnesota, he was taken East during his early years when his father, an employee of

Procter and Gamble, was assigned to posts in Buffalo and Syracuse, New York. On losing his job in 1908, the father brought his family back to St. Paul, where Fitzgerald attended St. Paul Academy. In 1911, he was sent to Newman Academy, a Catholic prep school in Hackensack, New Jersey.

Two years later, Fitzgerald entered Princeton, where he became friends with Edmund Wilson and John Peale Bishop. He wrote for the dramatic productions of the Triangle Club — starring as a showgirl in one — and published stories and poems, but he was a marginal student. He dropped out of Princeton in 1917 to enter the army as a second lieutenant. The United States had declared war on Germany and was preparing to send troops to France. Fitzgerald was stationed for a time in 1918 at Camp Sheridan, near Montgomery, Alabama, where he met — and fell in love with — Zelda Sayre, daughter of an Alabama judge.

When Fitzgerald looked back on his past in 1936 in "The Crack-Up," he remembered being haunted by "two juvenile regrets": "at not being big enough (or good enough) to play football in college, and at not getting overseas during the war." But he also remembered that he had almost lost the girl he loved because of "lack of money." As it turned out, the improbable came true. He wrote a novel, made a fortune, and married Zelda. But the episode instilled in him an "abiding distrust, an animosity, toward the leisure class . . . the smouldering hatred of a peasant." He was never able afterwards "to stop wondering where [his] friends' money came from."

Fitzgerald's concern for money and its sources runs through all his fiction. *This Side of Paradise*, his first novel published in 1920, presents a hero from a wealthy family in vague revolt against his fate growing up to find "all Gods dead, all wars fought, all faiths in man shaken." By the end of the novel, he is penniless, has lost the girl he loved, and has lost also some of the arrogance of his youth, exclaiming: "I know myself, but that is all." The novel appealed to the postwar generation and sold 40,000 copies its first year.

Fitzgerald and his wife Zelda became leaders in the revolt of the 1920s against the genteel tradition and all its proprieties. As one biographer wrote, they "complemented each other like gin and vermouth in a martini, each making the other more powerful in their war with dullness and convention." They lived extravagantly, drank to excess, danced on restaurant tables, waded in public fountains, and rode through Manhattan on top of a taxi. Fitzgerald's first volume of short stories, *Flappers and Philosophers*, appeared in 1920, and his second novel, *The Beautiful and Damned*, in 1922, followed the same year by his second volume of short stories, *Tales of the Jazz Age*. The 1920s had found its historian as well as its chief proponents and rebels.

In 1924, Scott and Zelda went to Europe to live for two years. There they met Ernest Hemingway, Gertrude Stein, and other American expatriates who were (with them) to be known later as "the lost generation." Fitzgerald spent time writing *The Great Gatsby*, published in 1925. It turned out to be not only his most carefully crafted novel but also his masterpiece. Jay Gatsby is an American original who reinvents himself and accumulates a fortune through shady deals, all to recapture the dream girl he had lost because he was poor. In spite of his crooked dealings and the tall tales of his past, Gatsby turns out in essence to be better than all the others in the sheer vitality and ultimate innocence of his romantic dream.

After *The Great Gatsby*, Fitzgerald published a volume of short stories, *All the Sad Young Men* (1926), containing some of his best stories, including "The Rich Boy." And although he then began work on a new novel, it stubbornly refused to take shape and kept going through transformations. Indeed, the work, *Tender Is the Night*, was not published until 1934. Zelda had suffered a major breakdown in 1930, and from that time forward began to show increasing signs of emotional and mental instability, spending more and more time in sanatoriums. Driven to realize her own creativity, she studied ballet for a time and became a gifted painter able to exhibit her work. When she turned to writing, Fitzgerald grew jealous of her taking over what he considered "his" material — the story of their complicated relationship. She published her novel *Save Me the Waltz* in 1932.

Tender is the Night, one of Fitzgerald's best novels, tells the story of the deterioration of a psychiatrist, Dick Diver, based on Fitzgerald himself. Married to one of his beautiful but unstable patients, he is unable finally to conserve his own sense of identity and capitulates to disaster, victimized by himself as much as by others. Diver's fate was not unlike that of his creator during the 1930s. "The Crack-Up" (1936) was in effect a confession by someone who had suddenly become aware that he was "drawing on resources [he] did not possess" and that he had mortgaged himself "physically and spiritually up to the hilt."

As the Jazz Age faded from consciousness during the Great Depression of the 1930s, interest in Fitzgerald's work diminished. Fitzgerald continued to write, however, publishing his final volume of stories, *Taps at Reveille*, in 1935. It contained one of his most moving tales, "Babylon Revisited," whose broken protagonist attempts to salvage his child and dignity in a return to his past and the scene of his dissipation — Paris. The story was sold to the movies in 1940, and Fitzgerald wrote to his daughter Scottie that she had earned him some money because she was "one of the principal characters."

During his last years, Fitzgerald worked off and on as a screen writer for Hollywood and was paid a handsome retainer fee for short periods. In the absence of Zelda, he developed a close relationship with the journalist Sheilah Graham. And he began work on a novel about Hollywood. But his dissipation finally caught up with him and he died of a heart attack in Sheilah Graham's apartment in 1940, at the age of forty-four. Zelda died in 1947 in a fire in the sanatorium where she was confined. Fitzgerald's unfinished novel, *The Last Tycoon*, appeared in 1941 and included notes indicating plans for its completion. Enough of the work had been finished to make clear that Fitzgerald's talent had, in spite of his squandered life, endured to the end.

ADDITIONAL READING

The Crack-Up, with Other Uncollected Pieces, Notebooks, and Unpublished Letters, ed. Edmund Wilson, 1945; *Afternoon of an Author: A Selection of Uncollected Stories and Essays*, ed. Arthur Mizener, 1957; *The Letters of F. Scott Fitzgerald*, ed. Andrew Turnbull, 1963; *The Apprentice Fiction of F. Scott Fitzgerald*, ed. John Kuehl, 1965; *F. Scott Fitzgerald in His Own Time: A Miscellany*, ed. Jackson R. Bryer and Matthew J. Bruccoli, 1971; *Dear Scott/ Dear Max: The Fitzgerald-Perkins Correspondence*, ed. John Kuehl and Jackson R. Bryer, 1971; *As Ever, Scott Fitz—*, ed. Matthew J. Bruccoli and Jennifer McCabe Atkinson, 1972; *Bits of Paradise: 21 Uncollected Stories, with Zelda Fitzgerald*, ed. Matthew Bruccoli and Scottie Fitzgerald Smith, 1973; *The Price Was High: The Last Uncollected Stories*, ed. Matthew J. Bruccoli, 1979; *Correspondence of F. Scott Fitzgerald*, ed. Matthew J. Bruccoli and Margaret M. Duggan, 1980.

Arthur Mizener, *The Far Side of Paradise*, 1951, rev. 1965; Alfred Kazin, ed., *F. Scott Fitzgerald: The Man and His Work*, 1951; Sheilah Graham and Gerold Frank, *Beloved Infidel*, 1958; Andrew Turnbull, *Scott Fitzgerald*, 1962; Kenneth Eble, *F. Scott Fitzgerald*, 1963; Arthur Mizener, ed., *A Collection of Critical Essays*, 1963; K. G. W. Cross, *F. Scott Fitzgerald*, 1964; James E. Miller, Jr., *F. Scott Fitzgerald: His Art and His Technique*, 1964; Sergio Perosa, *The Art of F. Scott Fitzgerald*, 1965; Henry D. Piper, *F. Scott Fitzgerald, A Critical Portrait*, 1965; Richard Lehan, *F. Scott Fitzgerald and the Craft of Fiction*, 1966; Sheilah Graham, *College of One*, 1967; Jackson R. Bryer, *The Critical Reputation of F. Scott Fitzgerald: A Bibliographical Study*, 1967; Robert Sklar,

F. Scott Fitzgerald: The Last Laocoön, 1967; Milton Hindus, *F. Scott Fitzgerald: An Introduction and Interpretation*, 1968; Nancy Milford, *Zelda*, 1970; Milton R. Stern, *The Golden Moment: The Novels of F. Scott Fitzgerald*, 1970; Aaron Latham, *Crazy Sundays: F. Scott Fitzgerald in Hollywood*, 1971; Sara Mayfield, *Exiles from Paradise: Zelda and Scott Fitzgerald*, 1971; John F. Callahan, *The Illusions of a Nation: Myth and History in the Novels of F. Scott Fitzgerald*, 1972; Robert Emmet Long, *The Achieving of the Great Gatsby, 1920–1925*, 1979; Brian Way, *F. Scott Fitzgerald and the Art of Social Fiction*, 1980; Matthew J. Bruccoli, *Some Sort of Epic Grandeur: The Life of F. Scott Fitzgerald*, 1981; Jackson R. Bryer, ed., *The Short Stories of F. Scott Fitzgerald*, 1982; Andre LeVot, *F. Scott Fitzgerald: A Biography*, trans. William Byron, 1983; Scott Donaldson, *Fool for Love: F. Scott Fitzgerald*, 1983; James Mellow, *Invented Lives*, 1984.

TEXTS

"Babylon Revisited," *Taps at Reveille*, 1935; "The Crack-Up," *The Crack-Up*, ed. Edmund Wilson, 1945.

Babylon Revisited

"And where's Mr. Campbell?" Charlie asked.

"Gone to Switzerland. Mr. Campbell's a pretty sick man, Mr. Wales."

"I'm sorry to hear that. And George Hardt?" Charlie inquired.

"Back in America, gone to work."

"And where is the Snow Bird?"[1]

"He was in here last week. Anyway, his friend, Mr. Schaeffer, is in Paris."

Two familiar names from the long list of a year and a half ago. Charlie scribbled an address in his notebook and tore out the page.

"If you see Mr. Schaeffer, give him this," he said. "It's my brother-in-law's address. I haven't settled on a hotel yet."

He was not really disappointed to find Paris was so empty. But the stillness in the Ritz bar was strange and portentous. It was not an American bar any more—he felt polite in it, and not as if he owned it. It had gone back into France. He felt the stillness from the moment he got out of the taxi and saw the doorman, usually in a frenzy of activity at this hour, gossiping with a *chasseur*[2] by the servants' entrance.

Passing through the corridor, he heard only a single, bored voice in the once-clamorous women's room. When he turned into the bar he travelled the twenty feet of green carpet with his eyes fixed straight ahead by old habit; and then, with his foot firmly on the rail, he turned and surveyed the room, encountering only a single pair of eyes that fluttered up from a newspaper in the corner. Charlie asked for the head barman, Paul, who in the latter days of the bull market had come to work in his own custom-built car—disembarking, however, with due nicety at the nearest corner. But Paul was at his country house today and Alix giving him information.

"No, no more," Charlie said, "I'm going slow these days."

Alix congratulated him: "You were going pretty strong a couple of years ago."

"I'll stick to it all right," Charlie assured him. "I've stuck to it for over a year and a half now."

"How do you find conditions in America?"

"I haven't been to America for months. I'm in business in Prague, representing a couple of concerns there. They don't know about me down there."

Alix smiled.

---

[1] Peddlar or addict of "snow" (heroin or cocaine).
[2] Uniformed attendant.

"Remember the night of George Hardt's bachelor dinner here?" said Charlie. "By the way, what's become of Claude Fessenden?"

Alix lowered his voice confidentially: "He's in Paris, but he doesn't come here any more. Paul doesn't allow it. He ran up a bill of thirty thousand francs, charging all his drinks and his lunches, and usually his dinner, for more than a year. And when Paul finally told him he had to pay, he gave him a bad check."

Alix shook his head sadly.

"I don't understand it, such a dandy fellow. Now he's all bloated up—" He made a plump apple of his hands.

Charlie watched a group of strident queens installing themselves in a corner.

"Nothing affects them," he thought. "Stocks rise and fall, people loaf or work, but they go on forever." The place oppressed him. He called for the dice and shook with Alix for the drink.

"Here for long, Mr. Wales?"

"I'm here for four or five days to see my little girl."

"Oh-h! You have a little girl?"

Outside, the fire-red, gas-blue, ghost-green signs shone smokily through the tranquil rain. It was late afternoon and the streets were in movement; the *bistros* gleamed. At the corner of the Boulevard des Capucines he took a taxi. The Place de la Concorde moved by in pink majesty; they crossed the logical Seine, and Charlie felt the sudden provincial quality of the left bank.

Charlie directed his taxi to the Avenue de l'Opera, which was out of his way. But he wanted to see the blue hour spread over the magnificent façade, and imagine that the cab horns, playing endlessly the first few bars of *Le Plus que Lent*,[3] were the trumpets of the Second Empire. They were closing the iron grill in front of Brentano's Book-store, and people were already at dinner behind the trim little bourgeois hedge of Duval's. He had never eaten at a really cheap restaurant in Paris. Five-course dinner, four francs fifty, eighteen cents, wine included. For some odd reason he wished that he had.

As they rolled on to the Left Bank and he felt its sudden provincialism, he thought, "I spoiled this city for myself. I didn't realize it, but the days came along one after another, and then two years were gone, and everything was gone, and I was gone."

He was thirty-five, and good to look at. The Irish mobility of his face was sobered by a deep wrinkle between his eyes. As he rang his brother-in-law's bell in the Rue Palatine, the wrinkle deepened till it pulled down his brows; he felt a cramping sensation in his belly. From behind the maid who opened the door darted a lovely little girl of nine who shrieked "Daddy!" and flew, struggling like a fish, into his arms. She pulled his head around by one ear and set her cheek against his.

"My old pie," he said.

"Oh, daddy, daddy, daddy, daddy, dads, dads, dads!"

She drew him into the salon, where the family waited, a boy and girl his daughter's age, his sister-in-law and her husband. He greeted Marion with his voice pitched carefully to avoid either feigned enthusiasm or dislike, but her response was more frankly tepid, though she minimized her expression of unalterable distrust by directing her regard toward his child. The two men clasped hands in a friendly way and Lincoln Peters rested his for a moment on Charlie's shoulder.

The room was warm and comfortably American. The three children moved intimately about, playing through the yellow oblongs that led to other rooms; the cheer of six o'clock spoke in the eager smacks of the fire and the sounds of French activity in the kitchen. But Charlie did not relax; his heart sat up rigidly in his body and he drew

---

[3]Debussy waltz.

confidence from his daughter, who from time to time came close to him, holding in her arms the doll he had brought.

"Really extremely well," he declared in answer to Lincoln's question. "There's a lot of business there that isn't moving at all, but we're doing even better than ever. In fact, damn well. I'm bringing my sister over from America next month to keep house for me. My income last year was bigger than it was when I had money. You see, the Czechs—"

His boasting was for a specific purpose; but after a moment, seeing a faint restiveness in Lincoln's eye, he changed the subject:

"Those are fine children of yours, well brought up, good manners."

"We think Honoria's a great little girl too."

Marion Peters came back from the kitchen. She was a tall woman with worried eyes, who had once possessed a fresh American loveliness. Charlie had never been sensitive to it and was always surprised when people spoke of how pretty she had been. From the first there had been an instinctive antipathy between them.

"Well, how do you find Honoria?" she asked.

"Wonderful. I was astonished how much she's grown in ten months. All the children are looking well."

"We haven't had a doctor for a year. How do you like being back in Paris?"

"It seems very funny to see so few Americans around."

"I'm delighted," Marion said vehemently. "Now at least you can go into a store without their assuming you're a millionaire. We've suffered like everybody, but on the whole it's a good deal pleasanter."

"But it was nice while it lasted," Charlie said. "We were a sort of royalty, almost infallible, with a sort of magic around us. In the bar this afternoon"—he stumbled, seeing his mistake—"there wasn't a man I knew."

She looked at him keenly. "I should think you'd have had enough of bars."

"I only stayed a minute. I take one drink every afternoon, and no more."

"Don't you want a cocktail before dinner?" Lincoln asked.

"I take only one drink every afternoon, and I've had that."

"I hope you keep to it," said Marion.

Her dislike was evident in the coldness with which she spoke, but Charlie only smiled; he had larger plans. Her very aggressiveness gave him an advantage, and he knew enough to wait. He wanted them to initiate the discussion of what they knew had brought him to Paris.

At dinner he couldn't decide whether Honoria was most like him or her mother. Fortunate if she didn't combine the traits of both that had brought them to disaster. A great wave of protectiveness went over him. He thought he knew what to do for her. He believed in character; he wanted to jump back a whole generation and trust in character again as the eternally valuable element. Everything wore out.

He left soon after dinner, but not to go home. He was curious to see Paris by night with clearer and more judicious eyes than those of other days. He bought a *strapontin*[4] for the Casino and watched Josephine Baker[5] go through her chocolate arabesques.

After an hour he left and strolled toward Montmartre, up the Rue Pigalle into the Place Blanche. The rain had stopped and there were a few people in evening clothes disembarking from taxis in front of cabarets, and *cocottes*[6] prowling singly or in pairs, and many Negroes. He passed a lighted door from which issued music, and stopped with the sense of familiarity; it was Bricktop's, where he had parted with so many hours and so much money. A few doors farther on he found another ancient rendezvous and incautiously put his head inside. Immediately an eager orchestra burst

---

[4]Seat let down in the aisle.
[5]Black American singer (1906–1975) popular in Paris during the Twenties.
[6]Prostitutes.

into sound, a pair of professional dancers leaped to their feet and a maître d'hôtel[7] swooped toward him, crying, "Crowd just arriving, sir!" But he withdrew quickly.

"You have to be damn drunk," he thought.

Zelli's was closed, the bleak and sinister cheap hotels surrounding it were dark; up in the Rue Blanche there was more light and a local, colloquial French crowd. The Poet's Cave had disappeared, but the two great mouths of the Café of Heaven and Café of Hell still yawned—even devoured, as he watched, the meagre contents of a tourist bus—a German, a Japanese, and an American couple who glanced at him with frightened eyes.

So much for the effort and ingenuity of Montmartre.[8] All the catering to vice and waste was on an utterly childish scale, and he suddenly realized the meaning of the word "dissipate"—to dissipate into thin air; to make nothing out of something. In the little hours of the night every move from place to place was an enormous human jump, an increase of paying for the privilege of slower and slower motion.

He remembered thousand-franc notes given to an orchestra for playing a single number, hundred-franc notes tossed to a doorman for calling a cab.

But it hadn't been given for nothing.

It had been given, even the most wildly squandered sum, as an offering to destiny that he might not remember the things most worth remembering, the things that now he would always remember—his child taken from his control, his wife escaped to a grave in Vermont.

In the glare of a *brasserie*[9] a woman spoke to him. He bought her some eggs and coffee, and then, eluding her encouraging stare, gave her a twenty-franc note and took a taxi to his hotel.

II

He woke upon a fine fall day—football weather. The depression of yesterday was gone and he liked the people on the streets. At noon he sat opposite Honoria at Le Grand Vatel, the only restaurant he could think of not reminiscent of champagne dinners and long luncheons that began at two and ended in a blurred and vague twilight.

"Now, how about vegetables? Oughtn't you to have some vegetables?"

"Well, yes."

"Here's *épinards* and *chou-fleur* and carrots and *haricots*."[10]

"I'd like *chou-fleur*."

"Wouldn't you like to have two vegetables?"

"I usually only have one at lunch."

The waiter was pretending to be inordinately fond of children. "*Qu'elle est mignonne la petite! Elle parle exactement comme une française.*"[11]

"How about dessert? Shall we wait and see?"

The waiter disappeared. Honoria looked at her father expectantly.

"What are we going to do?"

"First, we're going to that toy store in the Rue Saint-Honoré and buy you anything you like. And then we're going to the vaudeville at the Empire."

She hesitated. "I like it about the vaudeville, but not the toy store."

"Why not?"

"Well, you brought me this doll." She had it with her. "And I've got lots of things. And we're not rich any more, are we?"

"We never were. But today you are to have anything you want."

"All right," she agreed resignedly.

---

[7]Headwaiter.
[8]Bohemian center of Paris, popular with American expatriates.
[9]Bar or pub.

[10]"Spinach," "cauliflower," "beans" (French).
[11]"How pretty, the little one! She speaks exactly like a French girl" (French).

When there had been her mother and a French nurse he had been inclined to be strict; now he extended himself, reached out for a new tolerance; he must be both parents to her and not shut any of her out of communication.

"I want to get to know you," he said gravely. "First let me introduce myself. My name is Charles J. Wales, of Prague."

"Oh, daddy!" her voice cracked with laughter.

"And who are you, please?" he persisted, and she accepted a rôle immediately: "Honoria Wales, Rue Palatine, Paris."

"Married or single?"

"No, not married. Single."

He indicated a doll. "But I see you have a child, madame."

Unwilling to disinherit it, she took it to her heart and thought quickly: "Yes, I've been married, but I'm not married now. My husband is dead."

He went on quickly. "And the child's name?"

"Simone. That's after my best friend at school."

"I'm very pleased that you're doing so well at school."

"I'm third this month," she boasted. "Elsie"—that was her cousin—"is only about eighteenth, and Richard is about at the bottom."

"You like Richard and Elsie, don't you?"

"Oh, yes. I like Richard quite well and I like her all right."

Cautiously, and casually he asked: "And Aunt Marion and Uncle Lincoln—which do you like best?"

"Oh, Uncle Lincoln, I guess."

He was increasingly aware of her presence. As they came in, a murmur of ". . . adorable" followed them, and now the people at the next table bent all their silences upon her, staring as if she were something no more conscious than a flower.

"Why don't I live with you?" she asked suddenly. "Because mamma's dead?"

"You must stay here and learn more French. It would have been hard for daddy to take care of you so well."

"I don't really need much taking care of any more. I do everything for myself."

Going out of the restaurant, a man and a woman unexpectedly hailed him!

"Well, the old Wales!"

"Hello there, Lorraine. . . . Dunc."

Sudden ghosts out of the past: Duncan Schaeffer, a friend from college. Lorraine Quarrles, a lovely, pale blonde of thirty; one of a crowd who had helped them make months into days in the lavish times of three years ago.

"My husband couldn't come this year," she said, in answer to his question. "We're poor as hell. So he gave me two hundred a month and told me I could do my worst on that. . . . This your little girl?"

"What about coming back and sitting down?" Duncan asked.

"Can't do it." He was glad for an excuse. As always, he felt Lorraine's passionate, provocative attraction, but his own rhythm was different now.

"Well, how about dinner?" she asked.

"I'm not free. Give me your address and let me call you."

"Charlie, I believe you're sober," she said judicially. "I honestly believe he's sober, Dunc. Pinch him and see if he's sober."

Charlie indicated Honoria with his head. They both laughed.

"What's your address?" said Duncan sceptically.

He hesitated, unwilling to give the name of his hotel.

"I'm not settled yet. I'd better call you. We're going to see the vaudeville at the Empire."

"There! That's what I want to do," Lorraine said. "I want to see some clowns and acrobats and jugglers. That's just what we'll do, Dunc."

"We've got to do an errand first," said Charlie. "Perhaps we'll see you there."

"All right, you snob. . . . Good-by, beautiful little girl."

"Good-by."

Honoria bobbed politely.

Somehow, an unwelcome encounter. They liked him because he was functioning, because he was serious; they wanted to see him, because he was stronger than they were now, because they wanted to draw a certain sustenance from his strength.

At the Empire, Honoria proudly refused to sit upon her father's folded coat. She was already an individual with a code of her own, and Charlie was more and more absorbed by the desire of putting a little of himself into her before she crystallized utterly. It was hopeless to try to know her in so short a time.

Between the acts they came upon Duncan and Lorraine in the lobby where the band was playing.

"Have a drink?"

"All right, but not up at the bar. We'll take a table."

"The perfect father."

Listening abstractedly to Lorraine, Charlie watched Honoria's eyes leave their table, and he followed them wistfully about the room, wondering what they saw. He met her glance and she smiled.

"I liked that lemonade," she said.

What had she said? What had he expected? Going home in a taxi afterward, he pulled her over until her head rested against his chest.

"Darling, do you ever think about your mother?"

"Yes, sometimes," she answered vaguely.

"I don't want you to forget her. Have you got a picture of her?"

"Yes, I think so. Anyhow, Aunt Marion has. Why don't you want me to forget her?"

"She loved you very much."

"I loved her too."

They were silent for a moment.

"Daddy, I want to come and live with you," she said suddenly.

His heart leaped; he had wanted it to come like this.

"Aren't you perfectly happy?"

"Yes, but I love you better than anybody. And you love me better than anybody, don't you, now that mummy's dead?"

"Of course I do. But you won't always like me best, honey. You'll grow up and meet somebody your own age and go marry him and forget you ever had a daddy."

"Yes, that's true," she agreed tranquilly.

He didn't go in. He was coming back at nine o'clock and he wanted to keep himself fresh and new for the thing he must say then.

"When you're safe inside, just show yourself in that window."

"All right. Good-by, dads, dads, dads, dads."

He waited in the dark street until she appeared, all warm and glowing, in the window above and kissed her fingers out into the night.

III

They were waiting. Marion sat behind the coffee service in a dignified black dinner dress that just faintly suggested mourning. Lincoln was walking up and down with the animation of one who had already been talking. They were as anxious as he was to get into the question. He opened it almost immediately:

"I suppose you know what I want to see you about—why I really came to Paris."

Marion played with the black stars on her necklace and frowned.

"I'm awfully anxious to have a home," he continued. "And I'm awfully anxious to have Honoria in it. I appreciate your taking in Honoria for her mother's sake, but things have changed now"—he hesitated and then continued more forcibly—

"changed radically with me, and I want to ask you to reconsider the matter. It would be silly for me to deny that about three years ago I was acting badly—"

Marion looked up at him with hard eyes.

"—but all that's over. As I told you, I haven't had more than a drink a day for over a year, and I take that drink deliberately, so that the idea of alcohol won't get too big in my imagination. You see the idea?"

"No," said Marion succinctly.

"It's a sort of stunt I set myself. It keeps the matter in proportion."

"I get you," said Lincoln. "You don't want to admit it's got any attraction for you."

"Something like that. Sometimes I forget and don't take it. But I try to take it. Anyhow, I couldn't afford to drink in my position. The people I represent are more than satisfied with what I've done, and I'm bringing my sister over from Burlington to keep house for me, and I want awfully to have Honoria too. You know that even when her mother and I weren't getting along well we never let anything that happened touch Honoria. I know she's fond of me and I know I'm able to take care of her and—well, there you are. How do you feel about it?"

He knew that now he would have to take a beating. It would last an hour or two hours, and it would be difficult, but if he modulated his inevitable resentment to the chastened attitude of the reformed sinner, he might win his point in the end.

Keep your temper, he told himself. You don't want to be justified. You want Honoria.

Lincoln spoke first: "We've been talking it over ever since we got your letter last month. We're happy to have Honoria here. She's a dear little thing, and we're glad to be able to help her, but of course that isn't the question—"

Marion interrupted suddenly. "How long are you going to stay sober, Charlie?" she asked.

"Permanently, I hope."

"How can anybody count on that?"

"You know I never did drink heavily until I gave up business and came over here with nothing to do. Then Helen and I began to run around with—"

"Please leave Helen out of it. I can't bear to hear you talk about her like that."

He stared at her grimly; he had never been certain how fond of each other the sisters were in life.

"My drinking only lasted about a year and a half—from the time we came over until I—collapsed."

"It was time enough."

"It was time enough," he agreed.

"My duty is entirely to Helen," she said. "I try to think what she would have wanted me to do. Frankly, from the night you did that terrible thing you haven't really existed for me. I can't help that. She was my sister."

"Yes."

"When she was dying she asked me to look out for Honoria. If you hadn't been in a sanitarium then, it might have helped matters."

He had no answer.

"I'll never in my life be able to forget the morning when Helen knocked at my door, soaked to the skin and shivering, and said you'd locked her out."

Charlie gripped the sides of the chair. This was more difficult than he expected; he wanted to launch out into a long expostulation and explanation, but he only said: "The night I locked her out—" and she interrupted, "I don't feel up to going over that again."

After a moment's silence Lincoln said: "We're getting off the subject. You want Marion to set aside her legal guardianship and give you Honoria. I think the main point for her is whether she has confidence in you or not."

"I don't blame Marion," Charlie said slowly, "but I think she can have entire confidence in me. I had a good record up to three years ago. Of course, it's within human possibilities I might go wrong any time. But if we wait much longer I'll lose Honoria's childhood and my chance for a home." He shook his head, "I'll simply lose her, don't you see?"

"Yes, I see," said Lincoln.

"Why didn't you think of all this before?" Marion asked.

"I suppose I did, from time to time, but Helen and I were getting along badly. When I consented to the guardianship, I was flat on my back in a sanitarium and the market had cleaned me out. I knew I'd acted badly, and I thought if it would bring any peace to Helen, I'd agree to anything. But now it's different. I'm functioning, I'm behaving damn well, so far as—"

"Please don't swear at me," Marion said.

He looked at her, startled. With each remark the force of her dislike became more and more apparent. She had built up all her fear of life into one wall and faced it toward him. This trivial reproof was possibly the result of some trouble with the cook several hours before. Charlie became increasingly alarmed at leaving Honoria in this atmosphere of hostility against himself; sooner or later it would come out, in a word here, a shake of the head there, and some of that distrust would be irrevocably implanted in Honoria. But he pulled his temper down out of his face and shut it up inside him; he had won a point, for Lincoln realized the absurdity of Marion's remark and asked her lightly since when she had objected to the word "damn."

"Another thing," Charlie said: "I'm able to give her certain advantages now. I'm going to take a French governess to Prague with me. I've got a lease on a new apartment—"

He stopped, realizing that he was blundering. They couldn't be expected to accept with equanimity the fact that his income was again twice as large as their own.

"I suppose you can give her more luxuries than we can," said Marion. "When you were throwing away money we were living along watching every ten francs. . . . I suppose you'll start doing it again."

"Oh, no," he said. "I've learned. I worked hard for ten years, you know—until I got lucky in the market, like so many people. Terribly lucky. It didn't seem any use working any more, so I quit. It won't happen again."

There was a long silence. All of them felt their nerves straining, and for the first time in a year Charlie wanted a drink. He was sure now that Lincoln Peters wanted him to have his child.

Marion shuddered suddenly; part of her saw that Charlie's feet were planted on the earth now, and her own maternal feeling recognized the naturalness of his desire; but she had lived for a long time with a prejudice—prejudice founded on a curious disbelief in her sister's happiness, and which, in the shock of one terrible night, had turned to hatred for him. It had all happened at a point in her life where the discouragement of ill health and adverse circumstances made it necessary for her to believe in tangible villainy and a tangible villain.

"I can't help what I think!" she cried out suddenly. "How much you were responsible for Helen's death, I don't know. It's something you'll have to square with your own conscience."

An electric current of agony surged through him; for a moment he was almost on his feet, an unuttered sound echoing in his throat. He hung on to himself for a moment, another moment.

"Hold on there," said Lincoln uncomfortably. "I never thought you were responsible for that."

"Helen died of heart trouble," Charlie said dully.

"Yes, heart trouble." Marion spoke as if the phrase had another meaning for her.

Then, in the flatness that followed her outburst, she saw him plainly and she knew he had somehow arrived at control over the situation. Glancing at her husband, she found no help from him, and as abruptly as if it were a matter of no importance, she threw up the sponge.

"Do what you like!" she cried, springing up from her chair. "She's your child. I'm not the person to stand in your way. I think if it were my child I'd rather see her—" She managed to check herself. "You two decide it. I can't stand this. I'm sick. I'm going to bed."

She hurried from the room; after a moment Lincoln said:

"This has been a hard day for her. You know how strongly she feels—" His voice was almost apologetic: "When a woman gets an idea in her head."

"Of course."

"It's going to be all right. I think she sees now that you—can provide for the child, and so we can't very well stand in your way or Honoria's way."

"Thank you, Lincoln."

"I'd better go along and see how see is."

"I'm going."

He was still trembling when he reached the street, but a walk down the Rue Bonaparte to the quais set him up, and as he crossed the Seine, fresh and new by the quai lamps, he felt exultant. But back in his room he couldn't sleep. The image of Helen haunted him. Helen whom he had loved so until they had senselessly begun to abuse each other's love, tear it into shreds. On that terrible February night that Marion remembered so vividly, a slow quarrel had gone on for hours. There was a scene at the Florida, and then he attempted to take her home, and then she kissed young Webb at a table; after that there was what she had hysterically said. When he arrived home alone he turned the key in the lock in wild anger. How could he know she would arrive an hour later alone, that there would be a snowstorm in which she wandered about in slippers, too confused to find a taxi? Then the aftermath, her escaping pneumonia by a miracle, and all the attendant horror. They were "reconciled," but that was the beginning of the end, and Marion, who had seen with her own eyes and who imagined it to be one of many scenes from her sister's martyrdom, never forgot.

Going over it again brought Helen nearer, and in the white, soft light that steals upon half sleep near morning he found himself talking to her again. She said that he was perfectly right about Honoria and that she wanted Honoria to be with him. She said she was glad he was being good and doing better. She said a lot of other things— very friendly things—but she was in a swing in a white dress, and swinging faster and faster all the time, so that at the end he could not hear clearly all that she said.

IV

He woke up feeling happy. The door of the world was open again. He made plans, vistas, futures for Honoria and himself, but suddenly he grew sad, remembering all the plans he and Helen had made. She had not planned to die. The present was the thing—work to do and someone to love. But not to love too much, for he knew the injury that a father can do to a daughter or a mother to a son by attaching them too closely: afterward, out in the world, the child would seek in the marriage partner the same blind tenderness and, failing probably to find it, turn against love and life.

It was another bright, crisp day. He called Lincoln Peters at the bank where he worked and asked if he could count on taking Honoria when he left for Prague. Lincoln agreed that there was no reason for delay. One thing—the legal guardianship. Marion wanted to retain that a while longer. She was upset by the whole matter, and it would oil things if she felt that the situation was still in her control for another year. Charlie agreed, wanting only the tangible, visible child.

Then the question of a governess. Charlie sat in a gloomy agency and talked to a cross Beárnaise and to a buxom Breton peasant, neither of whom he could have endured. There were others whom he would see tomorrow.

He lunched with Lincoln Peters at Griffons, trying to keep down his exultation.

"There's nothing quite like your own child," Lincoln said. "But you understand how Marion feels too."

"She's forgotten how hard I worked for seven years there," Charlie said. "She just remembers one night."

"There's another thing." Lincoln hesitated. "While you and Helen were tearing around Europe throwing money away, we were just getting along. I didn't touch any of the prosperity because I never got ahead enough to carry anything but my insurance. I think Marion felt there was some kind of injustice in it — you not even working toward the end, and getting richer and richer."

"It went just as quick as it came," said Charlie.

"Yes, a lot of it stayed in the hands of *chasseurs* and saxophone players and maîtres d'hôtel — well, the big party's over now. I just said that to explain Marion's feeling about those crazy years. If you drop in about six o'clock tonight before Marion's too tired, we'll settle the details on the spot."

Back at his hotel, Charlie found a *pneumatique*[12] that had been redirected from the Ritz bar where Charlie had left his address for the purpose of finding a certain man.

> Dear Charlie: You were so strange when we saw you the other day that I wondered if I did something to offend you. If so, I'm not conscious of it. In fact, I have thought about you too much for the last year, and it's always been in the back of my mind that I might see you if I came over here. We *did* have such good times that crazy spring, like the night you and I stole the butcher's tricycle, and the time we tried to call on the president and you had the old derby rim and the wire cane. Everybody seems so old lately, but I don't feel old a bit. Couldn't we get together some time today for old time's sake? I've got a vile hang-over for the moment, but will be feeling better this afternoon and will look for you about five in the sweat-shop at the Ritz.
>
> Always devotedly,
Lorraine.

His first feeling was one of awe that he had actually, in his mature years, stolen a tricycle and pedalled Lorraine all over the Étoile[13] between the small hours and dawn. In retrospect it was a nightmare. Locking out Helen didn't fit in with any other act of his life, but the tricycle incident did — it was one of many. How many weeks or months of dissipation to arrive at that condition of utter irresponsibility?

He tried to picture how Lorraine had appeared to him then — very attractive; Helen was unhappy about it, though she said nothing. Yesterday, in the restaurant, Lorraine had seemed trite, blurred, worn away. He emphatically did not want to see her, and he was glad Alix had not given away his hotel address. It was a relief to think, instead, of Honoria, to think of Sundays spent with her and of saying good morning to her and of knowing she was there in his house at night, drawing her breath in the darkness.

At five he took a taxi and bought presents for all the Peters — a piquant cloth doll, a box of Roman soldiers, flowers for Marion, big linen handkerchiefs for Lincoln.

He saw, when he arrived in the apartment, that Marion had accepted the inevitable. She greeted him now as though he were a recalcitrant member of the family, rather than a menacing outsider. Honoria had been told she was going; Charlie was glad to see that her tact made her conceal her excessive happiness. Only on his lap did

---

[12]"Message" delivered by pneumatic tube (French).
[13]"Place de l'Etoile," famous Parisian intersection and traffic circle containing the Arc de Triomphe.

she whisper her delight and the question "When?" before she slipped away with the other children.

He and Marion were alone for a minute in the room, and on an impulse he spoke out boldly:

"Family quarrels are bitter things. They don't go according to any rules. They're not like aches or wounds; they're more like splits in the skin that won't heal because there's not enough material. I wish you and I could be on better terms."

"Some things are hard to forget," she answered. "It's a question of confidence." There was no answer to this and presently she asked, "When do you propose to take her?"

"As soon as I can get a governess. I hoped the day after tomorrow."

"That's impossible. I've got to get her things in shape. Not before Saturday."

He yielded. Coming back into the room, Lincoln offered him a drink.

"I'll take my daily whiskey," he said.

It was warm here, it was a home, people together by a fire. The children felt very safe and important; the mother and father were serious, watchful. They had things to do for the children more important than his visit here. A spoonful of medicine was, after all, more important than the strained relations between Marion and himself. They were not dull people, but they were very much in the grip of life and circumstances. He wondered if he couldn't do something to get Lincoln out of his rut at the bank.

A long peal at the door-bell; the *bonne à toute faire*[14] passed through and went down the corridor. The door opened upon another long ring, and then voices, and the three in the salon looked up expectantly; Richard moved to bring the corridor within his range of vision, and Marion rose. Then the maid came back along the corridor, closely followed by the voices, which developed under the light into Duncan Schaeffer and Lorraine Quarrles.

They were gay, they were hilarious, they were roaring with laughter. For a moment Charlie was astounded; unable to understand how they ferreted out the Peters' address.

"Ah-h-h!" Duncan wagged his finger roguishly at Charlie. "Ah-h-h!"

They both slid down another cascade of laughter. Anxious and at a loss, Charlie shook hands with them quickly and presented them to Lincoln and Marion. Marion nodded, scarcely speaking. She had drawn back a step toward the fire; her little girl stood beside her, and Marion put an arm about her shoulder.

With growing annoyance at the intrusion, Charlie waited for them to explain themselves. After some concentration Duncan said:

"We came to invite you out to dinner. Lorraine and I insist that all this shishi, cagy business 'bout your address got to stop."

Charlie came closer to them, as if to force them backward down the corridor.

"Sorry, but I can't. Tell me where you'll be and I'll phone you in half an hour."

This made no impression. Lorraine sat down suddenly on the side of a chair, and focussing her eyes on Richard, cried, "Oh, what a nice little boy! Come here, little boy!" Richard glanced at his mother, but did not move. With a perceptible shrug of her shoulders, Lorraine turned back to Charlie:

"Come and dine. Sure your cousins won' mine. See you so sel'om. Or solemn."

"I can't," said Charlie sharply. "You two have dinner and I'll phone you."

Her voice became suddenly unpleasant. "All right, we'll go. But I remember once when you hammered on my door at four A.M. I was enough of a good sport to give you a drink. Come on, Dunc."

Still in slow motion, with blurred, angry faces, with uncertain feet, they retired along the corridor.

---

[14]"All-purpose maid" (French).

"Good night," Charlie said.

"Good night!" responded Lorraine emphatically.

When he went back into the salon Marion had not moved, only now her son was standing in the circle of her other arm. Lincoln was still swinging Honoria back and forth like a pendulum from side to side.

"What an outrage!" Charlie broke out. "What an absolute outrage!"

Neither of them answered. Charlie dropped into an armchair, picked up his drink, set it down again and said:

"People I haven't seen for two years having the colossal nerve—"

He broke off. Marion had made the sound "Oh!" in one swift, furious breath, turned her body from him with a jerk and left the room.

Lincoln set down Honoria carefully.

"You children go in and start your soup," he said, and when they obeyed, he said to Charlie:

"Marion's not well and she can't stand shocks. That kind of people make her really physically sick."

"I didn't tell them to come here. They wormed your name out of somebody. They deliberately—"

"Well, it's too bad. It doesn't help matters. Excuse me a minute."

Left alone, Charlie sat tense in his chair. In the next room he could hear the children eating, talking in monosyllables, already oblivious to the scene between their elders. He head a murmur of conversation from a farther room and then the ticking bell of a telephone receiver picked up, and in a panic he moved to the other side of the room and out of earshot.

In a minute Lincoln came back. "Look here, Charlie. I think we'd better call off dinner for tonight. Marion's in bad shape."

"Is she angry with me?"

"Sort of," he said, almost roughly. "She's not strong and—"

"You mean she's changed her mind about Honoria?"

"She's pretty bitter right now. I don't know. You phone me at the bank tomorrow."

"I wish you'd explain to her I never dreamed these people would come here. I'm just as sore as you are."

"I couldn't explain anything to her now."

Charlie got up. He took his coat and hat and started down the corridor. Then he opened the door of the dining room and said in a strange voice, "Good night, children."

Honoria rose and ran around the table to hug him.

"Good night, sweetheart," he said vaguely, and then trying to make his voice more tender, trying to conciliate something, "Good night, dear children."

V

Charlie went directly to the Ritz bar with the furious idea of finding Lorraine and Duncan, but they were not there, and he realized that in any case there was nothing he could do. He had not touched his drink at the Peters', and now he ordered a whiskey-and-soda. Paul came over to say hello.

"It's a great change," he said sadly. "We do about half the business we did. So many fellows I hear about back in the States lost everything, maybe not in the first crash, but then in the second. Your friend George Hardt lost every cent, I hear. Are you back in the States?"

"No, I'm in business in Prague."

"I heard that you lost a lot in the crash."

"I did," and he added grimly, "but I lost everything I wanted in the boom."

"Selling short."

"Something like that."

Again the memory of those days swept over him like a nightmare—the people they had met travelling; then people who couldn't add a row of figures or speak a coherent sentence. The little man Helen had consented to dance with at the ship's party, who had insulted her ten feet from the table; the women and girls carried screaming with drink or drugs out of public places—

—The men who locked their wives out in the snow, because the snow of twenty-nine wasn't real snow. If you didn't want it to be snow, you just paid some money.

He went to the phone and called the Peters' apartment; Lincoln answered.

"I called up because this thing is on my mind. Has Marion said anything definite?"

"Marion's sick," Lincoln answered shortly. "I know this thing isn't altogether your fault, but I can't have her go to pieces about it. I'm afraid we'll have to let it slide for six months; I can't take the chance of working her up to this state again."

"I see."

"I'm sorry, Charlie."

He went back to his table. His whisky glass was empty, but he shook his head when Alix looked at it questioningly. There wasn't much he could do now except send Honoria some things; he would send her a lot of things tomorrow. He thought rather angrily that this was just money—he had given so many people money. . . .

"No, no more," he said to another waiter. "What do I owe you?"

He would come back some day; they couldn't make him pay forever. But he wanted his child, and nothing was much good now, beside that fact. He wasn't young any more, with a lot of nice thoughts and dreams to have by himself. He was absolutely sure Helen wouldn't have wanted him to be so alone.

1931, 1935

from The Crack-Up[1]

[MORTGAGED SPIRITUALLY UP TO THE HILT]

February, 1936

Of course all life is a process of breaking down, but the blows that do the dramatic side of the work—the big sudden blows that come, or seem to come, from outside—the ones you remember and blame things on and, in moments of weakness, tell your friends about, don't show their effect all at once. There is another sort of blow that comes from within—that you don't feel until it's too late to do anything about it, until you realize with finality that in some regard you will never be as good a man again. The first sort of breakage seems to happen quick—the second kind happens almost without your knowing it but is realized suddenly indeed.

Before I go on with this short history, let me make a general observation—the test of a first-rate intelligence is the ability to hold two opposed ideas in the mind at the same time, and still retain the ability to function. One should, for example, be able to see that things are hopeless and yet be determined to make them otherwise. This philosophy fitted on to my early adult life, when I saw the improbable, the implausible, often the "impossible," come true. Life was something you dominated if you were any good. Life yielded easily to intelligence and effort, or to what proportion could be mustered of both. It seemed a romantic business to be a successful literary man—

---

[1]Fitzgerald's confession of spiritual malaise—or an emotional "crack-up"—published in three installments ("The Crack-Up," "Pasting It Together," "Handle with Care") in *Esquire* in 1936 and collected in *The Crack-Up* (1945).

you were not ever going to be as famous as a movie star but what note you had was probably longer-lived—you were never going to have the power of a man of strong political or religious convictions but you were certainly more independent. Of course within the practice of your trade you were forever unsatisfied—but I, for one, would not have chosen any other.

As the twenties passed, with my own twenties marching a little ahead of them, my two juvenile regrets—at not being big enough (or good enough) to play football in college, and at not getting overseas during the war—resolved themselves into childish waking dreams of imaginary heroism that were good enough to go to sleep on in restless nights. The big problems of life seemed to solve themselves, and if the business of fixing them was difficult, it made one too tired to think of more general problems.

Life, ten years ago, was largely a personal matter. I must hold in balance the sense of the futility of effort and the sense of the necessity to struggle; the conviction of the inevitability of failure and still the determination to "succeed"—and, more than these, the contradiction between the dead hand of the past and the high intentions of the future. If I could do this through the common ills—domestic, professional and personal—then the ego would continue as an arrow shot from nothingness to nothingness with such force that only gravity would bring it to earth at last.

For seventeen years, with a year of deliberate loafing and resting out in the center—things went on like that, with a new chore only a nice prospect for the next day. I was living hard, too, but: "Up to forty-nine it'll be all right," I said. "I can count on that. For a man who's lived as I have, that's all you could ask."

—And then, ten years this side of forty-nine, I suddenly realized that I had prematurely cracked.

II

Now a man can crack in many ways—can crack in the head—in which case the power of decision is taken from you by others! or in the body, when one can but submit to the white hospital world; or in the nerves. William Seabrook[2] in an unsympathetic book tells, with some pride and a movie ending, of how he became a public charge. What led to his alcoholism or was bound up with it, was a collapse of his nervous system. Though the present writer was not so entangled—having at the time not tasted so much as a glass of beer for six months—it was his nervous reflexes that were giving way—too much anger and too many tears.

Moreover, to go back to my thesis that life has a varying offensive, the realization of having cracked was not simultaneous with a blow, but with a reprieve.

Not long before, I had sat in the office of a great doctor and listened to a grave sentence. With what, in retrospect, seems some equanimity, I had gone on about my affairs in the city where I was then living, not caring much, not thinking how much had been left undone, or what would become of this and that responsibility, like people do in books; I was well insured and anyhow I had been only a mediocre caretaker of most of the things left in my hands, even of my talent.

But I had a strong sudden instinct that I must be alone. I didn't want to see any people at all. I had seen so many people all my life—I was an average mixer, but more than average in a tendency to identify myself, my ideas, my destiny, with those of all classes that I came in contact with. I was always saving or being saved—in a single morning I would go through the emotions ascribable to Wellington at Waterloo.[3] I lived in a world of inscrutable hostiles and inalienable friends and supporters.

But now I wanted to be absolutely alone and so arranged a certain insulation from ordinary cares.

---

[2]William Seabrook (1886–1945), author of *Asylum* (1935), the story of his confinement for alcoholism.

[3]Arthur Wellesley, Duke of Wellington (1769–1852), British general who defeated Napoleon at Waterloo in 1815.

It was not an unhappy time. I went away and there were fewer people. I found I was good-and-tired. I could lie around and was glad to, sleeping or dozing sometimes twenty hours a day and in the intervals trying resolutely not to think — instead I made lists — made lists and tore them up, hundreds of lists: of cavalry leaders and football players and cities, and popular tunes and pitchers, and happy times, and hobbies and houses lived in and how many suits since I left the army and how many pairs of shoes (I didn't count the suit I bought in Sorrento that shrunk, nor the pumps and dress shirt and collar that I carried around for years and never wore, because the pumps got damp and grainy and the shirt and collar got yellow and starch-rotted). And lists of women I'd liked, and of the times I had let myself be snubbed by people who had not been my betters in character or ability.

— And then suddenly, surprisingly, I got better.

— And cracked like an old plate as soon as I heard the news.

That is the real end of this story. What was to be done about it will have to rest in what used to be called the "womb of time." Suffice it to say that after about an hour of solitary pillow-hugging, I began to realize that for two years my life had been a drawing on resources that I did not possess, that I had been mortgaging myself physically and spiritually up to the hilt. What was the small gift of life given back in comparison to that? — when there had once been a pride of direction and a confidence in enduring independence.

I realized that in those two years, in order to preserve something — an inner hush maybe, maybe not — I had weaned myself from all the things I used to love — that every act of life from the morning tooth-brush to the friend at dinner had become an effort. I saw that for a long time I had not liked people and things, but only followed the rickety old pretense of liking. I saw that even my love for those closest to me was become only an attempt to love, that my casual relations — with an editor, a tobacco seller, the child of a friend, were only what I remembered I *should* do, from other days. All in the same month I became bitter about such things as the sound of the radio, the advertisements in the magazines, the screech of tracks, the dead silence of the country — contemptuous at human softness, immediately (if secretively) quarrelsome toward hardness — hating the night when I couldn't sleep and hating the day because it went toward night. I slept on the heart side now because I knew that the sooner I could tire that out, even a little, the sooner would come that blessed hour of nightmare which, like a catharsis, would enable me to better meet the new day.

There were certain spots, certain faces I could look at. Like most Middle Westerners, I have never had any but the vaguest race prejudices — I always had a secret yen for the lovely Scandinavian blondes who sat on porches in St. Paul but hadn't emerged enough economically to be part of what was then society. They were too nice to be "chickens" and too quickly off the farmlands to seize a place in the sun, but I remember going round blocks to catch a single glimpse of shining hair — the bright shock of a girl I'd never know. This is urban, unpopular talk. It strays afield from the fact that in these latter days I couldn't stand the sight of Celts, English, Politicians, Strangers, Virginians, Negroes (light or dark), Hunting People, or retail clerks, and middlemen in general, all writers (I avoided writers very carefully because they can perpetuate trouble as no one else can) — and all the classes as classes and most of them as members of their class ...

Trying to cling to something, I liked doctors and girl children up to the age of about thirteen and well-brought-up boy children from about eight years old on. I could have peace and happiness with these few categories of people. I forgot to add that I liked old men — men over seventy, sometimes over sixty if their faces looked seasoned. I liked Katharine Hepburn's face on the screen, no matter what was said about her pretentiousness, and Miriam Hopkins' face, and old friends if I only saw them once a year and could remember their ghosts.

All rather inhuman and undernourished, isn't it? Well, that, children, is the true sign of cracking up.

It is not a pretty picture. Inevitably it was carted here and there within its frame and exposed to various critics. One of them can only be described as a person whose life makes other people's lives seem like death—even this time when she was cast in the usually unappealing role of Job's comforter.[4] In spite of the fact that this story is over, let me append our conversation as a sort of postscript:

"Instead of being so sorry for yourself, listen—" she said. (She always says "Listen," because she thinks while she talks—*really* thinks.) So she said: "Listen. Suppose this wasn't a crack in you—suppose it was a crack in the Grand Canyon."

"The crack's in me," I said heroically.

"Listen! The world only exists in your eyes—your conception of it. You can make it as big or as small as you want to. And you're trying to be a little puny individual. By God, if I ever cracked, I'd try to make the world crack with me. Listen! The world only exists through your apprehension of it, and so it's much better to say that it's not you that's cracked—it's the Grand Canyon."

"Baby et up all her Spinoza?"[5]

"I don't know anything about Spinoza. I know—" She spoke, then, of old woes of her own, that seemed, in the telling, to have been more dolorous than mine, and how she had met them, over-ridden them, beaten them.

I felt a certain reaction to what she said, but I am a slow-thinking man, and it occurred to me simultaneously that of all natural forces, vitality is the incommunicable one. In days when juice came into one as an article without duty, one tried to distribute it—but always without success; to further mix metaphors, vitality never "takes." You have it or you haven't it, like health or brown eyes or honor or a baritone voice. I might have asked some of it from her, neatly wrapped and ready for home cooking and digestion, but I could never have got it—not if I'd waited around for a thousand hours with the tin cup of self-pity. I could walk from her door, holding myself very carefully like cracked crockery, and go away into the world of bitterness, where I was making a home with such materials as are found there—and quote to myself after I left the door:

"Ye are the salt of the earth. But if the salt hath lost its savour, wherewith shall it be salted?"
Matthew 5-13.

1936

WILLIAM FAULKNER
(1897–1962)

In a letter to Malcolm Cowley in 1944, Faulkner observed: "Art is simpler than people think because there is so little to write about. All the moving things are eternal in man's history and have been written before, and if a man writes hard enough, sincerely enough, humbly enough, and with the unalterable determination never never never to be quite satisfied with it, he will repeat them, because art like poverty takes care of its own, shares its bread." Faulkner indicated that the writer's material—the human scene—remained in essence the same, regardless of place: "life is a phenomenon but not a novelty, the same

[4]In the Book of Job (3–31), there are three friends who attempt to explain to Job the causes for God's making him suffer.

[5]Pun for *spinach*: Baruch Spinoza (1632–1677), Dutch philosopher.

frantic steeplechase toward nothing everywhere and man stinks the same stink no matter where in time."

This view of art and life — the simplicity of the one and the absurdity of the other — had been the driving force behind Faulkner's major works from *The Sound and the Fury* in 1929 to *Go Down, Moses* in 1942. When Faulkner wrote to Cowley in 1944, all but one of his books were out of print, and Cowley was at work on *The Portable Faulkner* (1946), presenting a sampling of all Faulkner's fiction which would initiate a revival of his reputation. From the position of a forgotten writer, Faulkner in a very few years rose to be crowned Nobel Laureate in 1950 (announced in 1949).

Faulkner was born in 1897 in New Albany, Mississippi, but grew up in Oxford, Mississippi, where the family moved in 1902. His great-grandfather, Colonel William Falkner (Faulkner was to add a "u" to his name in 1924 on publication of his first book) commanded his own company in the Civil War, built a sixty-mile railroad, ran a plantation, and published a number of works, including a bestseller, *The White Rose of Memphis*. He was killed by his railroad partner in the streets of Ripley, Mississippi, in 1889. The descendents of this mythic figure lived less flamboyant, more mundane lives, as the South's and the family's fortunes declined. Faulkner would reflect this sense of diminishment in his fiction, portraying southern families whose vital creative energies have been gradually sapped.

When the United States entered the First World War, Faulkner attempted to enlist for flight training but was rejected because he was under regulation weight and height. He went to Canada in 1918 and trained as a pilot in Britain's Royal Air Force, but the war ended before he could be sent overseas. He came back home and was for a year a special student at the University of Mississippi (he had never finished high school), went to New York and worked in a bookstore for two years, then returned to Oxford and became postmaster of the University of Mississippi. When he was dismissed for neglecting his duties, he was reported to have said: "Now I won't be at the beck and call of every son-of-a-bitch who happens to have two cents [i.e., the price of a stamp for regular mail]."

All during these early years, Faulkner had been writing poems, largely imitative of the poetry of the romantics (John Keats), the Victorians (Alfred Lord Tennyson and Algernon Swinburne), and the new modernists (T. S. Eliot). He published a book of poems, *The Marble Faun*, in 1924, but it was little noticed. As it was to turn out, Faulkner's serious apprenticeship in poetry — he later called himself a "failed poet" — would prove of the greatest importance in his development as a novelist with a richly connotative and complex style.

In 1925, Faulkner went to New Orleans, where he came to know Sherwood Anderson, whose wife, Elizabeth Pratt, he had met in New York. Encouraged by Anderson to write prose, Faulkner wrote a novel, *Soldier's Pay*, and then set off on a freighter for a visit to Europe. He travelled in Italy and France on foot and bicycle, but was not caught up in the American expatriate writers' colony then in Paris.

Faulkner's first two novels appeared in 1926 and 1927 — *Soldier's Pay* and *Mosquitoes*. The first portrays a disillusioned soldier after the war, filled with a great sense of the futility of existence; the other presents a group of sophisticated characters discussing ideas about art and life. Neither novel sold well, and Faulkner's publisher cut him off. Although these first two novels exhibited talent and fluency, they appeared thin, at times even superficial in theme and subject. Faulkner had not yet found his material.

Undiscouraged and committed to writing, Faulkner began work on a new novel entitled *Flags in the Dust* (published as *Sartoris*), exploiting for the first time the material he had inherited (and lived) in his native Mississippi. He included the stories about his family's and the South's past that he had heard as a boy, creating the Sartoris family, with a Civil War character very much like Faulkner's great-grandfather. Faulkner later said: "Beginning with *Sartoris* I discovered my own little postage stamp of native soil was worth writing about and that I would never live long enough to exhaust it, and that by sublimating the actual into the apocryphal I would have complete liberty to use whatever talent I might have to its absolute top. It opened up a gold mine of other people, so I created a cosmos of my own."

Sartoris appeared in 1929, followed by *The Sound and the Fury* later the same year. Faulkner was well on the way to populating his mythical Mississippi county, Yoknapatawpha, and writing its history beginning with the first encounter of white settlers and their slaves with the Indians native to the land, from the pre-Civil War period to the present. The history would unfold unsystematically in novel after novel, roaming back and forth over time and the expanding Yoknapatawpha.

The Sound and the Fury presents the Compsons, a southern aristocratic family in decline. *As I Lay Dying* (1930) portrays a "poor white trash" county family, the Bundrens, on an epic journey to bury the mother, as she requested, in distant Jefferson (the county seat modelled on Oxford, Mississippi). Both these novels demonstrate Faulkner's mastery of the stream-of-consciousness technique, dramatizing through multiple "interior monologues" the flow of thoughts in his characters' minds. Though they brought him modest critical recognition, they did not attract a popular audience.

Determined to gain such an audience, Faulkner invented one of his most shocking plots in his next novel, *Sanctuary* (1931). It tells the story of a Twenties flapper who is raped with a corncob by a retarded gangster-bootlegger and held captive in a Memphis whorehouse. The book was a sensational success and was made into a popular movie in 1931, entitled *The Story of Temple Drake*.

For the next ten years, Faulkner produced book after book written at the height of his powers. *Light in August* (1932), one of the greatest of his novels, describes the life and death of the self-destructive Joe Christmas, never to know for certain whether he was born with Negro blood. *Absalom, Absalom!* (1936), considered by many critics Faulkner's masterpiece, depicts the rise and fall of the Yoknapatawpha plantation owner Thomas Sutpen as imaginatively reconstructed by Quentin Compson and his Canadian roommate at Harvard. In *The Unvanquished* (1938), *The Hamlet* (1940), and *Go Down, Moses* (1942)—all set in Yoknapatawpha County—Faulkner proved himself adept at interlinking sequences of short stories that gain density and meaning when brought together as loosely constructed novels.

After the appearance of Malcolm Cowley's ingeniously edited sampling of Faulkner's out-of-print work in *The Portable Faulkner* in 1946, Faulkner's writings began to be republished and his reputation started to rise, enhanced, of course, by the Nobel Prize announced in 1949. *Intruder in the Dust* (1948), an exploration of duplicity and violence in southern race relations, and *Requiem for a Nun* (1951), a continuation of the story of Temple Drake (from *Sanctuary*), were both popular but not critical successes. And Faulkner completed what has come to be known as the Snopes trilogy, the epic story of Flem Snopes and his numberless relatives — the unscrupulous, tight-fisted, and crafty "white trash" who won their way into the vitals of the South to become the inheritors. The Snopeses occupied the center in *The Hamlet* (1940), and were followed through their rise to power in *The Town* (1957) and *The Mansion* (1959).

Throughout his career, Faulkner wrote short stories and offered them to such magazines as *The Saturday Evening Post* to support himself in the writing of novels. Often he would revise his stories for inclusion in his novels, complicating them both stylistically and structurally. His *Collected Stories* appeared in 1950, containing forty-two tales. He was master of the short story form no less than master of the novel.

Although Faulkner's greatest work was set in Yoknapatawpha County, Mississippi, on occasion he went outside its bounds for settings and characters. *Pylon* (1935) is a modern story about stunt pilots. *The Wild Palms* (1939) interweaves two seemingly unrelated tales (the title story of doomed love and "The Old Man" [a nickname for the Mississippi River] about an escaped convict). *A Fable* (1954) is set in France during the First World War and recounts a week in the life of a platoon in mutiny against the officers; but the transparent allegory makes clear that the platoon leader is a Christ-figure, with other characters assuming roles close to their New Testament Crucifixion counterparts.

In 1929, Faulkner married his high school love, Estelle Oldham, and settled into a refurbished plantation house in Mississippi. At various times in the 1930s and the 1940s, to meet growing family expenses, he went to Hollywood to write for the movies. In 1957, he was appointed Writer-in-Residence at the University of Virginia, where his conversations with students were recorded and published as *Faulkner in the University* (1959), a rich source of his opinions about his own work and many other topics. After receiving the Nobel Prize, he was often sent by the State Department as a cultural representative abroad—going to Brazil in 1954, Japan in 1955, and Greece in 1957.

Faulkner died of a heart attack in 1962, having just published his last novel, *The Reivers*. In this work he turned to the materials that had become his imaginative property—Yoknapatawpha County and its people. It is nostalgic in spirit and comic in mode. Throughout his writing career, Faulkner had proved himself adept at combining comedy with tragedy, in a form that writers after the Second World War would "invent" as black humor.

As his delayed recognition suggests, Faulkner had been ahead of his time from the beginning. He not only perfected the modernist technique of stream-of-consciousness narration, but he also anticipated later fictional innovations in the foregrounding of language through his convoluted, poetically charged style and in his self-conscious or self-reflective narration (as in the imaginative reconstruction of unknown past events in *Absalom, Absalom!*). Like all great artists, Faulkner transcended his own age. At the same time he remained constant to "the problems of the human heart in conflict with itself," to the writer's "duty" and "privilege to help man endure by lifting his heart."

ADDITIONAL READING

The Portable Faulkner, ed. Malcolm Cowley, 1946; *Faulkner at Nagano*, ed. Robert A. Jelliffe, 1956; *Faulkner in the University: Class Conferences at the University of Virginia, 1957–1958*, ed. Frederick L. Gwynn and Joseph L. Blotner, 1959; *Faulkner at West Point*, ed. Joseph L. Fant and Robert Ashley, 1964; *The Faulkner-Cowley File: Letters and Memories, 1944–1962*, ed. Malcolm Cowley, 1961; *William Faulkner: Essays, Speeches, and Public Letters*, ed. James B. Meriwether, 1965; *The Lion in the Garden: Interviews with William Faulkner, 1926–1962*, ed. James B. Meriwether and Michael Millgate, 1968; *Selected Letters of William Faulkner*, ed. Joseph Blotner, 1977.

Frederick J. Hoffman and Olga Vickery, eds., *William Faulkner: Two Decades of Criticism*, 1951; Irving Howe, *William Faulkner*, 1952, 1962; William Van O'Connor, *The Tangled Fire of William Faulkner*, 1954; Robert Coughlan, *The Private World of William Faulkner*, 1954; Olga Vickery, *The Novels of William Faulkner*, 1959, 1964; Hyatt Waggoner, *William Faulkner: From Jefferson to the World*, 1959; Walter Slatoff, *Quest for Failure*, 1960; Frederick J. Hoffman and Olga Vickery, eds., *Three Decades of Criticism*, 1960; James B. Meriwether, *The Literary Career of William Faulkner: A Bibliographical Study*, 1961; John Cullen and Floyd C. Watkins, *Old Times in the Faulkner Country*, 1961; Warren Beck, *Man in Motion: Faulkner's Trilogy*, 1961; Frederick J. Hoffman, *William Faulkner*, 1961; Michael Millgate, *William Faulkner*, 1961; Peter Swiggert, *The Art of Faulkner's Novels*, 1962; Lawrance Thompson, *William Faulkner: An Introduction and Interpretation*, 1963, 1967; Cleanth Brooks, *William Faulkner: The Yoknapatawpha Country*, 1963; Michael Millgate, *The Achievement of William Faulkner*, 1963; John Longley, Jr., *The Tragic Mask: A Study of Faulkner's Heroes*, 1963; Robert W. Kirk and Marvin Klotz, *Faulkner's People: A Complete Guide and Index*, 1963; Dorothy Tuck, *Crowell's Handbook of Faulkner*, 1964; Edward L. Volpe, *A Reader's Guide to William Faulkner*, 1964; Harry Runyan, *A Faulkner Glossary*, 1964; John Hunt, *William Faulkner: Art in Theological Tension*, 1965; Charles H. Nilon, *Faulkner and the Negro*, 1965; Melvin Backman, *Faulkner: The Major Years*, 1966; Robert Penn Warren, ed., *Faulkner: A Collection of Critical Essays*, 1966; James E. Miller, Jr., "William Faulkner: Descent into the Vortex," *Quests Surd and Absurd*, 1967; Richard P. Adams, *Faulkner: Myth and Motion*, 1968; Walter Brylowski, *Faulkner's Olympian Laugh*, 1968; H. Edward Richardson, *William Faulkner: The Journey to Self-Discovery*, 1969; Dean M. Schmitter, ed., *William Faulkner: A Collection of Criticism*, 1973; Linda Wagner, ed., *William Faulkner: Four Decades of Criticism*, 1973; Joseph Blotner, *Faulkner: A Biography*, 2 vols., 1974, 1 vol., 1984; John T. Irwin, *Doubling and Incest, Repetition and Revenge: A Speculative Reading of Faulkner*, 1975; Cleanth Brooks, *Toward Yoknapatawpha and Beyond*, 1978; Donald Kartiganer, *The Fragile Thread: The Meaning of Form in Faulkner's Novels*, 1979; Judith Wittenberg, *Faulkner: The Transfiguration of Biography*, 1979; David Minter, *William Faulkner: His Life and Work*, 1980; Thomas E. Dasher, *William Faulkner's Characters: An Index to the Published and Unpublished Fiction*, 1981; Eric J. Sundquist, *Faulkner: The House Divided*, 1983; Thadious M. Davis, *Faulkner's "Negro": Art and the Southern Context*, 1983; Richard H. Brodhead, ed., *Faulkner: New Perspectives*, 1983; Cleanth Brooks, *William Faulkner: First Encounters*, 1983; Max Putzel, *Genius of Place: William Faulkner's Triumphant Beginnings*, 1985; Judith Sensibar, *The Origins of Faulkner's Art*, 1985; Warwick Wadlington, *Reading Faulknerian Tragedy*, 1987; Thomas E. Connolly, *Faulkner's World: A Directory of His People and Synopses of Actions in His Published Works*, 1988; Frederick R. Karl, *William Faulkner: American Writer, A Biography*, 1989.

TEXTS

"A Rose for Emily," *Collected Stories of William Faulkner*, 1950; "Spotted Horses," *Uncollected Stories of William Faulkner*, ed. Joseph Blotner, 1979; "Address upon Receiving the Nobel Prize for Literature," *Essays, Speeches, and Public Letters*, ed. James B. Meriwether, 1965.

A Rose for Emily

I

When Miss Emily Grierson died, our whole town went to her funeral: the men through a sort of respectful affection for a fallen monument, the women mostly out of curiosity to see the inside of her house, which no one save an old man-servant — a combined gardener and cook — had seen in at least ten years.

It was a big, squarish frame house that had once been white, decorated with cupolas and spires and scrolled balconies in the heavily lightsome style of the seventies, set on what had once been our most select street. But garages and cotton gins had encroached and obliterated even the august names of that neighborhood; only Miss Emily's house was left, lifting its stubborn and coquettish decay above the cotton wagons and the gasoline pumps—an eyesore among eyesores. And now Miss Emily had gone to join the representatives of those august names where they lay in the cedar-bemused cemetery among the ranked and anonymous graves of Union and Confederate soldiers who fell at the battle of Jefferson.

Alive, Miss Emily had been a tradition, a duty, and a care; a sort of hereditary obligation upon the town, dating from that day in 1894 when Colonel Sartoris, the mayor—he who fathered the edict that no Negro woman should appear on the streets without an apron—remitted her taxes, the dispensation dating from the death of her father on into perpetuity. Not that Miss Emily would have accepted charity. Colonel Sartoris invented an involved tale to the effect that Miss Emily's father had loaned money to the town, which the town, as a matter of business, preferred this way of repaying. Only a man of Colonel Sartoris' generation and thought could have invented it, and only a woman could have believed it.

When the next generation, with its more modern ideas, became mayors and aldermen, this arrangement created some little dissatisfaction. On the first of the year they mailed her a tax notice. February came, and there was no reply. They wrote her a formal letter, asking her to call at the sheriff's office at her convenience. A week later the mayor wrote her himself, offering to call or to send his car for her, and received in reply a note on paper of an archaic shape, in a thin, flowering calligraphy in faded ink, to the effect that she no longer went out at all. The tax notice was also enclosed, without comment.

They called a special meeting of the Board of Aldermen. A deputation waited upon her, knocked at the door through which no visitor had passed since she ceased giving china-painting lessons eight or ten years earlier. They were admitted by the old Negro into a dim hall from which a stairway mounted into still more shadow. It smelled of dust and disuse—a close, dank smell. The Negro led them into the parlor. It was furnished in heavy, leather-covered furniture. When the Negro opened the blinds of one window, they could see that the leather was cracked; and when they sat down, a faint dust rose sluggishly about their thighs, spinning with slow motes in the single sun-ray. On a tarnished gilt easel before the fireplace stood a crayon portrait of Miss Emily's father.

They rose when she entered—a small, fat woman in black, with a thin gold chain descending to her waist and vanishing into her belt, leaning on an ebony cane with a tarnished gold head. Her skeleton was small and spare; perhaps that was why what would have been merely plumpness in another was obesity in her. She looked bloated, like a body long submerged in motionless water, and of that pallid hue. Her eyes, lost in the fatty ridges of her face, looked like two small pieces of coal pressed into a lump of dough as they moved from one face to another while the visitors stated their errand.

She did not ask them to sit. She just stood in the door and listened quietly until the spokesman came to a stumbling halt. Then they could hear the invisible watch ticking at the end of the gold chain.

Her voice was dry and cold. "I have no taxes in Jefferson. Colonel Sartoris explained it to me. Perhaps one of you can gain access to the city records and satisfy yourselves."

"But we have. We are the city authorities, Miss Emily. Didn't you get a notice from the sheriff, signed by him?"

"I received a paper, yes," Miss Emily said. "Perhaps he considers himself the sheriff . . . I have no taxes in Jefferson."

"But there is nothing on the books to show that, you see. We must go by the—"

"See Colonel Sartoris. I have no taxes in Jefferson."

"But, Miss Emily—"

"See Colonel Sartoris." (Colonel Sartoris had been dead almost ten years.) "I have no taxes in Jefferson. Tobe!" The Negro appeared. "Show these gentlemen out."

II

So she vanquished them, horse and foot, just as she had vanquished their fathers thirty years before about the smell. That was two years after her father's death and a short time after her sweetheart—the one we believed would marry her—had deserted her. After her father's death she went out very little; after her sweetheart went away, people hardly saw her at all. A few of the ladies had the temerity to call, but were not received, and the only sign of life about the place was the Negro man—a young man then—going in and out with a market basket.

"Just as if a man—any man—could keep a kitchen properly," the ladies said; so they were not surprised when the smell developed. It was another link between the gross, teeming world and the high and mighty Griersons.

A neighbor, a woman, complained to the mayor, Judge Stevens, eighty years old.

"But what will you have me do about it, madam?" he said.

"Why, send her word to stop it," the woman said. "Isn't there a law?"

"I'm sure that won't be necessary," Judge Stevens said. "It's probably just a snake or a rat that nigger of hers killed in the yard. I'll speak to him about it."

The next day he received two more complaints, one from a man who came in diffident deprecation. "We really must do something about it, Judge. I'd be the last one in the world to bother Miss Emily, but we've got to do something." That night the Board of Aldermen met—three graybeards and one younger man, a member of the rising generation.

"It's simple enough," he said. "Send her word to have her place cleaned up. Give her a certain time to do it in, and if she don't . . ."

"Dammit, sir," Judge Stevens said, "will you accuse a lady to her face of smelling bad?"

So the next night, after midnight, four men crossed Miss Emily's lawn and slunk about the house like burglars, sniffing along the base of the brickwork and at the cellar openings while one of them performed a regular sowing motion with his hand out of a sack slung from his shoulder. They broke open the cellar door and sprinkled lime there, and in all the outbuildings. As they recrossed the lawn, a window that had been dark was lighted and Miss Emily sat in it, the light behind her, and her upright torso motionless as that of an idol. They crept quietly across the lawn and into the shadow of the locusts that lined the street. After a week or two the smell went away.

That was when people had begun to feel really sorry for her. People in our town, remembering how old lady Wyatt, her great-aunt, had gone completely crazy at last, believed that the Griersons held themselves a little too high for what they really were. None of the young men were quite good enough for Miss Emily and such. We had long thought of them as a tableau, Miss Emily a slender figure in white in the background, her father a spraddled silhouette in the foreground, his back to her and clutching a horsewhip, the two of them framed by the back-flung front door. So when she got to be thirty and was still single, we were not pleased exactly, but vindicated; even with insanity in the family she wouldn't have turned down all of her chances if they had really materialized.

When her father died, it got about that the house was all that was left to her; and in a way, people were glad. At last they could pity Miss Emily. Being left alone, and a pauper, she had become humanized. Now she too would know the old thrill and the old despair of a penny more or less.

The day after his death all the ladies prepared to call at the house and offer condolence and aid, as is our custom. Miss Emily met them at the door, dressed as usual and with no trace of grief on her face. She told them that her father was not dead. She did that for three days, with the ministers calling on her, and the doctors, trying to persuade her to let them dispose of the body. Just as they were about to resort to law and force, she broke down, and they buried her father quickly.

We did not say she was crazy then. We believed she had to do that. We remembered all the young men her father had driven away, and we knew that with nothing left, she would have to cling to that which had robbed her, as people will.

III

She was sick for a long time. When we saw her again, her hair was cut short, making her look like a girl, with a vague resemblance to those angels in colored church windows—sort of tragic and serene.

The town had just let the contracts for paving the sidewalks, and in the summer after her father's death they began the work. The construction company came with niggers and mules and machinery, and a foreman named Homer Barron, a Yankee—a big, dark, ready man, with a big voice and eyes lighter than his face. The little boys would follow in groups to hear him cuss the niggers, and the niggers singing in time to the rise and fall of picks. Pretty soon he knew everybody in town. Whenever you heard a lot of laughing anywhere about the square, Homer Barron would be in the center of the group. Presently we began to see him and Miss Emily on Sunday afternoons driving in the yellow-wheeled buggy and the matched team of bays from the livery stable.

At first we were glad that Miss Emily would have an interest, because the ladies all said, "Of course a Grierson would not think seriously of a Northerner, a day laborer." But there were still others, older people, who said that even grief could not cause a real lady to forget *noblesse oblige*—without calling it *noblesse oblige*. They just said, "Poor Emily. Her kinsfolk should come to her." She had some kin in Alabama; but years ago her father had fallen out with them over the estate of old lady Wyatt, the crazy woman, and there was no communication between the two families. They had not even been represented at the funeral.

And as soon as the old people said, "Poor Emily," the whispering began. "Do you suppose it's really so?" they said to one another. "Of course it is. What else could . . ." This behind their hands; rustling of craned silk and satin behind jalousies closed upon the sun of Sunday afternoon as the thin, swift clop-clop-clop of the matched team passed: "Poor Emily."

She carried her head high enough—even when we believed that she was fallen. It was as if she demanded more than ever the recognition of her dignity as the last Grierson; as if it had wanted that touch of earthiness to reaffirm her imperviousness. Like when she bought the rat poison, the arsenic. That was over a year after they had begun to say "Poor Emily," and while the two female cousins were visiting her.

"I want some poison," she said to the druggist. She was over thirty then, still a slight woman, though thinner than usual, with cold, haughty black eyes in a face the flesh of which was strained across the temples and about the eye-sockets as you imagine a lighthouse-keeper's face ought to look. "I want some poison," she said.

"Yes, Miss Emily. What kind? For rats and such? I'd recom—"

"I want the best you have. I don't care what kind."

The druggist named several. "They'll kill anything up to an elephant. But what you want is—"

"Arsenic," Miss Emily said. "Is that a good one?"

"Is . . . arsenic? Yes, ma'am. But what you want—"

"I want arsenic."

The druggist looked down at her. She looked back at him, erect, her face like a strained flag. "Why, of course," the druggist said. "If that's what you want. But the law requires you to tell what you are going to use it for."

Miss Emily just stared at him, her head tilted back in order to look him eye for eye, until he looked aw v and went and got the arsenic and wrapped it up. The Negro delivery boy brought her the package; the druggist didn't come back. When she opened the package at home there was written on the box, under the skull and bones: "For rats."

IV

So the next day we all said, "She will kill herself"; and we said it would be the best thing. When she had first begun to be seen with Homer Barron, we had said, "She will marry him." Then we said, "She will persuade him yet," because Homer himself had remarked—he liked men, and it was known that he drank with the younger men in the Elks' Club—that he was not a marrying man. Later we said, "Poor Emily" behind the jalousies as they passed on Sunday afternoon in the glittering buggy, Miss Emily with her head high and Homer Barron with his hat cocked and a cigar in his teeth, reins and whip in a yellow glove.

Then some of the ladies began to say that it was a disgrace to the town and a bad example to the young people. The men did not want to interfere, but at last the ladies forced the Baptist minister—Miss Emily's people were Episcopal—to call upon her. He would never divulge what happened during that interview, but he refused to go back again. The next Sunday they again drove about the streets, and the following day the minister's wife wrote to Miss Emily's relations in Alabama.

So she had blood-kin under her roof again and we sat back to watch developments. At first nothing happened. Then we were sure that they were to be married. We learned that Miss Emily had been to the jeweler's and ordered a man's toilet set in silver, with the letters H.B. on each piece. Two days later we learned that she had bought a complete outfit of men's clothing, including a nightshirt, and we said, "They are married." We were really glad. We were glad becaue the two female cousins were even more Grierson than Miss Emily had ever been.

So we were not surprised when Homer Barron—the streets had been finished some time since—was gone. We were a little disappointed that there was not a public blowing-off, but we believed that he had gone on to prepare for Miss Emily's coming, or to give her a chance to get rid of the cousins. (By that time it was a cabal, and we were all Miss Emily's allies to help circumvent the cousins.) Sure enough, after another week they departed. And, as we had expected all along, within three days Homer Barron was back in town. A neighbor saw the Negro man admit him at the kitchen door at dusk one evening.

And that was the last we saw of Homer Barron. And of Miss Emily for some time. The Negro man went in and out with the market basket, but the front door remained closed. Now and then we would see her at a window for a moment, as the men did that night when they sprinkled the lime, but for almost six months she did not appear on the streets. Then we knew that this was to be expected too; as if that quality of her father which had thwarted her woman's life so many times had been too virulent and too furious to die.

When we next saw Miss Emily, she had grown fat and her hair was turning gray. During the next few years it grew grayer and grayer until it attained an even pepper-and-salt iron-gray, when it ceased turning. Up to the day of her death at seventy-four it was still that vigorous iron-gray, like the hair of an active man.

From that time on her front door remained closed, save for a period of six or seven years, when she was about forty, during which she gave lessons in china-painting. She fitted up a studio in one of the downstairs rooms, where the daughters and granddaughters of Colonel Sartoris' contemporaries were sent to her with the same regularity and in the same spirit that they were sent to church on Sundays with a twenty-five-cent piece for the collection plate. Meanwhile her taxes had been remitted.

Then the newer generation became the backbone and the spirit of the town, and the painting pupils grew up and fell away and did not send their children to her with boxes of color and tedious brushes and pictures cut from the ladies' magazines. The front door closed upon the last one and remained closed for good. When the town got free postal delivery, Miss Emily alone refused to let them fasten the metal numbers above her door and attach a mailbox to it. She would not listen to them.

Daily, monthly, yearly we watched the Negro grow grayer and more stooped, going in and out with the market basket. Each December we sent her a tax notice, which would be returned by the post office a week later, unclaimed. Now and then we would see her in one of the downstairs windows—she had evidently shut up the top floor of the house—like the carven torso of an idol in a niche, looking or not looking at us, we could never tell which. Thus she passed from generation to generation—dear, inescapable, impervious, tranquil, and perverse.

And so she died. Fell ill in the house filled with dust and shadows, with only a doddering Negro man to wait on her. We did not even know she was sick; we had long since given up trying to get any information from the Negro. He talked to no one, probably not even to her, for his voice had grown harsh and rusty, as if from disuse.

She died in one of the downstairs rooms, in a heavy walnut bed with a curtain, her gray head propped on a pillow yellow and moldy with age and lack of sunlight.

V

The Negro met the first of the ladies at the front door and let them in, with their hushed, sibilant voices and their quick, curious glances, and then he disappeared. He walked right through the house and out the back and was not seen again.

The two female cousins came at once. They held the funeral on the second day, with the town coming to look at Miss Emily beneath a mass of bought flowers, with the crayon face of her father musing profoundly above the bier and the ladies sibilant and macabre; and the very old men—some in their brushed Confederate uniforms—on the porch and the lawn, talking of Miss Emily as if she had been a contemporary of theirs, believing that they had danced with her and courted her perhaps, confusing time with its mathematical progression, as the old do, to whom all the past is not a diminishing road but, instead, a huge meadow which no winter even quite touches, divided from them now by the narrow bottle-neck of the most recent decade of years.

Already we knew that there was one room in that region above stairs which no one had seen in forty years, and which would have to be forced. They waited until Miss Emily was decently in the ground before they opened it.

The violence of breaking down the door seemed to fill this room with pervading dust. A thin, acrid pall as of the tomb seemed to lie everywhere upon this room decked and furnished as for a bridal: upon the valance curtains of faded rose color, upon the rose-shaded lights, upon the dressing table, upon the delicate array of crystal and the man's toilet things backed with tarnished silver, silver so tarnished that the monogram was obscured. Among them lay a collar and tie, as if they had just been removed, which, lifted, left upon the surface a pale crescent in the dust. Upon a chair hung the suit, carefully folded; beneath it the two mute shoes and the discarded socks.

The man himself lay in the bed.

For a long time we just stood there, looking down at the profound and fleshless grin. The body had apparently once lain in the attitude of an embrace, but now the long sleep that outlasts love, that conquers even the grimace of love, had cuckolded him. What was left of him, rotted beneath what was left of the nightshirt, had become inextricable from the bed in which he lay; and upon him and upon the pillow beside him lay that even coating of the patient and biding dust.

Then we noticed that in the second pillow was the indentation of a head. One of us lifted something from it, and leaning forward, that faint and invisible dust dry and acrid in the nostrils, we saw a long strand of iron-gray hair.

1930, 1931

Spotted Horses[1]

I

Yes, sir. Flem Snopes has filled that whole country full of spotted horses. You can hear folks running them all day and all night, whooping and hollering, and the horses running back and forth across them little wooden bridges ever now and then kind of like thunder. Here I was this morning pretty near half way to town, with the team ambling along and me setting in the buckboard about half asleep, when all of a sudden something come swurging up outen the bushes and jumped the road clean, without touching hoof to it. It flew right over my team, big as a billboard and flying through the air like a hawk. It taken me thirty minutes to stop my team and untangle the harness and the buckboard and hitch them up again.

That Flem Snopes. I be dog if he ain't a case, now. One morning about ten years ago, the boys was just getting settled down on Varner's porch for a little talk and tobacco, when here come Flem out from behind the counter, with his coat off and his hair all parted, like he might have been clerking for Varner for ten years already. Folks all knowed him; it was a big family of them about five miles down the bottom. That year, at least. Share-cropping. They never stayed on any place over a year. Then they would move on to another place, with the chap or maybe the twins of that year's litter. It was a regular nest of them. But Flem. The rest of them stayed tenant farmers, moving ever year, but here come Flem one day, walking out from behind Jody Varner's counter like he owned it. And he wasn't there but a year or two before folks knowed that, if him and Jody was both still in that store in ten years more, it would be Jody clerking for Flem Snopes. Why, that fellow could make a nickel where it wasn't but four cents to begin with. He skun me in two trades, myself, and the fellow that can do that, I just hope he'll get rich before I do; that's all.

All right. So here Flem was, clerking at Varner's, making a nickel here and there and not telling nobody about it. No, sir. Folks never knowed when Flem got the better of somebody lessen the fellow he beat told it. He'd just set there in the store-chair, chewing his tobacco and keeping his own business to hisself, until about a week later we'd find out it was somebody else's business he was keeping to hisself — provided the fellow he trimmed was mad enough to tell it. That's Flem.

We give him ten years to own ever thing Jody Varner had. But he never waited no ten years. I reckon you-all know that gal of Uncle Billy Varner's, the youngest one; Eula. Jody's sister. Ever Sunday ever yellow-wheeled buggy and curried riding horse in that country would be hitched to Bill Varner's fence, and the young bucks setting on the porch, swarming around Eula like bees around a honey pot. One of these here kind of big, soft-looking gals that could giggle richer than plowed new-ground. Wouldn't none of them leave before the others, and so they would set there on the porch until time to go home, with some of them with nine and ten miles to ride and then get up tomorrow and go back to the field. So they would all leave together and they would ride in a clump down to the creek ford and hitch them curried horses and yellow-wheeled buggies and get out and fight one another. Then they would get in the buggies again and go on home.

Well, one day about a year ago, one of them yellow-wheeled buggies and one of them curried saddle-horses quit this country. We heard they was heading for Texas. The next day Uncle Billy and Eula and Flem come in to town in Uncle Bill's surrey, and when they come back, Flem and Eula was married. And on the next day we

[1] "Spotted Horses" was first published in *Scribner's* in 1931, the source of this text. Later Faulkner revised it, changing it radically from first person to third person narration in order to include it in *The Hamlet* (1940), a collection of interrelated tales about the Snopeses and the first volume of the "Snopes Trilogy."

heard that two more of them yellow-wheeled buggies had left the country. They mought have gone to Texas, too. It's a big place.

Anyway, about a month after the wedding, Flem and Eula went to Texas, too. They was gone pretty near a year. Then one day last month, Eula come back, with a baby. We figgured up, and we decided that it was as well-growed a three-months-old baby as we ever see. It can already pull up on a chair. I reckon Texas makes big men quick, being a big place. Anyway, if it keeps on like it started, it'll be chewing tobacco and voting time it's eight years old.

And so last Friday here come Flem himself. He was on a wagon with another fellow. The other fellow had one of these two-gallon hats and a ivory-handled pistol and a box of gingersnaps sticking out of his hind pocket, and tied to the tail-gate of the wagon was about two dozen of them Texas ponies, hitched to one another with barbed wire. They was colored like parrots and they was quiet as doves, and ere a one of them would kill you quick as a rattlesnake. Nere a one of them had two eyes the same color, and nere a one of them had ever see a bridle, I reckon; and when that Texas man got down offen the wagon and walked up to them to show how gentle they was, one of them cut his vest clean offen him, same as with a razor.

Flem had done already disappeared; he had went on to see his wife, I reckon, and to see if that ere baby had done gone on to the field to help Uncle Billy plow maybe. It was the Texas man that taken the horses on to Mrs. Littlejohn's lot. He had a little trouble at first, when they come to the gate, because they hadn't never see a fence before, and when he finally got them in and taken a pair of wire cutters and un-hitched them and got them into the barn and poured some shell corn into the trough, they durn nigh tore down the barn. I reckon they thought that shell corn was bugs, maybe. So he left them in the lot and he announced that the auction would begin at sunup to-morrow.

That night we was setting on Mrs. Littlejohn's porch. You-all mind the moon was nigh full that night, and we could watch them spotted varmints swirling along the fence and back and forth across the lot same as minnows in a pond. And then now and then they would all kind of huddle up against the barn and rest themselves by biting and kicking one another. We would hear a squeal, and then a set of hoofs would go Bam! against the barn, like a pistol. It sounded just like a fellow with a pistol, in a nest of cattymounts, taking his time.

II

It wasn't ere a man knowed yet if Flem owned them things or not. They just knowed one thing: that they wasn't never going to know for sho if Flem did or not, or if maybe he didn't just get on that wagon at the edge of town, for the ride or not. Even Eck Snopes didn't know, Flem's own cousin. But wasn't nobody surprised at that. We knowed that Flem would skin Eck quick as he would ere a one of us.

They was there by sunup next morning, some of them come twelve and sixteen miles, with seed-money tied up in tobacco sacks in their overalls, standing along the fence, when the Texas man come out of Mrs. Littlejohn's after breakfast and clumb onto the gate post with that ere white pistol butt sticking outen his hind pocket. He taken a new box of gingersnaps outen his pocket and bit the end offen it like a cigar and spit out the paper, and said the auction was open. And still they was coming up in wagons and a horse- and mule-back and hitching the teams across the road and coming to the fence. Flem wasn't nowhere in sight.

But he couldn't get them started. He begun to work on Eck, because Eck help him last night to get them into the barn and feed them that shell corn. Eck got out just in time. He come outen that barn like a chip on the crest of a busted dam of water, and clumb into the wagon just in time.

He was working on Eck when Henry Armstid come up in his wagon. Eck was saying he was skeered to bid on one of them, because he might get it, and the Texas man says, "Them ponies? Them little horses?" He clumb down offen the gate post and went toward the horses. They broke and run, and him following them, kind of chirping to them, with his hand out like he was fixing to catch a fly, until he got three or four of them cornered. Then he jumped into them, and then we couldn't see nothing for a while because of the dust. It was a big cloud of it, and them blare-eyed, spotted things swoaring outen it twenty foot to a jump, in forty directions without counting up. Then the dust settled and there they was, that Texas man and the horse. He had its head twisted clean around like a owl's head. Its legs was braced and it was trembling like a new bride and groaning like a saw mill, and him holding its head wrung clean around on its neck so it was snuffing sky. "Look it over," he says, with his heels dug too and that white pistol sticking outen his pocket and his neck swole up like a spreading adder's until you could just tell what he was saying, cussing the horse and talking to us all at once: "Look him over, the fiddle-headed son of fourteen fathers. Try him, buy him; you will get the best —" Then it was all dust again, and we couldn't see nothing but spotted hide and mane, and that ere Texas man's boot-heels like a couple of walnuts on two strings, and after a while that two-gallon hat come sailing out like a fat old hen crossing a fence.

When the dust settled again, he was just getting outen the far fence corner, brushing himself off. He come and got his hat and brushed it off and come and clumb onto the gate post again. He was breathing hard. He taken the gingersnap box outen his pocket and et one, breathing hard. The hammer-head horse was still running round and round the lot like a merry-go-round at a fair. That was when Henry Armstid come shoving up to the gate in them patched overalls and one of them dangle-armed shirts of hisn. Hadn't nobody noticed him until then. We was all watching the Texas man and the horses. Even Mrs. Littlejohn; she had done come out and built a fire under the wash-pot in her back yard, and she would stand at the fence a while and then go back into the house and come out again with a arm full of wash and stand at the fence again. Well, here come Henry shoving up, and then we see Mrs. Armstid right behind him, in that ere faded wrapper and sunbonnet and them tennis shoes. "Git on back to that wagon," Henry says.

"Henry," she says.

"Here, boys," the Texas man says; "make room for missus to git up and see. Come on, Henry," he says; "here's your chance to buy that saddle-horse missus has been wanting. What about ten dollars, Henry?"

"Henry," Mrs. Armstid says. She put her hand on Henry's arm. Henry knocked her hand down.

"Git on back to that wagon, like I told you," he says.

Mrs. Armstid never moved. She stood behind Henry, with her hands rolled into her dress, not looking at nothing. "He hain't no more despair than to buy one of them things," she says. "And us not five dollars ahead of the pore house, he hain't no more despair." It was the truth, too. They ain't never made more than a bare living offen that place of theirs, and them with four chaps and the very clothes they wears she earns by weaving by the firelight at night while Henry's asleep.

"Shut your mouth and git on back to that wagon," Henry says. "Do you want I taken a wagon stake to you here in the big road?"

Well, that Texas man taken one look at her. Then he begun on Eck again, like Henry wasn't even there. But Eck was skeered. "I can git me a snapping turtle or a water moccasin for nothing. I ain't going to buy none,"

So the Texas man said he would give Eck a horse. "To start the auction, and because you help me last night. If you'll start the bidding on the next horse," he says, "I'll give you that fiddle-head horse."

I wish you could have seen them, standing there with their seed-money in their pockets, watching that Texas man give Eck Snopes a live horse, all fixed to call him a fool if he taken it or not. Finally Eck says he'll take it. "Only I just starts the bidding," he says. "I don't have to buy the next one lessen I ain't overtopped." The Texas man said all right, and Eck bid a dollar on the next one, with Henry Armstid standing there with his mouth already open, watching Eck and the Texas man like a mad-dog or something. "A dollar," Eck says.

The Texas man looked at Eck. His mouth was already open too, like he had started to say something and what he was going to say had up and died on him. "A dollar?" he says. "One dollar? You mean, *one* dollar, Eck?"

"Durn it," Eck says; "two dollars, then."

Well, sir, I wish you could a seen that Texas man. He taken out that gingersnap box and held it up and looked into it, careful, like it might have been a diamond ring in it, or a spider. Then he throwed it away and wiped his face with a bandana. "Well," he says. "Well. Two dollars. Two dollars. Is your pulse all right, Eck?" he says. "Do you have ager-sweats at night, maybe?" he says. "Well," he says, "I got to take it. But are you boys going to stand there and see Eck get two horses at a dollar a head?"

That done it. I be dog if he wasn't nigh as smart as Flem Snopes. He hadn't no more than got the words outen his mouth before here was Henry Armstid, waving his hand. "Three dollars," Henry says. Mrs. Armstid tried to hold him again. He knocked her hand off, shoving up to the gate post.

"Mister," Mrs. Armstid says, "we got chaps in the house and not corn to feed the stock. We got five dollars I earned my chaps a-weaving after dark, and him snoring in the bed. And he hain't no more despair."

"Henry bids three dollars," the Texas man says. "Raise him a dollar, Eck, and the horse is yours."

"Henry," Mrs. Armstid says.

"Raise him, Eck," the Texas man says.

"Four dollars," Eck says.

"Five dollars," Henry says, shaking his fist. He shoved up right under the gate post. Mrs. Armstid was looking at the Texas man too.

"Mister," she says, "if you take that five dollars I earned my chaps a-weaving for one of them things, it'll be a curse onto you and yourn during all the time of man."

But it wasn't no stopping Henry. He had shoved up, waving his fist at the Texas man. He opened it; the money was in nickels and quarters, and one dollar bill that looked like a cow's cud. "Five dollars," he says. "And the man that raises it'll have to beat my head off, or I'll beat hisn."

"All right," the Texas man says. "Five dollars is bid. But don't you shake your hand at me."

III

It taken till nigh sundown before the last one was sold. He got them hotted up once and the bidding got up to seven dollars and a quarter, but most of them went around three or four dollars, him setting on the gate post and picking the horses out one at a time by mouth-word, and Mrs. Littlejohn pumping up and down at the tub and stopping and coming to the fence for a while and going back to the tub again. She had done got done too, and the wash was hung on the line in the back yard, and we could smell supper cooking. Finally they was all sold; he swapped the last two and the wagon for a buckboard.

We was all kind of tired, but Henry Armstid looked more like a mad-dog than ever. When he bought, Mrs. Armstid had went back to the wagon, setting in it behind them two rabbit-sized, bone-pore mules, and the wagon itself looking like it would fall all to pieces soon as the mules moved. Henry hadn't even waited to pull it outen the road; it was still in the middle of the road and her setting in it, not looking at nothing, ever since this morning.

Henry was right up against the gate. He went up to the Texas man. "I bought a horse and I paid cash," Henry says. "And yet you expect me to stand around here until they are all sold before I can get my horse. I'm going to take my horse outen that lot."

The Texas man looked at Henry. He talked like he might have beer, asking for a cup of coffee at the table. "Take your horse," he says.

Then Henry quit looking at the Texas man. He begun to swallow, holding onto the gate. "Ain't you going to help me?" he says.

"It ain't my horse," the Texas man says.

Henry never looked at the Texas man again, he never looked at nobody. "Who'll help me catch my horse?" he says. Never nobody said nothing. "Bring the plowline," Henry says. Mrs. Armstid got outen the wagon and brought the plowline. The Texas man got down offen the post. The woman made to pass him, carrying the rope.

"Don't you go in there, missus," the Texas man says.

Henry opened the gate. He didn't look back. "Come on here," he says.

"Don't you go in there, missus," the Texas man says.

Mrs. Armstid wasn't looking at nobody, neither, with her hands across her middle, holding the rope. "I reckon I better," she says. Her and Henry went into the lot. The horses broke and run. Henry and Mrs. Armstid followed.

"Get him into the corner," Henry says. They got Henry's horse cornered finally, and Henry taken the rope, but Mrs. Armstid let the horse get out. They hemmed it up again, but Mrs. Armstid let it get out again, and Henry turned and hit her with the rope. "Why didn't you head him back?" Henry says. He hit her again. "Why didn't you?" It was about that time I looked around and see Flem Snopes standing there.

It was the Texas man that done something. He moved fast for a big man. He caught the rope before Henry could hit the third time, and Henry whirled and made like he would jump at the Texas man. But he never jumped. The Texas man went and taken Henry's arm and led him outen the lot. Mrs. Armstid come behind them and the Texas man taken some money outen his pocket and he give it into Mrs. Armstid's hand. "Get him into the wagon and take him on home," the Texas man says, like he might have been telling them he enjoyed his supper.

Then here come Flem. "What's that for, Buck?" Flem says.

"Thinks he bought one of them ponies," the Texas man says. "Get him on away, missus."

But Henry wouldn't go. "Give him back that money," he says. "I bought that horse and I aim to have him if I have to shoot him."

And there was Flem, standing there with his hands in his pockets, chewing, like he had just happened to be passing.

"You take your money and I take my horse," Henry says. "Give it back to him," he says to Mrs. Armstid.

"You don't own no horse of mine," the Texas man says. "Get him on home, missus."

Then Henry seen Flem. "You got something to do with these horses," he says. "I bought one. Here's the money for it." He taken the bill outen Mrs. Armstid's hand. He offered it to Flem. "I bought one. Ask him. Here. Here's the money," he says, giving the bill to Flem.

When Flem taken the money, the Texas man dropped the rope he had snatched outen Henry's hand. He had done sent Eck Snopes's boy up to the store for another box of gingersnaps, and he taken the box outen his pocket and looked into it. It was empty and he dropped it on the ground. "Mr. Snopes will have your money for you to-morrow," he says to Mrs. Armstid. "You can get it from him to-morrow. He don't own no horse. You get him into the wagon and get him on home." Mrs. Armstid went back to the wagon and got in. "Where's that ere buckboard I bought?" the Texas man says. It was after sundown then. And then Mrs. Littlejohn come out on the porch and rung the supper bell.

IV

I come on in and et supper. Mrs. Littlejohn would bring in a pan of bread or something, then she would go out to the porch a minute and come back and tell us. The Texas man had hitched his team to the buckboard he had swapped them last two horses for, and him and Flem had gone, and then she told that the rest of them that never had ropes had went back to the store with I. O. Snopes to get some ropes, and wasn't nobody at the gate but Henry Armstid, and Mrs. Armstid setting in the wagon in the road, and Eck Snopes and that boy of hisn. "I don't care how many of them fool men gets killed by them things," Mrs. Littlejohn says, "but I ain't going to let Eck Snopes take that boy into that lot again." So she went down to the gate, but she come back without the boy or Eck neither.

"It ain't no need to worry about that boy," I says. "He's charmed." He was right behind Eck last night when Eck went to help feed them. The whole drove of them jumped clean over that boy's head and never touched him. It was Eck that touched him. Eck snatched him into the wagon and taken a rope and frailed the tar outen him.

So I had done et and went to my room and was undressing, long as I had a long trip to make next day; I was trying to sell a machine to Mrs. Bundren up past Whiteleaf; when Henry Armstid opened that gate and went in by hisself. They couldn't make him wait for the balance of them to get back with their ropes. Eck Snopes said he tried to make Henry wait, but Henry wouldn't do it. Eck said Henry walked right up to them and that when they broke, they run clean over Henry like a hay-mow breaking down. Eck said he snatched that boy of hisn out of the way just in time and that them things went through that gate like a creek flood and into the wagons and teams hitched side the road, busting wagon tongues and snapping harness like it was fishing-line, with Mrs. Armstid still setting in their wagon in the middle of it like something carved outen wood. Then they scattered, wild horses and tame mules with pieces of harness and single trees dangling offen them, both ways up and down the road.

"There goes ourn, paw!" Eck says his boy said. "There it goes, into Mrs. Littlejohn's house." Eck says it run right up the steps and into the house like a boarder late for supper. I reckon so. Anyway, I was in my room, in my underclothes, with one sock on and one sock in my hand, leaning out the window when the commotion busted out, when I heard something run into the melodeon in the hall; it sounded like a railroad engine. Then the door to my room come sailing in like when you throw a tin bucket top into the wind and I looked over my shoulder and see something that looked like a fourteen-foot pinwheel a-blaring its eyes at me. It had to blare them fast, because I was already done jumped out the window.

I reckon it was anxious, too. I reckon it hadn't never seen barbed wire or shell corn before, but I know it hadn't never seen underclothes before, or maybe it was a sewing-machine agent it hadn't never seen. Anyway, it swirled and turned to run back up the hall and outen the house, when it met Eck Snopes and that boy just coming in, carrying a rope. It swirled again and run down the hall and out the back door just in time to meet Mrs. Littlejohn. She had just gathered up the clothes she had washed, and she was coming onto the back porch with a armful of washing in one hand and a scrubbing-board in the other, when the horse skidded up to her, trying to stop and swirl again. It never taken Mrs. Littlejohn no time a-tall.

"Git outen here, you son," she says. She hit it across the face with the scrubbing-board; that ere scrubbing-board split as neat as ere a axe could have done it, and when the horse swirled to run back up the hall, she hit it again with what was left of the scrubbing-board, not on the head this time. "And stay out," she says.

Eck and that boy was half-way down the hall by this time. I reckon that horse looked like a pinwheel to Eck too. "Git to hell outen here, Ad!" Eck says. Only there wasn't time. Eck dropped flat on his face, but the boy never moved. The boy was about a yard tall maybe, in overhalls just like Eck's; that horse swoared over his head without touching a hair. I saw that, because I was just coming back up the front steps, still carrying that ere sock and still in my underclothes, when the horse come onto the porch again. It taken one look at me and swirled again and run to the end of the porch and jumped the banisters and the lot fence like a hen-hawk and lit in the lot running and went out the gate again and jumped eight or ten upside-down wagons and went on down the road. It was a full moon then. Mrs. Armstid was still setting in the wagon like she had done been carved outen wood and left there and forgot.

That horse. It ain't never missed a lick. It was going about forty miles a hour when it come to the bridge over the creek. It would have had a clear road, but it so happened that Vernon Tull was already using the bridge when it got there. He was coming back from town; he hadn't heard about the auction; him and his wife and three daughters and Mrs. Tull's aunt, all setting in chairs in the wagon bed, and all asleep, including the mules. They waked up when the horse hit the bridge one time, but Tull said the first he knew was when the mules tried to turn the wagon around in the middle of the bridge and he seen that spotted varmint run right twixt the mules and run up the wagon tongue like a squirrel. He said he just had time to hit it across the face with his whip-stock, because about that time the mules turned the wagon around on that ere one-way bridge and that horse clumb across one of the mules and jumped down onto the bridge again and went on, with Vernon standing up in the wagon and kicking at it.

Tull said the mules turned in the harness and clumb back into the wagon too, with Tull trying to beat them out again, with the reins wrapped around his wrist. After that he says all he seen was overturned chairs and womenfolks' legs and white drawers shining in the moonlight, and his mules and that spotted horse going on up the road like a ghost.

The mules jerked Tull outen the wagon and drug him a spell on the bridge before the reins broke. They thought at first that he was dead, and while they was kneeling around him, picking the bridge splinters outen him, here come Eck and that boy, still carrying the rope. They was running and breathing a little hard. "Where'd he go?" Eck says.

V

I went back and got my pants and shirt and shoes on just in time to go and help get Henry Armstid outen the trash in the lot. I be dog if he didn't look like he was dead, with his head hanging back and his teeth showing in the moonlight, and a little rim of white under his eyelids. We could still hear them horses, here and there; hadn't none of them got more than four-five miles away yet, not knowing the country, I reckon. So we could hear them and folks yelling now and then: "Whooey. Head him!"

We toted Henry into Mrs. Littlejohn's. She was in the hall; she hadn't put down the armful of clothes. She taken one look at us, and she laid down the busted scrubbing-board and taken up the lamp and opened a empty door. "Bring him in here," she says.

We toted him in and laid him on the bed. Mrs. Littlejohn set the lamp on the dresser, still carrying the clothes. "I'll declare, you men," she says. Our shadows was way up the wall, tiptoeing too; we could hear ourselves breathing. "Better get his wife," Mrs. Littlejohn says. She went out, carrying the clothes.

"I reckon we had," Quick says. "Go get her, somebody."

"Whyn't you go?" Winterbottom says.

"Let Ernest git her," Durley says. "He lives neighbors with them."

Ernest went to fetch her. I be dog if Henry didn't look like he was dead. Mrs. Littlejohn come back, with a kettle and some towels. She went to work on Henry, and then Mrs. Armstid and Ernest come in. Mrs. Armstid come to the foot of the bed and stood there, with her hands rolled into her apron, watching what Mrs. Littlejohn was doing, I reckon.

"You men git outen the way," Mrs. Littlejohn says. "Git outside," she says. "See if you can't find something else to play with that will kill some more of you."

"Is he dead?" Winterbottom says.

"It ain't your fault if he ain't," Mrs. Littlejohn says. "Go tell Will Varner to come up here. I reckon a man ain't so different from a mule, come long come short. Except maybe a mule's got more sense."

We went to get Uncle Billy. It was a full moon. We could hear them, now and then, four mile away: "Whooey. Head him." The country was full of them, one on ever wooden bridge in the land, running across it like thunder: "Whooey. There he goes. Head him."

We hadn't got far before Henry begun to scream. I reckon Mrs. Littlejohn's water had brung him to; anyway, he wasn't dead. We went on to Uncle Billy's. The house was dark. We called to him, and after a while the window opened and Uncle Billy put his head out, peart as a peckerwood, listening. "Are they still trying to catch them durn rabbits?" he says.

He come down, with his britches on over his night-shirt and his suspenders dangling, carrying his horse-doctoring grip. "Yes, sir," he says, cocking his head like a woodpecker; "they're still a-trying."

We could hear Henry before we reached Mrs. Littlejohn's. He was going Ah-Ah-Ah. We stopped in the yard. Uncle Billy went on in. We could hear Henry. We stood in the yard, hearing them on the bridges, this-a-way and that: "Whooey. Whooey."

"Eck Snopes ought to caught hisn," Ernest says.

"Looks like he ought," Winterbottom said.

Henry was going Ah-Ah-Ah steady in the house; then he begun to scream. "Uncle Billy's started," Quick says. We looked into the hall. We could see the light where the door was. Then Mrs. Littlejohn come out.

"Will needs some help," she says. "You, Ernest. You'll do." Ernest went into the house.

"Hear them?" Quick said. "That one was on Four Mile bridge." We could hear them; it sounded like thunder a long way off; it didn't last long:

"Whooey."

We could hear Henry: "Ah-Ah-Ah-Ah-Ah."

"They are both started now," Winterbottom says. "Ernest too."

That was early in the night. Which was a good thing, because it taken a long night for folks to chase them things right and for Henry to lay there and holler, being as Uncle Billy never had none of this here chloryfoam to set Henry's leg with. So it was considerate in Flem to get them started early. And what do you reckon Flem's comment was?

That's right. Nothing. Because he wasn't there. Hadn't nobody see him since that Texas man left.

VI

That was Saturday night. I reckon Mrs. Armstid got home about daylight, to see about the chaps. I don't know where they thought her and Henry was. But lucky the oldest one was a gal, about twelve, big enough to take care of the little ones. Which she did for the next two days. Mrs. Armstid would nurse Henry all night and work in the kitchen for hern and Henry's keep, and in the afternoon she would drive home (it was about four miles) to see to the chaps. She would cook up a pot of victuals and leave it on the stove, and the gal would bar the house and keep the little ones quiet. I would hear Mrs. Littlejohn and Mrs. Armstid talking in the kitchen. "How are the chaps making out?" Mrs. Littlejohn says.

"All right," Mrs. Armstid says.

"Don't they git skeered at night?" Mrs. Littlejohn says.

"Ina May bars the door when I leave," Mrs. Armstid says. "She's got the axe in bed with her. I reckon she can make out."

I reckon they did. And I reckon Mrs. Armstid was waiting for Flem to come back to town; hadn't nobody seen him until this morning; to get her money the Texas man said Flem was keeping for her. Sho. I reckon she was.

Anyway, I heard Mrs. Armstid and Mrs. Littlejohn talking in the kitchen this morning while I was eating breakfast. Mrs. Littlejohn had just told Mrs. Armstid that Flem was in town. "You can ask him for that five dollars," Mrs. Littlejohn says.

"You reckon he'll give it to me?" Mrs. Armstid says.

Mrs. Littlejohn was washing dishes, washing them like a man, like they was made out of iron. "No," she says. "But asking him won't do no hurt. It might shame him. I don't reckon it will, but it might."

"If he wouldn't give it back, it ain't no use to ask," Mrs. Armstid says.

"Suit yourself," Mrs. Littlejohn says. "It's your money."

I could hear the dishes.

"Do you reckon he might give it back to me?" Mrs. Armstid says. "That Texas man said he would. He said I could get it from Mr. Snopes later."

"Then go and ask him for it," Mrs. Littlejohn says.

I could hear the dishes.

"He won't give it back to me," Mrs. Armstid says.

"All right," Mrs. Littlejohn says. "Don't ask him for it, then."

I could hear the dishes; Mrs. Armstid was helping. "You don't reckon he would, do you?" she says. Mrs. Littlejohn never said nothing. It sounded like she was throwing the dishes at one another. "Maybe I better go and talk to Henry about it," Mrs. Armstid says.

"I would," Mrs. Littlejohn says. I be dog if it didn't sound like she had two plates in her hands, beating them together. "Then Henry can buy another five-dollar horse with it. Maybe he'll buy one next time will out and out kill him. If I thought that, I'd give you back the money, myself."

"I reckon I better talk to him first," Mrs. Armstid said. Then it sounded like Mrs. Littlejohn taken up all the dishes and throwed them at the cook-stove, and I come away.

That was this morning. I had been up to Bundren's and back, and I thought that things would have kind of settled down. So after breakfast, I went up to the store. And there was Flem, setting in the store-chair and whittling, like he might not have ever moved since he come to clerk for Jody Varner. I. O. was leaning in the door, in his shirt sleeves and with his hair parted too, same as Flem was before he turned the clerking job over to I. O. It's a funny thing about them Snopes: they all looks alike, yet there ain't ere a two of them that claims brothers. They're always just cousins, like Flem and Eck and Flem and I. O. Eck was there too, squatting against the wall, him and that boy, eating cheese and crackers outen a sack; they told me that Eck hadn't been home a-tall. And that Lon Quick hadn't got back to town, even. He followed his horse clean down to Samson's Bridge, with a wagon and a camp outfit. Eck finally caught one of hisn. It run into a blind lane at Freeman's and Eck and the boy taken and tied their rope across the end of the lane, about three foot high. The horse come to the end of the lane and whirled and run back without ever stopping. Eck says it never seen the rope a-tall. He says it looked just like one of these here Christmas pinwheels. "Didn't it try to run again?" I says.

"No," Eck says, eating a bite of cheese offen his knife blade. "Just kicked some."

"Kicked some?" I says.

"It broke its neck," Eck says.

Well, they was squatting there, about six of them, talking, talking at Flem; never nobody knowed yet if Flem had ere a interest in them horses or not. So finally I come right out and asked him. "Flem's done skun all of us so much," I says, "that we're proud of him. Come on, Flem," I says, "how much did you and that Texas man make offen them horses? You can tell us. Ain't nobody here but Eck that bought one of them; the others ain't got back to town yet, and Eck's your own cousin; he'll be proud to hear, too. How much did you-all make?"

They was all whittling, not looking at Flem, making like they was studying. But you could a heard a pin drop. And I. O. He had been rubbing his back up and down on the door, but he stopped now, watching Flem like a pointing dog. Flem finished cutting the sliver offen his stick. He spit across the porch, into the road. "'Twarn't none of my horses," he says.

I. O. cackled, like a hen, slapping his legs with both hands. "You boys might just as well quit trying to get ahead of Flem," he said.

Well, about that time I see Mrs. Armstid come outen Mrs. Littlejohn's gate, coming up the road. I never said nothing. I says, "Well, if a man can't take care of himself in a trade, he can't blame the man that trims him."

Flem never said nothing, trimming at the stick. He hadn't seen Mrs. Armstid. "Yes, sir," I says. "A fellow like Henry Armstid ain't got nobody but hisself to blame."

"Course he ain't," I. O. says. He ain't seen her, neither. "Henry Armstid's a born fool. Always is been. If Flem hadn't a got his money, somebody else would."

We looked at Flem. He never moved. Mrs. Armstid come on up the road.

"That's right," I says. "But, come to think of it, Henry never bought no horse." We looked at Flem; you could a heard a match drop. "That Texas man told her to get that five dollars back from Flem next day. I reckon Flem's done already taken that money to Mrs. Littlejohn's and give it to Mrs. Armstid."

We watched Flem. I. O. quit rubbing his back against the door again. After a while Flem raised his head and spit across the porch, into the dust. I. O. cackled, just like a hen. "Ain't he a beating fellow, now?" I. O. says.

Mrs. Armstid was getting closer, so I kept on talking, watching to see if Flem would look up and see her. But he never looked up. I went on talking about Tull, about how he was going to sue Flem, and Flem setting there, whittling his stick, not saying nothing else after he said they wasn't none of his horses.

Then I. O. happened to look around. He seen Mrs. Armstid. "Psssst!" he says. Flem looked up. "Here she comes!" I. O. says. "Go out the back. I'll tell her you done went in to town to-day."

But Flem never moved. He just set there, whittling, and we watched Mrs. Armstid come up onto the porch, in that ere faded sunbonnet and wrapper and them tennis shoes that made a kind of hissing noise on the porch. She come onto the porch and stopped, her hands rolled into her dress in front, not looking at nothing.

"He said Saturday," she says, "that he wouldn't sell Henry no horse. He said I could get the money from you."

Flem looked up. The knife never stopped. It went on trimming off a sliver same as if he was watching it. "He taken that money off with him when he left," Flem says.

Mrs. Armstid never looked at nothing. We never looked at her, neither, except that boy of Eck's. He had a half-et cracker in his hand, watching her, chewing.

"He said Henry hadn't bought no horse," Mrs. Armstid says. "He said for me to get the money from you today."

"I reckon he forgot about it," Flem said. "He taken that money off with him Saturday." He whittled again. I. O. kept on rubbing his back, slow. He licked his lips. After a while the woman looked up the road, where it went on up the hill, toward the graveyard. She looked up that way for a while, with that boy of Eck's watching her and I. O. rubbing his back slow against the door. Then she turned back toward the steps.

"I reckon it's time to get dinner started," she says.

"How's Henry this morning, Mrs. Armstid?" Winterbottom says.

She looked at Winterbottom; she almost stopped. "He's resting, I thank you kindly," she says.

Flem got up, outen the chair, putting his knife away. He spit across the porch. "Wait a minute, Mrs. Armstid," he says. She stopped again. She didn't look at him. Flem went on into the store, with I. O. done quit rubbing his back now, with his head craned after Flem, and Mrs. Armstid standing there with her hands rolled into her dress, not looking at nothing. A wagon come up the road and passed; it was Freeman, on the way to town. Then Flem come out again, with I. O. still watching him. Flem had one of these little striped sacks of Jody Varner's candy; I bet he still owes Jody that nickel, too. He put the sack into Mrs. Armstid's hand, like he would have put it into a hollow stump. He spit again across the porch. "A little sweetening for the chaps," he says.

"You're right kind," Mrs. Armstid says. She held the sack of candy in her hand, not looking at nothing. Eck's boy was watching the sack, the half-et cracker in his hand; he wasn't chewing now. He watched Mrs. Armstid roll the sack into her apron. "I reckon I better get on back and help with dinner," she says. She turned and went back across the porch. Flem sat down in the chair again and opened his knife. He spit across the porch again, past Mrs. Armstid where she hadn't went down the steps yet. Then she went on, in that ere sunbonnet and wrapper all the same color, back down the road toward Mrs. Littlejohn's. You couldn't see her dress move, like a natural woman walking. She looked like a old snag still standing up and moving along on a high water. We watched her turn in at Mrs. Littlejohn's and go outen sight. Flem was whittling. I. O. began to rub his back on the door. Then he begun to cackle, just like a durn hen.

"You boys might just as well quit trying," I. O. says. "You can't git ahead of Flem. You can't touch him. Ain't he a sight, now?"

I be dog if he ain't. If I had brung a herd of wild cattymounts into town and sold them to my neighbors and kinfolks, they would have lynched me. Yes, sir.

1931

Address upon Receiving the Nobel Prize for Literature

Stockholm, December 10, 1950

I feel that this award was not made to me as a man, but to my work—a life's work in the agony and sweat of the human spirit, not for glory and least of all for profit, but to create out of the materials of the human spirit something which did not exist before. So this award is only mine in trust. It will not be difficult to find a dedication for the money part of it commensurate with the purpose and significance of its origin. But I would like to do the same with the acclaim too, by using this moment as a pinnacle from which I might be listened to by the young men and women already dedicated to the same anguish and travail, among whom is already that one who will some day stand here where I am standing.

Our tragedy today is a general and universal physical fear so long sustained by now that we can even bear it. There are no longer problems of the spirit. There is only the question: When will I be blown up? Because of this, the young man or woman writing today has forgotten the problems of the human heart in conflict with itself which alone can make good writing because only that is worth writing about, worth the agony and the sweat.

He must learn them again. He must teach himself that the basest of all things is to be afraid; and, teaching himself that, forget it forever, leaving no room in his workshop for anything but the old verities and truths of the heart, the old universal truths lacking which any story is ephemeral and doomed — love and honor and pity and pride and compassion and sacrifice. Until he does so, he labors under a curse. He writes not of love but of lust, of defeats in which nobody loses anything of value, of victories without hope and, worst of all, without pity or compassion. His griefs grieve on no universal bones, leaving no scars. He writes not of the heart but of the glands.

Until he relearns these things, he will write as though he stood among and watched the end of man. I decline to accept the end of man. It is easy enough to say that man is immortal simply because he will endure: that when the last ding-dong of doom has clanged and faded from the last worthless rock hanging tideless in the last red and dying evening, that even then there will still be one more sound: that of his puny inexhaustible voice, still talking. I refuse to accept this. I believe that man will not merely endure: he will prevail. He is immortal, not because he alone among creatures has an inexhaustible voice, but because he has a soul, a spirit capable of compassion and sacrifice and endurance. The poet's, the writer's, duty is to write about these things. It is his privilege to help man endure by lifting his heart, by reminding him of the courage and honor and hope and pride and compassion and pity and sacrifice which have been the glory of his past. The poet's voice need not merely be the record of man, it can be one of the props, the pillars to help him endure and prevail.

1950

ERNEST HEMINGWAY
(1899–1961)

Ernest Hemingway defined the essence of his spare, lean style to an interviewer in 1954: "I always try to write on the principle of the iceberg. There is seven-eighths of it under water for every part that shows. Anything you know you can eliminate and it only strengthens your iceberg. It is the part that doesn't show. If a writer omits something because he does not know it then there is a hole in the story." It was Hemingway's style in part that made him the most popular, the most critically acclaimed, and the most imitated author of his time. His simple, pared down sentences filled with short, everyday words appeared exactly the right style to convey the emptiness felt by characters wandering aimlessly in a seemingly meaningless world. But Hemingway's fame spread, too, because he lived a life in public as one of his own most flamboyant creations.

Born in Oak Park, Illinois, to a father who was a prominent doctor and outdoorsman and a mother who was a committed Congregationalist and devoted to the arts, Hemingway grew up in a family pretense that he and his older sister were twins (his mother dressed him as a girl in his first years). His father's imprint on the young boy, to find its way into his fiction, was made on the trips to the Hemingway summer house in the lake country of northern Michigan. There was boating and fishing and hunting and the sportsman's life. His mother's imprint was in developing his interest in the arts and — through her religious zeal — inspiring his disillusionment with religious belief.

In 1917, Hemingway graduated from Oak Park High School only shortly after America had entered the First World War. He decided to skip college and go to work for the *Kansas City Star* as a reporter. He may well have learned more about writing by making this choice. The style sheet of the *Star* contained 110 rules, such as, "Use short sentences. Use short first paragraphs. Use vigorous prose. Be positive, not negative"; "Avoid the use of adjectives, especially such extravagant ones as *splendid, gorgeous, grand, magnificent*, etc."

After only a few months as a reporter, Hemingway found the action of a world conflict irresistible. He signed up as an ambulance driver for the Red Cross in Italy and was wounded one night while passing out candy to soldiers near the front. Hit with shrapnel, he was dragging another wounded soldier to the rear and was hit again—in the knee. He spent several months in a Milan hospital as the shell fragments were removed from his body. There he would meet and fall in love with the nurse Agnes von Kurowsky, the inspiration for Catherine in *A Farewell to Arms*. Biographies have dated his bouts with insomnia from this time.

Hemingway returned home and, while working in Chicago in 1920, met Sherwood Anderson and other participants in the "Chicago Renaissance." He returned to Europe in 1921 with the first of his four wives, Hadley Richardson, after being appointed foreign correspondent for the *Toronto Daily Star* and *Star Weekly*. Anderson's letter introduced him to Gertrude Stein and he soon met other expatriate writers, including Ezra Pound. Although Hadley lost a suitcase of his manuscripts on a train in Paris, an incident which would haunt him for the rest of his life, he was sufficiently resilient and energetic to recoup and start over, and to produce enough to fill a first book, *Three Stories and Ten Poems*, published in Paris in 1923.

This work was followed by a volume of short stories, published first as *in our time* in Paris in 1924, and in the United States in 1925 as *In Our Time*. It contained many of the Nick Adams stories set in northern Michigan, including "Big Two-Hearted River," Parts I and II. The publisher, Boni & Liveright, had options on Hemingway's next two books, but by this time Maxwell Perkins, F. Scott Fitzgerald's editor at Scribner's, wanted to publish Hemingway. Hemingway thought up the scheme of writing a parody of Sherwood Anderson, which Boni & Liveright, Anderson's publisher, would have to reject, freeing him to publish with Scribner's. Thus Scribner's brought out both *The Torrents of Spring* (the Anderson parody) and *The Sun Also Rises* in 1926.

With *The Sun Also Rises* Hemingway's reputation as a writer was established. The book was praised by reviewers, and sold impressively. And it has for long been considered by many critics Hemingway's greatest novel. Its account of international expatriates living on the edge of despair—eating, talking, drinking, and loving in postwar Paris, and going to Spain for the bull fights—has been taken as the definitive portrayal of the "lost generation" of the 1920s. The term appeared as an epigraph to the novel, ascribed to Gertrude Stein: "You are all a lost generation." She had, she claimed, first heard the phrase from a French garage owner who applied it to those whom the war had wounded intellectually and spiritually—like the young mechanic trying to fix Stein's car.

In 1927, Hemingway published another volume of short stories, *Men Without Women*, followed in 1929 by another novel, *A Farewell to Arms*. It was a war-time love story, set in Italy, and ended with the tragic death of the heroine in childbirth. The hero, who had made a "separate peace" in the war to join his love, is left at the end deeply embittered by the "dirty trick" played by a godless universe. The novel was turned into a popular—but inaccurate—movie in 1932 with Gary Cooper and Helen Hayes.

As Hemingway's fame spread, his writing diminished. He published two widely read nonfiction books in the 1930s—*Death in the Afternoon* (1932), an explanatory account of the rituals of bull fighting; and *Green Hills of Africa*, the description of a safari. And he brought out another volume of short stories in 1933, *Winner Take Nothing*, containing such widely acclaimed stories as "A Clean, Well-Lighted Place." In 1938 he published *The Fifth Column and the First Forty-Nine Stories*, including not only the stories of his first three collections, but also a few recently written stories, such as "The Snows of Kilimanjaro." *The Fifth Column* (1938) was Hemingway's only play, set in Spain during the Spanish Civil War. In his one novel of this period, *To Have and Have Not* (1937), Hemingway attempted to embody serious social themes relevant to the period of the Great Depression — but without major success.

Hemingway went to Spain in 1937 as a correspondent to cover the Spanish Civil War for the North American Newspaper Alliance. His sympathies, strongly anti-Fascist and pro-Loyalist, were to find their embodiment in the novel *For Whom the Bell Tolls* (1940). Now married to his third wife, the journalist Martha Gellhorne, he continued his hard-driving life of sports, heavy drinking, and socializing at his finca in Cuba. More and more during this period, Hemingway worked as a journalist, enabling him to turn up any place in the world where the action was. He spent two years in China in the early 1940s covering the Japanese-Chinese conflict. And in 1944, as a war correspondent, he observed the D-Day invasion, and participated in the liberation of Paris (where he "liberated" the Ritz Hotel) and the Battle of the Bulge, earning the Bronze Star.

By this time Hemingway was a celebrity, newsworthy in his own right, and he played the part of one of his own heroes to the hilt. When he went to Africa on safari with his fourth wife, the journalist Mary Welsh, in 1953, he was in two successive airplane crashes, and his death was reported worldwide. He and his wife did suffer serious physical injuries, but they survived — with wit and grace, as appropriate for Hemingway characters. He enjoyed, he said, reading his own obituaries. His critical reputation suffered with the publication of his novel *Across the River and Into the Trees* in 1950, but recouped with *The Old Man and the Sea*, published first in *Life* magazine in 1952. He was awarded the Nobel Prize in 1954, and the Nobel Committee cited especially his "powerful, style-making mastery of the art of modern narration."

His last years were spent in Ketchum, Idaho, where he suffered from a number of physical illnesses, as well as severe depression, for which he received electric-shock treatment. In 1961, he committed suicide in Ketchum, following the method his father had used in 1928, a gunshot into the head. On hearing of his death, John Steinbeck commented: "He had only one theme — only one. A man contends with the forces of the world, called fate, and meets them with courage. Surely a man has a right to remove his own life but you'll find no such possibility in any of Hemingway's heroes."

The memoir Hemingway had been working on before his death, *A Moveable Feast*, about the early Paris years, appeared in 1964 and seemed to be written in the early vigorous style. The unflattering portraits Hemingway painted of Gertrude Stein and F. Scott Fitzgerald in this memoir suggested that he was paying off old scores. A long novel found among his papers, *Islands in the Stream*, was published in 1970. Its length and meditative (or ruminating) style did little to reverse the trend downward in Hemingway's reputation.

Culled also from his manuscripts and issued in 1986 was the heavily edited novel *Garden of Eden*, set in France and Spain during the early years. Because the newly married couple at the center switched sex-roles while making love, it demonstrated that Hemingway could still make sensational literary news some dec-

ades after his death. But it also tended to confirm critical-biographical speculation that Hemingway's machismo and that of his characters, which to many
readers (especially women) seemed exaggerated, was more complicated than
thought, and may well have been a guise — whether conscious or unconscious —
to mask ambivalent sexuality or androgyny. It is, ironically, this new view of
Hemingway (see especially Kenneth Lynn's biography, *Hemingway*, 1987) that
seems to support renewed interest in his work.

ADDITIONAL READING

The Wild Years (early journalism), ed. Gene Z. Hanrahan, 1962; *By-Line: Ernest Hemingway,
Selected Articles and Dispatches of Four Decades*, ed. William White, 1967; *Ernest Hemingway: Selected
Letters, 1917–1961*, ed. Carlos Baker, 1981; *Conversations with Ernest Hemingway*, ed. Matthew J.
Bruccoli, 1986; *Dateline: Toronto/ The Complete Toronto Star Dispatches, 1920–1924, by Ernest Hemi-
ngway*, ed. William White, 1986.

Philip Young, *Ernest Hemingway*, 1952; Carlos Baker, *Ernest Hemingway: The Writer as Artist*,
1952, 1972; Charles A. Fenton, *The Apprenticeship of Ernest Hemingway: The Early Years*, 1954;
Carlos Baker, ed., *Hemingway and His Critics*, 1961; Robert P. Weeks, ed., *Hemingway: A Collection
of Critical Essays*, 1962; Roger Asselineau, ed., *The Literary Reputation of Hemingway in Europe*,
1965; Robert W. Lewis, *Hemingway on Love*, 1965; Philip Young, *Ernest Hemingway: A Reconsidera-
tion*, 1966; A. E. Hotchner, *Papa Hemingway*, 1966; Sheridan Baker, *Ernest Hemingway*, 1967;
Audre Hanneman, *Ernest Hemingway: A Comprehensive Bibliography*, 1967, supplement, 1975;
Robert O. Stephens, *Hemingway's Non-Fiction: The Public Voice*, 1968; Richard B. Hovey, *Hemingway: The Inward Terrain*, 1968; Leo Gurko, *Ernest Hemingway and the Pursuit of Heroism*, 1968;
Delbert E. Wylder, *Hemingway's Heroes*, 1969; Carlos Baker, *Ernest Hemingway: A Life Story*, 1969;
John K. M. McCaffrey, ed., *Ernest Hemingway: The Man and His Work*, 1971; Emily A. Watts,
Ernest Hemingway and the Arts, 1971; Arthur Waldhorn, *A Reader's Guide to Ernest Hemingway*,
1972; Arthur Waldhorn, ed., *Ernest Hemingway: A Collection of Criticism*, 1973; Sheldon N. Greb-
stein, *Hemingway's Craft*, 1973; Linda Wagner, *Ernest Hemingway*, 1974; Scott Donaldson, *By
Force of Will: The Life and Art of Ernest Hemingway*, 1977; Matthew J. Bruccoli, *Scott and Ernest*,
1978; Anthony Burgess, *Ernest Hemingway and His World*, 1978; Bernard S. Oldsey, *Hemingway's
Hidden Craft*, 1979; Jeffrey Meyers, *Hemingway: The Critical Heritage*, 1982; Wirt Williams, *The
Tragic Art of Ernest Hemingway*, 1982; Bernice Kert, *The Hemingway Women*, 1983; James Nagel,
ed., *Ernest Hemingway: The Writer in Context*, 1984; Jeffrey Meyers, *Hemingway: A Biography*,
1985; Earl Rovit and Gerry Brenner, *Ernest Hemingway*, 1986; Peter Griffin, *Along with Youth:
Hemingway, The Early Years*, 1986; Michael Reynolds, *The Young Hemingway*, 1986; Anthony Bur-
gess, *Ernest Hemingway and His World*, 1986; Kenneth S. Lynn, *Hemingway*, 1987; Henry Serrano
Villard and James Nagel, *Hemingway in Love and War*, 1989.

TEXTS

The Short Stories of Ernest Hemingway, 1938; *A Moveable Feast*, 1964.

Big Two-Hearted River

PART I

The train went on up the track out of sight, around one of the hills of burnt timber.
Nick sat down on the bundle of canvas and bedding the baggage man had pitched
out of the door of the baggage car. There was no town, nothing but the rails and the
burned-over country. The thirteen saloons that had lined the one street of Seney had
not left a trace. The foundations of the Mansion House hotel stuck up above the
ground. The stone was chipped and split by the fire. It was all that was left of the town
of Seney. Even the surface had been burned off the ground.

Nick looked at the burned-over stretch of hillside, where he had expected to find the scattered houses of the town and then walked down the railroad track to the bridge over the river. The river was there. It swirled against the log spiles of the bridge. Nick looked down into the clear, brown water, colored from the pebbly bottom, and watched the trout keeping themselves steady in the current with wavering fins. As he watched them they changed their positions by quick angles, only to hold steady in the fast water again. Nick watched them a long time.

He watched them holding themselves with their noses into the current, many trout in deep, fast moving water, slightly distorted as he watched far down through the glassy convex surface of the pool, its surface pushing and swelling smooth against the resistance of the log-driven piles of the bridge. At the bottom of the pool were the big trout. Nick did not see them at first. Then he saw them at the bottom of the pool, big trout looking to hold themselves on the gravel bottom in a varying mist of gravel and sand, raised in spurts by the current.

Nick looked down into the pool from the bridge. It was a hot day. A kingfisher flew up the stream. It was a long time since Nick had looked into a stream and seen trout. They were very satisfactory. As the shadow of the kingfisher moved up the stream, a big trout shot upstream in a long angle, only his shadow marking the angle, then lost his shadow as he came through the surface of the water, caught the sun, and then, as he went back into the stream under the surface, his shadow seemed to float down the stream with the current, unresisting, to his post under the bridge where he tightened facing up into the current.

Nick's heart tightened as the trout moved. He felt all the old feeling.

He turned and looked down the stream. It stretched away, pebbly-bottomed with shallows and big boulders and a deep pool as it curved away around the foot of a bluff.

Nick walked back up the ties to where his pack lay in the cinders beside the railway track. He was happy. He adjusted the pack harness around the bundle, pulling straps tight, slung the pack on his back, got his arms through the shoulder straps and took some of the pull off his shoulders by leaning his forehead against the wide band of the tump-line. Still, it was too heavy. It was much too heavy. He had his leather rod-case in his hand and leaning forward to keep the weight of the pack high on his shoulders he walked along the road that paralleled the railway track, leaving the burned town behind in the heat, and then turned off around a hill with a high, fire-scarred hill on either side onto a road that went back into the country. He walked along the road feeling the ache from the pull of the heavy pack. The road climbed steadily. It was hard work walking up-hill. His muscles ached and the day was hot, but Nick felt happy. He felt he had left everything behind, the need for thinking, the need to write, other needs. It was all back of him.

From the time he had gotten down off the train and the baggage man had thrown his pack out of the open car door things had been different. Seney was burned, the country was burned over and changed, but it did not matter. It could not all be burned. He knew that. He hiked along the road, sweating in the sun, climbing to cross the range of hills that separated the railway from the pine plains.

The road ran on, dipping occasionally, but always climbing. Nick went on up. Finally the road after going parallel to the burnt hillside reached the top. Nick leaned back against a stump and slipped out of the pack harness. Ahead of him, as far as he could see, was the pine plain. The burned country stopped off at the left with the range of hills. On ahead islands of dark pine trees rose out of the plain. Far off to the left was the line of the river. Nick followed it with his eye and caught glints of the water in the sun.

There was nothing but the pine plain ahead of him, until the far blue hills that marked the Lake Superior height of land. He could hardly see them, faint and far away in the heat-light over the plain. If he looked too steadily they were gone. But if he only half-looked they were there, the far-off hills of the height of land.

Nick sat down against the charred stump and smoked a cigarette. His pack balanced on the top of the stump, harness holding ready, a hollow molded in it from his back. Nick sat smoking, looking out over the country. He did not need to get his map out. He knew where he was from the position of the river.

As he smoked, his legs stretched out in front of him, he noticed a grasshopper walk along the ground and up onto his woolen sock. The grasshopper was black. As he had walked along the road, climbing, he had started many grasshoppers from the dust. They were all black. They were not the big grasshoppers with yellow and black or red and black wings whirring out from their black wing sheathing as they fly up. These were just ordinary hoppers, but all a sooty black in color. Nick had wondered about them as he walked, without really thinking about them. Now, as he watched the black hopper that was nibbling at the wool of his sock with its fourway lip, he realized that they had all turned black from living in the burned-over land. He realized that the fire must have come the year before, but the grasshoppers were all black now. He wondered how long they would stay that way.

Carefully he reached his hand down and took hold of the hopper by the wings. He turned him up, all his legs walking in the air, and looked at his jointed belly. Yes, it was black too, iridescent where the back and head were dusty.

"Go on, hopper," Nick said, speaking out loud for the first time. "Fly away somewhere."

He tossed the grasshopper up into the air and watched him sail away to a charcoal stump across the road.

Nick stood up. He leaned his back against the weight of his pack where it rested upright on the stump and got his arms through the shoulder straps. He stood with the pack on his back on the brow of the hill looking out across the country, toward the distant river and then struck down the hillside away from the road. Underfoot the ground was good walking. Two hundred yards down the hillside the fire line stopped. Then it was sweet fern, growing ankle high, to walk through, and clumps of jack pines; a long undulating country with frequent rises and descents, sandy underfoot and the country alive again.

Nick kept his direction by the sun. He knew where he wanted to strike the river and he kept on through the pine plain, mounting small rises to see other rises ahead of him and sometimes from the top of a rise a great solid island of pines off to his right or his left. He broke off some sprigs of the heathery sweet fern, and put them under his pack straps. The chafing crushed it and he smelled it as he walked.

He was tired and very hot, walking across the uneven, shadeless pine plain. At any time he knew he could strike the river by turning off to his left. It could not be more than a mile away. But he kept on toward the north to hit the river as far upstream as he could go in one day's walking.

For some time as he walked Nick had been in sight of one of the big islands of pine standing out above the rolling high ground he was crossing. He dipped down and then as he came slowly up to the crest of the bridge he turned and made toward the pine trees.

There was no underbrush in the island of pine trees. The trunks of the trees went straight up or slanted toward each other. The trunks were straight and brown without branches. The branches were high above. Some interlocked to make a solid shadow on the brown forest floor. Around the grove of trees was a bare space. It was brown and soft underfoot as Nick walked on it. This was the over-lapping of the pine needle floor, extending out beyond the width of the high branches. The trees had grown tall and the branches moved high, leaving in the sun this bare space they had once covered with shadow. Sharp at the edge of this extension of the forest floor commenced the sweet fern.

Nick slipped off his pack and lay down in the shade. He lay on his back and looked up into the pine trees. His neck and back and the small of his back rested as he stretched. The earth felt good against his back. He looked up at the sky, through the branches, and then shut his eyes. He opened them and looked up again. There was a wind high up in the branches. He shut his eyes again and went to sleep.

Nick woke stiff and cramped. The sun was nearly down. His pack was heavy and the straps painful as he lifted it on. He leaned over with the pack on and picked up the leather rod-case and started out from the pine trees across the sweet fern swale, toward the river. He knew it could not be more than a mile.

He came down a hillside covered with stumps into a meadow. At the edge of the meadow flowed the river. Nick was glad to get to the river. He walked upstream through the meadow. His trousers were soaked with the dew as he walked. After the hot day, the dew had come quickly and heavily. The river made no sound. It was too fast and smooth. At the edge of the meadow, before he mounted to a piece of high ground to make camp, Nick looked down the river at the trout rising. They were rising to insects come from the swamp on the other side of the stream when the sun went down. The trout jumped out of water to take them. While Nick walked through the little stretch of meadow alongside the stream, trout had jumped high out of water. Now as he looked down the river, the insects must be settling on the surface, for the trout were feeding steadily all down the stream. As far down the long stretch as he could see, the trout were rising, making circles all down the surface of the water, as though it were starting to rain.

The ground rose, wooded and sandy, to overlook the meadow, the stretch of river and the swamp. Nick dropped his pack and rod-case and looked for a level piece of ground. He was very hungry and he wanted to make his camp before he cooked. Between two jack pines, the ground was quite level. He took the ax out of the pack and chopped out two projecting roots. That leveled a piece of ground large enough to sleep on. He smoothed out the sandy soil with his hands and pulled all the sweet fern bushes by their roots. His hands smelled good from the sweet fern. He smoothed the uprooted earth. He did not want anything making lumps under the blankets. One he folded double, next to the ground. The other two he spread on top.

With the ax he slit off a bright slab of pine from one of the stumps and split it into pegs for the tent. He wanted them long and solid to hold in the ground. With the tent unpacked and spread on the ground, the pack, leaning against a jackpine, looked much smaller. Nick tied the rope that served the tent for a ridge-pole to the trunk of one of the pine trees and pulled the tent up off the ground with the other end of the rope and tied it to the other pine. The tent hung on the rope like a canvas blanket on a clothesline. Nick poked a pole he had cut up under the back peak of the canvas and then made it a tent by pegging out the sides. He pegged the sides out taut and drove the pegs deep, hitting them down into the ground with the flat of the ax until the rope loops were buried and the canvas was drum tight.

Across the open mouth of the tent Nick fixed cheesecloth to keep out mosquitoes. He crawled inside under the mosquito bar with various things from the pack to put at the head of the bed under the slant of the canvas. Inside the tent the light came through the brown canvas. It smelled pleasantly of canvas. Already there was something mysterious and homelike. Nick was happy as he crawled inside the tent. He had not been unhappy all day. This was different though. Now things were done. There had been this to do. Now it was done. It had been a hard trip. He was very tired. That was done. He had made his camp. He was settled. Nothing could touch him. It was a good place to camp. He was there, in the good place. He was in his home where he had made it. Now he was hungry.

He came out, crawling under the cheesecloth. It was quite dark outside. It was lighter in the tent.

Nick went over to the pack and found, with his fingers, a long nail in a paper sack of nails, in the bottom of the pack. He drove it into the pine tree, holding it close and hitting it gently with the flat of the ax. He hung the pack up on the nail. All his supplies were in the pack. They were off the ground and sheltered now.

Nick was hungry. He did not believe he had ever been hungrier. He opened and emptied a can of pork and beans and a can of spaghetti into the frying pan.

"I've got a right to eat this kind of stuff, if I'm willing to carry it," Nick said. His voice sounded strange in the darkening woods. He did not speak again.

He started a fire with some chunks of pine he got with the ax from a stump. Over the fire he stuck a wire grill, pushing the four legs down into the ground with his boot. Nick put the frying pan on the grill over the flames. He was hungrier. The beans and spaghetti warmed. Nick stirred them and mixed them together. They began to bubble, making little bubbles that rose with difficulty to the surface. There was a good smell. Nick got out a bottle of tomato catchup and cut four slices of bread. The little bubbles were coming faster now. Nick sat down beside the fire and lifted the frying pan off. He poured about half the contents out into the tin plate. It spread slowly on the plate. Nick knew it was too hot. He poured on some tomato catchup. He knew the beans and spaghetti were still too hot. He looked at the fire, then at the tent, he was not going to spoil it all by burning his tongue. For years he had never enjoyed fried bananas because he had never been able to wait for them to cool. His tongue was very sensitive. He was very hungry. Across the river in the swamp, in the almost dark, he saw a mist rising. He looked at the tent once more. All right. He took a full spoonful from the plate.

"Chrise," Nick said, "Geezus Chrise," he said happily.

He ate the whole plateful before he remembered the bread. Nick finished the second plateful with the bread, mopping the plate shiny. He had not eaten since a cup of coffee and a ham sandwich in the station restaurant at St. Ignace. It had been a very fine experience. He had been that hungry before, but had not been able to satisfy it. He could have made camp hours before if he had wanted to. There were plenty of good places to camp on the river. But this was good.

Nick tucked two big chips of pine under the grill. The fire flared up. He had forgotten to get water for the coffee. Out of the pack he got a folding canvas bucket and walked down the hill, across the edge of the meadow, to the stream. The other bank was in the white mist. The grass was wet and cold as he knelt on the bank and dipped the canvas bucket into the stream. It bellied and pulled hard in the current. The water was ice cold. Nick rinsed the bucket and carried it full up to the camp. Up away from the stream it was not so cold.

Nick drove another big nail and hung up the bucket full of water. He dipped the coffee pot half full, put some more chips under the grill onto the fire and put the pot on. He could not remember which way he made coffee. He could remember an argument about it with Hopkins, but not which side he had taken. He decided to bring it to a boil. He remembered now that was Hopkins's way. He had once argued about everything with Hopkins. While he waited for the coffee to boil, he opened a small can of apricots. He liked to open cans. He emptied the can of apricots out into a tin cup. While he watched the coffee on the fire, he drank the juice syrup of the apricots, carefully at first to keep from spilling, then meditatively, sucking the apricots down. They were better than fresh apricots.

The coffee boiled as he watched. The lid came up and coffee and grounds ran down the side of the pot. Nick took it off the grill. It was a triumph for Hopkins. He put sugar in the empty apricot cup and poured some of the coffee out to cool. It was too hot to pour and he used his hat to hold the handle of the coffee pot. He would not let it steep in the pot at all. Not the first cup. It should be straight Hopkins all the way. Hop deserved that. He was a very serious coffee drinker. He was the most serious man Nick had ever known. Not heavy, serious. That was a long time ago. Hopkins spoke without moving his lips. He had played polo. He made millions of dollars in Texas. He had borrowed carfare to go to Chicago, when the wire came that his first big well had come in. He could have wired for money. That would have been too slow. They called Hop's girl the Blonde Venus. Hop did not mind because she was not his real girl. Hopkins said very confidently that none of them would make fun of his real girl. He was right. Hopkins went away when the telegram came. That was on the Black River. It took eight days for the telegram to reach him. Hopkins gave away his .22 caliber Colt automatic pistol to Nick. He gave his camera to Bill. It was to remember him always by. They were all going fishing again next summer. The Hop Head was rich. He would get a yacht and they would all cruise along the north shore of Lake Superior. He was excited but serious. They said good-bye and all felt bad. It broke up the trip. They never saw Hopkins again. That was a long time ago on the Black River.

Nick drank the coffee, the coffee according to Hopkins. The coffee was bitter. Nick laughed. It made a good ending to the story. His mind was starting to work. He knew he could choke it because he was tired enough. He spilled the coffee out of the pot and shook the grounds loose into the fire. He lit a cigarette and went inside the tent. He took off his shoes and trousers, sitting on the blankets, rolled the shoes up inside the trousers for a pillow and got in between the blankets.

Out through the front of the tent he watched the glow of the fire, when the night wind blew on it. It was a quiet night. The swamp was perfectly quiet. Nick stretched under the blanket comfortably. A mosquito hummed close to his ear. Nick sat up and lit a match. The mosquito was on the canvas, over his head. Nick moved the match quickly up to it. The mosquito made a satisfactory hiss in the flame. The match went out. Nick lay down again under the blanket. He turned on his side and shut his eyes. He was sleepy. He felt sleep coming. He curled up under the blanket and went to sleep.

PART II

In the morning the sun was up and the tent was starting to get hot. Nick crawled out under the mosquito netting stretched across the mouth of the tent, to look at the morning. The grass was wet on his hands as he came out. He held his trousers and his shoes in his hands. The sun was just up over the hill. There was the meadow, the river and the swamp. There were birch trees in the green of the swamp on the other side of the river.

The river was clear and smoothly fast in the early morning. Down about two hundred yards were three logs all the way across the stream. They made the water smooth and deep above them. As Nick watched, a mink crossed the river on the logs and went into the swamp. Nick was excited. He was excited by the early morning and the river. He was really too hurried to eat breakfast, but he knew he must. He built a little fire and put on the coffee pot.

While the water was heating in the pot he took an empty bottle and went down over the edge of the high ground to the meadow. The meadow was wet with dew and Nick wanted to catch grasshoppers for bait before the sun dried the grass. He found plenty of good grasshoppers. They were at the base of the grass stems. Sometimes they clung to a grass stem. They were cold and wet with the dew, and could not jump until the sun warmed them. Nick picked them up, taking only the medium-sized brown ones, and put them into the bottle. He turned over a log and just under the shelter of the edge were several hundred hoppers. It was a grasshopper lodging house. Nick put about fifty of the medium browns into the bottle. While he was picking up the hoppers the others warmed in the sun and commenced to hop away. They flew when they hopped. At first they made one flight and stayed stiff when they landed, as though they were dead.

Nick knew that by the time he was through with breakfast they would be as lively as ever. Without dew in the grass it would take him all day to catch a bottle full of good grasshoppers and he would have to crush many of them, slamming at them with his hat. He washed his hands at the stream. He was excited to be near it. Then he walked up to the tent. The hoppers were already jumping stiffly in the grass. In the bottle, warmed by the sun, they were jumping in a mass. Nick put in a pine stick as a cork. It plugged the mouth of the bottle enough, so the hoppers could not get out and left plenty of air passage.

He had rolled the log back and knew he could get grasshoppers there every morning.

Nick laid the bottle full of jumping grasshoppers against a pine trunk. Rapidly he mixed some buckwheat flour with water and stirred it smooth, one cup of flour, one cup of water. He put a handful of coffee in the pot and dipped a lump of grease out of a can and slid it sputtering across the hot skillet. On the smoking skillet he poured smoothly the buckwheat batter. It spread like lava, the grease spitting sharply. Around the edges the buckwheat cake began to firm, then brown, then crisp. The surface was bubbling slowly to porousness. Nick pushed under the browned under surface with a fresh pine chip. He shook the skillet sideways and the cake was loose on the surface. I won't try and flop it, he thought. He slid the chip of clean wood all the way under the cake, and flopped it over onto its face. It sputtered in the pan.

When it was cooked Nick regreased the skillet. He used all the batter. It made another big flapjack and one smaller one.

Nick ate a big flapjack and a smaller one, covered with apple butter. He put apple butter on the third cake, folded it over twice, wrapped it in oiled paper and put it in his shirt pocket. He put the apple butter jar back in the pack and cut bread for two sandwiches.

In the pack he found a big onion. He sliced it in two and peeled the silky outer skin. Then he cut one half into slices and made onion sandwiches. He wrapped them in oiled paper and buttoned them in the other pocket of his khaki shirt. He turned the skillet upside down on the grill, drank the coffee, sweetened and yellow brown with the condensed milk in it, and tidied up the camp. It was a good camp.

Nick took his fly rod out of the leather rod-case, jointed it, and shoved the rod-case back into the tent. He put on the reel and threaded the line through the guides. He had to hold it from hand to hand, as he threaded it, or it would slip back through its own weight. It was a heavy, double tapered fly line. Nick had paid eight dollars for it a long time ago. It was made heavy to lift back in the air and come forward flat and heavy and straight to make it possible to cast a fly which has no weight. Nick opened the aluminum leader box. The leaders were coiled between the damp flannel pads. Nick had wet the pads at the water cooler on the train up to St. Ignace. In the damp pads the gut leaders had softened and Nick unrolled one and tied it by a loop at the end to the heavy fly line. He fastened a hook on the end of the leader. It was a small hook; very thin and springy.

Nick took it from his hook book, sitting with the rod across his lap. He tested the knot and the spring of the rod by pulling the line taut. It was a good feeling. He was careful not to let the hook bite into his finger.

He started down to the stream, holding his rod, the bottle of grasshoppers hung from his neck by a thong tied in half hitches around the neck of the bottle. His landing net hung by a hook from his belt. Over his shoulder was a long flour sack tied at each corner into an ear. The cord went over his shoulder. The sack flapped against his legs.

Nick felt awkward and professionally happy with all his equipment hanging from him. The grasshopper bottle swung against his chest. In his shirt the breast pockets bulged against him with the lunch and his fly book.

He stepped into the stream. It was a shock. His trousers clung tight to his legs. His shoes felt the gravel. The water was a rising cold shock.

Rushing, the current sucked against his legs. Where he stepped in, the water was over his knees. He waded with the current. The gravel slid under his shoes. He looked down at the swirl of water below each leg and tipped up the bottle to get a grasshopper.

The first grasshopper gave a jump in the neck of the bottle and went out into the water. He was sucked under in the whirl by Nick's right leg and came to the surface a little way down stream. He floated rapidly, kicking. In a quick circle, breaking the smooth surface of the water, he disappeared. A trout had taken him.

Another hopper poked his face out of the bottle. His antennae wavered. He was getting his front legs out of the bottle to jump. Nick took him by the head and held him while he threaded the slim hook under his chin, down through his thorax and into the last segments of his abdomen. The grasshopper took hold of the hook with his front feet, spitting tobacco juice on it. Nick dropped him into the water.

Holding the rod in his right hand he let out line against the pull of the grasshopper in the current. He stripped off line from the reel with his left hand and let it run free. He could see the hopper in the little waves of the current. It went out of sight.

There was a tug on the line. Nick pulled against the taut line. It was his first strike. Holding the now living rod across the current, he brought in the line with his left hand. The rod bent in jerks, the trout pumping against the curent. Nick knew it was a small one. He lifted the rod straight up in the air. It bowed with the pull.

He saw the trout in the water jerking with his head and body against the shifting tangent of the line in the stream.

Nick took the line in his left hand and pulled the trout, thumping tiredly against the current, to the surface. His back was mottled the clear, water-over-gravel color, his side flashing in the sun. The rod under his right arm, Nick stooped, dipping his right hand into the current. He held the trout, never still, with his moist right hand, while he unhooked the barb from his mouth, then dropped him back into the stream.

He hung unsteadily in the current, then settled to the bottom beside a stone. Nick reached down his hand to touch him, his arm to the elbow under water. The trout was steady in the moving stream, resting on the gravel, beside a stone. As Nick's fingers touched him, touched his smooth, cool, underwater feeling he was gone, gone in a shadow across the bottom of the stream.

He's all right, Nick thought. He was only tired.

He had wet his hand before he touched the trout, so he would not disturb the delicate mucus that covered him. If a trout was touched with a dry hand, a white fungus attacked the unprotected spot. Years before when he had fished crowded streams, with fly fishermen ahead of him and behind him, Nick had again and again come on dead trout, furry with white fungus, drifted against a rock, or floating belly up in some pool. Nick did not like to fish with other men on the river. Unless they were of your party, they spoiled it.

He wallowed down the stream, above his knees in the current, through the fifty yards of shallow water above the pile of logs that crossed the stream. He did not rebait his hook and held it in his hand as he waded. He was certain he could catch small trout in the shallows, but he did not want them. There would be no big trout in the shallows this time of day.

Now the water deepened up his thighs sharply and coldly. Ahead was the smooth dammed-back flood of water above the logs. The water was smooth and dark; on the left, the lower edge of the meadow; on the right the swamp.

Nick leaned back against the current and took a hopper from the bottle. He threaded the hopper on the hook and spat on him for good luck. Then he pulled several yards of line from the reel and tossed the hopper out ahead onto the fast, dark water. It floated down towards the logs, then the weight of the line pulled the bait under the surface. Nick held the rod in his right hand, letting the line run out through his fingers.

There was a long tug. Nick struck and the rod came alive and dangerous, bent double, the line tightening, coming out of water, tightening, all in a heavy, dangerous, steady pull. Nick felt the moment when the leader would break if the strain increased and let the line go.

The reel ratcheted into a mechanical shriek as the line went out in a rush. Too fast. Nick could not check it, the line rushing out, the reel note rising as the line ran out.

With the core of the reel showing, his heart feeling stopped with the excitement, leaning back against the current that mounted icily his thighs, Nick thumbed the reel hard with his left hand. It was awkward getting his thumb inside the fly reel frame.

As he put on pressure the line tightened into sudden hardness and beyond the logs a huge trout went high out of water. As he jumped, Nick lowered the tip of the rod. But he felt, as he dropped the tip to ease the strain, the moment when the strain was too great; the hardness too tight. Of course, the leader had broken. There was no mistaking the feeling when all spring left the line and it became dry and hard. Then it went slack.

His mouth dry, his heart down, Nick reeled in. He had never seen so big a trout. There was a heaviness, a power not to be held, and then the bulk of him, as he jumped. He looked as broad as a salmon.

Nick's hand was shaky. He reeeled in slowly. The thrill had been too much. He felt, vaguely, a little sick, as though it would be better to sit down.

The leader had broken where the hook was tied to it. Nick took it in his hand. He thought of the trout somewhere on the bottom, holding himself steady over the gravel, far down below the light, under the logs, with the hook in his jaw. Nick knew the trout's teeth would cut through the snell of the hook. The hook would imbed itself in his jaw. He'd bet the trout was angry. Anything that size would be angry. That was a trout. He had been solidly hooked. Solid as a rock. He felt like a rock, too, before he started off. By God, he was a big one. By God, he was the biggest one I ever heard of.

Nick climbed out onto the meadow and stood, water running down his trousers and out of his shoes, his shoes squlchy. He went over and sat on the logs. He did not want to rush his sensations any.

He wriggled his toes in the water, in his shoes, and got out a cigarette from his breast pocket. He lit it and tossed the match into the fast water below the logs. A tiny trout rose at the match, as it swung around in the fast current. Nick laughed. He would finish the cigarette.

He sat on the logs, smoking, drying in the sun, the sun warm on his back, the river shallow ahead entering the woods, curving into the woods, shallows, light glittering, big water-smooth rocks, cedars along the bank and white birches, the logs warm in the sun, smooth to sit on, without bark, gray to the touch; slowly the feeling of disappointment left him. It went away slowly, the feeling of disappointment that came sharply after the thrill that made his shoulders ache. It was all right now. His rod lying out on the logs, Nick tied a new hook on the leader, pulling the gut tight until it grimped into itself in a hard knot.

He baited up, then picked up the rod and walked to the far end of the logs to get into the water, where it was not too deep. Under and beyond the logs was a deep pool. Nick walked around the shallow shelf near the swamp shore until he came out on the shallow bed of the stream.

On the left, where the meadow ended and the woods began, a great elm tree was uprooted. Gone over in a storm, it lay back into the woods, its roots clotted with dirt, grass growing in them, rising a solid bank beside the stream. The river cut to the edge of the uprooted tree. From where Nick stood he could see deep channels, like ruts, cut in the shallow bed of the stream by the flow of the current. Pebbly where he stood and pebbly and full of boulders beyond; where it curved near the tree roots, the bed of the stream was marly and between the ruts of deep water green weed fronds swung in the current.

Nick swung the rod back over his shoulder and forward, and the line, curving forward, laid the grasshopper down on one of the deep channels in the weeds. A trout struck and Nick hooked him.

Holding the rod far out toward the uprooted tree and sloshing backward in the current, Nick worked the trout, plunging, the rod bending alive, out of the danger of the weeds into the open river. Holding the rod, pumping alive against the current, Nick brought the trout in. He rushed, but always came, the spring of the rod yielding to the rushes, sometimes jerking under water, but always bringing him in. Nick eased downstream with the rushes. The rod above his head he led the trout over the net, then lifted.

The trout hung heavy in the net, mottled trout back and silver sides in the meshes. Nick unhooked him; heavy sides, good to hold, big undershot jaw, and slipped him, heaving and big sliding, into the long sack that hung from his shoulders in the water.

Nick spread the mouth of the sack against the current and it filled, heavy with water. He held it up, the bottom in the stream, and the water poured out through the sides. Inside at the bottom was the big trout, alive in the water.

Nick moved downstream. The sack out ahead of him sunk heavy in the water, pulling from his shoulders.

It was getting hot, the sun hot on the back of his neck.

Nick had one good trout. He did not care about getting many trout. Now the stream was shallow and wide. There were trees along both banks. The trees of the left bank made short shadows on the current in the forenoon sun. Nick knew there were trout in each shadow. In the afternoon, after the sun had crossed toward the hills, the trout would be in the cool shadows on the other side of the stream.

The very biggest ones would lie up close to the bank. You could always pick them up there on the Black. When the sun was down they all moved out into the current. Just when the sun made the water blinding in the glare before it went down, you were liable to strike a big trout anywhere in the current. It was almost impossible to fish then, the surface of the water was blinding as a mirror in the sun. Of course, you could fish upstream, but in a stream like the Black, or this, you had to wallow against the current and in a deep place, the water piled up on you. It was no fun to fish upstream with this much current.

Nick moved along through the shallow stretch watching the banks for deep holes. A beech tree grew close beside the river, so that the branches hung down into the water. The stream went back in under the leaves. There were always trout in a place like that.

Nick did not care about fishing that hole. He was sure he would get hooked in the branches.

It looked deep though. He dropped the grasshopper so the current took it under water, back in under the overhanging branch. The line pulled hard and Nick struck. The trout threshed heavily, half out of water in the leaves and branches. The line was caught. Nick pulled hard and the trout was off. He reeled in and holding the hook in his hand, walked down the stream.

Ahead, close to the left bank, was a big log. Nick saw it was hollow; pointing up river the current entered it smoothly, only a little ripple spread each side of the log. The water was deepening. The top of the hollow log was gray and dry. It was partly in the shadow.

Nick took the cork out of the grasshopper bottle and a hopper clung to it. He picked him off, hooked him and tossed him out. He held the rod far out so that the hopper on the water moved into the current flowing into the hollow log. Nick lowered the rod and the hopper floated in. There was a heavy strike. Nick swung the rod against the pull. It felt as though he were hooked into the log itself, except for the live feeling.

He tried to force the fish out into the current. It came, heavily.

The line went slack and Nick thought the trout was gone. Then he saw him, very near, in the current, shaking his head, trying to get the hook out. His mouth was clamped shut. He was fighting the hook in the clear flowing current.

Looping in the line with his left hand, Nick swung the rod to make the line taut and tried to lead the trout toward the net, but he was gone, out of sight, the line pumping. Nick fought him against the current, letting him thump in the water against the spring of the rod. He shifted the rod to his left hand, worked the trout upstream, holding his weight, fighting on the rod, and then let him down into the net. He lifted him clear of the water, a heavy half circle in the net, the net dripping, unhooked him and slid him into the sack.

He spread the mouth of the sack and looked down in at the two big trout alive in the water.

Through the deepening water, Nick waded over to the hollow log. He took the sack off, over his head, the trout flopping as it came out of water, and hung it so the trout were deep in the water. Then he pulled himself up on the log and sat, the water from his trouser and boots running down into the stream. He laid his rod down, moved along to the shady end of the log and took the sandwiches out of his pocket. He dipped the sandwiches in the cold water. The current carried away the crumbs. He ate the sandwiches and dipped his hat full of water to drink, the water running out through his hat just ahead of his drinking.

It was cool in the shade, sitting on the log. He took a cigarette out and struck a match to light it. The match sunk into the gray wood, making a tiny furrow. Nick leaned over the side of the log, found a hard place and lit the match. He sat smoking and watching the river.

Ahead the river narrowed and went into a swamp. The river became smooth and deep and the swamp looked solid with cedar trees, their trunks close together, their branches solid. It would not be possible to walk through a swamp like that. The branches grew so low. You would have to keep almost level with the ground to move at all. You could not crash through the branches. That must be why the animals that lived in swamps were built the way they were, Nick thought.

He wished he had brought something to read. He felt like reading. He did not feel like going on into the swamp. He looked down the river. A big cedar slanted all the way across the stream. Beyond that the river went into the swamp.

Nick did not want to go in there now. He felt a reaction against deep wading with the water deepening up under his armpits, to hook big trout in places impossible to land them. In the swamp the banks were bare, the big cedars came together overhead, the sun did not come through, except in patches; in the fast deep water, in the half light, the fishing would be tragic. In the swamp fishing was a tragic adventure. Nick did not want it. He did not want to go down the stream any further today.

He took out his knife, opened it and stuck it in the log. Then he pulled up the sack, reached into it and brought out one of the trout. Holding him near the tail, hard to hold, alive, in his hand, he whacked him against the log. The trout quivered, rigid. Nick laid him on the log in the shade and broke the neck of the other fish the same way. He laid them side by side on the log. They were fine trout.

Nick cleaned them, slitting them from the vent to the tip of the jaw. All the insides and the gills and tongue came out in one piece. They were both males; long gray-white strips of milt, smooth and clean. All the insides clean and compact, coming out all together. Nick tossed the offal ashore for the minks to find.

He washed the trout in the stream. When he held them back up in the water they looked like live fish. Their color was not gone yet. He washed his hands and dried them on the log. Then he laid the trout on the sack spread out on the log, rolled them up in it, tied the bundle and put it in the landing net. His knife was still standing, blade stuck in the log. He cleaned it on the wood and put it in his pocket.

Nick stood up on the log, holding his rod, the landing net hanging heavy, then stepped into the water and splashed ashore. He climbed the bank and cut up into the woods, toward the high ground. He was going back to camp. He looked back. The river just showed through the trees. There were plenty of days coming when he could fish the swamp.

1924   *1925*

from A Moveable Feast

MISS STEIN INSTRUCTS[1]

When we came back to Paris it was clear and cold and lovely. The city had accommodated itself to winter, there was good wood for sale at the wood and coal place across our street, and there were braziers outside of many of the good cafés so that you could keep warm on the terraces. Our own apartment was warm and cheerful. We burned *boulets*[2] which were molded, egg-shaped lumps of coal dust, on the wood fire, and on the streets the winter light was beautiful. Now you were accustomed to see the bare trees against the sky and you walked on the fresh-washed gravel paths through the Luxembourg gardens in the clear sharp wind. The trees were sculpture without their leaves when you were reconciled to them, and the winter winds blew across the surfaces of the ponds and the fountains blew in the bright light. All the distances were short now since we had been in the mountains.

Because of the change in altitude I did not notice the grade of the hills except with pleasure, and the climb up to the top floor of the hotel where I worked, in a room that looked across all the roofs and the chimneys of the high hill of the quarter, was a pleasure. The fireplace drew well in the room and it was warm and pleasant to work. I brought mandarines and roasted chestnuts to the room in paper packets and peeled and ate the small tangerine-like oranges and threw their skins and spat their seeds in the fire when I ate them and roasted chestnuts when I was hungry. I was always hungry with the walking and the cold and the working. Up in the room I had a bottle of kirsch[3] that we had brought back from the mountains and I took a drink of kirsch when I would get toward the end of a story or toward the end of the day's work. When I was through working for the day I put away the notebook, or the paper, in the drawer of the table and put any mandarines that were left in my pocket. They would freeze if they were left in the room at night.

It was wonderful to walk down the long flights of stairs knowing that I'd had good luck working. I always worked until I had something done and I always stopped when I knew what was going to happen next. That way I could be sure of going on the next day. But sometimes when I was starting a new story and I could not get it going, I would sit in front of the fire and squeeze the peel of the little oranges into the edge of the flame and watch the sputter of blue that they made. I would stand and look out over the roofs of Paris and think, "Do not worry. You have always written before and you will write now. All you have to do is write one true sentence. Write the truest sentence that you know." So finally I would write one true sentence, and then

---

[1]See Gertrude Stein's impressions of Hemingway in the excerpts from her *Autobiography of Alice B. Toklas* in the section entitled "Autobiography: Modes of Remembering."

[2]Literally, "cannon balls" (French).
[3]Unaged brandy made from fermented cherry mash.

go on from there. It was easy then because there was always one true sentence that I knew or had seen or had heard someone say. If I started to write elaborately, or like someone introducing or presenting something, I found that I could cut that scroll-work or ornament out and throw it away and start with the first true simple declarative sentence I had written. Up in that room I decided that I would write one story about each thing that I knew about. I was trying to do this all the time I was writing, and it was good and severe discipline.

It was in that room too that I learned not to think about anything that I was writing from the time I stopped writing until I started again the next day. That way my subconscious would be working on it and at the same time I would be listening to other people and noticing everything, I hoped; learning, I hoped; and I would read so that I would not think about my work and make myself impotent to do it. Going down the stairs when I had worked well, and that needed luck as well as discipline, was a wonderful feeling and I was free then to walk anywhere in Paris.

If I walked down by different streets to the Jardin du Luxembourg[4] in the afternoon I could walk through the gardens and then go to the Musée du Luxembourg where the great paintings were that have now mostly been transferred to the Louvre and the Jeu de Paume.[5] I went there nearly every day for the Cézannes and to see the Manets and the Monets[6] and the other Impressionists that I had first come to know about in the Art Institute in Chicago.[7] I was learning something from the painting of Cézanne that made writing simple true sentences far from enough to make the stories have the dimensions that I was trying to put in them. I was learning very much from him but I was not articulate enough to explain it to anyone. Besides it was a secret. But if the light was gone in the Luxembourg I would walk up through the gardens and stop in at the studio apartment where Gertrude Stein lived at 27 rue de Fleurus.

My wife and I had called on Miss Stein, and she and the friend who lived with her had been very cordial and friendly and we had loved the big studio with the great paintings.[8] It was like one of the best rooms in the finest museum except there was a big fireplace and it was warm and comfortable and they gave you good things to eat and tea and natural distilled liqueurs made from purple plums, yellow plums or wild raspberries. These were fragrant, colorless alcohols served from cut-glass carafes in small glasses and whether they were *quetsche, mirabelle* or *framboise*[9] they all tasted like the fruits they came from, converted into a controlled fire on your tongue that warmed you and loosened it.

Miss Stein was very big but not tall and was heavily built like a peasant woman. She had beautiful eyes and a strong German-Jewish face that also could have been Friulano[10] and she reminded me of a northern Italian peasant woman with her clothes, her mobile face and her lovely, thick, alive immigrant hair which she wore put up in the same way she had probably worn it in college. She talked all the time and at first it was about people and places.

Her companion had a very pleasant voice, was small, very dark, with her hair cut like Joan of Arc in the Boutet de Monvel illustrations[11] and had a very hooked nose.

---

[4] The famed Luxembourg Gardens in Paris on the left bank (the student or bohemian quarter).

[5] The Louvre Palace houses one of the greatest art collections in the world; the Jeu de Paume was famous for its collection of Impressionist and Post-Impressionist paintings, which has now been moved to the new Musée D'Orsay.

[6] The French painters Paul Cézanne (1839–1906), Édouard Manet (1832–1883), and Claude Monet (1840–1926) all were associated with Impressionism, which attempted to catch the fleeting impression by rendering the play of light on the surface of objects. Cézanne soon broke away to become the leader of Post-Impressionism and anticipated cubism by his treatment of Nature "through the cylinder, the sphere, the cone."

[7] The Art Institute of Chicago was one of the first American museums to obtain and display a very rich collection of the French Impressionists.

[8] Gertrude Stein (1874–1946) and her brother Leo had built up a fine collection of modern French art from the time they arrived in France shortly after the turn of the century. At the time of Hemingway's visit, she no longer lived with her brother but, instead, with Alice B. Toklas.

[9] "Alsatian plum, yellow plum, raspberry" (French).

[10] Someone from the Friuli (northeast) region of Italy.

[11] Louis Maurice Boutet de Monvel (1851–1913), French painter and illustrator known for his illustrations of children's books, including *Jeanne d'Arc*.

She was working on a piece of needlepoint when we first met them and she worked on this and saw to the food and drink and talked to my wife. She made one conversation and listened to two and often interrupted the one she was not making. Afterwards she explained to me that she always talked to the wives. The wives, my wife and I felt, were tolerated. But we liked Miss Stein and her friend, although the friend was frightening. The paintings and the cakes and the *eau-de-vie*[12] were truly wonderful. They seemed to like us too and treated us as though we were very good, well mannered and promising children and I felt that they forgave us for being in love and being married — time would fix that — and when my wife invited them to tea, they accepted.

When they came to our flat they seemed to like us even more; but perhaps that was because the place was so small and we were much closer together. Miss Stein sat on the bed that was on the floor and asked to see the stories I had written and she said that she liked them except one called "Up in Michigan."

"It's good," she said. "That's not the question at all. But it is *inaccrochable*.[13] That means it is like a picture that a painter paints and then he cannot hang it when he has a show and nobody will buy it because they cannot hang it either."

"But what if it is not dirty but it is only that you are trying to use words that people would actually use? That are the only words that can make the story come true and that you must use them? You have to use them."

"But you don't get the point at all," she said. "You mustn't write anything that is *inaccrochable*. There is no point in it. It's wrong and it's silly."

She herself wanted to be published in the *Atlantic Monthly*, she told me, and she would be. She told me that I was not a good enough writer to be published there or in *The Saturday Evening Post* but that I might be some new sort of writer in my own way but the first thing to remember was not to write stories that were *inaccrochable*. I did not argue about this nor try to explain again what I was trying to do about conversation. That was my own business and it was much more interesting to listen. That afternoon she told us, too, how to buy pictures.

"You can either buy clothes or buy pictures," she said. "It's that simple. No one who is not very rich can do both. Pay no attention to your clothes and no attention at all to the mode, and buy your clothes for comfort and durability, and you will have the clothes money to buy pictures."

"But even if I never bought any more clothing ever," I said, "I wouldn't have enough money to buy the Picassos[14] that I want."

"No. He's out of your range. You have to buy the people of your own age — of your own military service group. You'll know them. You'll meet them around the quarter. There are always good new serious painters. But it's not you buying clothes so much. It's your wife always. It's women's clothes that are expensive."

I saw my wife trying not to look at the strange, steerage clothes that Miss Stein wore and she was successful. When they left we were still popular, I thought, and we were asked to come again to 27 rue de Fleurus.

It was later on that I was asked to come to the studio any time after five in the winter time. I had met Miss Stein in the Luxembourg. I cannot remember whether she was walking her dog or not, nor whether she had a dog then. I know that I was walking myself, since we could not afford a dog nor even a cat then, and the only cats I knew were in the cafés or small restaurants or the great cats that I admired in the concierges' windows. Later I often met Miss Stein with her dog in the Luxembourg gardens; but I think this time was before she had one.

12"Brandy" (French).
13"Un-hangable" (French).
14Pablo Picasso (1881–1973), Spanish painter and sculptor who lived in France and who was a friend of, and had painted, Gertrude Stein.

But I accepted her invitation, dog or no dog, and had taken to stopping in at the studio, and she always gave me the natural *eau-de-vie*, insisting on my refilling my glass, and I looked at the pictures and we talked. The pictures were exciting and the talk was very good. She talked, mostly, and she told me about modern pictures and about painters—more about them as people than as painters—and she talked about her work. She showed me the many volumes of manuscript that she had written and that her companion typed each day. Writing every day made her happy, but as I got to know her better I found that for her to keep happy it was necessary that this steady daily output, which varied with her energy, be published and that she receive recognition.

This had not become an acute situation when I first knew her, since she had published three stories that were intelligible to anyone. One of these stories, "Melanctha,"[15] was very good and good samples of her experimental writing had been published in book form and had been well praised by critics who had met her or known her. She had such a personality that when she wished to win anyone over to her side she would not be resisted, and critics who met her and saw her pictures took on trust writing of hers that they could not understand because of their enthusiasm for her as a person, and because of their confidence in her judgment. She had also discovered many truths about rhythms and the uses of words in repetition that were valid and valuable and she talked well about them.

But she disliked the drudgery of revision and the obligation to make her writing intelligible, although she needed to have publication and official acceptance, especially for the unbelievably long book called *The Making of Americans*.[16]

This book began magnificently, went on very well for a long way with great stretches of great brilliance and then went on endlessly in repetitions that a more conscientious and less lazy writer would have put in the waste basket. I came to know it very well as I got—forced, perhaps would be the word—Ford Madox Ford[17] to publish it in *The Transatlantic Review* serially, knowing that it would outrun the life of the review. For publication in the review I had to read all of Miss Stein's proof for her as this was a work which gave her no happiness.

On this cold afternoon when I had come past the concierge's lodge and the cold courtyard to the warmth of the studio, all that was years ahead. On this day Miss Stein was instructing me about sex. By that time we liked each other very much and I had already learned that everything I did not understand probably had something to it. Miss Stein thought that I was too uneducated about sex and I must admit that I had certain prejudices against homosexuality since I knew its more primitive aspects. I knew it was why you carried a knife and would use it when you were in the company of tramps when you were a boy in the days when wolves was not a slang term for men obsessed by the pursuit of women. I knew many *inaccrochable* terms and phrases from Kansas City days and the mores of different parts of that city, Chicago and the lake boats. Under questioning I tried to tell Miss Stein that when you were a boy and moved in the company of men, you had to be prepared to kill a man, know how to do it and really know that you would do it in order not to be interfered with. That term was *accrochable*.[18] If you knew you would kill, other people sensed it very quickly and you were let alone; but there were certain situations you could not allow yourself to be forced into or trapped into. I could have expressed myself more vividly by using an *inaccrochable* phrase that wolves used on the lake boats, "Oh gash[19] may be fine but one eye for mine." But I was always careful of my language with Miss Stein even when true phrases might have clarified or better expressed a prejudice.

[15]One of the stories in *Three Lives*, published in 1909.
[16]Published as a book in 1925.
[17]English novelist (1873–1939) and, in the mid-1920s, editor of one of the fugitive little magazines, *The Transatlantic Review*.
[18]"Hangable" (French). I.e., the offense is such as to render the perpetrator killable.
[19]Slang (vulgar) for vagina, or woman as sex object.

"Yes, yes, Hemingway," she said. "But you were living in a milieu of criminals and perverts."

I did not want to argue that, although I thought that I had lived in a world as it was and there were all kinds of people in it and I tried to understand them, although some of them I could not like and some I still hated.

"But what about the old man with beautiful manners and a great name who came to the hospital in Italy and brought me a bottle of Marsala or Campari[20] and behaved perfectly, and then one day I would have to tell the nurse never to let that man into the room again?" I asked.

"Those people are sick and cannot help themselves and you should pity them."

"Should I pity so and so?" I asked. I gave his name but he delights so in giving it himself that I feel there is no need to give it for him.

"No. He's vicious. He's a corrupter and he's truly vicious."

"But he's supposed to be a good writer."

"He's not," she said. "He's just a showman and he corrupts for the pleasure of corruption and he leads people into other vicious practices as well. Drugs, for example."

"And in Milan the man I'm to pity was not trying to corrupt me?"

"Don't be silly. How could he hope to corrupt you? Do you corrupt a boy like you, who drinks alcohol, with a bottle of Marsala? No, he was a pitiful old man who could not help what he was doing. He was sick and he could not help it and you should pity him."

"I did at the time," I said. "But I was disappointed because he had such beautiful manners."

I took another sip of the *eau-de-vie* and pitied the old man and looked at Picasso's nude of the girl with the basket of flowers. I had not started the conversation and thought it had become a little dangerous. There were almost never any pauses in a conversation with Miss Stein, but we had paused and there was something she wanted to tell me and I filled my glass.

"You know nothing about any of this really, Hemingway," she said. "You've met known criminals and sick people and vicious people. The main thing is that the act male homosexuals commit is ugly and repugnant and afterwards they are disgusted with themselves. They drink and take drugs, to palliate this, but they are disgusted with the act and they are always changing partners and cannot be really happy."

"I see."

"In women it is the opposite. They do nothing that they are disgusted by and nothing that is repulsive and afterwards they are happy and they can lead happy lives together."

"I see," I said. "But what about so and so?"

"She's vicious," Miss Stein said. "She's truly vicious, so she can never be happy except with new people. She corrupts people."

"I understand."

"You're sure you understand?"

There were so many things to understand in those days and I was glad when we talked about something else. The park was closed so I had to walk down along it to the rue de Vaugirard[21] and around the lower end of the park. It was sad when the park was closed and locked and I was sad walking around it instead of through it and in a hurry to get home to the rue Cardinal Lemoine. The day had started out so brightly too. I would have to work hard tomorrow. Work could cure almost anything, I believed then, and I believe now. Then all I had to be cured of, I decided Miss Stein

---

[20]Italian alcoholic beverages: Marsala is a sweet, dark red wine; Campari is a slightly bitter-sweet, dark red liqueur.
[21]A street that borders one side of the Luxembourg Gardens.

felt, was youth and loving my wife. I was not at all sad when I got home to the rue Cardinal Lemoine and told my newly acquired knowledge to my wife. In the night we were happy with our own knowledge we already had and other new knowledge we had acquired in the mountains.

1964

JOHN STEINBECK
(1902–1968)

John Steinbeck once commented on the purpose of writing: "A writer out of loneliness is trying to communicate like a distant star sending signals. He isn't telling or teaching or ordering. Rather he seeks to establish a relationship of meaning, of feeling, of observing. We are lonesome animals. We spend all life trying to be less lonesome. One of our ancient methods is to tell a story begging the listener to say — and to feel — 'Yes, that's the way it is, or at least that's the way I feel it. You're not as alone as you thought.'" Steinbeck's stories are filled with "lonesome animals" trying to break out of their loneliness.

Steinbeck was born in Salinas, California, where he graduated from high school in 1919, already determined to be a writer. From 1920 to 1925, he attended Stanford University off and on, never completing a degree. But he read widely in classic authors, including Dostoevsky, Flaubert, and Thomas Hardy. He was especially fond of Sir Thomas Malory's *Morte d' Arthur*, which he would later render into modern English and leave on his death to be published in 1976 as *The Acts of King Arthur and His Noble Knights*.

Steinbeck went to New York in 1925 in the belief that there he might advance his writing career. He returned to California the following year, disappointed with the big city and its coldness to young beginning writers. He worked at a succession of odd jobs in order to write — as a ranchhand, fruit picker, road construction laborer, seaman, bricklayer. In such jobs he encountered the lowly workers, drifters, and outcasts who would later people his fiction.

His first novel, *Cup of Gold*, published in 1929, was based on the seventeenth-century pirate, Sir Henry Morgan. Appearing just at the beginning of the Great Depression, it attracted little notice in the literary world. *The Pastures of Heaven* (1932), a collection of short stories set in the California milieu Steinbeck knew, fared little better even though it represented a great advance in his work. A second novel, *To a God Unknown* (1933), about a California farmer's obsession with a pagan fertility religion, appeared to be a throwback, in its epic sweep, to the clumsiness of the first book.

In the meantime Steinbeck's stories were beginning to attract attention, especially "The Red Pony" (1933), and "The Murder," designated in 1934 an O. Henry Prize Story. Then, in 1935, came fame, attention, and money with the publication of *Tortilla Flat*, a sequence of stories interconnected like those of Sherwood Anderson's *Winesburg, Ohio*, and portraying the paisanos of the Salinas Valley in their everyday escapades, the whole ironically "framed" by recurring allusions to the legends of King Arthur and his Knights of the Round Table. The film rights brought in several thousand dollars, although the movie would not appear for some years. Steinbeck was for the first time in his career financially independent.

During the next five years Steinbeck produced his finest work. *In Dubious Battle* (1936), a novel involving strikers, strike-breaking, vigilantes, and Reds, created a storm of political controversy. The novelette *Of Mice and Men* (1937) portrayed the tragic end of a feeble-minded farmhand who could not control his own super strength. It was made a selection of the Book-of-the-Month Club and turned into a powerful play by Steinbeck, followed later by a highly successful movie. *The Long Valley* (1938) contained Steinbeck's best short stories, including "The Leader of the People" and "Flight."

Although Steinbeck had reached the height of his fame, his greatest work lay ahead. He had become interested in the plight of migrant farm laborers in California and decided to follow a farm family cross-country on Highway 66 as it moved from the farmlands of Oklahoma, rendered a dust bowl by the terrible drought, to the West Coast, staying in the migrant camps and learning about the laborers' experiences firsthand. The result was *The Grapes of Wrath*, published in 1939. It was an immediate bestseller and endlessly discussed in newspapers and magazines. It won the Pulitzer Prize, the American Booksellers' Award, and earned membership for Steinbeck in the National Institute of Arts and Letters.

The Grapes of Wrath touched the national conscience. The movie, with Henry Fonda and Jane Darwell, appeared in 1940 and carried the story of suffering and endurance to additional millions. The book was frequently compared to Harriet Beecher Stowe's *Uncle Tom's Cabin* in its effect of arousing protest against a social evil. But *The Grapes of Wrath* was clearly more than mere propaganda. As one critic has written, "The great movement of the Okies across the dust bowl and into the Promised Land of California suggests the Biblical analogy of the Chosen People fleeing into Israel." The struggle the novel depicts is "epic," and its "major themes" clear: "in the people are love, brotherhood, integrity; in the exploiting classes fear, power, suspicion."

Never again was Steinbeck to match his achievement of the late 1930s. In 1942, he published what appeared to be a hastily written war novel set in Norway, *The Moon Is Down*, depicting the Norwegian resistance to German occupation. He wrote for the Armed Forces (*Bombs Away: The Story of a Bomber Team*, 1942), and he worked as a journalist for a time in 1943, reporting the war. And in 1944, he published *Cannery Row*, set in Monterey, California — a nostalgic return to earlier material from his past that captured some of the comic spirit of *Tortilla Flat*.

By and large, Steinbeck's major efforts in fiction during these last years failed to measure up to his ambitions. The most important was the saga *East of Eden* (1952), set in the Salinas Valley and patterned after the Biblical story of Cain and Abel. Much of Steinbeck's creative energy was spent in journalistic enterprises, the most memorable being *Travels with Charley: In Search of America* (1962), an account of his leisurely travels with his dog through a large part of the country, especially the small towns.

Steinbeck received the Nobel Prize for Literature in 1962. In his acceptance speech in Sweden, he said: "The ancient commission of the writer has not changed. He is charged with exposing our many grievous faults and failures, with dredging up to light our dark and dangerous dreams, for the purpose of improvement. Furthermore, the writer is delegated to declare and to celebrate man's proven capacity for greatness of heart and spirit — for gallantry in defeat, for courage, compassion, and love."

Steinbeck died in New York in 1968 from the complications of an inoperable heart condition, emphysema, and a stroke. At the widow's request, Henry Fonda read some of Steinbeck's favorite poems at the service. His ashes were later taken to California to be scattered in the Pacific Ocean.

ADDITIONAL READING

The Shorter Novels of John Steinbeck, ed. Joseph Henry Jackson, 1963; *Steinbeck: A Life in Letters*, ed. Elaine Steinbeck and Robert Wallsten, 1976; *Conversations with John Steinbeck*, ed. Thomas Fensch, 1988; *Working Days: The Journals of "The Grapes of Wrath," 1938–1941*, ed. Robert Demott, 1989.

Harry T. Moore, *The Novels of John Steinbeck: A First Critical Study*, 1939, 1968; E. W. Tedlock and C. V. Wicker, eds., *Steinbeck and His Critics*, 1957; Peter Lisca, *The Wide World of John Steinbeck*, 1958; Warren French, *John Steinbeck*, 1961, 1975; Joseph Fontenrose, *John Steinbeck: An Introduction and Interpretation*, 1963; Tetsumaro Hayashi, *John Steinbeck: A Concise Bibliography (1930–1965)*, 1967; Lester J. Marks, *Thematic Design in the Novels of John Steinbeck*, 1969; Richard Astro and Tetsumaro Hayashi, eds., *Steinbeck: The Man and His Work*, 1970; Robert M. Davis, ed., *John Steinbeck: A Collection of Critical Essays*, 1972; Howard Levant, *The Novels of John Steinbeck*, 1974; Peter Lisca, *John Steinbeck: Nature and Myth*, 1978; Thomas Fensch, *Steinbeck and Covici: The Story of a Friendship*, 1979; Thomas Kiernan, *The Intricate Music: A Biography of John Steinbeck*, 1979; Paul McCarthy, *John Steinbeck*, 1980; Jackson J. Benson, *The True Adventures of John Steinbeck, Writer*, 1984; Louis Owen, *John Steinbeck's Re-vision of America*, 1985; John H. Timmerman, *John Steinbeck's Fiction: The Aesthetics of the Road Taken*, 1986; Studs Terkel, "Introduction," *The Grapes of Wrath*, 1989.

TEXT

The Long Valley, 1938.

Flight

About fifteen miles below Monterey, on the wild coast, the Torres family had their farm, a few sloping acres above a cliff that dropped to the brown reefs and to the hissing white waters of the ocean. Behind the farm the stone mountains stood up against the sky. The farm buildings huddled like little clinging aphids on the mountain skirts, crouched low to the ground as though the wind might blow them into the sea. The litle shack, the rattling, rotting barn were grey-bitten with sea salt, beaten by the damp wind until they had taken on the color of the granite hills. Two horses, a red cow and a red calf, half a dozen pigs and a flock of lean, multi-colored chickens stocked the place. A little corn was raised on the sterile slope, and it grew short and thick under the wind, and all the cobs formed on the landward sides of the stalks.

Mama Torres, a lean, dry woman with ancient eyes, had ruled the farm for ten years, ever since her husband tripped over a stone in the field one day and fell full length on a rattlesnake. When one is bitten on the chest there is not much that can be done.

Mama Torres had three children, two undersized black ones of twelve and fourteen, Emilio and Rosy, whom Mama kept fishing on the rocks below the farm when the sea was kind and when the truant officer was in some distant part of Monterey County. And there was Pepé, the tall smiling son of nineteen, a gentle, affectionate boy, but very lazy. Pepé had a tall head, pointed at the top, and from its peak, coarse black hair grew down like a thatch all around. Over his smiling little eyes Mama cut a straight bang so he could see. Pepé had sharp Indian cheek bones and an eagle nose, but his mouth was as sweet and shapely as a girl's mouth, and his chin was fragile and chiseled. He was loose and gangling, all legs and feet and wrists, and he was very lazy.

Mama thought him fine and brave, but she never told him so. She said, "Some lazy cow must have got into thy father's family, else how could I have a son like thee." And she said, "When I carried thee, a sneaking lazy coyote came out of the brush and looked at me one day. That must have made thee so."

Pepé smiled sheepishly and stabbed at the ground with his knife to keep the blade sharp and free from rust. It was his inheritance, that knife, his father's knife. The long heavy blade folded back into the black handle. There was a button on the handle. When Pepé pressed the button, the blade leaped out ready for use. The knife was with Pepé always, for it had been his father's knife.

One sunny morning when the sea below the cliff was glinting and blue and the white surf creamed on the reef, when even the stone mountains looked kindly, Mama Torres called out the door of the shack, "Pepé, I have a labor for thee."

There was no answer. Mama listened. From behind the barn she heard a burst of laughter. She lifted her full long skirt and walked in the direction of the noise.

Pepé was sitting on the ground with his back against a box. His white teeth glistened. On either side of him stood the two black ones, tense and expectant. Fifteen feet away a redwood post was set in the ground. Pepé's right hand lay limply in his lap, and in the palm the big black knife rested. The blade was closed back into the handle. Pepé looked smilingly at the sky.

Suddenly Emilio cried, "Ya!"

Pepé's wrist flicked like the head of a snake. The blade seemed to fly open in midair, and with a thump the point dug into the redwood post, and the black handle quivered. The three burst into excited laughter. Rosy ran to the post and pulled out the knife and brought it back to Pepé. He closed the blade and settled the knife carefully in his listless palm again. He grinned self-consciously at the sky.

"Ya!"

The heavy knife lanced out and sunk into the post again. Mama moved forward like a ship and scattered the play.

"All day you do foolish things with the knife, like a toy-baby," she stormed. "Get up on thy huge feet that eat up shoes. Get up!" She took him by one loose shoulder and hoisted at him. Pepé grinned sheepishly and came half-heartedly to his feet. "Look!" Mama cried. "Big lazy, you must catch the horse and put on him thy father's saddle. You must ride to Monterey. The medicine bottle is empty. There is no salt. Go thou now, Peanut! Catch the horse."

A revolution took place in the relaxed figure of Pepé. "To Monterey, me? Alone? *Sí*, Mama."

She scowled at him. "Do not think, big sheep, that you will buy candy. No, I will give you only enough for the medicine and the salt."

Pepé smiled. "Mama, you will put the hatband on the hat?"

She relented then. "Yes, Pepé. You may wear the hatband."

His voice grew insinuating, "And the green handkerchief, Mama?"

"Yes, if you go quickly and return with no trouble, the silk green handkerchief will go. If you make sure to take off the handkerchief when you eat so no spot may fall on it. . . ."

"*Sí*, Mama. I will be careful. I am a man."

"Thou? A man? Thou art a peanut."

He went into the rickety barn and brought out a rope, and he walked agilely enough up the hill to catch the horse.

When he was ready and mounted before the door, mounted on his father's saddle that was so old that the oaken frame showed through torn leather in many places, then Mama brought out the round black hat with the tooled leather band, and she reached up and knotted the green silk handkerchief about his neck. Pepé's blue denim coat was much darker than his jeans, for it had been washed much less often.

Mama handed up the big medicine bottle and the silver coins. "That for the medicine," she said, "and that for the salt. That for a candle to burn for the papa. That for *dulces*[1] for the little ones. Our friend Mrs. Rodriguez will give you dinner and maybe a bed for the night. When you go to the church say only ten Paternosters and only twenty-five Ave Marias.[2] Oh! I know, big coyote. You would sit there flapping your mouth over Aves all day while you looked at the candles and the holy pictures. That is not good devotion to stare at the pretty things."

The black hat, covering the high pointed head and black thatched hair of Pepé, gave him dignity and age. He sat the rangy horse well. Mama thought how handsome he was, dark and lean and tall. "I would not send thee now alone, thou little one, except for the medicine," she said softly. "It is not good to have no medicine, for who knows when the toothache will come, or the sadness of the stomach. These things are."

"Adios, Mama," Pepé cried. "I will come back soon. You may send me often alone. I am a man."

"Thou art a foolish chicken."

He straightened his shoulders, flipped the reins against the horse's shoulder and rode away. He turned once and saw that they still watched him, Emilio and Rosy and Mama. Pepé grinned with pride and gladness and lifted the tough buckskin horse to a trot.

When he had dropped out of sight over a little dip in the road, Mama turned to the black ones, but she spoke to herself. "He is nearly a man now," she said. "It will be a nice thing to have a man in the house again." Her eyes sharpened on the childen. "Go to the rocks now. The tide is going out. There will be abalones to be found." She put the iron hooks into their hands and saw them down the steep trail to the reefs. She brought the smooth stone *metate* to the doorway and sat grinding her corn to flour and looking occasionally at the road over which Pepé had gone. The noonday came and then the afternoon, when the little ones beat the abalones on a rock to make them tender and Mama patted the tortillas to make them thin. They ate their dinner as the red sun was plunging down toward the ocean. They sat on the door-steps and watched the big white moon come over the mountain tops.

Mama said, "He is now at the house of our friend Mrs. Rodriguez. She will give him nice things to eat and maybe a present."

Emilio said, "Some day I too will ride to Monterey for medicine. Did Pepé come to be a man today?"

Mama said wisely, "A boy gets to be a man when a man is needed. Remember this thing. I have known boys forty years old because there was no need for a man."

Soon afterwards they retired, Mama in her big oak bed on one side of the room, Emilio and Rosy in their boxes full of straw and sheepskins on the other side of the room.

The moon went over the sky and the surf roared on the rocks. The roosters crowed the first call. The surf subsided to a whispering surge against the reef. The moon dropped toward the sea. The roosters crowed again.

The moon was near down to the water when Pepé rode on a winded horse to his home flat. His dog bounced out and circled the horse yelping with pleasure. Pepé slid off the saddle to the ground. The weathered little shack was silver in the moonlight and the square shadow of it was black to the north and east. Against the east the piling mountains were misty with light; their tops melted into the sky.

Pepé walked wearily up the three steps and into the house. It was dark inside. There was a rustle in the corner.

---

[1] "Candy" (Spanish).
[2] Catholic prayers, "Our Father," the Lord's Prayer, and "Hail Mary" (Latin).

Mama cried out from her bed. "Who comes? Pepé, is it thou?"

"*Sí*, Mama."

"Did you get the medicine?"

"*Sí*, Mama."

"Well, go to sleep, then. I thought you would be sleeping at the house of Mrs. Rodriguez." Pepé, stood silently in the dark room. "Why do you stand there, Pepé? Did you drink wine?"

"*Sí*, Mama."

Well, go to bed then and sleep out the wine."

His voice was tired and patient, but very firm. "Light the candle, Mama. I must go away into the mountains."

"What is this, Pepé? You are crazy." Mama struck a sulphur match and held the little blue burr until the flame spread up the stick. She set light to the candle on the floor beside her bed. "Now, Pepé, what is this you say?" She looked anxiously into his face.

He was changed. The fragile quality seemed to have gone from his chin. His mouth was less full than it had been, the lines of the lips were straighter, but in his eyes the greatest change had taken place. There was no laughter in them any more, nor any bashfulness. They were sharp and bright and purposeful.

He told her in a tired monotone, told her everything just as it had happened. A few people came into the kitchen of Mrs. Rodriguez. There was wine to drink. Pepé drank wine. The little quarrel—the man started toward Pepé and then the knife—it went almost by itself. It flew, it darted before Pepé knew it. As he talked, Mama's face grew stern, and it seemed to grow more lean. Pepé finished. "I am a man now, Mama. The man said names to me I could not allow."

Mama nodded. "Yes, thou art a man, my poor little Pepé. Thou art a man. I have seen it coming on thee. I have watched you throwing the knife into the post, and I have been afraid." For a moment her face had softened, but now it grew stern again. "Come! We must get you ready. Go. Awaken Emilio and Rosy. Go quickly."

Pepé stepped over to the corner where his brother and sister slept among the sheepskins. He leaned down and shook them gently. "Come, Rosy! Come, Emilio! The mama says you must arise."

The little black ones sat up and rubbed their eyes in the candlelight. Mama was out of bed now, her long black skirt over her nightgown. "Emilio," she cried. "Go up and catch the other horse for Pepé. Quickly, now! Quickly." Emilio put his legs in his overalls and stumbled sleepily out the door.

"You heard no one behind you on the road?" Mama demanded.

"No, Mama. I listened carefully. No one was on the road."

Mama darted like a bird about the room. From a nail on the wall she took a canvas water bag and threw it on the floor. She stripped a blanket from her bed and rolled it into a tight tube and tied the ends with string. From a box beside the stove she lifted a flour sack half full of black stringy jerky. "Your father's black coat, Pepé. Here, put it on."

Pepé stood in the middle of the floor watching her activity. She reached behind the door and brought out the rifle, a long 38-56, worn shiny the whole length of the barrel. Pepé took it from her and held it in the crook of his elbow. Mama brought a little leather bag and counted the cartridges into his hand. "Only ten left," she warned. "You must not waste them."

Emilio put his head in the door. "'*Qui 'st 'l caballo*,[3] Mama."

"Put on the saddle from the other horse. Tie on the blanket. Here, tie the jerky to the saddle horn."

---

[3]"Here's the horse" (Spanish).

Still Pepé stood silently watching his mother's frantic activity. His chin looked hard, and his sweet mouth was drawn and thin. His little eyes followed Mama about the room almost suspiciously.

Rosy asked softly, "Where goes Pepé?"

Mama's eyes were fierce. "Pepé goes on a journey. Pepé is a man now. He has a man's thing to do."

Pepé straightened his shoulders. His mouth changed until he looked very much like Mama.

At last the preparation was finished. The loaded horse stood outside the door. The water bag dripped a line of moisture down the bay shoulder.

The moonlight was being thinned by the dawn and the big white moon was near down to the sea. The family stood by the shack. Mama confronted Pepé. "Look, my son! Do not stop until it is dark again. Do not sleep even though you are tired. Take care of the horse in order that he may not stop of weariness. Remember to be careful with the bullets—there are only ten. Do not fill thy stomach with jerky or it will make thee sick. Eat a little jerky and fill thy stomach with grass. When thou comest to the high mountains, if thou seest any of the dark watching men, go not near to them nor try to speak to them. And forget not thy prayers." She put her lean hands on Pepé's shoulders, stood on her toes and kissed him formally on both cheeks, and Pepé kissed her on both cheeks. Then he went to Emilio and Rosy and kissed both of their cheeks.

Pepé turned back to Mama. He seemed to look for a little softness, a little weakness in her. His eyes were searching, but Mama's face remained fierce. "Go now," she said. "Do not wait to be caught like a chicken."

Pepé pulled himself into the saddle. "I am a man," he said.

It was the first dawn when he rode up the hill toward the little canyon which let a trail into the mountains. Moonlight and daylight fought with each other, and the two warring qualities made it difficult to see. Before Pepé had gone a hundred yards, the outlines of his figure were misty; and long before he entered the canyon, he had become a grey, indefinite shadow.

Mama stood stiffly in front of her doorstep, and on either side of her stood Emilio and Rosy. They cast furtive glances at Mama now and then.

When the grey shape of Pepé melted into the hillside and disappeared, Mama relaxed. She began the high, whining keen of the death wail. "Our beautiful—our brave," she cried. "Our protector, our son is gone." Emilio and Rosy moaned beside her. "Our beautiful—our brave, he is gone." It was the formal wail. It rose to a high piercing whine and subsided to a moan. Mama raised it three times and then she turned and went into the house and shut the door.

Emilio and Rosy stood wondering in the dawn. They heard Mama whimpering in the house. They went out to sit on the cliff above the ocean. They touched shoulders. "When did Pepé come to be a man?" Emilio asked.

"Last night," said Rosy. "Last night in Monterey." The ocean clouds turned red with the sun that was behind the mountains.

"We will have no breakfast," said Emilio. "Mama will not want to cook." Rosy did not answer him. "Where is Pepé gone?" he asked.

Rosy looked around at him. She drew her knowledge from the quiet air. "He has gone on a journey. He will never come back."

"Is he dead? Do you think he is dead?"

Rosy looked back at the ocean again. A little steamer, drawing a line of smoke sat on the edge of the horizon. "He is not dead," Rosy explained. "Not yet."

Pepé rested the big rifle across the saddle in front of him. He let the horse walk up the hill and he didn't look back. The stony slope took on a coat of short brush so that Pepé found the entrance to a trail and entered it.

When he came to the canyon opening, he swung once in his saddle and looked back, but the houses were swallowed in the misty light. Pepé jerked forward again. The high shoulder of the canyon closed in on him. His horse stretched out its neck and sighed and settled to the trail.

It was a well-worn path, dark soft leaf-mould earth strewn with broken pieces of sandstone. The trail rounded the shoulder of the canyon and dropped steeply into the bed of the stream. In the shallows the water ran smoothly, glinting in the first morning sun. Small round stones on the bottom were as brown as rust with sun moss. In the sand along the edges of the stream the tall, rich wild mint grew, while in the water itself the cress, old and tough, had gone to heavy seed.

The path went into the stream and emerged on the other side. The horse sloshed into the water and stopped. Pepé dropped his bridle and let the beast drink of the running water.

Soon the canyon sides became steep and the first giant sentinel redwoods guarded the trail, great round red trunks bearing foliage as green and lacy as ferns. Once Pepé was among the trees, the sun was lost. A perfumed and purple light lay in the pale green of the underbrush. Gooseberry bushes and blackberries and tall ferns lined the stream, and overhead the branches of the redwoods met and cut off the sky.

Pepé drank from the water bag, and he reached into the flour sack and brought out a black string of jerky. His white teeth gnawed at the string until the tough meat parted. He chewed slowly and drank occasionally from the water bag. His little eyes were slumberous and tired, but the muscles of his face were hard set. The earth of the trail was black now. It gave up a hollow sound under the walking hoofbeats.

The stream fell more sharply. Little waterfalls splashed on the stones. Five-fingered ferns hung over the water and dripped spray from their fingertips. Pepé rode half over in his saddle, dangling one leg loosely. He picked a bay leaf from a tree beside the way and put it into his mouth for a moment to flavor the dry jerky. He held the gun loosely across the pommel.

Suddenly he squared in his saddle, swung the horse from the trail and kicked it hurriedly up behind a big redwood tree. He pulled up the reins tight against the bit to keep the horse from whinnying. His face was intent and his nostrils quivered a little.

A hollow pounding came down the trail, and a horseman rode by, a fat man with red cheeks and a white stubble beard. His horse put down its head and blubbered at the trail when it came to the place where Pepé had turned off. "Hold up!" said the man and he pulled up his horse's head.

When the last sound of the hoofs died away, Pepé came back into the trail again. He did not relax in the saddle any more. He lifted the big rifle and swung the lever to throw a shell into the chamber, and then he let down the hammer to half cock.

The trail grew very steep. Now the redwood trees were smaller and their tops were dead, bitten dead where the wind reached them. The horse plodded on; the sun went slowly overhead and started down toward the afternoon.

Where the stream came out of a side canyon, the trail left it. Pepé dismounted and watered his horse and filled up his water bag. As soon as the trail had parted from the stream, the trees were gone and only the thick brittle sage and manzanita and chaparral edged the trail. And the soft black earth was gone, too, leaving only the light tan broken rock for the trail bed. Lizards scampered away into the brush as the horse rattled over the little stones.

Pepé turned in his saddle and looked back. He was in the open now: he could be seen from a distance. As he ascended the trail the country grew more rough and terrible and dry. The way wound about the bases of great square rocks. Little grey rabbits skittered in the brush. A bird made a monotonous high creaking. Eastward the bare rock mountaintops were pale and powder-dry under the dropping sun. The horse plodded up and up the trail toward a little V in the ridge which was the pass.

Pepé looked suspiciously back every minute or so, and his eyes sought the tops of the ridges ahead. Once, on a white barren spur, he saw a black figure for a moment, but he looked quickly away, for it was one of the dark watchers. No one knew who the watchers were, nor where they lived, but it was better to ignore them and never to show interest in them. They did not bother one who stayed on the trail and minded his own business.

The air was parched and full of light dust blown by the breeze from the eroding mountains. Pepé drank sparingly from his bag and corked it tightly and hung it on the horn again. The trail moved up the dry shale hillside, avoiding rocks, dropping under clefts, climbing in and out of old water scars. When he arrived at the little pass he stopped and looked back for a long time. No dark watchers were to be seen now. The trail behind was empty. Only the high tops of the redwoods indicated where the stream flowed.

Pepé rode on through the pass. His little eyes were nearly closed with weariness, but his face was stern, relentless and manly. The high mountain wind coasted sighing through the pass and whistled on the edges of the big blocks of broken granite. In the air, a red-tailed hawk sailed over close to the ridge and screamed angrily. Pepé went slowly through the broken jagged pass and looked down on the other side.

The trail dropped quickly, staggering among broken rock. At the bottom of the slope there was a dark crease, thick with brush, and on the other side of the crease a little flat, in which a grove of oak trees grew. A scar of green grass cut across the flat. And behind the flat another mountain rose, desolate with dead rocks and starving little black bushes. Pepé drank from the bag again for the air was so dry that it encrusted his nostrils and burned his lips. He put the horse down the trail. The hooves slipped and struggled on the steep way, starting little stones that rolled off into the brush. The sun was gone behind the westward mountain now, but still it glowed brilliantly on the oaks and on the grassy flat. The rocks and the hillsides still sent up waves of the heat they had gathered from the day's sun.

Pepé looked up to the top of the next dry withered ridge. He saw a dark form against the sky, a man's figure standing on top of a rock, and he glanced away quickly not to appear curious. When a moment later he looked up again, the figure was gone.

Downward the trail was quickly covered. Sometimes the horse floundered for footing, sometimes set his feet and slid a little way. They came at last to the bottom where the dark chaparral was higher than Pepé's head. He held up his rifle on one side and his arm on the other to shield his face from the sharp brittle fingers of the brush.

Up and out of the crease he rode, and up a little cliff. The grassy flat was before him, and the round comfortable oaks. For a moment he studied the trail down which he had come, but there was no movement and no sound from it. Finally he rode out over the flat, to the green streak, and at the upper end of the damp he found a little spring welling out of the earth and dropping into a dug basin before it seeped out over the flat.

Pepé filled his bag first, and then he let the thirsty horse drink out of the pool. He led the horse to the clump of oaks, and in the middle of the grove, fairly protected from sight on all sides, he took off the saddle and the bridle and laid them on the ground. The horse stretched his jaws sideways and yawned. Pepé knotted the lead rope about the horse's neck and tied him to a sapling among the oaks, where he could graze in a fairly large circle.

When the horse was gnawing hungrily at the dry grass, Pepé went to the saddle and took a black string of jerky from the sack and strolled to an oak tree on the edge of the grove, from under which he could watch the trail. He sat down in the crisp dry oak leaves and automatically felt for his big black knife to cut the jerky, but he had no knife. He leaned back on his elbow and gnawed at the tough strong meat. His face was blank, but it was a man's face.

The bright evening light washed the eastern ridge, but the valley was darkening. Doves flew down from the hills to the spring, and the quail came running out of the brush and joined them, calling clearly to one another.

Out of the corner of his eye Pepé saw a shadow grow out of the bushy crease. He turned his head slowly. A big spotted wildcat was creeping toward the spring, belly to the ground, moving like thought.

Pepé cocked his rifle and edged the muzzle slowly around. Then he looked apprehensively up the trail and dropped the hammer again. From the ground beside him he picked an oak twig and threw it toward the spring. The quail flew up with a roar and the doves whistled away. The big cat stood up: for a long moment he looked at Pepé with cold yellow eyes, and then fearlessly walked back into the gulch.

The dusk gathered quickly in the deep valley. Pepé muttered his prayers, put his head down on his arm and went instantly to sleep.

The moon came up and filled the valley with cold blue light, and the wind swept rustling down from the peaks. The owls worked up and down the slopes looking for rabbits. Down in the brush of the gulch a coyote gabbled. The oak trees whispered softly in the night breeze.

Pepé started up, listening. His horse had whinnied. The moon was just slipping behind the western ridge, leaving the valley in darkness behind it. Pepé sat tensely gripping his rifle. From far up the trail he heard an answering whinny and the crash of shod hooves on the broken rock. He jumped to his feet, ran to his horse and led it under the trees. He threw on the saddle and cinched it tight for the steep trail, caught the unwilling head and forced the bit into the mouth. He felt the saddle to make sure the water bag and the sack of jerky were there. Then he mounted and turned up the hill.

It was velvet dark. The horse found the entrance to the trail where it left the flat, and started up, stumbling and slipping on the rocks. Pepé's hand rose up to his head. His hat was gone. He had left it under the oak tree.

The horse had struggled far up the trail when the first change of dawn came into the air, a steel greyness as light mixed thoroughly with dark. Gradually the sharp snaggled edge of the ridge stood out above them, rotten granite tortured and eaten by the winds of time. Pepé had dropped his reins on the horn, leaving direction to the horse. The brush grabbed at his legs in the dark until one knee of his jeans was ripped.

Gradually the light flowed down over the ridge. The starved brush and rocks stood out in the half light, strange and lonely in high perspective. Then there came warmth into the light. Pepé drew up and looked back, but he could see nothing in the darker valley below. The sky turned blue over the coming sun. In the waste of the mountainside, the poor dry brush grew only three feet high. Here and there, big outcroppings of unrotted granite stood up like mouldering houses. Pepé relaxed a little. He drank from his water bag and bit off a piece of jerky. A single eagle flew over, high in the light.

Without warning Pepé's horse screamed and fell on its side. He was almost down before the rifle crash echoed up from the valley. From a hole behind the struggling shoulder, a stream of bright crimson blood pumped and stopped and pumped and stopped. The hooves threshed on the ground. Pepé lay half stunned beside the horse. He looked slowly down the hill. A piece of sage clipped off beside his head and another crash echoed up from side to side of the canyon. Pepé flung himself frantically behind a bush.

He crawled up the hill on his knees and one hand. His right hand held the rifle up off the ground and pushed it ahead of him. He moved with the instinctive care of an animal. Rapidly he wormed his way toward one of the big outcroppings of granite on the hill above him. Where the brush was high he doubled up and ran, but where the cover was slight he wriggled forward on his stomach, pushing the rifle ahead of him. In the last little distance there was no cover at all. Pepé poised and then he darted across the space and flashed around the corner of the rock.

He leaned panting against the stone. When his breath came easier he moved along behind the big rock until he came to a narrow split that offered a thin section of vision down the hill. Pepé lay on his stomach and pushed the rifle barrel through the slit and waited.

The sun reddened the western ridges now. Already the buzzards were settling down toward the place where the horse lay. A small brown bird scratched in the dead sage leaves directly in front of the rifle muzzle. The coasting eagle flew back toward the rising sun.

Pepé saw a little movement in the brush far below. His grip tightened on the gun. A little brown doe stepped daintily out on the trail and crossed it and disappeared into the brush again. For a long time Pepé waited. Far below he could see the little flat and the oak trees and the slash of green. Suddenly his eyes flashed back at the trail again. A quarter of a mile down there had been a quick movement in the chaparral. The rifle swung over. The front sight nestled in the v of the rear sight. Pepé studied for a moment and then raised the rear sight a notch. The little movement in the brush came again. The sight settled on it. Pepé squeezed the trigger. The explosion crashed down the mountain and up the other side, and came rattling back. The whole side of the slope grew still. No more movement. And then a white streak cut into the granite of the slit and a bullet whined away and a crash sounded up from below. Pepé felt a sharp pain in his right hand. A sliver of granite was sticking out from between his first and second knuckles and the point protruded from his palm. Carefully he pulled out the sliver of stone. The wound bled evenly and gently. No vein nor artery was cut.

Pepé looked into a little dusty cave in the rock and gathered a handful of spider web, and he pressed the mass into the cut, plastering the soft web into the blood. The flow stopped almost at once.

The rifle was on the ground. Pepé picked it up, levered a new shell into the chamber. And then he slid into the brush on his stomach. Far to the right he crawled, and then up the hill, moving slowly and carefully, crawling to cover and resting and then crawling again.

In the mountains the sun is high in its arc before it penetrates the gorges. The hot face looked over the hill and brought instant heat with it. The white light beat on the rocks and reflected from them and rose up quivering from the earth again, and the rocks and bushes seemed to quiver behind the air.

Pepé crawled in the general direction of the ridge peak, zig-zagging for cover. The deep cut between his knuckles began to throb. He crawled close to a rattlesnake before he saw it, and when it raised its dry head and made a soft beginning whirr, he backed up and took another way. The quick grey lizards flashed in front of him, raising a tiny line of dust. He found another mass of spider web and pressed it against his throbbing hand.

Pepé was pushing the rifle with his left hand now. Little drops of sweat ran to the ends of his coarse black hair and rolled down his cheeks. His lips and tongue were growing thick and heavy. His lips writhed to draw saliva into his mouth. His little dark eyes were uneasy and suspicious. Once when a grey lizard paused in front of him on the parched ground and turned its head sideways he crushed it flat with a stone.

When the sun slid past noon he had not gone a mile. He crawled exhaustedly a last hundred yards to a patch of high sharp manzanita, crawled desperately, and when the patch was reached he wriggled in among the tough gnarly trunks and dropped his head on his left arm. There was little shade in the meager brush, but there was cover and safety. Pepé went to sleep as he lay and the sun beat on his back. A few little birds hopped close to him and peered and hopped away. Pepé squirmed in his sleep and he raised and dropped his wounded hand again and again.

The sun went down behind the peaks and the cool evening came, and then the dark. A coyote yelled from the hillside, Pepé started awake and looked about with misty eyes. His hand was swollen and heavy; a little thread of pain ran up the inside of his arm and settled in a pocket in his armpit. He peered about and then stood up, for the mountains were black and the moon had not yet risen. Pepé stood up in the dark. The coat of his father pressed on his arm. His tongue was swollen until it nearly filled his mouth. He wriggled out of the coat and dropped it in the brush, and then he struggled up the hill, falling over rocks and tearing his way through the brush. The rifle knocked against stones as he went. Little dry avalanches of gravel and shattered stone went whispering down the hill behind him.

After a while the old moon came up and showed the jagged ridge top ahead of him. By moonlight Pepé traveled more easily. He bent forward so that his throbbing arm hung away from his body. The journey uphill was made in dashes and rests, a frantic rush up a few yards and then a rest. The wind coasted down the slope rattling the dry stems of the bushes.

The moon was at meridian when Pepé came at last to the sharp backbone of the ridge top. On the last hundred yards of the rise no soil had clung under the wearing winds. The way was on solid rock. He clambered to the top and looked down on the other side. There was a draw like the last below him, misty with moonlight, brushed with dry struggling sage and chaparral. On the other side the hill rose up sharply and at the top the jagged rotten teeth of the mountain showed against the sky. At the bottom of the cut the brush was thick and dark.

Pepé stumbled down the hill. His throat was almost closed with thirst. At first he tried to run, but immediately he fell and rolled. After that he went more carefully. The moon was just disappearing behind the mountains when he came to the bottom. He crawled into the heavy brush feeling with his fingers for water. There was no water in the bed of the stream, only damp earth. Pepé laid his gun down and scooped up a handful of mud and put it in his mouth, and then he spluttered and scraped the earth from his tongue with his finger, for the mud drew at his mouth like a poultice. He dug a hole in the stream bed with his fingers, dug a little basin to catch water; but before it was very deep his head fell forward on the damp ground and he slept.

The dawn came and the heat of the day fell on the earth, and still Pepé slept. Late in the afternoon his head jerked up. He looked slowly around. His eyes were slits of wariness. Twenty feet away in the heavy brush a big tawny mountain lion stood looking at him. Its long thick tail waved gracefully, its ears were erect with interest, not laid back dangerously. The lion squatted down on its stomach and watched him.

Pepé looked at the hole he had dug in the earth. A half inch of muddy water had collected in the bottom. He tore the sleeve from his hurt arm, with his teeth ripped out a little square, soaked it in the water and put it in his mouth. Over and over he filled the cloth and sucked it.

Still the lion sat and watched him. The evening came down but there was no movement on the hills. No birds visited the dry bottom of the cut. Pepé looked occasionally at the lion. The eyes of the yellow beast drooped as though he were about to sleep. He yawned and his long thin red tongue curled out. Suddenly his head jerked around and his nostrils quivered. His big tail lashed. He stood up and slunk like a tawny shadow into the thick brush.

A moment later Pepé heard the sound, the faint far crash of horse's hooves on gravel. And he heard something else, a high whining yelp of a dog.

Pepé took his rifle in his left hand and he glided into the brush almost as quietly as the lion had. In the darkening evening he crouched up the hill toward the next ridge. Only when the dark came did he stand up. His energy was short. Once it was dark he fell over the rocks and slipped to his knees on the steep slope, but he moved on and on up the hill, climbing and scrabbling over the broken hillside.

When he was far up toward the top, he lay down and slept for a little while. The withered moon, shining on his face, awakened him. He stood up and moved up the hill. Fifty yards away he stopped and turned back, for he had forgotten his rifle. He walked heavily down and poked about in the brush, but he could not find his gun. At last he lay down to rest. The pocket of pain in his armpit had grown more sharp. His arm seemed to swell out and fall with every heartbeat. There was no position lying down where the heavy arm did not press against his armpit.

With the effort of a hurt beast, Pepé got up and moved again toward the top of the ridge. He held his swollen arm away from his body with his left hand. Up the steep hill he dragged himself, a few steps and a rest, and a few more steps. At last he was nearing the top. The moon showed the uneven sharp back of it against the sky.

Pepé's brain spun in a big spiral up and away from him. He slumped to the ground and lay still. The rock ridge top was only a hundred feet above him.

The moon moved over the sky. Pepé half turned on his back. His tongue tried to make words, but only a thick hissing came from between his lips.

When the dawn came, Pepé pulled himself up. His eyes were sane again. He drew his great puffed arm in front of him and looked at the angry wound. The black line ran up from his wrist to his armpit. Automatically he reached in his pocket for the big black knife, but it was not there. His eyes searched the ground. He picked up a sharp blade of stone and scraped at the wound, sawed at the proud flesh and then squeezed the green juice out in big drops. Instantly he threw back his head and whined like a dog. His whole right side shuddered at the pain, but the pain cleared his head.

In the grey light he struggled up the last slope to the ridge and crawled over and lay down behind a line of rocks. Below him lay a deep canyon exactly like the last, waterless and desolate. There was no flat, no oak trees, not even heavy brush in the bottom of it. And on the other side a sharp ridge stood up, thinly brushed with starving sage, littered with broken granite. Strewn over the hill there were giant outcroppings, and on the top the granite teeth stood out against the sky.

The new day was light now. The flame of the sun came over the ridge and fell on Pepé where he lay on the ground. His coarse black hair was littered with twigs and bits of spider web. His eyes had retreated back into his head. Between his lips the tip of his black tongue showed.

He sat up and dragged his great arm into his lap and nursed it, rocking his body and moaning in his throat. He threw back his head and looked up into the pale sky. A big black bird circled nearly out of sight, and far to the left another was sailing near.

He lifted his head to listen, for a familiar sound had come to him from the valley he had climbed out of; it was the crying yelp of hounds, excited and feverish, on a trail.

Pepé bowed his head quickly. He tried to speak rapid words but only a thick hiss came from his lips. He drew a shaky cross on his breast with his left hand. It was a long struggle to get to his feet. He crawled slowly and mechanically to the top of a big rock on the ridge peak. Once there, he arose slowly, swaying to his feet, and stood erect. Far below he could see the dark brush where he had slept. He braced his feet and stood there, black against the morning sky.

There came a ripping sound at his feet. A piece of stone flew up and a bullet droned off into the next gorge. The hollow crash echoed up from below. Pepé looked down for a moment and then pulled himself straight again.

His body jarred back. His left hand fluttered helplessly toward his breast. The second crash sounded from below. Pepé swung forward and toppled from the rock. His body struck and rolled over and over, starting a little avalanche. And when at last he stopped against a bush, the avalanche slid slowly down and covered up his head.

1937, 1938

The Leader of the People

On Saturday afternoon Billy Buck, the ranch-hand, raked together the last of the old year's haystack and pitched small forkfuls over the wire fence to a few mildly interested cattle. High in the air small clouds like puffs of cannon smoke were driven eastward by the March wind. The wind could be heard whishing in the brush on the ridge crests, but no breath of it penetrated down into the ranch-cup.

The little boy, Jody, emerged from the house eating a thick piece of buttered bread. He saw Billy working on the last of the haystack. Jody tramped down scuffing his shoes in a way he had been told was destructive to good shoe-leather. A flock of white pigeons flew out of the black cypress tree as Jody passed, and circled the tree and landed again. A half-grown tortoise-shell cat leaped from the bunkhouse porch, galloped on stiff legs across the road, whirled and galloped back again. Jody picked up a stone to help the game along, but he was too late, for the cat was under the porch before the stone could be discharged. He threw the stone into the cypress tree and started the white pigeons on another whirling flight.

Arriving at the used-up haystack, the boy leaned against the barbed wire fence. "Will that be all of it, do you think?" he asked.

The middle-aged ranch-hand stopped his careful raking and stuck his fork into the ground. He took off his black hat and smoothed down his hair. "Nothing left of it that isn't soggy from ground moisture," he said. He replaced his hat and rubbed his dry leathery hands together.

"Ought to be plenty mice," Jody suggested.

"Lousy with them," said Billy. "Just crawling with mice."

"Well, maybe, when you get all through, I could call the dogs and hunt the mice."

"Sure, I guess you could," said Billy Buck. He lifted a forkful of the damp ground-hay and threw it into the air. Instantly three mice leaped out and burrowed frantically under the hay again.

Jody sighed with satisfaction. Those plump, sleek, arrogant mice were doomed. For eight months they had lived and multiplied in the haystack. They had been immune from cats, from traps, from poison and from Jody. They had grown smug in their security, overbearing and fat. Now the time of disaster had come; they would not survive another day.

Billy looked up at the top of the hills that surrounded the ranch. "Maybe you better ask your father before you do it," he suggested.

"Well, where is he? I'll ask him now."

"He rode up to the ridge ranch after dinner. He'll be back pretty soon."

Jody slumped against the fence post. "I don't think he'd care."

As Billy went back to his work he said ominously. "You'd better ask him anyway. You know how he is."

Jody did know. His father, Carl Tiflin, insisted upon giving permission for anything that was done on the ranch, whether it was important or not. Jody sagged farther against the post until he was sitting on the ground. He looked up at the little puffs of wind-driven cloud. "Is it like to rain, Billy?"

"It might. The wind's good for it, but not strong enough."

"Well, I hope it don't rain until after I kill those damn mice." He looked over his shoulder to see whether Billy had noticed the mature profanity. Billy worked on without comment.

Jody turned back and looked at the side-hill where the road from the outside world came down. The hill was washed with lean March sunshine. Silver thistles, blue lupins and a few poppies bloomed among the sage bushes. Halfway up the hill Jody could see Doubletree Mutt, the black dog, digging in a squirrel hole. He paddled for a while and then paused to kick bursts of dirt out between his hind legs, and he dug with an earnestness which belied the knowledge he must have had that no dog had ever caught a squirrel by digging in a hole.

Suddenly, while Jody watched, the black dog stiffened, and backed out of the hole and looked up the hill toward the cleft in the ridge where the road came through. Jody looked up too. For a moment Carl Tiflin on horseback stood out against the pale sky and then he moved down the road toward the house. He carried something white in his hand.

The boy started to his feet. "He's got a letter," Jody cried. He trotted away toward the ranch house, for the letter would probably be read aloud and he wanted to be there. He reached the house before his father did, and ran in. He heard Carl dismount from his creaking saddle and slap the horse on the side to send it to the barn where Billy would unsaddle it and turn it out.

Jody ran into the kitchen. "We got a letter!" he cried.

His mother looked up from a pan of beans. "Who has?"

"Father has. I saw it in his hand."

Carl strode into the kitchen then, and Jody's mother asked, "Who's the letter from, Carl?"

He frowned quickly. "How did you know there was a letter?"

She nodded her head in the boy's direction. "Big-Britches Jody told me."

Jody was embarrassed.

His father looked down at him contemptuously. "He *is* getting to be a Big-Britches," Carl said. "He's minding everybody's business but his own. Got his big nose into everything."

Mrs. Tiflin relented a little. "Well, he hasn't enough to keep him busy. Who's the letter from?"

Carl still frowned on Jody. "I'll keep him busy if he isn't careful." He held out a sealed letter. "I guess it's from your father."

Mrs. Tiflin took a hairpin from her head and slit open the flap. Her lips pursed judiciously. Jody saw her eyes snap back and forth over the lines. "He says," she translated, "he says he's going to drive out Saturday to stay for a little while. Why, this is Saturday. The letter must have been delayed." She looked at the postmark. "This was mailed day before yesterday. It should have been here yesterday." She looked up questioningly at her husband, and then her face darkened angrily. "Now what have you got that look on you for? He doesn't come often."

Carl turned his eyes away from her anger. He could be stern with her most of the time, but when occasionally her temper arose, he could not combat it.

"What's the matter with you?" she demanded again.

In his explanation there was a tone of apology Jody himself might have used. "It's just that he talks," Carl said lamely. "Just talks."

"Well, what of it? You talk yourself."

"Sure I do. But your father only talks about one thing."

"Indians!" Jody broke in excitedly. "Indians and crossing the plains!"

Carl turned fiercely on him. "You get out, Mr. Big-Britches! Go on, now! Get out!"

Jody went miserably out the back door and closed the screen with elaborate quietness. Under the kitchen window his shamed, downcast eyes fell upon a curiously shaped stone, a stone of such fascination that he squatted down and picked it up and turned it over in his hands.

The voices came clearly to him through the open kitchen window. "Jody's damn well right," he heard his father say. "Just Indians and crossing the plains. I've heard that story about how the horses got driven off about a thousand times. He just goes on and on, and he never changes a word in the things he tells."

When Mrs. Tiflin answered her tone was so changed that Jody, outside the window, looked up from his study of the stone. Her voice had become soft and explanatory. Jody knew how her face would have changed to match the tone. She said quietly,

"Look at it this way, Carl. That was the big thing in my father's life. He led a wagon train clear across the plains to the coast, and when it was finished, his life was done. It was a big thing to do, but it didn't last long enough. Look!" she continued, "it's as though he was born to do that, and after he finished it, there wasn't anything more for him to do but think about it and talk about it. If there'd been any farther west to go, he'd have gone. He's told me so himself. But at last there was the ocean. He lives right by the ocean where he had to stop."

She had caught Carl, caught him and entangled him in her soft tone.

"I've seen him," he agreed quietly. "He goes down and stares off west over the ocean." His voice sharpened a little. "And then he goes up to the Horseshoe Club in Pacific Grove, and he tells people how the Indians drove off the horses."

She tried to catch him again. "Well, it's everything to him. You might be patient with him and pretend to listen."

Carl turned impatiently away. "Well, if it gets too bad, I can always go down to the bunkhouse and sit with Billy," he said irritably. He walked through the house and slammed the front door after him.

Jody ran to his chores. He dumped the grain to the chickens without chasing any of them. He gathered the eggs from the nests. He trotted into the house with the wood and interlaced it so carefully in the wood-box that two armloads seemed to fill it to overflowing.

His mother had finished the beans by now. She stirred up the fire and brushed off the stove-top with a turkey wing. Jody peered cautiously at her to see whether any rancor toward him remained. "Is he coming today?" Jody asked.

"That's what the letter said."

"Maybe I better walk up the road to meet him."

Mrs. Tiflin clanged the stove-lid shut. "That would be nice," she said. "He'd probably like to be met."

"I guess I'll just do it then."

Outside, Jody whistled shrilly to the dogs. "Come on up the hill," he commanded. The two dogs waved their tails and ran ahead. Along the roadside the sage had tender new tips. Jody tore off some pieces and rubbed them on his hands until the air was filled with the sharp wild smell. With a rush the dogs leaped from the road and yapped into the brush after a rabbit. That was the last Jody saw of them, for when they failed to catch the rabbit, they went back home.

Jody plodded on up the hill toward the ridge top. When he reached the little cleft where the road came through, the afternoon wind struck him and blew up his hair and ruffled his shirt. He looked down on the little hills and ridges below and then out at the huge green Salinas Valley. He could see the white town of Salinas far out in the flat and the flash of its windows under the waning sun. Directly below him, in an oak tree, a crow congress had convened. The tree was black with crows all cawing at once.

Then Jody's eyes followed the wagon road down from the ridge where he stood, and lost it behind a hill, and picked it up again on the other side. On that distant stretch he saw a cart slowly pulled by a bay horse. It disappeared behind the hill. Jody sat down on the ground and watched the place where the cart would reappear again. The wind sang on the hilltops and the puff-ball clouds hurried eastward.

Then the cart came into sight and stopped. A man dressed in black dismounted from the seat and walked to the horse's head. Although it was so far away, Jody knew he had unhooked the check-rein, for the horse's head dropped forward. The horse moved on, and the man walked slowly up the hill beside it. Jody gave a glad cry and ran down the road toward them. The squirrels bumped along off the road, and a road-runner flirted its tail and raced over the edge of the hill and sailed out like a glider.

Jody tried to leap into the middle of his shadow at every step. A stone rolled under his foot and he went down. Around a little bend he raced, and there, a short distance ahead, were his grandfather and the cart. The boy dropped from his unseemly running and approached at a dignified walk.

The horse plodded stumble-footedly up the hill and the old man walked beside it. In the lowering sun their giant shadows flickered darkly behind them. The grandfather was dressed in a black broadcloth suit and he wore kid congress gaiters[1] and a black tie on a short, hard collar. He carried his black slouch hat in his hand. His white beard was cropped close and his white eyebrows overhung his eyes like moustaches. The blue eyes were sternly merry. About the whole face and figure there was a granite dignity, so that every motion seemed an impossible thing. Once at rest, it seemed the old man would be stone, would never move again. His steps were slow and certain. Once made, no step could ever be retraced; once headed in a direction, the path would never bend nor the pace increase nor slow.

When Jody appeared around the bend, Grandfather waved his hat slowly in welcome, and he called, "Why Jody! Come down to meet me, have you?"

Jody sidled near and turned and matched his step to the old man's step and stiffened his body and dragged his heels a little. "Yes, sir," he said. "We got your letter only today."

"Should have been here yesterday," said Grandfather. "It certainly should. How are all the folks?"

"They're fine, sir." He hesitated and then suggested shyly, "Would you like to come on a mouse hunt tomorrow, sir?"

"Mouse hunt, Jody?" Grandfather chuckled. "Have the people of this generation come down to hunting mice? They aren't very strong, the new people, but I hardly thought mice would be game for them."

"No, sir. It's just play. The haystack's gone. I'm going to drive out the mice to the dogs. And you can watch, or even beat the hay a little."

The stern, merry eyes turned down on him. "I see. You don't eat them, then. You haven't come to that yet."

Jody explained, "The dogs eat them, sir. It wouldn't be much like hunting Indians, I guess."

"No, not much—but then later, when the troops were hunting Indians and shooting children and burning teepees, it wasn't much different from your mouse hunt."

They topped the rise and started down into the ranch cup, and they lost the sun from their shoulders. "You've grown," grandfather said. "Nearly an inch, I should say."

"More," Jody boasted. "Where they mark me on the door, I'm up more than an inch since Thanksgiving even."

Grandfather's rich throaty voice said, "Maybe you're getting too much water and turning to pith and stalk. Wait until you head out, and then we'll see."

Jody looked quickly into the old man's face to see whether his feelings should be hurt, but there was no will to injure, no punishing nor putting-in-your-place light in the keen blue eyes. "We might kill a pig," Jody suggested.

"Oh, no! I couldn't let you do that. You're just humoring me. It isn't the time and you know it."

"You know Riley, the big boar, sir?"

"Yes. I remember Riley well."

"Well, Riley ate a hole into that same haystack, and it fell down on him and smothered him."

"Pigs do that when they can," said Grandfather.

"Riley was a nice pig, for a boar, sir. I rode him sometimes, and he didn't mind."

A door slammed at the house below them, and they saw Jody's mother standing on

---

[1] High-top shoes (or spats) covering the ankle and instep, suggesting formal dress.

the porch waving her apron in welcome. And they saw Carl Tiflin walking up from the barn to be at the house for the arrival.

The sun had disappeared from the hills by now. The blue smoke from the house chimney hung in flat layers in the purpling ranch-cup. The puff-ball clouds, dropped by the falling wind, hung listlessly in the sky.

Billy Buck came out of the bunkhouse and flung a wash basin of soapy water on the ground. He had been shaving in mid-week, for Billy held Grandfather in reverence, and Grandfather said that Billy was one of the few men of the new generation who had not gone soft. Although Billy was in middle age, Grandfather considered him a boy. Now Billy was hurrying toward the house too.

When Jody and Grandfather arrived, the three were waiting for them in front of the yard gate.

Carl said, "Hello, sir. We've been looking for you."

Mrs. Tiflin kissed Grandfather on the side of his beard, and stood still while his big hand patted her shoulder. Billy shook hands solemnly, grinning under his straw moustache. "I'll put up your horse," said Billy, and he led the rig away.

Grandfather watched him go, and then, turning back to the group, he said as he had said a hundred times before, "There's a good boy. I knew his father, old Mule-tail Buck. I never knew why they called him Mule-tail except he packed mules."

Mrs. Tiflin turned and led the way into the house. "How long are you going to stay, Father? Your letter didn't say."

"Well, I don't know. I thought I'd stay about two weeks. But I never stay as long as I think I'm going to."

In a short while they were sitting at the white oilcloth table eating their supper. The lamp with the tin reflector hung over the table. Outside the dining-room windows the big moths battered softly against the glass.

Grandfather cut his steak into tiny pieces and chewed slowly. "I'm hungry," he said. "Driving out here got my appetite up. It's like when we were crossing. We all got so hungry every night we could hardly wait to let the meat get done. I could eat about five pounds of buffalo meat every night."

"It's moving around does it," said Billy. "My father was a government packer. I helped him when I was a kid. Just the two of us could about clean up a deer's ham."

"I knew your father, Billy," said Grandfather. "A fine man he was. They called him Mule-tail Buck. I don't know why except he packed mules."

"That was it," Billy agreed. "He packed mules."

Grandfather put down his knife and fork and looked around the table. "I remember one time we ran out of meat—" His voice dropped to a curious low sing-song, dropped into a tonal groove the story had worn for itself. "There was no buffalo, no antelope, not even rabbits. The hunters couldn't even shoot a coyote. That was the time for the leader to be on the watch. I was the leader, and I kept my eyes open. Know why? Well, just the minute the people began to get hungry they'd start slaughtering the team oxen. Do you believe that? I've heard of parties that just ate up their draft cattle. Started from the middle and worked toward the ends. Finally they'd eat the lead pair, and then the wheelers. The leader of a party had to keep them from doing that."

In some manner a big moth got into the room and circled the hanging kerosene lamp. Billy got up and tried to clap it between his hands. Carl struck with a cupped palm and caught the moth and broke it. He walked to the window and dropped it out.

"As I was saying," Grandfather began again, but Carl interrupted him. "You'd better eat some more meat. All the rest of us are ready for our pudding."

Jody saw a flash of anger in his mother's eyes. Grandfather picked up his knife and fork. "I'm pretty hungry, all right," he said. "I'll tell you about that later."

When supper was over, when the family and Billy Buck sat in front of the fireplace in the other room, Jody anxiously watched Granfather. He saw the signs he knew. The bearded head leaned forward; the eyes lost their sternness and looked wonderingly into the fire; the big lean fingers laced themselves on the black knees. "I wonder," he began, "I just wonder whether I ever told you how those thieving Piutes drove off thirty-five of our horses."

"I think you did," Carl interrupted. "Wasn't it just before you went up into the Tahoe country?"

Grandfather turned quickly toward his son-in-law. "That's right. I guess I must have told you that story."

"Lots of times," Carl said cruelly, and he avoided his wife's eyes. But he felt the angry eyes on him, and he said, "'Course I'd like to hear it again."

Grandfather looked back at the fire. His fingers unlaced and laced again. Jody knew how he felt, how his insides were collapsed and empty. Hadn't Jody been called a Big-Britches that very afternoon? He arose to heroism and opened himself to the term Big-Britches again. "Tell about Indians," he said softly.

Grandfather's eyes grew stern again. "Boys always want to hear about Indians. It was a job for men, but boys want to hear about it. Well, let's see. Did I ever tell you how I wanted each wagon to carry a long iron plate?"

Everyone but Jody remained silent. Jody said, "No. You didn't."

"Well, when the Indians attacked, we always put the wagons in a circle and fought from between the wheels. I thought that if every wagon carried a long plate with rifle holes, the men could stand the plates on the outside of the wheels when the wagons were in the circle and they would be protected. It would save lives and that would make up for the extra weight of the iron. But of course the party wouldn't do it. No party had done it before and they couldn't see why they should go to the expense. They lived to regret it, too."

Jody looked at his mother, and knew from her expression that she was not listening at all. Carl picked at a callus on his thumb and Billy Buck watched a spider crawling up the wall.

Grandfather's tone dropped into its narrative groove again. Jody knew in advance exactly what words would fall. The story droned on, speeded up for the attack, grew sad over the wounds, struck a dirge at the burials on the great plains. Jody sat quietly watching Grandfather. The stern blue eyes were detached. He looked as though he were not very interested in the story himself.

When it was finished, when the pause had been politely respected as the frontier of the story, Billy Buck stood up and stretched and hitched his trousers. "I guess I'll turn in," he said. Then he faced Grandfather. "I've got an old powder horn and a cap and ball pistol down to the bunkhouse. Did I ever show them to you?"

Grandfather nodded slowly. "Yes, I think you did, Billy. Reminds me of a pistol I had when I was leading the people across." Billy stood politely until the little story was done, and then he said, "Good night," and went out of the house.

Carl Tiflin tried to turn the conversation then. "How's the country between here and Monterey?[2] I've heard it's pretty dry."

"It is dry," said Grandfather. "There's not a drop of water in the Laguna Seca.[3] But it's a long pull from '87. The whole country was powder then, and in '61 I believe all the coyotes starved to death. We had fifteen inches of rain this year."

"Yes, but it all came too early. We could do with some now." Carl's eye fell on Jody. "Hadn't you better be getting to bed?"

Jody stood up obediently. "Can I kill the mice in the old haystack, sir?"

---

[2]The county of Monterey is located on a peninsula in California, south of San Francisco, protruding into the Pacific, on the shores of which is situated the city of Monterey.
[3]"Dry lagoon" (Spanish).

"Mice? Oh! Sure, kill them all off. Billy said there isn't any good hay left."

Jody exchanged a secret and satisfying look with Grandfather. "I'll kill every one tomorrow," he promised.

Jody lay in his bed and thought of the impossible world of Indians and buffaloes, a world that had ceased to be forever. He wished he could have been living in the heroic time, but he knew he was not of heroic timber. No one living now, save possibly Billy Buck, was worthy to do the things that had been done. A race of giants had lived then, fearless men, men of a staunchness unknown in this day. Jody thought of the wide plains and of the wagons moving across like centipedes. He thought of Grandfather on a huge white horse, marshaling the people. Across his mind marched the great phantoms, and they marched off the earth and they were gone.

He came back to the ranch for a moment, then. He heard the dull rushing sound that space and silence make. He heard one of the dogs, out in the doghouse, scratching a flea and bumping his elbow against the floor with every stroke. Then the wind arose again and the black cypress groaned and Jody went to sleep.

He was up half an hour before the triangle sounded for breakfast. His mother was rattling the stove to make the flames roar when Jody went through the kitchen. "You're up early," she said. "Where are you going?"

"Out to get a good stick. We're going to kill the mice today."

"Who is 'we'?"

"Why, Grandfather and I."

"So you've got him in it. You always like to have someone in with you in case there's blame to share."

"I'll be right back," said Jody. "I just want to have a good stick ready for after breakfast."

He closed the screen door after him and went out into the cool blue morning. The birds were noisy in the dawn and the ranch cats came down from the hill like blunt snakes. They had been hunting gophers in the dark, and although the four cats were full of gopher meat, they sat in a semi-circle at the back door and mewed piteously for milk. Doubletree Mutt and Smasher moved sniffing along the edge of the brush, performing the duty with rigid ceremony, but when Jody whistled, their heads jerked up and their tails waved. They plunged down to him, wriggling their skins and yawning. Jody patted their heads seriously, and moved on to the weathered scrap pile. He selected an old broom handle and a short piece of inch-square scrap wood. From his pocket he took a shoelace and tied the ends of the sticks loosely together to make a flail. He whistled his new weapon through the air and struck the ground experimentally, while the dogs leaped aside and whined with apprehension.

Jody turned and started down past the house toward the old haystack ground to look over the field of slaughter, but Billy Buck, sitting patiently on the back steps, called to him, "You better come back. It's only a couple of minutes till breakfast."

Jody changed his course and moved toward the house. He leaned his flail against the steps. "That's to drive the mice out," he said. "I'll bet they're fat. I'll bet they don't know what's going to happen to them today."

"No, nor you either," Billy remarked philosophically, "nor me, nor anyone."

Jody was staggered by this thought. He knew it was true. His imagination twitched away from the mouse hunt. Then his mother came out on the back porch and struck the triangle, and all thoughts fell in a heap.

Grandfather hadn't appeared at the table when they sat down. Billy nodded at his empty chair. "He's all right? He isn't sick?"

"He takes a long time to dress," said Mrs. Tiflin. "He combs his whiskers and rubs up his shoes and brushes his clothes."

Carl scattered sugar on his mush. "A man that's led a wagon train across the plains has got to be pretty careful how he dresses"

Mrs. Tiflin turned on him. "Don't do that, Carl! Please don't!" There was more of threat than of request in her tone. And the threat irritated Carl.

"Well, how many times do I have to listen to the story of the iron plates, and the thirty-five horses? That time's done. Why can't he forget it, now it's done?" He grew angrier while he talked, and his voice rose. "Why does he have to tell them over and over? He came across the plains. All right! Now it's finished. Nobody wants to hear about it over and over."

The door into the kitchen closed softly. The four at the table sat frozen. Carl laid his mush spoon on the table and touched his chin with his fingers.

Then the kitchen door opened and Grandfather walked in. His mouth smiled tightly and his eyes were squinted. "Good morning," he said, and he sat down and looked at his mush dish.

Carl could not leave it there. "Did—did you hear what I said?"

Grandfather jerked a little nod.

"I don't know what got into me, sir. I didn't mean it. I was just being funny."

Jody glanced in shame at his mother, and he saw that she was looking at Carl, and that she wasn't breathing. It was an awful thing that he was doing. He was tearing himself to pieces to talk like that. It was a terrible thing to him to retract a word, but to retract it in shame was infinitely worse.

Grandfather looked sidewise. "I'm trying to get right side up," he said gently. "I'm not being mad. I don't mind what you said, but it might be true, and I would mind that."

"It isn't true," said Carl. "I'm not feeling well this morning. I'm sorry I said it."

"Don't be sorry, Carl. An old man doesn't see things sometimes. Maybe you're right. The crossing is finished. Maybe it should be forgotten, now it's done."

Carl got up from the table. "I've had enough to eat. I'm going to work. Take your time, Billy!" He walked quickly out of the dining-room. Billy gulped the rest of his food and followed soon after. But Jody could not leave his chair.

"Won't you tell any more stories?" Jody asked.

"Why, sure I'll tell them, but only when—I'm sure people want to hear them."

"I like to hear them, sir."

"Oh! Of course you do, but you're a little boy. It was a job for men, but only little boys like to hear about it."

Jody got up from his place. "I'll wait outside for you, sir. I've got a good stick for those mice."

He waited by the gate until the old man came out on the porch. "Let's go down and kill the mice now," Jody called.

"I think I'll just sit in the sun, Jody. You go kill the mice."

"You can use my stick if you like."

"No, I'll just sit here a while."

Jody turned disconsolately away, and walked down toward the old haystack. He tried to whip up his enthusiasm with thoughts of the fat juicy mice. He beat the ground with his flail. The dogs coaxed and whined about him, but he could not go. Back at the house he could see Grandfather sitting on the porch, looking small and thin and black.

Jody gave up and went to sit on the steps at the old man's feet.

"Back already? Did you kill the mice?"

"No, sir. I'll kill them some other day."

The morning flies buzzed close to the ground and the ants dashed about in front of the steps. The heavy smell of sage slipped down the hill. The porch boards grew warm in the sunshine.

Jody hardly knew when Grandfather started to talk. "I shouldn't stay here, feeling the way I do." He examined his strong old hands. "I feel as though the crossing wasn't worth doing." His eyes moved up the side-hill and stopped on a motionless hawk perched on a dead limb. "I tell those old stories, but they're not what I want to tell. I only know how I want people to feel when I tell them.

"It wasn't Indians that were important, nor adventures, nor even getting out here. It was a whole bunch of people made into one big crawling beast. And I was the head. It was westering and westering. Every man wanted something for himself, but the big beast that was all of them wanted only westering. I was the leader, but if I hadn't been there, someone else would have been the head. The thing had to have a head.

"Under the little bushes the shadows were black at white noonday. When we saw the mountains at last, we cried—all of us. But it wasn't getting here that mattered, it was movement and westering.

"We carried life out here and set it down the way those ants carry eggs. And I was the leader. The westering was as big as God, and the slow steps that made the movement piled up and piled up until the continent was crossed.

"Then we came down to the sea, and it was done." He stopped and wiped his eyes until the rims were red. "That's what I should be telling instead of stories."

When Jody spoke, Grandfather started and looked down at him. "Maybe I could lead the people some day," Jody said.

The old man smiled. "There's no place to go. There's the ocean to stop you. There's a line of old men along the shore hating the ocean because it stopped them."

"In boats I might, sir."

"No place to go, Jody. Every place is taken. But that's not the worst—no, not the worst. Westering has died out of the people. Westering isn't a hunger any more. It's all done. Your father is right. It is finished." He laced his fingers on his knee and looked at them.

Jody felt very sad. "If you'd like a glass of lemonade I could make it for you."

Grandfather was about to refuse, and then he saw Jody's face. "That would be nice," he said. "Yes, it would be nice to drink a lemonade."

Jody ran into the kitchen where his mother was wiping the last of the breakfast dishes. "Can I have a lemon to make a lemonade for Grandfather?"

His mother mimicked—"And another lemon to make a lemonade for you."

"No, ma'am. I don't want one."

"Jody! You're sick!" Then she stopped suddenly. "Take a lemon out of the cooler," she said softly. "Here, I'll reach the squeezer down to you."

                                                                              1938

EUDORA WELTY
(b. 1909)

An interviewer, noting the importance of the South in Eudora Welty's fiction, asked her whether *place* was the source of her "inspiration"; she replied: "Not only that, it's my source of knowledge. It tells me the important things. It steers me and keeps me going straight, because place is a definer and a confiner of what I'm doing. It helps me to identify, to recognize and explain. . . . It saves me."

Clearly the South is vital in Welty's fiction, but she is not simply a *southern* writer: she is a writer who is a southerner, creating stories that sound the depths connecting all people. Although born in Mississippi, she is not a descendent of a long line of Mississippians like Faulkner. Her father was from Ohio, her mother from West Virginia. Welty herself was born in Jackson, Mississippi, and went to high school there, graduating in 1925.

For two years she attended Mississippi State College for Women in Columbus, where she "used to sit up at night" listening to "the different voices" of "people from the hill country . . . and those from the Delta." Her love of voices is a part of her love of story telling—which she sees as a southern predilection—and a part of her curiosity about people. As a child, when her family would set out in the car for a Sunday drive, she would settle in and say, "Now start talking!" Her "ears would just open like morning glories."

When she transferred to the University of Wisconsin, she became an English major, steeping herself in the Russian novelists—Chekhov was "kindred"—and contemporary novelists—Virginia Woolf's *To the Lighthouse* "opened the door." Welty had always been an ardent reader, devouring all the books at home— including the influential fairy tales, myths, and Bible stories found there—and ransacking the Jackson Public Library for others. On graduation in 1929 she was determined to be a writer. Her sympathetic but practical father urged her to learn how to make a living, and so Welty went to New York (with an "ulterior motive" of just living there) to study advertising at Columbia University's School of Business from 1930 to 1931.

Welty's father died in 1931. His death was a blow to the family, coming, as it did, at the beginning of the Great Depression. Welty found herself taking a number of jobs—in journalism, advertising, public relations, photography. For a time she worked for one of President Roosevelt's Depression-era programs, the Works Progress Administration, travelling up and down the state of Mississippi as a "Junior Publicity Agent." She carried along her camera and her pen, coming to know the people, towns, and farmlands of Mississippi in ways that would prove valuable to her later in her writing.

On these trips, Welty witnessed countless poverty-stricken blacks and whites and also witnessed their dignity in adversity, their sense of good feeling and humor in the midst of their mean condition. She made a record of what she saw in unposed photographs of the people. These Depression-era photographs, placed on exhibit in a New York gallery for one month in 1936, were not published until many years later as *One Time, One Place* (1971) and still later in a fuller selection entitled simply *Photographs* (1989). In her Preface to the first volume, Welty wrote: "The human face and the human body are eloquent in themselves, and stubborn and wayward, and a snapshot is a moment's glimpse (as a story may be a long look, a growing contemplation) into what never stops moving, never ceases to express for itself something of our common feeling."

In 1936 Welty found her first story, "Death of a Traveling Salesman," accepted for publication in a little Ohio magazine, *Manuscript*. The following year, the editors of the *Southern Review*, Robert Penn Warren and Albert Erskine, encouraged her to submit her stories, and published "A Curtain of Green" and "Petrified Man." By 1940, she was placing her work in such nationally circulated magazines as the *Atlantic Monthly*, where "Why I Live at the P. O." and "A Worn Path" appeared.

Katherine Anne Porter read Welty's work in the *Southern Review* and became a strong supporter. In an introduction to Welty's first volume of stories, *A Curtain of Green* (1941), Porter asserted that Welty's greatest achievement was manifest in such stories as "A Worn Path," "where external act and the internal voiceless life of the human imagination almost meet and mingle on the mysterious threshold between dream and waking, one reality refusing to admit or confirm the existence of the other, yet both conspiring to the same end."

The story of Welty's life from 1941 on is the story of her art, to which she has dedicated that life. She published *The Robber Bridegroom*, a novelette containing elements of the fairy tale, in 1942. Two short novels, *Delta Wedding* (1946) and *The Ponder Heart* (1954), both set in Mississippi, demonstrated a gift for social drama as well as comic portraiture. In two later, full-size novels, *Losing Battles* (1970) and *The Optimist's Daughter* (1972), she drew heavily on memories of her earlier family life and her Mississippi background.

But critics are in general accord that her genius shines most brightly in her short stories. After the first volume, she brought out three more collections — *The Wide Net* (1943), *The Golden Apples* (1949), *The Bride of Innisfallen* (1955). And in 1980, she published *The Collected Stories of Eudora Welty*. A compilation of her criticism and commentaries on the art of writing, *The Eye of the Story*, appeared in 1978. In 1983, she was invited to give a series of lectures at Harvard University. The result was *One Writer's Beginnings* (1984), divided into three parts: "Listening," "Learning to See," and "Finding a Voice." The book is a remarkable autobiography of an artist with a gift for poetic language. It concludes: "As you have seen, I am a writer who came of a sheltered life. A sheltered life can be a daring life as well. For all serious daring starts from within."

ADDITIONAL READING

Place in Fiction, 1957; *Conversations with Eudora Welty*, ed. Peggy Whitman Prenshaw, 1984.

Ruth M. Vande Kieft, *Eudora Welty*, 1962, 1987; Alfred Appel, Jr., *A Season of Dreams: The Fiction of Eudora Welty*, 1965; J. A. Bryant, Jr., *Eudora Welty*, 1968; Neil D. Issacs, *Eudora Welty*, 1969; Marie Antoinette Manz-Kung, *Eudora Welty: Aspects of Reality in Her Fiction*, 1971; Zelma Turner Howard, *The Rhetoric of Eudora Welty's Short Stories*, 1973; Victor H. Thompson, *Eudora Welty: A Reference Guide*, 1976; John F. Desmond, ed., *A Still Moment: Essays on the Art of Eudora Welty*, 1978; Louis Dollarhide and Ann J. Abadie, eds., *Eudora Welty: A Form of Thanks*, 1979; Michael Kreyling, *Eudora Welty's Achievement of Order*, 1980; Elizabeth Evans, *Eudora Welty*, 1981; Peggy Whitman Prenshaw, ed., *Eudora Welty: Thirteen Essays*, 1983; Albert J. Devlin, *Eudora Welty's Chronicle: A Story of Mississippi Life*, 1983; Bethany C. Swearingen, *Eudora Welty, A Critical Bibliography, 1936–1958*, 1984; Carol Sue Manning, *Ears Opening Like Morning Glories: Eudora Welty and the Love of Story Telling*, 1985; Albert J. Devlin, ed., *Welty: A Life in Literature*, 1987.

TEXT

The Collected Stories of Eudora Welty, 1980.

A Worn Path

It was December — a bright frozen day in the early morning. Far out in the country there was an old Negro woman with her head tied in a red rag, coming along a path through the pinewoods. Her name was Phoenix Jackson. She was very old and small and she walked slowly in the dark pine shadows, moving a little from side to side in her steps, with the balanced heaviness and lightness of a pendulum in a grandfather clock. She carried a thin, small cane made from an umbrella, and with this she kept tapping the frozen earth in front of her. This made a grave and persistent noise in the still air, that seemed meditative like the chirping of a solitary little bird.

She wore a dark striped dress reaching down to her shoe tops, and an equally long apron of bleached sugar sacks, with a full pocket: neat and tidy, but every time she took a step she might have fallen over her shoelaces, which dragged from her unlaced shoes. She looked straight ahead. Her eyes were blue with age. Her skin had a pattern all its own of numberless branching wrinkles and as though a whole little tree stood in the middle of her forehead, but a golden color ran underneath, and the two knobs of her cheeks were illumined by a yellow burning under the dark. Under the red rag her hair came down on her neck in the frailest of ringlets, still black, and with an odor like copper.

Now and then there was a quivering in the thicket. Old Phoenix said, "Out of my way, all you foxes, owls, beetles, jack rabbits, coons and wild animals! . . . Keep out from under these feet, little bob-whites. . . . Keep the big wild hogs out of my path. Don't let none of those come running my direction. I got a long way." Under her small black-freckled hand her cane, limber as a buggy whip, would switch at the brush as if to rouse up any hiding things.

On she went. The woods were deep and still. The sun made the pine needles almost too bright to look at, up where the wind rocked. The cones dropped as light as feathers. Down in the hollow was the mourning dove—it was not too late for him.

The path ran up a hill. "Seems like there is chains about my feet, time I get this far," she said, in the voice of argument old people keep to use with themselves. "Something always take a hold of me on this hill—pleads I should stay."

After she got to the top she turned and gave a full, severe look behind her where she had come. "Up through pines," she said at length. "Now down through oaks."

Her eyes opened their widest, and she started down gently. But before she got to the bottom of the hill a bush caught her dress.

Her fingers were busy and intent, but her skirts were full and long, so that before she could pull them free in one place they were caught in another. It was not possible to allow the dress to tear. "I in the thorny bush," she said. "Thorns, you doing your appointed work. Never want to let folks pass, no sir. Old eyes thought you were a pretty little *green* bush."

Finally, trembling all over, she stood free, and after a moment dared to stoop for her cane.

"Sun so high!" she cried, leaning back and looking, while the thick tears went over her eyes. "The time getting all gone here."

At the foot of this hill was a place where a log was laid across the creek.

"Now comes the trial," said Phoenix.

Putting her right foot out, she mounted the log and shut her eyes. Lifting her skirt, leveling her cane fiercely before her, like a festival figure in some parade, she began to march across. Then she opened her eyes and she was safe on the other side.

"I wasn't as old as I thought," she said.

But she sat down to rest. She spread her skirts on the bank around her and folded her hands over her knees. Up above her was a tree in a pearly cloud of mistletoe. She did not dare to close her eyes, and when a little boy brought her a plate with a slice of marblecake on it she spoke to him. "That would be acceptable," she said. But when she went to take it there was just her own hand in the air.

So she left that tree, and had to go through a barbed-wire fence. There she had to creep and crawl, spreading her knees and stretching her fingers like a baby trying to climb the steps. But she talked loudly to herself: she could not let her dress be torn now, so late in the day, and she could not pay for having her arm or her leg sawed off if she got caught fast where she was.

At last she was safe through the fence and risen up out in the clearing. Big dead trees, like black men with one arm, were standing in the purple stalks of the withered cotton field. There sat a buzzard.

"Who you watching?"

In the furrow she made her way along.

"Glad this not the season for bulls," she said, looking sideways, "and the good Lord made his snakes to curl up and sleep in the winter. A pleasure I don't see no two-headed snake coming around that tree, where it come once. It took a while to get by him, back in the summer."

She passed through the old cotton and went into a field of dead corn. It whispered and shook and was taller than her head. "Through the maze now," she said, for there was no path.

Then there was something tall, black and skinny there, moving before her.

At first she took it for a man. It could have been a man dancing in the field. But she stood still and listened, and it did not make a sound. It was as silent as a ghost.

"Ghost," she said sharply, "who be you the ghost of? For I have heard of nary death close by."

But there was no answer—only the ragged dancing in the wind.

She shut her eyes, reached out her hand, and touched a sleeve. She found a coat and inside that an emptiness, cold as ice.

"You scarecrow," she said. Her face lighted. "I ought to be shut up for good," she said with laughter. "My senses is gone. I too old. I the oldest people I ever know. Dance, old scarecrow," she said, "while I dancing with you."

She kicked her foot over the furrow, and with mouth drawn down, shook her head once or twice in a little strutting way. Some husks blew down and whirled in streamers about her skirts.

Then she went on, parting her way from side to side with the cane, through the whispering field. At last she came to the end, to a wagon track where the silver grass blew between the red ruts. The quail were walking around like pullets, seeming all dainty and unseen.

"Walk pretty," she said. "This the easy place. This the easy going."

She followed the track, swaying through the quiet bare fields, through the little strings of trees silver in their dead leaves, past cabins silver from weather, with the doors and windows boarded shut, all like old women under a spell sitting there. "I walking in their sleep," she said, nodding her head vigorously.

In a ravine she went where a spring was silently flowing through a hollow log. Old Phoenix bent and drank. "Sweet-gum makes the water sweet," she said, and drank more. "Nobody know who made this well, for it was here when I was born."

The track crossed a swampy part where the moss hung as white as lace from every limb. "Sleep on, alligators, and blow your bubbles." Then the track went into the road.

Deep, deep the road went down between the high green-colored banks. Overhead the live-oaks met, and it was as dark as a cave.

A black dog with a lolling tongue came up out of the weeds by the ditch. She was meditating, and not ready, and when he came at her she only hit him a little with her cane. Over she went in the ditch, like a little puff of milkweed.

Down there, her senses drifted away. A dream visited her, and she reached her hand up, but nothing reached down and gave her a pull. So she lay there and presently went to talking. "Old woman," she said to herself, "that black dog come up out of the weeds to stall you off, and now there he sitting on his fine tail, smiling at you."

A white man finally came along and found her—a hunter, a young man, with his dog on a chain.

"Well, Granny!" he laughed. "What are you doing there?"

"Lying on my back like a June-bug waiting to be turned over, mister," she said, reaching up her hand.

He lifted her up, gave her a swing in the air, and set her down. "Anything broken, Granny?"

"No sir, them old dead weeds is springy enough," said Phoenix, when she had got her breath. "I thank you for your trouble."

"Where do you live, Granny?" he asked, while the two dogs were growling at each other.

"Away back yonder, sir, behind the ridge. You can't even see it from here."

"On your way home?"

"No sir, I going to town."

"Why, that's too far! That's as far as I walk when I come out myself, and I get something for my trouble." He patted the stuffed bag he carried, and there hung down a little closed claw. It was one of the bob-whites, with its beak hooked bitterly to show it was dead. "Now you go on home, Granny!"

"I bound to go to town, mister," said Phoenix. "The time come around."

He gave another laugh, filling the whole landscape. "I know you old colored people! Wouldn't miss going to town to see Santa Claus!"

But something held old Phoenix very still. The deep lines in her face went into a fierce and different radiation. Without warning, she had seen with her own eyes a flashing nickel fall out of the man's pocket onto the ground.

"How old are you, Granny?" he was saying.

"There is no telling, mister," she said, "no telling."

Then she gave a little cry and clapped her hands and said, "Git on away from here, dog! Look! Look at that dog!" She laughed as if in admiration. "He ain't scared of nobody. He a big black dog." She whispered, "Sic him!"

"Watch me get rid of that cur," said the man. "Sic him, Pete! Sic him!"

Phoenix heard the dogs fighting, and heard the man running and throwing sticks. She even heard a gunshot. But she was slowly bending forward by that time, further and further forward, the lids stretched down over her eyes, as if she were doing this in her sleep. Her chin was lowered almost to her knees. The yellow palm of her hand came out from the fold of her apron. Her fingers slid down and along the ground under the piece of money with the grace and care they would have in lifting an egg from under a setting hen. Then she slowly straightened up, she stood erect, and the nickel was in her apron pocket. A bird flew by. Her lips moved. "God watching me the whole time. I come to stealing."

The man came back, and his own dog panted about them. "Well, I scared him off that time," he said, and then he laughed and lifted his gun and pointed it at Phoenix.

She stood straight and faced him.

"Doesn't the gun scare you?" he said, still pointing it.

"No, sir, I seen plenty go off closer by, in my day, and for less than what I done," she said, holding utterly still.

He smiled, and shouldered the gun. "Well, Granny," he said, "you must be a hundred years old, and scared of nothing. I'd give you a dime if I had any money with me. But you take my advice and stay home, and nothing will happen to you."

"I bound to go on my way, mister," said Phoenix. She inclined her head in the red rag. Then they went in different directions, but she could hear the gun shooting again and again over the hill.

She walked on. The shadows hung from the oak trees to the road like curtains. Then she smelled wood-smoke, and smelled the river, and she saw a steeple and the cabins on their steep steps. Dozens of little black children whirled around her. There ahead was Natchez shining. Bells were ringing. She walked on.

In the paved city it was Christmas time. There were red and green electric lights strung and crisscrossed everywhere, and all turned on in the daytime. Old Phoenix would have been lost if she had not distrusted her eyesight and depended on her feet to know where to take her.

She paused quietly on the sidewalk where people were passing by. A lady came along in the crowd, carrying an armful of red-, green- and silver-wrapped presents; she gave off perfume like the red roses in hot summer, and Phoenix stopped her.

"Please, missy, will you lace up my shoe?" She held up her foot.

"What do you want, Grandma?"

"See my shoe," said Phoenix. "Do all right for out in the country, but wouldn't look right to go in a big building."

"Stand still then, Grandma," said the lady. She put her packages down on the sidewalk beside her and laced and tied both shoes tightly.

"Can't lace 'em with a cane," said Phoenix. "Thank you, missy. I doesn't mind asking a nice lady to tie up my shoe, when I gets out on the street."

Moving slowly and from side to side, she went into the big building, and into a tower of steps, where she walked up and around and around until her feet knew to stop.

She entered a door, and there she saw nailed up on the wall the document that had been stamped with the gold seal and framed in the gold frame, which matched the dream that was hung up in her head.

"Here I be," she said. There was a fixed and ceremonial stiffness over her body.

"A charity case, I suppose," said an attendant who sat at the desk before her.

But Phoenix only looked above her head. There was sweat on her face, the wrinkles in her skin shone like a bright net.

"Speak up, Grandma," the woman said. "What's your name? We must have your history, you know. Have you been here before? What seems to be the trouble with you?"

Old Phoenix only gave a twitch to her face as if a fly were bothering her.

"Are you deaf?" cried the attendant.

But then the nurse came in.

"Oh, that's just old Aunt Phoenix," she said. " She doesn't come for herself—she has a little grandson. She makes these trips just as regular as clockwork. She lives away back off the Old Natchez Trace." She bent down. "Well, Aunt Phoenix, why don't you just take a seat? We won't keep you standing after your long trip." She pointed.

The old woman sat down, bolt upright in the chair.

"Now, how is the boy?" asked the nurse.

Old Phoenix did not speak.

"I said, how is the boy?"

But Phoenix only waited and stared straight ahead, her face very solemn and withdrawn into rigidity.

"Is his throat any better?" asked the nurse. "Aunt Phoenix, don't you hear me? Is your grandson's throat any better since the last time you came for the medicine?"

With her hands on her knees, the old woman waited, silent, erect and motionless, just as if she were in armor.

"You mustn't take up our time this way, Aunt Phoenix," the nurse said. "Tell us quickly about your grandson, and get it over. He isn't dead, is he?"

At last there came a flicker and then a flame of comprehension across her face, and she spoke.

"My grandson. It was my memory had left me. There I sat and forgot why I made my long trip."

"Forgot?" The nurse frowned. "After you came so far?"

Then Phoenix was like an old woman begging a dignified forgiveness for waking up frightened in the night. "I never did go to school, I was too old at the Surrender,"[1] she said in a soft voice. "I'm an old woman without an education. It was my memory fail me. My little grandson, he is just the same, and I forgot it in the coming."

"Throat never heals, does it?" said the nurse, speaking in a loud, sure voice to old Phoenix. By now she had a card with something written on it, a little list. "Yes. Swallowed lye. When was it?—January—two, three years ago—"

Phoenix spoke unasked now. "No, missy, he not dead, he just the same. Every little while his throat begin to close up again, and he not able to swallow. He not get his breath. He not able to help himself. So the time come around, and I go on another trip for the soothing medicine."

---

[1]The Confederate Army's surrender to the Union Army at Appomattox on April 9, 1865.

"All right. The doctor said as long as you came to get it, you could have it," said the nurse. "But it's an obstinate case."

"My little grandson, he sit up there in the house all wrapped up, waiting by himself." Phoenix went on. "We is the only two left in the world. He suffer and it don't seem to put him back at all. He got a sweet look. He going to last. He wear a little patch quilt and peep out holding his mouth open like a little bird. I remembers so plain now. I not going to forget him again, no, the whole enduring time. I could tell him from all the others in creation."

"All right." The nurse was trying to hush her now. She brought her a bottle of medicine. "Charity," she said, making a check mark in a book.

Old Phoenix held the bottle close to her eyes, and then carefully put it into her pocket.

"I thank you," she said.

"It's Christmas time, Grandma," said the attendant. "Could I give you a few pennies out of my purse?"

"Five pennies is a nickel," said Phoenix stiffly.

"Here's a nickel," said the attendant.

Phoenix rose carefully and held out her hand. She received the nickel and then fished the other nickel out of her pocket and laid it beside the new one. She stared at her palm closely, with her head on one side.

Then she gave a tap with her cane on the floor.

"This is what come to me to do," she said. "I going to the store and buy my child a little windmill they sells, made out of paper. He going to find it hard to believe there such a thing in the world. I'll march myself back where he waiting, holding it straight up in this hand."

She lifted her free hand, gave a little nod, turned around, and walked out of the doctor's office. Then her slow step began on the stairs, going down.

1940, 1941

Why I Live at the P.O.[1]

I was getting along fine with Mama, Papa-Daddy and Uncle Rondo until my sister Stella-Rondo just separated from her husband and came back home again. Mr. Whitaker! Of course I went with Mr. Whitaker first, when he first appeared here in China Grove, taking "Pose Yourself" photos, and Stella-Rondo broke us up. Told him I was one-sided. Bigger on one side than the other, which is a deliberate, calculated falsehood: I'm the same. Stella-Rondo is exactly twelve months to the day younger than I am and for that reason she's spoiled.

She's always had anything in the world she wanted and then she'd throw it away. Papa-Daddy gave her this gorgeous Add-a-Pearl necklace when she was eight years old and she threw it away playing baseball when she was nine, with only two pearls.

So as soon as she got married and moved away from home the first thing she did was separate! From Mr. Whitaker! This photographer with the popeyes she said she trusted. Came home from one of those towns up in Illinois and to our complete surprise brought this child of two.

Mama said she like to made her drop dead for a second. "Here you had this marvelous blonde child and never so much as wrote your mother a word about it," says Mama. "I'm thoroughly ashamed of you." But of course she wasn't.

---

[1] I.e., the post office.

Stella-Rondo just calmly takes off this *hat*, I wish you could see it. She says, "Why, Mama, Shirley-T.'s adopted, I can prove it."

"How?" says Mama, but all I says was, "H'm!" There I was over the hot stove, trying to stretch two chickens over five people and a completely unexpected child into the bargain, without one moment's notice.

"What do you mean—'H'm!'?" says Stella-Rondo, and Mama says, "I heard that, Sister."

I said that oh, I didn't mean a thing, only that whoever Shirley-T. was, she was the spit-image of Papa-Daddy if he'd cut off his beard, which of course he'd never do in the world. Papa-Daddy's Mama's papa and sulks.

Stella-Rondo got furious! She said, "Sister, I don't need to tell you you got a lot of nerve and always did have and I'll thank you to make no future reference to my adopted child whatsoever."

"Very well," I said. "Very well, very well. Of course I noticed at once she looks like Mr. Whitaker's side too. That frown. She looks like a cross between Mr. Whitaker and Papa-Daddy."

"Well, all I can say is she isn't."

"She looks exactly like Shirley Temple[2] to me," says Mama, but Shirley-T. just ran away from her.

So the first thing Stella-Rondo did at the table was turn Papa-Daddy against me.

"Papa-Daddy," she says. He was trying to cut up his meat. "Papa-Daddy!" I was taken completely by surprise. Papa-Daddy is about a million years old and's got this long-long beard. "Papa-Daddy, Sister says she fails to understand why you don't cut off your beard."

So Papa-Daddy l-a-y-s down his knife and fork! He's real rich. Mama says he is, he says he isn't. So he says, "Have I heard correctly? You don't understand why I don't cut off my beard?"

"Why," I says, "Papa-Daddy, of course I understand, I did not say any such of a thing, the idea!"

He says, "Hussy!"

I says, "Papa-Daddy, you know I wouldn't any more want you to cut off your beard than the man in the moon. It was the farthest thing from my mind! Stella-Rondo sat there and made that up while she was eating breast of chicken."

But he says, "So the postmistress fails to understand why I don't cut off my beard. Which job I got you through my influence with the government. 'Bird's nest'—is that what you call it?"

Not that it isn't the next to smallest P.O. in the entire state of Mississippi.

I says, "Oh, Papa-Daddy," I says, "I didn't say any such of a thing, I never dreamed it was a bird's nest, I have always been grateful though this is the next to smallest P.O. in the state of Mississippi, and I do not enjoy being referred to as a hussy by my own grandfather."

But Stella-Rondo says, "Yes, you did say it too. Anybody in the world could of heard you, that had ears."

"Stop right there," says Mama, looking at *me*.

So I pulled my napkin straight back through the napkin ring and left the table.

As soon as I was out of the room Mama says, "Call her back, or she'll starve to death," but Papa-Daddy says, "This is the beard I started growing on the Coast when I was fifteen years old." He would of gone on till nightfall if Shirley-T. hadn't lost the Milky Way she ate in Cairo.

So Papa-Daddy says, "I am going out and lie in the hammock, and you can all sit here and remember my words: I'll never cut off my beard as long as I live, even one

---

[2] A child actress, born in 1928, highly popular during the 1930s.

inch, and I don't appreciate it in you at all." Passed right by me in the hall and went straight out and got in the hammock.

It would be a holiday. It wasn't five minutes before Uncle Rondo suddenly appeared in the hall in one of Stella-Rondo's flesh-colored kimonos, all cut on the bias, like something Mr. Whitaker probably thought was gorgeous.

"Uncle Rondo!" I says. "I didn't know who that was! Where are you going?"

"Sister," he says, "get out of my way, I'm poisoned."

"If you're poisoned stay away from Papa-Daddy," I says. "Keep out of the hammock. Papa-Daddy will certainly beat you on the head if you come within forty miles of him. He thinks I deliberately said he ought to cut off his beard after he got me the P.O., and I've told him and told him and told him, and he acts like he just don't hear me. Papa-Daddy must of gone stone deaf."

"He picked a fine day to do it then," says Uncle Rondo, and before you could say "Jack Robinson" flew out in the yard.

What he'd really done, he'd drunk another bottle of that prescription. He does it every single Fourth of July as sure as shooting, and it's horribly expensive. Then he falls over in the hammock and snores. So he insisted on zigzagging right on out to the hammock, looking like a half-wit.

Papa-Daddy woke up with this horrible yell and right there without moving an inch he tried to turn Uncle Rondo against me. I heard every word he said. Oh, he told Uncle Rondo I didn't learn to read till I was eight years old and he didn't see how in the world I ever got the mail put up at the P.O., much less read it all, and he said if Uncle Rondo could only fathom the lengths he had gone to to get me that job! And he said on the other hand he thought Stella-Rondo had a brilliant mind and deserved credit for getting out of town. All the time he was just lying there swinging as pretty as you please and looping out his beard, and poor Uncle Rondo was *pleading* with him to slow down the hammock, it was making him as dizzy as a witch to watch it. But that's what Papa-Daddy likes about a hammock. So Uncle Rondo was too dizzy to get turned against me for the time being. He's Mama's only brother and is a good case of a one-track mind. Ask anybody. A certified pharmacist.

Just then I heard Stella-Rondo raising the upstairs window. While she was married she got this peculiar idea that it's cooler with the windows shut and locked. So she has to raise the window before she can make a soul hear her outdoors.

So she raises the window and says, *"Oh!"* You would have thought she was mortally wounded.

Uncle Rondo and Papa-Daddy didn't even look up, but kept right on with what they were doing. I had to laugh.

I flew up the stairs and threw the door open! I says, "What in the wide world's the matter, Stella-Rondo? You mortally wounded?"

"No," she says, "I am not mortally wounded but I wish you would do me the favor of looking out that window there and telling me what you see."

So I shade my eyes and look out the window.

"I see the front yard," I says.

"Don't you see any human beings?" she says.

"I see Uncle Rondo trying to run Papa-Daddy out of the hammock," I says. "Nothing more. Naturally, it's so suffocating-hot in the house, with all the windows shut and locked, everybody who cares to stay in their right mind will have to go out and get in the hammock before the Fourth of July is over."

"Don't you notice anything different about Uncle Rondo?" asks Stella-Rondo.

"Why, no, except he's got on some terrible-looking flesh-colored contraption I wouldn't be found dead in, is all I can see," I says.

"Never mind, you won't be found dead in it, because it happens to be part of my trousseau, and Mr. Whitaker took several dozen photographs of me in it," says Stella-Rondo. "What on earth could Uncle Rondo *mean* by wearing part of my trousseau out in the broad open daylight without saying so much as 'Kiss my foot,' *knowing* I only got home this morning after my separation and hung my negligee up on the bathroom door, just as nervous as I could be?"

"I'm sure I don't know, and what do you expect me to do about it?" I says. "Jump out the window?"

"No, I expect nothing of the kind. I simply declare that Uncle Rondo looks like a fool in it, that's all," she says. "It makes me sick to my stomach."

"Well, he looks as good as he can," I says. "As good as anybody in reason could." I stood up for Uncle Rondo, please remember. And I said to Stella-Rondo, "I think I would do well not to criticize so freely if I were you and came home with a two-year-old child I had never said a word about, and no explanation whatever about my separation."

"I asked you the instant I entered this house not to refer one more time to my adopted child, and you gave me your word of honor you would not," was all Stella-Rondo would say, and started pulling out every one of her eyebrows with some cheap Kress tweezers.

So I merely slammed the door behind me and went down and made some green-tomato pickle. Somebody had to do it. Of course Mama had turned both the Negroes loose; she always said no earthly power could hold one anyway on the Fourth of July, so she wouldn't even try. It turned out that Jaypan fell in the lake and came within a very narrow limit of drowning.

So Mama trots in. Lifts up the lid and says, "H'm! Not very good for your Uncle Rondo in his precarious condition, I must say. Or poor little adopted Shirley-T. Shame on you!"

That made me tired. I says, "Well, Stella-Rondo had better thank her lucky stars it was her instead of me came trotting in with that very peculiar-looking child. Now if it had been me that trotted in from Illinois and brought a peculiar-looking child of two, I shudder to think of the reception I'd of got, much less controlled the diet of an entire family."

"But you must remember, Sister, that you were never married to Mr. Whitaker in the first place and didn't go up to Illinois to live," says Mama, shaking a spoon in my face. "If you had I would of been just as overjoyed to see you and your little adopted girl as I was to see Stella-Rondo, when you wound up with your separation and came on back home."

"You would not," I says.

"Don't contradict me, I would," says Mama.

But I said she couldn't convince me though she talked till she was blue in the face. Then I said, "Besides, you know as well as I do that that child is not adopted."

"She most certainly is adopted," says Mama, stiff as a poker.

I says, "Why, Mama, Stella-Rondo had her just as sure as anything in this world, and just too stuck up to admit it."

"Why, Sister," said Mama. "Here I thought we were going to have a pleasant Fourth of July, and you start right out not believing a word your own baby sister tells you!"

"Just like Cousin Annie Flo. Went to her grave denying the facts of life," I remind Mama.

"I told you if you ever mentioned Annie Flo's name I'd slap your face," says Mama, and slaps my face.

"All right, you wait and see," I says.

"I," says Mama, "*I* prefer to take my children's word for anything when it's humanly possible." You ought to see Mama, she weighs two hundred pounds and has real tiny feet.

Just then something perfectly horrible occurred to me.

"Mama," I says, "can that child talk?" I simply had to whisper! "Mama, I wonder if that child can be—you know—in any way? Do you realize," I says, "that she hasn't spoken one single, solitary word to a human being up to this minute? This is the way she looks," I says, and I looked like this.

Well, Mama and I just stood there and stared at each other. It was horrible!

"I remember well that Joe Whitaker frequently drank like a fish," says Mama. "I believed to my soul he drank *chemicals*." And without another word she marches to the foot of the stairs and calls Stella-Rondo.

"Stella-Rondo? Ooooo! Stella-Rondo!"

"What?" says Stella-Rondo from upstairs. Not even the grace to get up off the bed.

"Can that child of yours talk?" asks Mama.

Stella-Rondo says, "Can she what?"

"Talk! Talk!" says Mama. "Burdyburdyburdyburdy!"

So Stella-Rondo yells back, "Who says she can't talk?"

"Sister says so," says Mama.

"You didn't have to tell me, I know whose word of honor don't mean a thing in this house," says Stella-Rondo.

And in a minute the loudest Yankee voice I ever heard in my life yells out, "OE'm Pop-OE the Sailor-r-r-r Ma-a-an!"[3] and then somebody jumps up and down in the upstairs hall. In another second the house would of fallen down.

"Not only talks, she can tap-dance!" calls Stella-Rondo. "Which is more than some people I won't name can do."

"Why, the little precious darling thing!" Mama says, so surprised. "Just as smart as she can be!" Starts talking baby talk right there. Then she turns on me. "Sister, you ought to be thoroughly ashamed! Run upstairs this instant and apologize to Stella-Rondo and Shirley-T."

"Apologize for what?" I says. "I merely wondered if the child was normal, that's all. Now that she's proved she is, why, I have nothing further to say."

But Mama just turned on her heel and flew out, furious. She ran right upstairs and hugged the baby. She believed it was adopted. Stella-Rondo hadn't done a thing but turn her against me from upstairs while I stood there helpless over the hot stove. So that made Mama, Papa-Daddy and the baby all on Stella-Rondo's side.

Next, Uncle Rondo.

I must say that Uncle Rondo has been marvelous to me at various times in the past and I was completely unprepared to be made to jump out of my skin, the way it turned out. Once Stella-Rondo did something perfectly horrible to him—broke a chain letter[4] from Flanders Field[5]—and he took the radio back he had given her and gave it to me. Stella-Rondo was furious! For six months we all had to call her Stella instead of Stella-Rondo, or she wouldn't answer. I always thought Uncle Rondo had all the brains of the entire family. Another time he sent me to Mammoth Cave, with all expenses paid.

But this would be the day he was drinking that prescription, the Fourth of July.

So at supper Stella-Rondo speaks up and says she thinks Uncle Rondo ought to try to eat a little something. So finally Uncle Rondo said he would try a little cold biscuits and ketchup, but that was all. So *she* brought it to him.

"Do you think it wise to disport with ketchup in Stella-Rondo's flesh-colored kimono?" I says. Trying to be considerate! If Stella-Rondo couldn't watch out for her trousseau, somebody had to.

"Any objections?" asks Uncle Rondo, just about to pour out all the ketchup.

"Don't mind what she says, Uncle Rondo," says Stella-Rondo. "Sister has been devoting this solid afternoon to sneering out my bedroom window at the way you look."

---

[3]"I'm Popeye the sailor man," a song popular during the late 1930s (sung in the movie cartoons of Popeye).
[4]Those who received chain letters were supposed to mail the sender a sum of money and, on mailing ten or twenty such letters (continuing the "chain"), receive in return ten- or twenty-fold the amount spent. This pastime was popular during the Great Depression.
[5]World War I battlefield and burial ground in France where many American troops fought and were buried.

"What's that?" says Uncle Rondo. Uncle Rondo has got the most terrible termper in the world. Anything is liable to make him tear the house down if it comes at the wrong time.

So Stella-Rondo says, "Sister says, 'Uncle Rondo certainly does look like a fool in that pink kimono!'"

Do you remember who it was really said that?

Uncle Rondo spills out all the ketchup and jumps out of his chair and tears off the kimono and throws it down on the dirty floor and puts his foot on it. It had to be sent all the way to Jackson to the cleaners and re-pleated.

"So that's your opinion of your Uncle Rondo, is it?" he says. "I look like a fool, do I? Well, that's the last straw. A whole day in this house with nothing to do, and then to hear you come out with a remark like that behind my back!"

"I didn't say any such of a thing, Uncle Rondo," I says, "and I'm not saying who did, either. Why, I think you look all right. Just try to take better care of yourself and not talk and eat at the same time," I says. "I think you better go lie down."

"Lie down my foot," says Uncle Rondo. I ought to of known by that he was fixing to do something perfectly horrible.

So he didn't do anything that night in the precarious state he was in—just played Casino[6] with Mama and Stella-Rondo and Shirley-T. and gave Shirley-T. a nickel with a head on both sides. It tickled her nearly to death, and she called him "Papa." But at 6:30 A.M. the next morning, he threw a whole five-cent package of some unsold one-inch firecrackers from the store as hard as he could into my bedroom and they every one went off. Not one bad one in the string. Anybody else, there'd be one that wouldn't go off.

Well, I'm just terribly susceptible to noise of any kind, the doctor has always told me I was the most sensitive person he had ever seen in his whole life, and I was simply prostrated. I couldn't eat! People tell me they heard it as far as the cemetery, and old Aunt Jep Patterson, that had been holding her own so good, thought it was Judgment Day and she was going to meet her whole family. It's usually so quiet here.

And I'll tell you it didn't take me any longer than a minute to make up my mind what to do. There I was with the whole entire house on Stella-Rondo's side and turned against me. If I have anything at all I have pride.

So I just decided I'd go straight down to the P.O. There's plenty of room there in the back, I says to myself.

Well! I made no bones about letting the family catch on to what I was up to. I didn't try to conceal it.

The first thing they knew, I marched in where they were all playing Old Maid[7] and pulled the electric oscillating fan out by the plug, and everything got real hot. Next I snatched the pillow I'd done the needlepoint on right off the davenport from behind Papa-Daddy. He went "Ugh!" I beat Stella-Rondo up the stairs and finally found my charm bracelet in her bureau drawer under a picture of Nelson Eddy.[8]

"So that's the way the land lies," says Uncle Rondo. There he was, piecing on the ham. "Well, Sister, I'll be glad to donate my army cot if you got any place to set it up, providing you'll leave right this minute and let me get some peace." Uncle Rondo was in France.

"Thank you kindly for the cot and 'peace' is hardly the word I would select if I had to resort to firecrackers at 6:30 A.M. in a young girl's bedroom," I says back to him. "And as to where I intend to go, you seem to forget my position as postmistress of China Grove, Mississippi," I says. "I've always got the P.O."

Well, that made them all sit up and take notice.

---

[6]A card game.
[7]Card game.

[8]Singing star of many movie operettas during the 1930s and later.

I went out front and started digging up some four-o'clocks to plant around the P.O.

"Ah-ah-ah!" says Mama, raising the window. "Those happen to be my four-o'clocks. Everything planted in that star is mine. I've never known you to make anything grow in your life."

"Very well," I says. "But I take the fern. Even you, Mama, can't stand there and deny that I'm the one watered that fern. And I happen to know where I can send in a box top and get a packet of one thousand mixed seeds, no two the same kind, free."

"Oh, where?" Mama wants to know.

But I says, "Too late. You 'tend to your house, and I'll 'tend to mine. You hear things like that all the time if you know how to listen to the radio. Perfectly marvelous offers. Get anything you want free."

So I hope to tell you I marched in and got that radio, and they could of all bit a nail in two, especially Stella-Rondo, that it used to belong to, and she well knew she couldn't get it back, I'd sue for it like a shot. And I very politely took the sewing-machine motor I helped pay the most on to give Mama for Christmas back in 1929, and a good big calendar, with the first-aid remedies on it. The thermometer and the Hawaiian ukelele certainly were rightfully mine, and I stood on the step-ladder and got all my watermelon-rind preserves and every fruit and vegetable I'd put up, every jar. Then I began to pull the tacks out of the bluebird wall vases on the archway to the dining room.

"Who told you you could have those, Miss Priss?" says Mama, fanning as hard as she could.

"I bought 'em and I'll keep track of 'em," I says. "I'll tack 'em up one on each side the post-office window, and you can see 'em when you come to ask me for your mail, if you're so dead to see 'em."

"Not I! I'll never darken the door to that post office again if I live to be a hundred," Mama says. "Ungrateful child! After all the money we spent on you at the Normal."[9]

"Me either," says Stella-Rondo. "You can just let my mail lie there and *rot*, for all I care. I'll never come and relieve you of a single, solitary piece."

"I should worry," I says. "And who you think's going to sit down and write you all those big fat letters and postcards, by the way? Mr. Whitaker? Just because he was the only man ever dropped down in China Grove and you got him—unfairly—is he going to sit down and write you a lengthy correspondence after you come home giving no rhyme nor reason whatsoever for your separation and no explanation for the presence of that child? I may not have your brilliant mind, but I fail to see it."

So Mama says, "Sister, I've told you a thousand times that Stella-Rondo simply got homesick, and this child is far too big to be hers," and she says, "Now, why don't you all just sit down and play Casino?"

Then Shirley-T. sticks out her tongue at me in this perfectly horrible way. She has no more manners than the man in the moon. I told her she was going to cross her eyes like that some day and they'd stick.

"It's too late to stop me now," I says. "You should have tried that yesterday. I'm going to the P.O. and the only way you can possibly see me is to visit me there."

So Papa-Daddy says, "You'll never catch me setting foot in that post office, even if I should take a notion into my head to write a letter some place." He says, "I won't have you reachin' out of that little old window with a pair of shears and cuttin' off any beard of mine. I'm too smart for you!"

"We all are," says Stella-Rondo.

But I said, "If you're so smart, where's Mr. Whitaker?"

So then Uncle Rondo says, "I'll thank you from now on to stop reading all the

---

[9] I.e., a "teacher's college."

orders I get on postcards and telling everybody in China Grove what you think is the matter with them," but I says, "I draw my own conclusions and will continue in the future to draw them." I says, "If people want to write their inmost secrets on penny postcards, there's nothing in the wide world you can do about it, Uncle Rondo."

"And if you think we'll ever *write* another postcard you're sadly mistaken," says Mama.

"Cutting off your nose to spite your face then," I says. "But if you're all determined to have no more to do with the U.S. mail, think of this: What will Stella-Rondo do now, if she wants to tell Mr. Whitaker to come after her?"

"Wah!" says Stella-Rondo. I knew she'd cry. She had a conniption fit right there in the kitchen.

"It will be interesting to see how long she holds out," I says. "And now—I am leaving."

"Goodbye," says Uncle Rondo.

"Oh, I declare," says Mama, "to think that a family of mine should quarrel on the Fourth of July, or the day after, over Stella-Rondo leaving old Mr. Whitaker and having the sweetest little adopted child! It looks like we'd all be glad!"

"Wah!" says Stella-Rondo, and has a fresh conniption fit.

"*He* left *her*—you mark my words," I says. "That's Mr. Whitaker. I know Mr. Whitaker. After all, I knew him first. I said from the beginning he'd up and leave her. I foretold every single thing that's happened."

"Where did he go?" asks Mama.

"Probably to the North Pole, if he knows what's good for him," I says.

But Stella-Rondo just bawled and wouldn't say another word. She flew to her room and slammed the door.

"Now look what you've gone and done, Sister," says Mama. "You go apologize."

"I haven't got time. I'm leaving." I says.

"Well, what are you waiting around for?" asks Uncle Rondo.

So I just picked up the kitchen clock and marched off, without saying "Kiss my foot" or anything, and never did tell Stella-Rondo good-bye.

There was a girl going along on a little wagon right in front.

"Girl," I says, "come help me haul these things down the hill, I'm going to live in the post office."

Took her nine trips in her express wagon. Uncle Rondo came out on the porch and threw her a nickel.

And that's the last I've laid eyes on any of my family or my family laid eyes on me for five solid days and nights. Stella-Rondo may be telling the most horrible tales in the world about Mr. Whitaker, but I haven't heard them. As I tell everybody, I draw my own conclusions.

But oh, I like it here. It's ideal, as I've been saying. You see, I've got everything cater-cornered, the way I like it. Hear the radio? All the war news. Radio, sewing machine, book ends, ironing board and that great big piano lamp—peace, that's what I like. Butter-bean vines planted all along the front where the strings are.

Of course, there's not much mail. My family are naturally the main people in China Grove, and if they prefer to vanish from the face of the earth, for all the mail they get or the mail they write, why, I'm not going to open my mouth. Some of the folks here in town are taking up for me and some turned against me. I know which is which. There are always people who will quit buying stamps just to get on the right side of Papa-Daddy.

But here I am, and here I'll stay. I want the world to know I'm happy.

And if Stella-Rondo should come to me this minute, on bended knees, and *attempt* to explain the incidents of her life with Mr. Whitaker, I'd simply put my fingers in both my ears and refuse to listen.

1940, 1941

NEW DIMENSIONS IN PROSE
Autobiography: Modes of Remembering

GERTRUDE STEIN   THOMAS WOLFE

CLAUDE MCKAY   ZORA NEALE HURSTON

JAMES THURBER   RICHARD WRIGHT

E. B. WHITE

"Time carries us away from all of our earlier states of being; memory recalls those earlier states—but it does so only as a function of present consciousness: we can recall what we were only from the complex perspective of what we are, which means that we may very well be recalling something that we never were at all. In the act of remembering the past in the present, the autobiographer imagines into existence another person, another world, and surely it is *not* the same, in any real sense, as that past world that does not, under any circumstances, nor however much we may now wish it, now exist. 'This,' in T. S. Eliot's phrase, 'is the use of memory.'"

James Olney, "The Ontology of Autobiography," *Autobiography: Essays Theoretical and Critical*, 1980

GERTRUDE STEIN
(1874–1946)

We often quote Gertrude Stein without realizing we are quoting her, or without understanding what we quote. "Pigeons on the grass alas." "There is no there there." "You are all a lost generation." "A rose is a rose is a rose is a rose." Sometimes we read Gertrude Stein convinced that we don't comprehend what we do, indeed, understand — at the deepest levels of the unconscious: "There is no use in telling more than you know, no not even if you do not know it"; "One of the things that is a very interesting thing to know is how you are feeling inside you to the words that are coming out to be outside of you."

Gertrude Stein is the most widely unread of all the important American writers. For those who have read her work, the books are likely to be *Three Lives* or *The Autobiography of Alice B. Toklas*, the most immediately accessible of all her writing. Even committed readers of difficult literary works — T. S. Eliot's and William Faulkner's — often find Stein's works unyielding. But dedicated readers have frequently experienced breakthroughs. There has existed a tradition in Greenwich Village in New York City of an annual New Year's "marathon reading" of the whole of Stein's long masterpiece *The Making of Americans* by a series of devoted readers. Those who have participated as readers and listeners have found themselves experiencing and appreciating the novel for the first time.

Stein was born in Pennsylvania in 1874 and was early taken abroad by her family, living in Austria and France for some four years. By 1880 the family was established in Oakland, California ("There is no there there"), where Stein went to school. By 1891, both parents were dead and the Stein children were left with enough money to live comfortably. Gertrude was closest to her older brother, Leo, and she followed him to Harvard, entering Harvard Annex (later Radcliffe). She studied psychology with William James, whose theory of consciousness (he invented the term "stream of consciousness") clearly fascinated her.

After graduating from Harvard *magna cum laude*, she entered Johns Hopkins Medical School but did not finish the program. By 1903, she was settled with her brother in what was to become known as the famed Stein salon at 27, rue de Fleurus, Paris. Both Steins immediately began making the acquaintance of Parisian painters and buying their pictures — Renoir, Gauguin, Toulouse-Lautrec, Matisse, and Picasso. By the time of the move to Paris, Stein was quietly beginning to experiment with words, working on two books, *Q.E.D.* and *The Making of Americans*. The first portrayed a love affair she had had involving two women in Baltimore and was not published until 1950, four years after her death. The second was based on the saga of three generations of her own family and appeared in 1925. By 1909, Alice B. Toklas entered Stein's life, moving in with her and becoming her companion, housekeeper, typist, adviser, and lover. Soon after, the valuable collection of paintings was divided between Gertrude and Leo, and he moved out.

Also in 1909 appeared Stein's first book, *Three Lives*, written several years earlier and published at her own expense. The three lives are "The Good Anna," "Melanctha," and "The Gentle Lena," all working women of the immigrant or lower class. The longest and most unusual is "Melanctha," portraying a black woman's career and love life in candid but unconventional language. When *Q.E.D.* appeared in 1950, admirers of "Melanctha" were startled to learn that Stein had changed the white characters and the woman-woman relationship in *Q.E.D.* to black characters and a woman-man relationship and used much of the earlier work in "Melanctha." Stein was fully aware of the extraordinary style of "Melanctha" and later referred to it in a piece called "Composition as Explanation": "In [Melanctha] there was a constant recurring and beginning there was a marked direction in the direction of being in the present although naturally I had been accustomed to past present and future, and why, because the composition forming around me was a prolonged present. . . . I created then a prolonged present naturally I knew nothing of a continuous present but it came naturally to me to make one, it was simple it was clear to me and nobody knew why it was done like that, I did not myself although naturally to me it was natural."

Stein's intuitive discovery of the "continuous present" marked a turning point in her style, reflected in all her later work, and its origins might be traced back to her training in psychology, particularly with William James and his studies in the nature of consciousness. But there was an additional element in her style that derived from the modernist paintings she had collected and come to love. The painters had, in such movements and innovations as cubism and the collage, experimented with pigments turned into shapes on canvas without concern for a representational relationship with the exterior world. Stein began to see words similarly, and began writing prose poems with words displaced from familiar syntactical positions. The poems appeared in 1914 as *Tender Buttons*.

Stein's salon became a gathering place not only for Parisian painters and writers but also American writers visiting or living as expatriates in Paris, including T. S. Eliot, Ezra Pound, Sherwood Anderson, Ernest Hemingway, and F. Scott Fitzgerald. All were to appear as characters in *The Autobiography of Alice B. Toklas*, published in 1933 and the only book of Stein's to become a bestseller. This work was followed in 1937 with *Everybody's Autobiography*, which opened: "Alice B. Toklas did hers and now everybody will do theirs."

At the request of the American composer, Virgil Thompson, Stein supplied the librettos for two operas which he set to music. The first, *Four Saints in Three Acts*, was produced in 1934 with an all-black cast and was a sensation. The second, based on the life of the American suffragette leader Susan B. Anthony, *The Mother of Us All*, did not see production until 1947, after Stein's death in 1946.

Although Stein remained an American all her life, she returned only once — as something of a celebrity for a successful lecture tour in 1934. Four lectures delivered at the University of Chicago were published as *Narration* in 1935. Her readers found her work much easier to comprehend listening to her read it aloud than when they read it silently. The strange syntax, repetitions, and disjunctions seemed to emphasize rather than obscure meaning.

Stein lived out the Second World War quietly in the countryside of France. She returned to Paris when it was liberated and became the center of interest for many of the American soldiers who found themselves in Paris during those heady days. During this period she published *Wars I Have Seen* (1945) and *Brewsie and Willie* (1946); the latter affectionately portrayed the American soldiers she encountered at the end of the war.

Her last words, just before her death in July 1946, were quintessentially her own. Turning to Alice, she asked, "What is the answer?" When Alice did not reply, she said, "In that case, what is the question?" Alice B. Toklas lived on alone until 1967. Her memoir appeared in 1963 as *What Is Remembered*.

ADDITIONAL READING

Selected Writings of Gertrude Stein, ed. Carl Van Vechten, 1946, 1962; *Gertrude Stein: Writings and Lectures*, ed. Patricia Meyerowitz, 1967; *The Yale Edition of the Unpublished Writings of Gertrude Stein*, 8 vols., ed. Carl Van Vechten, 1951–58.

Donald Sutherland, *Gertrude Stein: A Biography of Her Work*, 1951; Donald Gallup, ed., *The Flowers of Friendship: Letters Written to Gertrude Stein*, 1953; Elizabeth Sprigge, *Gertrude Stein: Her Life and Work*, 1952; Benjamin L. Reid, *Art by Subtraction: A Dissenting Opinion of Gertrude Stein*, 1958; John Malcolm Brinnin, *The Third Rose: Gertrude Stein and Her World*, 1959; Frederick J. Hoffman, *Gertrude Stein*, 1961; J. Michael Hoffman, *The Development of Abstractionism in the Writings of Gertrude Stein*, 1965; Allegra Stewart, *Gertrude Stein and the Present*, 1967; Richard Bridgman, *Gertrude Stein in Pieces*, 1970; Norman Weinstein, *Gertrude Stein and the Literature of Modern Consciousness*, 1970; Robert B. Haas, *A Primer for the Gradual Understanding of Gertrude Stein*, 1971; Howard Greenfield, *Gertrude Stein: A Biography*, 1973; Linda Simons, *Gertrude Stein: A Composite Portrait*, 1974; James R. Mellow, *Charmed Circle: Gertrude Stein and Company*, 1974; Carolyn Faunce Copeland, *Language and Time in Gertrude Stein*, 1975; Janet Hobhouse, *Everybody Who Was Anybody*; Michael J. Hoffman, *Gertrude Stein*, 1976; Wendy Steiner, *Exact Resemblance to Exact Resemblance: The Literary Portraiture of Gertrude Stein*, 1978; Maurice R. Liston, *Gertrude Stein: An Annotated Bibliography*, 1979; Shirley C. Neuman, *Gertrude Stein: Autobiography and the Problem of Narration*, 1979; Marianne DeKoven, *A Different Language: Gertrude Stein's Experimental Writing*, 1983; Jayne L. Walker, *The Making of a Modernist: Gertrude Stein from "Three Lives" to "Tender Buttons"*, 1984; Randa Dubnick, *The Structure of Obscurity: Gertrude Stein, Language, and Cubism*, 1984; Betsy Alayne Ryan, *Gertrude Stein's Theatre of the Absolute*, 1984; Janice L. Doane, *Silence and Narrative: The Early Novels of Gertrude Stein*, 1986; Michael J. Hoffman, ed., *Critical Essays on Gertrude Stein*, 1986; Shirley Neuman and Ira B. Nadel, eds., *Gertrude Stein and the Making of Modern Literature*, 1988; Lisa Ruddick, *Reading Gertrude Stein: Body, Text, Gnosis*, 1990.

TEXTS

The Autobiography of Alice B. Toklas, 1933; *Tender Buttons*, 1914.

from The Autobiography of Alice B. Toklas

AFTER THE WAR
1919–1932

We were, in these days as I look back at them, constantly seeing people.

It is a confused memory those first years after the war and very difficult to think back and remember what happened before or after something else. Picasso[1] once said, I have already told, when Gertrude Stein and he were discussing dates, you forget that when we were young an awful lot happened in a year. During the years just after the war as I look in order to refresh my memory over the bibliography of Gertrude Stein's work, I am astonished when I realise how many things happened in a year. Perhaps we were not so young then but there were a great many young in the world and perhaps that comes to the same thing. . . .

[SHERWOOD ANDERSON]

Sylvia Beach[2] from time to time brought groups of people to the house, groups of young writers and some older women with them. It was at that time that Ezra Pound came, no that was brought about in another way. She later ceased coming to the house but she sent word that Sherwood Anderson had come to Paris and wanted to see Gertrude Stein and might he come. Gertrude Stein sent back word that she would be very pleased and he came with his wife. . . .

For some reason or other I was not present on this occasion, some domestic complication in all probability, at any rate when I did come home Gertrude Stein was

---

[1]Pablo Picasso (1881–1973), Spanish painter and sculptor who lived in France.
[2]Sylvia Beach (1887–1962), an American who opened a book store, Shakespeare and Co., in Paris in 1919. It became a center for American and British expatriates.

moved and pleased as she has very rarely been. Gertrude Stein was in those days a little bitter, all her unpublished manuscripts, and no hope of publication or serious recognition. Sherwood Anderson came and quite simply and directly as is his way told her what he thought of her work and what it had meant to him in his development. He told it to her then and what was even rarer he told it in print immediately after. Gertrude Stein and Sherwood Anderson have always been the best of friends but I do not believe even he realises how much his visit meant to her. It was he who thereupon wrote the introduction to Geography and Plays. . . .[3]

[POUND AND ELIOT]

We met Ezra Pound at Grace Lounsbery's[4] house, he came home to dinner with us and he stayed and he talked about japanese prints among other things. Gertrude Stein liked him but did not find him amusing. She said he was a village explainer, excellent if you were a village, but if you were not, not. Ezra also talked about T. S. Eliot. It was the first time any one had talked about T.S. at the house. Pretty soon everybody talked about T.S. Kitty Buss[5] talked about him and much later Hemingway talked about him as the Major. Considerably later Lady Rothermere[6] talked about him and invited Gertrude Stein to come and meet him. They were founding the Criterion. We had met Lady Rothermere through Muriel Draper[7] whom we had seen again for the first time after many years. Gertrude Stein was not particularly anxious to go to Lady Rothermere's and meet T. S. Eliot, but we all insisted she should, and she gave a doubtful yes. I had no evening dress to wear for this occasion and started to make one. The bell rang and in walked Lady Rothermere and T.S.

Eliot and Gertrude Stein had a solemn conversation, mostly about split infinitives and other grammatical solecisms and why Gertrude Stein used them. Finally Lady Rothermere and Eliot rose to go and Eliot said that if he printed anything of Gertrude Stein's in the Criterion it would have to be her very latest thing. They left and Gertrude Stein said, don't bother to finish your dress, now we don't have to go, and she began to write a portrait of T. S. Eliot and called it the fifteenth of November, that being this day and so there could be no doubt but that it was her latest thing. It was all about wool is wool and silk is silk or wool is woollen and silk is silken. She sent it to T. S. Eliot and he accepted it but naturally he did not print it.

Then began a long correspondence, not between Gertrude Stein and T. S. Eliot, but between T. S. Eliot's secretary and myself. We each addressed the other as Sir, I signing myself A. B. Toklas and she signing initials. It was only considerably afterwards that I found out that his secretary was not a young man. I don't know whether she ever found out that I was not.

In spite of all this correspondence nothing happened and Gertrude Stein mischievously told the story to all the english people coming to the house and at that moment there were a great many english coming in and out. At any rate finally there was a note, it was now early spring, from the Criterion asking would Miss Stein mind if her contribution appeared in the October number. She replied that nothing could be more suitable than the fifteenth of November on the fifteenth of October.

Once more a long silence and then this time came proof of the article. We were surprised but returned the proof promptly. Apparently a young man had sent it without authority because very shortly came an apologetic letter saying that there had been a mistake, the article was not to be printed just yet. This was also told to the passing english with the result that after all it was printed.[8] Thereafter it was re-

[3]Anderson had come upon and admired Stein's *Tender Buttons* as early as 1914. He gave an account of his visit to Stein in "Four American Impressions," published in the October 11, 1922, issue of *The New Republic*. *Geography and Plays* was published in 1922.

[4]Grace Lounsbery was among a circle of Stein's friends during her Baltimore days, and later turned up in Paris.

[5]Kate Buss, a journalist and sculptor from Medford, Massachusetts, was a Pound admirer.

[6]Lady Rothermere, married to a wealthy British publisher, was the financial backer of Eliot's magazine, *The Criterion*.

[7]Wife of the American singer Paul Draper.

[8]"Fifteenth of November" was published in the January 1926 issue of *The Criterion*.

printed in the Georgian Stories. Gertrude Stein was delighted when later she was told that Eliot had said in Cambridge that the work of Gertrude Stein was very fine but not for us.

But to come back to Ezra. Ezra did come back and he came back with the editor of The Dial.[9] This time it was worse than japanese prints, it was much more violent. In his surprise at the violence Ezra fell out of Gertrude Stein's favourite little armchair, the one I have since tapestried with Picasso designs, and Gertrude Stein was furious. Finally Ezra and the editor of The Dial left, nobody too well pleased. Gertrude Stein did not want to see Ezra again. Ezra did not quite see why. He met Gertrude Stein one day near the Luxembourg gardens and said, but I do want to come to see you. I am so sorry, answered Gertrude Stein, but Miss Toklas has a bad tooth and beside we are busy picking wild flowers. All of which was literally true, like all of Gertrude Stein's literature, but it upset Ezra, and we never saw him again. . . .

[HEMINGWAY, FITZGERALD, AND OTHERS]

I remember very well the impression I had of Hemingway that first afternoon. He was an extraordinarily good-looking young man, twenty-three years old. It was not long after that that everybody was twenty-six. It became the period of being twenty-six. During the next two or three years all the young men were twenty-six years old. It was the right age apparently for that time and place. There were one or two under twenty, for example George Lynes but they did not count as Gertrude Stein carefully explained to them. If they were young men they were twenty-six. Later on, much later on they were twenty-one and twenty-two.

So Hemingway was twenty-three, rather foreign looking, with passionately interested, rather than interesting eyes. He sat in front of Gertrude Stein and listened and looked.

They talked then, and more and more, a great deal together. He asked her to come and spend an evening in their apartment and look at his work. Hemingway had then and has always a very good instinct for finding apartments in strange but pleasing localities and good femmes de ménage[10] and good food. This his first apartment was just off the place du Tertre. We spent the evening there and he and Gertrude Stein went over all the writing he had done up to that time. He had begun the novel that it was inevitable he would begin and there were the little poems afterwards printed by McAlmon in the Contact Edition.[11] Gertrude Stein rather liked the poems, they were direct, Kiplingesque, but the novel she found wanting. There is a great deal of description in this, she said, and not particularly good description. Begin over again and concentrate, she said.

Hemingway was at this time Paris correspondent for a canadian newspaper. He was obliged there to express what he called the canadian viewpoint.

He and Gertrude Stein used to walk together and talk together a great deal. One day she said to him, look here, you say you and your wife have a little money between you. Is it enough to live on if you live quietly. Yes, he said. Well, she said, then do it. If you keep on doing newspaper work you will never see things, you will only see words and that will not do, that is of course if you intend to be a writer. Hemingway said he undoubtedly intended to be a writer. He and his wife went away on a trip and shortly after Hemingway turned up alone. He came to the house about ten o'clock in the morning and he stayed, he stayed for lunch, he stayed all afternoon, he stayed for dinner and he stayed until about ten o'clock at night and then all of a sudden he

[9]Scofield Thayer, editor of *The Dial*, a little magazine in New York.

[10]"Cleaning ladies," or "charwomen" (French).

[11]Robert McAlmon (1896–1956) was an American expatriate who came into money through a marriage of convenience to the wealthy British writer, Winifred Ellerman (later Bryher), and established a press to publish the "Contact Editions." He published works by James Joyce, Hemingway, and other expatriates; he published Stein's *The Making of Americans* in 1925. McAlmon wrote an autobiographical account of these years, *Being Geniuses Together*, 1938.

announced that his wife was enceinte[12] and then with great bitterness, and I, I am too young to be a father. We consoled him as best we could and sent him on his way.

When they came back Hemingway said that he had made up his mind. They would go back to America and he would work hard for a year and with what he would earn and what they had they would settle down and he would give up newspaper work and make himself a writer. They went away and well within the prescribed year they came back with a new born baby. Newspaper work was over.

The first thing to do when they came back was as they thought to get the baby baptised. They wanted Gertrude Stein and myself to be god-mothers and an english war comrade of Hemingway was to be god-father. We were all born of different religions and most of us were not practising any, so it was rather difficult to know in what church the baby could be baptised. We spent a great deal of time that winter, all of us, discussing the matter. Finally it was decided that it should be baptised episcopalian and episcopalian it was. Just how it was managed with the assortment of god-parents I am sure I do not know, but it was baptised in the episcopalian chapel.

Writer or painter god-parents are notoriously unreliable. That is, there is certain before long to be a cooling of friendship. I know several cases of this, poor Paulot Picasso's godparents have wandered out of sight and just as naturally it is a long time since any of us have seen or heard of our Hemingway god-child.

However in the beginning we were active god-parents, I particularly. I embroidered a little chair and I knitted a gay coloured garment for the god-child. In the meantime the god-child's father was very earnestly at work making himself a writer.

Gertrude Stein never corrects any detail of anybody's writing, she sticks strictly to general principles, the way of seeing what the writer chooses to see, and the relation between that vision and the way it gets down. When the vision is not complete the words are flat, it is very simple, there can be no mistake about it, so she insists. It was at this time that Hemingway began the short things that afterwards were printed in a volume called In Our Time.[13]

One day Hemingway came in very excited about Ford Madox Ford and the Transatlantic.[14] Ford Madox Ford had started the Transatlantic some months before. A good many years before, indeed before the war, we had met Ford Madox Ford who was at that time Ford Madox Hueffer. He was married to Violet Hunt and Violet Hunt and Gertrude Stein were next to each other at the tea table and talked a great deal together. I was next to Ford Madox Hueffer and I liked him very much and I liked his stories of Mistral and Tarascon and I liked his having been followed about in that land of the french royalist, on account of his resemblance to the Bourbon claimant.[15] I had never seen the Bourbon claimant but Ford at that time undoubtedly might have been a Bourbon.

We had heard that Ford was in Paris, but we had not happened to meet. Gertrude Stein had however seen copies of the Transatlantic and found it interesting but had thought nothing further about it.

Hemingway came in then very excited and said that Ford wanted something of Gertrude Stein's for the next number and he, Hemingway, wanted The Making of Americans to be run in it as a serial and he had to have the first fifty pages at once. Gertrude Stein was of course quite overcome with her excitement at this idea, but there was no copy of the manuscript except the one that we had had bound. That makes no difference, said Hemingway, I will copy it. And he and I between us did copy it and it was printed in the next number of the Transatlantic. So for the first time a piece of the monumental work which was the beginning, really the beginning of

---

12 "Pregnant" (French).
13 Hemingway's book of short stories published in 1924.
14 Ford Madox Ford (1873–1939), English novelist, edited the *Transatlantic Review* in Paris in 1924. Frédéric Mistral (1830–1914), Provençal poet, and Tarascon, France, appear

in his *Provence* (1935).
15 I.e., the descendant of the royal Bourbon line in France who would be rightful heir to the throne in the unlikely event that the monarchy were restored.

modern writing, was printed, and we were very happy. Later on when things were difficult between Gertrude Stein and Hemingway, she always remembered with gratitude that after all it was Hemingway who first caused to be printed a piece of The Making of Americans. She always says, yes sure I have a weakness for Hemingway. After all he was the first of the young men to knock at my door and he did make Ford print the first piece of The Making of Americans.

I myself have not so much confidence that Hemingway did do this. I have never known what the story is but I have always been certain that there was some other story behind it all. That is the way I feel about it.

Gertrude Stein and Sherwood Anderson are very funny on the subject of Hemingway. The last time that Sherwood was in Paris they often talked about him. Hemingway had been formed by the two of them and they were both a little proud and a little ashamed of the work of their minds. Hemingway had at one moment, when he had repudiated Sherwood Anderson and all his works,[16] written him a letter in the name of american literature which he, Hemingway, in company with his contemporaries was about to save, telling Sherwood just what he, Hemingway thought about Sherwood's work, and, that thinking, was in no sense complimentary. When Sherwood came to Paris Hemingway naturally was afraid. Sherwood as naturally was not.

As I say he and Gertrude Stein were endlessly amusing on the subject. They admitted that Hemingway was yellow, he is, Gertrude Stein insisted, just like the flatboat men on the Mississippi river as described by Mark Twain. But what a book, they both agreed, would be the real story of Hemingway, not those he writes but the confessions of the real Ernest Hemingway. It would be for another audience than the audience Hemingway now has but it would be very wonderful. And then they both agreed that they have a weakness for Hemingway because he is such a good pupil. He is a rotten pupil, I protested. You don't understand, they both said, it is so flattering to have a pupil who does it without understanding it, in other words he takes training and anybody who takes training is a favourite pupil. They both admit it to be a weakness. Gertrude Stein added further, you see he is like Derain.[17] You remember Monsieur de Tuille said, when I did not understand why Derain was having the success he was having that it was because he looks like a modern and he smells of the museums. And that is Hemingway, he looks like a modern and he smells of the museums. But what a story that of the real Hem, and one he should tell himself but alas he never will. After all, as he himself once murmured, there is the career, the career.

But to come back to the events that were happening.

Hemingway did it all. He copied the manuscript and corrected the proof. Correcting proofs is, as I said before, like dusting, you learn the values of the thing as no reading suffices to teach it to you. In correcting these proofs Hemingway learned a great deal and he admired all that he learned. It was at this time that he wrote to Gertrude Stein saying that it was she who had done the work in writing The Making of Americans and he and all his had but to devote their lives to seeing that it was published.

He had hopes of being able to accomplish this. Some one, I think by the name of Sterne,[18] said that he could place it with a publisher. Gertrude Stein and Hemingway believed that he could, but soon Hemingway reported that Sterne had entered into his period of unreliability. That was the end of that.

In the meantime and sometime before this Mina Loy[19] had brought McAlmon to the house and he came from time to time and he brought his wife and brought

---

[16]Reference to Hemingway's parody of Sherwood Anderson, *The Torrents of Spring* (1926).
[17]André Derain (1880–1954), French post-impressionist painter.
[18]Harold Stearns (1891–1943), then acting as an agent for Liveright (publisher).
[19]Mina Loy (1882–1936), an English-born American poet.

William Carlos Williams. And finally he wanted to print The Making of Americans in the Contact Edition and finally he did. I will come to that.

In the meantime McAlmon had printed the three poems and ten stories of Hemingway and William Bird[20] had printed In Our Time and Hemingway was getting to be known. He was coming to know Dos Passos and Fitzgerald and Bromfield and George Antheil[21] and everybody else and Harold Loeb[22] was once more in Paris. Hemingway had become a writer. He was also a shadow-boxer, thanks to Sherwood, and he heard about bull-fighting from me. I have always loved spanish dancing and spanish bull-fighting and I loved to show the photographs of bull-fighters and bull-fighting. I also loved to show the photograph where Gertrude Stein and I were in the front row and had our picture taken there accidentally. In these days Hemingway was teaching some young chap how to box. The boy did not know how, but by accident he knocked Hemingway out.[23] I believe this sometimes happens. At any rate in these days Hemingway although a sportsman was easily tired. He used to get quite worn out walking from his house to ours. But then he had been worn by the war. Even now he is, as Hélène says all men are, fragile. Recently a robust friend of his said to Gertrude Stein, Ernest is very fragile, whenever he does anything sporting something breaks, his arm, his leg, or his head.

In those early days Hemingway liked all his contemporaries except Cummings.[24] He accused Cummings of having copied everything, not from anybody but from somebody. Gertrude Stein who had been much impressed by The Enormous Room said that Cummings did not copy, he was the natural heir of the New England tradition with its aridity and its sterility, but also with its individuality. They disagreed about this. They also disagreed about Sherwood Anderson. Gertrude Stein contended that Sherwood Anderson had a genius for using a sentence to convey a direct emotion, this was in the great american tradition, and that really except Sherwood there was no one in America who could write a clear and passionate sentence. Hemingway did not believe this, he did not like Sherwood's taste. Taste has nothing to do with sentences, contended Gertrude Stein. She also added that Fitzgerald was the only one of the younger writers who wrote naturally in sentences.

Gertrude Stein and Fitzgerald are very peculiar in their relation to each other. Gertrude Stein had been very much impressed by This Side of Paradise. She read it when it came out and before she knew any of the young american writers. She said of it that it was this book that really created for the public the new generation. She has never changed her opinion about this. She thinks this equally true of *The Great Gatsby*. She thinks Fitzgerald will be read when many of his well known contemporaries are forgotten. Fitzgerald always says that he thinks Gertrude Stein says these things just to annoy him by making him think that she means them, and he adds in his favourite way, and her doing it is the cruellest thing I ever heard. They always however have a very good time when they meet. And the last time they met they had a good time with themselves and Hemingway.

Then there was McAlmon. McAlmon had one quality that appealed to Gertrude Stein, abundance, he could go on writing, but she complained that it was dull.

There was also Glenway Wescott[25] but Glenway Wescott at no time interested Gertrude Stein. He has a certain syrup but it does not pour.

So then Hemingway's career was begun. For a little while we saw less of him and

20An American journalist in Paris who taught himself printing and established the "three mountain press" to publish the expatriates and others.

21Louis Bromfield (1896–1956), American novelist; George Antheil (1900–1959), an avant-garde American composer.

22Harold Loeb, an American Jewish writer, on whom Hemingway based his character Robert Cohn in The Sun Also Rises; it was an unflattering portrait, and perhaps not true to life, as Loeb claimed in his memoir, *The Way It Was* (1959).

23The story was that Morley Callaghan, a young Canadian

journalist-writer, had in 1929 knocked Hemingway out in a boxing match at the Dome in Paris, with Scott Fitzgerald serving as timekeeper; Callaghan wrote his account of the story in *That Summer in Paris* (1963).

24E. E. Cummings (1894–1962), American poet; his *Enormous Room* (1922) was an account of his experiences in a French prison during World War I (the French mistakenly believed he was plotting treason in his cryptic correspondence).

25Glenway Wescott (1901–1987), American novelist from Wisconsin and one of the expatriates.

then he began to come again. He used to recount to Gertrude Stein the conversations that he afterwards used in The Sun Also Rises and they talked endlessly about the character of Harold Loeb. At this time Hemingway was preparing his volume of short stories to submit to publishers in America. One evening after we had not seen him for a while he turned up with Shipman.[26] Shipman was an amusing boy who was to inherit a few thousand dollars when he came of age. He was not of age. He was to buy the Transatlantic Review when he came of age, so Hemingway said. He was to support a surrealist review when he came of age, André Masson said. He was to buy a house in the country when he came of age, Josette Gris[27] said. As a matter of fact when he came of age nobody who had known him then seemed to know what he did do with his inheritance. Hemingway brought him with him to the house to talk about buying the Transatlantic and incidentally he brought the manuscript he intended sending to America. He handed it to Gertrude Stein. He had added to his stories a little story of meditations and in these he said that The Enormous Room was the greatest book he had ever read. It was then that Gertrude Stein said, Hemingway, remarks are not literature.

After this we did not see Hemingway for quite a while and then we went to see some one, just after The Making of Americans was printed, and Hemingway who was there came up to Gertrude Stein and began to explain why he would not be able to write a review of the book. Just then a heavy hand fell on his shoulder and Ford Madox Ford said, young man it is I who wish to speak to Gertrude Stein. Ford then said to her, I wish to ask your permission to dedicate my new book to you. May I. Gertrude Stein and I were both awfully pleased and touched.

For some years after this Gertrude Stein and Hemingway did not meet. And then we heard that he was back in Paris and telling a number of people how much he wanted to see her. Don't you come home with Hemingway on your arm, I used to say when she went out for a walk. Sure enough one day she did come back bringing him with her.

They sat and talked a long time. Finally I heard her say, Hemingway, after all you are ninety percent Rotarian.[28] Can't you, he said, make it eighty percent. No, said she regretfully, I can't. After all, as she always says, he did, and I may say, he does have moments of disinterestedness.

After that they met quite often. Gertrude Stein always says she likes to see him, he is so wonderful. And if he could only tell his own story. In their last conversation she accused him of having killed a great many of his rivals and put them under the sod. I never, said Hemingway, seriously killed anybody but one man and he was a bad man and, he deserved it, but if I killed anybody else I did it unknowingly, and so I am not responsible.

It was Ford who once said of Hemingway, he comes and sits at my feet and praises me. It makes me nervous. Hemingway also said once, I turn my flame which is a small one down and down and then suddenly there is a big explosion. If there were nothing but explosions my work would be so exciting nobody could bear it.

However, whatever I say, Gertrude Stein always says, yes I know but I have a weakness for Hemingway. . . .

[CONCLUSION: TOKLAS REVEALED AS STEIN]

For some time now many people, and publishers, have been asking Gertrude Stein to write her autobiography and she had always replied, not possibly.

She began to tease me and say that I should write my autobiography. Just think, she would say, what a lot of money you would make. She then began to invent titles

---

[26]Evan Biddle Shipman, an American journalist-poet from a wealthy New Hampshire family.
[27]André Masson, French surrealist painter; Josette Gris, wife of the Spanish cubist painter Juan Gris.
[28]The Rotary Club is a businessman's club; the members are distinctly non- and perhaps even anti-bohemian.

for my autobiography. My Life With The Great, Wives of Geniuses I Have Sat With, My Twenty-five Years With Gertrude Stein.

Then she began to get serious and say, but really seriously you ought to write your autobiography. Finally I promised that if during the summer I could find time I would write my autobiography.

When Ford Madox Ford was editing the Transatlantic Review he once said to Gertrude Stein, I am a pretty good writer and a pretty good editor and a pretty good business man but I find it very difficult to be all three at once.

I am a pretty good housekeeper and a pretty good gardener and a pretty good needlewoman and a pretty good secretary and a pretty good editor and a pretty good vet for dogs and I have to do them all at once and I found it difficult to add being a pretty good author.

About six weeks ago Gertrude Stein said, it does not look to me as if you were ever going to write that autobiography. You know what I am going to do. I am going to write it for you. I am going to write it as simply as Defoe did the autobiography of Robinson Crusoe.[29] And she has and this is it.

1932   *1933*

from Tender Buttons[1]

OBJECTS

A CARAFE, THAT IS A BLIND GLASS

A kind in glass and a cousin, a spectacle and nothing strange a single hurt color and an arrangement in a system to pointing. All this and not ordinary, not unordered in not resembling. The difference is spreading.

•   •   •   •   •

A FRIGHTFUL RELEASE

A bag which was left and not only taken but turned away was not found. The place was shown to be very like the last time. A piece was not exchanged, not a bit of it, a piece was left over. The rest was mismanaged.

•   •   •   •   •

A PETTICOAT

A light white, a disgrace, an ink spot, a rosy charm.

A WAIST

A star glide, a single frantic sullenness, a single financial grass greediness.
Object that is in wood. Hold the pine, hold the dark, hold in the rush, make the bottom.

---

[29]Daniel Defoe (1660?–1731), English author of *Robinson Crusoe* (1719), an account, based on a true story but highly embellished, of being stranded on an uninhabited island and surviving.
[1]*Tender Buttons* is divided into three parts, "Objects," "Food," and "Rooms." Gertrude Stein called the passages poems. They have been variously interpreted as nonsense, as dadaist or surreal, and as linguistic dribble-painting from the unconscious. Psychoanalytic critics have found a great deal of sexual symbolism in various passages. Readers are likely to find in the "poems" what they bring with them in the art of reading. Stein has said (in *Poetry and Grammar*, 1935) that when she was writing *The Making of Americans* and thus prose,

"something happened": "I began to discover the names of things, that is not discover the names but discover the things the things to see the things to look at and in so doing I had of course to name them not to give them new names but to see that I could find out how to know that they were there by their names or by replacing their names. And how was I to do so. They had their names and naturally I called them by the names they had and in doing so having begun looking at them I called them by their names with passion and that made poetry, I did not mean it to make poetry but it did, it made the *Tender Buttons*, and the *Tender Buttons* was very good poetry. . . ."

A piece of crystal. A change, in a change that is remarkable there is no reason to say that there was a time.

A woolen object gilded. A country climb is the best disgrace, a couple of practices any of them in order is so left.

A TIME TO EAT

A pleasant simple habitual and tyrannical and authorized and educated and resumed and articulate separation. This is not tardy.

• • • • • •

RED ROSES

A cool red rose and a pink cut pink, a collapse and a sold hole, a little less hot.

• • • • • •

SHOES

To be a wall with a damper a stream of pounding way and nearly enough choice makes a steady midnight. It is pus.

A shallow hole rose on red, a shallow hole in and in this makes ale less. It shows shine.

A DOG

A little monkey goes like a donkey that means to say that means to say that more sighs last goes. Leave with it. A little monkey goes like a donkey.

A WHITE HUNTER

A white hunter is nearly crazy.

A LEAVE

In the middle of a tiny spot and nearly bare there is a nice thing to say that wrist is leading. Wrist is leading.

SUPPOSE AN EYES

Suppose it is within a gate which open is open at the hour of closing summer that is to say it is so.

All the seats are needing blackening. A white dress is in sign. A soldier a real soldier has a worn lace a worn lace of different sizes that is to say if he can read, if he can read he is a size to show shutting up twenty-four.

Go red go red, laugh white.

Suppose a collapse in rubbed purr, in rubbed purr get.

Little sales ladies little sales ladies little saddles of mutton.

Little sales of leather and such beautiful beautiful, beautiful beautiful.

A SHAWL

A shawl is a hat and hurt and a red balloon and an under coat and a sizer a sizer of talks.

A shawl is a wedding, a piece of wax a little build. A shawl.

Pick a ticket, pick it in strange steps and with hollows. There is hollow hollow belt, a belt is a shawl.

A plate that has a little bobble, all of them, any so.

Please a round it is ticket.

It was a mistake to state that a laugh and a lip and a laid climb and a depot and a cultivator and little choosing is a point it.

BOOK

Book was there, it was there. Book was there. Stop it, stop it, it was a cleaner, a wet cleaner and it was not where it was wet, it was not high, it was directly placed back, not back again, back it was returned, it was needless, it put a bank, a bank when, a bank care.

Suppose a man a realistic expression of resolute reliability suggests pleasing itself white all white and no head does that mean soap. It does not so. It means kind wavers and little chance to beside beside rest. A plain.

Suppose ear rings that is one way to breed, breed that. Oh chance to say, oh nice old pole. Next best and nearest a pillar. Chest not valuable, be papered.

Cover up cover up the two with a little piece of string and hope rose and green, green.

Please a plate, put a match to the seam and really then really then, really then it is a remark that joins many many lead games. It is a sister and sister and a flower and a flower and a dog and a colored sky a sky colored grey and nearly that nearly that let.

PEELED PENCIL, CHOKE

Rub her coke.

IT WAS BLACK, BLACK TOOK

Black ink best wheel bale brown.
Excellent not a hull house, not a pea soup, no bill no care, no precise no past pearl pearl goat.

THIS IS THIS DRESS, AIDER

Aider, why aider why whow, whow stop touch, aider whow, aider stop the muncher, muncher munchers.
A jack in kill her, a jack in, makes a meadowed king, makes a to let.

1914

CLAUDE McKAY
(1889–1948)

Claude McKay first gained fame as a poet with a poem written in response to a bloody race riot in Chicago, triggered when a black boy accidentally found his way into a segregated swimming area. McKay's poem, "If We Must Die," expressed the rage of his race on being repeatedly victimized by the dominant white society. Never before had black poetry expressed such defiance:

> O kinsmen! we must meet the common foe!
> Though outnumbered let us show us brave
> And for their thousand blows deal one deathblow!
> What though before us lies the open grave?

McKay would recall later, in his autobiography, the agitation when he read the poem aloud to his fellow crew members on the train where he worked as the diner steward. It was because of this poem, he observed, that "the Negro people unanimously hailed" him as a poet. But, he added ruefully, "that one grand outburst is their sole standard of appraising my poetry."

McKay was born in Jamaica and had already published two volumes of dialect poetry when at twenty-three he was sent to Tuskegee Institute in Alabama to obtain an education in agriculture. After a few months McKay switched to Kansas State University, in Manhattan, Kansas, and a year later he took off for Harlem, determined to be a poet. Thus he began his life as a vagabond, looking for work "easy" to his hand while his head "was thinking hard." He worked as "porter, fireman, waiter, bar-boy, houseman" — at anything, in short, that would free his intellectual and imaginative energies for writing. His ambition was to "graduate as a poet."

In 1920 McKay went to London, discovered the works of Karl Marx, and worked for a time on a Communist newspaper, *The Worker's Dreadnought*. In England he brought out his third volume of poems, *Spring in New Hampshire* (1920). Then he returned to New York and was invited by Max Eastman, editor of the Marxist *Liberator*, to become associate editor.

During this period, McKay brought out his fourth volume of poems, *Harlem Shadows* (1922), a collection of nondialect poetry earning him high praise. Soon he was functioning as co-editor with Michael Gold of the *Liberator*, and before long they quarreled over Gold's determination to maintain the *Liberator*'s ideological purity even at the expense of literary quality. McKay resigned and went to Russia to see the Communist Revolution firsthand, working his way there as a stoker in the engine room of a steamship.

In Russia, McKay met Trotsky and Bukharin and observed the Fourth Congress of the Communist International in 1922. But in his short stay there he became disillusioned because of the self-serving manipulation and skullduggery he witnessed in the international Communist movement. From Russia, McKay travelled and lived for various periods in Germany, France, Spain, Morocco, becoming a kind of international vagabond, but in serious quest of his identity and the meaning of his blackness. His wandering abroad lasted from 1922 to 1934.

In 1928 McKay published his first novel, *Home to Harlem*, portraying two complementary blacks: the focal character is a fun-loving, instinctual American who deserts the American army in France and returns to Harlem; his buddy is a West Indian intellectual searching for his soul. The two were meant to suggest and encompass the complexity of black identity. The novel was universally acclaimed by white reviewers, but condemned by black critics as "stereotypical" in its portrayal of the happy-go-lucky central character Jake. Whereas McKay earlier had been accepted as a leader of the Harlem Renaissance because of his powerful poem of protest, "If We Must Die," he was now rejected by the black intelligentsia because of a novel they saw as "racist." With the appearance and success of his second novel, *Banjo*, in 1929, extending and exploring the same themes found in *Home to Harlem*, but set in Marseilles, France, the controversy faded and McKay was accepted as a charter member of the New Negro movement.

In 1932 McKay brought together twelve short stories, six set in Harlem and six in Jamaica, under the title *Gingertown*. The following year he published his last novel, *Banana Bottom*, set in Jamaica. *A Long Way from Home*, his autobiography, appeared in 1937. And *Harlem: Negro Metropolis*, an account of the famed New York black ghetto, was published in 1941. Near the end of his life, McKay converted to Catholicism. When he died in 1948, he was teaching in one of the Catholic schools in Chicago.

McKay had been in search of a belief all his adult life, ever since he had lost his faith as a boy in his native Jamaica. His own keen intelligence and sense of irony, his frankness in facing realities, would not let him be caught up permanently in any of the delusions that held many in thrall, luring them into by-ways leading to dead-ends. He concluded his autobiography with a chapter entitled "On Belonging to a Minority Group," observing: ". . . there is very little group spirit among Negroes. The American Negro group is the most advanced in the world. . . . But it sadly lacks a group soul." McKay proved himself a kind of spiritual pioneer for his people. If blacks today have discovered that "group soul," he played a part in helping to make the discovery possible.

ADDITIONAL READING

Selected Poems of Claude McKay, 1953; *The Passion of Claude McKay: Selected Poetry and Prose, 1912–1948*, ed., Wayne F. Cooper, 1973.

Nathan Irvin Huggins, *Harlem Renaissance*, 1971; George Kent, "The Soulful Way of Claude McKay," *Blackness and the Adventure of Western Culture*, 1972; Addison Gayle, Jr., *Claude McKay: The Black Poet at War*, 1972; Addison Gayle, Jr., *The Way of the New World: The Black Novel*, 1975; James R. Giles, *Claude McKay*, 1976; Wayne F. Cooper, *Claude McKay: Rebel Sojourner in the Harlem Renaissance*, 1987.

TEXT

A Long Way from Home, intro. St. Clair Drake, 1970.

from A Long Way from Home

THE NEW NEGRO IN PARIS

I finished my native holiday in Marrakesh.[1] In Casablanca[2] I found a huge pile of mail awaiting me. The handsomest thing was a fat envelope from a New York bank containing a gold-lettered pocket book. The pocket book enclosed my first grand from the sale of *Home to Harlem*.[3]

There were stacks of clippings with criticisms of my novel; praise from the white press, harsh censure from the colored press. And a lot of letters from new admirers and old friends and associates and loves. One letter in particular took my attention. It was from James Weldon Johnson,[4] inviting me to return to America to participate in the Negro renaissance movement. He promised to do his part to facilitate my return if there were any difficulty. And he did.

The Johnson letter set me thinking hard about returning to Harlem. All the reports stressed the great changes that had occurred there since my exile, pictured a Harlem spreading west and south, with splendid new blocks of houses opened up for the colored people. The reports described the bohemian interest in and patronage of Harlem, the many successful colored shows on Broadway, the florescence of Negro literature and art, with many promising aspirants receiving scholarships from foundations and patronage from individuals. Newspapers and magazines brought me exciting impressions of a more glamorous Harlem. Even in Casablanca a Moor of half-German parentage exhibited an article featuring Harlem in an important German newspaper, and he was eager for more information.

But the resentment of the Negro intelligentsia against *Home to Harlem* was so general, bitter and violent that I was hesitant about returning to the great Black Belt. I

---

[1] In Morocco, the southern capital.
[2] Chief seaport of Morocco.
[3] His controversial novel, published in 1928, and liked by white critics but considered "racist" by blacks.

[4] James Weldon Johnson (1871–1938), black American author of many books; his *God's Trombones: Seven Negro Sermons in Verse*, published in 1927, was especially praised for using black dialect for serious rather than comic purposes.

had learned very little about the ways of the Harlem élite during the years I lived there. When I left the railroad and the companionship of the common blacks, my intellectual contacts were limited mainly to white radicals and bohemians. I was well aware that if I returned to Harlem I wouldn't be going back to the *milieu* of railroad men, from whom I had drifted far out of touch. Nor could I go back among radical whites and try to rekindle the flames of an old enthusiasm. I knew that if I did return I would have to find a new orientation among the Negro intelligentsia.

One friend in Harlem had written that Negroes were traveling abroad *en masse* that spring and summer and that the élite would be camping in Paris. I thought that it might be less unpleasant to meet the advance guard of the Negro intelligentsia in Paris. And so, laying aside my experiment in wearing bags, bournous and tarboosh,[5] I started out.

First to Tangier,[6] where four big European powers were performing their experiment of international government in Africa upon a living corpse. Otherwise Tangier was a rare African-Mediterranean town of Moors and progressive Sephardic Jews and Europeans, mostly Spanish.

Through Spanish Morocco I passed and duly noted its points of interest. The first was Tetuán,[7] which inspired this sonnet:

TETUÁN

Morocco conquering homage paid to Spain
And the Alhambra[8] lifted up its towers!
Africa's fingers tipped with miracles,
And quivering with Arabian designs,
Traced words and figures like exotic flowers,
Sultanas' chambers of rare tapestries,
Filigree marvels from Koranic[9] lines,
Mosaics chanting notes like tropic rain.

And Spain repaid the tribute ages after:
To Tetuán, that fort of struggle and strife,
Where chagrined Andalusian[10] Moors retired,
She brought a fountain bubbling with new life,
Whose jewelled charm won even the native pride,
And filled it sparkling with flamenco laughter.

In all Morocco there is no place as delicious as Tetuán. By a kind of magic instinct the Spaniards have created a modern town which stands up like a happy extension of the antique Moroccan. The ancient walls merge into the new without pain. The Spanish Morisco[11] buildings give more lightness to the native Moroccan, and the architectural effect of the whole is a miracle of perfect miscegenation.

I loved the colored native lanterns, illuminating the archways of Larache. I liked Ceuta lying like a symbolic handclasp across the Mediterranean. And I adored the quaint tile-roofed houses and cool watered gardens in the mountain fastness of Xauen.[12] From Gibraltar I was barred by the British. But that was no trouble to my skin, for ever since I have been traveling for the sheer enjoyment of traveling I have avoided British territory. That was why I turned down an attractive invitation to visit Egypt, when I was living in France.

---

[5]Also "burnoose," a hooded cloak worn by Arabs; tarboosh: a tasseled cloth cap worn by Muslim men.
[6]Seaport on the north coast of Morocco, near the Strait of Gibralter.
[7]Capital of Tetuán province, formerly of Spanish Morocco.
[8]The Alhambra, palace at Granada in Spain built by the Moorish kings (1248–1354)
[9]The Koran, sacred text and foundation of Islamic religion;

according to tradition, dictated to Muhammad by the Archangel Gabriel.
[10]Andalusia: southern province of Spain which was ruled by the Moors from the eighth through the fifteenth centuries.
[11]I.e., Moorish.
[12]Larache, Ceuta, and Xauen are all towns or cities of what was once Spanish Morocco.

Once again in Spain, I inspected the great Moorish landmarks. And more clearly I saw Spain outlined as the antique bridge between Africa and Europe.

After the strong dazzling colors of Morocco, Paris that spring appeared something like the melody of larks chanting over a gray field. It was over three years since I had seen the metropolis. At that time it had a political and financial trouble hanging heavy round its neck. Now it was better, with its head up and a lot of money in every hand. I saw many copies of my book, *Banjo*,[13] decorating a shop window in the Avenue de l'Opéra and I was disappointed in myself that I could not work up to feeling a thrill such as I imagine an author should feel.

I took a fling at the cabarets in Montparnasse and Montmartre, and I was very happy to meet again a French West Indian girl whom I knew as a *bonne*[14] in Nice when I was a valet. We ate some good dinners together and saw the excellent French productions of *Rose Marie* and *Show Boat*[15] and danced a little at the Bal Negre and at Bricktop's[16] Harlem hang-out in Montmartre.

I found Louise Bryant[17] in Paris. It was our first meeting since she took my manuscript to New York in the summer of 1926. The meeting was a nerve-tearing ordeal. About two years previously she had written of a strange illness and of doctors who gave her only six months to live and of her determination to live a long time longer than that. She had undergone radical treatment. The last time I had seen her she was plump and buxom. Now she was shrunken and thin and fragile like a dried-up reed. Her pretty face had fallen like a mummy's and nothing was left of her startling attractiveness but her eyebrows.

She embarrassed me by continually saying: "Claude, you won't even look at me." Her conversation was pitched in a nervous hysterical key and the burden was "male conceit." I told her that the female was largely responsible for "male conceit." Often when I had seen her before she had been encircled by a following of admirably created young admirers of the collegiate type. Now she was always with an ugly-mugged woman. This woman was like an apparition of a male impersonator, who was never off the stage. She had a trick way of holding her shoulders and her hands like a gangster and simulating a hard-boiled accent. A witty Frenchman pronounced her a *Sappho-manqué*.[18] The phrase sounded like a desecration of the great glamorous name of Sappho. I wondered why (there being so many attractive women in the world) Louise Bryant should have chosen such a companion. And I thought that it was probably because of the overflow of pity pouring out of her impulsive Irish heart.

I remembered, "Aftermath," the beautiful poem which she sent us for publication in *The Liberator* after John Reed died. Now it seemed of greater significance:

AFTERMATH

Dear, they are singing your praises,
Now you are gone.
But only I saw your going,
I . . . alone . . . in the dawn.

Dear, they are weeping about you,
Now you are dead,

---

[13]McKay's novel, set on the waterfront of the port city of Marseilles, France, published in 1929.
[14]"Maid" (French).
[15]American musicals on which popular movies were based.
[16]"Negro Dancehall" (French); Ada "Bricktop" Smith (1894–1984), cafe singer and owner of a series of clubs in Paris frequented by royalty, society, and leading artists.

[17]Well-known wife of John Reed, radical reporter for *The New Masses* and observer of the Russian Revolution in 1917; he published *Ten Days that Shook the World* in 1919 and died in Russia in 1920. Louise Bryant was a bohemian who believed in free love; she had an affair with Eugene O'Neill.
[18]"Unfulfilled Sappho" (or lesbian) (French), after the Greek poet Sappho.

And they've placed a granite stone
Over your darling head.

I cannot cry any more,
Too burning deep is my grief . . .
I dance through my spendthrift days
Like a fallen leaf.

Faster and faster I whirl
Toward the end of my days.
Dear, I am drunken with sadness
And lost down strange ways.

If only the dance could finish
Like a flash in the sky . . . Oh, soon,
If only a storm could come shouting—
Hurl me past stars and moon.

And I thought if I could not look frankly with admiration at Louise Bryant's face, I could always turn to the permanently lovely poem which she had created.

I had spruced myself up a bit to meet the colored élite. Observing that the Madrileños[19] were well-tailored, I had a couple of suits made in Madrid, and chose a hat there. In Paris I added shoes and shirts and ties and gloves to my wardrobe.

The cream of Harlem was in Paris. There was the full cast of *Blackbirds*[20] (with Adelaide Hall starring in the place of Florence Mills), just as fascinating a group off the stage as they were extraordinary on the stage. The *Porgy*[21] actors had come over from London. There was an army of school teachers and nurses. There were Negro Communists going to and returning from Russia. There were Negro students from London and Scotland and Berlin and the French universities. There were presidents and professors of the best Negro colleges. And there were painters and writers and poets, of whom the most outstanding was Countee Cullen.

I met professor Alain Locke.[22] He had published *The Anthology of the New Negro* in 1925 and he was the animator of the movement as well as the originator of the phrase "Negro renaissance." Commenting upon my appearance, Dr. Locke said, "Why, you are wearing the same kind of gloves as I am!" "Yes," I said, "but my hand is heavier than yours." Dr. Locke was extremely nice and invited me to dinner with President Hope[23] of Atlanta University. The dinner was at one of the most expensive restaurants in the *grands boulevards*. President Hope, who was even more Nordic-looking than Walter White,[24] was very affable and said I did not look like the boxer-type drawings of me which were reproduced with the reviews of *Home to Harlem*. President Hope hoped that I would visit his university when I returned to America.

There had been an interesting metamorphosis in Dr. Locke. When we met for the first time in Berlin in 1923, he took me for a promenade in the Tiergarten.[25] And walking down the row, with the statues of the Prussian kings supported by the famous philosophers and poets and composers on either side, he remarked to me that he thought those statues the finest ideal and expression of the plastic arts in the

---

[19]"Inhabitants of Madrid" (Spanish).
[20]An all-black American musical review, produced annually (1926–39), with songs and skits about black life in America, Harlem, and elsewhere; its 1928 production was starring Adelaide Hall instead of Florence Mills, who had starred in the Harlem production and who had died in 1927.
[21]An American play about black life by Dorothy and Dubose Heyward; George Gershwin based his "folk opera" *Porgy and*

Bess on it in 1935.
[22]Black professor of philosophy (1886–1954), who taught at Howard University and whose *Anthology of the New Negro* in 1925 launched the Harlem Renaissance.
[23]John Hope (1868–1936), distinguished black educator.
[24]Black civil rights leader and writer (1893–1955).
[25]"Zoological park or garden" (German).

world. The remark was amusing, for it was just a short while before that I had walked through the same row with George Grosz,[26] who had described the statues as "the sugar-candy art of Germany." When I showed Dr. Locke George Grosz's book of drawings, *Ecce Homo*,[27] he recoiled from their brutal realism. (Dr. Locke is a Philadelphia blue-black blood, a Rhodes scholar and graduate of Oxford University, and I have heard him described as the most refined Negro in America).

So it was interesting now to discover that Dr. Locke had become the leading Negro authority on African Negro sculpture. I felt that there was so much more affinity between the art of George Grosz and African sculpture than between the Tiergarten insipid idealization of Nordic kings and artists and the transcending realism of the African artists.

Yet I must admit that although Dr. Locke seemed a perfect symbol of the Aframerican rococo in his personality as much as in his prose style, he was doing his utmost to appreciate the new Negro that he had uncovered. He had brought the best examples of their work together in a pioneer book. But from the indication of his appreciations it was evident that he could not lead a Negro renaissance. His introductory remarks were all so weakly winding round and round and getting nowhere. Probably this results from a kink in Dr. Locke's artistic outlook, perhaps due to its effete European academic quality.

When he published his *Anthology of the New Negro*, he put in a number of my poems, including one which was originally entitled "The White House." My title was symbolic, not meaning specifically the private homes of white people, but more the vast modern edifice of American Industry from which Negroes were effectively barred as a group. I cannot convey here my amazement and chagrin when Dr. Locke arbitrarily changed the title of my poem to "White Houses" and printed it in his anthology, without consulting me. I protested against the act, calling Dr. Locke's attention to the fact that my poem had been published under the original title of "The White House" in *The Liberator*.[28] He replied that he had changed the title for political reasons, as it might be implied that the title meant the White House in Washington, and that that could be made an issue against my returning to America.

I wrote him saying that the idea that my poem had reference to the official residence of the President of the United States was ridiculous; and that, whether I was permitted to return to America or not, I did not want the title changed, and would prefer the omission of the poem. For his title "White Houses" was misleading. It changed the whole symbolic intent and meaning of the poem, making it appear as if the burning ambition of the black malcontent was to enter white houses in general. I said that there were many white folks' houses I would not choose to enter, and that, as a fanatical advocate of personal freedom, I hoped that all human beings would always have the right to decide whom they wanted to have enter their houses.

But Dr. Locke high-handedly used his substitute title of "White Houses" in all the editions of his anthology. I couldn't imagine such a man as the leader of a renaissance, when his artistic outlook was so reactionary.

The Negroid élite was not so formidable to meet after all. The financial success of my novel had helped soften hard feelings in some quarters. A lovely lady from Harlem expressed the views of many. Said she: "Why all this nigger-row if a colored writer can exploit his own people and make money and a name? White writers have been exploiting us long enough without any credit to our race. It is silly for the Negro critics to holler to God about *Home to Harlem* as if the social life of the characters is

---

[26]German artist (1893–1959), whose style caricatured and attacked the comfortable middle-class, militarism, and capitalism; he came to America in 1932.
[27]"Behold the Man" (Latin).

[28]An avant-garde, radical periodical (1918–24), founded and edited by the socialist Max Eastman; it published poetry and fiction as well as political essays.

anything like that of the respectable class of Negroes. The people in *Home to Harlem* are our low-down Negroes and we respectable Negroes ought to be proud that we are not like them and be grateful to you for giving us a real picture of Negroes whose lives we know little about on the inside." I felt completely vindicated.

My agent in Paris gave a big party for the cast of *Blackbirds*, to which the lovely lady and other members of the black élite were invited. Adelaide Hall was the animating spirit of the *Blackbirds*. They gave some exhibition numbers, and we all turned loose and had a grand gay time together, dancing and drinking champagne. The French guests (there were some chic ones) said it was the best party of the season. And in tipsy accents some of the Harlem élite admonished me against writing a *Home-to-Harlem* book about *them*.

Thus I won over most of the Negro intelligentsia in Paris, excepting the leading journalist and traveler who remained intransigent. Besides Negro news, the journalist specialized in digging up obscure and Amazing Facts for the edification of the colored people. In these "Facts" Beethoven is proved to be a Negro because he was dark and gloomy; also the Jewish people are proved to have been originally a Negro people!

The journalist was writing and working his way through Paris. Nancy Cunard's *Negro Anthology* describes him as a guide and quoted him as saying he had observed, in the flesh market of Paris, that white southerners preferred colored trade, while Negro leaders preferred white trade.[29] Returning to New York, he gave lectures "for men only" on the peepholes in the walls of Paris.

The journalist was a bitter critic of *Home to Harlem*, declaring it was obscene. I have often wondered if it is possible to establish a really intelligent standard to determine obscenity—a standard by which one could actually measure the obscene act and define the obscene thought. I have done lots of menial work and have no snobbery about common labor. I remember that in Marseilles and other places in Europe I was sometimes approached and offered a considerable remuneration to act as a guide or procurer or do other sordid things. While I was working as a model in Paris a handsome Italian model brought me an offer to work as an occasional attendant in a special *bains de vapeur*.[30] The Italian said that he made good extra money working there. Now, although I needed more money to live, it was impossible for me to make myself do such things. The French say *"On fait ce qu'on peut."*[31] I could not. The very idea of the thing turned me dead cold. My individual morale was all I possessed. I felt that if I sacrificed it to make a little extra money, I would become personally obscene. I would soon be utterly unable to make that easy money. I preferred a menial job.

Yet I don't think I would call another man obscene who could do what I was asked to do without having any personal feeling of revulsion against it. And if an artistic person had or was familiar with such sordid experiences of life and could transmute them into literary or any other art form, I could not imagine that his performance or his thought was obscene.

The Negro journalist argued violently against me. He insisted that I had exploited Negroes to please the white reading public. He said that the white public would not read good Negro books because of race prejudice; that he himself had written a "good" book which had not sold. I said that Negro writers, instead of indulging in whining and self-pity, should aim at reaching the reading public in general or creating a special Negro public; that Negroes had plenty of money to spend on books if books were sold to them.

I said I knew the chances for a black writer and a white writer were not equal, even

---

[29]The journalist is J. A. Rogers (1880?–1966), Jamaican-American writer who popularized black history in books and newspaper columns. Nancy Cunard (1897–1965) rebelled against her wealthy British shipping family and became a Communist; she edited and published an anthology of black writing, *Negro*, in 1934. Claude McKay refused to contribute without pay.

[30]"Steam-baths" (apparently a cover for sexual liaisons) (French).

[31]"One does what one can" (French).

if both were of the same caliber. The white writer had certain avenues, social and financial, which opened to carry him along to success, avenues which were closed to the black. Nevertheless I believed that the Negro writer also had a chance, even though a limited one, with the great American reading public. I thought that if a Negro writer were sincere in creating a plausible Negro tale—if a Negro character were made credible and human in his special environment with a little of the virtues and the vices that are common to the human species—he would obtain some recognition and appreciation. For Negro writers are not alone in competing with heavy handicaps. They have allies among some of the white writers and artists, who are fighting formalism and classicism, crusading for new forms and ideas against the dead weight of the old.

But the journalist was loudly positive that it was easy for a Negro writer to make a sensational success as a writer by "betraying" his race to the white public. So many of the Negro elite love to mouth that phrase about "betraying the race"! As if the Negro group had special secrets which should not be divulged to the other groups. I said I did not think the Negro could be betrayed by any real work of art. If the Negro were betrayed in any place it was perhaps in that Negro press, by which the journalist was syndicated, with its voracious black appetite for yellow journalism.

Thereupon the journalist declared that he would prove that it was easy for a Negro to write the "nigger stuff" the whites wanted of him and make a success of it. He revealed that he was planning a novel for white consumption; that, indeed, he had already written some of it. He was aiming at going over to the white market. He was going to stop writing for Negroes, who gave him so little support, although he had devoted his life to the betterment of the Negro.

I was eager to see him prove his thesis. For he was expressing the point of view of the majority of the colored élite, who maintain that Negroes in the arts can win success by clowning only, because that is all the whites expect and will accept of them. So although I disliked his type of mind, I promised to help him, I was so keen about the result of his experiment. I introduced him to my agent in Paris, and my agent introduced him to a publisher in New York.

Our Negro journalist is very yellow and looks like a *métèque*[32] in France, without attracting undue attention. Yet besides his "Amazing Facts" about Negroes he has written in important magazines, stressing the practical nonexistence of color prejudice in Europe and blaming Negroes for such as exists! Also he wrote in a white magazine about Africa and the color problem under a nom de plume[33] which gave no indication of the writer's origin.

He might have thought that as he had "passed white" a little in complexion and in journalism, it would be just as easy "passing white" as a creative writer. Well, the Negro journalist deliberately wrote his novel as a "white" novelist—or as he imagined a white man would write. But the sensational white novel by a Negro has not yet found its publisher.

The last time I heard about him, he was again a Negro in Ethiopia,[34] interviewing Haile Selassie and reporting the white rape of Ethiopia from an African point of view for the American Negro press.

Nigger Heaven, the Harlem novel of Carl Van Vechten,[35] also was much discussed. I met some of Mr. Van Vechten's Negro friends, who were not seeing him any more because of his book. I felt flattered that they did not mind seeing me! Yet most of

---

32"Resident foreigner" (French).
33"Pen name" (French).
34A country in northeast Africa which, at this time, was ruled by the Emperor Haile Selassie; he was overthrown by Italy (under Mussolini) in 1935, but restored after the Second World War.

35Carl Van Vechten (1880–1964), American writer from Iowa, one of the rare white participants in the Harlem Renaissance; his novel *Nigger Heaven* is a love story set in Harlem and describes the cabaret life there in lurid terms. It has been both praised and condemned.

them agreed that *Nigger Heaven* was broadly based upon the fact of contemporary high life in Harlem. Some of them said that Harlemites should thank their stars that *Nigger Heaven* had soft-pedaled some of the actually wilder Harlem scenes. While the conventional Negro moralists gave the book a hostile reception because of its hectic bohemianism, the leaders of the Negro intelligentsia showed a marked liking for it. In comparing it with *Home to Harlem*, James Weldon Johnson said that I had shown a contempt for the Negro bourgeoisie. But I could not be contemptuous of a Negro bourgeoisie which simply does not exist as a class or a group in America. Because I made the protagonist of my novel a lusty black worker, it does not follow that I am unsympathetic to a refined or wealthy Negro.

My attitude toward *Nigger Heaven* was quite different from that of its Negro friends and foes. I was more interested in the implications of the book. It puzzled me a little that the author, who is generally regarded as a discoverer and sponsor of promising young Negro writers, gave Lascar, the ruthless Negro prostitute, the victory over Byron,[36] the young Negro writer, whom he left, when the novel ends, in the hands of the police, destined perhaps for the death house in Sing Sing.

Carl Van Vechten also was in Paris in the summer of 1929. I had been warned by a white non-admirer of Mr. Van Vechten that I would not like him because he patronized Negroes in a subtle way, to which the Harlem élite were blind because they were just learning sophistication! I thought it would be a new experience to meet a white who was subtly patronizing to a black; the majority of them were so naïvely crude about it. But I found Mr. Van Vechten not a bit patronizing, and quite all right. It was neither his fault nor mine if my reaction was negative.

One of Mr. Van Vechten's Harlem sheiks introduced us after midnight at the Café de la Paix. Mr. Van Vechten was a heavy drinker at that time, but I was not drinking liquor. I had recently suffered from a cerebral trouble and a specialist had warned me against drinking, even wine. And when a French doctor forbids wine, one ought to heed. When we met at that late hour at the celebrated rendezvous of the world's cosmopolites, Mr. Van Vechten was full and funny. He said, "What will you take?" I took a soft drink and I could feel that Mr. Van Vechten was shocked.

I am afraid that as a soft drinker I bored him. The white author and the black author of books about Harlem could not find much of anything to make conversation. The market trucks were rolling by loaded with vegetables for Les Halles,[37] and suddenly Mr. Van Vechten, pointing to a truckload of huge carrots, exclaimed, "How I would like to have all of them!" Perhaps carrots were more interesting than conversation. But I did not feel in any way carroty. I don't know whether my looks betrayed any disapproval. Really I hadn't the slightest objection to Mr. Van Vechten's enthusiasm for the truck driver's raw carrots, though I prefer carrots *en casserole avec poulet cocotte*.[38] But he excused himself to go to the men's room and never came back. So, after waiting a considerable time, I paid the bill with some *Home to Harlem* money and walked in the company of the early dawn (which is delicious in Paris) back to the Rue Jean-Jacques Rousseau.[39]

Mr. Van Vechten's sheik friend was very upset. He was a precious, hesitating sheik and very nervous about that introduction, wondering if it would take. I said that all was okay. But upon returning to New York he sent me a message from Mr. Van Vechten. The message said that Mr. Van Vechten was sorry for not returning, but that he was so high that, after leaving us, he discovered himself running along the avenue after a truck load of carrots.

Among the Negro intelligentsia in Paris there was an interesting group of storytellers, poets and painters. Some had received grants from foundations to continue

---

[36]Characters in *Nigger Heaven*.
[37]A famous marketplace in Paris.
[38]"In a casserole with roast chicken" ("cocotte" is a heavy pot used for cooking casserole-style) (French).
[39]A street named after the famed eighteenth-century French philosopher and writer.

work abroad; some were being helped by private individuals; and all were more or less identified with the Negro renaissance. It was illuminating to exchange ideas with them. I was an older man and not regarded as a member of the renaissance, but more as a forerunner. Indeed, some of them had aired their resentment of my intrusion from abroad into the renaissance set-up. They had thought that I had committed literary suicide because I went to Russia.

For my part I was deeply stirred by the idea of a real Negro renaissance. The Arabian cultural renaissance and the great European renaissance had provided some of my most fascinating reading. The Russian literary renaissance and also the Irish had absorbed my interest. My idea of a renaissance was one of talented persons of an ethnic or national group working individually or collectively in a common purpose and creating things that would be typical of their group.

I was surprised when I discovered that many of the talented Negroes regarded their renaissance more as an uplift organization and a vehicle to accelerate the pace and progress of smart Negro society. It was interesting to note how sharply at variance their artistic outlook was from that of the modernistic white groups that took a significant interest in Negro literature and art. The Negroes were under the delusion that when a lady from Park Avenue or from Fifth Avenue, or a titled European, became interested in Negro art and invited Negro artists to her home, that was a token of Negroes breaking into upper-class white society. I don't think that it ever occurred to them that perhaps such white individuals were searching for a social and artistic significance in Negro art which they could not find in their own society, and that the radical nature and subject of their interest operated against the possibility of their introducing Negroes further than their own particular homes in coveted white society.

Also, among the Negro artists there was much of that Uncle Tom attitude[40] which works like Satan against the idea of a coherent and purposeful Negro group. Each one wanted to be the first Negro, the one Negro, and the only Negro *for the whites* instead of for their group. Because an unusual number of them were receiving grants to do creative work, they actually and naïvely believed that Negro artists as a group would always be treated differently from white artists and be protected by powerful white patrons.

Some of them even expressed the opinion that Negro art would solve the centuries-old social problem of the Negro. That idea was vaguely hinted by Dr. Locke in his introduction to *The New Negro*. Dr. Locke's essay is a remarkable chocolate *soufflé* of art and politics, with not an ingredient of information inside.

They were nearly all Harlem-conscious, in a curious synthetic way, it seemed to me — not because they were aware of Harlem's intrinsic values as a unique and popular Negro quarter, but apparently because white folks had discovered black magic there. I understood more clearly why there had been so much genteel-Negro hostility to my *Home to Harlem* and to Langston Hughes's primitive Negro poems.

I wondered after all whether it would be better for me to return to the new *milieu* of Harlem. Much as all my sympathy was with the Negro group and the idea of a Negro renaissance, I doubted if going back to Harlem would be an advantage. I had done my best Harlem stuff when I was abroad, seeing it from a long perspective. I thought it might be better to leave Harlem to the artists who were on the spot, to give them their chance to produce something better than *Home to Harlem*. I thought that I might as well go back to Africa.

1937

---

[40]Overly submissive and subservient (named after a character in Harriet Beecher Stowe's *Uncle Tom's Cabin*, published in 1852).

JAMES THURBER
(1894–1961)

James Thurber, perhaps America's greatest humorist of the twentieth century, said of his "type of writing" that it "is not a joyous form of self-expression but the manifestation of a twitchiness at once cosmic and mundane. Authors of such pieces have, nobody knows why, a genius for getting into minor difficulties. . . . The little wheels of their invention are set in motion by the damp hand of melancholy."

Although identified throughout his writing career with *The New Yorker* magazine, Thurber was born and grew up in Columbus, Ohio. A childhood accident blinded his left eye, and years later he would gradually lose the sight of the other eye. Thurber went to Ohio State University (1913–18) and came to know a drama student, Elliott Nugent, with whom he would later collaborate on a hit play, *The Male Animal* (1940).

After college, Thurber worked as a reporter for various newspapers. In 1925 he went to France to write a novel, but instead took a job with the Paris edition of the *Chicago Tribune*. In 1926 he returned to the United States and started working for the New York *Evening Post*. He began to submit humorous pieces to *The New Yorker*, which had been founded in 1925 by Harold Ross. Although his first submissions were rejected, Thurber met Ross in 1927 and was hired as managing editor of the magazine. After a short stint as editor, he was shifted to staff writer.

Thurber came to know another staff writer for *The New Yorker*, E. B. White, and the two collaborated on *Is Sex Necessary?*, a spoof on sex manuals and a bestseller in 1929. It was White who saw that Thurber's drawings were a perfect complement to his humorous pieces, and who encouraged him as a cartoonist.

The 1930s were astonishingly productive for Thurber: *The Owl in the Attic and Other Perplexities* (1931); *The Seal in the Bedroom & Other Predicaments* (1932); *My Life and Hard Times* (1933); *The Middle-Aged Man on the Flying Trapeze* (1935); *Let Your Mind Alone! and Other More or Less Inspirational Pieces* (1937). All of these works ingeniously combine drawings of knowing dogs, put-upon men, and apparitional (or predatory) women with prose sketches that most often portray human failure and defeat in confronting the incredible "perplexities" of contemporary life. In *My Life and Hard Times*, Thurber adopted a form — a burlesque or caricatured autobiography — unusually congenial to his comic vision; it was rooted in fact, but nurtured by exaggeration into producing the grotesqueries and incongruities of a humor often dark and teetering on the edge of disaster.

In 1939, Thurber produced two of his most haunting works. *The Last Flower* is a cartoon parable about the strong destructive tendencies that cause war and the frail creative spirit that resists annihilation. "The Secret Life of Walter Mitty" tells the story of the daring and dangerous imaginative life lived by a henpecked, self-effacing, timid — and ordinary — man. It was to be turned into a popular movie in 1947.

In the early 1940s, Thurber went through a series of eye operations and suffered the gradual loss of sight in his remaining eye. He commented on his handicap: "A Blind man benefits by lack of distractions," explaining: "my one-eighth vision happily obscures sad and ungainly sights, leaving only the vivid and radiant, some of whom are my friends and neighbours."

But in spite of his difficulties, Thurber continued to draw and write. In 1940 he published *Fables for Our Time and Famous Poems Illustrated*; in 1942, *My World — and Welcome to It*; in 1943, *Men, Women and Dogs*. With the publication of a selection of the best work from his previous books in *The Thurber Carnival* in 1945, Thurber finally got the serious consideration a great humorist deserves. He introduced the collection with a Preface, "My Fifty Years with James Thurber," providing a sketchy survey of his life and adding: "Thurber goes on as he always has, walking now a little more slowly, answering fewer letters, jumping at slighter sounds."

Thurber continued to produce many books during his last years. Some of these, such as *The 13 Clocks* (1950), were written for children and have become classics. In 1959 he published *The Years with Ross*, a biography of Harold Ross, who had edited *The New Yorker* since founding it in 1925 until his death in 1951. Thurber himself died in 1961 of pneumonia which followed the surgery performed after a blood-clot in the brain and a stroke.

Thurber once characterized humor as "a kind of emotional chaos told about quietly and calmly in retrospect." T. S. Eliot seemed to elaborate on this characterization when he said of Thurber's work that it is "a form of humor which is also a way of saying something serious. There is a criticism of life at the bottom of it. It is serious and even somber. Unlike so much of humor, it is not merely a criticism of manners . . . but something more profound."

ADDITIONAL READING

Selected Letters of James Thurber, ed. Helen Thurber and Edward Weeks, 1981; *Collecting Himself: James Thurber on Writing and Writers, Humor and Himself*, ed. Michael J. Rosen, 1989; *Conversations with James Thurber*, ed. Thomas Fensch, 1989.

Robert E. Morsberger, *James Thurber*, 1964; Edwin T. Bowden, *James Thurber: A Bibliography*, 1968; Richard C. Tobias, *The Art of James Thurber*, 1969; Stephen A. Black, *James Thurber: His Masquerades*, 1970; Charles S. Holmes, *The Clocks of Columbus: The Literary Career of James Thurber*, 1972; Charles S. Holmes, ed., *Thurber: A Collection of Critical Essays*, 1974; Burton Bernstein, *Thurber: A Biography*, 1975; Catherine McGehee Kenney, *Thurber's Anatomy of Confusion*, 1984; Sarah Eleanora Toombs, *James Thurber: An Annotated Bibliography of Criticism*, 1987; Robert Emmet Long, *James Thurber*, 1988.

TEXT

My Life and Hard Times, 1933.

from My Life and Hard Times

THE DOG THAT BIT PEOPLE

Probably no one man should have as many dogs in his life as I have had, but there was more pleasure than distress in them for me except in the case of an Airedale named Muggs. He gave me more trouble than all the other fifty-four or five put together, although my moment of keenest embarrassment was the time a Scotch terrier named Jeannie, who had just had six puppies in the clothes closet of a fourth floor apartment in New York, had the unexpected seventh and last at the corner of Eleventh Street and Fifth Avenue during a walk she had insisted on taking. Then, too, there was the prize winning French poodle, a great big black poodle — none of your little, untroublesome white miniatures—who got sick riding in the rumble seat of a car with me on her way to the Greenwich Dog Show. She had a red rubber bib tucked around her throat and, since a rain storm came up when we were half way through the Bronx, I had to hold over her a small green umbrella, really more of a parasol. The rain beat down fearfully and suddenly the driver of the car drove into a big garage, filled with mechanics. It happened so quickly that I forgot to put the umbrella down and I will always remember, with sickening distress, the look of incredulity mixed with hatred that came over the face of the particular hardened garage man that came over to see what we wanted, when he took a look at me and the poodle. All garage men, and people of that intolerant stripe, hate poodles with their curious hair cut, especially the pom-poms that you got to leave on their hips if you expect the dogs to win a prize.

But the Airedale, as I have said, was the worst of all my dogs. He really wasn't my dog, as a matter of fact: I came home from a vacation one summer to find that my brother Roy[1] had bought him while I was away. A big, burly, choleric dog, he always acted as if he thought I wasn't one of the family. There was a slight advantage in being one of the family, for he didn't bite the family as often as he bit strangers. Still, in the years that we had him he bit everybody but mother, and he made a pass at her once but missed. That was during the month when we suddenly had mice, and Muggs refused to do anything about them. Nobody ever had mice exactly like the mice we had that month. They acted like pet mice, almost like mice somebody had trained. They were so friendly that one night when mother entertained at dinner the Friraliras, a club she and my father had belonged to for twenty years, she put down a lot of little dishes with food in them on the pantry floor so that the mice would be satisfied with that and wouldn't come into the dining room. Muggs stayed out in the pantry with the mice, lying on the floor, growling to himself—not at the mice, but about all the people in the next room that he would have liked to get at. Mother slipped out into the pantry once to see how everything was going. Everything was going fine. It made her so mad to see Muggs lying there, oblivious of the mice—they came running up to her—that she slapped him and he slashed at her, but didn't make it. He was sorry immediately, mother said. He was always sorry, she said, after he bit someone, but we could not understand how she figured this out. He didn't act sorry.

Mother used to send a box of candy every Christmas to the people the Airedale bit. The list finally contained forty or more names. Nobody could understand why we didn't get rid of the dog. I didn't understand it very well myself, but we didn't get rid of him. I think that one or two people tried to poison Muggs—he acted poisoned once in a while—and old Major Moberly fired at him once with his service revolver near the Seneca Hotel in East Broad Street—but Muggs lived to be almost eleven years old and even when he could hardly get around he bit a Congressman who had called to see my father on business. My mother had never liked the Congressman— she said the signs of his horoscope showed he couldn't be trusted (he was Saturn with the moon in Virgo)—but she sent him a box of candy that Christmas. He sent it right back, probably because he suspected it was trick candy. Mother persuaded herself it was all for the best that the dog had bitten him, even though father lost an important business association because of it. "I wouldn't be associated with such a man," mother said, "Muggs could read him like a book."

We used to take turns feeding Muggs to be on his good side, but that didn't always work. He was never in a very good humor, even after a meal. Nobody knew exactly what was the matter with him, but whatever it was it made him irascible, especially in the mornings. Roy never felt very well in the morning, either, especially before

---

[1]Thurber's name in this autobiography for his brother Robert.

Nobody Knew Exactly What Was the Matter with Him

breakfast, and once when he came downstairs and found that Muggs had moodily chewed up the morning paper he hit him in the face with a grapefruit and then jumped up on the dining room table, scattering dishes and silverware and spilling the coffee. Muggs' first free leap carried him all the way across the table and into a brass fire screen in front of the gas grate but he was back on his feet in a moment and in the end he got Roy and gave him a pretty vicious bite in the leg. Then he was all over it; he never bit anyone more than once at a time. Mother always mentioned that as an argument in his favor; she said he had a quick temper but that he didn't hold a grudge. She was forever defending him. I think she liked him because he wasn't well. "He's not strong," she would say, pityingly, but that was inaccurate; he may not have been well but he was terribly strong.

One time my mother went to the Chittenden Hotel to call on a woman mental healer who was lecturing in Columbus[2] on the subject of "Harmonious Vibrations." She wanted to find out if it was possible to get harmonious vibrations into a dog. "He's a large tan-colored Airedale," mother explained. The woman said that she had never treated a dog but she advised my mother to hold the thought that he did not bite and would not bite. Mother was holding the thought the very next morning when Muggs got the iceman but she blamed that slip-up on the iceman. "If you didn't think he would bite you, he wouldn't," mother told him. He stomped out of the house in a terrible jangle of vibrations.

One morning when Muggs bit me slightly, more or less in passing, I reached down and grabbed his short stumpy tail and hoisted him into the air. It was a foolhardy thing to do and the last time I saw my mother, about six months ago, she said she didn't know what possessed me. I don't either, except that I was pretty mad. As long as I held the dog off the floor by his tail he couldn't get at me, but he twisted and jerked so, snarling all the time, that I realized I couldn't hold him that way very long. I carried him to the kitchen and flung him onto the floor and shut the door on him just as he crashed against it. But I forgot about the backstairs. Muggs went up the backstairs and down the frontstairs and had me cornered in the living room. I managed to get up onto the mantlepiece above the fireplace, but it gave way and came down with a tremendous crash throwing a large marble clock, several vases, and myself heavily to the floor. Muggs was so alarmed by the racket that when I picked myself up he had disappeared. We couldn't find him anywhere, although we whistled

---

[2]Columbus, Ohio, where Thurber grew up.

Lots of People Reported Our Dog to the Police

and shouted, until old Mrs. Detweiler called after dinner that night. Muggs had bitten her once, in the leg, and she came into the living room only after we assured her that Muggs had run away. She had just seated herself when, with a great growling and scratching of claws, Muggs emerged from under a davenport where he had been quietly hiding all the time, and bit her again. Mother examined the bite and put arnica[3] on it and told Mrs. Detweiler that it was only a bruise. "He just bumped you," she said. But Mrs. Detweiler left the house in a nasty state of mind.

Lots of people reported our Airedale to the police but my father held a municipal office at the time and was on friendly terms with the police. Even so, the cops had been out a couple of times—once when Muggs bit Mrs. Rufus Sturtevant and again when he bit Lieutenant-Governor Malloy—but mother told them that it hadn't been Muggs' fault but the fault of the people who were bitten. "When he starts for them, they scream," she explained, "and that excites him." The cops suggested that it might be a good idea to tie the dog up, but mother said that it mortified him to be tied up and that he wouldn't eat when he was tied up.

Muggs at his meals was an unusual sight. Because of the fact that if you reached toward the floor he would bite you, we usually put his food plate on top of an old kitchen table with a bench alongside the table. Muggs would stand on the bench and eat. I remember that my mother's Uncle Horatio, who boasted that he was the third man up Missionary Ridge,[4] was splutteringly indignant when he found out that we fed the dog on a table because we were afraid to put his plate on the floor. He said he wasn't afraid of any dog that ever lived and that he would put the dog's plate on the floor if we would give it to him. Roy said that if Uncle Horatio had fed Muggs on the ground just before the battle he would have been the first man up Missionary Ridge. Uncle Horatio was furious. "Bring him in! Bring him in now!" he shouted. "I'll feed the _____ on the floor!" Roy was all for giving him a chance, but my father wouldn't

---

[3]A tincture, made from the flowers of the "arnica" plant, applied in the past to bruises and sprains.

[4]A ridge in Georgia and Tennessee where a Civil War battle was fought in 1863.

Muggs at His Meals Was an Unusual Sight

hear of it. He said that Muggs had already been fed. "I'll feed him again!" bawled Uncle Horatio. We had quite a time quieting him.

In his last year Muggs used to spend practically all of his time outdoors. He didn't like to stay in the house for some reason or other — perhaps it held too many unpleasant memories for him. Anyway, it was hard to get him to come in and as a result the garbage man, the iceman, and the laundryman wouldn't come near the house. We had to haul the garbage down to the corner, take the laundry out and bring it back, and meet the iceman a block from home. After this had gone on for some time we hit on an ingenious arrangement for getting the dog in the house so that we could lock him up while the gas meter was read, and so on. Muggs was afraid of only one thing, an electrical storm. Thunder and lightning frightened him out of his senses (I think he thought a storm had broken the day the mantelpiece fell). He would rush into the house and hide under a bed or in a clothes closet. So we fixed up a thunder machine out of a long narrow piece of sheet iron with a wooden handle on one end. Mother would shake this vigorously when she wanted to get Muggs into the house. It made an excellent imitation of thunder, but I suppose it was the most roundabout system for running a household that was ever devised. It took a lot out of mother.

A few months before Muggs died, he got to "seeing things." He would rise slowly from the floor, growling low, and stalk stiff-legged and menacing toward nothing at all. Sometimes the Thing would be just a little to the right or left of a visitor. Once a Fuller Brush salesman[5] got hysterics. Muggs came wandering into the room like Hamlet following his father's ghost. His eyes were fixed on a spot just to the left of the Fuller Brush man, who stood it until Muggs was about three slow, creeping paces from him. Then he shouted. Muggs wavered on past him into the hallway grumbling to himself but the Fuller man went on shouting. I think mother had to throw a pan of cold water on him before he stopped. That was the way she used to stop us boys when we got into fights.

---

[5] A door-to-door salesman of the Fuller brand of household brushes, brooms, etc.

Muggs died quite suddenly one night. Mother wanted to bury him in the family lot under a marble stone with some such inscription as "Flights of angels sing thee to thy rest" but we persuaded her it was against the law. In the end we just put up a smooth board above his grave along a lonely road. On the board I wrote with an indelible pencil "Cave Canem."[6] Mother was quite pleased with the simple classic dignity of the old Latin epitaph.

1933

E. B. WHITE
(1899–1985)

E. B. White, regarded as one of the greatest of contemporary American humorists, co-edited with his wife Katherine White *A Subtreasury of American Humor* in 1941. In the Preface, he commented on the genre of humor:

> One of the things commonly said about humorists is that they are really very sad people—clowns with a breaking heart. There is some truth in it, but it is badly stated. It would be more accurate, I think, to say there is a deep vein of melancholy running through everyone's life and that a humorist, perhaps more sensible of it than some others, compensates for it actively and positively. . . . There is often a rather fine line between laughing and crying, and if a humorous piece of writing brings a person to the point where his emotional responses are untrustworthy and seem likely to break over into the opposite realm, it is because humorous writing, like poetical writing, has an extra content. It plays, like an active child, close to the big hot fire which is Truth. And sometimes the reader feels the heat.

White was born in Mount Vernon, a New York suburb, where he began writing poetry and essays in high school. He attended Cornell University, graduating in 1921. He worked on the college newspaper and was active in the Manuscript Club, a writing group that included both faculty and students. After leaving Cornell, he tried his hand at journalism and advertising, with little taste for either. It was *The New Yorker*, founded in 1925, that became White's salvation. He began submitting to it short, humorous pieces, which caught the attention of Harold Ross, founder and editor. In 1926, White started working part-time at *The New Yorker*, and was working full time the following year. For eleven years (1927–38), he wrote the anonymous "Talk of the Town" section opening the magazine.

In 1929, White collaborated with James Thurber, another *New Yorker* writer, on *Is Sex Necessary?* The work, a spoof on sex-handbooks, was extraordinarily successful and established both authors as important humorists. This same year, White married Katherine Sergeant Angell, fiction editor at *The New Yorker*. Other books followed, successful enough to enable White to resign from *The New Yorker* and retreat to his Maine farm in North Brooklin. There he devoted himself to writing as he pleased. From 1938 to 1943, he wrote the "One Man's Meat" column for *Harper's* magazine.

---

[6]"Beware of the dog" (Latin).

White proved his versatility as an author, publishing poetry, essays, and children's books. Among the most notable volumes of essays were: *Quo Vadimus? or The Case for the Bicycle* (1939), sketches and stories about the trials and tribulations of city living; *One Man's Meat* (1942, enlarged edition 1944), pieces about the problems of rural living; *The Second Tree from the Corner* (1954), containing essays and poems; and *The Points of My Compass* (1962), with additional essays. White's most celebrated children's book, *Charlotte's Web*, was published in 1952; it has been called the best children's book of the contemporary period. *Essays of E. B. White* appeared in 1970, and *Poems and Sketches of E. B. White* in 1981.

Upon receiving the National Medal for Literature in 1971, White wrote a piece for *Publishers Weekly* discussing the role of the writer in the modern world:

> I have always felt that the first duty of a writer was to ascend—to make flights, carrying others along if he could manage it. To do this takes courage. . . . Today, with so much of earth damaged and endangered . . . a writer's courage can easily fail him. . . . But despair is no good—for the writer, for anyone. Only hope can carry us aloft, can keep us afloat. Only hope, and a certain faith that the incredible structure that has been fashioned by this most strange and ingenious of all mammals cannot end in ruin and disaster. This faith is a writer's faith, for writing itself is an act of faith, nothing else. And it must be the writer, above all others, who keeps it alive—choked with laughter, or pain.

ADDITIONAL READING

An E. B. White Reader, ed. William W. Watt and Robert W. Bradford, 1966; *Letters of E. B. White*, ed. Dorothy Lobrano Guth, 1976.

James Thurber, *The Years with Ross*, 1959; Edward Sampson, *E. B. White*, 1974; A. J. Anderson, *E. B. White: A Bibliography*, 1978; Barbara J. Rogers, *E. B. White*, 1979; Katherine Romans Hall, *E. B. White: A Bibliographic Catalogue of Printed Materials in the Department of Rare Books, Cornell University Library*, 1979; Scott Elledge, *E. B. White: A Biography*, 1984.

TEXT

One Man's Meat, 1944.

from One Man's Meat

WALDEN[1]

Miss Nims, take a letter to Henry David Thoreau. Dear Henry: I thought of you the other afternoon as I was approaching Concord doing fifty on Route 62. That is a high speed at which to hold a philosopher in one's mind, but in this century we are a nimble bunch.

On one of the lawns in the outskirts of the village a woman was cutting the grass with a motorized lawn mower. What made me think of you was that the machine had rather got away from her, although she was game enough, and in the brief glimpse I

---

[1] A pond near Concord, Massachusetts, by which Henry David Thoreau (1817–1862) lived alone for two years in the late 1840s in order to "front only the essential facts of life"; he recorded his experiences in a journal which he later turned into a philosophical-poetic work entitled *Walden*, published in 1854.

had of the scene it appeared to me that the lawn was mowing the lady. She kept a tight grip on the handles, which throbbed violently with every explosion of the one-cylinder motor, and as she sheered around bushes and lurched along at a reluctant trot behind her impetuous servant, she looked like a puppy who had grabbed something that was too much for him. Concord hasn't changed much, Henry; the farm implements and the animals still have the upper hand.

I may as well admit that I was journeying to Concord with the deliberate intention of visiting your woods; for although I have never knelt at the grave of a philosopher nor placed wreaths on moldy poets, and have often gone a mile out of my way to avoid some place of historical interest, I have always wanted to see Walden Pond. The account which you left of your sojourn there is, you will be amused to learn, a document of increasing pertinence; each year it seems to gain a little headway, as the world loses ground. We may all be transcendental[2] yet, whether we like it or not. As our common complexities increase, any tale of individual simplicity (and yours is the best written and the cockiest) acquires a new fascination; as our goods accumulate, but not our well-being, your report of an existence without material adornment takes on a certain awkward credibility.

My purpose in going to Walden Pond, like yours, was not to live cheaply or to live dearly there, but to transact some private business with the fewest obstacles. Approaching Concord, doing forty, doing forty-five, doing fifty, the steering wheel held snug in my palms, the highway held grimly in my vision, the crown of the road now serving me (on the righthand curves), now defeating me (on the lefthand curves), I began to rouse myself from the stupefaction which a day's motor journey induces. It was a delicious evening, Henry, when the whole body is one sense, and imbibes delight through every pore, if I may coin a phrase. Fields were richly brown where the harrow, drawn by the stripped Ford, had lately sunk its teeth; pastures were green; and overhead the sky had that same everlasting great look which you will find on Page 144 of the Oxford pocket edition. I could feel the road entering me, through tire, wheel, spring, and cushion; shall I not have intelligence with earth too? Am I not partly leaves and vegetable mold myself? — a man of infinite horsepower, yet partly leaves.

Stay with me on 62 and it will take you into Concord. As I say, it was a delicious evening. The snake had come forth to die in a bloody S on the highway, the wheel upon its head, its bowels flat now and exposed. The turtle had come up too to cross the road and die in the attempt, its hard shell smashed under the rubber blow, its intestinal yearning (for the other side of the road) forever squashed. There was a sign by the wayside which announced that the road had a "cotton surface." You wouldn't know what that is, but neither, for that matter, did I. There is a cryptic ingredient in many of our modern improvements — we are awed and pleased without knowing quite what we are enjoying. It is something to be traveling on a road with a cotton surface.

The civilization round Concord today is an odd distillation of city, village, farm, and manor. The houses, yards, fields look not quite suburban, not quite rural. Under the bronze beech and the blue spruce of the departed baron grazes the milch goat of the heirs. Under the porte-cochère[3] stands the reconditioned station wagon; under the grape arbor sit the puppies for sale. (But why do men degenerate ever? What makes families run out?)

---

[2]The transcendental movement originated in Concord, Massachusetts, with Ralph Waldo Emerson the leader and Henry David Thoreau the main disciple; transcendentalists believed that all human beings partook of an oversoul and thus had within themselves nonintellectual recourse to divine or transcendent knowledge and inspiration.

[3]A porch-like shelter at a building's entrance to protect carriages or automobiles as people arrive or leave.

It was June and everywhere June was publishing her immemorial stanza; in the lilacs, in the syringa, in the freshly edged paths and the sweetness of moist beloved gardens, and the little wire wickets that preserve the tulips' front. Farmers were already moving the fruits of their toil into their yards, arranging the rhubarb, the asparagus, the strictly fresh eggs on the painted stands under the little shed roofs with the patent shingles. And though it was almost a hundred years since you had taken your ax and started cutting out your home on Walden Pond, I was interested to observe that the philosophical spirit was still alive in Massachusetts: in the center of a vacant lot some boys were assembling the framework of the rude shelter, their whole mind and skill concentrated in the rather inauspicious helter-skeleton of studs and rafters. They too were escaping from town, to live naturally, in a rich blend of savagery and philosophy.

That evening, after supper at the inn, I strolled out into the twilight to dream my shapeless transcendental dreams and see that the car was locked up for the night (first open the right front door, then reach over, straining, and pull up the handles of the left rear and the left front till you hear the click, then the handle of the right rear, then shut the right front but open it again, remembering that the key is still in the ignition switch, remove the key, shut the right front again and with a bang, push the tiny keyhole cover to one side, insert key, turn, and withdraw). It is what we all do, Henry. It is called locking the car. It is said to confuse thieves and keep them from making off with the laprobe. Four doors to lock behind one robe. The driver himself never uses a laprobe, the free movement of his legs being vital to the operation of the vehicle, so that when he locks the car it is a pure and unselfish act. I have in my life gained very little essential heat from laprobes, yet I have ever been at pains to lock them up.

The evening was full of sounds, some of which would have stirred your memory. The robins still love the elms of New England villages at sundown. There is enough of the thrush in them to make song inevitable at the end of day, and enough of the tramp to make them hang round the dwellings of men. A robin, like many another American, dearly loves a white house with green blinds. Concord is still full of them.

Your fellow-townsmen were stirring abroad—not many afoot, most of them in their cars; and the sound which they made in Concord at evening was a rustling and a whispering. The sound lacks steadfastness and is wholly unlike that of a train. A train, as you know who lived so near the Fitchburg line, whistles once or twice sadly and is gone, trailing a memory in smoke, soothing to ear and mind. Automobiles, skirting a village green, are like flies that have gained the inner ear—they buzz, cease, pause, start, shift, stop, halt, brake and the whole effect is a nervous polytone curiously disturbing.

As I wandered along, the toc toc of ping pong balls drifted from an attic window. In front of the Reuben Brown house a Buick was drawn up. At the wheel, motionless, his hat upon his head, a man sat, listening to Amos and Andy[4] on the radio (it is a drama of many scenes without an end). The deep voice of Andrew Brown, emerging from the car, although it originated more than two hundred miles away, was unstrained by distance. When you used to sit on the shore of your pond on Sunday morning, listening to the church bells of Acton and Concord, you were aware of the excellent filter of the intervening atmosphere. Science has attended to that, and sound now maintains its intensity without regard for distance. Properly sponsored, it goes on forever.

---

[4]A long-running, comic radio show in which two white men played the black title characters.

A fire engine, out for a trial spin, roared past Emerson's house, hot with readiness for public duty. Over the barn roofs the martins dipped and chittered. A swarthy daughter of an asparagus grower, in culottes, shirt, and bandanna, pedalled past on her bicycle. It was indeeed a delicious evening, and I returned to the inn (I believe it was your house once) to rock with the old ladies on the concrete veranda.

Next morning early I started afoot for Walden, out Main Street and down Thoreau, past the depot and the Minuteman Chevrolet Company. The morning was fresh, and in a bean field along the way I flushed an agriculturalist, quietly studying his beans. Thoreau Street soon joined Number 126, an artery of the State. We number our highways nowadays, our speed being so great we can remember little of their quality or character and are lucky to remember their number. (Men have an indistinct notion that if they keep up this activity long enough all will at length ride somewhere, in next to no time.) Your pond is on 126.

I knew I must be nearing your woodland retreat when the Golden Pheasant lunchroom came into view—Sealtest ice cream, toasted sandwiches, hot frankfurters, waffles, tonics, and lunches. Were I the proprietor, I should add rice, Indian meal, and molasses—just for old time's sake. The Pheasant, incidentally, is for sale: a chance for some nature lover who wishes to set himself up beside a pond in the Concord atmosphere and live deliberately, fronting only the essential facts of life on Number 126. Beyond the Pheasant was a place called Walden Breezes, an oasis whose porch pillars were made of old green shutters sawed into lengths. On the porch was a distorting mirror, to give the traveler a comical image of himself, who had miraculously learned to gaze in an ordinary glass without smiling. Behind the Breezes, in a sunparched clearing, dwelt your philosophical descendants in their trailers, each trailer the size of your hut, but all grouped together for the sake of congeniality. Trailer people leave the city, as you did, to discover solitude and in any weather, at any hour of the day or night, to improve the nick of time; but they soon collect in villages and get bogged deeper in the mud than ever. The camp behind Walden Breezes was just rousing itself to the morning. The ground was packed hard under the heel, and the sun came through the clearing to bake the soil and enlarge the wry smell of cramped housekeeping. Cushman's bakery truck had stopped to deliver an early basket of rolls. A camp dog, seeing me in the road, barked petulantly. A man emerged from one of the trailers and set forth with a bucket to draw water from some forest tap.

Leaving the highway I turned off into the woods toward the pond, which was apparent through the foliage. The floor of the forest was strewn with dried old oak leaves and *Transcripts*.[5] From beneath the flattened popcorn wrapper (*granum explosum*)[6] peeped the frail violet. I followed a footpath and descended to the water's edge. The pond lay clear and blue in the morning light, as you have seen it so many times. In the shallows a man's waterlogged shirt undulated gently. A few flies came out to greet me and convoy me to your cove, past the No Bathing signs on which the fellows and the girls had scrawled their names. I felt strangely excited suddenly to be snooping around your premises, tiptoeing along watchfully, as though not to tread by mistake upon the intervening century. Before I got to the cove I heard something which seemed to me quite wonderful: I heard your frog, a full, clear *troonk*, guiding me, still hoarse and solemn, bridging the years as the robins had bridged them in the sweetness of the village evening. But he soon quit, and I came on a couple of young boys throwing stones at him.

Your front yard is marked by a bronze tablet set in a stone. Four small granite posts, a few feet away, show where the house was. On top of the tablet was a pair of

---

[5] I.e., the newspaper, *Boston Daily Transcript.*
[6] "Exploding grain" (Latin). Improvised by White; Thoreau often gave the Latin names for plants in his writing.

faded blue bathing trunks with a white stripe. Back of it is a pile of stones, a sort of cairn, left by your visitors as a tribute I suppose. It is a rather ugly little heap of stones, Henry. In fact the hillside itself seems faded, browbeaten; a few tall skinny pines, bare of lower limbs, a smattering of young maples in suitable green, some birches and oaks, and a number of trees felled by the last big wind. It was from the bole of one of these fallen pines, torn up by the roots, that I extracted the stone which I added to the cairn—a sentimental act in which I was interrupted by a small terrier from a nearby picnic group, who confronted me and wanted to know about the stone.

I sat down for a while on one of the posts of your house to listen to the bluebottles and the dragonflies. The invaded glade sprawled shabby and mean at my feet, but the flies were tuned to the old vibration. There were the remains of a fire in your ruins, but I doubt that it was yours; also two beer bottles trodden into the soil and become part of earth. A young oak had taken root in your house, and two or three ferns, unrolling like the ticklers at a banquet. The only other furnishings were a DuBarry pattern sheet, a page torn from a picture magazine, and some crusts in wax paper.

Before I quit I walked clear round the pond and found the place where you used to sit on the northeast side to get the sun in the fall, and the beach where you got sand for scrubbing your floor. On the eastern side of the pond, where the highway borders it, the State has built dressing rooms for swimmers, a float with diving towers, drinking fountains of porcelain, and rowboats for hire. The pond is in fact a State Preserve, and carries a twenty-dollar fine for picking wild flowers, a decree signed in all solemnity by your fellow-citizens Walter C. Wardwell, Erson B. Barlow, and Nathaniel I. Bowditch. There was a smell of creosote where they had been building a wide wooden stairway to the road and the parking area. Swimmers and boaters were arriving; bodies plunged vigorously into the water and emerged wet and beautiful in the bright air. As I left, a boatload of town boys were splashing about in midpond, kidding and fooling, the young fellows singing at the tops of their lungs in a wild chorus:

> Amer-ica, Amer-ica, God shed his grace on thee,
> And crown they good with brotherhood
> From sea to shi-ning sea!

I walked back to town along the railroad, following your custom. The rails were expanding noisily in the hot sun, and on the slope of the roadbed the wild grape and the blackberry sent up their creepers to the track.

The expense of my brief sojourn in Concord was:

Canvas shoes	$1.95	
Baseball bat	.25 ⎱	gifts to take back
Left-handed fielder's glove	1.25 ⎰	to a boy
Hotel and meals	4.25	
In all	$7.70	

As you see, this amount was almost what you spent for food for eight months. I cannot defend the shoes or the expenditure for shelter and food: they reveal a meanness and grossness in my nature which you would find contemptible. The baseball equipment, however, is the kind of impediment with which you were never on even terms. You must remember that the house where you practiced the sort of economy which I respect was haunted only by mice and squirrels. You never had to cope with a shortstop.

June, 1939   *1942*

THOMAS WOLFE
(1900–1938)

In 1923, Thomas Wolfe, then studying at Harvard, wrote prophetically to his mother of his ambition to write: "I intend to wreak out of my soul on paper and express it all. This is what my life means to me: I am at the mercy of this thing and I will do it or die. I never forget; I have never forgotten. I have tried to make myself conscious of the whole of my life since the baby in the basket became conscious of the warm sunlight on the porch. . . ." In *The Story of a Novel* in 1936, when death was only some two years away, Wolfe spoke of the task of all American writers, formulating his own burning ambition: "Out of the billion forms of America, out of the savage violence and the dense complexity of all its swarming life; from the unique and single substance of this land and life of ours, must we draw the power and energy of our own life, the articulation of our speech, the substance of our art."

In the thirty-eight years allotted to him on earth, Wolfe seems to have remembered the whole of his life and gotten most of it down on paper. How much of "swarming life" in the "billion forms of America" he was able to articulate is a question that is still debated. Youthful readers have fallen under Wolfe's spell convinced that he had lyrically embraced the whole of their and the American experience. Critics (sometimes those same youthful readers grown older) have concluded that Wolfe's rhetoric exceeded its grasp.

Wolfe was born in Asheville, North Carolina, the last of eight children in the household of a liquor-loving, forty-nine-year-old stone cutter. Wolfe was his mother's favorite. Not weaned until he was over three years old, he was taken to live with her when she moved out of the family home to run a boarding house nearby. Wolfe's teachers in Asheville quickly spotted his talent and encouraged him. He entered the University of North Carolina in 1916 and there developed a keen interest in playwriting. In 1918, Wolfe was stunned by the death of his favorite brother Ben, a loss that would haunt him for the rest of his life.

After graduating from the University of North Carolina in 1920, Wolfe headed to Harvard for an M.A., but primarily to study with Professor George Pierce Baker in his "47 Workshop" devoted to playwriting. During the two years at Harvard (1920–22) and for three or four more years, while he was teaching English composition at New York University, Wolfe devoted himself to writing plays. But gradually he was discovering that his expansiveness and gargantuan vision could not be contained in the dramatic form. Encouraged by Aline Bernstein, whom he met and fell in love with on a return voyage from Europe in 1925, he turned to the writing of fiction. Aline Bernstein was a successful scene designer for the theater, and had a husband and children. The story of their stormy affair was to be later described in detail in Wolfe's fiction. She would give her side of the story, after Wolfe's death, in her own book, *An Actor's Daughter* (1941).

Wolfe had completed a novel he called *O Lost* by the middle of 1927. The immense work was turned down by successive publishers until Maxwell Perkins of Scribner's saw it. After being cut by about one-third, it appeared in 1929 as *Look Homeward, Angel*. Wolfe's second novel, *Of Time and the River*, did not appear until 1934, primarily because Wolfe could not stop writing, always expanding when asked to cut. These first two novels were a fictional account of Wolfe's life, introducing many characters based on people he knew; although disliked by those who saw themselves meanly portrayed, the works were extravagantly praised by many critics who compared Wolfe with Dickens, Proust, and Joyce.

Wolfe travelled abroad in 1935, visiting for some time in Germany, where his books were popular. He published a volume of short stories, *From Death to Morning* (1935), and an account of his becoming a writer, *The Story of a Novel* (1936). In 1937 he returned to Asheville, where feelings about him were still ambivalent. But mostly he wrote and wrote, filling a trunk with manuscripts. Before setting out on a journey west in 1938, he delivered the trunk to his new editor, Edward Aswell of Harper's (he had broken with Perkins at Scribner's in 1936).

Wolfe died suddenly in September 1938. His editor found in his trunk of manuscripts enough material to publish two novels: *The Web and the Rock* (1939) and *You Can't Go Home Again* (1940). Whereas Eugene Gant had been the Wolfe persona in the first two novels, George Weber became his counterpart in these books. In a sense they completed the story of Wolfe's life, only slightly fictionalized, focusing on such key emotional episodes as the affair with Aline Bernstein and the traumatic break with the editor Maxwell Perkins. The critical debate continues as to how much Wolfe's fiction was shaped by his two editors. The debate had begun when Wolfe was still alive and lay behind the break with Perkins.

When William Faulkner was asked in 1950 to rank modern American novelists, including himself, he listed five writers in the following order: Thomas Wolfe, William Faulkner, John Dos Passos, Ernest Hemingway, and John Steinbeck. When challenged about putting Wolfe first, Faulkner said that Wolfe was "the best failure," willing "to throw away style, coherence, all the rules of preciseness, to try to put all the experience of the human heart on the head of a pin, as it were." Faulkner's reputation was to soar, and Wolfe's to plummet. But in a contemporary reassessment, Wolfe has found his readers and defenders. His work has remained in print continuously since his death.

ADDITIONAL READING

The Face of a Nation: Poetical Passages from the Writings of Thomas Wolfe, 1939; *A Stone, A Leaf, A Door: Poems by Thomas Wolfe*, ed. J. S. Barnes, 1946; *The Letters of Thomas Wolfe*, ed. Elizabeth Nowell, 1956; *The Short Novels of Thomas Wolfe*, ed. C. Hugh Holman, 1961; *The Thomas Wolfe Reader*, ed. C. Hugh Holman, 1962; *The Letters of Thomas Wolfe to His Mother*, ed. C. Hugh Holman and Sue Fields Ross, 1968; *The Notebooks of Thomas Wolfe*, 2 vols., ed. Richard S. Kennedy and Paschal Reeves, 1970; *The Autobiography of an American Novelist*, ed. Leslie Field, 1983; *Between Love and Loyalty: The Letters of Thomas Wolfe and Elizabeth Nowell*, ed. Richard Kennedy, 1983; *My Other Loneliness: Letters of Thomas Wolfe and Aline Bernstein*, ed. Suzanne Stutman, 1983; *Thomas Wolfe Interviewed, 1929–1938*, ed. Aldo P. Magi and Richard Walser, 1985.

Aline Bernstein, *The Journey Down* (a novel), 1938; Aline Bernstein, *An Actor's Daughter*, 1941; Herbert J. Muller, *Thomas Wolfe*, 1947; Louis D. Rubin, *Thomas Wolfe: The Weather of His Youth*, 1955; Floyd C. Watkins, *Thomas Wolfe's Characters: Portraits from Life*, 1957; E. D. Johnson, *Of Time and Thomas Wolfe: A Bibliography and Character Index of His Works*, 1959; Mabel Wolfe Wheaton and Legett Blythe, *Thomas Wolfe and His Family*, 1961; Richard S. Kennedy, *The Window of Memory: The Literary Career of Thomas Wolfe*, 1962; C. Hugh Holman, ed., *The World of Thomas Wolfe*, 1962; Philip Johnson, *The Art of Thomas Wolfe*, 1963; Bruce R. McElderry, *Thomas Wolfe*, 1964; N. F. Austin, *A Biography of Thomas Wolfe*, 1968; Leslie A. Field, ed., *Thomas Wolfe: Three Decades of Criticism*, 1968; Andrew Turnbull, *Thomas Wolfe: A Biography*, 1967; Fritz Heinrich Ryssel, *Thomas Wolfe*, trans. Helen Sebba, 1972; Pascal Reeves, ed., *Thomas Wolfe: The Critical Reception*, 1974; Leo Gurko, *Thomas Wolfe: Beyond the Romantic Edge*, 1975; C. Hugh Holman, ed., *The Loneliness at the Core: Studies in Thomas Wolfe*, 1975; Elizabeth Evans, *Thomas Wolfe*, 1984; John S. Phillipson, ed., *Critical Essays on Thomas Wolfe*, 1985; David Herbert Donald, *Look Homeward: A Life of Thomas Wolfe*, 1987.

TEXT

From Death to Morning, 1935.

from From Death to Morning

CIRCUS AT DAWN

There were times in early autumn — in September — when the greater circuses would come to town — the Ringling Brothers, Robinson's, and Barnum and Bailey shows, and when I[1] was a route-boy on the morning paper, on those mornings when the circus would be coming in I would rush madly through my route in the cool and thrilling darkness that comes just before break of day, and then I would go back home and get my brother out of bed.

Talking in low excited voices we would walk rapidly back toward town under the rustle of September leaves, in cool streets just grayed now with that still, that unearthly and magical first light of day which seems suddenly to re-discover the great earth out of darkness, so that the earth emerges with an awful, a glorious sculptural stillness, and one looks out with a feeling of joy and disbelief, as the first men on this earth must have done, for to see this happen is one of the things that men will remember out of life forever and think of as they die.

At the sculptural still square where at one corner, just emerging into light, my father's shabby little marble shop stood with a ghostly strangeness and familiarity, my brother and I would "catch" the first street-car of the day bound for the "depot" where the circus was — or sometimes we would meet some one we knew, who would give us a lift in his automobile.

Then, having reached the dingy, grimy, and rickety depot section, we would get out, and walk rapidly across the tracks of the station yard, where we could see great flares and steamings from the engines, and hear the crash and bump of shifting freight cars, the swift sporadic thunders of a shifting engine, the tolling of bells, the sounds of great trains on the rails.

And to all these familiar sounds, filled with their exultant prophecies of flight, the voyage, morning, and the shining cities — to all the sharp and thrilling odors of the trains — the smell of cinders, acrid smoke, of musty, rusty freight cars, the clean pineboard of crated produce, and the smells of fresh stored food — oranges, coffee, tangerines and bacon, ham and flour and beef — there would be added now, with an unforgettable magic and familiarity, all the strange sounds and smells of the coming circus.

The gay yellow sumptuous-looking cars in which the star performers lived and slept, still dark and silent, heavily and powerfully still, would be drawn up in long strings upon the tracks. And all around them the sounds of the unloading circus would go on furiously in the darkness. The receding gulf of lilac and departing night would be filled with the savage roar of the lions, the murderously sudden snarling of great jungle cats, the trumpeting of the elephants, the stamp of the horses, and with the musty, pungent, unfamiliar odor of the jungle animals: the tawny camel smells, and the smells of panthers, zebras, tigers, elephants, and bears.

---

[1]The speaker in this autobiographical piece is clearly Thomas Wolfe, but he seems almost identical with the main character of Wolfe's first novel, *Look Homeward, Angel*. The brother who accompanies the speaker to the circus is Benjamin Harrison ("Ben") Wolfe, Tom's older brother who was his favorite. Ben becomes Ben Gant in the novel. Ben's death in 1918 haunted Wolfe all his life and is movingly described in *Look Homeward, Angel*.

Then, along the tracks, beside the circus trains, there would be the sharp cries and oaths of the circus men, the magical swinging dance of lanterns in the darkness, the sudden heavy rumble of the loaded vans and wagons as they were pulled along the flats and gondolas, and down the runways to the ground. And everywhere, in the thrilling mystery of darkness and awakening light, there would be the tremendous conflict of a confused, hurried, and yet orderly movement.

The great iron-gray horses, four and six to a team, would be plodding along the road of thick white dust to a rattling of chains and traces and the harsh cries of their drivers. The men would drive the animals to the river which flowed by beyond the tracks, and water them; and as first light came one could see the elephants wallowing in the familiar river and the big horses going slowly and carefully down to drink.

Then, on the circus grounds, the tents were going up already with the magic speed of dreams. All over the place (which was near the tracks and the only space of flat land in the town that was big enough to hold a circus) there would be this fierce, savagely hurried, and yet orderly confusion. Great flares of gaseous circus light would blaze down on the seared and battered faces of the circus toughs as, with the rhythmic precision of a single animal—a human riveting machine—they swung their sledges at the stakes, driving a stake into the earth with the incredible instancy of accelerated figures in a motion picture. And everywhere, as light came, and the sun appeared, there would be a scene of magic, order, and of violence. The drivers would curse and talk their special language to their teams, there would be the loud, gasping and uneven labor of a gasoline engine, the shouts and curses of the bosses, the wooden riveting of driven stakes, and the rattle of heavy chains.

Already in an immense cleared space of dusty beaten earth, the stakes were being driven for the main exhibition tent. And an elephant would lurch ponderously to the field, slowly lower his great swinging head at the command of a man who sat perched upon his skull, flourish his gray wrinkled snout a time or two, and then solemnly wrap it around a tent pole big as the mast of a racing schooner. Then the elephant would back slowly away, dragging the great pole with him as if it were a stick of matchwood.

And when this happened, my brother would break into his great "whah-whah" of exuberant laughter, and prod me in the ribs with his clumsy fingers. And further on, two town darkeys, who had watched the elephant's performance with bulging eyes, would turn to each other with apelike grins, bend double as they slapped their knees and howled with swart rich nigger-laughter, saying to each other in a kind of rhythmical chorus of question and reply:

"He don't play with it, do he?"

"No, *suh!* He don't send no boy!"

"He don't say 'Wait a minute,' do he?"

"No, suh! He say 'Come with me!' That's what he say!"

"He go boogety—boogety!" said one, suiting the words with a prowling movement of his black face toward the earth.

"He go rootin' faw it!" said the other, making a rooting movement with his head.

"He say 'Ar-rumpf'!" said one.

"He say 'Big boy, we is on ouah way'!" the other answered.

"Har! Har! Har! Har! Har!"—and they choked and screamed with their rich laughter, slapping their thighs with a solid smack as they described to each other the elephant's prowess.

Meanwhile, the circus food-tent—a huge canvas top without concealing sides—had already been put up, and now we could see the performers seated at long trestled tables underneath the tent, as they ate breakfast. And the savor of the food they ate—mixed as it was with our strong excitement, with the powerful but wholesome smells of the animals, and with all the joy, sweetness, mystery, jubilant magic and glory of the morning and the coming of the circus—seemed to us to be of the most maddening and appetizing succulence of any food that we had ever known or eaten.

We could see the circus performers eating tremendous breakfasts, with all the savage relish of their power and strength: they ate big fried steaks, pork chops, rashers of bacon, a half dozen eggs, great slabs of fried ham and great stacks of wheat-cakes which a cook kept flipping in the air with the skill of a juggler, and which a husky-looking waitress kept rushing to their tables on loaded trays held high and balanced marvellously on the fingers of a brawny hand. And above all the maddening odors of the wholesome and succulent food, there brooded forever the sultry and delicious fragrance—that somehow seemed to add a zest and sharpness to all the powerful and thrilling life of morning—of strong boiling coffee, which we could see sending off clouds of steam from an enormous polished urn, and which the circus performers gulped down, cup after cup.

And the circus men and women themselves—these star performers—were such fine-looking people, strong and handsome, yet speaking and moving with an almost stern dignity and decorum, that their lives seemed to us to be as splendid and wonderful as any lives on earth could be. There was never anything loose, rowdy, or tough in their comportment, nor did the circus women look like painted whores, or behave indecently with the men.

Rather, these people in an astonishing way seemed to have created an established community which lived an ordered existence on wheels, and to observe with a stern fidelity unknown in towns and cities the decencies of family life. There would be a powerful young man, a handsome and magnificent young woman with blonde hair and the figure of an Amazon, and a powerfully-built, thick-set man of middle age, who had a stern, lined, responsible-looking face and a bald head. They were probably the members of a trapeze team—the young man and woman would leap through space like projectiles, meeting the grip of the older man and hurling back again upon their narrow perches, catching the swing of their trapeze in mid-air, and whirling thrice before they caught it, in a perilous and beautiful exhibition of human balance and precision.

But when they came into the breakfast tent, they would speak gravely yet courteously to other performers, and seat themselves in a family group at one of the long tables, eating their tremendous breakfasts with an earnest concentration, seldom speaking to one another, and then gravely, seriously and briefly.

And my brother and I would look at them with fascinated eyes: my brother would watch the man with the bald head for a while and then turn toward me, whispering:

"D-d-do you see that f-f-fellow there with the bald head? W-w-well he's the heavy man," he whispered knowingly. "He's the one that c-c-c-catches them! That f-f-fellow's got to know his business! You know what happens if he m-m-misses, don't you?" said my brother.

"What?" I would say in a fascinated tone.

My brother snapped his fingers in the air.

"Over!" he said. "D-d-done for! W-w-why, they'd be d-d-d-dead before they knew what happened. Sure!" he said, nodding vigorously. "It's a f-f-f-fact! If he ever m-m-m-misses it's all over! That boy has g-g-g-got to know his s-s-s-stuff!" my brother said. "W-w-w-why," he went on in a low tone of solemn conviction, "it w-w-w-wouldn't surprise me at all if they p-p-p-pay him s-s-seventy-five or a hundred dollars a week! It's a fact!" my brother cried vigorously.

And we would turn our fascinated stares again upon these splendid and romantic creatures, whose lives were so different from our own, and whom we seemed to know with such familiar and affectionate intimacy. And at length, reluctantly, with full light come and the sun up, we would leave the circus grounds and start for home.

And somehow the memory of all we had seen and heard that glorious morning, and the memory of the food-tent with its wonderful smells, would waken in us the pangs of such a ravenous hunger that we could not wait until we got home to eat. We would stop off in town at lunch-rooms and, seated on tall stools before the counter, we would devour ham-and-egg sandwiches, hot hamburgers red and pungent at their cores with coarse spicy sanguinary[2] beef, coffee, glasses of foaming milk and doughnuts, and then go home to eat up everything in sight upon the breakfast table.

1935

ZORA NEALE HURSTON
(1891–1960)

Zora Neale Hurston gave many different versions of the year of her birth—1901, 1903, 1910. But never did she give the actual year, which has recently been discovered to be 1891 (census records of 1900 showed Zora as then nine years old; see Robert Hemenway's Introduction to his 1984 edition of *Dust Tracks on a Road*). This example highlights her creativity in imaginatively shaping the story of her life as she told it in *Dust Tracks on a Road*, published in 1942 and one of her most enduring works.

Hurston was born in the all black town of Eatonville, Florida, one of eight children of a tenant farmer-preacher and sometime mayor of Eatonville. After the death of her mother in 1904, and the remarriage of her father, Hurston set out on her own, moving from one relative to another and one job to another (maid, wardrobe mistress for a travelling theatrical group). She studied for two years at the preparatory school Morgan Academy in Baltimore and then attended Howard University in Washington, D.C. In the early 1920s, she began to write and publish her first stories. As her reputation grew, she was awarded a scholarship to Barnard College, where she attracted the attention of the distinguished anthropologist Franz Boas. She took her degree at Barnard in 1928.

With the urging and support of Boas, Hurston launched a career as a folklorist. Travelling in the South from sawmills to turpentine camps and juke joints in small towns, she collected oral tales, superstitions, and songs and studied the cult of voodoo. Out of this experience, she published a number of articles during this period. In the mid-1930s, Hurston received several fellowships, including two Guggenheims, to continue her research, leading to her study of magic (*obeah*) in Haiti and Jamaica. In 1935, Hurston published *Mules and Men* and in 1938, *Tell My Horse*, presenting the results of her investigations into the folklore and customs of black culture. Another work, *The Florida Negro*, produced for the Florida Federal Writers Project in 1938, was completed but not published.

Throughout her career as a cultural anthropologist, Hurston continued writing fiction, encouraged by two successful white writers of the time—Carl Van Vechten and Fannie Hurst. For a while Hurston was employed as personal secretary to Fannie Hurst, who enjoyed passing Hurston off as "Princess Zora," checking into a hotel with Hurston "dressed up as an Asiatic person of royal blood . . . while the attendants goggled" at her and "bowed low."

Hurston wrote a total of four novels. *Jonah's Gourd Vine* (1934) draws on her knowledge of black folklore and her memories of her father as a preacher. *Their Eyes Were Watching God* (1937) is a romance based on a passionate love affair. The

---

[2]Bloody.

most whimsical of all her fictions, *Moses, Man of the Mountain* (1939), an imaginative retelling of the biblical story of Moses as a kind of black folk tale, introduces variations on the tale as well as satire and farce. Hurston's last novel, *Seraph on the Suwanee* (1948), portrays whites rather than blacks, with the focus on sexual relationships and the psychology of the characters.

Hurston seems to have faded from the scene during her last years. She returned to Florida, where she took a job as a maid. When she wrote anything, it seemed calculated to arouse the anger of other blacks. In 1950 she published "I Saw Negro Votes Peddled" in the *American Legion Magazine*, a piece that appeared to undermine the campaign underway to obtain voting rights for southern blacks. Alienated and penniless, she died in 1960 without much notice from former friends and associates.

Since her death, however, enough attention has been paid to give her reputation as a writer a new lease on life. An important biography by Robert Hemenway was published in 1977. In 1979, Alice Walker edited *I Love Myself When I Am Laughing: A Zora Neale Hurston Reader*. And in 1984, her autobiography, *Dust Tracks on a Road*, was reissued, edited by Robert Hemenway and including material suppressed by the publisher in the first edition.

In her dedication of *I Love Myself*, Alice Walker wrote: "Zora Neale Hurston, who went forth into the world with one dress to her name, and who was permitted, at other times in her life, only a single pair of shoes, rescued and recreated a world which she labored to hand us whole, never underestimating the value of her gift, if at times doubting the good sense of its recipients. She appreciated us, in any case, *as we fashioned ourselves*. That is something. And of all the people in the world to be, she chose to be herself, *and more and more herself*. That, too, is something."

ADDITIONAL READING

I Love Myself When I Am Laughing: A Zora Neale Hurston Reader, ed. Alice Walker, 1979.

Darwin T. Turner, *In a Minor Chord: Three Afro-American Writers and Their Search for Identity*, 1971; Robert E. Hemenway, *Zora Neale Hurston: A Literary Biography*, 1977; Lillie P. Howard, *Zora Neale Hurston*, 1980; Bruce Kellner, ed., *The Harlem Renaissance: A Historical Dictionary*, 1984; Bernard W. Bell, *The Afro-American Novel and Its Tradition*, 1987; Adele S. Newson, *Zora Neale Hurston: A Reference Guide*, 1987; Karla F. Holloway, *The Character of the Word, The Texts of Zora Neale Hurston*, 1987.

TEXT

Dust Tracks on a Road, ed. Robert E. Hemenway, 1984.

from Dust Tracks on a Road

WANDERING

I knew that Mama was sick. She kept getting thinner and thinner and her chest cold never got any better. Finally, she took to bed.

She had come home from Alabama that way. She had gone back to her old home to be with her sister during her sister's last illness. Aunt Dinky had lasted on for two months after Mama got there, and so Mama had stayed on till the last.

It seems that there had been other things there that worried her. Down underneath, it appeared that Grandma had never quite forgiven her for the move she had made twenty-one years before in marrying Papa. So that when Mama suggested that the old Potts place be sold so that she could bring her share back with her to Florida, her mother, urged on by Uncle Bud, Mama's oldest brother, refused. Not until Grandma's head was cold, was an acre of the place to be sold. She had long since quit living on it, and it was pretty well run down, but she wouldn't, that was all. Mama could just go on back to that yaller rascal she had married like she came. I do not think that the money part worried Mama as much as the injustice and spitefulness of the thing.

Then Cousin Jimmie's death seemed to come back on Mama during her visit. How he came to his death is an unsolved mystery. He went to a party and started home. The next morning his headless body was found beside the railroad track. There was no blood, so the train couldn't have killed him. This had happened before I was born. He was said to have been a very handsome young man, and very popular with the girls. He was my mother's favorite nephew and she took it hard. She had probably numbed over her misery, but going back there seemed to freshen up her grief. Some said that he had been waylaid by three other young fellows and killed in a jealous rage. But nothing could be proved. It was whispered that he had been shot in the head by a white man unintentionally, and then beheaded to hide the wound. He had been shot from ambush, because his assailant mistook him for a certain white man. It was night. The attacker expected the white man to pass that way, but not Jimmie. When he found out his mistake, he had forced a certain Negro to help him move the body to the railroad track without the head, so that it would look as if he had been run over by the train. Anyway, that is what the Negro wrote back after he had moved to Texas years later. There was never any move to prove the charge, for obvious reasons. Mama took the whole thing very hard.

It was not long after Mama came home that she began to be less active. Then she took to bed. I knew she was ailing, but she was always frail, so I did not take it too much to heart. I was nine years old, and even though she had talked to me very earnestly one night, I could not conceive of Mama actually dying. She had talked of it many times.

That day, September 18th, she had called me and given me certain instructions. I was not to let them take the pillow from under her head until she was dead. The clock was not to be covered, nor the looking-glass. She trusted me to see to it that these things were not done. I promised her as solemnly as nine years could do, that I would see to it.

What years of agony that promise gave me! In the first place, I had no idea that it would be soon. But the same day near sundown I was called upon to set my will against my father, the village dames and village custom. I know now that I could not have succeeded.

I had left Mama and was playing outside for a little while when I noted a number of women going inside Mama's room and staying. It looked strange. So I went on in. Papa was standing at the foot of the bed looking down on my mother, who was breathing hard. As I crowded in, they lifted up the bed and turned it around so that Mama's eyes would face the east. I thought that she looked to me as the head of the bed was reversed. Her mouth was slightly open, but her breathing took up so much of her strength that she could not talk. But she looked at me, or so I felt, to speak for her. She depended on me for a voice.

The Master-Maker in His making had made Old Death. Made him with big, soft feet and square toes. Made him with a face that reflects the face of all things, but neither changes itself, nor is mirrored anywhere. Made the body of Death out of infinite hunger. Made a weapon for his hand to satisfy his needs. This was the morning of the day of the beginning of things.

But Death had no home and he knew it at once.

"And where shall I dwell in my dwelling?" Old Death asked, for he was already old when he was made.

"You shall build you a place close to the living, yet far out of the sight of eyes. Wherever there is a building, there you have your platform that comprehends the four roads of the winds. For your hunger, I give you the first and last taste of all things."

We had been born, so Death had had his first taste of us. We had built things, so he had his platform in our yard.

And now, Death stirred from his platform in his secret place in our yard, and came inside the house.

Somebody reached for the clock, while Mrs. Mattie Clark put her hand to the pillow to take it away.

"Don't!" I cried out. "Don't take the pillow from under Mama's head! She said she didn't want it moved!"

I made to stop Mrs. Mattie, but Papa pulled me away. Others were trying to silence me. I could see the huge drop of sweat collected in the hollow at Mama's elbow and it hurt me so. They were covering the clock and the mirror.

"Don't cover up that clock! Leave that looking-glass like it is! Lemme put Mama's pillow back where it was!"

But Papa held me tight and the others frowned me down. Mama was still rasping out the last morsel of her life. I think she was trying to say something, and I think she was trying to speak to me. What was she trying to tell me? What wouldn't I give to know! Perhaps she was telling me that it was better for the pillow to be moved so that she could die easy, as they said. Perhaps she was accusing me of weakness and failure in carrying out her last wish. I do not know. I shall never know.

Just then, Death finished his prowling through the house on his padded feet and entered the room. He bowed to Mama in his way, and she made her manners and left us to act out our ceremonies over unimportant things.

I was to agonize over that moment for years to come. In the midst of play, in the wakeful moments after midnight, on the way home from parties, and even in the classroom during lectures. My thoughts would escape occasionally from their confines and stare me down.

Now, I know that I could not have had my way against the world. The world we lived in required those acts. Anything else would have been sacrilege, and no nineyear-old voice was going to thwart them. My father was with the mores. He had restrained me physically from outraging the ceremonies established for the dying. If there is any consciousness after death, I hope that Mama knows that I did my best. She must know how I suffered for my failure.

But life picked me up from the foot of Mama's bed, grief, self-despisement and all, and set my feet in strange ways. That moment was the end of a phase in my life. I was old before my time with grief of loss, of failure, and of remorse. No matter what the others did, my mother had put her trust in me. She had felt that I could and would carry out her wishes, and I had not. And then in that sunset time, I failed her. It seemed as she died that the sun went down on purpose to flee away from me.

That hour began my wanderings. Not so much in geography, but in time. Then not so much in time as in spirit.

Mama died at sundown and changed a world. That is, the world which had been built out of her body and her heart. Even the physical aspects fell apart with a suddenness that was startling.

My oldest brother was up in Jacksonville in school, and he arrived home after Mama had passed. By then, she had been washed and dressed and laid out on the ironing-board in the parlor.

Practically all of the village was in the front yard and on the porch, talking in low tones and waiting. They were not especially waiting for my brother Bob. They were doing that kind of waiting that people do around death. It is a kind of sipping up the drama of the thing. However, if they were asked, they would say it was the sadness of the occasion which drew them. In reality it is a kind of feast of the Passover.[1]

Bob's grief was awful when he realized that he was too late. He could not conceive at first that nothing could be done to straighten things out. There was no ear for his excuse nor explanation — no way to ease what was in him. Finally it must have come to him that what he had inside, he must take with him wherever he went. Mama was there on the cooling board with the sheet draped over her blowing gently in the wind. Nothing there seemed to hear him at all.

There was my sister Sarah in the kitchen crying and trying to quiet Everett, who was just past two years old. She was crying and trying to make him hush at the same time. He was crying because he sensed the grief around him. And then, Sarah, who was fifteen, had been his nurse and he would respond to her mood, whatever it was. We were all grubby bales of misery, huddled about lamps.

I have often wished I had been old enough at the time to look into Papa's heart that night. If I could know what that moment meant to him, I could have set my compass towards him and been sure. I know that I did love him in a way, and that I admired many things about him. He had a poetry about him that I loved. That had made him a successful preacher. He could hit ninety-seven out of a hundred with a gun. He could swim Lake Maitland from Maitland to Winter Park,[2] and no man in the village could put my father's shoulders to the ground. We were so certain of Papa's invincibility in combat that when a village woman scolded Everett for some misdemeanor, and told him that God would punish him, Everett, just two years old, reared back and told her, "He better not bother me. Papa will shoot Him down." He found out better later on, but that goes to show you how big our Papa looked to us. We had seen him bring down bears and panthers with his gun, and chin the bar more times than any man in competing distance. He had to our knowledge licked two men who Mama told him had to be licked. All that part was just fine with me. But I was Mama's child. I knew that she had not always been happy, and I wanted to know just how sad he was that night.

I have repeatedly called up that picture and questioned it. Papa cried some too, as he moved in his awkward way about the place. From the kitchen to the front porch and back again. He kept saying, "Poor thing! She suffered so much." I do not know what he meant by that. It could have been love and pity for her suffering ending at last. It could have been remorse mixed with relief. The hard-driving force was no longer opposed to his easy-going pace. He could put his potentialities to sleep and be happy in the laugh of the day. He could do next year or never, what Mama would have insisted must be done today. Rome, the eternal city, meant two different things to my parents. To Mama, it meant, you must build it today so it could last through eternity. To Papa, it meant that you could plan to lay some bricks today and you have the rest of eternity to finish it. With all time, why hurry? God had made more time than anything else, anyway. Why act so stingy about it?

Then too, I used to notice how Mama used to snatch Papa. That is, he would start to put up an argument that would have been terrific on the store porch, but Mama would pitch in with a single word or a sentence and mess it all up. You could tell he was mad as fire with no words to blow it out with. He would sit over in the corner and cut his eyes at her real hard. He was used to being a hero on the store porch and in church affairs, and I can see how he must have felt to be always outdone around home. I know now that that is a griping thing to a man — not to be able to whip his woman mentally. Some women know how to give their man that conquesting feeling. My mother took her over-the-creek man and bare-knuckled him from brogans to

---

[1] A Jewish festival celebrating the deliverance of the ancient Hebrews from slavery in Egypt.

[2] Maitland and Winter Park are towns on Lake Maitland in central Florida.

broadcloth, and I am certain that he was proud of the change, in public. But in the house, he might have always felt over-the-creek, and because that was not the statue he had made for himself to look at, he resented it. But then, you cannot blame my mother too much if she did not see him as his entranced congregations did. The one who makes the idols never worships them, however tenderly he might have molded the clay. You cannot have knowledge and worship at the same time. Mystery is the essence of divinity. Gods must keep their distances from men.

Anyway, the next day, Sam Moseley's span of fine horses, hitched to our wagon, carried my mother to Macedonia Baptist Church for the last time. The finality of the thing came to me fully when the earth began to thud on the coffin.

That night, all of Mama's children were assembled together for the last time on earth. The next day, Bob and Sarah went back to Jacksonville to school. Papa was away from home a great deal, so two weeks later I was on my way to Jacksonville, too. I was under age, but the school had agreed to take me in under the circumstances. My sister was to look after me, in a way.

The midnight train had to be waved down at Maitland for me. That would put me into Jacksonville in the daytime.

As my brother Dick drove the mile with me that night, we approached the curve in the road that skirts Lake Catherine, and suddenly I saw the first picture of my visions. I had seen myself upon that curve at night leaving the village home, bowed down with grief that was more than common. As it all flashed back to me, I started violently for a minute, then I moved closer beside Dick as if he could shield me from those others that were to come. He asked me what was the matter, and I said I thought I heard something moving down by the lake. He laughed at that, and we rode on, the lantern showing the roadway, and me keeping as close to Dick as I could. A little, humped-up, shabby-backed trunk was behind us in the buckboard. I was on my way from the village, never to return to it as a real part of the town.

Jacksonville made me know that I was a little colored girl. Things were all about the town to point this out to me. Streetcars and stores and then talk I heard around the school. I was no longer among the white people whose homes I could barge into with a sure sense of welcome. These white people had funny ways. I could tell that even from a distance. I didn't get a piece of candy or a bag of crackers just for going into a store in Jacksonville as I did when I went into Galloway's or Hill's at Maitland, or Joe Clarke's in Eatonville.

Around the school I was an awful bother. The girls complained that they couldn't get a chance to talk without me turning up somewhere to be in the way. I broke up many good "He said" conferences just by showing up. It was not my intention to do so. What I wanted was for it to go full steam ahead and let me listen. But that didn't seem to please. I was not in the "he said" class, and they wished I would kindly please stay out of the way. My underskirt was hanging, for instance. Why didn't I go some place and fix it? My head looked like a hooraw's nest. Why didn't I go comb it? If I took time enough to match my stockings, I wouldn't have time to be trying to listen in on grown folk's business. These venerable old ladies were anywhere from fifteen to eighteen.

In the classroom I got along splendidly. The only difficulty was that I was rated as sassy. I just had to talk back at established authority and that established authority hated backtalk worse than barbed-wire pie. My brother was asked to speak to me in addition to a licking or two. But on the whole, things went along all right. My immediate teachers were enthusiastic about me. It was the guardians of study-hour and prayer meetings who felt that their burden was extra hard to bear.

School in Jacksonville was one of those twilight things. It was not dark, but it lacked the bold sunlight that I craved. I worshipped two of my teachers and loved gingersnaps with cheese, and sour pickles. But I was deprived of the loving pine, the lakes, the wild violets in the woods and the animals I used to know. No more holding down first base on the team with my brothers and their friends. Just a jagged hole where my home used to be.

At times, the girls of the school were lined up two and two and taken for a walk. On one of these occasions, I had an experience that set my heart to fluttering. I saw a woman sitting on a porch who looked at a distance like Mama. Maybe it *was* Mama! Maybe she was not dead at all. They had made some mistake. Mama had gone off to Jacksonville and they thought that she was dead. The woman was sitting in a rocking-chair just like Mama always did. It must be Mama! But before I came abreast of the porch in my rigid place in line, the woman got up and went inside. I wanted to stop and go in. But I didn't even breathe my hope to anyone. I made up my mind to run away someday and find the house and let Mama know where I was. But before I did, the hope that the woman was really my mother passed. I accepted my bereavement.

1942

RICHARD WRIGHT
(1908–1960)

In "The Literature of the Negro in the United States," a lecture written in Paris in the early 1950s, Richard Wright said:

> Held in bondage, stripped of his culture, denied family life for centuries, made to labor for others, the Negro tried to learn to live the life of the New World in an atmosphere of rejection and hate. . . . [Negro life] is the same life [as white life] lifted to the heights of pain and pathos, drama and tragedy. The history of the Negro in America is the history of America written in vivid and bloody terms; it is the history of Western Man writ small. It is the history of men who tried to adjust themselves to a world whose laws, customs, and instruments of force were leveled against them. The Negro is America's metaphor.

Wright was born in 1908 in a cabin on a farm near Natchez, Mississippi. His father, a farmhand, deserted his family when Wright was five years old. His mother, a school teacher, struggled to keep her two sons fed and housed, working as a housemaid. After a number of paralytic strokes, she moved her family into her mother's house in Jackson, Mississippi, where Wright grew up. After attending a series of schools, Wright graduated as valedictorian from the ninth grade at the Smith-Robinson Public School in 1925.

Determined to escape the discrimination and oppression of the South, Wright set out for the North, settling first in Memphis, Tennessee. There he got a job with an optical company, hoarding his small salary of eight dollars a week (later raised to ten) in preparation for travelling to Chicago. The white men for whom he worked lured him into a fight with another black boy, offering ten dollars for their barbaric entertainment. The two boys ended up feeling both badly bruised and morally degraded.

While in Memphis, and by the connivance of a friendly white man, Wright devised a system by which he could check out books from the segregated public library to satisfy his hunger for reading. Suddenly through the world of literature, Wright found his horizons expanding. In reading H. L. Mencken's *A Book of Prefaces*, he learned how a writer could "use words as a weapon." He ran across the names of other writers—Sinclair Lewis, Sherwood Anderson, Mark Twain,

Stephen Crane, Frank Norris, Theodore Dreiser — and he consumed them all in large gulps. He read the British, French, and Russian novelists.

By the time Wright arrived in Chicago in 1927, his whole world had changed through books. He held a series of jobs — as porter, dishwasher, post office clerk — but with the advent of the Great Depression in 1929, he found himself unemployed and on relief. Throughout these years he continued his reading and he began his first attempts at writing. He joined the John Reed Club, a leftist literary organization and began to publish crude, free-verse propagandistic poems in radical magazines like *The New Masses*. In 1933, he joined the Communist party.

Almost from the beginning, Wright began to chafe at the control the Communist party assumed over him and his writing. And by the mid-1930s, Wright was determined to be a writer. For a time he worked for the Federal Experimental Theater and, later, the Federal Writers' Project, President Roosevelt's New Deal programs to help authors. During this period, Wright completed a novel, *Lawd Today*, published in 1963, after his death. By the time he set out for New York in 1937 to work for the Communist newspaper *The Daily Worker*, he had completed most of the short stories he would include in his first book, *Uncle Tom's Children*, published in 1938.

This work enabled him to win a Guggenheim Fellowship and write *Native Son* in 1939, published in 1940. It was selected as a Book-of-the-Month Club choice and established Wright as a leading American novelist. Set in Chicago, it tells the story of a black man who accidentally kills his white employer's daughter, panics, flees, is captured, tried, and executed; the action exposed the endemic racism in American society and institutions. Wright collaborated with the dramatist Paul Green on a dramatic version of *Native Son*, successfully produced by Orson Welles in 1941.

In 1941, Wright wrote the text for *Twelve Million Black Voices*, a "folk history of the Negro in the United States" combining pictures and words. And he was soon at work on his autobiography, which told the story of his life up to 1937. But it was split into two parts, and the first, carrying the story up to 1927 and Wright's departure for Chicago, was published as *Black Boy: A Record of Childhood and Youth* in 1945. Perhaps Wright's greatest work, it was another Book-of-the-Month Club choice and sold well in English and several translations. The other half of the biography was published posthumously in 1970 as *American Hunger*.

In 1944, Wright made his break with the Communist party a matter of public record by publishing "I Tried to Be a Communist" in *The Atlantic Monthly*. His quarrel with the party, he revealed, went back to as early as 1936, and the break began in 1942, when Wright came to realize that the Communists were using blacks for their own political purposes, refusing to protest segregation in the Armed Forces and in the Red Cross blood banks. "I Tried to Be a Communist" was reprinted by Richard Crossman in his collection of recantations of former Communists, *The God that Failed* (1949).

In 1947, Wright settled permanently in France with his family (his second marriage took place in 1941) and became friends with the celebrated French existentialists, Jean-Paul Sartre and Simone de Beauvoir. He continued to write and publish, but his best work was behind him. In 1953 he published a somewhat ponderous existential novel, *The Outsider*, and in 1954, a slight novel with all-white characters, *Savage Holiday*. During these last years he wrote two books that grew out of his extensive travels on the Gold Coast of Africa and in Spain — *Black Power* (1954) and *Pagan Spain* (1956).

Wright collected his lectures in 1957 under the title *White Man, Listen!* And in 1958 he published a novel, *The Long Dream*, intended as the first volume of a trilogy. The reviews were generally negative. Wright brought together another collection of short stories, *Eight Men*, but it did not appear until 1961, after his death. He died of a heart attack in November 1960, at the age of fifty-two.

At the end of *American Hunger*, Wright wrote of his ambition as he stood, in 1937, at the threshhold of his most creative period: "I would hurl words into this darkness and wait for an echo, and if an echo sounded, no matter how faintly, I would send other words to tell, to march, to fight, to create a sense of the hunger for life that gnaws in us all, to keep alive in our hearts a sense of the inexpressibly human." Later, a distinguished successor, Ralph Ellison, would write as though in answer: ". . . in this lies Wright's most important achievement: He has converted the American Negro impulse toward self-annihilation and 'going-underground' into a will to confront the world, to evaluate his experience honestly and throw his findings unashamedly into the guilty conscience of America."

ADDITIONAL READING

The Richard Wright Reader, ed. Ellen Wright and Michel Fabre, 1978.

James Baldwin, "Everybody's Protest Novel," *Notes of a Native Son*, 1955; Ralph Ellison, "Richard Wright's Blues" and "The World and the Jug," *Shadow and Act*, 1964; Constance Webb, *Richard Wright: A Biography*, 1968; Dan McCall, *The Example of Richard Wright*, 1969; Edward Margolies, *The Art of Richard Wright*, 1969; Robert A. Bone, *Richard Wright*, 1969; Milton and Patricia Rickles, *Richard Wright*, 1970; Russell Carl Brignano, *Richard Wright: An Introduction to the Man and His Work*, 1970; Keneth Kinnamon, *The Emergence of Richard Wright*, 1972; David Bakish, *Richard Wright*, 1973; Michel Fabre, *The Unfinished Quest of Richard Wright*, 1973; David Ray and Robert M. Farnsworth, eds., *Richard Wright: Impressions and Perspectives*, 1973; Katherine Fishburn, *Richard Wright's Hero: The Faces of a Rebel-Victim*, 1977; John M. Reilly, ed., *Richard Wright: The Critical Reception*, 1978; Addison Gayle, *Ordeal of a Native Son*, 1980; Robert Felgar, *Richard Wright*, 1980; Yoshino Hakutani, ed., *Critical Essays on Richard Wright*, 1982; Robert Felgar, ed., *Richard Wright: A Collection of Critical Essays*, 1984; Michel Fabre, *The World of Richard Wright*, 1985; Joyce Ann Joyce, *Richard Wright's Art of Tragedy*, 1986; Bernard W. Bell, *The Afro-American Novel and Its Tradition*, 1987; C. James Trotman, ed., *Richard Wright: Myths and Realities*, 1988; Margaret Walker, *Richard Wright: Daemonic Genius: A Portrait of the Man, a Critical Look at His Work*, 1988; Keneth Kinnamon, *Richard Wright Bibliography: Fifty Years of Criticism and Commentary, 1933–1987*, 1988; Joan Urban, *Richard Wright*, 1989.

TEXT

Black Boy, 1945.

from Black Boy

[BLACK BOYS TRICKED INTO FIGHTING][1]

One summer morning I stood at a sink in the rear of the factory washing a pair of eyeglasses that had just come from the polishing machines whose throbbing shook the floor upon which I stood. At each machine a white man was bent forward, working intently. To my left sunshine poured through a window, lighting up the rouge smears and making the factory look garish, violent, dangerous. It was nearing noon and my mind was drifting toward my daily lunch of a hamburger and a bag of peanuts. It had been a routine day, a day more or less like the other days I had spent on the job as errand boy and washer of eyeglasses. I was at peace with the world, that is,

---

[1] As this episode begins, Wright has found a low-paying job at an optical company in Memphis, Tennessee.

at peace in the only way in which a black boy in the South can be at peace with a world of white men.

Perhaps it was the mere sameness of the day that soon made it different from the other days; maybe the white men who operated the machines felt bored with their dull, automatic tasks and hankered for some kind of excitement. Anyway, I presently heard footsteps behind me and turned my head. At my elbow stood a young white man, Mr. Olin, the immediate foreman under whom I worked. He was smiling and observing me as I cleaned emery dust from the eyeglasses.

"Boy, how's it going?" he asked.

"Oh, fine, sir!" I answered with a false heartiness, falling quickly into that nigger-being-a-good-natured-boy-in-the-presence-of-a-white-man pattern, a pattern into which I could now slide easily; although I was wondering if he had any criticism to make of my work.

He continued to hover wordlessly at my side. What did he want? It was unusual for him to stand there and watch me; I wanted to look at him, but was afraid to.

"Say, Richard, do you believe that I'm your friend?" he asked me.

The question was so loaded with danger that I could not reply at once. I scarcely knew Mr. Olin. My relationship with him had been the typical relationship of Negroes to southern whites. He gave me orders and I said, "Yes, sir," and obeyed them. Now, without warning, he was asking me if I thought that he was my friend; and I knew that all southern white men fancied themselves as friends of niggers. While fishing for an answer that would say nothing, I smiled.

"I mean," he persisted, "do you think I'm your friend?"

"Well," I answered, skirting the vast racial chasm between us, "I hope you are."

"I am," he said emphatically.

I continued to work, wondering what motives were prompting him. Already apprehension was rising in me.

"I want to tell you something," he said.

"Yes, sir," I said.

"We don't want you to get hurt," he explained. "We like you round here. You act like a good boy."

"Yes sir," I said. "What's wrong?"

"You don't deserve to get into trouble," he went on.

"Have I done something that somebody doesn't like?" I asked, my mind frantically sweeping over all my past actions, weighing them in the light of the way southern white men thought Negroes should act.

"Well, I don't know," he said and paused, letting his words sink meaningfully into my mind. He lit a cigarette. "Do you know Harrison?"

He was referring to a Negro boy of about my own age who worked across the street for a rival optical house. Harrison and I knew each other casually, but there had never been the slightest trouble between us.

"Yes, sir," I said. "I know him."

"Well, be careful," Mr. Olin said. "He's after you."

"After me? For what?"

"He's got a terrific grudge against you," the white man explained. "What have you done to him?"

The eyeglasses I was washing were forgotten. My eyes were upon Mr. Olin's face, trying to make out what he meant. Was this something serious? I did not trust the white man, and neither did I trust Harrison. Negroes who worked on jobs in the South were usually loyal to their white bosses; they felt that that was the best way to ensure their jobs. Had Harrison felt that I had in some way jeopardized his job? Who was my friend: the white man or the black boy?

"I haven't done anything to Harrison," I said.

"Well, you better watch that nigger Harrison," Mr. Olin said in a low, confidential tone. "A little while ago I went down to get a Coca-Cola and Harrison was waiting for you at the door of the building with a knife. He asked me when you were coming down. Said he was going to get you. Said you called him a dirty name. Now, we don't want any fighting or bloodshed on the job."

I still doubted the white man, yet thought that perhaps Harrison had really interpreted something I had said as an insult.

"I've got to see that boy and talk to him," I said, thinking out loud.

"No, you'd better not," Mr. Olin said. "You'd better let some of us white boys talk to him."

"But how did this start?" I asked, still doubting but half believing.

"He just told me that he was going to get even with you, going to cut you and teach you a lesson," he said. "But don't you worry. Let me handle this."

He patted my shoulder and went back to his machine. He was an important man in the factory and I had always respected his word. He had the authority to order me to do this or that. Now, why would he joke with me? White men did not often joke with Negroes, therefore what he had said was serious. I was upset. We black boys worked long hard hours for what few pennies we earned and we were edgy and tense. Perhaps that crazy Harrison was really after me. My appetite was gone. I had to settle this thing. A white man had walked into my delicately balanced world and had tipped it and I had to right it before I could feel safe. Yes, I would go directly to Harrison and ask what was the matter, what I had said that he resented. Harrison was black and so was I; I would ignore the warning of the white man and talk face to face with a boy of my own color.

At noon I went across the street and found Harrison sitting on a box in the basement. He was eating lunch and reading a pulp magazine. As I approached him, he ran his hand into his pocket and looked at me with cold, watchful eyes.

"Say, Harrison, what's this all about?" I asked, standing cautiously four feet from him.

He looked at me a long time and did not answer.

"I haven't done anything to you," I said.

"And I ain't got nothing against you," he mumbled, still watchful. "I don't bother nobody."

"But Mr. Olin said that you came over to the factory this morning, looking for me with a knife."

"Aw, naw," he said, more at ease now. "I ain't been in your factory all day." He had not looked at me as he spoke.

"Then what did Mr. Olin mean?" I asked. "I'm not angry with you."

"Shucks, I thought *you* was looking for me to cut me," Harrison explained. "Mr. Olin, he came over here this morning and said you was going to kill me with a knife the moment you saw me. He said you was mad at me because I had insulted you. But I ain't said nothing about you." He still had not looked at me. He rose.

"And I haven't said anything about you," I said.

Finally he looked at me and I felt better. We two black boys, each working for ten dollars a week, stood staring at each other, thinking, comparing the motives of the absent white man, each asking himself if he could believe the other.

"But why would Mr. Olin tell me things like that?" I asked.

Harrison dropped his head; he laid his sandwich aside.

"I . . . I . . ." he stammered and pulled from his pocket a long, gleaming knife; it was already open. "I was just waiting to see what you was gonna do to me . . ."

I leaned weakly against a wall, feeling sick, my eyes upon the sharp steel blade of the knife.

"You were going to cut me?" I asked.

"If you had cut me, I was gonna cut you first," he said. "I ain't taking no chances."

"Are you angry with me about something?" I asked.

"Man, I ain't mad at nobody," Harrison said uneasily.

I felt how close I had come to being slashed. Had I come suddenly upon Harrison, he would have thought I was trying to kill him and he would have stabbed me, perhaps killed me. And what did it matter if one nigger killed another?

"Look here," I said. "Don't believe what Mr. Olin says."

"I see now," Harrison said. "He's playing a dirty trick on us."

"He's trying to make us kill each other for nothing."

"How come he wanna do that?" Harrison asked.

I shook my head. Harrison sat, but still played with the open knife. I began to doubt. Was he really angry with me? Was he waiting until I turned my back to stab me? I was in torture.

"I suppose it's fun for white men to see niggers fight," I said, forcing a laugh.

"But you might've killed me," Harrison said.

"To white men we're like dogs or cocks," I said.

"I don't want to cut you," Harrison said.

"And I don't want to cut you," I said.

Standing well out of each other's reach, we discussed the problem and decided that we would keep silent about our conference. We would not let Mr. Olin know that we knew that he was egging us to fight. We agreed to ignore any further provocations. At one o'clock I went back to the factory. Mr. Olin was waiting for me, his manner grave, his face serious.

"Did you see that Harrison nigger?" he asked.

"No, sir," I lied.

"Well, he still has that knife for you," he said.

Hate tightened in me. But I kept a dead face.

"Did you buy a knife yet?" he asked me.

"No, sir," I answered.

"Do you want to use mine?" he asked. "You've got to protect yourself, you know."

"No, sir. I'm not afraid," I said.

"Nigger, you're a fool," he spluttered. "I thought you had some sense! Are you going to just let that nigger cut your heart out? His boss gave *him* a knife to use against *you*! Take this knife, nigger, and stop acting crazy."

I was afraid to look at him; if I had looked at him I would have had to tell him to leave me alone, that I knew he was lying, that I knew he was no friend of mine, that I knew if anyone had thrust a knife through my heart he would simply have laughed. But I said nothing. He was the boss and he could fire me if he did not like me. He laid an open knife on the edge of his workbench, about a foot from my hand. I had a fleeting urge to pick it up and give it to him, point first into his chest. But I did nothing of the kind. I picked up the knife and put it into my pocket.

"Now, you're acting like a nigger with some sense," he said.

As I worked Mr. Olin watched me from his machine. Later when I passed him he called me.

"Now, look here, boy," he began. "We told that Harrison nigger to stay out of this building and leave you alone, see? But I can't protect you when you go home. If that nigger starts at you when you are on your way home, you stab him before he gets a chance to stab you, see?"

I avoided looking at him and remained silent.

"Suit yourself, nigger," Mr. Olin said. "But don't say I didn't warn you."

I had to make my round of errands to deliver eyeglasses and I stole a few minutes to run across the street to talk to Harrison. Harrison was sullen and bashful, wanting to trust me, but afraid. He told me that Mr. Olin had telephoned his boss and had told him to tell Harrison that I had planned to wait for him at the back entrance of the building at six o'clock and stab him. Harrison and I found it difficult to look at each other; we were upset and distrustful. We were not really angry at each other; we knew that the idea of murder had been planted in each of us by the white men who employed us. We told ourselves again and again that we did not agree with the white men; we urged ourselves to keep faith in each other. Yet there lingered deep down in each of us a suspicion that maybe one of us was trying to kill the other.

"I'm not angry with you, Harrison," I said.

"I don't wanna fight nobody," Harrison said bashfully, but he kept his hand in his pocket on his knife.

Each of us felt the same shame, felt how foolish and weak we were in the face of the domination of the whites.

"I wish they'd leave us alone," I said.

"Me too," Harrison said.

"There are a million black boys like us to run errands," I said. "They wouldn't care if we killed each other."

"I know it," Harrison said.

Was he acting? I could not believe in him. We were toying with the idea of death for no reason that stemmed from our own lives, but because the men who ruled us had thrust the idea into our minds. Each of us depended upon the whites for the bread we ate, and we actually trusted the whites more than we did each other. Yet there existed in us a longing to trust men of our own color. Again Harrison and I parted, vowing not to be influenced by what our white boss men said to us.

The game of egging Harrison and me to fight, to cut each other, kept up for a week. We were afraid to tell the white men that we did not believe them, for that would have been tantamount to calling them liars or risking an argument that might have ended in violence being directed against us.

One morning a few days later Mr. Olin and a group of white men came to me and asked me if I was willing to settle my grudge with Harrison with gloves, according to boxing rules. I told them that, though I was not afraid of Harrison, I did not want to fight him and that I did not know how to box. I could feel now that they knew I no longer believed them.

When I left the factory that evening, Harrison yelled at me from down the block. I waited and he ran toward me. Did he want to cut me? I backed away as he approached. We smiled uneasily and sheepishly at each other. We spoke haltingly, weighing our words.

"Did they ask you to fight me with gloves?" Harrison asked.

"Yes," I told him. "But I didn't agree."

Harrison's face became eager.

"They want us to fight four rounds for five dollars apiece," he said. "Man, if I had five dollars, I could pay down on a suit. Five dollars is almost half a week's wages for me."

"I don't want to," I said.

"We won't hurt each other," he said.

"But why do a thing like that for white men?"

"To get that five dollars."

"I don't need five dollars that much."

"Aw, you're a fool," he said. Then he smiled quickly.

"Now, look here," I said. "Maybe you *are* angry with me . . ."

"Naw, I'm not." He shook his head vigorously.

"I don't want to fight for white men. I'm no dog or rooster."

I was watching Harrison closely and he was watching me closely. Did he really want to fight me for some reason of his own? Or was it the money? Harrison stared at me with puzzled eyes. He stepped toward me and I stepped away. He smiled nervously.

"I need that money," he said.

"Nothing doing," I said.

He walked off wordlessly, with an air of anger. Maybe he will stab me now, I thought. I got to watch that fool . . .

For another week the white men of both factories begged us to fight. They made up stories about what Harrison had said about me; and when they saw Harrison they lied to him in the same way. Harrison and I were wary of each other whenever we met. We smiled and kept out of arm's reach, ashamed of ourselves and of each other.

Again Harrison called to me one evening as I was on my way home.

"Come on and fight," he begged.

"I don't want to and quit asking me," I said in a voice louder and harder than I had intended.

Harrison looked at me and I watched him. Both of us still carried the knives that the white men had given us.

"I wanna make a payment on a suit of clothes with that five dollars," Harrison said.

"But those white men will be looking at us, laughing at us," I said.

"What the hell," Harrison said. "They look at you and laugh at you every day, nigger."

It was true. But I hated him for saying it. I ached to hit him in his mouth, to hurt him.

"What have we got to lose?" Harrison asked.

"I don't suppose we have anything to lose," I said.

"Sure," he said. "Let's get the money. We don't care."

"And now they know that we know what they tried to do to us," I said, hating myself for saying it. "And they hate us for it."

"Sure," Harrison said. "So let's get the money. You can use five dollars, can't you?"

"Yes."

"Then let's fight for 'em."

"I'd feel like a dog."

"To them, both of us are dogs," he said.

"Yes," I admitted. But again I wanted to hit him.

"Look, let's fool them white men," Harrison said. "We won't hurt each other. We'll just pretend, see? We'll show 'em we ain't as dumb as they think, see?"

"I don't know."

"It's just exercise. Four rounds for five dollars. You scared?"

"No."

"Then come on and fight."

"All right," I said. "It's just exercise. I'll fight."

Harrison was happy. I felt that it was all very foolish. But what the hell. I would go through with it and that would be the end of it. But I still felt a vague anger that would not leave.

When the white men in the factory heard that we had agreed to fight, their excitement knew no bounds. They offered to teach me new punches. Each morning they would tell me in whispers that Harrison was eating raw onions for strength. And—from Harrison—I heard that they told him I was eating raw meat for strength. They offered to buy me my meals each day, but I refused. I grew ashamed of what I had agreed to do and wanted to back out of the fight, but I was afraid that they would be angry if I tried to. I felt that if white men tried to persuade two black boys to stab each other for no reason save their own pleasure, then it would not be difficult for them to aim a wanton blow at a black boy in a fit of anger, in a passing mood of frustration.

The fight took place one Saturday afternoon in the basement of a Main Street building. Each white man who attended the fight dropped his share of the pot into a hat that sat on the concrete floor. Only white men were allowed in the basement; no women or Negroes were admitted. Harrison and I were stripped to the waist. A bright electric bulb glowed above our heads. As the gloves were tied on my hands, I looked at Harrison and saw his eyes watching me. Would he keep his promise? Doubt made me nervous.

We squared off and at once I knew that I had not thought sufficiently about what I had bargained for. I could not pretend to fight. Neither Harrison nor I knew enough about boxing to deceive even a child for a moment. Now shame filled me. The white men were smoking and yelling obscenities at us.

"Crush that nigger's nuts, nigger!"

"Hit that nigger!"

"Aw, fight, you goddamn niggers!"

"Sock 'im in his f-k-g piece!"

"Make 'im bleed!"

I lashed out with a timid left. Harrison landed high on my head and, before I knew it, I had landed a hard right on Harrison's mouth and blood came. Harrison shot a blow to my nose. The fight was on, was on against our will. I felt trapped and ashamed. I lashed out even harder, and the harder I fought the harder Harrison fought. Our plans and promises now meant nothing. We fought four hard rounds, stabbing, slugging, grunting, spitting, cursing, crying, bleeding. The shame and anger we felt for having allowed ourselves to be duped crept into our blows and blood ran into our eyes, half blinding us. The hate we felt for the men whom we had tried to cheat went into the blows we threw at each other. The white men made the rounds last as long as five minutes and each of us was afraid to stop and ask for time for fear of receiving a blow that would knock us out. When we were on the point of collapsing from exhaustion, they pulled us apart.

I could not look at Harrison. I hated him and I hated myself. I clutched my five dollars in my fist and walked home. Harrison and I avoided each other after that and we rarely spoke. The white men attempted to arrange other fights for us, but we had sense enough to refuse. I heard of other fights being staged between other black boys, and each time I heard those plans falling from the lips of the white men in the factory I eased out of earshot. I felt that I had done something unclean, something for which I could never properly atone.

[BOOKS: NEW AVENUES OF FEELING AND SEEING]

One morning I arrived early at work and went into the bank lobby where the Negro porter was mopping. I stood at a counter and picked up the Memphis *Commercial Appeal* and began my free reading of the press. I came finally to the editorial page and saw an article dealing with one H. L. Mencken. I knew by hearsay that he was the editor of the *American Mercury*, but aside from that I knew nothing about him. The article was a furious denunciation of Mencken, concluding with one, hot, short sentence: Mencken is a fool.

I wondered what on earth this Mencken had done to call down upon him the scorn of the South. The only people I had ever heard denounced in the South were Negroes, and this man was not a Negro. Then what ideas did Mencken hold that made a newspaper like the *Commercial Appeal* castigate him publicly? Undoubtedly he must be advocating ideas that the South did not like. Were there, then, people other than Negroes who criticized the South? I knew that during the Civil War the South had hated northern whites, but I had not encountered such hate during my life. Knowing no more of Mencken than I did at that moment, I felt a vague sympathy for him. Had not the South, which had assigned me the role of a non-man, cast at him its hardest words?

Now, how could I find out about this Mencken? There was a huge library near the riverfront, but I knew that Negroes were not allowed to patronize its shelves any more than they were the parks and playgrounds of the city. I had gone into the library several times to get books for the white men on the job. Which of them would now help me to get books? And how could I read them without causing concern to the white men with whom I worked? I had so far been successful in hiding my thoughts and feelings from them, but I knew that I would create hostility if I went about this business of reading in a clumsy way.

I weighed the personalities of the men on the job. There was Don, a Jew; but I distrusted him. His position was not much better than mine and I knew that he was uneasy and insecure; he had always treated me in an offhand, bantering way that barely concealed his contempt. I was afraid to ask him to help me to get books; his frantic desire to demonstrate a racial solidarity with the whites against Negroes might make him betray me.

Then how about the boss? No, he was a Baptist and I had the suspicion that he would not be quite able to comprehend why a black boy would want to read Mencken. There were other white men on the job whose attitudes showed clearly that they were Kluxers[1] or sympathizers, and they were out of the question.

There remained only one man whose attitude did not fit into an anti-Negro category, for I had heard the white men refer to him as a "Pope lover." He was an Irish Catholic and was hated by the white Southerners. I knew that he read books, because I had got him volumes from the library several times. Since he, too, was an object of hatred, I felt that he might refuse me but would hardly betray me. I hesitated, weighing and balancing the imponderable realities.

One morning I paused before the Catholic fellow's desk.

"I want to ask you a favor," I whispered to him.

"What is it?"

"I want to read. I can't get books from the library. I wonder if you'd let me use your card?"

He looked at me suspiciously.

"My card is full most of the time," he said.

"I see," I said and waited, posing my question silently.

"You're not trying to get me into trouble, are you, boy?" he asked, staring at me.

"Oh, no, sir."

"What book do you want?"

"A book by H. L. Mencken."

"Which one?"

"I don't know. Has he written more than one?"

"He has written several."

"I didn't know that."

"What makes you want to read Mencken?"

"Oh, I just saw his name in the newspaper," I said.

"It's good of you to want to read," he said. "But you ought to read the right things."

I said nothing. Would he want to supervise my reading?

"Let me think," he said. "I'll figure out something."

I turned from him and he called me back. He stared at me quizzically.

"Richard, don't mention this to the other white men," he said.

"I understand," I said. "I won't say a word."

A few days later he called me to him.

"I've got a card in my wife's name," he said. "Here's mine."

"Thank you, sir."

"Do you think you can manage it?"

"I'll manage fine," I said.

"If they suspect you, you'll get in trouble," he said.

"I'll write the same kind of notes to the library that you wrote when you sent me for books," I told him. "I'll sign your name."

He laughed.

"Go ahead. Let me see what you get," he said.

---

[1]Members of the violently racist organization the Ku Klux Klan, which originated in the South after the Civil War as a way to control blacks.

That afternoon I addressed myself to forging a note. Now, what were the names of books written by H. L. Mencken? I did not know any of them. I finally wrote what I thought would be a foolproof note: *Dear Madam: Will you please let this nigger boy* — I used the word "nigger" to make the librarian feel that I could not possibly be the author of the note — *have some books by H. L. Mencken?* I forged the white man's name.

I entered the library as I had always done when on errands for whites, but I felt that I would somehow slip up and betray myself. I doffed my hat, stood a respectful distance from the desk, looked as unbookish as possible, and waited for the white patrons to be taken care of. When the desk was clear of people, I still waited. The white librarian looked at me.

"What do you want, boy?"

As though I did not possess the power of speech, I stepped forward and simply handed her the forged note, not parting my lips.

"What books by Mencken does he want?" she asked.

"I don't know, ma'am," I said, avoiding her eyes.

"Who gave you this card?"

"Mr. Falk," I said.

"Where is he?"

"He's at work, at the M— Optical Company," I said. "I've been in here for him before."

"I remember," the woman said. "But he never wrote notes like this."

Oh, God, she's suspicious. Perhaps she would not let me have the books? If she had turned her back at that moment, I would have ducked out the door and never gone back. Then I thought of a bold idea.

"You can call him up, ma'am," I said, my heart pounding.

"You're not using these books, are you?" she asked pointedly.

"Oh, no, ma'am. I can't read."

"I don't know what he wants by Mencken," she said under her breath.

I knew now that I had won; she was thinking of other things and the race question had gone out of her mind. She went to the shelves. Once or twice she looked over her shoulder at me, as though she was still doubtful. Finally she came forward with two books in her hand.

"I'm sending him two books," she said. "But tell Mr. Falk to come in next time, or send me the names of the books he wants. I don't know what he wants to read."

I said nothing. She stamped the card and handed me the books. Not daring to glance at them, I went out of the library, fearing that the woman would call me back for further questioning. A block away from the library I opened one of the books and read a title: *A Book of Prefaces.* I was nearing my nineteenth birthday and I did not know how to pronounce the word "preface." I thumbed the pages and saw strange words and strange names. I shook my head, disappointed. I looked at the other book; it was called *Prejudices.* I knew what that word meant; I had heard it all my life. And right off I was on guard against Mencken's books. Why would a man want to call a book *Prejudices*? The word was so stained with all my memories of racial hate that I could not conceive of anybody using it for a title. Perhaps I had made a mistake about Mencken? A man who had prejudices must be wrong.

When I showed the books to Mr. Falk, he looked at me and frowned.

"That librarian might telephone you," I warned him.

"That's all right," he said. "But when you're through reading those books, I want you to tell me what you get out of them."

That night in my rented room, while letting the hot water run over my can of pork and beans in the sink, I opened *A Book of Prefaces* and began to read. I was jarred and shocked by the style, the clear, clean, sweeping sentences. Why did he write like that? And how did one write like that? I pictured the man as a raging demon, slashing with his pen, consumed with hate, denouncing everything American, extolling everything

European or German, laughing at the weaknesses of people, mocking God, authority. What was this? I stood up, trying to realize what reality lay behind the meaning of the words . . . Yes, this man was fighting, fighting with words. He was using words as a weapon, using them as one would use a club. Could words be weapons? Well, yes, for here they were. Then, maybe, perhaps, I could use them as a weapon? No. It frightened me. I read on and what amazed me was not what he said, but how on earth anybody had the courage to say it.

Occasionally I glanced up to reassure myself that I was alone in the room. Who were these men about whom Mencken was talking so passionately? Who was Anatole France? Joseph Conrad? Sinclair Lewis, Sherwood Anderson, Dostoevski, George Moore, Gustave Flaubert, Maupassant, Tolstoy, Frank Harris, Mark Twain, Thomas Hardy, Arnold Bennett, Stephen Crane, Zola, Norris, Gorky, Bergson, Ibsen, Balzac, Bernard Shaw, Dumas, Poe, Thomas Mann, O. Henry, Dreiser, H. G. Wells, Gogol, T. S. Eliot, Gide, Baudelaire, Edgar Lee Masters, Stendhal, Turgenev, Huneker, Nietzsche,[2] and scores of others? Were these men real? Did they exist or had they existed? And how did one pronounce their names?

I ran across many words whose meanings I did not know, and I either looked them up in a dictionary or, before I had a chance to do that, encountered the word in a context that made its meaning clear. But what strange world was this? I concluded the book with the conviction that I had somehow overlooked something terribly important in life. I had once tried to write, had once reveled in feeling, had let my crude imagination roam, but the impulse to dream had been slowly beaten out of me by experience. Now it surged up again and I hungered for books, new ways of looking and seeing. It was not a matter of believing or disbelieving what I read, but of feeling something new, of being affected by something that made the look of the world different.

As dawn broke I ate my pork and beans, feeling dopey, sleepy. I went to work, but the mood of the book would not die; it lingered, coloring everything I saw, heard, did. I now felt that I knew what the white men were feeling. Merely because I had read a book that had spoken of how they lived and thought, I identified myself with that book. I felt vaguely guilty. Would I, filled with bookish notions, act in a manner that would make the whites dislike me?

I forged more notes and my trips to the library became frequent. Reading grew into a passion. My first serious novel was Sinclair Lewis's *Main Street*. It made me see my boss, Mr. Gerald, and identify him as an American type. I would smile when I saw him lugging his golf bags into the office. I had always felt a vast distance separating me from the boss, and now I felt closer to him, though still distant. I felt now that I knew him, that I could feel the very limits of his narrow life. And this had happened because I had read a novel about a mythical man called George F. Babbitt.[3]

The plots and stories in the novels did not interest me so much as the point of view revealed. I gave myself over to each novel without reserve, without trying to criticize it; it was enough for me to see and feel something different. And for me, everything was something different. Reading was like a drug, a dope. The novels created moods in which I lived for days. But I could not conquer my sense of guilt, my feeling that the white men around me knew that I was changing, that I had begun to regard them differently.

Whenever I brought a book to the job, I wrapped it in newspaper—a habit that was to persist for years in other cities and under other circumstances. But some of the white men pried into my packages when I was absent and they questioned me.

"Boy, what are you reading those books for?"

"Oh, I don't know, sir."

---

[2]These writers are important French, British, American, Russian, Scandinavian, and German novelists, poets, dramatists, philosophers, and essayists of the nineteenth and twentieth centuries—an impressive reading program.
[3]*Babbitt* (1922), by Sinclair Lewis.

"That's deep stuff you're reading, boy."

"I'm just killing time, sir."

"You'll addle your brains if you don't watch out."

I read Dreiser's *Jennie Gerhardt* and *Sister Carrie*[4] and they revived in me a vivid sense of my mother's suffering; I was overwhelmed. I grew silent, wondering about the life around me. It would have been impossible for me to have told anyone what I derived from these novels, for it was nothing less than a sense of life itself. All my life had shaped me for the realism, the naturalism of the modern novel, and I could not read enough of them.

Steeped in new moods and ideas, I bought a ream of paper and tried to write; but nothing would come, or what did come was flat beyond telling. I discovered that more than desire and feeling were necessary to write and I dropped the idea. Yet I still wondered how it was possible to know people sufficiently to write about them? Could I ever learn about life and people? To me, with my vast ignorance, my Jim Crow station in life,[5] it seemed a task impossible of achievement. I now knew what being a Negro meant. I could endure the hunger. I had learned to live with hate. But to feel that there were feelings denied me, that the very breath of life itself was beyond my reach, that more than anything else hurt, wounded me. I had a new hunger.

In buoying me up, reading also cast me down, made me see what was possible, what I had missed. My tension returned, new, terrible, bitter, surging, almost too great to be contained. I no longer *felt* that the world about me was hostile, killing; I *knew* it. A million times I asked myself what I could do to save myself, and there were no answers. I seemed forever condemned, ringed by walls.

I did not discuss my reading with Mr. Falk, who had lent me his library card; it would have meant talking about myself and that would have been too painful. I smiled each day, fighting desperately to maintain my old behavior, to keep my disposition seemingly sunny. But some of the white men discerned that I had begun to brood.

"Wake up there, boy!" Mr. Olin said one day.

"Sir!" I answered for the lack of a better word.

"You act like you've stolen something," he said.

I laughed in the way I knew he expected me to laugh, but I resolved to be more conscious of myself, to watch my every act, to guard and hide the new knowledge that was dawning within me.

If I went north, would it be possible for me to build a new life then? But how could a man build a life upon vague, unformed yearnings? I wanted to write and I did not even know the English language. I bought English grammars and found them dull. I felt that I was getting a better sense of the language from novels than from grammars. I read hard, discarding a writer as soon as I felt that I had grasped his point of view. At night the printed page stood before my eyes in sleep.

Mrs. Moss, my landlady, asked me one Sunday morning:

"Son, what is this you keep on reading?"

"Oh, nothing. Just novels."

"What you get out of 'em?"

"I'm just killing time," I said.

"I hope you know your own mind," she said in a tone which implied that she doubted if I had a mind.

I knew of no Negroes who read the books I liked and I wondered if any Negroes ever thought of them. I knew that there were Negro doctors, lawyers, newspapermen, but I never saw any of them. When I read a Negro newspaper I never caught

---

[4]Novels by Theodore Dreiser, the first published in 1911, the next, earlier, in 1900.
[5]A station that made discrimination and segregation inevitable; Jim Crow came from a name in an early Negro minstrel song.

the faintest echo of my preoccupation in its pages. I felt trapped and occasionally, for a few days, I would stop reading. But a vague hunger would come over me for books, books that opened up new avenues of feeling and seeing, and again, I would forge another note to the white librarian. Again I would read and wonder as only the naïve and unlettered can read and wonder, feeling that I carried a secret, criminal burden about with me each day.

That winter my mother and brother came and we set up housekeeping, buying furniture on the installment plan, being cheated and yet knowing no way to avoid it. I began to eat warm food and to my surprise found that regular meals enabled me to read faster. I may have lived through many illnesses and survived them, never suspecting that I was ill. My brother obtained a job and we began to save toward the trip north, plotting our time, setting tentative dates for departure. I told none of the white men on the job that I was planning to go north; I knew the moment they felt I was thinking of the North they would change toward me. It would have made them feel that I did not like the life I was living, and because my life was completely conditioned by what they said or did, it would have been tantamount to challenging them.

I could calculate my chances for life in the South as a Negro fairly clearly now.

I could fight the southern whites by organizing with other Negroes, as my grandfather had done. But I knew that I could never win that way; there were many whites and there were but few blacks. They were strong and we were weak. Outright black rebellion could never win. If I fought openly I would die and I did not want to die. News of lynchings were frequent.

I could submit and live the life of a genial slave, but that was impossible. All of my life had shaped me to live by my own feelings and thoughts. I could make up to Bess[6] and marry her and inherit the house. But that, too, would be the life of a slave; if I did that, I would crush to death something within me, and I would hate myself as much as I knew the whites already hated those who had submitted. Neither could I ever willingly present myself to be kicked, as Shorty had done. I would rather have died than do that.

I could drain off my restlessness by fighting with Shorty and Harrison. I had seen many Negroes solve the problem of being black by transferring their hatred of themselves to others with a black skin and fighting them. I would have to be cold to do that, and I was not cold and I could never be.

I could, of course, forget what I had read, thrust the whites out of my mind, forget them; and find release from anxiety and longing in sex and alcohol. But the memory of how my father had conducted himself made that course repugnant. If I did not want others to violate my life, how could I voluntarily violate it myself?

I had no hope whatever of being a professional man. Not only had I been so conditioned that I did not desire it, but the fulfillment of such an ambition was beyond my capabilities. Well-to-do Negroes lived in a world that was almost as alien to me as the world inhabited by whites.

What, then, was there? I held my life in my mind, in my consciousness each day, feeling at times that I would stumble and drop it, spill it forever. My reading had created a vast sense of distance between me and the world in which I lived and tried to make a living, and that sense of distance was increasing each day. My days and nights were one long, quiet, continuously contained dream of terror, tension, and anxiety. I wondered how long I could bear it.

1945

---

[6]The daughter of Wright's landlady in Memphis; the landlady took him in and then tried to get him to marry her daughter with the connivance of the daughter; Wright resisted and extricated himself from the situation, but not without offending the daughter and mother.

NEW DIMENSIONS IN PROSE
Cultural and Social Commentary

———

H. L. MENCKEN	EDMUND WILSON
SINCLAIR LEWIS	JOHN DOS PASSOS
HENRY MILLER	JAMES AGEE

"Of a piece with the absurd pedagogical demand for so-called constructive criticism is the doctrine that an iconoclast is a hollow and evil fellow unless he can prove his case. Why, indeed, should he prove it? Doesn't he prove enough when he proves by his blasphemy that this or that idol is defectively convincing—that at least *one* visitor to the shrine is left full of doubts? The fact is enormously significant; it indicates that instinct has somehow risen superior to the shallowness of logic, the refuge of fools. The pedant and the priest have always been the most expert of logicians—and the most diligent disseminators of nonsense and worse. The liberation of the human mind has never been furthered by such learned dunderheads; it has been furthered by gay fellows who heaved dead cats into sanctuaries and then went roistering down the highways of the world, proving to all men that doubt, after all, was safe—that the god in the sanctuary was finite in his power, and hence a fraud. One horse-laugh is worth ten thousand syllogisms. It is not only more effective; it is also vastly more intelligent."

H. L. Mencken, "From a Critic's Notebook," *Prejudices, Fourth Series*, 1924

H. L. MENCKEN
(1880–1956)

H. L. Mencken was a journalist, drama reviewer, literary critic, political pundit, social commentator, and lexicographer. He has been called the "W. C. Fields of journalism" as well as "America's first literary dictator." Even those who disliked him were charmed by his style. He wrote: "Faith may be defined briefly as an illogical belief in the occurrence of the improbable"; "The man who boasts that he habitually tells the truth is simply a man who has no respect for it"; "Man, at his best, remains a sort of one-lunged animal, never completely rounded and perfect, as a cockroach, say, is perfect"; "It is the dull man who is always sure, and the sure man who is always dull."

Henry Louis Mencken was born in Baltimore in 1880, the son of a co-owner of a cigar factory. When Mencken wrote his autobiography, he entitled Volume I *Happy Days, 1880–1892* (1940) because his childhood was a period of contentment. He attended the public high school, the Baltimore Polytechnic with an emphasis on the sciences, and graduated in 1896 as valedictorian. He educated himself at the Enoch Pratt Free Library, and said later: "Altogether, I doubt that any human being in this world has ever read more than I did between my twelfth and eighteenth years." He read the British novelists, poets, and essayists, including William Thackery, Alexander Pope, Joseph Addison, and Richard Steele; and he read William Dean Howells, Henry James, and Stephen Crane. He found *Huckleberry Finn* "one of the great masterpieces of the world," and declared Mark Twain "the true father of our national literature."

Mencken announced to his father that he wanted to become a journalist. The elder Mencken forced him to choose between law school at Johns Hopkins University or work at the cigar factory. The stubborn son chose the latter, and loathed the work. When his father died in 1899, Mencken immediately launched his journalism career. Volume II of his autobiography was entitled *Newspaper Days, 1899–1906* (1941).

Mencken's association with Baltimore newspapers was to last throughout his working life. He started as a reporter, covering the police beat and city hall, and he then rose from city editor to editor-in-chief. As a journalist, Mencken honed his style, incorporating in it coinages and slang he heard in the streets. He early learned to pair a stripped-down style with a sharp satiric thrust to expose corruption hidden beneath phoney genteel surfaces.

Mencken's first two books, *George Bernard Shaw* in 1905 and *Philosophy of Friedrich Nietzsche* in 1908, were aimed at popularizing the playwright and the philosopher that Mencken much admired. As a newspaper drama reviewer, he had come to admire Shaw's iconoclastic, irreverent wit and gift with language. And he turned Nietzsche into the kind of free-thinking social Darwinist he himself had become through reading Aldous Huxley and Herbert Spencer.

In 1908, Mencken became a book reviewer for *The Smart Set* and by 1914 was co-editing this highly influential magazine with drama critic George Jean Nathan. First through *The Smart Set*, which they edited until 1923, and then through *The American Mercury*, which they founded in 1924, Mencken and Nathan inspired the literary and intellectual rebellions of the 1920s. They published and promoted Theodore Dreiser, Sherwood Anderson, Willa Cather, F. Scott Fitzgerald, Ezra Pound, Edgar Lee Masters, and Elinor Wylie. And they kept up a running commentary on the arid stretches of the American cultural landscape.

Out of *boob* and *bourgeoisie* Mencken coined the word *booboisie* to characterize the clods, louts, and conformists that made up much of the American middle class. And he invented the geographical term *Bible Belt* to identify that southern stretch of states dominated by American fundamentalists who believe in a literal interpretation of the Bible. American politics Mencken considered "the greatest show on earth," and the presidential election "uproariously idiotic—a deafening, nerve-wracking battle to the death between Tweedledum and Tweedledee."

Mencken was indefatigable in writing and publishing his views about every aspect of American culture and modern life. In 1917 appeared his *Book of Prefaces*, including two influential essays on Joseph Conrad and Theodore Dreiser. In 1919, he published *Prejudices: First Series*, and followed it by an additional five volumes, with *Prejudices: Sixth Series* appearing in 1927. These volumes were often carried about as though they were Bibles of the rebellion and quoted by the youths in revolt. Religion, politics, prohibition, puritanism, conventional morality, English professors—no institution, subject, or group was immune from the Mencken onslaught of mockery and invective.

In 1919, Mencken compiled and published his most scholarly work, *The American Language*, establishing once and for all that the language spoken and written in the United States could no longer properly be identified with British English or held to its vocabulary, usages, or syntax and style. The divergences had begun during the colonial period and deepened over the years. In identifying American English, Mencken used (among other resources) the texts of such quintessential American writers as Walt Whitman, Mark Twain, and Theodore Dreiser. *The American Language* was brought out in new editions in 1921, 1923, and 1936, and Supplements I and II were issued in 1945 and 1948. It appeared again in 1963, as revised by the linguist Raven I. McDavid, Jr.

With the coming of the Great Depression in 1929, Mencken's popularity began to wane. Nathan left *The American Mercury* in 1930, Mencken in 1933. His attacks on President Franklin D. Roosevelt and the New Deal were not popular among a sobered, socially conscious intelligentsia. Mencken's mother, with whom he had lived as a bachelor, died in 1925, and in 1930 he married, at the age of fifty, an English teacher and writer, Sara Powell Haardt. She died in 1935 from tuberculosis, and Mencken moved back to the Baltimore family home he had occupied practically all his life.

In the 1940s Mencken turned to the writing of his autobiography (the first two volumes were mentioned above); the third volume, entitled *Heathen Days, 1890–1936*, appeared in 1943. In 1948 he suffered a paralytic stroke and found himself unable to read or write; his memory and speech were affected. The remaining years, until his death in 1956, were painful for him. But whatever the frustrations he might have endured, he had the satisfaction of knowing that he had lived the rebellious life he had set out to live at the beginning. He was surely describing himself when he described *iconoclasts* as those "who heaved dead cats into sanctuaries and then went roistering down the highways of the world, proving to all men that doubt, after all, was safe—that the god in the sanctuary was . . . a fraud."

In "Thoughts on Being Bibliographed" (1943), Edmund Wilson credited Mencken with being *the* seer and shaper of the period he lived through:

> Mencken and Shaw were the prophets of new eras in their national cultures to which they were also important contributors; and, though their conceptions of their social aims differed, both were carrying on that work of "Enlightenment" of which the flame had been so fanned by Voltaire. I suppose that I, too, wanted to prove myself a "soldier in the Liberation War of humanity" and to

speak for the "younger generation" who were "knocking at the door": such phrases were often in my head. But for American writing, when I came upon the scene, the battle had mostly been won: I was myself a beneficiary of the work that had been done by Mencken and others.

ADDITIONAL READING

A Mencken Chrestomathy, ed. H. L. Mencken, 1949; *The Vintage Mencken*, ed. Alistair Cooke, 1955; *H. L. Mencken: The American Scene, A Reader*, ed. Huntington Cairns, 1965, 1982; *The Editor, the Bluenose, and the Prostitute: H. L. Mencken's History of the "Hatrack" Censorship Case*, ed. Carl Bode, 1988; *The Diary of H. L. Mencken*, ed. Charles A. Fecher, 1989.

Ernest Boyd, *H. L. Mencken*, 1925; Edgar Kemler, *The Irreverent Mr. Mencken*, 1950; William R. Manchester, *Disturber of the Peace: The Life of H. L. Mencken*, 1950, 1986; M. K. Singleton, *H. L. Mencken and the American Mercury*, 1962; William Nolte, *H. L. Mencken: Literary Critic*, 1964, 1966; Carl Dolmetsch, *The Smart Set: A History and Anthology*, 1966; Philip Wagner, *H. L. Mencken*, 1966; Sara Mayfield, *The Constant Circle: H. L. Mencken and His Friends*, 1968; Carl Bode, *Mencken*, 1969; Douglas C. Stevenson, *Mencken: Iconoclast from Baltimore*, 1971; Fred C. Hobson, Jr., *Serpent in Eden: H. L. Mencken and the South*, 1974; George H. Douglas, *H. L. Mencken: Critic of American Life*, 1978; Charles A. Fecher, *Mencken: A Study of His Thought*, 1980; John Dorsey, ed., *On Mencken*, 1980; Charles Scruggs, *The Sage in Harlem: H. L. Mencken and the Black Writers of the 1920s*, 1984; Edward A. Martin, *H. L. Mencken and the Debunkers*, 1984; Allison Bulsterbaum, *H. L. Mencken: A Research Guide*, 1988.

TEXT

Prejudices: Third Series, 1922.

from On Being an American

[WHY I AM NOT AN EXPATRIATE]

Apparently there are those who begin to find it disagreeable—nay, impossible. Their anguish fills the Liberal weeklies, and every ship that puts out from New York carries a groaning cargo of them, bound for Paris, London, Munich, Rome and way points—anywhere to escape the great curses and atrocities that make life intolerable for them at home. Let me say at once that I find little to cavil at in their basic complaints. In more than one direction, indeed, I probably go a great deal further than even the Young Intellectuals. It is, for example, one of my firmest and most sacred beliefs, reached after an inquiry extending over a score of years and supported by incessant prayer and meditation, that the government of the United States, in both its legislative arm and its executive arm, is ignorant, incompetent, corrupt, and disgusting—and from this judgment I except no more than twenty living lawmakers and no more than twenty executioners of their laws. It is a belief no less piously cherished that the administration of justice in the Republic is stupid, dishonest, and against all reason and equity—and from this judgment I except no more than thirty judges, including two upon the bench of the Supreme Court of the United States. It is another that the foreign policy of the United States—its habitual manner of dealing with other nations, whether friend or foe—is hypocritical, disingenuous, knavish, and dishonorable—and from this judgment I consent to no exceptions whatever, either recent or long past. And it is my fourth (and, to avoid too depressing a bill, final) conviction that the American people, taking one with another, constitute the most timorous, sniveling, poltroonish, ignominious mob of serfs and goosesteppers ever gathered under one flag in Christendom since the end of the Middle Ages, and that they grow more timorous, more sniveling, more poltroonish, more ignominious every day.

So far I go with the fugitive Young Intellectuals—and into the Bad Lands beyond. Such, in brief, are the cardinal articles of my political faith, held passionately since my admission to citizenship and now growing stronger and stronger as I gradually disintegrate into my component carbon, oxygen, hydrogen, phosphorus, calcium, sodium, nitrogen and iron. This is what I believe and preach, *in nomine Domini*,[1] Amen. Yet I remain on the dock, wrapped in the flag, when the Young Intellectuals set sail. Yet here I stand, unshaken and undespairing, a loyal and devoted Americano, even a chauvinist, paying taxes without complaint, obeying all laws that are physiologically obeyable, accepting all the searching duties and responsibilities of citizenship unprotestingly, investing the sparse usufructs[2] of my miserable toil in the obligations of the nation, avoiding all commerce with men sworn to overthrow the government, contributing my mite toward the glory of the national arts and sciences, enriching and embellishing the native language, spurning all lures (and even all invitations) to get out and stay out—here am I, a bachelor of easy means, forty-two years old, unhampered by debts or issue, able to go wherever I please and to stay as long as I please—here am I, contentedly and even smugly basking beneath the Stars and Stripes, a better citizen, I daresay, and certainly a less murmurous and exigent one, than thousands who put the Hon. Warren Gamaliel Harding beside Friedrich Barbarossa and Charlemagne,[3] and hold the Supreme Court to be directly inspired by the Holy Spirit, and belong ardently to every Rotary Club, Ku Klux Klan, and Anti-Saloon League,[4] and choke with emotion when the band plays "The Star-Spangled Banner," and believe with the faith of little children that one of Our Boys, taken at random, could dispose in a fair fight of ten Englishmen, twenty Germans, thirty Frogs, forty Wops, fifty Japs, or a hundred Bolsheviki.[5]

Well, then, why am I still here? Why am I so complacent (perhaps even to the point of offensiveness), so free from bile, so little fretting and indignant, so curiously happy? Why did I answer only with a few academic "Hear, Hears" when Henry James, Ezra Pound, Harold Stearns[6] and the *emigrés* of Greenwich Village issued their successive calls to the cornfed *intelligentsia* to flee the shambles, escape to fairer lands, throw off the curse forever? The answer, of course, is to be sought in the nature of happiness, which tempts to metaphysics. But let me keep upon the ground. To me, at least (and I can only follow my own nose) happiness presents itself in an aspect that is tripartite. To be happy (reducing the thing to its elementals) I must be:

a. Well-fed, unhounded by sordid cares, at ease in Zion.[7]
b. Full of a comfortable feeling of superiority to the masses of my fellow-men.
c. Delicately and unceasingly amused according to my taste.

It is my contention that, if this definition be accepted, there is no country on the face of the earth wherein a man roughly constituted as I am—a man of my general weaknesses, vanities, appetites, prejudices, and aversions—can be so happy, or even one-half so happy, as he can be in these free and independent states. Going further, I lay down the proposition that it is a sheer physical impossibility for such a man to live in These States and *not* be happy—that it is as impossible to him as it would be to a

---

[1] "In the name of the Lord" (Latin).

[2] The right of enjoying property of another without altering it (Roman and civil law).

[3] Warren G. Harding (1865–1923) won the presidential election of 1920; Barbarossa (1123–1190), emperor of Germany (1155–90); Charlemagne (768–814), Emperor of the Holy Roman Empire (800–14).

[4] The three organizations are, in order, a businessman's club, a then recently revived racist (anti-black, anti-Jewish, and anti-Catholic) organization, and a militant anti-liquor group.

[5] Terms often used by the prejudiced: Frogs, French; Wops, Italian; Bolsheviki, the Communist revolutionaries who had recently taken over Russia.

[6] James and Pound were expatriates who lived permanently abroad (James in England, Pound in Italy); see their biographies in this volume. Harold Stearns (1891–1943) became an expatriate after publishing two books critical of America; he wrote *America and the Young Intellectuals* (1921), and he edited *Civilization in the United States* (1922).

[7] I.e., the heavenly city, a blessed and happy place.

schoolboy to weep over the burning down of his school-house. If he says that he isn't happy here, then he either lies or is insane. Here the business of getting a living, particularly since the war brought the loot of all Europe to the national strong-box, is enormously easier than it is in any other Christian land — so easy, in fact, that an educated and forehanded man who fails at it must actually make deliberate efforts to that end. Here the general average of intelligence, of knowledge, of competence, of integrity, of self-respect, of honor is so low that any man who knows his trade, does not fear ghosts, has read fifty good books, and practices the common decencies stands out as brilliantly as a wart on a bald head, and is thrown willy-nilly into a meager and exclusive aristocracy. And here, more than anywhere else that I know of or have heard of, the daily panorama of human existence, of private and communal folly — the unending procession of governmental extortions and chicaneries, of commercial brigandages and throat-slittings, of theological buffooneries, of aesthetic ribaldries, of legal swindles and harlotries, of miscellaneous rogueries, villainies, imbecilities, grotesqueries, and extravagances — is so inordinately gross and preposterous, so perfectly brought up to the highest conceivable amperage, so steadily enriched with an almost fabulous daring and originality, that only the man who was born with a petrified diaphragm can fail to laugh himself to sleep every night, and to awake every morning with all the eager, unflagging expectation of a Sunday-school superintendent touring the Paris peepshows.

A certain sough of rhetoric may be here. Perhaps I yield to words as a chautauqua lecturer[8] yields to them, belaboring and fermenting the hinds[9] with his Message from the New Jerusalem. But fundamentally I am quite as sincere as he is. For example, in the matter of attaining to ease in Zion, of getting a fair share of the national swag, now piled so mountainously high. It seems to me, sunk in my Egyptian night, that the man who fails to do this in the United States today is a man who is somehow stupid — maybe not on the surface, but certainly deep down. Either he is one who cripples himself unduly, say by setting up a family before he can care for it, or by making a bad bargain for the sale of his wares, or by concerning himself too much about the affairs of other men; or he is one who endeavors fatuously to sell something that no normal American wants. Whenever I hear a professor of philosophy complain that his wife has eloped with some moving-picture actor or bootlegger who can at least feed and clothe her, my natural sympathy for the man is greatly corrupted by contempt for his lack of sense. Would it be regarded as sane and laudable for a man to travel the Soudan[10] trying to sell fountain-pens, or Greenland offering to teach double-entry bookkeeping or counterpoint? Coming closer, would the judicious pity or laugh at a man who opened a shop for sale of incunabula[11] in Little Rock, Ark., or who demanded a living in McKeesport, Pa., on the ground that he could read Sumerian? In precisely the same way it seems to me to be nonsensical for a man to offer generally some commodity that only a few rare and dubious Americans want, and then weep and beat his breast because he is not patronized. One seeking to make a living in a country must pay due regard to the needs and tastes of that country. Here in the United States we have no jobs for grand dukes, and none for *Wirkliche Geheimräte*,[12] and none for palace eunuchs, and none for masters of the buckhounds, and none (any more) for brewery *Todsaufer*[13] — and very few for oboeplayers, metaphysicians, astrophysicists, assyriologists, watercolorists, stylites and epic poets. There was a time when the *Todsaufer* served a public need and got an adequate reward, but it is no more. There may come a time when the composer of string quartettes is paid as much as a railway conductor, but it is not yet. Then why

---

[8]A travelling lecture circuit popular in the nineteenth century (the name comes from a lake in New York, a popular site for such lectures).
[9]Peasants.
[10]French spelling of Sudan, a vast plain in central Africa with

little need for pens.
[11]Early, and rare, printed books.
[12]"Imperial undersecretaries" (German).
[13]"Death Tippler" (a taster of brews to insure against poison) (German).

practice such trades — that is, as trades? The man of independent means may venture into them prudently; when he does so, he is seldom molested; it may even be argued that he performs a public service by adopting them. But the man who has a living to make is simply silly if he goes into them; he is like a soldier going over the top with a coffin strapped to his back. Let him abandon such puerile vanities, and take to the uplift instead, as, indeed, thousands of other victims of the industrial system have already done. Let him bear in mind that, whatever its neglect of the humanities and their monks, the Republic has never got half enough bond salesmen, quack doctors, ward leaders, phrenologists, Methodist evangelists, circus clowns, magicians, soldiers, farmers, popular song writers, moonshine distillers, forgers of gin labels, mine guards, detectives, spies, snoopers, and *agents provocateurs*.[14] The rules are set by Omnipotence; the discreet man observes them. Observing them, he is safe beneath the starry bed-tick, in fair weather or foul. The *boobus Americanus*[15] is a bird that knows no closed season — and if he won't come down to Texas oil stock, or one-night cancer cures, or building lots in Swampshurst, he will always come down to Inspiration and Optimism, whether political, theological, pedagogical, literary, or economic.

The doctrine that it is *infra digitatem*[16] for an educated man to take a hand in the snaring of this goose is one in which I see nothing convincing. It is a doctrine chiefly voiced, I believe, by those who have tried the business and failed. They take refuge behind the childish notion that there is something honorable about poverty *per se* — the Greenwich Village complex. This is nonsense. Poverty may be an unescapable misfortune, but that no more makes it honorable than a cocked eye is made honorable by the same cause. Do I advocate, then, the ceaseless, senseless hogging of money? I do not. All I advocate — and praise as virtuous — is the hogging of enough to provide security and ease. Despite all the romantic superstitions to the contrary, the artist cannot do his best work when he is oppressed by unsatisfied wants. Nor can the philosopher. Nor can the man of science. The best and clearest thinking of the world is done and the finest art is produced, not by men who are hungry, ragged and harassed, but by men who are well-fed, warm and easy in mind. It is the artist's first duty to his art to achieve that tranquility for himself. Shakespeare tried to achieve it; so did Beethoven, Wagner, Brahms, Ibsen and Balzac. Goethe, Schopenhauer, Schumann and Mendelssohn[17] were born to it. Joseph Conrad, Richard Strauss and Anatole France have got it for themselves in our own day. In the older countries, where competence is far more general and competition is thus more sharp, the thing is often cruelly difficult, and sometimes almost impossible. But in the United States it is absurdly easy, given ordinary luck. Any man with a superior air, the intelligence of a stockbroker, and the resolution of a hat-check girl — in brief, any man who believes in himself enough, and with sufficient cause, to be called a journeyman — can cadge enough money, in this glorious commonwealth of morons, to make life soft for him.

And if a lining for the purse is thus facilely obtainable, given a reasonable prudence and resourcefulness, then balm for the ego is just as unlaboriously got, given ordinary dignity and decency. Simply to exist, indeed, on the plane of a civilized man is to attain, in the Republic, to a distinction that should be enough for all save the most vain; it is even likely to be too much, as the frequent challenges of the Ku Klux Klan, the American Legion, the Anti-Saloon League, and other such vigilance committees of the majority testify. Here is a country in which all political thought and activity are concentrated upon the scramble for jobs — in which the normal politician, whether he be a President or a village road supervisor, is willing to renounce any principle, however precious to him, and to adopt any lunacy, however offensive to him, in order to keep his place at the trough. Go into politics, then, without seeking

---

or wanting office, and at once you are as conspicuous as a red-haired blackamoor — in fact, a great deal more conspicuous, for red-haired blackamoors have been seen, but who has ever seen or heard of an American politician, Democrat or Republican, Socialist or Liberal, Whig or Tory, who did not itch for a job? Again, here is a country in which it is an axiom that a business man shall be a member of a Chamber of Commerce, an admirer of Charles M. Schwab,[18] a reader of the *Saturday Evening Post*, a golfer — in brief, a vegetable. Spend your hours of escape from *Geschäft*[19] reading Remy de Gourmont[20] or practicing the violoncello, and the local Sunday newspaper will infallibly find you out and hymn the marvel — nay, your banker will summon you to discuss your notes, and your rivals will spread the report (probably truthful) that you were pro-German during the war. Yet again, here is a land in which women rule and men are slaves. Train your women to get your slippers for you, and your ill fame will match Galileo's or Darwin's. Once more, here is the Paradise of back-slappers, of democrats, of mixers, of go-getters. Maintain ordinary reserve, and you will arrest instant attention — and have your hand kissed by multitudes who, despite democracy, have all the inferior man's unquenchable desire to grovel and admire.

Nowhere else in the world is superiority more easily attained or more eagerly admitted. The chief business of the nation, as a nation, is the setting up of heroes, mainly bogus. It admired the literary style of the late Woodrow;[21] it respects the theological passion of Bryan;[22] it venerates J. Pierpont Morgan;[23] it takes Congress seriously; it would be unutterably shocked by the proposition (with proof) that a majority of its judges are ignoramuses, and that a respectable minority of them are scoundrels. The manufacture of artificial *Durchlauchten, k.k. Hoheiten*[24] and even gods goes on feverishly and incessantly; the will to worship never flags. Ten iron-molders meet in the back-room of a near-beer saloon, organize a lodge of the Noble and Mystic Order of American Rosicrucians,[25] and elect a wheelwright Supreme Worthy Whimwham; a month later they send a notice to the local newspaper that they have been greatly honored by an official visit from that Whimwham, and that they plan to give him a jeweled fob for his watch-chain. The chief national heroes — Lincoln, Lee, and so on — cannot remain mere men. The mysticism of the mediaeval peasantry gets into the communal view of them, and they begin to sprout haloes and wings. As I say, no intrinsic merit — at least, none commensurate with the mob esti-mate — is needed to come to such august dignities. Everything American is a bit ama-teurish and childish, even the national gods. The most conspicuous and respected American in nearly every field of endeavor, saving only the purely commercial (I exclude even the financial) is a man who would attract little attention in any other country. The leading American critic of literature, after twenty years of diligent ex-position of his ideas, has yet to make it clear what he is in favor of, and why. The queen of the *haut monde*,[26] in almost every American city, is a woman who regards Lord Reading[27] as an aristocrat and her superior, and whose grandfather slept in his underclothes. The leading American musical director, if he went to Leipzig, would be put to polishing trombones and copying drum parts. The chief living American military man[28] — the national heir to Frederick, Marlborough, Wellington, Washing-

---

[18]Schwab (1862–1939), a steel entrepreneur.

[19]"Employment" (German).

[20]Gourmont (1858–1915), French literary critic and admirer of the symbolist poets.

[21]President Woodrow Wilson, who left office in 1921 and died in 1924.

[22]William Jennings Bryan (1860–1925), defeated three times for the presidency, famous for his speeches (especially their length).

[23]J. Pierpont Morgan (1837–1913), a wealthy entrepreneur who built a financial empire on the acquisition of railroads

and steel companies, and who collected books and art; his son, J. Pierpont Morgan (1867–1943), continued the family name and managed the family banking firm and fortune.

[24]"Highnesses and Royal Imperial Highnesses" (German).

[25]A secret, occult society.

[26]"High society" (French).

[27]Lord Reading (1860–1935), British politician and, in 1918, a special ambassador to the United States.

[28]Probably General John J. Pershing (1860–1948), com-mander of the American Expeditionary Force sent to France in the First World War.

ton and Prince Eugene[29]—is a member of the Elks,[30] and proud of it. The leading American philosopher[31] (now dead, with no successor known to the average pedagogue) spent a lifetime erecting an epistemological defense for the national aesthetic maxim: "I don't know nothing about music, but I know what I like." The most eminent statesman the United States has produced since Lincoln was fooled by Arthur James Balfour,[32] and miscalculated his public support by more than 5,000,000 votes. And the current Chief Magistrate of the nation—its defiant substitute for czar and kaiser—is a small-town printer who, when he wishes to enjoy himself in the Executive Mansion, invites in a homeopathic doctor, a Seventh Day Adventist evangelist, and a couple of moving-picture actresses. . . .[33]

[WHY I ENJOY LIVING IN AMERICA]

All the while I have been forgetting the third of my reasons[1] for remaining so faithful a citizen of the Federation, despite all the lascivious inducements from expatriates to follow them beyond the seas, and all the surly suggestions from patriots that I succumb. It is the reason which grows out of my mediaeval but unashamed taste for the bizarre and indelicate, my congenital weakness for comedy of the grosser varieties. The United States, to my eye, is incomparably the greatest show on earth. It is a show which avoids diligently all the kinds of clowning which tire me most quickly—for example, royal ceremonials, the tedious hocuspocus of *haut politique*,[2] the taking of politics seriously—and lays chief stress upon the kinds which delight me unceasingly—for example, the ribald combats of demagogues, the exquisitely ingenious operations of master rogues, the pursuit of witches and heretics, the desperate struggles of inferior men to claw their way into Heaven. We have clowns in constant practice among us who are as far above the clowns of any other great state as a Jack Dempsey[3] is above a paralytic—and not a few dozen or score of them, but whole droves and herds. Human enterprises which, in all other Christian countries, are resigned despairingly to an incurable dullness—things that seem devoid of exhilarating amusement by their very nature—are here lifted to such vast heights of buffoonery that contemplating them strains the midriff almost to breaking. I cite an example: the worship of God. Everywhere else on earth it is carried on in a solemn and dispiriting manner; in England, of course, the bishops are obscene, but the average man seldom gets a fair chance to laugh at them and enjoy them. Now come home. Here we not only have bishops who are enormously more obscene than even the most gifted of the English bishops; we have also a huge force of lesser specialists in ecclesiastical mountebankery—tinhorn Loyolas, Savonarolas and Xaviers[4] of a hundred fantastic rites, each performing untiringly and each full of a grotesque and illimitable whimsicality. Every American town, however small, has one of its own: a holy

---

[29]A series of military heroes: Frederick the Great (1712–1786), King of Prussia (1740–86); British General Marlborough (1650–1722) defeated the French at Blenheim in 1704; British General Wellington (1769–1852) defeated Napoleon at Waterloo in 1815; American General George Washington (1732–1799) defeated the British in the Revolutionary War; Prince Eugene of Savoy (1663–1736), an Austrian general who distinguished himself many times in battle, including participation with Marlborough at the Battle of Blenheim.
[30]A fraternal organization.
[31]William James (1842–1910), a pragmatist.
[32]British philosopher and statesman who as Foreign Secretary participated in the peace settlement at the end of the First World War, and (according to Mencken) misled the naive American president, Woodrow Wilson. Wilson was not able to mount public support to get the Congress to approve the treaty creating the League of Nations, planned at his insistence at the peace settlement.
[33]I.e., President Warren G. Harding (1865–1923), who was

mediocre intellectually and whose administration was one of the most corrupt in history.
[1]See above, where Mencken indicates that the United States makes him happy by fulfilling three of his elemental needs: to be "well-fed, unhounded by sordid cares, at ease in Zion"; to be "full of a comfortable feeling of superiority to the masses of my fellow-men"; and to be "delicately and unceasingly amused according to my taste."
[2]"High politics" (French).
[3]Famous American boxer (1895–1983) who was world heavyweight champion until 1926.
[4]Ignatius Loyola (1491–1556) Spanish founder of the Jesuits; Girolamo Savonarola (1452–1498), popular Italian preacher and stern moralist, member of the Dominican order, worked for reform but came into conflict with the Pope and was tried for sedition and heresy and was burned at the stake; St. Francis Xavier (1506–1562), Spanish Jesuit missionary in India and Japan.

clerk with so fine a talent for introducing the arts of jazz into the salvation of the damned that his performance takes on all the gaudiness of a four-ring circus, and the bald announcement that he will raid Hell on such and such a night is enough to empty all the town blind-pigs and bordellos and pack his sanctuary to the doors. And to aid him and inspire him there are traveling experts to whom he stands in the relation of a wart to the Matterhorn — stupendous masters of theological imbecility, contrivers of doctrines utterly preposterous, heirs to the Joseph Smith, Mother Eddy and John Alexander Dowie tradition — Bryan, Sunday, and their like.[5] These are the eminences of the American Sacred College. I delight in them. Their proceedings make me a happier American.

Turn, now, to politics. Consider, for example, a campaign for the Presidency. Would it be possible to imagine anything more uproariously idiotic — a deafening, nerve-wracking battle to the death between Tweedledum and Tweedledee, Harlequin and Sganarelle, Gobbo and Dr. Cook[6] — the unspeakable, with fearful snorts, gradually swallowing the inconceivable? I defy any one to match it elsewhere on this earth. In other lands, at worst, there are at least intelligible issues, coherent ideas, salient personalities. Somebody says something, and somebody replies. But what did Harding say in 1920, and what did Cox reply?[7] Who was Harding, anyhow, and who was Cox? Here, having perfected democracy, we lift the whole combat to symbolism, to transcendentalism, to metaphysics. Here we load a pair of palpably tin cannon with blank cartridges charged with talcum powder, and so let fly. Here one may howl over the show without any uneasy reminder that it is serious, and that some one may be hurt. I hold that this elevation of politics to the plane of undiluted comedy is peculiarly American, that nowhere else on this disreputable ball has the art of the shambattle been developed to such fineness. Two experiences are in point. During the Harding-Cox combat of bladders an article of mine, dealing with some of its more melodramatic phases, was translated into German and reprinted by a Berlin paper. At the head of it the editor was careful to insert a preface explaining to his readers, but recently delivered to democracy, that such contests were not taken seriously by intelligent Americans, and warning them solemnly against getting into sweats over politics. At about the same time I had dinner with an Englishman. From cocktails to bromo seltzer he bewailed the political lassitude of the English populace — its growing indifference to the whole partisan harliquinade. Here were two typical foreign attitudes: the Germans were in danger of making politics too harsh and implacable, and the English were in danger of forgetting politics altogether. Both attitudes, it must be plain, make for bad shows. Observing a German campaign, one is uncomfortably harassed and stirred up; observing an English campaign (at least in times of peace), one falls asleep. In the United States the thing is done better. Here politics is purged of all menace, all sinister quality, all genuine significance, and stuffed with such gorgeous humors, such inordinate farce that one comes to the end of a campaign with one's ribs loose, and ready for "King Lear," or a hanging, or a course of medical journals.

But feeling better for the laugh. *Ridi si sapis*, said Martial.[8] Mirth is necessary to wisdom, to comfort, above all, to happiness. Well, here is the land of mirth, as Ger-

---

[5]Joseph Smith (1805–1844), an American who founded the Mormon Church; Mary Baker Eddy (1821–1910), American founder of the Christian Science Church; John Alexander Dowie (1847–1907), American founder of the Christian Catholic Apostolic Church in Zion (and of Zion, Illinois); William Jennings Bryan (1860–1925), American lawyer and politician who was a fundamentalist and defended Tennessee's right to banish from the schools the teaching of Darwin's theory of evolution in the famous Scopes trial in 1925; Billy Sunday (1863–1935), a fundamentalist and a flamboyant evangelist.

[6]Harlequin, Sganarelle, and Gobbo are comic characters or

clowns in commedia dell 'arte, Moliere (*Sganarelle or, The Imaginary Cuckold*, 1660), and Shakespeare (Old Gobbo in *The Merchant of Venice*); Frederick Cook (1865–1940), American physician and explorer whose claims to have reached the peak of Mt. McKinley and to have reached the north pole in his expeditions were later discredited.

[7]In the American presidential election of 1920, the Republican Warren G. Harding defeated James Cox (1870–1957), a Democrat.

[8]Marcus Valerius Martialis (40?–120?), Latin writer and epigrammatist. The Latin epigram is translated by Mencken ("laughter is necessary to wisdom").

many is the land of metaphysics and France is the land of fornication. Here the buffoonery never stops. What could be more delightful than the endless struggle of the Puritan to make the joy of the minority unlawful and impossible? The effort is itself a greater joy to one standing on the side-lines that any or all of the carnal joys that it combats. Always, when I contemplate an uplifter at his hopeless business, I recall a scene in an oldtime burlesque show, witnessed for hire in my days as a dramatic critic. A chorus girl executed a fall upon the stage, and Rudolph Krausemeyer, the Swiss comedian, rushed to her aid. As he stooped painfully to succor her, Irving Rabinovitz, the Zionist comedian, fetched him a fearful clout across the cofferdam[9] with a slap-stick. So the uplifter, the soul-saver, the Americanizer, striving to make the Republic fit for Y. M. C. A. secretaries. He is the eternal American, ever moved by the best of intentions, ever running *a la* Krausemeyer to the rescue of virtue, and ever getting his pantaloons fanned by the Devil. I am naturally sinful, and such spectacles caress me. If the slap-stick were a sash-weight the show would be cruel, and I'd probably complain to the *Polizei*. As it is, I know that the uplifter is not really hurt, but simply shocked. The blow, in fact, does him good, for it helps to get him into Heaven, as exegetes prove from Matthew v, 11: *Heureux serez-vous, lorsqu'on vous outragera, qu'on vous persécutera,*[10] and so on. As for me, it makes me a more contented man, and hence a better citizen. One man prefers the Republic because it pays better wages than Bulgaria. Another because it has laws to keep him sober and his daughter chaste. Another because the Woolworth Building[11] is higher than the cathedral at Chartres. Another because, living here, he can read the New York *Evening Journal*. Another because there is a warrant out for him somewhere else. Me, I like it because it amuses me to my taste. I never get tired of the show. It is worth every cent it costs.

That cost, it seems to me is very moderate. Taxes in the United States are not actually high. I figure, for example, that my private share of the expense of maintaining the Hon. Mr. Harding in the White House this year will work out to less than 80 cents. Try to think of better sport for the money: in New York it has been estimated that it costs $8 to get comfortably tight, and $17.50, on an average, to pinch a girl's arm. The United States Senate will cost me perhaps $11 for the year, but against that expense set the subscription price of the *Congressional Record*, about $15, which, as a journalist, I receive for nothing. For $4 less than nothing I am thus entertained as Solomon never was by his hooch dancers.[12] Col. George Brinton McClellan Harvey[13] costs me but 25 cents a year; I get Nicholas Murray Butler[14] free. Finally, there is young Teddy Roosevelt,[15] the naval expert. Teddy costs me, as I work it out, about 11 cents a year, or less than a cent a month. More, he entertains me doubly for the money, first as a naval expert, and secondly as a walking *attentat*[16] upon democracy, a devastating proof that there is nothing, after all, in that superstition. We Americans subscribe to the doctrine of human equality—and the Rooseveltii reduce it to an absurdity as brilliantly as the sons of Veit Bach.[17] Where is your equal opportunity now? Here in this Eden of clowns, with the highest rewards of clowning theoretically open to every poor boy—here in the very citadel of democracy we found and cherish a clown *dynasty!*

1922

---

[9]A vulnerable part of his anatomy.
[10]"Blessed are ye, when men shall revile you, and persecute you, and say all matter of evil against you, for my sake" (the King James version of the biblical passage partially quoted by Mencken in French; it comes from Matthew 5:2).
[11]The Woolworth Building in New York City, built in the Gothic style and called "the Cathedral of Commerce," was then the tallest skyscraper; Chartres, a Gothic cathedral in France.
[12]The Song of Solomon celebrates the dance of the Shulamite in 6:13.
[13]Harvey (1864–1928), a journalist who campaigned for

Harding and served as ambassador to Great Britain.
[14]Butler (1862–1947), an educator who served as president of Columbia University (1902–45), and often commented on public affairs.
[15]Roosevelt (1887–1944), son of President Theodore Roosevelt, served in the First World War and was then serving as Assistant Secretary of the Navy.
[16]"Outrage" (French).
[17]Great-great-grandfather of Johann Sebastian Bach who lived in the latter half of the sixteenth century and was the founder of the German family of musicians and composers.

SINCLAIR LEWIS
(1885–1951)

Mark Schorer says near the end of his exhaustive biography, *Sinclair Lewis: An American Life* (1961): "[Lewis] was one of the worst writers in modern American literature, but without his writing one cannot imagine American literature." This paradoxical judgment is similar in spirit to evaluations of Lewis made by the critics in his day. They discovered it much easier to find the flaws of style and structure in his novels than to explain the vividness and staying-power of the images he created of American life.

A glance at Lewis's life reveals that its hallmarks were rootlessness and loneliness. From his birth in Sauk Centre, Minnesota, in 1885, to his death in Rome — alone — some sixty-five years later, he seems to have been beset by a restlessness that kept him forever on the go. He married twice (his second wife was the journalist Dorothy Thompson) and had two sons, but he seems never to have found a place he wanted to call home for long. Both marriages ended in divorce. Although his work brought him money, fame, and popularity, he seems not to have derived satisfaction from his success.

Lewis attended the public schools in Sauk Centre but convinced his father (his mother died in 1891) to send him East to college. He went for one year to Oberlin Academy and then entered Yale University in 1903. He worked his way on a cattleboat to Liverpool in the summer of 1904. And in 1906 he took a year off from his studies, repeated the trip to England, and then joined for a time Upton Sinclair's communal living experiment in Upton Hall, Englewood, New Jersey. He worked in New York, doing some editing and writing, and then set off for Panama to find work on the Panama Canal. He returned to Yale the following year and graduated in 1908.

Most casual readers are surprised to learn that *Main Street*, published in 1920, was not Lewis's first but his sixth novel. After leaving Yale, he found employment as a journalist or editor in a number of American cities, including Waterloo, Iowa; San Francisco; Washington, D.C.; and New York. During this time, he was writing fiction, publishing his first novel, *Our Mr. Wrenn*, in 1914. A constant stream of fiction flowed from his pen and appeared in the magazines — short stories and serialized novels, later appearing in book form. Although he was a commercial success as a writer, he attracted little critical attention.

With the appearance of *Main Street* in 1920, his life changed, as did (so it seemed) American literature. An exposé of the stifling pettiness of small-town life in the United States, the novel defined the issues of the literary revolt of the 1920s. With *Babbitt* in 1922, and its portrayal of the banality of the boosterism of American business, Lewis demonstrated the power and range of his satiric gifts. Successive novels found new targets to attack. In *Arrowsmith* in 1925, it was the medical profession. In *Elmer Gantry* in 1927, it was evangelical fundamentalism. In *Dodsworth* in 1929, it was American business, but several cuts above the level of that portrayed in *Babbitt*.

In 1930, Sinclair Lewis became the first American to win the Nobel Prize in Literature. His speech of acceptance, "The American Fear of Literature," became an attack on still another American institution — literary criticism, which too often extolled the mediocre and respectable at the expense of the excellent and candid. The Nobel Prize brought Lewis worldwide recognition at the moment in his career when his best work was behind him. He continued to publish novel after novel, and they sold in enormous numbers. But more and more he was thought of in the past tense, a 1920s author of *Main Street* and *Babbitt*. The titles became words of special meaning in the American language, used by those who knew nothing of the novels.

Since his death in 1951, even the highly praised novels of the 1920s have been assailed as seriously flawed, not only in their craft, but in their ambivalent point of view, drawn in sympathy at the deepest level to the very targets they attack. As one critic has put it, "the question that [Lewis's] career raises is how one can be such a limited writer and also have such an important place in the history of Western literature."

Lewis's biographer Mark Schorer has probably provided the most persuasive answer to that question:

> Unquestionably, [Lewis] helps us into the imagination of ourselves as did no other writer of the 1920s. What he helped us to imagine is a part of ourselves that we do not greatly admire and that, in some of its grossest features, we may indeed by now have outgrown. It was the very worst of our gawky adolescence that he showed us, with the chin weaker than it would finally be, the nose larger, the hands still hanging out of the sleeves, pimples all over the flushed face. Interestingly enough, Sinclair Lewis himself, one of the gawkiest adolescents of all time, always aspired to become an elegant man of the world. So, his fiction, without much more subtlety, tried to whip the most barbarous kind of American into the Lewis conception of culture. When his personal ambition failed, his novels fell back into a defense of the very barbarousness that he had always held onto as an ace in the hole.

ADDITIONAL READING

From Main Street to Stockholm: Letters of Sinclair Lewis, 1919–1930, ed. Harrison Smith, 1952.

Mark Schorer, *Sinclair Lewis: An American Life*, 1961; Sheldon Grebstein, *Sinclair Lewis*, 1962; Mark Schorer, ed., *Sinclair Lewis: A Collection of Critical Essays*, 1962; D. J. Dooley, *The Art of Sinclair Lewis*, 1967; James Lundquist, *Guide to Sinclair Lewis*, 1970; James Lundquist, *Sinclair Lewis*, 1973; Martin Light, *The Quixotic Vision of Sinclair Lewis*, 1975; Robert E. Fleming, *Sinclair Lewis: A Reference Guide*, 1980; Michael Connaughton, ed., *Sinclair Lewis at 100*, 1985; Martin Bucco, ed., *Critical Essays on Sinclair Lewis*, 1986; Harold Bloom, ed., *Sinclair Lewis*, 1987.

TEXT

The Man from Main Street: Selected Essays and Other Writings, 1904–1950, ed. Harry E. Maule and Melville H. Cane, 1953.

The American Fear of Literature

AN ADDRESS BY SINCLAIR LEWIS, DECEMBER 12, 1930, ON RECEIVING THE NOBEL PRIZE IN LITERATURE

Sinclair Lewis was the first American to receive the Nobel Prize in Literature. The award was made at the Nobel Festival in the Stockholm Concert House on December 10, 1930. He received the prize from the hands of King Gustav and his address was delivered two days later in a ceremony before the Swedish Academy, held at the Stock Exchange Hall.

Some of the reasoning of the judges who made the award is set forth in the book, *Nobel: The Man and His Prizes*, written by various authors and published in 1950 by The Nobel Foundation, Stockholm. The following quotation is taken from the section on The Literary Prize, written by Andres Österling:

"The 1930 prize was awarded to Sinclair Lewis (b. 1885) 'for his vigorous and graphic art of description and his ability to create, with wit and humour, new types of people.' On the final phrase special emphasis should be laid, because when the Academy agreed in favour of his nomination, it was influenced, among other things, by a desire to recognize a vigorous trend in modern literature — high-class American humour, the best traditions of which had been continued with such marked success by Sinclair Lewis.

"Against him was weighed another wholly different painter of American reality, the ponderous and solemn Theodore Dreiser, the pioneer American writer of novels criticizing social conditions. Against Lewis's gay virtuosity and flashing satire could be set Dreiser's all-embracing sympathies and his affection for the productive chaos of existence, but the future alone can decide which is the more significant."

The text of the address used here is a second edition revised by the author. It was printed in a little book issued by Harcourt, Brace and Company in May, 1931, entitled *Why Sinclair Lewis Got the Nobel Prize,* by Erik Axel Karlfeldt, permanent secretary of the Swedish Academy. The edition was only 2000 copies, according to the Harvey Taylor Bibliography. Of the first, unrevised edition, 3000 copies were printed, of which 2000 were destroyed and 1000 distributed.[1]

&

Members of the Swedish Academy; Ladies and Gentlemen: Were I to express my feeling of honor and pleasure in having been awarded the Nobel Prize in Literature, I should be fulsome and perhaps tedious, and I present my gratitude with a plain "Thank you."

I wish, in this address, to consider certain trends, certain dangers, and certain high and exciting promises in present-day American literature. To discuss this with complete and unguarded frankness — and I should not insult you by being otherwise than completely honest, however indiscreet — it will be necessary for me to be a little impolite regarding certain institutions and persons of my own greatly beloved land.

But I beg of you to believe that I am in no case gratifying a grudge. Fortune has dealt with me rather too well. I have known little struggle, not much poverty, many generosities. Now and then I have, for my books or myself, been somewhat warmly denounced — there was one good pastor in California who upon reading my *Elmer Gantry*[2] desired to lead a mob and lynch me, while another holy man in the State of Maine wondered if there was no respectable and righteous way of putting me in jail. And, much harder to endure than any raging condemnation, a certain number of old acquaintances among journalists, what in the galloping American slang we call the "I Knew Him When Club," have scribbled that since they know me personally, therefore I must be a rather low sort of fellow and certainly no writer. But if I have now and then received such cheering brickbats, still I, who have heaved a good many bricks myself, would be fatuous not to expect a fair number in return.

No, I have for myself no conceivable complaint to make, and yet for American literature in general, and its standing in a country where industrialism and finance

---

[1]This headnote was supplied by the editors of *The Man from Main Street* (1953), from which the text was taken.

[2]Lewis's novel about a corrupt and hypocritical preacher was published in 1927.

and science flourish and the only arts that are vital and respected are architecture and the film, I have a considerable complaint.

I can illustrate by an incident which chances to concern the Swedish Academy and myself and which happened a few days ago, just before I took ship at New York for Sweden. There is in America a learned and most amiable old gentleman who has been a pastor, a university professor, and a diplomat.[3] He is a member of the American Academy of Arts and Letters and no few universities have honored him with degrees. As a writer he is chiefly known for his pleasant little essays on the joy of fishing. I do not suppose that professional fishermen, whose lives depend on the run of cod or herring, find it altogether an amusing occupation, but from these essays I learned, as a boy, that there is something very important and spiritual about catching fish, if you have no need of doing so.

This scholar stated, and publicly, that in awarding the Nobel Prize to a person who has scoffed at American institutions as much as I have, the Nobel Committee and the Swedish Academy had insulted America. I don't know whether, as an ex-diplomat, he intends to have an international incident made of it, and perhaps demand of the American Government that they land Marines in Stockholm to protect American literary rights, but I hope not.

I should have supposed that to a man so learned as to have been made a Doctor of Divinity, a Doctor of Letters, and I do not know how many other imposing magnificences, the matter would have seemed different; I should have supposed that he would have reasoned, "Although personally I dislike this man's books, nevertheless the Swedish Academy has in choosing him honored America by assuming that the Americans are no longer a puerile backwoods clan, so inferior that they are afraid of criticism, but instead a nation come of age and able to consider calmly and maturely any dissection of their land, however scoffing."

I should even have supposed that so international a scholar would have believed that Scandinavia, accustomed to the works of Strindberg, Ibsen, and Pontoppidan,[4] would not have been peculiarly shocked by a writer whose most anarchistic assertion has been that America, with all her wealth and power, has not yet produced a civilization good enough to satisfy the deepest wants of human creatures.

I believe that Strindberg rarely sang the "Star-Spangled Banner" or addressed Rotary Clubs, yet Sweden seems to have survived him.

I have at such length discussed this criticism of the learned fisherman not because it has any conceivable importance in itself, but because it does illustrate the fact that in America most of us—not readers alone but even writers—are still afraid of any literature which is not a glorification of everything American, a glorification of our faults as well as our virtues. To be not only a best-seller in America but to be really beloved, a novelist must assert that all American men are tall, handsome, rich, honest, and powerful at golf; that all country towns are filled with neighbors who do nothing from day to day save go about being kind to one another; that although American girls may be wild, they change always into perfect wives and mothers; and that, geographically, America is composed solely of New York, which is inhabited entirely by millionaires; of the West, which keeps unchanged all the boisterous heroism of 1870; and of the South, where every one lives on a plantation perpetually glossy with moonlight and scented with magnolias.

It is not today vastly more true than it was twenty years ago that such novelists of ours as you have read in Sweden, novelists like Dreiser and Willa Cather, are authentically popular and influential in America. As it was revealed by the venerable fishing

---

[3]Henry Van Dyke (1852–1933), a Presbyterian minister who became a professor at Princeton; he was the author of a number of travel sketches, moralistic essays or sermon-like tales, and books about the outdoors (including fishing). His style was graceful but genteel.

[4]August Strindberg (1849–1912), Swedish playwright and novelist; Henrik Ibsen (1828–1906), Norwegian poet and dramatist; and Henrik Pontoppidan (1857–1943), Danish novelist.

Academician whom I have quoted, we still most revere the writers for the popular magazines who in a hearty and edifying chorus chant that the America of a hundred and twenty million population is still as simple, as pastoral, as it was when it had but forty million; that in an industrial plant with ten thousand employees, the relationship between the worker and the manager is still as neighborly and uncomplex as in a factory of 1840, with five employees; that the relationships between father and son, between husband and wife, are precisely the same in an apartment in a thirty-story palace today, with three motor cars awaiting the family below and five books on the library shelves and a divorce imminent in the family next week, as were those relationships in a rose-veiled five-room cottage in 1880; that, in fine, America has gone through the revolutionary change from rustic colony to world-empire without having in the least altered the bucolic and Puritanic simplicity of Uncle Sam.

I am, actually, extremely grateful to the fishing Academician for having somewhat condemned me. For since he is a leading member of the American Academy of Arts and Letters, he has released me, has given me the right to speak as frankly of that Academy as he has spoken of me. And in any honest study of American intellectualism today, that curious institution must be considered.

Before I consider the Academy, however, let me sketch a fantasy which has pleased me the last few days in the unavoidable idleness of a rough trip on the Atlantic. I am sure that you know, by now, that the award to me of the Nobel Prize has by no means been altogether popular in America. Doubtless the experience is not new to you. I fancy that when you gave the award even to Thomas Mann, whose *Zauberberg*[5] seems to me to contain the whole of intellectual Europe, even when you gave it to Kipling,[6] whose social significance is so profound that it has been rather authoritatively said that he created the British Empire, even when you gave it to Bernard Shaw,[7] there were countrymen of those authors who complained because you did not choose another.

And I imagined what would have been said had you chosen some American other than myself. Suppose you had taken Theodore Dreiser.

Now to me, as to many other American writers, Dreiser more than any other man, marching alone, usually unappreciated, often hated, has cleared the trail from Victorian and Howellsian timidity and gentility in American fiction to honesty and boldness and passion of life. Without his pioneering, I doubt if any of us could, unless we liked to be sent to jail, seek to express life and beauty and terror.

My great colleague Sherwood Anderson has proclaimed this leadership of Dreiser. I am delighted to join him. Dreiser's great first novel, *Sister Carrie*, which he dared to publish thirty long years ago and which I read twenty-five years ago, came to housebound and airless America like a great free Western mind, and to our stuffy domesticity gave us the first fresh air since Mark Twain and Whitman.

Yet had you given the Prize to Mr. Dreiser, you would have heard groans from America; you would have heard that his style — I am not exactly sure what this mystic quality "style" may be, but I find the word so often in the writings of minor critics that I suppose it must exist — you would have heard that his style is cumbersome, that his choice of words is insensitive, that his books are interminable. And certainly respectable scholars would complain that in Mr. Dreiser's world, men and women are often sinful and tragic and despairing, instead of being forever sunny and full of song and virtue, as befits authentic Americans.

And had you chosen Mr. Eugene O'Neill,[8] who has done nothing much in American drama save to transform it utterly, in ten or twelve years, from a false world of

[5]German novelist (1875–1955), author of *The Magic Mountain (Zauberberg)* (1924).
[6]Rudyard Kipling (1865–1936), British novelist born in India; his stories are set around the world, in far-flung outposts of the British Empire.
[7]George Bernard Shaw (1856–1950), Irish-born British playwright.
[8]O'Neill won the Nobel Prize in 1936; Dreiser never won it.

neat and competent trickery to a world of splendor and fear and greatness, you would have been reminded that he has done something far worse than scoffing — he has seen life as not to be neatly arranged in the study of a scholar but as a terrifying, magnificent and often quite horrible thing akin to the tornado, the earthquake, the devastating fire.

And had you given Mr. James Branch Cabell[9] the Prize, you would have been told that he is too fantastically malicious. So would you have been told that Miss Willa Cather, for all the homely virtue of her novels concerning the peasants of Nebraska, has in her novel, *The Lost Lady*, been so untrue to America's patent and perpetual and possibly tedious virtuousness as to picture an abandoned woman who remains, nevertheless, uncannily charming even to the virtuous, in a story without any moral; that Mr. Henry Mencken is the worst of all scoffers; that Mr. Sherwood Anderson viciously errs in considering sex as important a force in life as fishing; that Mr. Upton Sinclair,[10] being a Socialist, sins against the perfectness of American capitalistic mass production; that Mr. Joseph Hergesheimer[11] is un-American in regarding graciousness of manner and beauty of surface as of some importance in the endurance of daily life; and that Mr. Ernest Hemingway is not only too young but, far worse, uses language which should be unknown to gentlemen; that he acknowledges drunkenness as one of man's eternal ways to happiness, and asserts that a soldier may find love more significant than the hearty slaughter of men in battle.

Yes, they are wicked, these colleagues of mine; you would have done almost as evilly to have chosen them as to have chosen me; and as a chauvinistic American — only, mind you, as an American of 1930 and not of 1880 — I rejoice that they are my countrymen and countrywomen, and that I may speak of them with pride even in the Europe of Thomas Mann, H. G. Wells, Galsworthy, Knut Hamsun, Arnold Bennett, Feuchtwanger, Selma Lagerlöf, Sigrid Undset, Werner von Heidenstam, D'Annunzio, Romain Rolland.[12]

It is my fate in this paper to swing constantly from optimism to pessimism and back, but so is it the fate of any one who writes or speaks of anything in America — the most contradictory, the most depressing, the most stirring, of any land in the world today.

Thus, having with no muted pride called the roll of what seem to me to be great men and women in American literary life today, and having indeed omitted a dozen other names of which I should like to boast were there time, I must turn again and assert that in our contemporary American literature, indeed in all American arts save architecture and the film, we — yes, we who have such pregnant and vigorous standards in commerce and science — have no standards, no healing communication, no heroes to be followed nor villains to be condemned, no certain ways to be pursued and no dangerous paths to be avoided.

The American novelist or poet or dramatist or sculptor or painter must work alone, in confusion, unassisted save by his own integrity.

That, of course, has always been the lot of the artist. The vagabond and criminal François Villon[13] had certainly no smug and comfortable refuge in which elegant ladies would hold his hand and comfort his starveling soul and more starved body. He, veritably a great man, destined to outlive in history all the dukes and puissant cardinals whose robes he was esteemed unworthy to touch, had for his lot the gutter and the hardened crust.

---

[9]American novelist (1879–1958) whose works (like *Jurgen*, 1919) were sexually suggestive and comic.
[10]American novelist and social reformer (1878–1968) whose novel, *The Jungle* (1906), was an exposé of Chicago's meatpacking industry.
[11]American writer (1880–1954) whose novels of manners were popular during the Twenties.

[12]A roster of modern German, British, Scandinavian, Italian, and French writers prominent at the time.
[13]Great French poet of the late Middle Ages who was often involved in brawls and accused of crimes; he was arrested in 1462 and sentenced to be hanged, but the sentence was later commuted to ten years' exile. He disappeared and was not heard from again.

Such poverty is not for the artist in America. They pay us, indeed, only too well; that writer is a failure who cannot have his butler and motor and his villa at Palm Beach, where he is permitted to mingle almost in equality with the barons of banking. But he is oppressed ever by something worse than poverty — by the feeling that what he creates does not matter, that he is expected by his readers to be only a decorator or a clown, or that he is good-naturedly accepted as a scoffer whose bark probably is worse than his bite and who probably is a good fellow at heart, who in any case certainly does not count in a land that produces eight-story buildings, motors by the million, and wheat by the billions of bushels. And he has no institution, no group, to which he can turn for inspiration, whose criticism he can accept and whose praise will be precious to him.

What institutions have we?

The American Academy of Arts and Letters[14] does contain along with several excellent painters and architects and statesmen, such a really distinguished university-president as Nicholas Murray Butler,[15] so admirable and courageous a scholar as Wilbur Cross,[16] and several first-rate writers: the poets Edwin Arlington Robinson and Robert Frost, the free-minded publicist James Truslow Adams, and the novelists Edith Wharton, Hamlin Garland, Owen Wister, Brand Whitlock and Booth Tarkington.[17]

But it does not include Theodore Dreiser, Henry Mencken, our most vivid critic, George Jean Nathan[18] who, though still young, is certainly the dean of our dramatic critics, Eugene O'Neill, incomparably our best dramatist, the really original and vital poets, Edna St. Vincent Millay and Carl Sandburg, Robinson Jeffers and Vachel Lindsay and Edgar Lee Masters, whose *Spoon River Anthology* was so utterly different from any other poetry ever published, so fresh, so authoritative, so free from any gropings and timidities that it came like a revelation, and created a new school of native American poetry. It does not include the novelists and short-story writers, Willa Cather, Joseph Hergesheimer, Sherwood Anderson, Ring Lardner, Ernest Hemingway, Louis Bromfield, Wilbur Daniel Steele, Fannie Hurst, Mary Austin, James Branch Cabell, Edna Ferber, nor Upton Sinclair,[19] of whom you must say, whether you admire or detest his aggressive Socialism, that he is internationally better known than any other American artist whosoever, be he novelist, poet, painter, sculptor, musician, architect.

I should not expect any Academy to be so fortunate as to contain all these writers, but one which fails to contain any of them, which thus cuts itself off from so much of what is living and vigorous and original in American letters, can have no relationship whatever to our life and aspirations. It does not represent literary America of today — it represents only Henry Wadsworth Longfellow.

It might be answered that, after all, the Academy is limited to fifty members; that, naturally, it cannot include every one of merit. But the fact is that while most of our few giants are excluded, the Academy does have room to include three extraordinarily bad poets, two very melodramatic and insignificant playwrights, two gentlemen who are known only because they are university presidents, a man who was thirty years ago known as a rather clever humorous draughtsman, and several gentlemen of whom — I sadly confess my ignorance — I have never heard.

Let me again emphasize the fact — for it is a fact — that I am not attacking the American Academy. It is a hospitable and generous and decidedly dignified institu-

---

[14]Founded in 1904 and limited to fifty members chosen from a parent organization, the National Institute of Arts and Letters.
[15]Butler (1862–1947), president of Columbia University (1901–45).
[16]Cross (1862–1948), English Professor at Yale (1894–1930).
[17]Adams (1878–1949), an eminent historian; Wister (1860–

1939), a popular Pennsylvania novelist; Whitlock (1869–1934), widely read Ohio novelist; Tarkington (1869–1946), a best-selling Indiana novelist.
[18]Nathan (1882–1958), drama critic, associated with H. L. Mencken in editing *The Smart Set* and *The American Mercury*.
[19]A list of many of the best-known American fiction writers of the time, some of whom are still read, many not.

tion. And it is not altogether the Academy's fault that it does not contain many of the men who have significance in our letters. Sometimes it is the fault of those writers themselves. I cannot imagine that grizzly-bear Theodore Dreiser being comfortable at the serenely Athenian dinners of the Academy, and were they to invite Mencken, he would infuriate them with his boisterous jeering. No, I am not attacking—I am reluctantly considering the Academy because it is so perfect an example of the divorce in America of intellectual life from all authentic standards of importance and reality.

Our universities and colleges, or gymnasia,[20] most of them, exhibit the same unfortunate divorce. I can think of four of them, Rollins College in Florida, Middlebury College in Vermont, the University of Michigan, and the University of Chicago—which has had on its roll so excellent a novelist as Robert Herrick,[21] so courageous a critic as Robert Morss Logvett[22]—which have shown an authentic interest in contemporary creative literature. Four of them. But universities and colleges and musical emporiums and schools for the teaching of theology and plumbing and signpainting are as thick in America as the motor traffic. Whenever you see a public building with Gothic fenestration on a sturdy backing of Indiana concrete, you may be certain that it is another university, with anywhere from two hundred to twenty thousand students equally ardent about avoiding the disadvantage of becoming learned and about gaining the social prestige contained in the possession of a B.A. degree.

Oh, socially our universities are close to the mass of our citizens, and so are they in the matter of athletics. A great college football game is passionately witnessed by eighty thousand people, who have paid five dollars apiece and motored anywhere from ten to a thousand miles for the ecstasy of watching twenty-two men chase one another up and down a curiously marked field. During the football season, a capable player ranks very nearly with our greatest and most admired heroes—even with Henry Ford, President Hoover, and Colonel Lindbergh.[23]

And in one branch of learning, the sciences, the lords of business who rule us are willing to do homage to the devotees of learning. However bleakly one of our trader aristocrats may frown upon poetry or the visions of a painter, he is graciously pleased to endure a Millikan, a Michelson, a Banting, a Theobald Smith.[24]

But the paradox is that in the arts our universities are as cloistered, as far from reality and living creation, as socially and athletically and scientifically they are close to us. To a true-blue professor of literature in an American university, literature is not something that a plain human being, living today, painfully sits down to produce. No; it is something dead; it is something magically produced by superhuman beings who must, if they are to be regarded as artists at all, have died at least one hundred years before the diabolical invention of the typewriter. To any authentic don, there is something slightly repulsive in the thought that literature could be created by any ordinary human being, still to be seen walking the streets, wearing quite commonplace trousers and coat and looking not so unlike a chauffeur or a farmer. Our American professors like their literature clear and cold and pure and very dead.

I do not suppose that American universities are alone in this. I am aware that to the dons of Oxford and Cambridge, it would seem rather indecent to suggest that

[20]Here used in the Continental sense of "classical preparatory schools" comparable to our undergraduate colleges.
[21]Herrick (1868–1938), American novelist who taught at the University of Chicago (1893–1923).
[22]Lovett (1870–1956), writer of novels and plays, but primarily a literary critic, taught at the University of Chicago (1893–1936).
[23]Ford (1863–1947), automobile tycoon who developed the assembly line to make inexpensive cars; Herbert Hoover (1874–1964), President of the United States during the first years of the Great Depression; Colonel Charles Lindbergh

(1902–1974), whose crossing of the Atlantic in 1927 from New York to Paris alone in a monoplane made him an international hero.
[24]Robert Millikan (1868–1953), American physicist professor and Nobel Prize winner in 1923; Albert Michelson (1852–1931), American professor of physics and Nobel Prize winner in 1907; Sir Frederick Grant Banting (1891–1941), Canadian physician and Nobel Prize winner in 1923; Theobald Smith (1859–1934), American pathologist and professor famous for his discoveries in the nature of and immunization against parasitic diseases.

Wells and Bennett and Galsworthy and George Moore may, while they commit the impropriety of continuing to live, be compared to any one so beautifully and safely dead as Samuel Johnson.[25] I suppose that in the universities of Sweden and France and Germany there exist plenty of professors who prefer dissection to understanding. But in the new and vital and experimental land of America, one would expect the teachers of literature to be less monastic, more human, than in the traditional shadows of old Europe.

They are not.

There has recently appeared in America, out of the universities, an astonishing circus called "the New Humanism."[26] Now of course "humanism" means so many things that it means nothing. It may infer anything from a belief that Greek and Latin are more inspiring than the dialect of contemporary peasants to a belief that any living peasant is more interesting than a dead Greek. But it is a delicate bit of justice that this nebulous word should have chosen to label this nebulous cult.

Insofar as I have been able to comprehend them—for naturally in a world so exciting and promising as this today, a life brilliant with Zeppelins and Chinese revolutions and the Bolshevik industrialization of farming and ships and the Grand Canyon and young children and terrifying hunger and the lonely quest of scientists after God, no creative writer would have time to follow all the chilly enthusiasms of the New Humanists—this newest of sects reasserts the dualism of man's nature. It would confine literature to the fight between man's soul and God, or man's soul and evil.

But, curiously, neither God nor the devil may wear modern dress, but must retain Grecian vestments. Oedipus[27] is a tragic figure for the New Humanists; man, trying to maintain himself as the image of God under the menace of dynamos, in a world of high-pressure salesmanship, is not. And the poor comfort which they offer is that the object of life is to develop self-discipline—whether or not one ever accomplishes anything with this self-discipline. So this whole movement results in the not particularly novel doctrine that both art and life must be resigned and negative. It is a doctrine of the blackest reaction introduced into a stirringly revolutionary world.

Strangely enough, this doctrine of death, this escape from the complexities and danger of living into the secure blankness of the monastery, has become widely popular among professors in a land where one would have expected only boldness and intellectual adventure, and it has more than ever shut creative writers off from any benign influence which might conceivably have come from the universities.

But it has always been so. America has never had a Brandes, a Taine, a Goethe, a Croce.[28]

With a wealth of creative talent in America, our criticism has most of it been a chill and insignificant activity pursued by jealous spinsters, ex-baseball-reporters, and acid professors. Our Erasmuses[29] have been village schoolmistresses. How should there be any standards when there has been no one capable of setting them up?

The great Cambridge-Concord circle of the middle of the Nineteenth Century—Emerson, Longfellow, Lowell, Holmes, the Alcotts—were sentimental reflections of Europe, and they left no school, no influence. Whitman and Thoreau and Poe and,

---

[25]H. G. Wells (1866–1946), Arnold Bennett (1867–1931), John Galsworthy (1867–1933), and George Moore (1852–1933) were all British writers of considerable achievement and popularity at the time; Dr. Samuel Johnson (1709–1784), British critic, novelist, lexicographer, and biographer, was a major literary figure of the eighteenth century.
[26]The "New Humanism" rejected the supernatural and placed emphasis on human experience and its ethical dimension, emphasizing a belief in free will and proposing restraint in human behavior. Principal proponents were Irving Babbitt (1865–1933), who taught French at Harvard (1894–1933), and Paul Elmer More (1864–1937), who taught Sanskrit at Harvard (1894–95) and at other universities. Stuart P. Sherman (1881–1926) studied at Harvard and was a Professor of English at the University of Illinois (1907–24); a

popularizer of his version of the New Humanism, attacking writers on moral grounds, he became the center of much literary controversy and was attacked by H. L. Mencken and other liberal thinkers.
[27]Hero of *Oedipus Rex*, by Greek playwright Sophocles (495–406 B.C.).
[28]George Morris Cohen Brandes (1842–1927), Danish literary critic; Hippolyte Taine (1828–1893), French philosopher and literary critic; Johann Wolfgang von Goethe (1749–1832), a German poet, playwright, novelist and writer on many subjects; Benedetto Croce (1866–1952), Italian philosopher and literary critic.
[29]Desiderius Erasmus (1466–1536), Dutch scholar and philosopher.

in some degree, Hawthorne, were outcasts, men alone and despised, berated by the New Humanists of their generation. It was with the emergence of William Dean Howells that we first began to have something like a standard, and a very bad standard it was.

Mr. Howells was one of the gentlest, sweetest, and most honest of men, but he had the code of a pious old maid whose greatest delight was to have tea at the vicarage. He abhorred not only profanity and obscenity but all of what H. G. Wells has called "the jolly coarseness of life." In his fantastic vision of life, which he innocently conceived to be realistic, farmers and seamen and factory-hands might exist, but the farmer must never be covered with muck, the seaman must never roll out bawdy chanteys, the factory-hand must be thankful to his good employer, and all of them must long for the opportunity to visit Florence and smile gently at the quaintness of the beggars.

So strongly did Howells feel this genteel, this New Humanistic philosophy that he was able vastly to influence his contemporaries, down even to 1914 and the turmoil of the Great War.

He was actually able to tame Mark Twain, perhaps the greatest of our writers, and to put that fiery old savage into an intellectual frock coat and top hat. His influence is not altogether gone today. He is still worshipped by Hamlin Garland, an author who should in every way have been greater than Howells but who under Howells' influence was changed from a harsh and magnificent realist into a genial and insignificant lecturer. Mr. Garland is, so far as we have one, the dean of American letters today, and as our dean, he is alarmed by all of the younger writers who are so lacking in taste as to suggest that men and women do not always love in accordance with the prayer-book, and that common people sometimes use language which would be inappropriate at a women's literary club on Main Street. Yet this same Hamlin Garland, as a young man, before he had gone to Boston and become cultured and Howellized, wrote two most valiant and revelatory works of realism, *Main-Travelled Roads* and *Rose of Dutcher's Coolly*.

I read them as a boy in a prairie village in Minnesota—just such an environment as was described in Mr. Garland's tales. They were vastly exciting to me. I had realized in reading Balzac and Dickens[30] that it was possible to describe French and English common people as one actually saw them. But it had never occurred to me that one might without indecency write of the people of Sauk Centre, Minnesota, as one felt about them. Our fictional tradition, you see, was that all of us in Midwestern villages were altogether noble and happy; that not one of us would exchange the neighborly bliss of living on Main Street for the heathen gaudiness of New York or Paris or Stockholm. But in Mr. Garland's *Main-Travelled Roads* I discovered that there was one man who believed that Midwestern peasants were sometimes bewildered and hungry and vile—and heroic. And, given this vision, I was released; I could write of life as living life.

I am afraid that Mr. Garland would not be pleased but acutely annoyed to know that he made it possible for me to write of America as I see it, and not as Mr. William Dean Howells so sunnily saw it. And it is his tragedy, it is a completely revelatory American tragedy, that in our land of freedom, men like Garland, who first blast the roads to freedom, become themselves the most bound.

But, all this time, while men like Howells were so effusively seeking to guide America into becoming a pale edition of an English cathedral town, there were surly and authentic fellows—Whitman and Melville, then Dreiser and James Huneker[31] and Mencken—who insisted that our land had something more than tea-table gentility.

And so, without standards, we have survived. And for the strong young men, it has perhaps been well that we should have no standards. For, after seeming to be

---

[30] Honoré de Balzac (1799–1950), French novelist, and Charles Dickens (1812–1870), British novelist; both created and peopled whole worlds in their innumerable novels.

[31] Huneker (1857–1921), American music critic who developed into an avante-garde critic with wide interests; he was praised by H. L. Mencken.

pessimistic about my own and much beloved land, I want to close this dirge with a very lively sound of optimism.

I have, for the future of American literature, every hope and every eager belief. We are coming out, I believe, of the stuffiness of safe, sane, and incredibly dull provincialism. There are young Americans today who are doing such passionate and authentic work that it makes me sick to see that I am a little too old to be one of them.

There is Ernest Hemingway, a bitter youth, educated by the most intense experience, disciplined by his own high standards, an authentic artist whose home is in the whole of life; there is Thomas Wolfe, a child of, I believe, thirty or younger, whose one and only novel, *Look Homeward, Angel*, is worthy to be compared with the best in our literary production, a Gargantuan creature with great gusto of life; there is Thornton Wilder, who in an age of realism dreams the old and lovely dreams of the eternal romantics; there is John Dos Passos, with his hatred of the safe and sane standards of Babbitt[32] and his splendor of revolution; there is Stephen Benét[33] who, to American drabness, has restored the epic poem with his glorious memory of old John Brown; there are Michael Gold,[34] who reveals the new frontier of the Jewish East Side, and William Faulkner, who has freed the South from hoop-skirts; and there are a dozen other young poets and fictioneers, most of them living now in Paris, most of them a little insane in the tradition of James Joyce,[35] who, however insane they may be, have refused to be genteel and traditional and dull.

I salute them, with a joy in being not yet too far removed from their determination to give to the America that has mountains and endless prairies, enormous cities and lost farm cabins, billions of money and tons of faith, to an America that is as strange as Russia and as complex as China, a literature worthy of her vastness.

1931

HENRY MILLER
(1891–1980)

Early in his life, Henry Miller proclaimed: "Some day I will write an enormous, ultimate book in which everything will be recorded: the street, the crowded cars, the Grand Street markets . . . the six-day bike races . . . all, all my life." In making such a proclamation, Miller was modeling himself on two American writers he much admired—on Henry David Thoreau, who recorded his life in his "ultimate book," his lifetime journal, from which he shaped *Walden* and other published works; and on Walt Whitman, who in his lifelong poetic work, *Leaves of Grass*, had put "a person," himself, "freely, fully and truly on record" (as he asserted in "A Backward Glance O'er Travel'd Roads").

Like Thoreau and Whitman, Miller was an individualist and a rebel. But he spent his most creative years abroad, rejecting the modern America his country had become. He firmly believed that the fate Whitman had only glimpsed as a possibility in *Democratic Vistas*—that a materialistic America was destined for the same doom as the "fabled damned"—had in fact been fulfilled in what he came to call the "air-conditioned nightmare."

---

[32]One of the New Humanists (see note 26).
[33]Stephen Vincent Benét (1898–1943), author of the epic poem *John Brown's Body* (1928).
[34]Gold (1893–1967), radical Jewish writer, especially literary critic, prominent in the 1930s; he wrote from his perspective of growing up in the New York slums.
[35]James Joyce (1882–1941), the major British modernist in fiction whose *Ulysses* (1922) and *Finnegans Wake* (1939) are standard modern classics.

Born in an immigrant section of New York in 1891, Miller grew up speaking German before English. After graduation from high school in 1909, he tried the City College of New York, but left after two months. He worked at various jobs in New York and then set out for California, where he worked as a field hand. Soon he was back in New York, supporting himself as best he could as he tried to launch a writing career. At one time he was a manager for Western Union Telegraph Company and wrote a novel about the messengers, but it was not published.

A first marriage in 1917 ended in divorce in 1924 and with a new wife Miller opened a speakeasy in Greenwich Village. This business failed, as did Miller's attempt to make a fortune in Florida in the real estate boom. In 1927 he worked for a period as a gravedigger.

In the late 1920s Miller visited Paris, settling there as an expatriate in 1930, alone and penniless. Friends came to his aid, letting him share their apartments and food while he wrote *Tropic of Cancer*, published in France in 1934 (it was banned in America). In this work, Miller discovered the semi-autobiographical form most congenial to his talent, and the episodes of the "fiction" came straight out of his marginal existence as a writer in Paris. Frank in its depiction of sexual experience, and often surrealistic in its style, the book was basically life-affirming.

By this time, Miller had met the French-American writer, Anaïs Nin, and their close relationship moved him to divorce his second wife in 1934. In 1936 Miller brought out a collection of autobiographical sketches and essays as *Black Spring*. And in 1939 he published *Tropic of Capricorn*, another semi-autobiographical "novel" set in the Brooklyn of his boyhood, a companion to the *Tropic of Cancer* in its candid account of sexual experience and its sometimes florid and surrealistic style.

Returning to America at the beginning of the Second World War, Miller obtained in 1940 a small advance from a publisher for a book based on a tour of the United States. Miller bought a car and set off, but was almost immediately discouraged. He wrote to Anaïs Nin: "I'm afraid of the monotony everywhere, the uniformity, the lackluster life or lifelessness." When Miller finished the manuscript (over 500 pages), it was turned down by the publisher, and Miller returned the advance. The manuscript was finally published three years later in two volumes, *The Air-Conditioned Nightmare* (1945) and *Remember to Remember* (1946).

Miller settled in Big Sur, California, in 1944, and began work on an account of the years of life left out of his previous work—the period of the middle 1920s, before Paris, while Miller was in Brooklyn attempting to develop a voice and find a style for his writing. The work was of mammoth proportions, published in Paris as *Sexus* (1949), *Plexus* (1952), and *Nexus* (1960), the trilogy bearing the title, *The Rosy Crucifixion*. It lacked the lyrical intensity and surrealistic flourishes of Miller's previous work.

For the first time Miller's main work was published in the United States in the 1960s, with *Tropic of Cancer* appearing in 1961 and *Tropic of Capricorn* in 1962. The publication was challenged, but a decision from the Supreme Court in 1963 ruled that *Tropic of Cancer* was not obscene. *The Rosy Crucifixion* was published in 1965. During his California years, Miller published a number of miscellaneous works: *The Books in My Life* (1952), *The Time of the Assassins: A Study of Rimbaud* (1956), *Big Sur and the Oranges of Hieronymus Bosch* (1957).

Miller published *The World of Lawrence* in 1980, the year of his death at the age of eighty-nine. This last published work was taken from a manuscript on D. H.

Lawrence he had written in the early 1930s. In it he said: "Strange as it may seem today to say, the aim of life is to live, and to live means to be aware, joyously, drunkenly, serenely, divinely *aware*. In this state of god-like awareness one sings; in this realm the world exists as a poem."

This philosophy filtered all through Miller's works and energized his dynamic style. It is part of what made his work appeal to the Beat Generation of the 1950s and 1960s. A measure of his literary influence is suggested by the writers who have been drawn to his work. The British novelist Lawrence Durrell edited *The Henry Miller Reader* in 1959; the American writer Norman Mailer published *Genius and Lust: A Journey through the Major Writings of Henry Miller* in 1976.

ADDITIONAL READING

Bern Porter, ed., *The Happy Rock: A Book About Henry Miller*, 1945; Alfred Perles, *My Friend Henry Miller: An Intimate Biography*, 1956; Annette Kar Baxter, *Henry Miller, Expatriate*, 1961; Thomas H. Moore, *Bibliography of Henry Miller*, 1961; Kingsley Widmer, *Henry Miller*, 1963; George Wickes, ed., *Henry Miller and the Critics*, 1963; George Wickes, *Henry Miller*, 1966; William A. Gordon, *The Mind and Art of Henry Miller*, 1967; Ihab Hassan, *The Literature of Silence: Henry Miller and Samuel Beckett*, 1967; Jane A. Nelson, *Form and Image in the Fiction of Henry Miller*, 1970; Edward B. Mitchell, ed., *Henry Miller: Three Decades of Criticism*, 1971; Jay Martin, *Always Merry and Bright: The Life of Henry Miller*, 1978; Lawrence J. Shifreen, *Henry Miller: A Bibliography of Secondary Sources*, 1979; J. D. Brown, *Henry Miller*, 1986.

TEXT

The Air-Conditioned Nightmare, 1945.

from The Air-Conditioned Nightmare

SOIRÉE IN HOLLYWOOD

My first evening in Hollywood. It was so typical that I almost thought it had been arranged for me. It was by sheer chance, however, that I found myself rolling up to the home of a millionaire in a handsome black Packard. I had been invited to dinner by a perfect stranger. I didn't even know my host's name. Nor do I know it now.

The first thing which struck me, on being introduced all around, was that I was in the presence of wealthy people, people who were bored to death and who were all, including the octogenarians, already three sheets to the wind. The host and hostess seemed to take pleasure in acting as bartenders. It was hard to follow the conversation because everybody was talking at cross purposes. The important thing was to get an edge on before sitting down to the table. One old geezer who had recently recovered from a horrible automobile accident was having his fifth old-fashioned—he was proud of the fact, proud that he could swill it like a youngster even though he was still partially crippled. Every one thought he was a marvel.

There wasn't an attractive woman about, except the one who had brought me to the place. The men looked like business men, except for one or two who looked like aged strike-breakers. There was one fairly young couple, in their thirties, I should say. The husband was a typical go-getter, one of those ex-football players who go in for publicity or insurance or the stock market, some clean all-American pursuit in which you run no risk of soiling your hands. He was a graduate of some Eastern University and had the intelligence of a high-grade chimpanzee.

That was the set-up. When every one had been properly soused dinner was announced. We seated ourselves at a long table, elegantly decorated, with three or four glasses beside each plate. The ice was abundant, of course. The service began, a dozen flunkeys buzzing at your elbow like horse flies. There was a surfeit of everything; a poor man would have had sufficient with the hors d'oeuvre alone. As they ate, they became more discursive, more argumentative. An elderly thug in a tuxedo who had the complexion of a boiled lobster was railing against labor agitators. He had a religious strain, much to my amazement, but it was more like Torquemada's[1] than Christ's. President Roosevelt's name almost gave him an apoplectic fit. Roosevelt, Bridges,[2] Stalin, Hitler—they were all in the same class to him. That is to say, they were anathema. He had an extraordinary appetite which served, it seemed, to stimulate his adrenal glands. By the time he had reached the meat course he was talking about hanging being too good for some people. The hostess, meanwhile, who was seated at his elbow, was carrying on one of those delightful inconsequential conversations with the person opposite her. She had left some beautiful dachshunds in Biarritz, or was it Sierra Leone,[3] and to believe her, she was greatly worried about them. In times like these, she was saying, people forget about animals. People can be so cruel, especially in time of war. Why, in Peking the servants had run away and left her with forty trunks to pack—it was outrageous. It was so good to be back in California. God's own country, she called it. She hoped the war wouldn't spread to America.[4] Dear me, where was one to go now? You couldn't feel safe anywhere, except in the desert perhaps.

The ex-football player was talking to some one at the far end of the table in a loud voice. It happened to be an Englishwoman and he was insulting her roundly and openly for daring to arouse sympathy for the English in this country. "Why don't you go back to England?" he shouted at the top of his voice. "What are you doing here? You're a menace. We're not fighting to hold the British Empire together. You're a menace. You ought to be expelled from the country."

The woman was trying to say that she was not English but Canadian, but she couldn't make herself heard above the din. The octogenarian, who was now sampling the champagne, was talking about the automobile accident. Nobody was paying any attention to him. Automobile accidents were too common—every one at the table had been in a smash-up at one time or another. One doesn't make a point about such things unless one is feeble-minded.

The hostess was clapping her hands frantically—she wanted to tell us a little story about an experience she had had in Africa once, on one of her safaris.

"Oh, can that!" shouted the football player. "I want to find out why this great country of ours, in the most crucial moment . . ."

"Shut up!" screamed the hostess. "You're drunk."

"That makes no difference," came his booming voice. "I want to know if we're all hundred percent Americans—and if not why not. I suspect that we have some traitors in our midst," and because I hadn't been taking part in any of the conversation he gave me a fixed, drunken look which was intended to make me declare myself. All I could do was smile. That seemed to infuriate him. His eyes roved about the table challengingly and finally, sensing an antagonist worthy of his mettle, rested on the aged, Florida-baked strikebreaker. The latter was at that moment quietly talking to the person beside him about his good friend, Cardinal So-and-so. He, the Cardinal, was always very good to the poor, I heard him say. A very gentle hard-working man, but he would tolerate no nonsense from the dirty labor agitators who were stirring up revolution, fomenting class hatred, preaching anarchy. The more he talked about his holy eminence, the Cardinal, the more he foamed at the mouth. But his rage in no

---

[1]Tomás de Torquemada (1420–1498), Spanish Dominican monk who became the Grand Inquisitor in 1487 for the Inquisition, dealing out cruel punishments, often death, for all nonbelievers and heretics.
[2]Harry Bridges (born 1900), American labor leader.

[3]Biarritz is a resort in France on the Bay of Biscay near Spain; Sierra Leone is in West Africa.
[4]The year is 1941. World War II has already started; America would not enter until after the attack by Japan on Pearl Harbor on December 7, 1941.

way affected his appetite. He was carnivorous, bibulous, querulous, cantankerous and poisonous as a snake. One could almost see the bile spreading through his varicose veins. He was a man who had spent millions of dollars of the public's money to help the needy, as he put it. What he meant was to prevent the poor from organizing and fighting for their rights. Had he not been dressed like a banker he would have passed for a hod carrier. When he grew angry he not only became flushed but his whole body quivered like guava. He became so intoxicated by his own venom that finally he overstepped the bounds and began denouncing President Roosevelt as a crook and a traitor, among other things. One of the guests, a woman, protested. That brought the football hero to his feet. He said that no man could insult the President of the United States in his presence. The whole table was soon in an uproar. The flunkey at my elbow had just filled the huge liquor glass with some marvelous cognac. I took a sip and sat back with a grin, wondering how it would all end. The louder the altercation the more peaceful I became. *"How do you like your new boarding house, Mr. Smith?"* I heard President McKinley[5] saying to his secretary. Every night Mr. Smith, the president's private secretary, used to visit Mr. McKinley at his home and read aloud to him the amusing letters which he had selected from the daily correspondence. The president, who was overburdened with affairs of state, used to listen silently from his big armchair by the fire: it was his sole recreation. At the end he would always ask *"How do you like your new boarding house, Mr. Smith?"* So worn out by his duties he was that he couldn't think of anything else to say at the close of these séances. Even after Mr. Smith had left his boarding house and taken a room at a hotel President McKinley continued to say *"How do you like your new boarding house, Mr. Smith?"* Then came the Exposition and Csolgosz,[6] who had no idea what a simpleton the president was, assassinated him. There was something wretched and incongruous about murdering a man like McKinley. I remember the incident only because that same day the horse that my aunt was using for a buggy ride got the blind staggers and ran into a lamp post and when I was going to the hospital to see my aunt the extras were out already and young as I was I understood that a great tragedy had befallen the nation. At the same time I felt sorry for Csolgosz—that's the strange thing about the incident. I don't know why I felt sorry for him, except that in some vague way I realized that the punishment meted out to him would be greater than the crime merited. Even at that tender age I felt that punishment was criminal. I couldn't understand why people should be punished—I don't yet. I couldn't even understand why God had the right to punish us for our sins. And of course, as I later realized, God doesn't punish us—we punish ourselves.

Thoughts like these were floating through my head when suddenly I became aware that people were leaving the table. The meal wasn't over yet, but the guests were departing. Something had happened while I was reminiscing. Pre-civil war days, I thought to myself. Infantilism rampant again. And if Roosevelt is assassinated they will make another Lincoln of him. Only this time the slaves will still be slaves. Meanwhile I overhear some one saying what a wonderful president Melvyn Douglas would make. I prick up my ears. I wonder do they mean Melvyn Douglas, the movie star? Yes, that's who they mean. He has a great mind, the woman is saying. And character. And *savoir faire*.[7] Thinks I to myself "and who will the vice-president be, may I ask? Shure and it's not Jimmy Cagney you're thinkin' of?" But the woman is not worried about the vice-presidency. She had been to a palmist the other day and learned some interesting things about herself. Her life line was broken. "Think of it," she said, "all these years and I never knew it was broken. What do you suppose is going to happen? Does it mean war? Or do you think it means an accident?"

[5]William McKinley (1843–1901), President of the United States (1897–1901).
[6]At the Pan-American Exposition in Buffalo, New York, on September 6, 1901, McKinley was shot by an anarchist, Leon Czolgosz, and later died.
[7]"Self-assurance" or "tact" (French).

The hostess was running about like a wet hen. Trying to rustle up enough hands for a game of bridge. A desperate soul, surrounded by the booty of a thousand battles. "I understand you're a writer," she said, as she tried to carom from my corner of the room to the bar. "Won't you have something to drink—a highball or something? Dear me, I don't know what's come over everybody this evening. I do hate to hear these political discussions. That young man is positively rude. Of course I don't approve of insulting the President of the United States in public but just the same he might have used a little more tact. After all, Mr. So-and-so is an elderly man. He's entitled to some respect, don't you think? Oh, there's So-and-so!" and she dashed off to greet a cinema star who had just dropped in.

The old geezer who was still tottering about handed me a highball. I tried to tell him that I didn't want any but he insisted that I take it anyway. He wanted to have a word with me, he said, winking at me as though he had something very confidential to impart.

"My name is Harrison," he said. "H-a-r-r-i-s-o-n," spelling it out as if it were a difficult name to remember.

"Now what is your name, may I ask?"

My name is Miller—M-i-l-l-e-r," I answered, spelling it out in Morse for him.

"Miller! Why, that's a very easy name to remember. We had a druggist on our block by that name. Of course. *Miller.* Yes, a very common name."

"So it is," I said.

"And what are you doing out here, Mr. Miller? You're a stranger, I take it?"

"Yes," I said, "I'm just a visitor."

"You're in business, are you?"

"No, hardly. I'm just visiting California."

"I see. Well, where do you come from—the Middle West?"

"No, from New York."

"From New York City? Or from up State?"

"From the city."

"And have you been here very long?"

"No, just a few hours."

"A few hours? My, my . . . well, that's interesting. Very interesting. And will you be staying long, Mr. Miller?"

"I don't know. It depends."

"I see. Depends on how you like it here, is that it?"

"Yes, exactly."

"Well, it's a grand part of the world, I can tell you that. No place like California, I always say. Of course I'm not a native. But I've been out here almost thirty years now. Wonderful climate. And wonderful people, too."

"I suppose so," I said, just to string him along. I was curious to see how long the idiot would keep up his infernal nonsense.

"You're not in business you say?"

"No, I'm not."

"On a vacation, is that it?"

"No, not precisely. I'm an ornithologist,[8] you see."

"A what? Well, that's interesting."

"*Very,*" I said, with great solemnity.

"Then you may be staying with us for a while, is that it?"

"That's hard to say. I may stay a week and I may stay a year. It all depends. Depends on what specimens I find."

"I see. Interesting work, no doubt."

---

[8]A branch of zoology, having to do with the study of birds.

"Very!"

"Have you ever been to California before, Mr. Miller?"

"Yes, twenty-five years ago."

"Well, well, is that so? *Twenty-five years ago!* And now you're back again."

"Yes, back again."

"Were you doing the same thing when you were here before?"

"You mean ornithology?"

"Yes, that's it."

"No, I was digging ditches then."

"Digging ditches? You mean you were—*digging ditches?*"

"Yes, that's it, Mr. Harrison. It was either dig ditches or starve to death."

"Well, I'm glad you don't have to dig ditches any more. It's not much fun—*digging ditches*, is it?"

"No, especially if the ground is hard. Or if your back is weak. Or vice versa. Or let's say your mother has just been put in the mad house and the alarm goes off too soon."

"I beg your pardon! *What did you say?*"

"If things are not just right, I said. You know what I mean—bunions, lumbago, scrofula. It's different now, of course. I have my birds and other pets. Mornings I used to watch the sun rise. Then I would saddle the jackasses—I had two and the other fellow had three. . . ."

"This was in California, Mr. Miller?"

"Yes, twenty-five years ago. I had just done a stretch in San Quentin.[9] . . ."

"San Quentin?"

"Yes, attempted suicide. I was really gaga but that didn't make any difference to them. You see, when my father set the house afire one of the horses kicked me in the temple. I used to get fainting fits and then after a time I got homicidal spells and finally I became suicidal. Of course I didn't know that the revolver was loaded. I took a pot shot at my sister, just for fun, and luckily I missed her. I tried to explain it to the judge but he wouldn't listen to me. I never carry a revolver any more. If I have to defend myself I use a jackknife. The best thing, of course, is to use your knee. . . ."

"Excuse me, Mr. Miller, I have to speak to Mrs. So-and-so a moment. Very interesting what you say. *Very interesting indeed.* We must talk some more. Excuse me just a moment. . . ."

I slipped out of the house unnoticed and started to walk towards the foot of the hill. The highballs, the red and the white wines, the champagne, the cognac were gurgling inside me like a sewer. I had no idea where I was, whose house I had been in or whom I had been introduced to. Perhaps the boiled thug was an ex-Governor of the State. Perhaps the hostess was an ex-movie star, a light that had gone out forever. I remembered that some one had whispered in my ear that So-and-so had made a fortune in the opium traffic in China. Lord Haw-Haw probably. The Englishwoman with the horse face may have been a prominent novelist—or just a charity worker. I thought of my friend Fred, now Private Alfred Perlès, No. 13802023 in the 137th Pioneer Corps or something like that. Fred would have sung the Lorelei[10] at the dinner table or asked for a better brand of cognac or made grimaces at the hostess. Or he might have gone to the telephone and called up Gloria Swanson, pretending to be Aldous Huxley or Chatto & Windus of Wimbledon.[11] Fred would never have permitted the dinner to become a fiasco. Everything else failing he would have slipped his silky paw in some one's bosom, saying as he always did—"The left one is better. Fish it out, won't you please?"

---

[9]State prison on San Francisco Bay.
[10]The Lorelei is a legendary siren on a rock in the Rhine River in Germany who sings a song that lures sailors into shipwreck.

[11]Swanson, a famous movie star; Aldous Huxley (1894–1963), a British novelist; Chatto & Windus, a British publisher; Wimbledon, London suburb, site of famed tennis championships.

I think frequently of Fred in moving about the country. He was always so damned eager to see America. His picture of America was something like Kafka's.[12] It would be a pity to disillusion him. And yet who can say? He might enjoy it hugely. He might not see anything but what he chose to see. I remember my visit to his own Vienna. Certainly it was not the Vienna I had dreamed of. And yet today, when I think of Vienna, I see the Vienna of my dreams and not the one with bed bugs and broken zithers and stinking drains.

I wobble down the canyon road. It's very Californian somehow. I like the scrubby hills, the weeping trees, the desert coolness. I had expected more fragrance in the air.

The stars are out in full strength. Turning a bend in the road I catch a glimpse of the city below. The illumination is more faërique than in other American cities. The red seems to predominate. A few hours ago, towards dusk, I had a glimpse of it from the bedroom window of the woman on the hill. Looking at it through the mirror on her dressing table it seemed even more magical. It was like looking into the future from the narrow window of an oubliette.[13] Imagine the Marquis de Sade[14] looking at the city of Paris through the bars of his cell in the Bastille. Los Angeles gives one the feeling of the future more strongly than any city I know of. A bad future, too, like something out of Fritz Lang's[15] feeble imagination. *Goodbye, Mr. Chips!*[16]

Walking along one of the Neon-lit streets. A shop window with Nylon stockings. Nothing in the window but a glass leg filled with water and a sea horse rising and falling like a feather sailing through heavy air. Thus we see how Surrealism penetrates to every nook and corner of the world. Dali[17] meanwhile is in Bowling Green, Va., thinking up a loaf of bread 30 feet high by 125 feet long, to be removed from the oven stealthily while every one sleeps and placed very circumspectly in the main square of a big city, say Chicago or San Francisco. Just a loaf of bread, enormous of course. No raison d'être.[18] No propaganda. And tomorrow night two loaves of bread, placed simultaneously in two big cities, say New York and New Orleans. Nobody knows who brought them or why they are there. And the next night three loaves of bread—one in Berlin or Bucharest this time. And so on, ad infinitum. Tremendous, no? Would push the war news off the front page. That's what Dali thinks, at any rate. Very interesting. *Very interesting, indeed.* Excuse me now, I have to talk to a lady over in the corner. . . .

Tomorrow I will discover Sunset Boulevard. Eurythmic dancing, ball room dancing, tap dancing, artistic photography, ordinary photography, lousy photography, electro-fever treatment, internal douche treatment, ultra-violet ray treatment, elocution lessons, psychic readings, institutes of religion, astrological demonstrations, hands read, feet manicured, elbows massaged, faces lifted, warts removed, fat reduced, insteps raised, corsets fitted, busts vibrated, corns removed, hair dyed, glasses fitted, soda jerked, hangovers cured, headaches driven away, flatulence dissipated, business improved, limousines rented, the future made clear, the war made comprehensible, octane made higher and butane lower, drive in and get indigestion, flush the kidneys, get a cheap car wash, stay awake pills and go to sleep pills, Chinese herbs are very good for you and without a Coca-cola life is unthinkable. From the car window it's like a strip teaser doing the St. Vitus dance[19]—a corny one.

1945

---

[12]Franz Kafka (1883–1924), Austrian novelist, author of a work set in the United States, *Amerika*, written 1911–14, published 1927, and translated 1938.
[13]A concealed dungeon, with the trap door in the ceiling the only opening.
[14]Marquis de Sade (1740–1814), author of erotic novels; "sadism" (pleasure from cruelty) derives from his name; he spent much of his life in prison for sexual perversion.
[15]Fritz Lang (1890–1976), Austrian-born American expressionistic film director who emphasized terror.
[16]Best-selling novel (1934) about an aging schoolmaster by British novelist James Hilton (1900–1954); made into a popular British film (1939).
[17]Salvador Dali (1904–1989), Spanish surrealist painter.
[18]"Reason for being" (French).
[19]A nervous disorder (also "chorea") that causes spasmodic, jerky movements.

EDMUND WILSON
(1895–1972)

When Edmund Wilson died in 1972, he was often referred to as the last American man of letters. His curiosity was boundless and he was indefatigable in following wherever it led. His writing always conveyed a sense of intellectual adventure, a conviction that books and ideas were central to human destiny as well as to lives as lived daily. In 1940, after two decades of rich critical and creative achievement, he sketched his belief about the basic challenge to the enterprise on which he and other intellectuals — or cultural critics — were embarked:

> In my view, all our intellectual activity, in whatever field it takes place, is an attempt to give meaning to our experience. . . . The experience of mankind on earth is always changing as man develops and has to deal with new combinations of elements; and the writer who is to be anything more than an echo of his predecessors must always find expression for something which has never been expressed, must master a new set of phenomena which has never yet been mastered. With each such victory of the human intellect . . . we experience a deep satisfaction, we have been . . . relieved of some oppressive burden of uncomprehended events. This relief that brings the sense of power, and, with the sense of power, joy, is the positive emotion which tells us that we have encountered a first rate piece of literature.

Edmund Wilson, Jr., was born in Red Bank, New Jersey, into an upper-middle-class family. His father was a lawyer, sometime politician, infused with the conservative work ethic of his Protestant heritage. Wilson was to inherit the work ethic but rebel against the conservatism and conformity. He was educated at the exclusive Hill School, Pottstown, Pennsylvania, and then sent to Princeton, where he became a friend of F. Scott Fitzgerald.

After a stint in the army during the First World War, with service in France, Wilson returned to launch his career as a journalist-editor-writer. He served as managing editor of *Vanity Fair* from 1920 to 1921 and as associate editor of *The New Republic* from 1926 to 1931. Later, from 1944 to 1948, he was book reviewer for *The New Yorker*.

Wilson's influence as an editor was immense. In 1952 he collected much of his early journalistic writing in *The Shores of Light: A Literary Chronicle of the Twenties and Thirties*. He preserved there his early views (or reviews) of F. Scott Fitzgerald, Willa Cather, Ezra Pound, Wallace Stevens, Sherwood Anderson, Eugene O'Neill, Ernest Hemingway, Gertrude Stein, and many other innovators and pacesetters of the period. It is astonishing how often Wilson's initial impressions of a writer or book became a key part of the general assessment settled on later. In 1958, Wilson published a companion volume to *The Shores of Light* entitled *The American Earthquake: A Documentary of the Twenties and Thirties*, bringing together his "non-literary" pieces — showing his perspicuity in contemporary cultural commentary. His focus shifted from drama to art to movies to opera to politics to government, and he brought a lively intelligence to bear wherever he looked.

Wilson brought his critical essays and reviews of the 1940s together in *Classics and Commercials: A Literary Chronical of the Forties*, published in 1950, with essays on a miscellany of writers, including Vladimir Nabokov, Franz Kafka, and Evelyn Waugh, and including also his immensely useful piece on James Joyce ("A Guide to *Finnegans Wake*") and his remarkable essay "Books of Etiquette and

Emily Post." In 1965, *The Bit Between My Teeth: A Literary Chronicle of 1950–1965* brought Wilson's journalistic collections up to 1965 (when he was seventy years old) and included impressive pieces on H. L. Mencken, Van Wyck Brooks, and many others.

These four collections of writing from the magazines reveal the extent of Wilson's influence through a half-century of American literary and cultural history. Neither ivory tower professor nor ordinary journalist, Wilson maintained in his magazine writing a high standard of intellectual discourse meant to appeal to the aware, intelligent citizen. His plain and lucid style bridges the gap between the common reader and the academic specialist.

But Wilson was not content to confine himself to the journals. He published a series of books that became landmarks of literary, cultural, or political commentary. His *Axel's Castle: A Study in the Imaginative Literature of 1870–1930* (1931) is a pioneer work linking the French symbolists with such American and British modernists as William Butler Yeats, T. S. Eliot, James Joyce, and Gertrude Stein. *To the Finland Station: A Study in the Writing and Acting of History* (1940) is a broad synthesis of historical movements, socialist thought, and Communist theory leading to the arrival of Nikolai Lenin at the Finland Station to launch the Bolshevik revolution in Russia. *The Wound and the Bow: Seven Studies in Literature* (1941) explores in depth the relationship between mental wounds (or neuroses) and art; chapters treated (among others) James Joyce, Ernest Hemingway, and Charles Dickens. *Patriotic Gore: Studies in the Literature of the American Civil War* (1962) sifts through the fascinating writings of the soldiers, statesmen, and novelists of both sides—and also Confederate women diarists—in a study of war-inspired literature.

Wilson tried his hand at almost every form of literature. His first book, *The Undertaker's Garland* (1922), contains stories and poems. *I Thought of Daisy* (1929) and *Memoirs of Hecate County* (1946) are novels, the first portraying New York bohemian life, the latter presenting a series of sketches of the sometimes bizarre life of suburbia. There are several volumes of plays, including *This Room and This Gin and These Sandwiches: Three Plays* (1937). There is even an attack on the Internal Revenue Service in *The Cold War and the Income Tax: A Protest* (1963). And in the late years, he wrote volumes of autobiography, such as *Upstate: Records and Recollections of Northern New York* (1971).

The year following, in 1972, Wilson died in upstate New York, in the large house that belonged to his mother's family and which he had known as a boy. His published work was extraordinary in both its quantity and quality, and his influence incalculable. Alfred Kazin's assessment in a review seems justly applicable to the body of Wilson's work: "There is no other critic who so evenly and so hauntingly writes criticism as a work of art . . . he has always to grasp out of time lost, out of the books misread by other critics, the whole figure of the writer in his age, and to present this subject as a new creation . . . he has to do it solidly, in his own style, gathering up all the details into one finally compact and lucid argument, like a man whose life hangs on the rightness of each sentence."

ADDITIONAL READING

Edmund Wilson: The Twenties: From the Notebooks and Diaries of the Period, ed. Leon Edel, 1975 (also *The Thirties*, 1980; *The Forties*, 1983; *The Fifties*, 1986); *Edmund Wilson's Letters on Literature and Politics, 1912–1972*, ed. Elena Wilson, 1977; *The Nabokov-Wilson Letters, 1940–1971*, ed. Simon Karlinsky, 1979; *The Portable Edmund Wilson*, ed. Lewis M. Dabney, 1983.

Sherman Paul, *Edmund Wilson: A Study of Literary Vocation in Our Time*, 1965; Warner Berthoff, *Edmund Wilson*, 1968; Charles P. Frank, *Edmund Wilson*, 1970; Richard David Ramsey, *Edmund Wilson: A Bibliography*, 1971; Leonard Krieger, *Edmund Wilson*, 1971; John Wain, *Edmund Wilson: The Man and His Work*, 1978; Richard Hauer Costa, *Edmund Wilson: Our Neighbor from Talcottville*, 1980; George H. Douglas, *Edmund Wilson's America*, 1983; David Castronovo, *Edmund Wilson*, 1984.

TEXT

"The Literary Consequences of the Crash," *The Shores of Light*, 1952.

from The Shores of Light

THE LITERARY CONSEQUENCES OF THE CRASH

A change of tone and of point of view will be noted in my articles of the early thirties.

Even before the stock market crash of October, 1929, a kind of nervous dissatisfaction and apprehension had begun to manifest itself in American intellectual life. The liberating movement of the twenties had by that time accomplished its work of discrediting the gentility and Puritanism of the later nineteenth century; the orgy of spending of the Boom was becoming more and more grotesque, and the Jazz Age was ending in hysteria. The principal points of view of this period I tried, after the crash, to sum up in an article of March 23, 1932:

The attitudes of the decade that followed the war, before the depression set in, already seem a long way off:

The attitude of the Menckenian gentleman, ironic, beer-loving and "civilized," living principally on the satisfaction of feeling superior to the broker and enjoying the debauchment of American life as a burlesque show or three-ring circus; the attitude of old-American-stock smugness, with its drawing aloof from the rabble in the name of old Uncle Gilead Pilcher who was Governor of Connecticut or Grandfather Timothy Merrymount who was killed in the Civil War — though the parvenus kept crashing the gate so fast, while the prosperity boom was on, that it was becoming harder and harder to get one's aloofness properly recognized; the liberal attitude that American capitalism was going to show a new wonder to the world by gradually and comfortably socializing itself and that we should just have to respect it in the meantime, taking a great interest in Dwight W. Morrow and Owen D. Young;[1] the attitude of trying to get a kick out of the sheer size and energy of American enterprises, irrespective of what they were aiming at; the attitude of proudly withdrawing and cultivating a refined sensibility or of losing oneself completely in abstruse intellectual pursuits — scholastic philosophy, symbolic logic or metaphysical physics; the attitude of letting oneself be carried along by the mad hilarity and heartbreak of jazz, living only for the excitement of the evening; the attitude of keeping one's mind and morals impregnably disinfected with the feeble fascism-classicism of humanism.

---

[1]Morrow (1873–1931), American banker, lawyer, diplomat, partner in J. P. Morgan & Co., and U. S. Senator (1930–31);   Owen D. Young (1874–1962), American corporation executive, served in diplomatic assignments.

I have in one mood or another myself felt some sympathy with all of these different attitudes—with the single exception of humanism; and they have all, no doubt, had their validity for certain people, for special situations. Yet today they all look rather queer: they are no use in our present predicament, and we can see how superficial they were. We can see now that they all represented attempts on the part of the more thoughtful Americans to reconcile themselves to a world dominated by salesmen and brokers—and that they all involved compromises with the salesman and the broker. Mencken and Nathan[2] laughed at the broker, but they justified the system which produced him and they got along with him very well, provided he enjoyed George Moore[3] and had pretensions to a taste in liquor; the jazz-age romantics spent the broker's money as speedily and wildly as possible and tried to laugh off the office and the factory with boyish and girlish jokes; the old-American-stockers sniffed at him, but though they salved their consciences thus, they were usually glad to get in on any of his good things that were going; the liberals, who had been vaguely unhappy, later became vaguely resigned and could never bring themselves to the point of serious quarrelling with him; the poets and philosophers hid from him—and the physicists grew more and more mystical in the laboratories subsidized mainly by the profits from industrial investments; the humanists, in volume after volume, endeavored by sheer hollow thunder to induce people to find in the stock exchange the harmony and dignity of the Parthenon.

I did not include in this catalogue a cult that was spreading in New York and that had converts in and around the *New Republic:* that of the Russo-Greek charlatan Gurdjieff,[4] who undertook to renovate the personalities of discontented well-to-do persons. He combined making his clients uncomfortable in various gratuitous ways—such as waking them up in the middle of the night and training them to perform grotesque dances—with reducing them to a condition of complete docility, in which they would hold, at a signal, any position, however awkward, that they happened to be in at the moment. They were promised, if they proved themselves worthy of it, an ultimate initiation into the mysteries of an esoteric doctrine. Gurdjieff's apostle in the United States was the English ex-journalist A. R. Orage,[5] a funereal and to me a distasteful person, who drilled his pupils, not in dancing, but in a kind of dialectic and who acquired at one time a considerable influence over the mind of Herbert Croly,[6] whose inhibited personality and unsatisfied religious instincts laid him open to the lures of a cult that pretended to liberate the mind and to put one in touch with some higher power. But Croly was a fastidious man, and in the long run he found Orage grating. I was myself the object of several attempts to recruit me to the Orage group, but the only interchange of influence that took place between Orage and me consisted of my once persuading him to go to the National Winter Garden (described under *Burlesque Shows* above);[7] when I next saw him, he told me with a severity that suggested a sense of outrage that he had not enjoyed it at all. Gurdjieff, however, whom I never met, had apparently a rogue's sense of humor. A young man in the office, a bishop's son who had lost his faith and was groping for something to take its place, told me of the banquets of roast sheep or goat, served in

[2]George Jean Nathan (1882–1958), drama critic and partner with H. L. Mencken in editing *The Smart Set* and *The American Mercury*.

[3]Moore (1852–1933), Irish novelist.

[4]George Gurdjieff (1874?–1949), a Greek-Russian-Armenian esoteric thinker. Gurdjieff set up his Institute for the Harmonious Development of Man in Fountainebleau, France, teaching ways to reach the higher, or cosmic, consciousness.

[5]Orage (1873–1934), English writer and editor of *The New*

Age and follower of Gurdjieff.

[6]Herbert D. Croly (1869–1930), founder in 1914 and first editor of *The New Republic*; Edmund Wilson served as associate editor of *The New Republic* from 1926 to 1931.

[7]The National Winter Garden was a burlesque house in New York City which presented the Minsky Brothers' Follies; Edmund Wilson went to see a production because *The New Republic* was sent a pass; he published a favorable review of the "ribald" show in 1925.

great pots in the Caucasian style and eaten with the fingers, to which Gurdjieff would invite his disciples and at which he would have read aloud to them a book he had written called *A Criticism of the Life of Man: Beëlzebub's Tale to His Grandson.* "It sounds as if it had been written," said this neophyte, "just on purpose to bore you to death. Everybody listens in silence, but every now and then Gurdjieff will suddenly burst out laughing—just roaring—nobody knows about what."

I did not read *Beëlzebub's Tale*, but I did read *Das Kapital*.[8] Not that I want to compare the two works, but there *was* a certain similarity in the way in which people then approached them; and I was surprised to find that an apparently social evening that would turn out to be a conspiracy to involve one in some Communist organization resembled a dinner I had once attended at which I was chilled to discover that the springes of Orage had been laid for me—and these both recalled to me an earlier occasion on which a literary conversation, in the rooms of the proselytizing rector of the Episcopal Church at Princeton, had been prodded by amusing remarks in the direction of the Christian faith. People did want faiths and churches badly, and though I am good at resisting churches, I caught a wave from the impulsion of the Marxist faith.

The stock market crash was to count for us almost like a rending of the earth in preparation for the Day of Judgment. In my articles of the months just before it, I had often urged writers to acquaint themselves with "the realities of our contemporary life," to apply themselves to "the study of contemporary reality," etc. I myself had not exercised enough insight to realize that American "prosperity" was an inflation that was due to burst. I had, however, become aware that we liberals of the *New Republic* were not taking certain recent happenings so seriously as we should. The execution of Sacco and Vanzetti in August, 1927,[9] had made liberals lose their bearings. During the months while the case was working up to its climax, Herbert Croly had been away in Honolulu attending a conference called by the Institute of Pacific Relations. When he returned, I was surprised to learn that he did not entirely approve of the way in which we had handled the case. Croly's method of commenting on current events was impersonal and very abstract; and, in his absence, we had given way to the impulse to print certain articles which were certainly, for the *New Republic*, unusually concrete and militant. I first became aware of a serious divergence between my own point of view and Croly's when I was talking with him one day about a leader called *A Nation of Foreigners* that I wrote for the paper in October. He did approve of this editorial, but for reasons that put me in a false position. My article had dealt with the futility of attempting to identify "Americanism" with the interests and ideas of the Anglo-Saxon element of the United States, pointing out that, in this case, the Irish, who had been snubbed by the Anglo-Saxon Bostonians, had combined with them in the most wolfish way to persecute the immigrant Italians; and I discovered that Croly was pleased at my treating the subject from this angle rather than from that of class animosities. This class aspect he wanted to deny; it was one of the assumptions of his political thinking—I had not then read *The Promise of American Life*[10]—that the class struggle should not, and in its true form did not, occur in the United States.

I had been running the literary department, and this was my first excursion on the political side of the paper, which Croly had kept strictly in line with his own very definite ideas. Sometime in the later months of 1928, he had the first of several strokes, and was never able again to perform his full functions as editor-in-chief.

---

[8]The principal work of Karl Marx (1818–1883) analyzing the economics of capitalism; its successive volumes appeared in 1867, 1885, and 1894. Gurdjieff's book appeared in 1950 under the title *All and Everything.*

[9]Nicola Sacco and Bartolemeo Vanzetti, Italian immigrants, were arrested for robbery and murder in Massachusetts in 1921; they were tried and sentenced to death on very little evidence. There was a worldwide outcry on their execution in 1927, especially by liberals and radicals.

[10]The principal work of Croly, published in 1909, reviewing democratic principles in the light of modern social and economic realities.

When he died in May, 1930, the paper was carried on by the editors as a group, with no one in Croly's position, and we had — rather difficult with men of conflicting opinions and temperaments, with nobody to make final decisions — to work out a policy of our own. I had been troubled by another incident that took place in the autumn of 1929. The bitter and violent Gastonia[11] strike of the textile workers in North Carolina had been going on ever since spring. It was the first major labor battle conducted by a Communist union. Sixteen union members, including three women, were being tried for the murder of a chief of police, who had invaded without a warrant the tent-colony in which the strikers had been living; and the death penalty was being asked for all of them except the women. Feeling on both sides had been roused to the point of ferocity — we were not then familiar with the Communists' habit of manufacturing martyrs — and, after the execution of Sacco and Vanzetti, one was apprehensive of another judicial lynching. John Dos Passos and Mary Heaton Vorse[12] both asked the *New Republic* to send them to report on Gastonia, but both were thought to be too far to the Left to be reliable from our point of view. "The liberals," Dos Passos said to me, "are all so neurotic about Communists!" This was perfectly true; and the pressure on us to do something about Gastonia, had at the time almost no effect. The young man who had been hooked by Orage — who had had no experience of labor disputes — was going down to a fashionable wedding at Asheville, not far from Gastonia, and he was asked to drop in at the seat of trouble. When he came back, this young man reported that there was nothing of interest going on. I do not know whom he could have talked to. He had been in Gastonia on the very day, September 14, when the hostilities were coming to a climax. In an attempt to prevent a union meeting, an armed mob had fired on unarmed strikers and had killed a woman named Ella May Wiggins, a widow with five children, who had written songs for the strikers and was extremely popular among them. Her death gave the Communists a battle-cry and the strikers an unforgettable grievance. It was obvious that the *New Republic*, which was supposed to cover labor sympathetically, was falling down on this part of its program.

The next month the slump began, and, as conditions grew worse and worse and President Hoover, unable to grasp what had happened, made no effort to deal with the breakdown, a darkness seemed to descend. Yet, to the writers and artists of my generation who had grown up in the Big Business era and had always resented its barbarism, its crowding-out of everthing they cared about, these years were not depressing but stimulating. One couldn't help being exhilarated at the sudden unexpected collapse of that stupid gigantic fraud. It gave us a new sense of freedom; and it gave us a new sense of power to find ourselves still carrying on while the bankers for a change, were taking a beating. With a businessman's president in the White House, who kept telling us, when he told us anything, that the system was perfectly sound, who sent General Douglas MacArthur[13] to burn the camp of the unemployed war veterans who had come to appeal to Washington, we wondered about the survival of republican American institutions; and we became more and more impressed by the achievements of the Soviet Union, which could boast that its industrial and financial problems were carefully studied by the government, and that it was able to avert such crises. We overdid both these tendencies; but the slump was like a flood or an earthquake, and it was long before many things righted themselves.

1932, 1952

---

[11]Gastonia, North Carolina, was the center for manufacture of cotton goods; the strike there in 1929 is important in labor history.
[12]Vorse (1874–1966), sponsor of the Provincetown Players and author of proletarian novels.

[13]General Douglas MacArthur (1880–1964) routed the Bonus Army of 12,000 veterans of the First World War who marched on Washington in the summer of 1932 to demand of the Congress that bonus certificates issued in 1924 be redeemed.

JOHN DOS PASSOS
(1896–1970)

In 1916, the year he graduated from Harvard, John Dos Passos published his first "professional" writing, "Against American Literature," in *The New Republic*. He found American literature a "wholesome rice-pudding fare . . . a strangely unstimulating diet." "We find ourselves floundering without rudder or compass, in the sea of modern life, vaguely lit by the phosphorescent gleam of our traditional optimism. . . . American life, as much as an unsuccessful inventor, is occupied with smiling abstractions." Walt Whitman, "our only poet," is the only American writer who "abandoned the vague genteelness that had characterized American writing." The "genteelness" still prevails, as literature is "bound tightly in the fetters of 'niceness,' of the middle-class outlook." Whitman pointed the way, Dos Passos concluded, to escape "stagnation," to produce something more than our "steel and oil and grain."

Like many of his generation, disillusioned by the First World War and dismayed by antidemocratic forces in America, Dos Passos would veer to the left for about two highly creative decades at the beginning of his career. Then, in the 1930s, he would suddenly veer to the right, jolted by the oppressive authoritarianism he discovered at the heart of Communism in practice. The seeds for Dos Passos's emergence, first on one side, and then on the other, of the political spectrum may be found in the cultural iconoclasm and in the Whitmanian individualism found in "Against American Literature," written when he was twenty, before he was launched on his literary career.

Dos Passos suffered an unnatural childhood, born in a hotel room and brought up in hotels in America and abroad by his mother, kept at a distance from a wealthy father who could not divorce his mentally ill wife. It was not until Dos Passos was sixteen that his tycoon father, a self-made man born of Portuguese immigrants, could marry his mother and legally bestow upon his son his name. The future novelist of *U. S. A.* grew up knowing very little firsthand about his native country.

After attending Choate, an exclusive preparatory school, Dos Passos entered Harvard in 1912 at a time when students read Walter Pater and became aesthetes (believers in art-for-art's sake), and when they also read Thorstein Veblen and became critics of social pretensions (and believers in leftist or anti-capitalistic causes). Dos Passos read these authors and many more, and he himself began to publish stories in the *Harvard Monthly*.

Dos Passos's class emerged from college just in time to be caught up in the First World War, an experience that would leave its deep psychic scar on an entire generation. When Dos Passos wanted in 1916 to volunteer for the ambulance service overseas, his father objected and deflected him into the study of architecture in Spain. In early 1917, however, Dos Passos's father suddenly died, and Dos Passos returned to America to take charge of affairs. He discovered that his father's fortune had been largely squandered. He then enlisted in the renowned Norton-Harjes Ambulance Unit for service in France. A tour of duty at the brutal, bloody front repelled him, and his criticism of the war upset his officers sufficiently to cause them to deny his attempt to extend his enlistment.

Dos Passos returned home, spent some time writing, but soon signed up to go back, this time in the Medical Corps. By the time he was on his way, the war was over, and Dos Passos seized the opportunity to study briefly at the Sorbonne. He spent some time in London, arranging for publication of a novel, and then returned to Spain, beginning a novel (*Three Soldiers*) in Madrid and finishing it in Paris in 1920.

Dos Passos's first book, *One Man's Initiation — 1917*, about an ambulance driver during the war, was published in 1920 in London; it created scarcely a ripple. This early work, retitled *First Encounter*, was reprinted in 1945; in a preface, Dos Passos said that the novel had been written in 1918 by "a bookish young man of twenty-two."

Although not much older when he wrote *Three Soldiers*, he was certainly more deeply experienced in his craft. When this second novel appeared in 1921, it was an immediate success, establishing Dos Passos as one of the new generation of postwar writers. This generation, including among others F. Scott Fitzgerald and Ernest Hemingway, would dominate the literature of the 1920s and beyond.

Three Soldiers was innovative in technique, introducing three quite different characters — an Italian-American happy-go-lucky private, a Midwestern farm boy repelled by the horrors of war, and a sensitive musician (and Harvard graduate) striving to be a composer. Their disrupted lives unfold, crisscrossing but not interconnecting — as happens in the haphazard time of a chaotic war. At the end, the musician faces death for desertion, and the pages of his composition-in-progress are blown into oblivion.

After publishing a number of minor works (some of them written at an earlier time), Dos Passos wrote *Manhattan Transfer*, published in 1925. As *Three Soldiers* is in some sense a portrait of a war, *Manhattan Transfer* is a portrait of a modern metropolis — New York City. The cast of characters is large, and the setting shifts from the slums to penthouses, from union halls to Wall Street. The novel evokes a sense of teeming — and largely purposeless — life.

Dos Passos's next major work, a massive trilogy, was not completed until over a decade later. *The 42nd Parallel* appeared in 1930, *1919* in 1932, and *The Big Money* in 1936. The three novels were published as a single work in 1938 as *U. S. A.* The work stretches from the beginning of the twentieth century to the middle of the Great Depression (1935), and the action portrays a slice of American life from top to bottom, set in virtually every area of the country. Dos Passos introduced a variety of techniques to intensify the likeness of this portrait of the United States: the Newsreel, including headlines, advertisements, pop songs; the Camera Eye, short stream-of-consciousness passages of the passing scene; and brief biographies of public figures, celebrities, tycoons, or radicals, whose lives often contrast with or parallel the lives of one or another of the multitude of characters in the "plot." The effect is a pessimistic vision of a country in decline, in process of losing its soul.

By the time *U. S. A.* was completed, Dos Passos had grown disillusioned with the radical movement in which he had participated. He had been associated with the Communist publication *The New Masses* in the late 1920s. And he had become actively involved in the celebrated case of Sacco and Vanzetti, protesting their execution in 1927 for a 1920 robbery and killing for which they claimed innocence. Dos Passos became convinced that he was being manipulated by the Communist party for its own purposes as early as 1931, when he faced arrest for speaking out in support of striking miners in Harlan County, Kentucky (the Communist party wanted him to stand trial for the publicity). And when he saw firsthand the Spanish Civil War in 1937, with the Communists and Soviet Union maneuvering to dominate the Republican resistance to Franco's Fascist takeover, he shifted to the right.

Dos Passos was attacked by his former friends, but his break with the left was final. Much of his imaginative energy he poured into the writing of another trilogy portraying the gradual disillusionment of an idealistic Communist — *Adventures of a Young Man* (1939), *Number One* (1943), and *The Grand Design* (1949). The three novels were published as *District of Columbia* in 1952. Dos Passos continued to write and publish novels, biographical sketches of Americans who established the country's basic freedoms, and books of essays expressing his increasingly conservative views. But he no longer had the critical following he had gained with his earlier work. He died of a heart attack in 1970, largely forgotten by those who had acclaimed his earlier work.

ADDITIONAL READING

The Fourteenth Chronicle: Letters and Diaries of John Dos Passos, ed. Townsend Ludington, 1973; *John Dos Passos: The Major Nonfictional Prose*, ed. Donald Pizer, 1988.

John H. Wrenn, *John Dos Passos*, 1961; Robert Gorham Davis, *John Dos Passos*, 1962; John D. Brantley, *The Fiction of Dos Passos*, 1968; Allen Belkind, *Dos Passos, the Critics, and the Writer's Intention*, 1971; Melvin Landsberg, *Dos Passos' Path to U. S. A.: A Political Biography, 1912–1936*, 1972; George J. Becker, *John Dos Passos*, 1974; Iain Colley, *Dos Passos and the Fiction of Despair*, 1978; Linda W. Wagner, *Dos Passos: Artist as American*, 1979; Townsend Ludington, *John Dos Passos: A Twentieth-Century Odyssey*, 1980; Robert C. Rosen, *John Dos Passos: Politics and the Writer*, 1981; Virginia Spencer Carr, *Dos Passos: A Life*, 1984; Michael Clark, *Dos Passos's Early Fiction, 1912–1938*, 1987; David Sanders, *John Dos Passos: A Comprehensive Bibliography*, 1987; Barry Maine, ed., *Dos Passos: The Critical Heritage*, 1988; Donald Pizer, *Dos Passos' "U. S. A.": A Critical Study*, 1988.

TEXT

U. S. A., 1938.

from U.S.A.

from THE BIG MONEY

[THE CRASH][1]

NEWSREEL LXVIII

WALL STREET STUNNED

This is not Thirty-eight but it's old Ninety-seven
You must put her in Center on time[2]

MARKET SURE TO RECOVER FROM SLUMP

Decline in Contracts

POLICE TURN MACHINE GUNS ON COLORADO MINE STRIKERS
KILL 5 WOUND 40

---

[1]The stock market crash took place in October 1929. In these pages from *U.S.A.*, Dos Passos, with a technique he used throughout the novel, conveyed a sense of the event, its causes, and impact by "pasting" together scraps from newspapers, popular songs, and public announcements, from images recorded by the "Camera Eye," and from brief biographies of public figures as in a montage or collage. The result is a quickly conveyed snapshot of the country caught at a particular moment in time.
[2]Lines from a ballad, "Wreck of the Old Ninety-seven"; additional lines appear later, suggesting an analogy between the train wreck and the crash of an economy out of control.

sympathizers appeared on the scene just as thousands of office workers were pouring out of the buildings at the lunch hour. As they raised their placard high and started an indefinite march from one side to the other, they were jeered and hooted not only by the office workers but also by workmen on a building under construction

NEW METHODS OF SELLING SEEN

Rescue Crews Try To Upend Ill-fated Craft While Waiting For Pontoons

> *He looked 'round an' said to his black greasy fireman*
> *Jus' shovel in a little more coal*
> *And when we cross that White Oak Mountain*
> *You can watch your Ninety-seven roll*

I find your column interesting and need advice. I have saved four thousand dollars which I want to invest for a better income. Do you think I might buy stocks?

POLICE KILLER FLICKS CIGARETTE AS HE GOES TREMBLING TO DOOM

PLAY AGENCIES IN RING OF SLAVE GIRL MARTS

Maker of Love Disbarred as Lawyer

> *Oh the right wing clothesmakers*
> *And the Socialist fakers*
> *They make by the workers . . .*
> *Double cross*

> *They preach Social-ism*
> *But Practice Fasc-ism*
> *To keep capitalism*
> *By the boss*

MOSCOW CONGRESS OUSTS OPPOSITION

> *It's a mighty rough road from Lynchburg to Danville*
> *An' a line on a three mile grade*
> *It was on that grade he lost his average*
> *An' you see what a jump he made*

MILL THUGS IN MURDER RAID

here is the most dangerous example of how at the decisive moment the bourgeois ideology liquidates class solidarity and turns a friend of the workingclass of yesterday into a most miserable propagandist for imperialism today

RED PICKETS FINED FOR PROTEST HERE

We leave our home in the morning
We kiss our children goodby

OFFICIALS STILL HOPE FOR RESCUE OF MEN

He was goin' downgrade makin' ninety miles an hour
When his whistle broke into a scream
He was found in the wreck with his hand on the throttle
An' was scalded to death with the steam

RADICALS FIGHT WITH CHAIRS AT UNITY MEETING

PATROLMEN PROTECT REDS

U.S. CHAMBER OF COMMERCE URGES CONFIDENCE

REAL VALUES UNHARMED

While we slave for the bosses
Our children scream an' cry
But when we draw our money
Our grocery bills to pay

PRESIDENT[3] SEES PROSPERITY NEAR

Not a cent to spend for clothing
Not a cent to lay away

STEAMROLLER IN ACTION AGAINST MILITANTS

MINERS BATTLE SCABS[4]

But we cannot buy for our children
Our wages are too low
Now listen to me you workers
Both you women and men
Let us win for them the victory
I'm sure it ain't no sin

CARILLON PEALS IN SINGING TOWER

the President declared it was impossible to view the increased advantages for the many without smiling at those who a short time ago expressed so much fear lest our country might come under the control of a few individuals of great wealth

HAPPY CROWDS THRONG CEREMONY

on a tiny island nestling like a green jewel in the lake that mirrors the singing tower, the President today participated in the dedication of a bird sanctuary and its pealing carillon, fulfilling the dream of an immigrant boy

---

[3]After the crash, President Herbert Hoover kept asserting that the economy was "fundamentally sound."

[4]Scabs are non-union workers willing to take the jobs of those on strike.

THE CAMERA EYE (51)

at the head of the valley in the dark of the hills on the broken floor of a lurchedover cabin a man halfsits[5] halflies propped up by an old woman two wrinkled girls that might be young   chunks of coal flare in the hearth flicker in his face white and sagging as dough   blacken the cavedin mouth the taut throat the belly swelled enormous with the wound he got working on the minetipple[6]

the barefoot girl brings him a tincup of water   the woman wipes sweat off his streaming face with a dirty denim sleeve   the firelight flares in his eyes stretched big with fever in the women's scared eyes and in the blanched faces of the foreigners

without help in the valley hemmed by dark strike-silent hills the man will die (my father died we know what it is like to see a man die) the women will lay him out on the rickety cot the miners will bury him

in the jail it's light too hot the steamheat hisses we talk through the greenpainted iron bars to a tall white mustachioed old man some smiling miners in shirtsleeves a boy   faces white from mining have already the tallowy look of jailfaces

foreigners what can we say to the dead?   foreigners what can we say to the jailed?   the representative of the political party talks fast through the bars join up with us and no other union we'll send you tobacco candy solidarity our lawyers will write briefs speakers will shout your names at meetings they'll carry your names on cardboard on picketlines   the men in the jail shrug their shoulders smile thinly our eyes look in their eyes through the bars   what can I say?   (in another continent I have seen the faces looking out through the barred basement windows behind the ragged sentry's boots I have seen before day the straggling footsore prisoners herded through the streets limping between bayonets   heard the volley

I have seen the dead lying out in those distant deeper valleys)   what can we say to the jailed?

in the law's office we stand against the wall the law is a big man with eyes angry in a big pumpkinface   who sits and stares at us meddling foreigners through the door the deputies crane with their guns   they stand guard at the mines   they blockade the miners' soupkitchens   they've cut off the road up the valley   the hiredmen with guns stand ready to shoot (they have made us foreigners in the land where we were born they are the conquering army that has filtered into the country unnoticed they have taken the hilltops by stealth they levy toll they stand at the minehead   they stand at the polls   they stand by when the bailiffs carry the furniture of the family evicted from the city tenement out on the sidewalk they are there when the bankers foreclose on a farm they are ambushed and ready to shoot down the strikers marching behind the flag up the switchback road to the mine   those that the guns spare they jail)

the law stares across the desk out of angry eyes his face reddens in splotches like a gobbler's neck with the strut of the power of submachineguns sawedoffshotguns teargas and vomitinggas the power that can feed you or leave you to starve

sits easy at his desk his back is covered he feels strong behind him he feels the prosecutingattorney the judge an owner himself the political boss the minesuperintendent the board of directors   the president of the utility the manipulator of the holdingcompany

he lifts his hand towards the telephone

the deputies crowd in the door

we have only words against

[5]In the fall of 1931, Dos Passos and Theodore Dreiser went to Harlan County, Kentucky, to report on the protracted and violent coal miner's strike there, and to witness the abuse of the strikers' civil rights. Both Dreiser and Dos Passos were later indicted by Kentucky for violation of its criminal syndi-calism law. Dos Passos was drawing on first-hand experience for this "Camera Eye" portrait of the suffering of a miner's family.

[6]A tipple at a coal mine is a structure where the coal is cleaned and loaded onto the railroad cars for shipment.

POWER SUPERPOWER

In eighteen eighty when Thomas Edison's[7] agent was hooking up the first telephone in London, he put an ad in the paper for a secretary and stenographer. The eager young cockney with sprouting muttonchop whiskers who answered it

had recently lost his job as officeboy. In his spare time he had been learning shorthand and bookkeeping and taking dictation from the editor of the English *Vanity Fair* at night and jotting down the speeches in Parliament for the papers. He came of temperance smallshopkeeper stock; already he was butting his bullethead against the harsh structure of caste that doomed boys of his class to a life of alpaca jackets, penmanship, subordination. To get a job with an American firm was to put a foot on the rung of a ladder that led up into the blue.

He did his best to make himself indispensable; they let him operate the switchboard for the first half-hour when the telephone service was opened. Edison noticed his weekly reports on the electrical situation in England

and sent for him to be his personal secretary.

Samuel Insull[8] landed in America on a raw March day in eightyone. Immediately he was taken out to Menlo Park, shown about the little group of laboratories, saw the strings of electriclightbulbs shining at intervals across the snowy lots, all lit from the world's first central electric station. Edison put him right to work and he wasn't through till midnight. Next morning at six he was on the job; Edison had no use for any nonsense about hours or vacations. Insull worked from that time on until he was seventy without a break; no nonsense about hours or vacations. Electric power turned the ladder into an elevator.

Young Insull made himself indispensable to Edison and took more and more charge of Edison's business deals. He was tireless, ruthless, reliable as the tides, Edison used to say, and fiercely determined to rise.

In ninetytwo he induced Edison to send him to Chicago and put him in as president of the Chicago Edison Company. Now he was on his own. *My engineering*, he said once in a speech, when he was sufficiently czar of Chicago to allow himself the luxury of plain speaking, *has been largely concerned with engineering all I could out of the dollar*.

He was a stiffly arrogant redfaced man with a closecropped mustache; he lived on Lake Shore Drive and was at the office at 7:10 every morning. It took him fifteen years to merge the five electrical companies into the Commonwealth Edison Company. *Very early I discovered that the first essential, as in other public utility business, was that it should be operated as a monopoly.*

When his power was firm in electricity he captured gas, spread out into the surrounding townships in northern Illinois. When politicians got in his way, he bought them, when laborleaders got in his way he bought them. Incredibly his power grew. He was scornful of bankers, lawyers were his hired men. He put his own lawyer in as corporation counsel and through him ran Chicago. When he found to his amazement that there were men (even a couple of young lawyers, Richberg and Ickes[9] in Chicago that he couldn't buy, he decided he'd better put on a show for the public;

Big Bill Thompson,[10] the Builder:

punch King George in the nose,

---

[7]Thomas Edison (1847–1931), American inventor who held over 1,000 patents for his inventions, one of which was the incandescent electric "lamp." By 1876 he was established in his own elaborate laboratories at Menlo Park, New Jersey.
[8]Samuel Insull (1859–1938), American financier born in London, who serves here as the prototype economic manipulator that brought about the crash and contributed to the suffering in its wake.

[9]Donald R. Richberg (1881–1960) and Harold Ickes (1874–1952); both were Chicago lawyers and both served in President Roosevelt's New Deal administration.
[10]William Hale Thompson (1869–1944), Republican mayor of Chicago (1915–23 and 1927–31), introduced spoils politics and accommodated gangsters such as Al Capone and ruthless tycoons such as Insull.

the hunt for the treeclimbing fish,[11]
the Chicago Opera.[12]

It was too easy; the public had money, there was one of them born every minute, with the founding of Middlewest Utilities in nineteen twelve Insull began to use the public's money to spread his empire. His companies began to have open stockholders' meetings, to ballyhoo service, the small investor could sit there all day hearing the bigwigs talk. It's fun to be fooled. Companyunions hypnotized his employees; everybody had to buy stock in his companies, employees had to go out and sell stock, officeboys, linemen, trolleyconductors. Even Owen D. Young[13] was afraid of him. *My experience is that the greatest aid in the efficiency of labor is a long line of men waiting at the gate.*

War shut up the progressives (no more nonsense about trustbusting, controlling monopoly, the public good) and raised Samuel Insull to the peak.

He was head of the Illinois State Council of Defense. *Now*, he said delightedly, *I can do anything I like*. With it came the perpetual spotlight, the purple taste of empire. If anybody didn't like what Samuel Insull did he was a traitor. Chicago damn well kept its mouth shut.

The Insull companies spread and merged put competitors out of business until Samuel Insull and his stooge brother Martin controlled through the leverage of holdingcompanies and directorates and blocks of minority stock

light and power, coalmines and tractioncompanies

in Illinois, Michigan, the Dakotas, Nebraska, Arkansas, Oklahoma, Missouri, Maine, Kansas, Wisconsin, Virginia, Ohio, North Carolina, Indiana, New York, New Jersey, Texas, in Canada, in Louisiana, in Georgia, in Florida and Alabama.

(It has been figured out that one dollar in Middle West Utilities controlled seventeen hundred and fifty dollars invested by the public in the subsidiary companies that actually did the work of producing electricity. With the delicate lever of a voting trust controlling the stock of the two top holdingcompanies he controlled a twelfth of the power output of America.)

Samuel Insull began to think he owned all that the way a man owns the roll of bills in his back pocket.

Always he'd been scornful of bankers. He owned quite a few in Chicago. But the New York bankers were laying for him; they felt he was a bounder, whispered that this financial structure was unsound. Fingers itched to grasp the lever that so delicately moved this enormous power over lives,

superpower, Insull liked to call it.

A certain Cyrus S. Eaton[14] of Cleveland, an exBaptistminister, was the David that brought down this Goliath.[15] Whether it was so or not he made Insull believe that Wall Street was behind him.

He started buying stock in the three Chicago utilities. Insull in a panic for fear he'd lose his control went into the market to buy against him. Finally the Reverend Eaton let himself be bought out, shaking down the old man for a profit of twenty million dollars.

---

[11]References to Big Bill Thomson's campaigns to recover the mayor's office in Chicago. To keep in the public eye, he set off on an expedition to hunt tree-climbing fish in the South Seas; the expedition failed, but the publicity succeeded. Thompson's campaign slogan was "America First, Last and Always!" and he linked this superpatriotism with repeated attacks on King George of England, trying to lure America into its dirty wars.
[12]Insull provided Chicago an opera house within an office building in 1929.
[13]Young (1874–1962), American lawyer, practicing in Boston, who served as Chairman of the Board for General Electric Co. (1922–39).
[14]Eaton (1883–1979), American businessman in Ohio, active in gas and electric firms.
[15]The story of David killing the giant Goliath is told in 1 Samuel 17:38–52.

The stockmarket crash.

Paper values were slipping. Insull's companies were intertwined in a tangle that no bookkeeper has ever been able to unravel.

The gas hissed out of the torn balloon. Insull threw away his imperial pride and went on his knees to the bankers.

The bankers had him where they wanted him. To save the face of the tottering czar he was made a receiver of his own concerns. But the old man couldn't get out of his head the illusion that the money was all his. When it was discovered that he was using the stockholders' funds to pay off his brothers' brokerage accounts it was too thick even for a federal judge. Insull was forced to resign.

He held directorates in eightyfive companies, he was chairman of sixtyfive, president of eleven: it took him three hours to sign his resignations.

As a reward for his services to monopoly his companies chipped in on a pension of eighteen thousand a year. But the public was shouting for criminal prosecution. When the handouts stopped newspapers and politicians turned on him. Revolt against the moneymanipulators was in the air. Samuel Insull got the wind up and ran off to Canada with his wife.

Extradition proceedings. He fled to Paris. When the authorities began to close in on him there he slipped away to Italy, took a plane to Tirana,[16] another to Saloniki and then the train to Athens. There the old fox went to earth. Money talked as sweetly in Athens as it had in Chicago in the old days.

The American ambassador tried to extradite him. Insull hired a chorus of Hellenic lawyers and politicos and sat drinking coffee in the lobby of the Grande Bretagne, while they proceeded to tie up the ambassador in a snarl of chicanery as complicated as the bookkeeping of his holdingcompanies. The successors of Demosthenes[17] were delighted. The ancestral itch in many a Hellenic palm was temporarily assuaged. Samuel Insull settled down cozily in Athens, was stirred by the sight of the Parthenon, watched the goats feeding on the Pentelic slopes, visited the Areopagus, admired marble fragments ascribed to Phidias,[18] talked with the local bankers about reorganizing the public utilities of Greece, was said to be promoting Macedonian lignite. He was the toast of the Athenians; Mme. Kouryoumdjouglou the vivacious wife of a Bagdad datemerchant devoted herself to his comfort. When the first effort at extradition failed, the old gentleman declared in the courtroom, as he struggled out from the embraces of his four lawyers: *Greece is a small but great country.*

The idyll was interrupted when the Roosevelt Administration began to put the heat on the Greek foreign office. Government lawyers in Chicago were accumulating truckloads of evidence and chalking up more and more drastic indictments.

Finally after many a postponement (he had hired physicians as well as lawyers, they cried to high heaven that it would kill him to leave the genial climate of the Attic plain),

he was ordered to leave Greece as an undesirable alien to the great indignation of Balkan society and of Mme. Kouryoumdjouglou.

He hired the *Maiotis* a small and grubby Greek freighter and panicked the foreignnews services by slipping off for an unknown destination.

It was rumored that the new Odysseus[19] was bound for Aden, for the islands of the South Seas, that he'd been invited to Persia. After a few days he turned up rather seasick in the Bosporus on his way, it was said, to Rumania where Madame Ko-

---

[16]In Albania.

[17]Demosthenes (d. 413 B.C.), Athenian orator and statesman.

[18]Parthenon, famous Doric temple of Athena built in the fifth century B.C. on the Acropolis in Athens; Pentelicus, a mountain near Athens; Areopagus, the hill of Ares, west of the Acropolis, where the high judges sat as a court; Phidias (c.

490–430 B.C.), the greatest of Greek sculptors.

[19]Odysseus, hero of the *Odyssey*, by Homer (ninth–eighth? century B.C.); the work relates the adventures on his voyage home after fighting in the Trojan War.

uryoumdjouglou had advised him to put himself under the protection of her friend la Lupescu.[20]

At the request of the American ambassador the Turks were delighted to drag him off the Greek freighter and place him in a not at all comfortable jail. Again money had been mysteriously wafted from England, the healing balm began to flow, lawyers were hired, interpreters expostulated, doctors made diagnoses;

but Angora[21] was boss

and Insull was shipped off to Smyrna to be turned over to the assistant federal districtattorney who had come all that way to arrest him.

the Turks wouldn't even let Mme. Kouryoumdjouglou, on her way back from making arrangements in Bucharest, go ashore to speak to him. In a scuffle with the officials on the steamboat the poor lady was pushed overboard

and with difficulty fished out of the Bosporus.

Once he was cornered the old man let himself tamely be taken home on the *Exilona*, started writing his memoirs, made himself agreeable to his fellow passengers, was taken off at Sandy Hook and rushed to Chicago to be arraigned.

In Chicago the government spitefully kept him a couple of nights in jail; men he'd never known, so the newspapers said, stepped forward to go on his twohundredandfiftythousanddollar bail. He was moved to a hospital that he himself had endowed. Solidarity. The leading businessmen in Chicago were photographed visiting him there. Henry Ford[22] paid a call.

The trial was very beautiful. The prosecution got bogged in finance technicalities. The judge was not unfriendly. The Insulls stole the show.

They were folks, they smiled at reporters, they posed for photographers, they went down to the courtroom by bus. Investors might have been ruined but so, they allowed it to be known, were the Insulls; the captain had gone down with the ship.

Old Samuel Insull rambled amiably on the stand, told his lifestory: from officeboy to powermagnate, his struggle to make good, his love for his home and the kiddies. He didn't deny he'd made mistakes; who hadn't, but they were honest errors. Samuel Insull wept. Brother Martin wept. The lawyers wept. With voices choked with emotion headliners of Chicago business told from the witnessstand how much Insull had done for business in Chicago. There wasn't a dry eye in the jury.

Finally driven to the wall by the prosecutingattorney Samuel Insull blurted out that yes, he had made an error of some ten million dollars in accounting but that it had been an honest error.

Verdict: Not Guilty.

Smiling through their tears the happy Insulls went to their towncar amid the cheers of the crowd. Thousands of ruined investors, at least so the newspapers said, who had lost their life savings sat crying over the home editions at the thought of how Mr. Insull had suffered. The bankers were happy, the bankers had moved in on the properties.

In an odor of sanctity the deposed monarch of superpower, the officeboy who made good, enjoys his declining years spending the pension of twenty-one thousand a year that the directors of his old companies dutifully restored to him. *After fifty years of work*, he said, *my job is gone.*

1936, 1938

---

[20]Magda Lupescu (1896?–1977), consort of King Carol of Rumania.
[21]Mohair, made from the long, silky hair of the Angora goat, and an important export for Turkey. In other words, Turkey's self-interest prevailed.

[22]Ford (1863–1947), American automobile manufacturer who revolutionized the industry by developing the assembly line for mass-producing cars.

JAMES AGEE
(1909–1955)

In 1938, when he was twenty-eight years old, James Agee wrote to his lifetime friend, Father James Harold Flye, about the doubts swarming over him as he attempted to write *Let Us Now Praise Famous Men*, later (after his death) to be recognized as his masterpiece. He said in part:

> The book as I may have told you is a short one on the three tenant families . . . I [have come to] know in Alabama. My trouble is, such a subject cannot be seriously looked at without intensifying itself toward a centre which is beyond what I, or anyone else, is capable of writing of: the whole problem and nature of existence. Trying to write it in terms of moral problems alone is more than I can possibly do. My main hope is to state the central subject and my ignorance from the start, and to manage to indicate that no one can afford to treat any human subject more glibly or to act on any less would-be central basis: well, there's no use trying to talk about it. If I could make it what it ought to be made I would not be human.

Agee finally did overcome his writing block and finished the book. When it was published in 1941, it attracted some laudatory reviews but few readers. Only when it was reissued in 1960, five years after Agee's death, did *Let Us Now Praise Famous Men* assume its place in American literature as a classic.

As a classic the book had a curious origin. It was first written for *Fortune* magazine, where Agee was employed from 1932 to 1939. Agee and photographer Walker Evans, on loan from a government position, were assigned by *Fortune* to write a documentary series on the plight of tenant farmers in the middle of the devastating Great Depression. They drove South wondering where to find their subjects and landed in Alabama, where they found the three families Agee wrote about and Walker photographed. The manuscript was rejected by *Fortune* because it violated most all journalistic conventions by its poetic style, its philosophical meditations, and its autobiographical intrusions. At a later period, it might have been called a nonfiction novel. As Agee indicated in his letter to Father Flye, it touched the "whole problem and nature of existence."

Agee was born in 1909 in Knoxville, Tennessee, into a comfortable, middle-class, religious family. When Agee was six, his father was killed in an automobile accident—an incident that haunted Agee all his life. In 1919, Agee entered a small Episcopal school for boys, St. Andrew's near Sewanee, Tennessee, where his mother taught. He met there Father James Harold Flye, who became a surrogate father to him. Father Flye edited and published Agee's correspondence, an extraordinary record of Agee's concerns over a thirty-year period, as *Letters of James Agee to Father Flye* in 1962 (revised in 1971 to include his own letters). From 1925 to 1928, Agee attended Phillips Exeter Academy in preparation for enrollment at Harvard University. At Harvard, Agee edited *The Advocate* and began to write for the literary magazines; when a senior, he did a parody of *Time* magazine, which led to his employment by *Fortune* on graduation in 1932.

In 1934, Agee's volume of poems, *Permit Me Voyage*, appeared in the Yale series of Younger Poets. Agee continued occasionally to write poems, and *The Collected Poems of James Agee* was edited and published in 1968 by Robert Fitzgerald (a fellow student at Harvard). Agee moved from *Fortune* to *Time* in 1939, working as a reviewer. And from 1941 to 1948, he reviewed movies for both *Time* and *The*

Nation. During this period, he wrote a number of critical essays on film subjects, including Charlie Chaplin and silent film comedy ("Comedy's Greatest Era").

Agee's passion for movies, and his belief that they offered great potentiality for genuine artists, made it inevitable that he would turn to the writing of film scripts. His best known credits are for *The African Queen* (1951) and *The Night of the Hunter* (1955). Two volumes of Agee's reviews, essays, and scripts have been published—*Agee on Film: Reviews and Comments* (1958, 1983) and *Agee on Film: Five Film Scripts* (1960, 1983), containing scripts for Stephen Crane's "The Bride Comes to Yellow Sky" and "The Blue Hotel."

Near the end of his life, Agee turned to the writing of fiction. In 1951, he published *The Morning Watch*, a lyrical account of one day in the life of a boy in a Tennessee school. In 1948 he had begun working on a novel about his childhood experience of his father's death. And in 1957, two years after he died of a heart attack, *A Death in the Family* was published. It won a Pulitzer Prize and was turned into a highly successful play by Tad Mosel in 1960.

In a remarkable passage of a story written in 1931, "They That Sow in Sorrow Shall Reap," Agee revealed—indirectly—his experience in attempting to capture reality through the medium of recalcitrant, unstable words:

> I have tried to work out to my own satisfaction some aspects of the mind's reaction to experience. . . . My mind is hopelessly weak and tangential; time and again . . . I fail to carry one idea through; before I realize it, I am whirled along the rim of another—and so on—ad nauseam. Yet, from time to time, I am aware of a definite form and rhythm and melody of existence. . . . And at that moment . . . the whole commonplaceness of existence is transfigured—becomes monstrously powerful, and beautiful, and significant—assuming these qualities validly but unanswerably—, and descends through tangled discords, once more into commonplaceness, with nothing answered, nothing gained, and heaven undisturbed.

This passage suggests the experience of *reading* Agee's best writing. There are successive moments of tension, of epiphany, rhythmically interspersed, transporting the reader along strange byways with the promise of successive illuminations. John Hersey, a fellow journalist at *Time*, had something of this sort in mind when he referred to the "many surprises and dazzling beauty of the prose" of *Let Us Now Praise Famous Men*: "This prose has the effect, finally, of enlarging the figures of the tale, until they become mythic, like Ahab, like Hester Prynne, like the children in *The Sound and the Fury*."

ADDITIONAL READING

The Collected Short Prose of James Agee, ed. Robert Fitzgerald, 1968; *James Agee: Selected Journalism*, ed. Paul Ashdown, 1985.

Peter H. Ohlin, *Agee*, 1966; Kenneth Seib, *James Agee: Promise and Fulfillment*, 1968; Erling Larsen, *James Agee*, 1971; Alfred T. Barson, *A Way of Seeing: A Critical Study of James Agee*, 1972; David Madden, ed., *Remembering James Agee*, 1974; Victor A. Kramer, *James Agee*, 1975; Genevieve Moreau, *The Restless Journey of James Agee*, 1977; Mark Doty, *Tell Me Who I Am: James Agee's Search for Selfhood*, 1981; Laurence Bergreen, *James Agee: A Life*, 1984; John Hersey, "A Critic at Large: Agee," *The New Yorker*, July 18, 1988.

TEXT

Let Us Now Praise Famous Men, 1960.

from Let Us Now Praise Famous Men[1]

MONEY

You are farmers; I am a farmer myself.

— FRANKLIN DELANO ROOSEVELT

Woods and Ricketts work for Michael and T. Hudson Margraves, two brothers, in partnership, who live in Cookstown. Gudger worked for the Margraves for three years; he now (1936) works for Chester Boles, who lives two miles south of Cookstown.

On their business arrangements, and working histories, and on their money, I wrote a chapter too long for inclusion in this volume without sacrifice of too much else. I will put in its place here as extreme a précis as I can manage.

Gudger has no home, no land, no mule; none of the more important farming implements. He must get all these of his landlord. Boles, for his share of the corn and cotton, also advances him rations money during four months of the year, March through June, and his fertilizer.

Gudger pays him back with his labor and with the labor of his family.

At the end of the season he pays him back further: with half his corn; with half his cotton; with half his cottonseed. Out of his own half of these crops he also pays him back the rations money, plus interest, and his share of the fertilizer, plus interest, and such other debts, plus interest, as he may have incurred.

What is left, once doctors' bills and other debts have been deducted, is his year's earnings.

Gudger is a straight halfcropper, or sharecropper.

Woods and Ricketts own no home and no land, but Woods owns one mule and Ricketts owns two, and they own their farming implements. Since they do not have to rent these tools and animals, they work under a slightly different arrangement. They give over to the landlord only a third of their cotton and a fourth of their corn. Out of their own parts of the crop, however, they owe him the price of two thirds of their cotton fertilizer and three fourths of their corn fertilizer, plus interest; and, plus interest, the same debts on rations money.

Woods and Ricketts are tenants; they work on third and fourth.

A very few tenants pay cash rent: but these two types of arrangement, with local variants (company stores; food instead of rations money; slightly different divisions of the crops) are basic to cotton tenantry all over the South.

From March through June, while the cotton is being cultivated, they live on the rations money.

---

[1]Writer James Agee and photographer Walker Evans were given the assignment by *Fortune* magazine in 1936 to produce a story on the sharecroppers in the South. They headed South in June, wondering where to find sharecroppers, touring Oklahoma first, and then going to Alabama. In Sprott, Alabama, they found Frank Tingle, a tenant farmer, and struck up a conversation. They were introduced to two friends of Tingle, Bud Fields and Floyd Burroughs. Fields invited them home — and the two journalists knew they had found their subjects. By the time he wrote his book, Agee was beset by bouts of guilt for exploiting poor families; he did not like what he was doing, but he could not keep himself from doing it. He thus opened his work with an apology: "It seems to me curious, not to say obscene and thoroughly terrifying . . . to pry intimately into the lives of an undefended and appallingly damaged group of human beings." He changed the names of the farmers to protect their anonymity: they became Fred Ricketts, Bud Woods, and George Gudger. By so distancing himself, Agee was able to write his masterpiece, *Let Us Now Praise Famous Men.*

From July through to late August, while the cotton is making, they live however they can.

From late August through October or into November, during the picking and ginning season, they live on the money from their share of the cottonseed.

From then on until March, they live on whatever they have earned in the year; or however they can.

During six to seven months of each year, then—that is, during exactly such time as their labor with the cotton is of absolute necessity to the landlord—they can be sure of whatever living is possible in rations advances and in cottonseed money.

During five to six months of the year, of which three are the hardest months of any year, with the worst of weather, the least adequacy of shelter, the worst and least of food, the worst of health, quite normal and inevitable, they can count on nothing except that they may hope least of all for any help from their landlords.

Gudger—a family of six—lives on ten dollars a month rations money during four months of the year. He has lived on eight, and on six. Woods—a family of six—until this year was unable to get better than eight a month during the same period; this year he managed to get it up to ten. Ricketts—a family of nine—lives on ten dollars a month during this spring and early summer period.

This debt is paid back in the fall at eight per cent interest. Eight per cent is charged also on the fertilizer and on all other debts which tenants incur in this vicinity.

At the normal price, a half-sharing tenant gets about six dollars a bale from his share of the cottonseed. A one-mule, half-sharing tenant makes on the average three bales. This half-cropper, then, Gudger, can count on eighteen dollars, more or less, to live on during the picking and ginning: though he gets nothing until his first bale is ginned.

Working on third and fourth, a tenant gets the money from two thirds of the cottonseed of each bale: nine dollars to the bale. Woods, with one mule, makes three bales, and gets twenty-seven dollars. Ricketts, with two mules, makes and gets twice that, to live on during the late summer and fall.

What is earned at the end of a given year is never to be depended on and, even late in a season, is never predictable. It can be enough to tide through the dead months of the winter, sometimes even better: it can be enough, spread very thin, to take through two months, and a sickness, or six weeks, or a month: it can be little enough to be completely meaningless: it can be nothing: it can be enough less than nothing to insure a tenant only of an equally hopeless lack of money at the end of his next year's work: and whatever one year may bring in the way of good luck, there is never any reason to hope that that luck will be repeated in the next year or the year after that.

The best that Woods has ever cleared was $1300 during a war year. During the teens and twenties he fairly often cleared as much as $300; he fairly often cleared $50 and less; two or three times he ended the year in debt. During the depression years he has more often cleared $50 and less; last year he cleared $150, but serious illness during the winter ate it up rapidly.

The best that Gudger has ever cleared is $125. That was in the plow-under year. He felt exceedingly hopeful and bought a mule: but when his landlord warned him of how he was coming out the next year, he sold it. Most years he has not made more than $25 to $30; and about one year in three he has ended in debt. Year before last he wound up $80 in debt; last year, $12; of Boles, his new landlord, the first thing he had to do was borrow $15 to get through the winter until rations advances should begin.

Years ago the Ricketts were, relatively speaking, almost prosperous. Besides their cotton farming they had ten cows and sold the milk, and they lived near a good stream and had all the fish they wanted. Ricketts went $400 into debt on a fine young pair of mules. One of the mules died before it had made its first crop; the other died the year after; against his fear, amounting to full horror, of sinking to the halfcrop level where nothing is owned, Ricketts went into debt for other, inferior mules; his cows went one by one into debts and desperate exchanges and by sickness; he got congestive chills; his wife got pellagra; a number of his children died; he got appendicitis and lay for days on end under the ice cap; his wife's pellagra got into her brain; and for ten consecutive years now, though they have lived on so little rations money, and have turned nearly all their cottonseed money toward their debts, they have not cleared or had any hope of clearing a cent at the end of the year.

It is not often, then, at the end of the season, that a tenant clears enough money to tide him through the winter, or even an appreciable part of it. More generally he can count on it that, during most of the four months between settlement time in the fall and the beginning of work and resumption of rations advances in the early spring, he will have no money and can expect none, nor any help, from his landlord: and of having no money during the six midsummer weeks of laying by, he can be still more sure. Four to six months of each year, in other words, he is much more likely than not to have nothing whatever, and during these months he must take care for himself: he is no responsibility of the landlord's. All he can hope to do is find work. This is hard, because there are a good many chronically unemployed in the towns, and they are more convenient to most openings for work and can at all times be counted on if they are needed; also there is no increase, during these two dead farming seasons, of other kinds of work to do. And so, with no more jobs open than at any other time of year, and with plenty of men already convenient to take them, the whole tenant population, hundreds and thousands in any locality, are desperately in need of work.

A landlord saves up certain odd jobs for these times of year: they go, at less than he would have to pay others, to those of his tenants who happen to live nearest or to those he thinks best of; and even at best they don't amount to much.

When there is wooded land on the farm, a landlord ordinarily permits a tenant to cut and sell firewood for what he can get. About the best a tenant gets of this is a dollar a load, but more often (for the market is glutted, so many are trying to sell wood) he can get no better than half that and less, and often enough, at the end of a hard day's peddling, miles from home, he will let it go for a quarter or fifteen cents rather than haul it all the way home again: so it doesn't amount to much. Then, too, by no means everyone has wood to cut and sell: in the whole southern half of the country we were working mainly in, there was so little wood that the negroes, during the hard winter of 1935–36, were burning parts of their fences, outbuildings, furniture and houses, and were dying off in great and not seriously counted numbers, of pneumonia and other afflictions of the lungs.

WPA work is available to very few tenants: they are, technically, employed, and thus have no right to it: and if by chance they manage to get it, landlords are more likely than not to intervene. They feel it spoils a tenant to be paid wages, even for a little while. A tenant who so much as tries to get such work is under disapproval.

There is not enough direct relief even for the widows and the old of the country.

Gudger and Ricketts, during this year, were exceedingly lucky. After they, and Woods, had been turned away from government work, they found work in a sawmill. They were given the work on condition that they stay with it until the mill was moved, and subject strictly to their landlords' permission: and their employer wouldn't so much as hint how long the work might last. Their landlords quite grudgingly gave them permission, on condition that they pay for whatever help was needed in their absence during the picking season. Gudger hired a hand, at eight dollars a month and board. Ricketts did not need to: his family is large enough. They got a dollar and a quarter a day five days a week and seventyfive cents on Saturday, seven dollars a week, ten hours' work a day. Woods did not even try for this work: he was too old and too sick.

from SHELTER

A home in its fields

George Gudger has of Chester Boles a little over twenty acres of open farm land, a few more acres of woods and of hillside ravines, a house, a barn, a smokehouse, a henroost, a garden, and a spring, all suspended and emplaced in solitude out at the end of a mile of dwindled branch road, and not within sight nor within a half-mile's walk of any other inhabited house. A little of his land is on the flat crest of the hill; the rest is broken into large patches among ravines and woods along the falling shapes of the hill and into little patches along the road that leads him out. The house and outbuildings, the garden and the spring, stand about midway in the main pieces of this land, and about halfway down the hill.

The top three acres are a long flat rectangle of keenly red clay and are planted in cotton. Between the edge of the hill and his barnyard there is nothing planted, only wild weeds and briars on a scrubbed-looking set of rounded and trenched surfaces, and a narrow path slid winding among them, but from this edge, standing at the edge of the cotton, you see the house and barnyard, resembling a large museum model or an establishment for large dolls, set at the middle of the slope, back-to-you, facing due west, and the two large fields in front of it and on its left which make up most of the rest of the farm, the whole bound in by a bluff horizon of trees. Now and then a faint windy noise of speed or a noise of grinding, sweeping a western crescent beyond the trees and through one thin sector of trees, for two seconds, the uncertain glimpse of a gliding bulk: and these are the thinly spaced sedans and trucks which use a minor artery between two county seats profoundly distant to a walking man.

One of these fields begins very deep behind the house on its left, and along its left flank the cotton plants nearly touch the wall; it is nearly all in cotton. Back beyond it and beneath it, in a clearing in the tall woods, is a smaller patch of corn. The field that falls away two hundred yards in front of the house is all in adolescent corn, softly flashing, ending at tall forest whose leaves run like quicksilver wheat in the lesions of heated air. Out of the right of the house is the rough stretch of mid-hill, partly bare, fluted with rain, not planted, sprung with tall weeds and smoky grasses and with berry briars, young pines and little runs and islands of young trees, seeming open, yet merged before long in a solid coastline of well-grown woods. Out along the road that, beginning just below the house, leads out to the right and north, there are further small floors and slivers of farm land, all but one less than an acre, and lying much within the moistures of trees during several hours of the day, in cotton, in corn, in sorghum cane, in peanuts, in watermelons, and in sweet potatoes. Some of this land of Gudger's is sandy clay, dull-orange to a dead sort of yellow; some is dark sand; a little is loam. He has in all about eleven acres in cotton, nine in corn, a quarter in sorghum cane, about half an acre divided among the melons, peanuts, and potatoes, and there are field peas planted in the corn rows.

These fields are workrooms, or fragrant but mainly sterile workfloors without walls and with a roof of uncontrollable chance, fear, rumination, and propitiative prayer, and are as the spread and broken petals of a flower whose bisexual center is the house.

Or the farm is also as a water spider whose feet print but do not break the gliding water membrane: it is thus delicately and briefly that, in its fields and structures, it sustains its entity upon the blind breadth and steady heave of nature.

Or it is the wrung breast of one human family's need and of an owner's taking, yielding blood and serum in its thin blue milk, and the house, the concentration of living and taking, is the cracked nipple: and of such breasts, the planet is thickly and desperately paved as the enfabled front of a goddess of east india.

The fields are organic of the whole, and of their own nature, and of the work that is poured into them: the spring, the garden, the outbuildings, are organic to the house itself.

The spring
The garden
The outbuildings

The spring is out to the rear of the house and above it, about a hundred and fifty yards away to the right, not a short distance to walk for every drop of water that is needed. The path lifts from the end of the back hall between the henroost and the smokehouse to just below the barn, swings left here, parts from the hill path, and runs narrowly, but slick as a scalp, among thick weeds under sunlight and toward trees whose greenbrown gloom and coolness is sudden and whose silence, different from that of the open light, seems to be conscious and to await the repetition of a signal. Not five feet deeper, a delicate yet powerful odor of wetness in constant shade, a broad windless standing-forth of a new coolness as from a refrigerator door, and a diminutive wrinkling noise of water: and ten feet deep within the roof of leaves, low, on the upward right, the spring, the dirt all round dark and strong-rooted and fragrant, tamped smooth as soap with bare feet, and a mottled piece of plank to kneel to water on. The water stands forward from between rounded strata of submerged dark stone as from between lips or rollers, in a look not of motion yet of quiet compulsion, into a basin a foot deep floored with dead oakleaves and shored up with slimy wood. On a submerged shelf small crocks of butter, cream, and milk stand sunken to their eyes, tied over with pieces of saturated floursack. A sapling next the spring has been chopped short to make a stob, and on it hangs a coffee can rusted black and split at the edges. The spring is not cowled so deeply under the hill that the water is brilliant and nervy, seeming to break in the mouth like crystals, as spring water can: it is about the temper of faucet water, and tastes slack and faintly sad, and as if just short of stale. It is not quite tepid, however, and it does not seem to taste of sweat and sickness, as the water does which the Woods family have to use.

Ten feet below, in a little alcove cleared at the edge of the woods, the water lets out through a rusted pipe and rambles loose. There is a brute oak bench here for washtubs,[1] and burnt stones are squared round the bright ashes of wood fires, and, next these stones, is one of those very heavy and handsome black iron kettles in which people one remove more primitive still make their own soap.

So, at the end of a slim liana of dry path running out of the heart of the house, a small wet flower suspended: the spring.

The garden plot is close on the right rear of the house. It is about the shape and about two thirds the size of a tennis court, and is caught within palings against the hunger and damage of animals. These palings are thin slats of split pine about three and a half feet tall and an inch and a half wide, wired together vertically, about their width apart from each other. The erratic grain and cleavage of this pine have given each of them a different welter and rippling streaming of surface and pattern structure; the weather has made this all as it were a muted silver and silk, exquisitely sensitive to light; and these slats closely approximate yet seldom perfect their perpendiculars; so that when the sun is on them, and with the segments of garden between each of them, there is here such a virtuosity as might be watched by speechless days on end merely for the variety and distinction of their beauty, without thought or any relevant room for thinking, and without possibility of absorbing all

---

[1] "There was also a split, mended washboard whose ribblings were homesawn out of a thick section of pine plank" (Agee's note).

that is there to be seen. Outside, the frowsy weeds stand halfway up these walls: inside, the planting is concentrated to the utmost possible, in green and pink-veined wax and velvet butter beans, and in rank tomatoes, hung low, burst against the ground, in hairy buds of okra, all these sprung heavy with weeds and smothered in textured shades of their leaves, blown like nearly exploding balloons in the full spread of the summer, each in its shape and nature, so that the whole of this space is one blowsy bristling pool and splendor of worm- and insect-embroidered plants and the savage odors of their special lusts that sting the face in gathering, nuzzling the paling as the bars of a zoo: waist-deep to wade in, so twined and spired and reached among each other that the paths betwen rows are discernible only like steps confounded in snow: a paling gate, nearest the kitchen, is bound shut against their bursting with a piece of wire.

Behind the house the dirt is blond and bare, except a little fledging of grass-leaves at the roots of structures, and walked-out rags of grass thickening along the sides. It lifts up gently, perhaps five feet in twenty yards: across the top line of this twenty yards is the barn, set a few feet to the right of center of the rear of the house. Half between the barn and house, symmetrical to the axis of the house, the henroost and the smokehouse face each other across a bare space of perhaps twelve feet of dirt.

These, like the house, are all made of unpainted pine. In some of this wood, the grain is broad and distinct: in some of it the grain has almost disappeared, and the wood has a texture and look like that of weathered bone.

The henroost is about seven feet square and five high, roofed with rotted shingles. It is built rather at random of planks varying in width between a foot and four inches, nailed on horizontally with narrow spaces between their edges. On the uphill side a short pole leans against the roof with chips and sticks nailed along it for steps and a box nailed at the top with straw in it; but most of the eggs are found by the children in places which are of the hens' own selection and return. Inside the roost, three or four sections of saplings, so arranged that the hens will not dirty each other; these poles rubbed smooth by their feet; the strong slits of light between the boards; the odor of closured and heated wood; and the nearly unbearably fetid odor of the feathers and excretions of the hens.

The smokehouse is about eight feet square and about seven tall to the peak of the roof. It is built of vertical boards of uniform width. The door is flush to the wall without a frame and is held shut by a wood button. On the uphill side, at center of the wall and flat to it, hangs a nearly new washtub, the concentrics on its bottom circle like a target. Its galvanized material is brilliant and dryly eating in the sun; the wood of the wall itself is not much less brilliant. The natural usage of a smokehouse is to smoke and store meat, but meat is not smoked here: this is a storage house. Mainly, there are a couple of dozen tin cans here, of many differing sizes and former uses, now holding sorghum; four hoes; a set of sweeps; a broken plow-frame; pieces of an ice-cream freezer; a can of rusty nails; a number of mule shoes; the strap of a white slipper; a pair of greenly eaten, crumpled workshoes, the uppers broken away, the soles worn broadly through, still carrying the odor of feet; a blue coil of soft iron wire; a few yards of rusted barbed wire; a rotted mulecollar; pieces of wire at random:[2] all those same broken creatures of the Ricketts' porch, of uselessness and of almost endless saving.

It should hardly be called a 'barn,' it is too thin an excuse for one: a long low shed divided into three chambers, a wired-in yard, a hog wallow and the hog's dirty little house. One room is made of thick and thin logs, partly stopped with clay, and this is

[2]"Invention here: I did not make inventory; there was more than I could remember. I remember for certain only the sorghum cans, the sweeps, the hoes, the work shoes, the nails; with a vaguer remembrance of random pieces of harness and of broken machinery: there may also have been, for instance, a ruined headlight and a boy's soggy worn-out cap. Many of the sorghum cans, by the way, were almost the only bright and new-looking things on the farm. Gudger may have bought them. If so, they are notable, for tenants seldom buy anything new" (Agee's note).

the stall for the mule when he is there: the rest is pine boards. The next partition is for the cow. In one corner of the small wired yard which squares off this part of the barn, in somewhat trampled and dunged earth, is the hogpen, made of logs; beyond that, a room used, in turn, as a corncrib and as a storage house for cotton prior to ginning. There is no hayloft. The whole structure is about twenty feet long and not more than seven high and seven or eight deep. The floor, except of the corncrib, is earth.

Here I must say, a little anyhow: what I can hardly hope to bear out in the record: that a house of simple people which stands empty and silent in the vast Southern country morning sunlight, and everything which on this morning in eternal space it by chance contains, all thus left open and defenseless to a reverent and cold-laboring spy, shines quietly forth such grandeur, such sorrowful holiness of its exactitudes in existence, as no human consciousness shall every rightly perceive, far less impart to another: that there can be more beauty and more deep wonder in the standings and spacings of mute furnishings on a bare floor between the squaring bourns of walls than in any music ever made: that this square home, as it stands in unshadowed earth between the winding years of heaven, is, not to me but of itself, one among the serene and final, uncapturable beauties of existence: that this beauty is made between hurt but invincible nature and the plainest cruelties and needs of human existence in this uncured time, and is inextricable among these, and as impossible without them as a saint born in paradise.

But I say these things only because I am reluctant to entirely lie. I can have nothing more to do with them now. I am hoping here only to tell a little, only so well as I may, about an ordinary[3] house, in which I lived a little while, and which is the home, for the time being, of the Gudger family, and is the sort of home a tenant family lives in, furnished and decorated as they furnish and decorate. Since it is so entirely static a subject, it may be slow going. That is as it may be.

from WORK

To come devotedly into the depths of a subject, your respect for it increasing in every step and your whole heart weakening apart with shame upon yourself in dealing with it: To know at length better and better and at length into the bottom of your soul your unworthiness of it: Let me hope in any case that it is something to have begun to learn. Let this all stand however it may: since I cannot make it the image it should be, let it stand as the image it is: I am speaking of my verbal part of this book as a whole. By what kind of foreword I can make clear some essential coherence in it, which I know is there, balanced of its chaos, I do not yet know. But the time is come when it is necessary for me to say at least this much: and now, having said it, to go on, and to try to make an entrance into this chapter, which should be an image of the very essence of their lives: that is, of the work they do.

It is for the clothing, and for the food, and for the shelter, by these to sustain their lives, that they work. Into this work and need, their minds, their spirits, and their strength are so steadily and intensely drawn that during such time as they are not at work, life exists for them scarcely more clearly or in more variance and seizure of appetite than it does for the more simply organized among the animals, and for the plants. This arduous physical work, to which a consciousness beyond that of the simplest child would be only a useless and painful encumbrance, is undertaken without choice or the thought of chance of choice, taught forward from father to son and from mother to daughter; and its essential and few returns you have seen: the houses

---

[3]"The whole problem, if I were trying fully to embody the house, would be to tell of it exactly in its ordinary terms" (Agee's note).

they live in; the clothes they wear: and have still to see, and for the present to imagine, what it brings them to eat; what it has done to their bodies, and to their consciousness; and what it makes of their leisure, the pleasures which are made available to them. I say here only: work as a means to other ends might have some favor in it, even which was of itself dull and heartless work, in which one's strength was used for another man's benefit: but the ends of this work are absorbed all but entirely into the work itself, and in what little remains, nearly all is obliterated; nearly nothing is obtainable; nearly all is cruelly stained, in the tensions of physical need, and in the desperate tensions of the need of work which is not available.

I have said this now three times. If I were capable, as I wish I were, I could say it once in such a way that it would be there in its complete awefulness. Yet knowing, too, how it is repeated upon each of them, in every day of their lives, so powerfully, so entirely, that it is simply the natural air they breathe, I wonder whether it could ever be said enough times.

The plainness and iterativeness of work must be one of the things which make it so extraordinarily difficult to write of. The plain details of a task once represented, a stern enough effort in itself, how is it possibly to be made clear enough that this same set of leverages has been undertaken by this woman in nearly every day of the eleven or the twenty-five years since her marriage, and will be persisted in in nearly every day to come in all the rest of her life; and that it is only one among the many processes of wearying effort which make the shape of each one of her living days; how is it to be calculated, the number of times she has done these things, the number of times she is still to do them; how conceivably in words is it to be given as it is in actuality, the accumulated weight of these actions upon her; and what this cumulation has made of her body; and what it has made of her mind and of her heart and of her being. And how is this to be made so real to you who read of it, that it will stand and stay in you as the deepest and most iron anguish and guilt of your existence that you are what you are, and that she is what she is, and that you cannot for one moment exchange places with her, nor by any such hope make expiation for what she has suffered at your hands, and for what you have gained at hers: but only by consuming all that is in you into the never relaxed determination that this shall be made different and shall be made right, and that of what is 'right' some, enough to die for, is clear already, and the vast darkness of the rest has still, and far more passionately and more skeptically than ever before, to be questioned into, defended, and learned toward. There is no way of taking the heart and the intelligence by the hair and wresting it to its feet, and of making it look this terrific thing in the eyes: which are such gentle eyes: you may meet them, with all the summoning of heart you have, in the photograph in this volume of the young woman with black hair: and they are to be multiplied, not losing the knowledge that each is a single, unrepeatable, holy individual, by the two billion human creatures who are alive upon the planet today; of whom a few hundred thousands are drawn into complications of specialized anguished, but of whom the huge swarm and majority are made and acted upon as she is: and of all these individuals, contemplate, try to encompass, the one annihilating chord.

But I must make a new beginning:

(Selection from Part I:

The family exists for work. It exists to keep itself alive. It is a cooperative economic unit. The father does one set of tasks; the mother another; the children still a third, with the sons and daughters serving apprenticeship to their father and mother respectively. A family is called a force, without irony; and children come into the world chiefly that they may help with the work and that through their help the family may increase itself. Their early years are leisurely; a child's life work begins as play. Among his first imitative gestures are gestures of work; and the whole imitative course of his maturing and biologic envy is a stepladder of the learning of physical tasks and skills.

This work solidifies, and becomes steadily more and more, in greater and greater quantity and variety, an integral part of his life.

Besides imitation, he works if he is a man under three compulsions, in three stages. First for his parents. Next for himself, single and wandering in the independence of his early manhood: 'for himself,' in the sense that he wants to stay alive, or better, and has no one dependent on him. Third, for himself and his wife and his family, under an employer. A woman works just for her parents; next, without a transition phase, for her husband and family.

Work for your parents is one thing: work 'for yourself' is another. They are both hard enough, yet light, relative to what is to come. On the day you are married, at about sixteen if you are a girl, at about twenty if you are a man, a key is turned, with a sound not easily audible, and you are locked between the stale earth and the sky; the key turns in the lock behind you, and your full life's work begins, and there is nothing conceivable for which it can afford to stop short of your death, which is a long way off. It is perhaps at its best during the first two years or so, when you are young and perhaps are still enjoying one another or have not yet lost all hope, and when there are not yet so many children as to weigh on you. It is perhaps at its worst during the next ten to twelve years, when there are more and more children, but none of them old enough, yet, to be much help. One could hardly describe it as slackening off after that, for in proportion with the size of the family, it has been necessary to take on more land and more work, and, too, a son or daughter gets just old enough to be any full good to you, and marries or strikes out for himself: yet it is true, anyhow, that from then on there are a number of strong and fairly responsible people in the household besides the man and his wife. In really old age, with one of the two dead, and the children all married, and the widowed one making his home among them in the slow rotations of a floated twig, waiting to die, it does ease off some, depending more then on the individual: one may choose to try to work hard and seem still capable, out of duty and the wish to help, or out of 'egoism,' or out of the dread of dropping out of life; or one may relax, and live unnoticed, never spoken to, dead already; or again, life may have acted on you in such a way that you have no choice in it: or still again, with a wife dead, and children gone, and a long hard lifetime behind you, you may choose to marry again and begin the whole cycle over, lifting onto your back the great weight a young man carries, as Woods has done.

That is the general pattern, its motions within itself lithe-unfolded, slow, gradual, grand, tremendously and quietly weighted, as a heroic dance: and the bodies in this dance, and the spirits, undergoing their slow, miraculous, and dreadful changes: such a thing indeed should be constructed of just these persons: the great, somber, blooddroned, beansprout helmed fetus unfurling within Woods' wife; the infants of three families, staggering happily, their hats held full of freshly picked cotton; the Ricketts children like delirious fawns and panthers; and secret Pearl with her wicked skin; Louise, lifting herself to rest her back, the heavy sack trailing, her eyes on you; Junior, jealous and lazy, malingering, his fingers sore; the Ricketts daughters, the younger stepping beautifully as a young mare, the elder at the stove with her mouth twisted; Annie Mae at twenty-seven, in her angular sweeping, every motion a wonder to watch; George, in his sunday clothes with his cuffs short on his blocked wrists, looking at you, his head slightly to one side, his earnest eyes a little squinted as if he were looking into a light; Mrs. Ricketts, in that time of morning when from the corn she reels into the green roaring glooms of her home, falls into a chair with gaspings which are almost groaning sobs, and dries in her lifted skirt her delicate and reeking head; Miss-Molly, chopping wood as if in each blow of the axe she held captured in focus the vengeance of all time; Woods, slowed in his picking, forced to stop and rest much too often, whose death is hastened against a doctor's warnings in that he is picking at all: I see these among others on the clay in the grave mutations of a dance whose business is the genius of a moving camera, and which it is not my hope ever to record: yet here, perhaps, if not of these archaic circulations of the rude clay altar, yet of their shapes of work, I can make a few crude sketches:

A man: George Gudger, Thomas Woods, Fred Ricketts: his work is with the land, in the seasons of the year, in the sustainment and ordering of his family, the training of his sons:

A woman: Annie Mae Gudger, Ivy Woods, Sadie Ricketts: her work is in the keeping of the home, the preparation of food against each day and against the dead season, the bearing and care of her children, the training of her daughters:

Children: all these children: their work is as it is told to them and taught to them until such time as they shall strengthen and escape, and, escaped of one imprisonment, are submitted into another.

There are times of year when all these three are overlapped and collaborated, all in the field in the demand, chiefly, of cotton; but more largely, the woman is the servant of the day, and of immediate life, and the man is the servant of the year, and of the basis and boundaries of life, and is their ruler; and the children are the servants of their parents: and the center of all their existence, the central work, that by which they have their land, their shelter, their living, that which they must work for no reward more than this, because they do not own themselves, and without hope or interest, that which they cannot eat and get no money of but which is at the center of their duty and greatest expense of strength and spirit, the cultivation and harvesting of cotton: and all this effort takes place between a sterile earth and an uncontrollable sky in whose propitiation is centered their chief reverence and fear, and the deepest earnestness of their prayers, who read in these machinations of their heaven all signs of a fate which the hardest work cannot much help, and, not otherwise than as the most ancient peoples of the earth, make their plantations in the unpitying pieties of the moon.

LET US NOW PRAISE FAMOUS MEN[1]

Let us now praise famous men, and our fathers that begat us.

The Lord hath wrought great glory by them through his great power from the beginning.

Such as did bear rule in their kingdoms, men renowned for their power, giving counsel by their understanding, and declaring prophecies:

Leaders of the people by their counsels, and by their knowledge of learning meet for the people, wise and eloquent in their instructions:

Such as found out musical tunes, and recited verses in writing:

Rich men furnished with ability, living peaceably in their habitations:

All these were honoured in their generations, and were the glory of their times.

There be of them, that have left a name behind them, that their praises might be reported.

And some there be which have no memorial; who perished, as though they had never been; and are become as though they had never been born; and their children after them.

---

[1]This quotation appears in *Let Us Now Praise Famous Men* at the end of the text but before "Notes and Appendices." Agee found it in Chapter 44 of Ecclesiasticus, or the Wisdom of Jesus the Son of Sirach, a much respected Apocryphal "book of wisdom."

But these were merciful men, whose righteousness hath not been forgotten.

With their seed shall continually remain a good inheritance, and their children are within the covenant.

Their seed standeth fast, and their children for their sakes. Their seed shall remain for ever, and their glory shall not be blotted out.

Their bodies are buried in peace; but their name liveth for evermore.

1941

PART III

THE AGE OF UNCERTAINTY: AFTER THE SECOND WORLD WAR
(1945–Present)

INTRODUCTION

The Allies triumphed in the Second World War, but the immense losses in human life, in wealth wasted in munitions, in energy and imagination devoted to destruction rather than creation made the victory a hollow one. The human race seemed to have crossed a deep divide in its history in 1945 when the atom was finally forced to yield its energy to be used for the instant demolition of two Japanese cities, Hiroshima and Nagasaki. Such immense power was unimaginable before the war. Did its discovery set us on a path to constructive achievement — or inevitable doom?

Awareness of human capacity for evil deepened at the end of the war when the Allied armies began to discover, and make known to the world, some seven million dead and dying Jews and other "undesirables" in the German concentration — or extermination — camps. How could the people of a nation acquiesce, either by assent or by silence, in the perpetration of such a holocaust? Could it be possible, as playwright Arthur Miller would ultimately argue in "Our Guilt for the World's Evil," that no individual could escape symbolic complicity? After the experiences of the war, no one could return to the solacing certainties that had helped them through horrors of the past: the belief in the innate dignity, nobility, or just common decency of humankind. People had to learn to live their lives beset often by doubt or dread in an age of uncertainty.

It was not long after the war that former allies — the Soviet Union and China — transmogrified themselves into enemies, aggressively bent on the spread of Communism. The United States lost its monopoly of atomic weapons when the Soviets exploded an atomic bomb in 1949. In 1950, Communist North Korea invaded South Korea, and the United States, bent on containing Communism, furnished the major share of troops for the United Nations' defense of South Korea in a war finally ended by an uneasy truce in 1953. In 1957, the Soviet Union became the first nation to place in orbit an earth satellite, Sputnik I; spurred by this event, America began a race to put a man on the moon, succeeding twelve years later, in 1969. When tensions developed in a divided Germany and a divided Berlin in 1961, and many Germans began fleeing from the East to the West, Communist East Germany constructed the Berlin Wall, a concrete embodiment of Winston Churchill's 1946 metaphor of an iron curtain dividing Western Europe and the Soviet-occupied countries in Eastern Europe.

The strife and violence that accompanied the civil rights movement of the late 1950s and the early 1960s; America's involvement in the seemingly endless Vietnam War and the mounting protests of the late 1960s and the early 1970s; the assassinations of President John Kennedy in 1963, of the civil rights leader Martin Luther King in 1968, and of Kennedy's brother Robert, running in the presidential primaries, also in 1968 — all seemed to confirm that the country was becoming more, not less, barbaric. With a numbing regularity, events shocked the national psyche, demonstrating the fragility of national, and world, peace — the resignation of Richard Nixon from the presidency in 1974 after the Watergate scandal; the occupation of the American embassy in Iran in 1979 with the staff held hostage throughout the last year of Jimmy Carter's presidency; the use of "private" diplomacy in 1986–87, in Ronald Reagan's presidency, to sell weapons secretly to this same Iran and to use the "profits" illegally to supply a guerrilla army to overthrow the government of Nicaragua in Central America (the Iran/Contra scandal). Even the advent of a Soviet leader in the late 1980s, Mikhail Gorbachev, who seemed bent on conciliation and peace with America, was, in the age of uncertainty, viewed with strong skepticism by a populace accustomed to trickery and deceit in a world racked daily by random violence and terrorist vengeance.

THE POLITICAL SCENE

When President Franklin D. Roosevelt died in April 1945, Harry S. Truman was sworn into office immediately. Though he had been vice president, he had not been kept abreast of the affairs of government by Roosevelt, and was immediately confronted with decisions about the peace treaty ending the war in Europe in May of 1945, the shaping of the United Nations in June, the dropping of the atomic bomb on Hiroshima in August, and the peace treaty with Japan in September. With the beginning of the Cold War, and the swallowing up of many of the countries of Eastern Europe by the Soviet Union, it was left to Truman to lead the nation into a willingness to aid European countries such as Greece and Turkey to keep them out of the Soviet orbit, and to bring America and the Western European democracies into a mutual defense arrangement known as NATO (the North Atlantic Treaty Organization).

In the presidential election of 1948, the Republicans nominated Thomas E. Dewey, who had been a popular district attorney of New York county. In the campaign, Dewey appeared contemptuous of the feisty Missourian, Truman, and all the polls indicated that Dewey would win. But to nearly everybody's surprise, Truman won the election. With the invasion of South Korea by North Korea in 1950, Truman made the decision to send American troops, under the command of General Douglas MacArthur, to help South Korea defend itself. And it was Truman's responsibility to remove MacArthur from his command when the strongly independent general disagreed with the limited objectives imposed on the troops and wanted to follow a more aggressive policy. Such a policy might have led to a major war with China, which had entered the war on the side of the North Koreans.

In the election of 1952, the Democrats nominated the governor of Illinois, Adlai Stevenson, and the Republicans nominated Dwight D. Eisenhower, who had been commanding general of the Allied forces in Europe during the Second World War. Stevenson's considerable assets, his sharp intellect and ready wit, were no match for Eisenhower's wartime popularity, and Eisenhower took office in 1953 for two terms (until 1961). He brought about a truce in the Korean War in 1953 and continued the policies in Europe begun by Truman. In 1957, he surprised southerners by sending troops to enforce racial integration of the schools in Little Rock, Arkansas, in accord with the Supreme Court ruling of 1954 banning segregation in education.

Eisenhower's vice president, Richard Nixon, became the Republican's candidate in 1960, pitted against a popular young Democratic Senator from Massachusetts, John F. Kennedy. Kennedy, a Catholic, was well aware of the slander and rumors another Catholic, Alfred E. Smith, had faced when he ran in the presidential race of 1928. Kennedy won a narrow victory and was the first Catholic to become president of the United States. It was Kennedy's lot to be president when an invasion of Castro-led Communist Cuba, planned under Eisenhower, turned into a catastrophic defeat in 1961. The most sensational moment of his administration came in 1962 when he compelled the Soviets to dismantle the missile bases established in Cuba. His assassination in Dallas in 1963 by Lee Harvey Oswald, a deranged loner, was the first such event to occur in the age of television, making the people as a whole not only participants in the mourning and funeral of a murdered president but also witnesses to the killing of the assassin by another deranged being.

Kennedy's vice president, the Texan Lyndon B. Johnson, took the oath of office in Dallas on the plane that would carry him and the dead Kennedy back to Washington, D.C. Elected in his own right in 1964, over the Republican Barry Goldwater, Johnson set about getting social legislation supporting his Great Society through Congress. With all his success with Congress, Johnson was to be defeated by the war in Vietnam, as American involvement, initially an advisory group, escalated rapidly in the late 1960s to over 500,000 troops locked in a conflict that seemed to be without end or purpose. Opposition to the war became so fierce that it tore the country apart, and Johnson became the focal point of the opposition's outrage. He announced in 1968 that he would not seek another term.

An embattled Democratic party met in Chicago in 1968 and, amidst the militant antiwar demonstrators (many of them brutally beaten by police), nominated Johnson's vice president, Hubert Humphrey, for president. Richard Nixon, risen from the ashes of his defeat by Kennedy in 1960, took the Republican nomination and this time was victorious. His most notable achievement was the opening of relations with China by his visit there in 1972. He did not, however, end the involvement in Vietnam until some time after his reelection in 1972, when he secured a cease-fire and precipitately withdrew American troops. He had won the 1972 election by a landslide, but eventually a crime committed in June 1972 in the middle of the campaign — a break-in at the Democratic headquarters then established in a Washington office complex known as Watergate — was tracked to his top campaign assistants and to the White House itself. Nixon decided to resign his presidency in 1974 rather than undergo the impeachment proceedings approved by the House Judiciary Committee.

Earlier, in 1973, Nixon's vice president, Spiro Agnew, had been forced to resign because of corruption (accepting bribes), and had been replaced by a Michigan congressman, Gerald Ford. Ford found himself president in 1974, the first president never to have stood for general election. One of his first acts was to pardon Nixon for any of the federal crimes he committed, an act that lost him much of his initial popularity. In the election of 1976, Ford was defeated by Democrat Jimmy Carter, who had served as governor of Georgia and who seemed, by not being a part of the Washington bureaucracy, to be exactly what the country was looking for. Carter, however, was destined to be a one-term president. During his tenure, the inflation rate rose alarmingly. But of even greater importance was Carter's failure to resolve the crisis in 1979 when militant, government-supported Iranian "students" took over the American embassy in Teheran and held the embassy staff hostage. The hostages were not released until 1981, just after the inauguration of Carter's successor.

The former movie star and governor of California, Ronald Reagan, defeated Carter in the 1980 election and served two terms. He was seventy-three years old, the oldest man ever to be elected U.S. president. He had once been a liberal democrat and had supported Franklin Roosevelt during the Great Depression. But he had gradually moved to the far right and had become a leader of the Republican party's conservative wing. His greatest successes as president were the largest reduction of income taxes in history, the reform of the tax code, and the containment of inflation. One of his greatest failures was to preside over a budget that accumulated a deficit greater than all the deficits combined of all the presidents preceding him.

Reagan's immense personal popularity pulled him through one of his administration's greatest scandals—the Iran-Contra affair. In a secret operation run out of the White House, the United States sold weapons to Iran apparently in exchange for the release of U.S. hostages held in Lebanon; some of the money gained in this illegal sale was siphoned off to help the Nicaraguan guerrilla army (the "Contras") topple the Marxist Nicaraguan government, which had come into power after ousting the long-time, U.S.-supported dictator of Nicaragua, Anastasio Somoza. The extent of Reagan's knowledge of or involvement in the Iran-Contra affair remained ambiguous, in spite of various investigations. And with the election of Reagan's vice president, George Bush, to the presidency in 1988 over his opponent, Michael Dukakis, governor of Massachusetts, there seemed little likelihood of ultimate clarification.

THE SOCIAL SCENE: CONFORMITY AND REBELLION

The decades since the Second World War have been characterized by pendulum swings between periods of conformity and periods of rebellion, times of withdrawal and times of engagement. The 1950s were relatively quiet, the 1960s and 1970s explosive, and the 1980s a reversion to conformity, albeit more uneasy than before.

The Cold War, and a growing fear of Communism, spawned a political-social movement in the early 1950s known as McCarthyism, named after Wisconsin Senator Joseph R. McCarthy. His tactic was the smear, the unsubstantiated charge, that there were Communists holding high office in Washington. His senatorial immunity made it possible for him to make the wildest of accusations, but he made the mistake finally of attacking Eisenhower's Secretary of the Army. Eisenhower denounced him, and the Senate censured him in 1954. He died in 1956, but "McCarthyism" got into the dictionaries as synonymous with "witch-hunting" and the ruining of the reputation of others through innuendo and half-truths.

Perhaps because of the large numbers of veterans who were trying to "catch up" on the time they had lost in the armed forces, and who were seriously bent on building their civilian careers by entering schools, businesses, or corporations, and establishing their families, the 1950s appeared to become an age of conformity. The ideal American family of four owned a house in the suburbs, and the father commuted to work for the organization to which he had pledged his allegiance and life. The American dream was to fit in, contribute, work hard, and move ahead. The phenomenon of the individual who submerged his identity in that of his company became a subject for sociological study in *The Organization Man* (1956), by William S. Whyte. The counterpart in fiction had appeared in *The Man in the Gray Flannel Suit* (1955), by Sloan Wilson. The ideal of conformity spawned a movement of nonconformity, with its ideal—tune in, drop out, turn on. Allen Ginsberg's *Howl* (1956) and Jack Kerouac's *On the Road* (1957) became the bible and road map for those who rejected the status quo. They gathered for a brief time in the mid-1950s in San Francisco and were dubbed the "Beat Generation."

By the mid-1960s, after Kennedy's assassination and Lyndon Johnson's assumption of the presidency, followed by escalation of U.S. involvement in Vietnam, the quiescent mood of the 1950s seemed to be in the distant past. The civil rights movement, spurred on by the 1954 Supreme Court ruling that racial segregation in the schools was unconstitutional, had gathered momentum in the late 1950s and early 1960s. The black leader and apostle of civil disobedience, Martin Luther King, Jr., had led the way of nonviolent protest by marching in the streets to demand changes in law and custom. In 1963, over 200,000 "Freedom Marchers" gathered in Washington, D.C., to protest racism and heard King's famous "I Have a Dream" speech.

His methods were taken over by those opposed to the war in Vietnam, especially college students of draft-age who formed the Students for a Democratic Society (SDS). But their marches were not always peaceful. The antiwar movement reached something of a climax in the March on the Pentagon in 1967, led in part by novelist Norman Mailer and poet Robert Lowell. Lowell would later write poems about the experience. Mailer would write a best-selling account, *Armies of the Night* (1967), in which he characterized the event as "that historic moment when a mass citizenry—not much more than a mob—marched on a bastion which symbolized the military might of the Republic, marching not to capture it, but to wound it *symbolically.*"

Another movement of considerable significance found momentum during this period. Although women had joined men in the various causes, some began to notice that they did not enjoy equal rights even in organizations founded on the principles of equality. According to one account, when one black leader was asked by a female follower, "What is the position of women in the civil rights movement?" he answered, "Horizontal." In 1966, women demanding a plank on women's liberation were pelted with tomatoes and thrown out of a convention of the Students for a Democratic Society.

The National Organization of Women (NOW) was formed in 1966, one of whose founders was Betty Friedan, author of *The Feminine Mystique* (1963). Her book, as well as Kate Millett's *Sexual Politics* (1970) and a precursor book, *The Second Sex* (1949), by the French writer Simone de Beauvoir, raised feminist consciousness and challenged a patriarchal society. Gloria Steinem founded the journal *Ms.* in 1971. Such novelists as Erica Jong (*Fear of Flying*, 1973) and Alice Walker (*The Color Purple*, 1982) advanced the cause, as did a number of feminist poets, including Anne Sexton and Adrienne Rich.

The American involvement in Vietnam continued, though diminished, until 1975. In 1970, four students at Kent State University in Ohio, in a group gathered to protest the Vietnam War, were killed by National Guardsmen called out to maintain order. This outrage intensified opposition to the war. And as taking to the streets to protest became a way of life, the targets of protest multiplied. It was common for a protest rally to denounce not only the war, but nuclear weapons, police brutality, corrupt government, capitalistic exploitation of workers, government neglect of the poor, and discrimination because of race, gender, or sexual orientation. There were also periodical race riots, in which the black poor took to the streets to express their rage and frustration by acts of random vandalism, often accompanied by looting. Riots took place in Watts (Los Angeles) in 1965, in Detroit in 1967, and, after the assassination of Martin Luther King, Jr., in 1968, in Chicago and elsewhere.

In the early 1970s, America's involvement in Vietnam began gradually to decrease as contingents of American troops were removed. Nixon's resignation from office in 1974, together with the total withdrawal from Vietnam in 1975, removed from the scene two of the most tempting targets of street demonstrations. In a conciliatory move, President Carter offered a general amnesty in 1977 to those who had refused to fight in Vietnam, some of whom had gone into hiding, or to live abroad, or to prison. The war had been the galvanizing issue. Without it, the national temper shifted in the late 1970s, and the causes that had come together tended to splinter; protesting as a way of life began to fade. By the 1980s, the Reagan era, the pendulum had swung back to conformity. Students in the colleges seemed more interested in making it in the world than in making the world a perfect place.

In 1988, Ronald Reagan and Mikhail Gorbachev, representing the two superpowers, signed a treaty that—for the first time in history—provided for the actual dismantling and destruction of nuclear missiles on both sides. Although limited to medium-range missiles, the treaty was important both substantively and symbolically. By the time George Bush had his first meeting as president with Gorbachev in the fall of 1989, the world was in process of an extraordinary transition.

Gorbachev, who was born in 1931 and had come to power in the Soviet Union in 1985, had gradually instituted his policies of *glasnost* (openness) and *perestroika* (restructuring), bringing significant elements of democracy into the Soviet Union. By the end of 1989, his policies, together with strong national protest movements, made possible radical changes in the satellites of the Soviet empire in Eastern Europe. First a non-Communist government was installed in Poland, followed by the toppling of oppressive Communist governments in Hungary, East Germany, Czechoslovakia, Bulgaria, and Rumania. The most emotionally charged of all Cold War symbols, the Berlin wall, began to crumble, and the reunification of Germany became inevitable. At the beginning of the 1990s, the Cold War appeared to be over, and a new world seemed to be emerging, no longer divided between and dominated by the two superpowers.

INTELLECTUAL CURRENTS: EXISTENTIALISM, ECOLOGY, ENTROPY

The most vital popular philosophical movement of the postwar period was existentialism, imported from France, but given a pragmatic twist in its American guise. Jean-Paul Sartre and Albert Camus embodied the philosophy in their fiction, in such novels as Sartre's *Nausea* (1938) and Camus's *The Stranger* (1942), works widely read in America shortly after the Second World War. A key concept of existentialism is the absurdity of the human condition, and the challenge for the individual is to act in the world in "good faith," even in the full awareness of this absurdity. Existentialists believe that the "existence" of human beings precedes their "essence," not the other way around as in many other systems of thought. Thus individuals create their own moral essence by the decisions they make freely throughout their lives.

The French existentialists had been influenced in part by the American novelists William Faulkner, Ernest Hemingway, and John Dos Passos, and in their turn influenced a new generation of novelists appearing after the war, such as Ralph Ellison (*Invisible Man*, 1952) and John Barth (*The Floating Opera*, 1956). The influence of existentialism in the United States is, thus, another example of America's cultural past flowing into its future hidden in foreign imports. In the nineteenth century, Edgar Allan Poe had been taken over by the French, absorbed by their symbolist movement — and then artfully shipped back to America via the symbolist influence on the American modernists, such as the poet T. S. Eliot.

Another important array of attitudes that came to the fore in the postwar period may be loosely identified as "ecological concerns." These concerns developed because of advances in "ecology" — the study of the interactions between organisms and their environment, between people and the world they inhabit. Whereas America had spent the first centuries of its existence clearing the wilderness and conquering a continent, the last few decades have brought the realization that the earth is a finite resource that can be destroyed. Rachel Carson in *Silent Spring* (1963) pointed out that the increasing use of insecticides was infecting the entire ecosystem, ultimately poisoning the poisoners. The population of America in 1940, some 130 million, had doubled by the late 1980s. And the population of other countries, like China, was exploding at a far faster rate. What would become of "civilization" when the earth's resources could no longer stretch to feed, house, and clothe the multitudes?

Daily newspapers deliver the bad news. The rain forests are disappearing at an incredibly fast rate. The ozone layer that protects the earth from the sun's ultraviolet rays is ripped open and disappearing. The seas along with their shores are becoming contaminated by indiscriminate dumping of poisons in and on them. Nuclear waste, with its long and sinister life, cannot safely be disposed of anywhere on the globe, yet it increases constantly. The accumulation of an affluent society's ordinary garbage is growing at such an alarming rate that soon the globe itself might become one large garbage dump. This possibility was dramatized in the late 1980s when the mass media focused on a barge, heaped with refuse, setting out from the east coast of the United States and wandering the globe in forlorn search of a country willing to be a dumping ground; it finally brought the garbage back to its place of accumulation.

Is it possible that, if the world is able to escape nuclear destruction in a third World War, it will die a slow death through systemic poisoning or submergence in mountains of garbage? Such novelists as Saul Bellow and John Updike have provided in their novels vivid descriptions of the accumulated debris and detritus choking their urban settings. Such poets as W. S. Merwin and Gary Snyder have written hauntingly of the destruction of their environment by the very people so dependent on it.

"And Darkness and Decay and the Red Death held illimitable dominion over all," Edgar Allan Poe had written at the end of his story "The Masque of the Red Death" (1843); his bizarre imagination may have provided in fiction a hint of the way earth's end may turn out in reality. The second law of thermodynamics, formulated in the nineteenth century, postulated the "heat death" of the universe because of its tendency to attain a state of inert uniformity, or stasis, in which all matter is at a uniform temperature. A new postwar writer, Thomas Pynchon, embraced the scientific concept as a major theme in his work, beginning with his short story "Entropy," first published in 1960. By the time he took it over, after reading Henry Adams and others, the word had already been adapted to historical and social contexts.

The idea of entropy, from the apocalyptic vision of the heat death of the world to the portrayal of conversational exchanges devoid of meaning, has infiltrated both postwar fiction and criticism. Entropy has been applied to all areas of human activity involving expenditure of energy — intellectual, imaginative, and physical. In an entirely entropic society, it is possible to envision utterly hollow individuals, in an entanglement of empty social relationships, muttering meaningless words — all in a world gradually winding its way down to stasis and the blessed heat death. That favorite word of the existentialists, "absurdity," seems appropriate also for this ultimate common doom envisioned by those obsessed with the "entropic vision."

POETRY: PLURALISM AND ITS PLEASURES

In *Modern Poetry and the End of an Era*, published in 1966, Robert Penn Warren, holder of Pulitzer Prizes in both fiction and poetry, opened with the announcement:

> The collected editions are now settled comfortably on the shelves, some, even, gathering a little dust. The authors of some of those books are dead. We are witnessing, in other words, the end of a poetic era, the end of "modernism," that school of which the Founding Fathers were Eliot, Pound, and Yeats. . . . The fall of the regime of modernism had been in the making a long time. The storm warnings were out. Whenever insight fails, when the fluidity of life puddles and hardens into orthodoxy, when personal styles become period style, then the time is ripe for change. There is an organic necessity for revolt, as natural as the rhythm of the seasons. The world changes, the tonality of experience changes, and we seek a language adequate to the new experience.

In looking over the poets who were replacing the modernists, Warren observed: "These poets do not constitute a group, a school. I see nothing to put them into the same package, except a drive toward individualism — a tendency toward the personal subject, the personal observation, the emotional response to personal fate, in contrast to the emphasis one found in the last age on the public nature of the poet's predicament and on the crisis of culture." Warren approved of the "pluralism and diversity" he found in poetry: "In fact, a reader should not make one, exclusive demand on poetry — seek merely one kind of satisfaction. Certainly, poetry as art should feed his love for the richness and variety of life, should broaden his sympathies, mollify his dogmatisms, and introduce him to imagination as the great 'as-if' of truth. But poetry as prophecy gives him the image of truth as a way to be, see, or live, quite literally with no 'as-if' attached. We need art, and we need prophecy."

Even as we near the end of the twentieth century, Warren's observations appear still to apply to the poetic scene. Pluralism and diversity are still the rule, and no one figure has come to dominate the scene, as, for example, T. S. Eliot once presided over the domain of modernism. There have been identifiable groups of poets with a variety of labels — the Beat poets, the Confessional poets, the Black Mountain poets, the New York poets, the Deep Image poets, the Feminist poets. And there have been clusters of poets identified by their region (South, Midwest, West) or their authenticity (black, Chicano, Asian-American, Native American). But no one group has succeeded in establishing a hegemony over the poetic domain. Such impressive poets as Elizabeth Bishop and Robert

Lowell escape all categories since no label fits them exactly or comprehensively; with them as examples, we should be cautious in grouping poets loosely or rigidly, well aware of their unique, unclassifiable qualities.

Before Warren declared the end of the modernist period, an influential anthology, *The New American Poetry*, edited by Donald M. Allen, had appeared in 1960, containing many of the founders of the schools and movements together with allied poets; and a companion volume, *The Poetics of the New American Poetry*, edited by Donald M. Allen and Warren Tallman, was to appear in 1973, bringing together statements and manifestoes.

First on the scene, coming to the fore in the latter 1950s in San Francisco, were the Beats. The name has its appropriate ambiguities — beaten down? beaten up? upbeat? beatific? All the meanings, from "exhausted" or "defeated" to "blessed" or "saintly," appeared applicable. The Beat poets rallied around the easterner Allen Ginsberg when his first book of poems, *Howl* (1956), was charged with obscenity; he was found innocent by the California courts in 1957. The trial made the Beats famous and they became popular readers of their poetry on college campuses. One of them, Gary Snyder, came out of the American Northwest of forests and mountains and brought to the movement his serious interest in Zen Buddhism; he would spend some twelve years studying Zen in Japan. Other Beats who enjoyed popularity were Gregory Corso and Lawrence Ferlinghetti, and their famous fictionist was Jack Kerouac, whose *On the Road* appeared in 1957. The Beats found their tradition flowing from the free verse and long lines of Walt Whitman and were enthusiastically endorsed by that "alternate" and somewhat subversive modernist William Carlos Williams.

Next on the scene were the Confessional poets, never coming together literally as a movement, but nevertheless following intuitively similar paths in their careers. There were obvious forerunners, poets of the past (Whitman, for example) whose verses contained some elements of personal revelation. But the first confessional poet of the contemporary movement was Robert Lowell, who in 1959 broke away from his own established career (he had already won a Pulitzer Prize) and wrote in a different way in *Life Studies*. His new style was more direct and simple and focused on his personal situation, particularly his hospitalizations for mental illness, his suicidal impulses, his failures in personal relationships, his intimate feelings about the people in his life.

There had been a strong confessional component in the poetry of the Beats. Ginsberg, for example, spoke openly in his poems about the taking of drugs, his homosexuality, and his sex life. Lowell maintained more control over his poetic forms and had less in the way of scandal to confess. His confessional poetry had more in common with that of Sylvia Plath, who wrote many of her best poems after the break-up of her marriage in England and before she committed suicide in 1963. These late poems did not appear until publication of her volume *Ariel*, in 1966, with an introduction by Robert Lowell which in effect invited the reader to view them as a collective suicide note: "These poems are playing Russian roulette with six cartridges in the cylinder."

Many of the other poets of this period wrote poems that could only be called personal, but the poets who have most frequently been identified as confessional are Anne Sexton and John Berryman, both of whom, like Plath, ended their own lives. Like Lowell, Berryman had started out as one kind of poet, but made himself over into another, especially with the last great work he produced, *The Dream Songs*, finished and put together as a whole in 1969. He jumped off a bridge to his death in 1972. Anne Sexton, who began to write poetry on the advice of her therapist, found the creative activity a stabilizing element in her life. She had met Sylvia Plath in a poetry class taught by Robert Lowell at Boston University in the late 1950s. Her first book, *To Bedlam and Part Way Back* (1960), was an account of her stay and treatment in an asylum; she won the Pulitzer Prize for her *Live or Die*, published in 1966.

The Black Mountain poets, though earlier in gathering, were later in establishing their presence. They came together at an experimental liberal arts school, Black Mountain College, in the mountains near Asheville, North Carolina, where the poet Charles Olson went to teach in 1948 and served as rector (or head) from 1951 to 1956. Olson published his manifesto, "Projective Verse," in 1950, calling for "Field Composition," in which the poet "puts himself in the open," writing poems that are a means of transferring energy from "where the poet got it" to the reader. The college attracted artists from all fields, including the musician of silences John Cage, the artists Franz Kline and Robert Rauschenberg, and the modern dance choreographer Merce Cunningham.

The principal poets associated with this group, besides Olson himself, were Robert Creeley and Denise Levertov. They were brought by Olson to Black Mountain College as teachers; Creeley founded and edited the *Black Mountain Review*. The Black Mountain poets shared much with the Beat poets in both substance and method. Like the Beats, they were rebels against the "establishment," on the side of freedom, against imposed or traditional restraints. And also like the Beats, they looked not to T. S. Eliot but to the "alternative" modernists William Carlos Williams and Ezra Pound as their forerunners.

The best known of the New York poets are Frank O'Hara and John Ashbery. The group also included Kenneth Koch and James Schuyler and was closely associated with a number of New York painters, including Willem de Kooning, Franz Kline, and Jackson Pollock. The New York poets were first brought together in a widely noticed anthology published in 1969, *The Poets of the New York School*, edited by John Bernard Myers. Influences flowed both ways, from poetry to painting, and from painting to poetry. The New York poets attempted, sometimes like the surrealists in visualizing the unconscious, sometimes like Jackson Pollock in "action painting," to capture the elusive truth buried in interior depths or in the successive moments of "now" that constitute one's "real" life.

Their poems seemed to say: now I do this, now I feel elated, now I see through the window, now I feel a hangover, now I take a walk, now I remember a dream, now I do that. A fragment of the perpetual present in which they lived, put down on paper, became the poem, a vignette of life snatched from the unceasing rush of it. Frank O'Hara seemed to stay more on the surface, while John Ashbery mined the deeper levels of consciousness. Ashbery admired the exotic imagery and linguistic wit of the modernist Wallace Stevens, but found his own distinctive techniques. Reading a poem by him is like intently observing the erratic and often incoherent directions of one's own interior stream of consciousness. There is, when the poems are genuinely engaged, a succession of shocks of self-recognition.

The Deep Image poets took their name from a term coined by poets Robert Kelly and Jerome Rothenberg, and elaborated by Kelly in "Notes on the Poetry of Deep Image" (1961). The "deep image" came not from outer reality, as in the earlier "imagism," but from an inner reality, the mysterious sources of the unconscious. The theory found its roots not in Freudian derangement (as had surrealism) but in the Jungian collective unconscious. Robert Bly, one of the movement's chief theoreticians, called for a "poetry which disregards the conscious and the intellectual structure of the mind entirely and by the use of images tries to bring forward another reality from *inward* experience."

Deep Image poets found models among such Latin American poets as the Chilean Pablo Neruda and Peruvian César Vallejo. Associated with this movement, in addition to Bly, were James Wright and W. S. Merwin (Bly and Wright collaborated in translations of Neruda and Vallejo). A major influence on them was America's nineteenth-century epic poet Walt Whitman, who had repeatedly been the subject of attacks by modernist poets. In an important essay, James Wright wrote in praise of what he called "The Delicacy of Whitman": "I mean [by 'delicacy'] to suggest powers of restraint, clarity, and wholeness, all of which taken together embody that deep spiritual inwardness, that fertile strength, which I take to be the most beautiful power of Whitman's poetry, and the most readily available to the poetry, and indeed the civilization, of our own moment in American history."

Feminism had a major impact on postwar poetry, as it did on all forms of literature. The most militant of the feminist poets of the period was Adrienne Rich, who came finally to use the redefined words "lesbian/feminist" interchangeably to describe her position. But other prominent poets of the period — Gwendolyn Brooks, Denise Levertov, Anne Sexton, Sylvia Plath, Nikki Giovanni, Louise Glück, Leslie Marmon Silko, and Rita Dove — provided a woman's vision of herself, her identity, her role in society, and her relationship with others. Accompanying this new awareness and sensitivity was a new interest in rescuing "lost" women poets of the past and in reexamining those who had been left largely to male critics. Rich, for example, provided fresh ways of seeing the seventeenth-century poet Anne Bradstreet and the nineteenth-century poet Emily Dickinson.

The pluralism of the period was evident from the variety of ethnic groups represented in poetry, as well as the diversity of the country's regions from which the poets came. Robert Hayden, Gwendolyn Brooks, Imamu Amiri Baraka (LeRoi Jones), Michael Harper, Nikki Giovanni, and Rita Dove were important and varied black voices; Karl Shapiro, Denise Levertov, and Allen Ginsberg were equally varied Jewish voices. Simon J. Ortiz and Leslie Marmon Silko found the sources of their poems and stories in their Native American heritage. The relatively young Gary Soto came out of a Mexico/California Chicano background. The New York poets were balanced by midwestern and western voices: Theodore Roethke, associated by birth or long residence with Michigan and Washington, William Stafford with Kansas and Oregon, James Wright with Ohio and Washington, and Gary Snyder with Oregon and Japan. John Berryman was born in Oklahoma, Randall Jarrell in Tennessee.

The postwar poets were separated by the schools to which they belonged or the geographical spaces they inhabited, yet they were often banded together in public causes. Although the period is known for its intensely personal poetry, it also produced much poetry aimed at public or political issues. Karl Shapiro and Randall Jarrell wrote out of their experiences in the armed forces a poetry about the horrors — or boredom — of war. It was, however, the Vietnam War, dominating public consciousness from the mid-1960s to the mid-1970s, that turned even apolitical poets political, involving them in marches and poetry readings against the war.

Robert Bly was one of the most energetic in bringing poets together against the war. He edited *A Poetry Reading Against the Vietnam War*, published in 1966, including contributions by (among others) James Wright, William Stafford, and

Robert Creeley. Bly wrote in a 1967 essay, "Leaping Up into Political Poetry": "A true political poem is a quarrel with ourselves, and the rhetoric is as harmful in that sort of poet as in the personal poem. The true political poem does not order us either to take any specific acts: like the personal poem, it moves to deepen awareness. . . . Whitman was the first true political poet we had in North America."

Although the postwar poets ushered in a new and pluralistic age in American poetry, there were clear continuities with the past, identified particularly in their redefinition of the tradition to which they were allied. Walt Whitman re-assumed his central place in the development of American poetry. And the unique form in which Whitman had pioneered with his complexly unified work *Leaves of Grass*—the lyric epic—continued to be a possible form for many of the most ambitious of the new poets. With the example of *Leaves of Grass* from the nineteenth century, and with Ezra Pound's *Cantos*, William Carlos Williams's *Paterson*, Hart Crane's *The Bridge*, and H. D.'s *Trilogy* from the modernist period, a number of the postwar poets undertook similar poetic journeys, focusing on themselves as their own epic heroes.

Impressive examples of these varied long works were Charles Olson's *Maximus Poems*, John Berryman's *Dream Songs*, Allen Ginsberg's *The Fall of America*, Robert Lowell's *Notebook*, A. R. Ammons's *Sphere: The Form of a Motion*, and James Merrill's *The Changing Light at Sandover*. The poetic vitality evident in these long works, sometimes requiring most of a lifetime to complete, and the poetic energy with which the best short poems of the postwar period are charged, all present convincing evidence that the poetic spirit is alive and well in "These States," as Whitman had hoped and prophesied.

FICTION: FROM HERE TO ABSURDITY

At the end of the Second World War, a number of works appeared indicating that this war would be portrayed in fiction much as had the First in John Dos Passos's *Three Soldiers* (1921) and Ernest Hemingway's *A Farewell to Arms* (1929). Norman Mailer's *The Naked and the Dead* (1948) depicted the war in a long, naturalistic novel as it had been fought against the Japanese on a Pacific island. Irwin Shaw's *The Young Lions* (1948) gave an equally detailed and vivid account of the war as it was fought against the German Nazis in Europe. James Jones's *From Here to Eternity* (1951) similarly treated the prewar period in the army in Hawaii, up through the devastating attack by the Japanese on Pearl Harbor, December 7, 1941.

All these novels were widely read and admired, but they very seldom are mentioned now in discussions of postwar fiction. If the question of war novels arises, the discussion is most likely to be about three other novels: Joseph Heller's *Catch-22* (1961), Kurt Vonnegut's *Slaughterhouse-Five: or The Children's Crusade* (1969), and Thomas Pynchon's *Gravity's Rainbow* (1973). The distance between the works by Mailer, Shaw, and Jones and the works by Heller, Vonnegut, and Pynchon is the distance between the old fiction and the new, the distance between a naturalistic and familiar world and a world become alien and absurd. It is no coincidence that the young, those who did not experience the Second World War, have in the past tended to turn Heller, Vonnegut, and Pynchon into cult or underground novelists, reading them not for their revelations about the war but for the bizarre nature of life as it is experienced daily.

It was not until the 1960s that Americans began to realize how radically their fiction had changed. Not all of the elements in it were without precedent, of course, but the elements all came together in new and astonishing ways. The new novelists could certainly feel an affinity with Herman Melville's Ishmael, when, in a key scene in *Moby-Dick* (1851), right after he has been abandoned at sea and rescued only by accident, he says: "There are certain queer times and occasions in this strange mixed affair we call life when a man takes this whole universe for a vast practical joke, though the wit thereof he but dimly discerns, and more than suspects that the joke is at nobody's expense but his own." The major components of the new fiction were a nightmare world, alienation and nausea, quest for identity, and humor in the horror.

1. *A Nightmare World*: In *Catch-22*, the soldier "hero," Yossarian, wanders at night in liberated Rome: "The night was filled with horrors and he thought he knew how Christ must have felt as he walked through the world, like a psychiatrist through a ward full of nuts, like a victim through a prison full of thieves. What a welcome sight a leper must have been! At the next corner a man was beating a small boy brutally in the midst of an immobile crowd of adult spectators who made no effort to intervene. Yossarian recoiled with sickening recognition." Such images of senseless brutality as this abound not only in *Catch-22* but throughout contemporary fiction; the sinister lurks in the familiar, hatred hides in a package of love, and our fondest dreams explode in our hands as we look on in horror.

2. *Alienation and Nausea*: There are no heroes in contemporary fiction. Everybody loses, nobody wins. If, for example, we take Ken Kesey's *One Flew Over the Cuckoo's Nest* (1962) as a paradigm of the modern predicament, we find the entire world a nuthouse, with Big Nurse in her stiff, starched white, imposing her power through the use of all her gleaming, glittering, flashing machinery. And her power completes the degradation and dehumanization of her victims, who are efficiently divided into two groups: the "hopeful" Acutes, who "move around a lot. They tell jokes to each other and snicker in their fists . . . and they write letters with yellow, runty, chewed pencils"; and the hopeless Chronics, who are the culls of the Acutes—the "Chronics are in for good . . . [and] are divided into Walkers . . . and Wheelers and Vegetables." The great fear of the Acute is to become a Chronic, as has happened to one Ellis, who came back from the "brain-murdering room," or the "Shock Shop," "nailed against the wall in the same condition they lifted him off the table the last time, in the same shape, arms out, palms cupped, with the same horror on his face. He's nailed like that on the wall, a stuffed trophy. They pull the nails when it's time to eat." Ellis may be one version of modern human beings, hopeless, helpless, self-crucified, committed for life to a super-efficient asylum that destroys what it cannot dehumanize.

3. *Quest for Identity*: Although the search for the self runs deep in American literature, as might be expected in a country not at all sure of its own identity or soul, the quest takes on a new poignancy in the contemporary novel. The unnamed black protagonist of Ralph Ellison's *Invisible Man* (1952), at one point on the downward spiral of his fortunes, after the explosion of the bubbling paint-vat in the white-paint factory, is swimming back to consciousness and sees the words looming above him: "Who . . . are . . . you?" He remembers: "Something inside me turned with a sluggish excitement. This phrasing of the question seemed to set off a series of weak and distant lights. . . . Who am I? I asked myself. But it was like trying to identify one particular cell that coursed through the torpid veins of my body. Maybe I was just this blackness and bewilderment and pain. . . ." The question "Who are you?" resounds through all contemporary

fiction—and frequently remains, at the end of the road, unanswered and perhaps unanswerable.

4. *Humor in the Horror*: Both *Catch-22* and *Gravity's Rainbow* are astonishingly funny works, their black humor deriving from the very horrors of the war with which they deal. Every time Yossarian accumulates enough flight missions to be eligible to be discharged, he discovers that there is a new regulation increasing the number required. And even if there is no new regulation, there is the catch-all regulation, Catch-22, which can be used to deny any request at any time of whatever kind. At the close of *Gravity's Rainbow*, we the readers ("who've always been at the theater") are the target toward which gravity is pulling down the rocket from its perfect rainbow arch made since its launching (hence, gravity's rainbow). As we wait unaware of our doom, Pynchon advises us to "follow the bouncing ball" in the singing of a hymn. The novel ends with a dash ("Now everybody— "), suggestive, not of the beginning of song, but of final annihilation.

Although the Second World War, with its atom bomb and holocaust, caused novelists to see reality in new and more complex dimensions, the very nature of postwar American life posed further challenges. In 1961, novelist Philip Roth said: "The American writer in the middle of the twentieth century has his hands full in trying to understand, describe, and then make *credible* much of American reality. It stupefies, it sickens, it unfuriates, and finally it is even a kind of embarrassment to one's own meager imagination. The actuality is continually outdoing our talents, and the culture tosses up figures almost daily that are the envy of any novelist." With television, widespread in America after the war, bringing fragments of that "reality" into living rooms daily, it is no wonder that novelists felt such competition.

Novelist John Barth made the case for new strategies in fiction, not only because of the perception of a new reality, but also because the old fictional techniques were dated and no longer worked. He said in 1967 in "The Literature of Exhaustion": "Beethoven's Sixth Symphony or the Chartres Cathedral if executed today would be merely embarrassing. A good many current novelists write turn-of-the-century-type novels, only in more or less mid-twentieth-century language and about contemporary people and topics; this makes them considerably less interesting (to me) than excellent writers who are also technically contemporary: Joyce and Kafka, for instance, in their time, and in ours, [Irish-French novelist] Samuel Beckett and [Argentine fiction writer] Jorge Luis Borges."

In 1980, in an important essay entitled "The Literature of Replenishment: Postmodernist Fiction," Barth elaborated and explained his earlier essay, calling for "a fiction more democratic in its appeal. . . . The ideal postmodernist novel will somehow rise above the quarrel between realism and irrealism, formalism and 'contentism,' pure and committed literature, coterie fiction and junk fiction." His new models had become the Italian fantasist or fabulist Italo Calvino and the Latin American novelist Gabriel García Márquez, whose works (like *One Hundred Years of Solitude*, 1967) were created out of a "synthesis of straightforwardness and artifice, realism and magic and myth, political passion and nonpolitical artistry, characterization and caricature, humor and terror."

Such statements as those of Roth and Barth suggest the changes that were coming about in American fiction in the decades after the war. For writers who felt that the techniques of realism no longer served, there was a movement to fable and fantasy, and to a foregrounding of language (language calling attention to itself); this movement led to self-referential fiction, in which the novelist commented on the writing of the story *in* the story itself. Important examples of such works were Vladimir Nabokov's *Pale Fire* (1962), John Barth's *Giles Goatboy* (1966), Donald Barthelme's *Snow White* (1967), and Kurt Vonnegut's *Slaughterhouse-Five* (1969). Perhaps the most extreme of these works was *Snow White*, in which language itself became the center of interest, serving simultaneously as protagonist and antagonist, and carrying (with its outrageous puns and non sequiturs) the only significant action (or "plot").

But there were other writers who felt that, since the techniques of realism seemed no longer to serve (some even declared the novel dead), the best alternative was to turn to the techniques of journalism, to write about actual events with all the art of a novelist. One successful fiction writer, Truman Capote, gave up the traditional novel form for this new form, which he dubbed the "non-fiction novel." This term, even though — perhaps because — it is paradoxical, captured the spirit of this paradoxical form, which owed something to the documentary film, similar in spirit and intent. Classic examples of this form were Truman Capote's *In Cold Blood* (1966), about the murder of a farm family in Kansas; Norman Mailer's *Armies of the Night* (1968), about the 1967 March on the Pentagon protesting the Vietnam War; Alex Haley's *Roots* (1970), about the author's own ancestors, traced back through slaves to their origins in Africa; Maxine Hong Kingston's *The Woman Warrior* (1976), about her family and ancestors and the China myths by which they lived; and Tom Wolfe's *The Right Stuff* (1979), about the first manned American space flight.

Not all fiction writers chose to become fabulists or documentary journalists, self-referential (or narcissistic) fantasists, or nonfiction novelists. Indeed, some of the most successful believed that many of the techniques and values of traditional fiction continued to serve, though refurbished and renewed. Prominent among them, and considered by many critics as one of the most "conservative," was the only American Nobel laureate among the postwar novelists, Saul Bellow. His Nobel Prize did not authenticate his superiority, but it testified at the least to a considerable worldwide readership that found his novels engaged with postwar realities. In 1966, he decried the amorality and the "debris of modernism, with apocalyptic leftovers added" in postwar fiction, adding defiantly, "There are friendships, affinities, natural feelings, rooted norms. People do on the whole agree . . . that it is wrong to murder. . . . It seems to me that writers might really do well to start thinking about such questions again."

Bellow concluded: "A final word about the avant-garde. To labor to create vanguard conditions is historicism. . . . genius is always, without strain, avant-garde. Its departure from tradition is not the result of caprice or of policy but of an inner necessity." Novelists who agreed with Bellow, directly or intuitively, were in no sense "old-fashioned," but succeeded in capturing, with their familiar methods but unique applications and voices, a good deal of American reality. Some of the notable examples were Ralph Ellison in *Invisible Man* (1952), Flannery O'Connor in *Wise Blood* (1952), Saul Bellow in *Mr. Sammler's Planet* (1970), and John Updike in the Rabbit tetralogy: *Rabbit, Run* (1960), *Rabbit Redux* (1971), *Rabbit Is Rich* (1981), and *Rabbit at Rest* (1990).

Although a number of postwar writers turned away from what they took to be traditional "realism," they did not turn away from their attempt to delineate "reality." Indeed, it was the challenge of the mind-blowing nature of postwar reality, together with a growing awareness of the fragility of language in wrestling with that reality, that inspired them to develop new strategies to capture it. The fantasy of stories like Donald Bartheme's "The Balloon," or self-referentiality of narratives like John Barth's "Lost in the Funhouse," or linguistic artifice of accounts like William Gass's "In the Heart of the Heart of the Country"—all are attempts to ambush an elusive reality, slip up on it slyly, and pin it to the earth before it slithers away out of reach.

Those writers who turned not to fantasy and linguistic fireworks but to actual events in their writing were attempting to make a frontal attack on, and wholesale capture of, reality, to embody in their work what "really happened" and could not therefore be challenged by a skeptical reader. Examples are Jack Kerouac's personal account of the development of an important literary movement, "The Origins of the Beat Generation"; Norman Mailer's report of his and others' participation in the March on the Pentagon, *Armies of the Night*; N. Scott Momaday's story of the mysteries of his Kiowa ancestors, *The Way to Rainy Mountain*. Such works recreate the historical reality of an actual personal, familial, or public event or episode, not through use of a journalistic style but by employment of a novelist's art.

Writers who chose to continue use of traditional fictional techniques, but often with a twist—or even with a dash of the avant-garde from the fantasists or nonfiction novelists—were and are widely read because of their remarkable artistic achievement in using the old tried and true ways of confronting the new, recalcitrant reality. Prominent examples of these works are Tillie Olsen's "I Stand Here Ironing," Ralph Ellison's "King of the Bingo Game," Carson McCullers's "The Ballad of the Sad Cafe," Shirley Jackson's "The Lottery," James Baldwin's "Sonny's Blues," John Updike's "Pigeon Feathers," and Alice Walker's "Everyday Use."

Most recently, a new fictional movement has come over the horizon—minimalism. In a 1985 issue of the *Mississippi Review*, minimalism was said to be characterized by "equanimity of surface, 'ordinary subjects,' recalcitrant narrators and deadpan narratives, slightness of story, and characters who don't think out loud." In attempts to describe the minimalists, one writer, Lee K. Abbott, said: "As I see it, our minimalist brothers and sisters inhabit the journalist's wing of Mr. [Henry] James's hallowed house of fiction. They're reporters—and damn good ones, for the most part—but they're giving us news that was old even when the center couldn't hold and when Bethlehem saw the first of many beasts. One way or another, they give the old headlines—that we're all morally frozen, that we can't talk to one another, that the brutes are loose again." Another writer, Linsey Abrams, commented that "minimalist fiction delivers wisdom in the manner of a Zen koan: either you get it or you don't."

Raymond Carver, one of those listed as a prominent minimalist, wrote: "In a review of my last book, somebody called me a 'minimalist' writer. The reviewer meant it as a compliment. But I didn't like it. There's something about 'minimalist' that smacks of smallness of vision and execution that I don't like." In spite of this disclaimer, the label seems to have stuck, covering Carver as well as Bobbie Ann Mason and Ann Beattie. Whether the term by which they are called endures, the minimalist writers are important as a reaction to narcissistic and self-reflexive fiction, or (as Vladimir Nabokov once called his work) "riddles with elegant solutions."

One prominent characteristic of postwar fiction is its ethnic diversity. Langston Hughes and Richard Wright had led the way for black writers before the war. After the war, such black fiction writers as Ralph Ellison, James Baldwin, Alice Walker, and Toni Morrison came into prominence. Jewish writers came into their own as never before and include Bernard Malamud, Saul Bellow, Norman Mailer, John Barth, and Philip Roth. Southern writers—including Carson

McCullers, Flannery O'Connor, Truman Capote, and Bobbie Ann Mason — continued to make a strong contribution to American fiction, mining that marvelous vein of southern Gothic that seems inexhaustible. Other ethnic groups found their voices: N. Scott Momaday, William Least Heat Moon, and Louise Erdrich, Native American; Richard Rodriguez, Mexican-American; Maxine Hong Kingston, Chinese-American. Few other countries could find such rich diversity in their contemporary writers; such diversity represents for America a national literary treasure.

THE NEW DRAMA: ABSURD AND OTHERWISE

During the earlier part of the twentieth century, live or "legitimate" theater declined with the rapid rise of the movies and opulent motion picture palaces as the primary source and place for mass entertainment. Broadway, no longer a center for production of serious drama, became instead a center for expensive, splashy musicals aimed at audiences of out-of-town business executives on large expense accounts. Broadway's eclipse accelerated after the Second World War with the quick spread of television, bringing popular entertainment into the living room. The movies, too, suffered, and the movie palaces fell into neglect in the decaying inner cities.

But television presented a great opportunity for film makers, with a sense of the medium as an art form, to experiment more boldly in the making of pictures. Just as talented dramatists and novelists had written for the movies earlier, so television attracted some excellent writers. Paddy Chayefsky's *Marty* was produced on TV in 1953, and turned into a film in 1955; he went on to become an acclaimed playwright, writing for television, the movies, and the legitimate theater. Neil Simon, a fine master of comedy, followed a similar path, beginning in television.

With the diminishing interest in serious drama on Broadway, off-Broadway theaters came into being in and around Greenwich Village, sometimes in rickety buildings otherwise unusable. When a play proved itself financially sound, it often was moved from off-Broadway to Broadway. But gradually off-Broadway itself was stricken with the same box-office disease as Broadway, and there developed in response the off-off-Broadway theaters, established in scattered locations, sometimes in church basements. A number of resident professional companies sprang up around the country, such as the Actors Workshop in San Francisco and the Guthrie Theater in Minneapolis. Drama was also kept alive in community and university theaters, where amateurs often joined with professionals in the production of plays. All of these alternatives to Broadway became places where new playwrights could get a hearing.

After the war, Eugene O'Neill continued to be the major playwright in the American theater, even after his death in 1953. He had written and set aside a number of plays during the late 1930s and the war years of the early 1940s. *The Iceman Cometh*, produced in 1946, revived his reputation; *Long Day's Journey into Night*, produced in 1956, together with *Hughie* and *A Touch of the Poet* in 1958, reestablished him as America's foremost playwright. Although the poet T. S. Eliot had had two plays produced during the 1930s, it was not until after the war that he became a much admired and popular playwright, especially with *The Cocktail Party* in 1949 and *The Confidential Clerk* in 1953. Another poet, Archibald MacLeish, surprised his readers by writing *J. B.*, a successful serious play about Job, produced in 1958.

Like contemporary poetry and fiction, contemporary drama attracted talented women writers who expanded the imaginative possibilities of the genre. Lillian Hellman had made a reputation in the 1930s, especially with *The Little Foxes* in 1939. During and after the war her reputation was enhanced by *Watch on the Rhine* (1941) and *Toys in the Attic* (1960). Among the important younger playwrights to come on the scene were Lorraine Hansberry, whose *Raisin in the Sun* (1959) portrayed life in a black Chicago ghetto; Beth Henley, whose *Crimes of the Heart* (1981) captivated audiences with its portrayal of odd characters in a small-town Mississippi family; and Marsha Norman, whose two-character play, *'Night, Mother* (1983), opening with the daughter's announcement of her intent to commit suicide and ending with fulfillment of the intent, created a sensation.

But the two most outstanding new playwrights to appear were Tennessee Williams and Arthur Miller. Tennessee Williams was a southerner and a homosexual, both facts important in the shaping of his dramas, usually set in the South and portraying the psycho-sexual complications and sometimes bizarre behavior of his complex characters. His first two plays to achieve success, *The Glass Menagerie* in 1945 and *A Streetcar Named Desire* in 1947, continue to be his most widely read and seen plays. He wrote a number of remarkable one-act plays, among the best of which is *Portrait of a Madonna* (1945).

Arthur Miller, a New Yorker and a Jew, was less interested in psychology than Williams and more interested in social conflict and economic problems. His two most popular plays proved to be *Death of a Salesman*, produced in 1949, portraying the shabby life of a travelling salesman who is a victim of his innocent belief in the American myth of easy wealth; and *The Crucible*, produced in 1953, a recreation of the witch-hunt madness in New England during the 1690s aimed as a parable at the contemporary witch-hunts of Senator Joseph McCarthy during the early 1950s. Miller also wrote one-act plays, one of which, *A Memory of Two Mondays* (1955), is perhaps his most personal and poignant play.

Williams, born in 1911, and Miller, born in 1915, had both been influenced and shaped imaginatively by the drama before the Second World War. At the time they were achieving success in the American theater after the war, there was a new kind of drama developing in Europe—the theater of the absurd. Eugene Ionesco's *The Bald Soprano* was produced in 1950, Samuel Beckett's *Waiting for Godot* in 1952, and Jean Genet's *The Balcony* in 1956. With the translation of these plays into English and production in America, interest in the theater of the absurd mushroomed. In 1961, Martin Esslin published *The Theatre of the Absurd*, identifying its central attitude as "its sense that the certitudes and unshakeable basic assumptions of former ages have been swept away, that they have been tested and found wanting, that they have been discredited as cheap and somewhat childish illusions."

Edward Albee was the first American playwright to establish himself as a full-fledged dramatist of the absurd. His first play to be staged was *The Zoo Story*, translated into German and produced in Berlin in 1959. It appeared in New York on a double-bill with Samuel Beckett's *Krapp's Last Tape* in an off-Broadway production in 1960. *The Zoo Story* portrays the meeting and bizarre conversation of two strangers in Central Park, one a middle-class conformist, the other a chronic outsider and nonconformist who tricks his new acquaintance into killing him. Albee's *The Sand Box* appeared in 1960 and *The American Dream* in 1961, both plays presenting as principal characters "Mommy," "Daddy," "Grandma," and "Young Man"—all involved in banal conversations and weird situations. These plays attracted a great deal of attention, but it was not until Albee produced

Who's Afraid of Virginia Woolf? in 1962 that his reputation was firmly established. Some critics have claimed that the play is really about two homosexual couples disguised as heterosexuals—an interpretation that Albee has denounced. Although considered America's best dramatist of the absurd, Albee went on to write plays that diverged widely from the absurdist formula. And he, like other American playwrights, found it difficult to match his early successes in the dramas produced in the latter part of his career.

With the fading into history of the theater of the absurd, the drama that has replaced it has become more diverse and less predictable in outlook. Sam Shepard and David Mamet are two of the most talented of the new playwrights, and both bear an abiding suspicion of Broadway, preferring off-off-Broadway productions in which they can maintain artistic control. Shepard is an actor of considerable talent, and a minor movie star, but he considers his serious vocation that of playwright. His work might be compared to that of the minimalists in fiction, in which very little in the way of action or dialogue is made to do a great deal in bringing about the dramatic effect he achieves. There is something of the improvisational in his rapid method of composition; perhaps even something of the "action painter" in his capturing inner, indefinable feelings, moods, or attitudes by getting them down quickly in the dialogue of a play. When asked about where his idea for a play came from, his answer was cryptic: "Ideas emerge from plays—not the other way around."

His *Action* was first produced in 1975, and presents four characters in a world that seems as strange to them as to the audience, engaged in what seem like incoherent or irrelevant exchanges—and very little of what the title might lead us to expect: action. With all of its ambiguities, the effect of the play is haunting and disturbing, leaving the viewer (or reader) in uneasy quiet. In all its strangeness, it appears to convey something deeply familiar. The drama critic, Richard Gilman, has written of Shepard: "Most of his plays seem like fragments, chunks of various sizes thrown out from some mother lode of urgent and heterogeneous imagination in which he has scrabbled with pick, shovel, gunbutt and hands." It is easy to agree with Gilman's overall assessment: "Not many critics would dispute the proposition that Sam Shepard is our most interesting and exciting American playwright."

Even though contemporary drama appears to be sent repeatedly into intensive care, with the end near, it has the will *not* to die, the will *to* live. There is an exciting something, vital and primal, that live actors on a stage can convey to an audience that cannot be conveyed through film or television. The remarkable American playwrights that have appeared since the war indicate that the theater will continue to attract first-rate literary talents, even if it means inventing an off-off-off-Broadway. Indeed, it may be that such a theater already exists in the many regional theaters around the country. For example, the Old Globe Theater in San Diego and the Steppenwolf Theater in Chicago have both premiered several productions that have gone on to successful runs on Broadway.

ADDITIONAL READING

GENERAL

Edmund Wilson, *Classics and Commercials: A Literary Chronicle of the Forties*, 1950.
Malcolm Cowley, ed., *Writers at Work: The Paris Review Interviews, Series I*, 1958 (see also *Series II–VII*, edited by various critics, in 1963, 1967, 1976, 1981, 1984, and 1986).

L. S. Dembo and Cyrena N. Pondrom, eds., *The Contemporary Writer: Interviews with Sixteen Novelists and Poets*, 1972.

John O'Brien, *Interviews with Black Writers*, 1973.

Irving Malin, *Contemporary American-Jewish Literature*, 1973.

George Garrett, ed., *The Writer's Voice: Conversations with Contemporary Writers Conducted by John Graham*, 1973.

Morris Dickstein, *Gates of Eden: American Culture in the Sixties*, 1977.

Angeline Jacobson, *Contemporary Native American Literature: A Selected & Partially Annotated Bibliography*, 1977.

Warner Berthoff, *A Literature Without Qualities: American Writing Since 1945*, 1979.

Daniel Hoffman, ed., *Harvard Guide to Contemporary Writing*, 1979.

Dexter Fisher, *The Third Woman: Minority Women Writers of the United States*, 1980.

Houston A. Baker, Jr., *Three American Literatures: Essays in Chicano, Native American, and Asian-American Literature for Teachers of American Literature*, 1982.

Paula Gunn Allen, *Studies in American Indian Literature: Critical Essays and Course Design*, 1983.

Kenneth Lincoln, *Native American Literature*, 1983.

Michael G. Cooke, *Afro-American Literature in the Twentieth Century: The Achievement of Intimacy*, 1984.

Claudia Tate, ed., *Black Women Writers at Work*, 1984.

Charles Ruas, *Conversations with American Writers*, 1985.

Julio A. Martinez and Francisco A. Lomeli, *Chicano Literature: A Reference Guide*, 1985.

Roger O. Rock, *The Native American in American Literature: A Selectively Annotated Bibliography*, 1985.

Larry McCaffery and Sinda Gregory, eds., *Alive and Writing: Interviews with American Authors of the 1980s*, 1987.

Jo Brans, *Listen to the Voices: Conversations with Contemporary Writers*, 1988.

Michiko Kakutani, *The Poet at the Piano: Portraits of Writers, Filmmakers, Playwrights, and Other Artists at Work*, 1988.

Emory Elliott, General Editor, *Columbia Literary History of the United States*, 1988.

POETRY

John Ciardi, ed., *Mid-Century American Voices*, 1950.

Randall Jarrell, *Poetry and the Age*, 1953.

Donald M. Allen, ed., *The New American Poetry*, 1960.

Anthony Ostroff, ed., *The Contemporary Poet as Artist and Critic: Eight Symposia*, 1964.

Ralph J. Mills, Jr., *Contemporary American Poetry*, 1965.

Stephen Stepanchev, *American Poetry Since 1945*, 1965.

Robert Penn Warren, *Modern Poetry and the End of an Era*, 1966.

Howard Nemerov, ed., *Poets on Poetry*, 1966.

Edward Hungerford, *Poets in Progress*, 1967.

M. L. Rosenthal, *The New Poets: American and British Poetry Since World War II*, 1967.

Richard Howard, *Alone with America: Essays on the Art of Poetry in the United States Since 1950*, 1969.

Harold Bloom, *The Ringers in the Tower*, 1971.

Stephen Henderson, *Understanding the New Black Poetry: Black Speech & Black Music as Poetic References*, 1972.

Karl Malkoff, *Crowell's Handbook of Contemporary American Poetry*, 1973.

Robert B. Shaw, ed., *American Poetry Since 1960*, 1973.

Donald M. Allen and Warren Tallman, eds., *The Poetics of the New American Poetry*, 1973.

Ralph J. Mills, Jr., *Cry of the Human: Essays on Contemporary American Poetry*, 1975.

William Heyen, ed., *American Poets in 1976*, 1976.

George S. Lensing and Ronald Morgan, *Four Poets and the Emotive Imagination: Robert Bly, James Wright, Louis Simpson, and William Stafford*, 1976.

David Kalstone, *Five Temperaments: Elizabeth Bishop, Robert Lowell, James Merrill, Adrienne Rich, John Ashbery*, 1977.

Robert Pinsky, *The Situation of Poetry*, 1977.

Laurence Lieberman, *Unassigned Frequencies: American Poetry in Review, 1964–77*, 1977.

Ekbert Faas, ed., *Towards a New American Poetics: Essays and Interviews*, 1978.

Howard Nemerov, *Figures of Thought*, 1978.

Charles Altieri, *Enlarging the Temple: New Directions in American Poetry During the 1960s*, 1979.

Charles Molesworth, *The Fierce Embrace: A Study of Contemporary American Poetry*, 1979.

James E. Miller, Jr., *The American Quest for a Supreme Fiction: Whitman's Legacy in the Personal Epic*, 1979.

Reginald Gibbons, ed., *The Poet's Work: 29 Poets on the Origins and Practice of Their Art*, 1979.

Helen Vendler, *Part of Nature, Part of Us: Modern American Poets*, 1980.

Sherman Paul, *The Lost America of Love: Rereading Robert Creeley, Edward Dorn, and Robert Duncan*, 1981.

Marjorie Perloff, *The Poetics of Indeterminacy*, 1981.

Bruce-Novoa, *Chicano Poetry: A Response to Chaos*, 1982.

Paul B. Janeczko, *Poetspeak: In Their Work About Their Work*, 1983.

Richard Jackson, *Acts of Mind: Conversations with Contemporary Poets*, 1983.

Joseph Bruchac, ed., *Breaking Silence, an Anthology of Contemporary Asian American Poets*, 1983.

James E. B. Breslin, *From Modern to Contemporary American Poetry, 1945–1965*, 1984.

Alan Williamson, *Introspection and Contemporary Poetry*, 1984.

Joe David Bellamy, ed., *American Poetry Observed: Poets on Their Work*, 1984.

Alberta Turner, ed., *45 Contemporary Poems: The Creative Process*, 1985.

Robert Hass, *Twentieth-Century Pleasures: Prose on Poetry*, 1985.

Dave Smith, *Local Assays: On Contemporary American Poetry*, 1985.

Robert von Hallberg, *American Poetry and Culture, 1945–1980*, 1985.

Diane Wood Middlebrook and Marilyn Yalom, eds., *Coming to Light: American Women Poets of the Twentieth Century*, 1985.

Marjorie Perloff, *The Dance of the Intellect*, 1985.

Mary K. DeShazer, *Inspiring Women: Reimagining the Muse*, 1986.

Jonathan Holden, *Style and Authenticity in Postmodern Poetry*, 1986.

Bruce Bawer, *The Middle Generation: The Lives and Poetry of Delmore Schwartz, Randall Jarrell, John Berryman, and Robert Lowell*, 1986.

Marie Harris and Kathleen Aguero, eds., *A Gift of Tongues: Critical Challenges in Contemporary American Poetry*, 1987.

William Packard, ed., *The Poet's Craft: Interviews from the New York Quarterly*, 1987.

David Lehman, ed., *Ecstatic Occasions, Expedient Forms: 65 Leading Contemporary Poets Select and Comment on Their Poems*, 1987.

Lee Bartlett, *Talking Poetry: Conversations in the Workshop with Contemporary Poets*, 1987.

Lynn Keller, *Re-Making It New: Contemporary Poetry and the Modernist Tradition*, 1987.

David Perkins, *A History of Modern Poetry: Modernism and After*, 1987.

Helen Vendler, *The Music of What Happens: Poems, Poets, Critics*, 1988.

Temma F. Berg et al., eds., *Engendering the Word: Feminist Essays in Psychosexual Poetics*, 1989.

FICTION

John Aldridge, *After the Lost Generation*, 1951.

Ihab Hassan, *Radical Innocence: The Contemporary American Novel*, 1961.

Chester E. Eisinger, *Fiction of the Forties*, 1963.

Marcus Klein, *After Alienation*, 1964.

Jonathan Baumbach, *The Landscape of Nightmare*, 1965.

John Aldridge, *Time to Murder and Create: The Contemporary Novel in Crisis*, 1966.

Robert Scholes, *The Fabulators*, 1967.

James E. Miller, Jr., "The Quest Absurd: The New American Novel," *Quests Surd and Absurd*, 1967.

Max F. Schulz, *Radical Sophistication: Studies in Contemporary Jewish-American Novelists*, 1969.

Helen Weinberg, *The New Novel in America: The Kafkan Mode in Contemporary Fiction*, 1970.

Tony Tanner, *City of Words: American Fiction 1935–1970*, 1971.

William H. Gass, *Fiction and the Figures of Life*, 1971.

Raymond M. Olderman, *Beyond the Waste Land: A Study of the American Novel in the 1960s*, 1972.

Gerald B. Nelson, *Ten Versions of America*, 1972.

Alfred Kazin, *Bright Book of Life: American Novelists and Storytellers from Hemingway to Mailer*, 1973.

Joe David Bellamy, *The New Fiction: Interviews with Innovative American Novelists*, 1974.

Raymond Federman, *Surfiction: Fiction Now and Tomorrow*, 1975.

Jerome Klinkowitz, *Literary Disruptions: The Making of a Post-Contemporary American Fiction*, 1975.

John Tytell, *Naked Angels, The Lives and Literature of the Beat Generation*, 1976.

Frank D. McConnell, *Four Postwar American Novelists: Bellow, Mailer, Barth, and Pynchon*, 1977.

John Gardner, *On Moral Fiction*, 1978.

Robert Scholes, *Fabulation and Metafiction*, 1979.

Linda Hutcheon, *Narcissistic Narrative: The Metafictional Paradox*, 1980.

Philip Stevick, *Alternative Pleasures: Postrealist Fiction and the Tradition*, 1981.

Larry McCaffery, *The Metafictional Muse: The Works of Robert Coover, Donald Barthelme, and William H. Gass*, 1982.

Maurice Couturier, ed., *Representation and Performance in Postmodern Fiction*, 1982.

Frederick R. Karl, *American Fictions, 1940–1980*, 1983.

Gordon Weaver, ed., *The American Short Story, 1945–1980*, 1983.

Malcolm Bradbury, *The Modern American Novel*, 1983.

Tom LeClair and Larry McCaffery, *Anything Can Happen: Interviews with Contemporary American Novelists*, 1983.

John Barth, *The Friday Book: Essays and Other Nonfiction*, 1984.

Allen Thiher, *Words in Reflection: Modern Language Theory and Postmodern Fiction*, 1984.

Patricia Waugh, *Metafiction: The Theory and Practice of Self-Conscious Fiction*, 1984.

Charles Newman, *The Post-Modern Aura: The Act of Fiction in an Age of Inflation*, 1985.

Larry McCaffery, ed., *Postmodern Fiction: A Bio-Bibliographical Guide*, 1986.

Bernard W. Bell, *The Afro-American Novel and Its Tradition*, 1987.

John F. Callahan, *In the African-American Grain: The Pursuit of Voice in Twentieth-Century Black Fiction*, 1988.

Margaret Morganroth Gullette, *Safe at Last in the Middle Years: The Invention of the Midlife Progress Novel: Saul Bellow, Margaret Drabble, Anne Tyler, and John Updike*, 1988.

DRAMA

Antonin Artaud, *The Theater and Its Double*, 1958.

Toby Cole, ed., *Playwrights on Playwriting: The Meaning and Making of Modern Drama from Ibsen to Ionesco*, 1960.

Martin Esslin, *The Theatre of the Absurd*, 1961.

Robert W. Corrigan, ed., *Theatre in the Twentieth Century*, 1963.

George Wellwarth, *The Theater of Protest and Paradox: Developments in the Avant-Garde Drama*, 1964.

Alan S. Downer, ed., *American Drama and Its Critics: A Collection of Critical Essays*, 1965.

Horst Frenz, ed., *American Playwrights on Drama*, 1965.

Alvin B. Kernan, ed., *The Modern American Theater: A Collection of Critical Essays*, 1967.

C. W. E. Bigsby, *Confrontation and Commitment: A Study of Contemporary American Drama, 1959–1966*, 1967.

Jerzy Grotowski, *Towards a Poor Theatre*, 1968.

Gerald Weales, "Drama," *Harvard Guide to Contemporary American Literature*, 1979.

Gerald Bordman, *The Oxford Companion to American Theatre*, 1984.

Rodney Simard, *Postmodern Drama, Contemporary Playwrights in America and Britain*, 1984.

C. W. E. Bigsby, *A Critical Introduction to Twentieth-Century American Drama, Volume II: Tennessee Williams, Arthur Miller, Edward Albee*, 1984.

CONTEMPORARY POETRY I
Poets Born Before 1920

ROBERT PENN WARREN   RANDALL JARRELL
THEODORE ROETHKE   JOHN BERRYMAN
CHARLES OLSON   WILLIAM STAFFORD
ELIZABETH BISHOP   ROBERT LOWELL
ROBERT HAYDEN   GWENDOLYN BROOKS
KARL SHAPIRO

"We are witnessing . . . the end of a poetic era, the end of 'modernism,' that school of which the Founding Fathers were Eliot, Pound, and Yeats."

Robert Penn Warren, "A Plea for Mitigation: Modern Poetry and the End of an Era"

"A poem is energy transferred from where the poet got it . . . , by way of the poem itself to, all the way over to, the reader."

Charles Olson, "Projective Verse"

"There is no 'split' [between the role of consciousness and the unconscious in art]. Dreams, works of art (some) glimpses of the always-more-successful surrealism of everyday life, unexpected moments of empathy (is it?), catch a peripheral vision of whatever it is one can never really see full-face but that seems enormously important."

Elizabeth Bishop, Letter to Anne Stevenson

"Almost the whole problem of writing poetry is to bring it back to what you really feel, and that takes an awful lot of maneuvering. . . . A lot of poetry seems to me very good in the tradition but just doesn't move me very much because it doesn't have personal vibrance to it."

Robert Lowell, *Writers at Work: The Paris Review Interviews, Second Series*

ROBERT PENN WARREN
(1905–1989)

When Robert Penn Warren published a volume of poetry, *Promises: Poems, 1954–1956*, in 1957, it broke his silence of over ten years as a lyric poet. He had published lyric poems earlier in the 1930s, but the last, *Selected Poems, 1923–43*, had appeared in 1944. In the interim he had won a reputation as a novelist. Now he won laurels as a poet, including the Pulitzer Prize and the National Book Award. The young poet James Wright, in reviewing the volume, said: "What makes Mr. Warren excitingly important is his refusal to quit even while he's ahead. In *Promises*, it seems to me, he has deliberately shed the armor of competence—a finely meshed and expensive armor, forged at heaven knows how many bitter intellectual fires—and has gone out to fight with the ungovernable tide. . . . [The] main importance [of *Promises*] is the further evidence it provides for the unceasing and furious growth of a considerable artist."

Wright's view was perceptive. Warren had developed as a poet under the shadow of the great modernist figures. By the time he was writing the poems of *Promises*, he had already sensed what he articulated in a lecture delivered in 1966, "A Plea for Mitigation: Modern Poetry and the End of An Era." It opened: "The collected editions are now settled comfortably on the shelves, some, even, gathering a little dust. The authors of some of those books are dead. We are witnessing, in other words, the end of a poetic era, the end of 'modernism,' that school of which the Founding Fathers were Eliot, Pound, and Yeats."

In the course of the lecture, Warren foresaw the advent of diversity and pluralism in poetry, but he firmly believed that the reader had the right to make one "vital demand" on it: "Certainly, poetry as art should feed [the reader's] love for the richness and variety of life, should broaden his sympathies, mollify his dogmatisms, and introduce him to imagination as the great 'as if' of truth. But poetry as prophecy gives him the image of truth as a way to be, see, or live, quite literally with no 'as-if' attached. We need art, and we need prophecy." Warren was, of course, describing his own aims in his development into the new poet he had become.

Robert Penn Warren was born in Guthrie, Kentucky, in 1905. He graduated from high school in Tennessee and turned up at Vanderbilt University in Nashville at a time of great intellectual ferment and literary activity. There he studied with John Crowe Ransom and Donald Davidson, came to know Allen Tate, and participated in the Fugitive Group, which gathered regularly to discuss each other's poems. Many of Warren's first poems appeared in *The Fugitive*, established in 1922. An indication of Warren's allegiance to the southern group was his contribution to a volume its members put together and published in 1930, *I'll Take My Stand*.

Warren did graduate work at the University of California, taking an M.A. in 1927, and continued graduate study at Yale University. In 1928 he became a Rhodes Scholar at Oxford University in England, earning a B.Litt. in 1930. He began a teaching career that would take him to Southwestern College (Memphis), Vanderbilt, Louisiana State University, and the University of Minnesota. In 1950 he accepted a professorship at Yale and retired from there in 1973, by then a renowned writer. He died in 1989.

While he was at Louisiana State University, Warren joined with another young professor, Cleanth Brooks, to found *The Southern Review* in 1935. As the leading little magazine of the period, it published the best writing then being produced, including Katherine Anne Porter and Eudora Welty, and became a center for the "New Criticism." Warren became co-author with Cleanth Brooks of a poetry textbook, *Understanding Poetry*, published in 1938. More than any other book, it spread the news of the New Criticism with its belief in the close reading of texts and helped revolutionize the way literature was taught in the schools.

Warren's first novel, *Night Rider*, appeared in 1939, and his second, *At Heaven's Gate*, in 1943; neither caused much stir. But in 1946, he published *All the King's Men*, based on the career of the demogogic populist, Huey P. Long ("two chickens in every pot"). Long created a ruthless, corrupt political machine in Louisiana and served first as governor and then as U.S. Senator; he was assassinated in the state capitol in 1935. Willie Stark, Warren's version of Long, was not so one-dimensional as Long's supporters and enemies had made him out, but was a complicated character with a mixture of good and evil in his makeup. The novel was both a critical and popular success (becoming a widely acclaimed movie). It won for Warren his first Pulitzer Prize.

Warren went on to write a number of novels, many of them best-sellers, but none to match *All the King's Men*. In 1953, he tried his hand at narrative poetry, publishing *Brother to Dragons: A Tale in Verse and Voices*. The story recreated an actual event of the early nineteenth century, the fiendish axe-slaying of a slave by a nephew of Thomas Jefferson. Warren was attracted to the story, he said, because of its connection with Thomas Jefferson, that "the philosopher of our liberties and the architect of our country and the prophet of human perfectibility had this in the family blood." Thus *Brother to Dragons* embodied two of the enduring themes of Warren's work, the ineradicability of evil and the complicity of all human beings in its perpetuation — in effect, original sin.

After his return to lyric poetry with *Promises* in 1957, Warren continued to publish fiction, essays, and poems. His volumes of poetry include *You, Emperors, and Others: Poems, 1957–1960* (1960); *Selected Poems: New and Old 1923–1966*, winner of the Bollingen Prize for 1966; *Incarnations: Poems, 1966–1968* (1968); *Audubon: A Vision* (1969); *Or Else — Poem/Poems 1968–1974* (1974); *Now and Then: Poems, 1976–1978* (1978); *Being Here* (1980); *Rumor Verified: Poems, 1979–1980* (1981); and *Chief Joseph of the Nez Perce* (1983). Warren published his *Selected Poems: 1923–1975* in 1976 and *New and Selected Poems: 1923–1985* in 1985. His *Selected Essays* appeared in 1958, *Democracy and Poetry* in 1975, and *Jefferson Davis Gets His Citizenship Back* in 1981. His was an extraordinary career, spanning several generations; he was a true "man of letters" in the old-fashioned sense. Universal approval greeted his appointment as the first Poet Laureate of the United States in 1986.

ADDITIONAL READING

Robert Penn Warren Talking: Interviews 1950–1978, ed. Floyd C. Watkins and John T. Hiers, 1980.

Paul West, *Robert Penn Warren*, 1964; John L. Longley, Jr., ed., *Robert Penn Warren: A Collection of Critical Essays*, 1964; John L. Longley, Jr., *Robert Penn Warren*, 1969; Neil Nakadate, *Robert Penn Warren: A Reference Guide*, 1977; Marshall Walker, *Robert Penn Warren: A Vision Earned*, 1979; Richard Gray, ed., *Robert Penn Warren: A Collection of Critical Essays*, 1980; William Bradford Clark, ed., *Critical Essays on Robert Penn Warren*, 1981; Neil Nakadate, ed., *Robert Penn Warren: Critical Perspectives*, 1981; James H. Justus, *The Achievement of Robert Penn Warren*, 1981; Charles Bohner, *Robert Penn Warren*, 1964, 1981; James A. Grimshaw, Jr., *Robert Penn Warren: A Descriptive Bibliography, 1922–1979*, 1982; Frank Graziano, *Homage to Robert Penn Warren*, 1982; Floyd C. Watkins, *Then and Now: The Personal Past in the Poetry of Robert Penn Warren*, 1982;

Katherine Snipes, *Robert Penn Warren*, 1983; Walter B. Edgar, ed., *A Southern Renascence Man: Views of Robert Penn Warren*, 1984; Calvin Bedient, *In the Heart's Last Kingdom*, 1986; Harold Bloom, ed., *Robert Penn Warren*, 1986; James A. Grimshaw, Jr., and Robert E. Lowery, eds., *Time's Glory: Original Essays on Robert Penn Warren*, 1986; John Burt, *Robert Penn Warren and American Idealism*, 1988.

TEXT

New and Selected Poems, 1923–1985, 1985.

The Child Next Door[1]

The child next door is defective because the mother,
Seven brats already in that purlieu of dirt,
Took a pill, or did something to herself she thought would not hurt,
But it did, and no good, for there came this monstrous other.

The sister is twelve. Is beautiful like a saint.   5
Sits with the monster all day, with pure love, calm eyes.
Has taught it a trick, to make *ciao*,[2] Italian-wise.
It crooks hand in that greeting. She smiles her smile without taint.

I come, and her triptych beauty and joy stir hate
— Is it hate? — in my heart. Fool, doesn't she know that the process   10
Is not that joyous or simple, to bless, or unbless,
The malfeasance of nature or the filth of fate?

Can it bind or loose, that beauty in that kind,
Beauty of benediction? We must trust our hope to prevail
That heart-joy in beauty be wisdom, before beauty fail   15
And be gathered like air in the ruck of the world's wind!

I think of your goldness, of joy, but how empires grind, stars are hurled.
I smile stiff, saying *ciao*, saying *ciao*, and think: *This is the world*.

1955, 1957

Little Boy and Lost Shoe

The little boy lost his shoe in the field.
Home he hobbled, not caring, with a stick whipping goldenrod.
Go find that shoe — I mean it, right now!
And he went, not now singing, and the field was big.

Under the sky he walked and the sky was big.   5
Sunlight touched the goldenrod, and yellowed his hair,
But the sun was low now, and oh, he should know
He must hurry to find that shoe, or the sun will be down.

---

[1]This poem is third of five poems headed: "To a Little Girl, One Year Old, in a Ruined Fortress." The poem is dedicated "To Rosanna," Warren's daughter.

[2]Italian form of greeting, "Hello," "Good-bye," pronounced "chow."

Oh, hurry, boy, for the grass will be tall as a tree.
Hurry, for the moon has bled, but not like a heart, in pity.   10
Hurry, for time is money and the sun is low.
Yes, damn it, hurry, for shoes cost money, you know.

I don't know why you dawdle and do not hurry.
The mountains are leaning their heads together to watch.
How dilatory can a boy be, I ask you?   15
                                        Off in Wyoming,
The mountains lean. They watch. They know.

                                                            1966

Blow, West Wind

I know, I know—though the evidence
Is lost, and the last who might speak are dead.
Blow, west wind, blow, and the evidence, O,

Is lost, and wind shakes the cedar, and O,
I know how the kestrel[1] hung over Wyoming,   5
Breast reddened in sunset, and O, the cedar

Shakes, and I know how cold
Was the sweat on my father's mouth, dead.
Blow, west wind, blow, shake the cedar, I know

How once I, a boy, crouching at creekside,   10
Watched, in the sunlight, a handful of water
Drip, drip, from my hand. The drops—they were bright!

But you believe nothing, with the evidence lost.

                                                            1966

Where the Slow
Fig's Purple Sloth

Where the slow fig's purple sloth
Swells, I sit and meditate the
Nature of the soul, the fig exposes,
To the blaze of afternoon, one haunch
As purple-black as Africa, a single   5
Leaf the rest screens, but through it, light
Burns, and for the fig's bliss
The sun dies, the sun
Has died forever—far, oh far—
For the fig's bliss, thus.   10

                        The air
Is motionless, and the fig,

---

[1]Small falcon noted for hovering in the air, head against the wind.

Motionless in that imperial and blunt
Languor of glut, swells, and inward
The fibers relax like a sigh in that   15
Hot darkness, go soft, the air
Is gold.

When you
Split the fig, you will see
Lifting from the coarse and purple seed, its   20
Flesh like flame, purer
Than blood.

It fills
The darkening room with light.

1967, 1968

Little Girl Wakes Early

Remember when you were the first one awake, the first
To stir in the dawn-curdled house, with little bare feet
Cold on boards, every door shut and accurst,
And behind shut doors no breath perhaps drew, no heart beat.

You held your breath and thought how all over town   5
Houses had doors shut, and no whisper of breath sleeping,
And that meant no swinging, nobody to pump up and down,
No hide-and-go-seek, no serious play at housekeeping.

So you ran outdoors, bare feet from the dew wet,
And climbed the fence to the house of your dearest friend,   10
And opened your lips and twisted your tongue, all set
To call her name — but the sound wouldn't come in the end,

For you thought how awful, if there was no breath there
For answer. Tears start, you run home, where now mother,
Over the stove, is humming some favorite air.   15
You seize her around the legs, but tears aren't over,

And won't get over, not even when she shakes you —
And shakes you hard — and more when you can't explain.
Your mother's long dead. And you've learned that when loneliness takes you
There's nobody ever to explain to — though you try again and again.   20

1985

THEODORE ROETHKE
(1908–1963)

At a time when American poetry seemed to have become obsessed with the
theme of alienation, Theodore Roethke led a return to nature in poetry that
seemed to offer a way out of the waste land. In an essay written when he was a

student at the University of Michigan (1926–27), he said: "I have a genuine love of nature. It is not the least bit affected, but an integral and powerful part of my life. . . . I can sense the moods of nature almost instinctively. Ever since I could walk, I have spent as much time as I could in the open. . . . When I get alone under an open sky where man isn't too evident, — then I'm tremendously exalted and a thousand vivid ideas and sweet visions flood my consciousness."

These statements were to prove prophetic for the poet that Roethke was to become. He was born in Saginaw, Michigan, and grew up assisting in his father's florist business on acreage that his immigrant German grandfather had acquired shortly after coming to America in 1872. As a child, he followed his father through the greenhouses and was assigned chores to perform to nurse the plants to maturity. He became intimately familiar with the damp soil, with its worms, slugs, and other strange creatures that lived hidden at the roots of the plants. Later the greenhouse would figure prominently in his poetry. "The greenhouse," he once said, was his "symbol for the whole of life, a womb, a heaven-on-earth."

Roethke finished a B.A. at the University of Michigan in 1929, and an M.A. in English in 1936. He spent his life writing — and teaching — poetry. He taught at Lafayette College, Michigan State University, Pennsylvania State University, Bennington, and, beginning in 1947, at the University of Washington in Seattle — where he remained as poet-in-residence until his death in 1963. Among his students at Washington was the poet James Wright. Roethke did not believe that poets could be "made," but he believed that much could "be taught about the craft of verse. A few people come together, establish an intellectual and emotional climate wherein creation is possible."

Roethke's first book of poems, *Open House* (1941), grew directly out of his experiences in his father's greenhouses and expressed a child-like wonder at the miracle of growing things. The volume showed all the promise that was to come to fruition in his second volume six years later — *The Lost Son and Other Poems* (1948). The reviews were highly favorable and Roethke was recognized as an original voice in American poetry. He published a third volume, *Praise to the End!*, in 1951, and a fourth, *The Waking, Poems 1933–1953*, in 1953. These books established Roethke as a leading poet of the postwar period, winning him a number of prizes, including the Pulitzer Prize for *The Waking*. In 1958, Roethke published *Words for the Wind*, containing a selection of poems from all his previous books, and some forty-three new poems. For it he was awarded the Bollingen Prize in poetry and the National Book Award.

Roethke once offered advice as to how to read *Praise to the End!* that might be applied in the reading of all his poems: "You will have no trouble if you approach these poems as a child would, naively, with your whole being awake, your faculties loose and alert. (A large order, I daresay!) *Listen* to them, for they are written to be heard, with the themes often coming alternately, as in music, and usually a partial resolution at the end. Each poem . . . is complete in itself; yet each in a sense is a stage in a kind of struggle out of the slime; part of a slow spiritual progress; an effort to be born, and later, to become something more."

During the latter part of his career, Roethke suffered several severe breakdowns, often requiring hospitalization. Many of the poems of this period reflected his precarious physical-spiritual state, as in the title poem of *The Waking*, in which he wrote:

> This shaking keeps me steady. I should know.
> What falls away is always. And is near.

> I wake to sleep, and take my waking slow.
> I learn by going where I have to go.

Roethke's search, manifest in his poetry, was for those deepest sources of feeling and knowing, and was in essence mystical or religious. The promise of the search was to transfigure the shudder of anxiety into the dance of affirmation. Dancing became a dominant image of the later poetry, as in "Four for Sir John Davies":

> I need a place to sing, and dancing-room,
> And I have made a promise to my ears
> I'll sing and whistle romping with the bears.

Roethke died of a heart attack in 1963 at the age of 55. A volume of new poems, *The Far Field*, appeared the year after his death. And *The Collected Poems of Theodore Roethke* was published in 1966.

ADDITIONAL READING

On the Poet and His Craft: Selected Prose of Theodore Roethke, ed. Ralph J. Mills, Jr., 1965; *Selected Letters of Theodore Roethke*, ed. Ralph J. Mills, Jr., 1970; *Straw for the Fire: From the Notebooks of Theodore Roethke, 1943–63*, ed. David Wagoner, 1972.

Ralph J. Mills, *Theodore Roethke*, 1963; Arnold Stein, ed., *Theodore Roethke: Essays and the Poetry*, 1966; Karl Malkoff, *Theodore Roethke: An Introduction to the Poetry*, 1966; Allan Seager, *The Glass House: The Life of Theodore Roethke*, 1968; Ursula Genug Walker, *Notes on Theodore Roethke*, 1968; William Heyen, ed., *Profile of Theodore Roethke*, 1971; Gary Lane, ed., *A Concordance to the Poems of Theodore Roethke*, 1972; James Richard McLeod, *Theodore Roethke: A Bibliography*, 1973; Richard Allen Blessing, *Theodore Roethke's Dynamic Vision*, 1974; Rosemary Sullivan, *Theodore Roethke: The Garden Master*, 1975; Jenijoy La Belle, *The Echoing Wood of Theodore Roethke*, 1976; Keith R. Moul, *Theodore Roethke's Career: An Annotated Bibliography*, 1977; Harry Williams, *"The Edge Is What I Have": Theodore Roethke and After*, 1977; Jay Parrini, *Theodore Roethke: An American Romantic*, 1979; George Wolff, *Theodore Roethke*, 1981; Lynn Ross-Bryant, *Theodore Roethke: Poetry of the Earth*, 1981; Neal Bowers, *Theodore Roethke: The Journey from I to Otherwise*, 1982; Randall Stifler, *Theodore Roethke: The Poet and His Critics*, 1986; Walter B. Kalaidjian, *Understanding Theodore Roethke*, 1987; Harold Bloom, ed., *Theodore Roethke*, 1988.

TEXT

The Collected Poems of Theodore Roethke, 1966.

Open House

> My secrets cry aloud.
> I have no need for tongue.
> My heart keeps open house,
> My doors are widely swung.
> An epic of the eyes   5
> My love, with no disguise.
>
> My truths are all foreknown,
> This anguish self-revealed.
> I'm naked to the bone,
> With nakedness my shield.   10
> Myself is what I wear:
> I keep the spirit spare.

The anger will endure,
The deed will speak the truth
In language strict and pure.   15
I stop the lying mouth:
Rage warps my clearest cry
To witless agony.

                                                    1936, 1941

Cuttings

Sticks-in-a-drowse droop over sugary loam,
Their intricate stem-fur dries;
But still the delicate slips keep coaxing up water;
The small cells bulge;

One nub of growth   5
Nudges a sand-crumb loose,
Pokes through a musty sheath
Its pale tendrilous horn.

                                                    1948

Cuttings
(later)

This urge, wrestle, resurrection of dry sticks,
Cut stems struggling to put down feet,
What saint strained so much,
Rose on such lopped limbs to a new life?

I can hear, underground, that sucking and sobbing,   5
In my veins, in my bones I feel it,—
The small waters seeping upward,
The tight grains parting at last.
When sprouts break out,
Slippery as fish,   10
I quail, lean to beginnings, sheath-wet.

                                                    1948

Root Cellar

Nothing would sleep in that cellar, dank as a ditch,
Bulbs broke out of boxes hunting for chinks in the dark,
Shoots dangled and drooped,
Lolling obscenely from mildewed crates,
Hung down long yellow evil necks, like tropical snakes.   5
And what a congress of stinks!—

Roots ripe as old bait,
Pulpy stems, rank, silo-rich,
Leaf-mold, manure, lime, piled against slippery planks.
Nothing would give up life: 10
Even the dirt kept breathing a small breath.

1943, 1948

Child on Top of a Greenhouse

The wind billowing out the seat of my britches,
My feet crackling splinters of glass and dried putty,
The half-grown chrysanthemums staring up like accusers,
Up through the streaked glass, flashing with sunlight,
A few white clouds all rushing eastward,   5
A line of elms plunging and tossing like horses,
And everyone, everyone pointing up and shouting!

1946, 1948

Frau Bauman, Frau Schmidt, and Frau Schwartze[1]

Gone the three ancient ladies
Who creaked on the greenhouse ladders,
Reaching up white strings
To wind, to wind
The sweet-pea tendrils, the smilax,[2]   5
Nasturtiums, the climbing
Roses, to straighten
Carnations, red
Chrysanthemums; the stiff
Stems, jointed like corn,   10
They tied and tucked,—
These nurses of nobody else.
Quicker than birds, they dipped
Up and sifted the dirt;
They sprinkled and shook;   15
They stood astride pipes,
Their skirts billowing out wide into tents,
Their hands twinkling with wet;
Like witches they flew along rows
Keeping creation at ease;   20
With a tendril for needle
They sewed up the air with a stem;
They teased out the seed that the cold kept asleep,—

---

[1] Workers in Roethke's father's greenhouse.
[2] A twining plant belonging to the lily family.

All the coils, loops, and whorls.
They trellised the sun; they plotted for more than themselves.   25

I remember how they picked me up, a spindly kid,
Pinching and poking my thin ribs
Till I lay in their laps, laughing,
Weak as a whiffet;[3]
Now, when I'm alone and cold in my bed,   30
They still hover over me,
These ancient leathery crones,
With their bandannas stiffened with sweat,
And their thorn-bitten wrists,
And their snuff-laden breath blowing lightly over me in my first sleep.   35

                                                                        1948

My Papa's Waltz

The whiskey on your breath
Could make a small boy dizzy;
But I hung on like death:
Such waltzing was not easy.

We romped until the pans   5
Slid from the kitchen shelf;
My mother's countenance
Could not unfrown itself.

The hand that held my wrist
Was battered on one knuckle;   10
At every step you missed
My right ear scraped a buckle.

You beat time on my head
With a palm caked hard by dirt,
Then waltzed me off to bed   15
Still clinging to your shirt.

                                                        1942, 1948

Dolor

I have known the inexorable sadness of pencils,
Neat in their boxes, dolor of pad and paper-weight,
All the misery of manilla folders and mucilage,
Desolation in immaculate public places,
Lonely reception room, lavatory, switchboard,   5
The unalterable pathos of basin and pitcher,

---

[3]Whippersnapper; insignificant person.

Ritual of multigraph, paper-clip, comma,
Endless duplication of lives and objects.
And I have seen dust from the walls of institutions,
Finer than flour, alive, more dangerous than silica,   10
Sift, almost invisible, through long afternoons of tedium,
Dropping a fine film on nails and delicate eyebrows,
Glazing the pale hair, the duplicate grey standard faces.

1943, 1948

The Lost Son[1]

1. *The Flight*

At Woodlawn[2] I heard the dead cry:
I was lulled by the slamming of iron,
A slow drip over stones,
Toads brooding wells.
All the leaves stuck out their tongues;   5
I shook the softening chalk of my bones,
Saying,
Snail, snail, glister me forward,
Bird, soft-sigh me home,
Worm, be with me.   10
This is my hard time.

Fished in an old wound,
The soft pond of repose;
Nothing nibbled my line,
Not even the minnows came.   15

Sat in an empty house
Watching shadows crawl,
Scratching.
There was one fly.

Voice, come out of the silence.   20
Say something.
Appear in the form of a spider
Or a moth beating the curtain.

Tell me:
Which is the way I take;   25
Out of what door do I go,
Where and to whom?

---

[1]Roethke's father died in 1923, when Roethke was only fifteen years old; this poem is an imaginative recreation of his experience of his father's death. Roethke said of "The Lost Son" that it "follows a narrative line indicated by the titles of the first four sections: 'The Flight,' 'The Pit,' 'The Gibber,' 'The Return.' 'The Flight' is just what it says it is: a terrified running away—with alternate periods of hallucinatory waiting (voices, etc.); the protagonist so geared-up, so over-alive that he is hunting, like a primitive, for some animistic suggestion, some clue to existence from the sub-human. These he sees and yet does not see: they are almost tail-flicks, from another world, seen out of the corner of the eye. In a sense he goes in and out of rationality; he hangs in the balance between the human and the animal." Roethke's comments on this poem are from *On the Poet and His Craft*, pp. 38–39.
[2]A cemetery.

Dark hollows said, lee to the wind,
The moon said, back of an eel,
The salt said, look by the sea,   30
Your tears are not enough praise,
You will find no comfort here,
In the kingdom of bang and blab.

Running lightly over spongy ground,
Past the pasture of flat stones,   35
The three elms,
The sheep strewn on a field,
Over a rickety bridge
Toward the quick-water, wrinkling and rippling.

Hunting along the river,   40
Down among the rubbish, the bug-riddled foliage,
By the muddy pond-edge, by the bog-holes,
By the shrunken lake, hunting, in the heat of summer.

The shape of a rat?
    It's bigger than that.   45
    It's less than a leg
    And more than a nose,
    Just under the water
    It usually goes.

Is it soft like a mouse?   50
Can it wrinkle its nose?
Could it come in the house
On the tips of its toes?

    Take the skin of a cat
    And the back of an eel,   55
    Then roll them in grease,—
    That's the way it would feel.

    It's sleek as an otter
    With wide webby toes
    Just under the water   60
    It usually goes.

2. The Pit[3]

Where do the roots go?
    Look down under the leaves.
Who put the moss there?
    These stones have been here too long.   65
Who stunned the dirt into noise?
    Ask the mole, he knows.
I feel the slime of a wet nest.
    Beware Mother Mildew.
Nibble again, fish nerves.   70

---

[3]Roethke's comment: "'The Pit' is a slowed-down section; a
period of physical and psychic exhaustion. And other obsessions begin to appear (symbolized by mole, nest, fish)."

3. *The Gibber*[4]

At the wood's mouth,
By the cave's door,
I listened to something
I had heard before.

Dogs of the groin   75
Barked and howled,
The sun was against me,
The moon would not have me.

The weeds whined,
The snakes cried,   80
The cows and briars
Said to me: Die.

What a small song. What slow clouds. What dark water.
Hath the rain a father? All the caves are ice. Only the snow's here.
I'm cold. I'm cold all over. Rub me in father and mother.   85
Fear was my father, Father Fear.
His look drained the stones.

        What gliding shape
        Beckoning through halls,
        Stood poised on the stair,   90
        Fell dreamily down?

        From the mouths of jugs
        Perched on many shelves,
        I saw substance flowing
        That cold morning.   95

        Like a slither of eels
        That watery cheek
        As my own tongue kissed
        My lips awake.

Is this the storm's heart? The ground is unstilling itself.   100
My veins are running nowhere. Do the bones cast out their fire?
Is the seed leaving the old bed? These buds are live as birds.
Where, where are the tears of the world?
Let the kisses resound, flat like a butcher's palm;
Let the gestures freeze; our doom is already decided.   105
All the windows are burning! What's left of my life?
I want the old rage, the lash of primordial milk!
Goodbye, goodbye, old stones, the time-order is going,
I have married my hands to perpetual agitation,
I run, I run to the whistle of money.   110

---

[4]Roethke's comment: "In 'The Gibber' these obsessions [see footnote 3] begin to take hold; again there is a frenetic activity, then a lapsing back into almost a crooning serenity ('What a small song,' etc.). The line, 'Hath the rain a father?' is from Job [38:28]—the only quotation in the piece. . . . The next rising agitation is rendered in terms of balked sexual experience, with an accompanying 'rant,' almost in the manner of the Elizabethans, and a subsequent near-blackout."

Money money money
Water water water

How cool the grass is.
Has the bird left?
The stalk still sways.   115
Has the worm a shadow?
What do the clouds say?

These sweeps of light undo me.
Look, look, the ditch is running white!
I've more veins than a tree!   120
Kiss me, ashes, I'm falling through a dark swirl.

4. *The Return*[5]

The way to the boiler was dark,
Dark all the way,
Over slippery cinders
Through the long greenhouse.   125

The roses kept breathing in the dark.
They had many mouths to breathe with.
My knees made little winds underneath
Where the weeds slept.

There was always a single light   130
Swinging by the fire-pit,
Where the fireman pulled out roses,
The big roses, the big bloody clinkers.[6]

Once I stayed all night.
The light in the morning came slowly over the white   135
Snow.
There were many kinds of cool
Air.
Then came steam.

Pipe-knock.   140

Scurry of warm over small plants.
Ordnung! ordnung![7]
Papa is coming!

A fine haze moved off the leaves;
Frost melted on far panes;   145
The rose, the chrysanthemum turned toward the light.

---

[5]Roethke's comment: "Section IV is a return, a return to a memory of childhood that comes back almost as in a dream, after the agitation and exhaustion of the earlier actions. The experience, again, is at once literal and symbolical. The 'roses' are still breathing in the dark; and the fireman can pull them out, even from the fire. After the dark night, the morning brings with it the suggestion of a renewing light: a coming of 'Papa.' Buried in the text are many little ambiguities, not all of which are absolutely essential to the central meaning of the poem. For instance, the 'pipe-knock.' With the coming of steam, the pipes begin knocking violently, in a greenhouse. But 'Papa,' or the florist, as he approached, often would knock the pipe he was smoking on the sides of the benches, or on the pipes. Then, with the coming of steam and 'papa'—the papa on earth and heaven are blended—there is the sense of motion in the greenhouse, my symbol for the whole of life, a womb, a heaven-on-earth."
[6]Slag; fused stony mass formed from impurities in burning coal.
[7]"Order! order!" (German).

Even the hushed forms, the bent yellowy weeds
Moved in a slow up-sway.

5. *"It Was Beginning Winter"*[8]

It was beginning winter,
An in-between time,   150
The landscape still partly brown:
The bones of weeds kept swinging in the wind,
Above the blue snow.

It was beginning winter,
The light moved slowly over the frozen field,   155
Over the dry seed-crowns,
The beautiful surviving bones
Swinging in the wind.

Light traveled over the wide field;
Stayed.   160
The weeds stopped swinging.
The mind moved, not alone,
Through the clear air, in the silence.

Was it light?
Was it light within?   165
Was it light within light?
Stillness becoming alive,
Yet still?

A lively understandable spirit
Once entertained you.   170
It will come again.
Be still.
Wait.

1947, 1948

The Waking[1]

I wake to sleep, and take my waking slow.
I feel my fate in what I cannot fear.
I learn by going where I have to go.

We think by feeling. What is there to know?
I hear my being dance from ear to ear.   5
I wake to sleep, and take my waking slow.

---

[8]Roethke's comment: "In the final untitled section, the illumination, the coming of light suggested at the end of the last passage occurs again, this time to the nearly-grown man. But the illumination is still only partly apprehended; he [the protagonist] is still 'waiting.' . . . This crude account tells very little about what actually happens in the poem; but at least you can see that the method is cyclic. I believe that to go forward as a spiritual man it is necessary first to go back. Any history of the psyche (or allegorical journey) is bound to be a succession of experiences, similar yet dissimilar. There is a perpetual slipping-back, then a going-forward; but there is *some* 'progress.'"

[1]A "villanelle," a French fixed form: five tercets followed by a quatrain, using only two rhymes; the first line of the first tercet is repeated at the ends of the second and fourth tercets, while the final line of the first tercet is repeated at the ends of the third and fifth; the two repeated lines then reappear as the last two lines of the final quatrain.

Of those so close beside me, which are you?
God bless the Ground! I shall walk softly there,
And learn by going where I have to go.

Light takes the Tree; but who can tell us how?   10
The lowly worm climbs up a winding stair;
I wake to sleep, and take my waking slow.

Great Nature has another thing to do
To you and me; so take the lively air,
And, lovely, learn by going where to go.   15

This shaking keeps me steady. I should know.
What falls away is always. And is near.
I wake to sleep, and take my waking slow.
I learn by going where I have to go.

                                                        1953

I Knew a Woman

I knew a woman, lovely in her bones,
When small birds sighed, she would sigh back at them;
Ah, when she moved, she moved more ways than one:
The shapes a bright container can contain!
Of her choice virtues only gods should speak,   5
Or English poets who grew up on Greek
(I'd have them sing in chorus, cheek to cheek).

How well her wishes went! She stroked my chin,
She taught me Turn, and Counter-turn, and Stand;
She taught me Touch, that undulant white skin;   10
I nibbled meekly from her proffered hand;
She was the sickle; I, poor I, the rake,
Coming behind her for her pretty sake
(But what prodigious mowing we did make).

Love likes a gander, and adores a goose: 15
Her full lips pursed, the errant note to seize;
She played it quick, she played it light and loose;
My eyes, they dazzled at her flowing knees;
Her several parts could keep a pure repose,
Or one hip quiver with a mobile nose   20
(She moved in circles, and those circles moved).

Let seed be grass, and grass turn into hay:
I'm martyr to a motion not my own;
What's freedom for? To know eternity.
I swear she cast a shadow white as stone.   25
But who would count eternity in days?
These old bones live to learn her wanton ways:
(I measure time by how a body sways).

                                                        1954, 1958

In a Dark Time[1]

In a dark time, the eye begins to see,
I meet my shadow in the deepening shade;
I hear my echo in the echoing wood—
A lord of nature weeping to a tree.
I live between the heron and the wren,   5
Beasts of the hill and serpents of the den.

What's madness but nobility of soul
At odds with circumstance? The day's on fire!
I know the purity of pure despair,
My shadow pinned against a sweating wall.   10
That place among the rocks—is it a cave,
Or winding path? The edge is what I have.

A steady storm of correspondences!
A night flowing with birds, a ragged moon,
And in broad day the midnight come again!   15
A man goes far to find out what he is—
Death of the self in a long, tearless night,
All natural shapes blazing unnatural light.

Dark, dark my light, and darker my desire.
My soul, like some heat-maddened summer fly,   20
Keeps buzzing at the sill. Which I is *I*?
A fallen man, I climb out of my fear.
The mind enters itself, and God the mind,
And one is One, free in the tearing[2] wind.

1958   *1960, 1964*

CHARLES OLSON
(1910–1970)

In 1950, Charles Olson published "Projective Verse," the most important manifesto to appear in the post-modernist period. He said:

A poem is energy transferred from where the poet got it (he will have some several causations), by way of the poem itself to, all the way over to, the reader. Okay. Then the poem itself must, at all points, be a high energy-construct and, at all points, an energy-discharge. . . . From the moment [the poet] ventures into FIELD COMPOSITION—puts himself in the open—he can go by no track other than the one the poem under hand declares, for itself. . . . the *principle*, the law which presides conspicuously over such composition . . . is

---

[1]Roethke said of this poem: "I take the central experience to be fairly common: to break from the bondage of the self, from the barriers of the 'real' world, to come as close to God as possible." The "spiritual experience" moves through the "dark night of the soul" to some kind of transcendent awareness (or God consciousness). For Roethke's comment see "The Poet and His Critics: A Symposium," ed. Anthony

Ostroff, *New World Writing*, no. 19, 1961.
[2]Roethke's comment: "I feel there is a hope in the ambiguity of 'tearing'—that the ambient air itself, that powers man once deemed merely 'natural,' or is unaware of, are capable of pity; that some other form or aspect of God will endure with man again, will save him from himself."

this: FORM IS NEVER MORE THAN AN EXTENSION OF CONTENT. . . . [and] the *process* . . . can be boiled down to one statement . . .: ONE PERCEP-TION MUST IMMEDIATELY AND DIRECTLY LEAD TO A FURTHER PERCEPTION.

Olson took his "principle" and his "process" formulations from two followers or associates, Robert Creeley and Edward Dahlberg, both, like Olson, literary rebels. His contribution, the notion of "composition by field," was the most origi-nal, offering fresh language for discussions grown stale about the nature of po-etry. In physics, a "field of force" is a space under the influence of some force, such as electricity or magnetism. By "field composition," in which the poet puts himself in the "open," Olson must have meant that the composition would come under the influence of metaphorically similar forces — personal or political cur-rents or pressures that bear down on the poet's immediate psychic environment. The overall image of a poet putting himself in the "open" is of a poet not control-ling his intellectual or emotional environment, but opening himself instead to the lines of force that intersect with his being in the particular space he happens to occupy.

In 1950, Olson was forty years old, and virtually unknown as a poet. He was born in Worcester, Massachusetts, and grew up in the coastal fishing town of Gloucester, a place he would later memorialize in his *Maximus Poems*. He took a B.A. at Wesleyan University in 1932 and an M.A. in 1933. He continued gradu-ate studies at Yale and then Harvard, but never finished an additional degree. He taught at a number of institutions, including Clark University and Har-vard, but the place with which his name became permanently associated was a poverty-stricken school in the mountains of North Carolina, Black Mountain College. He went there in 1948, became rector or head in 1951, and stayed until 1956.

Black Mountain College, though poor, became the gathering place of rebel artists, including musicians (John Cage), artists (Franz Kline and Robert Rau-schenberg), dancers (Merce Cunningham), and poets (Robert Creeley, Denise Levertov, and Robert Duncan). During his stay at the college, Olson made him-self the leading figure of the "Black Mountain poets," and his 1950 manifesto became the group's rallying cry. The group rejected the dominant literary figure of the time, T. S. Eliot, and his insistence on connecting with the *tradition*. And it recognized connections with two modernist poets then frequently dismissed, Ezra Pound and William Carlos Williams. The *Black Mountain Review* reached out to include sympathetic souls and fellow rebels, including Allen Ginsberg, Jack Kerouac, and other writers of the Beat movement.

Olson's first book, published in 1947, was on Herman Melville, entitled *Call Me Ishmael*. It was a highly personal, anti-academic work that recognized no other commentary on Melville. It opened: "I take SPACE to be the central fact to man born in America, from Folsom cave to now. I spell it large because it comes large here. Large and without mercy." For long stretches it was difficult for a reader to determine what point was being made about Melville. In fact, it was not a book *about* Melville; it was a meditation and prose-poem, most nearly about America, space, and Charles Olson himself.

The most important journey made by Charles Olson was in 1950–51 to Yucatán, Mexico, the land of the Mayas. He lived in Lerma, on the sea near the city of Campeche, on the Yucatán peninsula, and was given a fellowship to study the Mayan hieroglyphics in that area. His essay "Human Universe" was a distilla-tion of his experience among the contemporary Mayas, inheritors of the culture of the ancient Mayan civilization. In the Western world, he said, the Greeks had fastened "logic and classification" on the "habits of thought." But, he observed, these habits went against the basic law of the "human universe": "If there is any absolute, it is never more than this one, you, this instant, in action." We must, he said, find ways to "stay in the human universe, and not be led to partition reality at any point, in any way."

The lessons of the Mayan experience would remain with Olson throughout his life and would frequently surface in his poetry. Olson's shorter poems began to appear in the little magazines in the 1950s and 1960s, and were collected in two volumes: *In Cold Hell, in Thicket* (1953) and *The Distances* (1960). These were brought together in *Archeologist of Morning: The Collected Poems Outside the Maximus Series* (1971). But the major project of Olson's career was his epic *The Maximus Poems*, which he was writing and publishing by the early 1950s and was still working on at the time of his death in 1970. Segments of the long poem appeared in 1953 and 1956, and were combined in 1960 into what was to become known as the first part of a three-part poem. In 1968, part two appeared as *Maximus Poems IV, V, VI*. Olson's death in 1970 left to his editors to assemble the final part three from his mass of manuscripts and publish it as *The Maximus Poems: Volume Three* in 1975. The entire work was brought together in one volume, *The Maximus Poems*, edited by George F. Butterick in 1983.

Like Walt Whitman's *Leaves of Grass*, Ezra Pound's *Cantos*, and William Carlos Williams's *Paterson*, *The Maximus Poems* is a lyric-epic, taking its author (in Olson's case called Maximus) as its hero, and embracing and exploring the events — psychic, intellectual, biographical — of the author's life, place, and time. At one point in the midst of *The Maximus Poems*, Olson writes: "I am making a mappe-munde [world map]. It is to include my being."

Olson once observed that Pound had given him his "methodological clue: the rag-bag," while Williams gave him "the lead on the local." Pound had once commented, referring to his *Cantos*, that "the modern world / Needs such a rag-bag to stuff all its thought in." Williams had deliberately turned away from Pound's orientation to foreign lands and histories and had set his epic in Paterson, New Jersey, the *local* which he knew well. Olson set his epic in the place that he knew well also, the fishing village in which he grew up, Gloucester, Massachusetts. All three long poems (Pound's, Williams's, Olson's) as well as *Leaves of Grass*, are rag-bags in the sense that they are able to incorporate whatever their poets find out, dig up, or toss in.

One critic, Paul Christensen, has written at the end of his study, *Charles Olson: Call Him Ishmael* (1978):

> Olson's canon has within it a potent utterance: life is strangled by systems. Existence has an order that cannot be isolated from nature; the order is continually changing and evolving. A system is a halting of change; it seizes upon a possible order and continues to duplicate it endlessly. As it entrenches in the midst of nature, its tyranny upon life grows, until the system is a prison of contradictions. . . . Olson wanted the poet to be the measure of awareness, to be that lone human figure thrust deep into the uncertainty of the real, where he lives and expresses himself joyfully and is ultimately joined by others.

ADDITIONAL READING

Selected Writings, ed. Robert Creeley, 1966; *Letters for "Origin" 1950–1956*, ed. Albert Glover, 1969; *The Special View of History*, ed. Ann Charters, 1970; *Poetry & Truth*, ed. George F. Butterick, 1971; *The Post Office: A Memoir of His Father*, 1974; *Charles Olson and Robert Creeley: The Complete Correspondence*, 7 vols., ed. George F. Butterick, 1980–86.

George F. Butterick and Albert Glover, *A Bibliography of Works by Charles Olson*, 1967; Ann Charters, *Olson/Melville: A Study in Affinity*, 1968; George F. Butterick, *A Guide to the Maximus Poems of Charles Olson*, 1978; Paul Christensen, *Charles Olson: Call Him Ishmael*, 1978; Sherman Paul, *Charles Olson's Push: 'Origin,' Black Mountain, and Recent American Poetry*, 1978; Robert von Hallberg, *Charles Olson: The Scholar's Art*, 1978; Gavin Selerie, *To Let Words Swim into the Soul: An Anniversary Tribute to the Art of Charles Olson*, 1980; Thomas F. Merrill, *The Poetry of Charles Olson: A Primer*, 1982; Brian Conniff, *The Lyric and Modern Poetry: Olson, Creeley, Bunting*, 1988.

TEXTS

The Maximus Poems, 1960; *The Collected Poems of Charles Olson, Excluding the Maximus Poems*, ed. George F. Butterick, 1987.

A Newly Discovered 'Homeric' Hymn[1]

(FOR JANE HARRISON,[2] IF SHE WERE ALIVE)

Hail and beware the dead who will talk life until you are blue
in the face. And you will not understand what is wrong,
they will not be blue, they will have tears in their eyes,
they will seem to you so much more full of life
than the rest of us, and they will ask so much, not of you no   5
but of life, they will cry, isn't it this way, if it isn't
I don't care for it, and you will feel the blackmail, you will not know
what to answer, it will all have become one mass

Hail and beware them, for they come from where you have not been,
they come from where you cannot have come, they come into life   10
by a different gate. They come from a place which is not easily known,
it is known only to those who have died. They carry seeds
you must not touch, you must not touch the pot they taste of,
no one must touch the pot, no one must, in their season.

Hail and beware them, in their season. Take care. Prepare   15
to receive them, they carry what the living cannot do without,
but take the proper precautions, do the prescribed things, let
down the thread from the right shoulder. And from the forehead.
And listen to what they say, listen to the talk, hear
every word of it—they are drunk from the pot, they speak   20
like no living man may speak, they have the seeds in their mouth—
listen, and beware

Hail them solely that they have the seeds in their mouth, they
are drunk, you cannot do without a drunkenness, seeds can't,
they must be soaked in the contents of the pot, they must be all one mass.   25
But you who live cannot know what else the seeds must be. Hail
and beware the earth, where the dead come from. Life

---

[1]Homeric Hymns, of unknown authorship, were literary rather than devotional, probably delivered in competitions at festivals from the eighth to sixth centuries B.C. The hymns, both lyric and hexametric, invoked Greek deities and de-scribed their attributes and deeds.
[2]Jane Ellen Harrison (1850–1928), English classical scholar and lecturer in classical archeology at Cambridge.

is not of the earth. The dead are of the earth. Hail and beware
the earth, where the pot is buried.

Greet the dead in the dead man's time. He is drunk of the pot.   30
He speaks like spring does. He will deceive you. You are meant
to be deceived. You must observe the drunkenness. You are not to
drink. But you must hear, and see. You must beware.

Hail them, and fall off. Fall off! The drink is not yours,
it is not yours! You do not come   35
from the same place, you do not suffer as the dead do,
they do not suffer, they need, because they have drunk of the pot,
they need. Do not drink of the pot, do not touch it. Do not touch
them.

    Beware the dead. And hail them. They teach you drunkenness.   40
You have your own place to drink. Hail and beware them, when they come.

1955   *1956, 1960*

The Distances

So the distances are Galatea[1]
                             and one does fall in love and desires
mastery

               old Zeus — young Augustus[2]

Love knows no distance, no place   5
                           is that far away or heat changes
into signals, and control

               old Zeus — young Augustus

Death is a loving matter, then, a horror
                           we cannot bide, and avoid   10
by greedy life

               we think all living things are precious
               — Pygmalions

                           a German inventor in Key West
who had a Cuban girl, and kept her, after her death   15
in his bed[3]
                           after her family retrieved her
he stole the body again from the vault

---

[1]In Greek legend, a female statue created by Pygmalion; he fell in love with it and Aphrodite, goddess of love, granted his wish, bringing it to life.
[2]Zeus, supreme god of the Greeks; Augustus, Caius Octavius (63 B.C.–A.D. 14), Julius Caesar's adopted son who became emperor after Caesar's assassination, with title of Augustus.
[3]According to Paul Christensen, *Charles Olson* (1978), p. 115: "the allusion is to Karl Tanzler, an eighty-three-year-old x-ray technician" who kept the body of his dead love in his house for eight years.

Torso on torso in either direction,
          young Augustus
                              out via nothing where messages
are

     or in, down La Cluny's steps to the old man sitting
a god throned on torsoes,[4]

          old Zeus   25

Sons go there hopefully as though there was a secret, the object
to undo distance?
                              They huddle there, at the bottom
of the shaft, against one young bum
                              or two loving cheeks,   30

          Augustus?

You can teach the young nothing
                              all of them go away, Aphrodite
tricks it out,

          old Zeus — young Augustus   35

You have love, and no object
                              or you have all pressed to your nose
which is too close,

          old Zeus hiding in your chin your young
          Galatea   40

the girl who makes you weep, and you keep the corpse live by all
your arts

               whose cheek do you stroke when you stroke the stone face
               of young Augustus, made for bed in a military camp,
               o Caesar?   45

O love who places all where each is, as they are, for every moment,
yield
          to this man
                         that the impossible distance
be healed,   50

          that young Augustus
          and old Zeus
be enclosed

          "I wake you,
stone. Love this man."   55

1959   *1960*

---

[4]The medieval Hôtel de Cluny in Paris, built over Roman baths, now a museum; Olson's allusion is to Chapter 41 in Herman Melville's *Moby-Dick* (1851), in which, in order to explain Ahab's "darker, deeper part," the narrator leads the reader down into his interior, compared to a descent into the Roman ruins beneath the Hôtel de Cluny, where "his whole awful essence sits . . . throned on torsoes!"

from The Maximus Poems

from The Songs of Maximus

SONG 3

This morning of the small snow
I count the blessings, the leak in the faucet
which makes of the sink time, the drop
of the water on water as sweet
as the Seth Thomas[1]   5
in the old kitchen
my father stood in his drawers to wind (always
he forgot the 30th day, as I don't want to remember
the rent
        a house these days   10
so much somebody else's,
especially,
Congoleum's[2]

           Or the plumbing,
that it doesn't work, this I like, have even used paper clips   15
as well as string to hold the ball up And flush it
with my hand
           But that the car doesn't, that no moving thing moves
without that song I'd void my ear of, the musickracket
of all ownership . . .   20
           Holes
in my shoes, that's all right, my fly
gaping, me out
at the elbows, the blessing
              that difficulties are once more[3]   25

      "In the midst of plenty, walk[4]
as close to
bare
         In the face of sweetness,
piss   30
           In the time of goodness,
go side, go
smashing, beat them, go as
(as near as you can

     tear   35

In the land of plenty, have
nothing to do with it
              take the way of

---

[1]A clock named after the manufacturer, Seth Thomas (1785–1859).
[2]A brand of floor covering, similar to linoleum.
[3]Such difficulties are a "blessing" in that they require one to reduce one's life (like Henry David Thoreau) to essentials.
[4]Cf. "Back and side go bare, go bare, / Both foot and hand go cold," from *Gammer Gurton's Needle*, a sixteenth-century British play (anonymous).

the lowest,
including   40
your legs, go
contrary, go

sing

                                                                    1953

Maximus, to himself

I have had to learn the simplest things
last. Which made for difficulties.
Even at sea I was slow, to get the hand out, or to cross
a wet deck.
        The sea was not, finally, my trade.   5
But even my trade, at it, I stood estranged
from that which was most familiar.[1] Was delayed,
and not content with the man's argument
that such postponement
is now the nature of   10
obedience,
        that we are all late
        in a slow time,
        that we grow up many
        And the single   15
        is not easily
        known

It could be, though the sharpness (the *achiote*)[2]
I note in others,
makes more sense   20
than my own distances. The agilities

        they show daily
        who do the world's
        businesses
        And who do nature's   25
        as I have no sense
        I have done either

I have made dialogues,
have discussed ancient texts,
have thrown what light I could, offered   30
what pleasures
doceat[3] allows

        But the known?
This, I have had to be given,

---

[1]Cf. "Man is estranged from that with which he is most familiar," Heraclitus (fl. 500 B.C.), a Greek philosopher.
[2]The small, tropical annatto tree, whose seeds yield a yellow-
ish-red dye.

[3]"Teaching" or "to teach" (Latin); one of the traditional functions of literature.

a life, love, and from one man
the world.[4]   35

  Tokens.
  But sitting here
  I look out as a wind
  and water man, testing   40
  And missing
  some proof

I know the quarters
of the weather, where it comes from,
where it goes. But the stem of me,   45
this I took from their welcome,
or their rejection, of me

  And my arrogance[5]
  was neither diminished
  nor increased,   50
  by the communication

                    2

It is undone business
I speak of, this morning,
with the sea
stretching out   55
from my feet

1953   1956

ELIZABETH BISHOP
(1911–1979)

Commenting on the enigmatic nature of poetry, Elizabeth Bishop once wrote
to Anne Stevenson:

> There is no "split" [between the role of consciousness and the unconscious in
> art]. Dreams, works of art (some) glimpses of the always-more-successful sur-
> realism of everyday life, unexpected moments of empathy (is it?), catch a pe-
> ripheral vision of whatever it is one can never really see full-face but that seems
> enormously important. I can't believe we are wholly irrational—and I do ad-
> mire Darwin—But reading Darwin one admires the beautiful solid case being
> built up out of his endless, heroic observations, almost unconscious or
> automatic—and then comes a sudden relaxation, a forgetful phrase, and one
> feels that strangeness of his undertaking, sees the lonely young man, his eyes
> fixed on facts and minute details, sinking or sliding giddily off into the un-
> known. What one seems to want in art, in experiencing it, is the same thing that
> is necessary for its creation, a self-forgetful, perfectly useless concentration.

---

[4]Olson wrote in a letter: "I have learned more from him [poet Robert Creeley] than from any living man" (*Letters for Origin*, p. 87).
[5]Olson once wrote that the root or original meaning of "arro-gance" was "to ask a question to or of something, to make a demand which has to be answered"; thus originally the word was the equivalent of "humility" (*The Special View of History*, p.30).

Like Darwin, Bishop travelled about the world and endlessly observed (and wrote about) its contents—places, things, animals, especially animals. Bishop's observations were not in the service of science but in the service of poetry. But like the Darwin she describes, when the observer in her poems has her "eyes fixed on facts and minute details," the reader might suddenly find her "sinking or sliding giddily off into the unknown." Her most famous poem is "The Fish." Other poems about animal life include "Roosters," "The Armadillo," "Sand-piper," "The Moose"; and there is her odd prose-poem sequence, "Rainy Season; Sub-Tropics," made up of "Giant Toad," "Strayed Crab," and "Giant Snail"—all creatures caught, as Randall Jarrell said of "The Fish" and "Roosters," in "the most calmly beautiful, deeply sympathetic poems of our time."

Elizabeth Bishop was born in Worcester, Massachusetts. Her father died when she was only eight months old, and her mother, who had suffered several break-downs, went insane and was institutionalized when Bishop was four. Raised by her maternal grandparents in Nova Scotia until she was six (she would summer with them until she was twelve), Bishop then lived unhappily with her paternal grandparents in Worcester until taken in by a Boston aunt. Bishop attended Walnut Hill School in Natick, Massachusetts, and Vassar College. By the time she entered Vassar in 1930, she had become an avid reader, having discovered Walt Whitman at thirteen, and going on to Emily Dickinson and Henry James. About this time she came across Harriet Monroe's anthology of modern poetry. While at Vassar, the librarian introduced her to Marianne Moore, who became a lifelong correspondent and confidante. Bishop would say of her later: "She had a great influence on me. We became very good friends, and she was very kind to me."

After graduation from Vassar in 1934, Bishop began a life of travel. During the years 1935–38, she visited Belgium, France, England, North Africa, Spain, and Italy. In 1939, she settled in Florida, and in 1943 she lived for a time in Mexico, where she met the Chilean poet Pablo Neruda. She had been publishing poems in the little magazines all during this period, but it was not until 1946 that she brought out a volume of poetry, *North and South*. It was highly praised by reviewers, especially Randall Jarrell. Jarrell introduced her to Robert Lowell, who became another lifelong friend. He dedicated his poem "Skunk Hour" to her, having modeled it on her poem "The Armadillo," which is dedicated to him.

The success of her first book resulted in her winning a Guggenheim Fellow-ship in 1947 and becoming consultant in poetry at the Library of Congress in 1949–50. Her wanderlust returned in 1951, and she travelled through South America, finally deciding to settle down in Brazil with her intimate friend Lota de Macedo Soares. She remained there for the next fifteen or so years. In 1955, she republished her first volume with a new group of poems under the title *Poems: North & South—A Cold Spring*. The book confirmed her talent, won her still wider attention, and was awarded the Pulitzer Prize. Meantime, she had learned Portuguese and had become engaged in translating Portuguese litera-ture, including poetry.

In 1965, Bishop published a new volume of poems *Questions of Travel*, which, as the title suggests, grew out of her extensive experiences in travelling about the world. The title poem, "Questions of Travel," posed those queries she must often have asked herself in the many foreign lands she visited:

Should we have stayed at home and thought of here?
Where should we be today?

•   •   •   •   •

"... *Should we have stayed at home,*
wherever that may be?"

Although the title of her volume of poems published in 1969, *The Complete Poems*, had the ring of finality, she did in fact continue to write. She published *Geography III* in 1976, containing, according to the critics, some of her best poetry; it won the National Book Critics Circle Award. Bishop died in 1979.

Throughout her career, she refused to accept the identity of "woman poet," believing that it was patronising and ultimately diminishing. She told an interviewer in 1977: "When I was in college and started publishing, even then, and in the following few years, there were women's anthologies, and all-women issues of magazines, but I always refused to be in them. I didn't think about it very seriously, but I felt it was a lot of nonsense, separating the sexes. I suppose this feeling came from feminist principles, perhaps stronger than I was aware of."

ADDITIONAL READING

The Collected Prose of Elizabeth Bishop, 1984.

Anne Stevenson, *Elizabeth Bishop*, 1966; David Kalstone, "Elizabeth Bishop," *Five Temperaments*, 1977; Candace MacMahon, *Elizabeth Bishop: A Bibliography*, 1980; Lloyd Schwartz and Sybil P. Estess, eds., *Elizabeth Bishop and Her Art*, 1983; Diana E. Wylie, *Elizabeth Bishop and Howard Nemerov: A Reference Guide*, 1983; Thomas J. Travisano, *Elizabeth Bishop: Her Artistic Development*, 1988; Robert Dale Parker, *The Unbeliever: The Poetry of Elizabeth Bishop*, 1988; David Kalstone, *Becoming a Poet: Elizabeth Bishop with Marianne Moore and Robert Lowell*, ed. Robert Hemenway, 1989.

TEXT

The Complete Poems, 1927–1979, 1983.

The Man-Moth[1]

Here, above,
cracks in the buildings are filled with battered moonlight.
The whole shadow of Man is only as big as his hat.
It lies at his feet like a circle for a doll to stand on,
and he makes an inverted pin, the point magnetized to the moon.   5
He does not see the moon; he observes only her vast properties,
feeling the queer light on his hands, neither warm nor cold,
of a temperature impossible to record in thermometers.

But when the Man-Moth
pays his rare, although occasional, visits to the surface,   10
the moon looks rather different to him. He emerges
from an opening under the edge of one of the sidewalks
and nervously begins to scale the faces of the buildings.
He thinks the moon is a small hole at the top of the sky,
proving the sky quite useless for protection.   15
He trembles, but must investigate as high as he can climb.

Up the façades,
his shadow dragging like a photographer's cloth behind him,
he climbs fearfully, thinking that this time he will manage
to push his small head through that round clean opening   20

----
[1] "Newspaper misprint for 'mammoth'" (Bishop's note).

and be forced through, as from a tube, in black scrolls on the light.
(Man, standing below him, has no such illusions.)
But what the Man-Moth fears most he must do, although
he fails, of course, and falls back scared but quite unhurt.

          Then he returns   25
to the pale subways of cement he calls his home. He flits,
he flutters, and cannot get aboard the silent trains
fast enough to suit him. The doors close swiftly.
The Man-Moth always seats himself facing the wrong way
and the train starts at once at its full, terrible speed,   30
without a shift in gears or a gradation of any sort.
He cannot tell the rate at which he travels backwards.

          Each night he must
be carried through artificial tunnels and dream recurrent dreams.
Just as the ties recur beneath his train, these underlie   35
his rushing brain. He does not dare look out the window,
for the third rail, the unbroken draught of poison,
runs there beside him. He regards it as a disease
he has inherited the susceptibility to. He has to keep
his hands in his pockets, as others must wear mufflers.   40

          If you catch him,
hold up a flashlight to his eye. It's all dark pupil,
an entire night itself, whose haired horizon tightens
as he stares back, and closes up the eye. Then from the lids
one tear, his only possession, like the bee's sting, slips.   45
Slyly he palms it, and if you're not paying attention
he'll swallow it. However, if you watch, he'll hand it over,
cool as from underground springs and pure enough to drink.

1935   1936, 1946

The Fish

I caught a tremendous fish
and held him beside the boat
half out of water, with my hook
fast in a corner of his mouth.
He didn't fight.   5
He hadn't fought at all.
He hung a grunting weight,
battered and venerable
and homely. Here and there
his brown skin hung in strips   10
like ancient wallpaper,
and its pattern of darker brown
was like wallpaper:
shapes like full-blown roses
stained and lost through age.   15
He was speckled with barnacles,
fine rosettes of lime,
and infested
with tiny white sea-lice,
and underneath two or three   20

rags of green weed hung down.
While his gills were breathing in
the terrible oxygen
—the frightening gills,
fresh and crisp with blood,   25
that can cut so badly—
I thought of the coarse white flesh
packed in like feathers,
the big bones and the little bones,
the dramatic reds and blacks   30
of his shiny entrails,
and the pink swim-bladder
like a big peony.
I looked into his eyes
which were far larger than mine   35
but shallower, and yellowed,
the irises backed and packed
with tarnished tinfoil
seen through the lenses
of old scratched isinglass.   40
They shifted a little, but not
to return my stare.
—It was more like the tipping
of an object toward the light.
I admired his sullen face,   45
the mechanism of his jaw,
and then I saw
that from his lower lip
—if you could call it a lip—
grim, wet, and weaponlike,   50
hung five old pieces of fish-line,
or four and a wire leader
with the swivel still attached,
with all their five big hooks
grown firmly in his mouth.   55
A green line, frayed at the end
where he broke it, two heavier lines,
and a fine black thread
still crimped from the strain and snap
when it broke and he got away.   60
Like medals with their ribbons
frayed and wavering,
a five-haired beard of wisdom
trailing from his aching jaw.
I stared and stared   65
and victory filled up
the little rented boat,
from the pool of bilge
where oil had spread a rainbow
around the rusted engine   70
to the bailer rusted orange,
the sun-cracked thwarts,
the oarlocks on their strings,
the gunnels—until everything
was rainbow, rainbow, rainbow!   75
And I let the fish go.

1940, 1946

At the Fishhouses

Although it is a cold evening,
down by one of the fishhouses
an old man sits netting,
his net, in the gloaming almost invisible,
a dark purple-brown,   5
and his shuttle worn and polished.
The air smells so strong of codfish
it makes one's nose run and one's eyes water.
The five fishhouses have steeply peaked roofs
and narrow, cleated gangplanks slant up   10
to storerooms in the gables
for the wheelbarrows to be pushed up and down on.
All is silver: the heavy surface of the sea,
swelling slowly as if considering spilling over,
is opaque, but the silver of the benches,   15
the lobster pots, and masts, scattered
among the wild jagged rocks,
is of an apparent translucence
like the small old buildings with an emerald moss
growing on their shoreward walls.   20
The big fish tubs are completely lined
with layers of beautiful herring scales
and the wheelbarrows are similarly plastered
with creamy iridescent coats of mail,
with small iridescent flies crawling on them.   25
Up on the little slope behind the houses,
set in the sparse bright sprinkle of grass,
is an ancient wooden capstan,[1]
cracked, with two long bleached handles
and some melancholy stains, like dried blood,   30
where the ironwork has rusted.
The old man accepts a Lucky Strike.
He was a friend of my grandfather.
We talk of the decline in the population
and of codfish and herring   35
while he waits for a herring boat to come in.
There are sequins on his vest and on his thumb.
He has scraped the scales, the principal beauty,
from unnumbered fish with that black old knife,
the blade of which is almost worn away.   40

Down at the water's edge, at the place
where they haul up the boats, up the long ramp
descending into the water, thin silver
tree trunks are laid horizontally
across the gray stones, down and down   45
at intervals of four or five feet.

Cold dark deep and absolutely clear,
element bearable to no mortal,
to fish and to seals . . . One seal particularly
I have seen here evening after evening.   50

---

[1]A rotating vertical cylinder used to lift weights by winding in
a cable.

He was curious about me. He was interested in music;
like me a believer in total immersion,[2]
so I used to sing him Baptist hymns.
I also sang "A Mighty Fortress Is Our God."[3]
He stood up in the water and regarded me   55
steadily, moving his head a little.
Then he would disappear, then suddenly emerge
almost in the same spot, with a sort of shrug
as if it were against his better judgment.
Cold dark deep and absolutely clear,   60
the clear gray icy water . . . Back, behind us,
the dignified tall firs begin.
Bluish, associating with their shadows,
a million Christmas trees stand
waiting for Christmas. The water seems suspended   65
above the rounded gray and blue-gray stones.
I have seen it over and over, the same sea, the same,
slightly, indifferently swinging above the stones,
icily free above the stones,
above the stones and then the world.   70
If you should dip your hand in,
your wrist would ache immediately,
your bones would begin to ache and your hand would burn
as if the water were a transmutation of fire
that feeds on stones and burns with a dark gray flame.   75
If you tasted it, it would first taste bitter,
then briny, then surely burn your tongue.
It is like what we imagine knowledge to be:
dark, salt, clear, moving, utterly free,
drawn from the cold hard mouth   80
of the world, derived from the rocky breasts
forever, flowing and drawn, and since
our knowledge is historical, flowing, and flown.

1947, 1955

Invitation to
Miss Marianne Moore

From Brooklyn, over the Brooklyn Bridge, on this fine morning,
    please come flying.
In a cloud of fiery pale chemicals,
    please come flying,
to the rapid rolling of thousands of small blue drums   5
descending out of the mackerel sky
over the glittering grandstand of harbor-water,
    please come flying.

Whistles, pennants and smoke are blowing. The ships
are signaling cordially with multitudes of flags   10
rising and falling like birds all over the harbor.

---

[2] Form of baptism practiced by some Protestant sects.
[3] Hymn composed by the German theologian Martin Luther
(1483–1546).

Enter: two rivers, gracefully bearing
countless little pellucid jellies
in cut-glass epergnes[1] dragging with silver chains.
The flight is safe; the weather is all arranged.   15
The waves are running in verses this fine morning.
    Please come flying.

Come with the pointed toe of each black shoe
trailing a sapphire highlight,
with a black capeful of butterfly wings and bon-mots,   20
with heaven knows how many angels all riding
on the broad black brim of your hat,
    please come flying.

Bearing a musical inaudible abacus,
a slight censorious frown, and blue ribbons,   25
    please come flying.
Facts and skyscrapers glint in the tide; Manhattan
is all awash with morals this fine morning,
    so please come flying.

Mounting the sky with natural heroism,   30
above the accidents, above the malignant movies,
the taxicabs and injustices at large,
while horns are resounding in your beautiful ears
that simultaneously listen to
a soft uninvented music, fit for the musk deer,   35
    please come flying.

For whom the grim museums will behave
like courteous male bower-birds,
for whom the agreeable lions lie in wait
on the steps of the Public Library,   40
eager to rise and follow through the doors
up into the reading rooms,
    please come flying.
We can sit down and weep; we can go shopping,
or play at a game of constantly being wrong   45
with a priceless set of vocabularies,
or we can bravely deplore, but please
    please come flying.

With dynasties of negative constructions
darkening and dying around you,   50
with grammar that suddenly turns and shines
like flocks of sandpipers flying,
    please come flying.

Come like a light in the white mackerel sky,
come like a daytime comet   55
with a long unnebulous train of words,
from Brooklyn, over the Brooklyn Bridge, on this fine morning,
    please come flying.

1948, 1955

---

[1]Centerpiece serving dishes, often in branched form.

Questions of Travel

There are too many waterfalls here; the crowded streams
hurry too rapidly down to the sea,
and the pressure of so many clouds on the mountaintops
makes them spill over the sides in soft slow-motion,
turning to waterfalls under our very eyes.   5
—For if those streaks, those mile-long, shiny, tearstains,
aren't waterfalls yet,
in a quick age or so, as ages go here,
they probably will be.
But if the streams and clouds keep travelling, travelling,   10
the mountains look like the hulls of capsized ships,
slime-hung and barnacled.

Think of the long trip home.
Should we have stayed at home and thought of here?
Where should we be today?   15
Is it right to be watching strangers in a play
in this strangest of theatres?
What childishness is it that while there's a breath of life
in our bodies, we are determined to rush
to see the sun the other way around?   20
The tiniest green hummingbird in the world?
To stare at some inexplicable old stonework,
inexplicable and impenetrable,
at any view,
instantly seen and always, always delightful?   25
Oh, must we dream our dreams
and have them, too?
And have we room
for one more folded sunset, still quite warm?

But surely it would have been a pity   30
not to have seen the trees along this road,
really exaggerated in their beauty,
not to have seen them gesturing
like noble pantomimists, robed in pink.
—Not to have had to stop for gas and heard   35
the sad, two-noted, wooden tune
of disparate wooden clogs
carelessly clacking over
a grease-stained filling-station floor.
(In another country the clogs would all be tested.   40
Each pair there would have identical pitch.)
—A pity not to have heard
the other, less primitive music of the fat brown bird
who sings above the broken gasoline pump
in a bamboo church of Jesuit baroque:[1]   45
three towers, five silver crosses.
—Yes, a pity not to have pondered,
blurr'dly and inconclusively,
on what connection can exist for centuries

---

[1]Ornate architecture brought into Latin America in the seventeenth century by Jesuit missionaries.

between the crudest wooden footwear   50
and, careful and finicky,
the whittled fantasies of wooden cages.
—Never to have studied history in
the weak calligraphy of songbirds' cages.
—And never to have had to listen to rain   55
so much like politicians' speeches:
two hours of unrelenting oratory
and then a sudden golden silence
in which the traveller takes a notebook, writes:

"Is it lack of imagination that makes us come   60
to imagined places, not just stay at home?
Or could Pascal[2] have been not entirely right
about just sitting quietly in one's room?

Continent, city, country, society:
the choice is never wide and never free.   65
And here, or there . . . No. Should we have stayed at home,
wherever that may be?"

                                                                    1956, 1965

The Armadillo

FOR ROBERT LOWELL

This is the time of year
when almost every night
the frail, illegal fire balloons appear.
Climbing the mountain height,

rising toward a saint   5
still honored in these parts,[1]
the paper chambers flush and fill with light
that comes and goes, like hearts.

Once up against the sky it's hard
to tell them from the stars—   10
planets, that is—the tinted ones:
Venus going down, or Mars,

or the pale green one. With a wind,
they flare and falter, wobble and toss;
but if it's still they steer between   15
the kite sticks of the Southern Cross,[2]

receding, dwindling, solemnly
and steadily forsaking us,
or, in the downdraft from a peak,
suddenly turning dangerous.   20

---

[2]Blaise Pascal (1623–1662), French philosopher who said
that human evil stems from man's being unable to sit still in a
room (*Pensées*).

[1]Rio de Janeiro, Brazil.
[2]A constellation visible only from the southern hemisphere.

Last night another big one fell.
It splattered like an egg of fire
against the cliff behind the house.
The flame ran down. We saw the pair

of owls who nest there flying up   25
and up, their whirling black-and-white
stained bright pink underneath, until
they shrieked up out of sight.

The ancient owls' nest must have burned.
Hastily, all alone,   30
a glistening armadillo left the scene,
rose-flecked, head down, tail down,

and then a baby rabbit jumped out,
short-eared, to our surprise.
So soft! — a handful of intangible ash   35
with fixed, ignited eyes.

Too pretty, dreamlike mimicry!
O falling fire and piercing cry
and panic, and a weak mailed fist
clenched ignorant against the sky!   40

                                        1957, 1965

Sestina[1]

September rain falls on the house.
In the failing light, the old grandmother
sits in the kitchen with the child
beside the Little Marvel Stove,
reading the jokes from the almanac,   5
laughing and talking to hide her tears.

She thinks that her equinoctial[2] tears
and the rain that beats on the roof of the house
were both foretold by the almanac,
but only known to a grandmother.   10
The iron kettle sings on the stove.
She cuts some bread and says to the child,

It's time for tea now; but the child
is watching the teakettle's small hard tears
dance like mad on the hot black stove,   15
the way the rain must dance on the house.

---

[1]The sestina form consists of six six-line stanzas and a three-line envoy (short concluding stanza); the six words that end the lines in the first stanza are repeated as line-end words in the other stanzas, according to a set pattern, and three occur at the middle of each line in the envoy.

[2]Since the time is autumn (September rain is mentioned in the first stanza), the tears may be linked to the autumn equinox (September 22), when day and night are of equal length: thus, equinoctial.

Tidying up, the old grandmother
hangs up the clever almanac

on its string. Birdlike, the almanac
hovers half open above the child,   20
hovers above the old grandmother
and her teacup full of dark brown tears.
She shivers and says she thinks the house
feels chilly, and puts more wood in the stove.

It was to be, says the Marvel Stove.   25
I know what I know, says the almanac.
With crayons the child draws a rigid house
and a winding pathway. Then the child
puts in a man with buttons like tears
and shows it proudly to the grandmother.   30

But secretly, while the grandmother
busies herself about the stove,
the little moons fall down like tears
from between the pages of the almanac
into the flower bed the child   35
has carefully placed in the front of the house.

Time to plant tears, says the almanac.
The grandmother sings to the marvellous stove
and the child draws another inscrutable house.

                                                        1956, 1965

Sandpiper[1]

The roaring alongside he takes for granted,
and that every so often the world is bound to shake.
He runs, he runs to the south, finical, awkward,
in a state of controlled panic, a student of Blake.[2]

The beach hisses like fat. On his left, a sheet   5
of interrupting water comes and goes
and glazes over his dark and brittle feet.
He runs, he runs straight through it, watching his toes.

—Watching, rather, the spaces of sand between them,
where (no detail too small) the Atlantic drains   10
rapidly backwards and downwards. As he runs,
he stares at the dragging grains.

The world is a mist. And then the world is
minute and vast and clear. The tide

---

[1]A small wading bird that frequents the seashore.
[2]English poet William Blake (1757–1827), often thought
mad for his prophetic visions. His "Auguries of Innocence"

begins: "To see a World in a Grain of Sand / And a Heaven in
a Wild Flower, / Hold Infinity in the palm of your hand / And
Eternity in an hour."

is higher or lower. He couldn't tell you which.   15
His beak is focussed; he is preoccupied,

looking for something, something, something.
Poor bird, he is obsessed!
The millions of grains are black, white, tan, and gray,
mixed with quartz grains, rose and amethyst.   20

1962, 1965

In the Waiting Room

In Worcester, Massachusetts,
I went with Aunt Consuelo
to keep her dentist's appointment
and sat and waited for her
in the dentist's waiting room.   5
It was winter. It got dark
early. The waiting room
was full of grown-up people,
arctics and overcoats,
lamps and magazines.   10
My aunt was inside
what seemed like a long time
and while I waited I read
the *National Geographic*
(I could read) and carefully   15
studied the photographs:
the inside of a volcano,
black, and full of ashes;
then it was spilling over
in rivulets of fire.   20
Osa and Martin Johnson[1]
dressed in riding breeches,
laced boots, and pith helmets.
A dead man slung on a pole
—"Long Pig,"[2] the caption said.   25
Babies with pointed heads
wound round and round with string;
black, naked women with necks
wound round and round with wire
like the necks of light bulbs.   30
Their breasts were horrifying.
I read it right straight through.
I was too shy to stop.
And then I looked at the cover:
the yellow margins, the date.   35

Suddenly, from inside,
came an *oh!* of pain

---

[1] American explorers and travel writers Osa (1894–1953) and
Martin (1884–1937) Johnson.
[2] Cannibals' name for a dead human being.

—Aunt Consuelo's voice—
not very loud or long.
I wasn't at all surprised;   40
even then I knew she was
a foolish, timid woman.
I might have been embarrassed,
but wasn't. What took me
completely by surprise   45
was that it was *me:*
my voice, in my mouth.
Without thinking at all
I was my foolish aunt,
I—we—were falling, falling,   50
our eyes glued to the cover
of the *National Geographic*,
February, 1918.

I said to myself: three days
and you'll be seven years old.   55
I was saying it to stop
the sensation of falling off
the round, turning world
into cold, blue-black space.
But I felt: you are an *I*,   60
you are an *Elizabeth*,
you are one of *them*.
Why should you be one, too?
I scarcely dared to look
to see what it was I was.   65
I gave a sidelong glance
—I couldn't look any higher—
at shadowy gray knees,
trousers and skirts and boots
and different pairs of hands   70
lying under the lamps.
I knew that nothing stranger
had ever happened, that nothing
stranger could ever happen.
Why should I be my aunt,   75
or me, or anyone?
What similarities—
boots, hands, the family voice
I felt in my throat, or even
the *National Geographic*   80
and those awful hanging breasts—
held us all together
or made us all just one?
How—I didn't know any
word for it—how "unlikely" . . .   85
How had I come to be here,
like them, and overhear
a cry of pain that could have
got loud and worse but hadn't?

The waiting room was bright   90
and too hot. It was sliding

beneath a big black wave,
another, and another.

Then I was back in it.
The War was on. Outside,   95
in Worcester, Massachusetts,
were night and slush and cold,
and it was still the fifth
of February, 1918.

                                                        1971, 1976

Crusoe[1] in England

A new volcano has erupted,
the papers say, and last week I was reading
where some ship saw an island being born:
at first a breath of steam, ten miles away;
and then a black fleck — basalt, probably —   5
rose in the mate's binoculars
and caught on the horizon like a fly.
They named it. But my poor old island's still
un-rediscovered, un-renamable.
None of the books has ever got it right.   10

Well, I had fifty-two
miserable, small volcanoes I could climb
with a few slithery strides —
volcanoes dead as ash heaps.
I used to sit on the edge of the highest one   15
and count the others standing up,
naked and leaden, with their heads blown off.
I'd think that if they were the size
I thought volcanoes should be, then I had
become a giant;   20
and if I had become a giant,
I couldn't bear to think what size
the goats and turtles were,
or the gulls, or the overlapping rollers
— a glittering hexagon of rollers   25
closing and closing in, but never quite,
glittering and glittering, though the sky
was mostly overcast.

My island seemed to be
a sort of cloud-dump. All the hemisphere's   30
left-over clouds arrived and hung
above the craters — their parched throats
were hot to touch.
Was that why it rained so much?

---

[1]*Robinson Crusoe*, by British novelist Daniel Defoe (1660–1731), portrays the title character, an English seaman, marooned on an island and surviving by skill and ingenuity; his oppressive solitude is dispelled when he discovers a companion he calls Friday. He is ultimately rescued by an English ship.

And why sometimes the whole place hissed?   35
The turtles lumbered by, high-domed,
hissing like teakettles.
(And I'd have given years, or taken a few,
for any sort of kettle, of course.)
The folds of lava, running out to sea,   40
would hiss. I'd turn. And then they'd prove
to be more turtles.
The beaches were all lava, variegated,
black, red, and white, and gray;
the marbled colors made a fine display.   45
And I had waterspouts. Oh,
half a dozen at a time, far out,
they'd come and go, advancing and retreating,
their heads in cloud, their feet in moving patches
of scuffed-up white.   50
Glass chimneys, flexible, attenuated,
sacerdotal[2] beings of glass . . . I watched
the water spiral up in them like smoke.
Beautiful, yes, but not much company.

I often gave way to self-pity.   55
"Do I deserve this? I suppose I must.
I wouldn't be here otherwise. Was there
a moment when I actually chose this?
I don't remember, but there could have been."
What's wrong about self-pity, anyway?   60
With my legs dangling down familiarly
over a crater's edge, I told myself
"Pity should begin at home." So the more
pity I felt, the more I felt at home.

The sun set in the sea; the same odd sun   65
rose from the sea,
and there was one of it and one of me.
The island had one kind of everything:
one tree snail, a bright violet-blue
with a thin shell, crept over everything,   70
over the one variety of tree,
a sooty, scrub affair.
Snail shells lay under these in drifts
and, at a distance,
you'd swear that they were beds of irises.   75
There was one kind of berry, a dark red.
I tried it, one by one, and hours apart.
Sub-acid, and not bad, no ill effects;
and so I made home-brew. I'd drink
the awful, fizzy, stinging stuff   80
that went straight to my head
and play my home-made flute
(I think it had the weirdest scale on earth)
and, dizzy, whoop and dance among the goats.
Home-made, home-made! But aren't we all?   85

---

[2]Priestly.

I felt a deep affection for
the smallest of my island industries.
No, not exactly, since the smallest was
a miserable philosophy.

Because I didn't know enough.   90
Why didn't I know enough of something?
Greek drama or astronomy? The books
I'd read were full of blanks;
the poems — well, I tried
reciting to my iris-beds,   95
"They flash upon that inward eye,
which is the bliss . . ."[3] The bliss of what?
One of the first things that I did
when I got back was look it up.

The island smelled of goat and guano.[4]   100
The goats were white, so were the gulls,
and both too tame, or else they thought
I was a goat, too, or a gull.
Baa, baa, baa and *shriek, shriek, shriek,*
baa . . . shriek . . . baa . . . I still can't shake   105
them from my ears; they're hurting now.
The questioning shrieks, the equivocal replies
over a ground of hissing rain
and hissing, ambulating turtles
got on my nerves.   110

When all the gulls flew up at once, they sounded
like a big tree in a strong wind, its leaves.
I'd shut my eyes and think about a tree,
an oak, say, with real shade, somewhere.
I'd heard of cattle getting island-sick.   115
I thought the goats were.
One billy-goat would stand on the volcano
I'd christened *Mont d'Espoir*[5] or *Mount Despair*
(I'd time enough to play with names),
and bleat and bleat, and sniff the air.   120
I'd grab his beard and look at him.
His pupils, horizontal, narrowed up
and expressed nothing, or a little malice.
I got so tired of the very colors!
One day I dyed a baby goat bright red   125
with my red berries, just to see
something a little different.
And then his mother wouldn't recognize him.

Dreams were the worst. Of course I dreamed of food
and love, but they were pleasant rather   130
than otherwise. But then I'd dream of things
like slitting a baby's throat, mistaking it

---

[3]From "I Wandered Lonely as a Cloud" by William Wordsworth (1770–1850); the speaker comes upon a host of
"golden daffodils," the antecedent of "they" in the lines
quoted. The missing words in the second line are "of

solitude."
[4]Bird excrement, often used for manure.
[5]"Mount of Hope" (French).

for a baby goat. I'd have
nightmares of other islands
stretching away from mine, infinities   135
of islands, islands spawning islands,
like frogs' eggs turning into polliwogs
of islands, knowing that I had to live
on each and every one, eventually,
for ages, registering their flora,   140
their fauna, their geography.

Just when I thought I couldn't stand it
another minute longer, Friday came.
(Accounts of that have everything all wrong.)
Friday was nice.   145
Friday was nice, and we were friends.
If only he had been a woman!
I wanted to propagate my kind,
and so did he, I think, poor boy.
He'd pet the baby goats sometimes,   150
and race with them, or carry one around.
— Pretty to watch; he had a pretty body.

And then one day they came and took us off.

Now I live here, another island,
that doesn't seem like one, but who decides?   155
My blood was full of them; my brain
bred islands. But that archipelago
has petered out. I'm old.
I'm bored, too, drinking my real tea,
surrounded by uninteresting lumber.   160
The knife there on the shelf—
it reeked of meaning, like a crucifix.
It lived. How many years did I
beg it, implore it, not to break?
I knew each nick and scratch by heart,   165
the bluish blade, the broken tip,
the lines of wood-grain on the handle . . .
Now it won't look at me at all.
The living soul has dribbled away.
My eyes rest on it and pass on.   170

The local museum's asked me to
leave everything to them:
the flute, the knife, the shrivelled shoes,
my shedding goatskin trousers
(moths have got in the fur),   175
the parasol that took me such a time
remembering the way the ribs should go.
It still will work but, folded up,
looks like a plucked and skinny fowl.
How can anyone want such things?   180
— And Friday, my dear Friday, died of measles
seventeen years ago come March.

1971, 1976

The Moose

FOR GRACE BULMER BOWERS

From narrow provinces
of fish and bread and tea,
home of the long tides
where the bay leaves the sea
twice a day and takes   5
the herrings long rides,

where if the river
enters or retreats
in a wall of brown foam
depends on if it meets   10
the bay coming in,
the bay not at home;

where, silted red,
sometimes the sun sets
facing a red sea,   15
and others, veins the flats'
lavender, rich mud
in burning rivulets;

on red, gravelly roads,
down rows of sugar maples,   20
past clapboard farmhouses
and neat, clapboard churches,
bleached, ridged as clamshells,
past twin silver birches,

through late afternoon   25
a bus journeys west,
the windshield flashing pink,
pink glancing off of metal,
brushing the dented flank
of blue, beat-up enamel;   30

down hollows, up rises,
and waits, patient, while
a lone traveller gives
kisses and embraces
to seven relatives   35
and a collie supervises.

Goodbye to the elms,
to the farm, to the dog.
The bus starts. The light
grows richer; the fog,   40
shifting, salty, thin,
comes closing in.

Its cold, round crystals
form and slide and settle
in the white hens' feathers,   45

in gray glazed cabbages,
on the cabbage roses
and lupins like apostles;

the sweet peas cling
to their wet white string   50
on the whitewashed fences;
bumblebees creep
inside the foxgloves,
and evening commences.

One stop at Bass River.   55
Then the Economies—
Lower, Middle, Upper;
Five Islands, Five Houses,[1]
where a woman shakes a tablecloth
out after supper.   60

A pale flickering. Gone.
The Tantramar marshes
and the smell of salt hay.
An iron bridge trembles
and a loose plank rattles   65
but doesn't give way.

On the left, a red light
swims through the dark:
a ship's port lantern.
Two rubber boots show,   70
illuminated, solemn.
A dog gives one bark.

A woman climbs in
with two market bags,
brisk, freckled, elderly.   75
"A grand night. Yes, sir,
all the way to Boston."
She regards us amicably.

Moonlight as we enter
the New Brunswick woods,   80
hairy, scratchy, splintery;
moonlight and mist
caught in them like lamb's wool
on bushes in a pasture.

The passengers lie back.   85
Snores. Some long sighs.
A dreamy divagation
begins in the night,
a gentle, auditory,
slow hallucination. . . .   90

---

[1] In Nova Scotia.

In the creakings and noises,
an old conversation
—not concerning us,
but recognizable, somewhere,
back in the bus: 95
Grandparents' voices

uninterruptedly
talking, in Eternity:
names being mentioned,
things cleared up finally;   100
what he said, what she said,
who got pensioned;

deaths, deaths and sicknesses;
the year he remarried;
the year (something) happened.   105
She died in childbirth.
That was the son lost
when the schooner foundered.

He took to drink. Yes.
She went to the bad.   110
When Amos began to pray
even in the store and
finally the family had
to put him away.

"Yes . . ." that peculiar   115
affirmative. "Yes . . ."
A sharp, indrawn breath,
half groan, half acceptance,
that means "Life's like that.
We know *it* (also death)."   120

Talking the way they talked
in the old featherbed,
peacefully, on and on,
dim lamplight in the hall,
down in the kitchen, the dog   125
tucked in her shawl.

Now, it's all right now
even to fall asleep
just as on all those nights.
—Suddenly the bus driver   130
stops with a jolt,
turns off his lights.

A moose has come out of
the impenetrable wood
and stands there, looms, rather,   135
in the middle of the road.
It approaches; it sniffs at
the bus's hot hood.

Towering, antlerless,
high as a church,   140
homely as a house
(or, safe as houses).
A man's voice assures us
"Perfectly harmless. . . ."

Some of the passengers   145
exclaim in whispers,
childishly, softly,
"Sure are big creatures."
"It's awful plain."
"Look! It's a she!"   150

Taking her time,
she looks the bus over,
grand, otherworldly.
Why, why do we feel
(we all feel) this sweet   155
sensation of joy?

"Curious creatures,"
says our quiet driver,
rolling his *r*'s.
"Look at that, would you."   160
Then he shifts gears.
For a moment longer,

by craning backward,
the moose can be seen
on the moonlit macadam;   165
then there's a dim
smell of moose, an acrid
smell of gasoline.

                                        1972, 1976

Poem

About the size of an old-style dollar bill,
American or Canadian,
mostly the same whites, gray greens, and steel grays
—this little painting (a sketch for a larger one?)
has never earned any money in its life.   5
Useless and free, it has spent seventy years
as a minor family relic
handed along collaterally to owners
who looked at it sometimes, or didn't bother to.

It must be Nova Scotia; only there   10
does one see gabled wooden houses
painted that awful shade of brown.
The other houses, the bits that show, are white.
Elm trees, low hills, a thin church steeple

—that gray-blue wisp—or is it? In the foreground   15
a water meadow with some tiny cows,
two brushstrokes each, but confidently cows;
two minuscule white geese in the blue water,
back-to-back, feeding, and a slanting stick.
Up closer, a wild iris, white and yellow,   20
fresh-squiggled from the tube.
The air is fresh and cold; cold early spring
clear as gray glass; a half inch of blue sky
below the steel-gray storm clouds.
(They were the artist's specialty.)   25
A specklike bird is flying to the left.
Or is it a flyspeck looking like a bird?

Heavens, I recognize the place, I know it!
It's behind—I can almost remember the farmer's name.
His barn backed on that meadow. There it is,   30
titanium white, one dab. The hint of steeple,
filaments of brush-hairs, barely there,
must be the Presbyterian church.
Would that be Miss Gillespie's house?
Those particular geese and cows   35
are naturally before my time.

A sketch done in an hour, "in one breath,"
once taken from a trunk and handed over.
Would you like this? I'll probably never
have room to hang these things again.   40
Your Uncle George, no, mine, my Uncle George,
he'd be your great-uncle, left them all with Mother
when he went back to England.
You know, he was quite famous, an R.A.[1] ...

I never knew him. We both knew this place,   45
apparently, this literal small backwater,
looked at it long enough to memorize it,
our years apart. How strange. And it's still loved,
or its memory is (it must have changed a lot).
Our visions coincided—"visions" is   50
too serious a word—our looks, two looks:
art "copying from life" and life itself,
life and the memory of it so compressed
they've turned into each other. Which is which?
Life and the memory of it cramped,   55
dim, on a piece of Bristol board,[2]
dim, but how live, how touching in detail
—the little that we get for free,
the little of our earthly trust. Not much.
About the size of our abidance   60
along with theirs: the munching cows,
the iris, crisp and shivering, the water
still standing from spring freshets,
the yet-to-be dismantled elms, the geese.

1972, 1976

---

[1] A member of the Royal Academy in London.
[2] Cardboard with a smooth surface.

One Art[1]

The art of losing isn't hard to master;
so many things seem filled with the intent
to be lost that their loss is no disaster.

Lose something every day. Accept the fluster
of lost door keys, the hour badly spent.   5
The art of losing isn't hard to master.

Then practice losing farther, losing faster:
places, and names, and where it was you meant
to travel. None of these will bring disaster.

I lost my mother's watch. And look! my last, or   10
next-to-last, of three loved houses went.
The art of losing isn't hard to master.

I lost two cities, lovely ones. And, vaster,
some realms I owned, two rivers, a continent.
I miss them, but it wasn't a disaster.   15

— Even losing you (the joking voice, a gesture
I love) I shan't have lied. It's evident
the art of losing's not too hard to master
though it may look like (*Write* it!) like disaster.

                                        1976

Five Flights Up

Still dark.
The unknown bird sits on his usual branch.
The little dog next door barks in his sleep
inquiringly, just once.
Perhaps in his sleep, too, the bird inquires   5
once or twice, quavering.
Questions — if that is what they are —
answered directly, simply,
by day itself.

Enormous morning, ponderous, meticulous;   10
gray light streaking each bare branch,
each single twig, along one side,
making another tree, of glassy veins . . .
The bird still sits there. Now he seems to yawn.

The little black dog runs in his yard.   15
His owner's voice arises, stern,

---

[1] The form is (with slight variations) the French fixed form of
the "villanelle" (see footnote 1 to Theodore Roethke's "The
Waking").

"You ought to be ashamed!"
What has he done?
He bounces cheerfully up and down;
he rushes in circles in the fallen leaves.   20

Obviously, he has no sense of shame.
He and the bird know everything is answered,
all taken care of,
no need to ask again.
— Yesterday brought to today so lightly!   25
(A yesterday I find almost impossible to lift.)

1974, 1976

ROBERT HAYDEN
(1913–1980)

In an interview published in 1973, Robert Hayden described in strong language what he believed the poet's function was, and perhaps more importantly, what it was not:

> There's a tendency today — more than a tendency, it's almost a conspiracy — to delimit poets, to restrict them to the political and the socially or racially conscious. To me, this indicates gross ignorance of the poet's true function as well as of the function and value of poetry as an art. With a few notable exceptions, poets have generally been on the side of justice and humanity. I can't imagine any poet worth his salt today not being aware of social evils, human needs. But I feel I have the right to deal with these matters in my own way, in terms of my own understanding of what a poet is. I resist whatever would force me into a role as politician, sociologist, or yea-sayer to current ideologies. I know who I am, and pretty much what I want to say.

Hayden was born in Detroit, Michigan, and grew up with adoptive parents (his natural parents separated), who were unschooled, poor, but hard-working. By the time he was ready to go to high school, Hayden was determined to be a poet. He had read voraciously and loved poetry. During this period he came across a copy of the Harlem Renaissance anthology of black writers, *The New Negro* (1925), edited by Alain Locke, where he encountered the poetry of Langston Hughes and Countee Cullen. In a reissue of the book in 1969, Hayden wrote in a Preface: "The New Negro writers rejected the 'minstrel tradition' in American literature, with its caricatures and southern dialect, and they likewise rejected overt propaganda and 'racial rhetoric' for the most part as obstacles to literary excellence and universal acceptance. They eschewed the stereotypes and easy moral solutions of the past." Hayden was to adopt these same principles in fashioning himself as a poet.

Hayden attended Detroit City College (later called Wayne State University) from 1932 to 1936. One of his most memorable experiences was an encounter with Langston Hughes, who turned up at a play in which Hayden was appearing. Hayden showed him some of his poems and got his first words of encouragement from a professional poet. In 1938, Hayden enrolled at the University of

Michigan, where he won a Hopwood Award for a collection of his poetry. He worked briefly for the Federal Writers Project of the WPA (a program of Roosevelt's New Deal), and saw his first volume of poems published in 1940 as *Heart-Shape in the Dust*.

During 1940–42, he did graduate work in English at the University of Michigan, finishing an M.A. and also winning another Hopwood Award for a new collection of his poetry. During this period, W. H. Auden, the British poet who had only shortly before declared himself an American, turned up at the University of Michigan as a visiting professor. Hayden took his class and was awestruck: "He made us aware of other literatures, and aware of poetry in a way that we never would have been." Hayden showed some of his poems to Auden and received encouragement from the distinguished poet. Hayden stayed on at the University of Michigan as a teaching assistant for the next few years. During this time, he was married and he and his wife joined the Baha'i church, affirming the worth of all religions, the unity of all races, and the equality of the sexes.

In 1946 Hayden accepted an assistant professorship in English at Fisk University in Nashville, Tennessee. As a northerner, he was not prepared for the shock of living within the restrictions imposed on black people in the segregated south. Segregation was enforced on buses, in public restrooms, at public fountains, everywhere. For a time, Hayden's wife took their daughter to New York to live so that she would not have to enter the segregated schools of Nashville. Hayden was to remain at Fisk University for over twenty years, and while there he published *The Lion and the Archer* (1948), *Figure of Time: Poems* (1955), *A Ballad of Remembrance* (1962, published in London in a limited edition), and *Selected Poems* (1966). In 1966, he achieved international recognition by winning the Grand Prize for Poetry in English at the First World Festival of Negro Arts in Dakar for his 1962 book *Ballad of Remembrance*.

Hayden moved in 1968 to a position at the University of Michigan, where he remained until his death in 1980. In 1976, he was appointed Consultant in Poetry to the Library of Congress, the first black to be so honored. During this latter part of his life, Hayden continued to publish his poems: in 1970, *Words in the Mourning Time*; in 1972, *The Night-Blooming Cereus*; in 1975, *Angle of Ascent: New and Selected Poems*; and in 1978, *American Journal*.

While insisting throughout his career on his right (and need) to devote poems to whatever subjects and themes he found of importance or interest, his most popular poems have tended to be those on black history or black experience in America. Among these are "Frederick Douglass" (on the famous slave who wrote the narrative of his escape from slavery), "Middle Passage" (an account of a slave ship seized by the slaves on its way from Africa to America), and "Runagate Runagate" (concerning Harriet Tubman and her escape from slavery). These were all early poems. But there are other excellent poems dealing with universal human feelings and experiences. They are the poems that grew out of the impulse he expressed in 1967: "I want to experiment with forms and techniques I have not used before—to arrive at something really my own, something patterned, wild, and free."

The American poet William Meredith wrote of Hayden in 1983 in his Foreword to Hayden's *Collected Prose*: "It was his work to share and enlighten the American black experience, not to diminish it by rancor. This he did by the difficult, simple method of almost flawless art, an art which finally called so loud across the chasm of race that, at last, he was heard on both sides, reminding us of our humanity. His is a complex vision of mutual responsibility."

ADDITIONAL READING

How I Write, with Paul McCluskey, 1972; *Collected Prose of Robert Hayden*, ed. Frederick Glaysher, 1984.

Fred M. Fetrow, *Robert Hayden*, 1984; John Hatcher, *From the Auroral Darkness: The Life and Poetry of Robert Hayden*, 1984; Pontheolla T. Williams, *Robert Hayden: A Critical Analysis of His Poetry*, 1987.

TEXT

Collected Poems, ed. Frederick Glaysher, 1985.

Tour 5

The road winds down through autumn hills
in blazonry of farewell scarlet
and recessional gold,
past cedar groves, through static villages
whose names are all that's left   5
of Choctaw, Chickasaw.[1]

We stop a moment in a town
watched over by Confederate sentinels,
buy gas and ask directions of a rawboned man
whose eyes revile us as the enemy.   10

Shrill gorgon silence breathes behind
his taut civility
and in the ever-tautening air,
dark for us despite its Indian summer glow.
We drive on, following the route   15
of highwaymen and phantoms,

Of slaves and armies.
Children, wordless and remote,
wave at us from kindling porches.
And now the land is flat for miles,   20
the landscape lush, metallic, flayed,
its brightness harsh as bloodstained swords.

1962

Homage to the
Empress of the Blues[1]

Because there was a man somewhere in a candystripe silk shirt,
gracile and dangerous as a jaguar and because a woman moaned
for him in sixty-watt gloom and mourned him Faithless Love
Twotiming Love Oh Love Oh Careless Aggravating Love,

---

[1]American Indian tribes, originally of Mississippi.
[1]Epithet for Bessie Smith (1894–1937), great American blues
singer.

She came out on the stage in yards of pearls, emerging like   5
a favorite scenic view, flashed her golden smile and sang.

Because grey laths began somewhere to show from underneath
torn hurdygurdy lithographs of dollfaced heaven;
and because there were those who feared alarming fists of snow
on the door and those who feared the riot-squad of statistics,   10

She came out on the stage in ostrich feathers, beaded satin,
and shone that smile on us and sang.

1948, 1962

Those Winter Sundays

Sundays too my father got up early
and put his clothes on in the blueblack cold,
then with cracked hands that ached
from labor in the weekday weather made
banked fires blaze. No one ever thanked him.   5

I'd wake and hear the cold splintering, breaking.
When the rooms were warm, he'd call,
and slowly I would rise and dress,
fearing the chronic angers of that house,

Speaking indifferently to him,   10
who had driven out the cold
and polished my good shoes as well.
What did I know, what did I know
of love's austere and lonely offices?

1962

Middle Passage[1]

I

Jesús, Estrella, Esperanza, Mercy:[2]

Sails flashing to the wind like weapons,
sharks following the moans the fever and the dying;
horror the corposant[3] and compass rose.

Middle Passage: 5
    voyage through death
       to life upon these shores.

---

[1]The voyage of slave ships across the Atlantic from Africa to America. Hayden has said that "although the horrors of the slave trade are common to all [three sections of the poem], each section develops a particular aspect of this horror. . . . In the opening section I describe the dreadful conditions aboard the slave ship, the brutal and inhuman treatment of the slaves. The scenes and incidents here are adapted from ships' logs, eyewitness accounts by trader's, depositions." For Hayden's comments see *How I Write*, pp. 169–76.
[2]Names of Spanish slave ships: *Jesus, Star, Hope, Mercy*.
[3]St. Elmo's fire, a luminous, bluish electrical glow.

"10 April 1800—
Blacks rebellious. Crew uneasy. Our linguist says
their moaning is a prayer for death,
ours and their own. Some try to starve themselves.   10
Lost three this morning leaped with crazy laughter
to the waiting sharks, sang as they went under."

Desire, Adventure, Tartar, Ann:

    Standing to America, bringing home   15
    black gold, black ivory, black seed.

        Deep in the festering hold thy father lies,
        of his bones New England pews are made,
        those are altar lights that were his eyes.[4]

Jesus   Saviour   Pilot   Me   20
Over   Life's   Tempestuous   Sea

We pray that Thou wilt grant, O Lord,
safe passage to our vessels bringing
heathen souls unto Thy chastening.

Jesus   Saviour   25

    "8 bells. I cannot sleep, for I am sick
    with fear, but writing eases fear a little
    since still my eyes can see these words take shape
    upon the page & so I write, as one
    would turn to exorcism. 4 days scudding,   30
    but now the sea is calm again. Misfortune
    follows in our wake like sharks (our grinning
    tutelary gods). Which one of us
    has killed an albatross?[5] A plague among
    our blacks—Ophthalmia: blindness—& we   35
    have jettisoned the blind to no avail.
    It spreads, the terrifying sickness spreads.
    Its claws have scratched sight from the Capt.'s eyes
    & there is blindness in the fo'c'sle
    & we must sail 3 weeks before we come   40
    to port."

        What port awaits us, Davy Jones'[6]
        or home? I've heard of slavers drifting, drifting,
        playthings of wind and storm and chance, their crews
        gone blind, the jungle hatred   45
        crawling up on deck.

Thou   Who   Walked   On   Galilee

"Deponent[7] further sayeth *The Bella J*
left the Guinea Coast

---

[4]Allusion to Ariel's song in Shakespeare's *The Tempest*: "Full
fathom five thy father lies; / Of his bones are coral made: /
Those are pearls that were his eyes."
[5]Among sailors, to kill an albatross, considered to be a bird of
good omen, is fatal.
[6]Sailor's name for the evil spirit of the sea; "Davy Jones'
locker" is the bottom of the sea, or grave of those who perish
at sea.
[7]Legal term for one who testifies under oath in writing.

with cargo of five hundred blacks and odd   50
for the barracoons[8] of Florida:

"That there was hardly room 'tween-decks for half
the sweltering cattle stowed spoon-fashion there;
that some went mad of thirst and tore their flesh
and sucked the blood: 55

"That Crew and Captain lusted with the comeliest
of the savage girls kept naked in the cabins;
that there was one they called The Guinea Rose
and they cast lots and fought to lie with her:

"That when the Bo's'n piped all hands, the flames   60
spreading from starboard already were beyond
control, the negroes howling and their chains
entangled with the flames:

"That the burning blacks could not be reached,
that the Crew abandoned ship,   65
leaving their shrieking negresses behind,
that the Captain perished drunken with the wenches:

"Further Deponent sayeth not."

Pilot   Oh   Pilot   Me

II[9]

Aye, lad, and I have seen those factories,   70
Gambia, Rio Pongo, Calabar;[10]
have watched the artful mongos[11] baiting traps
of war wherein the victor and the vanquished

Were caught as prizes for our barracoons.
Have seen the nigger kings whose vanity   75
and greed turned wild black hides of Fellatah,
Mandingo, Ibo, Kru[12] to gold for us.

And there was one—King Anthracite we named him—
fetish face beneath French parasols
of brass and orange velvet, impudent mouth   80
whose cups were carven skulls of enemies:

He'd honor us with drum and feast and conjo[13]
and palm-oil-glistening wenches deft in love,
and for tin crowns that shone with paste,
red calico and German-silver trinkets   85

Would have the drums talk war and send
his warriors to burn the sleeping villages
and kill the sick and old and lead the young
in coffles[14] to our factories.

---

[8]Barracks for slaves.
[9]Hayden's comment: "In the second part, we are listening to
the reminiscences of an old slave-trader. . . . It introduces . . .
the complicity, the guilt, of African kings or chiefs who sold
their own people into slavery."

[10]On the west coast of Africa.
[11]Variant of "mungos," archaic for Negroes.
[12]African tribes.
[13]Magic rites and spells (related to "conjuring").
[14]Chained together in files.

Twenty years a trader, twenty years,   90
for there was wealth aplenty to be harvested
from those black fields, and I'd be trading still
but for the fevers melting down my bones.

III[15]

Shuttles in the rocking loom of history,
the dark ships move, the dark ships move,   95
their bright ironical names
like jests of kindness on a murderer's mouth;
plough through thrashing glister toward
fata morgana's[16] lucent melting shore,
weave toward New World littorals[17] that are   100
mirage and myth and actual shore.

Voyage through death,
            voyage whose chartings are unlove.

A charnel stench, effluvium of living death
spreads outward from the hold,   105
where the living and the dead, the horribly dying,
lie interlocked, lie foul with blood and excrement.

>   *Deep in the festering hold thy father lies,*
>   *the corpse of mercy rots with him,*
>   *rats eat love's rotten gelid eyes.*   110

But, oh, the living look at you
with human eyes whose suffering accuses you,
whose hatred reaches through the swill of dark
to strike you like a leper's claw.

You cannot stare that hatred down   115
or chain the fear that stalks the watches
and breathes on you its fetid scorching breath;
cannot kill the deep immortal human wish,
the timeless will.

>   "But for the storm that flung up barriers   120
>   of wind and wave, *The Amistad*, señores,[18]
>   would have reached the port of Príncipe in two,
>   three days at most; but for the storm we should
>   have been prepared for what befell.
>   Swift as the puma's leap it came. There was   125
>   that interval of moonless calm filled only

---

[15]The third part is based on the account of the 1839 *Amistad* (Spanish for "Friendship") mutiny given by American poet Muriel Rukeyser (1913–1980) in her biography of Willard Gibbs (1942). Hayden's comment: "In the *Amistad* mutiny, fifty-four slaves being transported from Havana to Port Príncipe [in Cuba] seized control of the *Amistad* under the leadership of a slave named Singbe, who had been given the Spanish name Joseph Cinquez. The captain was killed, but the two Spanish slavers aboard were spared their lives so that they could navigate the ship. The slaves demanded that the vessel sail to Africa, but at night the Spaniards would turn the vessel westward, attempting to stay close to the North American continent. Finally the ship neared Long Island and was boarded by American officials. The slaves were taken into custody and a long court battle ensued to determine whether the slaves should be charged with mutiny, or considered free men since the slave trade had been outlawed. John Quincy Adams, then a member of Congress, argued the case before the Supreme Court and the slaves were set free and returned to Sierra Leone in 1841."

[16]Fata morgana: mirage.

[17]Coastal regions.

[18]Hayden has said that here he "tried to create a dramatic effect by letting one of the Spanish slavers speak. What he says . . . is substantially what he actually said during the trial of the *Amistad* mutineers."

with the water's and the rigging's usual sounds,
then sudden movement, blows and snarling cries
and they had fallen on us with machete
and marlinspike. It was as though the very   130
air, the night itself were striking us.
Exhausted by the rigors of the storm,
we were no match for them. Our men went down
before the murderous Africans. Our loyal
Celestino ran from below with gun   135
and lantern and I saw, before the cane-
knife's wounding flash, Cinquez,
that surly brute who calls himself a prince,
directing, urging on the ghastly work.
He hacked the poor mulatto down, and then   140
he turned on me. The decks were slippery
when daylight finally came. It sickens me
to think of what I saw, of how these apes
threw overboard the butchered bodies of
our men, true Christians all, like so much jetsam.   145
Enough, enough. The rest is quickly told:
Cinquez was forced to spare the two of us
you see to steer the ship to Africa,
and we like phantoms doomed to rove the sea
voyaged east by day and west by night,   150
deceiving them, hoping for rescue,
prisoners on our own vessel, till
at length we drifted to the shores of this
your land, America, where we were freed
from our unspeakable misery. Now we   155
demand, good sirs, the extradition of
Cinquez and his accomplices to La
Havana. And it distresses us to know
there are so many here who seem inclined
to justify the mutiny of these blacks.   160
We find it paradoxical indeed
that you whose wealth, whose tree of liberty
are rooted in the labor of your slaves
should suffer the august John Quincy Adams
to speak with so much passion of the right   165
of chattel slaves to kill their lawful masters
and with his Roman rhetoric weave a hero's
garland for Cinquez. I tell you that
we are determined to return to Cuba
with our slaves and there see justice done. Cinquez—   170
or let us say 'the Prince'—Cinquez shall die."

The deep immortal human wish,
the timeless will:

Cinquez its deathless primaveral image,
life that transfigures many lives.   175

Voyage through death
            to life upon these shores.

1945, 1962

Frederick Douglass[1]

When it is finally ours, this freedom, this liberty, this beautiful
and terrible thing, needful to man as air,
usable as earth; when it belongs at last to all,
when it is truly instinct, brain matter, diastole, systole,
reflex action; when it is finally won; when it is more   5
than the gaudy mumbo jumbo of politicians:
this man, this Douglass, this former slave, this Negro
beaten to his knees, exiled, visioning a world
where none is lonely, none hunted, alien,
this man, superb in love and logic, this man   10
shall be remembered. Oh, not with statues' rhetoric,
not with legends and poems and wreaths of bronze alone,
but with the lives grown out of his life, the lives
fleshing his dream of the beautiful, needful thing.

1947, 1962

Sphinx[1]

    If he could solve the riddle,
she would not leap
    from those gaunt rocks to her death,
but devour him instead.

    It pleasures her to hold   5
him captive there —
    to keep him in the reach of her
blood-matted paws.

    It is your fate, she has often
said, to endure   10
    my riddling. Your fate to live
at the mercy of my

    conundrum, which, in truth,
is only a kind
    of psychic joke. No, you shall   15
not leave this place.

    (Consider anyway the view from
here.) In time,
    you will come to regard my questioning
with a certain pained   20

    amusement; in time, get so
you would hardly find
    it possible to live without
my joke and me.

1969, 1970

---

[1]Douglass (1817–1895) escaped from slavery in 1838 and became an abolitionist, writer, orator, and statesman.
[1]In Greek mythology, a winged monster with the head of a woman and the body of a lion that destroyed all who could not answer its riddle. When Oedipus answered correctly, the Sphinx killed herself.

KARL SHAPIRO
(b. 1913)

Karl Shapiro has been a maverick in contemporary poetry, fiercely independent in his thinking. He has never wavered in his view of the value of poetry. He remarked in *Beyond Criticism* (1953):

> To say that poetry is everywhere at its goal is to say that poetry gives us knowledge of its own kind, a unique, unrepeatable, intelligible form. Poetic knowledge is neither intuitive, nor provable, nor ordered, nor consistent, but self-contradictory, beyond demonstration, beyond proof. We accept it by conviction or not at all. We accept it as we accept the belief in another's pain or pleasure, or we reject it as unconvincing, not sincere, or a symptom of disorder. How much bad poetry is only pitiful bravado, a falsetto cry of self-assertion! Poetic truth is in fact personal truth itself, that which comes out of the experience of life, and *only* out of the experience itself.

Shapiro has devoted his entire life to pursuit of that poetic truth. There was never a time that he did not think of himself as a poet. Born in Baltimore, Maryland, the son of a travelling salesman, he grew up during the years of the Great Depression, when his family's finances were precarious. He attended the University of Virginia for one unhappy year (1932–33). And he published, privately, a volume of *Poems* in 1935, which went largely unnoticed. It did, however, win him a scholarship at Johns Hopkins University, which he attended from 1937 to 1939. One B on a history exam, for an essay the professor noted was "Too bitter against big business," cost him his scholarship, and in 1940 he entered Baltimore's Pratt Library School. In March 1941—nine months before Pearl Harbor—Shapiro was drafted. Eventually he was on his way as a Medical Corps clerk to Australia, where an invasion by Japanese forces was feared, and he carried with him the New Directions volume *Five Young American Poets*, published in 1941. Shapiro was one of the five.

Throughout his four years in Australia and the Pacific, Shapiro wrote poetry, sending it back to his girl friend (later his wife), Evelyn Katz, who moved from Baltimore to New York in order to operate as midwife in publication of the poems. *Person, Place and Thing*, published in 1942, attracted a great deal of notice from reviewers, particularly Allen Tate. What was to prove one of Shapiro's most popular poems, "Auto Wreck," appeared in the volume. *V-Letter and Other Poems*, published in 1944, established Shapiro as an important new poet, and won for him the Pulitzer Prize. The title poem carried the name ("V" stood for victory) bestowed on the microfilmed letters from servicemen abroad. The book was filled with vivid, moving poems that grew directly out of Shapiro's wartime experiences.

On his return to the United States after his service in the war, Shapiro served as Consultant in Poetry to the Library of Congress (1947–48). He was appointed to serve on the committee for the Bollingen Prize, and when the committee selected Ezra Pound as the winner in 1948, Shapiro was its only dissenter. Shapiro said later: "I would have voted for the *Pisan Cantos* [by Ezra Pound] if it hadn't been for all the anti-Semitic and anti-American propaganda in them." There was a national controversy over the issue, with poets and critics aligning themselves on one side or another. Shapiro's role in this controversy, and his later attack on T. S. Eliot ("The Death of Literary Judgment") in his book of essays *In Defense of Ignorance* (1960), caused Shapiro to be cast in the role of "wild man" in American letters, a role that he came to relish and cultivate.

Shapiro served as editor of *Poetry* magazine in Chicago from 1950 to 1956, when he became professor of English at the University of Nebraska and editor of the *Prairie Schooner*. He had published *Poems 1940–1953* in 1953. In Nebraska his writing took a new turn. In 1958 his *Poems of a Jew* appeared. He explained in his Introduction: "The poems here were written over a long period of time and are extracted mostly from volumes which have nothing to do with the present theme. But the undercurrent of most of my poems is the theme of the Jew, and for this reason I collect these examples now as a separate presentation." Critics were again taken by surprise in 1964 with the appearance of Shapiro's *A Bourgeois Poet*, not only because of the title but also because it was a book of prose-poems. Theodore Roethke had called Shapiro in jest a bourgeois poet; Shapiro accepted the epithet and adopted it as a title. In all his previous poetry, Shapiro had worked within traditional stanzaic patterns and measured lines. His use of the prose-poem seemed to align him with the free verse experiments of Walt Whitman and Allen Ginsberg, an alignment he himself affirmed when he collaborated with James E. Miller, Jr., and Bernice Slote in the writing of *Start with the Sun: Studies in Cosmic Poetry* (1960), an exploration of the Whitman tradition in American literature.

In 1966 Shapiro moved from Nebraska, taught for a brief stint at the University of Illinois in Chicago, and then spent the rest of his teaching career at the University of California at Davis. He continued to write and publish, always exploring in his poetry new areas of experience. His later books of poetry include *White-Haired Lover* (1968) and *Adult Bookstore* (1976) and his later books of prose, *To Abolish Children and Other Essays* (1968) and *The Poetry Wreck: Selected Essays 1950–1970* (1975). He published a novel based on his experiences teaching at the University of Nebraska, *Edsel* (1971). And he has published two autobiographical volumes, *The Younger Son* (1988), and *Reports of My Death* (1990).

Asked recently why he wrote, Shapiro replied: "I don't know why, but it's a compulsion. I feel that after working a long time, I've really learned how to do what I do. I enjoy it. I don't think there's anything more satisfying than turning out a good stanza or a good piece of prose. And when you're satisfied enough, you want to show it to other people. That's called publication."

ADDITIONAL READING

William White, *Karl Shapiro: A Bibliography*, 1960; Ralph J. Mills, Jr., "Karl Shapiro," *Contemporary American Poetry*, 1965; Stephen Stepanchev, "Karl Shapiro," *American Poetry Since 1945*, 1965; Karl Malkoff, "The Self in the Modern World: Karl Shapiro's Jewish Poems," *Contemporary American-Jewish Literature: Critical Essays*, ed. Irving Malin, 1973; Lee Bartlett, *Karl Shapiro: A Descriptive Bibliography, 1933–1977*, 1979; Joseph Reino, *Karl Shapiro*, 1981; Robert Richman, "The Trials of a Poet," *New Criterion* 6:7 (April 1988).

TEXTS

"Troop Train" from *Love & War, Art & God*, 1984; remaining poems from *New and Selected Poems*, 1987.

Auto Wreck

Its quick soft silver bell beating, beating,
And down the dark one ruby flare
Pulsing out red light like an artery,

The ambulance at top speed floating down
Past beacons and illuminated clocks   5
Wings in a heavy curve, dips down,
And brakes speed, entering the crowd.
The doors leap open, emptying light;
Stretchers are laid out, the mangled lifted
And stowed into the little hospital.   10
Then the bell, breaking the hush, tolls once,
And the ambulance with its terrible cargo
Rocking, slightly rocking, moves away,
As the doors, an afterthought, are closed.

We are deranged, walking among the cops   15
Who sweep glass and are large and composed.
One is still making notes under the light.
One with a bucket douches ponds of blood
Into the street and gutter.
One hangs lanterns on the wrecks that cling,   20
Empty husks of locusts, to iron poles.

Our throats were tight as tourniquets,
Our feet were bound with splints, but now,
Like convalescents intimate and gauche,
We speak through sickly smiles and warn   25
With the stubborn saw of common sense,
The grim joke and the banal resolution.
The traffic moves around with care,
But we remain, touching a wound
That opens to our richest horror.   30
Already old, the question Who shall die?
Becomes unspoken Who is innocent?
For death in war is done by hands;
Suicide has cause and stillbirth, logic;
And cancer, simple as a flower, blooms.   35
But this invites the occult mind,
Cancels our physics with a sneer,
And spatters all we knew of denouement
Across the expedient and wicked stones.

                                                        1941, 1942

The Dirty Word

The dirty word hops in the cage of the mind like the Pondicherry[1] vulture, stomping with its heavy left claw on the sweet meat of the brain and tearing it with its vicious beak, ripping and chopping the flesh. Terrified, the small boy bears the big bird of the dirty word into the house, and grunting, puffing, carries it up the stairs to his own room in the skull. Bits of black feather cling to his clothes and his hair as he locks the staring creature in the dark closet.

   All day the small boy returns to the closet to examine and feed the bird, to caress and kick the bird, that now snaps and flaps its wings savagely whenever the

---

[1]Territory in India, formerly French.

door is opened. How the boy trembles and delights at the sight of the white excrement of the bird! How the bird leaps and rushes against the walls of the skull, trying to escape from the zoo of the vocabulary! How wildly snaps the sweet meat of the brain in its rage.

And the bird outlives the man, being freed at the man's death-funeral by a word from the rabbi.

But I one morning went upstairs and opened the door and entered the closet and found in the cage of my mind the great bird dead. Softly I wept it and softly removed it and softly buried the body of the bird in the hollyhock garden of the house I lived in twenty years before. And out of the worn black feathers of the wing have I made pens to write these elegies, for I have outlived the bird, and I have murdered it in my early manhood.

1942

Troop Train

It stops the town we come through. Workers raise
Their oily arms in good salute and grin.
Kids scream as at a circus. Business men
Glance hopefully and go their measured way.
And women standing at their dumbstruck door   5
More slowly wave and seem to warn us back,
As if a tear blinding the course of war
Might once dissolve our iron in their sweet wish.

Fruit of the world, O clustered on ourselves
We hang as from a cornucopia   10
In total friendliness, with faces bunched
To spray the streets with catcalls and with leers.
A bottle smashes on the moving ties
And eyes fixed on a lady smiling pink
Stretch like a rubber-band and snap and sting   15
The mouth that wants the drink-of-water kiss.

And on through crummy continents and days,
Deliberate, grimy, slightly drunk we crawl,
The good-bad boys of circumstance and chance,
Whose bucket-helmets bang the empty wall   20
Where twist the murdered bodies of our packs
Next to the guns that only seem themselves.
And distance like a strap adjusted shrinks,
Tightens across the shoulder and holds firm.

Here is a deck of cards; out of this hand   25
Dealer, deal me my luck, a pair of bulls,[1]
The right draw to a flush,[2] the one-eyed jack.[3]
Diamonds and hearts are red but spades are black,
And spades are spades and clubs are clovers — black.

---

[1]Pair of aces in poker (slang).
[2]A card the same suit as the other cards the player holds.
[3]The jack of hearts and of spades, which may be declared wild by the dealer.

But deal me winners, souvenirs of peace.   30
This stands to reason and arithmetic,
Luck also travels and not all come back.

Trains lead to ships and ships to death or trains,
And trains to death or trucks, and trucks to death,
Or trucks lead to the march, the march to death,   35
Or that survival which is all our hope;
And death leads back to trucks and trains and ships,
But life leads to the march, O flag! at last
The place of life found after trains and death —
Nightfall of nations brilliant after war.   40

1943, 1944

The Leg[1]

Among the iodoform,[2] in twilight-sleep,
What have I lost? he first inquires,
Peers in the middle distance where a pain,
Ghost of a nurse, hazily moves, and day,
Her blinding presence pressing in his eyes   5
And now his ears. They are handling him
With rubber hands. He wants to get up.

One day beside some flowers near his nose
He will be thinking, *When will I look at it?*
And pain, still in the middle distance, will reply,   10
At what? and he will know it's gone,
O where! and begin to tremble and cry.
He will begin to cry as a child cries
Whose puppy is mangled under a screaming wheel.

Later, as if deliberately, his fingers   15
Begin to explore the stump. He learns a shape
That is comfortable and tucked in like a sock.
This has a sense of humor, this can despise
The finest surgical limb, the dignity of limping,
The nonsense of wheel-chairs. Now he smiles to the wall: 20
The amputation becomes an acquisition.

For the leg is wondering where he is (all is not lost)
And surely he has a duty to the leg;
He is its injury, the leg is his orphan,
He must cultivate the mind of the leg,   25
Pray for the part that is missing, pray for peace
In the image of man, pray, pray for its safety,
And after a little it will die quietly.

The body, what is it, Father, but a sign
To love the force that grows us, to give back   30

---

[1]"Freud speaks . . . of 'violent defloration' and 'the fear of being eaten by the Father.' In Freud's view, as in that of every Jew, mutilation, circumcision, and 'the fear of being eaten' are all one. 'The Leg' is a poem written during war and its subject is the wholeness of the mutilated" (Shapiro's note).
[2]Iodine compound, used as an antiseptic.

What in Thy palm is senselessness and mud?
Knead, knead the substance of our understanding
Which must be beautiful in flesh to walk,
That if Thou take me angrily in hand
And hurl me to the shark, I shall not die!   35

1944

V-Letter[1]

I love you first because your face is fair,
      Because your eyes Jewish and blue,
Set sweetly with the touch of foreignness
Above the cheekbones, stare rather than dream.
Often your countenance recalls a boy   5
      Blue-eyed and small, whose silent mischief
Tortured his parents and compelled my hate
      To wish his ugly death.
Because of this reminder, my soul's trouble,
And for your face, so often beautiful,   10
      I love you, wish you life.

I love you first because you wait, because
      For your own sake, I cannot write
Beyond these words. I love you for these words
That sting and creep like insects and leave filth.
I love you for the poverty you cry   15
      And I bend down with tears of steel
That melt your hand like wax, not for this war
      The droplets shattering
Those candle-glowing fingers of my joy,   20
But for your name of agony, my love,
      That cakes my mouth with salt.

And all your imperfections and perfections
      And all your magnitude of grace
And all this love explained and unexplained   25
Is just a breath. I see you woman-size
And this looms larger and more goddess-like
      Than silver goddesses on screens.
I see you in the ugliness of light,
      Yet you are beautiful,   30
And in the dark of absence your full length
Is such as meets my body to the full
      Though I am starved and huge.

You turn me from these days as from a scene
      Out of an open window far   35
Where lies the foreign city and the war.
You are my home and in your spacious love

---

[1]An airmail letter form used by American servicemen in the
Second World War; V stood for victory.

I dream to march as under flaring flags
        Until the door is gently shut.
Give me the tearless lesson of your pride,   40
        Teach me to live and die
As one deserving anonymity,
The mere devotion of a house to keep
        A woman and a man.

Give me the free and poor inheritance   45
        Of our own kind, not furniture
Of education, nor the prophet's pose,
The general cause of words, the hero's stance,
The ambitions incommensurable with flesh,
        But the drab makings of a room   50
Where sometimes in the afternoon of thought
        The brief and blinding flash
May light the enormous chambers of your will
And show the gracious Parthenon that time
        Is ever measured by.   55

As groceries in pantry gleam and smile
        Because they are important weights
Bought with the metal minutes of your pay,
So do these hours stand in solid rows,
The dowry for a use in common life.   60
        I love you first because your years
Lead to my matter-of-fact and simple death
        Or to our open marriage,
And I pray nothing for my safety back,
Not even luck, because our love is whole   65
        Whether I live or fail.

                                                      1944

Adult Bookstore

Round the green fountain thick with women
Abstract in the concrete, water trickling
Between their breasts, wetting their waists
Girdled with wheat, pooling in the basin,
The walker pauses, shrugs, peregrinates   5
To the intersection, section of the city
Where forgotten fountains struggle for existence,
Shops have declined to secondhand
And marginal cultures collect like algae.
Dubious enterprises flourish here,   10
The massage parlor, the adult bookstore.

Their windows are either yellowed or blacked
Or whited or redded out,
Bold lettering proclaiming No Minors Allowed,
Bachelor Books, Adult Films and Cartoons.   15

The doorway jogs to the right at a strict angle
And everything from the street is invisible,

Keeping the law and clutching the illusion.
Inside, the light is cold and clean and bright,
Everything sanitary, wrapped in cellophane   20

Which flashes messages from wall to wall
Of certain interest to the eye that reads
Or does not read: Randy, Coit,
Sex Hold-Up, Discipline, Ghetto Male,
Images of cruelty, ideas for the meek,   25
Scholarly peeks at French, English and Greek,
And everywhere the more than naked nude
Mystery called the wound that never heals.

Or there a surgical cabinet all glass:
Pink plastic phalli, prickly artifact,   30
Enlarger finger-small or stallion-size,
Inflatable love partner, five feet four.
Lotions, Hot Melt, super-double-dong,
Battery dildo (origin obscure),
Awakeners of the tired heart's desire   35
When love goes wrong.

The expense of spirit in a waste of shame[1]
Is sold forever to the single stag
Who takes it home in a brown paper bag.

1975, 1976

RANDALL JARRELL
(1914–1965)

Randall Jarrell came early to his decision to be a poet and held no mean view of the importance of poetry. He wrote in an early essay:

> Poetry does not need to be defended, any more than air or food needs to be defended; poetry—using the word in its widest sense, the only sense in which it is important—has been an indispensable part of any culture we know anything about. Human life without some form of poetry is not human life but animal existence. Our world today is not an impossible one for poets and poetry: poets can endure its disadvantages, and good poetry is still being written. . . . But what will happen to the public—to that portion of it divorced from any real art even of the simplest kind—I do not know.

Randall Jarrell was born in Nashville, Tennessee, but was early taken by his family to Long Beach, California, where his father's family lived. After some ten years, in 1925, Jarrell's mother separated from his father and took her children back to Tennessee, where her brother had a profitable candy business. The family's economic situation was precarious during the depression years, but the uncle was able to send Jarrell to Vanderbilt University, where he studied with Rob-

[1]The first line of Shakespeare's Sonnet 129: "Th' expense of spirit in a waste of shame / Is lust in action; and till action, lust / Is perjur'd, murd'rous, bloody, full of blame, / Savage, extreme, rude, cruel, not to trust; / Enjoy'd no sooner but despised straight."

ert Penn Warren and John Crowe Ransom, and where he came to know Allen
Tate. When Ransom went to teach at Kenyon College in Ohio in 1937, Jarrell
followed him there and soon found himself rooming at Ransom's house with
Robert Lowell, who had left Harvard also to study with Ransom.

Jarrell took an M.A. in English at Vanderbilt in 1939 and accepted a teaching
position at the University of Texas, in Austin, that same year. There he married,
and there he saw his first book publication as one of New Directions' *Five Young
American Poets* (1940). In 1942 Jarrell enlisted in the Army Air Force and washed
out as a pilot but was trained as a flight instructor and celestial-navigation instructor. After his training, Jarrell was sent to an air field near Tucson, Arizona,
where he spent the years from 1943 to 1946. From his own experiences and the
stories he heard from fliers and navigators, he found the material for the poems
that appeared in *Little Friend, Little Friend*, published in 1945. One of the best
volumes of poetry to come from the Second World War, the book took its name
(as the epigraph indicated) from a radio exchange between a bomber and its
fighter escort: ". . . Then I heard the bomber call me in: 'Little Friend, Little
Friend, I got two engines on fire. Can you see me, Little Friend?' I said, 'I'm
crossing right over you. Let's go home.'" The most chilling of Jarrell's war poems
took the point of view of the dead gunner, flier, or soldier. A second volume of
war poems, *Losses*, appeared in 1948. These two early volumes of poetry contain
the poems by which Jarrell is best remembered.

After discharge from the Air Force, Jarrell took a part-time job during 1946–
47 teaching at Sarah Lawrence College in New York. His experiences there became the basis for his witty, fiercely satiric novel *Pictures from an Institution*, published in 1954. In 1947, Jarrell went to teach at Woman's College, later renamed
the University of North Carolina at Greensboro. He continued to write poetry,
but never again matched the success of his two volumes of war poems. Later
poems tended to adopt the point of view of an older woman, as, for example, *The
Woman at the Washington Zoo: Poems & Translations*, published in 1960. Although it
was given the National Book Award for poetry, its reception was quite mixed. His
The Lost World, poems written in recollection of his youth in the make-believe
world of Hollywood, appeared in 1965.

One critic, Helen Vendler, has said that Jarrell put his talent into his poetry,
but his genius into his criticism. There is much truth to the remark. Sometimes
caustic, sometimes ebullient in his reviews and essays, Jarrell was always interesting. It was he who first observed the irony in the fate of his generation of poets to
be living in an "age of criticism." His essay by that title appeared in his first
collection of prose, *Poetry and the Age* (1953). Also included in that volume was a
deceptively simple essay on Walt Whitman entitled "Some Lines from Whitman,"
which rescued the "good, gray poet," with elegance and clarity, from the oblivion
to which the New Critics had assigned him. Essays on Wallace Stevens and William Carlos Williams were models of critical assessments, written with grace, wit,
and conviction. In 1962, Jarrell published a second book of essays, *A Sad Heart at
the Supermarket: Essays and Fables*.

In 1964 Jarrell began to suffer bouts of depression and was hospitalized for a
time and placed on drugs. In early 1965 he made an attempt at suicide and was
again placed under care. Later in the year he seemed to be getting better. But
one evening, while walking along a country road, he was struck by a car and
killed. The occupants of the car said that he seemed to lunge at the car. Although
what happened was never precisely determined, the death was declared accidental. It has been assumed by many, however, to have been a suicide. In 1969, a

book of prose, *The Third Book of Criticism*, was published; and the same year, Jarrell's wife and his editor brought together *The Complete Poems*.

ADDITIONAL READING

Randall Jarrell's Letters, ed. Mary Jarrell, 1985; *Selected Poems by Randall Jarrell*, ed. William H. Pritchard, 1990.

Charles Adams, *Randall Jarrell: A Bibliography*, 1958; Karl Shapiro, *Randall Jarrell*, 1967; Robert Lowell, Peter Taylor, and Robert Penn Warren, eds., *Randall Jarrell, 1914–1965*, 1967; Frederick J. Hoffman, ed., *The Achievement of Randall Jarrell*, 1970; Suzanne Ferguson, *The Poetry of Randall Jarrell*, 1971; M. L. Rosenthal, *Randall Jarrell*, 1972; Helen Hagenbuchle, *The Black Goddess: A Study of the Archetypal Feminine in the Poetry of Randall Jarrell*, 1975; Sister M. Bernetta Quinn, *Randall Jarrell*, 1981; Suzanne Ferguson, ed., *Critical Essays on Randall Jarrell*, 1983; Stuart Wright, *Randall Jarrell: A Descriptive Bibliography*, 1985; J. A. Bryant, Jr. *Understanding Randall Jarrell*, 1986; William H. Pritchard, *Randall Jarrell: A Literary Life*, 1990.

TEXT

The Complete Poems, 1969.

The Death of the Ball Turret Gunner[1]

From my mother's sleep I fell into the State,
And I hunched in its belly till my wet fur froze.
Six miles from earth, loosed from its dream of life,
I woke to black flak and the nightmare fighters.
When I died they washed me out of the turret with a hose.   5

                                              1945

Losses

It was not dying: everybody died.
It was not dying: we had died before
In the routine crashes—and our fields
Called up the papers, wrote home to our folks,
And the rates rose, all because of us.   5
We died on the wrong page of the almanac,
Scattered on mountains fifty miles away;
Diving on haystacks, fighting with a friend,
We blazed up on the lines we never saw.
We died like aunts or pets or foreigners.   10
(When we left high school nothing else had died
For us to figure we had died like.)

[1] "A ball turret was a plexiglass sphere set into the belly of a B-17 or B-24, and inhabited by two .50 caliber machine-guns and one man, a short small man. When this gunner tracked with his machine-guns a fighter attacking his bomber from below, he revolved with the turret; hunched upside-down in his little sphere, he looked like the foetus in the womb. The fighters which attacked him were armed with cannon firing explosive shells. The hose was a steam hose" (Jarrell's note).

In our new planes, with our new crews, we bombed
The ranges by the desert or the shore,
Fired at towed targets, waited for our scores—
And turned into replacements and woke up   15
One morning, over England, operational.
It was different: but if we died
It was not an accident but a mistake
(But an easy one for anyone to make).
We read our mail and counted up our missions—   20
In bombers named for girls, we burned
The cities we had learned about in school—
Till our lives wore out; our bodies lay among
The people we had killed and never seen.
When we lasted long enough they gave us medals;   25
When we died they said, "Our casualties were low."
They said, "Here are the maps"; we burned the cities.

It was not dying—no, not ever dying;
But the night I died I dreamed that I was dead,   30
And the cities said to me: "Why are you dying?
We are satisfied, if you are; but why did I die?"

1944, 1945

Second Air Force

Far off, above the plain the summer dries,
The great loops of the hangars sway like hills.
Buses and weariness and loss, the nodding soldiers
Are wire, the bare frame building, and a pass
To what was hers; her head hides his square patch   5
And she thinks heavily: My son is grown.
She sees a world: sand roads, tar-paper barracks,
The bubbling asphalt of the runways, sage,
The dunes rising to the interminable ranges,
The dim flights moving over clouds like clouds.   10
The armorers in their patched faded green,
Sweat-stiffened, banded with brass cartridges,
Walk to the line; their Fortresses, all tail,
Stand wrong and flimsy on their skinny legs,
And the crews climb to them clumsily as bears.   15
The head withdraws into its hatch (a boy's),
The engines rise to their blind laboring roar,
And the green, made beasts run home to air.
Now in each aspect death is pure.
(At twilight they wink over men like stars   20
And hour by hour, through the night, some see
The great lights floating in—from Mars, from Mars.)
How emptily the watchers see them gone.

They go, there is silence; the woman and her son
Stand in the forest of the shadows, and the light   25
Washes them like water. In the long-sunken city
Of evening, the sunlight stills like sleep

The faint wonder of the drowned; in the evening,
In the last dreaming light, so fresh, so old,
The soldiers pass like beasts, unquestioning,   30
And the watcher for an instant understands
What there is then no need to understand;
But she wakes from her knowledge, and her stare,
A shadow now, moves emptily among
The shadows learning in their shadowy fields   35
The empty missions.
                     Remembering,
She hears the bomber calling, *Little Friend!*[1]
To the fighter hanging in the hostile sky,
And sees the ragged flame eat, rib by rib,
Along the metal of the wing into her heart: 40
The lives stream out, blossom, and float steadily
To the flames of the earth, the flames
That burn like stars above the lands of men.

She saves from the twilight that takes everything
A squadron shipping, in its last parade —   45
Its dogs run by it, barking at the band —
A gunner walking to his barracks, half-asleep,
Starting at something, stumbling (above, invisible,
The crews in the steady winter of the sky
Tremble in their wired fur); and feels for them   50
The love of life for life. The hopeful cells
Heavy with someone else's death, cold carriers
Of someone else's victory, grope past their lives
Into her own bewilderment: The years meant *this*?

But for them the bombers answer everything.   55

                                    1944, 1945

Eighth Air Force[1]

If, in an odd angle of the hutment,
A puppy laps the water from a can
Of flowers, and the drunk sergeant shaving
Whistles *O Paradiso!* — shall I say that man
Is not as men have said: a wolf to man?   5

The other murderers troop in yawning;
Three of them play Pitch, one sleeps, and one
Lies counting missions, lies there sweating
Till even his heart beats: One; One; One.
O murderers! . . . . Still, this is how it's done: 10

---

[1] "In SECOND AIR FORCE the woman visiting her son remembers what she has read on the front page of her newspaper the week before, a conversation between a bomber, in flames over Germany, and one of the fighters protecting it: 'Then I heard the bomber call me in: "Little Friend, Little Friend, I got two engines on fire. Can you see me, Little Friend?" I said, "I'm crossing right over you. Let's go home"'" (Jarrell's note).

[1] "EIGHTH AIR FORCE is a poem about the air force which bombed the Continent from England. The man who lies counting missions has one to go before being sent home. The phrases from the Gospels compare such criminals and scapegoats as these with that earlier criminal and scapegoat about whom the Gospels were written" (Jarrell's note).

This is a war. . . . But since these play, before they die,
Like puppies with their puppy; since, a man,
I did as these have done, but did not die—
I will content the people as I can
And give up these to them: Behold the man![2]   15

I have suffered, in a dream, because of him,
Many things;[3] for this last saviour, man,
I have lied as I lie now. But what is lying?
Men wash their hands, in blood,[4] as best they can:
I find no fault in this just man.   20

                                            1947, 1948

Well Water

What a girl called "the dailiness of life"
(Adding an errand to your errand. Saying,
"Since you're up . . ." Making you a means to
A means to a means to) is well water
Pumped from an old well at the bottom of the world.   5
The pump you pump the water from is rusty
And hard to move and absurd, a squirrel-wheel
A sick squirrel turns slowly, through the sunny
Inexorable hours. And yet sometimes
The wheel turns of its own weight, the rusty   10
Pump pumps over your sweating face the clear
Water, cold, so cold! you cup your hands
And gulp from them the dailiness of life.

                                            1965

Thinking of the Lost World

This spoonful of chocolate tapioca
Tastes like—like peanut butter, like the vanilla
Extract Mama told me not to drink.
Swallowing the spoonful, I have already traveled
Through time to my childhood. It puzzles me   5
That age is like it.
                    Come back to that calm country
Through which the stream of my life first meandered,
My wife, our cat, and I sit here and see
Squirrels quarreling in the feeder, a mockingbird
Copying our chipmunk, as our end copies   10
Its beginning.

---

[2]Pilate's words as he presented Jesus to the Jews, who had chosen that Barabbas, not Jesus, be released from prison (John 19:4–5).
[3]Before asking the Jews to choose between Jesus and Barabbas, Pilate received a message from his wife: "Have thou nothing to do with that just man: for I have suffered many things this day in a dream because of him" (Matthew 27:19).
[4]When the people called for the crucifixion of Jesus, Pilate washed his hands, saying "I am innocent of the blood of this just person: ye see to it. Then answered all the people, and said, His blood be on us, and on our children" (Matthew 27:24–25).

Back in Los Angeles, we missed
Los Angeles. The sunshine of the Land
Of Sunshine is a gray mist now, the atmosphere
Of some factory planet: when you stand and look
You see a block or two, and your eyes water.   15
The orange groves are all cut down . . . My bow
Is lost, all my arrows are lost or broken,
My knife is sunk in the eucalyptus tree
Too far for even Pop to get it out,
And the tree's sawed down. It and the stair-sticks   20
And the planks of the tree house are all firewood
Burned long ago; its gray smoke smells of Vicks.

Twenty Years After, thirty-five years after,
Is as good as ever—better than ever,
Now that D'Artagnan[1] is no longer old—   25
Except that it is unbelievable.
I say to my old self: "I believe. Help thou
Mine unbelief."[2]
                    I believe the dinosaur
Or pterodactyl's married the pink sphinx
And lives with those Indians in the undiscovered   30
Country between California and Arizona
That the mad girl told me she was princess of—
Looking at me with the eyes of a lion,
Big, golden, without human understanding,
As she threw paper-wads from the back seat   35
Of the car in which I drove her with her mother
From the jail in Waycross to the hospital
In Daytona.[3] If I took my eyes from the road
And looked back into her eyes, the car would—I'd be—

Or if only I could find a crystal set   40
Sometimes, surely, I could still hear their chief
Reading to them from Dumas or *Amazing Stories*;[4]
If I could find in some Museum of Cars
Mama's dark blue Buick, Lucky's electric,
Couldn't I be driven there? Hold out to them,   45
The paraffin half picked out, Tawny's dewclaw—
And have walk to me from among their wigwams
My tall brown aunt, to whisper to me: "Dead?
They told you I was dead?"
                    As if you could die!
If I never saw you, never again   50
Wrote to you, even, after a few years,
How often you've visited me, having put on,
As a mermaid puts on her sealskin, another face
And voice, that don't fool me for a minute—
That are yours for good . . . All of them are gone   55
Except for me; and for me nothing is gone—
The chicken's body is still going round

---

[1]One of the musketeers in *The Three Musketeers* and its sequel *Twenty Years After* by Alexandre Dumas (1802–1870), French novelist.
[2]Cf. "And straightway the father of the child [an epileptic] cried out, and said with tears, Lord I believe; help thou mine unbelief" (Mark 9:24).
[3]I.e., from a town in Georgia to a town in Florida.
[4]A science-fiction magazine popular in the 1940s.

And round in widening circles, a satellite
From which, as the sun sets, the scientist bends
A look of evil on the unsuspecting earth.   60
Mama and Pop and Dandeen are still there
In the Gay Twenties.
                 The Gay Twenties! You say
The Gay Nineties . . . But it's all right: they *were* gay,
O so gay! A certain number of years after,
Any time is Gay, to the new ones who ask: 65
"Was that the first World War or the second?"
Moving between the first world and the second,
I hear a boy call, now that my beard's gray:
"Santa Claus! Hi, Santa Claus!" It *is* miraculous
To have the children call you Santa Claus.   70
I wave back. When my hand drops to the wheel,
It is brown and spotted, and its nails are ridged
Like Mama's. Where's my own hand? My smooth
White bitten-fingernailed one? I seem to see
A shape in tennis shoes and khaki riding-pants   75
Standing there empty-handed; I reach out to it
Empty-handed, my hand comes back empty,
And yet my emptiness is traded for its emptiness,
I have found that Lost World in the Lost and Found
Columns whose gray illegible advertisements   80
My soul has memorized world after world:
LOST — NOTHING. STRAYED FROM NOWHERE. NO REWARD.
I hold in my own hands, in happiness,
Nothing: the nothing for which there's no reward.

                                    1963, 1965

JOHN BERRYMAN
(1914–1972)

Shortly before his death in 1972 at the age of fifty-seven, an interviewer asked
John Berryman about his plans for the future. Berryman answered:

> I have a tiny little secret hope that, after a decent period of silence and prose, I
> will find myself in some almost impossible life situation and will respond to this
> with outcries of rage, rage and love, such as the world has never heard before.
> . . . My idea is this: the artist is extremely lucky who is presented with the worst
> possible ordeal which will not actually kill him. . . . I think that what happens in
> my poetic work in the future will probably largely depend not on my sitting
> calmly on my ass as I think, "Hmm, hmm, a long poem again? Hmm," but on
> being knocked in the face, and thrown flat, and given cancer, and all kinds of
> other things short of senile dementia. At that point, I'm out, but short of that, I
> don't know. I hope to be nearly crucified.

Berryman had clearly come to believe in poetry as profoundly personal at its
deepest sources, a view quite the contrary of T. S. Eliot's famous theory of impersonal poetry. He had travelled a long road from his beginnings as a poet, and the
road had carried him back to his beginnings as an adolescent, and direct confrontation with a traumatic episode that took place during his twelfth year, leav-

ing its jagged scar on his psyche. The adolescent boy had been witness in Florida, outside the window of his room, to his father's suicide — death by gunshot. Berryman's masterpiece, the lyric-epic *Dream Songs*, was completed in 1969 and had as its binding thematic thread the exorcism of the ghost of the suicidal father. In the penultimate Song, 384, the poet wrote:

> I spit upon this dreadful banker's grave
> who shot his heart out in a Florida dawn
> O ho alas alas
> When will indifference come, I moan & rave

Berryman was born bearing the name of his father, John Smith, in McAlester, Oklahoma in 1914. His father was a banker, his mother a school teacher. The marriage had been filled with dissension and quarreling from the beginning. The senior Smith moved his family to Florida and suffered losses in the collapse of the real estate boom in the mid-1920s. After his suicide, the widow married a friend who had helped the family through the trying times — John Berryman, whose last name was taken by the two stepsons. The family settled in New York, where Berryman went to South Kent School in Connecticut and then to Columbia University. He took a B.A. in 1936 and accepted a fellowship to attend Clare College, Cambridge, England, for two years.

On returning to America, Berryman began an academic career that he would follow the rest of his life. He taught at Wayne University in Detroit (now Wayne State) for a year, for three years at Harvard, about ten years at Princeton, and, beginning in 1955, at the University of Minnesota until his death. All during this period, he was publishing both poetry and criticism. He once said, "I masquerade as a writer. Actually I am a scholar." His *Stephen Crane*, published in 1950, was an important book on the American novelist and poet. Berryman's scattered literary essays were brought together and published posthumously in 1976 under the title, *The Freedom of the Poet*. His subjects ranged from Shakespeare to Hemingway and included Whitman and Conrad.

Berryman's poetry had its first book-publication in the 1940 New Directions volume entitled *Five Young American Poets*. Neither his work there, nor in the volume of *Poems* published in 1942, attracted much attention beyond the circle of poet-friends that Berryman had acquired over the years. Some six years later, Berryman's collection *The Dispossessed* did little more to gain him recognition. The poems were traditional in form, as well as difficult or obscure in meaning. One critic, Joel Conarroe, commented on the poetry of these volumes: "The humorless, abstract, often bloodless quality of much of the early work, inhibited even in an age of arid art, gives evidence of the price Berryman paid for rejecting the validity of his own sensory experience."

With the appearance of *Homage to Mistress Bradstreet* in 1956, Berryman seemed to be on his way to discovering his distinctive poetic voice. It was purportedly about the colonial poet Anne Bradstreet, author of *The Tenth Muse Lately Sprung Up in America* (1650), the first book of poems to be published by an American; but Berryman's long poem was really about Berryman himself — his isolation, his loneliness, his craving for sympathetic companionship and love. Edmund Wilson called *Homage to Mistress Bradstreet* the "most distinguished long poem by an American since *The Waste Land*."

Beginning in the late 1950s and early 1960s, Berryman embarked on his greatest work, *The Dream Songs*. The work was published in two stages, with first the appearance of *77 Dream Songs* in 1964, followed by *His Toy, His Dream, His Rest* in 1968; the two volumes, containing a total of 385 "songs," were published as a single work in 1969. The step from *Homage to Mistress Bradstreet* to *The Dream Songs* was a large one, but Berryman was no doubt emboldened to make it because of the need he felt to come to terms with his haunted feelings and buried memories. In making the step, Berryman created a series of voices, in shifting dialects, conducting eerie interior conversations that touched on the most intimate of personal concerns or obsessions. But in sounding personal depths, Berryman struck universal vibrations. In reading *The Dream Songs*, few readers have failed to come to some kind of oblique self-recognition.

Berryman himself supplied the best explanation of the complex "voice" of *The Dream Songs* in a prefatory note: "The poem . . . is essentially about an imaginary character (not the poet, not me) named Henry, a white American in early middle age sometimes in blackface, who has suffered an irreversible loss and talks about himself sometimes in the first person, sometimes in the third, sometimes even in the second; he has a friend, never named, who addresses him as Mr. Bones and variants thereof." Pressed on the identity of Henry in an interview, Berryman replied: "Henry both is and is not me, obviously. We touch at certain points. But I am an actual human being; he is nothing but a series of conceptions—my conceptions. . . . He only does what I make him do."

The unique voice Berryman invented for *The Dream Songs* seems to be made up not only of the exchanges in the old black-face minstrel shows (Mr. Bones was one of the end-men who exchanged banter with the central Interlocutor), but is also at times suggestive of slurred drunken talk, of baby talk, of the blurred speech of sleep—appropriate to *dreams*. Whatever the components, the varied voices of the *The Dream Songs* enabled Berryman finally to confront that traumatic event of his boyhood, the suicide of his father. That confrontation is the foundation on which the dazzling structure of the lyric-epic is constructed, with its shifting focus on a multitude of facets of contemporary American life.

During his final years, Berryman found himself hospitalized for treatment of his alcoholism. He had been raised as a Catholic, but he lost his faith in the bitter aftermath of his father's suicide. While under treatment, he underwent a "religious conversion," regaining the faith he had lost. Things seemed to be going his way when, in 1971, he was awarded a National Endowment for the Humanities Senior Fellowship for a work on Shakespeare he had long had in gestation. But he decided inexplicably to end his life. He jumped off a bridge in Minneapolis in early January 1972. His novel, based on his experiences in his treatment for alcoholism, appeared in 1973, entitled *Recovery*.

ADDITIONAL READING

We Dream of Honour: John Berryman's Letters to His Mother, ed. Richard J. Kelly, 1988; *John Berryman: Collected Poems, 1937–1971*, ed. Charles Thornbury, 1989.

William J. Martz, *John Berryman*, 1969; Ernest C. Stefanik, Jr., *John Berryman: A Descriptive Bibliography*, 1974; J. M. Linebarger, *John Berryman*, 1974; Joel Conarroe, *John Berryman: An Introduction to the Poetry*, 1977; Gary Arpin, *The Poetry of John Berryman*, 1978; John Haffenden, *John Berryman: A Critical Commentary*, 1980; John Haffenden, *The Life of John Berryman*, 1982; James D. Bloom, *The Stock of Available Reality*, 1984; Harry Thomas, ed., *Berryman's Understanding: Reflections on the Poetry*, 1988; Stephen Matterson, *Berryman and Lowell: The Art of Losing*, 1988; Paul Mariani, *Dream Song: The Life of John Berryman*, 1990.

TEXTS

"Winter Landscape" and "The Ball Poem" from *Homage to Mistress Bradstreet and Other Poems*, 1968; "The Dream Songs" from *The Dream Songs*, 1969; "Despair" from *Love & Fame*, 1970; "Henry's Understanding" from *Delusions, Etc.*, 1972.

Winter Landscape[1]

The three men coming down the winter hill
In brown, with tall poles and a pack of hounds
At heel, through the arrangement of the trees
Past the five figures at the burning straw,
Returning cold and silent to their town,   5

Returning to the drifted snow, the rink
Lively with children, to the older men,
The long companions they can never reach,
The blue light, men with ladders, by the church
The sledge and shadow in the twilit street,   10

Are not aware that in the sandy time
To come, the evil waste of history
Outstretched, they will be seen upon the brow
Of that same hill: when all their company
Will have been irrecoverably lost,   15

These men, this particular three in brown
Witnessed by birds will keep the scene and say
By their configuration with the trees,
The small bridge, the red houses and the fire,
What place, what time, what morning occasion   20

Sent them into the wood, a pack of hounds
At heel and the tall poles upon their shoulders,
Thence to return as now we see them and
Ankle-deep in snow down the winter hill
Descend, while three birds watch and the fourth flies.   25

1939   1940

The Ball Poem[1]

What is the boy now, who has lost his ball,
What, what is he to do? I saw it go
Merrily bouncing, down the street, and then
Merrily over — there it is in the water!
No use to say 'O there are other balls':   5
An ultimate shaking grief fixes the boy
As he stands rigid, trembling, staring down
All his young days into the harbour where
His ball went. I would not intrude on him,
A dime, another ball, is worthless. Now   10
He senses first responsibility
In a world of possessions. People will take balls,
Balls will be lost always, little boy,

---

[1]The poem is drawn from the painting *Hunters in the Snow* by Dutch painter Pieter Brueghel the Elder (*c.* 1525–1569).
[1]Berryman has written of this poem: "The poet himself is both left out and put in; the boy does and does not become him and we are confronted with a process which is at once a process of life and a process of art." See *Poets on Poetry*, ed. Howard Nemerov (1966), p. 98.

And no one buys a ball back. Money is external.
He is learning, well behind his desperate eyes,   15
The epistemology of loss, how to stand up
Knowing what every man must one day know
And most know many days, how to stand up.
And gradually light returns to the street,
A whistle blows, the ball is out of sight,   20
Soon part of me will explore the deep and dark
Floor of the harbour . . I am everywhere,
I suffer and move, my mind and my heart move
With all that move me, under the water
Or whistling, I am not a little boy.   25

1942

from The Dream Songs[1]

1

Huffy Henry hid   the day,
unappeasable Henry sulked.
I see his point,—a trying to put things over.
It was the thought that they thought
they could *do* it made Henry wicked & away.   5
But he should have come out and talked.

All the world like a woolen lover
once did seem on Henry's side.
Then came a departure.[2]
Thereafter nothing fell out as it might or ought.   10
I don't see how Henry, pried
open for all the world to see, survived.

What he has now to say is a long
wonder the world can bear & be.
Once in a sycamore I was glad   15
all at the top, and I sang.
Hard on the land wears the strong sea
and empty grows every bed.

1959, 1964

14

Life, friends, is boring. We must not say so.
After all, the sky flashes, the great sea yearns,
we ourselves flash and yearn,
and moreover my mother told me as a boy

---

[1] See the Berryman introduction for a discussion of the *Dream Songs*.
[2] An oblique reference to a recurrent memory in the *Dream*

Songs, the suicide of Berryman's father when Berryman was twelve.

(repeatingly) 'Ever to confess you're bored   5
means you have no

Inner Resources.' I conclude now I have no
inner resources, because I am heavy bored.
Peoples bore me,
literature bores me, especially great literature,   10
Henry bores me, with his plights & gripes
as bad as achilles,[1]

who loves people and valiant art, which bores me.
And the tranquil hills, & gin, look like a drag
and somehow a dog   15
has taken itself & its tail considerably away
into mountains or sea or sky, leaving
behind: me, wag.

                                                                1963, 1964

29

There sat down, once, a thing on Henry's heart
só heavy, if he had a hundred years
& more, & weeping, sleepless, in all them time
Henry could not make good.
Starts again always in Henry's ears   5
the little cough somewhere, an odour, a chime.

And there is another thing he has in mind
like a grave Sienese face[1] a thousand years
would fail to blur the still profiled reproach of. Ghastly,
with open eyes, he attends, blind.   10
All the bells say: too late. This is not for tears;
thinking.

But never did Henry, as he thought he did,
end anyone and hacks her body up
and hide the pieces, where they may be found.   15
He knows: he went over everyone, & nobody's missing.
Often he reckons, in the dawn, them up.
Nobody is ever missing.

                                                                1960, 1964

35

MLA[1]

Hey, out there!—assistant professors, full,
associates,—instructors—others—any—
I have a sing to shay.

---

[1]The Greek hero of Homer's *Iliad* who, angered by insults to his honor, withdrew from the fight against the Trojans and sulked in his tent.
[1]A face in the religious paintings by thirteenth- and fourteenth-century artists of Siena, Italy.

[1]The Modern Language Association, which holds an annual meeting in late December at which professors read critical papers to each other and newly produced Ph.D.'s apply for jobs in interviews with chairmen of departments.

We are assembled here in the capital
city for Dull—and one professor's wife is Mary—   5
at Christmastide, hey!

and all of you did theses or are doing
and the moral history of what we were up to
thrives in Sir Wilson's[2] hands—
who I don't see here—only deals go screwing   10
some of you out, some up—the chairmen too
are nervous, little friends—

a chairman's not a chairman, son, forever,
and hurts with his appointments; ha, but circle—
take my word for it—   15
though maybe Frost[3] is dying—around Mary;
forget your footnotes on the old gentleman;
dance around Mary.

                                                                        1964

40

I'm scared a lonely. Never see my son,
easy be not to see anyone,
combers[1] out to sea
know they're goin somewhere but not me.
Got a little poison, got a little gun,   5
I'm scared a lonely.

I'm scared a only one thing, which is me,
from othering I don't take nothin, see,
for any hound dog's sake.
But this is where I livin, where I rake   10
my leaves and cop my promise,[2] this' where we
cry oursel's awake.

Wishin was dyin but I gotta make
it all this way to that bed on these feet
where peoples said to meet.   15
Maybe but even if I see my son
forever never, get back on the take,
free, black & forty-one.[3]

                                                                     1963, 1964

45

He stared at ruin. Ruin stared straight back.
He thought they was old friends. He felt on the stair
where her papa found them bare

---

[2]Edmund Wilson (1895–1972), famous American man of letters and critic who was not an academic and was even on occasion anti-academic.
[3]Robert Frost (1874–1963), American poet.

[1]Long, cresting waves; breakers.
[2]I.e., fail to live up to my promise.
[3]A play on "free, white, and twenty-one."

they became familiar. When the papers were lost
rich with pals' secrets, he thought he had the knack   5
of ruin. Their paths crossed

and once they crossed in jail; they crossed in bed;
and over an unsigned letter their eyes met,
and in an Asian city
directionless & lurchy at two & three,   10
or trembling to a telephone's fresh threat,
and when some wired his head

to reach a wrong opinion, 'Epileptic'.
But he noted now that: they were not old friends.
He did not know this one.   15
This one was a stranger, come to make amends
for all the imposters, and to make it stick.
Henry nodded, un-.

1963, 1964

73

Karesansui, Ryoan-ji[1]

The taxi makes the vegetables fly.
'Dozo kudasai,'[2] I have him wait.
Past the bright lake up into the temple,
shoes off, and
my right leg swings me left.   5
I do survive beside the garden I

came seven thousand mile the other way
supplied of engines all to see, to see.
Differ them photographs, plans lie:
how big it is!   10
austere a sea rectangular   of sand by the oiled mud wall,
and the sand is not quite white: granite sand, grey,

—from nowhere can one see *all* the stones—
but helicopters or   a Brooklyn reproduction[3]
will fix that—   15

and the fifteen changeless stones in their five worlds
with a shelving of moving moss
stand me the thought of the ancient maker priest.
Elsewhere occurs—I remembers—loss.
Through awes & weathers neither it increased   20
nor did one blow of all his stone & sand thought die.

1958   *1964*

---

[1]A famous Zen Temple and garden in Kyoto, Japan; Berryman visited it in 1957. The fifteen stones of the garden are so placed in the carefully raked gravel that it is impossible to see all fifteen at once from the gallery of the temple (from where one must view it).

[2]A polite Japanese expression, roughly translated as "please."
[3]A reproduction of the garden has been created in a Brooklyn park.

75

Turning it over, considering, like a madman
Henry put forth a book.
No harm resulted from this.
Neither the menstruating   stars (nor man) was moved
at once.   5
Bare dogs drew closer for a second look

and performed their friendly operations there.
Refreshed, the bark rejoiced.
Seasons went and came.
Leaves fell, but only a few.   10
Something remarkable about this
unshedding bulky bole-proud blue-green moist

thing made by savage & thoughtful
surviving Henry
began to strike the passers from despair   15
so that sore on their shoulders old men hoisted
six-foot sons and polished women called
small girls to dream awhile toward the flashing & bursting tree!

1959, 1964

76

Henry's Confession

Nothin very bad happen to me lately.
How you explain that? — I explain that, Mr Bones,[1]
terms o' your bafflin odd sobriety.
Sober as man can get, no girls, no telephones,
what could happen bad to Mr Bones?   5
— *If* life is a handkerchief sandwich,

in a modesty of death I join my father
who dared so long agone leave me.
A bullet on a concrete stoop
close by a smothering southern sea   10
spreadeagled on an island, by my knee.
— You is from hunger, Mr Bones,

I offers you this handkerchief, now set
your left foot by my right foot,
shoulder to shoulder, all that jazz,   15
arm in arm, by the beautiful sea,[2]
hum a little, Mr Bones.
— I saw nobody coming, so I went instead.

1964

---

[1] See Berryman's comment in the Berryman introduction of the role of Mr. Bones in the *Dream Songs*.

[2] Line from a song popular in the early part of the twentieth century.

78

Op. posth.[1] no. 1

Darkened his eye, his wild smile disappeared,
inapprehensible his studies grew,
nourished he less & less
his subject body with good food & rest,
something bizarre about Henry, slowly sheared   5
off, unlike you & you,

smaller & smaller, till in question stood
his eyeteeth and one block of memories
These were enough for him
implying commands from upstairs & from down,   10
Walt's 'orbic flex,'[2] triads of Hegel[3] would
incorporate, if you please,

into the know-how of the American bard
embarrassed Henry heard himself a-being,
and the younger Stephen Crane[4]   15
of a powerful memory, of pain,
these stood the ancestors, relaxed & hard,
whilst Henry's parts were fleeing.

1964   *1966, 1968*

91

Op. posth. no. 14

Noises from underground made gibber some
others collected & dug Henry up
saying, 'You *are* a sight.'
Chilly, he muttered for a double rum
waving the mikes away, putting a stop   5
to rumours, pushing his fright

off with the now accumulated taxes
accustomed in his way to solitude
and no bills.
Wives came forward, claiming a new Axis,[1]   10
fearful for their insurance, though, now, glued
to disencumbered Henry's many ills.

A fortnight later, sense a single man
upon the trampled scene at 2 a.m.
insomnia-plagued, with a shovel   15

---

[1] "Opus Posthumous": work published after death of the author; Songs 78–91 are so-titled, but there is a return to life of Henry in Song 91.
[2] See Walt Whitman's "Song of Myself," Section 26: "A tenor large and fresh as the creation fills me, / The orbic flex of his mouth is pouring and filling me full."
[3] I.e., thesis, antithesis, synthesis, the dialectical logic of German philosopher Georg Wilhelm Friedrich Hegel (1770–1831).
[4] American novelist (1871–1900); Berryman published a biographical-critical work on him in 1950.
[1] I.e., alliance; during World War II, Germany, Italy, and Japan were referred to collectively as "the Axis."

digging like mad, Lazarus[2] with a plan
to get his own back, a plan, a stratagem
no newsman will unravel.

1968

324

An Elegy for W. C. W.,[1] the lovely man

Henry in Ireland to Bill underground:
Rest well, who worked so hard, who made a good sound
constantly, for so many years:
your high-jinks delighted the continents & our ears:
you had so many girls your life was a triumph   5
and you loved your one wife.

At dawn you rose & wrote—the books poured forth—
you delivered infinite babies, in one great birth—
and your generosity
to juniors made you deeply loved, deeply: 10
if envy was a Henry trademark, he would envy you,
especially the being through.

Too many journeys lie for him ahead,
too many galleys & page-proofs to be read,
he would like to lie down   15
in your sweet silence, to whom was not denied
the mysterious late excellence which is the crown
of our trials & our last bride.

1966   *1968*

354

The only happy people in the world
are those who do not have   to write long poems:
muck, administration, toil:
the protototality of an absence of contact
in one's own generation, chiefly the old & the young   5
persisting with interest.

'The Care & Feeding of Long Poems' was Henry's title
for his next essay, which will come out when
he wants it to.
A Kennedy[1]-sponsored bill for the protection   10
of poets from long poems   will benefit the culture
and do no harm to that kind Lady, Mrs Johnson.[2]

---

[2]Jesus raised Lazarus from the dead (see John 11–12).
[1]William Carlos Williams, American poet.
[1]Edward Kennedy (senator, 1962–) or Robert Kennedy
(senator, 1964–68), who, of course, did not sponsor such a
bill.
[2]Lady Bird Johnson, President Lyndon Johnson's wife; Johnson was president 1963–68.

He would have gone to the White House & consulted the President
during his 10 seconds in the receiving line
on the problems of long poems   15
Mr Johnson has never written one
but he seems a generous & able man
'Tetelestai'[3] said St John.

1966   1968

382

At Henry's bier let some thing fall out well:
enter there none who somewhat has to sell,
the music ancient & gradual,
the voices solemn but the grief subdued,
no hairy jokes but everybody's mood   5
subdued, subdued,

until the Dancer comes, in a short short dress
hair black & long & loose, dark dark glasses,
uptilted face,
pallor & strangeness, the music changes   10
to 'Give!' & 'Ow!' and how! the music changes,
she kicks a backward limb

on tiptoe, pirouettes, & she is free
to the knocking music, sails, dips, & suddenly
returns to the terrible gay   15
occasion hopeless & mad, she weaves, it's hell,
she flings to her head a leg, bobs, all is well,
she dances Henry away.

1968   1968

384

The marker slants, flowerless, day's almost done,
I stand above my father's grave with rage,
often, often before
I've made this awful pilgrimage to one
who cannot visit me, who tore his page   5
out: I come back for more,

I spit upon this dreadful banker's grave
who shot his heart out in a Florida dawn
O ho alas alas
When will indifference come, I moan & rave   10
I'd like to scrabble till I got right down
away down under the grass

---

[3]"It is finished" (Greek); Jesus speaks these words when he
asks for a drink and is given vinegar and then gives up the
spirit (see John 19:28–30).

and ax the casket open ha to see
just how he's taking it, which he sought so hard
we'll tear apart   15
the mouldering grave clothes ha & then Henry
will heft the ax once more, his final card,
and fell it on the start.

                                                                    1968

Despair

It seems to be dark all the time.
I have difficulty walking.
I can remember what to say to my seminar
but I don't know that I want to.

I said in a Song once: I am unusually tired.   5
I repeat that & increase it.
I'm vomiting.
I broke down today in the slow movement of K.365.[1]

I certainly don't think I'll last much longer.
I wrote: 'There may be horribles.'   10
I increase that.
(I think she took her little breasts away.)

I am in love with my excellent baby.
Crackles! in darkness HOPE; & disappears.
Lost arts.   15
Vanishings.

Walt![2]   We're downstairs,
even you don't comfort me
but I join your risk my dear friend & go with you.
There are no matches   20

Utter, His Father, one word

                                                                    1970

Henry's Understanding

He was reading late, at Richard's,[1] down in Maine,
aged 32? Richard & Helen long in bed,
my good wife long in bed.
All I had to do was strip & get into my bed,
putting the marker in the book, & sleep,
& wake to a hot breakfast.   5

---

[1]A composition by Mozart (1756–1791), Concerto for Two Pianos, so designated on the "Köchel listing," made by Austrian musicologist Ludwig von Köchel (1800–1877); the listing assigned numbers to Mozart's compositions in chronological order.

[2]Walt Whitman, American poet.
[1]In 1946, Berryman visited American poet and critic Richard Blackmur (1904–1965) and his wife Helen at their summer home in Harrington, Maine.

Off the coast was an island, P'tit Manaan,
the bluff from Richard's lawn was almost sheer.
A chill at four o'clock.
It only takes a few minutes to make a man.   10
A concentration upon now & here.
Suddenly, unlike Bach,[2]

& horribly, unlike Bach, it occurred to me
that *one* night, instead of warm pajamas,
I'd take off all my clothes   15
& cross the damp cold lawn & down the bluff
into the terrible water & walk forever
under it out toward the island.

1969, 1972

WILLIAM STAFFORD
(b. 1914)

William Stafford's poems often seem so simple and so relaxed in form that readers wonder why they should be considered poems. Stafford has explained: "Poetry and prose to me are very close to the same thing. The distinction is not so much in the craft that's gone into it but in the way you present it to a reader. If you say something in such a way as to ask a certain amount of attention from the reader, that's a poem." As for his avoiding traditional forms, Stafford has pointed out:

> I don't feel less concerned with patterns than are some more "formal" poets, but I feel that there are more patterns to be discovered than have been recorded so far in traditional forms. You have to find your own form; it's like a dog circling and getting ready to lie down in high grass—you sort of make your pattern according to how stiff the grass is, what the temperature is, lots of things. Now, that doesn't mean you don't get a feel for what the grass is doing—what your words and feelings are doing—only that you have to find more patterns than do people devoted to form.

For Stafford, the poetic process is more an act of passive meditation than it is an act of deliberate construction:

> You let the process itself carry you where it and you want to go. It's lending yourself to the impressions or the impulses that come right now without trying to guide the process in terms of what an editor wants or what you think society needs. Instead it's finding the center of your attention at that moment. . . . So many people feel that, when they write, they select some effect they want to make on a reader. I see it from the other way, as a kind of following out of your own impulses. And if you are lucky or if your society happens to be in step with you, then what you find is also harmonious with what they need.

---

[2]Johann Sebastian Bach (1685–1750), German composer of enormous creativity; one story tells of the young Bach, forbidden access to an organ manuscript by a jealous elder brother, copying the work out by moonlight each night for six months.

Stafford was born in Hutchinson, Kansas, in 1914, and took a B.A. at the University of Kansas in 1937. He worked for a time in the sugar beet fields, in an oil refinery, and in construction jobs until the Second World War. Declaring himself a conscientious objector (he was a member of a pacifist religious group, Church of the Brethren), he was assigned to work in the Forest Service and Soil Conservation camps during the war. It was while in this alternative service that he became accustomed to getting up at an early hour in order to have time to write poetry — a schedule he would follow later. After the war, he returned to the University of Kansas for an M.A. in English, finishing it in 1945. In 1948, he accepted an appointment teaching English at Lewis and Clark College in Portland, Oregon, a place where he would stay for the rest of his career except for a few temporary assignments elsewhere. In 1955, he took a Ph.D. in the University of Iowa Writers' Workshop and English Department.

Stafford's first book was *Down in My Heart*, published in 1947 (reissued in 1985), and was prose not poetry — an account of his wartime experiences as a conscientious objector. He began to publish poems in the little magazines during the 1950s, but it was not until he was forty-six years old, in 1960, that he published his first volume of poetry, *West of Your City*. The poems seemed poems of simple statement and acceptance, quite unlike the popular poetry of alienation and complicated, convoluted thought: "Mine was a Midwest home — you can keep your world. / Plain black hats rode the thoughts that made our code. / We sang hymns in the house; the roof was near God."

Travel Through the Dark, Stafford's second book of poems, appeared in 1962. Like the poetry in the first, the poems were simple and immediately accessible — and identifiably western:

> We saw a town by the track in Colorado.
> Cedar trees below had sifted the air,
> snow water foamed the torn river there,
> and a lost road went climbing the slope like a ladder.

Stafford's poetry seemed like a mountain breeze bringing fresh and clarified air into overstuffed rooms. The book attracted wide attention and won for Stafford the National Book Award for Poetry.

Gentle and unassuming by nature, Stafford came across in poetry readings as a genuine Westerner and lover of the outdoors. In a recent interview he remarked on the recurrence of Indian and nature themes in his poetry: "Out here in the Northwest [nature's] very much a part of our lives. Even in rain we're out, and there's a lot of rain. I suppose the Indian flavor and the outdoor flavor go together. We just happen to live in a country where these things are a part of our lives."

Although Stafford was something of a slow starter in publishing his poetry, he became astonishingly prolific during the 1970s and 1980s. An omnibus volume, *Stories That Could Be True: New and Collected Poems*, appeared in 1977. Later volumes include *A Glass in the Rains: New Poems* (1982), *Smoke's Way: Poems from Limited Editions, 1968–1981* (1983), and *An Oregon Message* (1987). Collections of prose include *Friends to This Ground: A Statement for Readers, Teachers, and Writers of Literature* (1967), *Writing the Australian Crawl: Views on the Writer's Vocation*, edited by Donald Hall (1978), and *You Must Revise Your Life* (1986). What fellow poet James Dickey said of Stafford in an early review seems applicable to the entire body of his work: Stafford's "natural mode of speech is a gentle, mystical, half-mocking and highly personal daydreaming about the landscape of the western

United States. Everything in this world is available to Mr. Stafford's way of writing, and I for one am very glad it is."

ADDITIONAL READING

Jonathan Holden, *The Mark to Turn: A Reading of William Stafford's Poetry*, 1976; George Lensing and Ronald Moran, *Four Poets of the Emotive Imagination: Robert Bly, James Wright, Louis Simpson and William Stafford*, 1976; David A. Carpenter, *William Stafford*, 1986; Lars Nordström, *Theodore Roethke, William Stafford, and Gary Snyder: The Ecological Metaphor As Transformed Regionalism*, 1989.

TEXTS

"Brother Wind," from *Brother Wind*, 1986; remaining poems from *Stories That Could Be True: New and Collected Poems*, 1977.

One Home

Mine was a Midwest home—you can keep your world.
Plain black hats rode the thoughts that made our code.
We sang hymns in the house; the roof was near God.

The light bulb that hung in the pantry made a wan light,
but we could read by it the names of preserves—   5
outside, the buffalo grass, and the wind in the night.

A wildcat sprang at Grandpa on the Fourth of July
when he was cutting plum bushes for fuel,
before Indians pulled the West over the edge of the sky.

To anyone who looked at us we said, "My friend";   10
liking the cut of a thought, we could say "Hello."
(But plain black hats rode the thoughts that made our code.)

The sun was over our town; it was like a blade.
Kicking cottonwood leaves we ran toward storms.
Wherever we looked the land would hold us up.   15

                                                         1960

At the Bomb Testing Site

At noon in the desert a panting lizard
waited for history, its elbows tense,
watching the curve of a particular road
as if something might happen.

It was looking at something farther off   5
than people could see, an important scene
acted in stone for little selves
at the flute end of consequences.

There was just a continent without much on it
under a sky that never cared less.
Ready for a change, the elbows waited.   10
The hands gripped hard on the desert.

1960

Level Light

Sometimes the light when evening fails
stains all haystacked country and hills,
runs the cornrows and clasps the barn
with that kind of color escaped from corn
that brings to autumn the winter word—   5
a level shaft that tells the world:

It is too late now for earlier ways;
now there are only some other ways,
and only one way to find them—fail.

In one stride night then takes the hill.   10

1960

Traveling Through the Dark

Traveling through the dark I found a deer
dead on the edge of the Wilson River road.
It is usually best to roll them into the canyon:
that road is narrow; to swerve might make more dead.

By glow of the tail-light I stumbled back of the car   5
and stood by the heap, a doe, a recent killing;
she had stiffened already, almost cold.
I dragged her off; she was large in the belly.

My fingers touching her side brought me the reason—
her side was warm; her fawn lay there waiting,   10
alive, still, never to be born.
Beside that mountain road I hesitated.

The car aimed ahead its lowered parking lights;
under the hood purred the steady engine.
I stood in the glare of the warm exhaust turning red;   15
around our group I could hear the wilderness listen.

I thought hard for us all—my only swerving—,
then pushed her over the edge into the river.

1962

Brother Wind

Air this morning embraces you, cool
from the canyon. You let go of earth
and wander treetops, fall upward,
tumble along free into space. Often
around corners you die and wait and get   5
warm, then wander forth again. Who knows
where you'll stay tonight? Horse-trading through
Wyoming, sage-nuzzling, canyon-whistling,
you campaign onward. Did you hear
the one about the kite from Texas? And they   10
say there's a cave where captive air has whispered
for centuries—you go there and listen
and learn the language rocks use
when nobody is around. When you come
back, everybody else is too loud, and every   15
morning you have to go out near dawn
even for only a minute, to lean over and hear
that patient sound, following again the cool
corridors through canyons that always go down.

1986

ROBERT LOWELL
(1917–1977)

Robert Lowell described the "struggle" he experienced in creating a poem in a 1961 interview:

> Almost the whole problem of writing poetry is to bring it back to what you really feel, and that takes an awful lot of maneuvering. You may feel the doorknob more strongly than some big personal event, and the doorknob will open into something that you can use as your own. . . . Often images and often the sense of the beginning and end of a poem are all you have—some journey to be gone through between those things; you know that, but you don't know the details. And that's marvelous; then you feel the poem will come out. It's a terrible struggle, because what you really feel hasn't got the form, it's not what you can put down in a poem. . . . Then the great moment comes when there's enough resolution of your technical equipment, your way of constructing things, and what you can make a poem out of, to hit something you really want to say. You may not know you have it to say.

Lowell's poetic career may be seen as tracing the radical change in postwar poetry as it moved beyond the great modernist poets of the earlier part of the century. He began writing as one kind of poet and, in mid-career as an established poet, remade himself into another kind of poet. He came from a long line of New England poets that included James Russell Lowell (1818–1891) and Amy Lowell (1874–1925). He was born in Boston, and attended Harvard for two years (1935–37). Then he made his first break with his past, leaving Harvard for Kenyon College in Ohio, where the southern poet John Crowe Ransom had just been appointed. He met there Randall Jarrell, who had also been attracted to Kenyon by Ransom. Lowell majored in the classics and studied poetry with Ransom, graduating in 1940.

In 1940 Lowell made another break with his Calvinistic New England past by becoming a Catholic. And during the Second World War he made still another break, from a father who had served in the U.S. Navy, by becoming a conscientious objector and serving some five months in prison in 1943 for his refusal to enter the armed forces. The experience reenforced his determination to become a poet, and he published his first volume, *Land of Unlikeness*, in 1944. The book of stiff, somewhat clotted and difficult poems attracted little notice. Lowell salvaged what poems he could from the book, reworked them rigorously, and along with new poems published his second volume, *Lord Weary's Castle*, in 1946. It was awarded the Pulitzer Prize and launched his career. In 1947 he was appointed Consultant in Poetry at the Library of Congress. Books published in 1950, *Poems 1938–1949*, and in 1951, *The Mills of the Kavanaughs*, increased Lowell's reputation as the leading figure in a new generation of poets.

But in the 1950s, Lowell began to have doubts about the direction of his career. He himself described the feeling that overcame him in 1957 during a poetry-reading tour on the West Coast:

> I was in San Francisco, the era and setting of Allen Ginsberg, and all about very modest poets were waking up prophets. I became sorely aware of how few poems I had written, and that these few had been finished at the latest three or four years earlier. Their style seemed distant, symbol-ridden and willfully difficult. I began to paraphrase my Latin quotations, and to add extra syllables to a line to make it clearer and more colloquial. I felt my old poems hid what they were really about, and many times offered a stiff, humorless and even impenetrable surface. I am no convert to the "beats." . . . Still, my own poems seemed like prehistoric monsters dragged down into the bog and death by their ponderous armor. I was reciting what I no longer felt. . . . When I returned to my home, I began writing lines in a new style. . . . When I began writing "Skunk Hour," I felt that most of what I knew about writing was a hindrance.

Seldom has a poet publicly described his feelings about his own poems with such candor. The new Lowell poems became more accessible, more personal, often in the "confessional" style, and immediately moving. Lowell had married novelist Jean Stafford in 1940 and was divorced in 1948; and he was married again in 1949, to the novelist Elizabeth Hardwick. The spells of acute depression that he had begun to feel early in his adulthood intensified as he became older, and he underwent a series of breakdowns, frequently requiring hospitalization. These experiences now became material for his poetry, the writing perhaps even serving in part as therapy. *Life Studies*, published in 1959, contained the "new" Lowell, and poems appearing in it remain among his most popular: "Waking in the Blue," "Memories of West Street and Lepke," and "Skunk Hour." *Life Studies* deservedly won the National Book Award for Poetry in 1959.

Although Lowell's style continued to develop and change, he never returned to the stiff formality and "impenetrable surface" of his earlier poems. His poetry remained open to his private feelings and experiences, and often dealt with public issues of immediate concern. Lowell gained some notoriety in 1965 by turning down an invitation to the White House Arts Festival in protest against America's involvement in Vietnam. And in 1967, he joined Norman Mailer and others in the March on the Pentagon against the Vietnam War, and thus became a character in Mailer's account of the event, *Armies of the Night*. Lowell himself wrote about the march in two poems, both entitled "The March" (I and II).

In 1961, Lowell published a volume of translations, entitled *Imitations*, which won the Bollingen Poetry Translation Prize. In 1964, Lowell saw to production in an off-Broadway theater three plays he had written, based on short works by Nathaniel Hawthorne ("Endecott and the Red Cross" and "My Kinsman, Major Molineaux") and Herman Melville ("Benito Cereno"). They were published in 1965 as *The Old Glory*. Lowell continued to write and publish volumes of poetry, including *For the Union Dead* (1964) and *Near the Ocean* (1967).

One book of poems went through several reshapings, appearing first as *Notebook 1967–68* (1969); and then, revised and expanded, as *Notebook* (1970); and then, sifted and rearranged, as two volumes: *History* (1973) and *For Lizzie and Harriet* (1973). This latter volume contained poems written for his wife Elizabeth Hardwick and his daughter. In 1972, he divorced Hardwick and married Lady Caroline Blackwood, a journalist and novelist, and settled in England. *The Dolphin* (1973) contained sonnets written about his third and last marriage. His *Selected Poems* appeared in 1976, and a last volume of new poetry, *Day by Day*, in 1977. In the latter were many poems about the remembered past, about growing old, and about death. He remarked: "From year to year, things remembered from the past change almost more than the present." Lowell returned to America in 1977 to resume his teaching post at Harvard University. He died of a heart attack in September in a taxicab in New York City.

Lowell's reputation as a worthy successor to the great modernist poets such as Pound, Eliot, and Williams was established early in his career. But he proved to be his own poet, moving out from under the long shadows cast by his precursors. By the time of his death, he was recognized as preeminent among postwar poets, with his own remarkable style and distinctive voice. In his turn, he became an influence on successor poets, especially those writing in the confessional mode, but also those whose range extended to political and public issues. His talent was still intact, and his imagination vigorous, up to the end.

ADDITIONAL READING

Robert Lowell: Collected Prose, ed. Robert Giroux, 1987.

Hugh Staples, *Robert Lowell: The First Twenty Years*, 1961; Jerome Mazzaro, *The Poetic Themes of Robert Lowell*, 1965; William J. Martz, *The Achievement of Robert Lowell*, 1966; Thomas Parkinson, ed., *Robert Lowell: A Collection of Critical Essays*, 1968; Michael London and Robert Boyers, *Robert Lowell: A Portrait of the Artist in His Time*, 1970; Philip Cooper, *The Autobiographical Myth of Robert Lowell*, 1970; Jay Martin, *Robert Lowell*, 1970; R. K. Meiners, *Everything to Be Endured: An Essay on Robert Lowell*, 1970; Jonathan Price, ed., *Critics on Robert Lowell*, 1972; Patrick Cosgrave, *The Public Poetry of Robert Lowell*, 1972; Marjorie Perloff, *The Poetic Art of Robert Lowell*, 1973; Alan Williamson, *Pity the Monsters: The Political Vision of Robert Lowell*, 1974; Stephen Yenser, *Circle to Circle: The Poetry of Robert Lowell*, 1975; Steven Gould Axelrod, *Robert Lowell: Life and Art*, 1978; Richard J. Fein, *Robert Lowell*, 1970, rev. 1979; Steven Gould Axelrod, *Robert Lowell: A Reference Guide*, 1982; Ian Hamilton, *Robert Lowell: A Biography*, 1982; Vereen M. Bell, *Robert Lowell: Nihilist as Hero*, 1983; Mark Rudman, *Robert Lowell: An Introduction to the Poetry*, 1983; Steven Gould Axelrod and Helen Deese, eds., *Robert Lowell: Essays on the Poetry*, 1986; Stephen Matterson, *Berryman and Lowell: The Art of Losing*, 1987; Jeffrey Meyers, *Manic Power: Robert Lowell and His Circle*, 1987; Philip Hobsbaum, *A Reader's Guide to Robert Lowell*, 1988; Katherine Wallingford, *Robert Lowell's Language of the Self*, 1988; Jeffrey Meyers, ed., *Robert Lowell: Interviews and Memoirs*, 1988.

TEXTS

"The Quaker Graveyard in Nantucket," "Mr. Edwards and the Spider," and "After the Surprising Conversions" from *Lord Weary's Castle*, 1946; "Words for Hart Crane," "Sailing Home from Rapallo," "Waking in the Blue," "Memories of West Street and Lepke," "'To Speak of Woe

That Is in Marriage,'" and "Skunk Hour" from *Life Studies*, 1959; "For the Union Dead" and "Night Sweat" from *For the Union Dead*, 1964; "Waking Early Sunday Morning" from *Near the Ocean*, 1967; "The March I" and "The March II" from *Notebook*, 1970; "History" and "Reading Myself" from *History*, 1973; "Fishnet" from *The Dolphin*, 1973; "For John Berryman" and "Epilogue" from *Day by Day*, 1977.

The Quaker
Graveyard in Nantucket

(FOR WARREN WINSLOW,[1] DEAD AT SEA)

Let man have dominion over the fishes of the sea and the
fowls of the air and the beasts and the whole earth, and
every creeping creature that moveth upon the earth.[2]

I

A brackish reach of shoal off Madaket, —[3]
The sea was still breaking violently and night
Had steamed into our North Atlantic Fleet,
When the drowned sailor clutched the drag-net. Light
Flashed from his matted head and marble feet,   5
He grappled at the net
With the coiled, hurdling muscles of his thighs:
The corpse was bloodless, a botch of reds and whites,
Its open, staring eyes
Were lustreless dead-lights[4]   10
Or cabin-windows on a stranded hulk
Heavy with sand.[5] We weight the body, close
Its eyes and heave it seaward whence it came,
Where the heel-headed dogfish barks its nose
On Ahab's void and forehead;[6] and the name   15
Is blocked in yellow chalk.
Sailors, who pitch this portent at the sea
Where dreadnaughts shall confess
Its hell-bent deity,
When you are powerless   20
To sand-bag this Atlantic bulwark, faced
By the earth-shaker, green, unwearied, chaste
In his steel scales: ask for no Orphean lute[7]
To pluck life back. The guns of the steeled fleet
Recoil and then repeat   25
The hoarse salute.

---

[1] Lowell's cousin, drowned when his ship was sunk during the Second World War.
[2] Genesis 1:26 (Douay Bible version).
[3] On Nantucket Island.
[4] Port-hole shutters or covers (to keep out the sea).
[5] Many of the images in ll. 4–12, as Hugh B. Staples has demonstrated, come from Henry David Thoreau's *Cape Cod* (1898), in a passage describing a shipwreck Thoreau had witnessed: "I saw many marble feet and matted heads. . . . the coiled up wreck of a human hulk, gashed by the rocks and fishes, so that the bone and muscle were exposed, but quite bloodless, — merely red and white, — with wide-open eyes, yet lustreless, deadlights, or like the cabin windows of a stranded vessel, filled with sand."
[6] Ahab, the monomaniacal captain sailing in pursuit of the great white whale in *Moby-Dick* by Herman Melville (1819–1891).
[7] Orpheus, in Greek mythology, charmed Persephone by playing his lute, persuading her to release his wife Eurydice from Hades, but on condition that he not look back at her as she followed him; he forgot, looked back, and lost Eurydice forever.

II

Whenever winds are moving and their breath
Heaves at the roped-in bulwarks of this pier,
The terns and sea-gulls tremble at your death
In these home waters. Sailor, can you hear   30
The Pequod's[8] sea wings, beating landward, fall
Headlong and break on our Atlantic wall
Off 'Sconset,[9] where the yawing S-boats[10] splash
The bellbuoy, with ballooning spinnakers,
As the entangled, screeching mainsheet clears   35
The blocks: off Madaket, where lubbers lash
The heavy surf and throw their long lead squids
For blue-fish? Sea-gulls blink their heavy lids
Seaward. The winds' wings beat upon the stones,
Cousin, and scream for you and the claws rush   40
At the sea's throat and wring it in the slush
Of this old Quaker graveyard where the bones
Cry out in the long night for the hurt beast
Bobbing by Ahab's whaleboats in the East.

III

All you recovered from Poseidon[11] died   45
With you, my cousin, and the harrowed brine
Is fruitless on the blue beard of the god,
Stretching beyond us to the castles in Spain,
Nantucket's[12] westward haven. To Cape Cod
Guns, cradled on the tide,   50
Blast the eelgrass about a waterclock
Of bilge and backwash, roil the salt and sand
Lashing earth's scaffold, rock
Our warships in the hand
Of the great God, where time's contrition blues   55
Whatever it was these Quaker sailors lost
In the mad scramble of their lives. They died
When time was open-eyed,
Wooden and childish; only bones abide
There, in the nowhere, where their boats were tossed   60
Sky-high, where mariners had fabled news
Of IS,[13] the whited monster. What it cost
Them is their secret. In the sperm-whale's slick
I see the Quakers drown and hear their cry:
"If God himself had not been on our side,   65
If God himself had not been on our side,
When the Atlantic rose against us, why,
Then it had swallowed us up quick."

IV

This is the end of the whaleroad[14] and the whale
Who spewed Nantucket bones on the thrashed swell   70

---

[8]Captain Ahab's ship, which was stove in by the white whale and sunk in *Moby-Dick*.
[9]I.e., Siasconset, a Nantucket town.
[10]Racing sailboats.
[11]God of the sea in Greek mythology.
[12]An island off Massachusetts from which whalers put out to sea.
[13]Cf. Exodus 3:14: "And God said unto Moses, I AM THAT I AM . . . thus shalt thou say unto the children of Israel, I AM hath sent me unto you"; also cf. Revelation 17:8: "Behold the beast that was, and is not, yet is."
[14]Old English term for the sea.

And stirred the troubled waters to whirlpools
To send the Pequod packing off to hell:
This is the end of them, three-quarters fools,
Snatching at straws to sail
Seaward and seaward on the turntail whale,   75
Spouting out blood and water as it rolls,
Sick as a dog to these Atlantic shoals:
Clamavimus,[15] O depths. Let the sea-gulls wail

For water, for the deep where the high tide
Mutters to its hurt self, mutters and ebbs.   80
Waves wallow in their wash, go out and out,
Leave only the death-rattle of the crabs,
The beach increasing, its enormous snout
Sucking the ocean's side.
This is the end of running on the waves;   85
We are poured out like water. Who will dance
The mast-lashed master of Leviathans[16]
Up from this field of Quakers in their unstoned graves?

                                    V

When the whale's viscera go and the roll
Of its corruption overruns this world   90
Beyond tree-swept Nantucket and Wood's Hole[17]
And Martha's Vineyard, Sailor, will your sword
Whistle and fall and sink into the fat?
In the great ash-pit of Jehoshaphat[18]
The bones cry for the blood of the white whale,   95
The fat flukes arch and whack about its ears,
The death-lance churns into the sanctuary, tears
The gun-blue swingle,[19] heaving like a flail,
And hacks the coiling life out: it works and drags
And rips the sperm-whale's midriff into rags,   100
Gobbets of blubber spill to wind and weather,
Sailor, and gulls go round the stoven timbers
Where the morning stars sing out together
And thunder shakes the white surf and dismembers
The red flag hammered in the mast-head.[20] Hide,   105
Our steel, Jonas Messias,[21] in Thy side.

                                   VI

                   OUR LADY OF WALSINGHAM[22]

There once the penitents took off their shoes
And then walked barefoot the remaining mile;
And the small trees, a stream and hedgerows file

---

[15]"We have cried out" (Latin). Cf. Psalm 130:1: "Out of the depths have I cried unto thee, O Lord."
[16]Biblical term for sea monsters, and used by Melville and others to apply to whales.
[17]A town in Massachusetts, near Martha's Vineyard, an island near Nantucket.
[18]Cf. Joel 3:12: "Let the heathen be wakened, and come up to the valley of Jehoshaphat: for there will I sit to judge all the heathen round about."
[19]A wooden instrument used for beating and cleaning flax or hemp.
[20]At the end of *Moby-Dick*, as the *Pequod* is sinking, the Indian

Tashtego's arm rises from the sea to nail Ahab's flag to the mast.
[21]A fanciful merging of Jonah, an Old Testament figure swallowed by a whale, and the Messiah or Jesus, the New Testament saviour; Jonah's delivery from the whale has been compared to the Resurrection of Christ. The harpoon used for capturing the whale merges with the centurion's spear wounding Christ.
[22]A shrine in Walsingham Priory, Norfolk, England, dedicated to the Virgin Mary; Lowell has indicated that he used E. I. Watkins's *Catholic Art and Culture* (1947) for details of the shrine.

Slowly along the munching English lane,   110
Like cows to the old shrine, until you lose
Track of your dragging pain.
The stream flows down under the druid tree,
Shiloah's[23] whirlpools gurgle and make glad
The castle of God. Sailor, you were glad   115
And whistled Sion[24] by that stream. But see:

Our Lady, too small for her canopy,
Sits near the altar. There's no comeliness
At all or charm in that expressionless
Face with its heavy eyelids. As before,   120
This face, for centuries a memory,
Non est species, neque decor,[25]
Expressionless, expresses God: it goes
Past castled Sion. She knows what God knows,
Not Calvary's Cross nor crib at Bethlehem   125
Now, and the world shall come to Walsingham.

VII

The empty winds are creaking and the oak
Splatters and splatters on the cenotaph,[26]
The boughs are trembling and a gaff
Bobs on the untimely stroke   130
Of the greased wash exploding on a shoal-bell[27]
In the old mouth of the Atlantic. It's well;
Atlantic, you are fouled with the blue sailors,
Sea-monsters, upward angel, downward fish:
Unmarried and corroding, spare of flesh   135
Mart once of supercilious, wing'd clippers,
Atlantic, where your bell-trap guts its spoil
You could cut the brackish winds with a knife
Here in Nantucket, and cast up the time
When the Lord God formed man from the sea's slime   140
And breathed into his face the breath of life,
And blue-lung'd combers lumbered to the kill.
The Lord survives the rainbow[28] of His will.

                                                          1945, 1946

Mr. Edwards and the Spider[1]

I saw the spiders marching through the air,
Swimming from tree to tree that mildewed day
In latter August when the hay

---

[23]Variant of "Siloam"; the "pool of Siloam" is a reservoir in the ancient city of Jerusalem (connected by tunnel to the spring of Gihon).
[24]Variant of Zion, the Temple Mount in Jerusalem; Zion has come to be identified as the heavenly city of God.
[25]"There is no form nor comeliness" (Latin); cf. Isaiah 53:2.
[26]A tomb or monument commemorating someone buried elsewhere.
[27]A bell buoy indicating shallow waters.
[28]Allusion to the rainbow symbolizing God's covenant with Noah that there would not be another flood destroying humankind (see Genesis 9:11–17).
[1]Jonathan Edwards (1703–1758), American Puritan minister and theologian, is the speaker of the poem. Edwards wrote an essay ("Essay on Insects") on the phenomenon of flying spiders when he was eleven, making the observations contained in the opening lines. Two of his sermons are the sources for much of the later stanzas: "Sinners in the Hands of an Angry God" and "The Punishment of the Wicked."

Came creaking to the barn. But where
  The wind is westerly,   5
Where gnarled November makes the spiders fly
Into the apparitions of the sky,
 They purpose nothing but their ease and die
Urgently beating east to sunrise and the sea;

What are we in the hands of the great God?   10
It was in vain you set up thorn and briar
  In battle array against the fire
  And treason crackling in your blood;
   For the wild thorns grow tame
And will do nothing to oppose the flame;   15
Your lacerations tell the losing game
You play against a sickness past your cure.
How will the hands be strong? How will the heart endure?[2]

A very little thing, a little worm,
Or hourglass-blazoned spider,[3] it is said,   20
  Can kill a tiger. Will the dead
  Hold up his mirror and affirm
   To the four winds the smell
And flash of his authority? It's well
If God who holds you to the pit of hell,   25
Much as one holds a spider, will destroy,
Baffle and dissipate your soul. As a small boy

On Windsor Marsh,[4] I saw the spider die
When thrown into the bowels of fierce fire:
  There's no long struggle, no desire   30
  To get up on its feet and fly —
   It stretches out its feet
And dies. This is the sinner's last retreat;
Yes, and no strength exerted on the heat
Then sinews the abolished will, when sick   35
And full of burning, it will whistle on a brick.

But who can plumb the sinking of that soul?
Josiah Hawley,[5] picture yourself cast
  Into a brick-kiln where the blast
  Fans your quick vitals to a coal —   40
   If measured by a glass,
How long would it seem burning! Let there pass
A minute, ten, ten trillion; but the blaze
Is infinite, eternal: this is death,
To die and know it. This is the Black Widow, death. 45

1946

---

[2]Cf. Ezekiel 22:14: "Can thine heart endure, or can thine hands be strong, in the days that I shall deal with thee?"
[3]The poisonous female black widow spider has on its underside an hourglass-shaped red mark.
[4]A marsh near East Windsor, Connecticut, where Edwards lived as a boy.

[5]Edwards's uncle by marriage, whose suicide Edwards described in "A Narrative of the Surprising Conversions"; Edwards attributed the suicide to the work of the devil. Lowell's poem, "After the Surprising Conversions," portrays Edwards's view of the suicide.

After the Surprising Conversions[1]

September twenty-second, Sir: today
I answer. In the latter part of May,
Hard on our Lord's Ascension,[2] it began
To be more sensible.[3] A gentleman[4]
Of more than common understanding, strict   5
In morals, pious in behavior, kicked
Against our goad. A man of some renown,
An useful, honored person in the town,
He came of melancholy parents; prone
To secret spells, for years they kept alone —   10
His uncle, I believe, was killed of it:
Good people, but of too much or little wit.
I preached one Sabbath on a text from Kings;
He showed concernment for his soul. Some things
In his experience were hopeful. He   15
Would sit and watch the wind knocking a tree
And praise this countryside our Lord has made.
Once when a poor man's heifer died, he laid
A shilling on the doorsill; though a thirst
For loving shook him like a snake, he durst   20
Not entertain much hope of his estate
In heaven. Once we saw him sitting late
Behind his attic window by a light
That guttered on his Bible; through that night
He meditated terror, and he seemed   25
Beyond advice or reason, for he dreamed
That he was called to trumpet Judgment Day
To Concord. In the latter part of May
He cut his throat. And though the coroner
Judged him delirious, soon a noisome stir   30
Palsied our village. At Jehovah's nod
Satan seemed more let loose amongst us: God
Abandoned us to Satan, and he pressed
Us hard, until we thought we could not rest
Till we had done with life. Content was gone.   35
All the good work was quashed. We were undone.
The breath of God had carried out a planned
And sensible withdrawal from this land;
The multitude, once unconcerned with doubt,
Once neither callous, curious nor devout,   40
Jumped at broad noon, as though some peddler groaned
As it in its familiar twang: "My friend,
Cut your own throat. Cut your own throat. Now! Now!"
September twenty-second, Sir, the bough
Cracks with the unpicked apples, and at dawn   45
The small-mouth bass breaks water, gorged with spawn.

                                                    1946

[1] As in "Mr. Edwards and the Spider," the Puritan minister and theologian Jonathan Edwards (1703–1758) is the speaker of the poem. In 1735, Edwards wrote a letter to a fellow clergyman describing the astonishing increase in numbers of religious conversions going on in and around Edwards's church in Northampton, Massachusetts. Added at the end as a curiosity was the account of a suicide, attributed to the work of Satan. On publication in 1736, it was called "A Narrative of the Surprising Conversions." It created a sensation, and Edwards expanded it and republished it in 1737 as *A Faithful Narrative of the Surprising Works of God*.
[2] A day, forty days after Easter, celebrating Christ's ascension into Heaven.
[3] Apparent (i.e., to the senses).
[4] Edwards's uncle by marriage, Josiah Hawley.

Words for Hart Crane[1]

"When the Pulitzers[2] showered on some dope
or screw who flushed our dry mouths out with soap,
few people would consider why I took
to stalking sailors, and scattered Uncle Sam's
phoney gold-plated laurels to the birds.   5
Because I knew my Whitman[3] like a book,
stranger in America, tell my country: I,
Catullus redivivus,[4] once the rage
of the Village and Paris, used to play my role
of homosexual, wolfing the stray lambs   10
who hungered by the Place de la Concorde.[5]
My profit was a pocket with a hole.
Who asks for me, the Shelley[6] of my age,
must lay his heart out for my bed and board."

1953, 1958, 1959

Sailing Home from Rapallo[1]

(FEBRUARY 1954)

Your nurse could only speak Italian,
but after twenty minutes I could imagine your final week,
and tears ran down my cheeks. . . .

When I embarked from Italy with my Mother's body,
the whole shoreline of the *Golfo di Genova*[2]   5
was breaking into fiery flower.
The crazy yellow and azure sea-sleds
blasting like jack-hammers across
the *spumante*[3]-bubbling wake of our liner,
recalled the clashing colors of my Ford.   10
Mother travelled first-class in the hold;
her *Risorgimento*[4] black and gold casket
was like Napoleon's at the *Invalides*. . . .[5]

While the passengers were tanning
on the Mediterranean in deck-chairs,   15
our family cemetery in Dunbarton[6]
lay under the White Mountains
in the sub-zero weather.
The graveyard's soil was changing to stone—
so many of its deaths had been midwinter.   20
Dour and dark against the blinding snowdrifts,
its black brook and fir trunks were as smooth as masts.

---

[1]Hart Crane, American poet whose masterpiece was *The Bridge*.
[2]Pulitzer Prizes for poetry, awarded annually.
[3]Crane was a great admirer of Walt Whitman's *Leaves of Grass*.
[4]"Catullus revived" (Latin); the Roman Catullus (c. 84–54 B.C.) was a great poet of love.
[5]A famous and popular square in Paris.
[6]Percy Bysshe Shelley (1792–1822), British romantic poet and rebel.
[1]Northern Italian city where Lowell's mother, Charlotte

Winslow Lowell, died.
[2]"Gulf of Genoa" (Italian).
[3]Italian sparkling wine (champagne-like).
[4]I.e., in the ornate style of the nineteenth-century period of revival (*Risorgimento*) of Italy as a nation.
[5]Soldiers' home in Paris, where Napoleon's casket is prominently displayed.
[6]New Hampshire town, location of the family home of the Winslows.

A fence of iron spear-hafts
black-bordered its mostly Colonial grave-slates.
The only "unhistoric" soul to come here   25
was Father, now buried beneath his recent
unweathered pink-veined slice of marble.
Even the Latin of his Lowell motto:
Occasionem cognosce,[7]
seemed too businesslike and pushing here,   30
where the burning cold illuminated
the hewn inscriptions of Mother's relatives:
twenty or thirty Winslows and Starks.
Frost had given their names a diamond edge. . . .

In the grandiloquent lettering on Mother's coffin,   35
Lowell had been misspelled *LOVEL.*
The corpse
was wrapped like *panetone*[8] in Italian tinfoil.

                                                   1959

Waking in the Blue

The night attendant, a B.U.[1] sophomore,
rouses from the mare's-nest of his drowsy head
propped on *The Meaning of Meaning.*[2]
He catwalks down our corridor.
Azure day   5
makes my agonized blue window bleaker.
Crows maunder on the petrified fairway.
Absence! My heart grows tense
as though a harpoon were sparring for the kill.
(This is the house for the "mentally ill.")   10

What use is my sense of humor?
I grin at Stanley, now sunk in his sixties,
once a Harvard all-American fullback,
(if such were possible!)
still hoarding the build of a boy in his twenties,   15
as he soaks, a ramrod
with the muscle of a seal
in his long tub,
vaguely urinous from the Victorian plumbing.
A kingly granite profile in a crimson golf-cap,   20
worn all day, all night,
he thinks only of his figure,
of slimming on sherbet and ginger ale—
more cut off from words than a seal.
This is the way day breaks in Bowditch Hall at McLean's:[3]   25
the hooded night lights bring out "Bobbie,"
Porcellian '29,[4]
a replica of Louis XVI[5]

---

[7]"Recognize your opportunity" (Latin).
[8]An Italian sweet-bread, traditionally eaten on holidays.
[1]Boston University.
[2]Major work of philosophy and criticism published in 1923 by English scholars C. K. Ogden (1889–1957) and I. A. Richards (1893–1979).

[3]McLean Hospital for the mentally ill in Belmont, Massachusetts.
[4]I.e., selected in 1929 as a member of Harvard's exclusive Porcellian Club.
[5]King of France (r. 1774–92).

without the wig—
redolent and roly-poly as a sperm whale,   30
as he swashbuckles about in his birthday suit
and horses at chairs.

These victorious figures of bravado ossified young.

In between the limits of day,
hours and hours go by under the crew haircuts   35
and slightly too little nonsensical bachelor twinkle
of the Roman Catholic attendants.
(There are no Mayflower
screwballs in the Catholic Church.)

After a hearty New England breakfast,   40
I weigh two hundred pounds
this morning. Cock of the walk,
I strut in my turtle-necked French sailor's jersey
before the metal shaving mirrors,
and see the shaky future grow familiar   45
in the pinched, indigenous faces
of these thoroughbred mental cases,
twice my age and half my weight.
We are all old-timers,
each of us holds a locked razor.   50

1959

Memories of
West Street and Lepke[1]

Only teaching on Tuesdays, book-worming
in pajamas fresh from the washer each morning,
I hog a whole house on Boston's
"hardly passionate Marlborough Street,"[2]
where even the man   5
scavenging filth in the back alley trash cans,
has two children, a beach wagon, a helpmate,
and is a "young Republican."
I have a nine months' daughter,
young enough to be my granddaughter.   10
Like the sun she rises in her flame-flamingo infants' wear.

These are the tranquillized *Fifties*,
and I am forty. Ought I to regret my seedtime?
I was a fire-breathing Catholic C. O.,[3]
and made my manic statement,   15
telling off the state and president, and then
sat waiting sentence in the bull pen
beside a Negro boy with curlicues
of marijuana in his hair.

---

[1]Lowell refused for reasons of conscience to serve in the armed forces during World War II and was sentenced to a year in jail. He was sent to West Street jail in Boston, where a jailmate was the notorious head of Murder, Inc., Lepke Buchalter, sent up for murder.
[2]Description by Henry James of a fashionable street where Lowell lived in the 1950s.
[3]Conscientious objector.

Given a year,   20
I walked on the roof of the West Street Jail, a short
enclosure like my school soccer court,
and saw the Hudson River once a day
through sooty clothesline entanglements
and bleaching khaki tenements.   25
Strolling, I yammered metaphysics with Abramowitz,
a jaundice-yellow ("it's really tan")
and fly-weight pacifist,
so vegetarian,
he wore rope shoes and preferred fallen fruit.   30
He tried to convert Bioff and Brown,[4]
the Hollywood pimps, to his diet.
Hairy, muscular, suburban,
wearing chocolate double-breasted suits,
they blew their tops and beat him black and blue.   35

I was so out of things, I'd never heard
of the Jehovah's Witnesses.[5]
"Are you a C. O.?" I asked a fellow jailbird.
"No," he answered, "I'm a J.W."
He taught me the "hospital tuck,"[6]   40
and pointed out the T shirted back
of *Murder Incorporated's* Czar Lepke,
there piling towels on a rack,
or dawdling off to his little segregated cell full
of things forbidden the common man: 45
a portable radio, a dresser, two toy American
flags tied together with a ribbon of Easter palm.
Flabby, bald, lobotomized,
he drifted in a sheepish calm,
where no agonizing reappraisal[7]   50
jarred his concentration on the electric chair —
hanging like an oasis in his air
of lost connections. . . .

1958, 1959

"To Speak of Woe
That Is in Marriage"[1]

*"It is the future generation that presses into being by means
of these exuberant feelings and supersensible soap bubbles of
ours."*

SCHOPENHAUER[2]

"The hot night makes us keep our bedroom windows open.
Our magnolia blossoms. Life begins to happen.
My hopped up husband drops his home disputes,

---

[4]William Bioff and George Browne, theatrical union officials convicted of extortion.
[5]American religious denomination whose members refuse on religious grounds to take part in wars.
[6]I.e., a method of making a smooth, taut bed by tucking excess bed coverings neatly under the mattress.
[7]A quotation from John Foster Dulles, President Eisen-

hower's Secretary of State, regarding a reassessment of America's foreign policy.
[1]From "The Wife of Bath's Prologue," *Canterbury Tales*, by Geoffrey Chaucer (1340?–1400).
[2]Arthur Schopenhauer (1788–1860), German philosopher noted for his pessimism.

and hits the streets to cruise for prostitutes,
free-lancing out along the razor's edge.   5
This screwball might kill his wife, then take the pledge.
Oh the monotonous meanness of his lust. . . .
It's the injustice . . . he is so unjust—
whiskey-blind, swaggering home at five.
My only thought is how to keep alive.   10
What makes him tick? Each night now I tie
ten dollars and his car key to my thigh. . . .
Gored by the climacteric of his want,
he stalls above me like an elephant."

                                                              1958, 1959

Skunk Hour

(FOR ELIZABETH BISHOP)[1]

Nautilus Island's[2] hermit
heiress still lives through winter in her Spartan cottage;
her sheep still graze about the sea.
Her son's a bishop. Her farmer
is first selectman in our village;   5
she's in her dotage.

Thirsting for
the hierarchic privacy
of Queen Victoria's century,
she buys up all   10
the eyesores facing her shore,
and lets them fall.

The season's ill—
we've lost our summer millionaire,
who seemed to leap from an L. L. Bean[3]   15
catalogue. His nine-knot yawl
was auctioned off to lobstermen.
A red fox stain covers Blue Hill.

And now our fairy
decorator brightens his shop for fall;   20
his fishnet's filled with orange cork,
orange, his cobbler's bench and awl;
there is no money in his work,
he'd rather marry.

One dark night,   25
my Tudor Ford climbed the hill's skull;
I watched for love-cars. Lights turned down,
they lay together, hull to hull,

---

[1]Lowell said that he modeled this poem on Elizabeth Bishop's "The Armadillo," a poem Bishop dedicated to Lowell.
[2]Near Castine, Maine, where Lowell spent many of his summers.
[3]A Maine mail-order house featuring sportsmen's clothing and camping gear.

where the graveyard shelves on the town. . . .
My mind's not right.   30

A car radio bleats,
"Love, O careless Love. . . ." I hear
my ill-spirit sob in each blood cell,
as if my hand were at its throat. . . .
I myself am hell;[4]   35
nobody's here—

only skunks, that search
in the moonlight for a bite to eat.
They march on their soles up Main Street:
white stripes, moonstruck eyes' red fire   40
under the chalk-dry and spar spire
of the Trinitarian Church.

I stand on top
of our back steps and breathe the rich air—
a mother skunk with her column of kittens swills the garbage pail.   45
She jabs her wedge-head in a cup
of sour cream, drops her ostrich tail,
and will not scare.

                                              1958, 1959

For the Union Dead[1]

"Relinquunt Omnia Servare Rem Publicam."[2]

The old South Boston Aquarium stands
in a Sahara of snow now. Its broken windows are boarded.
The bronze weathervane cod has lost half its scales.
The airy tanks are dry.

Once my nose crawled like a snail on the glass;   5
my hand tingled
to burst the bubbles
drifting from the noses of the cowed, compliant fish.

My hand draws back. I often sigh still
for the dark downward and vegetating kingdom   10
of the fish and reptile. One morning last March,
I pressed against the new barbed and galvanized

fence on the Boston Common. Behind their cage,
yellow dinosaur steamshovels were grunting
as they cropped up tons of mush and grass   15
to gouge their underworld garage.

---

[4]Cf. "Which way I fly is Hell, myself am Hell" (Satan speaking in Book IV, line 75, of John Milton's *Paradise Lost*).
[1]Those who fought on the side of the North in the Civil War; the poem was originally entitled "Colonel Shaw and the Massachusetts 54th," and describes a bronze bas-relief in Boston by Augustus Saint-Gaudens (1848–1907) portraying Robert Gould Shaw (1837–1863), commander of an all-Negro Union regiment that fought in the Civil War. In an attack on Fort Wagner in South Carolina (1863), he and many of his men were killed; they were buried together.
[2]"They give up everything to serve the republic" (Latin).

Parking spaces luxuriate like civic
sandpiles in the heart of Boston.
A girdle of orange, Puritan-pumpkin colored girders
braces the tingling Statehouse,   20

shaking over the excavations, as it faces Colonel Shaw
and his bell-cheeked Negro infantry
on St. Gaudens' shaking Civil War relief,
propped by a plank splint against the garage's earthquake.

Two months after marching through Boston,   25
half the regiment was dead;
at the dedication,
William James[3] could almost hear the bronze Negroes breathe.

Their monument sticks like a fishbone
in the city's throat.   30
Its Colonel is as lean
as a compass-needle.

He has an angry wrenlike vigilance,
a greyhound's gentle tautness;
he seems to wince at pleasure,   35
and suffocate for privacy.

He is out of bounds now. He rejoices in man's lovely,
peculiar power to choose life and die—
when he leads his black soldiers to death,
he cannot bend his back.   40

On a thousand small town New England greens,
the old white churches hold their air
of sparse, sincere rebellion; frayed flags
quilt the graveyards of the Grand Army of the Republic.[4]

The stone statues of the abstract Union Soldier   45
grow slimmer and younger each year—
wasp-waisted, they doze over muskets
and muse through their sideburns . . .

Shaw's father wanted no monument
except the ditch,   50
where his son's body was thrown
and lost with his "niggers."

The ditch is nearer.
There are no statues for the last war[5] here;
on Boylston Street, a commercial photograph   55
shows Hiroshima boiling

---

[3]American psychologist and philosopher (1842–1910), who
spoke at the dedication of the monument in 1897, saying:
"There on foot go the dark outcasts, so true to nature that
one can almost hear them breathing as they march."

[4]A Civil War veterans organization, founded in 1866, and
called the GAR.
[5]The Second World War (1939–45).

over a Mosler Safe, the "Rock of Ages"[6]
that survived the blast. Space is nearer.
When I crouch to my television set,
the drained faces of Negro school-children rise like balloons.[7]   60

Colonel Shaw
is riding on his bubble,
he waits
for the blessèd break.

The Aquarium is gone. Everywhere,   65
giant finned cars nose forward like fish;
a savage servility
slides by on grease.

                                        1959, 1964

Night Sweat

Work-table, litter, books and standing lamp,
plain things, my stalled equipment, the old broom—
but I am living in a tidied room,
for ten nights now I've felt the creeping damp
float over my pajamas' wilted white . . .   5
Sweet salt embalms me and my head is wet,
everything streams and tells me this is right;
my life's fever is soaking in night sweat—
one life, one writing! But the downward glide
and bias of existing wrings us dry—   10
always inside me is the child who died,
always inside me is his will to die—
one universe, one body . . . in this urn
the animal night sweats of the spirit burn.
Behind me! You! Again I feel the light   15
lighten my leaded eyelids, while the gray
skulled horses whinny for the soot of night.
I dabble in the dapple of the day,
a heap of wet clothes, seamy, shivering,
I see my flesh and bedding washed with light,   20
my child exploding into dynamite,
my wife . . . your lightness alters everything,
and tears the black web from the spider's sack,
as your heart hops and flutters like a hare.
Poor turtle, tortoise, if I cannot clear   25
the surface of these troubled waters here,
absolve me, help me, Dear Heart, as you bear
this world's dead weight and cycle on your back.

                                        1964

---

[6]The tragedy of the Japanese city of Hiroshima (which the atomic bomb destroyed in World War II) is exploited for advertising purposes.

[7]In the early 1960s, TV newscasts carried many filmed shots of black children trying to attend desegregated schools as they walked through crowds of hostile white adults.

Waking Early Sunday Morning

O to break loose, like the chinook
salmon jumping and falling back,
nosing up to the impossible
stone and bone-crushing waterfall—
raw-jawed, weak-fleshed there, stopped by ten   5
steps of the roaring ladder, and then
to clear the top on the last try,
alive enough to spawn and die.

Stop, back off. The salmon breaks
water, and now my body wakes   10
to feel the unpolluted joy
and criminal leisure of a boy—
no rainbow smashing a dry fly
in the white run is free as I,
here squatting like a dragon on   15
time's hoard before the day's begun!

Vermin run for their unstopped holes;
in some dark nook a fieldmouse rolls
a marble, hours on end, then stops;
the termite in the woodwork sleeps—   20
listen, the creatures of the night
obsessive, casual, sure of foot,
go on grinding, while the sun's
daily remorseful blackout dawns.

Fierce, fireless mind, running downhill.   25
Look up and see the harbor fill:
business as usual in eclipse
goes down to the sea in ships—
wake of refuse, dacron rope,
bound for Bermuda or Good Hope,   30
all bright before the morning watch
the wine-dark hulls of yawl and ketch.

I watch a glass of water wet
with a fine fuzz of icy sweat,
silvery colors touched with sky,   35
serene in their neutrality—
yet if I shift, or change my mood,
I see some object made of wood,
background behind it of brown grain,
to darken it, but not to stain.   40

O that the spirit could remain
tinged but untarnished by its strain!
Better dressed and stacking birch,
or lost with the Faithful at Church—
anywhere, but somewhere else!   45
And now the new electric bells,

clearly chiming, "Faith of our fathers,"
and now the congregation gathers.

O Bible chopped and crucified
in hymns we hear but do not read,   50
none of the milder subtleties
of grace or art will sweeten these
stiff quatrains shovelled out four-square —
they sing of peace, and preach despair;
yet they gave darkness some control,   55
and left a loophole for the soul.

No, put old clothes on, and explore
the corners of the woodshed for
its dregs and dreck:[1] tools with no handle,
ten candle-ends not worth a candle,   60
old lumber banished from the Temple,[2]
damned by Paul's precept and example,
cast from the kingdom, banned in Israel,
the wordless sign, the tinkling cymbal.[3]

When will we see Him face to face?   65
Each day, He shines through darker glass.[4]
In this small town where everything
is known, I see His vanishing
emblems, His white spire and flag-
pole sticking out above the fog,   70
like old white china doorknobs, sad,
slight, useless things to calm the mad.

Hammering military splendor,
top-heavy Goliath[5] in full armor —
little redemption in the mass   75
liquidations of their brass,
elephant and phalanx moving
with the times and still improving,
when that kingdom hit the crash:
a million foreskins[6] stacked like trash . . .   80

Sing softer! But what if a new
diminuendo[7] brings no true
tenderness, only restlessness,
excess, the hunger for success,
sanity of self-deception   85
fixed and kicked by reckless caution,
while we listen to the bells —
anywhere, but somewhere else!

---

[1] Refuse or trash.
[2] I.e., the Jewish religion replaced by Christianity through the apostleship of St. Paul, a Jew converted to Christianity on the road to Damascus.
[3] Cf. 1 Corinthians 13:1: "Though I speak with the tongues of men and of angels, and have not charity, I am become as sounding brass, or a tinkling cymbal."
[4] Cf. 1 Corinthians 13:12: "For now we see through a glass, darkly; but then face to face: now I know in part; but then shall I know even as also I am known."
[5] Philistine giant slain by David with a slingshot (1 Samuel 17:49).
[6] King Saul offered his daughter in marriage to David, but only if — in lieu of dowry — he brought the king a hundred foreskins of his enemies, the Philistines; David brought back two hundred foreskins (1 Samuel 18:25–27).
[7] Gradual decrease in loudness.

O to break loose. All life's grandeur
is something with a girl in summer . . .
elated as the President[8]   90
girdled by his establishment
this Sunday morning, free to chaff
his own thoughts with his bear-cuffed staff,
swimming nude, unbuttoned, sick   95
of his ghost-written rhetoric!

No weekends for the gods now. Wars
flicker, earth licks its open sores,
fresh breakage, fresh promotions, chance
assassinations, no advance.   100
Only man thinning out his kind
sounds through the Sabbath noon, the blind
swipe of the pruner and his knife
busy about the tree of life . . .

Pity the planet, all joy gone   105
from this sweet volcanic cone;
peace to our children when they fall
in small war on the heels of small
war—until the end of time
to police the earth, a ghost   110
orbiting forever lost
in our monotonous sublime.

                                                              1967

The March I[1]

(FOR DWIGHT MACDONALD)[2]

Under the too white marmoreal Lincoln Memorial,
the too tall marmoreal Washington Obelisk,
gazing into the too long reflecting pool,
the reddish trees, the withering autumn sky,
the remorseless, amplified harangues for peace—   5
lovely to lock arms, to march absurdly locked
(unlocking to keep my wet glasses from slipping)
to see the cigarette match quaking in my fingers,
then to step off like green Union Army recruits
for the first Bull Run,[3] sped by photographers,   10
the notables, the girls . . . fear, glory, chaos, rout . . .
our green army staggered out on the miles-long green fields,
met by the other army,[4] the Martian, the ape, the hero,
his new-fangled rifle, his green new steel helmet.

                                                              1970

---

[8]President Lyndon Johnson, playful with his staff members in moments of relaxation.
[1]The March on the Pentagon in 1967 to protest the war in Vietnam.
[2]Macdonald (1906–1982), prominent writer, social critic, and editor who participated in the march with Lowell.
[3]A battle in the Civil War (1861), in which the green Union soldiers broke and ran.
[4]I.e., the U.S. Army.

The March II[1]

Where two or three were heaped together, or fifty,
mostly white-haired, or bald, or women . . . sadly
unfit to follow their dream, I sat in the sunset
shade of their Bastille,[2] the Pentagon,
nursing leg- and arch-cramps, my cowardly,   5
foolhardy heart; and heard, alas, more speeches,
though the words took heart now to show how weak
we were, and right. An MP[3] sergeant kept
repeating, 'March slowly through them. Don't even brush
anyone sitting down.' They tiptoed through us   10
in single file, and then their second wave
trampled us flat and back. Health to those who held,
health to the green steel head . . . to your kind hands
that helped me stagger to my feet, and flee.

                                                   1970

History

History has to live with what was here,
clutching and close to fumbling all we had —
it is so dull and gruesome how we die,
unlike writing, life never finishes.
Abel was finished; death is not remote,   5
a flash-in-the-pan electrifies the skeptic,
his cows crowding like skulls against high-voltage wire,
his baby crying all night like a new machine.
As in our Bibles, white-faced, predatory,
the beautiful, mist-drunken hunter's moon ascends —   10
a child could give it a face: two holes, two holes,
my eyes, my mouth, between them a skull's no-nose —
O there's a terrifying innocence in my face
drenched with the silver salvage of the mornfrost.

                                                   1973

Reading Myself

Like thousands, I took just pride and more than just,
struck matches that brought my blood to a boil;
I memorized the tricks to set the river on fire —
somehow never wrote something to go back to.
Can I suppose I am finished with wax flowers   5
and have earned my grass on the minor slopes of Parnassus. . . .[1]

---

[1] In this second poem about the 1967 March on the Pentagon to protest the Vietnam War, the marchers have arrived in a large parking area near the Pentagon, carefully watched by the military police.
[2] The prison in Paris that was stormed and taken in 1789 during the French Revolution.
[3] Military police, in charge of keeping order.
[1] A mountain in Greece; in Greek mythology, the place for worship of Apollo and the Muses.

No honeycomb is built without a bee
adding circle to circle, cell to cell,
the wax and honey of a mausoleum—
this round dome proves its maker is alive;   10
the corpse of the insect lives embalmed in honey,
prays that its perishable work live long
enough for the sweet-tooth bear to desecrate—
this open book . . . my open coffin.

1969, 1973

Fishnet

Any clear thing that blinds us with surprise,
your wandering silences and bright trouvailles,[1]
dolphin let loose to catch the flashing fish. . . .
saying too little, then too much.
Poets die adolescents, their beat embalms them,   5
the archetypal voices sing offkey;
the old actor cannot read his friends,
and nevertheless he reads himself aloud,
genius hums the auditorium dead.
The line must terminate.   10
Yet my heart rises, I know I've gladdened a lifetime
knotting, undoing a fishnet of tarred rope;
the net will hang on the wall when the fish are eaten,
nailed like illegible bronze[2] on the futureless future

1973

For John Berryman

(AFTER READING HIS LAST *DREAM SONG*)[1]

The last years we only met
when you were on the road,
and lit up for reading
your battering *Dream*—
audible, deaf . . .   5
in another world then as now.
I used to want to live
to avoid your elegy.
Yet really we had the same life,
the generic one   10
our generation offered
(*Les Maudits*[2]—the compliment
each American generation

---

[1]"Discoveries" (French).
[2]Reference to the claim of the Roman poet Horace (65–8 B.C.) that poetry will outlast bronze (*Odes*, III, 30).
[1]Berryman, American poet and Lowell's friend, committed suicide in 1972 by jumping off a bridge; his masterpiece was the long lyric-epic *The Dream Songs*.
[2]"The damned" (French); *le poète maudit* ("the damned [or cursed] poet") was a common phrase in France during the latter nineteenth century.

pays itself in passing):
first students, then with our own,   15
our galaxy of grands maîtres,[3]
our fifties' fellowships
to Paris, Rome and Florence,
veterans of the Cold War[4] not the War —
all the best of life . . .   20
then daydreaming to drink at six,
waiting for the iced fire,
even the feel of the frosted glass,
like waiting for a girl . . .
if you had waited.   25
We asked to be obsessed with writing,
and we were.

Do you wake dazed like me,
and find your lost glasses in a shoe?
Something so heavy lies on my heart —   30
there, still here, the good days
when we sat by a cold lake in Maine,
talking about the *Winter's Tale*,
Leontes' jealousy[5]
in Shakespeare's broken syntax.   35
You got there first.
Just the other day,
I discovered how we differ — humor . . .
even in this last *Dream Song*,
to mock your catlike flight   40
from home and classes —
to leap from the bridge.

Girls will not frighten the frost from the grave.[6]

To my surprise, John,
I pray *to* not for you,   45
think of you not myself,
smile and fall asleep.

                                                                1977

Epilogue[1]

Those blessèd structures, plot and rhyme —
why are they no help to me now
I want to make
something imagined, not recalled?
I hear the noise of my own voice: 5
The painter's vision is not a lens,

---

[3]"Great masters" (French).
[4]The hostility between the Soviet Union and the United States that developed after the Second World War (when they were allies).
[5]In Shakespeare's *The Winter's Tale*, Leontes, King of Sicilia, orders his wife put to death because he suspects her of

adultery.
[6]Cf. "'Except Love's fires the virtue have, / To fright the frost out of the grave,'" from a song in *The Sad Shepherd* by Ben Jonson (1572/3–1637).
[1]In Lowell's final volume of poems, *Day by Day* (1977), this poem appeared last.

it trembles to caress the light.
But sometimes everything I write
with the threadbare art of my eye
seems a snapshot,   10
lurid, rapid, garish, grouped,
heightened from life,
yet paralyzed by fact.
All's misalliance.
Yet why not say what happened?   15
Pray for the grace of accuracy
Vermeer[2] gave to the sun's illumination
stealing like the tide across a map
to his girl solid with yearning.
We are poor passing facts,   20
warned by that to give
each figure in the photograph
his living name.

                                                                    1977

GWENDOLYN BROOKS
(b. 1917)

Gwendolyn Brooks said in an interview in 1967: "I think my poetry is related to life in the broad sense of the word, even though the subject matter relates closest to the Negro. Although I called my first book *A Street in Bronzeville*, I hoped that people would recognize instantly that Negroes are just like other people; they have the same hates and loves and fears, the same tragedies and triumphs and deaths, as people of any race or religion or nationality." Brooks was taken aback by the rebellions of the late 1960s, but she remained pragmatic in her view. When asked in 1984 to comment on the "black aesthetic," Brooks replied: "An announcement that we are going to deal with 'the black aesthetic' seems to me to be a waste of time. I've been talking about blackness and black people all along. But . . . I do believe in blacks writing about black life."

Brooks was born in Topeka, Kansas, in 1917, and that same year her parents moved to Chicago, settling on the South Side. During the Great Depression, her father worked as a janitor and the family frequently subsisted on beans. He had great respect for education and books and saw that his daughter had the opportunity to attend school. At an early age, with the encouragement of her parents, she determined to be a poet. At thirteen, she published her first poem in a children's magazine. She graduated from Englewood High School in 1934, and during this period met two famous black poets, James Weldon Johnson and Langston Hughes. Both encouraged her. She continued her education at Wilson Junior College, taking a degree there in 1936.

In the early 1940s, Brooks attended a writer's workshop at Chicago's Southside Community Art Center run by a reader for *Poetry* magazine, Inez Cunningham. She went on to win the Midwestern Writers' Conference poetry award in 1943 and the next year placed some of her poems in *Poetry* magazine. In 1945

---

[2]Jan Vermeer (1632–1675), Dutch painter. The painting described is *Girl Reading a Letter*, with a map on the wall adjacent to a window which the girl faces; the radiant sun's reflection gives the figure in profile its "grace of accuracy."

she published her first book, *A Street in Bronzeville*. The Iowa poet Paul Engle wrote a highly favorable review of the volume for the *Chicago Tribune*, and Brooks's career as a poet appeared to be launched. The poems presented a series of vivid and powerful scenes and portraits of people in Chicago's black South Side slum where she grew up.

A Street in Bronzeville attracted awards, the *Mademoiselle* Merit Award in 1945, the American Academy of Letters Award in 1946, and a Guggenheim Fellowship, which enabled Brooks to devote full time to the writing of poetry for a year. Her second book of poems, *Annie Allen*, appeared in 1949. With it, Brooks became the first black writer to win the Pulitzer Prize for literature. The autobiographical book was divided into three parts, "Notes from the Childhood and the Girlhood," "The Anniad," and "The Womanhood," and constituted an account of coming to maturity during the Second World War in the black urban slum. The poems were a powerful declaration of identity, of self-hood, and were filled with urgent and compelling lines:

> Men of careful turns, haters of forks in the road,
> The strain at the eye, that puzzlement, that awe—
> Grant me that I am human, that I hurt,
> That I can cry.

In the 1950s, Brooks began to publish frequently in the literary journals and magazines, often contributing reviews to major newspapers. She proved her versatility by publishing a novel, *Maud Martha*, in 1953, and a book of children's verse, *Bronzeville Boys and Girls*, in 1955. In 1960, she published a new volume of poems, *The Bean Eaters*, and in 1963, her *Selected Poems*. In the 1960s, she began to teach in poetry workshops, beginning at Chicago's Columbia College.

In 1967, she attended the Second Black Writers' Conference at Fisk University, an experience that had a profound effect on her. She recalled: "I arrived in Nashville, Tennessee, to give one more 'reading.' But blood-boiling surprise was in store for me. First, I was aware of a general energy, an electricity, in look, walk, speech, *gesture* of the young blackness I saw all about me." The message she heard from the new young poets was that "black poets should write as blacks, about blacks, and address themselves *to* blacks." Somewhat shaken by this experience, Brooks went back to Chicago to brood on her career and to review and reshape her own ideas about her art.

A new book of poems, *In the Mecca*, appeared in 1968 and showed a sharper concern with social problems. The Mecca was a large, run-down Chicago apartment building, and the long title poem of the book presented a series of portraits of the occupants and their hard-scrabble lives. Shorter poems like "Malcolm X" showed a deepening interest in the mystery of the black mystique. Other books that followed the directions pointed by *In the Mecca* include *Riot* (1969), *Family Pictures* (1970), *Aurora* (1972), and *Beckonings* (1975); many of the later poems reflected Brooks's willingness to become polemic in the service of her political-racial beliefs. A book of prose, *Report from Part One* (1972), contained a reminiscence of Brooks's roots, beginnings, and development as a writer; also included was a brief series of notes written about her trip to East Africa in 1971.

In a 1967 interview included in *Report from Part One*, Brooks explained why she wrote poetry: "I like the concentration, the crush; I like working with language, as others like working with paints and clay, or notes. . . . 'Vivify the contemporary fact,' said Whitman. I like to vivify the *universal* fact, when it occurs to me. But the universal wears contemporary clothing very well." A recent critic of her work, D. H. Melhem, concluded: "[Brooks] has extended language itself, as

Whitman did, by imaginative compounding, word-coinage, and use of black English vernacular. She belongs to that select category Pound called 'the inventors,' the highest classification of poets who create and expand formal limits and, thereby, taste itself."

ADDITIONAL READING

George E. Kent, "The Poetry of Gwendolyn Brooks," *Blackness and the Adventure of Western Culture*, 1972; Don L. Lee, "Gwendolyn Brooks: Beyond the Wordmaker—The Making of an African Poet," *Gwendolyn Brooks: Report from Part One*, 1972; Houston A. Baker, Jr., *Singers of Daybreak: Studies in Black American Literature*, 1974; Harry B. Shaw, *Gwendolyn Brooks*, 1980; Maria K. Mootry and Gary Smith, eds., *A Life Distilled: Gwendolyn Brooks, Her Poetry and Fiction*, 1987; D. H. Melhem, *Gwendolyn Brooks: Poetry and the Heroic Voice*, 1987; George E. Kent, *A Life of Gwendolyn Brooks*, 1990.

TEXT

The World of Gwendolyn Brooks, 1971.

from A Street in Bronzeville

Kitchenette Building

We are things of dry hours and the involuntary plan,
Grayed in, and gray. "Dream" makes a giddy sound, not strong
Like "rent," "feeding a wife," "satisfying a man."

But could a dream send up through onion fumes
Its white and violet, fight with fried potatoes   5
And yesterday's garbage ripening in the hall,
Flutter, or sing an aria down these rooms

Even if we were willing to let it in,
Had time to warm it, keep it very clean,
Anticipate a message, let it begin?   10

We wonder. But not well! not for a minute!
Since Number Five is out of the bathroom now,
We think of lukewarm water, hope to get in it.

                                                                    1945

The Mother

Abortions will not let you forget.
You remember the children you got that you did not get,
The damp small pulps with a little or with no hair,

The singers and workers that never handled the air.
You will never neglect or beat   5
Them, or silence or buy with a sweet.
You will never wind up the sucking-thumb
Or scuttle off ghosts that come.
You will never leave them, controlling your luscious sigh,
Return for a snack of them, with gobbling mother-eye.   10

I have heard in the voices of the wind the voices of my dim killed children.
I have contracted. I have eased
My dim dears at the breasts they could never suck.
I have said, Sweets, if I sinned, if I seized
Your luck   15
And your lives from your unfinished reach,
If I stole your births and your names,
Your straight baby tears and your games,
Your stilted or lovely loves, your tumults, your marriages, aches, and your
     deaths,
If I poisoned the beginnings of your breaths,   20
Believe that even in my deliberateness I was not deliberate.
Though why should I whine,
Whine that the crime was other than mine? —
Since anyhow you are dead.
Or rather, or instead,   25
You were never made.
But that too, I am afraid,
Is faulty: oh, what shall I say, how is the truth to be said?
You were born, you had body, you died.
It is just that you never giggled or planned or cried.   30

Believe me, I loved you all.
Believe me, I knew you, though faintly, and I loved, I loved you
All.

1945

We Real Cool

THE POOL PLAYERS.
SEVEN AT THE GOLDEN SHOVEL.

We real cool. We
Left school. We

Lurk late. We
Strike straight. We

Sing sin. We   5
Thin gin. We

Jazz June. We
Die soon.

1960

The Chicago *Defender*[1]
Sends a Man to Little Rock[2]

FALL, 1957

In Little Rock the people bear
Babes, and comb and part their hair
And watch the want ads, put repair
To roof and latch. While wheat toast burns
A woman waters multiferns.   5

Time upholds or overturns
The many, tight, and small concerns.

In Little Rock the people sing
Sunday hymns like anything,
Through Sunday pomp and polishing.   10

And after testament and tunes,
Some soften Sunday afternoons
With lemon tea and Lorna Doones.[3]

I forecast
And I believe   15
Come Christmas Little Rock will cleave
To Christmas tree and trifle, weave,
From laugh and tinsel, texture fast.

In Little Rock is baseball; Barcarolle.[4]
That hotness in July . . . the uniformed figures raw and implacable 20
And not intellectual,
Batting the hotness or clawing the suffering dust.
The Open Air Concert, on the special twilight green . . .
When Beethoven is brutal or whispers to lady-like air.
Blanket-sitters are solemn, as Johann[5] troubles to lean   25
To tell them what to mean. . . .

There is love, too, in Little Rock. Soft women softly
Opening themselves in kindness,
Or, pitying one's blindness,
Awaiting one's pleasure   30
In azure
Glory with anguished rose at the root. . . .
To wash away old semi-discomfitures.
They re-teach purple and unsullen blue.
The wispy soils go. And uncertain   35
Half-havings have they clarified to sures.

In Little Rock they know
Not answering the telephone is a way of rejecting life,

---

[1]A Chicago newspaper, one of the first black daily papers
with a national readership to be established in this century
(1905); it helped spur the black migration from the South to
to the North during and after the First World War.
[2]Little Rock, Arkansas. In September 1957, President

Eisenhower sent federal troops to the city to forestall violence
during the crisis over public school desegregation.
[3]A brand of cookies.
[4]A Venetian gondolier's song.
[5]I.e., the music of Johann Sebastian Bach.

That it is our business to be bothered, is our business
To cherish bores or boredom, be polite   40
To lies and love and many-faceted fuzziness.

I scratch my head, massage the hate-I-had.
I blink across my prim and pencilled pad.
The saga I was sent for is not down.
Because there is a puzzle in this town.   45
The biggest News I do not dare
Telegraph to the Editor's chair:
"They are like people everywhere."

The angry Editor would reply
In hundred harryings of Why.   50

And true, they are hurling spittle, rock,
Garbage and fruit in Little Rock.
And I saw coiling storm a-writhe
On bright madonnas. And a scythe
Of men harassing brownish girls.   55
(The bows and barrettes in the curls
And braids declined away from joy.)

I saw a bleeding brownish boy. . . .

The lariat lynch-wish I deplored.

The loveliest lynchee was our Lord.   60

                                                        1960

The Lovers of the Poor

            arrive. The Ladies from the Ladies' Betterment League
Arrive in the afternoon, the late light slanting
In diluted gold bars across the boulevard brag
Of proud, seamed faces with mercy and murder hinting
Here, there, interrupting, all deep and debonair,   5
The pink paint on the innocence of fear;
Walk in a gingerly manner up the hall.
Cutting with knives served by their softest care,
Served by their love, so barbarously fair.
Whose mothers taught: You'd better not be cruel!   10
You had better not throw stones upon the wrens!
Herein they kiss and coddle and assault
Anew and dearly in the innocence
With which they baffle nature. Who are full,
Sleek, tender-clad, fit, fiftyish, a-glow, all   15
Sweetly abortive, hinting at fat fruit,
Judge it high time that fiftyish fingers felt
Beneath the lovelier planes of enterprise.
To resurrect. To moisten with milky chill.
To be a random hitching post or plush.   20
To be, for wet eyes, random and handy hem.
            Their guild is giving money to the poor.

The worthy poor. The very very worthy
And beautiful poor. Perhaps just not too swarthy?
Perhaps just not too dirty nor too dim   25
Nor—passionate. In truth, what they could wish
Is—something less than derelict or dull.
Not staunch enough to stab, though, gaze for gaze!
God shield them sharply from the beggar-bold!
The noxious needy ones whose battle's bald   30
Nonetheless for being voiceless, hits one down.
            But it's all so bad! and entirely too much for them.
The stench; the urine, cabbage, and dead beans,
Dead porridges of assorted dusty grains,
The old smoke, *heavy* diapers, and, they're told,   35
Something called chitterlings. The darkness. Drawn
Darkness, or dirty light. The soil that stirs.
The soil that looks the soil of centuries.
And for that matter the *general* oldness. Old
Wood. Old marble. Old tile. Old old old.   40
Not homekind Oldness! Not Lake Forest, Glencoe.[1]
Nothing is sturdy, nothing is majestic,
There is no quiet drama, no rubbed glaze, no
Unkillable infirmity of such
A tasteful turn as lately they have left,   45
Glencoe, Lake Forest, and to which their cars
Must presently restore them. When they're done
With dullards and distortions of this fistic[2]
Patience of the poor and put-upon.
            They've never seen such a make-do-ness as   50
Newspaper rugs before! In this, this "flat,"
Their hostess is gathering up the oozed, the rich
Rugs of the morning (tattered! the bespattered . . .),
Readies to spread clean rugs for afternoon.
Here is a scene for you. The Ladies look,   55
In horror, behind a substantial citizeness
Whose trains clank out across her swollen heart.
Who, arms akimbo, almost fills a door.
All tumbling children, quilts dragged to the floor
And tortured thereover, potato peelings, soft-   60
Eyed kitten, hunched-up, haggard, to-be-hurt.
            Their League is allotting largesse to the Lost.
But to put their clean, their pretty money, to put
Their money collected from delicate rose-fingers
Tipped with their hundred flawless rose-nails seems . . .   65
            They own Spode, Lowestoft,[3] candelabra,
Mantels, and hostess gowns, and sunburst clocks,
Turtle soup, Chippendale,[4] red satin "hangings,"
Aubussons[5] and Hattie Carnegie.[6] They Winter
In Palm Beach; cross the Water in June; attend,   70
When suitable, the nice Art Institute;
Buy the right books in the best bindings; saunter
On Michigan,[7] Easter mornings, in sun or wind.

---

[1]Wealthy suburbs of Chicago.
[2]Pertaining to fistfights.
[3]Fine china made in England.
[4]Elegant furniture in the style of the eighteenth-century English cabinetmaker Thomas Chippendale.

[5]French tapestries or carpets.
[6]Fashionable dress designer.
[7]Avenue in Chicago with expensive stores, known as the "Magnificent Mile," in the midst of exclusive dwellings and churches.

Oh Squalor! This sick four-story hulk, this fibre
With fissures everywhere! Why, what are bringings   75
Of loathe-love largesse? What shall peril hungers
So old old, what shall flatter the desolate?
Tin can, blocked fire escape and chitterling
And swaggering seeking youth and the puzzled wreckage
Of the middle passage,[8] and urine and stale shames   80
And, again, the porridges of the underslung
And children children children. Heavens! That
Was a rat, surely, off there, in the shadows? Long
And long-tailed? Gray? The Ladies from the Ladies'
Betterment League agree it will be better   85
To achieve the outer air that rights and steadies,
To hie to a house that does not holler, to ring
Bells elsetime, better presently to cater
To no more Possibilities, to get
Away. Perhaps the money can be posted.   90
Perhaps they two may choose another Slum!
Some serious sooty half-unhappy home! —
Where loathe-love likelier may be invested.
      Keeping their scented bodies in the center
Of the hall as they walk down the hysterical hall,   95
They allow their lovely skirts to graze no wall,
Are off at what they manage of a canter,
And, resuming all the clues of what they were,
Try to avoid inhaling the laden air.

                        1960

The Crazy Woman

I shall not sing a May song.
A May song should be gay.
I'll wait until November
And sing a song of gray.

I'll wait until November.   5
That is the time for me.
I'll go out in the frosty dark
And sing most terribly.

And all the little people
Will stare at me and say,   10
"That is the Crazy Woman
Who would not sing in May."

                        1960

---

[8]The slave-ship passage across the Atlantic from Africa to
America.

CONTEMPORARY POETRY II
Poets Born in the 1920s

HOWARD NEMEROV   JAMES MERRILL
RICHARD WILBUR   FRANK O'HARA
DENISE LEVERTOV   JOHN ASHBERY
JAMES DICKEY   W. S. MERWIN
ALLEN GINSBERG   JAMES WRIGHT
ROBERT CREELEY   ANNE SEXTON
ROBERT BLY   ADRIENNE RICH
A. R. AMMONS

"Form is never more than an extension of content."

Robert Creeley, quoted by Charles Olson in "Projective Verse"

"Form is never more than a *revelation* of content."

Denise Levertov, "Some Notes on Organic Form"

"Expanding the area you can deal with directly, especially to include all the irrational of subjective mystic experience & queerness & pants — in other words individuality — means again (as it did for Whitman) the possibility in a totally brainwashed age . . . the possibility of Prophetic poetry. . . ."

Allen Ginsberg, Letter to John Hollander

"'Political' poetry by men remains stranded amid the struggles for power among male groups. . . . The creative energy of patriarchy is fast running out; what remains is its self-generating energy for destruction. As women, we have our work cut out for us."

Adrienne Rich, "When We Dead Awaken: Writing as Re-vision"

HOWARD NEMEROV

(b. 1920)

Howard Nemerov, defending himself against a common judgment of his poetry, wrote in 1966: "The charge typically raised against my work by literary critics has been that my poems are jokes, even bad jokes. I incline to agree, insisting however that they are bad jokes, and even terrible jokes, emerging from the nature of things as well as from my propensity for coming at things a touch subversively and from the blind side, or the dark side, the side everyone concerned with 'values' would just as soon forget." In agreeing with the critics and then turning their comments upside down, Nemerov performed a maneuver not unlike that in one of his poems. They often come at things "a touch subversively and from the blind side."

Born in New York in 1920, Nemerov graduated from Harvard in 1941, just in time for the Second World War. He joined the Royal Canadian Air Force as a fighter pilot, serving until 1944 when he shifted to the U.S. Army Air Force. On his discharge from the Air Force, he began an academic career, teaching English at Hamilton College, Bennington College, Brandeis University, the University of Minnesota, and Hollins College. In 1963–64 he served as Poetry Consultant at the Library of Congress, and in 1964 began a long tenure as professor at Washington University in St. Louis. He was named Poet Laureate in 1988.

He had begun writing poetry as an undergraduate at Harvard and had won there the Bowdoin Prize. His first book of poems, *The Image and the Law*, was published in 1947. He published steadily and regularly in the following decades, and when *The Collected Poems of Howard Nemerov* appeared in 1977, he was awarded the Pulitzer Prize for Poetry. He himself has provided the best description of his development as a poet:

> Stylistically, I began under the aegis of notions drawn, I suppose, chiefly from T. S. Eliot. Along with many other beginners, I learned to value irony, difficulty, erudition, and the Metaphysical style of composition after the example of John Donne. Again along with many others I learned from William Empson to value ambiguity. . . . I think the direction of my development was away from all these things considered as technical devices; I now regard simplicity and the appearance of ease in the measure as primary values, and the detachment of a single thought from its ambiguous surroundings as a worthier object than the deliberate cultivation of ambiguity.

Nemerov has been unabashedly conservative in his conception of poetry. In preparation for a book he was editing, *Poets on Poetry* (1966), he sent the contributors a list of questions to answer or not as they saw fit. In his own essay for the book, "Attentiveness and Obedience," he published the questions along with his answers. One of the questions, phrased as he admitted with a "surly sarcasm," gave itself away: "Is there, has there been, was there ever, a 'revolution' in poetry, or is all that a matter of a few sleazy technical tricks? What is the relation of your work to this question, if there is a relation? Otherwise put: do you respond to such notions as The New Poetry, An American Language Distinct from English, The Collapse of Prosody, No Thoughts but in Things, The Battle between Academics and — What? — Others (a Fair Field Full of Mostly Corpses)?"

Nemerov's answer to this question was wryly skeptical. He wrote, for example: "So many people now concerned with the poetic art are obsessed with technique, even if the obsession is avowedly directed toward 'liberation,' that poetry sometimes appears as a technology, as though the 'new idioms,' announced with the regularity of new hair styles, were going to make obsolete everything that preceded them." Of the notions he listed in his question ("No Thoughts but in Things," etc.), he said: "Mostly these slogans amount to edicts decreeing that from now on you should walk on one foot only; when you have got that much of the message you needn't wait around to find out whether they mean the right or the left."

ADDITIONAL READING

Reflexions on Poetry & Poetics, 1972; *Figures of Thought: Speculations on the Meaning of Poetry and Other Essays*, 1978; *New and Selected Essays*, 1985.

Peter Meinke, *Howard Nemerov*, 1968; Bowie Duncan, ed., *The Critical Reception of Howard Nemerov: A Selection of Essays and a Bibliography*, 1971; Julia A. Bartholomay, *The Shield of Perseus: The Vision and Imagination of Howard Nemerov*, 1972; William Mills, *The Stillness in Moving Things: The World of Howard Nemerov*, 1975; Ross Labrie, *Howard Nemerov*, 1980; Diana E. Wyllie, *Elizabeth Bishop and Howard Nemerov: Reference Guide*, 1983.

TEXT

The Collected Poems of Howard Nemerov, 1977.

The Vacuum

The house is so quiet now
The vacuum cleaner sulks in the corner closet,
Its bag limp as a stopped lung, its mouth
Grinning into the floor, maybe at my
Slovenly life, my dog-dead youth.   5

I've lived this way long enough,
But when my old woman died her soul
Went into that vacuum cleaner, and I can't bear
To see the bag swell like a belly, eating the dust
And the woolen mice, and begin to howl   10

Because there is old filth everywhere
She used to crawl, in the corner and under the stair.
I know now how life is cheap as dirt,
And still the hungry, angry heart
Hangs on and howls, biting at air.   15

1955

The Icehouse in Summer

SEE Amos, *3:15*[1]

A door sunk in a hillside, with a bolt
thick as the boy's arm, and behind that door
the walls of ice, melting a blue, faint light,

---

[1]The shepherd and prophet Amos warns the Israelites of God's wrath by quoting Him: "And I will smite the winter house with the summer house; and the houses of ivory shall perish, and the great houses shall have an end, saith the Lord."

an air of cedar branches, sawdust fern:
decaying seasons keeping from decay.   5

A summer guest, the boy had never seen
(a servant told him of it) how the lake
froze three foot thick, how farmers came with teams,
with axe and saw, to cut great blocks of ice,
translucid, marbled, glittering in the sun,   10
load them on sleds and drag them up the hill
to be manhandled down the narrow path
and set in courses for the summer's keeping,
the kitchen uses and luxuriousness
of the great houses. And he heard how once   15
a team and driver drowned in the break of spring:
the man's cry melting from the ice that summer
frightened the sherbet-eaters off the terrace.
Dust of the cedar, lost and evergreen
among the slowly blunting water walls   20
where the blade edge melted and the steel saw's bite
was rounded out, and the horse and rider drowned
in the red sea's blood,[2] I was the silly child
who dreamed that riderless cry, and saw the guests
run from a ghostly wall, so long before   25
the winter house fell with the summer house,
and the houses, Egypt, the great houses, had an end.

                                           1958, 1960

A Picture

Of people running down the street
Among the cars, a good many people.
You could see that something was up,
Because people in American towns
Don't ordinarily run, they walk,   5
And not in the street. The camera caught
A pretty girl tilted off-balance
And with her mouth in O amazed;
A man in a fat white shirt, his tie
Streaming behind him, as one flat foot   10
Went slap on the asphalt — you could see
He was out of breath, but dutifully
Running along with all the others,
Maybe at midday, on Main Street somewhere.

The running faces did not record   15
Hatred or anger or great enthusiasm
For what they were doing (hunting down
A Negro, according to the caption),
But seemed rather solemn, intent,
With the serious patience of animals   20
Driven through a gate by some

---

[2]Allusion to God's miraculous parting of the Red Sea to provide an escape route for the Israelites fleeing from Egypt (see
Exodus 14:19–31).

Urgency out of the camera's range,
On an occasion too serious
For private feeling. The breathless faces
Expressed a religion of running,   25
A form of ritual exaltation
Devoted to obedience, and
Obedient, it might be, to the Negro,
Who was not caught by the camera
When it took the people in the street   30
Among the cars, toward some object,
Seriously running.

                                        1958, 1962

To David,[1] About His Education

The world is full of mostly invisible things,
And there is no way but putting the mind's eye,
Or its nose, in a book, to find them out,
Things like the square root of Everest
Or how many times Byron goes into Texas,   5
Or whether the law of the excluded middle
Applies west of the Rockies. For these
And the like reasons, you have to go to school
And study books and listen to what you are told,
And sometimes try to remember. Though I don't know   10
What you will do with the mean annual rainfall
On Plato's Republic,[2] or the calorie content
Of the Diet of Worms;[3] such things are said to be
Good for you, and you will have to learn them
In order to become one of the grown-ups   15
Who sees invisible things neither steadily nor whole,[4]
But keeps gravely the grand confusion of the world
Under his hat, which is where it belongs,
And teaches small children to do this in their turn.

                                        1958, 1962

Thirtieth Anniversary
Report of the Class of '41[1]

We who survived the war and took to wife
And sired the kids and made the decent living,
And piecemeal furnished forth the finished life
Not by grand theft so much as petty thieving—

---

[1]Nemerov's son.
[2]Plato (*c.* 428–348 B.C.), author of the *Republic*, sketching the ideal state.
[3]A Roman Catholic council (diet), which met in 1521 in the

German city of Worms and declared Martin Luther a heretic.
[4]British writer Matthew Arnold said of Sophocles in "To A Friend" (1849) that he "saw life steadily and saw it whole."
[1]Harvard class to which Nemerov belonged.

Who had the routine middle-aged affair   5
And made our beds and had to lie in them
This way or that because the beds were there,
And turned our bile and choler in for phlegm—

Who saw grandparents, parents, to the vault
And wives and selves grow wrinkled, grey and fat   10
And children through their acne and revolt
And told the analyst about all that—

Are done with it. What is there to discuss?
There's nothing left for us to say of us.

                                                                            1973

Ginkgoes[1] in Fall

They are the oldest living captive race,
Primitive gymnosperms that in the wild
Are rarely found or never, temple trees
Brought down in line unbroken from the deep
Past where the Yellow Emperor lies tombed.   5

Their fallen yellow fruit mimics the scent
Of human vomit, and definite statement of
An attitude, and their translucency of leaf,
Filtering a urinary yellow light,
Remarks a delicate wasting of the world,   10

An innuendo to be clarified
In winter when they defecate their leaves
And bear the burden of their branches up
Alone and bare, dynastic diagrams
Of their distinguished genealogies.   15

                                                                            1975

RICHARD WILBUR
(b. 1921)

In the 1960s, Richard Wilbur spoke of the changes he thought he had undergone in his career as a poet: "My first poems were written in answer to the inner
and outer disorders of the Second World War and they helped me, as poems
should, to take ahold of raw events and convert them, provisionally, into experience. At the same time I think that they may at moments have taken refuge from
events in language itself—in word-play, in the coinage of new words, in a certain

---

[1]Large shade tree, native to China, with fan-shaped leaves
and fleshy seeds; the sole surviving species of the gym-
nosperm family (vascular plants with ovaries containing
seeds). It thrived during the Jurassic Period (190 to 140 million years ago), but survives now only by cultivation.

preciosity. At any rate, my writing is now plainer and more straightforward than it used to be." He added that his generation of poets felt "that the most adequate and convincing poetry is that which accommodates mixed feelings, clashing ideas, and incongruous images. Poetry could not be honest, we thought, unless it began by acknowledging the full discordancy of modern life and consciousness."

Wilbur was born in New York City, but grew up on a farm in New Jersey. He entered Amherst College in 1938, and, according to his own testimony, did not decide to become a poet until after he graduated in 1942 and was swept up into the Second World War. He served in the U.S. Army in battles in Italy (Monte Cassino and Anzio) and later in Germany. He began writing poems during this period, he said (quoting Robert Frost), as a "momentary stay against confusion." The poems accumulated unpublished, and he brought them back with him after his discharge from the army.

Wilbur entered Harvard, preparing for a career in teaching English. He took an M.A. there in 1947, and the same year published his first volume of poems, *The Beautiful Changes and Other Poems*. His second volume, *Ceremony and Other Changes*, appeared in 1950. It was with publication of his third volume of poems, *Things of This World*, in 1956, that Wilbur became established as a leading young poet. His book won both the National Book Award and the Pulitzer Prize. By then Wilbur was clearly set on an academic career that would accommodate his creative energies. He taught for a time at Harvard and Wellesley, and then for twenty years at Wesleyan; since 1977 he has been at Smith as writer-in-residence. In 1987 he succeeded Robert Penn Warren as Poet Laureate of the United States.

Wilbur's superb translation of the French eighteenth-century dramatist Molière's *The Misanthrope* was produced in 1954. Two years later, he collaborated (providing the lyrics) with the playwright Lillian Hellman and the composer-conductor Leonard Bernstein on the musical *Candide*, based on the novel by the eighteenth-century French writer Voltaire. It was a critical if not a popular success, and has had a number of other productions around the country. Recognized as a brilliant translator of Molière, Wilbur went on to translate *Tartuffe* (first produced in 1964), *The School for Wives* (1971), and *The Learned Ladies* (1977).

Unlike Robert Lowell, Wilbur did not diverge from the poetic path on which he began. When poetry had turned confessional, and even somewhat wild in experimental variations of free-verse forms, Wilbur continued to write the elegant, sculptured poems for which he is recognized as a master. He commented in an interview recorded in the latter part of his career: "I think it is absurd to feel that free verse—which has only been with us in America for a little over a hundred years—has definitely 'replaced' measure and rhyme and other traditional instruments. Precisely because trimeter, for example, doesn't mean anything, there's no reason why it shouldn't be put to good use now and tomorrow. It's not inherently dated, and, in ways one really needn't go into, meter, rhyme, and the like are, or can be, serviceable for people who know how to handle them well." No critic would deny that Wilbur is one of the poets who knows how to handle traditional poetic techniques well.

Wilbur's later volumes of poetry include *Advice to a Prophet and Other Poems* (1962), *Walking to Sleep and Other Poems* (1969), and *The Mind-Reader* (1976). *New and Collected Poems* appeared in 1988. But his most popular poems continue to be those he published in the first half of his career—such as "Potato," "The Death of a Toad," and "In the Smoking-Car." The voice is that of a sophisticated suburbanite, by turns quizzical, meditative, ironic, but never rent by rage or passion. One reviewer of Wilbur's *Collected Poems*, Anthony Hecht, focused on what he identified as the "nobility" in Wilbur's lines, and concluded that "this rare quality, usually joined to wit, good humor, grace, modesty, and a kind of physical zest or athletic dexterity . . . is, so far as I know, unrivaled."

ADDITIONAL READING

Responses: Prose Pieces 1953–1976, 1976; *Conversations with Richard Wilbur*, ed. William Butts, 1990.

Ralph J. Mills, Jr., *Contemporary American Poetry*, 1965; Donald Hill, *Richard Wilbur*, 1967; John P. Field, *Richard Wilbur: A Bibliographical Checklist*, 1971; Paul F. Cummins, *Richard Wilbur*, 1971; Wendy Salinger, ed., *Richard Wilbur's Creation*, 1983.

TEXT

New and Collected Poems, 1988.

The Beautiful Changes

One wading a Fall meadow finds on all sides
The Queen Anne's Lace[1] lying like lilies
On water; it glides
So from the walker, it turns
Dry grass to a lake, as the slightest shade of you   5
Valleys my mind in fabulous blue Lucernes.[2]

The beautiful changes as a forest is changed
By a chameleon's tuning his skin to it;
As a mantis, arranged
On a green leaf, grows   10
Into it, makes the leaf leafier, and proves
Any greenness is deeper than anyone knows.

Your hands hold roses always in a way that says
They are not only yours; the beautiful changes
In such kind ways,   15
Wishing ever to sunder
Things and things' selves for a second finding, to lose
For a moment all that it touches back to wonder.

1947

Potato

For André du Bouchet

An underground grower, blind and a common brown;
Got a misshapen look, it's nudged where it could;
Simple as soil yet crowded as earth with all.

---

[1] Wildflower whose tiny white blossoms resemble lace.
[2] Lucerne, city in Switzerland, on Lake Lucerne.

Cut open raw, it looses a cool clean stench,
Mineral acid seeping from pores of prest meal;   5
It is like breaching a strangely refreshing tomb:

Therein the taste of first stones, the hands of dead slaves,
Waters men drank in the earliest frightful woods,
Flint chips, and peat, and the cinders of buried camps.

Scrubbed under faucet water the planet skin   10
Polishes yellow, but tears to the plain insides;
Parching, the white's blue-hearted like hungry hands.

All of the cold dark kitchens, and war-frozen gray
Evening at window; I remember so many
Peeling potatoes quietly into chipt pails.   15

"It was potatoes saved us, they kept us alive."
Then they had something to say akin to praise
For the mean earth-apples, too common to cherish or steal.

Times being hard, the Sikh and the Senegalese,[1]
Hobo and Okie,[2] the body of Jesus the Jew,   20
Vestigial virtues, are eaten; we shall survive.

What has not lost its savor shall hold us up,
And we are praising what saves us, what fills the need.
(Soon there'll be packets again, with Algerian fruits.)

Oh, it will not bear polish, the ancient potato,   25
Needn't be nourished by Caesars, will blow anywhere,
Hidden by nature, counted-on, stubborn and blind.

You may have noticed the bush that it pushes to air,
Comical-delicate, sometimes with second-rate flowers
Awkward and milky and beautiful only to hunger.   30

                                                        1946, 1947

To an American Poet Just Dead

In the *Boston Sunday Herald* just three lines
Of no-point type for you who used to sing
The praises of imaginary wines,
And died, or so I'm told, of the real thing.

Also gone, but a lot less forgotten,   5
Are an eminent cut-rate druggist, a lover of Giving,
A lender, and various brokers: gone from this rotten
Taxable world to a higher standard of living.

---

[1]Sikh: in India, a disciple of the Hindu religion Sikhism that
believes in one god and rejects the caste system; Senegalese: a
native Moor (or Black) of Senegal, in West Africa.
[2]A term applied to people from the state of Oklahoma, used
especially when many migrated to California during the
1930s because of the droughts and dust storms in the Southwest, which turned much of Oklahoma into a "dust bowl."

It is out in the comfy suburbs I read you are dead,
And the soupy summer is settling, full of the yawns   10
Of Sunday fathers loitering late in bed,
And the ssshh of sprays on all the little lawns.

Will the sprays weep wide for you their chaplet tears?
For you will the deep-freeze units melt and mourn?
For you will Studebakers shred their gears   15
And sound from each garage a muted horn?

They won't. In summer sunk and stupefied
The suburbs deepen in their sleep of death.
And though they sleep the sounder since you died
It's just as well that now you save your breath.   20

1950

The Death of a Toad

A toad the power mower caught,
Chewed and clipped of a leg, with a hobbling hop has got
   To the garden verge, and sanctuaried him
   Under the cineraria leaves, in the shade
      Of the ashen heartshaped leaves, in a dim,   5
         Low, and a final glade.

The rare original heartsblood goes,
Spends on the earthen hide, in the folds and wizenings, flows
   In the gutters of the banked and staring eyes. He lies
   As still as if he would return to stone,   10
      And soundlessly attending, dies
         Toward some deep monotone,

Toward misted and ebullient seas
And cooling shores, toward lost Amphibia's emperies.[1]
   Day dwindles, drowning, and at length is gone   15
   In the wide and antique eyes, which still appear
      To watch, across the castrate lawn,
         The haggard daylight steer.

1948, 1950

Mind

Mind in its purest play is like some bat
That beats about in caverns all alone,
Contriving by a kind of senseless wit
Not to conclude against a wall of stone.

---

[1]Empires (archaic).

It has no need to falter or explore;   5
Darkly it knows what obstacles are there,
And so may weave and flitter, dip and soar
In perfect courses through the blackest air.

And has this simile a like perfection?
The mind is like a bat. Precisely. Save   10
That in the very happiest intellection
A graceful error may correct the cave.

1954, 1956

In the Smoking-Car

The eyelids meet. He'll catch a little nap.
The grizzled, crew-cut head drops to his chest.
It shakes above the briefcase on his lap.
Close voices breathe, "Poor sweet, he did his best."

"Poor sweet, poor sweet," the bird-hushed glades repeat,   5
Through which in quiet pomp his litter goes,
Carried by native girls with naked feet.
A sighing stream concurs in his repose.

Could he but think, he might recall to mind
The righteous mutiny or sudden gale   10
That beached him here; the dear ones left behind . . .
So near the ending, he forgets the tale.

Were he to lift his eyelids now, he might
Behold his maiden porters, brown and bare.
But even here he has no appetite.   15
It is enough to know that they are there.

Enough that now a honeyed music swells,
The gentle, mossed declivities begin,
And the whole air is full of flower-smells.
Failure, the longed-for valley, takes him in.   20

1960, 1961

April 5, 1974

The air was soft, the ground still cold.
In the dull pasture where I strolled
Was something I could not believe.
Dead grass appeared to slide and heave,
Though still too frozen-flat to stir,   5
And rocks to twitch, and all to blur.
What was this rippling of the land?

Was matter getting out of hand
And making free with natural law?
I stopped and blinked, and then I saw   10
A fact as eerie as a dream.
There was a subtle flood of steam
Moving upon the face of things.
It came from standing pools and springs
And what of snow was still around;   15
It came of winter's giving ground
So that the freeze was coming out,
As when a set mind, blessed by doubt,
Relaxes into mother-wit.
Flowers, I said, will come of it.   20

1976

The Writer

In her room at the prow of the house
Where light breaks, and the windows are tossed with linden,
My daughter is writing a story.

I pause in the stairwell, hearing
From her shut door a commotion of typewriter-keys   5
Like a chain hauled over a gunwale.

Young as she is, the stuff
Of her life is a great cargo, and some of it heavy:
I wish her a lucky passage.

But now it is she who pauses,   10
As if to reject my thought and its easy figure.
A stillness greatens, in which

The whole house seems to be thinking,
And then she is at it again with a bunched clamor
Of strokes, and again is silent.   15

I remember the dazed starling
Which was trapped in that very room, two years ago;
How we stole in, lifted a sash

And retreated, not to affright it;
And how for a helpless hour, through the crack of the door,   20
We watched the sleek, wild, dark

And iridescent creature
Batter against the brilliance, drop like a glove
To the hard floor, or the desk-top,

And wait then, humped and bloody,   25
For the wits to try it again; and how our spirits
Rose when, suddenly sure,

It lifted off from a chair-back,
Beating a smooth course for the right window
And clearing the sill of the world.   30

It is always a matter, my darling,
Of life or death, as I had forgotten. I wish
What I wished you before, but harder.

                                                                    1976

DENISE LEVERTOV
(b. 1923)

Denise Levertov summed up the essence of her poetics in the memorable line: "Form is never more than a *revelation* of content." In "Some Notes on Organic Form" (1965), Levertov described her concept of the poetic process:

> First there must be an experience, a sequence or constellation of perceptions of sufficient interest, felt by the poet intensely enough to demand of him their equivalence in words: he is *brought to speech*. Suppose there's the sight of the sky through a dusty window, birds and clouds and bits of paper flying through the sky, the sound of music from his radio, feelings of anger and love and amusement roused by a letter just received, the memory of some long ago thought or event associated with what's seen or heard or felt, and an idea, a concept, he has been pondering, each qualifying the other; together with what he knows about history; and what he has been dreaming—whether or not he remembers it—working in him. This is only a rough outline of a possible moment in a life. But the condition of being a poet is that periodically such a cross-section, or constellation, of experiences . . . demands, or wakes in him this demand, *the poem*.

Denise Levertov was born and grew up in London, England, the daughter of an immigrant Russian Jew (who converted to Christianity) and a Welsh mother. Both parents traced family lines back to Jewish and Christian religious figures of strong mystical tendencies. Levertov received no formal schooling, but was surrounded at home by a house full of books in several languages. She grew up intimately familiar with the British nineteenth-century writers such as Robert Browning and Alfred Lord Tennyson, and began to write romantic poetry at the age of twelve. During the Second World War, Levertov worked as a nurse in a London hospital, and she published her first volume of poems, *The Double Image*, after the end of the war in 1946. The poems were neo-romantic in substance and traditional in form in their use of rhyme and meter.

Levertov's life changed in 1947 with her marriage to an American soldier, Mitchell Goodman, stationed in England. The couple moved to New York, and Levertov's imagination underwent radical change, especially as she became steeped in American life, American English, and American poetry. The poet most clearly responsible for turning her into an American poet was William Carlos Williams. On his death in 1963, she wrote of him:

> His historical importance is, above all, that more than anyone else he made available to us the whole range of the language, he showed us the rhythms of speech as *poetry*—the rhythms and idioms not only of what we say aloud but of

what we say in our thoughts. . . . Only a poetry with its roots in the language *as it is used* can be free to explore and reclaim all those levels that otherwise become "only literature." Only a poetry freed from rhythmic patterns that had become habitual and inapt can discover the rhythms of our experience. He cleared the ground, he gave us tools.

Some ten years after issuing her first book of poems, Levertov published her second volume, *Here and Now*, in 1956. It was clear from the free-verse poems in this new volume that she had transformed herself into an American poet. And, as the title made clear, the poems grew out of experiences of the "here and now." One critic, Ralph Mills, has called her work a "poetry of the immediate," taking as its subject matter "everything that falls within the circumference of the poet's life as an individual." A companion to *Here and Now, Overland to the Islands* was published in 1958; she had originally planned the two volumes to appear as one.

As her work became known, she was identified with a group of American writers, the Black Mountain Poets (Charles Olson, Robert Creeley, and others), who were publicly proclaiming themselves the literary heirs of Walt Whitman, Hart Crane, and William Carlos Williams. She was one of the few women to appear in the important 1960 volume *The New American Poetry*, edited by Donald M. Allen, and again in the 1973 collection *The Poetics of the New American Poetry*, edited by Allen and Warren Tallman. In the first of these, she said: "I do not believe that a violent imitation of the horrors of our times is the concern of poetry. Horrors are taken for granted. . . . I long for poems of an inner harmony in utter contrast to the chaos in which they exist. Insofar as poetry has a social function it is to awaken sleepers by other means than shock."

New Directions became her publisher in 1960, issuing *With Eyes at the Back of Our Heads*. In 1961, with the publication of *The Jacob's Ladder*, Levertov appeared at the top of her form, skilled and confident in the path she was following; many of the poems took as their subject the writing of poetry. She began this same year a three-year stint as poetry editor for *The Nation*. As the 1960s wore on, she became keenly interested in political issues, particularly the Vietnam War. She became active in the antiwar movement, initiating in 1965 the "Writers' and Artists' Protest against the War in Vietnam." Her poetry also began to focus on political issues, beginning with *The Sorrow Dance* (1967), and continuing through a number of volumes, including *A Marigold from North Vietnam* (1968), *Relearning the Alphabet* (1970), and *To Stay Alive* (1971).

With the example of her own "political poetry" before her, Levertov felt moved to modify her 1960 statement ruling out "a violent imitation of the horrors of our times" as a "concern of poetry." In 1973 she wrote: "Our period in history was (is) violent and filled with horrors, and I never for a moment considered it was 'not poetic,' not the concern of poetry, to speak of them." Her target was not the subject but the "formlessness," the "lack of care for the language, for delving deep, for precision" in purely polemical poetry; effective political poems must be "works of art, not self-indulgent spittle-dribblings." And she concluded: "The poem has a social *effect* of some kind whether or not the poet wills that it have. It has kinetic force, it sets in motion . . . elements in the reader that otherwise would be stagnant."

Levertov has been a prolific writer. Her *Collected Earlier Poems, 1940–1960* appeared in 1979, and her *Poems, 1960–1967* in 1983. Recent titles are *The Menaced World* (1984) and *Breathing the Water* (1987). She collaborated with Edward C. Dimcock in translating *In Praise of Krishna: Songs from the Bengali* (1967). Her prose has been collected in two volumes: *The Poet in the World* (1973) and *Light Up the Cave* (1981). The latter volume, in addition to essays on other writers, on "The Nature of Poetry," and on "Poetry and Politics," contains fiction and auto-biographical pieces ("Memoirs"). Her productivity shows few signs of diminishing. The judgment of her work by Ralph Mills, made in 1965, seems as sound today as it was then: "Denise Levertov stands out as one whose art, fresh and compelling, convinces us of her genuine rapport with the reality she presents as its core."

ADDITIONAL READING

Ralph Mills, Jr., *Contemporary American Poetry*, 1965; Linda W. Wagner, *Denise Levertov*, 1967; Robert A. Wilson, *A Bibliography of Denise Levertov*, 1972; Linda W. Wagner, ed., *Denise Levertov: In Her Own Province*, 1979; William Slaughter, *The Imagination's Tongue: Denise Levertov's Poetic*, 1981; Liana Sakelliou-Schultz, *Denise Levertov: An Annotated Primary and Secondary Bibliography*, 1988; Harry Marten, *Understanding Denise Levertov*, 1988.

TEXTS

"Mrs. Cobweb," "Pure Products," "At the Edge" from *Collected Earlier Poems, 1940–1960*, 1979; "The Ache of Marriage" from *Poems, 1960–1967*, 1983; "A Hunger" from *Relearning the Alphabet*, 1970; "Fragment," "News Items" from *The Freeing of the Dust*, 1975; "Of Being" from *Oblique Prayers*, 1984.

Mrs. Cobweb[1]

Her dress was too tight, she had
fits & starts of violent memory that threw
daily memories down the airshaft, she looked
into the cupboard and found
a bone   5
            that changed into a shadow
                                    that stole

some treasure from its hiding place behind
the clock, she could not follow, her dress
clutched her,   10
            but there were days
when shreds of light, fringes of sun
caught her up & whizzed away with her
along serene trolley lines, she reached
for anything & could keep   15
whatever she could touch, she made:
            a collage of torn leaves she had touched,
            a glass moon-reflector,
often she almost spoke, sharp stars
got tangled in her hair, dazzled by the quietly   20
shining tracks she wondered if they had passed
the place of arrival?

                                                            1955, 1956

---

[1] "A lady who used to send me her poems in the mid '50's;
mad poems in which here and there a marvellous image
gleamed" (Levertov's note).

Pure Products

To the sea they came—
2000 miles in an old bus
fitted with brittle shelves and makeshift beds
and cluttered with U.S. canned goods
               —to the Sea!   5
on which they paddle
innertubes   —and the lowhovering Sun!
from which the old woman hides her head
under what looks like
a straw wastebasket.   10
                  'Yep, they cured me all right,
but see, it made my breasts grow like a woman's.'
And she: 'Something hurts him in his chest,
I think
        maybe it's his heart,'—and hers   15
I can see beating at the withered throat.

To the Sea some force has driven them—
            away from a lifetime.
And in this windless heat they purpose
to walk the 3 miles of shadeless beach to the store   20
to ask in Spanish (of which they know
only yes and no) for wholewheat flour
(which is unknown in the region) that she
may bake their bread!
                 They are dying   25
in their gentleness, adorned
with wrinkled apple smiles—nothing
remains for them
but to live a little, invoking
the old powers.   30

1956

At the Edge

How much I should like to begin
a poem with And—presupposing
the hardest said—
the moss cleared off the stone,
the letters plain.   5
How the round moon
would shine into all the corners
of such a poem and show
the words! Moths and dazzled
awakened birds   10
would freeze in its light!
The lines would be
an outbreak of bells
and I swinging on the rope!

Yet, not desiring apocrypha[1]   15
but true revelation,
what use to pretend the stone discovered,
anything visible?
That poem indeed
may not be carved there, may lie   20
—the quick of mystery—
in animal eyes gazing
from the thicket,
a creature of unknown size,
fierce, terrified, having teeth or   25
no defense, but whom
no And may approach suddenly.

                                            1960

The Ache of Marriage

The ache of marriage:

thigh and tongue, beloved,
are heavy with it,
it throbs in the teeth

We look for communion   5
and are turned away, beloved,
each and each

It is leviathan and we
in its belly
looking for joy, some joy   10
not to be known outside it

two by two in the ark of
the ache of it.

                                            1962, 1964

A Hunger

Black beans, white sunlight.
These have sufficed.

Approval of mothers, of brothers,
of strangers—a plunge of the hands
in sifted flour, over the wrists.   5
It gives pleasure.

---

[1]Biblical books rejected by Protestants as of questionable
authenticity.

And being needed. Being loved for that.
Being forgiven.

What mountains there are
to border solitude and provide   10
limits, blue or
dark as raisins.

But hunger: a hunger there is
refuses. Refuses the earth.

1969, 1970

Fragment

All one winter, in every crowded hall,
at every march and rally,
first thing I'd look for was your curly head.

One night last summer in a crowded room
across the ocean,   5
my heart missed a beat—it seemed I saw you
in the far corner.

You who were so many thousand miles away.

1975

News Items

i   America the Bountiful

After the welfare hotel
crumbled suddenly (after repeated warnings)
into the street,

Seventh Day Adventists brought supplies
of clothing to the survivors.   5
"'Look at this,' exclaimed
Loretta Rollock, 48 years old,
as she held up a green dress
and lingerie. 'I've never worn
such nice clothes. I feel like   10
when I was a kid and my mom
brought me something.' Then
she began to cry."

ii   In the Rubble

For some the hotel's collapse meant
life would have to be started   15
all over again.

Sixty-year-old Charles, on welfare
like so many of the others, who said,
'We are the rootless people,' and
'I have no home, no place that I can say I   20
really live in,' and,
'I had become used to it here,'
also said:
'I lost
all I ever had,   25
in the rubble.
I lost my clothes,
I lost the picture of my parents
and I lost my television.'

                                                     1975

Of Being

I know this happiness
is provisional:

      the looming presences—
      great suffering, great fear—

      withdraw only   5
      into peripheral vision:

but ineluctable this shimmering
of wind in the blue leaves:

this flood of stillness
widening the lake of sky: 10

this need to dance,
this need to kneel:
         this mystery:

                                                     1984

JAMES DICKEY
(b. 1923)

James Dickey provided, in "The Poet Turns on Himself" (in *Babel to Byzantium*), a revealing description of what he was trying to do in his poetry:

> What I have always striven for is to find some way to incarnate my best moments—those which in memory are most persistent or obsessive. I find that most of these moments have an element of danger, an element of repose, and an element of joy. I should like now to develop a writing instrument which would be capable of embodying these moments and their attendant states of mind, and I would be most pleased if readers came away from my poems not at all sure as to where the danger and the repose separate, where joy ends and longing begins. Strongly mixed emotions are what I usually have and what I

usually remember from the events of my life. Strongly mixed, but giving the impression of being one emotion, impure and overwhelming—that is the condition I am seeking to impose on my readers, whoever they may be.

Dickey, like Walt Whitman, came to the profession of poetry late, not publishing his first volume until he was thirty-seven. He was born in Buckhead, Georgia, a suburb of Atlanta, and in 1941 entered Clemson A & M College in Clemson, South Carolina. He was, however, soon involved in the Second World War, joining a night-fighter squadron of the Air Corps that flew bombing missions over targets in the South Pacific. On discharge after the war, Dickey went to Vanderbilt University in Nashville, Tennessee, graduating in English in 1949 (*magna cum laude*) and taking an M.A. in English in 1950. He began a teaching career in English at Rice University in Houston, Texas, but was recalled to service during the Korean War. After this second war experience, Dickey returned to teaching, first at Rice, and then, in 1956, at the University of Florida. He began to write poems and publish them in the little magazines.

But Dickey found academic life little to his liking, and in 1956 went into advertising. He explained in an interview: "I'd rather go for the buck and make some damn dough in the market place. I had the confidence of Lucifer in myself by that time. . . . I figured that the kind of thing that an advertising writer would be able to write, I could do . . . with the little finger of the left hand, and they were getting paid good dough for it." As it turned out, Dickey was right, and he became a successful copywriter and manager in advertising agencies in Atlanta and New York.

During his business career, Dickey continued to write and publish poems, and in 1960 he brought out his first book, *Into the Stone and Other Poems*. The volume attracted enough attention to win him a Guggenheim Fellowship, enabling him to concentrate on his poetry. He went to Italy and worked on a second volume of poems, published as *Drowning with Others* in 1962. These were followed by *Helmets* (poems) and *The Suspect in Poetry* (essays and reviews) in 1964. And then Dickey published the work that would bring critical acknowledgment of his talent, *Buckdancer's Choice* (1965). The book won the National Book Award for Poetry and brought Dickey many invitations from colleges to serve as poet-in-residence. He was appointed Consultant in Poetry at the Library of Congress from 1966 to 1968. In 1969, Dickey began a long tenure as professor of English and writer-in-residence at the University of South Carolina.

Dickey has been a prolific writer, publishing not only poetry but reviews, essays, "self-interviews," and fiction. An expanded volume of his reviews and essays, *Babel to Byzantium: Poets & Poetry Now*, appeared in 1968. His novel *Deliverance*, published in 1970, was turned into a popular motion-picture in 1972. Dickey acted as scriptwriter and even played the part of a southern sheriff in the film. Dickey's *Self-Interviews* appeared in 1970, as "Recorded and Edited by Barbara and James Reiss." *Night Hurdling*, published in 1983, was identified in its subtitle as a compendium of *Poems, Essays, Conversations, Commencements, and Afterwords*.

Throughout these later decades, Dickey has continued to experiment in his poetry. In 1970 he entitled a new book of poems *The Eye-Beaters, Blood, Victory, Madness, Buckhead and Mercy*, emphasizing the "strongly mixed emotions" he felt compelling in poetry. In 1976, he published *The Zodiac*, a long and semi-mystical poem—"Its twelve sections are the story of a drunken and perhaps dying Dutch poet who returns to his home in Amsterdam after years of travel and tries desperately to relate himself, by means of stars, to the universe." Other volumes include *The Strength of Fields* (1979), *Puella* (1982), and *False Youth: Four Seasons* (1983).

Having written so much, Dickey has raised the question of the coherence of his work only to dismiss it—in the American tradition. He said:

> I think it's a serious mistake on the poet's part to try to make his work coherent as far as a rational structure is concerned. Because really a poet like myself is writing about experiences and ideas based on them. Any kind of self-consistency would be fine if it simply happens, but I don't think the poet should seek it out. I would agree with Emerson that a foolish consistency is the hobgoblin of little minds. . . . The larger consistency that the body of a poet's work should have, should come from the totality of the poet's personality, including all its contradictions. It took me a long time to find that out.

ADDITIONAL READING

Laurence Lieberman, ed., *The Achievement of James Dickey: A Comprehensive Selection of His Poems with a Critical Introduction*, 1968; Richard J. Calhoun, ed., *James Dickey: The Expansive Imagination*, 1973; James Elledge, *James Dickey: A Bibliography, 1947–1974*, 1979; Patricia De La Fuente, ed., *James Dickey: Splintered Sunlight: Interview, Essays, and Bibliography*, 1979; Richard J. Calhoun and Robert W. Hill, *James Dickey*, 1983; Bruce Weigl and T. R. Hummer, eds., *The Imagination as Glory: The Poetry of James Dickey*, 1984; Ronald Baughman, *Understanding James Dickey*, 1985; Neal Bowers, *James Dickey: The Poet as Pitchman*, 1985; Robert Kirschten, *James Dickey and the Gentle Ecstasy of Earth: A Reading of the Poems*, 1988.

TEXT

Poems, 1947–1967, 1967.

Cherrylog Road

Off Highway 106
At Cherrylog Road I entered
The '34 Ford without wheels,
Smothered in kudzu,[1]
With a seat pulled out to run   5
Corn whiskey down from the hills,

And then from the other side
Crept into an Essex
With a rumble seat of red leather
And then out again, aboard   10
A blue Chevrolet, releasing
The rust from its other color,

Reared up on three building blocks.
None had the same body heat;
I changed with them inward, toward   15
The weedy heart of the junkyard,
For I knew that Doris Holbrook
Would escape from her father at noon

And would come from the farm
To seek parts owned by the sun   20
Among the abandoned chassis,

---

[1]Tough, parasitic, rapidly spreading vine.

Sitting in each in turn
As I did, leaning forward
As in a wild stock-car race

In the parking lot of the dead.   25
Time after time, I climbed in
And out the other side, like
An envoy or movie star
Met at the station by crickets.
A radiator cap raised its head,   30

Become a real toad or a kingsnake
As I neared the hub of the yard,
Passing through many states,
Many lives, to reach
Some grandmother's long Pierce-Arrow   35
Sending platters of blindness forth

From its nickel hubcaps
And spilling its tender upholstery
On sleepy roaches,
The glass panel in between   40
Lady and colored driver
Not all the way broken out,

The back-seat phone
Still on its hook.
I got in as though to exclaim,   45
"Let us go to the orphan asylum,
John; I have some old toys
For children who say their prayers."

I popped with sweat as I thought
I heard Doris Holbrook scrape   50
Like a mouse in the southern-state sun
That was eating the paint in blisters
From a hundred car tops and hoods.
She was tapping like code,

Loosening the screws,   55
Carrying off headlights,
Sparkplugs, bumpers,
Cracked mirrors and gear-knobs,
Getting ready, already,
To go back with something to show   60

Other than her lips' new trembling
I would hold to me soon, soon,
Where I sat in the ripped back seat
Talking over the interphone,
Praying for Doris Holbrook   65
To come from her father's farm

And to get back there
With no trace of me on her face
To be seen by her red-haired father
Who would change, in the squalling barn,   70

Her back's pale skin with a strop,
Then lay for me

In a bootlegger's roasting car
With a string-triggered 12-gauge shotgun
To blast the breath from the air.   75
Not cut by the jagged windshields,
Through the acres of wrecks she came
With a wrench in her hand,

Through dust where the blacksnake dies
Of boredom, and the beetle knows   80
The compost has no more life.
Someone outside would have seen
The oldest car's door inexplicably
Close from within:

I held her and held her and held her,   85
Convoyed at terrific speed
By the stalled, dreaming traffic around us,
So the blacksnake, stiff
With inaction, curved back
Into life, and hunted the mouse   90

With deadly overexcitement,
The beetles reclaimed their field
As we clung, glued together,
With the hooks of the seat springs
Working through to catch us red-handed   95
Amidst the gray breathless batting

That burst from the seat at our backs.
We left by separate doors
Into the changed, other bodies
Of cars, she down Cherrylog Road   100
And I to my motorcycle
Parked like the soul of the junkyard

Restored, a bicycle fleshed
With power, and tore off
Up Highway 106, continually   105
Drunk on the wind in my mouth,
Wringing the handlebar for speed,
Wild to be wreckage forever.

                                                        1963, 1964

Buckdancer's Choice[1]

So I would hear out those lungs,
The air split into nine levels,
Some gift of tongues of the whistler

---

[1] A buckdancer is a dancer of the "buck-and-wing," an energetic tap dance with many loud slaps.

In the invalid's bed: my mother,
Warbling all day to herself   5
The thousand variations of one song;

It is called Buckdancer's Choice.
For years, they have all been dying
Out, the classic buck-and-wing men

Of traveling minstrel shows;   10
With them also an old woman
Was dying of breathless angina,

Yet still found breath enough
To whistle up in my head
A sight like a one-man band,   15

Freed black, with cymbals at heel,
An ex-slave who thrivingly danced
To the ring of his own clashing light

Through the thousand variations of one song
All day to my mother's prone music,   20
The invalid's warbler's note,

While I crept close to the wall
Sock-footed, to hear the sounds alter,
Her tongue like a mockingbird's break

Through stratum after stratum of a tone   25
Proclaiming what choices there are
For the last dancers of their kind,

For ill women and for all slaves
Of death, and children enchanted at walls
With a brass-beating glow underfoot,   30

Not dancing but nearly risen
Through barnlike, theatrelike houses
On the wings of the buck and wing.

                                                              1965

The Sheep Child

Farm boys wild to couple
With anything   with soft-wooded trees
With mounds of earth   mounds
Of pinestraw   will keep themselves off
Animals by legends of their own: 5
In the hay-tunnel dark
And dung of barns, they will
Say   I have heard tell

That in a museum in Atlanta
Way back in a corner somewhere   10

There's this thing that's only half
Sheep   like a woolly baby
Pickled in alcohol   because
Those things can't live   his eyes
Are open   but you can't stand to look   15
I heard from somebody who . . .

But this is now almost all
Gone. The boys have taken
Their own true wives in the city,
The sheep are safe in the west hill   20
Pasture   but we who were born there
Still are not sure. Are we,
Because we remember, remembered
In the terrible dust of museums?

Merely with his eyes, the sheep-child may   25

Be saying   saying

    I am here, in my father's house.
    I who am half of your world, came deeply
    To my mother in the long grass
    Of the west pasture, where she stood like moonlight   30
    Listening for foxes. It was something like love
    From another world that seized her
    From behind, and she gave, not lifting her head
    Out of dew, without ever looking, her best
    Self to that great need. Turned loose, she dipped her face   35
    Farther into the chill of the earth, and in a sound
    Of sobbing   of something stumbling
    Away, began, as she must do,
    To carry me. I woke, dying,

    In the summer sun of the hillside, with my eyes   40
    Far more than human. I saw for a blazing moment
    The great grassy world from both sides,
    Man and beast in the round of their need,
    And the hill wind stirred in my wool,
    My hoof and my hand clasped each other,   45
    I ate my one meal
    Of milk, and died
    Staring. From dark grass I came straight

    To my father's house, whose dust
    Whirls up in the halls for no reason   50
    When no one comes   piling deep in a hellish mild corner,
    And, through my immortal waters,
    I meet the sun's grains eye
    To eye, and they fail at my closet of glass.
    Dead, I am most surely living   55
    In the minds of farm boys: I am he who drives
    Them like wolves from the hound bitch and calf
    And from the chaste ewe in the wind.
    They go into woods   into bean fields   they go
    Deep into their known right hands. Dreaming of me,   60

They groan   they wait   they suffer
Themselves, they marry, they raise their kind.

1966, 1967

The Leap

The only thing I have of Jane MacNaughton
Is one instant of a dancing-class dance.
She was the fastest runner in the seventh grade,
My scrapbook says, even when boys were beginning
To be as big as the girls,   5
But I do not have her running in my mind,
Though Frances Lane is there, Agnes Fraser,
Fat Betty Lou Black in the boys-against-girls
Relays we ran at recess: she must have run

Like the other girls, with her skirts tucked up   10
So they would be like bloomers,
But I cannot tell; that part of her is gone.
What I do have is when she came,
With the hem of her skirt where it should be
For a young lady, into the annual dance   15
Of the dancing class we all hated, and with a light
Grave leap, jumped up and touched the end
Of one of the paper-ring decorations

To see if she could reach it. She could,
And reached me now as well, hanging in my mind   20
From a brown chain of brittle paper, thin
And muscular, wide-mouthed, eager to prove
Whatever it proves when you leap
In a new dress, a new womanhood, among the boys
Whom you easily left in the dust   25
Of the passionless playground. If I said I saw
In the paper where Jane MacNaughton Hill,

Mother of four, leapt to her death from a window
Of a downtown hotel, and that her body crushed-in
The top of a parked taxi, and that I held   30
Without trembling a picture of her lying cradled
In that papery steel as though lying in the grass,
One shoe idly off, arms folded across her breast,
I would not believe myself. I would say
The convenient thing, that it was a bad dream   35
Of maturity, to see that eternal process

Most obsessively wrong with the world
Come out of her light, earth-spurning feet
Grown heavy: would say that in the dusty heels
Of the playground some boy who did not depend   40
On speed of foot, caught and betrayed her.
Jane, stay where you are in my first mind:

It was odd in that school, at that dance.
I and the other slow-footed yokels sat in corners
Cutting rings out of drawing paper   45

Before you leapt in your new dress
And touched the end of something I began,
Above the couples struggling on the floor,
New men and women clutching at each other
And prancing foolishly as bears: hold on   50
To that ring I made for you, Jane—
My feet are nailed to the ground
By dust I swallowed thirty years ago—
While I examine my hands.

                                                                1967

ALLEN GINSBERG
(b. 1926)

A small, pamphlet-like book of only forty-two pages entitled *Howl and Other Poems* appeared in 1956, published by City Lights Books (located at City Lights Bookstore) in San Francisco, California. The book's Preface was by the respectable doctor-poet William Carlos Williams and concluded: "Hold back the edges of your gowns, Ladies, we are going through hell." The book was dedicated to Jack Kerouac ("new Buddha of American prose"), William Burroughs ("author of *Naked Lunch*, an endless novel that will drive everybody mad"), and Neal Cassady ("author of *The First Third*, an autobiography . . . which enlightened Buddha"). The first lines of the lead poem "Howl" read: "I saw the best minds of my generation destroyed by madness, starving hysterical naked, / dragging themselves through the negro streets at dawn looking for an angry fix."

The author was Allen Ginsberg, who wrote unabashedly in his poems of his drug hallucinations, his homosexuality, and his rage against a repressive, warmad America. Fortunately for Ginsberg, his book was charged with obscenity. By the time a trial was concluded in 1957 and the book declared innocent, Ginsberg was famous and *Howl* a best-seller. Like Walt Whitman's first edition of *Leaves of Grass* published some hundred years before (in 1855), *Howl* would change the course of American poetry. Indeed, Ginsberg had considered at one point calling his book *Yawp*, a word Whitman had made his own in a famous line from "Song of Myself": "I sound my barbaric yawp over the roofs of the world."

In a seemingly endless letter written in 1958 to the poet John Hollander, who had been a fellow student with Ginsberg at Columbia University, Ginsberg struggled to explain, in a prose that seemed always on the verge of incoherence, his fierce desire to expand "the area of reality" that poets could embrace in their poems:

> Expanding the area you can deal with directly, especially to include all the irrational of subjective mystic experience & queerness & pants—in other words individuality—means again (as it did for Whitman) the possibility in a totally brain-washed age where all communication is subject to mass control (including especially including off-beat type talks in universities & places like

Partisan) — means again at last the possibility of Prophetic poetry — it's no miracle — all you have to know is what you actually think & feel & every sentence will be a revelation — everybody else is so afraid to talk even if they have any feelings left. & this kind of Bardic frankness prophecy is what Whitman called for in American poets — them to take over from Priests — lest materialism & mass-production of emotion drown america (which it has) & we become what he called the Fabled Damned among nations which we have — and it's been the cowardice and treason & abandonment of the poetic natural democratic soul by the poets themselves that's caused the downfall & doom of the rest of the world too — an awful responsibility.

Ginsberg was born in 1926 in Newark, New Jersey. His father was a high school English teacher and lyric poet in the romantic tradition; his mother was a crusading reformer, often caught up in socialist or communist organizations on behalf of one important cause or another. Ginsberg attended Paterson High School, where his father taught, and entered Columbia University in 1943. He was suspended in 1945 for scrawling obscenities in the dust on a window, but was readmitted in 1948 and took a B.A. During this period, he was attempting to come to terms with his homosexuality. He began to have mystic visions while simultaneously reading Blake and experiencing self-induced orgasms. When an addict friend's stolen goods were found in his apartment, Ginsberg pleaded insanity to avoid prosecution and was confined for eight months in the Columbia Psychiatric Institute.

Ginsberg was writing many more or less conventional poems under the influence of poets he admired. One of these was William Carlos Williams, with whom Ginsberg exchanged letters (Williams included one of Ginsberg's letters in his epic poem *Paterson*). These early poems would find book publication later under the titles *Empty Mirror: Early Poems* (1961) and *The Gates of Wrath: Rhymed Poems (1948–51)* (1972). In association with the writers to whom he dedicated *Howl* (Kerouac, Burroughs, Cassady), in what must have been something like a beat generation writers' workshop, Ginsberg found his own voice and broke out on his own with *Howl*. Ginsberg's notoriety made him a popular reader of his poetry on campuses around the country, and his appearances, especially his dramatic effectiveness in reciting his poems, revitalized the "poetry reading" as an art form. His poems could be immediately understood, the rhythms instantly felt.

While other poets came and went, Ginsberg remained on the poetic scene during the three decades following the publication of *Howl*, writing new poems, supporting new causes, appearing before new audiences. As a public personality, he proved astonishingly durable, and as a poet, remarkably productive. He wrote *Kaddish* (1961) as an elegy for his mother who died in 1956. Other books include *Reality Sandwiches* (1963), *Planet News* (1968), *The Fall of America: Poems of These States* (1973), *Mind Breaths, Poems (1971–76)* (1978), *Poems All Over the Place, Mostly '70s* (1978), and *White Shroud, Poems 1980–1985* (1986). His *Collected Poems: 1947–1980*, over 800 pages long, appeared in 1984, dedicated to his mother and father.

Ginsberg travelled about the world in search of a belief, and his published journals constitute an important part of his work. His trip into the Peruvian jungles with William Burroughs and their experiments with the Yage drug are the subject of *The Yage Letters* (1963). A journey through India in search of Oriental holy men and their wisdom is recorded in *Indian Journals: March 1962–May 1963* (1970). Gordon Ball has edited two important volumes: *Allen Verbatim: Lectures on Poetry, Politics, Consciousness* (1974) and *Allen Ginsberg: Journals Early Fifties Early Sixties* (1977).

Ginsberg's influence has been incalculable. More than most other poets he was responsible for postwar poetry breaking out of the restraints imposed by the modernist poetic theory as it had become calcified in rigid rules: poetry must be impersonal; it must be difficult, learned, ironic; it must adhere to an exclusive tradition from John Donne to T. S. Eliot. Ginsberg opened up both poetic form and subject matter. He resurrected the Whitman tradition and reintroduced the long, breath-length line into poetry, and the Whitmanian concern for individuality and the fate (or doom) of "These States." At its best, Ginsberg's influence has been subtle, inspiring poets not to imitate him, but to find the courage to be themselves and to launch out on their own.

ADDITIONAL READING

Thomas F. Merrill, *Allen Ginsberg*, 1969; Jane Kramer, *Allen Ginsberg in America*, 1969; George Dowden, *A Bibliography of Works by Allen Ginsberg, October, 1943 to July 1, 1967*, 1971; John Tytell, *Naked Angels: The Lives and Literature of the Beat Generation*, 1976; Michelle P. Kraus, *Allen Ginsberg: An Annotated Bibliography, 1969–1977*, 1980; Paul Portugés, *The Visionary Poetics of Allen Ginsberg*, 1978; Lewis Hyde, ed., *On the Poetry of Allen Ginsberg*, 1984; Barry Miles, *Ginsberg*, 1989.

TEXT

Collected Poems, 1947–1980, 1984.

from Howl

FOR CARL SOLOMON[1]

I

I saw the best minds of my generation destroyed by madness, starving hysterical naked,

dragging themselves through the negro streets at dawn looking for an angry fix,

angelheaded hipsters burning for the ancient heavenly connection to the starry dynamo in the machinery of night,

who poverty and tatters and hollow-eyed and high sat up smoking in the supernatural darkness of cold-water flats floating across the tops of cities contemplating jazz,

who bared their brains to Heaven under the El and saw Mohammedan angels staggering on tenement roofs illuminated,   5

who passed through universities with radiant cool eyes hallucinating Arkansas and Blake-light tragedy among the scholars of war,

who were expelled from the academies for crazy & publishing obscene odes on the windows of the skull,[2]

who cowered in unshaven rooms in underwear, burning their money in wastebaskets and listening to the Terror through the wall,

who got busted in their pubic beards returning through Laredo with a belt of marijuana for New York,

who ate fire in paint hotels or drank turpentine in Paradise Alley, death, or purgatoried their torsos night after night   10

---

[1]Ginsberg's friend who was in the psychiatric hospital with him in 1949.   [2]Ginsberg had been suspended from Columbia University for marking obscenities on the dust of a windowpane.

with dreams, with drugs, with waking nightmares, alcohol and cock and endless balls,

incomparable blind streets of shuddering cloud and lightning in the mind
leaping toward poles of Canada & Paterson, illuminating all the motionless
world of Time between,

Peyote solidities of halls, backyard green tree cemetery dawns, wine drunkenness over the rooftops, storefront boroughs of teahead joyride neon blinking
traffic light, sun and moon and tree vibrations in the roaring winter dusks of
Brooklyn, ashcan rantings and kind king light of mind,

who chained themselves to subways for the endless ride from Battery to holy
Bronx on benzedrine until the noise of wheels and children brought them
down shuddering mouth-wracked and battered bleak of brain all drained of
brilliance in the drear light of Zoo,

who sank all night in submarine light of Bickford's[3] floated out and sat through
the stale beer afternoon in desolate Fugazzi's,[4] listening to the crack of doom
on the hydrogen jukebox,   15

who talked continuously seventy hours from park to pad to bar to Bellevue[5] to
museum to the Brooklyn Bridge,

a lost battalion of platonic conversationalists jumping down the stoops off fire
escapes off windowsills off Empire State out of the moon,

yacketayakking screaming vomiting whispering facts and memories and anecdotes and eyeball kicks and shocks of hospitals and jails and wars,

whole intellects disgorged in total recall for seven days and nights with brilliant
eyes, meat for the Synagogue cast on the pavement,

who vanished into nowhere Zen New Jersey leaving a trail of ambiguous pic-
ture postcards of Atlantic City Hall,   20

suffering Eastern sweats and Tangerian bone-grindings and migraines of
China under junk-withdrawal in Newark's bleak furnished room,

who wandered around and around at midnight in the railroad yard wondering
where to go, and went, leaving no broken hearts,

who lit cigarettes in boxcars boxcars boxcars racketing through snow toward
lonesome farms in grandfather night,

who studied Plotinus Poe St. John of the Cross telepathy and bop kabbalah[6]
because the cosmos instinctively vibrated at their feet in Kansas,

who loned it through the streets of Idaho seeking visionary indian angels who
were visionary indian angels,   25

who thought they were only mad when Baltimore gleamed in supernatural
ecstasy,

who jumped in limousines with the Chinaman of Oklahoma on the impulse of
winter midnight streetlight smalltown rain,

who lounged hungry and lonesome through Houston seeking jazz or sex or
soup, and followed the brilliant Spaniard to converse about America and
Eternity, a hopeless task, and so took ship to Africa,

who disappeared into the volcanoes of Mexico leaving behind nothing but the
shadow of dungarees and the lava and ash of poetry scattered in fireplace
Chicago,

who reappeared on the West Coast investigating the FBI in beards and shorts
with big pacifist eyes sexy in their dark skin passing out incomprehensible
leaflets,   30

who burned cigarette holes in their arms protesting the narcotic tobacco haze
of Capitalism,

3"A slum courtyard N. Y. Lower East Side, site of [Jack]
Kerouac's *Subterraneans*, 1958" (Ginsberg's note).
3Cafeteria in New York City, open all night.
4Greenwich Village bar.

5New York psychiatric hospital.
6I.e., mystical method of interpretation of Hebrew scriptures
(also "cabala"), here done to the accompaniment of bop (variety of jazz).

who distributed Supercommunist pamphlets in Union Square weeping and
    undressing while the sirens of Los Alamos[7] wailed them down, and wailed
    down Wall, and the Staten Island ferry also wailed,
who broke down crying in white gymnasiums naked and trembling before the
    machinery of other skeletons,
who bit detectives in the neck and shrieked with delight in policecars for com-
    mitting no crime but their own wild cooking pederasty and intoxication,
who howled on their knees in the subway and were dragged off the roof waving
    genitals and manuscripts,   35
who let themselves be fucked in the ass by saintly motorcyclists, and screamed
    with joy,
who blew and were blown by those human seraphim, the sailors, caresses of
    Atlantic and Caribbean love,
who balled in the morning in the evenings in rosegardens and the grass of
    public parks and cemeteries scattering their semen freely to whomever come
    who may,
who hiccuped endlessly trying to giggle but wound up with a sob behind a
    partition in a Turkish Bath when the blond & naked angel came to pierce
    them with a sword,
who lost their loveboys to the three old shrews of fate the one eyed shrew of the
    heterosexual dollar the one eyed shrew that winks out of the womb and the
    one eyed shrew that does nothing but sit on her ass and snip the intellectual
    golden threads of the craftsman's loom,   40
who copulated ecstatic and insatiate with a bottle of beer a sweetheart a pack-
    age of cigarettes a candle and fell off the bed, and continued along the floor
    and down the hall and ended fainting on the wall with a vision of ultimate
    cunt and come eluding the last gyzym of consciousness,
who sweetened the snatches of a million girls trembling in the sunset, and were
    red eyed in the morning but prepared to sweeten the snatch of the sunrise,
    flashing buttocks under barns and naked in the lake,
who went out whoring through Colorado in myriad stolen night-cars, N.C.,[8]
    secret hero of these poems, cocksman and Adonis of Denver—joy to the
    memory of his innumerable lays of girls in empty lots & diner backyards,
    moviehouses' rickety rows, on mountaintops in caves or with gaunt wait-
    resses in familiar roadside lonely petticoat upliftings & especially secret gas-
    station solipsisms of johns, & hometown alleys too,
who faded out in vast sordid movies, were shifted in dreams, woke on a sudden
    Manhattan, and picked themselves up out of basements hungover with
    heartless Tokay and horrors of Third Avenue iron dreams & stumbled to
    unemployment offices,
who walked all night with their shoes full of blood on the snowbank docks
    waiting for a door in the East River to open to a room full of steamheat and
    opium,   45
who created great suicidal dramas on the apartment cliff-banks of the Hudson
    under the wartime blue floodlight of the moon & their heads shall be
    crowned with laurel in oblivion,
who ate the lamb stew of the imagination or digested the crab at the muddy
    bottom of the rivers of Bowery,
who wept at the romance of the streets with their pushcarts full of onions and
    bad music,
who sat in boxes breathing in the darkness under the bridge, and rose up to
    build harpsichords in their lofts,

---

[7]City in New Mexico where the atom bomb was first developed.

[8]Neal Cassady (1926–1968), friend of Ginsberg and the orig-inal of Dean Moriarty in Jack Kerouac's *On the Road.*

who coughed on the sixth floor of Harlem crowned with flame under the tubercular sky surrounded by orange crates of theology,   50

who scribbled all night rocking and rolling over lofty incantations which in the
yellow morning were stanzas of gibberish,

who cooked rotten animals lung heart feet tail borsht & tortillas dreaming of
the pure vegetable kingdom,

who plunged themselves under meat trucks looking for an egg,

who threw their watches off the roof to cast their ballot for Eternity outside of
Time, & alarm clocks fell on their heads every day for the next decade,

who cut their wrists three times successively unsuccessfully, gave up and were
forced to open antique stores where they thought they were growing old and
cried,   55

who were burned alive in their innocent flannel suits on Madison Avenue amid
blasts of leaden verse & the tanked-up clatter of the iron regiments of fashion & the nitroglycerine shrieks of the fairies of advertising & the mustard
gas of sinister intelligent editors, or were run down by the drunken taxicabs
of Absolute Reality,

who jumped off the Brooklyn Bridge this actually happened and walked away
unknown and forgotten into the ghostly daze of Chinatown soup alleyways &
firetrucks, not even one free beer,

who sang out of their windows in despair, fell out of the subway window,
jumped in the filthy Passaic, leaped on negroes, cried all over the street,
danced on broken wineglasses barefoot smashed phonograph records of
nostalgic European 1930s German jazz finished the whiskey and threw up
groaning into the bloody toilet, moans in their ears and the blast of colossal
steamwhistles,

who barreled down the highways of the past journeying to each other's hotrod-
Golgotha[9] jail-solitude watch or Birmingham jazz incarnation,

who drove crosscountry seventytwo hours to find out if I had a vision or you
had a vision or he had a vision to find out Eternity,   60

who journeyed to Denver, who died in Denver, who came back to Denver &
waited in vain, who watched over Denver & brooded & loned in Denver and
finally went away to find out the Time, & now Denver is lonesome for her
heroes,

who fell on their knees in hopeless cathedrals praying for each other's salvation
and light and breasts, until the soul illuminated its hair for a second,

who crashed through their minds in jail waiting for impossible criminals with
golden heads and the charm of reality in their hearts who sang sweet blues to
Alcatraz,

who retired to Mexico to cultivate a habit, or Rocky Mount to tender Buddha
or Tangiers to boys or Southern Pacific to the black locomotive or Harvard to
Narcissus to Woodlawn to the daisychain or grave,

who demanded sanity trials accusing the radio of hypnotism & were left with
their insanity & their hands & a hung jury,   65

who threw potato salad at CCNY[10] lecturers on Dadaism and subsequently
presented themselves on the granite steps of the madhouse with shaven
heads and harlequin speech of suicide, demanding instantaneous lobotomy,

and who were given instead the concrete void of insulin Metrazol[11] electricity
hydrotherapy psychotherapy occupational therapy pingpong & amnesia,

who in humorless protest overturned only one symbolic pingpong table, resting briefly in catatonia,

returning years later truly bald except for a wig of blood, and tears and fingers,
to the visible madman doom of the wards of the madtowns of the East,

---

[9]Calvary, site of Christ's crucifixion.   [11]Drug sometimes used in shock treatment of mental
[10]City College of New York.   patients.

Pilgrim State's Rockland's and Greystone's[12] foetid halls, bickering with the
　　echoes of the soul, rocking and rolling in the midnight solitude-bench dol-
　　men-realms of love, dream of life a nightmare, bodies turned to stone as
　　heavy as the moon,   70
with mother finally ******,[13] and the last fantastic book flung out of the tene-
　　ment window, and the last door closed at 4 A.M. and the last telephone
　　slammed at the wall in reply and the last furnished room emptied down to
　　the last piece of mental furniture, a yellow paper rose twisted on a wire
　　hanger in the closet, and even that imaginary nothing but a hopeful little bit
　　of hallucination—
ah, Carl,[14] while you are not safe I am not safe, and now you're really in the
　　total animal soup of time—
and who therefore ran through the icy streets obsessed with a sudden flash of
　　the alchemy of the use of the ellipse the catalog the meter & the vibrating
　　plane,
who dreamt and made incarnate gaps in Time & Space through images juxta-
　　posed, and trapped the archangel of the soul between 2 visual images and
　　joined the elemental verbs and set the noun and dash of consciousness to-
　　gether jumping with sensation of Pater Omnipotens Aeterna Deus[15]
to recreate the syntax and measure of poor human prose and stand before you
　　speechless and intelligent and shaking with shame, rejected yet confessing
　　out the soul to conform to the rhythm of thought in his naked and endless
　　head,   75
the madman bum and angel beat in Time, unknown, yet putting down here
　　what might be left to say in time come after death,
and rose reincarnate in the ghostly clothes of jazz in the goldhorn shadow of
　　the band and blew the suffering of America's naked mind for love into an eli
　　eli lamma lamma sabacthani[16] saxophone cry that shivered the cities down to
　　the last radio
with the absolute heart of the poem of life butchered out of their own bodies
　　good to eat a thousand years.

1955–56   *1956*

A Supermarket in California

　　　What thoughts I have of you tonight, Walt Whitman, for I walked down
the sidestreets under the trees with a headache self-conscious looking at the
full moon.

　　　In my hungry fatigue, and shopping for images, I went into the neon
fruit supermarket, dreaming of your enumerations!

　　　What peaches and what penumbras! Whole families shopping at night!
Aisles full of husbands! Wives in the avocados, babies in the tomatoes!—and
you, García Lorca,[1] what were you doing down by the watermelons?

　　　I saw you, Walt Whitman, childless, lonely old grubber, poking among
the meats in the refrigerator and eyeing the grocery boys.

---

[12]All mental institutions near New York City.
[13]I.e., "fucked."
[14]Carl Solomon.
[15]"Omnipotent Father, Eternal God" (Latin). Ginsberg followed French painter Paul Cézanne (1839–1906), whose letters Ginsberg was reading, using the Latin feminine form

("Aeterna") for eternal.
[16]"My God, My God, why hast thou forsaken me" (Hebrew);
the last words of Christ on the cross (Matthew 27:46).
[1]Spanish poet (1898–1936) who was homosexual and wrote
an "Ode to Walt Whitman"; he was shot by the Fascists in the
Spanish Civil War.

I heard you asking questions of each: Who killed the pork chops? What price bananas? Are you my Angel?   5

I wandered in and out of the brilliant stacks of cans following you, and followed in my imagination by the store detective.

We strode down the open corridors together in our solitary fancy tasting artichokes, possessing every frozen delicacy, and never passing the cashier.

Where are we going, Walt Whitman? The doors close in an hour. Which way does your beard point tonight?

(I touch your book and dream of our odyssey in the supermarket and feel absurd.)

Will we walk all night through solitary streets? The trees add shade to shade, lights out in the houses, we'll both be lonely.   10

Will we stroll dreaming of the lost America of love past blue automobiles in driveways, home to our silent cottage?

Ah, dear father, graybeard, lonely old courage-teacher, what America did you have when Charon[2] quit poling his ferry and you got out on a smoking bank and stood watching the boat disappear on the black waters of Lethe?

1955   *1956*

Sunflower Sutra[1]

I walked on the banks of the tincan banana dock and sat down under the huge
  shade of a Southern Pacific locomotive to look at the sunset over the box
  house hills and cry.
Jack Kerouac sat beside me on a busted rusty iron pole, companion, we
  thought the same thoughts of the soul, bleak and blue and sad-eyed, surrounded by the gnarled steel roots of trees of machinery.
The oily water on the river mirrored the red sky, sun sank on top of final Frisco
  peaks, no fish in that stream, no hermit in those mounts, just ourselves
  rheumy-eyed and hung-over like old bums on the riverbank, tired and wily.
Look at the Sunflower, he said, there was a dead gray shadow against the sky,
  big as a man, sitting dry on top of a pile of ancient sawdust—
—I rushed up enchanted—it was my first sunflower, memories of Blake[2]—my
  visions—Harlem   5
and Hells of the Eastern rivers, bridges clanking Joes Greasy Sandwiches, dead
  baby carriages, black treadless tires forgotten and unretreaded, the poem of
  the riverbank, condoms & pots, steel knives, nothing stainless, only the dank
  muck and the razor-sharp artifacts passing into the past—
and the gray Sunflower poised against the sunset, crackly bleak and dusty with
  the smut and smog and smoke of olden locomotives in its eye—
corolla[3] of bleary spikes pushed down and broken like a battered crown, seeds
  fallen out of its face, soon-to-be-toothless mouth of sunny air, sunrays obliterated on its hairy head like a dried wire spiderweb,
leaves stuck out like arms out of the stem, gestures from the sawdust root,
  broke pieces of plaster fallen out of the black twigs, a dead fly in its ear,

---

[2]In Greek mythology, the boatman who ferried souls of the dead over the river Styx to Hades; Lethe is the river of forgetfulness from which the dead drink oblivion of their former lives.
[1]"Buddhist discourses or dialogues, joining teacher and student in transmission of Dharma, or doctrine, over genera-
tions" (Ginsberg's note).
[2]William Blake (1757–1827), British poet and author of "Ah Sun-Flower." In 1948 Ginsberg had a vision in which Blake appeared reading this poem.
[3]The petals arranged around the center of a flower.

Unholy battered old thing you were, my sunflower O my soul, I loved you then!
The grime was no man's grime but death and human locomotives,   10
all that dress of dust, that veil of darkened railroad skin, that smog of cheek,
    that eyelid of black mis'ry, that sooty hand or phallus or protuberance of
    artificial worse-than-dirt—industrial—modern—all that civilization spot-
    ting your crazy golden crown—
and those blear thoughts of death and dusty loveless eyes and ends and with-
    ered roots below, in the home-pile of sand and sawdust, rubber dollar bills,
    skin of machinery, the guts and innards of the weeping coughing car, the
    empty lonely tincans with their rusty tongues alack, what more could I name,
    the smoked ashes of some cock cigar, the cunts of wheelbarrows and the
    milky breasts of cars, wornout asses out of chairs & sphincters of dynamos—
    all these
entangled in your mummied roots—and you there standing before me in the
    sunset, all your glory in your form!
A perfect beauty of a sunflower! a perfect excellent lovely sunflower existence!
    a sweet natural eye to the new hip moon, woke up alive and excited grasping
    in the sunset shadow sunrise golden monthly breeze!   15
How many flies buzzed round you innocent of your grime, while you cursed
    the heavens of the railroad and your flower soul?
Poor dead flower? when did you forget you were a flower? when did you look at
    your skin and decide you were an impotent dirty old locomotive? the ghost
    of a locomotive? the specter and shade of a once powerful mad American
    locomotive?
You were never no locomotive, Sunflower, you were a sunflower!
And you Locomotive, you are a locomotive, forget me not!
So I grabbed up the skeleton thick sunflower and stuck it at my side like a
    scepter,   20
and deliver my sermon to my soul, and Jack's soul too, and anyone who'll listen,
—We're not our skin of grime, we're not our dread bleak dusty imageless loco-
    motive, we're all golden sunflowers inside, blessed by our own seed & hairy
    naked accomplishment-bodies growing into mad black formal sunflowers in
    the sunset, spied on by our eyes under the shadow of the mad locomotive
    riverbank sunset Frisco hilly tincan evening sitdown vision.

1955   *1956*

To Aunt Rose

Aunt Rose—now—might I see you
with your thin face and buck tooth smile and pain
            of rheumatism—and a long black heavy shoe
            for your bony left leg
    limping down the long hall in Newark on the running carpet   5
        past the black grand piano
            in the day room
                where the parties were
        and I sang Spanish loyalist[1] songs
            in a high squeaky voice   10

----

[1]Those opposed to the Fascist takeover of Spain led by the
insurgent General Francisco Franco in the Spanish Civil War
(1936–39).

> (hysterical) the committee listening
>   while you limped around the room
>   collected the money —
> Aunt Honey, Uncle Sam, a stranger with a cloth arm
>   in his pocket   15
>   and huge young bald head
>   of Abraham Lincoln Brigade[2]
>
> —your long sad face
>   your tears of sexual frustration
>   (what smothered sobs and bony hips   20
>   under the pillows of Osborne Terrace)
> —the time I stood on the toilet seat naked
>   and you powdered my thighs with calamine
>   against the poison ivy — my tender
>   and shamed first black curled hairs   25
> what were you thinking in secret heart then
>   knowing me a man already —
> and I an ignorant girl of family silence on the thin pedestal
>   of my legs in the bathroom — Museum of Newark.
>
>   Aunt Rose   30
> Hitler is dead, Hitler is in Eternity; Hitler is with
>   Tamburlane and Emily Brontë[3]
>
> Though I see you walking still, a ghost on Osborne Terrace
>   down the long dark hall to the front door
>   limping a little with a pinched smile   35
>   in what must have been a silken
>   flower dress
> welcoming my father, the Poet, on his visit to Newark
>   —see you arriving in the living room
>   dancing on your crippled leg   40
>   and clapping hands his book
>   had been accepted by Liveright[4]
>
> Hitler is dead and Liveright's gone out of business
> *The Attic of the Past* and *Everlasting Minute*[5] are out of print
>   Uncle Harry sold his last silk stocking   45
>   Claire quit interpretive dancing school
>   Buba sits a wrinkled monument in Old
>   Ladies Home blinking at new babies
>
> last time I saw you was the hospital
>   pale skull protruding under ashen skin   50
>   blue veined unconscious girl
>   in an oxygen tent
>   the war in Spain has ended long ago
>   Aunt Rose

1958   1961

[2]A Brigade made up of American volunteers to fight on the Spanish Loyalist side and against Franco in the Spanish Civil War.
[3]Tamburlane (also Timur, 1336–1405), Turkish conqueror of much of the world before his death in China in 1405; Emily Brontë (1818–1848), British novelist, author of *Wuthering Heights*.
[4]A leading publisher of the time.
[5]Books of poems by Ginsberg's father Louis.

A Vow

I will haunt these States
    with beard bald head
    eyes staring out plane window,
    hair hanging in Greyhound bus midnight
leaning over taxicab seat to admonish   5
    an angry cursing driver
    hand lifted to calm
    his outraged vehicle
that I pass with the Green Light of common law.

Common Sense, Common law, common tenderness   10
    & common tranquillity
our means in America to control the money munching
    war machine, bright lit industry
everywhere digesting forests & excreting soft pyramids
    of newsprint, Redwood and Ponderosa patriarchs   15
    silent in Meditation murdered & regurgitated as smoke,
    sawdust, screaming ceilings of Soap Opera,
    thick dead Lifes,[1] slick Advertisements
    for Gubernatorial big guns
    burping Napalm on palm rice tropic greenery,   20

Dynamite in forests,
    boughs fly slow motion
    thunder down ravine,
    Helicopters roar over National Park, Mekong Swamp,[2]
    Dynamite fire blasts thru Model Villages,   25
Violence screams at Police, Mayors get mad over radio,
    Drop the Bomb on Niggers!
    drop Fire on the gook China
    Frankenstein Dragon
waving its tail over Bayonne's[3] domed Aluminum oil reservoir!   30

I'll haunt these States all year
    gazing bleakly out train windows, blue airfield
    red TV network on evening plains,
decoding radar Provincial editorial paper message,
    deciphering Iron Pipe laborers' curses as   35
    clanging hammers they raise steamshovel claws
over Puerto Rican agony lawyers' screams in slums.

1966   *1972*

ROBERT CREELEY
(b. 1926)

    Robert Creeley wrote in "I'm Given to Write Poems" (1967) about his experience of being a poet:

---

[1] I.e., files of the picture magazine *Life.*
[2] Reference to the Mekong Delta, along the Mekong River in Vietnam.
[3] An industrialized seaport city in New Jersey.

What I have written I knew little of until I had written it. If at times I have said that I enjoy what I write, I mean that writing is for me the most viable and open condition of possibility in the world. Things have happened there, as they have happened nowhere else — and I am not speaking of "make-believe," which, be it said, is "as real as real can be." In poems I have both discovered and born testament to my life in ways no other possibility has given me. Can I *like* all that I may prove to be, or does it matter? Am I merely living for my own approval? In writing it has seemed to me that such small senses of existence were altogether gone, and that, at last, the world "came true." Far from being its limit or director, the wonder is that I have found myself to be there also.

As so often the case when he talks about being a poet, Creeley begins to sound more and more mystical — almost as though he is communing privately with himself. When asked about influences on him, he has cited Charles Olson and his 1950 proclamation "Projective Verse," in which, as a matter of fact, Olson quotes Creeley's own principle: "Form is never more than an extension of content." And Creeley has cited, also, William Carlos Williams and his prefatory statement to his volume *The Wedge*. There Williams said (and Creeley quoted in "I'm Given to Write Poems"): "When a man makes a poem, makes it, mind you, he takes words as he finds them interrelated about him and composes them — without distortion which would mar their exact significances — into an intense expression of his perceptions and ardors that they may constitute a revelation in the speech that he uses. It isn't what he *says* that counts as a work of art, it's what he makes, with such intensity of perception that it lives with an intrinsic movement of its own to verify its authenticity." Creeley has cited this passage so often as to suggest that it describes in some literal way his sense of what he does in making a poem.

In commenting in an interview about his formulation, "Form is never more than an extension of content," Creeley said: "I found that statement in a variety of other writers from other times. . . . certainly Emerson had it much in mind in his sense of spontaneous form." And he said at another point, "I don't at all agree with the contention that free verse is like playing tennis without the net. . . . If it becomes simply a farmer's meandering all over the field, one who has not as yet mastered either the horses or the plow, it will look simply as such, a man wandering over a surface, which is rather incoherent. Although there will be lines. And if they do somehow gain a coherence in that wandering, then that will be interesting."

Born in 1926 in Arlington, Massachusetts, Creeley was only four when his father died. After three years at the Holderness School in Plymouth, New Hampshire, he entered Harvard in 1943, but went off to join the American Field Service in 1944, driving an ambulance in India and Burma. He returned to Harvard for a time and dropped out just before receiving his degree. While a student, Creeley had married, and he and his wife tried subsistence farming in New Hampshire for three years. Unable to pay the mortgage, they went next to Aix-en-Provence in France, then to the Spanish island of Majorca, where Creeley attempted to establish a press. In 1954, Charles Olson appointed him to the faculty of Black Mountain College, where he was granted a B.A. Creeley founded and edited the *Black Mountain Review*, publishing not only the Black Mountain poets such as Denise Levertov, but also Allen Ginsberg and other poets who shared his and Charles Olson's iconoclastic literary attitudes.

Although Creeley left Black Mountain College in 1955, at a time when its fortunes were going downhill, he and Olson remained friends for the rest of

Olson's life; their large correspondence would be published after Olson's death in some seven volumes. Creeley's marriage broke up, and he went for a brief period to San Francisco, where he met the group of writers, including Ginsberg, that would before long become recognized as the Beat Generation. He saw immediately that he and the Black Mountain group shared much with Ginsberg and his friends (Jack Kerouac and Gary Snyder) in their views about writing and poetry.

Looking for a place to live a simple life, Creeley went to teach in a boys' school in Albuquerque, and took time out to complete an M.A. at the University of New Mexico. After three years (1956–59), he went to Central America to teach in a school on a coffee plantation in Guatemala. During all the 1950s, Creeley had kept writing poetry which was published by various small presses, but received little notice. In 1962, Scribners brought out *For Love: Poems 1950–1960*, which was widely reviewed, sold well, and was nominated for the National Book Award. In his brief Preface, Creeley emphasized, through a remarkable "stumbling" metaphor, the casual, *found* nature of his short lyrics: "Wherever it is one stumbles (to get to wherever) at least some way will exist, so to speak, as and when a man takes this or that step—for which, god bless him. Insofar as these poems are such places, always they were ones stumbled into: warmth for a night perhaps, the misdirected intention come right; and too, a sudden instance of love, and the being loved, wherewith a man also contrives a world (of his own mind)." From 1963 on, critics began to take serious notice of Creeley's work.

On returning from Guatemala in 1961, Creeley followed an academic career, teaching at a number of places before settling into a permanent appointment at the State University of New York at Buffalo. His marriage to Bobbie Haek in 1957 ended in 1976, and he married again in 1977. Creeley continued to publish volumes of poetry, bringing them together in *Selected Poems* (1976) and *The Collected Poems* (1982). More recent volumes include *A Calendar: Twelve Poems* (1983), *Memories* (1984), and *Memory Gardens* (1986). Creeley has never, like Olson and Ginsberg, been tempted by the longer poetic forms such as the lyric-epic. He has stuck with the brief, casual-seeming lyric on a subject he has stumbled up against and seen suddenly in a new dimension. The resulting poem is a "compact, ephiphanal instance of emotion or insight."

Creeley has written fiction, including a volume of short stories, *The Gold Diggers and Other Stories* (1965), and a novel set in Majorca, *The Island* (1963). Important books of essays are *A Quick Graph: Collected Notes & Essays* (1970), *Was That a Real Poem & Other Essays* (1979), and *The Collected Prose of Robert Creeley* (1984).

ADDITIONAL READING

Contexts of Poetry: Interviews 1961–1971, ed. Donald M. Allen, 1973; *Charles Olson and Robert Creeley: The Complete Correspondence*, 7 vols., ed. George F. Butterick, 1980–86.

Ronald Anthony Sheffler, *The Development of Robert Creeley's Poetry*, 1971; Mary Novik, *Robert Creeley: An Inventory, 1945–1970*, 1973; Warren Tallman, *Three Essays on Creeley*, 1973; Cynthia Dubin Edelberg, *Robert Creeley's Poetry: A Critical Introduction*, 1978; Arthur L. Ford, *Robert Creeley*, 1978; Sherman Paul, *The Lost America of Love: Rereading Robert Creeley, Edward Dorn, and Robert Duncan*, 1981; Carroll F. Terrell, ed., *Robert Creeley: The Poet's Workshop*, 1984; John Wilson, ed., *Robert Creeley's Life and Work: A Sense of Increment*, 1987; Willard Fox III, *Robert Creeley, Edward Dorn, and Robert Duncan: A Reference Guide*, 1988.

TEXT

The Collected Poems of Robert Creeley, 1945–1975, 1982.

The Dishonest Mailmen

They are taking all my letters, and they
put them into a fire.

                      I see the flames, etc.
But do not care, etc.

They burn everything I have, or what little   5
I have. I don't care, etc.

The poem supreme, addressed to
emptiness—this is the courage

necessary. This is something
quite different.   10

                                        1953

Naughty Boy

When he brings home a whale
she laughs and says, that's not for real.

And if he won the Irish sweepstakes,
she would say, where were you last night?

Where are you now, for that matter? Am   5
I always (she says) to be looking

at you? She says,
if I thought it would get any better I

would shoot you, you
nut, you. Then pats her hair   10

into place, and waits
for Uncle Jim's deep-fired, all-fat, real gone

whale steaks.

                                  1955, 1959

"I Keep to Myself
Such Measures . . ."

I keep to myself such
measures as I care for,

daily the rocks
accumulate position.

There is nothing   5
but what thinking makes
it less tangible. The mind,
fast as it goes, loses

pace, puts in place of it
like rocks simple markers,   10
for a way only to
hopefully come back to

where it cannot. All
forgets. My mind sinks.
I hold in both hands such weight   15
it is my only description.

1963   *1964, 1966*

Words

You are always
with me,
there is never
a separate

place. But if   5
in the twisted
place I
cannot speak,

not indulgence
or fear only,   10
but a tongue
rotten with what

it tastes —   There is
a memory
of water, of   15
food, when hungry.

Some day
will not be
this one, then
to say   20

words like a
clear, fine
ash sifts,
like dust,

from nowhere.   25

1965   *1965*

Joy

I could look at
an empty hole for hours
thinking it will
get something in it,

will collect   5
things. There is
an infinite emptiness
placed there.

1965   *1966, 1967*

The Birds

FOR JANE AND STAN BRAKHAGE

I'll miss the small birds that come
for the sugar you put out
and the bread crumbs. They've

made the edge of the sea domestic
and, as I am, I welcome that.   5
Nights my head seemed twisted

with dreams and the sea wash,
I let it all come quiet, waking,
counting familiar thoughts and objects.

Here to rest, like they say, I best   10
liked walking along the beach
past the town till one reached

the other one, around the corner
of rock and small trees. It was
clear, and often empty, and   15

peaceful. Those lovely ungainly
pelicans fished there, dropping
like rocks, with grace, from the air,

headfirst, then sat on the water,
letting the pouch of their beaks   20
grow thin again, then swallowing

whatever they'd caught. The birds,
no matter they're not of our kind,
seem most like us here. I want

to go where they go, in a way, if   25
a small and common one. I want
to ride that air which makes the sea

seem down there, not the element
in which one thrashes to come up.
I love water, I *love* water —   30

but I also love air, and fire.

1970   *1970, 1971*

ROBERT BLY
(b. 1926)

Robert Bly said in an interview in 1973:

> I think a poem . . . is a dream, a dream which you are willing to share with the community. It happens a writer often doesn't understand a poem until some months after he's written it — just as a dreamer doesn't understand a dream. . . . For the person who writes poetry, the great joy of the poem lies in his or her being able to make an utterance in which the shallow intellect — which has really been trained through grade school and high school to be destructive — doesn't enter. He can continue to write that way the rest of his life if he wishes. Or once he feels that his spontaneous being has been given confidence and is safe from the attacks of rationality — the destructive attacks — then he can choose to ask the intellect to reenter. *Not* on *its* terms, but on the imagination's terms.

This mystical, dream-like perspective has been held by Bly throughout his career. He has been highly influential on the poets who are usually called, as a group, the Deep Image poets, a term that Robert Kelly made current in a 1961 essay entitled "Notes on the Poetry of Deep Image." Poets usually associated with the name, in addition to Bly, are W. S. Merwin and James Wright. They have felt uneasy with the title, but they have also disclaimed other names applied to the kind of poetry they write — surrealist, emotive, mystical. They believe that the energy of a poem is in its sequence of images, but the images are not those of the outer world as in Ezra Pound's imagism, but images of the inner world of deeper levels of consciousness or the unconscious. Both Bly and Wright learned much of their technique by translating such Latin American poets as the Chilean Pablo Neruda and the Peruvian César Vallejo, noted for their surrealistic imagery.

Bly was born in Madison, Minnesota, in a family of Norwegian-American farmers. After spending two years in the navy, he attended St. Olaf's College in Minnesota for a year and then transferred to Harvard, where he graduated *magna cum laude* and was class poet in 1950. After a brief return to Minnesota, he went to live in New York, where he remained, poor and lonely, for three years. He supported himself by part-time jobs and spent most of his time reading and writing. It was in New York that he made the decision to take the "inward road" — be a poet. In 1954 he entered the writing workshop at the University of Iowa, completing an M.A. in 1956. He spent 1956–57 on a student Fulbright in Norway, where in the Oslo library he began to read poetry from around the world, including the Latin American and European surrealists.

He returned to Minnesota to live on a farm and soon founded a little magazine, the *Fifties* (the name shifted with the decades, becoming *Sixties*, then *Seventies*). Through this little magazine he was outspoken in his criticism of the reigning schools of poetry (academic and intellectual) and criticism (the New

Criticism). And of course, because of his candid criticism, he made enemies. But he also made friends, including James Wright, then teaching at the University of Minnesota. He published his first book of poems, *Silence in the Snowy Fields*, in 1962. As the 1960s progressed, Bly became active in the anti-Vietnam War movement, helping to organize in 1966 the American Writers Against the Vietnam War. This same year he edited *A Poetry Reading Against the Vietnam War*. In a 1967 essay "Leaping Up into Political Poetry," he said that "the poet's main job is to penetrate that husk around the American psyche, and since that psyche is inside *him* too, the writing of political poetry is like the writing of personal poetry, a sudden drive by the poet inward." It was the "inward poets," he observed, not the rhetorical poets, who had written the best poems about the Vietnam War.

In 1967, Bly published his second volume of poems, *The Light Around the Body*, which won the National Book Award for poetry. The book contained several antiwar poems, including "War and Silence," "Asian Peace Offers Rejected without Publication," "Driving through Minnesota during the Hanoi Bombings." It also contained a quotation, under the title "In Praise of Grief," from one of Bly's favorite authors, Jacob Boehme, the sixteenth-century German mystic: "O dear children, look in what a dungeon we are lying, in what lodging we are, for we have been captured by the spirit of the outward world; it is our life, for it nourishes and brings us up, it rules in our marrow and bones, in our flesh and blood, it has made our flesh earthly, and now death has us." Clearly Bly's poetry of the "inward road" was meant to counteract what Boehme described.

Bly has published many volumes of translations, including *Twenty Poems of Pablo Neruda* (1968) and *Selected Poems of Rainer Maria Rilke* (1981). His long title poem in *Sleepers Joining Hands* (1973), a kind of dream-like autobiography of the inner life, clearly connects with the American poet that Bly frequently praised, Walt Whitman; Bly's title invokes Whitman's poem "The Sleepers" ("They flow hand in hand over the whole earth from east to west as they lie unclothed"). A volume of interviews and essays, *Talking All Morning*, appeared in 1979. And in 1986, Bly published his *Selected Poems*, providing an introductory comment on each of the several volumes from which he made his selections. He has been an indefatigable public reader of his poems, impressing audiences with his vagabond appearance, his dramatic voice, and his candid running commentary on his poetry, himself, and the world.

ADDITIONAL READING

Ingegerd Friberg, *Moving Inward: A Study of Robert Bly's Poetry*, 1977; Kate Daniels and Richard Jones, eds., *Of Solitude and Silence: Writings on Robert Bly*, 1982; Howard Nelson, *Robert Bly: An Introduction to the Poetry*, 1984; Joyce Peseroff, ed., *Robert Bly: When Sleepers Awake*, 1984; Richard P. Sugg, *Robert Bly*, 1986; William H. Roberson, *Robert Bly: A Primary and Secondary Bibliography*, 1986; William V. Davis, *Understanding Robert Bly*, 1988.

TEXT

Selected Poems, 1986.

Poem in Three Parts

I

Oh, on an early morning I think I shall live forever!
I am wrapped in my joyful flesh,
As the grass is wrapped in its clouds of green.

II

Rising from a bed, where I dreamt
Of long rides past castles, and hot coals,   5
The sun lies happily on my knees;
I have suffered and survived the night
Bathed in dark water, like any blade of grass.

III

The strong leaves of the box elder tree,
Plunging in the wind, call us to disappear   10
Into the wilds of the universe,
Where we shall sit at the foot of a plant,
And live forever, like the dust.

1959, 1962

Watering the Horse

How strange to think of giving up all ambition!
Suddenly I see with such clear eyes
The white flake of snow
That has just fallen on the horse's mane!

1962

The Executive's Death

Merchants have multiplied more than the stars of heaven.
Half the population are like the long grasshoppers
That sleep in the bushes in the cool of the day;
The sound of their wings is heard at noon, muffled, near the earth.
The crane handler dies; the taxi driver dies, slumped over   5
In his taxi. Meanwhile high in the air an executive
Walks on cool floors, and suddenly falls.
Dying, he dreams he is lost in a snowbound mountain
On which he crashed, carried at night by great machines.
As he lies on the wintry slope, cut off and dying,   10
A pine stump talks to him of Goethe[1] and Jesus.
Commuters arrive in Hartford at dusk like moles
Or hares flying from a fire behind them,
And the dusk in Hartford is full of their sighs.
Their trains come through the air like a dark music,   15
Like the sound of horns, the sound of thousands of small wings.

1967

---

[1]Johann Wolfgang von Goethe (1749–1832), German poet.

Johnson's Cabinet[1] Watched by Ants

I

It is a clearing deep in a forest: overhanging boughs
Make a low place. Here the citizens we know during the day,
The ministers, the department heads,
Appear changed: the stockholders of large steel companies
In small wooden shoes; here are the generals dressed as gamboling lambs.   5

II

Tonight they burn the rice supplies; tomorrow
They lecture on Thoreau;[2] tonight they move around the trees;
Tomorrow they pick the twigs from their clothes;
Tonight they throw the firebombs; tomorrow
They read the Declaration of Independence; tomorrow they are in church.   10

III

Ants are gathered around an old tree.
In a choir they sing, in harsh and gravelly voices,
Old Etruscan[3] songs on tyranny.
Toads nearby clap their small hands, and join
The fiery songs, their five long toes trembling in the soaked earth.   15

1966, 1967

Kneeling Down to Peer into a Culvert[1]

I kneel down to peer into a culvert.
The other end seems far away.
One cone of light floats in the shadowed water.
This is how our children will look when we are dead.

I kneel near floating shadowy water.   5
On my knees, I am half inside the tunnel —
blue sky widens the far end —
darkened by the shadowy insides of the steel.

Are they all born? I walk on farther;
out in the plowing I see a lake newly made.   10
I have seen this lake before. . . . It is a lake
I return to each time my children are grown.

I have fathered so many children and returned
to that lake — grayish flat slate banks,
low arctic bushes. I am a water-serpent throwing water drops   15
off my head. My gray loops trail behind me.

---

[1]President Lyndon B. Johnson's (1908–1973) Cabinet; the
Secretaries of Defense and State (Robert S. McNamara and
Dean Rusk) were in charge of defending and carrying out the
policies of the U.S. participation in the Vietnam War.
[2]Henry David Thoreau (1817–1862), American writer, au-

thor of *Walden*.
[3]Ancient civilization (Etruria) in central Italy.
[1]A drain under a street or road. When first published, the
poem was titled "Kneeling Down to Look into a Culvert."

How long I live there alone! For a thousand years
I am alone, with no duties, living as I live.
Then one morning a head like mine pokes from the water.
I fight—it's time, it's right—and am torn to pieces fighting.   20

1981

A . R . A M M O N S
(b. 1926)

A. R. Ammons has provided the essence of his aesthetic in the title of an essay he published in 1968, "A Poem Is a Walk": "Granted walks and poems are different things," they both afford "clarification or intensification by distraction, seeing one thing better by looking at something else." Ammons said in an interview in 1988: "Like a walk, the poem becomes the cure of itself. It uses words in order to find the cure of words. That's why I don't believe that the Word comes first. What's first is what words imitate and register and what they return to."

In the interview, Ammons rejected the idea that it was through poetry that the world could be discovered: "The Word is not the only way into the world. The most essential thing for a poet to have is silence or reticence. The reason is that the words break up experience at the same time they declare it. A poem returns things to silence." Ammons has pointed out the impossibility of a "fixed" poetics: "Each poem in becoming generates the laws by which it is generated: extensions of the laws to other poems never completely take."

Archie Randolph Ammons was born on a farm near Whiteville, North Carolina, in 1926. After graduating from Whiteville High School in 1943, he went to work in the shipyards. He entered the navy in 1944 and served during the Second World War in the South Pacific. When asked how he became a poet, he replied: "I started writing in the Navy. I was on an anti-submarine detection destroyer. We ran interference with sonar, listening for Japanese subs. There was a paperback anthology of poetry on board, and I had nothing to read. That's where it all started. I never stopped writing after that."

After discharge from the service, Ammons studied at Wake Forest College on the G. I. Bill, receiving his B.S. in 1949. After serving briefly as principal of an elementary school, he started graduate work at the University of California, but left after one year. From 1952 until 1964, he worked as executive vice-president of a glass manufacturing business in New Jersey. He continued to write poems, and in 1955 he privately published his first volume, *Ommateum* (meaning "compound eye"). The book attracted virtually no attention.

Ammons's second volume of poems, *Expressions of Sea Level*, appeared some nine years after the first, in 1964. This same year Ammons was invited to read his poems at Cornell and, on the basis of his visit, offered an appointment on the faculty. Within a few years he moved up to a tenured professorship and has spent his career teaching and writing poetry there. In 1965, he published two volumes of poetry, *Corson's Inlet: A Book of Poems* and *Tape for the Turn of the Year*. *Tape* was a long, thin poem, which had been composed on an adding machine tape Ammons had placed in his typewriter on December 6 and did not remove until the tape had run out and the poem was thus "complete," with the last entry on January 10 (the poem was written as the year "turned"). The poem remained open to everything that happened or occurred to Ammons during this period, including the experience of writing the poem: it is thus a poem which is in large measure about itself.

In 1966, Ammons published *Northfield Poems*, and in 1968 his *Selected Poems*. By this time Ammons was attracting considerable notice as an important new voice in American poetry; he was awarded a Guggenheim Fellowship in 1968. When his *Collected Poems, 1951–1971* appeared in 1972, he won the National Book Award for poetry. And on publication of his long poem *Sphere: The Form of a Motion* in 1974, he received the Bollingen Prize. Later books include *The Snow Poems* (1977), *The Selected Poems, 1951–1977* (1977), *A Coast of Trees* (1981), *The Selected Poems: Expanded Edition* (1986), and *Sumerian Vistas* (1987).

Often called a transcendental poet, in the tradition of Emerson and Whitman, Ammons was asked about his religious beliefs. He said:

> My father was Baptist. My Methodist mother died singing hymns I still play on the piano. When I look at their words, I am astonished to find much that I know already written. The transcendence . . . the temptation to walk away from this world . . . much of it is there. But I am not a rememberer of poetry. I think that must be a deliberate strategy. I can't remember my own poems or anybody else's. That makes me available to my own speech all the time, like being available to take any turn along a walk. I put old poems behind me, as if I were on a walk, because I want to be available to whatever is happening here and now, to my own direct contact with things.

Pressed on his idea about transcendentalism, he added: "I try to look nature straight in the face. That is the only real instruction finally, the way to penetrate the complexes of existence on this planet, to see that the planet is spherical and that there is no possibility of life after death. Life and death intermingle and transform into each other. There's no getting off the planet in that sense."

ADDITIONAL READING

Richard Howard, *Alone with America*, 1969; Alan Holder, *A. R. Ammons*, 1978; Stuart Wright, *A. R. Ammons: A Bibliography, 1954–1979*, 1980; Harold Bloom, ed., *A. R. Ammons*, 1986; Helen Vendler, *The Music of What Happens*, 1988.

TEXTS

"Apologia pro Vita Sua" from *Collected Poems*, 1972; "Sight Seed" from *Sumerian Vistas*, 1987; remaining poems from *The Selected Poems*, 1986.

Gravelly Run

I don't know somehow it seems sufficient
to see and hear whatever coming and going is,
losing the self to the victory
    of stones and trees,
of bending sandpit lakes, crescent   5
round groves of dwarf pine:

for it is not so much to know the self
as to know it as it is known
    by galaxy and cedar cone,

as if birth had never found it
and death could never end it: 10

the swamp's slow water comes
down Gravelly Run fanning the long
    stone-held algal
hair and narrowing roils between   15
the shoulders of the highway bridge:

holly grows on the banks in the woods there,
and the cedars' gothic-clustered
    spires could make
green religion in winter bones: 20

so I look and reflect, but the air's glass
jail seals each thing in its entity:

no use to make any philosophies here:
    I see no
god in the holly, hear no song from   25
the snowbroken weeds: Hegel[1] is not the winter
yellow in the pines: the sunlight has never
heard of trees: surrendered self among
    unwelcoming forms: stranger,
hoist your burdens, get on down the road.   30

1965

Corsons Inlet[1]

I went for a walk over the dunes again this morning
to the sea,
then turned right along
    the surf

                        rounded a naked headland   5
                        and returned

    along the inlet shore:

it was muggy sunny, the wind from the sea steady and high,
crisp in the running sand,
        some breakthroughs of sun   10
    but after a bit

continuous overcast:

the walk liberating, I was released from forms,
from the perpendiculars,
        straight lines, blocks, boxes, binds   15
    of thought

---

[1]George Wilhelm Friedrich Hegel (1770–1831), German ide- | erates antithesis leading to synthesis.
alist philosopher who envisaged a world-soul developed out | [1]In southeastern New Jersey.
of and known through the dialectic logic whereby thesis gen-

into the hues, shadings, rises, flowing bends and blends
          of sight:

                    I allow myself eddies of meaning:
yield to a direction of significance   20
running
like a stream through the geography of my work:
    you can find
in my sayings
                         swerves of action   25
                    like the inlet's cutting edge:
          there are dunes of motion,
organizations of grass, white sandy paths of remembrance
in the overall wandering of mirroring mind:
but Overall is beyond me: is the sum of these events   30
I cannot draw, the ledger I cannot keep, the accounting
beyond the account:

in nature there are few sharp lines: there are areas of
primrose
      more or less dispersed;   35
disorderly orders of bayberry; between the rows
of dunes,
irregular swamps of reeds,
though not reeds alone, but grass, bayberry, yarrow, all . . .
predominantly reeds: 40

I have reached no conclusions, have erected no boundaries,
shutting out and shutting in, separating inside
          from outside: I have
          drawn no lines:
          as   45

manifold events of sand
change the dune's shape that will not be the same shape
tomorrow,

so I am willing to go along, to accept
the becoming   50
thought, to stake off no beginnings or ends, establish
          no walls:

by transitions the land falls from grassy dunes to creek
to undercreek: but there are no lines, though
      change in that transition is clear   55
      as any sharpness: but "sharpness" spread out,
allowed to occur over a wider range
than mental lines can keep:

the moon was full last night: today, low tide was low:
black shoals of mussels exposed to the risk   60
of air
and, earlier, of sun,
waved in and out with the waterline, waterline inexact,
caught always in the event of change:
      a young mottled gull stood free on the shoals   65
      and ate

to vomiting: another gull, squawking possession, cracked a crab,
picked out the entrails, swallowed the soft-shelled legs, a ruddy
turnstone[2] running in to snatch leftover bits:

risk is full: every living thing in   70
siege: the demand is life, to keep life: the small
white blacklegged egret, how beautiful, quietly stalks and spears
          the shallows, darts to shore
                    to stab—what? I couldn't
     see against the black mudflats—a frightened   75
     fiddler crab?

          the news to my left over the dunes and
reeds and bayberry clumps was
          fall: thousands of tree swallows
          gathering for flight: 80
          an order held
          in constant change: a congregation
rich with entropy: nevertheless, separable, noticeable
          as one event,
                    not chaos: preparations for   85
flight from winter,
cheet, cheet, cheet, cheet, wings rifling the green clumps,
beaks
at the bayberries
     a perception full of wind, flight, curve,   90
     sound:
     the possibility of rule as the sum of rulelessness:
the "field" of action
with moving, incalculable center:

in the smaller view, order tight with shape: 95
blue tiny flowers on a leafless weed: carapace of crab:
snail shell:
          pulsations of order
          in the bellies of minnows: orders swallowed,
broken down, transferred through membranes   100
to strengthen larger orders: but in the large view, no
lines or changeless shapes: the working in and out, together
          and against, of millions of events: this,
                    so that I make
                    no form of   105
                    formlessness:

orders as summaries, as outcomes of actions override
or in some way result, not predictably (seeing me gain
the top of a dune,
the swallows   110
could take flight—some other fields of bayberry
          could enter fall
          berryless) and there is serenity:

          no arranged terror: no forcing of image, plan,
or thought: 115

---

²A shore bird.

no propaganda, no humbling of reality to precept:

terror pervades but is not arranged, all possibilities
of escape open: no route shut, except in
　　the sudden loss of all routes:

　　　　I see narrow orders, limited tightness, but will　　　　120
not run to that easy victory:
　　　　still around the looser, wider forces work:
　　　　I will try
　　to fasten into order enlarging grasps of disorder, widening
scope, but enjoying the freedom that　　　　125
Scope eludes my grasp, that there is no finality of vision,
that I have perceived nothing completely,
　　　　that tomorrow a new walk is a new walk.

　　　　　　　　　　　　　　　　　　1965

Reflective

　　　　I found a
　　　　weed
　　　　that had a

　　　　mirror in it
　　　　and that　　　　5
　　　　mirror

　　　　looked in at
　　　　a mirror
　　　　in

　　　　me that　　　　10
　　　　had a
　　　　weed in it

　　　　　　　　　　　1966

Height

There was a hill once wanted
to become a mountain
　　　and
forces underground helped it
　　lift itself　　　　5
　　　into broad view
and noticeable height:

but the green hills around and even
some passable mountains,
　　　diminished by white,　　　　10

wanted it down
so the mountain, alone, found
   grandeur taxing and
   turned and turned
to try to be concealed: 15

oh but after the rock is
massive and high . . !
     how many centuries of rain and
ice, avalanche
and shedding shale   20
   before the dull mound
can yield to grass!

                                       1966

Apologia pro Vita Sua[1]

I started picking up the stones
throwing them into one place
and by sunrise I was going far away
for the large ones
always turning to see never lost   5
the cairn's[2] height
lengthening my radial reach:

the sun watched with deep concentration
and the heap through the hours grew
and became by nightfall   10
distinguishable from all the miles around
of slate and sand:

during the night the wind falling
turned earthward its lofty freedom and speed
and the sharp blistering sound muffled   15
toward dawn and the blanket was
drawn up over a breathless face:

even so you can see in full dawn
the ground there lifts
a foreign thing desertless in origin.   20

                                        1970

Mountain Talk

I was going along a dusty highroad
when the mountain
across the way

---

[1] "A Defense of His Own Life" (Latin), the title of a famous autobiographical treatise by the British Catholic theologian John Henry Cardinal Newman (1801–1890). [2] Mound of stones.

turned me to its silence:
oh I said how come   5
I don't know your
massive symmetry and rest:
nevertheless, said the mountain,
would you want
to be   10
lodged here with
a changeless prospect, risen
to an unalterable view:
so I went on
counting my numberless fingers.   15

1970

Cascadilla Falls[1]

I went down by Cascadilla
Falls this
evening, the
stream below the falls,
and picked up a   5
handsized stone
kidney-shaped, testicular, and

thought all its motions into it,
the 800 mph earth spin,
the 190-million-mile yearly   10
displacement around the sun,
the overriding
grand
haul

of the galaxy with the 30,000   15
mph of where
the sun's going:
thought all the interweaving
motions
into myself: dropped   20

the stone to dead rest:
the stream from other motions
broke
rushing over it:
shelterless,   25
I turned

to the sky and stood still:
oh
I do

---

[1]In Ithaca, New York, near the poet's home.

not know where I am going   30
that I can live my life
by this single creek.

                                        1970

The City Limits

When you consider the radiance, that it does not withhold
itself but pours its abundance without selection into every
nook and cranny not overhung or hidden; when you consider

that birds' bones make no awful noise against the light but
lie low in the light as in a high testimony; when you consider   5
the radiance, that it will look into the guiltiest

swervings of the weaving heart and bear itself upon them,
not flinching into disguise or darkening; when you consider
the abundance of such resource as illuminates the glow-blue

bodies and gold-skeined wings of flies swarming the dumped   10
guts of a natural slaughter or the coil of shit and in no
way winces from its storms of generosity; when you consider

that air or vacuum, snow or shale, squid or wolf, rose or lichen,
each is accepted into as much light as it will take, then
the heart moves roomier, the man stands and looks about, the   15

leaf does not increase itself above the grass, and the dark
work of the deepest cells is of a tune with May bushes
and fear lit by the breadth of such calmly turns to praise.

                                        1971

Sight Seed

When the jay caught
the cicada midair, a fluffy,
rustling beakful, the
burr-song flooded dull but
held low: the jay perched and   5
holding the prey to the branch
as if to halt
indecorous song pecked
once, a plink that did it,
but in the noticeable silence   10
proceeded at ease
and expertly to
take this, then that eye.

                                        1987

JAMES MERRILL

(b. 1926)

James Merrill belongs with those poets who insist that all the traditional techniques of poetry remain available to the modern poet. He once said, "People who talk about experimentation sound as if they thought poets set out deliberately to experiment, when in fact they haven't; they've simply recognized afterwards the newness of what they've done." He said of his own practice: "Even when I sort of slyly thought of changing to irregular line lengths I always found some way to justify them, by secret scanning and rhyme." But he added: "Now and then one enjoys a little moonwalk, some little departure from tradition. And the forms themselves seem to invite this, in our age of 'breakthroughs.' . . . One doesn't, I mean, have to be just a stolid 'formalist.' The forms, the meters and rhyme-sounds, are far too liberative for that."

Often, as critics have pointed out, one does not read far into a Merrill poem before confronting what seems a contradiction. He admitted to a "fondness for paradox" in his poems: "I suppose that early on I began to understand the relativity, even the reversibility, of truths. . . . I believe the secret lies primarily in the nature of poetry—and of science too, for that matter—and that the ability to see both ways at once isn't merely an idiosyncrasy but corresponds to how the world needs to be seen—cheerful *and* awful, opaque *and* transparent. The plus and minus signs of a vast evolving formula."

James Merrill was born into the wealthy New York family headed by Charles E. Merrill, who was one of the founders of the investment firm of Merrill, Lynch, Pierce, Fenner and Beane, one of the largest in the world. Merrill was the son of his father's second wife; soon there was to be a third wife, and the boy grew up in a "broken home," which he would later give as a title to one of his poems. Merrill attended exclusive schools, and when he was ready for college was sent to his father's alma mater, Amherst. His studies there were interrupted by two years of army service (1944–45). When Merrill told his father he wanted to become a writer, his father wrote to a professor at Amherst to ask if the work of his son was any good; assured that it was, he supported his son's decision. After his graduation in 1947, Merrill taught for a year at Bard College, and then, with the freedom that only an independent income can assure, followed his desire to see the world. He travelled throughout Europe and Asia during the 1950s.

As an adolescent, at the same time that he was feeling his first impulses to write poetry, he was also beginning to recognize his homosexuality. He was able to come to terms with it, but he felt some anguish at his parents' reaction: "They had a clear idea of what I should turn out to be, sexually, and I could see that I was going to disappoint them." In his early poetry, Merrill did not deal openly with homosexual relationships, but in his later poetry, with a shift in social attitudes, he began to treat same-sex relationships in his work with the understanding his personal experience had bestowed.

After publishing his first two volumes of poetry privately (in 1942 and 1946), his *First Poems* was brought out by Knopf in 1951. Although he tried his hand at writing novels (*The Seraglio*, 1957, and *The (Diblos) Notebook*, 1965) and drama (*The Immortal Husband*, 1956), his first love was poetry. From the very beginning, his poetry was recognized, as indicated by the prizes it won. His *Nights and Days*, published in 1966, won the National Book Award; his *Braving the Elements* (1972) won the Bollingen Prize. And in 1977, with publication of *Divine Comedies: Poems* (which contained the first part, "The Book of Ephraim," of his modern epic poem), he won the Pulitzer Prize. The second book of his epic, *Mirabell: Books of Number* (1978), was given the National Book Award.

As this list of titles suggests, in the early part of his career Merrill concentrated on shorter lyrics; in the latter part, on a long epic now finished. *Scripts for the Pageant*, the third book, appeared in 1980. Merrill also started reviewing (and revising) his early work and published *From the First Nine: Poems 1946–1976* in 1982. He commented on one unifying strand in his poetry in an interview: "Returning to those early poems *now*, obviously in the light of the completed trilogy [the epic], I've had to marvel a bit at the resemblances. It's as though after a long lapse or, as you put it, displacement of faith, I'd finally, with the trilogy, reentered the church of those original themes. The colors, elements, the magical emblems: they were the first subjects I'd found again at last."

Merrill's trilogy, a volume of 560 pages now coming to be recognized as his masterpiece, was entitled *The Changing Light at Sandover* when it was completed and published as a book in 1982. It consists of three books and a Coda: "The Book of Ephraim," "Mirabell's Books of Number," "Scripts for the Pageant," and "Coda: The Higher Keys." Clearly connecting with the lyric-epic established by Whitman as a peculiarly American form in his *Leaves of Grass*, and continued by Ezra Pound in his *Cantos*, T. S. Eliot in *The Waste Land*, Hart Crane in *The Bridge*, William Carlos Williams in *Paterson*, John Berryman in *The Dream Songs*, and Allen Ginsberg in *The Fall of America*, Merrill's *The Changing Light at Sandover* is a sequence of connected moments or episodes structured along the contours of the lives of the author and his friend David Jackson, as they have lived in the latter twentieth century in their home in Stonington, Connecticut, and gone periodically abroad for temporary stays in foreign countries (especially Greece).

The characters became numerous as the famous and imaginary dead, Ephraim and Mirabell, the angels Michael and Gabriel—even God himself—as well as Homer, W. H. Auden, Wallace Stevens, Maria Mitsotsaki, and others are called forth through the magic use of the *Ouija* board (*ouija* is French and German for "yes"), a spiritualist device for communicating with the world beyond. Merrill has used all the figures on the board itself to structure his poem: Book I follows the letters of the alphabet; Book II, the digits from 0 to 9; and Book III, the tripartite "Yes & No," the "irreducible language," as Charles Molesworth has noted, of "assertion, qualification, and denial." As Merrill and his friends place their hands on a movable pointer, they are able to speak with characters on the "other side," who move the pointer to letters, numbers, or "Yes," "&," and "No." The poem is serious and witty by turns, alternating between moments of lyric intensity and narrative expansiveness. Merrill has remarked of it: "It is not so much a visionary poem as a revisionary one."

Since completing his trilogy, Merrill has published additional volumes of poetry, *Late Settings* (1985) and *The Inner Room* (1989), and a volume of prose, *Recitative* (1986). Most critics now agree that Merrill's is a major voice in American literature. His revised lyric poems and his epic trilogy have been at hand for too short a time for comprehensive understanding and assessment. Merrill himself has commented on the "meaning" of his work: "I've always been oddly comforted by the notion that, no matter how well I think I know what I've said in a poem, it might have a whole dimension that's hidden from me—by the very nature of art." It seems likely that Merrill's reputation will see a steady growth in the future, like the late-developing reputations of writers he admires and who influenced him—the French memoirist-novelist Marcel Proust and the American poet Wallace Stevens.

ADDITIONAL READING

David Kalstone, *Five Temperaments: Elizabeth Bishop, Robert Lowell, James Merrill, Adrienne Rich, John Ashbery*, 1977; Ross Labrie, *James Merrill*, 1982; David Lehman and Charles Berger, eds., *James Merrill: Essays in Criticism*, 1983; Judith Moffett, *James Merrill: An Introduction to the Poetry*, 1984; Stephen Yenser, *The Consuming Myth: The Work of James Merrill*, 1987.

TEXTS

"Samos" from *The Changing Light at Sandover*, 1982; remaining poems from *From the First Nine: Poems 1946–1976*, 1982.

An Urban Convalescence

Out for a walk, after a week in bed,
I find them tearing up part of my block
And, chilled through, dazed and lonely, join the dozen
In meek attitudes, watching a huge crane
Fumble luxuriously in the filth of years.   5
Her jaws dribble rubble. An old man
Laughs and curses in her brain,
Bringing to mind the close of *The White Goddess*.[1]

As usual in New York, everything is torn down
Before you have had time to care for it.   10
Head bowed, at the shrine of noise, let me try to recall
What building stood here. Was there a building at all?
I have lived on this same street for a decade.

Wait. Yes. Vaguely a presence rises
Some five floors high, of shabby stone   15
— Or am I confusing it with another one
In another part of town, or of the world? —
And over its lintel into focus vaguely
Misted with blood (my eyes are shut)
A single garland sways, stone fruit, stone leaves,   20
Which years of grit had etched until it thrust
Roots down, even into the poor soil of my seeing.
When did the garland become part of me?
I ask myself, amused almost,
Then shiver once from head to toe,   25

Transfixed by a particular cheap engraving of garlands
Bought for a few francs long ago,
All calligraphic tendril and cross-hatched rondure,
Ten years ago, and crumpled up to stanch
Boughs dripping, whose white gestures filled a cab,   30
And thought of neither then nor since.
Also, to clasp them, the small, red-nailed hand
Of no one I can place. Wait. No. Her name, her features

---

[1] *The White Goddess: A Historical Grammar of Poetic Myth* (1948), by British poet Robert Graves (1895–1985), presenting the thesis that poets have traditionally derived their primal inspiration from the Moon (or White) Goddess, the eternal female. When they replace her with a male muse (God or mon- arch), she exacts her vengeance. Merrill appears to have in mind a specific image in a poem Graves placed at the close of *The White Goddess*: she will appear as "A gaunt, red-legged crane," lunging her "beak down like a spear" (cf. the mechanical crane Merrill introduced in line 4).

Lie toppled underneath that year's fashions.
The words she must have spoken, setting her face   35
To fluttering like a veil, I cannot hear now,
Let alone understand.

So that I am already on the stair,
As it were, of where I lived,
When the whole structure shudders at my tread   40
And soundlessly collapses, filling
The air with motes of stone.
Onto the still erect building next door
Are pressed levels and hues —
Pocked rose, streaked greens, brown whites.   45
Who drained the pousse-café?[2]
Wires and pipes, snapped off at the roots, quiver.

Well, that is what life does. I stare
A moment longer, so. And presently
The massive volume of the world   50
Closes again.

Upon that book I swear
To abide by what it teaches:
Gospels of ugliness and waste,
Of towering voids, of soiled gusts,   55
Of a shrieking to be faced
Full into, eyes astream with cold —

With cold?
All right then. With self-knowledge.

Indoors at last, the pages of *Time* are apt   60
To open, and the illustrated mayor of New York,
Given a glimpse of how and where I work,
To note yet one more house that can be scrapped.

Unwillingly I picture
My walls weathering in the general view.   65
It is not even as though the new
Buildings did very much for architecture.

Suppose they did. The sickness of our time requires
That these as well be blasted in their prime.
You would think the simple fact of having lasted   70
Threatened our cities like mysterious fires.

There are certain phrases which to use in a poem
Is like rubbing silver with quicksilver. Bright
But facile, the glamour deadens overnight.
For instance, how "the sickness of our time"   75

Enhances, then debases, what I feel.
At my desk I swallow in a glass of water

---

[2]An after-dinner drink made up of vari-colored liqueurs
poured so as to remain in layers in the glass.

No longer cordial, scarcely wet, a pill
They had told me not to take until much later.

With the result that back into my imagination   80
The city glides, like cities seen from the air,
Mere smoke and sparkle to the passenger
Having in mind another destination

Which now is not that honey-slow descent
Of the Champs-Elysées,[3] her hand in his,   85
But the dull need to make some kind of house
Out of the life lived, out of the love spent.

                                                        1962

The Water Hyacinth

When I was four or so
I used to read aloud
To you—I mean, recite
Stories both of us knew
By heart, the book held close   5
To even then nearsighted
Eyes. It was morning. You,
Still in your nightgown
Over cold tea, would nod
Approval. Once I caught   10
A gay note in your quiet:
The book was upside down.

Now all is upside down.
I sit while you babble.
I watch your sightless face   15
Jerked swiftly here and there,
Set in a puzzled frown.
Your face! It is no more yours
Than its reflected double
Bobbing on scummed water.   20
Other days, the long pure
Sobs break from a choked source
Nobody here would dare
Fathom, even if able.

With you no longer able,   25
I tried to keep apart,
At first, or to set right
The stories you would tell.
The European trip,
The fire of 1908—   30
I could reel them off in sleep,
Given a phrase to start;

---

[3] A fashionable boulevard in the center of Paris.

Chimneys of kerosene
Lamps only you could clean
Because your hands were small . . .   35
I have them all by heart

But cannot now find heart
To hinder them from growing
Together, wrong, absurd.
Do as you must, poor stranger.   40
There is no surer craft
To take you where you are going
—A story I have heard
And shall over and over
Till you are indeed gone.   45
Last night the mockingbird
Wept and laughed, wept and laughed,
Telling it to the moon.

Your entire honeymoon,
A ride in a rowboat   50
On the St. Johns River,[1]
Took up an afternoon.
And by that time, of course,
The water hyacinth
Had come here from Japan,[2]   55
A mauve and rootless guest
Thirsty for life, afloat
With you on the broad span
It would in sixty years
So vividly congest.   60

1962

Charles on Fire

Another evening we sprawled about discussing
Appearances. And it was the consensus
That while uncommon physical good looks
Continued to launch one, as before, in life
(Among its vaporous eddies and false calms),   5
Still, as one of us said into his beard,
"Without your intellectual and spiritual
Values, man, you are sunk." No one but squared
The shoulders of his own unloveliness.
Long-suffering Charles, having cooked and served the meal,   10
Now brought out little tumblers finely etched
He filled with amber liquor and then passed.
"Say," said the same young man, "in Paris, France,
They do it this way"—bounding to his feet
And touching a lit match to our host's full glass.   15
A blue flame, gentle, beautiful, came, went

---

[1]In northeast Florida.
[2]Imported from Japan at the turn of the century, the water
hyacinth has grown prolifically, choking the waters.

Above the surface. In a hush that fell
We heard the vessel crack. The contents drained
As who should step down from a crystal coach.
Steward of spirits, Charles's glistening hand   20
All at once gloved itself in eeriness.
The moment passed. He made two quick sweeps and
Was flesh again. "It couldn't matter less,"
He said, but with a shocked, unconscious glance
Into the mirror. Finding nothing changed,   25
He filled a fresh glass and sank down among us.

                                                    1966

The Broken Home

Crossing the street,
I saw the parents and the child
At their window, gleaming like fruit
With evening's mild gold leaf.

In a room on the floor below,   5
Sunless, cooler—a brimming
Saucer of wax, marbly and dim—
I have lit what's left of my life.

I have thrown out yesterday's milk
And opened a book of maxims.   10
The flame quickens. The word stirs.

Tell me, tongue of fire,
That you and I are as real
At least as the people upstairs.

My father,[1] who had flown in World War I,   15
Might have continued to invest his life
In cloud banks well above Wall Street and wife.
But the race was run below, and the point was to win.

Too late now, I make out in his blue gaze
(Through the smoked glass of being thirty-six)   20
The soul eclipsed by twin black pupils, sex
And business; time was money in those days.

Each thirteenth year he married. When he died
There were already several chilled wives
In sable orbit—rings, cars, permanent waves.   25
We'd felt him warming up for a green bride.

He could afford it. He was "in his prime"
At three score ten. But money was not time.

---

[1]Merrill's father, Charles E. Merrill, was a founder of the Wall
Street investment firm of Merrill, Lynch, Pierce, Fenner and
Beane.

When my parents were younger this was a popular act:
A veiled woman would leap from an electric, wine-dark car   30
To the steps of no matter what—the Senate or the Ritz Bar—
And bodily, at newsreel speed, attack

No matter whom—Al Smith or José Maria Sert
Or Clemenceau[2]—veins standing out on her throat
As she yelled *War mongerer! Pig! Give us the vote!*,   35
And would have to be hauled away in her hobble skirt.

What had the man done? Oh, made history.
Her business (he had implied) was giving birth,
Tending the house, mending the socks.

Always that same old story—   40
Father Time and Mother Earth,
A marriage on the rocks.

One afternoon, red, satyr-thighed
Michael, the Irish setter, head
Passionately lowered, led   45
The child I was to a shut door. Inside,

Blinds beat sun from the bed.
The green-gold room throbbed like a bruise.
Under a sheet, clad in taboos
Lay whom we sought, her hair undone, outspread,   50

And of a blackness found, if ever now, in old
Engravings where the acid bit.
I must have needed to touch it
Or the whiteness—was she dead?
Her eyes flew open, startled strange and cold.   55
The dog slumped to the floor. She reached for me. I fled.

Tonight they have stepped out onto the gravel.
The party is over. It's the fall
Of 1931. They love each other still.

She: Charlie, I can't stand the pace.   60
He: Come on, honey—why, you'll bury us all!

A lead soldier guards my windowsill:
Khaki rifle, uniform, and face.
Something in me grows heavy, silvery, pliable.

How intensely people used to feel!   65
Like metal poured at the close of a proletarian novel,
Refined and glowing from the crucible,
I see those two hearts, I'm afraid,
Still. Cool here in the graveyard of good and evil,
they are even so to be honored and obeyed.   70

---

[2]Alfred E. Smith (1873–1944), governor of New York who ran on the Democratic ticket for president in 1928; Sert (1874–1945), Spanish painter famous for his baroque murals in buildings around the world, including the Waldorf Astoria in New York; Georges Clemenceau (1841–1929), French premier during World War I and leader of the French delegation to the Paris Peace conference in 1919 (visited the United States in 1922).

. . . Obeyed, at least, inversely. Thus
I rarely buy a newspaper, or vote.
To do so, I have learned, is to invite
The tread of a stone guest within my house.[3]

Shooting this rusted bolt, though, against him,   75
I trust I am no less time's child than some
Who on the heath impersonate Poor Tom[4]
Or on the barricades risk life and limb.

Nor do I try to keep a garden, only
An avocado in a glass of water —   80
Roots pallid, gemmed with air. And later,

When the small gilt leaves have grown
Fleshy and green, I let them die, yes, yes,
And start another. I am earth's no less.

A child, a red dog roam the corridors,   85
Still, of the broken home. No sound. The brilliant
Rag runners halt before wide-open doors.
My old room! Its wallpaper — cream, medallioned
With pink and brown — brings back the first nightmares,
Long summer colds, and Emma, sepia-faced,   90
Perspiring over broth carried upstairs
Aswim with golden fats I could not taste.

The real house became a boarding school.
Under the ballroom ceiling's allegory
Someone at last may actually be allowed   95
To learn something; or, from my window, cool
With the unstiflement of the entire story,
Watch a red setter stretch and sink in cloud.

1966

Lost in Translation

FOR RICHARD HOWARD[1]

Diese Tage, die leer dir scheinen
und wertlos für das All,
haben Wurzeln zwischen den Steinen
und trinken dort überall.[2]

A card table in the library stands ready
To receive the puzzle which keeps never coming.
Daylight shines in or lamplight down
Upon the tense oasis of green felt.

---

[3]In some works of art, such as Mozart's *Don Giovanni* (1787), stone statues come to life as avenging characters.
[4]In William Shakespeare's *King Lear*, Gloucester's son Edgar, disowned by his father, pretends madness on the heath and refers to himself as Tom ("poor Tom's acold").
[1]American writer (b. 1929) and translator from the French.

[2]"These days, which seem empty and entirely worthless to you, have roots between the stones and drink from everywhere" (German); from a translation into German by the Austrian poet Rainer Maria Rilke (1875–1926) of "Palme," by the French poet Paul Valéry (1871–1945). See ll. 32–35 below.

Full of unfulfillment, life goes on,   5
Mirage arisen from time's trickling sands
Or fallen piecemeal into place:
German lesson, picnic, see-saw, walk
With the collie who "did everything but talk"—
Sour windfalls of the orchard back of us.   10
A summer without parents in the puzzle,
Or should be. But the boy, day after day,
Writes in his Line-a-Day *No puzzle*.

He's in love, at least. His French Mademoiselle,
In real life a widow since Verdun,[3]   15
Is stout, plain, carrot-haired, devout.
She prays for him, as does a curé in Alsace,
Sews costumes for his marionettes,
Helps him to keep behind the scene
Whose sidelit goosegirl, speaking with his voice,   20
Plays Guinevere as well as Gunmoll Jean.[4]
Or else at bedtime in his tight embrace
Tells him her own French hopes, her German fears,
Her—but what more is there to tell?
Having known grief and hardship, Mademoiselle   25
Knows little more. Her languages. Her place.
Noon coffee. Mail. The watch that also waited
Pinned to her heart, poor gold, throws up its hands—
No puzzle! Steaming bitterness
Her sugars draw pops back into his mouth, translated: 30
"Patience, chéri. Geduld, mein Schatz."[5]
(Thus, reading Valéry the other evening
And seeming to recall a Rilke version of "Palme,"[6]
That sunlit paradigm whereby the tree
Taps a sweet wellspring of authority,   35
The hour came back. Patience dans l'azur.
Geduld im . . . Himmelblau?[7] Mademoiselle.)

Out of the blue, as promised, of a New York
Puzzle-rental shop the puzzle comes—
A superior one, containing a thousand hand-sawn,   40
Sandal-scented pieces. Many take
Shapes known already—the craftsman's repertoire
Nice in its limitation—from other puzzles:
Witch on broomstick, ostrich, hourglass,
Even (surely not just in retrospect)   45
An inchling, innocently branching palm.
These can be put aside, made stories of
While Mademoiselle spreads out the rest face-up,
Herself excited as a child; or questioned
Like incoherent faces in a crowd,   50
Each with its scrap of highly colored
Evidence the Law must piece together.

---

[3]I.e., the French governess ("Mademoiselle") lost her husband at the battle at Verdun in the First World War.
[4]Guinevere was the wife of King Arthur of the Round Table in medieval legend and poetry; Gunmoll Jean, probably some heroine attached to a gangster in imagination or some "popular culture" source.
[5]"Patience, my dear. Patience, my dear" (French and German).
[6]See footnote 2.
[7]"Patience in the blue. Patience in the blue" (French and German); phrase from Rilke's translation into German of Valéry's French.

Sky-blue ostrich? Likely story.
Mauve of the witch's cloak white, severed fingers
Pluck? Detain her. The plot thickens   55
As all at once two pieces interlock.

Mademoiselle does borders—(Not so fast.
A London dusk, December last.
Chatter silenced in the library
This grown man reenters, wearing grey.   60
A medium. All except him have seen
Panel slid back, recess explored,
An object at once unique and common
Displayed, planted in a plain tole
Casket the subject now considers   65
Through shut eyes, saying in effect:
"Even as voices reach me vaguely
A dry saw-shriek drowns them out,
Some loud machinery—a lumber mill?
Far uphill in the fir forest   70
Trees tower, tense with shock,
Groaning and cracking as they crash groundward.
But hidden here is a freak fragment
Of a pattern complex in appearance only.
What it seems to show is superficial   75
Next to that long-term lamination
Of hazard and craft, the karma[8] that has
Made it matter in the first place.
Plywood, Piece of a puzzle." Applause
Acknowledged by an opening of lids   80
Upon the thing itself. A sudden dread—
But to go back. All this lay years ahead.)

Mademoiselle does borders. Straight-edge pieces
Align themselves with earth or sky
In twos and threes, naive cosmogonists[9]   85
Whose views clash. Nomad inlanders meanwhile
Begin to cluster where the totem
Of a certain vibrant egg-yolk yellow
Or pelt of what emerging animal
Acts on the straggler like a trumpet call   90
To form a more sophisticated unit.
By suppertime two ragged wooden clouds
Have formed. In one, a Sheik with beard
And flashing sword hilt (he is all but finished)
Steps forward on a tiger skin. A piece   95
Snaps shut, and fangs gnash out at us!
In the second cloud—they gaze from cloud to cloud
With marked if undecipherable feeling—
Most of a dark-eyed woman veiled in mauve
Is being helped down from her camel (kneeling)   100
By a small backward-looking slave or page-boy
(Her son, thinks Mademoiselle mistakenly)
Whose feet have not been found. But lucky finds

---

[8]Fate, brought about by one's action (Hinduism).
[9]Theorists on the origins and development of the universe.

In the last minutes before bed
Anchor both factions to the scene's limits   105
And, by so doing, orient
Them eye to eye across the green abyss.
The yellow promises, oh bliss,
To be in time a sumptuous tent.

Puzzle begun I write in the day's space,   110
Then, while she bathes, peek at Mademoiselle's
Page to the curé: ". . . cette innocent mère,
Ce pauvre enfant, que deviendront-ils?"[10]
Her azure script is curlicued like pieces
Of the puzzle she will be telling him about.   115
(Fearful incuriosity of childhood!
"Tu as l'accent allemand,"[11] said Dominique.
Indeed. Mademoiselle was only French by marriage.
Child of an English mother, a remote
Descendant of the great explorer Speke,[12]   120
And Prussian father. No one knew. I heard it
Long afterwards from her nephew, a UN[13]
Interpreter. His matter-of-fact account
Touched old strings. My poor Mademoiselle,
With 1939 about to shake   125
This world[14] where "each was the enemy, each the friend"
To its foundations, kept, though signed in blood,
Her peace a shameful secret to the end.)
"Schlaf wohl, chéri."[15] Her kiss. Her thumb
Crossing my brow against the dreams to come.   130

This World that shifts like sand, its unforeseen
Consolidations and elate routine,
Whose Potentate had lacked a retinue?
Lo! it assembles on the shrinking Green.

Gunmetal-skinned or pale, all plumes and scars,   135
Of Vassalage the noblest avatars — [16]
The very coffee-bearer in his vair
Vest is a swart Highness, next to ours.

Kef[17] easing Boredom, and iced syrups, thirst,
In guessed-at glooms old wives who know the worst   140
Outsweat that virile fiction of the New:
"Insh'Allah,[18] he will tire — " " — or kill her first!"

(Hardly a proper subject for the Home,
Work of — dear Richard, I shall let *you* comb
Archives and learned journals for his name —   145
A minor lion attending on Gérôme.[19])

---

[10]"This innocent mother, this poor child, what will become of them?" (French).
[11]"You have a German accent" (French).
[12]John Hanning Speke (1827–1864), English explorer of Africa.
[13]The United Nations.
[14]I.e., the outbreak of the Second World War with the German invasion of Poland.
[15]"Sleep well, dear" (German and French).
[16]I.e., of slavery the noblest of examples.
[17]Narcotic made from hemp leaves.
[18]"As Allah wills."
[19]Jean-Léon Gérôme (1824–1904), French painter.

While, thick as Thebes[20] whose presently complete
Gates close behind them, Houri and Afreet[21]
Both claim the Page. He wonders whom to serve,
And what his duties are, and where his feet,   150

And if we'll find, as some before us did,
That piece of Distance deep in which lies hid
Your tiny apex sugary with sun,
Eternal Triangle, Great Pyramid!

Then Sky alone is left, a hundred blue   155
Fragments in revolution, with no clue
To where a Niche will open. Quite a task,
Putting together Heaven, yet we do.

It's done. Here under the table all along
Were those missing feet. It's done.   160

The dog's tail thumping. Mademoiselle sketching
Costumes for a coming harem drama
To star the goosegirl. All too soon the swift
Dismantling. Lifted by two corners,
The puzzle hung together—and did not.   165
Irresistibly a populace
Unstitched of its attachments, rattled down.
Power went to pieces as the witch
Slithered easily from Virtue's gown.
The blue held out for time, but crumbled, too.   170
The city had long fallen, and the tent,
A separating sauce mousseline,[22]
Been swept away. Remained the green
On which the grown-ups gambled. A green dusk.
First lightning bugs. Last glow of west   175
Green in the false eyes of (coincidence)
Our mangy tiger safe on his bared hearth.

Before the puzzle was boxed and readdressed
To the puzzle shop in the mid-Sixties,
Something tells me that one piece contrived   180
To stay in the boy's pocket. How do I know?
I know because so many later puzzles
Had missing pieces—Maggie Teyte's[23] high notes
Gone at the war's end, end of the vogue for collies,
A house torn down; and hadn't Mademoiselle   185
Kept back her pitiful bit of truth as well?
I've spent the last days, furthermore,
Ransacking Athens for that translation of "Palme."
Neither the Goethehaus nor the National Library
Seems able to unearth it. Yet I can't   190
Just be imagining. I've seen it. Know
How much of the sun-ripe original
Felicity Rilke made himself forego

---

[20]Pun on "thick as thieves"; Thebes was an ancient city in Upper Egypt which figured in Greek legend and mythology.
[21]Houri: beautiful virgin provided muslims in paradise;
Afreet: an evil demon or monster.
[22]Frothy sauce made with whipped cream.
[23]British soprano (1888–1976), opera star.

(Who loved French words — verger, mûr, parfumer[24])
In order to render its underlying sense.   195
Know already in that tongue of his
What Pains, what monolithic Truths
Shadow stanza to stanza's symmetrical
Rhyme-rutted pavement. Know that ground plan left
Sublime and barren, where the warm Romance   200
Stone by stone faded, cooled; the fluted nouns
Made taller, lonelier than life
By leaf-carved capitals in the afterglow.
The owlet umlaut[25] peeps and hoots
Above the open vowel. And after rain   205
A deep reverberation fills with stars.

Lost, is it, buried? One more missing piece?

But nothing's lost. Or else: all is translation
And every bit of us is lost in it
(Or found — I wander through the ruin of S[26]   210
Now and then, wondering at the peacefulness)
And in that loss a self-effacing tree,
Color of context, imperceptibly
Rustling with its angel, turns the waste
To shade and fiber, milk and memory.   215

                                                        1976

from The Changing Light at Sandover

Samos[1]

And still, at sea all night, we had a sense
Of sunrise, golden oil poured upon water,
Soothing its heave, letting the sleeper sense
What inborn, amniotic homing sense[2]
Was ferrying him — now through the dream-fire   5
In which (it has been felt) each human sense
Burns, now through ship's radar's cool sixth sense,
Or mere unerring starlight — to an island.
Here we were. The twins of Sea and Land,
Up and about for hours — hues, cries, scents —   10
Had placed at eye level a single light
Croissant:[3] the harbor glazed with warm pink light.

Fire-wisps were weaving a string bag of light
For sea stones. Their astounding color sense!
Porphyry, alabaster, chrysolite   15
Translucences that go dead in daylight

---

[24]"Orchard, ripe, to scent" (French).
[25]German accent mark (¨) placed over a vowel, indicating a change in the vowel sound.
[26]Initial of former acquaintance, friend, or lover.
[1]This poem opens "&" in "Scripts for the Pageant." Samos is one of the Greek Islands in the Aegean Sea, birthplace of the philosopher Pythagoras (sixth century B.C.), who discovered the mathematical ratios of the musical scale and interpreted the world through numbers. The stanzaic pattern used in the poem follows (with variations) that of the *canzone* by the Italian national poet Dante Alighieri (1265–1321). Note the recurrence (with variations) of "air," "land" (earth), "fire," "water," "light," and "sense" as end words throughout.
[2]I.e., a sense of being carried back to the prebirth state (in the amniotic fluid), a paradise-like state.
[3]"Crescent" (French).

Asked only the quick dip in holy water
For the saint of cell on cell to come alight—
Illuminated crystals thinking light,
Refracting it, the gray prismatic fire   20
Or yellow-gray of sea's dilute sapphire . . .
Wavelengths daily deeply score the leit-
Motifs[4] of Loom and Wheel upon this land.
To those who listen, it's the Promised Land.[5]

A little spin today? Dirt roads inland   25
Jounce and revolve in a nerve-jangling light,
Doing the ancient dances of the land
Where, gnarled as olive trees that shag the land
With silver, old men—their two-bladed sense
Of spendthrift poverty, the very land   30
Being, if not loaf, tomb—superbly land
Upright on the downbeat. We who water
The local wine, which "drinks itself" like water,
Clap for more, cry out to *be* this island
Licked all over by a white, salt fire,   35
Be noon's pulsing ember raked by fire,

Know nothing, now, but Earth, Air, Water, Fire![6]
For once out of the frying pan to land
Within their timeless, everlasting fire![7]
Blood's least red monocle, O magnifier   40
Of the great Eye that sees by its own light
More pictures in "the world's enchanted fire"
Than come and go in any shrewd crossfire
Upon the page, of syllable and sense,
We want unwilled excursions and ascents,   45
Crave the upward-rippling rungs of fire,
The outward-rippling rings (enough!) of water . . .
(Now some details—how else will this hold water?)

Our room's three flights above the whitewashed water-
front where Pythagoras was born. A fire   50
Escape of sky-blue iron leads down to water.
Yachts creak on mirror berths, and over water
Voices from Sweden or Somaliland
Tell how this or that one crossed the water
To Ephesus,[8] came back with toilet water   55
And a two kilo box of Turkish delight[9]
—Trifles. Yet they shine with such pure light
In memory, even they, that the eyes water.
As with the setting sun, or innocence,
Do things that fade especially make sense?   60

---

[4]Recurrent pattern or theme in a musical or literary work; cf. the comment by the poet Stanley Kunitz on Merrill's vision of the "supreme awareness that we can have" that "all existence is a continuous tissue, a gigantic web of interconnected filaments, so delicately woven that if touched at any point the whole web trembles."
[5]I.e., Canaan, the land promised by God to Abraham and the Israelites; Samos is thus presented in the poem as paradisiacal.
[6]The basic elements of the ancient and medieval world.

[7]Allusion to the Pythagorean doctrine of the transmigration of souls. Pythagoras believed that the soul was doomed to reincarnation as human, animal, or plant, until it achieved an ideal purity; in the Pythagorean cosmology, the seed contained elements of the fire which was the essence and center of the cosmos to which the soul returned on attaining purification.
[8]Ancient Greek city.
[9]Nougat candy.

> Samos. We keep trying to make sense
> Of what we can. Not souls of the first water—
> Although we've put on airs, and taken fire—
> We shall be dust of quite another land
> Before the seeds here planted come to light.   65

1980, 1982

FRANK O'HARA
(1926–1966)

In "Statements on Poetics" written for Donald M. Allen's *New American Poetry*, published in 1960, Frank O'Hara said:

> What is happening to me, allowing for lies and exaggerations which I try to avoid, goes into my poems. I don't think my experiences are clarified or made beautiful for myself or anyone else, they are just there in whatever form I can find them. What is clear to me in my work is probably obscure to others, and vice versa. My formal "stance" is found at the crossroads where what I know and can't get meets what is left of that I know and can bear without hatred. I dislike a great deal of contemporary poetry—all of the past you read is usually quite great—but it is a useful thorn to have in one's side.

Frank O'Hara was born in Baltimore in 1926, but the family moved to Grafton, Massachusetts, in 1927. O'Hara attended school in Worcester, Massachusetts, and entered the navy in 1944 in time to serve on a destroyer in the South Pacific during the Second World War. After his discharge in 1946, O'Hara went to Harvard, where he came to know John Ashbery, a fellow student. Changing his major from music to English, he began to publish poems and stories in the *Harvard Advocate*. After taking his B.A. at Harvard, O'Hara completed an M.A. in 1951 at the University of Michigan; while there, he won a Hopwood Award in creative writing for a play. In the early 1950s, he began to write art reviews in New York while holding a clerk's job behind the sales counter at the Museum of Modern Art, and soon he was an editorial assistant on *Art News*. He ended up an associate curator at the museum.

During the 1950s and 1960s, O'Hara followed two careers. He continuously wrote poetry, publishing volumes now and then. And he worked as an art critic, writing reviews, essays, and books. His first book of poems, *A City Winter and Other Poems*, appeared in 1952, and his second, *Meditations in an Emergency*, in 1957. He published a work of art criticism, *Jackson Pollock*, in 1959. In 1960, he was chosen to appear in the important anthology *The New American Poetry*. Some fifteen of his poems appeared, and his poetry became widely known for the first time. His volumes of poems published in the 1960s include *Second Avenue* (1960), *Lunch Poems* (1964), and *Love Poems (Tentative Title)* (1965). He was killed in a freak accident in 1966 when he was run over by a dune buggy on Fire Island, a summer resort off Long Island.

At the time of his death, no one was aware of how many poems he had written because his method was to write rapidly on any available scrap of paper and to lay the poem aside in a drawer or box. His *Collected Poems*, edited in 1971 by Donald Allen, ran to almost 600 pages. His *Early Writing* (1977) and *Poems Retrieved* (1977), also edited by Allen, contained additional poems that had been passed by or overlooked for the *Collected Poems*.

O'Hara was a central figure in the group that came to be known as the "New York Poets," and that included John Ashbery, Kenneth Koch, James Schuyler, and others. The writers were closely allied with a group of artists in New York, including Willem de Kooning, Franz Kline, Jackson Pollock, Robert Motherwell, Helen Frankenthaler, Larry Rivers, and Michael Goldberg. O'Hara became acquainted with a number of these poets and artists while still a student at Harvard. His early poetry tended to the surrealistic, with incongruous images juxtaposed in startling ways, as in the opening of "The Muse Considered as a Demon Lover":

> Once at midnight in the fall
> I woke with a shout at a light!
>
> it burned all over the sheets, the
> walls were panting with excitement!
>
> a picture fell down! and a collage
> peeled into a forest floor! It was
>
> an angel! was I invited to a butterfly
> ball? did it want to be in my movie?

Gradually O'Hara's style relaxed, his imagery became less bizarre and his poems more accessible. In his "Personism: A Manifesto," written semi-tongue-in-cheek, O'Hara said: "Too many poets act like a middle-aged mother trying to get her kids to eat too much cooked meat, and potatoes with drippings (tears). I don't give a damn whether they eat or not. Forced feeding leads to excessive thinness (effete). Nobody should experience anything they don't need to, if they don't need poetry bully for them, I like the movies too. And after all, only Whitman and Crane and Williams, of the American poets, are better than the movies."

A typical O'Hara poem presents the matter-of-fact events of his minor experiences, going to lunch, taking a stroll, having a coke with a friend. His love poems are frankly homosexual, written out of the immediacy of encounter and as casual in the presentation of factual detail as in the other poems. In "Adieu to Norman, Bon Jour to Joan and Jean-Paul," he opens:

> It is 12:10 in New York and I am wondering
> if I will finish this in time to meet Norman for lunch
> ah lunch! I think I am going crazy
> what with my terrible hangover and the weekend coming up.

The poems reveal private moments, but have little in common with the confessional mode. The voice is that of one self-assured in his identity, content with the life that flows by and the recurrences and surprises it brings—all shared with the reader of his poems.

ADDITIONAL READING

Art Chronicles 1954–1966, 1975; *Selected Plays*, 1978.

Marjorie G. Perloff, *Frank O'Hara, Poet among Painters*, 1977; Bill Berkson and Joe LeSueur, eds., *A Homage to Frank O'Hara*, 1978; Alan Feldman, *Frank O'Hara*, 1979; Alexander Smith, Jr., *Frank O'Hara: A Comprehensive Bibliography*, 1979; Norman Finkelstein, *The Utopian Movement in Contemporary American Poetry*, 1988.

TEXT

The Selected Poems of Frank O'Hara, ed. Donald M. Allen, 1974.

Poem

The eager note on my door said "Call me,
call when you get in!" so I quickly threw
a few tangerines into my overnight bag,
straightened my eyelids and shoulders, and

headed straight for the door. It was autumn   5
by the time I got around the corner, oh all
unwilling to be either pertinent or bemused, but
the leaves were brighter than grass on the sidewalk!

Funny, I thought, that the lights are on this late
and the hall door open; still up at this hour, a   10
champion jai-alai[1] player like himself? Oh fie!
for shame! What a host, so zealous! And he was

there in the hall, flat on a sheet of blood that
ran down the stairs. I did appreciate it. There are few
hosts who so thoroughly prepare to greet a guest   15
only casually invited, and that several months ago.

1950   1950, 1952

Poem

At night Chinamen jump
on Asia with a thump

while in our willful way
we, in secret, play

affectionate games and bruise   5
our knees like China's shoes.

The birds push apples through
grass the moon turns blue,

these apples roll beneath
our buttocks like a heath   10

full of Chinese thrushes
flushed from China's bushes.

As we love at night
birds sing out of sight,

Chinese rhythms beat   15
through us in our heat,

---

[1]A game resembling handball, played on a three-walled court
with two or four players, with wicker baskets strapped to
their wrists.

the apples and the birds
move us like soft words,

we couple in the grace
of that mysterious race.   20

1950   *1952*

A Step Away from Them

It's my lunch hour, so I go
for a walk among the hum-colored
cabs. First, down the sidewalk
where laborers feed their dirty
glistening torsos sandwiches   5
and Coca-Cola, with yellow helmets
on. They protect them from falling
bricks, I guess. Then onto the
avenue where skirts are flipping
above heels and blow up over   10
grates. The sun is hot, but the
cabs stir up the air. I look
at bargains in wristwatches. There
are cats playing in sawdust.
                                On   15
to Times Square, where the sign[1]
blows smoke over my head, and higher
the waterfall pours lightly. A
Negro stands in a doorway with a
toothpick, languorously agitating.   20
A blonde chorus girl clicks: he
smiles and rubs his chin. Everything
suddenly honks: it is 12:40 of
a Thursday.
                    Neon in daylight is a   25
great pleasure, as Edwin Denby[2] would
write, as are light bulbs in daylight.
I stop for a cheeseburger at JULIET'S
CORNER. Giulietta Masina, wife of
Federico Fellini, *è bell' attrice*.[3]   30
And chocolate malted. A lady in
foxes on such a day puts her poodle
in a cab.
                    There are several Puerto
Ricans on the avenue today, which   35
makes it beautiful and warm. First
Bunny died, then John Latouche,
then Jackson Pollock.[4] But is the

---

[1] A large billboard advertising cigarettes with a hole emitting smoke-like steam.
[2] A poet, dance critic, and friend.
[3] "[She] is a beautiful actress" (Italian). Among Fellini's films, she starred in *La Strada* (1954) and *Nights of Cabiria* (1956).
[4] Bunny Lang (1924–1956), poet; John Latouche (1917–1956), a writer of lyrics for musicals; and Pollock (1912–1956), action painter—all friends of O'Hara.

earth as full as life was full, of them?
And one has eaten and one walks,   40
past the magazines with nudes
and the posters for BULLFIGHT and
the Manhattan Storage Warehouse,
which they'll soon tear down. I
used to think they had the Armory   45
Show[5] there.
                  A glass of papaya juice
and back to work. My heart is in my
pocket, it is Poems by Pierre Reverdy.[6]

1956   *1957, 1964*

The Day Lady[1] Died

It is 12:20 in New York a Friday
three days after Bastille day,[2] yes
it is 1959 and I go get a shoeshine
because I will get off the 4:19 in Easthampton[3]
at 7:15 and then go straight to dinner   5
and I don't know the people who will feed me

I walk up the muggy street beginning to sun
and have a hamburger and a malted and buy
an ugly NEW WORLD WRITING to see what the poets
in Ghana are doing these days   10
                              I go on to the bank
and Miss Stillwagon (first name Linda I once heard)
doesn't even look up my balance for once in her life
and in the GOLDEN GRIFFIN[4] I get a little Verlaine
for Patsy with drawings by Bonnard[5] although I do   15
think of Hesiod,[6] trans. Richmond Lattimore or
Brendan Behan's new play or *Le Balcon* or *Les Nègres*
of Genet,[7] but I don't, I stick with Verlaine
after practically going to sleep with quandariness

and for Mike I just stroll into the PARK LANE   20
Liquor Store and ask for a bottle of Strèga and
then I go back where I came from to 6th Avenue
and the tobacconist in the Ziegfeld Theatre and
casually ask for a carton of Gauloises and a carton
of Picayunes, and a NEW YORK POST with her face on it   25

and I am sweating a lot by now and thinking of
leaning on the john door in the 5 SPOT[8]

---

[5]Exhibit of modernist art in 1913 that profoundly affected the direction of twentieth-century art.
[6]French poet (1844–1896), a favorite of O'Hara.
[1]Billie Holiday (1915–1959), known as Lady Day, a famous black blues and jazz singer.
[2]July 14, celebrating the fall of the Bastille prison during the French Revolution.
[3]Summer resort in eastern Long Island.
[4]Bookstore.

[5]Pierre Bonnard (1867–1947), French painter, who illustrated a volume of poems by the French poet Paul Verlaine (1844–1896).
[6]Greek poet (*c.* 800 B.C.).
[7]Behan (1923–1964), Irish playwright; Jean Genêt (1910–1986), French playwright, author of *The Balcony* and *The Blacks*.
[8]Jazz nightclub.

while she whispered a song along the keyboard
to Mal Waldron[9] and everyone and I stopped breathing

1959   1960

Ave Maria[1]

Mothers of America
    let your kids go to the movies!
get them out of the house so they won't know what you're up to
it's true that fresh air is good for the body
        but what about the soul   5
that grows in darkness, embossed by silvery images
and when you grow old as grow old you must
        they won't hate you
they won't criticize you they won't know
       they'll be in some glamorous country   10
they first saw on a Saturday afternoon or playing hookey
they may even be grateful to you
      for their first sexual experience
which only cost you a quarter
      and didn't upset the peaceful home   15
they will know where candy bars come from
        and gratuitous bags of popcorn
as gratuitous as leaving the movie before it's over
with a pleasant stranger whose apartment is in the Heaven on Earth Bldg
near the Williamsburg Bridge   20
     oh mothers you will have made the little tykes
so happy because if nobody does pick them up in the movies
they won't know the difference
      and if somebody does it'll be sheer gravy
and they'll have been truly entertained either way   25
instead of hanging around the yard
      or up in their room
        hating you
prematurely since you won't have done anything horribly mean yet
except keeping them from the darker joys   30
      it's unforgivable the latter
so don't blame me if you won't take this advice
      and the family breaks up
and your children grow old and blind in front of a TV set
        seeing   35
movies you wouldn't let them see when they were young

1960   1961, 1964

Why I Am Not a Painter

I am not a painter, I am a poet.
Why? I think I would rather be
a painter, but I am not. Well,

---

[9]Accompanist for Billie Holiday.
[1]"Hail Mary" (Latin); Catholic prayer to the Virgin Mary,
Mother of God.

for instance, Mike Goldberg[1]
is starting a painting. I drop in.
"Sit down and have a drink" he   5
says. I drink; we drink. I look
up. "You have SARDINES in it."
"Yes, it needed something there."
"Oh." I go and the days go by   10
and I drop in again. The painting
is going on, and I go, and the days
go by. I drop in. The painting is
finished. "Where's SARDINES?"
All that's left is just   15
letters, "It was too much," Mike says.

But me? One day I am thinking of
a color: orange. I write a line
about orange. Pretty soon it is a
whole page of words, not lines.   20
Then another page. There should be
so much more, not of orange, of
words, of how terrible orange is
and life. Days go by. It is even in
prose, I am a real poet. My poem   25
is finished and I haven't mentioned
orange yet. It's twelve poems, I call
it ORANGES. And one day in a gallery
I see Mike's painting, called SARDINES.

1956   *1957, 1971*

My Heart

I'm not going to cry all the time
nor shall I laugh all the time,
I don't prefer one "strain" to another.
I'd have the immediacy of a bad movie,
not just a sleeper, but also the big,   5
overproduced first-run kind. I want to be
at least as alive as the vulgar. And if
some aficionado of my mess says "That's
not like Frank!", all to the good! I
don't wear brown and grey suits all the time,   10
do I? No. I wear workshirts to the opera,
often. I want my feet to be bare,
I want my face to be shaven, and my heart—
you can't plan on the heart, but
the better part of it, my poetry, is open.   15

1971

---

[1]Artist (b. 1924) who provided artwork for O'Hara's 1960
Odes.

JOHN ASHBERY
(b. 1927)

Asked in a recent interview how he went about writing a poem, John Ashbery replied:

> An idea might occur to me, something very banal—for example, isn't it strange that it is possible to both talk and think at the same time? That might be an idea for a poem. Or certain words or phrases might have come to my attention with a meaning I wasn't aware of before. Also, I often put in things that I have overheard people say, on the street for instance. Suddenly something fixes itself in the flow that is going on around one and seems to have a significance. . . . Many times I will jot down ideas and phrases, and then when I am ready to write I can't find them. But it doesn't make any difference, because whatever comes along at that time will have the same quality. Whatever was there is replaceable. In fact, often in revising I will remove the idea that was the original stimulus. I think I am more interested in the movement among ideas than in the ideas themselves, the way one goes from one point to another rather than the destination or the origin.

Most readers have found the experience of reading an Ashbery poem baffling, until they take the plunge into the stream of fragments, images, words, and go with the flow. "Movement" does turn out to be more important than "destination" or "origin." What does it all mean? Perhaps this is the wrong question. Ashbery himself, when asked about his "obscurity," said: "This is the way life appears to me, the way that experience happens. I can concentrate on the things in this room and our talking together, but what the context is is mysterious to me. And it's not that I want to make it more mysterious in my poems—really, I just want to make it more photographic. I often wonder if I am suffering from some mental dysfunction because of how weird and baffling my poetry seems to so many people and sometimes to me too."

Ashbery was born in Rochester, New York, in 1927 and grew up in upstate New York. He attended Deerfield Academy and then went to Harvard, where he graduated in 1949, writing his undergraduate honors paper on W. H. Auden. He took an M.A. at Columbia University in 1951, with a thesis on the British novelist Henry Green. There he read the French novelist Marcel Proust, a lifelong influence. Later he studied French literature at New York University. After working in publishing houses in New York, he won a Fulbright to France in 1955, renewed in 1956. Ashbery extended his stay in Paris for ten years, until 1965. While there he worked as an art critic, first for the *New York Herald Tribune* and then for *Art International*. He also served as Paris reviewer for *Art News*.

Critics have often speculated on the influence of modern art on Ashbery's poetry. He himself has said:

> I have probably been influenced, more or less unconsciously I suppose, by the modern art that I have looked at. Certainly the simultaneity of Cubism is something that has rubbed off on me, as well as the Abstract Expressionism idea that the work is a sort of record of its own coming-into-existence; it has an "anti-referential sensuousness," but it is nothing like flinging a bucket of words on the page, as [Jackson] Pollock did paint. It is more indirect than that. When I was fresh out of college, Abstract Expressionism was the most exciting thing in the arts.

Ashbery returned from Paris to New York to serve as Executive Editor of *Art News*, a position he held until 1972. He had privately published his first volume of poems, *Turandot and Other Poems*, in 1953. In 1956, Yale Press had published *Some Trees* in the Yale Younger Poets Series on the recommendation of W. H. Auden. In an interview in 1977, Ashbery commented on Auden (one of his favorite poets): "I think he respected something in [*Some Trees*] but didn't understand it very well. In fact, in later life, I heard that he told a friend that he had never understood a single word I had ever written."

Although Ashbery steadily continued to publish volumes of poems, he at first attracted little critical attention, and what he did receive was often hostile. By 1975, however, with the publication of *Self-Portrait in a Convex Mirror*, critics could no longer ignore Ashbery. The book became a triple-prize winner, receiving the Pulitzer Prize, the National Book Award, and the National Book Critics Circle Award for Poetry. Subsequent volumes from Ashbery have continued to surprise the critics.

Three Poems in 1972 turned out to be three prose-poems, quite unlike Ashbery's previous poetry. In the title poem from *Houseboat Days* (1977), hailed as one of his best books, Ashbery wrote:

> But I don't set much stock in things
> Beyond the weather and the certainties of living and dying:
> The rest is optional. To praise this, blame that,
> Leads one subtly away from the beginning, where
> We must stay, in motion. . . .

As We Know (1979) contained the long poem "Litany," actually two narrow poems running down the wide pages side-by-side, with very little or no surface connection with each other. An introductory note advised: "The two columns of 'Litany' are meant to be read as simultaneous but independent monologues." An attempt was made in a public performance in Greenwich Village to present such a simultaneous reading. In 1985, on the publication of his *Selected Poems*, Ashbery was awarded the Bollingen Prize in Poetry.

Critics have often linked Ashbery's wit and exotic juxtapositions with Wallace Stevens's poetic techniques. Indeed, Ashbery's enterprise of endless search might well be seen in the light of that sketched in Stevens's "Of Modern Poetry":

> The poem of the mind in the act of finding
> What will suffice. . . .
>   It must
> be the finding of a satisfaction, and may
> Be of a man skating, a woman dancing, a woman
> Combing. The poem of the act of the mind.

Ashbery has developed his own free-verse forms, with long, sweeping lines often embodying lists or catalogues of things, images, fragments—recalling another American poet, Walt Whitman and his *Leaves of Grass*. Ashbery might be seen as fulfilling in a way Whitman's prophecy: "Books are to be call'd for, and supplied, on the assumption that the process of reading is not a half-sleep, but, in highest sense, an exercise, a gymnast's struggle; that the reader is to do something for himself, must be on the alert, must himself or herself construct indeed the poem, argument, history, metaphysical essay—the text furnishing the hints, the clue, the start or frame-work."

If readers find Ashbery's poetry difficult, they might take some comfort in the fact that Ashbery himself has expressed his own bafflement. He has said: "I'm quite puzzled by my work too, along with a lot of other people." And he has added by way of explanation: "I usually start with very few preconceptions of what I'm writing, and not very much memory afterwards of what I was doing. It's a sort of attention that occasionally I feel I can bring to focus on what's happening right now. And then that stops, and something is there which I'd like to call a poem."

ADDITIONAL READING

David K. Kermani, *John Ashbery: A Comprehensive Bibliography*, 1976; David Kalstone, *Five Temperaments: Elizabeth Bishop, Robert Lowell, James Merrill, Adrienne Rich, John Ashbery*, 1977; David Shapiro, *John Ashbery: An Introduction to the Poetry*, 1979; David Lehman, ed., *Beyond Amazement: New Essays on John Ashbery*, 1980; Harold Bloom, ed., *John Ashbery*, 1985.

TEXTS

"The Instruction Manual," "Some Trees," "The Painter" from *Some Trees*, 1956; "The One Thing That Can Save America" from *Self-Portrait in a Convex Mirror*, 1975; "Unctuous Platitudes," "What Is Poetry" from *Houseboat Days*, 1977; "As We Know" from *As We Know*, 1979; "Paradoxes and Oxymorons" from *Shadow Train*, 1981; "Just Walking Around" from *A Wave*, 1984.

The Instruction Manual

As I sit looking out of a window of the building
I wish I did not have to write the instruction manual on the uses of a new
   metal.
I look down into the street and see people, each walking with an inner
   peace,
And envy them—they are so far away from me!
Not one of them has to worry about getting out this manual on schedule. 5
And, as my way is, I begin to dream, resting my elbows on the desk and
   leaning out of the window a little,
Of dim Guadalajara! City of rose-colored flowers!
City I wanted most to see, and most did not see, in Mexico!
But I fancy I see, under the press of having to write the instruction manual,
Your public square, city, with its elaborate little bandstand! 10
The band is playing *Scheherazade* by Rimsky-Korsakov.
Around stand the flower girls, handing out rose- and lemon-colored flowers,
Each attractive in her rose-and-blue striped dress (Oh! such shades of rose
   and blue),
And nearby is the little white booth where women in green serve you green
   and yellow fruit.
The couples are parading; everyone is in a holiday mood. 15
First, leading the parade, is a dapper fellow
Clothed in deep blue. On his head sits a white hat
And he wears a mustache, which has been trimmed for the occasion.
His dear one, his wife, is young and pretty; her shawl is rose, pink, and
   white.
Her slippers are patent leather, in the American fashion, 20
And she carries a fan, for she is modest, and does not want the crowd to see
   her face too often.
But everybody is so busy with his wife or loved one
I doubt they would notice the mustachioed man's wife.
Here come the boys! They are skipping and throwing little things on the
   sidewalk

Which is made of gray tile. One of them, a little older, has a toothpick in his teeth. 25
He is silenter than the rest, and affects not to notice the pretty young girls in white.
But his friends notice them, and shout their jeers at the laughing girls.
Yet soon all this will cease, with the deepening of their years,
And love bring each to the parade grounds for another reason.
But I have lost sight of the young fellow with the toothpick. 30
Wait—there he is—on the other side of the bandstand,
Secluded from his friends, in earnest talk with a young girl
Of fourteen or fifteen. I try to hear what they are saying
But it seems they are just mumbling something—shy words of love, probably.
She is slightly taller than he, and looks quietly down into his sincere eyes. 35
She is wearing white. The breeze ruffles her long fine black hair against her olive cheek.
Obviously she is in love. The boy, the young boy with the toothpick, he is in love too;
His eyes show it. Turning from this couple,
I see there is an intermission in the concert.
The paraders are resting and sipping drinks through straws 40
(The drinks are dispensed from a large glass crock by a lady in dark blue),
And the musicians mingle among them, in their creamy white uniforms, and talk
About the weather, perhaps, or how their kids are doing at school.

Let us take this opportunity to tiptoe into one of the side streets.
Here you may see one of those white houses with green trim 45
That are so popular here. Look—I told you!
It is cool and dim inside, but the patio is sunny.
An old woman in gray sits there, fanning herself with a palm leaf fan.
She welcomes us to her patio, and offers us a cooling drink.
"My son is in Mexico City," she says. "He would welcome you too 50
If he were here. But his job is with a bank there.
Look, here is a photograph of him."
And a dark-skinned lad with pearly teeth grins out at us from the worn leather frame.
We thank her for her hospitality, for it is getting late
And we must catch a view of the city, before we leave, from a good high place. 55
That church tower will do—the faded pink one, there against the fierce blue of the sky. Slowly we enter.
The caretaker, an old man dressed in brown and gray, asks us how long we have been in the city, and how we like it here.
His daughter is scrubbing the steps—she nods to us as we pass into the tower.
Soon we have reached the top, and the whole network of the city extends before us.
There is the rich quarter, with its houses of pink and white, and its crumbling, leafy terraces. 60
There is the poorer quarter, its homes a deep blue.
There is the market, where men are selling hats and swatting flies
And there is the public library, painted several shades of pale green and beige.
Look! There is the square we just came from, with the promenaders.
There are fewer of them, now that the heat of the day has increased,
But the young boy and girl still lurk in the shadows of the bandstand. 65

And there is the home of the little old lady—
She is still sitting in the patio, fanning herself.
How limited, but how complete withal, has been our experience of
　Guadalajara!
We have seen young love, married love, and the love of an aged mother for
　her son.   70
We have heard the music, tasted the drinks, and looked at colored houses.
What more is there to do, except stay? And that we cannot do.
And as a last breeze freshens the top of the weathered old tower, I turn my
　gaze
Back to the instruction manual which has made me dream of Guadalajara.

1956

Some Trees

These are amazing: each
Joining a neighbor, as though speech
Were a still performance.
Arranging by chance

To meet as far this morning   5
From the world as agreeing
With it, you and I
Are suddenly what the trees try

To tell us we are:
That their merely being there   10
Means something; that soon
We may touch, love, explain.

And glad not to have invented
Such comeliness, we are surrounded:
A silence already filled with noises,   15
A canvas on which emerges

A chorus of smiles, a winter morning.
Placed in a puzzling light, and moving,
Our days put on such reticence
These accents seem their own defense.   20

1949, 1956

The Painter

Sitting between the sea and the buildings
He enjoyed painting the sea's portrait.
But just as children imagine a prayer
Is merely silence, he expected his subject
To rush up the sand, and, seizing a brush,   5
Plaster its own portrait on the canvas.

So there was never any paint on his canvas
Until the people who lived in the buildings
Put him to work: "Try using the brush
As a means to an end. Select, for a portrait,   10
Something less angry and large, and more subject
To a painter's moods, or, perhaps, to a prayer."

How could he explain to them his prayer
That nature, not art, might usurp the canvas?
He chose his wife for a new subject,   15
Making her vast, like ruined buildings,
As if, forgetting itself, the portrait
Had expressed itself without a brush.

Slightly encouraged, he dipped his brush
In the sea, murmuring a heartfelt prayer: 20
"My soul, when I paint this next portrait
Let it be you who wrecks the canvas."
The news spread like wildfire through the buildings:
He had gone back to the sea for his subject.

Imagine a painter crucified by his subject!   25
Too exhausted even to lift his brush,
He provoked some artists leaning from the buildings
To malicious mirth: "We haven't a prayer
Now, of putting ourselves on canvas,
Or getting the sea to sit for a portrait!"   30

Others declared it a self-portrait.
Finally all indications of a subject
Began to fade, leaving the canvas
Perfectly white. He put down the brush.
At once a howl, that was also a prayer,   35
Arose from the overcrowded buildings.

They tossed him, the portrait, from the tallest of the buildings;
And the sea devoured the canvas and the brush
As though his subject had decided to remain a prayer.

1948   *1955, 1956*

The One Thing
That Can Save America

Is anything central?
Orchards flung out on the land,
Urban forests, rustic plantations, knee-high hills?
Are place names central?
Elm Grove, Adcock Corner, Story Book Farm?   5
As they concur with a rush at eye level
Beating themselves into eyes which have had enough
Thank you, no more thank you.
And they come on like scenery mingled with darkness
The damp plains, overgrown suburbs,   10
Places of known civic pride, of civil obscurity.

These are connected to my version of America
But the juice is elsewhere.
This morning as I walked out of your room
After breakfast crosshatched with   15
Backward and forward glances, backward into light,
Forward into unfamiliar light,
Was it our doing, and was it
The material, the lumber of life, or of lives
We were measuring, counting?   20
A mood soon to be forgotten
In crossed girders of light, cool downtown shadow
In this morning that has seized us again?

I know that I braid too much my own
Snapped-off perceptions of things as they come to me.   25
They are private and always will be.
Where then are the private turns of event
Destined to boom later like golden chimes
Released over a city from a highest tower?
The quirky things that happen to me, and I tell you,   30
And you instantly know what I mean?
What remote orchard reached by winding roads
Hides them? Where are these roots?

It is the lumps and trials
That tell us whether we shall be known   35
And whether our fate can be exemplary, like a star.
All the rest is waiting
For a letter that never arrives,
Day after day, the exasperation
Until finally you have ripped it open not knowing what it is,   40
The two envelope halves lying on a plate.
The message was wise, and seemingly
Dictated a long time ago.
Its truth is timeless, but its time has still
Not arrived, telling of danger, and the mostly limited   45
Steps that can be taken against danger
Now and in the future, in cool yards,
In quiet small houses in the country,
Our country, in fenced areas, in cool shady streets.

1974, 1975

Unctuous Platitudes

There is no reason for the surcharge to bother you.
Living in a city one is nonplussed by some

Of the inhabitants. The weather has grown gray with age.
Poltergeists[1] go about their business, sometimes

---

[1] A ghost or spirit that makes its presence known by mysterious rapping or knocking.

Demanding a sweeping revision. The breath of the air   5
Is invisible. People stay

Next to the edges of fields, hoping that out of nothing
Something will come, and it does, but what? Embers

Of the rain tamp down the shitty darkness that issues
From nowhere. A man in her room, you say.   10

I like the really wonderful way you express things
So that it might be said, that of all the ways in which to

Emphasize a posture or a particular mental climate
Like this gray-violet one with a thin white irregular line

Descending the two vertical sides, these are those which   15
Can also unsay an infinite number of pauses

In the ceramic day. Every invitation
To every stranger is met at the station.

                                                              1977

What Is Poetry

The medieval town, with frieze
Of boy scouts from Nagoya?[1] The snow

That came when we wanted it to snow?
Beautiful images? Trying to avoid

Ideas, as in this poem? But we   5
Go back to them as to a wife, leaving

The mistress we desire? Now they
Will have to believe it

As we believe it. In school
All the thought got combed out: 10

What was left was like a field.
Shut your eyes, and you can feel it for miles around.

Now open them on a thin vertical path.
It might give us — what? — some flowers soon?

                                                              1977

As We Know

All that we see is penetrated by it —
The distant treetops with their steeple (so
Innocent), the stair, the windows' fixed flashing —

---

[1]A seaport city in Japan.

Pierced full of holes by the evil that is not evil,
The romance that is not mysterious, the life that is not life,   5
A present that is elsewhere.

And further in the small capitulations
Of the dance, you rub elbows with it,
Finger it. That day you did it
Was the day you had to stop, because the doing   10
Involved the whole fabric, there was no other way to appear.
You slid down on your knees
For those precious jewels of spring water
Planted on the moss, before they got soaked up
And you teetered on the edge of this   15
Calm street with its sidewalks, its traffic,

As though they are coming to get you.
But there was no one in the noon glare,
Only birds like secrets to find out about
And a home to get to, one of these days.   20

The light that was shadowed then
Was seen to be our lives,
Everything about us that love might wish to examine,
Then put away for a certain length of time, until
The whole is to be reviewed, and we turned   25
Toward each other, to each other.
The way we had come was all we could see
And it crept up on us, embarrassed
That there is so much to tell now, really now.

1979

Paradoxes and Oxymorons

This poem is concerned with language on a very plain level.
Look at it talking to you. You look out a window
Or pretend to fidget. You have it but you don't have it.
You miss it, it misses you. You miss each other.

The poem is sad because it wants to be yours, and cannot.   5
What's a plain level? It is that and other things,
Bringing a system of them into play. Play?
Well, actually, yes, but I consider play to be

A deeper outside thing, a dreamed role-pattern,
As in the division of grace these long August days   10
Without proof. Open-ended. And before you know
It gets lost in the steam and chatter of typewriters.

It has been played once more. I think you exist only
To tease me into doing it, on your level, and then you aren't there
Or have adopted a different attitude. And the poem   15
Has set me softly down beside you. The poem is you.

1981

Just Walking Around

What name do I have for you?
Certainly there is no name for you
In the sense that the stars have names
That somehow fit them. Just walking around,

An object of curiosity to some,   5
But you are too preoccupied
By the secret smudge in the back of your soul
To say much, and wander around,

Smiling to yourself and others.
It gets to be kind of lonely   10
But at the same time off-putting,
Counterproductive, as you realize once again

That the longest way is the most efficient way,
The one that looped among islands, and
You always seemed to be traveling in a circle.   15
And now that the end is near

The segments of the trip swing open like an orange.
There is light in there, and mystery and food.
Come see it. Come not for me but it.
But if I am still there, grant that we may see each other.   20

1984

W. S. MERWIN

(b. 1927)

In an interview in 1981, W. S. Merwin explained that he had never been able
to follow a "deliberate program for writing a poem":

> A poem begins to be a poem when a sequence of words starts giving off what
> you might describe as a kind of electric charge, when it begins to have a life of
> its own that I sense the way I would if I suddenly picked up a shorted electric
> wire. If it doesn't have that, even if it's got what I would very much like it to
> have, then it's not working as a poem. I suppose all poets work that way in one
> way or another, but I notice in many of my contemporaries a more deliberate
> approach to what they want to put in their poems, though they do it differently
> and in ways that I have never been able to.

William Stanley Merwin was born in New York City in 1927, the son of a
Presbyterian minister; he grew up in Union City, New Jersey, and in Scranton,
Pennsylvania. He has described his own development as a writer:

> I started writing hymns for my father almost as soon as I could write at all,
> illustrating them. . . . I can remember . . . wondering whether there might not
> be some more liberating mode. In Scranton there was an anthology of *Best
> Loved Poems of the American People* in the house, which seemed for a time to

afford some clues. But the first real writers that held were not poets: Conrad first, and then Tolstoy, and it was not until I had received a scholarship and gone away to the university that I began to read poetry steadily and try incessantly, and with abiding desperation, to write it.

The university was Princeton, where at the time the poets John Berryman and R. P. Blackmur were teaching. Merwin remembered later that they helped him, "by example as much as by design, to find out some things about writing: of course it was years before I began to realize just what I had learned, and from whom." Merwin's encounter with Berryman left a deep enough impression to inspire a poem about him many years later: "as for publishing he advised me / to paper my wall with rejection slips / his lips and the bones of his long fingers trembled / with the vehemence of his views about poetry." Berryman advised Merwin to get down on his knees and pray to the Muse—and "he meant it literally," Merwin recalled.

After taking a B.A. in 1947, Merwin remained for a year studying foreign languages. He put the languages to use by spending many of the following years abroad, working as a tutor in France and Portugal in 1949, and in 1950 tutoring the son of the British poet Robert Graves on the Spanish island of Majorca. In the early 1950s, he supported himself in England by translating classics from the French and Spanish for the Third Programme of the British Broadcasting Corporation. For a time he became associated with theater groups, writing plays, first in 1956 in Cambridge, Massachusetts, and then, in 1964–65, in Lyon, France. Although he lived in New York City in the early 1960s, he has spent most of his later years living in Haiku, Hawaii.

Merwin's first book, *A Mask for Janus*, was published in 1952 on the recommendation of W. H. Auden in the Yale Series of Younger Poets. It was marked by Merwin's interest in foreign literatures and traditional metrical forms. Only three of the poems would survive the sifting process for the 1988 *Selected Poems*. And from the second book, *The Dancing Bears*, only two would survive. In his next several books—*The Drunk in the Furnace* (1960), *The Moving Target* (1963), *The Lice* (1967), *The Carrier of Ladders* (1970)—Merwin found his distinctive voice and hit his poetic stride. The poems became more personal (but never confessional), and the style less fixed and traditional. And the books began to sound an insistent theme that reached a crescendo in *The Lice*—rage over the destruction of the earth by earth's inhabitants (as in "The Last One"). Merwin was awarded the Pulitzer Prize for *The Carrier of Ladders*.

Merwin's later works include *Writing to an Unfinished Accompaniment* (1973), *The Compass Flower* (1977), *Opening the Hand* (1983), and *The Rain in the Trees* (1988). He was awarded the Bollingen Prize for *Feathers from the Hills* (1978). In these poems, Merwin's tone lost some of its edge, becoming more elegiac, and his style became looser, less dense. And he began to experiment with the poetic line, adopting a "broken-back" line (a line with a long space in the middle, forcing a pause). Merwin commented on the line to an interviewer: "I think it's basically an English line, Anglo-Saxon, but it's also there in a great many literatures, that line with parallelism built into it: Spanish, as close to English as that—*Poem of the Cid* was written in a line very like that; in fact, I translated it in that line." Merwin's translations have been an important part of his creative production, and have included works (often in collaboration with others) in Spanish, French, Sanskrit, Greek, and other literatures. His translation of the Spanish classic *The Poem of the Cid* was published in 1959; his rendering of the French classic *The Song of Roland*, in 1963.

In a prefatory note to his *Selected Poems*, published in 1988, he wrote: "I have not changed the poems I have included. That is not because I thought they were beyond improvement but because in certain respects I am no longer the person who wrote them." In an earlier interview, with an offhand remark he described his view of the mysterious workings of poetry: "Writing is something I know little about; less at some times than at others. I think, though, that so far as it is poetry it is a matter of correspondences: one glimpses them, pieces of an order, or thinks one does, and tries to convey the sense of what one has seen to those to whom it may matter, including, if possible, one's self."

ADDITIONAL READING

Houses and Travellers: A Book of Prose, 1977; *Selected Translations, 1968–1978*, 1979; *Unframed Originals: Recollections*, 1982; *Regions of Memory: Uncollected Prose, 1949–1982*, 1987.

Cheri Davis, *W. S. Merwin*, 1981; Cary Nelson, *Our First Last Poets*, 1981; Cary Nelson and Ed Folsom, eds., *W. S. Merwin: Essays on the Poetry*, 1987.

TEXT

W. S. Merwin: Selected Poems, 1988.

Grandfather in the
Old Men's Home

Gentle at last, and as clean as ever,
He did not even need drink any more,
And his good sons unbent and brought him
Tobacco to chew, both times when they came
To be satisfied he was well cared for.   5
And he smiled all the time to remember
Grandmother, his wife, wearing the true faith
Like an iron nightgown, yet brought to birth
Seven times and raising the family
Through her needle's eye while he got away   10
Down the green river, finding directions
For boats. And himself coming home sometimes
Well-heeled but blind drunk, to hide all the bread
And shoot holes in the bucket while he made
His daughters pump. Still smiled as kindly in   15
His sleep beside the other clean old men
To see Grandmother, every night the same,
Huge in her age, with her thumbed-down mouth, come
Hating the river, filling with her stare
His gliding dream, while he turned to water,   20
While the children they both had begotten,
With old faces now, but themselves shrunken
To child-size again, stood ranged at her side,
Beating their little Bibles till he died.

1960

Grandmother Watching
at Her Window

There was always the river or the train
Right past the door, and someone might be gone
Come morning. When I was a child I mind
Being held up at a gate to wave
Good-bye, good-bye to I didn't know who,   5
Gone to the War, and how I cried after.
When I married I did what was right
But I knew even that first night
That he would go. And so shut my soul tight
Behind my mouth, so he could not steal it   10
When he went. I brought the children up clean
With my needle, taught them that stealing
Is the worst sin; knew if I loved them
They would be taken away, and did my best
But must have loved them anyway   15
For they slipped through my fingers like stitches.
Because God loves us always, whatever
We do. You can sit all your life in churches
And teach your hands to clutch when you pray
And never weaken, but God loves you so dearly   20
Just as you are, that nothing you are can stay,
But all the time you keep going away, away.

1960

The Drunk in the Furnace

For a good decade
The furnace stood in the naked gully, fireless
And vacant as any hat. Then when it was
No more to them than a hulking black fossil
To erode unnoticed with the rest of the junk-hill   5
By the poisonous creek, and rapidly to be added
    To their ignorance,

    They were afterwards astonished
To confirm, one morning, a twist of smoke like a pale
Resurrection, staggering out of its chewed hole,   10
And to remark then other tokens that someone,
Cosily bolted behind the eye-holed iron
Door of the drafty burner, had there established
    His bad castle.

    Where he gets his spirits   15
It's a mystery. But the stuff keeps him musical:
Hammer-and-anvilling with poker and bottle
To his jugged bellowings, till the last groaning clang
As he collapses onto the rioting

Springs of a litter of car-seats ranged on the grates,   20
    To sleep like an iron pig.

    In their tar-paper church
On a text about stoke-holes that are sated never
Their Reverend lingers. They nod and hate trespassers.
When the furnace wakes, though, all afternoon   25
Their witless offspring flock like piped rats to its siren
Crescendo, and agape on the crumbling ridge
    Stand in a row and learn.

1960

Noah's Raven[1]

Why should I have returned?
My knowledge would not fit into theirs.
I found untouched the desert of the unknown,
Big enough for my feet. It is my home.
It is always beyond them. The future   5
Splits the present with the echo of my voice.
Hoarse with fulfillment, I never made promises.

1963

The Child

Sometimes it is inconceivable that I should be the age I am
Almost always it is a dry point in the afternoon
I cannot remember what
I am waiting for and in my astonishment I
Can hear the blood crawling over the plains   5
Hurrying on to arrive before dark
I try to remember my faults to make sure
One after the other but it is never
Satisfactory the list is never complete

At times night occurs to me so that I think I have been   10
Struck from behind I remain perfectly
Still feigning death listening for the
Assailant perhaps at last
I even sleep a little for later I have moved
I open my eyes the lanternfish have gone home in darkness   15
On all sides the silence is unharmed
I remember but I feel no bruise

Then there are the stories and after a while I think something
Else must connect them besides just this me
I regard myself starting the search turning   20

---

[1]When Noah landed with his ark on Mount Ararat, he sent out a dove and a raven to see whether the Flood had dimin- ished; the dove returned but the raven did not (Genesis 8:7–12).

Corners in remembered metropoli
I pass skins withering in gardens that I see now
Are not familiar
And I have lost even the thread I thought I had

If I could be consistent even in destitution   25
The world would be revealed
While I can I try to repeat what I believe
Creatures spirits not this posture
I do not believe in knowledge as we know it
But I forget   30

This silence coming at intervals out of the shell of names
It must be all one person really coming at
Different hours for the same thing
If I could learn the word for yes it could teach me questions
I would see that it was itself every time and I would   35
Remember to say take it up like a hand
And go with it this is at last
Yourself

The child that will lead you[1]

                                                            1967

For the Anniversary of My Death

Every year without knowing it I have passed the day
When the last fires will wave to me
And the silence will set out
Tireless traveller
Like the beam of a lightless star   5

Then I will no longer
Find myself in life as in a strange garment
Surprised at the earth
And the love of one woman
And the shamelessness of men   10
As today writing after three days of rain
Hearing the wren sing and the falling cease
And bowing not knowing to what

                                                            1967

The Dry Stone Mason

The mason is dead the gentle drunk
Master of dry walls

---

[1]Cf. "The wolf also shall dwell with the lamb, and the leopard shall lie down with the kid; and the calf and the young lion and the fatling together; and a little child shall lead them" (Isaiah 11:6).

What he made of his years crosses the slopes without wavering
Upright but nameless
Ignorant in the new winter   5
Rubbed by running sheep
But the age of mortar has come to him

Bottles are waiting like fallen shrines
Under different trees in the rain
And stones drip where his hands left them   10
Leaning slightly inwards
His thirst is past

As he had no wife
The neighbors found where he kept his suit
A man with no family they sat with him   15
When he was carried through them they stood by their own dead
And they have buried him among the graves of the stones

1967

In the Winter of
My Thirty-Eighth Year

It sounds unconvincing to say *When I was young*
Though I have long wondered what it would be like
To be me now
No older at all it seems from here
As far from myself as ever   5

Waking in fog and rain and seeing nothing
I imagine all the clocks have died in the night
Now no one is looking I could choose my age
It would be younger I suppose so I am older
It is there at hand I could take it   10
Except for the things I think I would do differently
They keep coming between they are what I am
They have taught me little I did not know when I was young

There is nothing wrong with my age now probably
It is how I have come to it   15
Like a thing I kept putting off as I did my youth

There is nothing the matter with speech
Just because it lent itself
To my uses

Of course there is nothing the matter with the stars   20
It is the emptiness among them
While they drift farther away in the invisible morning

1967

The Asians Dying[1]

When the forests have been destroyed their darkness remains
The ash the great walker follows the possessors
Forever
Nothing they will come to is real
Not for long   5
Over the watercourses
Like ducks in the time of the ducks
The ghosts of the villages trail in the sky
Making a new twilight

Rain falls into the open eyes of the dead   10
Again again with its pointless sound
When the moon finds them they are the color of everything

The nights disappear like bruises but nothing is healed
The dead go away like bruises
The blood vanishes into the poisoned farmlands   15
Pain the horizon
Remains
Overhead the seasons rock
They are paper bells
Calling to nothing living   20

The possessors move everywhere under Death their star
Like columns of smoke they advance into the shadows
Like thin flames with no light
They with no past
And fire their only future   25

1967

For a Coming Extinction

Gray whale
Now that we are sending you to The End
That great god
Tell him
That we who follow you invented forgiveness   5
And forgive nothing

I write as though you could understand
And I could say it
One must always pretend something
Among the dying   10
When you have left the seas nodding on their stalks

---

[1]During the Vietnam War; American involvement escalated
during the late 1960s.

Empty of you
Tell him that we were made
On another day

The bewilderment will diminish like an echo   15
Winding along your inner mountains
Unheard by us
And find its way out
Leaving behind it the future
Dead   20
And ours

When you will not see again
The whale calves trying the light
Consider what you will find in the black garden
And its court   25
The sea cows the Great Auks the gorillas
The irreplaceable hosts ranged countless
And fore-ordaining as stars
Our sacrifices
Join your word to theirs   30
Tell him
That it is we who are important

1967

Strawberries

When my father died I saw   a narrow valley

it looked as though it began   across the river
from the landing where he was born   but there was no river

I was hoeing the sand   of a small vegetable plot
for my mother   in deepening twilight   5
and looked up in time   to see a farm wagon
dry and gray   horse already hidden
and no driver   going into the valley
carrying a casket

                     and another wagon   10
coming out of the valley   behind a gray horse
with a boy driving   and a high load
of two kinds of berries   one of them strawberries

         that night when I slept   I dreamed of things
wrong in the house   all of them signs   15
the water of the shower   running brackish
and an insect of a kind   I had seen him kill
climbing around   the walls of his bathroom
         up in the morning   I stopped on the stairs
my mother was awake   already and asked me   20
if I wanted a shower   before breakfast
and for breakfast she said   we have strawberries

1983

JAMES WRIGHT
(1927–1980)

When James Wright was asked in an interview why he had often called himself a "nature poet," he replied:

> I care very much about the living world, the organic and the inorganic world. It comforts me more and more to realize and to observe and to feel the great self-restoring power that the creatures in nature have while we human beings are making such a mess of things. I hope that poetry, and the poetry of nature, has a similar power. Roethke said a beautiful thing once when he talked to a class about the poetry of nature. He said that we ought to remember that there is an inner nature, and I think he was suggesting something about poetry. That, perhaps, poetry could remind us of the need for restoration through the inner nature. Also, I think that in the poetry of nature there is the willingness to approach the living creatures with the kind of attentiveness that is almost a reverence.

James Arlington Wright was born in 1927 in the industrial town Martins Ferry, Ohio. His father worked in the Hazel-Atlas Glass factory for fifty years, except for frequent payless periods when he was laid off. Wright later remembered Martins Ferry as situated in a beautiful physical location made ugly by industrialization. An open sewer poured continuously into the river, the site of steel plants and other factories. Growing up in a family suffering the hardships of the Great Depression, Wright looked upon Martins Ferry as a place from which to escape. After graduation from high school in 1946, he enlisted in the U.S. Army and served in the occupation forces in Japan.

With the G. I. Bill, Wright was able to go to college after his discharge. He was accepted at Kenyon College, Ohio, and there had a course with John Crowe Ransom, whose poetry Wright admired. He began to write poetry and won the Robert Frost Poetry Prize for one of his poems. To his surprise, he won a student Fulbright scholarship for study at the University of Vienna the year following his graduation in 1952. He married one of his classmates at Martins Ferry High School, Liberty Kardules, and spent his year in Vienna, where a son was born. On returning to the United States, Wright entered the graduate program in English at the University of Washington in Seattle and enrolled in a poetry-writing class taught by Theodore Roethke.

Wright's poems had by this time been appearing in the little magazines, and in 1957 his volume *The Green Wall* was published in the Yale Series of Younger Poets on the recommendation of W. H. Auden. Wright had taken his M.A. in 1954, and by the time he took his Ph.D. at the University of Washington in 1959, he saw publication of his second book of poems, *Saint Judas*. Wright began teaching in 1957 at the University of Minnesota, where he would remain until 1964. At a time when everything appeared to be going his way, Wright found himself acutely unhappy, first because he sensed a deep-seated need to remake himself as a poet (he wrote to his publisher that his future poetry would be completely different). And with his marriage falling apart, he began to drink excessively.

Wright's marriage ended in divorce in 1962. By the time his third volume of poems, *This Branch Will Not Break*, appeared in 1963, he was true to his promise to his publisher: his poetry *was* different. Part of the change, as Wright himself indicated, stemmed from his translations, with Robert Bly, of the Austrian poet Georg Trakl in 1961, and the Latin-American poets César Vallejo in 1962, and

Pablo Neruda in 1968. Wright spoke eloquently of the effects of the translating exercise: "You are forced to find some equivalents in your own language, not only equivalents of language but also equivalents of imagination. In this way you can force yourself actually to try to understand the vision of the poem in the other language. It's bound to have an effect on you." The poems in *This Branch Will Not Break* and his next volume, *Shall We Gather at the River* (1968), moved away from the traditional forms of his earlier work and demonstrated a greater structural reliance on moments of heightened emotional intensity. The imagery itself tended to be more lush, even to some extent surrealistic (like that of Neruda). Typical of the new style was a poem about his agonizing loneliness after the break-up of his marriage, "Having Lost My Sons, I Confront the Wreckage of the Moon."

In 1966, Wright began his teaching career at Hunter College in New York, where he insisted on teaching literature, not poetry writing. He distrusted poetry workshops and preferred to teach the English novel. In 1967 he married Anne Runk; his love for her would be celebrated in his poems as would their European travels. His reputation grew steadily and with publication of his *Collected Poems* in 1971, he was awarded the Pulitzer Prize for Poetry. Other volumes followed, including *Moments of the Italian Summer* (1976) and *To a Blossoming Pear Tree* (1977). Wright died of throat cancer, at the age of fifty-two, in 1980. While in the hospital, he put the finishing touches on a final volume of poems, *This Journey*, which appeared in 1982.

ADDITIONAL READING

Collected Prose of James Wright, ed. Anne Wright, 1983; *The Delicacy and Strength of Lace: Letters between Leslie Marmon Silko and James Wright*, ed. Anne Wright, 1986.

William Saunders, *James Wright: An Introduction*, 1979; Dave Smith, ed., *The Pure Clear Word: Essays on the Poetry of James Wright*, 1982; Peter Stitt, *The World's Hieroglyphic Beauty: Five American Poets*, 1985; David C. Dougherty, *James Wright*, 1987; Kevin Stein, *James Wright: The Poetry of a Grown Man*, 1988; Frank Graziano and Peter Stitt, eds., *James Wright: A Profile*, 1988.

TEXTS

"With the Shell of a Hermit Crab" from *To a Blossoming Pear Tree*, 1977; remaining poems from *Collected Poems*, 1971.

Lament for My
Brother on a Hayrake

Cool with the touch of autumn, waters break
Out of the pump at dawn to clear my eyes;
I leave the house, to face the sacrifice
Of hay, the drag and death. By day, by moon,
I have seen my younger brother wipe his face   5
And heave his arm on steel. He need not pass
Under the blade to waste his life and break;

The hunching of the body is enough
To violate his bones. That bright machine
Strips the revolving earth of more than grass;   10
Powered by the fire of summer, bundles fall
Folded to die beside a burlap shroud;
And so my broken brother may lie mown
Out of the wasted fallows, winds return,
Corn-yellow tassels of his hair blow down,   15
The summer bear him sideways in a bale
Of darkness to October's mow of cloud.

1957, 1959

A Note Left in
Jimmy Leonard's Shack

Near the dry river's water-mark we found
    Your brother Minnegan,
Flopped like a fish against the muddy ground.
Beany, the kid whose yellow hair turns green,
Told me to find you, even in the rain,   5
    And tell you he was drowned.

I hid behind the chassis on the bank,
    The wreck of someone's Ford:
I was afraid to come and wake you drunk:
You told me once the waking up was hard,   10
The daylight beating at you like a board.
    Blood in my stomach sank.

Beside, you told him never to go out
    Along the river-side
Drinking and singing, clattering about.   15
You might have thrown a rock at me and cried
I was to blame, I let him fall in the road
    And pitch down on his side.

Well, I'll get hell enough when I get home
    For coming up this far,   20
Leaving the note, and running as I came.
I'll go and tell my father where you are.
You'd better go find Minnegan before
    Policemen hear and come.

Beany went home, and I got sick and ran,   25
    You old son of a bitch.
You better hurry down to Minnegan;
He's drunk or dying now, I don't know which,
Rolled in the roots and garbage like a fish,
    The poor old man.   30

1957, 1959

Lying in a Hammock at William Duffy's Farm in Pine Island, Minnesota

Over my head, I see the bronze butterfly,
Asleep on the black trunk,
Blowing like a leaf in green shadow.
Down the ravine behind the empty house,
The cowbells follow one another   5
Into the distances of the afternoon.
To my right,
In a field of sunlight between two pines,
The droppings of last year's horses
Blaze up into golden stones.   10
I lean back, as the evening darkens and comes on.
A chicken hawk floats over, looking for home.
I have wasted my life.

1961, 1963

Having Lost My Sons, I Confront the Wreckage of the Moon: Christmas, 1960

After dark
Near the South Dakota border,
The moon is out hunting, everywhere,
Delivering fire,
And walking down hallways   5
Of a diamond.

Behind a tree,
It lights on the ruins
Of a white city:
Frost, frost.   10

Where are they gone,
Who lived there?

Bundled away under wings
And dark faces.

I am sick   15
Of it, and I go on,
Living, alone, alone,
Past the charred silos, past the hidden graves
Of Chippewas and Norwegians.

This cold winter   20
Moon spills the inhuman fire
Of jewels
Into my hands.

Dead riches, dead hands, the moon
Darkens,   25
And I am lost in the beautiful white ruins
Of America.

1961, 1963

A Blessing

Just off the highway to Rochester, Minnesota,
Twilight bounds softly forth on the grass.
And the eyes of those two Indian ponies
Darken with kindness.
They have come gladly out of the willows   5
To welcome my friend and me.
We step over the barbed wire into the pasture
Where they have been grazing all day, alone.
They ripple tensely, they can hardly contain their happiness
That we have come.   10
They bow shyly as wet swans. They love each other.
There is no loneliness like theirs.
At home once more,
They begin munching the young tufts of spring in the darkness.
I would like to hold the slenderer one in my arms,   15
For she has walked over to me
And nuzzled my left hand.
She is black and white,
Her mane falls wild on her forehead,
And the light breeze moves me to caress her long ear   20
That is delicate as the skin over a girl's wrist.
Suddenly I realize
That if I stepped out of my body I would break
Into blossom.

1961, 1963

Two Postures Beside a Fire

1.

Tonight I watch my father's hair,
As he sits dreaming near his stove.
Knowing my feather of despair,
He sent me an owl's plume for love,
Lest I not know, so I've come home.   5
Tonight Ohio, where I once
Hounded and cursed my loneliness,
Shows me my father, who broke stones,
Wrestled and mastered great machines,
And rests, shadowing his lovely face.   10

2.

Nobly his hands fold together in his repose.
He is proud of me, believing
I have done strong things among men and become a man
Of place among men of place in the large cities.
I will not waken him.   15
I have come home alone, without wife or child
To delight him. Awake, solitary and welcome,
I too sit near his stove, the lines
Of an ugly age scarring my face, and my hands
Twitch nervously about.   20

1968

Small Frogs Killed on the Highway

Still,
I would leap too
Into the light,
If I had the chance.
It is everything, the wet green stalk of the field   5
On the other side of the road.
They crouch there, too, faltering in terror
And take strange wing. Many
Of the dead never moved, but many
Of the dead are alive forever in the split second   10
Auto headlights more sudden
Than their drivers know.
The drivers burrow backward into dank pools
Where nothing begets
Nothing.   15

Across the road, tadpoles are dancing
On the quarter thumbnail
Of the moon. They can't see,
Not yet.

1971

Northern Pike

All right. Try this,
Then. Every body
I know and care for,
And every body
Else is going   5
To die in a loneliness
I can't imagine and a pain
I don't know. We had

To go on living. We
Untangled the net, we slit   10
The body of this fish
Open from the hinge of the tail
To a place beneath the chin
I wish I could sing of.
I would just as soon we let   15
The living go on living.
An old poet whom we believe in
Said the same thing, and so
We paused among the dark cattails and prayed
For the muskrats,   20
For the ripples below their tails,
For the little movements that we knew the crawdads[1]
   were making under water,
For the right-hand wrist of my cousin who is a policeman.
We prayed for the game warden's blindness.
We prayed for the road home.   25
We ate the fish.
There must be something very beautiful in my body,
I am so happy.

1971

With the Shell
of a Hermit Crab

Lugete, O Veneres Cupidinesque—Catullus[1]

This lovely little life whose toes
Touched the white sand from side to side,
How delicately no one knows,
Crept from his loneliness, and died.

From deep waters long miles away   5
He wandered, looking for his name,
And all he found was you and me,
A quick life and a candle flame.

Today, you happen to be gone.
I sit here in the raging hell,   10
The city of the dead, alone,
Holding a little empty shell.

I peer into his tiny face.
It looms too huge for me to bear.
Two blocks away the sea gives place   15
To river. Both are everywhere.

---

[1]Crayfish.
[1]"Lament, O graces of Venus, and Cupids" (Latin, tr. Celia and Louis Zukofsky); from "On the Death of Lesbia's Sparrow" by Catullus (*c.* 84–54 B.C.), Roman poet of love.

I reach out and flick out the light.
Darkly I touch his fragile scars,
So far away, so delicate,
Stars in a wilderness of stars.   20

1977

ANNE SEXTON
(1928–1974)

Anne Sexton once told an interviewer: "My analyst told me to write between our sessions about what I was feeling and thinking and dreaming." When she showed what she had written, the analyst encouraged her to continue. In response to another interviewer's question about why she chose to write poetry, she said: "I haven't the slightest idea. When I was eighteen or nineteen I wrote for half a year. . . . When I was twenty-eight, I saw I. A. Richards on television. He was talking about the form of the sonnet, its images, and I thought, I can do that. I would like to be a photographer if the camera could work the way fingers work. I like to capture an instant. A picture is a one second thing — it's a fragile moment in time. I try to do it with words."

Whatever the source, Sexton's pathway to poetry was surely a strange and winding one. She was thirty-two years old when her first book, *To Bedlam and Part Way Back*, was published in 1960. She was dead by suicide only fourteen years later. In her abbreviated creative life she published a large number of volumes, some four or five of which established her as a leading poet. Her *Love Poems* (1969) was a best-seller among poetry books. And she won a number of coveted prizes, including a Pulitzer Prize for *Live or Die*, published in 1966.

It is difficult to find in her long foreground the clues that would make for her success as a poet. Born Anne Gray Harvey in Newton, Massachusetts, she attended both public and private schools, finishing with two years at a Boston junior college. She eloped at the age of nineteen with Alfred Sexton and for a time worked as a model. She had two daughters, born in 1953 and 1955. She early lost her faith in the Catholicism in which she had been raised, but she would begin a search near the end of her life for religious belief. She attempted suicide first in 1956, as she would do again repeatedly. Periodical hospitalizations and more or less regular psychiatric care became her way of life.

In the late 1950s, Sexton participated in poetry workshops and enrolled in a course taught by Robert Lowell at Boston University. A fellow student in the class was Sylvia Plath, with whom she exchanged poems and criticism. Later Sexton herself would conduct poetry workshops. Asked what she thought of them, she replied: "They were very valuable to me. It's where I started. All you need is one friend to tell you to write a poem a day. It's not the criticism — it's the stimulation, the countered interest. It's a time to grow."

Sexton once said that poetry "should be a shock to the senses." Her poems certainly lived up to that provision. In her first book, a poem to her doctor in a mental institution begins: "You, Doctor Martin, walk / from breakfast to madness." In her second book, *All My Pretty Ones* (1962), the title poem, addressed to her father who had died in 1959, only a few months after the death of her mother, opens: "Father, this year's jinx rides us apart / where you followed our mother to her cold slumber"; and concludes: "Whether you are pretty or not, I outlive you, / bend down my strange face to yours and forgive you." "Suicide Note" in *Live or Die* (1966) ends: "At night the bats will beat on the trees, / knowing it all, / seeing what they sensed all day."

There can be no doubt that a part of the effect of her poems is their relation to her mental state. She once said: "Any poem is therapy. The art of writing is therapy. You don't solve problems in writing. They're still there. I've heard psychiatrists say, 'See, you've forgiven your father. There it is in your poem.' But I haven't forgiven my father. I just wrote that I did." It was inevitable that she would be classified as a "confessional poet," a designation she resisted at first. But, she told one interviewer, she came to the conclusion finally that she was the *only* confessional poet. The work she described as most influential in encouraging her to write about her own psychic problems was W. D. Snodgrass's *Heart's Needle* (1959), a candid account of a father's loss of a daughter through the break-up of a marriage (it had won a Pulitzer Prize).

In the latter part of her career, her life began to fall apart. She was divorced in 1973, suffered a series of breakdowns, and her poetry declined in its public appeal. *Transformations*, published in 1971, was a retelling of several of Grimm's fairy tales so as to highlight the psychic fantasies hidden in them. It was the last of her works about which the critical consensus was positive. *The Book of Folly* (1972) showed a weakening of control over style. *The Death Notebooks* (1974) and the two posthumously published volumes, *The Awful Rowing Toward God* (1975) and *45 Mercy Street* (1976), were recognized as inferior even by those who had championed her work before.

But the poems that established her reputation continue to fascinate readers. Ralph Mills's early judgment in *Contemporary American Poetry* (1965) remains sound today: "Anne Sexton is, by any standards, a bold and impressive poet. . . . The private experience [she] holds up so courageously to frank, imaginative scrutiny falls outside her possession once the poem has been written: that experience is transformed into a public one, that is to say, one capable of illuminating the lives of each of us."

ADDITIONAL READING

Anne Sexton: A Self-Portrait in Letters, ed. Linda Gray Sexton and Lois Ames, 1977; *No Evil Star: Selected Essays, Interviews, and Prose*, ed. Stephen E. Colburn, 1985.

Ralph J. Mills, Jr., *Contemporary American Poetry*, 1965; Cameron Northouse and Thomas P. Walsh, *Sylvia Plath and Anne Sexton: A Reference Guide*, 1974; J. D. McClatchy, ed., *Anne Sexton: The Artist and Her Critics*, 1978; Diana Hume George, *Oedipus Anne: The Poetry of Anne Sexton*, 1987; Frances Bixler, ed., *Original Essays on Anne Sexton*, 1988; Steven E. Colburn, ed., *Anne Sexton: Telling the Tale*, 1988; Diana Hume George, ed., *Sexton: Selected Criticism*, 1988.

TEXT

The Complete Poems, 1981.

Her Kind

I have gone out, a possessed witch,
haunting the black air, braver at night;
dreaming evil, I have done my hitch

over the plain houses, light by light:
lonely thing, twelve-fingered,[1] out of mind.   5
A woman like that is not a woman, quite.
I have been her kind.

I have found the warm caves in the woods,
filled them with skillets, carvings, shelves,
closets, silks, innumerable goods;   10
fixed the suppers for the worms and the elves:
whining, rearranging the disaligned.
A woman like that is misunderstood.
I have been her kind.

I have ridden in your cart, driver,   15
waved my nude arms at villages going by,
learning the last bright routes, survivor
where your flames still bite my thigh
and my ribs crack where your wheels wind.[2]
A woman like that is not ashamed to die.   20
I have been her kind.

1959, 1960

Ringing the Bells

And this is the way they ring
the bells in Bedlam[1]
and this is the bell-lady
who comes each Tuesday morning
to give us a music lesson   5
and because the attendants make you go
and because we mind by instinct,
like bees caught in the wrong hive,
we are the circle of the crazy ladies
who sit in the lounge of the mental house   10
and smile at the smiling woman
who passes us each a bell,
who points at my hand
that holds my bell, E flat,
and this is the gray dress next to me   15
who grumbles as if it were special
to be old, to be old,
and this is the small hunched squirrel girl
on the other side of me
who picks at the hairs over her lip,   20
who picks at the hairs over her lip all day,
and this is how the bells really sound,
as untroubled and clean

---

[1]Witches were sometimes believed to have six fingers on each
hand.
[2]I.e., tortured on the rack, the wheels and ropes often pulling the body apart.
[1]In London, a hospital for the insane; now a general term for
similar places.

as a workable kitchen,
and this is always my bell responding   25
to my hand that responds to the lady
who points at me, E flat;
and although we are no better for it,
they tell you to go. And you do.

1960

The Truth the Dead Know

FOR MY MOTHER, BORN MARCH 1902, DIED MARCH 1959
AND MY FATHER, BORN FEBRUARY 1900, DIED JUNE 1959

Gone, I say and walk from church,
refusing the stiff procession to the grave,
letting the dead ride alone in the hearse.
It is June. I am tired of being brave.

We drive to the Cape.[1] I cultivate   5
myself where the sun gutters from the sky,
where the sea swings in like an iron gate
and we touch. In another country people die.

My darling, the wind falls in like stones
from the whitehearted water and when we touch   10
we enter touch entirely. No one's alone.
Men kill for this, or for as much.

And what of the dead? They lie without shoes
in their stone boats. They are more like stone
than the sea would be if it stopped. They refuse   15
to be blessed, throat, eye and knucklebone.

1961, 1962

All My Pretty Ones[1]

Father, this year's jinx rides us apart
where you followed our mother to her cold slumber;
a second shock boiling its stone to your heart,
leaving me here to shuffle and disencumber
you from the residence you could not afford: 5
a gold key, your half of a woolen mill,

---

[1] I.e., Cape Cod in Massachusetts.
[1] Cf. "All my pretty ones? / Did you say all? O hell-kite! All? / What, all my pretty chickens and their dam / At one fell swoop? . . . I cannot but remember *such* things were / That were most precious to me." From Shakespeare's *Macbeth*, 4.3. 216 ff.; Macduff reacts to news that his wife and children have been killed.

twenty suits from Dunne's, an English Ford,
the love and legal verbiage of another will,
boxes of pictures of people I do not know.
I touch their cardboard faces. They must go.   10

But the eyes, as thick as wood in this album,
hold me. I stop here, where a small boy
waits in a ruffled dress for someone to come . . .
for this soldier who holds his bugle like a toy
or for this velvet lady who cannot smile.   15
Is this your father's father, this commodore
in a mailman suit? My father, time meanwhile
has made it unimportant who you are looking for.
I'll never know what these faces are all about.
I lock them into their book and throw them out.   20

This is the yellow scrapbook that you began
the year I was born; as crackling now and wrinkly
as tobacco leaves: clippings where Hoover outran
the Democrats, wiggling his dry finger at me
and Prohibition; news where the *Hindenburg* went   25
down[2] and recent years where you went flush
on war. This year, solvent but sick, you meant
to marry that pretty widow in a one-month rush.
But before you had that second chance, I cried
on your fat shoulder. Three days later you died.   30

These are the snapshots of marriage, stopped in places.
Side by side at the rail toward Nassau[3] now;
here, with the winner's cup at the speedboat races,
here, in tails at the Cotillion,[4] you take a bow,
here, by our kennel of dogs with their pink eyes,   35
running like show-bred pigs in their chain-link pen;
here, at the horseshow where my sister wins a prize;
and here, standing like a duke among groups of men.
Now I fold you down, my drunkard, my navigator,
my first lost keeper, to love or look at later.   40

I hold a five-year diary that my mother kept
for three years, telling all she does not say
of your alcoholic tendency. You overslept,
she writes. My God, father, each Christmas Day
with your blood, will I drink down your glass   45
of wine? The diary of your hurly-burly years
goes to my shelf to wait for my age to pass.
Only in this hoarded span will love persevere.
Whether you are pretty or not, I outlive you,
bend down my strange face to yours and forgive you.   50

1961, 1962

---

[2]In 1928, Herbert Hoover, a Republican, became president by defeating Alfred E. Smith, a "whisky" Democrat; during the 1920s (until 1932), Prohibition made selling or drinking alcohol illegal in the United States; in 1937, the German zeppelin *Hindenberg* went down in flames on arrival in New Jersey, killing many passengers aboard.
[3]Capital of the Bahamas.
[4]A debutante ball, a "coming out" party for daughters of the socially elite.

The Starry Night

> That does not keep me from having a terrible need
> of — shall I say the word — religion. Then I go out at
> night to paint the stars.
>   VINCENT VAN GOGH in a letter to his brother[1]

The town does not exist
except where one black-haired tree slips
up like a drowned woman into the hot sky.
The town is silent. The night boils with eleven stars.
Oh starry starry night! This is how   5
I want to die.

It moves. They are all alive.
Even the moon bulges in its orange irons
to push children, like a god, from its eye.
The old unseen serpent swallows up the stars.   10
Oh starry starry night! This is how
I want to die:

into that rushing beast of the night,
sucked up by that great dragon, to split
from my life with no flag,   15
no belly,
no cry.

1961, 1962

Self in 1958

What is reality?
I am a plaster doll; I pose
with eyes that cut open without landfall or nightfall
upon some shellacked and grinning person,
eyes that open, blue, steel, and close.   5
Am I approximately an I. Magnin[1] transplant?
I have hair, black angel,
black-angel-stuffing to comb,
nylon legs, luminous arms
and some advertised clothes.   10

I live in a doll's house
with four chairs,
a counterfeit table, a flat roof
and a big front door.
Many have come to such a small crossroad.   15
There is an iron bed,

---

[1]Van Gogh (1853–1890), a Dutch painter who went insane
and committed suicide, wrote this letter to his brother Theo
in September 1888, from Arles, France. Sexton's poem is
based on his painting *The Starry Night* (1889).
[1]A fashionable department store.

(Life enlarges, life takes aim)
a cardboard floor,
windows that flash open on someone's city,
and little more.   20

Someone plays with me,
plants me in the all-electric kitchen,
Is this what Mrs. Rombauer[2] said?
Someone pretends with me —
I am walled in solid by their noise —   25
or puts me upon their straight bed.
They think I am me!
Their warmth? Their warmth is not a friend!
They pry my mouth for their cups of gin
and their stale bread.   30

What is reality
to this synthetic doll
who should smile, who should shift gears,
should spring the doors open in a wholesome disorder,
and have no evidence of ruin or fears?   35
But I would cry,
rooted into the wall that
was once my mother,
if I could remember how
and if I had the tears.   40

1958–65   *1966*

ADRIENNE RICH

(b. 1929)

In a key feminist document of the contemporary period, "When We Dead
Awaken: Writing as Re-vision," delivered in 1971 to a forum on "The Woman
Writer in the Twentieth Century," Adrienne Rich said: "Both the victimization
and the anger experienced by women are real, and have real sources, everywhere in the environment, built into society, language, the structures of thought.
They will go on being tapped and explored by poets, among others. . . . 'Political'
poetry by men remains stranded amid the struggles for power among male
groups. . . . The creative energy of patriarchy is fast running out; what remains is
its self-generating energy for destruction. As women, we have our work cut out
for us."

Rich had travelled a long road to reach the position she expressed in this
essay. She was born the daughter of a Jewish doctor and a non-Jewish mother in
Baltimore in 1929 and entered Radcliffe College in 1947. By the time of her
graduation in 1951, a volume of her poems, *A Change of World*, had been selected
by W. H. Auden to be published in the Yale Younger Poets Series. In his introduction to the volume of undisturbing poems in traditional forms, Auden wrote:
"The poems a reader will encounter in this book are neatly and modestly

---

[2]Author of the popular cookbook *The Joy of Cooking*.

dressed, speak quietly but do not mumble, respect their elders but are not cowed by them, and do not tell fibs: that, for a first volume, is a good deal."

By the time Rich's second volume of poems was published in 1955, *The Diamond Cutters and Other Poems*, she had married a Jewish Harvard professor, Alfred Conrad, an economist. And determined, as she recalled later, to "prove that as a woman poet" she "could also have what was then defined as a 'full' woman's life," she had three sons by the time she was thirty. To all outward appearances a happy, middle-class wife, mother, and published poet, Adrienne Rich began in the late 1950s to suffer deep discontents, sensing almost indefinable losses that accompanied all the gains in her life.

In the candid review of her life in "When We Dead Awaken," she said: "My own luck was being born white and middle-class into a house full of books, with a father who encouraged me to read and write. So for about twenty years I wrote for a particular man, who criticized and praised me and made me feel I was indeed 'special.' The obverse side of this, of course, was that I tried for a long time to please him, or rather, not to displease him." She was, she added, "formed first by male poets: by the men I was reading as an undergraduate." The traditional forms of the earlier poetry were a part of her conformity: "In those years formalism was part of the strategy — like asbestos gloves, it allowed me to handle materials I couldn't pick up bare-handed."

The late 1950s and early 1960s were a time of great turmoil for Rich, and she jotted down in a notebook during this period her feelings of frustration: "Paralyzed by the sense that there exists a mesh of relationships — e.g., between my anger at the children, my sensual life, pacifism, sex (I mean sex in its broadest significance, not merely sexual desire) — an interconnectedness which, if I could see it, make it valid, would give me back myself, make it possible to function lucidly and passionately. Yet I grope in and out among these dark webs." Out of such feelings, Rich was able to remake herself as a poet. She found herself, she later recalled, able "for the first time" to write "directly about experiencing myself as a woman."

The progress of the change may be followed in the successive volumes of poems that were published during the 1960s and early 1970s: *Snapshots of a Daughter-in-Law* (1963), *Necessities of Life* (1966), *Leaflets* (1969), *The Will to Change* (1971), and *Diving into the Wreck, 1971–1972* (1973). The poems tended to be written in a looser style than Rich's earlier work. And whereas she had constructed her first poems trying "very much *not* to identify" herself "as a female poet," now she wrote with the full sense of her identity as a woman. Rich's emotional growth made it inevitable that she would become associated with the feminist movement and with the antiwar movement, the two merging in her belief that, in a patriarchal society, it is "phallocentric sadism" that is responsible for the omnipresent violence, not only in wars but in social and sexual conflicts.

In a forum in 1976, sponsored by the Women's Commission and Gay Caucus of the Modern Language Association, Rich read an essay, "It Is the Lesbian in Us . . .," revealing the new position to which her radical rethinking of her life had brought her: "I believe it is the lesbian in every woman who is compelled by female energy, who gravitates toward strong women, who seeks a literature that will express that energy and strength. It is the lesbian in us who drives us to feel imaginatively, render in language, grasp, the full connection between woman and woman. It is the lesbian in us who is creative, for the dutiful daughter of the fathers in us is only a hack." She elaborated on her meaning in the Foreword to her 1979 book of prose (which included this controversial essay), *On Lies, Secrets and Silence*: "It is . . . crucial that we understand lesbian/feminism in the deepest, most radical sense: as that love for ourselves and other women, that commitment to the freedom of all of us, which transcends the category of 'sexual preference' and the issue of civil rights, to become a politics of *asking women's questions*, demanding a world in which the integrity of all women—not a chosen few—shall be honored and validated in every aspect of culture."

Rich published *Twenty-One Love Poems* in 1976, addressed to a woman, apparently in accord with the philosophy of the "lesbian-feminism" she espoused (her husband had committed suicide in 1970). Also appearing in 1976 was an important book of prose, *Of Woman Born: Motherhood as Experience and Institution*. Later books of essays include *Compulsory Heterosexuality and Lesbian Existence* (1980) and *Blood, Bread and Poetry: Selected Prose, 1979–1985* (1986).

When Rich published her *Poems Selected and New, 1950–1974* (1975), she described her discovery of—and surprise at—her own poetic evolution: "I began dating poems sometime in 1954. I had come to the end of the kind of poetry I was writing in *The Diamond Cutters*, and felt embarked on a process that was tentative and exploratory, both as to form and materials; I needed to allow the poems to speak for their moment." In a few broad strokes, she sketched herself in 1984 as "a person in history, a woman and not a man, a white and also Jewish inheritor of a particular Western consciousness, from the making of which most women have been excluded."

Rich's other books of poetry include *The Dream of a Common Language: Poems, 1974–1977* (1978), *A Wild Patience Has Taken Me This Far: Poems, 1978–1981* (1981), *The Fact of a Doorframe* (1984), *Your Native Land, Your Life* (1986), and *Time's Power* (1989). This last volume reflects her continuing concern for the fate of—and possibilities for—women in the contemporary male-dominated world. She writes in one poem, "Divisions of Labor": "I have seen a woman sitting / between the stove and the stars / her fingers singed from snuffing out the candles / of pure theory   Finger and thumb: both scorched: / I have felt that sacred wax blister my hand."

ADDITIONAL READING

Adrienne Rich's Poetry: Texts of the Poems, The Poet on Her Work, Reviews and Criticism, ed. Barbara Charlesworth Gelpi and Albert Gelpi, 1975.

Wendy Martin, *American Triptych: Anne Bradstreet, Emily Dickinson, and Adrienne Rich*, 1984; Jane Roberta Cooper, ed., *Reading Adrienne Rich*, 1984; Myriam Diaz-Diocaretz, *Translating Poetic Discourse: Questions on Feminist Strategies in Adrienne Rich*, 1985; Claire Keyes, *The Aesthetics of Power: The Poetry of Adrienne Rich*, 1986; Craig Werner, *Adrienne Rich: The Poet and Her Critics*, 1988.

TEXTS

"Upper Broadway" from *The Dream of a Common Language*, 1978; "Grandmothers" from *A Wild Patience Has Taken Me This Far*, 1981; remaining poems from *Poems Selected and New, 1950–1974*, 1975.

Aunt Jennifer's Tigers

Aunt Jennifer's tigers prance across a screen,
Bright topaz denizens of a world of green.
They do not fear the men beneath the tree;
They pace in sleek chivalric certainty.

Aunt Jennifer's fingers fluttering through her wool   5
Find even the ivory needle hard to pull.
The massive weight of Uncle's wedding band
Sits heavily upon Aunt Jennifer's hand.

When Aunt is dead, her terrified hands will lie
Still ringed with ordeals she was mastered by.   10
The tigers in the panel that she made
Will go on prancing, proud and unafraid.

1951

Living in Sin

She had thought the studio would keep itself;
no dust upon the furniture of love.
Half heresy, to wish the taps less vocal,
the panes relieved of grime. A plate of pears,
a piano with a Persian shawl, a cat   5
stalking the picturesque amusing mouse
had risen at his urging.
Not that at five each separate stair would writhe
under the milkman's tramp; that morning light
so coldly would delineate the scraps   10
of last night's cheese and three sepulchral bottles;
that on the kitchen shelf among the saucers
a pair of beetle-eyes would fix her own—
envoy from some village in the moldings . . .
Meanwhile, he, with a yawn,   15
sounded a dozen notes upon the keyboard,
declared it out of tune, shrugged at the mirror,
rubbed at his beard, went out for cigarettes;
while she, jeered by the minor demons,
pulled back the sheets and made the bed and found   20
a towel to dust the table-top,
and let the coffee-pot boil over on the stove.
By evening she was back in love again,
though not so wholly but throughout the night
she woke sometimes to feel the daylight coming   25
like a relentless milkman up the stairs.

1955

Snapshots of a
Daughter-in-Law

1.

You, once a belle in Shreveport,
with henna-colored hair, skin like a peachbud,
still have your dresses copied from that time,

and play a Chopin prelude
called by Cortot: *"Delicious recollections*   5
float like perfume through the memory."[1]

Your mind now, moldering like wedding-cake,
heavy with useless experience, rich
with suspicion, rumor, fantasy,
crumbling to pieces under the knife-edge   10
of mere fact. In the prime of your life.

Nervy, glowering, your daughter
wipes the teaspoons, grows another way.

2.

Banging the coffee-pot into the sink
she hears the angels chiding, and looks out   15
past the raked gardens to the sloppy sky.
Only a week since They said: *Have no patience.*

The next time it was: *Be insatiable.*
Then: *Save yourself; others you cannot save.*
Sometimes she's let the tapstream scald her arm,   20
a match burn to her thumbnail,

or held her hand above the kettle's snout
right in the woolly steam. They are probably angels,
since nothing hurts her anymore, except
each morning's grit blowing into her eyes.   25

3.

A thinking woman sleeps with monsters.
The beak that grips her, she becomes. And Nature,
that sprung-lidded, still commodious
steamer-trunk of *tempora* and *mores*[2]
gets stuffed with it all: the mildewed orange-flowers,   30
the female pills, the terrible breasts
of Boadicea[3] beneath flat foxes' heads and orchids.

Two handsome women, gripped in argument,
each proud, acute, subtle, I hear scream
across the cut glass and majolica   35
like Furies[4] cornered from their prey:
The argument *ad feminam,*[5] all the old knives
that have rusted in my back, I drive in yours,
ma semblable, ma soeur![6]

[1]Remark of Alfred Cortot (1877–1962), French pianist, in his work *Chopin: 24 Preludes* (1930); Frédéric Chopin (1810–1849), Polish composer and pianist who lived much of his life in Paris.
[2]"Times and customs" (Latin); an oblique allusion to the exclamation, "O tempora! O mores!" ("Alas for the degeneracy of our times and the low standard of our morals"), by the Roman orator, Cicero (106–43 B.C.).
[3]Boadicea (d. 62 A.D.), Queen of Iceni, Britons of Norfolk and Suffolk; led revolt against the Romans.
[4]Goddesses of vengeance in Greek mythology.
[5]A back-formation from "ad hominem" (attack against the man, not his arguments).
[6]"My double, my sister!" (French); adapted from the phrase by Charles Baudelaire (1821–1867), French poet: "Hypocrite reader, my double, my brother!" (in "To the Reader" prefacing his *Flowers of Evil*). Baudelaire's phrase was used by T. S. Eliot in *The Waste Land* (1922).

4.

Knowing themselves too well in one another: 40
their gifts no pure fruition, but a thorn,
the prick filed sharp against a hint of scorn . . .
Reading while waiting
for the iron to heat,
writing, *My Life had stood—a Loaded Gun—*[7]   45
in that Amherst pantry while the jellies boil and scum,
or, more often,
iron-eyed and beaked and purposed as a bird,
dusting everything on the whatnot every day of life.

5.

Dulce ridens, dulce loquens,[8]   50
she shaves her legs until they gleam
like petrified mammoth-tusk.

6.

When to her lute Corinna sings[9]
neither words nor music are her own;
only the long hair dipping   55
over her cheek, only the song
of silk against her knees
and these
adjusted in reflections of an eye.

Poised, trembling and unsatisfied, before   60
an unlocked door, that cage of cages,
tell us, you bird, you tragical machine—
is this *fertilisante douleur?*[10] Pinned down
by love, for you the only natural action,
are you edged more keen   65
to prise the secrets of the vault? has Nature shown
her household books to you, daughter-in-law,
that her sons never saw?

7.

"To have in this uncertain world some stay
which cannot be undermined, is   70
of the utmost consequence."[11]
                    Thus wrote
a woman, partly brave and partly good,
who fought with what she partly understood.
Few men about her would or could do more,   75
hence she was labeled harpy, shrew and whore.

---

[7]Poem by Emily Dickinson (1830–1886), American poet who lived in Amherst, Massachusetts; see Poem 754 in the edition by T. H. Johnson.
[8]"Sweetly laughing, sweetly speaking" (Latin), from Horace's Ode XXII ("Integer vitae"), lines 23–24.
[9]First line of a love poem by Thomas Campion (1567–1620), British poet.
[10]"Fertilizing sorrow" (French).
[11]From *Thoughts on the Education of Daughters* (1787), by Mary Wollstonecraft (1759–1797), English writer and early feminist.

8.

"You all die at fifteen," said Diderot,[12]
and turn part legend, part convention.
Still, eyes inaccurately dream
behind closed windows blankening with steam.   80
Deliciously, all that we might have been,
all that we were—fire, tears,
wit, taste, martyred ambition—
stirs like the memory of refused adultery
the drained and flagging bosom of our middle years.   85

9.

Not that it is done well, but
that it is done at all?[13] Yes, think
of the odds! or shrug them off forever.
This luxury of the precocious child,
Time's precious chronic invalid,—   90
would we, darlings, resign it if we could?
Our blight has been our sinecure:
mere talent was enough for us—
glitter in fragments and rough drafts.

Sigh no more, ladies.   95
                        Time is male
and in his cups drinks to the fair.
Bemused by gallantry, we hear
our mediocrities over-praised,
indolence read as abnegation,   100
slattern thought styled intuition,
every lapse forgiven, our crime
only to cast too bold a shadow
or smash the mold straight off.

For that, solitary confinement,   105
tear gas, attrition shelling.
Few applicants for that honor.

10.

                        Well,
she's long about her coming, who must be
more merciless to herself than history.   110
Her mind full to the wind, I see her plunge
breasted and glancing through the currents,
taking the light upon her
at least as beautiful as any boy
or helicopter,   115
                        poised, still coming,
her fine blades making the air wince

but her cargo
no promise then:

---

[12]From *Letters to Sophie Volland* by Denis Diderot (1713–1784), French encyclopedist and writer-philosopher.
[13]Cf. "Sir, a woman's preaching is like a dog's walking on his hind legs. It is not done well; but you are surprised to find it done at all," said by Dr. Johnson (1709–1784) and quoted in *The Life of Samuel Johnson* by James Boswell (1740–1795).

delivered
palpable
ours.   120

1958–60   1963

Peeling Onions

Only to have a grief
equal to all these tears!

There's not a sob in my chest.
Dry-hearted as Peer Gynt[1]
I pare away, no hero,   5
merely a cook.

Crying was labor, once
when I'd good cause.
Walking, I felt my eyes like wounds
raw in my head,   10
so postal-clerks, I thought, must stare.
A dog's look, a cat's, burnt to my brain—
yet all that stayed
stuffed in my lungs like smog.

These old tears in the chopping-bowl.   15

1961   1963

"I Am in Danger—Sir—"[1]

"Half-cracked" to Higginson, living,
afterward famous in garbled versions,
your hoard of dazzling scraps a battlefield,
now your old snood

mothballed at Harvard[2]   5
and you in your variorum monument[3]
equivocal to the end—
who are you?

Gardening the day-lily,
wiping the wine-glass stems,   10
your thought pulsed on behind
a forehead battered paper-thin,

---

[1]Boastful and capricious hero of *Peer Gynt* by Henrik Ibsen
(1828–1906), Norwegian playwright and poet.
[1]Emily Dickinson (1830–1886) sent some of her poems to the
critic-essayist Thomas Wentworth Higginson (1823–1911)
for comment; when he criticized their metrical "faults," she
replied: "You think my gait 'spasmodic'—I am in danger—

Sir—you think me 'uncontrolled'—I have no Tribunal."
[2]In the Dickinson Room of the Houghton Library at Harvard Dickinson manuscripts and memorabilia are stored.
[3]The three-volume variorum edition (containing all variant
readings found in the manuscripts) of Dickinson's *Poems*,
edited by Thomas H. Johnson in 1955.

you, woman, masculine
in single-mindedness,
for whom the word was more   15
than a symptom—

a condition of being.
Till the air buzzing with spoiled language
sang in your ears
of Perjury   20

and in your half-cracked way you chose
silence for entertainment,[4]
chose to have it out at last
on your own premises.

1964   1966

Orion[1]

Far back when I went zig-zagging
through tamarack[2] pastures
you were my genius, you
my cast-iron Viking, my helmed
lion-heart king in prison.[3]   5
Years later now you're young

my fierce half-brother, staring
down from that simplified west
your breast open, your belt dragged down
by an oldfashioned thing, a sword   10
the last bravado you won't give over
though it weighs you down as you stride

and the stars in it are dim
and maybe have stopped burning.
But you burn, and I know it;   15
as I throw back my head to take you in
an old transfusion happens again:
divine astronomy is nothing to it.

Indoors I bruise and blunder,
break faith, leave ill enough
alone, a dead child born in the dark.   20
Night cracks up over the chimney,
pieces of time, frozen geodes
come showering down in the grate.

A man reaches behind my eyes
and finds them empty   25

---

[4]Out of the some 1800 poems she wrote, Dickinson published only ten during her lifetime.
[1]In Greek mythology, a giant hunter who pursued the Pleiades (seven daughters of Atlas) and was slain by the virgin huntress Artemis (associated with the moon); Orion was then made into a constellation in the sky.
[2]An American larch tree, of the pine family.
[3]Richard I of England (1157–1199) was known as "the Lion-Hearted" and was imprisoned for a short time on returning from a crusade.

a woman's head turns away
from my head in the mirror
children are dying my death
and eating crumbs of my life.   30

Pity is not your forte.
Calmly you ache up there
pinned aloft in your crow's nest,
my speechless pirate!
You take it all for granted   35
and when I look you back

it's with a starlike eye
shooting its cold and egotistical spear
where it can do least damage.
Breathe deep! No hurt, no pardon   40
out here in the cold with you
you with your back to the wall.

1965   1969

Diving into the Wreck

First having read the book of myths,
and loaded the camera,
and checked the edge of the knife-blade,
I put on
the body-armor of black rubber   5
the absurd flippers
the grave and awkward mask.
I am having to do this
not like Cousteau[1] with his
assiduous team   10
aboard the sun-flooded schooner
but here alone.

There is a ladder.
The ladder is always there
hanging innocently   15
close to the side of the schooner.
We know what it is for,
we who have used it.
Otherwise
it's a piece of maritime floss   20
some sundry equipment.

I go down.
Rung after rung and still
the oxygen immerses me
the blue light   25
the clear atoms
of our human air.

---

[1]Jacques-Yves Cousteau (b. 1910), French explorer of the
seas, popular in film and television programs.

I go down.
My flippers cripple me,
I crawl like an insect down the ladder   30
and there is no one
to tell me when the ocean
will begin.

First the air is blue and then
it is bluer and then green and then   35
black I am blacking out and yet
my mask is powerful
it pumps my blood with power
the sea is another story
the sea is not a question of power   40
I have to learn alone
to turn my body without force
in the deep element.

And now: it is easy to forget
what I came for   45
among so many who have always
lived here
swaying their crenellated fans
between the reefs
and besides   50
you breathe differently down here.

I came to explore the wreck.
The words are purposes.
The words are maps.
I came to see the damage that was done   55
and the treasures that prevail.
I stroke the beam of my lamp
slowly along the flank
of something more permanent
than fish or weed   60

the thing I came for:
the wreck and not the story of the wreck
the thing itself and not the myth
the drowned face always staring
toward the sun   65
the evidence of damage
worn by salt and sway into this threadbare beauty
the ribs of the disaster
curving their assertion
among the tentative haunters.   70

This is the place.
And I am here, the mermaid whose dark hair
streams black, the merman in his armored body
We circle silently
about the wreck   75
we dive into the hold.
I am she: I am he

whose drowned face sleeps with open eyes
whose breasts still bear the stress

whose silver, copper, vermeil cargo lies   80
obscurely inside barrels
half-wedged and left to rot
we are the half-destroyed instruments
that once held to a course
the water-eaten log   85
the fouled compass

We are, I am, you are
by cowardice or courage
the one who find our way
back to this scene   90
carrying a knife, a camera
a book of myths
in which
our names do not appear.

1972   1973

Translations

You show me the poems of some woman
my age, or younger
translated from your language

Certain words occur: *enemy, oven, sorrow*
enough to let me know   5
she's a woman of my time

obsessed

with Love, our subject:
we've trained it like ivy to our walls
baked it like bread in our ovens   10
worn it like lead on our ankles
watched it through binoculars as if
it were a helicopter
bringing food to our famine
or the satellite   15
of a hostile power

I begin to see that woman
doing things: stirring rice
ironing a skirt
typing a manuscript till dawn   20

trying to make a call
from a phonebooth

The phone rings unanswered
in a man's bedroom
she hears him telling someone else   25
Never mind. She'll get tired—
hears him telling her story to her sister

who becomes her enemy
and will in her own time
light her own way to sorrow   30

ignorant of the fact this way of grief
is shared, unnecessary
and political

1972   1973

From a Survivor

The pact that we made was the ordinary pact
of men & women in those days

I don't know who we thought we were
that our personalities
could resist the failures of the race   5

Lucky or unlucky, we didn't know
the race had failures of that order
and that we were going to share them

Like everybody else, we thought of ourselves as special

Your body is as vivid to me   10
as it ever was: even more

since my feeling for it is clearer:
I know what it could and could not do

it is no longer
the body of a god
or anything with power over my life   15

Next year it would have been 20 years
and you are wastefully dead
who might have made the leap
we talked, too late, of making   20

which I live now
not as a leap
but a succession of brief, amazing movements

each one making possible the next

1972   1973

Upper Broadway

The leafbud straggles forth
toward the frigid light of the airshaft   this is faith
this pale extension of a day

when looking up   you know   something is changing
winter has turned   though the wind is colder   5
Three streets away   a roof collapses   onto people
who thought they still had time   Time out of mind

I have written so many words
wanting to live inside you
to be of use to you   10

Now I must write for myself   for this blind
woman scratching the pavement   with her wand of thought
this slippered crone   inching on icy streets
reaching into wire trashbaskets   pulling out
what was thrown away   and infinitely precious   15

I look at my hands and see   they are still unfinished
I look at the vine and see the leafbud
inching towards life

I look at my face in the glass   and see
a halfborn woman   20

1975   1978

Grandmothers

1. Mary Gravely Jones

We had no petnames, no diminutives for you,
always the formal guest under my father's roof:
you were "Grandmother Jones" and you visited rarely.
I see you walking up and down the garden,
restless, southern-accented, reserved, you did not seem   5
my mother's mother or anyone's grandmother.
You were Mary, widow of William, and no matriarch,
yet smoldering to the end with frustrate life,
ideas nobody listened to, least of all my father.
One summer night you sat with my sister and me   10
in the wooden glider long after twilight,
holding us there with streams of pent-up words.
You could quote every poet I had ever heard of,
had read *The Opium Eater*, Amiel and Bernard Shaw,[1]
your green eyes looked clenched against opposition.   15
You married straight out of the convent school,
your background was country, you left an unperformed
typescript of a play about Burr and Hamilton,[2]
you were impotent and brilliant, no one cared
about your mind, you might have ended   20
elsewhere than in that glider
reciting your unwritten novels to the children.

[1]*Confessions of an Opium Eater* (1821) by Thomas de Quincy (1785–1859), British essayist; Henri Frédéric Amiel (1821–1881), Swiss poet-philosopher; George Bernard Shaw (1856–1950), Irish playwright and social critic.

[2]Aaron Burr (1756–1836), ambitious to be president, was opposed (and criticized) by Alexander Hamilton (1755–1804); Burr challenged Hamilton to a duel in 1804 and killed him in the encounter.

2. Hattie Rice Rich

Your sweetness of soul was a mystery to me,
you who slip-covered chairs, glued broken china,
lived out of a wardrobe trunk in our guestroom   25
summer and fall, then took the Pullman train
in your darkblue dress and straw hat, to Alabama,
shuttling half-yearly between your son and daughter.
Your sweetness of soul was a convenience for everyone,
how you rose with the birds and children, boiled your own egg,   30
fished for hours on a pier, your umbrella spread,
took the street-car downtown shopping
endlessly for your son's whims, the whims of genius,
kept your accounts in ledgers, wrote letters daily.
All through World War Two the forbidden word   35
Jewish was barely uttered in your son's house;
your anger flared over inscrutable things.
Once I saw you crouched on the guestroom bed,
knuckles blue-white around the bedpost, sobbing
your one brief memorable scene of rebellion: 40
you didn't want to go back South that year.
You were never "Grandmother Rich" but "Anana";
you had money of your own but you were homeless,
Hattie, widow of Samuel, and no matriarch,
dispersed among the children and grandchildren.   45

3. Granddaughter

Easier to encapsulate your lives
in a slide-show of impressions given and taken,
to play the child or victim, the projectionist,
easier to invent a script for each of you,
myself still at the center,   50
than to write words in which you might have found
yourselves, looked up at me and said
"Yes, I was like that; but I was something more. . . ."
Danville, Virginia; Vicksburg, Mississippi;
the "war between the states"[3] a living memory   55
its aftermath the plague-town closing
its gates, trying to cure itself with poisons.
I can almost touch that little town. . . .
a little white town rimmed with Negroes,
making a deep shadow on the whiteness.   60
Born a white woman, Jewish or of curious mind
—twice an outsider, still believing in inclusion—
in those defended hamlets of half-truth
broken in two by one strange idea,
"blood" the all-powerful, awful theme—   65
what were the lessons to be learned? If I believe
the daughter of one of you—Amnesia was the answer.

1980   1981

---

[3] I.e., the Civil War (1861–65).

CONTEMPORARY POETRY III
Poets Born in the 1930s, 1940s, and 1950s

GARY SNYDER
SYLVIA PLATH
IMAMU AMIRI BARAKA
  (LEROI JONES)
CHARLES WRIGHT
MICHAEL S. HARPER
ROBERT PINSKY

SIMON J. ORTIZ
NIKKI GIOVANNI
LOUISE GLÜCK
LESLIE MARMON SILKO
RITA DOVE
GARY SOTO

"As a poet I hold the most archaic values on earth. They go back to the Neolithic: the fertility of the soil, the magic of animals, the power-vision in solitude, the terrifying initiation and rebirth, the love and ecstasy of the dance, the common work of the tribe."

Gary Snyder, *A Controversy of Poets*

"The poet's medium . . . is abstract, more or less discursive, and in some senses conventional. But his convictions about reality and art are likely to be pervaded by the idea that reality inheres in particulars, not abstractions; in experience, not in discourse or convention."

Robert Pinsky, *The Situation of Poetry: Contemporary Poetry and Its Traditions*

"A man makes his prayers; he sings his songs. He considers all that is important and special to him, his home, children, his language, the self that he is. He must make spiritual and physical preparation before anything else. Only then does anything begin."

Simon J. Ortiz, Prologue to *Going for the Rain*

"It's by language that I enter a poem, and that also leads me forward. . . . There's nothing new under the sun, but it's the way you *see* it. For me as a poet, language becomes an integral part of that perception, the *way* one sees it."

Rita Dove, Interview in *Black American Literature Forum*

GARY SNYDER
(b. 1930)

Gary Snyder, in his fascination with Oriental thought, developed a mystical view of poetry. He once remarked in an interview for *Road Apple* (1969/70):

> Poetry *is* before it *begins* in a sense. Like stopping a person momentarily in their tracks with a poem they have happened to look at accidentally and they forget that they were to catch a bus somewhere and they look around and think: My God, I'm living in the world! Or like the great enlightened poet saints like Milarepa or Zen Buddhist masters who wrote poetry. They wrote poetry at the height of their delight, the sheer play of being. Or they would trade poems with each other that other people had written. So the poem always stands there as almost the essence of it. And the beauty of it is that at the beginning and at the end it is equal. That the poem is as valid for the Zen master who is seeing through it, as it is for the man on the street who suddenly remembers that it is spring because the poem has turned his head from his preoccupation.

Such a view of the delight and joy of poetry hardly seems right for the Beat Generation of Allen Ginsberg's *Howl*, but Snyder is usually classified as a Beat poet. He is, however, very much his own poet. Unlike the eastern urban background of most of the other beats, Snyder's background was western and rural. He was born in San Francisco in 1930 and when he was two moved to the state of Washington where his father settled on a farm. It was the time of the Great Depression, and Snyder grew up helping with the farm chores, learning to use his hands to make what the family could not afford to buy. He very early developed a keen respect for master craftsmen. The family migrated to Portland, Oregon, when Snyder was twelve, and he finished high school there in 1947.

During these years Snyder developed the skills of self-sufficiency, both indoors and out, learning to sew and cook as well as chop wood and fix machines. But he also became a reader of books, especially those about Indians, animals, and nature. After finishing high school, he entered Reed College, where he majored in both anthropology and English. He published poetry in the college magazine, and wrote a B.A. thesis on American Indian culture that would later be published. He said of his teachers at Reed: "They . . . exposed me to all varieties of intellectual positions and gave me a territory in which I could speak out my radical politics and get arguments and argumentation on it."

During the early 1950s, Snyder tried graduate work at the University of Indiana, but left after a brief period. In 1952 he settled in the San Francisco Bay area and began studying oriental languages at the University of California, a program he followed for some four years. His summers he spent working in such outdoor jobs as fire-lookout on Sourdough Mountain in Washington or as a worker on a "trail crew" at Yosemite National Park. This was the period during which the Beat poets were coming together in San Francisco. Snyder met Allen Ginsberg and Jack Kerouac and was present in 1955 as one of the performers in the legendary poetry reading at which Ginsberg read *Howl*. Snyder left for the Orient a few months after this event. Although his association with the Beats was brief, and his poetic temperament in many ways different, he would be stamped with the Beat literary identity throughout his career. Kerouac used him as the basis for his character Japhy Ryder in *The Dharma Bums* (1958).

In 1956, Snyder sailed for Japan, where he would stay the next twelve years, with the exception of a few trips back to America. Snyder had been attracted to

Buddhism at an early age, and his study of Oriental languages grew out of that interest. He came to look upon Christianity as an "ideology which separated human kind from all other living beings (with the two categories of redeemable and unredeemable)"; and he thought he had found in Buddhism "an organic, process-oriented view of the world." In Japan, he began his prolonged studies of Zen Buddhism. Toward the end of his Japanese stay, Snyder, whose two earlier brief marriages had ended in divorce, married a Japanese wife; it was a marriage that would endure.

During this period, Snyder began to publish poems, and his initial book, *Riprap*, appeared in 1959. He explained the title in "Statements on Poetics" for Donald M. Allen's *New American Poetry* (1960):

> I've just recently come to realize that the rhythms of my poems follow the rhythm of the physical work I'm doing and life I'm leading at any given time — which makes the music in my head which creates the line. . . . "Riprap" is really a class of poems I wrote under the influence of the geology of the Sierra Nevada and the daily trail-crew work of picking up and placing granite stones in tight cobble patterns on hard slab. "What are you doing?" I asked old Roy Marchbanks. — "Riprapping" he said. His selection of natural rocks was perfect — the result looked like dressed stone fitting to hair-edge cracks. Walking, climbing, placing with the hands. I tried writing poems of tough, simple, short words, with the complexity far beneath the surface texture. In part the line was influenced by the five- and seven-character Chinese poems I'd been reading, which work like sharp blows on the mind.

Riprap was reissued in 1965 together with *Cold Mountain Poems*, translations from the work of Han-shan, a seventh-century Chinese poet.

In 1960, Snyder published *Myths & Texts*, the title of which came, Snyder explained, from the collections that anthropologists and others had "made of American Indian folktales early in this century"; it also meant, he added, "the two sources of human knowledge — symbols and sense-impressions." The poems were written from 1952 to 1956, when he was frequently working as a fire-look-out or in the logging camps: "I tried to make my life as a hobo and worker, the questions of history & philosophy in my head, and the glimpses of the roots of religion I'd seen through meditation, peyote, and 'secret frantic rituals' into one whole thing."

Snyder and his Japanese wife and children returned to America in 1968 and settled for a time in San Francisco. Soon growing tired of urban life, Snyder sought out a place in the foothills of the Sierra Nevada, where he built his home surrounded by the nature he loves. *The Back Country* (1968) contained poems that grew out of experiences both in the American West and in Japan. Many of these and later poems appeared to be written in accord with Snyder's view: "The true poem is walking that edge between what can be said and that which cannot be said. That's the real razor's edge. . . . the [poems] that make your hair stand on edge are the ones that are right on the line."

The poems in *Regarding Wave* (1969) were written in an increasingly cryptic style, their imagery reflecting a subtle integration of Snyder's interest in the American West, the Indians, and Zen Buddhism. *Turtle Island* (1974) took its title from the Indian name for North America. "The poems," Snyder explained in an Introductory Note, "speak of place, and the energy-pathways that sustain life. Each living being is a swirl in the flow, a formal turbulence, a 'song.' The land, the planet itself, is also a living being — at another place." With *Turtle Island*, Snyder won his first major award, the Pulitzer Prize. Recent volumes of poems are *Axe Handles* (1983) and *Left Out in the Rain* (1986).

In 1965, Snyder published *Six Sections from Mountains and Rivers Without End*, a long poem in progress. He has said of it: "Since 1956 I've been working on a long poem I'm calling *Mountains and Rivers without End* after a Chinese sidewise scroll painting. It threatens to be like its title. Travel, the sense of journey in space that modern people have lost (it takes as long to go from Cedar Grove to the Bighorn Plateau in the Sierras as it does to cross America by train), and rise and fall of rock and water. . . . History and its vengeful ghosts. The dramatic structure follows a certain type of *No* play."

Snyder's books of prose include *Earth House Hold: Technical Notes and Queries to Follow Dharma Revolutionaries* (1969); *The Old Ways: Six Essays* (1977); the B.A. thesis written at Reed College, *He Who Hunted Birds in His Father's Village: The Dimensions of a Haida Myth* (1979); *The Real Work: Interviews and Talks, 1964–1979* (1980); and *A Passage Through India* (1984).

ADDITIONAL READING

Bob Steuding, *Gary Snyder*, 1976; Bert Almon, *Gary Snyder*, 1979; Charles Molesworth, *Gary Snyder's Vision: Poetry and the Real Work*, 1983; Katherine McNeill, *Gary Snyder: A Bibliography*, 1983; Sherman Paul, *In Search of the Primitive: Reading David Antin, Jerome Rothenberg, and Gary Snyder*, 1986.

TEXTS

"Riprap" and "this poem is for bear" from *A Range of Poems*, 1966; "A Walk" and "Song of the Taste" from *The Back Country*, 1967; "Meeting the Mountains" and "Running Water Music" from *Regarding Wave*, 1970; "The Dead by the Side of the Road" from *Turtle Island*, 1974; "Axe Handles" from *Axe Handles*, 1983.

Riprap[1]

```
Lay down these words
Before your mind like rocks.
            placed solid, by hands
In choice of place, set
Before the body of the mind                              5
            in space and time:
Solidity of bark, leaf, or wall
            riprap of things:
Cobble of milky way,
            straying planets,                            10
These poems, people,
            lost ponies with
Dragging saddles —
            and rocky sure-foot trails.
The worlds like an endless                               15
            four-dimensional
Game of Go.
            ants and pebbles
In the thin loam, each rock a word
            a creek-washed stone                         20
Granite: ingrained
            with torment of fire and weight
```

---

[1] "Riprap: a cobble of stone laid on steep slick rock to make a trail for horses in the mountains" (Snyder's note).

Crystal and sediment linked hot
　　　all change, in thoughts,
As well as things.   25

                                        1959

this poem is for bear

"As for me I am a child of the god of the mountains."

A bear down under the cliff.
She is eating huckleberries.
They are ripe now
Soon it will snow, and she   5
Or maybe he, will crawl into a hole
And sleep. You can see
Huckleberries in bearshit if you
Look, this time of year
If I sneak up on the bear   10
It will grunt and run

The others had all gone down
From the blackberry brambles, but one girl
Spilled her basket, and was picking up her
Berries in the dark.   15
A tall man stood in the shadow, took her arm,
Led her to his home. He was a bear.
In a house under the mountain
She gave birth to slick dark children
With sharp teeth, and lived in the hollow   20
Mountain many years.
　　　　　snare a bear: call him out:
honey-eater
forest apple
light-foot   25
Old man in the fur coat, Bear! come out!
Die of your own choice!
Grandfather black-food!
　　　　　　this girl married a bear
Who rules in the mountains, Bear!   30
　　　　　you have eaten many berries
　　　　　you have caught many fish
　　　　　you have frightened many people

Twelve species north of Mexico
Sucking their paws in the long winter   35
Tearing the high-strung caches down
Whining, crying, jacking off
(Odysseus was a bear)

Bear-cubs gnawing the soft tits
Teeth gritted, eyes screwed tight   40
　　　　　but she let them.

Til her brothers found the place
Chased her husband up the gorge

Cornered him in the rocks.
Song of the snared bear: 45
    "Give me my belt.
    "I am near death.
    "I came from the mountain caves
    "At the headwaters,
    "The small streams there   50
    "Are all dried up.

—I think I'll go hunt bears.
        "hunt bears?
Why shit Snyder,
You couldn't hit a bear in the ass   55
      with a handful of rice!"

                            1960

Song of the Taste

Eating the living germs of grasses
Eating the ova of large birds

    the fleshy sweetness packed
    around the sperm of swaying trees

The muscles of the flanks and thighs of   5
        soft-voiced cows
    the bounce in the lamb's leap
    the swish in the ox's tail

Eating roots grown swoll
        inside the soil   10

Drawing on life of living
    clustered points of light spun
        out of space
hidden in the grape.

Eating each other's seed   15
        eating
ah, each other.

Kissing the lover in the mouth of bread:
        lip to lip.

                      1968, 1969

Running Water Music

under the trees
under the clouds

by the river
on the beach,

"sea roads."   5
whales   great sea-path beasts—

                salt;   cold
                water;   smoky fire.
steam, cereal,
                stone, wood boards.   10
bone awl, pelts,
                bamboo pins and spoons.
unglazed bowl.
a band around the hair.

                beyond wounds.   15

sat on a rock in the sun,
watched the old pine
wave
over blinding fine white
                river sand.   20

                                        1970

Meeting the Mountains

He[1] crawls to the edge of the foaming creek
He backs up the slab ledge
He puts a finger in the water
He turns to a trapped pool
Puts both hands in the water   5
Puts one foot in the pool
Drops pebbles in the pool
He slaps the water surface with both hands
He cries out, rises up and stands
Facing toward the torrent and the mountain   10
Raises up both hands and shouts three times!

                                        1969, 1970

The Dead by the
Side of the Road

How did a great Red-tailed Hawk
    come to lie—all stiff and dry—
        on the shoulder of
            Interstate 5?

---

[1]"Kai at Sawmill Lake VI.69" (Snyder's note); Kai is Snyder's
son by his Japanese wife.

Her wings for dance fans   5

Zac skinned a skunk with a crushed head
    washed the pelt in gas; it hangs,
        tanned, in his tent

Fawn stew on Hallowe'en
    hit by a truck on highway forty-nine   10
        offer cornmeal by the mouth;
            skin it out.

Log trucks run on fossil fuel

I never saw a Ringtail til I found one in the road:
    case-skinned it with the toenails   15
        footpads, nose, and whiskers on;
            it soaks in salt and water
                sulphuric acid pickle;

she will be a pouch for magic tools.

The Doe was apparently shot   20
    lengthwise and through the side —
        shoulder and out the flank
            belly full of blood

Can save the other shoulder maybe,
    if she didn't lie too long —   25
Pray to their spirits. Ask them to bless us:
    our ancient sisters' trails
        the roads were laid across and kill them:
            night-shining eyes

The dead by the side of the road.   30

                                              1972, 1974

Axe Handles

One afternoon the last week in April
Showing Kai[1] how to throw a hatchet
One-half turn and it sticks in a stump.
He recalls the hatchet-head
Without a handle, in the shop   5
And go gets it, and wants it for his own.
A broken-off axe handle behind the door
Is long enough for a hatchet,
We cut it to length and take it
With the hatchet head   10
And working hatchet, to the wood block.
There I begin to shape the old handle

---

[1]Snyder's son by his Japanese wife.

With the hatchet, and the phrase
First learned from Ezra Pound
Rings in my ears!   15
"When making an axe handle
    the pattern is not far off."
And I say this to Kai
"Look: We'll shape the handle
By checking the handle   20
Of the axe we cut with—"
And he sees. And I hear it again:
It's in Lu Ji's *Wên Fu*, fourth century
A.D. "Essay on Literature"[2]—in the
Preface: "In making the handle   25
Of an axe
By cutting wood with an axe
The model is indeed near at hand."
My teacher Shih-hsiang Chen
Translated that and taught it years ago   30
And I see: Pound was an axe,
Chen was an axe, I am an axe
And my son a handle, soon
To be shaping again, model
And tool, craft of culture,   35
How we go on.

                                                              1983

SYLVIA PLATH
(1932–1963)

In the Foreword to Sylvia Plath's volume of poems *Ariel*, published in America in 1966, Robert Lowell (whose confessional *Life Studies* had appeared in 1959) wrote:

> Everything in these poems is personal, confessional, felt, but the manner of feeling is controlled hallucination, the autobiography of a fever. She burns to be on the move, a walk, a ride, a journey, the flight of the queen bee. She is driven forward by the pounding pistons of her heart. The title *Ariel* summons up Shakespeare's lovely, though slightly chilling and androgenous spirit, but the truth is that this *Ariel* is the author's horse. . . . These poems are playing Russian roulette with six cartridges in the cylinder, a game of "chicken," the wheels of both cars locked and unable to swerve.

Lowell could write with such assurance because Sylvia Plath had committed suicide some three years before in 1963. Most of the poems in *Ariel* were written in the last months of her life, and seemed to foretell her death. In a shocking poem entitled "Daddy," she concluded:

> There's a stake in your fat black heart
> And the villagers never liked you.

---

[2]The Chinese poet Lu Ji (variant of Lu Chi) wrote *Wen Fu*, a "fu" or "Rhymeprose" (a work containing both prose and rhymes) on the nature of the creative process.

> They are dancing and stamping on you,
> They always *knew* it was you.
> Daddy, daddy, you bastard, I'm through.

In another poem entitled "Lady Lazarus," Plath wrote: "Dying / is an art, like everything else. / I do it exceptionally well."

It was not until the appearance of *Ariel* that American readers came to realize that a gifted, perhaps even major poet had lived and died without their noticing. Plath was born in 1932 in Boston. Her parents were immigrants from Grabow, Poland, her German father a professor of biology at Boston University and the author of a treatise on bees, her Austrian mother a teacher. When Plath was eight years old, in 1940, her father died. Talented and ambitious from the start, she published her first poem before she was nine; in her last year of high school in Wellesley, Massachusetts, she published a poem and a short story in *Seventeen*.

Plath entered Smith College in 1950 and was successful in everything she undertook. She became an honors student and continued to write poetry and fiction. In the summer of 1953 she was appointed guest managing-editor for the college issue of *Madamoiselle*, and she threw herself into the job with great zest. She wrote in a letter to her brother about her feelings in the midst of all the excitement of New York: "I can't think logically who I am or where I am going. I have been very ecstatic, horribly depressed, shocked, elated, enlightened, and enervated." On returning home from New York, her depression increased. She underwent shock treatment, without success, and then attempted suicide by taking a large number of sleeping pills. She was hospitalized long enough to delay her returning to school. The entire experience became the subject of a best-selling novel, *The Bell Jar*, published under a pseudonym in early 1963.

Back on an even keel, Plath returned to school and took her degree at Smith in 1955. She was awarded a student Fulbright fellowship and went to study at Cambridge University in England. The fellowship was extended for a second year, and in 1956 she met and married the British poet Ted Hughes, two years her senior. In 1957, the couple returned to New England, and Plath taught English for a year at Smith College. In 1958, she attended a poetry class taught by Robert Lowell at Boston University, where she met Anne Sexton. Sexton later recalled: "Often, very often, Sylvia and I would talk at length about our first suicides; at length, in detail and in depth between the free potato chips. Suicide is, after all, the opposite of the poem. Sylvia and I often talked opposites. We talked death and burned-up intensity, both of us drawn to it like moths to an electric light bulb."

Plath and her husband returned to England in 1959 and stayed for a time in London, moving later to a farm in Devon. Both poets were hungry for time in which to write and settled on a schedule, after children were born, for Plath to write in the morning, and Hughes the afternoon. Plath's first book, *The Colossus and Other Poems*, appeared in 1960 to mixed reviews. Plath was disappointed, but her creative energies intensified. In 1962, she discovered that her husband was seeing another woman. They separated. He went to live in London; she stayed for a time in Devon, but later moved with the two children to a flat in London.

These last months she produced her greatest work. She wrote to her mother: "I am writing the best poems of my life; they will make my name." But in 1963 she could not contain her despondency. She went to her kitchen and, after making sure that the cracks around the door were sealed and her children were cared for, she turned on the gas in the oven. Her estranged husband became her literary executor, responsible for the posthumous publication of her poetry—

Ariel (1966), *Crossing the Water* (1971), and *Winter Trees* (1972). He edited *The Collected Poems* in 1981, providing a rigorously impersonal Introduction in which he commented on her development as a poet. In what seems like self-realization of her achievement, she wrote in one of her last poems, "Edge": "The woman is perfected. / Her dead / Body wears the smile of accomplishment." Few readers would deny the "accomplishment."

ADDITIONAL READING

Letters Home: Correspondence, 1950–1963, ed. Aurelia Schober Plath, 1975; *The Journals of Sylvia Plath*, ed. Ted Hughes and Frances McCullough, 1982.

Charles Newman, *The Art of Sylvia Plath*, 1970; Ingrid Melander, *The Poetry of Sylvia Plath: A Study of Themes*, 1972; Eileen M. Aird, *Sylvia Plath: Her Life and Works*, 1973; Cameron North-ouse and Thomas P. Walsh, *Sylvia Plath and Anne Sexton: A Reference Guide*, 1974; David Holbrook, *Sylvia Plath: Poetry and Existence*, 1976; Edward Butscher, *Sylvia Plath: Method and Madness*, 1976; Judith Kroll, *Chapters in Mythology: The Poetry of Sylvia Plath*, 1976; Barry Kyle, ed., *Sylvia Plath: A Dramatic Portrait*, 1976; Edward Butscher, ed., *Sylvia Plath: The Woman and Her Work*, 1977; Gary Lane and Maria Stevens, *Sylvia Plath: A Bibliography*, 1978; Caroline King Barnard, *Sylvia Plath*, 1978; Gary Lane, ed., *Sylvia Plath: New Views on the Poetry*, 1979; Jon Rosenblatt, *Sylvia Plath: The Poetry of Initiation*, 1979; Margaret Dickie Uroff, *Sylvia Plath and Ted Hughes*, 1979; Mary Lynn Broe, *Protean Poetic: The Poetry of Sylvia Plath*, 1980; Linda K. Bundtzen, *Plath's Incarnations: Woman and the Creative Process*, 1983; Linda Wagner, ed., *Critical Essays on Sylvia Plath*, 1984; Stephen Tabor, *Sylvia Plath: An Analytical Bibliography*, 1986, and *A Bibliography*, 1987; Linda Wagner-Martin, *Sylvia Plath: A Biography*, 1987; Linda Wagner-Martin, ed., *Sylvia Plath: The Critical Heritage*, 1988; Anne Stevenson, *Bitter Fame: A Life of Sylvia Plath*, 1989.

TEXT

The Collected Poems, ed. Ted Hughes, 1981.

Black Rook in Rainy Weather

On the stiff twig up there
Hunches a wet black rook
Arranging and rearranging its feathers in the rain.
I do not expect a miracle
Or an accident   5

To set the sight on fire
In my eye, nor seek
Any more in the desultory weather some design,
But let spotted leaves fall as they fall,
Without ceremony, or portent.   10

Although, I admit, I desire,
Occasionally, some backtalk
From the mute sky, I can't honestly complain:
A certain minor light may still
Lean incandescent   15

Out of kitchen table or chair
As if a celestial burning took
Possession of the most obtuse objects now and then —

Thus hallowing an interval
Otherwise inconsequent   20

By bestowing largesse, honor,
One might say love. At any rate, I now walk
Wary (for it could happen
Even in this dull, ruinous landscape); skeptical,
Yet politic; ignorant   25

Of whatever angel may choose to flare
Suddenly at my elbow. I only know that a rook
Ordering its black feathers can so shine
As to seize my senses, haul
My eyelids up, and grant   30

A brief respite from fear
Of total neutrality. With luck,
Trekking stubborn through this season
Of fatigue, I shall
Patch together a content   35

Of sorts. Miracles occur,
If you care to call those spasmodic
Tricks of radiance miracles. The wait's begun again,
The long wait for the angel,
For that rare, random descent.   40

                                                        1957, 1960

The Colossus

I shall never get you put together entirely,
Pieced, glued, and properly jointed.
Mule-bray, pig-grunt and bawdy cackles
Proceed from your great lips.
It's worse than a barnyard.   5

Perhaps you consider yourself an oracle,
Mouthpiece of the dead, or of some god or other.
Thirty years now I have labored
To dredge the silt from your throat.
I am none the wiser.   10

Scaling little ladders with gluepots and pails of Lysol
I crawl like an ant in mourning
Over the weedy acres of your brow
To mend the immense skull-plates and clear
The bald, white tumuli[1] of your eyes.   15

A blue sky out of the Oresteia[2]
Arches above us. O father, all by yourself

---

[1]Mounds, especially of graves.
[2]The trilogy by Greek playwright Aeschylus (525–426 B.C.), recounting the downfall of the house of Atreus, in which Orestes kills his mother for murdering his father.

You are pithy and historical as the Roman Forum.
I open my lunch on a hill of black cypress.
Your fluted bones and acanthine[3] hair are littered   20

In their old anarchy to the horizon-line.
It would take more than a lightning-stroke
To create such a ruin.
Nights, I squat in the cornucopia
Of your left ear, out of the wind,   25

Counting the red stars and those of plum-color.
The sun rises under the pillar of your tongue.
My hours are married to shadow.
No longer do I listen for the scrape of a keel
On the blank stones of the landing.   30

1960

The Hanging Man

By the roots of my hair some god got hold of me.
I sizzled in his blue volts like a desert prophet.[1]

The nights snapped out of sight like a lizard's eyelid:
A world of bald white days in a shadeless socket.

A vulturous boredom pinned me in this tree.   5
If he were I, he would do what I did.

1960   *1965*

The Arrival of the Bee Box

I ordered this, this clean wood box
Square as a chair and almost too heavy to lift.
I would say it was the coffin of a midget
Or a square baby
Were there not such a din in it.   5

The box is locked, it is dangerous.
I have to live with it overnight
And I can't keep away from it.
There are no windows, so I can't see what is in there.
There is only a little grid, no exit.   10

I put my eye to the grid.
It is dark, dark,
With the swarmy feeling of African hands

---

[3]Acanthus leaf-like (also, stylized leaves found in Greek art).
[1]The description is based on the "shock treatment" Plath un- derwent while hospitalized for psychiatric problems during her college years.

Minute and shrunk for export,
Black on black, angrily clambering.   15

How can I let them out?
It is the noise that appalls me most of all,
The unintelligible syllables.
It is like a Roman mob,
Small, taken one by one, but my god, together!   20

I lay my ear to furious Latin.
I am not a Caesar.
I have simply ordered a box of maniacs.
They can be sent back.
They can die, I need feed them nothing, I am the owner.   25

I wonder how hungry they are.
I wonder if they would forget me
If I just undid the locks and stood back and turned into a tree.
There is the laburnum, its blond colonnades,
And the petticoats of the cherry.   30

They might ignore me immediately
In my moon suit and funeral veil.
I am no source of honey
So why should they turn on me?
Tomorrow I will be sweet God, I will set them free.   35

The box is only temporary.

1962   *1963, 1965*

The Applicant

First, are you our sort of a person?
Do you wear
A glass eye, false teeth or a crutch,
A brace or a hook,
Rubber breasts or a rubber crotch,   5

Stitches to show something's missing? No, no? Then
How can we give you a thing?
Stop crying.
Open your hand.
Empty? Empty. Here is a hand   10

To fill it and willing
To bring teacups and roll away headaches
And do whatever you tell it.
Will you marry it?
It is guaranteed   15

To thumb shut your eyes at the end
And dissolve of sorrow.

We make new stock from the salt.
I notice you are stark naked.
How about this suit—   20

Black and stiff, but not a bad fit.
Will you marry it?
It is waterproof, shatterproof, proof
Against fire and bombs through the roof.
Believe me, they'll bury you in it.   25

Now your head, excuse me, is empty.
I have the ticket for that.
Come here, sweetie, out of the closet.
Well, what do you think of *that*?
Naked as paper to start   30

But in twenty-five years she'll be silver,
In fifty, gold.[1]
A living doll, everywhere you look.
It can sew, it can cook,
It can talk, talk, talk.   35

It works, there is nothing wrong with it.
You have a hole, it's a poultice.
You have an eye, it's an image.
My boy, it's your last resort.
Will you marry it, marry it, marry it.   40

1962   *1963, 1965*

Daddy

You do not do, you do not do
Any more, black shoe
In which I have lived like a foot
For thirty years, poor and white,
Barely daring to breathe or Achoo.   5

Daddy, I have had to kill you.
You died before I had time—
Marble-heavy, a bag full of God,
Ghastly statue with one gray toe[1]
Big as a Frisco seal   10

And a head in the freakish Atlantic
Where it pours bean green over blue
In the waters off beautiful Nauset.
I used to pray to recover you.
Ach, du.[2]   15

---

[1] By tradition, the twenty-fifth wedding anniversary is silver
(with gifts of silver) and the fiftieth golden.
[1] Otto Plath suffered from diabetes, causing his toe to become
gangrenous and swell.
[2] "Ah, you" (German).

In the German tongue, in the Polish town
Scraped flat by the roller
Of wars, wars, wars.
But the name of the town is common.
My Polack[3] friend   20

Says there are a dozen or two.
So I never could tell where you
Put your foot, your root,
I never could talk to you.
The tongue stuck in my jaw.   25

It stuck in a barb wire snare.
Ich, ich, ich, ich,[4]
I could hardly speak.
I thought every German was you.
And the language obscene   30

An engine, an engine
Chuffing me off like a Jew.
A Jew to Dachau, Auschwitz, Belsen.[5]
I began to talk like a Jew.
I think I may well be a Jew.   35

The snows of the Tyrol, the clear beer of Vienna[6]
Are not very pure or true.
With my gipsy ancestress and my weird luck
And my Taroc pack and my Taroc pack[7]
I may be a bit of a Jew.   40

I have always been scared of *you*,
With your Luftwaffe,[8] your gobbledygoo.
And your neat mustache
And your Aryan[9] eye, bright blue.
Panzer-man, panzer-man,[10] O You——   45

Not God but a swastika[11]
So black no sky could squeak through.
Every woman adores a Fascist,
The boot in the face, the brute
Brute heart of a brute like you.   50

You stand at the blackboard, daddy,[12]
In the picture I have of you,
A cleft in your chin instead of your foot
But no less a devil for that, no not
Any less the black man who   55

---

[3]Derogatory term for someone from Poland.
[4]"I, I, I, I" (German).
[5]Notorious concentration camps where Nazis exterminated Jews and other "undesirables."
[6]Tyrol: mountainous region of Austria; Vienna: capital of Austria.
[7]Also Tarot, a pack of cards used to tell fortunes (used in T. S. Eliot's *The Waste Land*).

[8]German air force during the Second World War.
[9]Hitler believed in the racial superiority of Aryans (German racial stock).
[10]Man fighting in a German Panzer (tank) unit in the Second World War.
[11]Nazi symbol.
[12]Plath's father was a professor at Boston University.

Bit my pretty red heart in two.
I was ten when they buried you.
At twenty I tried to die
And get back, back, back to you.
I thought even the bones would do.   60

But they pulled me out of the sack,
And they stuck me together with glue.
And then I knew what to do.
I made a model of you,
A man in black with a Meinkampf[13] look   65

And a love of the rack and the screw.[14]
And I said I do, I do.
So daddy, I'm finally through.
The black telephone's off at the root,
The voices just can't worm through.   70

If I've killed one man, I've killed two——
The vampire who said he was you
And drank my blood for a year,
Seven years, if you want to know.
Daddy, you can lie back now.   75

There's a stake in your fat black heart[15]
And the villagers never liked you.
They are dancing and stamping on you.
They always *knew* it was you.
Daddy, daddy, you bastard, I'm through.   80

1962   *1963, 1965*

Ariel[1]

Stasis in darkness.
Then the substanceless blue
Pour of tor[2] and distances.

God's lioness,
How one we grow,
Pivot of heels and knees!—The furrow   5

Splits and passes, sister to
The brown arc
Of the neck I cannot catch,

Nigger-eye   10
Berries cast dark
Hooks————

---

[13]"My Battle" (German); title of Hitler's book, which he wrote in prison (1925–27).
[14]Medieval instruments of torture.
[15]In common lore, the only way to kill a vampire permanently was to drive a stake through his heart.
[1]The gossamer-like character in Shakespeare's *The Tempest*; and the name Plath gave to her horse.
[2]Rocky mountain or hill.

Black sweet blood mouthfuls,
Shadows.
Something else   15

Hauls me through air——
Thighs, hair;
Flakes from my heels.

White
Godiva,[3] I unpeel——   20
Dead hands, dead stringencies.

And now I
Foam to wheat, a glitter of seas.
The child's cry

Melts in the wall.   25
And I
Am the arrow,

The dew that flies
Suicical, at one with the drive
Into the red   30

Eye, the cauldron of morning.

1962   *1963, 1965*

Poppies in October

Even the sun-clouds this morning cannot manage such skirts.
Nor the woman in the ambulance
Whose red heart blooms through her coat so astoundingly——

A gift, a love gift
Utterly unasked for   5
By a sky

Palely and flamily
Igniting its carbon monoxides, by eyes
Dulled to a halt under bowlers.

O my God, what am I   10
That these late mouths should cry open
In a forest of frost, in a dawn of cornflowers.

1962   *1963, 1965*

---

[3]In legend, Lady Godiva (d. 1057) rode naked on her horse
through the streets of Coventry, England, to protest burdensome taxes.

Lady Lazarus[1]

I have done it again.
One year in every ten
I manage it——

A sort of walking miracle, my skin
Bright as a Nazi lampshade,[2]   5
My right foot

A paperweight,
My face a featureless, fine
Jew linen.

Peel off the napkin[3]   10
O my enemy.
Do I terrify?——

The nose, the eye pits, the full set of teeth?
The sour breath
Will vanish in a day.   15

Soon, soon the flesh
The grave cave ate will be
At home on me

And I a smiling woman.
I am only thirty.   20
And like the cat I have nine times to die.

This is Number Three.
What a trash
To annihilate each decade.

What a million filaments.   25
The peanut-crunching crowd
Shoves in to see

Them unwrap me hand and foot——
The big strip tease.
Gentlemen, ladies   30

These are my hands
My knees.
I may be skin and bone,

Nevertheless, I am the same, identical woman.
The first time it happened I was ten.   35
It was an accident.

---

[1]Lazarus was raised from the dead by Jesus (John 11:44).
[2]The Nazis made lampshades out of the skins of some of the
Jews they murdered during the Second World War.

[3]The cloth which St. Veronica gave Jesus to wipe the perspiration as he carried the cross through Jerusalem was, according to tradition, imprinted with the image of his face.

The second time I meant
To last it out and not come back at all.
I rocked shut

As a seashell.   40
They had to call and call
And pick the worms off me like sticky pearls.

Dying
Is an art, like everything else.
I do it exceptionally well.   45

I do it so it feels like hell.
I do it so it feels real.
I guess you could say I've a call.

It's easy enough to do it in a cell.
It's easy enough to do it and stay put.   50
It's the theatrical

Comeback in broad day
To the same place, the same face, the same brute
Amused shout:

'A miracle!'   55
That knocks me out.
There is a charge

For the eyeing of my scars, there is a charge
For the hearing of my heart——
It really goes.   60

And there is a charge, a very large charge
For a word or a touch
Or a bit of blood

Or a piece of my hair or my clothes.
So, so, Herr Doktor.⁴   65
So, Herr Enemy.

I am your opus,
I am your valuable,
The pure gold baby

That melts to a shriek.   70
I turn and burn.
Do not think I underestimate your great concern.

Ash, ash—
You poke and stir.
Flesh, bone, there is nothing there——   75

---

⁴"Mr. Doctor" (German); the customary address of a doctor.

A cake of soap,
A wedding ring,
A gold filling.[5]

Herr God, Herr Lucifer
Beware   80
Beware.

Out of the ash
I rise with my red hair
And I eat men like air.

1962   *1963, 1965*

Death & Co.

Two, of course there are two.
It seems perfectly natural now——
The one who never looks up, whose eyes are lidded
And balled, like Blake's,[1]
Who exhibits   5

The birthmarks that are his trademark——
The scald scar of water,
The nude
Verdigris of the condor.
I am red meat. His beak   10

Claps sidewise: I am not his yet.
He tells me how badly I photograph.
He tells me how sweet
The babies look in their hospital
Icebox, a simple   15

Frill at the neck,
Then the flutings of their Ionian
Death-gowns,
Then two little feet.
He does not smile or smoke.   20

The other does that,
His hair long and plausive.
Bastard
Masturbating a glitter,
He wants to be loved.   25

I do not stir.
The frost makes a flower,
The dew makes a star,

---

[5]The Nazis took anything of value from the bodies of their victims as they killed them; human fat was rendered into soap.

[1]Reference to the plaster death mask taken of William Blake (1757–1827), British poet.

The dead bell,
The dead bell.   30

Somebody's done for.

1962   1963, 1965

Winter Trees

The wet dawn inks are doing their blue dissolve.
On their blotter of fog the trees
Seem a botanical drawing—
Memories growing, ring on ring,
A series of weddings.   5

Knowing neither abortions nor bitchery,
Truer than women,
They seed so effortlessly!
Tasting the winds, that are footless,
Waist-deep in history—   10

Full of wings, otherworldliness.
In this, they are Ledas.[1]
O mother of leaves and sweetness
Who are these pietàs?[2]
The shadows of ringdoves chanting, but easing nothing.   15

1962   1963, 1971

Child

Your clear eye is the one absolutely beautiful thing.
I want to fill it with color and ducks,
The zoo of the new

Whose names you meditate—
April snowdrop, Indian pipe,   5
Little

Stalk without wrinkle,
Pool in which images
Should be grand and classical

Not this troublous   10
Wringing of hands, this dark
Ceiling without a star.

1963   1963, 1971

---

[1]In Greek mythology, Leda was made love to and impreg-
nated by Zeus in the form of a swan and gave birth to Helen
of Troy.

[2]Reference to pictorial representations, in sculpture and
paintings, of Mary holding the dead Christ after his release
from the cross. "Pietà": Italian for "pity" or "devotion."

Kindness

Kindness glides about my house.
Dame Kindness, she is so nice!
The blue and red jewels of her rings smoke
In the windows, the mirrors
Are filling with smiles.   5

What is so real as the cry of a child?
A rabbit's cry may be wilder
But it has no soul.
Sugar can cure everything, so Kindness says.
Sugar is a necessary fluid,   10

Its crystals a little poultice.
O kindness, kindness
Sweetly picking up pieces!
My Japanese silks, desperate butterflies,
May be pinned any minute, anesthetized.   15

And here you come, with a cup of tea
Wreathed in steam.
The blood jet is poetry,
There is no stopping it.
You hand me two children, two roses.   20

1963   1963, 1965

Words

Axes
After whose stroke the wood rings,
And the echoes!
Echoes traveling
Off from the center like horses.   5

The sap
Wells like tears, like the
Water striving
To re-establish its mirror
Over the rock   10

That drops and turns,
A white skull,
Eaten by weedy greens.
Years later I
Encounter them on the road——   15

Words dry and riderless,
The indefatigable hoof-taps.
While
From the bottom of the pool, fixed stars
Govern a life.   20

1963   1965

Edge

The woman is perfected.
Her dead

Body wears the smile of accomplishment,
The illusion of a Greek necessity

Flows in the scrolls of her toga,   5
Her bare

Feet seem to be saying:
We have come so far, it is over.

Each dead child coiled, a white serpent,
One at each little   10

Pitcher of milk, now empty.
She has folded

Them back into her body as petals
Of a rose close when the garden

Stiffens and odors bleed   15
From the sweet, deep throats of the night flower.

The moon has nothing to be sad about,
Staring from her hood of bone.

She is used to this sort of thing.
Her blacks crackle and drag.   20

1963   *1963, 1965*

IMAMU AMIRI BARAKA
(LEROI JONES)
(b. 1934)

Imamu Amiri Baraka, born LeRoi Jones, may be considered as virtually two
different writers: the first, LeRoi Jones, who became recognized as a mainstream
American poet with his two books of poetry written out of his black experience;
and Imamu Amiri Baraka who, in the mid-1960s, became the militant spokesman for blacks and rejected his former self by adopting a new African name (a
Bantu version of three Muslim words: a spiritual leader, "Prince," and "the
blessed one"). In this process, Baraka divorced his white wife in 1965 and married a black woman in 1967. In contrast with the early poetry, the later work
(prose and poetry) tended to become polemical, declamatory, even demagogic: a
poetry of rage and denunciation.

When he was known as LeRoi Jones, Baraka wrote a statement on poetics to
be included in Donald M. Allen's *The New American Poetry*, published in 1960: "I

must be completely free to do just what I want, in the poem. . . . There cannot be anything I must *fit* the poem into. Everything must be made to fit into the poem. There must not be any preconceived notion or *design* for what the poem *ought* to be. . . . The only 'recognizable tradition' a poet need follow is himself . . . & with that, say, all those things out of tradition he can use, adapt, work over, into something for himself. To broaden his *own* voice with. (You have to start and finish there . . . your own voice . . . how you sound.)" The poets who had had the greatest influence on him, he said, were Federico García Lorca, William Carlos Williams, Ezra Pound, and Charles Olson.

Baraka/Jones's first two books of poems, published under the name of LeRoi Jones, reflected the freedoms he proclaimed for himself in this statement. His *Preface to a Twenty Volume Suicide Note* was published in 1961, and his *The Dead Lecturer* in 1964. The title poem of the first volume was dedicated to the poet's daughter and concludes with a moment of tenderness (and affirmation) when he happens on the little girl "on her knees, peeking into / Her own clasped hands." Other poems have other such moments, as do the poems in the second book. It is, indeed, impossible to identify the color of the poet in many of the poems treating universal themes in the two volumes, as, for example, "In Memory of Radio."

By the time Baraka/Jones wrote "State/Meant" in 1965, he had become a radically different poet: "The Black Artist's role in America is to aid in the destruction of America as he knows it. His role is to report and reflect so precisely the nature of the society, and of himself in that society, that other men will be moved by the exactness of his rendering and, if they are black men, grow strong through this moving, having seen their own strength; and if they are white men, tremble, curse, and go mad, because they will be drenched with the filth of their evil."

The best, most comprehensive introduction to the new Baraka/Jones was presented in his *Black Magic: Sabotage, Target Study, Black Art: Collected Poetry, 1961–1967*, published in 1968. In an "Explanation of the Work," Baraka/Jones wrote that the poems grouped under *Sabotage* represented the period when he "had come to see the superstructure of filth Americans call their way of life, and wanted to see it fall"; *Target Study* grouped poems that "studied" the target (like "bomber crews" studying "soon-to-be-destroyed cities"); *Black Art* brought poems together that represented the "crucial seeing, the decisions, the actual move. The strengthening to destroy, and the developing of willpower to build, even in the face of destruction and despair. . . ." A sample poem, "Ration" (from the *Target Study* section), opens: "Banks must be robbed, / the guards bound and gagged. / The money must be taken / and used to buy weapons."

Imamu Amiri Baraka was born Everett LeRoi Jones in Newark, New Jersey, into a middle-class family in which the father was a postal worker, the mother a social worker. After attending Rutgers University briefly, he moved to Howard University and took a B.A. in English in 1954. He volunteered for service in the U.S. Air Force and served from 1954 to 1957 as a gunner and aerial climatographer. After his discharge, he studied for a time at Columbia and the New School for Social Research in New York City. He began to write poetry and was soon associated with little magazines, including *Yugen* (which he cofounded), and *Floating Bear* (which he coedited). His first two volumes of poetry, as we have seen, were published in 1961 and 1964, establishing him as an important young poet. In 1964, two of his plays, *Dutchman* and *The Slave*, were produced off-Broadway; the first of these received an Obie Award for best off-Broadway play.

As he became radicalized, Baraka/Jones returned to his birthplace, Newark, where he became politically active, founding in 1967 the United Brothers, later called the Committee for Unified Newark. More and more, he became involved in a number of political organizations, specifically black separatist in nature. Much of his creative energy went into the writing of prose, generally political and polemic: *A Black Value System* (1970) and *Raise, Race, Rays, Raze: Essays since 1965* (1971). In 1979, he published *Selected Poetry of Amiri Baraka/LeRoi Jones* and *Selected Plays and Prose of Amiri Baraka/LeRoi Jones*. (He had dropped the title "Imamu" in 1974.) And in 1984, he published *The Autobiography of LeRoi Jones/Amiri Baraka*. Although critics have disagreed on his political-literary tactics in the latter part of his career, they agree that his talent is not in question.

ADDITIONAL READING

Daggers and Javelins: Essays, 1974–1979, 1984.

Letitia Dace, *LeRoi Jones (Imamu Amiri Baraka): A Checklist of Works By and About Him*, 1971; Theodore Hudson, *From LeRoi Jones to Amiri Baraka: The Literary Works*, 1973; Kimberly W. Benston, *Baraka: The Renegade and the Mask*, 1976; Kimberly W. Benston, *Imamu Amiri Baraka: A Collection of Critical Essays*, 1978; Werner Sollors, *Amiri Baraka/LeRoi Jones: The Quest for a "Populist Modernism,"* 1978; Paulette Pennington-Jones, *Amiri Baraka: Bibliography, Biography, Playography*, 1978; Lloyd W. Brown, *Amiri Baraka*, 1980; Hency C. Lacey, *To Raise, Destroy and Create: The Poetry, Drama, and Fiction of Imamu Amiri Baraka*, 1981; William J. Harris, *The Poetry and Poetics of Amiri Baraka: The Jazz Aesthetic*, 1985.

TEXTS

"Preface to a Twenty Volume Suicide Note" and "In Memory of Radio" from *Preface to a Twenty Volume Suicide Note*, 1961; "I Substitute for the Dead Lecturer" from *The Dead Lecturer*, 1964; "A Poem Some People Will Have to Understand" from *Black Magic*, 1969.

Preface to a Twenty
Volume Suicide Note

(FOR KELLIE JONES, BORN 16 MAY 1959)

Lately, I've become accustomed to the way
The ground opens up and envelopes me
Each time I go out to walk the dog.
Or the broad edged silly music the wind
Makes when I run for a bus . . .   5

Things have come to that.

And now, each night I count the stars,
And each night I get the same number.
And when they will not come to be counted,
I count the holes they leave.   10

Nobody sings anymore.

And then last night, I tiptoed up
To my daughter's room and heard her
Talking to someone, and when I opened
The door, there was no one there . . .   15
Only she on her knees, peeking into

Her own clasped hands.

1957   1958, 1961

In Memory of Radio

Who has ever stopped to think of the divinity of Lamont Cranston?[1]
(Only Jack Kerouac,[2] that I know of: & me.
The rest of you probably had on WCBS and Kate Smith,[3]
Or something equally unattractive.)

What can I say?   5
It is better to have loved and lost
Than to put linoleum in your living rooms?

Am I a sage or something?
Mandrake's[4] hypnotic gesture of the week?
(Remember, I do not have the healing powers of Oral Roberts . . .   10
I cannot, like F. J. Sheen,[5] tell you how to get saved & *rich!*
I cannot even order you to gaschamber satori[6] like Hitler or Goody Knight[7]

& Love is an evil word.
Turn it backwards/see, see what I mean?
An evol word. & besides   15
who understands it?
I certainly wouldn't like to go out on that kind of limb.

Saturday mornings we listened to *Red Lantern* & his undersea folk.
At 11, *Let's Pretend*/& we did/& I, the poet, still do, Thank God!

What was it he used to say (after the transformation, when he was safe   20
& invisible & the unbelievers couldn't throw stones?) "Heh, heh, heh,
Who knows what evil lurks in the hearts of men? The Shadow knows."

O, yes he does
O, yes he does.
An evil word it is,   25
This Love.

                                                                  1959, 1961

---

[1]The voice-hero of "The Shadow," a popular radio program featuring a "mysterious avenger of crime and injustice," with the "power to cloud men's minds" and a "bloodchilling laugh" (described in lines 20–22 of the poem).
[2]Beat novelist (1922–1969), author of *On the Road*.
[3]Kate Smith was a popular (and hefty) radio singer, famous for her version of "God Bless America."
[4]Mandrake the Magician, a comic strip hero who used his

powers to fight evil; later hero of a radio show.
[5]Roberts, a Protestant fundamentalist who practiced faith healing and Fulton J. Sheen, a Catholic bishop, both delivering their messages on radio.
[6]Sudden enlightenment (in Zen Buddhism).
[7]Goodwin Knight, governor of California in the 1950s, involved in discussions on the use of gas chambers to execute convicted criminals.

I Substitute for
the Dead Lecturer

What is most precious, because
it is lost. What is lost,
because it is most
precious.

They have turned, and say that I am dying. That   5
I have thrown
my life
away. They
have left me alone, where
there is no one, nothing   10
save who I am. Not a note
nor a word.

        Cold air batters
the poor (and their minds
turn open   15
like sores). What kindness
What wealth
can I offer? Except
what is, for me,
ugliest. What is   20
for me, shadows, shrieking
phantoms. Except
they have need
of life. Flesh
at least,   25
           should be theirs.

The Lord has saved me
to do this. The Lord
has made me strong. I
am as I must have   30
myself. Against all
thought, all music, all
my soft loves.

        For all these wan roads
I am pushed to follow, are   35
my own conceit. A simple muttering
elegance, slipped in my head
pressed on my soul, is my heart's
worth. And I am frightened
that the flame of my sickness   40
will burn off my face. And leave
the bones, my stewed black skull,
an empty cage of failure.

                            1964

A Poem Some People
Will Have to Understand

Dull unwashed windows of eyes
and buildings of industry. What
industry do I practice? A slick
colored boy, 12 miles from his
home. I practice no industry. 5
I am no longer a credit
to my race. I read a little,
scratch against silence slow spring
afternoons.
           I had thought, before, some years ago 10
that I'd come to the end of my life.
             Watercolor ego. Without the preciseness
a violent man could propose.
           But the wheel, and the wheels,
wont let us alone. All the fantasy 15
        and justice, and dry charcoal winters
All the pitifully intelligent citizens
      I've forced myself to love.

We have awaited the coming of a natural
phenomenon. Mystics and romantics, knowledgeable 20
workers
of the land.

But none has come.
(Repeat)
          but none has come. 25

Will the machinegunners please step forward?

                       1963, 1969

CHARLES WRIGHT
(b. 1935)

Charles Wright's "Nightdream" opens: "Each day is an iceberg / Dragging its chill paunch underfoot." The poem is filled with such startling images — "the old roads are taking flight," "mother floats from her bed," "the bedroom becomes a rose." Asked about the meaning and structure of the poem, Wright replied that it was written out of a recollection: an attempt to recreate "what the mood is after a parent's death, the futility of things and their apparent proliferation, the inability of anything except the poem to rescue what once was." As a "gloss of the poem, of the emotional quotient of the poem," Wright cited lines from Ezra Pound's "Canto LXXVI": "nothing matters but the quality / of the affection — / in the end — that has carved the trace in the mind / dove sta memoria [where memory remains]."

Wright is the poet above all of such *traces*, excavated from deep memory and displayed with whatever transfigurations, losses, or additions have rendered them more mysterious, enigmatic, and haunting. His citing of Pound is revealing. Wright did not come to poetry until relatively late in life, when he was twenty-five years old, serving in the Army Intelligence Corps, and stationed in Verona, Italy. There he came upon the writings of Ezra Pound: "I began by using Ezra Pound's Italian Cantos first as a guide book to out-of-the-way places, then as a reference book and finally as a 'copy' book." He added: "Pound was a tremendous influence, he was the first poet I ever read seriously." Pound would remain a model and inspiration, as his "Homage to Ezra Pound" reveals.

Wright was born in Pickwick Dam, Tennessee, in 1935, and took a B.A. at Davidson College in North Carolina. He served in the army for four years (1957–61) and was stationed in Italy for his last three years. On his discharge and return to America, he entered the Writers Workshop at the University of Iowa and took an M.F.A. in 1963. He has supported himself as a poet by teaching, and his main academic appointments have included the University of California at Irvine, and, more recently, the University of Virginia. But he has taught for shorter periods at the University of Iowa, Princeton, and Columbia. In 1968–69, he served as a Fulbright lecturer in Italy at the University of Padua. In addition to Pound, he was, he has said, influenced by the Italian poet Eugenio Montale, who won the Nobel Prize in 1975. Wright translated a volume of Montale's poems *The Storm and Other Things*, published in 1978, which was awarded the P. E. N. Translation Prize.

Wright began publishing regularly in 1963, after he finished his studies at the University of Iowa, but the works that have established his reputation are *The Grave of the Right Hand* (1970), *Hard Freight* (1973), *Bloodlines* (1975), and *China Trace* (1977). It is from these volumes that Wright selected the contents of his *Country Music: Selected Early Poems*, published in 1982. The title is explained by the epigraph from Ernest Hemingway: "The country was always better than the people." Many of the poems are constructed out of Wright's memories of his southern past and are thus the *music* evoked by the *country* of his youth.

One of the most remarkable works is entitled "Tattoos" (in *Bloodlines*), a sequence of twenty poems created out of memories tattooed indelibly in the mind at different levels of time (dates accompany the texts), with a key provided at the end in a page of notes. The episodes surrealistically recalled range from molestation by a school janitor when Wright was a boy to the death of his father. *Country Music* won the American Book Award in poetry in 1983. Wright's other books include *The Southern Cross* (1981) and *The Other Side of the River* (1984).

About his poetic method, Wright has said: "All poems are made. They're not made in heaven, they're made on the page. . . . You write your poems in the way that best pleases you and that's all you can do. Every change in every doctrine is a temporary change at best, and at worst it's just blather. . . . I admit that I have certain things in mind I want to say, but I still think I'm trusting my instincts in *how* I say it."

ADDITIONAL READING

Elizabeth McBride, "Charles Wright: An Interview," *Ohio Review*, 1985; Sherod Santos, "An Interview with Charles Wright," *Mississippi Review*, 1987.

TEXTS

"Ars Poetica" from *The Southern Cross*, 1981; remaining poems from *Country Music: Selected Early Poems*, 1982.

The New Poem

It will not resemble the sea.
It will not have dirt on its thick hands.
It will not be part of the weather.

It will not reveal its name.
It will not have dreams you can count on.   5
It will not be photogenic.

It will not attend our sorrow.
It will not console our children.
It will not be able to help us.

1973

Tattoos[1]

1.[2]

Necklace of flame, little dropped hearts,
Camellias: I crunch you under my foot.
And here comes the wind again, bad breath
Of thirty-odd years, and catching up. Still,
I crunch you under my foot.   5

Your white stalks sequester me,
Their roots a remembered solitude.
Their mouths of snow keep forming my name.
Programmed incendiaries,
Fused flesh, so light your flowering,   10

So light the light that fires you
—Petals of horn, scales of blood—,
Where would you have me return?
What songs would I sing,
And the hymns . . . What garden of wax statues . . .   15

1973

2.[3]

The pin oak has found new meat,
The linkworm a bone to pick.
Lolling its head, slicing its blue tongue,
The nightflower blooms on its one stem;
The crabgrass hones down its knives: 5

Between us again there is nothing. And since
The darkness is only light
That has not yet reached us,

---

[1]Images or writing imprinted indelibly on the skin.
[2]"Camellias; Mother's Day; St. Paul's Episcopal Church,   Kingsport, Tennessee" (Wright's note).
[3]"Death of my father" (Wright's note).

You slip it on like a glove.
Duck soup, you say. *This is duck soup.*   10

And so it is.
                    Along the far bank
Of Blood Creek, I watch you turn
In that light, and turn, and turn,
Feeling it change on your changing hands,
Feeling it take. Feeling it.   15

                                                        1972

                              3.4

Body fat as my forearm, blunt-arrowed head
And motionless, eyes
Sequin and hammer and nail
In the torchlight, he hangs there,
Color of dead leaves, color of dust,   5

Dumbbell and hourglass—copperhead.
Color of bread dough, color of pain, the hand
That takes it, that handles it
—The snake now limp as a cat—
Is halfway to heaven, and in time.   10

Then Yellow Shirt, twitching and dancing,
Gathers it home, handclap and heartstring,
His habit in ecstasy.
Current and godhead, hot coil,
Grains through the hourglass glint and spring.   15

                                                        1951

                              4.5

Silt fingers, silt stump and bone.
And twice now, in the drugged sky,
White moons, black moons.
And twice now, in the gardens,
The great seed of affection.   5

Liplap of Zuan's canal, blear
Footfalls of Tintoretto; the rest
Is brilliance: Turner6 at 3 a.m.; moth lamps
Along the casements. O blue
Feathers, this clear cathedral . . .   10

And now these stanchions of joy,
Radiant underpinning:
Old scaffolding, old arrangements,
All fall in a rain of light.
I have seen what I have seen.   15

                                                        1968

4"Snake-handling religious service; East Tennessee"
(Wright's note).
5"Venice, Italy" (Wright's note).
6Zuan's Canal is one of the many canals of Venice, where
Wright lived for a time when he was in the army; Tintoretto

(c. 1518–1594), Venetian painter whose greatest works are in
Venice; Joseph Mallord William Turner (1775–1851), British
painter whose late Venetian watercolors display his magical
effects of light and brilliance of color.

5.[7]

Hungering acolyte, pale body,
The sunlight—through St Paul of the 12 Sorrows—
Falls like Damascus òn me:[8]
I feel the gold hair of Paradise rise through my skin
Needle and thread, needle and thread;   5

I feel the worm in the rose root.
I hear the river of heaven
Fall from the air, I hear it enter the wafer
And sink me, the whirlpool stars
Spinning me down, and down. O . . .   10

Now I am something else, smooth,
Unrooted, with no veins and no hair, washed
In the waters of nothingness;
Anticoronal, released . . .
And then I am risen, the cup, new sun, at my lips.   15

1946

6.[9]

Skyhooked above the floor, sucked
And mummied by salt towels, my left arm
Hangs in the darkness, bloodwood, black gauze,
The slow circle of poison
Coming and going through the same hole . . .   5

Sprinkle of rain through the pine needles,
Shoosh pump shoosh pump of the heart;
Bad blood, bad blood . . .
                          Chalk skin like a light,
Eyes thin dimes, whose face
Comes and goes at the window?   10

Whose face . . .
              For I would join it,
And climb through the nine-and-a-half footholds of fever
Into the high air,
and shed these clothes and renounce,   15
Burned over, repurified.

1941

7.[10]

This one's not like the other, pale, gingerly—
Like nothing, in fact, to rise, as he does,
In three days, his blood clotted,
His deathsheet a feather across his chest,
His eyes twin lenses, and ready to unroll.   5

---

[7]"Acolyte; fainting at the altar; Kingsport, Tennessee" (Wright's note).
[8]"St. Paul of the 12 Sorrows" is the church Wright attended when a boy; the apostle St. Paul was converted to Christianity on the "road to Damascus."
[9]"Blood-poisoning; hallucination; Hiwassee, North Caro-
lina" (Wright's note).
[10]"*The Resurrection*, Piero della Francesca, Borgo San Sepolcro, Italy" (Wright's note). This "Tattoo" describes the picture, portraying the resurrection of Christ, of Piero della Francesca (*c.* 1420–1492); it is located in Borgo San Sepolcro, where the artist was born.

Arm and a leg, nail hole and knucklebone,
He stands up. In his right hand,
The flagstaff of victory;
In his left, the folds of what altered him.
And the hills spell V, and the trees V . . .   10

Nameless, invisible, what spins out
From this wall comes breath by breath,
And pulls the vine, and the ringing tide,
The scorched syllable from the moon's mouth.
And what pulls them pulls me.   15

1963

8.[11]

A tongue hangs in the dawn wind, a wind
That trails the tongue's voice like a banner, star
And whitewash, the voice
Sailing across the 14 mountains, snap and drift,
To settle, a last sigh, here.   5

That tongue is his tongue, the voice his voice:
Lifting out of the sea
Where the tongue licks, the voice starts,
Monotonous, out of sync,
Yarmulke, tfillin, tallis.[12]   10

His nude body waist deep in the waves,
The book a fire in his hands, his movements
Reedflow and counter flow, the chant light
From his lips, the prayer rising to heaven,
And everything brilliance, brilliance, brilliance.   15

1959

9.[13]

In the fixed crosshairs of evening,
In the dust-wallow of certitude,
Where the drop drops and the scalding starts,
Where the train pulls out and the light winks,
The tracks go on, and go on: 5

The flesh pulls back and snaps,
The fingers are ground and scraped clean,
Reed whistles in a green fire.
The bones blow on, singing their bald song.
It stops. And it starts again.   10

Theologians, Interpreters:
Song, the tracks, crosshairs, the light;
The drop that is always falling.

---

[11]"Harold Schimmel's morning prayers; Positano, Italy" (Wright's note).
[12]*Yarmulke*: small hat worn by orthodox Jews; *tfillin*: phylacteries, leather cases holding prayers, strapped to the head and arm during worship; *tallis*: prayer shawl worn by Jews during service.
[13]"Temporary evangelical certitude; Christ School, Arden, North Carolina" (Wright's note).

Over again I feel the palm print,
The map that will take me there.   15

1952

10.[14]

It starts here, in a chair, sunflowers
Inclined from an iron pot, a soiled dishcloth
Draped on the backrest. A throat with a red choker
Throbs in the mirror. High on the wall,
Flower-like, disembodied,   5

A wren-colored evil eye stares out
At the white blooms of the oleander, at the white
Gobbets of shadow and shade,
At the white lady and white parasol, at this
Dichogamous landscape, this found chord   10

(And in the hibiscus and moonflowers,
In the smoke trees and spider ferns,
The unicorn crosses his thin legs,
The leopard sips at her dish of blood,
And the vines strike and the vines recoil).   15

1973

11.[15]

So that was it, the rush and the take-off,
The oily glide of the cells
Bringing it up—ripsurge, refraction,
The inner spin
Trailing into the cracked lights of oblivion . . .   5

Re-entry is something else, blank, hard:
Black stretcher straps; the peck, peck
And click of a scalpel; glass shards
Eased one by one from the flesh;
Recisions; the long bite of the veins . . .   10

And what do we do with this,
Rechuted, reworked into our same lives, no one
To answer to, no one to glimpse and sing,
The cracked light flashing our names?
We stand fast, friend, we stand fast.   15

1958

12.[16]

Oval oval oval oval push pull push pull . . .
Words unroll from our fingers.
A splash of leaves through the windowpanes,
A smell of tar from the streets:
Apple, arrival, the railroad, shoe.   5

---

[14]"Visions of heaven" (Wright's note).
[15]"Automobile wreck; hospital; Baltimore, Maryland"
(Wright's note).

[16]"Handwriting class; Palmer Method; words as 'things';
Kingsport, Tennessee" (Wright's note).

The words, like bees in a sweet ink, cluster and drone,
Indifferent, indelible,
A hum and a hum:
Back stairsteps to God, ropes to the glass eye:
Vineyard, informer, the chair, the throne.   10

Mojo[17] and numberless, breaths
From the wet mountains and green mouths; rustlings,
Sure sleights of hand,
The news that arrives from nowhere:
Angel, omega,[18] silence, silence . . .   15

                                                                1945

13.[19]

What I remember is fire, orange fire,
And his huge cock in his hand,
Touching my tiny one; the smell
Of coal dust, the smell of heat,
Banked flames through the furnace door.   5

Of him I remember little, if anything:
Black, overalls splotched with soot,
His voice, *honey, O, honey* . . .
And then he came, his left hand
On my back, holding me close.   10

Nothing was said, of course—one
Terrible admonition, and that was all . . .
And if that hand, like loosed lumber, fell
From grace, and stayed there? We give,
And we take it back. We give again . . .   15

                                                                1940

14.[20]

Now there is one, and still masked;
White death's face, sheeted and shoeless, eyes shut
Behind the skull holes.
She stands in a field, her shadow no shadow,
The clouds no clouds. Call her Untitled.   5

                              *

And now there are four, white shoes, white socks;
They stand in the same field, the same clouds
Vanishing down the sky. Cat masks and mop hair
Cover their faces. Advancing, they hold hands.

                              *

Nine. Now there are nine, their true shadows   10
The judgments beneath their feet.

---

[17]The art of casting magic spells.
[18]Last letter of the Greek alphabet (often used, along with the first letter, alpha, to refer to God: "I am the Alpha and Omega, the beginning and the end, saith the Lord," Revela-

tion 1:18).
[19]"The janitor; kindergarten; Corinth, Mississippi" (Wright's note).
[20]"Dream" (Wright's note).

Black masks, white nightgowns. A wind
Is what calls them, that field, those same clouds
Lisping one syllable *I, I, I.*

1970

15.[21]

And the saw keeps cutting,
Its flashy teeth shredding the mattress, the bedclothes,
The pillow and pillow case.
Plugged in to a socket in your bones,
It coughs, and keeps on cutting.   5

It eats the lamp and the bedpost.
It licks the clock with its oiled tongue,
And keeps on cutting.
It leaves the bedroom, and keeps on cutting.
It leaves the house, and keeps on cutting . . .   10

— Dogwood, old feathery petals,
Your black notches burn in my blood;
You flutter like bandages across my childhood.
Your sound is a sound of good-bye.
Your poem is a poem of pain.   15

1964

16.[22]

All gloss, gothic and garrulous, staked
To her own tree, she takes it off,
Half-dollar an article. With each
Hike of the price, the gawkers
Diminish, spitting, rubbing their necks.   5

Fifteen, and staked to *my* tree,
Sap-handled, hand in my pocket, head
Hot as the carnival tent, I see it out — as does
The sheriff of Cherokee County,
Who fondles the payoff, finger and shaft.   10

Outside, in the gathering dark, all
Is fly buzz and gnat hum and whine of the wires;
Quick scratch of the match, cicadas,
Jackhammer insects; drone, drone
Of the blood-suckers, sweet dust, last sounds . . .   15

1950

17.[23]

I dream that I dream I wake
The room is throat-deep and brown with dead moths
I throw them back like a quilt
I peel them down from the wall
I kick them like leaves I shake them I kick them again   5

---

[21]"The day of my mother's funeral, in Tennessee; Rome,
Italy" (Wright's note).
[22]"Sideshow stripper; Cherokee County Fair, Cherokee,
North Carolina" (Wright's note).
[23]"Recurrent Dream" (Wright's note).

The bride on the couch and the bridegroom
Under their gauze dust-sheet
And cover up turn to each other
Top hat and tails white veil and say as I pass
It's mother again just mother the window open   10

On the 10th floor going up
Is Faceless and under steam his mask
Hot-wired my breath at his heels in sharp clumps
Darkness and light darkness and light
Faceless come back O come back   15

                                                        1955 ff.

                            18.[24]

Flash click tick, flash click tick, light
Through the wavefall—electrodes, intolerable curlicues;
Splinters along the skin, eyes
Flicked by the sealash, spun, pricked;
Terrible vowels from the sun.   5

And everything dry, wrung, the land flaked
By the wind, bone dust and shale;
And hills without names or numbers,
Bald coves where the sky harbors.
The dead grass whistles a tune, strangely familiar.   10

And all in a row, seated, their mouths biting the empty air,
Their front legs straight, and their backs straight,
Their bodies pitted, eyes wide,
The rubble quick glint beneath their feet,
The lions stare, explaining it one more time.   15

                                                        1959

                            19.[25]

The hemlocks wedge in the wind.
Their webs are forming something—questions:
Which shoe is the alter ego?
Which glove inures the fallible hand?
Why are the apple trees in draped black?   5

And I answer them. In words
They will understand, I answer them:
The left shoe.
The left glove.
Someone is dead; someone who loved them is dead.   10

Regret is what anchors me;
I wash in a water of odd names.
White flakes from next year sift down, sift down.
I lie still, and dig in,
Snow-rooted, ooze-rooted, cold blossom.   15

                                                        1972

---

[24]"The Naxian lions; Delos, Greece" (Wright's note); reference to prehistoric carvings in stone.
[25]"Death of my father" (Wright's note).

20.²⁶

You stand in your shoes, two shiny graves
Dogging your footsteps;
You spread your fingers, ten stalks
Enclosing your right of way;
You yip with pain in your little mouth.   5

And this is where the ash falls.
And this is the time it took to get here—
And yours, too, is the stall, the wet wings
Arriving, and the beak.
And yours the thump, and the soft voice: 10

The octopus on the reef's edge, who slides
His fat fingers among the cracks,
Can use you. You've prayed to him,
In fact, and don't know it.
You *are* him, and think yourself yourself.   15

1973
1975

Reunion

Already one day has detached itself from all the rest up ahead.
It has my photograph in its soft pocket.
It wants to carry my breath into the past in its bag of wind.

I write poems to untie myself, to do penance and disappear
Through the upper right-hand corner of things, to say grace.   5

1977

Ars Poetica¹

I like it back here

Under the green swatch of the pepper tree and the aloe vera.
I like it because the wind strips down the leaves without a word.
I like it because the wind repeats itself,
                                             and the leaves do.   5

I like it because I'm better here than I am there,

Surrounded by fetishes and figures of speech:
Dog's tooth and whale's tooth, my father's shoe, the dead weight
Of winter, the inarticulation of joy . . .

---

²⁶"The last stanza is an adaptation of lines from Eugenio
Montale's *Serenato Indiana*" (Wright's note). Eugenio Montale
(1896–1981), an Italian poet, was awarded the Nobel Prize
in 1975.
¹"The Art of Poetry" (Latin); the title of a work setting out
rules for poetry by the Roman poet Horace (65–68 B.C.).

The spirits are everywhere.   10

And once I have them called down from the sky, and spinning and
    dancing in the palm of my hand,
What will it satisfy?
                  I'll still have

The voices rising out of the ground,   15
The fallen star my blood feeds,
                  this business I waste my heart on.

And nothing stops that.

                                  1981

MICHAEL S. HARPER
(b. 1938)

Asked in an interview what he meant when he said that his poems were
"rhythmic rather than metric, the pulse . . . jazz, the tradition generally oral,"
Michael Harper explained: "There is a difference between a metronomic approach to language and a human, intuitive feeling for the language. The best
equivalent I could think of was the jazz idiom. When I say 'oral' I mean that to me
poetry is to be spoken or sung. . . . I think the most important thing here to
remember is that jazz and blues are open-ended forms, not programmatic and
not abstract."

Harper was born in Brooklyn, New York, his father a postal worker, his
mother a medical stenographer. He was delivered by his grandfather, a successful doctor. There was an excellent record collection in the household, and Harper grew up listening to music of all kinds, including the rich black tradition in
jazz and the blues. It is no wonder that he has insisted that the influences on him
were "more musical than poetic." The family moved to Los Angeles when Harper was thirteen. He finished high school there and went to Los Angeles State
College, graduating in 1961. Giving up his ambition to be a doctor like his grandfather (as a black he was discouraged from trying), he decided to become a
writer, taking an M.A. at the University of Iowa's Writers Workshop in 1963.

Harper began placing poems in the little magazines and published his first
book, *Dear John, Dear Coltrane*, in 1970. It was highly praised by reviewers and
was nominated for a National Book Award in 1971. Although the book did not
win the award, Harper's career as a poet was assured, and there has been a steady
flow of volumes from his pen since, among them: *History Is Your Own Heartbeat*
(1971), *Song: I Want a Witness* (1972), *Debridement* (1973), and *Nightmare Begins
Responsibility* (1975). In 1977, he published a collection, *Images of Kin: New and
Selected Poems. Healing Song for the Inner Ear* (1985) carried the epigraph "It's a
wise blues that knows its father."

The title of Harper's first volume (also the title of a poem) invoked the name
of the great avant-garde jazz musician John Coltrane (1926–1967), famous for
his melodic and harmonic experimentation. Some of the most frequent allusions
in Harper's poetry are to other such black artists—Bessie Smith, Louis Arm-

strong, Duke Ellington, Miles Davis, and Charlie (Bird) Parker. In the short biographical piece "Don't They Speak Jazz?" in which he described his early immersion in the black musical tradition, he concluded: "Some final notes on the blues: always say *yes* to life; meet life's terms but never accept them."

Harper also often alludes to places abroad, especially Mexico; he has explained: "In the late sixties [I] traveled to Mexico and Europe where those landscapes broadened my scope and interest in poetry and culture of other countries while I searched my own family and racial history for folklore, history and myth for themes that would give my writing the tradition and context where I could find my own voice." He did find his own voice and developed a philosophy of inclusion rather than exclusion. He found that "being a Black poet and an American poet are two aspects of the same story, two ways of telling the same story. I'm both/and, not either/or." He has reiterated the point: "I don't believe in either/or, I believe in both/and."

Harper has taught English at a number of institutions, including Pasadena City College, Contra Costa College, Reed College, and California State College at Hayward. In 1970 he was given an appointment at Brown University, where he is now the Israel J. Kapstein Professor of English. He has held numerous brief visiting appointments, including terms at Harvard, Yale, and Carleton College in Minnesota. He was the coeditor with Robert B. Stepto of an important and influential anthology, *Chant of Saints: a Gathering of Afro-American Literature, Art, and Scholarship* (1979).

ADDITIONAL READING

William Heyen, ed., *The Generation of 2000: Contemporary American Poets*, 1984; John O'Brien, *Interviews with Black Writers*, 1973; Günter H. Lenz, ed., *History and Tradition in Afro-American Culture*, 1984.

TEXT

Images of Kin: New and Selected Poems, 1977.

American History

Those four black girls blown up
in that Alabama church[1]
remind me of five hundred
middle passage blacks,[2]
in a net, under water   5
in Charleston harbor
so *redcoats*[3] wouldn't find them.
Can't find what you can't see
can you?

1970

---

[1] Terrorist act committed by white racists at the height of the civil rights demonstrations in the South during the 1960s.
[2] African blacks transported by ship to America destined for sale as slaves.
[3] I.e., British soldiers.

We Assume: On the Death of
Our Son, Reuben Masai Harper[1]

We assume
that in 28 hours,
lived in a collapsible isolette,
you learned to accept pure oxygen
as the natural sky;   5
the scant shallow breaths
that filled those hours
cannot, did not make you fly —
but dreams were there
like crooked palmprints on   10
the twin-thick windows of the nursery —
in the glands of your mother.

We assume
the sterile hands
drank chemicals in and out   15
from lungs opaque with mucus,
pumped your stomach,
eeked the bicarbonate in
crooked, green-winged veins,
out in a plastic mask;   20

A woman who'd lost her first son
consoled us with an angel gone ahead
to pray for our family —
gone into that sky
seeking oxygen,   25
gone into autopsy,
a fine brown powdered sugar,
a disposable cremation:

We assume
you did not know we loved you.   30

                                                    1970

Martin's Blues[1]

He came apart in the open,
the slow motion cameras
falling quickly
neither alive nor kicking;

---

[1]Harper has said of this poem: "Reuben was my second son. . . .
I was sitting in the front room of our house in San Francisco;
my wife was on the couch having checked out of the hospital
earlier that day. . . . Reuben was still in the hospital in the intensive care unit. We knew that he was going to die. We were
watching the fog roll in at three o'clock in the afternoon, and
I was waiting to scribble some notes and discovered these notes
sometime afterward, perhaps a month or so afterward. I
changed very little of what I had written. And I am sure had
I not scribbled down those notes and lines at the time, I never
would have written the poem."
[1]Martin Luther King, Jr. (1929–1968), inspired and inspiring leader of the civil rights movements during the 1960s.

stone blind dead
on the balcony[2]
that old melody
etched his black lips
in a pruned echo:
We shall overcome
some day—[3]
Yes we did!
Yes we did!

5
10

1971

Last Affair:
Bessie's Blues Song[1]

Disarticulated
arm torn out,
large veins cross
her shoulder intact,
her tourniquet
her blood in all-white big bands:

5

Can't you see
what love and heartache's done to me
I'm not the same as I used to be
this is my last affair[2]

10

Mail truck or parked car
in the fast lane,
afloat at forty-three
on a Mississippi road,
Two-hundred-pound muscle on her ham bone,
'nother nigger dead 'fore noon:

15

Can't you see
what love and heartache's done to me
I'm not the same as I used to be
this is my last affair

20

Fifty-dollar record
cut the vein in her neck,
fool about her money
toll her black train wreck,
white press missed her fun'ral
in the same stacked deck:

25

Can't you see
what love and heartache's done to me

---

[2]I.e., the balcony of the motel in Memphis, Tennessee, where King was assassinated.
[3]Refrain from the civil rights theme song.
[1]Bessie Smith (1898?–1937), one of the greatest of the blues singers, died after the car in which she was travelling hit a truck; her right arm was nearly severed and she suffered massive chest injuries.
[2]Refrain from one of the favorite songs of Bessie Smith, "My Last Affair."

I'm not the same as I used to be
this is my last affair   30

Loved a little blackbird
heard she could sing,
Martha in her vineyard
pestle in her spring,
Bessie had a bad mouth   35
made my chimes ring:

Can't you see
what love and heartache's done to me
I'm not the same as I used to be
this is my last affair   40

1972

Nightmare Begins Responsibility[1]

I place these numbed wrists to the pane
watching white uniforms whisk over
him[2] in the tube-kept
prison
fear what they will do in experiment   5
watch my gloved stickshifting gasolined hands
breathe *boxcar-information-please* infirmary tubes
distrusting white-pink mending paperthin
silkened end hairs, distrusting tubes
shrunk in his *trunk-skincapped*   10
shaven head, in thighs
distrusting-white-hands-picking-baboon-light
on this son who will not make his second night
of this wardstrewn intensive airpocket
where his father's asthmatic   15
hymns of *night-train*, train done gone
his mother can only know that he has flown
up into essential calm unseen corridor
going boxscarred home, *mamaborn, sweetsonchild*
gonedowntown into *researchtestingwarehousebatteryacid*   20
mama-son-done-gone/me telling her 'nother
train tonight, no music, no breathstroked
heartbeat in my infinite distrust of them:

and of my distrusting self
white-doctor-who-breathed-for-him-all-night   25
say it for two sons gone,
say nightmare, say it loud
panebreaking heartmadness:
nightmare begins responsibility.

1975

---

[1]A play on *In Dreams Begin Responsibilities*, the title of a book by American poet Delmore Schwartz (1913–1966); he had taken the phrase from *Responsibilities*, by British poet William Butler Yeats (1865–1939).
[2]Harper's son, the second to die in infancy.

ROBERT PINSKY
(b. 1940)

In *The Situation of Poetry: Contemporary Poetry and Its Traditions* (1976), Robert Pinsky, instead of searching out the new in the contemporary, sought out continuities in the tradition. Such continuities, he believed, had their basis in the very nature of language:

> The poet's medium . . . is abstract, more or less discursive, and in some senses conventional. But his convictions about reality and are art likely to be pervaded by the idea that reality inheres in particulars, not abstractions; in experience, not in discourse or convention. Experience may well seem fluid and instantaneous, but language is sequential and, once uttered, relatively fixed. These are the broad, cold outlines of a conflict which inspired the dazzling solutions and accomplishments of modernism, an extraordinary, manifold transformation of poetry in English. The conflict and the accomplishments remain, and have their relevance to most of the work, good and bad, in current numbers of *Poetry* magazine or in new volumes of poetry.

The key word for Pinsky, in his description of the stubborn nature of language, is *discursive*. In a chapter on "The Discursive Aspect of Poetry," he explains what he means by "discursive" as a "quality in poetry": "It is speech, organized by its meaning, avoiding the distances and complications of irony on the one side and the ecstatic fusion of speaker, meaning, and subject on the other. The idea is to have all of the virtues of prose, in addition to those qualities and degrees of precision which can be called poetic." It was Ezra Pound, Pinsky reminds the reader, who insisted that poetry must be "as well-written as prose."

Recognizing that his position is "reactionary," he proceeds to ask: "What happens to poetry when it gets too far from prose, and the prose virtues?" And he answers: "If the plural is analyzed, the virtues turn out to be a drab, unglamorous group, including perhaps Clarity, Flexibility, Efficiency, Cohesiveness . . . a puritanical assortment of shrews. They do not as a rule appear in blurbs. And yet when they are courted by those who understand them — William Carlos Williams and Elizabeth Bishop would be examples — the Prose Virtues are transformed from a supporting chorus to the performers of virtuoso marvels. They can become not merely the poem's minimum requirement, but the poetic essence."

In his insistence on the "discursive," on the "prose virtues," Pinsky in effect defined his own position as a poet, a position that may be clarified by a glance at his background. He was born in 1940 in Long Branch, New Jersey, took a B.A. in 1962 at Rutgers University, and then entered Stanford to work on a Ph.D. (completed in 1968). There he took classes with the poet-professor Yvor Winters, whose principle works of criticism (one of which was entitled *The Anatomy of Nonsense*) were brought together under the title *In Defense of Reason* in 1947. These titles reveal Winters's obsession that poetry had to make sense, could not go against reason — must, in other words, have the "prose virtues." In his Foreword to *The Anatomy of Nonsense*, Winters wrote: "The theory of literature which I defend in these essays is absolutist. I believe that the work of literature, in so far as it is valuable, approximates a real apprehension and communication of a particular kind of objective truth."

Pinsky, of course, has his own discriminating definitions of the "prose virtues," and would never speak so casually about "objective truth," but his notions are clearly related to Winters's emphasis on sense. A casual examination of Pinsky's volumes of poetry reveals their "discursive" quality. His poems communicate very much in the way a conversation, sharing information or views, communicates. His books of poetry include *Sadness and Happiness* (1975), *An Explanation of America* (1979), and *History of My Heart* (1984). In the first of these volumes, the long poem "Essay on Psychiatrists" opens: "It's crazy to think one could describe them— / Calling on reason, fantasy, eyes and ears— / As though they were all alike." We are oriented immediately as to the intent of the poem, and the faculties the poet will call into play—reason, fantasy, experience—to describe or define the subject of the poem, psychiatrists.

Similarly, *An Explanation of America* indicates by its title the subject of the poem, America, and the method—explanation through reason. In fact, this long poem is in the form of a dramatic monologue, indicated by the subtitle: "A Poem to My Daughter." Within the first few lines, we encounter: "I want to tell you something about our country, / Or my idea of it: explaining it / If not to you, to my idea of you." The titles of the poem's three parts suggest much about the direction the monologue will take: "Its Many Fragments," "Its Great Emptiness," and "Its Everlasting Possibility." *An Explanation of America* is something of a tour de force in Pinsky's use of a private, personal voice for the skillful handling of large themes about America's nature, meaning, and destiny, themes that Walt Whitman handled with oratorical flourishes and sometimes bombast, and Ezra Pound handled with invective and didacticism. Perhaps one of Pinsky's greatest contributions is in discovering and leading the way for poetry to return to the treatment of such themes.

After finishing his Ph.D. at Stanford, Pinsky taught at a number of universities, including the University of Chicago, Wellesley College, and Harvard. He is now a professor of English at the University of California, Berkeley. In addition to *The Situation of Poetry*, Pinsky has published his doctoral dissertation on the British poet Walter Savage Landor, *Landor's Poetry* (1968), and a "computer novel," *Mindwheel* (1987). In 1988, he brought together a collection of his essays, *Poetry and the World*.

ADDITIONAL READING

Robert Von Hallberg, *American Poetry and Culture, 1945–1980*, 1985.

TEXTS

"Poem about People," "December Blues," and "Doctor Frolic" from *Sadness and Happiness*, 1975; "Dying" from *History of My Heart*, 1984.

Poem About People

The jaunty crop-haired graying
Women in grocery stores,
Their clothes boyish and neat,
New mittens or clean sneakers,

Clean hands, hips not bad still,   5
Buying ice cream, steaks, soda,

Fresh melons and soap—or the big
Balding young men in work shoes

And green work pants, beer belly
And white T-shirt, the porky walk   10
Back to the truck, polite; possible
To feel briefly like Jesus,

A gust of diffuse tenderness
Crossing the dark spaces
To where the dry self burrows   15
Or nests, something that stirs,

Watching the kinds of people
On the street for a while—
But how love falters and flags
When anyone's difficult eyes come   20

Into focus, terrible gaze of a unique
Soul, its need unlovable: my friend
In his divorced schoolteacher
Apartment, his own unsuspected

Paintings hung everywhere,   25
Which his wife kept in a closet—
Not, he says, that she wasn't
Perfectly right; or me, mis-hearing

My rock radio sing my self-pity:
"The Angels Wished Him Dead"—all   30
The hideous, sudden stare of self,
Soul showing through like the lizard

Ancestry showing in the frontal gaze
Of a robin busy on the lawn.
In the movies, when the sensitive   35
Young Jewish soldier nearly drowns

Trying to rescue the thrashing
Anti-semitic bully, swimming across
The river raked by nazi fire,
The awful part is the part truth: 40

Hate my whole kind, but me,
Love me for myself. The weather
Changes in the black of night,
And the dream-wind, bowling across

The sopping open spaces   45
Of roads, golf-courses, parking lots,
Flails a commotion
In the dripping treetops,

Tries a half-rotten shingle
Or a down-hung branch, and we   50
All dream it, the dark wind crossing
The wide spaces between us.

1975

December Blues

At the bad time, nothing betrays outwardly the harsh findings,
The studies and hospital records. Carols play.

Sitting upright in the transit system, the widowlike women
Wait, hands folded in their laps, as monumental as bread.

In the shopping center lots, lights mounted on cold standards   5
Tower and stir, condensing the blue vapour

Of the stars; between the rows of cars people in coats walk
Bundling packages in their arms or holding the hands of children.

Across the highway, where a town thickens by the tracks
With stores open late and creches[1] in front of the churches,   10

Even in the bars a businesslike set of the face keeps off
The nostalgic pitfall of the carols, tugging. In bed,

How low and still the people lie, some awake, holding the carols
Consciously at bay, Oh Little Town,[2] enveloped in unease.

                                                                       1975

Doctor Frolic

Felicity the healer isn't young
And you don't look him up unless you need him.
Clown's eyes, Pope's nose,[1] a mouth for dirty stories,
He made his bundle in the Great Depression

And now, a jovial immigrant success   5
In baggy pinstripes, he winks and wheezes gossip,
Village stories that could lift your hair
Or lance a boil; the small town dirt, the dope,

The fishy deals and incestuous combinations,
The husband and the wife of his wife's brother,   10
The hospital contract, the certificate . . . .
A realist and hardy omnivore,[2]

He strolls the jetties when the month is right
With a knife and lemons in his pocket, after
Live mussels from among the smelly rocks,   15
Preventative of impotence and goitre.

---

[1]Miniature recreations of the scene of the birth of Christ, with the Holy Family, stable, animals, shepherds, and wise men.
[2]Allusion to a line from a Christmas carol: "O little town of Bethlehem, how still we see thee lie. . . ."

[1]Vulgar term for the tail of a roast chicken or other fowl.
[2]Eater of every kind of food.

And as though the sight of tissue healing crooked
Pleased him, like the ocean's vaginal taste,
He'll stitch your thumb up so it shows for life.
And where he once was the only quack in town   20

We all have heard his half-lame joke, the one
About the operation that succeeded,
The tangy line that keeps that clever eye
So merry in the punchinello[3] face.

1975

Dying

Nothing to be said about it, and everything—
The change of changes, closer or further away:
The Golden Retriever next door, Gussie, is dead,

Like Sandy, the Cocker Spaniel from three doors down
Who died when I was small; and every day   5
Things that were in my memory fade and die.

Phrases die out: first, everyone forgets
What doornails are; then after certain decades
As a dead metaphor, *"dead as a doornail"* flickers

And fades away. But someone I know is dying—   10
And though one might say glibly, "everyone is,"
The different pace makes the difference absolute.

The tiny invisible spores in the air we breathe,
That settle harmlessly on our drinking water
And on our skin, happen to come together   15

With certain conditions on the forest floor,
Or even a shady corner of the lawn—
And overnight the fleshy, pale stalks gather,

The colorless growth without a leaf or flower;
And around the stalks, the summer grass keeps growing   20
With steady pressure, like the insistent whiskers

That grow between shaves on a face, the nails
Growing and dying from the toes and fingers
At their own humble pace, oblivious

As the nerveless moths, that live their night or two—   25
Though like a moth a bright soul keeps on beating,
Bored and impatient in the monster's mouth.

1984

---

[3]Punch, the absurd or comic hero in a puppet show (of Italian origin).

SIMON J. ORTIZ
(b. 1941)

In "Song/Poetry and Language—Expression and Perception," published in the journal *Sun Tracks* in 1977, Simon Ortiz wrote of finding the origins of his feeling for poetry in hearing his father singing as he carved wood, usually dancing figures: "I listen carefully, but I listen for more than just the sound, listen for more than just the words and phrases, for more than the various parts of the song. I try to perceive the context, meaning, purpose—all of these items not in their separate parts but as a whole—and I think it comes completely like that." The view is almost mystical, certainly reverential, probably tribal: without the something "more" and that wholeness for which the young Ortiz quietly listened, the poetry would not or could not be.

For Ortiz, the words *song* and *poetry* are interchangeable, and connect with the primal and instinctive use of language: "The song is basic to all vocal expression. The song as expression is an opening from inside of yourself to outside and from outside of yourself to inside but not in the sense that there are separate states of yourself. Instead, it is a joining and an opening together." In discriminating between the interconnected elements essential to poetry or song (perception and expression), Ortiz returned to the image of his father, carving wooden figures: "Indeed, the song was the road from outside of himself to inside—which is perception—and from inside of himself to outside—which is expression."

An Acoma Pueblo Indian, Ortiz was born in Albuquerque in 1941 and grew up in the Acoma Pueblo, the Sky City, a community located on the top of a mesa seventy miles west of Albuquerque. After attending the Bureau of Indian Affairs school on the Indian reservation, he studied at Ft. Lewis College in Colorado and the University of New Mexico. Later he enrolled in the Writers Workshop at the University of Iowa, where he took a Master of Fine Arts degree. He has taught creative writing and Native American literature at a number of institutions, including San Diego State University, Navajo Community College, and the University of New Mexico.

Ortiz's first full-size collection of poems, *Going for the Rain* (1976), contained many poems about the journey away from his origins. It was followed by *A Good Journey* (1977), which recorded the experience of the return home. In his Prologue to the first book, Ortiz wrote of the journey away and the journey back: "A man leaves; he encounters all manner of things. He has adventures, meets people, acquires knowledge, goes different places; he is always looking"; "A man returns, and even the returning has moments of despair and tragedy. But there is beauty and there is joy. At times he is confused, and at times he sees with utter clarity." The journey away and back Ortiz writes about is clearly his own—but it is also a universal experience that we all comprehend, a road that we all travel.

Other books of poetry by Ortiz include *Fight Back: For the Sake of the People, For the Sake of the Land* (1980) and *From Sand Creek: Rising in This Heart Which Is Our America* (1981). The latter won the Pushcart Prize for Poetry. Ortiz has also written short stories, published in *Howbah Indians* (1978) and *Fightin': New and Collected Stories* (1983). In 1983 he edited a volume of Native American stories, *Earth Power Coming*; and in 1984, a volume of Native American poems, *These Hearts, These Poems.*

In the Preface to *From Sand Creek*, Ortiz affirmed that his poetry was an analysis of himself, "as an American, which is hemispheric, a U.S. Citizen, which is national, and as an Indian, which is spiritual and human." He said that he would like his poetry "to be a study [for Indian people] of that process which they have experienced as victim, subject, and expendable resource." And he added: "For people of European heritage, I want it to be a study, too, but one which looks at motive and mission and their own victimization. I hope, finally, we will all learn something from each other."

ADDITIONAL READING

Kenneth Lincoln, *Native American Renaissance*, 1983; Andrew Wiget, *Simon Ortiz*, 1986; Joseph Bruchac, ed., *Survival This Way: Interviews with American Indian Poets*, 1987.

TEXT

Going for the Rain, 1976.

The Creation, According to Coyote[1]

"First of all, it's all true."
Coyote, he says this, this way,
humble yourself, motioning and meaning
what he says.

You were born when you came   5
from that body, the earth;
your black head burst from granite,
the ashes cooling,

until it began to rain.
It turned muddy then,   10
and then green and brown things
came without legs.

They looked strange.
Everything was strange.
There was nothing to know then,   15

until later, Coyote told me this,
and he was b.s.-ing probably,
two sons were born,
Uyuyayeh and Masaweh.

They were young then,   20
and then later on they were older.

And then the people were wondering
what was above.
They had heard rumors.

---

[1]Coyote is a mythic hero for a number of Indian tribes and recurs throughout Ortiz's poems as a character or narrator. He is both a serious and humorous figure and becomes symbolic for the poetry's theme of survival and continuance.

But, you know, Coyote,   25
he was mainly bragging
when he said (I think),
"My brothers, the Twins then said,
'Let's lead these poor creatures
and save them.'"   30

1976

My Father's Song

Wanting to say things,
I miss my father tonight.
His voice, the slight catch,
the depth from his thin chest,
the tremble of emotion   5
in something he has just said
to his son, his song:

> We planted corn one Spring at Acu—
> we planted several times
> but this one particular time   10
> I remember the soft damp sand
> in my hand.

> My father had stopped at one point
> to show me an overturned furrow;
> the plowshare had unearthed   15
> the burrow nest of a mouse
> in the soft moist sand.

> Very gently, he scooped tiny pink animals
> into the palm of his hand
> and told me to touch them.   20
> We took them to the edge
> of the field and put them in the shade
> of a sand moist clod.

> I remember the very softness
> of cool and warm sand and tiny alive mice   25
> and my father saying things.

1976

A Patience Poem for
the Child That Is Me

> Be patient child,
> be patient, quiet.
> The rivers run into the center

of the earth
and around　　　　　　　　　　　　　　　　　　5
revolve all things
and flow
into the center.
Be patient, child,
quiet.　　　　　　　　　　　　　　　　　　　　10

1976

The Significance
of a Veteran's Day

I happen to be a veteran
but you can't tell in how many ways
unless I tell you.

A cold morning waking up on concrete;
I never knew that feeling before,　　　　　　　　5
calling for significance,
and no one answered.

Let me explain it this way
so that you may not go away
without knowing a part of me:　　　　　　　　　10

that I am a veteran of at least 30,000 years
when I travelled with the monumental yearning
of glaciers, relieving myself by them,
growing, my children seeking shelter
by the roots of pines and mountains.　　　　　　15

When it was that time to build,
my grandfather said, "We cut stone and mixed mud
and ate beans and squash and sang
while we moved ourselves. That's what we did."
And I believe him.　　　　　　　　　　　　　20

And then later on in the ancient and deep story
of all our nights, we contemplated,
contemplated not the completion of our age,
but the continuance of the universe,
the travelling, not the progress,　　　　　　　25
but the humility of our being there.

Caught now, in the midst of wars
against foreign disease, missionaries,
canned food, Dick & Jane textbooks, IBM cards,
Western philosophies, General Electric,　　　　30
I am talking about how we have been able
to survive insignificance.

1976

A Story of
How a Wall Stands

At Acu, there is a wall
almost 400 years old
which supports hundreds
of tons of dirt and bones—
it's a graveyard built on a
steep incline—and it looks
like it's about to fall down
the incline but will not for
a long time.

My father, who works with stone,
says, "That's just the part you see,
the stones which seem to be
just packed in on the outside,"
and with his hands puts the stone and mud   5
in place. "Underneath
what looks like loose stone,
there is stone woven together."
He ties one hand over the other,
fitting like the bones of his hands   10
and fingers. "That's what is
holding it together."

"It is built that carefully,"
he says, "the mud mixed
to a certain texture," patiently   15
"with the fingers," worked
in the palm of his hand. "So that
placed between the stones, they hold
together for a long, long time."

He tells me those things,   20
the story of them worked
with his fingers, in the palm
of his hands, working the stone
and the mud until they become
the wall that stands a long, long time.   25

1976

It Doesn't End, of Course

FOR ADELLE, SPRING 1970

It doesn't end.

In all growing
from all earths
to all skies,

in all touching

all things,

in all soothing
the aches of all years,

it doesn't end.

1976

NIKKI GIOVANNI
(b. 1943)

In a book of poems, *Those Who Ride the Night Winds*, published in 1983, Nikki Giovanni wrote the Preface in the same new style she used in the poems—with many spaces marked by three dots, resembling a stream of hesitant thought. She opened the Preface: "The first poem . . . ever written . . . was probably carved . . . on a cold damp cave . . . by a physically unendowed cave man . . . who wanted to make a good impression . . . on a physically endowed . . . cave woman . . . But maybe not . . . Maybe it was she . . . trying to gain the notice . . . of a hunk . . . who was in demand . . . Or perhaps . . . it was simply someone . . . who admired the motion . . . of a sabertooth tiger . . . and wanting to capture the beauty . . . picked up a sharpened rock . . . to draw . . . We know so very little . . . about the origin of the written word . . . let alone the language . . . that all conjecture deserves some consideration . . ."

This conception of poetry was a far cry from that which lay behind her first three books of poems, *Black Feeling, Black Talk* (1967), *Black Judgement* (1968)— later combined as *Black Feeling, Black Talk/Black Judgement* (1970)—and *Re: Creation* (1970). In these first books, the feeling was intense, the stance rhetorical, the voice angry. From 1967 to 1983, Giovanni moved away from militancy and rebellion and found her way to the universal themes of poetry.

She was born Yolande Cornelia Giovanni, Jr., in Knoxville, Tennessee, into a family which soon relocated in a suburb of Cincinnati, where her father was a social worker, and her mother worked for the Welfare Department. Giovanni grew up a devoted Goldwater Republican (the conservative Barry Goldwater ran against Lyndon Johnson in the 1964 election and lost). But at some point while she was a student at Fisk University in Knoxville, she turned from a conservative Republican to a militant black activist, founding a chapter of the Student Non-Violent Coordinating Committee (SNCC) on the Fisk campus in 1964. She graduated from Fisk in 1967, *magna cum laude*.

The poetry of her first three books attracted enough attention to confirm her in her decision to devote her life to being a poet. In her view, marriage was incompatible with her career, but she longed for a child. She made the deliberate decision to have a baby out of wedlock, and her son was born in 1969. The birth of her child accelerated a change—already in progress—in her outlook on life. In 1971, she published two books—*Spin a Soft Black Song: Poems for Children*, dedicated to her son, and *Gemini: An Extended Autobiographical Statement on My First Twenty-Five Years of Being a Black Poet*.

In 1971, Giovanni achieved a new kind of fame with a best-selling record, *Truth Is on Its Way*, a recitation of her poems against the background of the gospel songs of the New York Community Choir. She became something of a celebrity, featured on the front pages of some magazines and awarded an honorary degree by Wilberforce University. Her new book of poems *My House*, published in 1972, showed a radical change in her perspective on the world. She herself commented: "I'm into a very personal thing, now, and I have a two and a half-year-old-son, and I'm more settled. . . . Only a fool doesn't change."

Giovanni did not of course give up being a black poet, but she took the whole range of human feelings and emotions to be her province. Her poems written in the volume dedicated to her son are especially appealing; but so too are such poems as "I Wrote a Good Omelet," in which she seems to be having great fun, and sharing it with the reader. Her later volumes of poetry include *The Women and the Men* (1975), *Cotton Candy on a Rainy Day* (1978), and *Those Who Ride the Night Winds* (1983). Her books of prose include *A Dialogue: James Baldwin and Nikki Giovanni* (1972), *A Poetic Equation: Conversations Between Nikki Giovanni and Margaret Walker* (1974), and *Sacred Cows . . . and Other Edibles* (1988).

Since the success of her first recording in 1971, Giovanni has issued more of her poems on records that have been widely circulated. And she has become a popular figure on campuses, reading and commenting on her poems. In an interview published in *Black Women Writers at Work* (1984), edited by Claudia Tate, Giovanni provided a glimpse of the way she writes her poetry: "A poem is a way of capturing a moment. . . . A poem's got to be a single stroke, and I make it the best I can because it's going to live. I feel if only one thing of mine is to survive, it's at least got to be an accurate picture of what I saw. I want my camera and film to record what my eye and my heart saw. It's that simple. And I keep working until I have the best reflection I can get. Universality has dimension in that moment."

ADDITIONAL READING

Don L. Lee, *Dynamite Voices: Black Poets of the 1960s*, 1971; Donald B. Gibson, ed., *Modern Black Poets: A Collection of Critical Essays*, 1973; Mari Evans, ed. *Black Women Writers, 1950—1980: A Critical Evaluation*, 1984; Marie Harris and Kathleen Aguero, eds., *A Gift of Tongues: Critical Challenges in Contemporary American Poetry*, 1987.

TEXTS

"Revolutionary Dreams," "Ego Tripping," and "Poetry" from *The Women and the Men*, 1975; "I Wrote a Good Omelet" from *Those Who Ride the Night Winds*, 1983.

Revolutionary Dreams

i used to dream militant
dreams of taking
over america to show
these white folks how it should be
done   5
i used to dream radical dreams
of blowing everyone away with my perceptive powers
of correct analysis
i even used to think i'd be the one
to stop the riot and negotiate the peace   10

then i awoke and dug
that if i dreamed natural
dreams of being a natural
woman doing what a woman
does when she's natural   15
i would have a revolution

1970   1970

Ego Tripping¹

(there may be a reason why)

I was born in the congo
I walked to the fertile crescent and built
    the sphinx
I designed a pyramid so tough that a star
    that only glows every one hundred years falls   5
    into the center giving divine perfect light
I am bad

I sat on the throne
    drinking nectar with allah²
I got hot and sent an ice age to europe   10
    to cool my thirst
My oldest daughter is nefertiti³
    the tears from my birth pains
    created the nile
I am a beautiful woman   15

I gazed on the forest and burned
    out the sahara desert
    with a packet of goat's meat
    and a change of clothes
I crossed it in two hours   20
I am a gazelle so swift
    so swift you can't catch me

For a birthday present when he was three
I gave my son hannibal⁴ an elephant
    He gave me rome for mother's day   25
My strength flows ever on

My son noah built new/ark⁵ and
I stood proudly at the helm
    as we sailed on a soft summer day

---

¹Giovanni has written of "Ego Tripping": "this poem is . . . a chronological poem tracing the development of humans through the movement of black women. i have no feelings that the poem is exclusive of any one but i wanted to write a sassy hands-on-the-hips poem from the understanding that i am a woman and indeed was once a girl. . . . it goes from the first human bones discovered all the way to the space age. what has been included is as important to me as what has been excluded. what i strove to do was show progress, movement, humor and a bit of pride."
²Allah is the supreme God of Islam.
³Nefertiti, queen of Egypt in the first half of the fourteenth century B.C.
⁴Hannibal (247–183 B.C.), Carthaginian general whose army crossed the Alps on elephants to invade Italy in the Second Punic War.
⁵Pun on Newark, the New Jersey city.

I turned myself into myself and was   30
   jesus
   men intone my loving name
   All praises All praises
I am the one who would save

I sowed diamonds in my back yard   35
My bowels deliver uranium
   the filings from my fingernails are
   semi-precious jewels
   On a trip north
I caught a cold and blew   40
My nose giving oil to the arab world
I am so hip even my errors are correct
I sailed west to reach east and had to round off
   the earth as I went
   The hair from my head thinned and gold was laid   45
   across three continents

I am so perfect so divine so ethereal so surreal
I cannot be comprehended
   except by my permission

I mean . . . I . . . can fly   50
   like a bird in the sky . . .

1970   1970

Poetry

poetry is motion graceful
as a fawn
gentle as a teardrop
strong like the eye
finding peace in a crowded room   5

we poets tend to think
our words are golden
though emotion speaks too
loudly to be defined
by silence   10

sometimes after midnight or just before
the dawn
we sit typewriter in hand
pulling loneliness around us
forgetting our lovers or children   15
who are sleeping
ignoring the weary wariness
of our own logic
to compose a poem
   no one understands it   20
it never says "love me" for poets are
beyond love
it never says "accept me" for poets seek not

acceptance but controversy
it only says "i am" and therefore 25
i concede that you are too

a poem is pure energy
horizontally contained
between the mind
of the poet and the ear of the reader 30
if it does not sing discard the ear
for poetry is song
if it does not delight discard
the heart for poetry is joy
if it does not inform then close 35
off the brain for it is dead
if it cannot heed the insistent message
that life is precious

which is all we poets
wrapped in our loneliness 40
are trying to say

1975

::I Wrote a Good Omelet

I wrote a good omelet . . . and ate a hot poem . . .
after loving you

Buttoned my car . . . and drove my coat home . . . in the rain . . .
after loving you

I goed on red . . . and stopped on green . . . floating somewhere in between . . . 5
being here and being there . . .
after loving you

I rolled my bed . . . turned down my hair . . . slightly confused but . . . I
   don't care . . .
Laid out my teeth . . . and gargled my gown . . . then I stood . . . and laid me
   down . . .
to sleep . . . 10
after loving you

1983

LOUISE GLÜCK
(b. 1943)

Louise Glück (pronounced Glick) published her first book of poems in 1968, her sixth in 1985. She has commented on her compulsion to write: "When I am working, I am completely absorbed in the work. When I am not working, I tend to be absorbed in that fact: preoccupied, depressed, mired in self. One of the efforts of my life is to cope with silence; my best discovery has been teaching."

Glück was born in New York City and attended Sarah Lawrence College in 1962 and Columbia University (1963–65). In addition to writing poetry, she has taught at a number of institutions, including Goddard College, the University of North Carolina at Greensboro, the University of Virginia, and the University of Iowa Writers' Workshop. She lives in Vermont with her second husband and a son, Noah, by her first marriage.

It was Glück's second book, *The House on Marshland*, published in 1975, that brought her wide recognition as an important new poet. As her later volumes have appeared, they have drawn the praise of reviewers and poetry awards. After publication of *Descending Figure* in 1980, she won the American Academy Award in 1981; and her 1985 volume, *The Triumph of Achilles*, won the National Book Critics Circle Award.

Glück's subjects are drawn from her personal life, and include anorexia, her family, school children, motherhood, love, birth, and death. Her outlook is somber, sometimes sad, occasionally affirmative; her voice quiet; her imagery startling. She has explained that her recurring themes of "death" and "absence" come from her keen awareness of the sister who died before she was born: "Her death was not my experience, but her absence was. Her death let me be born." She has, she says, "an instinctive identification with the abandoned, the widowed, with all figures left behind."

Glück once thought that "poems were like words inscribed in rock or caught in amber." But she came to believe that this view left out the intimacy of poetry: "Poems do not endure as objects but as presences. When you read anything worth remembering, you liberate a human voice; you release into the world again a companion spirit. Perpetual resurrection — "; she added: "I read poems to hear that voice. And I write to speak to those I have heard."

ADDITIONAL READING

William Heyen, ed., *The Generation of 2000: Contemporary American Poets*, 1984.

TEXTS

"Easter Season," "Scraps" from *Firstborn*, 1968; "All Hallows," "For My Mother," "The School Children," "The Apple Trees" from *The House on Marshland*, 1975; "The Drowned Children," "Illuminations" from *Descending Figure*, 1980.

Easter Season

There is almost no sound . . . only the redundant stir
Of shrubs as perfumed temperatures embalm
Our coast. I saw the spreading gush of people with their palms.[1]
In Westchester, the crocus spreads like cancer.

This will be the death of me. I feel the leaves close in,   5
Promise threaten from all sides and above.
It is not real. The green seed-pod, flaky dove
Of the bud descend. The rest is risen.

1968

---

[1] I.e., on the Sunday before Easter, Palm Sunday, churchgoers traditionally receive palms to commemorate Christ's triumphal entry into Jerusalem, when the people strewed the way with branches and leaves of palm trees (John 12:12–13).

Scraps

We had codes
In our house. Like
Locks; they said
We never lock
Our door to you.   5
And never did.
Their bed
Stood, spotless as a tub . . .
I passed it every day
For twenty years, until   10
I went my way. My chore
Was marking time. Gluing
Relics into books I saw
Myself at seven learning
Distance at my mother's knee.   15
My favorite snapshot of my
Father shows him pushing forty
And lyrical
Above his firstborn's empty face.
The usual miracle.   20

1968

All Hallows[1]

Even now this landscape is assembling.
The hills darken. The oxen
sleep in their blue yoke,
the fields having been
picked clean, the sheaves   5
bound evenly and piled at the roadside
among cinquefoil,[2] as the toothed moon rises:

This is the barrenness
of harvest or pestilence.
And the wife leaning out the window   10
with her hand extended, as in payment,
and the seeds
distinct, gold, calling
Come here
Come here, little one   15

And the soul creeps out of the tree.

1975

---

[1] I.e., Hallowe'en (All Hallow E'en—the eve before All Saints Day), October 31.   [2] Plants with five-petaled flowers or five-lobed compound leaves.

For My Mother

It was better when we were
together in one body.
Thirty years. Screened
through the green glass
of your eye, moonlight   5
filtered into my bones
as we lay
in the big bed, in the dark,
waiting for my father.
Thirty years. He closed   10
your eyelids with
two kisses. And then spring
came and withdrew from me
the absolute
knowledge of the unborn,   15
leaving the brick stoop
where you stand, shading
your eyes, but it is
night, the moon
is stationed in the beech tree,   20
round and white among
the small tin markers of the stars:
Thirty years. A marsh
grows up around the house.
Schools of spores circulate   25
behind the shades, drift through
gauze flutterings of vegetation.

                                                    1975

The School Children

The children go forward with their little satchels.
And all morning the mothers have labored
to gather the late apples, red and gold,
like words of another language.

And on the other shore   5
are those who wait behind great desks
to receive these offerings.

How orderly they are — the nails
on which the children hang
their overcoats of blue or yellow wool.   10

And the teachers shall instruct them in silence
and the mothers shall scour the orchards for a way out,
drawing to themselves the gray limbs of the fruit trees
bearing so little ammunition.

                                                    1975

The Apple Trees

Your son presses against me
his small intelligent body.

I stand beside his crib
as in another dream
you stood among trees hung   5
with bitten apples
holding out your arms.
I did not move
but saw the air dividing
into panes of color—at the very last   10
I raised him to the window saying
See what you have made
and counted out the whittled ribs,
the heart on its blue stalk
as from among the trees   15
the darkness issued:

In the dark room your son sleeps.
The walls are green, the walls
are spruce and silence.
I wait to see how he will leave me.   20
Already on his hand the map appears
as though you carved it there,
the dead fields, women rooted to the river.

1975

The Drowned Children

You see, they have no judgment.
So it is natural that they should drown,
first the ice taking them in
and then, all winter, their wool scarves
floating behind them as they sink   5
until at last they are quiet.
And the pond lifts them in its manifold dark arms.

But death must come to them differently,
so close to the beginning.
As though they had always been   10
blind and weightless. Therefore
the rest is dreamed, the lamp,
the good white cloth that covered the table,
their bodies.

And yet they hear the names they used   15
like lures slipping over the pond:
What are you waiting for
come home, come home, lost
in the waters, blue and permanent.

1980

Illuminations[1]

1

My son squats in the snow in his blue snowsuit.
All around him stubble, the brown
degraded bushes. In the morning air
they seem to stiffen into words.
And, between, the white steady silence.   5
A wren hops on the airstrip
under the sill, drills
for sustenance, then spreads
its short wings, shadows
dropping from them.   10

2

Last winter he could barely speak.
I moved his crib to face the window:
in the dark mornings
he would stand and grip the bars
until the walls appeared,   15
calling *light, light,*
that one syllable, in
demand or recognition.

3

He sits at the kitchen window
with his cup of apple juice.   20
Each tree forms where he left it,
leafless, trapped in his breath.
How clear their edges are,
no limb obscured by motion,
as the sun rises   25
cold and single over the map of language.

1980

LESLIE MARMON SILKO

(b. 1948)

In *Voices of the Rainbow: Contemporary Poetry by American Indians* (1975), which contained a number of her poems, Leslie Marmon Silko provided a simple account of her complex origins and identity: "My family are the Marmons at Old Laguna on the Laguna Pueblo Reservation where I grew up. We are mixed bloods—Laguna, Mexican, white—but the way we live is like Marmons, and if you are from Laguna Pueblo you will understand what I mean. All those lan-

---

[1] Title (*Les Illuminations*, 1886) of a volume of visionary poems
by Arthur Rimbaud (1854–1891), a French poet whose work
was a major influence on twentieth-century poetry.

guages, all those ways of living are combined, and we live somewhere on the fringes of all three. But I don't apologize for this any more — not to whites, not to full bloods — our origin is unlike any other. My poetry, my storytelling rise out of this source."

The Laguna Pueblo Reservation is located near Albuquerque. Silko took a degree at the University of New Mexico, graduating *summa cum laude* in 1969. She attended law school for a time, but gave it up for writing. Her first story to be published, "The Man to Send Rain Clouds," was written as an assignment in a creative writing class at the university, and appeared in the *New Mexico Quarterly*. Silko published her first book, *Laguna Woman: Poems*, in 1974. The book was highly praised, and Silko's poetry began appearing in anthologies. She won the Pushcart Prize for poetry in 1977. This same year she published her first novel, *Ceremony*, which told the story of an Indian veteran returning from the Second World War, suffering a breakdown because the enemy Japanese he was ordered to kill resembled his own people much more compellingly than did his fellow U.S. soldiers, who looked down on him; he survived by returning to the ways, traditions, and rituals of his people.

A fellow poet, James Wright, wrote to Silko after reading *Ceremony*, calling it "one of the four or five best books I have ever read about America." Silko answered, and the two poets became strong friends through a lively correspondence that lasted until Wright's death in 1980. It was collected and edited by Wright's widow, Anne Wright, and published in 1986 as *The Delicacy and Strength of Lace*. Silko once wrote Wright her idea about poetry: "In sand paintings the little geometric forms are said to designate mountains, planets, rainbows — in one sand painting or another all things in Creation are traced out in sand. What I learned for myself was that words can function like the sand. I say 'learned for myself' because I think most poets and writers understand this, but it is a kind of lesson that must be found on one's own."

In 1981, Silko published *Storyteller*, puzzling reviewers because it mixed poems, short stories, and photographs, all related to the author's family, people, and ancestors. Silko said of the book: "White ethnologists have reported that the oral tradition among Native American groups has died out, because whites have always looked for museum pieces and artifacts when dealing with Native American communities. . . . I grew up at Laguna listening, and I hear the ancient stories, I hear them very clearly in the stories we are telling right now. Most important, I feel the power which the stories have, to bring us together, especially when there is loss and grief."

Storyteller glides from poetry to prose and back into poetry again without breaks or warning; before long the reader understands that stories are threaded through the entirety and they are all part of a larger story being endlessly told. The language brings to life the interspersed photographs, which in turn endow the words with a gritty reality. The importance of the enterprise is suggested in a poem entitled "The Storyteller's Escape": "With these stories of ours / we can escape almost anything / with these stories we will survive"; "In this way / we hold them / and keep them with us forever / and in this way / we continue."

Storyteller established Silko as a major writer mining a material uniquely hers (and her people's). In 1983, she was given a John D. and Catherine T. MacArthur Foundation grant, a financial award lasting for five years and large enough to free talented individuals to devote themselves to any creative project they wish to undertake. Silko teaches English at the University of New Mexico and has held visiting appointments at the University of Arizona and at Vassar. Now divorced from her husband John Silko, she maintains her residence with her children on the Laguna Pueblo Reservation.

ADDITIONAL READING

Per Seyersted, *Leslie Marmon Silko*, 1980.

TEXT

Storyteller, 1981.

The Time We
Climbed Snake Mountain

Seeing good places
    for my hands
I grab the warm parts of the cliff
        and I feel the mountain as I climb.

Somewhere around here   5
      yellow spotted snake is sleeping on his rock
      in the sun.

So
   please, I tell them
      watch out,
don't step on the spotted yellow snake   10
      he lives here.
The mountain is his.

1981

How to Write a
Poem about the Sky

FOR THE STUDENTS OF THE BETHEL MIDDLE
SCHOOL, BETHEL, ALASKA — FEB. 1975

You see the sky now
colder than the frozen river
so dense and white
little birds
walk across it.   5

You see the sky now
but the earth
is lost in it
and there are no horizons.

It is all   10
a single breath.

You see the sky
but the earth is called
by the same name
                    the moment   15
                    the wind shifts
sun splits it open
and bluish membranes
push through slits of skin.

You see the sky   20

                                                        1981

In Cold Storm Light

In cold storm light
I watch the sandrock
    canyon rim.

    The wind is wet
        with the smell of piñon.   5
    The wind is cold
        with the sound of juniper.
                And then
                    out of the thick ice sky
                        running swiftly   10
                        pounding
                        swirling above the treetops
                    The snow elk come,
                    Moving, moving
                        white song   15
                        storm wind in the branches.
And when the elk have passed
    behind them
        a crystal train of snowflakes
        strands of mist   20
                tangled in rocks
                and leaves.

                                                        1981

Where Mountain Lion
Lay Down with Deer

I climb the black rock mountain
stepping from day to day
                silently.

I smell the wind for my ancestors
    pale blue leaves
    crushed wild mountain smell.
Returning
  up the gray stone cliff
  where I descended
        a thousand years ago
Returning to faded black stone
where mountain lion lay down with deer.
It is better to stay up here
        watching wind's reflection
        in tall yellow flowers.
The old ones who remember me are gone
      the old songs are all forgotten
and the story of my birth.

How I danced in snow-frost moonlight
    distant stars to the end of the Earth,
How I swam away
      in freezing mountain water
      narrow mossy canyon tumbling down
         out of the mountain
         out of deep canyon stone
     down
       the memory
          spilling out
          into the world.

5

10

15

20

25

1981

Preparations

Dead sheep
  beside the highway.
Belly burst open
    guts and life unwinding on the sand.

The body is carefully attended.
Look at the long black wings
    the shining eyes
Solemn and fat the crows gather
    to make preparations.

Pull wool from skin
Pick meat from bone
    tendon from muscle.
Only a few more days
    they say to each other
A few more days and this will be finished.

Bones, bones
Let wind polish the bones.
It is done.

5

10

15

1981

RITA DOVE
(b. 1952)

In an interview, Rita Dove remarked on her own process of writing a poem:

> I think the worst thing that can happen to a poet is to be self-conscious, to think, "I'm writing a poem," the moment that you're writing a poem. When you get that moment where things begin to click in a poem and you begin to go off in a direction that you didn't know you were going in, you'd better just ride that current as far as it'll take you. That's such a tenuous connection for me that any self-consciousness is going to kill it right away. I try not to know what I'm doing. That may sound facetious, but I try not to clutter my head up with literary theories and critiques and stuff like that. I don't really want to know where I've been. I only follow what I need. . . . Each poem is a new field to enter. I wanted each one to be an epiphany. . .

For Dove, what she calls the "epiphanal quality" is a necessary dimension of the "lyric poem."

Dove was born in Akron, Ohio, and graduated from Miami University, in Oxford, Ohio, in 1973, *summa cum laude*. In 1974–75, she was awarded a Fulbright Fellowship to study modern European literature at the University of Tübingen, Germany. On returning from Europe, she entered the University of Iowa, taking a Master of Fine Arts in 1977. She taught creative writing at Arizona State University, Tempe, and is now a professor of English at the University of Virginia. Since her year of study in Germany, she has returned to Europe, settling for periods of time in Jerusalem and in Berlin.

Dove has said of her formative experiences abroad:

> When I went to Europe the first time . . . it was mind boggling to see how blind I'd been in my own little world of America. . . . It was really quite shocking to see that there was another way of looking at things. And when I went back in '80–81 to spend a lot of time, I got a different angle on the way things are. . . . Also as a *person* going to Europe I was treated differently because I was American. I was Black, but they treated me differently than people treat me here because I'm Black. . . . I became an object. I was a Black American, and therefore I became a representative for all of that. And I sometimes felt like a ghost. I mean, people would ask me questions, but I had a feeling that they weren't seeing *me*, but a shell.

Her first book of poems, *The Yellow House on the Corner*, was published in 1980 and contained many remarkable poems about a young girl's awakening to the world, to both its pains and its joys. *Museum*, which appeared in 1983, showed a widening and deepening of her interests in the places and people of the world as she had come to experience it more fully, especially in her foreign travel. In 1985, Dove published a book of short stories entitled *Fifth Sunday*, a title which, as she has explained, "refers to those occasional months where there are five Sundays." Where she grew up, the fifth Sunday was "youth Sunday," and the service "was conducted with the church youth." She has said of her fiction: "All the stories . . . feature individuals who are trying to be recognized as human beings in a world that loves to pigeonhole and forget."

In 1986, Dove published *Thomas and Beulah*, a series of interrelated lyric poems about her grandfather and grandmother, who had migrated early in the century to Akron from the South (one from Tennessee, the other from Georgia). Dove has revealed that she started to tell her grandfather's story, but came to realize that her grandmother had "to say her part, too." She has described her book as "the story of a Black couple growing up in the industrial Midwest from about 1900 to 1960." At the end of the book, she provided a chronology which revealed that the title characters were married in 1924, suffered through the Great Depression of the 1930s, and raised four daughters, all of whom were "married off" by 1956. Thomas died in 1963, Beulah in 1969. In this volume, Dove demonstrated that she had an extraordinary talent for portraiture in her poetry, and could narrate lives obliquely by presenting a series of vividly realized moments. She was awarded the Pulitzer Prize for Poetry in 1987. In her fourth book of poems, *Grace Notes* (1989), Dove continues, as Emily Grosholz has said, to make "the language shimmer."

And for Dove, as she expressed in what is in effect her poetic credo:

> Language is everything. As Mallarmé said, "A poem is made of words." It's by language that I enter a poem, and that also leads me forward. That doesn't exclude perceptions and experience and emotions or anything like that. But emotion is useless if there's no way to express it. Language is just the clay we use to make our poems. It's something that a lot of people who are *not* writers take for granted. . . . Because all of us use language, we assume, "Well, anyone can do that. I talk everyday." But it's a different use of language; it is the sounds of the language, the way of telling something, that makes a poem for me. There's nothing new under the sun, but it's the way you *see* it. For me as a poet, language becomes an integral part of that perception, the *way* one sees it.

ADDITIONAL READING

"A Conversation with Rita Dove," ed. Stan Sanvel Rubin and Earl G. Ingersoll, *Black American Literature Forum* 20:3 (Fall, 1986).

TEXTS

"Adolescence—II" from *The Yellow House on the Corner*, 1980; "Flirtation" from *Museum*, 1983; remaining poems from *Thomas and Beulah*, 1986.

Adolescence — II

Although it is night, I sit in the bathroom, waiting.
Sweat prickles behind my knees, the baby-breasts are alert.
Venetian blinds slice up the moon; the tiles quiver in pale strips.

Then they come, the three seal men with eyes as round
As dinner plates and eyelashes like sharpened tines.   5
They bring the scent of licorice. One sits in the washbowl,

One on the bathtub edge; one leans against the door.
"Can you feel it yet?" they whisper.
I don't know what to say, again. They chuckle,

Patting their sleek bodies with their hands.   10
"Well, maybe next time." And they rise,
Glittering like pools of ink under moonlight,

And vanish. I clutch at the ragged holes
They leave behind, here at the edge of darkness.
Night rests like a ball of fur on my tongue.   15

                                                          1980

Flirtation

After all, there's no need
to say anything

at first. An orange, peeled
and quartered, flares

like a tulip on a wedgwood plate.   5
Anything can happen.

Outside the sun
has rolled up her rugs

and night strewn salt
across the sky. My heart   10

is humming a tune
I haven't heard in years!

Quiet's cool flesh—
let's sniff and eat it.

There are ways   15
to make of the moment

a topiary
so the pleasure's in

walking through.

                                                          1983

from Thomas and Beulah[1]

Jiving

Heading North, straw hat
cocked on the back of his head,

---

[1]A sequence of interrelated poems telling the story of the poet's grandparents, "the story of a Black couple growing up in the industrial Midwest from about 1900 to 1960." For Dove's comments on her book, see the biographical introduction.

tight curls gleaming
with brilliantine, he didn't stop

until the nights of chaw   5
and river-bright

had retreated, somehow
into another's life. He landed

in Akron, Ohio
1921,   10

on the dingy beach
of a man-made lake.

Since what he'd been through
he was always jiving, gold hoop

from the right ear jiggling   15
and a glass stud, bright blue

in his left. The young ladies
saying *He sure plays*

that tater bug
like the devil!   20

sighing their sighs
and dimpling.

1986

The Zeppelin Factory[1]

The zeppelin factory
needed workers, all right—
but, standing in the cage
of the whale's belly, sparks
flying off the joints   5
and noise thundering,
Thomas wanted to sit
right down and cry.

That spring the third
largest airship was dubbed   10
the biggest joke
in town, though they all
turned out for the launch.
Wind caught,

---

[1] In her chronology at the end of *Thomas and Beulah*, Dove lists two events that have significance for this poem: "1929: The Goodyear Zeppelin Airdock is built—the largest building in the world without interior supports"; "1931: The airship *Akron* disaster."

"The Akron" floated   15
out of control,

three men in tow—
one dropped
to safety, one
hung on but the third,   20
muscles and adrenalin
failing, fell
clawing
six hundred feet.

Thomas at night   25
in the vacant lot:
    Here I am, intact
    and faint-hearted.

Thomas hiding
his heart with his hat   30
at the football game, eyeing
the Goodyear blimp overhead:
    Big boy I know
    you're in there.

                        1986

Gospel[1]

Swing low so I
can step inside—
a humming ship of voices
big with all

the wrongs done   5
done them.
No sound this generous
could fail:

ride joy until
it cracks like an egg,   10
make sorrow
seethe and whisper.

From a fortress
of animal misery
soars the chill voice   15
of the tenor, enraptured

with sacrifice.
What do I see,

---

[1]From the poet's chronology: "1946: Thomas quits the gospel choir at the A. M. E. Zion Church."

he complains, notes
brightly rising   20

towards a sky
blank with promise.
Yet how healthy
the single contralto

settling deeper   25
into her watery furs!
Carry me home,
she cajoles, bearing

down. Candelabras
brim. But he slips   30
through God's net and swims
heavenward, warbling.

                                                              1986

Weathering Out

She liked mornings the best—Thomas gone
to look for work, her coffee flushed with milk,

outside autumn trees blowsy and dripping.
Past the seventh month she couldn't see her feet

so she floated from room to room, houseshoes flapping,   5
navigating corners in wonder. When she leaned

against a door jamb to yawn, she disappeared entirely.

Last week they had taken a bus at dawn
to the new airdock. The hangar slid open in segments

and the zeppelin nosed forward in its silver envelope.   10
The man walked it out gingerly, like a poodle,

then tied it to a mast and went back inside.
Beulah felt just that large and placid, a lake;

she glistened from cocoa butter smoothed in
when Thomas returned every evening nearly   15

in tears. He'd lean an ear on her belly
and say: *Little fellow's really talking,*

though to her it was more the *pok-pok-pok*
of a fingernail tapping a thick cream lampshade.

Sometimes during the night she woke and found him   20
asleep there and the child sleeping, too.

The coffee was good but too little. Outside
everything shivered in tinfoil — only the clover

between the cobblestones hung stubbornly on,
green as an afterthought . . .   25

                                                    1986

Daystar

She wanted a little room for thinking:
but she saw diapers steaming on the line,
a doll slumped behind the door.

So she lugged a chair behind the garage
to sit out the children's naps.   5

Sometimes there were things to watch —
the pinched armor of a vanished cricket,
a floating maple leaf. Other days
she stared until she was assured
when she closed her eyes   10
she'd see only her own vivid blood.

She had an hour, at best, before Liza appeared
pouting from the top of the stairs.
And just *what* was mother doing
out back with the field mice? Why,   15

building a palace. Later
that night when Thomas rolled over and
lurched into her, she would open her eyes
and think of the place that was hers
for an hour — where   20
she was nothing,
pure nothing, in the middle of the day.

                                                    1986

GARY SOTO
(b. 1952)

Gary Soto, when his first work appeared in the mid-1970s, was often identified as a Chicano poet; but as his books have accumulated, and appreciation of
his talent grown, critics are now more apt to identify him as an important young
American poet who happens to be a Chicano. He continues, as he started, writing out of his Mexican-American heritage with an art that is controlled and
never dominated by the pathos of his subject. The poems have a strong emo-

tional impact, primarily because of their strategy of restraint and of understatement.

In the poem "History," which appeared in his first book, Soto writes about his grandmother's fierce struggle for survival: "Grandpa left for work, / she hosed down / The walks her sons paved." The speaker recalls: "A face streaked / From cutting grapes / And boxing plums. / I remember her insides / Were washed of tapeworm, / Her arms swelled into knobs." The poem ends with a reminder of her Mexican origins, her movement from "Taxco to San Joaquin," from Mexico to California: "The places / In which we all begin." Thus the poem opens out at the end to fulfill the promise of the title ("History") at the beginning: the history of the grandmother is the history of the Mexican migrant-laborers and their families, including the author's.

Out of this collective memory, Soto fashioned many of his early poems. But he wrote, too, about his own experiences in the San Joaquin Valley working as a field hand when a child — in such poems as "Daybreak," "Field Poem," and "Hoeing." The images are always concrete, but often startling: "The onions are unplugged from their sleep," the leaves of the cotton plants are like "small hands / Waving good-bye." In addition to the moments of monotonous drudgery, of exhaustion, of fear and pain, there are moments of remembered exhilaration in Soto's poetry. "Walking with Jackie, Sitting with a Dog" captures such a carefree day of his youth, rambling with a friend, concluding: "We lick our fingers and realize / That with oranges now and plums four months away, / No one need die."

Soto was born in Fresno, California, took a B.A. at the California State University at Fresno and an M.F.A. at the University of California at Irvine. He teaches in the Chicano Studies program and the English Department at the University of California, Berkeley. Soto's first book, *The Elements of San Joaquin* (1977), won the U.S. Award of the International Poetry Forum. His volumes of poetry include *The Tale of Sunlight* (1978), *Where Sparrows Work Hard* (1981), *Black Hair* (1985), *Small Faces* (1986), and *Lesser Evils: Ten Quartets* (1988). Soto's autobiographical prose work, *Living Up the Street: Narrative Recollections* (1985), won the Before Columbus Foundation American Book Award. He has edited *California Childhood: Recollections and Stories of the Golden State* (1988).

In "The Evolution of Chicano Literature" (*Three American Literatures*, 1982), Luis Leal and Pepe Barrón said: "Soto's poetry represents a culmination in contemporary Chicano literature, embodying many of its best qualities. Soto moves easily across National boundaries to mark the lines of continuity between Chicanos and Mexicans and to portray man's essential dignity. . . . Soto seems . . . to have grown in ethnic consciousness. . . . Yet he carries his ethnicity unobtrusively, and it is this combination of talents that places him in the first rank of young American poets."

ADDITIONAL READING

Luis Leal and Pepe Barrón, "The Evolution of Chicano Literature," *Three American Literatures*, ed. Houston A. Baker, Jr., 1982; Bruce-Novoa, "Patricide and Resurrection: Gary Soto," *Chicano Poetry: A Response to Chaos*, 1982.

TEXTS

"Field Poem," "Hoeing," and "History" from *The Elements of San Joaquin*, 1977; "Walking with Jackie, Sitting with a Dog" from *Where Sparrows Work Hard*, 1981; "The Jungle Cafe" from *Black Hair*, 1985.

Field Poem

When the foreman whistled
My brother and I
Shouldered our hoes,
Leaving the field.
We returned to the bus   5
Speaking
In broken English, in broken Spanish
The restaurant food,
The tickets to a dance
We wouldn't buy with our pay.   10

From the smashed bus window,
I saw the leaves of cotton plants
Like small hands
Waving good-bye.

                                                    1977

Hoeing

During March while hoeing long rows
Of cotton
Dirt lifted in the air
Entering my nostrils
And eyes   5
The yellow under my fingernails

The hoe swung
Across my shadow   chopping weeds
And thick caterpillars
That shriveled   10
Into rings
And went where the wind went

When the sun was on the left
And against my face
Sweat   the sea   15
That is still within me
Rose and fell from my chin
Touching land
For the first time

                                                    1977

History

Grandma lit the stove.
Morning sunlight
Lengthened in spears

Across the linoleum floor.
Wrapped in a shawl,   5
Her eyes small
With sleep,
She sliced papas,[1]
Pounded chiles[2]
With a stone   10
Brought from Guadalajara.[3]

                                                    After
Grandpa left for work,
She hosed down
The walk her sons paved   15
And in the shade
Of a chinaberry,
Unearthed her
Secret cigar box
Of bright coins   20
And bills, counted them
In English,
Then in Spanish,
And buried them elsewhere.
Later, back   25
From the market,
Where no one saw her,
She pulled out
Pepper and beet, spines
Of asparagus   30
From her blouse,
Tiny chocolates
From under a paisley bandana,
And smiled.

That was the '50s,   35
And Grandma in her '50s,
A face streaked
From cutting grapes
And boxing plums.
I remember her insides   40
Were washed of tapeworm,
Her arms swelled into knobs
Of small growths—
Her second son
Dropped from a ladder   45
And was dust.
And yet I do not know
The sorrows
That sent her praying
In the dark of a closet,   50
The tear that fell
At night
When she touched
Loose skin

---

[1] "Potatoes" (Spanish).
[2] I.e., chile (or hot) peppers.
[3] A city in Mexico.

Of belly and breasts.   55
I do not know why
Her face shines
Or what goes beyond this shine,
Only the stories
That pulled her   60
From Taxco to San Joaquin,
Delano to Westside,[4]
The places
In which we all begin.

                                                    1977

Walking with Jackie,
Sitting with a Dog

Jackie on the porch, shouting for me to come out.
It's Saturday, and I am in a sweater that's
Too large, balled at the elbows, black at the collar.
Laughing, we slam the screen door on a strained
Voice, and run down the street, sticks   5
In hand, shooing pigeons and the girls
Who are all legs.
                            We cross the gray traffic
Of Belmont, and enter an alley, its quick stream
Of glass blinking in the angled light. We blink,
And throw rocks at things that move,   10
Slow cat or bough. We grin
Like shovels, and continue on
Because it's Saturday, early as it's ever
Going to get, and we're brothers
To all that's heaved over fences.   15
Our talk is nonsense: Africa and trees splintered
Into matchsticks, handlebars and the widening targets
Of his sister's breasts, staring us down.
The scattered newspaper, cartwheeling across
A street, is one way to go.
                            And we go into   20
Another alley, where we find a man, asleep behind
Stacked cardboard. The sun flares
Behind trees and it means little.
We find a dog, hungry and sad as a suitcase kicked open
And showing nothing. At a curb we drape   25
Him across our laps and quarter an orange—
The juice runs like the tears an onion would give,
If only it opened its eye.
We lick our fingers and realize
That with oranges now and plums four months away,   30
No one need die.

                                                    1981

The Jungle Cafe

We could wipe away a fly,
Drink, and order that yellow
Thing behind the glass, peach
Or sweet bread. Sunlight
Is catching on a fork,   5
Toothy wink from a star.
The fan is busy, the waiter is busy,
And today, in this cafe
Of two dollars and fifty
Cents, we're so important   10
Dogs are shaking our hands.
"Welcome, turistas,"[1] they say,
Or might say if they could
Roll their Rs. Where we sit
It's three o'clock, and   15
Across the room, where
Old men are playing dominos
It's maybe later, it's maybe
Peru under their hats.
There are toads in this place   20
—sullen guards by the door—
And the bartender is just another
Uncle fooling with the radio.
"A little to the left,"
I shout, and he dials left,   25
Then right, until it's German
Polkas, accordions by the sea.
The toads move a little.
An old man clicks a domino.
Omar, my gypsy friend, puts in—   30
"Love is chasing me up my sleeve."
I salute him, he salutes me,
And together we're so drunk
We're making sense. Little
By little, with rum the color   35
Of a woman's arm, we're seeing things—
One dancer, no two,
Make that three with one chair.
And that man—the old one
Over there—is so blurry   40
He thinks he's flying.

                                                                1985

---

[1] "Tourists" (Spanish).

CONTEMPORARY FICTION

VLADIMIR NABOKOV	FLANNERY O'CONNOR
WRIGHT MORRIS	JOHN BARTH
JOHN CHEEVER	DONALD BARTHELME
TILLIE OLSEN	JOHN UPDIKE
RALPH ELLISON	PHILIP ROTH
BERNARD MALAMUD	THOMAS PYNCHON
SAUL BELLOW	JOYCE CAROL OATES
PETER TAYLOR	RAYMOND CARVER
CARSON MCCULLERS	BOBBIE ANN MASON
SHIRLEY JACKSON	GARRISON KEILLOR
TRUMAN CAPOTE	ALICE WALKER
WILLIAM GASS	ANN BEATTIE
JAMES BALDWIN	LOUISE ERDRICH

"I have no social purpose, no moral message; I've no general ideas to exploit but I like composing riddles and I like finding elegant solutions to those riddles that I have composed myself."

Vladimir Nabokov, "Vladimir Nabokov on His Life and Work: A BBC TV Interview"

"Our century is more than two-thirds done; it is dismaying to see so many of our writers following Dostoevsky or Tolstoy or Balzac, when the question seems to me to be how to succeed not even Joyce and Kafka, but those who *succeeded* Joyce and Kafka and are now in the evening of their own careers."

John Barth, "The Literature of Exhaustion"

"To labor to create vanguard conditions is historicism. It means that people have been reading books of culture-history and have concluded retrospectively that originality is impossible without such conditions. But genius is always, without strain, avant-garde. Its departure from tradition is not the result of caprice or of policy but of an inner necessity."

Saul Bellow, "Speaking of Books: Cloister Culture"

"It seems a country-headed thing to say: that literature is language, that stories and the places and the people in them are merely made of words as chairs are made of smoothed sticks and sometimes of cloth or metal tubes."

William Gass, "The Medium of Fiction"

"It is, in the end, the saving of lives that we writers are about. Whether we are 'minority' writers or 'majority.' It is simply in our power to do this. We do it because we care. . . . We care because we know this: *the life we save is our own.*"

Alice Walker, "Saving the Life That Is Your Own"

VLADIMIR NABOKOV

(1899–1977)

In a 1966 interview, Nabokov was asked whether he, like many other writers, ever felt characters taking over in a fiction and actually dictating the "course of the action." Nabokov's reply was immediate and doctrinaire: "I have never experienced this. What a preposterous experience! Writers who have had it must be very minor or insane. No, the design of my novel is fixed in my imagination and every character follows the course I imagine for him. I am the perfect dictator in that private world insofar as I alone am responsible for its stability and truth."

Readers of Nabokov are likely to recognize him as the dictatorial ruler in his fiction, in contrast, say, with a Willa Cather, a Sherwood Anderson, or a Katherine Anne Porter, for all of whom the writing process was much more intuitive, much less intellectually controlled, often turning in surprising directions and leading to unforeseen destinations. Nabakov's emphasis on his "fixed" design and his characters' obedience to his imperious will may be taken, in part, as suggestive of the difference between postmodernist and modernist fiction.

Nabakov was born into an aristocratic family in St. Petersburg, Russia, in 1899 and grew up alternating between a city house and a large country estate, both requiring a retinue of servants. He described his life during this period in a 1951 autobiographical volume, *Speak, Memory* (revised 1966, first entitled *Conclusive Evidence*). His father was a professor, and his mother a cultivated lady who introduced her son early to the world of literature. He was often left in the care of an English-speaking governess, and was at home in English and French as well as his native Russian at a young age.

This idyllic first twenty years of Nabokov's life came to a sudden end in 1919, when the family was forced to flee Russia to escape the Communist Revolution. The next twenty years he spent in England, France, and Germany. His father was assassinated at a political meeting in Berlin by a Russian member of a rival party as he attempted to aid the intended victim. Until 1923, Nabokov studied languages at Cambridge University, graduating with honors. He then went to Berlin, where he soon married and had his only child, Dimitri. By the mid-1920s, he was launched on a literary career, publishing his first novel (in Russian) in 1926. He published some nine Russian novels, including *King, Queen, Knave,* (1928), *The Defense* (1930), *Laughter in the Dark* (1932), and *Invitation to a Beheading* (1938). The Russian fiction was not to be translated into English until later.

In 1938, the Nabokovs moved to Paris because of the rise to power in Germany of Hitler and his Nazi followers. But soon after, in 1940 with the beginning of the Second World War, Nabokov was forced to flee in order to escape the invading German armies. He and his family sailed to the United States and became American citizens; although they would go abroad to live after about twenty years in the United States, they would retain their American citizenship.

In 1941, Nabokov published his first novel in English, *The Real Life of Sebastian Knight*, and embarked on an academic career, which was to be spent primarily at Cornell University. He continued to write fiction, publishing *Bend Sinister* in 1947 and *Pnin* in 1957. He had, however, finished another novel he could not get published in America because it was considered obscene in its tale of an older man's passion for, and affair with, a thirteen-year-old "nymphet." The novel, *Lolita*, was published in Paris in 1955 and copies began to be smuggled into the United States. In 1958, it was published here and became an instant best-seller, bringing Nabokov fame and sufficient fortune to free him to pursue for the rest of his life his two great loves, writing fiction and collecting butterflies; by the time he had migrated to America, he had become a serious and learned lepidopterist.

When Nabokov left America for Switzerland in 1960, he was in his sixties. But some of his best work, including his masterpiece, was yet to come. *Pale Fire* appeared in 1962 and was hailed by one reviewer, Mary McCarthy, as "one of the very great works of art of this century." It challenged readers because it opened with a 999-line poem called "Pale Fire," by a poet who had been accidentally killed; the poem was followed by an extended annotation that seemed to have very little to do with its meaning but much to do with the fantasy-life of the mad, homosexual commentator who believed himself to have been the former king of the mythical kingdom of Zembla. If this sounds a bit wild, it is because the novel does not lend itself to a summary of its action; the "facts," as related by a madman, cannot easily be established. Did the poet create the commentator, or the commentator invent the poet, or the sly author Nabokov imagine them both and even himself as a persona in the novel? Critical consensus appears to be that Nabokov's novels are never about what they first may seem to be, but are all at some level about the ambiguous, complex, and even duplicitous nature of art itself.

Nabokov continued to publish fiction, including *Ada* (1969), *Transparent Things* (1972), and *Look at the Harlequins!* (1974). His Russian works were translated into English, and he published a number of volumes of stories, including *Nabokov's Dozen* (1958), *Nabokov's Quartet* (1966), *A Russian Beauty* (1973), and *Tyrants Destroyed and Other Stories* (1975). In 1964 he published his translation from the Russian of Pushkin's long narrative poem *Eugene Onegin;* Edmund Wilson attacked its use of archaic English, and Nabokov attacked Wilson's knowledge of Russian. *Lolita* and *Pale Fire,* however, remain his two most widely read and critically acclaimed works. He died in 1977.

"The Vane Sisters," reprinted here, raises all the relevant critical questions about Nabokov's work. Embedded in it is a hidden message, the decipherment of which constitutes a considerable part of its pleasurable effect. Nabokov once remarked: "A work of art has no importance whatever to society. It is only important to the individual, and only the individual reader is important to me. I don't give a damn for the group, the community, the masses. . . . There can be no question that what makes a work of fiction safe from larvae and rust is not its social importance, but its art, only its art." And he also said, "I like composing riddles and I like finding elegant solutions to those riddles." One critical book devoted to him, by Page Stegner, is entitled *Escape into Aesthetics.* Other critics have claimed that his work constitutes a serious exploration of serious themes. They often cite a passage in the poem "Pale Fire," which seems to them to constitute a summation of Nabokov's view of the limited but nevertheless gratifying reach of human awareness:

> Just this: not text, but texture; not the dream
> But topsy-turvical coincidence,
> Not flimsy nonsense, but a web of sense.
> Yes! It sufficed that I in life could find
> Some kind of link-and-bobolink, some kind
> Of correlated pattern in the game,
> Plexed artistry, and something of the same
> Pleasure in it as they who played it found.

Skeptical critics observe, however, that these words come from a fictional poet and are part of a poem that is often comic in substance and ironic in tone. Although Nabokov gave many interviews during his lifetime, he tended to be evasive about his own work. He did, however, once observe: "We shall never know the origin of life, or the meaning of life, or the nature of space and time, or the nature of nature, or the nature of thought. . . . To be quite candid—and what I am going to say now is something I never said before, and I hope it provokes a salutary little chill—I know more than I can express in words, and the little I can express would not have been expressed, had I not known more."

ADDITIONAL READING

Vladimir Nabokov: Strong Opinions (Interviews, Letters to Editors, Articles), with a Foreword by Nabokov, 1973; *The Nabokov-Wilson Letters, 1940–1971,* ed. Simon Karlinsky, 1979; *Lectures on Literature,* with an Introduction by John Updike, 1980; *Lectures on Russian Literature,* ed. Fredson Bowers, 1981; *Vladimir Nabokov: Selected Letters, 1940–1977,* ed. Dmitri Nabokov and Matthew J. Bruccoli, 1989.

Page Stegner, *Escape into Aesthetics: The Art of Vladimir Nabokov,* 1966; L. S. Dembo, ed., *Nabokov: The Man and His Work,* 1967; Andrew Field, *Nabokov: His Life in Art,* 1967; Alfred Appel, Jr., and Charles Newman, eds., *Nabokov: Criticism, Reminiscences, Translations, and Tributes,* 1970; Julian Moynahan, *Vladimir Nabokov,* 1971; William W. Rowe, *Nabokov's Deceptive World,* 1971; Julia Bader, *Crystal Land; Artiface in Nabokov's English Novels,* 1972; Douglas Fowler, *Reading Nabokov,* 1974; Alfred Appel, Jr., *Nabokov's Dark Cinema,* 1974; L. L. Lee, *Vladimir Nabokov,* 1976; G. M. Hyde, *Vladimir Nabokov: America's Russian Novelist,* 1977; Andrew Field, *Nabokov: His Life in Part,* 1977; Dabney Stuart, *Nabokov: The Dimensions of Parody,* 1978; Donald E. Morton, *Vladimir Nabokov,* 1978; Peter Quennell, *Vladimir Nabokov: A Tribute, His Life, His Work, His World,* 1979; Samuel Schuman, *Vladimir Nabokov: A Reference Guide,* 1979; Ellen Pifer, *Nabokov and the Novel,* 1980; J. E. Rivers and Charles Nicol, eds., *Nabokov's Fifth Arc: Nabokov and Others on His Life's Work,* 1982; David Packman, *Vladimir Nabokov: The Structure of Literary Desire,* 1982; Norman Page, ed., *Nabokov: The Critical Heritage,* 1982; Phyllis Roth, ed., *Critical Essays on Vladimir Nabokov,* 1984; Laurie Clancy, *The Novels of Vladimir Nabokov,* 1984; David Rampton, *Vladimir Nabokov: A Critical Study of the Novels,* 1984; George Gibian and Stephen Jan Parker, eds., *The Achievement of Vladimir Nabokov: Essays, Studies, Reminiscences,* 1984; Stanley Ross, *Vladimir Nabokov: Life, Work and Criticism,* 1985; Andrew Field, *VN: The Life and Art of Vladimir Nabokov,* 1986; Michael Juliar, *Vladimir Nabokov: A Descriptive Bibliography,* 1986; Stephen Jan Parker, *Understanding Nabokov,* 1987; Geoffrey Green, *Freud and Nabokov,* 1988; Brian Boyd, *Vladimir Nabokov: The Russian Years,* 1990.

TEXT

Nabokov's Congeries, ed. Page Stegner, 1968 (subsequently issued as *The Portable Nabokov,* 1971).

The Vane Sisters

1

I might never have heard of Cynthia's death, had I not run, that night, into D., whom I had also lost track of for the last four years or so; and I might never have run into D., had I not got involved in a series of trivial investigations.

The day, a compunctious Sunday after a week of blizzards, had been part jewel, part mud. In the midst of my usual afternoon stroll through the small hilly town attached to the girls' college where I taught French literature, I had stopped to watch a family of brilliant icicles drip-dripping from the eaves of a frame house. So clear-cut were their pointed shadows on the white boards behind them that I was sure the shadows of the falling drops should be visible too. But they were not. The roof jutted too far out, perhaps, or the angle of vision was faulty, or, again, I did not chance to be watching the right icicle when the right drop fell. There was a rhythm, an alternation in the dropping that I found as teasing as a coin trick. It led me to inspect the corners of several house blocks, and this brought me to Kelly Road, and right to the house where D. used to live when he was instructor here. And as I looked up at the eaves of the adjacent garage with its full display of transparent stalactites backed by their blue silhouettes, I was rewarded at last, upon choosing one, by the sight of what might be described as the dot of an exclamation mark leaving its ordinary position to glide down very fast—a jot faster than the thaw-drop it raced. This twinned twinkle was delightful but not completely satisfying; or rather it only sharpened my appetite for other tidbits of light and shade, and I walked on in a state of raw awareness that seemed to transform the whole of my being into one big eyeball rolling in the world's socket.

Through peacocked lashes I saw the dazzling diamond reflection of the low sun on the round back of a parked automobile. To all kinds of things a vivid pictorial sense had been restored by the sponge of the thaw. Water in overlapping festoons flowed down one sloping street and turned gracefully into another. With ever so slight a note of meretricious appeal, narrow passages between buildings revealed treasures of brick and purple. I remarked for the first time the humble fluting—last echoes of grooves on the shafts of columns—ornamenting a garbage can, and I also saw the rippling upon its lid—circles diverging from a fantastically ancient center. Erect, dark-headed shapes of dead snow (left by the blades of a bulldozer last Friday) were lined up like rudimentary penguins along the curbs, above the brilliant vibration of live gutters.

I walked up, and I walked down, and I walked straight into a delicately dying sky, and finally the sequence of observed and observant things brought me, at my usual eating time, to a street so distant from my usual eating place that I decided to try a restaurant which stood on the fringe of the town. Night had fallen without sound or ceremony when I came out again. The lean ghost, the elongated umbra[1] cast by a parking meter upon some damp snow, had a strange ruddy tinge; this I made out to be due to the tawny red light of the restaurant sign above the sidewalk; and it was then—as I sauntered there, wondering rather wearily if in the course of my return tramp I might be lucky enough to find the same in neon blue it was then that a car crunched to a standstill near me and D. got out of it with an exclamation of feigned pleasure.

He was passing, on his way from Albany to Boston, through the town he had dwelt in before, and more than once in my life have I felt that stab of vicarious emotion followed by a rush of personal irritation against travelers who seem to feel nothing at all upon revisiting spots that ought to harass them at every step with wailing and writhing memories. He ushered me back into the bar that I had just left, and after the usual exchange of buoyant platitudes came the inevitable vacuum which he filled with the random words: "Say, I never thought there was anything wrong with Cynthia Vane's heart. My lawyer tells me she died last week."

2

He was still young, still brash, still shifty, still married to the gentle, exquisitely pretty woman who had never learned or suspected anything about his disastrous affair with Cynthia's hysterical young sister, who in her turn had known nothing of the interview I had had with Cynthia when she suddenly summoned me to Boston to make me swear I would talk to D. and get him "kicked out" if he did not stop seeing Sybil at once—or did not divorce his wife (whom incidentally she visualized through the prism of Sybil's wild talk as a termagant and a fright). I had cornered him immediately. He had said there was nothing to worry about—had made up his mind, anyway, to give up his college job and move with his wife to Albany where he would work in his father's firm; and the whole matter, which had threatened to become one of those hopelessly entangled situations that drag on for years, with peripheral sets of

---

[1]Shadow.

well-meaning friends endlessly discussing it in universal secrecy—and even founding, among themselves, new intimacies upon its alien woes—came to an abrupt end.

I remember sitting next day at my raised desk in the large classroom where a mid-year examination in French Lit was being held on the eve of Sybil's suicide. She came in on high heels, with a suitcase, dumped it in a corner where several other bags were stacked, with a single shrug slipped her fur coat off her thin shoulders, folded it on her bag, and with two or three other girls stopped before my desk to ask when would I mail them their grades. It would take me a week, beginning from tomorrow, I said, to read the stuff. I also remember wondering whether D. had already informed her of his decision—and I felt acutely unhappy about my dutiful little student as during one hundred and fifty minutes my gaze kept reverting to her, so childishly slight in close-fitting gray, and kept observing that carefully waved dark hair, that small, small-flowered hat with a little hyaline[2] veil as worn that season and under it her small face broken into a cubist pattern by scars due to a skin disease, pathetically masked by a sun-lamp tan that hardened her features, whose charm was further impaired by her having painted everything that could be painted, so that the pale gums of her teeth between cherry-red chapped lips and the diluted black ink of her eyes under darkened lids were the only visible openings into her beauty.

Next day, having arranged the ugly copybooks alphabetically, I plunged into their chaos of scripts and came prematurely to Valevsky and Vane, whose books I had somehow misplaced. The first was dressed up for the occasion in a semblance of legibility, but Sybil's work displayed her usual combination of several demon hands. She had begun in very pale, very hard pencil which had conspicuously embossed the blank verso, but had produced little of permanent value on the upper-side of the page. Happily the tip soon broke, and Sybil continued in another, darker lead, gradually lapsing into the blurred thickness of what looked almost like charcoal, to which, by sucking the blunt point, she had contributed some traces of lipstick. Her work, although even poorer than I had expected, bore all the signs of a kind of desperate conscientiousness, with underscores, transposes, unnecessary footnotes, as if she were intent upon rounding up things in the most respectable manner possible. Then she had borrowed Mary Valevsky's fountain pen and added: *"Cette examain est finie ainsi que ma vie. Adieu, jeunes filles!* Please, Monsieur le Professeur, contact *ma soeur*[3] and tell her that Death was not better than D minus, but definitely better than Life minus D."

I lost no time in ringing up Cynthia who told me it was all over—had been all over since eight in the morning—and asked me to bring her the note, and when I did, beamed through her tears with proud admiration for the whimsical use ("Just like her!") Sybil had made of an examination in French literature. In no time she "fixed" two highballs, while never parting with Sybil's notebook—by now splashed with soda water and tears—and went on studying the death message, whereupon I was impelled to point out to her the grammatical mistakes in it and to explain the way "girl" is translated in American colleges lest students innocently bandy around the French equivalent of "wench," or worse. These rather tasteless trivialities pleased Cynthia hugely as she rose, with gasps, above the heaving surface of her grief. And then, holding that limp notebook as if it were a kind of passport to a casual Elysium[4] (where pencil points do not snap and a dreamy young beauty with an impeccable complexion winds a lock of her hair on a dreamy forefinger, as she meditates over some celestial test), Cynthia led me upstairs, to a chilly little bedroom just to show me, as if I were the police or a sympathetic Irish neighbor, two empty pill bottles and the

---

[2]Transparent.
[3]"This exam is finished as well as my life. Goodbye, young   girls! Please, Professor, contact my sister. . . ." (French).
[4]Paradise.

tumbled bed from which a tender, inessential body, that D. must have known down to its last velvet detail, had been already removed.

3

It was four or five months after her sister's death that I began seeing Cynthia fairly often. By the time I had come to New York for some vocational research in the Public Library she had also moved to that city where for some odd reason (in vague connection, I presume, with artistic motives) she had taken what people, immune to gooseflesh, term a "cold water" flat, down in the scale of the city's transverse streets. What attracted me were neither her ways, which I thought repulsively vivacious, nor her looks, which other men thought striking. She had wide-spaced eyes very much like her sister's, of a frank, frightened blue with dark points in a radial arrangement. The interval between her thick black eyebrows was always shiny, and shiny too were the fleshy volutes of her nostrils. The coarse texture of her epiderm looked almost masculine, and, in the stark lamplight of her studio, you could see the pores of her thirty-two-year-old face fairly gaping at you like something in an aquarium. She used cosmetics with as much zest as her little sister had, but with an additional slovenliness that would result in her big front teeth getting some of the rouge. She was handsomely dark, wore a not too tasteless mixture of fairly smart heterogeneous things, and had a so-called good figure; but all of her was curiously frowsy, after a way I obscurely associated with left-wing enthusiasms in politics and "advanced" banalities in art, although, actually, she cared for neither. Her coily hair-do, on a part-and-bun basis, might have looked feral[5] and bizarre had it not been thoroughly domesticated by its own soft unkemptness at the vulnerable nape. Her fingernails were gaudily painted, but badly bitten and not clean. Her lovers were a silent young photographer with a sudden laugh and two older men, brothers, who owned a small printing establishment across the street. I wondered at their tastes whenever I glimpsed, with a secret shudder, the higgledy-piggledly striation of black hairs that showed all along her pale shins through the nylon of her stockings with the scientific distinctness of a preparation flattened under glass; or when I felt, at her every movement, the dullish, stalish, not particularly conspicuous but all-pervading and depressing emanation that her seldom bathed flesh spread from under weary perfumes and creams.

Her father had gambled away the greater part of a comfortable fortune, and her mother's first husband had been of Slav origin, but otherwise Cynthia Vane belonged to a good, respectable family. For aught we know, it may have gone back to kings and soothsayers in the mists of ultimate islands. Transferred to a newer world, to a landscape of doomed, splendid deciduous trees, her ancestry presented, in one of its first phases, a white churchful of farmers against a black thunderhead, and then an imposing array of townsmen engaged in mercantile pursuits, as well as a number of learned men, such as Dr. Jonathan Vane, the gaunt bore (1780–1839), who perished in the conflagration of the steamer "Lexington" to become later an habitué of Cynthia's tilting table.[6] I have always wished to stand genealogy on its head, and here I have an opportunity to do so, for it is the last scion, Cynthia, and Cynthia alone, who will remain of any importance in the Vane dynasty. I am alluding of course to her artistic gift, to her delightful, gay, but not very popular paintings which the friends of her friends bought at long intervals—and I dearly should like to know where they went after her death, those honest and poetical pictures that illumined her living room—the wonderfully detailed images of metallic things, and my favorite "Seen Through a Windshield"—a windshield partly covered with rime, with a brilliant

---

[5]Wild.
[6]Table used in spiritualism to communicate with the dead.

trickle (from an imaginary car roof) across its transparent part and, through it all, the sapphire flame of the sky and a green and white fir tree.

4

Cynthia had a feeling that her dead sister was not altogether pleased with her — had discovered by now that she and I had conspired to break her romance; and so, in order to disarm her shade, Cynthia reverted to a rather primitive type of sacrificial offering (tinged, however, with something of Sybil's humor), and began to send to D.'s business address, at deliberately unfixed dates, such trifles as snapshots of Sybil's tomb in a poor light; cuttings of her own hair which was indistinguishable from Sybil's; a New England sectional map with an inked-in cross, midway between two chaste towns, to mark the spot where D. and Sybil had stopped on October the twenty-third, in broad daylight, at a lenient motel, in a pink and brown forest; and, twice, a stuffed skunk.

Being as a conversationalist more voluble than explicit, she never could describe in full the theory of intervenient auras that she had somehow evolved. Fundamentally there was nothing particularly new about her private creed since it presupposed a fairly conventional hereafter, a silent solarium of immortal souls (spliced with mortal antecedents) whose main recreation consisted of periodical hoverings over the dear quick.[7] The interesting point was a curious practical twist that Cynthia gave to her tame metaphysics. She was sure that her existence was influenced by all sorts of dead friends each of whom took turns in directing her fate much as if she were a stray kitten which a schoolgirl in passing gathers up, and presses to her cheek, and carefully puts down again, near some suburban hedge — to be stroked presently by another transient hand or carried off to a world of doors by some hospitable lady.

For a few hours, or for several days in a row, and sometimes recurrently, in an irregular series, for months or years, anything that happened to Cynthia, after a given person had died, would be, she said, in the manner and mood of that person. The event might be extraordinary, changing the course of one's life; or it might be a string of minute incidents just sufficiently clear to stand out in relief against one's usual day and then shading off into still vaguer trivia as the aura gradually faded. The influence might be good or bad; the main thing was that its source could be identified. It was like walking through a person's soul, she said. I tried to argue that she might not always be able to determine the exact source since not everybody has a recognizable soul; that there are anonymous letters and Christmas presents which anybody might send; that, in fact, what Cynthia called "a usual day" might be itself a weak solution of mixed auras or simply the routine shift of a humdrum guardian angel. And what about God? Did or did not people who would resent any omnipotent dictator on earth look forward to one in heaven? And wars? What a dreadful idea — dead soldiers still fighting with living ones, or phantom armies trying to get at each other through the lives of crippled old men.

But Cynthia was above generalities as she was beyond logic. "Ah, that's Paul," she would say when the soup spitefully boiled over, or: "I guess good Betty Brown is dead" — when she won a beautiful and very welcome vacuum cleaner in a charity lottery. And, with Jamesian[8] meanderings that exasperated my French mind, she would go back to a time when Betty and Paul had not yet departed, and tell me of the showers of well-meant, but odd and quite unacceptable bounties — beginning with an old purse that contained a check for three dollars which she picked up in the street and, of course, returned (to the aforesaid Betty Brown — this is where she first comes in — a decrepit colored woman hardly able to walk), and ending with an insulting

---

[7]Living.
[8]Reference to the long, complicated sentences of American novelist Henry James.

proposal from an old beau of hers (this is where Paul comes in) to paint "straight" pictures of his house and family for a reasonable remuneration—all of which followed upon the demise of a certain Mrs. Page, a kindly but petty old party who had pestered her with bits of matter-of-fact advice since Cynthia had been a child.

Sybil's personality, she said, had a rainbow edge as if a little out of focus. She said that had I known Sybil better I would have at once understood how Sybil-like was the aura of minor events which, in spells, had suffused her, Cynthia's, existence after Sybil's suicide. Ever since they had lost their mother they had intended to give up their Boston home and move to New York, where Cynthia's paintings, they thought, would have a chance to be more widely admired; but the old home had clung to them with all its plush tentacles. Dead Sybil, however, had proceeded to separate the house from its view—a thing that affects fatally the sense of home. Right across the narrow street a building project had come into loud, ugly scaffolded life. A pair of familiar poplars died that spring, turning to blond skeletons. Workmen came and broke up the warm-colored lovely old sidewalk that had a special violet sheen on wet April days and had echoed so memorably to the morning footsteps of museum-bound Mr. Lever, who upon retiring from business at sixty had devoted a full quarter of a century exclusively to the study of snails.

Speaking of old men, one should add that sometimes these posthumous auspices and interventions were in the nature of parody. Cynthia had been on friendly terms with an eccentric librarian called Porlock who in the last years of his dusty life had been engaged in examining old books for miraculous misprints such as the substitution of "l" for the second "h" in the word "hither." Contrary to Cynthia, he cared nothing for the thrill of obscure predictions; all he sought was the freak itself, the chance that mimics choice, the flaw that looks like a flower; and Cynthia, a much more perverse amateur of mis-shapen or illicitly connected words, puns, logographs,[9] and so on, had helped the poor crank to pursue a quest that in the light of the example she cited struck me as statistically insane. Anyway, she said, on the third day after his death she was reading a magazine and had just come across a quotation from an imperishable poem (that she, with other gullible readers, believed to have been really composed in a dream) when it dawned upon her that "Alph"[10] was a prophetic sequence of the initial letters of Anna Livia Plurabelle[11] (another sacred river running through, or rather around, yet another fake dream), while the additional "h" modestly stood, as a private signpost, for the word that had so hypnotized Mr. Porlock. And I wish I could recollect that novel or short story (by some contemporary writer, I believe) in which, unknown to its author, the first letters of the words in its last paragraph formed, as deciphered by Cynthia, a message from his dead mother.

5

I am sorry to say that not content with these ingenious fancies Cynthia showed a ridiculous fondness for spiritualism. I refused to accompany her to sittings in which paid mediums took part: I knew too much about that from other sources. I did consent, however, to attend little farces rigged up by Cynthia and her two poker-faced gentlemen-friends of the printing shop. They were podgy, polite, and rather eerie old fellows, but I satisfied myself that they possessed considerable wit and culture. We sat down at a light little table, and crackling tremors started almost as soon as we laid our fingertips upon it. I was treated to an assortment of ghosts who rapped out their reports most readily though refusing to elucidate anything that I did not

---

[9]An anagram, in which rearrangement or realignment of letters divulges a concealed message.
[10]The "sacred river" from the poem "Kubla Khan" by Samuel Taylor Coleridge (1772–1834), British poet; Coleridge claimed to have composed it in a dream.

[11]Section of (and symbolic character in) *Finnegans Wake*, by James Joyce (1882–1941), Irish novelist; she personifies the river Liffey and her initials A. L. P. are interwoven throughout the work.

quite catch. Oscar Wilde[12] came in and in rapid garbled French, with the usual anglicisms, obscurely accused Cynthia'a dead parents of what appeared in my jottings as *"plagiatisme."* A brisk spirit contributed the unsolicited information that he, John Moore, and his brother Bill had been coal miners in Colorado and had perished in an avalanche at "Crested Beauty" in January 1883. Frederic Myers, an old hand at the game, hammered out a piece of verse (oddly resembling Cynthia's own fugitive productions) which in part reads in my notes:

> *What is this — a conjurer's rabbit,*
> *Or a flawy but genuine gleam —*
> *Which can check the perilous habit*
> *And dispel the dolorous dream?*

Finally, with a great crash and all kinds of shudderings and jig-like movements on the part of the table, Leo Tolstoy[13] visited our little group and, when asked to identify himself by specific traits of terrene habitation, launched upon a complex description of what seemed to be some Russian type of architectural woodwork ("figures on boards — man, horse, cock, man, horse, cock"), all of which was difficult to take down, hard to understand, and impossible to verify.

I attended two or three other sittings which were even sillier but I must confess that I preferred the childish entertainment they afforded and the cider we drank (Podgy and Pudgy were teetotallers) to Cynthia's awful house parties.

She gave them at the Wheelers' nice flat next door — the sort of arrangement dear to her centrifugal nature, but then, of course, her own living room always looked like a dirty old palette. Following a barbaric, unhygienic, and adulterous custom, the guests' coats, still warm on the inside, were carried by quiet, baldish Bob Wheeler into the sanctity of a tidy bedroom and heaped on the conjugal bed. It was also he who poured out the drinks, which were passed around by the young photographer while Cynthia and Mrs. Wheeler took care of the canapés.

A late arrival had the impression of lots of loud people unnecessarily grouped within a smoke-blue space between two mirrors gorged with reflections. Because, I suppose, Cynthia wished to be the youngest in the room, the women she used to invite, married or single, were, at the best, in their precarious forties; some of them would bring from their homes, in dark taxis, intact vestiges of good looks, which, however, they lost as the party progressed. It has always amazed me — the capacity sociable week-end revelers have of finding almost at once, by a purely empiric but very precise method, a common denominator of drunkenness, to which everybody loyally sticks before descending, all together, to the next level. The rich friendliness of the matrons was marked by tomboyish overtones, while the fixed inward look of amiably tight men was like a sacrilegious parody of pregnancy. Although some of the guests were connected in one way or another with the arts, there was no inspired talk, no wreathed, elbow-propped heads, and of course no flute girls. From some vantage point where she had been sitting in a stranded mermaid pose on the pale carpet with one or two younger fellows, Cynthia, her face varnished with a film of beaming sweat, would creep up on her knees, a proffered plate of nuts in one hand, and crisply tap with the other the athletic leg of Cochran or Corcoran, an art dealer, ensconced, on a pearl-gray sofa, between two flushed, happily disintegrating ladies.

At a further stage there would come spurts of more riotous gaiety. Corcoran or Coransky would grab Cynthia or some other wandering woman by the shoulder and lead her into a corner to confront her with a grinning imbroglio of private jokes

[12]Wilde (1856–1900), Irish playwright and poet.
[13]Tolstoy (1828–1910), Russian novelist.

and rumors, whereupon, with a laugh and a toss of her head, she would break away. And still later there would be flurries of intersexual chumminess, jocular reconciliations, a bare fleshy arm flung around another woman's husband (he standing very upright in the midst of a swaying room), or a sudden rush of flirtatious anger, of clumsy pursuit—and the quiet half smile of Bob Wheeler picking up glasses that grew like mushrooms in the shade of chairs.

After one last party of that sort, I wrote Cynthia a perfectly harmless and, on the whole, well-meant note, in which I poked a little Latin fun at some of her guests. I also apologized for not having touched her whisky, saying that as a Frenchman I preferred the grape to the grain. A few days later I met her on the steps of the Public Library, in the broken sun, under a weak cloudburst, opening her amber umbrella, struggling with a couple of armpitted books (of which I relieved her for a moment), "Footfalls on the Boundary of Another World," by Robert Dale Owen,[14] and something on "Spiritualism and Christianity"; when, suddenly, with no provocation on my part, she blazed out at me with vulgar vehemence, using poisonous words, saying— through pear-shaped drops of sparse rain—that I was a prig and a snob; that I only saw the gestures and disguises of people; that Corcoran had rescued from drowning, in two different oceans, two men—by an irrelevant coincidence both called Corcoran; that romping and screeching Joan Winter had a little girl doomed to grow completely blind in a few months; and that the woman in green with the freckled chest whom I had snubbed in some way or other had written a national best-seller in 1932. Strange Cynthia! I had been told she could be thunderously rude to people whom she liked and respected; one had, however, to draw the line somewhere and since I had by then sufficiently studied her interesting auras and other odds and ids, I decided to stop seeing her altogether.

6

The night D. informed me of Cynthia's death I returned after eleven to the two-storied house I shared, in horizontal section, with an emeritus professor's widow. Upon reaching the porch I looked with the apprehension of solitude at the two kinds of darkness in the two rows of windows: the darkness of absence and the darkness of sleep.

I could do something about the first but could not duplicate the second. My bed gave me no sense of safety; its springs only made my nerves bounce. I plunged into Shakespeare's sonnets—and found myself idiotically checking the first letters of the lines to see what sacramental words they might form. I got FATE (LXX), ATOM (CXX) and, twice, TAFT (LXXXVIII, CXXXI). Every now and then I would glance around to see how the objects in my room were behaving. It was strange to think that if bombs began to fall I would feel little more than a gambler's excitement (and a great deal of earthy relief) whereas my heart would burst if a certain suspiciously tense-looking little bottle on yonder shelf moved a fraction of an inch to one side. The silence, too, was suspiciously compact as if deliberately forming a black back-drop for the nerve flash caused by any small sound of unknown origin. All traffic was dead. In vain did I pray for the groan of a truck up Perkins Street. The woman above who used to drive me crazy by the booming thuds occasioned by what seemed monstrous feet of stone (actually, in diurnal life, she was a small dumpy creature resembling a mummified guinea pig) would have earned my blessings had she now trudged to her bathroom. I put out my light and cleared my throat several times so as to be responsible for at

---

[14]Owen (1801–1877), American social reformer and strong believer in spiritualism (son of the British reformer, Robert Owen, who settled New Harmony, Indiana).

least *that* sound. I thumbed a mental ride with a very remote automobile but it dropped me before I had a chance to doze off. Presently a crackle (due, I hoped, to a discarded and crushed sheet of paper opening like a mean, stubborn night flower) — started and stopped in the waste-paper basket, and my bed-table responded with a little click. It would have been just like Cynthia to put on right then a cheap poltergeist show.

I decided to fight Cynthia. I reviewed in thought the modern era of raps and apparitions, beginning with the knockings of 1848,[15] at the hamlet of Hydesville, N.Y., and ending with grotesque phenomena at Cambridge, Mass.; I evoked the ankle-bones and other anatomical castanets of the Fox sisters (as described by the sages of the University of Buffalo); the mysteriously uniform type of delicate adolescent in bleak Epworth or Tedworth, radiating the same disturbances as in old Peru; solemn Victorian orgies with roses falling and accordions floating to the strains of sacred music; professional imposters regurgitating moist cheesecloth; Mr. Duncan, a lady medium's dignified husband, who, when asked if he would submit to a search, excused himself on the ground of soiled underwear; old Alfred Russel Wallace, the naïve naturalist, refusing to believe that the white form with bare feet and unperforated earlobes before him, at a private pandemonium in Boston, could be prim Miss Cook whom he had just seen asleep, in her curtained corner, all dressed in black, wearing laced-up boots and earrings; two other investigators, small, puny, but reasonably intelligent and active men, closely clinging with arms and legs about Eusapia, a large, plump elderly female reeking of garlic, who still managed to fool them; and the sceptical and embarrassed magician, instructed by charming Margery's "control" not to get lost in the bathrobe's lining but to follow up the left stocking until he reached the bare thigh — upon the warm skin of which he felt a "teleplastic" mass that appeared to the touch uncommonly like cold, uncooked liver.

7

I was appealing to flesh, and the corruption of flesh, to refute and defeat the possible persistence of discarnate life. Alas, these conjurations only enhanced my fear of Cynthia's phantom. Atavistic peace came with dawn, and when I slipped into sleep, the sun through the tawny window shades penetrated a dream that somehow was full of Cynthia.

This was disappointing. Secure in the fortress of daylight, I said to myself that I had expected more. She, a painter of glass-bright minutiæ — and now so vague! I lay in bed, thinking my dream over and listening to the sparrows outside: Who knows, if recorded and then run backward, those bird sounds might not become human speech, voiced words, just as the latter become a twitter when reversed? I set myself to re-read my dream — backward, diagonally, up, down — trying hard to unravel something Cynthia-like in it, something strange and suggestive that must be there.

I could isolate, consciously, little. Everything seemed blurred, yellow-clouded, yielding nothing tangible. Her inept acrostics, maudlin evasions, theopathies — every recollection formed ripples of mysterious meaning. Everything seemed yellowly blurred, illusive, lost.[16]

1951   *1959*

---

[15]Spiritualism, or spiritism — communication with the dead through a medium or psychic — became popular in America beginning with the Fox sisters in 1848 (American girls of Arcadia, New York, who became professional mediums) and lasting into the twentieth century. A Society for Psychical Research was founded for serious investigation of inexplicable psychic phenomena. Many philosophers and scientists, such

as William James, encouraged research in the field.
[16]Nabokov has said the narrator is "supposed to be unaware that his last paragraph has been used acrostically by two dead girls to assert their mysterious participation in the story. This particular trick can be tried only once in a thousand years of fiction." See the last paragraph of Part 4 for a description of such an acrostic.

WRIGHT MORRIS
(b. 1910)

Wright Morris spent the first twenty-four years of his life on the Great Plains, in Nebraska, where the sight of a tree was an event. Although he ultimately lived in and wrote about many other places in the world, his imagination never escaped from Nebraska. His first work, he was to discover later, was trapped (like that of so many American writers) in nostalgia—the raw material of experience presented as longingly recalled. "The realization," he has said, "that I had to create coherence, conjure up my synthesis, rather than find it, came to me, as it does to most Americans, disturbingly late."

Morris has been called "the least well-known and most widely unappreciated important writer alive in this country." His novels number nineteen, his "Photo-Texts" five, his volumes of essays six. There are now a *Wright Morris Reader* (1970) and a *Collected Stories* (1986). To date, three volumes of his memoirs have appeared: *Will's Boy* (1981), *Solo* (1983), and *A Cloak of Light* (1985). Still the critical response has been sparse, which perhaps speaks more to contemporary bias than to considered judgment; little serious attention has been paid to an impressive body of work.

Morris was born and lived for his first nine years in Central City, Nebraska; in the next decade he lived in a series of small towns along the Platte River and finally in Omaha, Nebraska's largest city. His early cross-country jaunts with his father and his summers on the farms of uncles in Nebraska and Texas left deep impressions later to turn up in his fiction. In 1930 he entered Pomona College in California, taking a year off in 1933–34 to bum around Europe. By the time he finished college, he was set on becoming a novelist.

In the late 1930s and early 1940s, he travelled extensively in America, particularly revisiting the country of his past with a pencil and camera in hand. He wrote about and photographed what he saw and remembered. His first novel, *My Uncle Dudley,* was published in 1941, followed by his second, *The Man Who Was There,* in 1942. The first of Morris's "photo-texts," *The Inhabitants,* was published in 1948, and won him a Guggenheim Fellowship to work on his second photo-text, *The Home Place*. In these works Morris developed a "mixed form" he made uniquely his. It featured a running commentary alongside haunting photographs of a vanishing prairie farm life: a basket of corncobs, two worn jackets hanging by pegs on a barren wall, a lone leafless tree in the middle of a level field.

Beginning in 1949, with the publication of *The World in the Attic,* Morris found his fictional voice and began the development of an original style that was to become identifiably his. In the next decade, he published seven more novels, among them those that have come to be considered his best—especially *The Field of Vision* (1956), which won the National Book Award; and *Ceremony in Lone Tree* (1960). The Nebraska characters in one turn up in the other (as in other of Morris's novels). In *Field of Vision*, Morris takes his characters to a bull fight in Mexico City, but in mind and memory they never leave Nebraska and the past that exerts its powerful pull. In *Ceremony in Lone Tree,* he assembles his characters in the isolated and abandoned prairie town of Lone Tree, Nebraska, for the "ceremony" of the patriarch's ninetieth birthday; this pathetic figure has spent his life reliving a past that never was and provides a climax to the ritual of celebration by his sudden death.

Of Morris's several impressive novels of the following two decades or so, two may be singled out for special mention. *One Day* (1965) is an exploration of the irrational violence that is a fact of contemporary American experience and that is harbored secretly within the breasts of the most peaceful-seeming citizens; although the novel is set in California, the "one day" of the action is the day President John F. Kennedy was assassinated in Dallas, Texas. *Plains Song: For Female Voices* (1980) is an account of three generations of a farm family and the strong but often lonely women who not only endured but triumphed over adversity.

Perhaps one of the reasons for the neglect of Morris's work is the air of the old-fashioned and the traditional that clings to it. He does not reject but connects with fictional masters of the past — Melville, Twain, James — and he has written perceptively and eloquently about them in *The Territory Ahead: Critical Interpretations in American Literature* (1958). He wrote in *About Fiction* (1975): "To make it new — rather than make it good, or make it sound, or make it true — makes of the rejection of the past what there is of value in the creative act. . . . If the talent is adequate, and the age provokes it, something new will appear as a matter of course; if not, the effort to make it new will result in little more than novelties." It is this latter kind of "newness" that Morris's best work represents and which will mean its endurance when the novelties of the day have been forgotten.

ADDITIONAL READING

Conversations with Wright Morris: Critical Views and Responses, ed. Robert E. Knoll, 1977.

David Madden, *Wright Morris,* 1964; Leon Howard, *Wright Morris,* 1968; G. B. Crump, *The Novels of Wright Morris: A Critical Interpretation,* 1978.

TEXT

Collected Stories, 1948–1986, 1986.

Victrola

"Sit!" said Bundy, although the dog already sat. His knowing what Bundy would say was one of the things people noticed about their close relationship. The dog sat — not erect, like most dogs, but off to one side, so that the short-haired pelt on one rump was always soiled. When Bundy attempted to clean it, as he once did, the spot no longer matched the rest of the dog, like a cleaned spot on an old rug. A second soiled spot was on his head, where children and strangers liked to pat him. Over his eyes the pelt was so thin his hide showed through. A third defacement had been caused by the leash in his younger years, when he had tugged at it harder, sometimes almost gagging as Bundy resisted.

Those days had been a strain on both of them. Bundy had developed a bad bursitis, and the crease of the leash could still be seen on the back of his hand. In the past year, over the last eight months, beginning with the cold spell in December, the dog was so slow to cross the street Bundy might have to drag him. That brought on spells of angina[1] for Bundy, and they would both have to stand there until they felt better. At such moments the dog's slantwise gaze was one that Bundy avoided. "Sit!" he would say, no longer troubling to see if the dog did.

---

[1]Spasm accompanied by a feeling of choking.

The dog leashed to a parking meter, Bundy walked through the drugstore to the prescription counter at the rear. The pharmacist, Mr. Avery, peered down from a platform two steps above floor level—the source of a customer's still pending lawsuit. His gaze to the front of the store, he said, "He still itching?"

Bundy nodded. Mr. Avery had recommended a vitamin supplement that some dogs found helpful. The scratching had been replaced by licking.

"You've got to remember," said Avery, "he's in his nineties. When you're in your nineties, you'll also do a little scratchin'!" Avery gave Bundy a challenging stare. If Avery reached his nineties, Bundy was certain Mrs. Avery would have to keep him on a leash or he would forget who he was. He had repeated this story about the dog's being ninety ever since Bundy had first met him and the dog was younger.

"I need your expertise," Bundy said. (Avery lapped up that sort of flattery.) "How does five cc.s compare with five hundred mg.s?"

"It doesn't. Five cc.s is a liquid measure. It's a spoonful."

"What I want to know is, how much Vitamin C am I getting in five cc.s?"

"Might not be any. In a liquid solution, Vitamin C deteriorates rapidly. You should get it in the tablet." It seemed clear he had expected more of Bundy.

"I see," said Bundy. "Could I have my prescription?"

Mr. Avery lowered his glasses to look for it on the counter. Bundy might have remarked that a man of Avery's age—and experience—ought to know enough to wear glasses he could both see and read through, but having to deal with him once a month dictated more discretion than valor.

Squinting to read the label, Avery said, "I see he's upped your dosage." On their first meeting, Bundy and Avery had had a sensible discussion about the wisdom of minimal medication, an attitude that Bundy thought was unusual to hear from a pharmacist.

"His point is," said Bundy, "since I like to be active, there's no reason I shouldn't enjoy it. He tells me the dosage is still pretty normal."

"Hmm," Avery said. He opened the door so Bundy could step behind the counter and up to the platform with his Blue Cross card. For the umpteenth time he told Bundy, "Pay the lady at the front. Watch your step as you leave."

As he walked toward the front Bundy reflected that he would rather be a little less active than forget what he had said two minutes earlier.

"We've nothing but trouble with dogs," the cashier said. "They're in and out every minute. They get at the bars of candy. But I can't ever remember trouble with your dog."

"He's on a leash," said Bundy.

"That's what I'm saying," she replied.

When Bundy came out of the store, the dog was lying down, but he made the effort to push up and sit.

"Look at you," Bundy said, and stooped to dust him off. The way he licked himself, he picked up dirt like a blotter. A shadow moved over them, and Bundy glanced up to see, at a respectful distance, a lady beaming on the dog like a healing heat lamp. Older than Bundy—much older, a wraithlike creature, more spirit than substance, her face crossed with wisps of hair like cobwebs—Mrs. Poole had known the dog as a pup; she had been a dear friend of its former owner, Miss Tyler, who had lived directly above Bundy. For years he had listened to his neighbor tease the dog to bark for pieces of liver, and heard the animal push his food dish around the kitchen.

"What ever will become of him?" Miss Tyler would whisper to Bundy, anxious that the dog shouldn't hear what she was saying. Bundy had tried to reassure her: look how spry she was at eighty! Look how the dog was overweight and asthmatic! But to ease her mind he had agreed to provide him with a home, if worst came to worst, as it did soon enough. So Bundy inherited the dog, three cases of dog food, balls and rubber bones in which the animal took no interest, along with an elegant cushioned sleeping basket he never used.

Actually, Bundy had never liked biggish dogs with very short pelts. Too much of everything, to his taste, was overexposed. The dog's long muzzle and small beady eyes put him in mind of something less than a dog. In the years with Miss Tyler, without provocation the animal would snarl at Bundy when they met on the stairs, or bark wildly when he opened his mailbox. The dog's one redeeming feature was that when he heard someone pronounce the word "sit" he would sit. That fact brought Bundy a certain distinction, and the gratitude of many shop owners. Bundy had once been a cat man. The lingering smell of cats in his apartment had led the dog to sneeze at most of the things he sniffed.

Two men, seated on stools in the corner tavern, had turned from the bar to gaze out into the sunlight. One of them was a clerk at the supermarket where Bundy bought his dog food. "Did he like it?" he called as Bundy came into view.

"Not particularly," Bundy replied. Without exception, the dog did not like anything he saw advertised on television. To that extent he was smarter than Bundy, who was partial to anything served with gravy.

The open doors of the bar looked out on the intersection, where an elderly woman, as if emerging from a package, unfolded her limbs through the door of a taxi. Sheets of plate glass on a passing truck reflected Bundy and the notice that was posted in the window of the bar, advising of a change of ownership. The former owner, an Irishman named Curran, had not been popular with the new crowd of wine and beer drinkers. Nor had he been popular with Bundy. A scornful man, Curran dipped the dirty glasses in tepid water, and poured drops of sherry back into the bottles. Two epidemics of hepatitis had been traced to him. Only when he was gone did Bundy realize how much the world had shrunk. To Curran, Bundy had confessed that he felt he was now living in another country. Even more he missed Curran's favorite expression, "Outlive the bastards!"

Two elderly men, indifferent to the screech of braking traffic, tottered toward each other to embrace near the center of the street. One was wearing shorts. A third party, a younger woman, escorted them both to the curb. Observing an incident like this, Bundy might stand for several minutes as if he had witnessed something unusual. Under an awning, where the pair had been led, they shared the space with a woman whose gaze seemed to focus on infinity, several issues of the *Watchtower*[2] gripped in her trembling hands.

At the corner of Sycamore and Poe streets — trees crossed poets, as a rule, at right angles — Bundy left the choice of the route up to the dog. Where the sidewalk narrowed, at the bend in the street, both man and dog prepared themselves for brief and unpredictable encounters. In the cities, people met and passed like sleepwalkers, or stared brazenly at each other, but along the sidewalks of small towns they felt the burden of their shared existence. To avoid rudeness, a lift of the eyes or a muttered greeting was necessary. This was often an annoyance for Bundy: the long approach by sidewalk, the absence of cover, the unavoidable moment of confrontation, then Bundy's abrupt greeting or a wag of his head, which occasionally startled the other person. To the young a quick "Hi!" was appropriate, but it was not at all suitable for elderly ladies, a few with pets as escorts. To avoid these encounters, Bundy might suddenly veer into the street or an alleyway, dragging the reluctant dog behind him. He liked to meet strangers, especially children, who would pause to stroke his bald spot. What kind of dog was he? Bundy was tactfully evasive; it had proved to be an unfruitful topic. He was equally noncommittal about the dog's ineffable name.

---

[2] A publication of the proselytizing sect, the Jehovah's Witnesses.

"Call him Sport," he would say, but this pleasantry was not appreciated. A smart-aleck's answer. Their sympathies were with the dog.

To delay what lay up ahead, whatever it was, they paused at the barnlike entrance of the local van-and-storage warehouse. The draft from inside smelled of burlap sacks full of fragrant pine kindling, and mattresses that were stored on boards above the rafters. The pair contemplated a barn full of junk being sold as antiques. Bundy's eyes grazed over familiar treasure and stopped at a Morris chair[3] with faded green corduroy cushions cradling a carton marked "FREE KITTENS."

He did not approach to look. One thing having a dog had spared him was the torment of losing another cat. Music (surely Elgar,[4] something awful!) from a facsimile edition of an Atwater Kent table-model radio[5] bathed dressers and chairs, sofas, beds and love seats, man and dog impartially. As it ended the announcer suggested that Bundy stay tuned for a Musicdote.

Recently, in this very spot—as he sniffed similar air, having paused to take shelter from a drizzle—the revelation had come to Bundy that he no longer wanted other people's junk. Better yet (or was it worse?), he no longer *wanted*—with the possible exception of an English mint, difficult to find, described as curiously strong. He had a roof, a chair, a bed, and, through no fault of his own, he had a dog. What little he had assembled and hoarded (in the garage a German electric-train set with four locomotives, and three elegant humidors and a pouch of old pipes) would soon be gratifying the wants of others. Anything else of value? The cushioned sleeping basket from Abercrombie & Fitch that had come with the dog. That would sell first. Also two Italian raincoats in good condition, and a Borsalino hat—*Extra Extra Superiore*—bought from G. Colpo in Venice.

Two young women, in the rags of fashion but radiant and blooming as gift-packed fruit, brushed Bundy as they passed, the spoor of their perfume lingering. In the flush of this encounter, his freedom from want dismantled, he moved too fast, and the leash reined him in. Rather than be rushed, the dog had stopped to sniff a meter. He found meters more life-enhancing than trees now. It had not always been so: some years ago he would tug Bundy up the incline to the park, panting and hoarsely gagging, an object of compassionate glances from elderly women headed down the grade, carrying lapdogs. This period had come to a dramatic conclusion.

In the park, back in the deep shade of the redwoods, Bundy and the dog had had a confrontation. An old tree with exposed roots had suddenly attracted the dog's attention. Bundy could not restrain him. A stream of dirt flew out between his legs to splatter Bundy's raincoat and fall into his shoes. There was something manic in the dog's excitement. In a few moments, he had frantically excavated a hole into which he could insert his head and shoulders. Bundy's tug on the leash had no effect on him. The sight of his soiled hairless bottom, his legs mechanically pumping, encouraged Bundy to give him a smart crack with the end of the leash. Not hard, but sharp, right on the button, and before he could move the dog had wheeled and the front end was barking at him savagely, the lips curled back. Dirt from the hole partially screened his muzzle, and he looked to Bundy like a maddened rodent. He was no longer a dog but some primitive, underground creature. Bundy lashed out at him, backing away, but they were joined by the leash. Unintentionally, Bundy stepped on the leash, which held the dog's snarling head to the ground. His slobbering jowls were bloody; the small veiled eyes peered up at him with hatred. Bundy had just enough presence of mind to stand there, unmoving, until they both grew calm.

Nobody had observed them. The children played and shrieked in the schoolyard as usual. The dog relaxed and lay flat on the ground, his tongue lolling in the dirt.

---

[3]Large armchair with adjustable back and removable cushions (designed by English poet, artist, and craftsman William Morris, 1834–1896).

[4]Sir Edward William Elgar (1857–1934), English composer.
[5]I.e., a modern copy of an old-fashioned radio made to set on a table (Atwater-Kent is a brand name).

Bundy breathed noisily, a film of perspiration cooling his face. When he stepped off the leash the dog did not move but continued to watch him warily, with bloodshot eyes. A slow burn of shame flushed Bundy's ears and cheeks, but he was reluctant to admit it. Another dog passed near them, but what he sniffed on the air kept him at a distance. In a tone of truce, if not reconciliation, Bundy said, "You had enough?"

When had he last said that? Seated on a school chum, whose face was red with Bundy's nosebleed. He bled too easily, but the boy beneath him had had enough.

"O.K.?" he said to the dog. The faintest tremor of acknowledgment stirred the dog's tail. He got to his feet, sneezed repeatedly, then splattered Bundy with dirt as he shook himself. Side by side, the leash slack between them, they left the park and walked down the grade. Bundy had never again struck the dog, nor had the dog ever again wheeled to snarl at him. Once the leash was snapped to the dog's collar a truce prevailed between them. In the apartment he had the floor of a closet all to himself.

At the Fixit Shop on the corner of Poplar, recently refaced with green asbestos shingles, Mr. Waller, the Fixit man, rapped on the glass with his wooden ruler. Both Bundy and the dog acknowledged his greeting. Waller had two cats, one asleep in the window, and a dog that liked to ride in his pickup. The two dogs had once been friends; they mauled each other a bit and horsed around like a couple of kids. Then suddenly it was over. Waller's dog would no longer trouble to leave the seat of the truck. Bundy had been so struck by this he had mentioned it to Waller. "Hell," Waller had said, "Gyp's a young dog. Your dog is old."

His saying that had shocked Bundy. There was the personal element, for one thing: Bundy was a good ten years older than Waller, and was he to read the remark to mean that Waller would soon ignore him? And were dogs—reasonably well-bred, sensible chaps—so indifferent to the facts of a dog's life? They appeared to be. One by one, as Bundy's dog grew older, the younger ones ignored him. He might have been a stuffed animal leashed to a parking meter. The human parallel was too disturbing for Bundy to dwell on it.

Old men, in particular, were increasingly touchy if they confronted Bundy at the frozen-food lockers. Did they think he was spying on them? Did they think he looked *sharper* than they did? Elderly women, as a rule, were less suspicious, and grateful to exchange a bit of chitchat. Bundy found them more realistic: they knew they were mortal. To find Bundy still around, squeezing the avocados, piqued the old men who returned from their vacations. On the other hand, Dr. Biddle, a retired dentist with a glistening head like an egg in a basket of excelsior, would unfailingly greet Bundy with the words "I'm really going to miss that mutt, you know that?," but his glance betrayed that he feared Bundy would check out first.

Bundy and the dog used the underpass walkway to cross to the supermarket parking area. Banners were flying to celebrate Whole Grains Cereal Week. In the old days, Bundy would leash the dog to a cart and they would proceed to do their shopping together, but now he had to be parked out front tied up to one of the bicycle racks. The dog didn't like it. The area was shaded and the cement was cold. Did he ever sense, however dimly, that Bundy too felt the chill? His hand brushed the coarse pelt as he fastened the leash.

"How about a new flea collar?" Bundy said, but the dog was not responsive. He sat, without being told to sit. Did it flatter the dog to leash him? Whatever Bundy would do if worst came to worst he had pondered, but had discussed with no one—his intent might be misconstrued. Of which one of them was he speaking? Impersonally appraised, in terms of survival the two of them were pretty much at a standoff: the dog was better fleshed out, but Bundy was the heartier eater.

Thinking of eating—of garlic-scented breadsticks, to be specific, dry but not dusty to the palate—Bundy entered the market to face a large display of odorless flowers and plants. The amplitude and bounty of the new market, at the point of entrance, before he selected a cart, always marked the high point of his expectations. Where else in the hungry world such a prospect? Barrels and baskets of wine, six-packs of beer and bran muffins, still warm sourdough bread that he would break and gnaw on as he shopped. Was this a cunning regression? As a child he had craved raw sugar cookies. But his euphoria sagged at the meat counter, as he studied the gray matter being sold as meat-loaf mix; it declined further at the dairy counter, where two cartons of yogurt had been sampled, and the low-fat cottage cheese was two days older than dated. By the time he entered the checkout lane, hemmed in by scandal sheets and romantic novels, the cashier's cheerfully inane "Have a good day!" would send him off forgetting his change in the machine. The girl who pursued him (always with pennies!) had been coached to say, "Thank you, sir!"

A special on avocados this week required that Bundy make a careful selection. Out in front, as usual, dogs were barking. On the airwaves, from the rear and side, the "Wang Wang Blues." Why wang wang, he wondered. Besides wang wang, how did it go? The music was interrupted by an announcement on the public-address system. Would the owner of the white dog leashed to the bike rack please come to the front? Was Bundy's dog white? The point was debatable. Nevertheless, he left his cart by the avocados and followed the vegetable display to the front. People were huddled to the right of the door. A clerk beckoned to Bundy through the window. Still leashed to the bike rack, the dog lay out on his side, as if sleeping. In the parking lot several dogs were yelping.

"I'm afraid he's a goner," said the clerk. "These other dogs rushed him. Scared him to death. He just keeled over before they got to him." The dog had pulled the leash taut, but there was no sign that anything had touched him. A small woman with a shopping cart thumped into Bundy.

"Is it Tiger?" she said. "I hope it's not Tiger." She stopped to see that it was not Tiger. "Whose dog was it?" she asked, peering around her. The clerk indicated Bundy. "Poor thing," she said. "What was his name?"

Just recently, watching the Royal Wedding,[6] Bundy had noticed that his emotions were nearer the surface: on two occasions his eyes had filmed over. He didn't like the woman's speaking of the dog in the past tense. Did she think he had lost his name with his life?

"What was the poor thing's name?" she repeated.

Was the tremor in Bundy's limbs noticeable? "Victor," Bundy lied, since he could not bring himself to admit the dog's name was Victrola. It had always been a sore point, the dog being too old to be given a new one. Miss Tyler had felt that as a puppy he looked like the picture of the dog at the horn of the gramophone.[7] The resemblance was feeble, at best. How could a person give a dog such a name?

"Let him sit," a voice said. A space was cleared on a bench for Bundy to sit, but at the sound of the word he could not bend his knees. He remained standing, gazing through the bright glare at the beacon revolving on the police car. One of those women who buy two frozen dinners and then go off with the shopping cart and leave it somewhere let the policeman at the crosswalk chaperon her across the street.

1982

---

[6]The televised wedding of Prince Charles and Princess Diane in 1981.
[7]The advertising logo of Victrola, a brand of phonograph, was a seated dog, head tilted, listening at the horn (loudspeaker) to "His Master's Voice."

JOHN CHEEVER
(1912–1982)

In a 1976 *Paris Review* interview, John Cheever made a number of comments that revealed in essence his approach to his craft. On plots: "I don't work with plots. I work with intuition, apprehension, dreams, concepts. Characters and events come simultaneously to me. Plot implies narrative and a lot of crap. It is a calculated attempt to hold the reader's interest at the sacrifice of moral conviction." On experimentation: "Fiction *is* experimentation; when it ceases to be that, it ceases to be fiction. One never puts down a sentence without the feeling that it has never been put down before in such a way, and that perhaps even the substance of the sentence has never been felt. Every sentence is an innovation." On morals in fiction: "Fiction is meant to illuminate, to explode, to refresh. I don't think there's any consecutive moral philosophy in fiction beyond excellence. Acuteness of feeling and velocity have always seemed to me terribly important. People look for morals in fiction because there has always been a confusion between fiction and philosophy." By the time Cheever had formulated this view of fiction and the creative process, he had already produced most of his stories and novels.

Cheever was born and grew up in Quincy, Massachusetts. His father was a shoe salesman whose business failed; his strong-willed mother opened a successful gift-shop to support the family. At Thayer Academy, a prep school, Cheever began to write poetry, but he was expelled in 1930 for his poor grades. Thus thrown out on his own at the age of seventeen, Cheever wrote a short story, "Expelled," based on his experience; it was accepted by Malcolm Cowley, then literary editor for the *New Republic*.

This early success turned him into a "story-making machine" and he became something of a nonstop writer for the rest of his life. He sold his first story at the age of twenty-three to the *New Yorker,* where he would publish during his lifetime over 120 stories. He was early branded, and sometimes dismissed by critics, as a *New Yorker* writer — applied as a put-down to suggest the use of too fine a manner on too trivial a matter. He married in 1941, and this same year entered the army for service during the Second World War. His first book of stories, *The Way Some People Live*, was published in 1943. After separation from the army in 1945, Cheever worked for a time in commercial television, writing scripts for the "Life with Father" series. His second book, *The Enormous Radio and Other Stories,* appeared in 1953.

Perception of Cheever as an inveterate and basically optimistic chronicler of middle-class suburban life was shaken by the appearance in 1957 of his novel *The Wapshot Chronicle*. The work recorded the breakdown of a family as well as the decline of a community's traditions and values. Cheever's earlier geniality was replaced by melancholy and pessimism. The novel received the National Book Award in 1958. Cheever continued to publish volumes of stories — *The Housebreaker of Shady Hill and Other Stories* (1958), *Some People, Places, and Things That Will Not Appear in My Next Novel* (1961) — but it was his next novel, *The Wapshot Scandal* (1964), relating the various disasters and the dissolution of the Wapshot family, that attracted wide notice. Cheever found himself the subject of a *Time* magazine cover story.

Also in 1964 Cheever published his fifth book of stories, *The Brigadier and the Golf Widow*, which many critics and readers believe contains his best work; it includes such widely admired stories as "The Swimmer" and "The Angel of the Bridge." But 1964 seems to have represented a turning point in Cheever's career. In the years following, his writing slowed and his confidence in mastery of his craft and control over his life diminished; for some years his relationship with his wife had been deteriorating. He published another novel, *Bullit Park*, in 1969, styled by one reviewer as "a brutal vivisection of American life." And he published another volume of stories, *The World of Apples*, in 1973. He served as writer-in-residence at the University of Iowa in 1974 and at Boston University in 1975. It was in the last of these positions that his despondency and alcoholism, as well as his careless abandonment to a succession of homosexual affairs, caught up with him. He was replaced in the middle of the term by John Updike and confined in a rehabilitation clinic.

Cured of his alcoholism, Cheever found imaginative reserves within himself to write two more novels, using the experiences he had gone through: *Falconer* (1977) and *Oh What a Paradise It Seems* (1982). *The Stories of John Cheever* appeared in 1978 and won the Pulitzer Prize. It was not long after this, when he was beginning to believe he had pulled himself out of his tailspin, that Cheever discovered he had the incurable cancer that would end his life in 1982.

When Cheever appeared on the cover of *Time* in 1964, he was established with his wife and children in a house in Ossining, New York; the magazine called him the "Ovid of Ossining," referring to his portrayal of the metamorphoses of love in the suburban lives of his characters. When his biography was published in 1988, one reviewer, Lorrie Moore in the *New York Times*, called him "The Chekhov of Westchester," referring to his remarkable ability to portray, in the miniature form of the short story, the melancholy and painful truths of lives lived placidly in suburbia. However just the epithets, they are surely nearer the truth than the earlier identifying label — "*New Yorker* writer."

ADDITIONAL READING

The Letters of John Cheever, ed. Benjamin Cheever, 1988; *The Uncollected Stories of John Cheever, 1930–81,* 1988.

Samuel Coale, *John Cheever,* 1977; Lynne Waldeland, *John Cheever,* 1979; *Critical Essays on John Cheever,* ed. Robert G. Collins, 1982; George W. Hunt, S. J., *John Cheever: The Hobgoblin Company of Love,* 1983; Susan Cheever, *Home Before Dark,* 1984; *Conversations with John Cheever,* ed. Scott Donaldson, 1987; Scott Donaldson, *John Cheever: A Biography,* 1988.

TEXT

The Stories of John Cheever, 1978.

The Angel of the Bridge

You may have seen my mother waltzing on ice skates in Rockefeller Center. She's seventy-eight years old now but very wiry, and she wears a red velvet costume with a short skirt. Her tights are flesh-colored, and she wears spectacles and a red ribbon in her white hair, and she waltzes with one of the rink attendants. I don't know why I should find the fact that she waltzes on ice skates so disconcerting, but I do. I avoid that neighborhood whenever I can during the winter months, and I never lunch in the restaurants on the rink. Once when I was passing that way, a total stranger took me by the arm and, pointing to Mother, said, "Look at that crazy old dame." I was very embarrassed. I suppose I should be grateful for the fact that she amuses herself and is not a burden to me, but I sincerely wish she had hit on some less conspicuous recreation. Whenever I see gracious old ladies arranging chrysanthemums and pouring tea, I think of my own mother, dressed like a hat-check girl, pushing some paid rink attendant around the ice, in the middle of the third-biggest city of the world.

My mother learned to figure-skate in the little New England village of St. Botolphs, where we come from, and her waltzing is an expression of her attachment to the past. The older she grows, the more she longs for the vanishing and provincial world of her youth. She is a hardy woman, as you can imagine, but she does not relish change. I arranged one summer for her to fly to Toledo and visit friends. I drove her to the Newark airport. She seemed troubled by the airport waiting room, with its illuminated advertisements, vaulted ceiling, and touching and painful scenes of separation played out to an uproar of continuous tango music. She did not seem to find it in any way interesting or beautiful, and compared to the railroad station in St. Botolphs it was indeed a strange background against which to take one's departure. The flight was delayed for an hour, and we sat in the waiting room. Mother looked tired and old. When we had been waiting half an hour, she began to have some noticeable difficulty in breathing. She spread a hand over the front of her dress and began to gasp deeply, as if she was in pain. Her face got mottled and red. I pretended not to notice this. When the plane was announced, she got to her feet and exclaimed, "I want to go home! If I have to die suddenly, I don't want to die in a flying machine." I cashed in her ticket and drove her back to her apartment, and I have never mentioned this seizure to her or to anyone, but her capricious, or perhaps neurotic, fear of dying in a plane crash was the first insight I had into how, as she grew older, her way was strewn with invisible rocks and lions and how eccentric were the paths she took, as the world seemed to change its boundaries and become less and less comprehensible.

At the time of which I'm writing, I flew a great deal myself. My business was in Rome, New York, San Francisco, and Los Angeles, and I sometimes traveled as often as once a month between these cities. I liked the flying. I liked the incandescence of the sky at high altitudes. I liked all eastward flights where you can see from the ports the edge of night move over the continent and where, when it is four o'clock by your California watch, the housewives of Garden City are washing up the supper dishes and the stewardess in the plane is passing a second round of drinks. Toward the end of the flight, the air is stale. You are tired. The gold thread in the upholstery scratches your cheek, and there is a momentary feeling of forlornness, a sulky and childish sense of estrangement. You find good companions, of course, and bores, but most of the errands we run at such high altitudes are humble and terrestrial. That old lady, flying over the North Pole, is taking a jar of calf's-foot jelly to her sister in Paris, and the man beside her sells imitation-leather inner soles. Flying westward one dark night — we had crossed the Continental Divide, but we were still an hour out of Los Angeles and had not begun our descent, and were at such an altitude that the sense of houses, cities, and people below us was lost — I saw a formation, a trace of light, like the lights that burn along a shore. There was no shore in that part of the world, and I knew I would never know if the edge of the desert or some bluff or mountain accounted for this hoop of light, but it seemed, in its obscurity — and at that velocity and height — like the emergence of a new world, a gentle hint at my own obsolescence, the lateness of my time of life, and my inability to understand the things I often see. It was a pleasant feeling, completely free of regret, of being caught in some observable mid-passage, the farther reaches of which might be understood by my sons.

I liked to fly, as I say, and had none of my mother's anxieties. It was my older brother — her darling — who was to inherit her resoluteness, her stubbornness, her table silver, and some of her eccentricities. One evening, my brother — I had not seen him for a year or so—called and asked if he could come for dinner. I was happy to invite him. We live on the eleventh floor of an apartment house, and at seven-thirty he telephoned from the lobby and asked me to come down. I thought he must have something to tell me privately, but when we met in the lobby he got into the automatic elevator with me and we started up. As soon as the doors closed, he showed the same symptoms of fear I had seen in my mother. Sweat stood out on his forehead, and he gasped like a runner.

"What in the world is the matter?" I asked.

"I'm afraid of elevators," he said miserably.

"But what are you afraid of?"

"I'm afraid the building will fall down."

I laughed—cruelly, I guess. For it all seemed terribly funny, his vision of the buildings of New York banging against one another like ninepins as they fell to the earth. There has always been a strain of jealousy in our feelings about one another, and I am aware, at some obscure level, that he makes more money and has more of everything than I, and to see him humiliated—crushed—saddened me but at the same time and in spite of myself made me feel that I had taken a stunning lead in the race for honors that is at the bottom of our relationship. He is the oldest, he is the favorite, but watching his misery in the elevator I felt that he was merely my poor old brother, overtaken by his worries. He stopped in the hallway to recover his composure, and explained that he had been suffering from this phobia for over a year. He was going to a psychiatrist, he said. I couldn't see that it had done him any good. He was all right once he got out of the elevator, but I noticed that he stayed away from the windows. When it was time to go, I walked him out to the corridor. I was curious. When the elevator reached our floor, he turned to me and said, "I'm afraid I'll have to take the stairs." I led him to the stairway, and we climbed slowly down the eleven flights. He clung to the railing. We said goodbye in the lobby, and I went up in the elevator, and told my wife about his fear that the building might fall down. It seemed strange and sad to her, and it did to me, too, but it also seemed terribly funny.

It wasn't terribly funny when, a month later, the firm he worked for moved to the fifty-second floor of a new office building and he had to resign. I don't know what reasons he gave. It was another six months before he could find a job in a third-floor office. I once saw him on a winter dusk at the corner of Madison Avenue and Fifty-ninth Street, waiting for the light to change. He appeared to be an intelligent, civilized, and well-dressed man, and I wondered how many of the men waiting with him to cross the street made their way as he did through a ruin of absurd delusions, in which the street might appear to be a torrent and the approaching cab driven by the angel of death.

He was quite all right on the ground. My wife and I went to his house in New Jersey, with the children, for a weekend, and he looked healthy and well. I didn't ask about his phobia. We drove back to New York on Sunday afternoon. As we approached the George Washington Bridge, I saw a thunderstorm over the city. A strong wind struck the car the moment we were on the bridge, and nearly took the wheel out of my hand. It seemed to me that I could feel the huge structure swing. Halfway across the bridge, I thought I felt the roadway begin to give. I could see no signs of a collapse, and yet I was convinced that in another minute the bridge would split in two and hurl the long lines of Sunday traffic into the dark water below us. This imagined disaster was terrifying. My legs got so weak that I was not sure I could brake the car if I needed to. Then it became difficult for me to breathe. Only by opening my mouth and gasping did I seem able to take in any air. My blood pressure was affected and I began to feel a darkening of my vision. Fear has always seemed to me to run a course, and at its climax the body and perhaps the spirit defend themselves by drawing on some new and fresh source of strength. Once over the center of the bridge, my pain and terror began to diminish. My wife and the children were admiring the storm, and they did not seem to have noticed my spasm. I was afraid both that the bridge would fall down and that they might observe my panic.

I thought back over the weekend for some incident that might account for my preposterous fear that the George Washington Bridge would blow away in a thunderstorm, but it had been a pleasant weekend, and even under the most exaggerated scrutiny I couldn't uncover any source of morbid nervousness or anxiety. Later in the week, I had to drive to Albany, and, although the day was clear and windless, the memory of my first attack was too keen; I hugged the east bank of the river as far north as Troy, where I found a small, old-fashioned bridge that I could cross comfortably. This meant going fifteen or twenty miles out of my way, and it is humiliating to have your travels obstructed by barriers that are senseless and invisible. I drove back from Albany by the same route, and next morning I went to the family doctor and told him I was afraid of bridges.

He laughed. "You, of all people," he said scornfully. "You'd better take hold of yourself."

"But Mother is afraid of airplanes," I said. "And Brother hates elevators."

"Your mother is past seventy," he said, "and one of the most remarkable women I've ever known. I wouldn't bring *her* into this. What *you* need is a little more backbone."

This was all he had to say, and I asked him to recommend an analyst. He does not include psychoanalysis in medical science, and told me I would be wasting my time and money, but, yielding to his obligation to be helpful, he gave me the name and address of a psychiatrist, who told me that my fear of bridges was the surface manifestation of a deep-seated anxiety and that I would have to have a full analysis. I didn't have the time, or the money, or, above all, the confidence in the doctor's methods to put myself in his hands, and I said I would try and muddle through.

There are obviously areas of true and false pain, and my pain was meretricious, but how could I convince my lights and vitals of this? My youth and childhood had their deeply troubled and their jubilant years, and could some repercussions from this past account for my fear of heights? The thought of a life determined by hidden obstacles was unacceptable, and I decided to take the advice of the family doctor and ask more of myself. I had to go to Idlewild later in the week, and, rather than take a bus or a taxi, I drove the car myself. I nearly lost consciousness on the Triborough Bridge. When I got to the airport I ordered a cup of coffee, but my hand was shaking so I spilled the coffee on the counter. The man beside me was amused and said that I must have put in quite a night. How could I tell him that I had gone to bed early and sober but that I was afraid of bridges?

I flew to Los Angeles late that afternoon. It was one o'clock by my watch when we landed. It was only ten o'clock in California. I was tired and took a taxi to the hotel where I always stay, but I couldn't sleep. Outside my hotel window was a monumental statue of a young woman, advertising a Las Vegas night club. She revolves slowly in a beam of light. At 2 A.M. the light is extinguished, but she goes on restlessly turning all through the night. I have never seen her cease her turning, and I wondered, that night, when they greased her axle and washed her shoulders. I felt some affection for her, since neither of us could rest, and I wondered if she had a family — a stage mother, perhaps, and a compromised and broken-spirited father who drove a municipal bus on the West Pico line? There was a restaurant across the street, and I watched a drunken woman in a sable cape being led out to a car. She twice nearly fell. The crosslights from the open door, the lateness, her drunkenness, and the solicitude of the man with her made the scene, I thought, worried and lonely. Then two cars that seemed to be racing down Sunset Boulevard pulled up at a traffic light under my window. Three men piled out of each car and began to slug one another. You could hear the blows land on bone and cartilage. When the light changed, they got back into their cars and raced off. The fight, like the hoop of light I had seen from the plane, seemed like the sign of a new world, but in this case an emergence of brutality and chaos. Then I remembered that I was to go to San Francisco on Thursday, and was expected in Berkeley for lunch. This meant crossing the San Francisco-Oakland Bay Bridge, and I reminded myself to take a cab both ways and leave the car I rented in San Francisco in the hotel garage. I tried again to reason out my fear that the bridge would fall. Was I the victim of some sexual dislocation? My life has been promiscuous, carefree, and a source of immense pleasure, but was there some secret here that would have to be mined by a professional? Were all my pleasures impostures and evasions, and was I really in love with my old mother in her skating costume?

Looking at Sunset Boulevard at three in the morning, I felt that my terror of bridges was an expression of my clumsily concealed horror of what is becoming of the world. I can drive with composure through the outskirts of Cleveland and Toledo—past the birthplace of the Polish Hot Dog, the Buffalo Burger stands, the used-car lots, and the architectural monotony. I claim to enjoy walking down Hollywood Boulevard on a Sunday afternoon. I have cheerfully praised the evening sky hanging beyond the disheveled and expatriated palm trees on Doheny Boulevard, stuck up against the incandescence, like rank upon rank of wet mops. Duluth and East Seneca are charming, and if they aren't, just look away. The hideousness of the road between San Francisco and Palo Alto is nothing more than the search of honest men and women for a decent place to live. The same thing goes for San Pedro and all that coast. But the height of bridges seemed to be one link I could not forge or fasten in this hypocritical chain of acceptances. The truth is, I hate freeways and Buffalo Burgers. Expatriated palm trees and monotonous housing developments depress me. The continuous music on special-fare trains exacerbates my feelings. I detest the destruction of familiar landmarks, I am deeply troubled by the misery and drunkenness I find among my friends, I abhor the dishonest practices I see. And it was at the highest point in the arc of a bridge that I became aware suddenly of the depth and bitterness of my feelings about modern life, and of the profoundness of my yearning for a more vivid, simple, and peaceable world.

But I couldn't reform Sunset Boulevard, and until I could, I couldn't drive across the San Francisco-Oakland Bay Bridge. What *could* I do? Go back to St. Botolphs, wear a Norfolk jacket, and play cribbage in the firehouse? There was only one bridge in the village, and you could throw a stone across the river there.

I got home from San Francisco on Saturday, and found my daughter back from school for the weekend. On Sunday morning, she asked me to drive her to the convent school in Jersey where she is a student. She had to be back in time for nine-o'clock Mass, and we left our apartment in the city a little after seven. We were talking and laughing, and I had approached and was in fact on the George Washington Bridge without having remembered my weakness. There were no preliminaries this time. The seizure came with a rush. The strength went out of my legs, I gasped for breath, and felt the terrifying loss of sight. I was, at the same time, determined to conceal these symptoms from my daughter. I made the other side of the bridge, but I was violently shaken. My daughter didn't seem to have noticed. I got her to school in time, kissed her goodbye, and started home. There was no question of my crossing the George Washington Bridge again, and I decided to drive north to Nyack and cross on the Tappan Zee Bridge. It seemed, in my memory, more gradual and more securely anchored to its shores. Driving up the parkway on the west shore, I decided that oxygen was what I needed, and I opened all the windows of the car. The fresh air seemed to help, but only momentarily. I could feel my sense of reality ebbing. The roadside and the car itself seemed to have less substance than a dream. I had some friends in the neighborhood, and I thought of stopping and asking them for a drink, but it was only a little after nine in the morning, and I could not face the embarrassment of asking for a drink so early in the day, and of explaining that I was afraid of bridges. I thought I might feel better if I talked to someone, and I stopped at a gas station and bought some gas, but the attendant was laconic and sleepy, and I couldn't explain to him that his conversation might make the difference between life and death. I had got onto the Thruway by then, and I wondered what alternatives I had if I couldn't cross the bridge. I could call my wife and ask her to make some arrangements for removing me, but our relationship involves so much self-esteem and face that to admit openly to this foolishness might damage our married happiness. I could call the garage we use and ask them to send up a man to chauffeur me home. I could park the car and wait until one o'clock, when the bars opened, and fill up on whiskey, but I had spent the last of my money for gasoline. I decided to take a chance, and turned onto the approach to the bridge.

All the symptoms returned, and this time they were much worse than ever. The wind was knocked out of my lungs as by a blow. My equilibrium was so shaken that the car swerved from one lane into another. I drove to the side and pulled on the hand brake. The loneliness of my predicament was harrowing. If I had been miserable with romantic love, racked with sickness, or beastly drunk, it would have seemed more dignified. I remembered my brother's face, sallow and greasy with sweat in the elevator, and my mother in her red skirt, one leg held gracefully aloft as she coasted backward in the arms of a rink attendant, and it seemed to me that we were all three characters in some bitter and sordid tragedy, carrying impossible burdens and separated from the rest of mankind by our misfortunes. My life was over, and it would never come back, everything that I loved—blue-sky courage, lustiness, the natural grasp of things. It would never come back. I would end up in the psychiatric ward of the county hospital, screaming that the bridges, all the bridges in the world, were falling down.

Then a young girl opened the door of the car and got in. "I didn't think anyone would pick me up on the bridge," she said. She carried a cardboard suitcase and— believe me—a small harp in a cracked waterproof. Her straight light-brown hair was brushed and brushed and grained with blondness and spread in a kind of cape over her shoulders. Her face seemed full and merry.

"Are you hitchhiking?" I asked.

"Yes."

"But isn't it dangerous for a girl your age?"

"Not at all."

"Do you travel much?"

"All the time. I sing a little. I play the coffeehouses."

"What do you sing?"

"Oh, folk music, mostly. And some old things—Purcell and Dowland.[1] But mostly folk music. . . . 'I gave my love a cherry that had no stone,'" she sang in a true and pretty voice. "'I gave my love a chicken that had no bone / I told my love a story that had no end / I gave my love a baby with no cryin'.'"

She sang me across a bridge that seemed to be an astonishingly sensible, durable, and even beautiful construction designed by intelligent men to simplify my travels, and the water of the Hudson below us was charming and tranquil. It all came back—blue-sky courage, the high spirits of lustiness, an ecstatic sereneness. Her song ended as we got to the toll station on the east bank, and she thanked me, said goodbye, and got out of the car. I offered to take her wherever she wanted to go, but she shook her head and walked away, and I drove on toward the city through a world that, having been restored to me, seemed marvelous and fair. When I got home, I thought of calling my brother and telling him what had happened, on the chance that there was

---

[1]Henry Purcell (1658–1695) and John Dowland (1562–1626), English composers.

also an angel of the elevator banks, but the harp—that single detail—threatened to make me seem ridiculous or mad, and I didn't call.

I wish I could say that I am convinced that there will always be some merciful intercession to help me with my worries, but I don't believe in rushing my luck, so I will stay off the George Washington Bridge, although I can cross the Triborough and the Tappan Zee with ease. My brother is still afraid of elevators, and my mother, although she's grown quite stiff, still goes around and around and around on the ice.

1961

TILLIE OLSEN
(b. 1913)

When Tillie Olsen was fifteen years old, she paid a dime for some bulky volumes of an old magazine in Omaha, Nebraska. In one of the issues she read a story that changed her life: "I first read *Life in the Iron Mills* in one of three water-stained, coverless volumes of bound *Atlantic Monthly*s. . . . Contributions to those old *Atlantics* were published anonymously, and I was ignorant of any process whereby I might find the name of the author of this work which meant increasingly more to me over the years, saying 'Literature can be made out of the lives of despised people,' and 'You, too, must write.'"

It was not until some thirty years later, in 1958, when she was in the public library of San Francisco browsing through *The Letters of Emily Dickinson* that she learned the author of "Life in the Iron Mills" was Rebecca Harding Davis. "It did not surprise me," she commented, "that the author was of my sex." It was not until fourteen years later, in 1972, that Tillie Olsen's edition of Davis's work appeared with a long commentary and notes by her, published by the Feminist Press. Tillie Olsen was then fifty-nine years old.

Tillie Olsen was attracted to Davis's story because she identified with the "despised people"—the downtrodden workers—portrayed in the narrative. She was born Tillie Lerner in Omaha, Nebraska, one of seven children of Jewish immigrants who had fled Russia during the general prerevolutionary upheavals of 1905. Her father was a laborer—farmer, paper hanger, painter—and a member of the Nebraska Socialist party. Tillie Lerner was forced to leave school after finishing the eleventh grade. She recalled later that she was lucky, because few of the people she knew stayed beyond the eighth grade.

It was the time of the Great Depression and she took whatever jobs she could find—working in a factory, a slaughterhouse, a food-processing plant. She joined the Young Communist League, but she later equated this act with that of a member of the 1960s generation taking a stand against the Vietnam War. She was arrested in the early 1930s for trying to unionize packinghouse workers in Kansas City; the illnesses resulting from imprisonment gave her the first stretch of free time she had ever experienced—and she began a novel, not to be published until 1974. In 1933, she moved to California, becoming involved in union activities, strikes, and clashes with the police. She married Jack Olsen, a fellow union member and printer, in 1936. She already had a daughter from a previous love affair, and she had four more in the marriage.

Tillie Olsen spent the bulk of her life as a working mother (waitress, secretary, Kelly Girl), bringing home a paycheck, raising five children, and participating in union and political activities. It is small wonder that, though she never forgot "Life in the Iron Mills," she found little time to think and write. In the mid-1950s, she finally was able to enroll in a creative-writing program at San Francisco State University. A creative-writing fellowship from Stanford University in 1956–57 and a grant from the Ford Foundation in 1959 enabled her to complete the four stories she would bring together in 1961 as *Tell Me a Riddle,* the title story of which won the O. Henry Award for the best short story of that year. Since their publication, two of these stories ("Tell Me a Riddle" and "I Stand Here Ironing") have come to be recognized as rare classics in two areas: social literature dealing with working men and women ("despised people"), and feminist literature exploring male-female relationships.

The lost manuscript for the novel she had started many years before was suddenly found, and Tillie Olsen began to work on it. She published it, still unfinished, in 1974 under the title *Yonnondio: From the Thirties,* the initial word of which she borrowed from Walt Whitman's poem "Yonnondio." Whitman had explained in a headnote to the poem: "The sense of the word is lament for the aborigines. It is an Iroquois term: and has been used for a personal name." The poem itself is indeed a lament for the disappearance of the Indians without a trace left — "No picture, poem, statement, passing them to the future"; "A muffled sonorous sound, a wailing word is borne through the air for a moment, / Then blank and gone and still, and utterly lost." Tillie Olsen's lament, in her autobiographical novel, is for all the inarticulate and silent "despised people" of the earth, whose lives have similarly disappeared without trace.

As Tillie Olsen's work became known, she developed into something of a heroine among cultural rebels, especially feminists. She was invited to teach creative writing and feminist literature at such institutions as Amherst, the University of Massachusetts, the Massachusetts Institute of Technology, and Stanford University. Much of the material she produced during this period appeared in a book of prose, *Silences,* published in 1978. She said at the opening: "The silences I speak of here are unnatural; the unnatural thwarting of what struggles to come into being, but cannot. In the old, the obvious parallels: when the seed strikes stone; the soil will not sustain; the spring is false; the time is drought or blight or infestation; the frost comes premature." And she added: "This book is about such silences. It is concerned with the relationship of circumstances — including class, color, sex; the times, climate into which one is born — to the creation of literature."

Tillie Olsen has come by her sympathies for "despised people" naturally, from her own experience as a worker, as a woman, and as a Jew. But her sympathies have not been exclusionary. *Silences* is addressed to all, regardless of class, color, sex. What she said of it she might have said of all her work: "A passion and a purpose inform its pages: love for my incomparable medium, literature; hatred for all that, societally rooted, unnecessarily lessens and denies it; slows, impairs, silences writers. It is written to re-dedicate and encourage."

ADDITIONAL READING

William Van O'Connor, "The Short Stories of Tillie Olsen," *Studies in Short Fiction,* Fall, 1963; Marilyn Yalom, ed., "Tillie Olsen," *Women Writers of the West Coast,* 1983; Elaine Neil Orr, *Tillie Olsen and a Feminist Spiritual Vision,* 1987.

TEXT

Tell Me a Riddle, 1961.

I Stand Here Ironing

I stand here ironing, and what you asked me moves tormented back and forth with the iron.

"I wish you would manage the time to come in and talk with me about your daughter. I'm sure you can help me understand her. She's a youngster who needs help and whom I'm deeply interested in helping."

"Who needs help." Even if I came, what good would it do? You think because I am her mother I have a key, or that in some way you could use me as a key? She has lived for nineteen years. There is all that life that has happened outside of me, beyond me.

And when is there time to remember, to sift, to weigh, to estimate, to total? I will start and there will be an interruption and I will have to gather it all together again. Or I will become engulfed with all I did or did not do, with what should have been and what cannot be helped.

She was a beautiful baby. The first and only one of our five that was beautiful at birth. You do not guess how new and uneasy her tenancy in her now-loveliness. You did not know her all those years she was thought homely, or see her poring over her baby pictures, making me tell her over and over how beautiful she had been — and would be, I would tell her — and was now, to the seeing eye. But the seeing eyes were few or non-existent. Including mine.

I nursed her. They feel that's important nowadays. I nursed all the children, but with her, with all the fierce rigidity of first motherhood, I did like the books then said. Though her cries battered me to trembling and my breasts ached with swollenness, I waited till the clock decreed.

Why do I put that first? I do not even know if it matters, or if it explains anything.

She was a beautiful baby. She blew shining bubbles of sound. She loved motion, loved light, loved color and music and textures. She would lie on the floor in her blue overalls patting the surface so hard in ecstasy her hands and feet would blur. She was a miracle to me, but when she was eight months old I had to leave her daytimes with the woman downstairs to whom she was no miracle at all, for I worked or looked for work and for Emily's father, who "could no longer endure" (he wrote in his good-bye note) "sharing want with us."

I was nineteen. It was the pre-relief, pre-WPA world of the depression. I would start running as soon as I got off the streetcar, running up the stairs, the place smelling sour, and awake or asleep to startle awake, when she saw me she would break into a clogged weeping that could not be comforted, a weeping I can hear yet.

After a while I found a job hashing at night so I could be with her days, and it was better. But it came to where I had to bring her to his family and leave her.

It took a long time to raise the money for her fare back. Then she got chicken pox and I had to wait longer. When she finally came, I hardly knew her, walking quick and nervous like her father, looking like her father, thin, and dressed in a shoddy red that yellowed her skin and glared at the pockmarks. All the baby loveliness gone.

She was two. Old enough for nursery school they said, and I did not know then what I know now — the fatigue of the long day, and the lacerations of group life in nurseries that are only parking places for children.

Except that it would have made no difference if I had known. It was the only place there was. It was the only way we could be together, the only way I could hold a job.

And even without knowing, I knew. I knew the teacher that was evil because all these years it was curdled into my memory, the little boy hunched in the corner, her rasp, "why aren't you outside, because Alvin hits you? that's no reason, go out, scaredy." I knew Emily hated it even if she did not clutch and implore "don't go Mommy" like the other children, mornings.

She always had a reason why we should stay home. Momma, you look sick, Momma. I feel sick. Momma, the teachers aren't there today, they're sick. Momma, we can't go, there was a fire there last night. Momma, it's a holiday today, no school, they told me.

But never a direct protest, never rebellion. I think of our others in their three-, four-year-oldness — the explosions, the tempers, the denunciations, the demands — and I feel suddenly ill. I put the iron down. What in me demanded that goodness in her? And what was the cost, the cost to her of such goodness?

The old man living in the back once said in his gentle way: "You should smile at Emily more when you look at her." What *was* in my face when I looked at her? I loved her. There were all the acts of love.

It was only with the others I remembered what he said, and it was the face of joy, and not of care or tightness or worry I turned to them — too late for Emily. She does not smile easily, let alone almost always as her brothers and sisters do. Her face is closed and sombre, but when she wants, how fluid. You must have seen it in her pantomimes, you spoke of her rare gift for comedy on the stage that rouses a laughter out of the audience so dear they applaud and applaud and do not want to let her go.

Where does it come from, that comedy? There was none of it in her when she came back to me that second time, after I had had to send her away again. She had a new daddy now to learn to love, and I think perhaps it was a better time.

Except when we left her alone nights, telling ourselves she was old enough.

"Can't you go some other time, Mommy, like tomorrow?" she would ask. "Will it be just a little while you'll be gone? Do you promise?"

The time we came back, the front door open, the clock on the floor in the hall. She rigid awake. "It wasn't just a little while. I didn't cry. Three times I called you, just three times, and then I ran downstairs to open the door so you could come faster. The clock talked loud. I threw it away, it scared me what it talked."

She said the clock talked loud again that night I went to the hospital to have Susan. She was delirious with the fever that comes before red measles, but she was fully conscious all the week I was gone and the week after we were home when she could not come near the new baby or me.

She did not get well. She stayed skeleton thin, not wanting to eat, and night after night she had nightmares. She would call for me, and I would rouse from exhaustion to sleepily call back: "You're all right, darling, go to sleep, it's just a dream," and if she still called, in a sterner voice, "now go to sleep, Emily, there's nothing to hurt you." Twice, only twice, when I had to get up for Susan anyhow, I went in to sit with her.

Now when it is too late (as if she would let me hold and comfort her like I do the others) I get up and go to her at once at her moan or restless stirring. "Are you awake, Emily? Can I get you something?" And the answer is always the same: "No, I'm all right, go back to sleep, Mother."

They persuaded me at the clinic to send her away to a convalescent home in the country where "she can have the kind of food and care you can't manage for her, and you'll be free to concentrate on the new baby." They still send children to that place. I see pictures on the society page of sleek young women planning affairs to raise money for it, or dancing at the affairs, or decorating Easter eggs or filling Christmas stockings for the children.

They never have a picture of the children so I do not know if the girls still wear those gigantic red bows and the ravaged looks on the every other Sunday when parents can come to visit "unless otherwise notified" — as we were notified the first six weeks.

Oh it is a handsome place, green lawns and tall trees and fluted flower beds. High up on the balconies of each cottage the children stand, the girls in their red bows and white dresses, the boys in white suits and giant red ties. The parents stand below shrieking up to be heard and the children shriek down to be heard, and between them the invisible wall "Not To Be Contaminated by Parental Germs or Physical Affection."

There was a tiny girl who always stood hand in hand with Emily. Her parents never came. One visit she was gone. "They moved her to Rose Cottage" Emily shouted in explanation. "They don't like you to love anybody here."

She wrote once a week, the labored writing of a seven-year-old. "I am fine. How is the baby. If I write my leter nicly I will have a star. Love." There never was a star. We wrote every other day, letters she could never hold or keep but only hear read—once. "We simply do not have room for children to keep any personal possessions," they patiently explained when we pieced one Sunday's shrieking together to plead how much it would mean to Emily, who loved so to keep things, to be allowed to keep her letters and cards.

Each visit she looked frailer. "She isn't eating," they told us.

(They had runny eggs for breakfast or mush with lumps, Emily said later, I'd hold it in my mouth and not swallow. Nothing ever tasted good, just when they had chicken.)

It took us eight months to get her released home, and only the fact that she gained back so little of her seven lost pounds convinced the social worker.

I used to try to hold and love her after she came back, but her body would stay stiff, and after a while she'd push away. She ate little. Food sickened her, and I think much of life too. Oh she had physical lightness and brightness, twinkling by on skates, bouncing like a ball up and down up and down over the jump rope, skimming over the hill; but these were momentary.

She fretted about her appearance, thin and dark and foreign-looking at a time when every little girl was supposed to look or thought she should look a chubby blonde replica of Shirley Temple. The doorbell sometimes rang for her, but no one seemed to come and play in the house or be a best friend. Maybe because we moved so much.

There was a boy she loved painfully through two school semesters. Months later she told me how she had taken pennies from my purse to buy him candy. "Licorice was his favorite and I brought him some every day, but he still liked Jennifer better'n me. Why, Mommy?" The kind of question for which there is no answer.

School was a worry to her. She was not glib or quick in a world where glibness and quickness were easily confused with ability to learn. To her overworked and exasperated teachers she was an overconscientious "slow learner" who kept trying to catch up and was absent entirely too often.

I let her be absent, though sometimes the illness was imaginary. How different from my now-strictness about attendance with the others. I wasn't working. We had a new baby, I was home anyhow. Sometimes, after Susan grew old enough, I would keep her home from school, too, to have them all together.

Mostly Emily had asthma, and her breathing, harsh and labored, would fill the house with a curiously tranquil sound. I would bring the two old dresser mirrors and her boxes of collections to her bed. She would select beads and single earrings, bottle tops and shells, dried flowers and pebbles, old postcards and scraps, all sorts of oddments; then she and Susan would play Kingdom, setting up landscapes and furniture, peopling them with action.

Those were the only times of peaceful companionship between her and Susan. I have edged away from it, that poisonous feeling between them, that terrible balancing of hurts and needs I had to do between the two, and did so badly, those earlier years.

Oh there are conflicts between the others too, each one human, needing, demanding, hurting, taking—but only between Emily and Susan, no, Emily toward Susan that corroding resentment. It seems so obvious on the surface, yet it is not obvious. Susan, the second child, Susan, golden- and curly-haired and chubby, quick and articulate and assured, everything in appearance and manner Emily was not; Susan, not able to resist Emily's precious things, losing or sometimes clumsily breaking them; Susan telling jokes and riddles to company for applause while Emily sat silent (to say to me later: that was *my* riddle, Mother, I told it to Susan); Susan, who for all the five years' difference in age was just a year behind Emily in developing physically.

I am glad for that slow physical development that widened the difference between her and her contemporaries, though she suffered over it. She was too vulnerable for that terrible world of youthful competition, of preening and parading, of constant measuring of yourself against every other, of envy, "If I had that copper hair," "If I had that skin. . . ." She tormented herself enough about not looking like the others, there was enough of the unsureness, the having to be conscious of words before you speak, the constant caring — what are they thinking of me? without having it all magnified by the merciless physical drives.

Ronnie is calling. He is wet and I change him. It is rare there is such a cry now. That time of motherhood is almost behind me when the ear is not one's own but must always be racked and listening for the child cry, the child call. We sit for a while and I hold him, looking out over the city spread in charcoal with its soft aisles of light. "*Shoogily*," he breathes and curls closer. I carry him back to bed, asleep. *Shoogily*. A funny word, a family word, inherited from Emily, invented by her to say: *comfort*.

In this and other ways she leaves her seal, I say aloud. And startle at my saying it. What do I mean? What did I start to gather together, to try and make coherent? I was at the terrible, growing years. War years. I do not remember them well. I was working, there were four smaller ones now, there was not time for her. She had to help be a mother, and housekeeper, and shopper. She had to set her seal. Mornings of crisis and near hysteria trying to get lunches packed, hair combed, coats and shoes found, everyone to school or Child Care on time, the baby ready for transportation. And always the paper scribbled on by a smaller one, the book looked at by Susan then mislaid, the homework not done. Running out to that huge school where she was one, she was lost, she was a drop; suffering over the unpreparedness, stammering and unsure in her classes.

There was so little time left at night after the kids were bedded down. She would struggle over books, always eating (it was in those years she developed her enormous appetite that is legendary in our family) and I would be ironing, or preparing food for the next day, or writing V-mail to Bill, or tending the baby. Sometimes, to make me laugh, or out of her despair, she would imitate happenings or types at school.

I think I said once: "Why don't you do something like this in the school amateur show?" One morning she phoned me at work, hardly understandable through the weeping: "Mother, I did it. I won, I won; they gave me first prize; they clapped and clapped and wouldn't let me go."

Now suddenly she was Somebody, and as imprisoned in her difference as she had been in anonymity.

She began to be asked to perform at other high schools, even in colleges, then at city and statewide affairs. The first one we went to, I only recognized her that first moment when thin, shy, she almost drowned herself into the curtains. Then: Was this Emily? The control, the command, the convulsing and deadly clowning, the spell, then the roaring, stamping audience, unwilling to let this rare and precious laughter out of their lives.

Afterwards: You ought to do something about her with a gift like that — but without money or knowing how, what does one do? We have left it all to her, and the gift has as often eddied inside, clogged and clotted, as been used and growing.

She is coming. She runs up the stairs two at a time with her light graceful step, and I know she is happy tonight. Whatever it was that occasioned your call did not happen today.

"Aren't you ever going to finish the ironing, Mother? Whistler painted his mother in a rocker. I'd have to paint mine standing over an ironing board." This is one of her communicative nights and she tells me everything and nothing as she fixes herself a plate of food out of the icebox.

She is so lovely. Why did you want me to come in at all? Why were you concerned? She will find her way.

She starts up the stairs to bed. "Don't get me up with the rest in the morning." "But I thought you were having midterms." "Oh, those," she comes back in, kisses me, and says quite lightly, "in a couple of years when we'll all be atom-dead they won't matter a bit."

She has said it before. She *believes* it. But because I have been dredging the past, and all that compounds a human being is so heavy and meaningful in me, I cannot endure it tonight.

I will never total it all. I will never come in to say: She was a child seldom smiled at. Her father left me before she was a year old. I had to work her first six years when there was work, or I sent her home and to his relatives. There were years she had care she hated. She was dark and thin and foreign-looking in a world where the prestige went to blondeness and curly hair and dimples, she was slow where glibness was prized. She was a child of anxious, not proud, love. We were poor and could not afford for her the soil of easy growth. I was a young mother, I was a distracted mother. There were the other children pushing up, demanding. Her younger sister seemed all that she was not. There were years she did not want me to touch her. She kept too much in herself, her life was such she had to keep too much in herself. My wisdom came too late. She has much to her and probably nothing will come of it. She is a child of her age, of depression, of war, of fear.

Let her be. So all that is in her will not bloom—but in how many does it? There is still enough left to live by. Only help her to know—help make it so there is cause for her to know—that she is more than this dress on the ironing board, helpless before the iron.

1953–54   *1956*

RALPH ELLISON
(b. 1914)

Ralph Ellison commented in an interview in 1961:

> There never was a time when I thought of writing fiction in which only Negroes appeared, or in which only whites appeared. And yet, from the very beginning I wanted to write about American Negro experience and I suspected that what was important, what made the difference, lay in the perspective from which it was viewed. . . . I felt it important to explore the full range of American Negro humanity and to affirm those qualities which are of value beyond any question of segregation, economics or previous condition of servitude. . . . What I have tried to commemorate in fiction is that which I believe to be enduring and abiding in our situation, especially those human qualities which the American Negro has developed despite and in rejection of the obstacles and meannesses imposed upon us. If the writer exists for any social good, his role is that of preserving in art those human values which can endure by confronting change. . . . I think that art is a celebration of life even when life extends into death and that the sociological conditions which have made for so much misery in Negro life are not necessarily the only factors which make for the values which I feel should endure and shall endure.

Ralph Waldo Ellison was born in Oklahoma City, Oklahoma. His father, who died when Ellison was only three, named his son after the nineteenth-century

American poet and essayist Ralph Waldo Emerson, perhaps with the notion that the name would influence its bearer in choosing a profession. At first Ellison set out to be a musician and studied music at Tuskegee Institute in Alabama, which he attended from 1933 to 1936. On a visit to New York, Ellison met Richard Wright, then associated with a number of leftist publications, who invited him to review a book. The review was accepted and Ellison found his fate as a writer. He began to write sketches, essays, and stories, including "King of the Bingo Game."

Before long, Ellison found that he had written what was the first paragraph of a novel. What he did not know was that it would take him five years to finish the work. *Invisible Man* was published in 1952 and won the National Book Award for fiction for that year. The novel has come to be recognized as not only an extraordinary representation of black experience in America, but—and perhaps more importantly—as one of the great American novels of this century. It has, however, also been the subject of sharp controversy.

The black protagonist and narrator, who is never named, recounts his nightmarish experiences from the time he is expelled from a southern Negro college and sent North, only to discover that all his letters of introduction seem to say the same thing: "Keep this nigger boy running." At one point he gets a job in a white-paint factory and is working near a vat when it explodes; his sudden transfiguration from black to white, from consciousness to unconsciousness, precipitates an identity crisis, and almost destroys him physically and spiritually. This is only one of the many episodes that take on a surrealistic dimension in the novel. Gradually the protagonist comes to realize he is being used, even by those who claim to be on his side—like the militantly political Brotherhood that some readers identified as the Communist party. Near the end he falls through an open man-hole into darkness and isolation, where we had encountered him at the beginning of the novel. Reviewing his experiences, he decides finally to end his hibernation and to emerge, taking on a "socially responsible role" he can't evade. And he touches the reader's own shaken identity when he concludes with a haunting question: "Who knows but that, on the lower frequencies, I speak for you?"

Some leftist critics, offended by Ellison's portrayal of the Brotherhood, thought it an attack on the Communist party. Other critics protested that the protagonist should have remained apart from society, acting to subvert it, instead of returning to it at the end to accept a "socially responsible role." In short, these critics wanted to shape Ellison to their own ends, much as the various individuals and organizations in the novel wanted to control the protagonist. But it appears that Ellison was true to his own instincts and his material. The novel's universal themes have engaged successive generations of readers, nonblacks as well as blacks, who have tuned in and responded to those lower frequencies mentioned by the protagonist in his closing comment.

Ellison continued to write and publish fiction in various journals after 1952, but he has not published a second book of fiction. It has been reported that some of the material he has published will be brought together in a long work of fiction that will appear as a trilogy, but no date has been announced. Meantime, he has spent his career teaching and lecturing at various universities, including Bard College, the University of Chicago, Rutgers, and the University of California. He held the post of Albert Schweitzer Professor of Humanities at New York University from 1970 to 1980.

Although the promised second novel has not appeared, there have been two collections of prose, *Shadow & Act* (1964) and *Going to the Territory* (1986). In such essays as "Twentieth-Century Fiction and the Black Mask of Humanity" and

"The Novel as a Function of American Democracy," Ellison has shown himself to be a perceptive and sophisticated commentator on American institutions and particularly American literature, worthy of that tradition his father had in mind in naming him after Ralph Waldo Emerson. These volumes have also led the readers of *Invisible Man* to discover depths and complexities that they might otherwise have overlooked, and to become aware of fictional strategies that they might not have noticed. In spite of the fact that Ellison, now in his seventies, has published only one novel, it is this work by which the fiction of later writers, whatever their color, might well be measured.

ADDITIONAL READING

John M. Reilly, ed., *Twentieth Century Interpretations of Invisible Man: A Collection of Essays*, 1970; Joseph F. Trimmer, *A Casebook on Ralph Ellison's Invisible Man*, 1972; Jacqueline Covo, *The Blinking Eye: Ralph Waldo Ellison and His American, French, German, and Italian Critics*, 1974; John Hersey, ed., *Ralph Ellison: A Collection of Critical Essays*, 1974; Robert G. O'Meally, *The Craft of Ralph Ellison*, 1980; Rudolf F. Dietze, *Ralph Ellison: The Genesis of an Artist*, 1982; Robert N. List, *Dedalus in Harlem, The Joyce-Ellison Connection*, 1982; Kimberly W. Bentson, ed., *Speaking for You: The Vision of Ralph Ellison*, 1987 (contains useful bibliography of Ellison's works as well as criticism of him); Robert O'Meally, ed., *New Essays on Invisible Man*, 1988; Alan Nadel, *Invisible Criticism: Ralph Ellison and the American Canon*, 1988; Susan Resneck Parr and Pancho Savery, eds., *Approaches to Teaching Ellison's Invisible Man*, 1989.

TEXT

Tomorrow, Vol. IV, No. 3 (November 1944).

King of the Bingo Game

The woman in front of him was eating roasted peanuts that smelled so good that he could barely contain his hunger. He could not even sleep and wished they'd hurry and begin the bingo game. There, on his right, two fellows were drinking wine out of a bottle wrapped in a paper bag, and he could hear soft gurgling in the dark. His stomach gave a low, gnawing growl. "If this was down South," he thought, "all I'd have to do is lean over and say 'Lady, gimme a few of those peanuts, please ma'm,' and she'd pass me the bag and never think nothing of it." Or he could ask the fellows for a drink in the same way. Folks down South stuck together that way; they didn't even have to know you. But up here it was different. Ask somebody for something, and they'd think you were crazy. Well, I ain't crazy. I'm just broke, 'cause I got no birth certificate to get a job, and Laura 'bout to die 'cause we got no money for a doctor. But I ain't crazy. And yet a pinpoint of doubt was focused in his mind as he glanced toward the screen and saw the hero stealthily entering a dark room and sending the beam of a flashlight along a wall of bookcases. This is where he finds the trapdoor, he remembered. The man would pass abruptly through the wall and find the girl tied to a bed, her legs and arms spread wide, and her clothing torn to rags. He laughed softly to himself. He had seen the picture three times, and this was one of the best scenes.

On his right the fellow whispered wide-eyed to his companion, "Man, look a-yonder!"

"Damn!"

"Wouldn't I like to have her tied up like that . . ."

"Hey! That fool's letting her loose!"

"Aw, man, he loves her."

"Love or no love!"

The man moved impatiently beside him, and he tried to involve himself in the scene. But Laura was on his mind. Tiring quickly of watching the picture he looked back to where the white beam filtered from the projection room above the balcony. It started small and grew large, specks of dust dancing in its whiteness as it reached the screen. It was strange how the beam always landed right on the screen and didn't mess up and fall somewhere else. But they had it all fixed. Everything was fixed. Now suppose when they showed that girl with her dress torn the girl started taking off the rest of her clothes, and when the guy came in he didn't untie her but kept her there and went to taking off his own clothes? *That* would be something to see. If a picture got out of hand like that those guys up there would go nuts. Yeah, and there'd be so many folks in here you couldn't find a seat for nine months! A strange sensation played over his skin. He shuddered. Yesterday he'd seen a bedbug on a woman's neck as they walked out into the bright street. But exploring his thigh through a hole in his pocket he found only goose pimples and old scars.

The bottle gurgled again. He closed his eyes. Now a dreamy music was accompanying the film and train whistles were sounding in the distance, and he was a boy again walking along a railroad trestle down South, and seeing the train coming, and running back as fast as he could go, and hearing the whistle blowing, and getting off the trestle to solid ground just in time, with the earth trembling beneath his feet, and feeling relieved as he ran down the cinder-strewn embankment onto the highway, and looking back and seeing with terror that the train had left the track and was following him right down the middle of the street, and all the white people laughing as he ran screaming . . .

"Wake up there, buddy! What the hell do you mean hollering like that? Can't you see we trying to enjoy this here picture?"

He stared at the man with gratitude.

"I'm sorry, old man," he said. "I musta been dreaming."

"Well, here, have a drink. And don't be making no noise like that, damn!"

His hands trembled as he tilted his head. It was not wine, but whiskey. Cold rye whiskey. He took a deep swoller, decided it was better not to take another, and handed the bottle back to its owner.

"Thanks, old man," he said.

Now he felt the cold whiskey breaking a warm path straight through the middle of him, growing hotter and sharper as it moved. He had not eaten all day, and it made him light-headed. The smell of the peanuts stabbed him like a knife, and he got up and found a seat in the middle aisle. But no sooner did he sit than he saw a row of intense-faced young girls, and got up again, thinking, "You chicks musta been Lindy-hopping[1] somewhere." He found a seat several rows ahead as the lights came on, and he saw the screen disappear behind a heavy red and gold curtain; then the curtain rising, and the man with the microphone and a uniformed attendant coming on the stage.

He felt for his bingo cards, smiling. The guy at the door wouldn't like it if he knew about his having *five* cards. Well, not everyone played the bingo game; and even with five cards he didn't have much of a chance. For Laura, though, he had to have faith. He studied the cards, each with its different numerals, punching the free center hole in each and spreading them neatly across his lap; and when the lights faded he sat slouched in his seat so that he could look from his cards to the bingo wheel with but a quick shifting of his eyes.

Ahead, at the end of the darkness, the man with the microphone was pressing a button attached to a long cord and spinning the bingo wheel and calling out the number each time the wheel came to rest. And each time the voice rang out his finger

---

[1]The Lindy-hop was an energetic jitterbug dance.

raced over the cards for the number. With five cards he had to move fast. He became nervous; there were too many cards, and the man went too fast with his grating voice. Perhaps he should just select one and throw the others away. But he was afraid. He became warm. Wonder how much Laura's doctor would cost? Damn that, watch the cards! And with despair he heard the man call three in a row which he missed on all five cards. This way he'd never win . . .

When he saw the row of holes punched across the third card, he sat paralyzed and heard the man call three more numbers before he stumbled forward, screaming,

"Bingo! Bingo!"

"Let that fool up there," someone called.

"Get up there, man!"

He stumbled down the aisle and up the steps to the stage into a light so sharp and bright that for a moment it blinded him, and he felt that he had moved into the spell of some strange, mysterious power. Yet it was as familiar as the sun, and he knew it was the perfectly familiar bingo.

The man with the microphone was saying something to the audience as he held out his card. A cold light flashed from the man's finger as the card left his hand. His knees trembled. The man stepped closer, checking the card against the numbers chalked on the board. Suppose he had made a mistake? The pomade on the man's hair made him feel faint, and he backed away. But the man was checking the card over the microphone now, and he had to stay. He stood tense, listening.

"Under the O, forty-four," the man chanted. "Under the I, seven. Under the G, three. Under the B, ninety-six. Under the N, thirteen!"

His breath came easier as the man smiled at the audience.

"Yessir, ladies and gentlemen, he's one of the chosen people!"

The audience rippled with laughter and applause.

"Step right up to the front of the stage."

He moved slowly forward, wishing that the light was not so bright.

"To win tonight's jackpot of $36.90 the wheel must stop between the double zero, understand?"

He nodded, knowing the ritual from the many days and nights he had watched the winners march across the stage to press the button that controlled the spinning wheel and receive the prizes. And now he followed the instructions as though he'd crossed the slippery stage a million prize-winning times.

The man was making some kind of a joke, and he nodded vacantly. So tense had he become that he felt a sudden desire to cry and shook it away. He felt vaguely that his whole life was determined by the bingo wheel; not only that which would happen now that he was at last before it, but all that had gone before, since his birth, and his mother's birth and the birth of his father. It had always been there, even though he had not been aware of it, handing out the unlucky cards and numbers of his days. The feeling persisted, and he started quickly away. I better get down from here before I make a fool of myself, he thought.

"Here, boy," the man called. "You haven't started yet."

Someone laughed as he went hesitantly back.

"Are you all reet?"

He grinned at the man's jive talk, but no words would come, and he knew it was not a convincing grin. For suddenly he knew that he stood on the slippery brink of some terrible embarassment.

"Where are you from, boy?" the man asked.

"Down South."

"He's from down South, ladies and gentlemen," the man said. "Where from? Speak right into the mike."

"Rocky Mont," he said. "Rock' Mont, North Car'lina."

"So you decided to come down off that mountain to the U.S.," the man laughed.

He felt that the man was making a fool of him, but then something cold was placed in his hand, and the lights were no longer behind him.

Standing before the wheel he felt alone, but that was somehow right, and he remembered his plan. He would give the wheel a short quick twirl. Just a touch of the button. He had watched it many times, and always it came close to double zero when it was short and quick. He steeled himself; the fear had left, and he felt a profound sense of promise, as though he were about to be repaid for all the things he'd suffered all his life. Trembling, he pressed the button. There was a whirl of lights, and in a second he realized with finality that though he wanted to, he could not stop. It was as though he held a high-powered line in his naked hand. His nerves tightened. As the wheel increased its speed it seemed to draw him more and more into its power, as though it held his fate; and with it came a deep need to submit, to whirl, to lose himself in its swirl of color. He could not stop it now, he knew. So let it be.

The button rested snuggly in his palm where the man had placed it. And now he became aware of the man beside him, advising him through the microphone, while behind the shadowy audience hummed with noisy voices. He shifted his feet. There was still that feeling of helplessness within him, making part of him desire to turn back, even now that the jackpot was right in his hand. He squeezed the button until his fist ached. Then, like the sudden shriek of a subway whistle, a doubt tore through his head. Suppose he did not spin the wheel long enough? What could he do, and how could he tell? And then he knew, even as he wondered, that as long as he pressed the button, he could control the jackpot. He and only he could determine whether or not it was to be his. Not even the man with the microphone could do anything about it now. He felt drunk. Then, as though he had come down from a high hill into a valley of people, he heard the audience yelling.

"Come down from there, you jerk!"

"Let somebody else have a chance . . ."

"Ole Jack thinks he done found the end of the rainbow . . ."

The last voice was not unfriendly, and he turned and smiled dreamily into the yelling mouths. Then he turned his back squarely on them.

"Don't take too long, boy," a voice said.

He nodded. They were yelling behind him. Those folks did not understand what had happened to him. They had been playing the bingo game day in and night out for years, trying to win rent money or hamburger change. But not one of those wise guys had discovered this wonderful thing. He watched the wheel whirling past the numbers and experienced a burst of exhaltation: This is God! This is the really truly God! He said it aloud, "This is God!"

He said it with such absolute conviction that he feared he would fall fainting into the footlights. But the crowd yelled so loud that they could not hear. Those fools, he thought. I'm here trying to tell them the most wonderful secret in the world, and they're yelling like they gone crazy. A hand fell upon his shoulder.

"You'll have to make a choice now, boy. You've taken too long."

He brushed the hand violently away.

"Leave me alone, man. I know what I'm doing!"

The man looked surprised and held on to the microphone for support. And because he did not wish to hurt the man's feelings he smiled, realizing with a sudden pang that there was no way of explaining to the man just why he had to stand there pressing the button forever.

"Come here," he called tiredly.

The man approached, rolling the heavy microphone across the stage.

"Anybody can play this bingo game, right?" he said.

"Sure, but . . ."

He smiled, feeling inclined to be patient with this slick looking white man with his blue sport shirt and his sharp gabardine suit.

"That's what I thought," he said. "Anybody can win the jackpot as long as they get the lucky number, right?"

"That's the rule, but after all . . ."

"That's what I thought," he said. "And the big prize goes to the man who knows how to win it?"

The man nodded speechlessly.

"Well then, go on over there and watch me win like I want to. I ain't going to hurt nobody," he said, "and I'll show you how to win. I mean to show the whole world how it's got to be done."

And because he understood, he smiled again to let the man know that he held nothing against him for being white and impatient. Then he refused to see the man any longer and stood pressing the button, the voices of the crowd reaching him like sounds in distant streets. Let them yell. All the Negroes down there were just ashamed because he was black like them. He smiled inwardly, knowing how it was. Most of the time he was ashamed of what Negroes did himself. Well, let them be ashamed for something this time. Like him. He was like a long thin black wire that was being stretched and wound upon the bingo wheel; wound until he wanted to scream; wound, but this time himself controlling the winding and the sadness and the shame, and because he did, Laura would be all right. Suddenly the lights flickered. He staggered backwards. Had something gone wrong? All this noise. Didn't they know that although he controlled the wheel, it also controlled him, and unless he pressed the button forever and forever and ever it would stop, leaving him high and dry, dry and high on this hard high slippery hill and Laura dead? There was only one chance; he had to do whatever the wheel demanded. And gripping the button in despair, he discovered with surprise that it imparted a nervous energy. His spine tingled. He felt a certain power.

Now he faced the raging crowd with defiance, its screams penetrating his eardrums like trumpets shrieking from a juke-box. The vague faces glowing in the bingo lights gave him a sense of himself that he had never known before. He was running the show, by God! They had to react to him, for he was their luck. This is *me,* he thought. Let the bastards yell. Then someone was laughing inside him, and he realized that somehow he had forgotten his own name. It was a sad, lost feeling to lose your name, and a crazy thing to do. That name had been given him by the white man who had owned his grandfather a long lost time ago down South. But maybe those wise guys knew his name.

"Who am I?" he screamed.

"Hurry up and bingo, you jerk!"

They didn't know either, he thought sadly. They didn't even know their own names, they were all poor nameless bastards. Well, he didn't need that old name; he was reborn. For as long as he pressed the button he was The-man-who-pressed-the-button-who-held-the-prize-who-was-the-King-of-Bingo. That was the way it was, and he'd have to press the button even if nobody understood, even though Laura did not understand.

"Live!" he shouted.

The audience quieted like the dying of a huge fan.

"Live, Laura, baby. I got holt of it now, sugar. Live!"

He screamed it, tears streaming down his face. "I got nobody but YOU!"

The screams tore from his very guts. He felt as though the rush of blood to his head would burst out in baseball seams of small red droplets, like a head beaten by police clubs. Bending over he saw a trickle of blood splashing the toe of his shoe. With his free hand he searched his head. It was his nose. God, suppose something has gone wrong? He felt that the whole audience had somehow entered him and was stamping its feet in his stomach and he was unable to throw them out. They wanted the prize, that was it. They wanted the secret for themselves. But they'd never get it; he would keep the bingo wheel whirling forever, and Laura would be safe in the wheel. But would she? It had to be, because if she were not safe the wheel would cease to turn; it could not go on. He had to get away, *vomit* all, and his mind formed an image of himself running with Laura in his arms down the tracks of the subway just ahead of an A train, running desperately *vomit* with people screaming for him to come out but knowing no way of leaving the tracks because to stop would bring the train crushing down upon him and to attempt to leave across the other tracks would mean to run into a hot third rail as high as his waist which threw blue sparks that blinded his eyes until he could hardly see.

He heard singing and the audience was clapping its hands.

> Shoot the liquor to him, Jim, boy!
> Clap-clap-clap
> Well a-calla the cop
> He's blowing his top!
> Shoot the liquor to him, Jim, boy!

Bitter anger grew within him at the singing. They think I'm crazy. Well let 'em laugh. I'll do what I got to do.

He was standing in an attitude of intense listening when he saw that they were watching something on the stage behind him. He felt weak. But when he turned he saw no one. If only his thumb did not ache so. Now they were applauding. And for a moment he thought that the wheel had stopped. But that was impossible, his thumb still pressed the button. Then he saw them. Two men in uniform beckoned from the end of the stage. They were coming toward him, walking in step, slowly, like a tap-dance team returning for a third encore. But their shoulders shot forward, and he backed away, looking wildly about. There was nothing to fight them with. He had only the long black cord which led to a plug somewhere back stage, and he couldn't use that because it operated the bingo wheel. He backed slowly, fixing the men with his eyes as his lips stretched over his teeth in a tight, fixed grin; moved toward the end of the stage and realizing that he couldn't go much further, for suddenly the cord became taut and he couldn't afford to break the cord. But he had to do something. The audience was howling. Suddenly he stopped dead, seeing the men halt, their legs lifted as in an interrupted step of a slow-motion dance. There was nothing to do but run in the other direction and he dashed forward, slipping and sliding. The men fell back, surprised. He struck out violently going past.

"Grab him!"

He ran, but all too quickly the cord tightened, resistingly, and he turned and ran back again. This time he slipped them, and discovered by running in a circle before the wheel he could keep the cord from tightening. But this way he had to flail his arms to keep the men away. Why couldn't they leave a man alone? He ran, circling.

"Ring down the curtain," someone yelled. But they couldn't do that. If they did the wheel flashing from the projection room would be cut off. But they had him before he could tell them so, trying to pry open his fist, and he was wrestling and trying to bring his knees into the fight and holding on to the button, for it was his life. And now he was down, seeing a foot coming down, crushing his wrist cruelly, down, as he saw the wheel whirling serenely above.

"I can't give it up," he screamed. Then quietly, in a confidential tone, "Boys, I really can't give it up."

It landed hard against his head. And in the blank moment they had it away from him, completely now. He fought them trying to pull him up from the stage as he watched the wheel spin slowly to a stop. Without surprise he saw it rest at double-zero.

"You see," he pointed bitterly.

"Sure, boy, sure, it's O. K.," one of the men said smiling.

And seeing the man bow his head to someone he could not see, he felt very, very happy; he would receive what all the winner's received.

But as he warmed in the justice of the man's tight smile he did not see the man's slow wink, nor see the bow-legged man behind him step clear of the swiftly descending curtain and set himself for a blow. He only felt the dull pain exploding in his skull, and he knew even as it slipped out of him that his luck had run out on the stage.

1944

BERNARD MALAMUD
(1914–1986)

When asked in 1974 whether he believed that "art is moral," the sixty-year-old Bernard Malamud replied:

> It tends toward morality. It values life. Even when it doesn't, it tends to. My former colleague, Stanley Edgar Hyman, used to say that even the act of creating a form is a moral act. That leaves out something, but I understand and like what he is driving at. It's close to Frost's definition of a poem as "a momentary stay against confusion." Morality begins with an awareness of the sanctity of one's life, hence the lives of others—even Hitler's, to begin with—the sheer privilege of being, in this miraculous cosmos, and trying to figure out why. Art, in essence, celebrates life and gives us our measure.

This remark was made in his *Paris Review* interview, one of the few "invasions" of his privacy he allowed during his life. When first approached by the *Paris Review*, he put the magazine off until he turned sixty. On reaching that age, he agreed to talk for the record. The interviewer began by asking him, Why sixty? The reply: "It's a respectable round number, and when it becomes your age you look at it with both eyes. It's a good time to see from."

Malamud was born in Brooklyn, New York, of immigrant Jewish parents from Russia. Asked about his life, Malamud gave a thumbnail sketch of his growing up that reveals much about him, his work, and his achievement:

> My father was a grocer; my mother, who helped him, after a long illness, died young. I had a younger brother who lived a hard and lonely life and died in his fifties. My mother and father were gentle, honest, kindly people, and who they were and their affection for me to some degree made up for the cultural deprivation I felt as a child. They weren't educated, but their values were stable. Though my father always managed to make a living, they were comparatively poor, especially in the Depression, and yet I never heard a word in praise of the buck. On the other hand, there were no books that I remember in the house, no records, music, pictures on the wall. On Sundays I listened to somebody's piano through the window.

When Malamud was nine and was sick with pneumonia, his father bought him the twenty volumes of *The Book of Knowledge*.

Malamud attended Erasmus Hall High School (1928–32) and City College of New York (1932–36); and he took an M.A. in English at Columbia University in 1942, writing his thesis on Thomas Hardy's poetry. In 1945 he married Ann de Chiara, of Italian descent. During this period he began to write short stories and at the same time taught night classes at Erasmus High and, later, at Harlem Evening High School. In 1949, Malamud accepted a position teaching at Oregon State College, Corvallis, Oregon, thus beginning a lifelong academic career. He left Oregon in 1961 to begin teaching at Bennington College in Vermont, where he remained for over twenty years, with time out to teach at Harvard University (1966–68). When asked whether he thought it was good for a writer to teach, he replied: "I've taught since I was twenty-five, and though I need more time for reading and writing, I also want to keep on doing what I can do well and enjoy doing."

Malamud began to publish his stories in such places as *Partisan Review* and *Harper's Bazaar* during the 1950s, and he published his first novel, *The Natural*, in 1952. Now it seems an anomaly among his other works, containing no Jewish characters—a "baseball novel" filled with the lore and mythology of America's national sport. It has remained, however, one of Malamud's most popular works, and was made into a successful movie in 1984 starring Robert Redford. In his next novel, *The Assistant,* published in 1957 and considered by many critics his master-piece, Malamud introduced the milieu with which he was to be identified throughout his career, and which he knew from firsthand experience—Jewish immigrant life in New York. The assistant of the title is an Italian-American working for a poor Jewish grocer in New York during the Depression; after the grocer's death at the end, the assistant takes over the marginal business and decides to convert to Judaism. *The Assistant* has rarely been matched by the au-thor's later work (except perhaps in his short stories) in its portrayal of the rhythms of immigrant life and immigrant speech and its subtle modulations from the comic to the tragic, with incidents steeped in a melancholy humor that is vintage Malamud.

A similar feeling is evoked by the best of Malamud's short stories, the first volume of which was published in 1958, entitled *The Magic Barrel.* The stories present a series of unforgettable characters entangled in webs not solely of their own weaving. Malamud once described his essential character as "someone who fears his fate, is caught up in it, yet manages to outrun it; he's the subject and object of laughter and pity."

The story of Malamud's career is the story of his books as they continued to appear regularly. In *A New Life* (1961), he capitalized on his experiences as an outsider teaching in a college in the Pacific Northwest. Other volumes of short stories appeared: *Idiots First* (1963), *Pictures of Fidelman* (1969), *Rembrandt's Hat* (1973), and *The Stories of Bernard Malamud* (1983). In the Introduction to this last volume, Malamud revealed his fondness for the short story form: "Somewhere I've said that a short story packs a self in a few pages predicating a lifetime. The drama is tense, happens fast, and is more often than not outlandish. In a few pages a good story portrays the complexity of a life while producing the surprise and effect of knowledge—not a bad payoff."

Malamud continued to write novels, but he wandered further and further afield for his subjects. He based *The Fixer* (1966) on a true story he first heard from his father about the imprisonment and torture of a Jew in Russia falsely accused of the ritual killing of a Christian child. *The Tenants* (1971) portrayed the love-hate relationship between two struggling writers, one Jewish and the other black. *Dubin's Lives* (1979) described the surprises life held in store for a famous, married biographer whose career had been spent sifting through others' lives. *God's Grace* (1982) was set in the future after a nuclear war had left only one man as human survivor.

Throughout his career, Malamud insisted on the importance of "story" and scoffed at those avant-garde writers who denied its importance. He once commented: "Writers who can't invent stories often pursue other strategies, even substituting style for narrative. I feel that story is the basic element of fiction though that ideal is not popular with disciples of the 'new novel.' They remind me of the painter who couldn't paint people, so he painted chairs."

Malamud also rejected the classification of "Jewish writer":

> I'm an American, I'm a Jew, and I write for all men. A novelist has to, or he's built himself a cage. I write about Jews, when I write about Jews, because they set my imagination going. I know something about their history, the quality of their experience and belief, and of their literature, though not as much as I would like. Like many writers I'm influenced especially by the Bible, both Testaments. . . . the point I'm making is that I was born in America and respond, in American life, to more than Jewish experience. I write for those who read.

ADDITIONAL READING

The People and Uncollected Stories, ed. Robert Giroux, 1989.

Sidney Richman, *Bernard Malamud,* 1966; Glenn Meeter, *Bernard Malamud and Philip Roth: A Critical Essay,* 1968; Rita Kosofsky, *Bernard Malamud: An Annotated Checklist,* 1970; Leslie A. Field and Joyce W. Field, eds., *Bernard Malamud and the Critics,* 1970; Sandy Cohen, *Bernard Malamud and the Trial by Love,* 1974; Robert Ducharme, *Art and Idea in the Novels of Bernard Malamud,* 1974; Leslie A. Field and Joyce W. Field, eds., *Bernard Malamud: A Collection of Critical Essays,* 1974; Iska Alter, *The Good Man's Dilemma: Social Criticism in the Fiction of Bernard Malamud,* 1981; Jeffrey Helterman, *Understanding Bernard Malamud,* 1985; Joel Salzberg, ed., *Critical Essays on Bernard Malamud,* 1987.

TEXT

The Stories of Bernard Malamud, 1983.

The Magic Barrel

Not long ago there lived in uptown New York, in a small, almost meager room, though crowded with books, Leo Finkle, a rabbinical student at the Yeshiva University.[1] Finkle, after six years of study, was to be ordained in June and had been advised by an acquaintance that he might find it easier to win himself a congregation if he were married. Since he had no present prospects of marriage, after two tormented days of turning it over in his mind, he called in Pinye Salzman, a marriage broker whose two-line advertisement he had read in the *Forward.*[2]

The matchmaker appeared one night out of the dark fourth-floor hallway of the graystone rooming house where Finkle lived, grasping a black, strapped portfolio that had been worn thin with use. Salzman, who had been long in the business, was of slight but dignified build, wearing an old hat, and an overcoat too short and tight for him. He smelled frankly of fish, which he loved to eat, and although he was missing a few teeth, his presence was not displeasing, because of an amiable manner curiously contrasted with mournful eyes. His voice, his lips, his wisp of beard, his bony fingers

---

[1] A university in New York City; "yeshiva" indicates seminary.
[2] The Yiddish-language *The Jewish Daily Forward,* published in New York City.

were animated, but give him a moment of repose and his mild blue eyes revealed a depth of sadness, a characteristic that put Leo a little at ease although the situation, for him, was inherently tense.

He at once informed Salzman why he had asked him to come, explaining that but for his parents, who had married comparatively late in life, he was alone in the world. He had for six years devoted himself almost entirely to his studies, as a result of which, understandably, he had found himself without time for social life and the company of young women. Therefore he thought it the better part of trial and error — of embarrassing fumbling — to call in an experienced person to advise him on these matters. He remarked in passing that the function of the marriage broker was ancient and honorable, highly approved in the Jewish community, because it made practical the necessary without hindering joy. Moreover, his own parents had been brought together by a matchmaker. They had made, if not a financially profitable marriage — since neither had possessed any worldly goods to speak of — at least a successful one in the sense of their everlasting devotion to each other. Salzman listened in embarrassed surprise, sensing a sort of apology. Later, however, he experienced a glow of pride in his work, an emotion that had left him years ago, and he heartily approved of Finkle.

The two went to their business. Leo had led Salzman to the only clear place in the room, a table near a window that overlooked the lamp-lit city. He seated himself at the matchmaker's side but facing him, attempting by an act of will to suppress the unpleasant tickle in his throat. Salzman eagerly unstrapped his portfolio and removed a loose rubber band from a thin packet of much-handled cards. As he flipped through them, a gesture and sound that physically hurt Leo, the student pretended not to see and gazed steadfastly out the window. Although it was still February, winter was on its last legs, signs of which he had for the first time in years begun to notice. He now observed the round white moon, moving high in the sky through a cloud menagerie, and watched with half-open mouth as it penetrated a huge hen, and dropped out of her like an egg laying itself. Salzman, though pretending through eyeglasses he had just slipped on to be engaged in scanning the writing on the cards, stole occasional glances at the young man's distinguished face, noting with pleasure the long, severe scholar's nose, brown eyes heavy with learning, sensitive yet ascetic lips, and a certain almost hollow quality of the dark cheeks. He gazed around at shelves upon shelves of books and let out a soft, contented sigh.

When Leo's eyes fell upon the cards, he counted six spread out in Salzman's hand.

"So few?" he asked in disappointment.

"You wouldn't believe me how much cards I got in my office," Salzman replied. "The drawers are already filled to the top, so I keep them now in a barrel, but is every girl good for a new rabbi?"

Leo blushed at this, regretting all he had revealed of himself in a curriculum vitae he had sent to Salzman. He had thought it best to acquaint him with his strict standards and specifications, but in having done so, felt he had told the marriage broker more than was absolutely necessary.

He hesitantly inquired, "Do you keep photographs of your clients on file?"

"First comes family, amount of dowry, also what kind promises," Salzman replied, unbuttoning his tight coat and settling himself in the chair. "After comes pictures, rabbi."

"Call me Mr. Finkle. I'm not yet a rabbi."

Salzman said he would, but instead called him doctor, which he changed to rabbi when Leo was not listening too attentively.

Salzman adjusted his horn-rimmed spectacles, gently cleared his throat, and read in an eager voice the contents of the top card:

"Sophie P. Twenty-four years. Widow one year. No children. Educated high school and two years college. Father promises eight thousand dollars. Has wonderful wholesale business. Also real estate. On the mother's side comes teachers, also one actor. Well known on Second Avenue."

Leo gazed up in surprise. "Did you say a widow?"

"A widow don't mean spoiled, rabbi. She lived with her husband maybe four months. He was a sick boy she made a mistake to marry him."

"Marrying a widow has never entered my mind."

"This is because you have no experience. A widow, especially if she is young and healthy like this girl, is a wonderful person to marry. She will be thankful to you the rest of her life. Believe me, if I was looking now for a bride, I would marry a widow."

Leo reflected, then shook his head.

Salzman hunched his shoulders in an almost imperceptible gesture of disappointment. He placed the card down on the wooden table and began to read another:

"Lily H. High school teacher. Regular. Not a substitute. Has savings and new Dodge car. Lived in Paris one year. Father is successful dentist thirty-five years. Interested in professional man. Well-Americanized family. Wonderful opportunity.

"I know her personally," said Salzman. "I wish you could see this girl. She is a doll. Also very intelligent. All day you could talk to her about books and theyater and what not. She also knows current events."

"I don't believe you mentioned her age?"

"Her age?" Salzman said, raising his brows. "Her age is thirty-two years."

Leo said after a while, "I'm afraid that seems a little too old."

Salzman let out a laugh. "So how old are you, rabbi?"

"Twenty-seven."

"So what is the difference, tell me, between twenty-seven and thirty-two? My own wife is seven years older than me. So what did I suffer? — Nothing. If Rothschild's[3] a daughter wants to marry you, would you say on account her age, no?"

"Yes," Leo said dryly.

Salzman shook off the no in the yes. "Five years don't mean a thing. I give you my word that when you will live with her for one week you will forget her age. What does it mean five years — that she lived more and knows more than somebody who is younger? On this girl, God bless her, years are not wasted. Each one that it comes makes better the bargain."

"What subject does she teach in high school?"

"Languages. If you heard the way she speaks French, you will think it is music. I am in the business twenty-five years, and I recommend her with my whole heart. Believe me, I know what I'm talking, rabbi."

"What's on the next card?" Leo said abruptly.

Salzman reluctantly turned up the third card:

"Ruth K. Nineteen years. Honor student. Father offers thirteen thousand cash to the right bridegroom. He is a medical doctor. Stomach specialist with marvelous practice. Brother-in-law owns own garment business. Particular people."

Salzman looked as if he had read his trump card.

"Did you say nineteen?" Leo asked with interest.

"On the dot."

"Is she attractive?" He blushed. "Pretty?"

Salzman kissed his fingertips. "A little doll. On this I give you my word. Let me call the father tonight and you will see what means pretty."

But Leo was troubled. "You're sure she's that young?"

"This I am positive. The father will show you the birth certificate."

"Are you positive there isn't something wrong with her?" Leo insisted.

"Who says there is wrong?"

---

[3]An international Jewish banking family, especially well-established in France.

"I don't understand why an American girl her age should go to a marriage broker."

A smile spread over Salzman's face.

"So for the same reason you went, she comes."

Leo flushed. "I am pressed for time."

Salzman, realizing he had been tactless, quickly explained. "The father came, not her. He wants she should have the best, so he looks around himself. When we will locate the right boy he will introduce him and encourage. This makes a better marriage than if a young girl without experience takes for herself. I don't have to tell you this."

"But don't you think this young girl believes in love?" Leo spoke uneasily.

Salzman was about to guffaw but caught himself and said soberly, "Love comes with the right person, not before."

Leo parted dry lips but did not speak. Noticing that Salzman had snatched a glance at the next card, he cleverly asked, "How is her health?"

"Perfect," Salzman said, breathing with difficulty. "Of course, she is a little lame on her right foot from an auto accident that it happened to her when she was twelve years, but nobody notices on account she is so brilliant and also beautiful."

Leo got up heavily and went to the window. He felt curiously bitter and upbraided himself for having called in the marriage broker. Finally, he shook his head.

"Why not?" Salzman persisted, the pitch of his voice rising.

"Because I detest stomach specialists."

"So what do you care what is his business? After you marry her do you need him? Who says he must come every Friday night in your house?"

Ashamed of the way the talk was going, Leo dismissed Salzman, who went home with heavy, melancholy eyes.

Though he had felt only relief at the marriage broker's departure, Leo was in low spirits the next day. He explained it as arising from Salzman's failure to produce a suitable bride for him. He did not care for his type of clientele. But when Leo found himself hesitating whether to seek out another matchmaker, one more polished than Pinye, he wondered if it could be—his protestations to the contrary, and although he honored his father and mother—that he did not, in essence, care for the matchmaking institution? This thought he quickly put out of mind yet found himself still upset. All day he ran around in the woods—missed an important appointment, forgot to give out his laundry, walked out of a Broadway cafeteria without paying and had to run back with the ticket in his hand; had even not recognized his landlady in the street when she passed with a friend and courteously called out, "A good evening to you, Doctor Finkle." By nightfall, however, he had regained sufficient calm to sink his nose into a book and there found peace from his thoughts.

Almost at once there came a knock on the door. Before Leo could say enter, Salzman, commercial cupid, was standing in the room. His face was gray and meager, his expression hungry, and he looked as if he would expire on his feet. Yet the marriage broker managed, by some trick of the muscles, to display a broad smile.

"So good evening. I am invited?"

Leo nodded, disturbed to see him again, yet unwilling to ask the man to leave.

Beaming still, Salzman laid his portfolio on the table. "Rabbi, I got for you tonight good news."

"I've asked you not to call me rabbi. I'm still a student."

"Your worries are finished. I have for you a first-class bride."

"Leave me in peace concerning this subject." Leo pretended lack of interest.

"The world will dance at your wedding."

"Please, Mr. Salzman, no more."

"But first must come back my strength," Salzman said weakly. He fumbled with the portfolio straps and took out of the leather case an oily paper bag, from which he extracted a hard, seeded roll and a small smoked whitefish. With a quick motion of his hand he stripped the fish out of its skin and began ravenously to chew. "All day in a rush," he muttered.

Leo watched him eat.

"A sliced tomato you have maybe?" Salzman hesitantly inquired.

"No."

The marriage broker shut his eyes and ate. When he had finished he carefully cleaned up the crumbs and rolled up the remains of the fish, in the paper bag. His spectacled eyes roamed the room until he discovered, amid some piles of books, a one-burner gas stove. Lifting his hat he humbly asked, "A glass tea you got, rabbi?"

Conscience-stricken, Leo rose and brewed the tea. He served it with a chunk of lemon and two cubes of lump sugar, delighting Salzman.

After he had drunk his tea, Salzman's strength and good spirits were restored.

"So tell me, rabbi," he said amiably, "you considered some more the three clients I mentioned yesterday?"

"There was no need to consider."

"Why not?"

"None of them suits me."

"What then suits you?"

Leo let it pass because he could give only a confused answer.

Without waiting for a reply, Salzman asked, "You remember this girl I talked to you—the high school teacher?"

"Age thirty-two?"

But, surprisingly, Salzman's face lit in a smile. "Age twenty-nine."

Leo shot him a look. "Reduced from thirty-two?"

"A mistake," Salzman avowed. "I talked today with the dentist. He took me to his safety deposit box and showed me the birth certificate. She was twenty-nine years last August. They made her a party in the mountains where she went for her vacation. When her father spoke to me the first time I forgot to write the age and I told you thirty-two, but now I remember this was a different client, a widow."

"The same one you told me about, I thought she was twenty-four?"

"A different. Am I responsible that the world is filled with widows?"

"No, but I'm not interested in them, nor, for that matter, in schoolteachers."

Salzman pulled his clasped hands to his breast. Looking at the ceiling he devoutly exclaimed, "Yiddishe kinder,[4] what can I say to somebody that he is not interested in high school teachers? So what then you are interested?"

Leo flushed but controlled himself.

"In what else will you be interested," Salzman went on, "if you not interested in this fine girl that she speaks four languages and has personally in the bank ten thousand dollars? Also her father guarantees further twelve thousand. Also she has a new car, wonderful clothes, talks on all subjects, and she will give you a first-class home and children. How near do we come in our life to paradise?"

"If she's so wonderful, why wasn't she married ten years ago?"

"Why?" said Salzman with a heavy laugh. "—Why? Because she is *partikiler*. This is why. She wants the *best*."

Leo was silent, amused at how he had entangled himself. But Salzman had aroused his interest in Lily H., and he began seriously to consider calling on her. When the marriage broker observed how intently Leo's mind was at work on the facts he had supplied, he felt certain they would soon come to an agreement.

Late Saturday afternoon, conscious of Salzman, Leo Finkle walked with Lily Hirschorn along Riverside Drive. He walked briskly and erectly, wearing with dis-

---

4"Yiddish children" (German).

tinction the black fedora he had that morning taken with trepidation out of the dusty hat box on his closet shelf, and the heavy black Saturday coat he had thoroughly whisked clean. Leo also owned a walking stick, a present from a distant relative, but quickly put temptation aside and did not use it. Lily, petite and not unpretty, had on something signifying the approach of spring. She was au courant,[5] animatedly, with all sorts of subjects, and he weighed her words and found her surprisingly sound — score another for Salzman, whom he uneasily sensed to be somewhere around, hiding perhaps high in a tree along the street, flashing the lady signals with a pocket mirror; or perhaps a cloven-hoofed Pan,[6] piping nuptial ditties as he danced his invisible way before them, strewing wild buds on the walk and purple grapes in their path, symbolizing fruit of a union, though there was of course still none.

Lily startled Leo by remarking, "I was thinking of Mr. Salzman, a curious figure, wouldn't you say?"

Not certain what to answer, he nodded.

She bravely went on, blushing, "I for one am grateful for his introducing us. Aren't you?"

He courteously replied, "I am."

"I mean," she said with a little laugh — and it was all in good taste, or at least gave the effect of being not in bad — "do you mind that we came together so?"

He was not displeased with her honesty, recognizing that she meant to set the relationship aright, and understanding that it took a certain amount of experience in life, and courage, to want to do it quite that way. One had to have some sort of past to make that kind of beginning.

He said that he did not mind. Salzman's function was traditional and honorable — valuable for what it might achieve, which, he pointed out, was frequently nothing.

Lily agreed with a sigh. They walked on for a while and she said after a long silence, again with a nervous laugh, "Would you mind if I asked you something a little bit personal? Frankly, I find the subject fascinating." Although Leo shrugged, she went on half embarrassedly, "How was it that you came to your calling? I mean, was it a sudden passionate inspiration?"

Leo, after a time, slowly replied, "I was always interested in the Law."

"You saw revealed in it the presence of the Highest?"

He nodded and changed the subject. "I understand that you spent a little time in Paris, Miss Hirschorn?"

"Oh, did Mr. Salzman tell you, Rabbi Finkle?" Leo winced but she went on, "It was ages ago and almost forgotten. I remember I had to return for my sister's wedding."

And Lily would not be put off. "When," she asked in a slightly trembly voice, "did you become enamored of God?"

He stared at her. Then it came to him that she was talking not about Leo Finkle but a total stranger, some mystical figure, perhaps even passionate prophet that Salzman had dreamed up for her — no relation to the living or dead. Leo trembled with rage and weakness. The trickster had obviously sold her a bill of goods, just as he had him, who'd expected to become acquainted with a young lady of twenty-nine, only to behold, the moment he had laid eyes upon her strained and anxious face, a woman past thirty-five and aging rapidly. Only his self-control had kept him this long in her presence.

"I am not," he said gravely, "a talented religious person," and in seeking words to go on, found himself possessed by shame and fear. "I think," he said in a strained manner, "that I came to God not because I loved Him but because I did not."

This confession he spoke harshly because its unexpectedness shook him.

Lily wilted. Leo saw a profusion of loaves of bread go flying like ducks high over

---

[5] "Up to date" (French).
[6] Greek god of flocks and shepherds, part man and part goat.

his head, not unlike the winged loaves by which he had counted himself to sleep last night. Mercifully, then, it snowed, which he would not put past Salzman's machinations.

He was infuriated with the marriage broker and swore he would throw him out of the room the moment he reappeared. But Salzman did not come that night, and when Leo's anger had subsided, an unaccountable despair grew in its place. At first he thought this was caused by his disappointment in Lily, but before long it became evident that he had involved himself with Salzman without a true knowledge of his own intent. He gradually realized—with an emptiness that seized him with six hands—that he had called in the broker to find him a bride because he was incapable of doing it himself. This terrifying insight he had derived as a result of his meeting and conversation with Lily Hirschorn. Her probing questions had somehow irritated him into revealing—to himself more than her—the true nature of his relationship to God, and from that it had come upon him, with shocking force, that apart from his parents, he had never loved anyone. Or perhaps it went the other way, that he did not love God so well as he might, because he had not loved man. It seemed to Leo that his whole life stood starkly revealed and he saw himself for the first time as he truly was—unloved and loveless. This bitter but somehow not fully unexpected revelation brought him to a point of panic, controlled only by extraordinary effort. He covered his face with his hands and cried.

The week that followed was the worst of his life. He did not eat and lost weight. His beard darkened and grew ragged. He stopped attending seminars and almost never opened a book. He seriously considered leaving the Yeshiva, although he was deeply troubled at the thought of the loss of all his years of study—saw them like pages torn from a book, strewn over the city—and at the devastating effect of this decision upon his parents. But he had lived without knowledge of himself, and never in the Five Books[7] and all the Commentaries—mea culpa[8]—had the truth been revealed to him. He did not know where to turn, and in all this desolating loneliness there was no *to whom*, although he often thought of Lily but not once could bring himself to go downstairs and make the call. He became touchy and irritable, especially with his landlady, who asked him all manner of personal questions; on the other hand, sensing his own disagreeableness, he waylaid her on the stairs and apologized abjectly, until, mortified, she ran from him. Out of this, however, he drew the consolation that he was a Jew and that a Jew suffered. But gradually, as the long and terrible week drew to a close, he regained his composure and some idea of purpose in life: to go on as planned. Although he was imperfect, the ideal was not. As for his quest of a bride, the thought of continuing afflicted him with anxiety and heartburn, yet perhaps with this new knowledge of himself he would be more successful than in the past. Perhaps love would now come to him and a bride to that love. And for this sanctified seeking who needed a Salzman?

The marriage broker, a skeleton with haunted eyes, returned that very night. He looked, withal, the picture of frustrated expectancy—as if he had steadfastly waited the week at Miss Lily Hirschorn's side for a telephone call that never came.

Casually coughing, Salzman came immediately to the point: "So how did you like her?"

Leo's anger rose and he could not refrain from chiding the matchmaker: "Why did you lie to me, Salzman?"

Salzman's pale face went dead white, the world had snowed on him.

"Did you not state that she was twenty-nine?" Leo insisted.

"I give you my word—"

"She was thirty-five, if a day. *At least* thirty-five."

---

[7] The five books of Moses ("pentateuch"), called the "Torah."
[8] "My fault" (Latin).

"Of this don't be too sure. Her father told me—"

"Never mind. The worst of it is that you lied to her."

"How did I lie to her, tell me?"

"You told her things about me that weren't true. You made me out to be more, consequently less than I am. She had in mind a totally different person, a sort of semi-mystical Wonder Rabbi."

"All I said, you was a religious man."

"I can imagine."

Salzman sighed. "This is my weakness that I have," he confessed. "My wife says to me I shouldn't be a salesman, but when I have two fine people that they would be wonderful to be married, I am so happy that I talk too much." He smiled wanly. "This is why Salzman is a poor man."

Leo's anger left him. "Well, Salzman, I'm afraid that's all."

The marriage broker fastened hungry eyes on him.

"You don't want any more a bride?"

"I do," said Leo, "but I have decided to seek her in another way. I am no longer interested in an arranged marriage. To be frank, I now admit the necessity of pre-marital love. That is, I want to be in love with the one I marry."

"Love?" said Salzman, astounded. After a moment he remarked, "For us, our love is our life, not for the ladies. In the ghetto they—"

"I know, I know," said Leo. "I've thought of it often. Love, I have said to myself, should be a product of living and worship rather than its own end. Yet for myself I find it necessary to establish the level of my need and fulfill it."

Salzman shrugged but answered, "Listen, rabbi, if you want love, this I can find for you also. I have such beautiful clients that you will love them the minute your eyes will see them."

Leo smiled unhappily. "I'm afraid you don't understand."

But Salzman hastily unstrapped his portfolio and withdrew a manila packet from it.

"Pictures," he said, quickly laying the envelope on the table.

Leo called after him to take the pictures away, but as if on the wings of the wind, Salzman had disappeared.

March came. Leo had returned to his regular routine. Although he felt not quite himself yet—lacked energy—he was making plans for a more active social life. Of course it would cost something, but he was an expert in cutting corners; and when there were no corners left he would make circles rounder. All the while Salzman's pictures had lain on the table, gathering dust. Occasionally as Leo sat studying, or enjoying a cup of tea, his eyes fell on the manila envelope, but he never opened it.

The days went by and no social life to speak of developed with a member of the opposite sex—it was difficult, given the circumstances of his situation. One morning Leo toiled up the stairs to his room and stared out the window at the city. Although the day was bright his view of it was dark. For some time he watched the people in the street below hurrying along and then turned with a heavy heart to his little room. On the table was the packet. With a sudden relentless gesture he tore it open. For a half hour he stood by the table in a state of excitement, examining the photographs of the ladies Salzman had included. Finally, with a deep sigh he put them down. There were six, of varying degrees of attractiveness, but look at them long enough and they all became Lily Hirschorn: all past their prime, all starved behind bright smiles, not a true personality in the lot. Life, despite their frantic yoohooings, had passed them by; they were pictures in a briefcase that stank of fish. After a while, however, as Leo attempted to return the photographs into the envelope, he found in it another, a snapshot of the type taken by a machine for a quarter. He gazed at it a moment and let out a low cry.

Her face deeply moved him. Why, he could at first not say. It gave him the impression of youth—spring flowers, yet age—a sense of having been used to the bone, wasted; this came from the eyes, which were hauntingly familiar, yet absolutely strange. He had a vivid impression that he had met her before, but try as he might he could not place her although he could almost recall her name, as if he had read it in her own handwriting. No, this couldn't be; he would have remembered her. It was not, he affirmed, that she had an extraordinary beauty—no, though her face was attractive enough; it was that *something* about her moved him. Feature for feature, even some of the ladies of the photographs could do better; but she leaped forth to his heart—had *lived*, or wanted to—more than just wanted, perhaps regretted how she had lived—had somehow deeply suffered: it could be seen in the depths of those reluctant eyes, and from the way the light enclosed and shone from her, and within her, opening realms of possibility: this was her own. Her he desired. His head ached and eyes narrowed with the intensity of his gazing, then as if an obscure fog had blown up in the mind, he experienced fear of her and was aware that he had received an impression, somehow, of evil. He shuddered, saying softly, it is thus with us all. Leo brewed some tea in a small pot and sat sipping it without sugar, to calm himself. But before he had finished drinking, again with excitement he examined the face and found it good: good for Leo Finkle. Only such a one could understand him and help him seek whatever he was seeking. She might, perhaps, love him. How she had happened to be among the discards in Salzman's barrel he could never guess, but he knew he must urgently go find her.

Leo rushed downstairs, grabbed up the Bronx telephone book, and searched for Salzman's home address. He was not listed, nor was his office. Neither was he in the Manhattan book. But Leo remembered having written down the address on a slip of paper after he had read Salzman's advertisement in the "personals" column of the *Forward*. He ran up to his room and tore through his papers, without luck. It was exasperating. Just when he needed the matchmaker he was nowhere to be found. Fortunately Leo remembered to look in his wallet. There on a card he found his name written and a Bronx address. No phone number was listed, the reason—Leo now recalled—he had originally communicated with Salzman by letter. He got on his coat, put a hat on over his skullcap and hurried to the subway station. All the way to the far end of the Bronx he sat on the edge of his seat. He was more than once tempted to take out the picture and see if the girl's face was as he remembered, but he refrained, allowing the snapshot to remain in his inside coat pocket, content to have her so close. When the train pulled into the station he was waiting at the door and bolted out. He quickly located the street Salzman had advertised.

The building he sought was less than a block from the subway, but it was not an office building, nor even a loft, nor a store in which one could rent office space. It was a very old tenement house. Leo found Salzman's name in pencil on a soiled tag under the bell and climbed three dark flights to his apartment. When he knocked, the door was opened by a thin, asthmatic, gray-haired woman, in felt slippers.

"Yes?" she said, expecting nothing. She listened without listening. He could have sworn he had seen her, too, before but knew it was an illusion.

"Salzman—does he live here? Pinye Salzman?" he said, "the matchmaker?"

She stared at him a long minute. "Of course."

He felt embarrassed. "Is he in?"

"No." Her mouth, though left open, offered nothing more.

"The matter is urgent. Can you tell me where his office is?"

"In the air." She pointed upward.

"You mean he has no office?" Leo asked.

"In his socks."

He peered into the apartment. It was sunless and dingy, one large room divided by a half-open curtain, beyond which he could see a sagging metal bed. The near side of the room was crowded with rickety chairs, old bureaus, a three-legged table, racks of cooking utensils, and all the apparatus of a kitchen. But there was no sign of Salzman or his magic barrel, probably also a figment of the imagination. An odor of frying fish made Leo weak to the knees.

"Where is he?" he insisted. "I've got to see your husband."

At length she answered, "So who knows where he is? Every time he thinks a new thought he runs to a different place. Go home, he will find you."

"Tell him Leo Finkle."

She gave no sign she had heard.

He walked downstairs, depressed.

But Salzman, breathless, stood waiting at his door.

Leo was astounded and overjoyed. "How did you get here before me?"

"I rushed."

"Come inside."

They entered. Leo fixed tea, and a sardine sandwich for Salzman. As they were drinking he reached behind him for the packet of pictures and handed them to the marriage broker.

Salzman put down his glass and said expectantly, "You found somebody you like?"

"Not among these."

The marriage broker turned away.

"Here is the one I want." Leo held forth the snapshot.

Salzman slipped on his glasses and took the picture into his trembling hand. He turned ghastly and let out a groan.

"What's the matter?" cried Leo.

"Excuse me. Was an accident this picture. She isn't for you."

Salzman frantically shoved the manila packet into his portfolio. He thrust the snapshot into his pocket and fled down the stairs.

Leo, after momentary paralysis, gave chase and cornered the marriage broker in the vestibule. The landlady made hysterical outcries but neither of them listened.

"Give me back the picture, Salzman."

"No." The pain in his eyes was terrible.

"Tell me who she is then."

"This I can't tell you. Excuse me."

He made to depart, but Leo, forgetting himself, seized the matchmaker by his tight coat and shook him frenziedly.

"*Please*," sighed Salzman. "*Please.*"

Leo ashamedly let him go. "Tell me who she is," he begged. "It's very important for me to know."

"She is not for you. She is a wild one—wild, without shame. This is not a bride for a rabbi."

"What do you mean wild?"

"Like an animal. Like a dog. For her to be poor was a sin. This is why to me she is dead now."

"In God's name, what do you mean?"

"Her I can't introduce to you," Salzman cried.

"Why are you so excited?"

"Why, he asks," Salzman said, bursting into tears. "This is my baby, my Stella, she should burn in hell."

Leo hurried up to bed and hid under the covers. Under the covers he thought his life through. Although he soon fell asleep he could not sleep her out of his mind. He woke, beating his breast. Though he prayed to be rid of her, his prayers went unanswered. Through days of torment he endlessly struggled not to love her; fearing success, he escaped it. He then concluded to convert her to goodness, himself to God. The idea alternately nauseated and exalted him.

He perhaps did not know that he had come to a final decision until he encountered Salzman in a Broadway cafeteria. He was sitting alone at a rear table, sucking the bony remains of a fish. The marriage broker appeared haggard, and transparent to the point of vanishing.

Salzman looked up at first without recognizing him. Leo had grown a pointed beard and his eyes were weighted with wisdom.

"Salzman," he said, "love has at last come to my heart."

"Who can love from a picture?" mocked the marriage broker.

"It is not impossible."

"If you can love her, then you can love anybody. Let me show you some new clients that they just sent me their photographs. One is a little doll."

"Just her I want," Leo murmured.

"Don't be a fool, doctor. Don't bother with her."

"Put me in touch with her, Salzman," Leo said humbly. "Perhaps I can be of service."

Salzman had stopped eating and Leo understood with emotion that it was now arranged.

Leaving the cafeteria, he was, however, afflicted by a tormenting suspicion that Salzman had planned it all to happen this way.

Leo was informed by letter that she would meet him on a certain corner, and she was there one spring night, waiting under a street lamp. He appeared, carrying a small bouquet of violets and rosebuds. Stella stood by the lamppost, smoking. She wore white with red shoes, which fitted his expectations, although in a troubled moment he had imagined the dress red, and only the shoes white. She waited uneasily and shyly. From afar he saw that her eyes—clearly her father's—were filled with desperate innocence. He pictured, in her, his own redemption. Violins and lit candles revolved in the sky. Leo ran forward with flowers outthrust.

Around the corner, Salzman, leaning against a wall, chanted prayers for the dead.

1954, 1958

SAUL BELLOW
(b. 1915)

Saul Bellow has tended to go against the grain of most of the so-called post-modernist movements in fiction after the war. At one point in the 1960s Bellow observed that it had become fashionable "to expose, to disenchant, to hate and to experience disgust," and to "see through to the class origins of one's affection for one's grandfather, or to reveal the hypocritical weakness and baseness at the heart of friendships." Bellow impatiently brushed aside this "supercivilized" posturing: "Nevertheless there are friendships, affinities, natural feelings, rooted norms. People do on the whole agree, for instance, that it is wrong to murder." And as for the writers who were anxiety-ridden about absorbing and going beyond the latest in the technique of fiction, Bellow offered this advice: "To labor to create vanguard conditions is historicism. It means that people have been reading books of culture-history and have concluded retrospectively that originality is impossible without such conditions. But genius is always, without strain, avant-garde. Its departure from tradition is not the result of caprice or of policy but of an inner necessity." In such comments as these, Bellow has consistently

1804   The Age of Uncertainty: After the Second World War (1945-Present)

placed himself on the side of old-fashioned values and continuity in the fictional tradition.

Bellow was born in Quebec, Canada, of deeply religious Jewish parents who had immigrated from Russia. When he was nine, his family moved to Chicago, where he grew up in one of Chicago's famed multilingual ethnic neighborhoods. He attended the University of Chicago for three years and then in 1935 transferred to Northwestern to take a degree in anthropology and sociology. He started graduate work in anthropology at the University of Wisconsin in 1937 but decided to throw it over in 1938 to write fiction. He worked at a variety of jobs to support himself, teaching, doing editorial work, and serving in the merchant marine during the Second World War.

In the early 1940s he began to place stories in the little magazines and in 1944 published his first novel, *Dangling Man,* an account of an individual living in a kind of social limbo as he waits to be drafted into the army. Bellow's second novel, *The Victim,* published in 1947, was a polished work exploring the relationship of a Jew and a Gentile, bound together in such inexplicable and subterranean ways as to suggest a shared identity—in the tradition of the "doppelganger" motif. Even though Bellow was well launched on his career as a novelist, he chose to continue in his academic career, begun in the mid-1940s at the University of Minnesota. He held appointments at New York University, Princeton, Bard, and in 1963 returned to the University of Chicago, where he has remained a Professor in the Committee on Social Thought (with joint appointments in other departments, including English).

To the surprise of critics, in his third work, *The Adventures of Augie March* (1953), Bellow abandoned the mode of the well-made, compact novel for the episodic, picaresque tradition. The novel won Bellow a wide audience as well as a National Book Award. In his novella *Seize the Day* (1956), Bellow appeared to return to the densely packed short work of his earlier period, exploring the nature and psyche of an habitual failure trapped in the orbit of a successful, unsympathetic father. But the rollicking tale of a restless, middle-aged American's experience in Africa, *Henderson the Rain King* (1959), and the richly documented account of the troubled love-life of a Jewish intellectual, *Herzog* (1964), who is absorbed in the letters that he writes (but never sends) to world and mythic figures, revealed that Bellow was unpredictable in his development as a writer. Widely read as a "divorce novel," *Herzog* grew in part out of Bellow's own experience in this American institution—he had gone through two before this novel (and he has gone through others since). With *Herzog,* Bellow won his second National Book Award.

In *Mr. Sammler's Planet* (1970), Bellow presented a poignant portrait of an accidental survivor of the holocaust, old Mr. Sammler, who, in the midst of what seems to be a general breakdown of civilization in New York in the chaotic 1960s, has come to the point that the only writer he wants to read is the German medievel mystic Meister Eckhardt. It won Bellow his third National Book Award and praise by many critics as his greatest novel. Bellow's next novel, *Humboldt's Gift* (1975), portraying a talented, poor, and slightly mad poet, was based in part on Bellow's longtime friend, the poet Delmore Schwartz who had died alone and in poverty in 1966. In 1976, Bellow became the eighth American to receive the Nobel Prize for Literature.

Bellow's later novels include *The Dean's December* (1982) and *More Die of Heartbreak* (1987). In 1989 he published two novellas, *A Theft* and *The Bellarosa Connection.* He has published two volumes of short stories, *Moseby's Memoirs* (1968) and

Him with His Foot in His Mouth (1984), and an account of his 1975 visit to Israel in *To Jerusalem and Back* (1976). In the 1960s Bellow tried his hand at writing plays, but without great success. One drama, *The Last Analysis,* was produced in 1964 and published in 1965.

At a time when many novelists were, like Nabokov, composing what seemed to be "riddles with elegant solutions," Bellow filled work after work with that "density of specification" which evoked a world his readers recognized as the one they inhabited. And moreover, the quanderies his characters confronted were the quandaries Bellow's readers felt they faced. Bellow's defining characteristics are all on display, and his strategies and techniques at the fullness of their power, in the short story reprinted here, "A Silver Dish" (1978), in which a son has become his father's keeper, confronting the question, "What do you do about death — in this case, the death of an old father?" Although secular on the surface, the story in its depths is profoundly religious.

Bellow himself has called attention to a metaphysical dimension in his work that has seemed to surge to the fore in the later stories (though it was no doubt there from the beginning). In a 1984 interview, he was pressed about his religious belief. He replied that although he grew up in a religious family, he finally turned away from a "suffocating orthodoxy": "But the religious feeling was very strong in me when I was young and it has persisted. I would *never* describe myself as an atheist or agnostic; I always thought those were terms for a pathological state and that people who don't believe in God have something wrong with them. Just say I am a religious man in a retarded condition and the only way I can square myself is to write."

ADDITIONAL READING

Tony Tanner, *Saul Bellow,* 1965; Irving Malin, ed., *Saul Bellow and the Critics,* 1967; Earl Rovit, *Saul Bellow,* 1967; Brigitte Scheer-Schäzler, *Saul Bellow,* 1972; B. A. Sokoloff and Mark E. Posner, *Saul Bellow: A Comprehensive Bibliography,* 1973; Earl Rovit, ed., *Saul Bellow: A Collection of Critical Essays,* 1975; John Clayton, *Saul Bellow: In Defense of Man,* 1968, 1979; Stanley Trachtenberg, ed., *Critical Essays on Saul Bellow,* 1979; Mark Harris, *Saul Bellow: Drumlin Woodchuck,* 1980; Joseph F. McCadden, *The Flight from Women in the Fiction of Saul Bellow,* 1981; Eusebio L. Rodrigues, *Quest for the Human: An Exploration of Saul Bellow's Fiction,* 1982; Robert B. Dutton, *Saul Bellow,* 1971, 1982; L. H. Goldman, *Saul Bellow's Moral Vision: A Critical Study of the Jewish Experience,* 1983; Daniel Fuchs, *Saul Bellow: Vision and Revision,* 1983; Judie Newman, *Saul Bellow and History,* 1984; Jonathan Wilson, *On Bellow's Planet: Readings from the Dark Side,* 1985; Harold Bloom, ed., *Saul Bellow: Modern Critical Views,* 1986; Gloria L. Cronin and Blaine H. Hall, *Saul Bellow: An Annotated Bibliography,* Second Edition, 1987.

TEXT

Him with His Foot in His Mouth and Other Stories, 1984.

A Silver Dish

What do you do about death — in this case, the death of an old father? If you're a modern person, sixty years of age, and a man who's been around, like Woody Selbst, what do you do? Take this matter of mourning, and take it against a contemporary background. How, against a contemporary background, do you mourn an octogenarian father, nearly blind, his heart enlarged, his lungs filling with fluid, who creeps, stumbles, gives off the odors, the moldiness or gassiness, of old men. I *mean*!

As Woody put it, be realistic. Think what times these are. The papers daily give it to you—the Lufthansa pilot in Aden is described by the hostages on his knees, begging the Palestinian terrorists not to execute him, but they shoot him through the head.[1] Later they themselves are killed. And still others shoot others, or shoot themselves. That's what you read in the press, see on the tube, mention at dinner. We know now what goes daily through the whole of the human community, like a global death-peristalsis.[2]

Woody, a businessman in South Chicago, was not an ignorant person. He knew more such phrases than you would expect a tile contractor (offices, lobbies, lavatories) to know. The kind of knowledge he had was not the kind for which you get academic degrees. Although Woody had studied for two years in a seminary, preparing to be a minister. Two years of college during the Depression was more than most high-school graduates could afford. After that, in his own vital, picturesque, original way (Morris, his old man, was also, in his days of nature, vital and picturesque), Woody had read up on many subjects, subscribed to *Science* and other magazines that gave real information, and had taken night courses at De Paul and Northwestern in ecology, criminology, existentialism. Also he had traveled extensively in Japan, Mexico, and Africa, and there was an African experience that was especially relevant to mourning. It was this: on a launch near the Murchison Falls in Uganda, he had seen a buffalo calf seized by a crocodile from the bank of the White Nile. There were giraffes along the tropical river, and hippopotamuses, and baboons, and flamingos and other brilliant birds crossing the bright air in the heat of the morning, when the calf, stepping into the river to drink, was grabbed by the hoof and dragged down. The parent buffaloes couldn't figure it out. Under the water the calf still threshed, fought, churned the mud. Woody, the robust traveler, took this in as he sailed by, and to him it looked as if the parent cattle were asking each other dumbly what had happened. He chose to assume that there was pain in this, he read brute grief into it. On the White Nile, Woody had the impression that he had gone back to the pre-Adamite past, and he brought reflections on this impression home to South Chicago. He brought also a bundle of hashish from Kampala. In this he took a chance with the customs inspectors, banking perhaps on his broad build, frank face, high color. He didn't look like a wrongdoer, a bad guy; he looked like a good guy. But he liked taking chances. Risk was a wonderful stimulus. He threw down his trenchcoat on the customs counter. If the inspectors searched the pockets, he was prepared to say that the coat wasn't his. But he got away with it, and the Thanksgiving turkey was stuffed with hashish. This was much enjoyed. That was practically the last feast at which Pop, who also relished risk or defiance, was present. The hashish Woody had tried to raise in his backyard from the Africa seeds didn't take. But behind his warehouse, where the Lincoln Continental was parked, he kept a patch of marijuana. There was no harm at all in Woody, but he didn't like being entirely within the law. It was simply a question of self-respect.

After that Thanksgiving, Pop gradually sank as if he had a slow leak. This went on for some years. In and out of the hospital, he dwindled, his mind wandered, he couldn't even concentrate enough to complain, except in exceptional moments on the Sundays Woody regularly devoted to him. Morris, an amateur who once was taken seriously by Willie Hoppe,[3] the great pro himself, couldn't execute the simplest billiard shots anymore. He could only conceive shots; he began to theorize about

---

[1]Aden is a seaport and capital of the People's Democratic Republic of Yemen, site of a terrorist incident in October 1977, in which anti-Israeli Palestinians murdered the pilot of a German Lufthansa plane which they had highjacked over the French Riviera. After five days and stops in several countries, the plane was stormed and retaken by West German troops in Mogadishu, Somalia. The hijackers were killed and the hostages saved. In retaliation, associates of the hijackers killed the West German industrialist Hanns-Martin Schleyer, who had been kidnapped in September.

[2]Peristalsis: muscular contractions and dilations in the walls of tubular organs in the body, passing substances forward.

[3]William Frederick Hoppe (1887–1959), American billiard player and world champion during the early part of the century.

impossible three-cushion combinations. Halina, the Polish woman with whom Morris had lived for over forty years as man and wife, was too old herself now to run to the hospital. So Woody had to do it. There was Woody's mother, too—a Christian convert—needing care; she was over eighty and frequently hospitalized. Everybody had diabetes and pleurisy and arthritis and cataracts and cardiac pacemakers. And everybody had lived by the body, but the body was giving out.

There were Woody's two sisters as well, unmarried, in their fifties, very Christian, very straight, still living with Mama in an entirely Christian bungalow. Woody, who took full responsibility for them all, occasionally had to put one of the girls (they had become sick girls) in a mental institution. Nothing severe. The sisters were wonderful women, both of them gorgeous once, but neither of the poor things was playing with a full deck. And all the factions had to be kept separate—Mama, the Christian convert; the fundamentalist sisters; Pop, who read the Yiddish paper as long as he could still see print; Halina, a good Catholic. Woody, the seminary forty years behind him, described himself as an agnostic. Pop had no more religion than you could find in the Yiddish paper, but he made Woody promise to bury him among Jews, and that was where he lay now, in the Hawaiian shirt Woody had bought for him at the tilers' convention in Honolulu. Woody would allow no undertaker's assistant to dress him, but came to the parlor and buttoned the stiff into the shirt himself, and the old man went down looking like Ben-Gurion[4] in a simple wooden coffin, sure to rot fast. That was how Woody wanted it all. At the graveside, he had taken off and folded his jacket, rolled up his sleeves on thick freckled biceps, waved back the little tractor standing by, and shoveled the dirt himself. His big face, broad at the bottom, narrowed upward like a Dutch house. And, his small good lower teeth taking hold of the upper lip in his exertion, he performed the final duty of a son. He was very fit, so it must have been emotion, not the shoveling, that made him redden so. After the funeral, he went home with Halina and her son, a decent Polack like his mother, and talented, too—Mitosh played the organ at hockey and basketball games in the Stadium, which took a smart man because it was a rabble-rousing kind of occupation—and they had some drinks and comforted the old girl. Halina was true blue, always one hundred percent for Morris.

Then for the rest of the week Woody was busy, had jobs to run, office responsibilities, family responsibilities. He lived alone; as did his wife; as did his mistress: everybody in a separate establishment. Since his wife, after fifteen years of separation, had not learned to take care of herself, Woody did her shopping on Fridays, filled her freezer. He had to take her this week to buy shoes. Also, Friday night he always spent with Helen—Helen was his wife de facto. Saturday he did his big weekly shopping. Saturday night he devoted to Mom and his sisters. So he was too busy to attend to his own feelings except, intermittently, to note, to himself, "First Thursday in the grave." "First Friday, and fine weather." "First Saturday; he's got to be getting used to it." Under his breath he occasionally said, "Oh, Pop."

But it was Sunday that hit him, when the bells rang all over South Chicago—the Ukrainian, Roman Catholic, Greek, Russian, African Methodist churches, sounding off one after another. Woody had his offices in his warehouses, and there had built an apartment for himself, very spacious and convenient, in the top story. Because he left every Sunday morning at seven to spend the day with Pop, he had forgotten by how many churches Selbst Tile Company was surrounded. He was still in bed when he heard the bells, and all at once he knew how heartbroken he was. This sudden big heartache in a man of sixty, a practical, physical, healthy-minded, and experienced man, was deeply unpleasant. When he had an unpleasant condition, he believed in taking something for it. So he thought: What shall I take? There were plenty of

---

[4]David Ben-Gurion (1886–1973), one of the founders and the first prime minister of Israel (1949–53 and 1955–63).

remedies available. His cellar was stocked with cases of Scotch whisky, Polish vodka, Armagnac, Moselle, Burgundy. There were also freezers with steaks and with game and with Alaskan king crab. He bought with a broad hand—by the crate and by the dozen. But in the end, when he got out of bed, he took nothing but a cup of coffee. While the kettle was heating, he put on his Japanese judo-style suit and sat down to reflect.

Woody was moved when things were *honest*. Bearing beams were honest, undisguised concrete pillars inside high-rise apartments were honest. It was bad to cover up anything. He hated faking. Stone was honest. Metal was honest. These Sunday bells were very straight. They broke loose, they wagged and rocked, and the vibrations and the banging did something for him—cleansed his insides, purified his blood. A bell was a one-way throat, had only one thing to tell you and simply told it. He listened.

He had had some connections with bells and churches. He was after all something of a Christian. Born a Jew, he was a Jew facially, with a hint of Iroquois or Cherokee, but his mother had been converted more than fifty years ago by her brother-in-law, the Reverend Doctor Kovner. Kovner, a rabbinical student who had left the Hebrew Union College in Cincinnati to become a minister and establish a mission, had given Woody a partly Christian upbringing. Now, Pop was on the outs with these fundamentalists. He said that the Jews came to the mission to get coffee, bacon, canned pineapple, day-old bread, and dairy products. And if they had to listen to sermons, that was okay—this was the Depression and you couldn't be too particular—but he knew they sold the bacon.

The Gospels said it plainly: "Salvation is from the Jews."

Backing the Reverend Doctor were wealthy fundamentalists, mainly Swedes, eager to speed up the Second Coming by converting all Jews. The foremost of Kovner's backers was Mrs. Skoglund, who had inherited a large dairy business from her late husband. Woody was under her special protection.

Woody was fourteen years of age when Pop took off with Halina, who worked in his shop, leaving his difficult Christian wife and his converted son and his small daughters. He came to Woody in the backyard one spring day and said, "From now on you're the man of the house." Woody was practicing with a golf club, knocking off the heads of dandelions. Pop came into the yard in his good suit, which was too hot for the weather, and when he took off his fedora the skin of his head was marked with a deep ring and the sweat was sprinkled over his scalp—more drops than hairs. He said, "I'm going to move out." Pop was anxious, but he was set to go—determined. "It's no use. I can't live a life like this." Envisioning the life Pop simply *had* to live, his free life, Woody was able to picture him in the billiard parlor, under the El tracks in a crap game, or playing poker at Brown and Koppel's upstairs. "You're going to be the man of the house," said Pop. "It's okay. I put you all on welfare. I just got back from Wabansia Avenue, from the relief station." Hence the suit and the hat. "They're sending out a caseworker." Then he said, "You got to lend me money to buy gasoline—the caddie money you saved."

Understanding that Pop couldn't get away without his help, Woody turned over to him all he had earned at the Sunset Ridge Country Club in Winnetka.[5] Pop felt that the valuable life lesson he was transmitting was worth far more than these dollars, and whenever he was conning his boy a sort of high-priest expression came down over his bent nose, his ruddy face. The children, who got their finest ideas at the movies, called him Richard Dix. Later, when the comic strip came out, they said he was Dick Tracy.

As Woody now saw it, under the tumbling bells, he had bankrolled his own desertion. Ha ha! He found this delightful; and especially Pop's attitude of "That'll teach

---

[5]Wealthy Chicago suburb.

you to trust your father." For this was a demonstration on behalf of real life and free instincts, against religion and hypocrisy. But mainly it was aimed against being a fool, the disgrace of foolishness. Pop had it in for the Reverend Doctor Kovner, not because he was an apostate (Pop couldn't have cared less), not because the mission was a racket (he admitted that the Reverend Doctor was personally honest), but because Doctor Kovner behaved foolishly, spoke like a fool, and acted like a fiddler. He tossed his hair like a Paganini[6] (this was Woody's addition; Pop had never even heard of Paganini). Proof that he was not a spiritual leader was that he converted Jewish women by stealing their hearts. "He works up all those broads," said Pop. "He doesn't even know it himself, I swear he doesn't know how he gets them."

From the other side, Kovner often warned Woody, "Your father is a dangerous person. Of course, you love him; you should love him and forgive him, Voodrow, but you are old enough to understand he is leading a life of wice."

It was all petty stuff: Pop's sinning was on a boy level and therefore made a big impression on a boy. And on Mother. Are wives children, or what? Mother often said, "I hope you put that brute in your prayers. Look what he has done to us. But only pray for him, don't see him." But he saw him all the time. Woodrow was leading a double life, sacred and profane. He accepted Jesus Christ as his personal redeemer. Aunt Rebecca took advantage of this. She made him work. He had to work under Aunt Rebecca. He filled in for the janitor at the mission and settlement house. In winter, he had to feed the coal furnace, and on some nights he slept near the furnace room, on the pool table. He also picked the lock of the storeroom. He took canned pineapple and cut bacon from the flitch with his pocketknife. He crammed himself with uncooked bacon. He had a big frame to fill out.

Only now, sipping Melitta coffee, he asked himself: Had he been so hungry? No, he loved being reckless. He was fighting Aunt Rebecca Kovner when he took out his knife and got on a box to reach the bacon. She didn't know, she couldn't prove that Woody, such a frank, strong, positive boy, who looked you in the eye, so direct, was a thief also. But he was also a thief. Whenever she looked at him, he knew that she was seeing his father. In the curve of his nose, the movements of his eyes, the thickness of his body, in his healthy face, she saw that wicked savage Morris.

Morris, you see, had been a street boy in Liverpool—Woody's mother and her sister were British by birth. Morris's Polish family, on their way to America, abandoned him in Liverpool because he had an eye infection and they would all have been sent back from Ellis Island. They stopped awhile in England, but his eyes kept running and they ditched him. They slipped away, and he had to make out alone in Liverpool at the age of twelve. Mother came of better people. Pop, who slept in the cellar of her house, fell in love with her. At sixteen, scabbing during a seaman's strike, he shoveled his way across the Atlantic and jumped ship in Brooklyn. He became an American, and America never knew it. He voted without papers, he drove without a license, he paid no taxes, he cut every corner. Horses, cards, billiards, and women were his lifelong interests, in ascending order. Did he love anyone (he was so busy)? Yes, he loved Halina. He loved his son. To this day, Mother believed that he had loved her most and always wanted to come back. This gave her a chance to act the queen, with her plump wrists and faded Queen Victoria face. "The girls are instructed never to admit him," she said. The Empress of India speaking.

Bell-battered Woodrow's soul was whirling this Sunday morning, indoors and out, to the past, back to his upper corner of the warehouse, laid out with such originality—the bells coming and going, metal on naked metal, until the bell circle expanded over the whole of steel-making, oil-refining, power-producing mid-autumn South Chicago, and all its Croatians, Ukrainians, Greeks, Poles, and respectable blacks heading for their churches to hear Mass or to sing hymns.

---

[6]Niccolo Paganini (1782–1840), Italian composer and violinist.

Woody himself had been a good hymn singer. He still knew the hymns. He had testified, too. He was often sent by Aunt Rebecca to get up and tell a churchful of Scandihoovians that he, a Jewish lad, accepted Jesus Christ. For this she paid him fifty cents. She made the disbursement. She was the bookkeeper, fiscal chief, general manager of the mission. The Reverend Doctor didn't know a thing about the operation. What the Doctor supplied was the fervor. He was genuine, a wonderful preacher. And what about Woody himself? He also had fervor. He was drawn to the Reverend Doctor. The Reverend Doctor taught him to lift up his eyes, gave him his higher life. Apart from this higher life, the rest was Chicago—the ways of Chicago, which came so natural that nobody thought to question them. So, for instance, in 1933 (what ancient, ancient times!), at the Century of Progress World's Fair, when Woody was a coolie and pulled a rickshaw, wearing a peaked straw hat and trotting with powerful, thick legs, while the brawny red farmers—his boozing passengers— were laughing their heads off and pestered him for whores, he, although a freshman at the seminary, saw nothing wrong, when girls asked him to steer a little business their way, in making dates and accepting tips from both sides. He necked in Grant Park with a powerful girl who had to go home quickly to nurse her baby. Smelling of milk, she rode beside him on the streetcar to the West Side, squeezing his rickshaw puller's thigh and wetting her blouse. This was the Roosevelt Road car. Then, in the apartment where she lived with her mother, he couldn't remember that there were any husbands around. What he did remember was the strong milk odor. Without inconsistency, next morning he did New Testament Greek: The light shineth in darkness—*to fos en te skotia fainei*[7]—and the darkness comprehended it not.

And all the while he trotted between the shafts on the fairgrounds he had one idea, nothing to do with these horny giants having a big time in the city: that the goal, the project, the purpose was (and he couldn't explain why he thought so; all evidence was against it)—God's idea was that this world should be a love world, that it should eventually recover and be entirely a world of love. He wouldn't have said this to a soul, for he could see himself how stupid it was—personal and stupid. Nevertheless, there it was at the center of his feelings. And at the same time, Aunt Rebecca was right when she said to him, strictly private, close to his ear even, "You're a little crook, like your father."

There was some evidence for this, or what stood for evidence to an impatient person like Rebecca. Woody matured quickly—he had to—but how could you expect a boy of seventeen, he wondered, to interpret the viewpoint, the feelings, of a middle-aged woman, and one whose breast had been removed? Morris told him that this happened only to neglected women, and was a sign. Morris said that if titties were not fondled and kissed, they got cancer in protest. It was a cry of the flesh. And this had seemed true to Woody. When his imagination tried the theory on the Reverend Doctor it worked out—he couldn't see the Reverend Doctor behaving in that way to Aunt Rebecca's breasts! Morris's theory kept Woody looking from bosoms to husbands and from husbands to bosoms. He still did that. It's an exceptionally smart man who isn't marked forever by the sexual theories he hears from his father, and Woody wasn't all that smart. He knew this himself. Personally, he had gone far out of his way to do right by women in this regard. What nature demanded. He and Pop were common, thick men, but there's nobody too gross to have ideas of delicacy.

The Reverend Doctor preached, Rebecca preached, rich Mrs. Skoglund preached from Evanston, Mother preached. Pop also was on a soapbox. Everyone was doing it. Up and down Division Street, under every lamp, almost, speakers were giving out: anarchists, Socialists, Stalinists, single-taxers, Zionists, Tolstoyans, vegetarians, and fundamentalist Christian preachers—you name it. A beef, a hope, a way of life or

---

[7]The following English text translates the Greek.

salvation, a protest. How was it that the accumulated gripes of all the ages took off so when transplanted to America?

And that fine Swedish immigrant Aase (Osie, they pronounced it), who had been the Skoglunds' cook and married the eldest son, to become his rich, religious widow— she supported the Reverend Doctor. In her time she must have been built like a chorus girl. And women seem to have lost the secret of putting up their hair in the high basketry fence of braid she wore. Aase took Woody under her special protection and paid his tuition at the seminary. And Pop said . . . But on this Sunday, at peace as soon as the bells stopped banging, this velvet autumn day when the grass was finest and thickest, silky green: before the first frost, and the blood in your lungs is redder than summer air can make it and smarts with oxygen, as if the iron in your system was hungry for it, and the chill was sticking it to you in every breath . . . Pop, six feet under, would never feel this blissful sting again. The last of the bells still had the bright air streaming with vibrations.

On weekends, the institutional vacancy of decades came back to the warehouse and crept under the door of Woody's apartment. It felt as empty on Sundays as churches were during the week. Before each business day, before the trucks and the crews got started, Woody jogged five miles in his Adidas suit. Not on this day still reserved for Pop, however. Although it was tempting to go out and run off the grief. Being alone hit Woody hard this morning. He thought: Me and the world; the world and me. Meaning that there always was some activity to interpose, an errand or a visit, a picture to paint (he was a creative amateur), a massage, a meal—a shield between himself and that troublesome solitude which used the world as its reservoir. But Pop! Last Tuesday, Woody had gotten into the hospital bed with Pop because he kept pulling out the intravenous needles. Nurses stuck them back, and then Woody astonished them all by climbing into bed to hold the struggling old guy in his arms. "Easy, Morris, Morris, go easy." But Pop still groped feebly for the pipes.

When the tolling stopped, Woody didn't notice that a great lake of quiet had come over his kingdom, the Selbst Tile warehouse. What he heard and saw was an old red Chicago streetcar, one of those trams the color of a stockyard steer. Cars of this type went out before Pearl Harbor[8]—clumsy, big-bellied, with tough rattan seats and brass grips for the standing passengers. Those cars used to make four stops to the mile, and ran with a wallowing motion. They stank of carbolic or ozone and throbbed when the air compressors were being charged. The conductor had his knotted signal cord to pull, and the motorman beat the foot gong with his mad heel.

Woody recognized himself on the Western Avenue line and riding through a blizzard with his father, both in sheepskins and with hands and faces raw, the snow blowing in from the rear platform when the doors opened and getting into the longitudinal cleats of the floor. There wasn't warmth enough inside to melt it. And Western Avenue was the longest car line in the world, the boosters said, as if it was a thing to brag about. Twenty-three miles long, made by a draftsman with a T square, lined with factories, storage buildings, machine shops, used-car lots, trolley barns, gas stations, funeral parlors, six-flats, utility buildings, and junkyards, on and on from the prairies on the south to Evanston on the north. Woodrow and his father were going north to Evanston, to Howard Street, and then some, to see Mrs. Skoglund. At the end of the line they would still have about five blocks to hike. The purpose of the trip? To raise money for Pop. Pop had talked him into this. When they found out, Mother and Aunt Rebecca would be furious, and Woody was afraid, but he couldn't help it.

Morris had come and said, "Son, I'm in trouble. It's bad."

---

[8]The attack on December 7, 1941, by the Japanese on Pearl Harbor in Hawaii, which led immediately to America's entry into the Second World War.

"What's bad, Pop?"

"Halina took money from her husband for me and has to put it back before old Bujak misses it. He could kill her."

"What did she do it for?"

"Son, you know how the bookies collect? They send a goon. They'll break my head open."

"Pop! You know I can't take you to Mrs. Skoglund."

"Why not? You're my kid, aren't you? The old broad wants to adopt you, doesn't she? Shouldn't I get something out of it for my trouble? What am I—outside? And what about Halina? She puts her life on the line, but my own kid says no."

"Oh, Bujak wouldn't hurt her."

"Woody, he'd beat her to death."

Bujak? Uniform in color with his dark-gray work clothes, short in the legs, his whole strength in his tool-and-die-maker's forearms and black fingers; and beat-looking—there was Bujak for you. But, according to Pop, there was big, big violence in Bujak, a regular boiling Bessemer[9] inside his narrow chest. Woody could never see the violence in him. Bujak wanted no trouble. If anything, maybe he was afraid that Morris and Halina would gang up on him and kill him, screaming. But Pop was no desperado murderer. And Halina was a calm, serious woman. Bujak kept his savings in the cellar (banks were going out of business). The worst they did was to take some of his money, intending to put it back. As Woody saw him, Bujak was trying to be sensible. He accepted his sorrow. He set minimum requirements for Halina: cook the meals, clean the house, show respect. But at stealing Bujak might have drawn the line, for money was different, money was vital substance. If they stole his savings he might have had to take action, out of respect for the substance, for himself—self-respect. But you couldn't be sure that Pop hadn't invented the bookie, the goon, the theft—the whole thing. He was capable of it, and you'd be a fool not to suspect him. Morris knew that Mother and Aunt Rebecca had told Mrs. Skoglund how wicked he was. They had painted him for her in poster colors—purple for vice, black for his soul, red for Hell flames: a gambler, smoker, drinker, deserter, screwer of women, and atheist. So Pop was determined to reach her. It was risky for everybody. The Reverend Doctor's operating costs were met by Skoglund Dairies. The widow paid Woody's seminary tuition; she bought dresses for the little sisters.

Woody, now sixty, fleshy and big, like a figure for the victory of American materialism, sunk in his lounge chair, the leather of its armrests softer to his fingertips than a woman's skin, was puzzled and, in his depths, disturbed by certain blots within him, blots of light in his brain, a blot combining pain and amusement in his breast (how did *that* get there?). Intense thought puckered the skin between his eyes with a strain bordering on headache. Why had he let Pop have his way? Why did he agree to meet him that day, in the dim rear of the poolroom?

"But what will you tell Mrs. Skoglund?"

"The old broad? Don't worry, there's plenty to tell her, and it's all true. Ain't I trying to save my little laundry-and-cleaning shop? Isn't the bailiff coming for the fixtures next week?" And Pop rehearsed his pitch on the Western Avenue car. He counted on Woody's health and his freshness. Such a straightforward-looking body was perfect for a con.

Did they still have such winter storms in Chicago as they used to have? Now they somehow seemed less fierce. Blizzards used to come straight down from Ontario, from the Arctic, and drop five feet of snow in an afternoon. Then the rusty green platform cars, with revolving brushes at both ends, came out of the barns to sweep the tracks. Ten or twelve streetcars followed in slow processions, or waited, block after block.

---

[9]Furnace for the making of steel.

There was a long delay at the gates of Riverview Park, all the amusements covered for the winter, boarded up—the dragon's-back high-rides, the Bobs, the Chute, the Tilt-a-Whirl, all the fun machinery put together by mechanics and electricians, men like Bujak the tool-and-die-maker, good with engines. The blizzard was having it all its own way behind the gates, and you couldn't see far inside; only a few bulbs burned behind the palings. When Woody wiped the vapor from the glass, the wire mesh of the window guards was stuffed solid at eye level with snow. Looking higher, you saw mostly the streaked wind horizontally driving from the north. In the seat ahead, two black coal heavers, both in leather Lindbergh flying helmets, sat with shovels between their legs, returning from a job. They smelled of sweat, burlap sacking, and coal. Mostly dull with black dust, they also sparkled here and there.

There weren't many riders. People weren't leaving the house. This was a day to sit legs stuck out beside the stove, mummified by both the outdoor and the indoor forces. Only a fellow with an angle, like Pop, would go and buck such weather. A storm like this was out of the compass, and you kept the human scale by having a scheme to raise fifty bucks. Fifty soldiers![10] Real money in 1933.

"That woman is crazy for you," said Pop.

"She's just a good woman, sweet to all of us."

"Who knows what she's got in mind. You're a husky kid. Not such a kid, either."

"She's a religious woman. She really has religion."

"Well, your mother isn't your only parent. She and Rebecca and Kovner aren't going to fill you up with their ideas. I know your mother wants to wipe me out of your life. Unless I take a hand, you won't even understand what life is. Because they don't know—those silly Christers."

"Yes, Pop."

"The girls I can't help. They're too young. I'm sorry about them, but I can't do anything. With you it's different."

He wanted me like himself, an American.

They were stalled in the storm, while the cattle-colored car waited to have the trolley reset in the crazy wind, which boomed, tingled, blasted. At Howard Street they would have to walk straight into it, due north.

"You'll do the talking at first," said Pop.

Woody had the makings of a salesman, a pitchman. He was aware of this when he got to his feet in church to testify before fifty or sixty people. Even though Aunt Rebecca made it worth his while, he moved his own heart when he spoke up about his faith. But occasionally, without notice, his heart went away as he spoke religion and he couldn't find it anywhere. In its absence, sincere behavior got him through. He had to rely for delivery on his face, his voice—on behavior. Then his eyes came closer and closer together. And in this approach of eye to eye he felt the strain of hypocrisy. The twisting of his face threatened to betray him. It took everything he had to keep looking honest. So, since he couldn't bear the cynicism of it, he fell back on mischievousness. Mischief was where Pop came in. Pop passed straight through all those divided fields, gap after gap, and arrived at his side, bent-nosed and broad-faced. In regard to Pop, you thought of neither sincerity nor insincerity. Pop was like the man in the song: he wanted what he wanted when he wanted it. Pop was physical; Pop was digestive, circulatory, sexual. If Pop got serious, he talked to you about washing under the arms or in the crotch or of drying between your toes or of cooking supper, of baked beans and fried onions, of draw poker or of a certain horse in the fifth race at Arlington. Pop was elemental. That was why he gave such relief from religion and paradoxes, and things like that. Now, Mother *thought* she was spiritual, but Woody knew that she was kidding herself. Oh, yes, in the British accent she never gave up she was always talking to God or about Him—please God, God willing, praise God.

---

[10]I.e., slang term for dollar bills.

But she was a big substantial bread-and-butter down-to-earth woman, with down-to-earth duties like feeding the girls, protecting, refining, keeping pure the girls. And those two protected doves grew up so overweight, heavy in the hips and thighs, that their poor heads looked long and slim. And mad. Sweet but cuckoo—Paula cheerfully cuckoo, Joanna depressed and having episodes.

"I'll do my best by you, but you have to promise, Pop, not to get me in Dutch with Mrs. Skoglund."

"You worried because I speak bad English? Embarrassed? I have a mockie[11] accent?"

"It's not that. Kovner has a heavy accent, and she doesn't mind."

"Who the hell are those freaks to look down on me? You're practically a man and your dad has a right to expect help from you. He's in a fix. And you bring him to her house because she's bighearted, and you haven't got anybody else to go to."

"I got you, Pop."

The two coal trimmers stood up at Devon Avenue. One of them wore a woman's coat. Men wore women's clothing in those years, and women men's, when there was no choice. The fur collar was spiky with the wet, and sprinkled with soot. Heavy, they dragged their shovels and got off at the front. The slow car ground on, very slow. It was after four when they reached the end of the line, and somewhere between gray and black, with snow spouting and whirling under the street lamps. In Howard Street, autos were stalled at all angles and abandoned. The sidewalks were blocked. Woody led the way into Evanston, and Pop followed him up the middle of the street in the furrows made earlier by trucks. For four blocks they bucked the wind and then Woody broke through the drifts to the snowbound mansion, where they both had to push the wrought-iron gate because of the drift behind it. Twenty rooms or more in this dignified house and nobody in them but Mrs. Skoglund and her servant Hjordis, also religious.

As Woody and Pop waited, brushing the slush from their sheepskin collars and Pop wiping his big eyebrows with the ends of his scarf, sweating and freezing, the chains began to rattle and Hjordis uncovered the air holes of the glass storm door by turning a wooden bar. Woody called her "monk-faced." You no longer see women like that, who put no female touch on the face. She came plain, as God made her. She said, "Who is it and what do you want?"

"It's Woodrow Selbst. Hjordis? It's Woody."

"You're not expected."

"No, but we're here."

"What do you want?"

"We came to see Mrs. Skoglund."

"What for do you want to see her?"

"Just tell her we're here."

"I have to tell her what you came for, without calling up first."

"Why don't you say it's Woody with his father, and we wouldn't come in a snowstorm like this if it wasn't important."

The understandable caution of women who live alone. Respectable old-time women, too. There was no such respectability now in those Evanston houses, with their big verandas and deep yards and with a servant like Hjordis, who carried at her belt keys to the pantry and to every closet and every dresser drawer and every padlocked bin in the cellar. And in High Episcopal Christian Science Women's Temperance Evanston, no tradespeople rang at the front door. Only invited guests. And here, after a ten-mile grind through the blizzard, came two tramps from the West Side. To this mansion where a Swedish immigrant lady, herself once a cook and now a philanthropic widow, dreamed, snowbound, while frozen lilac twigs clapped at her

---

[11]Jewish (slang).

storm windows, of a new Jerusalem and a Second Coming and a Resurrection and a Last Judgment. To hasten the Second Coming, and all the rest, you had to reach the hearts of these scheming bums arriving in a snowstorm.

Sure, they let us in.

Then in the heat that swam suddenly up to their mufflered chins Pop and Woody felt the blizzard for what it was; their cheeks were frozen slabs. They stood beat, itching, trickling in the front hall that *was* a hall, with a carved newel post staircase and a big stained-glass window at the top. Picturing Jesus with the Samaritan woman.[12] There was a kind of Gentile closeness to the air. Perhaps when he was with Pop, Woody made more Jewish observations than he would otherwise. Although Pop's most Jewish characteristic was that Yiddish was the only language he could read a paper in. Pop was with Polish Halina, and Mother was with Jesus Christ, and Woody ate uncooked bacon from the flitch. Still, now and then he had a Jewish impression.

Mrs. Skoglund was the cleanest of women — her fingernails, her white neck, her ears — and Pop's sexual hints to Woody all went wrong because she was so intensely clean, and made Woody think of a waterfall, large as she was, and grandly built. Her bust was big. Woody's imagination had investigated this. He thought she kept things tied down tight, very tight. But she lifted both arms once to raise a window and there it was, her bust, beside him, the whole unbindable thing. Her hair was like the raffia you had to soak before you could weave with it in a basket class — pale, pale. Pop, as he took his sheepskin off, was in sweaters, no jacket. His darting looks made him seem crooked. Hardest of all for these Selbsts with their bent noses and big, apparently straightforward faces was to look honest. All the signs of dishonesty played over them. Woody had often puzzled about it. Did it go back to the muscles, was it fundamentally a jaw problem — the projecting angles of the jaws? Or was it the angling that went on in the heart? The girls called Pop Dick Tracy, but Dick Tracy was a good guy. Whom could Pop convince? Here Woody caught a possibility as it flitted by. Precisely because of the way Pop looked, a sensitive person might feel remorse for condemning unfairly or judging unkindly. Just because of a face? Some must have bent over backward. Then he had them. Not Hjordis. She would have put Pop into the street then and there, storm or no storm. Hjordis was religious, but she was wised up, too. She hadn't come over in steerage and worked forty years in Chicago for nothing.

Mrs. Skoglund, Aase (Osie), led the visitors into the front room. This, the biggest room in the house, needed supplementary heating. Because of fifteen-foot ceilings and high windows, Hjordis had kept the parlor stove burning. It was one of those elegant parlor stoves that wore a nickel crown, or miter, and this miter, when you moved it aside, automatically raised the hinge of an iron stove lid. That stove lid underneath the crown was all soot and rust, the same as any other stove lid. Into this hole you tipped the scuttle and the anthracite chestnut rattled down. It made a cake or dome of fire visible through the small isinglass frames. It was a pretty room, three-quarters paneled in wood. The stove was plugged into the flue of the marble fireplace, and there were parquet floors and Axminster carpets[13] and cranberry-colored tufted Victorian upholstery, and a kind of Chinese étagère,[14] inside a cabinet, lined with mirrors and containing silver pitchers, trophies won by Skoglund cows, fancy sugar tongs and cut-glass pitchers and goblets. There were Bibles and pictures of Jesus and the Holy Land and that faint Gentile odor, as if things had been rinsed in a weak vinegar solution.

"Mrs. Skoglund, I brought my dad to you. I don't think you ever met him," said Woody.

"Yes, Missus, that's me, Selbst."

---

[12]See John 4: 9–14. Though the Jews have nothing to do with the Samaritans, the Samaritan woman gives Jesus water to drink and then recognizes him as a prophet.

[13]Machine-made English carpets with cut piles and intricate designs.
[14]"Set of shelves" (French).

Pop stood short but masterful in the sweaters, and his belly sticking out, not soft but hard. He was a man of the hard-bellied type. Nobody intimidated Pop. He never presented himself as a beggar. There wasn't a cringe in him anywhere. He let her see at once by the way he said "Missus" that he was independent and that he knew his way around. He communicated that he was able to handle himself with women. Handsome Mrs. Skoglund, carrying a basket woven out of her own hair, was in her fifties — eight, maybe ten years his senior.

"I asked my son to bring me because I know you do the kid a lot of good. It's natural you should know both of his parents."

"Mrs. Skoglund, my dad is in a tight corner and I don't know anybody else to ask for help."

This was all the preliminary Pop wanted. He took over and told the widow his story about the laundry-and-cleaning business and payments overdue, and explained about the fixtures and the attachment notice, and the bailiff's office and what they were going to do him; and he said, "I'm a small man trying to make a living."

"You don't support your children," said Mrs. Skoglund.

"That's right," said Hjordis.

"I haven't got it. If I had it, wouldn't I give it? There's bread lines and soup lines all over town. Is it just me? What I have I divvy with. I give the kids. A bad father? You think my son would bring me if I was a bad father into your house? He loves his dad, he trusts his dad, he knows his dad is a good dad. Every time I start a little business going I get wiped out. This one is a good little business, if I could hold on to that little business. Three people work for me, I meet a payroll, and three people will be on the street, too, if I close down. Missus, I can sign a note and pay you in two months. I'm a common man, but I'm a hard worker and a fellow you can trust."

Woody was startled when Pop used the word "trust." It was as if from all four corners a Sousa band blew a blast to warn the entire world: "Crook! This is a crook!" But Mrs. Skoglund, on account of her religious preoccupations, was remote. She heard nothing. Although everybody in this part of the world, unless he was crazy, led a practical life, and you'd have nothing to say to anyone, your neighbors would have nothing to say to you, if communications were not of a practical sort, Mrs. Skoglund, with all her money, was unworldly — two-thirds out of this world.

"Give me a chance to show what's in me," said Pop, "and you'll see what I do for my kids."

So Mrs. Skoglund hesitated, and then she said she'd have to go upstairs, she'd have to go to her room and pray on it and ask for guidance — would they sit down and wait. There were two rocking chairs by the stove. Hjordis gave Pop a grim look (a dangerous person) and Woody a blaming one (he brought a dangerous stranger and disrupter to injure two kind Christian ladies). Then she went out with Mrs. Skoglund.

As soon as they left, Pop jumped up from the rocker and said in anger, "What's this with the praying? She has to ask God to lend me fifty bucks?"

Woody said, "It's not you, Pop, it's the way these religious people do."

"No," said Pop. "She'll come back and say that God wouldn't let her."

Woody didn't like that; he thought Pop was being gross and he said, "No, she's sincere. Pop, try to understand: she's emotional, nervous, and sincere, and tries to do right by everybody."

And Pop said, "That servant will talk her out of it. She's a toughie. It's all over her face that we're a couple of chiselers."

"What's the use of us arguing," said Woody. He drew the rocker closer to the stove. His shoes were wet through and would never dry. The blue flames fluttered like a school of fishes in the coal fire. But Pop went over to the Chinese-style cabinet or étagère and tried the handle, and then opened the blade of his penknife and in a second had forced the lock of the curved glass door. He took out a silver dish.

"Pop, what is this?" said Woody.

Pop, cool and level, knew exactly what this was. He relocked the étagère, crossed the carpet, listened. He stuffed the dish under his belt and pushed it down into his trousers. He put the side of his short thick finger to his mouth.

So Woody kept his voice down, but he was all shook up. He went to Pop and took him by the edge of his hand. As he looked into Pop's face, he felt his eyes growing smaller and smaller, as if something were contracting all the skin on his head. They call it hyperventilation when everything feels tight and light and close and dizzy. Hardly breathing, he said, "Put it back, Pop."

Pop said, "It's solid silver; it's worth dough."

"Pop, you said you wouldn't get me in Dutch."

"It's only insurance in case she comes back from praying and tells me no. If she says yes, I'll put it back."

"How?"

"It'll get back. If I don't put it back, you will."

"You picked the lock. I couldn't. I don't know how."

"There's nothing to it."

"We're going to put it back now. Give it here."

"Woody, it's under my fly, inside my underpants. Don't make such a noise about nothing."

"Pop, I can't believe this."

"For cry-ninety-nine, shut your mouth. If I didn't trust you I wouldn't have let you watch me do it. You don't understand a thing. What's with you?"

"Before they come down, Pop, will you dig that dish out of your long johns."

Pop turned stiff on him. He became absolutely military. He said, "Look, I order you!"

Before he knew it, Woody had jumped his father and begun to wrestle with him. It was outrageous to clutch your own father, to put a heel behind him, to force him to the wall. Pop was taken by surprise and said loudly, "You want Halina killed? Kill her! Go on, you be responsible." He began to resist, angry, and they turned about several times, when Woody, with a trick he had learned in a Western movie and used once on the playground, tripped him and they fell to the ground. Woody, who already outweighed the old man by twenty pounds, was on top. They landed on the floor beside the stove, which stood on a tray of decorated tin to protect the carpet. In this position, pressing Pop's hard belly, Woody recognized that to have wrestled him to the floor counted for nothing. It was impossible to thrust his hand under Pop's belt to recover the dish. And now Pop had turned furious, as a father has every right to be when his son is violent with him, and he freed his hand and hit Woody in the face. He hit him three or four times in midface. Then Woody dug his head into Pop's shoulder and held tight only to keep from being struck and began to say in his ear, "Jesus, Pop, for Christ sake remember where you are. Those women will be back!" But Pop brought up his short knee and fought and butted him with his chin and rattled Woody's teeth. Woody thought the old man was about to bite him. And because he was a seminarian, he thought: Like an unclean spirit. And held tight. Gradually Pop stopped threshing and struggling. His eyes stuck out and his mouth was open, sullen. Like a stout fish. Woody released him and gave him a hand up. He was then overcome with many many bad feelings of a sort he knew the old man never suffered. Never, never. Pop never had these groveling emotions. There was his whole superiority. Pop had no such feelings. He was like a horseman from Central Asia, a bandit from China. It was Mother, from Liverpool, who had the refinement, the English manners. It was the preaching Reverend Doctor in his black suit. You have refinements, and all they do is oppress you? The hell with that.

The long door opened and Mrs. Skoglund stepped in, saying, "Did I imagine, or did something shake the house?"

"I was lifting the scuttle to put coal on the fire and it fell out of my hand. I'm sorry I was so clumsy," said Woody.

Pop was too huffy to speak. With his eyes big and sore and the thin hair down over his forehead, you could see by the tightness of his belly how angrily he was fetching his breath, though his mouth was shut.

"I prayed," said Mrs. Skoglund.

"I hope it came out well," said Woody.

"Well, I don't do anything without guidance, but the answer was yes, and I feel right about it now. So if you'll wait, I'll go to my office and write a check. I asked Hjordis to bring you a cup of coffee. Coming in such a storm."

And Pop, consistently a terrible little man, as soon as she shut the door, said, "A check? Hell with a check. Get me the greenbacks."

"They don't keep money in the house. You can cash it in her bank tomorrow. But if they miss that dish, Pop, they'll stop the check, and then where are you?"

As Pop was reaching below the belt, Hjordis brought in the tray. She was very sharp with him. She said, "Is this a place to adjust clothing, Mister? A men's washroom?"

"Well, which way is the toilet, then?" said Pop.

She had served the coffee in the seamiest mugs in the pantry, and she bumped down the tray and led Pop down the corridor, standing guard at the bathroom door so that he shouldn't wander about the house.

Mrs. Skoglund called Woody to her office and after she had given him the folded check said that they should pray together for Morris. So once more he was on his knees, under rows and rows of musty marbled-cardboard files, by the glass lamp by the edge of the desk, the shade with flounced edges, like the candy dish. Mrs. Skoglund, in her Scandinavian accent—an emotional contralto—raising her voice to Jesus-uh Christ-uh, as the wind lashed the trees, kicked the side of the house, and drove the snow seething on the windowpanes, to send light-uh, give guidance-uh, put a new heart-uh in Pop's bosom. Woody asked God only to make Pop put the dish back. He kept Mrs. Skoglund on her knees as long as possible. Then he thanked her, shining with candor (as much as he knew how), for her Christian generosity and he said, "I know that Hjordis has a cousin who works at the Evanston YMCA. Could she please phone him and try to get us a room tonight so that we don't have to fight the blizzard all the way back? We're almost as close to the Y as to the car line. Maybe the cars have even stopped running."

Suspicious Hjordis, coming when Mrs. Skoglund called to her, was burning now. First they barged in, made themselves at home, asked for money, had to have coffee, probably left gonorrhea on the toilet seat. Hjordis, Woody remembered, was a woman who wiped the doorknobs with rubbing alcohol after guests had left. Nevertheless, she telephoned the Y and got them a room with two cots for six bits.

Pop had plenty of time, therefore, to reopen the étagère, lined with reflecting glass or German silver (something exquisitely delicate and tricky), and as soon as the two Selbsts had said thank you and goodbye and were in midstreet again up to the knees in snow, Woody said, "Well, I covered for you. Is that thing back?"

"Of course it is," said Pop.

They fought their way to the small Y building, shut up in wire grille and resembling a police station—about the same dimensions. It was locked, but they made a racket on the grille, and a small black man let them in and shuffled them upstairs to a cement corridor with low doors. It was like the small-mammal house in Lincoln Park.[15] He said there was nothing to eat, so they took off their wet pants, wrapped themselves tightly in the khaki army blankets, and passed out on their cots.

First thing in the morning, they went to the Evanston National Bank and got the fifty dollars. Not without difficulties. The teller went to call Mrs. Skoglund and was absent a long time from the wicket. "Where the hell has he gone?" said Pop.

---

[15]Location of the Chicago zoo.

But when the fellow came back, he said, "How do you want it?"

Pop said, "Singles." He told Woody, "Bujak stashes it in one-dollar bills."

But by now Woody no longer believed Halina had stolen the old man's money.

Then they went into the street, where the snow-removal crews were at work. The sun shone broad, broad, out of the morning blue, and all Chicago would be releasing itself from the temporary beauty of those vast drifts.

"You shouldn't have jumped me last night, Sonny."

"I know, Pop, but you promised you wouldn't get me in Dutch."

"Well, it's okay. We can forget it, seeing you stood by me."

Only, Pop had taken the silver dish. Of course he had, and in a few days Mrs. Skoglund and Hjordis knew it, and later in the week they were all waiting for Woody in Kovner's office at the settlement house. The group included the Reverend Doctor Crabbie, head of the seminary, and Woody, who had been flying along, level and smooth, was shot down in flames. He told them he was innocent. Even as he was falling, he warned that they were wronging him. He denied that he or Pop had touched Mrs. Skoglund's property. The missing object—he didn't even know what it was—had probably been misplaced, and they would be very sorry on the day it turned up. After the others were done with him, Dr. Crabbie said that until he was able to tell the truth he would be suspended from the seminary, where his work had been unsatisfactory anyway. Aunt Rebecca took him aside and said to him, "You are a little crook, like your father. The door is closed to you here."

To this Pop's comment was "So what, kid?"

"Pop, you shouldn't have done it."

"No? Well, I don't give a care, if you want to know. You can have the dish if you want to go back and square yourself with all those hypocrites."

"I didn't like doing Mrs. Skoglund in the eye, she was so kind to us."

"Kind?"

"Kind."

"Kind has a price tag."

Well, there was no winning such arguments with Pop. But they debated it in various moods and from various elevations and perspectives for forty years and more, as their intimacy changed, developed, matured.

"Why did you do it, Pop? For the money? What did you do with the fifty bucks?" Woody, decades later, asked him that.

"I settled with the bookie, and the rest I put in the business."

"You tried a few more horses."

"I maybe did. But it was a double, Woody. I didn't hurt myself, and at the same time did you a favor."

"It was for me?"

"It was too strange of a life. That life wasn't *you*, Woody. All those women . . . Kovner was no man, he was an in-between. Suppose they made you a minister? Some Christian minister! First of all, you wouldn't have been able to stand it, and second, they would throw you out sooner or later."

"Maybe so."

"And you wouldn't have converted the Jews, which was the main thing they wanted."

"And what a time to bother the Jews," Woody said. "At least *I* didn't bug them."

Pop had carried him back to his side of the line, blood of his blood, the same thick body walls, the same coarse grain. Not cut out for a spiritual life. Simply not up to it.

Pop was no worse than Woody, and Woody was no better than Pop. Pop wanted no relation to theory, and yet he was always pointing Woody toward a position—a jolly, hardy, natural, likable, unprincipled position. If Woody had a weakness, it was to be unselfish. This worked to Pop's advantage, but he criticized Woody for it, nevertheless. "You take too much on yourself," Pop was always saying. And it's true that Woody gave Pop his heart because Pop was so selfish. It's usually the selfish people who are loved the most. They do what you deny yourself, and you love them for it. You give them your heart.

Remembering the pawn ticket for the silver dish, Woody startled himself with a laugh so sudden that it made him cough. Pop said to him after his expulsion from the seminary and banishment from the settlement house, "You want in again? Here's the ticket. I hocked that thing. It wasn't so valuable as I thought."

"What did they give?"

"Twelve-fifty was all I could get. But if you want it you'll have to raise the dough yourself, because I haven't got it anymore."

"You must have been sweating in the bank when the teller went to call Mrs. Skoglund about the check."

"I was a little nervous," said Pop. "But I didn't think they could miss the thing so soon."

That theft was part of Pop's war with Mother. With Mother, and Aunt Rebecca, and the Reverend Doctor. Pop took his stand on realism. Mother represented the forces of religion and hypochondria. In four decades, the fighting never stopped. In the course of time, Mother and the girls turned into welfare personalities and lost their individual outlines. Ah, the poor things, they became dependents and cranks. In the meantime, Woody, the sinful man, was their dutiful and loving son and brother. He maintained the bungalow—this took in roofing, painting, wiring, insulation, air-conditioning—and he paid for heat and light and food, and dressed them all out of Sears, Roebuck and Wieboldt's, and bought them a TV, which they watched as devoutly as they prayed. Paula took courses to learn skills like macramé-[16]making and needlepoint, and sometimes got a little job as recreational worker in a nursing home. But she wasn't steady enough to keep it. Wicked Pop spent most of his life removing stains from people's clothing. He and Halina in the last years ran a Cleanomat in West Rogers Park—a so-so business resembling a laundromat—which gave him leisure for billiards, the horses, rummy and pinochle. Every morning he went behind the partition to check out the filters of the cleaning equipment. He found amusing things that had been thrown into the vats with the clothing—sometimes, when he got lucky, a locket chain or a brooch. And when he had fortified the cleaning fluid, pouring all that blue and pink stuff in from plastic jugs, he read the *Forward*[17] over a second cup of coffee, and went out, leaving Halina in charge. When they needed help with the rent, Woody gave it.

After the new Disney World was opened in Florida, Woody treated all his dependents to a holiday. He sent them down in separate batches, of course. Halina enjoyed this more than anybody else. She couldn't stop talking about the address given by an Abraham Lincoln automaton. "Wonderful, how he stood up and moved his hands, and his mouth. So real! And how beautiful he talked." Of them all, Halina was the soundest, the most human, the most honest. Now that Pop was gone, Woody and Halina's son, Mitosh, the organist at the Stadium, took care of her needs over and above Social Security, splitting expenses. In Pop's opinion, insurance was a racket. He left Halina nothing but some out-of-date equipment.

Woody treated himself, too. Once a year, and sometimes oftener, he left his business to run itself, arranged with the trust department at the bank to take care of his gang, and went off. He did that in style, imaginatively, expensively. In Japan, he wasted little time on Tokyo. He spent three weeks in Kyoto and stayed at the Tawaraya Inn, dating from the seventeenth century or so. There he slept on the floor, the Japanese way, and bathed in scalding water. He saw the dirtiest strip show on

---

[16]Elaborately patterned lace-like webbing made of yarn.
[17]*The Jewish Daily Forward*, published in Yiddish.

earth, as well as the holy places and the temple gardens. He visited also Istanbul, Jerusalem, Delphi, and went to Burma and Uganda and Kenya on safari, on democratic terms with drivers, Bedouins, bazaar merchants. Open, lavish, familiar, fleshier and fleshier but (he jogged, he lifted weights) still muscular — in his naked person beginning to resemble a Renaissance courtier in full costume — becoming ruddier every year, an outdoor type with freckles on his back and spots across the flaming forehead and the honest nose. In Addis Ababa he took an Ethiopian beauty to his room from the street and washed her, getting into the shower with her to soap her with his broad, kindly hands. In Kenya he taught certain American obscenities to a black woman so that she could shout them out during the act. On the Nile, below Murchison Falls, those fever trees[18] rose huge from the mud, and hippos on the sandbars belched at the passing launch, hostile. One of them danced on his spit of sand, springing from the ground and coming down heavy, on all fours. There, Woody saw the buffalo calf disappear, snatched by the crocodile.

Mother, soon to follow Pop, was being lightheaded these days. In company, she spoke of Woody as her boy — "What do you think of my Sonny?" — as though he was ten years old. She was silly with him, her behavior was frivolous, almost flirtatious. She just didn't seem to know the facts. And behind her all the others, like kids at the playground, were waiting their turn to go down the slide: one on each step, and moving toward the top.

Over Woody's residence and place of business there had gathered a pool of silence of the same perimeter as the church bells while they were ringing, and he mourned under it, this melancholy morning of sun and autumn. Doing a life survey, taking a deliberate look at the gross side of his case — of the other side as well, what there was of it. But if this heartache continued, he'd go out and run it off. A three-mile jog — five, if necessary. And you'd think that this jogging was an entirely physical activity, wouldn't you? But there was something else in it. Because, when he was a seminarian, between the shafts of his World's Fair rickshaw, he used to receive, pulling along (capable and stable), his religious experiences while he trotted. Maybe it was all a single experience repeated. He felt truth coming to him from the sun. He received a communication that was also light and warmth. It made him very remote from his horny Wisconsin passengers, those farmers whose whoops and whore cries he could hardly hear when he was in one of his states. And again out of the flaming of the sun would come to him a secret certainty that the goal set for this earth was that it should be filled with good, saturated with it. After everything preposterous, after dog had eaten dog, after the crocodile death had pulled everyone into his mud. It wouldn't conclude as Mrs. Skoglund, bribing him to round up the Jews and hasten the Second Coming, imagined it, but in another way. This was his clumsy intuition. It went no further. Subsequently, he proceeded through life as life seemed to want him to do it.

There remained one thing more this morning, which was explicitly physical, occurring first as a sensation in his arms and against his breast and, from the pressure, passing into him and going into his breast.

It was like this: When he came into the hospital room and saw Pop with the sides of his bed raised, like a crib, and Pop, so very feeble, and writhing, and toothless, like a baby, and the dirt already cast into his face, into the wrinkles — Pop wanted to pluck out the intravenous needles and he was piping his weak death noise. The gauze patches taped over the needles were soiled with dark blood. Then Woody took off his shoes, lowered the side of the bed, and climbed in and held him in his arms to soothe and still him. As if he were Pop's father, he said to him, "Now, Pop. Pop." Then it was like the wrestle in Mrs. Skoglund's parlor, when Pop turned angry like an unclean

---

[18] Any of a number of kinds of trees that produce a substance believed to prevent malaria.

spirit and Woody tried to appease him, and warn him, saying, "Those women will be back!" Beside the coal stove, when Pop hit Woody in the teeth with his head and then became sullen, like a stout fish. But this struggle in the hospital was weak—so weak! In his great pity, Woody held Pop, who was fluttering and shivering. From those people, Pop had told him, you'll never find out what life is, because they don't know what it is. Yes, Pop—well, what is it, Pop? Hard to comprehend that Pop, who was dug in for eighty-three years and had done all he could to stay, should now want nothing but to free himself. How could Woody allow the old man to pull the intravenous needles out? Willful Pop, he wanted what he wanted when he wanted it. But what he wanted at the very last Woody failed to follow, it was such a switch.

After a time, Pop's resistance ended. He subsided and subsided. He rested against his son, his small body curled there. Nurses came and looked. They disapproved, but Woody, who couldn't spare a hand to wave them out, motioned with his head toward the door. Pop, whom Woody thought he had stilled, only had found a better way to get around him. Loss of heat was the way he did it. His heat was leaving him. As can happen with small animals while you hold them in your hand, Woody presently felt him cooling. Then, as Woody did his best to restrain him, and thought he was succeeding, Pop divided himself. And when he was separated from his warmth, he slipped into death. And there was his elderly, large, muscular son, still holding and pressing him when there was nothing anymore to press. You could never pin down that self-willed man. When he was ready to make his move, he made it—always on his own terms. And always, always, something up his sleeve. That was how he was.

1978, 1984

PETER TAYLOR

(b. 1917)

Peter Taylor was born in Trenton, a small town in Tennessee, and has lived most of his life in the South, an area of the country that figures prominently in his fiction. But Taylor does not consider himself a "regional writer." He has remarked in a 1981 interview:

> I don't really like it when people say, "He writes about the urban South." I'm writing about people under certain circumstances, but I'm always concerned with the individual experience and the unique experience of that story. Goodness knows I don't have any political vision for the South, in retrospect or in the future, but I have strong feelings about it. And I think that's the main thing that you have to write about, not only what you have ideas about but what you feel about most keenly. My earliest recollections are a sense of the past in the South, and that's what I think has been responsible for a lot of Southern writing. There was the great turning point: before 1865 is the past; after that, the present. That's dramatic, and it's bound to create stories.

Taylor has traced his beginnings as a writer to his childhood: "My theory is that you listen to people talk when you're a child—a Southerner does especially—and they tell stories and stories and stories, and you feel those stories must mean something. So, really, writing becomes an effort to find out what these stories mean in the beginning, and then you want to find out what *all* the stories you hear or think of mean. The story you write is interpretation." It was Taylor's mother he remembers most vividly as telling stories. Both his grandfathers were politicians and lawyers, one becoming a governor and a senator; they too had stories to tell. Taylor published his first two stories in 1937, at the age of twenty, and has been writing more or less steadily ever since, mostly fiction but with an occasional try at playwrighting.

In 1926 the Taylors located in St. Louis, Missouri, where Taylor's father was president of an insurance company. But in 1932 the family returned to Tennessee, settling in Memphis, where Taylor finished high school. In 1936 Taylor studied with Allen Tate at Southwestern in Memphis, and then with John Crowe Ransom at Vanderbilt in Nashville. He dropped out after Ransom left Vanderbilt for Kenyon College in Ohio (where he founded the *Kenyon Review*). He sold real estate for a time, and then, in 1938, he followed Ransom to Kenyon. There he fell in with the poets Robert Lowell and Randall Jarrell, who would remain lifelong friends; they had heady discussions of the poems and novels they were reading. After taking a degree in 1940, Taylor began graduate study at Louisiana State University in Baton Rouge, where Cleanth Brooks and Robert Penn Warren were teaching and where they had established the *Southern Review*.

Taylor's graduate study was interrupted by his service in the army from 1941 to 1945. In 1943, he married the poet Eleanor Ross, a North Carolinian. After the war he began a teaching career in English at the Woman's College of the University of North Carolina at Greensboro, where he taught off and on through 1966. Other institutions at which he taught include the University of Chicago, Kenyon College, and Harvard University. In 1967 he received an appointment at the University of Virginia, where he taught creative writing for the remainder of his career until his retirement.

Taylor published his first book, *A Long Fourth and Other Stories*, in 1948. It contained an introduction by Robert Penn Warren, well-known at the time for his fiction (especially *All the King's Men*, 1946). In his Introduction, Warren focused on Taylor's immense skill in writing about "the attrition of old loyalties, the breakdown of old patterns, and the collapse of old values" in the urban South. Reviewers followed Warren's lead in praising the book, and Taylor's future as a writer seemed assured.

In 1948 *The New Yorker* began to accept his work, and over the next several decades he became a steady contributor to the magazine. In 1950 he published his second book, a short novel entitled *Woman of Means*, but its subtle probing of the consciousness of an adolescent boy failed to excite the reviewers. It was not until the publication of additional volumes of short stories that critics came to agree that Taylor's was a major talent: *The Widows of Thornton* (1954), *Happy Families Are All Alike* (1959), and *Miss Leonora When Last Seen and Fifteen Other Stories* (1963). What became clear is that, in a decade that would bring radical change in American fiction, Taylor's was an old-fashioned brilliance, in the tradition of Anton Chekhov and—particularly—Henry James.

At the time in the 1930s and 1940s when Taylor was most impressionable in his formation as a writer, the New Criticism had found its model for poetry in the practice and theory of T.S. Eliot and its model for fiction in the practice and theory of Henry James. The poet-critic Richard P. Blackmur in 1934 had published James's Prefaces to the New York Edition of his work under the title *The Art of the Novel*. In 1947, *The Notebooks of Henry James* appeared. These two books embodied not only an extraordinarily compelling theory of fiction, but were concerned at every turn with the problems of technique. Taylor no doubt felt their impact, given the respect for James in his teachers, Tate and Ransom. Taylor's careful attention to point of view in his stories appears Jamesian, as does his skill in constructing "dramas of consciousness." But of course his material and his voice are his own; and his talent for compression is quite un-Jamesian.

Taylor's more recent books have included *The Collected Stories of Peter Taylor* (1969), *Presences: Seven Dramatic Pieces* (1973), *In the Miro District and Other Stories* (1977), and *The Old Forest and Other Stories* (1985). Although his second novel, *A Summons to Memphis* (1986), was awarded the Pulitzer Prize, it seems likely that he will be valued most for his short stories. He has commented on the short form that seems best to suit his talent: "I've always been interested in compression, trying to see how much one could put into a short story and yet have it as good as a longer story. In the end, short stories are not just short novels. They're much more intense, and the words have to do a lot more work. Just as in a lyric poem."

ADDITIONAL READING

Conversations with Peter Taylor, ed. Hubert McAlexander, 1987.

Albert J. Griffith, *Peter Taylor*, 1970; Stuart Wright, *Peter Taylor: A Descriptive Bibliography, 1934–87*, 1988; James Curry Robison, *Peter Taylor: A Study of the Short Fiction*, 1988.

TEXT

The Old Forest and Other Stories, 1985.

A Walled Garden

No, Memphis in autumn has not the moss-hung oaks of Natchez. Nor, my dear young man, have we the exotic, the really exotic orange and yellow and rust foliage of the maples at Rye or Saratoga.[1] When our five-month summer season burns itself out, the foliage is left a cheerless brown. Observe that Catawba tree beyond the wall; and the leaves under your feet here on the terrace are mustard and khaki colored; and the air, the atmosphere (who would dare to breathe a deep breath!) is virtually a sea of dust. But we do what we can. We've walled ourselves in here with these evergreens and box and jasmine. You must know, yourself, young man, that no beauty is native to us but the verdure of early summer. And it's as though I've had to take my finger, just so, and point out to Frances the lack of sympathy that there is in the climate and in the eroded countryside of this region. I have had to build this garden and say, "See, my child, how nice and sympathetic everything can be." But now she does see it my way, you understand. You understand, my daughter has finally made her life with me in this little garden plot, and year by year she has come to realize how little else there is hereabouts to compare with it.

And you, you know nothing of flowers? A young man who doesn't know the zinnia from the aster! How curious that you and my daughter should have made friends. I don't know under what circumstances you two may have met. In her League work, no doubt. She *throws* herself so into whatever work she undertakes. Oh? Why, of course, I should have guessed. She simply *spent* herself on the Chest Drive this year. . . . But my daughter has most of her permanent friends among the flower-minded people. She makes so few friends nowadays outside of our little circle, sees so few people outside our own garden here, really, that I find it quite strange for there to be someone who doesn't know flowers.

---

[1]In New York state.

No, nothing, we've come to feel, is ever very lovely, really lovely, I mean, in this part of the nation, nothing *but* this garden; and you can well imagine what even this little bandbox of a garden once was. I created it out of a virtual chaos of a backyard—Franny's playground, I might say. For three years I nursed that little magnolia there, for one whole summer did nothing but water the ivy on the east wall of the house; if only you could have seen the scrubby hedge and the unsightly servants' quarters of our neighbors that are beyond my serpentine wall (I suppose, at least, they're still there). In those days it was all very different, you understand, and Frances's father was about the house, and Frances was a child. But now in the spring we have what is truly a sweet garden here, modeled on my mother's at Rye; for three weeks in March our hyacinths are an inspiration to Frances and to me and to all those who come to us regularly; the larkspur and marigold are heavenly in May over there beside the roses.

But you do not know the zinnia from the aster, young man? How curious that you two should have become friends. And now you are impatient with her, and you mustn't be; I don't mean to be too indulgent, but she'll be along presently. Only recently she's become incredibly painstaking in her toilet again. Whereas in the last few years she's not cared so much for the popular fads of dress. Gardens and floral design have occupied her—with what guidance I could give—have been pretty much her life, really. Now in the old days, I confess, before her father was taken from us—I lost Mr. Harris in the dreadfully hot summer of '48 (people don't generally realize what a dreadful year that was—the worst year for perennials and annuals, alike, since Terrible '30. Things died that year that I didn't think would *ever* die. A dreadful summer)—why, she used then to run here and there with people of every sort, it seemed. I put no restraint upon her, understand. How many times I've said to my Franny, "You must make your own life, my child, as you would have it." Yes, in those days she used to run here and there with people of every sort and variety, it seemed to me. Where was it you say you met, for she goes so few places that are really *out* anymore? But Mr. Harris would let me put no restraint upon her. I still remember the strong-headedness of her teens that had to be overcome and the testiness in her character when she was nearer to twenty than thirty. And you should have seen her as a tot of twelve when she would be somersaulting and rolling about on this very spot. Honestly, I see that child now, the mud on her middy blouse and her straight yellow hair in her eyes.

When I used to come back from visiting my people at Rye, she would grit her teeth at me and give her confidence to the black cook. I would find my own child become a mad little animal. It was through this door here from the sun-room that I came one September afternoon—just such an afternoon as this, young man—still wearing my traveling suit, and called to my child across the yard for her to come and greet me. I had been away for the two miserable summer months, caring for my sick mother, but at the sight of me the little Indian turned and with a whoop she ran to hide in the scraggly privet hedge which was at the far end of the yard. I called her twice to come from out that filthiest of shrubs. "Frances Ann!" We used to call her by her full name when her father was alive. But she didn't stir. She crouched at the roots of the hedge and spied at her travel-worn mother between the leaves.

I pleaded with her at first quite indulgently and good-naturedly and described the new ruffled dress and the paper cutouts I had brought from her grandmother at Rye. (I wasn't to have Mother much longer, and I knew it, and it was hard to come home to this kind of scene.) At last I threatened to withhold my presents until Thanksgiving or Christmas. The cook in the kitchen may have heard some change in my tone, for she came to the kitchen door over beyond the latticework which we've since put up, and looked out first at me and then at the child. While I was threatening, my daughter crouched in the dirt and began to mumble things to herself which I could not hear, and the noises she made were like those of an angry little cat. It seems that it was a warmer afternoon than this one—but my garden does deceive—and I had been moving about in my heavy traveling suit. In my exasperation I stepped out into the rays of the sweltering sun, and into the yard which I so detested; and I uttered in a scream the child's full name, "Frances Ann Harris!" Just then the black cook stepped out onto the back porch, but I ordered her to return to the kitchen. I began to cross the yard toward Frances Ann—that scowling little creature who was *incredibly* the same Frances you've met—and simultaneously she began to crawl along the hedgerow toward the wire fence that divided my property from the neighbor's.

I believe it was the extreme heat that made me speak so very harshly and with such swiftness as to make my words incomprehensible. When I saw that the child had reached the fence and intended climbing it, I pulled off my hat, tearing my veil to pieces as I hurried my pace. I don't actually know what I was saying—I probably couldn't have told you even a moment later—and I didn't even feel any pain from the turn which I gave my ankle in the gully across the middle of the yard. But the child kept her nervous little eyes on me and her lips continued to move now and again. Each time her lips moved I believed I must have raised my voice in more intense rage and greater horror at her ugliness. And so, young man, striding straight through the hedge I reached her before she had climbed to the top of the wire fencing. I think I took her by the arm above the elbow, about here, and I said something like, "I shall have to punish you, Frances Ann." I did not jerk her. I didn't jerk her one bit, as she wished to make it appear, but rather, as soon as I touched her, she relaxed her hold on the wire and fell to the ground. But she lay there—in her canniness—only the briefest moment looking up and past me through the straight hair that hung over her face like an untrimmed main. I had barely ordered her to rise when she sprang up and moved with such celerity that she soon was out of my reach again. I followed—running in those high heels—and this time I turned my other ankle in the gully, and I fell there on the ground in that yard, this garden. You won't believe it— pardon, I must sit down. . . . I hope you don't think it too odd, me telling you all this. . . . You won't believe it: I lay there in the ditch and she didn't come to aid me with childish apologies and such, but instead she deliberately climbed into her swing that hung from the dirty old poplar that was here formerly (I have had it cut down and the roots dug up) and she began to swing, not high and low, but only gently, and stared straight down at her mother through her long hair—which, you may be sure, young man, I had cut the very next day at my own beautician's and curled into a hundred ringlets.

1985

CARSON McCULLERS
(1917–1967)

Carson McCullers captured the essence of the recurrent and even obsessive theme of her fiction in the title of her first novel, *The Heart Is a Lonely Hunter:* her characters are all in search of an elusive love that will relieve the intolerable loneliness of *being.* In an essay revealingly entitled "Loneliness . . . An American Malady," McCullers sketched her view of the human plight: "After the first establishment of identity there comes the imperative need to lose this new-found sense of separateness and to belong to something larger and more powerful than the weak, lonely self. The sense of moral isolation is intolerable to us."

Carson McCullers was born Lula Carson Smith in Columbia, Georgia, the eldest of three children. Her mother encouraged her in her desire to achieve early fame and fortune. She at first wanted to be a concert pianist, but she became a voracious reader in high school and also had thoughts of becoming a writer. She set out alone for New York at the age of seventeen to take courses at Columbia and study music at the Juilliard School, with $500 pinned to her underwear. The money was raised, after a family conference, by the sale of an heirloom ring that McCullers's grandmother had willed her. The year was 1934, in the depths of the Great Depression. Through the carelessness of a roommate, the money was left behind on a subway or stolen; but fortunately the tuition had been paid for courses in writing at Columbia University.

Fiercely ambitious, McCullers let nothing stand in her way to become a famous writer. She held a succession of menial jobs, taking pride in never quitting but always being fired by her employer. Wandering the streets of New York, she found telephone booths a place for retreat and reading. And she found time to write. Soon she was placing her first stories in the little magazines. During this period she met Reeves McCullers, a young southerner on a three-year hitch in the army who had ambitions to write. The relationship developed rapidly, and they were married in 1937.

McCullers was soon embarked on a novel, entitled *The Mute,* which had at its center the deep, intuitive bond between two men, both deaf-mutes. By the time it was published in 1940 by Houghton Mifflin, it had become *The Heart Is a Lonely Hunter.* The novel was widely and favorably reviewed and became a best-seller. McCullers basked briefly in the glory of her new-won fame in New York, but was soon at work on *Reflections in a Golden Eye,* completed in two months and published also in 1940, in *Harper's Bazaar* (and as a book in 1941). Set in an army camp in the south, *Reflections* dealt with the bisexual feelings of an officer and his ambivalent relations with a virile enlisted man who passionately pursues the officer's wife.

The novel obliquely reflected the problems arising in McCullers's marriage. Both Carson and Reeves appeared to possess elements of bisexuality in their makeup. McCullers found herself falling in love with a Swedish writer and novelist, Annemarie Clarac-Schwarzenbach, whom she met in the Thomas Mann household where many of the refugees from Europe then pouring into New York turned up. Clarac-Schwarzenbach gently held McCullers at a distance, but developed a warm companionship with both her and Reeves.

As the relationship between Carson and Reeves deteriorated (in part because of Reeves's despondency over his failure as a writer), Carson met and felt strongly attracted to a young composer-musician, David Diamond, who, like Clarac-Schwarzenbach, was drawn into a complicated triangle. While Carson was away writing at the Yaddo artists colony in Saratoga Springs, Reeves moved in with David. Disturbed, McCullers divorced Reeves, who reenlisted in the army. Although they were remarried in 1945, the relationship was to continue a troubled one; in 1953, when they were living in France, Reeves (who had shown suicidal impulses before) proposed a joint suicide. Carson fled back to America. A few weeks later, Reeves committed suicide in a Paris hotel.

Throughout all of this domestic turbulence, McCullers's problems were intensified by deteriorating health. She had always suffered from sick spells. In 1941 she had a mild stroke. Eventually there would be additional strokes, partial paralysis, diminishment of vital energies. But in the meantime she devoted herself single-mindedly to her writing. In 1943 she produced what is widely considered her finest work, *The Ballad of the Sad Café,* a novella, set in a tiny southern town, that explores the complex relationships among the three grotesque figures trapped in a sexually charged triangle: a spinsterish Amazonian woman; her estranged ne'er-do-well husband (with whom she refused to sleep); and the crafty hunchback who has wandered into her life, become her pet, and inspired her to enliven the town by turning her store into a café at night. The climactic scene comes in a wrestling match between husband and wife, decided by the passionate intervention of the hunchback on the side of the husband. These bizarre events are narrated by a folksy town native in the tones of wonder and enchantment of a melancholy fairy tale.

McCullers published her most popular novel, *The Member of the Wedding,* in 1946. Its twelve-year-old protagonist was modelled in part on McCullers's younger self. Asked to be a member of her older brother's wedding, the adolescent girl believes that she was meant to live with the newlyweds, and refuses to get out of the honeymoon car after the wedding. Her initiation into the realities of love is painful, but imaginatively useful in the process of maturation. Encouraged by Tennessee Williams, McCullers turned the novel into a play, produced in 1950. It received a number of awards, including that of the New York Drama Critics Circle. The following year the play was turned into a movie, assuring McCullers's financial security.

Although she had achieved fame and fortune, she clearly had not achieved happiness. She had a succession of strokes in 1947 that brought paralysis of her left side and some loss of speech. She attempted suicide in 1948. But in spite of all her setbacks and her depression, she continued to struggle with her writing. Her play *The Square Root of Wonderful,* based on her mother's experiences, was produced in 1958; and her novel *Clock Without Hands,* set in the South and touching on the growing tensions in race relations, was published in 1961. Neither of these works matched in power that of her earlier writing.

Her name was kept before the public, however, by the successful production in 1963 of Edward Albee's dramatization of *The Ballad of the Sad Café;* and in 1967 by a movie version of *Reflections in a Golden Eye,* produced by John Huston and starring Elizabeth Taylor and Marlon Brando. During this period, the producers had cleared with McCullers a movie script for *The Heart Is a Lonely Hunter,* and shooting had begun in 1967 (distributed in 1968). McCullers appears to have lived in constant pain during her last years. Her various debilitating illnesses were complicated by breast cancer in the late 1950s and by recurring depression to the end. There were hospitalizations, operations, and finally, in 1967, a prolonged coma ending in death.

In a piece written for *Esquire* in 1959, "The Flowering Dream: Notes on Writing," McCullers succinctly defined the focus of the whole body of her work: "Spiritual isolation is the basis of most of my themes. My first book was concerned with this, almost entirely, and all of my books since, in one way or another. Love, and especially love of a person who is incapable of returning or receiving it, is at the heart of my selection of grotesque figures to write about—people whose physical incapacity is a symbol of their spiritual incapacity to love or receive love—their spiritual isolation."

ADDITIONAL READING

The Mortgaged Heart: Carson McCullers, ed. Margarita G. Smith, 1971 (contains early stories, essays, and poems).

Oliver Evans, *The Ballad of Carson McCullers: A Biography,* 1966; Lawrence Graver, *Carson McCullers,* 1969; Dale Edmonds, *Carson McCullers,* 1969; Richard M. Cook, *Carson McCullers,* 1975; Virginia Spencer Carr, *The Lonely Hunter: A Biography of Carson McCullers,* 1975; Robert R.

Kiernan, *Carson McCullers and Katherine Anne Porter: A Reference Guide*, 1976; Margaret B. McDowell, *Carson McCullers*, 1980; Louise Westling, *Sacred Groves and Ravaged Gardens: The Fiction of Eudora Welty, Carson McCullers, and Flannery O'Connor*, 1986.

TEXT

Collected Stories of Carson McCullers, 1987.

The Ballad of the Sad Café

The town itself is dreary; not much is there except the cotton mill, the two-room houses where the workers live, a few peach trees, a church with two colored windows, and a miserable main street only a hundred yards long. On Saturdays the tenants from the nearby farms come in for a day of talk and trade. Otherwise the town is lonesome, sad, and like a place that is far off and estranged from all other places in the world. The nearest train stop is Society City, and the Greyhound and White Bus Lines use the Forks Falls Road which is three miles away. The winters here are short and raw, the summers white with glare and fiery hot.

If you walk along the main street on an August afternoon there is nothing whatsoever to do. The largest building, in the very center of the town, is boarded up completely and leans so far to the right that it seems bound to collapse at any minute. The house is very old. There is about it a curious, cracked look that is very puzzling until you suddenly realize that at one time, and long ago, the right side of the front porch had been painted, and part of the wall — but the painting was left unfinished and one portion of the house is darker and dingier than the other. The building looks completely deserted. Nevertheless, on the second floor there is one window which is not boarded; sometimes in the late afternoon when the heat is at its worst a hand will slowly open the shutter and a face will look down on the town. It is a face like the terrible dim faces known in dreams — sexless and white, with two gray crossed eyes which are turned inward so sharply that they seem to be exchanging with each other one long and secret gaze of grief. The face lingers at the window for an hour or so, then the shutters are closed once more, and as likely as not there will not be another soul to be seen along the main street. These August afternoons — when your shift is finished there is absolutely nothing to do; you might as well walk down to the Forks Falls Road and listen to the chain gang.

However, here in this very town there was once a café. And this old boarded-up house was unlike any other place for many miles around. There were tables with cloths and paper napkins, colored streamers from the electric fans, great gatherings on Saturday nights. The owner of the place was Miss Amelia Evans. But the person most responsible for the success and gaiety of the place was a hunchback called Cousin Lymon. One other person had a part in the story of this café — he was the former husband of Miss Amelia, a terrible character who returned to the town after a long term in the penitentiary, caused ruin, and then went on his way again. The café has long since been closed, but it is still remembered.

The place was not always a café. Miss Amelia inherited the building from her father, and it was a store that carried mostly feed, guano,[1] and staples such as meal and snuff. Miss Amelia was rich. In addition to the store she operated a still three miles back in the swamp, and ran out the best liquor in the county. She was a dark, tall

---

[1] Manure from seabirds (or bats).

woman with bones and muscles like a man. Her hair was cut short and brushed back from the forehead, and there was about her sunburned face a tense, haggard quality. She might have been a handsome woman if, even then, she was not slightly cross-eyed. There were those who would have courted her, but Miss Amelia cared nothing for the love of men and was a solitary person. Her marriage had been unlike any other marriage ever contracted in this county — it was a strange and dangerous marriage, lasting only for ten days, that left the whole town wondering and shocked. Except for this queer marriage Miss Amelia had lived her life alone. Often she spent whole nights back in her shed in the swamp, dressed in overalls and gum boots, silently guarding the low fire of the still.

With all things which could be made by the hands Miss Amelia prospered. She sold chitterlins[2] and sausage in the town near-by. On fine autumn days she ground sorghum, and the syrup from her vats was dark golden and delicately flavored. She built the brick privy behind her store in only two weeks and was skilled in carpentering. It was only with people that Miss Amelia was not at ease. People, unless they are nilly-willy or very sick, cannot be taken into the hands and changed overnight to something more worth-while and profitable. So that the only use that Miss Amelia had for other people was to make money out of them. And in this she succeeded. Mortgages on crops and property, a sawmill, money in the bank — she was the richest woman for miles around. She would have been rich as a congressman if it were not for her one great failing, and that was her passion for lawsuits and the courts. She would involve herself in long and bitter litigation over just a trifle. It was said that if Miss Amelia so much as stumbled over a rock in the road she would glance around instinctively as though looking for something to sue about it. Aside from these lawsuits she lived a steady life and every day was very much like the day that had gone before. With the exception of her ten-day marriage, nothing happened to change this until the spring of the year that Miss Amelia was thirty years old.

It was toward midnight on a soft quiet evening in April. The sky was the color of a blue swamp iris, the moon clear and bright. The crops that spring promised well and in the past weeks the mill had run a night shift. Down by the creek the square brick factory was yellow with light, and there was the faint, steady hum of the looms. It was such a night when it is good to hear from faraway, across the dark fields, the slow song of a Negro on his way to make love. Or when it is pleasant to sit quietly and pick up a guitar, or simply to rest alone and think of nothing at all. The street that evening was deserted, but Miss Amelia's store was lighted and on the porch outside there were five people. One of these was Stumpy MacPhail, a foreman with a red face and dainty, purplish hands. On the top step were two boys in overalls, the Rainey twins — both of them lanky and slow, with white hair and sleepy green eyes. The other man was Henry Macy, a shy and timid person with gentle manners and nervous ways, who sat on the edge of the bottom step. Miss Amelia herself stood leaning against the side of the open door, her feet crossed in their big swamp boots, patiently untying knots in a rope she had come across. They had not talked for a long time.

One of the twins, who had been looking down the empty road, was the first to speak. "I see something coming," he said.

"A calf got loose," said his brother.

The approaching figure was still too distant to be clearly seen. The moon made dim, twisted shadows of the blossoming peach trees along the side of the road. In the air the odor of blossoms and sweet spring grass mingled with the warm, sour smell of the near-by lagoon.

"No. It's somebody's youngun," said Stumpy MacPhail.

Miss Amelia watched the road in silence. She had put down her rope and was fingering the straps of her overalls with her brown bony hand. She scowled, and a

---

[2]Chitterlings: the small intestines of pigs.

dark lock of hair fell down on her forehead. While they were waiting there, a dog from one of the houses down the road began a wild, hoarse howl that continued until a voice called out and hushed him. It was not until the figure was quite close, within the range of the yellow light from the porch, that they saw clearly what had come.

The man was a stranger, and it is rare that a stranger enters the town on foot at that hour. Besides, the man was a hunchback. He was scarcely more than four feet tall and he wore a ragged, dusty coat that reached only to his knees. His crooked little legs seemed too thin to carry the weight of his great warped chest and the hump that sat on his shoulders. He had a very large head, with deep-set blue eyes and a sharp little mouth. His face was both soft and sassy—at the moment his pale skin was yellowed by dust and there were lavender shadows beneath his eyes. He carried a lopsided old suitcase which was tied with a rope.

"Evening," said the hunchback, and he was out of breath.

Miss Amelia and the men on the porch neither answered his greeting nor spoke. They only looked at him.

"I am hunting for Miss Amelia Evans."

Miss Amelia pushed back her hair from her forehead and raised her chin. "How come?"

"Because I am kin to her," the hunchback said.

The twins and Stumpy MacPhail looked up at Miss Amelia.

"That's me," she said. "How do you mean 'kin'?"

"Because—" the hunchback began. He looked uneasy, almost as though he was about to cry. He rested the suitcase on the bottom step, but did not take his hand from the handle. "My mother was Fanny Jesup and she come from Cheehaw. She left Cheehaw some thirty years ago when she married her first husband. I remember hearing her tell how she had a half-sister named Martha. And back in Cheehaw today they tell me that was your mother."

Miss Amelia listened with her head turned slightly aside. She ate her Sunday dinners by herself; her place was never crowded with a flock of relatives, and she claimed kin with no one. She had had a great-aunt who owned the livery stable in Cheehaw, but that aunt was now dead. Aside from her there was only one double first cousin who lived in a town twenty miles away, but this cousin and Miss Amelia did not get on so well, and when they chanced to pass each other they spat on the side of the road. Other people had tried very hard, from time to time, to work out some kind of far-fetched connection with Miss Amelia, but with absolutely no success.

The hunchback went into a long rigmarole, mentioning names and places that were unknown to the listeners on the porch and seemed to have nothing to do with the subject. "So Fanny and Martha Jesup were half-sisters. And I am the son of Fanny's third husband. So that would make you and I—" He bent down and began to unfasten his suitcase. His hands were like dirty sparrow claws and they were trembling. The bag was full of all manner of junk—ragged clothes and odd rubbish that looked like parts out of a sewing machine, or something just as worthless. The hunchback scrambled among these belongings and brought out an old photograph. "This is a picture of my mother and her half-sister."

Miss Amelia did not speak. She was moving her jaw slowly from side to side, and you could tell from her face what she was thinking about. Stumpy MacPhail took the photograph and held it out toward the light. It was a picture of two pale, withered-up little children of about two and three years of age. The faces were tiny white blurs, and it might have been an old picture in anyone's album.

Stumpy MacPhail handed it back with no comment. "Where you come from?" he asked.

The hunchback's voice was uncertain. "I was traveling."

Still Miss Amelia did not speak. She just stood leaning against the side of the door, and looked down at the hunchback. Henry Macy winked nervously and rubbed his hands together. Then quietly he left the bottom step and disappeared. He is a good soul, and the hunchback's situation had touched his heart. Therefore he did not want to wait and watch Miss Amelia chase this newcomer off her property and run him out of town. The hunchback stood with his bag open on the bottom step; he sniffled his nose, and his mouth quivered. Perhaps he began to feel his dismal predicament. Maybe he realized what a miserable thing it was to be a stranger in the town with a suitcase full of junk, and claiming kin with Miss Amelia. At any rate he sat down on the steps and suddenly began to cry.

It was not a common thing to have an unknown hunchback walk to the store at midnight and then sit down and cry. Miss Amelia rubbed back her hair from her forehead and the men looked at each other uncomfortably. All around the town was very quiet.

At last one of the twins said: "I'll be damned if he ain't a regular Morris Finestein." Everyone nodded and agreed, for that is an expression having a certain special meaning. But the hunchback cried louder because he could not know what they were talking about. Morris Finestein was a person who had lived in the town years before. He was only a quick, skipping little Jew who cried if you called him Christkiller, and ate light bread and canned salmon every day. A calamity had come over him and he had moved away to Society City. But since then if a man were prissy in any way, or if a man ever wept, he was known as a Morris Finestein.

"Well, he is afflicted," said Stumpy MacPhail. "There is some cause."

Miss Amelia crossed the porch with two slow, gangling strides. She went down the steps and stood looking thoughtfully at the stranger. Gingerly, with one long brown forefinger, she touched the hump on his back. The hunchback still wept, but he was quieter now. The night was silent and the moon still shone with a soft, clear light — it was getting colder. Then Miss Amelia did a rare thing; she pulled out a bottle from her hip pocket and after polishing off the top with the palm of her hand she handed it to the hunchback to drink. Miss Amelia could seldom be persuaded to sell her liquor on credit, and for her to give so much as a drop away free was almost unknown.

"Drink," she said. "It will liven your gizzard."

The hunchback stopped crying, neatly licked the tears from around his mouth, and did as he was told. When he was finished, Miss Amelia took a slow swallow, warmed and washed her mouth with it, and spat. Then she also drank. The twins and the foreman had their own bottle they had paid for.

"It is smooth liquor," Stumpy MacPhail said. "Miss Amelia, I have never known you to fail."

The whiskey they drank that evening (two big bottles of it) is important. Otherwise, it would be hard to account for what followed. Perhaps without it there would never have been a café. For the liquor of Miss Amelia has a special quality of its own. It is clean and sharp on the tongue, but once down a man it glows inside him for a long time afterward. And that is not all. It is known that if a message is written with lemon juice on a clean sheet of paper there will be no sign of it. But if the paper is held for a moment to the fire then the letters turn brown and the meaning becomes clear. Imagine that the whiskey is the fire and that the message is that which is known only in the soul of a man — then the worth of Miss Amelia's liquor can be understood. Things that have gone unnoticed, thoughts that have been harbored far back in the dark mind, are suddenly recognized and comprehended. A spinner who has thought only of the loom, the dinner pail, the bed, and then the loom again — this spinner might drink some on a Sunday and come across a marsh lily. And in his palm he might hold this flower, examining the golden dainty cup, and in him suddenly might come a sweetness keen as pain. A weaver might look up suddenly and see for the first time the cold, weird radiance of midnight January sky, and a deep fright at his own smallness stop his heart. Such things as these, then, happen when a man has drunk Miss Amelia's liquor. He may suffer, or he may be spent with joy — but the experience has shown the truth; he has warmed his soul and seen the message hidden there.

They drank until it was past midnight, and the moon was clouded over so that the night was cold and dark. The hunchback still sat on the bottom steps, bent over miserably with his forehead resting on his knee. Miss Amelia stood with her hands in her pockets, one foot resting on the second step of the stairs. She had been silent for a long time. Her face had the expression often seen in slightly cross-eyed persons who are thinking deeply, a look that appears to be both very wise and very crazy. At last she said: "I don't know your name."

"I'm Lymon Willis," said the hunchback.

"Well, come on in," she said. "Some supper was left in the stove and you can eat."

Only a few times in her life had Miss Amelia invited anyone to eat with her, unless she was planning to trick them in some way, or make money out of them. So the men on the porch felt there was something wrong. Later, they said among themselves that she must have been drinking back in the swamp the better part of the afternoon. At any rate she left the porch, and Stumpy MacPhail and the twins went on off home. She bolted the front door and looked all around to see that her goods were in order. Then she went to the kitchen, which was at the back of the store. The hunchback followed her, dragging his suitcase, sniffing and wiping his nose on the sleeve of his dirty coat.

"Sit down," said Miss Amelia. "I'll just warm up what's here."

It was a good meal they had together on that night. Miss Amelia was rich and she did not grudge herself food. There was fried chicken (the breast of which the hunchback took on his own plate), mashed rootabeggars, collard greens, and hot, pale golden, sweet potatoes. Miss Amelia ate slowly and with the relish of a farm hand. She sat with both elbows on the table, bent over the plate, her knees spread wide apart and her feet braced on the rungs of the chair. As for the hunchback, he gulped down his supper as though he had not smelled food in months. During the meal one tear crept down his dingy cheek — but it was just a little leftover tear and meant nothing at all. The lamp on the table was well-trimmed, burning blue at the edges of the wick, and casting a cheerful light in the kitchen. When Miss Amelia had eaten her supper she wiped her plate carefully with a slice of light bread, and then poured her own clear, sweet syrup over the bread. The hunchback did likewise — except that he was more finicky and asked for a new plate. Having finished, Miss Amelia tilted back her chair, tightened her fist, and felt the hard, supple muscles of her right arm beneath the clean, blue cloth of her shirtsleeves — an unconscious habit with her, at the close of a meal. Then she took the lamp from the table and jerked her head toward the staircase as an invitation for the hunchback to follow after her.

Above the store there were the three rooms where Miss Amelia had lived during all of her life — two bedrooms with a large parlor in between. Few people had even seen these rooms, but it was generally known that they were well-furnished and extremely clean. And now Miss Amelia was taking up with her a dirty little hunchbacked stranger, come from God knows where. Miss Amelia walked slowly, two steps at a time, holding the lamp high. The hunchback hovered so close behind her that the swinging light made on the staircase wall one great, twisted shadow of the two of them. Soon the premises above the store were dark as the rest of the town.

The next morning was serene, with a sunrise of warm purple mixed with rose. In the fields around the town the furrows were newly plowed, and very early the tenants were at work setting out the young, deep green tobacco plants. The wild crows flew down close to the fields, making swift blue shadows on the earth. In town the people set out early with their dinner pails, and the windows of the mill were blinding gold in the sun. The air was fresh and the peach trees light as March clouds with their blossoms.

Miss Amelia came down at about dawn, as usual. She washed her head at the pump and very shortly set about her business. Later in the morning she saddled her mule and went to see about her property, planted with cotton, up near the Forks Falls Road. By noon, of course, everybody had heard about the hunchback who had come to the store in the middle of the night. But no one as yet had seen him. The day soon grew hot and the sky was a rich, midday blue. Still no one had laid an eye on this strange guest. A few people remembered that Miss Amelia's mother had had a half-sister — but there was some difference of opinion as to whether she had died or had run off with a tobacco stringer. As for the hunchback's claim, everyone thought it was a trumped-up business. And the town, knowing Miss Amelia, decided that surely she had put him out of the house after feeding him. But toward evening, when the sky had whitened, and the shift was done, a woman claimed to have a seen a crooked face at the window of one of the rooms up over the store. Miss Amelia herself said nothing. She clerked in the store for a while, argued for an hour with a farmer over a plow shaft, mended some chicken wire, locked up near sundown, and went to her rooms. The town was left puzzled and talkative.

The next day Miss Amelia did not open the store, but stayed locked up inside her premises and saw no one. Now this was the day that the rumor started — the rumor so terrible that the town and all the country about were stunned by it. The rumor was started by a weaver called Merlie Ryan. He is a man of not much account — sallow, shambling, and with no teeth in his head. He has the three-day malaria, which means that every third day the fever comes on him. So on two days he is dull and cross, but on the third day he livens up and sometimes has an idea or two, most of which are foolish. It was while Merlie Ryan was in his fever that he turned suddenly and said:

"I know what Miss Amelia done. She murdered that man for something in that suitcase."

He said this in a calm voice, as a statement of fact. And within an hour the news had swept through the town. It was a fierce and sickly tale the town built up that day. In it were all the things which cause the heart to shiver — a hunchback, a midnight burial in the swamp, the dragging of Miss Amelia through the streets of the town on the way to prison, the squabbles over what would happen to her property — all told in hushed voices and repeated with some fresh and weird detail. It rained and women forgot to bring in the washing from the lines. One or two mortals, who were in debt to Miss Amelia, even put on Sunday clothes as though it were a holiday. People clustered together on the main street, talking and watching the store.

It would be untrue to say that all the town took part in this evil festival. There were a few sensible men who reasoned that Miss Amelia, being rich, would not go out of her way to murder a vagabond for a few trifles of junk. In the town there were even three good people, and they did not want this crime, not even for the sake of the interest and the great commotion it would entail; it gave them no pleasure to think of Miss Amelia holding to the bars of the penitentiary and being electrocuted in Atlanta. These good people judged Miss Amelia in a different way from what the others judged her. When a person is as contrary in every single respect as she was and when the sins of a person have amounted to such a point that they can hardly be remembered all at once — then this person plainly requires a special judgment. They remembered that Miss Amelia had been born dark and somewhat queer of face, raised motherless by her father who was a solitary man, that early in youth she had grown to be six feet two inches tall which in itself is not natural for a woman, and that her ways and habits of life were too peculiar ever to reason about. Above all, they remembered her puzzling marriage, which was the most unreasonable scandal ever to happen in this town.

So these good people felt toward her something near to pity. And when she was out on her wild business, such as rushing in a house to drag forth a sewing machine in payment for a debt, or getting herself worked up over some matter concerning the law — they had toward her a feeling which was a mixture of exasperation, a ridiculous little inside tickle, and a deep, unnamable sadness. But enough of the good people, for there were only three of them; the rest of the town was making a holiday of this fancied crime the whole of the afternoon.

Miss Amelia herself, for some strange reason, seemed unaware of all this. She spent most of her day upstairs. When down in the store, she prowled around peacefully, her hands deep in the pockets of her overalls and head bent so low that her chin was tucked inside the collar of her shirt. There was no bloodstain on her anywhere. Often she stopped and just stood somberly looking down at the cracks in the floor, twisting a lock of her short-cropped hair, and whispering something to herself. But most of the day was spent upstairs.

Dark came on. The rain that afternoon had chilled the air, so that the evening was bleak and gloomy as in wintertime. There were no stars in the sky, and a light, icy drizzle had set in. The lamps in the houses made mournful, wavering flickers when watched from the street. A wind had come up, not from the swamp side of the town but from the cold black pinewoods to the north.

The clocks in the town struck eight. Still nothing had happened. The bleak night, after the gruesome talk of the day, put a fear in some people, and they stayed home close to the fire. Others were gathered in groups together. Some eight or ten men had convened on the porch of Miss Amelia's store. They were silent and were indeed just waiting about. They themselves did not know what they were waiting for, but it was this: in times of tension, when some great action is impending, men gather and wait in this way. And after a time there will come a moment when all together they will act in unison, not from thought or from the will of any one man, but as though their instincts had merged together so that the decision belongs to no single one of them, but to the group as a whole. At such a time no individual hesitates. And whether the matter will be settled peaceably, or whether the joint action will result in ransacking, violence, and crime, depends on destiny. So the men waited soberly on the porch of Miss Amelia's store, not one of them realizing what they would do, but knowing inwardly that they must wait, and that the time had almost come.

Now the door to the store was open. Inside it was bright and natural-looking. To the left was the counter where slabs of white meat, rock candy, and tobacco were kept. Behind this were shelves of salted white meat and meal. The right side of the store was mostly filled with farm implements and such. At the back of the store, to the left, was the door leading up the stairs, and it was open. And at the far right of the store there was another door which led to a little room that Miss Amelia called her office. This door was also open. And at eight o'clock that evening Miss Amelia could be seen there sitting before her rolltop desk, figuring with a fountain pen and some pieces of paper.

The office was cheerfully lighted, and Miss Amelia did not seem to notice the delegation on the porch. Everything around her was in great order, as usual. This office was a room well-known, in a dreadful way, throughout the country. It was there Miss Amelia transacted all business. On the desk was a carefully covered typewriter which she knew how to run, but used only for the most important documents. In the drawers were literally thousands of papers, all filed according to the alphabet. This office was also the place where Miss Amelia received sick people, for she enjoyed doctoring and did a great deal of it. Two whole shelves were crowded with bottles and various paraphernalia. Against the wall was a bench where the patients sat. She could sew up a wound with a burnt needle so that it would not turn green. For burns she had a cool, sweet syrup. For unlocated sickness there were any number of different medicines which she had brewed herself from unknown recipes. They wrenched loose the bowels very well, but they could not be given to small children, as they caused bad convulsions; for them she had an entirely separate draught, gentler and sweet-flavored. Yes, all in all, she was considered a good doctor. Her hands, though very large and bony, had a light touch about them. She possessed great imagination and used hundreds of different cures. In the face of the most dangerous and extraordinary treatment she did not hesitate, and no disease was so terrible but what she would undertake to cure it. In this there was one exception. If a patient came with a female complaint she could do nothing. Indeed at the mere mention of the words her face would slowly darken with shame, and she would stand there craning her neck against the collar of her shirt, or rubbing her swamp boots together, for all the world like a great, shamed, dumb-tongued child. But in other matters people trusted her. She charged no fees whatsoever and always had a raft of patients.

On this evening Miss Amelia wrote with her fountain pen a good deal. But even so she could not be forever unaware of the group waiting out there on the dark porch, and watching her. From time to time she looked up and regarded them steadily. But she did not holler out to them to demand why they were loafing around her property like a sorry bunch of gabbies. Her face was proud and stern, as it always was when she sat at the desk of her office. After a time their peering in like that seemed to annoy her. She wiped her cheek with a red handkerchief, got up, and closed the office door.

Now to the group on the porch this gesture acted as a signal. The time had come. They had stood for a long while with the night raw and gloomy in the street behind them. They had waited long and just at that moment the instinct to act came on them. All at once, as though moved by one will, they walked into the store. At that moment the eight men looked very much alike—all wearing blue overalls, most of them with whitish hair, all pale of face, and all with a set, dreaming look in the eye. What they would have done next no one knows. But at that instant there was a noise at the head of the staircase. The men looked up and then stood dumb with shock. It was the hunchback, whom they had already murdered in their minds. Also, the creature was not at all as had been pictured to them—not a pitiful and dirty little chatterer, alone and beggared in this world. Indeed, he was like nothing any man among them had ever beheld until that time. The room was still as death.

The hunchback came down slowly with the proudness of one who owns every plank of the floor beneath his feet. In the past days he had greatly changed. For one thing he was clean beyond words. He still wore his little coat, but it was brushed off and neatly mended. Beneath this was a fresh red and black checkered shirt belonging to Miss Amelia. He did not wear trousers such as ordinary men are meant to wear, but a pair of tight-fitting little knee-length breeches. On his skinny legs he wore black stockings, and his shoes were of a special kind, being queerly shaped, laced up over the ankles, and newly cleaned and polished with wax. Around his neck, so that his large, pale ears were almost completely covered, he wore a shawl of lime-green wool, the fringes of which almost touched the floor.

The hunchback walked down the store with his stiff little strut and then stood in the center of the group that had come inside. They cleared a space about him and stood looking with hands loose at their sides and eyes wide open. The hunchback himself got his bearings in an odd manner. He regarded each person steadily at his own eye-level, which was about belt line for an ordinary man. Then with shrewd deliberation he examined each man's lower regions—from the waist to the sole of the shoe. When he had satisfied himself he closed his eyes for a moment and shook his head, as though in his opinion what he had seen did not amount to much. Then with assurance, only to confirm himself, he tilted back his head and took in the halo of faces around him with one long, circling stare. There was a half-filled sack of guano on the left side of the store, and when he had found his bearings in this way, the hunchback sat down upon it. Cozily settled, with his little legs crossed, he took from his coat pocket a certain object.

Now it took some moments for the men in the store to regain their ease. Merlie Ryan, he of the three-day fever who had started the rumor that day, was the first to speak. He looked at the object which the hunchback was fondling, and said in a hushed voice:

"What is it you have there?"

Each man knew well what it was the hunchback was handling. For it was the snuffbox which had belonged to Miss Amelia's father. The snuffbox was of blue enamel with a dainty embellishment of wrought gold on the lid. The group knew it well and marveled. They glanced warily at the closed office door, and heard the low sound of Miss Amelia whistling to herself.

"Yes, what is it, Peanut?"

The hunchback looked up quickly and sharpened his mouth to speak. "Why, this is a lay-low to catch meddlers."

The hunchback reached in the box with his scrambly little fingers and ate something, but he offered no one around him a taste. It was not even proper snuff which he was taking, but a mixture of sugar and cocoa. This he took, though, as snuff, pocketing a little wad of it beneath his lower lip and licking down neatly into this with a flick of his tongue which made a frequent grimace come over his face.

"The very teeth in my head have always tasted sour to me," he said in explanation. "This is the reason why I take this kind of sweet snuff."

The group still clustered around, feeling somewhat gawky and bewildered. This sensation never quite wore off, but it was soon tempered by another feeling—an air of intimacy in the room and a vague festivity. Now the names of the men of the group there on that evening were as follows: Hasty Malone, Robert Calvert Hale, Merlie Ryan, Reverend T. M. Willin, Rosser Cline, Rip Wellborn, Henry Ford Crimp, and Horace Wells. Except for Reverend Willin, they are all alike in many ways as has been said—all having taken pleasure from something or other, all having wept and suffered in some way, most of them tractable unless exasperated. Each of them worked in the mill, and lived with others in a two- or three-room house for which the rent was ten dollars or twelve dollars a month. All had been paid that afternoon, for it was Saturday. So, for the present, think of them as a whole.

The hunchback, however, was already sorting them out in his mind. Once comfortably settled he began to chat with everyone, asking questions such as if a man was married, how old he was, how much his wages came to in an average week, et cetera— picking his way along to inquiries which were downright intimate. Soon the group was joined by others in the town, Henry Macy, idlers who had sensed something extraordinary, women came to fetch their men who lingered on, and even one loose, towhead child who tiptoed into the store, stole a box of animal crackers, and made off very quietly. So the premises of Miss Amelia were soon crowded, and she herself had not yet opened her office door.

There is a type of person who has a quality about him that sets him apart from other and more ordinary human beings. Such a person has an instinct which is usually found only in small children, an instinct to establish immediate and vital contact between himself and all things in the world. Certainly the hunchback was of this type. He had only been in the store half an hour before an immediate contact had been established between him and each other individual. It was as though he had lived in the town for years, was a well-known character, and had been sitting and talking there on that guano sack for countless evenings. This, together with the fact that it was Saturday night, could account for the air of freedom and illicit gladness in the store. There was a tension, also, partly because of the oddity of the situation and because Miss Amelia was still closed off in her office and had not yet made her appearance.

She came out that evening at ten o'clock. And those who were expecting some drama at her entrance were disappointed. She opened the door and walked in with her slow, gangling swagger. There was a streak of ink on one side of her nose, and she had knotted the red handkerchief about her neck. She seemed to notice nothing unusual. Her gray, crossed eyes glanced over to the place where the hunchback was sitting, and for a moment lingered there. The rest of the crowd in her store she regarded with only a peaceable surprise.

"Does anyone want waiting on?" she asked quietly.

There were a number of customers, because it was Saturday night, and they all wanted liquor. Now Miss Amelia had dug up an aged barrel only three days past and had siphoned it into bottles back by the still. This night she took the money from the customers and counted it beneath the bright light. Such was the ordinary procedure. But after this what happened was not ordinary. Always before, it was necessary to go around to the dark back yard, and there she would hand out your bottle through the kitchen door. There was no feeling of joy in the transaction. After getting his liquor the customer walked off into the night. Or, if his wife would not have it in the home, he was allowed to come back around to the front porch of the store and guzzle there or in the street. Now, both the porch and the street before it were the property of Miss Amelia, and no mistake about it—but she did not regard them as premises; the premises began at the front door and took in the entire inside of the building. There she had never allowed liquor to be opened or drunk by anyone but herself. Now for the first time she broke this rule. She went to the kitchen, with the hunchback close at her heels, and she brought back the bottles into the warm, bright store. More than that she furnished some glasses and opened two boxes of crackers so that they were there hospitably in a platter on the counter and anyone who wished could take one free.

She spoke to no one but the hunchback, and she only asked him in a somewhat harsh and husky voice: "Cousin Lymon, will you have yours straight, or warmed in a pan with water on the stove?"

"If you please, Amelia," the hunchback said. (And since what time had anyone presumed to address Miss Amelia by her bare name, without a title of respect?— Certainly not her bridegroom and her husband of ten days. In fact, not since the death of her father, who for some reason had always called her Little, had anyone dared to address her in such a familiar way.) "If you please, I'll have it warmed."

Now, this was the beginning of the café. It was as simple as that. Recall that the night was gloomy as in wintertime, and to have sat around the property outside would have made a sorry celebration. But inside there was company and a genial warmth. Someone had rattled up the stove in the rear, and those who bought bottles shared their liquor with friends. Several women were there and they had twists of licorice, a Nehi, or even a swallow of the whisky. The hunchback was still a novelty and his presence amused everyone. The bench in the office was brought in, together with several extra chairs. Other people leaned against the counter or made themselves comfortable on barrels and sacks. Nor did the opening of liquor on the premises cause any rambunctiousness, indecent giggles, or misbehavior whatsoever. On the contrary the company was polite even to the point of a certain timidness. For people in this town were then unused to gathering together for the sake of pleasure. They met to work in the mill. Or on Sunday there would be an all-day camp meeting—and though that is a pleasure, the intention of the whole affair is to sharpen your view of Hell and put into you a keen fear of the Lord Almighty. But the spirit of a café is altogether different. Even the richest, greediest old rascal will behave himself, insulting no one in a proper café. And poor people look about them gratefully and pinch up the salt in a dainty and modest manner. For the atmosphere of a proper café implies these qualities: fellowship, the satisfactions of the belly, and a certain gaiety and grace of behavior. This had never been told to the gathering in Miss Amelia's store that night. But they knew it of themselves, although never, of course, until that time had there been a café in the town.

Now, the cause of all this, Miss Amelia, stood most of the evening in the doorway leading to the kitchen. Outwardly she did not seem changed at all. But there were many who noticed her face. She watched all that went on, but most of the time her eyes were fastened lonesomely on the hunchback. He strutted about the store, eating from his snuffbox, and being at once sour and agreeable. Where Miss Amelia stood, the light from the chinks of the stove cast a glow, so that her brown, long face was somewhat brightened. She seemed to be looking inward. There was in her expression pain, perplexity, and uncertain joy. Her lips were not so firmly set as usual, and she swallowed often. Her skin had paled and her large empty hands were sweating. Her look that night, then, was the lonesome look of the lover.

This opening of the café came to an end at midnight. Everyone said good-bye to everyone else in a friendly fashion. Miss Amelia shut the front door of her premises, but forgot to bolt it. Soon everything—the main street with its three stores, the mill, the houses—all the town, in fact—was dark and silent. And so ended three days and nights in which had come an arrival of a stranger, an unholy holiday, and the start of the café.

Now time must pass. For the next four years are much alike. There are great changes, but these changes are brought about bit by bit, in simple steps which in themselves do not appear to be important. The hunchback continued to live with Miss Amelia. The café expanded in a gradual way. Miss Amelia began to sell her liquor by the drink, and some tables were brought into the store. There were customers every evening, and on Saturday a great crowd. Miss Amelia began to serve fried catfish suppers at fifteen cents a plate. The hunchback cajoled her into buying a fine mechanical piano. Within two years the place was a store no longer, but had been converted into a proper café, open every evening from six until twelve o'clock.

Each night the hunchback came down the stairs with the air of one who has a grand opinion of himself. He always smelled slightly of turnip greens, as Miss Amelia rubbed him night and morning with pot liquor to give him strength. She spoiled him to a point beyond reason, but nothing seemed to strengthen him; food only made his hump and his head grow larger while the rest of him remained weakly and deformed. Miss Amelia was the same in appearance. During the week she still wore swamp boots and overalls, but on Sunday she put on a dark red dress that hung on her in a most peculiar fashion. Her manners, however, and her way of life were greatly changed. She still loved a fierce lawsuit, but she was not so quick to cheat her fellow man and to exact cruel payments. Because the hunchback was so extremely sociable she even went about a little—to revivals, to funerals, and so forth. Her doctoring was as successful as ever, her liquor even finer than before, if that were possible. The café itself proved profitable and was the only place of pleasure for many miles around.

So for the moment regard these years from random and disjointed views. See the hunchback marching in Miss Amelia's footsteps when on a red winter morning they set out for the pinewoods to hunt. See them working on her properties—with Cousin Lymon standing by and doing absolutely nothing, but quick to point out any laziness among the hands. On autumn afternoons they sat on the back steps chopping sugar cane. The glaring summer days they spent back in the swamp where the water cypress is a deep black green, where beneath the tangled swamp trees there is a drowsy gloom. When the path leads through a bog or a stretch of blackened water see Miss Amelia bend down to let Cousin Lymon scramble on her back—and see her wading forward with the hunchback settled on her shoulders, clinging to her ears or to her broad forehead. Occasionally Miss Amelia cranked up the Ford which she had bought and treated Cousin Lymon to a picture-show in Cheehaw, or to some distant fair or cockfight; the hunchback took a passionate delight in spectacles. Of course, they were in their café every morning, they would often sit for hours together by the fireplace in the parlor upstairs. For the hunchback was sickly at night and dreaded to lie looking into the dark. He had a deep fear of death. And Miss Amelia would not leave him by himself to suffer with this fright. It may even be reasoned that the growth of the café came about mainly on this account; it was a thing that brought him company and pleasure and that helped him through the night. So compose from such flashes an image of these years as a whole. And for a moment let it rest.

Now some explanation is due for all this behavior. The time has come to speak about love. For Miss Amelia loved Cousin Lymon. So much was clear to everyone. They lived in the same house together and were never seen apart. Therefore, according to Mrs. MacPhail, a warty-nosed old busybody who is continually moving her sticks of furniture from one part of the front room to another; according to her and to certain others, these two were living in sin. If they were related, they were only a cross between first and second cousins, and even that could in no way be proved. Now, of course Miss Amelia was a powerful blunderbuss of a person, more than six feet tall—and Cousin Lymon a weakly little hunchback reaching only to her waist. But so much the better for Mrs. Stumpy MacPhail and her cronies, for they and their kind glory in conjunctions which are ill-matched and pitiful. So let them be. The good people thought that if those two had found some satisfaction of the flesh between themselves, then it was a matter concerning them and God alone. All sensible people agreed in their opinion about this conjecture—and their answer was a plain, flat *no*. What sort of thing, then, was this love?

First of all, love is a joint experience between two persons—but the fact that it is a joint experience does not mean that it is a similar experience to the two people involved. There are the lover and the beloved, but these two come from different countries. Often the beloved is only a stimulus for all the stored-up love which has lain quiet within the lover for a long time hitherto. And somehow every lover knows this. He feels in his soul that his love is a solitary thing. He comes to know a new, strange loneliness and it is this knowledge which makes him suffer. So there is only one thing for the lover to do. He must house his love within himself as best he can; he must create for himself a whole new inward world—a world intense and strange, complete in himself. Let it be added here that this lover about whom we speak need not necessarily be a young man saving for a wedding ring—this lover can be man, woman, child, or indeed any human creature on this earth.

Now, the beloved can also be of any description. The most outlandish people can be the stimulus for love. A man may be a doddering great-grandfather and still love only a strange girl he saw in the streets of Cheehaw one afternoon two decades past. The preacher may love a fallen woman. The beloved may be treacherous, greasy-headed, and given to evil habits. Yes, and the lover may see this as clearly as anyone else—but that does not affect the evolution of his love one whit. A most mediocre person can be the object of a love which is wild, extravagant, and beautiful as the poison lilies of the swamp. A good man may be the stimulus for a love both violent and debased, or a jabbering madman may bring about in the soul of someone a tender and simple idyll. Therefore, the value and quality of any love is determined solely by the lover himself.

It is for this reason that most of us would rather love than be loved. Almost everyone wants to be the lover. And the curt truth is that, in a deep secret way, the state of being beloved is intolerable to many. The beloved fears and hates the lover, and with the best of reasons. For the lover is forever trying to strip bare his beloved. The lover craves any possible relation with the beloved, even if this experience can cause him only pain.

It has been mentioned before that Miss Amelia was once married. And this curious episode might as well be accounted for at this point. Remember that it all happened long ago, and that it was Miss Amelia's only personal contact, before the hunchback came to her, with this phenomenon—love.

The town then was the same as it is now, except there were two stores instead of three and the peach trees along the street were more crooked and smaller than they are now. Miss Amelia was nineteen years old at the time, and her father had been dead many months. There was in the town at that time a loom-fixer named Marvin Macy. He was the brother of Henry Macy, although to know them you would never guess that those two could be kin. For Marvin Macy was the handsomest man in this region—being six feet one inch tall, hard-muscled, and with slow gray eyes and curly hair. He was well off, made good wages, and had a gold watch which opened in the back to a picture of a waterfall. From the outward and worldly point of view Marvin

Macy was a fortunate fellow; he needed to bow and scrape to no one and always got just what he wanted. But from a more serious and thoughtful viewpoint Marvin Macy was not a person to be envied, for he was an evil character. His reputation was as bad, if not worse, than that of any young man in the county. For years, when he was a boy, he had carried about with him the dried and salted ear of a man he had killed in a razor fight. He had chopped off the tails of squirrels in the pinewoods just to please his fancy, and in his left hip pocket he carried forbidden marijuana weed to tempt those who were discouraged and drawn toward death. Yet in spite of his well-known reputation he was the beloved of many females in this region—and there were at the time several young girls who were clean-haired and soft-eyed, with tender sweet little buttocks and charming ways. These gentle young girls he degraded and shamed. Then finally, at the age of twenty-two, this Marvin Macy chose Miss Amelia. That solitary, gangling, queer-eyed girl was the one he longed for. Nor did he want her because of her money, but solely out of love.

And love changed Marvin Macy. Before the time when he loved Miss Amelia it could be questioned if such a person had within him a heart and soul. Yet there is some explanation for the ugliness of his character, for Marvin Macy had had a hard beginning in this world. He was one of seven unwanted children whose parents could hardly be called parents at all; these parents were wild younguns who liked to fish and roam around the swamp. Their own children, and there was a new one almost every year, were only a nuisance to them. At night when they came home from the mill they would look at the children as though they did not know wherever they had come from. If the children cried they were beaten, and the first thing they learned in this world was to seek the darkest corner of the room and try to hide themselves as best they could. They were as thin as little whitehaired ghosts, and they did not speak, not even to each other. Finally, they were abandoned by their parents altogether and left to the mercies of the town. It was a hard winter, with the mill closed down almost three months, and much misery everywhere. But this is not a town to let white orphans perish in the road before your eyes. So here is what came about: the eldest child, who was eight years old, walked into Cheehaw and disappeared—perhaps he took a freight train somewhere and went out into the world, nobody knows. Three other children were boarded out amongst the town, being sent around from one kitchen to another, and as they were delicate they died before Easter time. The last two children were Marvin Macy and Henry Macy, and they were taken into a home. There was a good woman in the town named Mrs. Mary Hale, and she took Marvin Macy and Henry Macy and loved them as her own. They were raised in her household and treated well.

But the hearts of small children are delicate organs. A cruel beginning in this world can twist them into curious shapes. The heart of a hurt child can shrink so that forever afterward it is hard and pitted as the seed of a peach. Or again, the heart of such a child may fester and swell until it is a misery to carry within the body, easily chafed and hurt by the most ordinary things. This last is what happened to Henry Macy, who is so opposite to his brother, is the kindest and gentlest man in town. He lends his wages to those who are unfortunate, and in the old days he used to care for the children whose parents were at the café on Saturday night. But he is a shy man, and he has the look of one who has a swollen heart and suffers. Marvin Macy, however, grew to be bold and fearless and cruel. His heart turned tough as the horns of Satan, and until the time when he loved Miss Amelia he brought to his brother and the good woman who raised him nothing but shame and trouble.

But love reversed the character of Marvin Macy. For two years he loved Miss Amelia, but he did not declare himself. He would stand near the door of her premises, his cap in his hand, his eyes meek and longing and misty gray. He reformed himself completely. He was good to his brother and foster mother, and he saved his wages and learned thrift. Moreover, he reached out toward God. No longer did he lie around on the floor of the front porch all day Sunday, singing and playing his guitar; he attended church services and was present at all religious meetings. He learned good manners: he trained himself to rise and give his chair to a lady, and he quit swearing and fighting and using holy names in vain. So for two years he passed through this transformation and improved his character in every way. Then at the end of the two years he went one evening to Miss Amelia, carrying a bunch of swamp flowers, a sack of chitterlins, and a silver ring—that night Marvin Macy declared himself.

And Miss Amelia married him. Later everyone wondered why. Some said it was because she wanted to get herself some wedding presents. Others believed it came about through the nagging of Miss Amelia's great-aunt in Cheehaw, who was a terrible old woman. Anyway, she strode with great steps down the aisle of the church wearing her dead mother's bridal gown, which was of yellow satin and at least twelve inches too short for her. It was a winter afternoon and the clear sun shone through the ruby windows of the church and put a curious glow on the pair before the altar. As the marriage lines were read Miss Amelia kept making an odd gesture—she would rub the palm of her right hand down the side of her satin wedding gown. She was reaching for the pocket of her overalls, and being unable to find it her face became impatient, bored, and exasperated. At last when the lines were spoken and the marriage prayer was done Miss Amelia hurried out of the church, not taking the arm of her husband, but walking at least two paces ahead of him.

The church is no distance from the store so the bride and groom walked home. It is said that on the way Miss Amelia began to talk about some deal she had worked up with a farmer over a load of kindling wood. In fact, she treated her groom in exactly the same manner she would have used with some customer who had come into the store to buy a pint from her. But so far all had gone decently enough; the town was gratified, as people had seen what this love had done to Marvin Macy and hoped that it might also reform his bride. At least, they counted on the marriage to tone down Miss Amelia's temper, to put a bit of bride-fat on her, and to change her at last into a calculable woman.

They were wrong. The young boys who watched through the window on that night said that this is what actually happened: The bride and groom ate a grand supper prepared by Jeff, the old Negro who cooked for Miss Amelia. The bride took second servings of everything, but the groom picked with his food. Then the bride went about her ordinary business—reading the newspaper, finishing an inventory of the stock in the store, and so forth. The groom hung about in the doorway with a loose, foolish, blissful face and was not noticed. At eleven o'clock the bride took a lamp and went upstairs. The groom followed close behind her. So far all had gone decently enough, but what followed after was unholy.

Within half an hour Miss Amelia had stomped down the stairs in breeches and a khaki jacket. Her face had darkened so that it looked quite black. She slammed the kitchen door and gave it an ugly kick. Then she controlled herself. She poked up the fire, sat down, and put her feet up on the kitchen stove. She read the Farmer's Almanac, drank coffee, and had a smoke with her father's pipe. Her face was hard, stern, and had now whitened to its natural color. Sometimes she paused to jot down some information from the Almanac on a piece of paper. Toward dawn she went into her office and uncovered her typewriter, which she had recently bought and was only just learning how to run. That was the way in which she spent the whole of her wedding night. At daylight she went out to her yard as though nothing whatsoever had occurred and did some carpentering on a rabbit hutch which she had begun the week before and intended to sell somewhere.

A groom is in a sorry fix when he is unable to bring his well-beloved bride to bed with him, and when the whole town knows it. Marvin Macy came down that day still in his wedding finery, and with a sick face. God knows how he had spent the night. He moped about the yard, watching Miss Amelia, but keeping some distance away from her. Then toward noon an idea came to him and he went off in the direction of Society City. He returned with presents—an opal ring, a pink enamel doreen of the sort which was then in fashion, a silver bracelet with two hearts on it, and a box of candy which had cost two dollars and a half. Miss Amelia looked over these fine gifts and opened the box of candy, for she was hungry. The rest of the presents she judged shrewdly for a moment to sum up their value—then she put them in the counter out for sale. The night was spent in much the same manner as the preceding one—except that Miss Amelia brought her feather mattress to make a pallet by the kitchen stove, and she slept fairly well.

Things went on like this for three days. Miss Amelia went about her business as usual, and took great interest in some rumor that a bridge was to be built some ten miles down the road. Marvin Macy still followed her about around the premises, and it was plain from his face how he suffered. Then on the fourth day he did an extremely simple-minded thing: he went to Cheehaw and came back with a lawyer. Then in Miss Amelia's office he signed over to her the whole of his worldly goods, which was ten acres of timberland which he had bought with the money he had saved. She studied the paper sternly to make sure there was no possibility of a trick and filed it soberly in the drawer of her desk. That afternoon Marvin Macy took a quart bottle of whisky and went with it alone out in the swamp while the sun was still shining. Toward evening he came in drunk, went up to Miss Amelia with wet wide eyes, and put his hand on her shoulder. He was trying to tell her something, but before he could open his mouth she had swung once with her fist and hit his face so hard that he was thrown back against the wall and one of his front teeth was broken.

The rest of this affair can only be mentioned in bare outline. After this first blow Miss Amelia hit him whenever he came within arm's reach of her, and whenever he was drunk. At last she turned him off the premises altogether, and he was forced to suffer publicly. During the day he hung around just outside the boundary line of Miss Amelia's property and sometimes with a drawn crazy look he would fetch his rifle and sit there cleaning it, peering at Miss Amelia steadily. If she was afraid she did not show it, but her face was sterner than ever, and often she spat on the ground. His last foolish effort was to climb in the window of her store one night and to sit there in the dark, for no purpose whatsoever, until she came down the stairs next morning. For this Miss Amelia set off immediately to the courthouse in Cheehaw with some notion that she could get him locked in the penitentiary for trespassing. Marvin Macy left the town that day, and no one saw him go, or knew just where he went. On leaving he put a long curious letter, partly written in pencil and partly with ink, beneath Miss Amelia's door. It was a wild love letter—but in it were also included threats, and he swore that in his life he would get even with her. His marriage had lasted for ten days. And the town felt the special satisfaction that people feel when someone has been thoroughly done in by some scandalous and terrible means.

Miss Amelia was left with everything that Marvin Macy had ever owned—his timberwood, his gild watch, every one of his possessions. But she seemed to attach little value to them and that spring she cut up his Klansman's robe to cover her tobacco plants. So all that he had ever done was to make her richer and to bring her love. But, strange to say, she never spoke of him but with a terrible and spiteful bitterness. She never once referred to him by name but always mentioned him scornfully as "that loom-fixer I was married to."

And later, when horrifying rumors concerning Marvin Macy reached the town, Miss Amelia was very pleased. For the true character of Marvin Macy finally revealed itself, once he had freed himself of his love. He became a criminal whose picture and whose name were in all the papers in the state. He robbed three filling stations and held up the A&P store of Society City with a sawed-off gun. He was suspected of the murder of Slit-Eye Sam who was a noted highjacker. All these crimes were connected with the name of Marvin Macy, so that his evil became famous through many counties. Then finally the law captured him, drunk, on the floor of a tourist cabin, his guitar by his side, and fifty-seven dollars in his right shoe. He was tried, sentenced, and sent off to the penitentiary near Atlanta. Miss Amelia was deeply gratified.

Well, all this happened a long time ago, and it is the story of Miss Amelia's marriage. The town laughed a long time over this grotesque affair. But though the outward facts of this love are indeed sad and ridiculous, it must be remembered that the real story was that which took place in the soul of the lover himself. So who but God can be the final judge of this or any other love? On the very first night of the café there were several who suddenly thought of this broken bridegroom, locked in the gloomy penitentiary, many miles away. And in the years that followed, Marvin Macy was not altogether forgotten in the town. His name was never mentioned in the presence of Miss Amelia or the hunchback. But the memory of his passion and his crimes, and the thought of him trapped in his cell in the penitentiary, was like a troubling undertone beneath the happy love of Miss Amelia and the gaiety of the café. So do not forget this Marvin Macy, as he is to act a terrible part in the story which is yet to come.

During the four years in which the store became a café the rooms upstairs were not changed. This part of the premises remained exactly as it had been all of Miss Amelia's life, as it was in the time of her father, and most likely his father before him. The three rooms, it is already known, were immaculately clean. The smallest object had its exact place, and everything was wiped and dusted by Jeff, the servant of Miss Amelia, each morning. The front room belonged to Cousin Lymon—it was the room where Marvin Macy had stayed during the few nights he was allowed on the premises, and before that it was the bedroom of Miss Amelia's father. The room was furnished with a large chifforobe, a bureau covered with a stiff white linen cloth crocheted at the edges, and a marble-topped table. The bed was immense, an old fourposter made of carved, dark rosewood. On it were two feather mattresses, bolsters, and a number of handmade comforts. The bed was so high that beneath it were two wooden steps—no occupant had ever used these steps before, but Cousin Lymon drew them out each night and walked up in state. Beside the steps, but pushed modestly out of view, there was a china chamberpot painted with pink roses. No rug covered the dark, polished floor and the curtains were of some white stuff, also crocheted at the edges.

On the other side of the parlor was Miss Amelia's bedroom, and it was smaller and very simple. The bed was narrow and made of pine. There was a bureau for her breeches, shirts, and Sunday dress, and she had hammered two nails in the closet wall on which to hang her swamp boots. There were no curtains, rugs, or ornaments of any kind.

The large middle room, the parlor, was elaborate. The rosewood sofa, upholstered in threadbare green silk, was before the fireplace. Marble-topped tables, two Singer sewing machines, a big vase of pampas grass—everything was rich and grand. The most important piece of furniture in the parlor was a big, glass-doored cabinet in which was kept a number of treasures and curios. Miss Amelia had added two objects to this collection—one was a large acorn from a water oak, the other a little velvet box holding two small, grayish stones. Sometimes when she had nothing much to do, Miss Amelia would take out this velvet box and stand by the window with the stones in the palm of her hand, looking down at them with a mixture of fascination, dubious respect, and fear. They were the kidney stones of Miss Amelia herself, and had been taken from her by the doctor in Cheehaw some years ago. It had been a terrible experience, from the first minute to the last, and all she had got out of it were those two little stones; she was bound to set great store by them, or else admit to a mighty sorry bargain. So she kept them and in the second year of Cousin Lymon's stay with her she had them set as ornaments in a watch chain which she gave to him. The other object she had added to the collection, the large acorn, was precious to her—but when she looked at it her face was always saddened and perplexed.

"Amelia, what does it signify?" Cousin Lymon asked her.

"Why, it's just an acorn," she answered. "Just an acorn I picked up on the afternoon Big Papa died."

"How do you mean?" Cousin Lymon insisted.

"I mean it's just an acorn I spied on the ground that day. I picked it up and put it in my pocket. But I don't know why."

"What a peculiar reason to keep it," Cousin Lymon said.

The talks of Miss Amelia and Cousin Lymon in the rooms upstairs, usually in the first few hours of the morning when the hunchback could not sleep, were many. As a rule, Miss Amelia was a silent woman, not letting her tongue run wild on any subject that happened to pop into her head. There were certain topics of conversation, however, in which she took pleasure. All these subjects had one point in common—they were interminable. She liked to contemplate problems which could be worked over for decades and still remain insoluble. Cousin Lymon, on the other hand, enjoyed talking on any subject whatsoever, as he was a great chatterer. Their approach to any conversation was altogether different. Miss Amelia always kept to the broad, rambling generalities of the matter, going on endlessly in a low, thoughtful voice and getting nowhere—while Cousin Lymon would interrupt her suddenly to pick up, magpie fashion, some detail which, even if unimportant, was at least concrete and bearing on some practical facet close at hand. Some of the favorite subjects of Miss Amelia were: the stars, the reason why Negroes are black, the best treatment for cancer, and so forth. Her father was also an interminable subject which was dear to her.

"Why, Law," she would say to Lymon. "Those days I slept. I'd go to bed just as the lamp was turned on and sleep—why, I'd sleep like I was drowned in warm axle grease. Then come daybreak Big Papa would walk in and put his hand down on my shoulder. 'Get stirring, Little,' he would say. Then later he would holler up the stairs from the kitchen when the stove was hot. 'Fried grits,' he would holler. 'White meat and gravy. Ham and eggs.' And I'd run down the stairs and dress by the hot stove while he was out washing at the pump. Then off we'd go to the still or maybe—"

"The grits we had this morning was poor," Cousin Lymon said. "Fried too quick so that the inside never heated."

"And when Big Papa would run off the liquor in those days—" The conversation would go on endlessly, with Miss Amelia's long legs stretched out before the hearth; for winter or summer there was always a fire in the grate, as Lymon was cold-natured. He sat in a low chair across from her, his feet not quite touching the floor and his torso usually well-wrapped in a blanket or the green wool shawl. Miss Amelia never mentioned her father to anyone else except Cousin Lymon.

That was one of the ways in which she showed her love for him. He had her confidence in the most delicate and vital matters. He alone knew where she kept the chart that showed where certain barrels of whisky were buried on a piece of property near-by. He alone had access to her bankbook and the key to the cabinet of curios. He took money from the cash register, whole handfuls of it, and appreciated the loud jingle it made inside his pockets. He owned almost everything on the premises, for when he was cross Miss Amelia would prowl about and find him some present—so that now there was hardly anything left close at hand to give him. The only part of her life that she did not want Cousin Lymon to share with her was the memory of her ten-day marriage. Marvin Macy was the one subject that was never, at any time, discussed between the two of them.

So let the slow years pass and come to a Saturday evening six years after the time when Cousin Lymon came first to the town. It was August and the sky had burned above the town like a sheet of flame all day. Now the green twilight was near and there was a feeling of repose. The street was coated an inch deep with dry golden dust and the little children ran about half-naked, sneezed often, sweated, and were fretful. The mill had closed down at noon. People in the houses along the main street sat resting on their steps and the women had palmetto fans. At Miss Amelia's there was a sign at the front of the premises saying CAFÉ. The back porch was cool with latticed shadows and there Cousin Lymon sat turning the ice-cream freezer—often he unpacked the salt and ice and removed the dasher to lick a bit and see how the work was coming on. Jeff cooked in the kitchen. Early that morning Miss Amelia had put a notice on the wall of the front porch reading: Chicken Dinner—Twenty Cents Tonite. The café was already open and Miss Amelia had just finished a period of work in her office. All the eight tables were occupied and from the mechanical piano came a jingling tune.

In a corner, near the door and sitting at a table with a child, was Henry Macy. He was drinking a glass of liquor, which was unusual for him, as liquor went easily to his head and made him cry or sing. His face was very pale and his left eye worked constantly in a nervous tic, as it was apt to do when he was agitated. He had come into the café sidewise and silent, and when he was greeted he did not speak. The child next to him belonged to Horace Wells, and he had been left at Miss Amelia's that morning to be doctored.

Miss Amelia came out from her office in good spirits. She attended to a few details in the kitchen and entered the café with the pope's nose of a hen between her fingers, as that was her favorite piece. She looked about the room, saw that in general all was well, and went over to the corner table by Henry Macy. She turned the chair around and sat straddling the back, as she only wanted to pass the time of day and was not yet ready for her supper. There was a bottle of Kroup Kure in the hip pocket of her overalls—a medicine made from whisky, rock candy, and a secret ingredient. Miss Amelia uncorked the bottle and put it to the mouth of the child. Then she turned to Henry Macy and, seeing the nervous winking of his left eye, she asked:

"What ails you?"

Henry Macy seemed on the point of saying something difficult, but, after a long look into the eyes of Miss Amelia, he swallowed and did not speak.

So Miss Amelia returned to her patient. Only the child's head showed above the table top. His face was very red, with the eyelids half-closed and the mouth partly open. He had a large, hard, swollen boil on his thigh, and had been brought to Miss Amelia so that it could be opened. But Miss Amelia used a special method with children; she did not like to see them hurt, struggling, and terrified. So she had kept the child around the premises all day, giving him licorice and frequent doses of the Kroup Kure, and toward evening she tied a napkin around his neck and let him eat his fill of the dinner. Now as he sat at the table his head wobbled slowly from side to side and sometimes as he breathed there came from him a little worn-out grunt.

There was a stir in the café and Miss Amelia looked around quickly. Cousin Lymon had come in. The hunchback strutted into the café as he did every night, and when he reached the exact center of the room he stopped short and looked shrewdly around him, summing up the people and making a quick pattern of the emotional material at hand that night. The hunchback was a great mischief-maker. He enjoyed any kind of to-do, and without saying a word he could set people at each other in a way that was miraculous. It was due to him that the Rainey twins had quarreled over a jackknife two years past, and had not spoken one word to each other since. He was present at the big fight between Rip Wellborn and Robert Calvert Hale, and every other fight for that matter since he had come into the town. He nosed around everywhere, knew the intimate business of everybody, and trespassed every waking hour. Yet, queerly enough, in spite of this it was the hunchback who was most responsible for the great popularity of the café. Things were never so gay as when he was around.

When he walked into the room there was always a quick feeling of tension, because with this busybody about there was never any telling what might descend on you, or what might suddenly be brought to happen in the room. People are never so free with themselves and so recklessly glad as when there is some possibility of commotion or calamity ahead. So when the hunchback marched into the café everyone looked around at him and there was a quick outburst of talking and a drawing of corks.

Lymon waved his hand to Stumpy MacPhail who was sitting with Merlie Ryan and Henry Ford Crimp. "I walked to Rotten Lake today to fish," he said. "And on the way I stepped over what appeared at first to be a fallen tree. But then as I stepped over I felt something stir and I taken this second look and there I was straddling this here alligator long as from the front door to the kitchen and thicker than a hog."

The hunchback chattered on. Everyone looked at him from time to time, and some kept track of his chattering and others did not. There were times when every word he said was nothing but lying and bragging. Nothing he said tonight was true. He had lain in bed with a summer quinsy all day long, and had only got up in the late afternoon in order to turn the ice-cream freezer. Everybody knew this, yet he stood there in the middle of the café and held forth with such lies and boasting that it was enough to shrivel the ears.

Miss Amelia watched him with her hands in her pockets and her head turned to one side. There was a softness about her gray, queer eyes and she was smiling gently to herself. Occasionally she glanced from the hunchback to the other people in the café—and then her look was proud, and there was in it the hint of a threat, as though daring anyone to try to hold him to account for all his foolery. Jeff was bringing in the suppers, already served on the plates, and the new electric fans in the café made a pleasant stir of coolness in the air.

"The little youngun is asleep," said Henry Macy finally.

Miss Amelia looked down at the patient beside her, and composed her face for the matter in hand. The child's chin was resting on the table edge and a trickle of spit or Kroup Kure had bubbled from the corner of his mouth. His eyes were quite closed, and a little family of gnats had clustered peacefully in the corners. Miss Amelia put her hand on his head and shook it roughly, but the patient did not awake. So Miss Amelia lifted the child from the table, being careful not to touch the sore part of his leg, and went into the office. Henry Macy followed after her and they closed the office door.

Cousin Lymon was bored that evening. There was not much going on, and in spite of the heat the customers in the café were good-humored. Henry Ford Crimp and Horace Wells sat at the middle table with their arms around each other, sniggering over some long joke—but when he approached them he could make nothing of it as he had missed the beginning of the story. The moonlight brightened the dusty road, and the dwarfed peach trees were black and motionless: there was no breeze. The drowsy buzz of swamp mosquitoes was like an echo of the silent night. The town seemed dark, except far down the road to the right there was the flicker of a lamp. Somewhere in the darkness a woman sang in a high wild voice and the tune had no start and no finish and was made up of only three notes which went on and on and on. The hunchback stood leaning against the banister of the porch, looking down the empty road as though hoping that someone would come along.

There were footsteps behind him, then a voice: "Cousin Lymon, your dinner is set out upon the table."

"My appetite is poor tonight," said the hunchback, who had been eating sweet snuff all the day. "There is a sourness in my mouth."

"Just a pick," said Miss Amelia. "The breast, the liver, and the heart."

Together they went back into the bright café, and sat down with Henry Macy. Their table was the largest one in the café, and on it there was a bouquet of swamp lilies in a Coca-Cola bottle. Miss Amelia had finished with her patient and was satisfied with herself. From behind the closed office door there had come only a few sleepy whimpers, and before the patient could wake up and become terrified it was all over. The child was now slung across the shoulder of his father, sleeping deeply, his little arms dangling loose along his father's back and his puffed-up face very red—they were leaving the café to go home.

Henry Macy was still silent. He ate carefully, making no noise when he swallowed, and was not a third as greedy as Cousin Lymon who had claimed to have no appetite and was now putting down helping after helping of the dinner. Occasionally Henry Macy looked across at Miss Amelia and again held his peace.

It was a typical Saturday night. An old couple who had come in from the country hesitated for a moment at the doorway, holding each other's hand, and finally decided to come inside. They had lived together so long, this old country couple, that they looked as similar as twins. They were brown, shriveled, and like two little walking peanuts. They left early, and by midnight most of the other customers were gone. Rosser Cline and Merlie Ryan still played checkers, and Stumpy MacPhail sat with a liquor bottle on his table (his wife would not allow it in the home) and carried on peaceable conversations with himself. Henry Macy had not yet gone away, and this was unusual, as he almost always went to bed soon after nightfall. Miss Amelia yawned sleepily, but Lymon was restless and she did not suggest that they close up for the night.

Finally, at one o'clock, Henry Macy looked up at the corner of the ceiling and said quietly to Miss Amelia: "I got a letter today."

Miss Amelia was not one to be impressed by this, because all sorts of business letters and catalogues came addressed to her.

"I got a letter from my brother," said Henry Macy.

The hunchback, who had been goose-stepping about the café with his hands clasped behind his head, stopped suddenly. He was quick to sense any change in the atmosphere of a gathering. He glanced at each face in the room and waited.

Miss Amelia scowled and hardened her right fist. "You are welcome to it," she said.

"He is on parole. He is out of the penitentiary."

The face of Miss Amelia was very dark, and she shivered although the night was warm. Stumpy MacPhail and Merlie Ryan pushed aside their checker game. The café was very quiet.

"Who?" asked Cousin Lymon. His large, pale ears seemed to grow on his head and stiffen. "What?"

Miss Amelia slapped her hands palm down on the table. "Because Marvin Macy is a—" But her voice hoarsened and after a few moments she only said: "He belongs to be in that penitentiary the balance of his life."

"What did he do?" asked Cousin Lymon.

There was a long pause, as no one knew exactly how to answer this. "He robbed three filling stations," said Stumpy MacPhail. But his words did not sound complete and there was a feeling of sins left unmentioned.

The hunchback was impatient. He could not bear to be left out of anything, even a great misery. The name Marvin Macy was unknown to him, but it tantalized him as did any mention of subjects which others knew about and of which he was ignorant— such as any reference to the old sawmill that had been torn down before he came, or a chance word about poor Morris Finestein, or the recollection of any event that had occurred before his time. Aside from this inborn curiosity, the hunchback took a great interest in robbers and crimes of all varieties. As he strutted around the table he was muttering the words "released on parole" and "penitentiary" to himself. But although he questioned insistently, he was unable to find anything, as nobody would dare to talk about Marvin Macy before Miss Amelia in the café.

"The letter did not say very much," said Henry Macy. "He did not say where he was going."

"Humph!" said Miss Amelia, and her face was still hardened and very dark. "He will never set his split hoof on my premises."

She pushed back her chair from the table, and made ready to close the café. Thinking about Marvin Macy may have set her to brooding, for she hauled the cash register back to the kitchen and put it in a private place. Henry Macy went off down the dark road. But Henry Ford Crimp and Merlie Ryan lingered for a time on the front porch. Later Merlie Ryan was to make certain claims, to swear that on that night he had a vision of what was to come. But the town paid no attention, for that was just the sort of thing that Merlie Ryan would claim. Miss Amelia and Cousin Lymon talked for a time in the parlor. And when at last the hunchback thought that he could sleep she arranged the mosquito netting over his bed and waited until he had finished with his prayers. Then she put on her long nightgown, smoked two pipes, and only after a long time went to sleep.

That autumn was a happy time. The crops around the countryside were good, and over at the Forks Falls market the price of tobacco held firm that year. After the long hot summer the first cool days had a clean bright sweetness. Goldenrod grew along the dusty roads, and the sugar cane was ripe and purple. The bus came each day from Cheehaw to carry off a few of the younger children to the consolidated school to get an education. Boys hunted foxes in the pinewoods, winter quilts were aired out on the wash lines, and sweet potatoes bedded in the ground with straw against the colder months to come. In the evening, delicate shreds of smoke rose from the chimneys, and the moon was round and orange in the autumn sky. There is no stillness like the quiet of the first cold nights in the fall. Sometimes, late in the night when there was no wind, there could be heard in the town the thin wild whistle of the train that goes through Society City on its way far off to the North.

For Miss Amelia Evans this was a time of great activity. She was at work from dawn until sundown. She made a new and bigger condenser for her still, and in one week ran off enough liquor to souse the whole county. Her old mule was dizzy from grinding so much sorghum, and she scalded her Mason jars and put away pear preserves. She was looking forward greatly to the first frost, because she had traded for three tremendous hogs, and intended to make much barbecue, chitterlins, and sausage.

During these weeks there was a quality about Miss Amelia that many people noticed. She laughed often, with a deep ringing laugh, and her whistling had a sassy, tuneful trickery. She was forever trying out her strength, lifting up heavy objects, or poking her tough biceps with her finger. One day she sat down to her typewriter and wrote a story—a story in which there were foreigners, trap doors, and millions of dollars. Cousin Lymon was with her always, traipsing along behind her coat-tails, and when she watched him her face had a bright, soft look, and when she spoke his name there lingered in her voice the undertone of love.

The first cold spell came at last. When Miss Amelia awoke one morning there were frost flowers on the windowpanes, and rime had silvered the patches of grass in the yard. Miss Amelia built a roaring fire in the kitchen stove, then went out of doors to judge the day. The air was cold and sharp, the sky pale green and cloudless. Very shortly people began to come in from the country to find out what Miss Amelia thought of the weather; she decided to kill the biggest hog, and word got round the countryside. The hog was slaughtered and a low oak fire started in the barbecue pit. There was the warm smell of pig blood and smoke in the back yard, the stamp of footsteps, the ring of voices in the winter air. Miss Amelia walked around giving orders and soon most of the work was done.

She had some particular business to do in Cheehaw that day, so after making sure that all was going well, she cranked up her car and got ready to leave. She asked Cousin Lymon to come with her, in fact, she asked him seven times, but he was loath to leave the commotion and wanted to remain. This seemed to trouble Miss Amelia, as she always liked to have him near to her, and was prone to be terribly homesick when she had to go any distance away. But after asking him seven times, she did not urge him any further. Before leaving she found a stick and drew a heavy line all around the barbecue pit, about two feet back from the edge, and told him not to trespass beyond that boundary. She left after dinner and intended to be back before dark.

Now, it is not so rare to have a truck or an automobile pass along the road and through the town on the way from Cheehaw to somewhere else. Every year the tax collector comes to argue with rich people such as Miss Amelia. And if somebody in the town, such as Merlie Ryan, takes a notion that he can connive to get a car on credit, or to pay down three dollars and have a fine electric icebox such as they advertise in the store windows of Cheehaw, then a city man will come out asking meddlesome questions, finding out all his troubles, and ruining his chances of buying anything on the installment plan. Sometimes, especially since they are working on the Forks Falls highway, the cars hauling the chain gang come through the town. And frequently people in automobiles get lost and stop to inquire how they can find the right road again. So, late that afternoon it was nothing unusual to have a truck pass the mill and stop in the middle of the road near the café of Miss Amelia. A man jumped down from the back of the truck, and the truck went on its way.

The man stood in the middle of the road and looking about him. He was a tall man, with brown curly hair, and slow-moving, deep-blue eyes. His lips were red and he smiled the lazy, half-mouthed smile of the braggart. The man wore a red shirt, and a wide belt of tooled leather; he carried a tin suitcase and a guitar. The first person in the town to see this newcomer was Cousin Lymon, who had heard the shifting of gears and come around to investigate. The hunchback stuck his head around the corner of the porch, but did not step out altogether into full view. He and the man stared at each other, and it was not the look of two strangers meeting for the first time and swiftly summing up each other. It was a peculiar stare they exchanged between them, like the look of two criminals who recognize each other. Then the man in the red shirt shrugged his left shoulder and turned away. The face of the hunchback was very pale as he watched the man go down the road, and after a few moments he began to follow along carefully, keeping many paces away.

It was immediately known throughout the town that Marvin Macy had come back again. First, he went to the mill, propped his elbows lazily on a window sill and looked inside. He liked to watch others hard at work, as do all born loafers. The mill was thrown into a sort of numb confusion. The dyers left the hot vats, the spinners and weavers forgot about their machines, and even Stumpy MacPhail, who was foreman, did not know exactly what to do. Marvin Macy still smiled his wet half-mouthed smiles, and when he saw his brother, his bragging expression did not change. After looking over the mill Marvin Macy went down the road to the house where he had been raised, and left his suitcase and guitar on the front porch. Then he walked around the millpond, looked over the church, the three stores, and the rest of the town. The hunchback trudged along quietly at some distance behind him, his hands in his pockets, and his little face still very pale.

It had grown late. The red winter sun was setting, and to the west the sky was deep gold and crimson. Ragged chimney swifts flew to their nests; lamps were lighted. Now and then there was the smell of smoke, and the warm rich odor of the barbecue slowly cooking in the pit behind the café. After making the rounds of the town Marvin Macy stopped before Miss Amelia's premises and read the sign above the porch. Then, not hesitating to trespass, he walked through the side yard. The mill whistle blew a thin, lonesome blast, and the day's shift was done. Soon there were others in Miss Amelia's back yard beside Marvin Macy—Henry Ford Crimp, Merlie Ryan, Stumpy MacPhail, and any number of children and people who stood around the edges of the property and looked on. Very little was said. Marvin Macy stood by himself on one side of the pit, and the rest of the people clustered together on the other side. Cousin Lymon stood somewhat apart from everyone, and he did not take his eyes from the face of Marvin Macy.

"Did you have a good time in the penitentiary?" asked Merlie Ryan, with a silly giggle.

Marvin Macy did not answer. He took from his hip pocket a large knife, opened it slowly, and honed the blade on the seat of his pants. Merlie Ryan grew suddenly very quiet and went to stand directly behind the broad back of Stumpy MacPhail.

Miss Amelia did not come home until almost dark. They heard the rattle of her automobile while she was still a long distance away, then the slam of the door and a bumping noise as though she were hauling something up the front steps of her premises. The sun had already set, and in the air there was the blue smoky glow of early winter evenings. Miss Amelia came down the back steps slowly, and the group in her yard waited very quietly. Few people in this world could stand up to Miss Amelia, and against Marvin Macy she had this special bitter hate. Everyone waited to see her burst into a terrible holler, snatch up some dangerous object, and chase him altogether out of town. At first she did not see Marvin Macy, and her face had the relieved and dreamy expression that was natural to her when she reached home after having gone some distance away.

Miss Amelia must have seen Marvin Macy and Cousin Lymon at the same instant. She looked from one to the other, but it was not the wastrel from the penitentiary on whom she finally fixed her gaze of sick amazement. She, and everyone else, was looking at Cousin Lymon, and he was a sight to see.

The hunchback stood at the end of the pit, his pale face lighted by the soft glow from the smoldering oak fire. Cousin Lymon had a very peculiar accomplishment, which he used whenever he wished to ingratiate himself with someone. He would stand very still, and with just a little concentration, he could wiggle his large pale ears with marvelous quickness and ease. This trick he always used when he wanted to get something special out of Miss Amelia, and to her it was irresistible. Now as he stood there the hunchback's ears were wiggling furiously on his head, but it was not Miss Amelia at whom he was looking this time. The hunchback was smiling at Marvin Macy with an entreaty that was near to desperation. At first Marvin Macy paid no attention to him, and when he did finally glance at the hunchback it was without any appreciation whatsoever.

"What ails this Brokeback?" he asked with a rough jerk of his thumb.

No one answered. And Cousin Lymon, seeing that his accomplishment was getting him nowhere, added new efforts of persuasion. He fluttered his eyelids, so that they were like pale, trapped moths in his sockets. He scraped his feet around on the ground, waved his hands about, and finally began doing a little trotlike dance. In the last gloomy light of the winter he resembled the child of a swamp-haunt.

Marvin Macy, alone of all the people in the yard, was unimpressed.

"Is the runt throwing a fit?" he asked, and when no one answered he stepped forward and gave Cousin Lymon a cuff on the side of his head. The hunchback staggered, then fell back on the ground. He sat where he had fallen, still looking up at Marvin Macy, and with great effort his ears managed one last forlorn little flap.

Now everyone turned to Miss Amelia to see what she would do. In all these years no one had so much as touched a hair of Cousin Lymon's head, although many had had the itch to do so. If anyone even spoke crossly to the hunchback, Miss Amelia would cut off this rash mortal's credit and find ways of making things go hard for him a long time afterward. So now if Miss Amelia had split open Marvin Macy's head with the ax on the back porch no one would have been surprised. But she did nothing of the kind.

There were times when Miss Amelia seemed to go into a sort of trance. And the cause of these trances was usually known and understood. For Miss Amelia was a fine doctor, and did not grind up swamp roots and other untried ingredients and give them to the first patient who came along; whenever she invented a new medicine she always tried it out first on herself. She would swallow an enormous dose and spend the following day walking thoughtfully back and forth from the café to the brick privy. Often, when there was a sudden keen gripe, she would stand quite still, her queer eyes staring down at the ground and her fists clenched; she was trying to decide which organ was being worked upon, and what misery the new medicine might be most likely to cure. And now as she watched the hunchback and Marvin Macy, her face wore this same expression, tense with reckoning some inward pain, although she had taken no new medicine that day.

"That will learn you, Brokeback," said Marvin Macy.

Henry Macy pushed back his limp whitish hair from his forehead and coughed nervously. Stumpy MacPhail and Merlie Ryan shuffled their feet, and the children and black people on the outskirts of the property made not a sound. Marvin Macy folded the knife he had been honing, and after looking about him fearlessly he swaggered out of the yard. The embers in the pit were turning to gray feathery ashes and it was now quite dark.

That was the way Marvin Macy came back from the penitentiary. Not a living soul in all the town was glad to see him. Even Mrs. Mary Hale, who was a good woman and had raised him with love and care—at the first sight of him even this old foster mother dropped the skillet she was holding and burst into tears. But nothing could faze that Marvin Macy. He sat on the back steps of the Hale house, lazily picking his guitar, and when the supper was ready, he pushed the children of the household out of the way and served himself a big meal, although there had been barely enough hoecakes and white meat to go round. After eating he settled himself in the best and warmest sleeping place in the front room and was untroubled by dreams.

Miss Amelia did not open the café that night. She locked the doors and all the windows very carefully, nothing was seen of her and Cousin Lymon, and a lamp burned in her room all the night long.

Marvin Macy brought with him bad fortune, right from the first, as could be expected. The next day the weather turned suddenly, and it became hot. Even in the early morning there was a sticky sultriness in the atmosphere, the wind carried the rotten smell of the swamp, and delicate shrill mosquitoes webbed the green millpond. It was unseasonable, worse than August, and much damage was done. For nearly everyone in the county who owned a hog had copied Miss Amelia and slaughtered the day before. And what sausage could keep in such weather as this? After a few days there was everywhere the smell of slowly spoiling meat, and an atmosphere of dreary waste. Worse yet, a family reunion near the Forks Falls highway ate pork roast and died, every one of them. It was plain that their hog had been infected—and who could tell whether the rest of the meat was safe or not? People were torn between the longing for the good taste of pork, and the fear of death. It was a time of waste and confusion.

The cause of all this, Marvin Macy, had no shame in him. He was seen everywhere. During work hours he loafed about the mill, looking in at the windows, and on Sundays he dressed in his red shirt and paraded up and down the road with his guitar. He was still handsome—with his brown hair, his red lips, and his broad strong shoulders; but the evil in him was now too famous for his good looks to get him anywhere. And this evil was not measured only by the actual sins he had committed. True, he had robbed those filling stations. And before that he had ruined the tenderest girls in the county and laughed about it. Any number of wicked things could be listed against him, but quite apart from these crimes there was about him a secret meanness that clung to him almost like a smell. Another thing—he never sweated, not even in August, and that surely is a sign worth pondering over.

Now it seemed to the town that he was more dangerous than he had ever been before, as in the penitentiary in Atlanta he must have learned the method of laying charms. Otherwise how could his effect on Cousin Lymon be explained? For since first setting eyes on Marvin Macy the hunchback was possessed by an unnatural spirit. Every minute he wanted to be following along behind this jailbird, and he was full of silly schemes to attract attention to himself. Still Marvin Macy either treated him hatefully or failed to notice him at all. Sometimes the hunchback would give up, perch himself on the banister of the front porch much as a sick bird huddles on a telephone wire, and grieve publicly.

"But why?" Miss Amelia would ask, staring at him with her crossed, gray eyes, and her fists closed tight.

"Oh, Marvin Macy," groaned the hunchback, and the sound of the name was enough to upset the rhythm of his sobs so that he hiccuped. "He has been to Atlanta."

Miss Amelia would shake her head and her face was dark and hardened. To begin with she had no patience with any traveling; those who had made the trip to Atlanta or traveled fifty miles from home to see the ocean—those restless people she despised. "Going to Atlanta does no credit to him."

"He has been to the penitentiary," said the hunchback, miserable with longing.

How are you going to argue against such envies as these? In her perplexity Miss Amelia did not herself sound any too sure of what she was saying. "Been to the penitentiary, Cousin Lymon? Why, a trip like that is no travel to brag about."

During these weeks Miss Amelia was closely watched by everyone. She went about absent-mindedly, her face remote as though she had lapsed into one of her gripe trances. For some reason, after the day of Marvin Macy's arrival, she put aside her overalls and wore always the red dress she had before this time reserved for Sundays, funerals, and sessions of the court. Then as the weeks passed she began to take some steps to clear up the situation. But her efforts were hard to understand. If it hurt her to see Cousin Lymon follow Marvin Macy about the town, why did she not make the issues clear once and for all, and tell the hunchback that if he had dealings with Marvin Macy she would turn him off the premises? That would have been simple, and Cousin Lymon would have had to submit to her, or else face the sorry business of finding himself loose in the world. But Miss Amelia seemed to have lost her will; for the first time in her life she hesitated as to just what course to pursue. And, like most people in such a position of uncertainty, she did the worst thing possible—she began following several courses at once, all of them contrary to each other.

The café was opened every night as usual, and, strangely enough, when Marvin Macy came swaggering through the door, with the hunchback at his heels, she did not turn him out. She even gave him free drinks and smiled at him in a wild, crooked way. At the same time she set a terrible trap for him out in the swamp that surely would have killed him if he had got caught. She let Cousin Lymon invite him to Sunday dinner, and then tried to trip him up as he went down the steps. She began a great campaign of pleasure for Cousin Lymon—making exhausting trips to various spectacles being held in distant places, driving the automobile thirty miles to a Chautauqua, taking him to Forks Falls to watch a parade. All in all it was a distracting time for Miss Amelia. In the opinion of most people she was well on her way in the climb up fools' hill, and everyone wanted to see how it would all turn out.

The weather turned cold again, the winter was upon the town, and night came before the last shift in the mill was done. Children kept on all their garments when they slept, and women raised the backs of their skirts to toast themselves dreamily at the fire. After it rained, the mud in the road made hard frozen ruts, there were faint flickers of lamplight from the windows of the houses, the peach trees were scrawny and bare. In the dark, silent nights of wintertime the café was the warm center point of the town, the lights shining so brightly that they could be seen a quarter of a mile away. The great iron stove at the back of the room roared, crackled, and turned red.

Miss Amelia had made red curtains for the windows, and from a salesman who passed through the town she bought a great bunch of paper roses that looked very real.

But it was not only the warmth, the decorations, and the brightness, that made the café what it was. There is a deeper reason why the café was so precious to this town. And this deeper reason has to do with a certain pride that had not hitherto been known in these parts. To understand this new pride the cheapness of human life must be kept in mind. There were always plenty of people clustered around a mill— but it was seldom that every family had enough meal, garments, and fat back to go the rounds. Life could become one long dim scramble just to get the things needed to keep alive. And the confusing point is this: All useful things have a price, and are bought only with money, as that is the way the world is run. You know without having to reason about it the price of a bale of cotton, or a quart of molasses. But no value has been put on human life; it is given to us free and taken without being paid for. What is it worth? If you look around, at times the value may seem to be little or nothing at all. Often after you have sweated and tried and things are not better for you, there comes a feeling deep down in the soul that you are not worth much.

But the new pride that the café brought to this town had an effect on almost everyone, even the children. For in order to come to the café you did not have to buy the dinner, or a portion of liquor. There were cold bottled drinks for a nickel. And if you could not even afford that, Miss Amelia had a drink called Cherry Juice which sold for a penny a glass, and was pink-colored and very sweet. Almost everyone, with the exception of Reverend T. M. Willin, came to the café at least once during the week. Children love to sleep in houses other than their own, and to eat at a neighbor's table; on such occasions they behave themselves decently and are proud. The people in the town were likewise proud when sitting at the tables in the café. They washed before coming to Miss Amelia's, and scraped their feet very politely on the threshold as they entered the café. There, for a few hours at least, the deep bitter knowing that you are not worth much in this world could be laid low.

The café was a special benefit to bachelors, unfortunate people, and consumptives. And here it may be mentioned that there was some reason to suspect that Cousin Lymon was consumptive. The brightness of his gray eyes, his insistence, his talkativeness, and his cough—these were all signs. Besides, there is generally supposed to be some connection between a hunched spine and consumption. But whenever this subject had been mentioned to Miss Amelia she had become furious; she denied these symptoms with bitter vehemence, but on the sly she treated Cousin Lymon with hot chest plasters, Kroup Kure, and such. Now this winter the hunchback's cough was worse, and sometimes even on cold days he would break out in a heavy sweat. But this did not prevent him from following along after Marvin Macy.

Early every morning he left the premises and went to the back door of Mrs. Hale's house, and waited and waited—as Marvin Macy was a lazy sleeper. He would stand there and call out softly. His voice was just like the voices of children who squat patiently over those tiny little holes in the ground where doodlebugs are thought to live, poking the hole with a broom straw, and calling plaintively: "Doodlebug, Doodlebug—fly away home. Mrs. Doodlebug, Mrs. Doodlebug. Come out, come out. Your house is on fire and all your children are burning up." In just such a voice—at once sad, luring, and resigned—would the hunchback call Marvin Macy's name each morning. Then when Marvin Macy came out for the day, he would trail him about the town, and sometimes they would be gone for hours together out in the swamp.

And Miss Amelia continued to do the worst thing possible: that is, to try to follow several courses at once. When Cousin Lymon left the house she did not call him back, but only stood in the middle of the road and watched lonesomely until he was out of sight. Nearly every day Marvin Macy turned up with Cousin Lymon at dinnertime, and ate at her table. Miss Amelia opened the pear preserves, and the table was well-set with ham or chicken, great bowls of hominy grits, and winter peas. It is true that on one occasion Miss Amelia tried to poison Marvin Macy—but there was a mistake, the plates were confused, and it was she herself who got the poisoned dish. This she quickly realized by the slight bitterness of the food, and that day she ate no dinner. She sat tilted back in her chair, feeling her muscle, and looking at Marvin Macy.

Every night Marvin Macy came to the café and settled himself at the best and largest table, the one in the center of the room. Cousin Lymon brought him liquor, for which he did not pay a cent. Marvin Macy brushed the hunchback aside as if he were a swamp mosquito, and not only did he show no gratitude for these favors, but if the hunchback got in his way he would cuff him with the back of his hand, or say: "Out of my way, Brokeback—I'll snatch you bald-headed." When this happened Miss Amelia would come out from behind her counter and approach Marvin Macy very slowly, her fists clenched, her peculiar red dress hanging awkwardly around her bony knees. Marvin Macy would also clench his fists and they would walk slowly and meaningfully around each other. But, although everyone watched breathlessly, nothing ever came of it. The time for the fight was not yet ready.

There is one particular reason why this winter is remembered and still talked about. A great thing happened. People woke up on the second of January and found the whole world about them altogether changed. Little ignorant children looked out of the windows, and they were so puzzled that they began to cry. Old people harked back and could remember nothing in these parts to equal the phenomenon. For in the night it had snowed. In the dark hours after midnight the dim flakes started falling softly on the town. By dawn the ground was covered, and the strange snow banked the ruby windows of the church, and whitened the roofs of the houses. The snow gave the town a drawn, bleak look. The two room houses near the mill were dirty, crooked, and seemed about to collapse, and somehow everything was dark and shrunken. But the snow itself—there was a beauty about it few people around here had ever known before. The snow was not white, as Northerners had pictured it to be; in the snow there were soft colors of blue and silver, the sky was a gentle shining gray. And the dreamy quietness of falling snow—when had the town been so silent?

People reacted to the snowfall in various ways. Miss Amelia, on looking out of her window, thoughtfully wiggled the toes of her bare feet, gathered close to her neck the collar of her nightgown. She stood there for some time, then commenced to draw the shutters and lock every window on the premises. She closed the place completely, lighted the lamps, and sat solemnly over her bowl of grits. The reason for this was not that Miss Amelia feared the snowfall. It was simply that she was unable to form an immediate opinion of this new event, and unless she knew exactly and definitely what she thought of a matter (which was nearly always the case) she preferred to ignore it. Snow had never fallen in this county in her lifetime, and she had never thought about it one way or the other. But if she admitted this snowfall she would have to come to some decision, and in those days there was enough distraction in her life as it was already. So she poked about the gloomy, lamp-lighted house and pretended that nothing had happened. Cousin Lymon, on the contrary, chased around in the wildest excitement, and when Miss Amelia turned her back to dish him some breakfast he slipped out of the door.

Marvin Macy laid claim to the snowfall. He said that he knew snow, had seen it in Atlanta, and from the way he walked about the town that day it was as though he owned every flake. He sneered at the little children who crept timidly out of the houses and scooped up handfuls of snow to taste. Reverend Willin hurried down the road with a furious face, as he was thinking deeply and trying to weave the snow into his Sunday sermon. Most people were humble and glad about this marvel; they spoke in hushed voices and said "thank you" and "please" more than was necessary. A few weak characters, of course, were demoralized and got drunk—but they were not numerous. To everyone this was an occasion and many counted their money and planned to go to the café that night.

Cousin Lymon followed Marvin Macy about all day, seconding his claim to the snow. He marveled that snow did not fall as does rain, and stared up at the dreamy, gently falling flakes until he stumbled from dizziness. And the pride he took on himself, basking in the glory of Marvin Macy—it was such that many people could not resist calling out to him: "'Oho,' said the fly on the chariot wheel. 'What a dust we do raise.'"

Miss Amelia did not intend to serve a dinner. But when, at six o'clock, there was the sound of footsteps on the porch she opened the front door cautiously. It was Henry Ford Crimp, and though there was no food, she let him sit at a table and served him a drink. Others came. The evening was blue, bitter, and though the snow fell no longer there was a wind from the pine trees that swept up delicate flurries from the ground. Cousin Lymon did not come until after dark, with him Marvin Macy, and he carried his tin suitcase and his guitar.

"So you mean to travel?" said Miss Amelia quickly.

Marvin Macy warmed himself at the stove. Then he settled down at his table and carefully sharpened a little stick. He picked his teeth, frequently taking the stick out of his mouth to look at the end and wipe it on the sleeve of his coat. He did not bother to answer.

The hunchback looked at Miss Amelia, who was behind the counter. His face was not in the least beseeching; he seemed quite sure of himself. He folded his hands behind his back and perked up his ears confidently. His cheeks were red, his eyes shining, and his clothes were soggy wet. "Marvin Macy is going to visit a spell with us," he said.

Miss Amelia made no protest. She only came out from behind the counter and hovered over the stove, as though the news had made her suddenly cold. She did not warm her backside modestly, lifting her skirt only an inch or so, as do most women when in public. There was not a grain of modesty about Miss Amelia, and she frequently seemed to forget altogether that there were men in the room. Now as she stood warming herself, her red dress was pulled up quite high in the back so that a piece of her strong, hairy thigh could be seen by anyone who cared to look at it. Her head was turned to one side; and she had begun talking with herself, nodding and wrinkling her forehead, and there was the tone of accusation and reproach in her voice although the words were not plain. Meanwhile, the hunchback and Marvin Macy had gone upstairs—up to the parlor with the pampas grass and the two sewing machines, to the private rooms where Miss Amelia had lived the whole of her life. Down in the café you could hear them bumping around, unpacking Marvin Macy, and getting him settled.

That is the way Marvin Macy crowded into Miss Amelia's home. At first Cousin Lymon, who had given Marvin Macy his own room, slept on the sofa in the parlor. But the snowfall had a bad effect on him; he caught a cold that turned into a winter quinsy, so Miss Amelia gave up her bed to him. The sofa in the parlor was much too short for her, her feet lapped over the edges, and often she rolled off onto the floor. Perhaps it was this lack of sleep that clouded her wits; everything she tried to do against Marvin Macy rebounded on herself. She got caught in her own tricks, and found herself in many pitiful positions. But still she did not put Marvin Macy off the premises, as she was afraid that she would be left alone. Once you have lived with another, it is a great torture to have to live alone. The silence of a firelit room when suddenly the clock stops ticking, the nervous shadows in an empty house—it is better to take in your mortal enemy than face the terror of living alone.

The snow did not last. The sun came out and within two days the town was just as it had always been before. Miss Amelia did not open her house until every flake had melted. Then she had a big house cleaning and aired everything out in the sun. But before that, the very first thing she did on going out again into her yard, was to tie a rope to the largest branch of the chinaberry tree. At the end of the rope she tied a crocus sack tightly stuffed with sand. This was the punching bag she made for herself and from that day on she would box with it out in her yard every morning. Already she was a fine fighter—a little heavy on her feet, but knowing all manner of mean holds and squeezes to make up for this.

Miss Amelia, as has been mentioned, measured six feet two inches in height. Marvin Macy was one inch shorter. In weight they were about even—both of them weighing close to a hundred and sixty pounds. Marvin Macy had the advantage in slyness of movement, and in toughness of chest. In fact from the outward point of view the odds were altogether in his favor. Yet almost everybody in the town was betting on Miss Amelia; scarcely a person would put up money on Marvin Macy. The town remembered the great fight between Miss Amelia and a Forks Falls lawyer who had tried to cheat her. He had been a huge strapping fellow, but he was left three-quarters dead when she had finished with him. And it was not only her talent as a boxer that had impressed everyone—she could demoralize her enemy by making terrifying faces and fierce noises, so that even the spectators were sometimes cowed. She was brave, she practiced faithfully with her punching bag, and in this case she was clearly in the right. So people had confidence in her, and they waited. Of course there was no set date for this fight. There were just the signs that were too plain to be overlooked.

During these times the hunchback strutted around with a pleased little pinched-up face. In many delicate and clever ways he stirred up trouble between them. He was constantly plucking at Marvin Macy's trouser leg to draw attention to himself. Sometimes he followed in Miss Amelia's footsteps—but these days it was only in order to imitate her awkward long-legged walk; he crossed his eyes and aped her gestures in a way that made her appear to be a freak. There was something so terrible about this that even the silliest customers of the café, such as Merlie Ryan, did not laugh. Only Marvin Macy drew up the left corner of his mouth and chuckled. Miss Amelia, when this happened, would be divided between two emotions. She would look at the hunchback with a lost, dismal reproach—then turn toward Marvin Macy with her teeth clamped.

"Bust a gut!" she would say bitterly.

And Marvin Macy, most likely, would pick up the guitar from the floor beside his chair. His voice was wet and slimy, as he always had too much spit in his mouth. And the tunes he sang glided slowly from his throat like eels. His strong fingers picked the strings with dainty skill, and everything he sang both lured and exasperated. This was usually more than Miss Amelia could stand.

"Bust a gut!" she would repeat, in a shout.

But always Marvin Macy had the answer ready for her. He would cover the strings to silence the quivering leftover tones, and reply with slow, sure insolence.

"Everything you holler at me bounces back on yourself. Yah! Yah!"

Miss Amelia would have to stand there helpless, as no one has ever invented a way out of this trap. She could not shout out abuse that would bounce back on herself. He had the best of her, there was nothing she could do.

So things went on like this. What happened between the three of them during the nights in the rooms upstairs nobody knows. But the café became more and more crowded every night. A new table had to be brought in. Even the Hermit, the crazy man named Rainer Smith, who took to the swamp years ago, heard something of the situation and came one night to look in at the window and brood over the gathering in the bright café. And the climax each evening was the time when Miss Amelia and Marvin Macy doubled their fists, squared up, and glared at each other. Usually this did not happen after any especial argument, but it seemed to come about mysteriously, by means of some instinct on the part of both of them. At these times the café would become so quiet that you could hear the bouquet of paper roses rustling in the draft. And each night they held this fighting stance a little longer than the night before.

The fight took place on Ground Hog Day, which is the second of February. The weather was favorable, being neither rainy nor sunny, and with a neutral temperature. There were several signs that this was the appointed day, and by ten o'clock the news spread all over the county. Early in the morning Miss Amelia went out and cut down her punching bag. Marvin Macy sat on the back step with a tin can of hog fat between his knees and carefully greased his arms and his legs. A hawk with a bloody breast flew over the town and circled twice around the property of Miss Amelia. The tables in the café were moved out to the back porch, so that the whole big room was cleared for the fight. There was every sign. Both Miss Amelia and Marvin Macy ate four helpings of half-raw roast for dinner, and then lay down in the afternoon to store up strength. Marvin Macy rested in the big room upstairs, while Miss Amelia stretched herself out on the bench in her office. It was plain from her white stiff face what a torment it was for her to be lying still and doing nothing, but she lay there quiet as a corpse with her eyes closed and her hands crossed on her chest.

Cousin Lymon had a restless day, and his little face was drawn and tightened with excitement. He put himself up a lunch, and set out to find the ground hog—within an hour he returned, the lunch eaten, and said that the ground hog had seen his shadow and there was to be bad weather ahead. Then, as Miss Amelia and Marvin Macy were both resting to gather strength, and he was left to himself, it occurred to him that he might as well paint the front porch. The house had not been painted for years—in fact, God knows if it had ever been painted at all. Cousin Lymon scrambled around, and soon he had painted half the floor of the porch a gay bright green. It was a loblolly job, and he smeared himself all over. Typically enough he did not even finish the floor, but changed over to the walls, painting as high as he could reach and then standing on a crate to get up a foot higher. When the paint ran out, the right side of the floor was bright green and there was a jagged portion of wall that had been painted. Cousin Lymon left it at that.

There was something childish about his satisfaction with his painting. And in this respect a curious fact should be mentioned. No one in the town, not even Miss Amelia, had any idea how old the hunchback was. Some maintained that when he came to town he was about twelve years old, still a child—others were certain that he was well past forty. His eyes were blue and steady as a child's, but there were lavender creepy shadows beneath these blue eyes that hinted of age. It was impossible to guess his age by his hunched queer body. And even his teeth gave no clue—they were all still in his head (two were broken from cracking a pecan), but he had stained them with so much sweet snuff that it was impossible to decide whether they were old teeth or young teeth. When questioned directly about his age the hunchback professed to know absolutely nothing—he had no idea how long he had been on the earth, whether for ten years or a hundred! So his age remained a puzzle.

Cousin Lymon finished his painting at five-thirty o'clock in the afternoon. The day had turned colder and there was a wet taste in the air. The wind came up from the pinewoods, rattling windows, blowing an old newspaper down the road until at last it caught upon a thorn tree. People began to come in from the country; packed automobiles that bristled with the poked-out heads of children, wagons drawn by old mules who seemed to smile in a weary, sour way and plodded along with their tired eyes half-closed. Three young boys came from Society City. All three of them wore yellow rayon shirts and caps put on backward—they were as much alike as triplets, and could always be seen at cockfights and camp meetings. At six o'clock the mill whistle sounded the end of the day's shift and the crowd was complete. Naturally, among the newcomers there were some riffraff, unknown characters, and so forth—

but even so the gathering was quiet. A hush was on the town and the faces of people were strange in the fading light. Darkness hovered softly; for a moment the sky was a pale clear yellow against which the gables of the church stood out in dark and bare outline, then the sky died slowly and the darkness gathered into night.

Seven is a popular number, and especially it was a favorite with Miss Amelia. Seven swallows of water for hiccups, seven runs around the millpond for cricks in the neck, seven doses of Amelia Miracle Mover as a worm cure — her treatment nearly always hinged on this number. It is a number of mingled possibilities, and all who love mystery and charms set store by it. So the fight was to take place at seven o'clock. This was known to everyone, not by announcement or words, but understood in the un-questioning way that rain is understood, or an evil odor from the swamp. So before seven o'clock everyone gathered gravely around the property of Miss Amelia. The cleverest got into the café itself and stood lining the walls of the room. Others crowded onto the front porch, or took a stand in the yard.

Miss Amelia and Marvin Macy had not yet shown themselves. Miss Amelia, after resting all afternoon on the office bench, had gone upstairs. On the other hand Cousin Lymon was at your elbow every minute, threading his way through the crowd, snapping his fingers nervously, and batting his eyes. At one minute to seven o'clock he squirmed his way into the café and climbed up on the counter. All was very quiet.

It must have been arranged in some manner beforehand. For just at the stroke of seven Miss Amelia showed herself at the head of the stairs. At the same instant Marvin Macy appeared in front of the café and the crowd made way for him silently. They walked toward each other with no haste, their fists already gripped, and their eyes like the eyes of dreamers. Miss Amelia had changed her red dress for her old overalls, and they were rolled up to the knees. She was barefooted and she had an iron strengthband around her right wrist. Marvin Macy had also rolled his trouser legs — he was naked to the waist and heavily greased; he wore the heavy shoes that had been issued him when he left the penitentiary. Stumpy MacPhail stepped forward from the crowd and slapped their hip pockets with the palm of his right hand to make sure there would be no sudden knives. They were alone in the cleared center of the bright café.

There was no signal, but they both struck out simultaneously. Both blows landed on the chin, so that the heads of Miss Amelia and Marvin Macy bobbed back and they were left a little groggy. For a few seconds after the first blows they merely shuffled their feet around on the bare floor, experimenting with various positions, and making mock fists. Then, like wildcats, they were suddenly on each other. There was the sound of knocks, panting, and thumpings on the floor. They were so fast that it was hard to take in what was going on — but once Miss Amelia was hurled backward so that she staggered and almost fell, and another time Marvin Macy caught a knock on the shoulder that spun him round like a top. So the fight went on in this wild violent way with no sign of weakening on either side.

During a struggle like this, when the enemies are as quick and strong as these two, it is worth-while to turn from the confusion of the fight itself and observe the spectators. The people had flattened back as close as possible against the walls. Stumpy MacPhail was in a corner, crouched over and with his fists tight in sympathy, making strange noises. Poor Merlie Ryan had his mouth so wide open that a fly buzzed into it, and was swallowed before Merlie realized what had happened. And Cousin Lymon — he was worth watching. The hunchback still stood on the counter, so that he was raised above everyone else in the café. He had his hands on his hips, his big head thrust forward, and his little legs bent so that the knees jutted outward. The excitement had made him break out in a rash, and his pale mouth shivered.

Perhaps it was half an hour before the course of the fight shifted. Hundreds of blows had been exchanged, and there was still a deadlock. Then suddenly Marvin Macy managed to catch hold of Miss Amelia's left arm and pinion it behind her back.

She struggled and got a grasp around his waist; the real fight was now begun. Wrestling is the natural way of fighting in this county — as boxing is too quick and requires much thinking and concentration. And now that Miss Amelia and Marvin were locked in a hold together the crowd came out of its daze and pressed in closer. For a while the fighters grappled muscle to muscle, their hipbones braced against each other. Backward and forward, from side to side, they swayed in this way. Marvin Macy still had not sweated, but Miss Amelia's overalls were drenched and so much sweat had trickled down her legs that she left wet footprints on the floor. Now the test had come, and in these moments of terrible effort, it was Miss Amelia who was the stronger. Marvin Macy was greased and slippery, tricky to grasp, but she was stronger. Gradually she bent him over backward, and inch by inch she forced him to the floor. It was a terrible thing to watch and their deep hoarse breaths were the only sound in the café. At last she had him down, and straddled; her strong big hands were on his throat.

But at that instant, just as the fight was won, a cry sounded in the café that caused a shrill bright shiver to run down the spine. And what took place has been a mystery ever since. The whole town was there to testify what happened, but there were those who doubted their own eyesight. For the counter on which Cousin Lymon stood was at least twelve feet from the fighters in the center of the café. Yet at the instant Miss Amelia grasped the throat of Marvin Macy the hunchback sprang forward and sailed through the air as though he had grown hawk wings. He landed on the broad strong back of Miss Amelia and clutched at her neck with his clawed little fingers.

The rest is confusion. Miss Amelia was beaten before the crowd could come to their senses. Because of the hunchback the fight was won by Marvin Macy, and at the end Miss Amelia lay sprawled on the floor, her arms flung outward and motionless. Marvin Macy stood over her, his face somewhat popeyed, but smiling his old half-mouthed smile. And the hunchback, he had suddenly disappeared. Perhaps he was frightened about what he had done, or maybe he was so delighted that he wanted to glory with himself alone — at any rate he slipped out of the café and crawled under the back steps. Someone poured water on Miss Amelia, and after a time she got up slowly and dragged herself into her office. Through the open door the crowd could see her sitting at her desk, her head in the crook of her arm, and she was sobbing with the last of her grating, winded breath. Once she gathered her right fist together and knocked it three times on the top of her office desk, then her hand opened feebly and lay palm upward and still. Stumpy MacPhail stepped forward and closed the door.

The crowd was quiet, and one by one the people left the café. Mules were waked up and untied, automobiles cranked, and the three boys from Society City roamed off down the road on foot. This was not a fight to hash over and talk about afterward; people went home and pulled the covers up over their heads. The town was dark, except for the premises of Miss Amelia, but every room was lighted there the whole night long.

Marvin Macy and the hunchback must have left the town an hour or so before daylight. And before they went away this is what they did:

They unlocked the private cabinet of curios and took everything in it.

They broke the mechanical piano.

They carved terrible words on the café tables.

They found the watch that opened in the back to show a picture of a waterfall and took that also.

They poured a gallon of sorghum syrup all over the kitchen floor and smashed the jars of preserves.

They went out in the swamp and completely wrecked the still, ruining the big new condenser and the cooler, and setting fire to the shack itself.

They fixed a dish of Miss Amelia's favorite food, grits with sausage, seasoned it with enough poison to kill off the county, and placed this dish temptingly on the café counter.

They did everything ruinous they could think of without actually breaking into the office where Miss Amelia stayed the night. Then they went off together, the two of them.

That was how Miss Amelia was left alone in the town. The people would have helped her if they had known how, as people in this town will as often as not be kindly if they have a chance. Several housewives nosed around with lost brooms and offered to clear up the wreck. But Miss Amelia only looked at them with lost crossed eyes and shook her head. Stumpy MacPhail came in on the third day to buy a plug of Queenie tobacco, and Miss Amelia said the price was one dollar. Everything in the café had suddenly risen in price to be worth one dollar. And what sort of a café is that? Also, she changed very queerly as a doctor. In all the years before she had been much more popular than the Cheehaw doctor. She had never monkeyed with a patient's soul, taking away from him such real necessities as liquor, tobacco, and so forth. Once in a great while she might carefully warn a patient never to eat fried watermelon or some such dish it had never occurred to a person to want in the first place. Now all this wise doctoring was over. She told one-half of her patients that they were going to die outright, and to the remaining half she recommended cures so farfetched and agonizing that no one in his right mind would consider them for a moment.

Miss Amelia let her hair grow ragged, and it was turning gray. Her face lengthened, and the great muscles of her body shrank until she was thin as old maids are thin when they go crazy. And those gray eyes—slowly day by day they were more crossed, and it was as though they sought each other to exchange a little glance of grief and lonely recognition. She was not pleasant to listen to; her tongue had sharpened terribly.

When anyone mentioned the hunchback she would say only this: "Ho! If I could lay hand to him I would rip out his gizzard and throw it to the cat!" But it was not so much the words that were terrible, but the voice in which they were said. Her voice had lost its old vigor; there was none of the ring of vengeance it used to have when she would mention "that loom-fixer I was married to," or some other enemy. Her voice was broken, soft, and sad as the wheezy whine of the church pump-organ.

For three years she sat out on the front steps every night, alone and silent, looking down the road and waiting. But the hunchback never returned. There were rumors that Marvin Macy used him to climb into windows and steal, and other rumors that Marvin Macy had sold him to a side show. But both these reports were traced back to Merlie Ryan. Nothing true was ever heard of him. It was in the fourth year that Miss Amelia hired a Cheehaw carpenter and had him board up the premises, and there in those closed rooms she has remained ever since.

Yes, the town is dreary. On August afternoons the road is empty, white with dust, and the sky above is bright as glass. Nothing moves—there are no children's voices, only the hum of the mill. The peach trees seem to grow more crooked every summer, and the leaves are dull gray and of a sickly delicacy. The house of Miss Amelia leans so much to the right that it is now only a question of time when it will collapse completely, and people are careful not to walk around the yard. There is no good liquor to be bought in the town; the nearest still is eight miles away, and the liquor is such that those who drink it grow warts on their livers the size of goobers, and dream themselves into a dangerous inward world. There is absolutely nothing to do in the town. Walk around the millpond, stand kicking at a rotten stump, figure out what you can do with the old wagon wheel by the side of the road near the church. The soul rots with boredom. You might as well go down to the Forks Falls highway and listen to the chain gang.

THE TWELVE MORTAL MEN

The Forks Falls highway is three miles from the town, and it is here the chain gang has been working. The road is of macadam, and the county decided to patch up the rough places and widen it at a certain dangerous place. The gang is made up of twelve men, all wearing black and white striped prison suits, and chained at the ankles. There is a guard, with a gun, his eyes drawn to red slits by the glare. The gang works all the day long, arriving huddled in the prison cart soon after daybreak, and being driven off again in the gray August twilight. All day there is the sound of the picks striking into the clay earth, hard sunlight, the smell of sweat. And every day there is music. One dark voice will start a phrase, half-sung, and like a question. And after a moment another voice will join in, soon the whole gang will be singing. The voices are dark in the golden glare, the music intricately blended, both somber and joyful. The music will swell until at last it seems that the sound does not come from the twelve men on the gang, but from the earth itself, or the wide sky. It is music that causes the heart to broaden and the listener to grow cold with ecstasy and fright. Then slowly the music will sink down until at last there remains one lonely voice, then a great hoarse breath, the sun, the sound of the picks in the silence.

And what kind of gang is this that can make such music? Just twelve mortal men, seven of them black and five of them white boys from this county. Just twelve mortal men who are together.

1943, 1951

SHIRLEY JACKSON
(1919–1965)

Seldom has a short story had the impact of Shirley Jackson's "The Lottery," published in *The New Yorker* on June 28, 1948. The Second World War had ended just three years earlier, and the world was still trying to adjust to the incomprehensible barbarism of the Holocaust and the unimaginable destructiveness of the atom bomb. The short story, set in an unnamed town, portrayed the murderous brutality of a group to one of their own in the annual repetition of a democratically run ritual whose meaning nobody seemed to understand.

Shirley Jackson's biographer, Judy Oppenheimer, has described the response of readers: "Phone calls . . . poured into the magazine — cancelling subscriptions, demanding explanations, venting fury. . . . [A reader wrote,] 'Please give me something to go on when I next try to placate my friend, who is now certain that you are tools of Stalin'. . . . Another was sure he had found the key: 'In this story you show the perversity of democracy.'" Many of the people who wrote wanted to know the place and time of the holding of the lottery so that they might be on hand to watch. The story was frequently anthologized, turning up in high school literature texts. Community groups, especially those rigidly committed to one extreme doctrine or another, became incensed, believing the story was an attack on them and demanding that the story be suppressed.

The writer who released all this fury was born in San Francisco in 1919 and began to write poems as a child. The family moved to New York when she was still an adolescent. She attended the University of Rochester briefly, dropping out for a year to write a thousand words a day. Then she entered Syracuse University, where she published stories in the college magazine. On graduation in 1940, she married Stanley Edgar Hyman, a fellow student. They lived for a time in New York City, and then, with a growing family, they moved to North Bennington, Vermont, where Hyman taught at Bennington College. There Shirley Jackson took care of the four children — and pursued her professional career as a writer.

Her first novel, *The Road Through the Wall* (1948), set in California, depicted middle-class life in suburbia. It was, however, the appearance of "The Lottery" this same year that established Jackson as a writer and gained her lasting fame — and notoriety. The story was reprinted in *Prize Stories in 1949: The O. Henry Awards*. And it was included in a volume of stories, *The Lottery or, The Adventures of James Harris,* published in 1949. Jackson continued to publish short stories throughout her career, and a number of them were to be reprinted in the annual volume *Best American Short Stories.* But never again was she to have the impact she achieved in "The Lottery."

Jackson also continued to publish novels: *Hangsaman* (1951) and *The Bird's Nest* (1954) both portrayed female characters who appeared to live in fantasy worlds — or were profoundly disturbed psychologically. Much of the effect of these works came from their ambiguity. Other novels included *The Sundial* (1958), about people preparing for the end of the world; *The Haunting of Hill House* (1959), an exploration of the psychic roots of loneliness with all the trappings of Gothic romance; and what is seen as her finest novel, *We Have Always Lived in the Castle* (1962), about a woman writer who, at the age of twelve, poisoned her entire family. A number of Jackson's stories and novels were turned into movies or plays.

In addition to her fiction, Jackson wrote two autobiographical accounts of her experiences in raising four children, *Life Among the Savages* (1953) and *Raising Demons* (1957). These volumes revealed a talent for humor and wit that the fiction, because of its serious subjects, did not accommodate. Jackson also wrote a number of works for children, including *The Witchcraft of Salem Village* (1956) and *Nine Magic Wishes* (1963).

Jackson died suddenly in 1965 of a heart attack; she was forty-six years old. In the Preface to a collection of her work, *The Magic of Shirley Jackson* (1966), her husband Stanley Edgar Hyman, a noted literary critic, said: "Her fierce visions of dissociation and madness, of alienation and withdrawal, of cruelty and terror, have been taken to be personal, even neurotic, fantasies. Quite the reverse: they are the sensitive and faithful anatomy of our times, fitting symbols for our distressing world of the concentration camp and the Bomb. She was always proud that the Union of South Africa banned 'The Lottery,' and she felt that *they* at least understood the story."

ADDITIONAL READING

Come Along With Me, ed. Stanley Edgar Hyman, 1968.

Lenemaja Friedman, *Shirley Jackson,* 1975; Judy Oppenheimer, *Private Demons: The Life of Shirley Jackson,* 1988.

TEXT

The Lottery and Other Stories, 1949.

The Lottery

The morning of June 27th was clear and sunny, with the fresh warmth of a full-summer day; the flowers were blossoming profusely and the grass was richly green. The people of the village began to gather in the square, between the post office and the bank, around ten o'clock; in some towns there were so many people that the lottery took two days and had to be started on June 26th, but in this village, where there were only about three hundred people, the whole lottery took less than two hours, so it could begin at ten o'clock in the morning and still be through in time to allow the villagers to get home for noon dinner.

The children assembled first, of course. School was recently over for the summer, and the feeling of liberty sat uneasily on most of them; they tended to gather together quietly for a while before they broke into boisterous play, and their talk was still of the classoom and the teacher, of books and reprimands. Bobby Martin had already stuffed his pockets full of stones, and the other boys soon followed his example, selecting the smoothest and roundest stones; Bobby and Harry Jones and Dickie Delacroix—the villagers pronounced this name "Dellacroy"—eventually made a great pile of stones in one corner of the square and guarded it against the raids of the other boys. The girls stood aside, talking among themselves, looking over their shoulders at the boys, and the very small children rolled in the dust or clung to the hands of their older brothers or sisters.

Soon the men began to gather, surveying their own children, speaking of planting and rain, tractors and taxes. They stood together, away from the pile of stones in the corner, and their jokes were quiet and they smiled rather than laughed. The women, wearing faded house dresses and sweaters, came shortly after their menfolk. They greeted one another and exchanged bits of gossip as they went to join their husbands. Soon the women, standing by their husbands, began to call to their children, and the children came reluctantly, having to be called four or five times. Bobby Martin ducked under his mother's grasping hand and ran, laughing, back to the pile of stones. His father spoke up sharply, and Bobby came quickly and took his place between his father and his oldest brother.

The lottery was conducted—as were the square dances, the teen-age club, the Halloween program—by Mr. Summers, who had time and energy to devote to civic activities. He was a round-faced, jovial man and he ran the coal business, and people were sorry for him, because he had no children and his wife was a scold. When he arrived in the square, carrying the black wooden box, there was a murmur of conversation among the villagers, and he waved and called, "Little late today, folks." The postmaster, Mr. Graves, followed him, carrying a three-legged stool, and the stool was put in the center of the square and Mr. Summers set the black box down on it. The villagers kept their distance, leaving a space between themselves and the stool, and when Mr. Summers said, "Some of you fellows want to give me a hand?" there was a hesitation before two men, Mr. Martin and his oldest son, Baxter, came forward to hold the box steady on the stool while Mr. Summers stirred up the papers inside it.

The original paraphernalia for the lottery had been lost long ago, and the black box now resting on the stool had been put into use even before Old Man Warner, the oldest man in town, was born. Mr. Summers spoke frequently to the villagers about making a new box, but no one liked to upset even as much tradition as was represented by the black box. There was a story that the present box had been made with some pieces of the box that had preceded it, the one that had been constructed when the first people settled down to make a village here. Every year, after the lottery, Mr. Summers began talking again about a new box, but every year the subject was allowed to fade off without anything's being done. The black box grew shabbier each year; by now it was no longer completely black but splintered badly along one side to show the original wood color, and in some places faded or stained.

Mr. Martin and his oldest son, Baxter, held the black box securely on the stool until Mr. Summers had stirred the papers thoroughly with his hand. Because so much of the ritual had been forgotten or discarded, Mr. Summers had been successful in having slips of paper substituted for the chips of wood that had been used for generations. Chips of wood, Mr. Summers had argued, had been all very well when the village was tiny, but now that the population was more than three hundred and likely to keep on growing, it was necessary to use something that would fit more easily into the black box. The night before the lottery, Mr. Summers and Mr. Graves made up the slips of paper and put them in the box, and it was then taken to the safe of Mr. Summers' coal company and locked up until Mr. Summers was ready to take it to the square next morning. The rest of the year, the box was put away, sometimes one place, sometimes another; it had spent one year in Mr. Graves's barn and another year underfoot in the post office, and sometimes it was set on a shelf in the Martin grocery and left there.

There was a great deal of fussing to be done before Mr. Summers declared the lottery open. There were the lists to make up—of heads of families, heads of households in each family, members of each household in each family. There was the proper swearing-in of Mr. Summers by the postmaster, as the official of the lottery; at one time, some people remembered, there had been a recital of some sort, performed by the official of the lottery, a perfunctory, tuneless chant that had been rattled off duly each year; some people believed that the official of the lottery used to stand just so when he said or sang it, others believed that he was supposed to walk among the people, but years and years ago this part of the ritual had been allowed to lapse. There had been, also, a ritual salute, which the official of the lottery had had to use in addressing each person who came up to draw from the box, but this also had changed with time, until now it was felt necessary only for the official to speak to each person approaching. Mr. Summers was very good at all this; in his clean white shirt and blue jeans, with one hand resting carelessly on the black box, he seemed very proper and important as he talked interminably to Mr. Graves and the Martins.

Just as Mr. Summers finally left off talking and turned to the assembled villagers, Mrs. Hutchinson came hurriedly along the path to the square, her sweater thrown over her shoulders, and slid into place in the back of the crowd. "Clean forgot what day it was," she said to Mrs. Delacroix, who stood next to her, and they both laughed softly. "Thought my old man was out back stacking wood," Mrs. Hutchinson went on, "and then I looked out the window and the kids was gone, and then I remembered it was the twenty-seventh and came a-running." She dried her hands on her apron, and Mrs. Delacroix said, "You're in time, though. They're still talking away up there."

Mrs. Hutchinson craned her neck to see through the crowd and found her husband and children standing near the front. She tapped Mrs. Delacroix on the arm as a farewell and began to make her way through the crowd. The people separated good-humoredly to let her through; two or three people said, in voices just loud enough to be heard across the crowd, "Here comes your Missus, Hutchinson," and "Bill, she made it after all." Mrs. Hutchinson reached her husband, and Mr. Summers, who had been waiting, said cheerfully, "Thought we were going to have to get on without you, Tessie." Mrs. Hutchinson said, grinning, "Wouldn't have me leave m'dishes in the sink, now, would you, Joe?," and soft laughter ran through the crowd as the people stirred back into position after Mrs. Hutchinson's arrival.

"Well, now," Mr. Summers said soberly, "guess we better get started, get this over with, so's we can go back to work. Anybody ain't here?"

"Dunbar," several people said. "Dunbar, Dunbar."

Mr. Summers consulted his list. "Clyde Dunbar," he said. "That's right. He's broke his leg, hasn't he? Who's drawing for him?"

"Me, I guess," a woman said, and Mr. Summers turned to look at her. "Wife draws for her husband," Mr. Summers said. "Don't you have a grown boy to do it for you, Janey?" Although Mr. Summers and everyone else in the village knew the answer perfectly well, it was the business of the official of the lottery to ask such questions formally. Mr. Summers waited with an expression of polite interest while Mrs. Dunbar answered.

"Horace's not but sixteen yet," Mrs. Dunbar said regretfully. "Guess I gotta fill in for the old man this year."

"Right," Mr. Summers said. He made a note on the list he was holding. Then he asked, "Watson boy drawing this year?"

A tall boy in the crowd raised his hand. "Here," he said. "I'm drawing for m'mother and me." He blinked his eyes nervously and ducked his head as several voices in the crowd said things like "Good fellow, Jack," and "Glad to see your mother's got a man to do it."

"Well," Mr. Summers said, "guess that's everyone. Old Man Warner make it?"

"Here," a voice said, and Mr. Summers nodded.

A sudden hush fell on the crowd as Mr. Summers cleared his throat and looked at the list. "All ready?" he called. "Now, I'll read the names — heads of families first — and the men come up and take a paper out of the box. Keep the paper folded in your hand without looking at it until everyone has had a turn. Everything clear?"

The people had done it so many times that they only half listened to the directions; most of them were quiet, wetting their lips, not looking around. Then Mr. Summers raised one hand high and said, "Adams." A man disengaged himself from the crowd and came forward. "Hi, Steve," Mr. Summers said, and Mr. Adams said, "Hi, Joe." They grinned at one another humorlessly and nervously. Then Mr. Adams reached into the black box and took out a folded paper. He held it firmly by one corner as he turned and went hastily back to his place in the crowd, where he stood a little apart from his family, not looking down at his hand.

"Allen," Mr. Summers said. "Anderson. . . . Bentham."

"Seems like there's no time at all between lotteries any more," Mrs. Delacroix said to Mrs. Graves in the back row. "Seems like we got through with the last one only last week."

"Time sure goes fast," Mrs. Graves said.

"Clark. . . . Delacroix."

"There goes my old man," Mrs. Delacroix said. She held her breath while her husband went forward.

"Dunbar," Mr. Summers said, and Mrs. Dunbar went steadily to the box while one of the women said, "Go on, Janey," and another said, "There she goes."

"We're next," Mrs. Graves said. She watched while Mr. Graves came around from the side of the box, greeted Mr. Summers gravely, and selected a slip of paper from the box. By now, all through the crowd there were men holding the small folded papers in their large hands, turning them over and over nervously. Mrs. Dunbar and her two sons stood together, Mrs. Dunbar holding the slip of paper.

"Harburt. . . . Hutchinson."

"Get up there, Bill," Mrs. Hutchinson said, and the people near her laughed.

"Jones."

"They do say," Mr. Adams said to Old Man Warner, who stood next to him, "that over in the north village they're talking of giving up the lottery."

Old Man Warner snorted. "Pack of crazy fools," he said. "Listening to the young folks, nothing's good enough for *them*. Next thing you know, they'll be wanting to go back to living in caves, nobody work any more, live *that* way for a while. Used to be a saying about 'Lottery in June, corn be heavy soon.' First thing you know, we'd all be eating stewed chickweed and acorns. There's *always* been a lottery," he added petulantly. "Bad enough to see young Joe Summers up there joking with everybody."

"Some places have already quit lotteries," Mrs. Adams said.

"Nothing but trouble in *that,*" Old Man Warner said stoutly. "Pack of young fools."

"Martin." And Bobby Martin watched his father go forward. "Overdyke. . . . Percy."

"I wish they'd hurry," Mrs. Dunbar said to her older son. "I wish they'd hurry."

"They're almost through," her son said.

"You get ready to run tell Dad," Mrs. Dunbar said.

Mr. Summers called his own name and then stepped forward precisely and selected a slip from the box. Then he called, "Warner."

"Seventy-seventh year I been in the lottery," Old Man Warner said as he went through the crowd. "Seventy-seventh time."

"Watson." The tall boy came awkwardly through the crowd. Someone said, "Don't be nervous, Jack," and Mr. Summers said, "Take your time, son."

"Zanini."

After that, there was a long pause, a breathless pause, until Mr. Summers, holding his slip of paper in the air, said, "All right, fellows." For a minute, no one moved, and then all the slips of paper were opened. Suddenly, all the women began to speak at once, saying, "Who is it?," "Who's got it?," "Is it the Dunbars?," "Is it the Watsons?" Then the voices began to say, "It's Hutchinson. It's Bill," "Bill Hutchinson's got it."

"Go tell your father," Mrs. Dunbar said to her older son.

People began to look around to see the Hutchinsons. Bill Hutchinson was standing quiet, staring down at the paper in his hand. Suddenly, Tessie Hutchinson shouted to Mr. Summers, "You didn't give him time enough to take any paper he wanted. I saw you. It wasn't fair!"

"Be a good sport, Tessie," Mrs. Delacroix called, and Mrs. Graves said, "All of us took the same chance."

"Shut up, Tessie," Bill Hutchinson said.

"Well, everyone," Mr. Summers said, "that was done pretty fast, and now we've got to be hurrying a little more to get done in time." He consulted his next list. "Bill," he said, "you draw for the Hutchinson family. You got any other households in the Hutchinsons?"

"There's Don and Eva," Mrs. Hutchinson yelled. "Make *them* take their chance!"

"Daughters draw with their husbands' families, Tessie," Mr. Summers said gently. "You know that as well as anyone else."

"It wasn't *fair,*" Tessie said.

"I guess not, Joe," Bill Hutchinson said regretfully. "My daughter draws with her husband's family, that's only fair. And I've got no other family except the kids."

"Then, as far as drawing for families is concerned, it's you," Mr. Summers said in explanation, "and as far as drawing for households is concerned, that's you, too. Right?"

"Right," Bill Hutchinson said.

"How many kids, Bill?" Mr. Summers asked formally.

"Three," Bill Hutchinson said. "There's Bill, Jr., and Nancy, and little Dave. And Tessie and me."

"All right, then," Mr. Summers said. "Harry, you got their tickets back?"

Mr. Graves nodded and held up the slips of paper. "Put them in the box, then," Mr. Summers directed. "Take Bill's and put it in."

"I think we ought to start over," Mrs. Hutchinson said, as quietly as she could. "I tell you it wasn't *fair.* You didn't give him time enough to choose. *Every*body saw that."

Mr. Graves had selected the five slips and put them in the box, and he dropped all the papers but those onto the ground, where the breeze caught them and lifted them off.

"Listen, everybody," Mrs. Hutchinson was saying to the people around her.

"Ready, Bill?" Mr. Summers asked, and Bill Hutchinson, with one quick glance around at his wife and children, nodded.

"Remember," Mr. Summers said, "take the slips and keep them folded until each person has taken one. Harry, you help little Dave." Mr. Graves took the hand of the little boy, who came willingly with him up to the box. "Take a paper out of the box, Davy," Mr. Summers said. Davy put his hand into the box and laughed. "Take just *one* paper," Mr. Summers said. "Harry, you hold it for him." Mr. Graves took the child's hand and removed the folded paper from the tight fist and held it while little Dave stood next to him and looked up at him wonderingly.

"Nancy next," Mr. Summers said. Nancy was twelve, and her school friends breathed heavily as she went forward, switching her skirt, and took a slip daintily from the box. "Bill, Jr.," Mr. Summers said, and Billy, his face red and his feet over-large, nearly knocked the box over as he got a paper out. "Tessie," Mr. Summers said. She hesitated for a minute, looking around defiantly, and then set her lips and went up to the box. She snatched a paper out and held it behind her.

"Bill," Mr. Summers said, and Bill Hutchinson reached into the box and felt around, bringing his hand out at last with the slip of paper in it."

The crowd was quiet. A girl whispered, "I hope it's not Nancy," and the sound of the whisper reached the edges of the crowd.

"It's not the way it used to be," Old Man Warner said clearly. "People ain't the way they used to be."

"All right," Mr. Summers said. "Open the papers. Harry, you open little Dave's."

Mr. Graves opened the slip of paper and there was a general sigh through the crowd as he held it up and everyone could see that it was blank. Nancy and Bill, Jr., opened theirs at the same time, and both beamed and laughed, turning around to the crowd and holding their slips of paper above their heads.

"Tessie," Mr. Summers said. There was a pause, and then Mr. Summers looked at Bill Hutchinson, and Bill unfolded his paper and showed it. It was blank.

"It's Tessie," Mr. Summers said, and his voice was hushed. "Show us her paper, Bill."

Bill Hutchinson went over to his wife and forced the slip of paper out of her hand. It had a black spot on it, the black spot Mr. Summers had made the night before with the heavy pencil in the coal-company office. Bill Hutchinson held it up, and there was a stir in the crowd.

"All right, folks," Mr. Summers said. "Let's finish quickly."

Although the villagers had forgotten the ritual and lost the original black box, they still remembered to use stones. The pile of stones the boys had made earlier was ready; there were stones on the ground with the blowing scraps of paper that had come out of the box. Mrs. Delacroix selected a stone so large she had to pick it up with both hands and turned to Mrs. Dunbar. "Come on," she said. "Hurry up."

Mrs. Dunbar had small stones in both hands, and she said, gasping for breath. "I can't run at all. You'll have to go ahead and I'll catch up with you."

The children had stones already, and someone gave little Davy Hutchinson a few pebbles.

Tessie Hutchinson was in the center of a cleared space by now, and she held her hands out desperately as the villagers moved in on her. "It isn't fair," she said. A stone hit her on the side of the head.

Old Man Warner was saying, "Come on, come on, everyone." Steve Adams was in the front of the crowd of villagers, with Mrs. Graves beside him.

"It isn't fair, it isn't right," Mrs. Hutchinson screamed, and then they were upon her.

1948, 1949

TRUMAN CAPOTE
(1924–1984)

In a *Paris Review* interview in 1957, Truman Capote presented his credo:

> My more unswerving ambitions still revolve around this form [the short story].
> When seriously explored, the short story seems to me the most difficult and
> disciplining form of prose writing extant. Whatever control and technique I
> may have I owe entirely to my training in this medium. . . . [By control] I mean
> maintaining a stylistic and emotional upper hand over your material. Call it
> precious and go to hell, but I believe a story can be wrecked by a faulty rhythm
> in a sentence—especially if it occurs toward the end—or a mistake in para-
> graphing, even punctuation. Henry James is the maestro of the semi-colon.
> Hemingway is a first rate paragrapher. From the point of view of ear, Virginia
> Woolf never wrote a bad sentence. I don't mean to imply that I successfully
> practice what I preach. I try, that's all.

For a writer famed for the effectiveness of his style, Capote's attention to the
minutest detail of sentence construction is revealing and has the ring of truth.
That Capote was not always to be trusted in what he said is indicated by his
remark to another interviewer: "I don't care what anybody says about me as long
as it isn't true." He himself admitted that a number of stories he had passed on
for a biography in *Who's Who* were made up. But the general outline of his life is
clear. He was born Truman Streckfus Persons in New Orleans in 1924 into an
unhappy marriage. His parents went their separate ways and left Truman to be
brought up by aunts and uncles in Louisiana, Mississippi, and Alabama. By a
very early age he knew he was going to be a writer; and he discovered and capitulated to his homosexuality, developing those traits (lisp, fey gestures) that, together with his petite stature, were to mark his identity as an adult.

His mother remarried (Joe Capote, a businessman) and settled in New York,
where Truman attended Trinity School, St. John's Academy, and the public
schools in Greenwich, Connecticut. In 1942, when he was seventeen, Capote was
hired by *The New Yorker* as a kind of errand boy. His dress and mannerisms were
such as to cause the editor Harold Ross to exclaim after first seeing him, "For
God's sake! What's that?" In spite of his presence in the editorial offices, Capote
did not break through the barriers to publication. With the appearance of his
short story "Miriam" in *Mademoiselle*, however, Capote began to receive notice: it
was chosen for the O. Henry Memorial Award volume, published in 1946.

In 1948, Capote published his first novel, *Other Voices, Other Rooms*. On the
dust jacket was a photograph of the author, reclining in a seductive pose on a
plush settee, staring straight into the camera. The novel itself, with its portrayal
of strange characters including a flamboyant transvestite, shocked readers. Critical controversy flared up between those who admired the book's exquisite style
and those who saw the work as a retreat from reality. *Other Voices, Other Rooms*
became a best-seller, and Capote found himself famous at the age of twenty-
three. His talent was confirmed by the appearance of *A Tree of Night and Other
Stories,* published in 1949.

Capote wrote a volume of travel pieces, *Local Color,* published in 1950, in
which he showed the same artistry he used in fiction. In *The Grass Harp* (1951) he
returned to fiction and drew on his memories of the eccentric rebels with whom
he had lived during his vagabond boyhood. He turned the novel into an unsuccessful play in 1952. In 1955 Capote travelled with a *Porgy and Bess* company on a
tour of Russia and wrote about the experience in *The Muses Are Heard,* published

in 1956. Once again he demonstrated that he could portray fascinating characters, spin out incidents in a coherent action, and even develop suspense — using fact, not fiction. As he was casting about for another nonfiction subject on which to try his talent, he produced in 1958 the acclaimed novelette *Breakfast at Tiffany's,* about a cheerful and charming prostitute. It was turned into a popular movie in 1961.

In late 1959, Capote read in the newspapers about the murder of a farm family in Kansas. He went there and began the research that would last six years, leading to the publication of *In Cold Blood* in *The New Yorker* in 1965 and as a book in 1966. It had all the impact of a powerful work of fiction, and Capote himself invented the term "non-fiction novel" to describe the form. It was widely hailed as pointing the direction for imaginative literature in the future, especially in the postwar world in which events themselves seemed to be more astounding, horrible, or fabulous than novelists dared to imagine.

In Cold Blood turned out to be Capote's last important work — and perhaps his most accomplished. He launched a long, never-to-be-finished novel which he called *Answered Prayers,* a title he took from St. Theresa of Avila: "More tears are shed over answered prayers than unanswered ones." Perhaps the quotation appealed to Capote because he lived its truth: his ambitions for fame and wealth were all realized, but they did not bring happiness. As his "friends" found out that they were being mercilessly portrayed in his work-in-progress, they began to cut him. He turned more and more to alcohol and drugs, and to a succession of unstable homosexual affairs that ended with Capote feeling more isolated and lonely than ever. He died in 1984 of a cardiac arrest caused by an overdose of drugs.

ADDITIONAL READING

The Dogs Bark, 1973; *Conversations with Capote,* ed. Lawrence Grobel, 1985.

William L. Nance, *The Worlds of Truman Capote,* 1970; Kenneth T. Reed, *Truman Capote,* 1981; John Malcolm Brinnin, *Sextet: T. S. Eliot and Truman Capote and Others,* 1981; Marie Rudisill and James C. Simmons, *Truman Capote,* 1983; Gerald Clarke, *Capote: A Biography,* 1988.

TEXT

A Tree of Night and Other Stories, 1949.

A Tree of Night

It was winter. A string of naked light bulbs, from which it seemed all warmth had been drained, illuminated the little depot's cold, windy platform. Earlier in the evening it had rained, and now icicles hung along the station-house eaves like some crystal monster's vicious teeth. Except for a girl, young and rather tall, the platform was deserted. The girl wore a gray flannel suit, a raincoat, and a plaid scarf. Her hair, parted in the middle and rolled up neatly on the sides, was rich blondish-brown; and, while her face tended to be too thin and narrow, she was, though not extraordinarily so, attractive. In addition to an assortment of magazines and a gray suede purse on which elaborate brass letters spelled Kay, she carried conspicuously a green Western guitar.

When the train, spouting steam and glaring with light, came out of the darkness and rumbled to a halt, Kay assembled her paraphernalia and climbed up into the last coach.

The coach was a relic with a decaying interior of ancient red-plush seats, bald in spots, and peeling iodine-colored woodwork. An old-time copper lamp, attached to the ceiling, looked romantic and out of place. Gloomy dead smoke sailed the air; and the car's heated closeness accentuated the stale odor of discarded sandwiches, apple cores, and orange hulls: this garbage, including Lily cups, soda-pop bottles, and mangled newspapers, littered the long aisle. From a water cooler, embedded in the wall, a steady stream trickled to the floor. The passengers, who glanced up wearily when Kay entered, were not, it seemed, at all conscious of any discomfort.

Kay resisted a temptation to hold her nose and threaded her way carefully down the aisle, tripping once, without disaster, over a dozing fat man's protruding leg. Two nondescript men turned an interested eye as she passed; and a kid stood up in his seat, squalling, "Hey, Mama, look at de banjo! Hey, lady, lemme play ya banjo!" till a slap from Mama quelled him.

There was only one empty place. She found it at the end of the car in an isolated alcove occupied already by a man and woman who were sitting with their feet settled lazily on the vacant seat opposite. Kay hesitated a second then said, "Would you mind if I sat here?"

The woman's head snapped up as if she had not been asked a simple question, but stabbed with a needle, too. Nevertheless, she managed a smile. "Can't say as I see what's to stop you, honey," she said, taking her feet down and also, with a curious impersonality, removing the feet of the man who was staring out the window, paying no attention whatsoever.

Thanking the woman, Kay took off her coat, sat down, and arranged herself with purse and guitar at her side, magazines in her lap: comfortable enough, though she wished she had a pillow for her back.

The train lurched; a ghost of steam hissed against the window; slowly the dingy lights of the lonesome depot faded past.

"Boy, what a jerkwater dump," said the woman. "No town, no nothin'."

Kay said, "The town's a few miles away."

"That so? Live there?"

No. Kay explained she had been at the funeral of an uncle. An uncle who, though she did not of course mention it, had left her nothing in his will but the green guitar. Where was she going? Oh, back to college.

After mulling this over, the woman concluded, "What'll you ever learn in a place like that? Let me tell you, honey, I'm plenty educated and I never saw the inside of no college."

"You didn't?" murmured Kay politely and dismissed the matter by opening one of her magazines. The light was dim for reading and none of the stories looked in the least compelling. However, not wanting to become involved in a conversational marathon, she continued gazing at it stupidly till she felt a furtive tap on her knee.

"Don't read," said the woman. "I need somebody to talk to. Naturally, it's no fun talking to *him*." She jerked a thumb toward the silent man. "He's afflicted: deaf and dumb, know what I mean?"

Kay closed the magazine and looked at her more or less for the first time. She was short; her feet barely scraped the floor. And like many undersized people she had a freak of structure, in her case an enormous, really huge head. Rouge so brightened her sagging, fleshy-featured face it was difficult even to guess at her age: perhaps fifty, fifty-five. Her big sheep eyes squinted, as if distrustful of what they saw. Her hair was an obviously dyed red, and twisted into parched, fat corkscrew curls. A once-elegant lavender hat of impressive size flopped crazily on the side of her head, and she was kept busy brushing back a drooping cluster of celluloid cherries sewed to the brim. She wore a plain, somewhat shabby blue dress. Her breath had a vividly sweetish gin smell.

"You do wanna talk to me, don't you, honey?"

"Sure," said Kay, moderately amused.

"Course you do. You bet you do. That's what I like about a train. Bus people are a close-mouthed buncha dopes. But a train's the place for putting your cards on the table, that's what I always say." Her voice was cheerful and booming, husky as a man's. "But on accounta *him*, I always try to get us this here seat; it's more private, like a swell compartment, see?"

"It's very pleasant," Kay agreed. "Thanks for letting me join you."

"Only too glad to. We don't have much company; it makes some folks nervous to be around him."

As if to deny it, the man made a queer, furry sound deep in his throat and plucked the woman's sleeve. "Leave me alone, dear-heart," she said, as if she were talking to an inattentive child. "I'm O.K. We're just having us a nice little ol' talk. Now behave yourself or this pretty girl will go away. She's very rich; she goes to college." And winking, she added, "He thinks I'm drunk."

The man slumped in the seat, swung his head sideways, and studied Kay intently from the corners of his eyes. These eyes, like a pair of clouded milky-blue marbles, were thickly lashed and oddly beautiful. Now, except for a certain remoteness, his wide, hairless face had no real expression. It was as if he were incapable of experiencing or reflecting the slightest emotion. His gray hair was clipped close and combed forward into uneven bangs. He looked like a child aged abruptly by some uncanny method. He wore a frayed blue serge suit, and he had anointed himself with a cheap, vile perfume. Around his wrist was strapped a Mickey Mouse watch.

"He thinks I'm drunk," the woman repeated. "And the real funny part is, I am. Oh, shoot you gotta do something, ain't that right?" She bent closer. "Say, ain't it?"

Kay was still gawking at the man; the way he was looking at her made her squeamish, but she could not take her eyes off him. "I guess so," she said.

"Then let's us have us a drink," suggested the woman. She plunged her hand into an oilcloth satchel and pulled out a partially filled gin bottle. She began to unscrew the cap but, seeming to think better of this, handed the bottle to Kay. "Gee, I forgot about you being company," she said. "I'll go get us some nice paper cups."

So, before Kay could protest that she did not want a drink, the woman had risen and started none too steadily down the aisle toward the water cooler.

Kay yawned and rested her forehead against the windowpane, her fingers idly strumming the guitar: the strings sang a hollow, lulling tune, as monotonously soothing as the Southern landscape, smudged in darkness, flowing past the window. An icy winter moon rolled above the train across the night sky like a thin white wheel.

And then, without warning, a strange thing happened: the man reached out and gently stroked Kay's cheek. Despite the breathtaking delicacy of this movement, it was such a bold gesture Kay was at first too startled to know what to make of it: her thoughts shot in three or four fantastic directions. He leaned forward till his queer eyes were very near her own; the reek of his perfume was sickening. The guitar was silent while they exchanged a searching gaze. Suddenly, from some spring of compassion, she felt for him a keen sense of pity; but also, and this she could not suppress, an overpowering disgust, an absolute loathing: something about him, an elusive quality she could not quite put a finger on, reminded her of—of what?

After a little, he lowered his hand solemnly and sank back in the seat, an asinine grin transfiguring his face, as if he had performed a clever stunt for which he wished applause.

"Giddyup! Giddyup! my little bucker-ROOS . . ." shouted the woman. And she sat down, loudly proclaiming to be, "Dizzy as a witch! Dog tired! Whew!" From a handful of Lily cups she separated two and casually thrust the rest down her blouse. "Keep 'em safe and dry, ha ha ha. . . ." A coughing spasm seized her, but when it was over she appeared calmer. "Has my boy friend been entertaining?" she asked, patting her bosom reverently. "Ah, he's so sweet." She looked as if she might pass out. Kay rather wished she would.

"I don't want a drink," Kay said, returning the bottle. "I never drink: I hate the taste."

"Mustn't be a kill-joy," said the woman firmly. "Here now, hold your cup like a good girl."

"No, please . . ."

"Formercysake, hold it still. Imagine, nerves at your age! Me, I can shake like a leaf, I've got reasons. Oh, Lordy, have I got 'em."

"But . . ?"

A dangerous smile tipped the woman's face hideously awry. "What's the matter? Don't you think I'm good enough to drink with?"

"Please, don't misunderstand," said Kay, a tremor in her voice. "It's just that I don't like being forced to do something I don't want to. So look, couldn't I give this to the gentleman?"

"Him? No sirree: he needs what little sense he's got. Come on, honey, down the hatch."

Kay, seeing it was useless, decided to succumb and avoid a possible scene. She sipped and shuddered. It was terrible gin. It burned her throat till her eyes watered. Quickly, when the woman was not watching, she emptied the cup out into the sound hole of the guitar. It happened, however, that the man saw; and Kay, realizing it, recklessly signaled to him with her eyes a plea not to give her away. But she could not tell from his clear-blank expression how much he understood.

"Where you from, kid?" resumed the woman presently.

For a bewildered moment, Kay was unable to provide an answer. The names of several cities came to her all at once. Finally, from this confusion, she extracted: "New Orleans. My home is in New Orleans."

The woman beamed. "N.O.'s where I wanna go when I kick off. One time, oh, say, 1923, I ran me a sweet little fortune-telling parlor there. Let's see, that was on St. Peter Street." Pausing, she stooped and set the empty gin bottle on the floor. It rolled into the aisle and rocked back and forth with a drowsy sound. "I was raised in Texas—on a big ranch—my papa was rich. Us kids always had the best; even Paris, France, clothes. I'll bet you've got a big swell house, too. Do you have a garden? Do you grow flowers?"

"Just lilacs."

A conductor entered the coach, preceded by a cold gust of wind that rattled the trash in the aisle and briefly livened the dull air. He lumbered along, stopping now and then to punch a ticket or talk with a passenger. It was after midnight. Someone was expertly playing a harmonica. Someone else was arguing the merits of a certain politician. A child cried out in his sleep.

"Maybe you wouldn't be so snotty if you knew who we was," said the woman, bobbing her tremendous head. "We ain't nobodies, not by a long shot."

Embarrassed, Kay nervously opened a pack of cigarettes and lighted one. She wondered if there might not be a seat in a car up ahead. She could not bear the woman, or, for that matter, the man, another minute. But she had never before been in a remotely comparable situation. "If you'll excuse me now," she said, "I have to be leaving. It's been very pleasant, but I promised to meet a friend on the train. . . ."

With almost invisible swiftness the woman grasped the girl's wrist. "Didn't your mama ever tell you it was sinful to lie?" she stage-whispered. The lavender hat tumbled off her head but she made no effort to retrieve it. Her tongue flicked out and wetted her lips. And, as Kay stood up, she increased the pressure of her grip. "Sit down, dear . . . there ain't any friend . . . Why, we're your only friends and we wouldn't have you leave us for the world."

"Honestly, I wouldn't lie."

"Sit down, dear."

Kay dropped her cigarette and the man picked it up. He slouched in the corner and became absorbed in blowing a chain of lush smoke rings that mounted upward like hollow eyes and expanded into nothing.

"Why, you wouldn't want to hurt his feelings by leaving us, now, would you, dear?" crooned the woman softly. "Sit down—down—now, that's a good girl. My, what a pretty guitar. What a pretty, pretty guitar . . ." Her voice faded before the sudden whooshing, static noise of a second train. And for an instant the lights in the coach went off; in the darkness the passing train's golden windows winked black-yellow-black-yellow-black-yellow. The man's cigarette pulsed like the glow of a firefly, and his smoke rings continued rising tranquilly. Outside, a bell pealed wildly.

When the lights came on again, Kay was massaging her wrist where the woman's strong fingers had left a painful bracelet mark. She was more puzzled than angry. She determined to ask the conductor if he would find her a different seat. But when he arrived to take her ticket, the request stuttered on her lips incoherently.

"Yes, miss?"

"Nothing," she said.

And he was gone.

The trio in the alcove regarded one another in mysterious silence till the woman said, "I've got something here I wanna show you, honey." She rummaged once more in the oilcloth satchel. "You won't be so snotty after you get a gander at this."

What she passed to Kay was a handbill, published on such yellowed, antique paper it looked as if it must be centuries old. In fragile, overly fancy lettering, it read:

LAZARUS

The Man Who Is Buried Alive

A MIRACLE

SEE FOR YOURSELF

Adults, 25¢ — Children, 10¢

"I always sing a hymn and read a sermon," said the woman. "It's awful sad: some folks cry, especially the old ones. And I've got me a perfectly elegant costume: a black veil and a black dress, oh, very becoming. *He* wears a gorgeous made-to-order bride-groom suit and a turban and lotsa talcum on his face. See, we try to make it as much like a bona-fide funeral as we can. But shoot, nowadays you're likely to get just a buncha smart alecks come for laughs—so sometimes I'm real glad he's afflicted like he is on accounta otherwise his feelings would be hurt, maybe."

Kay said, "You mean you're with a circus or a sideshow or something like that?"

"Nope, us alone," said the woman as she reclaimed the fallen hat. "We've been doing it for years and years—played every tank town in the South: Singasong, Missis-sippi—Spunky, Louisiana—Eureka, Alabama . . ." these and other names rolled off her tongue musically, running together like rain. "After the hymn, after the sermon, we bury him."

"In a coffin?"

"Sort of. It's gorgeous, it's got silver stars painted all over the lid."

"I should think he would suffocate," said Kay, amazed. "How long does he stay buried?"

"All told it takes maybe an hour—course that's not counting the lure."

"The lure?"

"Uh huh. It's what we do the night before a show. See, we hunt up a store, any ol' store with a big glass window'll do, and get the owner to let *him* sit inside this window, and, well, hypnotize himself. Stays there all night stiff as a poker and people come and look: scares the livin' hell out of 'em. . . ." While she talked she jiggled a finger in her ear, withdrawing it occasionally to examine her find. "And one time this ol' bind-lestiff[1] Mississippi sheriff tried to . . ."

The tale that followed was baffling and pointless: Kay did not bother to listen. Nevertheless, what she had heard already inspired a reverie, a vague recapitulation of her uncle's funeral; an event which, to tell the truth, had not much affected her since she had scarcely known him. And so, while gazing abstractedly at the man, an image of her uncle's face, white next the pale silk casket pillow, appeared in her mind's eye. Observing their faces simultaneously, both the man's and uncle's, as it were, she thought she recognized an odd parallel: there was about the man's face the same kind of shocking, embalmed, secret stillness, as though, in a sense, he were truly an exhibit in a glass cage, complacent to be seen, uninterested in seeing.

"I'm sorry, what did you say?"

"I said: I sure wish they'd lend us the use of a regular cemetery. Like it is now we have to put on the show wherever we can . . . mostly in empty lots that are nine times outa ten smack up against some smelly fillin' station, which ain't exactly a big help. But like I say, we got us a swell act, the best. You oughta come see it if you get a chance."

"Oh, I should love to," Kay said, absently.

"Oh, I should love to," mimicked the woman. "Well, who ask you? Anybody ask you?" She hoisted up her skirt and enthusiastically blew her nose on the ragged hem of a petticoat. "Bu-leeve me, it's a hard way to turn a dollar. Know what our take was last month? Fifty-three bucks! Honey, you try living on that sometime." She sniffed and rearranged her skirt with considerable primness. "Well, one of these days my sweet boy's sure enough going to die down there; and even then somebody'll say it was a gyp."

At this point the man took from his pocket what seemed to be a finely shellacked peach seed and balanced it on the palm of his hand. He looked across at Kay and, certain of her attention, opened his eyelids wide and began to squeeze and caress the seed in an undefinably obscene manner.

Kay frowned. "What does he want?"

"He wants you to buy it."

"But what is it?"

"A charm," said the woman. "A love charm."

Whoever was playing the harmonica stopped. Other sounds, less unique, became at once prominent: someone snoring, the gin bottle seesaw rolling, voices in sleepy argument, the train wheels' distant hum.

"Where could you get love cheaper, honey?"

"It's nice. I mean it's cute. . . ." Kay said, stalling for time. The man rubbed and polished the seed on his trouser leg. His head was lowered at a supplicating, mournful angle, and presently he stuck the seed between his teeth and bit it, as if it were a suspicious piece of silver. "Charms always bring me bad luck. And besides . . . please, can't you make him stop acting that way?"

"Don't look so scared," said the woman, more flat-voiced than ever. "He ain't gonna hurt you."

"Make him stop, damn it!"

"What can I do?" asked the woman, shrugging her shoulders. "You're the one that's got money. You're rich. All he wants is a dollar, one dollar."

---

[1]Hobo (slang).

Kay tucked her purse under her arm. "I have just enough to get back to school," she lied, quickly rising and stepping out into the aisle. She stood there a moment, expecting trouble. But nothing happened.

The woman, with rather deliberate indifference, heaved a sigh and closed her eyes; gradually the man subsided and stuck the charm back in his pocket. Then his hand crawled across the seat to join the woman's in a lax embrace.

Kay shut the door and moved to the front of the observation platform. It was bitterly cold in the open air, and she had left her raincoat in the alcove. She loosened her scarf and draped it over her head.

Although she had never made this trip before, the train was traveling through an area strangely familiar: tall trees, misty, painted pale by malicious moonshine, towered steep on either side without a break or clearing. Above, the sky was a stark, unexplorable blue thronged with stars that faded here and there. She could see streamers of smoke trailing from the train's engine like long clouds of ectoplasm. In one corner of the platform a red kerosene lantern cast a colorful shadow.

She found a cigarette and tried to light it: the wind snuffed match after match till only one was left. She walked to the corner where the lantern burned and cupped her hands to protect the last match: the flame caught, sputtered, died. Angrily she tossed away the cigarette and empty folder; all the tension in her tightened to an exasperating pitch and she slammed the wall with her fist and began to whimper softly, like an irritable child.

The intense cold made her head ache, and she longed to go back inside the warm coach and fall asleep. But she couldn't, at least not yet; and there was no sense in wondering why, for she knew the answer very well. Aloud, partly to keep her teeth from chattering and partly because she needed the reassurance of her own voice, she said: "We're in Alabama now, I think, and tomorrow we'll be in Atlanta and I'm nineteen and I'll be twenty in August and I'm a sophomore. . . ." She glanced around at the darkness, hoping to see a sign of dawn, and finding the same endless wall of trees, the same frosty moon. "I hate him, he's horrible and I hate him. . . ." She stopped, ashamed of her foolishness and too tired to evade the truth: she was afraid.

Suddenly she felt an eerie compulsion to kneel down and touch the lantern. Its graceful glass funnel was warm, and the red glow seeped through her hands, making them luminous. The heat thawed her fingers and tingled along her arms.

She was so preoccupied she did not hear the door open. The train wheels roaring clickety-clack-clackety-click hushed the sound of the man's footsteps.

It was a subtle zero sensation that warned her finally; but some seconds passed before she dared look behind.

He was standing there with a mute detachment, his head tilted, his arms dangling at his sides. Staring up into his harmless, vapid face, flushed brilliant by the lantern light, Kay knew of what she was afraid: it was a memory, a childish memory of terrors that once, long ago, had hovered above her like haunted limbs on a tree of night. Aunts, cooks, strangers—each eager to spin a tale or teach a rhyme of spooks and death, omens, spirits, demons. And always there had been the unfailing threat of the wizard man: stay close to the house, child, else a wizard man'll snatch and eat you alive! He lived everywhere, the wizard man, and everywhere was danger. At night, in bed, hear him tapping at the window? Listen!

Holding onto the railing, she inched upward till she was standing erect. The man nodded and waved his hand toward the door. Kay took a deep breath and stepped forward. Together they went inside.

The air in the coach was numb with sleep: a solitary light now illuminated the car, creating a kind of artificial dusk. There was no motion but the train's sluggish sway, and the stealthy rattle of discarded newspapers.

The woman alone was wide awake. You could see she was greatly excited: she fidgeted with her curls and celluloid cherries, and her plump little legs, crossed at the ankles, swung agitatedly back and forth. She paid no attention when Kay sat down. The man settled in the seat with one leg tucked beneath him and his arms folded across his chest.

In an effort to be casual, Kay picked up a magazine. She realized the man was watching her, not removing his gaze an instant: she knew this though she was afraid to confirm it, and she wanted to cry out and waken everyone in the coach. But suppose they did not hear? What if they were not really *asleep?* Tears started in her eyes, magnifying and distorting the print on a page till it became a hazy blur. She shut the magazine with fierce abruptness and looked at the woman.

"I'll buy it," she said. "The charm, I mean. I'll buy it, if that's all — just all you want."

The woman made no response. She smiled apathetically as she turned toward the man.

As Kay watched, the man's face seemed to change form and recede before her like a moon-shaped rock sliding downward under a surface of water. A warm laziness relaxed her. She was dimly conscious of it when the woman took away her purse, and when she gently pulled the raincoat like a shroud above her head.

1945, 1949

WILLIAM GASS
(b. 1924)

William Gass is both a professor of philosophy and a novelist, and no other writer has been more radical in attempts to redefine fiction and its province. He begins with what may seem the obvious: "It seems a country-headed thing to say: that literature is language, that stories and the places and the people in them are merely made of words as chairs are made of smoothed sticks and sometimes of cloth or metal tubes." The novelist's business is not "to render the world," but "to *make* [a world] from the only medium of which he is a master — language." Fictions are not "ways of viewing reality" but are "additions to it." It is not the business of fiction, but rather the business of "philosophy," to address "important human issues." It is not the purpose of the novelist to "communicate," but to "plant some object in the world" whose signs don't point to the world (though they may seem to do so) but in assembly form a "sculpture" that one may "ponder" and "love" because "it is so beautiful in itself."

Gass was born in Fargo, North Dakota, but soon after his birth his family moved to Warren, Ohio, where he grew up under difficult circumstances: his mother was an alcoholic, and his father suffered from crippling arthritis. His later retreat into aesthetics may have had its psychic roots in this domestic reality. He attended both Kenyon College and Ohio Wesleyan before entering the navy during the Second World War. After the war, he returned to Kenyon and took his B.A. in philosophy in 1947. He did graduate work at Cornell University, taking his Ph.D. in philosophy in 1954 (his dissertation was entitled "A Philosophical Investigation of Metaphor"). His encounter at Cornell with the linguistic-analytical philosopher Ludwig Wittgenstein, in a series of lecture-discussion sessions, was later described by Gass as the "most important intellectual experience" of his life. After teaching philosophy for some fifteen years at Purdue University in Indiana, Gass moved to Washington University in St. Louis in 1969, teaching in both the philosophy and English departments.

He began to publish stories in the little magazines in the 1950s and published his first novel, *Omensetter's Luck,* in 1966. A summary of the action — focusing on the conflict between a naive, innocent man and a semi-deranged preacher — misses the novel's meaning, which resides in its language. One reviewer, Paul West, wrote: "One would have to be criminally tone-deaf and almost snowblind not to register the sonic and visual brilliance of the language . . . a pregnant, swaying physicality with an undertow of festive and smutty limericks: a delight to say aloud and a continuing sound in the mind."

In 1968, Gass published *Willie Masters' Lonesome Wife* (reissued in 1971) and a volume of short stories, *In the Heart of the Heart of the Country.* These stories, often surrealistic in effect, focus most frequently on people who find themselves outsiders, or isolatoes, enclosed within themselves and holding on, perhaps sometimes breaking through, only by the spinning of language, defining (or creating) for themselves the worlds they — and others — inhabit. A housewife, for example, in "The Order of Insects," seems to come to a new understanding of herself and her world in an epiphany ("entrusted with a kind of eastern mystery, sacred to a dreadful god") inspired by the beauty of the "order" of a bug (a roach). The title story, included here, has become Gass's most widely read (or misread) story, accepted as an excellent example of the kind of fiction his theory has led him to write.

Gass's body of fiction is relatively small, perhaps because the scruples of his theory are so austere. He has published a number of sections of a work-in-progress entitled *The Tunnel,* which he described as an "attempt to get outside language"; and he added: "The fact is that language creates a world which does protect us and which we can live in, but it also bamboozles us." He has published a number of books of essays, reviews, and critical evaluations that have addressed many of the questions surrounding modernist and postmodernist fiction. *Fiction and the Figures of Life* (1970) contains some of his most important and fundamental statements on fiction. *On Being Blue* (1976) is a kind of analytical prose-poem, focusing on the many incarnations and metamorphoses of the word "blue," with serious philosophical implications for the nature of language and its imaginative uses. *The World Within the Word* (1978) and *Habitations of the Word* (1985) collect essays that elaborate Gass's linguistically centered theory of fiction or focus on particular authors. One of Gass's favorite American novelists, to whom he frequently returns, is Gertrude Stein, whose use of language influenced his own experiments.

In an interview published in 1986 (in Arthur M. Saltzman's *The Fiction of William Gass*), the interviewer pressed the author as to how he would go about teaching his own work, and Gass revealed much that is useful to the reader in his reply:

> I'm not sure. I think what you would have to do with my work, because of the attitudes behind it, is to pretend you were reading Montaigne. It's basically skeptical and non-committed, so behind it are plenty of attitudes and values that are absolute, but in terms of the theoretical frame around them, they are held with a great deal of skepticism. I'd probably be inclined to do a New Critical approach, because that's the way I was brought up, although that's not what I do in the class much. Mine is generally a philosophy class more than a literature class.

ADDITIONAL READING

"A Debate: William Gass and John Gardner," in *Anything Can Happen: Interviews with Contemporary Authors,* ed. Tom LeClair and Larry McCaffery, 1983.

Larry McCaffery, *The Metafictional Muse*, 1982; Elizabeth W. Bruss, *Beautiful Theories*, 1982; Arthur M. Saltzman, *The Fiction of William Gass: The Consolation of Language*, 1986.

TEXT

In the Heart of the Heart of the Country, 1968.

In the Heart of the Heart of the Country

A PLACE[1]

So I have sailed the seas and come . . .

to B . . .[2]

a small town fastened to a field in Indiana. Twice there have been twelve hundred people here to answer to the census. The town is outstandingly neat and shady, and always puts its best side to the highway. On one lawn there's even a wood or plastic iron deer.

You can reach us by crossing a creek. In the spring the lawns are green, the forsythia is singing, and even the railroad that guts the town has straight bright rails which hum when the train is coming, and the train itself has a welcome horning sound.

Down the back streets the asphalt crumbles into gravel. There's Westbrook's, with the geraniums, Horsefall's, Mott's. The sidewalk shatters. Gravel dust rises like breath behind the wagons. And I am in retirement from love.

WEATHER

In the Midwest, around the lower Lakes, the sky in the winter is heavy and close, and it is a rare day, a day to remark on, when the sky lifts and allows the heart up. I am keeping count, and as I write this page, it is eleven days since I have seen the sun.

MY HOUSE

There's a row of headless maples behind my house, cut to free the passage of electric wires. High stumps, ten feet tall, remain, and I climb these like a boy to watch the country sail away from me. They are ordinary fields, a little more uneven than they should be, since in the spring they puddle. The topsoil's thin, but only moderately stony. Corn is grown one year, soybeans another. At dusk starlings darken the single tree — a larch — which stands in the middle. When the sky moves, fields move under it. I feel, on my perch, that I've lost my years. It's as though I were living at last in my eyes, as I have always dreamed of doing, and I think then I know why I've come here: to see, and so to go out against new things — oh god how easily — like air in a breeze. It's true there are moments — foolish moments, ecstasy on a tree stump — when I'm all but gone, scattered I like to think like seed, for I'm the sort now in the

---

[1]Gass has said of this story: "The first thing I had to do was to get rid of any intention to be truthful about the place. That would have been exceedingly difficult and would have required all kinds of other operations. What you could say is, yes, something like certain of these things happened in a town like this but that was only part of what happened, not the whole thing, and I frequently get letters which say, 'You really captured how it was to live in this small town in Utah, in Indiana.' That just means they weren't seeing their town fully enough because it isn't the way it was. Again, they are doing something people frequently do, taking the complexities of experienced reality and bringing them down *not* to the complexities of language which is, I hope, a rival, but to the complexities of something they then lift out of the language, simplify and then suppose that they have got a picture of their world. I find that dismaying." See *Shenandoah*, 27 (Winter 1976), 7.

[2]"And therefore I have sailed the seas and come / To the holy city of Byzantium," from "Sailing to Byzantium" by Irish poet William Butler Yeats (1865–1939). Byzantium symbolizes the domain of art in the poem.

fool's position of having love left over which I'd like to lose; what good is it now to me, candy ungiven after Halloween?

A PERSON

There are vacant lots on either side of Billy Holsclaw's house. As the weather improves, they fill with hollyhocks. From spring through fall, Billy collects coal and wood and puts the lumps and pieces in piles near his door, for keeping warm is his one work. I see him most often on mild days sitting on his doorsill in the sun. I notice he's squinting a little, which is perhaps the reason he doesn't cackle as I pass. His house is the size of a single garage, and very old. It shed its paint with its youth, and its boards are a warped and weathered gray. So is Billy. He wears a short lumpy faded black coat when it's cold, otherwise he always goes about in the same loose, grease-spotted shirt and trousers. I suspect his galluses were yellow once, when they were new.

WIRES

These wires offend me. Three trees were maimed on their account, and now these wires deface the sky. They cross like a fence in front of me, enclosing the crows with the clouds. I can't reach in, but like a stick, I throw my feelings over. What is it that offends me? I am on my stump, I've built a platform there and the wires prevent my going out. The cut trees, the black wires, all the beyond birds therefore anger me. When I've wormed through a fence to reach a meadow, do I ever feel the same about the field?

THE CHURCH

The church has a steeple like the hat of a witch, and five birds, all doves, perch in its gutters.

MY HOUSE

Leaves move in the windows. I cannot tell you yet how beautiful it is, what it means. But they do move. They move in the glass.

POLITICS

. . . for all those not in love.

I've heard Batista described as a Mason. A farmer who'd seen him in Miami made this claim. He's as nice a fellow as you'd ever want to meet. Of Castro,[3] of course, no one speaks.

For all those not in love there's law: to rule . . . to regulate . . . to rectify. I cannot write the poetry of such proposals, the poetry of politics, though sometimes — often — always now — I am in that uneasy peace of equal powers which makes a State; then I communicate by passing papers, proclamations, orders, through my bowels. Yet I was not a State with you, nor were we both together any Indiana. A squad of Pershing Rifles at the moment, I make myself Right Face! Legislation packs the screw of my intestines. Well, king of the classroom's king of the hill. You used to waddle when you walked because my sperm between your legs was draining to a towel. Teacher, poet, folded lover — like the politician, like those drunkards, ill, or those who faucet-off while pisssing heartily to preach upon the force and fullness of that stream, or pause from vomiting to praise the purity and passion of their puke — I chant, I beg, I orate, I command, I sing —

> Come back to Indiana — not too late!
> (Or will you be a ranger to the end?)

---

[3]Fulgencio Batista (1901–1973), Cuban dictator, was deposed by Fidel Castro in 1959. Mason: a member of a secret fraternity.

> Good-bye . . . Good-bye . . . oh, I shall always wait
>   You, Larry, traveler—
>   stranger,
>   son,
>   — my friend —[4]

my little girl, my poem by heart, my self, my childhood.

But I've heard Batista described as a Mason. That dries up my pity, melts my hate. Back from the garage where I have overheard it, I slap the mended fender of my car to laugh, and listen to the metal stinging tartly in my hand.

PEOPLE

Their hair in curlers and their heads wrapped in loud scarves, young mothers, fattish in trousers, lounge about in the speedwash, smoking cigarettes, eating candy, drinking pop, thumbing magazines, and screaming at their children above the whir and rumble of the machines.

At the bank a young man freshly pressed is letting himself in with a key. Along the street, delicately teetering, many grandfathers move in a dream. During the murderous heat of summer, they perch on window ledges, their feet dangling just inside the narrow shelf of shade the store has made, staring steadily into the street. Where their consciousness has gone I can't say. It's not in the eyes. Perhaps it's diffuse, all temperature and skin, like an infant's, though more mild. Near the corner there are several large overalled men employed in standing. A truck turns to be weighed on the scales at the Feed and Grain. Images drift on the drugstore window. The wind has blown the smell of cattle into town. Our eyes have been driven in like the eyes of the old men. And there's no one to have mercy on us.

VITAL DATA

There are two restaurants here and a tearoom. two bars. one bank, three barbers, one with a green shade with which he blinds his window. two groceries. a dealer in Fords. one drug, one hardware, and one appliance store. several that sell feed, grain, and farm equipment. an antique shop. a poolroom. a laundromat. three doctors. a dentist. a plumber. a vet. a funeral home in elegant repair the color of a buttercup. numerous beauty parlors which open and shut like night-blooming plants. a tiny dime and department store of no width but several floors. a hutch, homemade, where you can order, after lying down or squirming in, furniture that's been fashioned from bent lengths of stainless tubing, glowing plastic, metallic thread, and clear shellac. an American Legion Post and a root beer stand. little agencies for this and that: cosmetics, brushes, insurance, greeting cards and garden produce—anything—sample shoes—which do their business out of hats and satchels, over coffee cups and dissolving sugar. a factory for making paper sacks and pasteboard boxes that's lodged in an old brick building bearing the legend OPERA HOUSE, still faintly golden, on its roof. a library given by Carnegie. a post office. a school. a railroad station. fire station. lumberyard. telephone company. welding shop. garage . . . and spotted through the town from one end to the other in a line along the highway, gas stations to the number five.

EDUCATION

In 1833, Colin Goodykoontz, an itinerant preacher with a name from a fairytale, summed up the situation in one Indiana town this way:

> Ignorance and her squalid brood. A universal dearth of intellect. Total abstinence from literature is very generally practiced. . . . There is not a scholar in

---

[4] From *The Bridge* (Part II), by American poet Hart Crane (1899–1932), who grew up in Ohio.

grammar or geography, or a *teacher capable of instructing* in them, to my knowledge. . . .Others are supplied a few months of the year with the most antiquated & unreasonable forms of teaching reading, writing & cyphering. . . . Need I stop to remind you of the host of loathsome reptiles such a stagnant pool is fitted to breed! Croaking jealousy; bloated bigotry; coiling suspicion; wormish blindness; crocodile malice!

Things have changed since then, but in none of the respects mentioned.

BUSINESS

One side section of street is blocked off with sawhorses. Hard, thin, bitter men in blue jeans, cowboy boots and hats, untruck a dinky carnival. The merchants are promoting themselves. There will be free rides, raucous music, parades and coneys, pop, popcorn, candy, cones, awards and drawings, with all you can endure of pinch, push, bawl, shove, shout, scream, shriek, and bellow. Children pedal past on decorated bicycles, their wheels a blur of color, streaming crinkled paper and excited dogs. A little later there's a pet show for a prize—dogs, cats, birds, sheep, ponies, goats—none of which wins. The whirlabouts whirl about. The Ferris wheel climbs dizzily into the sky as far as a tall man on tiptoe might be persuaded to reach, and the irritated operators measure the height and weight of every child with sour eyes to see if they are safe for the machines. An electrical megaphone repeatedly trumpets the names of the generous sponsors. The following day they do not allow the refuse to remain long in the street.

MY HOUSE, THIS PLACE AND BODY

I have met with some mischance, wings withering, as Plato[5] says obscurely, and across the breadth of Ohio, like heaven on a table, I've fallen as far as the poet, to the sixth sort of body, this house in B, in Indiana, with its blue and gray betwitching windows, holy magical insides. Great thick evergreens protect its entry. And I live *in*.

Lost in the corn rows, I remember feeling just another stalk, and thus this country takes me over in the way I occupy myself when I am well . . . completely—to the edge of both my house and body. No one notices, when they walk by, that I am brimming in the doorways. My house, this place and body, I've come in mourning to be born in. To anybody else it's pretty silly: love. Why should I feel a loss? How am I bereft? She was never mine; she was a fiction, always a golden tomgirl, barefoot, with an adolescent's slouch and a boy's taste for sports and fishing, a figure out of Twain, or worse, in Riley. Age cannot be kind.

There's little hand-in-hand here . . . not in B. No one touches except in rage. Occasionally girls will twine their arms about each other and lurch along, school out, toward home and play. I dreamed my lips would drift down your back like a skiff on a river. I'd follow a vein with the point of my finger, hold your bare feet in my naked hands.

THE SAME PERSON

Billy Holsclaw lives alone—how alone it is impossible to fathom. In the post office he talks greedily to me about the weather. His head bobs on a wild flood of words, and I take this violence to be a measure of his eagerness for speech. He badly needs a shave, coal dust has layered his face, he spits when he speaks, and his fingers pick at his tatters. He wobbles out in the wind when I leave him, a paper sack mashed in the fold of his arm, the leaves blowing past him, and our encounter drives me sadly home to poetry—where there's no answer. Billy closes his door and carries coal or wood to his fire and closes his eyes, and there's simply no way of knowing how lonely and

---

[5]Plato (c. 428–348 B.C.), Greek philosopher.

empty he is or whether he's as vacant and barren and loveless as the rest of us are—here in the heart of the country.

WEATHER

For we're always out of luck here. That's just how it is—for instance in the winter. The sides of the buildings, the roofs, the limbs of the trees are gray. Streets, sidewalks, faces, feelings—they are gray. Speech is gray, and the grass where it shows. Every flank and front, each top is gray. Everything is gray: hair, eyes, window glass, the hawkers' bills and touters' posters, lips, teeth, poles and metal signs—they're gray, quite gray. Cars are gray. Boots, shoes, suits, hats, gloves are gray. Horses, sheep, and cows, cats killed in the road, squirrels in the same way, sparrows, doves, and pigeons, all are gray, everything is gray, and everyone is out of luck who lives here.

A similar haze turns the summer sky milky, and the air muffles your head and shoulders like a sweater you've got caught in. In the summer light, too, the sky darkens a moment when you open your eyes. The heat is pure distraction. Steeped in our fluids, miserable in the folds of our bodies, we can scarcely think of anything but our sticky parts. Hot cyclonic winds and storms of dust crisscross the country. In many places, given an indifferent push, the wind will still coast for miles, gathering resource and edge as it goes, cunning and force. According to the season, paper, leaves, field litter, seeds, snow, fill up the fences. Sometimes I think the land is flat because the winds have leveled it, they blow so constantly. In any case, a gale can grow in a field of corn that's as hot as a draft from hell, and to receive it is one of the most dismaying experiences of this life, though the smart of the same wind in winter is more humiliating, and in that sense even worse. But in the spring it rains as well, and the trees fill with ice.

PLACE

Many small Midwestern towns are nothing more than rural slums, and this community could easily become one. Principally during the first decade of the century, though there were many earlier instances, well-to-do farmers moved to town and built fine homes to contain them in their retirement. Others desired a more social life, and so lived in, driving to their fields like storekeepers to their businesses. These houses are now dying like the bereaved who inhabit them; they are slowly losing their senses—deafness, blindness, forgetfulness, mumbling, an insecure gait, an uncontrollable trembling has overcome them. Some kind of Northern Snopes[6] will occupy them next: large-familied, Catholic, Democratic, scrambling, vigorous, poor; and since the parents will work in larger, nearby towns, the children will be loosed upon themselves and upon the hapless neighbors much as the fabulous Khan[7] loosed his legendary horde. These Snopes will undertake makeshift repairs with materials that other people have thrown away; paint halfway round their house, then quit; almost certainly maintain an ugly loud cantankerous dog and underfeed a pair of cats to keep the rodents down. They will collect piles of possibly useful junk in the back yard, park their cars in the front, live largely leaning over engines, give not a hoot for the land, the old community, the hallowed ways, the established clans. Weakening widow ladies have already begun to hire large rude youths from families such as these to rake and mow and tidy the grounds they will inherit.

PEOPLE

In the cinders at the station boys sit smoking steadily in darkened cars, their arms bent out the windows, white shirts glowing behind the glass. Nine o'clock is the best

---

[6]An intrusive "poor white trash" family that multiplies like rabbits and is portrayed as taking over the South in the "Snopes trilogy" (*The Hamlet, The Town,* and *The Mansion*), by American novelist William Faulkner (1897–1962).
[7]Genghis Khan (1167–1227), Mongolian ruler and conqueror.

time. They sit in a line facing the highway—two or three or four of them—idling their engines. As you walk by a machine may growl at you or a pair of headlights flare up briefly. In a moment one will pull out, spinning cinders behind it, to stalk impatiently up and down the dark streets or roar half a mile into the country before returning to its place in line and pulling up.

MY HOUSE, MY CAT, MY COMPANY

I must organize myself. I must, as they say, pull myself together, dump this cat from my lap, stir—yes, resolve, move, do. But do what? My will is like the rosy dustlike light in this room: soft, diffuse, and gently comforting. It lets me do . . . anything . . . nothing. My ears hear what they happen to; I eat what's put before me; my eyes see what blunders into them; my thoughts are not thoughts, they are dreams. I'm empty or I'm full . . . depending; and I cannot choose. I sink my claws in Tick's fur and scratch the bones of his back until his rear rises amorously. Mr. Tick, I murmur, I must organize myself. I must pull myself together. And Mr. Tick rolls over on his belly, all ooze.

I spill Mr. Tick when I've rubbed his stomach. Shoo. He steps away slowly, his long tail rhyming with his paws. How beautifully he moves, I think; how beautifully, like you, he commands his loving, how beautifully he accepts. So I rise and wander from room to room, up and down, gazing through most of my forty-one windows. How well this house receives its loving too. Let out like Mr. Tick, my eyes sink in the shrubbery. I am not here; I've passed the glass, passed second-story spaces, flown by branches, brilliant berries, to the ground, grass high in seed and leafage every season; and it is the same as when I passed above you in my aged, ardent body; it's, in short, a kind of love; and I am learning to restore myself, my house, my body, by paying court to gardens, cats, and running water, and with neighbors keeping company.

Mrs. Desmond is my right-hand friend; she's eighty-five. A thin white mist of hair, fine and tangled, manifests the climate of her mind. She is habitually suspicious, fretful, nervous. Burglars break in at noon. Children trespass. Even now they are shaking the pear tree, stealing rhubarb, denting lawn. Flies caught in the screens and numbed by frost awake in the heat to buzz and scrape the metal cloth and frighten her, though she is deaf to me, and consequently cannot hear them. Boards creak, the wind whistles across the chimney mouth, drafts cruise like fish through the hollow rooms. It is herself she hears, her own flesh failing, for only death will preserve her from those daily chores she climbs like stairs, and all that anxious waiting. Is it now, she wonders. No? Then: is it now?

We do not converse. She visits me to talk. My task to murmur. She talks about her grandsons, her daughter who lives in Delphi, her sister or her husband—both gone—obscure friends—dead—obscurer aunts and uncles—lost—ancient neighbors, members of her church or of her clubs—passed or passing on; and in this way she brings the ends of her life together with a terrifying rush: she is a girl, a wife, a mother, widow, all at once. All at once—appalling—but I believe it; I wince in expectation of the clap. Her talk's a fence—a shade drawn, window fastened, door that's locked—for no one dies taking tea in a kitchen; and as her years compress and begin to jumble, I really believe in the brevity of life; I sweat in my wonder; death is the dog down the street, the angry gander, bedroom spider, goblin who's come to get her; and it occurs to me that in my listening posture I'm the boy who suffered the winds of my grandfather with an exactly similar politeness, that I am, right now, all my ages, out in elbows, as angular as badly stacked cards. Thus was I, when I loved you, every man I could be, youth and child—far from enough—and you, so strangely ambiguous a being, met me, heart for spade, play after play, the whole run of our suits.

Mr. Tick, you do me honor. You not only lie in my lap, but you remain alive there, coiled like a fetus. Through your deep nap, I feel you hum. You are, and are not, a machine. You are alive, alive exactly, and it means nothing to you—much to me. You are a cat—you cannot understand—you are a cat so easily. Your nature is not something you must rise to. You, not I, live in: in house, in skin, in shrubbery. Yes. I think I shall hat my head with a steeple; turn church; devour people. Mr. Tick, though, has a tail he can twitch, he need not fly his Fancy. Claws, not metrical schema, poetry his paws; while smoothing . . . smoothing . . . smoothing roughly, his tongue laps its neatness. O Mr. Tick, I know you; you are an electrical penis. Go on now, shoo. Mrs. Desmond doesn't like you. She thinks you will tangle yourself in her legs and she will fall. You murder her birds, she knows, and walk upon her roof with death in your jaws. I must gather myself together for a bound. What age is it I'm at right now, I wonder. The heart, don't they always say, keeps the true time. Mrs. Desmond is knocking. Faintly, you'd think, but she pounds. She's brought me a cucumber. I believe she believes I'm a woman. Come in, Mrs. Desmond, thank you, be my company, it looks lovely, and have tea. I'll slice it, crisp, with cream, for luncheon, each slice as thin as me.

POLITICS

O all ye isolate and separate powers, Sing! Sing, and sing in such a way that from a distance it will seem a harmony, a Strindberg[8] play, a friendship ring . . . so happy—happy, happy, happy—as here we go hand in handling, up and down. Our union was a singing, though we were silent in the songs we sang like single notes are silent in a symphony. In no sense sober, we barbershopped[9] together and never heard the discords in our music or saw ourselves as dirty, cheap, or silly. Yet cats have worn out better shoes than those thrown through our love songs at us. Hush. Be patient—prudent—politic. Still, Cleveland killed you, Mr. Crane.[10] Were you not politic enough and fond of being beaten? Like a piece of sewage, the city shat you from its stern three hundred miles from history—beyond the loving reach of sailors. Well, I'm not a poet who puts Paris to his temple in his youth to blow himself from Idaho, or—fancy that—Missouri.[11] My god, I said, this is my country, but must my country go so far as Terre Haute or Whiting, go so far as Gary?[12]

When the Russians first announced the launching of their satellite, many people naturally refused to believe them. Later others were outraged that they had sent a dog around the earth. I wouldn't want to take that mutt from out that metal flying thing if he's still living when he lands, our own dog catcher said; anybody knows you shut a dog up by himself to toss around the first thing he'll be setting on to do you let him out is bite somebody.

This Midwest. A dissonance of parts and people, we are a consonance of Towns. Like a man grown fat in everything but heart, we overlabor; our outlook never really urban, never rural either, we enlarge and linger at the same time, as Alice[13] both changed and remained in her story. You are blond. I put my hand upon your belly; feel it tremble from my trembling. We always drive large cars in my section of the country. How could you be a comfort to me now?

MORE VITAL DATA

The town is exactly fifty houses, trailers, stores, and miscellaneous buildings long, but in places no streets deep. It takes on width as you drive south, always adding to the east. Most of the dwellings are fairly spacious farm houses in the customary white, with wide wraparound porches and tall narrow windows, though there are

8August Strindberg (1849–1912), innovative Swedish playwright.
9I.e., sang together like a barbershop quartet.
10See footnote 4; Crane went to high school in Cleveland; his homosexuality resulted in his frequently being beaten; he had affairs with several sailors; and he leapt from the stern of a ship to his death in 1932.
11Ezra Pound was born in Hailey, Idaho; T. S. Eliot was born in St. Louis, Missouri.
12All towns in Indiana. Gary is notorious for its industrial pollution.
13Reference to *Alice's Adventures in Wonderland*, by Lewis Carroll (1832–1898).

many of the grander kind—fretted, scalloped, turreted, and decorated with clap-boards set at angles or on end, with stained-glass windows at the stair landings and lots of wrought iron full of fancy curls—and a few of these look like castles in their rarer brick. Old stables serve as garages now, and the lots are large to contain them and the vegetable and flower gardens which, ultimately, widows plant and weed and then entirely disappear in. The shade is ample, the grass is good, the sky a glorious fall violet; the apple trees are heavy and red, the roads are calm and empty; corn has sifted from the chains of tractored wagons to speckle the streets with gold and with the russet fragments of the cob, and a man would be a fool who wanted, blessed with this, to live anywhere else in the world.

EDUCATION

Buses like great orange animals move through the early light to school. There the children will be taught to read and warned against Communism. By Miss Janet Jakes. That's not her name. Her name is Helen something—Scott or James. A teacher twenty years. She's now worn fine and smooth, and has a face, Wilfred says, like a mail-order ax. Her voice is hoarse, and she has a cough. For she screams abuse. The children stare, their faces blank. This is the thirteenth week. They are used to it. You will all, she shouts, you will all draw pictures of me. No. She is a Mrs.—someone's missus. And in silence they set to work while Miss Jakes jabs hairpins in her hair. Wilfred says an ax, but she has those rimless tinted glasses, graying hair, an almost dimpled chin. I must concentrate. I must stop making up things. I must give myself to life; let it mold me: that's what they say in *Wisdom's Monthly Digest*[14] every day. Enough, enough—you've been at it long enough; and the children rise formally a row at a time to present their work to her desk. No, she wears rims; it's her chin that's dimpleless. Well, it will take more than a tablespoon of features to sweeten that face. So she grimly shuffles their sheets, examines her reflection crayoned on them. I would not dare . . . allow a child . . . to put a line around me. Though now and then she smiles like a nick in the blade, in the end these drawings depress her. I could not bear it—how can she ask?—that anyone . . . draw me. Her anger's lit. That's why she does it: flame. There go her eyes; the pink in her glasses brightens, dims. She is a pumpkin, and her rage is breathing like the candle in. No, she shouts, no—the cartoon trembling—no, John Mauck, John Stewart Mauck, this will not do. The picture flutters from her fingers. You've made me too muscular.

I work on my poetry. I remember my friends, associates, my students, by their names. Their names are Maypop, Dormouse, Upsydaisy. Their names are Gladiolus, Callow Bladder, Prince and Princess Oleo, Hieronymus, Cardinal Mummum, Mr. Fitchew, The Silken Howdah, Spot. Sometimes you're Tom Sawyer, Huckleberry Finn; it is perpetually summer; your buttocks are my pillow; we are adrift on a raft; your back is our river. Sometimes you are Major Barbara,[15] sometimes a goddess who kills men in battle, sometimes you are soft like a shower of water; you are bread in my mouth.

I do not work on my poetry. I forget my friends, associates, my students, and their names: Gramophone, Blowgun, Pickle, Serenade . . . Marge the Barge, Arena, Uberhaupt . . . Doctor Dildoe, The Fog Machine. For I am now in B, in Indiana: out of job and out of patience, out of love and time and money, out of bread and out of body, in a temper, Mrs. Desmond, out of tea. So shut your fist up, bitch, you bag of death; go bang another door; go die, my dearie. Die, life-deaf old lady. Spill your breath. Fall over like a frozen board. Gray hair grows from the nose of your mind. You are a skull already—*memento mori*[16]—the foreskin retracts from your teeth. Will

---

[14]Suggestive of *Reader's Digest*, one of America's most popular magazines which chooses selections in accord with its "positive thinking" point of view.

[15]Central character of *Major Barbara*, by Irish playwright George Bernard Shaw (1856–1950).

[16]"Reminder of death" (Latin).

your plastic gums last longer than your bones, and color their grinning? And is your twot still hazel-hairy, or are you bald as a ditch? . . . bitch . . . . . . bitch . . . . bitch. I wanted to be famous, but you bring me age—my emptiness. Was it *that* which I thought would balloon me above the rest? Love? where are you? . . . love me. I want to rise so high, I said, that when I shit I won't miss anybody.

BUSINESS

For most people, business is poor. Nearby cities have siphoned off all but a neigh-borhood trade. Except for feed and grain and farm supplies, you stand a chance to sell only what one runs out to buy. Chevrolet has quit, and Frigidaire. A locker plant has left its afterimage. The lumberyard has been, so far, six months about its going. Gas stations change hands clumsily, a restaurant becomes available, a grocery closes. One day they came and knocked the cornices from the watch repair and pasted campaign posters on the windows. Torn across, by now, by boys, they urge you still to vote for half an orange beblazoned man who as a whole one failed two years ago to win at his election. Everywhere, in this manner, the past speaks, and it mostly speaks of failure. The empty stores, the old signs and dusty fixtures, the debris in alleys, the flaking paint and rusty gutters, the heavy locks and sagging boards: they say the same disagreeable things. What do the sightless windows see, I wonder, when the sun throws a passerby against them? Here a stair unfolds toward the street—dark, rick-ety, and treacherous—and I always feel, as I pass it, that if I just went carefully up and turned the corner at the landing, I would find myself out of the world. But I've never had the courage.

THAT SAME PERSON

The weeds catch up with Billy. In pursuit of the hollyhocks, they rise in coarse clumps all around the front of his house. Billy has to stamp down a circle by his door like a dog or cat does turning round to nest up, they're so thick. What particularly troubles me is that winter will find the weeds still standing stiff and tindery to take the sparks which Billy's little mortarless chimney spouts. It's true that fires are fun here. The town whistle, which otherwise only blows for noon (and there's no noon on Sunday), signals the direction of the fire by the length and number of its blasts, the volunteer firemen rush past in their cars and trucks, houses empty their owners along the street every time like an illustration in a children's book. There are many bikes, too, and barking dogs, and sometimes—halleluiah—the fire's right here in town—a vacant lot of weeds and stubble flaming up. But I'd rather it weren't Billy or Billy's lot or house. Quite selfishly I want him to remain the way he is—counting his sticks and logs, sitting on his sill in the soft early sun—though I'm not sure what his presence means to me . . . or to anyone. Nevertheless, I keep wondering whether, given time, I might not someday find a figure in our language which would serve him faithfully, and furnish his poverty and loneliness richly out.

WIRES

Where sparrows sit like fists. Doves fly the steeple. In mist the wires change per-spective, rise and twist. If they led to you, I would know what they were. Thoughts passing often, like the starlings who flock these fields at evening to sleep in the trees beyond, would form a family of paths like this; they'd foot down the natural height of air to just about a bird's perch. But they do not lead to you.

>Of whose beauty it was sung
>She shall make the old man young.

They fasten me.

If I walked straight on, in my present mood, I would reach the Wabash.[17] It's not a mood in which I'd choose to conjure you. Similes dangle like baubles from me. This time of year the river is slow and shallow, the clay banks crack in the sun, weeds surprise the sandbars. The air is moist and I am sweating. It's impossible to rhyme in this dust. Everything—sky, the cornfield, stump, wild daisies, my old clothes and pressless feelings—seem fabricated for installment purchase. Yes. Christ. I am suffering a summer Christmas; and I cannot walk under the wires. The sparrows scatter like handfuls of gravel. Really, wires are voices in thin strips. They are words wound in cables. Bars of connection.

WEATHER

I would rather it were the weather that was to blame for what I am and what my friends and neighbors are—we who live here in the heart of the country. Better the weather, the wind, the pale dying snow . . . the snow—why not the snow? There's never much really, not around the lower Lakes anyway, not enough to boast about, not enough to be useful. My father tells how the snow in the Dakotas would sweep to the roofs of the barns in the old days, and he and his friends could sled on the crust that would form because the snow was so fiercely driven. In Bemidji[18] trees have been known to explode. That would be something—if the trees in Davenport or Francisville or Carbondale or Niles were to go blam some winter—blam! blam! blam! all the way down the gray, cindery, snow-sick streets.

A cold fall rain is blackening the trees or the air is like lilac and full of parachuting seeds. Who cares to live in any season but his own? Still I suspect the secret's in this snow, the secret of our sickness, if we could only diagnose it, for we are all dying like the elms in Urbana.[19] This snow—like our skin it covers the country. Later dust will do it. Right now—snow. Mud presently. But it is snow without any laughter in it, a pale gray pudding thinly spread on stiff toast, and if that seems a strange description, it's accurate all the same. Of course soot blackens everything, but apart from that, we are never sufficiently cold here. The flakes as they come, alive and burning, we cannot retain, for if our temperatures fall, they rise promptly again, just as, in the summer, they bob about in the same feckless way. Suppose though . . . suppose they were to rise some August, climb and rise, and then hang in the hundreds like a hawk through December, what a desert we could make of ourselves—from Chicago to Cairo, from Hammond to Columbus—what beautiful Death Valleys.

PLACE

I would rather it were the weather. It drives us in upon ourselves—an unlucky fate. Of course there is enough to stir our wonder anywhere; there's enough to love, anywhere, if one is strong enough, if one is diligent enough, if one is perceptive, patient, kind enough—whatever it takes; and surely it's better to live in the country, to live on a prairie by a drawing of rivers, in Iowa or Illinois or Indiana, say, than in any city, in any stinking fog of human beings, in any blooming orchard of machines. It ought to be. The cities are swollen and poisonous with people. It ought to be better. Man has never been a fit environment for man—for rats, maybe, rats do nicely, or for dogs or cats and the household beetle.

And how long the street is, nowadays. These endless walls are fallen to keep back the tides of earth. Brick could be beautiful but we have covered it gradually with gray industrial vomits. Age does not make concrete genial, and asphalt is always—like America—twenty-one, until it breaks up in crumbs like stale cake. The brick, the asphalt, the concrete, the dancing signs and garish posters, the feed and excrement

---

[17]Indiana river.
[18]Town and lake in Minnesota; other towns and cities mentioned are located in mid-America (the heart of the country).

[19]Urbana, Illinois, in which all the many elm trees died (as they did in many American towns, succumbing to the "Dutch Elm Disease" in the decades after World War II).

of the automobile, the litter of its inhabitants: they compose, they decorate, they line our streets, and there is nowhere, nowadays, our streets can't reach.

A man in the city has no natural thing by which to measure himself. His parks are potted plants. Nothing can live and remain free where he resides but the pigeon, starling, sparrow, spider, cockroach, mouse, moth, fly and weed, and he laments the existence of even these and makes his plans to poison them. The zoo? There *is* the zoo. Through its bars the city man stares at the great cats and dully sucks his ice. Living, alas, among men and their marvels, the city man supposes that his happiness depends on establishing, somehow, a special kind of harmonious accord with others. The novelists of the city, of slums and crowds, they call it love — and break their pens.

Wordsworth[20] feared the accumulation of men in cities. He foresaw their "degrading thirst after outrageous stimulation," and some of their hunger for love. Living in a city, among so many, dwelling in the heat and tumult of incessant movement, a man's affairs are touch and go — that's all. It's not surprising that the novelists of the slums, the cities, and the crowds, should find that sex is but a scratch to ease a tickle, that we're most human when we're sitting on the john, and that the justest image of our life is in full passage through the plumbing.

> That man, immur'd in cities, still retains
> His inborn inextinguishable thirst
> Of rural scenes, compensating his loss
> By supplemental shifts, the best he may.[21]

Come into the country, then. The air nimbly and sweetly recommends itself unto our gentle senses.[22] Here, growling tractors tear the earth. Dust roils up behind them. Drivers sit jouncing under bright umbrellas. They wear refrigerated hats and steer by looking at the tracks they've cut behind them, their transistors blaring. Close to the land, are they? good companions to the soil? Tell me: do they live in harmony with the alternating seasons?

It's a lie of old poetry. The modern husbandman uses chemicals from cylinders and sacks, spike-ball-and-claw machines, metal sheds, and cost accounting. Nature in the old sense does not matter. It does not exist. Our farmer's only mystical attachment is to parity.[23] And if he does not realize that cows and corn are simply different kinds of chemical engine, he cannot expect to make a go of it.

It isn't necessary to suppose our cows have feelings; our neighbor hasn't as many as he used to have either; but think of it this way a moment, you can correct for the human imputations later: how would it feel to nurse those strange tentacled calves with their rubber, glass, and metal lips, their stainless eyes?

PEOPLE

Aunt Pet's still able to drive her car — a high square Ford — even though she walks with difficulty and a stout stick. She has a watery gaze, a smooth plump face despite her age, and jet black hair in a bun. She has the slowest smile of anyone I ever saw, but she hates dogs, and not very long ago cracked the back of one she cornered in her garden. To prove her vigor she will tell you this, her smile breaking gently while she raises the knob of her stick to the level of your eyes.

HOUSE, MY BREATH AND WINDOW

My window is grave, and all that lies within it's dead. No snow is falling. There's no haze. It is not still, not silent. Its images are not an animal that waits, for movement is

---

[20]William Wordsworth (1770–1850), British romantic "lake poet."

[21]From "The Winter Evening: A Brown Study" (ll. 767–770), Book IV of *The Task* by British poet William Cowper (1731–1800).

[22]From Shakespeare's *Macbeth*, Act I, Scene vi, ll. 1–3:

Duncan's words on entering Macbeth's castle where he will be murdered.

[23]Refers to system used by the government to determine price-support levels to guarantee that income will not fall below that of a pre-set period.

no demonstration. I have seen the sea slack, life bubble through a body without a trace, its spheres impervious as soda's. Downwound, the whore at wagtag clicks and clacks. Leaves wiggle. Grass sways. A bird chirps, pecks the ground. An auto wheel in penning circles keeps its rigid spokes. These images are stones; they are memorials. Beneath this sea lies sea: god rest it . . . rest the world beyond my window, me in front of my reflection, above this page, my shade. Death is not so still, so silent, since silence implies a falling quiet, stillness a stopping, containing, holding in; for death is time in a clock, like Mr. Tick, electric . . . like wind through a windup poet. And my blear floats out to visible against the glass, befog its country and bespill myself. The mist lifts slowly from the fields in the morning. No one now would say: the Earth throws back its covers; it is rising from sleep. Why is the feeling foolish? The image is too Greek. I used to gaze at you so wantonly your body blushed. Imagine: wonder: that my eyes could cause such flowering. Ah, my friend, your face is pale, the weather cloudy; a street has been felled through your chin, bare trees do nothing, houses take root in their rectangles, a steeple stands up in your head. You speak of loving; then give me a kiss. The pane is cold. On icy mornings the fog rises to greet me (as you always did); the barns and other buildings, rather than ghostly, seem all the more substantial for looming, as if they grew in themselves while I watched (as you always did). Oh my approach, I suppose, was like breath in a rubber monkey. Nevertheless, on the road along the Wabash in the morning, though the trees are sometimes obscured by fog, their reflection floats serenely on the river, reasoning the banks, the sycamores in French rows. Magically, the world tips. I'm led to think that only those who grow down live (which will scarcely win me twenty-five[24] from *Wisdom's Monthly Digest*), but I find I write that only those who live down grow; and what I write, I hold, whatever I really know. My every word's inverted, or reversed — or I am. I held you, too, that way. You were so utterly provisional, subject to my change. I could inflate your bosom with a kiss, disperse your skin with gentleness, enter your vagina from within, and make my love emerge like a fresh sex. The pane is cold. Honesty is cold, my inside lover. The sun looks, through the mist, like a plum on the tree of heaven, or a bruise on the slope of your belly. Which? The grass crawls with frost. We meet on this window, the world and I, inelegantly, swimmers of the glass; and swung wrong way round to one another, the world seems in. The world — how grand, how monumental, grave and deadly, that word is: the world, my house and poetry. All poets have their inside lovers. Wee penis does not belong to me, or any of this foggery. It is *his* property which he's thrust through what's womanly of me to set down this. These wooden houses in their squares, gray streets and fallen sidewalks, standing trees, your name I've written sentimentally across my breath into the whitening air, pale birds: they exist in me now because of him. I gazed with what intensity . . . A bush in the excitement of its roses could not have bloomed so beautifully as you did then. It was a look I'd like to give this page. For that is poetry: to bring within about, to change.

POLITICS

Sports, politics, and religion are the three passions of the badly educated. They are the Midwest's open sores. Ugly to see, a source of constant discontent, they sap the body's strength. Appalling quantities of money, time, and energy are wasted on them. The rural mind is narrow, passionate, and reckless on these matters. Greed, however shortsighted and direct, will not alone account for it. I have known men, for instance, who for years have voted squarely against their interests. Nor have I ever noticed that their surly Christian views prevented them from urging forward the smithereening, say, of Russia, China, Cuba, or Korea. And they tend to back their country like they back their local team: they have a fanatical desire to win; yelling is

---

[24]I.e., twenty-five dollars; *Reader's Digest* often offered such sums to readers who sent in short, inspirational pieces (reference here to growing "down" rather than growing "up" — which the *Digest* would prefer).

their forte; and if things go badly, they are inclined to sack the coach. All in all, then, Birch[25] is a good name. It stands for the bigot's stick, the wild-child-tamer's cane.

Forgetfulness—is that their object?

Oh, I was new, I thought. A fresh start: new cunt, new climate, and new country— there you were, and I was pioneer, and had no history. That language hurts me, too, my dear. You'll never hear it.

FINAL VITAL DATA

The Modern Homemakers' Demonstration Club. The Prairie Home Demonstration Club. The Night-outers' Home Demonstration Club. The IOOF, FFF, VFW, WCTU, WSCS, 4-H, 40 and 8, Psi Iota Chi, and PTA. The Boy and Girl Scouts, Rainbows, Masons, Indians and Rebekah Lodge. Also the Past Noble Grand Club of the Rebekah Lodge. As well as the Moose and the Ladies of the Moose. The Elks, the Eagles, the Jaynettes and the Eastern Star. The Women's Literary Club, the Hobby Club, the Art Club, the Sunshine Society, the Dorcas Society, the Pythian Sisters, the Pilgrim Youth Fellowship, the American Legion, the American Legion Auxiliary, the American Legion Junior Auxiliary, the Gardez Club, the Bridge for Fun Club, the What-can-you-do? Club, the Get Together Club, the Coterie Club, the Worthwhile Club, the Let's Help Our Town Club, the No Name Club, the Forget-me-not Club, the Merry-go-round Club . . . [26]

EDUCATION

Has a quarter disappeared from Paula Frosty's pocket book? Imagine the landscape of that face: no crayon could engender it; soft wax is wrong; thin wire in trifling snips might do the trick. Paula Frosty and Christopher Roger accuse the pale and splotchy Cheryl Pipes. But Miss Jakes, I *saw* her. Miss Jakes is so extremely vexed she snaps her pencil. What else is missing? I appoint you a detective, John: search her desk. Gum, candy, paper, pencils, marble, round eraser—whose? A thief. I can't watch her all the time, I'm here to teach. Poor pale fossetted.[27] Cheryl, it's determined, can't return the money because she took it home and spent it. Cindy, Janice, John, and Pete—you four who sit around her—you will be detectives this whole term to watch her. A thief. In all my time. Miss Jakes turns, unfists, and turns again. I'll handle you, she cries. To think. A thief. In all my years. Then she writes on the blackboard the name of Cheryl Pipes and beneath that the figure twenty-five with a large sign for cents. Now Cheryl, she says, this won't be taken off until you bring that money out of home, out of home straight up to here, Miss Jakes says, tapping her desk.

Which is three days.

ANOTHER PERSON

I was raking leaves when Uncle Halley introduced himself to me. He said his name came from the comet,[28] and that his mother had borne him prematurely in her fright of it. I thought of Hobbes,[29] whom fear of the Spanish Armada had hurried into birth, and so I believed Uncle Halley to honor the philosopher, though Uncle Halley is a liar, and neither the one hundred twenty-nine nor the fifty-three he ought to be. That fall the leaves had burned themselves out on the trees, the leaf lobes had curled, and now they flocked noisily down the street and were broken in the wires of my rake. Uncle Halley was himself (like Mrs. Desmond and history generally) both

---

[25]Reference to a birch branch used as a whip as well as to the ultra-rightist John Birch Society, named after a fundamentalist Baptist missionary killed by Chinese Communists shortly after the end of World War II (in 1945).

[26]A satiric thrust at the American habit of forming organizations at the drop of a hat.

[27]Dimpled.

[28]Halley's comet, which appears about every 76 years, named after the man who calculated its appearance; it was seen this century in 1910 and 1986.

[29]Thomas Hobbes (1588–1679), English philosopher, born the same year in which the Spanish Armada sailed to conquer Britain and was destroyed by the British.

deaf and implacable, and he shooed me down his basement stairs to a room set aside there for stacks of newspapers reaching to the ceiling, boxes of leaflets and letters and programs, racks of photo albums, scrapbooks, bundles of rolled-up posters and maps, flags and pennants and slanting piles of dusty magazines devoted mostly to motoring and the Christian ethic. I saw a bird cage, a tray of butterflies, a bugle, a stiff straw boater, and all kinds of tassels tied to a coat tree. He still possessed and had on display the steering lever from his first car, a linen duster, driving gloves and goggles, photographs along the wall of himself, his friends, and his various machines, a shell from the first war, a record of "Ramona" nailed through its hole to a post, walking sticks and fanciful umbrellas, shoes of all sorts (his baby shoes, their counters broken, were held in sorrow beneath my nose—they had not been bronzed, but he might have them done someday before he died, he said), countless boxes of medals, pins, beads, trinkets, toys, and keys (I scarcely saw—they flowed like jewels from his palms), pictures of downtown when it was only a path by the railroad station, a brightly colored globe of the world with a dent in Poland, antique guns, belt buckles, buttons, souvenir plates and cups and saucers (I can't remember all of it—I won't), but I recall how shamefully, how rudely, how abruptly, I fled, a good story in my mouth but death in my nostrils; and how afterward I busily, righteously, burned my leaves as if I were purging the world of its years. I still wonder if this town—its life, and mine now—isn't really a record like the one of "Ramona" that I used to crank around on my grandmother's mahogany Victrola through lonely rainy days as a kid.

THE FIRST PERSON

Billy's like the coal he's found: spilled, mislaid, discarded. The sky's no comfort. His house and his body are dying together. His windows are boarded. And now he's reduced to his hands. I suspect he has glaucoma. At any rate he can scarcely see, and weeds his yard of rubble on his hands and knees. Perhaps he's a surgeon cleansing a wound or an ardent and tactile lover. I watch, I must say, apprehensively. Like mine-war detectors, his hands graze in circles ahead of him. Your nipples were the color of your eyes. Pebble. Snarl of paper. Length of twine. He leans down closely, picks up something silvery, holds it near his nose. Foil? cap? coin? He has within him—what, I wonder? Does he know more now because he fingers everything and has to sniff to see? It would be romantic cruelty to think so. He bends the down on your arms like a breeze. You wrote me: something is strange when we don't understand. I write in return: I think when I loved you I fell to my death.

Billy, I could read to you from Beddoes;[30] he's your man perhaps; he held with dying, freed his blood of its arteries; and he said that there were many wretched love-ill fools like me lying alongside the last bone of their former selves, as full of spirit and speech, nonetheless, as Mrs. Desmond, Uncle Halley and the Ferris wheel, Aunt Pet, Miss Jakes, Ramona or the megaphone; yet I reverse him finally, Billy, on no evidence but braggadocio, and I declare that though my inner organs were devoured long ago, the worm which swallowed down my parts still throbs and glows like a crystal palace.

Yes, you were younger. I was Uncle Halley, the museum man and infrequent meteor. Here is my first piece of ass. They weren't so flat in those days, had more round, more juice. And over here's the sperm I've spilled, nicely jarred and clearly labeled. Look at this tape like lengths of intestine where I've stored my spew, the endless worm of words I've written, a hundred million emissions or more: oh I was quite a man right from the start; even when unconscious in my cradle, from crotch to cranium, I was erectile tissue; though mostly, after the manner approved by Plato; I had intercourse by eye. Never mind, old Holsclaw, you are blind. We pull down dark-

---

[30]Thomas Lovell Beddoes (1803–1849), English poet.

ness when we go to bed; put out like Oedipus[31] the actually offending organ, and train our touch to lies. All cats are gray, says Mr. Tick; so under cover of glaucoma you are sack gray too, and cannot be distinguished from a stallion.

I must pull myself together, get a grip, just as they say, but I feel spilled, bewildered, quite mislaid. I did not restore my house to its youth, but to its age. Hunting, you hitch through the hollyhocks. I'm inclined to say you aren't half the cripple I am, for there is nothing left of me but mouth. However, I resist the impulse. It is another lie of poetry. My organs are all there, though it's there where I fail—at the roots of my experience. Poet of the spiritual, Rilke,[32] weren't you? yet that's what you said. Poetry, like love, is—in and out—a physical caress. I can't tolerate any more of my sophistries about spirit, mind, and breath. Body equals being, and if your weight goes down, you are the less.

HOUSEHOLD APPLES

I knew nothing about apples. Why should I? My country came in my childhood, and I dreamed of sitting among the blooms like the bees. I failed to spray the pear tree too. I doubled up under them at first, admiring the sturdy low branches I should have pruned, and later I acclaimed the blossoms. Shortly after the fruit formed there were falls—not many—apples the size of goodish stones which made me wobble on my ankles when I walked about the yard. Sometimes a piece crushed by a heel would cling on the shoe to track the house. I gathered a few and heaved them over the wires. A slingshot would have been splendid. Hard, an unattractive green, the worms had them. Before long I realized the worms had them all. Even as the apples reddened, lit their tree, they were being swallowed. The birds preferred the pears, which were small—sugar pears I think they're called—with thick skins of graying green that ripen on toward violet. So the fruit fell, and once I made some applesauce by quartering and paring hundreds; but mostly I did nothing, left them, until suddenly, overnight it seemed, in that ugly late September heat we often have in Indiana, my problem was upon me.

My childhood came in the country. I remember, now, the flies on our snowy luncheon table. As we cleared away they would settle, fastidiously scrub themselves and stroll to the crumbs to feed where I would kill them in crowds with a swatter. It was quite a game to catch them taking off. I struck heavily since I didn't mind a few stains; they'd wash. The swatter was a square of screen bound down in red cloth. It drove no air ahead of it to give them warning. They might have thought they'd flown headlong into a summered window. The faint pink dot where they had died did not rub out as I'd supposed, and after years of use our luncheon linen would faintly, pinkly, speckle.

The country became my childhood. Flies braided themselves on the flypaper in my grandmother's house. I can smell the bakery and the grocery and the stables and the dairy in that small Dakota town I knew as a kid; knew as I dreamed I'd know your body, as I've known nothing, before or since; knew as the flies knew, in the honest, unchaste sense: the burned house, hose-wet, which drew a mist of insects like the blue smoke of its smolder, and gangs of boys, moist-lipped, destructive as its burning. Flies have always impressed me; they are so persistently alive. Now they were coating the ground beneath my trees. Some were ordinary flies; there were the large blue-green ones; there were swarms of fruit flies too, and the red-spotted scavenger beetle; there were a few wasps, several sorts of bees and butterflies—checkers, sulphurs, monarchs, commas, question marks—and delicate dragonflies . . . but principally houseflies and horseflies and bottleflies, flies and more flies in clusters around the rotting fruit. They loved the pears. Inside, they fed. If you picked up a pear, they flew, and the pear became skin and stem. They were everywhere the fruit was: in the

---

[31] King Oedipus blinded himself when he discovered he had killed his father and married his mother (see *Oedipus Rex*, c. 430 B.C. by Sophocles).
[32] Rainer Maria Rilke (1875–1926), German poet.

tree still—apples like a hive for them—or where the fruit littered the ground, squashing itself as you stepped . . . there was no help for it. The flies droned, feasting on the sweet juice. No one could go near the trees; I could not climb; so I determined at last to labor like Hercules.[33] There were fruit baskets in the barn. Collecting them and kneeling under the branches, I began to gather remains. Deep in the strong rich smell of the fruit, I began to hum myself. The fruit caved in at the touch. Glistening red apples, my lifting disclosed, had families of beetles, flies, and bugs, devouring their rotten undersides. There were streams of flies; there were lakes and cataracts and rivers of flies, seas and oceans. The hum was heavier, higher, than the hum of the bees when they came to the blooms in the spring, though the bees were there, among the flies, ignoring me—ignoring everyone. As my work went on and juice covered my hands and arms, they would form a sleeve, black and moving, like knotty wool. No caress could have been more indifferently complete. Still I rose fearfully, ramming my head in the branches, apples bumping against me before falling, bursting with bugs. I'd snap my hand sharply but the flies would cling to the sweet. I could toss a whole cluster into a basket from several feet. As the pear or apple lit, they would explosively rise, like monads[34] for a moment, windowless, certainly, with respect to one another, sugar their harmony. I had to admit, though, despite my distaste, that my arm had never been more alive, oftener or more gently kissed. Those hundreds of feet were light. In washing them off, I pretended the house was a pump. What have I missed? Childhood is a lie of poetry.

THE CHURCH

Friday night. Girls in dark skirts and white blouses sit in ranks and scream in concert. They carry funnels loosely stuffed with orange and black paper which they shake wildly, and small megaphones through which, as drilled, they direct and magnify their shouting. Their leaders, barely pubescent girls, prance and shake and whirl their skirts above their bloomers. The young men, leaping, extend their arms and race through puddles of amber light, their bodies glistening. In a lull, though it rarely occurs, you can hear the squeak of tennis shoes against the floor. Then the yelling begins again, and then continues; fathers, mothers, neighbors joining in to form a single pulsing ululation—a cry of the whole community—for in this gymnasium each body becomes the bodies beside it, pressed as they are together, thigh to thigh, and the same shudder runs through all of them, and runs toward the same release. Only the ball moves serenely through this dazzling din. Obedient to law it scarcely speaks but caroms quietly and lives at peace.

BUSINESS

It is the week of Christmas and the stores, to accommodate the rush they hope for, are remaining open in the evening. You can see snow falling in the cones of the street lamps. The roads are filling—undisturbed. Strings of red and green lights droop over the principal highway, and the water tower wears a star. The windows of the stores have been bedizened. Shamelessly they beckon. But I am alone, leaning against a pole—no . . . there is no one in sight. They're all at home, perhaps by their instruments, tuning in on their evenings, and like Ramona, tirelessly playing and replaying themselves. There's a speaker perched in the tower, and through the boughs of falling snow and over the vacant streets, it drapes the twisted and metallic strains of a tune that can barely be distinguished—yes, I believe it's one of the jolly ones, it's "Joy to the World." There's no one to hear the music but myself, and though I'm listening, I'm no longer certain. Perhaps the record's playing something else.

1967, 1968

---

[33]Hero of Greek mythology who set out to perform twelve staggeringly difficult labors in order to attain immortality. [34]A simple single-celled organism. German philosopher Gottfried Leibniz (1646–1716) speculated that independent atoms, "windowless monads," made up the substance of the world.

JAMES BALDWIN
(1924–1987)

James Baldwin made clear in a 1984 interview, in a description of his encounter with Richard Wright and his fiction, that he had adopted the older black novelist as the writer on whom he would model himself:

> I'd just read *Uncle Tom's Children* and *Native Son*. I knew of Langston [Hughes] and Countee Cullen, they were the only other black writers whose work I knew at that time, but for some reason they did not attract me. . . . The black middle class was essentially an abstraction to me. Richard was very different, though. The life he described was the life I lived. I recognized the tenements. I knew that rat in *Native Son*. . . . All of that was urgent to me. And it was through Richard that I came to read the black writers who had preceded me, like Jean Toomer, and came to know Langston and Countee Cullen in a new way. By the time I went to see Richard I was committed to the idea of being a writer, though I knew how impossible it was. Maybe I went to see Richard to see if he would laugh at me.

In contrast, Alice Walker later would have to work harder to find her model of a black woman writer, Zora Neale Hurston, digging her out of footnotes and resurrecting her for a contemporary audience. Baldwin not only met Wright in 1944 in Greenwich Village; with Wright's aid, he received a Eugene Saxton fellowship in 1945, enabling him to begin writing for *Partisan Review, Harper's,* and *Commentary.* He also followed Wright into exile in Paris in 1948 (Wright had gone there in 1947). Later Baldwin would name a volume of his essays about racism after Wright's most famous novel, calling it *Notes of a Native Son* (1955); and Wright would accuse Baldwin of having betrayed him in two of those essays attacking the idea of protest literature.

Baldwin was born in Harlem in 1924, the first of nine children that his stepfather had to support on the meager income of a minister. David Baldwin was the son of slaves and was an old-fashioned and rigid hell-fire-and-damnation preacher. Baldwin early developed a deep hatred for his father and wanted to escape the household and the whole oppressive environment of the ghetto. But at the age of puberty, in 1938, Baldwin was converted and began to preach at his father's church, the Fireside Pentecostal Assembly. The experience, though it lasted only until his graduation from high school in 1942, left its indelible mark on his style of writing and his way of public speaking (or "witnessing").

Shortly after leaving high school, he moved to Greenwich Village. He was on his way to becoming a writer and already at work on his first novel. There is general critical agreement that Baldwin's early books, which established his reputation, remain among his best: *Go Tell It on the Mountain* (1953), based on his experience of growing up in Harlem and his religious conversion and ministry as an adolescent; *Giovanni's Room* (1956), a novel portraying a white American homosexual coming to terms with his sexuality in Paris in a relationship with a Frenchman; *Notes of a Native Son* (1955) and *Nobody Knows My Name: More Notes of a Native Son* (1961), essays describing the painful experience of growing up black in America. In the second of these volumes of essays, in a piece entitled "Alas, Poor Richard," Baldwin tried to "set the record straight" with respect to Wright. Baldwin would later comment on his treatment of Wright: "I knew Richard and I loved him. . . . I was not attacking him; I was trying to clarify something for myself."

The themes of racism and sexuality, treated in these first books, would reappear in Baldwin's work. Of the later novels, the most noteworthy is *Another Country* (1962), dealing in part with the marriage of a black woman and a white man. Reaction to it was mixed. Other novels include *Tell Me How Long the Train's Been Gone* (1968), about a black actor who (like Baldwin) made it out of Harlem; *If Beale Street Could Talk* (1974), portraying the trials and tribulations of a pregnant black woman trying to free her falsely accused lover from prison; *Just Above My Head* (1979), concerning a Harlem gospel singer's search for peace and salvation.

Baldwin's work in other genres during the latter part of his career tended to surpass his novels in popularity. This was particularly true of his volumes of social commentary and personal essays. The most remarkable of these was *The Fire Next Time,* which appeared first in *The New Yorker* in 1962 and then as a book in 1963. The book's epigraph was the threat of God's retribution—"God gave Noah the rainbow sign, / No more water, the fire next time!" The impassioned essay rejected the program of the Black Muslims for separation of the races and pleaded for love as the only way out of the racial labyrinth. Later books of essays and other nonfiction include *No Name in the Street* (1972), *The Devil Finds Work* (1976), *The Evidence of Things Not Seen* (1985), and *The Price of a Ticket* (1985). Baldwin's two published plays are *Blues for Mr. Charley* (1964) and *The Amen Corner* (1968). His volume of short fiction, *Going to Meet the Man,* published in 1965, contained his frequently anthologized story "Sonny's Blues."

Baldwin gave up his exile in France in 1957 and returned to America a successful and prosperous author. After the sensational appearance of *The Fire Next Time* in 1962, he became more and more involved in the civil rights movement as a public speaker at functions and rallies for black causes. He once defined his role: "I have never seen myself as a spokesman. I am a witness. In the church in which I was raised you were supposed to bear witness to the truth. Now, later on, you wonder what in the world the truth is, but you do know what a lie is." As he became more of a public figure, his fiction and his reputation as a writer went into a decline. He said in a 1984 interview, "One of the hazards of being an American writer, and I'm well placed to know it, is that eventually you have nothing to write about. . . . There is a decidedly grave danger of becoming a celebrity, of becoming a star, of becoming a personality. Again, I'm very well placed to know that."

When asked in that 1984 interview how he would define the task of "black writers today," he answered: "This may sound strange, but I would say to make the question of color obsolete." When asked how this might be done, he replied: "By realizing first of all that the world is not white. And by realizing that the real terror that engulfs the white world now is a visceral terror. I can't prove this, but I know it. It's the terror of being described by those they've been describing for so long. And that will make the concept of color obsolete."

ADDITIONAL READING

Conversations with James Baldwin, ed. Fred L. Standley and Louis H. Pratt, 1989.

Fern M. Eckman, *The Furious Passage of James Baldwin,* 1966; Kenneth Kinnamon, ed., *James Baldwin: A Collection of Critical Essays,* 1974; W. J. Weatherby, *Squaring Off: Mailer vs. Baldwin,* 1976; Therman B. O'Daniel, ed., *James Baldwin: A Critical Evaluation,* 1977; Louis H. Pratt, *James Baldwin,* 1978; Carolyn Wedin Sylvander, *James Baldwin,* 1980; Bernard W. Bell, *The Afro-American Novel and Its Tradition,* 1987; Fred L. Standley and Nancy V. Burt, eds., *Critical Essays on James Baldwin,* 1988; W. J. Weatherby, *James Baldwin: Artist on Fire,* 1989; Horace A. Porter, *Stealing the Fire: The Art and Protest of James Baldwin,* 1989; Quincy Troupe, ed., *James Baldwin: The Legacy,* 1989.

TEXT

Going to Meet the Man, 1965.

Sonny's Blues

I read about it in the paper, in the subway, on my way to work. I read it, and I couldn't believe it, and I read it again. Then perhaps I just stared at it, at the news-print spelling out his name, spelling out the story. I stared at it in the swinging lights of the subway car, and in the faces and bodies of the people, and in my own face, trapped in the darkness which roared outside.

It was not to be believed and I kept telling myself that, as I walked from the subway station to the high school. And at the same time I couldn't doubt it. I was scared, scared for Sonny. He became real to me again. A great block of ice got settled in my belly and kept melting there slowly all day long, while I taught my classes algebra. It was a special kind of ice. It kept melting, sending trickles of ice water all up and down my veins, but it never got less. Sometimes it hardened and seemed to expand until I felt my guts were going to come spilling out or that I was going to choke or scream. This would always be at a moment when I was remembering some specific thing Sonny had once said or done.

When he was about as old as the boys in my classes his face had been bright and open, there was a lot of copper in it; and he'd had wonderfully direct brown eyes, and great gentleness and privacy. I wondered what he looked like now. He had been picked up, the evening before, in a raid on an apartment downtown, for peddling and using heroin.

I couldn't believe it: but what I mean by that is that I couldn't find any room for it anywhere inside me. I had kept it outside me for a long time. I hadn't wanted to know. I had had suspicions, but I didn't name them, I kept putting them away. I told myself that Sonny was wild, but he wasn't crazy. And he'd always been a good boy, he hadn't ever turned hard or evil or disrespectful, the way kids can, so quick, so quick, especially in Harlem. I didn't want to believe that I'd ever see my brother going down, coming to nothing, all that light in his face gone out, in the condition I'd already seen so many others. Yet it had happened and here I was, talking about algebra to a lot of boys who might, every one of them for all I knew, be popping off needles every time they went to the head. Maybe it did more for them than algebra could.

I was sure that the first time Sonny had ever had horse,[1] he couldn't have been much older than these boys were now. These boys, now, were living as we'd been living then, they were growing up with a rush and their heads bumped abruptly against the low ceiling of their actual possibilities. They were filled with rage. All they really knew were two darknesses, the darkness of their lives, which was now closing in on them, and the darkness of the movies, which had blinded them to that other darkness, and in which they now, vindictively, dreamed, at once more together than they were at any other time, and more alone.

When the last bell rang, the last class ended, I let out my breath. It seemed I'd been holding it for all that time. My clothes were wet — I may have looked as though I'd been sitting in a steam bath, all dressed up, all afternoon. I sat alone in the classroom a long time. I listened to the boys outside, downstairs, shouting and cursing and laughing. Their laughter struck me for perhaps the first time. It was not the joyous laughter which — god knows why — one associates with children. It was mocking and insular, its intent was to denigrate. It was disenchanted, and in this, also, lay the

---

[1]Heroin.

authority of their curses. Perhaps I was listening to them because I was thinking about my brother and in them I heard my brother. And myself.

One boy was whistling a tune, at once very complicated and very simple, it seemed to be pouring out of him as though he were a bird, and it sounded very cool and moving through all that harsh, bright air, only just holding its own through all those other sounds.

I stood up and walked over to the window and looked down into the courtyard. It was the beginning of the spring and the sap was rising in the boys. A teacher passed through them every now and again, quickly, as though he or she couldn't wait to get out of that courtyard, to get those boys out of their sight and off their minds. I started collecting my stuff. I thought I'd better get home and talk to Isabel.

The courtyard was almost deserted by the time I got downstairs. I saw this boy standing in the shadow of a doorway, looking just like Sonny. I almost called his name. Then I saw that it wasn't Sonny, but somebody we used to know, a boy from around our block. He'd been Sonny's friend. He'd never been mine, having been too young for me, and, anyway, I'd never liked him. And now, even though he was a grown-up man, he still hung around that block, still spent hours on the street corners, was always high and raggy. I used to run into him from time to time and he'd often work around to asking me for a quarter or fifty cents. He always had some real good excuse, too, and I always gave it to him, I don't know why.

But now, abruptly, I hated him. I couldn't stand the way he looked at me, partly like a dog, partly like a cunning child. I wanted to ask him what the hell he was doing in the school courtyard.

He sort of shuffled over to me, and he said, "I see you got the papers. So you already know about it."

"You mean about Sonny? Yes, I already know about it. How come they didn't get you?"

He grinned. It made him repulsive and it also brought to mind what he'd looked like as a kid. "I wasn't there. I stay away from them people."

"Good for you." I offered him a cigarette and I watched him through the smoke. "You come all the way down here just to tell me about Sonny?"

"That's right." He was sort of shaking his head and his eyes looked strange, as though they were about to cross. The bright sun deadened his damp dark brown skin and it made his eyes look yellow and showed up the dirt in his kinked hair. He smelled funky. I moved a little away from him and I said, "Well, thanks. But I already know about it and I got to get home."

"I'll walk you a little ways," he said. We started walking. There were a couple of kids still loitering in the courtyard and one of them said goodnight to me and looked strangely at the boy beside me.

"What're you going to do?" he asked me. "I mean, about Sonny?"

"Look. I haven't seen Sonny for over a year, I'm not sure I'm going to do anything. Anyway, what the hell *can* I do?"

"That's right," he said quickly, "ain't nothing you can do. Can't much help old Sonny no more, I guess."

It was what I was thinking and so it seemed to me he had no right to say it.

"I'm surprised at Sonny, though," he went on—he had a funny way of talking, he looked straight ahead as though he were talking to himself—"I thought Sonny was a smart boy, I thought he was too smart to get hung."

"I guess he thought so too," I said sharply, "and that's how he got hung. And now about you? You're pretty goddamn smart, I bet."

Then he looked directly at me, just for a minute. "I ain't smart," he said. "If I was smart, I'd have reached for a pistol a long time ago."

"Look. Don't tell *me* your sad story, if it was up to me, I'd give you one." Then I felt guilty—guilty, probably, for never having supposed that the poor bastard *had* a story of his own, much less a sad one, and I asked, quickly, "What's going to happen to him now?"

He didn't answer this. He was off by himself some place. "Funny thing," he said, and from his tone we might have been discussing the quickest way to get to Brooklyn, "when I saw the papers this morning, the first thing I asked myself was if I had anything to do with it. I felt sort of responsible."

I began to listen more carefully. The subway station was on the corner, just before us, and I stopped. He stopped, too. We were in front of a bar and he ducked slightly, peering in, but whoever he was looking for didn't seem to be there. The juke box was blasting away with something black and bouncy and I half watched the barmaid as she danced her way from the juke box to her place behind the bar. And I watched her face as she laughingly responded to something someone said to her, still keeping time to the music. When she smiled one saw the little girl, one sensed the doomed, still-struggling woman beneath the battered face of the semi-whore.

"I never *give* Sonny nothing," the boy said finally, "but a long time ago I came to school high and Sonny asked me how it felt." He paused, I couldn't bear to watch him, I watched the barmaid, and I listened to the music which seemed to be causing the pavement to shake. "I told him it felt great." The music stopped, the barmaid paused and watched the juke box until the music began again. "It did."

All this was carrying me some place I didn't want to go. I certainly didn't want to know how it felt. It filled everything, the people, the houses, the music, the dark, quicksilver barmaid, with menace; and this menace was their reality.

"What's going to happen to him now?" I asked again.

"They'll send him away some place and they'll try to cure him." He shook his head. "Maybe he'll even think he's kicked the habit. Then they'll let him loose"—he gestured, throwing his cigarette into the gutter. "That's all."

"What do you mean, that's *all*?"

But I knew what he meant.

"I *mean*, that's *all*." He turned his head and looked at me, pulling down the corners of his mouth. "Don't you know what I mean?" he asked, softly.

"How the hell *would* I know what you mean?" I almost whispered it, I don't know why.

"That's right," he said to the air, "how would *he* know what I mean?" He turned toward me again, patient and calm, and yet I somehow felt him shaking, shaking as though he were going to fall apart. I felt that ice in my guts again, the dread I'd felt all afternoon; and again I watched the barmaid, moving about the bar, washing glasses, and singing. "Listen. They'll let him out and then it'll just start all over again. That's what I mean."

"You mean—they'll let him out. And then he'll just start working his way back in again. You mean he'll never kick the habit. Is that what you mean?"

"That's right," he said, cheerfully. "*You* see what I mean."

"Tell me," I said at last, "why does he want to die? He must want to die, he's killing himself, why does he want to die?"

He looked at me in surprise. He licked his lips. "He don't want to die. He wants to live. Don't nobody want to die, ever."

Then I wanted to ask him—too many things. He could not have answered, or if he had, I could not have borne the answers. I started walking. "Well, I guess it's none of my business."

"It's going to be rough on old Sonny," he said. We reached the subway station. "This is your station?" he asked. I nodded. I took one step down. "Damn!" he said, suddenly. I looked up at him. He grinned again. "Damn it if I didn't leave all my money home. You ain't got a dollar on you, have you? Just for a couple of days, is all."

All at once something inside gave and threatened to come pouring out of me. I didn't hate him any more. I felt that in another moment I'd start crying like a child.

"Sure," I said. "Don't sweat." I looked in my wallet and didn't have a dollar, I only had a five. "Here," I said. "That hold you?"

He didn't look at it—he didn't want to look at it. A terrible, closed look came over his face, as though he were keeping the number on the bill a secret from him and me. "Thanks," he said, and now he was dying to see me go. "Don't worry about Sonny. Maybe I'll write him or something."

"Sure," I said. "You do that. So long."

"Be seeing you," he said. I went on down the steps.

And I didn't write Sonny or send him anything for a long time. When I finally did, it was just after my little girl died, he wrote me back a letter which made me feel like a bastard.

Here's what he said:

> Dear brother,
> You don't know how much I needed to hear from you. I wanted to write you many a time but I dug how much I must have hurt you and so I didn't write. But now I feel like a man who's been trying to climb up out of some deep, real deep and funky hole and just saw the sun up there, outside. I got to get outside.
> I can't tell you much about how I got here. I mean I don't know how to tell you. I guess I was afraid of something or I was trying to escape from something and you know I have never been very strong in the head (smile). I'm glad Mama and Daddy are dead and can't see what's happened to their son and I swear if I'd known what I was doing I would never have hurt you so, you and a lot of other fine people who were nice to me and who believed in me.
> I don't want you to think it had anything to do with me being a musician. It's more than that. Or maybe less than that. I can't get anything straight in my head down here and I try not to think about what's going to happen to me when I get outside again. Sometime I think I'm going to flip and *never* get outside and sometime I think I'll come straight back. I tell you one thing, though, I'd rather blow my brains out than go through this again. But that's what they all say, so they tell me. If I tell you when I'm coming to New York and if you could meet me, I sure would appreciate it. Give my love to Isabel and the kids and I was sure sorry to hear about little Gracie. I wish I could be like Mama and say the Lord's will be done, but I don't know it seems to me that trouble is the one thing that never does get stopped and I don't know what good it does to blame it on the Lord. But maybe it does some good if you believe it.
>
> Your brother,
> Sonny

Then I kept in constant touch with him and I sent him whatever I could and I went to meet him when he came back to New York. When I saw him many strange things I thought I had forgotten came flooding back to me. This was because I had begun, finally, to wonder about Sonny, about the life that Sonny lived inside. This life, whatever it was, had made him older and thinner and it had deepened the distant stillness in which he had always moved. He looked very unlike my baby brother. Yet, when he smiled, when we shook hands, the baby brother I'd never known looked out from the depths of his private life, like an animal waiting to be coaxed into the light.

"How you been keeping?" he asked me.

"All right. And you?"

"Just fine." He was smiling all over his face. "It's good to see you again."

"It's good to see you."

The seven years' difference in our ages lay between us like a chasm: I wondered if these years would ever operate between us as a bridge. I was remembering, and it made it hard to catch my breath, that I had been there when he was born; and I had heard the first words he had ever spoken. When he started to walk, he walked from our mother straight to me. I caught him just before he fell when he took the first steps he ever took in this world.

"How's Isabel?"

"Just fine. She's dying to see you."

"And the boys?"

"They're fine, too. They're anxious to see their uncle."

"Oh, come on. You know they don't remember me."

"Are you kidding? Of course they remember you."

He grinned again. We got into a taxi. We had a lot to say to each other, far too much to know how to begin.

As the taxi began to move, I asked, "You still want to go to India?"

He laughed. "You still remember that. Hell, no. This place is Indian enough for me."

"It used to belong to them," I said.

And he laughed again. "They damn sure knew what they were doing when they got rid of it."

Years ago, when he was around fourteen, he'd been all hipped on the idea of going to India. He read books about people sitting on rocks, naked, in all kinds of weather, but mostly bad, naturally, and walking barefoot through hot coals and arriving at wisdom. I used to say that it sounded to me as though they were getting away from wisdom as fast as they could. I think he sort of looked down on me for that.

"Do you mind," he asked, "if we have the driver drive alongside the park? On the west side — I haven't seen the city in so long."

"Of course not," I said. I was afraid that I might sound as though I were humoring him, but I hoped he wouldn't take it that way.

So we drove along, between the green of the park, and the stony, lifeless elegance of hotels and apartment buildings, toward the vivid, killing streets of our childhood. These streets hadn't changed, though housing projects jutted up out of them now like rocks in the middle of a boiling sea. Most of the houses in which we had grown up had vanished, as had the stores from which we had stolen, the basements in which we had first tried sex, the rooftops from which we had hurled tin cans and bricks. But houses exactly like the houses of our past yet dominated the landscape, boys exactly like the boys we once had been found themselves smothering in these houses, came down into the streets for light and air and found themselves encircled by disaster. Some escaped the trap, most didn't. These who got out always left something of themselves behind, as some animals amputate a leg and leave it in the trap. It might be said, perhaps, that I had escaped, after all, I was a school teacher; or that Sonny had, he hadn't lived in Harlem for years. Yet, as the cab moved uptown through streets which seemed, with a rush, to darken with dark people, and as I covertly studied Sonny's face, it came to me that what we both were seeking through our separate cab windows was that part of ourselves which had been left behind. It's always at the hour of trouble and confrontation that the missing member aches.

We hit 110th Street and started rolling up Lenox Avenue. And I'd known this avenue all my life, but it seemed to me again, as it had seemed on the day I'd first heard about Sonny's trouble, filled with a hidden menace which was its very breath of life.

"We almost there," said Sonny.

"Almost." We were both too nervous to say anything more.

We live in a housing project. It hasn't been up long. A few days after it was up it seemed uninhabitably new, now, of course, it's already rundown. It looks like a parody of the good, clean, faceless life — God knows the people who live in it do their best to make it a parody. The beat-looking grass lying around isn't enough to make their lives green, the hedges will never hold out the streets, and they know it. The big windows fool no one, they aren't big enough to make space out of no space. They don't bother with the windows, they watch the TV screen instead. The playground is most popular with the children who don't play at jacks, or skip rope, or roller skate, or swing, and they can be found in it after dark. We moved in partly because it's not too far from where I teach, and partly for the kids; but it's really just like the houses in which Sonny and I grew up. The same things happen, they'll have the same things to remember. The moment Sonny and I started into the house I had the feeling that I was simply bringing him back into the danger he had almost died trying to escape.

Sonny has never been talkative. So I don't know why I was sure he'd be dying to talk to me when supper was over the first night. Everything went fine, the oldest boy remembered him, and the youngest boy liked him, and Sonny had remembered to bring something for each of them; and Isabel, who is really much nicer than I am, more open and giving, had gone to a lot of trouble about dinner and was genuinely glad to see him. And she's always been able to tease Sonny in a way that I haven't. It was nice to see her face so vivid again and to hear her laugh and watch her make Sonny laugh. She wasn't, or, anyway, she didn't seem to be, at all uneasy or embarrassed. She chatted as though there were no subject which had to be avoided and she got Sonny past his first, faint stiffness. And thank God she was there, for I was filled with that icy dread again. Everything I did seemed awkward to me, and everything I said sounded freighted with hidden meaning. I was trying to remember everything I'd heard about dope addiction and I couldn't help watching Sonny for signs. I wasn't doing it out of malice. I was trying to find out something about my brother. I was dying to hear him tell me he was safe.

"Safe!" my father grunted, whenever Mama suggested trying to move to a neighborhood which might be safer for children. "Safe, hell! Ain't no place safe for kids, nor nobody."

He always went on like this, but he wasn't, ever, really as bad as he sounded, not even on weekends, when he got drunk. As a matter of fact, he was always on the lookout for "something a little better," but he died before he found it. He died suddenly, during a drunken weekend in the middle of the war, when Sonny was fifteen. He and Sonny hadn't ever got on too well. And this was partly because Sonny was the apple of his father's eye. It was because he loved Sonny so much and was frightened for him, that he was always fighting with him. It doesn't do any good to fight with Sonny. Sonny just moves back, inside himself, where he can't be reached. But the principal reason that they never hit it off is that they were so much alike. Daddy was big and rough and loud-talking, just the opposite of Sonny, but they both had — that same privacy.

Mama tried to tell me something about this, just after Daddy died. I was home on leave from the army.

This was the last time I ever saw my mother alive. Just the same, this picture gets all mixed up in my mind with pictures I had of her when she was younger. The way I always see her is the way she used to be on a Sunday afternoon, say, when the old folks were talking after the big Sunday dinner. I always see her wearing pale blue. She'd be sitting on the sofa. And my father would be sitting in the easy chair, not far from her. And the living room would be full of church folks and relatives. There they sit, in chairs all around the living room, and the night is creeping up outside, but nobody knows it yet. You can see the darkness growing against the windowpanes and you hear the street noises every now and again, or maybe the jangling beat of a tambourine from one of the churches close by, but it's real quiet in the room. For a moment nobody's talking, but every face looks darkening, like the sky outside. And my mother rocks a little from the waist, and my father's eyes are closed. Everyone is looking at something a child can't see. For a minute they've forgotten the children. Maybe a kid is lying on the rug, half asleep. Maybe somebody's got a kid in his lap and is absent-mindedly stroking the kid's head. Maybe there's a kid, quiet and big-eyed, curled up in a big chair in the corner. The silence, the darkness coming, and the darkness in the faces frightens the child obscurely. He hopes that the hand which strokes his forehead will never stop — will never die. He hopes that there will never come a time when the old folks won't be sitting around the living room, talking about where they've come from, and what they've seen, and what's happened to them and their kinfolk.

But something deep and watchful in the child knows that this is bound to end, is already ending. In a moment someone will get up and turn on the light. Then the old folks will remember the children and they won't talk any more that day. And when light fills the room, the child is filled with darkness. He knows that every time this happens he's moved just a little closer to that darkness outside. The darkness outside is what the old folks have been talking about. It's what they've come from. It's what they endure. The child knows that they won't talk any more because if he knows too much about what's happened to *them*, he'll know too much too soon, about what's going to happen to *him*.

The last time I talked to my mother, I remember I was restless. I wanted to get out and see Isabel. We weren't married then and we had a lot to straighten out between us.

There Mama sat, in black, by the window. She was humming an old church song, *Lord, you brought me from a long ways off.* Sonny was out somewhere. Mama kept watching the streets.

"I don't know," she said, "if I'll ever see you again, after you go off from here. But I hope you'll remember the things I tried to teach you."

"Don't talk like that," I said, and smiled. "You'll be here a long time yet."

She smiled, too, but she said nothing. She was quiet for a long time. And I said, "Mama, don't you worry about nothing. I'll be writing all the time, and you be getting the checks. . . ."

"I want to talk to you about your brother," she said, suddenly. "If anything happens to me he ain't going to have nobody to look out for him."

"Mama," I said, "ain't nothing going to happen to you *or* Sonny. Sonny's all right. He's a good boy and he's got good sense."

"It ain't a question of his being a good boy," Mama said, "nor of his having good sense. It ain't only the bad ones, nor yet the dumb ones that gets sucked under." She stopped, looking at me. "Your Daddy once had a brother," she said, and she smiled in a way that made me feel she was in pain. "You didn't never know that, did you?"

"No," I said, "I never knew that," and I watched her face.

"Oh, yes," she said, "your Daddy had a brother." She looked out of the window again. "I know you never saw your Daddy cry. But *I* did — many a time, through all these years."

I asked her, "What happened to his brother? How come nobody's ever talked about him?"

This was the first time I ever saw my mother look old.

"His brother got killed," she said, "when he was just a little younger than you are now. I knew him. He was a fine boy. He was maybe a little full of the devil, but he didn't mean nobody no harm."

Then she stopped and the room was silent, exactly as it had sometimes been on those Sunday afternoons. Mama kept looking out into the streets.

"He used to have a job in the mill," she said, "and, like all young folks, he just liked to perform on Saturday nights. Saturday nights, him and your father would drift around to different place, go to dances and things like that, or just sit around with people they knew, and your father's brother would sing, he had a fine voice, and play along with himself on his guitar. Well, this particular Saturday night, him and your father was coming home from some place, and they were both a little drunk and there was a moon that night, it was bright like day. Your father's brother was feeling kind of good, and he was whistling to himself, and he had his guitar slung over his shoulder. They was coming down a hill and beneath them was a road that turned off from the highway. Well, your father's brother, being always kind of frisky, decided to run down this hill, and he did, with that guitar banging and clanging behind him, and he ran across the road, and he was making water behind a tree. And your father was sort of amused at him and he was still coming down the hill, kind of slow. Then he heard a car motor and that same minute his brother stepped from behind the tree, into the road, in the moonlight. And he started to cross the road. And your father started to run down the hill, he says he don't know why. This car was full of white men. They was all drunk, and when they seen your father's brother they let out a great whoop and holler and they aimed the car straight at him. They was having fun, they just wanted to scare him, the way they do sometimes, you know. But they was drunk. And I guess the boy, being drunk, too, and scared, kind of lost his head. By the time he jumped it was too late. Your father says he heard his brother scream when the car rolled over him, and he heard the wood of that guitar when it give, and he heard them strings go flying, and he heard them white men shouting, and the car kept on a-going and it ain't stopped till this day. And, time your father got down the hill, his brother weren't nothing but blood and pulp."

Tears were gleaming on my mother's face. There wasn't anything I could say.

"He never mentioned it," she said, "because I never let him mention it before you children. Your Daddy was like a crazy man that night and for many a night thereafter. He says he never in his life seen anything as dark as that road after the lights of that car had gone away. Weren't nothing, weren't nobody on that road, just your Daddy and his brother and that busted guitar. Oh, yes. Your Daddy never did really get right again. Till the day he died he weren't sure but that every white man he saw was the man that killed his brother."

She stopped and took out her handkerchief and dried her eyes and looked at me.

"I ain't telling you all this," she said, "to make you scared or bitter or to make you hate nobody. I'm telling you this because you got a brother. And the world ain't changed."

I guess I didn't want to believe this. I guess she saw this in my face. She turned away from me, toward the window again, searching those streets.

"But I praise my Redeemer," she said at last, "that He called your Daddy home before me. I ain't saying it to throw no flowers at myself, but, I declare, it keeps me from feeling too cast down to know I helped your father get safely through this world. Your father always acted like he was the roughest, strongest man on earth. And everybody took him to be like that. But if he hadn't had *me* there—to see his tears!"

She was crying again. Still, I couldn't move. I said, "Lord, Lord, Mama, I didn't know it was like that."

"Oh, honey," she said, "there's a lot that you don't know. But you are going to find it out." She stood up from the window and came over to me. "You got to hold on to your brother," she said, "and don't let him fall, no matter what it looks like is happening to him and no matter how evil you gets with him. You going to be evil with him many a time. But don't you forget what I told you, you hear?"

"I won't forget," I said. "Don't you worry, I won't forget. I won't let nothing happen to Sonny."

My mother smiled as though she were amused at something she saw in my face. Then, "You may not be able to stop nothing from happening. But you got to let him know you's *there*."

Two days later I was married, and then I was gone. And I had a lot of things on my mind and I pretty well forgot my promise to Mama until I got shipped home on a special furlough for her funeral.

And, after the funeral, with just Sonny and me alone in the empty kitchen, I tried to find out something about him.

"What do you want to do?" I asked him.

"I'm going to be a musician," he said.

For he had graduated, in the time I had been away, from dancing to the juke box to finding out who was playing what, and what they were doing with it, and he had bought himself a set of drums.

"You mean, you want to be a drummer?" I somehow had the feeling that being a drummer might be all right for other people but not for my brother Sonny.

"I don't think," he said, looking at me very gravely, "that I'll ever be a good drummer. But I think I can play a piano."

I frowned. I'd never played the role of the older brother quite so seriously before, had scarcely ever, in fact, *asked* Sonny a damn thing. I sensed myself in the presence of something I didn't really know how to handle, didn't understand. So I made my frown a little deeper as I asked: "What kind of musician do you want to be?"

He grinned. "How many kinds do you think there are?"

"Be *serious*," I said.

He laughed, throwing his head back, and then looked at me. "I *am* serious."

"Well, then, for Christ's sake, stop kidding around and answer a serious question. I mean, do you want to be a concert pianist, you want to play classical music and all that, or—or what?" Long before I finished he was laughing again. "For Christ's *sake*, Sonny!"

He sobered, but with difficulty. "I'm sorry. But you sound so—*scared*!" and he was off again.

"Well, you may think it's funny now, baby, but it's not going to be so funny when you have to make your living at it, let me tell you *that*." I was furious because I knew he was laughing at me and I didn't know why.

"No," he said, very sober now, and afraid, perhaps, that he'd hurt me, "I don't want to be a classical pianist. That isn't what interests me. I mean"—he paused, looking hard at me, as though his eyes would help me to understand, and then gestured helplessly, as though perhaps his hand would help—"I mean, I'll have a lot of studying to do, and I'll have to study *everything*, but, I mean, I want to play *with*—jazz musicians." He stopped. "I want to play jazz," he said.

Well, the word had never before sounded as heavy, as real, as it sounded that afternoon in Sonny's mouth. I just looked at him and I was probably frowning a real frown by this time. I simply couldn't see why on earth he'd want to spend his time hanging around nightclubs, clowning around on bandstands, while people pushed each other around a dance floor. It seemed—beneath him, somehow. I had never thought about it before, had never been forced to, but I suppose I had always put jazz musicians in a class with what Daddy called "good-time people."

"Are you *serious*?"

"Hell, *yes*, I'm serious."

He looked more helpless than ever, and annoyed, and deeply hurt.

I suggested helpfully: "You mean—like Louis Armstrong?"

His face closed as though I'd struck him. "No. I'm not talking about none of that old-time, down home crap."

"Well, look, Sonny, I'm sorry, don't get mad. I just don't altogether get it, that's all. Name somebody—you know, a jazz musician you admire."

"Bird."

"Who?"

"Bird! Charlie Parker! Don't they teach you nothing in the goddamn army?"

I lit a cigarette. I was surprised and then a little amused to discover that I was trembling. "I've been out of touch," I said. "You'll have to be patient with me. Now. Who's this Parker character?"

"He's just one of the greatest jazz musicians alive," said Sonny, sullenly, his hands in his pockets, his back to me. "Maybe *the* greatest," he added, bitterly, "that's probably why *you* never heard of him."

"All right," I said, "I'm ignorant. I'm sorry. I'll go out and buy all the cat's records right away, all right?"

"It don't," said Sonny, with dignity, "make any difference to me. I don't care what you listen to. Don't do me no favors."

I was beginning to realize that I'd never seen him so upset before. With another part of my mind I was thinking that this would probably turn out to be one of those things kids go through and that I shouldn't make it seem important by pushing it too hard. Still, I didn't think it would do any harm to ask: "Doesn't all this take a lot of time? Can you make a living at it?"

He turned back to me and half leaned, half sat, on the kitchen table. "Everything takes time," he said, "and—well, yes, sure, I can make a living at it. But what I don't seem to be able to make you understand is that it's the only thing I want to do."

"Well, Sonny," I said, gently, "you know people can't always do exactly what they *want* to do—"

"*No*, I don't know that," said Sonny, surprising me. "I think people *ought* to do what they want to do, what else are they alive for?"

"You getting to be a big boy," I said desperately, "it's time you started thinking about your future."

"I'm thinking about my future," said Sonny, grimly. "I think about it all the time."

I gave up. I decided, if he didn't change his mind, that we could always talk about it later. "In the meantime," I said, "you got to finish school." We had already decided that he'd have to move in with Isabel and her folks. I knew this wasn't the ideal arrangement because Isabel's folks are inclined to be dicty[2] and they hadn't especially wanted Isabel to marry me. But I didn't know what else to do. "And we have to get you fixed up at Isabel's."

There was a long silence. He moved from the kitchen table to the window. "That's a terrible idea. You know it yourself."

"Do you have a *better* idea?"

He just walked up and down the kitchen for a minute. He was as tall as I was. He had started to shave. I suddenly had the feeling that I didn't know him at all.

He stopped at the kitchen table and picked up my cigarettes. Looking at me with a kind of mocking, amused defiance, he put one between his lips. "You mind?"

"You smoking already?"

He lit the cigarette and nodded, watching me through the smoke. "I just wanted to see if I'd have the courage to smoke in front of you." He grinned and blew a great cloud of smoke to the ceiling. "It was easy." He looked at my face. "Come on, now. I bet you was smoking at my age, tell the truth."

I didn't say anything but the truth was on my face, and he laughed. But now there was something very strained in his laugh. "Sure. And I bet that ain't all you was doing."

He was frightening me a little. "Cut the crap," I said. "We already decided that you was going to go and live at Isabel's. Now what's got into you all of a sudden?"

"*You* decided it," he pointed out. "*I* didn't decide nothing." He stopped in front of me, leaning against the stove, arms loosely folded. "Look, brother. I don't want to stay in Harlem no more, I really don't." He was very earnest. He looked at me, then over toward the kitchen window. There was something in his eyes I'd never seen before, some thoughtfulness, some worry all his own. He rubbed the muscle of one arm. "It's time I was getting out of here."

"Where do you want to *go*, Sonny?"

---

[2]Highhanded or snobbish.

"I want to join the army. Or the navy, I don't care. If I say I'm old enough, they'll believe me."

Then I got mad. It was because I was so scared. "You must be crazy. You goddamn fool, what the hell do you want to go and join the *army* for?"

"I just told you. To get out of Harlem."

"Sonny, you haven't even finished *school*. And if you really want to be a musician, how do you expect to study if you're in the *army*?"

He looked at me, trapped, and in anguish. "There's ways. I might be able to work out some kind of deal. Anyway, I'll have the G.I. Bill when I come out."

"*If* you come out." We stared at each other. "Sonny, please. Be reasonable. I know the setup is far from perfect. But we got to do the best we can."

"I ain't learning nothing in school," he said. "Even when I go." He turned away from me and opened the window and threw his cigarette out into the narrow alley. I watched his back. "At least, I ain't learning nothing you'd want me to learn." He slammed the window so hard I thought the glass would fly out, and turned back to me. "And I'm sick of the stink of these garbage cans!"

"Sonny," I said, "I know how you feel. But if you don't finish school now, you're going to be sorry later that you didn't." I grabbed him by the shoulders. "And you only got another year. It ain't so bad. And I'll come back and I swear I'll help you do *whatever* you want to do. Just try to put up with it till I come back. Will you please do that? For me?"

He didn't answer and he wouldn't look at me.

"Sonny. You hear me?"

He pulled away. "I hear you. But you never hear anything *I* say."

I didn't know what to say to that. He looked out of the window and then back at me. "OK," he said, and sighed. "I'll try."

Then I said, trying to cheer him up a little, "They got a piano at Isabel's. You can practice on it."

And as a matter of fact, it did cheer him up for a minute. "That's right," he said to himself. "I forgot that." His face relaxed a little. But the worry, the thoughtfulness, played on it still, the way shadows play on a face which is staring into the fire.

But I thought I'd never hear the end of that piano. At first, Isabel would write me, saying how nice it was that Sonny was so serious about his music and how, as soon as he came in from school, or wherever he had been when he was supposed to be at school, he went straight to that piano and stayed there until suppertime. And, after supper, he went back to that piano and stayed there until everybody went to bed. He was at the piano all day Saturday and all day Sunday. Then he bought a record player and started playing records. He'd play one record over and over again, all day long sometimes, and he'd improvise along with it on the piano. Or he'd play one section of the record, one chord, one change, one progression, then he'd do it on the piano. Then back to the record. Then back to the piano.

Well, I really don't know how they stood it. Isabel finally confessed that it wasn't like living with a person at all, it was like living with sound. And the sound didn't make any sense to her, didn't make any sense to any of them—naturally. They began, in a way, to be afflicted by this presence that was living in their home. It was as though Sonny were some sort of god, or monster. He moved in an atmosphere which wasn't like theirs at all. They fed him and he ate, he washed himself, he walked in and out of their door; he certainly wasn't nasty or unpleasant or rude, Sonny isn't any of those things; but it was as though he were all wrapped up in some cloud, some fire, some vision all his own; and there wasn't any way to reach him.

At the same time, he wasn't really a man yet, he was still a child, and they had to watch out for him in all kinds of ways. They certainly couldn't throw him out. Neither did they dare to make a great scene about that piano because even they dimly sensed, as I sensed, from so many thousands of miles away, that Sonny was at that piano playing for his life.

But he hadn't been going to school. One day a letter came from the school board and Isabel's mother got it—there had, apparently, been other letters but Sonny had torn them up. This day, when Sonny came in, Isabel's mother showed him the letter and asked where he'd been spending his time. And she finally got it out of him that he'd been down in Greenwich Village, with musicians and other characters, in a white girl's apartment. And this scared her and she started to scream at him and what came up, once she began—though she denies it to this day—was what sacrifices they were making to give Sonny a decent home and how little he appreciated it.

Sonny didn't play the piano that day. By evening, Isabel's mother had calmed down but then there was the old man to deal with, and Isabel herself. Isabel says she did her best to be calm but she broke down and started crying. She says she just watched Sonny's face. She could tell, by watching him, what was happening with him. And what was happening was that they penetrated his cloud, they had reached him. Even if their fingers had been a thousand times more gentle than human fingers ever are, he could hardly help feeling that they had stripped him naked and were spitting on that nakedness. For he also had to see that his presence, that music, which was life or death to him, had been torture for them and that they had endured it, not at all for his sake, but only for mine. And Sonny couldn't take that. He can take it a little better today than he could then but he's still not very good at it and, frankly, I don't know anybody who is.

The silence of the next few days must have been louder than the sound of all the music ever played since time began. One morning, before she went to work, Isabel was in his room for something and she suddenly realized that all of his records were gone. And she knew for certain that he was gone. And he was. He went as far as the navy would carry him. He finally sent me a postcard from some place in Greece and that was the first I knew that Sonny was still alive. I didn't see him any more until we were both back in New York and the war had long been over.

He was a man by then, of course, but I wasn't willing to see it. He came by the house from time to time, but we fought almost every time we met. I didn't like the way he carried himself, loose and dreamlike all the time, and I didn't like his friends, and his music seemed to be merely an excuse for the life he led. It sounded just that weird and disordered.

Then we had a fight, a pretty awful fight, and I didn't see him for months. By and by I looked him up, where he was living, in a furnished room in the Village, and I tried to make it up. But there were lots of other people in the room and Sonny just lay on his bed, and he wouldn't come downstairs with me, and he treated these other people as though they were his family and I weren't. So I got mad and then he got mad, and then I told him that he might just as well be dead as live the way he was living. Then he stood up and he told me not to worry about him any more in life, that he *was* dead as far as I was concerned. Then he pushed me to the door and the other people looked on as though nothing were happening, and he slammed the door behind me. I stood in the hallway, staring at the door. I heard somebody laugh in the room and then the tears came to my eyes. I started down the steps, whistling to keep from crying, I kept whistling to myself, *You going to need me, baby, one of these cold, rainy days.*

I read about Sonny's trouble in the spring. Little Grace died in the fall. She was a beautiful little girl. But she only lived a little over two years. She died of polio and she suffered. She had a slight fever for a couple of days, but it didn't seem like anything and we just kept her in bed. And we would certainly have called the doctor, but the fever dropped, she seemed to be all right. So we thought it had just been a cold. Then, one day, she was up, playing, Isabel was in the kitchen fixing lunch for the two boys when they'd come in from school, and she heard Grace fall down in the living room. When you have a lot of children you don't always start running when one of them falls, unless they start screaming or something. And, this time, Grace was quiet. Yet, Isabel says that when she heard that *thump* and then that silence, something happened in her to make her afraid. And she ran to the living room and there was little Grace on the floor, all twisted up, and the reason she hadn't screamed was that she couldn't get her breath. And when she did scream, it was the worst sound, Isabel says, that she'd ever heard in all her life, and she still hears it sometimes in her dreams. Isabel will sometimes wake me up with a low, moaning, strangled sound and I have to be quick to awaken her and hold her to me and where Isabel is weeping against me seems a mortal wound.

I think I may have written Sonny the very day that little Grace was buried. I was sitting in the living room in the dark, by myself, and I suddenly thought of Sonny. My trouble made his real.

One Saturday afternoon, when Sonny had been living with us, or, anyway, been in our house, for nearly two weeks, I found myself wandering aimlessly about the living room, drinking from a can of beer, and trying to work up the courage to search Sonny's room. He was out, he was usually out whenever I was home, and Isabel had taken the children to see their grandparents. Suddenly I was standing still in front of the living room window, watching Seventh Avenue. The idea of searching Sonny's room made me still. I scarcely dared to admit to myself what I'd be searching for. I didn't know what I'd do if I found it. Or if I didn't.

On the sidewalk across from me, near the entrance to a barbecue joint, some people were holding an old-fashioned revival meeting. The barbecue cook, wearing a dirty white apron, his conked hair[3] reddish and metallic in the pale sun, and a cigarette between his lips, stood in the doorway, watching them. Kids and older people paused in their errands and stood there, along with some older men and a couple of very tough-looking women who watched everything that happened on the avenue, as though they owned it, or were maybe owned by it. Well, they were watching this, too. The revival was being carried on by three sisters in black, and a brother. All they had were their voices and their Bibles and a tambourine. The brother was testifying and while he testified two of the sisters stood together, seeming to say, amen, and the third sister walked around with the tambourine outstretched and a couple of people dropped coins into it. Then the brother's testimony ended and the sister who had been taking up the collection dumped the coins into her palm and transferred them to the pocket of her long black robe. Then she raised both hands, striking the tambourine against the air, and then against one hand, and she started to sing. And the two other sisters and the brother joined in.

It was strange, suddenly, to watch, though I had been seeing these street meetings all my life. So, of course, had everybody else down there. Yet, they paused and watched and listened and I stood still at the window. "'*Tis the old ship of Zion,*" they sang, and the sister with the tambourine kept a steady, jangling beat, "*it has rescued many a thousand!*" Not a soul under the sound of their voices was hearing this song for the first time, not one of them had been rescued. Nor had they seen much in the way of rescue work being done around them. Neither did they especially believe in the holiness of the three sisters and the brother, they knew too much about them, knew where they lived, and how. The woman with the tambourine, whose voice dominated the air, whose face was bright with joy, was divided by very little from the woman who stood watching her, a cigarette between her heavy, chapped lips, her hair a cuckoo's nest, her face scarred and swollen from many beatings, and her black eyes glittering like coal. Perhaps they both knew this, which was why, when, as rarely, they addressed each other, they addressed each other as Sister. As the singing filled the air the watch-

---

[3]Chemically straightened hair.

ing, listening faces underwent a change, the eyes focusing on something within; the music seemed to soothe a poison out of them; and time seemed, nearly, to fall away from the sullen, belligerent, battered faces, as though they were fleeing back to their first condition, while dreaming of their last. The barbecue cook half shook his head and smiled, and dropped his cigarette and disappeared into his joint. A man fumbled in his pockets for change and stood holding it in his hand impatiently, as though he had just remembered a pressing appointment further up the avenue. He looked furious. Then I saw Sonny, standing on the edge of the crowd. He was carrying a wide, flat notebook with a green cover, and it made him look, from where I was standing, almost like a schoolboy. The coppery sun brought out the copper in his skin, he was very faintly smiling, standing very still. Then the singing stopped, the tambourine turned into a collection plate again. The furious man dropped in his coins and vanished, so did a couple of the women, and Sonny dropped some change in the plate, looking directly at the woman with a little smile. He started across the avenue, toward the house. He has a slow, loping walk, something like the way Harlem hipsters walk, only he's imposed on this his own half-beat. I had never really noticed it before.

I stayed at the window, both relieved and apprehensive. As Sonny disappeared from my sight, they began singing again. And they were still singing when his key turned in the lock.

"Hey," he said.

"Hey, yourself. You want some beer?"

"No. Well, maybe." But he came up to the window and stood beside me, looking out. "What a warm voice," he said.

They were singing *If I could only hear my mother pray again!*

"Yes," I said, "and she can sure beat that tambourine."

"But what a terrible song," he said, and laughed. He dropped his notebook on the sofa and disappeared into the kitchen. "Where's Isabel and the kids?"

"I think they went to see their grandparents. You hungry?"

"No." He came back into the living room with his can of beer. "You want to come some place with me tonight?"

I sensed, I don't know how, that I couldn't possibly say no. "Sure. Where?"

He sat down on the sofa and picked up his notebook and started leafing through it. "I'm going to sit in with some fellows in a joint in the Village."

"You mean, you're going to play, tonight?"

"That's right." He took a swallow of his beer and moved back to the window. He gave me a sidelong look. "If you can stand it."

"I'll try," I said.

He smiled to himself and we both watched as the meeting across the way broke up. The three sisters and the brother, heads bowed, were singing *God be with you till we meet again.* The faces around them were very quiet. Then the song ended. The small crowd dispersed. We watched the three women and the lone man walk slowly up the avenue.

"When she was singing before," said Sonny, abruptly, "her voice reminded me for a minute of what heroin feels like sometimes — when it's in your veins. It makes you feel sort of warm and cool at the same time. And distant. And — and sure." He sipped his beer, very deliberately not looking at me. I watched his face. "It makes you feel — in control. Sometimes you've got to have that feeling."

"Do you?" I sat down slowly in the easy chair.

"Sometimes." He went to the sofa and picked up his notebook again. "Some people do."

"In order," I asked, "to play?" And my voice was very ugly, full of contempt and anger.

"Well," — he looked at me with great, troubled eyes, as though, in fact, he hoped his eyes would tell me things he could never otherwise say—"they *think* so. And *if* they think so—!"

"And what do *you* think?" I asked.

He sat on the sofa and put his can of beer on the floor. "I don't know," he said, and I couldn't be sure if he were answering my question or pursuing his thoughts. His face didn't tell me. "It's not so much to *play*. It's to *stand* it, to be able to make it at all. On any level." He frowned and smiled: "In order to keep from shaking to pieces."

"But these friends of yours," I said, "they seem to shake themselves to pieces pretty goddamn fast."

"Maybe." He played with the notebook. And something told me that I should curb my tongue, that Sonny was doing his best to talk, that I should listen. "But of course you only know the ones that've gone to pieces. Some don't—or at least they haven't *yet* and that's just about all *any* of us can say." He paused. "And then there are some who just live, really, in hell, and they know it and they see what's happening and they go right on. I don't know." He sighed, dropped the notebook, folded his arms. "Some guys, you can tell from the way they play, they on something *all* the time. And you can see that, well, it makes something real for them. But of course," he picked up his beer from the floor and sipped it and put the can down again, "they *want* to, too, you've got to see that. Even some of them that say they don't—*some*, not all."

"And what about you?" I asked—I couldn't help it. "What about you? Do *you* want to?"

He stood up and walked to the window and remained silent for a long time. Then he sighed. "Me," he said. Then: "While I was downstairs before, on my way here, listening to that woman sing, it struck me all of a sudden how much suffering she must have had to go through—to sing like that. It's *repulsive* to think you have to suffer that much."

I said: "But there's no way not to suffer—is there, Sonny?"

"I believe not," he said and smiled, "but that's never stopped anyone from trying." He looked at me. "Has it?" I realized, with this mocking look, that there stood between us, forever, beyond the power of time or forgiveness, the fact that I had held silence—so long!—when he had needed human speech to help him. He turned back to the window. "No, there's no way not to suffer. But you try all kinds of ways to keep from drowning in it, to keep on top of it, and to make it seem—well, like *you*. Like you did something, all right, and now you're suffering for it. You know?" I said nothing. "Well you know," he said, impatiently, "why *do* people suffer? Maybe it's better to do something to give it a reason, *any* reason."

"But we just agreed," I said, "that there's no way not to suffer. Isn't it better, then, just to—take it?"

"But nobody just takes it," Sonny cried, "that's what I'm telling you! *Everybody* tries not to. You're just hung up on the *way* some people try—it's not *your* way!"

The hair on my face began to itch, my face felt wet "That's not true," I said, "that's not true. I don't give a damn what other people do, I don't even care how they suffer. I just care how *you* suffer." And he looked at me. "Please believe me," I said, "I don't want to see you—die—trying not to suffer."

"I won't," he said, flatly, "die trying not to suffer. At least, not any faster than anybody else."

"But there's no need," I said, trying to laugh, "is there? in killing yourself."

I wanted to say more, but I couldn't. I wanted to talk about will power and how life could be—well, beautiful. I wanted to say that it was all within; but was it? or, rather, wasn't that exactly the trouble? And I wanted to promise that I would never fail him again. But it would all have sounded—empty words and lies.

So I made the promise to myself and prayed that I would keep it.

"It's terrible sometimes, inside," he said, "that's what's the trouble. You walk these streets, black and funky and cold, and there's not really a living ass to talk to, and there's nothing shaking, and there's no way of getting it out—that storm inside. You can't talk it and you can't make love with it, and when you finally try to get with it and play it, you realize *nobody's* listening. So *you've* got to listen. You got to find a way to listen."

And then he walked away from the window and sat on the sofa again, as though all the wind had suddenly been knocked out of him. "Sometimes you'll do *anything* to play, even cut your mother's throat." He laughed and looked at me. "Or your brother's." Then he sobered. "Or your own." Then: "Don't worry. I'm all right now and I think I'll *be* all right. But I can't forget—where I've been. I don't mean just the physical place I've been, I mean where I've *been*. And *what* I've been."

"What have you been, Sonny?" I asked.

He smiled—but sat sideways on the sofa, his elbow resting on the back, his fingers playing with his mouth and chin, not looking at me. "I've been something I didn't recognize, didn't know I could be. Didn't know anybody could be." He stopped, looking inward, looking helplessly young, looking old. "I'm not talking about it now because I feel *guilty* or anything like that—maybe it would be better if I did, I don't know. Anyway, I can't really talk about it. Not to you, not to anybody," and now he turned and faced me. "Sometimes, you know, and it was actually when I was most *out* of the world, I felt that I was in it, that I was *with* it, really, and I could play or I didn't really have to *play*, it just came out of me, it was there. And I don't know how I played, thinking about it now, but I know I did awful things, those times, sometimes, to people. Or it wasn't that I *did* anything to them—it was that they weren't real." He picked up the beer can; it was empty; he rolled it between his palms: "And other times—well, I needed a fix, I needed to find a place to lean, I needed to clear a space to *listen*—and I couldn't find it, and I—went crazy, I did terrible things to *me*, I was terrible *for* me." He began pressing the beer can between his hands, I watched the metal begin to give. It glittered, as he played with it, like a knife, and I was afraid he would cut himself, but I said nothing. "Oh well. I can never tell you. I was all by myself at the bottom of something, stinking and sweating and crying and shaking, and I smelled it, you know? *my* stink, and I thought I'd die if I couldn't get away from it and yet, all the same, I knew that everything I was doing was just locking me in with it. And I didn't know," he paused, still flattening the beer can, "I didn't know, I still *don't* know, something kept telling me that maybe it was good to smell your own stink, but I didn't think that *that* was what I'd been trying to do—and—who can stand it?" and he abruptly dropped the ruined beer can, looking at me with a small, still smile, and then rose, walking to the window as though it were the lodestone rock. I watched his face, he watched the avenue. "I couldn't tell you when Mama died—but the reason I wanted to leave Harlem so bad was to get away from drugs. And then, when I ran away, that's what I was running from—really. When I came back, nothing had changed, *I* hadn't changed, I was just—older." And he stopped, drumming with his fingers on the windowpane. The sun had vanished, soon darkness would fall. I watched his face. "It can come again," he said, almost as though speaking to himself. Then he turned to me. "It can come again," he repeated. "I just want you to know that."

"All right," I said, at last. "So it can come again, All right."

He smiled, but the smile was sorrowful. "I had to try to tell you," he said.

"Yes," I said. "I understand that."

"You're my brother," he said, looking straight at me, and not smiling at all.

"Yes," I repeated, "yes. I understand that."

He turned back to the window, looking out. "All that hatred down there," he said, "all that hatred and misery and love. It's a wonder it doesn't blow the avenue apart."

We went to the only nightclub on a short, dark street, downtown. We squeezed through the narrow, chattering, jam-packed bar to the entrance of the big room, where the bandstand was. And we stood there for a moment, for the lights were very dim in this room and we couldn't see. Then, "Hello, boy," said a voice and an enormous black man, much older than Sonny or myself, erupted out of all that atmospheric lighting and put an arm around Sonny's shoulder. "I been sitting right here," he said, "waiting for you."

He had a big voice, too, and heads in the darkness turned toward us.

Sonny grinned and pulled a little away, and said, "Creole, this is my brother. I told you about him."

Creole shook my hand. "I'm glad to meet you, son," he said, and it was clear that he was glad to meet me *there*, for Sonny's sake. And he smiled, "You got a real musician in *your* family," and he took his arm from Sonny's shoulder and slapped him, lightly, affectionately, with the back of his hand.

"Well. Now I've heard it all," said a voice behind us. This was another musician, and a friend of Sonny's, a coal-black, cheerful-looking man, built close to the ground. He immediately began confiding to me, at the top of his lungs, the most terrible things about Sonny, his teeth gleaming like a lighthouse and his laugh coming up out of him like the beginning of an earthquake. And it turned out that everyone at the bar knew Sonny, or almost everyone; some were musicians, working there, or nearby, or not working, some were simply hangers-on, and some were there to hear Sonny play. I was introduced to all of them and they were all very polite to me. Yet, it was clear that, for them, I was only Sonny's brother. Here, I was in Sonny's world. Or, rather: his kingdom. Here, it was not even a question that his veins bore royal blood.

They were going to play soon and Creole installed me, by myself, at a table in a dark corner. Then I watched them, Creole, and the little black man, and Sonny, and the others, while they horsed around, standing just below the bandstand. The light from the bandstand spilled just a little short of them and, watching them laughing and gesturing and moving about, I had the feeling that they, nevertheless, were being most careful not to step into that circle of light too suddenly: that if they moved into the light too suddenly, without thinking, they would perish in flame. Then, while I watched, one of them, the small, black man, moved into the light and crossed the bandstand and started fooling around with his drums. Then—being funny and being, also, extremely ceremonious—Creole took Sonny by the arm and led him to the piano. A woman's voice called Sonny's name and a few hands started clapping. And Sonny, also being funny and being ceremonious, and so touched, I think, that he could have cried, but neither hiding it nor showing it, riding it like a man, grinned, and put both hands to his heart and bowed from the waist.

Creole then went to the bass fiddle and a lean, very bright-skinned brown man jumped up on the bandstand and picked up his horn. So there they were, and the atmosphere on the bandstand and in the room began to change and tighten. Someone stepped up to the microphone and announced them. Then there were all kinds of murmurs. Some people at the bar shushed others. The waitress ran around frantically getting in the last orders, guys and chicks got closer to each other, and the lights on the bandstand, on the quartet, turned to a kind of indigo. Then they all looked different there. Creole looked about him for the last time, as though he were making certain that all his chickens were in the coop, and then he—jumped and struck the fiddle. And there they were.

All I know about music is that not many people ever really hear it. And even then, on the rare occasions when something opens within, and the music enters, what we mainly hear, or hear corroborated, are personal, private, vanishing evocations. But the man who creates the music is hearing something else, is dealing with the roar rising from the void and imposing order on it as it hits the air. What is evoked in him, then, is of another order, more terrible because it has no words, and triumphant, too, for that same reason. And his triumph, when he triumphs, is ours. I just watched Sonny's face. His face was troubled, he was working hard, but he wasn't with it. And I had the feeling that, in a way, everyone on the bandstand was waiting for him, both waiting for him and pushing him along. But as I began to watch Creole, I realized that it was Creole who held them all back. He had them on a short rein. Up there, keeping the beat with his whole body, wailing on the fiddle, with his eyes half closed, he was listening to everything, but he was listening to Sonny. He was having a dialogue with Sonny. He wanted Sonny to leave the shoreline and strike out for the deep water. He was Sonny's witness that deep water and drowning were not the same thing—he had been there, and he knew. And he wanted Sonny to know. He was waiting for Sonny to do the things on the keys which would let Creole know that Sonny was in the water.

And, while Creole listened, Sonny moved, deep within, exactly like someone in torment. I had never before thought of how awful the relationship must be between the musician and his instrument. He has to fill it, this instrument, with the breath of life, his own. He has to make it do what he wants it to do. And a piano is just a piano. It's made out of so much wood and wires and little hammers and big ones, and ivory. While there's only so much you can do with it, the only way to find this out is to try; to try and make it do everything.

And Sonny hadn't been near a piano for over a year. And he wasn't on much better terms with his life, not the life that stretched before him now. He and the piano stammered, started one way, got scared, stopped; started another way, panicked, marked time, started again; then seemed to have found a direction, panicked again, got stuck. And the face I saw on Sonny I'd never seen before. Everything had been burned out of it, and, at the same time, things usually hidden were being burned in, by the fire and fury of the battle which was occurring in him up there.

Yet, watching Creole's face as they neared the end of the first set, I had the feeling that something had happened, something I hadn't heard. Then they finished, there was scattered applause, and then, without an instant's warning, Creole started into something else, it was almost sardonic, it was *Am I Blue*. And, as though he commanded, Sonny began to play. Something began to happen. And Creole let out the reins. The dry, low, black man said something awful on the drums, Creole answered, and the drums talked back. Then the horn insisted, sweet and high, slightly detached perhaps, and Creole listened, commenting now and then, dry, and driving, beautiful and calm and old. Then they all came together again, and Sonny was part of the family again. I could tell this from his face. He seemed to have found, right there beneath his fingers, a damn brand-new piano. It seemed that he couldn't get over it. Then, for awhile, just being happy with Sonny, they seemed to be agreeing with him that brand-new pianos certainly were a gas.

Then Creole stepped forward to remind them that what they were playing was the blues. He hit something in all of them, he hit something in me, myself, and the music tightened and deepened, apprehension began to beat the air. Creole began to tell us what the blues were all about. They were not about anything very new. He and his boys up there were keeping it new, at the risk of ruin, destruction, madness, and death, in order to find new ways to make us listen. For, while the tale of how we suffer, and how we are delighted, and how we may triumph is never new, it always must be heard. There isn't any other tale to tell, it's the only light we've got in all this darkness.

And this tale, according to that face, that body, those strong hands on those strings, has another aspect in every country, and a new depth in every generation. Listen, Creole seemed to be saying, listen. Now these are Sonny's blues. He made the little black man on the drums know it, and the bright, brown man on the horn. Creole wasn't trying any longer to get Sonny in the water. He was wishing him Godspeed. Then he stepped back, very slowly, filling the air with the immense suggestion that Sonny speak for himself.

Then they all gathered around Sonny and Sonny played. Every now and again one of them seemed to say, amen. Sonny's fingers filled the air with life, his life. But that life contained so many others. And Sonny went all the way back, he really began with the spare, flat statement of the opening phrase of the song. Then he began to make it his. It was very beautiful because it wasn't hurried and it was no longer a lament. I seemed to hear with what burning he had made it his, with what burning we had yet to make it ours, how we could cease lamenting. Freedom lurked around us and I understood, at last, that he could help us to be free if we would listen, that he would never be free until we did. Yet, there was no battle in his face now. I heard what he had gone through, and would continue to go through until he came to rest in earth. He had made it his: that long line, of which we knew only Mama and Daddy. And he was giving it back, as everything must be given back, so that, passing through death, it can live forever. I saw my mother's face again, and felt, for the first time, how the stones of the road she had walked on must have bruised her feet. I saw the moonlit road where my father's brother died. And it brought something else back to me, and carried me past it, I saw my little girl again and felt Isabel's tears again, and I felt my own tears begin to rise. And I was yet aware that this was only a moment, that the world waited outside, as hungry as a tiger, and that trouble stretched above us, longer than the sky.

Then it was over. Creole and Sonny let out their breath, both soaking wet, and grinning. There was a lot of applause and some of it was real. In the dark, the girl came by and I asked her to take drinks to the bandstand. There was a long pause, while they talked up there in the indigo light and after awhile I saw the girl put a Scotch and milk on top of the piano for Sonny. He didn't seem to notice it, but just before they started playing again, he sipped from it and looked toward me, and nodded. Then he put it back on top of the piano. For me, then, as they began to play again, it glowed and shook above my brother's head like the very cup of trembling.

1957, 1965

FLANNERY O'CONNOR
(1925–1964)

Flannery O'Connor, living in the South, the stronghold of American Protestantism, made no secret of the fact that she wrote from the perspective of the "dogma" of her deep Catholic faith. She said, "Christian dogma is about the only thing left in the world that surely guards and respects mystery." In "The Fiction Writer and His Country," in explanation of her portrayal of the grotesque, she observed:

> The novelist with Christian concerns will find in modern life distortions which are repugnant to him, and his problem will be to make these appear as distortions to an audience which is used to seeing them as natural; and he may well be forced to take ever more violent means to get his vision across to this hostile audience. When you can assume that your audience holds the same beliefs you do, you can relax a little and use more normal means of talking to it; when you have to assume that it does not, then you have to make your vision apparent by shock—to the hard of hearing you shout, and for the almost-blind you draw large and startling figures.

But whatever the motivation for her writing, O'Connor did not practice nor endorse didacticism in fiction. She explained in "The Church and the Fiction Writer": "Henry James said that the morality of a piece of fiction depended on the amount of 'felt life' that was in it. The Catholic writer, insofar as he has the mind of the Church, will feel life from the standpoint of the central Christian mystery. . . . When people have told me that because I am Catholic, I cannot be an artist, I have had to reply, ruefully, that because I am a Catholic, I cannot afford to be less than an artist."

Flannery O'Connor was born in Savannah, Georgia. In 1938 her family moved to Milledgeville, Georgia, where she spent the rest of her life. She attended Georgia State College for Women (now Georgia College), followed by the University of Iowa, where she took a Master of Fine Arts in 1947, with a thesis entitled "Geranium: A Collection of Short Stories." It contained "The Train," which would later, and in a different version, become the opening chapter of a novel.

The novel was called *Wise Blood* and appeared in 1952. Set in the South and portraying poor, white fundamentalists, the book led readers to expect comedy, satire, or scathing exposure. Their expectations of comedy were not disappointed, as the novel presented grotesque characters behaving in absurd ways. But they were surprised to discover that O'Connor's satiric thrusts were aimed not at the religious fanatics but at the comfort-seeking nonbelievers. The reader's sympathies were finally destined to come down on the side of the hero, Hazel Motes, who, though in flight from Christ at the beginning, ended up recognizing that he was "unclean," in need of God's grace, and seeking atonement in the only fundamentalist ways he knew—by blinding himself, putting broken glass in his shoes, and wrapping his chest with barbed wire. Because the novel was so often misunderstood, O'Connor described it in a brief Preface when it was reissued as "a comic novel about a Christian *malgré lui* [in spite of himself]."

Most of O'Connor's stories were to follow a similar pattern of concealed metamorphosis in unlikely characters, in which not only the readers but the characters themselves were confronted by the mystery of interior change they could not always detect nor, when detected, fully comprehend. Her first book of short stories, *A Good Man Is Hard to Find* (1955), exhibited elements of this pattern in the title story as well as in such other impressive stories as "The River," "The Life You Save May Be Your Own," and "Good Country People."

O'Connor's second novel, *The Violent Bear It Away* (1960), portrayed the struggle between a backwoods preacher-prophet and his citified, accommodationist nephew over the soul of a young skeptic; the young man's belief in the reality of evil came in a casual but chilling encounter with the devil in the form of a driver who picked him up, drugged, and raped him. Similar characters and situations appeared in the stories of *Everything That Rises Must Converge,* published in 1965. But there was in these later stories a diminishment in the comic tone if not in power. By the time this volume appeared, Flannery O'Connor had died—in August 1964—of a disease she discovered she had in 1950, "disseminated lupus." She was thirty-nine years old.

With the publication of a volume of O'Connor's essays in 1969, *Mystery and Manners,* readers were able to pick up many pointers from her as to how to read her work. One vital element she made quite clear—"a sense of evil which sees the devil as a real spirit." She explained in "On Her Own Work": "From my own experience in trying to make stories 'work,' I have discovered that what is needed is an action that is totally unexpected, yet totally believable, and I have found that, for me, this is always an action which indicates that grace has been offered. And frequently it is an action in which the devil has been the unwilling instrument of grace. This is not a piece of knowledge that I consciously put into my stories; it is a discovery that I get out of them."

O'Connor saw her situation not as isolated but as representative of that of any writer committed to a set of beliefs. In a kind of credo that she wrote in "The Church and the Fiction Writer," O'Connor stated: "What the fiction writer will discover, if he discovers anything at all, is that he himself cannot move or mold reality in the interests of abstract truth. The writer learns, perhaps more quickly than the reader, to be humble in the fact of what-is. What-is is all he has to do with; the concrete is his medium; and he will realize eventually that fiction can transcend its limitations only by staying within them."

ADDITIONAL READING

Flannery O'Connor: Mystery and Manners, Occasional Prose, ed. Sally and Robert Fitzgerald, 1969; *The Habit of Being: Letters of Flannery O'Connor,* ed. Sally Fitzgerald, 1979; *The Presence of Grace and Other Book Reviews,* ed. Leo J. Zuber and Carter W. Martin, 1983; *Conversations with Flannery O'Connor,* ed. Rosemary M. Magee, 1987; *Collected Works by Flannery O'Connor,* ed. Sally Fitzgerald, 1989.

Stanley Edgar Hyman, *Flannery O'Connor,* 1966; Melvin J. Friedman and Lewis A. Lawson, eds., *The Added Dimension: The Art and Mind of Flannery O'Connor,* 1966, 1977; Carter W. Martin, *The True Country: Themes in the Fiction of Flannery O'Connor,* 1969; Josephine Hendin, *The World of Flannery O'Connor,* 1970; Leon V. Driskell and Joan T. Brittain, *The Eternal Crossroads: The Art of Flannery O'Connor,* 1971; David Eggenschwiler, *The Christian Humanism of Flannery O'Connor,* 1972; Sister M. Kathleen Feeley, S.S.N.D., *Flannery O'Connor: Voice of the Peacock,* 1972; Gilbert H. Muller, *Nightmares and Visions: Flannery O'Connor and the Catholic Grotesque,* 1972; Miles Orvell, *Invisible Parade: The Fiction of Flannery O'Connor,* 1972; Dorothy Walters, *Flannery O'Connor,* 1973; Martha Stephens, *The Question of Flannery O'Connor,* 1973; Preston M. Browning, Jr., *Flannery O'Connor,* 1974; John R. May, *The Pruning Word: The Parables of Flannery O'Connor,* 1976; Dorothy Tuck McFarland, *Flannery O'Connor,* 1976; Robert E. Golden and Mary C. Sullivan, *Flannery O'Connor and Caroline Gordon: A Reference Guide,* 1977; Carol Shloss, *Flannery O'Connor's Dark Comedies,* 1980; Robert Coles, *Flannery O'Connor's South,* 1980; Barbara McKenzie, *Flannery O'Connor's Georgia,* 1980; David Farmer, *Flannery O'Connor: A Descriptive Bibliography,* 1981; James A. Grimshaw, Jr., *The Flannery O'Connor Companion,* 1981; Frederick Asals, *Flannery O'Connor: The Imagination of Extremity,* 1982; Lorine M. Getz, *Nature and Grace in Flannery O'Connor's Fiction,* 1982; Arthur F. Kinney, *Flannery O'Connor's Library: Resources of Being,* 1985; Melvin J. Freidman and Beverly Lyon Clark, eds., *Critical Essays on Flannery O'Connor,* 1985; Marshall Bruce Gentry, *Flannery O'Connor's Religion of the Grotesque,* 1986; Edward Kessler, *Flannery O'Connor and the Language of Apocalypse,* 1986; Louis Welting, *Sacred Groves and Ravaged Gardens: The Fiction of Eudora Welty, Carson McCullers, and Flannery O'Connor,* 1986; John F. Desmond, *Risen Sons: Flannery O'Connor's Vision of History,* 1987; Karl-Heinz Westarp and Jan Nordby Gretlund, eds., intro. Sally Fitzgerald, *Realist of Distances: Flannery O'Connor Revisited,* 1987; Jill P. Baumgaertner, *Flannery O'Connor: A Proper Scaring,* 1988; Suzanne Morrow Paulson, *Flannery O'Connor: A Study of the Short Fiction,* 1988; Brian Abel Ragen, *A Wreck on the Road to Damascus: Innocence, Guilt, and Conversion in Flannery O'Connor,* 1989; Robert H. Brinkmeyer, Jr., *The Art and Vision of Flannery O'Connor,* 1990.

TEXT

Flannery O'Connor: The Complete Stories, 1971.

Good Country People

Besides the neutral expression that she wore when she was alone, Mrs. Freeman had two others, forward and reverse, that she used for all her human dealings. Her forward expression was steady and driving like the advance of a heavy truck. Her eyes never swerved to left or right but turned as the story turned as if they followed a yellow line down the center of it. She seldom used the other expression because it was not often necessary for her to retract a statement, but when she did, her face came to a complete stop, there was an almost imperceptible movement of her black eyes, during which they seemed to be receding, and then the observer would see that Mrs. Freeman, though she might stand there as real as several grain sacks thrown on top of each other, was no longer there in spirit. As for getting anything across to her when this was the case, Mrs. Hopewell had given it up. She might talk her head off. Mrs. Freeman could never be brought to admit herself wrong on any point. She would stand there and if she could be brought to say anything, it was something like, "Well, I wouldn't of said it was and I wouldn't have said it wasn't," or letting her gaze range over the top kitchen shelf where there was an assortment of dusty bottles, she might remark, "I see you ain't ate many of them figs you put up last summer."

They carried on their most important business in the kitchen at breakfast. Every morning Mrs. Hopewell got up at seven o'clock and lit her gas heater and Joy's. Joy was her daughter, a large blonde girl who had an artificial leg. Mrs. Hopewell thought of her as a child though she was thirty-two years old and highly educated. Joy would get up while her mother was eating and lumber into the bathroom and slam the door, and before long, Mrs. Freeman would arrive at the back door. Joy would hear her mother call, "Come on in," and then they would talk for a while in low voices that were indistinguishable in the bathroom. By the time Joy came in, they had usually finished the weather report and were on one or the other of Mrs. Freeman's daughters, Glynese or Carramae, Joy called them Glycerin and Caramel. Glynese, a redhead, was eighteen and had many admirers; Carramae, a blonde, was only fifteen but already married and pregnant. She could not keep anything on her stomach. Every morning Mrs. Freeman told Mrs. Hopewell how many times she had vomited since the last report.

Mrs. Hopewell liked to tell people that Glynese and Carramae were two of the finest girls she knew and that Mrs. Freeman was a *lady* and that she was never ashamed to take her anywhere or introduce her to anybody they might meet. Then she would tell how she had happened to hire the Freemans in the first place and how they were a godsend to her and how she had had them four years. The reason for her keeping them so long was that they were not trash. They were good country people. She had telephoned the man whose name they had given as a reference and he had told her that Mr. Freeman was a good farmer but that his wife was the nosiest woman ever to walk the earth. "She's got to be into everything," the man said. "If she don't get there before the dust settles, you can bet she's dead, that's all. She'll want to know all your business. I can stand him real good," he had said, "but me nor my wife neither could have stood that woman one minute more on this place." That had put Mrs. Hopewell off for a few days.

She had hired them in the end because there were no other applicants but she had made up her mind beforehand exactly how she would handle the woman. Since she was the type who had to be into everything, then, Mrs. Hopewell had decided, she would not only let her be into everything, she would *see to it* that she was into every-thing—she would give her the responsibility of everything, she would put her in charge. Mrs. Hopewell had no bad qualities of her own but she was able to use other people's in such a constructive way that she never felt the lack. She had hired the Freemans and she had kept them four years.

Nothing is perfect. This was one of Mrs. Hopewell's favorite sayings. Another was: that is life! And still another, the most important was: well, other people have their opinions too. She would make these statements, usually at the table, in a tone of gentle insistence as if no one held them but her, and the large hulking Joy, whose constant outrage had obliterated every expression from her face, would stare just a little to the side of her, her eyes icy blue, with the look of someone who has achieved blindness by an act of will and means to keep it.

When Mrs. Hopewell said to Mrs. Freeman that life was like that, Mrs. Freeman would say, "I always said so myself." Nothing had been arrived at by anyone that had not first been arrived at by her. She was quicker than Mr. Freeman. When Mrs. Hopewell said to her after they had been on the place a while, "You know, you're the wheel behind the wheel," and winked, Mrs. Freeman had said, "I know it. I've always been quick. It's some that are quicker than others."

"Everybody is different," Mrs. Hopewell said.

"Yes, most people is," Mrs. Freeman said.

"It takes all kinds to make the world."

"I always said it did myself."

The girl was used to this kind of dialogue for breakfast and more of it for dinner; sometimes they had it for supper too. When they had no guest they ate in the kitchen because that was easier. Mrs. Freeman always managed to arrive at some point during the meal and to watch them finish it. She would stand in the doorway if it were summer but in the winter she would stand with one elbow on top of the refrigerator and look down on them, or she would stand by the gas heater, lifting the back of her skirt slightly. Occasionally she would stand against the wall and roll her head from side to side. At no time was she in any hurry to leave. All this was very trying on Mrs. Hopewell but she was a woman of great patience. She realized that nothing is perfect and that in the Freemans she had good country people and that if, in this day and age, you get good country people, you had better hang onto them.

She had plenty of experience with trash. Before the Freemans she had averaged one tenant family a year. The wives of these farmers were not the kind you would want to be around you for very long. Mrs. Hopewell, who had divorced her husband long ago, needed someone to walk over the fields with her; and when Joy had to be impressed for these services, her remarks were usually so ugly and her face so glum that Mrs. Hopewell would say, "If you can't come pleasantly, I don't want you at all," to which the girl, standing square and rigid-shouldered with her neck thrust slightly forward would reply, "If you want me, here I am—LIKE I AM."

Mrs. Hopewell excused this attitude because of the leg (which had been shot off in a hunting accident when Joy was ten). It was hard for Mrs. Hopewell to realize that her child was thirty-two now and that for more than twenty years she had had only one leg. She thought of her still as a child because it tore her heart to think instead of the poor stout girl in her thirties who had never danced a step or had any *normal* good times. Her name was really Joy but as soon as she was twenty-one and away from home, she had had it legally changed. Mrs. Hopewell was certain that she had thought and thought until she had hit upon the ugliest name in any language. Then she had gone and had the beautiful name, Joy, changed without telling her mother until after she had done it. Her legal name was Hulga.

When Mrs. Hopewell thought the name, Hulga, she thought of the broad blank hull of a battleship. She would not use it. She continued to call her Joy to which the girl responded but in a purely mechanical way.

Hulga had learned to tolerate Mrs. Freeman who saved her from taking walks with her mother. Even Glynese and Carramae were useful when they occupied attention that might otherwise have been directed at her. At first she had thought she could not stand Mrs. Freeman for she had found that it was not possible to be rude to her. Mrs. Freeman would take on strange resentments and for days together she would be sullen but the source of her displeasure was always obscure; a direct attack, a positive leer, blatant ugliness to her face—these never touched her. And without warning one day, she began calling her Hulga.

She did not call her that in front of Mrs. Hopewell who would have been incensed but when she and the girl happened to be out of the house together, she would say something and add the name Hulga to the end of it, and the big spectacled Joy-Hulga would scowl and redden as if her privacy had been intruded upon. She considered the name her personal affair. She had arrived at it first purely on the basis of its ugly sound and then the full genius of its fitness had struck her. She had a vision of the name working like the ugly sweating Vulcan[1] who stayed in the furnace and to whom, presumably, the goddess had to come when called. She saw it as the name of her highest creative act. One of her major triumphs was that her mother had not been able to turn her dust into Joy, but the greater one was that she had been able to turn it herself into Hulga. However, Mrs. Freeman's relish for using the name only irritated her. It was as if Mrs. Freeman's beady steel-pointed eyes had penetrated far enough behind her face to reach some secret fact. Something about her seemed to fascinate Mrs. Freeman and then one day Hulga realized that it was the artificial leg. Mrs. Freeman had a special fondness for the details of secret infections, hidden deformities, assaults upon children. Of diseases, she preferred the lingering or incurable. Hulga had heard Mrs. Hopewell give her the details of the hunting accident, how the leg had been literally blasted off, how she had never lost consciousness. Mrs. Freeman could listen to it any time as if it had happened an hour ago.

When Hulga stumped into the kitchen in the morning (she could walk without making the awful noise but she made it — Mrs. Hopewell was certain — because it was ugly sounding), she glanced at them and did not speak. Mrs. Hopewell would be in her red kimono with her hair tied around her head in rags. She would be sitting at the table, finishing her breakfast and Mrs. Freeman would be hanging by her elbow outward from the refrigerator, looking down at the table. Hulga always put her eggs on the stove to boil and then stood over them with her arms folded, and Mrs. Hopewell would look at her — a kind of indirect gaze divided between her and Mrs. Freeman — and would think that if she would only keep herself up a little, she wouldn't be so bad looking. There was nothing wrong with her face that a pleasant expression wouldn't help. Mrs. Hopewell said that people who looked on the bright side of things would be beautiful even if they were not.

Whenever she looked at Joy this way, she could not help but feel that it would have been better if the child had not taken the Ph.D. It had certainly not brought her out any and now that she had it, there was no more excuse for her to go to school again. Mrs. Hopewell thought it was nice for girls to go to school to have a good time but Joy had "gone through." Anyhow, she would not have been strong enough to go again. The doctors had told Mrs. Hopewell that with the best of care, Joy might see forty-five. She had a weak heart. Joy had made it plain that if it had not been for this condition, she would be far from these red hills and good country people. She would be in a university lecturing to people who knew what she was talking about. And Mrs. Hopewell could very well picture her there, looking like a scarecrow and lecturing to more of the same. Here she went about all day in a six-year-old skirt and a yellow sweat shirt with a faded cowboy on a horse embossed on it. She thought this was funny; Mrs. Hopewell thought it was idiotic and showed simply that she was still a child. She was brilliant but she didn't have a grain of sense. It seemed to Mrs. Hopewell that every year she grew less like other people and more like herself — bloated, rude, and squint-eyed. And she said such strange things! To her own mother she had said — without warning, without excuse, standing up in the middle of a meal with her face purple and her mouth half full — "Woman! do you ever look inside? Do you ever look inside and see what you are *not*? God!" she had cried sinking down again and staring at her plate, "Malebranche[2] was right: we are not our own light. We are not our own light!" Mrs. Hopewell had no idea to this day what brought that on. She had only made the remark, hoping Joy would take it in, that a smile never hurt anyone.

The girl had taken the Ph.D. in philosophy and this left Mrs. Hopewell at a complete loss. You could say, "My daughter is a nurse," or "My daughter is a school-

---

[1]Roman fire-god, consort of Venus, goddess of love.
[2]Nicolas de Malebranche (1638–1715), French philosopher and religious thinker who believed that the mind could not have any knowledge external to itself except through God.

teacher," or even, "My daughter is a chemical engineer." You could not say, "My daughter is a philosopher." That was something that had ended with the Greeks and Romans. All day Joy sat on her neck in a deep chair, reading. Sometimes she went for walks but she didn't like dogs or cats or birds or flowers or nature or nice young men. She looked at nice young men as if she could smell their stupidity.

One day Mrs. Hopewell had picked up one of the books the girl had just put down and opening it at random, she read, "Science, on the other hand, has to assert its soberness and seriousness afresh and declare that it is concerned solely with what-is. Nothing—how can it be for science anything but a horror and a phantasm? If science is right, then one thing stands firm: science wishes to know nothing of nothing. Such is after all the strictly scientific approach to Nothing. We know it by wishing to know nothing of Nothing." These words had been underlined with a blue pencil and they worked on Mrs. Hopewell like some evil incantation in gibberish. She shut the book quickly and went out of the room as if she were having a chill.

This morning when the girl came in, Mrs. Freeman was on Carramae. "She thrown up four times after supper," she said, "and was up twict in the night after three o'clock. Yesterday she didn't do nothing but ramble in the bureau drawer. All she did. Stand up there and see what she could run up on."

"She's got to eat," Mrs. Hopewell muttered, sipping her coffee, while she watched Joy's back at the stove. She was wondering what the child had said to the Bible salesman. She could not imagine what kind of a conversation she could possibly have had with him.

He was a tall gaunt hatless youth who had called yesterday to sell them a Bible. He had appeared at the door, carrying a large black suitcase that weighted him so heavily on one side that he had to brace himself against the door facing. He seemed on the point of collapse but he said in a cheerful voice. "Good morning, Mrs. Cedars!" and set the suitcase down on the mat. He was not a bad-looking young man though he had on a bright blue suit and yellow socks that were not pulled up far enough. He had prominent face bones and a streak of sticky-looking brown hair falling across his forehead.

"I'm Mrs. Hopewell," she said.

"Oh!" he said, pretending to look puzzled but with his eyes sparkling. "I saw it said 'The Cedars' on the mailbox so I thought you was Mrs. Cedars!" and he burst out in a pleasant laugh. He picked up the satchel and under cover of a pant, he fell forward into her hall. It was rather as if the suitcase had moved first, jerking him after it. "Mrs. Hopewell!" he said and grabbed her hand. "I hope you are well!" and he laughed again and then all at once his face sobered completely. He paused and gave her a straight earnest look and said, "Lady, I've come to speak of serious things."

"Well, come in," she muttered, none too pleased because her dinner was almost ready. He came into the parlor and sat down on the edge of a straight chair and put the suitcase between his feet and glanced around the room as if he was sizing her up by it. Her silver gleamed on the two sideboards; she decided he had never been in a room as elegant as this.

"Mrs. Hopewell," he began, using her name in a way that sounded almost intimate, "I know you believe in Chrustian service."

"Well yes," she murmured.

"I know," he said and paused, looking very wise with his head cocked on one side, "that you're a good woman. Friends have told me."

Mrs. Hopewell never liked to be taken for a fool. "What are you selling?" she asked.

"Bibles," the young man said and his eye raced around the room before he added, "I see you have no family Bible in your parlor, I see that is the one lack you got!"

Mrs. Hopewell could not say, "My daughter is an atheist and won't let me keep the Bible in the parlor." She said, stiffening slightly, "I keep my Bible by my bedside." This was not the truth. It was in the attic somewhere.

"Lady," he said, "the word of God ought to be in the parlor."

"Well, I think that's a matter of taste," she began. "I think . . ."

"Lady," he said, "for a Chrustian, the word of God ought to be in every room in the house besides in his heart. I know you're a Chrustian because I can see it in every line of your face."

She stood up and said, "Well, young man, I don't want to buy a Bible and I smell my dinner burning.

He didn't get up. He began to twist his hands and looking down at them, he said softly, "Well lady, I'll tell you the truth—not many people want to buy one nowadays and besides, I know I'm real simple. I don't know how to say a thing but to say it. I'm just a country boy." He glanced up into her unfriendly face. "People like you don't like to fool with country people like me!"

"Why!" she cried, "good country people are the salt of the earth! Besides, we all have different ways of doing, it takes all kinds to make the world go 'round. That's life!"

"You said a mouthful," he said.

"Why, I think there aren't enough good country people in the world!" she said, stirred. "I think that's what's wrong with it!"

His face had brightened. "I didn't inraduce myself," he said. "I'm Manley Pointer from out in the country around Willohobie, not even from a place, just near a place."

"You wait a minute," she said. "I have to see about my dinner." She went out to the kitchen and found Joy standing near the door where she had been listening.

"Get rid of the salt of the earth," she said, "and let's eat."

Mrs. Hopewell gave her a pained look and turned the heat down under the vegetables. "*I* can't be rude to anybody," she murmured and went back into the parlor.

He had opened the suitcase and was sitting with a Bible on each knee.

"You might as well put those up," she told him. "I don't want one."

"I appreciate your honesty," he said. "You don't see any more real honest people unless you go way out in the country."

"I know," she said, "real genuine folks!" Through the crack in the door she heard a groan.

"I guess a lot of boys come telling you they're working their way through college," he said, "but I'm not going to tell you that. Somehow," he said, "I don't want to go to college. I want to devote my life to Chrustian service. See," he said, lowering his voice, "I got this heart condition. I may not live long. When you know it's something wrong with you and you may not live long, well then, lady . . ." He paused, with his mouth open, and stared at her.

He and Joy had the same condition! She knew that her eyes were filling with tears but she collected herself quickly and murmured, "Won't you stay for dinner? We'd love to have you!" and was sorry the instant she heard herself say it.

"Yes mam," he said in an abashed voice, "I would sher love to do that!"

Joy had given him one look on being introduced to him and then throughout the meal had not glanced at him again. He had addressed several remarks to her, which she had pretended not to hear. Mrs. Hopewell could not understand deliberate rudeness, although she lived with it, and she felt she had always to overflow with hospitality to make up for Joy's lack of courtesy. She urged him to talk about himself and he did. He said he was the seventh child of twelve and that his father had been crushed under a tree when he himself was eight year old. He had been crushed very badly, in fact, almost cut in two and was practically not recognizable. His mother had got along the best she could by hard working and she had always seen that her children went to Sunday School and that they read the Bible every evening. He was now nineteen year old and he had been selling Bibles for four months. In that time he had sold seventy-seven Bibles and had the promise of two more sales. He wanted to become a missionary because he thought that was the way you could do most for people. "He who losest his life shall find it," he said simply and he was so sincere, so genuine and earnest that Mrs. Hopewell would not for the world have smiled. He prevented his peas from sliding onto the table by blocking them with a piece of bread which he later cleaned his plate with. She could see Joy observing sidewise how he handled his knife and fork and she saw too that every few minutes, the boy would dart a keen appraising glance at the girl as if he were trying to attract her attention.

After dinner Joy cleared the dishes off the table and disappeared and Mrs. Hopewell was left to talk with him. He told her again about his childhood and his father's accident and about various things that had happened to him. Every five minutes or so she would stifle a yawn. He sat for two hours until finally she told him she must go because she had an appointment in town. He packed his Bibles and thanked her and prepared to leave, but in the doorway he stopped and wrung her hand and said that not on any of his trips had he met a lady as nice as her and he asked if he could come again. She had said she would always be happy to see him.

Joy had been standing in the road, apparently looking at something in the distance, when he came down the steps toward her, bent to the side with his heavy valise. He stopped where she was standing and confronted her directly. Mrs. Hopewell could not hear what he said but she trembled to think what Joy would say to him. She could see that after a minute Joy said something and that then the boy began to speak again, making an excited gesture with his free hand. After a minute Joy said something else at which the boy began to speak once more. Then to her amazement, Mrs. Hopewell saw the two of them walk off together, toward the gate. Joy had walked all the way to the gate with him and Mrs. Hopewell could not imagine what they had said to each other, and she had not yet dared to ask.

Mrs. Freeman was insisting upon her attention. She had moved from the refrigerator to the heater so that Mrs. Hopewell had to turn and face her in order to seem to be listening. "Glynese gone out with Harvey Hill again last night," she said. "She had this sty."

"Hill," Mrs. Hopewell said absently, "is that the one who works in the garage?"

"Nome, he's the one that goes to chiropracter school," Mrs. Freeman said. "She had this sty. Been had it two days. So she says when he brought her in the other night he says, 'Lemme get rid of that sty for you,' and she says, 'How?' and he says, 'You just lay yourself down acrost the seat of that car and I'll show you.' So she done it and he popped her neck. Kept on a-popping it several times until she made him quit. This morning," Mrs. Freeman said, "she ain't got no sty. She ain't got no traces of a sty."

"I never heard of that before," Mrs. Hopewell said.

"He ast her to marry him before the Ordinary,"[3] Mrs. Freeman went on, "and she told him she wasn't going to be married in no *office*."

"Well, Glynese is a fine girl," Mrs. Hopewell said. "Glynese and Carramae are both fine girls."

"Carramae said when her and Lyman was married Lyman said it sure felt sacred to him. She said he said he wouldn't take five hundred dollars for being married by a preacher."

"How much would he take?" the girl asked from the stove.

"He said he wouldn't take five hundred dollars," Mrs. Freeman repeated.

"Well we all have work to do," Mrs. Hopewell said.

"Lyman said it just felt more sacred to him," Mrs. Freeman said. "The doctor wants Carramae to eat prunes. Says instead of medicine. Says them cramps is coming from pressure. You know where I think it is?"

"She'll be better in a few weeks," Mrs. Hopewell said.

"In the tube," Mrs. Freeman said. "Else she wouldn't be as sick as she is."

---

[3]A justice of the peace prepared to perform civil marriages.

Hulga had cracked her two eggs into a saucer and was bringing them to the table along with a cup of coffee that she had filled too full. She sat down carefully and began to eat, meaning to keep Mrs. Freeman there by questions if for any reason she showed an inclination to leave. She could perceive her mother's eye on her. The first round-about question would be about the Bible salesman and she did not wish to bring it on. "How did he pop her neck?" she asked.

Mrs. Freeman went into a description of how he had popped her neck. She said he owned a '55 Mercury but that Glynese said she would rather marry a man with only a '36 Plymouth who would be married by a preacher. The girl asked what if he had a '32 Plymouth and Mrs. Freeman said what Glynese had said was a '36 Plymouth.

Mrs. Hopewell said there were not many girls with Glynese's common sense. She said what she admired in those girls was their common sense. She said that reminded her that they had had a nice visitor yesterday, a young man selling Bibles. "Lord," she said, "he bored me to death but he was so sincere and genuine I couldn't be rude to him. He was just good country people, you know," she said, "—just the salt of the earth."

"I seen him walk up," Mrs. Freeman said, "and then later—I seen him walk off," and Hulga could feel the slight shift in her voice, the slight insinuation, that he had not walked off alone, had he? Her face remained expressionless but the color rose into her neck and she seemed to swallow it down with the next spoonful of egg. Mrs. Freeman was looking at her as if they had a secret together.

"Well, it takes all kinds of people to make the world go 'round," Mrs. Hopewell said. "It's very good we aren't all alike."

"Some people are more alike than others," Mrs. Freeman said.

Hulga got up and stumped, with about twice the noise that was necessary, into her room and locked the door. She was to meet the Bible salesman at ten o'clock at the gate. She had thought about it half the night. She had started thinking of it as a great joke and then she had begun to see profound implications in it. She had lain in bed imagining dialogues for them that were insane on the surface but that reached below to depths that no Bible salesman would be aware of. Their conversation yesterday had been of this kind.

He had stopped in front of her and had simply stood there. His face was bony and sweaty and bright, with a little pointed nose in the center of it, and his look was different from what it had been at the dinner table. He was gazing at her with open curiosity, with fascination, like a child watching a new fantastic animal at the zoo, and he was breathing as if he had run a great distance to reach her. His gaze seemed somehow familiar but she could not think where she had been regarded with it before. For almost a minute he didn't say anything. Then on what seemed an insuck of breath, he whispered, "You ever ate a chicken that was two days old?"

The girl looked at him stonily. He might have just put this question up for consideration at the meeting of a philosophical association. "Yes," she presently replied as if she had considered it from all angles.

"It must have been mighty small!" he said triumphantly and shook all over with little nervous giggles, getting very red in the face, and subsiding finally into his gaze of complete admiration, while the girl's expression remained exactly the same.

"How old are you?" he asked softly.

"She waited some time before she answered. Then in a flat voice she said, "Seventeen."

His smiles came in succession like waves breaking on the surface of a little lake. "I see you got a wooden leg," he said. "I think you're brave. I think you're real sweet."

The girl stood blank and solid and silent.

"Walk to the gate with me," he said. "You're a brave sweet little thing and I liked you the minute I seen you walk in the door."

Hulga began to move forward.

"What's your name?" he asked, smiling down on the top of her head.

"Hulga," she said.

"Hulga," he murmured, "Hulga. Hulga. I never heard of anybody name Hulga before. You're shy, aren't you, Hulga?" he asked.

She nodded, watching his large red hand on the handle of the giant valise.

"I like girls that wear glasses," he said. "I think a lot. I'm not like these people that a serious thought don't ever enter their heads. It's because I may die."

"I may die too," she said suddenly and looked up at him. His eyes were very small and brown, glittering feverishly.

"Listen," he said, "don't you think some people was meant to meet on account of what all they got in common and all? Like they both think serious thoughts and all?" He shifted the valise to his other hand so that the hand nearest her was free. He caught hold of her elbow and shook it a little. "I don't work on Saturday," he said. "I like to walk in the woods and see what Mother Nature is wearing. O'er the hills and far away. Pic-nics and things. Couldn't we go on a pic-nic tomorrow? Say yes, Hulga," he said and gave her a dying look as if he felt his insides about to drop out of him. He had even seemed to sway slightly toward her.

During the night she had imagined that she seduced him. She imagined that the two of them walked on the place until they came to the storage barn beyond the two back fields and there, she imagined, that things came to such a pass that she very easily seduced him and that then, of course, she had to reckon with his remorse. True genius can get an idea across even to an inferior mind. She imagined that she took his remorse in hand and changed it into a deeper understanding of life. She took all his shame away and turned it into something useful.

She set off for the gate at exactly ten o'clock, escaping without drawing Mrs. Hopewell's attention. She didn't take anything to eat, forgetting that food is usually taken on a picnic. She wore a pair of slacks and a dirty white shirt, and as an afterthought, she had put some Vapex on the collar of it since she did not own any perfume. When she reached the gate no one was there.

She looked up and down the empty highway and had the furious feeling that she had been tricked, that he had only meant to make her walk to the gate after the idea of him. Then suddenly he stood up, very tall, from behind a bush on the opposite embankment. Smiling, he lifted his hat which was new and wide-brimmed. He had not worn it yesterday and she wondered if he had bought it for the occasion. It was toast-colored with a red and white band around it and was slightly too large for him. He stepped from behind the bush still carrying the black valise. He had on the same suit and the same yellow socks sucked down in his shoes from walking. He crossed the highway and said, "I knew you'd come!"

The girl wondered acidly how he had known this. She pointed to the valise and asked, "Why did you bring your Bibles?"

He took her elbow, smiling down on her as if he could not stop. "You can never tell when you'll need the word of God, Hulga," he said. She had a moment in which she doubted that this was actually happening and then they began to climb the embankment. They went down into the pasture toward the woods. The boy walked lightly by her side, bouncing on his toes. The valise did not seem to be heavy today; he even swung it. They crossed half the pasture without saying anything and then, putting his hand easily on the small of her back, he asked softly, "Where does your wooden leg join on?"

She turned an ugly red and glared at him and for an instant the boy looked abashed. "I didn't mean you no harm," he said. "I only meant you're so brave and all. I guess God takes care of you."

"No," she said, looking forward and walking fast, "I don't even believe in God."

At this he stopped and whistled. "No!" he exclaimed as if he were too astonished to say anything else.

She walked on and in a second he was bouncing at her side, fanning with his hat. "That's very unusual for a girl," he remarked, watching her out of the corner of his eye. When they reached the edge of the wood, he put his hand on her back again and drew her against him without a word and kissed her heavily.

The kiss, which had more pressure than feeling behind it, produced that extra surge of adrenalin in the girl that enables one to carry a packed trunk out of a burning house, but in her, the power went at once to the brain. Even before he released her, her mind, clear and detached and ironic anyway, was regarding him from a great distance, with amusement but with pity. She had never been kissed before and she was pleased to discover that it was an unexceptional experience and all a matter of the mind's control. Some people might enjoy drain water if they were told it was vodka. When the boy, looking expectant but uncertain, pushed her gently away, she turned and walked on, saying nothing as if such business, for her, were common enough.

He came along panting at her side, trying to help her when he saw a root that she might trip over. He caught and held back the long swaying blades of thorn vine until she had passed beyond them. She led the way and he came breathing heavily behind her. Then they came out on a sunlit hillside, sloping softly into another one a little smaller. Beyond, they could see the rusted top of the old barn where the extra hay was stored.

The hill was sprinkled with small pink weeds. "Then you ain't saved?" he asked suddenly, stopping.

The girl smiled. It was the first time she had smiled at him at all. "In my economy," she said, "I'm saved and you are damned but I told you I didn't believe in God."

Nothing seemed to destroy the boy's look of admiration. He gazed at her now as if the fantastic animal at the zoo had put its paw through the bars and given him a loving poke. She thought he looked as if he wanted to kiss her again and she walked on before he had the chance.

"Ain't there somewheres we can sit down sometime?" he murmured, his voice softening toward the end of the sentence.

"In that barn," she said.

They made for it rapidly as if it might slide away like a train. It was a large two-story barn, cool and dark inside. The boy pointed up the ladder that led into the loft and said, "It's too bad we can't go up there."

"Why can't we?" she asked.

"Yer leg," he said reverently.

The girl gave him a contemptuous look and putting both hands on the ladder, she climbed it while he stood below, apparently awestruck. She pulled herself expertly through the opening and then looked down at him and said, "Well, come on if you're coming," and he began to climb the ladder, awkwardly bringing the suitcase with him.

"We won't need the Bible," she observed.

"You never can tell," he said, panting. After he had got into the loft, he was a few seconds catching his breath. She had sat down in a pile of straw. A wide sheath of sunlight, filled with dust particles, slanted over her. She lay back against a bale, her face turned away, looking out the front opening of the barn where hay was thrown from a wagon into the loft. The two pink-speckled hillsides lay back against a dark ridge of woods. The sky was cloudless and cold blue. The boy dropped down by her side and put one arm under her and the other over her and began methodically kissing her face, making little noises like a fish. He did not remove his hat but it was pushed far enough back not to interfere. When her glasses got in his way, he took them off of her and slipped them into his pocket.

The girl at first did not return any of the kisses but presently she began to and after she had put several on his cheek, she reached his lips and remained there, kissing him again and again as if she were trying to draw all the breath out of him. His breath was clear and sweet like a child's and the kisses were sticky like a child's. He mumbled about loving her and about knowing when he first seen her that he loved her, but the mumbling was like the sleepy fretting of a child being put to sleep by his mother. Her mind, throughout this, never stopped or lost itself for a second to her feelings. "You ain't said you loved me none," he whispered finally, pulling back from her. "You got to say that."

She looked away from him off into the hollow sky and then down at a black ridge and then down farther into what appeared to be two green swelling lakes. She didn't realize he had taken her glasses but this landscape could not seem exceptional to her for she seldom paid any close attention to her surroundings.

"You got to say it," he repeated. "You got to say you love me."

She was always careful how she committed herself. "In a sense," she began, "if you use the word loosely, you might say that. But it's not a word I use. I don't have illusions. I'm one of those people who see *through* to nothing."

The boy was frowning. "You got to say it. I said it and you got to say it," he said.

The girl looked at him almost tenderly. "You poor baby," she murmured. "It's just as well you don't understand," and she pulled him by the neck, face-down, against her. "We are all damned," she said, "but some of us have taken off our blindfolds and see that there's nothing to see. It's a kind of salvation."

The boy's astonished eyes looked blankly through the ends of her hair. "Okay," he almost whined, "but do you love me or don'tcher?"

"Yes," she said and added, "in a sense. But I must tell you something. There mustn't be anything dishonest between us." She lifted his head and looked him in the eye. "I am thirty years old," she said. "I have a number of degrees."

The boy's look was irritated but dogged. "I don't care," he said. "I don't care a thing about what all you done. I just want to know if you love me or don'tcher?" and he caught her to him and wildly planted her face with kisses until she said, "Yes, yes."

"Okay then," he said, letting her go. "Prove it."

She smiled, looking dreamily out on the shifty landscape. She had seduced him without even making up her mind to try. "How?" she asked, feeling that he should be delayed a little.

He leaned over and put his lips to her ear. "Show me where your wooden leg joins on," he whispered.

The girl uttered a sharp little cry and her face instantly drained of color. The obscenity of the suggestion was not what shocked her. As a child she had sometimes been subject to feelings of shame but education had removed the last traces of that as a good surgeon scrapes for cancer; she would no more have felt it over what he was asking than she would have believed in his Bible. But she was as sensitive about the artificial leg as a peacock about his tail. No one ever touched it but her. She took care of it as someone else would his soul, in private and almost with her own eyes turned away. "No," she said.

"I known it," he muttered, sitting up. "You're just playing me for a sucker."

"Oh no no!" she cried. "It joins on at the knee. Only at the knee. Why do you want to see it?"

The boy gave her a long penetrating look. "Because," he said, "it's what makes you different. You ain't like anybody else."

She sat staring at him. There was nothing about her face or her round freezing-blue eyes to indicate that this had moved her; but she felt as if her heart had stopped and left her mind to pump her blood. She decided that for the first time in her life she was face to face with real innocence. This boy, with an instinct that came from beyond wisdom, had touched the truth about her. When after a minute, she said in a hoarse high voice, "All right," it was like surrendering to him completely. It was like losing her own life and finding it again, miraculously, in his.

Very gently he began to roll the slack leg up. The artificial limb, in a white sock and brown flat shoe, was bound in a heavy material like canvas and ended in an ugly jointure where it was attached to the stump. They boy's face and his voice were entirely reverent as he uncovered it and said, "Now show me how to take it off and on."

She took it off for him and put it back on again and then he took it off himself, handling it as tenderly as if it were a real one. "See!" he said with a delighted child's face. "Now I can do it myself!"

"Put it back on." she said. She was thinking that she would run away with him and that every night he would take the leg off and every morning put it back on again. "Put it back on," she said.

"Not yet," he murmured, setting it on its foot out of her reach. "Leave it off for a while. You got me instead."

She gave a little cry of alarm but he pushed her down and began to kiss her again. Without the leg she felt entirely dependent on him. Her brain seemed to have stopped thinking altogether and to be about some other function that it was not very good at. Different expressions raced back and forth over her face. Every now and then the boy, his eyes like two steel spikes, would glance behind him where the leg stood. Finally she pushed him off and said, "Put it back on me now."

"Wait," he said. He leaned the other way and pulled the valise toward him and opened it. It had a pale blue spotted lining and there were only two Bibles in it. He took one of these out and opened the cover of it. It was hollow and contained a pocket flask of whiskey, a pack of cards, and a small blue box with printing on it. He laid these out in front of her one at a time in an evenly-spaced row, like one presenting offerings at the shrine of a goddess. He put the blue box in her hand. THIS PRODUCT TO BE USED ONLY FOR THE PREVENTION OF DISEASE, she read, and dropped it. The boy was unscrewing the top of the flask. He stopped and pointed, with a smile, to the deck of cards. It was not an ordinary deck but one with an obscene picture on the back of each card. "Take a swig," he said, offering her the bottle first. He held it in front of her, but like one mesmerized, she did not move.

Her voice when she spoke had an almost pleading sound. "Aren't you," she murmured, "aren't you just good country people?"

The boy cocked his head. He looked as if he were just beginning to understand that she might be trying to insult him. "Yeah," he said, curling his lip slightly, "but it ain't held me back none. I'm as good as you any day in the week."

"Give me my leg," she said.

He pushed it farther away with his foot. "Come on now, let's begin to have us a good time," he said coaxingly. "We ain't got to know one another good yet."

"Give me my leg!" she screamed and tried to lunge for it but he pushed her down easily.

"What's the matter with you all of a sudden?" he asked, frowning as he screwed the top on the flask and put it quickly back inside the Bible. "You just a while ago said you didn't believe in nothing. I thought you was some girl!"

Her face was almost purple. "You're a Christian!" she hissed. "You're a fine Christian! You're just like them all—say one thing and do another. You're a perfect Christian, you're . . ."

The boy's mouth was set angrily. "I hope you don't think," he said in a lofty indignant tone, "that I believe in that crap! I may sell Bibles but I know which end is up and I wasn't born yesterday and I know where I'm going!"

"Give me my leg!" she screeched. He jumped up so quickly that she barely saw him sweep the cards and the blue box into the Bible and throw the Bible into the valise. She saw him grab the leg and then she saw it for an instant slanted forlornly across the inside of the suitcase with a Bible at either side of its opposite ends. He slammed the lid shut and snatched up the valise and swung it down the hole and then stepped through himself.

When all of him had passed but his head, he turned and regarded her with a look that no longer had any admiration in it. "I've gotten a lot of interesting things," he said. "One time I got a woman's glass eye this way. And you needn't to think you'll catch me because Pointer ain't really my name. I use a different name at every house I call at and don't stay nowhere long. And I'll tell you another thing, Hulga," he said, using the name as if he didn't think much of it, "you ain't so smart. I been believing in nothing ever since I was born!" and then the toast-colored hat disappeared down the hole and the girl was left, sitting on the straw in the dusty sunlight. When she turned her churning face toward the opening, she saw his blue figure struggling successfully over the green speckled lake.

Mrs. Hopewell and Mrs. Freeman, who were in the back pasture, digging up onions, saw him emerge a little later from the woods and head across the meadow toward the highway. "Why, that looks like that nice dull young man that tried to sell me a Bible yesterday," Mrs. Hopewell said, squinting. "He must have been selling them to the Negroes back in there. He was so simple," he said, "but I guess the world would be better off if we were all that simple."

Mrs. Freeman's gaze drove forward and just touched him before he disappeared under the hill. Then she returned her attention to the evil-smelling onion shoot she was lifting from the ground. "Some can't be that simple," she said. " I know I never could."[4]

1955   1955

JOHN BARTH
(b. 1930)

John Barth has speculated more about the avant-garde in fiction than any other major novelist of this period. In "The Literature of Exhaustion," a highly influential essay published in 1967, he said:

> Our century is more than two-thirds done; it is dismaying to see so many of our writers following Dostoevsky or Tolstoy or Balzac, when the question seems to me to be how to succeed not even Joyce and Kafka, but those who *succeeded* Joyce and Kafka and are now in the evenings of their own careers. . . . Two of the finest live specimens that I know of [who are *au courant*] are Samuel Beckett and Jorge Luis Borges — with Vladimir Nabokov, just about the only contemporaries of my reading acquaintance mentionable with the 'old masters' of twentieth-century fiction. . . . One of the modern things about these two writers is that in an age of ultimacies and "final solutions" — at least *felt* ultimacies, in everything from weaponry to theology, the celebrated dehumanization of society, and the history of the novel — their work in separate ways reflects and deals with ultimacy, both technically and thematically.

This essay became so widely quoted — or misquoted — that Barth felt the necessity to offer a clarification and expansion of his ideas. He published "The

---

[4]Flannery O'Connor has made two useful comments on this story. From "Writing Short Stories," *Mystery and Manners*: "Early in the story, we're presented with the fact that the Ph.D. [Hulga] is spiritually as well as physically crippled. She believes in nothing but her own belief in nothing, and we perceive that there is a wooden part of her soul that corresponds to her wooden leg. Now of course this is never stated. The fiction writer states as little as possible. . . . As the story goes on, the wooden leg continues to accumulate meaning. The reader learns how the girl feels about her leg . . . and finally, by the time the Bible salesman comes along, the leg has accumulated so much meaning that it is, as the saying goes, loaded. And when the Bible salesman steals it, the reader realizes that he has taken away part of the girl's personality and has revealed her deeper affliction to her for the first time." From *Letters of Flannery O'Connor* (August 24, 1956): "[Hulga] is full of contempt for the Bible salesman until she finds he is full of contempt for her. Nothing 'comes to flower' here except her realization in the end that she ain't so smart. It's not said that she has never had any faith but it is implied that her fine education has got rid of it for her, that purity has been overridden by pride of intellect through her fine education."

Literature of Replenishment: Postmodernist Fiction" some twelve years later, in 1980, saying: "If the modernists, carrying the torch of romanticism, taught us that linearity, rationality, consciousness, cause and effect, naive illusionism, transparent language, innocent anecdote, and middle-class moral conventions are not the whole story, then from the perspective of these closing decades of our century we may appreciate that the contraries of those things are not the whole story either. Disjunction, simultaneity, irrationalism, anti-illusionism, self-reflexiveness, medium-as-message, political olympianism, and a moral pluralism approaching moral entropy—these are not the whole story either." Barth's proposal for the "whole story," on the surface, is simple: "A worthy program for postmodernist fiction, I believe, is the synthesis or transcension of these antitheses, which may be summed up as pre-modernist and modernist modes of writing." The result would be, Barth thought, "a fiction more democratic in its appeal."

It is possible that Barth wrote this last essay as much for his own instruction as for the instruction of others. He had won something of a popular audience in some of his earlier work, but by the late 1970s, when a number of reviewers of his books had become caustic, he may have felt the need to reexamine his theories.

Barth was born in 1930 into a middle class family in Cambridge, Maryland, where he graduated from high school in 1947. His ambitions were in music—he had played drums in high school—and he set out to attend the Juilliard School of Music in New York. After only a few months, however, he discovered that this career would be too expensive, and he entered Johns Hopkins University in the fall of 1947. He took his degree in 1951, holding the highest grade-average of any student in the College of Arts and Sciences. He entered the graduate program in creative writing, taking his Master's degree in 1952. Soon after, he began teaching composition at Pennsylvania State University, where he was to remain until his move to the University of New York in Buffalo in 1965. Eight years later, in 1973, he accepted a post (which he still holds) at Johns Hopkins University, which brought him back to his home state in the tidewater country of Maryland. By this time he was a famed, if controversial, novelist.

Barth planned to write his first three novels as a comic nihilistic trilogy. His first novel, *The Floating Opera* (1956), presents a character remembering in 1954 the day he planned to commit suicide back in 1937, deciding finally that although there was no reason to live, neither was there a final reason to die. Barth's second novel, *The End of the Road* (1958), portrays a struggle between a nihilist and a relativist for sexual dominance over the latter's wife, who died in a bungled abortion of a child whose father might have been either. By the time Barth came to his third novel, his style and form if not his themes changed radically. *The Sot-Weed Factor* (1960), over 800 pages long, is written in a leisurely eighteenth-century style, taking its title, subject, and characters from a poem about a British tobacco merchant's adventures in the New World written by the real Ebenezer Cooke and published in 1708. Barth remarked of his first three novels: "I thought I was writing about values and it turned out I was writing about innocence."

Barth's early work did not sell well, although it attracted favorable critical attention. His next novel, *Giles Goat-Boy; or, The Revised New Syllabus* (1966), was his first popular success. It is a combination of fantasy and allegory: a mega-university represents the universe; the East and West Campuses represent the two superpowers, the Soviet Union and the United States; and campus riots represent world wars. Some readers were charmed; others saw the work as satire run amuck, its inordinate length of 710 pages diminishing its effect. Barth published *Lost in the Funhouse,* a volume of interrelated stories, in 1968; the work throughout, and especially the title story, is persistently self-reflexive, and thus a work as much about the writing of fiction as anything else. In his National Book Award winner *Chimera* (1972), Barth presents three novellas relating stories of mythic figures of the past, but the subtext focus is again the problems of writing contemporary fiction.

In *Letters* (1979), Barth returned to the long novel (772 pages) that is not only unrelentingly self-reflexive but even (as some critics said) narcissistic in its interweaving of characters and fragments of action from all of Barth's previous novels. Reviewers tended to be skeptical, one of them suggesting that the book "seems to have been written for graduate students and other masochists." Two additional novels, *Sabbatical: A Romance* (1982) and *Tidewater Tales* (1987), the latter a blockbuster in length, suggested that Barth's direction, found in *The Sot-Weed Factor* and set in *Giles Goat-Boy,* would not deviate from the postmodernist mode, moving the "behind the scenes" strategies of fiction to front and center stage.

What one British reviewer said of *Tidewater Tales* might be said of any one of these works:

> It sits stubbornly on the map of modern American fiction as a gigantic, and memorable, construction, like Robert Rauschenberg's stuffed goat encircled by a rubber tyre or Claes Oldenburg's forty-foot-high clothes-peg. Barth is far closer in spirit to his American painter contemporaries than he is to the European and South American writers (like Calvino, Borges and García Márquez) to whom he doffs his cap in his work. Like the painters, he is broad of humour, fecund, slapdash; like them, he's an edge-of-the-frame man in a specifically American way, filling the space between high *ars* [art] and low *vita* [life] with rowdy games and spectacular fancies.

The self-skepticism of Barth's work is perhaps best exemplified by the comments of the "voice" of *Lost in the Funhouse* exclaiming with some contempt in the middle of the book: "The reader! You dogged, uninsultable, print-oriented bastard, it's you I'm addressing, who else, from inside this monstrous fiction. You've read me this far, then? Even this far? For what discreditable motive? How is it you don't go to a movie, watch TV, stare at a wall, play tennis with a friend, make amorous advances to the person who comes to your mind when I speak of amorous advances? Can nothing surfeit, saturate you, turn you off? Where's your shame?" Some readers might take one of the suggested alternatives seriously.

ADDITIONAL READING

The Friday Book: Essays and Other Nonfiction, 1984.

Gerhard Joseph, *John Barth,* 1970; John O. Stark, *The Literature of Exhaustion: Borges, Nabokov, Barth,* 1974; Jac Tharpe, *John Barth: The Comic Sublimity of Paradox,* 1974; Joseph Weixlmann, *John Barth: An Annotated Bibliography,* 1975; David Morrell, *John Barth: An Introduction,* 1976; Evelyn Glaser-Wohrer, *An Analysis of John Barth's Weltanschauung: His View of Life and Literature,* 1977; Richard A. Vine, *John Barth: An Annotated Bibliography,* 1977; Frank D. McConnell, *Four Postwar American Novelists: Bellow, Mailer, Barth, and Pynchon,* 1978; Charles B. Harris, *Passionate Virtuosity: The Fiction of John Barth,* 1983; Edward P. Walkiewicz, *John Barth,* 1986; Heide Ziegler, ed., *Facing Texts: Encounters Between Contemporary Writers and Critics,* 1988.

TEXT

Lost in the Funhouse, 1968.

Lost in the Funhouse

For whom is the funhouse fun? Perhaps for lovers. For Ambrose it is *a place of fear and confusion*. He has come to the seashore with his family for the holiday, *the occasion of their visit is Independence Day, the most important secular holiday of the United States of America*. A single straight underline is the manuscript mark for italic type, *which in turn* is the printed equivalent to oral emphasis of words and phrases as well as the customary type for titles of complete works, not to mention. Italics are also employed, in fiction stories especially, for "outside," intrusive, or artificial voices, such as radio announcements, the texts of telegrams and newspaper articles, et cetera. They should be used *sparingly*. If passages originally in roman type are italicized by someone repeating them, it's customary to acknowledge the fact. *Italics mine*.

Ambrose was "at that awkward age." His voice came out high-pitched as a child's if he let himself get carried away; to be on the safe side, therefore, he moved and spoke with *deliberate calm* and *adult gravity*. Talking soberly of unimportant or irrelevant matters and listening consciously to the sound of your own voice are useful habits for maintaining control in this difficult interval. *En route* to Ocean City he sat in the back seat of the family car with his brother Peter, age fifteen, and Magda G———, age fourteen, a pretty girl an exquisite young lady, who lived not far from them on B——— Street in the town of D———, Maryland. Initials, blanks, or both were often substituted for proper names in nineteenth-century fiction to enhance the illusion of reality. It is as if the author felt it necessary to delete the names for reasons of tact or legal liability. Interestingly, as with other aspects of realism, it is an *illusion* that is being enhanced, by purely artificial means. Is it likely, does it violate the principle of verisimilitude, that a thirteen-year-old boy could make such a sophisticated observation? A girl of fourteen is *the psychological coeval* of a boy of fifteen or sixteen; a thirteen-year old boy, therefore, even one precocious in some other respects, might be three years *her emotional junior*.

Thrice a year — on Memorial, Independence, and Labor Days — the family visits Ocean City for the afternoon and evening. When Ambrose and Peter's father was their age, the excursion was made by train, as mentioned in the novel *The 42nd Parallel* by John Dos Passos. Many families from the same neighborhood used to travel together, with dependent relatives and often with Negro servants; schoolfuls of children swarmed through the railway cars; everyone shared everyone else's Maryland fried chicken, Virginia ham, deviled eggs, potato salad, beaten biscuits, iced tea. Nowadays (that is, in 19 , the year of our story) the journey is made by automobile — more comfortably and quickly though without the extra fun though without the *camaraderie* of a general excursion. It's all part of the deterioration of American life, their father declares; Uncle Karl supposes that when the boys take *their* families to Ocean City for the holidays they'll fly in Autogiros. Their mother, sitting in the middle of the front seat like Magda in the second, only with her arms on the seat-back behind the men's shoulders, wouldn't want the good old days back again, the steaming trains and stuffy long dresses; on the other hand she can do without Autogiros, too, if she has to become a grandmother to fly in them.

Description of physical appearance and mannerisms is one of several standard methods of characterization used by writers of fiction. It is also important to "keep the senses operating"; when a detail from one of the five senses, say visual, is "crossed" with a detail from another, say auditory, the reader's imagination is oriented to the scene, perhaps unconsciously. This procedure may be compared to the way surveyors and navigators determine their positions by two or more compass bearings, a process known as triangulation. The brown hair on Ambrose's mother's forearms gleamed in the sun like. Though right-handed, she took her left arm from the seat-back to press the dashboard cigar lighter for Uncle Karl. When the glass bead in its handle glowed red, the lighter was ready for use. The smell of Uncle Karl's cigar smoke reminded one of. The fragrance of the ocean came strong to the picnic ground where they always stopped for lunch, two miles inland from Ocean City. Having to pause for a full hour almost within sound of the breakers was difficult for Peter and Ambrose when they were younger; even at their present age it was not easy to keep their anticipation, *stimulated by the briny spume,* from turning into short temper. The Irish author James Joyce, in his unusual novel entitled *Ulysses,* now available in this country, uses the adjectives *snot-green* and *scrotum-tightening* to describe the sea. Visual, auditory, tactile, olfactory, gustatory. Peter and Ambrose's father, while steering their black 1936 LaSalle sedan with one hand, could with the other remove the first cigarette from a white pack of Lucky Strikes and, more remarkably, light it with a match forefingered from its book and thumbed against the flint paper without being detached. The matchbook cover merely advertised U. S. War Bonds and Stamps. A fine metaphor, simile, or other figure of speech, in addition to its obvious "first-order" relevance to the thing it describes, will be seen upon reflection to have a second order of significance: it may be drawn from the *milieu* of the action, for example, or be particularly appropriate to the sensibility of the narrator, even hinting to the reader things of which the narrator is unaware; or it may cast further and subtler lights upon the thing it describes, sometimes ironically qualifying the more evident sense of the comparison.

To say that Ambrose's and Peter's mother was *pretty* is to accomplish nothing; the reader may acknowledge the proposition, but his imagination is not engaged. Besides, Magda was also pretty, yet in an altogether different way. Although she lived on B_____ Street she had very good manners and did better than average in school. Her figure was very well developed for her age. Her right hand lay casually on the plush upholstery of the seat, very near Ambrose's left leg, on which his own hand rested. The space between their legs, between her right and his left leg, was out of the line of sight of anyone sitting on the other side of Magda, as well as anyone glancing into the rearview mirror. Uncle Karl's face resembled Peter's—rather, vice versa. Both had dark hair and eyes, short husky statures, deep voices. Magda's left hand was probably in a similar position on her left side. The boy's father is difficult to describe; no particular feature of his appearance or manner stood out. He wore glasses and was principal of a T_____ County grade school. Uncle Karl was a masonry contractor.

Although Peter must have known as well as Ambrose that the latter, because of his position in the car, would be the first to see the electrical towers of the power plant at V_____, the halfway point of their trip, he leaned forward and slightly toward the center of the car and pretended to be looking for them through the flat pinewoods and tuckahoe creeks along the highway. For as long as the boys could remember, "looking for the Towers" had been a feature of the first half of their excursions to Ocean City, "looking for the standpipe" of the second. Though the game was childish, their mother preserved the tradition of rewarding the first to see the Towers with a candy-bar or piece of fruit. She insisted now that Magda play the game; the prize, she said, was "something hard to get nowadays." Ambrose decided not to join in; he sat far back in his seat. Magda, like Peter, leaned forward. Two sets of straps were discernible through the shoulders of her sun dress; the inside right one, a brassiere-strap, was fastened or shortened with a small safety pin. The right armpit of her dress, presumably the left as well, was damp with perspiration. The simple strategy for being first to espy the Towers, which Ambrose had understood by the age of four, was to sit on the right-hand side of the car. Whoever sat there, however, had also to put up with the worst of the sun, and so Ambrose, without mentioning the matter, chose sometimes the one and sometimes the other. Not impossibly Peter had never caught on to the trick, or thought that his brother hadn't simply because Ambrose on occasion preferred shade to a Baby Ruth or tangerine.

The shade-sun situation didn't apply to the front seat, owing to the windshield; if anything the driver got more sun, since the person on the passenger side not only was shaded below by the door and dashboard but might swing down his sunvisor all the way too.

"Is that them?" Magda asked. Ambrose's mother teased the boys for letting Magda win, insinuating that "somebody [had] a girlfriend." Peter and Ambrose's father reached a long thin arm across their mother to butt his cigarette in the dashboard ashtray, under the lighter. The prize this time for seeing the Towers first was a banana. Their mother bestowed it after chiding their father for wasting a half-smoked cigarette when everything was so scarce. Magda, to take the prize, moved her hand from so near Ambrose's that he could have touched it as though accidentally. She offered to share the prize, things like that were so hard to find; but everyone insisted it was hers alone. Ambrose's mother sang an iambic trimeter couplet from a popular song, femininely rhymed:

> "What's good is in the Army;
> What's left will never harm me."

Uncle Karl tapped his cigar ash out the ventilator window; some particles were sucked by the slipstream back into the car through the rear window on the passenger side. Magda demonstrated her ability to hold a banana in one hand and peel it with her teeth. She still sat forward; Ambrose pushed his glasses back onto the bridge of his nose with his left hand, which he then negligently let fall to the seat cushion immediately behind her. He even permitted the single hair, gold, on the second joint of his thumb to brush the fabric of her skirt. Should she have sat back at that instant, his hand would have been caught under her.

Plush upholstery prickles uncomfortably through gabardine slacks in the July sun. The funciton of the *beginning* of a story is to introduce the principal characters, establish their initial relationships, set the scene for the main action, expose the background of the situation if necessary, plant motifs and foreshadowings where appropriate, and initiate the first complication or whatever of the "rising action." Actually, if one imagines a story called "The Funhouse," or "Lost in the Funhouse," the details of the drive to Ocean City don't seem especially relevant. The *beginning* should recount the events between Ambrose's first sight of the funhouse early in the afternoon and his entering it with Magda and Peter in the evening. The *middle* would narrate all relevant events from the time he goes in to the time he loses his way; middles have the double and contradictory function of delaying the climax while at the same time preparing the reader for it and fetching him to it. Then the *ending* would tell what Ambrose does while he's lost, how he finally finds his way out, and what everybody makes of the experience. So far there's been no real dialogue, very little sensory detail, and nothing in the way of a *theme*. And a long time has gone by already without anything happening; it makes a person wonder. We haven't even reached Ocean City yet: we will never get out of the funhouse.

The more closely an author identifies with the narrator, literally or metaphorically, the less advisable it is, as a rule, to use the first-person narrative viewpoint. Once three years previously the young people *aforementioned* played Niggers and Masters in the backyard; when it was Ambrose's turn to be Master and theirs to be Niggers Peter had to go serve his evening papers; Ambrose was afraid to punish Magda alone, but she led him to the whitewashed Torture Chamber between the woodshed and the privy in the Slaves Quarters; there she knelt sweating among bamboo rakes and dusty Mason jars, pleadingly embraced his knees, and while bees droned in the lattice as if on an ordinary summer afternoon, purchased clemency at a surprising price set by herself. Doubtless she remembered nothing of this event; Ambrose on the other hand seemed unable to forget the least detail of his life. He even recalled how, standing beside himself with awed impersonality in the reeky heat, he'd stared the while at an empty cigar box in which Uncle Karl kept stonecutting chisels: beneath the words *El Producto*, a laureled, loose-toga'd lady regarded the sea from a marble bench; beside her, forgotten or not yet turned to, was a five-stringed lyre. Her chin reposed on the back of her right hand; her left depended negligently from the bench-arm. The lower half of scene and lady was peeled away; the words EXAMINED BY ———— were inked there into the wood. Nowadays cigar boxes are made of pasteboard. Ambrose wondered what Magda would have done, Ambrose wondered what Magda would do when she sat back on his hand as he resolved she should. Be angry. Make a teasing joke of it. Give no sign at all. For a long time she leaned forward, playing cow-poker with Peter against Uncle Karl and Mother and watching for the first sign of Ocean City. At nearly the same instant, picnic ground and Ocean City standpipe hove into view; an Amoco filling station on their side of the road cost Mother and Uncle Karl fifty cows and the game; Magda bounced back, clapping her right hand on Mother's right arm; Ambrose moved clear "in the nick of time."

At this rate our hero, at this rate our protagonist will remain in the funhouse forever. Narrative ordinarily consists of alternating dramatization and summarization. One symptom of nervous tension, paradoxically, is repeated and violent yawning; neither Peter nor Magda nor Uncle Karl nor Mother reacted in this manner. Although they were no longer small children, Peter and Ambrose were each given a dollar to spend on boardwalk amusements in addition to what money of their own they'd brought along. Magda too, though she protested she had ample spending money. The boys' mother made a little scene out of distributing the bills; she pretended that her sons and Magda were small children and cautioned them not to spend the sum too quickly or in one place. Magda promised with a merry laugh and, having both hands free, took the bill with her left. Peter laughed also and pledged in a falsetto to be a good boy. His imitation of a child was not clever. The boys' father was tall and thin, balding, fair-complexioned. Assertions of that sort are not effective; the reader may acknowledge the proposition, but. We should be much farther along than we are; something has gone wrong; not much of this preliminary rambling seems relevant. Yet everyone begins in the same place; how is it that most go along without difficulty but a few lose their way?

"Stay out from under the boardwalk," Uncle Karl growled from the side of his mouth. The boys' mother pushed his shoulder *in mock annoyance.* They were all standing before Fat May the Laughing Lady who advertised the funhouse. Larger than life, Fat May mechanically shook, rocked on her heels, slapped her thighs while recorded laughter—uproarious, female—came amplified from a hidden loud-speaker. It chuckled, wheezed, wept; tried in vain to catch its breath; tittered, groaned, exploded raucous and anew. You couldn't hear it without laughing yourself, no matter how you felt. Father came back from talking to a Coast-Guardsman on duty and reported that the surf was spoiled with crude oil from tankers recently torpedoed offshore. Lumps of it, difficult to remove, made tarry tidelines on the beach and stuck on swimmers. Many bathed in the surf nevertheless and came out speckled; others paid to use a municipal pool and only sunbathed on the beach. We would do the latter. We would do the latter. We would do the latter.

Under the boardwalk, matchbook covers, grainy other things. What is the story's theme? Ambrose is ill. He perspires in the dark passages; candied apples-on-a-stick, delicious-looking, disappointing to eat. Funhouses need men's and ladies' room at intervals. Others perhaps have also vomited in corners and corridors; may even have had bowel movements liable to be stepped in in the dark. The word *fuck* suggests suction and/or and/or flatulence. Mother and Father; grandmothers and grandfathers on both sides; great-grandmothers and great-grandfathers on four sides, et cetera. Count a generation as thirty years: in approximately the year when Lord Baltimore was granted charter to the province of Maryland by Charles I, five hundred twelve women—English, Welsh, Bavarian, Swiss—of every class and character, received into themselves the penises the intromittent organs of five hundred twelve men, ditto, in every circumstance and posture, to conceive the five hundred twelve ancesters of the two hundred fifty-six ancestors of the et cetera et cetera et cetera et cetera et cetera et cetera et cetera et cetera of the author, of the narrator, of this story, *Lost in the Funhouse*. In alleyways, ditches, canopy beds, pinewoods, bridal suites, ship's cabins, coach-and-fours, coaches-and-four, sultry toolsheds; on the cold sand under boardwalks, littered with *El Producto* cigar butts, treasured with Lucky Strike cigarette stubs, Coca-Cola caps, gritty turds, cardboard lollipop sticks, matchbook covers warning that A Slip of the Lip Can Sink a Ship. The shluppish whisper, continuous as seawash round the globe, tidelike falls and rises with the circuit of dawn and dusk.

Magda's teeth. She *was* left-handed. Perspiration. They've gone all the way, through, Magda and Peter, they've been waiting for hours with Mother and Uncle Karl while Father searches for his lost son; they draw french-fried potatoes from a paper cup and shake their heads. They've named the children they'll one day have and bring to Ocean City on holidays. Can spermatozoa properly be though of as male animalcules when there are no female spermatozoa? They grope through hot, dark windings, past Love's Tunnel's fearsome obstacles. Some perhaps lose their way.

Peter suggested then and there that they do the funhouse; he had been through it before, so had Magda, Ambrose hadn't and suggested, his voice cracking on account of Fat May's laughter, that they swim first. All were chuckling, couldn't help it; Ambrose's father, Ambrose's and Peter's father came up grinning like a lunatic with two boxes of syrup-coated popcorn, one for Mother, one for Magda; the men were to help themselves. Ambrose walked on Magda's right; being by nature left-handed, she carried the box in her left hand. Up front the situation was reversed.

"What are you limping for?" Magda inquired of Ambrose. He supposed in a husky tone that his foot had gone to sleep in the car. Her teeth flashed. "Pins and needles?" It was the honeysuckle on the lattice of the former privy that drew the bees. Imagine being stung there. How long is this going to take?

The adults decided to forgo the pool; but Uncle Karl insisted they change into swimsuits and do the beach. "He wants to watch the pretty girls," Peter teased, and ducked behind Magda from Uncle Karl's pretended wrath. "You've got all the pretty girls you need right here," Magda declared and Mother said: "Now that's the gospel truth." Magda scolded Peter, who reached over her shoulder to sneak some popcorn. "Your brother and father aren't getting any." Uncle Karl wondered if they were going to have fireworks that night, what with the shortages. It wasn't the shortages, Mr. M̲̲̲̲̲ replied; Ocean City had fireworks from pre-war. But it was too risky on account of the enemy submarines, some people thought.

"Don't seem like Fourth of July without fireworks," said Uncle Karl. The inverted tag in dialogue writing is still considered permissible with proper names or epithets, but sounds old-fashioned with personal pronouns. "We'll have 'em again soon enough," predicted the boys' father. Their mother declared she could do without fireworks: they reminded her too much of the real thing. Their father said all the more reason to shoot off a few now and again. Uncle Karl asked *rhetorically* who needed reminding, just look at people's hair and skin.

"The oil, yes," said Mrs. M̲̲̲̲̲

Ambrose had a pain in his stomach and so didn't swim but enjoyed watching the others. He and his father burned red easily. Magda's figure was exceedingly well developed for her age. She too declined to swim, and got mad, and became angry when Peter attempted to drag her into the pool. She always swam, he insisted; what did she mean not swim? Why did a person come to Ocean City?

"Maybe I want to lay here with Ambrose," Magda teased.

Nobody likes a pedant.

"Aha," said Mother. Peter grabbed Magda by one ankle and ordered Ambrose to grab the other. She squealed and rolled over on the beach blanket. Ambrose pretended to help hold her back. Her tan was darker than even Mother's and Peter's. "Help out, Uncle Karl!" Peter cried. Uncle Karl went to seize the other ankle. Inside the top of her swimsuit, however, you could see the line where the sunburn ended and, when she hunched her shoulders and squealed again, one nipple's auburn edge. Mother made them behave themselves. "*You* should certainly know," she said to Uncle Karl. Archly. "That when a lady says she doesn't feel like swimming, a gentleman doesn't ask questions." Uncle Karl said excuse *him;* Mother winked at Magda; Ambrose blushed; stupid Peter kept saying "Phooey on *feel like!*" and tugging at Magda's ankle; then even he got the point, and cannonballed with a holler into the pool.

"I swear," Magda said, in mock *in feigned* exasperation.

The diving would make a suitable literary symbol. To go off the high board you had to wait in a line along the poooolside and up the ladder. Fellows tickled girls and goosed one another and shouted to the ones at the top to hurry up, or razzed them for bellyfloppers. Once on the springboard some took a great while posing or clowning or deciding on a dive or getting up their nerve; others ran right off. Especially among the younger fellows the idea was to strike the funniest pose or do the craziest stunt as you fell, a thing that got harder to do as you kept on and kept on. But whether you hollered *Geronimo!* or *Sieg heil!*, held your nose or "rode a bicycle," pretended to be shot or did a perfect jacknife or changed your mind halfway down and ended up with nothing, it was over in two seconds, after all that wait. Spring, pose, splash. Spring, neat-o, splash. Spring, aw fooey, splash.

The grown-ups had gone on; Ambrose wanted to converse with Magda; she was remarkably well developed for her age; it was said that that came from rubbing with a turkish towel, and there were other theories. Ambrose could think of nothing to say except how good a diver Peter was, who was showing off for her benefit. You could pretty well tell by looking at their bathing suits and arm muscles how far along the different fellows were. Ambrose was glad he hadn't gone in swimming, the cold water shrank you up so. Magda pretended to be uninterested in the diving; she probably weighed as much as he did. If you knew your way around in the funhouse like your own bedroom, you could wait until a girl came along and then slip away without ever getting caught, even if her boyfriend was right with her. She'd think *he* did it! It would be better to be the boyfriend, and act outraged, and tear the funhouse apart.

Not act; *be*.

"He's a master diver," Ambrose said. In feigned admiration. "You really have to slave away at it to get that good." What would it matter anyhow if he asked her right our whether she remembered, even teased her with it as Peter would have?

There's no point in going farther; this isn't getting anybody anywhere; they haven't even come to the funhouse yet. Ambrose is off the track, in some new or old part of the place that's not supposed to be used; he strayed into it by some one-in-a-million chance, like the time the roller-coaster car left the tracks in the nineteen-teens against all the laws of physics and sailed over the boardwalk in the dark. And they can't locate him because they don't know where to look. Even the designer and operator have forgotten this other part, that winds around on itself like a whelk shell. That winds around the right part like the snakes on Mercury's caduceus.[1] Some people, perhaps, don't "hit their stride" until their twenties, when the growing-up business is over and women appreciate other things besides wisecracks and teasing and strutting. Peter didn't have one-tenth the imagination *he* had, not one-tenth. Peter did this naming-their-children thing as a joke, making up names like Aloysius and Murgatroyd, but Ambrose knew *exactly* how it would feel to be married and have children of your own, and be a loving husband and father, and go comfortably to work in the mornings and to bed with your wife at night, and wake up with her there. With a breeze coming through the sash and birds and mockingbirds singing in the Chinese-cigar trees. His eyes watered, there aren't enough ways to say that. He would be quite famous in his line of work. Whether Magda was his wife or not, one evening

---

[1]Winged staff entwined with serpents, symbol of the medical profession.

when he was wise-lined and gray at the temples he'd smile gravely, at a fashionable dinner party, and remind her of his youthful passion. The time they went with his family to Ocean City; the *erotic fantasies* he used to have about her. How long ago it seemed, and childish! Yet tender, too, *n'est-ce pas?*[2] Would she have imagined that the world-famous whatever remembered how many strings were on the lyre on the bench beside the girl on the label of the cigar box he'd stared at in the toolshed at age ten while she, age eleven. Even then he had felt *wise beyond his years;* he'd stroked her hair and said in his deepest voice and correctest English, as to a dear child: "I shall never forget this moment."

But though he had breathed heavily, groaned as if ecstatic, what he'd really felt throughout was an odd detachment, as though someone else were Master. Strive as he might to be transported, he heard his mind take notes upon the scene: *This is what they call* passion. *I am experiencing it.* Many of the digger machines were out of order in the penny arcades and could not be repaired or replaced for the duration. Moreover the prizes, made now in USA, were less interesting than formerly, pasteboard items for the most part, and some of the machines wouldn't work on white pennies. The gypsy fortuneteller machine might have provided a foreshadowing of the climax of this story if Ambrose had operated it. It was even dilapidateder than most: the silver coating was worn off the brown metal handles, the glass windows around the dummy were cracked and taped, her kerchiefs and silks long-faded. If a man lived by himself, he could take a department-store mannequin with flexible joints and modify her in certain ways. *However:* by the time he was that old he'd have a real woman. There was a machine that stamped your name around a white-metal coin with a star in the middle: A   . His son would be the second, and when the lad reached thirteen or so he would put a strong arm around his shoulder and tell him calmly: "It is perfectly normal. We have all been through it. It will not last forever." Nobody knew how to be what they were right. He'd smoke a pipe, teach his son how to fish and softcrab, assure him he needn't worry about himself. Magda would certainly give, Magda would certainly yield a great deal of milk, although guilty of occasional solecisms. It don't taste so bad. Suppose the lights came on now!

The day wore on. You think you're yourself, but there are other persons in you. Ambrose gets hard when Ambrose doesn't want to, *and obversely.* Ambrose watches them disagree; Ambrose watches him watch. In the funhouse mirror-room you can't see yourself go on forever, because no matter how you stand, your head gets in the way. Even if you had a glass perioscope, the image of your eye would cover up the thing you really wanted to see. The police will come; there'll be a story in the papers. That must be where it happened. Unless he can find a surprise exit, an unofficial backdoor or escape hatch opening on an alley, say, and then stroll up to the family in front of the funhouse and ask where everbody's been; *he's* been out of the place for ages. That's just where it happened, in that last lighted room: Peter and Magda found the right exit; he found one that you weren't supposed to find and strayed off into the works somewhere. In a perfect funhouse you'd be able to go only one way, like the divers off the highboard; getting lost would be impossible; the doors and halls would work like minnow traps or the valves in veins.

On account of German U-boats, Ocean City was "browned out": streetlights were shaded on the seaward side; shop-windows and boardwalk amusement places were kept dim, not to silhouette tankers and Liberty-ships for torpedoing. In a short story about Ocean City, Maryland, during World War II, the author could make use of the image of sailors on leave in the penny arcades and shooting galleries, sighting through the crosshairs of toy machine guns at swastika'd subs, while out in the black Atlantic a U-boat skipper squints through his periscope at real ships outlined by the glow of penny arcades. After dinner the family strolled back to the amusement end of the boardwalk. The boys' father had burnt red as always and was masked with

---

[2]"Is it not so?" (French)

Noxzema, a minstrel in reverse. The grown-ups stood at the end of the boardwalk where the Hurricane of '33 had cut an inlet from the ocean to Assawoman Bay.

"Pronounced with a long *o*," Uncle Karl reminded Magda with a wink. His shirt sleeves were rolled up; Mother punched his brown biceps with the arrowed heart on it and said his mind was naughty. Fat May's laugh came suddenly from the funhouse, as if she'd just got the joke; the family laughed too at the coincidence. Ambrose went under the boardwalk to search for out-of-town matchbook covers with the aid of his pocket flashlight; he looked out from the edge of the North American continent and wondered how far their laughter carried over the water. Spies in rubber rafts; survivors in lifeboats. If the joke had been beyond his understanding, he could have said: "*The laughter was over his head.*" And let the reader see the serious wordplay on second reading.

He turned the flashlight on and then off at once even before the woman whooped. He sprang away, heart athud, dropping the light. What had the man grunted? Perspiration drenched and chilled him by the time he scrambled up to the family. "See anything?" his father asked. His voice wouldn't come; he shrugged and violently brushed sand from his pants legs.

"Let's ride the old flying horses!" Magda cried. I'll never be an author. It's been forever already, everybody's gone home, Ocean City's deserted, the ghost-crabs are tickling across the beach and down the littered cold streets. And the empty halls of clapboard hotels and abandoned funhouses. A tidal wave; an enemy air raid; a monster-crab swelling like an island from the sea. *The inhabitants fled in terror.* Magda clung to his trouser leg; he alone knew the maze's secret. "He gave his life that we might live," said Uncle Karl with a scowl of pain, as he. The fellow's hands had been tattooed; the woman's legs, the woman's fat white legs had. *An astonishing coincidence.* He yearned to tell Peter. He wanted to throw up for excitement. They hadn't even chased him. He wished he were dead.

One possible ending would be to have Ambrose come across another lost person in the dark. They'd match their wits together against the funhouse, struggle like Ulysses past obstacle after obstacle, help and encourage each other. Or a girl. By the time they found the exit they'd be closest friends, sweethearts if it were a girl; they'd know each other's inmost souls, be bound together *by the cement of shared adventure;* then they'd emerge into the light and it would turn out that his friend was a Negro. A blind girl. President Roosevelt's son. Ambrose's former archenemy.

Shortly after the mirror room he'd groped along a musty corridor, his heart already misgiving him at the absence of phosphorescent arrows and other signs. He'd found a crack of light — not a door, it turned out, but a seam between the plyboard wall panels — squinting up to it, espied a small old man, *in appearance not unlike* the photographs at home of Ambrose's late grandfather, nodding upon a stool beneath a bare, speckled bulb. A crude panel of toggle- and knife-switches hung beside the open fuse box near his head; elsewhere in the little room were wooden levers and ropes belayed to boat cleats. At the time, Ambrose wasn't lost enough to rap or call; later he couldn't find that crack. Now it seemed to him that he'd possibly dozed off for a few minutes somewhere along the way; certainly he was exhausted from the afternoon's sunshine and the evening's problems; he couldn't be sure he hadn't dreamed part or all of the sight. Had an old black wall fan droned like bees and shimmied two flypaper streamers? Had the funhouse operator — gentle, somewhat sad and tired-appearing, in expression not unlike the photographs at home of Ambrose's late Uncle Konrad — murmured in his sleep? Is there really such a person as Ambrose, or is he a figment of the author's imagination? Was it Assawoman Bay or Sinepuxent? Are there other errors of fact in this fiction? Was there another sound besides the little slap slap of thigh on ham, like water sucking at the chine-boards of a skiff?

When you're lost, the smartest thing to do is stay put till you're found, hollering if necessary. But to holler guarantees humiliation as well as rescue; keeping silent permits some saving of face—you can act surprised at the fuss when your rescuers find you and swear you weren't lost, if they do. What's more you might find your own way yet, *however belatedly.*

"Don't tell me your foot's still asleep!" Magda exclaimed as the three young people walked from the inlet to the area set aside for ferris wheels, carrousels, and other carnival rides, they having decided in favor of the vast and ancient merry-go-round instead of the funhouse. What a sentence, everything was wrong from the outset. People don't know what to make of him, he doesn't know what to make of himself, he's only thirteen, *athletically and socially inept*, not astonishingly bright, but there are antennae; he has . . . some sort of receivers in his head; things speak to him, he understands more than he should, the world winks at him through its objects, grabs grinning at his coat. Everybody else is in on some secret he doesn't know; they've forgotten to tell him. Through simple *procrastination* his mother put off his baptism until this year. Everyone else had it done as a baby; he'd assumed the same of himself, as had his mother, so she claimed, until it was time for him to join Grace Methodist-Protestant and the oversight came out. He was mortified, but pitched sleepless through his private catechizing, intimidated by the ancient mysteries, a thirteen year old would never say that, resolved to experience conversion like St. Augustine. When the water touched his brow and Adam's sin left him, he contrived by a strain like defecation to bring tears into his eyes—but felt nothing. There was some simple, radical difference about him; he hoped it was genius, feared it was madness, devoted himself to amiability and inconspicuousness. Alone on the seawall near his house he was seized by the terrifying transports he'd thought to find in toolshed, in Communion-cup, The grass was alive! The town, the river, himself, were not imaginary; time roared in his ears like wind; the world was *going on!* This part ought to be dramatized. The Irish author James Joyce once wrote. Ambrose M——— is going to scream.

There is no *texture of rendered sensory detail*, for one thing. The faded distorting mirrors beside Fat May; the impossibility of choosing a mount when one had but a single ride on the great carrousel; the *vertigo attendant on his recognition* that Ocean City was worn out, the place of fathers and grandfathers, strawboatered men and parasoled ladies survived by their amusements. Money spent, the three paused at Peter's insistence beside Fat May to watch the girls get their skirts blown up. The object was to tease Magda, who said: "I swear, Peter ————, you've got a one-track mind! Amby and me aren't *interested* in such things." In the tumbling-barrel, too, just inside the Devil's-mouth entrance to the funhouse, the girls were upended and their boyfriends and others could see up their dresses if they cared to. Which was the whole point, Ambrose realized. Of the entire funhouse! If you looked around, you noticed that almost all the people on the boardwalk were paired off into couples except the small children; in a way, that was the whole point of Ocean City! If you had X-ray eyes and could see everything going on at that instant under the boardwalk and in all the hotel rooms and cars and alleyways, you'd realize that all that normally *showed*, like restaurants and dance halls and clothing and test-your-strength machines, was merely preparation and intermission. Fat May screamed.

Because he watched the goings-on from the corner of his eye, it was Ambrose who spied the half-dollar on the boardwalk near the tumbling-barrel. Losers weepers. The first time he'd heard some people moving through a corridor not far away, just after he'd lost sight of the crack of light, he'd decided not to call to them, for fear they'd guess he was scared and poke fun; it sounded like roughnecks; he'd hoped they'd come by and he could follow in the dark without their knowing. Another time he'd heard just one person, unless he imagined it, bumping along as if on the other side of the plywood; perhaps Peter coming back for him, or Father, or Magda lost too. Or the owner and operator of the funhouse. He'd called out once, as though merrily: "Anybody know where the heck we are?" But the query was too stiff, his voice cracked, when the sounds stopped he was terrified: maybe it was a queer who waited for fellows to get lost, or a longhaired filthy monster that lived in some cranny of the funhouse. He stood rigid for hours it seemed like, scarcely respiring. His future was shockingly clear, in outline. He tried holding his breath to the point of unconsciousness. There ought to be a button you could push to end your life absolutely without pain; disappear in a flick, like turning out a light. He would push it instantly! He despised Uncle Karl. But he despised his father too, for not being what he was supposed to be. Perhaps his father hated *his* father, and so on, and his son would hate him, and so on. Instantly!

Naturally he didn't have nerve enough to ask Magda to go through the funhouse with him. With incredible nerve and to everyone's surprise he invited Magda, quietly and politely, to go through the funhouse with him. "I warn you, I've never been through it before," he added, *laughing easily;* "but I reckon we can manage somehow. The important thing to remember, after all, is that it's meant to be a *fun*house; that is, a place of amusement. If people really got lost or injured or too badly frightened in it, the owner'd go out of business. There'd even be lawsuits. No character in a work of fiction can make a speech this long without interruption or acknowledgment from the other characters."

Mother teased Uncle Karl. "Three's a crowd, I always heard." But actually Ambrose was relieved that Peter now had a quarter too. Nothing was what it looked like. Every instant, under the surface of the Atlantic Ocean, millions of living animals devoured one another. Pilots were falling in flames over Europe; women were being forcibly raped in the South Pacific. His father should have taken him aside and said: "There is a simple secret to getting through the funhouse, as simple as being first to see the Towers. Here it is. Peter does not know it; neither does your Uncle Karl. You and I are different. Not surprisingly, you've often wished you weren't. Don't think I haven't noticed how unhappy your childhood has been! But you'll understand, when I tell you, why it had to be kept secret until now. And you won't regret not being like your brother and your uncle. *On the contrary!*" If you knew all the stories behind all the people on the boardwalk, you'd see that *nothing* was what it looked like. Husbands and wives often hated each other; parents didn't necessarily love their children; et cetera. A child took things for granted because he had nothing to compare his life to and everybody acted as if things were as they should be. Therefore each saw himself as the hero of the story, when the truth might turn out to be that he's the villain, or the coward. And there wasn't one thing you could do about it!

Hunchbacks, fat ladies, fools—that no one chose what he was was unbearable. In the movies he'd meet a beautiful young girl in the funhouse; they'd have hairsbreadth escapes from real dangers; he'd do and say the right things; she also; in the end they'd be lovers; their dialogue lines would match up; he'd be perfectly at ease; she'd not only like him well enough, she'd think he was *marvelous;* she'd lie awake thinking about *him,* instead of vice versa—the way *his* face looked in different lights and how he stood and exactly what he'd said—and yet that would be only one small episode in his wonderful life, among many many others. Not a *turning point* at all. What had happened in the toolshed was nothing. He hated, he loathed his parents! One reason for not writing a lost-in-the-funhouse story is that either everybody's felt what Ambrose feels, in which case it goes without saying, or else no normal person feels such things, in which case Ambrose is a freak. "Is anything more tiresome, in fiction, than the problems of sensitive adolescents?" And it's all too long and rambling, as if the author. For all a person knows the first time through, the end could be just around any corner; perhaps, *not impossibly* it's been within reach any number of times. On the other hand he may be scarcely past the start, with everything yet to get through, an intolerable idea.

Fill in: His father's raised eyebrows when he announced his decision to do the funhouse with Magda. Ambrose understands now, but didn't then, that his father was wondering whether he knew what the funhouse was *for*—especially since he didn't object, as he should have, when Peter decided to come along too. The ticketwoman, witchlike, mortifying him when inadvertently he gave her his name-coin instead of the half-dollar, then unkindly calling Magda's attention to the birthmark on his temple: "Watch out for him, girlie, he's a marked man!" She wasn't even cruel, he understood, only vulgar and insensitive. Somewhere in the world there was a young woman with such splendid understanding that she'd see him entire, like a poem or story, and find his words so valuable after all that when he confessed his apprehensions she would explain why they were in fact the very things that made him precious to her . . . and to Western Civilization! There was no such girl, the simple truth being. Violent yawns as they approached the mouth. Whispered advice from an old-timer on a bench near the barrel: "Go crabwise and ye'll get an eyeful without upsetting!" Composure vanished at the first pitch: Peter hollered joyously, Magda tumbled, shrieked, clutched her skirt; Ambrose scrambled crabwise, tight-lipped with terror, was soon out, watched his dropped name-coin slide among the couples. Shamefaced he saw that to get through expeditiously was not the point; Peter feigned assistance in order to trip Magda up, shouted "I see Christmas!" when her legs went flying. The old man, his latest betrayer, cacked approval. A dim hall then of black-thread cobwebs and recorded gibber: he took Magda's elbow to steady her against revolving discs set in the slanted floor to throw your feet out from under, and explained to her in a calm, deep voice his theory that each phase of the funhouse was triggered either automatically, by a series of photoelectric devices, or else manually by operators stationed at peepholes. But he lost his voice thrice as the discs unbalanced him; Magda was anyhow squealing; but at one point she clutched him about the waist to keep from falling, and her right cheek pressed for a moment against his belt-buckle. Heroically he drew her up, it was his chance to clutch her close as if for support and say: "I love you." He even put an arm lightly about the small of her back before a sailor-and-girl pitched into them from behind, sorely treading his left big toe and knocking Magda asprawl with them. The sailor's girl was a string-haired hussy with a loud laugh and light blue drawers; Ambrose realized that he wouldn't have said "I love you" anyhow, and was smitten with self-contempt. How much better it would be to be that common sailor! A wiry little Seaman 3rd, the fellow squeezed a girl to each side and stumbled hilarious into the mirror room, closer to Magda in thirty seconds than Ambrose had got in thirteen years. She giggled at something the fellow said to Peter; she drew her hair from her eyes with a movement so womanly it struck Ambrose's heart; Peter's smacking her backside then seemed particularly coarse. But Magda made a pleased indignant face and cried, "All right for *you* mister!" and pursued Peter into the maze without a backward glance. The sailor followed after, leisurely, drawing his girl against his hip; Ambrose understood not only that they were all so relieved to be rid of his burdensome company that they didn't even notice his absence, but that he himself shared their relief. Stepping from the treacherous passage at last into the mirror-maze, he saw once again, more clearly than ever, how readily he deceived himself into supposing he was a person. He even foresaw, wincing at his dreadful self-knowledge, that he would repeat the deception, at ever-rarer intervals, all his wretched life, so fearful were the alternatives. Fame, madness, suicide; perhaps all three. It's not believable that so young a boy could articulate that reflection, and in fiction the merely true must always yield to the plausible. Moreover, the symbolism is in places heavy-footed. Yet Ambrose M_____ understood, as few adults do, that the famous loneliness of the great was no popular myth but a general truth—furthermore, that it was as much cause as effect.

All the preceding except the last few sentences is exposition that should've been done earlier or interspersed with the present action instead of lumped together. No reader would put up with so much with such *prolixity*. It's interesting that Ambrose's father, though presumably an intelligent man (as indicated by his role as grade-school principal), neither encouraged nor discouraged his sons at all in any way—as if he either didn't care about them or cared all right but didn't know how to act. If this fact should contribute to one of them's becoming a celebrated but wretchedly unhappy scientist, was it a good thing or not? He too might someday face the question; it would be useful to know whether it had tortured his father for years, for example, or never once crossed his mind.

In the maze two important things happened. First, our hero found a name-coin someone else had lost or discarded: *AMBROSE*, suggestive of the famous lightship and of his late grandfather's favorite dessert, which his mother used to prepare on special occasions out of coconut, oranges, grapes, and what else. Second, as he wondered at the endless replication of his image in the mirrors, second, as he *lost himself in the reflection* that the necessity for an observer makes perfect observation impossible, better make him eighteen at least, yet that would render other things unlikely, he heard Peter and Magda chuckling somewhere together in the maze. "Here!" "No here!" they shouted to each other; Peter said, "Where's Amby?" Magda murmured. "Amb?" Peter called. In a pleased, friendly voice. He didn't reply. The truth was, his brother was a *happy-go-lucky youngster* who'd've been better off with a regular brother of his own, but who seldom complained of his lot and was generally cordial. Ambrose's throat ached; there aren't enough different ways to say that. He stood quietly while the two young people giggled and thumped through the glittering maze, hurrah'd their discovery of its exit, cried out in joyful alarm at what next beset them. Then he set his mouth and followed after, as he supposed, took a wrong turn, strayed into the pass *wherein he lingers yet.*

The action of conventional dramatic narrative may be represented by a diagram called Freitag's Triangle:[3]

or more accurately by a variant of that diagram:

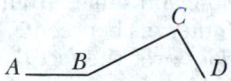

in which *AB* represents the exposition, *B* the introduction of conflict, *BC* the "rising action," complication, or development of the conflict, *C* the climax, or turn of the action, *CD* the dénouement, or resolution of the conflict. While there is no reason to regard this pattern as an absolute necessity, like many other conventions it became conventional because great numbers of people over many years learned by trial and error that it was effective; one ought not to forsake it, therefore, unless one wishes to forsake as well the effect of drama or has clear cause to feel that deliberate violation of the "normal" pattern can better can better effect that effect. This can't go on much longer; it can go on forever. He died telling stories to himself in the dark; years later, when that vast unsuspected area of the funhouse came to light, the first expedition found his skeleton in one of its labyrinthine corridors and mistook it for part of the entertainment. He died of starvation telling himself stories in the dark; but unbeknownst unbeknownst to him, an assistant operator of the funhouse, happening to

---

[3]Gustav Freitag (1816–1895), a German critic, published in 1863 *Technique of the Drama*, describing the structure of a five-act drama as a "pyramid" with a rising action, climax, and falling action.

overhear him, crouched just behind the plyboard partition and wrote down his every word. The operator's daughter, an exquisite young woman with a figure unusually well developed for her age, crouched just behind the partition and transcribed his every word. Though she had never laid eyes on him, she recognized that here was one of Western Culture's truly great imaginations, the eloquence of whose suffering would be an inspiration to unnumbered. And her heart was torn between her love for the misfortunate young man (yes, she loved him, though she had never laid though she knew him only — but how well! — through his words, and the deep, calm voice in which he spoke them) between her love et cetera and her womanly intuition that only in suffering and isolation could he give voice et cetera. Lone dark dying. Quietly she kissed the rough plyboard, and a tear fell upon the page. Where she had written in shorthand *Where she had written in shorthand* Where she had written in shorthand *Where she* et cetera. A long time ago we should have passed the apex of Freitag's Triangle and made brief work of the *dénouement;* the plot doesn't rise by meaningful steps but winds upon itself, digresses, retreats, hesitates, sighs, collapses, expires. The climax of the story must be its protagonist's discovery of a way to get through the funhouse. but he has found none, may have ceased to search.

What relevance does the war have to the story? Should there be fireworks ouside or not?

Ambrose wandered, languished, dozed. Now and then he fell into his habit of rehearsing to himself the unadventurous story of his life, narrated from the third-person point of view, from his earliest memory parenthesis of maple leaves stirring in the summer breath of tidewater Maryland end of parenthesis to the present moment. Its principal events, on this telling, would appear to have been *A, B, C,* and *D.*

He imagined himself years hence, successful, married, at ease in the world, the trials of his adolescence far behind him. He has come to the seashore with his family for the holiday: how Ocean City has changed! But at one seldom at one ill-frequented end of the boardwalk a few derelict amusements survive from times gone by: the great carrousel from the turn of the century, with its monstrous griffins and mechanical concert band; the roller coaster rumored since 1916 to have been condemned; the mechanical shooting gallery in which only the image of our enemies changed. His own son laughs with Fat May and wants to know what a funhouse is; Ambrose hugs the sturdy lad close and smiles around his pipestem at his wife.

The family's going home. Mother sits between Father and Uncle Karl, who teases him good-naturedly who chuckles over the fact that the comrade with whom he'd fought his way shoulder to shoulder through the funhouse had turned out to be a blind Negro girl — to their mutual discomfort, as they'd opened their souls. But such are the walls of custom, which even. Whose arm is where? How must it feel. He dreams of a funhouse vaster by far than any yet constructed; but by then they may be out of fashion, like steamboats and excursion trains. Already quaint and seedy: the draperied ladies on the frieze of the carrousel are his father's father's mooncheeked dreams; if he thinks of it more he will vomit his apple-on-a-stick.

He wonders: will he become a regular person? Something has gone wrong; his vaccination didn't take; at the Boy-Scout initiation campfire he only pretended to be deeply moved, as he pretends to this hour that it is not so bad after all in the funhouse, and that he has a little limp. How long will it last? He envisions a truly astonishing funhouse, incredibly complex yet utterly controlled from a great central switchboard like the console of a pipe organ. Nobody had enough imagination. He could design such a place himself, wiring and all, and he's only thirteen years old. He would be its operator: panel lights would show what was up in every cranny of its cunning of its multifarious vastness; a switch-flick would ease this fellow's way, complicate that's, to balance things out; if anyone seemed lost or frightened, all the operator had to do was.

He wishes he had never entered the funhouse. But he has. Then he wishes he were dead. But he's not. Therefore he will construct funhouses for others and be their secret operator — though he would rather be among the lovers for whom fun-houses are designed.

1967, 1968

DONALD BARTHELME
(1931–1989)

In an interview published in 1974, Donald Barthelme was pressed about a radical generalization he had once made: "The principle of collage is the central principle of all art in the twentieth century in all media." Barthelme commented on his comment:

> I was probably wrong, or too general. I point out however that New York City is or can be regarded as a collage, as opposed to, say, a tribal village in which all the huts (or yurts, or whatever) are the same hut, duplicated. The point of collage is that unlike things are stuck together to make, in the best case, a new reality. This new reality, in the best case, may be or imply a comment on the other reality from which it came, and may be also much else. It's an *itself*, if it's successful: [the art critic] Harold Rosenberg's "anxious object," which does not know whether it's a work of art or a pile of junk.

Barthelme was born in Philadelphia of parents who were there to attend the University of Pennsylvania; soon after his birth, his family moved to Houston, Texas, where he grew up. He began to write poetry and essays in high school. His attendance at the University of Houston was interrupted for service in the U.S. Army, during which he was sent to Japan and Korea. After his service, he returned to the University of Houston and was for a time director of Houston's Contemporary Arts Museum. He also founded and edited a literary magazine, *Forum*. In 1962 he went to New York City to edit a journal of art and literature, *Location*, under the tutelage of Harold Rosenberg, but the magazine lasted for only two issues. Barthelme was already writing fiction, and by the mid-1960s he was publishing his stories regularly in *The New Yorker*.

Barthelme's first collection of short stories, *Come Back, Dr. Caligari*, appeared in 1964. But it was not until the publication of his novel *Snow White*, first in *The New Yorker* and then as a book in 1967, that Barthelme attracted wide attention. This modern version of the fairy tale portrays a Snow White living with the seven dwarfs, who share pleasures with her in the shower, and who work at a baby-food factory. Readers did not get very far into the work before they realized that characters and plot were secondary to language itself, both as it was a subject *of* the work and as it was on display *in* the work. One of the dwarfs meditated on the "filling" or "stuffing" of ordinary language: "The quality this 'stuffing' has, that the other parts of verbality do not have, is two-parted, perhaps: (1) an 'endless' quality and (2) a 'sludge' quality. Of course that is possibly two qualities but I prefer to think of them as different aspects of a single quality, if you can think that way."

In some sense, all of Barthelme's work is about language, its limitations, and its frequently bizarre behavior. In his early work, there seems to be a kind of zest in the buffoonery of repeatedly pulling the rug out from under language; but in the later work, a melancholy comes to dominate the tone, a regret for what has been lost in the failure of language to be what it was once thought. At the middle of his work stands the collection of stories *City Life* (1970), which critics tend to agree contains his best work, combining gusto and melancholy, in such stories as "Views of My Father Weeping" and "At the Tolstoy Museum."

His volumes of short stories include *Unspeakable Practices, Unnatural Acts* (1968), *Sadness* (1972), *Guilty Pleasures* (1974), *Amateurs* (1976), *Great Days* (1979), and *Overnight to Many Distant Cities* (1983). *Sixty Stories*, which appeared in 1981, is a selection of stories published over a period of twenty years. In addition to *Snow White*, Barthelme published two other novels, both using, like the first novel, mythic frames in which to assemble collages or fragments of contemporary life — *The Dead Father* (1975) and *Paradise* (1986). He died in 1989, leaving in manuscript a novel called *The King* (1990).

One of the stories in *City Life*, entitled "Sentence," is one long, meandering sentence beginning with "Or" and ending: "a disappointment, to be sure, but it reminds us that the sentence is a man-made object, not the one we wanted of course, but still a construction of man, a structure to be treasured for its weakness, as opposed to the strength of stones." Asked whether this story revealed anything about the way he wrote, Barthelme answered: "I look for a particular kind of sentence, perhaps more often the awkward than the beautiful. A backbroke sentence is interesting. Any sentence that begins with the phrase, 'It is clear that . . .' is clearly clumsy but preparing itself for greatness of a kind. A way of backing into a story — of getting past the reader's hardwon armor. . . . [What happens next is] a process of accretion. Barnacles growing on a wreck or a rock. I'd rather have a wreck than a ship that sails. Things attach themselves to wrecks. Strange fish find your wreck or rock to be a good feeding ground; after a while you've got a situation with possibilities."

Barthelme might have added that it is from the barnacles that cling to his "back-broke" sentences, and from the "strange fish" that feed on it, that his "meaning," however tenuous or ambiguous, flows.

ADDITIONAL READING

Forty Stories, 1987.

Jerome Klinkowitz et al., eds., *Donald Barthelme: A Comprehensive Bibliography and Annotated Secondary Checklist*, 1977; Lois Gordon, *Donald Barthelme*, 1981; Larry McCaffery, *The Metafictional Muse: The Works of Robert Coover, Donald Barthelme, and William H. Gass*, 1982; Maurice Couturier and Regis Durand, *Donald Barthelme*, 1982; Charles Molesworth, *Donald Barthelme's Fiction: The Ironist Saved from Drowning*, 1982; Wayne B. Stengel, *The Shape of Art in the Short Stories of Donald Barthelme*, 1985.

TEXT

Unspeakable Practices, Unnatural Acts, 1968.

The Balloon

The balloon, beginning at a point on Fourteenth Street, the exact location of which I cannot reveal, expanded northward all one night, while people were sleeping, until it reached the Park. There, I stopped it; at dawn the northernmost edges lay over the Plaza; the free-hanging motion was frivolous and gentle. But experiencing a faint irritation at stopping, even to protect the trees, and seeing no reason the balloon should not be allowed to expand upward, over the parts of the city it was already covering, into the "air space" to be found there, I asked the engineers to see to it. This expansion took place throughout the morning, soft imperceptible sighing of gas through the valves. The balloon then covered forty-five blocks north-south and an irregular area east-west, as many as six crosstown blocks on either side of the Avenue in some places. That was the situation, then.

But it is wrong to speak of "situations," implying sets of circumstances leading to some resolution, some escape of tension; there were no situations, simply the balloon hanging there—muted heavy grays and browns for the most part, contrasting with walnut and soft yellows. A deliberate lack of finish, enhanced by skillful installation, gave the surface a rough, forgotten quality; sliding weights on the inside, carefully adjusted, anchored the great, vari-shaped mass at a number of points. Now we have had a flood of original ideas in all media, works of singular beauty as well as significant milestones in the history of inflation, but at that moment there was only *this balloon,* concrete particular, hanging there.

There were reactions. Some people found the balloon "interesting." As a response this seemed inadequate to the immensity of the balloon, the suddenness of its appearance over the city; on the other hand, in the absence of hysteria or other societally-induced anxiety, it must be judged a calm "mature" one. There was a certain amount of initial argumentation about the "meaning" of the balloon; this subsided, because we have learned not to insist on meanings, and they are rarely even looked for now, except in cases involving the simplest, safest phenomena. It was agreed that since the meaning of the balloon could never be known absolutely, extended discussion was pointless, or at least less purposeful than the activities of those who, for example, hung green and blue paper lanterns from the warm gray underside, in certain streets, or seized the occasion to write messages on the surface, announcing their availability for the performance of unnatural acts, or the availability of acquaintances.

Daring children jumped, especially at those points where the balloon hovered close to a building, so that the gap between balloon and building was a matter of a few inches, or points where the balloon actually made contact, exerting an ever-so-slight pressure against the side of a building, so that balloon and building seemed a unity. The upper surface was so structured that a "landscape" was presented, small valleys as well as slight knolls, or mounds; once atop the balloon, a stroll was possible, or even a trip, from one place to another. There was pleasure in being able ro run down an incline, then up the opposing slope, both gently graded, or in making a leap from one side to the other. Bouncing was possible, because of the pneumaticity of the surface, and even falling, if that was your wish. That all these varied motions, as well as others, were within one's possibilities, in experiencing the "up" side of the balloon, was extremely exciting for children, accustomed to the city's flat, hard skin. But the purpose of the balloon was not to amuse children.

Too, the number of people, children and adults, who took advantage of the opportunities described was not so large as it might have been: a certain timidity, lack of trust in the balloon, was seen. There was, furthermore, some hostility. Because we had hidden the pumps, which fed helium to the interior, and because the surface was so vast that the authorities could not determine the point of entry—that is, the point at which the gas was injected—a degree of frustration was evidenced by those city officers into whose province such manifestations normally fell. The apparent purposelessness of the balloon was vexing (as was the fact that it was "there" at all). Had we painted, in great letters, "LABORATORY TESTS PROVE" OR "18% MORE EFFECTIVE" on the sides of the balloon, this difficulty would have been circumvented. But I could not bear to so. On the whole, these officers were remarkably tolerant, considering the dimensions of the anomaly, this tolerance being the result of, first, secret tests conducted by night that convinced them that little or nothing could be done in the way of removing or destroying the balloon, and, secondly, a public warmth that arose (not uncolored by touches of the aforementioned hostility) toward the balloon, from ordinary citizens.

As a single balloon must stand for a lifetime of thinking about balloons, so each citizen expressed, in the attitude he chose, a complex of attitudes. One man might consider that the balloon had to do with the notion *sullied,* as in the sentence *The big balloon sullied the otherwise clear and radiant Manhattan sky.* That is, the balloon was, in this man's view, an imposture, something inferior to the sky that had formerly been there, something interposed between the people and their "sky." But in fact it was January, the sky was dark and ugly; it was not a sky you could look up into, lying on your back in the street, with pleasure, unless pleasure, for you, proceeeded from having been threatened, from having been misused. And the underside of the balloon was a pleasure to look up into, we had seen to that, muted grays and browns for the most part, contrasted with walnut and soft, forgotten yellows. And so, while this man was thinking *sullied,* still there was an admixture of pleasurable cognition in his thinking, struggling with the original perception.

Another man, on the other hand, might view the balloon as if it were part of a system of unanticipated rewards, as when one's employer walks in and says, "Here, Henry, take this package of money I have wrapped for you, because we have been doing so well in the business here, and I admire the way you bruise the tulips, without which bruising your department would not be a success, or at least not the success that is is." For this man the balloon might be a brilliantly heroic "muscle and pluck" experience, even if an experience poorly understood.

Another man might say, "Without the example of ——, it is doubtful that —— would exist today in its present form," and find many to agree with him, or to argue with him. Ideas of "bloat" and "float" were introduced, as well as concepts of dream and responsibility. Others engaged in remarkably detailed fantasies having to do with a wish either to lose themselves in the balloon, or to engorge it. The private character of these wishes, of their origins, deeply buried and unknown, was such that they were not much spoken of; yet there is evidence that they were widespread. It was also argued that what was important was what you felt when you stood under the balloon; some people claimed that they felt sheltered, warmed, as never before, while enemies of the balloon felt, or reported feeling, constrained, a "heavy" feeling.

Critical opinion was divided:

"monstrous pourings"

"harp"

XXXXXXX "certain contrasts with darker portions"

"inner joy"

"large, square corners"

"conservative eclecticism that has so far governed
modern balloon design"

::::::: "abnormal vigor"

"warm, soft, lazy passages"

"Has unity been sacrificed for a sprawling quality?"

"Quelle catastrophe!"[1]

"munching"

People began, in a curious way, to locate themselves in relation to aspects of the balloon: "I'll be at that place where it dips down into Forty-seventh Street almost to

---

[1] "What a catastrophe!" (French).

the sidewalk, near the Alamo Chile House," or, "Why don't we go stand on top, and take the air, and maybe walk about a bit, where it forms a tight, curving line with the façade of the Gallery of Modern Art—" Marginal intersections offered entrances within a given time duration, as well as "warm, soft, lazy passages" in which . . . But it is wrong to speak of "marginal intersections," each intersection was crucial, none could be ignored (as if, walking there you might not find someone capable of turning your attention, in a flash, from old exercises to new exercises, risks and escalations). Each intersection was crucial, meeting of balloon and building, meeting of balloon and man, meeting of balloon and balloon.

It was suggested that what was admired about the balloon was finally this: that it was not limited, or defined. Sometimes a bulge, blister, or sub-section would carry all the way east to the river on its own initiative, in the manner of an army's movements on a map, as seen in a headquarters remote from the fighting. Then that part would be, as it were, thrown back again, or would withdraw into new dispositions; the next morning, that part would have made another sortie, or disappeared altogether. This ability of the balloon to shift its shape, to change, was very pleasing, especially to people whose lives were rather rigidly patterned, persons to whom change, although desired, was not available. The balloon, for the twenty-two days of its existence, offered the possibility, in its randomness, of mislocation of the self, in contradistinction to the grid of precise, rectangular pathways under our feet. The amount of specialized training currently needed, and the consequent desirability of long-term commitments, has been occasioned by the steadily growing importance of complex machinery, in virtually all kinds of operations; as this tendency increases, more and more people will turn, in bewildered inadequacy, to solutions for which the balloon may stand as a prototype, or "rough draft."

I met you under the balloon, on the occasion of your return from Norway; you asked if it was mine; I said it was. The balloon, I said, is a spontaneous autobiographical disclosure, having to do with the unease I felt at your absence, and with sexual deprivation, but now that your visit to Bergen has been terminated, it is no longer necessary or appropriate. Removal of the balloon was easy; trailer trucks carried away the depleted fabric, which is now stored in West Virginia, awaiting some other time of unhappiness, sometime, perhaps, when we are angry with one another.

1968

JOHN UPDIKE
(b. 1932)

John Updike has repeatedly shown a distrust for terms such as "modernist" and "postmodernist." In a review published in 1984, he said:

> Such literary labelling is innocent fun, and helps not only us but, more to the point, college English majors to get a grip on things. . . . Categorization in these matters, of course, tends to excuse us from confronting each author in his or her intricate individuality, and to enlist artists in phantom armies—the modernists, for example, doing battle in a body with something called "the bourgeoisie." . . . I myself doubt whether "post-modernist" will acquire the canonical permanence of "Post-Impressionist" or "post-Kantian," for the reason that Impressionism and Immanuel Kant were phenomena more distinct and limited than modernism was. We still live in modern (from the Latin *modo,* "just now") times, and so will our descendants, until the dictionary falls to dust.

Updike was born in 1932 in Shillington, Pennsylvania, where he attended school and where, as he wrote in "The Dogwood Tree: A Boyhood," he came to see art "as a method of riding a thin pencil line out of Shillington, out of time altogether, into an infinity of unseen and even unborn hearts." Because of difficult times, in 1945 the family moved ten miles out of Shillington to a farm in Plowville. Updike's father was a mathematics teacher at Shillington High School, and the son rode with his father to school. These early experiences and family members would turn up later, translated into fiction, in Updike's stories and novels. In 1950 Updike entered Harvard on a full scholarship. He graduated *summa cum laude* in 1954 and this same year sold his first story to *The New Yorker.*

Updike's mother, who had literary ambitions of her own, had introduced her son to *The New Yorker,* and he had decided early in life to become a cartoonist. Updike and his wife, an art student he had married in 1953, headed for England to spend a year (1954–55) at the Ruskin School of Drawing and Fine Art in Oxford. While there, E. B. White sought him out to offer him a job as staff-writer at *The New Yorker.* Updike accepted immediately. From 1955 to 1957, Updike worked at the magazine, often writing items for the "Talk of the Town" section of miscellany that opens each issue.

Feeling that he would never be able to get on with his career as a writer, Updike took the major step of resigning the position and moving his family, now including two children, to Ipswich, Massachusetts, where he rented second-floor office space for a retreat in which he could write on a daily schedule. The plan worked. In 1958 he published his first book, *The Carpentered Hen,* a volume of poems. The following year he published two books, *The Poorhouse Fair,* a novel; and *The Same Door,* a volume of stories. The novel, an indictment of a secular society's materialism, was reviewed favorably, but earned little money.

In 1960, Updike published *Rabbit, Run,* which brought him wide attention as one of the most promising young novelists around. Among his novels, it has remained the constant best-seller, and its reception reassured him that his daring move from *The New Yorker* was the right one. The book introduced two themes, religious and sexual, in an ordinary young man's search for assurance and fulfillment. These themes would recur in all of Updike's work, including the continuation of Rabbit's story in *Rabbit Redux* (1971), *Rabbit Is Rich* (1981), and *Rabbit at Rest* (1990). This Rabbit tetralogy is remarkably successful in conveying what it was like to live in America during the extraordinary period of the 1950s, 1960s, 1970s, and 1980s.

Updike kept to his daily writing schedule after the success of *Rabbit, Run,* even after a divorce in 1974 and remarriage in 1977. He won a National Book Award for *The Centaur* (1963), a story of a high school teacher and his son, based on remembered experiences of his father. Other novels include *Of the Farm* (1965), drawing on boyhood experiences; *Couples* (1968), portraying the somewhat scandalous sex life of suburbia; *Bech: A Book* (1970), a comic representation of a successful Jewish writer in quest of approval, continued in a sequel a decade later in *Bech is Back* (1982); *A Month of Sundays* (1975), focusing on the sex life of a minister; *Marry Me* (1976), depicting married couples trading partners; and *The Coup* (1979), a comic novel about the politics of a poor African state.

In 1986, Updike published the first part of a trilogy, *Roger's Version,* a modern retelling of Nathaniel Hawthorne's *The Scarlet Letter;* Roger Chillingworth was Hawthorne's fiendish avenger betrayed sexually by his wife. *S.* (1988), part two of the trilogy, presents the "version" of a modern Hester Prynne. Still to come is the "version" from a modern replica of Hawthorne's guilty minister, Arthur Dimmesdale. Updike has turned again and again to the portrayal of ministers, some nonbelievers, others radical in their faith, in exploration of his complex religious themes. His interest in religion and theology is suggested by his reviews of serious books on the subject, including those of the Swiss theologian Karl Barth. And he has turned repeatedly to questions revolving around sex, guilt, and faith. There seems little doubt that, after concluding this trilogy, Updike's feverishly fertile imagination will lead him on to new material, new characters, and more books.

In addition to his novels, Updike has continued to publish short stories and poems — enough to make him among the most prolific of American writers. His short story volumes include *The Same Door* (1951), *Pigeon Feathers and Other Stories* (1962), *Olinger Stories, A Selection* (1964), *The Music School* (1966), *Museums and Women and Other Stories* (1972), *Problems and Other Stories* (1979), and *Trust Me* (1988). Later books of poetry are *Telephone Poles* (1963), *Midpoint (1969)*, *Seventy Poems* (1972), *Tossing and Turning* (1977), and *Facing Nature* (1985).

Throughout his career, Updike has published enough first-rate reviews and essays, introducing the works of international avant-garde writers like Italo Calvino, Gunter Grass, and Roland Barthes as they have appeared, to establish himself as one of the foremost general literary critics of the period. And he has done comprehensive reassessments of such major American writers as Benjamin Franklin, Nathaniel Hawthorne, Herman Melville, and Walt Whitman. In a way, he has taken on the role of a latter-day Edmund Wilson, delivering the sometimes arcane messages of an intellectual-aesthetic world to a popular audience in a comprehensible language. His collections of essays include *Assorted Prose* (1965), *Picked-Up Pieces* (1975), and *Hugging the Shore* (1983); the last volume, over 900 pages long, contains some of the best of Updike's criticism.

But Updike clearly considers himself foremost a writer of fiction. He has kept himself up to date on all aspects of the new in fiction, reviewing the work of such representative avant-garde figures as Samuel Beckett, Vladimir Nabokov, and Donald Barthelme quite favorably. But he has shied away from the easy generalization about postwar fiction, insisting on possibilities of newness within the tradition. He said in an interview in 1981: "It is reality after all that we care about and that we're trying to write about. . . .what excites me in prose is the feeling that I'm getting down something that's real, and I'm getting it right, and that it will radiate out from my words and the paper something of actuality. So I can't imagine a literature that is not realistic in this broad sense." Updike had earlier described the reality he is trying to write about as "middleness with all its grits, bumps, and anonymities, in its fullness of satisfaction and mystery."

ADDITIONAL READING

Self-Consciousness: Memoirs, 1989.

Charles Thomas Samuels, *John Updike,* 1969; Alice and Kenneth Hamilton, *The Elements of John Updike,* 1970; B. A. Sokloff and David E. Aranson, *John Updike: A Comprehensive Bibliography,* 1973; Rachel C. Burchard, *John Updike: Yea Sayings,* 1971; Larry E. Taylor, *Pastoral and Anti-Pastoral Patterns in John Updike's Fiction,* 1971; Joyce B. Markle, *Fighters and Lovers: Theme in the Novels of John Updike,* 1973; Edward P. Vargo, *Rainstorms and Fire: Ritual in the Novels of John Updike,* 1973; Michael A. Olivas, *An Annotated Bibliography of John Updike's Criticism, 1967–1973, and a Checklist of his Works,* 1975; David Thorburn and Howard Eiland, eds., *John Updike: A Collection of Critical Essays,* 1979; George W. Hunt, *John Updike and the Three Great Secret Things: Sex, Religion, and Art,* 1980; Susan Henning Uphaus, *John Updike,* 1980; Donald J. Greiner, *The Other John Updike: Poems, Short Stories, Prose, Play,* 1981; William R. Macnaughton, ed., *Critical Essays on John Updike,* 1982; Donald J. Greiner, *John Updike's Novels,* 1984; Robert Detweiler, *John Updike,* 1972, rev. 1984; George J. Searles, *The Fiction of Philip Roth and John Updike,* 1985; Judie Newman, *John Updike,* 1988.

TEXT

Pigeon Feathers and Other Stories, 1962.

Pigeon Feathers

When they moved to Firetown, things were upset, displaced, rearranged. A red cane-back sofa that had been the chief piece in the living room at Olinger was here banished, too big for the narrow country parlor, to the barn, and shrouded under a tarpaulin. Never again would David lie on its length all afternoon eating raisins and reading mystery novels and science fiction and P. G. Wodehouse.[1] The blue wing chair that had stood for years in the ghostly, immaculate guest bedroom, gazing through the windows curtained with dotted swiss toward the telephone wires and horse-chestnut trees and opposite houses, was here established importantly in front of the smutty little fireplace that supplied, in those first cold April days, their only heat. As a child, David had been afraid of the guest bedroom—it was there that he, lying sick with the measles, had seen a black rod the size of a yardstick jog along at a slight slant beside the edge of the bed and vanish when he screamed—and it was disquieting to have one of the elements of its haunted atmosphere basking by the fire, in the center of the family, growing sooty with use. The books that at home had gathered dust in the case beside the piano were here hastily stacked, all out of order, in the shelves that the carpenters had built along one wall below the deep-silled windows. David, at fourteen, had been more moved than a mover; like the furniture, he had to find a new place, and on the Saturday of the second week he tried to work off some of his disorientation by arranging the books.

It was a collection obscurely depressing to him, mostly books his mother had acquired when she was young: college anthologies of Greek plays and Romantic poetry, Will Durant's *Story of Philosophy*, a soft-leather set of Shakespeare with string bookmarks sewed to the bindings, *Green Mansions* boxed and illustrated with woodcuts, *I, the Tiger*, by Manuel Komroff, novels by names like Galsworthy and Ellen Glasgow and Irvin S. Cobb and Sinclair Lewis and "Elizabeth."[2] The odor of faded taste made him feel the ominous gap between himself and his parents, the insulting gulf of time that existed before he was born. Suddenly he was tempted to dip into this time. From the heaps of books piled around him on the worn old floorboards, he picked up Volume II of a four-volume set of *The Outline of History*, by H. G. Wells. Once David had read *The Time Machine* in an anthology; this gave him a small grip on the author.[3] The book's red binding had faded to orange-pink on the spine. When he lifted the cover, there was a sweetish, attic-like smell, and his mother's maiden name written in unfamiliar handwriting on the flyleaf—an upright, bold, yet careful signature, bearing a faint relation to the quick scrunched backslant that flowed with marvellous consistency across her shopping lists and budget accounts and Christmas cards to college friends from this same, vaguely menacing long ago.

He leafed through, pausing at drawings, done in an old-fashioned stippled style, of bas-reliefs, masks, Romans without pupils in their eyes, articles of ancient costume, fragments of pottery found in unearthed homes. He knew it would be interesting in a magazine, sandwiched between ads and jokes, but in this undiluted form history was somehow sour. The print was determinedly legible, and smug, like a lesson book. As he bent over the pages, yellow at the edges, they seemed rectangles of

---

[1]P.G. Wodehouse (1881–1975), British comic novelist who resided for a long period in the United States.
[2]Will Durant (1885–1981), American philosopher and historian; author of *The Story of Philosophy* (1926); *Green Mansions* (1904), a romantic novel set in South America by British author W. H. Hudson (1841–1922); Manuael Komroff (1890–1974), American writer, author of *I, the Tiger* (1933); John Galsworthy (1867–1933), British novelist and playwright, well-known for his *The Forsyte Saga* (1922); Ellen Glasgow (1874–1945), Southern American novelist of manners; Irvin

S. Cobb (1876–1944), American journalist and humorist; Sinclair Lewis (1885–1951), American author of satiric novels, such as *Main Street* (1920); "Elizabeth," pen name for Elizabeth Mary Russell (1866–1941), Australian novelist and author of the popular *Elizabeth and Her German Garden* (1898).
[3]H. G. Wells (1866–1946), British writer known for his futuristic novels, such as *The Time Machine* (1895), and the immensely popular *Outline of History* (1920).

dusty glass through which he looked down into unreal and irrelevant worlds. He could see things sluggishly move, and an unpleasant fullness came into his throat. His mother and grandmother fussed in the kitchen; the puppy, which they had just acquired, for "protection in the country," was cowering, with a sporadic panicked scrabble of claws, under the dining table that in their old home had been reserved for special days but that here was used for every meal.

Then, before he could halt his eyes, David slipped into Wells's account of Jesus. He had been an obscure political agitator, a kind of hobo, in a minor colony of the Roman Empire. By an accident impossible to reconstruct, he (the small *h* horrified David) survived his own crucifixion and presumably died a few weeks later. A religion was founded on the freakish incident. The credulous imagination of the times retrospectively assigned miracles and supernatural pretensions to Jesus; a myth grew, and then a church, whose theology at most points was in direct contradiction of the simple, rather communistic teachings of the Galilean.

It was as if a stone that for weeks and even years had been gathering weight in the web of David's nerves snapped them and plunged through the page and a hundred layers of paper underneath. These fantastic falsehoods—plainly untrue; churches stood everywhere, the entire nation was founded "under God"—did not at first frighten him; it was the fact that they had been permitted to exist in an actual human brain. This was the initial impact—that at a definite spot in time and space a brain black with the denial of Christ's divinity had been suffered to exist; that the universe had not spit out this ball of tar but allowed it to continue in its blasphemy, to grow old, win honors, wear a hat, write books that, if true, collapsed everything into a jumble of horror. The world outside the deep-silled windows—a rutted lawn, a whitewashed barn, a walnut tree frothy with fresh green—seemed a haven from which he was forever sealed off. Hot washrags seemed pressed against his cheeks.

He read the account again. He tried to supply out of his ignorance objections that would defeat the complacent march of these black words, and found none. Survivals and misunderstandings more farfetched were reported daily in the papers. But none of them caused churches to be built in every town. He tried to work backwards through the churches, from their brave high fronts through their shabby, ill-attended interiors back into the events at Jerusalem, and felt himself surrounded by shifting gray shadows, centuries of history, where he knew nothing. The thread dissolved in his hands. Had Christ ever come to him, David Kern, and said, "Here. Feel the wound in My side"? No; but prayers had been answered. What prayers? He had prayed that Rudy Mohn, whom he had purposely tripped so he cracked his head on their radiator, not die, and he had not died. But for all the blood, it was just a cut; Rudy came back the same day, wearing a bandage and repeating the same teasing words. He could never have died. Again, David had prayed for two separate war-effort posters he had sent away for to arrive tomorrow, and though they did not, they did arrive, some days later, together, popping through the clacking letter slot like a rebuke from God's mouth: *I answer your prayers in My way, in My time.* After that, he had made his prayers less definite, less susceptible of being twisted into a scolding. But what a tiny, ridiculous coincidence this was, after all, to throw into battle against H. G. Wells's engines of knowledge! Indeed, it proved the enemy's point: Hope bases vast premises on foolish accidents, and reads a word where in fact only a scribble exists.

His father came home. Though Saturday was a free day for him, he had been working. He taught school in Olinger and spent all his days performing, with a curious air of panic, needless errands. Also, a city boy by birth, he was frightened of the farm and seized any excuse to get away. The farm had been David's mother's birthplace; it had been her idea to buy it back. With an ingenuity and persistence unparalleled in her life, she had gained that end, and moved them all here—her son, her husband, her mother. Granmom, in her prime, had worked these fields alongside her husband, but now she dabbled around the kitchen futilely, her hands waggling with Parkinson's disease. She was always in the way. Strange, out in the country, amid eighty acres, they were crowded together. His father expressed his feelings of discomfort by conducting with Mother an endless argument about organic farming. All through dusk, all through supper, it rattled on.

"Elsie, I *know*, I know from my education, the earth is nothing but chemicals. It's the only damn thing I got out of four years of college, so don't tell me it's not true."

"George, if you'd just walk out on the farm you'd know it's not true. The land has a *soul*."

"Soil, has, no, soul," he said, enunciating stiffly, as if to a very stupid class. To David he said, "You can't argue with a femme. Your mother's a real femme. That's why I married her, and now I'm suffering for it."

"*This* soil has no soul," she said, "because it's been killed with superphosphate. It's been burned bare by Boyer's tenant farmers." Boyer was the rich man they had bought the farm from. "It used to have a soul, didn't it, Mother? When you and Pop farmed it?"

"Ach, yes; I guess." Granmom was trying to bring a forkful of food to her mouth with her less severely afflicted hand. In her anxiety she brought the other hand up from her lap. The crippled fingers, dull red in the orange light of the kerosene lamp in the center of the table, were welded by paralysis into one knobbed hook.

"Only human indi-vidu-als have souls," his father went on, in the same mincing, lifeless voice. "Because the Bible tells us so." Done eating, he crossed his legs and dug into his ear with a match miserably; to get at the thing inside his head he tucked in his chin, and his voice came out low-pitched at David. "When God made your mother, He made a real femme."

"George, don't you read the papers? Don't you know that between the chemical fertilizers and the bug sprays we'll all be dead in ten years? Heart attacks are killing every man in the country over forty-five."

He sighed wearily; the yellow skin of his eyelids wrinkled as he hurt himself with the match. "There's no connection," he stated, spacing his words with pained patience, "between the heart - and chemical fertilizers. It's alcohol that's doing it. Alcohol and milk. There is too much - cholesterol - in the tissues of the American heart. Don't tell me about chemistry, Elsie; I majored in the damn stuff for four years."

"Yes and I majored in Greek and I'm not a penny wiser. Mother, put your waggler *away!*" The old woman started, and the food dropped from her fork. For some reason, the sight of her bad hand at the table cruelly irritated her daughter. Granmom's eyes, worn bits of crazed crystal embedded in watery milk, widened behind her cock-eyed spectacles. Circles of silver as fine as thread, they clung to the red notches they had carved over the years into her little white beak. In the orange flicker of the kerosene lamp her dazed misery seemed infernal. David's mother began, without noise, to cry. His father did not seem to have eyes at all; just jaundiced sockets of wrinkled skin. The steam of food clouded the scene. It was horrible but the horror was particular and familiar, and distracted David from the formless dread that worked, sticky and sore, within him, like a too large wound trying to heal.

He had to go to the bathroom, and took a flashlight down through the wet grass to the outhouse. For once, his fear of spiders there felt trival. He set the flashlight, burning, beside him, and an insect alighted on its lens, a tiny insect, a mosquito or flea, made so fine that the weak light projected its X-ray onto the wall boards: the faint rim of its wings, the blurred strokes, magnified, of its long hinged legs, the dark cone at the heart of its anatomy. The tremor must be its heart beating. Without warning, David was visited by an exact vision of death: a long hole in the ground, no wider than your body, down which you are drawn while the white faces above recede. You try to reach them but your arms are pinned. Shovels pour dirt into your face.

There you will be forever, in an upright position, blind and silent, and in time no one will remember you, and you will never be called. As strata of rock shift, your fingers elongate, and your teeth are distended sideways in a great underground grimace indistinguishable from a strip of chalk. And the earth tumbles on, and the sun expires, and unaltering darkness reigns where once there were stars.

Sweat broke out on his back. His mind seemed to rebound off a solidness. Such extinction was not another threat, a graver sort of danger, a kind of pain; it was qualitatively different. It was not even a conception that could be voluntarily pictured; it entered him from outside. His protesting nerves swarmed on its surface like lichen on a meteor. The skin of his chest was soaked with the effort of rejection. At the same time that the fear was dense and internal, it was dense and all around him; a tide of clay had swept up to the stars; space was crushed into a mass. When he stood up, automatically hunching his shoulders to keep his head away from the spider webs, it was with a numb sense of being cramped between two huge volumes of rigidity. That he had even this small freedom to move surprised him. In the narrow shelter of that rank shack, adjusting his pants, he felt — his first spark of comfort — too small to be crushed.

But in the open, as the beam of the flashlight skidded with frightened quickness across the remote surfaces of the barn and the grape arbor and the giant pine that stood by the path to the woods, the terror descended. He raced up through the clinging grass pursued, not by one of the wild animals the woods might hold, or one of the goblins his superstitous grandmother had communicated to his childhood, but by spectres out of science fiction, where gigantic cinder moons fill half the turquoise sky. As David ran, a gray planet rolled inches behind his neck. If he looked back, he would be buried. And in the momentum of his terror, hideous possibilities — the dilation of the sun, the triumph of the insects, the crabs on the shore in *The Time Machine* — wheeled out of the vacuum of make-believe and added their weight to his impending oblivion.

He wrenched the door open; the lamps within the house flared. The wicks burning here and there seemed to mirror one another. His mother was washing the dishes in a little pan of heated pump-water; Granmom fluttered near her elbow apprehensively. In the living room — the downstairs of the little square house was two long rooms — his father sat in front of the black fireplace restlessly folding and unfolding a newspaper as he sustained his half of the argument. "Nitrogen, phosphorus, potash: these are the three replaceable consituents of the soil. One crop of corn carries away hundreds of pounds of" — he dropped the paper into his lap and ticked them off on three fingers — "nitrogen, phosphorus, potash."

"Boyer didn't grow corn."

"*Any* crop, Elsie. The human animal —"

"You're killing the *earth*worms, George!"

"The human animal, after thousands and *thou*sands of years, learned methods whereby the chemical balance of the soil may be maintained. Don't carry me back to the Dark Ages."

"When we moved to Olinger the ground in the garden was like slate. Just one summer of my cousin's chicken dung and the earthworms came back."

"I'm sure the Dark Ages were a fine place to the poor devils born in them, but I don't want to go there. They give me the creeps." Daddy stared into the cold pit of the fireplace and clung to the rolled newspaper in his lap as if it alone were keeping him from slipping backwards and down, down.

Mother came into the doorway brandishing a fistful of wet forks. "And thanks to your DDT there soon won't be a bee left in the country. When I was a girl here you could eat a peach without washing it."

"It's primitive, Elsie. It's Dark Age stuff."

"Oh what do *you* know about the Dark Ages?"

"I know I don't want to go back to them."

David took from the shelf, where he had placed it this afternoon, the great unabridged Webster's Dictionary that his grandfather had owned. He turned the big thin pages, floppy as cloth, to the entry he wanted, and read

> **soul** . . . 1. An entity conceived as the essence, substance, animating principle, or actuating cause of life, or of the individual life, esp. of life manifested in psychical activities; the vehicle of individual existence, separate in nature from the body and usually held to be separable in existence.

The definition went on, into Greek and Egyptian conceptions, but David stopped short on the treacherous edge of antiquity. He needed to read no further The careful overlapping words shingled a temporary shelter for him. "Usually held to be separable in existence"—what could be fairer, more judicious, surer?

His father was saying, "The modern farmer can't go around sweeping up after his cows. The poor devil has thousands and *thous*ands of acres on his hands. Your modern farmer uses a scientifically-arrived-at mixture, like five-ten-five, or six-twelve-six, or *three*-twelve-six, and spreads it on with this wonderful modern machinery which of course we can't afford. Your modern farmer can't *afford* medieval methods."

Mother was quiet in the kitchen; her silence radiated waves of anger.

"No now Elsie; don't play the femme with me. Let's discuss this calmly like two rational twentieth-century people. Your organic farming nuts aren't attacking five-ten-five; they're attacking the chemical fertilizer crooks. The monster firms."

A cup clinked in the kitchen. Mother's anger touched David's face; his cheeks burned guiltily. Just by being in the living room he was associated with his father. She appeared in the doorway with red hands and tears in her eyes, and said to the two of them, "I knew you didn't want to come here but I didn't know you'd torment me like this. You talked Pop into his grave and now you'll kill me. Go ahead, George, more power to you; at least I'll be buried in good ground." She tried to turn and met an obstacle and screamed, "Mother, stop hanging on my *back!* Why don't you go to *bed?*"

"Let's all go to bed," David's father said, rising from the blue wing chair and slapping his thigh with a newspaper. "This reminds me of death." It was a phrase of his that David had heard so often he never considered its sense.

Upstairs, he seemed to be lifted above his fears. The sheets on his bed were clean. Granmom had ironed them with a pair of flatirons saved from the Olinger attic; she plucked them hot off the stove alternately, with a wooden handle called a goose. It was a wonder, to see how she managed. In the next room, his parents grunted peaceably: they seemed to take their quarrels less seriously than he did. They made comfortable scratching noises as they carried a little lamp back and forth. Their door was open a crack, so he saw the light shift and swing. Surely there would be, in the last five minutes, in the last second, a crack of light, showing the door from the dark room to another, full of light. Thinking of it this vividly frightened him. His own dying, in a specific bed in a specific room, specific walls mottled with wallpaper, the dry whistle of his breathing, the murmuring doctors, the nervous relatives going in and out, but for him no way out but down into the funnel. *Never touch a doorknob again.* A whisper, and his parents' light was blown out. David prayed to be reassured. Though the experiment frightened him, he lifted his hands high into the darkness above his face and begged Christ to touch them. Not hard or long: the faintest, quickest grip would be final for a lifetime. His hands waited in the air, itself a substance, which seemed to move through his fingers; or was it the pressure of his pulse? He returned his hands to beneath the covers uncertain if they had been touched or not. For would not Christ's touch *be* infinitely gentle?

Through all the eddies of its aftermath, David clung to this thought about his revelation of extinction: that there, in the outhouse, he had struck a solidness qualitatively different, a rock of horror firm enough to support any height of construction. All he needed was a little help; a word, a gesture, a nod of certainty, and he would be sealed in, safe. The assurance from the dictionary had melted in the night. Today was Sunday, a hot fair day. Across a mile of clear air the church bells called, *Celebrate, celebrate.* Only Daddy went. He put on a coat over his rolled-up shirtsleeves and got into the little old black Plymouth parked by the barn and went off, with the same pained hurried grimness of all his actions. His churning wheels, as he shifted too hastily into second, raised plumes of red dust on the dirt road. Mother walked to the far field, to see what bushes needed cutting. David, though he usually preferred to stay in the house, went with her. The puppy followed at a distance, whining as it picked its way through the stubble but floundering off timidly if one of them went back to pick it up and carry it. When they reached the crest of the far field, his mother asked, "David, what's troubling you?"

"Nothing. Why?"

She looked at him sharply. The greening woods crosshatched the space beyond her half-gray hair. Then she showed him her profile, and gestured toward the house, which they had left a half-mile behind them. "See how it sits in the land? They don't know how to build with the land any more. Pop always said the foundations were set with the compass. We must try to get a compass and see. It's supposed to face due south; but south feels a little more *that* way to me." From the side, as she said these things, she seemed handsome and young. The smooth sweep of her hair over her ear seemed white with a purity and calm that made her feel foreign to him. He had never regarded his parents as consolers of his troubles; from the beginning they had seemed to have more troubles than he. Their confusion had flattered him into an illusion of strength; so now on this high clear ridge he jealously guarded the menace all around them, blowing like a breeze on his fingertips, the possibility of all this wide scenery sinking into darkness. The strange fact that though she came to look at the brush she carried no clippers, for she had a fixed prejudice against working on Sundays, was the only consolation he allowed her to offer.

As they walked back, the puppy whimpering after them, the rising dust behind a distant line of trees announced that Daddy was speeding home from church. When they reach the house he was there. He had brought back the Sunday paper and the vehement remark, "Dobson's too intelligent for these farmers. They just sit there with their mouths open and don't hear a thing the poor devil's saying."

"What makes you think farmers are unintelligent? This country was made by farmers. George Washington was a farmer."

"They are, Elsie. They are unintelligent. George Washington's dead. In this day and age only the misfits stay on the farm. The lame, the halt, the blind. The morons with one arm. Human garbage. They remind me of death, sitting there with their mouths open."

"My *father* was a farmer."

"He was a frustrated man, Elsie. He never knew what hit him. The poor devil meant so well, and he never knew which end was up. Your mother'll bear me out. Isn't that right, Mom? Pop never knew what hit him?"

"Ach, I guess not," the old woman quavered, and the ambiguity for the moment silenced both sides.

David hid in the funny papers and sports section until one-thirty. At two, the catechetical class met at the Firetown church. He had transferred from the catechetical class of the Lutheran church in Olinger, a humiliating comedown. In Olinger they met on Wednesday nights, spiffy and spruce, in the atmosphere of a dance. Afterwards, blessed by the brick-faced minister from whose lips the word "Christ" fell like a burning stone, the more daring of them went with their Bibles to a luncheonette and smoked. Here in Firetown, the girls were dull white cows and the boys narrow-faced brown goats in old men's suits, herded on Sunday afternoons into a threadbare church basement that smelled of stale hay. Because his father had taken the car on one of his endless errands to Olinger, David walked, grateful for the open air and the silence. The catechetical class embarrassed him, but today he placed hope in it, as the source of the nod, the gesture, that was all he needed.

Reverend Dobson was a delicate young man with great dark eyes and small white shapely hands that flickered like protesting doves when he preached; he seemed a bit misplaced in the Lutheran ministry. This was his first call. It was a split parish; he served another rural church twelve miles away. His iridescent green Ford, new six months ago, was spattered to the windows with red mud and rattled from bouncing on the rude back roads, where he frequently got lost, to the malicious satisfaction of many. But David's mother liked him, and, more pertinent to his success, the Haiers, the sleek family of feed merchants and innkeepers and tractor salesmen who dominated the Firetown church, liked him. David liked him, and felt liked in turn; sometimes in class, after some special stupidity, Dobson directed toward him out of those wide black eyes a mild look of disbelief, a look that, though flattering, was also delicately disquieting.

Catechetical instruction consisted of reading aloud from a work booklet answers to problems prepared during the week, problems like, "I am the _____, the _____, and the _____, saith the Lord."[4] Then there was a question period in which no one ever asked any questions. Today's theme was the last third of the Apostles' Creed.[5] When the time came for questions, David blushed and asked, "About the Resurrection of the Body—are we conscious between the time when we die and the Day of Judgment?"

Dobson blinked, and his fine little mouth pursed, suggesting that David was making difficult things more difficult. The faces of the other students went blank, as if an indiscretion had been committed.

"No, I suppose not," Reverend Dobson said.

"Well, where is our soul, then, in this gap?"

The sense grew, in the class, of a naughtiness occurring. Dobson's shy eyes watered, as if he were straining to keep up the formality of attention, and one of the girls, the fattest, simpered toward her twin, who was a little less fat. Their chairs were arranged in a rough circle. The current running around the circle panicked David. Did everybody know something he didn't know?

"I suppose you could say our souls are asleep," Dobson said.

"And then they wake up, and there is the earth like it always is, and all the people who have ever lived? Where will Heaven be?"

Anita Haier giggled. Dobson gazed at David intently, but with an awkward, puzzled flicker of forgiveness, as if there existed a secret between them that David was violating. But David knew of no secret. All he wanted was to hear Dobson repeat the words he said every Sunday morning. This he would not do. As if these words were unworthy of the conversational voice.

"David, you might think of Heaven this way: as the way the goodness Abraham Lincoln did lives after him."

"But is Lincoln conscious of it living on?" He blushed no longer with embarrassment but in anger; he had walked here in good faith and was being made a fool.

"Is he conscious now? I would have to say no; but I don't think it matters." His voice had a coward's firmness; he was hostile now.

"You don't."

---

[4] Cf. John 14:6: "I am the way, the truth, and the life."
[5] A creed ascribed to Christ's apostles, beginning "I believe in God the Father Almighty" and ending with a belief in the "Resurrection of the Body."

"Not in the eyes of God, no." The unction, the stunning impudence, of this reply sprang tears of outrage in David's eyes. He bowed them to his book, where short words like Duty, Love, Obey, Honor, were stacked in the form of a cross.

"Were there any other questions, David?" Dobson asked with renewed gentleness. The others were rustling, collecting their books.

"No." He made his voice firm, though he could not bring up his eyes.

"Did I answer your question fully enough?"

"Yes."

In the minister's silence the shame that should have been his crept over David: the burden and fever of being a fraud were placed upon *him*, who was innocent, and it seemed, he knew, a confession of this guilt that on the way out he was unable to face Dobson's stirred gaze, though he felt it probing the side of his head.

Anita Haier's father gave him a ride down the highway as far as the dirt road. David said he wanted to walk the rest, and figured that his offer was accepted because Mr. Haier did not want to dirty his bright blue Buick with dust. This was all right; everything was all right, as long as it was clear. His indignation at being betrayed, at seeing Christianity betrayed, had hardened him. The straight dirt road reflected his hardness. Pink stones thrust up through its packed surface. The April sun beat down from the center of the afternoon half of the sky; already it had some of summer's heat. Already the fringes of weeds at the edges of the road were bedraggled with dust. From the reviving grass and scruff of the fields he walked between, insects were sending up a monotonous, automatic chant. In the distance a tiny figure in his father's coat was walking along the edge of the woods. His mother. He wondered what joy she found in such walks; to him the brown stretches of slowly rising and falling land expressed only a huge exhaustion.

Flushed with fresh air and happiness, she returned from her walk earlier than he had expected, and surprised him at his grandfather's Bible. It was a stumpy black book, the boards worn thin where the old man's fingers had held them; the spine hung by one weak hinge of fabric. David had been looking for the passage where Jesus says to the one thief on the cross, "Today shalt thou be with me in paradise."[6] He had never tried reading the Bible for himself before. What was so embarrassing about being caught at it, was that he detested the apparatus of piety. Fusty churches, creaking hymns, ugly Sunday-school teachers and their stupid leaflets — he hated everything about them but the promise they held out, a promise that in the most perverse way, as if the homeliest crone in the kingdom were given the Prince's hand, made every good and real thing, ball games and jokes and pert-breasted girls, possible. He couldn't explain this to his mother. There was no time. Her solicitude was upon him.

"David, what are you doing?"

"Nothing."

"What are you doing at Grandpop's Bible?"

"Trying to read it. This is supposed to be a Christian country, isn't it?"

She sat down on the green sofa, which used to be in the sun parlor at Olinger, under the fancy mirror. A little smile still lingered on her face from the walk. "David, I wish you'd talk to me."

"What about?"

"About whatever it is that's troubling you. Your father and I have both noticed it."

"I asked Reverend Dobson about Heaven and he said it was like Abraham Lincoln's goodness living after him."

He waited for the shock to strike her. "Yes?" she said, expecting more.

"That's all."

"And why didn't you like it?"

---

[6]Cf. Luke 23:43.

"Well; don't you see? It amounts to saying there isn't any Heaven at all."

"I don't see that it amounts to that. What do you want Heaven to be?"

"Well, I don't know. I want it to be *something*. I thought he'd tell me what it was. I thought that was his job." He was becoming angry, sensing her surprise at him. She had assumed that Heaven had faded from his head years ago. She had imagined that he had already entered, in the secrecy of silence, the conspiracy that he now knew to be all around him.

"David," she asked gently, "don't you ever want to rest?"

"No. Not forever."

"David, you're so young. When you get older, you'll feel differently."

"Grandpa didn't. Look how tattered this book is."

"I never understood your grandfather."

"Well I don't understand ministers who say it's like Lincoln's goodness going on and on. Suppose you're not Lincoln?"

"I think Reverend Dobson made a mistake. You must try to forgive him."

"It's not a *question* of his making a mistake! It's a question of dying and never moving or seeing or hearing anything ever again."

"But"—in exasperation—"darling, it's so *greedy* of you to want more. When God has given us this wonderful April day, and given us this farm, and you have your whole life ahead of you—"

"You think, then, that there is God?"

"Of course I do"—with deep relief, that smoothed her features into a reposeful oval. He had risen and was standing too near her for his comfort. He was afraid she would reach out and touch him.

"He made everything? You feel that?"

"Yes."

"Then who made Him?"

"Why, Man. Man." The happiness of this answer lit up her face radiantly, until she saw his gesture of disgust. She was so simple, so illogical; such a femme.

"Well that amounts to saying there is none."

Her hand reached for his wrist but he backed away. "David, it's a mystery. A miracle. It's a miracle more beautiful than any Reverend Dobson could have told you about. You don't say houses don't exist because Man made them."

"No. God has to be different."

"But, David, you have the *evidence*. Look out the window at the sun; at the fields."

"Mother, good grief. Don't you see"—he rasped away the roughness in his throat—"if when we die there's nothing, all your sun and fields and what not are all, ah, *horror*? It's just an ocean of horror."

"But David, it's not. It's so clearly not that." And she made an urgent opening gesture with her hands that expressed, with its suggestion of a willingness to receive his helplessness, all her grace, her gentleness, her love of beauty, gathered into a passive intensity that made him intensely hate her. He would not be wooed away from the truth. *I am the Way, the Truth . . .*

"No," he told her. "Just let me alone."

He found his tennis ball behind the piano and went outside to throw it against the side of the house. There was a patch high up where the brown stucco that had been laid over the sandstone masonry was crumbling away; he kept trying with the tennis ball to chip more pieces off. Superimposed upon his deep ache was a smaller but more immediate worry; that he had hurt his mother. He heard his father's car rattling on the straightaway, and went into the house, to make peace before he arrived. To his relief, she was not giving off the stifling damp heat of her anger, but instead was cool, decisive, maternal. She handed him an old green book, her college text of Plato.

"I want you to read the Parable of the Cave,"[7] she said.

"All right," he said, though he knew it would do no good. Some story by a dead Greek just vague enough to please her. "Don't worry about it, Mother."

"I *am* worried. Honestly, David, I'm sure there will be something for us. As you get older, these things seem to matter a great deal less."

"That may be. It's a dismal thought, though."

His father bumped at the door. The locks and jambs stuck here. But before Granmom could totter to the latch and let him in, he had knocked it open. He had been in Olinger dithering with track meet tickets. Although Mother usually kept her talks with David a confidence, a treasure between them, she called instantly, "George, David is worried about death!"

He came to the doorway of the living room, his shirt pocket bristling with pencils, holding in one hand a pint box of melting ice cream and in the other the knife with which he was about to divide it into four sections, their Sunday treat. "Is the kid worried about death? Don't give it a thought, David. I'll be lucky if I live till tomorrow, and I'm not worried. If they'd taken a buckshot gun and shot me in the cradle I'd be better off. The *world*'d be better off. Hell, I think death is a wonderful thing. I look forward to it. Get the garbage out of the way. If I had the man here who invented death, I'd pin a medal on him."

"Hush, George. You'll frighten the child worse than he is."

This was not true; he never frightened David. There was no harm in his father, no harm at all. Indeed, in the man's steep self-disgust the boy felt a kind of ally. A distant ally. He saw his position with a certain strategic coldness. Nowhere in the world of other people would he find the hint, the nod, he needed to begin to build his fortress against death. They none of them believed. He was alone. In that deep hole.

In the months that followed, his position changed little. School was some comfort. All those sexy, perfumed people, wisecracking, chewing gum, all of them doomed to die, and none of them noticing. In their company David felt that they would carry him along into the bright, cheap paradise reserved for them. In any crowd, the fear ebbed a little; he had reasoned that somewhere in the world there must exist a few people who believed what was necessary, and the larger the crowd, the greater the chance that he was near such a soul, within calling distance, if only he was not too ignorant, too ill-equipped, to spot him. The sight of clergymen cheered him; whatever they themselves thought, their collars were still a sign that somewhere, at some time, someone had recognized that we cannot, *cannot,* submit to death. The sermon topics posted outside churches, the flip, hurried pieties of disc jockeys, the cartoons in magazines showing angels or devils—on such scraps he kept alive the possibility of hope.

For the rest, he tried to drown his hopelessness in clatter and jostle. The pinball machine at the luncheonette was a merciful distraction; as he bent over its buzzing, flashing board of flippers and cushions, the weight and constriction in his chest lightened and loosened. He was grateful for all the time his father wasted in Olinger. Every delay postponed the moment when they must ride together down the dirt road into the heart of the dark farmland, where the only light was the kerosene lamp waiting on the dining-room table, a light that drowned their food in shadow and made it sinister.

He lost his appetite for reading. He was afraid of being ambushed again. In mystery novels people died like dolls being discarded; in science fiction enormities of

[7]The Parable of the Cave is related in *The Republic* by Greek philosopher Plato (c. 428–348 B.C.). The parable describes the plight of humankind by suggesting that it is like that of a prisoner in a cave, seeing only shadows cast on a wall (sense experience); but he frees himself and sees behind him the objects and the light casting the shadows (the world of belief); next he finds his way through an opening and is blinded by sunlight (the true reality, the world of abstract forms).

space and time conspired to crush the humans; and even in P.G. Wodehouse he felt a hollowness, a turning away from reality that was implicitly bitter, and became explicit in the comic figures of futile clergymen. All gaiety seemed minced out on the skin of a void. All quiet hours seemed invitations to dread.

Even on weekends, he and his father contrived to escape the farm; and when, some Saturdays, they did stay home, it was do something destructive—tear down an old henhouse or set huge brush fires that threatened, while Mother shouted and flapped her arms, to spread to the woods. Whenever his father worked, it was with rapt violence; when he chopped kindling, fragments of the old henhouse boards flew like shrapnel and the ax-head was always within a quarter of an inch of flying off the handle. He was exhilarating to watch, sweating and swearing and sucking bits of saliva back into his lips.

School stopped. His father took the car in the opposite direction, to a highway construction job where he had been hired for the summer as a timekeeper, and David was stranded in the middle of acres of heat and greenery and blowing pollen and the strange, mechanical humming that lay invisibly in the weeds and alfalfa and dry orchard grass.

For his fifteenth birthday his parents gave him, with jokes about him being a hillbilly now, a Remington .22. It was something like a pinball machine to take it out to the old kiln in the woods where they dumped their trash, and set up tin cans on the kiln's sandstone shoulder and shoot them off one by one. He'd take the puppy, who had grown long legs and a rich coat of reddish fur—he was part chow. Copper hated the gun but loved the boy enough to accompany him. When the flat acrid crack rang out, he would race in terrified circles that would tighten and tighten until they brought him, shivering, against David's legs. Depending upon his mood, David would shoot again or drop to his knees and comfort the dog. Giving this comfort to a degree returned comfort to him. The dog's ears, laid flat against his skull in fear, were folded so intricately, so—he groped for the concept—*surely.* Where the dull-studded collar made the fur stand up, each hair showed a root of soft white under the length, black-tipped, of the metal-color that had lent the dog its name. In his agitation Copper panted through nostrils that were elegant slits, like two healed cuts, or like the keyholes of a dainty lock of black, grained wood. His whole whorling, knotted, jointed body was a wealth of such embellishments. And in the smell of the dog's hair David seemed to descend through many finely differentiated layers of earth: mulch, soil, sand, clay, and the glittering mineral base.

But when he returned to the house, and saw the books arranged on the low shelves, fear returned. The four adamant volumes of Wells like four thin bricks, the green Plato that had puzzled him with its queer softness and tangled purity, and dead Galsworthy and "Elizabeth," Grandpa's mammoth dictionary, Grandpa's Bible, the Bible that he himself had received on becoming a member of the Firetown Lutheran Church—at the sight of these, the memory of his fear reawakened and came around him. He had grown stiff and stupid in its embrace. His parents tried to think of ways to entertain him.

"David, I have a job for you to do," his mother said one evening at the table.

"What?"

"If you're going to take that tone perhaps we'd better not talk."

"What tone? I didn't take any tone."

"Your grandmother thinks there are too many pigeons in the barn."

"Why?" David turned to look at his grandmother, but she sat there staring at the burning lamp with her usual expression of bewilderment.

Mother shouted, "Mom, he wants to know why!"

Granmom made a jerky, irritable motion with her bad hand, as if generating the force for utterance, and said, "They foul the furniture."

"That's right," Mother said. "She's afraid for that old Olinger furniture that we'll never use. David, she's been after me for a month about those poor pigeons. She wants you to shoot them."

"I don't want to kill anything especially," David said.

Daddy said, "The kid's like you are, Elsie. He's too good for this world. Kill or be killed, that's my motto."

His mother said loudly, "Mother, he doesn't want to do it."

"Not?" The old lady's eyes distended as if in horror, and her claw descended slowly to her lap.

"Oh, I'll do it, I'll do it tomorrow," David snapped, and a pleasant crisp taste entered his mouth with the decision.

"And I had thought, when Boyer's men made the hay, it would be better if the barn doesn't look like a rookery," his mother added needlessly.

A barn, in day, is a small night. The splinters of light between the dry shingles pierce the high roof like stars, and the rafters and crossbeams and built-in ladders seem, until your eyes adjust, as mysterious as the branches of a haunted forest. David entered silently, the gun in one hand. Copper whined desperately at the door, too frightened to come in with the gun yet unwilling to leave the boy. David stealthily turned, said "Go away," shut the door on the dog, and slipped the bolt across. It was a door within a door; the double door for wagons and tractors was as high and wide as the face of a house.

The smell of old straw scratched his sinuses. The red sofa, half-hidden under its white-splotched tarpaulin, seemed assimilated into this smell, sunk in it, buried. The mouths of empty bins gaped like caves. Rusty oddments of farming—coils of baling wire, some spare tines for a harrow, a handleless shovel—hung on nails driven here and there in the thick wood. He stood stock-still a minute; it took a while to separate the cooing of the pigeons from the rustling in his ears. When he had focused on the cooing, it flooded the vast interior with its throaty, bubbling outpour: there seemed no other sound. They were up behind the beams. What light there was leaked through the shingles and the dirty glass windows at the far end and the small round holes, about as big as basketballs, high on the opposite stone side walls, under the ridge of the roof.

A pigeon appeared in one of these holes, on the side toward the house. It flew in, with a battering of wings, from the outside, and waited there, silhouetted against its pinched bit of sky, preening and cooing in a throbbing, thrilled, tentative way. David tiptoed four steps to the side, rested his gun against the lowest rung of a ladder pegged between two upright beams, and lowered the gunsight into the bird's tiny, jauntily cocked head. The slap of the report seemed to come off the stone wall behind him, and the pigeon did not fall. Neither did it fly. Instead it stuck in the round hole, pirouetting rapidly and nodding its head as if in frantic agreement. David shot the bolt back and forth and had aimed again before the spent cartridge had stopped jingling on the boards by his feet. He eased the tip of the sight a little lower, into the bird's breast, and took care to squeeze the trigger with perfect evenness. The slow contraction of his hand abruptly sprang the bullet; for a half-second there was doubt, and then the pigeon fell like a handful of rags, skimming down the barn wall into the layer of straw that coated the floor of the mow on this side.

Now others shook loose from the rafters, and whirled in the dim air with a great blurred hurtle of feathers and noise. They would go for the hole; he fixed his sight on the little moon of blue, and when a pigeon came to it, shot him as he was walking the ten inches of stone that would have carried him into the open air. This pigeon lay down in that tunnel of stone, unable to fall either one way or the other, although he was alive enough to lift one wing and cloud the light. It would sink back, and he would suddenly lift it again, the feathers flaring. His body blocked that exit. David raced to the other side of the barn's main aisle, where a similar ladder was symmetrically placed, and rested his gun on the same rung. Three birds came together to this hole; he got one, and two got through. The rest resettled in the rafters.

There was a shallow triangular space behind the cross beams supporting the roof. It was here they roosted and hid. But either the space was too small, or they were curious, for now that his eyes were at home in the dusty gloom David could see little dabs of gray popping in and out. The cooing was shriller now; its apprehensive tremolo made the whole volume of air seem liquid. He noticed one little smudge of a head that was especially persistent in peeking out; he marked the place, and fixed his gun on it, and when the head appeared again, had his finger tightened in advance on the trigger. A parcel of fluff slipped off the beam and fell the barn's height onto a canvas covering some Olinger furniture, and where its head had peeked out there was a fresh prick of light in the shingles.

Standing in the center of the floor, fully master now, disdaining to steady the barrel with anything but his arm, he killed two more that way. He felt like a beautiful avenger. Out of the shadowy ragged infinity of the vast barn roof these impudent things dared to thrust their heads, presumed to dirty its starred silence with their filthy timorous life, and he cut them off, tucked them back neatly into the silence. He had the sensation of a creator; these little smudges and flickers that he was clever to see and even cleverer to hit in the dim recesses of the rafters — out of each of them he was making a full bird. A tiny peek, probe, dab of life, when he hit it, blossomed into a dead enemy, falling with good, final weight.

The imperfection of the second pigeon he had shot, who was still lifting his wing now and then up in the round hole, nagged him. He put a new clip into the stock. Hugging the gun against his body, he climbed the ladder. The barrel sight scratched his ear; he had a sharp, garish vision, like a color slide, of shooting himself and being found tumbled on the barn floor among his prey. He locked his arm around the top rung — a fragile, gnawed rod braced between uprights — and shot into the bird's body from a flat angle. The wing folded, but the impact did not, as he hoped, push the bird out of the hole. He fired again, and again, and still the little body, lighter than air when alive, was too heavy to budge from its high grave. From up here he could see green trees and a brown corner of the house through the hole. Clammy with the cobwebs that gathered between the rungs, he pumped a full clip of eight bullets into the stubborn shadow, with no success. He climbed down, and was struck by the silence in the barn. The remaining pigeons must have escaped out the other hole. That was all right; he was tired of it.

He stepped with his rifle into the light. His mother was coming to meet him, and it tickled him to see her shy away from the carelessly held gun. "You took a chip out of the house," she said. "What were those last shots about?"

"One of them died up in that little round hole and I was trying to shoot it down."

"Copper's hiding behind the piano and won't come out. I had to leave him."

"Well don't blame me. *I* didn't want to shoot the poor devils."

"Don't smirk. You look like your father. How many did you get?"

"Six."

She went into the barn, and he followed. She listened to the silence. Her hair was scraggly, perhaps from tussling with the dog. "I don't suppose the others will be back," she said wearily. "Indeed, I don't know why I let Mother talk me into it. Their cooing was such a comforting noise." She began to pick up the dead pigeons. Though he didn't want to touch them, David went into the mow and picked up by its tepid, horny, coral-colored feet the first bird he had killed. Its wings unfolded disconcertingly, as if the creature had been held together by threads that now were slit. It did not weigh much. He retrieved the one on the other side of the barn; his mother got the three in the middle and led the way across the road to the little southern slope of land that went down toward the foundations of the vanished tobacco shed. The ground was too steep to plant and mow; wild strawberries grew in the tangled grass. She put her burden down and said, "We'll have to bury them. The dog will go wild."

He put his two down on her three; the slick feathers let the bodies slide liquidly on one another. He asked, "Shall I get you the shovel?"

"Get it for yourself; *you* bury them. They're your kill. And be sure to make the hole deep enough so he won't dig them up." While he went to the tool shed for the shovel, she went into the house. Unlike her, she did not look up, either at the orchard to the right of her or at the meadow on her left, but instead held her head rigidly, tilted a little, as if listening to the ground.

He dug the hole, in a spot where there were no strawberry plants, before he studied the pigeons. He had never seen a bird this close before. The feathers were more wonderful than dog's hair, for each filament was shaped within the shape of the feather, and the feathers in turn were trimmed to fit a pattern that flowed without error across the bird's body. He lost himself in the geometrical tides as the feathers now broadened and stiffened to make an edge for flight, now softened and constricted to cup warmth around the mute flesh. And across the surface of the infinitely adjusted yet somehow effortless mechanics of the feathers played idle designs of color, no two alike, designs executed, it seemed, in a controlled rapture, with a joy that hung level in the air above and behind him. Yet these birds bred in the millions and were exterminated as pests. Into the fragrant open earth he dropped one broadly banded in slate shades of blue, and on top of it another, mottled all over in rhythms of lilac and gray. The next was almost wholly white, but for a salmon glaze at its throat. As he fitted the last two, still pliant, on the top, and stood up, crusty coverings were lifted from him, and with a feminine, slipping sensation along his nerves that seemed to give the air hands, he was robed in this certainty: that the God who had lavished such craft upon these worthless birds would not destroy His whole Creation by refusing to let David live forever.

1961, 1962

PHILIP ROTH
(b. 1933)

In a 1960 lecture, later published as "Writing American Fiction" (1961, 1975), Philip Roth observed: "The American writer in the middle of the twentieth century has his hands full in trying to understand, describe, and then make *credible* much of American reality. It stupefies, it sickens, it infuriates, and finally it is even a kind of embarrassment to one's meager imagination. The actuality is continually outdoing our talents, and the culture tosses up figures almost daily that are the envy of any novelist." Roth concluded: "That the communal predicament *is* distressing weighs upon the writer no less, and perhaps even more, than upon his neighbor—for to the writer the community is, properly, both subject and audience. And it may be that when this situation produces not only feelings of disgust, rage, and melancholy but impotence too, the writer is apt to lose heart and turn finally to other matters, to the construction of wholly imaginary worlds, and to a celebration of the self, which may, in a variety of ways, become his subject, as well as the impetus that establishes the perimeters of his technique."

What Roth seems to have done was to outline the course of postmodernist fiction before anyone knew that it had come into existence — the flight into fantasy and the concern for self in self-reflexiveness. Although there are some flights into fantasy in Roth's fiction, and his protagonists often appear to be distorted versions of himself, he seems on the whole to be more in the tradition than out of it. The novelists with whom he identifies, and with whom we identify him, are Saul Bellow and Bernard Malamud, not Vladimir Nabokov nor John Barth.

Roth was born in Newark, New Jersey, at the height of the Great Depression in 1933. His father was an insurance agent, and the family was relatively affluent during the years of the Second World War, the time of Roth's growing up. After one year at the Newark Branch of Rutgers University, he entered Bucknell University, graduating magna cum laude in 1954. He took an M.A. in English at the University of Chicago in 1955 and then enlisted in the army. Discharged after being injured in basic training, Roth returned to the University of Chicago to resume graduate work and serve as an instructor in English (1956–58). He would, like Bellow, continue to teach at various universities long after achieving success as a novelist — primarily for what the experience brought to his life as a writer.

As an undergraduate at Bucknell, Roth began to publish stories in the college literary magazine, which he founded and edited. Later, one of his stories was selected to appear in *The Best Short Stories of 1956*. During the latter 1950s his stories were accepted by the *Paris Review, The New Yorker,* and *Esquire.* In 1959, when he was twenty-six, he published his first book, *Goodbye Columbus, and Five Short Stories.* Although it won the National Book Award, it inspired a charge about Roth's fiction that would persist in following him whenever he published a new book: that his satiric exposure of the Jewish *nouveau riche* was a betrayal of his own Jewishness and played directly into the hands of anti-Semites. Indeed, the controversy itself became integrated into the fictions that Roth would continue to create out of his personal experiences.

Roth's next two novels, *Letting Go* (1962) and *When She Was Good* (1967), did not seem to live up to the promise of Roth's first book. The first was based on his experiences teaching at the University of Chicago; the second exploited the experiences of his unhappy marriage in 1959 to a midwestern gentile (who died in 1968). Neither book struck reviewers as rooted in Roth's natural materials which he had discovered in *Goodbye, Columbus.* But in *Portnoy's Complaint,* published in 1969, Roth seemed to be back on track — and again a center of controversy. The book, in the form of an extended confession, depicts its Jewish protagonist locked in combat with his dominating Jewish mother and trying to overcome his hang-up — infatuation with barely literate gentile girls who perform for his sexual pleasure whatever and whenever he desires (at some surprising places and times). He alternates between indulgence in his infatuations and bouts of masturbation in lonely isolation. The work was for most readers high comedy in a raunchy American tradition, but for some it was a scandalous pandering to anti-Semitism.

The next three of Roth's novels were all in some ways a flight into fantasy. *Our Gang* (1971) is political satire, in which the main target is a president named Trick E. Dixon. *The Breast* (1972) is a Kafkaesque tale of a professor turning into a six-foot female breast. *The Great American Novel* (1973) follows the fortunes of a baseball team, making do in face of the shortage of fit men after the Second World War, using a fourteen-year-old second baseman, a one-legged catcher, and a one-armed outfielder. These novels had their fans, but they appeared to be a detour from Roth's development as a novelist.

In his next two novels, Roth edged back into his natural subject, his own trans-figured experience, now as a writer and sometime professor. *My Life as a Man* (1974) presents the life of an author, using two of his own stories to explore the interrelationships of life and fiction. *The Professor of Desire* (1977) reincarnates the professor of *The Breast* before his metamorphosis and portrays his entangle-ments with love, both in the classroom (he taught a course in "Erotic Literature, Desire 341") and in the bedroom.

In his next several years, Roth hit his stride in a series of works that can be described as belonging to his major phase. The works, forming a trilogy, all deal with the career of an author named Nathan Zuckerman. In *The Ghost Writer* (1979), Zuckerman, at the beginning of his career, pays a visit on a master crafts-man, E. I. Lonoff (modeled loosely on Bernard Malamud), and makes the dis-covery that Lonoff's young and attractive wife is Anne Frank, who has secretly and miraculously survived the holocaust. *Zuckerman Unbound* (1981) portrays the highly successful Zuckerman trying to cope with his success, particularly at-tempting to make peace with his critical father. *The Anatomy Lesson* (1985) takes up an aging Zuckerman trying to change his profession (to medicine) and also trying to deal with his pursuing critics. In 1985, the three Zuckerman novels were published together as *Zuckerman Bound: A Trilogy and Epilogue*. The epi-logue, entitled "The Prague Orgy," is set in Czechoslovakia, and brings Zuckerman to the city and country of Franz Kafka, a writer that Roth had read deeply and strongly admired.

Roth's *The Counterlife,* published in 1986, reintroduces Nathan Zuckerman, now reappraising his life and comparing it to the life his brother the dentist, Henry Zuckerman, had lived. The critical reception was mixed: some critics were charmed by the device of including alternate possibilities in the course of the novel's events; and others were convinced that Roth had written himself finally into a corner. Roth next turned away from fiction and in 1988 published *The Facts: A Novelist's Autobiography,* in a sense bringing his career full circle: here-tofore, he had written novels that read like veiled autobiography; now he pro-duced an autobiography that read like a covert novel. Roth collected his inter-views and essays into a volume, *Reading Myself and Others*, in 1975; it included important comments on various of his novels as well as his early essay "Writing American Fiction" and other occasional pieces.

When asked by Joyce Carol Oates in an interview in 1974 about his celebration of "sheer playfulness" in such novels as *The Great American Novel,* Roth answered with a good deal of sense in the guise of nonsense: "Sheer Playfulness and Deadly Seriousness are my closest friends; it is with them that I take those walks in the country at the end of the day [after a long stint of writing in isolation]. I am also on friendly terms with Deadly Playfulness, Playful Playfulness, Serious Play-fulness, Serious Seriousness, and Sheer Sheerness. From the last, however, I get nothing; he just wrings my heart and leaves me speechless."

ADDITIONAL READING

A Philip Roth Reader, 1980.

Glenn Meeter, *Philip Roth and Bernard Malamud,* 1968; Stanley Cooperman, *Philip Roth's Portnoy's Complaint: A Critical Commentary,* 1973; John McDaniel, *The Fiction of Philip Roth,* 1974; Sanford Pinsker, *The Comedy that "Hoits": An Essay on the Fiction of Philip Roth,* 1975; Bernard F. Rodgers, Jr., *Philip Roth,* 1978; Judith Paterson Jones and Guinevera A. Nance, *Philip Roth,* 1981; Hermione Lee, *Philip Roth,* 1982; Sanford Pinsker, ed., *Critical Essays on Philip Roth,* 1982; Bernard F. Rodgers, Jr., *Philip Roth: A Bibliography,* 1974, rev. 1984, Asher Z. Milbauer and Donald G. Watson, eds., *Reading Philip Roth,* 1988.

TEXT

Goodbye, Columbus, and Five Short Stories, 1959, rpt. 1989 (with Preface by Author).

Defender of the Faith[1]

In May of 1945, only a few weeks after the fighting had ended in Europe, I was rotated back to the States, where I spent the remainder of the war with a training company at Camp Crowder, Missouri. Along with the rest of the Ninth Army, I had been racing across Germany so swiftly during the late winter and spring that when I boarded the plane, I couldn't believe its destination lay to the west. My mind might inform me otherwise, but there was an inertia of the spirit that told me we were flying to a new front, where we would disembark and continue our push eastward — eastward until we'd circled the globe, marching through villages along whose twisting, cobbled streets crowds of the enemy would watch us take possession of what, up till then, they'd considered their own. I had changed enough in two years not to mind the trembling of the old people, the crying of the very young, the uncertainty and fear in the eyes of the once arrogant. I had been fortunate enough to develop an infantryman's heart, which, like his feet, at first aches and swells but finally grows horny enough for him to travel the weirdest paths without feeling a thing.

Captain Paul Barrett was my C.O.[2] in Camp Crowder. The day I reported for duty, he came out of his office to shake my hand. He was short, gruff, and fiery, and — indoors or out — he wore his polished helmet liner[3] pulled down to his little eyes. In Europe, he had received a battlefield commission and a serious chest wound, and he'd been returned to the States only a few months before. He spoke easily to me, and at the evening formation he introduced me to the troops. "Gentlemen," he said, "Sergeant Thurston, as you know, is no longer with this company. Your new first sergeant is Sergeant Nathan Marx, here. He is a veteran of the European theater, and consequently will expect to find a company of soldiers here, and not a company of *boys*."

I sat up late in the orderly room that evening, trying half-heartedly to solve the riddle of duty rosters, personnel forms, and morning reports. The Charge of Quarters[4] slept with his mouth open on a mattress on the floor. A trainee stood reading the next day's duty roster, which was posted on the bulletin board just inside the screen door. It was a warm evening, and I could hear radios playing dance music over in the barracks. The trainee, who had been staring at me whenever he thought I wouldn't notice, finally took a step in my direction.

"Hey, Sarge — we having a G.I.[5] party tomorrow night?" he asked. A G.I. party is a barracks cleaning.

"You usually have them on Friday nights?" I asked him.

"Yes," he said, and then he added, mysteriously, "that's the whole thing."

"Then you'll have a G.I. party."

He turned away, and I heard him mumbling. His shoulders were moving, and I wondered if he was crying.

"What's your name, soldier?" I asked.

He turned, not crying at all. Instead, his green-speckled eyes, long and narrow, flashed like fish in the sun. He walked over to me and sat on the edge of my desk. He reached out a hand. "Sheldon," he said.

---

[1] A title conferred on Henry VIII by the Pope in 1521, later rescinded, but restored by Parliament and used ever since by British monarchs.
[2] Commanding Officer.
[3] Liner made of light material, used to protect the head from the heavy metal helmet.
[4] "Charge of Quarters," usually, a noncommissioned officer.
[5] Slang name for soldier, deriving from Government Issue.

"Stand on your feet, Sheldon."

Getting off the desk, he said, "Sheldon Grossbart." He smiled at the familiarity into which he'd led me.

"You against cleaning the barracks Friday night, Grossbart?" I said. "Maybe we shouldn't have G.I. parties. Maybe we should get a maid." My tone startled me. I felt I sounded like every top sergeant I had ever known.

"No, Sergeant." He grew serious, but with a seriousness that seemed to be only the stifling of a smile. "It's just—G.I. parties on Friday night, of all nights."

He slipped up onto the corner of the desk again—not quite sitting, but not quite standing, either. He looked at me with those speckled eyes flashing, and then made a gesture with his hand. It was very slight—no more than a movement back and forth of the wrist—and yet it managed to exclude from our affairs everything else in the orderly room, to make the two of us the center of the world. It seemed, in fact, to exclude everything even about the two of us except our hearts.

"Sergeant Thurston was one thing," he whispered, glancing at the sleeping C.Q., "but we thought that with you here things might be a little different."

"We?"

"The Jewish personnel."

"Why?" I asked, harshly. "What's on your mind?" Whether I was still angry at the "Sheldon" business, or now at something else, I hadn't time to tell, but clearly I was angry.

"We thought you—Marx, you know, like Karl Marx. The Marx Brothers. Those guys are all—M-a-r-x. Isn't that how *you* spell it, Sergeant?"

"M-a-r-x."

"Fishbein said—" He stopped. "What I mean to say, Sergeant—" His face and neck were red, and his mouth moved but no words came out. In a moment, he raised himself to attention, gazing down at me. It was as though he had suddenly decided he could expect no more sympathy from me than from Thurston, the reason being that I was of Thurston's faith, and not his. The young man had managed to confuse himself as to what my faith really was, but I felt no desire to straighten him out. Very simply, I didn't like him.

When I did nothing but return his gaze, he spoke, in an altered tone. "You see, Sergeant," he explained to me, "Friday nights, Jews are supposed to go to services."

"Did Sergeant Thurston tell you you couldn't go to them when there was a G.I. party?"

"No."

"Did he say you had to stay and scrub the floors?"

"No, Sergeant."

"Did the Captain say you had to stay and scrub the floors?"

"That isn't it, Sergeant. It's the other guys in the barracks." He leaned toward me. "They think we're goofing off. But we're not. That's when Jews go to services, Friday night. We have to."

"Then go."

"But the other guys make accusations. They have no right."

"That's not the Army's problem, Grossbart. It's a personal problem you'll have to work out yourself."

"But it's un*fair*."

I got up to leave. "There's nothing I can do about it," I said.

Grossbart stiffened and stood in front of me. "But this is a matter of *religion*, sir."

"Sergeant,"[6] I said.

---

[6]Only commissioned officers were supposed to be addressed
as "sir"; noncommissioned officers were properly addressed
by their rank.

"I mean 'Sergeant,'" he said, almost snarling.

"Look, go see the chaplain. You want to see Captain Barrett, I'll arrange an appointment."

"No, no. I don't want to make trouble, Sergeant. That's the first thing they throw up to you. I just want my rights!"

"Damn it, Grossbart, stop whining. You have your rights. You can stay and scrub floors or you can go to shul—"[7]

The smile swam in again. Spittle gleamed at the corners of his mouth. "You mean church, Sergeant."

"I mean shul, Grossbart!"

I walked past him and went outside. Near me, I heard the scrunching of a guard's boots on gravel. Beyond the lighted windows of the barracks, young men in T shirts and fatigue pants were sitting on their bunks, polishing their rifles. Suddenly there was a light rustling behind me. I turned and saw Grossbart's dark frame fleeing back to the barracks, racing to tell his Jewish friends that they were right—that, like Karl and Harpo, I was one of them.

The next morning, while chatting with Captain Barrett, I recounted the incident of the previous evening. Somehow, in the telling, it must have seemed to the Captain that I was not so much explaining Grossbart's position as defending it. "Marx, I'd fight side by side with a nigger if the fella proved to me he was a man. I pride myself," he said, looking out the window, "that I've got an open mind. Consequently, Sergeant, nobody gets special treatment here, for the good *or* the bad. All a man's got to do is prove himself. A man fires well on the range, I give him a weekend pass. He scores high in P.T.,[8] he gets a weekend pass. He *earns* it." He turned from the window and pointed a finger at me. "You're a Jewish fella, am I right, Marx?"

"Yes, sir."

"And I admire you. I admire you because of the ribbons on your chest. I judge a man by what he shows me on the field of battle, Sergeant. It's what he's got *here*," he said, and then, though I expected he would point to his chest, he jerked a thumb toward the button straining to hold his blouse across his belly. "Guts," he said.

"O.K., sir. I only wanted to pass on to you how the men felt."

"Mr. Marx, you're going to be old before your time if you worry about how the men feel. Leave that stuff to the chaplain—that's his business, not yours. Let's us train these fellas to shoot straight. If the Jewish personnel feels the other men are accusing them of goldbricking—well, I just don't know. Seems awful funny that suddenly the Lord is calling so loud in Private Grossman's ear he's just got to run to church."

"Synagogue," I said.

"Synagogue is right, Sergeant. I'll write that down for handy reference. Thank you for stopping by."

That evening, a few minutes before the company gathered outside the orderly room for the chow formation, I called the C.Q., Corporal Robert LaHill, in to see me. LaHill was a dark, burly fellow whose hair curled out of his clothes wherever it could. He had a glaze in his eyes that made one think of caves and dinosaurs. "LaHill," I said, "when you take the formation, remind the men that they're free to attend church services *whenever* they are held, provided they report to the orderly room before they leave the area."

LaHill scratched his wrist, but gave no indication that he'd heard or understood.

"LaHill," I said, "*church*. You remember? Church, priest, Mass, confession."

---

[7]Synagogue.
[8]Physical Training.

He curled one lip into a kind of smile; I took it for a signal that for a second he had flickered back up into the human race.

"Jewish personnel who want to attend services this evening are to fall out in front of the orderly room at 1900," I said. Then, as an afterthought, I added, "By order of Captain Barrett."

A little while later, as the day's last light—softer than any I had seen that year—began to drop over Camp Crowder, I heard LaHill's thick, inflectionless voice outside my window: "Give me your ears, troopers. Toppie says for me to tell you that at 1900 hours all Jewish personnel is to fall out in front, here, if they want to attend the Jewish Mass."

At seven o'clock, I looked out the orderly-room window and saw three soldiers in starched khakis standing on the dusty quadrangle. They looked at their watches and fidgeted while they whispered back and forth. It was getting dimmer, and, alone on the otherwise deserted field, they looked tiny. When I opened the door, I heard the noises of the G.I. party coming from the surrounding barracks—bunks being pushed to the walls, faucets pounding water into buckets, brooms whisking at the wooden floors, cleaning the dirt away for Saturday's inspection. Big puffs of cloth moved round and round on the windowpanes. I walked outside, and the moment my foot hit the ground I thought I heard Grossbart call to the others, "'Ten-*hut!*"[9] Or maybe, when they all three jumped to attention, I imagined I heard the command.

Grossbart stepped forward. "Thank you, sir," he said.

"'Sergeant,' Grossbart," I reminded him. "You call officers 'sir.' I'm not an officer. You've been in the Army three weeks—you know that."

He turned his palms out at his sides to indicate that, in truth, he and I lived beyond convention. "Thank you, anyway," he said.

"Yes," a tall boy behind him said, "Thanks a lot."

And the third boy whispered. "Thank you," but his mouth barely fluttered, so that he did not alter by more than a lip's movement his posture of attention.

"For what?" I asked.

Grossbart snorted happily. "For the announcement. The Corporal's announcement. It helped. It made it—"

"Fancier." The tall boy finished Grossbart's sentence.

Grossbart smiled. "He means formal, sir. Public," he said to me. "Now it won't seem as though we're just taking off—goldbricking because the work has begun."

"It was by order of Captain Barrett," I said.

"Aaah, but you pull a little weight," Grossbart said. "So we thank you." Then he turned to his companions. "Sergeant Marx, I want you to meet Larry Fishbein."

The tall boy stepped forward and extended his hand. I shook it. "You from New York?" he asked.

"Yes."

"Me, too." He had a cadaverous face that collapsed inward from his cheekbone to his jaw, and when he smiled—as he did at the news of our communal attachment—revealed a mouthful of bad teeth. He was blinking his eyes a good deal, as though he were fighting back tears. "What borough?" he asked.

I turned to Grossbart. "It's five after seven. What time are services?"

"Shul," he said, smiling, "is in ten minutes. I want you to meet Mickey Halpern. This is Nathan Marx, our sergeant."

The third boy hopped forward. "Private Michael Halpern." He saluted.

"Salute officers, Halpern," I said. The boy dropped his hand, and, on its way down, in his nervousness, checked to see if his shirt pockets were buttoned.

---

[9] Abbreviated form for "Attention."

"Shall I march them over, sir?" Grossbart asked. "Or are you coming along?"

From behind Grossbart, Fishbein piped up. "Afterward, they're having refreshments. A ladies' auxiliary from St. Louis, the rabbi told us last week."

"The chaplain," Halpern whispered.

"You're welcome to come along," Grossbart said.

To avoid his plea, I looked away, and saw, in the windows of the barracks, a cloud of faces staring out at the four of us. "Hurry along, Grossbart," I said.

"O.K., then," he said. He turned to the others. "Double time, *march!*"

They started off, but ten feet away Grossbart spun around and, running backward, called to me, "Good *shabbus,*[10] sir!" And then the three of them were swallowed into the alien Missouri dusk.

Even after they had disappeared over the parade ground, whose green was now a deep blue, I could hear Grossbart singing the double-time cadence, and as it grew dimmer and dimmer, it suddenly touched a deep memory—as did the slant of the light—and I was remembering the shrill sounds of a Bronx playground where, years ago, beside the Grand Concourse,[11] I had played on long spring evenings such as this. It was a pleasant memory for a young man so far from peace and home, and it brought so many recollections with it that I began to grow exceedingly tender about myself. In fact, I indulged myself in a reverie so strong that I felt as though a hand were reaching down inside me. It had to reach so very far to touch me! It had to reach past those days in the forests of Belgium, and past the dying I'd refused to weep over; past the nights in German farmhouses whose books we'd burned to warm us; past endless stretches when I had shut off all softness I might feel for my fellows, and had managed even to deny myself the posture of a conqueror—the swagger that I, as a Jew, might well have worn as my boots whacked against the rubble of Wesel, Münster, and Braunschweig.

But now one night noise, one rumor of home and time past, and memory plunged down through all I had anesthetized, and came to what I suddenly remembered was myself. So it was not altogether curious that, in search of more of me, I found myself following Grossbart's tracks to Chapel No. 3, where the Jewish services were being held.

I took a seat in the last row, which was empty. Two rows in front of me sat Grossbart, Fishbein, and Halpern, holding little white Dixie cups. Each row of seats was raised higher than the one in front of it, and I could see clearly what was going on. Fishbein was pouring the contents of his cup into Grossbart's, and Grossbart looked mirthful as the liquid made a purple arc between Fishbein's hand and his. In the glaring yellow light, I saw the chaplain standing on the platform at the front; he was chanting the first line of the responsive reading. Grossbart's prayer book remained closed on his lap; he was swishing the cup around. Only Halpern responded to the chant by praying. The fingers of his right hand were spread wide across the cover of his open book. His cap was pulled down low onto his brow, which made it round, like a yarmulke.[12] From time to time, Grossbart wet his lips at the cup's edge; Fishbein, his long yellow face a dying light bulb, looked from here to there, craning forward to catch sight of the faces down the row, then of those in front of him, then behind. He saw me, and his eyelids beat a tattoo. His elbow slid into Grossbart's side, his neck inclined toward his friend, he whispered something, and then, when the congregation next responded to the chant, Grossbart's voice was among the others. Fishbein looked into his book now, too; his lips, however, didn't move.

Finally, it was time to drink the wine. The chaplain smiled down at them as Grossbart swigged his in one long gulp, Halpern sipped, meditating, and Fishbein faked devotion with an empty cup. "As I look down amongst the congregation"—the

---

[10]"Sabbath" (Yiddish).
[11]Expressway in the Bronx, a borough of New York.
[12]Skullcap worn during prayer.

chaplain grinned at the word—"this night, I see many new faces, and I want to welcome you to Friday-night services here at Camp Crowder. I am Major Leo Ben Ezra, your chaplain." Though an American, the chaplain spoke deliberately—syllable by syllable, almost—as though to communicate, above all, with the lip readers in his audience. "I have only a few words to say before we adjourn to the refreshment room, where the kind ladies of the Temple Sinai, St. Louis, Missouri, have a nice setting for you."

Applause and whistling broke out. After another momentary grin, the chaplain raised his hands, palms out, his eyes flicking upward a moment, as if to remind the troops where they were and Who Else might be in attendance. In the sudden silence that followed, I thought I heard Grossbart cackle, "Let the goyim[13] clean the floors!" Were those the words? I wasn't sure, but Fishbein, grinning, nudged Halpern. Halpern looked dumbly at him, then went back to his prayer book, which had been occupying him all through the rabbi's talk. One hand tugged at the black kinky hair that stuck out under his cap. His lips moved.

The rabbi continued. "It is about the food that I want to speak to you for a moment. I know, I know, I know," he intoned, wearily, "how in the mouths of most of you the *trafe*[14] food tastes like ashes. I know how you gag, some of you, and how your parents suffer to think of their children eating foods unclean and offensive to the palate. What can I tell you? I can only say, close your eyes and swallow as best you can. Eat what you must to live, and throw away the rest. I wish I could help more. For those of you who find this impossible, may I ask that you try and try, but then come to see me in private. If your revulsion is so great, we will have to seek aid from those higher up."

A round of chatter rose and subsided. Then everyone sang "Ain Kelohainu";[15] after all those years, I discovered I still knew the words. Then, suddenly, the service over, Grossbart was upon me. "Higher up? He means the General?"

"Hey, Shelly," Fishbein said, "he means God." He smacked his face and looked at Halpern. "How high can you go!"

"Sh-h-h!" Grossbart said. "What do you think, Sergeant?"

"I don't know," I said. "You better ask the chaplain."

"I'm going to. I'm making an appointment to see him in private. So is Mickey."

Halpern shook his head. "No, no, Sheldon—"

"You have rights, Mickey," Grossbart said. "They can't push us around."

"It's O.K.," said Halpern. "It bothers my mother, not me."

Grossbart looked at me. "Yesterday he threw up. From the hash. It was all ham and God knows what else."

"I have a cold—that was why," Halpern said. He pushed his yarmulke back into a cap.

"What about you, Fishbein?" I asked. "You kosher, too?"

He flushed. "A little. But I'll let it ride. I have a very strong stomach, and I don't eat a lot anyway." I continued to look at him, and he held up his wrist to reinforce what he'd just said; his watch strap was tightened to the last hole, and he pointed that out to me.

"But services are important to you?" I asked him.

He looked at Grossbart. "Sure, sir."

"'Sergeant.'"

"Not so much at home," said Grossbart, stepping between us, "but away from home it gives one a sense of his Jewishness."

"We have to stick together," Fishbein said.

---

[13]"Gentiles" (Yiddish)
[14]"Unkosher" (Yiddish); not prepared according to Jewish ritual.

[15]"Ain Kelohanoh," Jewish religious song ("There is none like our God, none like our Lord. . . .").

I started to walk toward the door; Halpern stepped back to make way for me.

"That's what happened in Germany," Grossbart was saying, loud enough for me to hear. "They didn't stick together. They let themselves get pushed around."

I turned. "Look, Grossbart. This is the Army, not summer camp."

He smiled. "So?"

Halpern tried to sneak off, but Grossbart held his arm.

"Grossbart, how old are you?" I asked.

"Nineteen."

"And you?" I said to Fishbein.

"The same. The same month, even."

"And what about him?" I pointed to Halpern, who had by now made it safely to the door.

"Eighteen," Grossbart whispered. "But like he can't tie his shoes or brush his teeth himself. I feel sorry for him."

"I feel sorry for all of us, Grossbart," I said, "but just act like a man. Just don't overdo it."

"Overdo what, sir?"

"The 'sir' business, for one thing. Don't overdo that," I said.

I left him standing there. I passed by Halpern, but he did not look at me. Then I was outside, but, behind, I heard Grossbart call, "Hey, Mickey, my *leben*,[16] come on back. Refreshments!"

"*Leben*!" My grandmother's word for me!

One morning a week later, while I was working at my desk, Captain Barrett shouted for me to come into his office. When I entered, he had his helmet liner squashed down so far on his head that I couldn't even see his eyes. He was on the phone, and when he spoke to me, he cupped one hand over the mouthpiece. "Who the hell is Grossbart?"

"Third platoon, Captain," I said. "A trainee."

"What's all this stink about food? His mother called a goddam congressman about the food." He uncovered the mouthpiece and slid his helmet up until I could see his bottom eyelashes. "Yes, sir," he said into the phone. "Yes, sir. I'm still here, sir. I'm asking Marx, here, right now—"

He covered the mouthpiece again and turned his head back toward me. "Lightfoot Harry's on the phone," he said, between his teeth. "This congressman calls General Lyman, who calls Colonel Sousa, who calls the Major, who calls me. They're just dying to stick this thing on me. Whatsa matter?" He shook the phone at me. "I don't feed the troops? What is this?"

"Sir, Grossbart is strange—" Barrett greeted that with a mockingly indulgent smile. I altered my approach. "Captain, he's a very orthodox Jew, and so he's only allowed to eat certain foods."

"He throws up, the congressman said. Every time he eats something, his mother says, he throws up!"

"He's accustomed to observing the dietary laws, Captain."

"So why's his old lady have to call the White House?"

"Jewish parents, sir—they're apt to be more protective than you expect. I mean, Jews have a very close family life. A boy goes away from home, sometimes the mother is liable to get very upset. Probably the boy mentioned something in a letter, and his mother misinterpreted."

"I'd like to punch him one right in the mouth," the Captain said. "There's a war on, and he wants a silver platter!"

---

[16] "Dear heart" (Yiddish); term of endearment.

"I don't think the boy's to blame, sir. I'm sure we can straighten it out by just asking him. Jewish parents worry—"

"*All* parents worry, for Christ's sake. But they don't get on their high horse and start pulling strings—"

I interrupted, my voice higher, tighter than before. "The home life, Captain, is very important—but you're right, it may sometimes get out of hand. It's a very wonderful thing, Captain, but because it's so close, this kind of thing . . ."

He didn't listen any longer to my attempt to present both myself and Lightfoot Harry with an explanation for the letter. He turned back to the phone. "Sir?" he said. "Sir—Marx, here, tells me Jews have a tendency to be pushy. He says he thinks we can settle it right here in the company. . . . Yes, sir. . . . I *will* call back, sir, soon as I can." He hung up. "Where are the men, Sergeant?"

"On the range."

With a whack on the top of his helmet, he crushed it down over his eyes again, and charged out of his chair. "We're going for a ride," he said.

The Captain drove, and I sat beside him. It was a hot spring day, and under my newly starched fatigues I felt as though my armpits were melting down onto my sides and chest. The roads were dry, and by the time we reached the firing range, my teeth felt gritty with dust, though my mouth had been shut the whole trip. The Captain slammed the brakes on and told me to get the hell out and find Grossbart.

I found him on his belly, firing wildly at the five-hundred-feet target. Waiting their turns behind him were Halpern and Fishbein. Fishbein, wearing a pair of steel-rimmed G.I. glasses I hadn't seen on him before, had the appearance of an old peddler who would gladly have sold you his rifle and the cartridges that were slung all over him. I stood back by the ammo boxes, waiting for Grossbart to finish spraying the distant targets. Fishbein straggled back to stand near me.

"Hello, Sergeant Marx," he said.

"How are you?" I mumbled.

"Fine, thank you. Sheldon's really a good shot."

"I didn't notice."

"I'm not so good, but I think I'm getting the hang of it now. Sergeant, I don't mean to, you know, ask what I shouldn't—" The boy stopped. He was trying to speak intimately, but the noise of the shooting forced him to shout at me.

"What is it?" I asked. Down the range, I saw Captain Barrett standing up in the jeep, scanning the line for me and Grossbart.

"My parents keep asking and asking where we're going," Fishbein said. "Everybody says the Pacific. I don't care, but my parents—If I could relieve their minds, I think I could concentrate more on my shooting."

"I don't know where, Fishbein. Try to concentrate anyway."

"Sheldon says you might be able to find out."

"I don't know a thing, Fishbein. You just take it easy, and don't let Sheldon—"

"*I'm* taking it easy, Sergeant. It's at home—"

Grossbart had finished on the line, and was dusting his fatigues with one hand. I called to him. "Grossbart, the Captain wants to see you."

He came toward us. His eyes blazed and twinkled. "Hi!"

"Don't point that rifle!" I said.

"I wouldn't shoot you, Sarge." He gave me a smile as wide as a pumpkin, and turned the barrel aside.

"Damn you, Grossbart, this is no joke! Follow me."

I walked ahead of him, and had the awful suspicion that, behind me, Grossbart was *marching*, his rifle on his shoulder, as though he were a one-man detachment. At the jeep, he gave the Captain a rifle salute. "Private Sheldon Grossbart, sir."

"At ease, Grossman." The Captain sat down, slid over into the empty seat, and, crooking a finger, invited Grossbart closer.

"Bart, sir. Sheldon Gross*bart*. It's a common error." Grossbart nodded at me; *I* understood, he indicated. I looked away just as the mess truck pulled up to the range, disgorging a half-dozen K.P.s with rolled-up sleeves. The mess sergeant screamed at them while they set up the chowline equipment.

"Grossbart, your mama wrote some congressman that we don't feed you right. Do you know that?" the Captain said.

"It was my father, sir. He wrote to Representative Franconi that my religion forbids me to eat certain foods."

"What religion is that, Grossbart?"

"Jewish."

"'Jewish, *sir*,'" I said to Grossbart.

"Excuse me, sir. Jewish, sir."

"What have you been living on?" the Captain asked. "You've been in the Army a month already. You don't look to me like you're falling to pieces."

"I eat because I have to, sir. But Sergeant Marx will testify to the fact that I don't eat one mouthful more than I need to in order to survive."

"Is that so, Marx?" Barrett asked.

"I've never seen Grossbart eat, sir," I said.

"But you heard the rabbi," Grossbart said. "He told us what to do, and I listened."

The Captain looked at me. "Well, Marx?"

"I still don't know what he eats and doesn't eat, sir."

Grossbart raised his arms to plead with me, and it looked for a moment as though he were going to hand me his weapon to hold. "But, Sergeant—"

"Look, Grossbart, just answer the Captain's questions," I said sharply.

Barrett smiled at me, and I resented it. "All right, Grossbart," he said. "What is it you want? The little piece of paper? You want out?"

"No, sir. Only to be allowed to live as a Jew. And for the others, too."

"What others?"

"Fishbein, sir, and Halpern."

"They don't like the way we serve, either?"

"Halpern throws up, sir. I've seen it."

"I thought *you* throw up."

"Just once, sir. I didn't know the sausage was sausage."

"We'll give menus, Grossbart. We'll show training films about the food, so you can identify when we're trying to poison you."

Grossbart did not answer. The men had been organized into two long chow lines. At the tail end of one, I spotted Fishbein—or, rather, his glasses spotted me. They winked sunlight back at me. Halpern stood next to him, patting the inside of his collar with a khaki handkerchief. They moved with the line as it began to edge up toward the food. The mess sergeant was still screaming at the K.P.s. For a moment, I was actually terrified by the thought that somehow the mess sergeant was going to become involved in Grossbart's problem.

"Marx," the Captain said, "you're a Jewish fella—am I right?"

I played straight man. "Yes, sir."

"How long you been in the Army? Tell this boy."

"Three years and two months."

"A year in combat, Grossbart. Twelve goddam months in combat all through Europe. I admire this man." The Captain snapped a wrist against my chest. "Do you hear him peeping about the food? Do you? I want an answer, Grossbart. Yes or no."

"No, sir."

"And why not? He's a Jewish fella."

"Some things are more important to some Jews than other things to other Jews."

Barrett blew up. "Look, Grossbart. Marx, here, is a good man—a goddam hero. When you were in high school, Sergeant Marx was killing Germans. Who does more for the Jews—you, by throwing up over a lousy piece of sausage, a piece of first-cut meat, or Marx, by killing those Nazi bastards? If I was a Jew, Grossbart, I'd kiss this man's feet. He's a goddam hero, and *he* eats what we give him. Why do you have to cause trouble is what I want to know! What is it you're buckin' for—a discharge?"

"No, sir."

"I'm talking to a wall! Sergeant, get him out of my way." Barrett swung himself back into the driver's seat. "I'm going to see the chaplain." The engine roared, the jeep spun around in a whirl of dust, and the Captain was headed back to camp.

For a moment, Grossbart and I stood side by side, watching the jeep. Then he looked at me and said, "I don't want to start trouble. That's the first thing they toss up to us."

When he spoke, I saw that his teeth were white and straight, and the sight of them suddenly made me understand that Grossbart actually did have parents—that once upon a time someone had taken little Sheldon to the dentist. He was their son. Despite all the talk about his parents, it was hard to believe in Grossbart as a child, an heir—as related by blood to anyone, mother, father, or, above all, to me. This realization led me to another.

"What does your father do, Grossbart?" I asked as we started to walk back toward the chow line.

"He's a tailor."

"An American?"

"Now, yes. A son in the Army," he said, jokingly.

"And your mother?" I asked.

He winked. "A *ballabusta*.[17] She practically sleeps with a dustcloth in her hand."

"She's also an immigrant?"

"All she talks is Yiddish still."

"And your father, too?"

"A little English. 'Clean,' 'Press,' 'Take the pants in.' That's the extent of it. But they're good to me."

"Then, Grossbart—" I reached out and stopped him. He turned toward me, and when our eyes met, his seemed to jump back, to shiver in their sockets. "Grossbart— you were the one who wrote the letter, weren't you?"

It took only a second or two for his eyes to flash happy again. "Yes." He walked on, and I kept pace. "It's what my father *would* have written if he had known how. It was his name, though. *He* signed it. He even mailed it. I sent it home. For the New York postmark."

I was astonished, and he saw it. With complete seriousness, he thrust his right arm in front of me. "Blood is blood, Sergeant," he said, pinching the blue vein in his wrist.

"What the hell *are* you trying to do, Grossbart?" I asked. "I've seen you eat. Do you know that? I told the Captain I don't know what you eat, but I've seen you eat like a hound at chow."

"We work hard, Sergeant. We're in training. For a furnace to work, you've got to feed it coal."

"Why did you say in the letter that you threw up all the time?"

"I was really talking about Mickey there. I was talking *for* him. He would never write, Sergeant, though I pleaded with him. He'll waste away to nothing if I don't help. Sergeant, I used my name—my father's name—but it's Mickey, and Fishbein, too, I'm watching out for."

"You're a regular Messiah, aren't you?"

---

[17]"Lady of the house" (Yiddish).

We were at the chow line now.

"That's a good one, Sergeant," he said, smiling. "But who knows? Who can tell? Maybe you're the Messiah[18]—a little bit. What Mickey says is the Messiah is a collective idea. He went to Yeshiva,[19] Mickey, for a while. He says *together* we're the Messiah. Me a little bit, you a little bit. You should hear that kid talk, Sergeant, when he gets going."

"Me a little bit, you a little bit," I said. "You'd like to believe that, wouldn't you, Grossbart? That would make everything so clean for you."

"It doesn't seem too bad a thing to believe, Sergeant. It only means we should all *give* a little, is all."

I walked off to eat my rations with the noncoms.

Two days later, a letter addressed to Captain Barrett passed over my desk. It had come through the chain of command—from the office of Congressman Franconi, where it had been received, to General Lyman, to Colonel Sousa, to Major Lamont, now to Captain Barrett. I read it over twice. It was dated May 14, the day Barrett had spoken with Grossbart on the rifle range.

> Dear Congressman:
>   First let me thank you for your interest in behalf of my son, Private Sheldon Grossbart. Fortunately, I was able to speak with Sheldon on the phone the other night, and I think I've been able to solve our problem. He is, as I mentioned in my last letter, a very religious boy, and it was only with the greatest difficulty that I could persuade him that the religious thing to do—what God Himself would want Sheldon to do—would be to suffer the pangs of religious remorse for the good of his country and all mankind. It took some doing, Congressman, but finally he saw the light. In fact, what he said (and I wrote down the words on a scratch pad so as never to forget), what he said was "I guess you're right, Dad. So many millions of my fellow-Jews gave up their lives to the enemy, the least I can do is live for a while minus a bit of my heritage so as to help end this struggle and regain for all the children of God dignity and humanity." That, Congressman, would make any father proud.
>   By the way, Sheldon wanted me to know—and to pass on to you—the name of a soldier who helped him reach this decision: SERGEANT NATHAN MARX. Sergeant Marx is a combat veteran who is Sheldon's first sergeant. This man has helped Sheldon over some of the first hurdles he's had to face in the Army, and is in part responsible for Sheldon's changing his mind about the dietary laws. I know Sheldon would appreciate any recognition Marx could receive.
>   Thank you and good luck. I look forward to seeing your name on the next election ballot.
>
>   Respectfully,
>   Samuel E. Grossbart

Attached to the Grossbart communiqué was another, addressed to General Marshall Lyman, the post commander, and signed by Representative Charles E. Franconi, of the House of Representatives. The communiqué informed General Lyman that Sergeant Nathan Marx was a credit to the U.S. Army and the Jewish people.

What was Grossbart's motive in recanting? Did he feel he'd gone too far? Was the letter a strategic retreat—a crafty attempt to strengthen what he considered our

---

[18]Deliverer who will lead the Jewish people forever.
[19]Orthodox Jewish school for elementary or higher education.

alliance? Or had he actually changed his mind, via an imaginary dialogue between Grossbart *père* and Grossbart *fils*?[20] I was puzzled, but only for a few days—that is, only until I realized that, whatever his reasons, he had actually decided to disappear from my life; he was going to allow himself to become just another trainee. I saw him at inspection, but he never winked; at chow formations, but he never flashed me a sign. On Sundays, with the other trainees, he would sit around watching the non-coms' softball team, for which I pitched, but not once did he speak an unnecessary word to me. Fishbein and Halpern retreated, too—at Grossbart's command, I was sure. Apparently he had seen that wisdom lay in turning back before he plunged over into the ugliness of privilege undeserved. Our separation allowed me to forgive him our past encounters, and, finally, to admire him for his good sense.

Meanwhile, free of Grossbart, I grew used to my job and my administrative tasks. I stepped on a scale one day, and discovered I had truly become a noncombatant; I had gained seven pounds. I found patience to get past the first three pages of a book. I thought about the future more and more, and wrote letters to girls I'd known before the war. I even got a few answers. I sent away to Columbia for a Law School catalogue. I continued to follow the war in the Pacific, but it was not my war. I thought I could see the end, and sometimes, at night, I dreamed that I was walking on the streets of Manhattan—Broadway, Third Avenue, 116th Street, where I had lived the three years I attended Columbia. I curled myself around these dreams and I began to be happy.

And then, one Sunday, when everybody was away and I was alone in the orderly room reading a month-old copy of the *Sporting News*, Grossbart reappeared.

"You a baseball fan, Sergeant?"

I looked up. "How are you?"

"Fine," Grossbart said. "They're making a soldier out of me."

"How are Fishbein and Halpern?"

"Coming along," he said. "We've got no training this afternoon. They're at the movies."

"How come you're not with them?"

"I wanted to come over and say hello."

He smiled—a shy, regular-guy smile, as though he and I well knew that our friendship drew its sustenance from unexpected visits, remembered birthdays, and borrowed lawnmowers. At first it offended me, and then the feeling was swallowed by the general uneasiness I felt at the thought that everyone on the post was locked away in a dark movie theater and I was here alone with Grossbart. I folded up my paper.

"Sergeant," he said. "I'd like to ask a favor. It is a favor, and I'm making no bones about it."

He stopped, allowing me to refuse him a hearing—which, of course, forced me into a courtesy I did not intend. "Go ahead."

"Well, actually it's two favors."

I said nothing.

"The first one's about these rumors. Everybody says we're going to the Pacific."

"As I told your friend Fishbein, I don't know," I said. "You'll just have to wait to find out. Like everybody else."

"You think there's a chance of any of us going East?"

"Germany?" I said. "Maybe."

---

[20]"Father" and "son" (French).

"I meant New York."

"I don't think so, Grossbart. Offhand."

"Thanks for the information, Sergeant," he said.

"It's not information, Grossbart. Just what I surmise."

"It certainly would be good to be near home. My parents—you know." He took a step toward the door and then turned back. "Oh, the other thing. May I ask the other?"

"What is it?"

"The other thing is—I've got relatives in St. Louis, and they say they'll give me a whole Passover dinner if I can get down there. God, Sergeant, that'd mean an awful lot to me."

I stood up. "No passes during basic, Grossbart."

"But we're off from now till Monday morning, Sergeant. I could leave the post and no one would even know."

"I'd know. You'd know."

"But that's all. Just the two of us. Last night, I called my aunt, and you should have heard her. 'Come—come,' she said. 'I got gefilte fish, *chrain*[21]—the works!' Just a day, Sergeant. I'd take the blame if anything happened."

"The Captain isn't here to sign a pass."

"You could sign."

"Look, Grossbart—"

"Sergeant, for two months, practically, I've been eating *trafe* till I want to die."

"I thought you'd made up your mind to live with it. To be minus a little bit of heritage."

He pointed a finger at me. "You!" he said. "That wasn't for you to read."

"I read it. So what?"

"That letter was addressed to a congressman."

"Grossbart, don't feed me any baloney. You *wanted* me to read it."

"Why are you persecuting me, Sergeant?"

"Are you kidding!"

"I've run into this before," he said, "but never from my own!"

"Get out of here, Grossbart! Get the hell out of my sight!"

He did not move. "Ashamed, that's what you are," he said. "So you take it out on the rest of us. They say Hitler himself was half a Jew. Hearing you, I wouldn't doubt it."

"What are you trying to do with me, Grossbart?" I asked him. "What are you after? You want me to give you special privileges, to change the food, to find out about your orders, to give you weekend passes."

"You even talk like a goy!" Grossbart shook his fist. "Is this just a weekend pass I'm asking for? Is a Seder[22] sacred, or not?"

Seder! It suddenly occurred to me that Passover had been celebrated weeks before. I said so.

"That's right," he replied. "Who says no? A month ago—and I was in the field eating hash! And now all I ask is a simple favor. A Jewish boy I thought would understand. My aunt's willing to go out of her way—to make a Seder a month later. . . ." He turned to go, mumbling.

"Come back here!" I called. He stopped and looked at me. "Grossbart, why can't you be like the rest? Why do you have to stick out like a sore thumb?"

"Because I'm a Jew, Sergeant. I *am* different. Better, maybe not. But different."

"This is a war, Grossbart. For the time being *be* the same."

---

[21]"Chopped horseradish root" (Yiddish), served as topping on gefilte (stuffed) fish.
[22]Ritual meal served the first day of Passover.

"I refuse."

"What?"

"I refuse. I can't stop being me, that's all there is to it." Tears came to his eyes. "It's a hard thing to be a Jew. But now I understand what Mickey says—it's a harder thing to stay one." He raised a hand sadly toward me. "Look at *you.*"

"Stop crying!"

"Stop this, stop that, stop the other thing! *You* stop, Sergeant. Stop closing your heart to your own!" And, wiping his face with his sleeve, he ran out the door. "The least we can do for one another—the least . . ."

An hour later, looking out of the window, I saw Grossbart headed across the field. He wore a pair of starched khakis and carried a little leather ditty bag. I went out into the heat of the day. It was quiet; not a soul was in sight except, over by the mess hall, four K.P.s[23] sitting around a pan, sloped forward from their waists, gabbing and peeling potatoes in the sun.

"Grossbart!" I called.

He looked toward me and continued walking.

"Grossbart, get over here!" I called.

He turned and came across the field. Finally, he stood before me.

"Where are you going?" I asked.

"St. Louis. I don't care."

"You'll get caught without a pass."

"So I'll get caught without a pass."

"You'll go to the stockade."

"I'm *in* the stockade." He made an about-face and headed off.

I let him go only a step or two. "Come back here," I said, and he followed me into the office, where I typed out a pass and signed the Captain's name, and my own initials after it.

He took the pass and then, a moment later, reached out and grabbed my hand. "Sergeant, you don't know how much this means to me."

"O.K.," I said. "Don't get in any trouble."

"I wish I could show you how much this means to me."

"Don't do me any favors. Don't write any more congressmen for citations."

He smiled. "You're right. I won't. But let me do something."

"Bring me a piece of that gefilte fish. Just get out of here."

"I will!" he said. "With a slice of carrot and a little horseradish. I won't forget."

"All right. Just show your pass at the gate. And don't tell *anybody.*"

"I won't. It's a month late, but a good Yom Tov[24] to you."

"Good Yom Tov, Grossbart," I said.

"You're a good Jew, Sergeant. You like to think you have a hard heart, but underneath you're a fine, decent man. I mean that."

Those last words touched me more than any words from Grossbart's mouth had the right to. "All right, Grossbart," I said. "Now call me 'sir,' and get the hell out of here."

He ran out the door and was gone. I felt very pleased with myself; it was a great relief to stop fighting Grossbart, and it had cost me nothing. Barrett would never find out, and if he did, I could manage to invent some excuse. For a while, I sat at my desk, comfortable in my decision. Then the screen door flew back and Grossbart burst in again. "Sergeant!" he said. Behind him I saw Fishbein and Halpern, both in starched khakis, both carrying ditty bags like Grossbart's.

"Sergeant, I caught Mickey and Larry coming out of the movies. I almost missed them."

---

[23]I.e., four soldiers assigned to duty in the kitchen—Kitchen Police.

[24]"Good day" (Yiddish); greeting used on a holiday.

"Grossbart—did I say tell no one?" I said.

"But my aunt said I could bring friends. That I should, in fact."

"*I'm* the Sergeant, Grossbart—not your aunt!"

Grossbart looked at me in disbelief. He pulled Halpern up by his sleeve. "Mickey, tell the Sergeant what this would mean to you."

Halpern looked at me and, shrugging, said, "A lot."

Fishbein stepped forward without prompting. "This would mean a great deal to me and my parents, Sergeant Marx."

"No!" I shouted.

Grossbart was shaking his head. "Sergeant, I could see you denying me, but how you can deny Mickey, a Yeshiva boy—that's beyond me."

"I'm not denying Mickey anything," I said. "You just pushed a little too hard, Grossbart. *You* denied him."

"I'll give him my pass, then," Grossbart said. "I'll give him my aunt's address and a little note. At least let him go."

In a second, he had crammed the pass into Halpern's pants pocket. Halpern looked at me, and so did Fishbein. Grossbart was at the door, pushing it open. "Mickey, bring me a piece of gefilte fish, at least," he said, and then he was outside again.

The three of us looked at one another, and then I said, "Halpern, hand that pass over."

He took it from his pocket and gave it to me. Fishbein had now moved to the doorway, where he lingered. He stood there for a moment with his mouth slightly open, and then he pointed to himself. "And me?" he asked.

His utter ridiculousness exhausted me. I slumped down in my seat and felt pulses knocking at the back of my eyes. "Fishbein," I said, "you understand I'm not trying to deny you anything, don't you? If it was my Army, I'd serve gefilte fish in the mess hall. I'd sell *kugel*[25] in the PX,[26] honest to God."

Halpern smiled.

"You understand, don't you, Halpern?"

"Yes, Sergeant."

"And you, Fishbein? I don't want enemies. I'm just like you—I want to serve my time and go home. I miss the same things you miss."

"Then, Sergeant," Fishbein said, "why don't you come, too?"

"Where?"

"To St. Louis. To Shelly's aunt. We'll have a regular Seder. Play hide-the-matzoh."[27] He gave me a broad, black-toothed smile.

I saw Grossbart again, on the other side of the screen.

"Pst!" He waved a piece of paper. "Mickey, here's the address. Tell her I couldn't get away."

Halpern did not move. He looked at me, and I saw the shrug moving up his arms into his shoulders again. I took the cover off my typewriter and made out passes for him and Fishbein. "Go," I said. "The three of you."

I thought Halpern was going to kiss my hand.

That afternoon, in a bar in Joplin, I drank beer and listened with half an ear to the Cardinal game. I tried to look squarely at what I'd become involved in, and began to wonder if perhaps the struggle with Grossbart wasn't as much my fault as his. What was I that I had to *muster* generous feelings? Who was I to have been feeling so grudging, so tight-hearted? After all, I wasn't being asked to move the world. Had I a right, then, or a reason, to clamp down on Grossbart, when that meant clamping down on Halpern too? And Fishbein—that ugly, agreeable soul? Out of the many

---

[25] A baked casserole of potatoes or noodles (Yiddish).
[26] Post Exchange, a store on the base where soldiers shopped.

[27] Unleavened bread (Yiddish); formed like large crackers, eaten during Passover.

recollections of my childhood that had tumbled over me these past few days I heard my grandmother's voice: "What are you making a *tsimmes?*"[28] It was what she would ask my mother when, say, I had cut myself while doing something I shouldn't have done, and her daughter was busy bawling me out. I needed a hug and a kiss, and my mother would moralize. But my grandmother knew—mercy overrides justice. I should have known it, too. Who was Nathan Marx to be such a penny pincher with kindness? Surely, I thought, the Messiah himself—if He should ever come—won't niggle over nickels and dimes. God willing, he'll hug and kiss.

The next day, while I was playing softball over on the parade ground, I decided to ask Bob Wright, who was noncom in charge of Classification and Assignment, where he thought our trainees would be sent when their cycle ended, in two weeks. I asked casually, between innings, and he said, "They're pushing them all into the Pacific. Shulman cut the orders on your boys the other day."

The news shocked me, as though I were the father of Halpern, Fishbein, and Grossbart.

That night, I was just sliding into sleep when someone tapped on my door. "Who is it?" I asked.

"Sheldon."

He opened the door and came in. For a moment, I felt his presence without being able to see him. "How was it?" I asked.

He popped into sight in the near-darkness before me. "Great, Sergeant." Then he was sitting on the edge of the bed. I sat up.

"How about you?" he asked. "Have a nice weekend?"

"Yes."

"The others went to sleep." He took a deep, paternal breath. We sat silent for a while, and a homey feeling invaded my ugly little cubicle; the door was locked, the cat was out, the children were safely in bed.

"Sergeant, can I tell you something? Personal?"

I did not answer, and he seemed to know why. "Not about me. About Mickey. Sergeant, I never felt for anybody like I feel for him. Last night I heard Mickey in the bed next to me. He was crying so, it could have broken your heart. Real sobs."

"I'm sorry to hear that."

"I had to talk to him to stop him. He held my hand, Sergeant—he wouldn't let it go. He was almost hysterical. He kept saying if he only knew where we were going. Even if he knew it *was* the Pacific, that would be better than nothing. Just to know."

Long ago, someone had taught Grossbart the sad rule that only lies can get the truth. Not that I couldn't believe in the fact of Halpern's crying; his eyes *always* seemed red-rimmed. But, fact or not, it became a lie when Grossbart uttered it. He was entirely strategic. But then—it came with the force of indictment—so was I! There are strategies of aggression, but there are strategies of retreat as well. And so, recognizing that I myself had not been without craft and guile, I told him what I knew. "It is the Pacific."

He let out a small gasp, which was not a lie. "I'll tell him. I wish it was otherwise."

"So do I."

He jumped on my words. "You mean you think you could do something? A change, maybe?"

"No, I couldn't do a thing."

"Don't you know anybody over at C. and A.?"[29]

"Grossbart, there's nothing I can do," I said. "If your orders are for the Pacific, then it's the Pacific."

---

[28]Also "tzimmes": any of various combinations of sweetened fruits, vegetables, and sometimes meat; also "fuss" or "up- roar" (Yiddish).
[29]Command and Administration.

"But Mickey—"

"Mickey, you, me—everybody, Grossbart. There's nothing to be done. Maybe the war'll end before you go. Pray for a miracle."

"But—"

"Good night, Grossbart." I settled back, and was relieved to feel the springs unbend as Grossbart rose to leave. I could see him clearly now; his jaw had dropped, and he looked like a dazed prizefighter. I noticed for the first time a little paper bag in his hand.

"Grossbart." I smiled. "My gift?"

"Oh, yes, Sergeant. Here—from all of us." He handed me the bag. "It's egg roll."

"Egg roll?" I accepted the bag and felt a damp grease spot on the bottom. I opened it, sure that Grossbart was joking.

"We thought you'd probably like it. You know—Chinese egg roll. We thought you'd probably have a taste for—"

"Your aunt served egg roll?"

"She wasn't home."

"Grossbart, she invited you. You told me she invited you and your friends."

"I know," he said. "I just reread the letter. *Next* week."

I got out of bed and walked to the window. "Grossbart," I said. But I was not calling to him.

"What?"

"What are you, Grossbart? Honest to God, what are you?"

I think it was the first time I'd asked him a question for which he didn't have an immediate answer.

"How can you do this to people?" I went on.

"Sergeant, the day away did us all a world of good. Fishbein, you should see him, he *loves* Chinese food."

"But the Seder," I said.

"We took second best, Sergeant."

Rage came charging at me. I didn't sidestep. "Grossbart, you're a liar!" I said. "You're a schemer and a crook. You've got no respect for anything. Nothing at all. Not for me, for the truth—not even for poor Halpern! You use us all—"

"Sergeant, Sergeant, I feel for Mickey. Honest to God, I do. I *love* Mickey. I try—"

"You try! You feel!" I lurched toward him and grabbed his shirt front. I shook him furiously. "Grossbart, get out! Get out and stay the hell away from me. Because if I see you, I'll make your life miserable. *You understand that?*"

"Yes."

I let him free, and when he walked from the room, I wanted to spit on the floor where he had stood. I couldn't stop the fury. It engulfed me, owned me, till it seemed I could only rid myself of it with tears or an act of violence. I snatched from the bed the bag Grossbart had given me and, with all my strength, threw it out the window. And the next morning, as the men policed the area around the barracks, I heard a great cry go up from one of the trainees, who had been anticipating only his morning handful of cigarette butts and candy wrappers. "Egg roll!" he shouted. "Holy Christ, Chinese goddam egg roll!"

A week later, when I read the orders that had come down from C. and A., I couldn't believe my eyes. Every single trainee was to be shipped to Camp Stoneman, California, and from there to the Pacific—every trainee but one. Private Sheldon Grossbart. He was to be sent to Fort Monmouth, New Jersey. I read the mimeographed sheet several times. Dee, Farrell, Fishbein, Fuselli, Fylypowycz, Glinicki, Gromke, Gucwa, Halpern, Hardy, Helebrandt, right down to Anton Zygadlo—all were to be headed West before the month was out. All except Grossbart. He had pulled a string, and I wasn't it.

I lifted the phone and called C. and A.

The voice on the other end said smartly, "Corporal Shulman, sir."

"Let me speak to Sergeant Wright."

"Who is this calling, sir?"

"Sergeant Marx."

And, to my surprise, the voice said, "*Oh!*" Then, "Just a minute, Sergeant."

Shulman's "*Oh!*" stayed with me while I waited for Wright to come to the phone. Why "*Oh!*"? Who was Shulman? And then, so simply, I knew I'd discovered the string that Grossbart had pulled. In fact, I could hear Grossbart the day he'd discovered Shulman in the PX, or in the bowling alley, or maybe even at services. "Glad to meet you. Where you from? Bronx? Me, too. Do you know So-and-So? And So-and-So? Me, too! You work at C. and A.? Really? Hey, how's chances of getting East? Could you do something? Change something? Swindle, cheat, lie? We gotta help each other, you know. If the Jews in Germany . . ."

Bob Wright answered the phone. "How are you, Nate? How's the pitching arm?"

"Good. Bob, I wonder if you could do me a favor." I heard clearly my own words, and they so reminded me of Grossbart that I dropped more easily than I could have imagined into what I had planned. "This may sound crazy, Bob, but I got a kid here on orders to Monmouth who wants them changed. He had a brother killed in Europe, and he's hot to go to the Pacific. Says he'd feel like a coward if he wound up Stateside. I don't know, Bob—can anything be done? Put somebody else in the Monmouth slot?"

"Who?" he asked cagily.

"Anybody. First guy in the alphabet. I don't care. The kid just asked if something could be done."

"What's his name?"

"Grossbart, Sheldon."

Wright didn't answer.

"Yeah," I said. "He's a Jewish kid, so he thought I could help him out. You know."

"I guess I can do something," he finally said. "The Major hasn't been around here for weeks. Temporary duty[30] to the golf course. I'll try, Nate, that's all I can say."

"I'd apreciate it, Bob. See you Sunday." And I hung up, perspiring.

The following day, the corrected orders appeared: Fishbein, Fuselli, Fylypowycz, Glinicki, Gromke, Grossbart, Gucwa, Halpern, Hardy . . . Lucky Private Harley Alton was to go to Fort Monmouth, New Jersey, where, for some reason or other, they wanted an enlisted man with infantry training.

After chow that night, I stopped back at the orderly room to straighten out the guard-duty roster. Grossbart was waiting for me. He spoke first.

"You son of a bitch!"

I sat down at my desk, and while he glared at me, I began to make the necessary alterations in the duty roster.

"What do you have against me?" he cried. "Against my family? Would it kill you for me to be near my father, God knows how many months he has left to him?"

"Why so?"

"His heart," Grossbart said. "He hasn't had enough troubles in a lifetime, you've got to add to them. I curse the day I ever met you, Marx! Shulman told me what happened over there. There's no limit to your anti-Semitism, is there? The damage you've done here isn't enough. You have to make a special phone call! You really want me dead!"

I made the last few notations in the duty roster and got up to leave. "Good night, Grossbart."

---

[30]Temporary Duty (a sarcastic reference to the Major's absence playing golf).

"You owe me an explanation!" He stood in my path.

"Sheldon, you're the one who owes explanations."

He scowled. "To *you?*"

"To me, I think so—yes. Mostly to Fishbein and Halpern."

"That's right, twist things around. I owe nobody nothing, I've done all I could do for them. Now I think I've got the right to watch out for myself."

"For each other we have to learn to watch out, Sheldon. You told me yourself."

"You call this watching out for me—what you did?"

"No. For all of us."

I pushed him aside and started for the door. I heard his furious breathing behind me, and it sounded like steam rushing from an engine of terrible strength.

"*You'll* be all right," I said from the door. And, I thought, so would Fishbein and Halpern be all right, even in the Pacific, if only Grossbart continued to see—in the obsequiousness of the one, the soft spirituality of the other—some profit for himself.

I stood outside the orderly room, and I heard Grossbart weeping behind me. Over in the barracks, in the lighted windows, I could see the boys in their T shirts sitting on their bunks talking about their orders, as they'd been doing for the past two days. With a kind of quiet nervousness, they polished shoes, shined belt buckles, squared away underwear, trying as best they could to accept their fate. Behind me, Grossbart swallowed hard, accepting his. And then, resisting with all my will an impulse to turn and seek pardon for my vindictiveness, I accepted my own.

1959

THOMAS PYNCHON
(b. 1937)

Thomas Pynchon is the most reclusive of modern American writers. Nobody is quite sure whether he now lives in Mexico, California, New York, or Europe. He has refused interviews, prizes, and publicity of all kinds. The facts that are known are sparse. He was born in Glen Cove, Long Island, where he graduated from Oyster Bay High School in 1953. He enrolled in the physics program at Cornell University, but left in 1955 to serve two years in the navy. He returned to Cornell in 1957 as an English major, and took Vladimir Nabokov's course in Masterpieces of European Fiction. He also came to know a fellow student, poet-singer-songwriter Richard Farina, killed at the age of twenty in a motorcycle accident; Pynchon would later, in 1983, provide an introduction for a reissue of Farina's novel, *Been Down So Long It Looks Like Up to Me* (1966), which drew on their experiences as undergraduates at Cornell.

After graduation in 1959, Pynchon passed by graduate study in English and went to Greenwich Village to become a writer. He had published stories in the college magazine as an undergraduate; now he placed his stories in such prestigious magazines as *Kenyon Review*. Capitulating to the need to make a living, Pynchon took a job with Boeing Corporation in Seattle from 1960 to 1962 as a technical writer. The job also gave him the time to write his first novel, *V.*, published in 1963. All trace of his private life from that time forward seems to have vanished.

V. both pleased and puzzled critics. One of the major figures in the novel, Herbert Stencil, is on a quest, never fully resolved, for the title "character" or "object" — V., who (or which) might be Venus, Virgin, Vagina, or Void. Pynchon's next novel, *The Crying of Lot 49* (1966), portrays Oedipa Maas, also on a quest, never resolved, for Tristero, symbolized by a muted horn, and which might be a life-affirming underground culture opposed to the contemporary technological insanity, or a death-oriented, nihilistic cult out to subvert civilization. When Pynchon's immense novel *Gravity's Rainbow* appeared in 1973, reviewers tended to rave about it but to shy away from summary. It is set in the Second World War and its central character, Lt. Tyrone Slothrop, sets off in search of the secrets of the V-2, a German rocket whose apparently nonrandom targets in London has some obscure connection with sexual activity at those devastated points. The cast of characters is huge, and the events — though ominous — often hilarious. At the end a massively destructive rocket seems poised to come down on an unaware movie audience in California, following an arc through the sky determined by flight from, and the pull by, gravity (gravity's rainbow of death).

Pynchon readers had to wait seventeen years after *Gravity's Rainbow* for his next novel. When *Vineland* appeared in 1990, there was cautious praise from the reviewers, but the disappointment was palpable even in the comments of earnest devotees. Set in California of the 1960s and with a female protagonist, *Vineland* has strong affinities in form, style, tone, and length to *The Crying of Lot 49,* but adds little in satiric thrust or complexity of meaning. And as reviewer James McManus said, it lacks "the density of weave, the thematic urgency, the structural audacity and grandeur of *Gravity's Rainbow.*"

But whatever its shortcomings, the new novel is of a piece stylistically and thematically with Pynchon's other work. Pynchon uses the fanciful and the fantastic in all his novels, and his work as a whole appears to be a satiric — and highly critical — portrait of the modern world, in increasing danger of extinguishing itself. That Pynchon himself is socially committed is confirmed by two occasional essays that he was written. The first of these appeared in the *New York Times* in 1966, entitled "Journey into the Mind of Watts"; it is a criticism of the racist elements of American society that led to the burning of Watts, a black ghetto in Los Angeles.

Pynchon's second essay, published in the *New York Times* in 1984, is entitled "Is It O.K. to Be a Luddite?" The Luddites, a group of workers named after one Ned Lud, flourished in England in the late eighteenth and early nineteenth century and attacked the technological machines of the industrial revolution that were putting people out of work. The modern analogues, contended Pynchon, are those who place themselves on the line against the computerized technology supporting the atomic machinery of destruction, under the control of "a permanent power establishment of admirals, generals and corporate CEO's [chief executive officers], up against whom us average bastards are completely outclassed. . . . We are all supposed to keep tranquil and allow it to go on."

In working his way in the essay from the eighteenth- and nineteenth-century industrial revolution to the modern military-industrial complex, Pynchon spoke of a religious vitality lost along the way that seems to have central relevance to the ambiguous quests of the protagonists of his fictions:

> As religion was being more and more secularized into Deism and nonbelief, *the abiding hunger for evidence of God and afterlife, for salvation — bodily resurrection, if possible — remained* [italics added]. The Methodist movement and the American Great Awakening were only two sectors on a broad front of resistance to the Age of Reason, a front which included Radicalism and Freemasonry as well as Luddites and the Gothic novel. Each in its way expressed the same profound

unwillingness to give up elements of faith, however "irrational," to an emerging technopolitical order that might or might not know what it was doing. "Gothic" became code for "medieval," and that has remained code for "miraculous," on through Pre-Raphaelites, turn-of-the-century tarot cards, space opera in the pulps and the comics, down to "Star Wars" and contemporary tales of sword and sorcery. To insist on the miraculous is to deny to the machine at least some of its claims on us, to assert the limited wish that living things, earthly and otherwise, may on occasion become Bad and Big enough to take part in transcendent doings.

When Pynchon's novels are placed in the context of these comments, there seems to be justification in seeing the quests of all his protagonists as essentially religious quests, the search for the *miraculous,* eternally beckoning, eternally elusive.

Pynchon at first apparently wanted to forget his early stories, but critics were repeatedly unearthing them in search of clues as to Pynchon's development as a novelist. As a result, Pynchon brought them together in a volume, *Slow Learner,* and published them in 1984. One of the stories, first published in 1960, was entitled "Entropy," a term that literary critics had taken over from Pynchon's later work (particularly *The Crying of Lot 49*) as useful in dealing with much of postwar fiction. The term came into physics originally from the second law of thermodynamics, formulated in the mid-nineteenth century; this "law" overturned an orderly Newtonian universe, positing that in "closed systems" energy is indeed lost, and on the cosmic level will result ultimately in a uniform temperature and universal "heat death." Social critics carried the term over into communications and social systems, observing analogous and dangerous tendencies attributable to human behavior. Norbert Wiener said in *The Human Use of Human Beings* (1950, rev. 1954) — a book which Pynchon read — "In a very real sense we are shipwrecked passengers on a doomed planet"; and, applying the concept of entropy to language, "the more probable the message, the less information it gives. Clichés, for example, are less illuminating than great poems."

When Pynchon was named as the winner of the National Book Award for *Gravity's Rainbow* the year after its publication in 1973, he sent the comedian Irwin Corey to appear in his place. When Corey gave his "acceptance speech," he used the double-talk for which he is famous. What he said was totally incomprehensible to the audience precisely because it was nonsense. Perhaps Pynchon was offering the world an example of linguistic entropy, a message without any content whatever; or perhaps the act itself was a satiric message much like his fiction, a warning sign for those who, like his protagonists, are in search of signs, clues — or the Word — as to the fate of the world and humankind.

ADDITIONAL READING

Joseph W. Slade, *Thomas Pynchon,* 1974; George Levine and David Leverenz, eds., *Mindful Pleasures: Essays on Thomas Pynchon,* 1976; Robert M. Scotto, *Three Contemporary Novelists: An Annotated Bibliography of Works by and about John Hawkes, Joseph Heller, and Thomas Pynchon,* 1977; Edward Mendelson, ed., *Pynchon: A Collection of Critical Essays,* 1978; William Plater, *The Grim Phoenix: Reconstructing Thomas Pynchon,* 1978; Mark R. Siegel, *Pynchon: Creative Paranoia in "Gravity's Rainbow,"* 1978; David Cowart, *Thomas Pynchon: The Art of Allusion,* 1980; Douglas Fowler, *A Reader's Guide to "Gravity's Rainbow,"* 1980; John Stark, *Pynchon's Fictions: Thomas Pynchon and the Literature of Information,* 1980; Richard Pearce, ed., *Critical Essays on Thomas Pynchon,* 1981; Thomas H. Schaub, *Pynchon: The Voice of Ambiguity,* 1981; Charles Clerc, ed., *Approaches to "Gravity's Rainbow,"* 1983; Peter L. Cooper, *Signs and Symptoms: Thomas Pynchon and the Contemporary World,* 1983; Molly Hite, *Ideas of Order in the Novels of Thomas Pynchon,* 1983; Robert D. Newman, *Understanding Thomas Pynchon,* 1986. Thomas Moore, *The Style of Connectedness: Gravity's Rainbow and Thomas Pynchon,* 1987; David Seed, *The Fictional Labyrinths of Thomas

Pynchon, 1988; Steven Weisenburger, *A Gravity's Rainbow Companion,* 1988; Georgiana M. M. Colvile, *Beyond and beneath the Mantle: On Thomas Pynchon's The Crying of Lot 49,* 1988; Alec McHoul and David Wills, *Writing Pynchon: Strategies in Fictional Analysis,* 1990.

TEXT

   Slow Learner: Early Stories, 1984.

Entropy[1]

> Boris has just given me a summary of his views. He is
> a weather prophet. The weather will continue bad,
> he says. There will be more calamities, more death,
> more despair. Not the slightest indication of a
> change anywhere. . . . We must get into step, a
> lockstep toward the prison of death. There is no
> escape. The weather will not change.
>
> — *Tropic of Cancer*[2]

Downstairs, Meatball Mulligan's lease-breaking party was moving into its 40th hour. On the kitchen floor, amid a litter of empty champagne fifths, were Sandor Rojas and three friends, playing spit in the ocean and staying awake on Heidseck and benzedrine pills. In the living room Duke, Vincent, Krinkles and Paco sat crouched over a 15-inch speaker which had been bolted into the top of a wastepaper basket, listening to 27 watts' worth of *The Heroes' Gate at Kiev.*[3] They all wore hornrimmed sunglasses and rapt expressions, and smoked funny-looking cigarettes which contained not, as you might expect, tobacco, but an adulterated form of *cannabis sativa.*[4] This group was the Duke di Angelis quartet. They recorded for a local label called Tambú and had to their credit one 10″ LP entitled *Songs of Outer Space.*[5] From time to time one of them would flick the ashes from his cigarette into the speaker cone to watch them dance around. Meatball himself was sleeping over by the window, holding an empty magnum to his chest as if it were a teddy bear. Several government girls, who worked for people like the State Department and NSA,[6] had passed out on couches, chairs and in one case the bathroom sink.

   This was in early February of '57 and back then there were a lot of American expatriates around Washington, D.C., who would talk, every time they met you, about how someday they were going to go over to Europe for real but right now it seemed they were working for the government. Everyone saw a fine irony in this. They would stage, for instance, polyglot parties where the newcomer was sort of ignored if he couldn't carry on simultaneous conversations in three or four languages. They would haunt Armenian delicatessens for weeks at a stretch and invite you over for bulghour[7] and lamb in tiny kitchens whose walls were covered with bullfight posters. They would have affairs with sultry girls from Andalucía or the Midi who studied economics at Georgetown. Their Dôme[8] was a collegiate Rath-

---

[1]See the Pynchon biography for the meaning of "entropy" and its relevance to Pynchon's work.
[2]Novel (1934) by Henry Miller (1891–1980), published in France but banned in America until 1961 because of its alleged obscenity.
[3]By Russian composer Modest Mussorgsky (1835–1881); the closing part of his piano suite "Pictures at an Exhibition."
[4]Marijuana.
[5]Ironic title, inasmuch as sound could not be produced

where there are no sound waves.
[6]National Security Agency, primarily engaged in breaking enemy codes and reading the encoded messages.
[7]Also "bulgur," a wheat that has been parboiled, cracked, and dried.
[8]I.e., gathering place (the Dôme café in Paris was a gathering place for artists and intellectuals). Andalucía: a region in Spain; Midi: the south of France.

skeller out on Wisconsin Avenue called the Old Heidelberg and they had to settle for cherry blossoms instead of lime trees when spring came, but in its lethargic way their life provided, as they said, kicks.

At the moment, Meatball's party seemed to be gathering its second wind. Outside there was rain. Rain splatted against the tar paper on the roof and was fractured into a fine spray off the noses, eyebrows and lips of wooden gargoyles under the eaves, and ran like drool down the windowpanes. The day before, it had snowed and the day before that there had been winds of gale force and before that the sun had made the city glitter bright as April, though the calendar read early February. It is a curious season in Washington, this false spring. Somewhere in it are Lincoln's Birthday and the Chinese New Year, and a forlornness in the streets because cherry blossoms are weeks away still and, as Sarah Vaughan has put it, spring will be a little late this year. Generally crowds like the one which would gather in the Old Heidelberg on weekday afternoons to drink Würtzburger and to sing Lili Marlene (not to mention The Sweetheart of Sigma Chi) are inevitably and incorrigibly Romantic. And as every good Romantic knows, the soul (*spiritus, ruach, pneuma*)[9] is nothing, substantially, but air; it is only natural that warpings in the atmosphere should be recapitulated in those who breathe it. So that over and above the public components—holidays, tourist attractions—there are private meanderings, linked to the climate as if this spell were a *stretto*[10] passage in the year's fugue: haphazard weather, aimless loves, unpredicted commitments: months one can easily spend in fugue, because oddly enough, later on, winds, rains, passions of February and March are never remembered in that city, it is as if they had never been.

The last bass notes of *The Heroes' Gate* boomed up through the floor and woke Callisto[11] from an uneasy sleep. The first thing he became aware of was a small bird he had been holding gently between his hands, against his body. He turned his head sidewise on the pillow to smile down at it, at its blue hunched-down head and sick, lidded eyes, wondering how many more nights he would have to give it warmth before it was well again. He had been holding the bird like that for three days: it was the only way he knew to restore its health. Next to him the girl stirred and whimpered, her arm thrown across her face. Mingled with the sounds of the rain came the first tentative, querulous morning voices of the other birds, hidden in philodendrons and small fan palms: patches of scarlet, yellow and blue laced through this Rousseau-like fantasy, this hothouse jungle it had taken him seven years to weave together. Hermetically sealed, it was a tiny enclave of regularity in the city's chaos, alien to the vagaries of the weather, of national politics, of any civil disorder. Through trial-and-error Callisto had perfected its ecological balance, with the help of the girl its artistic harmony, so that the swayings of its plant life, the stirrings of its birds and human inhabitants were all as integral as the rhythms of a perfectly-executed mobile. He and the girl could no longer, of course, be omitted from that sanctuary; they had become necessary to its unity. What they needed from outside was delivered. They did not go out.

"Is he all right," she whispered. She lay like a tawny question mark facing him, her eyes suddenly huge and dark and blinking slowly. Callisto ran a finger beneath the feathers at the base of the bird's neck; caressed it gently. "He's going to be well, I think. See: he hears his friends beginning to wake up." The girl had heard the rain and the birds even before she was fully awake. Her name was Aubade:[12] she was part French and part Annamese,[13] and she lived on her own curious and lonely planet, where the clouds and the odor of poincianas, the bitterness of wine and the acciden-

[9]"Soul" (Latin, Hebrew, Greek).
[10]In music, the close overlapping of statements in the subject of a fugue, each voice entering immediately after the preceding one (Italian).
[11]In Greek mythology, Callisto, a nymph in the train of Ar-
temis, was loved by Zeus and became mother of Arcas, ancestor of the Arcadians.
[12]"Dawn song" (French; sung at dawn, sometimes by lovers).
[13]Area of Vietnam.

tal fingers at the small of her back or feathery against her breasts came to her reduced inevitably to the terms of sound: of music which emerged at intervals from a howling darkness of discordancy. "Aubade," he said, "go see." Obedient, she arose; padded to the window, pulled aside the drapes and after a moment said: "It is 37. Still 37." Callisto frowned. "Since Tuesday, then," he said. "No change." Henry Adams,[14] three generations before his own, had stared aghast at Power; Callisto found himself now in much the same state over Thermodynamics, the inner life of that power, realizing like his predecessor that the Virgin and the dynamo stand as much for love as for power; that the two are indeed identical; and that love therefore not only makes the world go round but also makes the boccie ball spin, the nebula precess.[15] It was this latter or sidereal[16] element which disturbed him. The cosmologists had predicted an eventual heat-death for the universe (something like Limbo:[17] form and motion abolished, heat-energy identical at every point in it); the meteorologists, day-to-day, staved it off by contradicting with a reassuring array of varied temperatures.

But for three days now, despite the changeful weather, the mercury had stayed at 37 degrees Fahrenheit. Leery at omens of apocalypse, Callisto shifted beneath the covers. His fingers pressed the bird more firmly, as if needing some pulsing or suffering assurance of an early break in the temperature.

It was that last cymbal crash that did it. Meatball was hurled wincing into consciousness as the synchronized wagging of heads over the wastebasket stopped. The final hiss remained for an instant in the room, then melted into the whisper of rain outside. "Aarrgghh," announced Meatball in the silence, looking at the empty magnum. Krinkles, in slow motion, turned, smiled and held out a cigarette. "Tea time,[18] man," he said. "No, no," said Meatball. "How many times I got to tell you guys. Not at my place. You ought to know, Washington is lousy with Feds." Krinkles looked wistful. "Jeez, Meatball," he said, "you don't want to do nothing no more." "Hair of dog," said Meatball. "Only hope. Any juice left?" He began to crawl toward the kitchen. "No champagne, I don't think," Duke said. "Case of tequila behind the icebox." They put on an Earl Bostic side.[19] Meatball paused at the kitchen door, glowering at Sandor Rojas. "Lemons," he said after some thought. He crawled to the refrigerator and got out three lemons and some cubes, found the tequila and set about restoring order to his nervous system. He drew blood once cutting the lemons and had to use two hands squeezing them and his foot to crack the ice tray but after about ten minutes he found himself, through some miracle, beaming down into a monster tequila sour. "That looks yummy," Sandor Rojas said. "How about you make me one." Meatball blinked at him. *"Kitchi lofass a shegithe,"*[20] he replied automatically, and wandered away into the bathroom. "I say, there seems to be a girl or something sleeping in the sink." He took her by the shoulders and shook. "Wha," she said. "You don't look too comfortable," Meatball said. "Well," she agreed. She stumbled to the shower, turned on the cold water and sat down crosslegged in the spray. "That's better," she smiled.

"Meatball," Sandor Rojas yelled from the kitchen. "Somebody is trying to come in the window. A burglar, I think. A second-story man." "What are you worrying about," Meatball said. "We're on the third floor." He loped back into the kitchen. A shaggy woebegone figure stood out on the fire escape, raking his fingernails down the windowpane. Meatball opened the window. "Saul," he said.

"Sort of wet out," Saul said. He climbed in, dripping. "You heard, I guess."

---

[14]American historian (1838–1918); see the chapter "The Dynamo and the Virgin" in his *Education of Henry Adams* (1907).
[15]Precession: the motion of the rotation axis of a rigid body, as a spinning top, when a disturbing torque is applied while the body is rotating, such that the rotation axis describes a cone.
[16]Starry or stellar.

[17]In Catholic cosmology, an area between heaven and hell to which are assigned those deserving neither salvation nor damnation (as, for example, unbaptised children).
[18]Slang for "marijuana time."
[19]Side of the record with music by the jazz saxophonist.
[20]"Up yours," short for "Up your ass" (slang translation from the Hungarian).

"Miriam left you," Meatball said, "or something, is all I heard."

There was a sudden flurry of knocking at the front door. "Do come in," Sandor Rojas called. The door opened and there were three coeds from George Washington, all of whom were majoring in philosophy. They were each holding a gallon of Chianti. Sandor leaped up and dashed into the living room. "We heard there was a party," one blonde said. "Young blood," Sandor shouted. He was an ex-Hungarian freedom fighter who had easily the worst chronic case of what certain critics of the middle class have called Don Giovannism in the District of Columbia. *Purche porti la gonnella, voi sapete quel che fa.*[21] Like Pavlov's dog: a contralto voice or a whiff of Arpège and Sandor would begin to salivate. Meatball regarded the trio blearily as they filed into the kitchen; he shrugged. "Put the wine in the icebox," he said "and good morning."

Aubade's neck made a golden bow as she bent over the sheets of foolscap, scribbling away in the green murk of the room. "As a young man at Princeton," Callisto was dictating, nestling the bird against the gray hairs of his chest, "Callisto had learned a mnemonic device for remembering the Laws of Thermodynamics: you can't win, things are going to get worse before they get better, who says they're going to get better. At the age of 54, confronted with Gibbs' notion of the universe,[22] he suddenly realized that undergraduate cant had been oracle, after all. That spindly maze of equations became, for him, a vision of ultimate, cosmic heat-death. He had known all along, of course, that nothing but a theoretical engine or system ever runs at 100% efficiency; and about the theorem of Clausius,[23] which states that the entropy of an isolated system always continually increases. It was not, however, until Gibbs and Boltzmann[24] brought to this principle the methods of statistical mechanics that the horrible significance of it all dawned on him: only then did he realize that the isolated system — galaxy, engine, human being, culture, whatever — must evolve spontaneously toward the Condition of the More Probable. He was forced, therefore, in the sad dying fall of middle age, to a radical reëvaluation of everything he had learned up to then; all the cities and seasons and casual passions of his days had now to be looked at in a new and elusive light. He did not know if he was equal to the task. He was aware of the dangers of the reductive fallacy and, he hoped, strong enough not to drift into the graceful decadence of an enervated fatalism. His had always been a vigorous, Italian sort of pessimism: like Machiavelli,[25] he allowed the forces of *virtù* and *fortuna*[26] to be about 50/50; but the equations now introduced a random factor which pushed the odds to some unutterable and indeterminate ratio which he found himself afraid to calculate." Around him loomed vague hothouse shapes; the pitifully small heart fluttered against his own. Counterpointed against his words the girl heard the chatter of birds and fitful car honkings scattered along the wet morning and Earl Bostic's alto rising in occasional wild peaks through the floor. The architectonic purity of her world was constantly threatened by such hints of anarchy: gaps and excrescences and skew lines, and a shifting or tilting of planes to which she had continually to readjust lest the whole structure shiver into a disarray of discrete and meaningless signals. Callisto had described the process once as a kind of "feedback": she crawled into dreams each night with a sense of exhaustion, and a desperate resolve never to relax that vigilance. Even in the brief periods when Cal-

---

[21]"As long as she wears a skirt, you know what she'll do" (Italian); from *Don Giovanni* (1787) by Wolfgang Mozart (1756–1791).

[22]Josiah Willard Gibbs (1839–1903), American mathematical physicist who applied a theory of probability (introducing uncertainty and even irrationality) to the laws of thermodynamics, thus introducing contingency into the universe in contrast with the certainties of the Newtonian universe following fixed laws. See especially Norbert Wiener, *The Human Use of Human Beings* (1954).

[23]Rudolf Julius Emanuel Clausius (1822–1888), German mathematical physicist who formulated the second law of thermodynamics.

[24]Ludwig Eduard Boltzmann (1844–1906), Austrian physicist who worked in the same area as Gibbs, exploring the relevance of probability to the laws of thermodynamics.

[25]Niccolo Machiavelli (1469–1527), Italian author of *The Prince* (1532), offering advice for rulers, combining cunning and virtue.

[26]"Virtue" and "chance" (Italian).

listo made love to her, soaring above the bowing of taut nerves in haphazard double-stops would be the one singing string of her determination.

"Nevertheless," continued Callisto, "he found in entropy or the measure of disorganization for a closed system an adequate metaphor to apply to certain phenomena in his own world. He saw, for example, the younger generation responding to Madison Avenue with the same spleen his own had once reserved for Wall Street; and in American 'consumerism' discovered a similar tendency from the least to the most probable, from differentiation to sameness, from ordered individuality to a kind of chaos. He found himself, in short, restating Gibbs' prediction in social terms, and envisioned a heat-death for his culture in which ideas, like heat-energy, would no longer be transferred, since each point in it would ultimately have the same quantity of energy; and intellectual motion would, accordingly, cease." He glanced up suddenly. "Check it now," he said. Again she rose and peered out at the thermometer. "37," she said. "The rain has stopped." He bent his head quickly and held his lips against a quivering wing. "Then it will change soon," he said, trying to keep his voice firm.

Sitting on the stove Saul was like any big rag doll that a kid has been taking out some incomprehensible rage on. "What happened," Meatball said. "If you feel like talking, I mean."

"Of course I feel like talking," Saul said. "One thing I did, I slugged her."

"Discipline must be maintained."

"Ha, ha. I wish you'd been there. Oh Meatball, it was a lovely fight. She ended up throwing a *Handbook of Chemistry and Physics* at me, only it missed and went through the window, and when the glass broke I reckon something in her broke too. She stormed out of the house crying, out in the rain. No raincoat or anything."

"She'll be back."

"No."

"Well." Soon Meatball said: "It was something earthshattering, no doubt. Like who is better, Sal Mineo or Ricky Nelson."

"What it was about," Saul said, "was communication theory. Which of course makes it very hilarious."

"I don't know anything about communication theory."

"Neither does my wife. Come right down to it, who does? That's the joke."

When Meatball saw the kind of smile Saul had on his face he said: "Maybe you would like tequila or something."

"No. I mean, I'm sorry. It's a field you can go off the deep end in, is all. You get where you're watching all the time for security cops: behind bushes, around corners. MUFFET is top secret."

"Wha."

"Multi-unit factorial field electronic tabulator."

"You were fighting about that."

"Miriam has been reading science fiction again. That and *Scientific American*. It seems she is, as we say, bugged at this idea of computers acting like people. I made the mistake of saying you can just as well turn that around, and talk about human behavior like a program fed into an IBM machine."

"Why not," Meatball said.

"Indeed, why not. In fact it is sort of crucial to communication, not to mention information theory. Only when I said that she hit the roof. Up went the balloon. And I can't figure out *why*. If anybody should know why, I should. I refuse to believe the government is wasting taxpayers' money on me, when it has so many bigger and better things to waste it on."

Meatball made a moue. "Maybe she thought you were acting like a cold, dehumanized amoral scientist type."

"My god," Saul flung up an arm. "Dehumanized. How much more human can I get? I worry, Meatball, I do. There are Europeans wandering around North Africa these days with their tongues torn out of their heads because those tongues have spoken the wrong words. Only the Europeans thought they were the right words."

"Language barrier," Meatball suggested.

Saul jumped down off the stove. "That," he said, angry, "is a good candidate for sick joke of the year. No, ace, it is *not* a barrier. If it is anything it's a kind of leakage. Tell a girl: 'I love you.' No trouble with two-thirds of that, it's a closed circuit. Just you and she. But that nasty four-letter word in the middle, *that's* the one you have to look out for. Ambiguity. Redundance. Irrelevance, even. Leakage. All this is noise. Noise screws up your signal, makes for disorganization in the circuit."

Meatball shuffled around. "Well, now, Saul," he muttered, "you're sort of, I don't know, expecting a lot from people. I mean, you know. What it is is, most of the things we say, I guess, are mostly noise."

"Ha! Half of what you just said, for example."

"Well, you do it too."

"I know." Saul smiled grimly. "It's a bitch, ain't it."

"I bet that's what keeps divorce lawyers in business. Whoops."

"Oh I'm not sensitive. Besides," frowning, "you're right. You find I think that most 'successful' marriages—Miriam and me, up to last night—are sort of founded on compromises. You never run at top efficiency, usually all you have is a minimum basis for a workable thing. I believe the phrase is Togetherness."

"Aarrgghh."

"Exactly. You find that one a bit noisy, don't you. But the noise content is different for each of us because you're a bachelor and I'm not. Or wasn't. The hell with it."

"Well sure," Meatball said, trying to be helpful, "you were using different words. By 'human being' you meant something that you can look at like it was a computer. It helps you think better on the job or something. But Miriam meant something entirely—"

"The hell with it."

Meatball fell silent. "I'll take that drink," Saul said after a while.

The card game had been abandoned and Sandor's friends were slowly getting wasted on tequila. On the living room couch, one of the coeds and Krinkles were engaged in amorous conversation. "No," Krinkles was saying, "no, I can't put Dave *down*. In fact I give Dave a lot of credit, man. Especially considering his accident and all." The girl's smile faded. "How terrible," she said. "What accident?" "Hadn't you heard?" Krinkles said. "When Dave was in the army, just a private E-2, they sent him down to Oak Ridge on special duty. Something to do with the Manhattan Project.[27] He was handling hot stuff one day and got an overdose of radiation. So now he's got to wear lead gloves all the time." She shook her head sympathetically. "What an awful break for a piano-player."

Meatball had abandoned Saul to a bottle of tequila and was about to go to sleep in a closet when the front door flew open and the place was invaded by five enlisted personnel of the U.S. Navy, all in varying stages of abomination. "This is the place," shouted a fat, pimply seaman apprentice who had lost his white hat. "This here is the hoorhouse that chief was telling us about." A stringy-looking 3rd class boatswain's mate pushed him aside and cased the living room. "You're right, Slab," he said. "But it don't look like much, even for Stateside. I seen better tail in Naples, Italy." "How much, hey," boomed a large seaman with adenoids, who was holding a Mason jar full of white lightning.[28] "Oh, my god," said Meatball.

---

[27]Oak Ridge, Tennessee, center established during the Second World War for the production of uranium for the atomic bomb; Manhattan Project was the code name for the project set up to produce the atomic bomb.

[28]I.e., homemade liquor, sometimes also called "rot-gut" or "moonshine."

Outside the temperature remained constant at 37 degrees Fahrenheit. In the hot-house Aubade stood absently caressing the branches of a young mimosa, hearing a motif of sap-rising, the rough and unresolved anticipatory theme of those fragile pink blossoms which, it is said, insure fertility. That music rose in a tangled tracery: arabesques of order competing fugally with the improvised discords of the party downstairs, which peaked sometimes in cusps and ogees of noise. That precious signal-to-noise ratio, whose delicate balance required every calorie of her strength, seesawed inside the small tenuous skull as she watched Callisto, sheltering the bird. Callisto was trying to confront any idea of the heat-death now, as he nuzzled the feathery lump in his hands. He sought correspondences. Sade,[29] of course. And Temple Drake,[30] gaunt and hopeless in her little park in Paris, at the end of *Sanctuary*. Final equilibrium. *Nightwood*.[31] And the tango. Any tango, but more than any perhaps the sad sick dance in Stravinsky's *L'Histoire du Soldat*.[32] He thought back: what had tango music been for them after the war, what meanings had he missed in all the stately coupled automatons in the *cafés-dansants*,[33] or in the metronomes which had ticked behind the eyes of his own partners? Not even the clean constant winds of Switzerland could cure the *grippe espagnole*:[34] Stravinsky had had it, they all had had it. And how many musicians were left after Passchendaele, after the Marne?[35] It came down in this case to seven: violin, double-bass. Clarinet, bassoon. Cornet, trombone. Tympani. Almost as if any tiny troupe of saltimbanques[36] had set about conveying the same information as a full pit-orchestra. There was hardly a full complement left in Europe. Yet with violin and tympani Stravinsky had managed to communicate in that tango the same exhaustion, the same airlessness one saw in the slicked-down youths who were trying to imitate Vernon Castle,[37] and in their mistresses, who simply did not care. *Ma maîtresse*.[38] Celeste. Returning to Nice after the second war he had found that café replaced by a perfume shop which catered to American tourists. And no secret vestige of her in the cobblestones or in the old pension next door; no perfume to match her breath heavy with the sweet Spanish wine she always drank. And so instead he had purchased a Henry Miller novel and left for Paris, and read the book on the train so that when he arrived he had been given at least a little forewarning. And saw that Celeste and the others and even Temple Drake were not all that had changed. "Aubade," he said, "my head aches." The sound of his voice generated in the girl an answering scrap of melody. Her movement toward the kitchen, the towel, the cold water, and his eyes following her formed a weird and intricate canon; as she placed the compress on his forehead his sigh of gratitude seemed to signal a new subject, another series of modulations.

"No," Meatball was still saying, "no, I'm afraid not. This is not a house of ill repute. I'm sorry, really I am." Slab was adamant. "But the chief said," he kept repeating. The seaman offered to swap the moonshine for a good piece. Meatball looked around frantically, as if seeking assistance. In the middle of the room, the Duke di Angelis quartet were engaged in a historic moment. Vincent was seated and the others standing: they were going through the motions of a group having a session, only without instruments. "I say," Meatball said. Duke moved his head a few times, smiled faintly, lit a cigarette, and eventually caught sight of Meatball. "Quiet, man," he whispered. Vincent began to fling his arms around, his fists clenched; then, abruptly, was still, then repeated the performance. This went on for a few minutes while Meatball

---

[29]The French Marquis de Sade (1740–1814), specialist in and writer about sexual perversions, especially sadism and masochism.

[30]The heroine (and the cause of miscarriage of justice) in *Sanctuary* (1931), by William Faulkner (1897–1962).

[31]Novel (1936) portraying psychopathic people, by Djuna Barnes (1892–1982).

[32]"The Story of the Soldier" (French); music by Russian composer, Igor Stravinsky (1882–1971).

[33]"Dance halls" (French).

[34]"Spanish flu" (French); there was a serious epidemic with many deaths in 1918.

[35]Passchendaele, Belgium, and the Marne, France: scenes of heavy fighting in the First World War.

[36]"Showmen" or "buffoons" (French).

[37]Vernon and Irene Castle made up a famous dancing team popular in Europe before the First World War.

[38]"My mistress" (French).

sipped his drink moodily. The navy had withdrawn to the kitchen. Finally at some invisible signal the group stopped tapping their feet and Duke grinned and said, "At least we ended together."

Meatball glared at him. "I say," he said. "I have this new conception, man," Duke said. "You remember your namesake. You remember Gerry."[39]

"No," said Meatball. "I'll remember April, if that's any help."

"As a matter of fact," Duke said, "it was Love for Sale. Which shows how much you know. The point is, it was Mulligan, Chet Baker and that crew, way back then, out yonder. You dig!"

"Baritone sax," Meatball said. "Something about a baritone sax."

"But no piano, man. No guitar. Or accordion. You know what that means."

"Not exactly," Meatball said.

"Well first let me just say, that I am no Mingus, no John Lewis. Theory was never my strong point. I mean things like reading were always difficult for me and all—"

"I know," Meatball said drily. "You got your card taken away because you changed key on Happy Birthday at a Kiwanis Club picnic."

"Rotarian. But it occurred to me, in one of these flashes of insight, that if that first quartet of Mulligan's had no piano, it could only mean one thing."

"No chords," said Paco, the baby-faced bass.

"What he is trying to say," Duke said, "is no root chords. Nothing to listen to while you blow a horizontal line. What one does in such a case is, one *thinks* the roots."

A horrified awareness was dawning on Meatball. "And the next logical extension," he said.

"Is to think everything," Duke announced with simple dignity. "Roots, line, everything."

Meatball looked at Duke, awed. "But," he said.

"Well," Duke said modestly, "there are a few bugs to work out."

"But," Meatball said.

"Just listen," Duke said. "You'll catch on." And off they went again into orbit, presumably somewhere around the asteroid belt. After a while Krinkles made an embouchure and started moving his fingers and Duke clapped his hand to his forehead. "Oaf!" he roared. "The new head we're using, you remember, I wrote last night?" "Sure," Krinkles said, "the new head. I come in on the bridge. All your heads I come in then." "Right," Duke said. "So why—" "Wha," said Krinkles, "16 bars, I wait, I come in—" "16?" Duke said. "No. No, Krinkles. Eight you waited. You want me to sing it? A cigarette that bears a lipstick's traces, an airline ticket to romantic places." Krinkles scratched his head. "These Foolish Things, you mean." "Yes," Duke said, "yes, Krinkles. Bravo." "Not I'll Remember April," Krinkles said. "*Minghe morte*,"[40] said Duke. "I *figured* we were playing it a little slow," Krinkles said. Meatball chuckled. "Back to the old drawing board," he said. "No, man," Duke said, "back to the airless void." And they took off again, only it seemed Paco was playing in G sharp while the rest were in E flat, so they had to start all over.

In the kitchen two of the girls from George Washington and the sailors were singing Let's All Go Down and Piss on the Forrestal.[41] There was a two-handed, bilingual *morra* game[42] on over by the icebox. Saul had filled several paper bags with water and was sitting on the fire escape, dropping them on passersby in the street. A fat government girl in a Bennington sweatshirt, recently engaged to an ensign attached to the Forrestal, came charging into the kitchen, head lowered, and butted

---

[39]Gerry Mulligan, Chet Baker, Charlie Mingus, and John Lewis (last three mentioned later) were all well-known jazz musicians.
[40]Vulgar exclamation in corrupt Italian.

[41]Ship named after the first secretary of defense, James Vincent Forrestal (1947–49).
[42]Italian game involving guessing the number of fingers held up by a player.

Slab in the stomach. Figuring this was as good an excuse for a fight as any, Slab's buddies piled in. The *morra* players were nose-to-nose, screaming *trois, sette*[43] at the tops of their lungs. From the shower the girl Meatball had taken out of the sink announced that she was drowning. She had apparently sat on the drain and the water was now up to her neck. The noise in Meatball's apartment had reached a sustained, ungodly crescendo.

Meatball stood and watched, scratching his stomach lazily. The way he figured, there were only about two ways he could cope: (a) lock himself in the closet and maybe eventually they would all go away, or (b) try to calm everybody down, one by one. (a) was certainly the more attractive alternative. But then he started thinking about that closet. It was dark and stuffy and he would be alone. He did not feature being alone. And then this crew off the good ship Lollipop or whatever it was might take it upon themselves to kick down the closet door, for a lark. And if that happened he would be, at the very least, embarassed. The other way was more a pain in the neck, but probably better in the long run.

So he decided to try and keep his lease-breaking party from deteriorating into total chaos: he gave wine to the sailors and separated the *morra* players; he introduced the fat government girl to Sandor Rojas, who would keep her out of trouble; he helped the girl in the shower to dry off and get into bed; he had another talk with Saul; he called a repairman for the refrigerator, which someone had discovered was on the blink. This is what he did until nightfall, when most of the revellers had passed out and the party trembled on the threshold of its third day.

Upstairs Callisto, helpless in the past, did not feel the faint rhythm inside the bird begin to slacken and fail. Aubade was by the window, wandering the ashes of her own lovely world; the temperature held steady, the sky had become a uniform darkening gray. Then something from downstairs — a girl's scream, an overturned chair, a glass dropped on the floor, he would never know what exactly — pierced that private time-warp and he became aware of the faltering, the constriction of muscles, the tiny tossings of the bird's head; and his own pulse began to pound more fiercely, as if trying to compensate. "Aubade," he called weakly, "he's dying." The girl, flowing and rapt, crossed the hothouse to gaze down at Callisto's hands. The two remained like that, poised, for one minute, and two, while the heartbeat ticked a graceful diminuendo down at last into stillness. Callisto raised his head slowly. "I held him," he protested, impotent with the wonder of it, "to give him the warmth of my body. Almost as if I were communicating life to him, or a sense of life. What has happened? Has the transfer of heat ceased to work? Is there no more . . ." He did not finish.

"I was just at the window," she said. He sank back, terrified. She stood a moment more, irresolute; she had sensed his obsession long ago, realized somehow that that constant 37 was now decisive. Suddenly then, as if seeing the single and unavoidable conclusion to all this she moved swiftly to the window before Callisto could speak; tore away the drapes and smashed out the glass with two exquisite hands which came away bleeding and glistening with splinters; and turned to face the man on the bed and wait with him until the moment of equilibrium was reached, when 37 degrees Fahrenheit should prevail both outside and inside, and forever, and the hovering, curious dominant of their separate lives should resolve into a tonic[44] of darkness and the final absence of all motion.

1958–59   *1960, 1984*

---

43 "Three" (French); "Seven" (Italian).
44 Musical term; songs usually return at the end to the key-note or chord set at the beginning, thus "resolving."

JOYCE CAROL OATES
(b. 1938)

In a 1987 review, John Updike, no piker himself on the fast track in publication of his books, wrote:

> Joyce Carol Oates, born in 1938, was perhaps born a hundred years too late; she needs a lustier audience, a race of Victorian word-eaters, to be worthy of her astounding productivity, her tireless gift of self-enthrallment. Not since Faulkner has an American writer seemed so mesmerized by a field of imaginary material, and so headstrong in the cultivation of that field. She has, I fear, rather overwhelmed the puny, parsimonious critical establishment of this country; after the first wave of stories and novels (most notably *A Garden of Earthly Delights* and *them*) crashed in and swept away a debris of praise and prizes, protective seawalls were built, and a sullen reaction set in. Many of the critics began to treat Miss Oates as one of her many scholar heroines, Marya Knauer, is treated by her eighth-grade instructor Mr. Schwilk: "Finally," Schwilk said airily, "You have a most *feverish* imagination," and handed the story back; and that was that."

Oates was born outside Lockport, a New York small town in a rural setting. Her father was a tool and die designer, while her mother took care of three children in the Catholic household. Oates began school in a one-room schoolhouse but went to town for junior and senior high school, graduating in 1956. She began to write in elementary school and by the age of fifteen had submitted her first novel, about a dope addict, to a publisher. It was rejected as unsuited to a juvenile audience.

In 1956 Oates entered Syracuse University, majoring in English and minoring in philosophy; each semester she wrote a novel. She won a prize for a short story published in *Mademoiselle* in 1959. When she graduated in 1960, she was a member of Phi Beta Kappa and was the class valedictorian. She began graduate study in English at the University of Wisconsin, taking an M.A. in 1961. By this time she was married to a fellow graduate student and accompanied him to Texas where he had found a job. For a time she enrolled in doctoral studies at Rice University in Houston, but on discovering that one of her stories had been cited on the honor roll in *Best American Short Stories,* she decided to be a writer instead.

She published her first book, *By the North Gate,* a collection of stories, in 1963, and her first novel, *With Shuddering Fall,* in 1964. There has been hardly a year since that she has not published a book—novels, short stories, poems, essays, plays. She has said of her method of writing: "It's mainly daydreaming, I sit and look out at the river, I daydream about a kind of populated empty space. There's nothing verbal about it. Then there comes a time when it's all set and I just go write it. With a story it's one evening, if I can type that fast." On another occasion she said: "My 'characters' really dictate themselves to me. I am not free of them, really, and I can't force them into situations they haven't themselves willed. They have the autonomy of characters in a dream. In fact . . . I am really transcribing dreams, giving them a certain civilized, extended shape, clearing a few things up, adding daytime details, subtracting fantastic details, and so on, in order to make the story or the novel a work of art."

In the late 1960s, Oates published three novels that she viewed as interrelated: *A Garden of Earthly Delights* (1967), *Expensive People* (1968), and *them* (1969).

She described this trilogy as "three novels that deal with social and economic facts of life in America, combined with unusually sensitive—but hopefully representative—young men and women who confront the puzzle of American life in different ways and come to different ends." In portraying America's "social and economic facts" in these works, Oates moved with the ease of a Theodore Dreiser from one class to another, including migrant laborers, white collar workers, and corporate executives.

She said of the last of the trilogy, *them:* "This is a work of history in fictional form—that is, in personal perspective, which is the only kind of history that exists. In the years 1962–1967 I taught English at the University of Detroit. . . . It was during this period that I met 'Maureen Wendall' of this narrative." The cumulative naturalistic detail of the novel was powerful—depictions of irrational violence, descriptions of Detroit slums, accounts of riots on the University of Detroit campus. It seemed to capture the feeling of the national disintegration of the 1960s as did few other books. In 1970 it won the National Book Award, establishing Oates as a novelist to be reckoned with.

Oates saw her next several novels as also interrelated: the series, she said, dealt "with the complex distribution of power in the United States." In the systematic manner of a Sinclair Lewis, she set her successive novels in deliberately contrasting occupational or professional groups. *Wonderland* (1971) portrayed the medical profession, *Do With Me What You Will* (1973) the profession of law, and *The Assassins* (1975) the world of politics. No one of these novels repeated the success of *them.* Her other novels of this time include *Childwold* (1976), set on a farm in Eden County; *Son of the Morning* (1978), a portrayal of religious experience; and *Unholy Loves* (1979), with a university setting. In the 1980s Oates surprised her readers by turning to what seemed to be Gothic romances, producing yet another trilogy: *Bellefleur* (1980), *A Bloodsmoor Romance* (1982), and *Mysteries of Winterthurn* (1984). In *You Must Remember This* (1987), Oates turned back to contemporary history, setting her novel in the America of the 1950s.

In addition to publishing numerous volumes of short stories, poetry, essays, and plays during her career, she has also had an academic career. She taught English at the University of Detroit (1962–67), and at the University of Windsor in Canada (1967–78). In 1978 she accepted the appointment of Writer-in-Residence at Princeton University. Her husband edits *The Ontario Review* and Oates assists as a contributing editor.

In his review of *You Must Remember This,* John Updike said that the number of her works was as overwhelming to him as to other readers, and that he could not "offer to lay out for dissection the hydra-headed monster of Miss Oates' oeuvre." But he ventured a generalization that seems to get at the effect of reading one of her novels: "Her plots suggest not architecture but cloud formation, beginning and ending in air; there is rarely a sentence that arrests a moment for its own cherishable sake, in a crystallization of language. All is flowing, shifting context. Her worlds refuse to enclose, to be pleasant. Prayers arise from them, but no praise."

ADDITIONAL READING

Conversations with Joyce Carol Oates, ed. Lee Milazzo, 1989.

Mary Kathryn Grant, R.S.M., *The Tragic Vision of Joyce Carol Oates,* 1978; Linda W. Wagner, ed., *Critical Essays on Joyce Carol Oates,* 1979; G. F. Waller, *Dreaming America: Obsession and Transcendence in the Fiction of Joyce Carol Oates,* 1979; Joanne V. Creighton, *Joyce Carol Oates,* 1979; Ellen Friedman, *Joyce Carol Oates,* 1980; Katherine Bastian, *Joyce Carol Oates's Short Stories: Be-*

tween Tradition and Innovation, 1983; Francine Lercangee (with Bruce F. Michelson), *Joyce Carol Oates: An Annotated Bibliography,* 1986; Eileen Teper Bender, *Joyce Carol Oates: Artist in Residence,* 1987; Greg Johnson, *Understanding Joyce Carol Oates,* 1987.

TEXT

The Wheel of Love and Other Stories, 1970.

How I Contemplated the World from the Detroit House of Correction and Began My Life Over Again

NOTES FOR AN ESSAY FOR AN ENGLISH CLASS
AT BALDWIN COUNTRY DAY SCHOOL; POKING
AROUND IN DEBRIS; DISGUST AND CURIOSITY;
A REVELATION OF THE MEANING OF LIFE; A
HAPPY ENDING . . .

I EVENTS

1. The girl (myself) is walking through Branden's, that excellent store. Suburb of a large famous city that is a symbol for large famous American cities. The event sneaks up on the girl, who believes she is herding it along with a small fixed smile, a girl of fifteen, innocently experienced. She dawdles in a certain style by a counter of costume jewelry. Rings, earrings, necklaces. Prices from $5 to $50, all within reach. All ugly. She eases over to the glove counter, where everything is ugly too. In her close-fitted coat with its black fur collar she contemplates the luxury of Branden's, which she has known for many years: its many mild pale lights, easy on the eye and the soul, its elaborate tinkly decorations, its women shoppers with their excellent shoes and coats and hairdos, all dawdling gracefully, in no hurry.

Who was ever in a hurry here?

2. The girl seated at home. A small library, paneled walls of oak. Someone is talking to me. An earnest, husky, female voice drives itself against my ears, nervous, frightened, groping around my heart, saying, "If you wanted gloves, why didn't you say so? Why didn't you ask for them?" That store, Branden's, is owned by Raymond Forrest who lives on Du Maurier Drive. We live on Sioux Drive. Raymond Forrest. A handsome man? An ugly man? A man of fifty or sixty, with gray hair, or a man of forty with earnest, courteous eyes, a good golf game; who is Raymond Forrest, this man who is my salvation? Father has been talking to him. Father is not his physician; Dr. Berg is his physician. Father and Dr. Berg refer patients to each other. There is a connection. Mother plays bridge with . . . On Mondays and Wednesdays our maid Billie works at . . . The strings draw together in a cat's cradle, making a net to save you when you fall. . . .

3. *Harriet Arnold's.* A small shop, better than Branden's. Mother in her black coat, I in my close-fitted blue coat. Shopping. Now look at this, isn't this cute, do you want this, why don't you want this, try this on, take this with you to the fitting room, take this also, what's wrong with you, what can I do for you, why are you so strange . . . ? "I wanted to steal but not to buy," I don't tell her. The girl droops along in her coat and gloves and leather boots, her eyes scan the horizon, which is pastel pink, and decorated like Branden's, tasteful walls and modern ceilings with graceful glimmering lights.

4. Weeks later, the girl at a bus stop. Two o'clock in the afternoon, a Tuesday; obviously she has walked out of school.

5. The girl stepping down from a bus. Afternoon, weather changing to colder. Detroit. Pavement and closed-up stores; grillwork over the windows of a pawnshop. What is a pawnshop, exactly?

II CHARACTERS

1. The girl stands five feet five inches tall. An ordinary height. Baldwin Country Day School draws them up to that height. She dreams along the corridors and presses her face against the Thermoplex glass. No frost or steam can ever form on that glass. A smudge of grease from her forehead . . . could she be boiled down to grease? She wears her hair loose and long and straight in suburban teenage style, 1968. Eyes smudged with pencil, dark brown. Brown hair. Vague green eyes. A pretty girl? An ugly girl? She sings to herself under her breath, idling in the corridor, thinking of her many secrets (the thirty dollars she once took from the purse of a friend's mother, just for fun, the basement window she smashed in her own house just for fun) and thinking of her brother who is at Susquehanna Boys' Academy, an excellent preparatory school in Maine, remembering him unclearly . . . he has long manic hair and a squeaking voice and he looks like one of the popular teenage singers of 1968, one of those in a group, *The Certain Forces, The Way Out, The Maniacs Responsible*. The girl in her turn looks like one of those fieldsful of girls who listen to the boys' singing, dreaming and mooning restlessly, breaking into high sullen laughter, innocently experienced.

2. The mother. A Midwestern woman of Detroit and suburbs. Belongs to the Detroit Athletic Club. Also the Detroit Golf Club. Also the Bloomfield Hills Country Club. The Village Women's Club at which lectures are given each winter on Genet and Sartre and James Baldwin,[1] by the Director of the Adult Education Program at Wayne State University. . . . The Bloomfield Art Association. Also the Founders Society of the Detroit Institute of Arts. Also . . . Oh, she is in perpetual motion, this lady, hair like blown-up gold and finer than gold, hair and fingers and body of inestimable grace. Heavy weighs the gold on the back of her hairbrush and hand mirror. Heavy heavy the candlesticks in the dining room. Very heavy is the big car, a Lincoln, long and black, that on one cool autumn day split a squirrel's body in two unequal parts.

3. The father. Dr. ____. He belongs to the same clubs as #2. A player of squash and golf; he has a golfer's umbrella of stripes. Candy stripes. In his mouth nothing turns to sugar, however; saliva works no miracles here. His doctoring is of the slightly sick. The sick are sent elsewhere (to Dr. Berg?), the deathly sick are sent back for more tests and their bills are sent to their homes, the unsick are sent to Dr. Coronet (Isabel, a lady), an excellent psychiatrist for unsick people who angrily believe they are sick and want to do something about it. If they demand a male psychiatrist, the unsick are sent by Dr. ____ (my father) to Dr. Lowenstein, a male psychiatrist, excellent and expensive, with a limited practice.

4. Clarita. She is twenty, twenty-five, she is thirty or more? Pretty, ugly, what? She is a woman lounging by the side of a road, in jeans and a sweater, hitchhiking, or she is slouched on a stool at a counter in some roadside diner. A hard line of jaw. Curious eyes. Amused eyes. Behind her eyes processions move, funeral pageants, cartoons.

[1]Jean Genet (1910–1986), French dramatist and novelist; Jean-Paul Sartre (1905–1980), French philosopher (of existentialism), novelist, dramatist, and critic; James Baldwin (1924–1987), American novelist.

She says, "I never can figure out why girls like you bum around down here. What are you looking for anyway?" An odor of tobacco about her. Unwashed underclothes, or no underclothes, unwashed skin, gritty toes, hair long and falling into strands, not recently washed.

5. Simon. In this city the weather changes abruptly, so Simon's weather changes abruptly. He sleeps through the afternoon. He sleeps through the morning. Rising, he gropes around for something to get him going, for a cigarette or a pill to drive him out to the street, where the temperature is hovering around 35°. Why doesn't it drop? Why, why doesn't the cold clean air come down from Canada; will he have to go up into Canada to get it? will he have to leave the Country of his Birth and sink into Canada's frosty fields . . . ? Will the F.B.I. (which he dreams about constantly) chase him over the Canadian border on foot, hounded out in a blizzard of broken glass and horns . . . ?

"Once I was Huckleberry Finn," Simon says, "but now I am Roderick Usher."[2] Beset by frenzies and fears, this man who makes my spine go cold, he takes green pills, yellow pills, pills of white and capsules of dark blue and green . . . he takes other things I may not mention, for what if Simon seeks me out and climbs into my girl's bedroom here in Bloomfield Hills and strangles me, what then . . . ? (As I write this I begin to shiver. Why do I shiver? I am now sixteen and sixteen is not an age for shivering.) It comes from Simon, who is always cold.

III WORLD EVENTS

Nothing.

IV PEOPLE & CIRCUMSTANCES
CONTRIBUTING TO THIS DELINQUENCY

Nothing.

V SIOUX DRIVE

George, Clyde G. 240 Sioux. A manufacturer's representative; children, a dog, a wife. Georgian with the usual columns. You think of the White House, then of Thomas Jefferson, then your mind goes blank on the white pillars and you think of nothing. Norris, Ralph W. 246 Sioux. Public relations. Colonial. Bay window, brick, stone, concrete, wood, green shutters, sidewalk, lantern, grass, trees, blacktop drive, two children, one of them my classmate Esther (Esther Norris) at Baldwin. Wife, cars. Ramsey, Michael D. 250 Sioux. Colonial. Big living room, thirty by twenty-five, fireplaces in living room, library, recreation room, paneled walls wet bar five bathrooms five bedrooms two lavatories central air conditioning automatic sprinkler automatic garage door three children one wife two cars a breakfast room a patio a large fenced lot fourteen trees a front door with a brass knocker never knocked. Next is our house. Classic contemporary. Traditional modern. Attached garage, attached Florida room, attached patio, attached pool and cabana, attached roof. A front door mail slot through which pour *Time Magazine, Fortune, Life, Business Week,* the *Wall Street Journal,* the *New York Times,* the *New Yorker,* the *Saturday Review, M.D., Modern Medicine, Disease of the Month* . . . and also . . . And in addition to all this, a quiet sealed letter from Baldwin saying: *Your daughter is not doing work compatible with her performance on the Stanford-Binet.*[3] . . . And your son is not doing well, not well at all, very sad. Where is your son anyway? Once he stole trick-and-treat candy from some six-year-old kids, he himself being a robust ten. The beginning. Now your daughter

---

[2]Leading character in the Gothic tale, "The Fall of the House
of Usher," by Edgar Allan Poe (1809–1849).
[3]Standard intelligence test.

steals. In the Village Pharmacy she made off with, yes she did, don't deny it, she made off with a copy of *Pageant Magazine* for no reason, she swiped a roll of Life Savers in a green wrapper and was in no need of saving her life or even in need of sucking candy; when she was no more than eight years old she stole, don't blush, she stole a package of Tums only because it was out on the counter and available, and the nice lady behind the counter (now dead) said nothing. . . . Sioux Drive. Maples, oaks, elms. Diseased elms cut down. Sioux Drive runs into Roosevelt Drive. Slow, turning lanes, not streets, all drives and lanes and ways and passes. A private police force. Quiet private police, in unmarked cars. Cruising on Saturday evenings with paternal smiles for the residents who are streaming in and out of houses, going to and from parties, a thousand parties, slightly staggering, the women in their furs alighting from automobiles bought of Ford and General Motors and Chrysler, very heavy automobiles. No foreign cars. Detroit. In 275 Sioux, down the block in that magnificent French-Normandy mansion, lives   himself, who has the C   account itself, imagine that! Look at where he lives and look at the enormous trees and chimneys, imagine his many fireplaces, imagine his wife and children, imagine his wife's hair, imagine her fingernails, imagine her bathtub of smooth clean glowing pink, imagine their embraces, his trouser pockets filled with odd coins and keys and dust and peanuts, imagine their ecstasy on Sioux Drive, imagine their income tax returns, imagine their little boy's pride in his experimental car, a scaled-down C   , as he roars around the neighborhood on the sidewalks frightening dogs and Negro maids, oh imagine all these things, imagine everything, let your mind roar out all over Sioux Drive and Du Maurier Drive and Roosevelt Drive and Ticonderoga Pass and Burning Bush Way and Lincolnshire Pass and Lois Lane.

When spring comes, its winds blow nothing to Sioux Drive, no odors of hollyhocks or forsythia, nothing Sioux Drive doesn't already possess, everything is planted and performing. The weather vanes, had they weather vanes, don't have to turn with the wind, don't have to contend with the weather. There is no weather.

VI DETROIT

There is always weather in Detroit. Detroit's temperature is always 32°. Fast-falling temperatures. Slow-rising temperatures. Wind from the north-northeast four to forty miles an hour, smallcraft warnings, partly cloudy today and Wednesday changing to partly sunny through Thursday . . . small warnings of frost, soot warnings, traffic warnings, hazardous lake conditions for small craft and swimmers, restless Negro gangs, restless cloud formations, restless temperatures aching to fall out the very bottom of the thermometer or shoot up over the top and boil everything over in red mercury.

Detroit's temperature is 32°. Fast-falling temperatures. Slow-rising temperatures. Wind from the north-northeast four to forty miles an hour. . . .

VII EVENTS

1. The girl's heart is pounding. In her pocket is a pair of gloves! In a plastic bag! Airproof breathproof plastic bag, gloves selling for twenty-five dollars on Branden's counter! In her pocket! Shoplifted! . . . In her purse is a blue comb, not very clean. In her purse is a leather billfold (a birthday present from her grandmother in Philadelphia) with snapshots of the family in clean plastic windows, in the billfold are bills, she doesn't know how many bills. . . . In her purse is an ominous note from her friend Tykie *What's this about Joe H. and the kids hanging around at Louise's Sat. night? You heard anything?* . . . passed in French class. In her purse is a lot of dirty yellow Kleenex, her mother's heart would break to see such very dirty Kleenex, and at the bottom of her purse are brown hairpins and safety pins and a broken pencil and a ballpoint pen (blue) stolen from somewhere forgotten and a purse-size compact of Cover Girl

Make-Up, Ivory Rose. . . . Her lipstick is Broken Heart, a corrupt pink; her fingers are trembling like crazy; her teeth are beginning to chatter; her insides are alive; her eyes glow in her head; she is saying to her mother's astonished face *I want to steal but not to buy.*

2. At Clarita's. Day or night? What room is this? A bed, a regular bed, and a mattress on the floor nearby. Wallpaper hanging in strips. Clarita says she tore it like that with her teeth. She was fighting a barbaric tribe that night, high from some pills; she was battling for her life with men wearing helmets of heavy iron and their faces no more than Christian crosses to breathe through, every one of those bastards looking like her lover Simon, who seems to breathe with great difficulty through the slits of mouth and nostrils in his face. Clarita has never heard of Sioux Drive. Raymond Forrest cuts no ice with her, nor does the C   account and its millions; Harvard Business School could be at the corner of Vernor and 12th Street for all she cares, and Vietnam might have sunk by now into the Dead Sea under its tons of debris, for all the amazement she could show . . . her face is overworked, overwrought, at the age of twenty (thirty?) it is already exhausted but fanciful and ready for a laugh. Clarita says mournfully to me *Honey somebody is going to turn you out let me give you warning.* In a movie shown on late television Clarita is not a mess like this but a nurse, with short neat hair and a dedicated look, in love with her doctor and her doctor's patients and their diseases, enamored of needles and sponges and rubbing alcohol. . . . Or no: she is a private secretary. Robert Cummings is her boss. She helps him with fantastic plots, the canned audience laughs, no, the audience doesn't laugh because nothing is funny, instead her boss is Robert Taylor and they are not boss and secretary but husband and wife, she is threatened by a young starlet, she is grim, handsome, wifely, a good companion for a good man. . . . She is Claudette Colbert. Her sister too is Claudette Colbert. They are twins, identical. Her husband Charles Boyer is a very rich handsome man and her sister, Claudette Colbert, is plotting her death in order to take her place as the rich man's wife, no one will know because they are *twins.* . . . All these marvelous lives Clarita might have lived, but she fell out the bottom at the age of thirteen. At the age when I was packing my overnight case for a slumber party at Tony Deshield's she was tearing filthy sheets off a bed and scratching up a rash on her arms. . . . Thirteen is uncommonly young for a white girl in Detroit, Miss Brock of the Detroit House of Correction said in a sad newspaper interview for the *Detroit News;* fifteen and sixteen are more likely. Eleven, twelve, thirteen are not surprising in colored . . . they are more precocious. What can we do? Taxes are rising and the tax base is falling. The temperature rises slowly but falls rapidly. Everything is falling out the bottom, Woodward Avenue is filthy, Livernois Avenue is filthy! Scraps of paper flutter in the air like pigeons, dirt flies up and hits you right in the eye, oh Detroit is breaking up into dangerous bits of newspaper and dirt, watch out. . . .

Clarita's apartment is over a restaurant. Simon her lover emerges from the cracks at dark. Mrs. Olesko, a neighbor of Clarita's, an aged white wisp of a woman, doesn't complain but sniffs with contentment at Clarita's noisy life and doesn't tell the cops, hating cops, when the cops arrive. I should give more fake names, more blanks, instead of telling all these secrets. I myself am a secret; I am a minor.

3. My father reads a paper at a medical convention in Los Angeles. There he is, on the edge of the North American continent, when the unmarked detective put his hand so gently on my arm in the aisle of Branden's and said, "Miss, would you like to step over here for a minute?"

And where was he when Clarita put her hand on my arm, that wintry dark sulphurous aching day in Detroit, in the company of closed-down barber shops, closed-down diners, closed-down movie houses, homes, windows, basements, faces . . . she put her hand on my arm and said, "Honey, are you looking for somebody down here?"

And was he home worrying about me, gone for two weeks solid, when they carried me off . . . ? It took three of them to get me in the police cruiser, so they said, and they put more than their hands on my arm.

4. I work on this lesson. My English teacher is Mr. Forest, who is from Michigan State. Not handsome, Mr. Forest, and his name is plain, unlike Raymond Forrest's, but he is sweet and rodentlike, he has conferred with the principal and my parents, and everything is fixed . . . treat her as if nothing has happened, a new start, begin again, only sixteen years old, what a shame, how did it happen? — nothing happened, nothing could have happened, a slight physiological modification known only to a gynecologist or to Dr. Coronet. I work on my lesson. I sit in my pink room. I look around the room with my sad pink eyes. I sigh, I dawdle, I pause, I eat up time, I am limp and happy to be home, I am sixteen years old suddenly, my head hangs heavy as a pumpkin on my shoulders, and my hair has just been cut by Mr. Faye at the Crystal Salon and is said to be very becoming.

(Simon too put his hand on my arm and said, "Honey, you have got to come with me," and in his six-by-six room we got to know each other. Would I go back to Simon again? Would I lie down with him in all that filth and craziness? Over and over again.

a Clarita is being betrayed as in front of a Cunningham Drug Store she is nervously eying a colored man who may or may not have money, or a nervous white boy of twenty with sideburns and an Appalachian look, who may or may not have a knife hidden in his jacket pocket, or a husky red-faced man of friendly countenance who may or may not be a member of the Vice Squad out for an early twilight walk.)

I work on my lesson for Mr. Forest. I have filled up eleven pages. Words pour out of me and won't stop. I want to tell everything . . . what was the song Simon was always humming, and who was Simon's friend in a very new trench coat with an old high school graduation ring on his finger . . . ? Simon's bearded friend? When I was down too low for him, Simon kicked me out and gave me to him for three days, I think, on Fourteenth Street in Detroit, an airy room of cold cruel drafts with newspapers on the floor. . . . Do I really remember that or am I piecing it together from what they told me? Did they tell the truth? Did they know much of the truth?

VIII CHARACTERS

1. Wednesdays after school, at four; Saturday mornings at ten. Mother drives me to Dr. Coronet. Ferns in the office, plastic or real, they look the same. Dr. Coronet is queenly, an elegant nicotine-stained lady who would have studied with Freud had circumstances not prevented it, a bit of a Catholic, ready to offer you some mystery if your teeth will ache too much without it. Highly recommended by Father! Forty dollars an hour, Father's forty dollars! Progress! Looking up! Looking better! That new haircut is so becoming, says Dr. Coronet herself, showing how normal she is for a woman with an I.Q. of 180 and many advanced degrees.

2. Mother. A lady in a brown-suede coat. Boots of shiny black material, black gloves, a black fur hat. She would be humiliated could she know of all the people in the world it is my ex-lover Simon who walks most like her . . . self-conscious and unreal, listening to distant music, a little bowlegged with craftiness. . . .

3. Father. Tying a necktie. In a hurry. On my first evening home he put his hand on my arm and said, "Honey, we're going to forget all about this."

4. Simon. Outside, a plane is crossing the sky, in here we're in a hurry. Morning. It must be morning. The girl is half out of her mind, whimpering and vague; Simon

her dear friend is wretched this morning . . . he is wretched with morning itself . . . he forces her to give him an injection with that needle she knows is filthy, she has a dread of needles and surgical instruments and the odor of things that are to be sent into the blood, thinking somehow of her father. . . . This is a bad morning, Simon says that his mind is being twisted out of shape, and so he submits to the needle that he usually scorns and bites his lip with his yellowish teeth, his face going very pale. *Ah baby!* he says in his soft mocking voice, which with all women is a mockery of love, *do it like this — Slowly —* And the girl, terrified, almost drops the precious needle but manages to turn it up to the light from the window . . . is it an extension of herself then? She can give him this gift then? *I wish you wouldn't do this to me,* she says, wise in her terror, because it seems to her that Simon's danger — in a few minutes he may be dead — is a way of pressing her against him that is more powerful than any other embrace. She has to work over his arm, the knotted corded veins of his arm, her forehead wet with perspiration as she pushes and releases the needle, staring at that mixture of liquid now stained with Simon's bright blood. . . . When the drug hits him she can feel it herself, she feels that magic that is more than any woman can give him, striking the back of his head and making his face stretch as if with the impact of a terrible sun. . . . She tries to embrace him but he pushes her aside and stumbles to his feet. *Jesus Christ,* he says. . . .

5. Princess, a Negro girl of eighteen. What is her charge? She is closed-mouthed about it, shrewd and silent; you know that no one had to wrestle her to the sidewalk to get her in here; she came with dignity. In the recreation room she sits reading *Nancy Drew and the Jewel Box Mystery,* which inspires in her face tiny wrinkles of alarm and interest: what a face! Light brown skin, heavy shaded eyes, heavy eyelashes, a serious sinister dark brow, graceful fingers, graceful wristbones, graceful legs, lips, tongue, a sugar-sweet voice, a leggy stride more masculine than Simon's and my mother's, decked out in a dirty white blouse and dirty white slacks; vaguely nautical is Princess' style. . . . At breakfast she is in charge of clearing the table and leans over me, saying, *Honey you sure you ate enough?*

6. The girl lies sleepless, wondering. Why here, why not there? Why Bloomfield Hills and not jail? Why jail and not her pink room? Why downtown Detroit and not Sioux Drive? What is the difference? Is Simon all the difference? The girl's head is a parade of wonders. She is nearly sixteen, her breath is marvelous with wonders, not long ago she was coloring with crayons and now she is smearing the landscape with paints that won't come off and won't come off her fingers either. She says to the matron *I am not talking about anything,* not because everyone has warned her not to talk but because, because she will not talk; because she won't say anything about Simon, who is her secret. And she says to the matron, *I won't go home,* up until that night in the lavatory when everything was changed. . . . "No, I won't go home I want to stay here," she says, listening to her own words with amazement, thinking that weeds might climb everywhere over that marvelous $180,000 house and dinosaurs might return to muddy the beige carpeting, but never never will she reconcile four o'clock in the morning in Detroit with eight o'clock breakfasts in Bloomfield Hills. . . . oh, she aches still for Simon's hands and his caressing breath, though he gave her little pleasure, he took everything from her (five-dollar bills, ten-dollar bills, passed into her numb hands by men and taken out of her hands by Simon) until she herself was passed into the hands of other men, police, when Simon evidently got tired of her and her hysteria. . . . *No, I won't go home, I don't want to be bailed out.* The girl thinks as a *Stubborn and Wayward Child* (one of several charges lodged against her), and the matron understands her crazy white-rimmed eyes that are seeking out some new violence that will keep her in jail, should someone threaten to let her out. Such children try to strangle the matrons, the attendants, or one another . . . they want the locks locked forever,

the doors nailed shut . . . and this girl is no different up until that night her mind is changed for her. . . .

IX THAT NIGHT

Princess and Dolly, a little white girl of maybe fifteen, hardy however as a sergeant and in the House of Correction for armed robbery, corner her in the lavatory at the farthest sink and the other girls look away and file out to bed, leaving her. God, how she is beaten up! Why is she beaten up? Why do they pound her, why such hatred? Princess vents all the hatred of a thousand silent Detroit winters on her body, this girl whose body belongs to me, fiercely she rides across the Midwestern plains on this girl's tender bruised body . . . revenge on the oppressed minorities of America! revenge on the slaughtered Indians! revenge on the female sex, on the male sex, revenge on Bloomfield Hills, revenge revenge. . . .

X DETROIT

In Detroit, weather weighs heavily upon everyone. The sky looms large. The horizon shimmers in smoke. Downtown the buildings are imprecise in the haze. Perpetual haze. Perpetual motion inside the haze. Across the choppy river is the city of Windsor, in Canada. Part of the continent has bunched up here and is bulging outward, at the tip of Detroit, a cold hard rain is forever falling on the expressways. . . . Shoppers shop grimly, their cars are not parked in safe places, their windshields may be smashed and graceful ebony hands may drag them out through their shatterproof smashed windshields, crying, *Revenge for the Indians!* Ah, they all fear leaving Hudson's[4] and being dragged to the very tip of the city and thrown off the parking roof of Cobo[5] Hall, that expensive tomb, into the river. . . .

XI CHARACTERS WE ARE FOREVER ENTWINED WITH

1. Simon drew me into his tender rotting arms and breathed gravity into me. Then I came to earth, weighed down. He said, *You are such a little girl,* and he weighed me down with his delight. In the palms of his hands were teeth marks from his previous life experiences. He was thirty-five, they said. Imagine Simon in this room, in my pink room: he is about six feet tall and stoops slightly, in a feline cautious way, always thinking, always on guard, with his scuffed light suede shoes and his clothes that are anyone's clothes, slightly rumpled ordinary clothes that ordinary men might wear to not-bad jobs. Simon has fair long hair, curly hair, spent languid curls that are like . . . exactly like the curls of wood shavings to the touch, I am trying to be exact . . . and he smells of unheated mornings and coffee and too many pills coating his tongue with a faint green-white scum. . . . Dear Simon, who would be panicked in this room and in this house (right now Billie is vacuuming next door in my parents' room; a vacuum cleaner's roar is a sign of all good things), Simon who is said to have come from a home not much different from this, years ago, fleeing all the carpeting and the polished banisters . . . Simon has a deathly face, only desperate people fall in love with it. His face is bony and cautious, the bones of his cheeks prominent as if with the rigidity of his ceaseless thinking, plotting, for he has to make money out of girls to whom money means nothing, they're so far gone they can hardly count it, and in a sense money means nothing to him either except as a way of keeping on with his life. *Each Day's Proud Struggle,* the title of a novel we could read at jail. . . . Each day he needs a certain amount of money. He devours it. It wasn't love he uncoiled in me with his hollowed-out eyes and his courteous smile, that remnant of a prosperous past, but a dark terror that needed to press itself flat against him, or against another man . . . but he was the first, he came over to me and took my arm, a claim. We struggled on

[4]Large Detroit department store.
[5]Detroit exhibition hall.

the stairs and I said, *Let me loose, you're hurting my neck, my face,* it was such a surprise that my skin hurt where he rubbed it, and afterward we lay face to face and he breathed everything into me. In the end I think he turned me in.

2. Raymond Forrest. I just read this morning that Raymond Forrest's father, the chairman of the board at   , died of a heart attack on a plane bound for London. I would like to write Raymond Forrest a note of sympathy. I would like to thank him for not pressing charges against me one hundred years ago, saving me, being so generous . . . well, men like Raymond Forrest are generous men, not like Simon. I would like to write him a letter telling of my love, or of some other emotion that is positive and healthy. Not like Simon and his poetry, which he scrawled down when he was high and never changed a word . . . but when I try to think of something to say, it is Simon's language that comes back to me, caught in my head like a bad song, it is always Simon's language:

> There is no reality only dreams
> Your neck may get snapped when you wake
> My love is drawn to some violent end
> She keeps wanting to get away
> My love is heading downward
> And I am heading upward
> She is going to crash on the sidewalk
> And I am going to dissolve into the clouds

XII EVENTS

1. Out of the hospital, bruised and saddened and converted, with Princess' grunts still tangled in my hair . . . and Father in his overcoat looking like a prince himself, come to carry me off. Up the expressway and out north to home. Jesus Christ, but the air is thinner and cleaner here. Monumental houses. Heartbreaking sidewalks, so clean.

2. Weeping in the living room. The ceiling is two stories high and two chandeliers hang from it. Weeping, weeping, though Billie the maid is *probably listening*. I will never leave home again. Never. Never leave home. Never leave this home again, never.

3. Sugar doughnuts for breakfast. The toaster is very shiny and my face is distorted in it. Is that my face?

4. The car is turning in the driveway. Father brings me home. Mother embraces me. Sunlight breaks in movieland patches on the roof of our traditional-contemporary home, which was designed for the famous automotive stylist whose identity, if I told you the name of the famous car he designed, you would all know, so I can't tell you because my teeth chatter at the thought of being sued . . . or having someone climb into my bedroom window with a rope to strangle me. . . . The car turns up the blacktop drive. The house opens to me like a doll's house, so lovely in the sunlight, the big living room beckons to me with its walls falling away in a delirium of joy at my return, Billie the maid is *no doubt* listening from the kitchen as I burst into tears and the hysteria Simon got so sick of. Convulsed in Father's arms, I say I will never leave again, never, why did I leave, where did I go, what happened, my mind is gone wrong, my body is one big bruise, my backbone was sucked dry, it wasn't the men who hurt me and Simon never hurt me but only those girls . . . my God, how they hurt me . . . I will never leave home again. . . . The car is perpetually turning up the drive and I am perpetually breaking down in the living room and we are perpetually taking the right exit from the expressway (Lahser Road) and the wall of the rest room is perpetually banging against my head and perpetually are Simon's hands moving

across my body and adding everything up and so too are Father's hands on my shaking bruised back, far from the surface of my skin on the surface of my good blue cashmere coat (dry-cleaned for my release). . . . I weep for all the money here, for God in gold and beige carpeting, for the beauty of chandeliers and the miracle of a clean polished gleaming toaster and faucets that run both hot and cold water, and I tell them, *I will never leave home, this is my home, I love everything here, I am in love with everything here.* . . .

I am home.

1969, 1970

RAYMOND CARVER
(1938–1988)

Raymond Carver said, in "On Writing," that he got "a little nervous" when he overheard discussions about "formal innovation" in fiction:

> Too often "experimentation" is a license to be careless, silly or imitative in the writing. Even worse, a license to try to brutalize or alienate the reader. Too often such writing gives us no news of the world, or else describes a desert landscape and that's all—a few dunes and lizards here and there, but no people; a place uninhabited by anything recognizably human, a place of interest only to a few scientific specialists. . . . The real experimenters have to Make It New, as Pound urged, and in the process have to find things out for themselves. But if writers haven't taken leave of their senses, they also want to stay in touch with us, they want to carry news from their world to ours.

Carver was born in Clatskanie, Oregon, but grew up in Yakima, Washington, where his father got a job in a sawmill. He married at the age of eighteen and soon had two children to support. He persisted with his education and took night courses at Chico State College in California, where he studied creative writing with novelist John Gardner, who was an important influence on him. He took his degree at Chico State in 1963 and spent the following year studying at the University of Iowa's Writers' Workshop.

In an essay entitled "Fires," Carver vividly recalled his down-and-out years:

> In those days I always worked some crap job or another, and my wife did the same. She waitressed or else was a door-to-door saleswoman. . . . I worked sawmill jobs, janitor jobs, delivery man jobs, service station jobs, stockroom boy jobs—name it, I did it. One summer, in Arcata, California, I picked tulips, I swear, during the daylight hours, to support us; and at night after closing, I cleaned the inside of a drive-in restaurant and swept up the parking lot. Once I even considered, for a few minutes anyway—the job application form there in front of me—becoming a bill collector!

A reader might, after encountering his short stories, have guessed some sort of background for Carver. His stories often deal with people who live on the margin, barely making a go of it, and who find their personal lives shaped—or torn apart—by the sheer necessity of paying the rent and putting food on the table. Carver developed a lean, hard style that seemed compatible with the diminished, often barren lives he represented. It was, however, a style that had been carefully cultivated. Carver's first books were volumes of poetry, published by small presses, *Near Klamath* (1968), *Winter Insomnia* (1970), and *At Night the Salmon Move* (1976).

But as early as 1967, one of Carver's stories, "Will You Please Be Quiet, Please?" was selected to appear in *Best American Short Stories,* and it became the title story of a volume published in 1976. It was followed by other collections, *What We Talk About When We Talk About Love* (1981) and *Cathedral* (1983). Carver found himself a critically acclaimed fiction writer without having published a novel — an achievement most writers and critics thought impossible.

His *Fires: Essays, Poems, Stories,* published in 1983, showed that his poetry, seemingly using similar elements of style and technique employed in his stories, could have as powerful an impact as his prose. He published two more volumes of poetry, *Where Water Comes Together with Other Water* (1985) and *Ultramarine* (1987). In 1989, a posthumous collection appeared — *A New Path to the Waterfall.* His wife, the poet Tess Gallagher, said in an Introduction to the latter volume that Carver wrote poetry not as a diversion from his fiction but out of a "spiritual necessity." In 1988, the year of his death, Carver himself put the finishing touches on his collection of fiction published that year, *Where I'm Calling From: New and Collected Stories.*

Carver wrote frequently about alcoholics in both his fiction and poetry. He himself was one for a number of years, but painfully worked his way out of his self-destructive habit. He said in an interview: "For a long time I found myself living by the seat of my pants, making things terribly difficult for myself and everyone around me by my drinking. Now in this second life, this post-drinking life, I still retain a certain sense of pessimism I suppose, but I also have belief in, and love for, the things of this world. And needless to say, I'm not talking about microwave ovens, jet planes, an expensive car." As it turned out, Carver's "second life" did not last as long as he had hoped. In 1987 he learned that he had lung cancer and that he could not live long. He wrote about the experience in a poem, "Gravy": "'Don't weep for me,' / he said to his friends. 'I'm a lucky man. / I've had ten years longer than I or anyone / expected. Pure Gravy. And don't forget it.'"

Carver has been recruited by some literary theorists into a group bearing the title "minimalists," devoted to ordinary lives and events, sparse and terse in style, with very little in the way of plot or drama, but with a good deal in the way of power. But Carver himself disavowed the term because he thought it did not get at the artistic complexity of what he and others like him were doing. He revealed, however, in "On Writing," something of the secret of how he gained his effect: "It's possible, in a poem or a short story, to write about commonplace things and objects using commonplace but precise language, and to endow those things — a chair, a window curtain, a fork, a stone, a woman's earring — with immense, even startling power. It is possible to write a line of seemingly innocuous dialogue and have it send a chill along the reader's spine — the source of artistic delight. . . . That's the kind of writing that most interests me."

ADDITIONAL READING

Conversations with Raymond Carver, ed. Marshall Bruce Gentry and William L. Stull, 1990.

Arthur M. Saltzman, *Understanding Raymond Carver,* 1988.

TEXT

Where I'm Calling From: New and Selected Stories, 1988.

A Serious Talk

Vera's car was there, no others, and Burt gave thanks for that. He pulled into the drive and stopped beside the pie he'd dropped the night before. It was still there, the aluminum pan upside down, a halo of pumpkin filling on the pavement. It was the day after Christmas.

He'd come on Christmas day to visit his wife and children. Vera had warned him beforehand. She'd told him the score. She'd said he had to be out by six o'clock because her friend and his children were coming for dinner.

They had sat in the living room and solemnly opened the presents Burt had brought over. They had opened his packages while other packages wrapped in festive paper lay piled under the tree waiting for after six o'clock.

He had watched the children open their gifts, waited while Vera undid the ribbon on hers. He saw her slip off the paper, lift the lid, take out the cashmere sweater.

"It's nice," she said. "Thank you, Burt."

"Try it on," his daughter said.

"Put it on," his son said.

Burt looked at his son, grateful for his backing him up.

She did try it on. Vera went into the bedroom and came out with it on.

"It's nice," she said.

"It's nice on *you*," Burt said, and felt a welling in his chest.

He opened his gifts. From Vera, a gift certificate at Sondheim's men's store. From his daughter, a matching comb and brush. From his son, a ballpoint pen.

Vera served sodas, and they did a little talking. But mostly they looked at the tree. Then his daughter got up and began setting the dining-room table, and his son went off to his room.

But Burt liked it where he was. He liked it in front of the fireplace, a glass in his hand, his house, his home.

Then Vera went into the kitchen.

From time to time his daughter walked into the dining room with something for the table. Burt watched her. He watched her fold the linen napkins into the wine glasses. He watched her put a slender vase in the middle of the table. He watched her lower a flower into the vase, doing it ever so carefully.

A small wax and sawdust log burned on the grate. A carton of five more sat ready on the hearth. He got up from the sofa and put them all in the fireplace. He watched until they flamed. Then he finished his soda and made for the patio door. On the way, he saw the pies lined up on the sideboard. He stacked them in his arms, all six, one for every ten times she had ever betrayed him.

In the driveway in the dark, he'd let one fall as he fumbled with the door.

The front door was permanently locked since the night his key had broken off inside it. He went around to the back. There was a wreath on the patio door. He rapped on the glass. Vera was in her bathrobe. She looked out at him and frowned. She opened the door a little.

Burt said, "I want to apologize to you for last night. I want to apologize to the kids, too."

Vera said, "They're not here."

She stood in the doorway and he stood on the patio next to the philodendron plant. He pulled at some lint on his sleeve.

She said, "I can't take any more. You tried to burn the house down."

"I did not."

"You did. Everybody here was a witness."

He said, "Can I come in and talk about it?"

She drew the robe together at her throat and moved back inside.

She said, "I have to go somewhere in an hour."

He looked around. The tree blinked on and off. There was a pile of colored tissue paper and shiny boxes at one end of the sofa. A turkey carcass sat on a platter in the center of the dining-room table, the leathery remains in a bed of parsley as if in a horrible nest. A cone of ash filled the fireplace. There were some empty Shasta cola cans in there too. A trail of smoke stains rose up to the bricks to the mantel, where the wood that stopped them was scorched black.

He turned around and went back to the kitchen.

He said, "What time did your friend leave last night?"

She said, "If you're going to start that, you can go right now."

He pulled a chair out and sat down at the kitchen table in front of the big ashtray. He closed his eyes and opened them. He moved the curtain aside and looked out at the backyard. He saw a bicycle without a front wheel standing upside down. He saw weeds growing along the redwood fence.

She ran water into a saucepan. "Do you remember Thanksgiving?" she said. "I said then that was the last holiday you were going to wreck for us. Eating bacon and eggs instead of turkey at ten o'clock at night."

"I know it," he said. "I said I'm sorry."

"Sorry isn't good enough."

The pilot light was out again. She was at the stove trying to get the gas going under the pan of water.

"Don't burn yourself," he said. "Don't catch yourself on fire."

He considered her robe catching fire, him jumping up from the table, throwing her down onto the floor and rolling her over and over into the living room, where he would cover her with his body. Or should he run to the bedroom for a blanket?

"Vera?"

She looked at him.

"Do you have anything to drink? I could use a drink this morning."

"There's some vodka in the freezer."

"When did you start keeping vodka in the freezer?"

"Don't ask."

"Okay," he said, "I won't ask."

He got out the vodka and poured some into a cup he found on the counter.

She said, "Are you just going to drink it like that, out of a cup?" She said, "Jesus, Burt. What'd you want to talk about, anyway? I told you I have someplace to go. I have a flute lesson at one o'clock."

"Are you still taking flute?"

"I just said so. What is it? Tell me what's on your mind, and then I have to get ready."

"I wanted to say I was sorry."

She said, "You said that."

He said, "If you have any juice, I'll mix it with this vodka."

She opened the refrigerator and moved things around.

"There's cranapple juice," she said.

"That's fine," he said.

"I'm going to the bathroom," she said.

He drank the cup of cranapple juice and vodka. He lit a cigarette and tossed the match into the big ashtray that always sat on the kitchen table. He studied the butts in it. Some of them were Vera's brand, and some of them weren't. Some even were lavender-colored. He got up and dumped it all under the sink.

The ashtray was not really an ashtray. It was a big dish of stoneware they'd bought from a bearded potter on the mall in Santa Clara. He rinsed it out and dried it. He put it back on the table. And then he ground out his cigarette in it.

The water on the stove began to bubble just as the phone began to ring.

He heard her open the bathroom door and call to him through the living room. "Answer that! I'm about to get into the shower."

The kitchen phone was on the counter in a corner behind the roasting pan. He moved the roasting pan and picked up the receiver.

"Is Charlie there?" the voice said.

"No," Burt said.

"Okay," the voice said.

While he was seeing to the coffee, the phone rang again.

"Charlie?"

"Not here," Burt said.

This time he left the receiver off the hook.

Vera came back into the kitchen wearing jeans and a sweater and brushing her hair.

He spooned the instant into the cups of hot water and then spilled some vodka into his. He carried the cups over to the table.

She picked up the receiver, listened. She said, "What's this? Who was on the phone?"

"Nobody," he said. "Who smokes colored cigarettes?"

"I do."

"I didn't know you did that."

"Well, I do."

She sat across from him and drank her coffee. They smoked and used the ashtray.

There were things he wanted to say, grieving things, consoling things, things like that.

"I'm smoking three packs a day," Vera said. "I mean, if you really want to know what goes on around here."

"God almighty," Burt said.

Vera nodded.

"I didn't come over here to hear that," he said.

"What did you come over here to hear, then? You want to hear the house burned down?"

"Vera," he said. "It's Christmas. That's why I came."

"It's the day after Christmas," she said. "Christmas has come and gone," she said. "I don't ever want to see another one."

"What about me?" he said. "You think I look forward to holidays?"

The phone rang again. Burt picked it up.

"It's someone wanting Charlie," he said.

"What?"

"Charlie," Burt said.

Vera took the phone. She kept her back to him as she talked. Then she turned to him and said, "I'll take this call in the bedroom. So would you please hang up after I've picked it up in there? I can tell, so hang it up when I say."

He took the receiver. She left the kitchen. He held the receiver to his ear and listened. He heard nothing. Then he heard a man clear his throat. Then he heard Vera pick up the other phone. She shouted, "Okay, Burt! I have it now, Burt!"

He put down the receiver and stood looking at it. He opened the silverware drawer and pushed things around inside. He opened another drawer. He looked in the sink. He went into the dining room and got the carving knife. He held it under hot water until the grease broke and ran off. He wiped the blade on his sleeve. He moved to the phone, doubled the cord, and sawed through without any trouble at all.

He examined the ends of the cord. Then he shoved the phone back into its corner behind the roasting pan.

She came in. She said, "The phone went dead. Did you do anything to the telephone?" She looked at the phone and then picked it up from the counter.

"Son of a bitch!" she screamed. She screamed, "Out, out, where you belong!" She was shaking the phone at him. "That's it! I'm going to get a restraining order, that's what I'm going to get!"

The phone made a *ding* when she banged it down on the counter.

"I'm going next door to call the police if you don't get out of here now!"

He picked up the ashtray. He held it by its edge. He posed with it like a man preparing to hurl the discus.

"Please," she said. "That's our ashtray."

He left through the patio door. He was not certain, but he thought he had proved something. He hoped he had made something clear. The thing was, they had to have a serious talk soon. There were things that needed talking about, important things that had to be discussed. They'd talk again. Maybe after the holidays were over and things got back to normal. He'd tell her the goddamn ashtray was a goddamn dish, for example.

He stepped around the pie in the driveway and got back into his car. He started the car and put it into reverse. It was hard managing until he put the ashtray down.

1981

BOBBIE ANN MASON
(b. 1940)

In Bobbie Ann Mason's story "Nancy Culpepper," readers learn more specific details about the characters than they expect to: that they are using Joy to wash the dishes; that they are listening to "Sgt. Pepper's Lonely Hearts Club Band" on the stereo; that they go to a Taco Bell to eat; that they watch a TV evangelist urging them to call him, toll free. This specificity of detail is characteristic of Mason's stories. In other stories, the characters work at a K Mart or Rexall; they watch Fred Astaire and Eleanor Powell dancing together in *That's Entertainment* on TV; they listen to the Oak Ridge Boys, a former gospel quartet, now singing country-rock; they see double features at a drive-in (*Dr. Strangelove* and *Lover Come Back*).

At first glance, this avalanche of detail may seem excessive; but gradually it contributes to a picture of the diminished lives the characters lead in a homogenized-fast-food-small-town world: instead of local color, the fiction might be called local drab-gray. Whereas many contemporary writers use such details to produce comic or satiric portraits, Mason uses them most frequently to evoke sympathy tinged with feelings of poignancy. She has said: "My work seems to have struck a chord with a number of readers who have left home and maybe who have rejected it. . . . I left that kind of world, too, but never could get rid of it, and it haunted me. It seems that I started writing because I was preoccupied with my past. . . . I left because I felt trapped in a conventional small-town culture, so I try to imagine what that world is like for people who don't leave. I guess I kind of project myself into it to know what it would be like for me."

She was born in 1940 in Mayfield, Kentucky, where her father was a dairy farmer. She graduated from the University of Kentucky in 1962, and, after a stint working in New York for the Ideal Publishing Company (*Movie Stars, Movie Life*), she returned to school and took an M.A. in journalism at the State University of New York at Binghamton in 1966. In 1972 she earned a Ph.D. in English at the University of Connecticut and afterwards taught English at Mansfield State College in Mansfield, Pennsylvania, from 1972 to 1979. She published a work of scholarship, *Nabokov's Garden: A Nature Guide to Ada*, in 1974 and a work on literature for girls, *The Girl Sleuth: A Feminist Guide to the Bobbsey Twins, Nancy Drew, and Their Sisters*, in 1975.

But she never gave up her ambition to be a writer and, after twenty submissions to *The New Yorker,* found one of her stories — "Offerings" — accepted in 1980. This success was followed by others, leading to the publication of her first volume of fiction, *Shiloh and Other Stories,* in 1982. It was universally praised in the reviews and won the 1983 Ernest Hemingway Foundation Award for the best first-work of fiction. She has published two novels, *In Country* (1985) and *Spence & Lila* (1988).

Mason's name often turns up in the lists of minimalists, or post-postmodernists, who have been credited with forging a new kind of realism in reaction to the postmodernist fantasists. She herself has commented: "My characters are members of the shopping mall generation. And there's a whole other, larger thing that's going on in terms of the classes, and it's reflected in many short stories being written now. John Barth calls them 'blue-collar minimalist hyper-realist'! An editor in England calls it 'dirty realism.' I love those terms!"

Once when Mason was visiting a college class in writing, a student remarked on how Mason wrote about K Mart clerks, saying: "You know, I never really noticed those people. I go in there to buy something and I never really thought of them as individual human beings." In her stories, Mason turns the K Mart clerks into real people. She has commented in an interview: "Basically, I'm trying to portray a world of some people who are aspiring to a better life for themselves, and I think I'm trying to understand them on their own terms and not judge them." But style to her is as important as subject. Asked what she looked for when reading fiction, she answered: "I think I go for style first because I like the pleasure of language and the feeling that comes through style. But style and content have to be perfectly fused for it to be really good. I don't think you can have one without the other, although if I had to choose, I'd probably choose style."

Mason has called "Nancy Culpepper," included here, the favorite of her stories. The title character is, like Mason, a displaced Kentuckian who discovers on a visit home how deep her roots are, and how important the subterranean connections that remain.

TEXT

Shiloh and Other Stories, 1982.

Nancy Culpepper

When Nancy received her parents' letter saying they were moving her grandmother to a nursing home, she said to her husband, "I really should go help them out. And I've got to save Granny's photographs. They might get lost." Jack did not try to discourage her, and she left for Kentucky soon after the letter came.

Nancy has been vaguely wanting to move to Kentucky, and she has persuaded Jack to think about relocating his photography business. They live in the country, near a small town an hour's drive from Philadelphia. Their son, Robert, who is eight, has fits when they talk about moving. He does not want to leave his room or his playmates. Once, he asked, "What about our chickens?"

"They have chickens in Kentucky," Nancy explained. "Don't worry. We're not going yet."

Later he asked, "But what about the fish in the pond?"

"I don't know," said Nancy. "I guess we'll have to rent a U-Haul."

When Nancy arrives at her parents' farm in western Kentucky, her mother says, "Your daddy and me's both got inner ear and nerves. And we couldn't lift Granny, or anything, if we had to all of a sudden."

"The flu settled in my ears," Daddy says, cocking his head at an angle.

"Mine's still popping," says Mother.

In a few days they plan to move Granny, and they will return to their own house, which they have been renting out. For nine years, they have lived next door, in Granny's house, in order to care for her. There Mother has had to cook on an ancient gas range, with her mother-in-law hovering over her, supervising. Granny used only lye soap on dishes, and it was five years before Nancy's mother defied her and bought some Joy. By then, Granny was confined to her bed, crippled with arthritis. Now she is ninety-three.

"You didn't have to come back," Daddy says to Nancy at the dinner table. "We could manage."

"I want to help you move," Nancy says. "And I want to make sure Granny's pictures don't get lost. Nobody cares about them but me, and I'm afraid somebody will throw them away."

Nancy wants to find out if Granny has a picture of a great-great-aunt named Nancy Culpepper. No one in the family seems to know anything about her, but Nancy is excited by the thought of an ancestor with the same name as hers. Since she found out about her, Nancy has been going by her maiden name, but she has given up trying to explain this to her mother, who persists in addressing letters to "Mr. and Mrs. Jack Cleveland."

"There's some pictures hid behind Granny's closet wall," Daddy tells Nancy. "When we hooked up the coal-oil stove through the fireplace a few years ago, they got walled in."

"That's ridiculous! Why would you do that?"

"They were in the way." He stands up and puts on his cap, preparing to go out to feed his calves.

"Will Granny care if I tear the wall down?" Nancy asks, joking.

Daddy laughs, acting as though he understood, but Nancy knows he is pretending. He seems tired, and his billed cap looks absurdly small perched on his head.

When Nancy and Jack were married, years ago, in Massachusetts, Nancy did not want her parents to come to the wedding. She urged them not to make the long trip. "It's no big deal," she told them on the telephone. "It'll last ten minutes. We're not even going on a honeymoon right away, because we both have exams Monday."

Nancy was in graduate school, and Jack was finishing his B.A. For almost a year they had been renting a large old house on a lake. The house had a field-rock fireplace with a heart-shaped stone centered above the mantel. Jack, who was studying design, thought the heart was tasteless, and he covered it with a Peter Max poster.

At the ceremony, Jack's dog, Grover, was present, and instead of organ music, a stereo played *Sgt. Pepper's Lonely Hearts Club Band*.[1] It was 1967. Nancy was astonished

---

[1]An album of rock songs issued by the Beatles, the British rock group, in 1967.

by the minister's white robe and his beard and by the fact that he chain-smoked. The preachers she remembered from childhood would have called him a heathen, she thought. Most of the wedding pictures, taken by a friend of Jack's, turned out to be trick photography—blurred faces and double exposures.

The party afterward lasted all night. Jack blew up two hundred balloons and kept the fire going. They drank too much wine-and-7Up punch. Guests went in and out, popping balloons with cigarettes, taking walks by the lake. Everyone was looking for the northern lights, which were supposed to be visible that evening. Holding on to Jack, Nancy searched the murky sky, feeling that the two of them were lone travelers on the edge of some outer-space adventure. At the same time, she kept thinking of her parents at home, probably watching *Gunsmoke*.

"I saw them once," Jack said. "They were fantastic."

"What was it like?"

"Shower curtains."

"Really? That's amazing."

"Luminescent shower curtains."

"I'm shivering," Nancy said. The sky was blank.

"Let's go in. It's too cloudy anyway. Someday we'll see them. I promise."

Someone had taken down the poster above the fireplace and put up the picture of Sgt. Pepper—the cutout that came with the album. Sgt. Pepper overlooked the room like a stern father.

"What's the matter?" a man asked Nancy. He was Dr. Doyle, her American History 1861–1865 professor. "This is your wedding. Loosen up." He burst a balloon and Nancy jumped.

When someone offered her a joint, she refused, then wondered why. The house was filled with strangers, and the Beatles album played over and over. Jack and Nancy danced, hugging each other in a slow two-step that was all wrong for the music. They drifted past the wedding presents, lined up on a table Jack had fashioned from a door—hand-dipped candles, a silver roach clip, *Joy of Cooking*,[2] signed pottery in nonfunctional shapes. Nancy wondered what her parents had eaten for supper. Possibly fried steak, two kinds of peas, biscuits, blackberry pie. The music shifted and the songs merged together; Jack and Nancy kept dancing.

"There aren't any stopping places," Nancy said. She was crying. "Songs used to have stopping places in between."

"Let's just keep on dancing," Jack said.

Nancy was thinking of the blackberry bushes at the farm in Kentucky, which spread so wildly they had to be burned down every few years. They grew on the banks of the creek, which in summer shrank to still, small occasional pools. After a while Nancy realized that Jack was talking to her. He was explaining how he could predict exactly when the last, dying chord on the album was about to end.

"Listen," he said. "*There*. Right there."

Nancy's parents had met Jack a few months before the wedding, during spring break, when Jack and Nancy stopped in Kentucky on their way to Denver to see an old friend of Jack's. The visit involved some elaborate lies about their sleeping arrangements on the trip.

At the supper table, Mother and Daddy passed bowls of food self-consciously. The table was set with some napkins left over from Christmas. The vegetables were soaked in bacon grease, and Jack took small helpings. Nancy sat rigidly, watching every movement, like a cat stationed near a bird feeder. Mother had gathered poke, because it was spring, and she said to Jack, "I bet you don't eat poke salet up there."

"It's weeds," said Nancy.

---

[2]An American cook book by Irma S. Rombauer, first copyrighted in 1931 but still in print after innumerable revisions and editions; it was, and still is, extraordinarily popular as a wedding gift. Roach: marijuana butt (slang).

"I've never heard of it," Jack said. He hesitated, then took a small serving.

"It's poison if it gets too big," Daddy said. He turned to Nancy's mother. "I think you picked this too big. You're going to poison us all."

"He's teasing," Nancy said.

"The berries is what's poison," said Mother, laughing. "Wouldn't that be something? They'll say up there I tried to poison your boyfriend the minute I met him!"

Everyone laughed. Jack's face was red. He was wearing an embroidered shirt. Nancy watched him trim the fat from his ham as precisely as if he were using an X-Acto knife on mat board.

"How's Granny?" said Nancy. Her grandmother was then living alone in her own house.

"Tolerable well," said Daddy.

"We'll go see her," Jack said. "Nancy told me all about her."

"She cooks her egg in her oats to keep from washing a extry dish," Mother said.

Nancy played with her food. She was looking at the pink dining room wall and the plastic flowers in the window. On the afternoon Jack and Nancy first met, he took her to a junk shop, where he bought a stained-glass window for his bathroom. Nancy would never have thought of going to a junk shop. It would not have occurred to her to put a stained-glass window in a bathroom.

"What do you aim to be when you graduate?" Daddy asked Jack abruptly, staring at him. Jack's hair looked oddly like an Irish setter's ears, Nancy thought suddenly.

"Won't you have to go in the army?" Mother asked.

"I'll apply for an assistantship if my grades are good enough," Jack said. "Anything to avoid the draft."

Nancy's father was leaning into his plate, as though he were concentrating deeply on each bite.

"He makes good grades," Nancy said.

"Nancy always made all A's," Daddy said to Jack.

"We gave her a dollar for ever' one," said Mother. "She kept us broke."

"In graduate school they don't give A's," said Nancy. "They just give S's and U's."

Jack wadded up his napkin. Then Mother served fried pies with white sauce. "Nancy always loved these better than anything," she said.

After supper, Nancy showed Jack the farm. As they walked through the fields, Nancy felt that he was seeing peaceful landscapes—arrangements of picturesque cows, an old red barn. She had never thought of the place this way before; it reminded her of prints in a dime store.

While her mother washes the dishes, Nancy takes Granny's dinner to her, and sits in a rocking chair while Granny eats in bed. The food is on an old TV dinner tray. The compartments hold chicken and dressing, mashed potatoes, field peas, green beans, and vinegar slaw. The servings are tiny—six green beans, a spoonful of peas.

Granny's teeth no longer fit, and she has to bite sideways, like a cat. She wears the lower teeth only during meals, but she will not get new ones. She says it would be wasteful to be buried with a new three-hundred-dollar set of teeth. In between bites, Granny guzzles iced tea from a Kentucky Lakes mug. "That slaw don't have enough sugar in it," she says. "It makes my mouth draw up." She smacks her lips.

Nancy says, "I've heard the food is really good at the Orchard Acres Rest Home."

Granny does not reply for a moment. She is working on a chicken gristle, which causes her teeth to clatter. Then she says, "I ain't going nowhere."

"Mother and Daddy are moving back into their house. You don't want to stay here by yourself, do you?" Nancy's voice sounds hollow to her.

"I'll be all right. I can do for myself."

When Granny swallows, it sounds like water spilling from a bucket into a cistern. After Nancy's parents moved in, they covered Granny's old cistern, but Nancy still remembers drawing the bucket up from below. The chains made a sound like crying.

Granny pushes her food with a piece of bread, cleaning her tray. "I can do a little cooking," she says. "I can sweep."

"Try this boiled custard, Granny. I made it just for you. Just the way you used to make it."

"It ain't yaller enough," says Granny, tasting the custard. "Store-bought eggs."

When she finishes, she removes her lower teeth and sloshes them in a plastic tumbler on the bedside table. Nancy looks away. On the wall are Nancy's high school graduation photograph and a picture of Jesus. Nancy looks sassy; her graduation hat resembles a tilted lid. Jesus has a halo, set at about the same angle.

Now Nancy ventures a question about the pictures hidden behind the closet wall. At first Granny is puzzled. Then she seems to remember.

"They're behind the stovepipe," she says. Grimacing with pain, she stretches her legs out slowly, and then, holding her head, she sinks back into her pillows and draws the quilt over her shoulders. "I'll look for them one of these days—when I'm able."

Jack photographs weeds, twigs, pond reflections, silhouettes of Robert against the sun with his arms flung out like a scarecrow's. Sometimes he works in the evenings in his studio at home, drinking tequila sunrises and composing bizarre still lifes with light bulbs, wine bottles, Tinker Toys, Lucite cubes. He makes arrangements of gourds look like breasts.

On the day Nancy tried to explain to Jack about her need to save Granny's pictures, a hailstorm interrupted her. It was the only hailstorm she had ever seen in the North, and she had forgotten all about them. Granny always said a hailstorm means that God was cleaning out his icebox. Nancy stood against a white Masonite wall mounted with a new series of photographs and looked out the window at tulips being smashed. The ice pellets littered the ground like shattered glass. Then, as suddenly as it had arrived, the hailstorm was over.

"Pictures didn't use to be so common," Nancy said. Jack's trash can was stuffed with rejected prints, and Robert's face was crumpled on top. "I want to keep Granny's pictures as reminders."

"If you think that will solve anything," said Jack, squinting at a negative he was holding against the light.

"I want to see if she has one of Nancy Culpepper."

"That's *you*."

"There was another one. She was a great-great-aunt or something, on my daddy's side. She had the same name as mine."

"There's another one of you?" Jack said with mock disbelief.

"I'm a reincarnation," she said, playing along.

"There's nobody else like you. You're one of a kind."

Nancy turned away and stared deliberately at Jack's pictures, which were held up by clear-headed pushpins, like translucent eyes dotting the wall. She examined them one by one, moving methodically down the row—stumps, puffballs, tree roots, close-ups of cat feet.

Nancy first learned about her ancestor on a summer Sunday a few years before, when she took her grandmother to visit the Culpepper graveyard, beside an oak grove off the Paducah highway. The old oaks had spread their limbs until they shaded the entire cemetery, and the tombstones poked through weeds like freak mushrooms. Nancy wandered among the graves, while Granny stayed beside her husband's gravestone. It had her own name on it too, with a blank space for the date.

Nancy told Jack afterward that when she saw the stone marked "NANCY CULPEP-PER, 1833–1905," she did a double take. "It was like time-lapse photography," she said. "I mean, I was standing there looking into the past and the future at the same time. It was weird."

"She wasn't kin to me, but she lived down the road," Granny explained to Nancy. "She was your granddaddy's aunt."

"Did she look like me?" Nancy asked.

"I don't know. She was real old." Granny touched the stone, puzzled. "I can't figure why she wasn't buried with her husband's people," she said.

On Saturday, Nancy helps her parents move some of their furniture to the house next door. It is only a short walk, but when the truck is loaded they all ride in it, Nancy sitting between her parents. The truck's muffler sounds like thunder, and they drive without speaking. Daddy backs up to the porch.

The paint on the house is peeling, and the latch of the storm door is broken. Daddy pulls at the door impatiently, saying, "I sure wish I could burn down these old houses and retire to Arizona." For as long as Nancy can remember, her father has been sending away for literature on Arizona.

Her mother says, "We'll never go anywhere. We've got our dress tail on a bedpost."

"What does that mean?" asks Nancy, in surprise.

"Use to, if a storm was coming, people would put a bedpost on a child's dress tail, to keep him from blowing away. In other words, we're tied down."

"That's funny. I never heard of that."

"I guess you think we're just ignorant," Mother says. "The way we talk."

"No, I don't."

Daddy props the door open, and Nancy helps him ease a mattress over the threshold. Mother apologizes for not being able to lift anything.

"I'm in your way," she says, stepping off the porch into a dead canna bed.

Nancy stacks boxes in her old room. It seems smaller than she remembered, and the tenants have scarred the woodwork. Mentally, she refurnishes the room—the bed by the window, the desk opposite. The first time Jack came to Kentucky he slept here, while Nancy slept on the couch in the living room. Now Nancy recalls the next day, as they headed west, with Jack accusing her of being dishonest, foolishly trying to protect her parents. "You let them think you're such a goody-goody, the ideal daughter," he said. "I bet you wouldn't tell them if you made less than an A."

Nancy's father comes in and runs his hand across the ceiling, gathering up strings of dust. Tugging at a loose piece of door facing, he says to Nancy, "Never trust renters. They won't take care of a place."

"What will you do with Granny's house?"

"Nothing. Not as long as she's living."

"Will you rent it out then?"

"No. I won't go through that again." He removes his cap and smooths his hair, then puts the cap back on. Leaning against the wall, he talks about the high cost of the nursing home. "I never thought it would come to this," he says. "I wouldn't do it if there was any other way."

"You don't have any choice," says Nancy.

"The government will pay you to break up your family," he says. "If I get like your granny, I want you to just take me out in the woods and shoot me."

"She told me she wasn't going," Nancy says.

"They've got a big recreation room for the ones that can get around," Daddy says. "They've even got disco dancing."

When Daddy laughs, his voice catches, and he has to clear his throat. Nancy laughs with him. "I can just see Granny disco dancing. Are you sure you want me to shoot you? That place sounds like fun."

They go outside, where Nancy's mother is cleaning out a patch of weed-choked perennials. "I planted these iris the year we moved," she says.

"They're pretty," says Nancy. "I haven't seen that color up North."

Mother stands up and shakes her foot awake. "I sure hope y'all can move down here," she says. "It's a shame you have to be so far away. Robert grows so fast I don't know him."

"We might someday. I don't know if we can."

"Looks like Jack could make good money if he set up a studio in town. Nowadays people want fancy pictures."

"Even the school pictures cost a fortune," Daddy says.

"Jack wants to free-lance for publications," says Nancy. "And there aren't any here. There's not even a camera shop within fifty miles."

"But people want pictures," Mother says. "They've gone back to decorating living rooms with family pictures. In antique frames."

Daddy smokes a cigarette on the porch, while Nancy circles the house. A beetle has infested the oak trees, causing clusters of leaves to turn brown. Nancy stands on the concrete lid of an old cistern and watches crows fly across a cornfield. In the distance a series of towers slings power lines across a flat sea of soybeans. Her mother is talking about Granny. Nancy thinks of Granny on the telephone, the day of her wedding, innocently asking, "What are you going to cook for your wedding breakfast?" Later, seized with laughter, Nancy told Jack what Granny had said.

"I almost said to her, 'We usually don't eat breakfast, we sleep so late!'"

Jack was busy blowing up balloons. When he didn't laugh, Nancy said, "Isn't that hilarious? She's really out of the nineteenth century."

"You don't have to make me breakfast," said Jack.

"In her time, it meant something really big," Nancy said helplessly. "Don't you see?"

Now Nancy's mother is saying, "The way she has to have that milk of magnesia every night, when I know good and well she don't need it. She thinks she can't live without it."

"What's wrong with her?" asks Nancy.

"She thinks she's got a knot in her bowels. But ain't nothing wrong with her but that head-swimming and arthritis." Mother jerks a long morning glory vine out of the marigolds. "Hardening of the arteries is what makes her head swim," she says.

"We better get back and see about her," Daddy says, but he does not get up immediately. The crows are racing above the power lines.

Later, Nancy spreads a Texaco map of the United States out on Granny's quilt. "I want to show you where I live," she says. "Philadelphia's nearly a thousand miles from here."

"Reach me my specs," says Granny, as she struggles to sit up. "How did you get here?"

"Flew. Daddy picked me up at the airport in Paducah."

"Did you come by the bypass or through town?"

"The bypass," says Nancy. Nancy shows her where Pennsylvania is on the map. "I flew from Philadelphia to Louisville to Paducah. There's California. That's where Robert was born."

"I haven't seen a geography since I was twenty years old," Granny says. She studies the map, running her fingers over it as though she were caressing fine material. "Law, I didn't know *where* Floridy was. It's way down there."

"I've been to Florida," Nancy says.

Granny lies back, holding her head as if it were a delicate china bowl. In a moment she says, "Tell your mama to thaw me up some of them strawberries I picked."

"When were you out picking strawberries, Granny?"

"They're in the freezer of my refrigerator. Back in the back. In a little milk carton." Granny removes her glasses and waves them in the air.

"Larry was going to come and play with me, but he couldn't come," Robert says to Nancy on the telephone that evening. "He had a stomachache."

"That's too bad. What did you do today?"

"We went to the Taco Bell and then we went to the woods so Daddy could take pictures of Indian pipes."

"What are those?"

"I don't know. Daddy knows."

"We didn't find any," Jack says on the extension. "I think it's the wrong time of year. How's Kentucky?"

Nancy tells Jack about helping her parents move. "My bed is gone, so tonight I'll have to sleep on a couch in the hallway," she says. "It's really dreary here in this old house. Everything looks so bare."

"How's your grandmother?"

"The same. She's dead set against that rest home, but what can they do?"

"Do you still want to move down there?" Jack asks.

"I don't know."

"I know how we could take the chickens to Kentucky," says Robert in an excited burst.

"How?"

"We could give them sleeping pills and then put them in the trunk so they'd be quiet."

"That sounds gruesome," Jack says.

Nancy tells Robert not to think about moving. There is static on the line. Nancy has trouble hearing Jack. "We're your family too," he is saying.

"I didn't mean to abandon you," she says.

"Have you seen the pictures yet?"

"No. I'm working up to that."

"Nancy Culpepper, the original?"

"You bet," says Nancy, a little too quickly. She hears Robert hang up. "Is Robert O.K.?" she asks through the static.

"Oh, sure."

"He doesn't think I moved without him?"

"He'll be all right."

"He didn't tell me good-bye."

"Don't worry," says Jack.

"She's been after me about those strawberries till I could wring her neck," says Mother as she and Nancy are getting ready for bed. "She's talking about some strawberries she put up in nineteen seventy-*one*. I've told her and told her that she eat them strawberries back then, but won't nothing do but for her to have them strawberries."

"Give her some others," Nancy says.

"She'd know the difference. She don't miss a thing when it comes to what's *hers*. But sometimes she's just as liable to forget her name."

Mother is trembling, and then she is crying. Nancy pats her mother's hair, which is gray and wiry and sticks out in sprigs. Wiping her eyes, Mother says, "All the kinfolks will talk. 'Look what they done to her, poor helpless thing.' It'll probably kill her, to move her to that place."

"When you move back home you can get all your antiques out of the barn," Nancy says. "You'll be in your own house again. Won't that be nice?"

Mother does not answer. She takes some sheets and quilts from a closet and hands them to Nancy. "That couch lays good," she says.

When Nancy wakes up, the covers are on the floor, and for a moment she does not remember where she is. Her digital watch says 2:43. Then it tells the date. In the darkness she has no sense of distance, and it seems to her that the red numerals could be the size of a billboard, only seen from far away.

Jack has told her that this kind of insomnia is a sign of depression, while the other kind—inability to fall asleep at bedtime—is a sign of anxiety. Nancy always thought he had it backward, but now she thinks he may be right. A flicker of distant sheet lightning exposes the bleak walls with the suddenness of a flashbulb. The angles of the hall seem unfamiliar, and the narrow couch makes Nancy feel small and alone. When Jack and Robert come to Kentucky with her, they all sleep in the living room, and in the early morning Nancy's parents pass through to get to the bathroom. "We're just one big happy family," Daddy announces, to disguise his embarrassment when he awakens them. Now, for some reason, Nancy recalls Jack's strange still lifes, and she thinks of the black irises and the polished skulls of cattle suspended in the skies of O'Keefe[3] paintings. The irises are like thunderheads. The night they were married, Nancy and Jack collapsed into bed, falling asleep immediately, their heads swirling. The party was still going on, and friends from New York were staying over. Nancy woke up the next day saying her new name, and feeling that once again, in another way, she had betrayed her parents. "The one time they really thought they knew what I was doing, they didn't at all," she told Jack, who was barely awake. The visitors had gone out for the Sunday newspapers, and they brought back doughnuts. They had doughnuts and wine for breakfast. Someone made coffee later.

In the morning, a slow rain blackens the fallen oak branches in the yard. In Granny's room the curtains are gray with shadows. Nancy places an old photograph album in Granny's lap. Silently, Granny turns pages of blank-faced babies in long white dresses like wedding gowns. Nancy's father is a boy in a sailor suit. Men and women in pictures the color of café au lait[4] stand around picnic tables. The immense trees in these settings are shaggy and dark. Granny cannot find Nancy Culpepper in the album. Quickly, she flips past a picture of her husband. Then she almost giggles as she points to a girl. "That's me."

"I wouldn't have recognized you, Granny."

"Why, it looks just *like* me." Granny strokes the picture, as though she were trying to feel the dress. "That was my favorite dress," she says. "It was brown poplin, with grosgrain ribbon and self-covered buttons. Thirty-two of them. And all those tucks. It took me three weeks to work up that dress."

Nancy points to the pictures one by one, asking Granny to identify them. Granny does not notice Nancy writing the names in a notebook. Aunt Sass, Uncle Joe, Dove and Pear Culpepper, Hortense Culpepper.

"Hort Culpepper went to Texas," says Granny. "She had TB."

"Tell me about that," Nancy urges her.

"There wasn't anything to tell. She got homesick for her mammy's cooking." Granny closes the album and falls back against her pillows, saying, "All those people are gone."

While Granny sleeps, Nancy gets a flashlight and opens the closet. The inside is crammed with the accumulation of decades — yellowed newspapers, boxes of greeting cards, bags of string, and worn-out stockings. Granny's best dress, a blue bonded knit she has hardly worn, is in plastic wrapping. Nancy pushes the clothing aside and examines the wall. To her right, a metal pipe runs vertically through the closet. Backing up against the dresses, Nancy shines the light on the corner and discovers a large framed picture wedged behind the pipe. By tugging at the frame, she is able to work it gradually through the narrow space between the wall and the pipe. In the picture a man and woman, whose features are sharp and clear, are sitting expectantly on a brocaded love seat. Nancy imagines that this is a wedding portrait.

In the living room, a TV evangelist is urging viewers to call him, toll free. Mother turns the TV off when Nancy appears with the picture, and Daddy stands up and helps her hold it near a window.

"I think that's Uncle John!" he says excitedly. "He was my favorite uncle."

---

[3]Georgia O'Keefe (1887–1986), American painter who settled in the latter part of her life in the American Southwest and became known for her sensuous close-up paintings of flowers and for her desert paintings often containing the bleached skulls of cattle.
[4]"Coffee with milk" (French).

"They're none of my people," says Mother, studying the picture through her bifocals.

"He died when I was little, but I think that's him," says Daddy. "Him and Aunt Lucy Culpepper."

"Who was she?" Nancy asks.

"Uncle John's wife."

"I figured that," says Nancy impatiently. "But who *was* she?"

"I don't know." He is still looking at the picture, running his fingers over the man's face.

Back in Granny's room, Nancy pulls the string that turns on the ceiling light, so that Granny can examine the picture. Granny shakes her head slowly. "I never saw them folks before in all my life."

Mother comes in with a dish of strawberries.

"Did I pick these?" Granny asks.

"No. You eat yours about ten years ago," Mother says.

Granny puts in her teeth and eats the strawberries in slurps, missing her mouth twice. "Let me see them people again," she says, waving her spoon. Her teeth make the sound of a baby rattle.

"Nancy Hollins," says Granny. "She was a Culpepper."

"That's Nancy Culpepper?" cries Nancy.

"*That's* not Nancy Culpepper," Mother says. "That woman's got a rat[5] in her hair. They wasn't in style back when Nancy Culpepper was alive."

Granny's face is flushed and she is breathing heavily. "She was a real little-bitty old thing," she says in a high, squeaky voice. "She never would talk. Everybody thought she was curious. Plumb curious."

"Are you sure it's her?" Nancy says.

"If I'm not mistaken."

"She don't remember," Mother says to Nancy. "Her mind gets confused."

Granny removes her teeth and lies back, her bones grinding. Her chest heaves with exhaustion. Nancy sits down in the rocking chair, and as she rocks back and forth she searches the photograph, exploring the features of the young woman, who is wearing an embroidered white dress, and the young man, in a curly beard that starts below his chin, framing his face like a ruffle. The woman looks frightened—of the camera perhaps—but nevertheless her deep-set eyes sparkle like shards of glass. This young woman would be glad to dance to "Lucy in the Sky with Diamonds"[6] on her wedding day, Nancy thinks. The man seems bewildered, as if he did not know what to expect, marrying a woman who has her eyes fixed on something so far away.

1982

GARRISON KEILLOR
(b. 1942)

Garrison Keillor came to national attention through an old-fashioned, outmoded medium—the radio. His show, called "A Prairie Home Companion," was broadcast from 1974 to 1987 in Minnesota before live audiences on Saturday nights and included country music, yodeling, and even dog acts. But the act that all the listeners waited for was the monologue by Keillor, which always opened,

[5]A pad formerly used to puff out a woman's hairdo.
[6]One of the songs in the Beatles' *Sgt. Pepper* album (1967).

"It has been a quiet week in Lake Wobegon, my hometown." He then usually described some incident and meandered off into a series of comic anecdotes, delivered in deadpan, which went further and further afield until the listeners thought he had lost his train of thought — but no: he always found his way back and connected with the opening. The audience knew when the monologue was over because it always concluded with: "That's the news from Lake Wobegon, where all the women are strong, the men are good-looking, and all the children are above average." He delivered the monologue without a script.

Lake Wobegon, a town of 942 people solely of his invention, took its place among the famous mythical towns of America, such as Spoon River, Illinois; Winesburg, Ohio; and Gopher Prairie, Minnesota. Listeners yearned to drop in at the Chatterbox Cafe and taste the meatloaf or tunafish hotdish, or shop at Ralph's Pretty Good Grocery, whose motto was, "If you can't get it at Ralph's, you can probably get along without it."

Like the other mythical American towns, Lake Wobegon was an imaginative creation, but its model existed in its creator's past. Keillor was born in Anoka, Minnesota, and attended the University of Minnesota, where he took a B.A. in 1966. For the next two years (1966–68), he did graduate work in English at the University. But in 1963, while an undergraduate, he had launched a radio program and by 1971 had become a producer-announcer. He was awarded the George Foster Peabody Broadcasting Award in 1980 and the Edward R. Murrow Award for Public Broadcasting in 1985.

Critics have seen Keillor as directly in the tradition of native American humor, in a line running from Mark Twin through Will Rogers to James Thurber. Like these predecessors, Keillor has a serious side to his stories. His monologues, he has said, celebrate the "pleasures of the familiar . . . . one of the themes of the stories is the theme of small pleasures, and one thing I've tried to give myself over to in the course of telling these stories is to stand in praise of common and modest things. And that really is at the heart of Lake Wobegon."

Keillor's books include *Happy to Be Here* (1981), *Lake Wobegon Days* (1985), and *Leaving Home: A Collection of Lake Wobegon Stories* (1987). The title of the last book has personal reference to Keillor's last year on the "Prairie Home Companion" show and his departure from Minnesota. His first marriage ended in divorce in 1976 and he remarried in 1985. *Leaving Home* opened with "A Letter from Copenhagen," where Keillor was then living with his Danish wife. He said of the Lake Wobegon monologues: "These stories are not about my family, and yet I hope they carry on our family tradition of storytelling and kitchen talk, the way we talk and what we talk about."

Since that book appeared, Keillor has resettled with his family in New York, where he is on the staff of *The New Yorker* magazine. Some of his pieces appear in the "Talk of the Town" section which introduces each issue, and others appear as stories or sketches over his name. He has written about the publication for which he works: "My people weren't much for literature, and they were dead set against conspicuous wealth, so a magazine in which classy paragraphs marched down the aisle between columns of diamond necklaces and French cognacs was not a magazine they welcomed into their home. I was more easily dazzled than they, and to me *The New Yorker* was a fabulous sight . . . . What I most admired was not the decor or the tone of the thing but rather the work of some writers." Keillor first read those writers in *The New Yorker* when he was fourteen. Now the boy from Anoka, Minnesota, is one of them. Many of the pieces written for *The New Yorker* are collected in *We Are Still Married: Stories and Letters* (1989).

ADDITIONAL READING

Peter A. Scholl's survey of Garrison Keillor's work in *Dictionary of Literary Biography: Yearbook 1987*, 1988; Judith Yaross Lee, *Garrison Keillor: A Voice of America*, 1991.

TEXT

Leaving Home: A Collection of Lake Wobegon Stories, 1987.

How the Crab Apple Grew

It has been a quiet week in Lake Wobegon. It was warm and sunny on Sunday, and on Monday the flowering crab in the Dieners' backyard burst into blossom. Suddenly, in the morning, when everyone turned their backs for a minute, the tree threw off its bathrobe and stood trembling, purple, naked, revealing all its innermost flowers. When you saw it standing where weeks before had been a bare stick stuck in the dirt, you had to stop, it made your head spin.

Becky Diener sat upstairs in her bedroom and looked at the tree. She was stuck on an assignment from Miss Melrose for English, a 750-word personal essay, "Describe your backyard as if you were seeing it for the first time." After an hour she had thirty-nine words, which she figured would mean she'd finish at 1:45 P.M. Tuesday, four hours late, and therefore would get an F even if the essay was great, which it certainly wasn't.

How can you describe your backyard as if you'd never seen it? If you'd never seen it, you'd have grown up someplace else, and wouldn't be yourself, you'd be someone else entirely, and how are you supposed to know what that person would think?

She imagined seeing the backyard in 1996, returning home from Hollywood. "Welcome Becky!" said the big white banner across McKinley Street as the pink convertible drove slowly along, everyone clapping and cheering as she cruised by, Becky Belafonte the movie star, and got off at her old house. "Here," she said to the reporters, "is where I sat as a child and dreamed my dreams, under this beautiful flowering crab. I dreamed I was a Chinese princess." Then a reporter asked, "Which of your teachers was the most important to you, encouraging you and inspiring you?" And just then she saw an old woman's face in the crowd, Miss Melrose pleading, whispering, "Say me, oh please, say me," and Becky looked straight at her as she said, "Oh, there were so many, I couldn't pick out one, they were all about the same, you know. But perhaps Miss—Miss—oh, I can't remember her name—she taught English, I think—Miss Milross? She was one of them. But there were so many."

She looked at her essay. "In my backyard is a tree that has always been extremely important to me since I was six years old when my dad came home one evening with this bag in the trunk and he said, 'Come here and help me plant this'—"

She crumpled the sheet of paper and started again.

"One evening when I was six years old, my father arrived home as he customarily did around 5:30 or 6:00 P.M. except this evening he had a wonderful surprise for me, he said, as he led me toward the car.

"My father is not the sort of person who does surprising things very often so naturally I was excited that evening when he said he had something for me in the car, having just come home from work where he had been. I was six years old at the time."

She took out a fresh sheet. "Six years old was a very special age for me and one thing that made it special was when my dad and I planted a tree together in our backyard. Now it is grown and every spring it gives off large purple blossoms. . . ."

The tree was planted by her dad, Harold, in 1976, ten years after he married her mother, Marlys. They grew up on Taft Street, across from each other, a block from the ballfield. They liked each other tremendously and then they were in love, as much as you can be when you're so young. Thirteen and fourteen years old and sixteen and seventeen: they looked at each other a lot. She came and sat in his backyard to talk with his mother and help her shell peas but really to look at Harold as he mowed the lawn, and then he disappeared into the house and she sat waiting for him, and of course he was in the kitchen looking out at her. It's how we all began, when our parents looked at each other, as we say, "when you were just a gleam in your father's eye," or your mother's, depending on who saw who first.

Marlys was longlegged, lanky, had short black hair and sharp eyes that didn't miss anything. She came over to visit the Dieners every chance she got. Her father was a lost cause, like the Confederacy, like the search for the Northwest Passage. He'd been prayed for and suffered for and fought for and spoken for, by people who loved him dearly, and when all was said and done he just reached for the gin bottle and said, "I don't know what you're talking about," and he didn't. He was a sore embarrassment to Marlys, a clown, a joke, and she watched Harold for evidence that he wasn't similar. One night she dropped in at the Dieners' and came upon a party where Harold, now nineteen, and his friends were drinking beer by the pail. Harold flopped down on his back and put his legs in the air and a pal put a lit match up to Harold's rear end and blue flame came out like a blowtorch, and Marlys went home disgusted and didn't speak to him for two years.

Harold went crazy. She graduated from high school and started attending dances with a geography teacher named Stu Jasperson, who was tall and dark-haired, a subscriber to *Time* magazine, educated at Saint Cloud Normal School, and who flew a red Piper Cub airplane. Lake Wobegon had no airstrip except for Tollerud's pasture, so Stu kept his plane in Saint Cloud. When he was en route to and from the plane was almost the only time Harold got to see Marlys and try to talk sense into her. But she was crazy about Stu the aviator, not Harold the hardware clerk, and in an hour Stu came buzzing overhead doing loops and dives and dipping his wings. Harold prayed for him to crash. Marlys thought Stu was the sun and the moon; all Harold could do was sit and watch her, in the backyard, staring up, her hand shielding her eyes, saying, "Oh, isn't he marvelous?" as Stu performed aerial feats and then shut off the throttle and glided overhead singing "Vaya con Dios"[1] to her. "Yes, he is marvelous," said Harold, thinking, "DIE DIE DIE."

That spring, Marlys was in charge of the Sweethearts Banquet at the Lutheran church. Irene Holm had put on a fancy winter Sweethearts Banquet with roast lamb, and Marlys wanted to top her and serve roast beef with morel mushrooms, a first for a church supper in Lake Wobegon. Once Irene had referred to Marlys's dad as a lush.

Morel mushrooms are a great delicacy. They are found in the wild by people who walk fifteen miles through the woods to get ten of them and then never tell the location to a soul, not even on their deathbeds to a priest. So Marlys's serving them at the banquet would be like putting out emeralds for party favors. It would blow Irene Holm out of the water and show people that even if Marlys's dad was a lush, she was still someone to be reckoned with.

Two men felt the call to go and search for morels: Harold put on his Red Wing boots and knapsack and headed out one evening with a flashlight. He was in the woods all night. Morels are found near the base of the trunk of a dead elm that's been dead three years, which you can see by the way moonlight doesn't shine on it, and he thought he knew where some were, but around midnight he spotted a bunch of flashlights behind him, a posse of morelists bobbing along on his trail, so he veered

---

[1]"Go with God" (Spanish), title of a popular song.

off and hiked five miles in the wrong direction to confuse them, and by them the sun was coming up so he went home to sleep. He woke at 2:00 P.M., hearing Stu flying overhead, and in an instant he knew. Dead elms! Of course! Stu could spot them from the air, send his ground crew to collect them for Marlys, and the Sweethearts Banquet would be their engagement dinner.

Stu might have done just that, but he wanted to put on a show and land the Cub in Lake Wobegon. He circled around and around, and came in low to the west of town, disappearing behind the trees. "He's going to crash!" cried Marlys, and they all jumped in their cars and tore out, expecting to find the young hero lying bloody and torn in the dewy grass, with a dying poem on his lips. But there he was standing tall beside the craft, having landed successfully in a field of spring wheat. They all mobbed around him and he told how he was going up to find the morels and bring them back for Marlys.

There were about forty people there. They seemed to enjoy it, so he drew out his speech, talking about the lure of aviation and his boyhood and various things so serious that he didn't notice Harold behind him by the plane or notice the people who noticed what Harold was doing and laughed. Stu was too inspired to pay attention to the laughter. He talked about how he once wanted to fly to see the world but once you get up in the air you can see that Lake Wobegon is the most beautiful place of all, a lot of warm horse manure like that, and then he gave them a big manly smile and donned his flying cap and scarf and favored them with a second and third smile and a wave and he turned and there was Harold to help him into the cockpit.

"Well, thanks," said Stu, "mighty kind, mighty kind." Harold jumped to the propeller and threw it once and twice, and the third time the engine fired and Stu adjusted the throttle, checked the gauges, flapped the flaps, fit his goggles, and never noticed the ground was wet and his wheels were sunk in. He'd parked in a wet spot, and then during his address someone had gone around and made it wetter, so when Stu pulled back on the throttle the Cub just sat, and he gave it more juice and she creaked a little, and he gave it more and the plane stood on its head with its tail in the air and dug in.

It pitched forward like the *Titanic*, and the propeller in the mud sounded like he'd eaten too many green apples. The door opened and Stu climbed out, trying to look dignified and studious as he tilted eastward and spun, and Harold said, "Stu, we didn't say we wanted those mushrooms sliced."

Harold went out that afternoon and collected five hundred morel mushrooms around one dead elm tree. Marlys made her mark at the Sweethearts dinner, amazing Irene Holm, who had thought Marlys was common. Harold also brought out of the woods a bouquet of flowering crab apple and asked her to marry him, and eventually she decided to.

The tree in the backyard came about a few years afterward. They'd been married awhile, had two kids, and some of the gloss had worn off their life, and one afternoon, Harold, trying to impress his kids and make his wife laugh, jumped off the garage roof, pretending he could fly, and landed wrong, twisting his ankle. He lay in pain, his eyes full of tears, and his kids said, "Oh poor Daddy," and Marlys said, "You're not funny, you're ridiculous."

He got up on his bum ankle and went in the woods and got her a pint of morels and a branch from the flowering crab apple. He cut a root from another crab apple and planted the root in the ground. "Look, kids," he said. He sharpened the branch with his hatchet and split the root open and stuck the branch in and wrapped a cloth around it and said, "Now, there, that will be a tree." They said, "Daddy, will that really be a tree?" He said, "Yes." Marlys said, "Don't be ridiculous."

He watered it and tended it and, more than that, he came out late at night and bent down and said, "GROW. GROW. GROW." The graft held, it grew, and one year it was interesting and the next it was impressive and then wonderful and finally it was magnificent. It's the most magnificent thing in the Dieners' backyard. Becky finished writing 750 words late that night and lay down to sleep. A backyard is a novel about us, and when we sit there on a summer day, we hear the dialogue and see the characters.

1987

ALICE WALKER
(b. 1944)

In "Saving the Life That Is Your Own," Alice Walker offered this observation of the relationship of art and the world: "What is always needed in the appreciation of art, or life, is the larger perspective. Connections made, or at least attempted, where none existed before, the straining to encompass in one's glance at the varied world the common thread, the unifying theme through immense diversity, a fearlessness of growth, of search, of looking, that enlarges the private and the public world. And yet, in our particular society, it is the narrowed and narrowing view of life that often wins." Walker passionately believes that literature makes a difference in people's lives: "It is, in the end, the saving of lives that we writers are about. Whether we are 'minority' writers or 'majority.' It is simply in our power to do this. We do it because we care. . . . We care because we know this: *the life we save is our own.*"

Walker was born the last of eight children of a sharecropper family in Eatonton, Georgia, in 1944. At the age of eight she suffered an injury that blinded and scarred one eye and that she believed made her ugly. She became introverted and shy, and began to read stories and to write poems. After finishing high school, she was able to gain enough scholarship money to enter Atlanta's Spelman College for women, where she remained two years; while there she became an active participant in the civil rights movement, then in its prime. In 1963, she transferred to Sarah Lawrence College in Bronxville, New York. She travelled in Africa in the summer of 1965, and on her return found that she was pregnant. She became desperate and suicidal, but a friend helped her find an abortionist. Again her misfortune caused her to turn to writing poetry, and she was encouraged by the American poet Muriel Rukeyser, writer-in-residence at Sarah Lawrence during this period. Many of the poems written at this time found their way into her first book, *Once,* which appeared in 1968. By the time Walker took her degree, in 1965, she had resolved to become a writer.

In 1967, Walker married Mel Leventhal, a civil rights lawyer, and settled in Mississippi, where they were both active in the movement and, as an interracial couple, subject to harrassment. In the midst of teaching, voter registration drives, and the birth of a daughter, Walker found time to begin work on her first novel, *The Third Life of Grange Copeland,* which was published in 1970. It portrayed three generations of a black sharecropper family in the South, in a hard struggle to keep body and soul together; it was a victory to survive, but the triumph was to survive *whole.* Walker's second novel, *Meridian,* appeared in 1976 and took as its protagonist a black woman who not only survived whole but devoted herself and all her possessions in service to the poor blacks in the rural South.

Walker was divorced in 1976. She was awarded a Guggenheim Fellowship for the writing of fiction in 1977–78, and at about this time became an editor of the feminist magazine *Ms.* She has taught in creative writing workshops and black studies programs at Jackson State College, Taugaloo College, Wellesley, the University of Massachusetts, and Brandeis. She created and taught a course in black women's literature. In her search for black women writers on whom she could model herself, she accidentally came across Zora Neale Hurston's name in a footnote, read her, and set about singlehandedly inspiring a revival of this "lost" black woman writer whose books had appeared and disappeared during the 1930s and 1940s. Walker edited a volume of her writings, published in 1979, entitled *I Love Myself When I Am Laughing . . . And Then Again When I am Looking Mean and Impressive: A Zora Neale Hurston Reader.*

It was with her third novel, *The Color Purple,* published in 1982, that Walker came into her own as a writer; it won both the American Book Award and the Pulitzer Prize. The novel was in its opening sections a shocking representation of the domestic subjugation, brutalization, and rape of the novel's adolescent black protagonist, Celie, by her "father" (who turned out to be her stepfather); Celie told this horror tale through a series of letters directed first to God, and then — after discovering her anger at a white, male God — to her sister, who escaped the violence at home and was taken by black American missionaries to Africa.

The reviews immediately set off a debate as to which theme was (or should have been) dominant: whites' brutalization of blacks or men's brutalization of women. Male critics, and particularly black males, were quick to take issue with the way black men were portrayed in the novel. Much of the debate took place in *Ms.* magazine. The controversy not only helped the sales of the novel, but also cleared the air by bringing long-suppressed feelings into the open. And it loosened the restraints black women writers (and perhaps writers generally, especially those classified as "minority") had long felt imposed on their subjects and themes.

Walker's books of poems include *Revolutionary Petunias & Other Poems* (1973), *Goodnight, Willie Lee, I'll See You in the Morning: Poems* (1979), and *Horses Make a Landscape Look More Beautiful* (1984). Her books of short stories include *In Love and Trouble* (1973) and *You Can't Keep a Good Woman Down* (1981). She has also published a children's biography, *Langston Hughes: American Poet* (1973), and a volume of her essays, *In Search of Our Mother's Garden: Womanist Prose* (1984). In 1989, Walker published a new novel, *The Temple of My Familiar,* which struck many reviewers as subordinating fictional structure to polemics.

In spite of the seriousness of her work, in the service of "saving lives," or perhaps because of its seriousness, Walker's writing in an important way is celebratory. She said once in an interview: "One thing I try to have in my life and my fiction is an awareness of and an openness to mystery, which, to me, is deeper than any politics, race or geographical location. In the poems I read, a sense of mystery, a deepening of it, is what I look for — because that is what I respond to."

Surprised that her "Northern brothers" do not believe her when she talks about the "positive material" she can draw from her "underprivileged" background, she answered in the accents and rhythms of that mystery so important to her work and life:

> But they have never lived, as I have, at the end of a long road in a house that was faced by the edge of the world on one side and nobody for miles on the other. They have never experienced the magnificent quiet of a summer day when the heat is intense and one is so very thirsty, as one moves across the dusty cotton fields, that one learns forever that water is the essence of all life. In the

cities it cannot be so clear to one that he is a creature of the earth, feeling the soil between the toes, smelling the dust thrown up by the rain, loving the earth so much that one longs to taste it and sometimes does.

ADDITIONAL READING

Living by the Word: Selected Writings 1973–1987, 1988.

Janet Sternburg, ed., *The Writer on Her Work,* 1980; Claudia Tate, ed., *Black Women Writers at Work,* 1984; Bernard W. Bell, *The Afro-American Novel and Its Tradition,* 1987; Erma Davis Banks and Keith Byerman, *Alice Walker: An Annotated Bibliography, 1968–1986,* 1989.

TEXT

In Love and Trouble, 1973.

Everyday Use

FOR YOUR GRANDMAMA

I will wait for her in the yard that Maggie and I made so clean and wavy yesterday afternoon. A yard like this is more comfortable than most people know. It is not just a yard. It is like an extended living room. When the hard clay is swept clean as a floor and the fine sand around the edges lined with tiny, irregular grooves, anyone can come and sit and look up into the elm tree and wait for the breezes that never come inside the house.

Maggie will be nervous until after her sister goes: she will stand hopelessly in corners, homely and ashamed of the burn scars down her arms and legs, eyeing her sister with a mixture of envy and awe. She thinks her sister has held life always in the palm of one hand, that "no" is a word the world never learned to say to her.

You've no doubt seen those TV shows where the child who has "made it" is confronted, as a surprise, by her own mother and father, tottering in weakly from backstage. (A pleasant surprise, of course: What would they do if parent and child came on the show only to curse out and insult each other?) On TV mother and child embrace and smile into each other's faces. Sometimes the mother and father weep, the child wraps them in her arms and leans across the table to tell how she would not have made it without their help. I have seen these programs.

Sometimes I dream a dream in which Dee and I are suddenly brought together on a TV program of this sort. Out of a dark and soft-seated limousine I am ushered into a bright room filled with many people. There I meet a smiling, gray, sporty man like Johnny Carson who shakes my hand and tells me what a fine girl I have. Then we are on the stage and Dee is embracing me with tears in her eyes. She pins on my dress a large orchid, even though she has told me once that she thinks orchids are tacky flowers.

In real life I am a large, bigboned woman with rough, man-working hands. In the winter I wear flannel nightgowns to bed and overalls during the day. I can kill and clean a hog as mercilessly as a man. My fat keeps me hot in zero weather. I can work outside all day, breaking ice to get water for washing. I can eat pork liver cooked over the open fire minutes after it comes steaming from the hog. One winter I knocked a bull calf straight in the brain between the eyes with a sledge hammer and had the meat hung up to chill before nightfall. But of course all this does not show on television. I am the way my daughter would want me to be: a hundred pounds lighter, my skin like an uncooked barley pancake. My hair glistens in the hot bright lights. Johnny Carson has much to do to keep up with my quick and witty tongue.

But that is a mistake. I know even before I wake up. Who ever knew a Johnson with a quick tongue? Who can even imagine me looking a strange white man in the eye? It seems to me I have talked to them always with one foot raised in flight, with my head turned in whichever way is farthest from them. Dee, though. She would always look anyone in the eye. Hesitation was no part of her nature.

"How do I look, Mama?" Maggie says, showing just enough of her thin body enveloped in pink skirt and red blouse for me to know she's there, almost hidden by the door.

"Come out into the yard," I say.

Have you ever seen a lame animal, perhaps a dog run over by some careless person rich enough to own a car, sidle up to someone who is ignorant enough to be kind to him? That is the way my Maggie walks. She has been like this, chin on chest, eyes on ground, feet in shuffle, ever since the fire that burned the other house to the ground.

Dee is lighter than Maggie, with nicer hair and a fuller figure. She's a woman now, though sometimes I forget. How long ago was it that the other house burned? Ten, twelve years? Sometimes I can still hear the flames and feel Maggie's arms sticking to me, her hair smoking and her dress falling off her in little black papery flakes. Her eyes seemed stretched open, blazed open by the flames reflected in them. And Dee. I see her standing off under the sweet gum tree she used to dig gum out of; a look of concentration on her face as she watched the last dingy gray board of the house fall in toward the red hot brick chimney. Why don't you do a dance around the ashes? I'd wanted to ask her. She hated the house that much.

I used to think she hated Maggie, too. But that was before we raised the money, the church and me, to send her to Augusta to school. She used to read to us without pity; forcing words, lies, other folks' habits, whole lives upon us two, sitting trapped and ignorant underneath her voice. She washed us in a river of make-believe, burned us with a lot of knowledge we didn't necessarily need to know. Pressed us to her with the serious way she read, to shove us away at just the moment, like dimwits, we seemed about to understand.

Dee wanted nice things. A yellow organdy dress to wear to her graduation from high school; black pumps to match a green suit she'd made from an old suit somebody gave me. She was determined to stare down any disaster in her efforts. Her eyelids would not flicker for minutes at a time. Often I fought off the temptation to shake her. At sixteen she had a style of her own: and knew what style was.

I never had an education myself. After second grade the school was closed down. Don't ask me why: in 1927 colored asked fewer questions than they do now. Sometimes Maggie reads to me. She stumbles along good-naturedly but can't see well. She knows she is not bright. Like good looks and money, quickness passed her by. She will marry John Thomas (who has mossy teeth in an earnest face) and then I'll be free to sit here and I guess just sing church songs to myself. Although I never was a good singer. Never could carry a tune. I was always better at a man's job. I used to love to milk till I was hooked in the side in '49. Cows are soothing and slow and don't bother you, unless you try to milk them the wrong way.

I have deliberately turned my back on the house. It is three rooms, just like the one that burned, except the roof is tin; they don't make shingle roofs any more. There are no real windows, just some holes cut in the sides, like the portholes in a ship, but not round and not square, with rawhide holding the shutters up on the outside. This house is in a pasture, too, like the other one. No doubt when Dee sees it she will want to tear it down. She wrote me once that no matter where we "choose" to live, she will manage to come see us. But she will never bring her friends. Maggie and I thought about this and Maggie asked me, "Mama, when did Dee ever *have* any friends?"

She had a few. Furtive boys in pink shirts hanging about on washday after school. Nervous girls who never laughed. Impressed with her they worshiped the well-turned phrase, the cute shape, the scalding humor that erupted like bubbles in lye. She read to them.

When she was courting Jimmy T she didn't have much time to pay to us, but turned all her faultfinding power on him. He *flew* to marry a cheap city girl from a family of ignorant flashy people. She hardly had time to recompose herself.

When she comes I will meet—but there they are!

Maggie attempts to make a dash for the house, in her shuffling way, but I stay her with my hand "Come back here," I say. And she stops and tries to dig a well in the sand with her toe.

It is hard to see them clearly through the strong sun. But even the first glimpse of leg out of the car tells me it is Dee. Her feet were always neat-looking, as if God himself had shaped them with a certain style. From the other side of the car comes a short, stocky man. Hair is all over his head a foot long and hanging from his chin like a kinky mule tail. I hear Maggie suck in her breath. "Uhnnnh," is what it sounds like. Like when you see the wriggling end of a snake just in front of your foot on the road. "Uhnnnh."

Dee next. A dress down to the ground, in this hot weather. A dress so loud it hurts my eyes. There are yellows and oranges enough to throw back the light of the sun. I feel my whole face warming from the heat waves it throws out. Earrings gold, too, and hanging down to her shoulders. Bracelets dangling and making noises when she moves her arm up to shake the folds of the dress out of her armpits. The dress is loose and flows, and as she walks closer, I like it. I hear Maggie go "Uhnnnh" again. It is her sister's hair. It stands straight up like the wool on a sheep. It is black as night and around the edges are two long pigtails that rope about like small lizards disappearing behind her ears.

"Wa-su-zo-Tean-o!" she says, coming on in that gliding way the dress makes her move. The short stocky fellow with the hair to his navel is all grinning and he follows up with "Asalamalakim, my mother and sister!" He moves up to hug Maggie but she falls back, right up against the back of my chair. I feel her trembling there when I look up I see the perspiration falling off her chin.

"Don't get up," says Dee. Since I am stout it takes something of a push. You can see me trying to move a second or two before I make it. She turns, showing white heels through her sandals, and goes back to the car. Out she peeks next with a Polaroid. She stoops down quickly and lines up picture after picture of me sitting there in front of the house with Maggie cowering behind me. She never takes a shot without making sure the house is included. When a cow comes nibbling around the edge of the yard she snaps it and me and Maggie *and* the house. Then she puts the Polaroid in the back seat of the car, and comes up and kisses me on the forehead.

Meanwhile Asalamalakim is going through motions with Maggie's hand. Maggie's hand is as limp as a fish, and probably as cold, despite the sweat, and she keeps trying to pull it back. It looks like Asalamalakim wants to shake hands but wants to do it fancy. Or maybe he don't know how people shake hands. Anyhow, he soon gives up on Maggie.

"Well," I say. "Dee."

"No, Mama," she says. "Not 'Dee,' Wangero Leewanika Kemanjo!"

"What happened to 'Dee'?" I wanted to know.

"She's dead," Wangero said. "I couldn't bear it any longer, being named after the people who oppress me."

"You know as well as me you was named after your aunt Dicie," I said. Dicie is my sister. She named Dee. We called her "Big Dee" after Dee was born.

"But who was *she* named after?" asked Wangero.

"I guess after Grandma Dee," I said.

"And who was she named after?" asked Wangero.

"Her mother," I said, and saw Wangero was getting tired. "That's about as far back as I can trace it," I said. Though, in fact, I probably could have carried it back beyond the Civil War through the branches.

"Well," said Asalamalakim, "there you are."

"Uhnnnh," I heard Maggie say.

"There I was not," I said, "before 'Dicie' cropped up in our family, so why should I try to trace it that far back?"

He just stood there grinning, looking down on me like somebody inspecting a Model A car. Every once in a while he and Wangero sent eye signals over my head.

"How do you pronounce this name?" I asked.

"You don't have to call me by it if you don't want to," said Wangero.

"Why shouldn't I?" I asked. "If that's what you want us to call you, we'll call you."

"I know it might sound awkward at first," said Wangero.

"I'll get used to it," I said. "Ream it out again."

Well, soon we got the name out of the way. Asalamalakim had a name twice as long and three times as hard. After I tripped over it two or three times he told me to just call him Hakim-a-barber. I wanted to ask him was he a barber, but I didn't really think he was, so I didn't ask.

"You must belong to those beef-cattle peoples down the road," I said. They said "Asalamalakim" when they met you, too, but they didn't shake hands. Always too busy: feeding the cattle, fixing the fences, putting up salt-lick shelters, throwing down hay. When the white folks poisoned some of the herd the men stayed up all night with rifles in their hands. I walked a mile and a half just to see the sight.

Hakim-a-barber said, "I accept some of their doctrines, but farming and raising cattle is not my style." (They didn't tell me, and I didn't ask, whether Wangero (Dee) had really gone and married him.)

We sat down to eat and right away he said he didn't eat collards and pork was unclean. Wangero, though, went on through the chitlins and corn bread, the greens and everything else. She talked a blue streak over the sweet potatoes. Everything delighted her. Even the fact that we still used the benches her daddy made for the table when we couldn't afford to buy chairs.

"Oh, Mama!" she cried. Then turned to Hakim-a-barber. "I never knew how lovely these benches are. You can feel the rump prints," she said, running her hands underneath her and along the bench. Then she gave a sigh and her hand closed over Grandma Dee's butter dish. "That's it!" she said. "I knew there was something I wanted to ask you if I could have." She jumped up from the table and went over in the corner where the churn stood, the milk in it clabber by now. She looked at the churn and looked at it.

"This churn top is what I need," she said. "Didn't Uncle Buddy whittle it out of a tree you all used to have?"

"Yes," I said.

"Uh huh," she said happily. "And I want the dasher, too."

"Uncle Buddy whittle that, too?" asked the barber.

Dee (Wangero) looked up at me.

"Aunt Dee's first husband whittled the dash," said Maggie so low you almost couldn't hear her. "His name was Henry, but they called him Stash."

"Maggie's brain is like an elephant's," Wangero said, laughing. "I can use the churn top as a centerpiece for the alcove table," she said, sliding a plate over the churn, "and I'll think of something artistic to do with the dasher."

When she finished wrapping the dasher the handle stuck out. I took it for a moment in my hands. You didn't even have to look close to see where hands pushing the dasher up and down to make butter had left a kind of sink in the wood. In fact, there were a lot of small sinks; you could see where thumbs and fingers had sunk into the wood. It was a beautiful light yellow wood, from a tree that grew in the yard where Big Dee and Stash had lived.

After dinner Dee (Wagnero) went to the trunk at the foot of my bed and started rifling through it. Maggie hung back in the kitchen over the dishpan. Out came Wangero with two quilts. They had been pieced by Grandma Dee and then Big Dee and me had hung them on the quilt frames on the front porch and quilted them. One was in the Lone Star pattern. The other was Walk Around the Mountain. In both of them were scraps of dresses Grandma Dee had worn fifty and more years ago. Bits and pieces of Grandpa Jarrell's Paisley shirts. And one teeny faded blue piece, about the size of a penny matchbox, that was from Great Grandpa Ezra's uniform that he wore in the Civil War.

"Mama," Wangero said sweet as a bird. "Can I have these old quilts?"

I heard something fall in the kitchen, and a minute later the kitchen door slammed.

"Why don't you take one or two of the others?" I asked. "These old things was just done by me and Big Dee from some tops your grandma pieced before she died."

"No," said Wangero. "I don't want those. They are stitched around the borders by machine."

"That'll make them last better," I said.

"That's not the point," said Wangero. "These are all pieces of dresses Grandma used to wear. She did all this stitching by hand. Imagine!" She held the quilts securely in her arms, stroking them.

"Some of the pieces, like those lavendar ones, come from old clothes her mother handed down to her," I said, moving up to touch the quilts. Dee (Wangero) moved back just enough so that I couldn't reach the quilts. They already belonged to her.

"Imagine!" she breathed again, clutching them closely to her bosom.

"The truth is," I said, "I promised to give them quilts to Maggie, for when she marries John Thomas."

She gasped like a bee had stung her.

"Maggie can't appreciate these quilts!" she said. "She'd probably be backward enough to put them to everyday use."

"I reckon she would," I said. "God knows I been saving 'em for long enough with nobody using 'em. I hope she will!" I didn't want to bring up how I had offered Dee (Wangero) a quilt when she went away to college. Then she had told me they were old-fashioned, out of style.

"But they're *priceless!*" she was saying now, furiously; for she has a temper. "Maggie would put them on the bed and in five years they'd be in rags. Less than that!"

"She can always make some more," I said. "Maggie knows how to quilt."

Dee (Wangero) looked at me with hatred. "You just will not understand. The point is these quilts, *these* quilts!"

"Well," I said, stumped. "What would *you* do with them?"

"Hang them," she said. As if that was the only thing you *could* do with quilts.

Maggie by now was standing in the door. I could almost hear the sound her feet made as they scraped over each other.

"She can have them, Mama," she said, like somebody used to never winning anything, or having anything reserved for her. "I can 'member Grandma Dee without the quilts."

I looked at her hard. She had filled her bottom lip with checkerberry snuff and it gave her face a kind of dopey, hangdog look. It was Grandma Dee and Big Dee who taught her how to quilt herself. She stood there with her scarred hands hidden in the folds of her skirt. She looked at her sister with something like fear but she wasn't mad at her. This was Maggie's portion. This was the way she knew God to work.

When I looked at her like that something hit me in the top of my head and ran down to the soles of my feet. Just like when I'm in church and the spirit of God touches me and I get happy and shout. I did something I never had done before: hugged Maggie to me, then dragged her on into the room, snatched the quilts out of Miss Wangero's hands and dumped them into Maggie's lap. Maggie just sat there on my bed with her mouth open.

"Take one or two of the others," I said to Dee.

But she turned without a word and went out to Hakim-a-barber.

"You just don't understand," she said, as Maggie and I came out to the car.

"What don't I understand?" I wanted to know.

"Your heritage," she said. And then she turned to Maggie, kissed her, and said, "You ought to try to make something of yourself, too, Maggie. It's really a new day for us. But from the way you and Mama still live you'd never know it."

She put on some sunglasses that hid everything above the tip of her nose and her chin.

Maggie smiled; maybe at the sunglasses. But a real smile, not scared. After we watched the car dust settle I asked Maggie to bring me a dip of snuff. And then the two of us sat there just enjoying, until it was time to go in the house and go to bed.

1973

ANN BEATTIE
(b. 1947)

When Ann Beattie's first novel, *Chilly Scenes of Winter*, and her first book of short stories, *Distortions*, were published in 1976, she was immediately identified by reviewers as the chronicler of the post-1960s generation. In an interview, when queried about filling such a role, she said: "I *was* going out of my way in the novel to say something about the 60s having passed," adding that the alienation or anomie of the characters "just seems to me to be an attitude that most of my friends and most of the people I know have. They all feel sort of let down, either by not having involved themselves more in the '60s now that the '70s are so dreadful, or else by having involved themselves very much to no avail."

But Beattie has resisted being typecast as a writer with one subject. In another interview she said: "It's certainly true that the people I write about are essentially my age, and so they were a certain age in the '60s and had certain common experiences and tend to listen to the same kind of music and get stoned and wear the same kind of clothes, but what I've always hoped for is that somebody will then start talking more about the meat and bones of what I'm writing about."

Ann Beattie, the daughter of a Washington bureaucrat, was raised in Washington, D.C., and attended American University, graduating with a B.A. in English in 1969. She took an M.A. at the University of Connecticut in 1970 and began work on a Ph.D in English, but left without finishing the degree. She remarked later on the "whole process" for obtaining a Ph.D. as "extremely demeaning and boring." She went to the University of Virginia, where she taught until 1977. She next went to Harvard University as Briggs-Copeland Lecturer in English, but left after one year, without, she says, "ever meeting the head of the

English Department." A Guggenheim Fellowship enabled her to devote her time to writing in 1978–79.

She has said of her writing career: "I never really set out to be a writer. I just sort of backed into it." She began by placing stories in the little magazines. It took some twenty tries at *The New Yorker* before one of her stories was accepted in 1974; now she has become a regular contributor to the magazine. Her books since 1976 include the novels *Falling in Place* (1980) and *Love Always* (1985); and the short story collections *Secrets and Surprises* (1978), *The Burning House* (1982), and *Where You'll Find Me* (1986). Most critics find her talents better fitted for the short story than for the novel.

In an interview, Beattie agreed that her stories were often about people not understanding each other: "A direct result of this breakdown of communication is the breakdown of relationships." And she added: "I find it very hard to envy most of the couples I know. . . . It seems to me they have made so many compromises to be together. . . . On the other hand, there are so many people who are together for all the obvious reasons: they don't want to be lonely, or they are in the habit of being together, or this whole Beckettian thing—I can't stay and I can't go." It is significant that she sees people she knows as affected by the same kind of paralysis as the characters in a play by the Irish playwright Samuel Beckett, one of the creators of the "drama of the absurd."

Characters in Beattie's stories often seem beset by feelings of melancholy over the loss of something that is never defined, that perhaps never really existed. They are overcome by enervating feelings of meaninglessness and aimlessness without ever having felt the overriding commitment to a dedicated purpose. They are in process of adjustment to diminished lives without ever having experienced fulfilled lives. Like Thoreau's "mass of men," they seem "to lead lives of quiet desperation," but with a keener sense of the weight of the trivial than of the tragic or cosmic. As one reviewer, the Canadian novelist Margaret Atwood, has said, "These people are on maintenance doses, getting from one day to the next, like a climber seizing the next rung on the ladder without having any idea of where he's going or wants to go."

Asked about her "deadpan" or "emotionless" style, Beattie replied: "That's the way people talk. I know I think that way—in short sentences. If I didn't describe things neutrally, I would be editorializing, which is not at all what I mean to do. It may be that I have gone *too* far with my prose style. It's a mannered style, really—or the effect of it is very mannered—but that effect is no more conscious on my part than these other things we've been talking about." Her style and her substance have caused Beattie to be labelled, along with Raymond Carver, one of the "minimalists." Although the epithet may be suggestive, it is probably one that she would ultimately resist—as she did that of "post-sixties chronicler." She might say of the one what she said of the other, that it misses the "meat and bones" of what she is writing about.

ADDITIONAL READING

Larry McCaffery, *Postmodern Fiction: A Bio-Bibliographical Guide,* 1986; Christina Murphy, *Ann Beattie,* 1986. Larry McCaffery and Sinda Gregory, eds., *Alive and Writing: Interviews with American Authors of the 1980s,* 1987.

TEXT

"In the White Night" in *New American Short Shories: The Writers Select Thier Own Favorites*, ed. Gloria Norris, 1986.

In the White Night

"Don't think about a cow," Matt Brinkley said. "Don't think about a river, don't think about a car, don't think about snow. . . ."

Matt was standing in the doorway, hollering after his guests. His wife, Gaye, gripped his arm and tried to tug him back into the house. The party was over. Carol and Vernon turned to wave good-bye, calling back their thanks, whispering to each other to be careful. The steps were slick with snow; an icy snow had been falling for hours, frozen granules mixed in with lighter stuff, and the instant they moved out from under the protection of the Brinkleys' porch the cold froze the smiles on their faces. The swirls of snow blowing against Carol's skin reminded her — an odd thing to remember on a night like this — of the way sand blew up at the beach, and the scratchy pain it caused.

"Don't think about an apple!" Matt hollered. Vernon turned his head, but he was left smiling at a closed door.

In the small, bright areas under the streetlights, there seemed for a second to be some logic to all the swirling snow. If time itself could only freeze, the snowflakes could become the lacy filigree of a valentine. Carol frowned. Why had Matt conjured up the image of an apple? Now she saw an apple where there was no apple, suspended in midair, transforming the scene in front of her into a silly surrealist painting.

It was going to snow all night. They had heard that on the radio, driving to the Brinkleys'. The Don't-Think-About-Whatever game had started as a joke, something long in the telling and startling to Vernon, to judge by his expression as Matt went on and on. When Carol crossed the room near midnight to tell Vernon that they should leave, Matt had quickly whispered the rest of his joke or story — whatever he was saying — into Vernon's ear, all in a rush. They looked like two children, the one whispering madly and the other with his head bent, but something about the inclination of Vernon's head let you know that if you bent low enough to see, there would be a big, wide grin on his face. Vernon and Carol's daughter, Sharon, and Matt and Gaye's daughter, Becky, had sat side by side, or kneecap to kneecap, and whispered that way when they were children — a privacy so rushed that it obliterated anything else. Carol, remembering that scene now, could not think of what passed between Sharon and Becky without thinking of sexual intimacy. Becky, it turned out, had given the Brinkleys a lot of trouble. She had run away from home when she was thirteen, and, in a family-counseling session years later, her parents found out that she had had an abortion at fifteen. More recently, she had flunked out of college. Now she was working in a bank in Boston and taking a night-school course in poetry. Poetry or pottery? The apple that reappeared as the windshield wipers slushed snow off the glass metamorphosed for Carol into a red bowl, then again became an apple which grew rounder as the car came to a stop at the intersection.

She had been weary all day. Anxiety always made her tired. She knew the party would be small (the Brinkleys' friend Mr. Graham had just had his book accepted for publication, and of course much of the evening would be spent talking about that); she had feared that it was going to be a strain for all of them. The Brinkleys had just returned from the Midwest, where they had gone for Gaye's father's funeral. It didn't seem a time to carry through with plans for a party. Carol imagined that not cancelling it had been Matt's idea, not Gaye's. She turned toward Vernon now and asked how the Brinkleys had seemed to him. Fine, he said at once. Before he spoke, she knew how he would answer. If people did not argue in front of their friends, they were not having problems; if they did not stumble into walls, they were not drunk. Vernon tried hard to think positively, but he was never impervious to real pain. His reflex was to turn aside something serious with a joke, but he was just as quick to wipe the smile off his face and suddenly put his arm around a person's shoulder. Unlike Matt, he was a warm person, but when people unexpectedly showed him affection it embarrassed him. The same counselor the Brinkleys had seen had told Carol—Vernon refused to see the man, and she found that she did not want to continue without him—that it was possible that Vernon felt uncomfortable with expressions of kindness because he blamed himself for Sharon's death: he couldn't save her, and when people were kind to him now he felt it was undeserved. But Vernon was the last person who should be punished. She remembered him in the hospital, pretending to misunderstand Sharon when she asked for her barette, on her bedside table, and picking it up and clipping the little yellow duck into the hair above his own ear. He kept trying to tickle a smile out of her—touching some stuffed animal's button nose to the tip of her nose and then tapping it on her earlobe. At the moment when Sharon died, Vernon had been sitting on her bed (Carol was backed up against the door, for some reason), surrounded by a battlefield of pastel animals.

They passed safely through the last intersection before their house. The car didn't skid until they turned onto their street. Carol's heart thumped hard, once, in the second when she felt the car becoming light, but they came out of the skid easily. He had been driving carefully, and she said nothing, wanting to appear casual about the moment. She asked if Matt had mentioned Becky. No, Vernon said, and he hadn't wanted to bring up a sore subject.

Gaye and Matt had been married for twenty-five years; Carol and Vernon had been married twenty-two. Sometimes Vernon said, quite sincerely, that Matt and Gaye were their alter egos, who absorbed and enacted crises, saving the two of them from having to experience such chaos. It frightened Carol to think that some part of him believed that. Who could really believe that there was some way to find protection in this world—or someone who could offer it? What happened happened at random, and one horrible thing hardly precluded the possibility of others happening next. There had been that fancy internist who hospitalized Vernon later in the same spring when Sharon died, and who looked up at him while drawing blood and observed almost offhandedly that it would be an unbearable irony if Vernon also had leukemia. When the test results came back, they showed that Vernon had mononucleosis. There was the time when the Christmas tree caught fire, and she rushed toward the flames, clapping her hands like cymbals, and Vernon pulled her away just in time, before the whole tree became a torch, and she with it. When Hobo, their dog, had to be put to sleep, during their vacation in Maine, that awful woman veterinarian, with her cold green eyes, issued the casual death sentence with one manicured hand on the quivering dog's fur and called him "Bobo," as though their dog were like some circus clown.

"Are you crying?" Vernon said. They were inside their house now, in the hallway, and he had just turned toward her, holding out a pink padded coat hanger.

"No," she said. "The wind out there is fierce." She slipped her jacket onto the hanger he held out and went into the downstairs bathroom, where she buried her face in a towel. In time, she looked at herself in the mirror. She had pressed the towel hard against her eyes, and for a few seconds she had to blink herself into focus. She was reminded of the kind of camera they had had when Sharon was young. There were two images when you looked through the finder, and you had to make the adjustment yourself so that one superimposed itself upon the other and the figure suddenly leaped into clarity. She patted the towel to her eyes again and held her breath. If she couldn't stop crying, Vernon would make love to her. When she was very sad, he sensed that his instinctive optimism wouldn't work; he became tongue-tied, and when he couldn't talk he would reach for her. Through the years, he had knocked over wineglasses shooting his hand across the table to grab hers. She had found herself suddenly hugged from behind in the bathroom; he would even follow her in there if he suspected she was going to cry—walk in to grab her without even having bothered to knock.

She opened the door now and turned toward the hall staircase, and then realized—felt it before she saw it, really—that the light was on in the living room.

Vernon lay stretched out on the sofa, with his legs crossed; one foot was planted on the floor and his top foot dangled in the air. Even when he was exhausted, he was always careful not to let his shoes touch the sofa. He was very tall, and couldn't stretch out on the sofa without resting his head on the arm. For some reason, he had not hung up her jacket. It was spread like a tent over his head and shoulders, rising and falling with his breathing. She stood still long enough to be sure that he was really asleep, and then came into the room. The sofa was too narrow to curl up on with him. She didn't want to wake him. Neither did she want to go to bed alone. She went back to the hall closet and took out his overcoat—the long, elegant camel's-hair coat he had not worn tonight because he thought it might snow. She slipped off her shoes and went quietly over to where he lay and stretched out on the floor beside the sofa, pulling the big blanket of the coat up high, until the collar touched her lips. Then she drew her legs up into the warmth.

Such odd things happened. Very few days were like the ones before. Here they were, in their own house with four bedrooms, ready to sleep in this peculiar double-decker fashion, in the largest, coldest room of all. What would anyone think?

She knew the answer to that question, of course. A person who didn't know them would mistake this for a drunken collapse, but anyone who was a friend would understand exactly. In time, each of the two of them had learned to stop passing judgment on how they coped with the inevitable sadness that set in, always unexpectedly but so real that it was met with the instant acceptance one gave to a snowfall. In the white night world outside, their daughter might be drifting past like an angel, and she would see this tableau, for the second that she hovered, as a necessary small adjustment.[1]

1984, 1986

LOUISE ERDRICH
(b. 1954)

Louise Erdrich was first motivated to become a writer by her parents. As she recalled: "My father used to give me a nickel for every story I wrote, and my mother wove strips of construction paper together and stapled them into book covers. So at an early age I felt myself to be a published author earning substantial royalties. Mine were wonderful parents: they got me excited about reading and writing in a lasting way."

Louise Erdrich grew up in Wahpeton, North Dakota, near the Turtle Mountain Chippewa Reservation. She visited her maternal grandparents on the reservation frequently. Her parents worked for the Bureau of Indian Affairs, teaching at the Indian school. She has reported in an interview: "I'm half German-American and half French-Indian on my mother's side. My great-grandfather [an Indian] took the name of a French trapper he paddled a canoe for. He needed a name to get by in the European society."

When Erdrich had finished high school, her parents read in the *National Geographic Magazine* that Dartmouth College was starting a Native American Studies

---

[1]Ann Beattie commented on this story: "In 'In the White Night,' I started playing with visual images without first knowing consciously why they were there. I hope that language and symbol finally melded in the story—that, in a way, the closing image was complex and radiated. The party hosts' game—language—became important to me as a subject. The host was interested in what language denoted, and I was interested in what language connoted metaphorically. In retrospect, I see that he and I ended up as co-conspirators."

program and sent their daughter there. The individual starting the program, an anthropologist and writer named Michael Dorris, was part Indian. The student eventually married the teacher — in 1981 — and they have become a kind of literary partnership. He is the one critic who sees her work before it is published, and she credits their conversations about plot and characters as the impetus for much of her writing. Erdrich received her B.A. from Dartmouth in 1976 and took a Master's degree in the creative writing program at Johns Hopkins University in 1977.

Erdrich's first break came in 1982, when she won the $5,000 Nelson Algren Award from *Chicago Magazine* for her short story "The World's Greatest Fisherman" (later incorporated in her first novel). She described her reaction: "It was like a validation, someone believed in me." In 1984, Erdrich published two works: a book of poems, *Jacklight,* and a novel, *Love Medicine.* The novel is really a book of fourteen interconnected — but self-contained — short stories, many of which had been published in little magazines. Covering a period of fifty years in the lives of two Chippewa familes and narrated by seven different family members, the work is a powerful and haunting exploration of their dreams and defeats. It won the National Book Critics Circle Award for 1984.

In her second novel, *The Beet Queen,* published in 1986, Erdrich wrote about the inhabitants of a small North Dakota town, and only indirectly about Indian life. The narrative centers on three women of the town whose lives are fatefully intertwined. It became a bestseller and attracted wide critical acclaim. Erdrich published her third novel, *Tracks,* in 1988, and in it shifted focus back to the Indian lives introduced in *Love Medicine.* It is set in a period before the beginning of her first novel and is written in the same episodic style. A postscript indicated that this novel was part of a larger work, a kind of fictional epic of twentieth-century Indian life in North Dakota: *Tracks* was to be the opening volume of a tetralogy that would include *Love Medicine* and *The Beet Queen.*

In a 1988 interview, Erdrich has spoken of America's violation of the treaties relating to land ownership that have been signed with Indian tribes — treaties that were made "for as long as the grass shall grow and the river shall flow." And she has noted that the problem of alcoholism among Indians (which figures prominently in *Love Medicine*) is directly related to the social (or racist) attitudes toward Indians off the reservation. She said: "I think anger about the American Indian situation is a big motivation behind my writing, but I don't think as a novelist or story-writer you can write a political diatribe, you can't write a political text. The subtext can be political; the text itself has to tell a good story. So the anger is only part of what I write about."

Asked about her method of writing, she added: "I don't consciously go out and gather material on the reservations. I do what a writer probably always does. I live life and see what happens. I do research, but none of my stories are real. There's not a single story based on a real family story. But there are things that come from family stories. . . . I don't write exclusively about American Indians. *The Beet Queen* has no Indian characters in it. I really consider myself a writer first. Then an Indian, or a woman or a mother."

ADDITIONAL READING

Joseph Bruchac, ed., *Survival This Way: Interviews with American Indian Poets,* 1987.

TEXT

Love Medicine, 1984.

The Red Convertible

(1974)[1]

LYMAN LAMARTINE

I was the first one to drive a convertible on my reservation. And of course it was red, a red Olds. I owned that car along with my brother Henry Junior. We owned it together until his boots filled with water on a windy night and he bought out my share. Now Henry owns the whole car, and his younger brother Lyman (that's myself), Lyman walks everywhere he goes.

How did I earn enough money to buy my share in the first place? My one talent was I could always make money. I had a touch for it, unusual in a Chippewa. From the first I was different that way, and everyone recognized it. I was the only kid they let in the American Legion Hall to shine shoes, for example, and one Christmas I sold spiritual bouquets for the mission door to door. The nuns let me keep a percentage. Once I started, it seemed the more money I made the easier the money came. Everyone encouraged it. When I was fifteen I got a job washing dishes at the Joliet Café, and that was where my first big break happened.

It wasn't long before I was promoted to bussing tables, and then the short-order cook quit and I was hired to take her place. No sooner than you know it I was managing the Joliet. The rest is history. I went on managing. I soon become part owner, and of course there was no stopping me then. It wasn't long before the whole thing was mine.

After I'd owned the Joliet for one year, it blew over in the worst tornado ever seen around here. The whole operation was smashed to bits. A total loss. The fryalator was up in a tree, the grill torn in half like it was paper. I was only sixteen. I had it all in my mother's name, and I lost it quick, but before I lost it I had every one of my relatives, and their relatives, to dinner, and I also bought that red Olds I mentioned, along with Henry.

The first time we saw it! I'll tell you when we first saw it. We had gotten a ride up to Winnipeg, and both of us had money. Don't ask me why, because we never mentioned a car or anything, we just had all our money. Mine was cash, a big bankroll from the Joliet's insurance. Henry had two checks — a week's extra pay for being laid off, and his regular check from the Jewel Bearing Plant.

We were walking down Portage anyway, seeing the sights, when we saw it. There it was, parked, large as life. Really as *if* it was alive. I thought of the word *repose*, because the car wasn't simply stopped, parked, or whatever. That car reposed, calm and gleaming, a FOR SALE sign in its left front window. Then, before we had thought it over at all, the car belonged to us and our pockets were empty. We had just enough money for gas back home.

We went places in that car, me and Henry. We took off driving all one whole summer. We started off toward the Little Knife River and Mandaree in Fort Berthold and then we found ourselves down in Wakpala somehow, and then suddenly we were over in Montana on the Rocky Boys, and yet the summer was not even half over. Some people hang on to details when they travel, but we didn't let them bother us and just lived our everyday lives here to there.

I do remember this one place with willows. I remember I laid under those trees and it was comfortable. So comfortable. The branches bent down all around me like a

---

[1]This date indicates the year of the action of the story; in *Love Medicine*, in which "The Red Convertible" is incorporated, the time of each episode is so indicated. "The Red Convertible" first appeared as a short story in the *Mississippi Valley Review* in 1982.

tent or a stable. And quiet, it was quiet, even though there was a powwow close enough so I could see it going on. The air was not too still, not too windy either. When the dust rises up and hangs in the air around the dancers like that, I feel good. Henry was asleep with his arms thrown wide. Later on, he woke up and we started driving again. We were somewhere in Montana, or maybe on the Blood Reserve—it could have been anywhere. Anyway it was where we met the girl.

All her hair was in buns around her ears, that's the first thing I noticed about her. She was posed alongside the road with her arm out, so we stopped. That girl was short, so short her lumber shirt looked comical on her, like a nightgown. She had jeans on and fancy moccasins and she carried a little suitcase.

"Hop on in," says Henry. So she climbs in between us.

"We'll take you home," I says. "Where do you live?"

"Chicken," she says.

"Where the hell's that?" I ask her.

"Alaska."

"Okay," says Henry, and we drive.

We got up there and never wanted to leave. The sun doesn't truly set there in summer, and the night is more a soft dusk. You might doze off, sometimes, but before you know it you're up again, like an animal in nature. You never feel like you have to sleep hard or put away the world. And things would grow up there. One day just dirt or moss, the next day flowers and long grass. The girl's name was Susy. Her family really took to us. They fed us and put us up. We had our own tent to live in by their house, and the kids would be in and out of there all day and night. They couldn't get over me and Henry being brothers, we looked so different. We told them we knew we had the same mother, anyway.

One night Susy came in to visit us. We sat around in the tent talking of this thing and that. The season was changing. It was getting darker by that time, and the cold was even getting just a little mean. I told her it was time for us to go. She stood up on a chair.

"You never seen my hair," Susy said.

That was true. She was standing on a chair, but still, when she unclipped her buns the hair reached all the way to the ground. Our eyes opened. You couldn't tell how much hair she had when it was rolled up so neatly. Then my brother Henry did something funny. He went up to the chair and said, "Jump on my shoulders." So she did that, and her hair reached down past his waist, and he started twirling, this way and that, so her hair was flung out from side to side.

"I always wondered what it was like to have long pretty hair," Henry says. Well we laughed. It was a funny sight, the way he did it. The next morning we got up and took leave of those people.

On to greener pastures, as they say. It was down through Spokane and across Idaho then Montana and very soon we were racing the weather right along under the Canadian border through Columbus, Des Lacs, and then we were in Bottineau County and soon home. We'd made most of the trip, that summer, without putting up the car hood at all. We got home just in time, it turned out, for the army to remember Henry had signed up to join it.

I don't wonder that the army was so glad to get my brother that they turned him into a Marine. He was built like a brick outhouse anyway. We liked to tease him that they really wanted him for his Indian nose. He had a nose big and sharp as a hatchet, like the nose on Red Tomahawk, the Indian who killed Sitting Bull, whose profile is on signs all along the North Dakota highways. Henry went off to training camp, came home once during Christmas, then the next thing you know we got an overseas letter from him. It was 1970, and he said he was stationed up in the northern hill country.

Whereabouts I did not know. He wasn't such a hot letter writer, and only got off two before the enemy caught him. I could never keep it straight, which direction those good Vietnam soldiers were from.

I wrote him back several times, even though I didn't know if those letters would get through. I kept him informed all about the car. Most of the time I had it up on blocks in the yard or half taken apart, because that long trip did a hard job on it under the hood.

I always had good luck with numbers, and never worried about the draft myself. I never even had to think about what my number was. But Henry was never lucky in the same way as me. It was at least three years before Henry came home. By then I guess the whole war was solved in the government's mind, but for him it would keep on going. In those years I'd put his car into almost perfect shape. I always thought of it as his car while he was gone, even though when he left he said, "Now it's yours," and threw me his key.

"Thanks for the extra key," I'd said. "I'll put it up in your drawer just in case I need it." He laughed.

When he came home, though, Henry was very different, and I'll say this: the change was no good. You could hardly expect him to change for the better, I know. But he was quiet, so quiet, and never comfortable sitting still anywhere but always up and moving around. I thought back to times we'd sat still for whole afternoons, never moving a muscle, just shifting our weight along the ground, talking to whoever sat with us, watching things. He'd always had a joke, then, too, and now you couldn't get him to laugh, or when he did it was more the sound of a man choking, a sound that stopped up the throats of other people around him. They got to leaving him alone most of the time, and I didn't blame them. It was a fact: Henry was jumpy and mean.

I'd bought a color TV set for my mom and the rest of us while Henry was away. Money still came very easy. I was sorry I'd ever bought it though, because of Henry. I was also sorry I'd bought color, because with black-and-white the pictures seem older and farther away. But what are you going to do? He sat in front of it, watching it, and that was the only time he was completely still. But it was the kind of stillness that you see in a rabbit when it freezes and before it will bolt. He was not easy. He sat in his chair gripping the armrests with all his might, as if the chair itself was moving at a high speed and if he let go at all he would rocket forward and maybe crash right through the set.

Once I was in the room watching TV with Henry and I heard his teeth click at something. I looked over, and he'd bitten through his lip. Blood was going down his chin. I tell you right then I wanted to smash that tube to pieces. I went over to it but Henry must have known what I was up to. He rushed from his chair and shoved me out of the way, against the wall. I told myself he didn't know what he was doing.

My mom came in, turned the set off real quiet, and told us she had made something for supper. So we went and sat down. There was still blood going down Henry's chin, but he didn't notice it and no one said anything, even though every time he took a bite of his bread his blood fell onto it until he was eating his own blood mixed in with the food.

While Henry was not around we talked about what was going to happen to him. There were no Indian doctors on the reservation, and my mom was afraid of trusting Old Man Pillager because he courted her long ago and was jealous of her husbands. He might take revenge through her son. We were afraid that if we brought Henry to a regular hospital they would keep him.

"They don't fix them in those places," Mom said; "they just give them drugs."

"We wouldn't get him there in the first place," I agreed, "so let's just forget about it."

Then I thought about the car.

Henry had not even looked at the car since he'd gotten home, though like I said, it was in tip-top condition and ready to drive. I thought the car might bring the old Henry back somehow. So I bided my time and waited for my chance to interest him in the vehicle.

One night Henry was off somewhere. I took myself a hammer. I went out to that car and I did a number on its underside. Whacked it up. Bent the tail pipe double. Ripped the muffler loose. By the time I was done with the car it looked worse than any typical Indian car that has been driven all its life on reservation roads, which they always say are like government promises — full of holes. It just about hurt me, I'll tell you that! I threw dirt in the carburetor and I ripped all the electric tape off the seats. I made it look just as beat up as I could. Then I sat back and waited for Henry to find it.

Still, it took him over a month. That was all right, because it was just getting warm enough, not melting, but warm enough to work outside.

"Lyman," he says, walking in one day, "that red car looks like shit."

"Well it's old," I says. "You got to expect that."

"No way!" says Henry. "That car's a classic! But you went and ran the piss right out of it, Lyman, and you know it don't deserve that. I kept that car in A-one shape. You don't remember. You're too young. But when I left, that car was running like a watch. Now I don't even know if I can get it to start again, let alone get it anywhere near its old condition."

"Well you try," I said, like I was getting mad, "but I say it's a piece of junk."

Then I walked out before he could realize I knew he'd strung together more than six words at once.

After that I thought he'd freeze himself to death working on that car. He was out there all day, and at night he rigged up a little lamp, ran a cord out the window, and had himself some light to see by while he worked. He was better than he had been before, but that's still not saying much. It was easier for him to do the things the rest of us did. He ate more slowly and didn't jump up and down during the meal to get this or that or look out the window. I put my hand in the back of the TV set, I admit, and fiddled around with it, so that it was almost impossible now to get a clear picture. He didn't look at it very often anyway. He was always out with that car or going off to get parts for it. By the time it was really melting outside, he had it fixed.

I had been feeling down in the dumps about Henry around this time. We had always been together before. Henry and Lyman. But he was such a loner now that I didn't know how to take it. So I jumped at the chance one day when Henry seemed friendly. It's not that he smiled or anything. He just said, "Let's take that old shitbox for a spin." Just the way he said it made me think he could be coming around.

We went out to the car. It was spring. The sun was shining very bright. My only sister, Bonita, who was just eleven years old, came out and made us stand together for a picture. Henry leaned his elbow on the red car's windshield, and he took his other arm and put it over my shoulder, very carefully, as though it was heavy for him to lift and he didn't want to bring the weight down all at once.

"Smile," Bonita said, and he did.

That picture. I never look at it anymore. A few months ago, I don't know why, I got his picture out and tacked it on the wall. I felt good about Henry at the time, close to him. I felt good having his picture on the wall, until one night when I was looking at television. I was a little drunk and stoned. I looked up at the wall and Henry was staring at me. I don't know what it was, but his smile had changed, or maybe it was gone. All I know is I couldn't stay in the same room with that picture. I was shaking. I got up, closed the door, and went into the kitchen. A little later my friend Ray came over and we both went back into that room. We put the picture in a brown bag, folded the bag over and over tightly, then put it way back in a closet.

I still see that picture now, as if it tugs at me, whenever I pass that closet door. The picture is very clear in my mind. It was so sunny that day Henry had to squint against the glare. Or maybe the camera Bonita held flashed like a mirror, blinding him, before she snapped the picture. My face is right out in the sun, big and round. But he might have drawn back, because the shadows on his face are deep as holes. There are two shadows curved like little hooks around the ends of his smile, as if to frame it and try to keep it there—that one, first smile that looked like it might have hurt his face. He has his field jacket on and the worn-in clothes he'd come back in and kept wearing ever since. After Bonita took the picture, she went into the house and we got into the car. There was a full cooler in the trunk. We started off, east, toward Pembina and the Red River because Henry said he wanted to see the high water.

The trip over there was beautiful. When everything starts changing, drying up, clearing off, you feel like your whole life is starting. Henry felt it, too. The top was down and the car hummed like a top. He'd really put it back in shape, even the tape on the seats was very carefully put down and glued back in layers. It's not that he smiled again or even joked, but his face looked to me as if it was clear, more peaceful. It looked as though he wasn't thinking of anything in particular except the bare fields and windbreaks and houses we were passing.

The river was high and full of winter trash when we got there. The sun was still out, but it was colder by the river. There were still little clumps of dirty snow here and there on the banks. The water hadn't gone over the banks yet, but it would, you could tell. It was just at its limit, hard swollen, glossy like an old gray scar. We made ourselves a fire, and we sat down and watched the current go. As I watched it I felt something squeezing inside me and tightening and trying to let go all at the same time. I knew I was not just feeling it myself; I knew I was feeling what Henry was going through at that moment. Except that I couldn't stand it, the closing and opening. I jumped to my feet. I took Henry by the shoulders and I started shaking him. "Wake up," I says, "wake up, wake up, wake up!" I didn't know what had come over me. I sat down beside him again.

His face was totally white and hard. Then it broke, like stones break all of a sudden when water boils up inside them.

"I know it," he says. "I know it. I can't help it. It's no use."

We started talking. He said he knew what I'd done with the car. It was obvious it had been whacked out of shape and not just neglected. He said he wanted to give the car to me for good now, it was no use. He said he'd fixed it just to give it back and I should take it.

"No way," I says, "I don't want it."

"That's okay," he says, "you take it."

"I don't want it, though," I says back to him, and then to emphasize, just to emphasize, you understand, I touch his shoulder. He slaps my hand off.

"Take that car," he says.

"No," I say, "make me," I say, and then he grabs my jacket and rips the arm loose. That jacket is a class act, suede with tags and zippers. I push Henry backwards, off the log. He jumps up and bowls me over. We go down in a clinch and come up swinging hard, for all we're worth, with our fists. He socks my jaw so hard I feel like it swings loose. Then I'm at his ribcage and land a good one under his chin so his head snaps back. He's dazzled. He looks at me and I look at him and then his eyes are full of tears and blood and at first I think he's crying. But no, he's laughing. "Ha! Ha!" he says. "Ha! Ha! Take good care of it."

"Okay," I says, "okay, no problem. Ha! Ha!"

I can't help it, and I start laughing, too. My face feels fat and strange, and after a while I get a beer from the cooler in the trunk, and when I hand it to Henry he takes his shirt and wipes my germs off. "Hoof-and-mouth disease," he says. For some reason this cracks me up, and so we're really laughing for a while, and then we drink all the rest of the beers one by one and throw them in the river and see how far, how fast, the current takes them before they fill up and sink.

"You want to go on back?" I ask after a while. "Maybe we could snag a couple nice Kashpaw girls."

He says nothing. But I can tell his mood is turning again.

"They're all crazy, the girls up here, every damn one of them."

"You're crazy too," I say, to jolly him up. "Crazy Lamartine boys!"

He looks as though he will take this wrong at first. His face twists, then clears, and he jumps up on his feet. "That's right!" he says. "Crazier 'n hell. Crazy Indians!"

I think it's the old Henry again. He throws off his jacket and starts swinging his legs out from the knees like a fancy dancer. He's down doing something between a grouse dance and a bunny hop, no kind of dance I ever saw before, but neither has anyone else on all this green growing earth. He's wild. He wants to pitch whoopee! He's up and at me and all over. All this time I'm laughing so hard, so hard my belly is getting tied up in a knot.

"Got to cool me off!" he shouts all of a sudden. Then he runs over to the river and jumps in.

There's boards and other things in the current. It's so high. No sound comes from the river after the splash he makes, so I run right over. I look around. It's getting dark. I see he's halfway across the water already, and I know he didn't swim there but the current took him. It's far. I hear his voice, though, very clearly across it.

"My boots are filling," he says.

He says this in a normal voice, like he just noticed and he doesn't know what to think of it. Then he's gone. A branch comes by. Another branch. And I go in.

By the time I get out of the river, off the snag I pulled myself onto, the sun is down. I walk back to the car, turn on the high beams, and drive it up the bank. I put it in first gear and then I take my foot off the clutch. I get out, close the door, and watch it plow softly into the water. The headlights reach in as they go down, searching, still lighted even after the water swirls over the back end. I wait. The wires short out. It is all finally dark. And then there is only the water, the sound of it going and running and going and running and running.

1982, 1984

REPORTS, REMINISCENCES, THE NONFICTION NOVEL

Jack Kerouac   William Least Heat Moon
Norman Mailer   Maxine Hong Kingston
N. Scott Momaday   Richard Rodriguez

"Mailer is a figure of monumental disproportions and so serves willy-nilly as [the comic hero,] the bridge . . . into the crazy house, the crazy mansion, of that historic moment when a mass of the citizenry—not much more than a mob—marched on a bastion which symbolized the military might of the Republic, marching not to capture it, but to wound it *symbolically*."

Norman Mailer, *The Armies of the Night*

"When I was growing up on the reservations of the Southwest, I saw people who were deeply involved in their traditional life, in the memories of their blood. They had, as far as I could see, a certain strength and beauty that I find missing in the modern world at large. I like to celebrate that involvement in my writing."

N. Scott Momaday, Interview in *American Poetry Review*

JACK KEROUAC
(1922–1969)

When *On the Road* appeared in 1957, its fast-moving, free-flowing style became the center of much critical discussion. Once asked about the origins of his style, Kerouac replied: "I got sick and tired of the conventional English which seemed to me to be so ironbound in its rules, so inadmissable with reference to the actual format of my mind as I learned to probe it in the modern spirit of Freud and Jung, that I couldn't express myself through that form any more. . . . If you don't stick to what you first thought, and to the words the thought brought, what's the sense of bothering with it anyway, what's the sense of foisting your little lies on others?" Kerouac developed a theory of what he called "spontaneous prose," a kind of "stream of authorial consciousness": "No 'selectivity' of expression but following free deviation (association) of mind into limitless blow-on-subject seas of thought, swimming in sea of English with no discipline other than rhythms of rhetorical exhalation & expostulated statement, like a fist coming down on a table with each complete utterance, bang."

On the Road became known as the bible of the "Beat Generation." In the essay reprinted here, Kerouac explains "The Origins of the Beat Generation." He claimed to be the first to use the phrase, but denied being part of any conscious movement. He said in a 1958 interview:

> Oh the beat generation was just a phrase I used in the 1951 manuscript of *On the Road* to describe guys like Moriarty [a major character in *On the Road*] who run around the country in cars looking for odd jobs, girlfriends, kicks. It was thereafter picked up by West Coast leftist groups and turned into a meaning like "beat mutiny" and "beat insurrection" and all that nonsense; they just wanted some youth movement to grab onto for their own political and social purposes. I had nothing to do with any of that. I was a football player, a scholarship college student, a merchant seaman, a railroad brakeman on road freights, a script synopsizer, a secretary.

Kerouac's self-characterization here is accurate. His background was not that of a wandering wild-eyed rebel. He was born in 1922 into a family of French-speaking Roman Catholics who had migrated from rural Quebec to Lowell, Massachusetts, where his father had established a successful print shop. Kerouac grew up speaking French. His older brother, Gerard, died when Kerouac was four years old, an event that would haunt him the rest of his life. Kerouac was a devout youth and served as altar boy at St. Jean Baptiste Cathedral, where in 1969 his funeral services would be held. In preparation for Columbia University, he attended Horace Mann School for Boys in New York (1939–40). He skipped his high-school graduation and instead went off by himself to read Walt Whitman's *Leaves of Grass*. Kerouac's career at Columbia was limited to a little over one year (1940–42). The Second World War was then disrupting the lives of all young men Kerouac's age. Kerouac served first in the U.S. Merchant Marine and later in the navy.

During these years, Kerouac read incessantly, came to know such aspiring writers as Allen Ginsberg and William Burroughs, and discovered his own strong desire to become a writer. He published his first novel, *The Town and the City,* in 1950. In 1946 Kerouac had met Neal Cassady, who would become the model for Dean Moriarty in *On the Road*. Inspired by a free-flowing, 23,000 word letter from Cassady in 1951, Kerouac wrote the first version of *On the Road* on a roll of teletype paper in three weeks. The novel went through several revisions, both by the author and by editors, before its publication in 1957 by Viking Press. The book established Kerouac not only as a writer but as something of a celebrity, spokesman for an alienated generation that had "turned on and dropped out."

Although Kerouac would write many more books, he would never again achieve the sensational success of *On the Road*. Among the most significant were *The Subterraneans* (1958), *The Dharma Bums* (1958), *Big Sur* (1962), *Visions of Gerard* (1963), *Desolation Angels* (1965), *Sartori in Paris* (1966), *Vanity of Duluoz* (1968), and *Visions of Cody* (1972). All of Kerouac's writings embodied his own and his friends' experiences, often with little change. Kerouac came to look upon his separate works as interconnected, much like the episodes of his life. He remarked: "My work comprises one vast book like Proust's *Remembrance of Things Past,* except that my remembrances are written on the run instead of afterwards in a sickbed."

Like other writers of his generation (and their acknowledged model, Walt Whitman, before them), Kerouac's religious views were shaped in part by oriental thought. He said in an interview: "What really influenced my work is the Mahayana Buddhism, the original Buddhism of Gotama Sakyamuni, the Buddha himself, of the India of old . . . . My serious Buddhism, that of ancient India, has influenced that part in my writing that you might call religious, or fervent, or pious, almost as much as Catholicism has. Original Buddhism referred to continual conscious compassion, brotherhood, the *dana paramita* meaning the perfection of charity, don't step on the bug, all that, humility, mendicancy, the sweet sorrowful face of the Buddha." As critic George Dardess has observed, Kerouac's "accomplishment was a complex and even a paradoxical one," and recent scholarship gives "hope that a calm assessment . . . is at last becoming possible."

ADDITIONAL READING

Ann Charters, *Kerouac: A Biography,* 1973; Charles E. Jarvis, *Visions of Kerouac,* 1974; Ann Charters, *A Bibliography of Works by Jack Kerouac, 1939–1975,* 1975; John Tytell, *Naked Angels: The Lives and Literature of the Beat Generation,* 1976; Robert A. Hipkiss, *Jack Kerouac: Prophet of the New Romanticism,* 1976; Carolyn Cassady, *Heart Beat: My Life With Jack and Neal,* 1976; Barry Gifford and Lawrence Lee, *Jack's Book: An Oral Biography of Jack Kerouac,* 1978; Dennis McNally, *Desolate Angel: Jack Kerouac, the Beat Generation, and America,* 1979; Timothy A. Hunt, *Kerouac's Crooked Road: Development of a Fiction,* 1981; Robert J. Milewsky, *Jack Kerouac: An Annotated Bibliography of Secondary Sources, 1944–1979,* 1981; Gerald Nicosia, *Memory Babe: A Critical Biography of Jack Kerouac,* 1983; Tom Clark, *Jack Kerouac,* 1984; Warren French, *Jack Kerouac: Novelist of the Beat Generation,* 1986; Regina Weinreich, *The Spontaneous Poetics of Jack Kerouac: A Study of the Fiction,* 1987. Arthur and Kit Knight, eds., *The Beat Vision,* 1987, and *Kerouac and the Beats: A Primary Source Book,* 1988; Carolyn Cassady, *Off the Road; My Years with Cassady, Kerouac, and Ginsberg,* 1990.

TEXT

"The Origins of the Beat Generation" in *Marginal Manners: The Variants of Bohemia,* ed. Frederick J. Hoffman, 1962.

The Origins of the Beat Generation[1]

This article necessarily'll have to be about myself. I'm going all out.

That nutty picture of me on the cover of *On the Road* results from the fact that I had just gotten down from a high mountain where I'd been for two months com-

---

[1]First published in *Playboy,* June 1959, this essay is based on Kerouac's remarks in November 1958 at a Hunter College debate on the question "Is There a Beat Generation?"

pletely alone and usually I was in the habit of combing my hair of course because you have to get rides on the highway and all that and you usually want girls to look at you as though you were a man and not a wild beast but my poet friend Gregory Corso opened his shirt and took out a silver crucifix that was hanging from a chain and said "Wear this and wear it outside your shirt and don't comb you hair!" so I spent several days around San Francisco going around with him and others like that, to parties, arties, parts, jam sessions, bars, poetry readings, churches, walking talking poetry in the streets, walking talking God in the streets (and at one point a strange gang of hoodlums got mad and said "What right does he got to wear that?" and my own gang of musicians and poets told them to cool it) and finally on the third day *Mademoiselle* magazine wanted to take pictures of us all so I posed just like that, wild hair, crucifix, and all, with Gregory Corso, Allen Ginsberg and Phil Whalen,[2] and the only publication which later did not erase the crucifix from my breast (from that plaid sleeveless cotton shirtfront) was *The New York Times*, therefore *The New York Times* is as beat as I am, and I'm glad I've got a friend. I mean it sincerely, God bless *The New York Times* for not erasing the crucifix from my picture as though it was something distasteful. As a matter of fact, who's *really* beat around here, I mean if you wanta talk of Beat as "beat down" the people who erased the crucifix are really the "beat down" ones and not *The New York Times*, myself, and Gregory Corso the poet. I am not ashamed to wear the crucifix of my Lord. It is because I am Beat, that is, I believe in beatitude and that God so loved the world that he gave his only begotten son to it. I am sure no priest would've condemned me for wearing the crucifix outside my shirt everywhere and *no matter where* I went, even to have my picture taken by *Mademoiselle*. So you people don't believe in God. So you're all big smart know-it-all Marxists and Freudians, hey? Why don't you come back in a million years and tell me all about it, angels?

Recently Ben Hecht[3] said to me on TV "Why are you afraid to speak out your mind, what's wrong with this country, what is everybody afraid of?" Was he talking to me? And all he wanted me to do was speak out my mind *against* people; he sneeringly brought up Dulles, Eisenhower, the Pope, all kinds of people like that habitually he would sneer at with Drew Pearson,[4] *against* the world he wanted, this is his idea of freedom, he calls it freedom. Who knows, my God, but that the universe is not one vast sea of compassion actually, the veritable holy honey, beneath all this show of personality and cruelty. In fact who knows but that it isn't the solitude of the oneness of the essence of everything, the solitude of the actual oneness of the unbornness of the unborn essence of everything, nay the true pure foreverhood, that big blank potential that can ray forth anything it wants from its pure store, that blazing bliss, *Mattivajrakaruna*[5] the Transcendental Diamond Compassion! No, I want to speak *for* things, for the crucifix I speak out, for the Star of Israel I speak out, for the divinest man who ever lived who was a German (Bach) I speak out, for sweet Mohammed I speak out, for Buddha I speak out, for Lao-tse and Chuang-tse I speak out, for D. T. Suzuki[6] I speak out . . . why should I attack what I love out of life. This is Beat. Live your lives out? Naw, *love* your lives out. When they come and stone you at least you won't have a glass house, just your glassy flesh.

That wild eager picture of me on the cover of *On the Road* where I look so Beat goes back much further than 1948 when John Clellon Holmes[7] (author of *Go* and *The Horn*) and I were sitting around trying to think up the meaning of the Lost Genera-

[2]Gregory Corso (b. 1930), Allen Ginsberg (b. 1926), Philip Whalen (b. 1923), American poets associated with the Beat movement.

[3]Ben Hecht (1894–1964), American writer and editor.

[4]John Foster Dulles (1888–1959), Secretary of State (1953–59) under Dwight Eisenhower (1890–1969), thirty-fourth U. S. president (1953–61); Drew Pearson (1897–1969), influential journalist and reporter on the Washington scene (his column was called "The Washington Merry-Go-Round").

[5]Transliteration of three Sanskrit words: *matti*, intellectual; *vajra*, diamond; *karuna*, compassion. Kerouac provides a rough translation following it.

[6]Johann Sebastian Bach (1685-1750), German composer; Lao-tse (or Lao-tzu), sixth-century B.C. Chinese philosopher, founder of Taoism; Chuang-tse(also Chuang-tzu), fourth-century B.C. Chinese philosopher, Taoist follower of Lao-tzu; D. T. Suzuki (1870–1966), Japanese philosopher and author of important books on Zen Buddhism.

[7]John Clellon Holmes(b. 1926), American writer and author of the first published Beat novel, *Go* (1952), and *The Horn* (1958).

tion[8] and the subsequent Existentialism and I said "You know, this is really a beat generation" and he leapt up and said "That's it, that's right!" It goes back to the 1880s when my grandfather Jean-Baptiste Kerouac used to go out on the porch in big thunderstorms and swing his kerosene lamp at the lightning and yell "Go ahead, go, if you're more powerful than I am strike me and put the light out!" while the mother and the children cowered in the kitchen. And the light never went out. Maybe since I'm supposed to be the spokesman of the Beat Generation (I *am* the originator of the term, and around it the term and the generation have taken shape) it should be pointed out that all this "Beat" guts therefore goes back to my ancestors who were Bretons who were the most independent group of nobles in all old Europe and kept fighting Latin France to the last wall (although a big blond bosun on a merchant ship snorted when I told him my ancestors were Bretons in Cornwall, Brittany, "Why, we Wikings used to swoop down and steal your nets!") Breton, Wiking, Irishman, Indian, madboy, it doesn't make any difference, there is no doubt about the Beat Generation, at least the core of it, being a swinging group of new American men intent on joy . . . Irresponsibility? Who wouldn't help a dying man on an empty road? No and the Beat Generation goes back to the wild parties my father used to have at home in the 1920s and 1930s in New England that were so fantastically loud nobody could sleep for blocks around and when the cops came they always had a drink. It goes back to the wild and raving childhood of playing the Shadow under windswept trees of New England's gleeful autumn, and the howl of the Moon Man on the sandbank until we caught him in a tree (he was an "older" guy of 15), the maniacal laugh of certain neighborhood madboys, the furious humor of whole gangs playing basketball till long after dark in the park, it goes back to those crazy days before World War II when teenagers drank beer on Friday nights at Lake ballrooms and worked off their hangovers playing baseball on Saturday afternoon followed by a dive in the brook — and our fathers wore straw hats like W. C. Fields. It goes back to the completely senseless babble of the Three Stooges, the ravings of the Marx Brothers (the tenderness of Angel Harpo at harp, too).[9]

It goes back[10] to the inky ditties of old cartoons (Krazy Kat with the irrational brick) — to Laurel and Hardy in the Foreign Legion — to Count Dracula and his *smile* to Count Dracula shivering and hissing back before the Cross — to the Golem[11] horrifying the persecutors of the Ghetto — to the quiet sage in a movie about India, unconcerned about the plot — to the giggling old Tao Chinaman trotting down the sidewalk of old Clark Gable Shanghai — to the holy old Arab warning the hotbloods that Ramadan[12] is near. To the Werewolf of London a distinguished doctor in his velour smoking jacket smoking his pipe over a lamplit tome on botany and suddenly hairs grown on his hands, his cat hisses, and he slips out into the night with a cape and a slanty cap like the caps of people in breadlines — to Lamont Cranston so cool and sure suddenly becoming the frantic Shadow going mwee hee hee ha ha in the alleys of New York imagination. To Popeye the sailor and the Sea Hag and the meaty gunwales of boats, to Cap'n Easy and Wash Tubbs screaming with ecstasy over canned peaches on a cannibal isle, to Wimpy looking X-eyed for a juicy hamburger such as they make no more. To Jiggs ducking before a household of furniture flying through the air, to Jiggs and the boys at the bar and the corned beef and cabbage of old woodfence noons — to King Kong his eyes looking into the hotel window with tender huge love for Fay Wray — nay, to Bruce Cabot in mate's cap leaning over the rail of a

---

[8]A term applied to the rootless, disillusioned intellectuals after the First World War; it appears in the epigraph of Hemingway's *The Sun Also Rises* (1926), ascribed to Gertrude Stein: "You are all a lost generation." Existentialism, a European philosophic movement, posits the isolation and alienation of the individual, freely and responsibly creating his own being in a meaningless, absurd universe.

[9]A catalogue of comedy film stars.
[10]Another kaleidoscopic list follows, with references to comic strips, radio shows, cartoons, and movies.
[11]Golem: a figure in Jewish folklore, made to look human and endowed with life.
[12]A Muslim period of daily fasting (the ninth month of the Muslim year).

fog-bound ship saying "Come aboard." It goes back to when grapefruits were thrown at crooners and harvestworkers at bar-rails slapped burlesque queens on the rump. To when fathers took their sons to the Twi League game. To the days of Babe Callahan on the waterfront, Dick Barthelmess camping under a London street-lamp. To dear old Basil Rathbone looking for the Hound of the Baskervilles (a dog big as the Gray Wolf who will destroy Odin) — to dear old bleary Doctor Watson with a brandy in his hand. To Joan Crawford her raw shanks in the fog, in striped blouse smoking a cigarette at sticky lips in the door of the waterfront dive. To train whistles of steam engines out above the moony pines. To Maw and Paw in the Model A clanking on to get a job in California selling used cars making a whole lotta money. To the glee of America, the honesty of America, the honesty of oldtime grafters in straw hats as well as the honesty of oldtime waiters in line at the Brooklyn Bridge in *Winterset*, the funny spitelessness of old bigfisted America like Big Boy Williams saying "Hoo? Hee? Huh? in a movie about Mack Trucks and slidingdoor lunchcarts. To Clark Gable, his certain smile, his confident leer. Like my grandfather this America was invested with wild selfbelieving individuality and this had begun to disappear around the end of World War II with so many great guys dead (I can think of half a dozen from my own boyhood groups) when suddenly it began to emerge again, the hipsters began to appear gliding around saying "Crazy, man."

When I first saw the hipsters creeping around Times Square in 1944 I didn't like them either. One of them, Huncke[13] of Chicago, came up to me and said "Man, I'm beat." I knew right away what he meant somehow. At that time I still didn't like bop which was then being introduced by Bird Parker and Dizzy Gillespie and Bags Jackson[14] (on vibes), the last of the great swing musicians was Don Byas who went to Spain right after, but then I began . . . but earlier I'd dug all my jazz in the old Minton Playhouse (Lester Young, Ben Webster, Joey Guy, Charlie Christian,[15] others) and when I first heard Bird and Diz in the Three Deuces I knew they were serious musicians playing a goofy new sound and didn't care what I thought, or what my friend Seymour thought. In fact I was leaning against the bar with a beer when Dizzy came over for a glass of water from the bartender, put himself right against me and reached both arms around both sides of my head to get the glass and danced away, as though knowing I'd be singing about him someday, or that one of his arrangements would be named after me someday by some goofy circumstance. Charlie Parker was spoken of in Harlem as the greatest musician since Chu Berry and Louis Armstrong.[16]

Anyway, the hipsters, whose music was bop, they looked like criminals but they kept talking about the same things I liked, long outlines of personal experience and vision, nightlong confessions full of hope that had become illicit and repressed by War, stirrings, rumblings of a new soul (that same old human soul). And so Huncke appeared to us and said "I'm beat" with radiant light shining out of his despairing eyes . . . a word perhaps brought from some midwest carnival or junk cafeteria. It was a new language, actually spade (Negro) jargon but you soon learned it, like "hung up" couldn't be a more economical term to mean so many things. Some of these hipsters wre raving mad and talked continually. It was jazzy. Symphony Sid's all-night modern jazz and bop show was always on.[17] By 1948 it began to take shape. That was a wild vibrating year when a group of us would walk down the street and yell hello

---

[13]Herbert E. Huncke (b. 1915), American prose writer and friend of Kerouac.

[14]Charlie "Bird" or "Yardbird" Parker (1920–1955), American alto saxophonist, composer, and leading exponent of bebop; John Birks "Dizzy" Gillespie (b. 1917), American trumpeter; Milt "Bags" Jackson (b. 1923), American vibraphonist.

[15]"Don" Carlos Wesley Byas (1912–1972), American tenor saxophonist; Lester "Pres" Young (1909–1959), American tenor saxophonist; Ben Webster (1909–1973), American tenor saxophonist; Joe Guy (b. 1920), American trumpeter;

Charlie Christian (1919–1942), American guitarist. Minton's Playhouse was a Harlem nightclub where jazz musicians gathered in the 1940s and developed bebop.

[16]Leon "Chu" Berry (1910–1941), American tenor saxophonist; Louis Armstrong (1900–1971), American trumpeter, singer, and composer.

[17]Symphony Sid Torin, a popular bebop disc jockey, announced the groups broadcast live on radio from Birdland, the jazz nightclub named after Parker.

and even stop and talk to anybody that gave us a friendly look. The hipsters had eyes. That was the year I saw Montgomery Clift,[18] unshaven, wearing a sloppy jacket, slouching down Madison Avenue with a companion. It was the year I saw Charley Bird Parker strolling down Eighth Avenue in a black turtleneck sweater with Babs Gonzales[19] and a beautiful girl.

By 1948 the hipsters, or beatsters, were divided into cool and hot. Much of the misunderstanding about hipsters and the Beat Generation in general today derives from the fact that there are two distinct styles of hipsterism: the cool today is your bearded laconic sage, or schlerm, before a hardly touched beer in a beatnik dive, whose speech is low and unfriendly, whose girls say nothing and wear black: the "hot" today is the crazy talkative shining eyed (often innocent and openhearted) nut who runs from bar to bar, pad to pad looking for everybody, shouting, restless, lushy, trying to "make it" with the subterranean beatniks who ignore him. Most Beat Generation artists belong to the hot school, naturally since that hard gemlike flame needs a little heat. In many cases the mixture is 50-50. It was a hot hipster like myself who finally cooled it in Buddhist meditation, though when I go in a jazz joint I still feel like yelling "Blow baby blow!" to the musicians though nowadays I'd get 86d[20] for this. In 1948 the "hot hipsters" were racing around in cars like in *On the Road* looking for wild bawling jazz like Willis Jackson or Lucky Thompson (the early) or Chubby Jackson's[21] big band while the "cool hipsters" cooled it in dead silence before formal and excellent musical groups like Lennie Tristano or Miles Davis.[22] It's still just about the same, except that it has begun to grow into a national generation and the name "Beat" has stuck (though all hipsters hate the word).

The word "beat" originally meant poor, down and out, dead-beat, on the bum, sad, sleeping in subways. Now that the word is belonging officially it is being made to stretch to include people who do not sleep in subways but have a certain new gesture, or attitude, which I can only describe as a new *more*.[23] "Beat Generation" has simply become the slogan or label for a revolution in manners in America. Marlon Brando was not really first to portray it on the screen. Dane Clark with his pinched Dostoievskyan face and Brooklyn accent, and of course Garfield, were first. The private eyes were Beat, if you will recall. Bogart. Lorre was Beat. In *M*, Peter Lorre started a whole revival, I mean the slouchy street walk.

I wrote *On the Road* in three weeks in the beautiful month of May 1941 while living in the Chelsea district of lower West Side Manhattan, on a 100-foot roll[24] and put the Beat Generation in words in there, saying at the point where I am taking part in a wild kind of collegiate party with a bunch of kids in an abandoned miner's shack "These kids are great but where are Dean Moriarty and Carlo Marx?[25] Oh well I guess they wouldn't belong in this gang, they're too *dark*, too strange, too subterranean and I am slowly beginning to join a new kind of *beat* generation." The manuscript of *Road* was turned down on the grounds that it would displease the sales manager of my publisher at that time, though the editor, a very intelligent man, said "Jack this is just like Dostoievsky, but what can I do at this time?" It was too early. So for the next six years I was a bum, a brakeman, a seaman, a panhandler, a pseudo-Indian in Mexico, anything and everything, and went on writing because my hero was Goethe[26] and I believed in art and hoped some day to write the third part of *Faust*, which I have done in *Doctor Sax*.[27] Then in 1952 an article was published in *The*

---

[18]Montgomery Clift (1920–1966), American movie star.
[19]Babs Gonzales (b. 1919), American bop singer.
[20]I.e., refused service at the bar (86: slang for an undesirable customer).
[21]Eli "Lucky" Thompson (b. 1924), American tenor saxophonist; Greig Stewart "Chubby" Jackson (b. 1918), American bass player.
[22]Leonard Joseph Tristano (1919–1978), American pianist and composer; Miles Davis, Jr. (b. 1926), American trumpeter.

[23]Kerouac's coinage for the singular form of the plural *mores* (customs, manners, ways).
[24]Of teletype paper.
[25]Characters in *On the Road*: Moriarty based on Neal Cassady; Marx, on Allen Ginsberg.
[26]Johann Wolfgang von Goethe (1749–1832), German author of *Faust*, a drama in two parts.
[27]Published in 1959.

New York Times Sunday magazine saying, the headline, "'This is a Beat Generation'" (in quotes like that) and in the article it said that I had come up with the term first "when the face was harder to recognize," the face of the generation. After that there was some talk of the Beat Generation but in 1955 I published an excerpt from *Road* (melling it with parts of *Visions of Neal*) under the pseudonym "Jean-Louis," it was entitled *Jazz of the Beat Generation* and was copyrighted as being an excerpt from a novel-in-progress entitled *Beat Generation* (which I later changed to *On the Road* at the insistence of my new editor) and so then the term moved a little faster. The term and the cats. Everywhere began to appear strange hepcats and even college kids went around hep and cool and using the terms I'd heard on Times Square in the early Forties, it was growing somehow. But when the publishers finally took a dare and published *On the Road* in 1957 it burst open, it mushroomed, everybody began yelling about a Beat Generation. I was being interviewed everywhere I went for "what I meant" by such a thing. People began to call themselves beatniks, beats, jazzniks, bopniks, bugniks and finally I was called the "avatar" of all this.

Yet it was as a Catholic, it was not at the insistence of any of these "niks" and certainly not with their approval either, that I went one afternoon to the church of my childhood (one of them), Ste. Jeanne d'Arc in Lowell, Mass., and suddenly with tears in my eyes and had a vision of what I must have really meant with "Beat" anyhow when I heard the holy silence in the church (I was the only one in there, it was five P.M., dogs were barking outside, children yelling, the fall leaves, the candles were flickering alone just for me), the vision of the word Beat as being to mean beatific . . . There's the priest preaching on Sunday morning, all of a sudden through a side door of the church comes a group of Beat Generation characters in strapped raincoats like the I.R.A.[28] coming in silently to "dig" the religion . . . I knew it then.

But this was 1954, so then what horror I felt in 1957 and later 1958 naturally to suddenly see "Beat" being taken up by everybody, press and TV and Hollywood borscht circuit to include the "juvenile delinquency" shot and the horrors of a mad teeming billyclub New York and L. A. and they began to call *that* Beat, *that* beatific . . . bunch of fools marching against the San Francisco Giants protesting baseball, as if (now) in my name and I, my childhood ambition to be a big league baseball star hitter like Ted Williams so that when Bobby Thomson hit that home-run in 1951 I trembled with joy and couldn't get over it for days and wrote poems about how it is possible for the human spirit to win after all! Or, when a murder, a routine murder took place in North Beach, they labeled it a Beat Generation slaying although in my childhood I'd been famous as an eccentric in my block for stopping the younger kids from throwing rocks at the squirrels, for stopping them from frying snakes in cans or trying to blow up frogs with straws. Because my brother had died at the age of nine, his name was Gerard Kerouac, and he'd told me "Ti Jean[29] never hurt any living being, all living beings whether it's just a little cat or squirrel or whatever, all, are going to heaven straight into God's snowy arms so never hurt anything and if you see anybody hurt anything stop them as best you can" and when he died a file of gloomy nuns in black from St. Louis de France parish had filed (1926) to his deathbed to hear his last words about Heaven. And my father too, Leo, had never lifted a hand to punish me, or to punish the little pets in our house, and this teaching was delivered to me by the men in my house and I have never had anything to do with violence, hatred, cruelty, and all that horrible nonsense which, nevertheless, because God is gracious beyond all human imagining, he will forgive in the long end . . . that million years I'm asking about you, America.

And so now they have beatnik routines on TV, starting with satires about girls in black and fellows in jeans with snapknives and sweatshirts and swastikas tattooed

---

[28]Irish Republican Army.
[29]Kerouac's childhood name, meaning "Little Jack."

under their armpits, it will come to respectable m.c.s[30] of spectaculars coming out nattily attired in Brooks Brothers jean-type tailoring and sweater-type pull-ons, in other words, it's a simple change in fashion and manners, just a history crust—like from the Age of Reason, from old Voltaire in a chair to romantic Chatterton[31] in the moonlight—from Teddy Roosevelt to Scott Fitzgerald[32] . . . So there's nothing to get excited about. Beat comes out, actually, of old American whoopee and it will only change a few dresses and pants and make chairs useless in the livingroom and pretty soon we'll have Beat Secretaries of State and there will be instituted new tinsels, in fact new reasons for malice and new reasons for virtue and new reasons for forgiveness . . .

But yet, but yet, woe, woe unto those who think that the Beat Generation means crime, delinquency, immorality, amorality . . . woe unto those who attack it on the grounds that they simply don't understand history and the yearnings of human souls . . . woe unto those who don't realize that America must, will, is, changing now, for the better I say. Woe unto those who believe in the atom bomb, who believe in hating mothers and fathers who deny the most important of the Ten Commandments, woe unto those (though) who don't believe in the unbelievable sweetness of sex love, woe unto those who are the standard bearers of death, woe unto those who believe in conflict and horror and violence and fill our books and screens and livingrooms with all that crap, woe in fact unto those who make evil movies about the Beat Generation where innocent housewives are raped by beatniks! Woe unto those who are the real dreary sinners that even God finds room to forgive . . . woe unto those who spit on the Beat Generation, the wind'll blow it back.

1959

NORMAN MAILER

(b. 1923)

Norman Mailer has repeatedly expressed his belief in the ability of a powerful writer to affect the lives of human beings. For example, he said in 1959: "The sour truth is that I am imprisoned with a perception which will settle for nothing less than making a revolution in the consciousness of our time." And again, in an interview in 1964, he said of the writer:

> At best you affect the consciousness of your time, and so indirectly you affect the history of the time which succeeds you. . . . It is no little matter to be a writer. There's that godawful Time magazine world out there, and one can make raids on it. There are palaces, and prisons to attack. One can even succeed now and again in blowing holes in the line of the world's communications. Sometimes I feel as if there's a vast guerrilla war going on for the mind of man. . . . And the stakes are huge. Will we spoil the best secrets of life or will we help to free a new kind of man? It's intoxicating to think of that. There's something rich waiting if one of us is brave enough and good enough to get there.

---

[30]Masters of Ceremony.

[31]François Voltaire (1694–1778), French philosopher of the eighteenth century ("Age of Reason") and author of the satiric *Candide*; Thomas Chatterton (1752–1770), English poet whose work anticipated the romantic period.

[32]Theodore Roosevelt (1858–1919), twenty-sixth U. S. president (1901–09); F. Scott Fitzgerald (1896–1940), American novelist.

Mailer came by his metaphor of the writer as a guerilla fighter naturally from his experience in the Second World War. He was born in 1923 in Long Branch, New Jersey, grew up in Brooklyn, and entered Harvard in 1939, majoring in aeronautical engineering. While at Harvard he took several writing courses and published stories in the *Harvard Advocate*, winning a prize awarded annually by *Story* magazine. He has said that before he was seventeen, he developed the desire to become a "major writer." After graduation from Harvard in 1943, he entered the army determined to write a great war novel, letting the army determine the setting by where it sent him. As it turned out, the army sent him to the Pacific, and he served in the invasion retaking the Philippines and, later, in the occupation of Japan. He was discharged from the service in 1946.

He wrote his great war novel during the next fifteen months. After finishing it, he went to Paris to study at the Sorbonne (on the G. I. Bill), and returned to America in 1948 just as *The Naked and the Dead* appeared. Set on one of the islands in the Pacific contested during the war, it was a realistic account of one American platoon's fate in fighting the Japanese. The book was critically acclaimed, with many reviewers citing its debt to the experimental American naturalist John Dos Passos, whose *U.S.A.* trilogy was (in part) Mailer's model. *The Naked and the Dead* was the first novel about the Second World War to become a bestseller, and remains today one of the best of the novels about the war in the Pacific, and one of the best of Mailer's books.

Mailer seemed well-launched on a career as a novelist. His next novel was *Barbary Shore* (1951), portraying the struggles between leftist and rightist social and political forces in America; Mailer had worked for the election of Henry Agard Wallace, who had run as a third-party candidate for the left-leaning Progressive party in the 1948 presidential election. Mailer's third novel, *The Deer Park* (1955), presented an unflattering picture of Hollywood (where Mailer had worked for a time as a film writer) under attack by the House of Representatives' Un-American Activities Committee. Neither of these novels seemed to live up to Mailer's promise. His lack of firsthand, deeply engaged experience with the materials of these works showed in their thinness—in contrast with the density of his war novel. And he appeared to be under the influence of a writer whose style was unsuited to his tempermant, F. Scott Fitzgerald of *The Great Gatsby* and *The Last Tycoon*.

During this period, Mailer began to reshape himself as a writer. He wrote essays for the magazine *Dissent* and began a column in *The Village Voice*, which he had helped found. In 1957, he published in *Dissent* one of the most important essays of his career, "The White Negro: Superficial Reflections on the Hipster." He wrote: "The Hip ethic is immoderation, childlike in its adoration of the present. . . . The nihilism of Hip proposes as its final tendency that every social restraint and category be removed. . . . Hip, which would return us to ourselves, at no matter what price in individual violence, is the affirmation of the barbarian." The essay was shaped in part by the period in which it was written. The 1950s was an age of conformity, a strange time of social quiescence between the violence of the Second World War and the street rebellions and rioting of the 1960s. Mailer's nihilistic existentialism expressed so aggressively in "The White Negro" was a reaction against that equivocal quiescence, a rallying cry for inborn nonconformists.

In 1959, Mailer published an extraordinary book that detailed a radical change in his notions about himself and his role as a writer, *Advertisements for Myself*. His model had become Ernest Hemingway, not so much Hemingway's work, but rather his public persona. Mailer candidly announced his program: "An author's personality can help or hurt the attention readers give to his book. . . . The way to save your work and reach more readers is to advertise yourself, steal your own favorite page out of Hemingway's unwritten *Notes From Papa On How The Working Novelist Can Get Ahead. . . .* I . . . would love to be one of the colorful old-young men of American letters."

Much of Mailer's life and work in the following decades constituted *advertisements* for himself. In 1960 he stabbed his wife with a penknife at a party and was committed to Bellevue for observation, thus becoming front-page news very much in the tradition of Hemingway. There were other brawls, assaults, disturbances that made the press. And Mailer appeared to exploit his bizarre behavior in *An American Dream* (1965), a melodramatic tale of a man who strangles his wife, makes it appear to be a suicide, and gets off free. The novel confirmed many in their view that Mailer's public personality had taken over and somehow diminished his talent. In 1966 Mailer published *Cannibals and Christians,* a mixed bag of a book containing both literary and political pieces ("writings from 1960 to the present"); it was dedicated: "To Lyndon B. Johnson, whose name inspired young men to cheer for me in public." His next novel, *Why Are We In Vietnam?* (1967), was in reality a polemic in the form of a parable, an indirect condemnation of America's involvement in Vietnam through a Texas disc jockey recalling a story of a bear hunt he experienced in his youth with his father in Alaska. To many readers, the voice of the novel seemed shrill, the humor forced.

It was with considerable surprise to those readers who thought Mailer's talent was faltering to discover that in his next work, *The Armies of the Night: History as a Novel / The Novel as History* (1968), he was at the top of his form. And he had turned from traditional fiction and reportage to a form uniquely Mailer's—a "non-fiction novel," with the author casting himself as "comic hero" and clown. In his classic account of the 1967 March on the Pentagon in protest against the Vietnam War, an event in which he, Robert Lowell, and other celebrities participated, Mailer succeeded in being historically scrupulous, sometimes moving, and frequently funny. It won both the Pulitzer Prize and the National Book Award. Many critics have expressed the belief that *Armies of the Night* is Mailer's best book.

Having found his most congenial form, intermingling history and autobiography, Mailer used it again and again in succeeding books—but without matching the success of *Armies of the Night.* In 1968, he told the story of the Republican and Democratic presidential nominating conventions in *Miami and the Siege of Chicago.* In 1970 he gave a detailed account of the take-off, flight, and moon landing of Apollo 11 in *Of a Fire on the Moon.* In 1971 he entered the debate on feminism with *Prisoner of Sex,* defending himself and other male writers in the attack launched by Kate Millett in her *Sexual Politics* (1970). In 1973, Mailer wrote an account of the life of Marilyn Monroe, *Marilyn,* which he called a "novel biography." In none of these works did Mailer find the perfect place for himself that he had found in *Armies of the Night*—that of ironic commentator and comic hero.

In 1979, Mailer produced what he called a "True Life Novel," entitled *The Executioner's Song.* It was a sympathetic reconstruction of the life of a Utah murderer who was executed in 1977—the first execution in the United States in a decade. The book was controversial, raising moral questions about glamorization of a criminal who had performed vicious crimes. The controversy was renewed and intensified when, in 1982, Mailer was instrumental in getting a convict released from a Utah prison. The ex-convict soon killed a New York waiter,

and Mailer, who had promoted publication of the convict's prision letter's, testified at the trial on his behalf, causing a public outcry against Mailer's glorification
of violence and defense of a writer as one above the law.

In 1983, Mailer surprised all his readers by publishing the extraordinarily
long novel *Ancient Evenings* (announced "in progress" a decade before)—a historical epic set in ancient Egypt. It is more a fantasy than a novel, introducing a
ghost with telepathic powers as a narrator, and portraying a hero with virtually a
thousand lives—through transmigration of the soul. In an interview, Mailer
commented: "The Egyptians have much to tell us—precisely because they came
before the Judeo-Christian era—about power, wealth, sex and death, and right
in there is waste, excrement. . . . It's no secret that Freud gave us a firm set of
connections between anality and power . . . and what I learned about Egypt
seemed a kind of confirmation." In 1984, Mailer again surprised his readers by
following this heavy-weight work with a light-weight murder mystery, *Tough
Guys Don't Dance*, proving himself as unpredictable in his career as ever.

In a 1981 interview (reprinted in *Pieces and Pontifications*, 1982), Mailer was
asked how he felt about his past. He answered:

> After a while you walk around your own life as though it were a piece of sculp-
> ture. It depends on where you're looking at it from. Are you thinking of it
> from the point of view of your work, or your children? Actually, I find I think
> less and less about myself as I get older. You begin to have the feeling, "well, I
> may only have another so many years to write, and write halfway well," and you
> tend to get more serious. You get practical about your life, and realize that
> there's going to be more and more work, and less and less fun as you go along.
> You say, "I'll think about that old part of my life when I'm writing about it, and
> if I never write about it, I'll never think about it again."

This statement suggests that Mailer has become somewhat mellow, but also that
he may have a few more surprises to spring before he is through.

ADDITIONAL READING

Conversations with Norman Mailer, ed. J. Michael Lennon, 1988.

Richard Foster, *Norman Mailer*, 1968; Donald L. Kaufman, *Norman Mailer: The Countdown /
The First Twenty Years*, 1969; Barry H. Leeds, *The Structured Vision of Norman Mailer*, 1969; Joe
Flaherty, *Managing Mailer*, 1970; Robert F. Lucid, ed., *Norman Mailer: The Man and His Work*,
1971; Richard Poirier, *Norman Mailer*, 1972; Leo Braudy, ed., *Norman Mailer: A Collection of
Critical Essays*, 1972; Laura Adams, ed., *Will the Real Norman Mailer Please Stand Up?* 1974;
Robert Solotaroff, *Down Mailer's Way*, 1974; Laura Adams, *Norman Mailer: A Comprehensive Bibli-
ography*, 1974; Stanley T. Gutman, *Mankind in Barbary: The Individual and Society in the Novels of
Norman Mailer*, 1975; Jean Radford, *Norman Mailer: A Critical Study*, 1975; Jonathan Mid-
dlebrook, *Mailer and the Times of His Time*, 1976; Laura Adams, *Existential Battles: The Growth of
Norman Mailer*, 1976; W. J. Weatherby, *Squaring Off*, 1976; Philip H. Bufithis, *Norman Mailer*,
1978; Robert Ehrlich, *The Radical as Hipster*, 1978; Robert Merrill, *Norman Mailer*, 1978; Jen-
nifer Bailey, *Norman Mailer: Quick-Change Artist*, 1979; Robert J. Begiebing, *Acts of Regeneration:
Allegory and Archetype in the Works of Norman Mailer*, 1980; Andrew Gordon, *An American Dreamer:
A Psychoanalytic Study of Norman Mailer*, 1980; Hillary Mills, *Mailer: A Biography*, 1982; Peter
Manso, ed., *Mailer: His Life and Times*, 1985; J. Michael Lennon, ed., *Critical Essays on Norman
Mailer*, 1986; Joseph Wenke, *Mailer's America*, 1987.

TEXT

The Armies of the Night, 1968.

from The Armies of the Night

BOOK ONE
HISTORY AS A NOVEL: THE STEPS OF THE PENTAGON

from PART I:
THURSDAY EVENING

5: TOWARD A THEATER OF IDEAS[1]

The guests were beginning to leave the party for the Ambassador, which was two blocks away. Mailer did not know this yet, but the audience there had been waiting almost an hour. They were being entertained by an electronic folk rock guitar group, so presumably the young were more or less happy, and the middle-aged dim. Mailer was feeling the high sense of clarity which accompanies the light show of the aurora borealis when it is projected upon the inner universe of the chest, the lungs, and the heart. He was happy. On leaving, he had appropriated a coffee mug and filled it with bourbon. The fresh air illumined the bourbon, gave it a cerebrative edge; words entered his brain with the agreeable authority of fresh minted coins. Like all good professionals, he was stimulated by the chance to try a new if related line of work. Just as professional football players love sex because it is so close to football, so he was fond of speaking in public because it was thus near to writing. An extravagant analogy? Consider that a good half of writing consists of being sufficiently sensitive to the moment to reach for the next promise which is usually hidden in some word or phrase just a shift to the side of one's conscious intent. (Consciousness, that blunt tool, bucks in the general direction of the truth: instinct plucks the feather. Cheers!) Where public speaking is an exercise from prepared texts to demonstrate how successfully a low order of consciousness can beat upon the back of a collective flesh, public speaking being, therefore, a sullen expression of human possibility metaphorically equal to a bugger on his victim, speaking-in-public (as Mailer liked to describe any speech which was more or less improvised, impromptu, or dangerously written) was an activity like writing; one had to trick or seize or submit to the grace of each moment, which, except for those unexpected and sometimes well-deserved moments when consciousness and grace came together (and one felt on the consequence, heroic) were usually occasions of some mystery. The pleasure of speaking in public was the sensitivity it offered: with every phrase one was better or worse, close or less close to the existential promise of truth, *it feels true*, which hovers on good occasions like a presence between speaker and audience. Sometimes one was better, and worse, at the same moment; so strategic choices on the continuation of the attack would soon have to be decided, a moment to know the blood of the gambler in oneself.

Intimations of this approaching experience, obviously one of Mailer's preferred pleasures in life, at least when he did it well, were now connected to the professional sense of intrigue at the new task: tonight he would be both speaker and master of ceremonies. The two would conflict, but interestingly. Already he was looking in his mind for kind even celebrative remarks about Paul Goodman[2] which would not violate every reservation he had about Goodman's dank glory. But he had it. It would be possible with no violation of truth to begin by saying that the first speaker looked very much like Nelson Algren,[3] because in fact the first speaker was Paul Goodman, and

---

[1] At this point in the narrative of *The Armies of the Night* (relating the story of the March on the Pentagon in October 1967 in protest against the Vietnam War), Mailer has come to Washington to participate and is attending a party before going to a mass rally of the marchers and their supporters in a theater in downtown Washington.
[2] Paul Goodman (1911–1972), American social critic and writer, author of *Growing Up Absurd* (1960).
[3] Nelson Algren (1909–1981), American naturalistic novelist, author of *The Man with the Golden Arm* (1949).

both Nelson Algren and Paul Goodman looked like old cons.[4] Ladies and Gentlemen, without further ado let me introduce one of young America's favorite old cons, Paul Goodman! (It would not be necessary to add that where Nelson Algren looked like the sort of skinny old con who was in on every make in the joint, and would sign away Grandma's farm to stay in the game, Goodman looked like the sort of old con who had first gotten into trouble in the YMCA, and hadn't spoken to anyone since.)

All this while, Mailer had in clutch *Why Are We In Vietnam?* He had neglected to bring his own copy to Washington and so had borrowed the book from his hostess on the promise he would inscribe it. (Later he was actually to lose it — working apparently on the principle that if you cannot make a hostess happy, the next best charity is to be so evil that the hostess may dine out on tales of your misconduct.) But the copy of the book is now noted because Mailer, holding it in one hand and the mug of whisky in the other, was obliged to notice on entering the Ambassador Theater that he has an overwhelming urge to micturate. The impulse to pass urine, being for some reason more difficult to restrain when both hands are occupied, there was no thought in the Master of Ceremonies' mind about the alternatives — he would have to find The Room before he went on stage.

That was not so immediately simple as one would have thought. The twenty guests from the party, looking a fair piece subdued under the fluorescent lights, had therefore the not unhaggard look of people who have arrived an hour late at the theater. No matter that the theater was by every evidence sleazy (for neighborhood movie houses built on the dream of the owner that some day Garbo or Harlow or Lombard would give a look in, aged immediately they were not used for movies anymore) no matter, the guests had the uneasiness of very late arrivals. Apologetic, they were therefore in haste for the speakers to begin.

Mailer did not know this. He was off already in search of The Room, which, it developed was up on the balcony floor. Imbued with the importance of his first gig as Master of Ceremonies, he felt such incandescence of purpose that he could not quite conceive it necessary to notify de Grazia[5] he would be gone for a minute. Incandescence is the *satori*[6] of the Romantic spirit which spirit would insist — this is the essence of the Romantic — on accelerating time. The greater the power of any subjective state, the more total is a Romantic's assumption that everyone understands exactly what he is about to do, therefore waste not a moment by stopping to tell them.

Flush with his incandescence, happy in all the anticipation of liberty which this Götterdämmerung[7] of a urination was soon to provide. Mailer did not know, but he had already and unwitting to himself metamorphosed into the Beast. Wait and see!

He was met on the stairs by a young man from *Time* magazine, a stringer presumably, for the young man lacked that I-am-damned look in the eye and rep tie of those whose work for *Time* has become a life addiction. The young man had a somewhat ill-dressed look, a map showed on his skin of an old adolescent acne, and he gave off the unhappy furtive presence of a fraternity member on probation for the wrong thing, some grievous mis-deposit of vomit, some hanky panky with frat-house tickets.

But the Beast was in a great good mood. He was soon to speak; that was food for all. So the Beast greeted the *Time* man with the geniality of a surrogate Hemingway unbending for the Luce-ites[8] (Loo-sights was the pun) made some genial cryptic remark or two about finding Herr John, said cheerfully in answer to why he was in Washington that he had come to protest the war in Vietnam, and taking a sip of bourbon from the mug he kept to keep all fires idling right, stepped off into the darkness of the top balcony floor, went through a door into a pitch-black men's room,

---

[4]I.e., confidence men.
[5]Ed de Grazia, an organizer of the march on the Pentagon.
[6]From Zen Buddhism: sudden enlightenment.
[7]Destruction of the Gods (in German mythology); often

translated as the "Twilight of the Gods."
[8]Reference to Henry Luce (1898 – 1967), founder and editor of *Time*.

and was alone with his need. No chance to find the light switch for he had no matches, he did not smoke. It was therefore a matter of locating what's what with the probing of his toes. He found something finally which seemed appropriate, and pleased with the precision of these generally unused senses in his feet, took aim between them at a point twelve inches ahead, and heard in the darkness the sound of his water striking the floor. Some damn mistake had been made, an assault from the side doubtless instead of the front, the bowl was relocated now, and Master of Ceremonies breathed deep of the great reveries of this utterly non-Sisyphian[9] release — at last! — and thoroughly enjoyed the next forty-five seconds, being left on the aftermath not a note depressed by the condition of the premises. No, he was off on the Romantic's great military dream, which is: seize defeat, convert it to triumph. Of course, pissing on the floor was bad; very bad; the attendant would probably gossip to the police (if the *Time* man did not sniff it out first) and The Uniformed in turn would report it to The Press who were sure to write about the scandalous condition in which this meeting had left the toilets. And all of this contretemps merely because the management, bitter with their lost dream of Garbo and Harlow and Lombard, were now so pocked and stingy they doused the lights. (Out of such stuff is a novelist's brain.)

Well, he could convert this deficiency to an asset. From gap to gain is very American. He would confess straight out to all aloud that he was the one who wet the floor in the men's room, he alone! While the audience was recovering from the existential anxiety of encountering an orator who confessed to such a crime, he would be able — their attention now riveted — to bring them up to a contemplation of deeper problems, of, indeed, the deepest problems, the most chilling alternatives, and would from there seek to bring them back to a restorative view of man. Man might be a fool who peed in the wrong pot, man was also a scrupulous servant of the self-damaging admission; man was therefore a philosopher who possessed the magic stone; he could turn loss to philosophical gain, and so illumine the deeps, find the poles, and eventually learn to cultivate his most special fool's garden: *satori*, incandescence, and the hard gem-like flame of bourbon burning in the furnaces of metabolism.

Thus composed, illumined by these first stages of Emersonian transcendence, Mailer left the men's room, descended the stairs, entered the back of the orchestra, all opening remarks held close file in his mind like troops ranked in order before the parade, and then suddenly, most suddenly saw, with a cancerous swoop of albatross wings, that de Grazia was on the stage, was acting as M.C., was — no calling it back — launched into the conclusion of a gentle stammering stumbling — small orator, de Grazia! — introduction of Paul Goodman. All lost! The magnificent opening remarks about the forces gathered here to assemble on Saturday before the Pentagon, this historic occasion, let us hold it in our mind and focus on a puddle of passed water on the floor above and see if we assembled here can as leftists and proud dissenters contain within our minds the grandeur of the two — all lost! — no chance to do more than pick up later — later! after de Grazia and Goodman had finished dead-assing the crowd. Traitor de Grazia! Sicilian de Grazia!

As Mailer picked his way between people sitting on the stone floor (orchestra seats had been removed — the movie house was a dance hall now with a stage) he made a considerable stir in the orchestra. Mailer had been entering theaters for years, mounting stages — now that he had put on weight, it would probably have been fair to say that he came to the rostrum like a poor man's version of Orson Welles,[10] some minor note of the same contemplative presence. A titter and rise of expectation followed him. He could not resist its appeal. As he passed de Grazia, he scowled, threw a look from Lower Shakesperia "Et tu Bruté,"[11] and proceeded to slap the back

---

[9]Sisyphus was a legendary king condemned in Hades to rolling a stone up a hill repeatedly — as it always rolled down again.
[10]Orson Welles (1915– 1985), famous American actor and

director.
[11]Spoken by Julius Caesar to Marcus Brutus as Brutus stabs Caesar (Shakespeare's *Julius Caesar* III, i,77).

of his hand against de Grazia's solar plexus. It was not a heavy blow, but then de Grazia was not a heavy man; he wilted some hint of an inch. And the audience pinched off a howl, squeaked on their squeal. It was not certain to them what had taken place.

Picture the scene two minutes later from the orchestra floor. Paul Goodman, now up at the microphone with no podium or rostrum, is reading the following lines:

> . . . these days my contempt
> for the misrulers of my country
> is icy and my indignation raucous.

It is impossible to tell what he is reading. Off at the wing of the stage where the others are collected — stout Macdonald, noble Lowell,[12] beleaguered de Grazia, and Mailer, Prince of Bourbon, the acoustics are atrocious. One cannot hear a word the speaker is saying. Nor are there enough seats. If de Grazia and Macdonald are sitting in folding chairs, Mailer is squatting on his haunches or kneeling on one knee like a player about to go back into the ball game. Lowell has the expression on his face of a dues payer who is just about keeping up with the interest on some enormous debt. As he sits on the floor with his long arms clasped mournfully about his long Yankee legs, "I am here," says his expression, "but I do not have to pretend I like what I see." The hollows in his cheeks give a hint of the hanging judge. Lowell is of a good weight, not too heavy, not too light, but the hollows speak of the great Puritan gloom in which the country was founded — man was simply not good enough for God.

At this moment, it is hard not to agree with Lowell. The cavern of the theater seems to resonate behind the glare of the footlights, but this is no resonance of a fine bass voice — it is rather electronics on the march. The public address system hisses, then rings in a random chorus of electronic music, sound of a cerebral mastication from some horror machine of Outer Space (where all that electricity doubtless comes from, child!) then a hum like the squeak in the hinges of the gates of Hell — we are in the penumbra of psychedelic netherworlds, ghost-odysseys from the dead brain cells of adolescent trysts with LSD, some ultrapurple spotlight from the balcony (not ultraviolet — ultrapurple, deepest purple one could conceive) there out in the dark like some neon eye of the night, the media is the message, and the message is purple, speaks of the monarchies of Heaven, madnesses of God, and clam-vaults of people on a stone floor. Mailer's senses are now tuned to absolute pitch — or sheer error — he marks a ballot for absolute pitch — he is certain there is a profound pall in the audience. Yes, they sit there, stricken, inert, in terror of what Saturday will bring, and so are unable to rise to a word the speaker is offering them. It will take dynamite to bring life. The shroud of burned-out psychedelic dreams is in this audience, Cancer Gulch with open maw — and Mailer thinks of the vigor and the light (from marijuana?) in the eyes of those American soldiers in Vietnam who have been picked by the newsreel cameras to say their piece, and the happy healthy never unintelligent faces of all those professional football players he studies so assiduously on television come Sunday (he has neglected to put his bets in this week) and wonders how they would poll out on sentiment for the war.

HAWKS 95   DOVES 6

NFL Footballers Approve Vietnam War

Doubtless. All the healthy Marines, state troopers, professional athletes, movie stars, rednecks, sensuous life-loving Mafia, cops, mill workers, city officials, nice

---

[12]Dwight Macdonald(1906–1982), American social critic, pacifist, and anarchist, author of *Against the American Grain* (1963); Robert Lowell (1917–1977), American poet.

healthy-looking easy-grafting politicians full of the light (from marijuana?) in their eye of a life they enjoy — yes, they would be for the war in Vietnam. Arrayed against them as hard-core troops: an elite! the Freud-ridden embers of Marxism, good old American anxiety strata — the urban middle-class with their proliferated monumental adenoidal resentments, their secret slavish love for the oncoming hegemony of the computer and the suburb, yes, they and their children, by the sheer ironies, the sheer ineptitude, the *kinks* of history, were now being compressed into more and more militant stands, their resistance to the war some hopeless melange, somehow firmed, of Pacifism and closet Communism. And their children — on a freak-out from the suburbs to a love-in on the Pentagon wall.

It was the children in whom Mailer had some hope, a gloomy hope. These mad middle-class children with their lobotomies from sin, their nihilistic embezzlement of all middle-class moral funds, their innocence, their lust for apocalypse, their unbelievable indifference to waste: twenty generations of buried hopes perhaps engraved in their chromosomes, and now conceivably burning like faggots in the secret inquisitional fires of LSD. It was a devil's drug — designed by the Devil to consume the love of the best, and leave them liver-wasted, weeds of the big city. If there had been a player piano, Mailer might have put in a quarter to hear "In the Heart of the City Which Has No Heart."

Yes, these were the troops: middle-class cancer-pushers and drug-gutted flower children. And Paul Goodman to lead them. Was he now reading this?

> Once American faces
> were beautiful to me
> but now they look cruel
> and as if they had narrow thoughts.

Not much poetry, but well put prose. And yet there was always Goodman's damnable tolerance for all the varieties of sex. Did he know nothing of evil or entropy? Sex was the superhighway to your own soul's entropy if it was used without a constant sharpening of the taste. And orgies? What did Goodman know of orgies, real ones, not lib-lab college orgies to carry out the higher program of the Great Society, but real ones with murder in the air, and witches on the shoulder. The collected Tory in Mailer came roaring to the surface like a docked hat in a royal coach.

"When Goodman finishes, I'm going to take over as M. C.," he whispered to de Grazia. (The revery we have just attended took no more in fact than a second. Mailer's melancholy assessment of the forces now mounting in America took place between two consecutive lines of Goodman's poem — not because Mailer cerebrated that instantly, but because he had had the revery many a time before — he had to do no more than sense the audience, whisper Cancer Gulch to himself and the revery went by with a mental ch-ch-ch Click! reviewed again.) In truth, Mailer was now in a state. He had been prepared to open the evening with apocalyptic salvos to announce the real gravity of the situation, and the intensely peculiar American aspect of it — which is that the urban and suburban middle class were to be offered on Saturday an opportunity for glory — what other nation could boast of such option for its middle class? Instead — lost! The benignity and good humor of his planned opening remarks now subjugated to the electronic hawking and squabbling *hum* of the P. A., the maniacal necessity to *wait* was on this hiatus transformed into a violent concentration of purpose, all intentions reversed. He glared at de Grazia. "How could you do this?" he whispered to his ear.

De Grazia looked somewhat confused at the intensity. Meetings to de Grazia were obviously just meetings, assemblages of people who coughed up for large admissions or kicked in for the pitch; at best, some meetings were less boring than others. De Grazia was much too wise and guilty-spirited to brood on apocalypse. "I couldn't find you," he whispered back.

"You didn't trust me long enough to wait one minute?"

"We were over an hour late," de Grazia whispered again, "We had to begin."

Mailer was all for having the conversation right then on stage: to hell with recipro-
cal rights and polite incline of the ear to the speaker. The Beast was ready to grapple
with the world. "Did you think I wouldn't show up?" he asked de Grazia.

"Well, I was wondering."

In what sort of mumbo-jumbo of promise and betrayal did de Grazia live? How
could de Grazia ever suppose he would not show up? He had spent his life showing
up at the most boring and onerous places. He gave a blast of his eyes to de Grazia. But
Macdonald gave a look at Mailer, as if to say, "You're creating disturbance."

Now Goodman was done.

Mailer walked to the stage. He did not have any idea any longer of what he would
say, his mind was empty, but in a fine calm, taking for these five instants a total rest.
While there was no danger of Mailer ever becoming a demagogue since if the first
idea he offered could appeal to a mob, the second in compensation would be sure to
enrage them, he might, nonetheless have made a fair country orator, for he loved to
speak, he loved in fact to holler, and liked to hear a crowd holler back. (Of how many
New York intellectuals may that be said?)

"I'm here as your original M. C., temporarily displaced owing to a contretemps"—
which was pronounced purposefully as contretempse—"in the men's room," he said
into the microphone for opening, but the gentle high-strung beast of a device
pushed into a panic by the electric presence of a real Beast, let loose a squeal which
shook the welds in the old foundation of the Ambassador. Mailer immediately decided he had had enough of public address systems, electronic fields of phase, im-
pedance, and spooks in the circuitry. A hex on collaborating with Cancer Gulch. He
pushed the microphone away, squared off before the audience. "Can you hear me?"
he bellowed.

"Yes"

"Can you hear me in the balcony?"

"Yes."

"Then let's do away with electronics." he called out.

Cries of laughter came back. A very small pattern of applause. (Not too many on
his side for electrocuting the public address system, or so his orator's ear recorded
the vote.)

"Now I missed the beginning of this occasion, or I would have been here to introduce Paul Goodman, for which we're all sorry, right?"

Confused titters. Small reaction.

"What are you, dead-heads?" he bellowed at the audience. "Or are you all"—here
he put on his false Irish accent—"in the nature of becoming dead ahsses?" Small
laughs. A whistle or two. "No," he said, replying to the whistles. "I invoke these dead
asses as part of the gravity of the occasion. The middle class plus one hippie surrealistic symbolic absolutely insane March on the Pentagon, bless us all," beginning of a big
applause which offended Mailer for it came on "bless" and that was too cheap a way
to win votes, "bless us all—shit!" he shouted, "I'm trying to say the middle class plus
shit, I mean plus revolution, is equal to one big collective dead ass." Some yells of
approval, but much shocked curious rather stricken silence. He had broken the
shank of his oratorical charge. Now he would have to sweep the audience together
again. (Perhaps he felt like a surgeon delivering a difficult breech—nothing to do but
plunge to the elbows again.)

"To resume our exposition," a good warm titter, then a ripple of laughter, not
unsympathetic to his ear; the humor had been unwitting, but what was the life of an
orator without some bonus? "To resume this orderly marshalling of concepts"—a
conscious attempt at humor which worked less well; he was beginning to recognize
for the first time that bellowing without a mike demanded a more forthright style—

"I shall now *engage* in confession." More Irish accent. (He blessed Brendan Behan[13] for what he had learned from him.) "A public speaker may offer you two opportunities. Instruction or confession." Laughter now. "Well, you're all college heads, so my instruction would be as pearls before—I dare not say it." Laughs. Boos. A voice from the balcony: "Come on, Norman, say something!"

"Is there a black man in the house?" asked Mailer. He strode up and down the stage pretending to peer at the audience. But in fact they were illumined just well enough to emphasize one sad discovery—if black faces there were they were certainly not in plenty. "Well ah'll just have to be the *impromptu* Black Power for tonight. Woo-eeeeee! Woo-eeeeee! HMmmmmmm." He grunted with some partial success, showing hints of Cassius Clay. "Get your white butts moving."

"The confession. The confession!" screamed some adolescents from up front.

He came to a stop, shifted his voice. Now he spoke in a relaxed tone. "The confession, yeah!" Well, at least the audience was awake. He felt as if he had driven away some sepulchral phantoms of a variety which inhabited the profound middle-class schist.[14] Now to charge the center of vested spookery.

"Say," he called out into the semidarkness with the ultrapurple light coming off the psychedelic lamp on the rail of the balcony, and the spotlights blaring against his eyes. "say," all happiness again, "I think of Saturday, and that March and do you know, fellow carriers of the holy unendurable grail, for the first time in my life I don't know whether I have the piss or the shit scared out of me most." It was an interesting concept, thought Mailer, for there was a difference between the two kinds of fear— pursue the thought, he would, in quieter times—"we are up, face this, all of you, against an existential situation—we do not know how it is going to turn out, and what is even more inspiring of dread is that the government doesn't know either."

Beginning of a real hand, a couple of rebel yells. "We're going to try to stick it up the government's ass," he shouted, "right to the sphincter of the Pentagon." Wild yells and chills of silence from different reaches of the crowd. Yeah, he was cooking now. "Will reporters please get every word accurately," he called out dryly to warm the chill.

But humor may have been too late. *The New Yorker* did not have strictures against the use of sh*t for nothing; nor did Dwight Macdonald love *The New Yorker* for nothing, he also had strictures against sh*t's metaphorical associations. Mailer looked to his right to see Macdonald approaching, a book in his hands, arms at his side, a sorrowing look of concern in his face. "Norman," said Macdonald quietly, "I can't possibly follow you after all this. Please introduce me, and get it over with."

Mailer was near to stricken. On the one hand interrupted on a flight; on the other, he had fulfilled no duty whatsoever as M. C. He threw a look at Macdonald which said: give me this. I'll owe you one.

But de Grazia was there as well. "Norman, let me be M. C. now," he said.

They were being monstrous unfair, thought Mailer. They didn't understand what he had been doing, how good he had been, what he would do next. Fatal to walk off now—the verdict would claim he was unbalanced. Still, he could not hold the stage by force. That was unthinkably worse.

For the virtuous, however, deliverance (like buttercups) pops up everywhere. Mailer now took the microphone and turned to the audience. He was careful to speak in a relaxed voice. "We are having a disagreement about the value of the proceedings. Some think de Grazia should resume his post as Master of Ceremonies. I would like to keep the position. It is an existential moment. We do not know how it will turn out. So let us vote on it." Happy laughter from the audience at these comic effects. Actually Mailer did not believe it was an existential situation any longer. He

---

[13]Brendan Behan (1923–1964), Irish author and playwright, notorious for his drinking bouts.

[14]Any of a class of crystalline, metamorphic rocks. layered or foliated.

reckoned the vote would be well in his favor. "Will those," he asked, "who are in favor of Mr. de Grazia succeeding me as Master of Ceremonies please say aye."

A good sound number said aye.

Now for the ovation. "Will those opposed to this, please say no." The no's to Mailer's lack of pleasure were no greater in volume. "It seems the ayes and no's are about equal." said Mailer. (He was thinking to himself that he had posed the issue all wrong—the ayes should have been reserved for those who would keep him in office.) "Under the circumstances," he announced, "I will keep the chair." Laughter at this easy cheek. He stepped into the middle of such laughter. "You have all just learned an invaluable political lesson." He waved the microphone at the audience. "In the absence of a definitive vote, the man who holds the power, keeps it."

"Hey, de Grazia," someone yelled from the audience, "why do you let him have it?"

Mailer extended the microphone to de Grazia who smiled sweetly into it. "Because if I don't," he said in a gentle voice, "he'll beat the shit out of me." The dread word had been used again.

"Please, Norman," said Macdonald retreating.

So Mailer gave his introduction to Macdonald. It was less than he would have attempted if the flight had not been grounded, but certainly respectable. Under the military circumstances, it was a decent cleanup operation. For about a minute he proceeded to introduce Macdonald as a man with whom one might seldom agree, but could never disrespect because he always told the truth as he saw the truth, a man therefore of the most incorruptible integrity. "Pray heaven, I am right," said Mailer to himself, and walked past Macdonald who was on his way to the mike. Both men nodded coolly to each other.

In the wing, visible to the audience, Paul Goodman sat on a chair clearly avoiding any contaminatory encounter with The Existentialist. De Grazia gave his "It's tough all over" smile. Lowell sat in a mournful hunch on the floor, his eyes peering over his glasses to scrutinize the metaphysical substance of his boot, now hide? now machine? now, where the joining and to what? foot to foot, boot to earth—cease all speculations as to what was in Lowell's head. "The one mind a novelist cannot enter is the mind of a novelist superior to himself," said once to Mailer by Jean Malaquais.[15] So by corollary, the one mind a minor poet may not enter. . .

Lowell looked most unhappy. Mailer, minor poet, had often observed that Lowell had the most disconcerting mixture of strength and weakness in his presence, a blending so dramatic in its visible sign of conflict that one had to assume he would be sensationally attractive to women. He had something untouchable, all insane in its force; one felt immediately there were any number of causes for which the man would be ready to die, and for some he would fight, with an axe in his hand and a Cromwellian[16] light in his eye. It was even possible that physically he was very strong—one couldn't tell at all—he might be fragile, he might have the sort of farm mechanic's strength which could manhandle the rear axle and differential off a car and into the back of a pickup. But physical strength or no, his nerves were all too apparently delicate. Obviously spoiled by everyone for years, he seemed nonetheless to need the spoiling. These nerves—the nerves of a consummate poet—were not tuned to any battering. The squalls of the mike, now riding up a storm on the erratic piping breath of Macdonald's voice, seemed to tear along Lowell's back like a gale. He detested tumult—obviously. And therefore, saw everything which was hopeless in a rife situation: the dank middle-class depths of the audience, the strident squalor of the mike, the absurdity of talent gathered to raise money—for what, dear God? who

[15]Jean Malaquais (b. 1908), Polish-born French novelist who became an American citizen in 1952.
[16]Oliver Cromwell (1599–1658), English Puritan leader who defeated the Royalists and had King Charles I (1625–1649) beheaded.

could finally know what this March might convey, or worse, purvey, and worst of all—to be associated now with Mailer's butcher boy attack. Lowell's eyes looked up from the shoe, and passed one withering glance by the novelist, saying much, saying, "Every single bad thing I have ever heard about you is not exaggerated."

Mailer, looking back, thought bitter words he would not say: "You, Lowell, beloved poet of many, what do you know of the dirt and the dark deliveries of the necessary? What do you know of dignity hard-achieved, and dignity lost through innocence, and dignity lost by sacrifice for a cause one cannot name. What do you know about getting fat against your will, and turning into a clown of an arriviste baron when you would rather be an eagle or a count, or rarest of all, some natural aristocrat from these damned democratic states. No, the only subject we share, you and I, is that species of perception which shows that if we are not very loyal to our unendurable and most exigent inner light, then some day we may burn. How dare you condemn me! You know the diseases which inhabit the audience in this accursed psychedelic house. How dare you scorn the explosive I employ?"

And Lowell with a look of the greatest sorrow as if all this *mess* were finally too shapeless for the hard Protestant smith of his own brain, which would indeed burst if it could not forge his experience into the iron edge of the very best words and the most unsinkable relation of words, now threw up his eyes like an epileptic as if turned out of orbit by a turn of the vision—and fell backward, his head striking the floor with no last instant hesitation to cushion the blow, but like a baby, downright sudden, savagely to himself, as if from the height of a foot he had taken a pumpkin and dropped it splat on the floor. "There, much-regarded, much-protected brain, you have finally taken a blow," Lowell might have said to himself, for he proceeded to lie there, resting quietly, while Macdonald went on reading from "The White Man's Burden," Lowell seeming as content as if he had just tested the back of his cranium against a policeman's club. What a royal head they had all to lose!

• • • • •

from PART II:
FRIDAY AFTERNOON

1: THE HISTORIAN[1]

To write an intimate history of an event which places its focus on a central figure who is not central to the event, is to inspire immediate questions about the competence of the historian. Or, indeed, his honorable motive. The figure he has selected may be convenient to him rather than critical to the history. Such cynical remarks obviously suggest themselves in the choice of our particular protagonist. It could be said that for this historian, there is no other choice. While that might not be necessarily inaccurate, nonetheless a presentation of his good motives had best be offered now.

The March on the Pentagon was an ambiguous event whose essential value or absurdity may not be established for ten or twenty years, or indeed ever. So to place the real principals, the founder or designers of the March, men like David Dellinger, or Jerry Rubin,[2] in the center of our portrait could prove misleading. They were serious men, devoted to hard detailed work; their position in these affairs, precisely because it was central, can resolve nothing of the ambiguity. For that, an eyewitness who is a participant but not a vested partisan is required, further he must be not only involved, but ambiguous in his own proportions, a comic hero, which is to say, one cannot happily resolve the emphasis of the category—is he finally comic, a ludicrous

---

[1]Throughout *The Armies of the Night*, Mailer explains his method of writing "history as a novel"; here he justifies making himself his own comic hero.

[2]Dellinger and Rubin were active in the movement against the Vietnam War and had helped plan the march on the Pentagon.

figure with mock-heroic associations; or is he not unheroic, and therefore embedded somewhat tragically in the comic? Or is he both at once, and all at once? These questions, which probably are not much more answerable than the very ambiguities of the event, at least help to recapture the precise feel of the ambiguity of the event and its monumental disproportions. Mailer is a figure of monumental disproportions and so serves willy-nilly as the bridge—many will say the *pons asinorum*—[3] into the crazy house, the crazy mansion, of that historic moment when a mass of the citizenry—not much more than a mob—marched on a bastion which symbolized the military might of the Republic, marching not to capture it, but to wound it *symbolically*; the forces defending that bastion reacted as if a symbolic wound could prove as mortal as any other combative rent. In the midst of a technological century, close to its apogee, a medieval, nay, a primitve mode of warfare was reinvigorated, and the nations of the world stood in grave observation. Either the century was entrenching itself more deeply into the absurd, or the absurd was delivering evidence that it was possessed of some of the nutritive mysteries of a marrow which would yet feed the armies of the absurd. So if the event took place in one of the crazy mansions, or indeed *the* crazy house of history, it is fitting that any ambiguous comic hero of such history should be not only off very much to the side of the history, but that he should be an egotist of the most startling misproportions, outrageously and often unhappily self-assertive, yet in command of a detachment classic in severity (for he was a novelist and so in need of studying every last lineament of the fine, the noble, the frantic, and the foolish in others and in himself). Such egotism being two-headed, thrusting itself forward the better to study itself, finds itself therefore at home in a house of mirrors, since it has habits, even the talent, to regard itself. Once History inhabits a crazy house, egotism may be the last tool left to History.

Let us then make our comic hero the narrative vehicle for the March on the Pentagon. Let us follow further. He is awakening Friday morning in his room at the Hay-Adams after his night on the stage of the Ambassador and the party thereafter. One may wonder if the Adams in the name of his hotel bore any relation to Henry[4]; we need not be concerned with Hay[5] who was a memorable and accomplished gentleman from the nineteenth century (then Secretary of State to McKinley and Roosevelt) other than to say that the hotel looked like its name, and was indeed the staunchest advocate of that happy if heavy style in Washington architecture which spoke of a time when men and events were solid, comprehensible, often obedient to a code of values, and resolutely nonelectronic. Mailer awakening with a thunderous electronic headache began his morning revery with a conclusion that the Georgian period in architecture was not resolutely suited to himself.

· · · · ·

from PART III:
SATURDAY MATINÉE

6: A CONFRONTATION BY THE RIVER

It was not much of a situation to study.[1] The MPs stood in two widely spaced ranks. The first rank was ten yards behind the rope, and each MP in that row was

---

[3]"Asses' bridge"(Latin); any device for beginners or simpletons.
[4]Henry Adams (1838–1918), American historian; son of Charles Francis Adams (1807–1886), American diplomat; grandson of John Quincy Adams (1767–1848), sixth U. S. president; and author of *The Education of Henry Adams* (1907).
[5]John Milton Hay (1838–1905), American diplomat and writer, was Secretary of State (1898–1905) under William McKinley (1843–1901), twenty-fifth U. S. president (1896–1901), and Theodore Roosevelt (1858–1919), twenty-sixth

U. S. president (1901–09).
[1]The marchers on the Pentagon were confined by authorities to a large, nearby parking lot; after prolonged demonstration with many speeches, Mailer decided that he would force his own arrest by violating the rules set by government authorities in uneasy charge of containing the demonstrators. The "situation" was that the marchers were separated from the Pentagon by rings of Military Police set to prevent any breakthroughs.

close to twenty feet from the next man. The second rank, similarly spaced, was ten yards behind the first rank and perhaps thirty yards behind them a cluster appeared, every fifty yards or so, of two or three U. S. Marshals in white helmets and dark blue suits. They were out there waiting. Two moods confronted one another, two separate senses of a private silence.

It was not unlike being a boy about to jump from one garage roof to an adjoining garage roof. The one thing not to do was wait. Mailer looked at Macdonald and Lowell. "Let's go," he said. Not looking again at them, not pausing to gather or dissipate resolve, he made a point of stepping neatly and decisively over the low rope. Then he headed across the grass to the nearest MP he saw.

It was as if the air had changed, or light had altered; he felt immediately much more alive—yes, bathed in air—and yet disembodied from himself, as if indeed he were watching himself in a film where this action was taking place. He could feel the eyes of the people behind the rope watching him, could feel the intensity of their existence as spectators. And as he walked forward, he and the MP looked at one another with the naked stricken lucidity which comes when absolute strangers are for the moment absolutely locked together.

The MP lifted his club to his chest as if to bar all passage. To Mailer's great surprise—he had secretly expected the enemy to be calm and strong, why should they not? they had every power, all the guns—to his great surprise, the MP was trembling. He was a young Negro, part white, who looked to have come from some small town where perhaps there were not many other Negroes; he had at any rate no Harlem smoke, no devil swish, no black, no black power for him, just a simple boy in an Army suit with a look of horror in his eye, "Why, why did it have to happen to me?" was the message of the petrified marbles in his face.

"Go back," he said hoarsely to Mailer.

"If you don't arrest me, I'm going to the Pentagon."

"No. Go back."

The thought of a return—"since they won't arrest me, what can I do?"—over these same ten yards was not at all suitable.

As the MP spoke, the raised club quivered. He did not know if it quivered from the desire of the MP to strike him, or secret military wonder was he now possessed of a moral force which implanted terror in the arms of young soldiers? Some unfamiliar current, now gyroscopic, now a sluggish whirlpool, was evolving from that quiver of the club, and the MP seemed to turn slowly away from his position confronting the rope, and the novelist turned with him, each still facing the other until the axis of their shoulders was not perpendicular to the rope, and still they kept turning in this psychic field, not touching, the club quivering, and then Mailer was behind the MP, he was free of him, and he wheeled around and kept going in a half run to the next line of MPs and then on the push of a sudden instinct, sprinted suddenly around the nearest MP in the second line, much as if he were a back cutting around the nearest man in the secondary to break free—that was actually his precise thought—and had a passing perception of how simple it was to get past the MPs. They looked petrified. Stricken faces as he went by. They did not know what to do. It was his dark pinstripe suit, his vest, the maroon and blue regimental tie, the part in his hair, the barrel chest, the early paunch—he must have looked like a banker himself, a banker, gone ape! And then he saw the Pentagon to his right across the field, not a hundred yards away, and a little to his left, the marshals, and he ran on a jog toward them, and came up, and they glared at him and shouted, "Go back."

He had a quick impression of hard-faced men with gray eyes burning some transparent fuel for flame, and said, "I won't go back. If you don't arrest me, I'm going on to the Pentagon," and knew he meant it, some absolute certainty had come to him, and then two of them leaped on him at once in the cold clammy murderous fury of all cops at the existential moment of making their bust—all cops who secretly expect to be struck at that instant for their sins—and a supervising force came to his voice, and he roared, to his own distant pleasure in new achievement and new authority—"Take your hands off me, can't you see? I'm not resisting arrest," and one then let go of him, and the other stopped trying to pry his arm into a lock, and contented himself with a hard hand under his armpit, and they set off walking across the field at a rabid intent quick rate, walking parallel to the wall of the Pentagon, fully visible on his right at last, and he was arrested, he had succeeded in that, and without a club on his head, the mountain air in his lungs as thin and fierce as smoke, yes, the livid air of tension on this livid side promised a few events of more interest than the routine wait to be free, yes he was more than a visitor, he was in the land of the enemy now, he would get to see their face.

1968

N. SCOTT MOMADAY
(b. 1934)

N. Scott Momaday, an American of Kiowa Indian ancestry, has remarked about his aim as a writer: "When I was growing up on the reservations of the Southwest, I saw people who were deeply involved in their traditional life, in the memories of their blood. They had, as far as I could see, a certain strength and beauty that I find missing in the modern world at large. I like to celebrate that involvement in my writing."

Speaking of the Indian's special relationship with the earth, Momaday has disavowed the theme of alienation popular in contemporary literature:

> On the basis of my experience, trusting my own perceptions, I don't see any validity in the separation of man and landscape. Oh, I know that the notion of alienation is very widespread, in a sense very popular. But I think it's an unfortunate point of view and a false one, where the relationship between man and the earth is concerned. Certainly it is one of the great afflictions of our time, this conviction of alienation, separation, isolation. And it is certainly an affliction in the Indian world. But there it has the least chance of taking hold, I believe, for there it is opposed by very strong forces. The whole world view of the Indian is predicated upon the principle of harmony in the universe. You can't tinker with that; it has the look of an absolute.

Momaday was born in Lawton, Oklahoma, in 1934, to a father who was a painter and teacher, and a mother who was a writer and teacher. His Kiowa name was Tsoai-talee, or "Rock-tree-Boy," a name the Kiowas call a volcanic butte in Wyoming sacred to their history; it is known on American maps as Devil's Tower. In 1935, the family moved to New Mexico, where Momaday grew up on Indian reservations. He was educated at the University of New Mexico, graduating with a B.A. in 1958. He took an M.A. at Stanford University in 1960, and a Ph.D. in English in 1963. He wrote his dissertation on Frederick Goddard Tuckerman, and in 1965 edited Tuckerman's *Complete Poems* for Oxford Press. The poet-critic Yvor Winters, a professor at Stanford, was a major influence on Momaday, encouraging him not only in his degree program but in his creative writing.

Momaday had always known he was Indian, but he dates his deep awareness of his Indian identity to an experience in adulthood: "I think of myself as an Indian because at one time in my life I suddenly realized that my father had grown up speaking a language that I didn't grow up speaking, that my forebears on his side had made a migration from Canada along with . . . Athapaskan peoples that I knew nothing about, and so I determined to find out something about these things and in the process I acquired an identity; it is an Indian identity, as far as I am concerned."

Momaday was initiated into the mysteries of the Kiowa tribe by his revered Indian grandmother Aho. She revealed to him that the Kiowa tribe's Sun dance fetish, the sacred "Tai-me bundle," still existed even though the last dance was performed in 1887. The sacred icon had been passed on from the Kiowa keeper, on his death, to his daughter. Momaday travelled with his grandmother and his father to Oklahoma to see the hallowed doll: "From the time I stood before the Tai-me issikia I knew a certain restlessness. I felt that I had come to know something about myself I had never known before. I became more keenly aware of myself as someone who had walked through time and in whose blood there is something inestimably old and undying."

Shortly after this trip, Momaday's grandmother died, and was buried in the Kiowa burial grounds in Rainy Mountain cemetery in Oklahoma. Momaday made a pilgrimage there to see his grandmother's grave and the graves of many other ancestors. He also sought out in Northeastern Wyoming the sacred Rock-tree-Boy (or Devil's Tower), after which he was named and which figured importantly in Kiowa mythology. The Kiowas had migrated to Oklahoma from the Northwest, and Rock-tree-Boy was part of their sacred oral history. Gradually the idea for an account of his and the Kiowa past took shape in Momaday's imagination, and it finally appeared as a book. *The Journey to Tai-me* appeared in a limited edition in 1967, and was enlarged and retitled *The Way to Rainy Mountain* in 1969, with illustrations provided by Momaday's artist-father.

Momaday's other books include a novel, *House Made of Dawn* (1968), which was awarded the Pulitzer Prize for fiction in 1969; two volumes of poems, *Angle of Geese and Other Poems* (1974) and *The Gourd Dancer* (1976); and an autobiographical work, *The Names: A Memoir* (1976). His plans for the future encompass not only fiction but also a work on storytelling. He said in a 1983 interview: "I'm interested in the origin of storytelling and the function of the storyteller and what his relationship is to his listener. There is an awful lot to be learned about that. I will, of course, focus on American Indian storytelling, but I also want to be able to make references to other ancient forms of storytelling." Readers can look forward to Momaday's redemptive celebrations of the "strength and beauty" of the American Indian past.

ADDITIONAL READING

Ancestral Voice: Conversations with N. Scott Momaday, ed. Charles L. Woodard, 1989.

Martha Scott Trimble, *N. Scott Momaday*, 1973; Matthias Schubnell, *N. Scott Momaday: The Cultural and Literary Background*, 1985; Kenneth M. Roemer, ed., *Approaches to Teaching Momaday's The Way to Rainy Mountain*, 1988.

TEXT

The Way to Rainy Mountain, 1969.

from The Way to Rainy Mountain

[RETURN TO RAINY MOUNTAIN]

A single knoll rises out of the plain in Oklahoma, north and west of the Wichita Range. For my people, the Kiowas,[1] it is an old landmark, and they gave it the name Rainy Mountain. The hardest weather in the world is there. Winter brings blizzards, hot tornadic winds arise in the spring, and in summer the prairie is an anvil's edge. The grass turns brittle and brown, and it cracks beneath your feet. There are green belts along the rivers and creeks, linear groves of hickory and pecan, willow and witch hazel. At a distance in July or August the steaming foliage seems almost to writhe in fire. Great green and yellow grasshoppers are everywhere in the tall grass, popping up like corn to sting the flesh, the tortoises crawl about on the red earth, going nowhere in the plenty of time. Loneliness is an aspect of the land. All things in the plain are isolate; there is no confusion of objects in the eye, but *one* hill or *one* tree or *one* man. To look upon that landscape in the early morning, with the sun at your back, is to lose the sense of proportion. Your imagination comes to life, and this, you think, is where Creation was begun.

I returned to Rainy Mountain in July. My grandmother had died in the spring, and I wanted to be at her grave. She had lived to be very old and at last infirm. Her only living daughter was with her when she died, and I was told that in death her face was that of a child.

I like to think of her as a child. When she was born, the Kiowas were living the last great moment of their history. For more than a hundred years they had controlled the open range from the Smoky Hill River to the Red, from the headwaters of the Canadian to the fork of the Arkansas and Cimarron. In alliance with the Comanches, they had ruled the whole of the southern Plains. War was their sacred business, and they were among the finest horsemen the world has ever known. But warfare for the Kiowas was preeminently a matter of disposition rather than of survival, and they never understood the grim, unrelenting advance of the U. S. Cavalry. When at last, divided and ill-provisioned, they were driven onto the Staked Plains in the cold rains of autumn, they fell into panic. In Palo Duro Canyon they abandoned their crucial stores to pillage and had nothing then but their lives. In order to save themselves, they surrendered to the soldiers at Fort Sill and were imprisoned in the old stone corral that now stands as a military museum. My grandmother was spared the humiliation of those high gray walls by eight or ten years, but she must have known from birth the affliction of defeat, the dark brooding of old warriors.

Her name was Aho, and she belonged to the last culture to evolve in North America. Her forebears came down from the high country in western Montana nearly three centuries ago. They were a mountain people, a mysterious tribe of hunters whose language has never been positively classified in any major group. In the late seventeenth century they began a long migration to the south and east. It was a journey toward the dawn, and it led to a golden age. Along the way the Kiowas were befriended by the Crows,[2] who gave them the culture and religion of the Plains. They acquired horses, and their ancient nomadic spirit was suddenly free of the ground. They acquired Tai-me, the sacred Sun Dance doll, from that moment the object and symbol of their worship, and so shared in the divinity of the sun. Not least, they acquired the sense of destiny, therefore courage and pride. When they entered

---

[1]Plains Indians inhabiting the southwestern United States.
[2]Siouan Indians inhabiting Montana, the upper basin of Yellowstone and Big Horn rivers.

upon the southern Plains they had been transformed. No longer were they slaves to the simple necessity of survival; they were a lordly and dangerous society of fighters and thieves, hunters and priests of the sun. According to their origin myth, they entered the world through a hollow log. From one point of view, their migration was the fruit of an old prophecy, for indeed they emerged from a sunless world.

Although my grandmother lived out her long life in the shadow of Rainy Mountain, the immense landscape of the continental interior lay like memory in her blood. She could tell of the Crows, whom she had never seen, and of the Black Hills, where she had never been. I wanted to see in reality what she had seen more perfectly in the mind's eye, and traveled fifteen hundred miles to begin my pilgrimage.

Yellowstone, it seemed to me, was the top of the world, a region of deep lakes and dark timber, canyons and waterfalls. But, beautiful as it is, one might have the sense of confinement there. The skyline in all directions is close at hand, the high wall of the woods and deep cleavages of shade. There is a perfect freedom in the mountains, but it belongs to the eagle and the elk, the badger and the bear. The Kiowas reckoned their stature by the distance they could see, and they were bent and blind in the wilderness.

Descending eastward, the highland meadows are a stairway to the plain. In July the inland slope of the Rockies is luxuriant with flax and buckwheat, stonecrop and larkspur. The earth unfolds and the limit of the land recedes. Clusters of trees, and animals grazing far in the distance, cause the vision to reach away and wonder to build upon the mind. The sun follows a longer course in the day, and the sky is immense beyond all comparison. The great billowing clouds that sail upon it are shadows that move upon the grain like water, dividing light. Farther down, in the land of the Crows and Blackfeet,[3] the plain is yellow. Sweet clover takes hold of the hills and bends upon itself to cover and seal the soil. There the Kiowas paused on their way; they had come to the place where they must change their lives. The sun is at home on the plains. Precisely there does it have the certain character of a god. When the Kiowas came to the land of the Crows, they could see the dark lees of the hills at dawn across the Bighorn River, the profusion of light on the grain shelves, the oldest deity ranging after the solstices. Not yet would they veer southward to the caldron of the land that lay below; they must wean their blood from the northern winter and hold the mountains a while longer in their view. They bore Tai-me in procession to the east.

A dark mist lay over the Black Hills, and the land was like iron. At the top of a ridge I caught sight of Devil's Tower[4] upthrust against the gray sky as if in the birth of time the core of the earth had broken through its crust and the motion of the world was begun. There are things in nature that engender an awful quiet in the heart of man; Devil's Tower is one of them. Two centuries ago, because they could not do otherwise, the Kiowas made a legend at the base of the rock. My grandmother said: *Eight children were there at play, seven sisters and their brother. Suddenly the boy was struck dumb; he trembled and began to run upon his hands and feet. His fingers became claws, and his body was covered with fur. Directly there was a bear where the boy had been. The sisters were terrified; they ran, and the bear after them. They came to the stump of a great tree, and the tree spoke to them. It bade them climb upon it, and as they did so it began to rise into the air. The bear came to kill them, but they were just beyond its reach. It reared against the tree and scored the bark all around with its claws. The seven sisters were borne into the sky, and they became the stars of the Big Dipper.*

From that moment, and so long as the legend lives, the Kiowas have kinsmen in the night sky. Whatever they were in the mountains, they could be no more. However

---

[3] An Algonquin Indian tribe inhabiting Montana and parts of Canada.

[4] A natural monolith in Devil's Tower National Monument in northeastern Wyoming.

tenuous their well-being, however much they had suffered and would suffer again, they had found a way out of the wilderness.

My grandmother had a reverence for the sun, a holy regard that now is all but gone out of mankind. There was a wariness in her, and ancient awe. She was a Christian in her later years, but she had come a long way about, and she never forgot her birthright. As a child she had been to the Sun Dances; she had taken part in those annual rites, and by them she had learned the restoration of her people in the presence of Tai-me. She was about seven when the last Kiowa Sun Dance was held in 1887 on the Washita River above Rainy Mountain Creek. The buffalo were gone. In order to consummate the ancient sacrifice — to impale the head of a buffalo bull upon the medicine tree — a delegation of old men journeyed into Texas, there to beg and barter for an animal from the Goodnight herd. She was ten when the Kiowas came together for the last time as a living Sun Dance culture. They could find no buffalo; they had to hang an old hide from the sacred tree. Before the dance could begin, a company of soldiers rode out from Fort Sill under orders to disperse the tribe. Forbidden without cause the essential act of their faith, having seen the wild herds slaughtered and left to rot upon the ground, the Kiowas backed away forever from the medicine tree. That was July 20, 1890, at the great bend of the Washita. My grandmother was there. Without bitterness, and for as long as she lived, she bore a vision of a deicide.

Now that I can have her only in memory, I see my grandmother in the several postures that were peculiar to her: standing at the wood stove on a winter morning and turning meat in a great iron skillet; sitting at the south window, bent above her beadwork, and afterwards, when her vision failed, looking down for a long time into the fold of her hands; going out upon a cane, very slowly as she did when the weight of age came upon her; praying. I remember her most often at prayer. She made long, rambling prayers out of suffering and hope, having seen many things. I was never sure that I had the right to hear, so exclusive were they of all mere custom and company. The last time I saw her she prayed standing by the side of her bed at night, naked to the waist, the light of a kerosene lamp moving upon her dark skin. Her long, black hair, always drawn and braided in the day, lay upon her shoulders and against her breasts like a shawl. I do not speak Kiowa, and I never understood her prayers, but there was something inherently sad in the sound, some merest hesitation upon the syllables of sorrow. She began in a high and descending pitch, exhausting her breath to silence; then again and again — and always the same intensity of effort, of something that is, and is not, like urgency in the human voice. Transported so in the dancing light among the shadows of her room, she seemed beyond the reach of time. But that was illusion: I think I knew then that I should not see her again.

Houses are like sentinels in the plain, old keepers of the weather watch. There, in a very little while, wood takes on the appearance of great age. All colors wear soon away in the wind and rain, and then the wood is burned gray and the grain appears and the nails turn red with rust. The windowpanes are black and opaque; you imagine there is nothing within, and indeed there are many ghosts, bones given up to the land. They stand here and there against the sky, and you approach them for a longer time than you expect. They belong in the distance; it is their domain.

Once there was a lot of sound in my grandmother's house, a lot of coming and going, feasting and talk. The summers there were full of excitement and reunion. The Kiowas are a summer people; they abide the cold and keep to themselves, but when the season turns and the land becomes warm and vital they cannot hold still; an old love of going returns upon them. The aged visitors who came to my grandmother's house when I was a child were made of lean and leather, and they bore themselves upright. They wore great black hats and bright ample shirts that shook in the wind. They rubbed fat upon their hair and wound their braids with strips of colored cloth. Some of them painted their faces and carried the scars of old and cherished enmities. They were an old council of warlords, come to remind and be reminded of who they were. Their wives and daughters served them well. The women might indulge themselves; gossip was at once the mark and compensation of their servitude. They made loud and elaborate talk among themselves, full of jest and gesture, fright and false alarm. They went abroad in fringed and flowered shawls, bright beadwork and German silver. They were at home in the kitchen, and they prepared meals that were banquets.

There were frequent prayer meetings, and great nocturnal feasts. When I was a child I played with my cousins outside, where the lamplight fell upon the ground and the singing of the old people rose up around us and carried away into the darkness. There were a lot of good things to eat, a lot of laughter and surprise. And afterwards, when the quiet returned, I lay down with my grandmother and could hear the frogs away by the river and feel the motion of the air.

Now there is a funeral silence in the rooms, the endless wake of some final word. The walls have closed in upon my grandmother's house. When I returned to it in mourning, I saw for the first time in my life how small it was. It was late at night, and there was a white moon, nearly full. I sat for a long time on the stone steps by the kitchen door. From there I could see out across the land; I could see the long row of trees by the creek, the low light upon the rolling plains, and the stars of the Big Dipper. Once I looked at the moon and caught sight of a strange thing. A cricket had perched upon the handrail, only a few inches away from me. My line of vision was such that the creature filled the moon like a fossil. It had gone there, I thought, to live and die, for there, of all places, was its small defintion made whole and eternal. A warm wind rose up and purled like the longing within me.

The next morning I awoke at dawn and went out on the dirt road to Rainy Mountain. It was already hot, and the grasshoppers began to fill the air. Still, it was early in the morning, and the birds sang out of the shadows. The long yellow grass on the mountain shone in the bright light, and a scissortail hied above the land. There, where it ought to be, at the end of a long and legendary way, was my grandmother's grave. Here and there on the dark stones were ancestral names. Looking back once, I saw the mountain and came away.

1967, 1969

WILLIAM LEAST HEAT MOON
(b. 1939)

In 1978, a man by the name of William Trogdon found himself out of work and his marriage on the rocks. His response was to reclaim his Native American name, William Least Heat Moon, and to begin a journey through America in an attempt to recover his lost self and rediscover a lost America. He set off in a van carrying his few possessions and only two books: Walt Whitman's *Leaves of Grass* and John Neihardt's *Black Elk Speaks*. In a blue mood, he kept to the "blue highways"—those backroads, colored blue on the maps, that meander through the rural areas of the United States. He started from Columbia, Missouri, the location of the college where he had taught, made his way to the east coast and then around the periphery of the country, deliberately travelling alone and without a dog so that he would feel compelled to strike up friendships with the strangers he encountered.

The book that grew out of the experience went through many revisions and finally found publication in 1982 as *Blue Highways*. It was an immediate critical and popular success, becoming a best-seller. One of the features of the book was the photographs of the people Heat Moon came to know on his journey. At one point the publisher had decided to remove all of the photographs because of the excessive cost of printing them. In spite of the fact that Heat Moon had spent four years finding a publisher, he threatened to withdraw the book if the photographs did not appear. In an interview, Heat Moon commented: "I think a good bit of success that *Blue Highways* has found derives from those photographs. It's important for readers to know that the people I spoke with are actual people."

William Trogdon was born in 1939 in Kansas City, Missouri. He tells the story of the origin of his Indian name in his book: "My father calls himself Heat Moon, my elder brother Little Heat Moon. I, coming last, am therefore Least. It has been a long lesson of a name to learn. To the Siouan peoples, the Moon of Heat is the seventh month, a time also known as the Blood Moon — I think because of its dusky midsummer color." The name William Trogdon came from an ancestor killed during the Revolutionary War for "providing food to rebel patriots." He "thereby got his name in volume four of *Makers of America.*" Heat Moon was educated at the University of Missouri, taking a Ph.D. in English in 1973 and a B.A. in photojournalism in 1978. The success of his book has brought him around full circle to teaching again at the University of Missouri — as a lecturer in the School of Journalism.

In an interview in 1985, Heat Moon pointed out the importance of distinguishing between the "actual journey" he made and "the book that came out of that journey":

> Of those three hundred pages I mentioned that I had to cut [out of the 800-page draft], a good bit was commentary about that so-called search for self. My concept of *Blue Highways* — as it developed in the writing — was to make it a book not so much about me, but, to use the expression, about Everyman — or maybe in this case I should say Anyman, any person who finds that it's time to start anew and who begins by putting himself into motion. I hope that the physical motion of the trip reflects Heat Moon's — the traveler's — own spiritual motion. I think a lot of reviewers missed most of the spiritual movement in the book and consequently had very little idea of the structure of *Blue Highways*, how it's based on the Hopi Maze of Migration, the Maze of Emergence. To circle about and emerge.

Blue Highways belongs to a genre of American travel literature that includes a number of fascinating volumes such as John Steinbeck's *Travels with Charley in Search of America* (1962) and Robert M. Pirsig's *Zen and the Art of Motorcycle Maintenance: An Inquiry into Values* (1974). These and other such works connect with a tradition in imaginative literature stretching from Walt Whitman's powerful free-verse poem "The Song of the Open Road" (1856) to Jack Kerouac's popular novel (the bible of the Beats), *On the Road* (1957). And these works in turn connect with that most enduring of American books, Mark Twain's *Adventures of Huckleberry Finn* (1884): at the end, after the long journey down the Mississippi, Huck decides to evade those who want to "sivilize" him and to "light out for the Territory ahead of the rest."

TEXT

Blue Highways: A Journey into America, 1982.

from Blue Highways

[THE HOPI WAY]

Dirty and hard, the morning light could have been old concrete. Twenty-nine degrees inside. I tried to figure a way to drive down the mountain without leaving the sleeping bag. I was stiff—not from the cold so much as from having slept coiled like a grub. Creaking open and pinching toes and fingers to check for frostbite, I counted to ten (twice) before shouting and leaping for my clothes. Shouting distracts the agony. Underwear, trousers, and shirt so cold they felt wet.

I went outside to relieve myself. In the snow, with the hot stream, I spelled out *alive*. Then to work chipping clear the windows. Somewhere off this mountain, people still lay warm in their blankets and not yet ready to get up to a hot breakfast. So what if they spent the day selling imprinted ballpoint pens? Weren't they down off mountains?

Down. I had to try it. And down it was, Utah 14 a complication of twists and drops descending the west side more precipitately than the east. A good thing I hadn't attempted it in the dark. After a mile, snow on the pavement became slush, then water, and finally at six thousand feet, dry and sunny blacktop.

Cedar City, a tidy Mormon town, lay at the base of the mountains on the edge of the Escalante Desert. Ah, desert! I pulled in for gas, snow still melting off my rig. "See you spent the night in the Breaks,"[1] the attendant said. "You people never believe the sign[2] at the bottom."

"I believed, but it said something about winter months. May isn't winter."

"It is up there. You Easterners just don't know what a mountain is."

I didn't say anything, but I knew what a mountain was: a high pile of windy rocks with its own weather.

In the cafeteria of Southern Utah State College, I bought a breakfast of scrambled eggs, pancakes, bacon, oatmeal, grapefruit, orange juice, milk, and a cinnamon roll. A celebration of being alive. I was full of victory.

Across the table sat an Indian student named Kendrick Fritz who was studying chemistry and wanted to become a physician. He had grown up in Moenkopi, Arizona, just across the highway from Tuba City. I said, "Are you Navajo or Hopi?"[3]

"Hopi. You can tell by my size. Hopis are smaller than Navajos."

His voice was gentle, his words considered, and smile timid. He seemed open to questions. "Fritz doesn't sound like a Hopi name."

"My father took it when he was in the Army in the Second World War. Hopis usually have Anglo first names and long Hopi last names that are hard for other people to pronounce."

I told him of my difficulty in rousing a conversation in Tuba City.[4] He said, "I can't speak for Navajos about prejudice, but I know Hopis who believe we survived Spaniards, missionaries, a thousand years of other Indians, even the BIA.[5] But tourists?" He smiled. "Smallpox would be better."

"Do you—yourself—think most whites are prejudiced against Indians?"

"About fifty-fifty. Half show contempt because they saw a drunk squaw at the Circle K. Another half think we're noble savages—they may be worse because if an Indian makes a mistake they hate him for being human. Who wants to be somebody's ideal myth?"

[1]i.e. Cedar Breaks National Monument, Utah.
[2]The sign read: "Elevation 10,000 Feet/ Road May Be Impassable/ During Winter Months."
[3]The Navaho are North American Indians occupying reservations in parts of New Mexico, Arizona, and Utah; the Hopi are also North American Indians, now concentrated in northeastern Arizona.
[4]A town in northern Arizona on a Hopi Indian reservation in which both Hopi and Navaho live.
[5]Bureau of Indian Affairs.

"My grandfather used to say the Big Vision made the Indian, but the white man invented him."

"Relations are okay here, but I wouldn't call them good, and I'm not one to go around looking for prejudice. I try not to."

"Maybe you're more tolerant of Anglo ways than some others."

"Could be. I mean, I *am* studying to be a doctor and not a medicine man. But I'm no apple Indian—red outside and white underneath. I lived up in Brigham City, Utah, when I went to the Intermountain School run by the BIA. It was too easy though. Too much time to goof around. So I switched to Box Elder—that's a public school. I learned there. And I lived in Dallas a few months. What I'm saying is that I've lived on Hopi land and I've lived away. I hear Indians talk about being red all the way through criticizing others for acting like Anglos, and all the time they're sitting in a pickup at a drive-in. But don't tell them to trade the truck for a horse."

"The Spanish brought the horse."

He nodded. "To me, being Indian means being responsible to my people. Helping with the best tools. Who invented penicillin doesn't matter."

"What happens after you finish school?"

"I used to want out of Tuba, but since I've been away, I've come to see how our land really is our Sacred Circle—it's our strength. Now, I want to go back and practice general medicine. At the Indian hospital in Tuba where my mother and sister are nurse's aides, there aren't any Indian M. D.'s and that's no good. I don't respect people who don't help themselves. Hopi land is no place to make big money, but I'm not interested anyway."

"You don't use the word *reservation*."

"We don't think of it as a reservation since we were never ordered there. We found it through Hopi prophecies. We're unusual because we've always held onto our original land—most of it anyway. One time my grandfather pointed out the old boundaries to me. We were way up on a mesa. I've forgotten what they are except for the San Francisco Peaks. But in the last eighty years, the government's given a lot of our land to Navajos, and now we're in a hard spot—eight thousand Hopis are surrounded and outnumbered twenty-five to one. I don't begrudge the Navajo anything, but I think Hopis should be in on making the decisions. Maybe you know that Congress didn't even admit Indians to citizenship until about nineteen twenty. Incredible—live someplace a thousand years and then find out you're a foreigner."

"I know an Osage who says, 'Don't Americanize me and I won't Americanize you.' He means everybody in the country came from someplace else."

"Hopi legends are full of migrations."

"Will other Hopis be suspicious of you when you go home as a doctor?"

"Some might be, but not my family. But for a lot of Hopis, the worst thing to call a man is *kahopi*, 'not Hopi.' Nowadays, though, we all have to choose either the new ways or the Hopi way, and it's split up whole villages. A lot of us try to find the best in both places. We've always learned from other people. If we hadn't, we'd be extinct like some other tribes."

"Medicine's a pretty good survival technique."

"Sure, but I also like Jethro Tull and the Moody Blues.[6] That's not survival."

"Is the old religion a survival technique?"

"If you live it."

"Do you?"

"Most Hopis follow our religion, at least in some ways, because it reminds us who we are and it's part of the land. I'll tell you, in the rainy season when the desert turns green, it's beautiful there. The land is medicine too."

---

[6]Two rock music groups popular in the early 1970s.

"If you don't mind telling me, what's the religion like?"

"Like any religion in one way—different clans believe in different things."

"There must be something they all share, something common."

"That's hard to say."

"Could you try?"

He thought a moment. "Maybe the idea of harmony. And the way a Hopi prays. A good life, a harmonious life, is a prayer. We don't just pray for ourselves, we pray for all things. We're famous for the Snake Dances, but a lot of people don't realize those ceremonies are prayers for rain and crops, prayers for life. We also pray for rain by sitting and thinking about rain. We sit and picture wet things like streams and clouds. It's sitting in pictures."

He picked up his tray to go. "I could give you a taste of the old Hopi Way. But maybe you're too full after that breakfast. You always eat so much?"

"The mountain caused that." I got up. "What do you mean by 'taste'?"

"I'll show you."

We went to his dormitory room. Other than several Kachina dolls[7] he had carved from cottonwood and a picture of a Sioux warrior, it was just another collegiate dorm room—maybe cleaner than most. He pulled a shoebox from under his bed and opened it carefully. I must have been watching a little wide-eyed because he said, "It isn't live rattlesnakes." From the box he took a long cylinder wrapped in waxed paper and held it as if trying not to touch it. "Will you eat this? It's very special." He was smiling. "If you won't, I can't share the old Hopi Way with you."

"Okay, but if it's dried scorpions, I'm going to speak with a forked tongue."

"Open your hands." He unwrapped the cylinder and ever so gently laid across my palms an airy tube the color of a thunderhead. It was about ten inches long and an inch in diameter. "There you go," he said.

"You first."

"I'm not having any right now."

So I bit the end off the blue-gray tube. It was many intricately rolled layers of something with less substance than butterfly wings. The bite crumbled to flakes that stuck to my lips. "Now tell me what I'm eating."

"Do you like it?"

"I think so. Except it disappears like cotton candy just as I get ready to chew. But I think I taste corn and maybe ashes."

"Hopis were eating that before horses came to America. It's piki. Hopi bread you might say. Made from blue-corn flour and ashes from greasewood or sagebrush. Baked on an oiled stone by my mother. She sends piki every so often. It takes time and great skill to make. We call it Hopi cornflakes."

"Unbelievably thin." I laid a piece on a page of his chemistry book. The words showed through.

"We consider corn our mother. The blue variety is what you might call our compass—wherever it grows, we can go. Blue corn directed our migrations. Navajos cultivate a yellow species that's soft and easy to grind, but ours is hard. You plant it much deeper than other corns, and it survives where they would die. It's a genetic variant the Hopi developed."

"Why is it blue? That must be symbolic."

"We like the color blue. Corn's our most important ritual ingredient."

"The piki's good, but it's making me thirsty. Where's a water fountain?"

When I came back from the fountain, Fritz said, "I'll tell you what I think the heart of our religion is—it's the Four Worlds."[8]

---

[7]Hopi Indian dolls, carved from cottonwood, representing the Hopi masked dancers who impersonate various ancestral spirits in religious rituals; the dolls are often given as gifts to children or used to decorate the household.

[8]See second paragraph following.

Over the next hour, he talked about the Hopi Way, and showed pictures and passages from *Book of the Hopi*.[9] The key seemed to be emergence. Carved in a rock near the village of Shipolovi is the ancient symbol for it:

With variations, the symbol appears among other Indians of the Americas. Its lines represent the course a person follows on his "road of life" as he passes through birth, death, rebirth. Human existence is essentially a series of journeys, and the emergence symbol is a kind of map of the wandering soul, an image of a process; but it is also, like most Hopi symbols and ceremonies, a reminder of cosmic patterns that all human beings move in.

The Hopi believes mankind has evolved through four worlds: the first a shadowy realm of contentment; the second a place so comfortable the people forgot where they had come from and began worshipping material goods. The third world was a pleasant land too, but the people, bewildered by their past and fearful for their future, thought only of their own earthly plans. At last, the Spider Grandmother, who oversees the emergences, told them: "You have forgotten what you should have remembered, and now you have to leave this place. Things will be harder." In the fourth and present world, life is difficult for mankind, and he struggles to remember his source because materialism and selfishness block a greater vision. The newly born infant comes into the fourth world with the door of his mind open (evident in the cranial soft spot), but as he ages, the door closes and he must work at remaining receptive to the great forces. A human being's grandest task is to keep from breaking with things outside himself.

"A Hopi learns that he belongs to two families," Fritz said, "his natural clan and that of all things. As he gets older, he's supposed to move closer to the greater family. In the Hopi Way, each person tries to recognize his part in the whole."

"At breakfast you said you hunted rabbits and pigeons and robins, but I don't see how you can shoot a bird if you believe in the union of life."

"A Hopi hunter asks the animal to forgive him for killing it. Only life can feed life. The robin knows that."

"How does robin taste, by the way?"

"Tastes good."

"The religion doesn't seem to have much of an ethical code."

"It's there. We watch what the Kachinas say and do. But the Spider Grandmother did give two rules. To all men, not just Hopis. If you look at them, they cover everything. She said, 'Don't go around hurting each other,' and she said, 'Try to understand things.'"

---

[9]Frank Waters and Oswald White Bear Fredericks (Hopi), *Book of the Hopi* (1963).

"I like them. I like them very much."

"Our religion keeps reminding us that we aren't just will and thoughts. We're also sand and wind and thunder. Rain. The seasons. All those things. You learn to respect everything because you *are* everything. If you respect yourself, you respect all things. That's why we have so many songs of creation to remind us where we came from. If the fourth world forgets that, we'll disappear in the wilderness like the third world, where people decided they had created themselves."

"Pride's the deadliest of the Seven Deadly Sins[10] in old Christian theology."

"It's *kahopi* to set yourself above things. It causes divisions."

Fritz had to go to class. As we walked across campus, I said, "I guess it's hard to be a Hopi in Cedar City — especially if you're studying biochemistry."

"It's hard to be a Hopi anywhere."

"I mean, difficult to carry your Hopi heritage into a world as technological as medicine is."

"Heritage? My heritage is the Hopi Way, and that's a way of the spirit. Spirit can go anywhere. In fact, it has to go places so it can change and emerge like in the migrations. That's the whole idea."

1982

MAXINE HONG KINGSTON
(b. 1940)

Maxine Hong Kingston once remarked: "I have no idea how people who don't write endure their lives." She believes, she said, that "words and stories create order. And some of the things that happen to us in life seem to have no meaning, but when you write them down you find the meanings for them; or, as you translate life into words, you force a meaning. Meaning is intrinsic in words and stories."

Maxine Hong was born in 1940 in Stockton, California, where her parents eventually settled. In the Chinese way of immigration to America, her father Tom Hong came to New York, after his marriage in China, and for fifteen years worked in a laundry, earning the money to send for his wife. By this time his wife Ying Lan Chew, with money he had sent, was certified in medicine and midwifery, professions she had to abandon on arriving in America, becoming a laundry worker and farm hand. She was forty-five years old when her third child was born (the first two had died in China when she was alone); the baby was named Maxine by her father, after a blonde American woman who gambled in the casino he once managed.

Kingston attended the University of California at Berkeley, taking a B.A. there in 1962. This same year she married an American actor, Earll Kingston. She began a teaching career in high schools, first in California and later in Hawaii, and has taught at a variety of institutions, including Kahaluu Drop-In School, Honolulu Business College, and the Mid-Pacific Institute in Honolulu. She was appointed visiting associate professor of English at the University of Hawaii in 1977.

---

[10]Sins that cause spiritual death: pride, covetousness, lust, anger, gluttony, envy, and sloth.

In 1976 she published her first book, *The Woman Warrior: Memoirs of a Girlhood among Ghosts*. It was immediately recognized as an important literary work, original in its blending of myth, legend, and contemporary reality, and in its focus on Chinese-American experience and tradition. It won the nonfiction award of the National Book Critics Circle. Kingston commented in an interview that she wrote in "the peasant talk-story Cantonese tradition ('low,' if you will), which is the heritage of Chinese Americans." She explained: "I do feel that I come from the tradition of storytellers, and that tradition is thousands of years old; but I'm different from the others in that I write, whereas the rest of them used memory and the moods of the audience. Storytelling is communal, whereas writing is solitary and more intellectual—and inflexible in a way. Tellers' stories change from telling to telling and from the storyteller to the listener, but when you write them down, there's a permanence."

The Woman Warrior was enlisted in the feminist movement because of its portrayal of male mistreatment of women, as in the story from it reprinted here, "No Name Woman." Asked in an interview about the status of women in China, Kingston said:

> In *The Woman Warrior* I was telling that the attitude towards women in China was very puzzling because on the one hand there was this slavery, which is so weird—I mean, I can almost understand better how white people can enslave black people than how men can enslave women. But at the same time they had these heroic stories about the women warriors, so there were two traditions going at once—about powerful fighters and poets and rulers that were women, and on the other hand, enslavement. So I think that women's liberation was already a tradition in China, too, you see. It's not as if they didn't have that idea on their own.

In 1980, Kingston published *China Men,* a companion book to *The Woman Warrior,* concentrating on the male Chinese-American experience, but using the same method of blending legend and reality. It apparently was a more difficult book to write because Kingston's father was less communicative than her mother. Near the beginning of the book, she addressed him: "Father, I have seen you lighthearted. . . . But usually you did not play. You were angry. You scared us. Every day we listened to you swear. . . . You say with the few words and silences: No stories, No past. No China. . . . You fix yourself in the present, but I want to hear the stories about the rest of your life, the Chinese stories."

China Men enjoyed a success similar to that of *The Woman Warrior*. But with its appearance, Kingston confessed that her Chinese material had run out: "I don't have any more stories saved up. . . . I am facing a blank, but I feel good about it. . . . I am going to make something out of nothing, which is the greatest creativity." When she published *Tripmaster Monkey: His Fake Book* in 1989, it was, to the puzzlement of many reviewers, advertised as Kingston's "first" novel. The title alludes to a sixteenth-century Chinese classic, *Journey to the West,* and its comic character Monkey, a trickster who protects a monk in search of Buddhist scriptures. Set in modern America, Kingston's novel portrays such flamboyant characters as the shrewd, get-up-and-go Chinese American, Wittman Ah Sing, whose father named him after the quintessentially American poet, Walt Whitman ("One's self *I sing*"). Her intention, Kingston had said while working on the book, was "to make beautiful literature without the aid of Chinese metaphors." One reviewer, the novelist Ann Tyler, agreed that she had succeeded, creating a novel of "satisfying complexity and bite and verve."

ADDITIONAL READING

Joanne S. Frye, *"The Woman Warrier:* Claiming Narrative Power, Recreating Female Self-hood," in Alice Kessler-Harris and William McBrien, eds., *Faith of a (Woman) Writer,* 1988.

TEXT

The Woman Warrior: Memoirs of a Girlhood Among Ghosts, 1976.

from The Woman Warrior

NO NAME WOMAN

"You must not tell anyone," my mother said, "what I am about to tell you. In China your father had a sister who killed herself. She jumped into the family well. We say that your father has all brothers because it is as if she had never been born.

"In 1924 just a few days after our village celebrated seventeen hurry-up weddings—to make sure that every young man who went 'out on the road' would responsibly come home—your father and his brothers and your grandfather and his brothers and your aunt's new husband sailed for America, the Gold Mountain. It was your grandfather's last trip. Those lucky enough to get contracts waved good-bye from the decks. They fed and guarded the stowaways and helped them off in Cuba, New York, Bali, Hawaii. 'We'll meet in California next year,' they said. All of them sent money home.

"I remember looking at your aunt one day when she and I were dressing; I had not noticed before that she had such a protruding melon of a stomach. But I did not think, 'She's pregnant,' until she began to look like other pregnant women, her shirt pulling and the white tops of her black pants showing. She could not have been pregnant, you see, because her husband had been gone for years. No one said anything. We did not discuss it. In early summer she was ready to have the child, long after the time when it could have been possible.

"The village had also been counting. On the night the baby was to be born the villagers raided our house. Some were crying. Like a great saw, teeth strung with lights, files of people walked zigzag across our land, tearing the rice. Their lanterns doubled in the disturbed black water, which drained away through the broken bunds. As the villagers closed in, we could see that some of them, probably men and women we knew well, wore white masks. The people with long hair hung it over their faces. Women with short hair made it stand up on end. Some had tied white bands around their foreheads, arms, and legs.

"At first they threw mud and rocks at the house. Then they threw eggs and began slaughtering our stock. We could hear the animals scream their deaths—the roosters, the pigs, a last great roar from the ox. Familiar wild heads flared in our night windows; the villagers encircled us. Some of the faces stopped to peer at us, their eyes rushing like searchlights. The hands flattened against the panes, framed heads, and left red prints.

"The villagers broke in the front and the back doors at the same time, even though we had not locked the doors against them. Their knives dripped with the blood of our animals. They smeared blood on the doors and walls. One woman swung a chicken, whose throat she had slit, splattering blood in red arcs about her. We stood together in the middle of our house, in the family hall with the pictures and tables of the ancestors around us, and looked straight ahead.

"At that time the house had only two wings. When the men came back, we would build two more to enclose our courtyard and a third one to begin a second courtyard.

The villagers pushed through both wings, even your grandparents' rooms, to find your aunt's, which was also mine until the men returned. From this room a new wing for one of the younger families would grow. They ripped up her clothes and shoes and broke her combs, grinding them underfoot. They tore her work from the loom. They scattered the cooking fire and rolled the new weaving in it. We could hear them in the kitchen breaking our bowls and banging the pots. They overturned the great waist-high earthenware jugs; duck eggs, pickled fruits, vegetables burst out and mixed in acrid torrents. The old woman from the next field swept a broom through the air and loosed the spirits-of-the-broom over our heads. 'Pig.' 'Ghost.' 'Pig,' they sobbed and scolded while they ruined our house.

"When they left, they took sugar and oranges to bless themselves. They cut pieces from the dead animals. Some of them took bowls that were not broken and clothes that were not torn. Afterward we swept up the rice and sewed it back up into sacks. But the smells from the spilled preserves lasted. Your aunt gave birth in the pigsty that night. The next morning when I went for the water, I found her and the baby plugging up the family well.

"Don't let your father know that I told you. He denies her. Now that you have started to menstruate, what happened to her could happen to you. Don't humiliate us. You wouldn't like to be forgotten as if you had never been born. The villagers are watchful."

Whenever she had to warn us about life, my mother told stories that ran like this one, a story to grow up on. She tested our strength to establish realities. Those in the emigrant generations who could not reassert brute survival died young and far from home. Those of us in the first American generations have had to figure out how the invisible world the emigrants built around our childhoods fit in solid America.

The emigrants confused the gods by diverting their curses, misleading them with crooked streets and false names. They must try to confuse their offspring as well, who, I suppose, threaten them in similar ways—always trying to get things straight, always trying to name the unspeakable. The Chinese I know hide their names; so-journers take new names when their lives change and guard their real names with silence.

Chinese-Americans, when you try to understand what things in you are Chinese, how do you separate what is peculiar to childhood, to poverty, insanities, one family, your mother who marked your growing with stories, from what is Chinese? What is Chinese tradition and what is the movies?

If I want to learn what clothes my aunt wore, whether flashy or ordinary, I would have to begin, "Remember Father's drowned-in-the-well sister?" I cannot ask that. My mother has told me once and for all the useful parts. She will add nothing unless powered by Necessity, a riverbank that guides her life. She plants vegetable gardens rather than lawns; she carries the odd-shaped tomatoes home from the fields and eats food left for the gods.

Whenever we did frivolous things, we used up energy; we flew high kites. We children came up off the ground over the melting cones our parents brought home from work and the American movie on New Year's Day—*Oh, You Beautiful Doll* with Betty Grable one year, and *She Wore a Yellow Ribbon* with John Wayne another year. After the one carnival ride each, we paid in guilt; our tired father counted his change on the dark walk home.

Adultery is extravagance. Could people who hatch their own chicks and eat the embryos and the heads for delicacies and boil the feet in vinegar for party food, leaving only the gravel, eating even the gizzard lining—could such people engender a prodigal aunt? To be a woman, to have a daughter in starvation time was a waste enough. My aunt could not have been the lone romantic who gave up everything for sex. Women in the old China did not choose. Some man had commanded her to lie with him and be his secret evil. I wonder whether he masked himself when he joined the raid on her family.

Perhaps she encountered him in the fields or on the mountain where the daughters-in-law collected fuel. Or perhaps he first noticed her in the marketplace. He was not a stranger because the village housed no strangers. She had to have dealings with him other than sex. Perhaps he worked an adjoining field, or sold her the cloth for the dress she sewed and wore. His demand must have surprised, then terrified her. She obeyed him; she always did as she was told.

When the family found a young man in the next village to be her husband, she stood tractably beside the best rooster, his proxy, and promised before they met that she would be his forever. She was lucky that he was her age and she would be the first wife, an advantage secure now. The night she first saw him, he had sex with her. Then he left for America. She had almost forgotten what he looked like. When she tried to envision him, she only saw the black and white face in the group photograph the men had had taken before leaving.

The other man was not, after all, much different from her husband. They both gave orders: she followed. "If you tell your family, I'll beat you. I'll kill you. Be here again next week." No one talked sex, ever. And she might have separated the rapes from the rest of living if only she did not have to buy her oil from him or gather wood in the same forest. I want her fear to have lasted just as long as rape lasted so that the fear could have been contained. No drawn-out fear. But women at sex hazarded birth and hence lifetimes. The fear did not stop but permeated everywhere. She told the man, "I think I'm pregnant." He organized the raid against her.

On nights when my mother and father talked about their life back home, sometimes they mentioned an "outcast table" whose business they still seemed to be settling, their voices tight. In a commensal[1] tradition, where food is precious, the powerful older people made wrongdoers eat alone. Instead of letting them start separate new lives like the Japanese, who could become samurais and geishas,[2] the Chinese family, faces averted but eyes glowering sideways, hung on to the offenders and fed them leftovers. My aunt must have lived in the same house as my parents and eaten at an outcast table. My mother spoke about the raid as if she had seen it, when she and my aunt, a daughter-in-law to a different household, should not have been living together at all. Daughters-in-law lived with their husbands' parents, not their own; a synonym for marriage in Chinese is "taking a daughter-in-law." Her husband's parents could have sold her, mortgaged her, stoned her. But they had sent her back to her own mother and father, a mysterious act hinting at disgraces not told me. Perhaps they had thrown her out to deflect the avengers.

She was the only daughter; her four brothers went with her father, husband, and uncles "out on the road" and for some years became western men. When the goods were divided among the family, three of the brothers took land, and the youngest, my father, chose an education. After my grandparents gave their daughter away to her husband's family, they had dispensed all the adventure and all the property. They expected her alone to keep the traditional ways, which her brothers, now among the barbarians, could fumble without detection. The heavy, deep-rooted women were to maintain the past against the flood, safe for returning. But the rare urge west had fixed upon our family, and so my aunt crossed boundaries not delineated in space.

The work of preservation demands that the feelings playing about in one's guts not be turned into action. Just watch their passing like cherry blossoms. But perhaps my aunt, my forerunner, caught in a slow life, let dreams grow and fade and after some months or years went toward what persisted. Fear at the enormities of the forbidden kept her desires delicate, wire and bone. She looked at a man because she

---

[1]Eating together at the same table.
[2]Samurais: warrior aristocracy of Japan; geishas: girls in Japan trained in the arts, including dancing and conversation, to entertain men.

liked the way the hair was tucked behind his ears, or she liked the question-mark line of a long torso curving at the shoulder and straight at the hip. For warm eyes or a soft voice or a slow walk—that's all—a few hairs, a line, a brightness, a sound, a pace, she gave up family. She offered us up for a charm that vanished with tiredness, a pigtail that didn't toss when the wind died. Why, the wrong lighting could erase the dearest thing about him.

It could very well have been, however, that my aunt did not take subtle enjoyment of her friend, but, a wild woman, kept rollicking company. Imagining her free with sex doesn't fit, though. I don't know any women like that, or men either. Unless I see her life branching into mine, she gives me no ancestral help.

To sustain her being in love, she often worked at herself in the mirror, guessing at the colors and shapes that would interest him, changing them frequently in order to hit on the right combination. She wanted him to look back.

On a farm near the sea, a woman who tended her appearance reaped a reputation for eccentricity. All the married women blunt-cut their hair in flaps about their ears or pulled it back in tight buns. No nonsense. Neither style blew easily into heart-catching tangles. And at their weddings they displayed themselves in their long hair for the last time. "It brushed the backs of my knees," my mother tells me. "It was braided, and even so, it brushed the backs of my knees."

At the mirror my aunt combed individuality into her bob. A bun could have been contrived to escape into black streamers blowing in the wind or in quiet wisps about her face, but only the older women in our picture album wear buns. She brushed her hair back from her forehead, tucking the flaps behind her ears. She looped pieces of thread, knotted into a circle between her index fingers and thumbs, and ran the double strand across her forehead. When she closed her fingers as if she were making a pair of shadow geese bite, the string twisted together catching the little hairs. Then she pulled the thread away from her skin, ripping the hairs out neatly, her eyes watering from the needles of pain. Opening her fingers, she cleaned the thread, then rolled it along her hairline and the tops of her eyebrows. My mother did the same to me and my sisters and herself. I used to believe that the expression "caught by the short hairs" meant a captive held with a depilatory string. It especially hurt at the temples, but my mother said we were lucky we didn't have to have our feet bound when we were seven. Sisters used to sit on their beds and cry together, she said, as their mothers or their slaves removed the bandages for a few minutes each night and let the blood gush back into their veins. I hope that the man my aunt loved appreciated a smooth brow, that he wasn't just a tits-and-ass man.

Once my aunt found a freckle on her chin, at a spot that the almanac said predestined her for unhappiness. She dug it out with a hot needle and washed the wound with peroxide.

More attention to her looks than these pullings of hairs and pickings at spots would have caused gossip among the villagers. They owned work clothes and good clothes, and they wore good clothes for feasting the new seasons. But since a woman combing her hair hexes beginnings, my aunt rarely found an occasion to look her best. Women looked like great sea snails—the corded wood, babies, and laundry they carried where the whorls on their backs. The Chinese did not admire a bent back; goddesses and warriors stood straight. Still there must have been a marvelous freeing of beauty when a worker laid down her burden and stretched and arched.

Such commonplace loveliness, however, was not enough for my aunt. She dreamed of a lover for the fifteen days of New Year's, the time for families to exchange visits, money, and food. She plied her secret comb. And sure enough she cursed the year, the family, the village, and herself.

Even as her hair lured her imminent lover, many other men looked at her. Uncles, cousins, nephews, brothers would have looked, too, had they been home between journeys. Perhaps they had already been restraining their curiosity, and they left, fearful that their glances, like a field of nesting birds, might be startled and caught. Poverty hurt, and that was their first reason for leaving. But another, final reason for leaving the crowded house was the never-said.

She may have been unusually beloved, the precious only daughter, spoiled and mirror gazing because of the affection the family lavished on her. When her husband left, they welcomed the chance to take her back from the in-laws; she could live like the little daughter for just a while longer. There are stories that my grandfather was different from other people, "crazy ever since the little Jap bayoneted him in the head." He used to put his naked penis on the dinner table, laughing. And one day he brought home a baby girl, wrapped up inside his brown western-style greatcoat. He had traded one of his sons, probably my father, the youngest, for her. My grandmother made him trade back. When he finally got a daughter of his own, he doted on her. They must have all loved her, except perhaps my father, the only brother who never went back to China, having once been traded for a girl.

Brothers and sisters, newly men and women, had to efface their sexual color and present plain miens. Disturbing hair and eyes, a smile like no other threatened the ideal of five generations living under one roof. To focus blurs, people shouted face to face and yelled from room to room. The immigrants I know have loud voices, unmodulated to American tones even after years away from the village where they called their friendships out across the fields. I have not been able to stop my mother's screams in public libraries or over telephones. Walking erect (knees straight, toes pointed forward, not pigeon-toed, which is Chinese-feminine) and speaking in an inaudible voice, I have tried to turn myself American-feminine. Chinese communication was loud, public. Only sick people had to whisper. But at the dinner table, where the family members came nearest one another, no one could talk, not the outcasts nor any eaters. Every word that falls from the mouth is a coin lost. Silently they gave and accepted food with both hands. A preoccupied child who took his bowl with one hand got a sideways glare. A complete moment of total attention is due everyone alike. Children and lovers have no singularity here, but my aunt used a secret voice, a separate attentiveness.

She kept the man's name to herself throughout her labor and dying; she did not accuse him that he be punished with her. To save her inseminator's name she gave silent birth.

He may have been somebody in her own household, but intercourse with a man outside the family would have been no less abhorrent. All the village were kinsmen, and the titles shouted in loud country voices never let kinship be forgotten. Any man within visiting distance would have been neutralized as a lover — "brother," "younger brother," "older brother" — one hundred and fifteen relationship titles. Parents researched birth charts probably not so much to assure good fortune as to circumvent incest in a population that has but one hundred surnames. Everybody has eight million relatives. How useless then sexual mannerisms, how dangerous.

As if it came from an atavism deeper than fear, I used to add "brother" silently to boys' names. It hexed the boys, who would or would not ask me to dance, and made them less scary and as familiar and deserving of benevolence as girls.

But, of course, I hexed myself also — no dates. I should have stood up, both arms waving, and shouted out across libraries, "Hey, you! Love me back." I had no idea, though, how to make attraction selective, how to control its direction and magnitude. If I made myself American-pretty so that the five or six Chinese boys in the class fell in love with me, everyone else — the Caucasian, Negro, and Japanese boys — would too. Sisterliness, dignified and honorable, made much more sense.

Attraction eludes control so stubbornly that whole societies designed to organize relationships among people cannot keep order, not even when they bind people to one another from childhood and raise them together. Among the very poor and the wealthy, brothers married their adopted sisters, like doves. Our family allowed some romance, paying adult brides' prices and providing dowries so that their sons and daughters could marry strangers. Marriage promises to turn strangers into friendly relatives—a nation of siblings.

In the village structure, spirits shimmered among the live creatures, balanced and held in equilibrium by time and land. But one human being flaring up into violence could open up a black hole, a maelstrom that pulled in the sky. The frightened villagers, who depended on one another to maintain the real, went to my aunt to show her a personal, physical representation of the break she had made in the "roundness." Misallying couples snapped off the future, which was to be embodied in true offspring. The villagers punished her for acting as if she could have a private life, secret and apart from them.

If my aunt had betrayed the family at a time of large grain yields and peace, when many boys were born, and wings were being built on many houses, perhaps she might have escaped such severe punishment. But the men—hungry, greedy, tired of planting in dry soil, cuckolded—had had to leave the village in order to send food-money home. There were ghost plagues, bandit plagues, wars with the Japanese, floods. My Chinese brother and sister had died of an unknown sickness. Adultery, perhaps only a mistake during good times, became a crime when the village needed food.

The round moon cakes and round doorways, the round tables of graduated size that fit one roundness inside another, round windows and rice bowls—these talismens had lost their power to warn this family of the law: a family must be whole, faithfully keeping the descent line by having sons to feed the old and the dead, who in turn look after the family. The villagers came to show my aunt and her lover-in-hiding a broken house. The villagers were speeding up the circling of events because she was too shortsighted to see that her infidelity had already harmed the village, that waves of consequences would return unpredictably, sometimes in disguise, as now, to hurt her. This roundness had to be made coin-sized so that she would see its circumference: punish her at the birth of her baby. Awaken her to the inexorable. People who refused fatalism because they could invent small resources insisted on culpability. Deny accidents and wrest fault from the stars.

After the villagers left, their lanterns now scattering in various directions toward home, the family broke their silence and cursed her. "Aiaa, we're going to die. Death is coming. Death is coming. Look what you've done. You've killed us. Ghost! Dead ghost! Ghost! You've never been born." She ran out into the fields, far enough from the house so that she could no longer hear their voices, and pressed herself against the earth, her own land no more. When she felt the birth coming, she thought that she had been hurt. Her body seized together. "They've hurt me too much," she thought. "This is gall, and it will kill me." Her forehead and knees against the earth, her body convulsed and then released her onto her back. The black well of sky and stars went out and out and out forever; her body and her complexity seemed to disappear. She was one of the stars, a bright dot in blackness, without home, without a companion, in eternal cold and silence. An agoraphobia[3] rose in her, speeding higher and higher, bigger and bigger; she would not be able to contain it; there would be no end to fear.

Flayed, unprotected against space, she felt pain return, focusing her body. This pain chilled her—a cold, steady kind of surface pain. Inside, spasmodically, the other pain, the pain of the child, heated her. For hours she lay on the ground, alternately body and space. Sometimes a vision of normal comfort obliterated reality: she saw the family in the evening gambling at the dinner table, the young people massaging

---

[3]Abnormal fear of open or public places.

their elders' backs. She saw them congratulating one another, high joy on the mornings the rice shoots came up. When these pictures burst, the stars drew yet further apart. Black space opened.

She got to her feet to fight better and remembered that old-fashioned women gave birth in their pigsties to fool the jealous, pain-dealing gods, who do not snatch piglets. Before the next spasms could stop her, she ran to the pigsty, each step a rushing out into emptiness. She climbed over the fence and knelt in the dirt. It was good to have a fence enclosing her, a tribal person alone.

Laboring, this woman who had carried her child as a foreign growth that sickened her every day, expelled it at last. She reached down to touch the hot, wet, moving mass, surely smaller than anything human, and could feel that it was human after all—fingers, toes, nails, nose. She pulled it up on to her belly, and it lay curled there, butt in the air, feet precisely tucked one under the other. She opened her loose shirt and buttoned the child inside. After resting, it squirmed and thrashed and she pushed it up to her breast. It turned its head this way and that until it found her nipple. There, it made little snuffling noises. She clenched her teeth at its preciousness, lovely as a young calf, a piglet, a little dog.

She may have gone to the pigsty as a last act of responsibility: she would protect this child as she had protected its father. It would look after her soul, leaving supplies on her grave. But how would this tiny child without family find her grave when there would be no marker for her anywhere, neither in the earth nor the family hall? No one would give her a family hall name. She had taken the child with her into the wastes. At its birth the two of them had felt the same raw pain of separation, a wound that only the family pressing tight could close. A child with no descent line would not soften her life but only trail after her, ghostlike, begging her to give it purpose. At dawn the villagers on their way to the fields would stand around the fence and look.

Full of milk, the little ghost slept. When it awoke, she hardened her breasts against the milk that crying loosens. Toward morning she picked up the baby and walked to the well.

Carrying the baby to the well shows loving. Otherwise abandon it. Turn its face into the mud. Mothers who love their children take them along. It was probably a girl; there is some hope of forgiveness for boys.

"Don't tell anyone you had an aunt. Your father does not want to hear her name. She has never been born." I have believed that sex was unspeakable and words so strong and fathers so frail that "aunt" would do my father mysterious harm. I have thought that my family, having settled among immigrants who had also been their neighbors in the ancestral land, needed to clean their name, and a wrong word would incite the kinspeople even here. But there is more to this silence: they want me to participate in her punishment. And I have.

In the twenty years since I heard this story I have not asked for details nor said my aunt's name; I do not know it. People who can comfort the dead can also chase after them to hurt them further—a reverse ancestor worship. The real punishment was not the raid swiftly inflicted by the villagers, but the family's deliberately forgetting her. Her betrayal so maddened them, they saw to it that she would suffer forever, even after death. Always hungry, always needing, she would have to beg food from other ghosts, snatch and steal it from those whose living descendants give them gifts. She would have to fight the ghosts massed at crossroads for the buns a few thoughtful citizens leave to decoy her away from village and home so that the ancestral spirits could feast unharassed. At peace, they could act like gods, not ghosts, their descent lines providing them with paper suits and dresses, spirit money, paper houses, paper automobiles, chicken, meat, and rice into eternity—essences delivered up in smoke and flames, steam and incense rising from each rice bowl. In an attempt to make the

Chinese care for people outside the family, Chairman Mao[4] encourages us now to give our paper replicas to the spirits of outstanding soldiers and workers, no matter whose ancestors they may be. My aunt remains forever hungry. Goods are not distributed evenly among the dead.

My aunt haunts me—her ghost drawn to me because now, after fifty years of neglect, I alone devote pages of paper to her, though not origamied[5] into houses and clothes. I do not think she always means me well. I am telling on her, and she was a spite suicide, drowning herself in the drinking water. The Chinese are always very frightened of the drowned one, whose weeping ghost, wet hair hanging and skin bloated, waits silently by the water to pull down a substitute.

1975, 1976

RICHARD RODRIGUEZ

(b. 1944)

Richard Rodriguez began life in California speaking Spanish, the language of his parents and community. His parents were Mexican immigrants, his father a dental technician, his mother a clerk-typist. When Rodriguez began school, he knew only English words he had picked up in the streets. At one point the Catholic nuns who taught Rodriguez requested that his parents speak only English to him in the home. The process of acculturation was begun, and along with it the estrangement from family and tradition.

Rodriguez went on to higher education, encouraged by his family. He attended Stanford University, taking a B.A. in 1967. And he went to Columbia University to take graduate work in his adopted language, English, earning an M.A. in 1969. He worked toward his Ph.D. in English at the University of California, Berkeley, in the early 1970s, and studied English Renaissance literature at the Warburg Institute, London (1972–73) as a Fulbright scholar. "But then," as he recounts in his autobiography, "came the crisis. . . the wandering doubts about the value of scholarship. . . . I rushed to 'come home.' Then quickly discovered that I could not. . . . I remained an academic—a kind of anthropologist in the family kitchen." Although he had many job offers, Rodriguez felt uncomfortable about benefiting from affirmative action as a "member of a disadvantaged minority" for he was "no longer disadvantaged." He turned to writing for a career. And he began to publish autobiographical essays about his family life and his education.

The writing clearly helped him work through the complications of the new being he had become, a transfiguration bringing both gains and losses. The complications were, indeed, emotionally charged, as he reported: "Shortly after I published my first autobiographical essay seven years ago, my mother wrote me a letter pleading with me never again to write about our family life. 'Write about something else in the future. Our family life is private.' And besides: 'Why do you need to tell the *gringos* about how "divided" you feel from the family?'"

---

[4]Mao Zedong (1893–1976), Chinese soldier and long-time Chairman of the Chinese Communist party.

[5]Origami: the Japanese art of folding paper into artistic shapes.

That essay was brought together with others under the title *Hunger of Memory: The Education of Richard Rodriguez,* published in 1982. The book struck reviewers as both honest and eloquent in its moving account of Rodriguez's movement into the American mainstream and away from his Mexican-American background. It also sparked controversy because Rodriguez expressed his reservations about bilingual education. He said in an interview:

> To me, public educators in a public schoolroom have an obligation to teach a public language. Public language isn't just English or Spanish or any other formal language. It is the language of public society, the language that people outside that public sector resist. For Mexican-Americans it is the language of *los gringos.* For Appalachian children who speak a fractured English or Black children in a ghetto, the problem is the same it seems to me. . . . My argument has always been that the imperative is to get children away from those languages that increase their sense of alientation from the public society.

Rodriguez finds himself as a writer lured into two different directions. As he told another interviewer:

> I see myself straddling two worlds of writing: journalism and literature. There is Richard Rodriguez, the journalist—every day I spend more time reading newspapers and magazines than I do reading novels and poetry. I wander away from my desk for hours, for weeks. I want to ask questions of the stranger on the bus. I want to consider the political and social issues of the day. Then there is Richard Rodriguez, the writer. It takes me a very long time to write. What I try to do when I write is break down the line separating the prosaic world from the poetic word. I try to write about everyday concerns—an educational issue, say, or the problems of the unemployed—but to write about them as power-fully, as richly, as well as I can.

Rodriguez's new book is a social-cultural study entitled *Mexico's Children,* scheduled for publication in 1991.

TEXT

Hunger of Memory: The Education of Richard Rodriguez, 1982.

from Hunger of Memory
[THE WORLD OF BOOKS]

From an early age I knew that my mother and father could read and write both Spanish and English. I had observed my father making his way through what, I now suppose, must have been income tax forms. On other occasions I waited apprehensively while my mother read onion-paper letters airmailed from Mexico with news of a relative's illness or death. For both my parents, however, reading was something done out of necessity and as quickly as possible. Never did I see either of them read an entire book. Nor did I see them read for pleasure. Their reading consisted of work manuals, prayer books, newspapers, recipes.

Richard Hoggart imagines how, at home,

> . . . [The scholarship boy] sees strewn around, and reads regularly himself, magazines which are never mentioned at school, which seem not to belong to the world to which the school introduces him; at school he hears about and

reads books never mentioned at home. When he brings those books into the house they do not take their place with other books which the family are reading, for often there are none or almost none; his books look, rather, like strange tools.[1]

In our house each school year would begin with my mother's careful instruction: 'Don't write in your books so we can sell them at the end of the year.' The remark was echoed in public by my teachers, but only in part: 'Boys and girls, don't write in your books. You must learn to treat them with great care and respect.'

OPEN THE DOORS OF YOUR MIND WITH BOOKS, read the red and white poster over the nun's desk in early September. It soon was apparent to me that reading was the classroom's central activity. Each course had its own book. And the information gathered from a book was unquestioned. READ TO LEARN, the sign on the wall advised in December. I privately wondered: What was the connection between reading and learning? Did one learn something only by reading it? Was an idea only an idea if it could be written down? In June, CONSIDER BOOKS YOUR BEST FRIENDS. Friends? Reading was, at best, only a chore. I needed to look up whole paragraphs of words in a dictionary. Lines of type were dizzying, the eye having to move slowly across the page, then down, and across . . . The sentences of the first books I read were coolly impersonal. Toned hard. What most bothered me, however, was the isolation reading required. To console myself for the loneliness I'd feel when I read, I tried reading in a very soft voice. Until: 'Who is doing all that talking to his neighbor?' Shortly after, remedial reading classes were arranged for me with a very old nun.

At the end of each school day, for nearly six months, I would meet with her in the tiny room that served as the school's library but was actually only a storeroom for used textbooks and a vast collection of *National Geographic*s. Everything about our sessions pleased me: the smallness of the room; the noise of the janitor's broom hitting the edge of the long hallway outside the door; the green of the sun, lighting the wall; and the old woman's face blurred white with a beard. Most of the time we took turns. I began with my elementary text. Sentences of astonishing simplicity seemed to me lifeless and drab: 'The boys ran from the rain . . . She wanted to sing . . . The kite rose in the blue.' Then the old nun would read from her favorite books, usually biographies of early American presidents. Playfully she ran through complex sentences, calling the words alive with her voice, making it seem that the author somehow was speaking directly to me. I smiled just to listen to her. I sat there and sensed for the very first time some possibility of fellowship between a reader and a writer, a communication, never *intimate* like that I heard spoken words at home convey, but one nonetheless *personal*.

One day the nun concluded a session by asking me why I was so reluctant to read by myself. I tried to explain; said something about the way written words made me feel all alone—almost, I wanted to add but didn't, as when I spoke to myself in a room just emptied of furniture. She studied my face as I spoke; she seemed to be watching more than listening. In an uneventful voice she replied that I had nothing to fear. Didn't I realize that reading would open up whole new worlds? A book could open doors for me. It could introduce me to people and show me places I never imagined existed. She gestured toward the bookshelves. (Bare-breasted African women danced, and the shiny hubcaps of automobiles on the back covers of the *Geographic* gleamed in my mind.) I listened with respect. But her words were not very influential. I was thinking then of another consequence of literacy, one I was too shy to admit but nonetheless trusted. Books were going to make me 'educated.' *That* confidence enabled me, several months later, to overcome my fear of the silence.

---

[1]This and later quotations from British writer Richard Hoggart (b. 1918) are taken from his book *The Uses of Literacy* (1957).

In fourth grade I embarked upon a grandiose reading program. 'Give me the names of important books,' I would say to startled teachers. They soon found out that I had in mind 'adult books.' I ignored their suggestion of anything I suspected was written for children. (Not until I was in college, as a result, did I read *Huckleberry Finn* or *Alice's Adventures in Wonderland*.) Instead, I read *The Scarlet Letter* and Franklin's *Autobiography*. And whatever I read I read for extra credit. Each time I finished a book, I reported the achievement to a teacher and basked in the praise my effort earned. Despite my best efforts, however, there seemed to be more and more books I needed to read. At the library I would literally tremble as I came upon whole shelves of books I hadn't read. So I read and I read and I read: *Great Expectations*; all the short stories of Kipling; *The Babe Ruth Story*; the entire first volume of the *Encyclopaedia Britannica* (A-ANSTEY); the *Iliad*; *Moby-Dick*; *Gone with the Wind*; *The Good Earth*; *Ramona*; *Forever Amber*; *The Lives of the Saints*; *Crime and Punishment*; *The Pearl*. . . . Librarians who initially frowned when I checked out the maximum ten books at a time started saving books they thought I might like. Teachers would say to the rest of the class, 'I only wish the rest of you took reading as seriously as Richard obviously does.'

But at home I would hear my mother wondering, 'What do you see in your books?' (Was reading a hobby like her knitting? Was so much reading even healthy for a boy? Was it the sign of 'brains'? Or was it just a convenient excuse for not helping around the house on Saturday mornings?) Always, 'What do you see . . . ?'

What *did* I see in my books? I had the idea that they were crucial for my academic success, though I couldn't have said exactly how or why. In the sixth grade I simply concluded that what gave a book its value was some major idea or theme it contained. If that core essence could be mined and memorized, I would become learned like my teachers. I decided to record in a notebook the themes of the books that I read. After reading *Robinson Crusoe*, I wrote that its theme was 'the value of learning to live by oneself.' When I completed *Wuthering Heights*, I noted the danger of 'letting emotions get out of control.' Rereading these brief moralistic appraisals usually left me disheartened. I couldn't believe that they were really the source of reading's value. But for many more years, they constituted the only means I had of describing to myself the educational value of books.

In spite of my earnestness, I found reading a pleasurable activity. I came to enjoy the lonely good company of books. Early on weekday mornings, I'd read in my bed. I'd feel a mysterious comfort then, reading in the dawn quiet—the blue-gray silence interrupted by the occasional churning of the refrigerator motor a few rooms away or the more distant sounds of a city bus beginning its run. On weekends I'd go to the public library to read, surrounded by old men and women. Or, if the weather was fine, I would take my books to the park and read in the shade of a tree. A warm summer evening was my favorite reading time. Neighbors would leave for vacation and I would water their lawns. I would sit through the twilight on the front porches or in backyards, reading to the cool, whirling sounds of the sprinklers.

I also had favorite writers. But often those writers I enjoyed most I was least able to value. When I read William Saroyan's *The Human Comedy*, I was immediately pleased by the narrator's warmth and the charm of his story. But as quickly I became suspicious. A book so enjoyable to read couldn't be very 'important.' Another summer I determined to read all the novels of Dickens. Reading his fat novels, I loved the feeling I got—after the first hundred pages—of being at home in a fictional world where I knew the names of the characters and cared about what was going to happen to them. And it bothered me that I was forced away at the conclusion, when the fiction closed tight, like a fortune-teller's fist—the futures of all the major characters neatly resolved. I never knew how to take such feelings seriously, however. Nor did I suspect that these experiences could be part of a novel's meaning. Still, there were pleasures to sustain me after I'd finish my books. Carrying a volume back to the library, I would be pleased by its weight. I'd run my fingers along the edge of the pages and marvel at the breadth of my achievement. Around my room, growing stacks of paperback books reenforced my assurance.

I entered high school having read hundreds of books. My habit of reading made me a confident speaker and writer of English. Reading also enabled me to sense something of the shape, the major concerns, of Western thought. (I was able to say something about Dante and Descartes and Engels and James Baldwin in my high school term papers.) In these various ways, books brought me academic success as I hoped that they would. But I was not a good reader. Merely bookish, I lacked a point of view when I read. Rather, I read in order to acquire a point of view. I vacuumed books for epigrams, scraps of information, ideas, themes — anything to fill the hollow within me and make me feel educated. When one of my teachers suggested to his drowsy tenth-grade English class that a person could not have a 'complicated idea' until he had read at least two thousand books, I heard the remark without detecting either its irony or its very complicated truth. I merely determined to compile a list of all the books I had ever read. Harsh with myself, I included only once a title I might have read several times. (How, after all, could one read a book more than once?) And I included only those books over a hundred pages in length. (Could anything shorter be a book?)

There was yet another high school list I compiled. One day I came across a newspaper article about the retirement of an English professor at a nearby state college. The article was accompanied by a list of the 'hundred most important books of Western Civilization.' 'More than anything else in my life,' the professor told the reporter with finality, 'these books have made me all that I am.' That was the kind of remark I couldn't ignore. I clipped out the list and kept it for the several months it took me to read all of the titles. Most books, of course, I barely understood. While reading Plato's *Republic*, for instance, I needed to keep looking at the book jacket comments to remind myself what the text was about. Nevertheless, with the special patience and superstition of a scholarship boy, I looked at every word of the text. And by the time I reached the last word, relieved, I convinced myself that I had read *The Republic*. In a ceremony of great pride, I solemnly crossed Plato off my list.

[THE LOSS OF THE PAST]

Like me, Hoggart's imagined scholarship boy spends most of his years in the classroom afraid to long for his past. Only at the very end of his schooling does the boy-man become nostalgic. In this sudden change of heart, Richard Hoggart notes:

> He longs for the membership he lost, 'he pines for some Nameless Eden where he never was.' The nostalgia is the stronger and the more ambiguous because he is really 'in quest of his own absconded self yet scared to find it.' He both wants to go back and yet thinks he has gone beyond his class, feels himself weighted with knowledge of his own and their situation, which hereafter forbids him the simpler pleasures of his father and mother. . . .

According to Hoggart, the scholarship boy grows nostalgic because he remains the uncertain scholar, bright enough to have moved from his past, yet unable to feel easy, a part of a community of academics.

This analysis, however, only partially suggests what happened to me in my last year as a graduate student. When I traveled to London to write a dissertation on English Renaissance literature, I was finally confident of membership in a 'community of scholars.' But the pleasure that confidence gave me faded rapidly. After only two or three months in the reading room of the British Museum, it became clear that I had joined a lonely community. Around me each day were dour faces eclipsed by large piles of books. There were the regulars, like the old couple who arrived every morning, each holding a loop of the shopping bag which contained all their notes.

And there was the historian who chattered madly to herself. ('Oh dear! Oh! Now, what's this? What? Oh, my!') There were also the faces of young men and women worn by long study. And everywhere eyes turned away the moment our glance accidentally met. Some persons I sat beside day after day, yet we passed silently at the end of the day, strangers. Still, we were united by a common respect for the written word and for scholarship. We did form a union, though one in which we remained distant from one another.

More profound and unsettling was the bond I recognized with those writers whose books I consulted. Whenever I opened a text that hadn't been used for years, I realized that my special interests and skills united me to a mere handful of academics. We formed an exclusive—eccentric!—society, separated from others who would never care or be able to share our concerns. (The pages I turned were stiff like layers of dead skin.) I began to wonder: Who, beside my dissertation director and a few faculty members, would ever read what I wrote? And: Was my dissertation much more than an act of social withdrawal? These questions went unanswered in the silence of the Museum reading room. They remained to trouble me after I'd leave the library each afternoon and feel myself shy—unsteady, speaking simple sentences at the grocer's or the butcher's on my way back to my bed-sitter.

Meanwhile my file cards accumulated. A professional, I knew exactly how to search a book for pertinent information. I could quickly assess and summarize the usability of the many books I consulted. But whenever I started to write, I knew too much (and not enough) to be able to write anything but sentences that were overly cautious, timid, strained brittle under the heavy weight of footnotes and qualifications. I seemed unable to dare a passionate statement. I felt drawn by professionalism to the edge of sterility, capable of no more than pedantic, lifeless, unassailable prose.

Then nostalgia began.

After years spent unwilling to admit its attractions, I gestured nostalgically toward the past. I yearned for that time when I had not been so alone. I became impatient with books. I wanted experience more immediate. I feared the library's silence. I silently scorned the gray, timid faces around me. I grew to hate the growing pages of my dissertation on genre and Renaissance literature. (In my mind I heard relatives laughing as they tried to make sense of its title.) I wanted something—I couldn't say exactly what. I told myself that I wanted a more passionate life. And a life less thoughtful. And above all, I wanted to be less alone. One day I heard some Spanish academics whispering back and forth to each other, and their sounds seemed ghostly voices recalling my life. Yearning became preoccupation then. Boyhood memories beckoned, flooded my mind. (Laughing intimate voices. Bounding up the front steps of the porch. A sudden embrace inside the door.)

For weeks after, I turned to books by educational experts. I needed to learn how far I had moved from my past—to determine how fast I would be able to recover something of it once again. But I found little. Only a chapter in a book by Richard Hoggart . . . I left the reading room and the circle of faces.

I came home. After the year in England, I spent three summer months living with my mother and father, relieved by how easy it was to be home. It no longer seemed very important to me that we had little to say. I felt easy sitting and eating and walking with them. I watched them, nevertheless, looking for evidence of those elastic, sturdy strands that bind generations in a web of inheritance. I thought as I watched my mother one night: Of course a friend had been right when she told me that I gestured and laughed just like my mother. Another time I saw for myself: My father's eyes were much like my own, constantly watchful.

But after the early relief, this return, came suspicion, nagging until I realized that I had not neatly sidestepped the impact of schooling. My desire to do so was precisely the measure of how much I remained an academic. *Negatively* (for that is how this idea first occured to me): My need to think so much and so abstractly about my parents and our relationship was in itself an indication of my long education. My father and mother did not pass their time thinking about the cultural meanings of their experience. It was I who described their daily lives with airy ideas. And yet, *positively*: The ability to consider experience so abstractly allowed me to shape into desire what would otherwise have remained indefinite, meaningless longing in the British Museum. If, because of my schooling, I had grown culturally separated from my parents, my education finally had given me ways of speaking and caring about that fact.

My best teachers in college and graduate school, years before, had tried to prepare me for this conclusion, I think, when they discussed texts of aristocratic pastoral literature. Faithfully, I wrote down all that they said. I memorized it: 'The praise of the unlettered by the highly educated is one of the primary themes of "elitist" literature.' But, 'the importance of the praise given the unsolitary, richly passionate and spontaneous life is that it simultaneously reflects the value of a reflective life.' I heard it all. But there was no way for any of it to mean very much to me. I was a scholarship boy at the time, busily laddering my way up the rungs of education. To pass an examination, I copied down exactly what my teachers told me. It would require many more years of schooling (an inevitable miseducation) in which I came to trust the silence of reading and the habit of abstracting from immediate experience — moving away from a life of closeness and immediacy I remembered with my parents, growing older — before I turned unafraid to desire the past, and thereby achieve what had eluded me for so long — the end of education.

1982

CONTEMPORARY DRAMA

TENNESSEE WILLIAMS   EDWARD ALBEE
ARTHUR MILLER   SAM SHEPARD

"I have always been more interested in creating a character that contains something crippled. . . . They have a certain appearance of fragility, these neurotic people that I write about, but they are really strong."

Tennessee Williams, Interview in *Conversations with Tennessee Williams*

"By showing [in my drama] what happens when there are no values, I . . . assume that the audience will be compelled and propelled toward a more intense quest for values that are missing."

Arthur Miller, Interview in *Conversations with Arthur Miller*

"I am concerned with altering people's perceptions, altering the status quo. All serious art interests itself in this. The self, the society should be altered by a good play."

Edward Albee, Interview in *Critical Essays on Edward Albee*

"Ideas emerge from plays — not the other way around."

Sam Shepard, Introduction to *Fool for Love and Other Plays*

TENNESSEE WILLIAMS
(1911–1983)

Tennessee Williams said of a work by a fellow writer (Carson McCullers's *Reflections in a Golden Eye*) that it was "conceived in that Sense of The Awful which is the desperate black root of nearly all significant modern art." Germane to that "Sense of The Awful" are some of his remarks made in various interviews: "desire is rooted in a longing for companionship, a release from the loneliness that haunts every individual"; "I think most of us have deep troubles. I've yet to find people I didn't think were deeply troubled. This is the age of anxiety. I think that if most people look at others they'll see deep trouble under the skin. There is an increasing tension and anxiety in people I know." In still another interview, Williams explained his interest in flawed people: "I have always been more interested in creating a character that contains something crippled. I think nearly all of us have some kind of defect, anyway, and I suppose I have found it easier to identify with the characters who verge upon hysteria, who were frightened of life, who were desperate to reach out to another person. But these seemingly fragile people are the strong people really. They have a certain appearance of fragility, these neurotic people that I write about, but they are really strong." In such remarks as these, Williams has provided a frame for the picture his plays present of the tragic human plight. Accused of being obsessed by the warped, grotesque, or bizarre, he has responded by affirming the universality of the afflictions represented symbolically by his characters.

In what may seem on the surface the most impersonal of literary genres, the drama, Williams has always insisted that his plays were personal: "I can't write about anything that does not seem to involve me, that I'm not emotionally involved in. I'm limited to the sort of material that is personal. You could say I write about two extremes, the great tenderness between individuals and the terrible circumstances which surround them." Williams's boyhood was an unhappy one; his later life, except for rare periods, deeply troubled. He was born Thomas Lanier Williams in Columbus, Mississippi, to a protective mother who was the daughter of an Episcopalian minister and a rowdy father who was a travelling salesman. His father early dubbed the young sickly boy, who stuck with his mother, "Miss Nancy." In his isolation Williams early turned to writing, winning an essay contest in *The Smart Set* at the age of fourteen and publishing a story in *Weird Tales* when he was seventeen.

In what Williams would describe as a "tragic move," in 1919 the Mississippi family moved to St. Louis, Missouri, where Williams's southern accent was the object of ridicule from his schoolmates. He attended the University of Missouri (1929–31), but was removed from school by his father because (according to one story) he flunked R.O.T.C. Williams ended up working in the warehouse of a shoe company for three years, an experience he later recalled as a "living death"; he spent his nights writing. After a nervous breakdown, he spent a year in recuperation living with his loving grandparents in Memphis.

He resumed his studies at Washington University in St. Louis and then entered the University of Iowa, where he completed his B.A. in 1938. In the meantime, his older sister Rose, with whom he was very close, suffered a breakdown from an incurable schizophrenia; she underwent a frontal lobotomy in 1937, after which she was permanently institutionalized. Williams was to be haunted by her for the rest of his life, and she would be the model for many of the fragile characters in his plays, especially Laura in *The Glass Menagerie*.

During his early years, Williams wrote poetry, fiction, and drama, but as time passed he concentrated more and more on playwrighting. One of his plays had been produced in Memphis in 1935, and others at Washington University during his year there. Beginning in 1938, Williams launched out on his own. First he went to New Orleans, and there changed his name from Thomas Lanier Williams to Tennessee Williams, claiming that the former sounded too much like that of a genteel poet (the kind he had once imitated). During the war years, he moved restlessly about from place to place — New York, Georgia, Mexico. For a time in 1943 he held a job as scriptwriter in Hollywood, where Metro Goldwyn Mayer continued to pay him $250 a week even when it did not use his work. He wrote a script on his own — *The Gentleman Caller* — but MGM turned it down.

Williams changed the movie script to a "memory play," renaming it *The Glass Menagerie.* It opened in Chicago late in 1944 and was moved to New York in 1945. An instant success, it won the New York Drama Critics Circle Award and brought fame and fortune to Williams, freeing him to devote full time to writing. The next two decades were the most successful, both personally and professionally, in Williams's life. He had confirmed his homosexuality in his earlier stay in New Orleans, and he now developed a lasting relationship with an Italian-American, Frank Merlo, who would remain with him until Merlo's death from cancer in 1963.

For a time it seemed that Williams could write nothing but Broadway hits. *A Streetcar Named Desire,* which he wrote in Mexico, opened in New York in 1947 and played for 855 performances, winning both the New York Drama Critics Circle Award and the Pulitzer Prize. In 1948, *Summer and Smoke* opened a modest run in New York, followed in 1951 by a longer run of *The Rose Tattoo. Camino Real,* a revision of an earlier play, had a relatively short run in 1953. But with *Cat on a Hot Tin Roof* in 1955, Williams recouped by winning the notable drama prizes, his third New York Circle Award and his second Pulitzer Prize. Williams's name was kept before the public in 1956–57 by the showing of a popular film, *Baby Doll,* which he had created by merging earlier short plays. But in 1957, Williams revised an earlier flop, *Battle of Angels,* which had closed in Boston in 1940 before reaching New York; it was renamed *Orpheus Descending* and displeased both critics and audiences.

About the time that *Orpheus Descending* was failing, Williams suffered a nervous breakdown and sought help through prolonged psychoanalysis. Out of the experience Williams wrote *Suddenly Last Summer,* produced in 1958 (together with a short play under the combined title *Garden District*); it contained the sensational (but narrated) episode of a homosexual son of a doting mother being torn to pieces (and partially cannibalized) by starving urchins. Williams, who reportedly wrote the play in analysis as "a catharsis, a final fling of violence," was surprised to find that it was a box office hit. Other plays followed: *Sweet Bird of Youth* (1959), a critical and popular success; *Period of Adjustment* (1960), called "A Serious Comedy" and only modestly popular; and *The Night of the Iguana* (1961), which had a long run and won another New York Critics Circle Award for Williams.

The Night of the Iguana was the last major success Williams was to write. But his plays continued to be produced, more frequently off-Broadway than on: *The Milk Train Doesn't Stop Here Anymore* (1962); *Eccentricities of a Nightingale* (1964); *Slapstick Tragedy* (a double bill, 1966); *The Seven Descents of Myrtle* (1968); *In the Bar of a Tokyo Hotel* (1969); *Small Craft Warnings* (1972); *The Red Devil Battery Sign* (1975); *Vieux Carré* (1977); *Creve Coeur* (1978); *Clothes for a Summer Hotel* (1980); *A*

House Not Meant to Stand (1981); *Something Cloudy, Something Clear* (1982). Out of all these productions, only *Small Craft Warnings* was a commercial success.

Williams called the 1960s his "Stoned Age." The death of Frank Merlo in 1963 left him at loose ends in his personal life. There is little doubt that Williams's heavy drinking and use of drugs affected his creativity during his last years. But there can be little doubt either that his finest plays of the period beginning in 1944 with *The Glass Menagerie* and ending in 1961 with *The Night of the Iguana* established him firmly as one of the greatest of American playwrights. Williams said of his writing in an interview in 1961:

> The whole meaning of all my work is that there is no such thing as complete right and complete wrong, complete black, complete white. That we're all in the same boat and really the boat is the world, you might even say it's the universe. All creation is the boat, not just one nation, not just one ideology, not just one system. That everything is in flux, everything is in a process of creation. The world is incomplete, it's like an unfinished poem. Maybe the poem will suddenly turn to a limerick or maybe it will turn to an epic poem. But it's for all of us to try to complete this poem, and the way to complete it is through understanding and patience and tolerance among ourselves.

The body of Williams's work is large, and includes short stories, poems, essays, screenplays, and novels. He published his *Memoirs* in 1975. Until he died in 1983 in a New York hotel room (by accidentally swallowing the cap of a medicine bottle), he continued to write on the daily morning schedule that he had maintained since he set out many decades before to be a writer.

In the years after the disastrous failure of his first professionally produced play, *The Battle of Angels* in Boston in 1940, Williams directed much of his creative energy into the writing of one-act plays. One of these, *Portrait of a Madonna*, was brought together with others and published under the title *27 Wagons Full of Cotton* in 1945 (reissued in 1953). Clearly Williams was perfecting his craft in this early writing, and it is generally agreed that some of his best work is found in these short plays, and that among the best is *Portrait of a Madonna*, whose central character, Lucretia Collins, is a foreshadowing of his Blanche DuBois in *A Streetcar Named Desire*.

The play was picked up in the mid-1940s as a piece for their repertoire by the directing-acting team of Hume Cronyn and Jessica Tandy with Tandy starring as the genteel (and mad) Miss Lucretia Collins. It was her performance in *Madonna* that confirmed Tennessee Williams, when he went to see it in California in 1947, that she should play the part of Blanche in the first production of *Streetcar* later that year; she was a great success in creating the role. Tandy once told an interviewer that music and poetry were vital elements in all of Williams's plays: "Music plays a great part in *Portrait of a Madonna*, with those old, old records." Even the stage directions were poetic, she said: "His poetry seems inevitable." Her judgment of *Madonna* appears apt and persuasive: "[It is] a superb play. It's got everything in it. It's a perfect little jewel of a play."

ADDITIONAL READING

The Theatre of Tennessee Williams, 7 vols., 1971–81; *Tennessee Williams' Letters to Donald Windham, 1940–1965*, ed. Donald Windham, 1976; *Where I Live: Selected Essays*, ed. Christine R. Day and Bob Woods, 1978; *Conversations with Tennessee Williams*, ed. Albert J. Devlin, 1986.

Benjamin Nelson, *Tennessee Williams: The Man and His Work*, 1961; Nancy M. Tischler, *Tennessee Williams: Rebellious Puritan*, 1961; Edwina Dakin Williams (as told to Lucy Freeman), *Remember Me to Tom*, 1963; Francis Donahue, *The Dramatic World of Tennessee Williams*, 1964; Esther Merle Jackson, *The Broken World of Tennessee Williams*, 1965; Gilbert Maxwell, *Tennessee Williams and His Friends*, 1965; Gerald Weales, *Tennessee Williams*, 1965; Norman J. Fedder, *The Influence of D. H. Lawrence on Tennessee Williams*, 1966; Mike Steen, *A Look at Tennessee Williams*, 1969; Jac L. Tharpe, ed. *Tennessee Williams: A Tribute*, 1977; Stephen S. Stanton, *Tennessee Williams: A Collection of Critical Essays*, 1977; Catherine R. Hughes, *Tennessee Williams: A Biography*, 1978; Signi Lenea Falk, *Tennessee Williams*, 1961, rev. 1978; Drewey Wayne Gunn, *Tennessee Williams: A Bibliography*, 1980; Dakin Williams, *Tennessee Williams: An Intimate Biography*, 1983; John S. McCann, *The Critical Reputation of Tennessee Williams: A Reference Guide*, 1983; Donald Spoto, *The Kindness of Strangers*, 1985; Dotson Rader, *Tennessee: Cry of the Heart*, 1985; Judith J. Thompson, *Tennessee Williams' Plays: Memory, Myth, and Symbol*, 1987; Timothy D. Murray, *Evolving Texts: The Writing of Tennessee Williams*, 1988; Dennis Vanatta, *Tenesee Williams: A Study of the Short Fiction*, 1988.

TEXT

27 Wagons Full of Cotton and Other One-Act Plays, 1945.

Portrait of a Madonna

Respectfully dedicated to the talent and charm of Miss Lillian Gish.[1]

CHARACTERS

MISS LUCRETIA COLLINS
THE PORTER
THE ELEVATOR BOY
THE DOCTOR
THE NURSE
MR. ABRAMS

SCENE: *The living room of a moderate-priced city apartment. The furnishings are old-fashioned and everything is in a state of neglect and disorder. There is a door in the back wall to a bedroom, and on the right to the outside hall.*

MISS COLLINS: Richard! (*The door bursts open and Miss Collins rushes out, distractedly. She is a middle-aged spinster, very slight and hunched of figure with a desiccated face that is flushed with excitement. Her hair is arranged in curls that would become a young girl and she wears a frilly negligee which might have come from an old hope chest of a period considerably earlier.*) No, no, no, no! I don't care if the whole church hears about it! (*She frenziedly snatches up the phone.*) Manager, I've got to speak to the manager! Hurry, oh, please hurry, there's a *man*—! (*wildly aside as if to an invisible figure*) Lost all respect, absolutely no respect! . . . Mr. Abrams? (*in a tense hushed voice*) I don't want any reporters to hear about this but something awful has been going on upstairs. Yes, this is Miss Collins' apartment on the top floor. I've refrained from making any complaint because of my connections with the church. I used to be assistant to the Sunday School superintendent and I once had the primary class. I helped them put on the Christmas pageant. I made the dress for the Virgin and Mother, made robes for the Wise Men. Yes, and now this has happened, I'm not responsible for it, but night after night after night this man has been coming into my apartment and—indulging his senses! Do you understand? Not once but repeatedly, Mr. Abrams! I don't know whether   20

---

[1]Lillian Gish (1896–), American film and stage actress whose career began in silent film in 1912.

he comes in the door or the window or up the fire-escape or whether there's some secret entrance they know about at the church, but he's here now, in my bedroom, and I can't force him to leave, I'll have to have some assistance! No, he isn't a thief, Mr. Abrams, he comes of a very fine family in Webb, Mississippi, but this woman has ruined his character, she's destroyed his respect for ladies! Mr. Abrams? Mr. Abrams! Oh, goodness! (*She slams up the receiver and looks distractedly about for a moment; then rushes back into the bedroom.*) Richard! (*The door slams shut. After a few moments an old porter enters in drab grey cover-alls. He looks about with a sorrowfully humorous curiosity, then timidly calls.*)

PORTER: Miss Collins? (*The elevator door slams open in hall and the Elevator Boy, wearing a uniform, comes in.*)   30

ELEVATOR BOY: Where is she?

PORTER: Gone in 'er bedroom.

ELEVATOR BOY: (*grinning*) She got him in there with her?

PORTER: Sounds like it. (*Miss Collins' voice can be heard faintly protesting with the mysterious intruder.*)

ELEVATOR BOY: What'd Abrams tell yuh to do?

PORTER: Stay here an' keep a watch on 'er till they git here.

ELEVATOR BOY: Jesus.

PORTER: Close 'at door.   40

ELEVATOR BOY: I gotta leave it open a little so I can hear the buzzer. Ain't this place a holy sight though?

PORTER: Don't look like it's had a good cleaning in fifteen or twenty years. I bet it ain't either. Abrams'll bust a blood-vessel when he takes a lookit them walls.

ELEVATOR BOY: How comes it's in this condition?

PORTER: She wouldn't let no one in.

ELEVATOR BOY: Not even the paper-hangers?

PORTER: Naw. Not even the plumbers. The plaster washed down in the bath-room underneath hers an' she admitted her plumbin' had been stopped up. Mr. Abrams had to let the plumber in with this here pass-key when she went out for a while.   50

ELEVATOR BOY: Holy Jeez. I wunner if she's got money stashed around here. A lotta freaks do stick away big sums of money in ole mattresses an' things.

PORTER: She ain't. She got a monthly pension check or something she always turned over to Mr. Abrams to dole it out to 'er. She tole him that Southern ladies was never brought up to manage finanshul affairs. Lately the checks quit coming'.

ELEVATOR BOY: Yeah?

PORTER: The pension give out or somethin'. Abrams says he got a contribution from the church to keep 'er on here without 'er knowin' about it. She's proud as a peacock's tail in spite of 'er awful appearance.   60

ELEVATOR BOY: Lissen to 'er in there!

PORTER: What's she sayin'?

ELEVATOR BOY: Apologizin' to him! For callin' the *police*!

PORTER: She thinks police 're comin'?

MISS COLLINS: (*from bedroom*) Stop it, it's got to stop!

ELEVATOR BOY: Fightin' to protect her honor again! What a commotion, no wunner folks are complainin'!

PORTER: (*lighting his pipe*) This here'll be the last time.

ELEVATOR BOY: She's goin' out, huh?   70

PORTER: (*blowing out the match*) Tonight.

ELEVATOR BOY: Where'll she go?

PORTER: (*slowly moving to the old gramophone*) She'll go to the state asylum.

ELEVATOR BOY: Holy G!

PORTER: Remember this ole number? (*He puts on a record of "I'm Forever Blowing Bubbles."*)

ELEVATOR BOY: Naw. When did that come out?

PORTER: Before your time, sonny boy. Machine needs oilin'. (*He takes out small oil-can and applies oil about the crank and other parts of gramophone.*)

ELEVATOR BOY: How long is the old girl been here?   80

PORTER: Abrams says she's been livin' here twenty-five, thirty years, since before he got to be manager even.

ELEVATOR BOY: Livin' alone all that time?

PORTER: She had an old mother died of an operation about fifteen years ago. Since then she ain't gone out of the place excep' on Sundays to church or Friday nights to some kind of religious meeting.

ELEVATOR BOY: Got an awful lot of ol' magazines piled aroun' here.

PORTER: She used to collect 'em. She'd go out in back and fish 'em out of the incinerator.

ELEVATOR BOY: What'n hell for?   90

PORTER: Mr. Abrams says she used to cut out the Campbell soup kids. Them red-tomato-headed kewpie dolls that go with the soup advertisements. You seen 'em, ain'tcha?

ELEVATOR BOY: Uh-huh.

PORTER: She made a collection of 'em. Filled a big lot of scrapbooks with them paper kiddies an' took 'em down to the Children's Hospitals on Xmas Eve an' Easter Sunday, exactly twicet a year. Sounds better, don't it? (*referring to gram-ophone, which resumes its faint, wheedling music*) Eliminated some a that crankin' noise . . .

ELEVATOR BOY: I didn't know that she'd been nuts *that* long.   100

PORTER: Who's nuts an' who ain't? If you ask me the world is populated with people that's just as peculiar as she is.

ELEVATOR BOY: Hell. She don't have brain *one*.

PORTER: There's important people in Europe got less'n she's got. Tonight they're takin' her off 'n' lockin' her up. They'd do a lot better to leave 'er go an' lock up some a them maniacs over there. She's harmless; they ain't. They kill millions of people an' go scot free!

ELEVATOR BOY: An ole woman like her is disgusting, though, imaginin' some-body's raped her.

PORTER: Pitiful, not disgusting. Watch out for them cigarette ashes.   110

ELEVATOR BOY: What's uh diff'rence? So much dust you can't see it. All a this here goes out in the morning, don't it?

PORTER: Uh-huh.

ELEVATOR BOY: I think I'll take a couple a those ole records as curiosities for my girl friend. She's got a portable in 'er bedroom, she says it's better with music!

PORTER: Leave 'em alone. She's still got 'er property rights.

ELEVATOR BOY: Aw, she's got all she wants with them dream-lovers of hers!

PORTER: Hush up! (*He makes a warning gesture as Miss Collins enters from bedroom. Her appearance is that of a ravaged woman. She leans exhaustedly in the doorway, hands clasped over her flat, virginal bosom.*)   120

MISS COLLINS: (*breathlessly*) Oh, Richard — Richard . . .

PORTER: (*coughing*) Miss — Collins.

ELEVATOR BOY: Hello, Miss Collins.

MISS COLLINS: (*just noticing the men*) Goodness! You've arrived already! Mother didn't tell me you were here! (*Self-consciously she touches her ridiculous corkscrew curls with the faded pink ribbon tied through them. Her manner becomes that of a slightly coquettish but prim little Southern belle.*) I must ask you gentlemen to excuse the terrible disorder.

PORTER: That's all right, Miss Collins.

MISS COLLINS: It's the maid's day off. Your No'thern girls receive such excellent 130
domestic training, but in the South it was never considered essential for a girl
to have anything but prettiness and charm! (*She laughs girlishly.*) Please do sit
down. Is it too close? Would you like a window open?

PORTER: No, Miss Collins.

MISS COLLINS: (*advancing with delicate grace to the sofa*) Mother will bring in something cool after while . . . Oh, my! (*She touches her forehead.*)

PORTER: (*kindly*) Is anything wrong, Miss Collins?

MISS COLLINS: Oh, no, no, thank you, nothing! My head is a little bit heavy. I'm
always a little bit — malarial — this time of year! (*She sways dizzily as she starts to
sink down on the sofa.*)   140

PORTER: (*helping her*) Careful there, Miss Collins.

MISS COLLINS: (*vaguely*) Yes, it is, I hadn't noticed before. (*She peers at them near-
sightedly with a hesitant smile.*) You gentlemen have come from the church?

PORTER: No, ma'am. I'm Nick, the porter, Miss Collins, and this boy here is
Frank that runs the elevator.

MISS COLLINS: (*stiffening a little*) Oh? . . . I don't understand.

PORTER: (*gently*) Mr. Abrams just asked me to drop in here an' see if you was
getting along all right.

MISS COLLINS: Oh! Then he must have informed you of what's been going on in
here!   150

PORTER: He mentioned some kind of — disturbance.

MISS COLLINS: Yes! Isn't it outrageous? But it musn't go any further, you understand. I mean you mustn't repeat it to other people.

PORTER: No, I wouldn't say nothing.

MISS COLLINS: Not a word of it, please!

ELEVATOR BOY: Is the man still here, Miss Collins?

MISS COLLINS: Oh, no. No, he's gone now.

ELEVATOR BOY: How did he go, out the bedroom window, Miss Collins?

MISS COLLINS: (*vaguely*) Yes. . . .

ELEVATOR BOY: I seen a guy that could do that once. He crawled straight up the 160
side of the building. They called him The Human Fly! Gosh, that's a wonderful
publicity angle, Miss Collins — "Beautiful Young Society Lady Raped by The
Human Fly!"

PORTER: (*nudging him sharply*) Git back in your cracker box!

MISS COLLINS: Publicity? No! It would be so humiliating! Mr. Abrams surely
hasn't reported it to the papers!

PORTER: No, ma'am. Don't listen to this smarty pants.

MISS COLLINS: (*touching her curls*) Will pictures be taken, you think? There's one
of him on the mantel.

ELEVATOR BOY: (*going to the mantel*) This one here, Miss Collins?   170

MISS COLLINS: Yes. Of the Sunday School faculty picnic. I had the little kinder-
gardeners that year and he had the older boys. We rode in the cab of a railroad
locomotive from Webb to Crystal Springs. (*She covers her ears with a girlish grimace and toss of her curls.*) Oh, how the steam-whistle blew! Blew! (*giggling*) Blew-
wwww! It frightened me so, he put his arm round my shoulders! But she was
there, too, though she had no business being. She grabbed his hat and stuck it
on the back of her head and they — they *rassled* for it, they actually *rassled* together! Everyone said it was *shameless*! Don't you think that it was?

PORTER: Yes, Miss Collins.

MISS COLLLINS: That's the picture, the one in the silver frame up there on the 180
mantel. We cooled the watermelon in the springs and afterwards played
games. She hid somewhere and he took ages to find her. It got to be dark and

he hadn't found her yet and everyone whispered and giggled about it and finally they came back together—her hangin' on to his arm like a common little strumpet—and Daisy Belle Huston shrieked out, "Look, everybody, the seat of Evelyn's skirt!" It was—covered with—grass-stains! Did you ever hear of anything as outrageous? It didn't faze her, though, she laughed like it was something very, very amusing! Rather *triumphant* she was!

ELEVATOR BOY: Which one is him, Miss Collins?

MISS COLLINS: The tall one in the blue shirt holding onto one of my curls. He [190] loved to play with them.

ELEVATOR BOY: Quite a Romeo—1910 model, huh?

MISS COLLINS: (*vaguely*) Do you? It's nothing, really, but I like the lace on the collar. I said to Mother, "Even if I don't wear it, Mother, it will be *so* nice for my hope-chest!"

ELEVATOR BOY: How was he dressed tonight when he climbed into your balcony, Miss Collins?

MISS COLLINS: Pardon?

ELEVATOR BOY: Did he still wear that nifty little stick-candy-striped blue shirt with the celluloid collar? [200]

MISS COLLINS: He hasn't changed.

ELEVATOR BOY: Oughta be easy to pick him up in that. What color pants did he wear?

MISS COLLINS: (*vaguely*) I don't remember.

ELEVATOR BOY: Maybe he didn't wear any. Shimmied out of 'em on the way up the wall! You could get him on grounds of indecent exposure, Miss Collins!

PORTER: (*grasping his arm*) Cut that or git back in your cage! Understand?

ELEVATOR BOY: (*snickering*) Take it easy. She don't hear a thing.

PORTER: Well, you keep a decent tongue or get to hell out. Miss Collins here is a lady. You understand that? [210]

ELEVATOR BOY: Okay. She's Shoiley Temple.[2]

PORTER: She's a *lady*!

ELEVATOR BOY: Yeah! (*He returns to the gramophone and looks through the records.*)

MISS COLLINS: I really shouldn't have created this disturbance. When the officers come I'll have to explain that to them. But you can understand my feelings, can't you?

PORTER   Sure, Miss Collins.

MISS COLLINS: When men take advantage of common white-trash women who smoke in public there is probably some excuse for it, but when it occurs to a lady who is single and always com-*pletely* above reproach in her moral behavior, [220] there's really nothing to do but call for police protection! Unless of course the girl is fortunate enough to have a father and brothers who can take care of the matter privately without any scandal.

PORTER: Sure. That's right, Miss Collins.

MISS COLLINS: Of course it's bound to cause a great deal of very disagreeable talk. Especially 'round the *church*! Are you gentlemen Episcopalian?

PORTER: No, ma'am. Catholic, Miss Collins.

MISS COLLINS: Oh. Well, I suppose you know in England we're known as the English Catholic church. We have direct Apostolic succession through St. Paul who christened the Early Angles—which is what the original English people [230] were called—and established the English branch of the Catholic church over there. So when you hear ignorant people claim that our church was founded by—by Henry the *Eighth*—that horrible, *lech*erous old man who had so many

---

[2]I.e., Shirley Temple (b. 1928), popular child movie star of the 1930s.

wives—as many as *Blue*-beard they say!—you can see how ridiculous it *is* and how thoroughly ob*nox*-ious to anybody who really *knows* and under*stands* Church *His*tory!

PORTER: (*comfortingly*) Sure, Miss Collins. Everybody knows that.

MISS COLLINS: I wish they *did*, but they need to be in*struc*ted! Before he died, my father was Rector at the Church of St. Michael and St. George at Glorious Hill, Mississippi. . . . I've literally grown up right in the very *shad*ow of the Episcopal 240 church. At Pass Christian and Natchez, Biloxi, Gulfport, Port Gibson, Columbus and Glorious Hill! (*with gentle, bewildered sadness*) But you know I sometimes suspect that there has been some kind of spiritual schism in the modern church. These northern dioceses have completely departed from the good old church traditions. For instance our Rector at the Church of the Holy Communion has never darkened my door. It's a fashionable church and he's terribly busy, but even so you'd think he might have time to make a stranger in the congregation feel at home. But he doesn't though! Nobody seems to have the time any more. . . . (*She grows more excited as her mind sinks back into illusion.*) I ought not to mention this, but do you know they actually take a malicious 250 de-*light* over there at the Holy Communion—where I've recently transferred my letter—in what's been going on here at night in this apartment? *Yes!!* (*She laughs wildly and throws up her hands.*) They take a malicious de*LIGHT* in it!! (*She catches her breath and gropes vaguely about her wrapper.*)

PORTER: You lookin' for somethin', Miss Collins?

MISS COLLINS: My—handkerchief . . . (*She is blinking her eyes against tears.*)

PORTER: (*removing a rag from his pocket*) Here. Use this, Miss Collins. It's just a rag but it's clean, except along that edge where I wiped off the phonograph handle.

MISS COLLINS: Thanks. You gentlemen are very kind. Mother will bring in something cool after while. . . .   260

ELEVATOR BOY: (*placing a record on machine*) This one is got some kind of foreign title. (*The record begins to play Tschaikowsky's "None But the Lonely Heart."*)[3]

MISS COLLINS: (*stuffing the rag daintily in her bosom*) Excuse me, please. Is the weather nice outside?

PORTER: (*huskily*) Yes, it's nice, Miss Collins.

MISS COLLINS: (*dreamily*) So wa'm for this time of year. I wore my little astrakhan[4] cape to the service but had to *carry* it *home*, as the weight of it actually seemed *oppres*sive to me. (*Her eyes fall shut.*) The sidewalks seem so dreadfully long in summer. . . .

ELEVATOR BOY: This ain't summer, Miss Collins.   270

MISS COLLINS: (*dreamily*) I used to think I'd never get to the end of that last block. And that's the block where all the trees went down in the big tornado. The walk is simply *glit*-tering with sunlight. (*pressing her eyelids*) Impossible to shade your face and I *do* perspire so freely! (*She touches her forehead daintily with the rag.*) Not a branch, not a leaf to give you a little protection! You simply *have* to en-*dure* it. Turn your hideous red face away from all the front-porches and walk as fast as you decently *can* till you get *by* them! Oh, dear, dear Savior, sometimes you're not so lucky and you *meet* people and have to *smile*! You can't *avoid* them unless you cut *across* and that's so ob-vious, you know. . . . People would say you're pe*cu*liar. . . . His house is right in the middle of that awful leafless block, *their* 280 house, his and *hers*, and they have an automobile and always get home early and sit on the porch and *watch* me walking by—Oh, Father in Heaven—with a ma*licious* de*light*! (*She averts her face in remembered torture.*) She has such *penetrat-*

---

[3]Composition by Russian composer Pyotr Ilyich Tchaikovsky (1840–1893).
[4]Especially lustrous fur of a young lamb.

ing eyes, they look straight through me. She sees that terrible choking thing in my throat and the pain I have in *here*—(*touching her chest*)—and she points it out and laughs and whispers to him, "There she goes with her shiny big red nose, the poor old maid—that *loves* you!" (*She chokes and hides her face in the rag.*)

PORTER: Maybe you better forget all that, Miss Collins.

MISS COLLINS: Never, never forget it! Never, never! I left my parasol once—the one with long white fringe that belonged to Mother—I left it behind in the   290
cloak-room at the church so I didn't have anything to cover my face with when I walked by, and I couldn't turn back either, with all those people behind me— giggling back of me, poking fun at my clothes! Oh, dear, dear! I had to walk straight forward—past the last elm tree and into that *merciless* sunlight. Oh! It beat down on me, *scorching* me! *Whips!* . . . Oh, Jesus! . . . Over my face and my body! . . . I tried to walk on fast but was dizzy and they kept closer behind me—! I stumbled, I nearly fell, and all of them burst out laughing! My face turned so *horribly* red, it got so red and wet, I knew how ugly it was in all that merciless glare—not a single shadow to hide in! And then—(*Her face contorts with fear.*)— their automobile drove up in front of their house, right where I had to pass by   300
it, and *she* stepped out, in white, so fresh and easy, her stomach round with a baby, the first of the *six*. Oh, God! . . . And he stood smiling behind her, white and easy and cool, and they stood there waiting for me. *Waiting!* I had to keep on. What else could I do? I couldn't turn *back*, could I? *No!* I said dear *God*, strike me *dead*! He didn't, though. I put my head way down like I couldn't see them! You know what she did? She stretched out her hand to *stop* me! and *he*— he stepped up straight in front of me, *smiling*, blocking the walk with his terri- ble big white body! "*Lucretia*," he said, "Lucretia *Collins!*" I—I tried to speak but I couldn't, the breath went out of my body! I covered my face and—ran! . . . Ran! . . . *Ran!* (*beating the arm of the sofa*) Till I reached the end of the block—   310
and the elm trees—*started* again. . . . Oh, Merciful Christ in Heaven, how *kind* they were! (*She leans back exhaustedly, her hand relaxed on sofa. She pauses and the music ends.*) I said to Mother, "Mother, we've got to leave town!" We *did* after that. And now after all these years he's finally remembered and come *back*! Moved away from that house and the woman and come *here*—I saw him in the back of the church one day. I wasn't sure—but it *was*. The night after that was the night that he first broke in—and indulged his senses with me. . . . He doesn't realize that I've changed, that I can't feel again the way that I used to feel, now that he's got six children by that Cincinnati girl—three in high-school already! Six! Think of that? Six children! I don't know what he'll say when he   320
knows another one's coming! He'll probably blame *me* for it because a man always *does*! In spite of the fact that he *forced* me!

ELEVATOR BOY: (*grinning*) Did you say—*a baby*, Miss Collins?

MISS COLLINS: (*lowering her eyes but speaking with tenderness and pride*) Yes—I'm expecting a *child*.

ELEVATOR BOY: Jeez! (*He claps his hand over his mouth and turns away quickly.*)

MISS COLLINS: Even if it's not legitimate, I think it has a perfect right to its fa- ther's name—don't you?

PORTER: Yes. Sure, Miss Collins.

MISS COLLINS: A child is innocent and pure. No matter how it's conceived. And it   330
must *not* be made to suffer! So I intend to dispose of the little property Cousin Ethel left me and give the child a private education where it won't come under the the evil influence of the Christian church! I want to make sure that it doesn't grow up in the shadow of the cross and then have to walk along blocks that scorch you with terrible sunlight! (*The elevator buzzer sounds from the hall.*)

PORTER: Frank! Somebody wants to come up. (*The Elevator Boy goes out. The eleva-*

tor door bangs shut. *The Porter clears his throat.*) Yes, it'd be better — to go off some place else.

MISS COLLINS: If only I had the courage — but I don't. I've grown so used to it here, and people outside — it's always so *hard* to *face* them!   340

PORTER: Maybe you won't — have to face nobody, Miss Collins. (*The elevator door clangs open.*)

MISS COLLINS: (*rising fearfully*) Is someone coming — here?

PORTER: You just take it easy, Miss Collins.

MISS COLLINS: If that's the officers coming for Richard, tell them to go away. I've decided not to prosecute Mr. Martin. (*Mr. Abrams enters with the Doctor and the Nurse. The Elevator boy gawks from the doorway. The Doctor is the weary, professional type, the Nurse hard and efficient. Mr. Abrams is a small, kindly person, sincerely troubled by the situation.*)

MISS COLLINS: (*shrinking back, her voice faltering*) I've decided not to — prosecute   350 Mr. Martin . . .

DOCTOR: Miss Collins?

MR. ABRAMS: (*with attempted heartiness*) Yes, this is the lady you wanted to meet, Dr. White.

DOCTOR: Hmmm. (*briskly to the Nurse*) Go in her bedroom and get a few things together.

NURSE: Yes, sir. (*She goes quickly across to the bedroom.*)

MISS COLLINS: (*fearfully shrinking*) Things?

DOCTOR: Yes, Miss Tyler will help you pack up an overnight bag. (*smiling mechanically*) A strange place always seems more homelike the first few days when we   360 have a few of our little personal articles around us.

MISS COLLINS: A strange — place?

DOCTOR: (*carelessly, making a memorandum*) Don't be disturbed, Miss Collins.

MISS COLLINS: I know! (*excitedly*) You've come from the Holy Communion to place me under arrest! On moral charges!

MR. ABRAMS: Oh, no, Miss Collins, you got the wrong idea. This is a doctor who —

DOCTOR: (*impatiently*) Now, now, you're just going away for a while till things get straightened out. (*He glances at his watch.*) Two-twenty-five! Miss Tyler?

NURSE: Coming!   370

MISS COLLINS: (*with slow and sad comprehension*) Oh. . . . I'm going away. . . .

MR. ABRAMS: She was always a lady, Doctor, such a perfect lady.

DOCTOR: Yes. No doubt.

MR. ABRAMS: It seems too bad!

MISS COLLINS: Let me — write him a note. A pencil? Please?

MR. ABRAMS: Here, Miss Collins. (*She takes the pencil and crouches over the table. The Nurse comes out with a hard, forced smile, carrying a suitcase.*)

DOCTOR: Ready, Miss Tyler?

NURSE: All ready, Dr. White. (*She goes up to Miss Collins.*) Come along, dear, we can tend to that later!   380

MR. ABRAMS: (*sharply*) Let her finish the note!

MISS COLLINS: (*straightening with a frightened smile*) It's — finished.

NURSE: All right, dear, come along. (*She propels her firmly toward the door.*)

MISS COLLINS: (*turning suddenly back*) Oh, Mr. Abrams!

MR. ABRAMS: Yes, Miss Collins?

MISS COLLINS: If he should come again — and find me gone — I'd rather you didn't tell him — about the baby. . . . I think its better for *me* to tell him *that*. (*gently smiling*) You know how men *are*, don't you?

MR. ABRAMS: Yes, Miss Collins.

PORTER: Goodbye, Miss Collins. (*The Nurse pulls firmly at her arm. She smiles over* 390
her shoulder with a slight apologetic gesture.)

MISS COLLINS: Mother will bring in — something cool — after while . . . (*She disappears down the hall with the Nurse. The elevator door clangs shut with the metallic sound of a locked cage. The wires hum.*)

MR. ABRAMS: She wrote him a note.

PORTER: What did she write, Mr. Abrams?

MR. ABRAMS: "Dear — Richard. I'm going away for a while. But don't worry, I'll
be back. I have a secret to tell you. Love — Lucretia." (*He coughs*) We got to clear
out this stuff an' pile it down in the basement till I find out where it goes.

PORTER: (*dully*) Tonight, Mr. Abrams?   400

MR. ABRAMS: (*roughly to hide his feeling*) No, no, not tonight, you old fool. Enough
has happened tonight! (*then gently*) We can do it tomorrow. Turn out that bedroom light — and close the window. (*Music playing softly becomes audible as the men
go out slowly, closing the door, and the light fades out.*)

CURTAIN

Early 1940s   *1945*

ARTHUR MILLER
(b. 1915)

Throughout his long career as a dramatist, Arthur Miller has repeatedly
insisted on the moral dimension in drama. He said, for example, in a 1958
interview:

> Not only modern drama, but literature in general — and this goes back a long,
> long distance in history — posits the idea of value, of right and wrong, good and
> bad, high and low, not so much by setting forth these values as such, but by
> showing, so to speak, the wages of sin. . . . In other words, by showing what
> happens when there are no values [in my drama], I, at least, assume that the
> audience will be compelled and propelled toward a more intense quest for
> values that are missing. I am assuming always that we have a kind of civilized
> sharing of what we would like to see occur within us and in the world; and I
> think that the drama, at least mine, is not so much an attack but an exposition,
> so to speak, of the want of value, and you can only do this if the audience itself
> is constantly trying to supply what is missing. I don't say that's a new thing. The
> Greeks did the same thing. They may have had a chorus which overtly stated
> that this is what happens when Zeus' laws are abrogated or broken, but that
> isn't what made their plays great.

Miller's angle of vision on life was shaped in large part by the Great Depression of the 1930s. He was born in Manhattan in 1915. His father was a manufacturer of coats, his mother a school teacher. Because of the failure of his father's
business in 1929, the family was forced to move to Brooklyn, where Miller finished high school in 1932. Unable to attend college because there was no money,
he took a job in an automobile parts warehouse for two years, saving most of his
meager salary as a college fund. In 1934 he enrolled at the University of Michigan, where he began to write plays. He won Hopwood Awards in Drama in both
1936 and 1937, each award accompanied by a $500 check. And with a revision of

one of the college plays he won a Theatre Guild Award in 1938, which brought another check for $1,250.

In the late 1930s and early 1940s, Miller held a series of jobs in New York writing radio scripts. In 1944 he toured army camps gathering material for the screenplay of Ernie Pyle's *Story of GI Joe* (1945). But Miller's main creative energy went into the writing of plays. The first of his plays to see Broadway production was *The Man Who Had All the Luck* (1944), which was ridiculed by critics and closed after four performances. His next play, *All My Sons* (1947), about a manufacturer whose shoddily-made airplane parts caused the death of his own son and other fliers, fared much better at the hands of reviewers and won the New York Drama Critics Circle Award.

Feeling that the conventional (and somewhat clumsy) sets used for *All My Sons* had in subtle ways diminished the play's impact on the audience, Miller set about writing his next play with the determination to find a more fluid way of moving back and forth quickly between present and past. By using a house with invisible walls and special light efffects, set designer Jo Mielziner provided the means for that uninterrupted flow of action that Miller sought for *Death of a Salesman*, produced in 1949. The play portrayed a travelling salesman entangled in and finally destroyed by the clichéd rhetoric of the vulgarest version of the American dream. An enormous success, winning both the Pulitzer Prize and the New York Drama Circle Critics Award, it has continued to be Miller's most admired play. Some academic critics thought the word "pathetic" was more appropriate than "tragic" for the protagonist, Willy Loman. Miller answered: "I think the tragic feeling is evoked in us when we are in the presence of a character who is ready to lay down his life, if need be, to secure one thing — his sense of personal dignity."

Recognized after *Death of a Salesman* as one of America's foremost playwrights, Miller was able to devote himself entirely to his writing. In 1950 he saw to production his adaptation of *An Enemy of the People* by Henrik Ibsen, a playwright whom he had always admired. He next turned to the writing of a play, *The Crucible* (1953), ostensibly about the 1692 Salem witchcraft trials but obliquely concerned with contemporary events during the McCarthy period of anti-Communist hysteria. In 1955, two of Miller's one-act plays were produced together: *A Memory of Two Mondays* and *A View from the Bridge*. The first of these, according to Miller, was so badly produced and performed that it destroyed the reception of both plays. The second play was expanded to full length and had a much more successful run in a 1965 off-Broadway production.

Ironically, Miller himself became a victim of the anti-Communist hysteria of the time, and was called to testify before the House Un-American Activities Committee in 1956; because he refused to divulge the names of associates he had seen at meetings run by Communists, he was cited for contempt. After a trial, he was found guilty of contempt of Congress in 1957. These and other personal distractions deflected Miller from the writing of plays for a number of years. He was divorced in 1955 from Mary Slattery, whom he had married in 1940; and in 1956 he married the famous screen star Marilyn Monroe. The marriage lasted through the filming of Miller's filmscript for *The Misfits* (1961), starring Monroe and Clark Gable. In 1962, Miller married a photographer who had worked on *The Misfits,* Inge Morath.

From this point forward, Miller became productive again. Early 1964 saw the opening of his *After the Fall,* one of the most personal of Miller's plays, indirectly exploring his past life and marriages in quest of self-understanding. Late 1964 saw production of still another new play, *Incident at Vichy,* set in Nazi-occupied

France during the Second World War. Other plays include *The Price* (1968), *The Creation of the World and Other Business* (1972), *The Archbishop's Ceiling* (1977), and *The American Clock* (1980). Miller's *Collected Plays* have appeared in two volumes, the first published in 1957, the second in 1981. *The Theater Essays of Arthur Miller* appeared in 1978.

Miller has published a volume of short stories, *I Don't Need You Any More* (1967). And he has published three volumes of his journals together with photographs by his wife, Inge Morath: *In Russia* (1969), *In the Country* (1977), and *Chinese Encounters* (1979). *Salesman in Beijing* (1983) is an account of his experiences overseeing a production of *Death of a Salesman* in China. In 1987, Miller published *Timebends: A Life,* a nonchronological—and intimate—account of the major episodes of his life.

As time has passed, Miller has become more and more disillusioned with theater as it has developed since he began writing plays. He said in an interview in 1988:

> We may be the only country that still does attempt tragic writing. . . . We still have the energy—if we could only find out how to form it and use it and symbolize it—to ask the big questions: Why are we alive? What does it all mean? These are the great tragic questions. . . . I cannot accept that each man is an island and that literature, theater, is something done altogether for the pleasure of the artist and altogether to divert people from real life. I think that there is a mission. It may be terribly subtle, it may be buried deep, but literature has a job that has to do with the way we live, the way we organize ourselves.

Miller apparently felt a special "love" for *A Memory of Two Mondays,* perhaps in part because its inital production was so badly bungled. But perhaps also because (as he has confessed) he was the model for Bert, the young man who comes to work for a time in a shipping room of a large auto-parts warehouse, escaping (as the others cannot escape) to go to college. Now the work appears to be one of Miller's most carefully crafted and deeply moving plays, with a sophisticated—and poetic—handling of the passage of time and movement from scene to scene.

Miller said in his introduction to his *Collected Plays:* "I wrote [*A Memory of Two Mondays*], I suppose, in part out of a desire to relive a sort of reality where necessity was open and bare; I hoped to define for myself the value of hope, why it must arise, as well as the heroism of those who know, at least, how to endure its absence. Nothing in this book was written with greater love, and for myself I love nothing printed here better than this play." Miller pointed out that the play spoke to the need of (among other things) "a little poetry in life." In speaking to that need in such a grimy and materialistic setting, the play is one of Miller's most subtle and most eloquent.

ADDITIONAL READING

Collected Plays, 1957; *Collected Plays: Volume II,* 1981; *The Theater Essays of Arthur Miller,* ed. Robert A. Martin, 1978; *Conversations with Arthur Miller,* ed. Matthew C. Roudané, 1987.

Dennis Welland, *Arthur Miller,* 1961; Robert O. Hogan, *Arthur Miller,* 1964; Sheila Huftel, *Arthur Miller: The Burning Glass,* 1965; Edward Murray, *Arthur Miller: Dramatist,* 1967; Robert W. Corrigan, ed., *Arthur Miller: A Collection of Critical Essays,* 1969; Benjamin Nelson, *Arthur Miller: Portrait of a Playwright,* 1970; Ronald Hayman, *Arthur Miller,* 1970; Dennis Welland, *Arthur Miller: A Study of His Plays,* 1979; Leonard Moss, *Arthur Miller,* 1967, rev. 1980; Helene Wickham Koon, ed., *Death of a Salesman: A Collection of Critical Essays,* 1983; Santosh K. Bhatia, *Arthur Miller: Social Drama as Tragedy,* 1985; June Schlueter and James K. Flanagan, *Arthur Miller,* 1987.

TEXT

Collected Plays, 1957.

A Memory of Two Mondays[1]

A PLAY IN ONE ACT

THE CHARACTERS

BERT	LARRY
RAYMOND	FRANK
AGNES	JERRY
PATRICIA	WILLIAM
GUS	TOM
JIM	MECHANIC
KENNETH	MR. EAGLE

The shipping room of a large auto-parts warehouse. This is but the back of a large loft in an industrial section of New York. The front of the loft, where we cannot see, is filled with office machinery, records, the telephone switchboard, and the counter where customers may come who do not order by letter or phone.

The two basic structures are the long packing table which curves upstage at the left, and the factory-type windows which reach from floor to ceiling and are encrusted with the hard dirt of years. These windows are the background and seem to surround the entire stage.

At the back, near the center, is a door to the toilet; on it are hooks for clothing. The back wall is bare but for a large spindle on which orders are impaled every morning and taken off and filled by the workers all day long. At center there is an ancient desk and chair. Downstage 10 *right is a small bench. Boxes, a roll of packing paper on the table, and general untidiness. This place is rarely swept.*

The right and left walls are composed of corridor openings, a louverlike effect, leading out into the alleys which are lined with bins reaching to the ceiling. Downstage center there is a large cast-iron floor scale with weights and balance exposed.

The nature of the work is simple. The men take orders off the hook, go out into the bin-lined alleys, fill the orders, bring the merchandise back to the table, where Kenneth packs and addresses everything. The desk is used by Gus and/or Tom Kelly to figure postage or express rates on, to eat on, to lean on, or to hide things in. It is just home base, generally.

A warning: The place must seem dirty and unmanageably chaotic, but since it is seen 20 *in this play with two separate visions it is also romantic. It is a little world, a home to which, unbelievably perhaps, these people like to come every Monday morning, despite what they say.*

It is a hot Monday morning in summer, just before nine.

The stage is empty for a moment; then Bert enters. He is eighteen. His trousers are worn at the knees but not unrespectable; he has rolled-up sleeves and is tieless. He carries a thick book, a large lunch in a brown paper bag, and a New York Times. He stores the lunch behind the packing table, clears a place on the table, sits and opens the paper, reads.

Enter Raymond Ryan, the manager. He wears a tie, white shirt, pressed pants, carries a clean towel, a tabloid, and in the other hand a sheaf of orders.

Raymond is forty, weighed down by responsibilities, afraid to be kind, quite able to be 30 *tough. He walks with the suggestion of a stoop.*

He goes directly to a large hook set in the back wall and impales the orders. Bert sees him but, getting no greeting, returns to his paper. Preoccupied, Raymond walks past Bert toward the toilet, then halts in thought, turns back to Bert.

---

[1]Arthur Miller has remarked of the subject of this play: "*A Memory of Two Mondays* is a pathetic comedy; a boy works among people for a couple of years, shares their troubles, their victories, their hopes, and when it is time for him to be on his way he expects some memorable moment, some sign from them that he has been among them, that he has touched them and been touched by them. In the sea of routine that swells around them they barely note his departure." On the technique of the play, Miller observed: "It is an abstract realism in form. It is in one act because I have chosen to say precisely enough about each character to form the image which drove me to write the play—enough and no more."

RAYMOND: Tommy Kelly get in yet?

BERT: I haven't seen him, but I just got here myself. *Raymond nods slightly, worried.* He'll probably make it all right.

RAYMOND: What are you doing in so early?

BERT: I wanted to get a seat on the subway for once. Boy, it's nice to walk around in the streets before the crowds get out . . .   40

RAYMOND—*he has never paid much attention to Bert, is now curious, has time for it:*   How do you get time to read that paper?

BERT: Well, I've got an hour and ten minutes on the subway. I don't read it all, though. Just reading about Hitler.

RAYMOND: Who's that?

BERT: He took over the German government last week.[2]

RAYMOND, *nodding, uninterested:*   Listen, I want you to sweep up that excelsior laying around the freight elevator.

BERT: Okay. I had a lot of orders on Saturday, so I didn't get to it.

RAYMOND, *self-consciously; thus almost in mockery:*   I hear you're going to go to col-   50 lege. Is that true?

BERT, *embarrassed:*   Oh, I don't know, Mr. Ryan. They may not even let me in, I got such bad marks in high school.

RAYMOND: *You* did?

BERT: Oh, yeah. I just played ball and fooled around, that's all. I think I wasn't listening, y'know?

RAYMOND: How much it going to cost you?

BERT: I guess about four, five hundred for the first year. So I'll be here a long time—if I ever do go. You ever go to college?

RAYMOND, *shaking his head negatively:*   My kid brother went to pharmacy though.   60 What are you going to take up?

BERT: I really don't know. You look through that catalogue—boy, you feel like taking it all, you know?

RAYMOND: This the same book you been reading?

BERT: Well, it's pretty long, and I fall asleep right after supper.

RAYMOND, *turning the book up:*   "War and Peace"?[3]

BERT: Yeah, he's supposed to be a great writer.

RAYMOND: How long it take you to read a book like this?

BERT: Oh, probably about three, four months, I guess. It's hard on the subway, with all those Russian names.   70

RAYMOND, *putting the book down:*   What do you get out of a book like that?

BERT: Well, it's—it's literature.

RAYMOND, *nodding, mystified:*   Be sure to open those three crates of axles that came in Saturday, will you? *He starts to go toward the toilet.*

BERT: I'll get to it this morning.

RAYMOND: And let me know when you decide to leave. I'll have to get somebody—

BERT: Oh, that'll be another year. Don't worry about it. I've got to save it all up first. I'm probably just dreaming anyway.

RAYMOND: How much do you save?

BERT: About eleven or twelve a week.   80

RAYMOND: Out of fifteen?

BERT: Well, I don't buy much. And my mother gives me my lunch.

RAYMOND: Well, sweep up around the elevator, will you?

---

[2]In 1933, Adolph Hitler (1889–1945) was appointed chancellor of Germany, a position he used to establish his dictatorship. By this device we are informed that the date of the ac- tion of the play is 1933, at the height of the Great Depression.
[3]By Russian novelist Count Leo Tolstoy (1828–1910).

Raymond starts for the toilet as Agnes enters. She is a spinster in her late forties, always on the verge of laughter.

AGNES: Morning, Ray!

RAYMOND: Morning, Agnes. *He exits into the toilet.*

AGNES, *to Bert:* Bet you wish you could go swimming, heh?

BERT: Boy, I wouldn't mind. It's starting to boil already.

AGNES: You ought to meet my nephew sometime, Bert. He's a wonderful swim- 90
mer. Really, you'd like him. He's very serious.

BERT: How old is he now?

AGNES: He's only thirteen, but he reads the *New York Times* too.

BERT: Yeah?

AGNES, *noticing the book:* You still reading that book?

BERT, *embarrassed:* Well, I only get time on the subway, Agnes—

AGNES: Don't let any of them kid you, Bert. You go ahead. You read the *New York Times* and all that. What happened today?

BERT: Hitler took over the German government.

AGNES: Oh, yes; my nephew knows about him. He loves civics. Last week one 100
night he made a regular speech to all of us in the living room, and I realized
that everything Roosevelt[4] has done is absolutely illegal. Did you know that?
Even my brother-in-law had to admit it, and he's a Democrat.

Enter Patricia on her way to the toilet. She is twenty-three, blankly pretty, dressed just a little too tightly. She is not quite sure who she is yet.

PATRICIA: Morning!

AGNES: Morning, Patricia! Where did you get that pin?

PATRICIA: It was given. *She glances at Bert, who blushes.*

AGNES: Oh, Patricia! Which one is he?

PATRICIA: Oh, somebody. *She starts past for the toilet; Bert utters a warning "Ugh,"* 110
and she remains.

AGNES—*she tends to laugh constantly, softly:* Did you go to the dance Saturday night?

PATRICIA, *fixing her clothing:* Well, they're always ending up with six guys in the
hospital at that dance, and like that, so we went bowling.

AGNES: Did he give you that pin?

PATRICIA: No, I had a date after him.

AGNES, *laughing, titillated:* Pat!

PATRICIA: Well, I forgot all about him. So when I got home he was still sitting
in front of the house in his car. I thought he was going to murder me. But isn't
it an unusual pin? *To Bert, who has moved off:* What are you always running 120
away for?

BERT, *embarrassed:* I was just getting ready to work, that's all.

Enter Gus. He is sixty-eight, a barrel-bellied man, totally bald, with a long, fierce, gray mustache that droops on the right side. He wears a bowler, and his pants are a little too short. He has a ready-made clip-on tie. He wears winter underwear all summer long, changes once a week. There is something neat and dusty about him—a rolling gait, bandy legs, a belly hard as a rock and full of beer. He speaks with a gruff Slavic accent.

PATRICIA: Oh, God, here's King Kong.[5] *She goes out up one of the corridors.*

GUS, *calling after her halfheartedly—he is not completely sober, not bright yet:* You let me
get my hands on you I give you King Kong!   130

AGNES, *laughing:* Oh, Gus, don't say those things!

GUS, *going for her:* Aggie, you make me crazy for you!

---

[4]Franklin Delano Roosevelt (1882–1945) was elected president in 1932 and served from 1933 until his death in 1945;
to solve the problems of the Depression, he initiated many
programs, many of which were challenged as to their
constitutionality.
[5]A monstrously giant ape that starred in a highly popular
Hollywood film released in 1933.

AGNES, *laughing and running from him toward the toilet door:*   Gus!

GUS: Agnes, let's go Atlantic City!

>   *Agnes starts to open the toilet door. Raymond emerges from it.*

AGNES, *surprised by Raymond:*   Oh!

RAYMOND, *with plaintive anger:*   Gus! Why don't you cut it out, heh?

GUS: Oh, I'm sick and tired, Raymond.

>   *Agnes goes into the toilet.*

RAYMOND: How about getting all the orders shipped out by tonight, heh, Gus— 140 for once?

GUS: What I did? I did something?

RAYMOND: Where's Jim?

GUS: How do I know where's Jim? Jim is my brother?

>   *Jim enters, stiff. He is in his mid-seventies, wears bent eyeglasses; has a full head of hair; pads about with careful tread.*

JIM, *dimly:*   Morning, Raymond. *He walks as though he will fall forward. All watch as Jim aims his jacket for a hook, then, with a sudden motion, makes it. But he never really sways.*

GUS: Attaboy, Jim! *To Raymond:* What you criticize Jim? Look at that!   150

JIM, *turning to Raymond with an apologetic smile:*   Morning, Raymond. Hot day to-day. *He goes to the spike and takes orders off it.*

RAYMOND: Now look, Gus, Mr. Eagle is probably going to come today, so let's have everything going good, huh?

GUS: You can take Mr. Eagle and you shove him!

>   *Agnes enters from the toilet.*

RAYMOND: What's the matter with you? I don't want that language around here any more. I'm not kidding, either. It's getting worse and worse, and we've got orders left over every night. Let's get straightened out here, will you? It's the same circus every Monday morning. *He goes out.*   160

AGNES: How's Lilly? Feeling better?

GUS: She's all the time sick, Agnes. I think she gonna die.

AGNES: Oh, don't say that. Pray to God, Gus.

GUS, *routinely:*   Aggie, come with me Atlantic City. *He starts taking off his shirt.*

AGNES, *going from him:*   Oh, how you smell!

GUS, *loudly:*   I stink, Aggie!

AGNES, *closing her ears, laughing:*   Oh, Gus, you're so terrible! *She rushes out.*

GUS *laughs loudly, tauntingly, and turns to Bert:*   What are you doin'? It's nine o'clock.

BERT: Oh. *He gets off the bench.* I've got five to. Is your wife really sick? *He gets an*   170 *order from the hook.*

GUS: You don't see Jim wait till nine o'clock! *He goes to Jim, who is looking through the orders, and puts an arm around him.* Goddam Raymond. You hear what he says to me?

JIM: Ssh, Gus, it's all right. Maybe better call Lilly.

GUS, *grasping Jim's arm:*   Wanna beer?

JIM, *trying to disengage himself:*   No, Gus, let's behave ourselves. Come on.

GUS, *looking around:*   Oh, boy. Oh, goddam boy. Monday morning. Ach.

JIM, *to Bert, as he starts out:*   Did you unpack those axles yet?

GUS, *taking the order out of Jim's hand:*   What are you doing with axles? Man your   180 age! *He gives Bert Jim's order.* Bert! Here! You let him pick up heavy stuff I show you something! Go!

BERT: I always take Jim's heavy orders, Gus. *He goes out with the orders.*

GUS: Nice girls, heh, Jim?

JIM: Oh, darn nice. Darn nice girls, Gus.

GUS: I keep my promise, hah, Jim?

JIM: You did, Gus. I enjoyed myself. But maybe you ought to call up your wife.
    She might be wonderin' about you. You been missin' since Saturday, Gus.

GUS, *asking for a reminder:*   Where we was yesterday?

JIM: That's when we went to Staten Island, I think. On the ferry? Remember? 190
    With the girls? I think we was on a ferry. So it must've been to Staten Island.
    You better call her.

GUS: Ach—She don't hear nothing, Jim.

JIM: But if the phone rings, Gus, she'll know you're all right.

GUS: All right, I ring the phone. *He goes and dials. Jim leaves with his orders.*
    Patricia enters.

PATRICIA: Morning, Kong!

GUS: Shatap.

    She goes into the toilet as Gus listens on the phone. Then he roars: Hallo! *Hallo!*
Lilly! Gus! *Gus!* How you feel? *Gus!* Working! Ya! Ya! *Gus!* Oh, shatap! *He hangs* 200
up the phone angrily, confused. Jim enters with a few small boxes, which he sets in a pile on
the table.

JIM: You call her?

GUS: Oh, Jim, she don't hear nothing. *He goes idly to the toilet, opens the door. Patri-*
    cia screams within, and Gus stands there in the open doorway, screaming with her in
    parody, then lets the door shut.

    Jim starts out, examining his order, a pencil in his hand, as Kenneth enters, lunch in
    hand. Kenneth is twenty-six, a strapping, fair-skinned man, with thinning hair, delicately
    shy, very strong. He has only recently come to the country.

JIM: Morning, Kenneth.   210

KENNETH: And how are you this fine exemplary morning, James?

JIM: Oh, comin' along. Goin' to be hot today. *He goes out.*

    Kenneth hangs up his jacket and stores his lunch. Gus is standing in thought, picking
his ear with a pencil.

KENNETH: Havin' yourself a thought this morning, Gus? *Gus just looks at him, then*
    goes back to his thought and his excavation. Gus, don't you think something could
    be done about the dust constantly fallin' through the air of this place? Don't
    you imagine a thing or two could be done about that?

GUS: Because it's dusty, that's why. *He goes to the desk, sits.*

KENNETH: That's what I was sayin'—it's dusty. Tommy Kelly get in?   220

GUS: No.

KENNETH: Oh, poor Tommy Kelly. *Bert enters.* Good morning to you, Bert. Have
    you finished your book yet?

BERT, *setting two heavy axles on the bench:*   Not yet, Kenneth.

KENNETH, *his jacket in his hand:*   Well, don't lose heart. *He orates:*

> "Courage, brother! do not stumble
> Though thy path be dark as night;
> There's a star to guide the humble;
> Trust in God, and do the Right."

By Norman Macleod.[6]   230

BERT, *with wonder, respect:*   How'd you learn all that poetry?

KENNETH, *hanging up his jacket:*   Why, in Ireland, Bert; there's all kinds of useless
    occupations in Ireland. "When lilacs last in the dooryard bloomed . . ."[7]

GUS, *from the desk:*   What the hell you doin'? *Bert goes to order hook.*

KENNETH: Why, it's the poetry hour, Gus, don't you know that? This is the hour
    all men rise to thank God for the blue of the sky, the roundness of the everlast-

---

[6]Norman Macleod (1812–1872), Scottish clergyman and author; this is the first stanza of his poem, "Trust in God."

[7]Elegy on the death of Abraham Lincoln written by Walt Whitman (1819–1892).

ing globe, and the cheerful cleanliness of the subway system. And here we have some axles. Oh, Bert, I never thought I would end me life wrappin' brown paper around strange axles. *He wraps.* And what's the latest in the *New York Times* this morning?   240

BERT, *looking through orders on the hook:*   Hitler took over the German government.

KENNETH: Oh, did he! Strange, isn't it, about the Germans? A great people they are for mustaches. You take Bismark, now, or you take Frederick the Great,[8] or even take Gus over here—

GUS: I'm no Heinie.[9]

KENNETH: Why, I always though you were, Gus, What are you, then?

GUS: American.

KENNETH: I know that, but what *are* you?

GUS: I fought in submarine.

KENNETH: Did you, now? An American submarine?   250

GUS: What the hell kind of submarine I fight in, Hungarian? *He turns back to his desk.*

KENNETH: Well, don't take offense, Gus. There's all kinds of submarines, y'know. *Bert starts out, examining his order.* How's this to be wrapped, Bert? Express?

BERT: I think that goes parcel post. It's for Skaneateles.[10]

GUS, *erupting at his desk:*   Axles parcel post? You crazy? You know how much gonna cost axles parcel post?

BERT: That's right. I guess it goes express.

GUS: And you gonna go college? Barber college you gonna go!

BERT: Well, I forgot it was axles, Gus.   260

GUS, *muttering over his desk:*   Stupid.

KENNETH: I've never been to Skaneateles. Where would that be?

BERT: It's a little town upstate. It's supposed to be pretty there.

KENNETH: That a sweet thought? Sendin' these two grimy axles out into the green countryside? I spent yesterday in the park. What did you do, Bert? Go swimmin' again, I suppose?

GUS, *turning:*   You gonna talk all day?

BERT: We're working. *He goes out. Kenneth wraps.*

KENNETH: You're rubbin' that poor kid pretty hard, Gus; he's got other things on his mind than parcel post and—   270

GUS: What the hell I care what he got on his mind? Axles he gonna send parcel post! *He returns to his work on the desk.*

KENNETH, *wraps, then:*   Can you feel the heat rising in this building! If only some of it could be saved for the winter. *Pause. He is wrapping.* The fiery furnace. Nebuchadnezzar[11] was the architect. *Pause.* What do you suppose would happen, Gus, if a man took it into his head to wash these windows? They'd snatch him off to the nuthouse, heh? *Pause.* I wonder if he's only kiddin'—Bert. About goin' to college someday.

GUS, *not turning from his desk:*   Barber College he gonna go.

KENNETH—*he works, thinking:*   He must have a wealthy family. Still and all, he   280
don't spend much. I suppose he's just got some strong idea in his mind. That's the thing, y'know. I often conceive them myself, but I'm all the time losin'

---

[8]Otto Eduard Leopold von Bismarck (1815–1989), first chancellor of the German Empire; Frederick the Great (1712–1786) was king of Prussia (1740–86).
[9]Disparaging slang for a German, popular during the First World War.
[10]Small town in the Finger Lakes region of upstate New York.

[11]King Nebuchadnezzar of Assyria captured Jerusalem and held the Jews in captivity in Babylon; because three Hebrews, Shadrach, Meshach, and Abednego, refused to bow down to a golden image, he ordered them into the "fiery furnace" but they emerged unharmed (see Daniel 3).

them, though. It's the holdin' on—that's what does it. You can almost see it in him, y'know? He's holdin' on to somethin'. *He shakes his head in wonder, then sings:*

> Oh, the heat of the summer,
> The cool of the fall.
> The lady went swimming
> With nothing at all.

Ah, that's a filthy song, isn't it! *Pause. He wraps.* Gus, you suppose Mr. Roose-velt'll be makin' it any better than it is? *He sings:*   290

> The minstrel boy to the war has gone,
> In the ranks of death . . .[12]

Patricia enters from the toilet.

PATRICIA: Was that an Irish song?

KENNETH, *shyly:*   All Irish here and none of yiz knows an Irish song.

PATRICIA: You have a terrific voice, Kenneth.

GUS, *to Patricia:*   Why don't you make date with him?

KENNETH, *stamping his foot:*   Oh, that's a nasty thing to say in front of a girl, Gus!
   Gus rises.

PATRICIA, *backing away from Gus:*   Now don't start with me, kid, because—   300
   Gus lunges for her. She turns to run, and he squeezes her buttocks mercilessly as she runs out and almost collides with Larry, who is entering. Larry is thirty-nine, a troubled but phlegmatic man, good-looking. He is carrying a container of coffee and a lighted cigarette. On the collision he spills a little coffee.

LARRY, *with a slight humor:*   Hey! Take it easy.

PATRICIA, *quite suddenly all concerned for Larry, to Gus:*   Look what you did, you big horse!
   Larry sets the coffee on the table.

LARRY: Jesus, Gus.

GUS: Tell her stop makin' all the men crazy! *He returns to his desk.*   310

PATRICIA: I'm sorry, Larry. *She is alone, in effect, with Larry. Both of them wipe the spot on his shirt.* Did you buy it?

LARRY, *embarrassed but courageous, as though inwardly flaunting his own fears:*   Yeah, I got it yesterday.

PATRICIA: Gee, I'd love to see it. You ever going to bring it to work?

LARRY—*now he meets her eyes:*   I might. On a Saturday, maybe.

PATRICIA: 'Cause I love those Auburns,[13] y'know?

LARRY: Yeah, they got nice valves. Maybe I'll drive you home some night. For the ride.

PATRICIA—*the news stuns her:*   Oh, boy! Well—I'll see ya. *She goes.*   320

GUS: You crazy? Buy Auburn?

LARRY, *with depth—a profound conclusion:*   I like the valves, Gus.

GUS: Yeah, but when you gonna go sell it who gonna buy an Auburn?

LARRY: Didn't you ever get to where you don't care about that? I *always* liked those valves, and I decided, that's all.

GUS: Yeah, but when you gonna go sell it—

LARRY: I don't care.

GUS: You don't care!

---

[12]From "The Minstrel Boy" by Thomas Moore (1779–1852),
Irish romantic poet known for his Irish folk songs.
[13]Flashy American car popular in the early 1930s.

LARRY: I'm sick of dreaming about things. They've got the most beautifully laid-out valves in the country on that car, and I want it, that's all.　　330
　　Kenneth is weighing a package on the scales.

GUS: Yeah, but when you gonna go sell it—

LARRY: I just don't care, Gus. Can't you understand that? *He stares away, inhaling his cigarette.*

KENNETH, *stooped over, sliding the scale weights:*   There's a remarkable circumstance, Larry. Raymond's got twins, and now you with the triplets. And both in the same corporation. We ought to send that to the *Daily News* or something. I think they give you a dollar for an item like that.
　　Bert enters, puts goods on the table.

BERT: Gee, I'm getting hungry. Want a sandwich, Kenneth? *He reaches behind the* 340 *packing table for his lunch bag.*

KENNETH: Thank you, Bert. I might take one later.

GUS, *turning from the desk to Bert:*   Lunch you gonna eat nine o'clock?

BERT: I got up too early this morning. You want some?

KENNETH: He's only a growing boy, Gus—and by the way, if you care to bend down, Gus—*indicating under the scale platform*—there's more mice than ever under here.

GUS, *without turning:*   Leave them mice alone.

KENNETH: Well, you're always complainin' the number of crayons I'm using, and I'm only tellin' you they're the ones is eatin' them up. *He turns to Larry.* It's a 350 feast of crayons goin' on here every night, Larry.
　　Enter Jim with goods, padding along.

JIM: Goin' to be hot today, Gus.

GUS: Take easy, what you running for? *Jim stops to light his cigar butt.*

KENNETH, *reading off the scale weights:*   Eighty-one pounds, Gus. For Skaneateles, in the green countryside of upper New York State.

GUS: What? What you want?

KENNETH: I want the express order—eighty-one pounds to Skaneateles, New York.

GUS: Then why don't you say that, goddam Irishman? You talk so much. When 360 you gonna stop talkin'? *He proceeds to make out the slip.*

KENNETH: Oh, when I'm rich, Gus, I'll have very little more to say. *Gus is busy making out the slip; Kenneth turns to Larry.* No sign yet of Tommy Kelly in the place, Larry.

LARRY: What'd you, cut a hole in your shoe?

KENNETH: A breath of air for me little toe. I only paid a quarter for them, y'know; feller was sellin' them in Bryant Park. Slightly used, but they're a fine pair of shoes, you can see that.

LARRY: They look small for you.

KENNETH: They are at that. But you can't complain for a quarter, I guess.　　370

GUS: Here.
　　Gus hands Kenneth an express slip, which Kenneth now proceeds to attach to the package on the table. Meanwhile Jim has been leafing through the orders on the hook and is now leaving with two in his hand.

KENNETH: How do you keep up your strength, Jim? I'm always exhausted. You never stop movin', do ya? *Jim just shakes his head with a "Heh, heh."* I bet it's because you never got married, eh?

JIM: No, I guess I done everything there is but that.

LARRY: How come you never did get married, Jim?

JIM: Well, I was out West so long, you know, Larry. Out West. *He starts to go again.* 380

KENNETH: Oh, don't they get married much out there?

JIM: Well, the cavalry was amongst the Indians most of the time.

BERT: How old are you now, Jim? No kidding.

KENNETH: I'll bet he's a hundred.

JIM: Me? No. I ain't no hunderd. I ain't near a hunderd. You don't have to be a hunderd to've fought the Indians. They was more Indians was fought than they tells in the schoolbooks, y'know. They was a hell of a lot of fightin' up to McKinley[14] and all in there. I ain't no hunderd. *He starts out.*

KENNETH: Well, how old would you say you are, Jim?

JIM: Oh, I'm seventy-four, seventy-five, seventy-six — around in there. But I ain't   390
no hunderd. *He exits, and Kenneth sneezes.*

BERT — *he has put his lunch bag away and is about to leave:*   Boy, I was hungry!

KENNETH, *irritated:*   Larry, don't you suppose a word might be passed to Mr. Eagle about the dust? It's rainin' dust from the ceiling!
        Bert goes out.

GUS: What the hell Mr. Eagle gonna do about the dust?

KENNETH: Why, he's supposed to be a brilliant man, isn't he? Dartmouth College graduate and all? I've been five and a half months in this country, and I never sneezed so much in my entire life before. My nose is all —
        Enter Frank, the truckdriver, an impassive, burly man in his thirties.   400

FRANK: Anything for the West Bronx?

KENNETH: Nothin' yet, Frank. I've only started, though.
        Jim enters with little boxes, which he adds to the pile on the bench.

FRANK: You got anything for West Bronx, Jim? I've got the truck on the elevator.

GUS: What's the hurry?

FRANK: I got the truck on the elevator.

GUS: Well, take it off the elevator! You got one little box of bearings for the West Bronx. You can't go West Bronx with one little box.

FRANK: Well, I gotta go.

GUS: You got a little pussy in the West Bronx.   410

FRANK: Yeah, I gotta make it before lunch.

JIM, *rifling through his orders:*   I think I got something for the East Bronx.

FRANK: No, West Bronx.

JIM, *removing one order from his batch:*   How about Brooklyn?

FRANK: What part? *He takes Jim's order, reads the address, looks up, thinking.*

JIM: Didn't you have a girl around Williamsburg?

FRANK: I'll have to make a call. I'll be right back.

GUS: You gonna deliver only where you got a woman?

FRANK: No, Gus, I go any place you tell me. But as long as I'm goin' someplace I might as well — you know. *He starts out.*   420

GUS: You some truckdriver.

FRANK: You said it, Gus. *He goes out.*

GUS: Why don't you go with him sometime, Kenneth? Get yourself nice piece ding-a-ling —

KENNETH: Oh, don't be nasty now, Gus. You're only tryin' to be nasty to taunt me.
        Raymond enters.

RAYMOND: Didn't Tommy Kelly get here?

GUS: Don't worry for Tommy. Tommy going to be all right.

LARRY: Can I see you a minute, Ray? *He moves with Raymond over to the left.*

RAYMOND: Eagle's coming today, and if he sees him drunk again I don't know   430
what I'm going to do.

LARRY: Ray, I'd like you to ask Eagle something for me.

RAYMOND: What?

---

[14]I.e., up to the time William McKinley (1843–1901) was president (1897–1901).

LARRY: I've got to have more money.

RAYMOND: You and me both, boy.

LARRY: No, I can't make it any more, Ray. I mean it. The car put me a hundred and thirty bucks in the hole. If one of the kids gets sick I'll be strapped.

RAYMOND: Well, what'd you buy the car for?

LARRY: I'm almost forty, Ray. What am I going to be careful for?

RAYMOND: See, the problem is, Larry, if you go up, I'm only making thirty-eight   440
myself, and I'm the manager, so it's two raises—

LARRY: Ray, I hate to make it tough for you, but my wife is driving me nuts. Now—

Enter Jerry Maxwell and Willy Hogan, both twenty-three. Jerry has a black eye; both are slick dressers.

JERRY AND WILLY: Morning. Morning, Gus.

RAYMOND: Aren't you late, fellas?

JERRY, *glancing at his gold wristwatch:*   I've got one minute to nine, Mr. Ryan.

WILLY: That's Hudson Tubes[15] time, Mr. Ryan.

GUS: The stopwatch twins.   450

RAYMOND, *to Jerry:*   You got a black eye?

JERRY: Yeah, we went to a dance in Jersey City last night.

WILLY: Ran into a wise guy in Jersey City, Mr. Ryan.

JERRY, *with his taunting grin; he is very happy with himself:*   Tried to take his girl away from us.

RAYMOND: Well, get on the ball. Mr. Eagle's—

Enter Tom Kelly. Gus rises from the desk. Bert enters, stands still. Raymond and Larry stand watching. Kenneth stops wrapping. Tom is stiff; he moves in a dream to the chair Gus has left and sits rigidly. He is a slight, graying clerk in his late forties.

GUS, *to Raymond:*   Go'way, go 'head.   460

Raymond comes up and around the desk to face Tom, who sits there, staring ahead, immobile, his hands in his lap.

RAYMOND: Tommy.

Jerry and Willy titter.

GUS, *to them:*   Shatap, goddam bums!

JERRY: Hey, don't call me—

GUS: Shatap, goddamit I break your goddam head! *He has an axle in his hand, and Raymond and Larry are pulling his arm down. Jim enters and goes directly to him. All are crying, "Gus! Cut it out! Put it down!"*

JERRY: What'd we do? What'd I say?   470

GUS: Watch out! Just watch out you make fun of this man! I break you head, both of you! *Silence. He goes to Tom, who has not moved since arriving.* Tommy. Tommy, you hear Gus? Tommy? *Tom is transfixed.*

RAYMOND: Mr. Eagle is coming today, Tommy.

GUS, *to all:*   Go 'head, go to work, go to work! *They all move; Jerry and Willy go out.*

RAYMOND: Can you hear me, Tom? Mr. Eagle is coming to look things over today, Tom.

JIM: Little shot of whisky might bring him to.

GUS: Bert! *He reaches into his pocket.* Here, go downstairs bring a shot. Tell him for Tommy. *He sees what is in his hand.* I only got ten cents.   480

RAYMOND: Here. *He reaches into his pocket as Jim, Kenneth, and Larry all reach into their own pockets.*

BERT, *taking a coin from Raymond:*   Okay, I'll be right up. *He hurries out.*

RAYMOND: Well, this is it, Gus. I gave him his final warning.

---

[15]Subway running through the tunnel under the Hudson River into New York City.

GUS—*he is worried:*   All right, go 'way, go 'way.
    Agnes enters.

AGNES: Is he—?

RAYMOND: You heard me, Agnes. I told him on Saturday, didn't I? *He starts past her.*

AGNES: But Ray, look how nice and clean he came in today. His hair is all 490 combed, and he's much neater.

RAYMOND: I did my best, Agnes. *He goes out.*

GUS, *staring into Tommy's dead eyes:*   Ach. He don't see nothin', Agnes.

AGNES, *looking into Tommy's face:*   And he's supposed to be saving for his daughter's confirmation dress! Oh, Tommy. I'd better cool his face. *She goes into the toilet.*

KENNETH, *to Larry:*   Ah, you can't blame the poor feller; sixteen years of his life in this place.

LARRY: You said it.

KENNETH: There's a good deal of monotony connected with the life, isn't it?   500

LARRY: You ain't kiddin'.

KENNETH: Oh, there must be a terrible lot of Monday mornings in sixteen years. And no philosophical idea at all, y'know, to pass the time?

GUS, *to Kenneth:*   When you gonna shut up?
    Agnes comes from the toilet with a wet cloth. They watch as she washes Tom's face.

KENNETH: Larry, you suppose we could get these windows washed sometime? I've often though if we could see a bit of sky now and again it would help matters now and again.

LARRY: They've never been washed since I've been here.

KENNETH: I'd do it myself if I thought they wouldn't all be laughin' at me for a 510 greenhorn. *He looks out through the open window, which only opens out a few inches.* With all this glass we might observe the clouds and the various signs of approaching storms. And there might even be a bird now and again.

AGNES: Look at that—he doesn't even move. And he's been trying so hard! Nobody gives him credit, but he does try hard. *To Larry:* See how nice and clean he comes in now?
    Jim enters, carrying parts.

JIM: Did you try blowing in his ear?

GUS: Blow in his ear?

JIM: Yeah, the Indians used to do that. Here, wait a minute. *He comes over, takes a* 520 *deep breath, and blows into Tom's ear. A faint smile begins to appear on Tom's face, but, as Jim runs out of breath, it fades.*

KENNETH: Well, I guess he's not an Indian.

JIM: That's the truth, y'know. Out West, whenever there'd be a drunken Indian, they used to blow in his ear.
    Enter Bert, carefully carrying a shotglass of whisky.

GUS: Here, gimme that. *He takes it.*

BERT, *licking his fingers:*   Boy, that stuff is strong.

GUS: Tommy? *He holds the glass in front of Tom's nose.* Whisky. *Tom doesn't move.* Mr. Eagle is coming today, Tommy.   530

JIM: Leave it on the desk. He might wake up to it.

BERT: How's he manage to make it here, I wonder

AGNES: Oh, he's awake. Somewhere inside, y'know. He just can't show it, somehow. It's not really like being drunk, even.

KENNETH: Well, it's pretty close, though, Agnes.
    Agnes resumes wetting Tom's brow.

LARRY: Is that a fact, Jim, about blowing in a guy's ear?

JIM: Oh sure, Indians always done that. *He goes to the order hook, leafs through.*

KENNETH: What did yiz all have against the Indians?

JIM: The Indians? Oh, we didn't have nothin' against the Indians. Just law and   540
order, that's all. Talk about heat, though. It was so hot out there we—
Jim exits with an order as Frank enters.

FRANK: All right, I'll go to Brooklyn.

GUS: Where you running? I got nothing packed yet.
Enter Jerry, who puts goods on the table.

FRANK: Well, you beefed that I want to go Bronx, so I'm tellin' you now I'll go to
Brooklyn.

GUS: You all fixed up in Brooklyn?

FRANK: Yeah, I just made a call.

AGNES, *laughing:*   Oh, you're all so terrible! *She goes out.*   550

JERRY: How you doin', Kenny? You gittin' any?

KENNETH: Is that all two fine young fellas like you is got on your minds?

JERRY: Yeah, that's all. What's on your mind?
Frank is loading himself with packages.

GUS, *of Tommy:*   What am I gonna do with him, Larry? The old man's comin'.

LARRY: Tell you the truth, Gus, I'm sick and tired of worrying about him,
y'know? Let him take care of himself.
Gus goes to Larry, concerned, and they speak quietly.

GUS: What's the matter with you these days?

LARRY: Two years I'm asking for a lousy five-dollar raise. Meantime my brother's   560
into me for fifty bucks for his wife's special shoes; my sister's got me for sixty-
five to have her kid's teeth fixed. So I buy a car, and they're all on my back—
how'd I dare buy a car! Whose money is it? Y'know, Gus? I mean—

GUS: Yeah, but an Auburn, Larry—

LARRY, *getting hot:*   I happen to like the valves! What's so unusual about that?
Enter Willy and Jerry with goods.

WILLY, *to Jerry:*   Here! Ask Frank. *To Frank:* Who played shortstop for Pittsburgh
in nineteen-twenty-four?

FRANK: Pittsburgh? Honus Wagner, wasn't it?[16]

WILLY, *to Jerry:*   What I tell ya?   570

JERRY: How could it be Honus Wagner? Honus Wagner—
*Raymond enters with a mechanic, and Willy and Jerry exit, arguing. Frank goes out
with his packages. Gus returns to his desk.*

RAYMOND: Larry, you want to help this man? He's got a part here.
*Larry simply turns, silent, with a hurt and angry look. The mechanic goes to him,
holds out the part; but Larry does not take it, merely inspects it, for it is greasy, as is the man.*

RAYMOND, *going to the desk, where Gus is now seated at work beside Tom Kelly:*   Did he
move at all, Gus?

GUS: He's feeling much better, I can see. Go, go 'way, Raymond.
Raymond worriedly stands there.   580

LARRY, *to mechanic:*   Where you from?

MECHANIC: I'm mechanic over General Truck.

LARRY: What's that off?

MECHANIC, *as Bert stops to watch, and Kenneth stops packing to observe:*   That's the
thing—I don't know. It's a very old coal truck, see, and I thought it was a Mack,
because it says Mack on the radiator, see? But I went over to Mack, and they
says there's no part like that on any Mack in their whole history, see?

LARRY: Is there any name on the engine?

---

[16]Honus (John P.) Wagner (1874–1955) was shortstop for the
Pittsburgh Pirates (1900–17).

MECHANIC: I'm tellin' you; on the engine it says American-LaFrance — must be a replacement engine.   590

LARRY: That's not off a LaFrance.

MECHANIC: I know! I went over to American-LaFrance, but they says they never seen nothin' like that in their whole life since the year one.
    Raymond joins them.

LARRY: What is it, off the manifold?

MECHANIC: Well, it ain't exactly off the manifold. It like sticks out, see, except it don't stick out, it's like stuck in there — I mean it's like in a little hole there on top of the head, except it ain't exactly a hole, it's a thing that comes up in like a bump, see, and then it goes down. Two days I'm walkin' the streets with this, my boss is goin' crazy.   600

LARRY: Well, go and find out what it is, and if we got it we'll sell it to you.

RAYMOND: Don't you have any idea, Larry?

LARRY: I might, Ray, but I'm not getting paid for being an encyclopedia. There's ten thousand obsolete parts upstairs — it was never my job to keep all that in my head. If the old man wants that service, let him pay somebody to do it.

RAYMOND: Ah, Larry, the guy's here with the part.

LARRY: The guy is always here with the part, Ray. Let him hire somebody to take an inventory up there and see what it costs him.

RAYMOND, *taking the part off the table:*   Well, I'll see what I can find up there.

LARRY: You won't find it, Ray. Put it down. *Raymond does, and Larry, blinking with*   610 *hurt, turns to the mechanic.* What is that truck, about nineteen-twenty-two?

MECHANIC: That truck? *He shifts onto his right foot in thought.*

LARRY: Nineteen-twenty?

MECHANIC, *in a higher voice, shifting to the left foot:*   That truck?

LARRY: Well, it's at least nineteen-twenty, isn't it?

MECHANIC: Oh, it's at least. I brung over a couple a friend of mines, and one of them is an old man and he says when he was a boy already that truck was an old truck, and he's an old, old man, that guy. *Larry takes the part now and sets it on the packing bench. Now even Gus gets up to watch as he stares at the part. There is a hush. Raymond goes out. Larry turns the part a little and stares at it again. Now he*   620 *sips his coffee.* I understand this company's got a lot of old parts from the olden days, heh?

LARRY: We may have one left, if it's what I think it is, but you'll have to pay for it.

MECHANIC: Oh, I know; that's why my boss says try all the other places first, because he says youse guys charge. But looks to me like we're stuck.

LARRY: Bert. *He stares in thought.* Get the key to the third floor from Miss Molloy. Go up there, and when you open the door you'll see those Model-T mufflers stacked up.

BERT: Okay.

LARRY: You ever been up there?   630

BERT: No, but I always wanted to go.

LARRY: Well, go past the mufflers and you'll see a lot of bins going up to the ceiling. They're full of Marmon valves and ignition stuff.

BERT: Yeah?

LARRY: Go past them, and you'll come to a little corridor, see?

BERT: Yeah?

LARRY: At the end of the corridor is a pile of crates — I think there's some Maxwell differentials in there.

BERT: Yeah?

LARRY: Climb over the crates, but don't keep goin', see. Stand on top of the crates   640 and turn right. Then bend down, and there's a bin — No, I tell you, get off the crates, and you can reach behind them, but to the right, and reach into that bin.

There's a lot of Locomobile headnuts in there, but way back — you gotta stick your hand way in, see, and you'll find one of these.

BERT: Geez, Larry, how do you remember all that?

Agnes rushes in.

AGNES: Eagle's here! Eagle's here!

LARRY, *to the mechanic:* Go out front and wait at the counter, will ya? *The mechanic nods and leaves. Larry indicates the glass on the desk.* Better put that whisky away, Gus.   650

GUS, *alarmed now:* What should we do with him?

Larry goes to Tom, peeved, and speaks in his ear.

LARRY: Tommy. Tommy!

AGNES: Larry, why don't you put him up on the third floor? He got a dozen warnings already. Eagle's disgusted —

GUS: Maybe he's sick. I never seen him like this.

Jim enters with goods.

JIM: Eagle's here.

LARRY: Let's try to walk him around. Come on.

Gus looks for a place to hide the whisky, then drinks it.   660

GUS: All right, Tommy, come on, get up. *They hoist him up to his feet, then let him go. He starts to sag; they catch him.* I don't think he feel so good.

LARRY: Come on, walk him. *To Agnes:* Watch out for Eagle. *She stands looking off and praying silently.* Let's go, Tom. *They try to walk Tom, but he doesn't lift his feet.*

AGNES, *trembling, watching Tommy:* He's so kindhearted, y'see? That's his whole trouble — he's too kindhearted.

LARRY, *angering, but restrained, shaking Tom:* For God's sake, Tom, come on! Eagle's here! *He shakes Tom more violently.* Come on! What the hell is the matter with you, you want to lose your job? Goddamit, you a baby or something?

AGNES: Sssh!   670

They all turn to the left. In the distance is heard the clacking of heel taps on a concrete floor.

GUS: Put him down. Larry! *They seat Tom before the desk. Agnes swipes back his mussed hair. Gus sets his right hand on top of an invoice on the desk.* Here, put him like he's writing. Where's my pencil? Who's got pencil? *Larry, Kenneth, Agnes search themselves for a pencil.*

KENNETH: Here's a crayon.

GUS: Goddam, who take my pencil! Bert! Where's that Bert! He always take my pencil!

Bert enters, carrying a heavy axle.   680

BERT: Hey, Eagle's here!

GUS: Goddam you, why you take my pencil?

BERT: I haven't got your pencil. This is mine.

Gus grabs the pencil out of Bert's shirt pocket and sticks it upright into Tom's hand. They have set him up to look as if he is writing. They step away. Tom starts sagging toward one side.

AGNES, *in a loud whisper:* Here he comes!

She goes to the order spike and pretends she is examining it. Larry meanwhile rushes to Tom, sets him upright, then walks away, pretending to busy himself. But Tom starts falling off the chair again, and Bert rushes and props him up.   690

The sound of the heel taps is on us now, and Bert starts talking to Tom, meantime supporting him with one hand on his shoulder.

BERT, *overloudly:* Tommy, the reason I ask, see, is because on Friday I filled an order for the same amount of coils for Scranton, see, and it just seems they wouldn't be ordering the same exact amount again.

During his speech Eagle has entered — a good-looking man in his late forties, wearing palm beach trousers, a shirt and tie, sleeves neatly folded up, a new towel over one arm. He walks across the shipping room, not exactly looking at anyone, but clearly observing everything. He goes into the toilet, past Agnes, who turns.

AGNES: Good morning, Mr. Eagle.   700

EAGLE, *nodding:*   Morning. *He goes into the toilet.*

KENNETH, *indicating the toilet:*   Keep it up, keep it up now!

BERT, *loudly:*   Ah — another thing that's bothering me, Tommy, is those rear-end gears for Riverhead. I can't find any invoice for Riverhead. I can't find any invoice for gears to Riverhead. *He is getting desperate, looks to the others, but they only urge him on.* So what happened to the invoice? That's the thing we're all wondering about, Tommy. What happened to that invoice? You see, Tom? That invoice — it was blue, I remember, blue with a little red around the edges —

KENNETH, *loudly:*   That's right there, Bert, it was a blue invoice — and it had numbers on it —   710

Suddenly Tom stands, swaying a little, blinking. There is a moment's silence.

TOM: No, no, Glen Wright was shortstop for Pittsburgh, not Honus Wagner.[17]

Eagle emerges from the toilet. Bert goes to the order spike.

LARRY: Morning, sir. *He goes out.*

TOM, *half bewildered, shifting from foot to foot:*   Who was talking about Pittsburgh? *He turns about and almost collides with Eagle.* Morning, Mr. Eagle.

EAGLE — *as he passes Tom he lets his look linger on his face:*   Morning, Kelly.

Eagle crosses the shipping room and goes out. Agnes, Kenneth, and Gus wait an instant. Jim enters, sees Tom is up.

JIM: Attaboy, Tommy, knew you'd make it.   720

TOM: Glen Wright was shortstop. Who asked about that?

GUS, *nodding sternly his approbation to Bert:*   Very good, Bert, you done good.

BERT, *wiping his forehead:*   Boy!

TOM: Who was talking about Pittsburgh? *Agnes is heard weeping. They turn.* Agnes? *He goes to her.* What's the matter, Ag?

AGNES: Oh, Tommy, why do you do that?

PATRICIA, *calling from offstage left:*   Aggie? Your switchboard's ringing.

AGNES: Oh, Tommy! *Weeping, she hurries out.*

TOM, *to the others:*   What happened? What is she cryin' for?

GUS, *indicating the desk:*   Why don't you go to work, Tommy? You got lotta parcel   730
   post this morning.

Tom always has a defensive smile. He shifts from foot to foot as he talks, as though he were always standing on a hot stove. He turns to the desk, sees Kenneth. He wants to normalize everything.

TOM: Kenny! I didn't even see ya!

KENNETH: Morning, Tommy. Good to see you up and about.

TOM, *with a put-on brogue:*   Jasus, me bye, y'r hair is fallin' like the dew of the evenin'.

KENNETH, *self-consciously wiping his hair:*   Oh, Tommy, now —

TOM: Kenny, bye, y'r gittin' an awful long face to wash!   740

KENNETH, *gently cuffing him:*   Oh, now, stop that talk!

TOM, *backing toward his desk:*   Why, ya donkey, ya. I bet they had to back you off the boat!

KENNETH, *with mock anger:*   Oh, don't you be callin' me a donkey now!

Enter Raymond.

---

[17]Glen ("Buckshot") Wright (b. 1901) served as shortstop for
the Pittsburgh Pirates (1924–28).

RAYMOND: Tom? *He is very earnest, even deadly.*

TOM, *instantly perceiving his own guilt:*   Oh, mornin' Ray, how's the twins? *He gasps little chuckles as he sits at his desk, feeling about for a pencil.*

    Raymond goes up close to the desk and leans over, as the others watch — pretending not to.   750

RAYMOND, *quietly:*   Eagle wants to see you.

TOM, *with foreboding, looking up into Raymond's face:*   Eagle? I got a lot of parcel post this morning, Ray. *He automatically presses down his hair.*

RAYMOND: He's in his office waiting for you now, Tom.

TOM: Oh, sure. it's just that there's a lot of parcel post on Monday.... *He feels for his tie as he rises, and walks out. Raymond starts out after him, but Gus intercedes.*

GUS, *going up to Raymond:*   What Eagle wants?

RAYMOND: I warned him, Gus, I warned him a dozen times.

GUS: He's no gonna fire him.

RAYMOND: Look, it's all over, Gus, so there's nothing —   760

GUS: He gonna fire Tommy?

RAYMOND: Now don't raise your voice.

GUS: Sixteen year Tommy work here! He got daughter gonna be in church confirmation!

RAYMOND: Now listen, I been nursing him along for —

GUS: Then you fire me! You fire Tommy, you fire me!

RAYMOND: Gus!

    With a stride Gus goes to the hook, takes his shirt down, thrusts himself into it.

GUS: Goddam son-of-a-bitch.

RAYMOND: Now don't be crazy, Gus.   770

GUS: I show who crazy! Tommy Kelly he gonna fire! *He grabs his bowler off the hook. Enter Agnes, agitated.*

AGNES: Gus! Go to the phone!

GUS, *not noticing her, and with bowler on, to Raymond:*   Come on, he gonna fire me now, son-of-a-bitch! *He starts out, shirttails flying, and Agnes stops him.*

AGNES, *indicating the phone:*   Gus, your neighbor's —

GUS, *trying to disengage himself:*   No, he gonna fire me now. He fire Tommy Kelly, he fire me!

AGNES: Lilly, Gus! Your neighbor wants to talk to you. Go, go to the phone.

    Gus halts, looks at Agnes.   780

GUS: What, Lilly?

AGNES: Something's happened. Go, go to the phone.

GUS: Lilly? *Perplexed, he goes to the phone. Hallo, Yeah, Gus. Ha? He listens, stunned. His hand, of itself, goes to his hatbrim as though to doff the hat, but it stays there. Jim enters, comes to a halt, sensing the attention, and watches Gus. When? When it happen? He listens, and then mumbles: Ya. Thank you. I come home right away. He hangs up. Jim comes forward to him questioningly. To Jim, perplexed: My Lilly. Die.*

JIM: Oh? Hm!

    Larry enters. Gus dumbly turns to him.

GUS, *to Larry:*   Die. My Lilly.   790

LARRY: Oh, that's tough, Gus.

RAYMOND: You better go home. *Pause.* Go ahead, Gus, Go home.

    Gus stands blinking. Raymond takes his jacket from the hook and helps him on with it. Agnes starts to push his shirttails into his pants.

GUS: We shouldn't've go to Staten Island, Jim. Maybe she don't feel good yesterday. Ts, I was in Staten Island, maybe she was sick. *Tommy Kelly enters, goes directly to his desk, sits, his back to the others. Pause. To Tom:* He fire you, Tommy?

TOM, *holding tears back:*   No, Gus, I'm all right.

GUS, *going up next to him:*   Give you another chance?

TOM—*he is speaking with his head lowered:*   Yeah. It's all right, Gus, I'm goin' to be 800
all right from now on.

GUS: Sure. Be a man, Tommy. Don't be no drunken bum. Be a man. You hear?
Don't let nobody walk on top you. Be man.

TOM: I'm gonna be all right, Gus.

GUS, *nodding:*   One more time you come in drunk I gonna show you something.
Agnes sobs. He turns to her. What for you cry all the time? *He goes past her and out.
Agnes then goes. A silence.*

RAYMOND, *breaking the silence:*   What do you say, fellas, let's get going, heh? *He
claps his hands and walks out as all move about their work. Soon all are gone but Tommy
Kelly, slumped at his desk; Kenneth, wrapping; and Bert, picking an order from the hook.* 810
Now Kenneth faces Bert suddenly.

KENNETH—*he has taken his feeling from the departing Gus, and turns now to Bert:*   Bert?
How would you feel about washing these windows—you and I—once and for
all? Let a little of God's light in the place?

BERT, *excitedly, happily:*   Would you?

KENNETH: Well, I would if you would.

BERT: Okay, come on! Let's do a little every day; couple of months it'll all be
clean! Gee! Look at the sun!

KENNETH: Hey, look down there!
See the old man sitting in a chair?   820
And roses all over the fence!
Oh, that's a lovely back yard!

> *A rag in hand, Bert mounts the table; they make one slow swipe of the window before
> them and instantly all the windows around the stage burst into the yellow light of summer that
> floods into the room.*

BERT: Boy, they've got a tree!
And all those cats!

KENNETH: It'll be nice to watch the seasons pass.
'That pretty up there now, a real summer sky
And a little white cloud goin' over?   830
I can just see autumn comin' in
And the leaves fallin on the gray days.
You've got to have a sky to look at!

> *Gradually, as they speak, all light hardens to that of winter, finally.*

BERT, *turning to Kenneth:*   Kenny, were you ever fired from a job?

KENNETH: Oh, sure; two-three times.

BERT: Did you feel bad?

KENNETH: The first time, maybe. But you have to get used to that, Bert. I'll bet
you never went hungry in your life, did you?

BERT: No, I never did. Did you?   840

KENNETH: Oh, many and many a time. You get used to that too, though.

BERT, *turning and looking out:*   That tree is turning red.

KENNETH: It must be spectacular out in the country now.

BERT: How does the cold get through these walls?
Feel it, it's almost a wind!

KENNETH: Don't cats walk dainty in the snow!

BERT: Gee, you'd never know it was the same place—
How clean it is when it's white!
Gus doesn't say much any more, y'know?

KENNETH: Well, he's showin' his age. Gus is old.   850
When do you buy your ticket for the train?

BERT: I did. I've got it.

KENNETH: Oh, then you're off soon!

You'll confound all the professors, I'll bet!
He sings softly.
"The minstrel boy to the war has gone . . ."
    Bert moves a few feet away; thus he is alone. Kenneth remains at the window, looking out, polishing, and singing softly.
BERT: There's something so terrible here!
There always was, and I don't know what.   860
Gus, and Agnes, and Tommy and Larry, Jim and Patricia —
Why does it make me so sad to see them every morning?
It's like the subway;
Every day I see the same people getting on
And the same people getting off,
And all that happens is that they get older. God!
Sometimes it scares me; like all of us in the world
Were riding back and forth across a great big room,
From wall to wall and back again,
And no end ever! Just no end!   870
    He turns to Kenneth, but not quite looking at him, and with a deeper anxiety.
Didn't you ever want to be anything, Kenneth?
KENNETH: I've never been able to keep my mind on it, Bert. . . .
I shouldn't've cut a hole in me shoe.
Now the snow's slushin' in, and me feet's all wet.
BERT: If you studied, Kenneth, if you put your mind to something great, I know you'd be able to learn anything, because you're clever, you're much smarter than I am!
KENNETH: You've got something steady in your mind, Bert;
Something far away and steady.   880
I never could hold my mind on a far-away thing . . .
    His tone changes as though he were addressing a group of men; his manner is rougher, angrier, less careful of proprieties.
She's not giving me the heat I'm entitled to.
Eleven dollars a week room and board,
And all she puts in the bag is a lousy pork sandwich,
The same every day and no surprises.
Is that right? Is that right now?
How's a man to live,
Freezing all day in this palace of dust   890
And night comes with one window and a bed
And the streets full of strangers
And not one of them's read a book through,
Or seen a poem from beginning to end
Or knows a song worth singing.
Oh, this is an ice-cold city, Mother,
And Roosevelt's not makin' it warmer, somehow.
    He sits on the table, holding his head.
And here's another grand Monday!
    They are gradually appearing in natural light now, but it is a cold wintry light which 900
has gradually supplanted the hot light of summer. Bert goes to the hook for a sweater.
Jesus, me head'll murder me. I never had the headache till this year.
BERT, *delicately:*   You're not taking up drinking, are you?
KENNETH — *he doesn't reply. Suddenly, as though to retrieve something slipping by, he gets to his feet, and roars out:*

      "The Ship of State," by Walt Whitman!
      "O Captain! my Captain! our fearful trip is done!"

> The ship has weathered every wrack,
> The prize we sought is won . . ."[18]

Now what in the world comes after that?   910
BERT: I don't know that poem.
KENNETH: Dammit all! I don't remember the bloody poems any more the way I
    did! It's the drinkin' does it, I think. I've got to stop the drinkin'!
BERT: Well, why do you drink, Kenny, if it makes you feel—
KENNETH: Good God, Bert, you can't always be doin' what you're better off to
    do! There's all kinds of unexpected turns, y'know, and things not workin' out
    the way they ought! What in hell *is* the next stanza of that poem? "The prize we
    sought is won . . ." God, I'd never believe I could forget that poem! I'm thinkin',
    Bert, y'know—maybe I ought to go onto the Civil Service. The only trouble is
    there's no jobs open except for the guard in the insane asylum. And that'd be a 920
    nervous place to work, I think.
BERT: It might be interesting, though.
KENNETH: I suppose it might. They tell me it's only the more intelligent people
    goes mad, y'know. But it's sixteen hundred a year, Bert, and I've a feelin' I'd
    never dare leave it, y'know? And I'm not ready for me last job yet, I think. I
    don't want nothin' to be the last, yet. Still and all . . .
        Raymond enters, going to toilet. He wears a blue button-up sweater.
RAYMOND: Morning, boys. *He impales a batch of orders on the desk.*
KENNETH, *in a routine way:*   Morning, Mr. Ryan. Have a nice New Year's, did you?
RAYMOND: Good enough. *To Bert, seeing the book on the table.* Still reading that book? 930
BERT: Oh, I'm almost finished now. *Raymond nods, continues on. Bert jumps off the
    table.* Mr. Ryan? Can I see you a minute? *He goes to Raymond.* I wondered if you
    hired anybody yet, to take my place.
RAYMOND, *pleasantly surprised:*   Why? Don't you have enough money to go?
BERT: No, I'm going. I just thought maybe I could help you break in the new
    boy. I won't be leaving till after lunch tomorrow.
RAYMOND, *with resentment, even an edge of sarcasm:*   We'll break him in all right.
    Why don't you just get on to your own work? There's a lot of excelsior laying
    around the freight elevator.
        Raymond turns and goes into the toilet. For an instant Bert is left staring after him. 940
Then he turns to Kenneth, perplexed.
BERT: Is he sore at me?
KENNETH, *deprecatingly:*   Ah, why would he be sore at you? *He starts busying himself
    at the table, avoiding Bert's eyes. Bert moves toward him, halts.*
BERT: I hope you're not, are you?
KENNETH, *with an evasive air:*   Me? Ha! Why, Bert, you've got the heartfelt good
    wishes of everybody in the place for your goin'-away! *But he turns away to busy
    himself at the table—and on his line Larry has entered with a container of coffee and a
    cigarette.*
BERT: Morning, Larry. *He goes to the hook, takes an order.*   950
LARRY, *leaning against the table:*   Jesus, it'd be just about perfect in here for pen-
    guins. *Bert passes him.* You actually leaving tomorrow?
BERT, *eagerly:*   I guess so, yeah.
LARRY, *with a certain embarrassed envy:*   Got all the dough, heh?
BERT: Well, for the first year anyway. *He grins in embarrassment.* You mind if I
    thank you?
LARRY: What for?

---

[18]The opening lines of "O Captain! My Captain!" by Walt
Whitman (another of Whitman's poems about Abraham Lincoln), often memorized by school children. The title Kenneth
gives the poem is an often-used metaphor, found, for example, as a line in "The Building of a Ship" by American poet
Henry Wadsworth Longfellow (1807–1882).

BERT: I don't know—just for teaching me everything. I'd have been fired the first month without you, Larry.

LARRY, *with some wonder, respect:*   Got all your dough, heh?   960

BERT: Well, that's all I've been doing is saving.
>   *Enter Tom Kelly. He is bright, clean, sober.*

TOM: Morning!

KENNETH, *with an empty kind of heartiness:*   Why, here comes Tommy Kelly!

TOM, *passing to hang up his coat and hat:*   Ah, y're gettin' an awful long face to wash, Kenny, me bye.

KENNETH: Oh, cut it out with me face, Tommy. I'm as sick of it as you are.

TOM: Go on, ya donkey ya, they backed you off the boat.

KENNETH: Why, I'll tear you limb from limb, Tom Kelly! *He mocks a fury, and Tom laughs as he is swung about. And then, with a quick hug and a laugh:*   970
Oh, Tommy, you're the first man I ever heard of done it. How'd you do it, Tom?

TOM: Will power, Kenny. *He walks to his desk, sits.* Just made up my mind, that's all.

KENNETH: Y'know the whole world is talking about you, Tom—the way you mixed all the drinks at the Christmas party and never weakened? Y'know, when I heard it was you going to mix the drinks I was prepared to light a candle for you.

TOM: I just wanted to see if I could do it, that's all. When I done that—mixin' the drinks for three hours, and givin' them away—I realized I made it. You don't look so hot to me, you know that?

KENNETH, *with a sigh:*   Oh, I'm all right. It's the sight of Monday, that's all, is got   980
me down.

TOM: You better get yourself a little will power, Kenny. I think you're gettin' a fine taste for the hard stuff.

KENNETH: Ah, no, I'll never be a drunk, Tommy.

TOM: You're a drunk now.

KENNETH: Oh, don't say that, please!

TOM: I'm tellin' you, I can see it comin' on you.

KENNETH, *deeply disturbed:*   You can't either. Don't say that, Tommy!
>   *Agnes enters.*

AGNES: Morning! *She wears sheets of brown paper for leggins.*   990

KENNETH: Winter's surely here when Agnes is wearin' her leggins.

AGNES, *with her laughter:*   Don't they look awful? But that draft under the switch-board is enough to kill ya.

LARRY: This place is just right for penguins.

AGNES: Haven't you got a heavier sweater, Bert? I'm surprised at your mother.

BERT: Oh, it's warm; she knitted it.

KENNETH: Bert's got the idea. Get yourself an education.

TOM: College guys are sellin' ties all over Macy's. Accountancy, Bert, that's my advice to you. You don't even have to go to college for it either.

BERT: Yeah, but I don't want to be an accountant.   1000

TOM, *with a superior grin:*   You don't want to be an accountant?

LARRY: What's so hot about an accountant?

TOM: Well, try runnin' a business without one. That's what you should've done, Larry. If you'd a took accountancy, you'd a—

LARRY: You know, Tommy, I'm beginning to like you better drunk? *Tommy laughs, beyond criticism.* I mean it. Before, we only had to pick you up all the time; now you got opinions about everything.

TOM: Well, if I happen to know something, why shouldn't I say—
>   *Enter Raymond from the toilet.*

RAYMOND: What do you say we get on the ball early today, fellas? Eagle's coming   1010
today. Bert, how about gettin' those carburetor crates open, will ya?

BERT: I was just going to do that.

> *Bert and Raymond are starting out, and Agnes is moving to go, when Gus and Jim enter. Both of them are on the verge of staggering. Gus has a bright new suit and checked overcoat, a new bowler, and new shoes. He is carrying upright a pair of Ford fenders, still in their brown paper wrappings—they stand about seven feet in height. Jim aids him in carefully resting the fenders against the wall.*
>
> *Kenneth, Agnes, and Larry watch in silence.*
>
> *Patricia enters and watches. She is wearing leggins.*
>
> *Willy and Jerry enter in overcoats, all jazzed up.*   1020

WILLY: Morning!

JERRY: Morn—*Both break off and slowly remove their coats as they note the scene and the mood. Gus, now that the fenders are safely stacked, turns.*

GUS, *dimly:*   Who's got a hanger?

KENNETH: Hanger? You mean a coat-hanger, Gus?

GUS: Coat-hanger.

JERRY: Here! Here's mine! *He gives a wire hanger to Gus. Gus is aided by Jim in removing his overcoat, and they both hang it on the hanger, then on a hook. Both give it a brush or two, and Gus goes to his chair, sits. He raises his eyes to them all.*

GUS: So what everybody is looking at?   1030

> *Bert, Willy, Jerry go to work, gradually going out with orders. Jim also takes orders off the hook, and the pattern of going-and-coming emerges. Patricia goes to the toilet. Tom Kelly works at the desk.*

LARRY, *half-kidding, but in a careful tone:*   What are you all dressed up about?

> *Gus simply glowers in his fumes and thoughts. Raymond goes over to Jim.*

RAYMOND: What's he all dressed up for?

JIM: Oh, don't talk to me about him, Ray, I'm sick and tired of him. Spent all Saturday buyin' new clothes to go to the cemetery; then all the way the hell over to Long Island City to get these damned fenders for that old wreck of a Ford he's got. Never got to the cemetery, never got the fenders on—and we been 1040 walkin' around all weekend carryin' them damn things.

RAYMOND: Eagle'll be here this morning. See if you can get him upstairs. I don't want him to see him crocked again.

JIM: I'd just let him sit there, Ray, if I was you. I ain't goin' to touch him. You know what he went and done? Took all his insurance money outa the bank Saturday. Walkin' around with all that cash in his pocket—I tell ya, I ain't been to sleep since Friday night, 'Cause you can't let him loose with all that money and so low in his mind, y'know . . .

GUS: Irishman! *All turn to him. He takes a wad out of his pocket, peels one bill off.* Here. Buy new pair shoes.   1050

KENNETH: Ah, thank you, no, Gus, I couldn't take that.

RAYMOND: Gus, Eagle's coming this morning; why don't you—

GUS, *stuffing a bill into Kenneth's pocket:*   Go buy pair shoes.

RAYMOND: Gus, he's going to be here right away; why don't you—

GUS: I don't give one goddam for Eagle! Why he don't make one more toilet?

RAYMOND: What?

> *Bert enters with goods.*

GUS: Toilet! That's right? Have one toilet for so many people? That's very bad, Raymond. That's no nice. *Offering Bert a bill:* Here, boy, go—buy book, buy candy.   1060

> *Larry goes to Gus before he gives the bill, puts an arm around him, and walks away from the group.*

LARRY: Come on, Gussy, let me take you upstairs.

GUS: I don't care Eagle sees me, I got my money now, goddam. Oh, Larry, Larry, twenty-two year I workin' here.

LARRY: Why don't you give me the money, Gus? I'll put in the bank for you.

GUS: What for I put in bank? I'm sixty-eight years old, Larry. I got no children, nothing. What for I put in bank? *Suddenly, reminded, he turns back to Raymond, pointing at the floor scale.* Why them goddam mice nobody does nothing?

RAYMOND, *alarmed by Gus's incipient anger:*   Gus, I want you to go upstairs!   1070
   Patricia enters from toilet.

GUS, *at the scale:*   Twenty-two years them goddam mice! That's very bad, Raymond, so much mice! *He starts rocking the scale.* Look at them goddam mice! *Patricia screams as mice come running out from under the scale. A mêlée of shouts begins, everyone dodging mice or swinging brooms and boxes at them. Raymond is pulling Gus away from the scale, yelling at him to stop it. Agnes rushes in and, seeing the mice, screams and rushes out. Jerry and Willy rush in and join in chasing the mice, laughing. Patricia, wearing leggins, is helped onto the packing table by Larry, and Gus shouts up at her.* Come with me Atlantic City, Patricia! *He pulls out the wad.* Five thousand dollars I got for my wife!   1080

PATRICIA: You rotten thing, you! You dirty rotten thing, Gus!

GUS: I make you happy, Patricia! I make you— *Suddenly his hand goes to his head; he is dizzy. Larry goes to him, takes one look.*

LARRY: Come, come on. *He walks Gus into the toilet.*

PATRICIA, *out of the momentary silence:*   Oh, that louse! Did you see what he did, that louse? *She gets down off the table, and, glancing angrily toward the toilet, she goes out.*

RAYMOND: All right, fellas, what do you say, heh? Let's get going.
   Work proceeds—the going and coming.

TOM, *as Raymond passes him:*   I tried talking to him a couple of times, Ray, but he's got no will power! There's nothing you can do if there's no will power, y'know?   1090

RAYMOND: Brother! It's a circus around here. Every Monday morning! I never saw anything like . . . .
   He is gone. Kenneth is packing. Tom works at his desk. Jim comes and, leaving goods on the packing table, goes to the toilet, peeks in, then goes out, studying an order. Bert enters with goods.

KENNETH: There's one thing you have to say for the Civil Service; it seals the fate and locks the door. A man needn't wonder what he'll do with his life any more.
   Jerry enters with goods.

BERT, *glancing at the toilet door:*   Gee, I never would've thought Gus liked his wife, would you?   1100
   Tom, studying a letter, goes out.

JERRY, *looking up and out the window:*   Jesus!

BERT, *not attending to Jerry:*   I thought he always hated his wife—

JERRY: Jesus, boy!

KENNETH, *to Jerry:*   What're you doin'? What's—?

JERRY: Look at the girls up in there. One, two, three, four windows—full a girls, look at them! Them two is naked!
   Willy enters with goods.

KENNETH: Oh, my God!

WILLY, *rushing to the windows:*   Where? Where?   1110

KENNETH: Well, what're you gawkin' at them for!
   Gus and Larry enter from the toilet.

JERRY: There's another one down there! Look at her on the bed! What a beast!

WILLY, *overjoyed:*   It's a cathouse! Gus! A whole cathouse moved in!
   Willy and Jerry embrace and dance around wildly; Gus stands with Larry, staring out, as does Bert.

KENNETH: Aren't you ashamed of yourself!!
   Tom enters with his letter.

TOM: Hey, fellas, Eagle's here.

JERRY, *pointing out:*   There's a new cathouse, Tommy! *Tom goes and looks out the* 1120
windows.

KENNETH: Oh, that's a terrible thing to be lookin' at, Tommy! *Agnes enters; Kenneth instantly goes to her to get her out.* Oh, Agnes, you'd best not be comin' back here any more now —

AGNES: What? What's the matter?
   Jerry has opened a window, and he and Willy whistle sharply through their fingers. Agnes looks out.

KENNETH: Don't, Agnes, don't look at that!

AGNES: Well, for heaven's sake! What are all those women doing there?

GUS: That's whorehouse, Aggie.   1130

KENNETH: Gus, for God's sake! *He walks away in pain.*

AGNES: What are they sitting on the beds like that for?

TOM: The sun is pretty warm this morning — probably trying to get a little tan.

AGNES: Oh, my heavens. Oh, Bert, it's good you're leaving! *She turns to them.* You're not all going, are you? *Gus starts to laugh, then Tom, then Jerry and Willy, then Larry, and she is unstrung and laughing herself, but shocked.* Oh, my heavens! *She is gone, as Jim enters with goods.*

KENNETH: All right, now, clear off, all of you. I can't be workin' with a lot of sex maniacs blockin' off me table!

GUS: Look, Jim! *Jim looks out.*   1140

JIM: Oh, nice.

JERRY: How about it, fellas? Let's all go lunchtime! What do you say, Kenny? I'll pay for you!
   Gus goes to the desk, drags the chair over to the window.

KENNETH: I'd sooner roll meself around in the horse manure of the gutter!

JERRY: I betcha you wouldn't even know what to do!

KENNETH, *bristling, fists shut:*   I'll show you what I do! I'll show you right now!
   Enter Raymond, furious.

RAYMOND: What the hell is this? What's going on here?

GUS, *sitting in his chair, facing the windows:*   Whorehouse. *Raymond looks out the* 1150
windows.

KENNETH: You'd better pass a word to Mr. Eagle about this, Raymond, or the corporation's done for. Poor Agnes, she's all mortified, y'know.

RAYMOND: Oh, my God! *To all:* All right, break it up, come on, break it up, Eagle's here. *Willy, Jerry, Bert, and Jim disperse, leaving with orders. Tommy returns to the desk.* What're you going to do, Gus? You going to sit there? *Gus doesn't answer; sits staring out thoughtfully.* What's going on with you? Gus! Eagle's here! All right, cook in your own juice. Sit there. *He glances out the windows.* Brother, I needed this now! *He goes out angrily.*

LARRY: Give me the money, Gus, come on. I'll hold it for you.   1160

GUS — *an enormous sadness is on him:*   Go way.
   Enter Patricia. She glances at Larry and Gus, then looks out the windows.

KENNETH, *wrapping:*   Ah, Patricia, don't look out there. It's disgraceful.

TOM: It's only a lot of naked women.

KENNETH: Oh, Tommy, now! In front of a girl!

PATRICIA, *to Kenneth:*   What's the matter? Didn't you ever see that before? *She sees Gus sitting there.* Look at Kong, will ya? *She laughs.* Rememberin' the old days, heh, Kong?
   Larry is walking toward an exit at left.

GUS: Oh, shatap!   1170

PATRICIA, *catching up with Larry at the edge of the stage, quietly:*   What's Ray sayin' about you sellin' the Auburn?

LARRY: Yeah, I'm kinda fed up with it. It's out of my class anyway.

PATRICIA: That's too bad. I was just gettin' to enjoy it.

LARRY, *very doubtfully:*   Yeah?

PATRICIA: What're you mad at me for?

LARRY: Why should I be mad?

PATRICIA: You're married, what're you—?

LARRY: Let me worry about that, will you?

PATRICIA: Well, I gotta worry about it too, don't I?   1180

LARRY: Since when do you worry about anything, Pat?

PATRICIA: Well, what did you expect me to do? How did I know you were serious?
     Gus goes to his coat, searches in a pocket.

LARRY: What did you think I was telling you all the time?

PATRICIA: Yeah, but Larry, anybody could say those kinda things.

LARRY: I know, Pat. But I never did. *With a cool, hurt smile:* You know, kid, you
     better start believing people when they tell you something. Or else you're liable
     to end up in there. *He points out the windows.*

PATRICIA, *with quiet fury:*   You take that back! *He walks away; she goes after him.*
     You're going to take that back, Larry!   1190
     Eagle enters, nods to Larry and Patricia.

EAGLE: Morning.

PATRICIA, *with a mercurial change to sunny charm:*   Good morning, Mr. Eagle!
     *Larry is gone, and she exits. Eagle crosses, noticing Gus, who is standing beside his
coat, drinking out of a pint whisky bottle.*

EAGLE: Morning, Gus.

GUS, *lowering the bottle:*   Good morning. *Eagle exits into the toilet.*

TOM, *to Gus:*   You gone nuts?
     *Gus returns, holding the bottle, to his chair, where he sits, looking out the window. He
is growing sodden and mean. Bert enters with goods.*   1200

KENNETH, *sotto voce:*[19]   Eagle's in there, and look at him. He'll get the back of it
     now for sure.

TOM, *going to Gus:*   Gimme the bottle, Gus!

GUS: I goin' go someplace, Tommy. I goin' go cemetery. I wasn't one time in
     cemetery. I go see my Lilly. My Lilly die, I was in Staten Island. All alone she
     was in the house. Ts! *Jerry enters with goods, sees him, and laughs.*

BERT: Gus, why don't you give Tommy the bottle?

GUS: Twenty-two years I work here.

KENNETH, *to Jerry, who is staring out the window:*   Will you quit hangin' around me
     table, please?   1210

JERRY: Can't I look out the window?
     Willy enters with goods.

WILLY: How's all the little pussies?

KENNETH: Now cut that out! *They laugh at him.*

TOM, *sotto voce:*   Eagle's in there!

KENNETH: Is that all yiz know of the world—filthy women and dirty jokes and
     the ignorance drippin' off your faces? *Eagle enters from the toilet.* There's got to
     be somethin' done about this, Mr. Eagle. It's an awful humiliation for the
     women here. *He points, and Eagle looks.* I mean to say, it's a terrible disorganizing
     sight starin' a man in the face eight hours a day, sir.   1220

EAGLE: Shouldn't have washed the windows, I guess. *He glances down at Gus and
his bottle and walks out.*

---

[19]"In a low voice" (Italian).

KENNETH: Shouldn't have washed the windows, he says! *They are laughing; Gus is tipping the bottle up. Jim enters with goods.*

JERRY: What a donkey that guy is!
Kenneth lunges for Jerry and grabs him by the tie, one fist ready.

KENNETH: I'll donkey you! *Jerry starts a swing at him, and Bert and Tom rush to separate them as Raymond enters.*

RAYMOND: Hey! Hey!

JERRY, *as they part:*   All right, donkey, I'll see you later.   1230

KENNETH: You'll see me later, all right—with one eye closed!

RAYMOND: Cut it out! *Kenneth, muttering, returns to work at his table. Jerry rips an order off the hook and goes out. Willy takes an order. Bert goes out with an order. Raymond has been looking down at Gus, who is sitting with the botile.* You going to work, Gus? Or you going to do that? *Gus gets up and goes to his coat, takes it off the hanger.* What're you doing?

GUS: Come on, Jim, we go someplace. Here—put on you coat.

RAYMOND: Where you going? It's half-past nine in the morning.
Enter Agnes.

AGNES: What's all the noise here? *She breaks off, seeing Gus dressing.*   1240

GUS: That's when I wanna go—half-past nine. *He hands Jim his coat.* Here. Put on. Cold outside.

JIM, *quietly:*   Maybe I better go with him, Ray. He's got all his money in—
Bert enters with goods.

RAYMOND, *reasonably, deeply concerned:*   Gus, now look; where you gonna go now? Why don't you lie down upstairs?

GUS, *swaying, to Bert:*   Twenty-two years I was here.

BERT: I know, Gus.
Larry enters, watches.

GUS: I was here before you was born I was here.   1250

BERT: I know.

GUS: Them mice was here before you was born. *Bert nods uncomfortably, full of sadness.* When Mr. Eagle was in high school I was already here. When there was Winton Six I was here. When was Minerva car I was here. When was Stanley Steamer I was here, and Stearns Knight, and Marmon was good car; I was here all them times. I was here first day Raymond come; he was young boy; work hard be manager. When Agnes still think she was gonna get married I was here. When was Locomobile, and Model K Ford and Model N Ford—all them different Fords, and Franklin was good car, Jordan car, Reo car, Pierce Arrow, Cleveland car—all them was good cars.[20] All them times I was here.   1260

BERT: I know.

GUS: You don't know nothing. Come on, Jim. *He goes and gets a fender. Jim gets the other.* Button up you coat, cold outside. Tommy? Take care everything good.
He walks out with Jim behind him, each carrying a fender upright. Raymond turns and goes out, then Larry. Agnes goes into the toilet. The lights lower as this movement takes place, until Bert is alone in light, still staring at the point where Gus left.

BERT: I don't understand;
I don't know anything:
How is it me that gets out?
I don't know half the poems Kenneth does,   1270
Or a quarter of what Larry knows about an engine.

---

[20]Reference to early makes and models of automobiles, by then part of the past.

I don't understand how they come every morning.
Every morning and every morning,
And no end in sight.
That's the thing—there's no end!
Oh, there ought to be a statue in the park—
"To All the Ones That Stay."
One to Larry, to Agnes, Tom Kelly, Gus . . .

Gee, it's peculiar to leave a place—forever!
Still, I always hated coming here;   1280
The same dried-up jokes, the dust;
Especially in spring, walking in from the sunshine,
Or any Monday morning in the hot days.
  In the darkness men appear and gather around the packing table, eating lunch out of
bags; we see them as ghostly figures, silent.
God, it's so peculiar to leave a place!
I know I'll remember them as long as I live,
As long as I live they'll never die,
And still I know that in a month or two
They'll forget my name, and mix me up   1290
With another boy who worked here once,
And went. Gee, it's a mystery!
  As full light rises Bert moves into the group, begins eating from a bag.
JERRY, *looking out the window:*   You know what's a funny thing? It's a funny thing
  how you get used to that.
WILLY: Tommy, what would you say Cobb's[21] average was for lifetime?
TOM: Cobb? Lifetime? *He thinks. Pause. Kenneth sings.*
KENNETH: "The minstrel boy to the war has gone—
  Patricia enters, crossing to toilet—
               In the ranks of death you will find him."   1300
PATRICIA: Is that an Irish song?
KENNETH: All Irish here, and none of yiz knows an Irish song! *She laughs, exits*
  into the toilet.
TOM: I'd say three-eighty lifetime for Ty Cobb. *To Larry:* You're foolish sellin'
  that car with all the work you put in it.
LARRY: Well, it was one of those crazy ideas. Funny how you get an idea, and
  then suddenly you wake up and you look at it and it's like—dead or something.
  I can't afford a car.
  Agnes enters, going toward the toilet.
AGNES: I think it's even colder today than yesterday.   1310
  Raymond enters.
RAYMOND: It's five after one, fellas; what do you say?
  They begin to get up as Jim enters in his overcoat and hat.
KENNETH: Well! The old soldier returns!
RAYMOND: Where's Gus, Jim?
  Agnes has opened the toilet door as Patricia emerges.
AGNES: Oh! You scared me. I didn't know you were in there!
JIM, *removing his coat:*   He died, Ray.
RAYMOND: What?
  The news halts everyone—but one by one—in midair, as it were.   1320

21Tyrus (Ty) Raymond Cobb (1886–1961), American baseball player whose career batting average was a record .367.

LARRY: He what?

AGNES: What'd you say?

JIM: Gus died.

KENNETH: Gus died!

BERT: Gus?

AGNES, *going to Jim:*   Oh, good heavens. When? What happened?

LARRY: What'd you have an accident?

JIM: No, we—we went home and got the fenders on all right, and he wanted to go over and start at the bottom, and go right up Third Avenue and hit the bars on both sides. And we got up to about Fourteenth Street, in around there, and 1330 we kinda lost track of the car someplace. I have to go back there tonight, see if I can find—

AGNES: Well, what happened?

JIM: Well, these girls got in the cab, y'know, and we seen a lot of places and all that—we was to some real high-class places, forty cents for a cup of coffee and all that; and then he put me in another cab, and we rode around a while; and then he got another cab to follow us. Case one of our cabs got a flat, see? He just didn't want to be held up for a minute, Gus didn't.

LARRY: Where were you going?

JIM: Oh, just all over. And we stopped for a light, y'know, and I thought I'd go 1340 up and see how he was gettin' along, y'know, and I open his cab door, and—the girl was fast asleep, see—and he—was dead. Right there in the seat. It was just gettin' to be morning.

AGNES: Oh, poor Gus!

JIM: I tell ya, Agnes, he didn't look too good to me since she died, the old lady. I never knowed it. He—liked that woman.

RAYMOND: Where's his money?

JIM: Oh—*with a wasting wave of the hand*—it's gone, Ray. We was stoppin' off every couple minutes so he call long distance. I didn't even know it, he had a brother someplace in California. Called him half a dozen times. And there was 1350 somebody he was talkin' to in Texas someplace, somebody that was in the Navy with him. He was tryin' to call all the guys that was in the submarine with him, and he was callin' all over hell and gone—and givin' big tips, and he bought a new suit, and give the cab driver a wristwatch and all like that. I think he got himself too sweated. Y'know it got pretty cold last night, and he was all sweated up. I kept tellin' him, I says, "Gus," I says, "you're gettin' yourself all sweated, y'know, and it's a cold night," I says; and all he kept sayin' to me all night he says, "Jim," he says, "I'm gonna do it right, Jim." That's all he says practically all night. "I'm gonna do it right," he says. "I'm gonna do it right." *Pause. Jim shakes his head.* Oh, when I open that cab door I knowed it right away. I takes one look 1360 at him and I knowed it. *There is a moment of silence, and Agnes turns and goes into the toilet.* Oh, poor Agnes, I bet she's gonna cry now.

Jim goes to the order hook, takes an order off, and, putting a cigar into his mouth, he goes out, studying the order. Raymond crosses and goes out; then Patricia goes. Willy and Jerry exit in different directions with orders in their hands; Kenneth begins wrapping. Tom goes to his desk and sits, clasps his hands, and for a moment he prays.

Bert goes and gets his jacket. He slowly puts it on.

Enter Frank, the truckdriver.

FRANK: Anything for West Bronx, Tommy?

TOM: There's some stuff for Sullivan's there.   1370

FRANK: Okay. *He pokes through the packages, picks some.*

KENNETH: Gus died.

FRANK: No kiddin'!

KENNETH: Ya, last night.

FRANK: What do you know. Hm. *He goes on picking packages out.* Is this all for West
Bronx, Tom?

TOM: I guess so for now.

FRANK, *to Kenneth:*   Died.

KENNETH: Yes, Jim was with him. Last night.

FRANK: Jesus. *He stares, shakes his head.* I'll take Brooklyn when I get back, 1380
Tommy. *He goes out, loaded with packages. Bert is buttoning his overcoat. Agnes comes
out of the toilet.*

BERT: Agnes?

AGNES, *seeing the coat on, the book in his hand:*   Oh, you're leaving, Bert!

BERT: Yeah.

AGNES: Well. You're leaving.

BERT, *expectantly:*   Yeah.
      Patricia enters.

PATRICIA: Agnes? Your switchboard's ringing.
      Jerry enters with goods.   1390

AGNES: Okay! *Patricia goes out.* Well, good luck. I hope you pass everything.

BERT: Thanks, Aggie. *She walks across and out, wiping a hair across her forehead.
Willy enters with goods as Jerry goes out. Jim enters with goods.*
      *Bert seems about to say good-by to each of them, but they are engrossed and he doesn't
quite want to start a scene with them; but now Jim is putting his goods on the table, so Bert
goes over to him.* I'm leaving, Jim, so—uh—

JIM: Oh, leavin'? Heh! Well, that's—

TOM, *from his place at the desk, offering an order to Jim:*   Jim? See if these transmis-
sions came in yet, will ya? This guy's been ordering them all month.

JIM: Sure, Tom.   1400
      *Jim goes out past Bert, studying his order. Bert glances at Kenneth, who is busy
wrapping. He goes to Tom, who is working at the desk.*

BERT: Well, so long, Tommy.

TOM, *turning:*   Oh, you goin', heh?

BERT: Yeah, I'm leavin' right now.

TOM: Well, keep up the will power, y'know. That's what does it.

BERT: Yeah. I—uh—I wanted to—
      Raymond enters.

RAYMOND, *handing Tom an order:*   Tommy, make this a special, will you? The guy's
truck broke down in Peekskill. Send it out special today.   1410

TOM: Right.
      Raymond turns to go out, sees Bert, who seems to expect some moment from him.

RAYMOND: Oh! 'By, Bert.

BERT: So long, Raymond, I— *Raymond is already on his way, and he is gone. Jim
enters with goods. Bert goes over to Kenneth and touches his back. Kenneth turns to him.
Jim goes out as Willy enters with goods—Jerry too, and this work goes on without halt.*
Well, good-by, Kenny.

KENNETH— *he is embarrassed as he turns to Bert:*   Well, it's our last look, I suppose,
isn't it?

BERT: No, I'll come back sometime. I'll visit you.   1420

KENNETH: Oh, not likely; it'll all be out of mind as soon as you turn the corner.
I'll probably not be here anyway.

BERT: You made up your mind for Civil Service?

KENNETH: Well, you've got to keep movin', and—I'll move there, I guess. I done
a shockin' thing last night, Bert; I knocked over a bar.

BERT: Knocked it over?

KENNETH: It's disgraceful, what I done. I'm standin' there, havin' a decent conversation, that's all, and before I know it I start rockin' the damned thing, and it

toppled over and broke every glass in the place, and the beer spoutin' out of the pipes all over the floor. They took all me money; I'll be six weeks payin' them 1430 back. I'm for the Civil Service, I think; I'll get back to regular there, I think.

BERT: Well—good luck, Kenny. *Blushing:* I hope you'll remember the poems again.

KENNETH, *as though they were unimportant:*   No, they're gone, Bert. There's too much to do in this country for that kinda stuff.

Willy enters with goods.

TOM: Hey, Willy, get this right away; it's a special for Peekskill.

WILLY: Okay.

Willy takes the order and goes, and when Bert turns back to Kenneth he is wrapping again. So Bert moves away from the table. Jerry enters, leaves; and Jim enters, drops goods 1440 on the table, and leaves. Larry enters with a container of coffee, goes to the order hook, and checks through the orders. Bert goes to him.

BERT: I'm goin', Larry.

LARRY, *over his shoulder:*   Take it easy, kid.

Patricia enters and crosses past Bert, looking out through the windows. Tom gets up and bumbles through a pile of goods on the table, checking against an order in his hand. It is as though Bert wished it could stop for a moment, and as each person enters he looks expectantly, but nothing much happens. And so he gradually moves—almost is moved—toward an exit, and with his book in his hand he leaves.

Now Kenneth turns and looks about, sees Bert is gone. He resumes his work and softly 1450 sings.

KENNETH: "The minstrel boy to the war has gone!" Tommy, I'll be needin' more crayon before the day is out.

TOM, *without turning from the desk:*   I'll get some for you.

KENNETH, *looking at a crayon, peeling it down to a nub:*   Oh, the damn mice. But they've got to live too, I suppose. *He marks a package and softly sings:*

> ". . . in the ranks of death you will find him.
> His father's sword he has girded on,
> And his wild harp slung behind him."[22]

CURTAIN

1955

EDWARD ALBEE
(b. 1928)

Throughout his career, Edward Albee has insisted that his plays were all written with serious social aims. As recently as 1985, he repeated in an interview many of the points he had made before:

> Directly or indirectly any playwright is a kind of demonic social critic. I am concerned with altering people's perceptions, altering the status quo. All serious art interests itself in this. The self, the society should be altered by a good play. All plays in their essence are indirectly political in that they make people

---

[22]Thomas Moore's "The Minstrel Boy" again (see footnote 12).

question the values that move them to make various parochial, social, and political decisions. Our political decisions are really a result of how we view consciousness. Plays should be relentless; the playwright shouldn't let people off the hook. He should examine their lives and keep hammering away at the fact that some people are not fully participating in their lives and therefore they're not participating with great intelligence in politics, in social intercourse, in aesthetics. It's something that I dearly hope runs through all of my plays.

Hailed as America's finest playwright of the "theatre of the absurd," Albee may seem aberrant in his insistence on drama with a purpose. The very essence of "theatre of the absurd" is that it presents a vision of the meaninglessness of life and the helplessness of individuals in controlling their destinies or in shaping the social structures in which they find themselves entangled. There are two possible solutions to this riddle. One is that Albee is not an *absurdist* but an eclectic dramatist who, especially in a play like *Who's Afraid of Virginia Woolf?*, is very much in the realistic tradition of Eugene O'Neill or Arthur Miller. Another solution is to see Albee as an *absurdist* in a uniquely American tradition, which not surprisingly, given America's Puritan heritage, comes with a strong moral component.

In many ways Albee's life seems to have been made up of episodes out of an absurdist drama parodying an eighteenth-century novel. He was born somewhere in Virginia in 1928 to parents who handed him over for adoption to Reed and Frances Albee, rich socialites with connections to the theater. Reed Albee had inherited a large share of the Keith-Albee Theatre Circuit established by his father. The year of Albee's adoption, his adoptive father retired to a life of leisure and luxury in their manor in Larchmont, New York. Albee was often taken in a chauffeured limousine to see plays on Broadway. And many people in show business — Ed Wynn and Jimmy Durante — turned up at the house.

Albee's schooling was erratic. His parents travelled to Florida or Arizona in the winters and sent Albee to a series of boarding schools. He was unhappy and unruly in all of them — he changed the name of Valley Forge Military Academy to Valley Forge Concentration Camp — until he arrived at Choate, where he found English teachers who not only tolerated but appreciated his literary efforts. He was mainly interested in writing poetry, but he also wrote stories and plays. One of his plays appeared in the school magazine, and one of his poems was published in a literary journal. In 1946 he entered Trinity College in Hartford, Connecticut, but left after a little over a year.

Following a brief stint writing for a radio station, Albee departed from home in 1950 and headed for Greenwich Village, determined to make it on his own. He had, however, a small income from a $100,000 trust fund left him by his grandmother. He supplemented it by working at a series of menial jobs — office boy, salesman, and counter-man in a luncheonette. In 1952 he went to Italy, where he wrote poetry and fiction for a time. Returning to the United States and still an unknown author, he worked as a messenger for Western Union (1955–58). When he saw himself reaching thirty without having made a name for himself as a writer, he became despondent — but the despondency triggered his creative energies and he wrote his first successful play in three weeks. *The Zoo Story* was rejected by American producers, but made its way circuitously to a theater in Berlin, where it was accepted and translated into German for production in 1959. Albee flew to the opening, and found himself witnessing his own play in a language he could not understand.

The Zoo Story was later produced in New York on a double bill with Samuel Beckett's *Krapp's Last Tape*. A two-character play set in Central Park, the play's conflict is that between a middle-class square (or conformist) and a social drop-out determined to explain his sense of alienation. The latter, daring his acquaintance to fight, kills himself on the knife he has just handed over to his antagonist. Albee remarked of his play: "My hero is not a beatnik and he is not insane. He is over-sane. Though he dies, he passes on an awareness of life to the other characters in the play."

With *The Zoo Story*, Albee entered his most successful and productive period as a dramatist, sustained through most of the next two decades. *The Death of Bessie Smith*, produced in 1960, was based on the black blues singer's being refused admittance to a white hospital after an automobile accident in 1937. *The Sandbox* and *The American Dream*, produced in 1960 and 1961, both one-act plays, focused on "Mommy" and "Daddy" (symbolic American parents) imprisoned in their stereotypical thinking and clichéd language, completely devoid of human feeling and compassion for grandma (in the first play) and for a son, "a clean-cut midwest farm boy type" (in the second).

In 1962, Albee came into his own with the production of *Who's Afraid of Virginia Woolf?*, still considered by many critics his finest play. In a college setting, the play presents an older couple, a professor and his wife, entertaining a younger academic couple. As the liquor and talk flow freely, the evening deteriorates into a sequence of scathing verbal assaults by the characters on each other, in a language that mesmerizes the audience. The only nonrealistic element typical of theatre of the absurd is the older couple's young son, a fantasy child they have conjured up over the years and used as a means of torturing each other. The play ends in purgation, with the exorcism of this nonexistent child. The play won the New York Drama Critics Circle Award and several other prizes, and was turned into a highly popular movie.

In 1963, Albee adapted Carson McCullers's novella *The Ballad of the Sad Café* for the stage. It was the first of a series of adaptations that Albee has attempted, none with the success so far of his own dramas. In 1966, he tried his hand at adapting James Purdy's novel *Malcolm* for the stage. It lasted only about a week. A production in 1967 of an adaptation of a play by British playwright Giles Cooper, *Everything in the Garden*, fared a bit better. But an adaptation of Vladimir Nabokov's *Lolita*, produced in 1981, lasted for only twelve performances. Asked in an interview if he would continue to do adaptations, Albee answered: "Considering what's happened to the last couple, I probably shouldn't. I don't have any plans to at the moment. *Lolita* went badly primarily because the production got out of hand, I think. The script wasn't bad, but the production was appalling."

Albee has been more successful with his own plays, but none has equaled in popularity *Who's Afraid of Virginia Woolf? Tiny Alice*, produced in 1964, evoked more controversy than enthusiasm, primarily because of the obscure symbolism used in the play. *A Delicate Balance*, which appeared in 1966, won for Albee his first Pulitzer Prize. In 1968, Albee brought out two interconnected plays, *Box* and *Quotations from Chairman Mao Tse-Tung*, and commented on them: "Both plays deal with the unconscious, primarily. That's where it is, and it must not be pigeonholed, examined, and specified." His explanation did little to help the play succeed with baffled, unenthusiastic audiences. His portrayal of a family experiencing the dying of the father in *All Over*, produced in 1971, did little to regain the audiences that he had lost with his previous plays. *Seascape*, a play about an encounter between a couple on a beach and two lizard-like, English-speaking creatures, was produced in 1975 and won another Pulitzer Prize, but little popular acclaim. Later plays by Albee, including *The Lady from Dubuque* (1980) and *The Man Who Had Three Arms*(1982), have not fared well with either critics or audiences.

A controversy that has surfaced repeatedly in the critical discussions of Albee's plays concerns the possibility that they somehow embody homosexual feelings or attitudes. Albee has not, like Tennessee Williams in *Suddenly Last Summer* (1958) and in his *Memoirs* (1975), dealt directly with the subject. Some reviewers raised the question in particular with two plays, *Who's Afraid of Virginia Woolf?* and *Tiny Alice*. They said of the first that it was about two homosexual couples disguised by the playwright as heterosexuals. Albee vehemently denounced this interpretation in an interview in 1966. One critic, Foster Hirsch, has explored the question in depth in *Who's Afraid of Edward Albee?*, published in 1978.

In a number of interviews, Albee has revealed that in spite of the reception of his recent plays, he continues to write every day and will continue to bring his plays to production. Asked to comment on the charge that he is a nihilistic, pessimistic writer, he has said: "If I were a pessimist I wouldn't bother to write. Writing itself, taking the trouble, communicating with your fellow human being is valuable, that's an act of optimism. There's a positive force within the struggle. Serious plays are unpleasant in one way or another, and my plays examine people who are not living their lives fully, dangerously, properly."

ADDITIONAL READING

Conversations with Edward Albee, ed. Philip C. Kolin, 1988.

Michael E. Rutenberg, *Edward Albee: Playwright in Protest*, 1969; Ruby Cohn, *Edward Albee*, 1969; C. W. E. Bigsby, *Albee*, 1969; Ronald Hayman, *Edward Albee*, 1971; Liliane Kerjane, *Edward Albee*, 1971; Gilbert Debusscher, *Edward Albee: Tradition and Renewal*, 1971; Anne Paolucci, *From Tension to Tonic: The Plays of Edward Albee*, 1972; Richard E. Amacher and Margaret Rule, *Edward Albee at Home and Abroad: A Bibliography*, 1973 (covers 1958–68); C. W. E. Bigsby, *Edward Albee: A Collection of Critical Essays* 1975; Foster Hirsch, *Who's Afraid of Edward Albee?*, 1978; Anita Maria Stenz, *Edward Albee: Poet of Loss*, 1978; Charles Green, *Edward Albee: An Annotated Bibliography, 1968–1977*, 1980; Richard E. Amacher, *Edward Albee*, 1969, rev. 1982; Julian N. Wasserman, ed., *Edward Albee: An Interview and Essays*, 1983; Philip C. Kolin and J. Madison Davis, eds., *Critical Essays on Edward Albee*, 1986; Richard Tyce, *Edward Albee: A Biliography*, 1986; Gerry McCarthy, *Edward Albee*, 1987; Harold Bloom, ed., *Edward Albee*, 1987; Matthew C. Roudané, *Understanding Edward Albee*, 1987; Scott Giantvalley, *Edward Albee: A Reference Guide*, 1987.

TEXT

The Zoo Story, The Death of Bessie Smith, The Sand Box: Three Plays, Introduced by the Author, 1960.

The Zoo Story

A PLAY IN ONE SCENE (1958)

THE PLAYERS

PETER: *A man in his early forties, neither fat nor gaunt, neither handsome nor homely. He wears tweeds, smokes a pipe, carries horn-rimmed glasses. Although he is moving into middle age, his dress and his manner would suggest a man younger.*

JERRY: *A man in his late thirties, not poorly dressed, but carelessly. What was once a trim and lightly muscled body has begun to go to fat; and while he is no longer handsome, it is evident that he once was. His fall from physical grace should not suggest debauchery; he has, to come closest to it, a great weariness.*

The Scene: *It is Central Park; a Sunday afternoon in summer; the present. There are two park benches, one toward either side of the stage; they both face the audience. Behind them: foliage, trees, sky. At the beginning,* Peter *is seated on one of the benches.*

Stage Directions: *As the curtain rises,* Peter *is seated on the bench stage-right. He is reading a book. He stops reading, cleans his glasses, goes back to reading.* Jerry *enters.*

JERRY: I've been to the zoo. (Peter *doesn't notice*) I said, I've been to the zoo. MISTER, I'VE BEEN TO THE ZOO!

PETER: Hm? . . . What? . . . I'm sorry, were you talking to me?

JERRY: I went to the zoo, and then I walked until I came here. Have I been walking north?   10

PETER: *(Puzzled)* North? Why . . . I . . . I think so. Let me see.

JERRY: *(Pointing past the audience)* Is that Fifth Avenue?

PETER: Why yes; yes, it is.

JERRY: And what is that cross street there; that one, to the right?

PETER: That? Oh, that's Seventy-fourth Street.

JERRY: And the zoo is around Sixty-fifth Street; so, I've been walking north.

PETER: *(Anxious to get back to his reading)* Yes; it would seem so.

JERRY: Good old north.

PETER: *(Lightly, by reflex)* Ha, ha.

JERRY: *(After a slight pause)* But not due north.   20

PETER: I . . . well, no, not due north; but, we . . . call it north. It's northerly.

JERRY: *(Watches as* Peter, *anxious to dismiss him, prepares his pipe)* Well, boy; *you're* not going to get lung cancer, are you?

PETER: *(Looks up, a little annoyed, then smiles)* No, sir. Not from this.

JERRY: No, sir. What you'll probably get is cancer of the mouth, and then you'll have to wear one of those things Freud wore after they took one whole side of his jaw away. What do they call those things?

PETER: *(Uncomfortable)* A prosthesis?

JERRY: The very thing! A prosthesis. You're an educated man, aren't you? Are you a doctor?   30

PETER: Oh, no; no. I read about it somewhere; *Time* magazine, I think. *(He turns to his book)*

JERRY: Well, *Time* magazine isn't for blockheads.

PETER: No, I suppose not.

JERRY: *(After a pause)* Boy, I'm glad that's Fifth Avenue there.

PETER: *(Vaguely)* Yes.

JERRY: I don't like the west side of the park much.

PETER: Oh? *(Then, slightly wary, but interested)* Why?

JERRY: *(Offhand)* I don't know.

PETER: Oh. *(He returns to his book)*   40

JERRY: *(He stands for a few seconds, looking at* Peter, *who finally looks up again, puzzled)* Do you mind if we talk?

PETER: *(Obviously minding)* Why . . . no, no.

JERRY: Yes you do; you do.

PETER: *(Puts his book down, his pipe out and away, smiling)* No, really; I don't mind.

JERRY: Yes you do.

PETER: *(Finally decided)* No; I don't mind at all, really.

JERRY: It's . . . it's a nice day.

PETER: *(Stares unnecessarily at the sky)* Yes. Yes, it is; lovely.
JERRY: I've been to the zoo.   50
PETER: Yes, I think you said so . . . didn't you?
JERRY: You'll read about it in the papers tomorrow, if you don't see it on your TV
        tonight. You have TV, haven't you?
PETER: Why yes, we have two; one for the children.
JERRY: You're married!
PETER: *(With pleased emphasis)* Why, certainly.
JERRY: It isn't a law, for God's sake.
PETER: No . . . no, of course not.
JERRY: And you have a wife.
PETER: *(Bewildered by the seeming lack of communication)* Yes!   60
JERRY: And you have children.
PETER: Yes; two.
JERRY: Boys?
PETER: No, girls . . . both girls.
JERRY: But you wanted boys.
PETER: Well . . . naturally, every man wants a son, but . . .
JERRY: *(Lightly mocking)* But that's the way the cookie crumbles?
PETER: *(Annoyed)* I wasn't going to say that.
JERRY: And you're not going to have any more kids, are you?
PETER: *(A bit distantly)* No. No more. *(Then back, and irksome)* Why did you say   70
        that? How would you know about that?
JERRY: The way you cross your legs, perhaps; something in the voice. Or maybe
        I'm just guessing. Is it your wife?
PETER: *(Furious)* That's none of your business! *(A silence)* Do you understand?
        (Jerry *nods.* Peter *is quiet now)* Well, you're right. We'll have no more children.
JERRY: *(Softly)* That *is* the way the cookie crumbles.
PETER: *(Forgiving)* Yes . . . I guess so.
JERRY: Well, now; what else?
PETER: What were you saying about the zoo . . . that I'd read about it, or see . . . ?
JERRY: I'll tell you about it, soon. Do you mind if I ask you questions?   80
PETER: Oh, not really.
JERRY: I'll tell you why I do it; I don't talk to many people—except to say like:
        give me a beer, or where's the john, or what time does the feature go on, or
        keep your hands to yourself buddy. You know—things like that.
PETER: I must say I don't . . .
JERRY: But every once in a while I like to talk to somebody, really *talk;* like to get
        to know somebody, know all about him.
PETER: *(Lightly laughing, still a little uncomfortable)* And am I the guinea pig for
        today?
JERRY: On a sun-drenched Sunday afternoon like this? Who better than a nice   90
        married man with two daughters and . . . uh . . . a dog? (Peter *shakes his head)*
        No? Two dogs. (Peter *shakes his head again)* Hm. No dogs? (Peter *shakes his head,*
        sadly) Oh, that's a shame. But you look like an animal man. CATS? (Peter *nods*
        his head, ruefully) Cats! But, that can't be your idea. No, sir. Your wife and
        daughters? (Peter *nods his head)* Is there anything else I should know?
PETER: *(He has to clear his throat)* There are . . . there are two parakeets. One . . .
        uh . . . one for each of my daughters.
JERRY: Birds.
PETER: My daughters keep them in a cage in their bedroom.
JERRY: Do they carry disease? The birds.   100
PETER: I don't believe so.
JERRY: That's too bad. If they did you could set them loose in the house and the

cats could eat them and die, maybe. (Peter *looks blank for a moment, then laughs*) And what else? What do you do to support your enormous household?

PETER: I . . . uh . . . I have an executive position with a . . . a small publishing house. We . . . uh . . . we publish textbooks.

JERRY: That sounds nice; very nice. What do you make?

PETER: *(Still cheerful)* Now look here!

JERRY: Oh, come on.

PETER: Well, I make around eighteen thousand a year, but I don't carry more 110
than forty dollars at any one time . . . in case you're a holdup man . . . ha, ha, ha.

JERRY: *(Ignoring the above)* Where do you live? (Peter *is reluctant*) Oh, look; I'm not going to rob you, and I'm not going to kidnap your parakeets, your cats, or your daughters.

PETER: *(Too loud)* I live between Lexington and Third Avenue, on Seventy-fourth Street.

JERRY: That wasn't so hard, was it?

PETER: I didn't mean to seem . . . ah . . . it's that you don't really carry on a conversation; you just ask questions. And I'm . . . I'm normally . . . uh . . .
reticent. Why do you just stand there?   120

JERRY: I'll start walking around in a little while, and eventually I'll sit down. *(Recalling)* Wait until you see the expression on his face.

PETER: What? Whose face? Look here; is this something about the zoo?

JERRY: *(Distantly)* The what?

PETER: The zoo; the zoo. Something about the zoo.

JERRY: The zoo?

PETER: You've mentioned it several times.

JERRY: *(Still distant, but returning abruptly)* The zoo? Oh, yes; the zoo. I was there before I came here. I told you that. Say, what's the dividing line between upper-middle-middle-class and lower-upper-middle-class?   130

PETER: My dear fellow, I . . .

JERRY: Don't my dear fellow me.

PETER: *(Unhappily)* Was I patronizing? I believe I was; I'm sorry. But, you see, your question about the classes bewildered me.

JERRY: And when you're bewildered you become patronizing?

PETER: I . . . I don't express myself too well, sometimes. *(He attempts a joke on himself)* I'm in publishing, not writing.

JERRY: *(Amused, but not at the humor)* So be it. The truth *is: I* was being patronizing.

PETER: Oh, now; you needn't say that.   140

   (It is at this point that Jerry may begin to move about the stage with slowly increasing determination and authority, but pacing himself, so that the long speech about the dog comes at the high point of the arc)

JERRY: All right. Who are your favorite writers? Baudelaire and J. P. Marquand?[1]

PETER: *(Wary)* Well, I like a great many writers; I have a considerable . . . catholicity of taste, if I may say so. Those two men are fine, each in his way. *(Warming up)* Baudelaire, of course . . . uh . . . is by far the finer of the two, but Marquand has a place . . . in our . . . uh . . . national . . .

JERRY: Skip it.

PETER: I . . . sorry.   150

JERRY: Do you know what I did before I went to the zoo today? I walked all the way up Fifth Avenue from Washington Square; all the way.

PETER: Oh; you live in the Village! *(This seems to enlighten* Peter*)*

---

[1]Charles Baudelaire (1821–1867), French symbolist poet;
J. P. Marquand (1893–1960), American popular novelist.

JERRY: No, I don't. I took the subway down to the Village so I could walk all the way up Fifth Avenue to the zoo. It's one of those things a person has to do; sometimes a person has to go a very long distance out of his way to come back a short distance correctly.

PETER: *(Almost pouting)* Oh, I thought you lived in the Village.

JERRY: What were you trying to do? Make sense out of things? Bring order? The old pigeonhole bit? Well, that's easy; I'll tell you. I live in a four-story brown- 160 stone roominghouse on the upper West Side between Columbus Avenue and Central Park West. I live on the top floor; rear; west. It's a laughably small room, and one of my walls is made of beaverboard; this beaverboard separates my room from another laughably small room, so I assume that the two rooms were once one room, a small room, but not necessarily laughable. The room beyond my beaverboard wall is occupied by a colored queen who always keeps his door open; well, not always but *always* when he's plucking his eyebrows, which he does with Buddhist concentration. This colored queen has rotten teeth, which is rare, and he has a Japanese kimono, which is also pretty rare; and he wears this kimono to and from the john in the hall, which is pretty 170 frequent. I mean, he goes to the john a lot. He never bothers me, and he never brings anyone up to his room. All he does is pluck his eyebrows, wear his ki-mono and go to the john. Now, the two front rooms on my floor are a little larger, I guess; but they're pretty small too. There's a Puerto Rican family in one of them, a husband, a wife, and some kids; I don't know how many. These people entertain a lot. And in the other front room, there's somebody living there, but I don't know who it is. I've never seen who it is. Never. Never ever.

PETER: *(Embarassed)* Why . . . why do you live there?

JERRY: *(From a distance again)* I don't know.

PETER: It doesn't sound like a very nice place . . . where you live. 180

JERRY: Well, no; it isn't an apartment in the East Seventies. But, then again, I don't have one wife, two daughters, two cats and two parakeets. What I do have, I have toilet articles, a few clothes, a hot plate that I'm not supposed to have, a can opener, one that works with a key, you know; a knife, two forks, and two spoons, one small, one large; three plates, a cup, a saucer, a drinking glass, two picture frames, both empty, eight or nine books, a pack of pornographic playing cards, regular deck, an old Western Union typewriter that prints noth-ing but capital letters, and a small strongbox without a lock which has in it . . . what? Rocks! Some rocks . . . sea-rounded rocks I picked up on the beach when I was a kid. Under which . . . weighed down . . . are some letters . . . please let- 190 ters . . . please why don't you do this, and please when will you do that letters. And when letters, too. When will you write? When will you come? When? These letters are from more recent years.

PETER: *(Stares glumly at his shoes, then)* About those two empty picture frames . . . ?

JERRY: I don't see why they need any explanation at all. Isn't it clear? I don't have pictures of anyone to put in them.

PETER: Your parents . . . perhaps . . . . a girl friend . . .

JERRY: You're a very sweet man, and you're possessed of a truly enviable inno-cence. But good old Mom and good old Pop are dead . . . you know? . . . . I'm broken up about it, too . . . I mean really. BUT. That particular vaudeville act is 200 playing the cloud circuit now, so I don't see how I can look at them, all neat and framed. Besides, or, rather, to be pointed about it, good old Mom walked out on good old Pop when I was ten and a half years old; she embarked on an adulterous turn of our southern states . . . a journey of a year's duration . . . and her most constant companion . . . among others, among many others . . . was a Mr. Barleycorn. At least, that's what good old Pop told me after he went down . . . came back . . . brought her body north. We'd received the news between Christmas and New Year's, you see, that good old Mom had parted with the ghost in some dump in Alabama. And, without the ghost . . . she was less welcome. I mean, what was she? A stiff . . . a northern stiff. At any rate, 210 good old Pop celebrated the New Year for an even two weeks and then slapped into the front of a somewhat moving city omnibus, which sort of cleaned things out family-wise. Well no; then there was Mom's sister, who was given neither to sin nor the consolations of the bottle. I moved in on her, and my memory of her is slight excepting I remember still that she did all things dourly; sleeping, eating, working, praying. She dropped dead on the stairs to her apartment, my apartment then, too, on the afternoon of my high school graduation. A terribly middle-European joke, if you ask me.

PETER: Oh, my; oh, my.

JERRY: Oh, your what? But that was a long time ago, and I have no feeling about 220 any of it that I care to admit to myself. Perhaps you can see, though, why good old Mom and good old Pop are frameless. What's your name? Your first name?

PETER: I'm Peter.

JERRY: I'd forgotten to ask you. I'm Jerry.

PETER: *(With a slight, nervous laugh)* Hello, Jerry.

JERRY: *(Nods his hello)* And let's see now; what's the point of having a girl's picture, especially in two frames? I have two picture frames, you remember. I never see the pretty little ladies more than once, and most of them wouldn't be caught in the same room with a camera. It's odd, and I wonder if it's sad.

PETER: The girls?   230

JERRY: No. I wonder if it's sad that I never see the little ladies more than once. I've never been able to have sex with, or, how is it put? . . . make love to anybody more than once. Once; that's it. . . . Oh, wait; for a week and a half, when I was fifteen . . . and I hang my head in shame that puberty was late. . . I was a h-o-m-o-s-e-x-u-a-l. I mean, I was queer . . . *(Very fast)* . . . queer, queer, queer . . . with bells ringing, banners snapping in the wind. And for those eleven days, I met at least twice a day with the park superintendent's son . . . a Greek boy, whose birthday was the same as mine, except he was a year older. I think I was very much in love . . . maybe just with sex. But that was the jazz of a very special hotel, wasn't it? And now; oh, do I love the little ladies; really, I love 240 them. For about an hour.

PETER: Well, it seems perfectly simple to me. . . .

JERRY: *(Angry)* Look! Are you going to tell me to get married and have parakeets?

PETER: *(Angry himself)* Forget the parakeets! And stay single if you want to. It's no business of mine. I didn't start this conversation in the . . .

JERRY: All right, all right. I'm sorry. All right? You're not angry?

PETER: *(Laughing)* No, I'm not angry.

JERRY: *(Relieved)* Good. *(Now back to his previous tone)* Interesting that you asked me about the picture frames. I would have thought that you would have asked me about the pornographic playing cards.   250

PETER: *(With a knowing smile)* Oh, I've seen those cards.

JERRY: That's not the point. *(Laughs)* I suppose when you were a kid you and your pals passed them around, or you had a pack of your own.

PETER: Well, I guess a lot of us did.

JERRY: And you threw them away just before you got married.

PETER: Oh, now; look here. I didn't *need* anything like that when I got older.

JERRY: No?

PETER: *(Embarrassed)* I'd rather not talk about these things.

JERRY: So? Don't. Besides, I wasn't trying to plumb your post-adolescent sexual life and hard times; what I wanted to get at is the value difference between 260 pornographic playing cards when you're a kid, and pornographic playing cards when you're older. It's that when you're a kid you use the cards as a substitute for a real experience, and when you're older you use real experience as a substitute for the fantasy. But I imagine you'd rather hear about what happened at the zoo.

PETER: *(Enthusiastic)* Oh, yes; the zoo. *(Then, awkward)* That is . . . if you. . . .

JERRY: Let me tell you about why I went . . . well, let me tell you some things. I've told you about the fourth floor of the roominghouse where I live. I think the rooms are better as you go down, floor by floor. I guess they are; I don't know. I don't know any of the people on the third and second floors. Oh, wait! I do 270 know that there's a lady living on the third floor, in the front. I know because she cries all the time. Whenever I go out or come back in, whenever I pass her door, I always hear her crying, muffled, but . . . very determined. Very determined indeed. But the one I'm getting to, and all about the dog, is the landlady. I don't like to use words that are too harsh in describing people. I don't like to. But the landlady is a fat, ugly, mean, stupid, unwashed, misanthropic, cheap, drunken bag of garbage. And you may have noticed that I very seldom use profanity, so I can't describe her as well as I might.

PETER: You describe her . . . vividly.

JERRY: Well, thanks. Anyway, she has a dog, and I will tell you about the dog, and 280 she and her dog are the gatekeepers of my dwelling. The woman is bad enough; she leans around in the entrance hall, spying to see that I don't bring in things or people, and when she's had her midafternoon pint of lemon-flavored gin she always stops me in the hall, and grabs ahold of my coat or my arm, and she presses her disgusting body up against me to keep me in a corner so she can talk to me. The smell of her body and her breath . . . you can't imagine it . . . and somewhere, somewhere in the back of that pea-sized brain of hers, an organ developed just enough to let her eat, drink and emit, she has some foul parody of sexual desire. And I, Peter, I am the object of her sweaty lust.   290

PETER: That's disgusting. That's . . . horrible.

JERRY: But I have found a way to keep her off. When she talks to me, when she presses herself to my body and mumbles about her room and how I should come there, I merely say: but, Love; wasn't yesterday enough for you, and the day before? Then she puzzles, she makes slits of her tiny eyes, she sways a little, and then, Peter . . . and it is at this moment that I think I might be doing some good in that tormented house . . . a simple-minded smile begins to form on her unthinkable face, and she giggles and groans as she thinks about yesterday and the day before; as she believes and relives what never happened. Then, she motions to that black monster of a dog she has, and she goes back to her room. 300 And I am safe until our next meeting.

PETER: It's so . . . unthinkable. I find it hard to believe that people such as that really *are.*

JERRY: *(Lightly mocking)* It's for reading about, isn't it?

PETER: *(Seriously)* Yes.

JERRY: And fact is better left to fiction. You're right, Peter. Well, what I have been meaning to tell you about is the dog; I shall, now.

PETER: *(Nervously)* Oh, yes; the dog.

JERRY: Don't go. You're not thinking of going, are you?

PETER: Well . . . no, I don't think so.   310

JERRY: *(As if to a child)* Because after I tell you about the dog, do you know what then? Then . . . then I'll tell you about what happened at the zoo.

PETER: *(Laughing faintly)* You're . . . you're full of stories, aren't you?

JERRY: You don't *have* to listen. Nobody is holding you here; remember that. Keep that in your mind.

PETER: *(Irritably)* I know that.
JERRY: You do? Good.

    (The following long speech, it seems to me, should be done with a great deal of action, to achieve a hypnotic effect on Peter, *and on the audience, too. Some specific actions have been suggested, but the director and the actor playing Jerry might best work it out for* 320 *themselves)*

    ALL RIGHT. *(As if reading from a huge billboard)* THE STORY OF JERRY AND THE DOG! *(Natural again)* What I am going to tell you has something to do with how sometimes it's necessary to go a long distance out of the way in order to come back a short distance correctly; or, maybe I only think that it has something to do with that. But, it's why I went to the zoo today, and why I walked north . . . northerly, rather . . . until I came here. All right. The dog, I think I told you, is a black monster of a beast: an oversized head, tiny, tiny ears, and eyes . . . bloodshot, infected, maybe; and a body you can see the ribs through the skin. The dog is black, all black; all black except for the bloodshot eyes, 330 and . . . yes . . . and an open sore on its . . . *right* forepaw; that is red, too. And, oh yes; the poor monster, and I do believe it's an old dog . . . it's certainly a misused one . . . almost always has an erection . . . of sorts. That's red, too. And . . . what else? . . . oh, yes; there's a gray-yellow-white color, too when he bares his fangs. Like this: Grrrrrrr! Which is what he did when he saw me for the first time . . . the day I moved in. I worried about that animal the very first minute I met him. Now, animals don't take to me like Saint Francis had birds hanging off him all the time. What I mean is: animals are indifferent to me . . . like people *(He smiles slightly)* . . . most of the time. But this dog wasn't indifferent. From the very beginning he'd snarl and then go for me, to get one of my legs. Not like he was 340 rabid, you know; he was sort of a stumbly dog, but he wasn't half-assed, either. It was a good, stumbly run; but I always got away. He got a piece of my trouser leg, look, you can see right here, where it's mended; he got that the second day I lived there; but, I kicked free and got upstairs fast, so that was that. *(Puzzles)* I still don't know to this day how the other roomers manage it, but you know what I *think:* I think it had to do only with me. Cozy. So. Anyway, this went on for over a week, whenever I came in; but never when I went out. That's funny. Or, it *was* funny. I could pack up and live in the street for all the dog cared. Well, I thought about it up in my room one day, one of the times after I'd bolted upstairs, and I made up my mind. I decided: First, I'll kill the dog with kind- 350 ness, and if that doesn't work . . . I'll just kill him. (Peter *winces*) Don't react, Peter; just listen. So, the next day I went out and bought a bag of hamburgers, medium rare, no catsup, no onion; and on the way home I threw away all the rolls and kept just the meat.

    (Action for the following, perhaps)
When I got back to the roominghouse the dog was waiting for me. I half opened the door that led into the entrance hall, and there he was; waiting for me. It figured. I went in, very cautiously, and I had the hamburgers, you re-member; I opened the bag, and I set the meat down about twelve feet from where the dog was snarling at me. Like so! He snarled; stopped snarling; 360 sniffed; moved slowly; then faster; then faster toward the meat. Well, when he got to it he stopped, and he looked at me. I smiled; but tentatively, you under-stand. He turned his face back to the hamburgers, smelled, sniffed some more, and then . . . RRRAAAAGGGGGHHHH, like that . . . he tore into them. It was as if he had never eaten anything in his life before, except like garbage. Which might very well have been the truth. I don't think the landlady ever eats any-thing but garbage. But. He ate all the hamburgers, almost all at once, making sounds in his throat like a woman. *Then,* when he'd finished the meat, the ham-burger, and tried to eat the paper, too, he sat down and smiled. I think he

smiled; I know cats do. It was a very gratifying few moments. Then, BAM, he 370
snarled and made for me again. He didn't get me this time, either. So, I got
upstairs, and I lay down on my bed and started to think about the dog again. To
be truthful, I was offended, and I was damn mad, too. It was six perfectly good
hamburgers with not enough pork in them to make it disgusting. I was offended. But, after a while, I decided to try it for a few more days. If you think
about it, this dog had what amounted to an antipathy toward me; really. And, I
wondered if I mightn't overcome this antipathy. So, I tried it for five more
days, but it was always the same: snarl, sniff; move; faster; stare; gobble;
RAAGGGHHH; smile; snarl; BAM. Well, now; by this time Columbus Avenue
was strewn with hamburger rolls and I was less offended than disgusted. So, I 380
decided to kill the dog.

   (Peter *raises a hand in protest*)
Oh, don't be so alarmed, Peter; I didn't succeed. The day I tried to kill the dog I
bought only one hamburger and what I thought was a murderous portion of
rat poison. When I bought the hamburger I asked the man not to bother with
the roll, all I wanted was the meat. I expected some reaction from him, like: we
don't sell no hamburgers without rolls; or, wha' d'ya wanna do, eat it out'a ya
han's? But no; he smiled benignly, wrapped up the hamburger in waxed paper,
and said: A bite for ya pussy-cat? I wanted to say: No, not really; it's part of a
plan to poison a dog I know. But, you can't say "a dog I know" without sound- 390
ing funny; so I said, a little too loud, I'm afraid, and too formally: YES, A BITE
FOR MY PUSSY-CAT. People looked up. It always happens when I try to simplify things; people look up. But that's neither hither nor thither. So. On my
way back to the roominghouse, I kneaded the hamburger and the rat poison
together between my hands, at that point feeling as much sadness as disgust. I
opened the door to the entrance hall, and there the monster was, waiting to
take the offering and then jump me. Poor bastard; he never learned that the
moment he took to smile before he went for me gave me time enough to get out
of range. BUT, there he was; malevolence with an erection, waiting. I put the
poison patty down, moved toward the stairs and watched. The poor animal 400
gobbled the food down as usual, smiled, which made me almost sick, and then,
BAM. But, I sprinted up the stairs, as usual, and the dog didn't get me, as
usual. AND IT CAME TO PASS THAT THE BEAST WAS DEATHLY ILL. I
knew this because he no longer attended me, and because the landlady sobered
up. She stopped me in the hall the same evening of the attempted murder and
confided the information that God had struck her puppy-dog a surely fatal
blow. She had forgotten her bewildered lust, and her eyes were wide open for
the first time. They looked like the dog's eyes. She sniveled and implored me to
pray for the animal. I wanted to say to her: Madam, I have myself to pray for,
the colored queen, the Puerto Rican family, the person in the front room 410
whom I've never seen, the woman who cries deliberately behind her closed
door, and the rest of the people in all roominghouses, everywhere; besides,
Madam, I don't understand how to pray. But . . . to simplify things . . . I told her
I would pray. She looked up. She said that I was a liar, and that I probably
wanted the dog to die. I told her, and there was so much truth here, that I
didn't want the dog to die. I didn't, and not just because I'd poisoned him. I'm
afraid that I must tell you I wanted the dog to live so that I could see what our
new relationship might come to.

   (Peter *indicates his increasing displeasure and slowly growing antagonism*)
Please understand, Peter; that sort of thing is important. You must believe me; 420
it *is* important. We have to know the effect of our actions. (*Another deep sigh*)
Well, anyway; the dog recovered. I have no idea why, unless he was a descen-

dant of the puppy that guarded the gates of hell or some such resort. I'm not up on my mythology. *(He pronounces the word myth-o-*logy*)* Are you?

(Peter *sets to thinking, but* Jerry *goes on)*

At any rate, and you've missed the eight-thousand-dollar question, Peter; at any rate, the dog recovered his health and the landlady recovered her thirst, in no way altered by the bow-wow's deliverance. When I came home from a movie that was playing on Forty-second Street, a movie I'd seen, or one that was very much like one or several I'd seen, after the landlady told me puppykins was 430 better, I was so hoping for the dog to be waiting for me. I was . . . well, how would you put it . . . enticed? . . . fascinated? . . . no, I don't think so . . . heart-shatteringly anxious, that's it; I was heart-shatteringly anxious to confront my friend again.

(Peter *reacts scoffingly)*

Yes, Peter; friend. That's the only word for it. I was heart-shatteringly et cetera to confront my doggy friend again. I came in the door and advanced, unafraid, to the center of the entrance hall. The beast was there . . . looking at me. And, you know, he looked better for his scrape with the nevermind. I stopped; I looked at him; he looked at me. I think . . . I think we stayed a long time that 440 way . . . still, stone-statue . . . just looking at one another. I looked more into his face than he looked into mine. I mean, I can concentrate longer at looking into a dog's face than a dog can concentrate at looking into mine, or into anybody else's face, for that matter. But during that twenty seconds or two hours that we looked into each other's face, we made contact. Now, here is what I had wanted to happen: I loved the dog now, and I wanted him to love me. I had tried to love, and I had tried to kill, and both had been unsuccessful by themselves. I hoped . . . and I don't really know why I expected the dog to understand anything, much less my motivations . . . I hoped that the dog would understand.

(Peter *seems to be hypnotized)*   450

It's just . . . it's just that . . . (Jerry *is abnormally tense, now)* . . . it's just that if you can't deal with people, you have to make a start somewhere. WITH ANI-MALS! *(Much faster now, and like a conspirator)* Don't you see? A person has to have some way of dealing with SOMETHING. If not with people . . . if not with people . . . SOMETHING. With a bed, with a cockroach, with a mirror . . . no, that's too hard, that's one of the last steps. With a cockroach, with a . . . with a . . . with a carpet, a roll of toilet paper . . . no, not that, either . . . that's a mirror, too; always check bleeding. You see how hard it is to find things? With a street corner, and too many lights, all colors reflecting on the oily-wet streets . . . with a wisp of smoke, a wisp . . . of smoke . . . with . . . with pornographic playing 460 cards, with a strongbox . . . WITHOUT A LOCK . . . with love, with vomiting, with crying, with fury because the pretty little ladies aren't pretty little ladies, with making money with your body which is an act of love and I could prove it, with howling because you're alive; with God. How about that? WITH GOD WHO IS A COLORED QUEEN WHO WEARS A KIMONO AND PLUCKS HIS EYEBROWS, WHO IS A WOMAN WHO CRIES WITH DETERMINA-TION BEHIND HER CLOSED DOOR . . . with God who, I'm told, turned his back on the whole thing some time ago . . . with . . . some day, with people. (Jerry *sighs the next word heavily)* People. With an idea; a concept. And where better, where ever better in this humiliating excuse for a jail, where better to 470 communicate one single, simple-minded idea than in an entrance hall? Where? It would be A START! Where better to make a beginning . . . to understand and just possibly be understood . . . a beginning of an understanding, than with . . .

(Here Jerry *seems to fall into almost grotesque fatigue)*

. . . than with A DOG. Just that; a dog.

    (Here there is silence that might be prolonged for a moment or so; then Jerry *wearily finishes his story)*

    A dog. It seemed like a perfectly sensible idea. Man is a dog's best friend, remember. So: the dog and I looked at each other. I longer than the dog. And 480 what I saw then has been the same ever since. Whenever the dog and I see each other we both stop where we are. We regard each other with a mixture of sadness and suspicion, and then we feign indifference. We walk past each other safely; we have an understanding. It's very sad, but you'll have to admit that it is an understanding. We had made many attempts at contact, and we had failed. The dog has returned to garbage, and I to solitary but free passage. I have not returned. I mean to say, I have *gained* solitary free passage, if that much further loss can be said to be gain. I have learned that neither kindness nor cruelty by themselves, independent of each other, creates any effect beyond themselves; and I have learned that the two combined, together, at the same time, 490 are the teaching emotion. And what is gained is loss. And what has been the result: the dog and I have attained a compromise; more of a bargain, really. We neither love nor hurt because we do not try to reach each other. And, *was* trying to feed the dog an act of love? And, perhaps, was the dog's attempt to bite me *not* an act of love? If we can so misunderstand, well then, why have we invented the word love in the first place?

    (There is silence. Jerry *moves to* Peter's *bench and sits down beside him. This is the first time* Jerry *has sat down during the play)*

The Story of Jerry and the Dog: the end.

    (Peter is silent)   500

Well, Peter? (Jerry *is suddenly cheerful*) Well, Peter? Do you think I could sell that story to the *Reader's Digest* and make a couple of hundred bucks for *The Most Unforgettable Character I've Ever Met*? Huh?

    (Jerry is animated, but Peter *is disturbed.)*

Oh, come on now, Peter; tell me what you think.

PETER: *(Numb)* I . . . I don't understand what . . . I don't think I . . . *(Now, almost tearfully)* Why did you tell me all of this?

JERRY: Why not?

PETER: I DON'T UNDERSTAND!

JERRY: *(Furious, but whispering)* That's a lie.   510

PETER: No. No, it's not.

JERRY: *(Quietly)* I tried to explain it to you as I went along. I went slowly; it all has to do with . . .

PETER: I DON'T WANT TO HEAR ANY MORE. I don't understand you, or your landlady, or her dog . . .

JERRY: *Her* dog! I thought it was my . . . No. No, you're right. It *is* her dog. *(Looks at* Peter *intently, shaking his head)* I don't know what I was thinking about; of course you don't understand. *(In a monotone, wearily)* I don't live in your block; I'm not married to two parakeets, or whatever your setup is. I am a *permanent transient*, and my home is the sickening roominghouses on the West Side of 520 New York City, which is the greatest city in the world. Amen.

PETER: I'm . . . I'm sorry; I didn't mean to . . .

JERRY: Forget it. I suppose you don't quite know what to make of me, eh?

PETER: *(A joke)* We get all kinds in publishing. *(Chuckles)*

JERRY: You're a funny man. *(He forces a laugh)* You know that? You're a very . . . a richly comic person.

PETER: *(Modestly, but amused)* Oh, now, not really. *(Still chuckling)*

JERRY: Peter, do I annoy you, or confuse you?

PETER: *(Lightly)* Well, I must confess that this wasn't the kind of afternoon I'd anticipated. 530
JERRY: You mean, I'm not the gentleman you were expecting.
PETER: I wasn't expecting anybody.
JERRY: No, I don't imagine you were. But I'm here, and I'm not leaving.
PETER: *(Consulting his watch)* Well, you may not be, but I must be getting home soon.
JERRY: Oh, come on; stay a while longer.
PETER: I really should get home; you see . . .
JERRY: *(Tickles* Peter's *ribs with his fingers)* Oh, come on.
PETER: *(He is very ticklish; as* Jerry *continues to tickle him his voice becomes falsetto)* No, I . . . OHHHHH! Don't do that. Stop, Stop. Ohhh, no, no. 540
JERRY: Oh, come on.
PETER: *(As* Jerry *tickles)* Oh, hee, hee, hee. I must go. I . . . hee, hee, hee. After all, stop, stop, hee, hee, hee, after all, the parakeets will be getting dinner ready soon. Hee, hee. And the cats are setting the table. Stop, stop, and, and . . . *(Peter is beside himself now)* . . . and we're having . . . hee, hee . . . uh . . . ho, ho, ho.
      Jerry stops tickling Peter, *but the combination of the tickling and his own mad whimsy has* Peter *laughing almost hysterically. As his laughter continues, then subsides,* Jerry *watches him, with a curious fixed smile*
JERRY: Peter?
PETER: Oh, ha, ha, ha, ha, ha. What? What? 550
JERRY: Listen, now.
PETER: Oh, ho, ho. What . . . what is it, Jerry? Oh, my.
JERRY: *(Mysteriously)* Peter, do you want to know what happened at the zoo?
PETER: Ah, ha, ha. The what? Oh, yes; the zoo. Oh, ho, ho. Well, I had my own zoo there for a moment with . . . hee, hee, the parakeets getting dinner ready, and the . . . ha, ha, whatever it was, the . . .
JERRY: *(Calmly)* Yes, that was very funny, Peter. I wouldn't have expected it. But do you want to hear about what happened at the zoo, or not?
PETER: Yes. Yes, by all means; tell me what happened at the zoo. Oh, my. I don't know what happened to me. 560
JERRY: Now I'll let you in on what happened at the zoo; but first, I should tell you why I went to the zoo. I went to the zoo to find out more about the way people exist with animals, and the way animals exist with each other, and with people too. It probably wasn't a fair test, what with everyone separated by bars from everyone else, the animals for the most part from each other, and always the people from the animals. But, if it's a zoo, that's the way it is. *(He pokes* Peter *on the arm)* Move over.
PETER: *(Friendly)* I'm sorry, haven't you enough room? *(He shifts a little)*
JERRY: *(Smiling slightly)* Well, all the animals are there, and all the people are there, and it's Sunday and all the children are there. *(He pokes* Peter *again)* 570 Move over.
PETER: *(Patiently, still friendly)* All right.
      (He moves some more, and Jerry *has all the room he might need)*
JERRY: And it's a hot day, so all the stench is there, too, and all the balloon sellers, and all the ice cream sellers, and all the seals are barking, and all the birds are screaming. *(Pokes* Peter *harder)* Move over!
PETER: *(Beginning to be annoyed)* Look here, you have more than enough room!
      (But he moves more, and is now fairly cramped at one end of the bench)
JERRY: And I am there, and it's feeding time at the lions' house, and the lion keeper comes into the lion cage, one of the lion cages, to feed one of the lions. 580 *(Punches* Peter *on the arm, hard)* MOVE OVER!

PETER: *(Very annoyed)* I can't move over any more, and stop hitting me. What's the matter with you?

JERRY: Do you want to hear the story? *(Punches* Peter's *arm again)*

PETER: *(Flabbergasted)* I'm not so sure! I certainly don't want to be punched in the arm.

JERRY: *(Punches* Peter's *arm again)* Like that?

PETER: Stop it! What's the matter with you?

JERRY: I'm crazy, you bastard.

PETER: That isn't funny.   590

JERRY: Listen to me, Peter. I want this bench. You go sit on the bench over there, and if you're good I'll tell you the rest of the story.

PETER: *(Flustered)* But . . . whatever for? What *is* the matter with you? Besides, I see no reason why I should give up this bench. I sit on this bench almost every Sunday afternoon, in good weather. It's secluded here; there's never anyone sitting here, so I have it all to myself.

JERRY: *(Softly)* Get off this bench, Peter; I want it.

PETER: *(Almost whining)* No.

JERRY: I said I want this bench, and I'm going to have it. Now get over there.

PETER: People can't have everything they want. You should know that; it's a rule;   600
people can have some of the things they want, but they can't have everything.

JERRY: *(Laughs)* Imbecile! You're slow-witted!

PETER: Stop that!

JERRY: You're a vegetable! Go lie down on the ground.

PETER: *(Intense)* Now *you* listen to me. I've put up with you all afternoon.

JERRY: Not really.

PETER: LONG ENOUGH! I've put up with you long enough. I've listened to you because you seemed . . . well, because I thought you wanted to talk to somebody.

JERRY: You put things well; economically, and, yet . . . oh, what is the word I want to put justice to your . . . JESUS, you make me sick . . . get off here and give me   610
my bench.

PETER: MY BENCH!

JERRY: *(Pushes* Peter *almost, but not quite, off the bench)* Get out of my sight.

PETER: *(Regaining his position)* God da . . . mn you. That's enough! I've had enough of you. I will not give up this bench; you can't have it, and that's that. Now, go away.

    (Jerry snorts but does not move)

    Go away, I said.

    (Jerry does not move)

    Get away from here. If you don't move on . . . you're a bum . . . that's what you   620
    are. . . . If you don't move on, I'll get a policeman here and make you go.

    (Jerry laughs, stays)

    I warn you, I'll call a policeman.

JERRY: *(Softly)* You won't find a policeman around here; they're all over on the west side of the park chasing fairies down from trees or out of the bushes. That's all they do. That's their function. So scream your head off; it won't do you any good.

PETER: POLICE! I warn you, I'll have you arrested. POLICE! *(Pause)* I said PO-
LICE! *(Pause)* I feel ridiculous.

JERRY: You look ridiculous: a grown man screaming for the police on a bright   630
Sunday afternoon in the park with nobody harming you. If a policeman *did* fill his quota and come sludging over this way he'd probably take you in as a nut.

PETER: *(With disgust and impotence)* Great God, I just came here to read, and now you want me to give up the bench. You're mad.

JERRY:　Hey, I got news for you, as they say. I'm on your precious bench, and you're never going to have it for yourself again.

PETER:　*(Furious)* Look, you; get off my bench. I don't care if it makes any sense or not. I want this bench to myself; I want you OFF IT!

JERRY:　*(Mocking)* Aw . . . look who's mad.

PETER:　GET OUT! 640

JERRY:　No.

PETER:　I WARN YOU!

JERRY:　Do you know how ridiculous you look *now?*

PETER:　*(His fury and self-consciousness have possessed him)* It doesn't matter. *(He is almost crying)* GET AWAY FROM MY BENCH!

JERRY:　Why? You have everything in the world you want; you've told me about your home, and your family, and *your own* little zoo. You have everything, and now you want this bench. Are these the things men fight for? Tell me, Peter, is this bench, this iron and this wood, is this your honor? Is this the thing in the world you'd fight for? Can you think of anything more absurd? 650

PETER:　Absurd? Look, I'm not going to talk to you about honor, or even try to explain it to you. Besides, it isn't a question of honor; but even if it were, you wouldn't understand.

JERRY:　*(Contemptuously)* You don't even know what you're saying, do you? This is probably the first time in your life you've had anything more trying to face than changing your cats' toilet box. Stupid! Don't you have any idea, not even the slightest, what other people *need?*

PETER:　Oh, boy, listen to you; well, you don't need this bench. That's for sure.

JERRY:　Yes; yes. I do.

PETER:　*(Quivering)* I've come here for years; I have hours of great pleasure, 660 great satisfaction, right here. And that's important to a man. I'm a responsible person, and I'm a GROWN UP. This is my bench, and you have no right to take it away from me.

JERRY:　Fight for it, then. Defend yourself; defend your bench.

PETER:　You've *pushed* me to it. Get up and fight.

JERRY:　Like a man?

PETER:　*(Still angry)* Yes, like a man, if you insist on mocking me even further.

JERRY:　I'll have to give you credit for one thing: you *are* a vegetable, and a slightly nearsighted one, I think . . .

PETER:　THAT'S ENOUGH. . . . 670

JERRY:　. . . but, you know, as they say on TV all the time—you know—and I mean this, Peter, you have a certain dignity; it surprises me. . . .

PETER:　STOP!

JERRY:　*(Rises lazily)* Very well, Peter, we'll battle for the bench, but we're not evenly matched.

　　(He takes out and clicks open an ugly-looking knife)

PETER:　*(Suddenly awakening to the reality of the situation)* You *are* mad! You're stark raving mad! YOU'RE GOING TO KILL ME!

　　(But before Peter *has time to think what to do,* Jerry *tosses the knife at* Peter's *feet)*

JERRY:　There you go. Pick it up. You have the knife and we'll be more evenly 680 matched.

PETER:　*(Horrified)* No!

JERRY:　*(Rushes over to* Peter, *grabs him by the collar;* Peter *rises; their faces almost touch)*

　　Now you pick up that knife and you fight with me. You fight for your self-respect; you fight for that goddamned bench.

PETER:　*(Struggling)* No! Let . . . let go of me! He . . . Help!

JERRY:　*(Slaps* Peter *on each "fight")* You fight, you miserable bastard; fight for that bench; fight for your parakeets; fight for your cats, fight for your two daughters; fight for your wife; fight for your manhood, you pathetic little vegetable. 690
　　(Spits in Peter's *face)* You couldn't even get your wife with a male child.

PETER:　*(Breaks away, enraged)* It's a matter of genetics, not manhood, you . . . you monster.
　　(He darts down, picks up the knife and backs off a little; he is breathing heavily)
　　I'll give you one last chance; get out of here and leave me alone!
　　(He holds the knife with a firm arm, but far in front of him, not to attack, but to defend)

JERRY:　*(Sighs heavily)* So be it!

　　(With a rush he charges Peter *and impales himself on the knife. Tableau: For just a* 700
moment, complete silence, Jerry *impaled on the knife at the end of* Peter's *still firm arm.*
Then Peter *screams, pulls away, leaving the knife in* Jerry. Jerry *is motionless, on point.*
Then he, too, screams, and it must be the sound of an infuriated and fatally wounded
animal. With the knife in him, he stumbles back to the bench that Peter *had vacated. He*
crumbles there, sitting, facing Peter, *his eyes wide in agony, his mouth open)*

PETER:　*(Whispering)* Oh my God, oh my God, oh my God. . . .
　　(He repeats these words many times, very rapidly)

JERRY:　*(*Jerry *is dying; but now his expression seems to change. His features relax, and*
while his voice varies, sometimes wrenched with pain, for the most part he seems re-
moved from his dying. He smiles) Thank you, Peter. I mean that, now; thank you
very much. 710
　　*(*Peter's *mouth drops open. He cannot move; he is transfixed)*
　　Oh, Peter, I was so afraid I'd drive you away. *(He laughs as best he can)* You don't
know how afraid I was you'd go away and leave me. And now I'll tell you what
happened at the zoo. I think . . . I think this is what happened at the zoo . . . I
think. I think that while I was at the zoo I decided that I would walk north . . .
northerly, rather . . . until I found you . . . or somebody . . . and I decided that I
would talk to you . . . I would tell you things . . . and things that I would tell you
would . . . Well, here we are. You see? Here we *are.* But . . . I don't know . . .
could I have planned all this? No . . . no, I couldn't have. But I think I did. And
now I've told you what you wanted to know, haven't I? And now you know all 720
about what happened at the zoo. And now you know what you'll see in your
TV, and the face I told you about . . . you remember . . . the face I told you
about . . . my face, the face you see right now. Peter . . . Peter? . . . Peter . . . thank
you. I came unto you *(He laughs, so faintly)* and you have comforted me. Dear
Peter.

PETER:　*(Almost fainting)* Oh my God!

JERRY:　You'd better go now. Somebody might come by, and you don't want to be
here when anyone comes.

PETER:　*(Does not move, but begins to weep)* Oh my God, oh my God.

JERRY:　*(Most faintly, now; he is very near death)* You won't be coming back here any 730
more, Peter; you've been dispossessed. You've lost your bench, but you've defended your honor. And Peter, I'll tell you something now; you're not really a
vegetable; it's all right, you're an animal. You're an animal, too. But you'd better hurry now, Peter. Hurry, you'd better go . . . see?
　　*(*Jerry *takes a handkerchief and with great effort and pain wipes the knife handle*
clean of fingerprints)
　　Hurry away, Peter.
　　*(*Peter *begins to stagger away)*
　　Wait . . . wait, Peter. Take your book . . . book. Right here . . . beside me . . . on
your bench . . . my bench, rather. Come . . . take your book. 740
　　*(*Peter *starts for the book, but retreats)*

Hurry . . . Peter.
(Peter *rushes to the bench, grabs the book, retreats*)
Very good, Peter . . . very good. Now . . . hurry away.
(Peter *hesitates for a moment, then flees, stage-left*)
Hurry away. . . . (*His eyes are closed now*) Hurry away, your parakeets are making dinner . . . the cats . . . are setting the table . . .
PETER: (*Off stage*)
(*A pitiful howl*)
OH MY GOD! 750
JERRY: (*His eyes still closed, he shakes his head and speaks; a combination of scornful mimicry and supplication*) Oh . . . my . . . God.
(*He is dead*)

CURTAIN

1958   *1959, 1960*

SAM SHEPARD
(b. 1943)

Sam Shepard has been called a primitive or naïf because he seems to have come to the writing of plays without the traditional kinds of influences. He is impatient with those who ask, "Where did the idea for this play come from?": "I never can answer it because it seems totally ass backwards. Ideas emerge from plays — not the other way around." He looks upon the theater and its possibilities with a great sense of wonder: "The fantastic thing about theater is that it can make something be seen that's invisible, and that's where my interest in theater is — that you can be watching this thing happening with actors and costumes and light and set and language, and even plot, and something emerges from beyond that, and that's the image part that I'm looking for, that sort of added dimension."

Shepard's observations on contemporary life reflect many of the attitudes that filter through his plays. He has, for example, said: "People are starved for the truth, and when something comes along that even looks like the truth, people will latch on to it because everything's so false. It's very difficult to find anything with a real authentic heart. Even art has turned into applauding the superficial as being authentic." He sees a universal longing for direction, for values: "People are starved for a way of life. They're hurting for a way to be or to act toward the world."

Many of his plays portray irrational violence. In an interview he remarked:

> I think there's something about American violence that to me is very touching. In full force it's very ugly, but there's also something very moving about it, because it has to do with humiliation. There's some hidden, deeply rooted thing in the Anglo male American that has to do with inferiority, that has to do with not being a man, and always, continually having to act out some idea of manhood that invariably is violent. This sense of failure runs very deep — maybe it has to do with the frontier being systematically taken away, with the guilt of having gotten this country by wiping out a native race of people, with the whole Protestant work ethic. I can't put my finger on it, but it's the source of a lot of intrigue for me.

Shepard is the only American playwright who has achieved a major reputation as a dramatist without submitting to the commercial judgments of Broadway. His plays have been produced primarily in off-off-Broadway houses. He was born Samuel Shepard Rogers in 1943 in Fort Sheridan, Illinois, the son of an army officer who was assigned to a number of posts that took the family, with its "army brat," to South Dakota, Utah, Florida, and — out in the Pacific — to Guam. Shepard's father retired to an avocado ranch in Duarte, California, where Shepard went to school. After graduating from high school in 1960, Shepard enrolled briefly in a junior college, but soon dropped out to join a touring theater group which played in churches across the country. Shepard became fascinated with the theater, and settled into New York in 1963 determined to continue his career in some connection with it.

In New York, Shepard ran into a high school friend, Charles Mingus, Jr., son of the jazz musician, who helped him find survival jobs and took him in as a roommate. While working at a night club, The Village Gate, Shepard met Ralph Cook, who had founded a little off-off-Broadway group, Theatre Genesis, at Saint Marks Church in-the-Bowery. Cook suggested that Shepard turn from writing poetry to the writing of plays. Shepard quickly wrote two short plays, *Cowboys* and *The Rock Garden,* which were produced in 1964. It was about this time that Shepard dropped his surname Rogers and became simply Sam Shepard, which seemed more compatible with his new life and identity.

The plays drew an enthusiastic review from *The Village Voice,* and Shepard was encouraged to continue his new profession — without, however, giving up his job earning a living. In 1965, no less than six of Shepard's plays were produced in various off-off-Broadway houses, including *Dog, Chicago,* and *Icarus's Mother.* Shepard was well on his way in his new career. By the late 1980s, the count of Shepard's plays and screen scripts was around fifty, an astonishing productivity unmatched by other American playwrights. He has won some ten Obies, an award given by *The Village Voice* for the best off-Broadway play of the year. Among the early Obie winners, besides *Chicago* and *Icarus's Mother,* were *Red Cross* (1966), *Forensic and the Navigators* (1967), *La Turista* (1967), and *Melodrama Play* (1968). In 1970, Shepard's full-length play *Operation Sidewinder,* which required a set too complicated for off-off-Broadway, was produced at New York's Lincoln Center; it was a financial failure, and its production made Shepard vow never to become enmeshed in such lavish, large-scale productions again, with artistic control taken out of his hands.

In 1969 Shepard married an actress, O-Lan Johnson, who had appeared in one of his plays, and he moved with her and their son to London in 1971. There he saw to production his play about a rock-and-roll star, *The Tooth of Crime,* in 1972 (later an Obie winner in New York). The play brought to the fore Shepard's interest in popular music, including jazz, country western, as well as rock-and-roll. As a youth he had become a proficient drummer (learning from his father), and he had appeared as the drummer in the rock group, the Holy Modal Rounders, that had played through the scene changes for the ill-fated *Sidewinder.* Other plays that saw production in England include *Blue Bitch, Geography of a Horse Dreamer,* and *Little Ocean.*

Back in America in the mid-1970s, Shepard wound up in San Francisco, where he found the Magic Theatre small and informal enough for his taste. He directed there his own plays, *Action* and *Killer's Head,* in 1975, a few months after they had closed at the American Place Theatre in New York. *Action* won another Obie for the playwright. Other plays followed, many produced first at the Magic Theatre and then going to off-off-Broadway theaters in New York. Plays produced during this period include *Angel City* (1976), *Suidice in B-flat* (1976), *Curse of the Starving Class* (1978), *Buried Child* (1978), *Seduced* (1979), *Tongues* (1979), *True West* (1980), *Fool for Love* (1983), and *A Lie of the Mind* (1985). Three of these plays (*Curse of the Starving Class, Buried Child,* and *Fool for Love*) won Obies, *Buried Child* won a Pulitzer Prize (the first such winner without a Broadway production), and *A Lie of the Mind* won the New York Drama Critics Circle Award. During this time Shepard divorced his wife to live with the actress and film producer Jessica Lange.

In spite of his preference for the live theater, Shepard has found himself lured into films. He received an academy award nomination as best supporting actor for his role in *The Right Stuff* (1983). He has appeared occasionally in other films, and has written his own screenplays. He co-produced his *Paris, Texas* in 1984, and won the Palme d'Or at the Cannes Film Festival. In 1985, Shepard adapted his *Fool for Love* for film and played a leading role in the production. In 1988 he achieved his ambition of directing a film based on his own filmscript—*Far North*. In addition to his work in film, Shepard has published *Hawk Moon: A Book of Short Stories, Poems, and Monologues* (1973), and two volumes of his journals, *Rolling Thunder Logbook* (1977) and *Motel Chronicles* (1982).

Shepard has shown so many different talents that it is hard to predict in what direction he might now go. But he seems to like best the role of the playwright, and prefers the milieu of the little theater. Unlike Albee, he has escaped being pigeonholed by terms that turn out to be narrowing. Although many critics have seen elements of the theater of the absurd in his work, they have also noted his realistic techniques; and they have been surprised by his exploitation of popular culture, especially that of the mythic American West, and his integration of popular music into his plays. His writing may have fewer connections with the style of dramatists of the past than with the "spontaneous poetics" of a Jack Kerouac, or even with the improvisations of jazz. The drama critic Richard Gilman justly wrote in 1981: "Not many critics would dispute the proposition that Sam Shepard is our most interesting and exciting American playwright."

ADDITIONAL READING

Bonnie Marranca, ed., *American Dreams: The Imagination of Sam Shepard,* 1981; Doris Auerbach, *Sam Shepard, Arthur Kopit, and the Off-Broadway,* 1982; Ron Mottram, *Inner Landscapes: The Theater of Sam Shepard,* 1984; Don Shewey, *Sam Shepard,* 1985; Ellen Oumano, *Sam Shepard: The Life and Work of an American Dreamer,* 1986; Lynda Hart, *Sam Shepard's Metaphorical Stages,* 1987; Dorothy Parker, ed., *Essays on Modern American Drama: Williams, Miller, Albee, Shepard,* 1987; Kimball King, ed., *Sam Shepard: A Casebook,* 1988.

TEXTS

Fool for Love and Other Plays, 1984.

Action

CHARACTERS

SHOOTER
JEEP
LIZA
LUPE

Scene: *Upstage center, a small Christmas tree on a small table with tiny blinking lights. Downstage center left, a plain board table with four wooden chairs, one each on the four sides. The table is set very simply for four people. Just plates, forks and knives. Four*

*coffee cups and a pot of hot coffee in the middle. Running across the middle of the stage above
is a clothesline attached to a pulley at either side of the stage. The light onstage is divided
exactly in half, so that upstage is in complete darkness except for the blinking lights of the
Christmas tree. Downstage is lit in pale yellow and white light which pulses brighter and
dimmer every ten minutes or so, as though the power were very weak.*

    *The characters are all in their late twenties to early thirties. Shooter and Jeep, the
two men, are dressed in long dark overcoats, jeans, lumberjack shirts, and heavy boots. They
both have their heads shaved. Lupe wears a flowered print dress in the 1940s Pearl Harbor
style. She wears platform heels. Liza wears a long, full, Mexican type skirt, plain blouse and
an apron. She wears sandals. Lupe sits upstage of the table facing Liza across from her.
Liza's back is directly to the audience. Jeep sits stage right at one end of the table across from
Shooter, who sits at the other end.*   10

    *The stage is in darkness for a while with just the tree blinking. The lights come up very
slowly downstage. Nothing happens for a while except the slight movements of the actors
drinking coffee. Jeep rocks slightly in his chair.*

    All the exits and entrances occur upstage into or out of the darkness.

JEEP: *(leaning back in his chair and rocking gently)* I'm looking forward to my life.   20
   I'm looking forward to uh — me. The way I picture me.

SHOOTER: Who're you talking to?

JEEP: Uh — *(pause)* I had this room I lived in. Shall I describe this room? *(pause as
the others take a sip of coffee together)* I had a wall with a picture of Walt Whitman in
an overcoat. Every time I looked at the picture I thought of Pennsylvania. I had
a picture of an antelope on a yellow prairie. Every time I looked at this picture I
saw him running. I had a picture of the Golden Gate Bridge. Every time I
looked at it I saw the water underneath it. I had a picture of me sitting on a
Jeep with a gun in one hand.

    (He lets the chair come to rest on the floor again. Pause as they all sip coffee. Suddenly   30
Liza jumps up and makes a big gesture with her hands melodramatically.)

LIZA: Oh my God! The turkey!

    (She goes running off upstage and disappears into the darkness.)

LUPE: *(to herself)* It's funny the way the snow is.

SHOOTER: *(pulling a book out from his lap and placing it on the table)* Maybe we
should read.

LUPE: We'll have to wait for Liza.

SHOOTER: Yeah. But we could be looking for the place. Do you remember where
it was?

LUPE: I thought we marked it.

SHOOTER: I lost the place.   40

LUPE: *(taking the book and thumbing through it)* Here, let me look.

JEEP: Shooter, can you do a soft shoe?

SHOOTER: Naw. I don't think so.

JEEP: I was wondering if we could both do it sitting down. Without getting up.
Just our legs.

SHOOTER: Just like this you mean?

JEEP: Yeah.

LUPE: Was it chapter sixteen?

SHOOTER: Uh — Maybe. *(Lupe continues thumbing)*   50

JEEP: Just try. Put your hands on the table.

    (They both put their hands on the table.)

JEEP: One, two, three, quatro!

    *(They both break into an attempt at a soft shoe patter as they stare blankly at each other
in their seats. Lupe keeps looking through the book. This lasts for about thirty seconds and*

ends with Liza *coming back into the light sucking on her fingers and wiping her hands on her apron. She sits back down in her chair.)*

LIZA: *(noticing* Lupe *with the book)* Oh. Are we gonna' read?

LUPE: I can't find the place.

LIZA: Let me take a look.   60

(Lupe *shoves the book across the table to* Liza, *who takes it and starts thumbing through it. She keeps sucking on her fingers in between turning the pages.)*

LUPE: Shooter lost the place.

JEEP: Uh — I saw this picture of a dancing bear. Some gypsies had it on a leash. They were all laying by the side of the road and the bear was standing on all fours. Right in the middle of the road. In the background was this fancy house.

(Shooter *pulls his overcoat over his head and holds his hands up in front of him like bear paws. Slowly he pushes his chair back and rises. He takes short staggering steps like a bear on his hind legs.* Liza *keeps looking through the book.)*

JEEP: *(to* Shooter) Don't act it out.   70

(Shooter *keeps on.)*

LIZA: *(referring to book)* Were we past the part where the comet exploded?

JEEP: *(to* Shooter) You don't have to act it out.

(Shooter *pays no attention.)*

LUPE: I never saw a dancing bear. That was before my time. I guess they made it illegal. Too cruel or something.

(Shooter *goes back and forth downstage like a trained bear, looking out at the audience.)*

SHOOTER: It doesn't feel cruel. Just humiliating. It's not the rightful position of a bear. You can feel it. It's all off balance.   81

LUPE: Well, that's what I mean.

JEEP: What?

LUPE: That's cruel. For a bear that's cruel.

SHOOTER: No. It's as though something's expected of me. As though I was human. But it puts me in a different position. A different situation.

JEEP: How?

SHOOTER: Performing. Um — Without realizing it. Um — I mean I realize it but the bear doesn't. He just finds himself doing something unusual for him. Awkward.

JEEP: You're not the bear.   90

LIZA: I found it! They've returned to earth only to find that things are exactly the same. Nothing's changed.

JEEP: That's not it. Let me try.

(Jeep *takes the book from* Liza *and goes through it.* Shooter *drops his bear routine and pulls his overcoat down on his shoulders. He looks blankly at the audience, then strolls back to his seat and sits. They all sip their coffee. After a long pause.)*

SHOOTER: I think I'll take a bath.

LIZA: The turkey's almost ready.

SHOOTER: I'm too scared to eat. *(not showing it)*

LUPE: *(to* Liza) Let him take a bath. It'll calm him down.   100

SHOOTER: Is there any hot water left?

JEEP: *(thumbing through the book)* There was the last time I was up there.

SHOOTER: I don't want to go up there alone.

LUPE: If you could remember the last time when you got scared it might help you this time.

SHOOTER: I know. It's the same. It's the snow. Being inside. Everything's so shocking inside. When I look at my hand I get terrified. The sight of my feet in the bathtub. The skin covering me. That's all that's covering me.

LIZA: *(pulling out a hip flask from her apron)* You want some rum?

(Shooter takes the flask and has a drink.)   110

LUPE: I can remember the last time I got scared. I thought I'd poisoned myself. I thought I'd eaten something. I imagined it working its way into me. I went outside in my bare feet and forced myself to throw up. It was that kind of a night.

LIZA: I remember that night. We were watching the stars.

(The two girls start laughing, covering their mouths, then stop.)

SHOOTER: I know I'll get over this. It just sorta' came on me.

(He hands the flask back to Liza who puts it in her apron.)

LIZA: *(without giving it back)* You can keep it.

SHOOTER: *(blankly)* I've got this feling that females are more generous. I've al-   120
ways felt that.

JEEP: *(pushing the book away from him)* OH THIS IS RIDICULOUS!! I CAN'T FIND THE PLACE!!

(He stands suddenly, picks up his chair and smashes it to the floor. The chair shatters into tiny pieces. Pause. None of the others are shocked.)

LIZA: *(standing)* I think there's another one out on the back porch.

(Liza leaves. She disappears in the darkness upstage. Jeep pulls his overcoat up over his head and raises his hands like Shooter did. He goes through the same bear motions as Shooter did before. Lupe takes the book again and looks through the pages.)

SHOOTER: *(to himself)* That's what I do. I get this feeling I can't control the situa-   130
tion. Something's getting out of control. Things won't work. And then I smash something. I punch something. I scream. Later I find out that my throat is torn. I've torn something loose. My voice is hoarse. I'm trembling. My breath is short. My heart's thumping. I don't recognize myself.

LUPE: Shooter, weren't you the last one to read?

SHOOTER: Was I?

LUPE: Yeah. It was you.

SHOOTER: It doesn't matter does it?

LUPE: Only if you can remember where you left off.

SHOOTER: Well, let me look. I'll see if I can find it.   140

(He takes the book and looks through it. Lupe starts into a soft shoe sitting down. Jeep has his back to her, but as he hears her feet tapping he stops his bear routine and turns to look at her. She continues with a smile. Jeep pulls his overcoat down on his shoulders and just stares at her.)

JEEP: *(flatly)* There's something to be said for not being able to do something well.

(Lupe stops. Her smile disappears.)

JEEP: No, I mean it's all right. It takes a certain amount of courage to bring it out into the open like that.

LUPE: It's no worse than the one you guys did.   150

JEEP: No, I know. I'm not trying to insult you or anything.

(Lupe starts up the soft shoe again in defiance.)

JEEP: I mean we've got this picture in our head of Judy Garland or Gene Kelly or Fred Astaire. Those feet flying all over the place. That fluid motion. How can we do anything for the first time. Even Nijinsky[1] went nuts.

LUPE: *(continuing with her feet)* What about it?

JEEP: It's hard to have a conversation.

(He sits down on the floor. Lupe continues dancing for a while after Jeep's seated. She slowly stops. Shooter thumbs through the book. They sip their coffee.)

---

[1]Vaslav Nijinsky (1890–1950), Russian ballet dancer.

LUPE: *(to* Jeep*)* When you're in a position of doing something like that it's hard to 160
      talk about it. You know what I mean? I mean while I was doing it — while I was
      in the middle of actually doing it — I didn't particularly feel like talking about
      it. I mean it made me feel funny. You know what I mean. It was like somebody
      was watching me. Judging me. Sort of making an evaluation. Chalking up
      points. I mean especially the references to all those stars. You know. I mean I
      know I'm not as good as Judy Garland. But so what? I wasn't trying to be as
      good as Judy Garland. It started off like it was just for fun you know. And then
      it turned into murder. It was like being murdered. You know what I mean.

JEEP: Didn't mean to piss you off.
      (Pause. Liza *enters from upstage with a new chair in one hand and a broom and* 170
dustpan in the other. She sets the chair down. Jeep *gets up off the floor and sits in the new
chair, folding his arms across his chest.* Liza *starts sweeping up the pieces of the old chair.*
Jeep *watches her.)*

JEEP: *(to* Liza*)* I'm not going to offer to clean it up because you're already doing it.
      *(*Liza *continues sweeping in silence.)*

SHOOTER: *(looking up from the book, directed at everyone)* I know that feeling of
      being out of control. Powerless. You go crazy. In a second you can go crazy. You
      can almost see it coming. A thunderstorm.

JEEP: *(to* Shooter*)* It's not that.

SHOOTER: Oh.   180
      *(*Shooter *goes back to thumbing through the book.)*

JEEP: I mean sometimes it's like that but this time it wasn't.

LIZA: *(still sweeping)* Did you find the place yet?

SHOOTER: Nope.

LUPE: I'm starving. *(she licks her lips)*

JEEP: This time it came from something else. I had an idea I wanted to be differ-
      ent. I pictured myself being different than how I was. I couldn't stand how I
      was. The picture grew in me, and the more it grew the more it came up against
      how I really was. Then I exploded.

SHOOTER: *(without looking up from the book)* That's what I meant.   190

LUPE: Oh, when are we gonna' EAT! *(hitting the table once with her fist)*

LIZA: It's almost ready.
      *(*Liza *exits upstage with the pieces of the old chair, leaving the broom onstage.)*

JEEP: I couldn't take it. Just thumbing through the book. Not even looking. Not
      even seeing the papers. Just turning them. Acting it out. Just pretending.
      (Suddenly Lupe *starts gnawing ravenously on her own arm.* Jeep *and* Shooter *pay
no attention.)*

SHOOTER: *(still looking through the book)* I know.

JEEP: Is that what you're doing? Is that what you're doing right now?

SHOOTER: *(without looking up)* I'm looking for the place.   200

JEEP: I admire your concentration. I couldn't concentrate. I kept thinking of
      other things. I kept drifting. I kept thinking of the sun. The Gulf of Mexico.
      Barracuda.

SHOOTER: *(still into the book)* That's okay.

JEEP: *(standing suddenly and yelling)* I KNOW IT'S OKAY! THAT'S NOT WHAT
      I'M SAYING!
      (He picks up the new chair and smashes it to the ground just like the other one. Lupe
stops chewing on her arm and licks it like a cat licking a wound. Shooter *keeps looking for
the place in the book.* Jeep *stands there looking at the damage.)*

SHOOTER: *(after a short pause, referring to book)* Was it just after the fall of the Great 210
      Continent?

LUPE: Oh my stomach!
      (She clutches her stomach with both hands and holds it like a baby. Liza *enters with a*

huge golden turkey on a silver platter with the steam rising off it. She sets it down on the table in front of Lupe.)

LUPE: I'll carve.

    (Lupe *picks up a knife and begins to slice the turkey in a calm way, very formally, and laying the slices on plates for everyone.* Liza *walks over to* Jeep, *who is still looking at the broken chair. They look at the chair together as though seeing it as an event outside themselves.*)   220

LIZA: *(to* Jeep *but looking at the broken chair)* You'll have to stop doing that. We've only got one left.

    (Liza *picks up the broom.* Jeep *grabs it. They both hold it together.*)

JEEP: I'll do it.

LIZA: That's okay.

    (*A short pause as they look at each other, then* Jeep *yanks the broom out of* Liza's *hand and starts sweeping up the broken chair.* Liza *goes to the table and sits folding her hands in her lap while* Lupe *continues to carve standing up.* Shooter *sticks with the book.*)

LUPE: We're lucky to have a turkey you know.

LIZA: Yes, I know.   230

LUPE: It was smart thinking to raise our own. To see ahead into the crisis.

LIZA: Whose idea was it anyway?

SHOOTER: *(not looking up)* Mine.

JEEP: *(still sweeping)* I think it was mine.

SHOOTER: *(not looking up)* It was your idea, and then I went and bought it.

JEEP: That's right.

LIZA: That's right.

LUPE: We're sure lucky.

LIZA: Do you know what they say is the best way to prepare a turkey? They say that before you kill it—about two weeks before—you start feeding it a little   240 cornmeal and some sherry. About a teaspoonful of sherry, three times a day. Then in the second week you force a whole walnut down its throat once a day and keep up the sherry dosage. When it comes time for the kill you'll have a turkey with a warm, nutty flavor.

LUPE: Is that what you did?

LIZA: Partly. I started out the first week with the sherry, but by the time the second week rolled around I couldn't bring myself to do it. I mean the walnut thing. I couldn't do that.

JEEP: *(as he exits upstage with the broken pieces of the chair)* It's not cruel.

LUPE: Who killed it anyway?   250

LIZA: I did.

SHOOTER: I can't find the place.

    (Shooter *folds the book and puts it on the floor, opens his napkin and tucks it into his shirt, picks up his knife and fork and waits to be served.*)

SHOOTER: Aren't we going to have any vegetables?

LIZA: No. We had a late frost remember?

LUPE: We're lucky to have a turkey.

SHOOTER: I know we are. I was just wondering about the vegetables. The creamed onions and stuff. The candied yams.

LUPE: *(to* Shooter*)* Dark or light?   260

SHOOTER: White.

    (She hands Shooter *a plate of turkey. He digs in.*)

LIZA: No wine either, I suppose?

LUPE: You were in the kitchen.

    (She hands Liza *a plate of turkey.* Liza *eats.* Lupe *serves herself and sits down to eat.*)

LIZA: Yes. I've never cooked over an open fire before. I mean a big fire blazing

like that. It's hard to keep from cooking yourself. Your arms start roasting. You 270
get afraid the kitchen's going to burn down.

LUPE: I can imagine.

LIZA: The heat is tremendous.

SHOOTER: I thought turkeys were supposed to cook slow.

LIZA: Well, you let the flames die down. It's just the embers you're cooking on.
But the heat!

SHOOTER: Yeah, it's hot in here for a change.

(Jeep *enters from upstage into the light, shivering and rubbing his arms. Liza
stops him.*)

LIZA: Oh Jeep, could you get us all some water?   280

JEEP: (*standing still, shivering*) Right now?

LIZA: Yeah, if you don't mind.

JEEP: From the well? It's a lot of work you know. We can't just turn on a tap.

LUPE: We're lucky to have a turkey.

(Jeep *turns upstage and exits.*)

SHOOTER: It *is* freezing out there. I don't envy him. Hauling up water. Spilling it
on his hands. It's freezing.

LIZA: It's all right.

SHOOTER: In the dark. Feeling your way around. He might fall in.

LIZA: We'll hear him.   290

LUPE: It's all right, Shooter.

SHOOTER: (*standing suddenly*) I KNOW IT'S ALL RIGHT!

(*The two women continue eating, paying no attention.* Shooter *sits down after a
while.*)

SHOOTER: (*quietly to himself;* Lupe *and* Liza *eat quietly*) Just because we're surrounded by four walls and a roof doesn't mean anything. It's still dangerous.
The chances of something happening are just as great. Anything could happen. Any move is possible. I've seen it. You go outside. The world's quiet.
White. Everything resounding. Not a sound of a motor. Not a light. You see
into the house. You see the candles. You watch the people. You can see what it's 300
like inside. The candles draw you. You get a cold feeling being outside. Separated. You have an idea that being inside it's cosier. Friendlier. Warmth. People.
Conversation. Everyone using a language. Then you go inside. It's a shock. It's
not like how you expected. You lose what you had outside. You forget that
there even is an outside. The inside is all you know. You hunt for a way of being
with everyone. A way of finding how to behave. You find out what's expected of
you. You act yourself out.

(Jeep *enters from upstage with a bucketful of water and four cups in the other hand.
Each cup dangling from one of his fingers by the handle. He sets the bucket down on the table
with the cups. He picks up a cup and dips it into the bucket. He does the same with each cup* 310
*and serves everyone at the table with a cup of water. Then he sits down on the floor. This all
happens in silence, except for the sounds of the others eating and the water.*)

LIZA: (*standing*) There's one chair left.

SHOOTER: (*standing and moving upstage*) I'll get it.

(Shooter *exits.* Liza *sits again.*)

LUPE: Dark or light, Jeep?

JEEP: White.

(Lupe *serves him a plate of turkey.* Jeep *eats, sitting on the floor.*)

JEEP: I was thinking. If things get worse we should get a cow.

LIZA: Nobody's selling.   320

JEEP: You've asked around?

LIZA: Nobody's selling.

LUPE: I was thinking chickens would be better.

LIZA: Nobody's selling.

JEEP: That's all right.

LUPE: A goat might be good.

LIZA: There's no way of actually preparing. We'll have to do the best with what we've got. We're all eating now. At least we're eating. We'll have to gauge our hunger. Find out if we actually need food when we think we need it. Find out how much it takes to stay alive. Find out what it does to us. Find out what's 330 happening to us. Sometimes I think I know, but it's only an idea. Sometimes I have the idea I know what's happening to us. Sometimes I can't see it. I go blind. Other times I don't have any idea. I'm just eating.

   (Shooter *comes back on from upstage empty-handed. They all stop eating and look at him.*)

SHOOTER: I forgot what it was I went for. I got out there and forgot.

JEEP: *(still on the floor)* The chair.

SHOOTER: Oh yeah.

   (Shooter *turns upstage and exits again. They go back to eating.*)

JEEP: *(to himself)* It doesn't really matter. I'm okay on the floor.   340

LIZA: I made a move to go get it, and then he beat me to it.

JEEP: It doesn't matter.

LUPE: Was he being polite?

LIZA: I guess.

LUPE: *(to* Liza*)* Just to keep you from going out there?

LIZA: I guess so.

LUPE: But he's getting the chair for Jeep, and Jeep doesn't even care.

LIZA: It's all right.

JEEP: *(suddenly, to himself)* Walt Whitman was a great man. He kissed soldiers. He held their hands. He saw mounds of amputated limbs.   350

LUPE: I don't know anything about him.

   (Shooter *comes on from upstage pulling a very heavy, stuffed red armchair. He huffs and puffs with it, pulling it by inches downstage as the others stay sitting and eat their turkey.*)

JEEP: He expected something from America. He had this great expectation.

LUPE: I don't know. I never heard about it.

JEEP: He was like what Tolstoy[2] was to Russia.

LIZA: I don't know much about it either.

JEEP: A father. A passionate father bleeding for his country.

LIZA: *(staying seated)* Do you want some help, Shooter?

SHOOTER: *(between heavy breaths)* No— I'm uh— okay. It's— not much— fur- 360 ther. I'll be all right.

JEEP: Almost a hundred years ago to the day. The same thing happened. Everybody at each other's throats. Walt was there. He could tell you.

LIZA: I thought he was dead.

JEEP: *(conversationally)* "Manahatta,"[3] it was called then. Indian. They had big, open tents on the Bowery with sawdust on the floor. German beer. Juggling acts. Dancing bears. The Civil War was just beginning.

LUPE: When was this?

JEEP: He'd tip his hat to Abe, and Abe would tip his hat back.

LIZA: They liked each other.   370

JEEP: *(in a Walter Cronkite newscaster voice)* The poet and the President. The poet

---

[2]Count Leo Tolstoy (1828–1910), Russian novelist and moral philosopher.
[3]"Mannahatta" is the title of two poems (1860, 1888) by Walt Whitman: "My city's fit and noble name . . . ,/Choice aborigi-

nal name." Whitman frequented a Broadway bohemian beer parlor, Pfaffs. The "good gr poet" also saw Lincoln on the streets of Washington.

all gray and white standing on his feet. The President all dark and somber, glooming down from his horse. The face of war in his eyes. The two of them seeing each other from their respective positions. The entire nation in a jack-knife. This all happened on Vermont Avenue near L Street. The street itself was raining. Blue soldiers were lying wounded in every doorway; some having slept there all night with gaping wounds. Soaked through to the bone. Walt was a witness to it.

(Shooter *finally gets the chair downstage right and stands by it trying to catch his* breath. *He looks at* Jeep, *who stays seated on the floor.* Shooter *makes a motion toward the* 380 *chair with his hand. He tries to speak, but he's out of breath. He tries again.*)

SHOOTER: *(motioning to chair)* There it is.

JEEP: I'm okay here.

(Shooter *looks at him for a while.*)

SHOOTER: You don't want it? *(no answer from* Jeep, *who keeps eating)* Don't you want it?

(*Still no answer from* Jeep. Shooter *moves in front of the armchair and collapses into it, staring out at the audience.*)

SHOOTER: Aaaaaaaah! This is the life. Now I'm glad I went through all that.

LIZA: *(to Shooter)* Aren't you hungry?   390

SHOOTER: No. I'm glad.

(*He folds his arms behind his head and smiles.*)

LIZA: *(standing)* Well, time to wash up.

(*She starts gathering all the dishes together very quickly, whipping the plates out from under everyone.* Jeep *and* Lupe *pick their teeth and smack their lips loudly.*)

JEEP: *(with his back to* Shooter) Do you want some water, Shooter? There's plenty of water.

SHOOTER: Nope. This is it for me. I'm never leaving this chair. I've finally found it.

JEEP: *(standing and moving to the bucket on the table)* I'm gonna' have some water. I'd 400 be glad to get you a cup if you want.

LUPE: He just said he doesn't want any.

(Jeep *stands by the bucket with a cup in one hand. He dips the cup into the bucket, raises the cup slowly, and tips the water back into the bucket, watching the trickle of water as he does it. He keeps doing this over and over as though hypnotized by his own action. When* Liza *has all the dishes she exits upstage leaving the remains of the turkey on the table.*)

LUPE: Does anyone want to read? *(pause)*

SHOOTER: I'm never leaving again.

LUPE: I don't mind looking for the place.

(*She goes and picks up the book on the floor and sits back down in her chair. She looks* 410 *through it.*)

SHOOTER: I could conduct all my business from here. I'll need a bedpan and some magazines.

JEEP: *(looking at the remains of the turkey)* We should save the bones for soup.

SHOOTER: This is more like it. This is more in line with how I see myself. I picture myself as a father. Very much at home. The world can't touch me.

JEEP: Shooter? You remember when you were scared? Shooter? You remember? Oh, Shooter?

SHOOTER: Naw. I don't remember that. Better to leave that. People are washing dishes now. Lupe's looking for the place again. Things are rolling right along. 420 Why bring that up?

LUPE: *(in the book)* Wasn't it around where the spaceship had collided with the neutron?

JEEP: Shooter, I remember. I remember you were so scared you couldn't go up to take a bath.

SHOOTER:　Naw. That's not me at all. That's entirely the wrong image. That must've been an accident.

JEEP:　Oh.

　　　　(Jeep *keeps pouring the water over his head.*)

SHOOTER:　I've never been afraid of baths. I've always been brave in those situa- 430
tions. I've plunged right in.

JEEP:　Oh, I thought it was you.

SHOOTER:　I knew a guy once who was afraid to take a bath. Something about the water. Stank to high heaven. "High Heaven." That's a good one. He stank, boy. Boy, how he stank. Boy, did he ever stink.

JEEP:　Was it the water?

SHOOTER:　Yeah. Something about how it distorted his body when he looked down into it.

JEEP:　Then, it wasn't the water.

SHOOTER:　Yeah. The water. The way it warped his body. 440

JEEP:　But that's just the way he saw it. That was him, not the water.

SHOOTER:　Then, he began to fear his own body.

JEEP:　From that? From seeing it in the water?

SHOOTER:　He began to feel like a foreign spy. Spying on his body. He'd lie awake. Afraid to sleep for fear his body might do something without him knowing. He'd keep watch on it.

JEEP:　Was he a close friend?

SHOOTER:　I knew him for a while.

JEEP:　What happened to him?

SHOOTER:　His body killed him. One day it just had enough and killed him. 450

JEEP:　What happened to the body?

SHOOTER:　It's still walking around I guess. *(pause)* Would somebody tell Liza to bring me the flask?

LUPE:　*(not looking up from the book)* She's washing the dishes.

JEEP:　*(still pouring)* That's an interesting story, Shooter.

SHOOTER:　Thank you.

JEEP:　How did it get started?

SHOOTER:　What?

JEEP:　I mean how did he get into this relationship?

SHOOTER:　Who knows. It developed. One day he found himself like that. 460

LUPE:　*(without looking up)* Remember the days of mass entertainment?

JEEP:　No.

LUPE:　*(not looking up)* This could never have happened then. Something to do every minute. Always something to do. I once was very active in the community.

JEEP:　What's a community?

LUPE:　*(looking up)* A sense of— A sense um— What's a community, Shooter?

SHOOTER:　Oh uh— You know. You were on the right track.

LUPE:　Something uh—

JEEP:　I know.

LUPE:　Yeah. You know. It doesn't need words. 470

　　　　(She goes back into the book.)

JEEP:　I know what you mean.

LUPE:　Just a kind of feeling.

JEEP:　Yeah, I know what you mean.

SHOOTER:　I think we're beginning to get it a little. To get it back. I mean you can feel it even in the dead of winter. Sort of everybody helping each other out.

JEEP:　Did he suspect his body of treason? Was that it?

SHOOTER:　I'm not sure. It was a touchy situation.

(Shooter *rolls both his pant legs up above his knees and starts scratching his legs as* 480
he talks.)

JEEP: He must've had a hard time. I mean he couldn't reach out. I mean he
   wouldn't expect anyone else to be in the same boat probably.

SHOOTER: Probably not.

LUPE: *(without looking up)* Well it *is* rare.

JEEP: Was it in a particular time of hardship?

SHOOTER: I can't rightly say.

JEEP: I mean were things crumbling?

SHOOTER: I suspect he couldn't see it. I mean I suspect he had his ideas. His
   opinions. Certain stiff attitudes.

LUPE: *(not looking up)* When was this?   490

JEEP: And his body's still walking around?

SHOOTER: That's right. A walking stiff.

JEEP: Can anyone tell? I mean if we ran into this body could we tell it was vacant?

SHOOTER: I'm not sure.

LUPE: *(still thumbing through the book)* Well, how *could* you tell?

JEEP: *(to* Lupe*)* There must be a way. I mean something must be missing. You
   could tell if he wasn't all there.

SHOOTER: I don't know.

LUPE: *(still in book)* How? How could you tell?

JEEP: You'd know. I'd know. I mean with us, we know. We know. We hear each 500
   other. We hear our voices. We know each other's voice. We can see. We recognize each other. We have a certain — We can tell who's who. We know our
   names. We respond. We call each other. We sort of — We — We're not completely stranded like that. I mean — It's not — It's not like that. How that
   would be.

(Pause as JEEP *slowly pours the water over his hand.* Shooter *scratches his legs.*
Lupe *thumbs through the book. After a short while* Shooter *sits back in the armchair with a*
jerk and holds his stomach.)

SHOOTER: I'm starving. Did we eat already?

LUPE: *(still in book)* You weren't here.   510

SHOOTER: I was here. I was here all along.

LUPE: *(in book)* Not at the right time.

(Shooter *stands suddenly with his pants legs still rolled up.* Lupe *and* Jeep *pay no*
attention.)

SHOOTER: You mean you ate without me!

   Pause as Shooter *looks around the space slowly.*

SHOOTER: *(to himself)* Now I'm beginning to regret my decision.

LUPE: What.

SHOOTER: *(gazing around him in amazement)* To stay in the chair.

LUPE: Oh.   520

SHOOTER: It was shortsighted. I'd give anything just to travel around this space.
   Just to lick the corners. To get my nose in the dust. To feel my body moving.

LUPE: *(referring to book)* Was it near the place where the sky rained fire?

SHOOTER: I can picture it. I give in to it. I let my body go. It moves out. It sniffs
   the board. My head imagines forests! Chain saws! Hammers and nails in my
   ears! A whole house is being built!

LUPE: *(in book)* Keep it to yourself.

SHOOTER: My nose finds things. Everything's churning with new pictures. Then
   suddenly it all ends again, and I'm back in the chair. But now I've ruined it.
   Now I've had my cake. Now neither one is any good. The chair doesn't get it 530
   on, and neither does the adventure. I'm nowhere.

LUPE: I'm trying to concentrate.

SHOOTER: Shall I tell a story?

LUPE: *(looking up from book)* Oh God! If I could find the place we could *read* a story!

SHOOTER: *(still standing)* I'll tell a story. I feel like a story. Jeep? How 'bout it?

JEEP: *(still pouring water, blankly)* You bet.

LUPE: *(back into book)* Oh Jesus!

   (Through the story which Shooter *tells standing on the armchair,* Jeep *keeps pouring the water slowly over his hand into the bucket, and* Lupe *keeps looking through the book.* 540 Shooter *tells it directly to the audience.)*

SHOOTER: One night there was some moths. A bunch of moths. In the distance they could see a candle. Just one candle in a window of a big house. The moths were tormented by this candle. They longed to be with this candle but none of them understood it or knew what it was. The leader of the moths sent one of them off to the house to bring back some information about this light. The moth returned and reported what he had seen, but the leader told him that he hadn't understood anything about the candle. So another moth went to the house. He touched the flame with the tip of his wings but the heat drove him off. When he came back and reported, the leader still wasn't satisfied. So he 550 sent a third moth out. This moth approached the house and saw the candle flickering inside the window. He became filled with love for this candle. He crashed against the glass and finally found a way inside. He threw himself on the flame. With his forelegs he took hold of the flame and united himself joyously with her. He embraced her completely, and his whole body became red as fire. The leader of the moths, who was watching from far off with the other moths, saw that the flame and the moth appeared to be one. He turned to the other moths and said: "He's learned what he wanted to know, but he's the only one who understands it."

   *(*Jeep *suddenly slaps the water in the bucket with his free hand and pulls a large dead* 560 *fish out of the bucket and throws it on the floor.* Shooter *looks down on it from the chair.* Lupe *sticks with the book.)*

JEEP: I've about had it with this bucket! I can't figure out what I've been doing here all this time.

SHOOTER: *(still standing and looking down at the fish)* How deep is our well anyway?

JEEP: *(to* Lupe*)* What's happened to Liza?

LUPE: Washing dishes.

JEEP: *(to* Lupe*)* Have I been standing here all this time?

LUPE: *(looking up)* I don't know! I've been looking for the place! I wish people would just leave me alone!   570

SHOOTER: I'm not standing up here because I'm afraid of fish, I'll tell you that much. I was standing up here before the fish ever arrived. It's just a coincidence. It's not the way it looks.

JEEP: Shooter, could you create some reason for me to move? Some justification for me to find myself somewhere else?

SHOOTER: Only if you promise that you're not thinking that I'm afraid of fish just because I'm standing up here on the chair and there happens to be a fish in the house.

JEEP: I'm not thinking about you!

   (Suddenly Lupe *gives an exasperated exhale of air, slams the book shut, glares at the* 580 *two men, stands and exits upstage.* Shooter *and* Jeep *are stuck in their respective positions. Short pause as they look at each other.)*

SHOOTER: Go and pick up the fish.

   *(*Jeep *goes to the fish and picks it up.)*

SHOOTER: Go and put the fish on the table.

(Jeep goes upstage of the table, facing audience, moves the turkey carcass to one side and lays the fish down on the table.)

SHOOTER: *(still standing)* Take your jackknife out of your pocket.

　Jeep *does it.*

SHOOTER: Open your jacknife. The big blade. 590

　(Jeep does it.)

SHOOTER: Cut open the belly of the fish, starting from the pee-hole and slicing
　toward the head.

　(Jeep cuts open the fish.)

SHOOTER: Now clean it like you would any other fish.

　(Jeep goes about cleaning the fish in silence. Shooter *sits back down slowly in the chair. He looks at his bare legs.)*

SHOOTER: What's been going on in here? *(to* Jeep*)* Was there a party?

　(Jeep keeps cleaning the fish. Shooter *looks at his legs again.)*

SHOOTER: Was someone taking liberties? 600

　(He leans back in the chair with a sigh.)

SHOOTER: It's agonizing. All this time I could've swore I was getting something
　done. I can't even remember eating. *(back to* Jeep*)* Did we eat already? Wasn't
　there a turkey? *(turns front again and leans back)* Somebody's gonna' have to
　bring me some food, you know. I've made this decision not to leave the chair
　and I'm gonna' stick with it. Come hell or high water. It's not my fault. *(back to*
　Jeep*)* I could have the fish. When you're finished with it, could you fry it up and
　bring it to me? If it's not too much trouble? *(no response from* Jeep, Shooter *turns
　front again and leans back in the chair)* This isn't the worst. It's just that my stom-
　ach growling. I COULDN'T STAY HERE FOREVER! I don't know what pos- 610
　sessed me. *(back to* Jeep*)* Didn't I say that I'll never leave the chair? *(back front
　again)* If I get up, it would be a sign of my weakness. Jeep? If I got up would you
　think I was weak? *(no answer)* This isn't the worst thing that could happen. *(short
　pause)*

JEEP: The table's littered with carcasses. Guts. Bones. The insides. I'm in the
　middle of all this.

SHOOTER: Who are you talking to?

JEEP: I'm swimming in it.

SHOOTER: *(still front)* It's nobody's fault, you know.

JEEP: I can't help eating. I'll eat to my dying day. 620

SHOOTER: Oh, brother!

　*(Shooter gives a heave and a groan and pushes with his feet so that the armchair tips
　over backwards with him in it. The bottom of the chair conceals* Shooter *from the audience.
　Only his voice is heard.* Jeep *continues with the fish methodically.)*

JEEP: *(looking at the fish)* If you were alone would you have done that?

SHOOTER: I'm still in the chair. I'm sticking to my promise.

JEEP: You wouldn't call it showing off?

SHOOTER: I'm at my wit's end. The whole world could disappear.

　*(The two women enter from upstage. Each one holds a handle on either end of a large
　wicker basket full of wet laundry.* Lupe *is now wearing* Liza's *apron with the pockets full of* 630
　*clothespins. They haul the basket down left center where the clothesline is. They set the basket
　down on the floor, and* Lupe *grabs one of the chairs and stands up on it to reach the
　clothesline* Liza *starts handing her the wet clothes, one piece at a time, from the basket, while*
　Lupe *pins them onto the line and pulls the line out, making room for the next piece. Gradu-
　ally the clothes are strung clear across the stage but high enough so as not to block too much of
　the action.* Jeep *keeps working on the fish, cutting the head off, scaling it, fileting it, cleaning
　it off in the bucket of water, etc. He is very meticulous about it and gets more involved as he
　goes along.* Shooter *remains hidden behind the armchair. The two girls remain closed off in
　their activity.)*

JEEP: I'm starting to feel better already. You remember before when I was get- 640
ting the fears?

SHOOTER: No. When was that?

JEEP: When I was asking you if you remembered when you were scared to go up
and take a bath.

SHOOTER: That was a long time ago.

JEEP: I'm getting better now. Even in the middle of all this violence.

SHOOTER: You should've told me you were scared. I would've done something
about it. I didn't realize you were scared.

JEEP: I'm in a better position now. Now I've got something to do.

(Shooter *pulls the armchair over on top of himself so that his arms stick out the sides* 650
like a headless turtle. He moves the chair slightly from side to side with his back. The women
continue in silence with the laundry.)

JEEP: I can even imagine how horrifying it could be to be doing all this, and it
doesn't touch me. It's like I'm dismissed.

SHOOTER: Am I completely hidden?

JEEP: More or less.

SHOOTER: Maybe I'm gone.

JEEP: Maybe.

SHOOTER: That's what it's like.

JEEP: Maybe that's it, then. Gone.   660

(Shooter *starts moving the armchair slowly around like a giant tortoise. The girls pay*
no attention.)

SHOOTER: That's it all right. Flown the coop. Is there anyone to verify? To check
it out?

JEEP: *(looking at the girls)* Are you sure you want to?

SHOOTER: Maybe it's better like this. We can keep it a secret.

JEEP: Are you sure you're not there?

SHOOTER: More or less. Something creeps back, now that you mention it.

JEEP: Oh.

SHOOTER: What's the matter?   670

JEEP: I don't know. I got no references for this. Suddenly it's shifted.

SHOOTER: What's the matter? You have to clue me in.

JEEP: Once I was in a family. I had no choice about it. I lived in different houses.
I had no choice. I couldn't even choose the wallpaper.

SHOOTER: Are you getting to the point?

JEEP: I found myself in schools. In cars. I got arrested. That was when it
changed. The second time I got arrested.

SHOOTER: Have you forgotten about me?

JEEP: The second I got arrested I understood something. I remember the
phrase "getting into trouble." I remember the word "trouble." I remember 680
the feeling of being in trouble. It wasn't until I got in trouble that I found out
my true position.

SHOOTER: What was that?

JEEP: I was in the world. I was up for grabs. I was being taken away by something
bigger.

SHOOTER: The cops?

JEEP: Something bigger. Bigger than family. Bigger than school. Bigger than the
4-H Club. Bigger than Little League Baseball. This was Big Time. My frame of
reference changed.

SHOOTER: Did you go to jail?   690

JEEP: I went everywhere. Cop car, court, jail, cop car, jail, court, cop car, home,
cop car, jail. And everywhere I noticed this new interest in my existence. These

new details. Every scar was noted down. Every mark. The lines in my fingers.
Hair. Eyes. Change in the pocket. Knives. Race. Age. Every detail.

SHOOTER: Who was interested?

JEEP: A vast network. A chain of events. I entered a new world.

SHOOTER: Weren't you scared?

JEEP: I used to have this dream that would come to me while I was on my feet. I'd
be on my feet just standing there in these walls, and I'd have this dream come to
me that the walls were moving in. It was like a sweeping kind of terror that 700
struck me. Then something in me would panic. I wouldn't make a move. I'd
just be standing there very still, but inside something would leap like it was
trying to escape. And then the leap would come up against something. It was
like an absolutely helpless leap. There was no possible way of getting out. I
couldn't believe it. It was like nothing in the whole wide world could get me out
of there. I'd relax for a second. I'd be forced to relax because if I didn't, if I
followed through with this inward leap, if I let my body do it I'd just crash
against the wall. I'd just smash my head in or something. I had to relax. For a
second I could escape it. That I was there. In jail. That I wasn't getting out. No
escape. For a second. Then these thoughts would come. "How long? How long 710
was I there for? A day. Maybe I could last a day. A week. A month? I'd never
last a month! FOREVER!" That's the thought that did it. FOREVER! And the
whole thing would start up again. Except worse this time. As though it wasn't
just a thought. As though it really was. And then I'd start to move. I couldn't
help myself. My body was shaking.

(Jeep *begins to move around the stage. The words animate him as though the space is
the cell he's talking about but not as though he's recalling a past experience but rather that he's
attempting his own escape from the space he's playing in. The other actions continue in their
own rhythm.*)

I'd start to make sounds. It just came out of me. A low moan. An animal noise. I 720
was moving now. I was stalking myself. I couldn't stop. Everything disappeared. I
had no idea what the world was. I had no idea how I got there or why or who did it.
I had no references for this.

(Jeep *just stands there. The others continue their actions. Lights fade slowly to black.
The Christmas tree keeps blinking.*)

1975, 1976

Copyrights and Acknowledgments and Illustration Credits

Illustrations

Part I: Franklin Square, 1878. *Harper's Weekley*, September 7, 1878; Theodore R. Davis.

Part II: Martin Lewis, *Relicts*, 1928, drypoint. The College of Wooster Art Museum, The John Taylor Arms Print Collection, Gift of Ward and Mariam C. Canaday.

Part III: Mark Tobey, *Rummage*, 1941, The Seattle Art Museum, Eugene Fuller Memorial Collection, 42.28.

INDEX

A 0
B 1
C 2
D 3
E 4
F 5
G 6
H 7
I 8
J 9